BRITISH MUSEUM. *Dept. of printed books.*

GENERAL CATALOGUE

OF

PRINTED BOOKS

Photolithographic edition

to 1955

Volume 35

CASTELN—CERE

PUBLISHED BY

THE TRUSTEES OF THE BRITISH MUSEUM

LONDON 1965

Printed in England by
Balding + Mansell, London and Wisbech
© *The Trustees of the British Museum, 1965*

CASTELNAU, FRANCIS L. DE LAPORTE, *Count de*. *See* LAPORTE.

——, LOUIS JOSEPH AMABLE DE RICHARD, *Baron de*. *See* RICHARD.

CASTELNAU ( ) *Baron de*. Réflexions ou Lettres du Baron de Castelnau à Lady Sophie F * * *; sur le gout; sur les livres; sur les philosophes, *etc.* pp. viii. 219 [220]. *J. de Boffe: Londres*, 1786. 8º.
713. b. 15.
The text on p. [217] and p. [220], i.e. the outer form of the last sheet, is wanting.

CASTELNAU (ALBERT) Les Médicis. 2 tom. *Paris*, 1879. 8º.
10629. ee. 19.

—— La Question religieuse. pp. 257. *Paris*, 1861. 12º.
4015. aa. 8.

—— Zanzara. (La Renaissance en Italie.) 2 tom. *Paris; Bruxelles* [printed], 1860. 8º.
12513. aaa. 36.

CASTELNAU (ALEXANDRE WESTPHAL) *See* WESTPHAL-CASTELNAU.

CASTELNAU (ALFRED WESTPHAL) *See* WESTPHAL-CASTELNAU.

CASTELNAU (AMABLE) Les Citoyens Castelnau, Trouille, Bergevin et Babin, à la Convention nationale. [Replying to attacks on the Commune of Brest.] pp. 7.
F. 949. (10.)

CASTELNAU (C.) Considérations sur la nostalgie, *etc.* [A thesis.] pp. 23. *Paris*, 1806. 4º.
1182. g. 8. (35.)

CASTELNAU (ÉDOUARD DE CURIÈRES DE) *See* CURIÈRES DE CASTELNAU (Noël M. J. E. de)

CASTELNAU (GABRIEL DE) *Marquis*. Essai sur l'histoire ancienne et moderne de la nouvelle Russie . . . Avec cartes, vues, plans . . . Seconde édition. 3 tom. *Paris*, 1827. 8º.
9455. bb. 20.

CASTELNAU (H. DE) Affaire Pierre Bonaparte, ou le Meurtre d'Auteuil. [By H. de Castelnau?] Avec portraits du prince Pierre Bonaparte & de Victor Noir, et nombreuses gravures, *etc.* pp. 177. 1870. 8º. *See* BONAPARTE (P. N.) *Prince*.
5425. aaa. 11.

CASTELNAU (HENRI DE) De l'interdiction des aliénés. Mémoire, *etc.* pp. xiii. 202. *Paris*, 1860, *etc.* 8º.
5405. f. 8.

—— Sur un projet de caisse de prévoyance et de caisse de secours pour les pharmaciens de France imaginé par M. Dorvault, *etc.* pp. 69. *Paris*, 1859. 8º.
7679. a. 8.

CASTELNAU (HENRI LOUIS) Faculté de Droit de Paris. Thèse pour la licence. pp. 58. *Paris*, 1860. 8º.
5406. c. 6. (5.)

CASTELNAU (HENRI PIERRE JEAN ABDON) *See* GIRARD (G.) La Vie et les souvenirs du général Castelnau, *etc.* 1930. 8º.
10655. a. 38.

CASTELNAU (JACQUES THOMAS DE)

—— Le Club des Jacobins, 1789–1795. pp. 255. *Paris*, 1947. 8º.
09226. e. 32.

—— Fouquier Tinville. Le pourvoyeur de l'échafaud. pp. 251. [*Paris*, 1937.] 8º.
010655. aa. 4.

—— Un Grand journaliste du siècle dernier: Hippolyte de Villemessant. *In:* Les Œuvres libres. Nouvelle série. no. 36. pp. 133–194. 1949. 8º.
12208. ee. 261.

CASTELNAU (JACQUES THOMAS DE)

—— Madame Tallien, révolutionnaire, favourite, princesse. pp. 253. [*Paris*,] 1938. 8º.
010655. aa. 34.

—— Marat, "l'ami du peuple," 1744–1793. pp. 255. [*Paris*,] 1939. 8º.
010655. bb. 18.

—— Le Maréchal de Saxe. Amours et batailles. pp. 254. [*Paris*,] 1937. 8º.
010709. de. 47.

—— Le Paris de Charles V, 1364–1380. [With a map.] pp. 158. pl. VIII. *Paris*, 1930. 8º.
010168. f. 33.

—— Les Petits métiers de Paris. pp. 156. *Paris*, 1952. 8º.
10175. b. 36

CASTELNAU (JEAN LOUIS) Essai sur les anévrysmes spontanés externes en général; thèse, *etc.* pp. 43. *Paris*, 1834. 4º.
1184. f. 15. (11.)

CASTELNAU (JUNIUS) Bibliographie du Languedoc en général, du département de l'Hérault et de la ville de Montpellier en particulier. pp. 116. 1859. *See* MONTPELLIER.—*Société Archéologique de Montpellier. Mémoires, etc.* vol. 4. 1840, *etc.* 4º.
Ac. 5317.

—— De la poésie descriptive, ou Discours en réponse à cette question proposée par la Société Hollandaise des Lettres . . . "Donner une dissertation sur ce qui constitue l'essence . . . de la poésie descriptive" . . . Précédé d'une introduction par M. Saint-René Taillandier. pp. xxxi. 180. *Paris*, 1859. 8º.
11825. d. 21.

CASTELNAU (L.) *Capitaine de la Garde nationale*. Simple avis touchant la réorganisation de la Garde nationale pp. 8. *Paris*, 1848. 8º.
8827. e. 49. (1.)

CASTELNAU (L.) *Professeur de mathématiques*. *See* FRIZON (P. L.) Note sur quelques opuscules mathématiques inédits de feu P. L. Frizon, par L. Castelnau. [With the text.] 1864. 8º.
8530. bbb. 26. (3.)

—— Cours de mathématiques appliquées à l'usage des candidats aux emplois d'agents secondaires et de conducteurs des ponts et chaussées, *etc.* 4 pt. *Paris*, 1866. 8º.
8530. g. 21.

—— Études pratiques sur les mathématiques appliquées . . . Deuxième édition, revue et augmentée, *etc.* [With folding plates.] pp. 54. *Paris*, 1856. 8º. **8531. d. 2.**

CASTELNAU (MAURICE FRANÇOIS DE) *Count d'Albignac*. *See* CASTELNAU (P. F. M. de)

CASTELNAU (MICHEL DE) *Docteur en droit*. *See* CURIÈRES DE CASTELNAU (M. de) *Marquis*.

CASTELNAU (MICHEL DE) *Seigneur de Mauvissière*. *See* HUBAULT (G.) Ambassade de Michel de Castelnau en Angleterre, 1575–1585, *etc.* [1856.] 8º. **9210. dd. 10.**

—— *See* LA RAMÉE (P. de) Traicté des Façons & Coustumes des anciens Gaulloys, traduit . . . par M. de Castelnau. 1559. 8º.
7706. aa. 28.

—— —— 1581. 8º.
1058. b. 2. (1.)

—— Les Mémoires de Messire Michel de Castelnau . . . Ausquelles sont traictées les choses plus remarquables, qu'il a veuës & negotiées en France, Angleterre, & Escosse soubs les Rois François II. & Charles IX. tant en temps de paix qu'en temps de guerre. [With a portrait.] pp. 479 *C. Chappelet: Paris*, 1621. 4º.
1197. i. 16.

—— Les Mémoires de Messire Michel de Castelnau . . . illustrez et augmentez de plusieurs commentaires & manuscrits . . . servans à donner la vérité de l'histoire des

CASTELNAU (MICHEL DE) *Seigneur de Mauvissière.*

règnes de François II. Charles IX. & Henry III. et de la régence & du gouvernement de Catherine de Medicis. Avec . . . l'histoire généalogique de la maison de Castelnau . . . par J. Le Laboureur . . . Nouvelle édition, révûë . . . et augmentée. [Edited by Jean Godefroy.] 3 tom. *Bruxelles,* 1731. fol. **187. f. 5–7.**

—— [Another copy.] **G. 11399.**

—— [Another edition.] pp. 504. *Paris,* 1823. 8°. [*Collection complète des mémoires relatifs à l'histoire de France, etc.* sér. 1. tom. 33.] **909. f. 11.**

—— [Another edition.] 1836. *See* PANTHÉON. Panthéon littéraire. (Choix de chroniques et mémoires sur l'histoire de France.) 1835, *etc.* 8°. **12200. p. 1/21.**

—— [Another edition.] 1838. *See* MICHAUD (J. F.) and POUJOULAT (J. J. F.) Nouvelle collection des mémoires pour servir à l'histoire de France, *etc.* sér. 1. tom. 9. 1836, *etc.* 8°. **805. e. 9.**

—— Memoirs of the Reigns of Francis II. and Charles IX. of France. Containing a particular account of the three first civil wars raised and carried on by the Huguenots in that Kingdom . . . Done into English by a Gentleman *etc.* pp. 426. *London,* 1724. fol. **596. i. 9**

—— Extrait des Mémoires de Messire Michel de Castelnau. —Extrait des additions aux Mémoires de Messire M. de Castelnau, par Monsieur le Laboureur, *etc. See* JEBB (Samuel) De vita & rebus gestis . . . Mariæ Scotorum Reginæ, *etc.* vol. 2. 1725. fol. **1321. l. 2.**

CASTELNAU (PAUL) Quelques considérations sur l'hygiène d'une partie de la population de la Haute-Garonne. Thèse, *etc.* pp. 64. *Montpellier,* 1864. 4°. **7379. f. 7. (1.)**

CASTELNAU (PHILIPPE FRANÇOIS MAURICE DE) *Count d'Albignac. See* SAUZEY (J. C. A. F.) De Munich à Vilna à l'état-major du Corps bavarois de la Grande Armée en 1812. D'après les " Papiers du général d'Albignac," *etc.* 1911. 8°. **09077. f. 46.**

CASTELNAU (PHILIPPE JOSEPH BOILEAU DE) *See* BOILEAU DE CASTELNAU.

CASTELNAU (PIERRE DE) *See* ROULLET DE LA BOUILLERIE (F. A.) successively *Bishop of Carcassonne* and *Archbishop of Perga.* Le Bienheureux Pierre de Castelnau et les Albigeois au XIIIᵉ siècle. 1867. 12°. **4867. aaa. 19.**

CASTELNAU (RAIMOND BOILEAU DE) *See* BOILEAU DE CASTELNAU.

CASTELNAU-BUCHER (RICHARD HUBERT LESTOQ DE) *See* BUCHER (R. H. L. de C.)

CASTELNAUDARI (ARNAUT VIDAL DE) *See* VIDAL DE CASTELNAUDARI.

CASTELNAUDARY. Un Monsieur de Castelnaudary. Vaudeville en un acte, par MM * * *, de Nimes. pp. xvi. *Nimes,* 1861. 4°. **11739. g. 89. (2.)**

CASTELNAUDARY (DOMINIQUE DE) *See* DOMINIQUE, *de Castelnaudary, Capuchin.*

CASTELNAU D'ESSENAULT (GUILLAUME DE) *Marquis. See* BAUREIN (J.) Variétés bordeloises . . . Avec . . . une table alphabétique et détaillée par M. le marquis de Castelnau d'Essenault. 1876, *etc.* 8°. **10171. ff. 17.**

CASTELNAU-MONTRATIER (BERTRAND DE MONTFAVÈS DE) *Cardinal. See* MONTFAVÈS (B. dє)

CASTELNAUT, HENRI NOMPAR DE CAUMONT, *Marquis de. See* CAUMONT (H. N. de) *Duke de La Force.*

CASTELNOU ( ) *See* SCHULER (F.) Ma double vie d'officier français et espion allemand. Autobiographie présentée, traduite et annotée par M. Castelnou. 1939. 8°. **010655. f. 29.**

CASTELNOU (JOAN DE)

—— Le Sirventés de Joan de Castelnou. [Edited, with a French translation by A. Pagès.] *In:* Bibliothèque méridionale. sér. 1. tom. 25. pp. 117–139. 1945. 8°. **12238. ee. 4/25.**

CASTELNOV, ALONSO DE CARDONA Y BORJA, *Marquis de. See* CARDONA Y BORJA.

CASTELNOVO. *See* CASTELNUOVO.

CASTELNOVO (GIROLAMO DA) Composizioni latine di Girolamo da Castelnovo, vicentino, le quali copiate sopra un manoscritto della Comunale di Verona son poste a luce nelle nozze Da Schio-Marcello. [Edited by Cesare Cavattoni.] pp. 47. *Verona,* 1864. 8°. **010910. dd. 44. (1.)**

CASTELNOVO (LEO DI) *pseud.* [i.e. *Count* LEOPOLDO GIOVANNI BATTISTA CARLO PULLÉ.] *See also* PULLÉ (L. G. B. C.) *Count.*

—— Un Cuor morto. Comedia in tre atti. pp. 98. *Milano,* 1871. 8°. **11715. e. 17.**

—— Fior d'Alpe. Opera in tre atti, *etc.* [In verse.] pp. 61. *Milano,* [1894.] 8°. **11725. c. 23. (4.)**

CASTELNUOVO. Copia d'una letera nouamēte venuta a Venetia, de la crudelissima rotta, e gran battaglia, fatta sotto Castel Nouo . . . 1539. [*Venice?* 1539.] 4°. **1312. b. 37.**

—— Coplas sobre Castil Nouo hechas por vn soldado q̄ esta captiuo en Constantinopla. [With a woodcut.] [1539?] 4°. **C. 62. c. 11.**

CASTELNUOVO ( ) *See* GATTESCHI (D.) Manuale di diritto pubblico e privato ottomano . . . Edito per cura dei sigg. Castelnuovo e Leoncavallo. 1865. 8°. **05319. k. 25.**

CASTELNUOVO (ALBERTO DE ORESTIS DI) *See* ORESTIS DI CASTELNUOVO.

CASTELNUOVO (ENRICO) *Novelist.*

—— *See* TENNYSON (A.) *Baron Tennyson.* [*Selections and Extracts.*] Il Primo diverbio . . . Traduzione di E. Castelnuovo. [1886.] 8°. **11602. gg. 19. (3.)**

—— I Coniugi Varedo. Romanzo. pp. 436. *Milano,* 1899. 8°. **12471. l. 10.**

—— La Contessina. Racconto. pp. 254. *Milano,* 1881. 8°. **12471. e. 22.**

—— Dal primo piano alla soffitta. Romanzo. pp. 320. *Milano,* 1883. 8°. **12471. e. 32.**

—— Due convinzioni. Romanzo. pp. 388. *Milano,* 1885. 8°. **12471. g. 27.**

—— Figurine veneziane. Disegni di G. Fattori e G. Micheli. [Tales.] pp. 92. *Livorno,* 1904. 16°. **12471. de. 10.**

—— I Moncalvo. Romanzo. pp. 339. *Milano,* 1908. 8°. **12471. tt. 31.**

—— Natalia, ed altri racconti. pp. 352. *Milano,* 1899. 8°. **12471. k. 39.**

CASTELNUOVO (ENRICO) *Novelist.*

—— [A reissue.] *Milano*, 1902. 8°.　　　**12471**. s. **9.**

—— Nell' andare al ballo, ed altri racconti . . . Terza edizione. pp. 166. *Venezia*, 1899. 8°.
　　　　　　　　　　　12470. bbb. **15.**

—— Nella bottega del cambiavalute. Romanzo. pp. 330. *Milano*, 1895. 8°.　　　**12471**. i. **16.**

—— Nella lotta. Romanzo. pp. 343. *Milano*, 1880. 8°.
　　　　　　　　　　　12471. ee. **35.**

—— Prima di partire. Nuovi racconti. pp. 362. *Milano*, 1890. 8°.　　　**12471**. d. **40.**

—— [Racconti e bozzetti.] Clarina's Staatsstreich . . . Uebersetzt von P. Dorosa.—Ein Sonnenstrahl . . . Uebersetzt von A. Dulk.—Der Schwager meiner Schwägerin . . . Uebersetzt von P. Dorosa. [Three tales from "Racconti e bozzetti."] 1878. *See* HEYSE (P.) Italienische Novellisten, *etc.* Bd. 5. 1877, *etc.* 8°.　**12471**. cc. **48.**

—— Reminiscenze e fantasie. pp. 397. *Milano*, 1886. 8°.
　　　　　　　　　　　12471. g. **34.**

—— Il Ritorno dell'Aretusa. [Tales.] pp. 376. *Milano*, 1901. 8°.　　　**12471**. s. **3.**

—— Sorrisi e lagrime. Nuovi racconti. pp. 346. *Milano*, 1882. 8°.　　　**12471**. e. **28.**

—— Sulla laguna. [With a portrait.] pp. 198. *Catania*, 1900. 8°.　　　**12472**. aa. **21.**
"*Semprevivi.*" *Biblioteca popolare contemporanea.* no. 11.

—— Ultime novelle. pp. 346. *Milano*, 1906. 8°.
　　　　　　　　　　　12471. t. **21.**

—— Novelle . . . With notes and a vocabulary by Rev. A. C. Clapin . . . Authorised edition. pp. 99. *Hachette & Co.: London*, [1891.] 8°. [*Biblioteca italiana.*]　　　**12225**. a. **17/2.**

—— Am Fenster. Eine Novelle. Uebersetzt von Konrad Telmann.—Spiritus Indocilis. Uebersetzt von Wilhelm Lange.—Lampo und Carmela. Uebersetzt von Wilhelm Lange. *See* ITALIAN STORY BOOK. Italienisches Novellenbuch, *etc.* 1882. 8°.　　**12471**. d. **1.**

CASTELNUOVO (GIACOMO DI) Roma di Mussolini. Primo decennale della rivoluzione fascista. A cura di G. di Castelnuovo. [With illustrations.] pp. 196. *Roma*, 1932. fol.　　　**20087**. b. **10.**
A special number of "Opere pubbliche."

CASTELNUOVO (GUIDO) Lezioni di geometria analitica. Quinta edizione. pp. viii. 605. *Milano*, 1922. 8°.
　　　　　　　　　　　08531. i. **7.**

—— La Probabilité dans les différentes branches de la science. pp. 61. *Paris*, 1937. 8°. [*Philosophie et histoire de la pensée scientifique.* no. 2.]　　W.P. **11413/2.**

—— Ricerche di geometria della retta nello spazio a quattro dimensioni, *etc.* pp. 47. [1891.] *See* VENICE.—*Imperiale Regio Istituto Veneto, etc.* Atti, *etc.* ser. 7. tom. 2. 1889, *etc.* 8°.　　　Ac. **110.**

—— Ricerche generali sopra i sistemi lineari di curve piane, *etc.* 1892. *See* TURIN.—*Accademia delle Scienze.* Memorie, *etc.* ser. 2. tom. 42. 1839, *etc.* 4°.　Ac. **2816.**

—— Sulle congruenze del terzo ordine dello spazio a quattro dimensioni. Seconda memoria. 1888. *See* VENICE.—*Imperiale Regio Istituto Veneto, etc.* Atti, *etc.* ser. 6. tom. 6. 1882, *etc.* 8°.　　　Ac. **110.**

CASTELNUOVO (GUIDO)

—— Vito Volterra e la sua opera scientifica. [With a portrait.] pp. 30. *Roma*, 1947. 8°. [*Atti della Accademia Nazionale dei Lincei. Rendiconto dell'adunanza generale.* vol. 5. fasc. 1.]　　　Ac. **102/13.**

CASTELO (MARÍA)

—— *See* ZAVALA (S.) and CASTELO (M.) Fuentes para la historia del trabajo en Nueva España, *etc.* 1939, *etc.* 8°.
　　　　　　　　　　　9771. s. **25.**

CASTELO BRANCO (CAMILO) *Viscount de Correia-Botelho. See* CASTELLO BRANCO (C.)

CASTELO BRANCO (HOLBECHE)

—— Hitler não é uma causa. A propósito de "O Espírito inglês," notas e comentários do Sr. Dr. Tomaz Ribeiro Colaço. pp. 15. *Lisboa*, 1940. 8°.　**8029**. g. **1.** (3.)

—— A Vitória das Potências do Eixo evitará a miséria e a anarquia na Europa. pp. 29. *Lisboa*, 1941. 8°.
　　　　　　　　　　　8029. g. **3.** (11.)

CASTELO BRANCO (J.)

—— *See* FOLEY (Thomas) *Able Seaman on the "Doric Star".* Prisioneiro no "Altmark". . . . Tradução de J. Castelo Branco. 1940. 8°.　　**9100**. a. **118.**

—— *See* KELTON (Gerald) [Wheels Beneath.] Luta de Espiões. Versão de J. Castelo Branco. 1939. 8°.
　　　　　　　　　　　012646. a. **63.**

—— *See* WADE (Henry) *pseud.* O 13.º Barão. The High Sheriff. Versão portuguesa por J. Castelo Branco. 1940. 8°.　　　**012641**. n. **142.**

—— *See* WILLIAMSON (Charles N.) [Honeymoon Hate.] Lua de—Fel. Tradução de J. Castelo Branco. 1939. 8°.
　　　　　　　　　　　012642. s. **44.**

CASTELO-BRANCO (MANUEL JOAQUIM CARDOZO) *See* CARDOZO CASTELO-BRANCO.

CASTELO BRANCO CHAVES (　　　　)

—— Eça de Queiroz visto por quem o conheceu. Prefácio e coordenação de Castelo Branco Chaves. pp. 64. *Lisboa*, [1944.] 8°.　　　**010632**. aa. **6.**

CASTELOT (ANDRÉ)

—— Le Duc de Berry et son double mariage. D'après des documents inédits. [With portraits.] pp. 333. *Paris*, 1951. 8°.　　　**010664**. m. **71.**
Part of the series "Présence de l'histoire."

—— Les Grandes heures des cités et châteaux de la Loire. Nouvelle édition revue et corrigée. [With plates.] pp. 232. *Paris*, 1953. 8°.　　　**010171**. n. **32.**

—— Louis XVII. L'énigme résolue. [With a portrait.] pp. 315. *Bruxelles*, 1947. 8°.　　　**010655**. h. **31.**

—— Le Mariage de Marie-Antoinette. *In:* Les Œuvres libres. Nouvelle série. no. 83. pp. 173–206. 1953. 8°.
　　　　　　　　　　　12208. ee. **208.**

—— Varennes. Le roi trahi. [With illustrations.] pp. 246. *Paris*, [1951.] 8°.　　　**9210**. e. **26.**
Part of a series entitled "La Grande et la petite histoire."

CASTELOT (E.) *See* SPENCER (Herbert) [*Principles of Ethics.*] Justice . . . Traduit par M. E. Castelot, *etc.* 1903. 8°.　　　**8410**. l. **10.**

CASTELOT (E.)

—— See SPENCER (Herbert) [*Principles of Ethics.*] La Morale des différents peuples et la morale personnelle . . . Traduction de M. É. Castelot . . . M. E. M. Saint-Léon. 1896. 8°.   **8408. dd. 9.**

—— See SPENCER (Herbert) [*Principles of Ethics.*] Le Rôle moral de la bienfaisance. Traduction de M. E. Castelot . . . et M. E. M. Saint-Léon. 1895. 8°.
8408. dd. 5.

CASTELOT (FRANÇOIS JOLLIVET) See JOLLIVET CASTELOT.

CASTELPLANIO (LODOVICO DI) See LODOVICO, da Castelplanio, Franciscan.

CASTELS (R.) Castelar segun la Frenología. pp. 14. Madrid, 1874. 8°.   **10602.** i. 5. (11.)

CASTELSEPRIO.—Church of Santa Maria.

—— Santa Maria di Castelseprio. [By G. P. Bognetti, G. Chierici and A. de Capitani d'Arzago.] pp. 739. pl. xc. Milano, 1948. 4°.   **L.R. 300. bb. 6.**

CASTELUCCHIO (PAULINO) See CASTELVECCHIO.

CASTELVECCHIO (L. P. DE) See BARZINI (L.) Pekin to Paris . . . Translated by L. P. de Castelvecchio, etc. 1907. 8°.   **010026.** i. 27.

—— See WORDSWORTH (John) *Bishop of Salisbury.* Breve descrizione della Chiesa Anglicana . . . Tradotta dall'inglese per cura di L. P. de Castelvecchio, etc. 1909. 8°.
4705. de. 36.

CASTELVECCHIO (PAULINO) See TASSONI (A.) Count. La Secchia rapita, etc. [Edited by P. Castelvecchio.] 1670. 12°.   **11429. aa. 39.**

—— —— [1680?] 12°.   **11429. aa. 41.**

CASTELVECCHIO (RICCARDO) pseud. [i.e. Count GIULIO CESARE BALDASSARE LEOPOLDO PULLÉ.] See also PULLÉ (G. C. B. L.) Count.

—— [Un Episodio del 1793.] 'Επεισοδιον της Γαλλικης 'Επαναστασεως του έτους 1793. Τα θυματα της Γαλλικης δημοκρατιας. Δραμα εἰς πραξεις πεντε του συγγραφεως Ρ. Καστελβεκιου. Ὑπο Παντολεοντος Α. Τσικνοπουλου. 'Εκ του 'Ιταλικου. pp. 70. 'Εν Σμυρνη, 1869. 8°.
11758. e. 13. (4.)

—— Esopo. Commedia in quattro atti. [In verse.] pp. 90. Milano, 1877. 8°.   **11715. bbb. 11.**

—— [Frine.] Phryne. A drama in four acts and a prologue with an introduction. By Democritus—Castelvecchio [i.e. translated and edited by Democritus, pseudonym of Frederick A. Laidlaw, from the Italian of Castelvecchio]. pp. 78. *University Press: Watford, London,* 1900. 8°.
11781. h. 33.

CASTELVERD (PAUL ÉMILE DE) Mémorial militaire des Français. [With plates and maps.] pp. iii. 533. *Paris,* 1846. 8°.   **1319. e. 3.**

CASTELVERO, GIUSEPPE MARIA ROBERTI, Count di. See ROBERTI.

CASTELVETERE (BERNARDO DA) See BERNARDO, da Castelvetere.

CASTELVETERE (FRANCESCO DI) See FRANCESCO, di Castelvetere, Dominican.

CASTELVETRANO.—Biblioteca Comunale. Notazione bibliografica degli incunabuli conservati nella Biblioteca Comunale di Castelvetrano. pp. 24. *Reggio d'Emilia,* 1935. 8°. [*Pubblicazioni della Scuola di Bibliografia Italiana.* no. 32.]   **Ac.9530.**

CASTELVETRANO.—Biblioteca Comunale.

—— [Another copy.] Notazione bibliografica degli incunabuli, etc. *Reggio d'Emilia,* 1935. 8°.   **11898. d. 50.**

CASTELVETRI (GIACOPO) See CASTELVETRO.

CASTELVETRO (GIACOMO) See CASTELVETRO (Giacopo)

CASTELVETRO (GIACOPO) Son of Giovanni Maria Castelvetro. See PETRARCA (F.) [*Canzoniere.—Italian.*] Le Rime del Petrarca breuemente sposte per Lodouico Casteluetro. [Edited by G. Castelvetro.] 1582. 4°.
638. h. 6.

CASTELVETRO (GIACOPO) Son of Nicolò Castelvetro. See ERASTUS (T.) Varia opuscula medica, etc. [Edited by G. Castelvetro.] 1590. fol.   **40. f. 13. (2.)**

—— See GUARINI (G. B.) Il Pastor fido, etc. [Edited by G. Castelvetro. 1591. 12°.   **1071. a. 20. (2.)**

—— See PORTA (G. B. della) of Naples. De furtiuis literarum notis, etc. [Edited by G. Castelvetro.] 1591. 4°.
787. e. 33.

—— See ROSENBERG (Eleanor) Giacopo Castelvetro, Italian Publisher in Elizabethan London, and his Patrons, etc. [1943.] 8°.   **10635. e. 30.**

—— See STELLA (J. C.) Iulii Caesaris Stellae . . . Columbeidos libri priores duo. [Edited by G. Castelvetro.] 1585. 4°.   **837. g. 14. (1.)**

CASTELVETRO (GIOVANNI MARIA) See CASTELVETRO (L.) Correttione d'alcune cose del Dialogo delle Lingue di Benedetto Varchi. [Edited by G. M. Castelvetro.] 1572. 4°.   **627. g. 7.**

CASTELVETRO (LODOVICO) See also DUBBIOSO, Accademico, pseud. [i.e. L. Castelvetro.]

—— See ARISTOTLE. [*Poetica.—Greek and Italian.*] Poetica d'Aristotile vulgarizzata, et sposta per L. Casteluetro. 1570. 4°.   **C. 76. b. 8.**

—— —— 1576. 4°.   **75. d. 7.**

—— See CAPASSO (D. A.) Note critiche su la polemica tra Annibal Caro e Ludovico Castelvetro. 1897. 8°.
011852. h. 2.

—— See CAVAZZUTI (G.) Lodovico Castelvetro. 1903. 8°.
10633. g. 5.

—— See CHARLTON (Henry B.) Castelvetro's Theory of Poetry. 1913. 8°. [*Publications of the University of Manchester. Comparative Literature Series.* no. 1.]
Ac. 2671/12.

—— See DANTE ALIGHIERI. [*Divina Commedia.—Italian.—Inferno.*] Sposizione di L. Castelvetro a XXIX canti dell' Inferno dantesco, etc. 1886. 4°.   **11420. i. 2.**

—— See MUZIO (G.) *Giustinopolitano.* Battaglie di Hieronimo Mutio (per difesa dell'Italica lingua) . . . Con vn trattato, intitolato la Varchina: doue si correggono . . . non pochi errori del Varchi, del Casteluetro, etc. 1582. 8°.
627. d. 14.

—— —— 1743. 8°.   **627. d. 15.**

—— See PETRARCA (F.) [*Canzioniere.—Italian.*] Le Rime del Petrarca breuemente sposte per L. Casteluetro. 1582. 4°.   **638. h. 6.**

—— —— 1756. 4°.   **638. i. 6.**

—— —— 1832. 8°.   **1070. m. 13.**

—— —— 1837. 8°.   **1463. g. 6.**

—— See SANDONNINI (T.) Lodovico Castelvetro e la sua famiglia, etc. 1882. 8°.   **10631. df. 54.**

CASTELVETRO (LODOVICO)

—— Opere varie critiche . . . non più stampate, colla vita dell'autore scritta dal sig. proposto Lodovico Antonio Muratori. [Edited by Filippo Argellati. With a portrait.] pp. 326. *Berna* [*Milan*], 1727. 4°. **71. c. 11.**

—— Correttione d'alcune cose del Dialogo delle Lingue di Benedetto Varchi, et vna giunta al primo libro delle Prose di Pietro Bembo, doue si ragiona della vulgar lingua. [Edited by Giovanni Maria Castelvetro.] pp. 290. [*P. Perna:*] *Basilæa*, 1572. 4°. **627. g. 7.**

—— [Another copy.] **72. c. 21.**

—— Correzione d'alcune cose nel Dialogo delle lingue di Benedetto Varchi. pp. 129. *See* VARCHI (B.) L'Ercolano, *etc.* tom. 2. 1744. 8°. **627. d. 23, 24.**

—— [Another edition.] *See* VARCHI (B.) L'Ercolano, *etc.* 1846. 8°. **1331. f. 16.**

—— Giunta fatta al ragionamento degli articoli et de' verbi di Messer Pietro Bembo [contained in his "Prose," bk. 3.] [By L. Castelvetro.] ff. 90. 1563. 4°. *See* BEMBO (P.) *Cardinal.* [*Prose.—Appendix.*] **12942. c. 4.**

—— [Another edition.] 1643. 4°. [*Degli autori del ben parlare per secolari e religiosi opere diverse.* pt. 1. tom. 3.] *See* BEMBO (P.) *Cardinal.* [*Prose.—Appendix.*] **836. e. 8.**

—— Le Giunte di L. Castelvetro, non solo quelle che prima vedevansi stampate separatamente, ma ancora alcune altre, che conservansi manuscritte nella libreria del ·.. Duca di Modona. *See* BEMBO (P.) *Cardinal.* [*Prose.*] Le Prose di M. Pietro Bembo, *etc.* 1714. 4°. **627. f. 11.**

—— Lettera . . . a M. Antonio Modona a · Brissello del lustro e dell'Olimpiada, con altre lettere del medesimo autore. 1752. *See* CALOGIERÀ (A.) Raccolta d'opuscoli scientifici, *etc.* tom. 47. 1728, *etc.* 12°. **247. c. 16.**

—— Lettera . . . scritta a M. Guasparro Calori a Roma del traslatare. 1747. *See* CALOGIERÀ (A.) Raccolta d'opuscoli scientifici, *etc.* tom. 37. 1728, *etc.* 12°. **247. c. 6.**

—— Ragione d'alcune cose segnate nella canzone d'Annibal Caro, Venite al'ombra de gran gigli d'oro. [By L. Castelvetro.] ff. 116. [1559.] 4°. *See* CARO (A.) **1089. m. 6. (2.)**

—— Di M. Lodouico Casteluetro Ragioni d'alcune cose segnate nella Canzone di Messer Annibal Caro. Venite a l'ombra de gran Gigli d'oro. ff. 176. FEW MS. NOTES. *Appresso A. Arriuabene: Venetia*, 1560. 8°. **1071. e. 26. (1.)**

—— [Another copy.] **240. f. 23.**

—— [Another edition.] ff. 180. 1573. 8°. *See* CARO (A.) **11805. aa. 18.**

—— Apologia de gli academici di Banchi di Roma, contra M. Lodouico Casteluetro da Modena. In forma d'uno Spaccio di Maestro Pasquino. Con alcune opere del Predella, del Buratto, di Ser Fedocco. In difesa de la seguente Canzone del Commendatore Annibal Caro, *etc.* [By Annibale Caro, replying to Lodovico Castelvetro's criticisms of his poem "Venite all' ombra dei gran gigli d'oro".] pp. 268. *Seth Viotto: Parma*, 1558. 4°. **1089. m. 7.**

—— [Another copy.] **1089. m. 6. (1.)**

—— [Another copy.] **72. c. 4.**

CASTELVETRO (LODOVICO)

—— [Another edition.] Spaccio di Maestro Pasquino romano a Messer Lodouico Casteluetro da Modena, *etc.* pp. 120. *Seth Viotto: Parma*, 1573. 8°. **1071. e. 26. (2.)** *The index has a separate titlepage reading "Apologia de gli academici di Banchi di Roma, etc."*

—— [Another copy.] **1458.a.25.**

—— Apologia degli academici di Banchi di Roma contro M. Lodovico Castelvetro da Modena, *etc.* [Edited by R. Bondi.] pp. 201. *Firenze*, 1819. 8°. **1440. h. 9.**

—— Difesa della Vita di Lodovico Castelvetro. [By L. A. Muratori. A reply to the criticisms of G. Fontanini in "Dell'eloquenza italiana," on Muratori's "Vita di Castelvetro."] pp. 62. [1730?] 4°. **112. b. 29.**

CASTELVÌ (AGOSTINO DI) *Marquis de Laconi.* *See* CASTELVÍ Y LANÇA (Agustín)

CASTELVI (JOSEF DELITALA Y) *See* DELITALA Y CASTELVI.

CASTELVITREUS (JACOBUS) *See* CASTELVETRO (Giacopo)

CASTELVÍ Y LANÇA (AGUSTÍN) *Marquis dę Laconi.*

—— *See* SCANO (D.) Donna Francesca di Zatrillas, marchesa di Laconi e di Sietefuentes. Notizie sugli avvenimenti che nel 1668 culminarono con gli omicidi del marchese di Laconi don Agostino di Castelvì e del marchese di Camarassa don Manuele Gomez de los Cobos, vicerè di Sardegna. [With genealogical tables.] 1946. 8°. [*Archivio storico sardo.* vol. 23. fasc. 1/4.] **Ac. 6501.**

—— *See* SPAIN. [*Laws, etc.—*IV. Charles II., *King.* 1665–1700.] *Begin.* Don Carlos segundo por la gracia de Dios, Rey de Castilla, *etc.* [Proclamations for the apprehension of Francisca de Castelvi, Marchioness de Laconi, charged with the murder of the Marquis de Laconi.] [1669.] fol. **704. h. 16. (14.)**

CASTELVÍ Y LANÇA (FRANCISCA DE) *Marchioness de Laconi.*

—— *See* SCANO (D.) Donna Francesca di Zatrillas, marchesa di Laconi e di Sietefuentes. Notizie sugli avvenimenti che nel 1668 culminarono con gli omicidi del marchese di Laconi don Agostino di Castelvì e del marchese di Camarassa don Manuelle Gomez de los Cobos, vicerè di Sardegna. 1946. 8°. [*Archivio storico sardo.* vol. 23. fasc. 1/4.] **Ac. 6501.**

—— *See* SPAIN. [*Laws, etc.—*IV. Charles II., *King.* 1665–1700.] *Begin.* Don Carlos segundo por la gracia de Dios, Rey de Castilla, *etc.* [Proclamations for the apprehension of Francisca de Castelvi, Marchioness de Laconi, charged with the murder of the Marquis de Laconi.] [1669.] fol. **704. h. 16. (14.)**

CASTENBAUER (STEPHAN) *the Elder.* Artickel wider Doctor Steffan Castenpaur. Eingelegt, auch was er darauf geantwort hat, *etc.* [*H. Steyner: Augsburg,*] 1523. 4°. **3906. e. 26.**

—— [Another edition.] [*Augsburg ?*] 1523. 4°. **3905. d. 87.**

—— Ain köstlicher gutter notwendiger Sermon, võ Sterbē wie sich der mensch darzu schicken soll mit etlichen Schlüssredē vom leyden Christi, *etc.* [*H. Steyner: Augsburg,*] 1523. 4°. **3905. d. 97.**

CASTENBAUER (STEPHAN) *the Younger.* *See* HEYDEN (S.) Kurtzer . . . Vnterricht von Heiliger Christlicher Lahr . . . Verdeutschet durch Stephanum Agricolam [i.e. S. Castenbauer]. 1551. 8°. **3906. aaa. 131.**

CASTENBAUER (STEPHAN) *the Younger.*

—— *See* MANSFELD, *Pastors in.* Der Prediger in der herrschafft Mansfelt antwort auff Stephani Agricole . . . aussgegangene schlussreden vnd schmeschrifften, *etc.* 1553. 4°.   **3906. i. 32. (7.)**

—— *See* MEIER (Georg) *Professor of Theology at Wittenberg.* Historia von S. Pauli . . . leben . . . Verdeudscht durch M. Stephanum Agricolam. 155[6]. 8°. **1016. f. 32. (2.)**

—— *See* NOGUERA (J.) De ecclesia Christi ab haereticorum conciliabulis dinoscenda præclari libri duo, *etc.* [Edited by S. Castenbauer.] 1560. fol.   **4520. f. 8. (1.)**

—— *See* SPANGENBERG (C.) Wider die böse Sieben ins Teufels Karnöffelspiel. (Wider den Gottlosen Apostaten Stephanum Agricolam.) 1562. 4°.   **3906. h. 115.**

CASTENDYCK (ELSA)

—— *See* STONE (Sybil A.) Children in the Community . . . [By] S. A. Stone, E. Castendyck, *etc.* 1946. 8°. [*Federal Security Agency. Social Security Administration. Children's Bureau. Publication.* no. 317.]   **A.S. 79.**

CASTENDYK (HERMANN) Das Infanterie-Regiment " Herzog Ferdinand von Braunschweig "—8. Westfälisches Nr. 57—in Weltkriege. Nach den amtlichen Kriegstage-büchern und persönlichen Aufzeichnungen bearbeitet . . . Mit 7 Karten, *etc.* pp. 104.   *Oldenburg, Berlin,* 1926. 8°.   [*Erinnerungsblätter deutscher Regimenter. Truppenteile des ehemaligen preussischen Kontingents.* Bd. 161.]   **8836. e. 1/161.**

—— Das Kgl. Preuss. Infanterie-Regiment " Herzog Ferdinand von Braunschweig "—8. Westfälisches Nr. 57—im Weltkrieg, 1914-1918. Nach amtlichen Unterlagen und Aufzeichnungen von Mitkämpfern bearbeitet. [With plates and maps.] pp. 230.   *Oldenburg,* 1936. 8°. [*Erinnerungsblätter deutscher Regimenter. Truppenteile des ehemaligen preussischen Kontingents.* Bd. 364.]   **8836. e. 1/364.**

CASTENFELT (TORSTEN)

—— Toothbrushing and Massage in Periodontal Disease. An experimental clinical histologic study. (Translated by Stanley Vernon.) [A thesis. With plates.] pp. 115. *Stockholm,* 1952. 8°.   **07611. l. 10.**

CASTENHOLZ (A.) Die Belagerung von Belfort im Jahre 1870, 71, *etc.* [With maps and plans.] 4 Tl. *Berlin,* 1875-78. 8°.   **9079. cc. 31.**

CASTENHOLZ (WILLIAM BURTIS) The Control of Distribution Costs and Sales. pp. viii. 194. *Harper & Bros.: New York & London,* 1930. 8°.   **08245. k. 48.**

CASTENIUS (HULDERICUS) *pseud.* [i.e. CHRISTIANUS BECMANUS.] *See also* BECMANUS (C.)

—— D. Matthiæ Höe neun vnd neunzig vnverschämbte handtgreiffliche Vnwarheiten, vnd vndoctorische, elende Schützereyen, mit welchen er die Reformierten . . . bey dem einfältigen Mann in den schweren Verdacht zu setzen sich bearbeitet . . . Zur Rettung der Reformierten Kirchen Vnschuldt . . . an den Tag gegeben durch H. Castenium. pp. 361. 1621. 4°.   **3907. b. 1.**

CASTENPAUR (STEPHAN) *See* CASTENBAUER.

CASTENS (A.) Über " Eins ist Noth," " Unum Necessarium " von J. A. Comenius. Vortrag. pp. 22. *Znaim,* 1892. 8°. [*Comenius-Studien.* Hft. 4.] **4888. c. 19.**

CASTENS (A.)

—— Was muss uns veranlassen, im Jahre 1892 das Andenken des A. Comenius festlich zu begehen ? Vortrag. pp. 24. *Znaim,* 1892. 8°. [*Comenius-Studien.* Hft. 1.]   **4888. c. 19.**

CASTENS (C.) De Oost-Indische Maatschappij van Administratie en Lijfrente . . . Derde brochure. Een woord over het door de directie . . . aan hare crediteuren voorgestelde accord, *etc.* pp. 47. *Rotterdam,* 1871. 8°.   **8023. f. 22. (6.)**

CASTENS (HERBERT ERNEST) An Investigation of the Soil Conditions in Compartment 1, Bwet Reserve, Prome Division, with reference to the dying off of Tectona grandis. pp. 14. *Rangoon,* 1927. 8°.   [*Burma Forest Bulletin.* no. 18.]   **I.S. BU. 151/8.**

CASTENS (MAURITIUS) De meretricibus currum Achab abluentibus, 1 Regum XXII. 38. *See* HASE (T.) and IKEN (C.) Thesaurus novus theologico-philologicus, *etc.* pt. 1. 1732. fol.   **L.16.f.2.**

—— De præsagiis locustarum incertis et falsis, *etc. Praes.* J. C. Örtlob. pp. 31. *Lipsiæ,* [1713.] 4°.   **B. 435. (5.)**

—— De Zacharia, Barachiæ filio, ad Matth. xxiii. v. 35. *See* HASE (T.) and IKEN (C.) Thesaurus novus theologico-philologicus, *etc.* pt. 2. 1732. fol.   **L.16.f.2.**

CASTENSEN (MATURIN) *See* MADSEN (J.) Magister Maturin Castensen, et Tidsbillede fra det attende Aarhundredes første Halvdel. 1906. 8°. [*Fra Ribe Amt.* no. 4.]   **Ac. 7645.**

CASTENSKIOLD (CHR. C. L. VON) *See* COPENHAGEN.— *Kongeligt Dansk Genealogisk og Heraldisk Selskab.* Lexicon over Adelige Familier, *etc.* (Supplement ved C. C. L. v. Castenskiold.) [1780, *etc.*] 4°.   **1328. c. 8.**

CASTER (ANDREW) Pearl Island . . . [A novel.] Illustrated by Florence Scovel Shinn. pp. v. 267. *Harper & Bros.: New York & London,* 1903. 8°.   **012707. aa. 33.**

CASTER (G. VAN) Histoire des rues de Malines et de leurs monuments. pp. xxxii. 380. *Malines,* 1882. 8°.   **10271. bbb. 11.**

—— Malines. Guide historique et description des monuments, *etc.* pp. 165. *Bruges,* [1887.] 8°.   **10271. aaa. 17.**

CASTER (HEINRICH) Die Histologie nach ihrem neuesten Standpunkte, *etc.* pp. 128. *Berlin,* 1874. 8°.   **7407. aa. 19.**

CASTER (KENNETH EDWARD)

—— *See* VON ENGELN (Oscar D.) and CASTER (K. E.) Geology. 1952. 8°.   **7112. bb. 3.**

——   A Devonian Fauna from Colombia . . . Including stratigraphic notes by Axel A. Olsson. pp. 192. pl. 14. *Ithaca, N.Y.,* 1939. 8°. [*Bulletins of American Paleontology.* vol. 24. no. 83.]   **Ac. 2692. g/12.**

CASTER (MARCEL)

—— *See* CLEMENT, *of Alexandria.* [*Stromata.*] Les Stromates . . . Traduction et notes de M. Caster. 1951, *etc.* 8°.   **W.P. A. 481/30.**

——   Études sur Alexandre ou le Faux prophète de Lucien. [With the Greek text and a French translation. By M. Caster.] pp. lxv. 102. 1938. 8°. *See* LUCIAN, *of Samosata.* [*Alexander seu Pseudomantis.*]   **11311. i. 2.**

CASTER (Marcel)

—— Lucien et la pensée religieuse de son temps. [With a bibliography.] pp. 412. *Paris*, 1937. 8°.
11311. i. 1.

CASTÉRA (Constantin) *See* Erasmus (D.) [*Two or more Works.—French.*] Œuvres d'Érasme. (Publiées par les soins de C. Castéra.) 1933, *etc.* 8°. **11409. l. 37.**

—— Le Livre de Diogène le cynique. [With illustrations.] pp. 408. *Paris*, 1950. 8°. **10608. df. 41.**

CASTÉRA (Jacques) Essai sur l'ophtalmie. Thèse, *etc.* pp. 25. *Montpellier*, 1833. 4°. **1181. f. 17. (15.)**

CASTÉRA (Jean Henri) *See* Barrow (*Sir* John) *Bart.* Voyage en Chine . . . Suivi de la relation de l'ambassade envoyée en 1719 à Peking . . . Traduits de l'anglais, avec des notes, par J. Castéra. [1805.] 8°.
566. d. 10, 11.

—— *See* Browne (William George) Nouveau voyage dans la Haute et Basse Égypte, la Syrie, le Dar-Four . . . Traduit de l'anglais . . . par J. Castéra. 1800. 8°.
1046. h. 17, 18.

—— *See* Bruce (James) *the Traveller.* Voyage en Nubie et en Abyssinie . . . Traduit . . . par M. Castéra. 1790, *etc.* 4°. **10096. gg. 19.**

—— *See* Bruce (James) *the Traveller.* Voyage aux sources du Nil en Nubie et en Abyssinie . . . Traduit . . . par J. H. Castéra. 1790, *etc.* 8°. **10096. ee. 22.**

—— *See* Catharine II., *Empress of Russia.* [*Two or more Works.*] Théâtre de l'Hermitage, *etc.* [Edited by J. H. Castéra.] [1799.] 8°. **86. d. 13, 14.**

—— *See* China. Voyage en Chine et en Tartarie de l'ambassade de Lord Macartney, *etc.* [An abridgment by Count A. Mahé de la Bourdonnais of J. H. Castéra's translation of " Travels in China," by Sir John Barrow.] [1896.] 8°. **010057. f. 38.**

—— *See* Kippis (Andrew) Vie du capitaine Cook, traduite de l'anglois [by J. H. Castéra]. 1789. 8°. **1202. f. 5.**

—— *See* Mackenzie (*Sir* Alexander) Tableau historique et politique du commerce des pelleteries dans le Canada . . . Traduit . . . par J. Castéra, *etc.* 1807. 8°.
1304. h. 12.

—— *See* Marshall (Edmund) *Vicar of Charing.* Edmond et Eléonora . . . Traduit de l'anglais, par un homme qui aime les mœurs simples [i.e. J. H. Castéra]. 1797. 12°.
12808. u. 18.

—— *See* Rennell (James) Description historique et géographique de l'Indostan . . . Traduite . . . par J. B. Boucheseiche . . . à laquelle on a joint des Mélanges d'histoire et de statistique sur l'Inde, traduits par J. Castéra, *etc.* 1800. 8°. **571. d. 27.**

—— *See* Staunton (*Sir* George L.) *Bart.* Voyage dans l'intérieur de la Chine, et en Tartarie, fait . . . par Lord Macartney . . . Traduit . . . avec des notes, par J. Castéra, *etc.* 1804. 8°. **566. d. 8.**

—— *See* Symes (Michael) Relation de l'ambassade anglaise envoyée en 1795 dans le royaume d'Ava . . . Suivie d'un Voyage fait, en 1798, à Colombo . . . et à la baie de Da Lagoa . . . Traduits . . . avec des notes, par J. Castéra. 1800. 8°. **10057. c. 2.**

—— *See* Turner (Samuel) *Captain in the East India Company's Service.* Ambassade au Thibet et au Boutan . . . Traduit . . . avec des notes par J. Castéra, *etc.* 1800. 8°. **566. d. 15.**

—— Odes. pp. 116. *Amsterdam*, 1785. 12°.
1065. a. 37.

CASTÉRA (Jean Henri)

—— Vie de Catherine II, Impératrice de Russie. [By J. H. Castéra.] Avec six portraits gravés en taille-douce. 2 tom. 1797. 8°. *See* Catharine II., *Empress of Russia.* [*Appendix.*—I. *Biography.—General.*]
151. c. 12, 13.

—— [Another edition.] Histoire de Catherine II, Impératrice de Russie . . . Avec seize portraits ou cartes, gravés en taille-douce [including a portrait of the author]. 3 tom. *Paris*, an VIII [1800]. 8°. **151. c. 9–11.**

—— The History of the Reigns of Peter III. and Catharine II. of Russia. Translated from the French [of J. H. Castéra's " Vie de Catherine II "] and enlarged with explanatory notes, *etc.* 2 vol. 1798. 8°. *See* Peter III., *Emperor of Russia.* [*Appendix.*—I. *Biography.—General.*]
9455. c. 23.

—— The Life of Catharine II., Empress of Russia. An enlarged translation from the French [of J. H. Castéra, by W. Tooke]. With seven portraits . . . and a correct map of the Russian Empire. 3 vol. 1798. 8°. *See* Catharine II., *Empress of Russia.* [*Appendix.*—I. *Biography.—General.*] **10790. cc. 28.**

—— The third edition, with considerable improvements. 3 vol. 1799. 8°. *See* Catharine II., *Empress of Russia.* [*Appendix.*—I. *Biography.—General.*] **989. b. 18–20.**

—— The fourth edition, with great additions and a copious index. 3 vol. 1800. 8°. *See* Catharine II., *Empress of Russia.* [*Appendix.*—I. *Biography.—General.*]
1200. f. 12–14.

—— The fifth edition, with great additions and a copious index, *etc.* 3 vol. 1800. 8°. *See* Catharine II., *Empress of Russia.* [*Appendix.*—I. *Biography.—General.*]
610. h. 24.

—— History of Catharine II. Empress of Russia . . . Translated from the French by Henry Hunter . . . Embellished with thirteen portraits, *etc.* pp. 579. *J. Stockdale: London*, 1800. 8°. **1200. f. 27.**

—— Geheime Lebens- und Regierungsgeschichte Katharinens der Zweiten, Kaiserin von Russland . . . Aus dem Französischen [of J. H. Castéra] . . . Mit sechs Porträts. 2 Bd. 1798. 8°. *See* Catharine II., *Empress of Russia.* [*Appendix.*—I. *Biography.—General.*] **10790. c. 21.**

—— Zweyte, verbesserte Ausgabe. 2 Bd. 1798. 8°. *See* Catharine II., *Empress of Russia.* [*Appendix.*—I. *Biography.—General.*] **10790. bb. 11.**

—— Leben Katharinens der Zweiten . . . Aus dem Französischen [of J. H. Castéra]. Bd. 1, 2. 1798. 8°. *See* Catharine II., *Empress of Russia.* [*Appendix.*—I. *Biography.—General.*] **1200. b. 6.**

CASTÉRA (Jean Pierre Paul) Essai sur les accidens qui peuvent compliquer l'opération de la taille par l'appareil latéral, et sur la manière de les prévenir ou de les combattre, *etc.* pp. 98. *Paris*, 1802. 8°. **1182. b. 8. (5.)**

CASTÉRA (Louis Adrien Duperron de) *See* Duperron de Castéra.

CASTÉRA (Noël) *See also* Pornin (   ) *Ex-commandant en chef des Montagnards, pseud.* [i.e. N. Castéra ?]

—— *See* Miot (J.) Réponse aux deux libelles : les Conspirateurs, et la Naissance de la République, *etc.* [Edited by N. Castéra.] 1850. 12°. **1320. a. 31.**

—— Le Triomphe de la liberté, ou Histoire . . . de la Révolution des 22, 23, et 24, février, 1848 . . . Ornée des portraits de tous les membres du gouvernement provisoire, *etc.* pp. 252. *Paris*, [1848.] 12°.
1319. b. 4.

Imperfect ; wanting the portraits.

CASTÉRA (Romain) Thèse pour le doctorat en médecine, *etc.* (Questions sur diverses branches des sciences médicales.) pp. 25. *Paris*, 1842. 4º. [*Collection des thèses soutenues à la Faculté de Médecine de Paris. An* 1842. tom. 3.] **7371. c. 17.**

CASTERAN (   ) Second numéro. Liberté. Égalité. Les Hommes de sang démasqués, ou les Meneurs du Club de Bordeaux, dénoncés à la Convention nationale, au réprésentant Threillard, et à l'opinion publique. [Signed by Casteran and others.] pp. 19. [*Paris*, 1795.] 4º. **F. 47*. (3.)**

—— Troisième numero. Tableau expositif présenté au représentans du peuple Boussion et Treilhard, envoyé à la Convention nationale et aux principales communes de la République par les citoyens Casteran, Dutasta, *etc.* pp. 8. [*Paris*, 1795?] 4º. **F. 4. (47*.)**

CASTERAN (Adolphe) Du typhus des camps observé en Crimée pendant le siége de Sébastopol. Thèse, *etc.* pp. 35. *Montpellier*, 1856. 4º. **7379. c. 20. (3.)**

CASTÉRAN (Almire) De la variole au point de vue de son traitement. Thèse, *etc.* pp. 38. *Montpellier*, 1855. 4º. **7379. c. 14. (3.)**

CASTERAN (Augustin) L'Algérie d'aujourd'hui. 20 illustrations hors texte. pp. 213. *Alger-Mustapha*, 1905. 8º. **010095. de. 47.**

—— L'Algérie française de 1884 à nos jours, *etc.* pp. vii. 310. *Paris*, [1900.] 8º. **010097. f. 40.**

—— Madame de Rennecy. Pièce en 3 actes, *etc.* pp. 48. *Alger*, 1890. 8º. **11740. cc. 1. (8.)**

—— Les Troubles d'Alger. pp. 70. *Alger*, 1898. 8º. **09004. aaa. 6. (6.)**

CASTERAN (Bernard) Dissertation sur la pyrosis ou fer chaud, *etc.* pp. 51. *Paris*, 1821. 4º. **1183. f. 13. (30.)**

CASTERAN (Étienne Auguste Eléonor) Considérations sur quelques points relatifs à l'aménorrhée. Tribut académique, *etc.* pp. 28. *Montpellier*, 1837. 4º. **1181. h. 10. (3.)**

CASTERAN (J. M.) De l'apoplexie pulmonaire. pp. 68. *Paris*, 1869. 4º. [*Collection des thèses soutenues à la Faculté de Médecine de Paris. An* 1869. tom. 3.] **7373. k. 9.**

CASTERAS (Marcel)

—— Recherches sur la structure du versant nord des Pyrénées centrales et orientales. pp. 525. pl. ix. *Paris & Liége*, 1933. 8º. [*Bulletin des Services de la carte géologique de la France et des topographies souterraines.* tom. 37. no. 189.] **7108.g.4.**

CASTERAS (Paul de) La Révolution en province. Histoire de la Révolution française dans le pays de Foix, et dans l'Ariége. pp. 424. *Paris*, 1876. 8º. **9226. i. 1.**

—— La Société toulousaine à la fin du dix-huitième siècle. L'ancien régime et la Révolution. pp. viii. 363. *Toulouse*, 1891. 8º. **010171. e. 8.**

CASTÉRAS-VILLEMARTIN (Jacques Adolphe Marie Pons François de Paule) *Viscount.* Historique du 16e Régiment de Dragons . . . Illustrations en couleurs, par M. le lieutenant Rozat de Mandres. pp. 208. *Paris*, 1892. 4º. **8825. g. 32.**

CASTÉRÉS (Paul) Des grossesses extra-utérines. Thèse, *etc.* pp. 74. *Montpellier*, 1876. 4º. **7379. k. 14. (8.)**

CASTERET (Norbert) Ten Years Under the Earth . . . Translated and edited by Barrows Mussey. [An abridgment of "Dix ans sous terre" and "Au fond des gouffres." With illustrations, including portraits.] pp. xx. 283. *Greystone Press: New York*, [1938.] 8º. **2249. g. 13.**

—— [Another edition.] pp. xv. 240. *J. M. Dent & Sons: London*, 1939. 8º. **07108. b. 32.**

—— Ten Years under the Earth. (Translated and edited by Burrows Massey [or rather, by Barrows Mussey].) pp. 200. pl. 32. *Penguin Books: Harmondsworth*, 1952. 8º. [*Penguin Books.* no. 846.] **12208. a. 1/846.**

—— Au fond des gouffres. [An account of subterranean exploration. With illustrations and a portrait.] pp. xvi. 293. *Paris*, 1936. 8º. **07108. a. 23.**

—— Dans les glaces souterraines les plus élevées du monde. Album illustré de 18 héliogravures. pp. 93. *Paris*, 1953. 4º. **7112. c. 27.**

—— Dix ans sous terre. Campagnes d'un explorateur solitaire. [An account of archeological exploration in the Pyrenees. With plates, including portraits.] pp. 314. *Paris*, 1933. 8º. **07704. de. 54.**

—— E-A. Martel, explorateur du monde souterrain. [With plates.] pp. 232. [*Paris*,] 1950. 8º. **10666. c. 4.**

—— [Exploration.] Cave Men New and Old . . . Translated by R. L. G. Irving. With . . . plates [including portraits]. pp. xiii. 178. *J. M. Dent & Sons: London*, 1951. 8º. **07106. e. 55.**

—— [Mes cavernes.] My Caves . . . Translated by R. L. G. Irving. With 26 illustrations [including a portrait], *etc.* pp. xi. 172. *J. M. Dent & Sons: London*, 1947. 8º. **7111. b. 42.**

—— Ténèbres. [With illustrations.] pp. xiii. 274. *Paris*, 1952. 8º. **7111. de. 6.**

—— [Ténèbres.] The Darkness under the Earth, *etc.* [With plates, including portraits.] pp. xiv. 168. *J. M. Dent & Sons: London*, 1954. 8º. **7112. aa. 30.**

—— [Trente ans sous terre.] The Descent of Pierre Saint-Martin . . . Translated by John Warrington, *etc.* [With plates, including portraits.] pp. xi. 160. *J. M. Dent & Sons: London*, 1955. 8º. **7922. f. 3.**

CASTERLÉ. *See* Casterlee.

CASTERLEE. Coutumes de Casterlé. *Dutch & Fr.* 1878. *See* Longé (G. P. de) Coutumes du pays et duché de Brabant. Quartier d'Anvers, *etc.* tom. 7. 1870, *etc.* 4º. **5686.g.1/1b.**

CASTERMANS (Auguste) Parallèle des maisons de Bruxelles et des principales villes de la Belgique, construites depuis 1830 jusqu'à nos jours, représentées en plans, élévations, coupes & détails intérieurs et extérieurs, mesurées et dessinées par A. Castermans, *etc.* 2 sér. *Paris, Liége*; [*Liége* printed], [1856–67.] fol. **1264.h.26.**

CASTERTON.—*School for Clergymen's Daughters.* Tenth [*etc.*] Report of the School for Clergymen's Daughters at Casterton, for the year 1837 (1838, 1841, 1842, 1845, 1853). *Kirkby Lonsdale*, 1838[–54]. 8º. **8367. e. 11.**

CASTET (   ) Quelques considérations sur les oreillons. Thèse, *etc.* pp. 64. *Montpellier*, 1876. 4º. **7379. k. 14. (14.)**

CASTET (C. DE) Considérations sur les corps fibreux utérins dans la grossesse et l'accouchement. pp. 42. *Paris*, 1874. 4°. [*Collection des thèses soutenues à la Faculté de Médecine de Paris.* An 1874. tom. 3.]
7374. a. 8.

CASTET (JEAN) *See* BUK (P.) La Tragédie tchécoslovaque de septembre 1938 à mars 1939 . . . Traduit par H. Jacob et J. Castet, *etc.* 1939. 8°. **09315. df. 61.**

CASTET (PIERRE HIPPOLYTE DE) Dissertation sur les tumeurs blanches ou lymphatiques des articulations en général; thèse, *etc.* pp. 23. *Paris*, 1833. 4°.
1184. f. 3. (26.)

CASTETBERT (B. H. M.) De la bronchotomie et de ses indications; thèse, *etc.* pp. 32. *Paris*, 1834. 4°.
1184. f. 9. (15.)

CASTETBIEILH (J.) Des caractères chimiques que présente l'urine dans certaines affections de l'appareil urinaire, *etc.* pp. 29. *Paris*, 1839. 4°. [*Collection des thèses soutenues à la Faculté de Médecine de Paris.* An 1839. tom. 3.] **7371. a. 3.**

CASTETPIVERT (ANDRÉ ALEXANDRE DE) Essai sur les maladies aiguës de poitrine connues sous le nom de pleurésie et de péripneumonie. Thèse, *etc.* pp. 28. *Montpellier*, 1836. 4°. **1181. g. 16. (24.)**

CASTETS (   ) Lettres sur la propagation de la culture des graines oléagineuses à messieurs les agriculteurs des Hautes-Pyrénées . . . Première lettre. Le Colza, sa culture, *etc.* pp. 8. *Tarbes*, [1863.] 4°.
7055. h. 13.

CASTETS (FERDINAND) *See* ALAMANNI (L.) *the Elder.* I Dodici canti. Épopée romanesque du XVIe siècle. Par F. Castets. 1908. 8°. [*Publications de la Société pour l'étude des langues romanes.* tom. 22.]
Ac. 9809/6.

—— *See* AYMON. [*Les Quatres fils Aymon.—Poetical Versions. —French.*] Les Quatre fils Aymon. [Edited by F. Castets.] 1906, *etc.* 8°. [*Revue des langues romanes.* sér. 5. tom. 9 ; sér. 6. tom. 2.] **Ac. 9809/2.**

—— *See* AYMON. [*Les Quatre fils Aymon.—Poetical Versions. —French.*] La Chanson des Quatre fils Aymon . . . Avec introduction, description des manuscrits, notes au texte et principales variantes, appendice où sont complétés l'examen et la comparaison des manuscrits et des diverses rédactions, par F. Castets. 1909. 8°. [*Publications de la Société pour l'étude des langues romanes.* tom. 24.]
Ac. 9809/6.

—— *See* CHARLES I., *Emperor of the West.* CHARLEMAGNE. [*Biography.*] Iter Hierosolymitanum, ou Voyage de Charlemagne à Jérusalem et à Constantinople, *etc.* [Edited by F. Castets.] 1892. 8°. [*Revue des langues romanes.* sér. 4. tom. 6.] **Ac. 9809/2.**

—— *See* DURANTE, *Ser.* Il Fiore . . . Texte inédit publié avec fac-simile, introduction et notes par F. Castets. 1881. 8°. [*Publications spéciales de la Société pour l'étude des langues romanes.* no. 9.] **Ac. 9809/6.**

—— *See* MAUGIST, *d'Aigremont.* Maugis d'Aigremont, Chanson de geste. [Edited by F. Castets.] 1892. 8°. [*Revue des langues romanes.* sér. 4. tom. 6.] **Ac. 9809/2.**

—— *See* TURPIN, *Archbishop of Rheims.* Turpini historia Karoli Magni et Rotholandi. Texte revu et complété . . . par F. Castets. 1880. 8°. [*Publications spéciales de la Société pour l'étude des langues romanes.* no. 7.]
Ac. 9809/6.

—— Bourdaloue. (Essai.) pp. 773. *Montpellier*, 1904 [1900, 04]. 8°. [*Académie des Sciences et Lettres de Montpellier. Mémoires de la section des lettres.* sér. 2. tom. 4.] **Ac. 378.**

CASTETS (FERDINAND)

—— Cyrano de Bergerac. Conférence, *etc.* pp. 53. *Montpellier*, 1900. 8°. **010662. k. 48.**

—— Eschine l'orateur. Thèse, *etc.* pp. xv. 187. *Nîmes*, 1872. 8°. **10606. g. 12.**

—— [A reissue.] Eschine. Étude historique et littéraire. pp. xlii. 191. *Paris*, 1875. 8°. **11312. h. 1.** *With the addition of an introduction. The appendix is of a different setting-up.*

—— Le VIe centenaire de Béatrix, 1290–1890. Leçon faite à la Faculté des Lettres de Montpellier. pp. 54. *Montpellier*, 1891. 8°. **11421. c. 24. (6.)**

CASTETS (FERDINAND) and **BERTHELÉ** (JOSEPH)

—— Notice sur les anciens inventaires des archives municipales de Montpellier. *See* MONTPELLIER. Archives de la ville de Montpellier, *etc.* tom. 1. 1895, *etc.* 4°. **10167. v.**

CASTETS (J.) *See* ROZ (F.) De erroribus Nestorianorum . . . Inédit latin-syriaque . . . retrouvé par le P. Castets, *etc.* 1928. 8°. [*Orientalia Christiana.* no. 40.]
Ac. 2002. bb.

—— Fr. Enrique Enriquez, " the Second Column of Xavier's Indian Mission." pp. 47. *Indian Catholic Truth Society: Trichinopoly*, 1926. 8°. **20018. f. 7.**

—— Logic. Inductive, deductive, and definition. pp. xix. 626. xxx. *St. Joseph's College Press: Trichinopoly*, 1905. 8°. **8467. de. 3.**

—— La Mission du Maduré. [With plates and maps.] pp. 93. *St. Joseph's Industrial School Press: Trichinopoly*, 1924. 8°. **20001. f. 35.**

—— The Madura Mission. [With plates and maps.] pp. 88. *St. Joseph's Industrial School Press: Trichinopoly*, 1924. 8°. **20017. i. 44.**

CASTEX (A.) *Professeur à l'Institut Électrotechnique de l'Université de Grenoble. See* BERGEON (P.) and CASTEX (A.) Lignes électriques aériennes, *etc.* 1919. 8°.
8764. aa. 31.

CASTEX (ADOLPHE)

—— Considérations sur les expertises médico-légales en matière d'aliénation mentale, *etc.* pp. 109. *Strasbourg*, 1868. 4°. [*Collection générale des dissertations de la Faculté de Médecine de Strasbourg.* sér. 3. tom. 5.]
7381.*f.

CASTEX (ANDRÉ)

—— *See* INTERNATIONAL MEDICAL CONGRESS. [Paris, 1900.] XIIIe Congrès international de médecine . . . Comptes rendus, *etc.* (vol. 13. Section d'otologie. Comptes rendus publiés par A. Castex.) [1901.] 8°. **Ac. 3699/12.**

—— Hygiène de la voix parlée et chantée. pp. 219. *Paris*, [1894.] 8°. [*Encyclopédie scientifique des aide-mémoire, etc.*] **08709. f. 31.**

—— Maladies du larynx, du nez et des oreilles . . . Troisième édition entièrement refondue et considérablement augmentée, *etc.* pp. vii. 1191. pl. IV. *Paris*, 1907 [1906]. 8°. **7616. ee. 17.**

CASTEX (EDMOND) Résistance électrique des tissus et du corps humain à l'état normal et pathologique. pp. 76. *Montpellier*, 1892. 8°. **07305. k. 14. (6.)**

CASTEX (GEORGES HUBERT DE) *See* HUBERT DE CASTEX.

CASTEX (J. J.) *de Fos, Haute-Garonne.* Questions de thèse tirées au sort. Sciences médicales, *etc.* pp. 22. *Montpellier*, 1840. 4º.   **1181**. i. **18**. (**7**.)

CASTEX (JACQUES JASON) Quelques considérations sur la fièvre typhoïde. pp. 54.   *Paris*, 1848. 4º. [*Collection des thèses soutenues à la Faculté de Médecine de Paris.* An 1848. tom. 3.]   **7372**. b. **6**.

CASTEX (LAURENT JEAN LÉON) Essai sur la cautérisation actuelle. Thèse, *etc.* pp. 31. *Montpellier*, 1851. 4º.
7379. b. **3**. (**20**.)

CASTEX (LOUIS HONORÉ) Essai sur l'avortement, *etc.* pp. 26. *Montpellier*, VII. R.F. [1799.] 4º.
1180. d. **4**. (**6**.)

CASTEX (MARIANO RAFAEL)

—— Algo de lo que la ciencia y la humanidad deben a la medicina británica. (Publicado en " La Prensa Médica Argentina.") pp. 16. 1941. 8º.   **7661**. b. **4**.

CASTEX (MAURICE DE) *See* CHAVANE (J. M.) Les Grands régiments disparus . . . Histoire du 11e Cuirassiers . . . Illustré par M. M. de Castex. 1889. 8º.   **8824**. i. **31**.

—— *See* OLLONE (C. A. M. C. d') Historique du 10e Régiment de Dragons . . . Illustration par M. de Castex, *etc.* 1893. 8º.   **8824**. k. **34**.

CASTEX (PIERRE GEORGES)

—— *See* BALZAC (H. de) [*Single Works.*] Mademoiselle du Vissard, ou la France sous le Consulat . . . Texte établi par P. G. Castex. 1950. 8º.   **12519**. e. **16**.

—— *See* VILLIERS DE L'ISLE-ADAM (J. M. M. P. A. de) *Count.* Reliques. Textes inédits réunis et présentés par P.-G. Castex. 1954. 8º.   **012359**. a. **49**.

—— Le Conte fantastique en France de Nodier à Maupassant. pp. 466. *Paris*, [1951.] 8º.   **11861**. f. **26**.

CASTEX (PIERRE JULES) De l'hémoptysie considérée au point de vue de l'étiologie et du diagnostic. Thèse, *etc.* pp. 59. *Montpellier*, 1860. 4º.   **7379**. e. **7**. (**7**.)

CASTEX (RAOUL VICTOR PATRICE) *See* DENIS DE RIVOYRE (C. L. M. C.) Histoire de la guerre navale 1914–1918. Avec une préface du capitaine de frégate Castex, *etc.* 1922. 8º.   **09084**. d. **2**.

—— De Gengis-Khan à Staline, ou les Vicissitudes d'une manœuvre stratégique, 1205–1935. pp. 188.   *Paris*, 1935. 8º.   **9058**. df. **36**.

—— L'Envers de la guerre de course. La vérité sur l'enlèvement du convoi de St.-Eustache par Lamotte-Picquet, avril—mai, 1781. [With a map.] pp. 55.   *Paris*, [1912.] 8º.   **09004**. dd. **11**. (**6**.)

—— Les Idées militaires de la Marine du XVIIIme siècle. De Ruyter à Suffren. [With plans.] pp. 371.   *Paris*, [1911.] 8º.   **08806**. g. **12**.

—— Jaunes contre blancs. Le problème militaire indochinois. Préface de M. François Deloncle. pp. 149. *Paris*, [1905.] 8º.   **8821**. g. **5**.

—— La Manœuvre de La Praya 16 avril 1781. Étude politique, stratégique et tactique, d'après des nombreux documents inédits. [With maps.] pp. 416.   *Paris*, 1912. 8º.   **8808**. f. **6**.

—— Le Péril japonais en Indo-Chine. Réflexions politiques et militaires. pp. 36. *Paris*, [1904.] 8º.   **8022**. cc. **51**.

—— Questions d'état-major. 2 tom. pp. 664.   *Paris*, [1923, 25.] 8º.   **08806**. g. **41**.

CASTEX (RAOUL VICTOR PATRICE)

—— Les Rivages indo-chinois. Étude économique et maritime. pp. xiv. 327. *Paris*, 1904. 8º.   **010057**. i. **28**.

—— Synthèse de la guerre sous-marine. De Pontchartrain à Tirpitz. pp. vi. 228. *Paris*, 1920. 8º. **09083**. dd. **22**.

—— Théories stratégiques. 5 tom. *Paris*, 1929–35. 8º.
8803. d. **10**.

—— Nouvelle édition revue et augmentée. [With maps.] tom. 1, 2. *Paris*, 1937, 39. 8º.   **8836**. dd. **8**.

CASTEX (RAYMOND) Sainte Livrade. Étude historique et critique sur sa vie, son martyre, ses reliques et son culte. pp. 258. *Lille*, 1890. 8º.   **4829**. e. **31**.

CASTI (ENRICO) L'Aquila degli Abruzzi ed il pontificato di Celestino V. *See* AQUILA, *City of.*—*Società di storia patria, etc.* Celestino V., *etc.* 1894. 8º.   **4856**. g. **17**.

—— Biblioteca provinciale Salvatore Tommasi nell'Aquila degli Abruzzi. Relazione finale . . . 1885–86. pp. 16. [1886.] 8º. *See* AQUILA, *City of.*—*Biblioteca provinciale Salvatore Tommasi.*   **011902**. k. **29**. (**2**.)

—— Dum honori et memoriae Sancti Ioannis a Capistrano qui . . . a Turcarum obsidione Albam Graecam liberavit Capistranenses tam magni civis . . . quingentesimum diei natalis anniversarium . . . concelebrant, Henrici Casti epinicion. pp. 3. *Aquilae*, 1885. 8º.
11409. gg. **28**. (**2**.)

CASTI (GIOVANNI BATTISTA) *See also* SQUARCIAFICO, *da Cogliariccia, Barbicazzita, pseud.* [i.e. G. B. Casti ?]

—— *See* BERGH (Herman van den) Giambattista Casti . . . L'homme et l'œuvre, *etc.* [With a portrait.] 1951. 8º.
10634. k. **28**.

—— Opere varie. [With a portrait.] 6 tom.   *Parigi*, 1821. 12º.   **11431**. aa. **8**.

—— Poesie liriche e drammatiche. 2 tom.   *Filadelfia*, 1803. 12º.   **640**. c. **31**.
The imprint is fictitious.

—— Melodrammi giocosi. [With a portrait.] pp. ix. 251. vii. *Milano*, 1824. 16º.   **639**. a. **38**.
Vol. 23 *of " Raccolta di poeti classici italiani antichi e moderni."*

—— Raccolta completa delle novelle galanti di G. B. Casti, *etc.* pp. vi. 337. *Brusselles*, 1827. 8º. **11436**. cc. **37**.

—— Opere scelte. *See* ITALIAN PARNASSUS. Parnaso italiano, *etc.* 1843. 8º.   **11422**. ff. **11**.

—— Epistolario inedito, curato dal prof. Quirino Ficari. pp. 83. *Montefiascone*, 1921. 8º.   **010905**. e. **53**.

—— Gli Animali parlanti, poema epico diviso in ventisei canti . . . Vi sono in fine aggiunti quattro Apologhi del medesimo autore non appartenenti al poema. 3 tom. *Parigi*, 1802. 8º.   **1063**. k. **1–3**.

—— [Another copy.] F.P.   G. **10839–41**.

—— [Another edition.] Con una spiegazione delle voci difficili, *etc.* 2 tom. *L. da Ponte: Londra*, 1803. 12º.
11431. bb. **16**.

—— [Another edition.] 3 tom. *Parigi*, 1820. 12º.
11431. cc. **41**.

—— [Another edition.] pp. 633.   *C. F. Molini: London*, 1822. 12º.   **11429**. c. **5**.

CASTI (GIOVANNI BATTISTA)

—— The Court of Beasts: translated from the Animali Parlanti of Giambattista Casti: a poem in seven cantos. [Translated by William S. Rose.] pp. 110. *W. Bulmer & Co.: London,* 1816. 12º. **11642. e. 18.**

—— [Another edition.] The Court and Parliament of Beasts, freely translated . . . by William Stewart Rose. pp. 119. *John Murray: London,* 1819. 8º.
993. e. 34. (4.)

—— Les Animaux parlans, poëme épique en vingt-six chants . . . Traduit en français, et en prose, par M. P. P. * * * [i.e. P. Paganel.] 3 tom. *Liége,* 1818. 12º.
11429. a. 26.

—— Die redenden Thiere. Ein episches Gedicht in sechsundzwanzig Gesängen . . . Aus dem Italiänischen übersetzt. [Translated by Carl J. L. Iken.] 3 Bd. *Bremen,* 1817. 8º. **11436. ee. 1.**

—— Los Animales parlantes: poema . . . vertido del italiano en rima castellana por Don Luis Maneyro. Segunda edicion. pp. 368. *Havre,* 1853. 8º. **11436. bbb. 48.**

—— L'Ane, apologue imité de Casti. [A prose translation by T. Vero of " L'Asino," one of the " Apologhi " published with " Gli Animali parlanti."] *See* VERO (T.) Luxure et mysticisme de François de Sales, *etc.* 1851. 16º.
4061. a. 27.

—— I Dormienti. *See* RACCOLTA. Raccolta di melodrammi giocosi, *etc.* 1826. 8º. **12201.p.1/345.**

—— La Grotta di Trofonio. *See* RACCOLTA. Raccolta di melodrammi giocosi, *etc.* 1826. 8º.**12201.p.1/345.**

—— Trofons Zauberhöle. Ein komisches Singspiel . . . Aus dem Italiänischen [of G. B. Casti] übersetzt von C. G. N. [i.e. C. G. Neefe], *etc.* pp. 77. 1787. 8º. *See* TROPHONIUS. **11747. de. 7. (5.)**

—— Notice sur Don Juan, drame bouffon en deux actes. Paroles de l'abbé Casti [or rather, by L. da Ponte], musique de Mozart. [By Victor E. P. Chasles. Extracted from " Les Beautés de l'opéra."] pp. 31. [*Paris,* 1845.] 4º.
Hirsch **3804.**

—— [Novelle.] Raccolta di poesie, o siano Novelle galanti del signore Ab * C * * * * [i.e. G. B. Casti]. [12 tales.] 2 tom. 1790. 8º. *See* C * * * * (Ab *) *Signore.*
11431. bbb. 22.

—— [Another edition.] Novelle galanti, in ottava rima, dell'Ab . . . C . . . [i.e. G. B. Casti.] Nuova edizione, corretta, e ricorretta. pp. 306. 1793. 8º. *See* C . . ., *Ab . . ..* **80. k. 29.**

—— Novelle galanti. [18 tales.] 2 tom. *Milano,* 1802. 12º. **11426. bb. 3.**

—— Novelle. [48 tales. With a portrait.] 6 tom. *Parigi,* anno IX [1801]. 16º. **011483. de. 39.**

—— [Another edition.] 3 vol. *Parigi,* 1804. 8º.
1081. m. 20–22.

—— Novelle, *etc.* [A selection.] pp. 245. *Firenze,* 1905. 8º. **11429. b. 60.**

—— The Happy Man's Shirt and the Magic Cap. Imitated from the Italian [i.e. from " La Camicia dell' uomo felice," and " Il Berretto magico " two of the " Novelle " of G. B. Casti. By John P. Collier. In verse]. pp. 16. 1850. 4º. *See* MAN. **11431. f. 31.**

—— La Papesse. Nouvelle en trois parties et en vers . . . traduite en français pour la première fois. Texte italien en regard avec les notes et pièces justificatives. (Notice sur l'abbé Casti par Ginguené.) pp. xix. 224. *Paris,* 1878. 12º. **11474. bb. 10.**

CASTI (GIOVANNI BATTISTA)

—— The Origin of Rome and of the Papacy. A poem, translated from the Italian [i.e. from " L'Origine di Roma," one of the " Novelle "], by Deuteros Whistlecraft, Gent. *Holyoake & Co.: London,* [1860.] 12º.
11431. c. 13.

—— Il Poema tartaro di Giambattista Casti. 2 tom. *Filadelfia,* 1803. 12º. **1489. m. 66.**
The imprint is false.

—— [Another copy.] **1063. f. 9.**
Imperfect; wanting tom. 2.

—— [Another edition.] 2 tom. *Milano,* 1803. 12º.
1063. f. 10.

—— [Another edition.] 2 tom. *Genova,* 1804. 12º.
1063. f. 11, 12.

—— Poesie liriche, *etc.* pp. vii. 192. *Firenze,* 1769. 4º.
1474. c. 16.

—— Poesie liriche . . . Quinta edizione con aggiunte. pp. 210. *Adrianopoli* [*Torino*], 1794. 12º.
1062. a. 19.

—— Poesie. [Selections from the " Poesie liriche."] pp. 61. *Pisa,* 1817. 8º. **1463. a. 1. (7.)**

—— Prima la musica e poi le parole. *See* RACCOLTA. Raccolta di melodrammi giocosi, *etc.* 1826. 8º.
12201.p.1/345.

—— Il Re Teodoro in Venezia. *See* RACCOLTA. Raccolta di melodrammi giocosi, *etc.* 1826. 8º.**12201.p.1/345.**

—— [Another edition.] *See* ITALIAN CLASSICAL THEATRE. Teatro classico italiano, *etc.* 1829. 8º. **1464. k. 9.**

—— Il Rè Teodoro in Venezia. A new comic opera, in two acts, as performed at the King's Theatre, *etc.* *Ital. & Eng.* pp. iv. 12–109. 1787. 8º. *See* THEODORE [Théodore Étienne de Neuhoff], *King of Corsica.* **907. k. 1. (8.)**

—— Il Rè Teodoro in Venezia. Drama eroicomico, *etc.* (König Theodor in Venedig, *etc.*) *Ital. & Ger.* pp. 211. 1787. 8º. *See* THEODORE [Théodore Étienne de Neuhoff], *King of Corsica.* **11715. de. 9.**

—— Li Tre Giulj. Sonetti. pp. 104. *Napoli,* 1814. 8º.
11431. e. 19.

—— The Trè Giuli. Translated [by Montagu Montagu] . . . [In verse.] With a memoir of the author, and some account of his other works. pp. xxxii. 208. *J. Hatchard & Son: London,* 1826. 8º. **1063. k. 4.**

—— The Three Groats . . . A new edition. With numismatic notes. By M. Montagu. pp. 272. *Henry Starie: London,* 1841. 8º. **1063. k. 5.**

—— Canzonette. [Selected poems.] *See* CARDUCCI (G. A. G.) [*Single Works.*] Poeti erotici del secolo XVIII, *etc.* 1868. 16º. **11420. a. 2.**

CASTI (HENRICUS) *See* CASTI (Enrico)

CASTIAU (A. O.) De la galvano-caustique thermique. pp. 47. *Paris,* 1870. 4º. [*Collection des thèses soutenues à la Faculté de Médecine de Paris.* An 1870. tom. 2.]
7373. l. 10.

CASTIAU (ADELSON JOSEPH ADOLPHE) Lettres démocratiques. (Avec une biographie de l'auteur [by L. P. Bertrand].) pp. 138. *Bruxelles,* 1886. 16º.
8051. a. 58.

—— Souveraineté nationale et suffrage universel. L'impot et l'armée. pp. 49. *Bruxelles & Liége,* 1867. 8º.
8008. ee. 17.

CASTIAU (LEO. J.) Evolution of the Milk Diet; or, the Elixir of youth. Scientific lessons, etc. pp. 23. [*Calgary*, 1920.] 8°. **7406. ff. 27.**

CASTIAU (NESTOR J. B. P.) Coup d'œil sur la gangrène dite spontanée; thèse, etc. pp. 22. *Paris*, 1834. 4°. **1184. f. 5. (22.)**

CASTIAUX (J.) Documents pour servir à l'étude de la méthode aspiratrice. pp. 192. *Lille*, 1873. 4°. [*Collection des thèses soutenues à la Faculté de Médecine de Paris. An* 1873. tom. 4.] **7373. o.**

CASTIEAU (WILLIAM) See DICTIONARIES. [*Arts and Sciences, etc.—English.*] The Modern Dictionary of Arts and Sciences . . . The astronomical, mechanical, and every other branch of the mathematics, by W. Castieau, etc. 1774. 8°. **12221. a. 7.**

CASTIELLA. *See* CASTILE.

CASTIELLO. *See* CASTELLO.

CASTIELLO (JAIME) A Humane Psychology of Education, etc. pp. xxiii. 254. *Sheed & Ward: London*, 1937. 8°. **8312. bb. 3.**

CASTIER (ÉDOUARD HENRI) Étude clinique sur le sarco-cèle tuberculeux. pp. 47. *Paris*, 1866. 4°. [*Collection des thèses soutenues à la Faculté de Médecine de Paris. An* 1866. tom. 3.] **7373. g. 6.**

CASTIER (JULES) *See* KIPLING (Rudyard) [*Single Works.*] [The Five Nations.] Les Cinq nations . . . Traduction en vers de J. Castier. 1920. 8°. **011483. b. 68.**

—— *See* MAUROIS (A.) *K.B.E.* General Bramble . . . Translated . . . by J. Castier and R. Boswell. 1921. 8°. **012547. c. 37.**

—— *See* WILDE (Oscar F. O'F. W.) Le Crime de Lord Arthur Savile, suivi d'autres contes . . . Traduction de J. Castier. 1954. 8°. **12650. a. 87.**

—— Rather Like. Some endeavours to assume the mantles of the great, etc. pp. 292. *Herbert Jenkins: London*, 1920 [1919]. 8°. **12330. tt. 20.**

CASTIGA MATTI. Il Castiga Matti, ouero Quaderni morali in lingua venetiana, ne' quali si contengono naturali, euangeliche, apostoliche, e sante sferzate al pazzo peccatore, etc. [By Domenico Babli.] pp. 48. *G. A. Remondinj: Venetia & Passano* [sic], [1700 ?] 12°. **1071. c. 3. (5.)**

CASTIGATION. A Castigation for the Sectarians. The Vision of Heresies; and other poems: by a Catholic priest. pp. 72. *Keating, Brown & Co.: London*, 1834. 12°. **T. 1529. (8.)**

CASTIGATOR, *pseud.* Dreams and Realities; or, John Bull awakened to a sense of his danger, and cautioned against poisonous drugs and nostrums recommended by advertising quacks . . . By Castigator. pp. 28. *W. Kidd: London*, [1835 ?] 12°. **T. 2082. (5.)**

—— The Mendicity Society Unmasked in a letter to the managers, wherein is shown the real character of this pretended benevolent society, as developed in the proceedings of its Begging Letter Committee. [Signed: Castigator.] pp. 50. *W. C. Wright: London*, 1825. 8°. **T. 1082. (10.)**

—— Notoriety; or, Fashionables unveiled, a tale for the haut-ton. Interspersed with elegant and original anecdotes . . . By Castigator. 3 vol. *Sherwood, Neeley & Jones; Earle & Taylor: London*, 1812. 12°. **12611. d. 5.**

CASTIGATOR, *pseud.* [i.e. CHARLES DIBDIN, *the Elder.*] The Lion and the Water-Wagtail: a mock heroic poem, in three cantos. By Castigator. pp. 174. *Sherwood, Neely, & Jones: London*, 1809. 12°. **11687. a. 43.**

CASTIGATOR, *pseud.* [i.e. ROSWELL MARSH.] Col. Fremont and his Slanderers. [A letter to the editor of the " New York Herald." Signed: Castigator.] [*New York*, 1856.] *s. sh.* fol. **1850. c. 6. (59*.)** *A newspaper cutting. Mutilated; wanting the signature.*

CASTIGATOR, *pseud.* [i.e. WILLIAM NAYLOR.] *See* CRITICOS, *pseud.*, and CASTIGATOR, *pseud.* The Visions of Sapience, etc. 1815. 8°. **3936. g. 3. (1.)**

CASTIGLIA (BENEDETTO) Abolizione della guerra internazionale. Relazione e progetto di legge presentato alla Camera de' Deputati del Parlamento Italiano. pp. 16. [*Florence*, 1868.] 8°. **8033. aa. 24.**

—— Al Nuovo Organo delle scienze dell'umanità proemio. pp. 420. *Palermo*, 1841. 8°. **8465. d. 16.**

—— Armamento difensivo. Progetto di legge presentato alla Camera de' Deputati del Parlamento Italiano. pp. 12. *Firenze*, 1868. 12°. **8824. bb. 31.**

—— Arnaldo di Brescia, o l'Eresia dei Papi, con un indirizzo alla Cristianità. pp. 80. *Milano*, 1860. 8°. **3901. f. 40. (3.)**

—— Cattolicismo: pervertimenti, verità, avvenire. (Estratto dalla Rivista contemporanea nazionale italiana.) pp. 43. *Torino*, 1868. 8°. **3902. g. 42. (2.)**

—— La Clef de la Divine Comédie. *See infra*: Dante Alighieri, ou, le Problème de l'humanité au moyen âge.

—— Conversione della polizia assoldata in polizia cittadina e gratuita. Progetto di legge presentato alla Camera de' Deputati del Parlamento Italiano. pp. 14. *Firenze*, 1868. 8°. **5326. a. 31. (2.)**

—— Cronichetta teatrale dell'està dell'anno 1839 in Palermo. Pubblicata da Benedetto Castiglia [or rather, written by him]. [With an article by him, entitled " Emilia Hallez nella Beatrice di Tenda."] pp. 72. *Palermo*, 1839. 8°. **12226. d. 14. (10.)**

—— Dante Alighieri, ou, le Problème de l'humanité au moyen âge. Lettres à M. de Lamartine. pp. 78. *Paris*, 1857. 8°. **11422. ff. 30. (1.)**

—— [Another edition.] La Clef de la Divine Comédie du Dante Alighieri . . . Nouvelle édition. pp. 78. *Paris*, 1865. 8°. **11420. g. 25.**

—— Dell'istruzione e del libro vivente. Primi schiarimenti. pp. 8. 90. *Roma*, 1874. 8°. **8311. eee. 22.**

—— L'Essenza del cattolicismo. I doveri d'Italia. pp. 19. *Firenze*, 1866. 8°. **3900. i. 54.**

—— Redenzione. Primo annuncio. pp. xx. 98. *Roma*, [1872.] 8°. **4375. dd. 11.**

—— La Riforma della libertà. Discorso, etc. pp. 33. *Firenze*, 1868. 8°. **8033. aaa. 13.**

—— Il Riordinamento, la confederazione latina, la capitale, le garantie al Pontificato. Programma. pp. 11. *Firenze*, 1870. 8°. **8033. aa. 52. (8.)**

CASTIGLIA (GIAMBATTISTA) Il Mio congedo: opuscoli. pp. 238. *Palermo*, 1844. 8°. **12225. c. 2.**

CASTIGLIA (GIUSEPPE) Sulla tomba di Giuseppe Mazzini. Canto. pp. 11. *Sassari*, 1872. 8°. **11436. ee. 52. (7.)**

CASTIGLIA (SALVATORE) Le Stazioni navali del regno d'Italia 2 pt. *Torino*, 1861. 8°. **8805. dd. 39. (2.)**

CASTIGLIANO (ALBERTO) Monografie e pubblicazioni diverse. pp. 152. pl. III. *Torino*, 1889. 8°.
8704. eee. 35.

—— Théorie de l'équilibre des systèmes élastiques et ses applications. pp. 480. pl. xv. *Turin*, 1879, 80. 8°.
08766. bb. 19.

—— Elastic Stresses in Structures. Translated . . . by Ewart S. Andrews, *etc.* pp. xx. 360. pl. xv. *Scott, Greenwood & Son: London*, 1919. 8°. **08767. k. 32.**

CASTIGLIANO (S. GORDON)

—— Oral Cancer. *In:* BURKET (Lester W.) Oral Medicine, *etc.* pp. 467–516. [1952.] 8°. **07611. k. 68.**

CASTIGLIO (FERDINANDO DEL) *See* CASTILLO (Hernando del) *Dominican Friar.*

CASTIGLIONCHIO (BERNARDO DA) Epistola di messer Bernardo da Castiglionchio a messer Lapo suo padre. *See* CASTIGLIONCHIO (L. da) Epistola o sia ragionamento dı messer Lapo da Castiglionchio, *etc.* 1753. 4°.
1316. h. 4.

CASTIGLIONCHIO (FRANCESCO DA) Lettera . . . sopra alla coronazione del re Carlo III, re di Cicilia e di Gerusalem. —Copia d'una lettera . . . per messer Francesco d'Alberto da Castiglionchio al detto Alberto suo padre a lui significando la morte di messer Lapo da Castiglionchio, *etc. See* CASTIGLIONCHIO (L. da) Epistola o sia ragionamento di messer Lapo da Castiglionchio, *etc.* 1753. 4°.
1316. h. 4.

CASTIGLIONCHIO (LAPO DA) [Allegationes.] *Begin.* [fol. 2 *recto:*] [N]on obstante constitutiōe facta per capitulum uacante sede penali et iurata de diminuendo caritatiuo subsidio poterit postea exigi allātio .xx. ʒ xxi., *etc. End.* [fol. 131 *verso:*] Finis Allegationū eximii dñi Lapi de Castelho, *etc.* ꝑ *Iohannem Reinhardi: rome,* die xiiii. mensis may, 1474. fol. **IC. 17711.**
132 *leaves, ff.* 1 *and* 18 *blank. Without signatures. Double columns, 54 lines to a column.*

—— [Another edition.] Allegationes Lapi. 𝕲.𝔏.
ꝑ *Paganinū de paganinis: Venetijs,* die .xxvij. mēsis Iulij, 1498. fol. **IC. 23298.**
70 *leaves,* 9–70 *numbered* 1–62. *Sig.* A⁸ a–i⁶ k⁸. *Double columns,* 68 *lines to a column.*

—— [Another edition.] Allegationes iur. vtr. monarcæ Domini Lapi de Castiglionchio . . . Ab infinitis erroribus per D. Quintilianum Mandosium . . . purgatæ, et cum eiusdem . . . additionibus . . . Additis insuper nonnullis Allegationibus . . . eiusdem Lapi, & aliorum, quæ in antiquis editionibus non habebantur, *etc.* ff. 170.
FEW MS. NOTES. *Apud I. Variscum & socios: Venetiis,* 1571. fol. **5035. f. 11. (1.)**

—— Epistola o sia ragionamento di messer Lapo da Castiglionchio . . . colla vita del medesimo composta dall'abate Lorenzo Mehus. Si aggiungono alcune lettere di Bernardo suo figliuolo e di Francesco di Alberto suo nipote. Con un appendice di antichi documenti. pp. lx. 222. *Bologna*, 1753. 4°. **1316. h. 4.**

—— [Another copy.] **88. k. 6.**

—— Tractatus de canonica portione ʒ de quarta, *etc. See* TRACTATUS. Primum [*etc.*] volumen tractatuum ex variis iuris interpretibus collectorum. vol. 15. 1549. fol. **5305. i.**

—— Tractatus hospitalitatis. *See* TRACTATUS. Primum [*etc.*] volumen tractatuum ex variis iuris interpretibus collectorum. vol. 15. 1549. fol. **5305. i.**

CASTIGLIONCHIO (LAPO DA)

—— [Another edition.] *See* TRACTATUS. Tractatus vniuersi iuris, *etc.* tom. 14. 1584. fol. **499. g. 9.**

CASTIGLIONE, FILIPPO BACILE, *Baron di. See* BACILE.

——, FRANCESCO GONZAGA, *Marquis di. See* GONZAGA.

——, PIERRE FRANÇOIS CHARLES AUGEREAU, *Duke de. See* AUGEREAU.

——, VIRGINIA VERASIS, *Countess di. See* VERASIS.

CASTIGLIONE-ALDOVRANDI, ADÈLE COLONNA, *Duchess di. See* COLONNA.

CASTIGLIONE-COLONNA, ADÈLE COLONNA, *Duchess di. See* COLONNA (A.) *Duchess di Castiglione-Aldovrandi.*

CASTIGLIONE DEL LAGO, FULVIO DELLA CORNIA, *Duke di. See* CORNIA.

CASTIGLIONE FIORENTINO.—*Biblioteca Comunale.*

—— Castiglione Fiorentino. Biblioteca comunale. [By G. Mischi and A. Nunziati.] *In:* Inventari dei manoscritti delle biblioteche d'Italia. vol. 26, 44. 1918, 30. 8°.
011900. dd. 20/26, 44.

CASTIGLIONE, *Family of. See* BEFFA NEGRINI (A.) Elogi historici di alcuni personaggi della famiglia Castigliona, *etc.* 1606. 4°. **10631. bb. 40.**

—— *See* CASTIGLIONE (M.) De origine, rebus gestis, ac priuilegijs gentis Castilioneæ . . . commentaria. 1596. 4°. **9903. d. 17.**

CASTIGLIONE (CATELINI DA) *See* CATELINI DA CASTIGLIONE.

CASTIGLIONE (A. P.) *See* CASTIGLIONE (B.) *Count.* [*Libro del Cortegiano.*] Il Cortegiano, or the Courtier . . . And a new version of the same into English . . . To which is prefix'd, the life of the author. By A. P. Castiglione. 1727. 4°. **31. e. 1.**

CASTIGLIONE (ALESSANDRO GONZAGA) calling himself *Duke of Mantua. See* GONZAGA-CASTIGLIONE.

CASTIGLIONE (ANGELO) Orazione . . . detta nell'essequie del reverendissimo vescovo di Verona Gian Matteo Giberto il giorno dī S. Silvestro dell'anno MDXLIII., *etc. See* GIBERTI (G. M.) *Bishop of Verona.* Jo. Matthaei Giberti . . . opera, *etc.* 1733. 4°. **696. m. 21.**

CASTIGLIONE (BALDASSARE) *Count.*

WORKS.

—— Opere volgari e latine . . . Novellamente raccolte, ordinate, ricorrette, ed illustrate . . . da Gio. Antonio, e Gaetano Volpi, *etc.* (Vita del conte Baldessar Castiglione, descritta da Bernardino Marliani, *etc.*) [With a portrait.] pp. xxxii. 436. *Padova*, 1733. 4°.
527. l. 20.

—— [Another copy.] **31. d. 3.**

—— Opere. vol. 1. Il Cortegiano . . . publicato per cura del conte Carlo Baudi di Vesme. pp. viii. 398. *Firenze*, 1854. 12°. **8406. e. 32.**
No more published.

TWO OR MORE WORKS.

—— Poesie volgari, e latine . . . corrette, illustrate, ed accresciute di varie cose inedite (dal abate Pierantonio Serassi). Aggiuntevi alcune rime e lettere di Cesare Gonzaga. (Notizie intorno al conte Baldessar Castiglione. —Notizie intorno a Cesare Gonzaga.—V. Cl. Cajetani Vulpii Adnotationes quædam selectæ . . . ad Balthassaris Castilionii Carmina.) pp. lxvi [xlvi]. 240. *Roma*, 1760. 12°. **678. a. 20.**

CASTIGLIONE (BALDASSARE) *Count.*

—— Lettere . . . ora per la prima volta date in luce e con annotazioni storiche illustrate dall'abate Pierantonio Serassi. (Lettera di Gio. Alfonso Valdes . . . in difesa del suo Dialogo sopra il sacco di Roma [in Spanish, with an Italian translation] con la risposta del conte B. Castiglione. —Stanze pastorali del conte B. Castiglione e del signor Cesare Gonzaga.—Balthassaris Castilionii . . . Carmina, aucta et illustrata.) 2 vol. *Padova*, 1769, 71. 4°.
636. i. 24.

LETTERS.

—— Lettere. *See* ZANETTI (F.) Lettere di diuersi huomini illustri, *etc.* 1603. 8°. **1084. e. 10.**

—— Due lettere inedite. [Instructions on the printing and distribution of the "Libro del Cortegiano."] (Estratto dall'Indicatore modenese.) pp. 7. [1851.] 4°.
10825. c. 30.

—— Lettere diplomatiche . . . cavate dagli autografi dell' Archivio storico dei Gonzaga in Mantova. [Edited by Count F. Contin.] pp. 27. *Padova*, 1875. 8°.
10910. l. 1.

—— Traduzione di quattro lettere latine del conte Baldassar Castiglione col testo a fronte, seguita da quattro altre originali italiane del medesimo autore. Con note. [With a portrait.] pp. 106. *Milano*, 1826. 8°. **1454. k. 6.**

—— Balthasaris Castilionii Ad Henricum Angliæ Regem epistola de uita et gestis Guidubaldi vrbini Ducis. *Per O. Petrutium: Forosempronii*, 1513. 4°. **1199. c. 3.**

—— Congettura che una lettera creduta di Baldessar Castiglione sia di Raffaello d'Urbino. (Discorso letto alla Reale Accademia fiorentina dall'abate Daniele Dᵣ Francesconi.) [With the text of the letter, which was addressed to Pope Leo X.] pp. 118. *Firenze*, 1799. 8°. **T. 2274. (2.)**

—— Lettera . . . a Federico Gonzaga, marchese di Mantova, ora per la prima volta messa in pubblico da Antonenrico Mortara. pp. 16. *Casalmaggiore*, 1851. 8°.
10910. g. 6.

—— Risposta . . . alla Lettera del Segretario Valdés. *See* VALDÉS (A.) Lettera di Gio: Alfonso Valdes . . . in difesa del suo diálogo sopra il sacco di Roma, *etc.* 1860. 8°. [*VALDES (J.)* Diálogo de la Lengua, *etc.*] **3902. f. 6.**

CARMINA.

—— Bald. Castilionis Cleopatra.—Bald. Castilionis Elegia.— Bald. Castilionis Elegiæ II. *See* SANNAZARO (J.) [*Latin Works.*] Actij Synceri Sannazarij de partu Virginis libri III, *etc.* 1533. 8°. **1070. d. 33.**

—— Balthassaris Castilioni Carminum liber. *See* CARMINA. Carmina quinque illustrium poetarum, *etc.* 1548. 8°.
1070. c. 13. (3.)

—— [Another edition.] *See* CARMINA. Carmina quinque illustrium poetarum, *etc.* 1549. 8°. **G. 9836.**

—— [Another edition.] *See* CARMINA. Carmina quinque illustrium poetarum, *etc.* 1552. 8°. **1070. d. 17.**

—— [Another edition.] *See* CARMINA. Carmina quinque illustrium poetarum, *etc.* 1552. 16°. **238. l. 33.**

—— [Another edition.] *See* CARMINA. Carmina quinque illustrium poetarum, *etc.* 1558. 8°. **G. 9837.**

—— [Another edition.] *See* TOSCANUS (J. M.) Carmina illustrium poetarum Italorum, *etc.* tom. I. 1576, *etc.* 16°. **686. a. 15.**

—— [Another edition.] *See* GHERUS (R.) *pseud.* Delitiæ CC. Italorum poetarum, *etc.* vol. 1. pt. 2. 1608. 16°.
238. i. 2.

CASTIGLIONE (BALDASSARE) *Count.* [CARMINA.]

—— Baltassaris Castilioni Alcon.—Eiusdem Cleopatra. *See* LABBÉ (P.) Heroicæ poeseos deliciæ, *etc.* 1646. 12°.
1213. k. 23.

—— [Poems.] *Lat.* 1719. *See* ITALIAN POETS. Carmina illustrium poetarum Italorum. tom. 3. 1719, *etc.* 8°.
657. a. 18.

—— Balthassaris Castilionii Carminum liber. *See* FRACASTORO (G.) Hieronymi Fracastorii et Marci Antonii Flaminii Carmina, *etc.* 1740. 12°. **1213. e. 12.**

—— [Poems.] *Lat.* 1740. *See* ITALIANS. Selecta poemata Italorum qui latine scripserunt, *etc.* vol. 2. 1740. 8°.
1213. e. 4.

—— Balthassaris Castilionii Carminum liber. *See* CARMINA. Carmina quinque illustrium poetarum, *etc.* 1753. 8°.
78. c. 1.

—— Balthassaris Castilionii Carminum liber. *See* FRACASTORO (G.) Hieronymi Fracastorii et Marci Antonii Flaminii Carmina, *etc.* 1782. 12°. **11405. a. 14.**

—— Balthasaris Castilionii Poemata. *See* ITALIANS. Poemata selecta Italorum, *etc.* 1808. 8°.
11405. d. 24.

—— Aus den lateinischen Gedichten des Balthasar Castiglione. *Lat. & Ger. See* BUDIK (P. A.) Leben und Wirken der vorzüglichsten lateinischen Dichter des XV.–XVIII. Jahrhunderts, *etc.* Bd. 2. 1828. 8°. **817. c. 12.**

—— [Ad puellam in litore ambulantem.] Versione d'una elegia di Baldassare Castiglione ad una fanciulla che passeggia sul lido del mare. *Lat. & Ital.* pp. 13. *Treviso*, 1815. 12°. **T. 2291. (5.)**

—— Hippolitæ Taurellæ . . . Epistola ad maritum suum Balthasarem Castilionem apud Leonem X. Ponti. Rom. oratorem. [By B. Castiglione.] 1558. 8°. [*MORATA (O. F.)* Olympiæ Fuluiæ Moratæ . . . Latina et Græca . . . monumenta, *etc.*] *See* CASTIGLIONE (I.)
1213. e. 18.

—— [Another edition.] 1562. 8°. [*MORATA (O. F.)* Olympiæ Fuluiæ Moratæ . . . orationes, *etc.*] *See* CASTIGLIONE (I.)
630. b. 28.

—— [Another edition.] 1570. 8°. [*MORATA (O. F.)* Olympiæ Fuluiæ Moratæ . . . opera, *etc.*] *See* CASTIGLIONE (I.)
630. b. 3.

—— [Another edition.] 1580. 8°. [*MORATA (O. F.)* Olympiæ Fuluiæ Moratæ . . . opera, *etc.*] *See* CASTIGLIONE (I.)
630. b. 4.

—— Poetischer Brief der Hippolyta Taurella an ihren Gatten Balthasar Castiglione in Rom. [By B. Castiglione.] *Lat. & Ger.* 1819. 8°. [*BRAUN (G. C.)* Des Leonardo da Vinci Leben und Kunst, *etc.*] *See* CASTIGLIONE (I.)
1402. f. 32.

—— Poetical Epistle from Hippolita Taurella . . . to her husband Balthazar Castiglione. [By B. Castiglione, but here attributed to Olympia Fulvia Morata. Translated into English verse by Amelia Gillespie Smyth.] *See* MORATA (O. F.) Olympia Morata, her Times, *etc.* 1834. 8°. **489. a. 26.**

—— Versione d'un elegia di Baldassare Castiglione (nella quale l'autore finge, che sua moglie Ippolita gli scriva), pubblicata in occasione delle . . . nozze del N. U. Leonardo Dolfin colla N. D. Lugrezia Boldù. [Translated into Italian verse by P. A. Paravia.] pp. 10. *Treviso*, 1817. 8°. **T. 2269. (7.)**

CASTIGLIONE (BALDASSARE) *Count.*

LIBRO DEL CORTEGIANO.

—— Il Libro del Cortegiano. *Nelle case d'Aldo Romano, & d'Andrea d'Asola: Venetia*, 1528. fol.   **674. k. 15.**
With the arms of Madame de Pompadour stamped on the binding.

—— [Another copy.]   **31. g. 9.**
With a portrait of the author inserted.

—— [Another copy.]   **G. 2458.**

—— [Another edition.]   *Per li heredi di P. di Giunta: Firenze*, 1528. 8°.   **722. a. 30.**

—— [Another edition.]   *Per A. di Viotti: Parma*, 1530. 8°.
1388. a. 47.

—— [Another edition.] COPIOUS MS. NOTES AND CORRECTIONS [by G. Rosati as Revisor to the Inquisition in Florence]. ff. 107 [207].   *Per li heredi di P. di Giunta: Firenze*, 1531. 8°.   **C. 28. a. 4.**

—— [Another edition.] ff. 7. 215.   *Nelle case delli heredi d'Aldo Romano et d'Andrea d'Asola: Venetia*, 1533. 8°.
C. 16. g. 10.
The foliation is irregular.

—— [Another copy.]   **G. 9871.**

—— [Another edition.] ff. 129 [209].   *Per B. Giunti: Firenze*, 1537. 8°.   **8408. aa. 26.**
The foliation of the last two quires is irregular.

—— [Another edition.] Nouamente reuisto. *Nella casa di G. Paduano, ad instantia del Nobile homo M. F. Torresano d'Asola: Vinegia*, 1538. 8°.   **722. a. 33.**

—— [Another edition.] Nuouamente stampato, et con somma diligenza reuisto. ff. 195. *In casa de' figliuoli di Aldo: Vinegia*, 1541. 8°.   **C. 20. a. 14. (1.)**

—— [Another edition.] Nuouamente stampato, & con somma diligentia reuisto, *etc.* ff. 191. *Appresso G. Giolito di Ferrarii: Vinetia*, 1544. 8°.   **C. 69. a. 7.**

—— [Another edition.] Nuouamente ristampato. *Nelle case de figlioli di Aldo: Venetia*, 1545. fol. **G. 2457. (1.)**
In this copy are inserted three sonnets in MS., *the first beginning " Consenti, o Mar di bellezza," the second addressed by F. Melchiori to Tasso, the third a reply by Tasso, the last two in the authors' autograph, and with their signatures.*

—— [Another edition.] Di nuouo rincontrato con l'originale scritto di mano de l'auttore, *etc.* ff. 195. *In casa de' figliuoli di Aldo: Vinegia*, 1547. 8°.   **1030. c. 6.**

—— [Another edition.] Il Cortegiano . . . Nouamente stampato, et . . . reuisto, *etc.* pp. 366. *Appresso G. Giolito de Ferrari & Fratelli: Vinegia*, 1551. 12°.
12470. aa. 24. (3.)

—— [Another edition.] Il Libro del Cortegiano . . . Nuouamente . . . corretto, & reuisto per il Dolce, secondo l'essemplare del proprio autore. ff. 204. *Appresso G. Giolito de Ferrari & Fratelli: Vinegia*, 1552. 8°.
1030. c. 7.

—— [Another edition.] Il Cortegiano . . . Di nuouo rincontrato con l'originale scritto di mano de l'autore, *etc.* pp. 457. *Appresso G. Rouillio: Lyone*, 1553. 16°.
231. k. 37.

CASTIGLIONE (BALDASSARE) *Count.* [LIBRO DEL CORTEGIANO.]

—— [Another edition.] Il Libro del Cortegiano . . . Nuouamente . . . reuisto per M. Lodouico Dolce . . . e nel margine apostillato, *etc.* pp. 416. *Appresso G. Giolito de' Ferrari: Vinegia*, 1556. 8°.   **231. k. 4.**

—— [Another edition.] Nuouamente . . . riuisto & corretto, secondo l'esemplare del proprio autore. ff. 220. *Per B. Fagiani: Venetia*, 1559. 8°.   **1030. c. 8.**

—— [Another edition.] Nuouamente . . . reuisto per M. Lodouico Dolce . . . Con l'aggiunta de gli argomenti per ciascun libro, *etc.* pp. 416. *Appresso G. Giolito de' Ferrari: Vinegia*, 1560. 8°.   **8404. aaa. 18.**

—— [Another edition.] Il Cortegiano . . . Reuisto per M. Lodouico Dolce, *etc.* [Without the "Argomenti."] pp. 494. *Appresso G. Rouillio: Lyone*, 1562. 16°.
C. 46. a. 22.
With the monogram of Nicolas Fouquet stamped on the covers.

—— [Another edition.] Nuouamente . . . reuisto per M. Lodouico Dolce . . . Con l'aggiunta de gli argomenti per ciascun libro, *etc.* pp. 475. *Appresso G. Caualcalouo: Venetia*, 1565. 12°.   **527. b. 34.**

—— [Another edition. Without the "Argomenti."] ff. 220. *Appresso D. Farri: Venetia*, 1568. 8°.   **1030. c. 9.**

—— [Another edition.] Nuouamente . . . reuisto per M. Lodouico Dolce . . . Con l'aggiunta de gli argomenti per ciascun libro, *etc.* pp. 475. *Appresso D. Farri: Vinegia*, 1574. 12°.   **12470. aaa. 6.**

—— [Another edition.] Riueduto, & corretto da Antonio Ciccarelli da Fuligni, *etc.* (Vita del conte Baldessar Castiglione. [By B. Marliani.]) ff. 212. *Appresso B. Basa: Venetia*, 1584. 8°.   **8410. e. 26.**

—— [Another edition.] Il Libro del Cortegiano del conte Baldessar Castiglione. Colla vita di lui scritta dal sig. abate Pierantonio Serassi. [The text as published by G. A. and G. Volpi in their edition of Castiglione's "Opere." With the notes of A. Ciccarelli on bk. 4, and with a portrait.] pp. xxiv. 352. *Padova*, 1766. 4°.
721. i. 15.

—— [Another edition.] (Vita del conte Baldessar Castiglione scritta dall' abate Pierantonio Serassi.) [With a portrait.] 2 vol. *Milano*, 1803. 8°. [*Collezione de' classici italiani.* vol. 67, 68.]   **12201.p.1/67, 68.**

—— [Another edition.] Edizione formata sopra quella d' Aldo, 1528, riscontrata con altre, delle più riputate, *etc.* (Vita del conte Baldessar Castiglione scritta dall'abate Pierantonio Serassi.) pp. vii. 562. *Milano*, 1822. 8°.
8403. b. 28.

—— [Another edition.] Il Cortegiano . . . Con prefazione di Giulio Salvadori. pp. xxxvi. 496. *Firenze*, 1884. 32°.
8410. aaa. 26.

—— [Another edition.] Annotato e illustrato da Vittorio Cian. pp. xxvi. 442. *Firenze*, 1894. 8°.   **08407. l. 1.**

—— (Nuova tiratura.) *Firenze*, 1908. 8°.   **08407. k. 14.**

—— Seconda edizione accresciuta e corretta. [With a portrait.] pp. xxi. 544. *Firenze*, 1910. 8°.
08407. k. 31.

—— Il Libro del Cortegiano . . . A cura di Vittorio Cian. (Quarta edizione riveduta e corretta.) pp. xii. 552. *Firenze*, 1947. 8°.   **2042. c.**

—— Le Parfait courtisan . . . es deux langues . . . De la traduction de Gabriel Chapuis. *Ital. & Fr.* pp. 660. *T. Ancelin, pour L. Cloquemin: Lyon*, 1580. 8°.
1030. c. 3.
The date in the colophon is 1579.

CASTIGLIONE (BALDASSARE) *Count.* [LIBRO DEL CORTEGIANO.]

—— [Another edition.] pp. 678. *Par N. Bonfons: Paris,* 1585. 8°. **1030. c. 4.**

—— The Courtier . . . Done into English by Thomas Hobby. *Ital., Fr. & Eng.* 𝕭.𝕷. MS. NOTES. *Printed by Iohn Wolfe: London,* 1588. 8°. **G. 16579.**

—— Il Cortegiano, or the Courtier : written by Conte B. Castiglione. And a new version of the same into English. Together with several of his celebrated pieces, as well Latin as Italian, both in prose and verse. To which is prefix'd, the life of the author. By À. P. Castiglione. [With a portrait.] *Ital. & Eng.* pp. 508. *Printed for the Editor: London,* 1727. 4°. **31. e. 1.**

—— The Courtyer . . . done into Englyshe by Thomas Hoby. 𝕭.𝕷. *Imprinted by wyllyam Seres: London,* 1561. 4°. **230. l. 17.**

—— [Another copy.] **1030. c. 13.** *Mutilated.*

—— [Another edition.] 𝕭.𝕷. *Imprinted by Henry Denham: London,* 1577. 4°. **8404. ccc. 25.**

—— [Another copy.] 𝕭.𝕷. **643. c. 69.** *Imperfect ; wanting the titlepage.*

—— [Another edition.] 𝕭.𝕷. *Printed by Thomas Creede: London,* 1603. 4°. **8403. d. 20.** *With spurious autographs of Shakespeare, forged by Samuel W. H. Ireland.*

—— The Courtier . . . Translated [by Robert Samber] from the original. 2 pt. *A. Bettesworth, etc.: London,* 1724. 8°. **8407. dd. 43.**

—— The Courtier . . . Translated [by Robert Samber] from the Italian original, *etc.* pp. xxi. 336. *E. Curll: London,* 1729. 8°. *A reissue of the edition of 1724.* **8407. e. 28.**

—— The Book of the Courtier . . . Done into English by Sir Thomas Hoby, anno 1561. With an introduction by Walter Raleigh. pp. lxxxvii. 377. *David Nutt: London,* 1900. 8°. [*Tudor Translations.* vol. 23.] **12211. pp. 1/10.**

—— [Another edition.] The Courtyer . . . Done into Englyshe by Thomas Hoby. (The work edited by Janet E. Ashbee, and carried out under the supervision of C. R. Ashbee.) pp. 391. *Edward Arnold: London,* 1900. 4°. **C. 99. f. 4.**

—— The Book of the Courtier . . . Translated from the Italian and annotated by Leonard Eckstein Opdycke. With seventy-one portraits and fifteen autographs, *etc.* pp. xiii. 439. *C. Scribner's Sons: New York,* 1901. 4°. **Tab. 443. c. 4.**

—— [Another copy, with a different titlepage.] *Duckworth & Co.: London; C. Scribner's Sons: New York; [printed in U.S.A.,]* 1902. 4°. **Tab. 443. c. 5.**

—— The Book of the Courtier . . . Done into English by Sir Thomas Hoby, *etc.* pp. xviii. 324. *J. M. Dent & Sons: London & Toronto; E. P. Dutton & Co.: New York,* [1928.] 8°. [*Everyman's Library.*] **12206.p.1/608.**

—— The Book of the Courtier. An epitome with annotations. *See* HARE (Christopher) *pseud.* Courts & Camps of the Italian Renaissance, *etc.* 1908. 8°. **9166. aa. 18.**

CASTIGLIONE (BALDASSARE) *Count.* [LIBRO DEL CORTEGIANO.]

—— Le Courtisan . . . Nouuellement reueu et corrige. [Translated by J. Colin, and edited by E. Dolet.] 2 pt. *F. Iuste: Lyon,* 1538. 8°. **C. 40. b. 23.**

—— [Another edition.] Le premier(—quatriesme) liure du Courtisan . . . Reduict de langue Ytalicque en Francoys [by J. Colin]. 4 pt. *Paris,* 1540. 8°. **731. a. 40.**

—— [Another edition.] Le Courtisan . . . nouuellement reueu, & corrigé. [Translated by J. Colin.] ff. 296. *N. du Chemin: Paris,* 1545. 16°. **C. 65. b. 9.**

—— Balthasaris Castilionis Comitis De Curiali siue Aulico Libri quatuor, ex Italico sermone in Latinum conuersi. Bartholomæo Clerke . . . interprete, *etc.* pp. 563. *Apud Iohannem Dayum: Londini,* 1571. 8°. **8403. b. 29.**

—— [Another edition.] Nouissimè æditi. pp. 297. FEW MS. NOTES. *Apud Thomam Dawson: Londini,* 1585. 8°. **8406. aaa. 13.**

—— [Another edition.] Nouissimè editi. pp. 297. [*Eliot's Court Press ;*] *Impensis Georg. Bishop: Londini,* 1593. 8°. **8410. aaaa. 43.**

—— [Another edition.] Nouissimè editi. pp. 260. *Impensis Georgij Bishop: Londini,* 1603. 8°. **1030. c. 10.**

—— [Another edition.] Quibus additus est in fine Aula Dialogus (Gulielmi Insulani Menapij) . . . Editio . . . reuisa, emendata & à multis mendis repurgata. pp. 295. *Ex officina Thomæ Adams; [printed by Richard Field]: Londini,* 1612. 8°. **1030. c. 11.**

—— [Another edition.] Quibus accessit De Aula dialogus Gulielmi Insulani Menapii . . . in quo partim refelluntur . . . partim attenuantur criminationes in Aulam Æneæ Syluii & Vlderici Hutteni, *etc.* pp. 395. MS. NOTES. *Sumptibus hæredum L. Zetzneri: Argentorati,* 1619. 8°. **8407. aaa. 13.**

—— Balthasaris Castilionis Comitis Libri IV. de curiali . . . interprete Bartholomaeo Clerke. Recensuit Samuel Drake. pp. 297. *Typis Academicis: Cantabrigiæ,* 1713. 8°. **1030. c. 12.**

—— Libro llamado el cortesano traduzido agora nueuamente en nuestro vulgar Castellano por Boscan. Con sus anotaciones por las margenes. 𝕲.𝕷. ff. cxliiij. *Por P. Touans, acosta del . . . varon guillermo d'Milles: Salamāca,* 1540. 4°. **C. 20. b. 10.**

—— [Another edition.] 𝕲.𝕷. ff. cxl. [*J. Cromberger: Seville,*] 1542. 4°. **C. 63. c. 28.**

—— [Another edition.] El Cortesano, traduzido por Boscan . . . nueuamente agora corregido. ff. 247. *En casa de la Biuda de M. Nutio: Anuers,* 1561. 8°. **C. 62. aa. 10.**

—— [Another edition.] ff. 294. *Impresso por F. Fernādez de Cordaua: Valladolid,* 1569. 8°. **8408. aa. 1.**

—— Los Cuatro Libros del Cortesano . . . Traduzidos en lengua castellana por Boscan. Edicion dirigida por D. Antonio María Fabié. pp. lxix. 581. *Madrid,* 1873. 8°. [*Libros de Antaño.* tom. 3.] **12230. bbb. 7.**

—— B. Castiglione. El Cortesano. Traducción de ʳuan Boscán. Estudio preliminar de M. Menéndez y Pelayo. pp. lxiv. 447. *Madrid,* 1942. 8°. [*Revista de filología española.* anejo 25.] **Ac. 145. c/5. (2.)**

CASTIGLIONE (BALDASSARE) *Count.* [LIBRO DEL CORTEGIANO.]

Appendix.

—— *See* BOTTARI (E.) Baldassare Castiglione e il suo Libro del Cortigiano. Studio. 1874. 8º. **11825. i. 13.**

—— —— 1877. 8º. [*Annali della R. Scuola Normale Superiore di Pisa.* vol. 2.] **Ac. 47. (a.)**

—— *See* FUCILLA (Joseph G.) The Role of the Cortegiano in the second part of Don Quijote. [1950.] 8º. **11865. k. 23.**

—— [For editions of " Dworzanin," by Ł. Górnicki, based on the " Libro del Cortegiano " :] *See* GÓRNICKI (Ł.)

—— *See* LOOS (Erich) Baldassare Castigliones " Libro del cortigiano." Studien zur Tugendauffassung des Cinquecento. [With a bibliography.] 1955. 8º. **P.P. 5044. ad. (2.)**

—— *See* MOHINĪMOHANA BHAṬṬACHĀRYA. " Courtesy " in Shakespeare, *etc.* [With special reference to the influence of Castiglione's " Libro del cortegiano."] 1940. 8º. **11767. b. 32.**

RIME.

—— Rime. 1787. *See* RUBBI (A.) Parnaso italiano, *etc.* tom. 26. 1784, *etc.* 8º. **240. g. 26.**

STANZE PASTORALI.

—— [For the " Stanze pastorali " or " Egloga " by B. Castiglione and C. Gonzaga, sometimes attributed to Castiglione alone :] *See infra:* WORKS WRITTEN IN COLLABORATION.

WORKS WRITTEN IN COLLABORATION.

—— Stanze pastorali, del Conte Baldesar Castiglione, et del Signor Cesare Gonzaga, con le Rime di M. Anton Giacomo Corso. [Edited by A. G. Corso.] ff. 112. *Aldi filii: Vinegia*, 1553. 8º. **674. a. 31.**
With the arms and monogram of Jacques Auguste de Thou and his first wife, Marie Barbançon stamped on the binding.

—— [Another edition.] Egloga. [By B. Castiglione and C. Gonzaga, but here attributed to Castiglione alone.] 1785. *See* RUBBI (A.) Parnaso italiano, *etc.* tom. 16. 1784, *etc.* 8º. **240. g. 16.**

SELECTIONS.

—— Le Più belle pagine di Baldassare Castiglione. Scelte da Giovanni Comisso. [With a portrait.] pp. v. 268. *Milano*, 1929. 12º. [*Le più belle pagine degli scrittori italiani.* vol. 48.] **012226. a. 1/48.**

APPENDIX.

—— *See* BENINI (G. V.) Elogio del più virtuoso cavaliere italiano del secolo sedecessimo (Baldessar Castiglione). 1781. 8º. **10630. c. 33. (5.)**

—— —— [1782.] 8º. [*RUBBI (A.) Elogj italiani.* tom. 4.] **276. g. 21.**

—— *See* CARTWRIGHT, afterwards ADY (Julia) Baldassare Castiglione . . . his life and letters, 1478–1529. [With portraits.] 1908. 8º. **10633. dd. 3.**

—— *See* CIAN (V.) Un Illustre nunzio pontificio del Rinascimento. Baldassar Castiglione. 1951. 8º. **012211. b. 1/156.**

CASTIGLIONE (BALDASSARE) *Count.* [APPENDIX.]

—— *See* CIAN (V.) La Lingua di Baldassare Castiglione. 1942. 8º. **W.P. 7475/3.**

—— *See* CIAN (V.) Nel mondo di Baldassarre Castiglioni. Documenti illustrati. 1942. 8º. [*Archivio storico lombardo.* nuova serie. anno 7. fasc. 1/4.] **Ac. 6525.**

—— *See* CURCIO BUFARDECI (G.) Su la vita letteraria del Conte Baldessare Castiglione, *etc.* 1900. 8º. **10632. c. 59.**

—— *See* FERRI (G.) *of Longiano.* Baltassaris Castilionii elogium, *etc.* 1780. 4º. **542. f. 26. (5.)**

—— *See* FONTANA (G.) Di Baldassare Castiglione. Lettura scolastica. 1871. 8º. **10631. e. 42. (13.)**

—— *See* HARE (Christopher) *pseud.* Courts & Camps of the Italian Renaissance : being a mirror of the life and times of . . . Count Baldassare Castiglione, *etc.* [With a portrait.] 1908. 8º. **9166. aa. 18.**

—— *See* MARTINATI (C.) Notizie storico-biografiche intorno al conte Baldassare Castiglione, *etc.* 1890. 8º. [*Pubblicazioni del R. Istituto di Studi superiori pratici in Firenze. Sezione di filosofia e filologia.* no. 19.] **Ac. 8848.**

—— *See* ROEDER (Ralph) The Man of the Renaissance. Four lawgivers . . . Castiglione, *etc.* [With a portrait.] 1933. 8º. **010662.bbb.36.**

—— *See* RUBBI (A.) Elogj italiani. (Elogio del conte Baldessar Castiglione, *etc.*) [1782.] 8º. **276. g. 21.**

—— *See* SCHRINNER (W.) Castiglione und die englische Renaissance. 1939. 8º. **012213.y.1/234.**

CASTIGLIONE (BONAVENTURA) Gallorum Insubrum antiquae sedes. pp. 133. *I. A. Castillioneus: Mediolani,* 1541. 4º. **566. f. 32.**

—— [Another edition.] *See* ITALY. [*Appendix.—History.*] Italiæ illustratæ . . . scriptores varii, *etc.* 1600. fol. **592. g. 1.**

—— [Another edition.] 1691. *See* ROBERTI (G.) Miscellanea italica erudita. vol. 2. [1690, *etc.*] 4º. **590. d. 11.**

—— [Another edition.] *See* GRAEVIUS (J. G.) Thesaurus antiquitatum et historiarum Italiæ, *etc.* tom. 1. pt. 1. 1704, *etc.* fol. **L.R.302.a.2/1.**

CASTIGLIONE (CARLO LOVERA DI) *See* LOVERA DI CASTIGLIONE.

CASTIGLIONE (FRANCESCO) Francisci Castilionensis Martyrium Antonianum, seu beati Antonii, vulgo Antonini de Ripolis ordinis Prædicatorum, *etc.* pp. xii. 31. *See* ORSI (G. A.) *Cardinal.* Dissertatio apologetica, *etc.* 1728. 4º. **4825. e. 20.**

—— Vita btī Antonij archiepiscopi florentini ordinis predicatorum. *See* ANTONINUS [Forciglioni], *Saint, Archbishop of Florence.* [*Trialogus de duobus discipulis.*] Jesus. In hoc volumine continentur infrascripti tractatus Primo deuotissimus trialogus . . . de duobus discipulis, *etc.* 1495. 8º. **IA. 24222.**

—— [Another edition.] *See* ANTONINUS [Forciglioni], *Saint, Archbishop of Florence.* [*Summa Theologica.*] Sancti Antonini . . . Summa theologica, *etc.* pt. 1. 1740. fol. **1242.k.12.**

CASTIGLIONE (GIAMBATISTA) Dissertazioni due, l'una sopra il rito di pregare per l'Imperatore usato nella Chiesa Ambrosiana : l'altra sopra il jus metropolitico della medesima Chiesa. 2 pt. *Milano*, 1771. 4°.
3475. i. 5.

—— Sentimenti di S. Carlo Borromeo intorno agli spettacoli. pp. xii. 220. *Bergamo*, 1759. 4°. **11795. f. 28.**

CASTIGLIONE (GIOVANNI) *Cardinal.* Johannis . . . Cardinalis Castillionæi, Auximatium et Cingulanorum episcopi, ad cleros, ordines, populosque utriusque dioecesis litteræ pastorales. pp. xiv. *Romæ*, 1808. 4°.
1356. k. 5. (36.)

—— [Another copy.] **898. g. 1. (11.)**

CASTIGLIONE (GIOVANNI ANTONIO) Gli Honori de gli antichi disciplinati, *etc.* (Gli Honori del sacro tempio di S. Catherina al ponte de' Fabbri di Porta Ticinese di Milano. Con la vita . . . di S. Gottardo Vescouo, e del glorioso Arciuescouo Thomaso Crasso, e'l martirio di S. Catherina vergine, *etc.*) 2 pt. *G. B. Bidelli : Milano*, 1622. 8°. **4785. cc. 18.**

—— Mediolanenses antiquitates ex vrbis parœcijs collectæ, ichnographicis ipsarum tabulis, recentibus rerum memorijs, varijs ecclesiasticis ritibus auctę & illustratę, *etc.* pp. 288. *I. B. Bidell : Mediolani*, 1625. 4°. **795. k. 10.**

—— [Another edition.] 1704. *See* GRAEVIUS (J. G.) Thesaurus antiquitatum et historiarum Italiæ, *etc.* tom. 3. pt. 1. 1704, *etc.* fol. **L.R.302.a.2/3.**

CASTIGLIONE (GIOVANNI BATTISTA) Difesa del capitan Gio. Battista Castiglione . . . intorno alla relatione del Mag. Simone Nuttio da Fossembrone, Podestà di Lucca. pp. 133. *G. Pauoni : Genoua*, 1603. 4°. **172. a. 19.**
The date in the colophon is 1604.

CASTIGLIONE (GIOVANNI BATTISTA DA) I Luoghi difficili del Petrarcha nuouamente dichiarati. ff. 66. *Per G. A. di Nicolini & Fratelli : Vinegia*, 1532. 8°.
11421. aa. 14.

CASTIGLIONE (GIOVANNI BENEDETTO)

—— *See* BLUNT (*Sir* Anthony F.) *K.C.V.O.* The Drawings of G. B. Castiglione & Stefano della Bella in the Collection of Her Majesty the Queen at Windsor Castle. [A catalogue, with reproductions.] 1954. 4°. **W.P. 3764/5.**

CASTIGLIONE (GIOVANNI FRANCESCO MAURO MELCHIORRE SALVEMINI DI) *See* SALVEMINI DI CASTIGLIONE.

CASTIGLIONE (GIOVANNI STEFANO) *See* SORBA (P. L.) La Giustizia del voto del M. Bernardo Vadorno . . . esposta al Senato . . . in confutazione di una risposta contraria [by G. S. Castiglione] intitolata Le Bilancie d'Astrea. 1712. fol. **501. g. 19. (10.)**

CASTIGLIONE (GIROLAMO)

—— *See* RAMONDINO (F.) Un Incunabulo rarissimo. Il Fiore de terra sancta, di Girolamo Castiglione. [On the edition printed at Messina by Georg Ricker.] 1942. 8°. **11898. c. 14.**

CASTIGLIONE (GIUSEPPE) *Doctor Juris. See* CASTALIO (Josephus)

CASTIGLIONE (GIUSEPPE) *Jesuit. See* B * * * * DE MALPIÈRE (D.) La Chine. Mœurs, usages, costumes . . . d'après les dessins originaux du père Castiglione, *etc.* 1825, *etc.* fol. **1782. c. 10.**

CASTIGLIONE (GOFFREDO) *See* CELESTINE IV., *Pope.*

CASTIGLIONE (IPPOLITA) Hippolitæ Taurellæ . . . Epistola ad maritum suum Balthasarem Castilionem apud Leonem x. Ponti. Rom. oratorem. [By Count B. Castiglione.] *See* MORATA (O. F.) Olympiæ Fuluiæ Moratæ . . . Latina et Græca . . . monumenta, *etc.* 1558. 8°.
1213. e. 18.

—— [Another edition.] *See* MORATA (O. F.) Olympiæ Fuluiæ Moratæ . . . Orationes, *etc.* 1562. 8°.
630. b. 28.

—— [Another edition.] *See* MORATA (O. F.) Olympiæ Fuluiæ Moratæ . . . Opera, *etc.* 1570. 8°.
630. b. 3.

—— [Another edition.] *See* MORATA (O. F.) Olympiæ Fuluiæ Moratæ . . . Opera, *etc.* 1580. 8°.
630. b. 4.

—— Poetischer Brief der Hippolyta Taurella an ihren Gatten Balthasar Castiglione in Rom. [By Count B. Castiglione.] *Lat. & Ger. See* BRAUN (G. C.) Des Leonardo da Vinci Leben und Kunst, *etc.* 1819. 8°. **1402. f. 32.**

CASTIGLIONE (IRENE DELLA ROCCA) *Countess. See* ROCCA CASTIGLIONE.

CASTIGLIONE (JACOMO) *See* CASTALIO (J.) Oratione . . . nell' essequie dell'illustrissimo . . . signor Gio. Francesco Aldobrandini . . . Tradotta di latino . . . da I. Castiglione. 1602. 4°. **10630. e. 13. (4.)**

—— Trattato dell'inondatione del Teuere . . . doue si discorre delle caggioni, e remedij suoi . . . Con vna relatione del diluuio di Roma del 1598, *etc.* pp. 77. *Appresso G. Facciotto, adistantia di G. Martinelli : Roma*, 1599. 8°.
446. a. 18. (1.)

CASTIGLIONE (LUIGI GONZAGA DI) *Prince. See* GONZAGA DI CASTIGLIONE.

CASTIGLIONE (MATTEO) De Origine, rebus gestis, ac priuilegijs gentis Castilioneæ . . . commentaria. pp. 136. *Apud I. B. Hugolinum : Venetijs*, 1596. 4°.
9903. d. 17.

CASTIGLIONE (PIETRO MARIA) Petri Mariæ Castillionæi . . . Admiranda naturalia ad renum calculos curandos. pp. 224. *Ex Apotheca G. Ferioli : Mediolani*, 1622. 8°.
1189. d. 27.
Cropped.

CASTIGLIONE (SABA DA) *See* MASSAROLI (I.) Fra Sabba da Castiglione e i suoi ricordi, *etc.* 1889. 8°. [*Archivio storico lombardo.* Anno 16.] **Ac. 6525.**

—— *See* PASOLINI-ZANELLI (G.) *Count.* Un Cavaliere di Rodi [i.e. Saba da Castiglione] ed un pittore del secolo XVI [i.e. G. Pennacchi]. 1893. 8°. **10630. c. 47.**

—— *See* VALGIMIGLI (G. M.) Frata Sabba da Castiglione . . . Cenni biografici, *etc.* 1870. 8°. **10604. g. 1. (2.)**

—— Novella . . . nuouamente stampata. pp. v. 12. *Lucca*, 1865. 8°. **12470. f. 27. (8.)**
One of an edition of sixty copies.

—— Ricordi, ouero Ammaestramenti . . . ne quali con prudenti, e christiani discorsi si ragiona di tutte le materie honorate, che si ricercano a vn vero gentil'huomo, *etc.* ff. 135. *Per P. Gherardo : Vinegia*, 1554. 4°.
232. h. 4.

—— [Another edition.] pp. 298. *Appresso di G. A. de gli Antonij : Milano*, 1559. 8°. **851. b. 6.**

—— [Another edition.] Di nuouo corretti, et ristampati . . . Et appresso breuemente e descritta la vita dell'auttore, *etc.* ff. 148 [150]. *Per P. Gerardo : Venetia*, 1560. 4°.
851. i. 20.
The date in the colophon is 1559.

CASTIGLIONE (SABA DA)

—— [Another edition.] Di nuouo ristampati, e con diligentia riueduti & emendati. ff. 152. FEW MS. NOTES. *Per G. Bonadio & Domenico F. & C.: Venetia*, 1562. 4º.
627. i. 6. (2.)

—— [Another edition.] ff. 298. *Appresso G. Bariletto: Venetia*, 1567. 8º.
1030. c. 14.

—— [Another edition.] ff. 292. *Appresso M. Bonelli: Venetia*, 1574. 8º.
1030. c. 15.

CASTIGLIONE (SALVATORE J.)

—— *See* CROCE (Benedetto) Politics and Morals. Translated . . . by S. J. Castiglione. 1946. 8º.
8009. b. 46.

CASTIGLIONE (VALERIANO) *See* SCOTO (L.) Il Gelone . . . Con le allegorie dell'abbate Castiglioni, *etc.* 1656. 4º.
11715. h. 35.

—— *See* TESAURO (E.) *Count.* Del regno d'Italia sotto i barbari epitome . . . Con le annotationi dell'abbate D. V. Castiglione. 1664. fol.
183. f. 14.

—— —— 1667. 12º.
9150. b. 17.

—— —— 1672. 12º.
9150. a. 45.

—— A Madama Reale Christiana di Francia, Duchessa di Sauoia, Reina di Cipro . . . Nella festa annuale della sua nascita. [A complimentary letter.] *[Torino*, 1642.] 4º.
T. 71*. (2.)

—— Le Pompe torinesi nel ritorno dell'Altezza Reale di Carlo Emanuele II. Duca di Savoia . . . descritte. (Oda del signor Ercole Agostino Berò . . . per il medesimo ingresso.) pp. 29. *G. G. Rustis: Torino*, 1645. 4º.
9930. e. 23.

—— Statista regnante . . . Accresciuto in questa terza impressione di una lettera discorsiua, spettante all'opera scritta dall'auttore a' politici. pp. 323. *G. D. Tarino: Torino*, 1630. 12º.
1477. cc. 10

CASTIGLIONE (VINCENZO) *See* SALLUSTIUS CRISPUS (C.) [*Works.—Latin.*] C. Crispi Salustii . . . Opera . . . Omnia . . . Cum . . . commentariis . . . V. Castilionei, *etc.* 1564. fol.
1307. l. 9.

—— —— 1710. 4º.
53. c. 3.

—— —— 1742. 4º.
587. h. 2.

CASTIGLIONE-HUMANI (VINCENZO)

—— L'Essenza giuridica del matrimonio. 1948. *See* ROME. —*The City.—Istituto Italiano di Studi Legislativi.* Annuario di diritto comparato e di studi legislativi, *etc.* vol. 23. fasc. 3. [1927, *etc.*] 8º.
Ac. 2104.

CASTIGLIONI (ALBERTO) Recuerdo de la Revolucion en Buenos Aires . . . julio de 1890. [With portraits.] pp. 152. *Buenos Aires*, 1890. 8º.
9772. aa. 15.

CASTIGLIONI (ALOYSIUS) *See* CASTIGLIONI (Luigi) *of Florence.*

CASTIGLIONI (ARTURO) *See* ALBERTIS (G. de) *da Capodistria.* Il Libro della Pestilenza di G. de Albertis, *etc.* [Edited by A. Castiglioni.] 1924. 8º. [*Archeografo triestino.* ser. 3. vol. 11.]
Ac. 6548.

—— *See* BLASI (J. de) Giacomo Leopardi . . . Letture tenute . . . da A. Castiglioni [and others], *etc.* 1938. 8º.
11860. f. 20.

—— Adventures of the Mind . . . Translated . . . by V. Gianturco. [With plates.] pp. xiv. 402. *Sampson Low, Marston & Co.: London*, [1947.] 8º.
4507. c. 19.

CASTIGLIONI (ARTURO)

—— Incantesimo e magia. pp. 468. pl. 75. *Milano*, 1934. 8º.
8610. d. 41.

—— Leonardo da Vinci, anatomista y fisiólogo. Versión del italiano por Mario Spinetti-Dini. [With plates, including a portrait.] pp. 37. *Mérida*, 1952. 8º. [*Publicaciones de la Universidad de los Andes. Dirección de Cultura.* no. 22.]
Ac. 1907. c.

—— Neo-Hippocratic Tendency of Contemporary Medical Thought. [With plates.] *New York*, 1934. 8º. [*Medical Life.* vol. 41. no. 3.]
P.P. 2894. da.

—— The Renaissance of Medicine in Italy . . . The Hideyo Noguchi Lectures. [With a portrait.] pp. xiv. 91. *Baltimore*, 1934. 8º. [*Publications of the Institute of the History of Medicine, Johns Hopkins University.* ser. 3. vol. 1.]
Ac. 2689. eb.

—— Storia della medicina. pp. xi. 959. pl. III. *Milano*, 1927. 8º.
7679. dd. 20.

—— Nuova edizione, riveduta e ampliata. pp. xxvii. 825. pl. VIII. *Milano*, 1936. 8º.
07680. dd. 18.

—— A History of Medicine. Translated . . . and edited by E. B. Krumbhaar . . . Second edition, revised and enlarged. [With a bibliography.] pp. xxx. 1192. lxi. *Alfred A. Knopf: New York*, 1947. 8º. **2024. e.**
A slip bearing the imprint, Routledge and Kegan Paul: London, has been pasted over the original imprint.

—— [Another copy.] A History of Medicine, *etc.* *New York*, 1947. 8º.
7682. d. 19.

CASTIGLIONI (BRUNO)

—— *See* ALBANIA. L'Albania, *etc.* [By B. Castiglioni, F. Milone and A. Sestini.] 1943. 8º.
10008. n. 3.

CASTIGLIONI (CAMILLO) Die Sammlung C. Castiglioni, Wien . . . Eingeleitet und beschrieben von Otto von Falke. pp. 167. pl. 106. *Berlin*, 1930. 4º.
7803. s. 3.

CASTIGLIONI (CARLO)

—— What to say in Italian, *etc.* pp. 127. *George Newnes: London*, 1946. 8º.
12942. aaa. 45.

CASTIGLIONI (CARLO) *Dottore dell' Ambrosiana.*

—— *See* CRIBELLUS (H.) *Mediolanensis.* Oratio parentalis in laudem Blancae Mariae Sfortiae Vicecomitis . . . A cura di C. Castiglioni. 1938. fol. [*MURATORI (L. A.) Rerum italicarum scriptores.* tom. 25. pt. 2.]
9168. l.

—— *See* FLAMMA (G. de la) Gualvanei de la Flamma . . . Opusculum de rebus gestis ab Azone, Luchino et Johanne Vicecomitibus . . . A cura di C. Castiglioni. 1938. fol. [*MURATORI (L. A.) Rerum italicarum scriptores.* tom. 12. pt. 4.]
9168. l.

—— *See* LANDULPHUS, *the Younger, de Sancto Paulo.* Landulphi Junioris . . . Historia Mediolanensis . . . A cura di C. Castiglioni. 1934. fol. [*MURATORI (L. A.) Rerum italicarum scriptores.* tom. 5. pt. 3.]
9168. l.

—— *See* RUBEUS (A.) Oratio . . . in laudem Johannis Galeatii Sfortiae Vicecomitis, Mediolani Ducis. A cura di C. Castiglioni. 1938. fol. [*MURATORI (L. A.) Rerum italicarum scriptores.* tom. 25. pt. 2.]
9168. l.

CASTIGLIONI (CARLO) *Dottore dell' Ambrosiana.*

—— *See* SABA (A.) Storia dei papi, *etc.* (vol. 2. Da Bonifacio VIII a Pio XI. [By C. Castiglioni.]) 1936. 4º.
20010. d. 30.

—— Il Cardinale Federico Borromeo, *etc.* [With plates, including portraits.] pp. xviii. 295. *Torino,* 1931. 8º.
4863. g. 21.

—— Napoleone e la Chiesa milanese, dal 1783 al 1818, *etc.* [With plates.] pp. 280. *Milano,* 1933. 8º.
10655. h. 30.

CASTIGLIONI (CARLO OTTAVIO) *Count. See* BIBLE.—*Corinthians.* [*Polyglott.*] Ulphilae gothica versio Epistolae Divi Pauli ad Corinthios secundae, quam . . . cum interpretatione, adnotationibus . . . edidit C. O. Castillionaeus. 1839. 4º.
689. g. 8.

—— *See* BIONDELLI (B.) Elogio del conte Carlo Ottavio Castiglioni, *etc.* [With a portrait.] 1856. 8º.
10631. f. 21.

—— *See* ULPHILAS, *Bishop of the Goths.* Ulphilae partium ineditarum in Ambrosianis palimpsestis ab Angelo Maio repertarum specimen, conjunctis curis ejusdem Maii et C. O. Castillionaei editum. 1819. 4º. **1216. k. 4. (1.)**

—— Considerazioni intorno al regime da adottarsi dai popoli della parte orientale dell'Alta Italia. pp. 32. *Milano,* 1848. 8º.
8032. e. 16.

—— Dell'uso cui erano destinati i vetri con epigrafi cufiche, e della origine, estensione e durata di esso. Memoria. (Inserita nel Giornale dell'I. R. Instituto ec.) pp. 67. pl. III. *Milano,* 1847. 4º.
7707. g. 29.

—— Mémoire géographique et numismatique sur la partie orientale de la Barbarie appelée Afrikia par les Arabes, suivi de recherches sur les Berbères Atlantiques, anciens habitans de ces contrées. pp. 127. *Milan,* 1826. 8º.
805. dd. 11.

—— Monete cufiche dell'I. R. Museo di Milano. [By Count C. O. Castiglioni. Edited by G. Cattaneo.] pp. xcii. 385. pl. XVIII. 1819. 4º. *See* MILAN.—*Imperiale Reale Museo di Milano.* **603. k. 2.**

CASTIGLIONI (CESARE) I Manicomj provinciali nel regno d'Italia, e l'organizzazione e amministrazione loro. Considerazioni. pp. 38. *Milano,* 1865. 4º. **7686. k. 7.**

CASTIGLIONI (FEDERICO) Della fisica educazione dei fanciulli. Dissertazione medico-politica. pp. 64. *Milano,* 1834. 8º. **1178. c. 12.**

CASTIGLIONI (FRANCESCO) *Marquis. See* OBIZZI (P. E. degli) *Marquis.* L'Atestis : poema . . . con gli argomenti del sig. march. F. Castiglioni, *etc.* 1642. 4º.
11429. ee. 11.

CASTIGLIONI (FRANCESCO XAVERIO) *See* PIUS VIII., *Pope.*

CASTIGLIONI (GIAN LUIGI CORNAGGIA MEDICI) *Count. See* CORNAGGIA-MEDICI-CASTIGLIONI.

CASTIGLIONI (GIOVANNI) *See* SALVEMINI DI CASTIGLIONE (G. F. M. M.)

CASTIGLIONI (GIOVANNI BATTISTA) *See* ESORTAZIONE. Vna Essortatione al Timor di Dio [attributed to Jacobus Acontius], *etc.* [Edited, with a dedicatory preface to Queen Elizabeth, by G. B. Castiglioni.] [1580 ?] 8º.
C. 53. b. 14.

CASTIGLIONI (ISAAC CHAYIM) *See* CASTIGLIONI (Vittorio)

CASTIGLIONI (LUIGI) *of Florence.* Collectanea graeca. pp. xiv. 303. *Pisis,* 1911. 8º. **11313. r. 6.**

—— Studi alessandrini. 1. Arianna e Teseo. pp. 60. 1908. *See* PISA.—*Reale Scuola Normale Superiore.* Annali, *etc.* Filosofia e filologia. vol. 21. 1871, *etc.* 8º.
Ac. 47. (a.)

—— Studi intorno alla storia del testo dell'Anabasi di Senofonte. *Milano,* 1932. fol. [*Memorie del R. Istituto Lombardo di Scienze e Lettere.* Classe di lettere, *etc.* vol. 24. fasc. 3.] **Ac. 110/5.**

—— Studi intorno alle fonti e alla composizione delle Metamorfosi di Ovidio. pp. iv. 385. 1907. *See* PISA.—*Reale Scuola Normale Superiore.* Annali, *etc.* Filosofia e filologia. vol. 20. 1871, *etc.* 8º.
Ac. 47. (a.)

—— Studi intorno alle " Storie filippiche " di Giustino. pp. vii. 152. *Napoli,* 1925. 8º. [*Biblioteca di Μουσειον.* vol. 3.] **20092. c. 5/3.**

CASTIGLIONI (LUIGI) *Patrizio Milanese.* Viaggio negli Stati Uniti dell'America Settentrionale, fatto negli anni 1785, 1786, e 1787 . . . Con alcune osservazioni sui vegetabili più utili di quel paese. [With plates.] 2 tom. *Milano,* 1790. 8º. **980. g. 25, 26.**

CASTIGLIONI (MANLIO)

—— *See* GARGIULO (A.) Scritti di estetica. A cura di M. Castiglioni. 1952. 8º. **07813. de. 17.**

—— Il Poema eroico di Federico Nietzsche. pp. 382. *Torino,* 1924. 8º. [*Letterature moderne.* vol. 8.] **11876. m. 1/8.**

CASTIGLIONI (PIETRO) *See* ITALY. [*Collections of Laws, etc.*] Codice sanitario del regno d'Italia, o Raccolta completa di leggi, decreti, regolamenti e circolari riguardanti la sanità interna, con noti e commenti . . . Opera compilata dal dottor P. Castiglioni. 1868. 8º.
5326. cc. 7.

—— *See* ITALY.—*Ministero dell'Interno.* Onore reso ai benemeriti della salute pubblica, relazione del Regio Ministro e nomi loro, con . . . considerazioni statistiche del cav P. Dr Castiglioni, *etc.* 1869. 8º. **10631. b. 40.**

—— Circoscrizioni amministrativa, giudiziaria, elettorale e diocesana, e dizionario dei comuni del regno d'Italia, comprese le provincie venete, *etc.* pp. vi. 242. *Firenze,* 1867. 4º. **10129. i. 5.**

—— Della monarchia parlamentare e dei diritti e doveri del cittadino secondo lo Statuto e le leggi del Piemonte. Trattato popolare con una appendice contenente lo Statuto, le ultime leggi organiche e politiche, *etc.* 2 vol. *Milano,* 1859, 60. 12º. **8032. c. 20.**

—— Della popolazione di Roma dalle origini ai nostri tempi. *See* ITALY.—*Istituto Centrale di Statistica.* Monografia della città di Roma, *etc.* pt. 2. 1878. 4º. **S. H. 401/2.**

CASTIGLIONI (VALERIANO) *See* CASTIGLIONE.

CASTIGLIONI (VITTORIO) *See* MISHNĀH. משיות . . . Mishnaiot . . . Con traduzione italiana, proemio e note illustrative di V. Castiglioni, *etc.* 1893. 8º.
01911. b. 13.

—— Saggi di pedagogia. Prima serie, *etc.* pp. viii. 139. *Torino,* 1895. 8º. **8311. c. 29.**

CASTIGO. Entremez intitulado : O Castigo da Ambiçaõ, ou O Velho avarento, enganado, e desenganado. [In verse.] pp. 16. *Lisboa,* 1771. 8º. **11726. bb. 45. (21.)**

—— Castigo de algunas mentiras, en el manifiesto de muchas verdades. [On the textile industry.] pp. 11. [1728 ?] fol. **1322. l. 2. (25.)**

CASTIGO.

—— Saynete, intitulado El Castigo de la Miseria. [In verse.] pp. 12. *Madrid*, 1791. 4°. 1342. f. 5. (32.)

—— [Another issue.] *Madrid*, 1791. 4°. [*Coleccion de Saynetes, etc.* tom. 2.] 11725. c. 21.

—— [Another edition.] pp. 12. *Barcelona*, [1830?] 4°. 11726. g. 5. (11.)

—— El Castigo de un Zeloso. Entremes. [In verse. By F. de Castro, or J. J. López de Castro?] *See* GARCÍA DE LA HUERTA (V. A.) Theatro Hespañol. pt. 4. 1785. 8°. 243. b. 19.

—— [Another edition.] Entremes nuevo: El Castigo de un Zeloso. [By F. de Castro, or J. J. López de Castro?] pp. 16. [1800?] 8°. 11725. aa. 2. (16.)

—— [Another copy.] 11726. aa. 4. (14.)

—— Romance nuevo. El Castigo del Asecino. Por F. O. [1830?] 4°. *See* O., F. 11450. f. 26. (15.)

—— El Castigo mas Piadoso, al Sobervio mas Cruel. Comedia famosa, de un ingenio de esta Corte. pp. 32. *Sevilla*, [1730?] 4°. 11726. f. 19.

—— Justo Castigo de los Revolucionarios Aprehendidos. [Signed: J. M. y G.] 1822. *s. sh.* fol. *See* M. Y G., J. 9770. k. 6. (122.)

—— El Mas inaudito, y exemplar castigo, que la Divina Magestad de Dios executó en dos mal entretenidos mancebos . . . Sucedió en la villa de Morales, *etc.* [In verse.] *J. Cabeças: Sevilla*, 1675. 4°. 811. e. 51. (18.)

CASTIGOS.
Castigos y dotrinas que un sabio daua á sus hijas. *See* KNUST (H.) Dos Obras didácticas y dos leyendas sacadas de manuscritos de la Biblioteca del Escorial. 1878. 8°. Ac. 8886/17.

CASTIL-BLAZE ( ) *See* BLAZE (F. H. J.) calling himself CASTIL-BLAZE.

CASTILE.

LAWS.

I. GENERAL COLLECTIONS.

—— *See* ARIAS DE BALBOA (V.) *Bishop of Plasencia.* Las Glosas de Arias de Balboa al Fuero Real de Castilla. [Edited by J. Cerdá Ruiz-Funes.] 1951, 52. 8°. [*Anuario de historia del derecho español.* tom. 21/22.] Ac. 145. c/15.

—— [Ordenanzas reales.] *Begin.* [fol. 4 *recto*:] enel nonbre [*sic*] de dios trino en personas ז vno en esneçia [*sic*] Aqui comiença la tabla delos libros ז titulos desta copilaçiõ de leyes que mandaron fazer ז copilar los muy altos ז muy poderosos prïçipes el Rey don fernando ז la Reyna doña ysabel nr̃os señores de todas las leyes ז pragmaticas fechas ז ordenadas por los rreyes de gloriosa memoria ante pasados, *etc. End.* [fol. 262 *recto*:] por mandado delos . . . prinçipes rrey dõ fernando ז rreyna doña ysabel . . . cõpuso este libro de leyes el doctor alfonso diaz de montaluo, *etc.* 𝕲.𝕴. [*Alvaro de*] *castro*: *huepte*, a onze dias del mes de nouïebre, 1484. fol. IB. 53402.
265 *leaves, ff.* 1–3, 161 (q 8), 229 (u 8) *and* 263–265 *blank; ff.* 10–86 *numbered* IIII–LXXX. *Sig.* [*⁶] a¹⁰ b¹⁰ c¹⁰⁺¹ d–i¹⁰ l–n¹⁰ o⁸ O⁸ p¹⁰ q⁸ r¹⁰ [¹⁰ S¹⁰ t¹² T⁸ v¹⁰ u⁸ x¹⁰ y¹⁰ J⁸ z⁸. *Double columns,* 41 *lines to a column. Imperfect; wanting ff.* 7 (a 1), 88 (i 1) *and the blank leaves* 1, 229 *and* 263–265.

CASTILE. [LAWS.—I. GENERAL COLLECTIONS.]

—— *Begin.* [fol. 3 *recto*:] enel nonbre de dios trino en psonas ז vno en esençia. Aqui comiença la tabla delos libros ז tiulos [*sic*] desta copilaçion de l̃yes q̄ mandaron fazer ז copilar . . . El rrey don fernãdo. E la rreyna doña ysabel nr̃os señores de todas las leyes. ז p̄agmaticas fechas ז ordenadas por los rreyes de gl̃iosa memoria ante pasados, *etc.* [fol. 314 *verso*:] por mãdado. delos . . . prinçipes rrey don fernãdo ז reina doña ysabel . . . ꝓpuso este libro. de leyes. El doctor alfonso diaz de motaluo [*sic*], *etc.* 𝕲.𝕴. [*Alvaro de*] *Castro*: *huepte*, a veĩte ז tres dias dl̃ mes de agosto, 1485. fol. IB. 53405.
316 *leaves, ff.* 1, 2, 132 (n 12), 254 (x 12) *and* 316 *blank. Sig.* [*⁸] a¹² b⁸ B⁶ c–h¹⁰ y¹⁰ l¹⁰ m¹⁰ n¹² o–q¹⁰ r⁸ r¹² [¹⁰ i¹⁰ s–u¹⁰ v¹⁰ x¹² z¹⁰ ã¹⁰ A–C¹⁰ D¹². *Double columns,* 35–38 *lines to a column. Without the blank leaf* 254 (x 12).

—— *Begin.* [fol. 1 *recto*:] [I]Ncipit secunda copilatio legum Et ordinationum regni castelle que a regibus hyspanie in generalibus curijs condite et promulgate fuerunt Vsque ad . . . Regem fernandũ Et . . . Reginam Helisabet . . . copilate et abreuiate per egregium doctorem Alfonsum de mõtaluo . . . Et de ydiomate in latinũ trãslate. Incipit prohemiũ feliciter. 𝕲.𝕴. [*Printer of Antonius Nebrissensis, Introductiones Latinae: Salamanca*, c. 1485.] fol. IB. 52807.
232 *leaves. Sig.* a–i k l–n¹⁰ o¹² p¹⁰ A–H¹⁰. 33 *lines of text to a page.*

—— *Begin.* [fol. 1 *verso*:] Enel nombre de dios trino en personas ז vno en esẽçia aqui comiença la tabla delos libros ז titulos desta copilaçion de leyes, *etc.* [fol. 4 *verso*:] Por mandado delos . . . prinçipes Rey don fernando ז Reyna doña ysabel . . . cõpuso este libro de leyes el doctor alfonso diaz de montaluo, *etc.* 𝕲.𝕴. *Por fadrigue aleman* [*i.e. Friedrich Biel*]: *burgos*, a veynte ז q̄tro dias de setiẽbre, 1488. fol. IB. 53216.
266 *leaves, ff.* 3 *and* 266 *blank; ff.* 5–265 *numbered* I–CCLX. *Without signatures. Double columns,* 35 *lines to a column.*

—— [fol. 1 *recto*:] [Reportoriũ Montalui.] [fol. 5 *recto*:] Incipit secũda cõpilatio legũ et ordinationũ regni Castelle: que a regibus Hyspanie in generalibus curijs cõdite ז promulgate fuerunt: vsꝗ ad Serenissimũ ז inuictissimũ dñm regẽ Ferdinãdũ ז Serenissimã reginã Helisabeth dñam nostraz eius cõiugem: laboriose ז vtiliter cõpilate ז abreuiate per Egregiũ doctorẽ Alfonsũ de Montaluo: dictorũ dñorum regũ auditorẽ ז sui consilij: ז de ydeomate in latinum trãslate. FEW MS. NOTES. 𝕲.𝕴. ff. cxxxiiij. *cura ז diligẽcia Meynardi· hungut alemani. et Stanislay polonij: in ciuitate Hyspalẽsi*, iiiij. ydus februarij [10 Feb.], 1496. fol. IB. 52400.
138 *leaves. Sig.* a–p⁸ q⁶ r⁸. *Double columns,* 45 *lines to a column. Imperfect; wanting the first quire of four leaves, signed* ✠. *Previous edition* c. 1485.

—— Leyes. del. estilo y declaraciones sobre. las leyes. del fuero. 𝕲.𝕴. [*Leonhard Hutz & Lope Sanz:*] *salamãca*, a diez dias de hebrero, 1497. fol. Add. MS. 9929. ff. 2–37.
36 *leaves. Sig.* a–f⁶. *Double columns,* 51, 52 *lines to a column.*

—— Ordenanças reales por las quales primeramẽte se hã de librar todos los pleytos ciuiles ז criminales, *etc.* [fol. 4 *recto*:] Por mandado delos . . . principes Rey don Fernando ז Reyna doña ysabel nuestros señores. Compuso este libro de leyes el doctor Alfonso diaz de montaluo, *etc.* 𝕲.𝕴. *Salamãca*, a veynte ז nueue de Março, 1500. fol. Add. MS. 9929. ff. 48–221.
174 *leaves,* 2–174 *so numbered. Sig.* a–x⁸ y⁶. 48 *lines to a column. Previous edition* 1488.

—— Leyes des estillo. y declaraciones sobre las leyes del fuero. *I. Gysser aleman de Silgenstad: Salamanca*, 1502. fol. C. 54. f. 21.
Previous edition 1497.

CASTILE. [Laws.—i. General Collections.]

—— [Another edition.] **G.ℜ.** *I. Varela de Salamanca:*
Toledo, 1511. fol. C. **63**. k. **14**.

—— [Another copy.] **I.B.52842.(5.)**

—— [Another edition.] **G.ℜ.** ff. xxiiii. *R. de Petras:*
Toledo, 1525. fol. **503**. g. **12**.

—— [Another edition.] **G.ℜ.** ff. xxx. MS. NOTES.
[*J. de Junta: Salamanca,* 1540?] fol. **503**. g. **13**.

—— Ordenáças reales d' Castilla por las quales primeramente
se an de librar todos los pleytos ciuiles ꝛ criminales. E los
q̃ porellas no se fallarē determinados se an d' librar por las
otras leyes ꝛ fueros ꝛ derechos. Nueuamēte corregidas,
etc. **G.ℜ.** ff. cxvii. *J. de Junta: Salamanca,* 1541. fol.
5383. gg. **7**.
Previous edition 1500.

—— Las Leyes del Estilo,.*etc.* **G.ℜ.** ff. xxx. [*J. de Junta:*
Salamanca, 1545?] fol. **503**. g. **14**.
Previous edition 1502.

—— Solenne repertorium, seu secunda compilatio legum
Montalui, seu glossa super leges ordinationū. Regni
nuperrime in lucem æditum subtiliterꝗ Emēdatum et in
pluribus copiosæ Additum. ff. cxxxiii. *in officina*
typographica Petri de Castro: Salmanticæ, 1549. fol.
503. g. **9**.
Previous edition 1496.

—— [Another edition.] **G.ℜ.** ff. xxvii. [*J. de Junta:*
Salamanca,] 1550. fol. **5384**. gg. **10**.

—— [Another copy.] **502**. g. **10**. (2.)

—— Ordenanças reales de Castilla, por las quales . . . se
han de librar y juzgar todos los pleytos ciuiles y criminales
(recopiladas por Alonso Diaz de Montaluo), nueuamēte
glossadas . . . con las aplicaciones de los fueros de
Aragon, y ordenanças de Portugal: por . . . Diego Perez,
etc. coll. 1572. FEW MS. NOTES. *I. M. a Terranoua,*
expensis I. Moreni: Salmanticæ, 1560. fol.
5385. ee. **9**.
Previous edition 1541. The date in the colophon is 1559.

—— Las Leyes del Estilo, *etc.* ff. 28. MS. NOTE.
I. B. de Terranoua: Salamanca, 1569. fol.
501. g. **1**. (2.)
Previous edition 1550. *The upper margin and part of the*
text are mutilated.

—— [Another copy.] G. **4303**. (2.)

—— [Ordenanzas reales.] Commentaria in quatuor priores
(posteriores) libros ordinationum regni Castellæ, authore
Doctore Didaco Perez de Salamanca . . . Nunc denuò
in hac secunda editione recognita, *etc.* [With the Spanish
text.] 2 vol. **G.ℜ.** *In ædibus D. à Portonarijs, expensis*
V. à Portonarijs: Salmanticæ, 1575, 74. fol. **1237**. f. **7**.
Previous edition 1560, 69.

—— El Fuero Viejo de Castilla, sacado, y comprobado con
el exemplar de la misma obra, que exîste en la Real
Biblioteca de esta Corte, y con otros MSS. Publicanlo con
notas historicas, y legales los doctores D. Ignacio
Jordan de Asso y del Rio, y D. Miguel de Manuel y
Rodriguez. pp. lvi. 143. *Madrid,* 1771. fol.
24. f. **6**. (1.)

—— Ordenanzas Reales de Castilla. Recopiladas, y com-
puestas por . . . Alonso Diaz de Montalvo. Glosadas
por . . . Diego Perez, y adicionadas por el mismo autor
en los lugares que concuerdan con las leyes de la nueva
recopilacion. 3 tom. *Madrid,* 1779, 80. fol. **710**. l. **4–6**.
Previous edition 1575, 74.

CASTILE. [Laws.—i. General Collections.]

—— El Fuero Real de España . . . hecho por el noble rey
Don Alonso IX: glosado por . . . Alonso Diaz de
Montalvo. Asimismo por un sabio doctor de la Uni-
versidad de Salamanca addicionado, y concordado con las
siete partidas, y leyes del Regno, *etc.* (Las Leyes del
Estilo, *etc.*) 2 tom. *Madrid,* 1781. fol. **707**. h. **30**.
Imperfect; wanting pp. 67–70 of tom. 2.

—— Opúsculos legales del Rey Don Alfonso el Sabio. (El
Espéculo ó Espejo de todos los derechos.—El Fuero real,
las Leyes de los Adelantados mayores, las Nuevas y el
Ordenamiento de las Tafurerias; y por apéndice las
Leyes del estilo.) 2 tom. 1836. 4°. *See* MADRID.—*Real*
Academia de la Historia. **710**. k. **5**.

—— El Fuero Viejo de Castilla. [Previous edition 1771.]
See SPAIN. [*Laws, etc.*—i.] Los Códigos Españoles, *etc.*
tom. 1. 1847, *etc.* 4°. **5384**. h. **8**.

—— Libro de los Fueros de Castiella. Publicado por Galo
Sánchez. [From a MS. in the Bibliothèque Nationale.]
pp. xvi. 166. 1924. 8°. *See* BARCELONA.—*Universidad*
de Barcelona.—Facultad de Derecho. Ac. **136**. b.

—— Kastilische Fazañas. a. Aus dem Libro de los Fueros de
Castiella. (b. Aus dem Fuero Viejo, Buch i.).—Fuero viejo
de Castiella, Libro ii. *Span. & Ger. See* WOHLHAUPTER
(E.) Altspanisch-gotische Rechte, *etc.* 1936. 8°.
[*Germanenrechte.* Bd. **12**.] Ac. **2121**.

II. CHRONOLOGICAL SERIES.

ALPHONSO VI. [1072–1109.]

—— Fuero de Miranda de Ebro. Edición crítica, versión y
estudio. [By Francisco Cantera Burgos. With facsimiles and a map.] pp. 189. pl. IV. *Madrid,* 1945. 8°.
05385. l. **9**.

ALPHONSO VIII., *King.* 1158–1214.]

—— Der Prinzgemahl. Ein pactum matrimoniale aus dem
Jahre 1188. [The text of the marriage treaty between
Frederick Barbarossa and Alphonso VIII. of Castile, with a
facsimile and commentary.] pp. 111. 1950. 8°. [*Quellen*
und Studien zur Verfassungsgeschichte des Deutschen Reiches
in Mittelalter und Neuzeit. Bd. 8. Hft. 1.] *See* RASSOW
(P.) **9325**. h. **3/23**.

ALPHONSO IX., *King.* [1188–1230.]

—— El Fuero de Coria. Estudio histórico-jurídico por José
Maldonado y Fernández del Torco . . . Transcripción y
fijación del texto por Emilio Sáez, *etc.* [With facsimiles
and a map.] pp. cclxxxii. 157. pl. v. 1949. 8°. *See*
MADRID.—*Instituto de Estudios de Administración Local.*
05385. l. **10**.

ALPHONSO X., *King,* called *the Wise.* [1252–1284.]

—— " Ordenamientos de posturas y otros capítulos generales"
otorgados a la ciudad de Burgos por el rey Alfonso X, *etc.*
[Decrees dated 12 Oct. 1252 and 15 Feb. 1258, with introductory essays and notes by Ismael García Rámila.] *In:*
Hispania. tom. 5. no. 19–21. 1945. 8°. Ac. **132**. e/**11**.

——[Fuero Real de España.] Foro Real gloxado de Spagna.
[With the Latin gloss of Alonzo Diaz de Montalvo.
With a woodcut.] **G.ℜ.** *Arte Simonis de Luere:*
Impensis Andree Torresani: in Venetiarum vrbe, p̄die
idus Ianuarij [12 Jan.], 1500. fol. IC. **24662**.
160 leaves, ff. 62 *and* 160 *blank,* 2–151 *numbered* ii–cl, cl.
Sig. a–c⁸ d⁶ e–s⁸ t¹⁰ (ij–iiij)⁸. *Double columns,* 84 *lines of*
gloss enclosing the text to a column. With the device of
Torresanus.

—— Fuero Real de España: Diligētemēte hecho por el noble Rey dō Alōso. ix. Glosado por . . . Alonzo Diaz de mōtaluo. Assimesmo por vn sabio doctor de la vniuersidad de Salamanca addicionado y concordado con las Siete partidas. y Leyes d'l reyno: dando a cada ley la addicion que conuenia. **G.L.** ff. cclxiii. *J. de Junta: Burgos*, 1541. fol. **5385. ee. 4.**

—— [Another copy.] C. **20. e. 4.**

—— [Another edition.] [Edited by Christoforus de Avila.] **G.L.** ff. cclxiii. *G. de Milles ; por P. de castro impressor: Medina del campo*, 1544. fol. **503. g. 17.**

—— [Another edition.] ff. cclxiii. few ms. notes. *Apud G. de Millis: [Medina del Campo,]* 1547. fol. **502. g. 10. (1.)**
The date in the colophon is 1543.

—— [Another edition.] ff. 263. *I. B. de Terranoua: Salamanca*, 1569. fol. **501. g. 1. (1.)**

—— [Another copy.] G. **4303. (1.)**
With an additional leaf containing corrections of errata in the "Fuero Real" and in the "Leyes del estilo" published in the same year.

—— [Another edition.] *See supra :* Laws.—i. *General Collections.* El Fuero Real de España, *etc.* 1781. fol. **707. h. 30.**

—— [Another edition.] *See* Spain. [*Laws, etc.—i.*] Los Códigos Españoles, *etc.* tom. 1. 1847, *etc.* 4º. **5384. h. 8.**

—— Fuero real de Afonso x, o Sábio. Versão portuguesa do século xiii. Publicada e comentada por Alfredo Pimenta. pp. xi. 459. *Instituto para a Alta Cultura: Lisboa*, 1946. 8º. **05385. l. 14.**

—— *See* López Ortiz (J.) La Colección conocida con el titulo " Leyes nuevas " y atribuida a Alfonso x el Sabio. 1945. 8º. [*Anuario de historia del derecho español.* tom. 16.] Ac. **145. c/15.**

—— [Las Siete Partidas.] *Begin.* [fol. 1 *verso:*] Aqui comiençan los titulos dela primera Partida. *End.* [fol. 424 *recto:*] Aquestas siete Partidas fizo collegir el muy excelente Rey don Alfonso el nono . . . paresçio alos Serenissimos ז muy altos ז muy poderosos don Fernando ז doña ysabel Rey ז Reyna de Castilla ז de Leon de Aragon ז de Siçilia זc. que se deuiessen poner enlos lugares conuenientes delos capitulos delas principales leyes que enestas siete partidas se contienē las adiçiones del Doctor de Montaluo, *etc.* **G.L.** *por Meynardo Ungut Alamano, ז Lançalao Polono conpañeros: Seuilla*, veynte ז cinco dias del mes de otubre, 1491. fol. IB. **52358.**
424 *leaves, ff.* 74 (R 6), 146 (u 8), 147 (aa 1), 248 (oo 6), 249 (A 1), 335 (AA 1) *and* 424 (l 10) *blank. Sig.* a–g⁸ h–k⁶ m–u⁸ ; aa² bb–mm⁸ nn⁶ oo⁶ ; A¹⁰ B–D⁸ E⁴ G–M⁸ ; AA–KK⁸ LL¹⁰. *Double columns,* 62 *lines to a column.*

—— *Begin.* [fol. 1 *recto:*] Primera partida. *End.* [fol. 479 *verso:*] Las siete partidas quel serenissimo ז muy excellēte señor don Alfonso rey de Castilla ז de Leon . . . fizo ז mando conpilar ז reduzir a muy prouechosa brueidad de todas las principales fuerças iudiciales por . . . aprobados iurisconsultos. Fueron impressas en . . . Seuilla . . . Uan en estas siete partidas las adiciones ז cōcordanças fechas por el doctor de montaluo. **G.L.** *paulo de colonia ז Iohañes pegniczer ז Magno ז Thomas compañeros alamanes: Seuilla*, a. xxiiij. dias de deziembre, 1491. fol. IB. **52327.**
480 *leaves, ff.* 88 (l 8), 172 (ll 6), 284 (ooo 8), 382 (G 6), 426 (FF 6) *and* 480 (GGG 6) *blank. Sig.* a–l⁸ ; aa–ii⁸ kk⁶ ll⁶ ; aaa–ooo⁸ ; aaaa¹⁰ bbbb–dddd⁸ eeee¹⁰ ; A–F⁸ G⁶ ; AA–DD⁸ EE⁶ FF⁶ ; AAA–FFF⁸ GGG⁶. *Double columns,* 52 *lines to a column.*

—— Repertorio muy copioso de el Texto y Leyes de las Siete Partidas, agora en esta vltima impression, hecho por . . . Gregorio Lopez de Touar, va por su abecedario. (Omnes fere tituli tam iuris ciuilis quam canonici leguntur in istis Septem Partitarum legibus, quod sequens tabula demōstrat . . . ædita . . . per . . . Gregorium Lopez à Touar.—Index. seu Repertorium materiarum ac vtriusque iuris decisionum quæ in singulis septem Partitarum glossis continentur . . . concinnatum per . . . Gregorium Lopez à Touar.) 3 pt. *D. de Portenarijs: Salamanca*, 1576. fol. **1891. f. 12.**
The date in the colophon of pt. 3 is 1577.

—— Las Siete Partidas de las leyes del sabio Rey Don Alonso el nono, glosadas por . . . Gregorio Lopez de Touar. (Reportorio de las siete partidas.—Index materiarum.) 9 pt. *I. Hasrey: Madrid*, 1611, 10. fol. C. **74. i. 7.**
The titlepage is mutilated.

—— [Another edition.] Cotejadas con varios codices antiguos por la Real Academia de la Historia. 3 tom. 1807. 4º. *See* Madrid.—*Real Academia de la Historia.* **503. f. 14–16.**

—— [Another edition.] 4 tom. *Madrid*, 1829–31. fol. **710. l. 11–14.**

—— [Another edition.] Estractadas por . . . Ignacio Velasco Perez, *etc.* pp. 671. 94. *Madrid*, 1843. 4º. **5385. c. 2.**

—— [Another edition.] 4 tom. *Madrid*, 1843, 44. 4º. **1238. g. 7, 8.**

—— [Another edition.] 5 tom. *Paris*, 1843, 44. 4º. **1239. f. 1.**

—— [Another edition.] 1848. *See* Spain. [*Laws, etc.—i.*] Códigos Españoles, *etc.* tom. 2. 1847, *etc.* 4º. **5384. h. 8.**

—— [Another edition.] Nuevamente comentadas y concordadas con los demas códigos y con las leyes . . . y sentencias del Tribunal Supremo publicadas hasta el dia, por . . . Clemente Fernandez Elías, con la colaboracion del Lic. D. José Ximenez Torres, y vertida la glosa al castellano por D. Antonio Perez Romeo. 2 tom. *Madrid*, 1877. 16º. **5384. aa. 19.**

—— Compendio del derecho publico y comun de España, o de las leyes de las Siete Partidas colocado en orden natural por Vicente Vizcaino Perez. 4 tom. *Madrid*, 1784. 8º. **503. a. 25–28.**

—— Compendio de las leyes de las Siete Partidas . . . Por . . . Vicente Vizcaino Perez . . . Primera edicion corregida y aumentada . . . por el L. D. J. A. E. [A prospectus.] pp. 11. *México*, 1835. 4º. **9770. bb. 23. (40.)**

—— *See* Perez Mozun (Diego) Diccionario alfabético y ortográfico de las voces, que en sus siete célebres partidas usó el Rey Don Alonso el Sabio. 1790, *etc.* 4º. **503. c. 23. (1.)**

—— Alphonso xi., *King.* [1312–1350.] El Ordenamiento de Leyes, que D. Alfonso xi. hizo en las Cortes de Alcalá de Henares el año de mil trescientos y quarenta y ocho. Publicanlo con notas, y un discurso sobre el estado, y condicion de los Judios en España, los doctores D. Ignacio Jordan de Asso y del Rio, y D. Miguel de Manuel y Rodriguez. pp. xxxiv. 158. *Madrid*, 1774. fol. **24. f. 6. (2.)**

—— [Another edition.] pp. xxx. 139. *Madrid*, 1847. 4º. **1238. g. 13**

CASTILE. [LAWS.—II. CHRONOLOGICAL SERIES.]

—— [Another edition.] *See* SPAIN. [*Laws, etc.—*i.] Los Códigos Españoles, *etc.* tom. 1. 1847, *etc.* 4°. **5384. h. 8.**

—— HENRY IV., *King.* [1454–1474.] *Begin.* Don Enrique, por la gracia de Dios Rey de Castilla, *etc.* [Granting the city and marquisate of Astorga to Alvaro Pérez Osorio, Count de Trastamara, in return for his services. 16 July 1465.] [*Madrid*, 1645.] fol. **1324. k. 15. (1.)**

—— JOANNA, *Queen.* [1504–1516.] [Las Leyes de Toro.] Quaderno delas leyes y nueuas decisiones fechas ⁊ ordenadas enla cibdad de Toro sobre las dudas de derecho, *etc.* [7 March 1505.] G.L. [*Salamanca?* 1505?] fol. **Add. MS. 9929. ff. 250–257.**

—— Quaderno delas leyes y nueuas decisiones sobre las dubdas de derecho que continuamente soliã y suelen ocurrir en estos reynos, en q̃ auia mucha diuersidad de opiniones entre los doctores y letrados destos reynos, *etc.* G.L. [*R. de Petras: Toledo*, 1525.] fol. **T. 92*. (1.)**

—— Las Leyes de Toro glosadas. Vtilis ⁊ aurea glosa dñi Didaci Castelli . . . super leges Tauri feliciter incipit. [With the text.] ff. clxiiii. *In officina I. Iunctę: Burgis*, 1527. fol. **503. g. 15.**

—— [Another copy.] MS. NOTES. **5385. ee. 24. (1.)**

—— Quaderno de las leyes y nueuas decisiones fechas . . . en la cibdad de Toro sobre las dudas de derecho, *etc.* G.L. MS. NOTES. [*R. de Petras: Toledo*, 1530?] fol. **5385. ee. 24. (2.)**

—— Glosemata: legum Tauri quas vulg⁹ de Toro appellat . . . a J. lopez de Palacios ruuios . . . elucubrata atꝗ digesta foeliciter incipiunt. [With the text. Edited by Alphonsus Perez de Bivero.] G.L. ff. cxii. MS. NOTES. *Expensis I. de Junta: in florentissima Salmanticensi academia*, 1542. fol. **5385. ee. 10.** *Slightly cropped.*

—— Las leyes de Toro glosadas. Vtilis ⁊ aurea glosa domini Didaci Castelli . . . super leges Tauri. Nuper ab eodem recognita additis insuper . . . doctissimis ac necessarijs additionib⁹ ⁊ glosis, *etc.* G.L. ff. ccxxvj. *In officina I. juncte: Salmanticē. vrbe*, 1544. fol. **507. g. 23.**

—— Quaderno de las leyes y nueuas decisiones, hechas y ordenadas en la ciudad de Toro sobre las dudas de derecho . . . Con la glosa de Miguel de Cifuētes, *etc.* G.L. ff. l. MS. NOTES. *P. de Castro: Medina del Campo*, 1546. fol. **T. 92*. (2.)**

—— Glosa de Miguel de Cifuentes sobre las leyes de Toro. Quaderno de las leyes y nueuas decisiones, hechas y ordenadas en la ciudad de Toro, *etc.* G.L. ff. l. *Por M. y F. del Canto; a costa de J. Moreno: Medina del Campo*, 1555. fol. **T. 92*. (3.)**

—— Opus praeclarum et vtilissimum super legibus Tauri . . . per Antonium Gomez, *etc.* [With the text.] ff. 323. *Excudebat A. à Portonarijs: Salmanticæ*, 1560. fol. **498. h. 16.**

—— Quaderno de las Leyes y nueuas decisiones hechas y ordenadas en la ciudad de Toro, *etc.* ff. 8. *Impresso en casa de P. Lasso a costa de M. Perez: Salamanca*, 1591. 4°. **5383. ff. 25. (1.)**

—— Dr. Antonij Gomezij . . . Ad leges Tauri. commentarius. Cui accesserunt Doctoris Diegi Gomezij . . . annotationes vtilissimæ, & pernecessariæ, *etc.* pp. 590. MS. NOTES. *Apud P. & I. Belleros: Antuerpiae*, 1617. fol. **1480. c. 9.**

CASTILE. [LAWS.—II. CHRONOLOGICAL SERIES.]

—— Comentario critico-juridico-literal á las ochenta y tres leyes de Toro; su autor Don Sancho de Llamas y Molina, *etc.* [With the text.] 2 tom. *Madrid*, 1827. fol. **710. l. 10.**

—— Tercera edicion, ilustrada con notas y adiciones . . . por Don José Vicente y Caravantes. 2 tom. *Madrid*, 1853. 8°. **5385. d. 11.**

—— [Another edition.] Por Don J. F. Pacheco. (tom. 2 por D. J. Gonzalez y Serrano.) 2 tom. *Madrid*, 1862, 76. 8°. **5385. cc. 7.**

—— Quinta edicion . . . por Don José Vicente y Caravantes. 2 tom. *Madrid*, 1875. 8°. **5385. cc. 1.**

—— *See* CIFUENTES (M. de) Noua lectura siue declaratio legū Taurinarū, *etc.* 1536. fol. **5383. ff. 5.**

—— Ordenãças nueuamēte hechas: sobre el obraje de los Paños: Lanas: Bonetes: ⁊ Sombreros, *etc.* [1 June, 1511.] G.L. [*R. de Petras: Toledo*, 1525?] fol. **C. 63. m. 12. (3.)**

—— [Another edition.] [1525?] fol. **IB.52842.(3.)** *Imperfect; wanting all after fol.* xii.

—— [Another edition.] G.L. ff. 12. MS NOTES. *J. de Ayala: Toledo*, 1544. fol. **C. 62. f. 5. (2.)**

—— [Another edition.] G.L. ff. xxiii. *In casa de I. d'Brocar; venden se en casa de Salzedo: Alcala de Henares*, 1552. fol. **Add. MS. 9931. ff. 311–330.**

———

—— Las Prematicas, Ordenanças, Ley, y Facultad dada por sus magestades [Ferdinand and Isabella, to the merchants of Burgos, granted also by Joanna of Castile] por privilegio especial, a la vniversidad de la contratacion de los fiel, y consules de la muy noble villa de Bilbao. *I. de Lorza: Bilbao*, [1670?] fol. **503. g. 29. (2.)**

OFFICIAL BODIES.

CONSEJO DE CASTILLA.

—— *See* SPAIN.

CORTES.

—— Cortes celebradas en los reynados de D. Sancho IV y de D. Fernando IV. Publicanlas con algunas observaciones los doctores D. Ignacio Jordan de Asso y del Rio, y D. Miguel de Manuel y Rodriguez. pp. 42. *Madrid*, 1775. fol. **8042. l. 13.**

—— [Another copy.] **24. f. 6. (3.)**

—— Coleccion de Cortes de los reynos de Leon y de Castilla. 1836–45. 4°. *See* LEON, *Kingdom of.—Cortes.* **1445. k. 8.**

—— Actas de las Córtes de Castilla, publicadas por acuerdo del Congreso de los Diputados, á propuesta de su comision de Gobierno interior. Tomo primero [*etc.*]. Contiene las de Madrid, celebradas el año 1563 [*etc.*]. *Madrid*, 1877, 62– . fol. **S. o. 12.** *Wanting tom.* 17, 19, 32–43, 46–48.

—— Cortes de los antiguos reinos de Leon y Castilla, *etc.* 5 tom. 1883–1903. 4°. *See* LEON, *Kingdom of.—Cortes.* **1859. b. 10.**

JUNTA DE LAS COMUNIDADES DE CASTILLA.

—— Proyecto de la Constitucion de la Junta de las Comunidades de Castilla. [Edited by Luis de Usoz y Rio.] pp. 13. *Valladolid*, 1842. 8°. **1389. f. 33. (2.)**

CASTILE. [Official Bodies.]

Patronato de Castilla.

—— El Patronato de Castilla y la presentación de diócesis en tiempo de Felipe II, *etc.* [Documents. Edited by M. Lasso de la Vega López de Tejada Zayas y Quintanilla, Marquis del Saltillo.] *In:* Boletín de la Real Academia de la Historia. tom. 123. pp. 419–522. 1948. 8°.
Ac. 6630/7.

APPENDIX.

—— Censo de poblacion de las provincias y partidos de la corona de Castilla en el siglo XVI. Con varios apendices para completar la del resto de la peninsula en el mismo siglo, *etc.* [Edited by Tomas Gonzalez.] pp. 399. *Madrid*, 1829. fol.
573. l. 7.

—— Coleccion de las Cronicas y Memorias de los Reyes de Castilla. 7 tom. *Madrid*, 1779–87. 4°.
179. d 6-12.

—— [Another copy.] **L.P.**
G. 6276-82.

—— Comedia nueva, primera parte, el miralo todo, en Castilla en Napoles, y en Sicilia. De un Sevillano Ingenio. [In verse.] pp. 32. *Salamanca*, [1730?] 4°.
11726. f. 63.

—— [Another edition.] [1750?] 4°.
T. 1734. (5.)

—— Compendio general de las contribuciones, y gastos, que ocasionan todos los efectos, frutos, caudales, y demás, que se trafican entre los reynos de Castilla, y America, *etc.* pp. 158. *Cadiz*, 1762. 4°.
8244. b. 48.

—— Fuentes para la historia de Castilla, por los PP. Benedictinos de Silos. *See* DOMINIC [Manso], *Saint, Benedictine Abbey of, at Silos.*

—— Historia del Bastardo de Castilla en Africa, ó el Castillo del Diablo. pp. 24. *Madrid*, 1857. 4°.
12330. h. 24. (2.)

—— [Another edition.] pp. 24. *Madrid*, [1881?] 4°.
12330. l. 6. (10.)

—— *Begin.* Lo Mas importante que oy ay que remediar en estos Reynos de la Corona de Castilla, *etc.* (Esta relacion, aunque parte della se a Lado antes, aora va ampliada, y con nuevas advertencias.) On the state of the Spanish currency.] 2 pt. [1630?] fol.
1322. l. 12. (63.)

—— The Pilgrime of Casteele. [Translated from Lope de Vega's "El Peregrino en su patria."] pp. 150. *By John Norton: London*, 1621. 4°.
C. 57. e. 23.

—— [Another edition.] pp. 150. *Edw. All-de for J. N.* [*John Norton*]; *solde by Tho. Dewe: London*, 1623. 4°.
12612. c. 7.

—— Resumen, y extracto de los sacrilegios . . . que por las informaciones autenticas, executad..., de orden de los Ordinarios Eclesiasticos de los Obispados de Siguença, Cuenca, Osma, y Arçobispado de Toledo, se justifica, averse cometido por los soldados y tropas del Archiduque . . . en las dos ocasiones, que internaron en este Reyno de Castilla en los años de 1706 y 1710. pp. 74. *Madrid*, [1711.] 4°.
T. 1302. (8.)

—— *Begin.* Señor. Los Libreros de los Reinos de Castilla dizen, *etc.* [A petition to the King asking for relief from the tax on books.] [1636?] fol.
1322. l. 3. (32.)

—— *Begin.* Señor. Siendo tan notoria la enfermedad que con la moneda de vellō padecen los Reynos desta Corona de Castilla, *etc.* (El assumpto deste discurso es, *etc.*) [Two letters to the King, on the currency question.] 2 pt. [1630?] fol.
1322. l. 12. (47.)

CASTILE. [Appendix.]

—— Souvenirs archéologiques des Castilles et du Midi français. Quelques jours de voyage en Espagne 1869. pp. 446. *Tulle*, 1874. 8°.
7708. aaa. 8.

CASTILE, *Province of.—Augustine Monks. Begin.* Estos discursos, que se escriven, è imprimen, es precisso, que tengan algun fin honesto, *etc.* [A memorial relating to the prolongation of the Provincial Chapter.] ff. 8. [1683?] fol.
4783. e. 1. (20.)

—— *Begin.* Hase procurado, y deseado ceñir este resumen, *etc.* [A memorial relating to the prolongation of the Provincial Chapter.] [1683?] fol.
4783. e. 1. (17.)

—— *Begin.* Ilustrᵐᵒ Señor. Los Maestros Fr. Pedro de Ortega . . . Fr. Luis Criado, *etc.* [A memorial relating to the prolongation of the Provincial Chapter.] [1683?] fol.
4783. e. 1. (18.)

—— Verdadera Noticia de lo que ha passada en orden à un breue, que por orden de su santidad, y su sagrada congregacion de regulares expidiò el . . . Nuncio de España, mandando dilatar vn año el capitulò provincial y sus oficios en la provincia de Castilla de la orden de N. P. S. Agustin, *etc.* ff. 8. [1683?] fol.
4783. e. 1. (19.)

—— *Carmelite Monks. Begin.* Ni la modestia religiosa permite que en puntos de descredito publico se calle, *etc.* [Relating to the authority of the Provincial Chapter.] [1680?] fol.
4783. e. 1. (29.)

—— *Franciscans.* Causa de S. Francisco. Razones por la pura y simple obseruancia de su regla, sin dispensacion, tam in capite, quam in membris. En orden a que no subsistan vnas letras, de que intenta valerse el Obispo de Ouiedo . . . A. de Salizanes, por continuarse General . . . Presentalo a la reyna . . . su prouincia de Castilla, junta en difinitorio. ff. 16. [1668?] fol. 4783. e. 3. (9.)

—— Por la causa de S. Francisco. Verdad contra la espumosa cauilacion de vna Relacion sin firma, ni autor, que intenta macularla. ff. 6. [1669?] fol.
4783. e. 3. (11.)

CASTILE AND LEON. Este libro se llama doctrinal delos caualleros En q̄ estā copiladas ciertas leys E ordenāças q̄ estā enlos fueros E partidas delos rreynos de castilla E de leon tocantes alos caualleros, *etc.* 1487. fol. *See* DOCTRINAL.
I.B.53211.

—— *Begin.* Los Libreros de los Reynos de Castilla y Leon . . . dizen, que si bien V.S. como prototypo verdadero que los representa, *etc.* [A petition for relief from the tax on books.] ff. 4. [1635?] fol. 1322. l. 3. (31.)

—— *Begin.* Señor. Los Libreros de los Reynos de Castilla, y Leon, *etc.* [A petition for relief from the tax on books.] ff. 4. [*Granada?* 1635?] fol.
1322. l. 9. (9.)

—— [Another copy.]
1322. l. 3. (30.)

—— *Begin.* Señor. Pusieron en las Reales manos de V. Magestad los libreros de Castilla, y Leon vna Suplica, *etc.* [A petition for relief from the tax on books.] ff. 4. [*Granada*, 1635?] fol.
1322. l. 9. (6.)

—— *Estado Eclesiastico.* Informacion de derecho en favor del Estado Ecclesiastico destos reynos de Castilla, y Leon, para que los Monasterios, y todos los que tienen priuilegios de no dezmar, tienen obligacion de contribuyr en los dozientos y cincuenta mil ducados, cō que el Estado Eclesiastico sirue a su Magestad por razon del Escusado. ff. 8. [*Madrid*, 1597.] fol.
1322. k. 14. (15.)

—— Por el Estado Ecclesiastico, y santa congregazion de la corona de Castilla, y de Leon, sobre la forma de las pagas del subsidio y escusado, con que sirve el clero de estos reynos a su Magestad. pp. 78. [1630?] fol.
1322. k. 14. (21.)

CASTILE AND LEON.

—— *Begin.* Señor. La Congregacion de las Santas Iglesias de Castilla y Leon, dize, *etc.* [A petition to the King of Spain against the exemption of a certain religious house from tithes, and the sale of offices to the prejudice of the Church.] ff. 6. [1640?] fol. **1322. k. 14. (1.)**

—— *Begin.* Señor. La Congregacion del Estado Eclesiastico de las Santas Iglesias de Castilla y Leon: dize, *etc.* [A protest against the sale of certain offices claimed to be under the jurisdiction of the Church.] ff. 6. [1640?] fol. **1322. k. 14. (3.)**

CASTILE, LEON AND GRANADA, *United Kingdoms of.* *See* SPAIN.

CASTILE (PEARL)

—— *See* BROOKES (Henry S.) A Text-book of Surgical Nursing. By H. S. Brookes . . . and P. Castile, *etc.* 1940 [1945]. 8°. **07688. e. 51.**

CASTILETI (JOANNES) *See* GUYOT (Jean) called CASTILETI.

CASTILHO (ALEXANDRE MAGNO DE) *See* CASTILHO BARRETO DA NORONHA (J. F. de) and CASTILHO (A. M. de) Formules pour la mnémonisation des souverains Pontifes, *etc.* 1835. 8°. **4570. aaa. 13.**

—— *See* CASTILHO BARRETO DA NORONHA (J. F. de) and CASTILHO (A. M. de) Traité de mnémotechnie, *etc.* 1833. 8°. **8471. bbb. 69.**

—— *See* EPHEMERIDES. Almanach de Lembranças para 1851, [*etc.*] [1851–61 edited by A. M. de Castilho, 1862–72 by A. M. de Castilho and A. X. Rodrigues Cordeiro.] 1853, *etc.* 12°. **P.P. 2387. b.**

—— Études historico-géographiques. Première étude sur les colonnes ou monuments commémoratifs des découvertes portugaises en Afrique, *etc.* pp. 62. *Lisbonne*, 1869. 8°. **10096. gg. 14.**

CASTILHO (ANTONIO FELICIANO DE) *Viscount de Castilho.*
See CERVANTES SAAVEDRA (M. de) [*Don Quixote.—Portuguese.*] O Engenhoso Fidalgo Dom Quichote de la Mancha . . . Traductores Viscondes de Castilho e de Azevedo, *etc.* 1876, *etc.* fol. **Cerv. 353.**

—— *See* G., T. Literatura Portuguesa. [A biographical notice of A. F. de Castilho.] 1837. 4°. **1444. e. 8. (14.)**

—— *See* GALLEANO-RAVARA (A.) Album Italo-Portuguez. [With an introduction by A. F. de Castilho.] 1853. 8°. **11452.aaa.29.**

—— *See* GOETHE (J. W. von) [*Faust.—Tl. 1.—Portuguese.*] Fausto. Poema dramatico trasladado [by A. F. de Castilho], *etc.* 1882. 8°. **11745. h. 9.**

—— *See* GOETHE (J. W. von) [*Faust.—Tl. 1.—Selections.—German and Portuguese.*] O Faust de Goethe e a traducção do Visconde de Castilho. Por J. de Vasconcellos. [With selected passages in Castilho's translation, in the original, and in a literal translation by J. de Vasconcellos.] 1872. 8°. **11745. ee. 6.**

—— *See* LATINO COELHO (J. M.) Escritos literários e políticos, *etc.* (Garrett e Castilho.) [1917, *etc.*] 8°. **W.P. 6060.**

—— *See* MALHEIRO DIAS (A.) Castilho e Quental. Reflexões sobre a actual questão litteraria. 1866. 8°. **011840. h. 53. (3.)**

—— *See* MOLIÈRE (J.B.P.de) [*Two or more Works.—Portuguese.*] Theatro de Molière. Primeira(—sexta e ultima) tentativa vertida . . . ao Portuguez [by A. F. de Castilho], *etc.* 1870, *etc.* 8°. **11736. cc. 6.**

CASTILHO (ANTONIO FELICIANO DE) *Viscount de Castilho.*

—— *See* OVIDIUS NASO (P.) [*Amores.—Portuguese.*] Os Amores . . . Traducção paraphrastica . . . por A. F. de Castilho, *etc.* 1858. 8°. **11385. f. 34.**

—— *See* OVIDIUS NASO (P.) [*Ars Amatoria.—Portuguese.*] Arte de amar . . . Traducção . . . por A. F. de Castilho, *etc.* 1862. 8°. **11355. cc. 12.**

—— *See* OVIDIUS NASO (P.) [*Fasti.—Latin and Portuguese.*] Os Fastos . . . Com traducção em verso portuguez por A. F. de Castilho. 1862. 8°. **11375. g. 17.**

—— *See* OVIDIUS NASO (P.) [*Metamorphoses.—Portuguese.*] As Metamorphóses . . . Poema . . . vertido em Portuguez por A. F. de Castilho. 1841. 8°. **11375. aa. 27.**

—— *See* PERIODICAL PUBLICATIONS.—*Lisbon.* Revista universal Lisbonense, *etc.* (Redigido por A. F. de Castilho, *etc.*) 1842, *etc.* 4°. **P.P. 4128.**

—— *See* PINTO DE CAMPOS (J.) Jerusalem. [With a preface by A. F. de Castilho.] 1874. 8°. **10077. l. 26.**

—— *See* QUENTAL (A. do) Bom-senso e bom-gusto. Carta ao excellentissimo señor A. F. de Castilho. [Occasioned by Castilho's letter on the literary school of Coimbra, printed with M. Pinheiro Chagas' " Poema da Mocidade."] 1865. 8°. **11826. d. 45. (3.)**

—— *See* RIBEIRO (T.) D. Jayme ou A dominação de Castella. Poema . . . com uma conversação preambular pelo senhor A. C. de Castilho. 1862. 8°. **11453. cc. 9.**

—— *See* RIBEIRO (T.) D. Jayme . . . Com uma conversação preambular pelo senhor A. F. de Castilho. 1863. 8°. **11452. bbb. 44.**

—— *See* RIBEIRO (T.) Elogio historico de Antonio Feliciano de Castilho, *etc.* [With a portrait.] 1877. 8°. **10601. d. 5. (4.)**

—— *See* RIBEIRO SARAIVA (A.) Saraiva e Castilho a proposito de Ovidio. [1862.] 8°. **12230. aaa. 10.**

—— *See* SHAKESPEARE (W.) [*Midsummer Night's Dream.—Portuguese.*] Sonho d'uma Noite de S. João. [Translated by A. F. de Castilho.] 1874. 8°. **11766. bb. 7.**

—— *See* TEIXEIRA DE VASCONCELLOS (A. A.) Os Senhores A. A. Teixeira de Vasconcellos, A. F. de Castilho e A. Osorio de Vasconcellos sobre a questão Coimbrã. 1866. 8°. **8304. b. 20. (6.)**

—— Adjuste de contas com os adversarios do Metodo Português. pp. 110. *Coimbra*, 1854. 16°. **12942. aaa. 22. (1.)**

—— Camões. Estudo historico-poetico liberrimamente fundado sobre um drama francez dos senhores Victor Perrot e Armand Du Mesnil. pp. 300. *Ponta Delgada*, 1849. 8°. **11452. c. 28.**

—— 2ª edição, copiosamente accrescentada nas notas. 3 tom. *Lisboa*, 1863. 18°. **11452. bbb. 23.**

—— Cartas de Echo e Narciso . . . seguidas de differentes peças, relativas ao mesmo objecto . . . Terceira edição . . . augmentada. pp. 224. *Coimbra*, 1836. 12°. **1161. b. 38. (2.)**

—— Nova edição, *etc.* pp. 149. *Pernambuco*, 1837. 12°. **11452. ee. 16.**

—— Diretorio para os senhores professores das escolas primarias pelo Metodo Português. pp. 57 [59]. FEW MS. NOTES. *Coimbra*, 1854. 16°. **8355. a. 35. (6.)**

—— Elogio historico do sócio Augusto Federico de Castilho, *etc.* *See* CASTILHO (Augusto F. de) Practicas Religiosas, *etc.* 1866. 8°. **4407. h. 18.**

CASTILHO (Antonio Feliciano de) *Viscount de Castilho.*

—— Epicedio na sentida morte da augustissima senhora D. Maria 1., Rainha fidelissima. pp. 23. *Lisboa,* 1816. 8°. **11452. c. 23.**

—— Epistola a sua magestade a senhora imperatriz do Brazil D. Teresa. [In verse.] pp. 19. *Coimbra,* 1856. 8°. **11452. cc. 20.**

—— Estreias poetico-musicaes para o anno liij. Por A. F. de Castilho e F. N. dos Santos Pinto. [With musical notes.] pp. 62. *Lisboa,* 1853. 8°. **11452. c. 25.**

—— Excavações poeticas. pp. 294. *Lisboa,* 1844. 8°. **11452. g. 23.**

—— [Another copy.] **11452. h. 6.**

—— A Faustissima exaltação de sua magestade fidelissima o senhor D. João vi. ao trono. Poema. pp. 82. *Lisboa,* 1818. 8°. **11452. c. 24.**

—— [Another copy.] **9180. ccc. 5. (12.)** *This copy contains a portrait of the author.*

—— Felicidade pela Instrucção. pp. 117. *Lisboa,* 1854. 8°. **11726. bb. 56. (3.)**

—— Methodo Portuguez Castilho . . . 4ª edição. pp. 142. *Lisboa,* 1857. 8°. **12942. aaa. 23. (4.)**

—— Mil e um mysterios, romance dos romances. tom. 1. pp. 285. *Lisboa,* 1845. 8°. **12491. g. 4.** *No more published.*

—— A Noite do Castello, e Os Ciumes do Bardo. Poemas, seguidos da Confissão de Amelia traduzida de Melle Delfine Gay. pp. xxii. 200. *Lisboa,* 1836. 12°. **1161. b. 38. (1.)**

—— O Outono. Collecção de poesias. pp. xxxv. 274. *Lisboa,* 1863. 8°. **11452. c. 27.**

—— A Primavera. Collecção de poemetos. pp. 181. *Lisboa,* 1822. 8°. **11452. a. 19.**

—— Segunda edição . . . accrescentada. pp. 330. *Lisboa,* 1837. 12°. **1161. b. 37.**

—— Quadros historicos de Portugal. [Plates, with descriptive letterpress.] pp. 58. *Lisboa,* 1838. fol. **648. c. 6.**

—— Recueil de souvenirs du cours de mnémotechnie de M. de Castilho. pp. xvi. 160. *Saint-Malo,* 1831. 8°. **8311. c. 4.**

—— Recueil des questions auxquelles M. de Castilho s'engage à répondre dans ses séances publiques de mnémotechnie. pp. 159. *Saint-Germain,* 1832. 8°. **8307. ee. 47.**

—— Taboada de Multiplicação Mnemonisada, *etc.* [*Lisbon?* 1851?] *s. sh.* fol. **806. k. 15. (147.)**

—— Tosquia d'un Camelo. Carta a todos os mestres das aldeas e das cidades. pp. 52. *Lisboa,* 1853. 8°. **10909. c. 25. (1.)**

—— Tratado de Metrificação Portugueza . . . 2ª edição correcta e augmentada. pp. xii. 156. *Lisboa,* 1858. 8°. **12943. bb. 7.**

—— Tratado de Mnemonica, ou Methodo facilimo para decorar muito em pouco tempo. pp. xix. 220. *Lisboa,* 1851. 8°. **8309. a. 25.**

—— Tributo Portuguez, á memoria do Libertador [i.e. Don Pedro]. pp. 97. *Lisboa,* 1836. 16°. **10632. a. 33.**

CASTILHO (Antonio Feliciano de) *Viscount de Castilho,* and **CASTILHO BARRETO E NORONHA** (José Feliciano de)

—— Livraria Classica Portugueza. Excerptos de todos os principaes Auctores Portuguezes de boa nota, assim prosadores como poetas. 25 tom. *Lisboa,* 1845-47. 16°. **12231. aa. 2.** *Imperfect; wanting pp.* 129-144 *of tom.* 12, *and pp.* 57-64 *of tom.* 16.

—— [Another edition.] tom. 1-8, 11-13. *Rio de Janeiro: Paris* [printed], 1865-75. 8°. **12231. e. 9.**

—— Tributo á memoria de sua majestade . . . Pedro Quinto o muito amado. pp. 127. *Rio de Janeiro,* 1862. 8°. **10632. cc. 14.**

CASTILHO (Artur)

—— Alguns aspectos agrícolas da Beira-Douro. Conferência, *etc.* pp. 39. *Porto,* 1952. 8°. **7082. b. 6.**

CASTILHO (Augusto de)

—— *See* Marques Santos (V.) Augusto de Castilho na Zambézia. 1952. 8°. [*Colecção Pelo império.* no. 125.] **S.L. 200/21.**

—— *See* Portugal. [*Appendix.*] Portugal e Brazil. Conflicto diplomatico. i. O processo . . . do capitão de fragata A. de Castilho, *etc.* 1894, *etc.* 8°. **8180. h. 35.**

—— Relatorio da Viagem da Corveta Mindello de Lisboa a Loanda pela Madeira, S. Thiago e S. Thomé . . . 1891-1892. pp. 77. 1892. fol. *See* Portugal.—*Navy.* **10497. ff. 44.**

CASTILHO (Augusto Frederico de) Practicas Religiosas . . . Precedido de um elogio historico por Antonio F. de Castilho. pp. xiv. 122. *Rio de Janeiro,* 1866. 8°. **4407. h. 18.**

CASTILHO (Eugenio de) *See* Dickens (Charles) [*Single Tales and Plays.*] Canticos do Natal. Traducção de E. de Castilho. 1873. 16°. **012601. ee. 73.**

CASTILHO (Francisco Alves da Silva) *See* Alves da Silva Castilho.

CASTILHO (Guilherme de)

—— António Nobre. [With plates, including portraits.] pp. 330. *Lisboa,* 1950. 8°. **10634. i. 61.**

CASTILHO (José Feliciano de) *See* Castilho Barreto e Noronha.

CASTILHO (Julio de) *See* Ferreira (A.) Antonio Ferreira, poeta quinhentista. [Selections.] Estudos biographico-litterarios por J. de Castilho. 1875. 8°. [*Livraria Classica, etc.* vol. 11-13.] **12231. e. 9/11-13.**

—— *See* Porto-Carrero (R. de) Lisboa, Coimbra e Porto e a questão litteraria. A carta do sr. A. do Quental ante os srs. Pinheiro Chagas . . . e J. de Castilho, *etc.* 1866. 8°. **011840. h. 53. (2.)**

—— D. Ignez de Castro. Drama em cinco actos e em verso. pp. xxiii. 356. *Rio de Janeiro; Paris* [printed], 1875. 12°. **11726. aaa. 1.**

—— Lisboa Antiga. 7 tom. *Lisboa,* 1879-1890. 8°. **10162. b. 1.**

—— Primeiros Versos. pp. 213. *Rio de Janeiro; Paris* [printed], 1867. 8°. **11452. b. 8.**

CASTILHO (JULIO DE)

—— A Ribeira de Lisboa. Descripção historica, *etc.*
pp. xxii. 750. *Lisboa*, 1893. 8°.   **10162. i. 2.**

CASTILHO (LUIZ DE) Industria assucareira. Estudo da
fabricação pelo processo da diffusão na usina Duquerry
em Guadelupe . . . Notas relativas á cultura da canna
nesses paizes. pp. 111. *Rio de Janeiro*, 1889. 8°.
    07942. k. 23. (1.)

CASTILHO (PEDRO DE) *Bishop of Leiria.* Constituçoens
Synodaes do Bispado de Leiria. Feytas, & ordenadas
em synodo pello Senhor Dom P. de Castilho, *etc.*
ff. 136. 1601. 4°. *See* LEIRIA, *Diocese of.* **5107. ee. 17.**

CASTILHO BARRETO (ADRIANO ERNESTO DE) As
Vinte e cinco Prisões. tom. 1. pp. 208.   *Lisboa*,
1845. 16°.   **10632. a. 30.**
No more published.

CASTILHO BARRETO E NORONHA (JOSÉ FELI-
CIANO DE) *See also* BETTENCOURT (Abel C. de) *pseud.*
[i.e. J. F. de Castilho Barreto e Noronha.]

—— *See* CASTILHO (A. F. de) *Viscount de Castilho*, and
CASTILHO BARRETO E NORONHA (J. F. de) Livraria
Classica Portugueza, *etc.* 1845, *etc.* 16°. **12231.aa.2.**

—— —— 1865, *etc.* 8°.   **12231. e. 9.**

—— *See* CASTILHO (A. F. de) *Viscount de Castilho*, and
CASTILHO BARRETO E NORONHA (J. F. de) Tributo á
memoria de . . . Pedro Quinto, *etc.* 1862. 8°.
    10632. cc. 14.

—— *See* FRANCO DE ALMEIDA (T.) O Brazil e a Inglaterra,
ou o Trafico de Africanos. Precedido de uma Carta do
conselheiro J. F. de Castilho Barreto e Noronha.
1868. 8°.   **8156. aaa. 27.**

—— A Aguia no ovo e nos astros, sive a Eschola Coimbrã
na sua aurora e em seo zenith . . . Por um Lisboeta
convertido [i.e. J. F. Castilho Barreto e Noronha]. (Primeira parte.) pp. 34. 1866. 8°. *See* COIMBRA SCHOOL.
    11826. d. 45. (4.)

—— Dissertation sur la nostalgie ; thèse, *etc.* pp. 31. *Paris*,
1831. 4°.   **1184. d. 16. (29.)**

—— A Escola Coimbrã. Cartas . . . ao Correio Mercantil
do Rio de Janeiro. 2 pt. *Lisboa*, 1866. 8°.
    011824. f. 41.

—— Estudo sobre o Missal de Estevam Gonçalves. pp. 41.
Rio de Janeiro, 1874. 8°.   **7807. k. 17. (2.)**

—— Grinalda da Arte de amar. *See* OVIDIUS NASO (P.)
[*Ars Amatoria.—Portuguese.*] Arte de Amar, *etc.*
1862. 8°.   **11355. cc. 12.**

—— A Grinalda Ovidiana, appendice á paraphrase dos Amores.
See OVIDIUS NASO (P.) [*Amores.—Portuguese.*] Os
Amores, *etc.* 1858. 8°.   **11385. f. 34.**

—— Relatorio á cerca da Bibliotheca Nacional de Lisboa e
mais estabelecimentos annexos. 4 tom.   *Lisboa*,
1844, 45. 8°.   **824. f. 5, 6.**

CASTILHO BARRETO E NORONHA (JOSÉ FELI-
CIANO DE) and **CASTILHO** (ALEXANDRE MAGNO DE)

——   Formules
pour la mnémonisation des souverains Pontifes et des
Conciles généraux. pp. 55. *Bordeaux*, 1835. 8°.
    4570. aaa. 13

CASTILHO BARRETO E NORONHA (JOSÉ FELI-
CIANO DE) and **CASTILHO** (ALEXANDRE MAGNO DE)

—— Traité de mnémotechnie, ou exposition des principes de
cet art, et de ses principales applications. pp. xvi. 230.
Paris, 1833. 8°.   **8471. bbb. 69.**

CASTILHON (JEAN) *See* MARITI (G.) Voyages dans
l'Isle de Chypre, la Syrie et la Palestine . . . traduits de
l'italien [by J. Castilhon ?]. 1791. 8°. **280. e. 29, 30.**

—— *See* PERIODICAL PUBLICATIONS.—*Liége.* Journal encyclopédique, *etc.* [By J. Castilhon and others.]
[1756, *etc.*] 12°.   **251. a–i.**

—— *See* PERIODICAL PUBLICATIONS.—*Paris.* Journal des
beaux-arts et des sciences, *etc.* [1774–75 by J. and J. L.
Castilhon.] 1768, *etc.* 12°.   **P.P. 1890.**

—— *See* PERIODICAL PUBLICATIONS.—*Paris.* Le Nécrologe
des hommes celèbres de France, *etc.* [By J. Castilhon
and others.] 1767, *etc.* 12°.   **612. d. 10–18.**

—— *See* ROBINET (J. B. R.) Dictionnaire universel des
sciences, *etc.* [Compiled with the assistance of J. Castilhon
and others.] 1777, *etc.* 4°.   **64. c. 1.**

—— *See* TURPIN DE CRISSÉ (L.) *Count*, and CASTILHON (J.)
Amusemens philosophiques et litteraires de deux amis,
etc. 1756. 12°.   **8403. d. 30. (1.)**

—— —— 1764. 12°.   **12331. a. 31.**

—— Histoire de Jean de Calais, sur de nouveaux mémoires.
[By J. Castilhon.] pp. 120. 1770. 12°. *See* JEAN, *de
Calais.*   **276. e. 16.**

—— Histoire de Jean de Calais. Par M * * * [i.e. J. Castil-
hon]. Dixième édition. pp. 32. [1820?] 12°. *See* M * * *.
    12430. aa. 2. (5.)

—— Histoire de Robert le Diable, duc de Normandie, et
de Richard sans peur, son fils. [By J. Castilhon.]
pp. xiii. 243. 1769. 8°. *See* ROBERT, *le Diable.*
    12410. aaa. 12.

CASTILHON (JEAN LOUIS) *See* PERIODICAL PUBLICA-
TIONS.—*Liége.* Journal encyclopédique. [From 1770 by
J. L. Castilhon and others.] [1756, *etc.*] 12°. **251. a–i.**

—— *See* PERIODICAL PUBLICATIONS.—*Paris.* Journal des
beaux-arts et des sciences, *etc.* [1774, 75 by J. and J. L.
Castilhon.] 1768, *etc.* 12°.   **P.P. 1890.**

—— *See* PLUTARCH. [*Moralia.—French.*] Essais de philosophie et de morale, en partie traduits librement et en partie
imités de Plutarque ; par M. L. Castilhon. 1770. 8°.
    231. f. 18.

—— *See* PLUTARCH. [*Moralia.—Abridgments and Selections.*]
De l'influence de la vertu et du vice sur le bonheur et le
malheur. Réflexions tirées de Plutarque. 1769. 8°.
[*Le Temple du bonheur, etc.* tom. 1.]   **231. e. 1.**

—— Considérations sur les causes physiques et morales de la
diversité du génie, des mœurs, et du gouvernement des
nations. Tiré en partie d'un ouvrage anonyme [entitled
" L'Esprit des Nations," by F. I. Espiard de La Borde].
pp. xix. 579. *Bouillon*, 1769. 8°.   **8005. df. 8.**

—— [Another edition.] 3 tom. *Bouillon*, 1770. 8°.
    521. b. 30.

—— Essai sur les erreurs et les superstitions. Par M. L. C . . .
[i.e. J. L. Castilhon]. pp. 411. 1765. 12°. *See* C . . .,
M. L.   **8631. aaa. 14.**

—— Nouvelle édition . . . augmentée. 2 tom.
Francfort, 1766. 8°.   **4506. b. 7.**

CASTILHON (Jean Louis)

—— Zingha, reine d'Angola. Histoire africaine, *etc.* 2 pt. *Bouillon*, 1769. 12º. **012548. e. 4.**

CASTILHON (Pierre) Convention nationale. Compte des dépenses faites par P. Castilhon envoyé au Havre . . . par décret du 8 ventose dernier. pp. 2. [*Paris*,] an III [1795]. 8º. **F. 1552. (26.)**

CASTILHOS GOYCOCHÊA (Luiz Felippe de)
—— À margen da filosofia das ciências. pp. iv. 267. *Rio de Janeiro*, 1953. 8º. **8476. aa. 20.**

CASTILIAN AUTHORS. Coleccion de autores selectos Latinos y Castellanos. *See* Latin Authors.

CASTILIAN BROTHERS. The Castilian Brothers; Chateaubriant; Waldemar; three tragedies: and the Rose of Sicily, a drama. [Each in verse.] By the author of "Ginevra" [i.e. F. A. H. Terrell], *etc.* pp. 278. *Kegan Paul & Co.: London*, 1883. 8º. **11781. cc. 54.**

CASTILIAN DICTIONARY.

—— Dictionario castellano . . . Dictionnaire François. Dictionari catala, *etc.* [By Pedro Lacavalleria.] *Pere Lacavalleria: Barcelona*, 1642. *obl.* 8º. **629. a. 5.**

CASTILIAN-INDIAN CATECHISM.

—— Pequeño catecismo castellano-indio—araucano . . . Nueva edición [of "Pequeño catecismo castellano-indio para enseñar la doctrina cristiana á los indios, *etc.*"] hecha por Rodolfo R. Schuller. 1707. 8º. **03504. ff. 18. (1.)**

CASTILIAN LANGUAGE. Coleccion de refranes y locuciones familiares de la lengua castellana . . . Por F. V. y M. B. 1841. 8º. *See* V., F., and B., M. **12305. c. 39.**

—— Declamacion contra los abusos introducidos en el Castellano . . . Siguela una disertacion sobre la lengua castellana, y la antecede un dialogo que explica el designio de la obra. [By Josef de Vargas y Ponce.] pp. xxvi. 214. *Madrid*, 1793. 4º. **829. e. 35.**

—— Diccionario de la lengua castellana . . . Compuesto por la Real Academia Española. *See* Madrid.—*Real Academia Española.*

—— Diccionario de la lengua castellana, redactado sobre la última edicion del de la Academia . . . por D. y M. 1846. 16º. Apéndice. Verbos irregulares de la lengua castellana. Puestos en órden alfabético por D. 1846. 16º. *See* D. and M. **829. a. 23.**

—— Diccionario de sinónimos de la lengua castellana, por una sociedad de literatos. [By Pedro María de Olive as far as E, and continued by Santos López Pelegrín.] pp. iii. 162. *Paris*, 1853. 4º. **12943. g. 4.** *This work was also issued as a part of the "Nuevo diccionario de la lengua castellana," entered below.*

—— Diccionario portátil de la lengua castellana segun la Academia Española, el mas completo de los publicados hasta el dia. pp. 1061. *Paris*, 1862. 8º. **12942. ccc. 1.**

—— Nuevo diccionario de la lengua castellana, que comprende la última edicion del de la Academia Española. Aumentado con cerca de 100,000 voces pertenecientes á las ciencias . . . Con un suplemento que contiene el diccionario de la rima [by Juan Peñalver] y el de sinónimos [by Pedro María de Olive as far as E, and continued by Santos López Pelegrín]. Por una sociedad literaria. 3 pt. *Paris*, [1853.] fol. **12943. h. 2.** *The "Diccionario de sinónimos" was also issued separately.*

CASTILIAN LANGUAGE.

—— Nuevo diccionario de la lengua castellana . . . Por D. R. B. 1856. 8º. *See* B., D. R. **12943. b. 29.**

—— [Nuevo diccionario de la lengua castellana.] Novísimo diccionario de la lengua castellana que comprende la última edicion íntegra del publicado por la Academia Española y cerca de cien mil voces, acepciones, frases y locuciones añalidas por una Sociedad de Literatos. Aumentado con un suplemento . . . y seguido del Diccionario de sinónimos de D. Pedro M. de Olive [completed by Santos López Pelegrín] y del Diccionario de la rima de D. Juan Peñalver. 3 pt. *Paris*, 1873. fol. **12942. k. 5.**

—— Novísimo Diccionario de la lengua castellana, *etc.* 3 pt. *Paris*, 1891 [1890]. fol. **12943. k. 1.**

—— [A reissue.] Nuevo diccionario de la lengua castellana, *etc.* 3 pt. *Paris*, 1873. fol. **12942. k. 1.**

—— Refranes de la Lengua Castellana. 2 pt. *Barcelona*, 1815. 8º. **12304. b. 21.**

—— Rhetorica en lengua castellana, en la qual se pone muy en breue lo necessario para saber bien hablar y escreuir; y conoscer quien habla, y escriue bien . . . Por vn frayle de la orden de sant Hieronymo. **G.L.** ff. cxvii. *En casa de I. de Brocar: Alcala de Henares*, 1541. 4º. **C. 63. f. 22.**

—— Soneto joco-serio al miserable estado á que se ve reducida la lengua castellana. [Signed: F. Ll., i.e. Felipe Llédías.] 1831. *s. sh.* 4º. *See* Ll., F. **1870. d. 1. (249****.)**

CASTILIAN MARTYRS. The Castilian Martyrs. A tale of the sixteenth century. pp. 95. *R.T.S.: London*, [1857.] 12º. **4419. c. 24.**

CASTILIAN ORTHOGRAPHY. Orthographia Castellana, *etc.* [Signed: A. F., i.e. A. de Fonseca.] [1660?] 12º. *See* F., A. **627. c. 36.**

CASTILIAN POETRY. Tesoro de la Poesía Castellana. Siglo 15–19. 5 tom. *Madrid*, 1877, 74–76. 16º. [*Biblioteca Universal.* tom. 30, 17–18, 20, 22.] **739. a. 17, 18, 20, 22 & 30.**

CASTILIAN PROVERBS.

—— Refranes Castellanos y Sentencias de los Santos Padres. Texto del siglo XVII publicado por . . . Antonio Palau y Dulcet. [A reprint of the Spanish part of "Recueil des plvs belles sentences des pères de l'église. En Latin, en François & en Espagnol," *etc.*] pp. 32. *Barcelona*, 1928. 8º. **3670. df. 27.**

CASTILIANS. Castellanos y Vascongados. Tratado breve de una disputa y diferencia que hubo entre dos amigos, el uno castellano de Búrgos y el otro vascongado en la villa de Potosí, reino del Perú. Documento hasta ahora inédito, publicado por Z * . . .. pp. 290. *Madrid*, 1876. 8º. **8042. b. 13.**

CASTILIAN-ZAPOTEC VOCABULARY.

—— Vocabulario castellano-zapoteco. Publicado por la Junta Colombina de México. Con motivo de la celebración del cuarto centenario del descubrimiento de América. [An edition of an anonymous manuscript of the eighteenth century.] pp. iii. 222. 1893. fol. *See* Mexico.—*Junta Colombina.* **12907. h. 11.**

—— [Another copy.] **12907. h. 12.**

CASTILIO (Baldessar) *Count. See* Castiglione.

CASTILIO (DONATUS) *See* CORRADUS (Q. M.) Q. M. Corradi . . . De lingua latina . . . libri XIII, *etc.* [Edited by D. Castilio.] 1575. 4°. **12932. cc. 11.**

CASTILIONAEUS (GASPAR) *Admiral of France. See* COLIGNY.

CASTILIONAEUS (JOANNES ANTONIUS) *See* CASTIGLIONE (Giovanni A.)

CASTILIONAEUS (SABBAS) *See* CASTIGLIONE (Saba da)

CASTILIONE (FRANCISCUS COTTA À) *See* COTTA À CASTILIONE.

CASTILIONEUS (BONAVENTURA) *See* CASTIGLIONE.

CASTILIONEUS (FRANCISCUS) *See* CASTIGLIONE (Francesco)

CASTILIONEUS (MATTHAEUS) *See* CASTIGLIONE (Matteo)

CASTILIONEUS (VINCENTIUS) *See* CASTIGLIONE (Vincenzo)

CASTILIONIUS (GULIELMUS PHILANDER) *See* PHILANDER (G.)

CASTILIONUS (ANGELUS) *See* CASTIGLIONE (Angelo)

CASTILLA. *See* CASTILE.

CASTILLA (DE) *See* MARY, *the Blessed Virgin.* [*Churches and Institutions.*]—Alençon.—*Monastère de la Visitation.* Notice sur le Monastère de la Visitation d'Alençon, 1689–1694 . . . avec annotations de MM. de Castilla, L. Duval, *etc.* 1915. 8°. **04782. h. 30.**

CASTILLA (A. DELGADO) *See* DELGADO CASTILLA.

CASTILLA (ALFONSO TORRES DE) *See* TORRES DE CASTILLA.

CASTILLA (ALONSO DE) *of Seville.* Discreto, y nuevo romance en que se declara, y dà cuenta de la peregrina, y tragica historia . . . de Don Alonso de Castilla. [In verse.] *Valencia,* [1750?] 4°. **T. 1957. (92.)**

CASTILLA (ALONSO VERDUGO Y) *Count de Torrepalma. See* VERDUGO Y CASTILLA.

CASTILLA (ANDRES CRIADO DE) *See* CRIADO DE CASTILLA.

CASTILLA (ANTONIA DE RIBA DE NEIRA Y) *See* XAEN Y MEDRANO (A. de)

CASTILLA (ANTONIO DE) *See* CASTILLO (A. del)

CASTILLA (DIEGO DE) Copias de cartas escritas por Don D. de Castilla . . . para el Ilustrisimo Señor Presidente de Castilla. ff. 6. [1655?] fol. **1322. k. 13. (6.)**

—— *Begin.* Señor. Don Diego de Castilla, Señor de la Casa de Castilla, *etc.* [A memorial to the King praying that the title of Marquis should be conferred on him.] [1622.] fol. **T. 16*. (28.)**

—— *Begin.* Lo que está verificado y prouado, *etc.* [A further memorial praying for the title of Marquis.] [1623?] fol. **1324. i. 2. (108.)**

CASTILLA (EDUARDO SANCHEZ DE) *See* SANCHEZ DE CASTILLA.

CASTILLA (ETHEL) The Australian Girl, and other verses. (Second edition.) pp. 64. *Elkin Mathews: London,* 1914. 8°. **011649. eee. 42.**

CASTILLA (FERNANDO DE LEÓN Y) *Marquis del Muni. See* LEÓN Y CASTILLA.

CASTILLA (FRANCISCO DE) Delos tratados de philosophia moral en coplas de dõ F. de Castilla. Los siguientes. El prohemio de su theorica de virtudes. Los prouerbios. Inquisicion dela felicidad enmetaphora. La Satirica lamentacion de humanidad. Otras cosas de deuocion, *etc.* **G.𝔏.** *A. d'Burgos: Seuilla,* 1546. fol. **G. 11370.**

—— Fabula de Acteon . . . Tercetos. 1773. *See* LOPEZ DE SEDANO (J. J.) Parnaso Español, *etc.* tom. 7. 1768, *etc.* 8°. **242. k. 34.**

—— Oracion panegyrica gratulatoria a las familias santissimas, que celebraron la beatificacion del . . . padre San Juan de La Cruz. *See* CEBREROS (D.) Sevilla festiva, *etc.* 1676. 4°. **486. c. 4. (2.)**

—— [Theorica de virtudes, *etc.*] Pratica de las virtudes de los buenos reyes despaña en coplas de arte mayor. pt. 2. **G.𝔏.** *G. Costilla: Murcia,* 1518. fol. **C. 63. i. 11.** *Imperfect; wanting pt.* 1 *entitled "Theorica de virtudes."*

—— Theorica de virtudes en coplas, y con cõmento, compuesta por don F. de Castilla y otras obras suyas en metro, *etc.* (Pratica de las virtudes de los buenos Reyes Despaña en coplas de arte mayor.) **G.𝔏.** 2 pt. *A. Millan: Caragoça,* 1552. 4°. **C. 37. e. 1.**

CASTILLA (GABRIEL SANCHEZ DE) *See* SANCHEZ DE CASTILLA.

CASTILLA (IGNACIO DE) *See* SPAIN. [*Laws, etc.*—II. *Roads.*] Código y manual de construccion . . . de los caminos vecinales . . . Arreglado por D. I. de Castilla. 1848. 8°. **5385. d. 12.**

CASTILLA (J. GERONIMO MURO DE) *See* MURO DE CASTILLA.

CASTILLA (JOANNES) Lectio rethorica in honorem D. Isidori . . . in ipso solemnis suæ festivitatis vespere . . . habita . . . A. à Nat. D. M.DCC.XV. pp. 16. [*Seville,* 1715.] 4°. **1474. b. 55. (1.)** *Cropped.*

CASTILLA (JOSÉ JOAQUÍN CAICEDO) *See* CAICEDO CASTILLA.

CASTILLA (JUAN DE PEDRAZA Y) *See* PEDRAZA Y CASTILLA.

CASTILLA (JULIAN DE) The English Conquest of Jamaica. An account of what happened in the island . . . from May 20 . . . 1655 . . . up to July 3 . . . 1656 . . . Translated from the original MS. in the Archives of the Indies and edited . . . by Irene A. Wright. pp. vi. 32. *London.* 1923 [1924]. 8°. [*Camden Miscellany.* vol. 13.] **Ac. 8113/39.**

CASTILLA (JULIÁN CHAVE Y) *See* CHAVE Y CASTILLA.

CASTILLA (LUIS) *See* CASSO Y FERNÁNDEZ (F. de) Trabajos forenses. Acusación presentada ante la Sala de lo Criminal de la Audiencia de Sevilla, á nombre de D. L. Castilla, en causa seguida por delito de parricidio por envenenamiento de su hijo, *etc.* 1892. 8°. **5384. ff. 10.**

CASTILLA (MANUEL CASADO Y SANCHEZ DE) *See* CASADO Y SANCHEZ DE CASTILLA.

CASTILLA (MANUEL ROMERO DE) *See* ROMERO DE CASTILLA.

CASTILLA (MODESTO) Historia de la Junta de Defensa de Galicia. pp. 533. *La Coruña,* 1894. 8°. **9180. dd. 16.**

CASTILLA (PATRICIO BUENO DE) *See* BUENO DE CASTILLA.

CASTILLA (PEDRO JOSÉ BRAVO DE LAGUNAS Y) *See* BRAVO DE LAGUNAS Y CASTILLA.

CASTILLA (PEDRO RAMON ROMERO DE TERREROS TREBUESTO DAVALOS OCHOA Y) *Count de Regla*. *See* ROMERO DE TERREROS TREBUESTO DAVALOS CASTILLA.

CASTILLA (PEDRO ROMERO DE TERREROS OCHOA Y) *Count de Regla*. *See* ROMERO DE TERREROS OCHOA Y CASTILLA.

CASTILLA (RAFAEL BUSTOS Y) *Marquess de Corvera*. *See* BUSTOS Y CASTILLA.

CASTILLA (RAMÓN) *President of the Peruvian Republic*.

—— [For official documents issued by Ramón Castilla as President of the Peruvian Republic :] *See* PERU.—Castilla (R.) *President*.

—— Biografía del gran Mariscal peruano Ramón Castilla, escrita por un amigo suyo imparcial [i.e. J. G. Valdivia]. [A facsimile of the edition of 1873. With a portrait.] pp. 24. *In :* Biblioteca de la República. vol. 4. 1953. 8°. **W.P. c. 406/4.**

CASTILLA (TOMÁS ROMERO DE) *See* ROMERO DE CASTILLA.

CASTILLA BENAVIDES (ANTONIO) Curso completo de caligrafia general, o Nuevo sistema de enseñanza del arte de escribir. pp. 244. *Madrid*, 1866. 8°. **1269. d. 3.**

—— Laminas. fol. **1269. d. 4.**

—— Practica de la Enseñanza. 12 cuadernos. *obl.* 8°. **1295. h. 31.**

CASTILLA DE LA CUEVA Y BENABIDEZ (JUAN DE) *Begin.* Señor, Don Juan de Castilla dela Cueua y Benabidez, *etc.* [A memorial to the King, setting forth the services of the memorialist's ancestors and praying for the office of governor of Almeria.] [1650?] fol. **1324. i. 2. (110.)**

CASTILLA MUÑIZ (GERONYMO MANUEL DE) El Principe de los Sabios. Poema comico, que en las solemnes fiestas que el ardiente zelo de los alumnos del Colegio Mayor de Santo Thomas de Aquino . . . consagra al mismo Angelico Doctor, se ha de representar por dichos alumnos, *etc.* pp. 42. *Sevilla*, [1735.] 4°. **11726. e. 16. (3.)**

CASTILLA PORTUGAL (M.) La República Argentina, su historia, geografia, *etc.* pp. 64. *Barcelona*, 1897. 8°. **010480. ff. 2.**

CASTILLA Y CEREZUELA (THOMASA DE) *See* ANTONY, *of Padua, Saint.* Nuevo y curioso romance, q̃ trata de dos portentosos milagros q̃ ha obrado . . . S. Antonio de Padua con . . . Doña Thomasa de Castilla y Cerezuela, *etc.* [1755?] 4°. **12330. l. 14. (18.)**

—— —— 1762. 4°. **T. 1958. (12.)**

—— —— [1790?] 4°. **11450. f. 28. (2.)**

CASTILLA Y DE AGUAYO (JUAN DE) El Perfecto Regidor. ff. 205. *C. Bonardo : Salamanca*, 1586. 8°. **1141. a. 32.**

CASTILLA Y GUTIERREZ (ANTONIO) Historia de un Gato Negro. pp. 127. *Madrid*, 1874. 8°. **12490. bbb. 1.**

CASTILLE. *See* CASTILE.

CASTILLE (C. H.) *See* PERRIER (Ferdinand) La Syrie sous le gouvernement de Méhémet Ali . . . Ouvrage précédé d'une introduction par C. H. Castille. 1842. 8°. **1434. g. 4.**

CASTILLE (HIPPOLYTE) *See also* ALCESTE, *pseud.* [i.e. H. Castille ?]

—— *See* MAFFRE (J.) Les Ennemis du Pape confondus. [In reference to the attacks of A. Grandguillot, J. H. Michon, H. Castille and others on the Temporal Power.] 1860. 12°. **4051. aa. 23.**

—— *See* MIRECOURT (Eugène de) *pseud.* Les Contemporains. (pt. 53. Hippolyte Castille.) 1855, *etc.* 16°. **10662. a. 28.**

—— Blanche d'Orbe, précédé d'un essai sur Clarisse Harlowe et La Nouvelle Héloise. 2 tom. *Paris*, 1859. 12°. **12514. cc. 9.**

—— L'Excommunication. pp. 31. *Paris*, 1860. 8°. **8033. d. 18. (1.)**

—— Histoire de la seconde République française. 4 tom. *Paris*, 1854–56. 8°. **9230. c. 26.**

—— Histoire de soixante ans, *etc.* 4 tom. *Paris*, 1859–63. 8°. **9230. dd. 17.**

—— Les Hommes et les moeurs en France sous le règne de Louis-Philippe. pp. xii. 383. *Paris*, 1853. 8°. **1322. d. 21.**

—— Napoléon III et le clergé . . . Quatrième édition. pp. 31. *Paris*, 1860. 8°. **4051. f. 10.**

—— Le Pape et l'Encyclique [of 19 Jan. 1860]. pp. 32. *Paris*, 1860. 8°. **4051. f. 9.**

—— Parallèle entre César, Charlemagne et Napoléon. L'empire et la démocratie, philosophie de la légende impériale. pp. 341. *Paris*, 1858. 8°. **8006. d. 12.**

—— Portraits politiques (et historiques) au dix-neuvième siècle. 50 pt. *Paris*, 1856–58. 16°. **10603. a. 18.**

—— —— sér. 2. 30 pt. *Paris*, 1859–62. 16°. **10603. a. 19.**

—— Questions actuelles. La quatrième dynastie [of France]. pp. 32. *Paris*, 1861. 8°. **8052. f. 55. (3.)**

CASTILLE (NICOLAS DE) *See* JEANNIN (P.) Les Négotiations de monsieur le President Jeannin. [Edited by N. de Castille.] 1656. fol. **594. i. 3.**

—— —— 1682. fol. **187. e. 4.**

CASTILLEJO (CHRISTOVAL DE) *See* NICOLAY (Clara L.) The Life and Works of Christóbal de Castillejo, *etc.* 1910. 8°. **Ac. 2692. p/10a.**

—— Las Obras de Christoual de Castillejo. Corregidas y emendadas por mãdado del Consejo de la Santa . . . Inquisicion. pp. 912. *P. Cosin : Madrid*, 1573. 8°. **011451. e. 28.** *Cropped.*

—— [Another edition.] [Edited by Pedro Bellero.] ff. 372. *M. Nutio : Anuers*, 1598. 12°. **243. a. 36.**

—— [Another copy, with a different titlepage.] **G. 10917.**

—— Obras, *etc.* [Edited by Ramón Fernández, pseudonym of Pedro Estala.] 2 tom. *Madrid*, 1792. 8°. [*Colección del Parnaso español.* tom. 12, 13.] **242. i. 24, 25.**

—— Obras . . . Prólogo, edición y notas de J. Domínguez Bordona. 4 vol. *Madrid*, 1926–28. 8°. **011451. h. 43.** *Part of the "Clásicos Castellanos." The wrapper of vol. 4 bears the date 1929.*

—— Poesías. 1854. *See* ARIBAU (B. C.) Biblioteca de Autores Españoles, *etc.* tom. 32. 1849, *etc.* 8°. **12232. f. 1/32.**

CASTILLEJO (CHRISTOVAL DE)

—— Diálogo sobre las Mujeres. Sermon de Amores. [In verse.] pp. 165. *Madrid*, 1878. 16°. [*Biblioteca Universal*. tom. 39.] **739. a. 39.**

—— Dialogo de Mugeres. Interlocutores. Alethio. Fileno. [By C. de Castillejo.] 𝕲.𝕷. 1544. 4°. *See* ALETHIO.
G. 11036.

—— Dialogo que habla de las condiciones de las mugeres. [By C. de Castillejo.] *See* ULLOA (A. de) Processo de cartas de amores, *etc.* 1553. 8°.
C.57.b.1.

—— Dialogo de mugeres, 1544. Wieder abgedruckt von Ludwig Pfandl. 1921. *See* PERIODICAL PUBLICATIONS.— *Paris*. Revue Hispanique, *etc.* tom. 52, no. 122. 1894, *etc.* 8°. **P.P. 4331. aea.**

—— Sermon de amores del maestro buē talāte llamado fray · Nidel dela orden d'l fristel. [By C. de Castillejo.] Agora nueuamente corregido y enmēdada. 𝕲.𝕷. 1542. 4°. *See* BUEN TALANTE, *pseud.* **C. 63. g. 29.**

CASTILLEJO (FEDERICO FERNÁNDEZ) *See* FERNÁNDEZ CASTILLEJO.

CASTILLEJO (FERNANDO MANUEL DE) *See* HELIODORUS, *Bishop of Tricca*. La Nueva Cariclea, o nueva traduccion de la novela de Theagenes y Cariclea . . . [Translated by] F. M. de Castillejo. 1722. 4°. **11340. c. 6.**

CASTILLEJO (JOSÉ)

—— Britain as the Centre of European Reconstruction, *etc.* pp. 35. [*Newcastle-upon-Tyne*, 1940.] 8°. [*Earl Grey Memorial Lecture*. no. 22.] Ac. **2671. g.**

—— La Educación en Inglaterra. pp. xxii. 674. *Madrid*, 1919. 8°. **08364. g. 1.**

—— [Another edition.] pp. 355. *Madrid*, 1930. 8°.
08364. de. 44.

—— Education and Revolution in Spain. Being three Joseph Payne Lectures for 1936, *etc.* pp. 26. *London*, 1937. 8°. [*University of London Institute of Education. Studies and Reports.* no. 12.] Ac. **2666. e.**

—— Wars of Ideas in Spain. Philosophy, politics and education, *etc.* pp. x. 167. *John Murray: London*, 1937. 8°. **08042. aa. 36.**

CASTILLEJO (JUAN PAEZ DE VALENÇUELA Y) *See* PAEZ DE VALENÇUELA Y CASTILLEJO.

CASTILLEJOS, FERNANDO DE LA QUADRA SALCEDO, *Marquis de los. See* QUADRO SALCEDO.

CASTILLEJOS (JOSÉ MARÍA ÁLVAREZ Y) *See* ÁLVAREZ Y CASTILLEJOS.

CASTILLERO (ANDRES) *See* BENJAMIN (Judah P.) In the United States District Court . . . California. The United States, vs. Andres Castillero . . . Claim for the mine and lands of New Almaden, *etc.* 1860. 8°.
6615. bb. 3.

—— In the United States District Court, Northern District of California. The United States vs. Andres Castillero "New Almaden." Transcript of the Record, *etc.* 4 vol. *Whitton, Towne & Co.: San Francisco*, 1859–61. 8°.
6643. d. 2.

CASTILLERO REYES (ERNESTO DE JESÚS)

—— La Causa Inmediata de la Emancipación de Panamá. Historia de los orígenes, la formación y el rechazo por el Senado Colombiano, del tratado Herran-Hay. [With plates, including portraits.] pp. viii. 184. *Panamá*, 1933. 8°. [*Publicaciones de la Academia Panameña de la Historia.*] Ac. **8580.**

CASTILLERO REYES (ERNESTO DE JESÚS)

—— El Doctor Manuel Amador Guerrero, Prócer de la Independencia y Primer Presidente de la República de Panamá. [With plates, including a portrait.] pp. 24. *Panamá*, 1933. 8°. **010885. f. 16.**

—— Dr. Rafael Lasso de la Vega, prelado, legislador y prócer, *etc.* [With a portrait.] pp. 86. *Panamá*, 1952. 8°. 1764-1831. **10899. de. 24.** *Panameños ilustres.* vol. 5.

—— Historia de la comunicación interoceánica y de su influencia en la formación y en el desarrollo de la entidad nacional panameña, *etc.* pp. xiv. 444. *Panamá*, [1939.] 8°. **9770. e. 6.**

—— Historia de los símbolos de la patria panameña. pp. 57. *Panamá*, [1946.] 8°. [*Publicaciones de la Biblioteca Nacional.* no. 5.] **W.P. 3299/3.**

—— La Universidad Interamericana. Historia de sus antecedentes y fundación. pp. 334. *Panamá*, 1943. 8°. [*Publicaciones de la Biblioteca Nacional.* no. 2.]
W.P. 3299/5.

CASTILLION (JOANNES BAPTISTA LUDOVICUS DE) Sacra Belgii chronologia, *etc.* pp. 544. *Bruxellis*, 1719. 8°.
1112. d. 9.

CASTILLIONAEUS (CAROLUS OCTAVIUS) *Count. See* CASTIGLIONI (Carlo O.)

CASTILLIONAEUS (JOANNES) *Cardinal. See* SALVEMINI DI CASTIGLIONE (G. F. M. M.)

CASTILLIONAEUS (PETRUS MARIA) *See* CASTIGLIONE (Pietro M.)

CASTILLIONEUS (BONAVENTURA) *See* CASTIGLIONE.

CASTILLIONEUS (FRANCISCUS) *See* CASTIGLIONE (Francesco)

CASTILLIONEUS (FRANCISCUS XAVERIUS) *Cardinal. See* PIUS VIII., *Pope.*

CASTILLIONEUS (GASPAR) *See* COLIGNY.

CASTILLIONEUS (JOANNES) *See* SALVEMINI DI CASTIGLIONE (G. F. M. M.)

CASTILLIONIUS (BALTHASSAR) *Count. See* CASTIGLIONE.

CASTILLO ( ) *See* MENDEZ (J. de D.) Contestacion a la protesta que contra el acuerdo del Vᵉ Cabildo . . . de la Catedral de Carácas . . . han publicado los Sʳᵉˢ . . . Sucre . . . y Castillo. [1864.] 8°. **4183. cc. 23.**

CASTILLO (ABEL ROMEO) Los Gobernadores de Guayaquil del siglo XVIII . . . Con 15 láminas, *etc.* pp. xii. 397. *Madrid*, 1931. 8°. **9770. ppp. 7.**

CASTILLO (ALBERTO DEL)

—— De la Puerta del Ángel a la Plaza de Lesseps. Ensayo de biología urbana, 1821–1945. pp. 521. pl. 96. *Barcelona*, 1945. 8°. **010171. s. 13.** *Part of the "Colección Barcelona y su historia."*

—— La Maquinista Terrestre y Marítima, personaje histórico, 1855–1955. [With plates.] pp. 574. *Barcelona*, 1955. 4°.
8223. g. 34.

—— El Neoeneolítico. *In:* MENÉNDEZ PIDAL (R.) Historia de España. tom. 1. vol. 1. pp. 487–714. 1947. 4°.
W.P. 12807.

CASTILLO (ALPHONSO DEL) A Collection of the Historical Notices and Poems in the Alhamrā of Granada. [Compiled by A. del Castillo.] pp. xxi. *See* SHAKESPEAR (John) *Writer on Hindustani*. The History of the Mahometan Empire in Spain, *etc.* 1816. 4°. **179. g. 16.**

CASTILLO (ANDRÉS RUIZ) *See* RUIZ CASTILLO.

CASTILLO (ANDRÉS SANZ DEL) *See* SANZ DEL CASTILLO.

CASTILLO (ANDRES V.) Spanish Mercantilism. Gerónimo de Uztáriz—economist, *etc.* [A thesis.] pp. ix. 193. *New York*, 1930. 8º.   **8230. ff. 12.**

CASTILLO (ANTONIO DE) and **AGUILERA** (JOSÉ G.) Fauna fosil de la Sierra de Catorce, San Luis Potosi. pp. 55. *México*, 1895. fol.   [*Instituto Geológico de México*. Boletin, num. 1.]   **LAS.F.35.**

CASTILLO (ANTONIO DEL) Auto sacramental al Nacimiento del Hijo de Dios. Loa sacramental al nacimiento de Christo. *See* AUTOS. Autos sacrementales, *etc.* 1675. 4º.   **11726. d. 8.**

—— [Another edition.] Auto al Nacimiento del Hijo de Dios, los Ángeles Encontrados. [In verse.] Loa para este auto. *Barcelona*, [1800?] 4º.   **11726. e. 3. (11.)**

—— El Devoto Peregrino, Viage de Tierra Santa. [With maps.] pp. 511. *Imprenta Real: Madrid*, 1656. 4º.
566. g. 19.

The titlepage is engraved.

—— [Another edition.] ff. 320. *Toledo*, [1660?] 8º.
1048. a. 5.

—— [Another edition.] [With plates.] pp. 683. 43. *A. Mureto: Paris*, 1664. 4º.   **148. c. 20.**

—— Nueva edicion, *etc.* pp. 408. *Madrid*, 1864. 8º.
4411. bb. 7.

CASTILLO (ANTONIO CANOVAS DEL) *See* CANOVAS DEL CASTILLO.

CASTILLO (ANTONIO DIAZ DEL) *See* DIAZ DE CASTILLO.

CASTILLO (ANTONIO JOSÉ)

—— Reforma Universitaria, *etc.* [An address.] pp. 24. *Caracas*, 1940. 8º.   **08385. bb. 43.**

CASTILLO (ANTONIO MORALES) *See* MORALES CASTILLO (A.)

CASTILLO (BALTASAR YAÑEZ DEL) *See* YAÑEZ DEL CASTILLO.

CASTILLO (BALTHASAR DEL) *Franciscan Friar.* Luz, y Guia de los Ministros Evangelicos, *etc.* *Span. & Mex.* 2 pt. *J. J. Guillena: México*, 1694. 4º.   **4402. n. 29.**

CASTILLO (BENJAMÍN E. DEL) Mitre íntimo y anecdótico. pp. 88. *Buenos Aires*, 1920. 8º.   **10884. a. 2.**

CASTILLO (BERNAL DIAZ DEL) *See* DIAZ DEL CASTILLO.

CASTILLO (CAMILO GARCÍA DE POLAVIEJA Y DEL) *Marquis de Polavieja. See* GARCÍA DE POLAVIEJA Y DEL CASTILLO.

CASTILLO (CARLOS) *See* BOGGS (Ralph S.) and CASTILLO (C.) Leyendas Épicas de España, *etc.* [1935.] 8º.
W.P. 13317/1.

—— *See* BOND (Otto F.) and CASTILLO (C.) Chicago Spanish Series, *etc.* 1931, *etc.* 8º.   Ac. **2691.** d/50.

—— *See* BOND (O. F.) and CASTILLO (C.) The Heath-Chicago Spanish Series, *etc.* 1935, *etc.* 8º. W.P. **13317.**

—— *See* CHICAGO.—*University of Chicago.* The University of Chicago Junior College Series. Spanish, *etc.* (O. F. Bond and C. Castillo, editors.) 1928, *etc.* 8º.
Ac. **2691.** d/35. (C. **1.**)

CASTILLO (CARLOS)

—— *See* PÉREZ GALDÓS (B.) La Nela. An adaptation of B. Pérez Galdós' "Marianela." By C. Castillo . . . and C. F. Sparkman, *etc.* 1932. 8º.   . Ac. **2691.** d/50. (3.)

—— *See* SPARKMAN (C. F.) and CASTILLO (C.) Beginning Spanish, *etc.* 1931. 8º.   Ac. **2691.** d/50. (1.)

—— —— 1934. 8º.   Ac. **2691.** d/50. (8.)

—— *See* SPARKMAN (C. F.) and CASTILLO (C.) Paso a Paso, *etc.* [1938.] 8º.   **12944. c. 1.**

—— *See* SPARKMAN (C. F.) and CASTILLO (C.) Repasemos. A Spanish review grammar, *etc.* 1932. 8º.
Ac. **2691.** d/50. (4.)

—— Antología de la Literatura Mexicana. Introducción, selecciones y critica de C. Castillo, *etc.* pp. xvi. 424. *University of Chicago Press: Chicago*, 1944. 8º.
12230. h. 3.

—— Lecturas introductorias. pp. xi. 139.   *Chicago*, 1928. 8º. [*University of Chicago Junior College Series*. Spanish.]   Ac. **2691.** d/35. (C. **1.**)

CASTILLO (CARLOS) and **BOND** (OTTO FERDINAND)

—— The University of Chicago Spanish Dictionary . . . Concise Spanish-English and English-Spanish dictionary of words and phrases . . . Compiled by C. Castillo & O. F. Bond . . . With the assistance of Barbara M. García. (Diccionario inglés-español y español-inglés.) pp. xxxvi. 226. xvii. 251. [1948.] 8º.   *See* CHICAGO.— *University of Chicago.* [*Miscellaneous Publications*.]
12944. e. 4.

—— The University of Chicago Spanish Dictionary . . . Compiled by C. Castillo & O. F. Bond . . . with the assistance of B. M. Garcia. (7th printing.) [A reduced photographic reprint of the edition of 1948.] 2 pt. *Pocket Books: New York*, 1955. 8º.   **12944. de. 20.** *Cardinal Edition.* no. C 122.

CASTILLO (CARLOS) and **LEAL** (LUIS)

—— De buen humor. Edited and annotated by C. Castillo . . . and L. Leal. pp. iv. 60.   *D. C. Heath & Co.: Boston*, [1954.] 8º. [*Graded Spanish Readers.* bk. 1: alternate.]
W.P. 13317/3a. (7.)

CASTILLO (CARLOS) and **SPARKMAN** (COLLEY FREDWARD)

—— España en América. Segundas lecturas. [With "Cuaderno."] 2 pt. *Chicago*, 1933. 8º.   [*Chicago Spanish Series*.]   . Ac. **2691.** d/50. (6.)

—— Graded Spanish Readers. (bk. 1–10 edited by C. Castillo and C. F. Sparkman.)

  bk. 1. De Todo un Poco. pp. vi. 56. [1936.]
W.P. 13317/3. (1.)

  bk. 2. Sigamos Leyendo. pp. iv. 58. [1936.]
W.P. 13317/3. (2.)

  bk. 3. La Buenaventura y otros cuentos. pp. v. 56. [1937.]
W.P. 13317/3. (3.)

  bk. 4. Aventuras de Gil Blas. pp. iv. 60. [1937.]
W.P. 13317/3. (4.)

  bk. 5. La Gitanilla. By M. de Cervantes Saavedra. pp. iv. 60. [1937.]
W.P. 13317/3. (5.)

  bk. 6. Un Vuelo a México. pp. v. 58. [1938.]
W.P. 13317/3. (6.)

  bk. 7. De México a Guatemala. pp. iv. 60. [1939.]
W.P. 13317/3. (7.)

  bk. 8. En Guatemala. pp. iii. 58. [1940.]
W.P. 13317/3. (8.)

  bk. 9. Volando por Sudamérica. pp. iii. 59. [1941.]
W.P. 13317/3. (9.)

  bk. 10. Un Vuelo sobre los Andes. pp. iv. 68. [1942.]
W.P. 13317/3. (10.)

  bk. 1—Alternate. Cuentecitos. Retold and adapted from the Spanish of Vicente Riva Palacio by Luis Leal. pp. iv. 50. [1944.]   **W.P. 13317/3a. (1.)**

  bk. 2—Alternate. Periquillo. By José Joaquín Fernández de Lizardi. Adapted and edited by Luis Leal. pp. iv. 58. [1946.]   **W.P. 13317/3a. (2.)**

CASTILLO (Carlos) and **SPARKMAN** (Colley Fredward)

> bk. 3—Alternate. Cuentos del Alto Perú. Adapted and edited by Willis Knapp Jones. pp. iv. 52. [1947.]
> W.P. **13317/3a**. (3.)

> bk. 6—Alternate. Cuatro cuentos rioplatenses. Adapted and edited by Glenn Barr. pp. iv. 60. [1950.]
> W.P. **13317/3a**. (6.)

> bk. 7—Alternate. De buen humor. Edited and annotated by Carlos Castillo . . . and Luis Leal. pp. iv. 60. [1954.]
> W.P. **13317/3a**. (7.)

D. C. Heath & Co.: Boston, [1936– .] 8°. [*Heath-Chicago Spanish Series.*] W.P. **13317/3**.

—— Primeras Lecturas Españolas. pp. xi. 144. *Chicago*, 1931. 8°. [*Chicago Spanish Series.*]
Ac. **2691**. d/50. (2.)

CASTILLO (Cárlos del) Carta . . . al director de " La Independencia " de Nueva York con motivo de su artículo editorial . . . titulado " ¡ La tea ! ¡ Y siempre la tea ! " pp. 86. *Wertheimer, Lea y Cia : Lóndres*, 1875. 8°. **1414**. c. 80. (4.)

—— Carta . . . al director de " La Independencia " de Nueva York respondiendo á su artículo editorial . . . titulado " Digamos algo sobre nuestros asuntos." pp. 28. *Wertheimer, Lea y Cia. : Lóndres*, 1874. 8°.
1414. c. 80. (3.)

CASTILLO (Cristóbal del) Fragmentos de la obra general sobre Historia de los Mexicanos escrita en lengua náuatl por Cristóbal del Castillo á fines del siglo xvi. Los tradujo al castellano F. del Paso y Troncoso. *Florencia*, 1908. 8°. **09004**. dd. 18. (2.)

—— *See* Paso y Troncoso (F. del) Histoire mexicaine de Cristobal del Castillo. 1902. 8°.
09004. dd. 18. (1.)

CASTILLO (Diego del) called *de Villa Sante. See* Castile.
—Joanna, *Queen.* Las Leyes de Toro glosadas . . . Glosa dñi D. Castelli . . . super leges Tauri feliciter incipit. 1527. fol. **503**. g. 15.

—— *See* Castile.—Joanna, *Queen.* Vtilis ꝗ aurea glosa . . . super leges Tauri, *etc.* 1544. fol. **507**. g. 23.

—— Tractatus de duello. (Remedio de desafios, vulgarizado del tractado d' duello . . . por un servidor de los . . . marqueses de Pescara, *etc.*) G.L. *Lat. & Span. Per D. A. Ranotum : Taurini*, 1525. 4°. **231**. i. 26.

—— [Another copy.] C. **62**. c. 13.

—— [Another copy.] G. **2313**.
> *The titlepage and fourth leaf are cropped.*

—— [Another edition.] *See* Tractatus. Primum [*etc.*] volumen tractatuum, *etc.* vol. 12. 1549. fol. **5305**. i.

—— [Another edition.] *See* Tractatus. Tractatus vniversi iuris, *etc.* tom. 12. 1584. fol. **499**. g. 6.

—— Tratado de cuentas . . . Enel qual se contiene que cosa es cuēta : y a quiē : y como an de dar la cuenta los tutores : y otros administradores de bienes agenos, *etc.* G.L. ff. xxviii. *J. de Junta : Salamanca*, 1542. 4°.
C. **63**. g. 30.

—— [Another edition.] Obra . . . agora nueuamente addicionada por el mesmo autor. G.L. ff. xxxvii. *J. de Junta : Salmanca*, 1[5]51. 4°. **8504**. c. 17.

CASTILLO (Diego del) *Don.* Don Diego del Castillo. Dàse quenta de los amorosos lances, y reñidas pendencias, que tuvo este principal cavallero en defensa de una dama. Primera parte. (Segunda parte. Nuevo y curioso romance, en que se dà fin à los amores de Don Diego del Castillo.) [In verse.] 2 pt. *Valencia*, [1758 ?] 4°.
T. **1958**. (21.)

CASTILLO (Diego del) *Don.*

—— [Another edition.] Nuevo y curioso romance, en que se da cuenta de los amores de D. Diego del Castillo, *etc.* 2 pt. *Málaga*, [1790 ?] 4°. **11450**. f. 28. (6.)

CASTILLO (Diego del) *Jesuit.* Stromas politicos y morales, en que . . . se pinta al hombre varonil, en su perfeccion natural, *etc.* pp. 444. *Valladolid*, 1729. 8°.
8009. c. 31.

CASTILLO (Diego Enriquez del) *See* Enriquez del Castillo.

CASTILLO (Diego Ramos del) *See* Ramos del Castillo.

CASTILLO (Diego Xarava de) *See* Xarava de Castillo.

CASTILLO (Domingo B.)

—— Aspectos de la Cuestión Monetaria en Venezuela. pp. 86. *Caracas*, 1938. 8°. **8222**. b. 22.

CASTILLO (E. Drake del) *See* Drake del Castillo.

CASTILLO (Eduardo)

—— *See* Céspedes (A. M.) Duelo lírico. [Poems by A. M. Céspedes and E. Castillo, attacking one another.] [c. 1952.] 8°. **11453**. e. 52.

CASTILLO (Eladio A. del)

—— Discurso de recepción del Dr. Eladio A. del Castillo . . . y contestación por E. Macías Mujica . . . Tema : La astronomía americana en sus orígenes. Estudio particular de ella referente a Venezuela, *etc.* pp. 38. 1945. 8°. *See* Barquisimeto, *City of.*—*Centro Histórico Larense.*
12302. bb. 156.

—— Recuerdos y letras larenses. [With a portrait.] pp. 23. *El Tocuyo*, 1945. 8°. **12360**. ee. 19.
La Quincena literaria. no. 9.

CASTILLO (Emilio Canovas del) *See* Canovas del Castillo.

CASTILLO (Enrique Loynaz del) *See* Loynaz del Castillo (E.)

CASTILLO (Fernando del) *Compiler of the Cancionero general.* Cancionero general (de muchas y diuersas obras de todos : o de los principales trobadores despaña : ansi antiguos como modernos : en deuocion : en moralidad : en amores : en burlas . . . copilado enmēdado y corregido por . . . F. del Castillo) nueuamēte añadido. G.L. ff. cciii. *I. de Villaquiran : Toledo*, 1520. fol. C. **20**. d. 3.

—— [Another edition.] Agora nuevamēte añadido, *etc.* G.L. ff. 205. *R. d' Petras : Toledo*, 1527. fol.
G. **11359**.

—— [Another edition.] Eñsta ultima impression . . . emēdado. G.L. ff. 207. *J. Cromberger : Seuilla*, 1535. fol.
G. **11360**.

—— [Another edition.] ff. ccccii. 1557. 8°. *See* Cancionero. C. **30**. d. 21.

—— [Another edition.] ff. ccclxxxvi. 1573. 8°. *See* Cancionero. C. **20**. b. 33.

—— [Another edition.] 2 tom. 1882. 8°. *See* Madrid.—*Sociedad de Bibliófilos Españoles.* Ac. **8886/21**.

—— [A facsimile of the edition of 1520.] ff. cciii. 1904. fol. *See* New York.—*Hispanic Society of America.*
K.T.C. **20**. b. 10.

CASTILLO (Fernando del) *Dominican Friar. See* Castillo (Hernando del)

CASTILLO (Fernando Paz) *See* Paz Castillo.

CASTILLO (Florencio María del) *See* Decaen ( ) *Lithographer.* Mexico y sus Alrededores, *etc.* [With an introductory chapter by F. M. del Castello.] 1855, *etc.* fol. **1780. b. 13.**

—— Obras de Don Florencio M. del Castillo. Novelas cortas. [With a biographical sketch by A. Villaseñor y Villaseñor.] pp. xxii. 509. *México,* 1902. 8°. **12231. cc. 20.**

CASTILLO (Francisco de) *of Murcia.* Dialogo entre la miseria humana y el cōsuelo, *etc. See* Cancionero. Cancionero General, *etc.* 1573. 8°. **C. 20. b. 33.**

CASTILLO (Francisco del) *Jesuit, of Lima. See* Buendía (J. de) Vida admirable . . . del Venerable y Apostolico Padre F. del Castillo, *etc.* 1693. 4°. **4985. df. 15.**

—— *See* Rome, *Church of.—Congregatio Rituum.* Limana. Beatificationis et canonizationis ven. servi Dei P. Francisci de Castillo . . . Positio super virtutibus in specie. 1910. fol. **5035. aa. 48.**

—— *See* Vargas Ugarte (R.) Vida del Venerable Padre F. del Castillo, *etc.* [With a portrait.] 1946. 8°. **4885. de. 25.**

CASTILLO (Francisco del) *of Cadiz.* Migaias Caydas de la Mesa de los Santos y Doctores de la Iglesia, colegidas y aplicadas a todos los Evangelios de la Quaresma. ff. 280. pp. 84. ms. notes. *Por N. de Assiayn ; acosta de I. de Bonilla : Pamplona,* 1619. 8°. **4408. cc. 13.**

CASTILLO (Francisco Bezerra del) *See* Bezerra del Castillo.

CASTILLO (Francisco Fernández del) *See* Fernández del Castillo.

CASTILLO (Francisco Joseph del) *Bishop of Sebaste. See* Tineo Hebia (G. J.) Al Rey nuestro Señor. Por el . . . Dean y Cavildo de la . . . Iglesia Cathedral de . . . Oviedo. En respuesta al manifiesto . . . en que . . . Don F. J. del Castillo . . . declara, y funda los honores . . . y Silla . . . que pretende se le debe comunicar, por el Dean, y Cabildo, en dicha Santa Iglesia, *etc.* 1719. fol. **5107. ff. 1. (5.)**

CASTILLO (Gerardo Brown) *See* Brown Castillo (G.)

CASTILLO (Gerónimo de Castro y) *See* Castro y Castillo.

CASTILLO (Gerónimo del) Compendio Histórico-Poético de la Vida . . . de Juana de Aza, Madre del Patriarca Santo Domingo de Guzman. pp. 34. *Madrid,* 1829. 8°. **12231. e. 13. (2.)**

CASTILLO (Giovanni del) *Canon of the Cathedral of Santiago, Chile. See* Castillo (Juan del) *Canon, etc.*

CASTILLO (Gonçalo de) Para que se compela . . . S. Gomez Rendon . . . á la obseruancia de la sentencia, en que se le manda se case c n J. de Valdes. ff. 4. [*Mexico,* 1650?] fol. **5125. ee. 1. (2.)**

—— Para que si executadas todas las penas de derecho en S. Gomez Rendon, por su rebeldia perseuerare en ella quod absit nunquam possit absolui, nisi prius præcesserit partis offensæ satisfactio : docent sequentes juris Pontificii constitutiones irrefragabiles. ff. 6. [*Mexico,* 1650?] fol. **5125. ee. 1. (3.)**

CASTILLO (Gonzalo Rodríguez) *See* Rodríguez Castillo.

CASTILLO (Guillermo Céspedes del) *See* Céspedes del Castillo.

CASTILLO (Hernando del) *Compiler of the " Cancionero General." See* Castillo (Fernando del)

33—23

CASTILLO (Hernando del) *Dominican Friar.* Primera parte de la Historia General de Sancto Domingo y de su Orden de Predicadores. ff. 514. *F. Sanchez : Madrid,* 1584. fol. **490. i. 2.**

—— Primera (segunda) parte de la Historia General de Santo Domingo, y de su Orden de Predicadores. (Tercera parte de la Historia general de Sancto Domingo por Ioan Lopez.) 3 pt. *Per F. Fernandez de Cordoūa : Valladolid,* 1612, 13. fol. **490. i. 3, 4.**

—— Dell'historia generale di S. Domenico et dell'ordine suo de' Predicatori . . . Tradotta nella nostra Italiana lingua dal . . . Padre Timotheo Bottoni. [pt. 2 translated by Filippo Pigafetta.] 2 pt. *Appresso F. Giunti : Venetia ; Fiorenza,* 1589, 96. fol. **1232. h. 4.**

CASTILLO (Ignacio del) Elementos de Retórica. Obra postuma . . . Dalos á luz el Dr. D. J. E. Fernandez, *etc.* pp. 95. *México,* 1812. 12°. **11824. a. 15.**

CASTILLO (Ignacio B. del)

—— Catálogo de seudónimos, anagramas, iniciales, etc. de escritores mexicanos y de extranjeros incorporados a las letras mexicanas. *In :* Boletín de la Biblioteca Nacional. [Mexico.] tom. 4. no. 4. pp. 31–48. 1953. 8°. **Ac. 9739. (1.)**

CASTILLO (J. Ruiz) *See* Ruiz-Castillo.

CASTILLO (J. Vidal) *See* Vidal Castillo.

CASTILLO (Jacinto del) Primera (segunda) parte de Don Jacinto del Castillo, y Doña Leonora de la Rosa, naturales de la Ciudad de la Coruña, del reyno de Galicia, *etc.* [A ballad.] *Madrid,* [1760?] 4°. **T. 1958. (7.)**

—— [Another edition.] pp. 8. *Madrid,* 1846. 4°. **11450. f. 23. (15.)**

—— [Another edition.] *Barcelona,* [1850?] 4°. **11450. f. 26. (67.)**

—— [Another edition.] *Córdoba,* [1850?] 4°. **11450. f. 28. (33.)**

—— [Another edition.] pp. 8. *Madrid,* 1858. 4°. **11450. f. 25. (12.)**

—— [Another edition.] *Barcelona,* 1859. 4°. **11450. f. 27. (79.)**

CASTILLO (Jacobus à) *See* Castillo (Diego del) called *De Villa Sante.*

CASTILLO (Jesús Rodríguez del) *See* Rodríguez del Castillo.

CASTILLO (Joannes de) Tractatus quo continentur summe necessaria, tàm de anatome quàm de vulneribus et ulceribus. pp. 345. few ms. notes. *Apud D. Garcia Morras : Matriti,* 1683. fol. **548. k. 12.**

CASTILLO (Joaquín del) La Ciudadela Inquisitorial de Barcelona, ó las víctimas immoladas en las aras del atroz despotismo del Conde de España . . . Tercera edicion. pp. 354. *Barcelona,* 1840. 8°. **1445. b. 13.**

CASTILLO (John) Awd Isaac, the Steeple Chase, and other poems; with a glossary of the Yorkshire dialect. pp. 199. *Horne & Richardson: Whitby*, 1843. 8°.
11641. df. 35.

—— The Bard of the Dales: or, Poems and miscellaneous pieces, partly in the Yorkshire Dialect. pp. 184. *John Hughes: London*, 1850. 12°.
11646. a. 46.

—— [Another edition.] With a life of the author, written by himself. pp. xii. 360. *W. F. Pratt: Stokesley*, 1858. 12°.
11642. de. 54.

—— Poems in the North Yorkshire Dialect . . . Edited, with a memoir and glossary by George Markham Tweddell. pp. 76. *The Editor: Stokesley*, 1878. 8°.
11644. ee. 1.

—— A Specimen of the Bilsdale Dialect; or, Two poems on Isaac Telltruth and Sammy Standfast. [Edited by John Nelson.] pp. 32. *J. Metcalfe: Northallerton*, [1831.] 12°.
T. 1368. (3.)

CASTILLO (José) Observaciones á la defensa de D. Juan Iñigues que ha dado á luz el sr. lic. D. J. M. Revuelta, *etc.* pp. 24. *[San Luis Potosi?]* 1865. 8°.
6785. b. 1. (11.)

CASTILLO (José de Arango y) *See* Arango y Castillo.

CASTILLO (Jose del) *Poet.*

—— *See* Del Castillo (J.)

CASTILLO (José González) *See* González Castillo.

CASTILLO (José María) El Pais de la Gracia. Cuentos de mil colores, escenas populares, *etc.* pp. 255. *Bilbao*, 1888. 8°.
4414. ee. 23.

CASTILLO (José María del) [For official documents issued by J. M. del Castillo as Secretario de Estado y del Despacho de Hacienda to the Republic of Colombia:] *See* Colombia, *Republic of.* [1819–31.]—*Despacho de Hacienda.*

—— *See* Mexico. [*Appendix.*] Apuntes para la Historia de la Guerra entre Mexico y los Estados-Unidos. (Redactores—Alcaraz . . . Castillo, *etc.*) 1848. 4°.
9771. f. 20.

CASTILLO (José R. del) Historia de la Revolución social de México. Primera etapa. pp. 320. *México*, 1915. 8°.
9771. e. 19.
No more published.

—— Juarez, la Intervencion y el Imperio. Refutación á la obra "El Verdadero Juarez," de Bulnes. pp. 462. *Mexico*, 1904. 8°.
9772. df. 18.
The date on the wrapper is 1905.

CASTILLO (Juan) *See* Perez Gavilan (J. A.) Defensa legal que del impreso titulado: Muy pronto llamará á nana el autor de la sotana, del que salió responsable . . . J. Castillo, pronunció . . . J. A. Perez Gavilan, *etc.* 1834. 4°.
9770. bb. 23. (9.)

CASTILLO (Juan del) *Canon of the Cathedral of Santiago, Chile.* Vita della Venerabile Marianna di Gesù de Paredes e Flores, *etc.* pp. xvi. 235. *Roma*, 1776. 4°.
4864. ee. 16.

CASTILLO (Juan del) *Captain. See* Cardenas (J. de) *Duke de Maqueda.* Recopilacion de las heroycas hazañas . . . del . . . Duque de Maqueda . . . y del Capitan Iuã del Castillo, *etc.* 1619. fol.
9181. g. 1. (8.)

CASTILLO (Juan del) *Consejero de Hazienda. Begin.* Señor. [A statement addressed to the King by J. del Castillo, in a question of precedence between himself as a Consejero de Hazienda and A. Chumazero as an Alcalde de Corte.] ff. 25. ms. notes. *[Madrid?* 1650?] fol.
1322. l. 1. (35.)

CASTILLO (Juan del) *Coronel de Caballeria. See* Castillo y Rodriguez.

CASTILLO (Juan del) *Dramatist, of Cadiz. See* Gonzalez del Castillo (Juan Ignacio)

CASTILLO (Juan del) *Dramatist, of Madrid.* Comedia famosa. Las Amazonas de España, y prodigio de Castilla. [In verse.] *[Madrid?]* 1701. 4°.
11728. b. 94.

—— Comedia famosa. Los Esclavos de su esclava, y hacer bien nunca se pierde. [In verse.] *Madrid*, 1745. 4°.
11728. b. 95.

—— [Another edition.] pp. 36. *Salamanca*, [1750?] 4°.
11728. i. 17. (2.)

—— Descripcion del feliz . . . arribo à esta corte de nuestros . . . Monarcas D. Phelipe v. y Maria Luisa Gabriela, y Don Luis Fernando, Principe de las Asturias el dia 15. de Noviembre 1711. Prevenciones . . . magnificas con que fueron recibidos sus Magestades, y Alteza, por la . . . villa de Madrid, *etc.* ff. 8. *[Madrid*, 1711.] 4°. **T. 1303. (40.)**

CASTILLO (Juan del) *of the Society of Jesus. See* González Pintado (G.) Los Mártires Jesuítas de las Misiones del Paraguay . . . Juan del Castillo. [With a portrait.] 1934. 8°.
20003. f. 60.

—— *See* Rome, *Church of.—Congregatio Rituum.* Bonaëren. Beatificationis seu declarationis martyrii . . . Joannis del Castillo . . . Positio super introductione causae. 1932. fol.
5052. f. 48.

—— *See* Rome, *Church of.—Congregatio Rituum.—Sectio Historica.* Bonaëren. Beatificationis seu declarationis martyrii servorum Dei . . . Joannis del Castillo [and others] . . . Informatio de serie documentorum ad causam pertinentium . . . Summarium de vita et martyrio . . . Dubia, *etc.* 1923. fol.
5035. aa. 74.

CASTILLO (Juan del) *Pharmacopola.* Pharmacopoea, vniuersa medicamenta in officinis pharmaceuticis vsitata complectens & explicans. ff. 335. *Apud I. de Borja: Gadibus*, 1622. 4°.
546. f. 5.

CASTILLO (Juan Cessati del) *See* Cessati del Castillo.

CASTILLO (Juan de Torres) *See* Torres Castillo.

CASTILLO (Juan Fernández del) *See* Fernández del Castillo.

CASTILLO (Juan Ignacio Gonzalez del) *See* Gonzalez del Castillo.

CASTILLO (Juan Manuel Álvarez del) *See* Álvarez del Castillo.

CASTILLO (Julian del) Historia de los Reyes Godos que vinieron de la Scitia de Europa contra el Imperio Romano, y a España: y la succession dellos hasta Philippe segundo Rey de España. ff. clviii. *P. de Iunta: Burgos*, 1582. fol.
C. 75. d. 17.

—— [Another copy.] **G. 4288. (1.)**

—— [Another edition.] Cõ adiciones de todos tiempos hasta el del Catolico dõ Filipe IIII., por Geronimo de Castro y Castillo, *etc.* pp. 461 [491]. *L. Sanchez: Madrid*, 1624. fol.
180. f. 16.

CASTILLO (LEONARDO DEL) Viage del Rey Nuestro Señor Don Felipe Quarto el Grande, a la Frontera de Francia. Funciones Reales del Desposorio, y entregas de la . . . Infante de España Doña Maria Teresa de Austria. Vistas de sus Magestades Catolica, Señora Reyna Christianissima Madre, y Señor Duque de Anjou. Solemne Iuramento de la Paz, etc. [With plates, including portraits.] pp. 296. *Imprenta Real: Madrid*, 1667. 4°.
9930. d. 30.

CASTILLO (LUIS) El Tollo, i su aprovechamiento industrial. pp. 8. [*Santiago de Chile*,] 1906. 8°.
7002. h. 21. (3.)

CASTILLO (LUIS) and VERGARA (ZACARIAS)

—— Apuntes Biolójicos e Industriales sobre la Ostra de Chile. pp. 59. 1907. 8°. See CHILE.—*Ministerio de Industria y Obras Públicas.—Sección de Aguas y Bosques.*
7001. r. 2. (2.)

CASTILLO (LUIS DEL) *Camarero del Duque de Medinasidonia.* See VELASCO MEDINILLA (P. de) Memorial del pleyto criminal que trata P. de Velasco Medinilla mandado de Su Magestad . . . con el Marques de Ayamonte, preso por Don L. del Castillo, etc. [1646 ?] fol.
1322. l. 11. (23.)

CASTILLO (LUIS DEL) *Writer on Russia.* Compendio Cronológico de la Historia y del Estado Actual del Imperio Ruso. pp. 250. *Madrid*, 1796. 4°. **9454. bb. 12.**

—— Observaciones sobre el Comercio del Mar Negro, con especificacion del que los Españoles pueden hacer allí ventajosamente. pp. 55. *Madrid*, 1828. 4°.
08227. i. 46.

CASTILLO (LUIS MARÍA) Discurso pronunciado el 14 de Diciembre de 1862 en la Capilla de la Universidad de Mérida, despues de la distribucion de premios, etc. pp. 22. *Mérida*, 1862. 8°. **8355. df. 2.**

CASTILLO (LUYS DEL) [Poems.] See CASTILLO (F. del) *Compiler of the "Cancionero general."* Cancionero general, etc. 1520. fol. **C. 20. d. 3.**

—— Obras. See CANCIONERO. Cancionero general, etc. 1573. 8°. **C. 20. b. 33.**

CASTILLO (MANUEL DEL) *Capitán de fregata.*

—— See O'SCANLAN (T.) Diccionario marítimo español, etc. [Revised by M. del Castillo.] 1831. 4°. **717. h. 17.**

CASTILLO (MANUEL) *Director del Instituto General y Técnico de Cáceres.* See LUNA (Alvaro de) *Constable of Castile and Leon.* Libro de las Claras e Virtuosas Mugeres . . . Edición crítica por Don M. Castillo. 1908. 8°.
10633. ccc. 5.

—— La Clasificación Bibliográfica Decimal. Exposición del sistema y traducción directa de las tablas generales del mismo. pp. 70. 1897. 8°. [*Office International de Bibliographie. Publication.* no. 13.] See DEWEY (Melvil) [*Decimal Classification.—Abridgments and Adaptations.*]
11908. d. 2.

CASTILLO (MANUEL SAMANIEGO DEL) See SAMANIEGO DEL CASTILLO.

CASTILLO (MARÍA DEL) See SIERRA (M. de la)

CASTILLO (MARÍA DEL) *Expert on Cookery.*

—— Cocina mexicana. pp. 141. *México*, 1953. 8°.
7940. b. 29.

CASTILLO (MARIANO ALONSO Y) See ALONSO Y CASTILLO.

CASTILLO (MARTIN DEL) See BIBLE.—*Susannah.* [*Latin.*] Crisis Danielica: sive Susanna littera et conceptibus illustrata, à calumnia liberata . . . Ad caput XIII. Danielis . . . Per . . . M. del Castillo, etc. 1658. fol.
1214. k. 10.

CASTILLO (MARTIN DEL)

—— Arte Hebraispano . . . Grammatica de la Lengua Santa en Idioma Castellano, etc. pp. 336. *F. Anisson: Leon de Francia*, 1676. 8°. **63. l. 28.**

—— Γραμματικη της Γλωσσης Ἑλληνικης ἐν τῃ διαλεκτῳ Ἰβηρικῃ . . . Grammatica de la Lengua Griega en Idioma Español, etc. pp. 557. *F. Anisson: Leon de Francia*, 1678. 8°. **236. g. 4.**

—— El Humano Seraphin y Único Llagado, tratado apologético, de como solo . . . S. Francisco entre todos los Santos de la Iglesia, goza y possee las llagas . . . cruentas, reales, y visibles de nuestro Señor Jesu Christo, etc. See SANCHEZ ARROYO (P.) Diálogo traumático regular, etc. 1690. 4°. **1225. e. 13.**

CASTILLO (NICETO ALCALÁ ZAMORA Y) See ALCALÁ ZAMORA Y CASTILLO.

CASTILLO (PEDRO AGUSTIN DEL) See CASTILLO RUIZ DE VERGARA.

CASTILLO (PEDRO ALCÁNTARA) See ALCÁNTARA CASTILLO.

CASTILLO (PEDRO FERNÁNDEZ DEL) See FERNÁNDEZ DEL CASTILLO.

CASTILLO (PEDRO PABLO DEL) See HOOD (Guillermo) Prontuario de Legislacion Venezolana . . . revisto . . . por P. P. del Castillo, etc. 1846. 8°. **6785. aa. 20.**

—— Canto fúnebre . . . dedicado al Señor J. A. Maitin, en obsequio a la memoria de su esposa . . . L. A. Sosa. pp. 7. *Valencia* [*Venezuela*], 1851. 8°. **11450. bbb. 30.**

—— El 19 de Abril, ó un verdadero patriota. Comedia en dos actos. pp. 31. *Caracas*, 1842. 12°.
11726. aa. 31. (1.)

—— El Fanatismo Druida ó la Sacerdotisa. Drama en tres actos en verso suelto. pp. 93. *Caracas*, 1839. 8°.
11450. c. 48.

CASTILLO (PEDRO RAMIREZ DEL) See RAMIREZ DEL CASTILLO.

CASTILLO (PEDRO SANZ DEL) See SANZ DEL CASTILLO.

CASTILLO (PELAYO) El que nace para ochavo . . . Proverbio en un acto y en verso . . . Segunda edicion. pp. 33. *Madrid*, 1868. 8°. **11726. bbb. 25. (10.)**

CASTILLO (PETRUS DEL) See CASTILLO Y ARTIGA (D. del) successively *Bishop of Truxillo*, and *Archbishop of Bogotá.* D.D. D. del Castillo et Artiga . . . Alphabetum Marianum, opus posthumum, per . . . P. del Castillo . . . collectum & elaboratum, etc. 1669. 4°. **4061. dd. 2.**

CASTILLO (RAFAEL DEL) See also CARRILLO (Álvaro) pseud. [i.e. R. del Castillo.]

—— See CARRERAS (L.) Los Malos Novelistas Españoles generalizados en M. Fernandez y Gonzales . . . R. del Castillo, etc. 1867. 8°. **11824. h. 29. (4.)**

—— La Ambicion de una Muger. Drama en tres actos, etc. pp. 15. *Madrid*, [1861 ?] 4°. **11725. h. 27.**

—— Amor de Padre, ó Secretos de Familia. Novela de costumbres. [With plates.] pp. 615. *Barcelona, Madrid*, 1864. 8°. **12490. k. 5.**
With an additional titlepage, engraved.

—— Ampliacion a la Hipotesis sobre la Naturaleza del Sol. pp. 23. *Madrid*, 1852. 8°. **8715. bb. 33.**

CASTILLO (Rafael del)

—— El Calzetin de Marco Antonio. Comedia en un acto, *etc.* pp. 7. *Madrid*, 1860. 4°. **11725. h. 26.**

—— El Campanero de San Pablo, novela historica. [With plates.] pp. 527. *Barcelona*, 1862. 8°. **12490. i. 13.**

—— Gran Diccionario geográfico, estadístico é histórico de España y sus provincias, de Cuba, Puerto Rico, Filipinas y posesiones de Africa . . . Esta obra se publica bajo la direccion de D. R. del Castillo. 4 tom. *Barcelona*, 1889–92. fol. **10160. g. 1.**

—— Las Hijas de Eva. Novela de costumbres. (Segunda edicion ilustrada con láminas.) pp. 478. *Barcelona*, 1864. 8°. **12491. h. 8.**
The date on the wrapper is 1865.

—— El Honor de España, episodios de la guerra de Marruecos. Novela historica . . . Edicion ilustrada, *etc.* pp. 972. *Madrid*, 1859. 8°. **12491. g. 18.**

—— Los Misterios Catalanes, ó el Obrero de Barcelona. Novela de costumbres. [With plates, including a portrait.] pp. 585. *Madrid; Barcelona*, 1862. 4°. **12490. i. 12.**

—— Palacio por Dentro y el Pueblo por Fuera. Novela historica . . . ilustrada, *etc.* pp. 504. *Madrid*, 1860. 8°. **12490. e. 19.**

—— Los Pobres de Barcelona. Drama en seis cuadros y un prologo, *etc.* pp. 22. *Madrid*, 1865. 4°. **11725. h. 28.**

—— Los Polvos de la Madre Celestina. Novela historica. pp. 512. *Mexico*, 1866. 4°. **12489. i. 2.**

—— El Trapero de Madrid. Novela de costumbres. pt. 1. pp. 729. *Madrid*, 1861. 8°. **12491. g. 32.**

CASTILLO (Raffaele del) Carlo Alberto. Biografia. [With portraits.] pp. 322. *Vicenza*, 1938. 8°. **10633. pp. 44.**

—— L'Ultimo sovrano romantico: Napoleone iii. [With plates, including portraits.] pp. 413. *Milano*, 1933. 8°. **10655. ppp. 17.**

CASTILLO (Ramon del) Recopilacion de Secretos y Procedimientos sumamente provechosos à la agricultura è industria pecuaria y otros de utilidad y recreo. pp. 208. *Madrid*, 1855. 8°. **7073. c. 9.**

CASTILLO (Ricardo del) *pseud. See* Rubio (Darío)

CASTILLO (Sebastiana del) Sebastiana del Castillo. Nuevo, y curioso romance, en que se declaran las atrocidades de Sebastiana del Castillo, *etc.* *Valencia*, [1760?] 4°. **T. 1957. (3.)**

—— [Another edition.] [1820?] 4°. **1072. g. 27. (6.)**

—— [Another edition.] *Valladolid*, [1830?] 4°. **11451. ee. 39. (46.)**

—— [Another edition.] *Barcelona*, [1845?] 4°. **11450. f. 26. (34.)**

—— [Another edition.] *Barcelona*, 1858. 4°. **11450. f. 27. (64.)**

—— [Another edition.] *Madrid*, 1859. 4°. **11450. f. 25. (84.)**

CASTILLO (Vicente Sancho del) Carta al señor D. J. C. Bruna en respuesta á su libro titulado: El Juego ante la verdad, *etc.* pp. 48. *Madrid*, 1895. 8°. **8410. f. 8. (2.)**

—— Le Lion de Flandre. Épisode historique en vers et en trois actes . . . D'après l'ouvrage de Henri Conscience. pp. v. 94. *Namur*, 1912. 8°. **11735. g. 29.**

CASTILLO (Vicente Sancho del)

—— Les Véritables Grands d'Espagne. Osius, évêque de Cordoue, 256–357. Étude historique. pp. xiv. 183. *Namur*, 1898. 8°. **4863. df. 7.**

CASTILLO (Vicente Sancho del) and **BRAVO Y MOLTÓ** (Emilio)

—— Baile de trajes en casa de los Duques de Fernan-Nuñez . . . Apuntes tomados por Don V. S. del Castillo y Don E. Bravo y Molto. pp. 63. *Madrid*, 1884. 4°. **7915. f. 12. (1.)**

CASTILLO ALONSO (Gonzalo del) Derecho Político y Constitucional Comparado. Comentarios a la constitución española, 9 diciembre 1931 . . . Tercera edición. pp. 462. *Barcelona*, 1932. 8°. **5384. ee. 7.**

CASTILLO ANDRACA Y TAMAYO (Francisco)

—— Obras . . . Introducción y notas de Rubén Vargas Ugarte. pp. xxxiv. 299. *Lima*, 1948. 8°. **11452. h. 29.**

Clásicos peruanos. vol. 2.

CASTILLO BRAVO (Consuelo del)

—— *See* Spain.—*Ministerio de Asuntos Exteriores.—Biblioteca.* Catálogo de la Biblioteca del Ministerio de Asuntos Exteriores. Por F. Ruiz Morcuende . . . Con la colaboración de . . . C. del Castillo Bravo. 1941, *etc.* 8°. **11915. b. 12.**

CASTILLO CALDERON (Franciscus de) Exorcismus pneumatis macrocosmi physico-theologicus, contra Ethnicos philosophos pseudo-trismegistos & Anti-Platones, *etc.* pp. 254. *Typis G. Czernoch: Pragæ*, 1677. 4°. **8461. aaa. 14.**

CASTILLO DE AZA (Zenón)

—— Trujillo, benefactor de la Iglesia . . . En el primer aniversario del Concordato. pp. 13. *Ciudad Trujillo*, 1955. 8°. **8181. b. 19.**

CASTILLO DE BOBADILLA (Gerónimo) *See* Miranda (L. de) El Fiscal [G. Castillo de Bobadilla] y el Concejo . . . de Navia. Con L. de Miranda, y A. Peréz de Navia, *etc.* [1605?] fol. **1322. l. 6. (7.)**

—— *See* Miranda (L. de) Memorial de las escripturas presentadas en el acuerdo por L. de Miranda, y consortes, en el pleyto q̄ con ellos trata el Fiscal y villa de Navia, *etc.* [1606?] fol. **1322. l. 6. (5.)**

—— *See* Miranda (L. de) Memorial del pleyto entre el Fiscal de su Magestad y el Concejo . . . de la villa de Navia con L. de Miranda y A. Lopez, *etc.* [1606?] fol. **1322. l. 6. (4.)**

—— *See* Miranda (L. de) Por Lope de Miranda y consortes. Con el Fiscal de su Magestad y villa de Navia. [1606?] fol. **1322. l. 6. (6.)**

—— *See* Teran ( ) *Doctor.* De Luys de Escobar y cõsortes sobre su hidalguia. Con el Fiscal, *etc.* 1604. fol. **1322. l. 4. (26.)**

—— El Licenciado Castillo de Bobadilla . . . y el Concejo de la villa de Villalon. Con Bernaue y Gaspar de Grajal y L. de Escovar hermanos, y A. A. de Grajal su primo. ff. 22. *Medina del Campo*, 1604. fol. **1322. l. 4. (27.)**

—— El Licenciado Castillo de Bobadilla . . . y el Concejo y vezinos de la villa de Navia, y J. de Castillon, y D. Fuertes y Sierra . . . con L. de Miranda . . . y A. Lopez Volaño, y A. Perez Baamonde, *etc.* ff. 18. *Medina del Campo*, 1604. fol. **1322. l. 6. (3.)**

CASTILLO DE BOBADILLA (GERÓNIMO)

—— Política para Corregidores y Señores de Vassallos, en tiempo de paz, y de guerra : y para perlados en lo espiritual, y temporal entre legos, iuezes de comission, regidores, abogados y otros oficiales publicos : y de las iurisdicciones, preeminencias, residencias y salarios dellos : y de lo locante à las de ordenes y cavalleros dellas. 2 vol. *L. Sanchez : Madrid*, 1597. fol.   **1479. dd. 5.**

—— [Another edition.] 2 tom. *S. de Cormellas : Barcelona*, 1624. fol.   **5383. gg. 2.**

—— [Another edition.] 2 tom. *Madrid*, 1775. fol.
   24. f. 1, 2.

CASTILLO DE GONZÁLEZ (AURELIA) *See* XENES (N.) Poesías. [Edited by A. Castillo de González.] 1915. 8°.
   011451. g. 88.

—— Fábulas . . . Con un prólogo de P. de Biedma. pp. 103. *Cadiz*, 1879. 8°.   **11450. c. 16.**

CASTILLO DE LUCAS (ANTONIO)

—— Folklore oftalmológico, *etc.* [With illustrations.] pp. 37. *Barcelona*, 1944. 8°.   **7612. b. 39.**
   Colección de publicaciones médicas histórico-artísticas. no. 14.

—— Refranes de Medicina, o Relacionados con ella por el pueblo, seleccionados, con breves notas, de las colecciones paremiológicas de Rodríguez Marín y el maestro Correas por el doctor A. Castillo de Lucas. Añádense al final los refranes que publicó en 1616 el doctor Sorapán de Rieros. pp. 225. *Madrid*, 1936. 8°.   **12306. ppp. 1.**

CASTILLO DE VILLA SANCTE (JACOBUS) *See* CASTILLO (Diego del) called DE VILLA SANTE.

CASTILLO-ELEJABEYTIA (DICTINIO DE)

—— La Canción de los pinos. pp. 73. *Madrid*, 1945. 8°.
   11453. e. 11.
   Colección Adonais. no. 17.

—— Lirios de Compostela. [With a portrait.] pp. 249. *Murcia*, 1949. 8°.

—— Vocabulario de los poemas gallegos de Lirios de Compostela. [*Murcia*, 1949.] 8°.   **11453. c. 39.**

CASTILLO FIEL, CARLOS, *Count de. See* CRESPO Y GIL-DELGADO.

CASTILLO I OROSCO (EUJENIO DEL) *See* CASTILLO Y OROSCO.

CASTILLO LEDÓN (LUIS) *See* GRANJA (J. de la) Epistolario. Con un estudio biográfico preliminar por L. Castillo Ledón, *etc.* 1937. 8°.   **010921. f. 3.**

—— Antigua Literatura Indigena Mexicana. Estudio y arreglo de L. Castillo Ledon, *etc.* pp. xv. 61. *México*, 1917. 8°.   **011853. p. 52.**

—— El Chocolate. [With plates.] pp. vi. 30. *México*, 1917. 16°.   **07077. de. 18.**

—— La Conquista y Colonización Española en México. Su verdadero carácter. pp. 82. *México*, 1932. 8°.
   9772. pp. 16.

—— El Museo Nacional de Arqueología, Historia y Etnografía, 1825–1925, *etc.* pp. 127. 1924. 8°. *See* MEXICO.— *Museo Nacional, etc.*   **07702.bb.26.**

CASTILLO LÓPEZ (ÁNGEL DEL)

—— Notas y comentarios a la historia antigua de La Coruña. [With plates.] pp. 52. *La Coruña*, 1948. 8°.
   9171. a. 7.

CASTILLO LÓPEZ (ÁNGEL DEL)

—— El Patrimonio Artístico de Galicia. Conferencia, *etc.* pp. 45.   *La Coruña*, 1926. 8°.   **07806. h. 80.**

CASTILLO MANTILLA Y COSSIO (GABRIEL DE) Laverintho poetico, texido de noticias naturales, históricas, y gentilicas, ajustadas a consonantes para el exercicio de la poesia. pp. 765.   *M. Alvarez : Madrid*, 1691. 4°.   **11451. f. 15.**

CASTILLON, LOUIS PERREAU, *Seigneur de. See* PERREAU.

CASTILLON (A.) *Professor at Sainte-Barbe.* Chasses aux Indes . . . Illustrées . . . par V. Adam. pp. 46. *Paris*, 1861. *obl.* 4°.   **1780. a. 36.**

—— Chasses en Afrique . . . Illustrées . . . par V. Adam. pp. 38. *Paris*, [1858.] *obl.* 4°.   **1780. a. 35.**

—— Nouvelle chasse aux papillons . . . Illustrée, *etc.* pp. 396. *Paris*, [1858.] 8°.   **12512. i. 3.**

—— Récréations chimiques . . . Ouvrage illustré . . . par H. Castelli, et faisant suite aux Récréations physiques du même auteur. pp. 377. *Paris*, 1866. 8°.
   12206. k. 5. (1.)

—— Récréations physiques. Ouvrage illustré . . . par Castelli. pp. 367. *Paris*, 1861. 8°.   **12206. i. 10. (2.)**

—— Deuxième édition. pp. 332. *Paris*, 1863. 8°.
   12206. i. 11. (2.)

CASTILLON (ANTOINE) Sermons sur les dimanches et fêtes de l'Avent, *etc.* 1844. *See* MIGNE (J. P.) Collection intégrale et universelle des orateurs sacrés, *etc.* tom. 2. 1844, *etc.* 4°.   **3676. a. 1.**

—— Sermons choisis. *See* LINGENDES (C. de) Sermons choisis de Lingendes, Castillon et Fromentières. 1830. 12°.   **4424. f. 40.**

CASTILLON (BALTHAZAR DE) *See* CASTIGLIONE (Baldassare) *Count.*

CASTILLON (FRANÇOIS) Dénonciation d'un plan de contre-révolution faite par M. Castillon commandant de la Garde Nationale de Cette, à la municipalité de la même ville, *etc.* pp. 6. *Paris*, [1790.] 8°.   **F. 53**. (36.)**

—— [Another copy.]   **F. 976. (4.)**

CASTILLON (FRÉDÉRIC ADOLPHE MAXIMILIEN GUSTAVE DE) *See* EUCLID. [*Elementa.*] Elémens de géométrie . . . Traduction nouvelle par F. de Castillon, *etc.* 1767. 8°.
   8530. a. 12.

—— *See* HULSHOFF (A.) Discours sur les penchans . . . traduit du hollandois en françois [by F. A. M. G. de Castillon]. 1769. 4°.   **8405. g. 14. (2.)**

—— *See* PERIODICAL PUBLICATIONS.—*Berlin.* Journal littéraire dédié au roy, *etc.* [Edited by F. A. M. G. de Castillon and others.] 1772, *etc.* 12°.   **266. c. 7.**

—— Recherches sur une Providence particulière. Onderzoek noopens eene Byzondere Voorzienigheid. *Fr. & Dutch.* 1782. *See* HAARLEM.—*Teyler's Stichting.* Verhandlingen raakende den natuurlyken en geopenbaarden Godsdienst, *etc.* dl. 2. 1781, *etc.* 4°.   **Ac. 942.**

CASTILLON (H.) Histoire des populations pyrénéennes, du Nébouzan et du pays de Comminges, depuis les temps les plus anciens jusqu'à la révolution de 89. 2 tom. *Toulouse, Paris*, 1842. 8°.   **1443. i. 7.**

—— Histoire du Comté de Foix depuis les temps anciens jusqu'à nos jours, avec notes, chartes, *etc.* 2 tom. *Toulouse*, 1852. 8°.   **10171. cc. 12.**

CASTILLON (JEAN) *See* CASTILHON.

CASTILLON (JEAN FRANÇOIS ANDRÉ LEBLANC DE) *See* LEBLANC DE CASTILLON.

CASTILLON (JEAN FRANÇOIS ANTOINE MARIE) Souvenirs du Premier Empire et de la Restauration . . . Publié par H. Duméril. 1889. *See* TOULOUSE.—*Académie des Sciences, Inscriptions et Belles-Lettres. Mémoires.* sér. 9. tom. 1. 1874, *etc.* 8º. Ac. 555.

CASTILLON (JEAN FRANÇOIS SALVEMINI DE) *See* SALVEMINI DI CASTIGLIONE (Giovanni F. M. M.)

CASTILLON (JEAN LOUIS) *See* CASTILHON.

CASTILLON (JUAN DE) *See* CASTRILLON.

CASTILLON (MERLE DE) *See* BORDE (C.) Œuvres diverses, *etc.* [Edited by M. de Castillon.] 1783. 8º. 12236. cc. 2.

CASTILLON (RICHARD)

—— Les Réparations allemandes. Deux expériences : 1919–1932, 1945–1952, *etc.* pp. 197. *Paris*, 1953. 4º. 8074. k. 29.

CASTILLON DE SAINT-VICTOR (MARIE ÉMILIEN DE) Historique du 5e régiment de Hussards . . . Gravures . . . par . . . H. de Bouillé, *etc.* pp. 210. 1889. fol. *See* FRANCE.—*Army.—5e Régiment de Hussards.* 8825. h. 14.

CASTILLON DU PERRON (MARGUERITE)

—— La Princesse Mathilde. Un règne féminin sous le second empire, *etc.* pp. 310. *Paris*, 1953. 8º. 10667. dd. 7. *Part of the series " Présence de l'histoire."*

CASTILLO NEGRETE (EMILIO DEL) Galería de Oradores de México en el siglo XIX. [Biographical sketches and speeches; with portraits.] tom. 1–3. *México*, 1877–80. 4º. 010881. g. 6. *No more published.*

—— Historia militar de México en el siglo XIX. tom. 1, 2. *México*, 1883. 8º. 9772. p. 11. *No more published.*

—— México en el Siglo XIX, o sea su historia desde 1800 hasta la época presente. [With portraits.] 6 tom. *México*, 1875–81. 4º. 9772. f. 7.

CASTILLO NEGRETE (JOSÉ DEL) Discurso . . . en el Aniversario de nuestra Independencia Nacional, *etc.* pp. 14. *Guadalajara* [*Mexico*], 1854. 8º. 12301. d. 7. (11.)

CASTILLONNOIS (BALTASAR) *Count. See* CASTIGLIONE (Baldassare)

CASTILLO QUINTERO (JOSÉ MARÍA DEL) Ataque á la libertad de imprenta por un padre de la patria [i.e. J. M. del Castillo Quintero as attorney for J. M. Morón y Molína in an action against G. Rodriguez.] 1827. 4º. *See* RODRIGUEZ (Gabriel) *Profesor de Farmácia en Puebla.* 8180. bb. 32.

CASTILLO QUINTERO (JUAN NEPOMUCENO DEL) *See* MEXICO.—*Cámara de Diputados.* Certificacion expedida por acuerdo de la Cámara . . . al diputado J. N. del Castillo Quintero de algunos de los hechos ocurridos en las sesiones secretas sobre la ley de provision de Canongías. [Dated : 16 May 1831.] 1831. 4º. L.A.S.527/25.(2.)

CASTILLO RUIZ DE VERGARA (PEDRO AGUSTÍN DEL) Descripcion historica y geografica de las Islas de Canaria. pp. xvii. 354. *Santa Cruz de Tenerife*, 1848 [1847, 48]. 8º. [*Biblioteca Isleña.*] 12231. e. 16.

CASTILLOS. Todos hacemos Castillos en el aire. Comedia en cuatro actos. pp. 40. *Madrid*, 1818. 4º. 1342. e. 1. (38.)

CASTILLO SOLÓRZANO (ALONSO DEL)

—— *See* DUNN (Peter N.) Castillo Solórzano, and the decline of the Spanish novel. 1952. 8º. W.P. 5736/11.

—— *See* GARCÍA SORIANO (J.) Los Dos " Don Quijotes." Investigaciones acerca de la génesis de " El Ingenioso Hidalgo " y quién pudo ser Avellaneda. [Suggesting that " Alonso Fernández de Avellaneda " is the pseudonym of Alonso del Castillo Solórzano.] 1944. 8º. 11866. cc. 16.

—— La Dicha Merecida.—El Pretendiente Oculto, y Casamiento Efectuado. 1785. *See* COLECCION. Coleccion de novelas, *etc.* tom. 6. 1794, 85, *etc.* 8º. 243. e. 22.

—— La Inclinacion Española.—El Disfrazado.—Mas Puede Amor que la Sangre.—Escarmiento de Atrevidos. 1788. *See* COLECCION. Coleccion de novelas, *etc.* tom. 3. 1794, 85, *etc.* 8º. 243. e. 19.

—— El Amor por la Piedad.—El Soberbio Castigado.—El Defensor contra sí.—La Duquesa de Mantua. 1789. *See* COLECCION. Coleccion de novelas, *etc.* tom. 7. 1794, 85, *etc.* 8º. 243. e. 23.

—— La Garduña de Sevilla.—La Inclinacion Española.—El Disfrazado. 1847. *See* SPANISH AUTHORS. Coleccion de los mejores autores Españoles. tom. 37. 1835, *etc.* 8º. 12230. h. 1/37.

—— La Garduña de Sevilla, y Anzuelo de las Bolsas.—La Inclinacion Española.—El Disfrazado. 1854. *See* ARIBAU (B. C.) Biblioteca de autores Españoles, *etc.* tom. 33. 1849, *etc.* 8º. 12232.f.1/33.

—— Comedia famosa titulada El Mayorazgo Figura.—Comedia famosa titulada el Marqués del Cigarral. 1858. *See* ARIBAU (B. C.) Biblioteca de autores Españoles, *etc.* tom. 45. 1849, *etc.* 8º. 12232.f.1/45.

—— Las Harpías en Madrid y Tiempo de Regocijo. Novelas . . . publicadas con una introducción por Don E. Cotarelo y Mori. pp. xxiv. 435. *Madrid*, 1907. 8º. 12489. b. 7.

—— The Duchess pf Mantua.—The Mask. *See* ROSCOE (Thomas) The Spanish Novelists, *etc.* vol. 3. 1832. 12º. N. 907.

—— Los Alivios de Casandra, *etc.* ff. 191. *I. Romeu : Barcelona*, 1640. 8º. 12490. aaaa. 8.

—— Les Divertissemens de Cassandre et de Diane, ou les Nouvelles de Castillo et de Taleyro, *etc.* [Translated, with a dedicatory epistle, by —— Vanel.] 3 tom. pp. 239. *J. Jombert : Paris*, 1685. 12º. 1072. f. 30.

—— Los Amantes Andaluzes. Historia entretenida, prosas y versos. ff. 221. *S. de Cormellas : Barcelona*, 1633. 8º. 12490. b. 8.

—— Aventuras del Bachiller Trapaza, *etc.* ff. 157. *P. Verges a costa de P. Alfay : Çaragoça*, 1637. 8º. 12490. df. 14.

—— [Another edition.] pp. 270. *Madrid*, [1905.] 8º. 12489. d. 40.

—— 't Leeven en bedrijff van den Doorsleepen Bedrieger, meester van bedrogh en fieltery . . . Uyt het Spaans vertaalt door G. D. B. [i.e. G. de Bay.] pp. 304. *A. de Wees : Amsterdam*, 1657. 12º. 12491. a. 6.

CASTILLO SOLÓRZANO (ALONSO DEL)

—— Epitome de la Vida y Hechos del inclito Rey Don Pedro de Aragon, tercero deste nombre, etc. pp. 224. *D. Dormer: Zaragoça, 1639. 8°.* **10632. aa. 11.**

—— Fiestas del Iardin. Que contienen tres comedias, y quatro nouelas. pp. 559. *S. Esparsa, a costa de F. Pincinali: Valencia, 1634. 8°.* **12304. d. 41.**

—— La Garduña de Seuilla, y Ançuelo de las Bolsas. ff. 192. *S. de Cormellas: Barcelona, 1644. 8°.* **243. e. 32.**

—— Quarta Impres. ff. 192. *Madrid, 1733. 8°.* **1075. d. 8.**

—— Nueva edicion adornado con . . . grabados, etc. pp. 279. *Madrid, 1844. 8°.* **12490. g. 6.**

—— Edición y notas de Federico Ruiz Morcuende. pp. 312. *Madrid, 1922. 8°.* **12490. tt. 24.**

—— La Garduña de Sevilla, etc. [An abridgment of the novel by A. del Castillo Solorzano.] 1846. 4°. *See* SEVILLE. **12330. h. 23. (7.)**

—— La Picara; or, the Triumphs of female subtility, display'd in the artifices and impostures of a beautiful woman . . . originally a Spanish relation [i.e. "La Garduña de Sevilla"] enriched with three pleasant novels. Render'd into English [from the French version] with some alterations and additions, by J. Davies of Kidwelly. pp. 304. *John Starkey: London, 1665. 8°.* **12490. b. 38.**

—— The Life of Donna Rosina. A novel . . . Originally a Spanish relation [i.e. "La Garduña de Sevilla," by A. del Castillo Solorzano] . . . Done into English by . . . E. W. [i.e. Edward Waldron, or rather, John Davies of Kidwelly.] pp. 157. [1700?] 12°. *See* ROSINA, Donna. **12489. a. 5.**

—— The Spanish Rogues: being the history of Donna Rosina, a notorious cheat, and her accomplices. Translated by Edward Waldron . . . Thirteenth edition. [An abridged and slightly altered edition of "La Pícara," a translation by John Davies of Kidwelly of "La Garduña de Sevilla," by A. del Castillo Solorzano.] pp. 180. 1792. 12°. *See* SPANISH ROGUES. **12492. bb. 1.**

—— The Spanish Pole-Cat; or, the Adventures of Seniora Rufina; in four books . . . Begun to be translated by Sir R. L'Estrange; and finish'd by Mr. Ozell. pp. 394. *Printed for E. Curll & W. Taylor: London, 1717. 12°.* **12490. aaa. 15.**

—— The second edition. pp. 394. *H. Curll: London, 1727. 12°.* **12490. aaaa. 22.**

—— Het Leven van Ruffine, of het Weseltje van Sivilien, etc. pp. 439. *Amsterdam, 1725. 8°.* **12350. b. 24.**

—— La Fouyne de Seville, ou l'Hameçon des bourses. Traduit de l'espagnol (par feu Monsieur Douville [i.e. Antoine Le Métel d'Ouville, or rather, by François de Métel de Boisrobert?]). pp. 592. *L. Bilaine: Paris, 1661. 8°.* **C. 71. b. 10.**

—— [Another edition.] Histoire et avantures de Dona Rufine, fameuse Courtisane de Seville, etc. 2 tom. *La Haye, 1743. 12°.* **244. b. 45.**

—— The Perfidious Mistress.—The Metamorphos'd Lover.—The Impostour out-witted.—The Amorous Miser.—The Pretended Alchymist. [Stories from "La Garduña de Sevilla" translated by Sir Roger L'Estrange.] *See* SPANISH DECAMERON. The Spanish Decameron, etc. 1687. 8°. **12490. bbb. 24.**

CASTILLO SOLÓRZANO (ALONSO DEL)

—— The Perfidious Mistress.—The Metamorphos'd Lover.—The Imposture out-witted.—The Amorous Miser.—The Pretended Alchemist. [From "La Garduña de Sevilla." Translated by Sir R. L'Estrange.] *In:* The Spanish Decameron, etc. pp. 183–319. [c. 1700.] 8°. **12492. bb. 29.**

—— —— *In:* The Spanish Decameron, etc. pp. 242–432. 1712. 8°. **12492. bb. 29a.**

—— [Another edition.] *See* SPANISH DECAMERON. The Spanish Decameron, etc. 1720. 12°. **12490. c. 32.**

—— Three Ingenious Spanish Novels [from "La Garduña de Sevilla"]: namely, I. The Loving Revenge . . . II. The Lucky Escape . . . III. The Witty Extravagant . . . render'd into French . . . Translated . . . by a Person of Quality. The second edition. [The translator's preface signed: J. D., i.e. John Davies of Kidwelly.] pp. 162. *E. Tracy: London, 1712. 12°.* **12499. aaaa. 9.**

—— Historia de Marco Antonio y Cleopatra ultima Reyna de Egypto . . . Segunda impresion. pp. 271. *Madrid, 1736. 8°.* **10605. aa. 12.**

—— Huerta de Valencia. Prosas y versos en las Academias de ella. [With an introduction by Eduardo Juliá Martínez.] pp. xl. 322. 1944. 8°. *See* MADRID.—*Sociedad de Bibliófilos Españoles.* **Ac. 8886/49.**

—— Jornadas Alegres, etc. ff. 224. *J. Gonçalez: Madrid, 1626. 8°.* **G. 10168.**

—— [Another edition.] pp. 363. *Madrid, 1909. 8°.* **12489. p. 18.**

—— Lisardo enamorado . . . Prólogo y notas de Eduardo Juliá y Martínez. pp. 331. *Madrid, 1947. 8°.* [Biblioteca selecta de clásicos españoles. ser. 2. vol. 3.] **Ac. 144/5.**

—— El Marques del Zigarral. Comedia famosa. MS. NOTE [by J. R. Chorley]. [*Lisbon*, 1647.] 4°. **11728. h. 8. (23.)** *A fragment.*

—— [Another edition.] 1679. *See* SPAIN. [*Appendix.—Miscellaneous.*] Primera parte de comedias escogidas, etc. vol. 46. 1652, etc. 4°. **11725. d. 5.**

—— [Another edition.] Comedia famosa, El Marques del Cigarral. De Don A. Moreto [or rather, A. del Castillo Solorzano]. [1705?] 4°. *See* MORETO Y CABAÑA (A.) **11728. e. 25.**

—— [Another edition.] Comedia famosa, El Marques del Cigarral. De Don A. Moreto [or rather, A. del Castillo Solorzano]. [1730?] 4°. *See* MORETO Y CABAÑA (A.) **11728. h. 8. (24.)**

—— Niña de los Embustes, Teresa de Manzanares . . . Con introducción y notas de Don Emilio Cotarelo y Mori. pp. xcv. 340. *Madrid, 1906. 8°.* **12489. ee. 39.**

—— Noches de Placer. Novelas . . . reimpresas con una advertencia de Don Emilio Cotarelo y Mori. pp. xi. 438. *Madrid, 1906. 8°.* **12489. ee. 41.**

—— Las Pruebas en la Muger. 1788. *See* COLECCION. Coleccion de novelas, etc. tom. 5. 1794, 84, etc. 8°. **243. e. 21.**

—— La Quinta de Laura, que contiene seis novelas entretenidas . . . Tercera impression. pp. 272. *Madrid, 1732. 8°.* **12491. a. 7.**

—— Sagrario de Valencia en quien se incluyen las vidas de los illustres Santos hijos suyos y del Reyno. ff. 159. *S. Esparsa: Valencia, 1635. 8°.* **4824. aa. 29.**

CASTILLO SOLÓRZANO (ALONSO DEL)

—— Sala de Recreacion. [With a preface by Joseph Alfay.] pp. 352. *Por los herederos de P. Lanaja y Lamarca, a costa de I. Alfay: Zaragoça*, 1649. 8°. C. 57. k. 6.

—— Tardes Entretenidas, en seis novelas . . . Publicadas por Don Emilio Cotarelo y Mori. pp. 403. *Madrid,* 1908. 8°. 12489. ee. 47.

—— Varios y Honestos Entretenimientos. En varios entremeses, y pasos apasibles, *etc.* pp. 162. *J. Garses: Mexico*, 1625. 8°. C. 63. a. 27.

—— Victoria de Norlingen, y el Infante en Alemania, comedia [1652?] *See* SPAIN. [*Appendix.—Miscellaneous.*] Primera parte de comedias escogidas, *etc.* vol. 28. 1652, *etc.* 4°. 11725. c. 7.

CASTILLO SOTOMAYOR (JOANNES DEL) D. Ioannis

del Castillo Sotomayor . . . Opera omnia, sive quotidianarum controversiarum iuris tomi octo . . . Quibus accesserunt Io. Pauli Melij . . . additiones & observationes ad Tractatum de alimentis, cum decisionibus S.R.R. ad materiam facientibus . . . cum summariis et indicibus, *etc.* 8 tom. *Sumptibus L. Anisson: Lugduni,* 1667. fol.

—— Repertorium generale rerum . . . quae in libris octo quotidianarum controversiarum J. del Castillo Sotomayor . . . continentur opera et . . . studio Nicolai Antonii, *etc. Apud Anissonios, J. Posuel & C. Rigaud: Lugduni*, 1686. fol. 5385. f. 2.

—— [Another edition.] tom. 1–10. *Coloniæ Allobrogum,* 1753, 52, 53. fol. 5385. g. 2. *Imperfect ; wanting tom.* 11.

CASTILLO TORRE (JOSÉ) El P.N.R. [i.e. Partido

Nacional Revolucionario] de México. Como debe entenderse la razón de su origen y su función como instituto político de la revolución mexicana. pp. 19. *México,* 1933. 4°. [*Del México actual.* no. 3.] L.A.S. 541/10.

CASTILLOU (HENRY)

—— The Brigand. *See* infra : Le Feu de l'Etna.

—— L'Escadron Toba. Nouvelle. *In:* Les Œuvres libres. Nouvelle série. no. 31. pp. 165–198. 1948. 8°. 12208. ee. 256.

—— [Le Feu de l'Etna.] The Brigand. (Translated by Mervyn Savill.) pp. 253. *Staples Press: London, New York,* 1953. 8°. 12519. e. 71.

—— Seigneur du nord. Roman inédit, *etc.* 3 pt. *Paris,* 1950. 8°. [*France Illustration. Supplément théâtral et littéraire.* no. 59–61.] P.P. 4283. m. (1.)

—— [Thaddéa.] Thaddëa. (Translated by Mervyn Savill.) pp. 252. *Staples Press: London, New York,* 1954. 8°. 012550. pp. 46.

CASTILLO-VALERO (FRANCISCO DEL) Observaciones

Criticas sobre el Codigo Penal de España. pp. 117. *Madrid*, 1860. 8°. 5385.aaa.39.(6.)

CASTILLO VELASCO (JOSÉ MARÍA DEL) Apunta

mientos para el Estudio del Derecho Constitucional Mexicano. pp. v. 860. *México*, 1871. 8°. 6784. e. 9.

CASTILLO Y ARTIGA (DIEGO DEL) successively *Bishop

of Truxillo* and *Archbishop of Bogotá.* D.D. Didaci del Castillo et Artiga . . . Alphabetum Marianum, opus posthumum, per . . . Petrum del Castillo . . . collectum & elaboratum . . . Nunc primum prodit. pp. 524. *L. Anisson: Lugduni*, 1669. 4°. 4061. dd. 2.

CASTILLO Y ARTIGA (DIEGO DEL) successively *Bishop

of Truxillo* and *Archbishop of Bogotá.*

—— De ornatu, et vestibus Aaronis, siue Commentarii litterales, et morales in caput xxviii. Exodi . . . Nunc primum prodit. [With the text.] pp. 478. *L. Anisson: Lugduni,* 1655. fol. 3165. g. 7.

CASTILLO Y AYENSA (JOSÉ DEL) *See* ANACREON.

[*Greek and Spanish.*] Ancreonte, Safo y Tirteo. Traducidos . . . en prosa y verso por Don J. del Castillo y Ayensa. 1832. 8°. 11450. d. 14.

—— Historia Critica de las Negociaciones con Roma desde la Muerte del Rey D. Fernando vij. 2 tom. *Madrid,* 1859. 8°. 9180. g. 18.

—— *See* PANDO FERNANDEZ DE PINEDO (M.) *Marquis de Miraflores.* Impugnacion á algunas aserciones de la obra publicada por J. del Castillo y Ayensa con el titulo " Historia critica de las negociaciones con Roma desde la muerte del Rey Don Fernando VII." 1859. 8°. 8042. d. 66. (4.)

CASTILLO Y CÁMARA (JULIAN) and ARGAIZ

(BASILIO MARÍA DE) El Coronel y Teniente-coronel del Batallon 1° de milicia local de Merida, á sus subordinados. [Dated : 30 Oct. 1828.] [*Merida in Yucatan,* 1828.] *s. sh.* fol. 9770. k. 9. (81.)

CASTILLO Y CLOS (ANTONIO MARÍA DEL) Exposicion

que hace al . . . Monarca . . . Fernando VII de Borbon . . . de la antigüedad, prodigios, épocas en que ha salido en rogativas públicas, y acaecimientos para poner en salvo de los enemigos acatólicos la imágen de María Santísima de Atocha, *etc.* pp. 16. *Madrid*, 1823. 4°. 9180. ccc. 10. (6.)

CASTILLO Y GALLEGOS (LORENZO DEL) Por Hiero-

nimo de Ablitas contra el Fiscal de su Magestad. [A pleading.] MS. NOTES. [1625?] fol. 1322. l. 10. (28.)

CASTILLO Y JIMENEZ (JOSÉ M.) El Katipunan ó

el filibusterismo en Filipinas, *etc.* pp. 396. *Madrid*, 1897. 8°. 9055. bbb. 21.

CASTILLO Y LANZAS (JOAQUIN M. DE) Arenga Cívica

que en memoria del glorioso grito de Dolores pronunció en la plaza de Veracruz en 16 de Setiembre de 1839, aniversario de él, el C. J. M. de Castillo y Lanzas, *etc.* pp. 16. *Veracruz*, 1839. 8°. 12301. d. 6. (18.)

CASTILLO Y LLATA (JOSEFA MARÍA DEL) *Countess de

la Sierra Gorda. See* NUÑEZ (F.) *of Michoacan.* Oracion fúnebre . . . con motivo de las . . . exêquias celebradas por la buena memoria del Sr. D. J. A. del Castillo y Llata, Conde de la Sierragorda . . . Danle á luz . . . la señora Condesa viuda, y . . . D. M. Samaniego del Castillo. 1818. 4°. 4985. de. 6. (2.)

—— *See* PEREZ VELASCO (A.) Elogio histórico del Señor Don J. A. del Castillo y Llata, Conde . . . de Sierragorda . . . Dado á luz por . . . su esposa, Doña J. M. de Escandon, Condesa de Sierragorda, *etc.* 1818. 4°. 4985. de. 6. (3.)

CASTILLO Y LLATA (JUAN ANTONIO DEL) *Count de la

Sierra Gorda. See* NUÑEZ (F.) *of Michoacan.* Oracion fúnebre . . . con motivo de las . . . exêquias, celebradas por la buena memoria del Sr. D. J. A. del Castello y Llata, *etc.* 1818. 4°. 4985. de. 6. (2.)

—— *See* PEREZ VELASCO (A.) Elogio histórico del Señor Don J. A. del Castillo y Llata, *etc.* 1818. 4°. 4985. de. 6. (3.)

CASTILLO Y NEGRETE (MANUEL DEL) [For official

documents issued by M. del Castillo y Negrete as Captain-General of the Philippines :] *See* PHILIPPINE ISLANDS.—Castillo y Negrete (M. del) *Captain-General.*

CASTILLO Y OCSIERO (MARIANO) *See* EPHEMERIDES. El Firmamento . . . calendario zaragozano . . . arreglado para toda España por . . . Don M. Castillo y Ocsiero. 1892, *etc.* 8º.   P.P. **2389**. led.

CASTILLO Y OLIVAS (PEDRO MARÍA DEL) Dialogos Españoles-Árabes, ó Guia de la conversacion Mogharbi, *etc.* pp. 110.ʹ *Madrid*, 1860. *obl.* 8º.   **12906**. a. **2**.

CASTILLO Y OROSCO (EUJENIO DEL) Vocabulario Páez-Castellano, catecismo, nociones gramaticales i dos pláticas . . . con adiciones, correcciones i un vocabulario castellano-paez por Ezequiel Uricoechea. pp. xxiv. 123. *Paris*, 1877. 8º. [*Coleccion lingüística Americana.* tom. 2.]   **12907**. dd. **17**.

CASTILLO Y QUARTIELLERS (RODOLFO DEL) La Medicación oleosa en tiempo de los Faraones. El aceite de ricino. (Publicado en la Revista de Medicina y Cirugía prácticas.) pp. 19. *Madrid*, 1908. 8º.   **07702**. c. **7**. (**4**.)

—— [Another copy.]   **7307**. bb. **6**. (**4**.)

—— Momificación y embalsamiento en tiempo de los Faraones. (Publicado en la Revista de Medicina y Cirugía prácticas.) pp. 20. *Madrid*, 1909. 8º.   **07702.g.10.**

—— [Another copy.]   **07702**. c. **12**. (**5**.)

—— Objetos egipcios encontrados en Tarragona . . . Publicado en el Boletin de la Real Academia de la Historia, *etc.* pp. 16. *Madrid*, 1909. 8º.   **07702**. c. **7**. (**7**.)

—— [La Oftalmología en Tiempo de los Romanos.] Die Augenheilkunde in der Römerzeit . . . Autorisierte Übersetzung aus dem Spanischen von Dr. Max Neuburger . . . Mit 26 Textfiguren. pp. vii. 137. *Leipzig & Wien*, 1907. 8º.   **07610**. f. (**9**.)

—— Recuerdo de un viaje a Egipto. Origen del Egipto . . . Memoria leída en la Real Academia de la Historia y publicada en su " Boletín." pp. 21. *Madrid*, 1908. 8º.   **010097**. l. **2**. (**2**.)

CASTILLO Y RADA (JOSÉ MARÍA DEL)
—— [For official documents issued by J. M. del Castillo y Rada as Minister of the Columbian Treasury:] *See* COLOMBIA. [Republic of Colombia, 1886– .]—*Ministerio de Hacienda.*

CASTILLO Y RODRIGUEZ (JUAN DEL) Encontraron las Españas la piedra filosofal. Proyecto presentado á las Córtes, *etc.* pp. 12. *México*, 1820. 4º.   **9770**. bb. **3**. (**26**.)
Cropped.

CASTILLO Y SORIANO (JOSÉ DEL) *See* CUENCA (C. L. de) and CASTILLO Y SORIANO (J. del) La Divina Zarzuela. Ensayo general cómico-lírico, *etc.* 1885. 8º.   **11728**. bbb. **13**. (**2**.)

—— El Abogado-consultor de la Mujer, *etc.* pp. 383. *Madrid*, 1899. 8º.   **05385**. ee. **1**.

—— Contra Soberbia Humildad. Cuadro en un acto y en verso, *etc.* pp. 23. *Madrid*, 1878. 12º.   **11728**. aaa. **4**.

—— Dos Horas de Exposicion. Apuntes cómicos de la de Pinturas de 1876. pp. 47. *Madrid*, 1876. 12º.   **11450**. aaa. **6**.

—— Núñez de Arce. Apuntes para su biografía. pp. 259. *Madrid*, 1904. 8º.   **10633**. e. **7**.

CASTILLO YURRITA (ALBERTO DEL) *See* CUYÁS ARMENGOL (Arturo) Diccionario Inglés-Español . . . Cuidadosamente revisado . . . por Antonio Cuyás Armengol y A. del Castillo Yurrita, *etc.* 1927. 16º.   **012942**. a. **18**.

CASTILLO YURRITA (ALBERTO DEL)
—— La Cultura del Vaso Campaniforme. Su origen y extensión en Europa. pp. 216. pl. CCVI. II. 1928. 8º. *See* BARCELONA.—*Universidad de Barcelona.—Facultad de Filosofía y Letras.*   Ac. **136**. c. (**1**.)

CASTIMONIUS (PAMPHILUS) *pseud.* Das politische Hof-Mädgen, d.i. allerhand neue, selzame und wunderliche Griffgen, welche von etlichen Frauen-Zimmer, sich in die Höhe zu bringen . . . practiciret worden . . . an den Tag gegeben von Pamphilo Castimonio. pp. 231. *Freistadt an der Gehl*, 1686. 12º.   **1204**. a. **17**. (**3**.)

CASTIN (JOANNES VILLA) *See* JOANNES [Villa-Castin], *a Nativitate.*

CASTIÑEIRAS (JULIO R.)
—— ·Algunos aspectos de la obra de Joaquín V. González. Introducción al vol. XX de las " Obras completas de Joaquín V. González," *etc.* [With a portrait.] pp. 70. 1938. 8º. *See* LA PLATA.—*Universidad Nacional.*   **11868**. bb. **1**.

—— Entrega de la Presidencia de la Universidad al Doctor Juan Carlos Rébora. Discurso del presidente saliente Ing. J. R. Castiñeiras. pp. 14. 1938. 8º. *See* LA PLATA.—*Universidad Nacional.*   Ac. **2694**. f/4. (**2**.)

CASTINELLI (GIOVANNI) Elogio funebre del Cavaliere Fran. Spannocchi Piccolomini, *etc.* pp. 10. *Firenze*, 1823. 8º.   **4865**. e. **42**. (**5**.)

CASTINELLI (RIDOLFO) *See* MAYER (Enrico) Alla memoria di Ridolfo Castinelli, *etc.* 1859. 8º.   **10631**. e. **33**.

CASTING. A Casting up of Accounts of certain Errors, *etc.* [The Epistle signed : W. T.] 1603. 8º. *See* T., W.   **698**. d. **20**. (**2**.)

CASTIRONICAL. The Castironical. *See* ENGLAND.— *Army.—Infantry.—London Regiment*, 6th *Battalion (City of London Rifles).*

CASTL, *Saint. See* CASTULUS.

CASTLE. The Castle and the Abbey. A Christmas tale. pp. 102. *J. V. Hall & Son: Maidstone*, 1846. 12º.   **012611**. h. **30**.

—— The Castle, East of the Sun and West of the World. A story from the Old Danish. *See* HOWITT (Mary) The Golden Casket, *etc.* [1861.] 8º.   **12804**. c. **31**.

—— [Another edition.] *See* HOWITT (William) Luke Barnicott, *etc.* [1866.] 8º.   **12806**. ee. **20/5**.

—— The Castle of Infamy. A poetical vision. In two parts. [ʌ William Combe.] pp. 80. *J. Bew: London*, 1780. 4º.   **11632**. f. **10**.
 {*Sometimes attributed to*

—— The Castle of Insolence. A poem. [By Richard B. Exton.] pp. 36. MS. NOTES. *Privately printed : Ipswich*, 1836. 12º.   **11644**. aaa. **51**.
Interleaved.

—— Here begynneth the castell of laboure. [Translated from the ' Chasteau de Labour ' of Pierre Gringore by Alexander Barclay. With woodcuts.] 𝔅.𝔏.   *Richarde Pynson : [London*, 1505 ?] 4º.   Huth. **29**.

—— [Another edition.] *Begin.* ANd than whan don is this assaut, *etc.* 𝔊.𝔏. [*Antoine Vérard : Paris*, 1505 ?] 4º.   C. **59**. ff. **4**.
A fragment, consisting of one unsigned leaf, from an apparently otherwise unknown edition. 29 lines to a page. With a woodcut headpiece showing " pacience " and " yre."

CASTLE.

—— [Another edition.] The Castell of Laboure. 𝔅.𝔏. [*Wynken de Worde: London*, 1510?] 4°. C. **21. c. 21.** *Imperfect; wanting some leaves at the end.*

—— The castell of loue, translated out of Spanishe [i.e. from D. de San Pedro's " Carcel de Amor "] in to Englyshe, by Iohan Bourchier knyght, lorde Bernis, at the instaunce of the lady Elizabeth Carew, late wyfe to syr Nicholas Carew knyght. The whiche boke treateth of the loue betwene Leriano and Laureola doughter to the kynge of Masedonia. 𝔅.𝔏. *Iohan Turke: London*, [1549?] 8°. C. **57. aa. 36.**

—— [Another edition.] [Edited, with additions, by Andrew Spigurnell.] 𝔅.𝔏. *Robert Wyer for Richarde Kele:* [*London*, 1550?] 8°. G. **10332.**

—— [For " The Castle of Perseverance " one of the mediaeval mysteries known as the " Macro Plays ":] *See* MACRO PLAYS.

—— The Castle of the Mist. [A tale. By the author of " My Lady Molly."] pp. 204. *William Stevens: London*, [1901.] 8°. [*Family Story-Teller.* no. 156.] **012600. ee. 156.**

—— The Enchanted Castle; or the Sleeping Beauty in the wood. A drama, in three acts. pp. 24. *London*, [1822.] 12°. [*Hodgson's Juvenile Drama.*] **840. b. 34. (9.)**

—— The Old Castle, and other stories. pp. 61. *Nelson & Sons: London*, 1881. 8°. **12804. gg. 29.**

—— The Solitary Castle. A romance of the eighteenth century. By the author of The Village of Martindale. 2 vol. *W. Lane: London*, 1789. 12°. **12611. a. 23.**

—— The White Castle; or, the Island of solitude. A Gothic romance. To which is added, the Cabinet; or, Fatal curiosity. An Arabian romance. pp. 36. *See* TELL TALE. The Tell Tale, *etc.* vol. 1. [1803.] 12°. **12614. aaa. 35. (1.)**

CASTLE ACRE.—*Church of St. James.*

—— Castle Acre Parish Church, *etc.* [Signed: A. Bek.] [1936.] *obl.* 8°. *See* BEK (Anthony H.) **10361. a. 23.**

Priory.

—— Castle Acre Priory. [An abridgment of the illustrated guide by F. J. E. Raby and P. K. B. Reynolds.] *London*, 1946. 8°. [*Ministry of Works. Ancient Monuments Inspectorate. Ancient Monuments and Historic Buildings. Leaflet Guides.*] **B.S. 46/32. (26.)**

CASTLE AVON. Castle Avon. By the author of " Emilia Wyndham " [i.e. Anne Marsh, afterwards Marsh-Caldwell], *etc.* 3 vol. *Colburn & Co.: London*, 1852. 8°. **12626. e. 13.**

—— [Another edition.] 2 vol. *Bernhard Tauchnitz: Leipzig*, 1852. 8°. [*Collection of British Authors.* vol. 249, 50.] **12267.a.1/212.**

—— [Another edition.] pp. 352. *Thomas Hodgson: London*, [1855.] 8°. [*Parlour Library.* vol. 122.] **12600. bb.**

CASTLE BAYNARD, *Ward of, London.* The Greeting of the Ward of Castle Baynard to its Alderman, the Rt. Hon. Sir T. Vansittart Bowater, Baronet, Lord Mayor of London, 10th November, 1913. pp. 70. *London*, [1913.] 4°. **10349. r. 3.**

CASTLE BAYNARD, *Ward of, London.*

—— *Begin.* To the Right Honourable the Lords Spiritual and Temporal, in Parliament Assembled, *etc.* (Petition of the Freemen Householders of the Ward of Castle . . . Baynard to both Houses of Parliament, for a repeal of the Statute of Geo. 1st. or such parts of it as effect their Elective Franchises.) pp. 3. [*London*, 1825?] fol. **1850. c. 5. (130*.)**

CASTLE BROMWICH.—*Castle Bromwich Golf Club.* Castle Bromwich Golf Club . . . Official handbook. [With illustrations.] pp. 18. *New Centurion Publishing & Publicity Co.: Derby & Cheltenham*, [1934.] 8°. **7916. eee. 16.**

CASTLE BUILDERS. The Castle Builders; or, the Deferred confirmation. By the author of " Heartsease " [i.e. Charlotte M. Yonge], *etc.* pp. 351. *J. & C. Mozley: London*, 1854. 18°. **4417. b. 12.**

—— [Another edition.] pp. 300. *D. Appleton & Co.: New York*, 1855. 12°. **12805. bbb. 15.**

—— The Castle-Builders; or, the History of William Stephens . . . A political novel . . . [By Thomas Stephens.] The second edition, with large additions. pp. xv. 320. *E. Cabe, etc.: London*, 1759. 8°. **12613. c. 25.**

CASTLE CARY.

—— Official Guide to the Parish of Castle Cary, Somerset. With map and illustrations. pp. 16. *Home Publishing Co.: Croydon*, [1949– .] 8°. **010368. r. 22.** —— *Various editions.*

CASTLE CARY VISITOR. *See* PERIODICAL PUBLICATIONS.—*Castle Cary.*

CASTLE DAMOURAY. *See* DAMOURAY, *Castle.*

CASTLE DONINGTON.

—— The Official Guide to Castle Donington, Leicestershire. With map and photographs. pp. 16. *Home Publishing Co.: Croydon*, [1950.] 8°. **010368. w. 28.**

CASTLE DONINGTON, *Rural District of.*

—— Castle Donington Rural District, Leicestershire. The official guide, *etc.* *Ed. J. Burrow & Co.: Cheltenham & London*,.[1953–] 8°. **10353. g. 37.** *Various editions.*

CASTLE DOUGLAS.—*High School.*

—— The Forward. June, 1920—June, 1939. *Castle Douglas*, 1920–39. 8°. **P.P. 6202. l.**

CASTLE EDEN. The Registers of Castle Eden, in the county of Durham. Baptisms, 1661–1812. Marriages, 1698–1794. Burials, 1696–1812. Transcribed and edited by the rector, Rev. F. G. J. Robinson, M.A. Indexed by A. E. & G. M. F. Wood. pp. viii. 40. *Sunderland*, 1914. 8°. [*Publications of the Durham and Northumberland Parish Register Society.* vol. 29.] **Ac. 8084/28.**

—— *Friendly Society.* Abstract of the Rules, Orders, and Regulations, for the government of the Castle-Eden Friendly Society. pp. 27. *F. Humble & Co.: Durham*, 1820. 8°. **8282. ff. 7. (3.)**

CASTLE FIEND. The Castle Fiend; or, the Fate of the loved and the lost. An old English romance. pp. iv. 84. *E. Lloyd: London*, [1847.] 8°. **12621. g. 16.**

CASTLE-GATE. The Wanton Wife of Castle-Gate: or, The Boat-mans Delight. To its own proper new tune. [A Song.] 𝔅.𝔏. *For Alex. Milbourn, W. Onely, T. Thackeray: [London*, 1700?] *s. sh.* fol. Rox. II. **496.**

CASTLE HILL CHURCH, *Northampton.* *See* NORTHAMPTON.—*Doddridge Chapel.*

CASTLE HILL MAGAZINE. *See* FOLKESTONE.—*Currie Schools.*

CASTLE HOWARD. Castle Howard: its Antiquity and History. The ancestral home of the Howards, *etc.* [Reprinted from John Preston Neale's "Views of the Seats of Noblemen and Gentlemen, *etc.*"] pp. 19. *Mitre Press: London,* [1931.] 8°.   **010352. b. 11.**

—— A Descriptive Catalogue of the Pictures at Castle Howard. pp. 16. *J. Gibson: Malton,* 1814. 8°.   **10347. de. 9. (5.)**

—— [Another edition.] pp. 18.   *R. W. Snow: Malton,* 1821. 12°.   **7857. a. 35. (1.)**

—— The Mausoleum at Castle Howard. Five plates, engraved by Henry Moses. Edited by C. H. Tatham.] [*London ?*] 1812. 4°.   **559*. b. 15.**

—— [Another copy.]   **191. b. 10.**

—— Another copy.]   **G. 13893.**

CASTLE HOWELL SCHOOL. *See* LANCASTER.

CASTLE HYDE. Beauty's of Castle Hyde. (Shannon and Chesapeak.) [Songs.]   *E. Hodge's* [sic]: *London,* [1860 ?] *s. sh.* 4°.   **C. 116. i. 1. (224.)**

CASTLE LINE. Castle Line. Views of the Fleet. pp. 32. [*London,* 1892.] 4°.   **10498. b. 17.**

—— Castle Line Handbook and Emigrant's Guide to South Africa. pp. 175.   *D. Currie & Co.: London,* 1888. 8°.   **10097. bb. 34.**

—— Handbook of Information for Passengers. pp. 65. *D. Currie & Co.: London,* 1893. 8°.   **10498. a. 25.**

CASTLE MONTHLY. *See* PERIODICAL PUBLICATIONS.—*Nottingham.*

CASTLE MUSEUM. *See* YORK.

CASTLE PRESS.

—— Castle Press Seasonal Flower Books. *See* HATFIELD (Audrey W.) *Seasonal Flower Books.*

CASTLE RACKRENT. Castle Rackrent, an Hibernian tale. Taken from facts, and from the manners of the Irish squires, before the year 1782. [By Maria Edgeworth.] pp. xliv. 182. *J. Johnson: [London,]* 1800. 8°.   **12611. f. 4.**

—— Castle Rackrent, *etc.* [By Maria Edgeworth.] pp. xliv. 182. *P. Wogan, etc.: Dublin,* 1800. 12°.   **012635. b. 83.**

—— The second edition. pp. xvi. 214. *J. Johnson: London,* 1800. 8°.   **N. 2494.**

—— [Another copy.]   **G. 17765.**

—— The third edition. pp. xii. 190. *P. Wogan & W. Porter: Dublin,* 1802. 12°.   **12613. b. 12.**

CASTLE READERS.

—— The Castle Readers.   *Frederick Warne: London & New York,* [1950– .] 8°.   **W.P. 68.**

CASTLE RISING.

—— The Guide to Castle Rising. pp. 8.   *West Norfolk & King's Lynn Newspaper Co.: King's Lynn,* 1925. 8°.   **7824. a. 1.**

CASTLE SAINT LAURE. Castle St. Laure. A tale. 2 vol. *Saunders & Otley: London,* 1853. 8°.   **12627. e. 13.**

CASTLE SHANE. *See* ARDGLASS.—*Jordan's Castle.*

CASTLE SPECTRE. The Castle Spectre. *See* PERIODICAL PUBLICATIONS.—*Aberdeen.*

CASTLE SQUARE PRESBYTERIAN CHURCH MONTHLY TREASURY. *See* CARNARVON.—*Castle Square Presbyterian Church.*

CASTLE STREET, *Church of. See* LONDON.—III. *French Protestant Church.—Church of Hungerford Market, afterwards of Castle Street.*

CASTLE TAVERN, *Paternoster Row.—Musical Society.* The By-Laws of the Musical Society at the Castle-Tavern, in Pater Noster Row. pp. 16. [*London,* 1731.] 8°.   **557*. d. 43. (2.)**

—— The Laws of the Musical Society, at the Castle Tavern, in Pater-Noster Row. pp. 24. *London,* 1750. 8°.   **7895. a. 39.**

CASTLE WARD, *Rural District.*

—— Official Guide to the Castle Ward Rural District, Northumberland, *etc.* (Castle Ward Rural District, Northumberland. The official guide.)   *Home Publishing Co.: Croydon,* [1949– .] 8°.   **010368. r. 6.** *Various editions.*

CASTLE'S GUIDE TO THE FRUIT, VEGETABLE AND ALLIED TRADES. *See* DIRECTORIES.—*Fruit Trade.*

CASTLE'S WHOLESALE AND RETAIL LIST OF THE FISHING AND ALLIED TRADES. *See* DIRECTORIES.—*Fish Trade.*

CASTLE (AGNES) Christ the Consoler. A collection of prayers for the bereaved by war compiled by Agnes Egerton Castle. pp. xiv. 123.   *Burns & Oates: London,* [1916.] 16°.   **03456. df. 1.**

—— My Little Lady Anne. pp. 153.   *John Lane: London; Henry Altemus: Philadelphia,* 1896. 8°.   [*Pierrot's Library.* vol. 2.]   **C. 109. aa. 24/2.**

—— Pinkina & Bunny Cony; or, the Faithless fair. A rabbit drama in three acts. pp. 32.   *Sheldon Press: London,* [1933.] 8°.   [*Parish Plays.* no. 53.]   **W.P. 467/53.**

CASTLE (AGNES) and **CASTLE** (EGERTON)

——   The Bath Comedy. pp. xx. 243. *Macmillan & Co.: London,* 1900. 8°.   **012641. aaa. 44.**

—— [Another edition.] Illustrated by H. M. Brock. pp. vi. 138.   *Amalgamated Press: [London,* 1908.] 8°. [*Daily Mail Sixpenny Novels.* no. 48.]   **012604. e. 29.**

—— [Another edition.] pp. 260.   *Hodder & Stoughton: London,* [1915.] 8°.   **012621. k. 28.**

—— The Black Office, and other chapters of romance. pp. xii. 306. *John Murray: London,* 1917. 8°.   **NN. 4600.**

—— Chance the Piper. [Tales.] pp. x. 320.   *Smith, Elder & Co.: London,* 1913. 8°.   **NN. 918.**

—— The Chartered Adventurer: being some episodes in the life of Mr. Terence O'Flaherty and his friend Lord Marlowe. pp. 256. *Skeffington & Son: London,* [1919.] 8°.   **NN. 5404.**

—— Count Raven. pp. 282.   *Cassell & Co.: London,* 1916. 8°.   **NN. 3868.**

CASTLE (Agnes) and **CASTLE** (Egerton)

—— Diamond Cut Paste. pp. 341. *John Murray: London,* 1909. 8°. **012623.b.36.**

—— [Another edition.] pp. 319. *Nisbet & Co.: London,* 1915. 8°. **12600. h. 47.**

—— Enchanted Casements. pp. 288. *Hutchinson & Co.: London,* [1923.] 8°. **NN. 8851.**

—— Flower o' the Orange, and other stories. pp. 310. *Methuen & Co.: London,* 1908. 8°. **012627. aa. 27.**

—— Forlorn Adventurers. pp. 348. *Methuen & Co.: London,* 1915. 8°. **NN. 2319.**

—— [Another edition.] pp. 470. *Paris,* [1915.] 8°. [*Nelson's Continental Library.* no. 7.] **012604. a. 1/7.**

—— French Nan, *etc.* pp. xiv. 216. *Smith Elder & Co.: London,* 1905. 8°. **012631. dd. 39.**

—— [Another edition.] pp. 272. *London,* [1909.] 8° [*Nelson's Library.*] **12202.y.1/49.**

—— The Golden Barrier. pp. vi. 361. *Methuen & Co.: London,* 1913. 8°. **NN. 1131.**

—— The Grip of Life. pp. 393. *Smith, Elder & Co.: London,* 1912. 8°. **NN. 420.**

—— The Hope of the House. pp. viii. 339. *Cassell & Co.: London,* 1915. 8°. **NN. 2918.**

—— " If Youth but knew ! " . . . With illustrations by Lancelot Speed. pp. xv. 348. *Smith, Elder & Co.: London,* 1906. 8°. **012632. d. 33.**

—— [Another edition.] pp. 288. *London,* [1907.] 8°. [*Nelson's Library.*] **12202.y.1/12.**

—— [Another edition.] pp. 288. *T. Nelson & Sons: London,* [1928.] 8°. **012604. b. 40.**

—— Incomparable Bellairs. pp. liv. 289. *F. A. Stokes Co.: New York,* 1903. 8°. **012707. a. 20.**

—— [Another edition.] pp. xxiii. 301. *Archibald Constable: London,* 1904. 8°. **012629. bb. 37.**

—— [Another edition.] pp. 281. *London,* [1907.] 8°. [*Nelson's Library.*] **12202.y.1/180.**

—— John Seneschal's Margaret. pp. 320. *Hodder & Stoughton: London,* [1920.] 8°. **NN. 6705.**

—— Kitty and Others. pp. 277. *Hutchinson & Co.: London,* [1922.] 8°. **NN. 7845.**

—— Little Hours in Great Days. [Life in England during the European War, 1914–19.] pp. 272. *Constable & Co.: London,* [1919.] 8°. **012350. df. 77.**

—— A Little House in War Time. pp. xx. 275. *Constable & Co.: London,* 1915. 8°. **012352. de. 3.**

—— The Lost Iphigenia. pp. 316. *Smith, Elder & Co.: London,* 1911. 8°. **012618. c. 2.**

—— Love gilds the Scene, and women guide the plot. pp. viii. 339. *Smith, Elder & Co.: London,* 1912. 8°. **NN. 104.**

—— [Another edition.] pp. 154. *London,* [1914.] 8°. [*Newnes' Sixpenny Copyright Novels.*] **012604.f.1/218.**

—— Minniglen. pp. 348. *John Murray: London,* 1918. 8°. **NN. 5095.**

—— Minuet and Foxtrot. pp. 287. *Hutchinson & Co.: London,* [1922.] 8°. **NN. 8281.**

CASTLE (Agnes) and **CASTLE** (Egerton)

—— My Merry Rockhurst. Some episodes in the life of Viscount Rockhurst, a friend of the King, at one time Constable of His Majesty's Tower, *etc.* pp. viii. 311. *Smith, Elder & Co.: London,* 1907. 8°. **012627. aa. 26.**

—— [Another edition.] pp. 253. *London,* [1913.] 8°. [*Everett's Library.*] **12209.k.1/59.**

—— [Another edition.] pp. 253. *George Newnes: London,* [1920.] 8°. **012603. de. 62.**

—— New Wine. pp. vi. 317. *W. Collins, Sons & Co.: London,* [1919.] 8°. **NN. 5815.**

—— Our Sentimental Garden . . . Illustrated by Charles Robinson. pp. 304. *William Heinemann: London,* 1914. 8°. **012354. ff. 51.**

—— Pamela Pounce. A tale, *etc.* pp. 317. *Hodder & Stoughton: London,* [1921.] 8°. **NN. 7320.**

—— Panther's Cub. pp. 512. *T. Nelson & Sons: London,* 1910. 8°. **012618. c. 3.**

—— Panther's Cub. pp. 380. *T. Nelson & Sons: London & Edinburgh,* [1912.] 8°. [*Nelson's Library.*] **12202. y. 1/253.**

—— The Pride of Jennico, *etc.* pp. 346. *R. Bentley & Son: London,* 1898. 8°. **012623. f. 17.**

—— [Another edition.] pp. 341. *Macmillan & Co.: London ; Norwood, Mass.* [printed], 1899. 8°. **12618. d. 32.**

—— [Another edition.] pp. 246. *J. M. Dent & Sons: London,* [1915.] 8°. [*The Wayfarer's Library.*] **012206.i.1/68.**

—— Romances in Red. pp. 314. *Hodder & Stoughton: London,* [1921.] 8°. **NN. 7096.**

—— Rose of the World. pp. 379. *Smith, Elder & Co.: London,* 1905. 8°. **012631. aaa. 18.**

—— [Another edition.] Illustrated by Hal Hurst. pp. v. 118. *Amalgamated Press: London,* [1908.] 8° [*Daily Mail Sixpenny Novels.* no. 31.] **012604. e.1/12**

—— [Another edition.] pp. 380. *London,* [1911.] 8°. [*Nelson's Library.*] **12202.y.1/102.**

—— [Another edition.] pp. 380. *T. Nelson & Sons: London,* [1920.] 8°. **012603. df. 23.**

—— The Secret Orchard. pp. vii. 316. *Macmillan & Co.: London,* 1901. 8°. **012639. aaa. 44.**

—— [A reissue.] *Cassell & Co.: London,* [1916.] 8°. **012602. i. 4.**

—— [Another edition.] Illustrated by C. D. Williams. pp. vii. 349. *McLeod & Allen: Toronto,* 1901. 8°. **012622. k. 10.**

—— [Another edition.] Illustrated by Hal Hurst. pp. vi. 154. *Amalgamated Press: [London,* 1908.] 8°. [*Daily Mail Sixpenny Novels.* no. 59.] **012604.e.1/40.**

—— The Star Dreamer. pp. 436. *A. Constable & Co.: London,* 1903. 8°. **012638. bb. 22.**

—— [Another edition.] Illustrated by J. R. Skelton. pp. vi. 170. *Amalgamated Press: London,* [1907.] 8°. [*Daily Mail Sixpenny Novels.* no. 15.] **012604.e.1/4.**

—— [Another edition.] pp. 382. *John Long: London,* 1924. 8°. **NN. 10246.**

CASTLE (AGNES) and **CASTLE** (EGERTON)

—— The Third Year in the Little House. pp. 279.
Hutchinson & Co.: London, 1917. 8°. **012352. e. 34.**

—— To the Tune of Little Red Heels. pp. 12.
Ward, Lock & Co.: London, 1903. 8°. **012630. m. 19.**

—— The Ways of Miss Barbara. pp. vi. 307. *Smith,
Elder & Co.: London*, 1914. 8°. **NN. 2318.**

—— The Wind's Will. pp. vi. 344. *Cassell & Co.: London*,
1916. 8°. **NN. 3588.**

—— Wolf-Lure. pp. 337. *Cassell & Co.: London*, 1917. 8°.
NN. 4530.

—— Wroth. pp. 371. *Smith, Elder & Co.: London*,
1908. 8°. **012625. aaa. 17.**

—— [Another edition.] pp. 158. *London*, [1912.] 8°.
[*Newnes' Sixpenny Copyright Novels.*]
012604.f.1/179.

CASTLE (AGNES EGERTON) *See* CASTLE (Agnes)

CASTLE (ALFRED WATKINS) Reader and Guide for New
Americans. 2 bk. *Macmillan Co.: New York*, 1924. 8°.
12825. e. 28.

CASTLE (ALICE)

—— Notes on the Church of St. Mary, Bishopsbourne, Kent.
Compiled by Miss A. Castle. pp. 8. *Gibbs & Sons:
Canterbury*, 1931. 8°. **1879. cc. 11. (39.)**

CASTLE (ANGELINE L.) *See* ARMSTRONG (Richard) No
Cause to Mourn for the Pious Dead. A sermon preached
. . . at the funeral of Angelina L. wife of S. N. Castle, an
assistant missionary, *etc.* 1841. 8°. **4985. cc. 46. (4.)**

CASTLE (ARTHUR) Phrénologie spiritualiste. Nouvelles
études de psychologie appliquée. pp. vii. 408. *Paris*,
1862. 8°. **7410. bb. 17.**

CASTLE (BARBARA)

—— Are Controls Necessary ? pp. 38. *Education Committee
of the London Co-operative Society: London*, 1947. 8°.
[*Co-operative Discussion Group Outlines.* no. 6.]
W.P. 6271/6.

CASTLE (C. F.) Boat Building. A new method for the
amateur. pp. 26. *C. F. Castle: Marlow*, [1937.] 8°.
8805. df. 32.

CASTLE (CHARLES)

—— Dogs. [With plates.] pp. 96. *W. & G. Foyle: London*,
1950. 8°. **7295. p. 25.**

—— Scientific Dog Management and Breeding. [With plates.]
pp. 128. *Nicholas Kaye: London*, 1951. 8°.
7296. aa. 43.

CASTLE (CHARTLEY) *pseud.* Harold Overdon, Ashore and
Afloat. pp. iv. 328. *Saunders, Otley & Co.: London*,
1862. 12°. **12632. k. 4.**

—— John Woodburn, Royal Navy. pp. viii. 304.
Saunders, Otley & Co.: London, 1861. 12°. **12632. i. 5.**

CASTLE (CORA SUTTON) A Statistical Study of Eminent
Women. pp. vii. 90. *Science Press: New York*,
1913. 8°. [*Archives of Psychology.* no. 27.]
P.P. 1247. gb.

CASTLE (DENNIS) *pseud.* [JOHN RIDLEY BROWN.]

—— Medallion Puppet Book (Medallion ' Western ' Puppet
Book). (Author: Dennis Castle. Designer: Darby
Headley.) 6 pt. *Medallion Press: London*, [1950, 53.] 4°.
12837. p. 21.

CASTLE (DON) Do Your Own Time. [A novel.] pp. 288
Arthur Barker: London, 1938. 8°. **NN. 28980.**

CASTLE (DOUGLAS) *pseud.* [i.e. JOHN RIDLEY BROWN.]

—— Arctic Assignment, *etc.* pp. 255. *Blackie & Son:
London & Glasgow*, [1952.] 8°. **12826. l. 50.**

—— The Brotherhood of the Tortoise . . . Illustrated by
Douglas Relf. pp. 255. *Blackie & Son: London &
Glasgow*, [1952.] 8°. **12832. k. 19.**

—— " Calling Base 10 " . . . Illustrated by Terence T.
Cuneo. [A tale.] pp. 176. *Blackie & Son: London &
Glasgow*, [1943.] 8°. **12827. ee. 26.**

—— " Calling Base 10 " . . . Edited and adapted by
Geoffrey G. Bond. pp. 168. *Blackie & Son: Glasgow
& Edinburgh*, 1948. 8°. [*Life and Adventure Series.
Boys' Section.* no. 1.] **W.P. 13289. a/1.**

—— The Cockney of Lisbon . . . Illustrated by Imre Hof-
bauer. pp. 253. *Blackie & Son: London & Glasgow*,
[1953.] 8°. **NNN. 3818.**

—— East of Algiers . . . Illustrated by Ellis Silas. pp. 288.
Blackie & Son: London & Glasgow, [1951.] 8°.
12833. ff. 39.

—— The Hounds of Caprozzi . . . Illustrated by M. Finlay.
pp. 256. *Blackie & Son: London & Glasgow*, [1947.] 8°.
12829. c. 18.

—— The Hounds of Caprozzi . . . Illustrated by M. Mackinlay.
pp. 256. *Blackie & Son: London & Glasgow*, [1955.] 8°.
12837. h. 14.

—— The Moor of Marrakesh . . . Illustrated by F. Stocks
May. pp. 224. *Blackie & Son: London & Glasgow*,
[1948.] 8°. **12831. b. 32.**

—— The Pirates of the Dezertas . . . Illustrated by Anthony
Barclay. pp. 256. *Blackie & Son: London & Glasgow*,
[1948.] 8°. **12831. b. 31.**

—— Storm over the Adriatic . . . Illustrated by R. G.
Campbell. pp. 255. *Blackie & Son: London & Glasgow*,
[1949.] 8°. **12832. e. 65.**

—— The Sword of Adventure . . . Illustrated by Warwick
W. Lendon. pp. 255. *Blackie & Son: London & Glasgow*,
[1951.] 8°. **12834. c. 13.**

CASTLE (E.) Should you, my Heart, relent. Song.
E. Castle: Newcastle-on-Tyne, 1895. s. sh. 8°.
1865. c. 8. (18.)
Typewritten.

CASTLE (E. F.)

—— *See* FAVELL (Archibald J.) Practical Bookkeeping and
Accounts. (Second edition. Revised by E. F. Castle.)
1949. 8°. **08230. b. 61.**

CASTLE (EDGAR BRADSHAW) *See* NEW EDUCATION FEL-
LOWSHIP. The Coming of Leisure . . . Edited by E. B.
Castle, A. K. C. Ottaway, *etc.* 1935. 8°. **8287. cc. 51.**

—— Better Thinking. How to make the most of your mind.
pp. 47. *University of London Press: London*, 1939. 8°.
8471. df. 17.

—— Building the New Age. pp. 156. *Rich & Cowan:
London*, [1945.] 8°. [*Needs of Today Series.* no. 26.]
W.P. 7580/26.

CASTLE (EDGAR BRADSHAW)

—— Education and World Citizenship. pp. 20.   *Council for Education in World Citizenship: London*, [1947.] 8°.
8288. df. **85.**

—— Fathers and Sons. pp. 160.   *University of London Press: London*, 1931. 8°.
08308. a. **12.**

—— People in School. pp. vii. 180.   *William Heinemann: London*, 1953 [1954]. 8°.
08311. h. **129.**
Part of " The Heinemann Education Series."

—— Reconciliation in Palestine . . . Reprinted . . . from " The Hibbert Journal," *etc.* pp. 11.   *Palestine Watching Committee of the Society of Friends: London*, 1945. 8°.
8024. b. **21.**

—— The Undivided Mind. pp. 102.   *G. Allen & Unwin: London*, 1941. 8°. [*Swarthmore Lecture.* 1941.]
W.P. **9910/35.**

—— Why Christian Education ? pp. 24.   *Edinburgh House Press: London*, 1942. 8°. [*World Issues.* no. 13.]
W.P. **13520/13.**

CASTLE (EDUARD) *See* ECKERMANN (J. P.) Gespräche mit Goethe . . . Herausgegeben . . . von . . . E. Castle, *etc.* [1916.] 8°.
010704. e. **2.**

—— *See* NAGL (J. W.) and ZEIDLER (J.) Deutsch-Oester-reichische Litteraturgeschichte . . . Herausgegeben von Dr. J.W. Nagl und J. Zeidler (E. Castle). [1897, *etc.*] 8°.
011851. f. **52.**

—— *See* RAIMUND (F.) Sämtliche Werke . . . Herausgegeben von F. Brukner und E. Castle. [1925, *etc.*] 8°.
20002. bb. **42.**

—— *See* SCHURZ (A. X.) Lenaus Leben . . . Erneut und erweitert von E. Castle. 1913, *etc.* 8°. [*Schriften des Literarischen Vereins in Wien.* no. 18, *etc.*]   Ac. **8970.**

—— *See* SCHWARZENBERG (Friedrich ron) *Prince.* Aus dem Wanderbuche eines verabschiedeten Lanzknechtes . . . Herausgegeben von E. Castle. 1925. 8°.
010025. ee. **17.**

—— Carl Künzels ' Schilleriana.' Briefe an Schiller und Schillers Familienmitglieder nach den Abschriften im Besitz des Wiener Goethe-Vereins. Herausgegeben von E. Castle, *etc.* [With a " Gesamtinventar von Carl Künzels ' Schilleriana ' nach seinen eigenen Listen."] pp. 202. *Wien*, 1955. 8°. [*Österreichische Akademie der Wissenschaften. Sitzungsberichte.* Bd. 229. Phil.-hist. Klasse. Abh. 3.]   Ac. **810/6.**

—— Der Dichter des " Soldatenbüchleins " [Josef Christian von Zedlitz]. 1898. *See* VIENNA.—*Grillparzer Gesell-schaft.* Jahrbuch, *etc.* Jahrg. 8. 1891, *etc.* 8°.
Ac. **8972.**

—— Festschrift zum 200. Geburtstag Goethes. Heraus-gegeben . . . von E. Castle. [With a portrait.] pp. 164. *Wien*, [1949.] 8°.   [*Chronik des Wiener Goethe-Vereins.* Bd. 52, 53.]   Ac. **9434.**

—— In Goethes Geist. Vorträge und Aufsätze. pp. xv. 414. *Wien & Leipzig*, 1926. 8°.
011840. dd. **16.**

—— Lenau und die Familie Löwenthal. Briefe und Gespräche, Gedichte und Entwürfe . . . Vollständiger Abdruck nach den Handschriften. Ausgabe, Einleitung und Anmerkungen von Prof. Dr. E. Castle. Mit zehn Bildnissen und fünf Schriftproben. 2 vol. pp. xcii. 634. *Leipzig*, 1906. 8°.
010920. i. **23.**

—— Nikolaus Lenau. Zur Jahrhundertfeier seiner Geburt . . . Mit neun Bildnissen und einer Schriftprobe. pp. viii. 120. *Leipzig*, 1902. 8°.
10708. df. **43.**

CASTLE (EDWARD J.) *F.R.H.S.* *See* WRIGHT (Walter P.) and CASTLE (E. J.) First Steps in Gardening, *etc.* 1906. 8°.
7054. df. **29.**

—— *See* WRIGHT (Walter P.) and CASTLE (E. J.) Pictorial Practical Flower Gardening, *etc.* 1905. 8°.
07029. i. **14.**

—— *See* WRIGHT (Walter P.) and CASTLE (E. J.) Pictorial Practical Potato Growing, *etc.* 1906. 8°.
07075. df. **14.**

—— The Unheated Greenhouse, *etc.* pp. 20.   *Agricultural & Horticultural Association: London*, [1910.] 8°. [*One & All Garden Books.* no. 24.]   07031.**df.58/24.**

CASTLE (EDWARD JAMES) *See* CASTLE (Henry J.) Prac-tical Remarks on the Principles of Rating . . . (Second edition.) By H. J. Castle . . . assisted by E. J. Castle. 1869. 8°.
6425. e. **1.**

—— The Law of Commerce in Time of War, with particular reference to the respective rights and duties of belligerents and neutrals. pp. x. 150.   *W. Maxwell & Son: London*, 1870. 8°.
6835. bb. **21.**

—— A Practical Treatise on the Law of Rating. pp. xxvi. 521.   *Stevens & Sons: London*, 1879. 8°.
6426. df. **4.**

—— Second edition. pp. xxviii. 570.   *Stevens & Sons: London*, 1886. 8°.
6425. df. **11.**

—— Third edition. pp. xlvii. 655.   *Stevens & Sons: London*, 1895. 8°.
6426. df. **24.**

—— Fourth edition. pp. l. 601.   *Stevens & Sons: London*, 1903. 8°.
6425. h. **24.**

—— Shakespeare, Bacon, Jonson and Greene. A study. pp. viii. 352.   *Sampson, Low & Co.: London*, 1897. 8°.
11763. dd. **1.**

CASTLE (EDWARDINA WILMOT) Nina Castle. Extracts from her letters & journals from West Africa, with a short sketch of her life. Compiled by Emily Symons. [With a portrait.] pp. viii. 130.   *Marshall Bros.: London*, [1904.] 8°.
4907. f. **45.**

CASTLE (EGERTON) [For works written by E. Castle in collaboration with Agnes Castle :] *See* CASTLE (Agnes) and CASTLE (Egerton)

—— *See* JERNINGHAM (Hon. Frances) *Lady.* The Jerning-ham Letters . . . Edited, with notes, by E. Castle, *etc.* 1896. 8°.
010910. b. **1.**

—— *See* MEEHAN (John F.) More Famous Houses of Bath & District . . . With an introduction by E. Castle, *etc.* 1906. 8°.
010360. l. **10.**

—— *See* MONTAIGNE (M. de) Thoughts from Montaigne . . . Foreword by E. Castle. 1904. 8°.
12239. de. **1.**

—— *See* STEVENSON (Robert L.) Le Roman du Prince Othon. Traduit . . . par E. Castle. 1896. 8°.
12603. f. **24.**

—— " La Bella " and others. Being certain stories recol-lected by E. Castle [and one by Agnes Castle]. pp. vi. 320. *Cassell & Co.: London*, 1892. 8°.   012634. k. **31.**

—— [A reissue.] pp. vi. 320.   *Macmillan & Co.: London*, 1901. 8°.
012622. ee. **39.**

—— Biblioteca artis dimicatoriæ. *See* POLLOCK (Walter H.) Fencing, *etc.* 1889. 4°.   K.T.C. **103. a. 1/9.**

—— Bibliotheca artis dimicatoriæ. *See* POLLOCK (Walter H.) Fencing . . . With a complete bibliography of the art by E. Castle, *etc.* 1890. 8°.   7913. pp. **1/26.**

CASTLE (Egerton)

—— —— 1893. 8°.   7913. pp. **1/11.**

—— Consequences. A novel. 3 vol.   *R. Bentley & Son:*
London, 1891. 8°.   **012640. l. 3.**

—— New edition. pp. vi. 406.   *R. Bentley & Son: London,*
1898. 8°.   **12618. ccc. 25.**

—— English Book-Plates. An illustrated handbook for
students of ex-libris. pp. xiii. 249.   *G. Bell & Sons:*
London, 1892. 8°.   K.T.C. **8. a. 5.**

—— [Another edition.] pp. xx. 352.   *G. Bell & Sons:*
London, 1893. 8°.   K.T.C. **8. a. 13.**

—— The Light of Scarthey. A romance. pp. viii. 503.
Osgood & Co.: London, [1895.] 8°.   **012628. m. 50.**

—— [Another edition.] pp. xxiv. 503.   *Macmillan & Co.:*
London, 1901. 8°.   **012622. ee. 40.**

—— Marshfield the Observer, and the Death-Dance. Studies
of character & action. pp. 356.   *Macmillan & Co.:*
London, 1900. 8°.   **012641. dd. 23.**

—— Schools and Masters of Fence, from the Middle Ages to
the Eighteenth Century. With . . . a bibliography, *etc.*
pp. lii. 254. pl. vi.   *G. Bell & Sons: London,*
1885 [1884]. 4°.   **7907. i. 12.**

—— A new and revised edition. pp. lxxviii. 355. pl. vi.
G. Bell & Sons: London, 1892. 8°.   **2270. cc. 13.**

—— L'Escrime et les escrimeurs depuis le moyen âge juqu'au
xviiie siècle . . . Traduit de l'anglais par Albert Fier-
lants. pp. xlvii. 281. pl. vi. *Paris*, 1888. 4°.
                7908. f. 15.

—— 'Young April.' pp. xiii. 406.   *Macmillan & Co.:*
London, 1899. 8°.   **012643. k. 31.**

—— [Another edition.]   pp. 377.   *London*, [1917.]   8°.
[*Nelson's Library*.]   **12202.y.1/246.**

CASTLE (*Mrs.* Egerton) *See* Castle (Agnes)

CASTLE (Eric Frank)

—— Practical Bookkeeping and Accounts, advanced stage.
pp. 448. *University Tutorial Press: London*, 1951. 8°.
                8219. c. 42.

—— Principles of Accounts. pp. 240.   *University*
Tutorial Press: London, 1954. 8°.   **08218. bb. 21.**

CASTLE (Ernest V.) Marion Boyde. An every-day
romance. pp. 143.   *Digby, Long & Co.: London,*
[1893.] 8°.   **012634. g. 51.**

CASTLE (F. R.) *See* Thomas (Harry H.) Tomatoes and
Salads. By H. H. Thomas . . . assisted by F. R. Castle,
etc. 1917. 8°.   **07029. i. 65.**

—— *See* Thomas (Harry H.) Vegetable Growing for Amateurs. By H. H. Thomas . . . assisted by F. R. Castle,
etc. [1916.] 8°.   **07029. k. 65.**

—— *See* Thomas (Harry H.) Vegetable Growing for Amateurs. By H. H. Thomas, assisted by F. R. Castle, *etc.*
1953. 8°.   W.P. b. **125/1.**

—— Tomatoes: and how to grow them . . . Edited by
T. W. Sanders . . . Illustrated. pp. 93.   *W. H. &*
L. Collingridge: London, [1911.] 8°.   **07077. ee. 22.**

—— Fourth edition. pp. 92.   *W. H. & L. Collingridge:*
London, [1917.] 8°. [*Practical Books on Food Production.*]
                07073.ee.28/2.

CASTLE (F. R.)

—— Fifth edition.   pp. 92.   *W. H. & L. Collingridge:*
London, [1921.] 8°.   **07078. de. 53.**

—— Sixth edition.   pp. 96.   *W. H. & L. Collingridge:*
London, [1925.] 8°.   **07029. eee. 106.**

—— [Another edition.] Revised by A. J. Macself . . .
Seventh edition. pp. 96.   *W. H. & L. Collingridge:*
London, [1928.] 8°.   **07075. df. 30.**

—— [Another edition.] Edited by A. J. Macself . . . Eighth
edition. pp. viii. 84.   *W. H. & L. Collingridge: London,*
[1932.] 8°.   **07028. cc. 7.**

CASTLE (Florence) *See* Herrick (Robert) *the Poet.*
Flower Poems . . . Illustrated with twelve coloured
plates by F. Castle. [1905.] 8°.   **012203. g. 12/2.**

CASTLE (Frances Mundy) *See also* Whitehouse (P.)
pseud. [i.e. F. M. Castle.]

—— A Young Woman grows up. pp. 320.   *Arrowsmith:*
London, 1928. 8°.   NN. **14633.**

CASTLE (Frank) *M.I.M.E.*

——   An Elementary Course in Practical
Physics. pp. 226. *London*, 1899. 8°. [*Nelson's School*
& College Series.]   **12202. cc. 3/137.**

—— Elementary Practical Mathematics. pp. x. 401.
Macmillan & Co.: London, 1899. 8°.   **08533. df. 8.**

—— [Another edition.] Elementary Practical Mathematics
for Technical Students. pp. x. 395.   *Macmillan & Co.:*
London, 1903. 8°.   **08548. ff. 7.**

—— Elementary Practical Mathematics for Technical Students . . . New and revised edition by F. G. W. Brown.
pp. x. 436. *Macmillan & Co.: London*, 1942. 8°.
                08535. de. 10.

—— Five-Figure Logarithmic and other Tables. pp. 58.
Macmillan & Co.: London, 1909. 8°.   **8548. d. 62.**

—— Five-Figure Logarithmic and other Tables. (With
additions.) pp. 60. *Macmillan & Co.: London*, 1920. 8°.
                08548. k. 19.

—— Four-Figure Mathematical Tables. pp. 48.
Macmillan & Co.: London, 1923. 8°.   **08548. e. 82.**

—— Logarithmic and other Tables for Schools. pp. 36.
Macmillan & Co.: London, 1908. 8°.   **8507. e. 23. (1.)**

—— [Another edition.] pp. 34.   *Macmillan & Co.: London,*
1938. 8°.   **08548. aa. 27.**

—— Machine Construction and Drawing. pp. viii. 275.
Macmillan & Co.: London, 1905. *obl.* 8°.   **8765. a. 56.**

—— [Another edition.] pp. viii. 289.   *Macmillan & Co.:*
London, 1922. *obl.* 8°.   **8764. de. 9.**

—— A Manual of Machine Design. pp. ix. 351.
Macmillan & Co.: London, 1919. 8°.   **8763. aa. 5.**

—— A Manual of Practical Mathematics. pp. xi. 541.
Macmillan & Co.: London, 1903. 8°.   **08533. e. 28.**

—— [Another edition.] [Revised by F. G. W. Brown.]
pp. xi. 624. *Macmillan & Co.: London*, 1934. 8°.
                8505. de. 32.

—— Mathematical Tables for Ready Reference. pp. 14.
Macmillan & Co.: London, 1902. 8°.   **08548. de. 8.**

—— Practical Arithmetic and Mensuration. pp. viii. 249.
Macmillan & Co.: London, 1908. 8°.   **08533. ee. 85.**

CASTLE (Frank) *M.I.M.E.*

—— Practical Arithmetic and Mensuration . . . New and revised edition by F. G. W. Brown. pp. viii. 264. *Macmillan & Co.: London*, 1942. 8º. **08535. df. 119.**

—— Practical Mathematics for Beginners. pp. ix. 313. *Macmillan & Co.: London*, 1901. 8º. **08533. e. 14.**

—— Key to Practical Mathematics for Beginners. pp. vi. 226. *Macmillan & Co.: London*, 1903. 8º. **08533. df. 47.**

—— Workshop Arithmetic. pp. viii. 172. *Macmillan & Co.: London*, 1915. 8º. **08532. de. 4.**

—— Workshop Mathematics. 2 pt. *Macmillan & Co.: London*, 1900. 8º. **08533. df. 28.**

—— *See* Brown (Frederick G. W.) Elementary Mathematics for Workshop Students. Founded upon Castle's "Workshop Mathematics." 1945. 8º. **08535. aaa. 64.**

CASTLE (Frank) *Novelist.*

—— Move along, Stranger, *etc.* pp. 184. *Fawcett Publications: [London*, 1954.] 8º. **12733. e. 2.** *Gold Medal Books.* no. 48.

CASTLE (Frederick Albert) *See* Wood (George B.) Wood's Household Practice of Medicine, Hygiene and Surgery . . . Edited by F. A. Castle, *etc.* 1881. 8º. **7390. i. 6.**

CASTLE (George) *M.D.* The Chymical Galenist : a treatise wherein the practise of the ancients is reconcil'd to the new discoveries in the theory of physick . . . In which are some reflections upon a book [by M. N., i.e. Marchamont Nedham], intituled, Medela Medicinæ. pp. 196. *Sarah Griffin for Henry Twyford & Timothy Twyford: London*, 1667. 8º. **1038. f. 25.** *Imperfect ; wanting the last leaf.*

CASTLE (George) *Writer of Verse.* Poems. pp. 32. *A. H. Stockwell: London*, [1937.] 8º. **11655. g. 14.**

CASTLE (Harold) *See* Berthe (A.) Life of St. Alphonsus de' Liguori . . . Edited in English by H. Castle. 1905. 8º . **4830. e. 7.**

—— Church History and Church Government. pp. 32. *Catholic Truth Society: London*, [1905.] 8º. **3938.gg.19.(5.)**

CASTLE (Harold George)

—— The Boy's Book of Motor Racing. [With illustrations.] pp. 152. *Guilford Press: London*, 1954. 4º. **8774. ff. 9.**

—— The Boy's Book of Motor Racing. [With illustrations.] pp. 152. *Guilford Press: London*, 1955. 8º. **7920. bb. 59.**

—— The Boy's Book of the Air. Edited by H. G. Castle. [With illustrations.] pp. 152. *Guilford Press: London*, 1954. 8º. **8774. ff. 10.** *An earlier edition is entered under* Boy.

—— The Boy's Book of the Air. Edited by H. G. Castle. [With illustrations.] pp. 152. *Guilford Press: London*, 1955. 8º. **12836. l. 21.**

—— Britain's Motor Industry . . . Consulting editor : Lieut.-Col. D. C. McLagan. [With illustrations.] pp. 328. *Clerke & Cockeran: London*, 1950. 4º. **08773. dd. 2.**

—— The Children's Book of the Circus. [With illustrations.] pp. 204. *Clerke & Cockeran: London*, 1948. 8º. **11797. ee. 31.**

CASTLE (Harold George)

—— Racing Review . . . Edited by H. G. Castle. pp. 95. *Newservice: London*, [1947.] 8º. **7917. e. 46.**

CASTLE (Henry) Cholera. Being practical rules for arresting its progress. pp. 32. *Longman & Co.: London*, 1848. 8º. **1166. g. 33. (3.)**

CASTLE (Henry) *pseud.* [i.e. E. H. Wilcox.] *See also* Wilcox (E. H.)

—— *See* Hurd (*Sir* Archibald S.) and Castle (H.) German Sea-Power, *etc.* 1913. 8º. **08806. c. 1.**

CASTLE (Henry Anson) The Army Mule and other war sketches . . . With illustrations by J. W. Vawter. pp. 269. *Bowen-Merrill Co.: Indianapolis & Kansas City*, 1898. 8º. **012314. f. 82.**

CASTLE (Henry James) *See* Simms (Frederick W.) A Treatise on the Principal Mathematical Drawing Instruments . . . Together with a description of the theodolite by Mr. H. J. Castle, *etc.* 1845. 12º. **1393. c. 13.**

—— Contributive Value a necessary Element in the parochial principle of Railway Assessments, what it is, and how it can be measured. pp. 63. *W. Maxwell; Shaw & Sons: London*, 1854. 8º. **8276. c. 14.**

—— Elementary Text Book for young surveyors and levellers, with copious field notes, plans and diagrams, *etc.* pp. xiv. 185. pl. 2. *Simpkin, Marshall & Co.: London*, 1846. 12º. **1394. b. 6.**

—— [Another edition.] pp. xiv. 185. pl. 2. *Simpkin, Marshall & Co.: London*, 1856. 8º. **8505. b. 18.**

—— A Few Words to the Shareholders of the Eastern Counties Railway Company. pp. 24. *Effingham Wilson: London*, [1851.] 8º. **8235. c. 24.**

—— Practical Remarks upon the Union Assessment Committee Act, 1862, showing how to apply the principles contained therein to the proper and uniform assessment of railway, gas, and water works, *etc.* pp. viii. 128. *W. Maxwell; Shaw & Sons: London*, 1863. 8º. **6425. bb. 9.**

—— (Second edition.) By H. J. Castle . . . assisted by Edward James Castle. pp. xvii. 163. *W. Maxwell & Son; Shaw & Sons: London*, 1869. 8º. **6425. e. 1.**

—— A Treatise on Land Surveying and Levelling, illustrated by copious field notes, plans, and diagrams . . . With . . . an appendix of tables of logarithms, *etc.* pp. xv. 284. 63. *Simpkin, Marshall & Co.: London*, 1842. 8º. **1394. h. 13.**

—— [Another edition.] pp. xvi. 309. 63. *Simpkin, Marshall & Co.: London*, 1845. 8º. **1394. h. 14.**

—— Railway Curves . . . With plates, *etc.* [Extracted from the 1845 edition of "A Treatise on Land Surveying and Levelling."] pp. 29. *W. Hughes: [London*, 1845.] 8º. **8767. bbb. 3. (11.)**

CASTLE (Horace) The Doctrine of Protection to Domestic Industries examined. pp. 39. *H. C. Baird & Co.: Philadelphia*, 1888. 8º. **08229. f. 31. (4.)**

CASTLE (Irene) *See* Castle (Vernon) and Castle (Irene) Modern Dancing, *etc.* 1914. 8º. **7913. cc. 38.**

—— My Husband (Vernon Castle), *etc.* [With extracts from his letters. With plates, including portraits.] pp. xii. 264. *John Lane: London ; New York* printed, 1919. 8º. **010855. b. 10.**

CASTLE (IVOR)

—— *See* BECKLES (Gordon) *pseud.* Coronation Souvenir Book. 1937 . . . Art editor: I. Castle. 1937. 4°.
10805. k. 35.

—— *See* SALUSBURY (Frederick G. H.) King Emperor's Jubilee . . . Art editor, I. Castle. 1935. 4°.
10805. k. 21.

CASTLE (J.) *Writer of Verse.*

—— Memories of Youthful Days. Told in verse, rhymed & unrhymed. For children. pp. 15. *Arthur H. Stockwell: Ilfracombe*, 1946. 8°.
11658. aaa. 111.

CASTLE (JEFFERY LLOYD)

—— Satellite E One. [A novel.] pp. 190. *Eyre & Spottiswoode: London*, 1954. 8°. **NNN. 5408.**

CASTLE (JOHN) *Artist.*

—— Journal von der Ao. 1736 aus Orenburg zu dem Abul Geier Chan der Kirgis-Caysack Tartarischen Horda . . . vollbrachten Reise, *etc.* pp. 144. 1784. *See* RUSSIA. [*Appendix.—History and Politics.*] Materialien zu der Russischen Geschichte, *etc.* 1777, *etc.* 8°.
1194. c. 4.

CASTLE (JOHN) *Assistant Priest, St. Giles, Cambridge.*

—— Cambridge Churchmen. An account of the Anglo-Catholic tradition at Cambridge. [With plates.] pp. 16. *A. R. Mowbray & Co.: Cambridge*, 1951. 8°.
.4708. b. 23.

—— Northern Churches. pp. 16. *Cambridge Express Printing Co.: Cambridge*, 1950. 8°. **4695. bb. 32.**

CASTLE (JOHN) *pseud.* [i.e. RONALD CHARLES PAYNE and JOHN WILLIAMS GARROD],

—— The Password is Courage. [An account of the experiences of Sergeant-Major Charles Coward in German prisoner-of-war camps and the concentration camp at Auschwitz. With plates, including portraits.] pp. 224. *Souvenir Press: London*, 1954. 8°. **9103. b. 22.**

CASTLE (JOSEPH) *M.A.*

—— Dungeness Ballads. pp. 39. *H. D. & B. Headley: Ashford*, 1887. 8°. **11647. df. 57.**

—— Queenborough and its Church . . . Reprinted from the " Sheerness Guardian." pp. 54. *Rigg, Allen & Co.: Sheerness*, 1907. 8°. **010358. ee. 38.**

CASTLE (JOSEPH) *Translator.*

—— *See* ERENBURG (I. G.) The Ninth Wave. (Translated by T. Shebunina and J. Castle.) 1955. 8°.
W.P. D. 504/1.

CASTLE (LEONARD) Church Music of To-day. A collection of articles on church music. The " Church Music Review " for 1933. Edited by L. Castle. pp. 32. *Church Music Review: London*, [1933.] 8°. **7894. ppp. 7.**

CASTLE (LEONARD JAMES) Mathematics, Science, and Drawing for the preliminary technical course . . . Fully illustrated. pp. vii. 149. *G. Routledge & Sons: London*, 1913. 8°. [*Broadway Text-Books of Technology.*]
012209.aaa.3/3.

CASTLE (LEWIS) *See* PERIODICAL PUBLICATIONS.—*London.* The Chrysanthemum Annual . . . Edited by L. Castle. [1889, *etc.*] 8°. **P.P. 2488. eh**

CASTLE (LEWIS)

—— Cactaceous Plants: their history and culture. With numerous illustrations. pp. 93. *Horticultural Press: London*, 1884. 8°. **7033. cc. 2.**

—— Flower Gardening for amateurs in town, suburban and country gardens. With a chapter on the greenhouse. pp. xii. 236. *Swan Sonnenschein & Co.: London*, 1888. 8°. **07028. e. 4.**

—— Orchids: a review of their structure and history, illustrated. pp. 59. *The Author: London*, [1885.] 8°.
7073. de. 6. (3.)

—— [Another edition.] pp. 104. *Journal of Horticulture: London*, [1886.] 8°. **7030. b. 3.**

—— Plums for Profit . . . Edited by Rev. E. Bartrum, *etc.* pp. 16. *S.P.C.K.: London*, 1897. 16°. [*Helpful Hints for Hard Times.*] **4430. aa. 7/18.**

CASTLE (M. E.)

—— *See* FOOT (Arthur S.) and LOVETT (J. F.) Electric Fencing. (Revised by M. E. Castle and C. Line.) 1953. 8°. [*Ministry of Agriculture and Fisheries. Bulletin. no. 147.*] **B.S. 3/75.**

CASTLE (MABEL WING)

—— My Mother's Reminiscences. By Elinor Castle Nef. A memorial to M. W. Castle, *etc.* [Edited by John U. Nef. With portraits.] pp. 75. 1954. 8°. *See* NEF (Elinor C.) **10891. b. 44.**

CASTLE (MARCELLUS PURNELL)

—— *See* LONDON.—III. *Royal Philatelic Society.* The London Philatelist . . . Editor: M. P. Castle, *etc.* 1892, *etc.* 8°.
P.P. 1424. aqb.

CASTLE (MARGARET S.) In the Land of Nod. pp. 39. *Sir I. Pitman & Sons: London*, 1937. 8°. **20059. e. 15.**

CASTLE (MARGARETHE) *See* RAIMUND (F.) Sämtliche Werke, *etc.* (Bd. 1, 2. Ferdinand Raimunds dramatische Dichtungen. Herausgegeben von M. Castle und E. Castle.) [1925, *etc.*] 8°. **20002. bb. 42.**

CASTLE (MARIAN)

—— Deborah. pp. 304. *Frederick Muller: London*, 1951 [1952]. 8°. **12701. c. 18.**

—— The Golden Fury. [A novel.] pp. 329. *Frederick Muller: London*, 1950. 8°. **12730. f. 27.**

CASTLE (MARIE LOUISE EGERTON) *See* DANTE ALIGHIERI. [*Divina Commedia.—English.*] The Divine Comedy . . . Translated by the Rev. H. F. Cary, M.A. Revised, with an introduction, by M.-L. E. Castle, *etc.* 1910. 8°.
2504. m. 4.

—— Dante. [With portraits.] pp. 110. *London*, 1907. 8°. [*Bell's Miniature Series of Poets.*] **10855.a.1/14.**

—— Italian Literature. pp. vii. 400. *Herbert & Daniel: London*, [1911.] 8°. **011850. ee. 42.**

CASTLE (MICHAEL) *See* DÉTAIN (C.) *Phrenologist.* Appréciation phrénologique de Monsieur Triat. Extrait d'une conférence donnée par le Dr Castle, *etc.* 1859. 8°.
7410. cc. 23. (5.)

—— Die Phrenologie . . . Mit zwei Tafeln Abbildungen. pp. xii. 436. *Stuttgart*, 1845. 8°. **7410. d. 16.**

—— Phrenologische Analyse des Charakters des Herrn Dr Justinus Kerner . . . Mit einem Briefe des Herrn Dr Kerner über das Werk an den Verfasser und einem Vorwort von Dr. Gustav Scheve. Mit Kerner's Bildniss. pp. xxvi. 74. *Heidelberg*, 1844. 8°. **7410. d. 4.**

CASTLE (MICHAEL)

—— Phrenologische Untersuchung des Doktor David Friedrich Strauss, durch allgemeine phrenologische und philosophische Anmerkungen erläutert, nebst einer Antikritik auf Dr. Scheve's Bemerkungen über Seite 57 der Analyse des Charakters Dr. Justinus Kerner's. pp. viii. 133. *Heilbronn*, 1844. 8°. **1403. h. 1. (2.)**

CASTLE (MOLLY)

—— New Winds are Blowing. [A novel.] pp. 250. *Sampson Low, Marston & Co.: London*, [1947.] 8°. **NN. 37123.**

—— Round the World with an Appetite. (A record of dishes from my travels.) pp. 254. *Hodder & Stoughton: London*, 1936. 8°. **7941. p. 20.**

—— This Is Where We Came In. pp. 256. *Hutchinson & Co.: London*, [1939.] 8°. **NN. 30708.**

CASTLE (NINA) *See* CASTLE (Edwardina W.)

CASTLE (PAT) Angling Holidays in Scotland. Where to fish and where to stay. [With plates.] pp. viii. 126. *Oliver & Boyd: Edinburgh, London*, 1937. 8°. **07908. e. 47.**

—— Angling Secrets. [Revised and enlarged edition of "Descriptive Angling."] pp. 116. *Oliver & Boyd: Edinburgh, London*, 1948. 8°. **7919. aa. 63.**

—— Descriptive Angling. pp. viii. 91. *Oliver & Boyd: Edinburgh, London*, 1935. 8°. **7916. eee. 40.**

—— The Scottish Fishing Guide. [With a map.] pp. xxii. 136. *W. & A. K. Johnston: Edinburgh*, [1933.] 8°. **7916. de. 5.**

—— Trout and how to catch them. pp. viii. 70. *Oliver & Boyd: Edinburgh*, 1920. 8°. **7904. ee. 7.**

—— Third edition. pp. viii. 77. *Oliver & Boyd: Edinburgh, London*, 1938. 8°. **07290. e. 39.**

—— Trout and How to Catch Them. (Fourth edition.) pp. viii. 79. *Oliver & Boyd: Edinburgh, London*, 1942. 8°. **7917. a. 36.**

—— [A reissue.] Trout and How to Catch Them. (Fourth edition, reprinted.) *Edinburgh, London*, 1946. 8°. **7918. aa. 59.**

—— Where to Fish in Scotland. [With plates, including a portrait.] pp. viii. 90. *Oliver & Boyd: Edinburgh, London*, 1931. 8°. **7916. aa. 14.**

CASTLE (PHILIP) Lysis, aet. XIII. XIV. XV. A memory. [Poems.] *Privately printed: London*, 1924. 8°. **011645. e. 143.**

CASTLE (R. F.) *See* CASTLE (F. R.)

CASTLE (R. LEWIS) Beans. pp. 20. *Agricultural & Horticultural Association: London*, [1908.] 8°. [*One & All Garden Books*. no. 17.] **07031.df.58/17.**

—— The Book of Market Gardening. pp. xi. 171. *John Lane: London; New York*, 1906. 8°. [*Handbooks of Practical Gardening*. vol. 27.] **7030. ppp. 27.**

—— Mushrooms. pp. 20. *Agricultural & Horticultural Association: London*, [1910.] 8°. [*One & All Garden Books*. no. 29.] **07031.df.58/29.**

CASTLE (REGINALD WINGFIELD) *See* MYERS (Alfred E. C.) and CASTLE (R. W.) " Prepare for Action ! " *etc.* [1908.] 16°. **8823. a. 61.**

—— [1909.] 16°. **8823. a. 62.**

CASTLE (RICHARD) An Essay toward supplying the City of Dublin with Water. pp. 32. *Syl. Pepyat: Dublin*, 1735. 8°. **900. g. 30. (7.)**

CASTLE (RICHARD BASIL TREVOR) and **BRAY** (FRANK SEWELL) Liquidator's Time Table in a Winding Up by the Court. pp. 24. *Gee & Co.: London*, 1934. fol. **6405. k. 16.**

CASTLE (RONALD B.)

—— Chapbook. Edited by Ronald Castle. no. 20, 21. March, June 1948. *Wellington*, 1948. 4°. **P.P. 6228. maa.**

—— Fleeting Music. [Poems.] pp. 47. *Wright & Carman: Wellington, N.Z.*, 1937. 8°. **11655. g. 18.**

CASTLE (SIDNEY) A Monograph on the Fox-Terrier . . . Revised and partly re-written by Theo: Marples . . . Fifth edition. pp. 96. pl. XXXII. *" Our Dogs " Publishing Co.: Manchester*, [1925.] 8°. **07294. g. 49.**

—— [Another edition.] A new section on wire-haired fox-terriers by Mrs. M. V. Hughes. Sixth edition, revised. pp. 119. pl. XXIX. *" Our Dogs " Publishing Co.: Manchester*, [1932.] 8°. **07295. eee. 70.**

CASTLE (SYDNEY E.) Metal Casements, old & new. [With plates.] pp. 40. *International Casement Co.: Liverpool, Jamestown, N.Y.*, [1914.] 16°. **07816. e. 13.**

CASTLE (THOMAS) *See* BARTON (Benjamin H.) and CASTLE (T.) The British Flora Medica, *etc.* 1837, *etc.* 8°. **724. f. 15, 16.**

—— —— 1877. 8°. **07509. f. 22.**

—— *See* BLUNDELL (James) Observations on some of the more Important Diseases of Women . . . Edited by T. Castle. 1837. 8°. **1177. c. 15.**

—— *See* BLUNDELL (James) The Principles and Practice of Obstetricy . . . To which are added notes and illustrations. By T. Castle. 1834. 8°. **1177. i. 13.**

—— *See* LONDON.—III. *Royal College of Physicians.* A Translation of the Pharmacopœia Londinensis of MDCCCXXXVI. With descriptive and explanatory notes on the Materia Medica, etc. By T. Castle. 1837. 32°. **777. a. 39.**

—— —— 1838. 32°. **7509. de. 28.**

—— Essay on Poisons ; embracing their symptoms, treatment, tests . . . To which is added, an appendix, or means for treating cases of suspended animation. Sixth edition, illustrated, *etc.* pp. vi. 135. pl. 21. *E. Cox: London*, 1834. 32°. **7509. a. 1.**

—— An Introduction to Medical Botany, *etc.* pp. 172. pl. III. *E. Cox: London*, 1829. 12°. **972. a. 31.**

—— An Introduction to Systematical and Physiological Botany. Illustrated with explanatory engravings. pp. xviii. 285. *E. Cox: London*, 1829. 12°. **972. a. 30.**

—— Lexicon Pharmacopœlium, or a Pharmacopœial Dictionary ; containing the London Pharmacopœia of MDCCCXXIV, in Latin and English, *etc.* pp. xx. 327. *E. Cox & Son ; W. Simpkin & R. Marshall: London*, 1826. 8°. **778. b. 35.**

—— The Linnæan Artificial System of Botany, illustrated and explained. In three parts, *etc.* [With plates.] pp. 30. *E. Cox: London*, 1836. 4°. **T. 80*. (20.)**

CASTLE (THOMAS)

—— A Manual of Modern Surgery, founded upon the principles and practice lately taught by Sir Astley Cooper Bart. . . . and Joseph Henry Green . . . Embellished with a portrait of Sir Astley Cooper. Edited by T. Castle. (Practical notes selected from a series of lectures.) pp. x. 334. *E. Cox & Son: London,* 1828. 12º.
782. e. 14.

—— The third edition, considerably enlarged, *etc.* pp. xi. 515. *E. Cox: London,* 1831. 12º.
782. e. 16.

—— Fifth edition. Considerably enlarged, *etc.* [The " Preface to the reprint " signed : E., i.e. C. C. Egerton.] pp. ix. 542. *W. Rushton & Co.: Calcutta,* 1839. 12º.
1189. g. 9.

—— A Table for finding the commencements, characteristics, and regular inflexions of Greek Verbs, *etc.* pp. 3. *J. & J. J. Deighton: Cambridge; Whittaker, Treacher & Arnot: London,* 1832. 4º.
12923. ff. 3.

CASTLE (TUDOR RALPH) The Gentle Shepherd, and other poems. pp. 91. *Grant Richards: London,* 1908. 8º.
11647. ff. 51.

CASTLE (VERNON) *See* CASTLE (Irene) My Husband (Vernon Castle), *etc.* [With extracts from his letters. With plates, including portraits.] 1919. 8º.
010855. b. 10.

CASTLE (VERNON) and **CASTLE** (IRENE)

—— Modern Dancing . . . With many illustrations from photographs and moving pictures of the newest dances for which the authors posed. Introduction by Elisabeth Marbury. pp. 175. *Harper & Bros.: New York & London,* 1914. 8º.
7913. cc. 38.

CASTLE (*Mrs.* VERNON) *See* CASTLE (Irene)

CASTLE (WALTER FRANCIS RAPHAEL) *See* CAMUS (Jean) Surgeon. Physical and Occupational Re-education of the Maimed . . . Translation by W. F. Castle, *etc.* 1918. 8º.
8357. c. 21.

CASTLE (WILFRED THOMAS FROGGATT) *See* CASTLE (Wilfrid T. F.)

CASTLE (WILFRID THOMAS FROGGATT) An English Parish Church of 1740 . . . A history and description of Saint Peter's Congleton, Cheshire, *etc.* [With plates.] pp. 43. *British Publishing Co.: Gloucester & London,* [1933.] 8º.
07815. a. 84.

—— Grand Turk. An historical outline of life and events . . . during the last years of the Ottoman Empire and the first years of the Turkish Republic, *etc.* [With plates and a bibliography.] pp. 170. *Hutchinson & Co.: London,* [1943.] 8º.
09136. aa. 3.

—— Syrian Pageant. The history of Syria and Palestine, 1000 B.C. to A.D. 1945 . . . With 16 illustrations, *etc.* pp. 184. *Hutchinson & Co.: London,* [1948.] 8º.
09059. cc. 22.

CASTLE (WILLIAM) *See* CASTELL.

CASTLE (WILLIAM BOSWORTH) Lectures on the Anaemias and Vital Deficiencies, *etc.* pp. 145. 1939. 8º. *See* MELBOURNE.—*Melbourne Permanent Postgraduate Committee.*
07630. df. 15.

CASTLE (WILLIAM BOSWORTH) and **MINOT** (GEORGE RICHARD)

—— Pathological Physiology and Clinical Description of the Anemias . . . Edited by Henry A. Christian . . . Reprinted from Oxford Loose-Leaf Medicine. [With a bibliography.] pp. ix. 205. *Oxford University Press: New York,* [1936.] 8º. [*Oxford Medical Publications.*]
20036.a.1/587.

CASTLE (WILLIAM C.) and **GOW** (J. B.) Exercises in Elementary Book-keeping. pp. viii. 158. *Macdonald & Evans: London,* 1928. 8º.
8222.aa.22.

CASTLE (WILLIAM ERNEST) *See* MACCURDY (Hansford) and CASTLE (W. E.) Selection and Cross-breeding in relation to the Inheritance of Coat-pigments and Coat-patterns in Rats and Guinea-pigs. 1907. 8º. [*Carnegie Institution of Washington.* Publication no. 70.]
Ac. 1866.

—— *See* MACDOWELL (E. C.) Size Inheritance in Rabbits. With a prefatory note and appendix by W. E. Castle. 1914. 8º. [*Carnegie Institution of Washington.* Publication no. 196.]
Ac. 1866.

—— Contributions to the Genetics of the Domestic Rabbit. [By] W. E. Castle and Paul B. Sawin. [With plates.] pp. 50. *Washington,* 1932. 8º. [*Carnegie Institution of Washington.* Publication no. 427.]
Ac. 1866.

—— The Early Embryology of Ciona intestinalis, Flemming, (L.) [With plates.] *Cambridge, Mass.,* 1896. 8º. [*Bulletin of the Museum of Comparative Zoology at Harvard College.* vol. 27. no. 7.]
Ac. 1736/2.

—— Genetic Studies of Rabbits and Rats. pp. 54. pl. 2. *Washington,* 1922. 8º. [*Carnegie Institution of Washington.* Publication no. 320.]
Ac. 1866.

—— Genetics and Eugenics. A text-book for students of biology and a reference book for animal and plant breeders. (Third impression.) [With a bibliography and plates.] pp. vi. 357. *Harvard University Press: Cambridge* [*Mass.*], 1916. 8º.
7001. s. 19.
The verso of the titlepage bears the date 1917.

—— Second edition. pp. viii. 434. *Harvard University Press: Cambridge, Mass.,* 1924. 8º.
07001. g. 25.

—— Fourth revised edition. pp. x. 474. *Harvard University Press: Cambridge, Mass.,* 1930. 8º. **2026.d.**

—— [Another copy.]
7002. bb. 25.

—— The Genetics of Domestic Rabbits, *etc.* [With plates.] pp. vi. 31. *Harvard University Press: Cambridge, Mass.,* 1930. 8º.
07294. ff. 37.

—— Heredity in relation to Evolution and Animal Breeding. pp. xii. 184. *D. Appleton & Co.: New York & London,* 1911. 8º.
7001. dd. 7.

—— Heredity of Coat Characters in Guinea-Pigs and Rabbits. pp. 78. pl. 6. *Washington,* 1905. 8º. [*Carnegie Institution of Washington.* Publication no. 23.]
Ac. 1866.

—— Mammalian Genetics. pp. viii. 169. *Harvard University Press: Cambridge, Mass.,* 1940. 8º.
07209. c. 16.

—— Manual for a Laboratory Course in Genetics, to accompany the textbook Mammalian Genetics by William E. Castle. pp. 21. *Harvard University Press: Cambridge, Mass.,* 1940. 8º.
07209. cc. 10.

—— The Origin of a Polydactylus Race of Guinea-Pigs. 1906. *See* WASHINGTON, D.C.—*Carnegie Institution.* [Publications.] no. 49. 1902, *etc.* 8º, *etc.*
Ac. 1866.

—— Outline for a Laboratory Course in Genetics, *etc.* pp. 33. *Harvard University Press: Cambridge, Mass.,* 1924. 8º.
07001. g. 27.

—— Reversion in Guinea-Pigs and its explanation. 1913. *See* WASHINGTON, D.C.—*Carnegie Institution.* [Publications.] no. 179. 1902, *etc.* 8º, *etc.*
Ac. 1866.

—— Studies of Colour Inheritance and of Linkage in Rabbits. *See* CONTRIBUTIONS. Contributions to a Knowledge of Inheritance in Mammals. 1926. 8º. [*Carnegie Institution of Washington.* Publication no. 337.]
Ac. 1866.

CASTLE (WILLIAM ERNEST)

—— Studies of Heredity in Rabbits, Rats, and Mice. pp. 56. pl. 3. *Washington*, 1919. 8°. [*Carnegie Institution of Washington.* Publication no. 288.]   Ac. **1866**.

—— Studies of Inheritance in Guinea-Pigs and Rats. By W. E. Castle and Sewall Wright. pp. iv. 192. pl. 7. *Washington*, 1916. 8°. [*Carnegie Institution of Washington.* Publication no. 241.]   Ac. **1866**.

—— Studies of Inheritance in Rabbits. By W. E. Castle, in collaboration with H. E. Walter, R. C. Mullenix, and S. Cobb. pp. 69. pl. 4. *Washington*, 1909. 8°. [*Carnegie Institution of Washington.* Publication no. 114.]   Ac. **1866**.

CASTLE (WILLIAM ERNEST) and **FORBES** (ALEXANDER) *Biologist.*

——   Heredity of Hair-Length in Guinea-Pigs and its bearing on the theory of pure gametes. pp. 14. 1906. *See* WASHINGTON, D.C. —*Carnegie Institution.* [Publications.] no. 49. 1902, *etc.* 8°, *etc.*   Ac. **1866**.

CASTLE (WILLIAM ERNEST) and **PHILLIPS** (JOHN CHARLES)

——   On Germinal Transplantation in Vertebrates. [With a bibliography.] pp. 26. pl. 2. *Washington*, 1911. 8°. [*Carnegie Institution of Washington.* Publication no. 144.]   Ac. **1866**.

—— Piebald Rats and Selection. An experimental test of the effectiveness of selection and of the theory of gametic purity in Mendelian crosses. pp. 56. pl. 3. *Washington*, 1914. 8°. [*Carnegie Institution of Washington.* Publication no. 195.]   Ac. **1866**.

CASTLE (WILLIAM MACCOY FITZGERALD) Sketch of the City of Iquique, Chili, South America, *etc.* pp. 54. *R. W. Stevens: Plymouth*, 1887. 8°.   **10480**. df. **1**. (3.)

CASTLE (WILLIAM RICHARDS) Hawaii Past and Present . . . With illustrations and a map. pp. xii. 242. *Dodd, Mead & Co.: New York*, 1913. 8°.   **10480**. aaa. **26**.

—— John Watson Foster, Secretary of State, June 29, 1892, to February 23, 1893. [With a portrait.] 1928. *See* BEMIS (Samuel F.) The American Secretaries of State, *etc.* vol. 8. 1927, *etc.* 8°.   **10880**. s. **3/8**.

—— Wake Up, America. A plea for the recognition of our individual and national responsibilities. pp. vii. 111. *Dodd, Mead & Co.: New York*, 1916. 8°. **08175**. a. **10**.

CASTLEBAR, Co. Mayo.

—— Castlebar, Co. Mayo. The official guide, *etc.* pp. 32. *E. J. Burrow & Co.: Cheltenham & London*, [1927.] 8°. **10354**. a. **196**.

CASTLEBURY. The Cobler of Castlebury. A musical entertainment in two acts. [By Charles Stuart.] As it is performed at the Theatre Royal, *etc.* pp. v. 35. *G. Kearsley: London*, [1779.] 8°.   **11777**. c. **17**.

CASTLECOOLE.

—— Castlecoole, Enniskillen, *etc.* [Signed: R. F., i.e. Henry R. Fedden. With plates.] 1952. 8°. *See* F., R. W.P. c. **200/9**.

CASTLEDEN (GEORGE) Conscience: an essay in blank verse. Being a sequel to "Woburn Park." [By G. Castleden.] pp. xi. 188. 1842. 12°. *See* CONSCIENCE. **11646**. aa. **63**.

CASTLEDEN (GEORGE)

—— Lays of Home. 3 no. pp. 144. *Partridge & Oakey: London*, 1850, 51. 12°.   **11647**. b. **94**.

—— A Memorial of the Woburn Exhibition. pp. 46. *Dodd & Peeling: Woburn*, 1854. 8°.   **12355**. b. **39**.

—— Woburn Park. A fragment, in rural rhyme. [By G. Castleden.] pp. 63. 1839. 16°. *See* WOBURN PARK. **11647**. a. **28**.

—— Second edition, with additions. pp. xii. 168. 1840. 12°. *See* WOBURN PARK.   **11647**. aa. **76**.

—— [Another copy.]   **11646**. aa. **68**.

CASTLEDINE (F. M.)

—— *See* PERIODICAL PUBLICATIONS.—*Nottingham.* The Castle Monthly . . . Editor: F. M. Castledine. 1942, *etc.* 8°.   P.P. **6065**. fc.

CASTLEDINE (W.) The Comprehensive Cash Book: plain and concise book-keeping and the income tax made easy. *C. W. Page: London*, 1884. 8°.   **8503**. ee. **46**.

—— The Comprehensive Cash Book: plain and concise book-keeping and the income tax made easy. *C. W. Page: Sidcup*, [1912.] 8°.   **8222**. aa. **18**.

CASTLEFORD.

—— Castleford, West Riding, Yorks. The official guide, *etc.* (Castleford. The official handbook.) *E. J. Burrow & Co.: Cheltenham*, [1931– .] 8°.   **10354**. a. **197**. *Various editions.*

                    Urban District Council.—*Housing Committee.*
—— The Council Tenants' Handbook, *etc.* *British Publishing Co.: Gloucester*, [1940– .] 8°.   W.P. **10169**. *Various editions.*

CASTLEFORD "GAZETTE" GENERAL ILLUSTRATED ALMANACK. *See* EPHEMERIDES.

CASTLEHAVEN, JAMES, *Earl of.* [1617–1684.] *See* TOUCHET.

——, MARGARET, *Lady.* *See* FOULIS (M.) *Lady.*

——, MERVYN, *Earl of.* [1592?–1631.] *See* TOUCHET.

CASTLEKNOCK.—*Castleknock College.* The Castleknock College Chronicle. no. 31. June, 1916.   *Dublin*, 1916. 4°.   P.P. **6180**. ii.

CASTLEKNOCK COLLEGE. *See* CASTLEKNOCK.

CASTLEM----, *Countess of.* The Gracious Answer of the most Illustrious Lady of Pleasure, the Countess of Castlem---- (Castlemain) to the Poor-Whores Petition. [1668.] *s. sh.* fol. *See* PALMER (Barbara) *Duchess of Cleveland.*   C. **45**. k. **4**. (5.)

CASTLEMAINE, BARBARA, *Countess of.* *See* PALMER (Barbara) *Duchess of Cleveland.*

——, ROGER, *Earl of.* *See* PALMER.

CASTLEMAINE DIRECTORY. The Castlemaine Directory, Almanac, and Book of General Information. *See* DIRECTORIES.—*Castlemaine, Victoria.*

CASTLEMAN (ALFRED L.) The Army of the Potomac. Behind the scenes. A diary of unwritten history, *etc.* pp. 288. *Strickland & Co.: Milwaukee*, 1863. 8°. **9604**. aaa. **24**.

CASTLEMAN (HENRY C. F.) Oliver. pp. 318.
John Long: London, 1909. 8°.   **012625. aaa. 18.**

—— That Moving Finger. pp. 274.   *Greening & Co.:*
London, 1905. 8°.   **012632. aa. 10.**

—— " What God hath Cleansed." pp. 300.
W. Westall & Co.: London, 1918. 8°.   **NN. 5096.**

CASTLEMAN (JOHN) *Vicar of South Petherton. See*
CASTELMAN.

CASTLEMAN (JOSIAH HAMILTON) *See* ARNOLD (M.)
[*Single Works.*] Matthew Arnold's Sohrab and Rustum.
Edited with an introduction and notes by J. H. Castle-
man. [1907.] 8°.   **12274. g. 12/6.**

—— *See* BULWER, *afterwards* BULWER LYTTON (Edward
G. E. L.) *Baron Lytton.* [*Novels.—Single Novels.*] The
Last Days of Pompeii . . . Edited with an introduction
and notes by J. H. Castleman. 1916. 8°.
          12199. a. 1/88.

—— *See* GRAY (Thomas) *the Poet.* [*Poetical Works.—Selections.*] Elegy written in a Country Church-yard, and other
poems . . . Edited, with an introduction and notes, by
J. H. Castleman. 1918. 16°.   **12199. a. 1/97.**

—— *See* LONGFELLOW (H. W.) Tales of a Wayside Inn . . .
Edited, with an introduction and notes, by J. H. Castleman. 1916. 8°.   **12199. a. 1/93.**

—— *See* SCOTT (*Sir* W.) *Bart.* [*Kenilworth.*] Kenilworth
. . . Edited with, an introduction and notes, by J. H.
Castleman. 1918. 8°.   **12199. a. 1/99.**

CASTLEMAN (JUSTUS COLLINS) *See* ARNOLD (Matthew)
[*Selections.*] Sohrab and Rustum, and other poems . . .
Edited by J. C. Castleman, *etc.* 1936. 8°. **W.P. 7624/2.**

—— *See* THACKERAY (W. M.) [*The English Humourists
of the Eighteenth Century.*] English Humorists . . .
Edited, with an introduction and notes, by J. C. Castleman. 1910. 8°.   **12199. a. 1/69.**

CASTLEMON (HARRY) *pseud.* [*i.e.* CHARLES AUSTIN
FOSDICK.] The Gunboat Series. Books for boys, by a
Gunboat Boy. 6 vol.
          1. Frank the Young Naturalist. 1869.
          2. Frank on a Gunboat. 1865.
          3. Frank in the Woods. 1869.
          4. Frank on the Prairie. 1869.
          5. Frank before Vicksburg. 1869.
          6. Frank on the Lower Mississippi. 1867.
R. W. Carroll & Co.: Cincinnati, 1869, 65–69. 8°.
          12804. g. 24.
Each volume has an additional titlepage, lithographed.

—— Joe Wayring at Home; or the Adventures of a fly-rod.
pp. 413. *Porter & Coates: Philadelphia*, [1886.] 8°.
          12704. m. 12.

—— Rolling-Stone Series. 2 vol.
          1. Tom Newcombe; or, the Boy of bad habits. 1869.
          3. No Moss: or, the Career of a rolling stone. 1871.
R. W. Carroll & Co.: Cincinnati, 1869, 71. 8°.
          12707. e. 13.
Imperfect; wanting vol. 2, entitled: " Go Ahead."

—— The Sportsman's Club among the Trappers. pp. 296.
Porter & Coates: Philadelphia, [1874.] 12°.
          12703. ee. 12.

CASTLEN (EPPIE BOWDRE) Autumn Dreams. By
Chiquita (E. B. Castlen). [With a portrait.] pp. 108.
D. Appleton & Co.: New York, 1870. 12°.
          11688. c. 22.

CASTLEREAGH, ROBERT, *Viscount. See* STEWART (R.)
Marquis of Londonderry.

CASTLEROSSE, VALENTINE EDWARD CHARLES, *Viscount.*
See BROWNE.

CASTLES. " Castles ": the new parlour game. Directions and rules. pp. 7. [*London ?*] 1884. 16°.
          7913. a. 49.

—— Castles and Manor-Houses. Illustrated, *etc.* pp. 127.
Odhams Press: London, 1951. 8°.   **07822. f. 25.**

—— Castles in the Air; or, Whims of my aunt. A novel.
By the authoress of " Dunethvin," *etc.* 3 vol. *Baldwin,
Cradock & Joy: London*, 1818. 12°.   **N. 1857.**

CASTLES (FRANK) Drawing Room Monologues. pp. 48.
Samuel French: London; S. French & Son: New York,
[1886.] 8°.   **12331. g. 27. (3.)**

CASTLETON. Peveril of the Peak. A handbook to
Castleton and its neighbourhood, *etc.* pp. 56. *J. C. Bates:
Buxton*, 1873. 8°.   **10360. aa. 85.**

CASTLETON, GRACE, *Viscountess. See* SAUNDERSON.

CASTLETON, *Moffat, pseud.* The Little Book [i.e. the
Bible]: true and all true . . . By Castleton, Moffat.
Second edition. pp. 96. *A. M. Grieve: Moffat*, 1930. 8°.
          03127. de. 60.

CASTLETON, *pseud.* [i.e. JANE MACDONALD ROGERS ?]
The Testimony of the Gods. An essay on the evidences
of history and experience that the greatest men of all
ages have acknowledged their beliefs in a great first cause.
By Castleton. pp. 115.   *Shum & Bonnett: London*,
1881. 8°.   **4018. h. 17.**

CASTLETON (ALBERT GEORGE) Karjo the Kidnapper.
pp. 29.   *Edinburgh House Press: London*, 1935. 8°.
[*Boys' Torch Adventure Library.* no. 84.]   **W.P. 9273.**

—— On the Roof of the World. Sam Pollard of China.
pp. 32.   *Edinburgh House Press: London*, 1938. 8°.
[*Eagle Books.* no. 9.]   **W.P. 8172/9.**

—— Rough, Tough and Far Away. (James Huston Edgar,
1872–1936.) pp. 32.   *Edinburgh House Press: London*,
1942. 8°. [*Eagle Books.* no. 44.]   **W.P. 8172/44.**

CASTLETON (ANN)

—— Bracken Had a Secret . . . [A tale.] Illustrated by
G. R. Day. pp. 224.   *Blackie & Son: London &
Glasgow*, [1947.] 8°.   **12829. c. 13.**

—— Gen finds a Family . . . With illustrations by Andrew
Wilson. pp. 226. *Hollis & Carter: London*, 1949. 8°.
          12832. ee. 34.

—— The Secret of Storm Abbey . . . Illustrated by S. Van
Abbé. pp. 224. *Hollis & Carter: London*, 1946. 8°.
          12821. dd. 82.

—— That Holiday at School . . . Illustrated by S. Van
Abbé. pp. v. 214. *Hollis & Carter: London*, 1949. 8°.
          12832. f. 10.

—— The Witch's Wood . . . Illustrated by F. Stockmay.
pp. 240. *Blackie & Son: London & Glasgow*, [1948.] 8°.
          12832. h. 24.

CASTLETON (FERDINAND) Ferdinand Castleton. A novel. 3 vol. *T. & W. Boone: London*, 1851. 12º.
12624. d. 5.

CASTLETON (HENRY) An Epithalamium. Being stanzas on the most auspicious nuptials of the Right Honourable the Marquess of Carmarthen, and the Lady Elizabeth Harley . . . By Mr. H. C. [i.e. H. Castleton.] pp. 6. 1712. fol. *See* C., H., *Mr.*
11632. i. 3.

CASTLETON (M.) Your Furniture. pp. 41. *M. Castleton: Birmingham*, [1927.] 16º. **07942. a. 45.**

CASTLETON (ROBERT) Adventures of an Actor. A novel. pp. 306. *Methuen & Co.: London*, 1911. 8º.
012634. p. 16.

—— A Study in Sepia. A novel. pp. 320. *Greening & Co.: London*, 1909. 8º. **012625. aaa. 19.**

CASTLETON (SAMUEL) *See* TATTON (John) A Journall of a Voyage made by the Pearle to the East Indies [under S. Castleton in 1612]. 1625. fol. [*Purchas his Pilgrimes.* pt. 1.]
213. d. 2.

—— *See* TATTON (John) Reys na Oost-Indien, van Kapiteyn S. Castleton . . . Gedaan in het jaar 1612, *etc.* 1707. 8º. [*Aa* (*P. van der*) *Naaukeurige versameling der gedenkwaardigste zee en land-reisen, etc.* vol. 98.]
979. f. 2. (1.)

—— —— 1727. fol. [*Aa* (*P. van der*) *De Aanmerkenswaardigste . . . zee- en landreizen der Portugeezen, etc.* dl. 6.]
566. l. 7.

—— *See* TATTON (John) Hauptmann Castletons Fahrt nach Priaman. 1612. 1747. 4º. [*SCHWABE* (*J. J.*) *Allgemeine Historie der Reisen.* Bd. 1.] **10025. dd.**

CASTLETOWN.

—— The " Borough " Guide to Castletown, Isle of Man. Including a map of the Isle of Man, *etc.* pp. 56. *E. J. Burrow: Cheltenham*, [1910.] 8º. **10354. a. 198.**

—— Castletown; Isle of Man. The official guide, *etc. Ed. J. Burrow & Co.: Cheltenham & London*, [1951– .] 8º.
010368. r. 87.

Various editions.

Grammar School.

—— The Old Grammar School of Castletown. *Norris Modern Press:* [*Douglas, c.* 1950.] 4º. **1879. c. 11. (104.)**

King William's College.

—— King William's College Register. 1833–1904. Compiled and arranged by H. S. Christopher. pp. vi. 381. *J. Maclehose & Sons: Glasgow*, 1905. 8º. **8367. bb. 10.**

—— King William's College Register, 1833–1927. Compiled under the direction of Major K. S. S. Henderson. pp. xxxii. 498. *Glasgow*, 1928. 8º. **08364. f. 59.**

—— The Barrovian, the King William's College Magazine. New series. *Douglas*, 1880– . 8º. **P.P. 6148. i.** *Imperfect; wanting no.* 15, 116. *No.* 1–19 *are mutilated.*

—— General Knowledge Papers, 1905–1953. Prepared for King William's College, *etc.* pp. 256. *Cresset Press: London*, 1954. 8º. **8369. de. 61.**

King William's College.—King William's College Society.

—— List of Members. 1948/49, *etc.* [*Douglas*, 1949– .] 8º.
P.P. 6202. la.

CASTLETOWN, BERNARD EDWARD BARNABY, *Baron. See* FITZPATRICK.

CASTLETOWN BREWERY LTD.

—— Touring the Island. An introduction to the Isle of Man and to the hotels of the Castletown Brewery Ltd. [With illustrations and a map.] pp. 56. *Ed. J. Burrow & Co.: Cheltenham & London*, [1954.] 8º. **010390. e. 65.**

CASTLEY (T.) Antiquarian Speculations, consisting of essays and dissertations, on various subjects. pp. ix. 599. *Sudbury*, 1817. 8º. **7706. cc. 15.**

CASTLING (HARRY) *See* HARRINGTON ( ) and CASTLING (H.) Push that Watch away, *etc.* [1893.] 4º.
1875. d. 9. (8.)

—— *See* MILLS (A. J.) *Writer of Verse*, and CASTLING (H.) In the Shade of the Old Apple Tree, *etc.* [1906.] 4º.
1875. d. 9. (96.)

CASTLING (HARRY) and **MILLS** (A. J.)

—— " Starve her, Joe " . . . Parody on " Navaho." *Francis, Day & Hunter: London*, [1905.] *s. sh.* fol. **1875. d. 9. (28.)**

CASTNER-KELLNER ALKALI CO. [Pamphlets on chemical products.] 6 pt. *Liverpool*, [1924, 25.] 8º.
8899. k. 17.

CASTNER (CASPARUS) *See* CASTNER (Gaspar)

CASTNER (GASPAR) *See* NOEL (François) *Jesuit*, and CASTNER (G.) Memoriale circa veritatem . . . facti, cui innititur decretum . . . Alexandri VII . . . permissivum rituum Sinensium, *etc.* [1703.] 4º. **700. i. 12. (5.)**

—— Relatio sepulturæ magno Orientis apostolo S. Francisco Xauerio erectæ in insula Sanciano anno sæculari MDCC. ff. 30. [*Macao ?* 1700.] 8º. **G. 6359.** *The numeration of the leaves is in Chinese. Printed from woodblock in cursive characters.*

—— Bericht . . . von der Grab-Statt des Heil. Indianer-Apostels S. Francisci Xaverii . . . auf der Insel Sanciano . . . Nebst einer Landkarten über besagte Insel, *etc.* 1729. *See* JESUITS. [*Letters from Missions.*] Allerhand so lehr- als geist-reiche Brief, Schrifften und Reis-Beschreibungen, *etc.* Bd. 2. Tl. 14. 1728, *etc.* fol.
4767. g. 3.

CASTNER (GEOFFREY) *See* FISHE (Vida) and CASTNER (G.) Outline of Proposition concerning the Foundation of a National Centre for the Arts, Music and Drama. [1938.] 8º. **11797. d. 9.**

CASTNER (J.) *Hauptmann.*

—— *See* BERDROW (Wilhelm) Buch der Erfindungen . . . Unter Mitwirkung von Prof. Dr. Lassar-Cohn und Hauptmann a.D. J. Castner bearbeitet von W. Berdrow. [With plates.] [1907.] 4º. **08710. dd. 39.**

CASTNER (JODOCUS) De obitu incomparabilis uiri, D. Henrici Loriti Glareani . . . epicedion, et epigrammata quædam funebria . . . Accesserunt nonnulla alia diuersorum in eiusdem obitum epitaphia. pp. 39. *Per I. Oporinum: Basileæ*, 1563. 4º. **837. h. 3. (28.)**

CASTNER (JOHANN) Wie man sich in pestilentzischen sterbsleuffen vor der vergifftung bewaren möge, vnd dargegen den vergifften mit artzney wider helffen, ein klare vnterrichtung sampt andern natürlichen nottürfften, *etc. Bey I. Petreio: Nürnberg*, 1542. 4º. **7560. de. 5.**

CASTNER (JOHANNES LEONHARDUS JOACHIMUS) Dissertatio inauguralis de restitutione in integrum, *etc.* pp. 64. *Typis viduæ Winterbergerianæ: Altdorffii*, [1669.] 4º.
897. d. 4. (9.)

CASTNER (Julius) Militär-Lexikon . . . Heerwesen und Marine aller Länder, mit besonderer Berücksichtigung des Deutschen Reichs, *etc.* pp. 384. *Leipzig*, 1882. 8°. **8823. k. 17.**

—— [Another copy.] **12222. a. 5.**

—— Das Schiesspulver in seinen Beziehungen zur Entwickelung der gezogenen Geschütze . . . Erweiterter Sonderabdruck aus der Wochenschrift " Prometheus," *etc.* pp. 29. *Berlin*, 1892. 8°. **M.L. b. 107. (1.)**

CASTO (Antonio del) Sogno di Fiorindo sopra l'origini della lingua toscana. pp. 216. *C. & F. Bindi: Firenze*, 1692. 4°. **627. f. 32.**

—— [Another copy.] **12942. c. 3.**

—— Vita della B. Berta de Conti Alberti . . . Monaca nel . . . Monistero di S. Felicita di Firenze. pp. 172. *I. Nauesi: Firenze*, 1685. 8°. **1231. a. 8.**

CASTO (Julius) Italy and the Italian Question. pp. 32. *The Author: London*, 1852. 8°. **8033. e. 2. (1.)**

CASTOIEMENT. *See* Châtiment.

CASTOLDI (Domenico) *See* Vittorj (G.) Modo di puntare le scritture volgari e latine . . . Fatto ristampare con qualche aggionta da D. Castoldi. 1738. 8°. **12942. a. 37.**

ČASTOLOVSKY (V. K.) *See* Nestroy (J.) Pěkné nadělení! Fraška . . . dle Nestroje od V. K. Častolovského, *etc.* 1877. 8°. [*Divadelní Ochotník . . . Nové sbírky.* sv. 140.] **11758. p. 16. (10.)**

CASTON (Alfred de) Constantinople en 1869. Histoire des hommes et des choses. pp. 418. *Paris*, 1868. 8°. **8028. cc. 43.**

The date on the wrapper is 1869.

—— Les Français sur le Rhin. La France devant l'opinion publique. pp. 24. *Paris*, 1870. 8°. **8051. df. 3.**

—— Les Marchands de miracles. Histoire de la superstition humaine. pp. 338. *Paris*, 1864. 12°. **8630. cc. 17.**

—— Tartuffe spirite. Roman de mœurs contemporaines. pp. 320. *Paris*, 1866. 8°. **12515. k. 9.**

—— Les Tricheurs. Scènes de jeu. pp. 270. *Paris*, 1863. 12°. **12352. bbbb. 22.**

—— Les Vendeurs de bonne aventure. pp. 317. *Paris*, 1866. 8°. **12516. c. 4.**

CASTON (Moses) *See* Sibree (John) *Independent Minister*, and Caston (M.) Independency in Warwickshire, *etc.* 1855. 8°. **4707. b. 13.**

—— Independency in Bristol: with brief memorials of its churches and pastors. pp. viii. 257. *Ward & Co.: London*, 1860. 8°. **4715. b. 11.**

CASTONIER (Edgar)

—— *See* Copenhagen.—*Kongelige Danske Geografiske Selskab.* Geografisk Tidsskrift, *etc.* (Bd. 27. Hft. 4.—Bd. 34. Hft. 3. Redigeret af E. Castonier.) 1877, *etc.* 4°, *etc.* **Ac. 6109.**

CASTONIER (Elizabeth)

—— Emily the Toad . . . With illustrations by Mariel Deans. pp. 56. *Collins: London, Glasgow*, [1944.] 8°. **12828. a. 23.**

—— The Eternal Front. [An account of Christian opposition in the occupied countries of Europe.] pp. 125. *J. Clarke & Co.: London*, [1942.] 8°. **8029. a. 82.**

CASTONIER (Elizabeth)

—— Jim the Goat . . . With illustrations by Mariel Deans. pp. 56. *Collins: London, Glasgow*, [1942.] 8°. **12827. b. 7.**

—— Lolly the Bat . . . With illustrations by Mariel Deans. pp. 56. *Collins: London, Glasgow*, [1944.] 8°. **12828. a. 24.**

—— Shippy the Tortoise . . . With illustrations by Mariel Deans. pp. 56. *Collins: London, Glasgow*, [1942.] 8°. **12827. b. 4.**

CASTONNET (Gustave) De l'ophthalmie catarrhale; thèse, *etc.* pp. 24. *Paris*, 1834. 4°. **1184. f. 12. (1.)**

CASTONNET DES FOSSES (Henri Louis) *See* Bernier (F.) Lettres de François Bernier. [Reprinted from the " Journal des savants," 1688.] Par H. Castonnet des Fosses. 1890. 8°. **010910. cc. 3. (1.)**

—— A travers la Perse. Conférence, *etc.* pp. 22. *Lille*, 1891. 8°. **10077. i. 21. (5.)**

—— L'Abyssinie et les Italiens. pp. 394. *Paris*, 1897. 12°. **9060. bb. 2.**

—— L'Annam au moyen âge . . . Extrait de la Revue libérale. pp. 60. *Angers*, 1889. 8°. **9004. l. 33. (4.)**

—— La Chine industrielle et commerciale. Conférence . . . Extrait du Bulletin de la Société de Géographie de Lyon. pp. 35. *Lyon*, 1888. 8°. **08227. k. 31. (4.)**

—— La Chute de Dupleix, ses causes et ses conséquences . . . Extrait du Bulletin de la Société de Géographie de Tours. pp. 55. *Angers*, 1888. 8°. **9004. dd. 5. (4.)**

—— La Colonisation de la Guyane française. *In:* Mémoires de la Société d'Agriculture, Sciences et Arts d'Angers. sér. 4. tom. 2. pp. 91–140. 1889. 8°. **Ac. 245.**

—— Le Commerce du Japon . . . Extrait du Bulletin de la Société de Géographie de Tours. pp. 28. *Angers*, 1889. 8°. **08227. i. 29. (3.)**

—— La Crète et l'hellénisme. pp. 212. *Paris*, 1897. 12°. **8027. aa. 15.**

—— Cuba & Puerto-Rico. Conférence, *etc.* pp. 24. *Lille*, 1889. 8°. **08227. g. 21. (5.)**

—— Dupleix; ses dernières luttes dans l'Inde . . . Extrait des Annales de l'Extrême Orient et de l'Afrique. pp. 46. *Paris*, 1889. 8°. **9010. h. 6. (3.)**

—— La France dans l'Extrême Orient. L'Inde française avant Dupleix. pp. 265. *Paris*, 1887. 8°. **9056. ff. 19.**

—— La France, l'Angleterre & l'Italie dans la Mer Rouge. Conférence . . . Extrait du Bulletin de la Société de Géographie de Lille. pp. 24. *Lille*, 1889. 8°. **8026. i. 6. (6.)**

—— François Bernier, ses voyages dans l'Inde . . . Extrait de la Revue de l'Anjou. pp. 78. *Angers*, 1888. 8°. **010057. k. 3.**

—— La Boullaye Le Gouz. Sa vie et ses voyages. (Extrait de la Revue de l'Anjou.) pp. 55. *Angers*, 1891. 8°. **10601. ff. 6. (6.)**

—— La Macédoine et la politique de l'Autriche en Orient . . . Extrait du Bulletin de la Société de Géographie commerciale de Saint-Nazaire. pp. 35. *Lyon*, 1889. 8°. **8028. de. 22. (4.)**

CASTONNET DES FOSSES (HENRI LOUIS)

—— Le Pèlerinage de la Mecque, ses influences politiques & commerciales. Conférence, *etc.* pp. 40. *Angers*, 1889. 8°. **4503. bb. 22. (9.)**

—— La Perte d'une colonie. La révolution de Saint Domingue. pp. vi. 380. *Paris*, 1893. 8°. **9771. aaa. 2.**

—— Les Petities Antilles françaises. (Extrait des Mémoires de la Société nationale d'Agriculture, Sciences et Arts d'Angers.) pp. 43. *Angers*, 1890. 8°. **10480. df. 1. (4.)**

—— Pierre Poivre. Sa vie & ses voyages . . . Extrait du Bulletin de la Société de Géographie de Lyon. pp. 54. *Lyon*, 1889. 8°. **10601. ff. 6. (2.)**

—— Les Relations de la Chine et de l'Annam. 1890. *See* PARIS.—*Société Académique Indo-chinoise.* Annales de l'Extrême Orient, *etc.* (Bulletin, *etc.* sér. 2. tom. 3.) 1878, *etc.* 8°. **Ac. 8812/3.**

—— Les Relations de La France avec la Perse . . . Extrait du Bulletin de la Société de Géographie de Tours. pp. 52. *Angers*, 1889. 8°. **9004. dd. 5. (4.)**

—— Le Siège de Lyon en 1793. *In:* Mémoires de la Société d'Agriculture, Sciences et Arts d'Angers. sér. 4. tom. 6. pp. 119–158. 1892. 8°. **Ac. 245.**

—— La Tunisie. Conférence . . . Extrait du Bulletin de la Société de Géographie de Lille. pp. 20. *Lille*, 1892. 8°. **010095. i. 22. (5.)**

CASTONUS, *Archbishop of Milan.* [For the proceedings of the provincial synod held by Castonus in 1311 as Archbishop of Milan:] *See* MILAN, *Ecclesiastical Province of.—Provincial Council.* [1311.]

CASTOR. [For works relating to Castor and Pollux:] *See* DIOSCURI.

CASTOR, *Bacularius, pseud.* Num candidato muneris sacri liceat esse pellito ? Tractatuli historici politici fragmenta Dresdae inventa. Edidit Castor, Bacularius. *Dresdae*, 1857. 16°. **7743. a. 12.**

CASTOR, *H.M.S.*

—— H.M.S. Castor. Grand Fleet Destroyer Flotillas, 1915–1918. Souvenir of a war commission. [With plates.] pp. 43. *Printed for private circulation: Glasgow*, 1919. 4°. **9082. dd. 9.**

CASTOR, *Père.*
—— Père Castor's Wild Animal Books. *See* LIDA, *pseud.*

CASTOR, *pseud.* A Century of Foxhunting with the Warwickshire Hounds, being a sketch history of the hunt from 1791 to 1891. By Castor. [Reprinted from the " Banbury Guardian."] pp. xi. 206. *John Potts: Banbury; E. Marlborough & Co.: London*, 1891. 8°. **7908. ee. 17.**

CASTOR, *Rhodius. See* BORNEMANN (L.) De Castoris Chronicis Diodori Siculi fonte ac norma, *etc.* 1878. 4°. **836. i. 19. (14.)**

—— *See* SCHWARTZ (E.) Die Königslisten des Eratosthenes und Kastor, *etc.* 1895. 4°. [*Abhandlungen der k. Gesellschaft der Wissenschaften zu Göttingen. Phil.-hist. Klasse.* Bd. 40.] **Ac. 670.**

—— Castoris Reliquiæ. [Historical fragments.] *See* HERODOTUS. [*Greek and Latin.*] Ἡρόδοτος. Herodoti Historiarum libri IX, *etc.* 1844. 8°. **011306.c.4.**

CASTOR, *Rhodius.*

—— Καστορος Ῥοδιου . . . Περι μετρων ῥητορικων. [Suppositious.] 1834. *See* WALZ (C.) Rhetores Graeci, *etc.* vol. 3. 1832, *etc.* 8°. **834. m. 8.**

—— [Another edition.] Pseudo-Castoris excerpta rhetorica edidit Guilelmus Studemund. pp. 26. *See* BRESLAU.—*Universitas Vratislaviensis.* [*Programmes, etc.*] Universitati Bononiensi octavorum saecularium diem festum . . . celebranti gratulatur Universitas Vratislaviensis Viadrina, *etc.* 1888. 4°. **11315. i. 40.**

CASTOR (A.) Travaux de navigation et de chemins de fer. Recueil d'appareils à vapeur employés dans ces constructions . . . Précédé d'un rapport sur les travaux de fondation du Pont du Rhin . . . par M. Baude. [Introduction and letterpress to pl. I–XIX.] pp. xii. 127. *Paris*, 1861. 8°. **8766. dd. 2.**

—— [Plates.] pl. XIX. *Paris*, 1861. fol. **1802. c. 8.**

—— Recueil d'appareils à vapeur employés aux travaux de navigation et de chemins de fer. Travaux nouveaux. [Letterpress to pl. XX–XXIV.] pp. 52. *Paris*, 1867. 8°. **8766. dd. 1.**

—— Planches. pl. XXIV. *Paris*, 1867. fol. **14000. i. 12.**

Pl. I–XIX are duplicates of those in " Travaux de navigation et de chemins de fer," 1861.

CASTOR (CLAUDE HAY) *See* STRAHAN (James A.) and KENRICK (G. H. B.) A Digest of Equity . . . Third edition. By J. A. Strahan . . . assisted by C. H. Castor. 1913. 8°. **6145. v. 6.**

CASTOR (J. J.) L'Interprète provençal, contenant un choix de 15,000 termes provençaux, les plus utiles, expliqués en français, *etc.* pp. xviii. 292. *Apt*, 1843. 12°. **12950. bb. 19.**

CASTOR (RICHARD HENDERSON) Further Notes on Plague. pp. 8. *Akyab Orphan Press: Akyab*, 1898. 8°. **07306. df. 15. (4.)**

—— Nomenclature of Diseases in Burmese. pp. x. 54. 1922. 8°. *See* BURMA. [*Miscellaneous Public Documents, etc.*] **I.S. BU. 149/11.**

—— Report on Cases of Œdema at Myingyan and Prevalence of Intestinal Parasites in Bassein Jail. pp. 5. 1913. fol. *See* BURMA.—*Prison Department.* **I.S. BU. 13/11.**

CASTORANI (RAPHAËL) De la kératite et de ses suites. pp. viii. 147. *Paris*, 1856. 8°. **7610. b. 14.**

—— Mémoire sur l'extraction linéaire externe simple et combinée de la cataracte, *etc.* pp. 106. *Paris*, 1874. 8°. **7611. g. 23.**

CASTORANO (CAROLUS HORATII À) *See* HORATII (C.) à Castorano.

CASTOREAN TRACTS. Castorean Tracts. no. 1, 2.
    1. Sin laid on Christ, *etc.* pp. 16. 1832.
    2. The Tower of Babel, *etc.* (By R. M. Beverley.) pp. 20. 1833.

Simpkin & Marshall: London, 1832, 33. 12°. **T. 1899. (2, 3.)**

CASTORENA (J. JESÚS)

—— ... De campanario o Democalotlán. Drama, *etc.* [With illustrations.] *In:* América. Revista antológica. época nueva. no. 60. pp. 225–303. 1949. 8°. **P.P. 4107. bgd.**

CASTORENA URSUA Y GOYENECHE (JUAN IGNACIO
MARIA DE)

—— *See* JUANA INÉS, *de la Cruz, of the Convento de San
Jerónimo, Mexico* [J. A. de Asbaxe]. Fama, y Obras
posthumas, *etc.* [Edited by J. I. M. de Castorena Ursua
y Goyeneche.] 1700. 4°. **11450. ee. 51.**

—— *See* PERIODICAL PUBLICATIONS.—Mexico.—*Gazeta de
México.* Gacetas de México . . . desde 1° de enero hasta
fin de junio de 1722. [Published by J. I. de Castorena y
Ursúa.] 1855. 8°. [*Documentos para la historia de
México.* ser. 2. tom. 4, 5.] **9771. bbb. 23.**

—— *See* PERIODICAL PUBLICATIONS.—Mexico.—*Gazeta de
México.* Gacetas de México. Castorena y Ursúa, 1722—
Sahagún de Arévalo, 1728 a 1742, *etc.* 1949, *etc.* 8°.
P.P. 4071. ddb.

—— El Minero mas feliz, que halló el thesoro escondido de la
virtud en el campo florido de la religion . . . Oracion
funebre a el siervo de Dios Fray Juan de Angulo . . .
Sacalo a luz . . . D. Phelipe Suarez de Estrado y Villa-
Real, *etc.* pp. 28. *Mexico,* 1728. 4°. **4985. de. 5. (9.)**
Slightly cropped.

CASTORI (BERNARDINO) Institutione ciuile e christiana
per vno, che desideri viuere tanto in corte, come altroue
honoratamente, e christianamente. pp. 225 [825].
A. Zannetti: Roma, 1622. 4°. **8408. g. 4.**
The titlepage is engraved.

CASTORI (COSTANTINO) Il Diritto di estradizione. 1886.
See MODENA.— *Accademia di Scienze, Lettere ed
Arti.* Memorie. ser. 2. vol. 4. 1833, *etc.* 4°. Ac. 92.

CASTORIA, JOANNES, *Bishop of. See* NEERCASSEL (J. de)

CASTORINA (DOMENICO) Il Fantasma al passo perico-
loso.—I Perollo e i Luna di Sciacca.—Il Moro. 1848.
See BROFFERIO (A.) Tradizioni italiane, *etc.* vol. 2.
1847, *etc.* 8°. **12470. g. 38.**

—— Quattrocento mila lire, ovvero il Castello delle donne.
—Massaniello.—Emma e Corrado.—La Fuggitiva.—
Torquato ed Eleonora. 1849. *See* BROFFERIO (A.) Tra-
dizioni italiane, *etc.* vol. 3. 1847, *etc.* 8°. **12470. g. 38.**

—— Maria.—Ermengarda.—La Penitente. 1850. *See*
BROFFERIO (A.) Tradizioni italiane, *etc.* vol. 4.
1847, *etc.* 8°. **12470. g. 38.**

—— Cartagine distrutta. Poema epico. 4 tom. *Catania,*
1835–40. 8°. **11436. f. 23.**

CASTORINA (EMANUELE)

—— L'Atticismo nell'evoluzione del pensiero di Cicerone.
pp. 302. *Catania,* 1952. 8°. **11311. e. 39.**

CASTORINA (PASQUALE) *See* COCO (Vitus) Elogio del
P. D. Vito M. Amico e Satella . . . pubblicato . . . con
note illustrative e documenti inediti pel can. P. Castorina.
1884. 8°. **4867. dd. 12.**

—— *See* JOANNES, *de Procida.* Il Vespro Siciliano. Cronaca
siciliana anonima intitolata "Lu Rebellamentu di
Sichilia " . . . Codice cartaceo del secolo XVII esistente
nell'Archivio Municipale di Catania. Per la prima volta
pubblicata, tradotta ed annotata dal Can. P. Castorina.
1882. 8°. **9167. i. 11.**

—— *See* MARY, *the Blessed Virgin.—Churches and Institutions.—Licodia Eubea.—Santa Maria di Licodia.* Un
Codice membranaceo del secolo XIII della Biblioteca
Benedettina di Catania. Con un saggio di studii paleo-
grafici sulle Costituzioni benedettine in lingua volgare
antica de' due monasteri benedettini di Santa Maria di
Licodia e S. Nicolò l'Arena. Or la prima volta pubblicate
per intiero dall'originale. Per cura del can. P. Castorina.
1876. 8°. **11903. d. 8.**

CASTORINA (PASQUALE)

—— Catania e Dante Alighieri, ovvero uno Sguardo retrospet-
tivo di anni seicento, la Cronaca di F. Atanasio di Aci, ed
una Società Catanese di storia patria. pp. 217.
Catania, 1883. 8°. **11420. g. 7.**

—— [Another copy.] **10151. dd. 5.**

—— Elogio storico di monsignor Salvatore Ventimiglia,
vescovo di Catania. Con documenti inediti e note illustrative. pp. lvi. 244. *Catania,* 1888. 8°.
4865. ff. 25.

—— Intorno ad una prima edizione di Q. Orazio Flacco.
Cenni bibliografici. pp. 22. *Catania,* 1887. 8°.
011903. m. 12. (5.)

—— I Platamoni in Catania e un cimelio architettonico del
secolo XIV relativo agli stessi. Discorso storico-artistico.
pp. 51. *Catania,* 1881. 8°. **7806. df. 16.**

CASTORISME. Le Castorisme. Voilà l'ennemi ! Par
un Vrai Conservateur. pp. 16. *Montréal,* 1892. 8°.
8154. bb. 32. (6.)

CASTORIUS. [For editions of the "Tabula Peutinge-
riana " attributed to Castorius :] *See* PEUTINGER (C.)

CASTORIUS (ALOYSIUS) *See* VALIERO (A.) *Cardinal.*
Augustini S. E. Cardinalis Valerii . . . De acolythorum
disciplina libri duo. [Edited by A. Castorius.]
1836. 8°. **1219. i. 12.**

CASTORP (HINRICH) *See* NEUMANN (Gerhard) Hinrich
Castorp. Ein Lübecker Bürgermeister aus der zweiten
Hälfte des 15. Jahrhunderts. 1932. 8°. **W.P. 1374/11.**

CASTORPH (LUDWIG) Offenes Sendschreiben an den
Verfasser der sechs Fragen an die deutsche Nation katho-
lischen Theils wegen religiös-kirchlicher Selbstständigkeit.
Beantwortet in einem Sendschreiben an dieselbe von
Karl Friedrich Theodul. pp. vi. 106. *Mannheim,*
1844. 8°. **3910. d. 11.**

—— Die Trierer Rock- und Glaubens-Revolution, oder :
Souvenir für den Ex-Priester Herr Johannes Ronge und
seine Verehrer. pp. 24. *Achern,* 1845. 8°.
3910. cc. 23.

CASTOVIUS (ERICUS) *See* UPMARCK (J.) Oratio
parentalis in obitum . . . Haquini Spegel, *etc.* (De vita
et morte . . . Erici Castovii, *etc.*) 1729. 8°. [NETTEL-
BLADT (*C. von*) *Memoria virorum in Suecia eruditissimo-
rum rediviva, etc.* pt. 2.] **617. d. 10.**

—— —— 1737. 8°. [*Collectio orationum funebrium in
memoriam virorum eruditorum edita.*] **236. a. 17.**

CASTRA (PETRUS DE) *Archbishop of Bourges.* Epistolæ
Petri Bituricensis archiepiscopi. 1808. *See* BOUQUET
(M.) Recueil des historiens des Gaules, *etc.* tom. 15.
1738, *etc.* fol. **Circ. 8–9. b.**

CASTRACANE (CASTRUCCIUS) De cathedra Romana
Sancti Petri principis Apostolorum, oratio, *etc.* pp. xv.
Romæ, [1804.] 4°. **T. 78*. (2.)**

—— [Another copy.] **1356. k. 4. (23.)**

CASTRACANE DEGLI ANTELMINELLI (FRANCESCO
SAVERIO) *Count.* Intorno ad alcune carte nautiche dei
secoli XIV, XV e XVI. (Estratto dagli Atti dell'Accademia
Pontificia de' Nuovi Lincei.) pp. 4. *Roma,*
1883. 4°. **10001. g. 3.**

CASTRACANE DEGLI ANTELMINELLI (Francesco Saverio) Count.

—— Report on the Diatomaceæ collected by H. M. S. Challenger during the years 1873–1876. pp. iii. 178. pl. xxx. *London*, 1886. 4°. [Thomson (Sir C. W.) *Report on the scientific results of the voyage of H.M.S. Challenger, etc.* Botany. vol. 2.] **1825. aa.**

CASTRACANI DEGLI ANTELMINELLI (Castruccio) *Duke of Lucca.* See Castruccio.

CASTRACANIUS (Franciscus) Tractatus de Societatbus [sic], quae fiunt super officiis Romanæ Ecclesiæ. pp. 209. *Apud hæredem M. Amadori: Romæ*, 1590. 4°.
Legg. 123.

CASTRAEUS (Sillacius) See La Châtre (J. de) *Sieur de Sillac.*

CASTRAPORCELLI (Taddeo) *pseud.* Replica . . . alla risposta di Giammaria Mastripieri [i.e. "Risposta a un libercolo intitolato 'Lettera d'un ecclesiastico italiano diretta a monsig. S. de' Ricci vescovo di Pistoja e Prato, 1786'"]. pp. 71. [*Genoa? 1787.*] 4°. **1352. c. 5.**

CASTRAS (Auguste Geneviève Valentin Davezac de) See Davezac de Castras.

CASTRAVILLA (Ridolfo) *pseud.* Discorso . . . nel quale si mostra l'imperfettione della Commedia di Dante. Contra al Dialogo delle lingue del Varchi. *See* Bulgarini (B.) Annotazioni . . . sopra la prima parte della Difesa, fatta da M. I. Mazzoni, *etc.* 1608. 4°.
638. h. 19. (2.)

—— I Discorsi di Ridolfo Castravilla contro Dante e di Filippo Sassetti in difesa di Dante. A cura di Mario Rossi. pp. 118. *Città di Castello*, 1897. 8°. [*Collezione di opuscoli danteschi inediti o rari.* vol. 40–41.]
011420. a. 1/28.

CASTRE (Ernest) Le Conseil Général des Bouches-du-Rhône. Analyses et extraits des délibérations, 1800–1838. Dictionnaire biographique, 1800–1912. pp. x. 343. 1912. 8°. *See* Bouches-du-Rhône, *Département des.* —*Conseil Général.* **9231. ccc. 10.**

CASTRECA BRUNETTI (Enrico) *See* Monti (V.) Lettere inedite di V. Monti . . . e di altri. [Edited by E. Castreca Brunetti.] 1846. 8°. **1454. e. 3.**

CASTREJON ( ) Viva Augustin 1°. [On the entry of Iturbide into Mexico.] [*Mexico?* 1822.] *s. sh.* 4°. **9770. bb. 13. (51.)**

CASTRÉN (Eric) Historisk och oeconomisk beskrifning öfwer Cajanaborgs-län, *etc.* Praes. P. Kalm. pp. 78. *Åbo*, [1754.] 4°. **B. 669. (15.)**

—— [Another copy.] **150. b. 16. (1.)**

CASTRÉN (Erik Johannes Sakari)

—— Kansainvälinen oikeusseuraanto, *etc.* pp. xix. 280. *Jakaja*, 1950. 8°. **6956. c. 29.** *Suomalaisen Lakimiesyhdistyksen julkaisuja.* ser. B. no. 38.

—— The Present Law of War and Neutrality. pp. 630. *Helsinki*, 1954. 8°. [*Suomalaisen Tiedeakatemian toimituksia.* ser. B. tom. 85.] **Ac. 1094. c.**

CASTRÉN (Fredrik Alfred) *See* Cervantes Saavedra (M. de) [*Don Quixote.—Finnish.—Abridgments.*] Michaël Cervanteen Don Quixote de la Mancha . . . nuorisoa varten vapaasti toimitti Aug. Th. Paban. Vanhemman, jo loppuun myydyn suomennoksen toinen painos, jonka korjaili F. A. C. [i.e. F. A. Castrén.] 1896. 8°. **12489. aaa. 44.**

CASTRÉN (Gunnar)

—— *See* Helsinki.—*Helsingfors Universitetet.* Helsingin Yliopiston alkuajoilta. (Toimituskunta: G. Suolahti . . . G. Castrén, *etc.*) 1928. 4°. **Ac. 1095/5.**

—— *See* Hirn (Y.) Festskrift tillägnad Yrjö Hirn, *etc.* (Redaktionskommitté: G. Castrén, K. S. Laurila, H. Ruin.) 1930. 8°. **012359. d. 13.**

—— *See* Levertin (O. I.) Sveriges national-litteratur, 1500–1900. (vol. 25. utgifvet under medverkan af G. Castrén.) 1907, *etc.* 8°. **011852. cc. 1.**

—— *See* Runeberg (J. L.) Samlade skrifter av Johan Ludvig Runeberg. Under redaktion av G. Castrén och M. Lamm. 1933, *etc.* 8°. [*Svenska författare.* 16.] **Ac. 9070.**

—— *See* Runeberg (J. L.) Runebergs brev till Emilie Björkstén. Utgivna av G. Castrén. 1940. 8°. [*Skrifter utgivna av Svenska Litteratursällskapet i Finland.* no. 281. *Historiska och litteraturhistoriska studier.* no. 16.] **Ac. 9082.**

—— *See* Runeberg (J. L.) Runebergs brev till Emilie Björkstén. Utgivna av G. Castrén. 1940. 8°. **10922. cc. 22.**

—— *See* Söderhjelm (T.) Uppsatser och kritiker. [Edited by J. W. Söderhjelm and G. Castrén.] 1908. 8°. **011852. i. 80.**

—— *See* Sylwan (O.) Svenska litteraturens historia. Av F. Böök, G. Castrén, *etc.* 1919, *etc.* 8°. **011851. dd. 48.**

—— Bröderna Gösta och Carl Lundahl. 1940. *See* Helsingfors.—*Svenska Litteratursällskapet i Finland.* Skrifter, *etc.* no. 281. 1866, *etc.* 8°. **Ac. 9082.**

—— G. Bernard Shaw. [With a portrait.] *Swed.* pp. 53. *Helsingfors*, 1906. 8°. **11853. ss. 23.**

—— Gustav Philip Creutz. [With a portrait.] pp. 92. *Stockholm*, 1949. 8°. **010761. aa. 3.** *Part of a series entitled "Svenska författare."*

—— Herman Kellgren. Ett bidrag till 1840- och 1850-talens kulturhistoria. [With a portrait.] pp. 428. *Helsingfors*, 1945. 8°. [*Skrifter utgivna av Svenska Litteratursällskapet i Finland.* no. 302.] **Ac. 9082.**

—— Johan Ludvig Runeberg. [With a portrait.] pp. 93. *Stockholm*, 1950. 8°. **10798. aa. 22.** *Part of the series "Svenska författare."*

—— Norden i den franska litteraturen. pp. 270. *Helsingfors*, 1910. 8°. **11852. s. 27.**

—— Stormaktstidens diktning. Studier. pp. 220. *Helsingfors*, 1907. 8°. **11851. s. 5.**

—— Werner Söderhjelm som teaterkritiker. *In:* Skrifter utgivna av Svenska Litteratursällskapet i Finland. no. 338. Historiska och litteraturhistoriska studier. no. 29. pp. 41–94. 1953. 8°. **Ac. 9082.**

—— Festskrift tillägnad Gunnar Castrén den 27 december 1938. [With a portrait.] pp. 426. *Helsingfors*, 1938. 8°. [*Skrifter utgivna av Svenska Litteratursällskapet i Finland.* no. 271.] **Ac. 9082.**

CASTRÉN (Jonas) *See* Hultin (T.) Taistelun mies. Piirteitä Jonas Castrénin elämästä ja toiminnasta. 1927. 4°. **010795. d. 18.**

—— Mikä on oikea ohjelma suomalaisuuden asiassa? Suoritusta "Finland" in ja hra A. Meurman'in kanssa. pp. 35. *Jywäskylässä*, 1887. 8°. **8093. bb. 18. (1.)**

CASTRÉN (KAARLE ALFRED) Muistelmia wuosien 1808–1809 sodasta. pp. 160. *Helsingissä, 1865.* 8°.
9454. cc. 17.

CASTRÉN (KAARLO) Kiveliön suuri herättäjä Lars Levi Laestadius. Elämäkerta . . . 26 kuvaa. Toinen painos. [With a portrait.] pp. 277. *Helsingissä, 1934.* 8°.
20043. a. 30.

—— Punaisten hirmutyöt vapaussodan aikana . . . Toinen painos. pp. 116. *Helsinki, 1926.* 8°.   9456. a. 56.

—— De Rödas våldsdåd under Frihetskriget, *etc.* [With portraits.] pp. 97. *Helsingfors, 1926.* 8°.
9456. aa. 17.

CASTRÉN (LIISA)

—— Adolf Ivar Arwidsson, *etc.* [With portraits.] *Helsingissä, 1944– .* 8°.   W.P. 9193.

—— Adolf Ivar Arwidsson isänmaallisena herättäjänä . . . Mit einem Auszug in deutscher Sprache. [With a portrait.] pp. 441. *Helsinki, 1951.* 8°. [*Historiallisia tutkimuksia.* no. 35.]   Ac. 7814/8.

—— J. L. Runebergs handskrifter. Systematisk förteckning. pp. 72. *In:* Skrifter utgivna av Svenska Litteratursällskapet i Finland. vol. 326. 1949. 8°.   Ac. 9082.

CASTRÉN (LISA) *See* CASTRÉN (Liisa)

CASTREN (MATTHIAS) Dissertatio academica de præjudiciis amovendis, *etc.* *Praes.* H. G. Porthan. pp. 24. *Aboæ,* [1785.] 4°.   817. c. 23. (12.)

CASTRÉN (MATTHIAS ALEXANDER) *See* BORG (C. G.) Matthias Alexander Castrén, *etc.* [With a list of his writings.] 1853. 8°.   10795. e. 36. (4.)

—— *See* KALEVALA. Kalevala. Öfversatt af M. A. Castrén. 1841. 8°.   11586. ee. 62.

—— De affixis personalibus linguarum altaicarum. Dissertatio. pp. 76. *Helsingforsiæ, 1850.* 4°.   1332. g. 10.

—— Elementa grammatices syrjaenae. pp. viii. 166. *Helsingforsiae, 1844.* 8°.   829. f. 30.

—— Elementa grammatices tscheremissæ. pp. xi. 75. *Kuopio, 1845.* 8°.   1333. f. 46.

—— Föredrag . . . Hållet i Universitetets Solennitetssal, den 9 november 1849. (Hvar låg det finska folkets vagga?) *See* HELSINGFORS. Litterära soiréer i Helsingfors, *etc.* 1849, *etc.* 8°.   11826. f. 3.

—— Några dagar i Lappland. *See* GROT (Ya. K.) Calender till minne af Kejserliga Alexanders-Universitetets andra secularfest, *etc.* 1842. 8°.   8357. h. 7.

—— Нѣсколько дней въ Лапландіи. [Translated by Ya. K. Grot.] *See* GROT (Ya. K.) Альманахъ въ память двухсотлѣтняго юбилея Императорскаго Александровскаго Университета, *etc.* 1842. 8°.   8357. f. 46.

—— M. Alexander Castrén's Nordische Reisen und Forschungen. Im Auftrage der Kaiserlichen Akademie der Wissenschaften herausgegeben von Anton Schiefner. 12 Bd.

    1. Reiseerinnerungen aus den Jahren 1838–1844 . . . Mit dem Bildniss des Verfassers und vier Samojedenporträts. pp. xiv. 308. 1853.
    2. Reiseberichte und Briefe aus den Jahren 1845–1849 . . . Mit drei lithographirten Beilagen. pp. x. 527. 1856.
    3. Vorlesungen über die finnische Mythologie . . . Aus dem schwedischen übertragen und mit Anmerkungen begleitet von A. Schiefner. pp. xii. 340. 1853.
    4. Ethnologische Vorlesungen über die altaischen Völker, nebst samojedischen Märchen und tatarischen Heldensagen, *etc.* pp. xviii. 257. 1857.

CASTRÉN (MATTHIAS ALEXANDER)

    5. Kleinere Schriften. [Translated from " Smärra afhandlingar " and " Tillfälliga uppsattser."] pp. x. 382. 1862.
    6. Versuch einer ostjakischen Sprachlehre, nebst kurzem Wörterverzeichniss. [With a portrait.] pp. ix. 102. 1849.
    [6*.] Zweite verbesserte Auflage. pp. xiv. 125. 1858.
    7. Grammatik der samojedischen Sprachen. pp. xxiv. 608. 1854.
    8. Wörterverzeichnisse aus den samojedischen Sprachen. [With " Sprachproben."] pp. xxxiv. 404. 1855.
    9. Grundzüge einer tungusischen Sprachlehre, nebst kurzem Wörterverzeichniss. pp. xvi. 139. 1856.
    10. Versuch einer burjatischen Sprachlehre, nebst kurzem Wörterverzeichniss. pp. xv. 244. 1857.
    11. Versuch einer koibalischen und karagassischen Sprachlehre, nebst Wörterverzeichnissen aus den tatarischen Mundarten des minussischen Kreises. pp. xix. 210. 1857.
    12. Versuch einer jenissei-ostjakischen und kottischen Sprachlehre, nebst Wörterverzeichnissen aus den genannten Sprachen. pp. xix. 264. 1858.

1853, 49–62. 8°. *See* RUSSIA.—*Академия Наук СССР.*
Ac. 1125/166.

—— Nordiska resor och forskningar. [Bd. 2 edited by B. O. Schauman, bd. 3–6 by C. G. Borg.] 6 bd.

    1. Reseminnen från åren 1838–1844. [With plates, including a portrait, and a map.] pp. 320. 1852.
    2. Reseberättelser och bref åren 1845–49. [With a plate and a map.] pp. xii. 463. 1855.
    3. Föreläsningar i finsk mytologi. pp. 332. 1853.
    4. Ethnologiska föreläsningar öfver altaiska folken ; samt samojediska och tatariska sagor. pp. xviii. 284. 1857.
    5. Smärre afhandlingar och akademiska dissertationer. pp. vii. 293. 1858.
    6. Tillfällige uppsatser. [With a life of M. A. Castrén, signed : J. V. S., i.e. J. V. Snellman.] pp. lxxviii. 160. 1870.

Helsingfors, 1852–70. 8°.   10027. e. 12.

—— M. A. Castrén'in elämä ja matkustukset, nuorisolle kerrotut. Ynnä kolme piirustusta A. Edelfelt'ilta [including a portrait] sekä kartta. [Adapted by Erik O. Edlund from " Reseminnen från åren 1838–1844 " and " Reseberättelser och bref åren 1845–1849." Translated by Pekka Väyrynen.] pp. 219. *Helsingissä, 1878.* 8°.
010795. e. 11.

—— Samojedische Volksdichtung. Gesammelt von M. A. Castrén. Herausgegeben von T. Lehtisalo. pp. xxv. 350. *Helsinki, 1940.* 8°. [*Suomalais-ugrilaisen Seuran toimituksia.* no. 83.]   Ac. 9081/3.

—— Vom Einflusse des Accents in der lappländischen Sprache . . . Aus den Mémoires de l'Académie Impériale des Sciences . . . besonders abgedruckt. pp. 44. *St. Petersburg, 1845.* 4°.   1333. k. 2.

—— Памяти М. А. Кастрена к 75-летию дня смерти. [With a portrait and a bibliography.] pp. 141. *Ленинград, 1927.* 8°. [*Очерки по истории знаний.* no. 2.]   Ac. 1125/119.

CASTRÉN (OLA) De sociala strömningarna i Frankrike på Ludvig XIV:s tid. Akademisk avhandling, *etc.* pp. iv. 383. *Helsingfors, 1911.* 8°.   09210. e. 23.

CASTRÉN (OLAVI) Bernhard von Clairvaux. Zur Typologie des mittelalterlichen Menschen. pp. 382. *Lund, 1938.* 8°.   20043. c. 37.

—— Die Bibeldeutung Calvins. pp. 159. *Helsinki, 1946.* 8°. [*Suomalaisen Tiedeakatemian toimituksia.* sarja B. nid. 56. no. 3.]   Ac. 1094. c.

CASTRÉN (PAAVO)

—— Über subkutane Leberrisse und das hepatorenale Syndrom. [Translated by Lilli Löfqvist.] pp. 176. *Helsinki, 1946.* 8°. [*Acta chirurgica scandinavica.* vol. 93. suppl. 105.]   P.P. 3081. b. (1.)

CASTRÉN (Reino)

—— Laatokan-Suomenlahden kanavasuunnitelma ja Venäjän kanavarakennus Vienanmeri-Itämeri. Liikennetaloudellinen tutkimus. [With maps.] pp. 111. *Helsinki,* 1933. 8º. **08809. b. 8.**

CASTRÉN (Robert) Skildringar ur Finlands nyare historia . . . Första samlingen. pp. 391. *Helsingfors,* 1882 [1881, 82]. 8º. **9455. cc. 28.**
Published in parts.

CASTRENSIS (Franciscus) *See* Castro (Francisco de) M.D.

CASTRENSIS (Jacobus Albertus) *See* Bible.—*Epistles.* [*Latin.*] Divi Thomæ Aquinatis . . . in omnes Beati Pauli Apostoli Epistolas commentaria. Adnotationibus illustrata, quibus antea nunquam: ac mendis non paucis . . . repurgata, labore atque industria F. I. A. Castrensis, *etc.* 1548. fol. **3627. ff. 6.**

CASTRENSIS (Nicolaus) *Bishop of Middelburg. See* Castro (Nicolaas de)

CASTRENSIS (Paulus) *See* Paulus, de Castro.

CASTRENSIS (Robertus) *See* Robertus, *Retenensis.*

CASTRENSIS (Stephanus) *See* Rodrigues de Castro (Estevam)

CASTRES. Les Declarations faites par les consuls & habitans des villes de Castres, Montauban, Briateste . . . & autres villes des Comtez d'Albigeois, de Lauraguais, & de Foix, sur leurs resolutions de demeurer en vne ferme obeyssance au seruice du Roy ; contre les armes & entreprises, tant du Roy de la grande Bretagne, que de celles du Duc de Rohan . . . Auec la lettre des consuls de Montauban au Roy. pp. 35. *E. Richer : Paris,* [1627.] 8º. **1193. h. 17. (12.)**

—— Inventaire-sommaire des archives communales de la ville de Castres—Tarn—antérieures à 1790. [Edited by M. Estadieu.] 11 pt. *Castres,* 1881. 4º. [*Collection des inventaires-sommaires des archives communales, etc.*] **S. 148. b. 2. (2.)**

—— Cantiques de Castres, en langue languedocienne et française. Nouvelle édition, revue, corrigée et augmentée, *etc.* pp. 111. *Castres,* [1800 ?] 8º. **11498. bb. 51.**

—— Collection des pièces relatives à la procédure instruite sur les événemens qui ont eu lieu dans la Commune de Castres et lieux circonvoisins . . . depuis le 1er Germinal an 5. pp. 208. An 6 [1798]. 4º. **F. 33*. (6.)**

—— Précis sur l'accusation de conspiration imputée à des habitans de Castres, Réalmont & Labruyere. Aux citoyens jurés de jugement. pp. 20. *Toulouse,* [1798 ?] 4º. **F. 44*. (5.)**

Musée Goya.

—— Exposition : Histoire et iconographie du catharisme, *etc.* [A catalogue.] pp. 30. [*Castres,*] 1955. 8º. **7960. i. 60.**

—— *Société des Amis du Vieux Pays Castrais.* Histoire de Castres et de son abbaye de Charlemagne à la guerre des Albigeois. [By Louis de Lacger. With plates.] pp. 172. [*Castres,*] 1937. 8º. **20043. d. 8.**

CASTRES.

—— *Société Littéraire et Scientifique.* Procès-verbaux des séances, *etc.* 6 vol. *Castres,* 1857–67. 8º. Ac. **306.**

—— Concours de 1860. Éloge de Pellisson par Mlle Mélanie Gibaudan, *etc.* pp. 39. *Toulouse,* 1861. 8º. **10660. bb. 37. (6.)**

CASTRES, Guy, *Bishop of.* [1383–1385.] *See* Roye (G. de) successively *Bishop of Verdun, of Castres, etc.*

——, Honoré, *Bishop of.* [1705–1736.] *See* Quiqueran de Beaujeu (H. de) successively *Bishop of Oléron* and *of Castres.*

——, Jean Sébastien, *Bishop of.* [1773–1801.] *See* Barral (J. S. de)

CASTRES (DE) *Count.* Essai d'une reconnaissance militaire sur le Bassin du Danube, *etc.* [With a map.] 2 pt. 1826, 28. *See* France.—*Ministère de la Guerre.* Mémorial du Dépôt général de la Guerre, *etc.* tom. 3, 4. 1826, *etc.* 4º. **818. l. 8.**

CASTRES (Abraham) *See* Ways. Ways and Means for suppressing Beggary and Relieving the Poor . . . Translated from the Italian [by A. Castres]. 1726. 4º. **713. h. 1. (1.)**

CASTRES (Antoine Sabatier de) *See* Sabatier (A.) de *Castres.*

CASTRES (G. H. F. de) Allgemeiner Grundriss der französischen Literaturgeschichte von ihrem Entstehen bis zum Sturze Louis Philippe's. pp. x. 288. *Leipzig,* 1854. 8º. **11851. dd. 8.**

—— Chefs d'oeuvre lyriques de la France ; accompagnés de notes historiques, biographiques et philologiques et précédés d'un abrégé de poétique. pp. vi. 154. *Leipzig,* 1854. 8º. **11481. c. 42. (1.)**

—— Diccionario Español-Aleman para uso de los escritorios de comercio. Spanisch-Deutsches Comtoir-Lexikon . . . Mit den analogen französischen, englischen und italienischen Redensarten verglichen. pp. iv. 107. *Hamburg,* 1860. 8º. **12943. cc. 5. (5.)**

—— Dictionnaire général des marchandises français-allemand-anglais-italien. (Allgemeines Waaren-Lexikon, *etc.*) pp. viii. 584. *Francfort,* 1858. 8º. **8244. c. 66.**

—— Etymologik, oder Theorie der Wortbildung der französischen Sprache, nach den Ergebnissen der neuern Sprachforschung, *etc.* pp. xii. vi–viii. 197. *Leipzig,* 1851. 8º. **1331. d. 24.**

—— Handels- und Correspondenz-Wörterbuch : französisch, englisch, deutsch. Zugleich Supplement zu allen französischen und englischen Handelscorrespondenzen namentlich denen von C. Munde und Fr. Noback. pp. vi. 184. *Leipzig,* 1860. 8º. **12901. c. 4.**

CASTRES (Marc Alexandre Caminade de) *See* Caminade de Castres.

CASTRESANA (Luis de)

—— La Muerte viaja sola. [With a portrait.] pp. 360. [*Madrid,* 1953.] 8º. **12487. pp. 16.** "La Nave." no. 11.

CASTRES DU CRENAY (DE) *Mr., pseud.* [i.e. Pierre Quesnel.] Almanach du Diable, contenant des prédictions très-curieuses & absolument infaillibles ; pour l'année MDCCXXXVII. Nouvelle édition, augmenté des plusieurs fautes qui ne sont point dans les precedentes editions. (Clef des predictions carminifiques de l'Almanach du diable.—La critique & contre-critique de l'Almanach du diable pour l'année MDCCXXXVII.) 3 pt. *Aux Enfers,* [1740 ?] 24º. **12330. a. 9.**

CASTRICIUS (HENRICUS) *See* GELDORPIUS (H.) *Castricius*.

CASTRICQUE (PAUL AUGUSTE MASUI) *See* MASUI-CASTRICQUE.

CASTRICUS (JACOBUS)

—— Jacobi Castrici . . . De sudore epıdemiali quem anglicum vocant ad medicos Gandenses epistola . . . Luteciae . . . 1529. *See* GRUNER (C. G.) Scriptores de sudore anglico superstites, *etc.* 1847. 8º. . **7561. h. 48.**

CASTRIES.—*St. Mary's College.*

—— Report on the Examination on the Lower Forms of St. Mary's College, July, 1935. pp. 4. [*Castries*, 1935.] fol. C.S. F. **244/2.**

CASTRIES, ARMAND CHARLES AUGUSTIN DE LA CROIX, *Duke de. See* LA CROIX.

——, CLAIRE CLÉMENCE HENRIETTE CLAUDINE DE LA CROIX, *Duchess de. See* LA CROIX.

CASTRIES (CHARLES EUGÈNE GABRIEL DE) *Marquis, Marshal of France. See* BOUILLON, *l'Hôtel*. Les Petits soupers et les nuits de l'Hôtel Bouill - n [i.e. Bouillon]. Lettre . . . au sujet des récréations de M. de C - stri - s [i.e. C. E. G. de Castries], *etc.* 1783. 8º. **1094. h. 6.**

—— *See* FOURNIER L'HÉRITIER (C.) Aux représentans de la nation. Dénonciation contre M. le maréchal de Castries, *etc.* [1790.] 4º. F. **48*. (8.)**

—— Lettres. *See* DAUDET (E.) Histoire de l'Emigration. Coblentz, *etc.* [1890.] 8º. **9226.c.19.**

—— Recueil de lettres aristocratiques trouvées chez M. de Castries . . . Mises au jour par une société de patriotes, *etc.* pp. 24. [*Paris*,] 1790. 12º. R. **199. (15.)**

CASTRIES (HENRY DE) *Count. See* 'ABD AL-RAHMĀN IBN MUHAMMAD, *al-Majdūb*. Les Gnomes de Sidi Abd Er-Rahman el-Medjedoub. [Edited, with a translation, by H. de Castries.] 1896. 8º. **14579. c. 38.**

—— *See* DAMPIERRE (J.. de) *Marquis*. Henry de Castries et Charles de Foucauld. [With a portrait.] 1938. 8º. [*FOUCAULD* (C. E. de) *Viscount*. *Lettres à Henry de Castries.*] **010921. pp. 6.**

—— *See* MOROCCO. Une Description du Maroc sous le regne de Moulay Ahmed el-Mansour, *etc.* (Copia do emperio e reinos dos Xarifes, *etc.*) [Edited, with a translation, by H. de Castries.] 1909. 8º. **10094. ee. 21.**

—— *See* MOROCCO. [French Zone.]—*Direction Générale de l'Instruction Publique, des Beaux-Arts et des Antiquités*. Au Maroc avec le colonel de Castries. Exposition commémorative du cinquantenaire de la collection des Sources inédits de l'histoire du Maroc, *etc.* [1955.] 8º. S. w. **158.**

—— L'Islam. Impressions et études . . . Deuxième édition. pp. 359. *Paris*, 1896. 8º. **4504. aa. 5.**

—— Moulay Ismail et Jacques II. Une apologie de l'Islam par un Sultan du Maroc. [With a French translation of two letters from Moulay Ismail to James II., and five plates.] pp. 120. *Paris*, 1903. 8º. **4503. g. 33.**

—— Les Sources inédites de l'histoire du Maroc de 1530 à 1845. Par le comte H. de Castries. (Publiées par Pierre de Cenival. Philippe de Cossé Brissac.) (Collection de lettres, documents et mémoires.)

    sér. 1. Dynastie Saadienne. **9062. dd. 1/1.**
      Archives et bibliothèques de France. 3 tom. 1905-11.
      9062. dd. 1/1. (1.)

CASTRIES (HENRY DE) *Count.*

    —— Bibliographie et index général. [With a genealogical table.] pp. 66. 1926. **9062. dd. 1/1. (1a.)**
    Archives et bibliothéques des Pays-Bas. (Bibliographie.—Index.) 6 tom. 1906-23. **9062. dd. 1/1. (2.)**
    Archives et bibliothèques d'Angleterre. (Bibliographie.—Index.) 3 tom. 1918-35. **9062. dd. 1/1. (3.)**
    Archives et bibliothèques d'Espagne. 1921- . **9062. dd. 1/1. (4.)**
    Archives et bibliothèques de Portugal. (tom. 2. pt. 1. Publié par David Lopes et Robert Ricard.—pt. 2. Par Pierre de Cenival, D. Lopes, et R. Ricard.—tom. 3, 4. Par R. Ricard.) 1934- . **9062. dd. 1/1. (5.)**
    sér. 2. Dynastie Filalienne. **9062. dd. 1/2.**
    Archives et bibliothèques de France. 1922- . **9062. dd. 1/2. (1.)**

    —— Bibliographie et index alphabétique. 1954- . **9062. dd. 1/2. (1a.)**

    Paris, 1905- . 8º. **9062. dd. 1.**

—— [Another copy ot ser. 1. Portugal. tom. 3.] Les Sources inédites de l'histoire du Maroc, *etc.* F.P. *Paris*, 1948. 8º. **9060. i. 3.**

CASTRIES (L. R. DE POGEY) *See* POGEY-CASTRIES.

CASTRIFRANCANUS (ALBERTUS) Alberti Castrifrancani Oratio habita in funere Vrbani Bellunensis e Minoritana familia vnius. *Per B. de Vitalibus:* [*Venice*,] 1524. 4º. **10630. d. 24.**

CASTRILLO (DIEGO NUÑEZ DE) *See* NUÑEZ DE CASTRILLO.

CASTRILLO (GAUDENCIO) *See* HOSPITAL (J.) *Bishop of Cauna*. Notas y Escenas de Viaje . . . Prólogo del R. P. Fr. G. Castrillo. 1914. 8º. **10058. r. 2.**

—— El Comercio en el Extremo Oriente, *etc.* pp. xi. 354. *Madrid*, 1918. 8º. **08223. h. 34.**

CASTRILLO (HERNANDO) Magia Natural, o Ciencia de filosofia oculta . . . Primera parte, donde se trata de los secretos que pertenecen a las partes de la tierra. ff. 224. *D. P. Estupiñan: Trigueros*, 1649. 4º. **719. f. 14.** *No more published.*

—— [Another edition.] Historia y Magia Natural, *etc.* pp. 342. *J. G. Infanzon: Madrid*, 1692. 4º. **8630. g. 14.**

CASTRILLO (VICENTE) *See* GUERAU DE ARELLANO Y PUCHADES (V.) Leve indicio del placèr, que, à la ciudad de Valencia, le ha causado la eleccion de Corrector General de todo el Orden de los Minimos . . . a favor del Rmo V. Castrillo, *etc.* 1788. 4º. **4866. b. 23.**

—— Vita del Beato Giovanni de Ribera, Patriarca di Antiochia, *etc.* [With a portrait.] pp. 165. *Roma*, 1797. 4º. **4866. g. 18.**

CASTRILLO (VINCENZO) *See* CASTRILLO (Vicente)

CASTRILLO HERNÁNDEZ (GONZALO) *See* ELÚSTIZA (J. B. de) and CASTRILLO HERNÁNDEZ (G.) Antología Musical, *etc.* 1933. 4º. **M.F.1176.cc.**

—— Estudio sobre el Canto Popular Castellano, *etc.* [With musical notes.] pp. ix. xvi. 137. 4. *Palencia*, 1925. 8º. **07896. h. 10.**

CASTRILLON (ANTONIO) Oracion fúnebre panegyrica . . . con que la gratitud de la nobilisima ciudad de San Tiago de Queretaro sintiò la muerte de su . . . bienhechor el Sr. D. Juan Antonio de Urrutia, Arana, Guerrero y Davila . . . Marquès de la Villa del Villar de la Aguila, *etc.* [With a plate.] pp. 54. *México*, 1744. 4º. **4985. df. 6.**

CASTRILLÓN (F. E.) *See* AYOS. Los Dos Ayos. Comedia . . . Traducida P. D. F. E. C. [i.e. F. E. Castrillón], *etc.* 1808. 4º. **1342. e. 6. (2.)**

—— *See* ROJAS ZORRILLA (F. de) Abre el Ojo . . . Comedia . . . refundida por F. E. Castrillon. 1814. 4º. **1342. e. 6. (46.)**

CASTRILLÓN (F. E.)

—— See SORDO. El Sordo en la Posada. Drama en dos actos en verso. Traducido del frances . . . por D. F. E. C. [i.e. F. E. Castrillón.] 1808. 4º.   **1342. e. 6. (1.)**

—— See SUEÑO. El Sueño . . . Nueva traduccion en verso. Por D. F. E. Castrillon. 1808. 4º.   **1342. e. 6. (45.)**

—— Teatro de D. F. E. Castrillon. 2 tom.

> tom. 1. El Distraido, comedia en dos actos: escrita en francés por Regnard y traducida . . . por D. F. E. Castrillon.
> La Dorotea, comedia original en tres actos.
> El Reconciliador, comedia en tres actos escrita en francés por el C. Demoystier, y traducida . . . por D. F. E. Castrillon.
> tom. 2. Marica la del Puchero, comedia en tres actos, refundida por D. F. E. Castrillon.
> El Opresor de su Familia, comedia en quatro actos. Traducida del francés.
> Aviso a los Casados, comedia en tres actos.
> Mentira contra Mentira, comedia original en dos actos.

Madrid, 1804, o8. 8º.   **11725. a. 17.**

—— Al Patriotismo y Valor de los Defensores de Fernando y la España. [In verse.] pp. 14. [*Madrid*, 1810?] 4º.   **11451. bbb. 6. (3.)**

—— Defensa de Valencia y Castigo de Traydores. Comedia . . . en quatro actos. [In verse.] pp. 30.   *Madrid*, [1810?] 4º.   **1444. e. 7. (11.)**

—— El Divorcio por Amor. Comedia en tres actos, en verso, *etc.* pp. 31. *Madrid*, 1808. 4º.   **1342. e. 6. (34.)**

—— Las Quatro Columnas del Trono Español, opereta alegórica . . . en celebridad de los dias de . . . Fernando vij., *etc.* pp. 23. *Cádiz*, [1809.] 4º.   **11725. ee. 8. (5.)**

CASTRILLON (FRANCISCO ORUETA Y) successively *Bishop of Truxillo* and *Archbishop of Lima. See* ORUETA Y CASTRILLON.

CASTRILLON (JUAN DE) *See* CASTILLO DE BOBADILLA (G.) El Licenciado Castillo de Bobadilla . . . y el Concejo y vezinos de la villa de Navia, y J. de Castillon . . . con L. de Miranda, *etc.* 1604. fol.   **1322. l. 6. (3.)**

CASTRILLÓN (MANUEL FREIRE)   *See* FREIRE (CASTRILLÓN (M.)

CASTRILLON (SEBASTIAN DE) Sermon septimo que predicò en las fiestas de San Francisco de Borja el R. Padre Fr. S. de Castrillon, *etc. See* MEXICO. [*Jesuits.*] Festivo aparato, *etc.* 1672. 4º.   **C. 63. b. 36.**

CASTRILLO TARDAJOS (SALVADOR) La Huelga Laboral. Contribución al estudio de la huelga laboral como institución jurídico-social, *etc.* pp. 176. *Santander*, 1935. 8º.   **05385. ee. 11.**

CASTRILLO Y SANTOS (JUAN) Ante el Drama de la Reforma Constitucional. pp. 236. *Madrid*, 1935. 8º.   **08042. aa. 34.**

—— Apuntes para la Historia de la Ruina de España. pp. 94. *Madrid*, 1919. 8º.   **8042. h. 10.**

—— Cuatro Años de Experiencia Republicana 1931–1935. pp. 318. *Madrid*, 1935. 8º.   **8042. k. 28.**

—— La Orientación de la República. pp. 205. *Madrid*, 1933. 8º.   **08042. a. 49.**

—— Revolución en España, *etc.* pp. 244.   *Buenos Aires*, 1938. 8º.   **9180. r. 15.**

CASTRIMENIANO (NEVALCO) *pseud.* [i.e. GIUSEPPE ERCOLANI.] Rime. 1717. *See* ROME.—*The City.— Arcadia.* Rime degli Arcadi, *etc.* tom. 5, 7. 1716, *etc.* 8º.   **240. k. 8, 10**

CASTRINGIUS (LUDOVICUS) Dissertatio inauguralis obstetricio-chirurgica de rationibus sectionem caesaream in usum vocandi, *etc.* pp. 63. *Jenae*, 1791. 8º.   **T. 637. (14.)**

CASTRINGIUS (LUDOVICUS) and **STUCKE** (CASPAR HEINRICH)

—— Ueber den Schwelmer Gesundbrunnen. pp. 248.   *Dortmund*, 1800. 8º.   **1171. i. 32.**

CASTRIOT (GEORGE) *Prince of Epirus*, called *Scanderbeg. See* GEORGE [Castriota], *Prince, etc.*

CASTRIOTA (CASSANDRA) *Marchioness d'Atripalda. See* SANNAZARO (J.) [*Italian Works.*] Un Divorzio ai tempi di Leone x., *etc.* [Letters of Sannazaro on the divorce of C. Castriota.] 1887. 8º.   **10909. ccc. 26.**

CASTRIOTA (PIER LUIGI) Accademia in occasione delle pubbliche feste per la fausta nascita del Real Primogenito di sua Maestà Siciliana [i.e. Charles Joseph Titus, son of Ferdinand I., King of the Two Sicilies] rappresentata da' Signori Convittori del Collegio Reale delle Scuole Pie di Puglia sotto la direzione del P. P. L. Castriota. (Prefazione del Signor D. Basilio Fiore.) pp. 48. *Napoli*, 1775. 4º.   **10600. bbb. 9. (1.)**

CASTRIOTA CARRAFA (GIOVANNA) *Duchess di Nocera. See* MONTI (S. de') Rime et versi in lode della . . . Dna G. Castriota Carrafa, *etc.* 1585. 4º.   **11426. d. 50.**

CASTRIOTA SCANDERBECH, *Family of.*

—— *See* PADIGLIONE (C.) Di Giorgio Castriota Scanderbech e de' suoi discendenti, *etc.* 1879. 4º.   **10606. g. 13.**

CASTRIOTA SCANDERBECH (GIORGIO) *Prince of Epirus. See* GEORGE [Castriota], *Prince of Epirus*, called *Scanderbeg.*

CASTRIOTA SCANDERBEG (FEDERICO) Difesa del Cagliari presso la Commissione delle Prede e de' Naufragi. [Signed: F. Castriota, Genno Damora, Raffe Damora. With an appendix of documents.] 2 pt.   [*Naples*, 1858.] 4º.   **6825. f. 14.**

—— Parere . . . nella causa del March. Gio. Pietro Campana. *See* CAMPANA (G. P.) *Marquis de Cavelli.* Pareri di celebri giureconsulti, *etc.* [1858?] 4º.   **5326. g. 19.**

CASTRIOTO (FELIX ANTONIO) *See* PERIODICAL PUBLICATIONS.—*Lisbon.* Jornal enciclopedico . . . destinado para instrucção geral, *etc.* [July 1779 edited by F. A. Castrioto.] 1779, *etc.* 8º.   **P.P.1419.d.**

CASTRIOTO (JORGE) *Prince of Epirus*, called SCANDERBEG. *See* GEORGE [Castriota], *Prince, etc.*

CASTRIOTTO, *Prince of Albania. See* ZANNOWICH (S.) calling himself CASTRIOTTO, *Prince of Albania.*

CASTRIOTTO (GEORGE) *Prince of Epirus*, called *Scanderbeg. See* GEORGE [Castriota], *Prince, etc.*

CASTRIOTTO (JACOMO FUSTO) *See* MAGGI (G.) Della fortificatione delle città, di M. Girolamo Maggi, e del capitan I. Castriotto, *etc.* 1564. fol.   **535. l. 19.**

CASTRIQUE (LOUIS J. A.) In the Privy Council. On appeal from the Royal Court of Appeal of the island of Malta. Between Louis J. A. Castrique, Appellant, and G. Buttigeig, Respondent. Case for Respondent. pp. 4. *Woodfall & Kinder: London*, [1855.] fol.   **1487.z.12.(1.)**

CASTRIQUE (Louis J. A.)

—— In the Privy Council. On appeal from the Royal Court of the island of Malta. Between Louis J. A. Castrique, Appellant; and Giuseppe Buttigieg, Respondent. Appendix. pp. 45. [*London*, 1855.] fol.
1487.z.12.(3.)

—— In the Privy Council. On appeal from the Royal Court of the island of Malta and its dependencies. Louis J. A. Castrique, Appellant; versus Giuseppe Buttigieg, Respondent. Appellant's case. pp. 2, [*London*, 1855.] fol. **1487.z.12.(2.)**

CASTRITIUS (Matthias) Matthiæ Castritij . . . De heroicis uirtutibus, memorabilibus factis, dictis & exemplis Principum Germaniæ, libri v. pp. 391. *Per I. Oporinum: Basileæ*, 1565. 8°. **1200. a. 5.**

CASTRIUM. *See* Campania, *Macedonia*.

CASTRO, *Tuscany*, Hieronymus, *Bishop of*. [1543–1574.] *See* Machabaeus.

——, Michael, *Bishop of*. [1469–1478?] *See* Canensius.

CASTRO, *Family of*. *See* Castro (C. de) Grundriss der Geschichte der Familie de Castro. 1934. 8°.
09915. d. 31.

——, *Family of, of the Pays de Waes*. *See* Sanchez de Castro, *Family of*.

CASTRO ( ) Correspondencia veridica entre dos amigos. [The letters signed " Castro " and " Nuñez," respectively.] [A political pamphlet.] pp. 20. [1811.] 4°. **636. g. 16. (4.)**

CASTRO (Bermudez de) *Licenciado*. *See* Bermudez de Castro.

CASTRO (Borja) *Doutor en Mathematicas*. *See* Borja Castro.

CASTRO (Ferreira de) *Novelist*. *See* Ferreira de Castro (J. M.)

CASTRO (A. M. Miranda e) *See* Miranda e Castro.

CASTRO (A. M. Simões de) *See* Simões de Castro (A. M.)

CASTRO (Abraham de) *See* Jashar, *Book of*. [Tōlĕdhōth Ādhām, commonly called Šĕpher hai-yāshār. In a Judæo-Spanish version by A. de Castro.] [1823.] 8°.
1955. b. 32.

CASTRO (Adolfo de) *See* Castro y Rossi.

CASTRO (Affonso de) As Possessões Portuguezas na Oceania. [With maps.] pp. xxi. 460. *Lisboa*, 1867. 8°. **10028. e. 25.**

CASTRO (Agnes de) *See* Castro (Inez de)

CASTRO (Agustin Angel) Carrera literaria y relacion de méritos del presbítero D. Agustin Angel Castro, *etc.* [An autobiographical sketch.] pp. 11. *México*, 1850. 8°. **10882. c. 30. (10.)**

CASTRO (Agustín María de)

—— Misioneros agustinos en el Extremo Oriente, 1565–1780. Osario venerable . . . Edición, introducción y notas por el P. M. Merino. pp. xl. 518. *Madrid*, 1954. 8°.
4768. ee. 14.
Biblioteca " Missionalica Hispanica." ser. B. vol. 6.

CASTRO (Alberto Osorio de) *See* Osorio de Castro.

CASTRO (Alejandro de) Apuntes y detalles que pueden ser útiles á quien escriba la historia de los acontecimientos en España desde 1873 hasta el dia. pp. 45. *Madrid*, 1877. 8°. **8042. g. 5. (4.)**

CASTRO (Alejandro Sánchez) *See* Sánchez Castro (A.)

CASTRO (Alfonso) Discursos Parlamentarios en los años de 1936–1937–1938. pp. 209. *Bogotá*, 1938. 8°.
012301. m. 6.

CASTRO (Alfonso de) *See* Castro (Alphonsus à)

CASTRO (Alfonsus de) *See* Castro (Alphonsus à)

CASTRO (Alfredo Carlos Franco de) *See* Franco de Castro.

CASTRO (Alonso Francisco Moreno y) *See* Moreno y Castro.

CASTRO (Alonso Nuñez de) *See* Nuñez de Castro.

CASTRO (Alóysio de)

—— Faculdade de Medicina do Rio de Janeiro. These apresentada . . . pelo Dr. A. de Castro . . . Das desordens da marcha e seu valor clinico, *etc.* pp. ix. 244. *Rio de Janeiro*, 1904. 4°. **7380. a. 5. (1.)**

CASTRO (Alphonsus à)

—— *See* Olarte (T.) Alfonso de Castro, *etc.* 1946. 8°.
10635. m. 16.

—— Opera . . . videlicet, Aduersus omnes hæreses lib. quatuordecim, De iusta punitione hæreticorum lib. tres, De potestate legis pœnalis lib. duo. [Edited by R. Trehetus.] coll. 1932. *Apud M. Sonnium: Parisiis*, 1571. fol. **472. f. 2.**

—— Opera . . . videlicet, Adversus omnes hæreses . . . De justa punitione hæreticorum . . . De potestate legis pœnalis . . . Super psalmum Miserere mei Deus homeliæ vigentiquinque . . . Super psalmum Beati quorum remissæ sunt iniquitates, vigintiquatuor . . . omnia ab auctore jam postremo . . . recognita, ac pluribus locis illustrata, *etc.* 2 tom. *Matriti*, 1773. fol. **L.16.c.5.**

—— Fr. Alfonsi de Castro . . . Aduersus omnes hereses lib. XIIII. In quibus recēsentur & reuincūtur omnes hereses quarum memoria extat, quę ab apostolorum tempore ad hoc vsqͩ seculum in ecclesia ortæ sunt. ff. ccxi. *Vęnundantur I. Badio & I. Roigny:* [*Paris*,] 1534. fol.
3835. g. 1.

—— [Another edition.] Nunc demum diligentius recogniti . . . Loca insuper aliquot in quibus D. Erasmi Rot. libri caute sunt legendi. (XXI. Articuli Anabaptistarum monasteriensium, per Doctorem Ioannem Cochleum confutati.) ff. ccxiii. *M. Nouesianus: Coloniæ*, 1539. fol.
C. 82. h. 10.

—— [Another edition.] Postremùm summa cura aucti & recogniti. ff. 177. *Apud A. Gyrault: Parisiis*, 1543. fol.
3845. a. 3.

—— [Another edition.] Opus hoc denuo ab auctore ipso recognitū est, & multis ab eo locis . . . auctum, *etc.* pp. 1231. *Ad signum spei: Venetiis*, 1546. 8°. **857. f. 1.**

—— [Another edition.] ff. 443. *Typis I. Withagij; in ædibus viduæ & hæredum I. Stelsij: Antuerpiæ*, 1565. fol.
3836. bb. 14.

—— Fr. Alphonsi de Castro . . . Aduersus omnes hæreses liber duodecimus. pp. 7. 1698. *See* Rocaberti (J. T. de) *Archbishop of Valencia*. Bibliotheca maxima pontificia, *etc.* tom. 2. 1698, *etc.* fol. **484. e. 1.**

CASTRO (Alphonsus à)

—— Questions préliminaires, pour servir d'introduction à l'Histoire des hérésies, tirées de l'ouvrage d'Alphonse de Castro. [A translation of " Adversus omnes haereses," lib. 1.] *See* Hermant (J.) Histoire des hérésies, *etc.* tom. 1. 1727, *etc.* 8º.　　　　　**4533. a. 7.**

—— Alphonsi à Castro . . . De impia sortilegarum, maleficarum, & lamiarum hæresi, earúmque punitione, opusculum. *See* Malleus. Malleus maleficarum, *etc.* tom. 2. pt. 2. 1669. 4º.　　　　　**719. i. 18.**

—— Fratris Alfonsi a Castro De iusta hæreticorum punitione libri tres, *etc.* ff. 226. *I. Giunta: Salmanticæ,* 1547. fol.　　　　　**697. l. 17.**

—— [Another edition.] Nunc recens accurate recogniti. ff. 367. *Ad signum spei: Venetiis,* 1549. 8º. **5063. a. 14.**

—— F. Alfonsi à Castro . . . De potestate legis pœnalis libri duo, *etc.* ff. 269.　　*A. de Portonariis: Salmanticæ,* 1551. fol.　　　　　**501. h. 4.**

—— Fr. Alfonsi a Castro . . . de Potestate Legis pœnalis, Libri duo. Opus hoc nunc denuò ab Autore ipso recognitum est, & multis locis ab eo emendatum, & locupletatum. Cum Indice copiosissimo, & Sacræ scripturæ Autoritatibus. ff. 324.　　　*In ædibus Viduæ & Hæredum Ioan. Stelsii: Antuerpiæ,* 1568. 8º.　　　　　**1472. a. 31.**
The last twenty leaves are mutilated.

—— Fratris Alfonsi a Castro . . . Homiliæ vigĩtiquattuor . . . super psalmũ, Beati quoꝗ remisse sunt iniquitates. [With the text.] ff. cxxxiiii. 1540. 8º.　*See* Bible.— *Psalms.—Selections.* [*Latin.—Single Psalms.—*xxxii. (31.)]
　　　　　　　　　　　C. 63. d. 26.

CASTRO (Alphonsus de) *See* Porta (S. de) Sermones . . . visi ꝫ emendati per fratrem A. de castro, *etc.* 1512. fol.　　　　　**C. 63. l. 10.**

CASTRO (Alvaro Gómez de) *See* Gómez de Castro.

CASTRO (Amador de) *See* Scott (*Sir* W.) *Bart.* [*Rob Roy.*] Rob Roy. Traducido . . . por D. A. de Castro. 1896. 8º.　　　　　**012613. ee. 1.**

CASTRO (Américo) *See* Bible. [*Spanish.*] Biblia Medieval Romanceada . . . Edición de A. Castro, A. Millares Carlo, *etc.* 1927, *etc.* 8º.　　　　**Ac. 2694. a.**

—— *See* Gómez de Quevedo Villegas (F.)　[*Works.*] Quevedo. [With an introduction by A. Castro.] 1911, *etc.* 8º.　　　　　**12231. b. 10.**

—— *See* Gómez de Quevedo Villegas (F.)　[*Separate Works.*] Historia de la Vida del Buscón . . . Prólogo y notas de A. Castro. [1919.] 8º.　**012200. k. 6/23.**

—— *See* Gómez de Quevedo Villegas (F.)　[*Separate Works.*] El Buscón . . . Nuevo texto, editado y comentado por A. Castro. 1927, *etc.* 8º.　**W.P. 9594.**

—— *See* Guevara (A. de) successively *Bishop of Guadix* and *of Mondoñedo.* El Villano del Danubio y otros fragmentos. With an introductory essay by A. Castro. 1945. 8º.
　　　　　　　　　　　Ac. 1833/11.

—— *See* Meyer-Luebke (W.) Introducción al estudio de la lingüística romance. Traduccion . . . por A. Castro. 1914. 8º.　[*Publicaciones de la Revista de Filología Española.* vol. 1.]　　　**Ac.145.b/9.**

—— *See* Molina (Tirso de) *pseud.* Obras. [vol. 1. With an introduction by A. Castro.] 1910, *etc.* 8º.
　　　　　　　　　　　W.P. 3734.

CASTRO (Américo)

—— *See* Rennert (H. A.) and Castro (A.)　Vida de Lope de Vega, *etc.* 1919. 8º.　　　　**10634. ee. 9.**

—— *See* Rojas Zorrilla (F. de)　Cada qual lo que le toca, y La Viña de Nabot. Publicadas por A. Castro. 1917. 8º. [*Teatro Antiguo Español.* vol. 2.]　　**Ac.-145. b/17.**

—— *See* Vega Carpio (L. F. de)　[*Plays.*]　Fuente Ovejuna . . . Edición . . . revisada por A. Castro. 1919. 8º.
　　　　　　　　　　　11726. a. 53.

—— *See* Vega Carpio (L. F. de)　[*Miscellaneous Works.*] La Dorotea . . . Edición de A. Castro. 1913. 8º.
　　　　　　　　　　　11725. bb. 18.

—— Aspectos del vivir hispánico. Espiritualismo, mesianismo, actitud personal en los siglos xiv al xvi. (Artículos publicados en la Revista de Filología Hispánica de Buenos Aires con el título de Lo hispánico y el erasmismo.) pp. 168. *Santiago de Chile,* 1949. 8º.　**12360. d. 41.**

—— El Enfoque histórico y la no hispanidad de los Visigodos. *In:* Nueva revista de filología hispánica. año. 3. no. 3. pp. 217–263. 1949. 8º.　　　　**Ac. 2693. ce.**

—— La Enseñanza del Español en España. pp. 108. *Madrid,* 1922. 8º.　　　　　**012942. a. 13.**

—— The Structure of Spanish History . . . Translated by Edmund L. King. (Based on España en su historia.) [With plates.] pp. xiii. 689.　*Princeton University Press: Princeton,* 1954. 8º.　　　　**9196. b. 26.**

—— Glosarios latino-españoles de la edad media. pp. lxxxvii. 378. *Madrid,* 1936. 8º. [*Revista de filología española.* anejo 22.]　　　**Ac. 145. c/5. (2.)**

—— Lengua, Enseñanza y Literatura. Esbozos. pp. 334. *Madrid,* 1924. 8º.　　　　　**012942. a. 16.**

—— La Peculiaridad Lingüística Rioplatense y su sentido histórico. pp. 159. *Buenos Aires,* 1941. 8º.
　　　　　　　　　　　12943. c. 33.

—— El Pensamiento de Cervantes. pp. 406.　　*Madrid,* 1925. 8º. [*Revista de Filología Española.* Anejo 6.]
　　　　　　　　　Ac.145.c/5.(2.)

—— Santa Teresa y otros ensayos, *etc.* pp. 278. *Santander,* 1929. 8º.　　　　　**4830. ff. 22.**

CASTRO (Américo) and **ONÍS** (Federico de)

——　　　　　　　　　 Fueros Leoneses de Zamora, Salamanca, Ledesma y Álba de Tormes. Edición y estudio de A. Castro y F. de Onís. 1. Textos. pp. 339. 1916. 8º.　*See* Madrid.—*Junta para Ampliación de Estudios e Investigaciones Científicas.—Centro de Estudios Históricos.*　　　　　**9181. v. 9.**

CASTRO (André de Mello de)　*See* Mello de Castro.

CASTRO (André Meyrelles de Tavora do Canto e) *See* Meyrelles de Tavora do Canto e Castro.

CASTRO (Andrés Máspero)　*See* Máspero Castro.

CASTRO (Angel Molina y)　*See* Molina y Castro.

CASTRO (Anjel Maria Morales)　*See* Morales Castro.

CASTRO (Antonio)　*See* Castro Leal.

CASTRO (Antonio de) *Colonel.* Proclama del Sr. Coronel Castro á los leales soldados del numero Cuatro de Caballeria del Ejercito Libertador.　*Mexico,* [1823.] *s. sh.* fol.　　　　**9770. k. 6. (173.)**

CASTRO (ANTONIO DE) *Dramatist*. *See* CASTRO (Pedro A. de)

CASTRO (ANTONIO DE) *Jesuit*. Fisonomia de la Virtud, y del Vicio al natural, sin colores, ni artificios. pt. 1. pp. 392. *I. de Rueda: Valladolid*, 1676. 4º.
1232. c. 36.
Imperfect; wanting pt. 2, published at Burgos in 1678. Slightly mutilated.

CASTRO (ANTONIO DE) *Licenciado*. Allegationes Canonicæ, cum suis decissionibus [*sic*] . . . in lucem æditis, et nouiter auctis per Dom Ioannem de Castro Gallego, *etc.* pp. 448. *B. de Villa-Diego: Matriti*, 1689. fol.
5035. h. 5.

—— Informacion en derecho, sobre ciertas nulidades que tuuo el Capitulo Prouincial de Lima, del orden de Nuestra Señora de la Merced, que se celebrò à siete de Setiembre de 1643. ff. 6. [*Madrid*, 1644?] fol. 4783. e. 1. (6.)

—— Por Don Ioseph de Saauedra, Marques de Ribas. Con Doña T. M. Arias de Saauedra, Marquesa de Malagon. Sobre el condado de Castellar. [By A. de Castro.] ff. 14. [1650?] fol. *See* RAMIREZ DE SAAVEDRA Y ULLOA (J.) *Marquis de Rivas*. 1322. k. 15. (23.)

CASTRO (ANTONIO MANUEL LOPES VIEIRA DE) *See* LOPES VIEIRA DE CASTRO.

CASTRO (ANTONIO MARTÍNEZ DE) *See* MARTÍNEZ DE CASTRO.

CASTRO (ANTONIO PEDRO)

—— *See* SARMIENTO (B.) Rasgos de la vida de Domingo F. Sarmiento. Por su hermana Bienvenida. Advertencia y biografia de A. P. Castro, *etc.* 1946. 8º. [*Publicaciones del Museo Histórico Sarmiento.* ser. 2. no. 14.]
Ac. 1900. e. (4.)

—— *See* SARMIENTO (D. F.) *President of the Argentine Republic*. " Diario de gastos " . . . Estudio y ordenamiento por Antonio P. Castro. 1950. 8º. [*Publicaciones del Museo Histórico Sarmiento.* ser. 4. no. 2.] Ac. 1900. e.

—— *See* SARMIENTO (D. F.) *President of the Argentine Republic*. [Discurso presentado para su recepción en el Instituto Istórico de Francia.] Sarmiento en el Instituto Histórico de Francia. Discurso sobre San Martín y Bolívar . . . Estudio y ordenamiento por Antonio P. Castro. 1951. 8º. [*Publicaciones del Museo Histórico Sarmiento.* ser. 4. no. 3.] Ac. 1900. e.

—— *See* SARMIENTO (D. F.) *President of the Argentine Republic*. Epistolario entre Sarmiento y Posse . . . Aclaraciones y biografia por A. P. Castro. 1946, etc. 8º. [*Publicaciones del Museo Histórico Sarmiento.* ser. 5. no. 1 Ac. 1900. e.

—— *See* SARMIENTO (D. F.) *President of the Argentine Republic*. Sarmiento visita a Urquiza . . . Correspondencia inédita. [Edited by A. P. Castro.] 1953. 8º.
10899. de. 11.

—— Las Bibliotecas del Museo Sarmiento. Reseña e índice de su contenido. Estudio y ordenamiento por A. P. Castro. [With illustrations.] pp. 27. *Buenos Aires*, 1946. 8º. [*Publicaciones del Museo Histórico Sarmiento.* ser. 1. no. 3.] Ac. 1900. e. (1.)

—— Nueva historia de Urquiza, industrial, comerciante y ganadero. 4ª edición corregida y aumentada. pp. 124. *Buenos Aires*, 1953. 8º. 10899. de. 10.

—— Salas Belin Sarmiento inauguradas el 29 de setiembre de 1945 en el Museo Histórico Sarmiento. Discurso, *etc.* [A biographical study of Augusto Belin Sarmiento. With illustrations, including a portrait.] pp. 29. *Buenos Aires*, 1945. 8º. [*Publicaciones del Museo Histórico Sarmiento.* ser. 2. no. 13.] Ac. 1900. e. (3.)

35-5*

CASTRO (ANTONIO PEDRO)

—— San Martín y Sarmiento. Conferencia, *etc.* [With illustrations, including a portrait and facsimiles.] pp. 64. *Buenos Aires*, 1947. 8º. [*Publicaciones del Museo Histórico Sarmiento.* ser. 2. no. 16.] Ac. 1900. e. (5.)

—— San Martín y Sarmiento. Conferencia . . . 2ª edición corregida y aumentada. [With plates, including a portrait of Sarmiento, and a map.] pp. 67. *Buenos Aires*, 1950. 8º. [*Publicaciones del Museo Histórico Sarmiento.* ser. 2. no. 19.] Ac. 1900. e.

—— Tres capítulos en la vida de Urquiza, *etc.* pp. 35. *Concordia, Entre Rios*, 1945. 8º. 10899. aa. 7.

CASTRO (ANTONIO PORRUA Y FERNÁNDEZ DE) *See* PORRUA Y FERNÁNDEZ DE CASTRO.

CASTRO (ANTONIO THOMAS DA SILVA LEITÃO E) *Bishop of Angola and the Congo*. *See* SILVA LEITÃO E CASTRO.

CASTRO (ANTONIUS DE) Impugnatoriū . . . cōtra Wesselum. *See* WESSEL (Joannes) *Gansfortius*. Wesseli Epistola aduersus M. Engelbertum Leydensem, *etc.* [1522.] 4º. 477. a. 41. (2.)

CASTRO (AUGUSTO DE)
Full name: AUGUSTO DE CASTRO SAMPAIO CÔRTE REAL.

—— Imagens da Europa vista da minha janela. [On twentieth century European problems.] pp. 168. *Lisboa*, 1936. 8º. 012359. de. 30.

CASTRO (AUGUSTO MENDES SIMÕES DE) *See* MENDES SIMÕES DE CASTRO (A.)

CASTRO (AUGUSTO OLYMPIO VIVEIROS DE) *See* VIVEIROS DE CASTRO.

CASTRO (AURELIO RUIZ) *See* RUIZ CASTRO.

CASTRO (BALTAZAR ORÓBIO DE) *See* ORÓBIO DE CASTRO (B.)

CASTRO (BARTHOLOMAEUS DE) Oratio ad Vrbanum VIII Pont. Max. cum Philippi IV Catholici Regis nomine . . . D. Fernandus Afan de Ribera, Alcalá Dux . . . eidem Summo Pontifici obedientiam prǫstaret. Habita . . . die 29. Iulij, anni 1625. (Responsio Ioannis Ciampoli.) pp. 15. *Typis I. Mascardi: Romæ*, 1625. 4º.
805. d. 46.

—— [Another edition.] pp. 15. *H. Meresius: Moguntiæ*, 1625. 4º. 697. f. 46.

CASTRO (BARTOLOME DE) *Begin*. El Capitan Bartolome de Castro dize, *etc.* [A memorial of Castro's services in the Spanish Navy.] [1645?] *s. sh.* fol.
1324. i. 2. (114.)

CASTRO (BENEDICTUS À) *See also* CASTELLUS (Philotheus) *pseud.* [i.e. B. à Castro.]

—— Disputatio medica de apoplexia, *etc.* Praes. A. E. Vorstius. *Ex officina Z. Smetii: Lugduni Batavorum*, 1621. 4º. 1185. g. 2. (13.)

—— Benedicti à Castro . . . Monomachia, sive Certamen medicum, quo verus in febre synocho putrida cum cruris inflammatione medendi usus per venæ sectionem in brachio demonstratur, *etc.* pp. 88. *Typis J. Rebenlini: Hamburgi*, 1647. 4º. 551. b. 47.

CASTRO (BENITO DE) *Begin*. En la pretension que el Estado Eclesiastico destos Reynos de Castilla y Leon tiene, de que la nueua declaracion hecha por Clemente Octauo . . . para que contribuyan en la gracia del subsidio de las galeras las capellanias amouibles ad nutū, como las perpetuas collatiuas, *etc.* ff. 8. [1640?] fol.
1322. k. 14. (5.)

CASTRO (Benito de)

—— *Begin.* En el pleyto de Subsidio, entre el Rector y Colegio de la Compañia de Iesus, de la ciudad de Palencia, con el Dean y Cabildo y Clero de la santa yglesia de la dicha ciudad y su obispado. Por parte de los dichos Dean, Cabildo y Clero, *etc.* ff. 19. ms. notes.
[1630?] fol. **1322. k. 14. (27.)**

CASTRO (Bento de Oliveira Cardoso e) *Viscount de Villa-Moura.* See Oliveira Cardoso e Castro.

CASTRO (Bento Madeyra de) *See* Madeyra de Castro.

CASTRO (Bernardo Jozé d'Abrantes e) *See* Abrantes e Castro.

CASTRO (C.) *Mexican Artist. See* Decaen (J.) México y sus Alrededores. Coleccion de monumentos, trajes y paisajes dibujados al natural y litografiados por . . . C. Castro, *etc.* 1855, *etc.* fol. **1780. b. 13.**

CASTRO (C. de) *Ingegnere capo nel R. Corpo delle Miniere.* Descrizione geologico-mineraria della zona argentifera del Sarrabus, Sardegna . . . Con . . . una carta, *etc.*
pp. x. 68. pl. vi. *Roma,* 1890. 8°. [*Memorie descrittive della carta geologica d'Italia.* vol. 5.] **07106. k.**

—— Le Miniere di mercurio del Monte Amiata, *etc.*
pp. 203. pl. xv. *Roma,* 1914. 8°. [*Memorie descrittive della carta geologica d'Italia.* vol. 16.] **07106. k.**

CASTRO (C. de) *Ingegnere capo nel R. Corpo delle Miniere,* and **PILOTTI** (C.)
—— I Giacimenti di lignite della Toscana.
pp. viii. 216. pl. xix. *Roma,* 1933. 8°. [*Memorie descrittive della carta geologica d'Italia.* vol. 23.] **07106. k.**

CASTRO (Carlos de) Grundriss der Geschichte der Familie de Castro. [With illustrations.] pp. 23.
[*Berlin,*] 1934. 8°. **09915.d.31.**

CASTRO (Carlos Bermudez de) *See* Bermudez de Castro.

CASTRO (Carlos J. Larraín de) *See* Larraín de Castro.

CASTRO (Carlos María de) Apuntes acerca de los Empedrados de Madrid, *etc.* pp. 96. pl. 12. *Madrid,* 1857. 8°. [*Revista de Obras Publicas.* tom. 2.]
P.P. 1803. s.

CASTRO (Carlos Pereira de) *See* Pereira de Castro.

CASTRO (Carmen)
—— Marcel Proust, o el vivir escribiendo. pp. 157. *Madrid,* 1952. 8°. **11869. ff. 34.**

CASTRO (Catarino) Honduras en la prima centuria. Nuestra vida política, diplomática, militar y cultural de los primeros cien años, 1821–1921, *etc.* [With plates.] pp. 129. *Tegucigalpa,* 1921. 8°. **9773. g. 3.**

CASTRO (Christophorus de) *See* Bible.—*Minor Prophets.* [*Latin.*] R.P. Christophori Castri . . . Commentariorum in duodecim prophetas libri duodecim, *etc.* 1615. fol. **L.17.f.1.**

—— *See* Bible.—*Jeremiah.* [*Latin.*] R. Patris Christophori a Castro . . . Commentariorum in Ieremiæ prophetias, Lamentationes, et Baruch, libri sex, *etc.* 1609. fol.
L.17.c.9.

—— Historia Deiparæ Virginis Mariæ, ad veritatem collecta et veterum patrum testimoniis comprobata, *etc.*
pp. 433 [734]. *Typis B. Liffij ; sumptibus Z. Palthenij : Moguntiæ,* 1610. 8°. **861. d. 6.**

CASTRO (Christophorus de)

—— [Another edition.] 1862. *See* Bourassé (J. J.) Summa aurea de laudibus beatissimæ Virginis Mariæ, *etc.* tom. 2. 1862, *etc.* 4°. **4807. f. 12.**

CASTRO (Cipriano) *President of Venezuela.* [For official documents issued by Cipriano Castro as President of the Venezuelan Republic.] *See* Venezuela.—Castro (C.) *President.*

—— *See* Guerrero (E. C.) Campaña Heroica. Estudio histórico-militar de la campaña dirigida en Venezuela por el general Cipriano Castro . . . en 1899. 1903. 8°.
9771. df. 28.

—— *See* Tello Mendoza (R.) Complemento. (Todas las peripecias del General C. Castro.) 1903. 8°. **8180. l. 7.**

—— *See* Tello Mendoza (R.) Viaje del general Cipriano Castro . . . en Abril y Mayo de 1905. [With a portrait.] 1905. fol. **10880. i. 18.**

—— Comentarios a los mensajes del general Cipriano Castro. Homenaje de justicia al restaurador de Venezuela, *etc.* pp. 36. *Caracas,* 1905. 8°. **8180. f. 57.**

—— Documentos del General Cipriano Castro. vol. 4. *Caracas,* 1905. 8°. **10899. d. 3.**
Imperfect ; wanting all other volumes.

CASTRO (Claudio Corrêa e) *See* Corrêa e Castro (C.)

CASTRO (Cristóbal de) *Historical Writer. See* Castro Gutiérrez (C. de)

CASTRO (Cristóbal de) *Vicario del Monasterio de Santo Domingo de Chincha,* and **ORTEGA MOREJÓN** (Diego de) Relaçion y declaraçion del modo que este valle de Chincha y sus comarcanos se governavan antes que oviese Yngas y despues que los vuo hasta que los christianos entraron en esta tierra, 1558. (Bearbeitet von Wilhelm Petersen.) *Span. & Ger. See* Trimborn (H.) Quellen zur Kulturgeschichte des präkolumbischen Amerika, *etc.* [1936.] 8°. [*Studien zur Kulturkunde.* Bd. 3.] **Ac. 659.**

CASTRO (Cristóbal Martínez de) *See* Martínez de Castro.

CASTRO (Curt de)

—— *See* Mattsson (A.) Untersuchungen zur Epigrammsammlung des Agathias. [Translated by C. de Castro.] 1942. 8°. **11313. g. 60.**

CASTRO (Damaso Calbo y Rochina de) *See* Calbo y Rochina de Castro.

CASTRO (Damian Antonio de Lemos Faria e) *See* Lemos Faria e Castro.

CASTRO (David de) Vislumbres. [Poems.] pp. 305. *Porto,* 1876. 8°. **11452. aaaa. 21.**

CASTRO (David Henriques de)

—— Keur van grafsteenen op de Nederl.-Portug.-Israël. begraafplaats te Ouderkerk aan den Amstel met beschrijving en biographische aanteekeningen. Met inleiding: Een en ander over deze en de vroegere begraafplaats der Nederl.-Portug.-Israël. gemeente te Amsterdam . . . Eerste bundel. (Auswahl von Grabsteinen, *etc.*) [The translator's preface signed : E. M. With a plan.]
Dutch & Ger. pp. xi. 125. pl. xv. *Leiden,* 1883. fol.
1707. c. 6.

No more published.

—— [Another copy.] Keur van grafsteenen, *etc.* *Leiden,* 1883. fol. **1941. d. 10.**

CASTRO (David Henriques de)

—— 1675–1875. De Synagoge der Portugeesch-Israelietische Gemeente te Amsterdam. Tot inleiding : Eenige geschiedkundige aanteekeningen betreffende de vroegere bedehuizen dezer gemeente. Een gedenkschrift, *etc.* pp. 66. lxxvii. *'s Gravenhage*, 1875. 8º.   **4516**. bb. **9.**

CASTRO (Diego de) Metodi per calcolare gli indici della criminalità. pp. 119. *Torino*, 1934. 8º. [*Università di Torino. Memorie dell'Istituto Giuridico.* ser. 2. no. 25.] Ac. **2308.**

—— Il Problema di Trieste. Genesi e sviluppi della questione giuliana in relazione agli avvenimenti internazionali, 1943–1952, *etc.* pp. xvi. 679. *Bologna*, 1953. 8º.   **9171.** c. **8.**

—— Trieste. Cenni riassuntivi sul problema giuliano nell'ultimo decennio. [With maps.] pp. xv. 236. *Bologna*, 1953. 8º.   **8033.** cc. **27.**

CASTRO (Diego Antonio Cernadas y) *See* Cernadas y Castro.

CASTRO (Diego di Sandoval di) *See* Sandoval di Castro.

CASTRO (Diego Lopez de) *See* Lopez de Castro.

CASTRO (Dinis de Mello de) *See* Mello de Castro.

CASTRO (Domingo de) *See* Periodical Publications.— *Madrid.* La Caza, *etc.* [Edited by D. de Castro.] 1866, *etc.* 8º.   P.P. **4092.** k.

CASTRO (E.) *See* Snell (Harold F. K.) and Castro (E.) First Spanish Course for Seniors, *etc.* [1934.] 8º.   **012942.** aa. **24.**

CASTRO (Eduardo de Sá Pereira de) *See* Sá Pereira de Castro.

CASTRO (Estevam Rodrigues de) *See* Rodrigues de Castro.

CASTRO (Eugénio de)

—— *See* Goethe (J. W. von) [*Selections.—German and Portuguese.*] Poesias de Gœthe. [Translated by E. de Castro.] 1931. 4º. [*Obras poéticas de E. de Castro.* vol. 7.]   **12233.** ff. **1/7.**

—— *See* Lopes de Sousa (P.) Diario da Navegação . . . Commentado por E. de Castro, *etc.* 1927. 8º.   **10482.** ff. **17.**

—— *See* Olivero (F.) Sull'opera poetica di Eugénio de Castro. 1950. 8º.   **11869.** r. **10.**

—— *See* Periodical Publications.—*Coimbra.* Arte . . . Directores E. de Castro & M. da Silva Gayo, *etc.* 1895, *etc.* 8º.   P.P. **4123.** ea.

—— *See* Ramos (F.) Eugénio de Castro e a Poesia Nova, *etc.* 1943. 8º.   **11865.** dd. **8.**

—— Oaristos. Horas, *etc.* (Versión castellana de Juan G. Olmedilla.) pp. xlvi. 155. *Madrid*, 1922. 8º.   **012352.** a. **17.**

—— Obras poéticas de Eugénio de Castro. [With portraits.] vol. 1–8.
   1. Oaristos. Horas. Silva. pp. 201.
   2. Interlúnio. Belkiss. Tirésias. pp. 218.
   3. Sagramor. pp. 224.
   4. Salomé. A Nereide de Harlém. O Rei Galaor. Saüdades do Céu. pp. 182.
   5. Constança. Depois da ceifa. A Sombra do quadrante. pp. 184.
   6. O Anel de Polícrates. A Fonte do sátiro. pp. 180.
   7. Poesias de Gœthe. O Filho pródigo. O Cavaleiro das mãos irresistíveis. pp. 167.
   8. Camaféus romanos. A Tentação de S. Macário. Canções desta negra vida. pp. 183.

Lisboa, 1927–40. 8º.   **12233.** ff. **1.**
Printed on blue paper. Imperfect ; wanting vol. 9, 10 ;

CASTRO (Eugénio de)

—— Ao Divino Joño de Deus. *In :* Deus (J. de) Poesias. pp. 7–14. 1896. 8º.   **11453.** e. **56.**

—— Belkiss, Rainha de Sabá, d'Axum e do Hymiar. [A drama.] pp. 204. *Coimbra*, 1894. 8º.   **11728.** aa. **8.**

—— Belkiss . . . Traduzione dal portoghese di Vittorio Pica, preceduta da un saggio critico. [With a portrait.] pp. xliv. 208. *Milano*, 1896. 12º.   **11728.** de. **4.**

—— A Caixinha das cem conchas. pp. 36.   *Lisboa*, 1923. 8º.   **11453.** ee. **6.**

—— Camafeus romanos. pp. 92. *Lisboa*, 1921. 8º.   **11453.** ee. **7.**

—— Canções desta Negra Vida. pp. 120. *Coimbra*, 1922. 8º.   **011451.** ff. **33.**

—— Cartas de torna-viagem . . . Primeiro volume. pp. 308. *Lisboa*, 1925. 8º.   **11869.** aa. **37.** *Wanting all after vol. 1.*

—— Chamas duma caudeia velha. pp. 120.   *Lisboa*, 1925. 8º.   **11453.** ee. **8.**

—— Cravos de Papel. pp. 154. *Coimbra*, 1922. 8º.   **011451.** ff. **31.**

—— Descendo a encosta. pp. 162. *Lisboa*, 1924. 8º.   **11453.** ee. **9.**

—— Éclogas. pp. 46. *Lisboa*, 1929. 8º.   **11453.** ee. **32.**

—— Geographia Linguistica e Cultura Brasileira. Ensaio. pp. 277. *Rio de Janeiro*, 1937. 8º.   **10482.** i. **20.**

—— Guia de Coimbra . . . Publicação oficial da Sociedade de Defesa e Propaganda de Coimbra. [With plates and a map.] pp. 103. *Coimbra*, [c. 1910.] 8º.   **10163.** de. **21.**

—— Interlunio. Poesias. pp. 74. *Coimbra*, 1894. 8º.   **11452.** bbb. **13.**

—— O Melhor retrato de João de Deus. [With a portrait.] pp. 14. *Lisboa*, 1906. 8º.   **10635.** m. **26.**

—— Sagramor. Poema. pp. 126. *Coimbra*, 1895. 8º.   **11726.** i. **10.**

—— Salomé y otros poemas. Traducción en verso de Francisco Villaespesa. Con un estudio-prólogo de Rubén Darío. pp. 167. *Madrid*, 1914. 8º.   **011451.** ee. **75.**

—— La Sombra del Cuadrante . . . Traducción de Francisco Villaespesa. pp. 111. *Madrid*, [1916.] 8º.   **011451.** f. **70.**

—— A Tentação de São Macário. pp. 58.   *Lisboa*, 1922. 8º.   **11453.** ee. **10.**

—— Tiresias. Ecloga. pp. 14. *Coimbra*, 1895. 8º.   **011451.** eee. **12. (2.)**

CASTRO (Eugenio Díaz) *See* Díaz Castro (E.)

CASTRO (Ezechiele di) afterwards (Petrus à)

—— ————   *See* Ponce de Santa Cruz (A.) De impedimentis magnorum auxiliorum in morborum curatione lib. iii. . . . Secundis curis emendatiores è Museo Petri à Castro. 1652. 12º.   **774.** a. **23.**

CASTRO (Ezechiele di) afterwards (Petrus à)

—— Amphitheatrum medicum, in quo morbi omnes quibus imposita sunt nomina ab animalibus raro spectaculo debellantur . . . Liber primus. pp. 52. *Apud F. Rubeum: Veronæ,* 1646. 8°.
544. c. 17.

—— Bibliotheca medici eruditi. pp. 78. *Typis I. B. Pasouati: Patauii,* 1654. 12°. 1168. a. 3.

—— [Another edition.] Nunc primum ab Andrea Pasta . . . recensita, atque aucta, *etc.* pp. 164. *Bergomi,* 1742. 8°.
551. a. 23.

—— Il Colostro, discorso aggiunto alla Ricoglitrice di Scipion Mercurio, *etc.* pp. 31. *F. di Rossi: Verona,* 1642. 4°. [Mercurio (S.) *La Commare, o Raccoglitrice, etc.*] 778. g. 7.

—— [Another edition.] pp. 31. *F. de' Rossi: Verona,* 1645. 4°. [Mercurio (S.) *La Commare, o Raccoglitrice, etc.*] 1477. c. 22.

—— Petri à Castro . . . Febris maligna puncticularis aphorismis delineata. [Edited by J. G. Volckamer.] pp. 269. *Ex officinâ Endterorum Iun: Norimbergæ,* 1652. 12°.
1166. d. 19. (3.)

—— [Another edition.] [Edited by C. Moia.] pp. 256. *M. C. Bolzettæ impensis: Patauij,* 1653. 12°.
1168. a. 29. (1.)
The titlepage is engraved.

—— Ignis lambens, historia medica, prolusio physica, rarum pulchrescentis naturæ specimen, *etc.* pp. 198. *Apud F. Rubeum: Veronæ,* 1642. 8°. 774. c. 11.

—— Imber aureus, siue Chilias aphorismorum ex libris Epidemiων Hippocratis, eorumque doctissimis Francisci Vallesij Commentariis extracta, *etc.* pp. 203. *Typis Rubeanis: Veronæ,* 1652. 12°. 540. a. 36.

—— Pestis Neapolitana, Romana et Genuensis annorum 1656. & 1657. fideli narratione delineata et commentarijs illustrata. pp. 263. *Typis Rubeanis: Veronæ,* 1657. 12°.
1167. b. 8.

CASTRO (F. de) *Ayudante del Laboratorio de Investigaciones Biológicas, Madrid.* See Ramón y Cajal (S.) and Castro (F. de) Elementos de Técnica micrográfica del sistema nervioso. 1933. 8°. 07641. df. 19.

CASTRO (F. F.) Hannover. Jorge Federico Alejandro. *See* Herrero (J. B.) Reyes Contemporáneos, *etc.* 1854. tom. 3. 1855, *etc.* 4°. 9077. h. 12.

CASTRO (F. Pérez) *See* Pérez Castro.

CASTRO (F. Ramos de) *See* Ramos de Castro.

CASTRO (Farruco de) *See* Castro (Francisco de) *Actor.*

CASTRO (Federico de) *See* Castro y Fernández.

CASTRO (Felipe Fernández de) *See* Fernández de Castro.

CASTRO (Felippe Ferreira d'Araujo e) *See* Ferreira d'Araujo e Castro.

CASTRO (Fernanda de) *See* Ferro (A.) Salazar . . . Traduit . . . par F. de Castro, *etc.* 1934. 8°.
20009. f. 61.

—— *See* Oliveira Salazar (A. de) Une Révolution dans la paix. Traduction de F. de Castro, *etc.* 1937. 8°.
08042. aa. 42.

CASTRO (Fernanda de)

—— Mariazinha em África. Romance infantil. Nova versão. pp. 193. *Lisboa,* [c. 1940.] 8°. 12492. e. 9.
Biblioteca das crianças. no. 1.

—— Raiz funda. Romance. pp. 251. *Lisboa,* [1950?] 8°.
12492. bbb. 27.

—— Trinta e nove poemas. pp. 206. *Lisboa,* 1941. 8°.
011451. h. 77.
One of the " Edicões Ocidente."

CASTRO (Fernando de) *Historian.*

—— *See* Cervantes Saavedra (M. de) [*Don Quixote.—Spanish.—Abridgments.*] El Quijote de los Niños . . . Abreviado por un entusiasto de su autor [F. de Castro]. 1856. 8°. 12491. b. 22.

—— —— 1870. 8°. Cerv. 63.

—— —— 1885. 8°. Cerv. 69.

—— —— 1897. 8°. Cerv. 77.

—— *See* Cervantes Saavedra (M. de) [*Don Quixote.—Spanish.—Abridgments.*] El Quijote para Todos, abreviado y anotado por un entusiasta de su autor [F. de Castro]. 1856. 8°. 12491. d. 31.

—— *See* Dozy (R. P. A.) Historia de los Musulmanes Españoles . . . Traducida y anotada por F. de Castro. 1877. 8°. 9181. c. 8.

—— *See* Labra (R. M. de) Propagandistas y Educadores. D. Fernando de Castro, *etc.* 1888. 8°.
10604. e. 17. (3.)

—— *See* Zschokke (J. H. D.) La Noche de Santa Walpurgis, novela . . . traducida . . . por F. de Castro. 1855. 8°.
12552. h. 24.

—— Compendio razonado de historia general. (Continuado por D. Manuel Sales y Ferré.) 4 tom. *Madrid,* 1863–75. 8°. 9006. ccc. 8.

—— Discurso acerca de los caracteres históricos de la Iglesia Española, leido ante la Real Academia de la Historia . . . Segunda edicion. pp. 166. *Madrid,* 1866. 8°.
4867. b. 13.

—— *See* Torre y Velez (A. de la) El Discurso del Académico de la historia Señor Don F. Castro del 7 de Enero de este año, examinado á la luz de la sana doctrina, *etc.* 1866. 4°. 9006. ccc. 5.

—— Historia antigua, para uso de los institutos y colegios de segunda enseñanza . . . Segunda edicion corregida y mejorada. pp. xii. 128. *Madrid,* 1850. 8°.
9007. c. 35.

—— Historia de la edad media, para uso de los institutos y colegios de segunda enseñanza . . . Segunda edicion corregida y mejorada. pp. xv. 358. *Madrid,* 1850. 8°.
9007. c. 33.

—— Historia moderna, para uso de los institutos y colegios de segunda enseñanza . . . Segunda edicion corregida y mejorada. pp. xv. 288. *Madrid,* 1850. 8°. 9007. c. 34.

—— Historia profana general, y particular de España . . . Sexta edicion. [A revised edition of " Historia antigua," " Historia de la edad media," and " Historia moderna," together with a fourth section entitled " Historia de España."] pp. xxiv. 638. *Madrid,* 1859. 8°.
9007. b. 11.

—— [Another edition.] Sexta edicion, *etc.* pp. vii. 583. *Paris,* 1859. 12°. 9007. b. 10.

CASTRO (FERNANDO DE) *Theosophist.*

—— *See* BESANT (Annie) [*Single Works.*] Introdução ao Yoga . . . Tradução de F. de Castro. 1922. 8°.
4507. aa. 11.

—— *See* BESANT (Annie) [*Single Works.*] O Mundo de Amanhã. Tradução de F. de Castro. 1926. 8°.
4506. de. 40.

—— *See* BESANT (Annie) [*Selections.*] Conferências Teosóficas . . . Compilaçao e versão de F. de Castro. 1926. 8°.
4507. aa. 19.

—— *See* LEADBEATER (Charles W.) Os Servidores da Raça Humana Actual . . . Tradução de F. de Castro. 1926. 8°.
4505. g. 39.

CASTRO (FERNANDO ALVIA DE) *See* ALVIA DE CASTRO.

CASTRO (FERNANDO DE ANDRADE Y) *See* ANDRADE Y CASTRO.

CASTRO (FRANCISCO DE) *Actor.* Primera(—tercera) parte de Alegria comica explicada en diferentes assumptos jocosos. 3 pt. *Zaragoça,* 1702. 8°.
243. a. 9.

—— [Another edition.] Primera (segunda) parte de Alegria comica, *etc. Zaragoça,* 1702. 8°. **11725. aa. 12.**
Pt. 2 is another copy of pt. 2 of the preceding.

—— Libro nuevo de Entremeses, intitulado Cómico Festejo. tom. 1. *Madrid,* 1742. 8°. **11725. aa. 13.**
Imperfect ; wanting pp. 1–2 of tom. 1, and tom. 2 entitled " Chistes del gusto, por varios Ingenios."

—— Entremes de las Burlas del figonero. (Bayle nuevo de la batalla.) pp. 28. [1750 ?] 4°. **11726. e. 1. (6.)**

—— El Castigo de un Zeloso. Entremes. [By F. de Castro ? or J. J. Lopez de Castro ?] 1785. 8°. [*GARCÍA DE LA HUERTA* (*V. A.*) *Theatro Español.* pt. 4.] *See* CASTIGO.
243. b. 19.

—— [Another edition.] Entremes nuevo : El Castigo de un Zeloso. pp. 16. [1800 ?] 8°. *See* CASTIGO.
11725. aa. 2. (16.)

—— [Another copy.] Entremes nuevo : El Castigo de un Zeloso. [By F. de Castro, or J. J. López de Castro ?] [1800 ?] 8°. *See* CASTIGO. **11726. aa. 4. (14.)**

—— Entremes intitulado : De los quatro toreadores. [By F. de Castro.] [1840 ?] 8°. *See* TOREADORES.
11725. aa. 3. (43.)

—— Entremes de Francisco que tienes. [By F. de Castro.] pp. 8. [1770 ?] 8°. *See* FRANCISCO. **11725. aa. 1. (16.)**

—— Poesias varias, que en la soledad de su retraimiento escrivio F. de Castro, *etc. Madrid,* 1710. 4°.
8042. bbb. 60. (26.)

CASTRO (FRANCISCO DE) *Bishop of Guarda.*

—— *See* JOHN IV., *King of Portugal.* El-Rei Don João IV e a Inquisição. [Correspondence between the King and the Inquisitor General, F. de Castro. Edited by A. Baião. With plates, including portraits.] 1942. fol. [*Anais.* vol. 6.]
Ac. 6683. b/2.

—— Constituições synodaes do Bispado da Guarda [promulgated by F. de Castro], impressas por ordem do excellentissimo . . . senhor Bernardo Antonio de Mello Osorio, Bispo da Guarda . . . Terceira impressão. pp. 812. 1759. fol. *See* GUARDA, *Diocese of.* **5107. ff. 13.**

CASTRO (FRANCISCO DE) *Bishop of Guarda.*

—— Oraçoens funebres nas exequias que o Tribunal do Santo Officio fez ao . . . Bispo D. Francisco de Castro, Inquisidor Gèral, *etc.* [By Manoel Ferreira, Nuno da Cunha and Antonio Vel.] pp. 100. *Officina Craesbeckiana : Lisboa,* 1654. 4°. **851. k. 17. (4.)**

CASTRO (FRANCISCO DE) *Jesuit, of Mexico.* La Octava maravilla, y sin segundo milagro de Mexico, perpetuado en las Rosas de Guadalupe, y escrito heroycamente en octavas por el P. F. de Castro ; adjunta à las Espinas de la Passion del Hombre Dios, discurridas en el mismo metro por el P. Juan Carnero, *etc.* 2 pt. *Mexico,* 1729. 8°. **11451. a. 11.**

CASTRO (FRANCISCO DE) *Jesuit, of Ocaña.* Martyrium Petri Elcii . . . ex epistola P. F. de Castro . . . ex hispanico idiomate in latinum conuersa. *See* CAMPIAN (Edmund) Martyrium R. P. Edmundi Campiani, *etc.* 1582. 8°. **4903. c. 24.**

CASTRO (FRANCISCO DE) *Lector de Theologia en el Colegiu de S. Buenaventura de Sevilla.* Idea virtuosa, oracion funebre panegirica a las honrras, que celebro el venerable Orden Tercero de Penitencia de N. P. S. Francisco . . . a . . . Isabel de la Cruz, *etc.* pp. 26. *J. F. de Blas : Sevilla,* [1695.] 4°. **4865. dd. 20. (12.)**

CASTRO (FRANCISCO DE) *Poet. See* LOPEZ DE CASTRO (F. de P.)

CASTRO (FRANCISCO DE) *Rector del Hospital de Juan de Dios de Granada.* Historia de la vida y sanctas obras de Iuan de Dios, y de la institucion de su orden, y principio de su hospital. ff. 112. *R. Rabut : Granada,* 1588. 8°.
4866. a. 13.

—— Vita B. Ioannis a Deo . . . Item Petri Peccatoris, eiusdem ordinis religiosi . . . Latinitate donata ab Arnoldo de Raisse. pp. 215. *Typis I. de Fampoux : Duaci,* 1623. 12°. **1121. b. 14.**

—— Vita Beati Ioannis Dei Ordinis patrum curantium infirmos fundatoris et Statuta eiusdem . . . à Martino Serro . . . latino idiomate donata. Addita est Vita Sancti Ioannis Calibitæ (auctore Simone Metaphraste) . . . Vna cum summorum Pontificum testimonijs ac priuilegijs eidem ordini donatis. (Vita Petri Peccatoris.) pp. 254. *Typis W. Ederi : Ingolstadij,* 1625. 4°.
4827. c. 13.

—— Istoria della vita e opere sante di Giovanni di Dio . . . Tradotto . . . dal R. M. Gio. Francesco Bordini . . . Aggiuntoui in fine la Vita del beato Giouanni Calouita (scritta da Simeone Metafraste, tradotta dal Reu. Padre G. F. Bondini [*sic*].) ff. 91. *B. Grassi : Roma,* 1587. 8°.
4867. a. 17.

CASTRO (FRANCISCO DE) *Son of Estevam Rodrigues de Castro. See* RODRIGUES DE CASTRO (E.) Castigationes exegeticæ, *etc.* [Edited by F. de Castro.] 1640. fol.
539. i. 11. (2.)

—— *See* RODRIGUES DE CASTRO (E.) Stephani Roderici Castrensis . . . Medicæ consultationes. [Edited by F. de Castro.] 1644. 4°. **1165. f. 6.**

—— *See* RODRIGUES DE CASTRO (E.) D. Stephani Roderici Castrensis . . . Posthuma de causa continente disceptatio. [Edited by F. de Castro.] 1641. 8°. **775. b. 16. (1.)**

—— *See* RODRIGUES DE CASTRO (E.) D. Stephani Roderici Castrensis . . . Posthuma de epilepsia disceptatio. [Edited by F. de Castro.] 1640. 8°. **775. b. 16. (2.)**

CASTRO (Francisco de) *Son of Estevam Rodrigues de Castro.*

—— *See* Rodrigues de Castro (E.) D. Stephani Roderici Castrensis . . . Posthuma de plenitudine disceptatio. [Edited by F. de Castro.] 1641. 8°. **775. b. 16.** (4.)

—— *See* Rodrigues de Castro (E.) D. Stephani Roderici Castrensis . . . Posthuma de spiritibus disceptatio, *etc.* [Edited by F. de Castro.] 1641. 8°. **775. b. 16.** (3.)

—— *See* Rodrigues de Castro (E.) Pythagoras, *etc.* [Edited by F. de Castro.] 1651. 12°. **527. a. 9.** (2.)

—— *See* Rodrigues de Castro (E.) D. Stephani Roderici Castrensis . . . Syntaxis prædictionum medicarum, *etc.* [Edited by F. de Castro.] 1661. 4°. **545. g. 13.**

—— *See* Rodrigues de Castro (E.) D. S. Roderici Castrensis . . . Tractatus de natura muliebri, *etc.* [Edited by F. de Castro.] 1668. 4°. **1173. h. 1.** (1.)

—— Metamorfosis a lo moderno en varios epigrammas . . . con vna cancion del Chaos, y delas quatro edades del mundo, *etc.* pp. 101. *A. Maffi [Massi] y L. Landi : Florençia,* 1641. 8°. **11451. a. 10.**

CASTRO (Francisco Antonio de) Alcides alegorico. Idea, con que celebro la Escuela de estudiantes del Colegio de San Pablo de esta Ciudad de Burgos, la feliz victoria, que consiguieron las armas de . . . Phelipe Quinto . . . en los campos de Villa-Viciosa, *etc.* pp. 12. *Burgos,* [1710.] 4°. **T. 1303.** (37.)

—— Laureola sacra de la vida y martyrio del Venerable Padre Diego Luis de Sanvitores, primer apostol de las Islas Marianas, *etc.* [A poem.] pp. 236. *Madrid,* 1723. 8°. **1072. e. 24.**

CASTRO (Francisco de Cordova y) *See* Cordova y Castro.

CASTRO (Francisco de Mello de) *See* Mello de Castro.

CASTRO (Francisco de Paula Lopez de) *See* Lopez de Castro.

CASTRO (Francisco García y García de) *See* García y García de Castro.

CASTRO (Francisco Javier de) *See* Alba y Martín (R.) Memoria sobre el cólera morbo asiático . . . Tema . . . precedido de una introducción por D. F. J. de Castro. 1884. 8°. **7561. bb. 2.**

CASTRO (Francisco Paulo de Portugal e) *Marquis de Valença. See* Portugal e Castro.

CASTRO (Francisco Sanchez de) *See* Sanchez de Castro.

CASTRO (Franciscus de) *Plovacensis.* Della fondazione e storia dell'antica città di Plubium. *Lat. See* Genoa, *Republic of.*—Doria (N.) *Doge.* Testo ed illustrazione di un codice cartaceo del secolo xv, *etc.* 1859. 8°. **6835. c. 18.**

CASTRO (Franciscus de Caldas Pereyra et) *See* Caldas Pereyra et Castro.

CASTRO (Frederico Augusto Franco de) *See* Franco de Castro.

CASTRO (G. E. de) *See* Donoso Cortés (J. F. M. M. de la S.) *Marquis de Valdegamas.* Saggio sul cattolicismo, liberalismo e socialismo. Versione preceduta da un cenno sulla vita e le opere dell'autore di G. E. de Castro. 1854. 8°. **4051. c. 15.**

CASTRO (G. E. de)

—— *See* Donoso Cortés (J. F. M. M. de la S.) *Marquis de Valdegamas.* Essay on Catholicism, Liberalism and Socialism . . . To which is prefixed a sketch of the life and works of the author from the Italian of G. E. de Castro, *etc.* 1862. 8°. **3902. bbb. 30.**

CASTRO (Gabriel Pereira de) *See* Pereira de Castro.

CASTRO (Gaspar Martínez de) *See* Martínez de Castro.

CASTRO (Genoveva de)

—— Pájaro de barro. Poemas. pp. 60. *Caracas,* 1942. 16°. **11453. a. 16.**

CASTRO (Gentil José de) *See* Celso de Assis Figueiredo (A.) *Count.* Visconde de Ouro Preto, *etc.* [Containing a reprint of " O Assassinato do Coronel Gentil de Castro."] 1929. 8°. [*Revista do Instituto Historico e Geographico Brasileiro.* tom. 103.] **P.P. 3937.**

—— —— 1935. 8°. **010886. g. 28.**

CASTRO (Gerónimo Osorio de) *See* Osorio de Castro.

CASTRO (Gerónimo Perez de) *See* Perez de Castro.

CASTRO (Giacomo de) De l'inflammation des parties constituant l'articulation du genou, et du diagnostic différentiel des tumeurs de cette région ; thèse, *etc.* pp. 46. *Paris,* 1836. 4°. **1184. h. 2.** (7.)

CASTRO (Gil Lopez de Armesto y) *See* Lopez de Armesto y Castro.

CASTRO (Giovanni de) Arnaldo da Brescia e la rivoluzione romana del xii secolo, *etc.* pp. viii. 567. *Livorno,* 1875. 8°. **4605. aa. 3.**

—— La Caduta del Regno Italico. Narrazione desunta da testimonianze contemporanee e da documenti inediti o poco noti, *etc.* pp. 346. *Milano,* 1882. 8°. **9166. bbb. 23.**

—— Fulvio Testi e le corti italiane nella prima metà del xvii secolo, con documenti inediti, *etc.* pp. 268. *Milano,* 1875. 8°. **10631. bbb. 18.**

—— Milano e la Repubblica Cisalpina giusta le poesie, le caricature ed altre testimonianze dei tempi, *etc.* pp. 412. *Milano,* 1879. 8°. **8033. e. 3.**

—— Milano e le cospirazioni lombarde, 1814–1820, giusta le poesie, le caricature, i diari e altre testimonianze dei tempi, *etc.* pp. 448. *Milano,* 1892. 8°. **9165. bbb. 4.**

—— Milano nel settecento, giusta le poesie, le caricature e altre testimonianze dei tempi, *etc.* pp. 420. *Milano,* 1887. 8°. **11824. df. 39.**

—— Il Mondo secreto. [A history of secret societies.] 9 vol. *Milano,* 1864. 8°. [*Daelli (G.) Biblioteca nuova.*] **12226. aaa. 7.**

—— Patria, *etc. See infra :* Sommario della storia d'Italia, *etc.*

—— Patriottismo lombardo, 1818–1820. Notizie desunte da diari e testimonianze contemporanee. 1889. *See* Milan. —*Società Storica Lombarda.* Archivio storico lombardo. anno 16. fasc. 2. 1874, *etc.* 8°. **Ac. 6525.**

—— Piccola storia d'Italia dalle origini fino al 1870, *etc.* pp. 230. *Milano,* 1885. 8°. **9166. b. 25.**

—— I Popoli dell' antico Oriente. Sommario. 2 vol. *Milano,* 1878. 8°. **9055. bbb. 4.**

CASTRO (Giovanni de)

—— I Processi di Mantova e il 6 febbrajo 1853, *etc.* pp. 604. *Milano*, 1893. 8°. **9167**. f. **1**.

—— Proverbi italiani illustrati . . . Con un discorso di Niccoló Tommaseo. pp. xi. 238. *Milano*, 1858. 8°.
12304. c. **7**.

—— Sommario della storia d'Italia . . . ad uso delle scuole normali e techniche, *etc.* pt. 1. pp. 196. *Milano*, 1881. 8°. **9166**. c. **10**.
Imperfect ; wanting pt. 2 and 3.

—— [A reissue.] Patria. Sommario di storia nazionale dai tempi più antichi fino alla morte di Vittorio Emanuele ii. 3 pt. *Milano*, 1882. 8°. **9166**. bbb. **21**.

—— Storia d'Italia dal 1799 al 1814. pp. x. 326. *Milano*, 1881. 4°. [*VILLARI* (P.) Storia politica d'Italia. vol. 7.]
9167.1.1/4.

—— Storia di un cannone. Notizie sulle armi da fuoco . . . Con 33 incisioni. pp. 319. *Milano*, 1866. 8°.
8823. b. **40**.

—— La Storia nella poesia popolare milanese, tempi vecchi, *etc.* pp. 168. *Milano*, 1879. 8°. **11850**. l. **5**.

—— Teresa Confalonieri, con documenti inediti. 1893. *See* MILAN.—*Società Storica Lombarda.* Archivio storico lombardo. anno 20. fasc. 3. 1874, *etc.* 8°. Ac. **6525**.

—— Ugo Foscolo. [With a portrait.] pp. 86. *Torino*, 1863. 16°. [*I Contemporanei italiani.* pt. 62.]
10631. a. **58**. (2.)

—— Vecchie Utopie. Note, *etc.* pp. 312. *Milano*, 1895. 8°.
011824. g. **53**.

CASTRO (Giovanni di) *Viceroy of India. See* CASTRO (João de)

CASTRO (Guilherme Gilberto de) Variadissima Collecção de contos populares portuguezes, ou Curiosa escolha de vinte e cinco contos modernos colligidos dos melhores authores portuguezes que n'este genero teem escripto . . . Por G. G. de Castro. [By the editor and others.] 19 pt. *Porto*, 1887. 8°. **12430**. bbb. **13**.

CASTRO (Guillem de) *See* CASTRO Y BELLVIS (Guillén de)

CASTRO (Gulielmus à) *See* BORCHT (Willem van der)

CASTRO (Helder de)

—— A quem pertence Moçambique. [With illustrations and a map.] pp. 30. [*Lisbon ?* 1943 ?] *obl.* 8°.
8029. g. **1**. (18.)

CASTRO (Henrique de) Don Henriquez [*sic*] de Castro : or, the Conquest of the Indies. A Spanish novel. [By F. Loubayssin de la Marca.] Translated out of Spanish, by a person of honour. pp. 167. *R. Bentley : London*, 1692. 12°. [*Modern Novels.* vol. 6.] **12410**. c. **23**.

CASTRO (Henrique José de) Lauso : tragedia. pp. 107. *Lisboa*, 1790. 8°. **11726**. bb. **44**. (1.)

—— Priamo : tragedia. pp. 77. *Lisboa*, 1786. 8°.
11726. bb. **44**. (2.)

—— A Verdadeira rezão demonstrada como lei universal e base firme e unica de hum perfeito contrato social em vinte e duas cartas . . . escriptas em reposta a hum seu amigo, *etc.* 2 pt. *Lisboa*, 1824. 4°. **8406**. ff. **13**.

CASTRO (Henriquez de) *See* CASTRO (Henrique de)

CASTRO (Horacio de) Don Juan de Lanuza, Justicia Mayor de Aragón. pp. 183. *Madrid*, [1935.] 8°.
20010. e. **28**.

CASTRO (Ignacio de) Relacion de la fundacion de la Real Audiencia del Cuzco en 1788 y de las fiestas con que esta grande . . . ciudad celebró este honor. Escribela . . . I. de Castro . . . la saca a luz . . . Sebastian de la Paliza, *etc.* (Dissertatio de populorum regimine præstantissimo.) pp. 287. *Madrid*, 1795. 8°. **9930**. e. **31**.

CASTRO (Ilefonso de) Begin. A lo que V.S. dessea saber, que cosas sean en las que he visto reparar, y dificultar a cerca desta contribucion delos quinientos cuentos que pide su Magestad, y que salida he hallado yo a ellas, dire breuemente, *etc.* [A memorial, signed I. de Castro, answering the city of Seville's objections to this grant.] [*Seville?* 1597 ?] fol. Add. MS. **9936**. ff. **303, 304**.

CASTRO (Inez de) *See* ARAUJO (J. de) Bibliographia Inesiana. 1897. 8°. **11902**. e. **23**. (2.)

—— *See* ARAUJO (J. de) Ignês de Castro, notas de bibliographia, *etc.* 1897. 8°. **011900**. g. **13**. (3.)

—— *See* CORNIL (S.) Inès de Castro. Contribution à l'étude du développement littéraire du thème dans les littératures romanes, *etc.* 1952. 8°. [*Académie Royale de Belgique. Classe des lettres et des sciences morales et politiques. Mémoires. Collection in-8°.* tom. 47. fasc. 2.]
Ac. **985/4**. (1.)

—— *See* DOMINGUES (M.) Inês de Castro na vida de D. Pedro. Evocação histórica. 1953. 8°. **10635**. i. **39**.

—— *See* FERNANDES THOMAZ (A.) Ignez de Castro. Iconografia. História. Litteratura. 1880. 8°. **12356**. t. **44**.

—— *See* FIGUEIREDO (A. de) D. Pedro e D. Inês, *etc.* 1914. 8°. **9181**. bbb. **26**.

—— *See* LOPES VIEIRA (A.) Inês de Castro na poesia e na lenda. Conferencia, *etc.* 1913. 8°. **11869**. d. **18**.

—— *See* MICHAELIS DE VASCONCELLOS (C.) A Saudade Portuguesa. Divagações filológicas e literar-históricas em volta de Inês de Castro, *etc.* 1922. 8°. **012942**. bb. **42**.

—— *See* RAUMER (F. L. G. von) Drei Portugiesinnen. Ines, Marie und Leonore. 1850. 8°. [*Historisches Taschenbuch.* Folge 3. Jahrg. 2.] P.P. **3625**.

—— Agnes de Castro, a tragedy . . . Written by a Young Lady [i.e. Catherine Trotter, afterwards Cockburn]. pp. 47. *H. Rhodes : London*, 1696. 4°. **644**. i. **65**.

—— [Another copy.] **81**. c. **13**. (1.)

—— Agnes de Castro : or, the Force of generous love. Written in French by a Lady of Quality [i.e. J. B. de Brilhac]. Made English by Mrs. Behn. pp. 63. *For William Canning : London*, 1688. 8°. **1073**. e. **25**.

—— The Fatal Beauty of Agnes de Castro [by J. B. de Brilhac] ; taken out of the History of Portugal. Made English out of French by P. B. G. [i.e. Peter Bellon, Gent.]. pp. 102. *R. Bentley : London*, 1688. 12°. [*Modern Novels.* vol. 5.] **12410**. c. **22**.

—— The History of Agnes de Castro. (Written . . . by Mrs. Aphra Behn [or rather, translated by her from the French of J. B. de Brilhac].) *See* GRIFFITH (Elizabeth) A Collection of Novels, *etc.* vol. 3. 1777. 12°. **12614**. cc. **14**.

CASTRO (INEZ DE)

—— Histoire d'Agnès de Castro, traduite de l'anglois (de Madame Behn [i.e. from her translation from the French of J. B. de Brilhac].) *See* LYTTELTON (George) *Baron Lyttelton.* Romans, *etc.* 1761. 8º.　　**1456. b. 1.**

—— [Another edition.] 1775. *See* MÉLANGES. Mélanges de littérature, de morale, et de physique. tom. 6. 1775, *etc.* 12º.　　**121. b. 17.**

—— Ignez de Castro: a tragedy . . . By the author of " Rural Sonnets." pp. vi. 100.　　*H. Hurst: London,* 1846. 8º.　　**1344. k. 42.**

—— Ines de Castro. A musical drama in two acts, *etc.* *Ital. & Eng.* pp. 55. *Da Ponte: London,* [1799.] 8º. **907. k. 3. (10.)**

—— Inez, a tragedy. [By Charles Symmons.] pp. vi. 124. *London,* 1796. 8º.　　**643. f. 4. (1.)**

—— [Another copy.]　　　　　　**T. 159. (5.)**

—— Nova Castro, tragedia. Segunda edição, correcta e augmentada. [By J. B. Gomes.] pp. 103.　　*Lisboa,* 1813. 16º.　　**11728. bb. 5.**

—— Sonetos a Dona Ignez de Castro. pp. 15.　　*Lisboa,* 1784. 4º.　　**11454. c. 5.**

—— Sonetos a D. Ignez de Castro. Segunda ediçaõ. pp. 32. *Lisboa,* 1824. 16º.　　**11452. aa. 23.**

—— Tragedia de Dona Ignez de Castro. [In verse.] pp. 31. *Lisboa,* 1772. 4º.　　**11728. g. 43. (8.)**

—— [Another edition.] pp. 31. [*Lisbon,* 1855 ?] 4º. **11726. g. 11. (5.)**

—— Tragedia muy sentida e elegante de Dona Ines de Castro, aqual foy representada na cidade de Coimbra. Agora nouamente acrescentada. [By A. Ferreira.] *Manoel de Lira: [Lisbon,* 1587.] 8º.　　**C. 125. a. 10.** *The bottom outer margin of the titlepage has been repaired and the last two figures of the date supplied in MS.*

—— Verdadera Relacion, en que se refiere la historia desgraciada de Doña Inès de Castro, Cuello de Garza de Portugal. [In verse.] *Valencia,* [1760 ?] 4º. **T. 1957. (66.)**

CASTRO (J.) *Writing-Master.* Grammatica Anglo-Lusitanica & Lusitano-Anglica; or, a New Grammar English and Portuguese and Portuguese and English . . . The second edition. 2 pt. *W. Meadows; E. Comyns: London,* 1751. 8º.　　**12943. bbb. 7.**

—— The fifth edition, revised and corrected by A. de Paz. pp. x. 407. *T. Davies: London,* 1770. 8º.　**627. e. 25.**

—— The Merchant's Assistant and Clerk's Instructor, *etc.* pp. 52. *Printed for the Author: London,* 1742. 8º. **530. c. 15. (3.)**

CASTRO (J. DE) *Chevalier de la Légion d'Honneur. See* GARCIA AYUSO (F.) L'Étude de la philologie dans ses rapports avec le sanscrit . . . traduit . . . par J. de Castro. 1884. 8º.　　**12902. e. 27.**

CASTRO (J. DE ALBUQUERQUE E) *See* ALBUQUERQUE E CASTRO.

CASTRO (J. C. LIMA E) *See* LIMA E CASTRO.

CASTRO (J. E. HENRIQUES) L'Hygiène dans la nourriture et dans la gymnastique. pp. 32. *Paris,* [1860.] 12º. **7391. b. 11.**

CASTRO (J. F. FERREIRA DE)　　*See* FERREIRA DE CASTRO.

CASTRO (J. RAFAEL DE) La Cuestion Mexicana, ó Esposicion de las causas que hacian indispensables la intervencion europea y el restablecimiento de la monarquia en México, *etc.* pp. 88. *Mexico,* 1864. 4º. **8179. bb. 17.**

CASTRO (JACOBO DE) *M.D. See* CASTRO SARMENTO (Jacob de)

CASTRO (JACOBO DE) *Padre de la Provincia de Santiago. See* JOSÉ, *de Madrid.* Examen de la Verdad en el Fiel de la Razon: respuesta à otra respuesta antiprologetica, appologetica, chronologica y sumulistica, que diò a la prensa . . . J. de Castro, *etc.* 1732. fol. **T. 20*. (7.)**

CASTRO (JESÚS AGUSTÍN) *See* MÁRQUEZ (J. M.) El Veintiuno. Hombres de la Revolución . . . Apuntes sobre el General de División J. A. Castro, *etc.* [1916.] 8º. **9773. bb. 2.**

CASTRO (JOANNES À) *See* BORCHT (J. van der)

CASTRO (JOANNES DE) Methodus cantus ecclesiastici graeco-slavici . . . Accedit Enchiridion Canticorum eiusdem ecclesiae ab eodem auctore concinnatum. pp. xviii. 228. *Romae,* 1881. 8º.　　**M.F. 969.**

CASTRO (JOANNES NUÑEZ DE) *See* NUÑEZ DE CASTRO.

CASTRO (JOÃO DE) *Poet.*

—— Portugal amoroso. Episódios românticos . . . 2ª edição. pp. 382. *Lisboa,* 1945. 8º.　　**12492. dd. 26.**

CASTRO (JOÃO DE) *Portuguese Historian.* Discurso da Vida do . . . Rey Dom Sebastiam nosso senhor o Encuberto des do seu nacimēto tee o presente, *etc.* (Aiunta do discurso precedente.) 2 pt. *M. Verac: Paris,* 1602. 8º. **1195. a. 3. (2.)**

CASTRO (JOÃO DE) *Viceroy of India.* [For editions of the " Vida de D. João de Castro " by Jacinto Freire de Andrade:] *See* FREIRE DE ANDRADE (J.)

—— *See* NUNES (L.)　Crónica de Dom João de Castro, *etc.* 1936. 8º.　　**20010. f. 19.**

—— *See* SANCEAU (Elaine) Knight of the Renaissance. D. João de Castro. Soldier, sailor, scientist, and viceroy of India, 1500–1548. [1949.] 8º.　　**10632. v. 33.**

—— Primeiro Roteiro da Costa da India; desde Goa até Dio: narrando a viagem que fez o Vice-Rei D. Garcia de Noronha em soccorro desta ultima cidade. 1538-1539. . . . Segundo MS. autographo. Publicado por Diogo Köpke, *etc.* [With plates, including facsimiles and a portrait.] pp. xliv. xii. 284. *Porto,* 1843. 8º. **Maps.12.d.39.**

—— Mappas. *Porto,* 1843. *obl.* ſol. **Maps.145.c.26.**

—— Roteiro de Lisboa à Goa . . . Annotado por João de Andrade Corvo. pp. xv. 428. pl. xv. 1882. 8º. *See* LISBON.—*Academia das Sciencias de Lisboa.* **10027. f. 5.**

—— Observações Magneticas. Roteiro de Lisboa a Goa, 1538. pp. 16. *Berlin,* 1898. 4º. [*HELLMAN* (G.) *Neudrucke von Schriften und Karten über Meteorologie und Erdmagnetismus, etc.* no. 10.]　　**8755. dd. 36.**

—— Roteiro, em que se contem a viagem que fizeram os Portuguezes no anno de 1541, partindo da nobre cidade de Goa atee Soez . . . Com o sitio, e pintura de todo o Syno Arabico . . . Tirado a luz pela primeira vez do manuscrito original, e acrescentado com o Itinerarium Maris Rubri [i.e. " Joannis de Castro Sinus Arabici accurata descriptio," an abridged version of the " Roteiro "] . . . pelo Doutor Antonio Nunes de Carvalho, *etc.* [With plates, including a portrait.] pp. xiv. ix. 334.　*Paris,* 1833. 8º.　　**Maps.28.b.49.**

CASTRO (João de) *Vicerou of India.*

—— [Atlas.] pl. xv. [*Paris*, 1833.] fol. **Maps.32.d.3.**

—— [Another copy.] **1046. g. 22.**
Imperfect ; wanting the atlas.

—— [Another copy.] **1046. g. 19.**
Imperfect ; wanting the atlas.

—— Naauwkeurig verhaal van een reys door Portugijsen uyt Indeen gedaan na Soez . . . Met schoone Kopere platen, *etc.* pp. 78. *Leyden*, 1706. 8°. [*Aa* (*P. van der*) *Bookseller. Naaukeurige versameling der gedenkwaardigste zee en land reysen, etc.* vol. 50.] **979. e. 14. (4.)**

—— [Another edition.] coll. 44. *Leyden*, 1706. fol. [*Aa* (*P. van der*) *Bookseller. De Aanmerkenswaardigste . . . zee- en landreizen der Portugeezen, etc.* dl. 4.] **566. l. 8.**

—— Le Routier de Dom Joam de Castro. L'exploration de la Mer Rouge par les Portugais en 1541. Traduit du portugais d'après le manuscrit du British Museum, avec une introduction historique et des notes critiques de géographie par A. Kammerer, *etc.* pp. vi. 202. pl. xxv. *Paris*, 1936. 8°. **Maps.29.b.64.**

—— Reise des Don Stephano de Gama aus Goa nach Suez, *etc. See* Schwabe (J. J.) Allgemeine Historie der Reisen, *etc.* Bd. 1. 1747, *etc.* 4°. **10025. dd.**

—— Joannis de Castro Sinus Arabici, seu Maris Rubri, itinerarium. *See* Matthaeus (Antonius) *Jurist, Third of the Name.* Veteris ævi analecta, *etc.* tom. 2. 1738. 4°. **156. e. 2.**

—— Summario delle cose successe à Don Giouanni di Castro . . . tanto nelle guerre contra lo Ydalcaaon Signore della terra ferma qual è presso alla città di Guoa, come anche principalmente nella uittoria . . . che hebbe rõpendo l'esercito del Rè di Cãbaia, *etc. A. Blado : Roma*, 1549. 4°. **C. 32. e. 22.**

—— Extracts on Magnetic Observations from Log-Books of João de Castro, 1538–1539 and 1541. [Translated by J. de Sampaio Ferrez.] [1944.] *See* Harradon (Harry D.) Some Early Contributions to the History of Geomagnetism. pt. 7. [1943, *etc.*] 8°. **08756. d. 64/5.**

CASTRO (João Bautista de) *See also* Jesam Baratta (Custodio) *pseud.* [i.e. J. B. de Castro.]

—— Mappa de Portugal, *etc.* 5 pt. *Lisboa*, 1745–58. 8°. **10160. aa. 22.**

—— [Another edition.] 3 tom. *Lisboa*, 1762-63. 4°. **281. e. 5-7.**

—— Roteiro terrestre de Portugal, *etc.* pp. 216. *Lisboa*, 1748. 8°. **10161. a. 21.**

—— [Another edition.] Pelo Padre J. B. de C. [i.e. J. B. de Castro] . . . Quinta edição. pp. xv. 190. 1814. 8°. *See* C., J. B. de, *Padre.* **10162. aa. 3.**

—— Vida do glorioso patriarca S. Joseph, estrahida, e reduzida a compendio do que escrevêrão os Sagrados Evangelistas, Santos Padres e varões pios. pp. 352. *Lisboa*, 1761. 4°. **4825. aaa. 13.**

CASTRO (João José de)

—— Dissertação . . . Da paralysia radial—peripherica, *etc.* pp. 73. *Rio de Janeiro*, 1903. 4°. **7379. n. 4. (2.)**

CASTRO (João Vicente Leite de) *See* Leite de Castro.

CASTRO (Joaquim Machado de) *See* Machado de Castro.

CASTRO (Joaquim Pereira Pimenta de) *See* Pereira Pimenta de Castro.

CASTRO (José de) *Ethnographer.*

—— Estudos etnográficos. Coordenados por D. José de Castro. [With plates.]
vol. 1. Aveiro. [By J. de Castro.] 1943–

1943. 4°. *See* Lisbon.—*Instituto para a Alta Cultura.* **W.P. 14219.**

CASTRO (José de) *of Funchal.*

—— As Victimas d'el-rei. Historia dos processos movidos contra os persequidos politicos da Ilha da Madeira, desde 29 de junho de 1884 até ao anno de 1885. pp. 83. *Lisboa*, 1885. 8°. **8042. d. 4. (1.)**

CASTRO (José de) *of the Portuguese Academy of History.*

—— Portugal em Roma. 2 vol. *Lisboa*, 1939. 8°. **4606. aa. 24.**

—— Portugal no Concílio de Trento. 6 vol. *Lisboa*, 1944–46. 8°. **4626. c. 1.**

CASTRO (José de) *Priest.*

—— O Cardial nacional. [Biographies of Portuguese members of the Sacred College of Cardinals.] pp. 456. 1943. 8°. *See* Portugal.—*Ministério do Ultramar.—Agência Geral do Ultramar.* **4856. l. 16.**

CASTRO (José Agustín de) *Begin.* De Don Josef Agustin de Castro. [Verses on Napoleon and Ferdinand vii.] [*Mexico ?* 1808.] 4°. **11451. bbb. 6. (7.)**

—— Elogio métrico al Señor General D. Felix María Calleja. [*Mexico*,] 1812. 4°. **11451. bbb. 45. (12.)**

—— Sentimientos de la América, justamente dolorida en la . . . muerte del Exmo. Señor Conde de Galvez, su Virey, *etc.* [A poem.] pp. 6. *México*, 1786. 4°. **11450. bbb. 31.**

—— El Triumfo del Silencio. Cancion heroica, que al glorioso martirio del . . . protector del sigilo sacramental San Juan Nepomuceno, decia Don J. A. de Castro . . . Sácalo á luz el señor Conde de Miravalle, *etc.* pp. 67. *México*, 1786. 4°. **11450. d. 20.**

CASTRO (José Antonio de Azevedo) *See* Azevedo Castro.

CASTRO (José Antonio de Magalhães) *See* Magalhães Castro.

CASTRO (José Antonio Fernández de) *See* Fernández de Castro.

CASTRO (José Boado y) *See* Boado y Castro.

CASTRO (José Carlos de Faria e) *See* Faria e Castro.

CASTRO (José de Antequera y) *See* Antequera y Castro.

CASTRO (José Ignacio de) El Comandante accidental del 6° Batallon de linea, á sus subordinados. [Dated : 7 Nov. 1828.] [*Merida in Yucatan*, 1828.] *s. sh.* fol. **9770. k. 9. (83.)**

CASTRO (José Joaquim de) *See* Lopes Cardozo Machado (J.) Apologia da agoa de Inglaterra da real fabrica de J. J. de Castro, *etc.* 1812. 4°. **9180. ccc. 7. (11.)**

—— *See* Paiva (M. J. H. de) Memoria sobre a excellencia, virtudes, e uso medicinal da verdadeira agua de Inglaterra . . . . actualmente preparada por J. J. de Castro, *etc.* 1816. 4°. **9180. ccc. 7. (10.)**

CASTRO (José Julian de) *See* Lopez de Castro.

CASTRO (José Luciano de) *See* Pereira Corte Real de Castro.

CASTRO (José Maria Ferreira de) *See* Ferreira de Castro.

CASTRO (José Medina di) *See* Medina di Castro.

CASTRO (José Miguel João de Portugal e) *Marquis de Valença. See* Portugal e Castro.

CASTRO (José Ramón)
—— Archivo General de Navarra. Catálogo de la Sección de Comptos. Documentos . . . Por J. R. Castro. 1952– . 8º. *See* Navarre. [Spain.]—*Archivo General.*
W.P. c. **319.**

—— Ensayo de una Biblioteca Tudelana, *etc.* (Conjunto de trabajos impresos en Tudela o publicados por Tudelanos fuera de su ciudad natal.) pp. xvi. 292. *Tudela,* 1933. 4º. **11911. dd. 8.**

—— El Matrimonio de Pedro IV de Aragón y María de Navarra. *In:* Estudios de edad media de la corona de Aragón. vol. 3. pp. 55–156. 1949. 8º. W.P. **13495/3.**

CASTRO (José Soriano de) *See* Soriano de Castro.

CASTRO (José Teixeira de) *See* Teixeira de Castro.

CASTRO (José Villa-Amil y) *See* Villa-Amil y Castro.

CASTRO (Josef Agustin de) *See* Castro (José A. de)

CASTRO (Joseph de) *See* Clare, *of Assisi, Saint.* Primera Regla de . . . Santa Clara de Assis . . . Pónense algunas breves notas al fin . . . Obra Posthuma de el R. P. Fr. J. Castro, *etc.* 1756. 4º. **858. h. 4.**

—— *See* Ximenez de Arellano (M.) Tiernos recuerdos, que excitan el llanto . . . por la muerte del Rev. Padre Fr. J. de Castro, *etc.* 1753. 4º. **4985. df. 7.**

—— Viage de America á Roma. [In verse.] pp. 156. *México,* 1745. 8º. **11450. aaa. 31.**

CASTRO (Joseph de Escobar Salmeron y) *See* Escobar Salmeron y Castro.

CASTRO (Joseph Fernández de) *See* Fernández de Castro.

CASTRO (Joseph Geronymo Sanchez de) *See* Sanchez de Castro.

CASTRO (Joseph Rodriguez de) *See* Rodriguez de Castro.

CASTRO (Josué de)

—— [Geografia da fome.] Geography of Hunger, *etc.* [Translated by George Reed and G. Robert Stange.] pp. 288. *Victor Gollancz: London,* 1952. 8º. **8285. w. 55.**

—— [Geografia da fome.]
Geográfia głodu. (Tłumaczył Roman Kutyłowski.) pp. 283. *Warszawa.* 1954. 8º. **8290. h. 19.**

CASTRO (Jozé Joaquin de) *See* Castro (José J. de)

CASTRO (Juan de) *Dominican.* Manifiesto en que el Maestro Fray Iuan de Castro . . . dà quenta, *etc.* [On the importation of negro slaves into the Spanish possessions in the Indies.] ff. 16. [*Madrid,* 1667.] fol.
1324. i. 3. (5.)

CASTRO (Juan de) *Dominican.*

—— Medio para sanar la Monarquia de España, *etc.* [By J. de Castro.] ff. 7. [*Madrid,* 1668.] fol. *See* Spain. [*Appendix.—History and Politics.*] **1324. i. 3. (10.)**

—— Ordinationes generales. (Ordinationes generales prouintiæ Sanctissimi Rosarii Philippinarum. Factæ per admodum Reuerendum patrem fratrem Ioãnem de Castro.) Incunable filipino de 1604. Facsímile del ejemplar existente en la Biblioteca del Congreso, Washington. Con un ensayo histórico-bibliográfico por Fr. J. Gayo Aragón, O.P. pp. 77. 1954. 8º. *See* Dominicans.
4626. b. 3.

—— Para el entero conocimiento de la causa, que destruye, y acaba . . . la Monarquia de España . . . y para la possibilidad, y facilidad del remedio a tãtos daños, y exequibilidad de todos los efectos, que en mi memorial, y copia de efectos tengo propuesto, pongo a la letra los instrumentos siguientes. ff. 5 [6]. [*Madrid,* 1669.] fol.
1324. i. 3. (9.)

—— Quinto papel. Medio general para sanar, conseruar, y aumentar la Monarquia. ff. 9. [*Madrid,* 1669.] fol.
1324. i. 3. (6.)

—— Respuesta del P. M. Fr. Iuan de Castro a las ficciones con que Domingo Grillo pretende obscurecer la verdad en vn papel descompuesto, que ha sacado impresso para que darse con muchas cantidades de la real hazienda, que deue de su assiento. 2 pt. [*Madrid,* 1670.] fol.
1324. i. 3. (14.)

—— Sabido el comercio que la Europa tiene en las Indias, de quenta de los estrangeros, es razon que tengamos noticia del retorno que se saca de las Indias, en frutos, fuera del oro, plata, perlas, y esmeraldas, *etc.* ff. 6. [*Madrid,* 1669 ?] fol. **1324. i. 3. (11.)**

—— *Begin.* Señora, El Maestro Fr. Iuan de Castro, *etc.* [A memorial relating to the financial administration of the Spanish colonies.] [*Madrid ?* 1668.] *s. sh.* fol.
1324. i. 3. (8.)

—— *Begin.* Señora. El Maestro Fray Iuan de Castro, *etc.* [A second memorial relating to the financial administration of the Spanish colonies.] ff. 10. [*Madrid ?* 1669.] fol.
1324. i. 3. (12.)

CASTRO (Juan de) *Historical Writer.* El Emperador Maximiliano y su augusta esposa la Emperatriz Carlota. Datos para su vida, *etc.* [With portraits.] pp. 31. *Madrid,* 1867. 8º. **10703. cc. 50. (6.)**

CASTRO (Juan de) *Military Writer. See* Castro Gutiérrez.

CASTRO (Juan de) *Musician. See* Castro (Joannes de)

CASTRO (Juan de) *Translator. See* Checchetelli (G.) Il Saltimbanco. Dramma lirico, *etc.* (Traduccion de D. J. de Castro.) 1859. 8º. **11714. aaa. 16. (5.)**

CASTRO (Juan A. de) Un Marido de Lance, pieza en un acto. pp. 7. *See* Museo. Museo dramático ilustrado. tom. 1. 1863, *etc.* 4º. **2298. i. 2.**

CASTRO (Juan Bautista) Discursos leidos en la Academia Venezolana . . . en la recepción pública del . . . Dr. D. J. B. Castro . . 1893. (Discurso leido por D. J. B. Castro. Discurso leido por D. M. A. Saluzzo.) pp. 44. *Carácas,* 1893. 8º. **12301. h. 5. (5.)**

CASTRO (Juan Blas de) *See* Blas de Castro.

CASTRO (Juan de Salinas y) *See* Salinas y Castro.

CASTRO (Juan Francisco)

—— Sarmiento y los ferrocarriles argentinos. Disertación, *etc.* pp. 45. *Buenos Aires*, 1950. 8º. [*Publicaciones del Museo Histórico Sarmiento.* ser. 2. no. 20.]
Ac. **1900**. e.

CASTRO (Juan Gilabert) *See* Gilabert Castro.

CASTRO (Juan José) Treatise on the South American Railways and the great International Lines, *etc.* pp. 601. pl. 15. 1893. 4º. *See* Uruguay.—*Ministerio de Fomento.* **8245**. gg. **20**.

CASTRO (Juan Joseph de Araujo y) *See* Araujo y Castro.

CASTRO (Juan Lagarto de) *See* Lagarto de Castro.

CASTRO (Juan Modesto)

—— Froilán Urrutia. Novela. pp. 254. *Santiago, Chile,* 1942. 8º. **12492**. cc. **18**.

CASTRO (Juan Moreno y) *Marquis de Valle-Ameno. See* Moreno y Castro.

CASTRO (Juan Muñoz y) *See* Muñoz y Castro.

CASTRO (Juan Paez de) *See* Paez de Castro.

CASTRO (Judocus à) F. Iudoci à Castro . . . Deca-chordum morale de decem virtutibus immaculatæ Virginis Annuntiatæ, per tractatus & discursus prædicabiles distinctum, *etc.* 2 pt. *Ex officina plantiniana B. Moreti: Antuerpiæ*, 1635. 4º. **4807**. eee. **3**.

CASTRO (Julian) Confesion de Julian Castro, y Sentencia de la Nacion Venezolana. Año de 1858. [A poem.] pp. 28. [*Caracas,*] 1858. 8º. **11450**. dd. **28**.

CASTRO (Julio) La Voz Apasionada. Poesías. [With plates.] pp. 219. *Madrid*, 1932. 4º. **20001**. dd. **44**.

CASTRO (Julio de Mello de) *See* Mello de Castro.

CASTRO (Julio Luxardo de) *See* Luxardo de Castro.

CASTRO (Leon de) *See* Nuñez de Guzman (F.) Refranes, o Proverbios en romance, *etc.* (Prologo del Maestro Leon.) 1555. fol. **635**. l. **11**.

—— —— 1578. 12º. **12304**. aaa. **40**.

—— —— 1602. 12º. **11451**. a. **27**.

—— —— 1619. 4º. **1075**. m. **11**.

—— —— 1621. 4º. **1075**. k. **9**.

—— —— 1804, *etc.* 8º. **89**. k. **5**.

—— Apologeticus pro lectione apostolica, et euangelica, pro vulgata Diui Hieronymi, pro translatione LXX virorum, proque omni ecclesiastica lectione : contra earum obtrecta-tores. pp. 715. *Hæredes M. Gastij: Salmanticæ,* 1585. fol. **3125**. g. **3**.

CASTRO (Lesmes Sanchez de) *See* Sanchez de Castro.

CASTRO (Lincoln de) Etiopia. Terra, uomini e cose . . . Seconda edizione. [With plates.] pp. vii. 336. *Milano*, 1936. 8º. **010093**. e. **5**.

—— Nella Terra dei Negus. Pagine raccolte in Abissinia, *etc.* [With plates.] 2 tom. *Milano*, 1915. 8º. **010097**. l. **21**.

CASTRO (Lourenço da Mesquita Pimentel Sotto-Maior e) *See* Mesquita Pimentel Sotto-Maior e Castro.

CASTRO (Luciano de)

—— A Questão do Amazonas nos tratados de Paris e de Madrid—1797 e 1801. [With plates, including maps.] pp. 135. *Pôrto*, 1945. 4º. **9773**. v. **24**.
Part of a series entitled " Colecção histórica publicada sob a direcção de Damião Peres."

CASTRO (Luis de) *Agrónomo.*

—— La Producción y el Cultivo del Trigo en Portugal. Conferencia . . . Traducida y anotada con datos concernientes a nuestro pais por José Cascon. pp. 93. *Salamanca*, 1895. 8º. **7075**. a. **18**. (6.)

CASTRO (Luís de) *of the Coimbra University Library.*

—— *See* Mendes.Simões de Castro (A.) Catálogo de Manu-scritos, Códices 1 a 250 . . . Reimpressão, introdução e notas por L. de Castro. 1940. 8º. Ac. **2699**. ba/2.

CASTRO (Luis Abarca de Bolea y) *Marquis de Torres. See* Abarca de Bolea y Castro.

CASTRO (Luis Bermúdez de) *See* Bermúdez de Castro.

CASTRO (Luis Carlos Pereira de) *See* Pereira de Castro.

CASTRO (Luis de Salazar y) *See* Salazar y Castro.

CASTRO (Luis Pereira de) *See* Pereira de Castro.

CASTRO (Luís Vieira de) *See* Vieira de Castro.

CASTRO (Luiz de Moraes e) *See* Moraes e Castro.

CASTRO (Luiz Joaquim de Oliveira e) *See* Oliveira e Castro.

CASTRO (Luiz Meirelles do Canto e) *See* Meirelles do Canto e Castro.

CASTRO (Mafalda de)

—— Botões de rosa. Primeiros versos. pp. 45. *Lisboa,* 1923. 8º. **11453**. ee. **11**.

CASTRO (Manuel de) Historia de un pequeño funcionario. Novela. pp. 164. *Montevideo*, 1928. 8º. **12488**. r. **12**.

CASTRO (Manuel Antonio de)

—— Prontuario de práctica forense. Reedición facsimilar. Con apéndice documental. Noticia preliminar de Ricardo Levene. pp. xxvii. 264. 42. *Buenos Aires*, 1945. 8º. **6786**. dd. **9**.
Colección de textos y documentos para la historia del derecho agentino. no. 4.

CASTRO (Manuel Bautista de) *See* Salazar y Castro (L. de) Examen Castellano de la Crisis Griega, con que el R. P. Fr. M. B. de Castro intentò establecer el Instituto Bethlemitico, *etc.* 1736. 4º. **4784**. ee. **31**.

CASTRO (Manuel Bermúdez de) *See* Bermúdez de Castro.

CASTRO (Manuel Fernández de) *See* Fernández de Castro.

CASTRO (Manuel Sanchez de) *See* Sanchez de Castro.

CASTRO (Manuel Sousa de) *See* Sousa de Castro.

CASTRO (Marcos de) Versos prohibidos. pp. 76. *Rio de Janeiro*, 1898. 16º. **011451**. e. **62**.

CASTRO (Margherita Morreale de) *See* Morreale de Castro.

CASTRO (María Antonia) La Casada que hoy es Monja sin licencia del marido. O Indicacion sobre la nulidad de la profesion religiosa que ha recibido hoy en el convento de Santa Isabel Doña M. A. Castro, etc. pp. 4. *México,* 1826. 4º. **8180. bbb. 20. (10.)**

CASTRO (María de los Angeles América Bernabela) *See* María Ana [Castro], *de Jesús.*

CASTRO (María Teresa Oliveros de) *See* Oliveros de Castro (M. T.)

CASTRO (Mariano Perez de) *See* Perez de Castro.

CASTRO (Martha de)

—— La Arquitectura barroca del virreinato del Perú. Tesis . . . Separata de la revista "Universidad de la Habana." pp. 87. pl. xxv. *Habana,* [1945.] 8º. **07822. bb. 29.**

—— Estudio Crítico de las Ideas Pedagógicas de John Dewey. Tesis, *etc.* [With a portrait.] pp. 133. *Habana,* 1939. 8º. **8312. bb. 45.**

CASTRO (Martin de Bolea y) *See* Bolea y Castro.

CASTRO (Mathieu de) *Bishop of Chrysopolis* and *Apostolic Vicar of India. See* Castro Malo (Matthaeus de)

CASTRO (Michael Gomes de) *See* Gomes de Castro.

CASTRO (Miguel de) Vida del soldado español Miguel de Castro, 1593–1611, escrito por él mismo, y publicada por A. Paz y Mélia. pp. ix. 232. *Barcelona; Madrid,* 1900. 8º. [*Bibliotheca Hispanica.* no. 2.] **12231. ddd. 12.**

CASTRO (Miguel Bermúdez de) *See* Bermúdez de Castro.

CASTRO (Miguel de Mello e) *See* Mello e Castro (M. de)

CASTRO (Miguel Lucio Francisco de Portugal e) *See* Portugal e Castro.

CASTRO (Moacir Werneck de) *See* Werneck de Castro.

CASTRO (Modesto de) Pláticas doctrinales tomadas de varios libros predicables, vertidas en idioma tagalo, y predicadas por . . . M. de Castro. pp. 249. *Manila,* 1864. 4º. **4424. k. 5.**

CASTRO (Moses Orobio à) *See* Orobio à Castro.

CASTRO (Narciso Varela de) *See* Varela de Castro.

CASTRO (Nicolaas de) *Bishop of Middelburg. See* Goossens (T.J.A.) Franciscus Sonnius in de pamfletten, *etc.* (D. Francisci Sonnii . . . aduersus nouos episcopos in Inferiori Germania factos, querela . . . 1567. Eorundem Defensio, triduo post scripto exhibita: autore, ut putatur, Nicalao [*sic*] Castrensi. [A satire, by H. Geldorpius?]). 1917. 8º. **4886. k. 7.**

—— *See* Weytsen (Q.) Nauwkeurig verhaal . . . van de aanstellinge des Eerwaardigen Heeren, N. de Castro, tot eersten bisschop van Middelburch, *etc.* 1757. 8º. **3925. e. 41.**

CASTRO (Nicolas de) Acsiomas Militares ó Mácsimas de la Guerra, *etc.* [A poem. Followed by "Discurso que pronunció D. Manuel Micheltorena."] pp. 64. *México,* 1840. 8º. **11450. aa. 27.**

—— [Another edition.] 1877. *See* Sbarbi (J. M.) El Refranero General Español, *etc.* tom. 8. 1874, *etc.* 8º. **12227. bb. 14.**

CASTRO (Nicolas Fernandez de) *See* Fernandez de Castro.

CASTRO (Olegario Herculano d' Aquino e) *See* Aquino e Castro.

CASTRO (Oscar)

—— Comarca del jazmín, y sus mejores cuentos. pp. 167. *Santiago de Chile,* 1953. 8º. **12493. cc. 24.** *Colección de autores chilenos.* vol. 5.

—— La Vida simplemente. Novela. pp. 396. *Santiago,* 1951. 8º. **12493. cc. 26.**

CASTRO (P. Fuentes) *See* Fuentes Castro.

CASTRO (Paulus de) *See* Paulus, *de Castro.*

CASTRO (Pedro de) *Archbishop of Granada. See* Granada, *City of.* Relacion breue de las reliquias que se hallaron en la ciudad de Granada, *etc.* [With a certificate by P. de Castro.] 1608, *etc.* fol. **604.l.13.**

CASTRO (Pedro de) *Canónigo de la Metropolitana de Sevilla.* Defensa de la Tortura y leyes patrias que la establecieron: e inpugnacion del tratado que escribio contra ella . . . Alfonso Maria de Acevedo. pp. xxviii. 256. *Madrid,* 1778. 4º. **5383. e. 24.**

—— Juicio sobre la Antigüedad de las Letras y de otras cosas de la vida civil . . . Á un erudito que las tenia por invencion de los Egipcios. [A reply to J. G. Wachter's anonymous "Naturae et scripturae concordia."] pp. 292. *Madrid,* 1800. 8º. **11825. aaa. 17.**

CASTRO (Pedro de) *Capitan.* Causas eficientes y accidentales del Fluxo, y Refluxo del Mar . . . Explicanse con ilustracion muchos discursos, que hizo D. Francisco de Seyxas y Lobera en su Teatro Naual, *etc.* pp. 276. *M. Ruiz de Murga: Madrid,* 1694. 4º. **537. g. 42.**

CASTRO (Pedro de) *Cavallero Andaluz. See* Botello de Moraes y Vasconcelos (F.) El Nuevo Mundo, poemma heroyco . . . con las alegorias de Don P. de Castro, *etc.* 1701. 4º. **1064. i. 19.**

CASTRO (Pedro Andrés de) Ortografía y Reglas de la Lengua Tagalog, acomodadas a sus propios caracteres . . . Reproducción del ms. ordenada por Antonio Graíño. pp. ix. 95. *Madrid,* 1930. 8º. **12911. ff. 5.**

CASTRO (Pedro Antonio de) Los Martires de Cordova, comedia famosa. [In verse.] [1650?] 4º. **1072. h. 6. (2.)**

—— [Another edition.] *Valladolid,* [1750?] 4º. **11728. b. 96.**

—— [Another copy.] ms. note [by J. R. Chorley]. **11728. i. 11. (2.)**

CASTRO (Pedro Antonio Perez de) *See* Perez de Castro.

CASTRO (Pedro Martínez de) *See* Martínez de Castro.

CASTRO (Petrus à) *See* Castro (Ezechiele di) afterwards (Petrus à)

CASTRO (Plácido R.)

—— La Saudade y el arte en los pueblos célticos, *etc.* pp. 50. *Vigo,* 1928. 8º. **11869. aa. 27.**

CASTRO (Rafael Fernández de Castro y) *See* Fernández de Castro y Castro.

CASTRO (Rafael García y García de) *See* García y García de Castro.

CASTRO (Raimundo de) *See* Castro y Bachiller.

CASTRO (Raúl Silva) *See* Silva-Castro.

CASTRO (RICARDO) *of Medellin, Colombia.* Páginas Históricas Colombianas. pp. 538. ii. *Medellin [Colombia],* 1912. 8º. **9770. c. 14.**

CASTRO (RICARDO) *Teniente Coronel.* Recopilacion de Leyes, Decretos Supremos i Circulares vijentes concernientes a la Cuardia [*sic*] Nacional desde el 3 de Deciembre [*sic*] de 1835 á 14 de Diciembre de 1872. pp. xi. 196. 1873. 8º. *See* CHILI. [*Laws, etc.*] **6784. b. 2.**

CASTRO (RICARDO MORALES DE) *See* MORALES DE CASTRO.

CASTRO (RODERICUS À) Roderici à Castro . . . De universa mulierum medicina, novo et antehac a nemine tentato ordine, opus absolutissimum, *etc.* 2 pt. *In officina Frobeniana; typis P. de Ohr: Hamburgi,* 1603. fol. **787. m. 36.**

—— [Another copy of pt. 1.] **544. i. 4. (1.)**

—— [A reissue of pt. 2.] *Hamburgi,* 1604. fol. **544. i. 4. (1*.)**

—— Quinta editio, auctior et emendatior. 2 pt. *Sumptibus S. Noethen: Coloniæ Agrippinæ,* 1689. 4º. **778. c. 6.**

—— Roderici à Castro . . . Medicus politicus, sive de officiis medico-politicis tractatus, *etc.* pp. 277. *Ex bibliopolio Frobeniano: Hamburgi,* 1614. 4º. **1038. k. 8.**

—— [Another edition.] pp. 277. *Ex bibliopolio Z. Hertelii: Hamburgi,* 1662. 4º. **1038. g. 5.**

—— Tractatus brevis de natura, et causis pestis, quæ hoc anno M.D.XCVI. Hamburgensem civitatem affligit, *etc.* *J. Lucius Junior: Hamburgi,* 1596. 4º. **1167. f. 11. (6.)**

CASTRO (RODOLFO BARÓN) *See* BARÓN CASTRO.

CASTRO (ROSALÍA) *See* CASTRO DE MURGUÍA.

CASTRO (S. RANGEL DE) *See* RANGEL DE CASTRO.

CASTRO (S. V. DE) Cholera in Egitto nel 1883, sua origine e misure igieniche e quarantenarie, con tavole grafiche. pp. 68. *Milano,* 1884. 8º. **7306. cc. 17. (3.)**

CASTRO (SALVADOR BERMÚDEZ DE) *See* BERMÚDEZ DE CASTRO.

CASTRO (SALVADOR ROCAFULL Y) *See* ROCAFULL Y CASTRO.

CASTRO (SATURNINO FERNÁNDEZ DE) *See* FERNÁNDEZ DE CASTRO.

CASTRO (SEBASTIAN GONZÁLEZ DE) *See* GONZÁLEZ DE CASTRO.

CASTRO (SIMÃO DA SILVA FERRAZ DE LIMA E) *Count de Renduffe. See* SILVA FERRAZ DE LIMA E CASTRO.

CASTRO (THOMAS) *See* ORTON (Arthur) calling himself *Sir* ROGER CHARLES DOUGHTY TICHBORNE, *Bart.*

CASTRO (TOMÁS DE JESÚS)
—— Esbozos críticos. pp. 159. *San Juan de Puerto Rico,* 1945. 8º. **11867. g. 29.**

CASTRO (TORQUATO)
—— Da tutela processual dos contratos preliminares. pp. 28. *Florença,* 1950. 8º. **05385. n. 12.**

CASTRO (VENANCIO MARÍA FERNÁNDEZ DE) *See* FERNÁNDEZ DE CASTRO.

CASTRO (VICENTE ANTONIO DE) *See* PERIODICAL PUBLICATIONS.—*Havanna.* La Cartera Cubana. Director V. A. de Castro. 1838, *etc.* 8º. **P.P. 4085. f.**

CASTRO (VICENTE SANTIAGO SÁNCHEZ DE) *Bishop of Santander. See* SÁNCHEZ DE CASTRO.

CASTRO (VINCENZO G. DE)

—— *See* DONOSO CORTES (J. F. M. M. de la S.) *Marquis de Valdegamas.* Saggio sul cattolicismo, liberalismo, e socialismo, *etc.* [Translated by V. de Castro.] 1854. 8º. **4051. c. 15.**

—— *See* FICKER (F.) [Literaturgeschichte der Griechen und Römer.] Storia della letteratura latina, preceduta da un parallelo fra le lettere greche e latine per V. de Castro, *etc.* 1865. 8º. **11852. b. 10.**

—— *See* GAZZETTI (F.) and CASTRO (V. de) Amore. Letture educative, *etc.* 1885. 8º. **8355. aa. 17.**

—— *See* PYRKER (J. L.) successively *Bishop of Zips, Patriarch of Venice* and *Archbishop of Erlau.* [Perlen der heiligen Vorzeit.] Gemme dell' Antico Testamento . . . Prima versione di V. de Castro, *etc.* 1848. 4º. **11436. k. 36.**

—— *See* RIO (A. F.) Leonardo da Vinci e la sua scuola . . . Prima traduzione con note di V. G. de Castro. 1856. 8º. **7856. aaa. 19.**

—— Al sesto Congresso Internazionale di Statistica in Firenze proposta d'una società di statistica italiana. pp. 31. *Milano,* 1867. 8º. **8226. bb. 64. (11.)**

—— Asilo e scuola coordinati secondo i principii e i metodi razionali. Aggiuntavi la Relazione sul tema XI. del Congresso Pedagogico di Palermo. pp. xvi. 96. *Milano,* 1877. 8º. **8310. e. 1.**

—— Corso di estetica, letto nell' Università di Padova . . . 1844-45. vol. 1. *Milano,* 1849. 8º. **11825. f. 7.** *Imperfect; wanting vol. 2.*

—— Del bello. [With a portrait.] pp. viii. 358. *Milano,* 1858. 8º. **11826. d. 19.**

—— *Begin.* Genova, 2 luglio 1848. Genovesi! *etc.* [A political address.] [*Genoa,* 1848.] *s. sh.* fol. **804. k. 13. (284.)**

CASTRO AGUILAR (PEDRO) and **FERRER DE M.** (GABRIEL) La Despoblación del Agro en México. pp. 23. [*Merida, Yucatan,*] 1939. 8º. **8288. h. 26.**

CASTRO ALBARRÁN (A. DE) El Derecho a la Rebeldía, *etc.* pp. xv. 469. *Madrid,* 1934. 8º. **8004. df. 22.**

—— Este es el Cortejo . . . Heroes y mártires de la cruzada española. pp. 303. *Salamanca,* 11 año triunfal [1938]. 8º. **9181. pp. 2.**

—— Guerra Santa. El Sentido Católico del Movimiento Nacional Español. pp. 247. *Burgos,* 1938. 8º. **9180. t. 32.**

CASTRO ALONSO (MANUEL DE) La Cremación é inhumación de los cadáveres ante la ciencia y la religión. pp. 151. *Barcelona,* [1903.] 8º. **7406. de. 34.**

—— La Moralidad del Quijote. pp. v. 171. *Valladolid,* 1906. 8º. **11853. r. 15.**

CASTRO ALVES (ANTÔNIO)

—— Espumas Fluctuantes. Poesias. Terceira edicção . . . augmentada. pp. 242. *Bahia,* 1878. 8º. **11452. ee. 1.**

—— Espumas fluctuantes . . . Illustrações de Santa Rosa. pp. 204. 1947. 4º. *See* RIO DE JANEIRO.—*Sociedade dos Cem Bibliófilos do Brasil.* **C.106.1.2.**

CASTRO ALVES (Antônio)

—— Espumas flutuantes . . . Prefácio de Agripino Grieco. pp. xxi. 235. *Rio de Janeiro*, 1947. 8°. [*Biblioteca popular brasileira*. no. 23.] W.P. **11936/23.**

—— Poesias escolhidas. Edição comemorativa do centenário do nascimento do poeta 1847–1947. Seleção, prefácio e notas de Homero Pires. [With plates, including portraits.] pp. xxix. 463. *Rio de Janeiro*, 1947. 8°. **11453. d. 24.**

CASTRO ANDRADE Y PORTUGAL (Pedro Antonio Fernández de) 10*th Count de Lemos. See* Fernández de de Castro Andrade y Portugal.

CASTRO BAREA (Pedro) Los Aragonitas de España.
pp. 112. pl. xvi. *Madrid*, 1919. 8°. [*Trabajos del Museo Nacional de Ciencias Naturales*. Serie geológica. no. 24.] Ac. **2828.**

CASTRO BARRETTO (   )

—— Povoamento e população. Política populacional brasileira. pp. 411. *Rio de Janeiro*, 1951. 8°. [*Coleção documentos brasileiros*. no. 68.] W.P. **585/68.**

CASTROBELLO (Augusto de) El Pernales (Francisco Ríos Gonzalez). Historia de este célebre bandido . . . Edición profusamente ilustrada. pp. 125. *Barcelona, Buenos Áires*, 1907. 8°. **10631. aaa. 24.**

CASTRO BOEDO (Emilio) Conferencia de actualidad predicada por el Dr. E. Castro Boedo. pp. 8. *Buenos Aires*, 1874. 8°. **4487. i. 2.**

—— Un Documento inédito para la historia de la Iglesia argentina. [A letter to Dr. Adolfo Saldías, relating to liberty of religious opinion. Printed from the manuscript of 1877.] Reproducida de "La Reforma." pp. 11. *Buenos Aires*, 1913. 8°. **4744. aaa. 8.**

—— Estudios sobre la navegacion del Bermejo y colonizacion del Chaco, *etc.* [With a map.] 2 tom. pp. vii. 275. *Buenos Aires*, 1873. 8°. **10480. bbb. 34.**

CASTRO CABEZA DE VACA Y QUIÑONES (Pedro de) *Archbishop of Granada and Seville. See* Heredia Barnuevo (D. N. de) Mystico ramillete . . . del . . . origén . . . vida y . . . fama posthuma . . . de . . . P. de Castro, *etc.* 1741. fol. **4855. f. 6.**

CASTRO CALPE (Antonio) Deontologiá médica en las tendencias sexuales de los célibes. pp. xvi. 175. *Madrid*, 1927. 8°. **07580. b. 17.**

CASTRO CANTO E MELLO (Domitila de) *Marchioness de Santos. See* Rangel (A.) Dom Pedro Primeiro e a Marquesa de Santos, *etc.* [With portraits.] 1928. 8°. **10633. w. 6.**

CASTROCARO (Franciscus de) *See* Franciscus, *de Castrocaro.*

CASTRO CARREIRA (Liberato de) Historia financeira e orçamentaria do imperio do Brazil desde a sua fundação, *etc.* pp. 796. *Rio de Janeiro*, 1889. 8°. **8225. eee. 36.**

CASTRO DE LA FAYETTE (Levindo) Novo Diccionario Inglez-Portuguez e Portuguez-Inglez, *etc.* (New Dictionary of the Portuguese and English Languages.) 2 pt. *Pariz*, 1892. 16°. **12942. ccc. 11.**

—— Novo Vocabulario Universal da Lingua Portugueza, *etc.* pp. vi. 1172. *Paris*, [1889.] 8°. **12942. ccc. 20.**

CASTRO DELGADO (Enrique)

—— J'ai perdu la foi à Moscou. Traduit et adapté de l'espagnol par Jean Talbot. pp. 350. [*Paris*,] 1950. 8°. **10293. aaa. 22.**

CASTRO DE MURGUÍA (Rosalía)

—— *See* Azambuja (M. da G.) Evocação de Rosalia de Castro, *etc.* 1955. 8°. P.P. **4123.** bc/1. (45.)

—— *See* González Besada (A.) Rosalía Castro. Notas biográficas. [1916.] 8°. **10633. d. 20.**

—— *See* Murguía (M.) Los Precursores . . . Rosalía Castro. 1885. 8°. [*Biblioteca Gallega*. tom. 1.] **12231. g.**

—— *See* Vales Failde (J.) Rosalía de Castro. 1906. 8°. **11853. pp. 30.**

—— Obras completas . . . Prólogo de Manuel Murguía. 4 tom. *Madrid*, 1909–11. 8°. **012230. aaa. 2.**

—— El Caballero de las Botas Azules. Cuento extraño. pp. xxxiii. 313. *Lugo*, 1867. 8°. **12491. k. 2.**

—— Cantares Gallegos. Nueva edicion, corregida y aumentada. pp. xi. 230. *Madrid*, 1872. 8°. **11450. de. 43.**

—— Beside the River Sar. Selected poems from En las orillas del Sar. Translated . . . with annotations and a preface by S. Griswold Morley. [With plates including a portrait.] *Span. & Eng.* pp. xv. 151. *University of California Press : Berkeley*, 1937. 8°. **011451. i. 4.**

—— Follas Novas. Versos en gallego . . . precedidos de un prólogo por Emilio Castelar. pp. xxviii. 271. *Madrid ; Habana*, 1880. 8°. **11450. ee. 21.**

—— 7 ensayos sobre Rosalía. [By various authors. With a portrait.] pp. 170. *Vigo*, 1952. 8°. **11869. h. 7.**

CASTRO DE OLIVEIRA (Armando)

—— Faculdade de Medicina do Rio de Janeiro. These apresentada . . . pelo Dr. A. Castro de Oliveira . . . Das suppurações peri-pharyngeanas e seu tratamento cirurgico, *etc.* pp. 52. *Rio de Janeiro*, 1903. 4°. **7379. n. 4. (1.)**

CASTRO DE SALINAS (Juan) *See* Plutarch.—[*Vitae Parallelae.—Spanish.*] Las Vidas de los ilustres y excellentes varones Griegos y Romanos . . . nueuamente traduzidas en Castellano por J. Castro de Salinas. 1562. fol. **10605. i. 5.**

CASTRO DE TORRES (   ) *Capitan.* Panegírico al Chocolate. Segunda edicion publicada por . . . Manuel Perez de Guzman, Marqués de Jerez de los Caballeros. [In verse.] pp. 30. *Sevilla*, 1887. 8°. **11451. bbb. 9. (5.)**

No. 19 of an edition of twenty copies.

CASTRO E ALMEIDA (Eduardo de) *See* Leite de Vasconcellos (J.) Defensão do Museu Etnologico Português contra as argüições que um Sr. Deputado (Eduardo de Almeida) lhe fez no Parlamento. 1913. 8°.

7871.c.12.

—— *See* Mesquita de Figueiredo (A.) Museu Etnologico Português. Contestação e replica ao folheto [by J. Leite de Vasconcellos] intitulado : " Defensão do Museu Etnologico Português contra as argüições que um Sr. Deputado (E. de Almeida) lhe fez no Parlamento." 1914. 8°.

7706. g. 34.

—— Archivo de Marinha e Ultramar. Inventario . . . Madeira e Porto Santo. 2 vol. 1907, 09. fol. *See* Lisbon.—*Bibliotheca Nacional.—Arquivo de Marinha e Ultramar.* **11908. l.**

—— Inventario dos documentos relativos ao Brasil existentes no Archivo de Marinha e Ultramar, *etc.* 1913– . 8°. [*Annaes da Bibliotheca Nacional do Rio de Janeiro*. vol. 31, 32, 34, 36, 37, 46, 50, *etc.*] *See* Lisbon.—*Bibliotheca Nacional.—Arquivo de Marinha e Ultramar.* Ac. **9205.**

—— [Another issue of pt. 1–6.] Ac. **9205/3.**

CASTRO E ALMEIDA (VIRGINIA DE) *See* EANNES (G.) *de Zurara.* Conquests & Discoveries of Henry the Navigator . . . Edited [and abridged] by V. de Castro e Almeida, *etc.* 1936. 8º. **20029. aaa. 15.**

—— Les Grands navigateurs et colons portugais du xve et du xvie siècles. Anthologie des écrits de l'époque par V. de Castro e Almeida. *Paris,* [1934– .] 8º.
W.P. 11729.

—— Vie de Camoens. Le poète des "Lusiades" et le Portugal de son temps, *etc.* [With plates, including a portrait.] pp. x. 192. *Paris,* [1935.] 8º. **20013. f. 12.**

CASTRO E AZEVEDO (ANTONIO MARIA DE) Nova farça. O Medico fingido e a doente namorada. pp. 20. *Lisboa,* 1831. 4º. **11728. g. 46. (16.)**

—— Acto intitulado Santo Antonio livrando seu pae do patibulo. pp. 16. *Lisboa,* 1857. 4º. **11728. g. 46. (29.)**

—— [Another edition.] pp. 16. *Lisboa,* 1862. 4º. **11728. g. 46. (31.)**

CASTRO E AZEVEDO (LUÍZA MARIA DE)
—— Bibliografia Vicentina. [Compiled by L. M. de Castro e Azevedo.] pp. xii. 1002. 1942. 8º. *See* LISBON.— *Bibliotheca Nacional.* **11925. b. 33.**

—— [Another copy.]
Bibliografia Vicentina. pp. xii. 1002. 1942. 8º. *See* LISBON.—*Bibliotheca Nacional.* **11926. aaa. 16.**

—— Exposição horaciana. Catálogo. [With facsimiles.] pp. xii. 358. 1937. 8º. *See* LISBON.—*Biblioteca Nacional.* **11926. f. 26.**

CASTRO E MENDONÇA (FRANCISCO DE ASSIS) A Dynastia e a Revolução de Setembro, ou Nova exposição da Questão Portugueza da successão. Por C. V., e S. C. [i.e. F. de A. Castro e Mendonça.] pp. viii. 191. 1840. 8º. *See* V., C., and C., S. **8042. bbb. 30.**

—— Memoria historica ácerca da perfida e traiçoeira amizade ingleza . . . por F. A. de S. C. [i.e. F. de A. Castro e Mendonça.] pp. 261. 1840. 8º. *See* C., F. A. de S. **8042. a. 44.**

CASTRO E NORONHA (AHARO PIREZ DE) *Bishop of Portalegre. See* PIREZ DE CASTRO E NORONHA.

CASTRO E SOUSA (ANTONIO DAMASO DE) Carta dirigida a Salustio, amador de antiguidades. pp. vii. 35. *Lisboa,* 1839. 8º. **10162. cc. 1. (1.)**

—— Descripção do Palacio Real na villa de Cintra que ali teem os Ses Reis de Portugal. pp. 38. *Lisboa,* 1838. 8º. **10160. b. 20.**

—— Descripçaõ do Real Mosteiro de Belem, com a noticia de sua fundaçaõ. [With a portrait of King Manuel xiv.] pp. 74. *Lisboa,* 1840. 8º. **4625. c. 10.**

—— Os Dous Requerimentos. [Praying the Portuguese government to order the erection in the National Arsenal of a statue in honour of Prince Henry of Portugal, and to authorise the removal of the remains of Vasco da Gama from Vidigueira to Lisbon.] pp. 19. *Lisboa,* 1859. 8º. **1298. c. 8.**

—— Fac Similes das Assignaturas dos Senhores Reis, Rainhas, e Infantes que tem governado este Reino de Portugal até hoje. Copiados de varios documentos originaes existentes no Archivo Real, *etc. Lisboa,* 1848. 8º. **10632. c. 35.**

—— Hospício dos Caetanos, actual Conservatório Nacional. (II edição.) [An off-print from "Cinzas de Lisboa," ser. 5.] pp. 32. *Lisboa,* 1954. 8º. **4625. b. 59.**

CASTRO E SOUSA (ANTONIO DAMASO DE)

—— Noticia ácerca dos antigos coches da Casa Real. Segunda impressão. pp. 12. *Lisboa,* 1858. 8º. **7943. cc. 23.**

—— Origem da Guarda Real dos Alabardeiros hoje Archeiros no paço. pp. 23. *Lisboa,* 1849. 8º. **1444. h. 9. (4.)**

—— Origem da Procissão de Nossa Senhora com a invocação da Saude, que é costume celebrar-se todos os annos n'esta cidade de Lisboa. pp. 13. *Lisboa,* 1857. 8º.
4625. b. 28.

CASTRO ESTEVES (RAMÓN DE)
—— *See* BUENOS AYRES.—*Instituto Argentino de Cultura Histórica.* La Obra de Ramón de Castro Esteves. Homenaje del Instituto Argentino de Cultura Histórica a su fundador y presidente. [With a portrait.] [1952.] 8º. **1878. d. 12. (49.)**

—— Historia de Correos y Telégrafos de la República Argentina . . . Por R. de Castro Esteves . . . Tomo I. Desde la época precolombiana hasta los orígenes del correo en el Río de la Plata, *etc.* pp. 192. 1934. 8º. *See* ARGENTINE REPUBLIC.—*Dirección General de Correos.* **20010. d. 7.**

—— Inquisiciones acerca de Rosas y su época. Con un ensayo sobre "La República Argentina ante la desmembración de su territorio." pp. 117. *Buenos Aires,* 1927. 8º. **10884. aa. 24.**

—— Oración a la bandera. [With a portrait.] *Buenos Aires,* [c. 1952.] 8º. **1851. c. 19. (60.)**

—— Rosas ante la Historia, *etc.* pp. 164. *Buenos Aires,* 1931. 8º. **10885. aa. 18.**

CASTRO FARIA (L. DE)
—— As Exposições de antropologia e arqueologia do Museu Nacional. Conferência L. de Castro Faria. pp. 18. pl. 16. 1949. 8º. *See* RIO DE JANEIRO.—*Museu Nacional.* **10009. v. 16.**

CASTRO FEIJO (ANTONIO JOAQUIM DE) *See* FEIJO (A.)

CASTRO FERNANDES (ANTÓNIO DE)

—— Princípios fundamentais da organização corporativa portuguesa. pp. 110. *Lisboa,* 1944. 8º. **8288. b. 101.**

CASTRO FERNÁNDEZ (HÉCTOR ALFREDO) calling himself "MARIZANCENE."

—— Teatro, *etc.* (Fragata Bar. Drama en tres actos. Versión castellana de L. Vives.—Juego limpio. Pieza dramática en un acto. [Translated by M. R. P. de Bonilla.] —Una Noche, esta noche . . . Drama en un acto. Versión castellana de R. R. Odin.) pp. 163. *San José, Costa Rica,* 1952. 8º. **11729. d. 6.**

—— Aguas negras . . . Drama en tres actos. Traducción de María Rosa Picado Ch. y Abelardo Bonilla. pp. 171. *San José, Costa Rica,* 1947. 8º. **11729. d. 7.**

CASTRO FIGUEROA Y SALAZAR (PEDRO DE) *Duke de la Conquista. See* CASTRO Y ASCARRAGA (P. de) Relacion del nacimiento y servicios . . . de . . . D. P. de Castro Figueroa y Salazar, *etc.* [1757.] 8º. **278. b. 33.**

—— [For official documents issued by the Duke de la Conquista as Viceroy of Mexico :] *See* MEXICO. [*Laws, etc.*—II.]—Castro Figueroa y Salazar (P. de) *Duke de la Conquista, Viceroy.* [1740, 41.]

CASTRO FIGUEROA Y SALAZAR (PEDRO DE) *Duke de la Conquista.*

—— *See* SPAIN.—*Consejo de las Indias.* Copia de la Sentencia dada por el . . . Consejo . . . en los Autos de Residencia del Excelentissimo señor don P. de Castro Figueroa y Salazar, Duque de la Conquista . . . de los empleos que sirvió de Virrey, Governador y Capitan General de la Nueva-España, *etc.* [1745.] fol. **9770. k. 5. (1.)**

CASTROFINI (FRANCESCO SAVERIO) Il Disinganno, ossia la Nera setta farisaica sconfitta dalle proprie armi. pp. x. 123. *Potenza*, 1877. 8º. **4380. cc. 6.**

CASTRO GALLEGO (JOANNES DE) *See* CASTRO (Antonio de) *Licenciado.* Allegationes Canonicæ, cum suis decissionibus [*sic*] . . . in lucem æditis, et nouiter auctis, per Don I. de Castro Gallego, *etc.* 1689. fol. **5035. h. 5.**

CASTRO-GIL (MANUEL) *See* HOYOS Y VINENT (A. de) Las Hogueras de Castilla . . . Evocaciones y ensayos líricos . . . Los ilustró . . . Castro-Gil. 1922. fol. **C. 62. i. 20.**

CASTROGIOVANNI (GIOVANNI) *See* DANTE ALIGHIERI. [*Divina Commedia.—Italian.*] La Divina Commedia . . . nuovamente illustrata ed esposta e renduta in facile prosa per G. Castrogiovanni. 1858. 8º. **11421. h. 21.**

—— *See* DANTE ALIGHIERI. [*Divina Commedia.—Inferno.—Selections and Extracts.—Italian.*] Squarci scelti dallo Inferno di Dante spiegati e commentati . . . per G. Castrogiovanni, *etc.* 1873. 8º. **11422. bbb. 1.**

—— Fraseologia poetica e dizionario generale della Divina Commedia. pp. 340. *Palermo*, 1858. 8º. **11421. i. 9.**

CASTROGIOVANNI TIPALDI (I.) I Sovrani in Sicilia nel 1881. Cronica. pp. xv. 474. *Palermo*, 1881. 8º. **9930. dd. 27.**

CASTRO GIRONA (ALBERTO) *See* FARFÁN DE LOS GODOS (G.) and GONZÁLEZ G. DE SANTIAGO (P.) Por los Fueros de la Verdad. Aclaraciones necesarias para la historia de los sucesos de Valencia. Apéndice y notas del General Castro Girona. [1930.] 8º. **9181. b. 34.**

CASTRO GUISASOLA (FLORENTINO)

—— El Enigma del vascuence ante las lenguas indeuropeas. pp. 289. *Madrid*, 1944. 8º. [*Revista de filología española.* anejo 30.] **Ac. 145. c/5. (2.)**

—— Observaciones sobre las Fuentes Literarias de " La Celestina." pp. 194. *Madrid*, 1924. 8º. [*Revista de Filología Española.* anejo 5.] **Ac. 145. c/5. (2.)**

CASTRO GUTIÉRREZ (CRISTÓBAL DE)

—— *See* SPAIN.—*Congreso de los Diputados.* Antología de las Cortes de 1820. Arreglada por C. de Castro. 1910. 4º. **9181. aa. 6.**

—— Felipe III. Idea de un príncipe político cristiano. [With a portrait.] pp. 254. *Madrid*, 1944. 8º. **10633. s. 46.**

—— Mujeres del Imperio, *etc.* *Madrid*, 1941– . 8º. **W.P. 2740.**

—— Provincia de Álava. pp. 232. pl. 95. *Madrid*, 1915. 4º. [*Catálogo Monumental de España.*] **W.P. 5031/1.**

—— Novelas escogidas, *etc.* [With a portrait.] pp. 586. *Madrid*, 1944. 16º. **12490. de. 13.**

CASTRO GUTIÉRREZ (CRISTÓBAL DE)

—— Santo Toribio de Mogrovejo. La conquista espiritual de América. pp. 228. *Madrid*, 1944. 8º. **4824. c. 13.**

CASTRO GUTIÉRREZ (JUAN DE) Los Factores del triunfo en la guerra moderna . . . 2ª edición, *etc.* pp. xxii. 325. *Madrid*, 1918. 8º. **08821. a. 54.**

CASTRO LEAL (ANTONIO)

—— *See* DÍAZ MIRÓN (S.) Poesías completas. Edición y prólogo de A. Castro Leal. 1952. 8º. **11454. b. 27.**

—— *See* GARCÍA ICAZBALCETA (J.) Don Fray Juan de Zumárraga . . . Edición de R. Aguayo Spencer y A. Castro Leal. 1947. 8º. **4869. a. 19.**

—— *See* RIVA PALACIO Y GUERRERO (V.) Martín Garatuza . . . Edición y prólogo de Antonio Castro Leal. 1945. 8º. **12492. b. 33.**

—— *See* RUIZ DE ALARCÓN Y MENDOZA (J.) La Verdad sospechosa. Biografía, prólogo y notas de A. Castro Leal. 1944. 8º. **12214. ee. 1/13.**

—— *See* URBINA Y SÁNCHEZ (L. G.) Poesías completas . . . Edición y prólogo de Antonio Castro Leal. 1946. 8º. **11453. bb. 33.**

—— Las Cien Mejores Poesías —Líricas—Mejicanas. Escogidas por A. Castro Leal, M. Toussaint y Ritter, A. Vázquez del Mercado. pp. xxii. 335. *Méjico*, 1914. 16º. **011451. e. 82.** *Part of the " Biblioteca de la Sociedad Hispánica de Méjico."*

—— Nueva edición refundida por A. Castro Leal. pp. xxx. 284. *México*, 1935. 12º. **20012. e. 2.**

—— Dos Palabras sobre las Ideas y sobre el Arte de George Bernard Shaw. *See* SHAW (George B.) [*Single Plays.*] [Overruled.] Vencidos, *etc.* 1917. 16º. **11783. a. 56.**

—— La Poesía mexicana moderna. Antología, estudio preliminar y notas de A. Castro Leal. pp. xxxix. 537. *México*, 1953. 8º. **11453. e. 48.** *Letras mexicanas.* vol. 12.

CASTRO LES (VICENTE) Noticiero-Guía de Madrid (1905). Arreglado por un Reporter.—Guide pratique de Madrid. —Avec l'itinéraire, en français, pour visiter Madrid en trois jours . . . Dirigido por D. V. Castro Les, *etc.* [With a map.] pp. 239. *Madrid*, [1905.] 8º. **10162. aaa. 16.**

CASTRO LOPES (A. DE) Le Soleil, comment se forme sa lumière, ce qu'elle est ; l'éther ; taches et éruptions solaires ; magnétisme terrestre ; aurores boréales. Prélection, *etc.* pp. 35. *Rio de Janeiro*, 1886. 8º. **8562. eee. 39. (6.)**

CASTRO LÓPEZ (MANUEL) El Tercio de Galicia en la defensa de Buenos Aires. Documentos inéditos [largely by P. A. Cerviño]. Con un prólogo de M. Castro López. [With plates.] pp. xxvi. 149. *Buenos Aires*, 1911. 8º. **9770. f. 28.**

CASTRO MALO (MATTHAEUS DE) *Bishop of Chrysopolis.*

—— *See* COMBALUZIER (F.) Mathieu de Castro, vicaire apostolique d'Idalcan, Pegu et Golconde, 1638–1658. 1943. 8º. [*Revue d'histoire ecclésiastique.* tom. 39. no. 1.] **Ac. 2646/3.**

—— *See* GHESQUIÈRE (T.) Mathieu de Castro, premier vicaire apostolique aux Indes, *etc.* 1937. 8º. [*Bibliothèque de la Revue d'histoire ecclésiastique.* fasc. 20.] **Ac. 2646/10.**

CASTRO MARCOS (MIGUEL DE) Asturias, país de amor y tierra de fuego, *etc.* folleto 1. pp. 89. *Madrid,* 1918. 8°. **10162. e. 40.**
No more published.

—— El Ministerio de Instrucción Pública bajo la dominación roja, *etc.* pp. 236. *Madrid,* 1939. 8°. **8356. p. 6.**

CASTRO MARSIACO (HENRICUS DE) *Abbot of Clairvaux, Cardinal. See* HENRICUS, *Abbot of Clairvaux, etc.*

CASTRO-MAYA (R. DE)

—— Catalogue de la bibliothèque de M. R. de C.-M. [i.e. R. de Castro-Maya], *etc.* [With plates.] pp. 42. 1932. fol. *See* C.-M., R. de, *M., Membre de la Société " Les Cent Bibliophiles."* **11912. dd. 63.**

CASTROMEDIANO DI LIMBURG (SIGISMONDO) *Duke di Morciano. See* LECCE.—*Commissione Conservatrice dei Monumenti Storici e di Belle Arti di Terra d'Otranto.* Relazione per gli anni 1874–75 (pello anno 1875) del duca S. Castromediano. 1875, *etc.* 8°. **Ac. 5226.**

—— *See* MAGGIULLI (L.) and CASTROMEDIANO DI LIMBURG (S.) *Duke di Morciano.* Le Iscrizioni messapiche, raccolte dai cav. L. Maggiulli e duca S. Castromediano, *etc.* 1871. 8°. **7707. de. 3.**

—— Carceri e galere politiche. Memorie, *etc.* 2 vol. *Lecce,* 1895. 8°. **10629. dd. 31.**

—— La Chiesa di S. Maria di Cerrate nel contado di Lecce. Ricerche. pp. 31. *Lecce,* 1877. 8°. **4534. e. 3. (5.)**

—— Delle monete d'oro trovate a Cursi, Terra d'Otranto. Ricerche e descrizione. pp. 38. *Lecce,* 1885. 8°. **7757. f. 28. (4.)**

—— Due Capitoli tolti alle Memorie del duca S. Castromediano. pp. 71. *Lecce,* 1886. 8°. **9004. gg. 9. (5.)**

CASTRO MORAES SARMENTO (ANTONIO DE) Hum Grito ao Padre Macedo. [Signed: A. C. M. S., i.e. A. de Castro Moraes Sarmento.] pp. 18. 1822. 4°. *See* S., A. C. M. **8042. e. 5. (1.)**

—— O Maçonismo confundido, ou Juizo critico sobre a analyse de todos os cathecismos maçonicos. [Signed: A. C. M. S., i.e. A. de Castro Moraes Sarmento.] pp. 42. 1822. 4°. *See* S., A. C. M. **4784. aaa. 6.**

CASTRONE (MATHILDE DE) *See* CASTRONE MARCHESI.

CASTRONE (SALVATORE DE) *See* JESUITISM. Il Gesuitismo fedelmente descritto secondo la sua natura . . . Tradotto . . . da S. de Castrone. 1887. 8°. **4091. h. 14.**

CASTRONE (SALVATORE DE) *Musician. See* CASTRONE MARCHESI (S. de)

CASTRONE MARCHESI (MATHILDE DE) Erinnerungen aus meinem Leben . . . Mit Porträt. pp. vi. 104. *Wien,* 1877. 8°. **10708. cc. 9.**

—— [Another edition, enlarged.] Aus meinem Leben. pp. viii. 246. *Düsseldorf,* [1889.] 8°. **10706. c. 45.**

—— Marchesi and Music: passages from the life of a famous singing-teacher, *etc.* [With portraits.] pp. xiv. 301. *Harper & Bros.: London & New York,* 1897. 8°. **010707. i. 31.**

CASTRONE MARCHESI (SALVATORE DE) *See* WAGNER (W. R.) [*Der Fliegende Holländer.*] L'Olandese dannato . . . Translated into Italian by Salvatore de C. Marchesi, *etc.* [1870.] 8°. **11779. b. 5. (4.)**

CASTRONE MARCHESI (SALVATORE DE)

—— Abenteuer und Erlebnisse des kleinen Hans. Ein Bilderbuch mit Musik und Gesang für Kinder. Mit 12 Illustrationen von Julius Koch . . . Deutsche Uebersetzung von Wolfgang Müller von Königswinter. pp. 40. *Leipzig,* 1868. 4°. **12806. i. 19.**

—— A Vademecum for Singing-Teachers and Pupils. pp. 49. *G. Schirmer: New York,* 1902. 8°. **7899. f. 27.**

CASTRONERIE. Castronerie d'un filosofo positivista, *etc.* [Signed: P. P.] 1882. 8°. *See* P., P. **8463. ccc. 17. (3.)**

CASTRONIUS (BENEDICTUS MARIA) Horographia universalis, seu Sciatericorum omnium planorum . . . pro quovis horologio . . . uniformis atque universalis doctrina . . . in tres digesta libros quibus triplex accessit Appendix: de nautica scientiâ, de militari architecturâ, ac de temporum januâ. *Panormi,* 1728. fol. **48. e. 14.**

CASTRONOVO (FERNANDO DE ZÁRATE Y) *See* ZÁRATE Y CASTRONOVO (F. de)

CASTRONOVO (GIUSEPPE) Erice oggi Monte San Giuliano in Sicilia. Memorie storiche. 2 pt. *Palermo,* 1872, 75. 8°. **10130. df. 11.**
The wrapper of pt. 1 bears the date 1873.

CASTRO NOVO (GUIGO DE) *General of the Carthusians. See* GUIGO.

CASTRONOVO (TOMASO D'AVERSA E) *See* AVERSA E CASTRONOVO.

CASTRONOVO (VINCENTIUS BANDELLUS DE) *See* BANDELLUS (V.) *de Castronovo.*

CASTRONOVO (VITO) *See* CASTRONOVO (Giuseppe)

CASTRO NUNES (JOÃO DE)

—— A Base antroponímica AREN[T]- numa inscrição figulina do Museu de Arganil. pp. 12. *Arganil,* 1952. 8°. **07708. n. 3.**
One of the " Publicações do Museu da Câmara Municipal de Arganil."

—— Um Machado de talão, de tipo galaico, na Beira-Alta interior. pp. 9. *Arganil,* 1952. 8°. **07705. s. 9.**
One of the " Publicações do Museu da Câmara Municipal de Arganil."

CASTRO NUNES (JOAQUIM ANTONIO DE) Compendio da grammatica da lingoa nacional . . . extrahido de diversos autores . . . Quinta edição augmentada, *etc.* pp. 104. *Recife,* 1861. 8°. **12943. a. 20.**

—— Elementos de arithmetica extrahido de varios autores . . . Segunda edição. 2 pt. *Recife,* 1865. 8°. **8506. aaa. 25.**

CASTRONUÑO. Las Ordenanzas de Castronuno (1467). *See* PUYOL Y ALONSO (J.) Las Hermandades de Castilla y León, *etc.* 1913. 8°. **9181. f. 6.**

CASTRONUOVO, *Sicily.* Statuto, capitoli e privilegi della città di Castronuovo di Sicilia, *etc.* (Pubblicati dall'avv. L. Tirritto.) 1877. *See* PALERMO.—*Società Siciliana per la Storia Patria.* Documenti, *etc.* ser. 2. vol. 1. fasc. 2. 1876, *etc.* 8°. **Ac. 6537.**

CASTRO OSÓRIO (JOÃO DE)

—— O Além-mar na literatura portuguesa—época dos descobrimentos. pp. 272. *Lisboa,* 1948. 8°. **11869. p. 11.**

CASTRO OSÓRIO (João de)

—— Gonzaga e a justiça. Confrontação de Baltasar Gracián e Tomás António Gonzaga. Um argumento novo sobre a autoria das " Cartas chilenas." pp. 78. *Lisboa,* 1950. 8°. [*Ocidente.* Suplemento.]
P.P. **4123**. bc/**1**. (**23**.)
Published in parts.

CASTRO OSSORIO (Rodrigo de) *Cardinal, Archbishop of Seville.*

—— Las Jornadas del Cardenal. [The text of a ms., here attributed to Luis Vélez de Guevara, in the library of the Real Academia de la Historia, containing an account of a journey through Spain made in 1598 by R. de Castro Ossorio. With an introduction.] Discurso leído por . . . A. Cotarelo Valledor . . . y contestación del . . . Señor D. Eloy Bullón y Fernández, *etc.* [With a portrait.] pp. 102. 1944. 8°. *See* MADRID.—*Real Academia de la Historia.* Ac. **6630/36**.

CASTRO-PALAO (Ferdinand de)

—— R.P. Ferdinandi de Castro-Palao . . . operis moralis, de virtutibus, et vitiis contrariis, in varios tractatus . . . distributi, pars prima (—septima) . . . Recentior et accuratior editio, cui accessit index locupletissimus . . . opera & studio N. J. B. Dantoine. 7 vol. *Sumptibus Anisson & Joannis Posuel: Lugduni,* 1700. fol. **3678**. h. **3**.

CASTRO PENCELLÍN Y VARONA (Juan) Cadena de Oro, *etc.* [In verse.] [1780?] 4°. **11450**. h. **6**. (**32**.)

CASTRO PERDIGÃO (Domingos de) O que se deve comer. Adaptação do systema de alimentação vegetariana para uso dos brazileiros. pp. 135. x. *Maranhão,* 1918. 8°. **07942**. d. **34**.

—— O que se deve lêr. Vade-mecum bibliographico. pp. 348. vi. *S. Luiz do Maranhão,* 1922. 16°. **11902**. a. **58**.

CASTRO PEREIRA SODRÉ (Pedro de) La Vérité sur le Brésil, *etc.* pp. 36. *Genève,* 1897. 8°. **8179**. c. **44**. (**6**.)

CASTRO PIRES DE LIMA (Fernando de)

—— A Nau Catrineta. Ensaio de interpretação histórica, *etc.* pp. 182. *Lisboa,* 1954. 8°. **10498**. tt. **36**.

CASTRO RAMÍREZ (Manuel) *See* Pasos Arana (M.) and Álvarez (E.) *of Managua.* El Laudo de su Majestad Alfonso xiii frente al derecho internacional, *etc.* [A reply to a pamphlet with the same title by M. Castro Ramírez, R. Arrieta Rossi and E. Córdoba.] 1938. 8°. **6784**. b. **33**.

CASTRO RAMOS (Manuel) *See* Figueroa (P. P.) El Periodista Martir, M. Castro Ramos, *etc.* 1884. 8°. **10601**. e. **3**. (**1**.)

CASTRO SABORÍO (Luis)

—— *See* Costa Rica. [*Laws.*—i.] Biblioteca de derecho vigente en Costa Rica, Dirigida por . . . L. Castro Saborío. 1913, *etc.* 8°. **6785**. e. **20**.

CASTRO SANTA ANNA (José Manuel de) Diario de Sucesos Notables . . . de 1752 a 1758. 1854. *See* Mexico. [*Appendix.*] Documentos para la Historia de Méjico. sér. i. tom. 4-6. 1853, *etc.* 8°. **9771**. bbb. **22**.

CASTRO SARMENTO (Jacob de)

—— *See* Esaguy (A. d') Jacob de Castro Sarmento. Notas relativas à sua vida e à sua obra, *etc.* [With a portrait and facsimile titlepages.] 1946. 8°. **10634**. l. **16**.

CASTRO SARMENTO (Jacob de)

—— *See* Esaguy (A. d') A Page from the Portuguese History of Medicine. Dr. Jacob or Henrique de Castro Sarmento. 1946. 8°. **7681**. d. **30**.

—— *See* Esaguy (A. d') Nótulas relativas ás Agoas de Inglaterra, inventadas pelo Dr. Jacob de Castro Sarmento, *etc.* 1931. 8°. **07680**. aa. **8**.

—— *See* Paiva (M. J. H. de) Memoria sobre a excellencia . . . e uso medicinal da . . . Agua de Inglaterra da invenção do Dr. J. de Castro Sarmento, *etc.* 1816. 4°. **9180**. ccc. **7**. (**10**.)

—— A Dissertation on the Method of Inoculating the Small-Pox ; with critical remarks on the several authors who have treated of this disease. By J. C. M. D. [i.e. Jacob de Castro Sarmento.] pp. 48. 1721. 8°. *See* C., J., *M.D.* **1174**. h. **21**. (**5**.)

—— [Another copy.] T. **374**. (**1**.)

—— [Another copy.] T. **433**. (**4**.)

—— Dissertationes in novam, tutam ac utilem methodum inoculationis, seu transplantationis variolarum. Prima methodus auctoritate Regiæ Majestatis Brittanicæ comprobata, publicata cum criticis notis in varios autores de hoc morbo scribentes à J. à Castro . . . Altera methodus prælecta à Gualtero Harris. Tertia byzantina dicta . . . ventilata ab Antonio Le Duc. pp. 117. *Lugduni Batavorum,* 1722. 8°. T. **340**. (**3**.)
Imperfect ; wanting pp. 47, 48.

—— Dissertatio in novam, tutam, ac utilem methodum inoculationis, seu transplantationis variolarum . . . Editio secunda. pp. 40. *Londini,* 1722. 8°. **1174**. h. **21**. (**6**.)

—— [Another edition.] *See* Morton (Richard) *M.D.* Richardi Morton . . . Opera medica, *etc.* tom. 2. 1737. 4°. **542**. e. **9, 10**.

—— Do uso, e abuso das minhas Agoas de Inglaterra . . . Pello inventor das mesma aguas. pp. xxxiv. 288. *Guilherme Strahan: Londres,* 1756. 8°. **955**. k. **32**.

—— Materia Medica Physico-Historico-Mechanica. Reyno mineral. Parte i. Ediçam nova . . . a que se accrescentam por continuaçam desta obra . . . Reynos vegetavel e animal. Parte ii. [With a portrait.] pp. li. 580. *Guilherme Strahan: Londres,* 1758. 4°. **462**. k. **12**.

—— Sermam funebre as deploraveis memorias do muy reverendo . . . David Netto, *etc.* pp. 11. 64. F.P. *Londres,* 5488 [1728]. 8°. **702**. d. **25**.

CASTRO SILVA (José Vicente) Oración funebre en elogio a la memoria del ilmo. y rvmo. Sr. Dr. Manuel José Mosquera, Arzobispo de Bogotá, *etc.* pp. 17. [*Bogotá,* 1936.] 8°. **12301**. r. **50**.

—— Sermones y Discursos. pp. 152. *Bogotá,* 1937. 8°. [*Biblioteca Aldeana de Colombia.* no. 77.] **12213**. b. **1/77**.

CASTRO SOFFIA (Joaquín) *See* Santiago [*Chile.*].—*Casa de Orates.* Casa de Orates de Santiago. Actas de la junta directiva, *etc.* [With an introduction by J. C. Soffia.] 1901. 8°. **8180**. d. **1**.

CASTRO TARTAZ (David de)

—— *See* Jews.—*Service Books.*—*Feastday Prayers.*—*Portuguese Rite.* [*Spanish.*] Orden de Ros-Asanah y Kipur por estilo seguido, y corriente, conforme se uza en este Kahal Kados. Nuevamente corregido . . . por D. Tartas. 5455 [1695.] 8°. **1971**. aaa. **22**.

CASTRO TARTAZ (David de) Sermoẽs que pregaraõ os doctos ingenios do K. K. de Talmud Torah, desta cidade de Amsterdam, no alegre estreamento, & publica celebridade da Esnoga que se consagrou a Deos, *etc.* [Edited, with a prologue and dedications by D. de Castro Tartaz. With plates.] pp. 155. *D. de Castro Tartaz: Amsterdam*, 5435 [1675]. 4º. **4034. m. 40.**

CASTRO TELES DE MENEZES DE VASCON-CELLOS DE BETTENCOURT DE FREITAS-BRANCO (Alfredo Antonio) *Viscount de Porto da Cruz.*

—— Notas & comentários para a história literária da Madeira. 3 vol. *Funchal*, 1949–53. 8º. **11871. r. 25.**

CASTRO-TERREÑO, Prudencio de Guadalfajara, *Duke de. See* Guadalfajara.

CASTRO TITO CUSSI YUPANGUI (Diego de) *Inca of Peru.* Relación de la conquista del Perú y hechos del Inca Manco ii . . . Notas biográficas y concordancias del texto por Horacio H. Urteaga . . . Biografía de Tito Cusi Yupangui por Carlos A. Romero. pp. xxxiii. 151. *Lima*, 1916. 8º. [*Colección de libros y documentos referentes a la historia del Perú.* tom. 2.] **9772. ppp. 21.**

CASTRO TRESPALACIOS (Pedro)

—— Proyectos de leyes presentados a la consideración de la Honorable Cámara de Representantes por el Honorable Representante Doctor Pedro Castro Trespalacios, por la circunscripción electoral del Depto. del Magdalena. pp. 30. 1937. 8º. *See* Colombia. [Republic of Colombia, 1886– .]—*Congreso.* [*Proyectos de Ley.*] **L.A.S. 381/40.**

CASTRO VACA Y QUIÑONES (Pedro de) *Arch-bishop of Granada and Seville. See* Castro Cabeza de Vaca y Quiñones.

CASTROVERDE.—*Concejo. See* Leon, *Spain, City of.* —*Cathedral Church.*—*Chapter.* El Dean y Cabildo de la Santa Yglesia Catedral de Leon. Con el Concejo y vezinos de la villa de Castrouerde. [1630?] fol. **1322. l. 6. (10.)**

CASTROVERDE (Joseph de Llétor) *See* Llétor Castroverde.

CASTROVERDE Y CABRERA (Jorge Alfredo de)

—— *See* Congreso Panamericano de Medicina Legal, Odontología Legal y Criminología. Primer Congreso Panamericano de Medicina Legal, Odontología Legal y Criminologia, *etc.* (Memoria preparada por J. A. de Castroverde.) [With a portrait.] 1946. 8º. **7682. d. 34.**

CASTROVIDO (Roberto) *See* Tato y Amat (M.) Sol y Ortega y la política contemporánea . . . Epílogo de D. R. Castrovido, *etc.* 1914. 8º. **10632. s. 3.**

CASTROVIEJO (José María)

—— Rías bajas of Galicia. [Translated by D. MacDermott. With plates and a map.] pp. 34. *Noguer: Barcelona*, 1953. 8º. **10163. e. 16.**

—— —— Supplement of Useful Information to the Guide to the Rías bajas of Galicia. pp. 10. [*Barcelona*, 1953.] 8º. **10163. e. 16.** *Part of the series entitled "Andar y ver. Guides to Spain."*

CASTROVINCI (Eroteide Rossi) *See* Rossi Castro-vinci.

CASTROVOL (Pétrus de) *See* Petrus, *de Castrovol.*

CASTROXERIS (Juan Garcias de) *See* Garcias de Castroxeris.

CASTRO Y AGUILA (Tomas de) Antidoto, y remedio vnico de daños publicos ; conservacion y restauracion de monarchias. Discurso legal, y politico. ff. 238. *V. Aluarez de Mariz: Antequera*, 1649. 4º. **522. d. 36.**

CASTRO Y AÑAYA (Pedro de) Auroras de Diana. pp. 339. *M. Dias: Coimbra*, 1654. 8º. **1072. f. 17.**

CASTRO Y ASCARRAGA (Pedro de) Relacion del nacimiento y servicios de . . . D. P. de Castro, Figueroa y Salazar . . . Virrey y Capitàn General . . . del Reyno de Nueva España. [Certified by Pedro Gordillo.] ff. 28. [*Madrid*, 1757.] 8º. **278. b. 33.** *The titlepage is preceded by 3 ff. of introductory matter.*

CASTRO Y BACHILLER (Raimundo de) A la Memoria de un maestro de maestros en el centenario de su muerte. Presbítero José Agustín Caballero. Discurso. pp. 27. *Habana*, [1937.] 8º. **012301. m. 1.**

—— Autopsia Médico-Legal . . . Publicado en la revista "Vida Nueva," *etc.* pp. 47. *Habana*, 1937. 8º. **6095. pp. 9.**

—— La Delincuencia infantil desde el punto de vista jurídico . . . Publicado en Revista Bimestre Cubana, *etc.* pp. 19. *Habana*, 1929. 8º. **6057. tt. 3.**

—— — Determinación de la Fecha de la Muerte en Cuba, *etc.* pp. 22. *Habana*, 1937. 8º. **6095. pp. 8.**

CASTRO Y BARBEYTO (Benito Francisco de) Diccionario histórico-portatil de las órdenes religiosas y militares, y de las congregaciones regulares y seculares, que han existido en varias partes del mundo hasta el dia hoy, *etc.* 2 tom. *Madrid*, 1792, 93. 4º. **4784. aaa. 1.**

CASTRO Y BARCELO (Francisco) Discurso que sobre los principales puntos de la frenología pronunció en el Salon de Actos de Minería . . . el Sr. D. F. Castro y Barcelo. Edicion de la Sinceridad. pp. 36. *México*, 1851. 12º. **7410. a. 68.**

CASTRO Y BARROS (Pedro Ignacio de) [For official documents issued by P. I. de Castro y Barros as President of the Congress of the United Provinces of Rio de la Plata :] *See* Plata, *River, United Provinces of the.* —*Congreso Nacional.* [1816–1820.]

CASTRO Y BELLVIS (Guillén de) *See* Fox, after-wards Vassall (Henry R.) *3rd Baron Holland.* Some Account of the Lives and writings of Lope Felix de Vega Carpio and Guillen de Castro. 1817. 8º. **1064. k. 10.**

—— *See* Martínez y Martínez (F.) Don Guillém de Castro no pudo ser Alonso Fernández de Avellaneda. Rèplica al folleto de D. Emilio Cotarelo y Mori "Sobre el Quijote de Avellaneda y acerca de su autor verdadero." 1935. 8º. **11857. d. 15.**

—— *See* Roca Franquesa (J. M.) Un Dramaturgo de la edad de oro : Guillén de Castro. Notas a un sector de su teatro. 1944. 8º. [*Revista de filología española.* tom. 28. cuaderno 4.] **Ac. 145. c/5.**

—— Obras. [Edited, with an introduction, by E. Juliá Martínez.] tom. 1–3. *Madrid*, 1925–27. 8º. [*Biblioteca selecta de clásicos españoles.* ser. 2.] **Ac. 144/5. (1.)**

—— Comedia del Amor Constante.—Famosa Comedia del Cauallero Bouo. 2 pt. *See* Valencia, *Spain, City of.* Doze comedias famosas, de quatro poetas naturales de la . . . ciudad de Valencia, *etc.* 1609. 4º. **C. 63. b. 44.**

—— [Another edition.] *See* Valencia, *Spain, City of.* Doze comedias famosas, *etc.* pt. 1. 1614, *etc.* 4º. **11725. cc. 10.**

CASTRO Y BELLVIS (Guillén de)

—— Comedia famosa de las Mocedades del Cid, primera (segunda) parte.—Famosa comedia de el Amor Constante. —Comedia famosa de la Piedad en la Justicia.—Comedia de el Narciso en su Opinion.—Comedia de la Fuerza de la Costumbre.—Los mal Casados de Valencia. 1857. *See* Aribau (B. C.) Biblioteca de Autores Españoles. tom. 43. 1849, *etc.* 8º. **12232.f.1/43.**

—— La Tragedia por los Celos.—Quien no se aventura. 1878. *See* Ramirez de Arellano (F.) *Marquis de la Fuensanta del Valle*, and Rayon (J. S.) Coleccion de libros españoles raros ó curiosos. tom. 12. 1871, *etc.* 8º. **12230. aa.**

—— Del Tao de San Anton. Comedia famosa. (El Renegado Arrepentido. Comedia famosa.) *See* Schaeffer (A.) Ocho comedias desconocidas, *etc.* 1887. 8º. [*Coleccion de Autores Españoles.* tom. 47.] **12230.bb.6/47.**

—— Comedia famosa. Allà van Leyes, donde quieren Reyes. 1662. *See* Spain. [*Appendix.—Miscellaneous.*] Primera [*etc.*] parte de comedias escogidas de los mejores de España. pt. 16. 1652, *etc.* 4º. **11725. b. 16.**

—— [Another edition.] ms. note [by J. R. Chorley]. [1700?] 4º. **11728. h. 8. (1.)**

—— Comedia famosa, Las Canas en el Papel, y Dudoso en la Venganza. De Don Pedro Calderon [or rather, by G. de Castro y Bellvis]. 1661. 4º. [*Primera [etc.] parte de comedias escogidas de los mejores ingenios de España.* pt. 14.] *See* Calderón de la Barca (P.) [*Doubtful or Supposititious Works.*] **11725. b. 14.**

—— [Another edition.] ff. 16. [1700?] 4º. *See* Calderón de la Barca (P.) [*Doubtful or Supposititious Works.*] **87. b. 1. (5.)**

—— [Another edition.] [1720?] 4º. *See* Calderón de la Barca (P.) [*Doubtful or Supposititious Works.*] **11728. h. 15. (8.)**

—— [Another edition.] [1750?] 4º. *See* Calderón de la Barca (P.) [*Doubtful or Supposititious Works.*] **11728. a. 78.**

—— Comedia del Conde de Irlos. [1620?] 4º. **C. 63. g. 7.**

—— Don Quixote de la Mancha. [1700?] 4º. **T. 1736. (4.**

—— Donde no està su Dueño està su Duelo. Comedia famosa. [1750?] 4º. **T. 1736. (2.)**

—— Los Enemigos Hermanos, comedia famosa. [1700?] 4º. **1072. h. 6. (1.)**

—— Engañarse engañando, comedia famosa. [1710?] 4º. **T. 1736. (3.)**

—— Ingratitud por Amor. Comedia . . . Edited, with an introduction, by Hugo A. Rennert. pp. 120. *Philadelphia*, 1899. 8º. [*Publications of the University of Pennsylvania.* Series in Philology, Literature and Archaeology. vol. 7. no. 1.] **Ac. 2692. p/2.**

—— Los Mal Casados de Valencia. 1838. *See* Spanish Authors. Coleccion de los Mejores Autores Españoles. tom. 10. 1835, *etc.* 8º. **12230. h. 1/10.**

—— [Another edition.] *See* Spanish Theatre. Coleccion Selecta del Antiguo Teatro Español, *etc.* 1854. 8º. **2298. i. 3.**

—— Comedia famosa, Las Marauillas de Babilonia. *See* Spain. [*Appendix.—Miscellaneous.*] Flor de las meiores doce comedias de los mayores ingenios de España, *etc.* 1652. 4º. **C. 34. i. 27**

CASTRO Y BELLVIS (Guillén de)

—— Comedia famosa : Las Mocedades del Cid. Primera parte. pp. 34. *Madrid*, [1780?] 4º. **11728. h. 8. (2.)**

—— [Another edition.] pp. 36. *Valencia*, 1796. 4º. **11728. c. 1. (1.)**

—— [Another copy.] **1342. e. 6. (47.)**

—— Première partie des Mocedades del Cid . . . publiée d'après l'édition princeps, avec une étude critique sur la vie et les œuvres de l'auteur, un commentaire et des poésies inédites, par E. Mérimée. pp. cxvii. 165. *Toulouse*, 1890. 8º. [*Bibliothèque méridionale* sér. 1. tom. 2.] **12238. ee. 4/2.**

—— La Jeunesse du Cid, *etc.* [A prose translation, by H. J. J. Lucas, of the first part of "Las Mocedades del Cid." *See* Lucas (Hippolyte J. J.) Documents relatifs. à l'histoire du Cid. 1860. 8º. **10633. g. 25.**

—— Comedia famosa : Las Mocedades del Cid. Segunda parte. pp. 37. *Madrid*, 1780. 4º. **11728. h. 8. (3.)**

—— [Another copy.] **11728. c. 1. (2.)**

—— [Another edition.] pp. 36. *Valencia*, 1796. 4º. **1342. e. 6. (48.)**

—— Las Mocedades del Cid. Primera (segunda) parte. *See* Michaelis de Vasconcellos (C.) Tres Flores del Teatro Antiguo Español. 1870. 8º. [*Coleccion de Autores Españoles.* tom. 27.] **12230.bb.6/27.**

—— [Another edition.] Reimpresion conforme a la original publicada en Valencia 1621. [With a preface by W. Foerster.] pp. viii. 214. *Bonn*, 1878. 8º. **11725. bb. 2.**

—— [Another edition.] pp. 190. *Chatto & Windus: London; J. H. E. Heitz: Strassburg; printed in Germany*, 1907. 16º. [*Bibliotheca Romanica.* no. 37–39.] **012207.f.22/16.**

—— [Another edition.] Edición y notas de Víctor Sáid Armesto. pp. xxix. 286. *Madrid*, 1913. 8º. **11725. de. 30.**

—— Las Mocedades del Cid. Edición, estudio y notas por Eduardo Julía Martínez, *etc.* pp. 135. *Zaragoza*, [1940.] 8º. **11729. aa. 16.**

—— La Jeunesse du Cid, première et seconde parties. [A prose translation, with a comparison of the Cid of G. de Castro and of P. Corneille, by V. L. S. M. Angliviel de la Beaumelle.] 1823. *See* Chefs-d'œuvre. Chefs-d'œuvre des théâtres étrangers, *etc.* tom. 16. 1822, *etc.* 8º. **1342. h. 16.**

—— *See* Bilderdijk (W.) [*Single Works.*] Bydragen tot de tooneelpoëzy. (Over het Spaansche treurspel van Don Guillem de Castro : De Heldendaden van den Cid.) 1823. 8º. **1209. d. 21.**

—— *See* Fée (A. L. A.) Études sur l'ancien théâtre espagnol. Lestro is Cid, Guillen de Castro, Corneille, Diamante, *etc.* 1873. 12º. **2306. a. 7.**

—— *See* Jachino (G.) Il Cid di Guglielmo De Castro e di Pietro Corneille, *etc.* 1890. 8º. **011824. f. 32. (6.)**

—— El Nieto de su Padre, comedia famosa. 1658. *See* Spain. [*Appendix.—Miscellaneous.*] Primera [*etc.*] parte de comedias escogidas de los mejores de España. vol. 10. 1652, *etc.* 4º. **11725. b. 10.**

—— Comedia famosa. La Piedad en la Justicia. 1666. *See* Spain. [*Appendix.—Miscellaneous.*] Primera [*etc.*] parte de comedias escogidas de los meiores ingenios de España. vol. 26. 1652, *etc.* 4º. **11725. c. 5.**

CASTRO Y BELLVIS (GUILLÉN DE)

—— Comedia famosa. El Prodigio de los Montes, y Martir del Cielo. *See* AUTOS. Autos Sacramentales, *etc.*
1655. 4º.   **1072. l. 2.**

—— [Another edition.] *Madrid*, 1729. 4º.
                                    11728. h. 8. (4.)

—— [Another copy.]   **11728. c. 2.**
The titlepage is slightly mutilated.

CASTRO Y BRAVO (FEDERICO DE)

—— Derecho civil de España. Segunda edición, *etc.*
Madrid, 1949– . 8º.   **W.P. c. 269.**

——   Las Naos Españolas
en la carrera de las Indias. Armadas y flotas en la segunda mitad del siglo XVI. pp. 284. *Madrid*, 1927. 8º.
                                    08806. a. 44.

CASTRO Y CALVO (JOSÉ MARÍA)

—— *See* JOHN EMMANUEL, *Infant of Spain, Grandson of Saint Ferdinand.* Libro de la caza. Edición de José María Castro y Calvo. 1945. 8º.   **7921. a. 23.**

—— *See* VERDAGUER (J.) Jacinto Verdaguer. Prólogo y selección de J. M. Castro y Calvo. 1945. 8º.
                                    11869. d. 40.

—— El Arte de gobernar en las obras de Don Juan Manuel. pp. 426. *Barcelona*, 1945. 8º.   **Ac. 132. c/10**

CASTRO Y CASALEIZ (ANTONIO DE) *See* WALLS Y MERINO (M.) La Extradición y el procedimiento judicial internacional en España . . . Precedido de una monografía de la extradición por D. A. de Castro y Casaleiz. 1905. 8º.   **06955. e. 1.**

—— Estudios de Derecho internacional privado. Conflictos de nacionalidad. Condición del extranjero ; heimathlosat ; naturalización y naturalizaciones criminales ; libertad de expatriación ó de emigración, *etc.* pp. 303. *Madrid*, 1900. 8º.   **06955. g. 29.**

CASTRO Y CASTILLO (GERONIMO DE) *See* CASTILLO (J. del) Historia de los Reyes Godos, que vinieron de la Scythia de Europa, contra el Imperio Romano ; y a España . . . por I. del Castillo, proseguida desde su principio cõ adiciones de todos tiempos hasta el del dõ Filipe IIII., por G. de Castro y Castillo, *etc.* 1624. fol.
                                    180. f. 16.

CASTRO Y DE LA CUEVA (BELTRAN DE) *See* VALAGUER Y SALZEDO (P.) Relacion de lo que hizo Don B. de Castro, y de la Cueua en la entrada de Iuan de Aquines ingles por el estrecho de Magallanes, *etc.*
[1594.] 8º.   **C. 32. a. 23.**

CASTRO Y ESPEJO (LEÓN) Zootecnia aplicada á la economía rural y doméstica. pp. 288.   *Madrid*, 1865. 8º.   **7294. cc. 12.**

CASTRO Y FERNÁNDEZ (FEDERICO DE) *See* SOLOMON BEN JUDAH ABEN GABIROL. La Fuente de la Vida. Traducida . . . por F. de Castro y Fernández. [1902.] 8º.   **14540. b. 33.**

—— Cervantes y la Filosofía Española. pp. 50.   *Sevilla*, 1870. 8º.   **011852. i. 12. (1.)**

—— [Another copy.]   **Cerv. 595.**

—— Recuerdo Biográfico del doctor Don Rafael Alvarez Sanchez Surga. *See* ALVAREZ SANCHEZ SURGA (R.) Obras. 1873. 8º.   **12231. f. 14**

CASTRO Y FRANGANILLO (CARLOS A. DE) *See* ABELA Y SAINZ DE ANDINO (E.) Memoria sobre el estado de la agricultura en la provincia de Madrid . . . Precedida del informe redactado por . . . C. A. de Castro y Franganillo. 1876. 8º.   **7078. dd. 2.**

CASTRO Y HERNANDEZ (MAGDALENO DE) Nacionalismo, Humanismo y Civilización. La constitución interna de España y la ideología catalanista. pp. 366. *Madrid*, 1922. 8º.   **08042. a. 13.**

CASTRO Y JARILLO (ANTONIO DE) La Sala de Goya del Museo de la Real Academia de San Fernando. [With illustrations.] 1930. 8º. *See* MADRID.—*Real Academia de San Fernando, etc.*   **Ac. 4521/11. (2.)**

CASTRO Y LOPEZ (JOSÉ DE) *See* VEGA INCLAN (M. de la) Relacion histórica de la última campaña del Marqués del Duero. Homenaje . . . que tributan . . . M. de la Vega Inclan . . . J. de Castro y Lopez, *etc.* 1874. 8º.
                                    9180. ff. 17

CASTRO Y MENA (RODRIGO) Oracion funebre á las reales exequias del rey . . . Carlos II., *etc. See* BUENDIA (J. de) Parentacion Real, *etc.* 1701. 4º. **10631. bbb. 44.**

CASTRO Y ORDOÑEZ (R.) *See* VINA (J. de la) Galería de Contemporáneos. Retratos fotográficos por R. Castro y Ordoñez, *etc.* [1860, *etc.*] 16º.
                                    10632. aa. 13.

CASTRO Y OROZCO ALVAREZ COGOLLOS (JOSÉ DE) *Marquis de Gerona.. See* MANRESA Y NAVARRO (J. M.) Instruccion del procedimiento civil, con respecto a la real jurisdiccion ordinaria, *etc.* (Reformas judiciales del Excmo Señor Marques de Gerona.). 1853. 8º.
                                    5385. b. 21.

—— *See* SPAIN. [*Laws, etc.*—III. *Penal Code.*] Código penal reformado . . . con notas y observaciones . . . por J. de Castro y Orozco, *etc.* 1850. 8º.   **5385. c. 15.**

—— Obras Poeticas y Literarias. 2 tom.   *Madrid*, 1864, 65. 8º.   **12230. aa. 5.**

—— Fr. Luis de Leon, ó el Siglo y el claustro. Melodrama en cuatro actos y en diferentes metros. pp. 95.   *Madrid*, 1837. 8º. [*Galeria Dramatica.* vol. 4.]
                                    1342. f. 10. (1.)

CASTRO Y PADILLA (MANUEL DE) Relacion del nueuo descubrimiento de las minas ricas del assiento de san Miguel de Oruro de la prouincia de Paria, juridicion de la Real Audiencia de la Plata, y villa de San Felipe de Austria, que en ella fundò el licenciado don M. de Castro y Padilla, *etc.* ff. 8. [1630 ?] fol.   **725. k. 18. (8.)**

—— [Another copy.]   **725. k. 18. (11.)**

CASTRO Y PARA (FEDERICO) De la leucocythémie. pp. 28. *Paris*, 1868. 4º. [*Collection des thèses soutenues à la Faculté de Médecine de Paris.* An 1868. tom. 3.]
                                    7373. i. 7.

CASTRO Y ROSSI (ADOLFO DE) *See* ABREU (Pedro de) Historia del Saqueo de Cadiz . . . en 1596, *etc.* [Edited by A. de Castro y Rossi.] 1866. 8º.   **9180. ee. 1.**

—— *See* CALDERON DE LA BARCA (P.) [*Poems.*] Poesias . . . Con anotaciones, y un discurso . . . sobre los plagios, que . . . cometio Le Sage, al escribir su Gil Blas de Santillana ; por A. de Castro. 1845. 12º.   **11451. d. 9.**

—— *See* CERVANTES SAAVEDA (M. de) [*Works.—Spanish.*] Varias Obras inéditas . . . sacadas de códices de la Biblioteca Colombina, con nuevas ilustraciones sobre la vida del autor y el Quijote, por . . . A. de Castro. 1874. 8º.   **12230. e. 1.**

CASTRO Y ROSSI (Adolfo de)

—— *See* Gonzalez del Castillo (J. J.) Sainetes . . . con un discurso sobre este género de composiciones por A. de Castro. 1845, *etc.* 12°. [*Galería Dramatica Gaditana.* tom. 1–4.] **11726. d. 12.**

—— *See* Herrero (J. B.) Reyes Contemporaneos, *etc.* (tom. 1. Hollanda. Guillermo III. [By A. de Castro y Rossi.]) 1855, *etc.* 4°. **9077. h. 12.**

—— *See* Vinajeras (A.) Ideas, *etc.* [Edited by A. de Castro y Rossi.] 1862. 8°. **11475. e. 29.**

—— Biografía del . . . Señor D. Fray Domingo de Silos Moreno, obispo que fué de Cádiz. pp. 128. *Cadiz,* 1853. 8°. **4855. a. 12.**
Imperfect ; wanting the portrait.

—— El Buscapié. Opúsculo inédito que en defensa de la primera parte del Quijote escribió Míguel de Cervantes Saavedra. Publicado con notas históricas, críticas i bibliográficas por Don Adolfo de Castro [the real author of the whole book]. pp. xix. 194. 1848. 12°. *See* Cervantes Saavedra (M. de) [*Don Quixote.—Appendix.—Criticism.*] **12490. c. 20.**

—— [Another copy.] Cerv. **441.**

—— [Another copy.] copious ms. notes [by Rawdon Brown]. C. **60. h. 6.**

—— [Another edition.] *See* Cervantes Saavedra (M. de) [*Don Quixote.—Spanish.—Pt. I., II.*] El Ingenioso Hidalgo Don Quijote de la Mancha . . . Novisima edicion clásica, *etc.* 1850. 8°. **12490. k. 9.**

—— Obra corregida y aumentada en esta cuarta edicion. pp. 34. [1851.] 8°. *See* Cervantes Saavedra (M. de) [*Doubtful or Soppositicious Works.*] Cerv. **618.**

—— [Another edition.] *See* Cervantes Saavedra (M. de) [*Don Quixote.—Spanish.—Pt. I., II.*] El Ingenioso Hidalgo Don Quijote de la Mancha . . . Novísima edicion clásica, *etc.* 1851. 4°. C. **60. n. 5.**

—— [Another edition.] *See* Cervantes Saavedra (M. de) [*Don Quixote.—Spanish.—Pt. I., II.*] El Ingenioso Hidalgo Don Quijote de la Mancha, *etc.* 1865. 8°. **12490. k. 8.**

—— [Another edition.] *See* Cervantes Saavedra (M. de) [*Don Quixote.—Spanish.—Pt. I., II.*] El Ingenioso Hidalgo Don Quijote de la Mancha . . . Novísima edición, *etc.* 1887. 8°. **12491. l. 28.**

—— El Buscapié. Cosas escondidas en la primera parte de Don Quijote de la Mancha. [By A. de Castro y Rossi.] Con 50 notas de E. H. pp. 99. [1905.] 8°. *See* Cervantes Saavedra (M. de) [*Don Quixote.—Appendix.—Criticism.*] **11851. aa. 7.**

—— El Buscapié. By Miguel de Cervantes [or rather by A. de Castro] . . . Translated with a life of the author [i.e. of Cervantes] and some account of his work, by Thomasina Ross. pp. xii. 235. 1849. 12°. *See* Cervantes Saavedra (M. de) [*Don Quixote.—Appendix.—Criticism.*] **12490. e. 9.**

—— [Another copy.] ms. notes [by Rawdon Brown]. C. **60. h. 5.**

—— [Another copy, with a longer list of errata.] Cerv. **442.**

—— The ' Squib ' or Searchfoot: an unedited little work which Miguel de Cervantes Saavedra wrote in defence of the first part of the Quijote. Published [or rather written] by Don Adolfo de Castro . . . Translated . . . by a Member of the University of Cambridge. pp. xv. 79. 1849. 8°. *See* Cervantes Saavedra (M. de) [*Don Quixote.—Appendix.—Criticism.*] **12490. e. 16.**

CASTRO Y ROSSI (Adolfo de)

—— *See* Barrera y Leirado (C. A. de la) El Cachetero del Buscapié, *etc.* [Resumen de las pruebas de hecho y de las razones críticas que evidencian la falsedad del '' Buscapié.'') 1916. 8°. **011853. r. 4.**

—— *See* Bo-Vaina, *el Bachiller, pseud.* El Buscapié del Buscaruido de Don A. de Castro, *etc.* 1851. 8°. **9180. d. 2. (4.)**

—— *See* C.-P., J. B. Carta al editor del Buscapié (A. de Castro y Rossi), *etc.* [1848.] 12°. **12491. aa. 15.**

—— *See* Gallardo (B. J.) Zapatazo a Zapatilla, i a su falso Buscapié un puntillazo : juguete crítico-burlesco . . . En carta a los redactores de La Ilustrazion, con varios rasgos sueltos de ótras sobre la falsificazion de El Buscapié, qe Adolfillo de Castro nos qiere vender como de Zervantes. 1851. 8°. Cerv. **536.**

—— Cadiz en la Guerra de la Independencia. Cuadro histórico . . . Segunda edicion. pp. 201. *Cadiz,* 1864. 8°. **9180. bb. 14.**

—— Cadiz y la primera expedicion de Colon. Refutaciones al Sr. Asencio [i.e. to his article in '' La España Moderna '' entitled: '' La carta de C. Colón con la relación del descubrimiento del Nuevo Mundo '']. pp. 33. *Cadiz,* 1891. 8°. **9004. c. 18. (1.)**

—— Camoens morimundo [*sic*] y la sombra de Ignês de Castro. *See* Araujo (J. de) Ignês de Castro : notas de bibliographia, *etc.* 1897. 8°. **011900. g. 13. (3.)**

—— Combates de Toros en España y Francia. pp. 104. *Madrid,* [1889.] 8°. **7907. aa. 63.**

—— El Conde-Duque de Olivares y el Rey Felipe IV. 2 pt. *Cadiz,* 1846. 8°. **10632. d. 3.**

—— Curiosidades bibliográficas, coleccion escogida de obras raras de amenidad y erudicion con apuntes biográficos de los diferentes autores. pp. xxiv. 556. *Madrid,* 1855. 8°. [*Biblioteca de Autores Españoles,* tom. 36.]
12232.f.1/36.

—— El Despuntar del Dia, escena de muerte y vida. Monólogo. pp. 16. *Puerto de Santa María,* 1876. 8°. **11725. ee. 10. (5.)**

—— Discurso acerca de las costumbres públicas y privadas de los Españoles en el siglo XVII. fundado en el estudio de las comedias de Calderon. Premidao por la Real Academia de Ciencias Morales y Políticas, *etc.* pp. 173. *Madrid,* 1881. 8°. **11840. l. 26.**

—— La Epistola Moral á Fabio no es de Rioja. Descubrimiento de su autor verdadero (A. Fernandez de Andrada). pp. 79. *Cádiz,* 1875. 8°. **11840. f. 10. (1.)**

—— Estudios prácticos de buen decir y de arcanidades del habla española, con un escrito sin verbo, otro sin nombres, otró con nombres y verbos solos y otro sin nombres y verbos. pp. 343. *Cádiz,* 1879. 8°. **12941. df. 4.**

—— Examen filosófico sobre las principales causas de la decadencia de España. pp. vii. 158. *Cádiz,* 1852. 4°. **9180. e. 9.**

—— History of Religious Intolerance in Spain : or, an Examination of some of the causes which led to that nation's decline . . . Translated from the Spanish . . . by Thomas Parker. [With a portrait.] pp. xxiv. 227. *W. & F. G. Cash: London,* 1853. 8°. **4625. d. 14.**

—— Filosofia de la Muerte. pp. 95. *Cádiz,* 1856. 16°. **8407. a. 17.**

CASTRO Y ROSSI (Adolfo de)

—— La Gota de Rocio, escena de muerte y vida. Monólogo. [In verse.] pp. 15. *Puerto de Santa María*, 1876. 8º.
11450. ee. 13.

—— Historia de Cádiz y su Provincia desde los remotos tiempos hasta 1814. pp. xvi. 826. *Cádiz*, 1858. 8º.
10161. e. 22.

—— Historia de la muy noble, muy leal y muy heróica Ciudad de Cádiz. pp. 144. xliv. *Cádiz*, 1845. 8º.
10160. b. 8.

—— Historia de la muy noble, muy leal y muy ilustre Ciudad de Xerez de la Frontera. 2 pt. *Cádiz*, 1845. 8º.
10160. e. 29.

—— Historia de la venida del Ingles sobre Cádiz en 1625. pp. 20. *Cádiz*, 1844. 12º.
1444. a. 6. (1.)

—— Historia de los Judios en España desde los tiempos de su establecimiento hasta principios del presente siglo, *etc.* pp. 224. 29. *Cádiz*, 1847. 8º.
4515. c. 10.

—— The History of the Jews in Spain, from the time of their settlement in that country till the commencement of the present century . . . Translated by the Rev. Edward D. G. M. Kirwan. pp. vii. 276. *John Deighton: Cambridge*, 1851. 8º.
4515. c. 11.

—— Historia de los Protestantes Españoles y de su Persecucion por Felipe II. pp. 460. *Cádiz*, 1851. 4º.
4625. d. 11.

—— The Spanish Protestants, and their Persecution by Philip II . . . Translated . . . by Thomas Parker. pp. lxiv. 386. *Charles Gilpin: London*, 1851. 16º.
4625. a. 5.

—— Una Joya Desconocida de Calderon [i.e. " La Adultera Penitente," attributed to him by the writer]; estudio acerca de ella . . . Segunda edicion. pp. 48. *Cádiz*, 1881. 8º.
11840. f. 17. (2.)

—— Libro de los Galicismos. pp. 143. *Madrid*, [1898.] 8º.
12941. d. 17.

—— Memoria sobre la ilegitimidad del Centon Epistolario (del Bachiller Fernan-Gomez de Cibdareal) y sobre su autor verdadero. [Attributing it to Gil Gonzalez de Avila.] pp. 22. *Cádiz*, 1857. 8º.
10921. c. 24.

—— Obras escogidas de filósofos, con un discurso preliminar del . . . Señor Don A. de Castro. pp. cl. 611. *Madrid*, 1873. 8º. [*Biblioteca de Autores Españoles.* tom. 65.]
12232.f.1/65.

—— Poetas líricos de los siglos XVI y XVII, coleccion ordenada por Don A. de Castro. 2 tom. *Madrid*, 1854, 59. 8º. [*Biblioteca de Autores Españoles.* tom. 32, 42.]
12232.f.1/32.42.

—— La Última Novela Ejemplar de Cervantes. [The story of his last days.] pp. 30. *Cádiz*, 1872. 8º. *Cerv. 559.*

—— Vidas de Niños Célebres. pp. vi. 101. *Cádiz*, 1865. 8º.
10603. aaa. 5.

CASTRO Y SERRANO (José de) *See* Zea (Francisco)
Poet. Obras, *etc.* (Prologo biográfico por D. J. de Castro y Serrano.) 1858. 8º.
12230. e. 16.

—— Obras literarias. 3 tom. *Madrid*, 1887. 8º.
12231. h. 7.

—— La Capitana Cook. Estudio de viajes. pp. 216. *Madrid*, 1871. 12º.
12491. e. 17.

CASTRO Y SERRANO (José de)

—— Cartas Trascendentales escritas á un amigo de confianza . . . Segunda edicion. sér. 1. pp. 250. *Madrid*, 1863. 8º.
8405. bb. 37.

—— Cervantes. pp. 58. *Madrid*, 1904. 16º.
10630. a. 52.

—— Cuadros Contemporáneos. pp. 411. *Madrid*, 1871. 8º.
12354. g. 15.

—— Los Cuartetos del Conservatorio : breves consideraciones sobre la música clásica. pp. 218. *Madrid*, 1866. 16º.
7896. a. 24.

—— España en Londres ; correspondencias sobre la Exposicion Universal de 1862. pp. 438. *Madrid*, 1862. 8º.
10349. bb. 24.

—— Segunda edicion. pp. 458. *Madrid*, 1867. 8º.
7957. de. 11.

CASTRO ZAMBRANO (Franciscus de)

—— Oratio pro certamine litterario Mexicanae Academiae in proclamatione Caroli Quarti, Hispaniarum Regis, *etc.* *See* Mexico, *City of.*—*Universidad Nacional Autónoma de Mexico.* Obras de Eloquencia, *etc.* 1791. 4º.
10632. bbb.

CASTRO ZAMORENSE (Alfonso de) *See* Castro (Alphonsus à)

CASTRUCCI (Giacomo) Tesoro letterario di Ercolano, ossia la Reale officina dei papiri ercolanesi.
pp. vii. 36. pl. XVII. *Napoli*, 1852. 4º. **813. h. 26.**

—— Seconda edizione accresciuta. pp. vi. 38. pl. xx. *Napoli*, 1855. 4º.
7708. e. 1. (6.)

—— [Verses in Latin, Greek and Italian on the death of the Marchioness Anna Maria Caracciolo.] pp. 15. [1850?] 8º.
11426. ccc. 17. (15.)

CASTRUCCI (Giovanni Paolo Matthia) Descrittione
del ducato d'Aluito nel regno di Napoli, *etc.* *C. Cauallo: Napoli*, 1686. 8º. **662. a. 15.**
Imperfect; wanting all after p. 140.

CASTRUCCI (Jacobus) *See* Castrucci (Giacomo)

CASTRUCCI (Niccolò) Vita del Beato Ambrogio Traversari da Portico di Romagna, *etc.* (Supplemento storico.) 2 pt. *Lucca*, 1722. 4º. **4827. c. 14.**

CASTRUCCI (Pietro) La Settimana istorica, ouero le
Felicità et infelicità occorse alli rè, regni, stati, republiche, famiglie, città e popoli più rinomati del mondo in ciascun' giorno della settimana. pp. 627. *A. Faostini: Todi*, 1655. 4º. **581. e. 19.**

CASTRUCCI (Pietro Cecconi Fantoni) *See* Cecconi Fantoni Castrucci.

CASTRUCCI (Sebastiano Fantoni) *See* Fantoni Castrucci.

CASTRUCCI DE VERNAZZA (Manuel) Viaje practicado desde el Callao hasta las misiones de las dos tribus de infieles, Záparos y Gívaros. pp. 44. *Lima*, 1849. 4º.
10481. de. 1.

CASTRUCCIO [Castracani degli Antelminelli], *Duke of Lucca.* [For editions and translations of Macchiavelli's Life of Castruccio Castracani published with editions of " Il Principe " :] *See* Macchiavelli (N.) [*Smaller Collections.*]

—— *See* Macchiavelli (N.) [*Minor Works.*] The Life of Castruccio Castracani of Lucca. Translated from the Italian original, *etc.* 1721. 12º. [*A Select Collection of Novels, etc.* vol. 6.] **12410. c. 17.**

CASTRUCCIO [CASTRACANI DEGLI ANTELMINELLI], *Duke of Lucca.*

—— *See* MACCHIAVELLI (N.) [*Minor Works.*] L'Histoire de Castruccio Castracani, *etc.* 1571. 12°.　**10629. a. 6.**

—— *See* MANUZIO (A.) *the Younger.* Le Attioni di Castruccio Castracane, *etc.* 1590. 4°.　**612. g. 11.**

—— —— 1820. 8°.　**10631. df. 18.**

—— —— 1843. 8°.　**1450. e. 26.**

——*See* SFORZA (G.) Castruccio Castracani degli Antelminelli e gli altri Lucchesi di parte Bianca in esilio, 1300–1314, *etc.* 1892. 4°. [*Memorie della Reale Accademia delle Scienze di Torino.* ser. 2. tom. 42. pt. 2.]　　　　Ac. **2816.**

—— *See* SFORZA (G.) Castruccio Castracani degli Antelminelli in Lunigiana. Ricerche storiche. 1891. [*Atti delle Reali Deputazioni di Storia Patria per le Provincie Modenesi e Parmensi.* ser. 3. vol. 6. pt. 2.]　　Ac. **6520.**

—— *See* TEGRIMUS (N.)　*Begin.* [fol. 2 *recto :*] Ad. illustriss. ac. excellentiss. ducum. Ludouicum Mariam. Sfortiam. Vicecom. Mediolani. Ducem. Nicolai Tegrimi . . . in Castruccii Ducis vitam. praefatio. [fol. 4 *recto :*] Castruccii Antelminelli. Castracani. Lucensis. Ducis. vita. 1496. fol.　　　　　　　　　　　　　　　　IA. **32269.**

—— *See* TEGRIMUS (N.) Vita Castrucci Antelminelli Lucensis ducis ab anno 1301 usque ad 1328, *etc.* 1727. fol. [*MURATORI (L. A.) Rerum Italicarum scriptores, etc.* tom. 11.]　　　　　　　**L.1.h.1/11.**

—— —— 1742. 4°.　**662. e. 10.**

—— *See* TEGRIMUS (N.)　Le Vite di Castruccio Castracani . . . di M. N. Tegrimo . . . e del minore Scipione . . . di M. A. Bendinelli, *etc.* 1556. 8°.　**275. a. 42. (1.)**

—— *See* WINKLER (F.) Castruccio Castracani, *etc.* 1897. 8°.　　　　　　　　　　　　　　　**09010. d. 1/9.**

—— Castruccio Castracani degli Antelminelli. Miscellanea di studi storici e letterari edita dalla Reale Accademia Lucchese. pp. 409. pl. XIII. *Firenze,* 1934. 8°. [*Atti della R. Accademia Lucchese di Scienze, Lettere ed Arti.* Nuova serie. tom. 3.]　　　　　　Ac. **58.**

—— Vita di Castruccio Castracani Antelminelli, signore di Lucca. pp. 52. *Livorno,* 1760. 4°.　**277. f. 40.**

CASTRUCCIO (LUIS)　*See* INGEGNIEROS (J.) El Envenenador Castruccio. Estudio psicopatológico. 1910. 8°.　　　　　　　　　　　**6055. eee. 17. (6.)**

CASTRUCCIO (RODOLFO) Der Bruch des Kahnbeins des Carpus. [With plates.] 1907. *See* BRUNS (P. von) Mittheilungen aus der chirurgischen Klinik zu Tübingen, *etc.* (Beiträge zur klinischen Chirurgie, *etc.*) Bd. 53. Hft. 1. 1886, *etc.* 8°.　　　**P.P.2927.aa.**

CASTRUCCIUS CASTRACANUS, *Antelminellus, Duke of Lucca. See* CASTRUCCIO [Castracani degli Antelminelli].

CASTRUM.

—— Castrum peregrini. *See* PERIODICAL PUBLICATIONS.— *Amsterdam.*

—— Castrum peregrini. [A volume in memory of Percy Gothein, Vincent Weijand, Liselotte von Gandersheim.] *See* DU CHATTEL (R. van Rossum)

CASTRUM FIDARDUM. *See* CASTELFIDARDO.

CASTRUNOVU (TUMASI D'AVERSA E) *See* AVERSA E CASTRONOVO (Tommaso d')

CASTRUP (JOHANNES J.) *Praes.* Theses porrò philologicas de methodo disciplinarum . . . offert J. J. Castrup. *Resp.* J. Wicher. *Havniæ,* [1709.] 4°.　**8307. f. 18.**

CÁSTULO DE ALATRISTE (MIGUEL) Discurso sobre la cronología para el estudio de la historia. pp. 48. *México,* 1844. 8°.　　　　**9008. bbb. 23. (1.)**

CASTULUS, *Saint. See* KREITMAN (M.) Histori von dem Fürtreffenlichen Ritter und . . . Martyr S. Castl, *etc.* 1584. 8°.　　　　　　　**4827. aa. 34.**

——, *Monastery of, in Moosburg.* Einführung und Beleuchtung des Codex traditionum Monasterii Sti. Castuli in Moosburg. Von M. Frhrn. von Freyberg. [With the text of the Codex.] pp. 119. lxxv. *München,* 1840. 4°. [*Abhandlungen der k. bayerischen Akademie der Wissenschaften.* Hist. Classe. Bd. 2.]　　Ac. **713/5.**

CASTUS, *Saint and Martyr. See* POLLIDORI (G. B.) Vita et antiqua monimenta Sancti Pardi . . . animadversionibus criticis illustrata . . . in iis agitur etiam de SS. Primiano . . . et Casto, *etc.* 1741. 4°.　　　　　　　　　　　　**663. d. 22. (1.)**

CASTYNE (ODA VAN DE)

—— L'Architecture privée en Belgique dans les centres urbains aux XVIᵉ et XVIIᵉ siècles. [With illustrations.] pp. 356. *Bruxelles,* 1934. 4°. [*Académie royale de Belgique. Mémoires.* Collection in-4°. Classe des Beaux-Arts. sér. 2. tom. 4. fasc. 1.]　　Ac. **985/50. (4.)**

—— [Another issue.]　　　L'Architecture privée en Belgique dans les centres urbains au XVIᵉ et XVIIᵉ siècles. (Extrait des Mémoires publiés par l'Académie Royale de Belgique, Classe des Beaux-Arts, Collection in-4°.) *Bruxelles,* 1934. 4°.　　　　　**7817. s. 22.**

CASU ADAMI (GIUSEPPE) La Pescatrice. Dramma lirico, *etc.* [In verse.] pp. 83. *Sassari,* 1867. 16°.　　　　　　　　　　　**11715. aa. 63. (3.)**

CASUAL. That Reminds me. [Anecdotes.] By " Casual." *Civil & Military Gazette Press : Lahore,* [1922.] 8°.　　　　　　　　　　　**012316. df. 24.**

CASUAL CLUB. *See* LONDON.—III.

CASUALTY, *pseud.* " Contemptible." By " Casualty." pp. vi. 226.　　*William Heinemann : London,* 1916. 8°. [*Soldiers' Tales of the Great War.*]　**9081. c. 1/2.**

CASUALTY SIMULATION.

—— Casualty Simulation. *See* ENGLAND.—*Casualties Union.* Casualties Union Journal.

CASUCCHI (NICCOLÒ)　*See* MONTAPERTI (N.)

CASUCCINI (OTTAVIO BONCI)　*See* BONCI CASUCCINI.

CASUCCINI (PIETRO BONCI)　*See* BONCI CASUCCINI.

CASUIST. The Casuist. A collection of cases in moral and pastoral theology. (Made up chiefly of cases that appeared in The Homiletic Monthly.)　3 vol. *J. F. Wagner : New York,* 1906–10. 8°.　**03558. ff. 9.**

CASULÁ (CARLOS) Causa de la Calle del Fucar, sobre homicidio perpetrado en la persona de Doña Vicenta Calza . . . Defensa de Don Carlos Casula por Don Simon Santos Lerin. pp. xix. 152. *Madrid,* 1864. 4°.　　　　　　　　　　　　　**5384. g. 3.**

CASULA (JUANE BATTISTA) *See* JESUS CHRIST. [*De Imitatione Christi.—Italian Dialects.*] De S. Imitassione de Cristos liberos battor. Tradussione Sardu-Logudoresa de J. B. Casula. 1871. 16°.　　I.X. Ital. Dial. **1.**

CASULANUS (PROTUS) De lingua, quà maximum est morborum acutorum signum, opus. pp. 144. *Apud P. Cecconcellium: Florentiæ*, 1621. 4º. **775. f. 2. (1.)**

ČAŠULE (KOLE)
—— Народен херој Страшо Пинџур. [With a portrait.] pp. 66. *Скопje*, 1950. 8º. **10798. de. 9.**

—— Народен херој Страшо Пинџур. [With a portrait.] pp. 97. *Скопje*, 1951. 8º. **10790. de. 66.**

CASULIS (JACOBUS DE) *See* CESSOLIS.

CASULLI (ANTONIO) *See* ARCOLEO (G.) Le Opere di Giorgio Arcoleo. (A cura di G. Paulucci di Calboli e A. Casulli.) 1929, *etc.* 8º. **012227.c.15.**

—— Giorgio Arcoleo. Con ritratto e bibliografia. II edizione. pp. 130. *Roma*, 1914. 8º. **10633. a. 17.**

CASUS. Casus conscientiæ ex Neo-confessario, seu methodo ritè obeundi munus confessarii, resolvendi. (Literæ et constitutiones Apostolicæ . . . quæ . . . clerum . . . concernunt.) [By Joannes Reuter.] pp. 194. *Coloniæ Agrippinæ*, 1758. 8º. **848. d. 24. (2.)**

—— Casus Papales. *See* PAPAL CASES.

—— Casus Penitentiales. *See* PAPAL CASES.

—— *Begin*. [fol. 1 *recto:*] Casus per modum questionis proponitur. 7 est talis. Vtrum liceat pueros ante pubertatis annos ad religionis ingressum inducere, *etc*. *End*. [fol. 12 *verso:*] Loppo zierrixee humilis seruitor vester. [By Gerardus de Elten.] ***G.A.*** [*Arnold ther Hoernen: Cologne*, 1480?] 4º. **IA. 3235.**
12 *leaves. Sig.* (I–VI)¹². 27 *lines to a page.*

—— Casus Placitorum and Reports of Cases in the King's Courts, 1272–1278. Edited with an introduction by William Huse Dunham. pp. xciv. 141. 176. *Bernard Quaritch: London*, 1952. 4º. [*Publications of the Selden Society.* vol. 69.] **Ac. 2176.**

CASUS (JOANNES) *See* CASE (John)

CASUS (MAXIMUS) Oberlehrer zu Druntenheim, pseud. [i.e. JEANNE MARIE VON GAYETTE, afterwards GAYETTE-GEORGENS.] Die Nebelscheuche . . . Dritte Auflage. 2 pt. *Berlin*, 1869. 16º. **12331. aaa. 43.**
Pt. 2 is of the second edition.

CASUTT (JOANN DE) Fuorma dilg Dreig Civil a Criminal, sco quel ven manaus enten ilg . . . cumin da Lgiont a da la Foppa, sco era enten ilg lud. singiuradi da Sax. Ansembel cun las fuormas dilg Sarament ca ven daus ad ün Mistral ad Oberkeit, *etc.* pp. 40. *Cuera*, 1731. 4º. **885. f. 31. (3.)**

CASVERA ( ) Abbé. I^er(–IIme) Noël. [By the Abbé Casvera.] pp. 4. [1845.] 8º. *See* NOËL. **11498. f. 2.**

CASWALL (ALFRED) *See* AUSTRALIAN SQUATTER. Hints from the Journal of an Australian Squatter . . . Edited . . . by A. Caswall. 1843. 8º. **1431. d. 16.**

—— A Letter to Edward Lytton Bulwer . . . on the present crisis, in answer to his Letter to a late Cabinet Minister . . . To which is added the address from Sir Robert Peel to his constituents. Second edition. pp. 38. *J. Hatchard & Son: London*, 1835. 8º. **T. 1602. (5.)**

—— A Treatise on Copyholds, containing the practical duties of the steward, bailiff, and other manorial officers, and remarks on copyhold enfranchisement, *etc.* pp. 67. *Simpkin, Marshall & Co.: London*, 1840. 12º. **6305. de. 5.**

CASWALL (ALFRED)
—— Third edition . . . Also the late Copyhold Act IV. and V. Vict. 35, with synopsis, analysis, notes and index. pp. xii. 204. 31. 11. *C. Reader: London*, 1841. 12º. **1380. c. 29.**

CASWALL (CHARLES) The Physiology of the Organ of Hearing deduced from its anatomy, *etc.* pp. x. 116. *Henry Wix: London*, 1833. 8º. **1186. d. 11.**

CASWALL (EDWARD) *See also* QUIZ, *pseud.* [i.e. E. Caswall.]

—— *See also* SCRIBLERUS, *Redivivus, pseud.* [i.e. E. Caswall.]

—— *See* BIBLE.—*Gospels.*—*Selections.* [*English.*] Verba Verbi. The words of Jesus arranged in order of time . . . by E. Caswall. 1855. 16º. **3050. a. 24.**

—— *See* NEWMAN (John H.) *Cardinal.* The Dream of Gerontius . . . Together with a biographical sketch of the Reverend John—Joseph—Gordon . . . compiled from details by the Reverend E. Caswall, *etc.* 1909. fol. **L.R.404.g.9.**

—— *See* PETIT (Pierre A). Love for Holy Church. From the French . . . By E. Caswall. 1862. 12º. **4409. bb. 45.**

—— *See* ROULLET DE LA BOUILLERIE (F. A.) successively *Bishop of Carcassonne* and *Archbishop of Perga.* Hours at the Altar . . . Edited by E. Caswall, *etc.* 1860. 12º. **4327. b. 58.**

—— The Art of Pluck, being a treatise after the fashion of Aristotle, writ for the use of students in the Universities. To which is added, Fragments from the examination papers. By Scriblerus Redivivus (E. Caswell [*sic*]). Twelfth edition. pp. xii. 62. *J. Vincent: Oxford*, 1874. 8º. **8365. aa. 21.**

—— New edition. pp. xvi. 75. *Bliss, Sands & Foster: London*, 1893. 8º. **8365. aaa. 9.**

—— The Catholic's Latin Instructor in the principal Church Offices and Devotions, *etc.* pp. viii. 273. *Burns & Oates: London*, 1897. 8º. **2274. c. 34.**

—— The Child's Manual: forty days' meditations on the chief truths of religion as contained in the Church Catechism. pp. xii. 97. *James Burns: London*, 1846. 16º. **1354. a. 19.**

—— Confraternity Manual of the Most Precious Blood. pp. 32. 1861. 16º. *See* JESUS CHRIST.—*Confraternity of the Most Precious Blood.* **3456. aa. 77. (7.)**

—— Devotions for Confession and Communion including Visits to the Blessed Sacrament. Edited by E. Caswall. [Chiefly extracted from " Les Délices des âmes pieuses."] pp. viii. 315. *James Burns: London*, 1849. 32º. **3455. aaaa. 19.**

—— The Altar Manual; or, Devotions for Confession and Communion . . . Third edition. pp. vii. 307. *James Duffy: Dublin*, 1859. 12º. **4327. b. 15.**

—— Hymns and Poems, original and translated . . . Second edition. pp. xii. 496. *Burns, Oates & Co.; Basil Montagu Pickering: London*, 1873. 16º. **3440. bb. 10.**

—— Hymns & Poems, original & translated . . . A new edition, with a biographical preface by Edward Bellasis. pp. 16. v–xii. 496. *Burns & Oates: London*, 1908. 8º. **11611. df. 19.**

—— Lyra Catholica: containing all the Breviary and Missal hymns, with others from various sources. Translated by E. Caswall. pp. xxxi. 311. 1849. 16º. *See* LITURGIES.—*Latin Rite.* [*Hymnals.*—I. *General.—English.*] **3434. a. 29.**

CASWALL (Edward)

—— [Another edition.] pp. 576. 1851. 12⁰. *See* LITURGIES. —*Latin Rite.* [*Hymnals.*—I. *General.*—*English.*]
3436. f. 43.

—— [Another edition.] pp. xxxi. 311. 1884. 32⁰. *See* LITURGIES.—*Latin Rite.* [*Hymnals*—I. *General.*— *English.*]
3438. ee. 16.

—— A Catholic Hymn-Book, for schools and private use. (Selected from "Lyra Catholica . . . translated by E. Caswall.") pp. 80. [1850?] 32⁰. *See* LITURGIES.— *Latin Rite.*—*Hymnals.*—I. [*English.*] **03440. de. 16.**

—— The Masque of Mary, and other poems. pp. xi. 391. *Burns & Lambert: London*, 1858 [1857]. 8⁰. **11650. c. 4.**

—— [Another edition.] pp. xi. 391. *Burns & Oates: London*, [1887.] 8⁰. **11652. d. 11.**

—— A May Pageant, and other poems. pp. 159. *Burns, Lambert & Co.: London*, 1865–[1864]. 18⁰.
11647. a. 17.

—— The Tale of Tintern. A May pageant . . . A new edition. pp. 142. *Burns & Oates: London*, [1907.] 8⁰.
011651. h. 59.

—— Morals from the Churchyard; in a series of cheerful fables. With illustrations by H. K. Browne. [The preface signed: E. C., i.e. E. Caswall.] pp. viii. 120. 1838. 16⁰. *See* C., E. **1210. g. 26.**

—— Sermons on the Seen and Unseen. pp. xii. 316. *James Burns: London*, 1846. 8⁰. **1358. g. 43.**

—— The Tale of Tintern, *etc. See* supra: A May Pageant, *etc.*

CASWALL (George) The Trifler, a satire inscribed to Lord —. [In verse.] pp. 23. *W. Flexney: London*, 1767. 4⁰. **11631. f. 5.**

CASWALL (Henry) *See* NEVILLE (William L.) Journal of a Voyage from Plymouth to Sierra Leone . . . Edited by H. Caswall. 1858. 12⁰. [*West Indian Church Association, etc.* Occasional Paper. no. 3.] **4766. bbb. 21.**

—— America, and the American Church. [With plates.] pp. xviii. 368. *J. G. & F. Rivington: London*, 1839. 12⁰.
792. g. 4.

—— Second edition. pp. xii. 400. *J. & C. Mozley: London*, 1851. 8⁰. **4745. de. 2.**

—— Samuel Gunn, the Lay-Reader. From the Rev. H. Caswall's "America and American Church." pp. 34. *Church Book Society: New York*, 1861. 12⁰. **4986. a. 7.**

—— The American Church and the American Union. pp. x. 300. *Saunders, Otley & Co.: London*, 1861. 8⁰.
4745. c. 26.

—— A Brief Account of the Method of Synodical Action in the American Church, *etc.* pp. 14. *J. Hatchard & Son: London*, 1851. 8⁰. **4745. c. 34. (4.)**

—— The City of the Mormons: or, Those days at Nauvoo, in 1842. pp. 82. *J. G. F. & J. Rivington: London*, 1842. 8⁰. **1369. b. 41.**

—— Didascalus; or, the Teacher: a Christmas present to the parents of England. [In verse.] pp. 31. *F. & J. Rivington: London*, 1850. 8⁰. **11645. a. 74. (11.)**

—— An Epitome of the History of the American Episcopal Church. pp. 24. *J. Clarke & Co.: Lexington*, 1836. 8⁰.
4745. aa. 13.

CASWALL (Henry)

—— The Jerusalem Chamber: or, Convocation and its possibilities. pp. 62. *F. & J. Rivington: London*, 1852. 8⁰. **4326. d. 19.**

—— The Jubilee [of the Society for the Propagation of the Gospel in Foreign Parts]; or, What I saw and heard in London on the 15th and 16th of June 1852. pp. 15. *F. & J. Rivington: London*, 1852. 8⁰. **4705. a. 19.**

—— (Second edition.) The Last Week of the Jubilee, *etc.* pp. 15. *F. & J. Rivington: London*, 1852. 8⁰.
4108. de. 15. (9.)

—— Liberty, Equality and Fraternity the Inheritance of Englishmen. A sermon, *etc.* pp. 16. *F. & J. Rivington, London*, 1848. 16⁰. **4475. cc. 26.**

—— The Martyr of the Pongas: being a memoir of the Rev. Hamble James Leacock, *etc.* [With a portrait.] pp. xvi. 294. *Rivingtons: London*, 1857. 8⁰. **4986. d. 18.**

—— Mormonism and its Author: or, a Statement of the doctrines of "The Latter Day Saints." pp. 16. *S.P.C.K.: London*, 1852. 12⁰. **4745. a. 26.**

—— A Pilgrimage to Canterbury in 1852. pp. 35. *F. & J. Rivington: London*, 1852. 8⁰.
10003. bbb. 25. (1.)

—— Progress of the Pongas Mission in Western Africa, during 1859 (1860-63, 65). Edited by the Rev. H. Caswall. *London*, 1860–66. 12⁰. [*West Indian Church Association, etc.* Occasional Paper. no. 4–9, 11.] **4766. bbb. 21.**

—— The Prophet of the Nineteenth Century [i.e. Joseph Smith]; or, the Rise, progress, & present state of the Mormons, or Latter-day Saints. To which is appended, an analysis of the Book of Mormon. pp. xx. 277. *J. G. F. & J. Rivington: London*, 1843. 12⁰. **1369. h. 8.**

—— Scotland and the Scottish Church. pp. x. 156. *J. H. Parker: Oxford*, 1853. 8⁰. **4735. aa. 49.**

—— Synodal Action necessary to the Church. A letter to the Right Hon. W. E. Gladstone. pp. 127. *J. & C. Mozley: London*, 1852. 12⁰. **4326. d. 18.**

—— The Western World revisited. pp. xvi. 351. *J. H. Parker: Oxford*, 1854. 8⁰. **4745. a. 43.**

—— The Wrongs and Claims of Africans. A sermon, *etc.* pp. 11. *Bell & Daldy: London*, 1863. 12⁰.
4478. aa. 18.

CASWALL (Thomas) The Shield of Faith; a short treatise on the Church; to which is added, the Profession of Faith according to the Bull of Pope Pius IV. Translated from the Cœleste Palmetum, by T. Caswall. pp. 48. *James Burns: London*, [1849.] 16⁰. **3938. aa. 44.**

CASWELL. Caswell, a paradox. [A novel.] 2 vol. *T. Fisher Unwin: London*, 1887. 8⁰. **12611. k. 9.**

CASWELL (Albert Edward) Experimental Physics. A laboratory manual. pp. ix. 181. *Macmillan Co.: New York*, 1928. 8⁰. **08710. c. 37.**

—— An Outline of Physics. pp. xiv. 773. *Macmillan Co.: New York*, 1928. 8⁰. **08710. c. 24.**

CASWELL (Alexis) *See* WAYLAND (Francis) *the Elder.* The Death of the Believer. A sermon, *etc.* [With a biographical sketch of E. L. Caswell by A. Caswell.] 1850. 8⁰. **4985. e. 58. (8.)**

—— Address before the American Association for the Advancement of Science. pp. 26. *Joseph Lovering: Cambridge* [*Mass.*], 1859. 8⁰. **8704. e. 25. (1.)**

CASWELL (ALEXIS)

—— Lectures on Astronomy. [An extract from " Smithsonian Lectures on Astronomy."] [*Washington*, 1860?] 8º. **8561. c. 61. (4.)**

—— Meteorological Observations made at Providence, R.I. extending over a period of twenty-eight years and a half, from December, 1831, to May, 1860. pp. iv. 179. *Washington*, 1859. 4º. [*Smithsonian Contributions to Knowledge.* vol. 12.] **Ac. 1875.**

—— Results of Meteorological Observations made at Providence, R.I. . . . from Dec., 1831, to Dec., 1876. [With charts.] pp. xiv. 247. *Washington*, 1882. 4º. [*Smithsonian Contributions to Knowledge.* vol. 24.] **Ac. 1875.**

CASWELL (ANNE) *See* ORR (Mary) *pseud.* [i.e. A. Caswell.]

CASWELL (ANNIE GRAY) Susann of Sandy Point, *etc.* pp. viii. 229. *Longmans & Co.: London; printed in U.S.A.*, 1930. 8º. **A.N. 493.**

CASWELL (D. J.) The Outward and Visible Sign. A new and attractive method of teaching religious truths, and especially applied to the teaching of the Church Catechism, *etc.* pp. 71. *Caswell Publishing Co.: Brantford, Canada*, 1891. 8º. **3506. ee. 6.**

CASWELL (EDWARD) *See* CASWALL.

CASWELL (EDWARD C.) *See* HENIUS (J.) Maisie's Music . . . Designed and pictured by E. C. Caswell. [1910.] 4º. **M. g. 1173.**

—— *See* MACBRIDE (Robert M.) Spanish Towns and People . . . With pictures by E. C. Caswell. 1926. 8º. **10162. i. 29.**

CASWELL (EDWARD SAMUEL) *See* STRICKLAND, afterwards TRAILL (Catharine P.) The Backwoods of Canada . . . Introduction by E. S. Caswell, *etc.* [1929.] 8º. **010470. aaa. 15.**

—— Canadian Singers and their Songs. A collection of portraits and autograph poems. Compiled by E. S. Caswell. pp. 157. *McClelland & Stewart: Toronto*, [1919.] 8º. **011604. k. 7.**

CASWELL (EDWARD THOMPSON) *See* SEMELEDER (F.) Rhinoscopy and Laryngoscopy . . . Translated . . . by E. T. Caswell, *etc.* 1866. 8º. **7510. cc. 19.**

CASWELL (ESTHER LOIS) *See* WAYLAND (Francis) *the Elder*. The Death of the Believer. A sermon, preached . . after the decease of Mrs. E. L. Caswell. [With a biographical sketch by A. Caswell.] 1850. 8º. **4985. e. 58. (8.)**

CASWELL (FLORENCE ANNIE) *See* GOODWIN (Lavinia S.) The Little Helper: a memoir of F. A. Caswell. 1867. 8º. **4986. aa. 13.**

CASWELL (GEORGE) *See* SMITH (Samuel) *Ordinary of Newgate*. The Confession of George Caswell Gent. executed . . . for the murther of Andrew Hickson, *etc.* 1691. *s. sh.* fol. **L.R.404.n.5.(51.)**

CASWELL (GEORGE HENRY)

—— Insects on Growing Crops at University College Ibadan. pp. 68. [*Ibadan*,] 1954. 4º. [*University College Ibadan. Faculty of Agriculture and Veterinary Science. Division of Agricultural Entomology. Divisional Reports.* no. 1.] **Ac. 2700. ie.**

Reproduced from typewriting.

CASWELL (HARRIET S.) Our Life among the Iroquois Indians. pp. xiii. 321. *Congregational Publishing Society: Boston & Chicago*, [1892.] 8º. **4767. ccc. 17.**

CASWELL (HOLLIS LELAND)

—— The American High School: its responsibility and opportunity. Hollis L. Caswell, editor, *etc.* pp. viii. 264. *Harper & Bros.: New York & London*, [1946.] 8º. [*Eighth Yearbook of the John Dewey Society.*] **Ac. 1819.**

—— City School Surveys. An interpretation and appraisal, *etc.* [A thesis.] pp. vi. 130. *Teachers College, Columbia University: New York*, 1929. 8º. **20019. f. 34.**

—— Developing the Design of the Curriculum.—Administrative Considerations in Curriculum Development. *See* RUGG (Harold O.) Democracy and the Curriculum, *etc.* [1939.] 8º. [*Third Year Book of the John Dewey Society.*] **Ac. 1819.**

—— Education in the Elementary School. pp. xiv. 321. *American Book Co.: New York*, [1942.] 8º. [*American Education Series.*] **W.P. 6365/31.**

The second edition is entered under CASWELL (H. L.) *and* FOSHAY (A. W.)

CASWELL (HOLLIS LELAND) *and* CAMPBELL (DOAK SHERIDAN)

—— Curriculum Development. [With a bibliography.] pp. xvii. 600. *American Book Co.: New York*, [1935.] 8º. **8311. cc. 52.**

—— Readings in Curriculum Development. pp. xvii. 753. *American Book Co.: New York*, [1937.] 8º. [*American Education Series.*] **W.P. 6365/23.**

CASWELL (HOLLIS LELAND) *and* FOSHAY (ARTHUR WELLESLEY)

—— Education in the Elementary School. Second edition. pp. xvii. 406. *American Book Co.: New York*, [1950.] 8º. [*American Education Series.*] **W.P. 6365/33.**

The first edition is entered under CASWELL (H. L.)

CASWELL (JESSE) Elementary Lessons. Designed to assist Siamese in the acquisition of the English language . . . With an appendix by Rev. D. B. Bradley. 7th edition. pp. 70. *Bradley's Press: Bangkok*, 1881. 12º. **12981. aaa. 67.**

CASWELL (JOHN) *Colonel*. Sporting Rifles and Rifle Shooting . . . Illustrated. pp. xviii. 283. *D. Appleton & Co.: New York, London*, 1920. 8º. **07905. k. 43.**

CASWELL (JOHN) *M.A.* A Brief, but full, Account of the Doctrine of Trigonometry, both plain and spherical. pp. 17. *John Playford: London; for Richard Davis: Oxford*, 1685. fol. **528. n. 20. (9.)**

—— [Another copy.] **8531. g. 1. (2.)**

CASWELL (JOHN) *Vice-President of St. Wilfrid's College*. *See* BIRMINGHAM, *Archdiocese of*. Almanack for the Diocese of Birmingham. Edited by Rev. W. Greaney and Rev. J. Caswell. [1884.] 8º. **P.P. 2484. fa.**

CASWELL (JOHN H.) Microscopic Petrography of the Black Hills of Dakota. *See* UNITED STATES OF AMERICA. —*Geographical and Geological Survey of the Rocky Mountain Region*. Report on the Geology . . . of the Black Hills of Dakota, *etc.* 1880. 4º. **A.S. 206/4.**

CASWELL (LILLEY BREWER) Brief History of the Massachusetts Agricultural College. pp. 72. *Amherst*, 1917. 8º. [*Massachusetts Agricultural College Semicentennial Publications.* no. 1.] **Ac. 3526.**

CASWELL (Mina Holway) Ministry of Music. The life, of William Rogers Chapman. [With plates, including portraits.] pp. xviii. 467. *Southworth-Anthoensen Press: Portland, Me.,* 1938. 4⁰.   **7897. w. 29.**

CASWELL (Samuel) All About Coal. pp. 28. *Bemrose & Sons: Derby & London,* [1888.] 4⁰.
                                   07109. g. 10.

ČASY.

—— Časy. Verše F. Halase, V. Holana, K. Jílka, J. Seiferta. pp. 6. *Kulturní Zápisník: v Londýně,* 1941. 4⁰.
                                   11585. m. 23.

CAT. A Maruelous Hystory intitulede, Beware the Cat. Conteynyng diuerse wounderfull and incredible matters, *etc.* [The preface signed: G. B., i.e. Gulielmus Baldwin.] 1570. 8⁰. *See* B., G.   **C. 60. b. 8.**

—— [Another edition.] Beware the Cat, 1570. An exceedingly rare and curious rhapsody, *etc.* 1864. 4⁰. *See* B., G.   **12316. c. 29.**

—— The Cat. *See* Periodical Publications.—*Bishop Auckland.*

—— Cat and Dog; or, Memoirs of Puss and the Captain. A story founded on fact. By the author of " The Doll and her Friends," " Letters from Madras " [i.e. Julia C. Maitland], *etc.* pp. 99.   *Grant & Griffith: London,* 1854 [1853]. 8⁰.   **12806. b. 59.**

—— Cat and Dog . . . [By Julia C. Maitland.] Second edition, *etc.* pp.99.   *Grant & Griffith: London,* 1854. 8⁰.
                                   12837. ff. 71.

—— Cat and Dog; or, Memoirs of Puss and the Captain . . . By the author of " The Doll and her Friends " [i.e. Julia C. Maitland] . . . Eighth edition, *etc.* [With plates.] pp. 100. *Griffith & Farran: London,* 1866. 8⁰.
                                   12816. a. 77.

—— The Cat and her Cousins. True stories . . . about the feline animals. By the author of " Curious Facts about Animals," *etc.* pp. 165.   *Seeley, Jackson & Halliday: London,* 1871 [1870]. 8⁰.   **7284. aa. 15.**

—— The Cat and her Kittens. By the author of " The Conceited Pig." pp. 32.   *Joseph Masters: London,* 1848. 16⁰.   **4415. a. 68. (2.)**

—— The Cat and the Mouse. Illustrated by Alice B. Woodward. *Blackie & Son: London,* [1899.] *obl.* 4⁰.
                                   12809. o. 20

—— A Cat may look upon a King. [A satirical account of the life and character of King James I., with preliminary notices of former English monarchs since the Conquest. By Sir Anthony Weldon.] pp. 105.   *For William Roybould: London,* 1652 [1653]. 16⁰.   **E. 1408. (2.)**

—— [Another edition. With a continuation to date.] pp. 59. *Amsterdam* [*London*], 1714. 8⁰.   **G. 3267.**

—— [Another edition.] 1815. *See* Somers (John) *Baron Somers.* A Collection of Scarce and Valuable Tracts, *etc.* vol. 13. 1809, *etc.* 4⁰.   **750. g. 13.**

—— A Cat may look upon a King. [By Sir Anthony Weldon.] (Answer'd paragraph by paragragh [*sic*]). pp. 24. *R. Mathard: London,* [1720 ?] 12⁰.   **8133. a. 12.**

—— The Cat's Concert. [In verse. With illustrations by William Mulready ?] *C. Chapple: London,* [1808 ?] 16⁰.
                                   C. 40. a. 57. (9.)
Engraved throughout.

—— The Cat's Party, the Donkey's Party, and the Dog's Party. Three laughable tales. [In verse.] pp. 17. *Dean & Son: London,* [1857.] 16⁰.   **12807. b. 45.**

CAT.

—— How to keep a Cat in health. By two friends of the race. [i.e. Mrs. F. P. Cotton and G. J. K. Ouseley.] pp. 24. [*London,* 1901.] 8⁰.   **07293. g. 48.**

—— Hush Cat from under the Table. To which are added, Tweedside. Live and Love. The Goblet of Wine. Castle Berry. The Venus of Longford. [Songs.] pp. 7. *Monaghan,* 1787. 8⁰.   **11622. df. 34. (29.)**

—— Only a Cat's Tale. By E. M. B. 1881. 8⁰. *See* B., E. M.   **12803. dd. 15.**

—— Quite a Nice Cat, and other sketches, *etc.* [By various authors.] pp. 93.   *London, New York,* [1927.] 8⁰. [*French's Acting Edition.*]   **11791. t. 1/92.**

—— " Send not a Cat for Lard." [A political satire.] By a person who knows the habits of cats. pp. 16. *Bemrose & Sons: London,* [1884.] 16⁰.   **12314. b. 57.**

—— When the Cat's away, the Mice may play. A fable, humbly inscrib'd to Dr. Sw - - t. [A reply to the satire on Marlborough entitled " The Fable of the Widow and her Cat." In verse.] pp. 4.   *A. Baldwin: London,* [1712.] fol.   **644. m. 14. (20.)**

—— [Another copy.] When the Cat's away, the Mice may play, *etc. London,* [1712.] fol.   **Ashley 4976.**

—— Where's the Cat. [A political satire.] pp. 36. *W. H. Allen & Co.: London,* 1886. 8⁰.
                                   12331. g. 26. (2.)

—— The White Cat. [A fairy tale, translated and abridged from the French of the Countess d'Aulnoy.] Illustrated by J. W. pp. 24. **L.P.**   *W. Blackwood & Sons: Edinburgh & London,* 1847. 4⁰.   **551. f. 14.**

—— The White Cat, and Riquet with the Tuft. [After the Countess d'Aulnoy and Perrault.] pp. 40. *George Newnes: London,* [1906.] 8⁰.   **12410. ff. 26.**

—— The White Cat. With the Earl of Grosvenor's Ass. [Satires in verse; the first, upon Queen Caroline, the second upon Robert Grosvenor, 1st Marquis of Westminster, and others. With illustrations by G. Cruikshank.] ms. notes. pp. 26.   *W. Wright: London,* 1821. 8⁰.   **C.131.d.13.(13.)**

—— [Another copy.]   **G. 18952. (29.)**

CAT, *pseud.* [i.e. Anna Garreau.] Aïcha. [Signed: Cat.] pp. 316. *Paris,* 1890. 18⁰.   **012547. k. 64.**

—— Au sortir du couvent. [A novel.] Par Cat. pp. 259. *Paris,* 1894. 12⁰.   **012550. f. 2.**

CAT, *pseud.* [i.e. Stanisław Mackiewicz] *See* Mackiewicz (S.)

CAT AND DOG STORIES. Cat and Dog Stories, as told to one another. pp. 32.   *W. Swan Sonnenschein & Co.: London,* [1883.] 4⁰.   **12810. d. 31.**

—— [Another edition.] pp. 62.   *W. Swan Sonnenschein & Co.: London,* [1884.] 16⁰.   **12810. a. 12.**

CAT BOOK. My Cat Book. pp. 96.   *C. H. Kelly: London,* [1905.] 4⁰.   **12813. s. 7.**

CAT GOSSIP. *See* Periodical Publications.—*London.*

CAT WORLD. The Cat World. *See* Periodical Publications.—*London.*

CAT (Édouard) A travers le désert. pp. 253.   *Paris,* [1892.] 8⁰.   **10096. i. 12.**

CAT (Édouard)

—— Charles Quint. pp. 63. *Paris*, [1883.] 8º.
10703. aa. 11.

—— De Caroli v. in Africa rebus gestis. pp. ii. 101. *Alger*,
1891. 8º. [*Publications de l'École Supérieure des Lettres
d'Alger.* no. 7.] Ac. **5350/2.**

—— Découvertes et explorations du xvie au xixe siècle, *etc.*
pp. 279. *Paris*, 1892. 8º. **10026. k. 15.**

—— Essai sur la province romaine de Maurétanie césarienne.
[With maps.] pp. xvi. 314. *Paris*, 1891. 8º.
07704. f. 17.

—— Essai sur la vie et les ouvrages du chroniqueur Gonzalo
de Ayora, suivi de fragments inédits de sa chronique.
pp. 59. *Alger*, 1890. 8º. [*Publications de l'École
Supérieure des Lettres d'Alger.* no. 3.] Ac. **5350/2.**

—— Les Grandes découvertes maritimes du treizième au
seizième siècle. pp. 300. *Paris*, 1882. 18º.
10024. aaa. 18.

—— Miguel Cervantès. [A biography. With a portrait.]
pp. 220. *Paris*, [1892.] 8º. **10631. ee. 47.**

—— [Another copy.] Cerv. **560.**

—— Mission bibliographique en Espagne. Rapport, *etc.*
(Documents espagnols sur l'Afrique du Nord. [Collected
and edited by É. Cat.]) pp. 148. *Alger*, 1891. 8º. [*Publications de l'École Supérieure des Lettres d'Alger.* no. 8.]
Ac. **5350/2.**

—— Notice sur la carte de l'Ogôoue. pp. 68. *Alger*,
1890. 8º. [*Publications de l'École Supérieure des Lettres
d'Alger.* no. 1.] Ac. **5350/2.**

—— Petite histoire de l'Algérie, Tunisie, Maroc. 2 tom.
Alger, 1888, 91. 8º. **9061. de. 33.**

CAT (J. H. François) Considérations générales sur l'état
physiologique de la femme, après l'accouchement
naturel et sur les soins qu'elle réclame soit qu'elle se livre
ou non à l'allaitement. Thèse, *etc.* pp. 51.
Montpellier, 1839. 4º. **1181. i. 9. (6.)**

CAT (Joseph) De la syphilis infantile. Thèse, *etc.* pp. 36.
Montpellier, 1868. 4º. **7379. h. 5. (11.)**

CATÁ (Alfonso Hernández) *See* Hernández Catá.

CATABAPTISTAE. *See* Anabaptists.

CATACAZY (Constantine) *See* Katakazes.

CATACOMB.

—— The Catacomb. *See* Periodical Publications —
London.

CATÁ DE CALELLA (José Antonio) Vida portentosa
de . . . Santa Rosa de Santa María, vulgo Santa Rosa de
Lima. Arreglada para esta edición á vista de los manu-
scritos . . . del Rdo. P. Fr. J. A. Catá de Calella, *etc.*
pp. 403. *Barcelona*, 1886. 8º. **4828. de. 14.**

CATAFAGO (Joseph) An English and Arabic Dictionary,
in two parts; Arabic and English, and English and
Arabic. pp. xii. 1060. *Bernard Quaritch: London*,
1858. 8º. **12904. d. 25**

—— Second edition, carefully corrected, improved, and
enlarged, *etc.* pp. viii. 1096. *Bernard Quaritch:
London*, 1873. 8º. **012904. g. 30.**
Imperfect; wanting pp. v, vi.

CÀ TAGLIAPIERA (Nicolo da) *See* Tagliapiera (N.)

CATAIN (Riobéard Ó) *See* Kane (Robert) *of Rahona
Lodge, Carrigaholt.*

CATALÁ (Auguste) Des perforations intestinales qui
surviennent dans le cours des fièvres typhoïdes; thèse, *etc.*
pp. 49. *Paris*, 1835. 4º. **1184. g. 7. (8.)**

CATALÁ (B. Febrer y) *See* Febrer y Catalá.

CATALÁ (José Barranco y) *See* Barranco y Catalá.

CATALÁ (Josef Berní y) *See* Berní y Catalá.

CATALÁ (Melchor de Palau y) *See* Palau y Catalá.

CATALÁ (Ramón A.) *See* Loveira y Chirino (C.) Un
Gran Ensayista Cubano: Fernando Lles. Discurso . . .
leído por . . . C. Loveira y Chirino . . . Divagaciones
sobre la novela, discurso . . . por . . . R. A. Catalá.
1926. 8º. Ac. **1908/4. (6.)**

—— *See* Remos y Rubio (J.N.J.) El Genio de Esteban Bor-
rero Echeverría . . . Discurso . . . leído por . . . Juan J.
Remos . . . Discurso de contestación por . . . R. A.
Catalá. 1930. 8º. Ac. **1908/4. (11.)**

CATALA (René)

—— Contribution à l'étude des effets optiques sur les ailes
des papillons, *etc.* [With illustrations.] pp. 78. *Paris*,
1949. 8º. [*Encyclopédie entomologique.* sér. A. no. 25.]
7297. p. 4/25.

CATALA (Valentin) Essai sur l'hygiène des gens de lettres.
pp. 143. *Paris*, 1857. 4º. [*Collection des thèses soutenues
à la Faculté de Médecine de Paris.* An 1857. tom. 3.]
7373. a. 3.

CATALÀ (Víctor) *pseud.* [i.e. Caterina Albert i Paradís.]

—— Obres completes. (Pròleg de Manuel de Montoliu.)
[With a portrait.] pp. lxxix. 1499. *Barcelona*, 1951. 8º.
12231. pp. **75.**
Biblioteca Excelsa. no. 9.

—— Dramas Rurals, *etc.* pp. viii. 296.
Barcelona, 1902. 8º. **12489. h. 38.**

—— Marines. pp. 121. *Barcelona*, [1929.] 8º.
12493. a. 17.
Les ales esteses. vol. 1.

—— Mosaic. iii. Impressions literàries sobre temes domèstics.
pp. 232. *Barcelona*, 1946. 8º. **12361. de. 4.**

CATALAN

—— Vocabulari català-alemany de l'any 1502. Edició fac-
símil segons l'únic exemplar conegut, acompanyada de la
transcripció, d'un estudi preliminar i d'registres alfa-
bètics per Pere Barnils. [The authorship here attributed
to J. Rosembach.] pp. xxxviii. 203. *Barcelona*, 1916. 8º.
[*Biblioteca filològica de l'Institut de la Llengua Catalana.*
no. 7.] Ac. **138. d/2.**

CATALAN ANTHOLOGY.

—— Antologia catalana. Les vint millors poesies dels vint
poetes més grands, *etc.* pp. 112. *Barcelona*, 1932. 8º.
11453. a. 60.

CATALAN ART. Catalan Art from the Ninth to the
Fifteenth Centuries. [Plates, with introductory essays
by various writers. Edited by C. Zervos.] 1937. fol.
See Zervos (C.) **7809. v. 34.**

CATALAN AUTHORS.

—— Autors catalans antics.

1. Historiografia. A cura de R. d'Alòs-Moner. pp. 195. 1932.

Barcelona, 1932. 8°. **12232. a. 14.**
Crestomaties Barcino. vol. 1. *Imperfect ; wanting all after pt.* 1.

CATALAN BANKING. La Cuenta Corriente de Efectos
o Valores de un Sector de la Banca Catalana. Su repercusión en el crédito y en la economía . . . Según los dictámenes emitidos por los . . . señores Rodríguez Sastre, Garrigues, Sánchez Román, Goicoechea, Miñana y Clemente de Diego. Seguidos de un estudio sobre la cuenta de efectos y el mercado libre de valores de Barcelona, por don Agustín Peláez. pp. 587. 1936. 8°.
See MADRID.—*Colegio de Agentes de Cambio u Bolsa de Madrid,* **8233. cc. 7.**

CATALAN - CASTILIAN - LATIN - FRENCH - ITALIAN DICTIONARY.

—— Diccionari catalá-castellá-llatí-frances-italiá. Per una societat de Catalans. 2 tom. *Barcelona,* 1839. 8°.
1331. g. 3, 4.

CATALAN CHAPBOOKS. *See* also SPANISH CHAPBOOKS.

—— [A collection of thirty-six chapbooks in Catalan verse.] *Barcelona,* [1790 ?–1835 ?] 4°. **11451. ee. 7.**

—— [A collection of 393 Catalan chapbooks, for the most part " goigs," or religious verses in honour of Jesus Christ, the Blessed Virgin Mary and other saints.] *Barcelona, etc.,* [1800 ?–75 ?] fol. **1875. a. 26.**

—— [A collection of Catalan chapbooks, in verse.] [*Barcelona, Lleyda, Reus,* 1823–86.] 4°. **11450. h. 21.**

CATALAN CHRONICLES. Crónicas Catalanas. 3 pt.
Barcelona, 1858. 8°. **12490. h. 20.**

CATALAN CUSTOMS. Quadros de costums catalanas.
Entrega 1, 3–8. *Barcelona,* 1869. 8°. **11725. g. 20. (3.)**

CATALAN EPIGRAMS. Mil y un Epigramas Catalans.
Colecció . . . recopilada . . . per una societat literaria e ilustrada ab retratos d'alguns dels principals autors. pp. 347. *Barcelona,* 1878. 8°. **11450. g. 10.**

CATALAN HOUSE.

—— Projecte de Reglament per un Casal Catala. [By P. Clua Coll.] Edicio corregida. pp. 44. *New York,* [1945.] 12°. **8042. a. 78.**

CATALAN LANGUAGE. Canciones en Catalan y
Castellano para cantar en los Belenes. pp. 16.
Barcelona, [1890 ?] 32°. **886. a. 23. (2.)**

—— Catalan. Two talks on the Catalan language, *etc.* pp. 7. *Linguaphone Institute: London,* [1935 ?] 8°. [*Linguaphone Miniature Language Series.*] **012902.n.14/2.**

—— Diccionari de la Llengua Catalana ab la correspondencia castellana. Nova edició, enciclopèdica il-lustrada, *etc.* [With maps and illustrations.] 3 vol. *Barcelona,* [1920.] 8°. **012941. dd. 1.**

—— [Another edition.] Diccionari enciclopèdic de la llengua cataiana amb la correspondència castellana. Nova edició, *etc.* 4 vol. *Barcelona,* 1930–35. 8°. **12943. t. 14.**
Each volume was published in parts.

CATALAN PAINTING. La Peinture catalane à la
fin du moyen âge. Conférences faites à la Sorbonne en 1931 par MM. Duran i Sanpere, Henri Focillon, Folch i Torrès, Fr. Martorell, Nicolau d'Olwer, René Schneider, M. Trens, Soler i March. pp. 140. pl. xxv. *Paris,* 1933. 4°. [*Bibliothèque d'art catalan. Publications.* no. 3.] **Ac. 442. f.**

—— La Pintura Catalana Contemporània. [Plates, with an introduction.] pp. 16. *Barcelona,* 1931. 4°.
L.R.294.b.8.

CATALAN PLAYS. [A collection of fifty short plays in
Catalan, " saynetes," " juguetes " and " entremeses."] *Barcelona, etc.,* 1850–69. 4°. **11726. g. 23.**

CATALAN PROVERBS.

—— Diccionario de refranes catalanes, y castellanos, recopilados y publicados por D. J. A. X. y F. 1878. 8°. [*SBARBI (J. M.)* *El Refranero general español etc.* tom. 9.] *See* X. y F., D. J. A. **12227. bb. 14.**

CATALAN RAGMAN. El Trapero Catalan. Tonadilla
bilingüe entre Jan y Paca. pp. 8. *Barcelona,* 1855. 4°.
11726. g. 5. (26.)

CATALAN SHEPHERDESS. Diálogo de un Oficial
y una Pastora Catalana. [In verse.] *Barcelona,* [1845 ?] 4°. **11450. f. 29. (6.)**

—— Nuevo Diálogo entre un Oficial y una Pastora Catalana. [In verse.] *Barcelona,* 1857. 4°. **11450. f. 29. (13.)**

CATALAN SONGBOOK. El Cancionero Catalán de
la Universidad de Zaragoza. Exhumado y anotado por . . . M. Baselga y Ramírez, *etc.* pp. 419. *Zaragoza,* 1896. 8°. **11450. dd. 9.**

CATALAN TRUTH. Appuy de la verité catalane op-
pugnée par un libelle, qui commence, La Justification royale. (Apoyos de la verdad catalana, *etc.*) Span. & Fr. pp. 87. *See* CATALONIA. [*Appendix.*] Histoire de tout ce qui s'est passé en la Catalogne, etc. 1642. 4°.
1060. i. 28.

CATALAN UNIVERSITY STUDIES. Estudis Uni-
versitaris Catalans. *See* BARCELONA.—*Institució Patxot.*

CATALAN VENGEANCE. La Venganza Catalana,
la Espedicion de Oriente. pp. 19. *Barcelona,* 1864. 4°.
12491. e. 31.

CATALAN WOMAN. *Begin.* La Catalana punita. Cru-
delissimo e maraviglioso caso seguito nella città di Barcellona . . . Tradotto dallo spagnolo in italiano dal P. Maestro Fulgentio Bozzolini, *etc.* [In verse.] pp. 12. [*Todi ?* 1795 ?] 12°. **11426. b. 75. (11.)**

—— [Another copy.] **11426. b. 74. (21.)**

—— [Another edition.] *Napoli,* 1798. 12°.
1071. c. 24. (13.)

—— [Another edition.] pp. 12. [*Lucca ?* 1815 ?] 12°.
1071. c. 19. (6.)

—— [Another edition.] pp. 12. [*Lucca ?* 1820 ?] 12°.
1071. c. 22. (20.)

—— [Another edition.] pp. 12. [*Lucca ?* 1825 ?] 12°.
11429. b. 57. (14.)

—— [Another edition.] [*Naples ?* 1825 ?] 12°.
1072. b. 20. (1.)

CATALAN (A.) Comentarios á la Constitucion Federal
Suiza del 29 de Mayo de 1874. (Traducidos del frances por Vicente Coronado.) pp. 117. *Carácas,* 1879. 8°.
8180. h. 19. (3.)

CATALAN (Antoine de) Les Indirects. Types administratifs. pp. 205. *Poitiers*, 1887. 12⁰.   **12331. d. 35.**

CATALAN (Arnaut) Le Poesie del trovatore Arnaut Catalan. Introduzione, testi, traduzione, note. [Edited by Ferruccio Blasi.] pp. xxix. 62.   *Firenze*, 1937. 8⁰. [*Biblioteca dell' Archivum Romanicum.* ser. 1. vol. 24.]
P.P. **4884. dba.**

CATALAN (Étienne) Études sur Montaigne, analyse de sa philosophie. pp. 350. *Paris*, 1846. 12⁰. **1249. a. 2.**

—— Miroir des sages et des fous . . . Préface de Louis Ulbach. pp. xix. 340. *Paris*, 1862. 12⁰.   **8408. e. 2.**

CATALAN (Eugène Charles) *See* Langlebert (J.) and Catalan (E. C.) Nouveau manuel des aspirants au baccalaureat ès sciences, *etc.* 1858, *etc.* 8⁰.
10006. c. 22.

—— *See* Momenheim (L.) and Catalan (E. C.) Solutions des problèmes de mathématiques et de physique, *etc.* [1853?] 8⁰.   **8529. a. 8.**

—— L'Article 757. Application de l'algèbre au Code civil. pp. 16. *Paris*, 1862. 8⁰.   **5425. aaa. 13.**

—— Mélanges mathématiques. 3 tom. *Liége*, 1885–88. 8⁰. [*Mémoires de la Société Royale des Sciences de Liége.* sér. 2. tom. 12, 13, 15.]   Ac. **2961.**

—— Mémoire en réponse à la question suivante : trouver les lignes de courbure du lieu des points dont la somme des distances à deux droites qui se coupent est constante. 1865. *See* Brussels.—*Académie Royale des Sciences, etc.* [*Memoirs and Proceedings.*] Mémoires sur les questions proposées, *etc.* tom. 32. 1818, *etc.* 4⁰.   Ac. **985/6.**

—— Mémoire sur la transformation des séries et sur quelques intégrales définies. 1867. *See* Brussels.—*Académie Royale des Sciences, etc.* [*Memoirs and Proceedings.*] Mémoires sur les questions proposées, *etc.* tom. 33. 1818, *etc.* 4⁰.   Ac. **985/6.**

—— Mémoire sur une transformation géométrique et sur la surface des ondes. pp. 63. 1871. *See* Brussels.—*Académie Royale des Sciences, etc.* [*Memoirs and Proceedings.*] Nouveaux mémoires, *etc.* tom. 38. 1820, *etc.* 4⁰.
Ac. **985/7.**

—— Note sur un problème d'analyse indéterminée . . . Extrait des Atti dell'Accademia Pontificia de' Nuovi Lincei, *etc.* pp. 9. *Rome*, 1866. 4⁰.   **8531. ee. 27. (3.)**

—— Notions d'astronomie. pp. 192. *Paris*, [1860?] 16⁰.
12206. b. 10.

—— Nouvelles notes d'algèbre et d'analyse. pp. 98. 1892. *See* Brussels.—*Académie Royale des Sciences, etc.* [*Memoirs and Proceedings.*] Nouveaux mémoires, *etc.* tom. 48. 1820, *etc.* 4⁰.   Ac. **985/7.**

—— Recherches sur la constante G, et sur les intégrales Eulériennes. pp. 51. *St.-Pétersbourg*, 1883. 4⁰. [*Mémoires de l'Académie Impériale des Sciences de St.-Pétersbourg.* ser. 7. tom. 31. no. 3.]   Ac. **1125/3.**

—— Recherches sur quelques produits indéfinis et sur la constante G. pp. 28. 1893. *See* Brussels.—*Académie Royale des Sciences, etc.* [*Memoirs and Proceedings.*] Nouveaux mémoires, *etc.* tom. 51. 1820, *etc.* 4⁰.
Ac. **985/7.**

—— *Begin.* République Française . . . Aux électeurs du département de la Seine. [An address by E. C. Catalan on his offering himself as a candidate for the representation of the Department in the National Assembly. Dated 25 March 1848.] [*Paris*, 1848.] *s. sh.* fol.
1850. d. 5. (63.)

—— [Another copy.]   **1850. d. 5. (64.)**

CATALAN (Eugène Charles)

—— Sur la transformation des variables dans les intégrales multiples, *etc.* pp. 47. 1841. *See* Brussels.—*Académie Royale des Sciences, etc.* [*Memoirs and Proceedings.*] Mémoires sur les questions proposées, *etc.* tom. 14. 1818, *etc.* 4⁰.   Ac. **985/6.**

—— Théorèmes et problèmes de géometrie élémentaire . . . Troisième édition, revue et augmentée. pp. xlvi. 339. pl. 15. *Paris*, 1858. 8⁰.   **8529. d. 32.**

—— Traité élémentaire de géométrie descriptive. [With "Atlas."] pt. 1. *Paris*, 1857. 8⁰.   **8529. d. 2.** *Imperfect; wanting pt.* 2.

CATALÁN (Giovanni Francesco Marco y) *Cardinal.* *See* Marco y Catalán.

CATALAN (Henry) *pseud.* [i.e. Henry Dupuy-Maznel.]

—— [Le Cas de Sœur Angèle.] Sœur Angèle and the Embarrassed Ladies. [A novel.] pp. 176.   *Sheed & Ward: London & New York*, 1955. 8⁰.   **12513. tt. 50.**

CATALÁN (Julián López) *See* López Catalán.

CATALÁN (M. A.) Investigaciones sobre las rayas últimas en los espectros de arco de los elementos. 1918. *See* Madrid.—*Instituto Nacional de Ciencias Fisico-naturales.*—*Laboratorio de Investigaciones Físicas.* Trabajos, *etc.* no. 46. 1918, *etc.* 8⁰.   Ac. **2828. c.**

CATALÁN (Manuel Jiménez) *See* Jiménez Catalán.

CATALÁN (Marco A. Galindo) *See* Galindo Catalán.

CATALÁN (Miguel A.)

—— *See* Russell (Henry N.) and Moore (C. E.) The Arc Spectrum of Iron-Fe 1. Part I. Analysis of the Spectrum. Based on the work of many investigators and including unpublished studies by M. A. Catalán, *etc.* 1944. 4⁰. [*Transactions of the American Philosophical Society.* New ser. vol. 34. pt. 1.]   Ac. **1830/3.**

CATALÁN (Nicolás) *Begin.* Señor: Si el que subscribe esta representacion fuese un gefe desconocido, *etc.* [A petition recounting his services and requesting military advancement.] *México*, 1824. fol.   **9770. k. 8. (134.)**

CATALÁN (Victoriano Lillo) *See* Lillo Catalán.

CATALANA. *See* Catalan Woman.

CATALANA (Terencio) Entremes del Zapatero, y Don Terencio Catalana. pp. 8. [*Valencia?* 1770?] 16⁰.
11726. aa. 1. (6.)

CATALANES. *See* Catalans.

CATALANI (Angelica) *See* Simpson (Arthur) Secret Memoirs of Madame Catalani. 1811. 8⁰.   **1343. g. 7.**

—— I Giudizj dell' Europa intorno alla signora Catalani, ossia articoli concernenti il merito musicale di lei, tratti dalle più riputate opere periodiche di Londra, Parigi, Berlino . . . preceduti da un breve compendio della sua vita. Seconda edizione corretta ed accresciuta. pp. 50. *Milano*, 1816. 8⁰.   Hirsch **2847.**

—— Kurze Lebensbeschreibung der Madame Angelica Catalani aus ganz authentischen Quellen gezogen. pp. 22. *Berlin*, 1816. 8⁰.   **10601. e. 1. (1.)**

CATALANI (Benedetta) *See* Lacaita (*Sir* G. F.) Memoria per la signora M. G. Passeggio . . . contro . . . le signore M. e B. Catalani, *etc.* 1851. 8⁰.
5373. i. 47. (28.)

CATALANI (G.) *See* GREEKS. The Modern Greeks. By G. Catalani, T. P. Armstrong, *etc.* 1939. 8°.
010007. e. 51.

CATALANI (GIUSEPPE) *See* COUNCILS OF THE CHURCH. Sacrosancta Concilia Oecumenica, prolegomenis et commentariis illustrata . . . Auctore J. Catalano. 1736, *etc.* fol. 5005. e. 7.

—— *See* JEROME, *Saint.* [*Epistolae.—Selections.*] Sancti Hieronymi . . . Epistolae . . . notis illustratae à J. Catalani, *etc.* 1831. 12°. 3627. aa. 21.

—— *See* LITURGIES.—*Latin Rite.—Pontificals.*—I. Pontificale Romanum . . . prolegomenis et commentariis illustratum. Auctore J. Catalano. 1738, *etc.* fol. 3356. d. 7.

—— —— 1851, *etc.* 4°. 3355. c. 8.

—— *See* LITURGIES.—*Latin Rite.—Pontificals.*—I. [*Appendix.*] Cæremoniale Episcoporum . . . commentariis illustratum . . . cura et studio J. Catalani. 1744. fol. 3356. e. 8.

—— —— 1860. 4°. 3395. ee. 13.

—— *See* LITURGIES.—*Latin Rite.—Rituals.*—I. Rituale Romanum . . . perpetuis commentariis exornatum . . . Auctore J. Catalano. 1757. fol. 1219. m. 11.

—— —— 1760. fol. 3356. d. 8.

—— *See* MURATORI (L. A.) Annali d'Italia . . . Colle prefazioni critiche di G. Catalani, *etc.* 1752, *etc.* 8°. 1057. c. 1–24.

—— —— 1762, *etc.* 4°. 9150. gg.

—— *See* PATRICIUS PICCOLOMINEUS (A.) *Bishop of Pienza and Montalcino.* Sacrarum cæremoniarum . . . Sanctæ Romanæ Ecclesiæ libri tres . . . Nunc . . . tandem . . . innumeris . . . mendis purgati, & commentariis aucti . . . auctore J. Catalano. 1750, *etc.* fol. L.18.h.6.

—— *See* SAENZ DE AGUIRRE (J.) *Cardinal.* Collectio maxima conciliorum omnium Hispaniæ . . . Editio altera . . . novis additionibus aucta . . . auctore J. Catalano. 1753, *etc.* fol. 7. e. 5.

—— De codice Sancti Euangelii, atque servatis in ejus lectione, & usu vario ritibus, libri III., *etc.* pp. 238. *Romæ,* 1733. 4°. 697. i. 1.

—— De magistro sacri palatii apostolici libri duo. [Founded upon the "Syllabus magistrorum sacri palatii apostolici" by V. M. Fontana.] pp. xvi. 232. *Romæ,* 1751. 4°. 1229. d. 2.

CATALANI (JORDANUS) *Bishop of Columbum. See* JORDANUS, *Catalani.*

CATALANI (LUIGI) La Chiesa di S. Angelo in Formis alle falde del Monte Tifata fuori Capua antica. Ricerche. pp. 15. *Napoli,* 1844. 8°. 7702. c. 3. (4.)

—— I Palazzi di Napoli. Ricerche. pp. xvii. 49. *Napoli,* 1845. 8°. 10130. dd. 1.

CATALANI (MADDALENA) *See* LACAITA (*Sir* G. F.) Memoria per la signora M. G. Passeggio . . . contro . . . le signore M. e B. Catalani, *etc.* 1851. 8°. 5373. i. 47. (28.)

CATALANI (MICHELE) *See* PIUS II., *Pope.* Pius II. Pont. Max. a calumniis vindicatus ternis retractationibus ejus, *etc.* (Æneae Sylvii . . . de rebus Basileae gestis stante vel dissoluto Concilio commentarius . . . in lucem editus cura M. Catalani, *etc.*) 1823. 8°. 1365. e. 6.

—— De ecclesia Firmana ejusque episcopis et archiepiscopis commentarius. (Appendix monumentorum.) pp. viii. 399. *Firmi,* 1783. 4°. 658. i. 12.

CATALANI (MICHELE)

—— De vita et scriptis Dominici Capranicae cardinalis . . . commentarius. Accedit appendix monumentorum, *etc.* pp. 328. [*Fermo,*] 1793. 4°. 4868. k. 9.

—— Della origine dei Piceni . . . Dissertazione seconda. *See* COLUCCI (G.) Delle antichità picene. tom. 1. 1786, *etc.* fol. 659. l. 1.

—— Memorie della zecca fermana illustrate. 1783. *See* ZANETTI (G. A.) Nuova raccolta delle monete, *etc.* tom. 3. 1775, *etc.* fol. 603. i. 11.

—— Origini e antichità fermane. pp. vii. 95. *Fermo,* 1778. 4°. 658. h. 14.

—— [Another edition.] 1788. *See* COLUCCI (G.) Delle antichità picene. tom. 2. 1786, *etc.* fol. 659. l. 2.

CATALANI DE SÉVÉRAC (JOURDAIN) *Bishop of Columbum. See* JORDANUS, *Catalani.*

CATALÁN LATORRE (AGUSTÍN) El Beato Juan de Avila ; su tiempo, su vida y sus escritos, y la literatura mística en España. pp. viii. 208. *Zaragoza,* 1894. 8°. 4866. de. 17.

CATALÁN MENÉNDEZ-PIDAL (DIEGO) and **GALMÉS DE FUENTES** (ALVARO)

—— La Vida de un romance en el espacio y el tiempo. *In:* Revista de filología española. anejo 60. pp. 143–301. 1954. 8°. Ac. 145. c/5. (2.)

CATALANO (ANDREA) De venerabili Eucharistia carminum libri quatuor, cum notis et animadversionibus. 4 tom. *Panormi,* 1832, 33. 8°. 11405. c. 15.

CATALANO (ERRICO) *See* MURAV'EV-APOSTOL (I. M.) Viaggio per la Tauride fatto nel 1820, *etc.* [Edited by E. Catalano.] 1833. 8°. 10290. d. 37.

CATALANO (FRANCESCO CAN.) Sambartolomeo in Galdo al consiglio provinciale di Benevento ed al Parlamento nazionale italiano. pp. 15. *Napoli,* 1861. 8°. 8033. c. 40. (7.)

CATALANO (FRANCO)

—— *See* SANCTIS (Francesco de) *Professor in the University of Naples.* Opere. (vol. 7. La Scuola liberale e la scuola democratica. A cura di F. Catalano.) 1952, *etc.* 8°. 12227. eee. 1/99.

—— Aspetti della vita economico-sociale della Lombardia nel secolo XVIII. *In:* Nuova rivista storica. anno 38. fasc. 1. pp. 25–78. 1954. 8°. P.P. 3556. ne.

—— Il Vicerè Caracciolo e la Sicilia alla fine del secolo XVIII. *In:* Belfagor. anno 7. no. 4, 5. 1952. 8°. P.P. 4188. ia.

CATALANO (GAETANO)

—— Le Ultime vicende della Legazia Apostolica di Sicilia. Dalla controversia liparitana alla legge delle guarentigie, 1711–1871. pp. ix. 232. *Catania,* 1950. 8°. 9150. r. 16. *Università di Catania. Pubblicazioni della Facoltà di Giurisprudenza.* no. 13.

CATALANO (GIULIO ANTONIO) *See* CATALANO (N.) Fiume del Terrestre Paradiso . . . Oue si ragguaglia il mondo nella verità dell'antica forma d'habito de' Frati Minori . . . Dato alle stampe dal P. M. G. A. Catalano, *etc.* 1652. 4°. 1364. k. 9.

CATALANO (M. C.) *M.A., Instructor in Italian and Spanish in the University of Toronto.* Italian Conversation for Schools and Colleges. pp. vi. 76. *Copp, Clark Co.: Toronto,* [1915.] 8°. **12941. pp. 1.**

CATALANO (MICHELE) *See* ARIOSTO (L.) [*Commedie.*] Le Commedie . . . A cura di M. Catalano. 1933. 8°. **20001. d. 9.**

—— *See* SABBADINI (R.) L'Università di Catania nel secolo XV. (Appendice. Per cura del prof. M. Catalano-Tirrito.) 1898, *etc.* fol. **8356. l. 15.**

—— Lezioni di letteratura italiana. Questioni dantesche. pp. 79. *Messina,* [1951.] 8°. **11871. tt. 2.**

—— Lucrezia Borgia, Duchessa di Ferrara. Con nuovi documenti, note critiche e un ritratto inedito. pp. 105. *Ferrara,* [1920.] 8°. **10634. b. 5.**

—— Nuovi documenti sul Panormita tratti dagli archivi palermitani. *See* BECCADELLI (A.) *Panormita.* Ottanta lettere inedite del Panormita, *etc.* 1910. 8°. **Ac. 6504/2.**

—— L'Università di Catania nel Rinascimento, 1434–1600. *In:* Storia della Università di Catania, *etc.* pp. 1–98. 1934. 8°. **Ac. 2600/2.**

—— Vita di Ludovico Ariosto ricostruita su nuovi documenti. [With a portrait.] 2 vol. *Genève; Firenze* [printed], 1930, 31. 8°. [*Biblioteca dell' " Archivum Romanicum."* ser. 1. vol. 15.] **P.P. 4884. dba.**

CATALANO (MICHELE C.) L'Era del Pacifico. I problemi dell'Estremo Oriente. Contributo dell'Italia alla loro soluzione. pp. xi. 340. *Milano,* 1939. 8°. **20043. bb. 18.**

—— Orme d'Italia nell'Estremo Oriente, *etc.* pp. 143. *Bologna,* 1937. 8°. [*Italiani nel mondo.*] **9171.c.1/8.**

CATALANO (NICCOLÒ) Fiume del Terrestre Paradiso diuiso in quattro capi, o discorsi. Trattato difensiuo . . . Oue si ragguaglia il mondo nella verità dell'antica forma d'habito de' Frati Minori . . . Dato alle stampe dal P. M. G. A. Catalano, *etc.* pp. 592. *A. Massi: Fiorenza,* 1652. 4°. **1364. k. 9.**

CATALANO (SILVIO)

—— *See* CARRÀ (C. D.) 12 opere di Carlo Carrà presentate da S. Catalano, *etc.* [1945.] fol. **L.R. 298. dd. 5.**

CATALANO-TIRRITO (MICHELE) *See* CATALANO.

CATALANS. Aristarco ó Censura de la Proclamacion Católica de los Catalanes. [1640?] 4°. *See* ARISTARCO. **9180. cc. 10.**

—— The Case of the Catalans considered. pp. 32. *J. Baker: London,* 1714. 8°. **B. 624. (2.)**

—— [Another copy.] **E. 2004. (4.)**

—— [Another copy.] **114. l. 44.**

—— La Deffence des Catalans, ou l'on void le juste suiet qu'ils ont eu de se retirer de la domination du Roy d'Espagne. Avec les droicts du Roy sur la Catalogne et le Roussillon. (Remonstrance aux peuples de Flandre; avec les droicts du Roy sur leurs Prouinces.) [By Charles Sorel.] pp. 349. *N. de Sercy: Paris,* 1642. 8°. **8042. aa. 27.**

—— The Deplorable History of the Catalans, from their first engaging in the war to the time of their reduction, *etc.* pp. 98. *J. Baker: London,* 1714. 8°. **9072. aa. 1. (1.)**

CATALANUS (ARNOLDUS) *See* ARNALDUS, *de Villa Nova.*

CATALANUS (JOSEPHUS) *See* CATALANI (Giuseppe)

CATALANUS (LAURENTIUS) *See* CATELAN.

CATALANUS (MICHAEL) *See* CATALANI (Michele)

CATALANUS (PETRUS) R.P. Petri Catalani . . . Universi juris theologico-moralis corpus integrum. 2 tom. *Venetiis,* 1728. fol. **1227. e. 7, 8.**

CATALAT (SIMON ARGOTE Y) *See* ARGOTE Y CATALAT.

CATALAUNUM. *See* CHÂLONS-SUR-MARNE.

CATALAUNUS (STAZIUS TRUGUS) *pseud.,* [i.e. LAZARO AGUSTINO COTTA.] *See* MACHANEUS (D.) Verbani Lacus, locorumque adjacentium chorographica descriptio: a Stazio Trugo Catalauno literis consignata in speciem commentarii ad lucubratiunculam D. Macanei. 1699. 4°. **178. h. 21.**

CATALÁ Y GAVILÁ (JUAN BAUTISTA) *See* DONOSO CORTÉS (J. F. M. M. de la S.) *Marquis de Valdegamas.* Discursos parlamentarios . . . Notas y observaciones de D. J. B. Catalá y Gavilá. 1915. 8°. **012301. df. 11.**

CATALDE (DE) Mémoires de Monsieur le comte de Claize. pp. 540. *Amsterdam,* 1738. 8°. **837. a. 16.**

—— Le Paysan gentilhomme, ou Avantures de M. Ransav, avec son voyage aux Isles Jumelles. pp. 284. *La Haye,* 1738. 12°. **12511. a. 10.**

CATALDI (NICOLA M.) Aletio illustrata, o siano Ricerche istorico-critiche sull'antica distrutta città di Aletio nella penisola salentina. pp. 83. *Napoli,* 1841. 8°. **7705. bb. 27. (3.)**

CATALDI (PABLO) *See* URQUIZA (E. de) Pablo Cataldi grabó para el General Urquiza, *etc.* 1927. 8°. **7756. c. 36.**

CATALDI (PIETRO ANTONIO) *See also* ANNOTIO (Perito) *pseud.* [i.e. P. A. Cataldi.]

—— *See* DANTI (E.) *Bishop of Alatri.* Primo volume dell'vso et fabbrica dell'astrolabio, *etc.* (Anemografia . . . Tradotto di latino . . . da M. P. Cattani.) 1578. 4°. **50. b. 7.**

—— Algebra discorsiua numerale, et lineale, doue discorrendo con il giudicio naturale si inuentano le regole alle equationi algebratiche, & il modo da esequire le operationi loro in numeri & in linee. pp. 43. *S. Bonomi: Bologna,* 1618. fol. **8532. f. 20.**

—— Due lettioni . . . doue si mostra come si troui la grandezza delle superficie rettilinee, *etc.* pp. 32. *B. Cochi: Bologna,* 1613. 4°. **8534. bb. 25. (6.)**

—— Due lettioni . . . fatte nell'Academia del Dissegno di Perugia, *etc.* MS. NOTES. *G. Rossi: Bologna,* 1577. 4°. **7855. bb. 16.**

—— Elementi delle quantità irrationali' o inesplicabili, necessarij alle operationi geometriche, algebratiche, & altre doue si tratta di numeri, & linee in qual si voglia scienza, ò arte, *etc.* pp. 35. *S. Bonomi: Bologna,* 1620. fol. **8532. f. 23.**

—— [Another copy.] **8534. ee. 21. (6.)**

—— Nuoua algebra proportionale, doue si mostra la inuentione della radice cuba di molti binomij, quali gl'illustri scrittori teneuano non potere essere cubi, et anco delli trinomij con molte considerationi intorno à simili quantità. pp. 51. *S. Bonomi: Bologna,* 1619. fol. **8532. f. 22.**

CATALDI (Pietro Antonio)

—— Operetta d'ordinanze quadre di terreno, & di gente, & altre . . . Di P. A. C. [i.e. P. A. Cataldi.] pp. 16.
1618. 4°. *See* C., P. A.   **8534. bb. 25.** (5.)

—— Opusculum de lineis rectis æquidistantibus et non æquidistantibus. pp. 35.   *Apud hæredes I. Rossij:*
Bononiæ, 1603. 4°.   **530. f. 3.** (1.)

—— [Another copy.]   **8534. bb. 25.** (2.)

—— Operetta delle linee rette equidistanti et non equi-distanti. (Aggiunta.) 2 pt. pp. 72.   *Gli heredi*
di G. Rossi: Bologna, 1603, 04. 4°. **8534. bb. 25.** (1, 3.)

—— Regola della quantita, ò cosa di cosa. pp. 32.
S. Bonomi: Bologna, 1618. fol.   **8532. f. 21.**

—— [Another copy.]   **8534. ee. 21.** (5.)

—— Tauola del leuar del sole et del mezo di per ciascun giorno dell'anno. Calculata . . . da P. A. C. [i.e. P. A. Cataldi.] 1587. *s. sh.* fol. *See* EPHEMERIDES.
                                             1882. c. 1. (166.)

—— Trattato de' numeri perfetti. pp. 48.   *Gli heredi*
di G. Rossi: Bologna, 1603. 4°.   **8506. d. 18.**

—— [Another copy.]   **8534. bb. 25.** (4.)
Imperfect; wanting pp. 41–48.

—— Trattato del modo breuissimo di trouare la radice quadra delli numeri, et regole da approssimarsi di con-tinuo al vero nelle radici de' numeri non quadrati, con le cause, et inuentioni loro, et anco il modo di pigliarne la radice cuba, applicando il tutto alle operationi militari, et altre. pp. 140.   *B. Cochi: Bologna,* 1613. fol.
                                             8534. ee. 21. (4.)

—— Trattato dell'algebra proportionale, doue si mostrano le inuentioni de i primi capitoli, ò equationi d'essa. pp. 76.
Gli heredi di G. Rossi: Bologna, 1610. fol.
                                             8534. ee. 21. (2.)

—— Trattato della quadratura del cerchio doue si esamina vn nuouo modo di quadrarlo per numeri et insieme si mostra come, dato vn rettilineo, si formi un curuilineo eguale ad esso dato, *etc.* pp. 55.   *B. Cochi: Bologna,* 1612. fol.
                                             531. n. 14. (2.)

—— [Another copy.]   **8534. ee. 21.** (3.)

CATALDI (Prospero) *See* GENTA (G. F.) Panegirico in lode del . . . vescovo, e martire S. Emidio . . . Dato alla luce da P. Cataldi, *etc.* 1741. fol.   **4828. e. 8.**

CATALDINO (José) *See* XARQUE (F.) *Dean of Albarracín.* Vida apostolica del . . . Padre José Cataldino, *etc.*
1664. 4°.   **4867. b. 52.**

CATALDINUS, *de Boncompagnis. See* BONCOMPAGNIS.

CATALDO, *Siciliano. See* BELANDO (V.) *called* CATALDO.

CATALDO (Pietro Antonio) *See* CATALDI.

CATALDUS, *Saint, Bishop of Taranto. See* MORONE (Bartolomeo) *of Taranto.* Vita et miracula S. Cataldi, *etc.*
1614. 4°. [MORONE (Bonaventura) *Cataldiados . . .*
libri sex.]   **1224. i. 9.**

—— *See* MORONE (Bartolomeo) *of Taranto.* Vita e miracoli di S. Cataldo, *etc.* 1779, *etc.* 12°.   **4863.bbb.30.**

—— Prophetia sancti Cataldi episcopi tarentini, reperta anno domini .MCCCCLXXXXII. in ecclesia tarentina uiuĕte adhuc & regnante Ferdinando alphonsi primi filio nuper autem mĕse maio in lucē edita per fratres sancte Marie Montis oliueti a quibus īuenta fuit in sicilia in bibliotecha [*sic*] regis alfonsi secundi cum morienti illi interfuissent.
[*Bartolommeo di Libri: Florence,* 1497 ?] 4°. IA. **27337.**
2 leaves. Sig. a². *34 lines to a page.*

CATALDUS (Petrus Antonius) *See* CATALDI (Pietro A.)

CATALINA. [For Saints, Sovereigns and Princesses of Sovereign Houses of this name:] *See* CATHARINE.

CATALINA (Juan)

—— *See* CATALINA (M.) Biografías de los distinguidos actores D. Manuel y D. Juan Catalina. 1862. 8°. [DIEZ (*M.*) *La Perla del teatro español, etc.*] **10632. bb. 46.** (2.)

—— Entre un Cabo y un Sargento. Apropósito en un acto, *etc.* pp. 20. *Madrid,* [1863.] 8°.   **11726. bbb. 26.** (4.)

—— Llueven Sobrinos ! ! ! Apropósito original en un acto e en verso, *etc.* pp. 12. *Madrid,* 1851. 4°.
                                             11725. h. 29.

—— La Trompa de Eustaquio, sordera en un acto, *etc.* pp. 26.
Madrid, 1867. 8°.   **11726. bbb. 29.** (2.)

CATALINA (Manuel) *See* MORETO Y CABAÑA (A.) El Licenciado Vidriera. Comedia . . . refundida por D. M. Catalina. 1852. 8°.   **11726. b. 49.**

—— Biografías de los distinguidos actores D. Manuel y D. Juan Catalina. pp. 22. *In:* DIEZ (M.) La Perla del teatro español, *etc.* 1862. 8°.   **10632. bb. 46.** (2.)

CATALINA (Mariano) *See* ALARCÓN (P. A. de) Novelas cortas . . . Primera serie. Biografía del autor [signed: M. Catalina]. 1881, *etc.* 8°.   **12230. b. 19.**

—— *See* CERVANTES SAAVEDRA (M. de) [*Novelas.—Spanish.*] Novelas, *etc.* [Edited by M. C., i.e. Mariano Catalina.] 1883. 16°.   **12231. aa. 4.**

—— *See* ROMANCERO. Romancero Selecto, *etc.* [Edited by M. C., i.e. Mariano Catalina.] 1883. 16°.
                                             12231. aa. 5.

—— *See* VEGA CARPIO (L. F. de) [*Miscellaneous Works.*] La Dorotea, *etc.* [Edited by M. C., i.e. Mariano Catalina.] 1886. 16°.   **12231. aa. 6.**

—— No hay buen fin por mal camino. Drama en tres actos y en verso, *etc.* pp. 83. *Madrid,* 1874. 8°.
                                             11728. bbb. 3. (5.)

—— La Poesía Lírica en el Teatro antiguo. Colección de trozos escogidos. 11 tom. *Madrid,* 1909–13. 8°.
                                             011451. h. 52.

—— Poesías, Cantares y Leyendas . . . Con un prólogo de . . . M. Cañete. pp. xxxviii. 324. *Madrid,* 1879. 8°.
                                             11450. bb. 9.

CATALINA (Severo) *See* CATALINA DEL AMO.

CATALINA DEL AMO (Severo) *See* BARCO (L. del) Diccionario Español de la Sagrada Escritura, *etc.* [With a preface by S. Catalina del Amo.] 1862. 4°.
                                             3129. g. 14.

—— Obras. 6 tom. *Madrid,* 1876–78. 8°.
                                             12230. aaa. 14.

—— La Legislacion Mosáica. Discurso, *etc.* pp. 16.
Madrid, 1857. 8°.   **5063. d. 1.**

—— La Mujer. Apuntes para un libro . . . [With a preface by Ramon de Campoamor y Campoosorio.] Segunda edicion aumentada. pp. xv. 288. *Madrid,* 1861. 8°.
                                             8415. dd. 10.

—— Roma, obra póstuma . . . Precede una noticia de la vida . . . del Señor Catalina . . . por D. Francisco Cutanda. pp. lxvii. 754. 1873. 8°.   *See* MADRID.—
Real Academia Española.   **10131. dd. 25.**

CATALINA DEL AMO (Severo)

—— La Verdad del Progreso. pp. viii. 330. *Madrid,* 1862. 8º. **8042. h. 5.**

—— [Another edition.] *Mejico,* 1864. fol. Hendon.
Imperfect ; wanting all after p. 62.

CATALINA GARCÍA (Juan) *See* Aguilera y Gamboa
(E. de) *Marquis de Cerralbo.* Discursos leídos ante la Real Academia de la Historia en la recepción pública del Excelentísimo Sr. D. E. de Aguilera y Gamboa, *etc.* (El Arzobispo D. Rodrigo Ximénez de Rada y el Monasterio de Santa María de Huerta.—Contestación del Excmo. Sr. D. J. Catalina García.) 1908. 8º.
4605. ff. 15.

—— *See* Aguilera y Gamboa (E. de) *Marquis de Cerralbo.* Del Hogar Castellano, *etc.* [With an introduction by J. Catalina García.] [1914.] 8º. **9181. b. 21.**

—— *See* José, *de Sigüenza.* Historia de la Orden de San Jerónimo . . . Publicada con un elogio de Fr. José de Sigüenza por D. J. Catalina García. 1907, *etc.* 8º.
012199. k. 1/8.

—— *See* Liñan y Eguizabal (J. de) *Count de Doña Marina.* Don Juan Catalina Garcia, *etc.* 1911. 8º.
10604. f. 22. (3.)

—— *See* Spain. [*Appendix.—Topography and Travels.*] Relaciones topográficas de España . . . con notas y aumentos de D. Juan Catalina Garcia. 1903, *etc.* 8º. [*Memorial Histórico Español.* tom. 41–47.] Ac. **6630.**

—— Biblioteca de escritores de la provincia de Guadalajara, y bibliografía de la misma hasta el siglo xix. pp. xii. 799. *Madrid,* 1899. 8º. **2330. f. 6.**

—— Castilla y Leon durante los reinados de Pedro i., Enrique ii., Juan i. y Enrique iii. tom. 1.
pp. xxxviii. 502. *Madrid,* 1893. 8º. [*Cánovas del Castillo (A.) Historia general de España, etc.*]
9181. ff. 1.

—— Datos bibliográficos sobre la Sociedad Económica Matritense. pp. 165. *Madrid,* 1877. 8º.
11902. aa. 29.

—— Ensayo de una Tipografía Complutense. pp. xii. 673. *Madrid,* 1889. 8º. **11899. h. 34.**

—— *See* Fernández (Benigno) Impresos de Alcalá en la Biblioteca del Escorial. Con adiciones y correcciones á la obra " Ensayo de una Tipografía Complutense " [by J. Catalina García], *etc.* 1916. 8º.
11908. c. 37.

—— Inventario de las antiguedades y objetos de arte que posee la Real Academia de la Historia. [By J. Catalina García.] pp. 146. 1903. 8º. *See* Madrid.—*Real Academia de la Historia.* **07708. k. 13.**

—— El Segundo Matrimonio del primer Marqués del Cenete. *See* Menéndez y Pelayo (M.) Homenaje á Menéndez y Pelayo, *etc.* vol. 2. 1899. 8º. **011852. i. 53.**

CATALISANO (Gennaro) Grammatica-armonica fisico-matematica ragionata su i veri principj fondamentali teorico-pratici, *etc.* pp. xxxii. 165. pl. xv. *Roma,* 1781. 4º. **7896. g. 22.**

—— [Another copy.] Grammatico-armonica fisico-matematica ragionata, *etc.* *Roma,* 1781. 4º. Hirsch i. **106.**

CATALOGERS. *See* Cataloguers.

CATALOGHI.

—— Cataloghi dei musei e gallerie d'Italia. *See* Italy.—*Ministero della Pubblica Istruzione.—Direzione Generale delle Antichità e Belle Arti.*

CATALOGNE. *See* Catalonia.

CATALOGNE (Gérard de) Une Génération. [Essays on François Mauriac, Jean Giraudoux, and others.] pp. 273. *Paris,* 1930. 8º. **11822. p. 29.**

—— Henry Bataille, ou le Romantisme de l'instinct. Fragments. pp. 70. *Paris,* 1925. 8º. **011840. a. 66.**

—— Le Message de Thomas Hardy . . . Avec un portrait, *etc.* [With " Le Carnet critique " by various authors.] pp. 188. *Paris,* 1928. 8º. **011840. d. 65.**

—— Notre révolution, *etc.* 3 tom.
  1. Tragédie dans le monde. pp. 212. 1941.
  2. Hommes et doctrines du vingtième siècle. pp. 176. 1941.
  3. Entretiens dans la tourmente. pp. 169. 1944.
Montréal, 1941, 44. 8º. **09062. s. 23.**

—— [Another copy of tom. 1, 2.] Notre révolution. *Montréal,* 1941. 8º. **08052. a. 86.**

CATALOGO. *See also* Catalogues.

—— Catálogo de la exposición de libros mexicanos de historia, *etc.* 1949. 8º. *See* Congreso de Historiadores de Mexico y los Estados Unidos.

—— Catálogo de revistas españolas. *See* Madrid.—*Instituto de Cultura Hispánica.—Departamento de Información.*

—— Catalogo dei cataloghi del libro italiano. *See* Italy.—*Società Generale delle Messaggerie Italiane, etc.*

—— Catalogo di spropositi. *See* Periodical Publications.—*Modena.* Strenna pel nuovo anno.

—— Catalogo ecclesiastico per la città e diocesi di Mantova. *See* Periodical Publications.—*Mantua.*

—— Catálogo general de la librería español e hispanoamericana. *See* Spain.—*Cámaras Oficiales del Libro.*

—— Catalogo generale della libreria italiana. *See* Milan.—*Associazione Tipografico-Libraria Italiana.*

—— Catalogo generale delle opere musicali, teoriche o pratiche, manoscritte o stampate, di autori vissuti sino ai primi decenni del secolo xix, esistenti nelle biblioteche e negli archivi d'Italia. *See* International Musical Society.—*Italian Section.*

—— Catálogo monumental de España. *See* Spain.—*Ministerio de Instrucción Publica y Bellas Artes.*

CATÁLOGOS.

—— Catálogos. Sua importância bibliográphica. [With a chronological list of Portuguese book catalogues.] *In :* Boletim da Sociedade de Biblióphilos Barbosa Machado. vol 2. pp. 89–184. 1913. 8º. Ac. **9547. b.**

—— Catálogos de la música antigua conservada en España. *See* Spain.—*Consejo Superior de Investigaciones Científicas.—Instituto Español de Musicologia.*

CATALOGŬ. Catalogŭ mensual al librăriei romăne. *See* Periodical Publications.—*Bucharest.*

CATALOGUE. *See also* Catalogues.

CATALOGUE.

—— Catalogue annuel de la librairie française. *See* PERIODICAL PUBLICATIONS.—*Paris.*

—— Catalogue félibréen, *etc. See* PERIODICAL PUBLICATIONS. —*Marseilles.*

—— Catalogue général des manuscrits des bibliothèques publiques de la France. 1885- . *See* FRANCE.—*Ministère de l'Instruction Publique.*

—— Catalogue général des manuscrits des bibliothèques publiques des départements. 1849-85. *See* FRANCE.— *Ministère de l'Instruction Publique.*

—— Catalogue illustré du Salon, *etc. See* PARIS.—*Salon.* Salon de 1879. Catalogue illustre, *etc.*

—— Catalogue mensuel de toutes les publications musicales de la France, la Belgique et la Suisse, *etc. See* PERIODICAL PUBLICATIONS.—*Vevey.*

—— The Catologue [*sic*] of Contented Cuckolds, *etc.* [A ballad.] 𝔅.𝔏. [*London*, 1670?] *s. sh.* fol.
C. **40**. m. **9.** (59.)

—— [Another edition.] 𝔅.𝔏. *London*, [1685?] *s. sh.* fol.
Rox. II. **43.**

—— Catalogue of London Periodicals, *etc. See* PERIODICAL PUBLICATIONS.—*London.*

—— Catalogue of Modern Chemical Apparatus. *See* DIRECTORIES.—*Chemical Apparatus.*

—— A Catalogue of Scientific Apparatus, for lecture and laboratory use, *etc. See* DIRECTORIES.—*Scientific Apparatus.*

—— Catalogue of the Active Volcanoes of the World. *See* INTERNATIONAL UNION OF GEODESY AND GEOPHYSICS.— *Association of Vulcanology.*

—— Catalogue périodique de médailles et monnaies grecques, romaines, du moyen âge, *etc. See* PERIODICAL PUBLICATIONS.—*Paris.*

CATALOGUERS.

—— Catalogers' and Classifiers' Yearbook. *See* UNITED STATES OF AMERICA.—*American Library Association.— Catalog Section.*

CATALOGUES.

This heading includes only anonymous catalogues. Catalogues of collections both public and private are entered under the heading appropriate to the collection. Sale catalogues not containing the name of the owner of the collection are entered under the name of the auctioneer when this is given. Other catalogues which contain the name of a compiler are entered under the compiler's name.

The " Index librorum prohibitorum " is entered under ROME, *Church of. Anonymous works with this title not published officially are entered below.*

The heading is arranged chronologically. In each year dated sale catalogues are entered first in order of dates and are followed by other catalogues published during the year, in alphabetical order.

—— [A MS. catalogue of Spanish comedies.] 2 pt. 4º.
11725. g. **19.**

CATALOGUES.

—— *Begin.* Cupiētes emere libros infra notatos venient ad hospiciuӡ subnotatum Venditorem habituri largissimum, *etc.* [An advertisement of the "Summa Antonini" and other books printed or sold by Anton Koberger.] 𝔊.𝔏. [*Anton Koberger: Nuremberg*, 1480?] *s. sh.* fol.
IC. **7195.**
Printed on one side of the leaf only. 3 lines of large type and 48 of small, on the left side.

—— *Begin.* witlik sy alleñ luden dat hir sind to kope desse nagheschreuene boke in dudesch. Is dat ienigen behegelik is desse nageschreuene boke alle edder etlike to kopen de mach kamē in de stede edder herberge hir na gescreuē he schal vinden enen milden verkoper. [*Lucas Brandis: Lubeck?* 1495?] *s. sh.* fol.
IB. **9829.**
Printed on one side of the leaf only. 4 lines of large type, 31 lines of small.

—— Catalogus Academiarum totius orbis Christiani. *Excudebant Hæredes P. Seitzij: Witebergæ*, 1554. 8º.
731. a. **18.**

—— Nouus index librorum prohibitorum et suspensorum. *Apud E. Viotum: Parmæ*, 1580. *s. sh.* fol.
1865. c. **10.** (4.)

—— Index librorum prohibitorum, gedruckt zu Parma 1580, nach dem einzigen bekannten Exemplare herausgegeben und erläutert von Dr. Fr. Heinrich Reusch. pp. 43. *Bonn*, 1889. 8º.
011902. h. **29.** (7.)

—— Catalogus testium veritatis, *etc.* (Ab Illyrico collectus.) 1597. 4º. *See* FLACIUS (M.) *Illyricus.*
850. l. **2.**

—— Jaggard's Catalogue of English Books [i.e. " A Catalogue of such English Bookes, as lately have bene, and now are in Printing for Publication. From the ninth day of October, 1618. untill Easter Terme, next ensuing."] [Edited by] Oliver M. Willard. Reprinted from Stanford Studies in Language and Literature. 1941. 8º.
11916. c. **51.**

—— Bibliotheca exotica, siue, Catalogus officinalis librorum peregrinis linguis usualibus scriptorum . . . omnium quotquot in officinis bibliopolarum indagari potuerunt, & in Nundinis Francofurtensibus prostant, ac venales habentur. La bibliothèque universail, contenant le catalogue de tous les livres . . . imprimes ce siecle passè, aux langues Françoise, Italienne, Espaignole, & autres, *etc.* pp. 302. *Par B. Ostern: Frankfourt*, 1625. 4º.
S.C. **549.** (1.)

—— A Catalogue of Certaine bookes, which haue beene published, and—by authoritie—printed in England, both in Latine and English, since the yeare 1626. vntill Nouember this present yeare 1631, *etc.* [*Thomas Cotes:*] *London*, 1631. 4º.
C. **120.** b. **14.**

—— A Catalogue of such Testimonies in all ages as plainly evidence Bishops and Presbyters to be both one, equall and the same in jurisdiction, office, dignity . . . by divine law and institution, and their disparity to be a meere humane ordinance, *etc.* pp. 23. 1637. 4º.
108. c. **8.**
The date has been altered in ink to 1641.

—— Catalogus librorum in diversis Italiæ locis emptorum, anno 1636 . . . Qui Londini in Cæmeterio sancti Pauli ad Insigne Rosæ prostant venales. pp. 58. *Typis Iohannis Legatt: Londini*, 1637. 4º.
C. **118.** c. **5.** (5.)

—— [Another copy.]
821. h. **56.**
Imperfect; wanting all after p. 46.

—— Catalogue de livres. pp. 56. [1650?] 4º.
S.C. **847.** (10.)

CATALOGUES.

—— Catalogus etlicher sehr alten Bücher, welche neulich in Irrland auff einem alten eroberten Schlosse in einer Bibliothec gefunden worden. [A jeu d'esprit.] 1650. 4°.
12331. bbb. 31.
Later edition 1666.

—— Bibliotheca Parliamenti. Libri Theologi [*sic*], Politici, Historici, qui prostant venales in Vico vulgo vocato Little-Britain. Done into English for the Assembly of Divines. [A satire.] pp. 6. *Printed at London,* 1653. 4°.
E. 693. (19.)

—— Bibliotheca Parliamenti. Libri Theologici, Politici, Historici, qui prostant venales in Vico vulgo vocato Little-Britain. Classis secunda. Done into English for the Assembly of Divines. [A satire.] pp. 7. [*London,*] 1653. 4°.
E. 702. (8.)

—— Bibliotheca Anti-Ianseniana, siue Catalogus piorum eruditorumque scriptorum, qui Corn. Iansenii . . . & Iansenianorum hæreses . . . oppugnarunt. Cum præludiis historiæ, et cribratione farraginis Iansenisticæ. [By Philippe Labbe.] pp. 104. *Ex officina Cramosiana: Parisiis,* 1654. 4°.
860. l. 17.

—— An exact and perfect Catalogue of all playes that are printed. *See* G., T., M^r *of Arts.* The Careles Shepherdess, a tragi-comedy, *etc.* 1656. 4°.
644. e. 21.

—— [A catalogue of books.] [1658 ?] 4°.
S.C. 853. (2.)
Imperfect ; wanting the titlepage and all after p. 192.

—— A Catalogue of New Books, by way of supplement to the former. Being such as have been printed from that time, till Easter-term, 1660. [The epistle dedicatory signed : W. L., i.e. W. London ?] 1660. 4°. *See* L., W.
E.1025.(17.)

—— A True, perfect, and exact Catalogue of all the Comedies, Tragedies, Tragi-Comedies, Pastorals, Masques and Interludes, that were ever yet printed and published, till this present year 1661., *etc.* pp. 16. [*London,* 1661.] 4°.
641. g. 1.

—— Catalogus universalis. Hoc est: Designatio omnium librorum, qui . . . Nundinis . . . Francofurtensibus & Lipsiensibus . . . prodierunt, *etc.* 1664–1759. 4°.
[Continued as :]
Allgemeines Verzeichniss derer Bücher, welche in der Frankfurter und Leipziger Ostermesse (Michaelmesse) . . . aufgeleget worden sind. 1760–1850. 4° & 8°.
[Continued as :]
Mess Katalog. Verzeichniss der Bücher, Zeitschriften u. Landkarten welche . . . im Gebiete des deutschen Buchhandels erschienen sind, *etc.* 1851–60. 8°. *See* PERIODICAL PUBLICATIONS.—*Leipsic.*
P.P. 6513. c.

—— Livres reliez a vandre. MS. NOTES. [1665 ?] 4°.
S.C. 847. (9.)

—— Catalogus etlicher sehr alten Bücher, welche newlich in Irrlandt auff einem alten eroberten Schlosse in einer Bibliothec gefunden worden. 1666. 4°. **11904. bb. 30.**
Previous edition 1650 ; *later edition* 1925.

—— Mercurius Librarius, or, a Catalogue of books printed and published in Michaelmass-Term, 1668(—Easter-Term, 1669 ; Michaelmas-Term, 1669). [no. 1 edited by John Starkey ; no. 2, 3, 5 edited by John Starkey and Robert Clavell.] no. 1–2, 5. [1668–69.] fol. *See* STARKEY (John)
821. ee. 38. (1.)

—— A Catalogue of Books printed and published at London in Easter-Term, 1670 (—Trinity Term, 1674). [Edited by Robert Clavell.] no. 1–18. [1670–74.] fol.

CATALOGUES.

—— Michaelmas Term, 1674 (—Trinity-Term, 1680). no. 1–24. [1674–80.] fol.

—— Michaelmas-Term, 1680 (—Trinity-Term, 1695). no. 1–57. 1680–[95.] fol.

—— Hillary-Term, 169⅚ (—Easter and Trinity Terms, 1709). no. 1–52. [1696–1709.] fol.
See PERIODICAL PUBLICATIONS.—*London.*
821. ee. 38. (2.) & 821. ee. 39. (1.)

—— Cimeliarchium venale, seu Thesaurus antiquissimorum numorum [*sic*], in honorem & memoriam consulum, III. virorum, familiarumque romanorum imperatorum . . . Stuttgardiæ . . . nunc promercalis. *Typis J. W. Rösslini: Stuttgardiæ,* 1670. 12°.
603. a. 1. (1.)
The titlepage is slightly mutilated.

—— Catalogus Electorum, Principum, Heroum, Comitum, Baronum, Nobilium, necnon aliorum . . . virorum, qui huic designationi interfuerunt. [A list of those present at the election and coronation of Maximilian II at Frankfort in 1562.] *See* SCHARDIUS (S.) Schardius redivivus, *etc.* tom. 3. 1673. fol.
9366. l. 6.

—— Libri medici in Germania (in Belgio, in Italia, in Gallia) impressi. pp. 8. [1675 ?] 8°.
820. c. 1. (4*.)

—— Catalogus lapidum pretiosorum, achatum, onycum . . . Nec non numismatum græcorum, romanorum . . . maxima impensa congestorum. pp. 197. *Amstelodami,* 1677. 12°.
603. a. 36. (1.)
Later edition 1688.

—— Catalogus librorum ex bibliotheca nobilis cujusdam Angli [i.e. Robert Greville, 4th Baron Brooke], qui ante paucos annos in humanis esse desiit. Accesserunt libri eximii theologi, D. Gabrielis Sangar . . . Adjectis theologi alterius . . . libris selectioribus. Quorum omnium auctio habebitur Londini 2° die Decembris . . . 1678, *etc.* pp. 98. [*London,*] 1678. 4°. **C.120.c.2.(8.)**

—— [Another copy.] MS. PRICES.
11906. e. 8.

—— [A catalogue of books for sale. With a note in MS., " De la Bibliotheque de monsieur Gaumont qui a esté vendue a Rouen 1678."] MS. PRICES. 2 pt. [1678 ?] 8°.
S.C. 834. (18.)
Imperfect ; wanting all before p. 3 of the first part.

—— Catalogus cujuscunque facultatis & linguæ librorum, abhinc 2 a 3 annorum spatio in Germania, Gallia, & Belgio, &c. novissime impressorum singulis semestribus continuandus. 16 pt. *Apud Janssonio-Waesbergios: Amstelædami,* 1678–84. 4°.
820. f. 2.
A copy of " Semestre vicesimum secundum," 1686, is entered separately below.

—— [Another copy of " Semestre sextum."]
821. h. 1. (3*.)

—— [Another copy of " Semestre septimum."] **821. h. 59.**

—— A Catalogue of two Choice and Considerable Libraries of Books, Latin and English, of two eminent and learned men deceased ; are to be exposed to sale by way of auction, at Mr. Bridges's Coffe-House in Popes-Head Alley . . . the 22^d day of this instant November, 1680. [A sale of books from the stock of Abel Roper.] pp. 19. 13–72. [*London,* 1680.] 4°.
S.C. 1035. (12.)

—— A Compleat Catalogue of all the Stitch'd Books and Single Sheets printed since the first discovery of the popish Plot, September 1678., to January 16⁷⁹⁄₈₀. To which is added a Catalogue of all His Majesties proclamations, speeches, and declarations, with the Orders of the King and Council, and what Acts of Parliament have been published since the Plot. pp. 32. [*J. R. :*] *London,* 1680. 4°.
128. a. 3. (1.)

CATALOGUES.

—— A Continuation of the Compleat Catalogue of Stitch'd Books and Single Sheets, &c. . . . From the 1st. of January 16$\frac{79}{80}$. to the 25th. of June. 1680, *etc.*
pp. 22. MS. NOTES AND PRICES. ✓   [*J. R.:*] *London,*
1680. 4°. ✓[*probably by Narcissus Luttrell*].**128**. a. **3**. (**2**.)
Interleaved.

—— A second Continuation of the Compleat Catalogue of Stitch'd Books and Single Sheets . . . from the 24th of June to Michaelmas Term 1680, *etc.*
pp. 16. MS. NOTES AND PRICES.   *J. R.: London,*
1680. 4°. [*probably by Narcissus Luttrell*]. **128**. a. **3**. (**3**.)
Interleaved.

—— A General Catalogue of all the stitch'd Books and Single Sheets &c. printed the two last years, commencing from the first discovery of the Popish Plot—September 1678.— and continued to Michaelmas Term 1680, *etc.* [A reissue in one volume of " A Compleat Catalogue of all the Stitch'd Books " and its two continuations.] 3 pt.
J. R.: London, 1680. 4°.   **T. 935**. (**1**.)

—— An Exact Catalogue of all the Comedies, Tragedies, Tragi-comedies . . . that were ever yet printed and published, till this present year 1680. pp. 16. *L. Lichfield for Nicholas Cox: Oxon,* 1680. 4°.   **641**. g. **2**. (**1**.)

—— Catalogo de Comedias de los Mejores Ingenios de España. 1681. *See* SPAIN. [*Appendix.—Miscellaneous.*] Primera [*etc.*] Parte de Comedias escogidas, *etc.*
1652, *etc.* 4°.   **11725**. d. **8**.

—— Catalogus variorum Librorum Theologicorum, Juridicorumque . . . Quorum auctio habebitur . . . secundo die Aprilis, 1683. [A sale of books belonging to Samuel Wilson.] pp. 10. MS. PRICES. 1683. 4°.
   821. i. **3**. (**6**.)

—— Catalogus librorum, varii generis, & idiomatis . . . quorum auctio publicè habebitur, anno 1683. d. 30. April. In ædibus And: Botticher, *etc.* pp. 104.   *Typis G. Rebenlini: Hamburgi,* [1683.] 8°.   S.C. **53**. (**1**.)

—— A Catalogue of the Libraries of two Eminent Persons [John Gellibrand and Thomas Simmons], consisting of choice English books . . . which will be sold by way of auction at Tunbridge-Wells . . . the 8. day of August, 1684. pp. 6. [1684.] 4°.   **821**. i. **4**. (**4**.)

—— Catalogus variorum librorum ex bibliothecis selectissimis doctissim. virorum nuperrime defunctorum quorum auctio habebitur . . . 19 die Octobris, 1685. [A sale of books from the stock of Thomas Parkhurst.] pp. 88. 1685. 4°.
   821. i. **4**. (**12**.)

—— [Another copy.]   **11906**. c. **55**.

—— A Catalogue of Several Sorts of Bibles, Testaments, Common Prayers . . . that are to be exposed to sale . . . the 10th of December, 1685. [1685.] *s. sh.* fol.
   821. i. **4**. (**18**.)

—— A Catalogue of a Remainder of Several Sorts of Bibles, Testaments, Common Prayers . . . lately expos'd to sale, by way of auction, *etc.* [10 Dec. 1685.]
1685. *s. sh.* fol.   **821**. i. **4**. (**19**.)

—— A Catalogue of Choice Books, chiefly Civil Law. Will be exposed to sale by way of auction . . . the 25th of February 1685 [o.s.]. [1686.] *s. sh.* fol.
   821. i. **4**. (**22**.)

—— Bibliotheca Anglicana : or, a Collection of choice English Books . . . will be exposed to sale, by way of auction . . . the fifth of May, 1686, *etc.* MS. PRICES. [1686.] 4°.
   821. i. **6**. (**2**.)

CATALOGUES.

—— Bibliotheca medica, et mathematica anglo-latina. Cujusdam Med. Doct. Claris. nuperrime defuncti . . . Quorum auctio habebitur . . . 30 die Augusti 1686. pp. 24. [1686.] 4°.   **821**. i. **6**. (**7**.)

—— A Catalogue containing Variety of English Books in Divinity, History . . . which will be exposed to sale by way of auction . . . the 20th of this instant December, 1686. pp. 48. [1686.] 4°.   S.C. **1039**. (**5**.)

—— [Another copy.]   **821**. i. **6**. (**10**.)

—— Catalogi librorum novissime impressorum, semestre vicesimum secundum à mense Ianuario usque ad mensem Iulii 1686. pp. 16. [*Amsterdam,* 1686.] 4°.
   S.C. **296**. (**3**.)
Imperfect ; wanting the titlepage. Catalogued from the caption-title. A copy of pt. 1–17, 1678–84, is entered above.

—— A Catalogue of Choice English Books . . . Which will be exposed to sale, by way of auction . . . the 10th day of January, 168$\frac{6}{7}$, *etc.* pp. 24. 24. 1686 [1687]. 4°.
   821. i. **6**. (**11**.)

—— Pinacotheca archetiparum imaginum. Raccolta volante d'intagli curiosi . . . A Collection of excellent prints and drawings, to be sold .xiii. Februar. M.DC.LXXXVIII, *etc.* pp. 18. [1688.] 8°.   S.C. **268**. (**2**.)

—— Catalogus lapidum pretiosorum, achatum, onycum . . . Nec non numismata [*sic*] græcorum, romanorum . . . maxima impensa congestorum. pp. 197.   *J. de Wees: Amstelodami,* 1688. 12°.   **603**. a. **36**. (**2**.)
Previous edition 1677.

—— A Collection of Original Drawings and Prints of the Most Eminent Masters of Europe. Together with several curious volumes of statues . . . Will be sold by auction . . . the fourth of this instant May, 1689, *etc.* pp. 4.
[*London,* 1689.] 4°.   **1402**. g. **1**. (**1**.)

—— A Curious Collection of Paintings, Drawings, and Prints by the best masters. Will be sold by auction . . . the 31st of this instant May, 1689, *etc.* pp. 6. [*London,* 1689.] 4°.   **1402**. g. **1**. (**2**.)

—— A Curious Collection of Paintings and Drawings, by the best masters. With several books of prints . . . Will be sold by auction . . . the 14th of this instant June, 1689, *etc.* [*London,* 1689.] 4°.   **1402**. g. **1**. (**3**.)

—— A Curious Collection of Paintings, Drawings, and Prints, by the best masters. With several books of Roman antiquities . . . Will be sold by auction the 21st of this instant June, 1689, *etc.* [*London,* 1689.] 4°.
   1402. g. **1**. (**4**.)

—— A Collection of Paintings, Drawings, and Prints, by the best masters. With several volumes of Mr. Ogilby's Atlas, &c. Will be sold by auction . . . the 28th of this instant June, 1689, *etc.* [*London,* 1689.] 4°.
   1402. g. **1**. (**5**.)

—— A Collection of Prints and Paintings, by the best masters ; with several engraven copper plates. Will be sold by auction . . . the 2d of this instant July, 1689, *etc.* [*London,* 1689.] 4°.   **1402**. g. **1**. (**6**.)

—— A Collection of Prints and Paintings, by the best masters ; with several volumes of Ogilby's Atlas. Will be sold by auction . . . the 5th of this instant July, 1689, *etc.* [*London,* 1689.] 4°.   **1402**. g. **1**. (**7**.)

—— A Collection of Prints and Paintings, by the best masters ; with several volumes of Ogilby's Atlas. Will be sold by auction . . . the 12th of this instant July, 1689, *etc.* [*London,* 1689.] 4°.   **1402**. g. **1**. (**8**.)

CATALOGUES.

—— A Collection of Prints and Paintings, by the best masters ; with several volumes of Ogilby's Atlas. Will be sold by auction . . . the 19th of this instant July, 1689, *etc.* [*London*, 1689.] 4º. **1402. g. 1. (9.)**

—— A Collection of Prints and Paintings, by the best masters ; with several volumes of Ogilby's Atlas. Will be sold by auction . . . the 26th of this instant July, 1689, *etc.* [*London*, 1689.] 4º. **1402. g. 1. (10.)**

—— A Catalogue of Prints and Paintings, by the best masters ; with several volumes of Ogilby's works. Will be sold by auction the 2d of this instant August, 1689, *etc.* [*London*, 1689.] 4º. **1402. g. 1. (11.)**

—— A Catalogue of very good English and Latin Books which will be sold by auction . . . the ninth of September, 1689 . . . at the Three half Moons in St. Paul's Church-Yard, *etc.* pp. 26. 4. [*London*, 1689.] 4º. **S.C. 1035. (4.)**

—— A Collection of Paintings by the best masters. Will be sold by auction . . . the 25th. of Septemb. 1689, *etc.* pp. 6. [*London*, 1689.] 4º. **1402. g. 1. (13.)**

—— A Collection of Paintings and Limnings, by the best masters : will be sold by auction . . . 1st of November, 1689, at Tom's Coffee-House, *etc.* pp. 4. [*London*, 1689.] 4º. **1402. g. 1. (14.)**

—— A Collection of Paintings by the best masters. Will be sold by auction . . . the 6th. of Novemb. 1689. At the Outropers-Office in the West-End of the Royal-Exchange, *etc.* pp. 9. [*London*, 1689.] 4º. **1402. g. 1. (15.)**

—— A Collection of Paintings & Limnings by the best masters : will be sold by auction . . . the 6th, and . . . 7th of this instant December, 1689. at the King's-Arms-Tavern . . . in the Strand, *etc.* pp. 5. [*London*, 1689.] 4º. **1402. g. 1. (16.)**

—— A Collection of Paintings by the best masters. Will be sold by auction . . . the 16th. and . . . 17th. of this instant Decemb. 1689. At the Outropers-Office in the West-End of the Royal Exchange, *etc.* pp. 9. [*London*, 1689.] 4º. **1402. g. 1. (17.)**

—— A Catalogue of All the Discourses published against Popery, during the Reign of James II. by the Members of the Church of England, and by the Non-conformists. With the names of the authors of them. [By Edward Gee.] pp. 34. *R. Baldwin : London*, 1689. 4º. **T. 1982. (3.)**

—— [Another copy.] MS. NOTES AND ADDITIONS. **125. k. 6.**

Interleaved.

—— A Collection of Paintings & Limnings by the best masters, &c. Will be sold by auction . . . the 29th, and . . . 31st of this instant January, 16$\frac{89}{90}$. at the Barbadoes Coffee-House in Exchange-Alley, *etc.* pp. 7. [*London*, 1690.] 4º. **1402. g. 1. (18.)**

—— A Collection of Paintings & Limnings by the best masters, &c. Will be sold by auction . . . the 7th, and . . . 8th of this instant February, 16$\frac{89}{90}$ at the Barbadoes Coffee-House in Exchange-Alley, *etc.* pp. 7. [*London*, 1690.] 4º. **1402. g. 1. (19.)**

—— A Collection of Paintings by the best masters. Will be sold by auction . . . the 26th of February 16$\frac{89}{90}$. At the Outropers-Office in the West End of the Royal Exchange, *etc.* pp. 16 [14]. [*London*, 1690.] 4º. **1402. g. 1. (21.)**

CATALOGUES.

—— A Collection of Paintings of several rare masters. Will be sold by auction . . . at the West End of Exeter change . . . the 3d. of April [1690], *etc.* pp. 8. [*London*, 1690.] 4º. **1402. g. 1. (23.)**

—— Bibliotheca selecta, seu catalogus librorum cujusdam generosi nuper defuncti . . . Quorum auctio habenda est Londini apud Rolles's Coffee-House . . . die lunæ septimo Aprilis 1690. pp. 7. [*London*, 1690.] 4º. **126. d. 2. (2.)**

—— At Exeter Change. A Collection of Paintings of several rare masters. Will be sold by auction . . . the 15th. day of April [1690], *etc.* pp. 4. [*London*, 1690.] 4º. **1402. g. 1. (24.)**

—— A Collection of Paintings, amongst them several originals of the best masters, will be sold by an auction at the further end of the Middle Exchange in the Strand . . . the 29th. of April [1690], *etc.* pp. 8. [*London*, 1690.] 4º. **1402. g. 1. (25.)**

—— At the West-end of Exeter Change. A Curious Collection of Three Hundred and Odd Paintings . . . Will be sold by an auction . . . the 5th. day of May [1690], *etc.* pp. 8. [*London*, 1690.] 4º. **1402. g. 1. (27.)**

—— A Collection of Paintings, many of them originals . . . will be sold by auction . . . the 12th. of this instant May 1690 . . . at the Blue-Balcony in Red-Lyon Street. pp. 6. [*London*, 1690.] 4º. **1402. g. 1. (28.)**

—— At the West-end of Exeter Change. A Curious Collection of One Hundred and odd Paintings . . . Will be sold be auction . . . the 19th. day of May [1690], *etc.* pp. 7. [*London*, 1690.] 4º. **1402. g. 1. (29.)**

—— A Curious Collection of Paintings, of several rare masters, will be sold by auction, at the Middle Exchange . . . in the Strand . . . the 26th. of this instant May [1690], *etc.* pp. 8. [*London*, 1690.] 4º. **1402. g. 1. (31.)**

—— A Collection of Paintings, by the best masters. Will be sold by auction . . . the 27th. May, 1690 . . . In the Outropers-Office in the West-End of the Royal Exchange, *etc.* pp. 13. [*London*, 1690.] 4º. **1402. g. 1. (32.)**

—— A Collection of Paintings, *etc.* [A sale catalogue, dated, in MS., 26 June 1690.] pp. 4. [1690.] 4º. **1402. g. 1. (36.)**

—— A Collection of Curious Original Paintings, and other fine copies . . . Will be sold by auction . . . the 8th of July, 1690 . . . at the King's-Head-Tavern . . . in Southwark, *etc.* pp. 7. [*London*, 1690.] 4º. **1402. g. 1. (38.)**

—— A Collection of Pictures with several fine prints . . . will be sold by auction, at the Cannary-House near the East End of Exeter Change . . . the sixteenth of August [1690], *etc.* pp. 4. [*London*, 1690.] 4º. **1402. g. 1. (43.)**

—— Catalogus selectorum librorum . . . à viro quodam illustri, p. m. comparatorum. Quorum auctio . . . habebitur die Septembr. & seqq. pp. 301. *H. Brendecke : Hamburgi*, 1690. 8º. **S.C. 77.**

—— A Curious Collection of Painting, of the most famous, antient and modern masters in Europe . . . will be exposed to sale by auction . . . the 24th. of this instant September [1690], at the House of Mr. Smith . . . in York-street, *etc.* pp. 13. [*London*, 1690.] 4º. **1402. g. 1. (47.)**

CATALOGUES.

—— At the Kings Arms Tavern, over against St. Clement's-Church in the Strand, will be sold by way of auction, a Curious Collection of Original Paintings . . . formerly belonging to a person of quality. The sale will begin . . . the 16th of October [1690], *etc.* pp. 7. [*London*, 1690.] 4°.   **1402. g. 1. (49.)**

—— At the Kings-Arms Tavern, over-against St. Clements Church in the Strand, will be sold by way of auction the 11th. of this instant November [1690]. A curious collection of original paintings, *etc.* pp. 10.   [*London*, 1690.] 4°.   **1402. g. 1. (52.)**

—— A Collection of Paintings, and several other Curiosities. By the best masters. Will be sold by auction . . . the 25th of this instant November, 1690 . . . in the Out-ropers-Office in the West-End of the Royal Exchange, *etc.* pp. 10. [*London*, 1690.] 4°.   **1402. g. 1. (56.)**

—— At the Kings-Arms Tavern over-against St. Clements Church in the Strand, will . . . be exposed to sale Several Original Paintings, and other fine copies . . . the 9th of this instant Decemb. 1690, *etc.* pp. 8. [*London*, 1690.] 4°.   **1402. g. 1. (59.)**

—— A Miscellaneous Catalog of mean, vulgar, cheap and simple experiments. pp. 3.   *Joseph Ray:* [*Dublin*, 1690 ?] fol.   **536. m. 25.**

—— At the Kings-Arms Tavern, over-against St. Clements Church in the Strand, will . . . be exposed to sale several original paintings, and other fine copies the 13th. of this instant January, $16\frac{90}{91}$, *etc.* pp. 8. [*London*, 1691.] 4°.   **1402. g. 1. (61.)**

—— An Extraordinary Collection of Paintings, and several other Curiosities. By the best masters. Will be sold by auction . . . the 20th of this instant January, $16\frac{90}{91}$ . . . in the Auction-Office in the West-End of the Royal Exchange, *etc.* pp. 18. [*London*, 1691.] 4°.   **1402. g. 1. (63.)**

—— A Collection of Curious Pictures, viz. Paintings and Limnings, by the best masters. Will be sold by auction . . . the 27th. instant [27 January 1691] . . . at the Blew-Balcony in Red-Lyon-street, *etc.* pp. 9. [*London*, 1691.] 4°.   **1402. g. 1. (65.)**

—— [Another copy.]   **1402. g. 1. (70.)**

—— At the Kings-Arms Tavern, over-against St. Clements Church in the Strand, will . . . be exposed to sale Several Original Paintings, and other fine copies . . . the 5th. of this instant February, $16\frac{90}{91}$, *etc.* pp. 8. [*London*, 1691.] 4°.   **1402. g. 1. (68.)**

—— At the Marine-Coffee-House in Castle-Alley in Birchin-Lane in Cornhil . . . the 26th of this instant February, $169\frac{0}{1}$ . . . sold by auction . . . all sorts of rich Point, lac'd, plain, mens and childrens cravats and neckcloths; as also ladies, &c. night-rails, *etc.* pp. 8.   [*London*, 1691.] 4°.   **S.C. 462. (3.)**

—— At the Kings-Arms Tavern, over-against St. Clements Church in the Strand, wil [*sic*] . . . be exposed to sale a Curious Collection of Original Paintings, and other fine copies . . . the third of this instant March, $16\frac{90}{91}$, *etc.* pp. 11. [*London*, 1691.] 4°.   **1402. g. 1. (71.)**

—— A Collection of Pictures, with some curious books of prints, history, &c. to be sold by auction . . . the ninth instant [9 March 1691], and the following day . . . at John's Coffee-House . . . in Cheapside. pp. 4. [*London*, 1691.] 4°.   **1402. g. 1. (73.)**

CATALOGUES.

—— A Curious Collection of Paintings and Limnings . . . Will be exposed to sale, by way of mineing—a method of sale not hitherto used in England— . . . the 12th . . . 13th, and . . . 14th, of this instant March [1691], at Mrs. Smythers Coffee-House in Thames-street, *etc.* pp. 9. [*London*, 1691.] 4°.   **1402. g. 1. (74.)**

—— At the Green Dragon next to Northumberland-House at Charing Cross, will be exposed to sale, by auction, a Curious Collection of Original Paintings . . . the 24th of this instant March [1691] . . . also a parcel of prints set off in water-colours. pp. 8. [*London*, 1691.] 4°.   **1402. g. 1. (75.)**

—— Catalogus variorum librorum in linguis & facultatibus omnigenis insignium, sive bibliotheca . . . doctissimi cujusdam generosi nuperrime defuncti. Cui præfigitur Bibliorum polyglotton D. Ducis Lauderdaliensis . . . sylloge illustrissima . . . Quorum auctio habebitur apud Tom's Coffee-House . . . 26 Martii [1691], *etc.* 3 pt. [*London*, 1691.] 4°.   **821. i. 9.**
    Imperfect; wanting pp. 17–28 *of the first part.*

—— A Curious Collettion [*sic*] of Paintings and Limnings . . . Will be exposed to sale, by way of auction . . . the 30th. and . . . 31st. of this instant March, and . . . April the 1st, 2d and 3d [1691], at Smythers Coffee-House in Thames-street, *etc.* pp. 10. [*London*, 1691.] 4°.   **1402. g. 1. (76.)**

—— At the Kings-Arms Tavern, over against St. Clements Church in the Strand, will . . . be exposed to sale a Curious Collection of Original Paintings, and other fine copies . . . the first of April, 1691, *etc.* pp. 11. [*London*, 1691.] 4°.   **1402. g. 1. (77.)**

—— The Great Sale of Original Paintings, that were design'd to be expos'd on Tuesday next, in Easter Week, at the New Auction-Room . . . Charles-street, Covent-Garden, will not be sold till Friday, in the same week [17 April 1691], *etc.* pp. 10. [*London*, 1691.] 4°.   **1402. g. 1. (78.)**

—— A Catalogue of Very Good Latin, French, and English Books . . . which will be sold by auction: the sale to begin on . . . the 20th. of April, 1691 . . . at Rolls's Coffee-House, *etc.* pp. 16. [*London*, 1691.] 4°.   **821. i. 9. (3.)**

—— An Extraordinary Collection of Paintings, and several other Curiosities, by the best masters. Will be now sold by auction . . . the 5th. of this instant May, 1691 . . . in the Auction-Office in the West-end of the Royal Exchange, *etc.* pp. 12. [*London*, 1691.] 4°.   **1402. g. 1. (79.)**

—— At the Canary-House, near the East End of Exeter Change . . . will be exposed to sale several Original Paintings, and other fine copies . . . the 7th. of this instant May 1691, *etc.* pp. 4. [*London*, 1691.] 4°.   **1402. g. 1. (81.)**

—— A Curious Collection of Paintings will be sold by auction at the Duke of Glocesters Coffee-House at Charing-Cross . . . the 22d. of May [1691]. pp. 4.   [*London*, 1691.] 4°.   **1402. g. 1. (84.)**

—— A Catalogue of Latin and English Books, to be sold by auction . . . the 29th. of May, 1691 . . . to booksellers only, at Clerks Coffee-House . . . in Smithfield. pp. 4. [*London*, 1691.] 4°.   **821. i. 9. (8.)**

—— At the Canary-House, near the East End of Exeter Change . . . Will be exposed to sale a Curious Collection of Paintings, being most of them the furniture of J. D.'s house . . . the sale will begin . . . the 8th. of this instant June, 1691, *etc.* pp. 8. [1691.] 4°. *See* D., J.   **1402. g. 1. (85.)**

CATALOGUES.

—— At the West End of Exeter Change above Stairs in the Strand, will be sold by way of auction, a Curious Collection of Pictures . . . the 24th. day of this instant June [1691], *etc.* pp. 8. [*London*, 1691.] 4°.   **1402. g. 1. (89.)**

—— A Catalogue of Excellent English Books in Divinity, History . . . which will be sold by auction : the sale begins . . . the 29th of June, 1691 . . . at John's Coffee-House . . . in Cheapside. pp. 10 [12]. [*London*, 1691.] 4°.   **821. i. 9. (11.)**

—— At the Canary-House, near the East End of Exeter Change . . . Will be exposed to sale a Curious Collection of Paintings . . . the 2d, of this instant July [1691], *etc.* pp. 7. [*London*, 1691.] 4°.   **1402. g. 1. (91.)**

—— A Catalogue of Books in folio, consisting of Fathers, Latin and English, Commentaries on the Bible . . . which will be sold by auction . . . the 31th. of July, 1691 . . . at Tom's Coffee-House adjoyning to Ludgate. pp. 4. [*London*, 1691.] 4°.   **821. i. 9. (13.)**

—— This Catalogue with many other scarce and good books . . . will be sold by auction to booksellers only . . . the twenty eighth of September, 1691 . . . at the Blew Anchor-Inn in Little Brittain. [*London*, 1691.] *s. sh.* 4°.   **821. i. 9. (17.)**

—— A Catalogue of Choice and Valuable Books . . . Which will be exposed to sale by way of auction . . . the 1st. of October, 1691. at Roll's Coffee-House in St. Paul's Church Yard, *etc.* pp. 12. [*London*, 1691.] 4°.   **821. i. 9. (18.)**

—— Libri theol. histor. & miscel. in octavo & duod. [A sale catalogue. Between 1 and 5 Oct. 1691 ?] pp. 4. [1691 ?] 4°.   **821. i. 9. (19.)**

—— A Catalogue of Divinity, History, Physick, Mathematical Books, &c. in Latin, French and English, will be sold by auction. The sale will begin . . . the seventh of Oct. 1691 . . . at Toms Coffee-House adjoyning to Ludgate, *etc.* coll. 30. [*London*, 1691.] 4°.   **821. i. 9. (22.)**

—— [Another copy.]   S.C. **1035. (17.)**

—— At the Bell-Tavern over against the Gate-House in Kings-Street Westminster. Will be exposed to sale a Curious Collection of Paintings . . . the 13th. 14th. 15th. and 16th. of this instant October, 1691, *etc.* pp. 8. [*London*, 1691.] 4°.   **1402. g. 1. (93.)**

—— An Extraordinary Collection of Pictures, will be continued to be sold by auction, at Batson's Coffee-House near Popes-Head Ally . . . the 21st. of October [1691], *etc.* [*London*, 1691.] *s. sh.* 4°.   **1402. g. 1. (94.)**

—— A Curious Collection of Paintings, and several Other Curiosities . . . Will be now sold by auction . . . the 22th. of this instant Octob. 1691 . . . in the Auction-Office in the West-end of the Royal Exchange, *etc.* pp. 7. [*London*, 1691.] 4°.   **1402. g. 1. (95.)**

—— An Extraordinary Collection of Pictures, will be continued to be sold by auction, at Batsons's Coffee-House near Popes-Head Ally . . . The sale will begin . . . the 30th. of this instant October [1691], *etc.* [*London*, 1691.] *s. sh.* 4°.   **1402. g. 1. (97.)**

—— At the West End of Exeter Change above Stairs in the Strand, will be exposed to sale a Curious Collection of Original Paintings, and other fine copies . . . the 2d. . . . 3d. . . . 6th. and . . . 7th. of November next, 1691, *etc.* [*London*, 1691.] 4°.   **1402. g. 1. (98.)**
Imperfect ; wanting all after p. 4.

CATALOGUES.

—— A Collection of Curious Paintings . . . will be sold by auction . . . the sixth and seventh of this instant November, 1691 . . . At the Long Dog in the New Palace-Yard, *etc.* pp. 6. [*London*, 1691.] 4°.   **1402. g. 1. (99.)**

—— Bibliotheca selectissima librorum omnigenorum . . . Quos . . . sibi procuravit Londinensis quidam generosus [here identified in a MS. note as D. Lapthorne]. Quorum auctio habebitur Londini in ædibus Nigri Leonis prope australem porticum Ecclesiæ Cathedralis Paulinæ . . . nono die Novembris, 1691. pp. 124. [*London*,] 1691. 4°.   S.C. **1033. (1.)**

—— [Another copy.]   **821. i. 9. (26.)**

—— An Extraordinary Collection of Original Pictures will be sold by auction, at the Three-Tun Tavern in Witch-street . . . the ninth of this instant November, 1691, *etc.* pp. 8. [*London*, 1691.] 4°.   **1402. g. 1. (100.)**

—— An Extraordinary Collection of Pictures, and other incomparable curiosities . . . will be sold by auction, at Batsons's Coffee-House near Popes-Head Ally . . . The sale begins . . . the 12th. of November [1691], *etc.* [*London*, 1691.] *s. sh.* 4°.   **1402. g. 1. (102.)**

—— At the West End of Exeter Change above Stairs in the Strand, will be exposed to sale a Curious Collection of Original Paintings . . . the 18th. . . . 19th. and . . . 20th. of this instant November, 1691, *etc.* [*London*, 1691.] 4°.   **1402. g. 1. (104.)**
Imperfect ; wanting all after p. 4.

—— A Curious Collection of Paintings, being most originals . . . Will be sold by auction, at the Spanish-Coffee-House, at the corner of Bromley-Street in Holbourn . . . the 27th of this instant November, 1691, *etc.* pp. 4. [*London*, 1691.] 4°.   **1402. g. 1. (106.)**

—— An Extraordinary Collection of Pictures, and other curiosities ; will be sold by auction, at Batsons's Coffee-House near Popes-Head Ally . . . The sale begins . . . the 2d. of December [1691], *etc.* [*London*, 1691.] *s. sh.* 4°.   **1402. g. 1. (107.)**

—— An Extraordinary Collection of Pictures, and other curiosities ; will be sold by auction, at Batsons's Coffee-House near Popes-Head Ally . . . The sale continues . . . the 7th. of December, *etc.* [*London*, 1691.] *s. sh.* 4°.   **1402. g. 1. (108.)**
The numeration of the lots in the catalogue begins with no. 701.

—— At the New Auction House in Drury-lane . . . on the 7th. . . . 9th. and . . . 11th. of this instant December [1691] . . . will be sold a Curious Collection of Paintings, *etc.* [*London*, 1691.] *s. sh.* 4°.   **1402. g. 1. (109.)**

—— A Curious Collection of Paintings . . . Will be expos'd to sale . . . December 11th. [1691] . . . at the Vendu . . . in Charles-street, *etc.* pp. 7. [*London*, 1691.] 4°.   **1402. g. 1. (112.)**

—— A Catalogue of Ancient and modern Musick Books, both vocal and instrumental, with divers treatises about the same, and several musical instruments . . . which will be sold at Dewing's Coffee-House in Popes-Head Alley . . . December the 17th, 1691. pp. 16. [*London*, 1691.] 8°.   **821. i. 9. (27.)**

—— A Curious Collection of Paintings and other curiosities ; will be sold by auction at the Barbadoes Coffee-House in Exchange Alley . . . The sale begins . . . the 21st of December [1691], *etc.* pp. 2. [*London*, 1691.] *s. sh.* 4°.   **1402. g. 1. (114.)**

CATALOGUES.

—— A Curious Collection of Paintings, being most originals . . . Will be sold by auction . . . at the Canary-House, near the East-End of Exeter-Exchange, in the Strand . . . the 29th of this instant December, 1691, *etc.* (An Appendix to the Auction of Paintings . . . exposed to sale at the Canary-House . . . the 30th and 31th of this instant Decemb. 1691.) pp. 8. [*London,* 1691.] 4⁰.
1402. g. 1. (115.)

—— A Curious Collection of Paintings, being most originals : will be sold by auction, at the Canary-House, near the East-End of Exeter-Exchange, in the Strand . . . the 7th of this instant January, 1691 [o.s]., *etc.* pp. 4. [*London,* 1692.] 4⁰. **1402. g. 1. (116.)**
The numeration of the lots in this catalogue continues that of the catalogue dated 29 Dec. 1691.

—— A Continuation of the Curious Collection of Paintings and other Curiosities ; will be sold by auction at the Barbadoes Coffee-House in Exchange Alley . . . the 14th of January [1692], and the two following days, *etc.* [*London,* 1692.] *s. sh.* 4⁰. **1402. g. 1. (117.)**
The numeration of the lots in this catalogue begins with no. 234.

—— At the Outropers-Office, in the Royal Exchange . . . the 26th. and 27th. of this instant January [1692] . . . will be continued the Sale by Auction of Pictures, Cabinets, *etc.* pp. 8. [*London,* 1692.] 4⁰. **1402. g. 1. (121.)**
The numeration of the lots in this catalogue begins with no. 190.

—— An Extraordinary Collection of Pictures, and other incomparable Curiosities . . . will be sold by auction, at Batsons's Coffee-House, near Popes-Head Ally . . . The sale begins . . . the 3d. of February [1692], *etc.* [*London,* 1692.] *s. sh.* 4⁰. **1402. g. 1. (122.)**

—— A Continuation of the Curious Collection of Paintings, &c. by the best masters . . . will be sold by auction at the Barbadoes Coffee-House in Exchange Alley . . . the 4th of this instant February [1692], *etc.* [*London,* 1692.] *s. sh.* 4⁰. **1402. g. 1. (123.)**
The numeration of the lots in this catalogue begins with no. 801.

—— At the Venduë next Bedford-Gate in Charles-street Covent Garden the Great Collection of Paintings will continue to be expos'd by auction . . . the 8th. instant [8 Feb. 1692] . . . and every Munday following till May. [*London,* 1692.] *s. sh.* fol. **1402. g. 1. (125.)**
The numeration of the lots in this catalogue begins with no. 201.

—— An Extraordinary Collection of Pictures, and other incomparable Curiosities . . . will be sold by auction, at Batsons's Coffee-House, near Popes-Head Ally . . . The sale begins . . . the 25th. of February, *etc.* [*London,* 1692.] *s. sh.* 4⁰. **1402. g. 1. (128.)**

—— A Curious Collection of Paintings . . . and Several Other Curiosities. Will be sold by auction . . . the 17th. 18th. and 19th. of this instant March, 16$\frac{91}{92}$ . . . in the Outropers-Office in the West-end of the Royal Exchange. pp. 10. [*London,* 1692.] 4⁰. **1402. g. 1. (130.)**

—— An Extraordinary Collection of Pictures, will be sold by auction, at Batsons's Coffee-House, near Popes-Head Ally . . . The sale begins . . . the 23d. of this instant March [1692], *etc.* [*London,* 1692.] *s. sh.* 4⁰.
1402. g. 1. (131.)

CATALOGUES.

—— A Curious Collection of Paintings, this present Wednesday the 23th. of this instant March [1692] . . . will be be [*sic*] continued the sale by auction of a curious collection of pictures . . . at the Outropers-Office in the West-end of the Royal Exchange, *etc.* [*London,* 1692.] 4⁰.
1402. g. 1. (132.)
The numeration of the lots in this catalogue begins with no. 322.

—— Catalogus librorum theol. jurid. . . . qui auctione ad d. 5 Sept. et seqq. 1692. constituta, in ædibus B. D. Kirchhofii . . . vendentur. [*C. Neumann* :] *Hamburgi,* [1692.] 8⁰. **822. a. 42. (2.)**
Cropped.

—— Catalogus librorum tam antiquorum quam recentium in omni facultate insignium. Quorum auctio . . . Oxoniæ habenda est Novemb. 9. 1692, *etc.* MS. PRICES. [1692.] 4⁰. **821. i. 2. (7.)**

—— Appendix librorum quorum auctio habenda est prope Templum Beatæ Mariæ, Nov. 28. 1692. [1692.] 4⁰. **821. i. 2. (8.)**

—— A Collection of Excellent English Books . . . To be sold by auction, at Batson's Coffee-house . . . the 23d day of May, 1693, *etc.* pp. 24. [*London,* 1693.] 4⁰. **S.C. 1035. (7.)**

—— Bibliotheca insignis : or, a Catalogue of excellent Greek, Latin and English books . . . Which will be sold by auction at Rolls's Auction House in Petty Canons-Hall . . . June 12. 1693. pp. 27. [*London,* 1693.] 4⁰. **S.C. 1035. (9.)**

—— Catalogus variorum, & in omni facultate, & lingua insignium librorum, præcipuè juridicorum. Quorum auctio habebitur Bredæ . . . ad diem Augusti 1693. pp. 16. *C. Seldenslach : Bredæ,* 1693. 4⁰. **S.C. 296. (1.)**
The figure 29 has been supplied in MS. in the blank space in the title.

—— A Catalogue of Books of the Newest Fashion, to be sold by auction at the Whiggs Coffee-House, at the Sign of the Jackanapes in Prating-Alley, near the Deanry of St. Paul's. pp. 8. MS. NOTES. [*London,* 1693.] 4⁰. **8122. e. 10.**
Later editions 1745, 1810.

—— Liste de livres nouvellement imprimés en Hollande, & se trouvent à Amsterdam. 1693. pp. 8. [*Amsterdam,* 1693.] 4⁰. **S.C. 1034. (3.)**

—— Bibliotheca instructissima : or, a Catalogue of Greek, Latin and English books, in all faculties : which will be sold by auction . . . the 13th of December, 1694. at Rolls's Auction house, in Petty-Canons-Hall, *etc.* pp. 20. [*London,* 1694.] 4⁰. **S.C. 1035. (10.)**

—— [A sale catalogue of miscellaneous books.] pp. 94. [1695 ?] 12⁰. **S.C. 13.**
Imperfect ; wanting the titlepage.

—— Catalogus librorum, historici, litteratores, antiquarii, numismatici, aliique miscellanei in folio (in quarto, in octavo, in duodecimo). pp. 46. [1695 ?] 8⁰. **S.C. 117. (1.)**

—— Catalogus librorum tam antiquorum quam recentium in omni facultate insignium. Quorum auctio . . . Oxoniæ habenda est Maij 5. 1696, *etc.* [1696.] 4⁰. **821. i. 2. (9.)**

CATALOGUES.

—— A Catalogue of Books printed in England since the . . . Fire of London in 1666. to the end of Michaelmas Term, 1695. With an abstract of the general bills of mortality since 1660 . . . The fourth edition. pp. 127. *For R. Clavel ; Benj. Tooke: London,* 1696. fol.
11905. b. 27.

—— [Another copy.] **823. k. 5.**

—— [Another copy.] **129. e. 2.**
Previous editions, compiled by R. Clavell, are entered under CLAVELL (*Robert*).

—— Catalogus librorum lingu. & facultat. diversorum [*sic*], quorum auctio publica habebitur in ædibus Rectoris prope Scholam Div. Virginis ad d. Julii ann: MDCXCVII. pp. 36. *Literis B. Danielis Eichhornii Viduæ: Hafniæ,* 1697.] 4°. S.C. **236. (1.)**
The titlepage is cropped. The figure 19 *has been supplied in* MS. *in the blank space in the title.*

—— Catalogus van verscheyde soorten van orangie, limoen, jasmijn . . . en laurier-boomen, en seer veele raare Africaanse en uytheemse boom, en by-gewassen . . . welke verkocht sullen werden op de plaats over het Haagsche Posthuys, op de Heere-Wegh, buyten Haarlem . . . den 1. en 2 October, 1697, *etc. By d'Erfg. van O. B. Smient: Amsterdam,* 1697. 4°. **1044. f. 39.**

—— Catalogus variorum insignium & rarissimorum, in omni materiâ linguâ & facultate, librorum . . . Quorum auctio instituetur in ædibus Ankelmannianis . . . die 5. Decembris & seqq. anno 1698. *Typis F. C. Greflingeri: Hamburgi,* [1698.] 8°. S.C. **53. (2.)**

—— Catalogue nouveau de toute sorte de livres françois, pour l'année 1698. qui se trouvent à Amsterdam. pp. 49 [40]. [*Amsterdam,* 1698.] 12°. S.C. **45. (2.)**

—— Catalogus universalis librorum, in omni facultate, linguaque insignium . . . non solum ex catalogis bibliothecarum Bodleianæ, Lugduno-Batavæ . . . sed etiam ex omnibus fere aliis prælo impressis . . . collectus. [By John Hartley.] 2 vol. *Apud Joannem Hartley: Londini,* 1699. 8°. **619. b. 4, 5.**
Later edition 1701.

—— [Another copy.] **125. b. 9, 10.**

—— Catalogus vieler raren gebundenen theologischen, juristischen . . . Bücher, so am 23. Augusti und folgende Tage in Hamburg in öffentlicher Auction verkaufft werden sollen, *etc.* [*Hamburg,*] 1700. 8°. S.C. **53. (3.)**

—— [A catalogue of a collection of books.] pp. 184. [*Amsterdam ?* 1700 ?] 8°. S.C. **117. (2.)**
Imperfect ; wanting the titlepage.

—— [A catalogue of books, issued probably by a bookseller in the Netherlands.] pp. 351. [1700 ?] 4°.
S.C. **853. (3.)**
Imperfect ; wanting the titlepage.

—— [A sale catalogue of books.] [*Hamburg ?* 1700 ?] 8°.
S.C. **146. (2.)**
Imperfect ; wanting the titlepage.

—— Catalogue des livres françois. [1700 ?] 8°.
S.C. **73. (7.)**
Imperfect ; wanting all after p. 40.

—— A Catalogue of Books in English, Latin, Greek, &c. in all volumes ; which will be sold where attendance will be given for about 10 days, *etc.* pp. 7. [1700 ?] 4°.
821. i. 2. (6.)

CATALOGUES.

—— A Catalogue of Valuable and Choice Books, being the collections of a person of eminent quality, and a learned Divine deceased . . . Which will be sold by retail . . . at Howson's Coffee-House in Devereux-Court . . . The sale will begin . . . the 17th. instant, *etc.* [*London,* 1700 ?] 8°. **820. c. 1. (2.)**
Imperfect ; wanting all after p. 48. *Cropped.*

—— A Continuation of a Catalogue of Ladies, to be set up by auction, on Monday the 6th of this instant July . . . By E. Cl - - - - r, Auctioner, that sold the young Heiress in Q - - - - street. [1700 ?] *s. sh.* fol. *See* CL - - - - R (E.) **816. m. 19. (20.)**

—— A Curious Collection of Original Paintings will be sold by auction at the Hen and Chickens in Bedford-Street, Covent Garden. Collected by an ingenious gentleman in Surrey . . . The sale begins on Thursday next at 2 in the afternoon, *etc.* [*London,* 1700 ?] *s. sh.* fol.
Cup. **645. e. 5. (14.)**

—— Medici. (Libri philophici [*sic*].—Philologi, poetæ, oratores & litteratores.—Mathematici, musici, artifices & militares.) [A catalogue of books.] pp. 86. [1700 ?] 4°.
S.C. **848.**

—— A Collection of Paintings, Japan-work, and several other Rarities, lately belonging to a Person of Quality deceased, will be sold by auction . . . on Thursday the sixth of February, *etc.* pp. 8. [*London,* 1701 ?] 4°.
Cup. **645. e. 5. (11.)**

—— Catalogus librorum varii generis: quorum auctio haberi incipiet Hauniæ, anni 1701 die   Aprilis: in ædibus Mag. Johannis Brunsmanni, *etc. Hafniæ,* [1701.] 4°.
S.C. **236. (2.)**
The titlepage is cropped.

—— Catalogus universalis librorum, in omni facultate, linguaque insignium . . . non solum ex catalogis bibliothecarum Bodleianæ, Lugduno-Batavæ . . . sed etiam ex omnibus fere aliis prælo impressis . . . collectus. Cum indice authorum alphabetico. [By John Hartley.] 2 vol. *Apud Joannem Hartley: Londini,* 1701. 8°.
011902. i. 19.
Previous edition 1699.

—— Catalogus librorum miscellaneorum, quorum auctio habebitur in ædibus Nicolai Svensøns . . . die 24. Julii anno 1702. *Hafniæ,* [1702.] 4°. S.C. **236. (4.)**

—— Catalogus variarum facultatum linguarumq; librorum, quorum auctio . . . in ædibus Viduæ beati Hamstenii . . . habebitur d. 16 Octobris ao. 1702. [*Copenhagen,* 1702.] 4°. S.C. **236. (5.)**

—— Catalogus scriptorum, ab Helvetiis ac Fœderatis Reformatæ Religionis, añis quinquaginta posterioribus seculi decimi septimi, editorum . . . Editio secunda, *etc.* [By Vincentius Paravicinus.] 1702. 8°. *See* PARAVICINUS (Vincentius) *the Younger.* **272. a. 37.**

—— Bibliotheca exquisitissima librorum omnis generis facultatum atque scientiarum â viro quodam celeberrimo . . . collecta . . . Quæ die 18. seqq. Augusti, anni hujus M.DCC.IV. in ædibus Gremannianis . . . auctionis lege præsenti pecunia pluris licitantibus cedet. 3 pt. *Lipsiæ,* 1704. 8°. S.C. **175.**

—— Verzeichniss unterschiedener sonderbaren Sachen und Curiositäten so in dem Cabinet eines gewissen Privati in Altenburg zu befinden. 1705. 4°. **7709. b. 18.**

CATALOGUES.

—— Catalogus librorum, theolog. & philosoph. qui sub hasta publica die 14 Sept. 1706 in ædibus à beata Vidua Catharina Hennings nuperrimè relictis . . . vendentur. *Hafniæ*, [1706.] 4º.   S.C. **236**. (6.)
Cropped.

—— Catalogus insignium & rarissimorum in omni facultate materiá & linguá librorum . . . Quorum? [*sic*] auctio habebitur in ædibus de Munt. ad diem 4. Novembris 1706. *Noviomagi*, 1706. 4º.   S.C. **458**.

—— Catalogus librorum, quorum. auctio habebitur in ædibus Pastoris Primarii ad Templum Divæ Virginis Hafniensis d. 1707. [*Copenhagen*, 1707.] 4º.   S.C. **236**. (7.)
The date " 2 May " has been supplied in MS. in the blank space on the titlepage.

—— Catalogus librorum, quorum est auctio habenda in ædibus Jani Drejeri Machæropæi in platea, Store Færge-Stræde dicta, die   Junii 1707, *etc. Hafniæ*, [1707.] 8º.
S.C.48/7.
The figure 13 has been supplied in MS. in the blank space on the titlepage and the word " Junii " altered to " Julii."

—— Librorum variarum facultatum, linguarum ac scientiarum maximè juridicarum auctio juxta præsentem catalogum in platea Wilschdorffiana, in der Frau Ehrlichen Hause die 7. Novembr. . . . instituta literarum patronis . . . signivicbtur [*sic*]. *Dresdæ*, 1707. 8º.
10602. aa. **32**. (2.)

—— Catalogus bibliothecæ selectæ theologicæ, philosophicæ & philologicæ distrahendæ auctione publica Hamburgi loco consueto . . . auf den Reventher . . . die   et sqq. anni 1708. [*Hamburg*, 1708.] 8º.   S.C. **124**. (3.)

—— Catalogus librorum varii generis, quorum auctio publica habebitur . . . Hafniæ propè Arcem Regiam in ædibus vulgò, Den gamle Guarde-Stall. ad d. 18. Junii. 1708, *etc. Hafniæ*, [1708.] 8º.   S.C. **48**. (8.).

—— [Another copy.]   S.C. **97**. (1.)

—— Catalogus librorum imprimis historicorum . . . Qui auctione publica . . . Gluckstadii in ædibus Domini Consulis a Woltereck, d.   Julii. anno 1708. distrahentur. *Tychopoli*, [1708.] 8º.   S.C. **41**. (1.)

—— Catalogus librorum theologico-juridico-historicorum, variorumque manuscriptorum, auctione publica Gluckstadii in ædibus beati Dn. Hassen . . . anno 1708. die distrahendorum. pp. 71.   [*Glückstadt*, 1708.] 8º.
S.C. **97**. (9.)
The date " 26 Novembr." has been supplied in MS. in the blank space in the title.

—— A New Catalogue of Books and Small Tracts against Vice and Immorality, *etc.* 1708. 8º.   *See* DOWNING (Joseph) *Bookseller.*   **1477**. aa. **2**. (2.)

—— Catalogus librorum nitide compactorum varii generis . . . qui auctione publica Gluckstadii in ædibus Hr. Capitain Eggers anno 1709. die   Januarii distrahentur. *Tychopoli*, [1709.] 8º.   S.C. **41**. (2.)
The figure 2 has been supplied in MS. in the blank space in the title.

—— Catalogus librorum theologicorum, juridicorum & historicorum, qui auctione publica Gluckstadii in ædibus Bibliopolæ Regii anno 1709. die   Septembr. distrahentur. *Gluckstadii*, [1709.] 8º.   S.C. **41**. (3.)
The figure 9 has been supplied in MS. in the blank space in the title.

CATALOGUES.

—— Bibliothecæ quondam instructissimæ . . . libri aliqui selectissimi . . . Quorum auctio instituenda erit in ædibus Dni. Senioris, in cœmit. ad D. Cathar. die Nov. xxv. & seqq. MS. NOTES AND PRICES. *Hamburgi*, 1709. 8º.
S.C. **124**. (4.)
Interleaved.

—— Catalogue, des livres imprimez à Paris, & dans quelques autres villes du Royaume, pendant le cours de l'année 1707, avec leurs prix, les noms des autheurs, *etc. See* EPHEMERIDES. Almanach bibliographique pour l'an MDCCIX, *etc.* 1709. 12º.   P.P. **6450**.

—— At the Rose-Tavern without Temple-bar . . . April 3. 1710. . . . will be sold by auction, choice medals, lately collected by a Gentleman, in his travels thro' Turkey, *etc.* pp. 4. [*London*, 1710.] fol.   **603**. l. **31**. (5.)

—— [Another copy.]   **603**. l. **31**. (7.)
Mutilated.

—— Catalogus vieler curieusen, raren . . . Bücher . . . Welche den 28. Aprilis anni 1710. auf. dem Reventher . . . durch öffentlichen Aussruff . . . sollen verkaufft werden. pp. 110. [*Hamburg*, 1710.] 8º. S.C. **124**. (5.)

—— Specification der köstlichen Tapisserien, Kleidern, Spitzen, Schildereyen und Spiegeln, so auf dem Embeckschen Hause den 21 Maji anno 1710. sollen verkauffet werden. *Hamburg*, [1710.] 8º.   S.C. **127**. (3*.)

—— [A sale catalogue of books.] pp. 127. [1710?] 8º.
S.C. **143**. (1.)
Imperfect ; wanting the titlepage.

—— [A sale catalogue of books.] pp. 32. [1710?] 8º.
S.C. **143**. (2.)
Imperfect ; wanting the titlepage.

—— Catalogus bibliothecæ cujusdam instructissimæ continentis libros varios . . . Quorum auctio . . . instituetur Hamburgi in Templi cathedralis loco, vulgò Reventher dicto, ad diem 16. Martii 1711. pp. 384.   [*Hamburg*, 1711.] 8º.   S.C. **120**. (1.)

—— Catalogus vieler curieusen, raren, nützlichen und wohl conditionnirten Bücher . . . Welche d. 27. Aprilis 1711. auff dem Reventher . . . durch öffentlichen Ausruff sollen verkauffet werden. pp. 134.   [*Hamburg*,] 1711. 8º.   S.C. **120**. (2.)

—— Catalogus librorum ministri cujusdam Verbi Divini . . . qui publica auctionis lege . . . distrahentur in ædibus Antonii Beckers . . . ad diem 14. Sept. seqq. anni 1711, *etc.* pp. 37. *Hamburgi*, [1711.] 8º.
S.C. **120**. (3.)

—— Catalogus variorum & insignium librorum, quorum auctio . . . instituetur die xxx. Septembr. MDCCXI. in der grossen Becker-Strassen. pp. 66. *Hamburgi*, [1711.] 8º.
S.C. **120**. (4.)

—— Catalogus bibliothecæ v. cujusdam instructissimæ omnis facultatis . . . libros exhibentis. Qui die 17. Febr: 1712. . . . Hamburgi publicæ auctionis more . . . in Templi Cathedralis loco vulgò Reventher dicto . . . venum exponentur. pp. 96. *Hamburgi*, 1712. 8º.
S.C. **124**. (7.)

—— A Catalogue of Extraordinary Original Pictures, by several eminent masters : to be sold by auction, at Elliot's Coffee-House in Stafford-street . . . on Thursday next, being the 3d of April 1712, *etc.* [*London*, 1712.] *s. sh.* fol.
Cup. **645**. e. **5**. (7.)

CATALOGUES.

—— A Catalogue of a Curious Collection of Ancient Roman Medals . . . Which will be sold by auction, at the Rose-Tavern without Temple-bar . . . the fourth day of June, 1712, *etc.* pp. 2. [*London*, 1712.] *s. sh.* fol.
603. l. **31**. (4.)

—— [Another copy.] **603**. l. **31**. (11.)

—— A Catalogue of Original Pictures, being the collection of a Person of Quality deceas'd, will be sold by auction at Harris's Coffee-House in Ormond Street . . . on . . . the 5th of this instant June, 1712, *etc.* [1712.] *s. sh.* fol.
L.R. 305. a. **7**. (10.)

—— Catalogus librorum in quacunque & materia & lingua . . . insignium. Ein Verzeichniss von allerhand raren . . . Büchern, welche sollen verkaufft werden, in der Heinsischen Behausung, auff dem Holländischen Broock den 7. Novemb. anno 1712. [*Hamburg?* 1712.] 8º.
S.C. 124. (8.)
Imperfect ; wanting all after sig. D.

—— A Catalogue of Several Gold, Silver, Copper and Tin Medals, Rings, and several other pieces of antiquity, which will begin to be sold by auction, at the Old King's Head at the Corner of Chancery Lane . . . the of this instant February. pp. 2. [*London*, 1713?] *s. sh.* fol.
603. l. **31**. (8.)
The words " Queens Head & Rose Tavern " have been substituted in MS. *for " Old King's Head " and the figure 27 supplied in the blank space in the title.*

—— A Collection of True Roman Medals, Silver and Brass . . . from before Julius Cæsar to Justinian . . . N.B. These medals are mentioned in the Catalogue of Rich Houshold Goods, Numb. VIII. Lot. 54, 55, 61, and are to be sold in Arlington-Street the 4th of May next. [*London*, 1713?] *s. sh.* fol. **603**. l. **31**. (12.)

—— A Catalogue of Extraordinary Original Pictures: by several of the most celebrated masters, most part lately brought from beyond sea ; to be sold by auction on Friday, the 8th day of May, 1713, at the Rainbow and Dove, near Durham Yard, in the Strand, *etc.* [*London*, 1713.] *s. sh.* fol. Cup. **645**. e. **5**. (3.)

—— A True and Exact Catalogue of All the Plays that were ever yet printed in the English tongue ; with the authors names against each play . . . and continued down to October, 1713. (Continuation of the following Catalogue of Plays to October, 1715 . . . Sold by W. Mears, *etc.*) *Printed for W. Mears:* [*London*,] 1713, [15.] 4º.
11903. f. **24**.

—— Catalogus, variorum . . . librorum . . . quorum auctio . . . instit: Hamb. die 25 Jun. 1714. in Templi cathedralis loco vulgò Reventher dicto, *etc.* 2 pt. *Hamburgi*, 1714. 8º. **S.C. 109**.
The date in the title has been altered in MS. *to " 9 Julij."*

—— Catalogus librorum medico-phisicorum . . . a viro arte & praxi medica . . . celeberrimo . . . relictorum, qui distrahentur. [1714.] 8º. **S.C. 115**. (3.)
The date " 20 Aug. 1714 " has been supplied in MS.

—— Catalogus variorum librorum . . . quorum auctio instituetur Hamburgi d. 27. Augusti 1714. in ædibus pastoralibus ad d. Jacobi, *etc.* pp. 29. [*Hamburg*, [1714.] 8º.
S.C. 115. (1.)

—— Catalogus librorum quorum auctio habebitur in ædibus Dni. Hans Willemsen in platea vulgo Skidenstrædet dicta d. 12. Novembr. seq. 1714, *etc.* pp. 213. *Havniæ*, [1714.] 8º. **S.C. 47**.

CATALOGUES.

—— Catalogus librorum, selectissimorum varii generis quorum auctio habebitur Glückstadii anno 1714. d. 4. Decembr. pp. 134. MS. PRICES. [*Glückstadt*, 1714.] 8º.
S.C. 113.
The titlepage bears the MS. *note, " Libri B. Simon: Gerckens."*

—— Catalogue des principaux historiens, avec des remarques critiques sur la bonté de leurs ouvrages & sur le choix des meilleures éditions. [By N. Lenglet du Fresnoy.] Nouvelle édition . . . revuë & augmentée de plusieurs livres & remarques, par J. B. Mencke. *Lipsic*, 1714. 8º. **9007**. aaaa. **10**.

—— Catalogus verschiedener juristischer, historischer und philologischer . . . Bücher eines weiland königl. Ministri, welche . . . durch eine kleine Lotterey von 701. Lossen in . . . Glückstadt distrahiret werden sollen, *etc.* pp. 92. *Hamburg*, 1714. 8º. **S.C. 115**. (2.)

—— The Monthly Catalogue. [Books published in London, May to December 1714.] no. 1–8. 1714, [15.] fol. *See* PERIODICAL PUBLICATIONS.—*London*. **821**. ee. **39**. (2.)

—— Designatio librorum varii argumenti & idiomatis, qui publico auctionis . . . ritu . . . die & seqq: Februarii . . . MDCCXV. in ædibus pastoralibus Jacobæis distrabentur. [A sale catalogue of the library of Johann Riemer.] pp. 106. *Hamburgi*, [1715.] 8º. **S.C. 94**. (3.)
The figure XXV *has been supplied in* MS. *in the blank space in the title.*

—— Catalogus librorum, selectissimorum . . . quorum auctio . . . habebitur Hamburgi in ædibus Mattfeldianis . . . 1715 d. & seqq., *etc.* pp. 93. [*Hamburg*,] 1715. 8º.
S.C. 115. (5.)
The date 4 Mar. has been supplied in MS. *in the blank space in the title.*

—— Catalogus bibliothecæ cujusdam eximiæ, libros juridicos, polit. . . . exhibentis. Quorum auctio . . . habebitur Hamburgi die 26. Martii & seqq. anni 1715. in Templi Cathedralis loco vulgò Reventher dicto. pp. 215. [*Hamburg*,] 1715. 8º. **S.C. 115**. (4.)

—— A Catalogue of the Library of an eminent Counsellor, lately deceas'd . . . Will be sold by auction, at the Temple-Change Coffee-House in Fleet street . . . the first day of June next, *etc.* pp. 16. [*London*, 1715?] 8º.
T. 1812. (15.)

—— Catálogus librorum, qui publica auctione distrahentur Itzehoæ in ædibus viduæ B. Præpositi Johan. Hieron: â Petkum . . . die XXV. Junii et sequent. a. M.DCC.XV. pp. 110. *Tychopoli*, [1715.] 8º. **S.C. 41**. (5.)

—— Catalogus einer auserlesenen raren Bibliothec . . . Welche durch öffentlichen Ausruff . . . d. 23. Septembr. an. 1715. in Herings Hause, vorn aufm Schiffbauer-Brock . . . sollen verkauffet werden. pp. 254. *Hamburg*, 1715. 8º. **S.C. 74**.

—— Catalogus variorum & insignium . . . librorum. Quorum auctio . . . instituetur Hamburgi die 5. Maji, anni 1716. in Templi Cathedralis Refectorio, *etc.* pp. 274. *Hamburgi*, [1716.] 8º. **S.C. 106**.

—— Verzeichniss verschiedener meist juristischer . . . Bücher . . . Welche den 11. May 1716. zu Glückstadt in des Herrn Wilhelm Selcken Behausung durch öffentlige auction sollen verkauffet werden. pp. 52. [*Glückstadt*, 1716.] 8º. **S.C. 41**. (6.)

CATALOGUES.

—— Catalogus verschiedener theologischer, philosophischer . . . Bücher, welche in des Herrn Alardi . . . Behausung, durch eine öffentliche Auction den   Julii ao. 1716. distrahiret werden sollen. *Hamburger Berg*, [1716.]
S.C. **169**. (3.)
The figure 27 has been supplied in MS. *in the blank space in the title.*

—— A Catalogue of Medals, from Julius Cæsar to the Emperor Heraclius, *etc.* pp. 36. *W. Mears ; J. Brown: London*, 1716. 4⁰. **603**. b. **1**. (3.)

—— A Catalogue of Valuable Books in several faculties and languages . . . of a Clergyman, and another gentleman deceased . . . which will begin to be sold, the 7. May, 1717 . . . at W. Mears. [*London*, 1717.] 8⁰.
128. i. **1**. (5.)

—— Catalogus allerhand auserlesener Bücher . . . Deren öffentliche Verkauffung wird seyn in der Schiffer-Gesellschafft, den 24. Maji, anno 1717. MS. PRICES. *Hamburg*, 1717. 8⁰. S.C. **169**. (4.)

—— Catalogus librorum egregiorum, cumprimis in facultate theologica, medic., philol. qui publica auctione distrahentur in ædibus Matthiæ Hauschildt, in platea, quæ vocatur Neueburg, die 7. Junii, anno 1717. pp. 315. *Hamburgi*, [1717.] 8⁰. S.C. **112**.

—— Catalogus variorum & insignium . . . librorum . . . qui publica auctione distrahentur die   August. anno 1717. *Hamburgi*, 1717. 8⁰. S.C. **168**. (4.)
The figure 16 has been supplied in MS. *in the blank space in the title.*

—— Catalogus variorum librorum, majori ex parte theologicorum, qui publico auctionis more . . . venales exponuntur, in ædibus Selkianis Tychopoli d.   Octobr. ao. . . . MDCCXVII. [*Glückstadt*, 1717.] 8⁰.
S.C. **127**. (1.)
The figure 25 has been supplied in MS. *in the blank space in the title.*

—— Catalogus variorum & insignium librorum . . . Qui in domicilio Mentzeriano publico . . . auctionis ritu distrahentur. Hamburgi, die 15. Aug. 1718. pp. 61. *Hamb.*, [1718.] 8⁰. S.C. **169**. (1.)

—— Catalogus librorum, variarum facultatum, auctionis lege ad d. III. Octob. MDCCXVIII. in platea dicta Rödingsmarckt et ædibus B. Lic. Hilckens distrahendorum. pp. 80. *Hamburgi*, [1718.] 8⁰. S.C. **169**. (2.)

—— Catalogus librorum, quorum auctio erit Gluckstadij d.   Octobr. 1718. in ædibus Dn. Consiliarii Wulffii, *etc.* pp. 78. [*Glückstadt*, 1718.] 8⁰. S.C. **127**. (2.)
The date in the title has been altered in MS. *to 2 Nov.*

—— Catalogus variorum . . . librorum, quorum auctio publica . . . instituetur Hamburgi die   anni 1719. in der Frau Doctorin Schrödern Behausung, *etc.*
MS. NOTES AND PRICES. [*Hamburg*,] 1719. 8⁰.
S.C. **127**. (3.)
Interleaved. The date 9 Jan. has been supplied in MS. *in the blank space in the title.*

—— [A sale catalogue of books.] [1720 ?]   S.C. **144**. (1.)
Imperfect ; wanting the titlepage.

—— [A sale catalogue of books.] 2 pt. [1720 ?] 8⁰.
S.C. **144**. (2.)
Imperfect ; wanting the titlepage.

—— [A sale catalogue of books.] pp. 48. [1720 ?] 8⁰.
S.C. **326**. (15.)
Imperfect ; wanting all before p. 9.

CATALOGUES.

—— [A catalogue of books.] [1720 ?] *12⁰*. S.C. **550**. (15.)
Imperfect ; wanting the titlepage.

—— [A sale catalogue of books.] pp. 250. [*Glückstadt ?* 1720 ?] 8⁰. S.C. **127**. (4.)
Imperfect ; wanting the titlepage.

—— A Catalogue of Books . . . Which are to be sold, at Tom's Coffee-House in Villar's Street . . . the 15th. instant. pp. 22. MS. PRICES. [*London*, 1720 ?] 8⁰.
S.C. **834**. (21.)

—— Catalogus von den raresten Büchern und Manuscriptis, welche bishero in der Historia Litteraria noch nicht zum Vorschein kommen, *etc.* [By — Wohlrab. A catalogue of imaginary works.] pp. 102. *Franckfurth & Leipzig*, 1720. 8⁰. **820**. d. **7**.

—— Inventario de' libri di diverse materie. pp. 73. [1720 ?] 8⁰. S.C. **251**. (3.)

—— Catalogus von einer auserlesenen theologischen und philologischen Bibliothec, welche den 30. Septembr. 1721 alhier in Hamburg in der Johannes-Schule . . . soll verauctioniret werden. pp. 260. [*Hamburg*, 1721.] 8⁰. S.C. **208**.

—— Books : being a curious collection of architecture, antiquity . . . which will begin to be sold by auction at Manwearings Coffee-house . . . in Fleet-street . . . the 5th of this instant December, 1722, *etc.* pp. 16. [*London*, 1722.] 8⁰. **128**. i. **2**. (11.)

—— Catalogus librorum, omnis generis facultatum . . . Publica auctione distrahendor., in ædibus prope molam vulgô die Poggen-Mühle . . . die novellis publicis indicando. pp. 332. *Hamburgi*, 1722. 8⁰. S.C. **158**.

—— Bibliotheca antiquaria & politica : being a catalogue of the library of a very great statesman deceased . . . Which will begin to be sold . . . at Dick's Coffee-House . . . in Covent-Garden . . . the 21st of May, 1723, *etc.* pp. 56. [*London*, 1723.] 8⁰. **128**. i. **3**. (6.)

—— [A sale catalogue of books, issued by W. Mears 22 Nov. 1723.] pp. 48. [*London*, 1723.] 8⁰. **128**. i. **3**. (8*.)
Imperfect ; wanting the titlepage.

—— Verzeichnüss einiger rarer Bücher. [By Georg Serpilius.] pp. 360. *Franckfurt & Leipzig*, 1723. 8⁰. **821**. b. **8**.

—— Catalogus insignium librorum. Being a catalogue of valuable books, part of the stock of a bookseller lately deceased . . . Which will begin to be sold . . . at the sign of the Fan near the Fountain Tavern in the Strand . . . the 8th of February, 1724–5. pp. 36. [*London*, 1725.] 8⁰. **128**. i. **4**. (6.)

—— [A sale catalogue of books.] 2 pt. [1725 ?] 8⁰.
S.C. **190**. (2.)

—— A Catalogue of a Very Valuable Collection of Books and Prints of antiquities . . . Will be sold by auction on Wednesday the 13th, and Thursday the 14th, *etc.* pp. 8. [*London*, 1725 ?] 8⁰. S.C. **222**. (5.)

—— Catalogus nummorum. pp. 126. 13. [*Amsterdam ?* 1725 ?] 8⁰. S.C. **468**. (1.)
Imperfect ; wanting the titlepage.

—— A Catalogue of the Common and Statute Law-Books of this Realm, with some others relating thereunto, to Michaelmas Term, 1725, *etc.* pp. 92. *J. Walthoe: London*, 1726. 12⁰. **510**. a. **32**. (1.)

—— A Compleat Catalogue of all the Plays that were ever yet printed in the English language . . . Continued to this present year, 1726. The second edition. pp. 104. *W. Mears: London*, 1726. 12⁰. **641**. a. **15**.

CATALOGUES.

—— [Another copy.]   **641**. f. **18**. (**1**.)
Imperfect ; wanting the titlepage.

—— Catalogus bibliothecæ omnium facultatum, præcipue vero historico-philologicos . . . libros complexæ qui d. xx. Aprilis & seqq. anno MDCCXXVIII. Luneburgi in ædibus prope Templum Div. Johan. vulgo im Rectorat . . . divendentur, *etc.* pp. 284. *Luneburgi,* 1728. 8º.
     11902. a. **44**.

—— A Catalogue of . . . Original Pictures, painted by the most famous masters, which are now to be sold. (These . . . pictures belong'd . . . to the . . . Princes of Barberini at Rome, *etc.*) [*London,* 1730 ?] *s. sh.* fol.
     C. 116. i. **4**. (**73**.)

—— Gatalogus [*sic*] numismatum, aureor. argent. æreor. &c. regum et urbium græcorum familiarum roman. . . . Item nummorum . . . modernorum. 2 pt. [1730 ?] 8º.
     602. a. **37**. (**2**.)
Apparently part of a larger catalogue.

—— Catalogus plantarum, tum exoticarum tum domesticarum, quæ in hortis haud procul a Londino sitis in venditionem propagantur . . . By a Society of Gardeners. 1730. fol. *See* LONDON.—III. *Society of Gardeners.*
     452. h. **2**.

—— Catalogus librorum theologicorum, iuridicorum . . . item numismatum . . . nec non iconum aeri incisarum, quae singula auctionis lege . . . a. MDCCXXXII. d. x. Martii seqq. Lipsiae distrahenda venum exponentur. pp. 173. MS. PRICES. [*Leipsic,* 1732.] 8º.
     S.C. **166**. (**2**.)

—— Catalogus librorum theologicorum, iuridicorum . . . nec non iconum aeri incisarum, quae singula auctionis lege . . . a. MDCCXXXII. d. 1. Decembr. seqq. Lipsiae distrahenda venum exponentur. pp. 114. MS. PRICES. [*Leipsic,* 1732.] 8º.
     S.C. **166**. (**3**.)

—— A True and Exact Catalogue of All the Plays and other Dramatick Pieces, that were ever yet printed in the English tongue . . . continu'd down to April 1732. pp. 35. MS. NOTES. *W. Feales: London,* 1732. 12º.
     641. f. **18**. (**2**.)

—— Catalogus bibliothecæ historico-philologicæ, quæ die 27. Aprilis & sequentibus anni 1733 . . . Luneburgi . . . im Rectorat . . . diuendetur. [Including books from the Library of Sylvester Kundtmann.] pp. 426. *Luneburgi,* [1733.] 8º.
     S.C. **194**.

—— Bibliotheca exquisitissima. Sive catalogus selectorum . . . librorum, quorum auctio habebitur in ædibus defuncti . . . ad diem 19 Aprilis, 1734. & seq., *etc.* pp. 107. MS. PRICES.
     269. i. **12**. (**1**.)

—— Catalogus nitidissimæ Bibliothecæ, continentis juridicos, historicos . . . accedunt & manuscripta nonnulla, ad historiam Germaniæ inferioris spectantia. Horum auctio habebitur in Aula Magna . . . Die 22 & 23 November 1734. pp. 43 [34]. [1734.] 8º.
     269. i. **12**. (**4**.)

—— [A sale catalogue of books, priced. Issued by Richard Montagu ?] pp. 32. [1735 ?] 8º.   S.C. **541**. (**3***.)
Imperfect ; wanting the titlepage.

—— [A sale catalogue of books, priced. Issued by Richard Montagu ?] pp. 32. [1735 ?] 8º.   S.C. **541**. (**3****.)
Imperfect ; wanting the titlepage.

—— [Another copy.]   S.C. **541**. (**5**.)
Imperfect ; wanting the titlepage.

CATALOGUES.

—— Catalogue des livres de M. * * * * [identified in a MS. note as — Du Cange]. pp. 177. [*Paris ?* 1735 ?] 8º.
     S.C. **217**.

—— Catalogus librorum rarissimorum, ab artis typographicæ inventoribus, aliisque ejusdem artis principibus, ante annum millesimum quingentesimum excusorum, *etc.* [A catalogue of books from the library of Joseph Smith.] [*Venice,* 1737.] 8º.
     821. c. **29**.

—— [Another copy.]   G. **407**.

—— Catalogus theologischer, juristischer . . . Bücher und Disputationen, wobey einige Hamburgensia und Manuscripta, welche . . . den 17. Martii 1738. in dem . . . Manckenschen Hause öffentlich an die Meistbietenden verkauffet werden sollen. pp. 156. *Hamburg,* [1738.] 8º.
     11902. aa. **6**.

—— [A sale catalogue of books.] pp. 196. [1740 ?] 8º.
     128. i. **5**. (**1**.)
Imperfect ; wanting all before p. iii.

—— [Tom. 1. pt. 3 of a sale catalogue of books.] pp. 146. [1740 ?] 8º.
     S.C. **122**.

—— Catalogus librorum omnis generis exquisitissimorum . . . nec non dissertationum . . . imprimis manuscriptorum rarissimorum . . . Hamburgi d.1. Augusti a. MDCCXL in platea, hinter S. Petri dicta, nahe beym Alster-Thor, publica auctionis lege . . . distrahendorum. 4 pt. [*Hamburg,* 1740.] 8º.
     130. k. **22**.

—— Catalogi lapidum Veronensium mantissa. pp. 12. pl. IV. *Veronæ,* 1740. 4º.   **661**. f. **19**. (**4**.)
In this copy the two leaves containing pp. 9–12 are in duplicate.

—— Bibliotheca selectissima seu catalogus omnis generis librorum . . . Hi libri auctione publicè distrahendi venum exponentur die 11. & seqq. Novembris 1743. in ædibus Petri Mortier, *etc.* [A sale catalogue of the library of Baron Schomberg.] 2 tom. *Amstelodami,* 1743. 8º.
     269. d. **6, 7**.

—— Καταλογος βιβλιων ἑλληνικων χειρι γραφεντων ἀγνωστου βιβλιοθηκης. (Catalogus librorum MSS. graecorum incertae bibliothecae. Phil. Elmio . . . interprete.) *Gr. & Lat.* pp. 224. 1743. *See* LAMI (G.) *Deliciae eruditorum, etc.* tom. 13. pt. 1. 1736, *etc.* 8º.   **246**. c. **35**.

—— A Catalogue of Books, of the newest fashion, to be sold by auction, at the Whigs Coffee-House, *etc.* [A reprint of the edition of 1693.] 1745. *See* HARLEIAN MISCELLANY. The Harleian Miscellany, *etc.* vol. 5. 1744, *etc.* 4º.
     185. a. **9**.

—— Catalogue of Curious but Prohibited Books, &c. chiefly modern : being the collection of a very eminent statesman, an officer in the Customs, well known to the present great political world. Now upon sale . . . for the benefit of George Briton, a poor fatherless orphan. [A political satire.] pp. 7. *T. Lion:* [*London,*] [1745 ?] fol.
     620. i. **43**.
Cropped.

—— A Catalogue of English Printers, from the year 1471 to 1600; most of them at London. [By Joseph Ames.] pp. 4. [*Joseph Ames: London,* 1745 ?] *obl.* 4º.
     C.119.c.3.
A proof, with corrections in MS.

—— A Catalogue of Curiosities, chiefly theatrical, which are to be sold by auction, *etc.* [The dedicatory epistle signed : Peter Skewball.] 1748. 8º. *See* SKEWBALL (Peter) *pseud.*
     641. f. **18**. (**5**.)

CATALOGUES.

—— Catalogus numismatum tam graecorum quam romanorum ex omni aere . . . quae veris antiquitatum aestimatoribus . . . offert possessor. pp. 256. *Gottingae*, 1754. 8°. **1103**. b. **26**. (**4**.)

—— Catalogus dissertationum et tractatuum Reformationem Noricam illustrantium, *etc.* pp. 127. *Altdorfii Noricorum*, 1755. 8°. **820**. d. **3**. *Interleaved*.

—— Catalogus librorum italicorum, latinorum, et manuscriptorum . . . per triginta annorum spatium Liburni collectorum. pp. 663. *Liburni*, 1756. 8°. **011902**. e. **18**.

—— Catalogus librorum A. C. D. A. [i.e. of Archibald Campbell, Duke of Argyle]. 1758. 4°. *See* A., A. C. D. **821**. g. **8**.

—— [Another copy.] **123**. i. **8, 9**.

—— Table alphabétique des dictionnaires, en toutes sortes de langues & sur toutes sortes de sciences & d'arts. [By J. B. Durey de Noinville. With " Question sur les dictionnaires," by C. Bellet.] pp. iv. 90. *Paris*, 1758. 8°. **T. 2073**. (**1**.)

—— Numophylacium, continens apparatum splendidum nummorum antiquiorum aeque ac recentiorum aureorum, argenteorum . . . e totius Europae, inprimis Sueciae regionibus conquisitorum, quod Hamburgi die xxix. Octobris anni MDCCLIX. sub hasta distrahetur. (Münz-Cabinet, welches einen herrlichen Vorrath sowohl alte. als neuer Münzen . . . in sich fasset, *etc.*) *Lat.* 2 pt, pp. 221. [*Hamburg*, 1759.] 8°. **1103**. b. **15**. (**1**.)

—— Catalogue of Pictures and Drawings in the Holbein-Chamber, at Strawbery-Hill. [By Horace Walpole, Earl of Orford.] pp. 8. [*Strawberry-Hill*,] 1760. 8°. **688**. c. **28**. (**2**.)

—— Catalogue de livres en feuilles . . . et plusieurs manuscrits . . . Lesquels se vendront . . . le 23 août 1762, & jours suivans, *etc.* pp. 277. 1762. 8°. *See* HONDT. (Pieter de) *Libraire*. **S.C. 805**. (**1**.)

—— Catalogue hebdomadaire : ou Liste des livres, estampes, cartes, ordonnances, édits, déclarations, arrêts, qui sont mis en vente chaque semaine, tant en France qu'en pays étrangers. 1763–89. 8°. *See* PERIODICAL PUBLICATIONS.—*Paris*. **P.P. 6455**.

—— A Catalogue of all the English Books that have been published for these sixty years past, to the present time, with the prices affixed. Any of which that are in print may be had of . pp. 59. *London*, 1764. 8°. **011901**. h. **21**. *Later edition* 1766.

—— Catalogue d'une bibliothèque incomparable, composée de livres anciens & modernes . . . Catalogus van eene uytmuntende bibliotheek, *etc.* tom. 3. MS. NOTES AND PRICES. [1765 ?] 8°. **822**. d. **24**. *Imperfect ; wanting tom.* 1, 2.

—— A Catalogue of the Paintings, Sculptures, Architecture, Models, Drawings, Engravings, &c., now exhibiting by the body of artists associated for the relief of their distressed brethren, their widows and children : at Mr. Moreing's Great Room in Maiden Lane, Covent Garden. pp. 12. *James Harrison : London*, 1765. 4°. **S.C. 1034**. (**19**.)

—— Catalogus dissertationum, quæ ad illustrandas res svecicas faciunt, præsertim in argumentis historicis, ecclesiasticis, juridicis, *etc.* [By Petrus Cederhamm.] pp. 214. *Holmiæ*, 1765. 4°. **271**. f. **1**.

CATALOGUES.

—— A Complete Catalogue of Modern Books published from the beginning of this century, to the present time, with the prices affixed. To which is added, a catalogue of the school books now in general use. Any books in the following catalogue, that are now in print, may be had . . . of . pp. 92. *London*, 1766. 8°. **11900**. c. **32**. (**1**.) *Earlier edition* 1764 ; *later edition* 1767.

—— A New and Correct Catalogue of all the English Books which have been printed from the year 1700, to the present time, with their prices. To which is added, a complete list of law books, for the same period, likewise all the school books now in use. Any article, that is in print, may be had of . pp. 108. *London*, 1767. 8°. **11900**. c. **32**. (**2**.) *Earlier edition* 1766.

—— Siciliae veterum populorum & urbium regum quoque et tyrannorum numismata, quae Panormi exstant in quodam privato cimelio. pp. lxvii. *Panormi*, 1767. 8°. **116**. h. **25**.

—— Catalogue d'une belle collection de livres ecclésiastiques, juridiques, historiques et autres. Qui se venderont publiquement . . . le 8. février 1768. & jours suivans, *etc.* pp. 54. *Anvers*, [1768.] 8°. **8079**. aa. **8**. (**2**.)

—— In Roma sotto la Panettaria di Monte Cavallo, a Strada Nova vi sono le seguenti machine metamatiche [*sic*] dilettevoli. pp. iv. [*Rome*, 1770.] 8°. **1230**. d. **20**. (**110**.)

—— Catalogus cochlidum atque concharum, summo studio collectarum. pp. 61. *Lipsiae*, 1772. 8°. **972**. e. **14**. (**2**.)

—— Vollständiger Catalogus einer Suiten Mineralien-Sammlung . . . aus allen Ländern Europens und den übrigen Welttheilen . . . gesammlet. pp. 301. *Leipzig*, 1772. 8°. **972**. e. **14**. (**1**.)

—— Catalogue d'une riche collection de tableaux . . . du cabinet de M*** [identified in a MS. note as J. D. Lempereur]. Dont la vente se fera . . . 24 mai 1773, *etc.* pp. iv. 159. MS. PRICES. 1773. 8°. *See* M***. **562**. e. **20**. (**1**.)

—— Catalogue systématique et raisonné d'une superbe collection d'objets des trois règnes de la nature . . . Le tout rassemblé par * * [i.e. — van Zuylen van Nyevelt], dont la vente se fera le 9 novembre 1773 & jours suivans . . . à Amsterdam, par . . . N. Blinkvliet, Ph. v. d. Schley et P. Posthumus, *etc.* (Systematisch-beredeneerde naamlyst van eene uitmuntende verzameling, *etc.*) [Compiled by F. C. Meuschen.] *Fr. & Dutch.* pp. xii. 400. [*Amsterdam*, 1773.] 8°. **956**. g. **6**.

—— The London Catalogue of Books in all Languages, Arts and Sciences, that have been printed in Great Britain, since the year M.DCC. properly classed . . . With their sizes and prices, *etc.* [Compiled by William Bent.] pp. 144. *London*, 1773. 8°. **128**. k. **9** *Interleaved*.

—— Catalogue des curiosités naturelles, qui composent le cabinet de M. de * * * [i.e. — Beost] et dont la vente se fera à Paris . . . le lundi 4 juillet 1774 & jours suivans, *etc.* [By J. B. L. de Romé de Lisle.] pp. viii. 295. *Paris*, 1774. 8°. **955**. d. **26**.

—— Books printed by the Booksellers of London and Westminster, in different sizes and prices ; of which there remains a large stock on hand : with the number of years an impression of each is in selling. pp. 4. [*London*, 1774.] fol. **215**. i. **4**. (**97**.)

CATALOGUES.

—— A Catalogue of the Plants, growing Wild in the Environs of London. [By William Curtis.] pp. 40. *London,* 1774. 8°. **B. 116. (4.)**

—— Catalogue raisonné d'une collection de médailles. [By C. A. von Schachmann.] pp. 162. *Leipzig,* 1774. 4°. **679. e. 34.**

—— [Another copy.] **603. h. 11.**

—— Catalogue d'une belle collection de tableaux, desseins, estampes, livres d'estampes et livres, du cabinet de M. * * * [i.e. P. H. Souchay?] Dont la vente se fera le mercredi 4 janvier 1775, & jours suivans . . . Par F. C. Joullain, fils. pp. 92. MS. NOTES OF PRICES. *Paris,* 1774. 8°. **562. e. 19. (3.)**

—— Catalogue des livres de feu M. de * * * dont la vente se fera . . . 6 mars 1775, *etc.* 2 pt. MS. PRICES. *Paris,* 1775. 8°. **269. h. 23. (3.)**

—— Catalogue d'une belle collection de tableaux, sculptures, desseins, estampes encadrées & en feuilles, livres d'estampes, livres & autres objets de curiosité. Provenant du cabinet de M. * * * [i.e. Philippe Caffieri]. Dont la vente se fera . . . le mardi 10 octobre 1775, pp. 55. *Paris,* 1775. 8°. **562. e. 19. (4.)**

—— [A collection of sale catalogues of estates chiefly in Suffolk.] 69 pt. 1775–1830. fol. **10351. i. 8.**

—— Notice des pricipaux [*sic*] articles qui composent le cabinet de M. * * *. Dont la vente se fera . . . 4 mars 1776, *etc.* pp. 11. MS. PRICES. **269. h. 23. (6.)**

—— Catalogue de tableaux, italiens, françois, hollandois, et autres. Dessins & estampes sous verre, dont la vente se fera le lundi 17 février 1777, & jours suivans, *etc.* pp. 86. MS. PRICES. *Paris,* 1777. 8°. **562. e. 20. (2.)**

—— Magazin des Estamps, 1777. A Catalogue of a . . . Collection of Historical Prints, English and Foreign Portraits . . . The whole now selling, at the Magazin des Estamps, *etc.* pp. vii. 232. [*London,* 1777.] 8°. **56. b. 29. (2.)**

—— A Catalogue of Plants copied from Nature in Paper Mosaick, finished in the year 1778, and disposed in alphabetical order, according to the . . . names of Linnæus. [By Mary Delany.] ff. 47. [1778.] 8°. **B. 100. (2.)** *Printed on one side of the leaf only.*

—— Magazin des Estamps, 1778. A Catalogue of a . . . Collection of Prints, Drawings, and Books of Prints . . . The whole . . . now selling at the Magazin des Estamps, *etc.* pp. 244. [*London,*] 1778. 8°. **1266. b. 36. (1.)**

—— A General Catalogue of Books in all Languages, Arts, and Sciences, that have been printed in Great Britain, published in London, since the year M.DCC. to the present time, *etc.* [Compiled by William Bent.] pp. 152. *London,* 1779. 8°. **11903. bb. 45.**

—— [Another copy.] **618. f. 20. (1.)**

—— Catalogue des livres choisis dans les différentes bibliothèques des ci-devant Jésuites des Pays-Bas . . . dont la vente se fera à Bruxelles . . . le 4 du mois septembre 1780, *etc.* pp. x. 302. *Bruxelles,* [1780.] 8°. **123. e. 7.**

—— A Catalogue of a Large and Curious Collection of Prints, Drawings, and Books of Prints . . . The whole now selling . . . at No. 28, in the Hay-market. pp. 49. [*London,* 1780?] 8°. **1266. b. 36. (2.)**

CATALOGUES.

—— Catalogue of Sarum and York Missals. [Reprinted from vol. 2 of " British Topography " by Richard Gough.] pp. 43. MS. NOTES. [*London,* 1780.] 4°. **3395. e. 8.** *Interleaved.*

—— Catalogus librorum qui venales erunt Patavii anno 1780. (Catalogo de' libri che saranno posti in vendita nella città di Padova l'anno 1780.—Catalogue de livres qui seront mis en vente à Padoue dans l'annèe 1780.) [A sale catalogue of books from the library of M. G. Cornaro, Bishop of Vicenza?] 3 vol. [*Padua,* 1780.] 8°. **269. b. 29–31.**

—— Catalogus supellectilis cuiusdam librorum septentrionalium cuius partes duæ priores . . . publica auctionis lege venum dabuntur Hafniæ in ædibus Jungianis . . . die 2. et seqq. Aprilis 1781. 2 pt. *Hafniæ,* [1781.] 8°. **269. d. 19.**

—— Appendix of aanhangzel, behoorende tot de Catalogus van een . . . inboedel, welke . . . verzaameld is, door den Heer G. R. [i.e. George III., King of Great Britain and Ireland], zullende alles . . . by executie, verkogt worden, binnen Londen, in de maanden Mey of Juny deezes jaars, *etc.* [1781.] 8°. *See* R., G. **934. f. 5. (8*.)**

—— An Appendix to the General Catalogue of Books printed in the year MDCCLXXIX: containing alphabetical and classical lists of the books published in London since that time, to the end of the year MDCCLXXX, *etc.* [Compiled by William Bent.] pp. 10. *London,* 1781. 8°. **618. f. 20. (2.)**

—— Catalogo di libri che restano esposti alla vendita in Padova coi loro prezzi. pp. xv. 671. [*Padua,* 1781.] **269. d. 26.** *Imperfect ; wanting all before p. iii.*

—— Inventaris van een uitmuntend partytje goederen, waar onder veelerlei bybelgeschiedenissen, by een gebragt door eenige inwooners van London . . . om de penningen, daarvoor komende, te gebruiken ter redding van den insolventen boedel, des Heeren G. R. [i.e. George III., King of Great Britain and Ireland.] [A skit.] pp. 16. [*Amsterdam,* 1781.] 8°. **934. f. 5. (8.)**

—— Catalogue des livres de la bibliothèque de M. le baron d'H * * [i.e. — d'Heisse] dont la vente se fera le . . . 22 juillet 1782, *etc.* 1782. 8°. *See* H * *, *M. le Baron de.* **11901. aaa. 20.**

—— A Catalogue of near Ten Thousand Volumes of Curious and Scarce Books, in which are included a good Collection in Divinity . . . and a . . . collection of tracts . . . collected by Dr. Mead . . . Which will begin selling August 1, 1783 . . . at No. 27. Snow Hill, *etc.* 3 pt. [*London,* 1783.] 8°. **128. k. 13. (3.)** *The date on the titlepage has been altered in MS. to "September 1."*

—— Beredeneerde Catalogus eener verzameling van schilderyen, der eerste meesters van Nederland (verzameld door Mr. C. W. V.). [By L. P. van de Spiegel?] [1783.] 8°. *See* V., C. W., *Mr.* **934. f. 5. (12.)**

—— Catalogue for 1783. [A priced catalogue of books prints and maps.] pp. 259. [1783.] 8°. **S.C. 715. (4.)** *Imperfect ; wanting the titlepage.*

—— Catalogue raisonnée [*sic*] d'une collection de tableaux peints par les plus fameux artistes de ce paix. [A political satire. By R. M. C. van Goens?] pp. 32. *En Hollande,* 1783. 4°. **934. f. 5. (14.)**

—— Beredeneerde catalogus, van eene uitmuntende verzameling schilderyen door de vermaardste Nederlandsche meesters, uit het Fransch vertaald. [A translation of " Catalogue raisonnée d'une collection de tableaux peints par les plus fameux artistes de ce paix " by R. M. C. van Goens?] pp. 37. *In Holland*, 1783. 8°.
934. f. 5. (13.)

—— Litteratur der Musik, oder Anleitung zur Kenntnis der vorzüglichen musikalischen Bücher . . . Herausgegeben von einem Liebhaber der Musik [i.e. J. S. Gruber]. pp. 56. *Nürnberg*, 1783. 8°.
Hirsch I. 658.

—— Catalogue systématique et raisonné, ou description du magnifique cabinet appartenant ci-devant à M. le C. de *** [i.e. Count de la Tour d'Auvergne] . . . Par M. de *** [i.e. — de Favanne de Montcerville]. pp. xii. 558. *Paris*, 1784. 8°.
956. h. 34.

—— [Another copy.] MS. PRICES.
956. g. 9.

—— [Another copy.]
45. d. 1.

—— Catalogue des livres rares et précieux de M. *** . . . Dont la vente se fera . . . 7 mars 1785, *etc.* pp. 155. *Paris*, 1785. 8°.
S.C. 807. (5.)

—— A Catalogue of a Collection of Pictures . . . Which will be sold by auction, by Mr. Greenwood . . . the 16th of June, 1785, *etc.* pp. 8. *H. Reynell: [London*, 1785.] 4°.
7805. e. 5. (20.)

—— Catalogue de diamans roses et autres, rubis, emeraudes . . . dont la vente se fera . . . le 21 juillet 1785 . . . à Bruxelles, *etc.* pp. 17. *Bruxelles*, 1785. 4°.
7805. e. 5. (22.)

—— Catalogue d'une collection de tableaux de plusieurs grands maîtres . . . provenant des maisons religieuses supprimées aux Pays-Bas, dont la vente se fera au Couvent des ci-devant Riches Claires à Bruxelles . . . La vente commencera le 12 du mois de septembre [1785], *etc.* pp. 38. *Bruxelles*, 1785. 4°.
7805. e. 5. (21.)

—— Catalogue de livres rares dont la vente se fera . . . 13 mars 1786 . . . Par Guillaume de Bure. [A sale catalogue of the library of — Le Camus de Limare.] pp. xii. 259. MS. PRICES. *Paris*, 1786. 8°.
11903. bb. 45.

—— A General Catalogue of Books in all Languages, Arts, and Sciences, printed in Great Britain, and published in London, from the year MDCC to MDCCLXXXVI, *etc.* [Compiled by William Bent.] pp. 168. *W. Bent: London*, 1786. 8°.
Circ. 90. a.

—— [Another copy.]
11900. bbb. 31. (1.)

—— Catalogue des livres rares et singuliers provenans du cabinet de M. *** [i.e. — Mars], dont la vente se fera . . . 19 novembre 1787, *etc.* pp. 180. MS. PRICES. *Paris*, 1787. 8°.
11903. bb. 35. (4.)

—— Catalogue d'une collection de tableaux de differents maîtres de l'école Flamande, dont la vente se fera aux premiers jours. pp. 7. [1787?] 8°.
117. b. 55.

—— Catalogue des noms des peintres compris en ce precieux recueil des tableaux, statué [*sic*], estampes, desseins . . . Le tout recuelli [*sic*] . . . par N. N . . ., dont la vent [*sic*] se fera . . . à Anvers . . . 30 août 1788, *etc.* [1788.] 8°. *See* N . . ., N.
117. a. 54.

—— A Modern Catalogue of Books printed in Great Britain and published in London, since the year MCCLXXXV [*sic*] to the present time . . . with their sizes and prices. [Compiled by William Bent.] pp. 23. *W. Bent: London*, 1788. 4°.
11900. bbb. 31. (2.)

—— [Another copy.]
11900. c. 32. (4.)

—— Catalogue des livres choisis et bien conditionnés du cabinet de M *** [i.e. — d'Angard]. Dont la vente se fera . . . 9 mars 1789, *etc.* [Compiled by J. F. Née de la Rochelle.] pp. 20. 316. 1789. 8°. *See* M*** 269. i. 6.

—— Bibliotheca Americana ; or, a Chronological catalogue of . . . books, pamphlets, state papers, &c. upon the subject of North and South America . . . With an introductory discourse on the present state of literature in those countries. pp. 271. *J. Debrett: London*, 1789. 4°.
[By LEMAN THOMAS REDE, the Elder.] 11901. cc. 23.

—— [Another copy.]
619. k. 22.

—— [Another copy.] FEW MS. ADDITIONS.
125. e. 4.

—— [Another copy.]
G. 325.

—— *See* SHERMAN (Stuart C.) Leman Thomas Rede's Bibliotheca Americana, *etc.* 1947. 8°.
11900. bbb. 98.

—— Catalogue. (Catalogue d'une collection de tableaux de différens maîtres des écoles flamandes, dont la vente se fera au premier jour.) [A satire.] pp. 8. [*Paris*, 1789?] 8°.
F. 463. (1.)

—— Catalogue des ouvrages relatifs aux États Generaux, qui ont paru depuis l'arrêt du Conseil du mois de juillet 1788. pp. 59. 1789. 8°.
R. 54. (9.)

—— Catalogue raisonné des ouvrages qui parurent en 1614 et 1615, à l'occasion des États. pp. 43. 1789. 8°.
F. 371. (5.)

—— Liste abrégée des ouvrages saisis depuis la liberté de la presse. [A satire.] pp. 4. [1789?] 8°. F.R. 14. (4.)

—— Notice intéressante et curieuse des ouvrages satyriques, qui parurent à l'époque des États-Généraux tenus en 1614, *etc.* [By the Marquis L. A. Caraccioli.] pp. 19. 1789. 8°.
F.R. 15. (4.)

—— A Select Catalogue of German Books ; with the subject of each in English. And an appendix of the best editions of the classics, and some French books, published in Germany. pp. 76. *Prince & Cooke: Oxford*, 1789. 8°.
272. k. 6.

—— An Arranged Catalogue of the Several Publications which have appeared, relating to the enlargement of the toleration of Protestant-Dissenting-Ministers ; and the repeal of the Corporation and Test-Acts . . . from the year M.DCC.LXXII, to M.DCC.XC, inclusive. pp. 31. *J. Johnson: London*, 1790. 8°.
126. i. 9.

—— Catalogi librorum specimen. [A catalogue of a portion of the library of J. J. Spalding. Compiled by himself.] pp. 76. [1790.] 8°.
11903. bb. 52.
One of an edition of twenty-five copies.

—— A Catalogue of Tracts. [A catalogue of the collection of Catharine Macaulay, afterwards Graham.] pp. 199. 1790. 8°.
126. a. 15.

—— Catalogus plantarum. [1790?] 8°. B. 71. (1.)

—— Naamlijst, van uitgekomen boeken, kaarten, prentwerken, enz. Jan. 1790–1854, no. 12. *'s Gravenhage; Amsterdam*, 1790–1854. 8°.
P.P. 6510.
The title is taken from the special titlepage for each volume ; the title of the separate parts reads : " Lijst van nieuw uitgekomen boeken." Imperfect ; wanting no. 5–12 of 1842, the whole of 1843, no. 1–9 of 1844 and the special titlepages and indexes for dl. 11, 1839–43, and dl. 13, 1849–53.

CATALOGUES.

—— The London Catalogue of Books, selected from the General Catalogue published in MDCCLXXXVI, and including the additions and alterations to September MDCCXCI, etc. [Compiled by William Bent.] pp. 160. *W. Bent: London*, 1791. 8º. **11900**. c. **32**. (5.)

—— Notice de livres rares, la plupart imprimés dans le quinziéme siècle, dont la vente se fera . . . le 16 janvier, 1792, etc. pp. 52. *Paris*, [1791.] 8º. **270**. d. **11**.

—— Verzeichniss einer auserlesenen Samlung medicinischer, chirurgischer, zur Naturhistorie gehöriger . . . und anderer Bücher, welche am 13 und folgenden Tagen des Febr. 1792 . . . sollen verkauft . . . werden. pp. 102. *Göttingen*, 1791. 8º. **T. 466**. (5.)

—— Catalogue des livres, estampes, manuscrits, et collections de pièces détachées de la bibliothèque de M. * * *. Contenant environ 13,000 volumes . . . dont la vente commencera . . . 16 avril 1792, etc. 2 pt. 1792. 8º. *See M***. **129**. i. **16**. (3.)

—— A Catalogue of a Valuable Museum consisting of . . . cameos, and intaglios, rings . . . the property of a gentleman, deceased . . . January 28th, 1793, etc. pp. 8. [*London*, 1793.] 4º. **7805**. e. **5**. (40.)

—— Collection de minéraux étrangers, dont la majeure partie est de Sibérie, et une suite de coquilles, belle machine électrique, et autres pièces de physique, et différens objets de l'art: qui seront vendus . . . le lundi 25 mars 1793, etc. pp. 35. *Paris*, 1793. 8º. **F.R. 451**. (25.) *Imperfect; wanting pp. 17–35.*

—— [Another copy.] **F.R. 451**. (26.) *Imperfect; wanting the first two leaves and pp. 9–24.*

—— A Catalogue of Modern Law Books; being a Supplement to Bibliotheca Legum Angliæ [of John Worrall]: containing a catalogue of law-publications, from Hilary Term 1788 to Trinity Term 1794, etc. [The advertisement signed: E. B., i.e. Edward Brooke.] 1794. 12º. *See* B., E. **518**. a. **17**.

—— [Six cuttings from American newspapers, containing advertisements of American booksellers.] [1795?] **11900**. b. **20**. (7.)

—— Neues Repertorium von seltenen Büchern und Schriften. [The preface signed: W., i.e. G. E. Waldau.] 1795–97. 8º. *See* W. **820**. b. **25**.

—— Systematisches Verzeichniss der in der medicinischen, physicalischen, chemischen und naturhistorischen Literatur in den Jahren 1785 bis 1790. (1791 bis 1795.) herausgekommenen deutschen und ausländischen Schriften. Mit Nachweisung der in den vornehmsten kritischen Journalen von ihnen enthaltenen Recensionen, auch Anzeige vieler in periodischen Schriften zerstreuten einzelnen Abhandlungen. [A separate issue of sections of "Allgemeines Repertorium der Literatur."] 2 pt. *Jena; Weimar*, 1795, 99. 4º. **551**. f. **2**.

—— A Catalogue of the Splendid Library . . . of a Nobleman . . . which will be sold by auction . . . April 18th, 1796, etc. pp. 34. MS. PRICES. [*London*,] 1796. 8º. **125**. b. **8**. *Interleaved.*

—— Catalogo de'capi d'opera di pittura, scultura, antichità, libri, storia naturale, ed altre curiosità trasportati dall' Italia in Francia. pp. xxxii. *Venezia*, 1799. 4º. **T. 64***. (2.)

CATALOGUES.

—— Catalogue of the Italian Pictures, lately brought from Rome, and now exhibited in the Great Room, Whitcomb Street, Leicester Square. March, 1799. pp. 59. *G. Hayden: London*, [1799.] 4º. **B. 744**. (6.)

—— The London Catalogue of Books, with their sizes and prices. Corrected to September MDCCXCIX. (An appendix to the London Catalogue of Books: containing the new publications . . . since August 1799 to the end of the year 1800.) [Compiled by William Bent.] 2 pt. pp. 182. *W. Bent: London*, 1799, 1800. 8º. **11900**. c. **31**. (1.)

—— Catalogue d'une collection d'empreintes en soufre de médailles grecques et romaines. pp. viii. 79. *Paris*, an 8 [1800]. 8º. **1043**. h. **13**. (18.)

—— A Catalogue of Modern Law Books; being a supplement to Bibliotheca Legum Angliæ [of J. Worrall]: containing a catalogue of law publications from Hilary Term 1788 to Hilary Term 1800, etc. [The Advertisement signed: E. B., J. R., i.e. Edward Brooke and J. Rider.] 1800. 12º. *See* B., E. **518**. a. **19**.

—— Feuille indicative des vacations de la vente du 30 messidor an x [19 July 1802]. pp. 23. [*Paris*, 1802.] 8º. **562**. e. **27**. (5.)

—— Catalogus insectorum, quæ Viennae Austriae die ix. et sequentibus Novembris MDCCCII. auctionis lege distrahuntur. [*Vienna*, 1802.] 8º. **T. 846**. (3.)

—— Feuille de distribution des articles qui doivent composer chaque vacation de la vente du 28 germinal an XI [18 April 1803], etc. pp. 16. [*Paris*, 1803.] 8º. **562**. e. **27**. (4.)

—— Catalogue des livres précieux, singuliers et rares, tant imprimés que manuscrits, qui composaient la bibliothèque de M. * * [i.e. D. M. Méon], dont la vente se fera . . . le 15 novembre 1803, etc. pp. xxiv. 522. 4. *Paris*, 1803. 8º. **821**. f. **19**.

—— An Account of the Statues, Busts, Bass-Relieves, Cinerary Urns, and other ancient marbles, and paintings, at Ince. Collected by H. B. [i.e. Henry Blundell.] pp. 331. 1803. 4º. *See* B., H. **742**. f. **5**.

—— Catalogue de tableaux, vendus à Bruxelles, depuis l'année 1773; avec les noms de maîtres, etc. pp. 320. *Bruxelles*, [1803?] 8º. **1422**. f. **15**.

—— The Modern Catalogue of Books, with their sizes and prices, and the names of the publishers: containing the books which have been published in London since the year 1792, etc. [Compiled by William Bent.] pp. 88. *W. Bent: London*, 1803. 8º. **11900**. c. **31**. (2.)

—— [A collection of sale catalogues of autographs, manuscripts, books, etc. from the years 1804–1863, bound chronologically in 13 volumes, each volume containing an index in MS.] 13 vol. [1804–63.] 8º. **S.C. 670–682**.

—— Catalogue de livres, en partie, rares, singulier [*sic*] . . . dont la vente se fera . . . 18 novembre 1805, etc. pp. 336. *Paris*, 1805. 8º. **269**. k. **38**.

—— The New London Catalogue of Books, with their sizes and prices. Containing the books which have been published . . . Since the London Catalogue of 1800. [Compiled by William Bent.] pp. 76. *W. Bent: London*, 1805. 8º. **11900**. c. **37**. (1.)

—— Catalogue des livres rares et précieux de M. * * * [identified in a MS. note as — Chardin]. Dont la vente se fera . . . 27 janvier 1806, etc. [The catalogue by G. de Bure.] pp. vi. 215. MS. PRICES. *Paris*, 1806. 8º. **270**. d. **8**.

CATALOGUES.

—— Catalogue. [A catalogue of the library of Sir F. M. Eden, compiled by himself.] pp. 277. 1806. 8º.
821. i. 17.

—— [Another copy.]
124. e. 6.

—— A Catalogue of Modern Law Books, being a supplement to Bibliotheca Legum Angliæ [of J. Worrall], containing a catalogue of law publications from Hilary Term, 1788, to Michaelmas Term, 1805. [By John Clarke.] pp. 114.
W. Clarke & Sons: London, 1806. 8º.
518. a. 20.

—— Catalogue des livres manuscrits et imprimés, des peintures, dessins et estampes du cabinet de M. L . . . [i.e. — Lamy], dont la vente se fera . . . 11 janvier 1808, *etc.* pp. vii. 424. 72. MS. PRICES. 1807. 8º.   *See*
L . . ., M.
269. d. 4.

—— Allmän catalog öfver de uti Sverige och Finland år 1802. (1803.) utkomna böcker och skrifter, *etc.* 1808. 8º.
See SWEDEN.—*Boktryckeri-Societeten.*
11904. e. 30.

—— Catalogue des livres rares et précieux . . . provenant du cabinet de M. F. D. [i.e. Firmin Didot.] pp. ii. 124.
1808. 8º. *See* D., M. F.
269. d. 5. (1.)

—— Symbola et emblemata. [A catalogue of the collection of George Spencer Churchill, 5th Duke of Marlborough.] pp. 12. *Brettell & Co.: London*, 1808. 4º.
11904. h. 36.

—— Notice de tableaux et dessins, anciens et modernes, du cabinet de M. * * * [identified in a MS. note as — Giusta], dont la vente se fera . . . 7 et 8 février 1809, *etc. pp. 10, M.S. PRICES, Paris.* 1809. 8º.   562. e. 28. (1.)

—— Catalogue de tableaux de diverses écoles, composant le cabinet de M. de C . . . . . . n [identified in a MS. note as — de Châtillon], dont la vente se fera 10 février 1809, *etc.* pp. 14. MS. PRICES. [1809.] 8º. *See* C . . . . N
(M. de)
562. e. 28. (2.)

—— Catalogue d'une belle collection de tableaux, de diverse. écoles, dont la vente se fera . . . 10 juillet 1809, *etc.* [The collection ascribed in a MS. note to M. Clisoriuss] pp. 14. MS. PRICES. [*Paris*, 1809.] 8º. 562. e. 28. (7.)

—— Catalogue d'une belle collection de tableaux, de diverses écoles provenant du cabinet de M * * *, dont la vente se fera . . . 16 octobre 1809, *etc.* pp. 27. MS. PRICES. 1809. 8º. *See* M * * *.
7854. cc. 32. (1.)

—— Catalogue d'une belle collection de tableaux, de diverses écoles, dessins et autres objets, d'après le départ de M * * * [identified in a MS. note as — Clisorius], dont la vente se fera . . . 6 novembre 1809, *etc.* pp. 16. MS. PRICES. [1809.] 8º. *See* M * * *. 562. e. 28. (9.)

—— Liste d'une jolie collection de tableaux venant de l'étranger, dont la vente se fera les vendredi 17 et samedi 18 novembre 1809, *etc.* pp. 12. MS. PRICES. [*Paris*,] 1809. 12º.
7855. b. 45. (1.)

—— Catalogue d'une jolie collection de tableaux anciens et modernes, provenant du cabinet de M * * * [identified in a MS. note as — Hazard], dont la vente . . . se fera . . . 27 . . . 28 et . . . 29 novembre 1809, *etc.* pp. 16.
MS. PRICES. [1809.] 8º. *See* M * * *.
7854. ccc. 20. (1.)

—— Catalogue d'une collection de tableaux anciens et modernes, provenant du cabinet de M. * * * * [identified in a MS. note as — Laneuville and — Giusta], dont la vente . . . se fera le 11 décembre 1809, *etc.* pp. 16.
MS. PRICES. [*Paris*, 1809.] 8º.   7854. ccc. 20. (2.)

CATALOGUES.

—— Catalogue des livres composant le cabinet de M. C . . . M . . . . pp. 88. 1809. 8º. *See* M . . . ., C . . ., M.
269. d. 5. (2.)

—— Catalogue d'une nombreuse collection de tableaux des grands maîtres de différentes écoles, dont la vente se fera . . . le lundi 26 février 1810, *etc.* pp. 38.
MS. NOTES AND PRICES. [*Paris*,] 1810. 8º.
7854. ccc. 19. (3.)

—— Catalogue d'une collection de tableaux, par differens maîtres des écoles d'Italie, de France et de Flandres, dont la vente se fera . . . 26 mars 1810, *etc.* [A sale catalogue of pictures from the collections of — Dufresne and M. Didot.] pp. 35. MS. NOTES AND PRICES. [*Paris*,] 1810. 8º.
7854. ccc. 19. (2.)

—— Selecta artis typographicæ monumenta, sivè Catalogus librorum seculo xvᵒ impressorum . . . qui pro adjectis in margine pretiis . . . publica auctionis lege divendentur d. 18. Jun. [1810], *etc.* pp. 80. *Turici Helvet.*, 1810. 8º.
T. 859. (13.)

—— Catalogue d'une magnifique collection de livres . . . Comme aussi une collection des desseins, estampes, plans et cartes. Dont la vente . . . se fera . . . le 3e septembre, 1810 . . . à Amsterdam, *etc.* (Catalogus van eene uitmuntende verzameling . . . boeken, *etc.*) pp. 63. MS. NOTES AND PRICES. [*Amsterdam*, 1810.] 8º.
812. d. 38. (1.)

Interleaved.

—— Catalogue d'une jolie collection de tableaux de diverses écoles, et autres objets, provenant du cabinet d'un amateur, dont la vente se fera . . . 12 novembre 1810, *etc.* pp. 15. MS. NOTES AND PRICES. [*Paris*, 1810.] 8º.
7854. cc. 32. (4.)

—— Catalogue d'une belle collection de tableaux des trois écoles, dont la vente se fera . . . 26 novembre 1810, *etc.* [The collection ascribed in a MS. note to — Hazard.] pp. 16. MS. NOTES AND PRICES. [*Paris*,] 1810. 8º.
7854. cc. 35. (1.)

—— A Catalogue of Books, of the newest fashion; to be sold by auction, at the Whigs' Coffee House, *etc.* [A reprint of the edition of 1693.] 1810. *See* HARLEIAN MISCELLANY. The Harleian Miscellany, *etc.* vol. 5.
1808, *etc.* 4º.   **2072.g.**

—— Notice d'une jolie collection de tableaux des trois écoles, dessins, gouaches . . . dont la vente se fera . . . les 14 et 15 janvier 1811, *etc.* [The collection ascribed in a MS. note to — Billaudet.] pp. 12. MS. NOTES AND PRICES. [*Paris*, 1811.] 8º.   7854. ccc. 19. (13.)
The date in the title has been altered in MS. *to* "13 et 14 janvier 1812."

—— Catalogue d'une collection de bons tableaux des trois écoles; dont la vente se fera . . . 21 janvier 1811, *etc.* [The collection ascribed in a MS. note to — Irlande and another.] pp. 16. MS. PRICES. [*Paris*,] 1811. 8º.
562. e. 29. (1.)

—— Notice d'une collection de tableaux des trois écoles, dont la vente se fera le 18 février 1811, *etc.* pp. 22.
MS. NOTES AND PRICES. [*Paris*,] 1811. 8º.
7854. cc. 32. (9.)

—— Notice d'une collection de bons tableaux des écoles italienne, flamande et hollandaise, estampes, et autres objets; provenants du cabinet de Mʳ D. S. G., artiste; dont la vente se fera . . . 25 mars 1811, *etc.* pp. 16.
MS. PRICES. 1811. 8º. *See* G., D. S., Mʳ, *Artiste.*
562. e. 29. (4.)

CATALOGUES.

—— Catalogue d'une collection de tableaux flamands et hollandais, provenant du cabinet de M*** [identified in a MS. note as — Hazard], dont la vente se fera . . . premier avril 1811, etc. pp. 16. MS. NOTES AND PRICES. 1811. 8°. See M***. **7854. ccc. 20. (5.)**

—— Notice d'une collection de bons tableaux des écoles flamande, hollandaise et italienne, bronzes, dorures . . . provenants du cabinet de Mr D. S. J., artiste [identified in a MS. note as — Brient]; dont la vente aura lieu . . . 4 avril 1811, etc. pp. 19. MS. PRICES. 1811. 8°. See J., D. S., Mr., Artiste. **562. e. 29. (5.)**

—— Notice d'une réunion de tableaux des trois écoles, belle suite de gravures . . . dont la vente . . . se fera . . . 27 mai 1811, etc. pp. 18. MS. NOTES AND PRICES. [Paris,] 1811. 8°. **7854. ccc. 19. (8.)**

—— Catalogue d'une jolie collection de tableaux français, flamands et hollandais . . . dont la vente se fera . . . 3 et 4 juin 1811, etc. pp. 24. MS. NOTES AND PRICES. [Paris,] 1811. 8°. **7854. cc. 32. (8.)**

—— Catalogue d'une jolie collection de tableaux de diverses écoles, dessins, estampes . . . dont la vente se fera . . . 21 novembre 1811, etc. pp. 15. MS. NOTES AND PRICES. [Paris, 1811.] 8°. **7854. cc. 32. (7.)**

—— Vente d'une collection de tableaux hollandais et flamands . . . provenant du cabinet de M*** [identified in a MS. note as — Irlande]. Les 3 et 4 décembre 1811, etc. pp. 14. MS. NOTES AND PRICES. 1811. 8°. See M***. **7854. ccc. 20. (7.)**

—— Catalogue d'une collection de jolis tableaux, bronzes . . . provenants du cabinet de M. J. B. [identified in a MS. note as J. Barbier.] Dont la vente se fera . . . 5, 6 et 7 décembre 1811, etc. pp. 15. FEW MS. NOTES AND PRICES. 1811. 8°. See B., M. J. **7854. cc. 32. (6.)**

—— Catalogue d'une riche collection de tableaux des écoles d'Italie, de France, de Flandre et de Hollande . . . Dont la vente . . . aura lieu . . . 9 décembre 1811, etc. [The collection ascribed in a MS. note to — Paillet.] pp. iv. 42. MS. NOTES AND PRICES. [Paris,] 1811. 8°. **7854. bb. 47. (6.)**

—— Feuille indicative des articles qui composeront les vacations dans la vente du 9 décembre 1811. [The collection attributed in a MS. note to — Paillet.] pp. 8. MS. NOTES AND PRICES. [Paris, 1811.] 8°. **7854. bb. 47. (7.)**

—— [Another copy.] **562. e. 27. (3.)**

—— Catalogue d'une très-jolie collection de tableaux des trois écoles . . . provenant du cabinet de M.*** [identified in a MS. note as — Irlande]; dont la vente se fera . . . les 26, 27 et 28 décembre 1811, etc. pp. 16. MS. NOTES AND PRICES. 1811. 8°. See M.***. **7854. ccc. 20. (6.)**

—— [A sale catalogue of books.] pp. xiv. 669. [Vienna, 1811.] 8°. **S.C. 234. (2.)**
Imperfect; wanting all before p. vii.

—— Catalogue de livres précieux, manuscrits et imprimés sur peau-vélin, du cabinet de M. ** [i.e. — Chardin]. pp. vi. 179. Paris, 1811. 8°. **270. d. 7.**

—— A Catalogue of Books on Angling; with some brief notices of several of their authors. [By Sir Henry Ellis.] pp. 21. T. Bensley: London, 1811. 8°. **B. 705. (4.)**

—— [Another copy.] MS. NOTES [by William White, of Crickhowell, and Joseph Haslewood]. T. Bensley: London, 1811. 8°. **11900. d. 23. (1.)**
Interleaved.

CATALOGUES.

—— The London Catalogue of Books, with their sizes and prices. Corrected to August MDCCCXI. [Compiled by William Bent.] pp. 239. W. Bent: London, 1811. 8°. **Circ. 90. a.**

—— Catalogue d'une collection précieuse de tableaux des trois écoles, composant le cabinet de M. de S.... [variously identified as — de Serréville and — de Séréville], dont la vente . . . aura lieu . . . 22 janvier 1812, etc. pp. iv. 62. MS. NOTES AND PRICES. 1811. 8°. See S...., DE, M. **7854. ccc. 19. (4.)**

—— Feuille indicative des articles qui composeront les vacations dans la vente du cabinet de M. de S. *** [identified in a MS. note as — de Serréville]. [22–24 Jan. 1812.] pp. 7. MS. NOTES AND PRICES. [1812.] 8°. See S. ***, M. de. **7855. aaa. 41. (1.)**

—— Catalogue d'une collection de tableaux des trois écoles, provenant du cabinet de M..*** [identified in a MS. note as — Irlande]; dont la vente se fera . . . les 28 et 29 janvier 1812, etc. pp. 11. MS. NOTES AND PRICES. 1812. 8°. See M..***. **7854. ccc. 19. (10.)**

—— Notice d'une collection de tableaux des écoles flamande et hollandaise, rassemblés en pays étranger, par M. P. F. Dont la vente se fera . . . les 13, 14 et 15 février 1812, etc. pp. 16. MS. PRICES. [1812.] 8°. See F., M. P. **562. e. 29. (8.)**

—— Notice d'une collection de dessins précieux de l'école ancienne et moderne, et de quelques tableaux; dont la vente se fera . . . le 5 mars 1812, etc. pp. 16. MS. NOTES AND PRICES. [Paris,] 1812. 8°. **7854. ccc. 19. (12.)**

—— Catalogue d'une collection de tableaux composant le cabinet de M. ***, peintre [identified in a MS. note as — Loué], dont la vente se fera . . . 2 novembre 1812, etc. pp. 23. FEW MS. PRICES. [Paris,] 1812. 8°. **7854. ccc. 19. (11.)**

—— Catalogue d'une collection de tableaux de diverses écoles, provenant du cabinet de M. *** [identified in a MS. note as — Barrois], dont la vente se fera . . . 5 novembre 1812, etc. pp. 15. MS. NOTES AND PRICES. [Paris,] 1812. 8°. **7854. ccc. 19. (9.)**

—— Catalogue d'une collection de tableaux des trois écoles. Dessins, estampes . . . dont la vente se fera . . . 9 novembre 1812, etc. [The catalogue compiled by J. B. P. Lebrun.] pp. 28. MS. NOTES AND PRICES. [Paris,] 1812. 18°. **7854. cc. 37. (2.)**

—— A Modern Catalogue of Books, with their sizes and prices: containing the books that have been published in London . . . from August 1811 to September 1812. [Compiled by William Bent.] pp. 24. W. Bent. London, 1812. 8°. **11900. c. 31. (4.)**

—— Catalogue d'une précieuse collection de tableaux des trois écoles . . . dont la vente se fera . . . 25 et . . . 26 janvier 1813, etc. [The collection ascribed in a MS. note to — Jamard.] pp. 32. MS. NOTES AND PRICES. Paris, 1813. 8°. **7854. cc. 32. (14.)**

—— Catalogue d'une collection variée de tableaux de diverses écoles, provenant de l'étranger, dont la vente se fera . . . 18, 19 et 20 février 1813, etc. pp. 16. MS. NOTES AND PRICES. [Paris,] 1813. 8°. **7854. cc. 35. (8.)**

—— Notice d'un cabinet, consistant en tableaux par divers bons maîtres des trois écoles, dont la vente se fera . . . 26 et . . . 27 février 1813, etc. [The collection ascribed in a MS. note to Théophile Barrois.] pp. 31. MS. PRICES. Paris, 1813. 8°. **562. e. 29. (11.)**

CATALOGUES.

—— Catalogue d'un cabinet de tableaux des trois écoles . . . dont la vente se fera . . . 11 du courant [11 April 1813], *etc.* pp. 22. MS. NOTES AND PRICES. [*Paris*,] 1813. 8°.
7854. cc. 34. (5.)

—— Vente, Hotel de Bullion, grande salle, les 25, 26 et 27 octobre 1813 . . . d'une collection de tableaux, dessins, *etc.* pp. 16. MS. NOTES AND PRICES. *Paris*, 1813. 8°.
7854. cc. 37. (3.)

—— Notice d'une jolie collection de tableaux des trois écoles, composant le cabinet d'un artiste [identified in a MS. note as — Ropiquet]. La vente s'en fera . . . 30 novembre, et 1er décembre 1813, *etc.* pp. 16. MS. NOTES AND PRICES. [*Paris*,] 1813. 8°.
7855. aaa. 41. (2.)

—— Catalogue des livres imprimés sur vélin, avec date, depuis 1457 jusqu'en 1472. [By J. B. B. Van Praet.] 2 pt. pp. 543. *Paris*, 1813. fol.
C. 70. i. 10.
One of an edition of eight copies privately printed.

—— Notice des tableaux composant le cabinet de M. * * * *, artiste. La vente s'en fera . . . 14 et . . . 15 mars 1814, *etc.* pp. 12. MS. NOTES AND PRICES. [*Paris*, 1814.] 8°.
7854. cc. 32. (16.)

—— Catalogue d'une très-jolie collection de tableaux des trois écoles, composant le cabinet d'un artiste [identified in a MS. note as J. M. Simon]. La vente . . . s'en fera les . . . 3, et . . . 4 octobre [1814], *etc.* pp. 20. MS. PRICES. *Paris*, 1814. 8°.
562. e. 31. (2.)

—— Notice de tableaux de toutes les écoles, dont la vente se fera . . . les 18, 19 et 20 octobre [1814], *etc.* pp. 16. MS. NOTES AND PRICES. *Paris*, 1814. 8°.
562. e. 31. (3.)

—— Catalogue de tableaux des trois écoles, et autres objets curieux . . . composant le cabinet de M. de S. La vente s'en fera . . . les 26 et 27 octobre [1814], *etc.* pp. 16. MS. NOTES AND PRICES. 1814. 8°. *See* S., M. de.
7854. cc. 32. (17.)

—— Notice d'un joli cabinet de tableaux, italiens, flamands et hollandais . . . dont la vente se fera . . . les 3 et 4 novembre [1814], *etc.* [The collection ascribed in a MS. note to J. A. Barbier.] pp. 15. MS. NOTES AND PRICES. *Paris*, 1814. 8°.
562. e. 31. (4.)

—— Notice de tableaux des trois écoles, composant le cabinet de M * * *. Dont la vente . . . se fera les 4 et 5 novembre [1814], *etc.* pp. 15. MS. PRICES. 1814. 8°. *See* M * * *.
562. e. 31. (5.)

—— Catalogue d'estampes anciennes et modernes . . . portefeuilles de pièces en feuilles . . . après le décès de M. D * * * [identified in a MS. note as — Dalogny]. Par F. L. Regnault-Delalande. Cette vente se fera le mardi 8 novembre [1814], *etc.* pp. 22. MS. PRICES. [1814.] 8°. *See* D * * *, M.
562. e. 31. (6.)

—— Notice d'une collection de tableaux, dont la vente aura lieu . . . 14 novembre 1814, *etc.* [The collection ascribed in a MS. note to — Celotti.] pp. 8. MS. NOTES AND PRICES. [*Paris*,] 1814. 8°.
562. e. 31. (8.)

—— Notice de jolis tableaux de toutes les écoles, dont la vente se fera . . . 15 et . . . 16 novembre [1814], *etc.* pp. 16. MS. NOTES AND PRICES. [*Paris*,] 1814. 8°.
562. e. 31. (9.)

—— Notice d'une charmante collection de tableaux, la plus grande partie provenant de l'étranger, dont la vente se fera . . . 18 et 19 novembre, 1814, *etc.* pp. 8. MS. NOTES AND PRICES. [*Paris*, 1814.] 8°.
562. e. 31. (10.)

CATALOGUES.

—— Catalogue d'une collection de tableaux de diverses écoles, gravures sous verre et en feuilles . . . provenant du cabinet d'un amateur [identified in a MS. note as — Lavoisière], dont la vente se fera . . . les 21, 22, 23 et 24 novembre 1814, *etc.* pp. 38. MS. NOTES AND PRICES. pp. 38. [*Paris*, 1814.] 8°.
562. e. 31. (11.)

—— Catalogue d'une collection de tableaux, des trois écoles Dont la vente . . . se fera . . . 5 . . . 6 et . . . 7 décembre 1814, *etc.* pp. 31. MS. NOTES AND PRICES. [*Paris*,] 1814. 8°.
562. e. 31. (12.)

—— Catalogue des tableaux, bronzes, pendules . . . composant le cabinet d'un artiste, dont la vente publique se fera . . . les 9 et 10 décembre [1814], *etc.* MS. NOTES AND PRICES. [*Paris*,] 1814. 8°.
562. e. 31. (13.)

—— Notice d'une collection variée de tableaux . . . dont la vente se fera . . . 12, 13 et 14 décembre 1814, *etc.* pp. 15. MS. NOTES AND PRICES. [*Paris*, 1814.] 8°.
562. e. 31. (14.)

—— Notice des tableaux formant le cabinet de M. * * * [identified in a MS. note as — Collin], dont la vente . . . se fera . . . le 24 décembre 1814, *etc.* pp. 7. MS. NOTES AND PRICES. [*Paris*,] 1814. 8°.
7854. cc. 31. (5.)

—— [A collection of miscellaneous sale catalogues from the years 1814–1865. With a few MS. notes by Sir George Smart.] 8 vol. [*London*, 1814–65.]
C. 61. h. 1. (1–109.)

—— The London Catalogue of Books, with their sizes and prices. MDCCXIV. [Compiled by William Bent.] pp. 259. *W. Bent: London*, [1814.] 8°.
11900. c. 31. (5.)

—— [Another copy.] L. P.
618. h. 18.

—— Notice des livres de la bibliothèque de M. C * * *., homme de lettres . . . Dont la vente se fera . . . 2 janvier 1815, *etc.* pp. 23. 1814. 8°. *See* C * * *, M., *Homme de lettres et membre de plusieurs sociétés savantes.*
S.C. 533.

—— Catalogue d'une collection de tableaux des écoles italienne, flamande, hollandaise, et française . . . dont la vente se fera . . . 16 janvier 1815, *etc.* [The collection ascribed in a MS. note to — Français.] pp. 21. MS. NOTES AND PRICES. [*Paris*, 1815.] 8°.
7806. aaa. 30.

—— Notice d'un cabinet intéressant de tableaux des trois écoles ; dont la vente s'en [*sic*] fera . . . 23 janvier 1815, *etc.* [The collection ascribed in a MS. note to — Montigneul.] pp. 12. MS. NOTES AND PRICES. [*Paris*,] 1815. 8°.
7854. cc. 34. (8.)

—— Catalogue d'une petite collection de jolis tableaux des différentes écoles, dont la vente sera faite . . . 24 et . . . 25 janvier 1815, *etc.* pp. 20. MS. PRICES. [*Paris*,] 1815. 8°.
7855. aaa. 7.

—— Notice d'une collection de tableaux anciens et modernes, de diverses écoles, dont la vente se fera . . . 27 et 28 février 1815, *etc.* pp. 8. MS. NOTES AND PRICES. [*Paris*, 1815.] 8°.
7854. cc. 34. (9.)

—— Catalogue d'une collection de tableaux, dont la vente se fera . . . le 1er mars 1815, *etc.* pp. 18. MS. NOTES AND PRICES. *Paris*, 1815. 8°.
7854. cc. 34. (7.)

—— Vente de dessins modernes, encadrés, estampes en feuilles . . . du cabinet de M. * * *, dont la vente se fera . . . 13 mars, *etc.* pp. 36. MS. NOTES AND PRICES. *Paris*, 1815. 8°.
7854. d. 30. (5.)
The date in the title has been altered in MS. to " 13 janvier 1817."

CATALOGUES.

—— Catalogue des livres rares et précieux de la bibliothèque de M * * * [i.e. D. M. Méon ?], dont la vente se fera . . . 10 avril [1815], *etc.* pp. vii. 207. 1815. 8º. *See* M * * *.
270. i. 25.

—— Catalogue des livres et collections concernant l'histoire de France . . . et à différentes époques, et plus particulièrement pendant la Révolution de 1789 à 1811 à vendre à l'amiable, en un seul lot. [August 1815.] pp. 60. *Paris*, 1815. 8º.
269. i. 3.

—— Notice des tableaux des trois écoles, dont la vente se fera . . . 7 août 1815, *etc.* pp. 8. FEW MS. NOTES AND PRICES. [*Paris*, 1815.] 8º.
7854. cc. 37. (7.)

—— Vente pour cause de départ, d'une collection de tableaux capitaux, de l'école italienne . . . La vente aura lieu les 4 et 5 septembre 1815, *etc.* pp. 8. MS. NOTES AND PRICES. [*Paris*, 1815.] 8º.
7854. cc. 37. (8.)

—— Catalogue des tableaux et pierres gravées composant le cabinet de feue Mᵐᵉ la baronne de V * * * ez ; dont la vente se fera . . . 19 et . . . 20 septembre 1815, *etc.* pp. 29. MS. NOTES AND PRICES. 1815. 8º. *See* V * * * EZ, *Mme. la baronne de.*
7854. cc. 32. (19.)

—— Catalogue d'une collection précieuse de tableaux des trois écoles, dessins et estampes . . . composant le cabinet de M. D * * * [identified in a MS. note as — Dutaillis], dont la vente aura lieu le 27 novembre 1815, *etc.* [The catalogue compiled by A. Perignon.] pp. 24. MS. NOTES AND PRICES. [1815.] 8º. *See* D * * *, M.
7806. aaa. 23.

—— Catalogue de tableaux des trois écoles, bronzes, gravures . . . dont la vente se fera . . . le 11 et 12 décembre 1815, *etc.* pp. 27. MS. NOTES AND PRICES. *Paris*, 1815. 8º.
7854. cc. 37. (6.)

—— Catalogue d'un bon choix de livres bien conditionnés du cabinet de M. De * * *, dont la vente aura lieu . . . 18 décembre [1815], *etc.* pp. 22. *Paris*, 1815. 8º.
130. k. 6. (11.)

—— Catalogo de' capi d'opera di pittura, scultura . . . trasportati dall'Italia in Francia. Seconda edizione, fatta su quella di Venezia del 1799. pp. 32. *Milano*, [1815 ?] 8º.
1422. g. 5.

—— Catalogue d'une précieuse collection de tableaux des trois écoles, dessins, beaux bronzes . . . La vente aura lieu . . . 10 et . . . 11 janvier 1816, *etc.* pp. 23. MS. NOTES AND PRICES. [*Paris*, 1816.] 8º.
562. e. 33. (2.)

—— Catalogue d'une collection de tableaux des trois écoles rassemblés . . . par M. D. B * * * [identified in a MS. note as D. Bénard]. La vente . . . s'en fera les 17 et 17 janvier [1816], *etc.* pp. ii. 28. MS. NOTES AND PRICES. 1816. 8º. *See* B * * *, M. D.
7854. cc. 32. (20.)

—— Catalogue d'une agréable collection de tableaux anciens et modernes, composant le cabinet de M. * * * . . . qui seront vendus . . . les 6 et 7 février 1816, *etc.* pp. 22. MS. NOTES AND PRICES. [*Paris*, 1816.] 8º.
562. e. 33. (8.)

—— Notice d'une collection de tableaux des écoles d'Italie et de France, composant le cabinet de M. F * * * [identified in a MS. note as — Francillon]. Le lundi 12 février 1816, *etc.* pp. 16. MS. NOTES AND PRICES. [1816.] 8º. *See* F * * *, M.
7855. aaa. 41. (3.)

—— Notice de bons tableaux, dont la vente se fera . . . 21 et . . . 22 février 1816, *etc.* pp. 7. MS. NOTES AND PRICES. [*Paris*, 1816.] 8º.
562. e. 33. (9.)

CATALOGUES.

—— Catalogue de tableaux, estampes et bronzes, composant le cabinet de M. P * * * [identified in a MS. note as — Perrin]. Dont la vente se fera les 4 et 5 mars 1816 . . . Ledit catalogue rédigé par Ch. Élie. pp. iv. 39. MS. PRICES. 1816. 8º. *See* P * * *, M.
562. e. 33. (10.)

—— Catalogue d'une collection de tableaux des trois écoles . . . le tout provenant du cabinet de M. M. * * * de N. * * *. Dont la vente aura lieu les 6, 7, 8 et 9 mars 1816, *etc.* pp. 36. MS. PRICES. [1816.] 8º. *See* N. * * *, M. M. * * * de.
562. e. 33. (11.)

—— Notice d'une collection de 33 tableau, provenant du cabinet de M. * * *, dont la vente aura lieu le 16 mars 1816, *etc.* pp. ii. 7. MS. NOTES AND PRICES. [*Paris*,] 1816. 8º.
562. e. 33. (14.)

—— Catalogue d'une collection de tableaux des trois écoles, provenant du cabinet de M. C. * * * [identified in a MS. note as — Constantin]. Par A. Pérignon . . . Dont la vente aura lieu les . . . 18 et 19 mars 1816, *etc.* pp. ii. 31. MS. PRICES. 1816. 8º. *See* C. * * *, M.
562. e. 33. (15.)

—— Notice d'une collection de tableaux des diverses écoles . . . provenant du cabinet de Mʳ * * * . . . 22 . . . 23 mars 1816, *etc.* pp. 10. MS. NOTES AND PRICES. [*Paris*, 1816.] 8º.
562. e. 33. (16.)

—— [Another copy.] MS. NOTES AND PRICES.
562. e. 33. (17.)

—— Catalogue d'une collection de jolis tableaux des peintres anciens et modernes . . . provenant du cabinet de M. * * * [identified in a MS. note as — de Livri] dont la vente . . . aura lieu le 25 mars [1816], *etc.* pp. ii. 6–23. MS. NOTES AND PRICES. 8º. *Paris,*
562. e. 33. (18.)

—— [Another copy.] MS. NOTES AND PRICES.
7854. d. 30. (11.)

—— Notice d'une collection de tableaux agréables, et la plupart modernes, dont la vente aura lieu le lundi 25 [25 March 1816], *etc.* [The collection ascribed in a MS. note to — Bonneuil.] pp. 10. MS. NOTES AND PRICES. [*Paris*, 1816.] 8º.
562. e. 33. (21.)

—— Catalogue d'une réunion de tableaux français, italiens, espagnols et flamands, dont la vente se fera les 28 et 29 mars [1816], *etc.* [The collection ascribed in a MS. note to — Quittet.] pp. 14. MS. NOTES AND PRICES. [*Paris*, 1816.] 8º.
562. e. 33. (20.)

—— Catalogue d'une réunion de tableaux français, italiens, espagnols et flamands, dont la vente se fera les 1 et 2 avril [1816], *etc.* pp. 14. MS. NOTES AND PRICES. [*Paris*, 1816.] 8º.
562. e. 34. (1.)

—— Catalogue d'une collection de tableaux, anciens et modernes, provenant du cabinet de M. P. * * * [identified in a MS. note as — Bonneuil], dont la vente se fera . . . le . . . 8 avril 1816, *etc.* pp. 8. MS. NOTES AND PRICES. [1816.] 8º. *See* P. * * *, M.
562. e. 34. (3.)

—— Notice de tableaux, estampes, dessins . . . dont la vente se fera . . . 23 et . . . 24 avril 1816, *etc.* pp. 8. MS. PRICES. [*Paris*, 1816.] 8º.
562. e. 34. (4.)

—— Catalogue de tableaux des trois écoles, composant la collection de M * * *, dont la vente . . . se fera . . . le . . . 27 mai [1816], *etc.* pp. 16. MS. NOTES AND PRICES. 1816. 8º. *See* M * * *.
562. e. 34. (6.)

CATALOGUES.

—— Notice de bons tableaux, dont la vente se fera . . . 15 juin 1816, *etc.* [The collection ascribed in a MS. note to — Barbier and — Streicker.] pp. 8. MS. NOTES AND PRICES. [*Paris*, 1816.] 8º. **562. e. 34. (9.)**

—— Catalogue de tableaux des trois écoles, statues, bustes . . . le tout provenant de l'ameublement et décoration de la maison de M. * * * [identified in a MS. note as Cardinal Fesch] . . . La vente . . . sera fait . . . le 17 de juin 1816, *etc.* pp. XII. 70. MS. NOTES AND PRICES. *Paris*, [1816.] 8º. **562. e. 34. (11.)**

—— Catalogue de tableaux, et autres objects de curiosité et d'ameublement, qui seront publiquement exposés le 1ᵉʳ septembre 1816 . . . et dont la vente aura lieu . . . 2, et . . . 3 du même mois, *etc.* pp. 16. MS. NOTES AND PRICES. [*Paris*, 1817.] 8º. **562. e. 35. (1.)**

—— Notice des tableaux provenant du cabinet d'un artiste . . . On commencera la vente . . . 16 septembre [1816], *etc.* pp. 8. MS. NOTES AND PRICES. [*Paris*,] 1816. 8º. **562. e. 35. (2.)**

—— Catalogue d'une collection de tableaux, des écoles hollandaise, flamande et française, composant le cabinet de M. * * *.. [identified in a MS. note as — Bonneuil and — Delamotte], dont la vente . . . se fera . . . 30 septembre et . . . 1ᵉʳ octobre 1816, *etc.* pp. 15. MS. NOTES AND PRICES. [*Paris*,] 1816. 8º. **7854. cc. 31. (6.)**

—— Notice de bons tableaux, dont la vente se fera . . . 7 octobre 1816, *etc.* [The collection ascribed in a MS. note to — Streicker]. pp. 4. MS. NOTES AND PRICES. [*Paris*, 1816.] 8º. **562. e. 35. (3.)**

—— Catalogue d'une collection de tableaux de différens maîtres des trois écoles, dont la vente se fera . . . 21 et . . . 22 octobre 1816, *etc.* [The collection ascribed in a MS. note to — Laville.] pp. 16. MS. NOTES AND PRICES. [*Paris*,] 1816. 8º. **562. e. 35. (5.)**

—— Notice de tableaux des trois écoles, composant le cabinet de M * * * [identified in a MS. note as — Rolland], dont la vente . . . aura lieu . . . les . . . 28 et . . . 29 octobre [1816], *etc.* pp. 15. MS. NOTES AND PRICES. 1816. 8º. *See* M * * *. **562. e. 35. (6.)**

—— Catalogue d'une jolie collection de tableaux des écoles française, flamande et hollandaise, dont la vente aura lieu . . . 4 et 5 novembre 1816, *etc.* pp. 16. MS. NOTES AND PRICES. [*Paris*,] 1816. 8º. **562. e. 35. (7.)**

—— Notice d'une collection de tableaux de différens maîtres, des écoles française, flamande et hollandaise, provenant du cabinet de M. F. [i.e. — Fossard?]; la vente . . . aura lieu . . . 9 novembre 1816, *etc.* pp. 8. 1816. 8º. *See* F., M. **7855. aaa. 41. (4.)**

—— Catalogue d'une belle collection de tableaux et dessins des écoles hollandaise, flamande, et française . . . dont la vente aura lieu . . . 11 et 12 novembre 1816, *etc.* pp. IV. 28. MS. NOTES AND PRICES. [*Paris*,] 1816. 8º. **562. e. 35. (9.)**

—— A Catalogue of Books, with their sizes and prices: containing the books that have been published . . . since the London Catalogue of Books, 1814, to September, 1816. [Compiled by William Bent.] pp. 35. *W. Bent: London*, 1816. 8º. **11900. c. 31. (6.)**

CATALOGUES.

—— A Catalogue raisonné of the Pictures now exhibiting at Pall Mall. 1816. 4º. *See* LONDON.—III. *British Institution for promoting the Fine Arts.* **7855. f. 7.**

—— Neu durchgesehenes Verzeichniss der verbothenen deutschen Bücher. pp. 350. *Wien*, 1816. 4º. **823. g. 11.**

—— Catalogue de dessins anciens et modernes; composant le cabinet de Mʳ F. D. Par Henry . . . Ces dessins seront exposés . . . les 19 . . . 20 et . . . 21 de janvier 1817 . . . ils seront vendus les . . . 22 et . . . 23 suivans, *etc.* pp. 24. MS. NOTES AND PRICES. [1817.] 8º. *See* D., F., Mʳ. **562. e. 36. (3.)**

—— Catalogue d'une collection de tableaux de différens maîtres des écoles italienne, flamande et française . . . provenant du cabinet de M. B * * *. (Par M. La Neuville.) La vente se fera les . . . 27 . . . 28 janvier 1817, *etc.* pp. 16. MS. NOTES AND PRICES. 1817. 8º. *See* B * * *, M. **562. e. 36. (5.)**

—— Catalogue d'une précieuse collection de tableaux italiens, flamands et français, la plupart formant le cabinet de M. le lieut-gén. Baron Th. [identified in a MS. note as Baron Thiébault.] Dont la vente . . . se fera les 25 & 26 février 1817, *etc.* pp. 50. MS. NOTES AND PRICES. *Paris*, 1817. 8º. **562. e. 36. (10.)**

—— Catalogue de tableaux et autres objets de curiosité, formant le cabinet de M. de C. [identified in a MS. note as M. de Franqueville Colcaute.] Dont la vente . . . se fera le . . . 3 mars [1817], *etc.* pp. 15. MS. NOTES AND PRICES. [1817.] 8º. *See* C., M. de. **562. e. 36. (12.)**

—— Notice d'une collection de jolis tableaux des trois écoles . . . terres cuites, bronzes . . . et différens autres articles de curiosité, provenant du cabinet de M. B. * * *, et après son départ, dont la vente aura lieu le . . . 3 mars 1817, *etc.* pp. II. 11. 1817. 8º. *See* B. * * *, M. **562. e. 36. (13.)**

—— Catalogue d'une collection de tableaux de différens maîtres des écoles italienne, flamande et française; statues et bustes en marbre statuaire, provenant du cabinet de M. B. * * *. La vente se fera les . . . 10 . . . 11 mars 1817, *etc.* pp. 16. MS. NOTES AND PRICES. 1817. 8º. *See* B. * * *, M. **562. e. 36. (14.)**

—— Catalogue d'une collection de tableaux, dessins et estampes, par différens maîtres, provenant du cabinet de M. . . . ., dont la vente se fera les 10 et 11 mars 1817, *etc.* pp. 16. MS. NOTES AND PRICES. [*Paris*,] 1817. 8º. **562. e. 36. (15.)**

—— Notice de tableaux des trois écoles, provenant du cabinet de Mr. E. * * * [identified in a MS. note as Charles Élie]. Dont la vente se fera les . . . 17 et . . . 18 mars 1817, *etc.* pp. 16. MS. NOTES AND PRICES. 1817. 8º. *See* E. * * *, Mr. **562. e. 36. (17.)**

—— Notice d'une collection de tableaux des trois écoles, provenant de l'atelier et cabinet d'un artiste [identified in a MS. note as — Armenaud], dont la vente se fera . . . 21 mars 1817, *etc.* MS. NOTES AND PRICES. pp. 8. [*Paris*,] 1817. 8º. **562. e. 36. (18.)**

—— Catalogue de tableaux des écoles d'Italie, de Flandres, de Hollande et de France . . . dont la vente aura lieu . . . 25 mars 1817, *etc.* pp. 31. MS. NOTES AND PRICES. [*Paris*,] 1817. 8º. **562. e. 36. (19.)**

—— Notice d'une collection de tableaux, figures, bustes . . . composant le cabinet d'un artiste [identified in a MS. note as — Vautier]; dont la vente aura lieu . . . 25 mars [1817], *etc.* pp. 8. MS. NOTES AND PRICES. [*Paris*, 1817.] 8º. **562. e. 58. (20.)**

CATALOGUES.

—— Notice d'une collection de tableaux, figures . . . et vases en marbre statuaire, et autres articles de curiosité, composant le cabinet d'un artiste [identified in a MS. note as — Wautier]; dont la vente aura lieu le . . . 25 mars [1817], *etc.* pp. 8. MS. NOTES AND PRICES. [*Paris,* 1817.] 8°.　　　　　　　　　**562. e. 36. (20.)**

—— Notice d'une collection de tableaux de différens maîtres des écoles italienne, flamande et française; provenant du cabinet de M. L*** [identified in a MS. note as — Laville]. La vente se fera les . . . 27 et . . . 28 mars 1817, *etc.* pp. 8. MS. NOTES AND PRICES. 1817. 8°. *See* L***, M.　　　　　　**562. e. 36. (21.)**

—— Notice de bons tableaux, dont la vente se fera . . . 7 avril 1817, *etc.* pp. 7. MS. NOTES AND PRICES. [*Paris,*] 1817. 8°.　　　　　　　**562. e. 37. (1.)**

—— Catalogue d'une collection précieuse . . . de tableaux des trois écoles, dessins et aquarelles . . . composant le cabinet de M. L*** [identified in a MS. note as — La Perrière] dont la vente aura lieu . . . le . . . 14 avril 1817 . . . Ledit catalogue rédigé, pour la partie des tableaux par A. Pérignon . . . et pour celle des bronzes et curiosités, par A. Coquille. pp. iii. 69. MS. NOTES AND PRICES. 1817. 8°. *See* L***, M.　　　　　**562. e. 37. (2.)**

—— Catalogue d'une collection de tableaux de différens maîtres des écoles italienne, flamande et française; de vues de Naples peints à la gouache . . . provenant de la collection de M. de R***. Dont la vente aura lieu le . . . 22 avril 1817, *etc.* (Par M. La Neuville.) pp. 24. MS. NOTES AND PRICES. 1817. 8°. *See* R***, M. de.　　　　　　　　　　　**562. e. 37. (4.)**

—— Tableaux. Le Guaspre, *etc.* [Pp. 1, 2 of a sale catalogue of pictures. A MS. note reads: " mai 1817. Inconnu."] [*Paris,* 1817?] 8°.　　**562. e. 37. (8.)**

—— Notice d'une collection de tableaux des différentes écoles . . . dont la vente aura lieu . . . 12 mai 1817, *etc.* pp. *10.* MS. NOTES AND PRICES. *Paris,* 1817. 8°. *pp. 9, 10 are misbound.*　　**562. e. 37. (9.)**

—— Notice de quarante tableaux (tous ayant fait partie et ayant orné la galerie de Monseigneur le cardinal F . . . . . . [i.e. Cardinal Fesch.]) Dont la vente se fera au comptant, le . . . 7 juillet [1817], *etc.* pp. 16. MS. NOTES AND PRICES. 1817. 8°. *See* F . . . . . ., *Monseigneur le Cardinal.*　　　　　　　　**562. e. 37. (14.)**

—— Notice des tableaux, bas reliefs, et porcelaines, dont la vente aura lieu . . . le . . . 28 juillet 1817 . . . après le départ de M. G . . . . . pp. 8. MS. NOTES AND PRICES. [1817.] 8°. *See* G . . . . ., M.　　**562. e. 37. (16.)**

—— Notice d'une collection peu nombreuse, mais d'un joli choix de tableaux des trois écoles . . . dont la vente aura lieu . . . 9 septembre [1817], *etc.* [The collection ascribed in a MS. note to — Streicker.] MS. NOTES AND PRICES. *Paris,* [1817.] 8°.　　　　　　　　　**562. e. 37. (18.)**

—— Vente d'une collection de tableaux, des trois écoles, composant le cabinet de Mr. C*** [identified in a MS. note as — Chartier], dont la vente se fera . . . 10 et . . . 11 septembre 1817, *etc.* pp. 8. MS. NOTES AND PRICES. 1817. 8°. *See* C***, *Mr.*　　**562. e. 37. (19.)**

—— Catalogue de tableaux venant de l'étranger, dont plusieurs du premier ordre. La vente de ces tableaux se fera . . . 16 septembre 1817, *etc.* pp. 12. MS. NOTES AND PRICES. [*Paris,* 1817.] 8°.　　　　　　　**562. e. 36. (16.)**

CATALOGUES.

—— Catalogue de tableaux anciens et modernes, composant le riche cabinet de M. le chevalier M., Consul de S. M. en pays étranger [identified in a MS. note as — Mimo] . . . Par Henry . . . Ces tableaux seront vendus les . . . 14 . . . 15 et . . . 16 octobre 1817, *etc.* pp. 47. MS. NOTES AND PRICES. [1817.] 8°. *See* M., *M. le Chevalier, Consul de S.M. en pays étranger.*　　　　　　　　**562. e. 37. (21.)**

—— Catalogue d'une réunion précieuse de tableaux des écoles italienne, espagnole, française et flamande. Cette vente se fera . . . 20 octobre [1817], *etc.* pp. 20. MS. NOTES AND PRICES. *Paris,* 1817. 8°.　　　　　**562. e. 37. (22.)**

—— Catalogue d'une nombreuse collection de tableaux des trois écoles, bustes et figures antiques . . . et autres curiosités, provenant du cabinet de feu M. D*** , Homme de lettres [identified in a MS. note as — Dubé] . . . dont la vente aura lieu les 27, 28, 29, 30 et 31 octobre 1817, *etc.* pp. 51. MS. NOTES AND PRICES. 1817. 8°. *See* D***, M., *Homme de Lettres.*　　　　　**562. e. 37. (23.)**

—— Catalogue d'un cabinet de tableaux des trois écoles, dessins, estampes . . . provenant d'un amateur de province; dont la vente se fera les 3, 4 et 5 novembre 1817, *etc.* [The collection ascribed in a MS. note to — Roux and — Ropiquet.] pp. 22. MS. NOTES AND PRICES. [*Paris,*] 1817. 8°.　　**562. e. 38. (1.)**

—— Notice de tableaux des trois écoles, meubles de curiosité . . . dont la vente se fera le 6 novembre 1817, *etc.* pp. 8. MS. NOTES AND PRICES. [*Paris,*] 1817. 8°.　　　　　　　**562. e. 38. (2.)**

—— Catalogue d'une collection de tableaux anciens et modernes, gouaches, aquarelles et dessins. Cette vente aura lieu . . . 7 et . . . 8 novembre [1817], *etc.* [The collection ascribed in a MS. note to — Giroult.] pp. 16. MS. NOTES AND PRICES. [*Paris,*] 1817. 8°.　　　　　　　**562. e. 38. (3.)**

—— Catalogue d'une collection de tableaux des écoles d'Italie, de Hollande et de France . . . recueils d'antiquités, etc., provenant du cabinet de M. S***, ancien Payeur-Général à Milan, et après son décès, dont la vente aura lieu les . . . 10, 11 et 12 novembre 1817, *etc.* pp. 23. MS. NOTES AND PRICES. 1817. 8°. *See* S***, M., *Ancien Payeur-Général à Milan.*　　**562. e. 38. (4.)**

—— Catalogue de tableaux hollandais et flamands, porcelaine de Sèvres et pierres gravées, provenant des voyages de M. J.-L. B . . . [identified in a MS. note as J.-L. Barbier.] (Par Ch. Paillet.) Dont la vente aura lieu les 24 et 25 novembre 1817, *etc.* pp. ii. 20. MS. NOTES AND PRICES. 1817. 8°. *See* B . . ., M. J. L.　　**562. e. 38. (7.)**

—— Catalogue de bonnes estampes, anciennes et modernes, encadrées et en feuilles, vignettes, portraits et recueils, du cabinet de M. B.*** [identified in a MS. note as — Boulle]. Par F-L. Regnault-Delalande. Cette vente se fera le . . . 27 novembre [1817], *etc.* pp. 28. MS. PRICES. 1817. 8°. *See* B.***, M.　　　　　　　　　　**562. e. 38. (8.)**

—— Catalogue d'une collection de tableaux des différentes écoles, dont la vente aura lieu . . . 4 et . . . 5 décembre 1817, *etc.* pp. 27. MS. NOTES AND PRICES. [*Paris,*] 1817. 8°.　　　　　**562. e. 38. (11.)**

—— Catalogue d'une riche collection de tableaux des différentes écoles anciennes et modernes . . . dont la vente se fera . . . 15 . . . 16 et . . . 17 décembre 1817, *etc.* pp. 38. [*Paris,*] 1817. 8°.　　**7854. cc. 32. (22.)**

CATALOGUES.

—— Catalogue de tableaux tout récemment apportés de l'étranger et qui seront vendus . . . 19 et 20 décembre 1817, *etc.* pp. 14. MS. NOTES AND PRICES. *Paris*, 1817. 8º. **562. e. 38. (18.)**
A slip bearing the date " 24 décembre " in MS. has been pasted over the original date in the title.

—— Notice d'une réunion agréable de tableaux de différens maîtres des trois écoles . . . dont la vente se fera . . . 19 et 20 décembre 1817, *etc.* [The collection ascribed in a MS. note to —Meunier.] pp. 16. MS. NOTES AND PRICES. *Paris*, 1817. 8º. **562. e. 38. (16.)**

—— Notice des tableaux, pendules et autres meubles dont la vente sera faite, après le décès de M. le marquis de L. B * * * [identified in a MS. note as the Marquis de La Baume Pluvinel] . . . les . . . 26 et 27 décembre 1817, *etc.* pp. 8. MS. NOTES AND PRICES. 1817. 8º. *See* L. B * * *, *M. le Marquis de.* **562. e. 38. (19.)**

—— [Another copy.] MS. NOTES AND PRICES.
562. e. 38. (20.)

—— Notice d'une collection peu nombreuse, mais d'un joli choix, de tableaux des trois écoles . . . dont la vente aura lieu . . . 29 et . . . 30 décembre 1817, *etc.* pp. 8. MS. NOTES AND PRICES. *Paris*, 1817. 8º.
562. e. 38. (21.)

—— Catalogue d'une collection de pièces relatives à la Revolution française, avant et depuis 1789, jusqu'à l'an XII inclusivement. pp. 31. *Paris*, 1817. 8º. **821. f. 28. (3.)**

—— Vente d'une collection de tableaux, des trois écoles . . . et autres objets de curiosité, provenans du cabinet de Mr. le Comte de * * * . . . dont la vente se fera les . . . 5 . . . 6 . . . 7 et . . . 8 janvier 1818, *etc.* pp. 18. MS. NOTES AND PRICES. *Paris*, 1818. 8º.
562. e. 39. (2.)

—— Catalogue de dessins, gouaches et aquarelles des écoles d'Italie, des Pays-Bas et de France, composant le cabinet de M. D * * * . . . Par F. Sallé . . . Cette vente aura lieu . . . le . . . 19 janvier 1818, *etc.* pp. 16. MS. NOTES AND PRICES. 1818. 8º. *See* D * * *, M.
562. e. 39. (4.)

—— Notice des curiosités idiennes, chinoises, et turques; ainsi que des tableaux . . . et autres objets d'art, composant le cabinet de M * * * [identified in a MS. note as Charles François de Riffardeau, Duke de Rivière], dont la vente se fera les 20, 21, 22 et 23 janvier 1818, *etc.* pp. 38. MS. NOTES AND PRICES. 1817. 8º. *See* M * * *.
562. e. 36. (4.)

—— [Another copy.] **562. e. 39. (5.)**

—— Catalogue d'une collection de jolis tableaux anciens et modernes, dont la vente aura lieu les 30 et 31 janvier 1818, *etc.* [The collection ascribed in a MS. note to — Bécard.] pp. 27. MS. NOTES AND PRICES. *Paris*, 1818. 8º.
562. e. 39. (7.)

—— Notice de tableaux des trois écoles, dont la vente se fera les 16 et 17 février [1818], *etc.* pp. 24. MS. NOTES AND PRICES. *Paris*, 1818. 8º. **562. e. 39. (11.)**

—— Catalogue d'une charmante collection de tableaux, la plupart modernes, dont l'exposition publique aura lieu 22 février 1818 . . . et la vente . . . 23 et . . . 24 du même mois, *etc.* pp. iv. 28. MS. NOTES AND PRICES. *Paris*, 1818. 8º. **562. e. 39. (13.)**

—— Notice d'une collection peu nombreuse de tableaux anciens et modernes . . . dont la vente aura lieu . . . 2 et . . . 3 mars 1818, *etc.* pp. 8. MS. NOTES AND PRICES. *Paris*, 1818. 8º. **562. e. 39. (16.)**

CATALOGUES.

—— Notice d'une jolie collection de tableaux, des trois écoles, et autres objets . . . composant le cabinet de M. F. B. [identified in a MS. note as F. Boudin.] Par M. Henry . . . La vente . . . se fera . . . les . . . 4 et . . . 5 mars [1818], *etc.* pp. 38. MS. NOTES AND PRICES. 1818. 8º. *See* B., F., M. **562. e. 39. (14.)**

—— Notice des curiosités chinoises et indiennes, ainsi que des peintures et dessins encadrés, provenant en grande partie du cabinet de M. l'abbé de T * * *, dont la vente se fera les 8, 9, 10 et 11 mars 1818, *etc.* pp. 31. MS. NOTES AND PRICES. 1818. 8º. *See* T * * *, *M. l'Abbé.*
562. e. 39. (18.)

—— Catalogue de tableaux, dessins et estampes encadrées, dont la vente aura lieu, après le départ de M. le comte de T * * * . . . le . . . 16 mars 1818, *etc.* pp. 8. MS. NOTES AND PRICES. [1818.] 8º. *See* T * * *, *M. le Comte de.* **562. e. 39. (20.)**

—— Notice de tableaux, miniatures, dessins, mosaïques de Florence . . . dont la vente se fera . . . 16 et . . . 17 mars 1818, *etc.* pp. 32. MS. NOTES AND PRICES. *Paris*, 1818. 8º. **562. e. 39. (21.)**

—— Catalogue d'une belle collection de tableaux, de différens maîtres des écoles flamande, française et hollandaise, provenant du cabinet de M. * * * [identified in a MS. note as — Fossard and — Bareira]. La vente . . . aura lieu le . . . 23 mars [1818], *etc.* pp. 10. MS. NOTES AND PRICES. [*Paris*,] 1818. 8º. **562. e. 39. (22.)**

—— Catalogue d'une précieuse collection de tableaux . . . bronzes . . . et différens objets de curiosités, formant la réunion des deux cabinets de M. D * * * [identified in a MS. note as — Drouillet] et de M. de B * * * [identified in a MS. note as — de Bertinval.] Rédigé par Ches Paillet . . . La vente aura lieu le . . . 24 mars 1818, *etc.* pp. 32. MS. NOTES AND PRICES. 1818. 8º. *See* D * * *, M.
562. e. 39. (23.)

—— Notice de quelques tableaux et estampes, marbre, pendules dorées, dont la vente aura lieu . . . 6 avril [1818], *etc.* pp. 8. MS. NOTES AND PRICES. pp. 8. *Paris*, 1818. 8º. **562. e. 41. (1.)**

—— Catalogue de tableaux des trois écoles, dessins, estampes . . . dont la vente s'en [*sic*] fera . . . 20 avril 1818, *etc.* pp. 22. MS. NOTES AND PRICES. [*Paris*,] 1818. 8º. **562. e. 41. (4.)**

—— Catalogue d'une collection précieuse et du plus beau choix, de tableaux des trois écoles, dont la vente se fera . . . 11 mai [1818], *etc.* pp. iv. 20. MS. NOTES AND PRICES. *Paris*, 1818. 8º. **562. e. 41. (6.)**

—— Catalogue d'une collection de jolis tableaux des écoles hollandaise, flamande et française . . . et autres objets de curiosité, qui composaient le cabinet de feu M. * * *, ancien chef au Trésor royal, dont la vente aura lieu les . . . 25 et . . . 26 mai 1818, *etc.* pp. 16. MS. NOTES AND PRICES. *Paris*, 1818. 8º. **562. e. 41. (9.)**

—— Catalogue d'une rare . . . collection de vases antiques . . . et d'objets de haute curiosité . . . le tout provenant du célèbre cabinet de M. D * * * [identified in a MS. note as — Durand]. La vente aura lieu les 25, 26 et 27 mai 1818, *etc.* pp. 23. MS. NOTES AND PRICES. 1818. 8º. *See* D * * *, M. **562. e. 41. (10.)**

—— Catalogue d'une précieuse collection de tableaux, dessins, pierres gravées . . . composant le cabinet de feu M. * * *, dont la vente, après son décès, se fera, le . . . 15 septembre 1818, *etc.* pp. 25. MS. NOTES AND PRICES. *Paris*, 1818. 8º. **562. e. 41. (14.)**

CATALOGUES.

—— Notice de bons tableaux anciens et modernes, dont la vente se fera . . . 5 et . . . 6 octobre 1818, *etc.* [The collection ascribed in a MS. note to — Streicker.] pp. 6. MS. NOTES AND PRICES. [*Paris*, 1818.] 8º.
562. e. 41. (19.)

—— Notice d'un choix de jolis tableaux hollandais, flamands, italiens et français, estampes et objets de curiosité, dont la vente aura lieu . . . 12 et . . . 13 octobre 1818, *etc.* pp. 18. MS. NOTES AND PRICES. *Paris*, 1818. 8º.
562. e. 41. (18.)

—— Catalogue d'une jolie collection de tableaux, la plupart des écoles flamande et hollandaise, appartenant à M. J. L. B * * * [identified as J. A. L. Barbier]. Dont la vente aura lieu les 19 et 20 octobre 1818, *etc.* (Par Ch^{es} Paillet.) pp. 23. 1818. 8º. *See* B * * *, M. J. L.
562. e. 41. (21.)

—— Catalogue d'une collection du plus beau choix en tableaux de toutes les écoles . . . appartenant à M. R * * *; dont la vente aura lieu . . . le . . . 20 octobre 1818, *etc.* pp. 64. MS. NOTES AND PRICES. 1818. 8º. *See* R * * *, M.
562. e. 40. (4.)

—— Catalogue des tableaux, porcelaines, pendules . . . composant le cabinet de M. B. . . . t, ancien avocat au parlement de Normandie . . . dont la vente aura lieu les . . . 23 et . . . 24 octobre 1818, *etc.* pp. 16. MS. NOTES AND PRICES. [1818.] 8º. *See* B. . . . T, M., *Ancien avocat au parlement de Normandie*.
562. e. 41. (22.)

—— Notice de tableaux de diverses écoles et bons maîtres . . . dont la vente se fera . . . 3 et . . . 4 novembre 1818, *etc.* pp. 14. MS. NOTES AND PRICES. [*Paris*,] 1818. 8º.
562. e. 40. (1.)

—— Notice de jolis tableaux de differentes écoles, gravures et dessins, dont la vente se fera les 5 et 6 novembre 1818, *etc.* [The collection ascribed in a MS. note to — Couturier.] pp. 8. MS. NOTES AND PRICES. *Paris*, 1818. 8º.
562. e. 40. (2.)

—— Notice d'un choix précieux de dessins de l'école moderne et d'estampes anciennes et autres . . . qui composaient le cabinet de M. D . . . . . [identified in a MS. note as — Devoix.] Par F.-L. Regnault-Delalande. Cette vente se fera . . . le . . . 9 novembre 1818, *etc.* pp. 16. MS. NOTES AND PRICES. 1818. 8º. *See* D . . . . ., M.
562. e. 40. (3.)

—— Notice des ouvrages de fonds et autres, provenant du magasin d'estampes de M. * * * [identified in a MS. note as — Cornuet and — Aubert], dont la vente aura lieu . . . les . . . 9 . . . 10 et . . . 11 novembre 1818, *etc.* pp. 8. MS. NOTES AND PRICES. *Paris*, 1818. 8º.
562. e. 40. (6.)

—— Catalogue d'une jolie collection de tableaux, anciens et modernes, appartenants à M. B * * *, doreur . . . dont la vente se fera . . . les . . . 16 et . . . 17 novembre 1818 . . . Par le ministère de Mm. Bonnefons de Vialle . . . Henry, *etc.* pp. 26. MS. NOTES AND PRICES. 1818. 8º. *See* B * * *, M., *Doreur.*
562. e. 40. (8.)

—— Catalogue d'une belle collection de tableaux, la plupart de maîtres hollandais et d'habiles peintres français modernes, composant le cabinet de M. R. de L * * *. Dont la vente aura lieu le 18 novembre [1818] . . . Ledit catalogue, rédigé par M. Laneuville, *etc.* pp. 32. MS. NOTES AND PRICES. 1818. 8º. *See* L * * *, M. R. de.
562. e. 40. (9.)

CATALOGUES.

—— Catalogue d'une belle collection de tableaux, dessins, gouaches . . . dont la vente aura lieu . . . 24 . . . 25 et . . . 26 novembre 1818, *etc.* [The collection ascribed in a MS. note to Giroult.] pp. 36. MS. NOTES AND PRICES. pp. 36. *Paris*, 1818. 12º.
562. e. 40. (11.)

—— Catalogue des livres très précieux, manuscrits et imprimés sur vélin, de premières éditions, etc. de M * * * [identified in a MS. note as D. M. Méon], dont la vente se fera . . . 26 novembre [1818], *etc.* pp. 16. 1818. 8º. *See* M * * *.
821. f. 28. (4.)

—— Catalogue d'une collection de jolis tableaux, des écoles flamande, hollandaise et française . . . dont la vente aura lieu . . . 7 et . . . 8 décembre 1818, *etc.* [The collection ascribed in a MS. note to — Simon and — Varoque.] pp. 16. MS. NOTES AND PRICES. *Paris*, 1818. 8º.
562. e. 40. (13.)

—— Catalogue d'une belle et nombreuse collection de tableaux, des écoles hollandaise et flamande . . . recuillie [*sic*] par Mr. J. L. M * * * [identified in a MS. note as J. L. Masson] . . . La vente . . . se fera . . . les . . . 21, 22, 23 et 24 décembre 1818 . . . Rédigé par Ch. Paillet, *etc.* pp. 35. MS. NOTES AND PRICES. 1818. 8º. *See* M * * *, J. L., M^r.
562. e. 40. (15.)

—— Notice de tableaux, gravures encadrées et en feuilles, dessins . . . dont la vente . . . se fera . . . 28 et . . . 29 décembre [1818], *etc.* [The collection ascribed in a MS. note to T. de Jolimont.] pp. 8. MS. NOTES AND PRICES. [*Paris*,] 1818. 8º.
562. e. 40. (16.)

—— A Catalogue of the Most Eminently Venerable Relics of the Roman Catholic Church . . . which are to be disposed of by auction, at the Church of Saint Peter's at Rome, the 1st of June, 1753, by order of the Pope, for the benefit of a young Gentleman of great rank . . . Reprinted from the edition of 1752, and edited by Josephus Tela. pp. 31. *J. Souter: London*, 1818. 8º.
3901. ee. 22. (2.)

Later edition 1866.

—— Choix de dessins précieux des plus habiles maîtres de différentes écoles, du cabinet de M. B . . . . . [identified in a MS. note as — Brunet], *etc.* pp. 12. 1818. 8º. *See* B . . . . ., M.
562. e. 40. (17.)

—— The Modern London Catalogue of Books, with their sizes, prices, and publishers. Containing the books published in London . . . since the year 1800 to October 1818. [Compiled by William Bent.] pp. 199. *William Bent: London*, 1818. 8º.
618. f. 23.

—— Notice d'une collection de très-beaux tableaux, dont la vente se fera . . . 14 et . . . 15 janvier 1819, *etc.* [The collection ascribed in a MS. note to — Streicker.] pp. 8. MS. NOTES AND PRICES. *Paris*, 1819. 8º.
562. e. 42. (3.)

—— Catalogue d'une jolie collection de tableaux, la plupart de l'école moderne; dont la vente se fera . . . 18 et . . . 19 janvier 1819, *etc.* pp. 32. MS. NOTES AND PRICES. *Paris*, [1819.] 8º.
562. e. 42. (4.)

—— Notice de tableaux, dessins . . . et autres objets de curiosité, dont la vente aura lieu les 1 et 2 février [1819], *etc.* [The collection ascribed in a MS. note to — Foret.] pp. 12. MS. NOTES AND PRICES. *Paris*, 1819. 8º.
562. e. 42. (7.)

—— Notice d'une collection de jolis tableaux, dont la vente se fera . . . 18 février 1819, *etc.* [The collection ascribed in a MS. note to — Goutmann and — Fontalard.] pp. 7. MS. NOTES AND PRICES. [*Paris*,] 1819. 8º.
562. e. 42. (13.)

CATALOGUES.

—— Catalogue d'une collection du meilleur choix de tableaux . . . provenant du cabinet de M. de C. Dont la vente aura lieu, le 1er. mars [1819], *etc.* pp. 18.   MS. NOTES AND PRICES. 1819. 8°. *See* C., M. de.   **562. e. 42. (23.)**

—— Catalogue d'une collection de tableaux des écoles anciennes et modernes, dont la vente se fera . . . 8 et . . . 9 mars 1819, *etc.* pp. 18.   MS. NOTES AND PRICES. [*Paris,*] 1819. 8°.   **562. e. 42. (17.)**

—— Notice d'une très belle collection . . . d'objets d'arts antiques et modernes . . . le tout provenant du château et de la galerie de la M * * * * * * * * * [i.e. the collection of the Empress Josephine at Malmaison] dont la vente . . . se fera le 15 mars 1819, *etc.* pp. 7.
MS. NOTES AND PRICES. [1819.] 8°. *See* M * * * * * * * * *.   **562. e. 42. (20.)**

—— Catalogue d'une jolie collection de bons tableaux . . . composant le cabinet de Monsieur de L * * *, dont la vente se fera les . . . 5 et . . . 6 avril [1819], *etc.* pp. 18.
MS. NOTES AND PRICES. 1819. 8°.   *See* L * * *, *Monsieur de.*   **562. e. 42. (24.)**

—— Catalogue de tableaux précieux, figure antique, fort vase en porphire . . . qui seront vendus . . . 20 avril [1819], *etc.* pp. 8.   MS. NOTES AND PRICES.   [*Paris,*] 1819. 8°.   **562. e. 42. (29.)**

—— Notice des tableaux, gouaches, gravures et curiosités, dont la vente . . . aura lieu . . . le . . . 21 avril 1819 . . . La présente notice rédigée par Mr. M., *etc.* pp. 15. MS. NOTES AND PRICES. 1819. 8°. *See* M., *Mr.*   **562. e. 42. (30.)**

—— Notice d'une collection de tableaux et de quelques objets de curiosités, composant le cabinet de M. T., et dont la vente se fera . . . le . . . 22 avril [1819], *etc.* pp. 12. MS. NOTES AND PRICES. 1819. 8°. *See* T., M.   **562. e. 42. (31.)**

—— **Notice de tableaux, dont la vente se fera** . . . 23 et . . . 24 avril 1819, *etc.* pp. 15. MS. NOTES AND PRICES. [*Paris,*] 1819. 8°.   **562. e. 42. (32.)**

—— Notice d'un choix précieux de dessins du cabinet de M. A * * * [identified in a MS. note as — Aubert]. Par F.-L. Regnault-Delalande. Cette vente se fera . . . le . . . 28 avril [1819], *etc.* pp. 11. MS. NOTES AND PRICES. 1819. 8°. *See* A * * *, M.   **562. e. 42. (35.)**

—— Catalogue d'une belle et nombreuse collection de tableaux . . . et autres objets de curiosité recueillis par Mr. J. L. M * * * [identified in a MS. note as J. L. Masson] . . . La vente de cette collection . . . se fera . . . le . . . 4 mai 1819, *etc.* pp. 32. MS. NOTES AND PRICES. 1819. 8°. *See* M * * *, J. L., *Mr.*   **562. e. 43. (1.)**

—— Catalogue d'un beau choix d'estampes . . . recueils sur la peinture, sur l'antiquité, etc., du cabinet de M. Ch. S . . . . Par F. L. Regnault-Delalande. Cette vente se fera le . . . 11 mai [1819], *etc.* pp. vii. 56. MS. NOTES AND PRICES. 1819. 8°. *See* S . . . . (Ch.)   **562. e. 43. (3.)**

—— **Catalogue d'une riche collection de tableaux, bronzes, pendules . . . dont la vente se fera** . . . 12 . . . 13 mai, 1819, *etc.* pp. 27. MS. NOTES AND PRICES. [*Paris,* 1819.] 8°.   **562. e. 43. (4.)**

—— Notice des tableaux qui seront vendus d'après le décès de M. * * * [identified in a MS. note as Madame de Souville] . . . le . . . 8 juillet 1819, *etc.* pp. 8.   MS. NOTES AND PRICES. *Paris,* 1819. 8°.   **562. e. 43. (5.)**

CATALOGUES.

—— Notice des curiosités, consistant en tableaux et miniatures . . . sculptures et bronzes . . . etc. ; le tout recueilli par M. * * * [identified in a MS. note as — Celotti.] La vente de ces objets aura lieu les 30, 31 août et 1er. septembre 1819, *etc.* pp. 36. MS. NOTES AND PRICES. [*Paris,* 1819.] 8°.   **562. e. 43. (7.)**

—— Notice de tableaux anciens et modernes, qui seront vendus . . . les . . . 4 et . . . 5 octobre [1819], *etc.* pp. 19. MS. NOTES AND PRICES. [*Paris,*] 1819. 8°.   **562. e. 43. (8*.)**

—— Notice de tableaux anciens et modernes, qui seront vendus . . . les . . . 11 et . . . 12 octobre 1819, *etc.* pp. 17. MS. NOTES AND PRICES. *Paris,* 1819. 8°.   **562. e. 43. (10.)**

—— Catalogue d'une collection de tableaux des écoles hollandaise et flamande . . . bustes et statues . . . provenant du cabinet de M * * *, dont la vente aura lieu le . . . 2 novembre 1819, *etc.* pp. 24. MS. NOTES AND PRICES. 1819. 8°. *See* M * * *.   **562. e. 43. (9.)**

—— Catalogue d'une jolie collection de tableaux de l'école hollandaise et flamande . . . La vente aura lieu . . . 13 décembre 1819, *etc.* [The collection ascribed in a MS. note to — Barbier.] pp. 27. MS. NOTES AND PRICES. [*Paris,*] 1819. 8°.   **562. e. 43. (13.)**

—— Catalogue d'une jolie réunion de tableaux des trois écoles, estampes montées et en feuilles, vitraux . . . dont la vente aura lieu . . . 24 décembre [1819], *etc.* pp. 14. MS. NOTES AND PRICES. *Paris,* [1819.] 8°.   **562. e. 43. (15.)**

—— Notice d'une précieuse collection de tableaux . . . dont l'exposition publique aura lieu . . . 25 décembre [1819] . . . et . . . 26 . . . et dont la vente . . . aura lieu . . . 27 et . . . 28, lendemain et surlendemain de l'exposition. [The collection ascribed in a MS. note to F. Didot.] pp. 38. MS. NOTES AND PRICES. [*Paris,*] 1819. 8°.   **562. e. 43. (16.)**

—— [Another copy.]   **562. e. 43. (17.)**

—— Notice d'une collection de tableaux par différens maitres des trois écoles . . . provenant du cabinet d'un étranger ; dont . . . la vente . . . se fera . . . 10 et . . . 11 janvier [1820], *etc.* pp. 20. MS. NOTES AND PRICES. *Paris,* 1820. 8°.   **562. e. 44. (1.)**

—— Vente d'une belle collection de tableaux . . . des écoles italienne, hollandaise, flamande et française, gouaches, dessins . . . formant le cabinet de M. B * * * [identified in a MS. note as — Bareirat] . . . dont la vente se fera . . . 3 et 4 février [1820], *etc.* (Par M. Laneuville.) pp. 23. MS. NOTES AND PRICES. 1820. 8°. *See* B * * *, M.   **562. e. 44. (5.)**

—— Notice de quelques tableaux, dessins . . . et autres objets de curiosité, provenant du cabinet de M. B * * *. de Montpellier, dont la vente aura lieu . . . les . . . 4 et 5 février [1820], *etc.* pp. 7. MS. NOTES AND PRICES. 1820. 8°. *See* B * * *, M., *de Montpellier.* **562. e. 44. (6.)**

—— Notice de tableaux des trois écoles . . . dont la vente aura lieu . . . 21 février 1820, *etc.* [The collection ascribed in a MS. note to — Boulade.] pp. 9 [6]. MS. NOTES AND PRICES. [*Paris,* 1820.] 8°.   **562. e. 44. (8.)**

—— Notice d'une collection de dessins et estampes . . . planches gravées . . . dont la vente aura lieu . . . 1er et 2 mars [1820], *etc.* [The collection ascribed in a MS. note to J. de Claussin.] pp. 15. MS. NOTES AND PRICES. [*Paris,* 1820.] 8°.   **562. e. 44. (13.)**

CATALOGUES.

—— Catalogue d'une collection précieuse . . . de tableaux des écoles italienne, hollandaise, flamande et française, composant le cabinet de M. d. D * * * [identified in a MS. note as C. M. P. A. d'Albert, Duke de Chevreuse], dont la vente se fera le 21 mars [1820], etc. (Par M. Laneuville.) pp. 43. MS. NOTES AND PRICES. 1820. 8º. *See* D * * *, *M. d.*   562. e. **44.** (**10.**)

—— Notice des tableaux provenant du cabinet de M. le Ch. de B . . . ., dont la vente se fera . . . les 23 et 24 mars 1820, etc. (Par Ch. Élie.) pp. 14. MS. NOTES AND PRICES. [1820.] 8º. *See* B . . . ., *M. le Ch. de.*   562. e. **44.** (**12.**)

—— Catalogue d'un cabinet de dessins précieux des trois écoles . . . La vente . . . aura lieu . . . 4 avril 1820, etc. [The collection ascribed in a MS. note to — Durand.] pp. 24. MS. NOTES AND PRICES. [*Paris,* 1820.] 8º.
562. e. **45.** (**1.**)

—— Notice de tableaux anciens et modernes, et de quelques livres concernant les arts, dont la vente aura lieu les . . . 10 et . . . 11 avril 1820, etc. [The collection ascribed in a MS. note to — Simon, — Henri and others.] pp. 20. MS. PRICES. [*Paris,*] 1820. 8º.   562. e. **45.** (**4.**)

—— Notice des tableaux et dessins composant le cabinet de M. G***, et qui serout vendus . . . le jeudi 25 mai 1820, etc. MS. NOTES AND PRICES. [1820.] 8º. *See* G***, M.
562. e. **45.** (**9.**)

—— Catalogue de tableaux des écoles d'Italie, de Hollande et de Flandre ; dont la vente, par suite de la faillite de MM. B*****. et compagnie, aura lieu . . . les . . . 29 et . . . 30 mai 1820, etc. MS. PRICES. 1820. 8º. *See* B***** ET COMPAGNIE, *MM.*   562. e. **45.** (**10.**)

—— Notice de tableaux composant le cabinet de M. le Cᵗᵉ de S*** . ; dont la vente se fera . . . les 6, 7 et 8 juin 1820, etc. [The collection ascribed in a MS. note to — Derepar, —Laville, — Durand, — Streicker and others.] 1820. 8º. *See* S***, *M. le Cᵗᵉ de.*   562. e. **45.** (**11.**)

—— Catalogue de tableaux italiens et hollandais, bronzes, mosaïque . . . La vente aura lieu . . . 27 et . . . 28 novembre 1820, etc. [The collection ascribed in a MS. note to —Barbier.] pp. 16. MS. NOTES AND PRICES. [*Paris,* 1820.] 8º.   562. e. **47.** (**2.**)

—— [A sale catalogue of books.] pp. 27. *W. Bulmer & Co.: London,* [1820?] 12º.   S.C. **234.** (**5.**)

—— Bibliotheca Americo-Septentrionalis : being a choice collection of books in various languages, relating to the history, climate . . . &c. of North America . . . Collection d'ouvrages, etc. [By D. B. Warden.] pp. 147. *Paris,* 1820. 8º.   619. d. **28.**

—— [Another copy.] MS. NOTES.   619. d. **41.**

—— A Catalogue of Books, with their sizes, prices, and publishers. Containing the books published in London . . . since the London Catalogue of Books 1818, or from October 1818 to October 1820. [Compiled by William Bent.] pp. 32. *William Bent: London,* 1820. 8º.
618. f. **24.** (**1.**)

—— A Descriptive Catalogue of a Collection of Cabinet Medallions, in oriental alabaster, supposed to be of the fourteenth century. Containing correct copies of the original sculptures on the four triumphal arches, erected in Rome, in honor of the Emperors Septimius Severus, Constantine, Titus, and Marcus Aurelius. pp. 12. *J. W. Marriott: Taunton,* [1820?] 12º.   **7755. aa. 4.**

—— [Another edition.] pp. 11.   *Marriott: Taunton,* [1820?] 8º.   **7875. a. 11.**

CATALOGUES.

—— Catalogue de dessins anciens et modernes . . . gouaches et aquarelles . . . dont la vente aura lieu . . . 22 et . . . 23 janvier 1821, etc. [The collection ascribed in a MS. note to F. Sallé.] pp. 18. MS. NOTES AND PRICES. [*Paris,*] 1821. 8º.   562. e. **48.** (**1.**)

—— Catalogue d'un choix de dix-neuf tableaux capitaux et de premier ordre . . . dont la vente aura lieu . . . 7 mai [1821], etc. [The collection ascribed in a MS. note to — Fabre.] pp. 12. MS. NOTES AND PRICES. *Paris,* 1821. 8º.   562. e. **49.** (**7.**)

—— Notice de tableaux, porcelaines, meubles de Boules et de Riesner . . . dont la vente . . . aura lieu . . . 8 mai 1821, etc. pp. 15. MS. NOTES AND PRICES. [*Paris,*] 1821. 8º.   562. e. **49.** (**8.**)

—— Notice de tableaux, anciens et modernes, de différentes écoles, qui seront vendus . . . les 4 et 5 juin 1821, etc. [The collection ascribed in a MS. note to — Muller and — Zarmante.] pp. 12. MS. NOTES AND PRICES. [*Paris,* 1821.] 8º.   562. e. **49.** (**12.**)

—— Catalogue de tableaux des différentes écoles . . . dont la vente se fera . . . 2 juillet 1821, etc. [The collections ascribed in a MS. note to — Pommier and — Dubois.] pp. 23. MS. NOTES AND PRICES. [*Paris,*] 1821. 8º.
562. e. **49.** (**14.**)

—— Notice d'une collection de bons tableaux des trois écoles, provenant du cabinet de M***, dont la vente se fera . . . les . . . 13 et 14 août 1821, etc. pp. 15. MS. PRICES. 1821. 8º. *See* M***.   562. e. **49.** (**16.**)

—— Notice de tableaux des trois écoles, dont la vente se fera le 15 octobre 1821, etc.
pp. 14. MS. NOTES AND PRICES. [*Paris,*] 1821. 8º.   562. e. **49.** (**21.**)

—— [Another edition.] Notice de tableaux des trois écoles dont la vente se fera le 15 octobre 1821, etc. pp. 15. MS. PRICES. [*Paris,*] 1821. 8º.   562. e. **49.** (**20.**)

—— Notice de tableaux des trois écoles, et richement embordurés, dont la vente aura lieu . . . 24 octobre 1821, etc.
pp. 4. MS. PRICES. *Paris,* 1821. 8º.
562. e. **50.** (**1.**)

—— Catalogue de tableaux et de dessins de différentes écoles, dont la vente se fera . . . 20 novembre 1821, etc. [The collection ascribed in a MS. note to — Gouin.] pp. 16. MS. PRICES. [*Paris,* 1821.] 8º.   562. e. **50.** (**4.**)

—— Catalogue d'une riche et agréable collection de tableaux, dont l'exposition publique aura lieu . . . 23 . . . novembre 1821 . . . et la vente . . . 26 . . . 27, et . . . 28 dudit mois, etc. pp. 60. 3. MS. NOTES AND PRICES. [*Paris,*] 1821. 8º.   562. e. **50.** (**8.**)

—— Catalogue d'une collection de tableaux de différentes écoles . . . dont l'exposition publique aura lieu . . . 9 décembre 1821 . . . et la vente . . . 10 dudit mois, etc. pp. 32. MS. NOTES AND PRICES. *Paris,* 1821. 8º.
562. e. **50.** (**11.**)

—— Catalogue de pierres gravées antiques et modernes, meubles de Boule, porcelaines . . . composant la collection de feu M***. Cette vente se fera le 10 décembre 1821, et jour suivant, etc. pp. 19. MS. PRICES. [1821.] 8º. *See* M***.   562. e. **50.** (**12.**)

CATALOGUES.

—— Catalogue de tableaux des trois écoles, tapisseries et porcelaines ; dont partie est dépendant de la succession de feu M. Julian . . . La vente aura lieu les . . . 12 et . . . 13 décembre 1821, *etc.* [The remainder of the collection ascribed in a MS. note to —Leblanc.] pp. 12. MS. PRICES. *Paris*, 1821. 8°.   **562. e. 50. (13.)**

—— Catalogo dei più celebri intagliatori in legno ed in rame, e capiscuola di diverse età e nazioni. Con alcune notizie sull'arte e sui metodi dell'intagliare, *etc.* pp. 63. pl. x. *Milano*, 1821. 8°.   **7855. f. 33. (1.)**

—— Catalogue d'une nombreuse et intéressante collection de tableaux . . . recueillis . . . par M. le comte de L. F. [i.e. Count de La Forest ?] dont l'exposition publique aura lieu les 4, 5 et 6 de janvier 1822 . . . et la vente . . . le lundi 7 du même mois, et jours suivants, *etc.* pp. 59. MS. PRICES. 1821. 8°. *See* L. F., *M. le Comte de.*   **562. e. 51. (1.)**

—— Notice de tableaux des trois écoles, armes, groupe en biscuit, et autres objets composant le cabinet de feu M. le lieutenant-général comte de S*** [i.e. Count de Sugny], dont la vente aura lieu . . . le samedi 26 janvier 1822, *etc.* 1822. 8°. *See* S***, *M. le Lieutenant-Général Comte de.*   **562. e. 51. (3.)**

—— Catalogue de tableaux italiens, flamands et hollandais, dont la vente aura lieu . . . 28 et . . . 29 janvier 1822, *etc.* pp. 16. MS. NOTES AND PRICES. *Paris*, 1822. 8°.   **562. e. 51. (4.)**

—— Notice d'une collection de tableaux des diverses écoles, dont la vente, par suite de la liquidation de M*** [identified in a MS. note as — Blanc], se fera . . . les . . . 25, et . . . 26 février 1822, *etc.* pp. 7. MS. PRICES. *Paris*, 1822. 8°.   **562. e. 51. (8.)**

—— Catalogue de tableaux anciens et modernes . . . dessins, gouaches et curiosités ; dont la vente se fera . . . 25 mars 1822, *etc.* pp. 23. MS. NOTES AND PRICES. *Paris*, 1822. 8°.   **562. e. 51. (12.)**

—— Catalogue des dessins, croquis, gouaches, gravures et tableaux . . . provenant du cabinet de M. le chevalier A***. La vente aura lieu les . . . 1er et . . . 2 avril 1822, *etc.* 1822. 8°. *See* A***, *M. le Chevalier.*   **562. e. 51. (15.)**

—— Notice sommaire de tableaux anciens et modernes, dont la vente, après le décès de M***, aura lieu le mercredi 24 avril 1822, *etc.* pp. 7. MS. PRICES. 1822. 8°. *See* M***.   **562. e. 51. (19.)**

—— Catalogue de tableaux hollandais, flamands et français, provenant du cabinet de M.*** [identified in a MS. note as — Delormery], dont la vente aura lieu le 25 avril 1822, *etc.* pp. 8. MS. PRICES. *Paris*, 1822. 8°.   **562. e. 51. (20.)**

—— Notice abrégée de quelques tableaux et dessins des maîtres anciens et modernes . . . dont partie ayant anciennement garni le château du feu duc de Pinthièvre . . . Cette vente aura lieu les . . . [28] et . . . 29 avril [1822], *etc.* pp. 11. MS. NOTES. [*Paris*,] 1822. 8°.   **562. e. 51. (21.)**

—— Catalogue des sculptures . . . tableaux . . . dessins . . . qui composent la collection de M. le comte de P***. La vente . . . se fera . . . les 6 et 7 mai [1822], *etc.* [The collection ascribed in a MS. note to the Count de Plainval. Also attributed to the Count de Pourtalès, i.e. Count J. A. de Pourtalès-Gorgier ?] 1822. 8°. *See* P***, *M. le Comte de.*   **562. e. 51. (22.)**

CATALOGUES.

—— Notice d'une jolie collection de tableaux anciens et modernes, formant le cabinet de M***, dont la vente aura lieu le mardi 21 mai [1822], *etc.* pp. 10. MS. PRICES. [1822.] 8°. *See* M***   **562. e. 51. (23.)**

—— Notice d'une petite collection de tableaux des trois écoles, estampes montées, etc., provenant du cabinet de M.*** . . . dont la vente se fera . . . les . . . 24 et . . . 25 juillet 1822, *etc.* pp. 8. MS. PRICES. *Paris*, 1822. 8°.   **562. e. 51. (29.)**

—— Catalogue de tableaux et croquis, dont la vente aura lieu après le décès d'un peintre [identified in a MS. note as J. Truchot] . . . 28 octobre 1822, *etc.* pp. 7. MS. NOTES AND PRICES. *Paris*, 1822. 8°.   **562. e. 52. (4.)**

—— Catalogue de tableaux anciens et modernes, estampes, gouaches, aquarelles et dessins d'album, dont partie provient du cabinet de M. G*** formé en 1795. La vente se fera les . . . 28 . . . et . . . 29 octobre 1822, *etc.* [The collection ascribed in a MS. note to — Gervais, marchand de chevaux, and to — Guévillers, amateur.] pp. 18. MS. NOTES AND PRICES. *Paris*, 1822. 8°.   **562. e. 52. (5.)**

—— Catalogue d'une collection de tableaux des écoles flamande et hollandaise, et de l'école française ancienne et moderne ; dont 23 tableaux de M. Demarne font partie. Cette vente aura lieu le lundi 4 novembre 1822, *etc.* pp. 25. MS. PRICES. *Paris*, 1822. 8°.   **562. e. 52. (7.)**

—— Catalogue d'un bon choix d'estampes . . . par les plus célèbres graveurs modernes . . . dont la plus grande partie proviennent du cabinet et des planches de fonds de MM. Volpato et Morghen. Dont la vente se fera le mercredi 6 novembre 1822 et jours suivans, *etc.* pp. 24. MS. PRICES. *Paris*, 1822. 8°.   **562. e. 52. (8.)**

—— Catalogue de tableaux des trois écoles, dessins, estampes . . . dont la vente aura lieu . . . 11 et . . . 12 novembre, 1822, *etc.* [The collection ascribed in a MS. note to — Sallé, — Montigneul and — Simon.] pp. 24. MS. NOTES AND PRICES. [*Paris*,] 1822. 8°.   **562. e. 52. (9.)**

—— Notice de tableaux des trois écoles, dessins et estampes . . . dont la vente aura lieu . . . 13 novembre [1822], *etc.* [The collection ascribed in a MS. note to — Terray, — Rond and others.] pp. 15. MS. NOTES AND PRICES. [*Paris*, 1822.] 8°.   **562. e. 52. (10.)**

—— Catalogue d'une agréable collection de tableaux anciens et modernes, dont l'exposition publique aura lieu . . . 17 novembre 1822 . . . et la vente . . . 18 et . . . 19, *etc.* pp. 28. MS. NOTES AND PRICES. [*Paris*, 1822.] 8°.   **562. e. 52. (11.)**

—— Catalogue d'une collection de bons tableaux des trois écoles . . . aquarelles, miniatures et pastels, provenant du cabinet d'un amateur étranger . . . dont la vente se fera . . . 21 et . . . 22 novembre 1822, *etc.* pp. 20. MS. NOTES AND PRICES. *Paris*, 1822. 8°.   **562. e. 52. (13.)**

—— Catalogue d'une riche collection de tableaux . . . suivi d'une notice d'objets curieux . . . Tous ces objets seront vendus . . . 27 . . . 28 . . . 29 novembre 1822, *etc.* [The collection ascribed in a MS. note to — Lafontaine.] pp. 25. MS. NOTES AND PRICES. [*Paris*, 1822.] 8°.   **562. e. 52. (16.)**

—— Catalogue d'une nombreuse collection de tableaux italiens, dont l'exposition publique aura lieu . . . 22 décembre [1822] . . . et la vente . . . 23 . . . 24 et jours suivants, *etc.* pp. 18. MS. NOTES AND PRICES. [*Paris*,] 1822. 8°.   **562. e. 52. (19.)**

CATALOGUES.

—— The London Catalogue of Books, with their sizes, prices, and publishers. Containing the books published in London . . . since the year 1800 to October 1822. [Compiled by William Bent.] pp. 239. *William Bent : London,* 1822. 8º. **618. f. 24. (2.)**

—— Catalogue d'une collection de tableaux des diverses écoles, dont la vente . . . se fera le lundi 20 janvier 1823, *etc.* pp. 12. MS. PRICES. *Paris,* 1823. 8º. **562. e. 53. (1.)**

—— Catalogue d'une collection intéressante de bons tableaux de plusieurs écoles . . . provenant du cabinet de M. le comte de *** [identified in a MS. note as Count de Montesquiou], dont la vente se fera . . . le lundi 3 février 1823, et jours suivans, *etc.* pp. 21. MS. PRICES. *Paris,* 1823. 8º. **562. e. 53. (2.)**

—— Catalogue d'une collection choisie de tableaux de diverses écoles . . . provenant du cabinet d'un amateur étranger, dont la vente se fera . . . 14 février [1823], *etc.* pp. 23. MS. NOTES AND PRICES. *Paris,* 1823. 8º. **562. e. 53. (3.)**

—— Catalogue de tableaux anciens et modernes, de différentes écoles, italiens, flamands et français, gouaches, dessins et curiosités ; dont la vente se fera . . . le lundi soir 17 février [1823] et jours suivants, *etc.* pp. 20. MS. NOTES AND PRICES. [*Paris,*] 1823. 8º. **562. e. 53. (4.)**

—— Notice d'une jolie collection de tableaux anciens et modernes, des trois écoles . . . un meuble très riche . . . vendus à l'enchère . . . 3 mars 1823, *etc.* pp. 15. MS. NOTES AND PRICES. *Paris,* 1823. 8º. **562. e. 53.**

—— Catalogue d'une belle collection d'un nombre considérable de bons tableaux . . . dont la vente se fera . . . 4 mars 1823, *etc.* pp. 48. *Paris,* 1823. 8º. **562. e. 53. (9.)**

—— Catalogue d'une belle collection d'un nombre considérable de bons tableaux des écoles italienne, expagnole, flamande, française et allemande . . . dont la vente se fera . . . 4 mars 1823, *etc.* pp. 51. MS. NOTES AND PRICES. pp. 51. *Paris,* 1823. 8º. **562. e. 53. (8.)**

—— Catalogue d'une collection choisie d'agréables tableaux . . . dont la vente se fera le lundi 10 mars [1823] et jours suivans, *etc.* [The collection ascribed in a MS. note to — Delanjeac, i.e. Égide L. E. J. de l'Espinasse de Langeac ?] pp. 20. MS. PRICES. *Paris,* 1823. 8º. **562. e. 53. (11.)**

—— Notice de tableaux, gouaches et dessins, dont la vente se fera les 13 et 14 mars [1823], *etc.* pp. 32. MS. NOTES AND PRICES. *Paris,* 1823. 8º. **562. e. 24. (7.)**

—— Notice de tableaux, gouaches et dessins, dont la vente se fera les 13 et 14 mars [1823], *etc.* pp. 32. MS. PRICES. *Paris,* 1823. 8º. **562. e. 53. (13.)**

—— Catalogue de tableaux et de dessins de différentes écoles, d'estampes et planches gravées, dont la vente se fera 17 mars 1823, *etc.* pp. 11. MS. NOTES AND PRICES. [*Paris,* 1823.] 8º. **562. e. 53. (14.)**

—— Notice d'une jolie collection de tableaux anciens et modernes, des trois écoles, dont plusieurs non vendus du catalogue de la vente Saint-Victor . . . et vendus . . . le lundi 23 mars 1823, *etc.* pp. 15. MS. PRICES. *Paris,* 1823. 8º. **562. e. 53. (7.)**
The date in the title has been altered in MS. to 3 March 1823.

CATALOGUES.

—— Catalogue de tableaux anciens et modernes, objets d'art et curiosités . . . dont la vente se fera le 31 mars et 1er avril 1823, *etc.* pp. 20. MS. NOTES AND PRICES. [*Paris,* 1823.] 8º. **562. e. 53. (18.)**

—— Notice des antiquités égyptiennes, grecques et romaines . . . qui seront vendus . . . 31 mars, et 1 avril 1823, *etc.* pp. 15. MS. NOTES AND PRICES. *Paris,* 1823. 8º. **562. e. 53. (19.)**

—— Catalogue d'une jolie collection de tableaux . . . dessins et curiosités, dont la vente se fera . . . 21 avril 1823, *etc.* pp. 23. MS. NOTES AND PRICES. [*Paris,*] 1823. 8º. **562. e. 53. (23.)**

—— Notice de bons tableaux de diverses écoles . . . provenant de la belle collection de M.*** de Reims ; dont la vente se fera . . . le . . . 28 avril [1823], le . . . 29, et jours suivans, *etc.* pp. 24. MS. PRICES. *Paris,* 1823. 8º. **562. e. 53. (22.)**

—— Catalogue de tableaux de l'école française moderne, dessins et gravures . . . composant le cabinet de M. A. L . . . . . . [identified in a MS. note as A. Lapeyrière], dont la vente se fera la jeudi 9 octobre 1823, et jours suivans, *etc.* 1823. 8º. *See* L . . . . . ., M. A. **562. e. 54. (4.)**

—— Catalogue d'une jolie collection de tableaux italiens, flamands, hollandais et français, dont l'exposition publique aura lieu dimanche 2 novembre 1823 . . . et la vente . . . le lundi, 3, et jours suivants, *etc.* pp. 23. MS. PRICES. *Paris,* 1823. 8º. **562. e. 54. (7.)**

—— Catalogue d'une riche et nombreuse collection de tableaux . . . provenant du cabinet de M.*** [identified in a MS. note as — de Langeac, i.e. Égide L. E. J. de l'Espinasse de Langeac ?] ; dont la vente se fera les . . . 10, 11 et 12 novembre [1823], *etc.* pp. 44. MS. PRICES. [*Paris,*] 1823. 8º. **562. e. 54. (8.)**

—— Notice de tableaux, dessins, et autres objets de curiosités, dont la vente . . . aura lieu les . . . 17 et . . . 18 novembre 1823, *etc.* pp. 14. MS. PRICES. *Paris,* 1823. 8º. **562. e. 54. (11.)**

—— Notice d'une jolie collection de tableaux peints par de bons maîtres, de diverses écoles, dont la vente se fera . . . 24 novembre 1823, *etc.* [The collection ascribed in a MS. note to — Lébe.] pp. 16. MS. NOTES AND PRICES. *Paris,* 1823. 8º. **562. e. 54. (10.)**

—— Catalogue de tableaux, anciens et modernes, des trois écoles . . . dont la vente aura lieu, le jeudi 27 novembre 1823, et jours suivants, *etc.* pp. 35. MS. PRICES. *Paris,* 1823. 8º. **562. e. 54. (12.)**

—— Catalogue de tableaux et de dessins de différentes écoles, dont la vente se fera . . . 1er . . . 2 . . . 3 décembre 1823, *etc.* [The collection ascribed in a MS. note to — Gouin.] pp. 15. MS. NOTES AND PRICES. [*Paris,* 1823.] 8º. **562. e. 54. (14.)**

—— Notice de tableaux, anciens et modernes, dessins, gouaches, miniatures . . . dont une partie provient du cabinet de M. de l'H. de l'Hille . . . La vente aura lieu, le lundi 8 décembre 1823, *etc.* [The remainder of the collection ascribed in a MS. note to — Gérard.] pp. 15. MS. PRICES. *Paris,* 1823. 8º. **562. e. 54. (15.)**

—— Notice de tableaux, bronzes, émaux de Limoges . . dont la vente se fera . . . 18 . . . 19 et . . . 20 décembre [1823], *etc.* pp. 8. MS. NOTES AND PRICES. *Paris,* 1823. 8º. **562. e. 54. (17.)**

CATALOGUES.

—— Catalogue d'une collection de tableaux de choix . . . formant le cabinet de M. C**. B*** [identified in a MS. note as C. Beaufort], dont la vente se fera . . . le . . . 19 et le . . . 20 décembre 1823, etc. [A part of the collection ascribed in a MS. note to — Desaint.] 1823. 8º. *See* B***, C**, M. **562. e. 54. (17*.)**

—— Catalogue de tableaux des trois écoles, composant le cabinet d'un amateur d'une des principales villes de France; dont la vente aura lieu . . . 22 et . . . 23 décembre 1823, etc. pp. 40. MS. PRICES. [Paris,] 1823. 8º. **562. e. 54. (18.)**

—— Catalogue de la bibliothèque d'un amateur, avec des notes, etc. [The compiler's preface signed: L. F. A. G.] 1823. 8º. *See* G., L. F. A. **619. g. 40.**

—— Notice d'une jolie collection de tableaux des diverses écoles . . . de miniatures . . . et de dessins . . . dont la vente se fera . . . 23 janvier [1824], etc. [The collection ascribed in a MS. note to — Blancheton, Mad, Laforest and others.] pp. 15. MS. NOTES AND PRICES. Paris, 1824. 8º. **562. e. 55. (5.)**

—— Catalogue de tableaux précieux . . . bronzes, terres cuites . . . qui seront vendus . . . 26 janvier 1824, etc. pp. 14. MS. NOTES AND PRICES. Paris, 1824. 8º. **562. e. 55. (7.)**

—— Catalogue d'une jolie collection de tableaux, des trois écoles, dessins et curiosités, dont la vente se fera . . . le 2 février 1824, etc. pp. 22. MS. NOTES AND PRICES. Paris, 1824. 8º. **562. e. 55. (8.)**

—— Notice de tableaux, dessins, aquarelles et estampes, provenant du cabinet de M***, dont la vente aura lieu les . . . 5 et . . . 6 février 1824, etc. [The collection ascribed in a MS. note to — Chazal and others.] pp. 12. MS. PRICES. 1824. 8º. *See* M***. **562. e. 55. (10.)**

—— Catalogue d'une riche et nombreuse collection de tableaux . . . provenant du cabinet de M.*** [identified in a MS. note as — de Lanjeac, i.e. Égide L. E. J. de l'Espinasse de Langeac ?] dont la vente se fera les . . . 16 et . . . 17 février [1824], etc. pp. 42. MS. PRICES. Paris, 1824. 8º. **562. e. 55. (13.)**

—— Catalogue de jolis tableaux modernes, gouaches, dessins et croquis composant le cabinet de M***, dont la vente aura lieu les . . . 17 et . . . 18 février 1824, etc. pp. 12. MS. PRICES. 1824. 8º. *See* M***. **562. e. 55. (14.)**

—— Notice de tableaux . . . curiosités, gravures et dessins. Dont l'exposition aura lieu le 18 février 1824 . . . et la vente le même jour, etc. pp. 16. MS. NOTES AND PRICES. Paris, 1824. 8º. **562. e. 55. (14.)**

—— Notice de statues, bustes, bas-reliefs, bronzes . . . le tout provenant de la décoration de la maison de M.*** . . . et devant être vendu . . . le 15 mars 1824, et jours suivans, etc. [The collection ascribed in a MS. note to — Feschs, i.e. Cardinal Fesch.] pp. 31. MS. PRICES. Paris, [1824.] 8º. **562. e. 55. (18.)**

—— Catalogue d'une jolie collection de tableaux, des trois écoles, dessins et estampes, dont la vente se fera . . . le 29 mars 1824, etc. pp. 16. MS. NOTES AND PRICES. Paris, 1824. 8º. **562. e. 56. (5.)**

—— Catalogue des livres imprimés et manuscrits . . . composant la bibliothèque de M. B. D. G. Dont la vente se fera . . . 29 mars 1824, etc. pp. 212. 1824. 12º. *See* G., M. B. D. **S.C. 548.**

CATALOGUES.

—— Catalogue d'une nombreuse et intéressante collection composée de tableaux des grands maîtres . . . provenant du cabinet d'un amateur étranger; dont la vente se fera . . . 17 mai [1824], etc. pp. 28. MS. NOTES AND PRICES. [Paris,] 1824. 8º. **562. e. 56. (9.)**

—— Catalogue d'une jolie collection composée en grande partie de tableaux des artistes modernes . . . provenant du cabinet de M. le chevalier de D***. Dont la vente se fera . . . le lundi 24 mai 1824 et jours suivans, etc. 1824. 8º. *See* D***, M. le Chevalier de. **562. e. 56. (10.)**

—— Catalogue d'une très-jolie collection de tableaux . . . des trois écoles; dessins et estampes précieuses, dont la vente se fera . . . 9 juin 1824, etc. pp. 16. MS. NOTES AND PRICES. [Paris,] 1824. 8º. **562. e. 56. (13.)**

—— Notice d'une collection peu nombreuse de tableaux modernes . . . La plupart de ces objets d'arts proviennent du cabinet de Madame la princesse O . . ., . . . dont la vente se fera le lundi 21 juin [1824], etc. pp. 10. MS. NOTES AND PRICES. Paris, 1824. 8º. **562. e. 56. (16.)**

—— Notice de tableaux et estampes, provenant du cabinet de M. G*** [identified in a MS. note as — Gosse], dont la vente aura lieu . . . le lundi . . . 28 juin 1824, etc. 1824. 8º. *See* G***, M. **562. e. 56. (17.)**

—— Notice de tableaux anciens et modernes, dessins, gouaches . . . dont la vente aura lieu . . . 11 octobre 1824, etc. [The collection ascribed in a MS. note to — Gérard and others.] pp. 13. MS. NOTES AND PRICES. [Paris,] 1824. 8º. **562. e. 57. (1.)**

—— Catalogue d'une collection intéressante de tableaux des trois écoles . . . dont la vente se fera . . . les 25 et 26 octobre 1824, etc. pp. 19. MS. NOTES AND PRICES. [Paris,] 1824. 8º. **562. e. 57. (2.)**

—— Catalogue d'une collection du meilleur choix de tableaux des diverses écoles . . . et . . . de l'école française moderne, parmi lesquels sont des tableaux de M. Laurent, M Demarne . . . dont la vente se fera . . . les 3 et . . . 4 novembre 1824, etc. pp. 16. MS. PRICES. [Paris,] 1824. 8º. **562. e. 57. (4.)**

—— Catalogue abrégé de tableaux des diverses écoles, dessins, bronzes et autres objets de curiosité; qui seront exposés le dimanche 7 novembre 1824 . . . et vendus . . . les . . . 8 et . . . 9 dudit mois, etc. pp. 16. MS. PRICES. [Paris,] 1824. 8º. **562. e. 57. (5.)**

—— Catalogue de tableaux anciens et modernes, provenant du cabinet de Mr T. de B., dont la vente aura lieu les 19 et 20 novembre [1824], etc. 1824. 8º. *See* B., T. de, Mr. **562. e. 57. (8.)**

—— Notice d'une jolie collection de tableaux des trois écoles . . . dont la vente . . . aura lieu . . . 23 décembre 1824, etc. pp. 15. MS. NOTES AND PRICES. [Paris, 1824.] 8º. **562. e. 57. (14.)**

—— A Catalogue of Books, with their sizes, prices, and publishers. Containing the works published in London . . . since the London Catalogue of 1822, or from October 1822 to October 1824. [Compiled by Robert Bent.] pp. 44. *Hurst, Robinson & Co.: London*, 1824. 8º. **618. f. 25.**

—— A Descriptive Catalogue of a Collection of Pictures, comprehending specimens of all the various schools of painting: belonging to [Sir Abraham Hume, Bart.] pp. vii. 47. *W. Nicol: London*, 1824. 4º. **7855. i. 4.** *Presentation copy from the 3rd Earl Brownlow to Sir Guy Sebright, Bart., with a binding inscribed: "1876. Catalogue of Pictures, Ashridge."*

CATALOGUES.

—— Catalogue de bons tableaux anciens et modernes, dessins et estampes . . . composant la collection de M. le baron de S*****, dont la vente, après son décès, aura lieu . . . les 14 et 15 janvier 1825, *etc.* 1825. 8°. *See* S*****, *M. le Baron de.* **562. e. 58. (1.)**

—— Catalogue de tableaux et dessins . . . dont la vente aura lieu les lundi 17 janvier 1825, et jours suivants, *etc.* [The collection ascribed in a MS. note to —— Denaples, —— Dusommerat, i.e. Alexandre Du Sommerard?, —— Coutant and others.] pp. 23. MS. PRICES. [*Paris*,] 1825. 8°. **562. e. 58. (2.)**

—— Catalogue d'une collection d'antiquités grecques et romaines, tableaux . . . qui seront vendus . . . 31 janvier [1825], *etc.* [The collection ascribed in a MS. note to —— Dufourni and others.] pp. 12. MS. NOTES AND PRICES. *Paris*, 1825. 8°. **562. e. 58. (4.)**

—— Catalogue d'une collection intéressante de tableaux des trois écoles . . . dont la vente se fera . . . les 21 et 22 février 1825, *etc.* pp. 15. MS. NOTES AND PRICES. [*Paris*,] 1825. 8°. **562. e. 58. (7.)**

—— Catalogue d'une magnifique collection de tableaux de premier ordre . . . accompagnés d'un choix . . . de manuscrits et de livres imprimés sur vélin : dont la vente se fera . . . 28 février 1825, *etc.* [The collection ascribed in a MS. note to the Count de Woronzoff, —— Zenard and —— Lerouge.] pp. 42. MS. PRICES. *Paris*, [1825.] 8°. **562. e. 58. (10.)**

—— [Another copy.] **7854. cc. 38. (2.)**

—— Catalogue des antiquités, tableaux, bronzes . . . qui seront vendus . . . le 28 février [1825], *etc.* pp. 20. *Paris*, 1825. 8°. **562. e. 58. (11.)**

—— Notice de tableaux et estampes, dont la vente aura lieu après le décès de Mme Des C*** . . . les . . . 2 et . . . 3 mars 1825, *etc.* 1825. 8°. *See* DES C***, *Mme.* **562. e. 58. (12.)**

—— Catalogue d'un choix précieux de manuscrits et de livres . . . dont la vente se fera le jeudi 3 mars 1825 et jours suivants, *etc.* [The collection ascribed in a MS. note to Prince Woronzoff and others.] pp. ii. 60. MS. PRICES. *Paris*, 1825. 8°. **562. e. 58. (12*.)**

—— Catalogue de tableaux, dessins, estampes . . . dont la vente se fera . . . 7 . . . 8 . . . 9 Mars 1825, *etc.* [The collection ascribed in a MS. note to —— Gouyn.] pp. 15. MS. NOTES AND PRICES. [*Paris*, 1825.] 8°. **562. e. 58. (13.)**

—— Catalogue d'un cabinet de tableaux, des écoles anciennes et modernes . . . dont la vente se fera . . . 28 . . . 29 [March 1825], *etc.* [The collection ascribed in a MS. note to —— Roux.] pp. 34. MS. NOTES AND PRICES. *Paris*, 1825. 8°. **562. e. 58. (18.)**

—— Notice de tableaux et dessins, la plupart de l'école française moderne, dont la vente aura lieu . . . 25 avril 1825, *etc.* pp. 11. MS. NOTES AND PRICES. [*Paris*,] 1825. 8°. **562. e. 59. (9.)**

—— Catalogue d'une nombreuse et intéressante collection de tableaux . . . recueillis en pays étrangers, dont la vente aura lieu . . . 27 juin 1825, *etc.* [The collection ascribed in a MS. note to —— Laneuville.] pp. 26. MS. NOTES AND PRICES. *Paris*, 1825. 8°. **562. e. 60. (4.)**

CATALOGUES.

—— Second Day's Sale, Wednesday, August 21, *etc.* [An auction catalogue of prints, water colour drawings and paintings.] pp. 4. [1825?] 8°. **11900. bb. 42. (7.)**

—— Notice de tableaux . . . gouaches, aquarelles . . . dont la vente aura lieu . . . 14 et . . . 15 novembre [1825], *etc.* pp. 12. MS. NOTES AND PRICES. **562. e. 50. (10.)**

—— Notice d'une collection de jolis tableaux et dessins modernes de l'école française, dont la vente aura lieu . . . 17 novembre [1825], *etc.* pp. 13. MS. NOTES AND PRICES. *Paris*, 1825. 8°. **562. e. 60. (11.)**

—— Catalogue d'une collection intéressante de tableaux des trois écoles . . . dont la vente aura lieu le 18 et 19 novembre 1825, *etc.* [The collection ascribed in a MS. note to —— Simon.] pp. 14. MS. NOTES AND PRICES. [*Paris*,] 1825. 8°. **562. e. 60. (15.)** *The date in the title has been altered in MS. to 28 and 29 Nov. 1825.*

—— Notice de tableaux anciens et modernes des trois écoles ; de dessins anciens . . . de quelques estampes et objets de curiosité ; dont la vente . . . aura lieu . . . 24 et . . . 25 novembre, [1825], *etc.* pp. 8. MS. NOTES AND PRICES. [*Paris*,] 1825. 8°. **562. e. 60. (14.)**

—— Notice des sculptures, pierres gravées, antiques et modernes . . . tableaux et dessins, qui seront vendus . . . les 30 novembre et 1er décembre 1825, *etc.* [The collection ascribed in a MS. note to —— Dubois.] pp. 10. MS. NOTES AND PRICES. [*Paris*,] 1825. 8°. **562. e. 60. (16.)**

—— Catalogue d'une magnifique collection de tableaux des plus grands maîtres . . . dont la vente se fera . . . 6 décembre 1825, *etc.* pp. 33. MS. NOTES AND PRICES. [*Paris*,] 1825. 8°. **562. e. 61. (20.)** *The date in the title has been altered in MS. to 29 Mar. 1826. Another issue with a titlepage bearing the date " 29 mars 1826 " is entered below.*

—— Notice d'une vente de tableaux des diverses écoles . . . dont la vente se fera . . . 12 et . . . 13 décembre 1825, *etc.* [The collection ascribed in a MS. note to —— Forget.] pp. 13. MS. NOTES AND PRICES. [*Paris*,] 1825. 8°. **562. e. 60. (20.)**

—— Catalogue d'une très-jolie collection de tableaux . . . gouaches, aquarelles et gravures, dont la vente se fera . . . les . . . 26 . . . 27, et . . . 28 décembre, 1825, *etc.* [The collection ascribed in a MS. note to —— Barrois, —— Drouillé, —— Dupointet and others.] pp. 21. MS. NOTES AND PRICES. [*Paris*, 1825.] 8°. **562. e. 60. (23.)**

—— [A sale catalogue of books.] [1825?] 8°. **899. f. 1. (6.)** *Imperfect ; wanting the titlepage.*

—— Catalogue d'une très-belle collection de tableaux des trois écoles, provenant du cabinet d'un amateur [identified in a MS. note as —— Brottier] ; dont la vente se fera . . . 16 . . . et . . . 17 janvier [1826], *etc.* pp. 21. MS. NOTES AND PRICES. [*Paris*,] 1826. 8°. **562. e. 61. (1.)**

—— Notice d'une collection intéressante de tableaux anciens et modernes des trois écoles, dont la vente se fera les 13 et 14 février 1826, *etc.* pp. 12. MS. NOTES AND PRICES. *Paris*, 1826. 8°. **562. e. 61. (6.)**

CATALOGUES.

—— Catalogue de tableaux modernes, dessins, estampes et bronzes du cabinet de M*** [identified in a MS. note as — Lovia]. La vente aura lieu les . . . 18 et . . . 19 février 1826, *etc.* pp. 16. MS. NOTES AND PRICES. 1826. 8º. *See* M***.   **562. e. 61. (8.)**

—— Notice de tableaux . . . objets de curiosité, gravures et miniatures, dont la vente aura lieu . . . 20 et 21 février [1826], *etc.* pp. 16. MS. NOTES AND PRICES. [*Paris,*] 1826. 8º.   **562. e. 61. (10.)**

—— Notice de tableaux des écoles flamande et française dont la vente se fera . . . 23 février 1826, *etc.* [The collection ascribed in a MS. note to — Doussin.] pp. 10. MS. NOTES AND PRICES. [*Paris,*] 1826. 8º.
562. e. 61. (11.)

—— Vente consistant en cent cinquante tableaux environ . . . objets de curiosité en tous genres, qui se fera . . . les 27, 28 février 1826, *etc.* [The collection ascribed in a MS. note to — Delaroque.] pp. 26. MS. NOTES AND PRICES. [*Paris,*] 1825. 8º.   **562. e. 61. (12.)**

—— Notice des superbes tableaux de galerie, en exposition publique . . . et dont la vente . . . sera annoncée, *etc.* pp. 8. MS. NOTES AND PRICES. [*Paris,* 1826.] 8º.
562. e. 61. (19.)
The date 20 *Mar.* 1826 *has been added in* MS.

—— Catalogue d'une magnifique collection de tableaux des plus grands maîtres . . . dont la vente se fera . . . 29 mars 1826, *etc.*
pp. 33. MS. NOTES AND PRICES.
[*Paris,*] 1826. 8º.   **562. e. 61. (21.)**
Another issue with a titlepage bearing the date " 6 *décembre* 1825 " *is entered above.*

—— Notice des bronzes, tableaux, et autres objets d'arts, et beaux meubles, dont la vente . . . aura lieu le mercredi 29 mars 1826, *etc.* pp. 8. [*Paris,*] 1826. 8º.
562. e. 61. (22.)

—— Catalogue d'une jolie collection de tableaux de diverses écoles, provenant du cabinet d'un amateur. Dont la vente se fera le 3 avril 1826, *etc.* pp. 26. MS. NOTES AND PRICES. *Paris,* 1826. 8º.   **562. e. 62. (1.)**

—— Catalogue d'une agréable collection de tableaux anciens et modernes . . . dont l'exposition publique aura lieu . . . 9 avril [1826] . . . et qui seront vendus . . . 10 et . . . 11 du même mois, *etc.* pp. 27. MS. NOTES AND PRICES. *Paris,* 1826. 8º.   **7854. d. 30. (12.)**

—— Catalogue d'une collection de tableaux . . . dessins, gravures . . . et autres objets d'arts . . . après le décès de M*** (M. G***) . . . dont la vente se fera . . . le mardi 11 avril 1826, et jours suivants, *etc.* 1826. 8º. *See* G***., M., *Ancien Avoué.*   **562. e. 62. (5.)**

—— Notice de tableaux et estampes, bronzes antiques . . . divers objets curieux, provenant du cabinet de M. le baron de la B*** . . . dont la vente aura lieu . . . le lundi 17 avril [1826] et jours suivans, *etc.* 1826. 8º. *See* LA B*** (de) *Baron.*   **562. e. 62. (8.)**

—— Catalogue des pierres gravées, antiques et modernes . . . et autres objets curieux, qui seront vendus . . . le 24 avril 1826, *etc.* pp. 19. MS. NOTES AND PRICES. *Paris,* 1826. 8º.   **562. e. 62. (11.)**

—— Notice de tableaux . . . et quelques estampes, provenant du cabinet de M.*** (M. B***) [identified in a MS. note as — Boursault, i.e. J. F. Boursault Malherbe], dont la vente aura lieu . . . les . . . 27, et . . . 28 avril [1826], *etc.* [Part of the collection also ascribed in a MS. note to — Claussin.] 1826. 8º. *See* B***, M.   **562. e. 62. (14.)**

CATALOGUES.

—— Notice d'une collection d'estampes encadrées, en feuilles et en recueils, lythographies et dessins, dont la vente se fera . . . 11 et . . . 12 mai [1826], *etc.* [The collection ascribed in a MS. note to — Piéri Bénard.] pp. 14. MS. NOTES AND PRICES. [*Paris,*] 1826. 8º.
562. e. 62. (19.)

—— Notice de tableaux, gravures, porcelaines et objets de curiosité, dont la vente aura lieu après le décès de M. le Vte de C . . . . le lundi 3 juillet 1826, *etc.* 1826. 8º. *See* C . . . ., M. *le* Vte *de.*   **562. e. 63. (1.)**

—— Catalogue d'une très-belle collection de bons tableaux des trois écoles, meubles de boule, ivoires . . . dont la vente aura lieu les 23 et 24 octobre [1826], *etc.* [The collection ascribed in a MS. note to — Brottier.] pp. 18. MS. NOTES AND PRICES. [*Paris,*] 1826. 8º.
562. e. 63. (2.)

—— Notice de tableaux des trois écoles, et dessins anciens et modernes . . . dont la vente aura lieu . . . 30 et . . . 31 octobre 1826, *etc.*
pp. 16.   MS. NOTES AND
PRICES. [*Paris,*] 1826. 8º.   **562. e. 63. (3.)**

—— Notice abrégée d'une collection de bons tableaux anciens et modernes, dont la vente aura lieu . . . 6 et . . . 7 novembre 1826, *etc.* [The collection ascribed in a MS. note to — Pérignon.] pp. 15. [*Paris,*] 1826. 8º.
562. e. 63. (5.)

—— Notice de tableaux, gravures et dessins, dont la vente se fera . . . 15 et 16 novembre 1826, *etc.* pp. 15. MS. PRICES. [*Paris,*] 1826. 8º.   **562. e. 62. (6.)**

—— Catalogue d'une collection de tableaux de diverses écoles ancienne et moderne, dessins, gouaches . . . provenant du cabinet d'un amateur, dont la vente se fera . . . 22 . . . 23, et . . . 24 novembre 1826, *etc.* pp. 26. MS. NOTES AND PRICES. [*Paris,*] 1826. 8º.
562. e. 63. (11.)

—— Catalogue d'une collection agréable de tableaux précieux, anciens et modernes, dessins, estampes et bronzes, dont la vente aura lieu . . . 30 novembre [1826], *etc.* [The collection ascribed in a MS. note to — Delanjeac and others.] pp. 24. MS. NOTES AND PRICES. [*Paris,*] 1826. 8º.
562. e. 63. (14.)

—— Catalogue d'une charmante collection de tableaux, des différentes écoles anciennes et modernes, dont l'exposition aura lieu . . . 13 décembre [1826], *etc.* pp. 17. MS. NOTES AND PRICES. [*Paris,*] 1826. 8º.
562. e. 63. (18.)

—— Notices d'objets de haute curiosité, mosaïques, camées, sculptures en ivoire, et autres, qui seront vendus . . . 18 au 20 décembre 1826. pp. 4. MS. NOTES AND PRICES. [*Paris,* 1826.] 8º.   **562. e. 63. (21.)**

—— Notice de beaux livres et de quelques manuscrits précieux, sur vélin . . . dont la vente se fera les . . . 18 et . . . 19 décembre [1826], *etc.* pp. 16. MS. PRICES. *Paris,* 1826. 8º.   **562. e. 63. (20.)**

—— Notice de tableaux, dessins et curiosités, dont la vente se fera les . . . 20 et 21 décembre 1826, *etc.* pp. 8. MS. PRICES. *Paris,* 1826. 8º.   **562. e. 63. (22.)**

—— Notice des tableaux anciens et modernes, dessins et croquis . . . dont la vente se fera . . . 26 . . . 27 décembre 1826, *etc.* pp. 7. MS. NOTES AND PRICES. [*Paris,*] 1826. 8º.   **562.e.63.(24.)**

CATALOGUES.

—— Catalogue de tableaux des différentes écoles anciennes et modernes, dont la vente aura lieu . . . 15 et . . . 16 janvier 1827, *etc.* pp. 15. MS. NOTES AND PRICES. [*Paris,*] 1827. 8°.   **562. e. 64. (3.)**

—— Catalogue d'une collection intéressante de bons tableaux des trois écoles; dont la vente se fera . . . 22 et . . . 23 janvier 1827, *etc.* pp. 15. MS. NOTES AND PRICES. [*Paris,*] 1827. 8°.   **562. e. 64. (5.)**

—— Catalogue d'une collection intéressante de tableaux, curiosités . . . dont la vente aura lieu . . . 1er mars [1827], *etc.* pp. 8. MS. NOTES AND PRICES.   [*Paris,*] 1827. 8°.   **562. e. 64. (11.)**

—— Catalogue d'une collection de tableaux venant d'Italie . . . La vente en aura lieu . . . 6 . . . 7 et . . . 8 mars [1827], *etc.* pp. 24. MS. NOTES AND PRICES.   [*Paris,*] 1827. 8°.   **562. e. 64. (12.)**

—— Notice d'une collection intéressante de tableaux des trois écoles, dont la vente aura lieu les 28 et 29 mars 1827, *etc.* [The collection ascribed in a MS. note to — Barois.] pp. 8. MS. NOTES AND PRICES. [*Paris,*] 1827. 8°.   **562. e. 64. (18.)**

—— Notice de tableaux anciens et modernes, et quelques estampes, médaillons . . . dont la vente aura lieu . . . 9 avril 1827, *etc.*   pp. 6. MS. NOTES AND PRICES. [*Paris,*] 1827. 8°.   **562. e. 65. (1.)**

—— Catalogue d'une jolie collection de tableaux des trois écoles, de dessins, estampes . . . dont la vente . . . aura lieu . . . 9 et 10 avril [1827], *etc.* pp. 31. MS. NOTES AND PRICES. [*Paris,*] 1827. 8°.   **562. e. 65. (3.)**

—— Notice de tableaux anciens et modernes, dont la vente aura lieu . . . 17, et . . . 18 avril [1827], *etc.* [The collection ascribed in a MS. note to — Duvalcamus.] pp. 10. MS. NOTES AND PRICES. [*Paris,*] 1827. 8°.   **562. e. 65. (5.)**

—— Catalogue d'une belle collection de tableaux, des trois écoles anciennes et modernes; meubles . . . dont la vente aura lieu . . . 23 et 24 avril [1827], *etc.* [The collection ascribed in a MS. note to — Roux.] pp. 52. MS. NOTES AND PRICES. [*Paris,*] 1827. 8°.   **562. e. 65. (8.)**

—— Catalogue d'une riche collection de tableaux . . . et d'objets de haute curiosité . . . dont la vente se fera . . . 30 avril [1827], *etc.* pp. 47. MS. NOTES AND PRICES. *Paris,* 1827. 8°.   **562. e. 65. (10.)**

—— Notice de livres, tableaux, gouaches, estampes . . . objets divers, dont la vente aura lieu par suite du départ de M. M*** [identified in a MS. note as — Monnier,] le . . . 28 et . . . 29 mai 1827, *etc.* 1827. 8°. *See* M***, M.   **562. e. 65. (11.)**

—— Catalogue d'une jolie collection de tableaux italiens, espagnols, flamands et français, dont la vente se fera . . . 29 octobre 1827, *etc.* pp. 15. MS. NOTES AND PRICES. [*Paris,*] 1827. 8°.   **562. e. 66. (5.)**

—— Catalogue d'une intéressante collection de tableaux des écoles hollandaise, flamande et française. L'exposition publique aura lieu . . . 7 novembre [1827] . . . La vente en sera faite . . . 8, et . . . 9 du même mois, *etc.* pp. 30. MS. NOTES AND PRICES. [*Paris,*] 1827. 8°.   **562. e. 66. (7.)**

CATALOGUES.

—— Catalogue d'une belle collection de tableaux de différentes écoles, et de quelques dessins, provenant du cabinet d'un prince; dont la vente aura lieu . . . 16 novembre 1827, *etc.* pp. 16. MS. NOTES AND PRICES. [*Paris,*] 1827. 8°.   **562. e. 66. (9.)**

—— Notice de curiosités après cessation de commerce de M. B***, et d'une collection de tableaux anciens et modernes des trois écoles dont la vente aura lieu . . . les 19 et 20 novembre 1827, *etc.* [The collection of pictures ascribed in a MS. note to Simonnet and — Gremillé.] 1827. 8°. *See* B***, M.   **562. e. 66. (10.)**

—— Notice de tableaux anciens et modernes, des trois écoles, dont la vente aura lieu les . . . 30 novembre et . . . 1er décembre 1827, *etc.* pp. 11. MS. PRICES.   [*Paris,*] 1827. 8°.   **562. e. 66. (12*.)**

—— Catalogue des tableaux précieux des trois écoles, composant le cabinet de M. B*** . . . La vente . . . aura lieu le lundi 3 décembre 1827, *etc.* 1827. 8°. *See* B***, M.   **562. e. 66. (13.)**

—— Catalogue d'une jolie collection de tableaux, dessins et gravures modernes, composant le cabinet de M. Bea***, dont la vente aura lieu les . . . 3 et . . . 4 décembre 1827, *etc.* 1827. 8°. *See* BEA*** (   )   **562. e. 66. (15.)**

—— Catalogue d'une belle collection de tableaux italiens, espagnols, flamands et français, composant le cabinet de feu M. S . . . [identified in a MS. note as — Souyns] dont la vente se fera . . . les . . . 3 . . . 4 . . . 5 . . . 6 et . . . 7 décembre 1827, *etc.* 1827. 8°. *See* S . ., M.   **562. e. 66. (14.)**

—— Notice d'une collection de tableaux anciens et principalement de modernes, dont la vente se fera . . . 10 et 11 décembre 1827, *etc.*   pp. 9. MS. NOTES AND PRICES. [*Paris,*] 1827. 8°.   **562. e. 66. (17.)**

—— Notice de tableaux, modernes et anciens, dessins, gravures, coquilles et curiosités, dont la vente aura [lieu] les 13 et 14 décembre 1827, *etc.* pp. 7. MS. PRICES. [*Paris,*] 1827. 8°.   **562. e. 66. (18.)**

—— Notice de tableaux des trois écoles anciennes et modernes, dont la vente se fera . . . 24 décembre 1827, *etc.* pp. 8. MS. NOTES AND PRICES. pp. 8. [*Paris,*] 1827. 8°.   **562. e. 66. (21.)**

—— Notice de quelques tableaux et dessins, anciens et modernes, lots d'estampes, cahiers de lithographie . . . dont la vente aura lieu . . . 26, et . . . 27 décembre 1827, *etc.* pp. 8. MS. NOTES AND PRICES.   [*Paris,*] 1827. 8°.   **562. e. 66. (22.)**

—— The London Catalogue of Books, with their sizes, prices, and publishers. Containing the books published in London . . . since the year 1800 to March 1827. [Compiled by Robert Bent.] pp. 308. *Longman & Co.:* *London,* 1827. 8°.   **618. f. 21. (1.)**

—— [Another copy.]   **11900. c. 24. (1.)**

—— Catalogue d'une intéressante collection de tableaux . . . L'exposition publique aura lieu . . . 27 janvier [1828] . . . La vente en sera faite . . . 28, et . . . 29 du même mois, *etc.*   pp. 20. MS. NOTES AND PRICES. [*Paris,*] 1828. 8°.   **562. e. 67. (2.)**

—— Notice d'une jolie collection de tableaux anciens et modernes, dessins encadrés, gouaches . . . dont la vente aura lieu, après décès de M.*** [identified in a MS. note as — Boisau] . . . les . . . 28, 29 et 30 janvier 1828, *etc.* pp. 10. MS. PRICES. [*Paris,*] 1828. 8°.   **562. e. 67. (4.)**

—— Notice de tableaux des trois écoles, dont la vente aura lieu . . . 7 et . . . 8 février 1828, *etc.* [The collection ascribed in a MS. note to — Fournier and others.] pp. 10. MS. NOTES AND PRICES. [*Paris,*] 1828. 8º.

562. e. 67. (8.)

—— Notice abrégée de tableaux, gouaches, dessins et gravures, dont la vente aura lieu . . . 28 . . . et . . . 29 février 1828, *etc.* pp. 10. MS. NOTES AND PRICES. [*Paris,*] 1828. 8º.

562. e. 67. (10.)

—— Catalogue de tableaux . . . dessins, gouaches, aquarelles et miniatures ; estampes . . . tabatières et bijoux . . . dont la vente aura lieu par suite du décès de M. V*** [identified in a MS. note as — Vigneron] . . . le lundi 3 mars 1828, et jours suivans, *etc.* 1828. 8º. *See* V***, *M.*

562. e. 67. (13.)

—— Notice de tableaux anciens et modernes, pendules, candelabres . . . dont la vente aura lieu . . . 10 et . . . 11 mars 1828, *etc.* pp. 108 [8]. MS. NOTES AND PRICES. [*Paris,*] 1828. 8º.

562. e. 67. (14.)

—— Catalogue de tableaux, dessins, bronzes, estampes, recueils et livres, provenant du cabinet et de la bibliothèque de M*** [identified in a MS. note as — Maillard], dont la vente aura lieu les . . . 13 . . . 14 et . . . 15 mars 1828, *etc.* pp. 19. MS. PRICES. 1828. 8º. *See* M***.

562. e. 67. (16.)

—— Notice de tableaux, dessins, gouaches . . . provenant du cabinet d'un artiste, dont la vente aura lieu . . . 17 et . . . 18 mars 1828, *etc.* pp. 16. MS. NOTES AND PRICES. [*Paris,*] 1828. 8º.

562.e.67.(17.)

—— Catalogue de tableaux précieux des trois écoles ; provenant de la galerie de M. le général T***, de Moscou, dont la vente aura lieu . . . le vendredi 21 mars [1828], *etc.* 1828. 8º. *See* T***, *M. le Général, de Moscou.*

562. e. 67. (20.)

—— Catalogue de tableaux précieux, composant la collection de madame P***. et de M. le chevalier D*** [identified in a MS. note as Madame Paumier and — Dubois] . . . dont la vente aura lieu le . . . 26 et le . . . 27 mars 1828, *etc.* 1828. 8º. *See* P***, *Madame.*

562. e. 68. (15.)

—— Catalogue abrégé d'une collection intéressante de bons tableaux des trois écoles, anciennes et modernes, et de curiosités, dont la vente aura lieu . . . 31 mars et . . . 1er avril 1828, *etc.* pp. 18. MS. NOTES AND PRICES. [*Paris,*] 1828. 8º.

562. e. 68. (1.)

—— Notice de quelques tableaux anciens et modernes, provenant de madame H***, et d'une suite de trois cents dessins, par Nicolle . . . dont la vente aura lieu le . . . 31 mars et . . . 1er avril 1828, *etc.* 1828. 8º. *See* H***, *Madame.*

562. e. 67. (24.)

—— Catalogue de tableaux anciens des trois écoles, et de quelques modernes ; dessins et gravures, dont la vente aura lieu . . . 14 et . . . 15 avril 1828, *etc.* pp. 16. MS. NOTES AND PRICES. [*Paris,*] 1828. 8º.

562. e. 68. (3.)

—— Vente, après décès de M***, d'une collection de tableaux des trois écoles anciennes et modernes . . . dont la vente aura lieu le vingt-un avril [1828], *etc.* pp. 12. MS. PRICES. 1828. 8º. *See* M***.

562. e. 68. (7.)

—— Catalogue de peintures chinoises et persanes . . . de bronzes, laques et porcelaines de la Chine . . . dont la vente aura lieu les 22, 23, 24, 25 et 26 avril 1828, *etc.* pp. 37. MS. NOTES AND PRICES. [*Paris,*] 1828. 8º.

562.e.68.(4.)

—— Notice de tableaux anciens et modernes, estampes, dessins . . . dont la vente aura lieu . . . 28, et . . . 29 avril 1828, *etc.* pp. 8. MS. NOTES AND PRICES. [*Paris,*] 1828. 8º.

562. e. 68. (5.)

—— Notice de tableaux anciens et modernes des trois écoles, dont la vente aura lieu . . . 5 mai 1828, *etc.* pp. 8. MS. NOTES AND PRICES. [*Paris,*] 1828. 8º.

562. e. 68. (9.)

—— Notice alphabétique d'un choix de tableaux originaux de maîtres célèbres . . . et de portraits d'après nature . . . provenans de la collection de M. M.-A. D. [identified in a MS. note as M.-A. Didot], dont la vente aura lieu . . . les 6, 7 et 8 mai [1828], *etc.* 1828. 8º. *See* D., M.-A., *M.*

562. e. 68. (10.)

—— Notice d'une collection de tableaux de différentes écoles . . . dont la vente aura lieu . . . les . . . 10 et . . . 11 septembre 1828, *etc.* [The collection ascribed in a MS. note to — Paumier and others.] pp. 16. MS. PRICES. *Paris,* 1828. 8º.

562. e. 68. (17.)

—— Catalogue d'une collection intéressante de tableaux des trois écoles . . . gouaches, dessins . . . dont la vente aura lieu les 13 et 14 octobre 1828, *etc.* [The collection ascribed in a MS. note to — Bon and — Laurent.] pp. 24. MS. NOTES AND PRICES. [*Paris,*] 1828. 8º.

562. e. 69. (1.)

—— Notice abrégée de tableaux, anciens et modernes, des trois écoles, dont la vente aura lieu . . . 24 octobre 1828, *etc.* pp. 4. MS. NOTES AND PRICES. [*Paris,*] 1828. 8º.

562. e. 69. (4.)

—— Pour cause de départ. Vente de tableaux, tous bien encadrés, qui aura lieu . . . 27 octobre 1828, *etc.* pp. 4. MS. NOTES AND PRICES. [*Paris,* 1828.] 8º.

562. e. 69. (3.)

—— Catalogue d'une collection de plus de 1200 tableaux de différentes écoles . . . dont la vente aura lieu . . . 5 novembre 1828, *etc.* [The collection ascribed in a MS. note to — Legain.] pp. 146. MS. NOTES AND PRICES. *Paris,* 1828. 8º.

562. e. 69. (6.)

—— Catalogue de tableaux anciens et modernes, des trois écoles, dont la vente aura lieu . . . 10 et . . . 11 novembre 1828, *etc.* pp. 14. MS. NOTES AND PRICES. [*Paris,*] 1828. 8º.

562. e. 69. (7.)

—— Catalogue de dessins, tableaux, estampes . . . dont la vente aura lieu . . . 24 et . . . 25 novembre 1828, *etc.* pp. 12. MS. NOTES AND PRICES. [*Paris,*] 1828. 8º.

562. e. 69. (9.)

—— Catalogue d'une belle et nombreuse collection de tableaux. Composant le cabinet d'un amateur [identified in a MS. note as the Duke de Montmorenci] . . . dont la vente se fera . . . 24 . . . 25 . . . 26 et . . . 27 novembre [1828], *etc.* pp. 54. MS. NOTES AND PRICES. *Paris,* 1828. 8º.

562. e. 69. (8.)

—— Catalogue d'une intéressante collection de tableaux . . . la vente en sera faite . . . 1er et . . . 2 décembre [1828], *etc.* pp. 20. MS. NOTES AND PRICES. *Paris,* 1828. 8º.

562. e. 69. (10.)

—— Catalogue de tableaux, bronzes, vases étrusques . . . formant le cabinet de M*** [identified in a MS. note as — Rosiert.] Il sera fait de ces objets une vente . . . les 1er et 2 décembre 1828, *etc.* 1828. 8º. *See* M***.

562. e. 69. (12.)

CATALOGUES.

—— Catalogue d'une jolie collection de tableaux ... provenant du cabinet de M. L ...... [identified in a MS. note as — Lemerle] dont la vente aura lieu le 2 décembre 1828, etc. 1828. 8º. *See* L ....., M.   **562. e. 69. (11.)**

—— Catalogue d'une intéressante collection de bons tableaux anciens, des trois écoles ... provenant du cabinet d'un étranger, dont la vente aura lieu ... 4 décembre 1828, *etc.* pp. 15. MS. NOTES AND PRICES. [*Paris,*] 1828. 8º.   **562. e. 69. (13.)**

—— Notice de tableaux anciens et modernes, des trois écoles, dont la vente aura lieu ... 5 et ... 6 décembre 1828, *etc.* pp. 8. MS. NOTES AND PRICES.   [*Paris,*] 1828. 8º.   **562. e. 69. (14.)**

—— Catalogue de tableaux des écoles anciennes et modernes, dessins, émaux ... dont la vente aura lieu ... 8 et ... 9 décembre 1828, *etc.* pp. 28. MS. NOTES AND PRICES. [*Paris,*] 1828. 8º.   **562. e. 69. (16.)**

—— Catalogue d'une collection intéressante et peu nombreuse de tableaux précieux, d'antiquités, d'objets d'arts ... Ces objets ... seront vendus ... les 15 et 16 décembre 1828, *etc.* pp. 22. MS. NOTES AND PRICES. [*Paris,*] 1828. 8º.   **562. e. 69. (19.)**

—— Catalogue d'une belle collection de tableaux des plus grands maîtres des trois écoles, dont la vente aura lieu ... 15 ... 16 et ... 17 décembre 1828, *etc.*

pp. 19. MS. NOTES AND PRICES. [*Paris,*] 1828. 8º.   **562. e. 69. (18.)**

—— Catalogue des armes orientales, curiosités, tableaux, gravures et planches gravées, composant le cabinet de M***, et dont la vente aura lieu les ... 22 et ... 23 décembre 1828, *etc.* pp. 15. MS. PRICES. 1828. 8º. *See* M***.   **562. e. 69. (21.)**

—— Notice de tableaux anciens et modernes ... dont la vente aura lieu ... 24 décembre 1828, *etc.* pp. 13. MS. NOTES AND PRICES. [*Paris,*] 1828. 8º.   **562. e. 69. (22.)**

—— A Catalogue raisonné of the Select Collection of Engravings of an Amateur [i.e. Thomas Wilson]. pp. 279. xii. *C. Richards: London,* 1828. 4º.   **787. i. 27.**

—— Catalogue d'une collection intéressante de tableaux anciens des trois écoles, bronzes, marbres précieux ... dont la vente aura lieu ... 5 janvier 1829, *etc.* [The collection ascribed in a MS. note to — Montigneul.] pp. 19. MS. NOTES AND PRICES. [*Paris,*] 1829. 8º.   **562. e. 70. (1.)**

—— Notice abrégée de tableaux anciens et modernes, dont la vente aura lieu ... 9 et 10 janvier 1829, *etc.* pp. 8. MS. NOTES AND PRICES. [*Paris,*] 1829. 8º.   **562. e. 70. (2.)**

—— Catalogue de tableaux des diverses écoles, et la plupart nouvellement apportés de l'étranger. La vente ... sera faite ... 12 et ... 13 janvier 1829, *etc.* pp. 17. MS. NOTES AND PRICES. [*Paris,*] 1829. 8º.   **562. e. 70. (4.)**

—— Catalogue de tableaux, dessins, gravures ... dont la vente aura lieu ... 19 et ... 20 janvier 1829, *etc.* pp. 4. MS. NOTES AND PRICES. [*Paris,* 1829.] 8º.   **562. e. 70. (10.)**

—— Notice abrégée de tableaux anciens et modernes, des trois écoles; curiosités ... dont la vente aura lieu ... 26 et ... 27 janvier 1829, *etc.* pp. 11. MS. NOTES AND PRICES. [*Paris,*] 1829. 8º.   **562. e. 70. (11.)**

CATALOGUES.

—— Catalogue abrégé d'une collection intéressante de bons tableaux anciens des trois écoles, provenant du cabinet d'un amateur étranger [identified in a MS. note as — Coltone]; et dont la vente aura lieu ... 5 et ... 6 février 1829, *etc.* pp. 15. MS. NOTES AND PRICES. [*Paris,*] 1829. 8º.   **562. e. 70. (12.)**

—— Catalogue d'une collection intéressante de tableaux, anciens et modernes; principalement des écoles flamandes et hollandaises. Dont la vente aura lieu ... 9 et ... 10 février 1829, *etc.*

pp. 16. MS. NOTES AND PRICES. [*Paris,*] 1829. 8º.   **562. e. 70. (14.)**

—— Catalogue d'une jolie collection de tableaux modernes, dont la vente sera faite ... 9 et 10 février 1829, *etc.*

pp. 16. MS. NOTES AND PRICES. [*Paris,*] 1829. 8º.   **562. e. 70. (13.)**

—— Notice de tableaux anciens et modernes, bronzes, ivoires ... dont la vente aura lieu ... 16 et ... 17 février 1829, *etc.* pp. 8. MS. NOTES AND PRICES. [*Paris,*] 1829. 8º.   **562. e. 70. (15.)**

—— Catalogue de tableaux anciens des trois écoles, provenant du cabinet d'un amateur étranger [i.e. — Coltone ?], et dont la vente ... aura lieu ... 23 et ... 24 février 1829, *etc.* pp. 16. MS. NOTES AND PRICES. [*Paris,*] 1829. 8º.   **562. e. 70. (16.)**

—— Catalogue de livres anciens et modernes, d'autographes et de gravures, de la bibliothèque de M*** ... dont la vente aura lieu le lundi 9 mars 1829, et jours suivans, *etc.* MS. PRICES. 1829. 8º. *See* M***.   **562. e. 70. (19*.)**

—— Catalogue de tableaux des trois écoles, dessins et estampes ... dont la vente aura lieu ... 9 et ... 10 mars 1829, *etc.* [The collection ascribed in a MS. note to — de Livry and others.] pp. 19. MS. NOTES AND PRICES. [*Paris,*] 1829. 8º.   **562. e. 70. (20.)**

—— Par continuation, Vente de tableaux et de curiosités ... 9 et 10 mars 1829, *etc.*

pp. 14. MS. NOTES AND PRICES. [*Paris,*] 1829. 8º.   **562. e. 70. (18.)**

—— Catalogue de tableaux des trois écoles, et de quelques dessins anciens, dont la vente aura lieu ... 16 et ... 17 mars 1829, *etc.* pp. 20. MS. NOTES AND PRICES. [*Paris,*] 1829. 8º.   **562. e. 70. (21.)**

—— Notice abrégée de tableaux anciens et modernes, de gravures ... dont la vente aura lieu ... 18 et 19 mars 1829, *etc.* pp. 8. MS. NOTES AND PRICES. [*Paris,*] 1829. 8º.   **562. e. 70. (22.)**

—— Catalogue d'une collection intéressante de bons tableaux anciens et modernes des trois écoles, provenant du cabinet d'un amateur [identified in a MS. note as — Vernois], dont la vente aura lieu ... 30 et ... 31 mars 1829, *etc.* pp. 19. MS. NOTES AND PRICES. [*Paris,*] 1829. 8º.   **562. e. 70. (27.)**

—— Catalogue de tableaux des trois écoles, de trente-quatre gravures de la bataille d'Austerlitz de M. Godefroy ... un très-beau Christ en ivoire ... dont la vente aura lieu ... 2 et ... 3 avril 1829, *etc.* pp. 15. MS. NOTES AND PRICES. [*Paris,*] 1829. 8º.   **562. e. 71. (1.)**

—— Catalogue de tableaux anciens et modernes des trois écoles, meubles curieux, bronzes ... dont la vente aura lieu ... 6 et ... 7 avril 1829, *etc.* [The collection ascribed in a MS. note to — Terray.] MS. NOTES AND PRICES. pp. 19. [*Paris,*] 1829. 8º.   **562. e. 71. (3.)**

CATALOGUES.

—— Notice d'une collection de tableaux anciens et modernes et de curiosités, dont la vente aura lieu . . . 13 et . . . 14 avril 1829, *etc.* pp. 12. MS. NOTES AND PRICES. [*Paris,*] 1829. 8º.   **562. e. 71. (5.)**

—— Catalogue d'une précieuse collection d'objets d'art et de curiosité de la Chine et du Japon . . . dont la vente aura lieu les 22, 23, 24 avril 1829, *etc.* [The collection ascribed in a MS. note to — Monticoul.] pp. 35. MS. NOTES AND PRICES. [*Paris,*] 1829. 8º.   **562. e. 71. (6.)**

—— Catalogue d'une précieuse collection de tableaux anciens . . . dont la vente aura lieu . . . 28 et . . . 29 avril 1829, *etc.* [The collection ascribed in a MS. note to Ve. Paumier.] pp. 17. MS. NOTES AND PRICES. [*Paris,*] 1829. 8º.   **562. e. 71. (8.)**

—— [Another copy.] MS. NOTES AND PRICES.
562. e. 71. (10.)

—— Catalogue de tableaux précieux, tant anciens que modernes, des trois écoles, et d'objets de curiosité, dont la vente aura lieu . . . 26 et . . . 27 octobre 1829, *etc.*

pp. 28. MS. NOTES AND PRICES.
[*Paris,*] 1829. 8º.   **562. e. 72. (3.)**

—— Catalogue d'une intéressante collection de tableaux anciens et modernes . . . La vente en sera faite . . . 16 et . . . 17 novembre [1829], *etc.*
pp. 19. MS. NOTES
AND PRICES. [*Paris,*] 1829. 8º.   **562. e. 72. (4.)**

—— Catalogue de tableaux précieux des trois écoles, dont la vente aura lieu . . . 19 et . . . 20 novembre 1829, *etc.* pp. 19. MS. NOTES AND PRICES. [*Paris,*] 1829. 8º.
562. e. 72. (5.)

—— Catalogue d'une collection de tableaux . . . provenant du cabinet d'un amateur, dont la vente aura lieu . . . 23 et . . . 24 novembre 1829, *etc.* pp. 25. MS. NOTES AND PRICES. *Paris,* 1829. 8º.
562. e. 72. (6.)

—— Catalogue d'une collection intéressante de bons tableaux anciens et modernes des trois écoles, meubles . . . provenant du cabinet de feu M. H*** . . . et dont la vente aura lieu . . . les . . . 30 novembre et . . . 1er décembre 1829, *etc.* [The collection ascribed in a MS. note to Vve. Helie.] 1829. 8º. *See* H***, *M., Architecte.*   **562. e. 72. (9.)**

—— Catalogue d'une collection précieuse de tableaux anciens et modernes des trois écoles, et d'objets curieux . . . composant le cabinet d'un amateur distingué du midi de la France, et dont la vente aura lieu . . . 3 . . . 4 et . . . 5 décembre 1829, *etc.* pp. 16. MS. NOTES AND PRICES. [*Paris,*] 1829. 8º.   **562. e. 72. (10.)**

—— Notice abrégée de tableaux et curiosités, dont la vente aura lieu . . . 7 et . . . 8 décembre 1829, *etc.* pp. 7. MS. NOTES AND PRICES. [*Paris,*] 1829. 8º.
562. e. 72. (12.)

—— Notice d'une collection de tableaux originaux de l'école flamande, provenant du cabinet d'un amateur étranger. La vente se fera . . . 10 et . . . 11 décembre [1829], *etc.* pp. 21. MS. NOTES AND PRICES. [*Paris,*] 1829. 8º.
562. e. 72. (13.)

—— Catalogue d'une nombreuse et très-belle collection de médailles et monnaies modernes, curiosités, antiquités . . . provenant du cabinet de M.***. Dont la vente . . . aura lieu . . . les 21, 22, 23, 24, 26, 28 et 29 décembre 1829, *etc.* pp. 62. MS. PRICES. *Paris,* 1829. 8º.
562. e. 72. (19.)

CATALOGUES.

—— Catalogue de tableaux anciens et modernes, dont la vente aura lieu . . . 24 décembre 1829, *etc.* pp. 12. [*Paris,*] 1829. 8º.   **562. e. 72. (18.)**

—— A Supplement to the London Catalogue of Books, published in March 1827, containing all the new works and new editions . . . from that period to June 1829, *etc.* [Compiled by Robert Bent.] pp. 47. *Longman & Co.: London,* 1829. 8º.   **618. f. 21. (2.)**

—— [Another copy.]   **11900. c. 24. (2.)**

—— Catalogue de la collection de tableaux de S. Exc. M. le comte de *** . . . dont la vente . . . aura lieu . . . le mardi 12 janvier 1830, *etc.* pp. 30. *Paris,* 1829. 8º.
562. e. 70. (3.)

—— Catalogue de tableaux, gouaches, dessins, fixés . . . du cabinet de M.***, dont la vente aura lieu les . . . 18 et . . . 19 janvier 1830, *etc.* pp. 21. *Paris,* 1830. 8º.
562. e. 73. (1.)

—— Notice d'une collection intéressante de bons tableaux des trois écoles, porcelaines de Chine et de Sèvres . . . dont la vente aura lieu . . . 18 et . . . 19 janvier 1830, *etc.* pp. 14. [*Paris,*] 1830. 8º. **562. e. 73. (2.)**

—— Catalogue de tableaux anciens et modernes, et autres objets divers de curiosité, dont la vente aura lieu . . . 20 . . . 21 et . . . 22 janvier 1830, *etc.* pp. 20. [*Paris,*] 1830. 8º.   **562. e. 73. (3.)**

—— Catalogue d'une jolie collection de tableaux des trois écoles . . . dessins et gravures, meubles . . . formant le cabinet de M.****, dont la vente aura lieu les . . . 25 et . . . 26 janvier 1830, *etc.* pp. 18. [*Paris,*] 1830. 8º.
562. e. 73. (4*.)

—— Notice de tableaux, dessins et estampes . . . provenant de la succession du cabinet de M. le comte de * * *. Dont la vente aura lieu . . . 25 janvier 1830, *etc.* pp. 16. MS. NOTES AND PRICES. [*Paris,*] 1830. 8º.
562. e. 73. (4.)

—— Notice de tableaux et dessins anciens des trois écoles, d'estampes et recueils divers provenant du cabinet de M.****. Dont la vente aura lieu, par suite de son décès . . . les . . . 28 et . . . 29 janvier 1830, *etc.* pp. 15. [*Paris,*] 1830. 8º.   **562. e. 73. (5.)**

—— Catalogue de tableaux de choix, la plupart flamands et hollandais, provenant du cabinet d'un amateur [identified in a MS. note as — Aubert], et dont la vente aura lieu . . . 1er février 1830, *etc.* pp. 15. MS. NOTES AND PRICES. [*Paris,*] 1830. 8º.   **562. e. 73. (6.)**

—— Catalogue des objets chinois et anglais, dont la vente aura lieu . . . 25 . . . 26 et . . . 27 février 1830, *etc.* pp. 27. *Paris,* 1830. 8º.   **562. e. 73. (9.)**

—— Notice d'une collection de tableaux anciens et modernes des trois écoles, dont la vente aura lieu . . . 1er et . . . 2 mars 1830, *etc.* pp. 13. MS. NOTES AND PRICES. [*Paris,*] 1830. 8º.   **562. e. 73. (12.)**

—— Notice de tableaux anciens et modernes, miniatures, aquarelles et dessins, dont la vente aura lieu . . . 8 et . . . 9 mars 1830, *etc.* pp. 13. MS. NOTES AND PRICES. [*Paris,*] 1830. 8º.   **562. e. 73. (13.)**

—— Catalogue d'une jolie collection de tableaux et dessins modernes, armures anciennes . . . provenant du cabinet d'un amateur, dont la vente aura lieu . . . 15 et . . . 16 mars [1830], *etc.* pp. 15. MS. NOTES AND PRICES. [*Paris,* 1830.] 8º.   **562. e. 73. (18.)**

CATALOGUES.

—— Notice d'une collection intéressante de tableaux anciens et modernes des trois écoles . . . dont la vente aura lieu . . . 15 et . . . 16 mars 1830, *etc.* pp. 12. MS. NOTES AND PRICES. [*Paris,*] 1830. 8º. 562. e. 73. (16.)

—— Catalogue d'une collection intéressante de tableaux anciens et modernes . . . dont la vente aura lieu . . . 29 et . . . 30 mars 1830, *etc.* pp. 18. MS. NOTES AND PRICES. [*Paris,*] 1830. 8º. 562. e. 73. (25.)

—— Catalogue d'une précieuse collection d'objets d'art en antiquités égyptiennes, grecques et romaines, bronzes florentins . . . dont la vente aura lieu . . . 2 et . . . 3 avril 1830, *etc.* pp. 24. MS. NOTES AND PRICES. [*Paris,*] 1830. 8º. 562. e. 74. (1.)

—— Notice de quelques tableaux des diverses écoles . . . provenant la plupart du cabinet de M.***, anglais ; et collection d'objets de Chine et des Indes ; dont la vente aura lieu le lundi 5 avril [1830] et jours suivans, *etc.* pp. 11. MS. PRICES. *Paris,* 1830. 8º. 562. e. 74. (2.)

—— Catalogue de statues, bustes, chimères . . . dont la vente . . . aura lieu . . . 14 et . . . 15 avril 1830, *etc.* pp. 14. MS. NOTES AND PRICES. [*Paris,*] 1830. 8º. 562. e. 74. (5.)

—— Notice de livres en feuilles, brochés et reliés, dont la vente se fera les . . . 19 . . . 20 et . . . 21 avril 1830, *etc.* pp. 23. *Paris,* 1830. 8º. 562. e. 74. (9.)

—— Catalogue de tableaux anciens et modernes, dessins, gravures . . . dont la vente aura lieu . . . 22 et . . . 23 avril [1830], *etc.* pp. 19. [*Paris,*] 1830. 8º. 562. e. 74. (10.)

—— Catalogue d'une collection unique d'une grande quantité de tableaux peints sur verre . . . de plusieurs mécaniques à musique . . . et de divers objets d'optique ; dont la vente aura lieu . . . 26 . . . 27 avril 1830, *etc.* pp. 23. MS. NOTES AND PRICES. [*Paris,*] 1830. 8º. 562. e. 74. (12.)

—— Catalogue d'une jolie collection de tableaux anciens et modernes, des trois écoles, dont la vente aura lieu . . . 3 et . . . 4 mai 1830, *etc.* pp. 20. MS. NOTES AND PRICES. [*Paris,*] 1830. 8º. 562. e. 74. (13.)

—— Catalogue de bons tableaux des écoles anciennes et modernes, dont la vente aura lieu . . . 10 et . . . 11 mai 1830, *etc.* pp. 19. [*Paris,*] 1830. 8º. 562. e. 74. (15.)

—— [Another copy.] MS. NOTES AND PRICES. 562. e. 74. (16.)

—— Catalogue de tableaux anciens, choisis dans les diverses écoles, et formant le riche cabinet de M. le duc de C*** [identified in a MS. note as the Duke de Caraman], *etc.* [Catalogue of a sale due to take place on 10–12 May, 1830.] 1830. 8º. *See* C***, *M. le Duc de.* 562. e. 74. (17.)

—— Catalogue des tableaux et dessins provenant du cabinet de M. d'H***, dont la vente aura lieu les . . . 17 . . . 18 et . . . 19 mai 1830, *etc.* 1830. 8º. *See* H***, *M. d'.* 562. e. 74. (19.)

—— Notice d'une collection de tableaux anciens . . . dont la vente aura lieu . . . 17 et . . . 18 mai 1830, *etc.* pp. 12. [*Paris,*] 1830. 8º. 562. e. 74. (20.)

—— Catalogue de tableaux anciens et modernes, et objets d'art et de curiosité, dont la vente aura lieu . . . les . . . 21 et . . . 22 juin 1830, *etc.* pp. 8. [*Paris,*] 1830. 8º. 562. e. 74. (23.)

CATALOGUES.

—— Collectio numorum graecorum romanorumque ad artis historiam illustrandam instructa. pp. 47. [1830 ?] 8º. 7755. aaa. 18.

—— List of Objects. [A list of objects for the microscope.] [*Privately printed : Middle Hill ?* 1830 ?] *s. sh.* 8º. Tab. 436. a. 1. (2.)

—— Catalogue de tableaux capitaux . . . une grande quantité d'objets de curiosité . . . dont la vente aura lieu . . . les 22, 23, 24 et 25 février 1831, *etc.* pp. 28. [*Paris,*] 1831. 8º. 562. e. 75. (3.)

—— Auctions-Verzeichniss von Naturalien, Mineralien, Alterthümern . . . welche den 31 Oktober [1831] . . . denen Meistbietenden überlassen werden sollen, *etc.* pp. 44. *Camenz,* 1831. 8º. 7805. a. 11. *The date in the title has been altered in* MS. *to* " 29 Oktober."

—— Catalogue d'une riche et belle collection de tableaux . . . provenant du cabinet de M. C., amateur, de Lyon [— Coulet], dont la vente aura lieu . . . les . . . 15 . . . 16 et . . . 17 novembre 1831, *etc.* 1831. 8º. *See* C., M., *Amateur, de Lyon.* 562. e. 75. (7.)

—— Bibliotheca Americana, being a choice collection of Books relating to North and South America and the West-Indies, including voyages to the Southern Hemisphere, maps, engravings and medals. [By David B. Warden.] pp. 138. *Paul Renouard : Paris,* 1831. 8º. 619. d. 42. *Later edition* 1840.

—— The London Catalogue of Books, with their sizes, prices, and publishers. Containing the books published in London . . . Since the year 1810 to February 1831. [Compiled by Robert Bent.] pp. 335. *Robert Bent : London,* 1831. 8º. Circ. 90. a.

—— [Another copy.] 618. f. 22. (1.)

—— Oriental Manuscripts purchased in Turkey. [A catalogue of the collection of John Lee.] pp. 22. *R. Watts : London,* 1831. 4º. 823. cc. 15. *Later edition* 1840.

—— Catalogue d'une belle collection de tableaux anciens et modernes, des trois écoles . . . dont la vente aura lieu . . . 13 et . . . 14 février 1832, *etc.* pp. 20. [*Paris,*] 1832. 8º. 562. e. 76. (1.)

—— Catalogue d'une nombreuse collection de tableaux anciens et modernes . . . dont la vente aura lieu . . . 5 . . . 6 et . . . 7 novembre 1832, *etc.* pp. 16. [*Paris,*] 1832. 8º. 562. e. 76. (7.)

—— Vente de tableaux, dessins, gravures avant la lettre . . . 28 . . . 29 et . . . 30 janvier 1833, *etc.* pp. 17. *Paris,* 1833. 8º. 7854. d. 31. (7.)

—— Catalogue d'une belle collection de tableaux italiens, flamands et françois, des écoles ancienne et moderne . . . dont la vente aura lieu . . . 27 et . . . 28 février [1833], *etc.* pp. viii. 32. [*Paris,*] 1833. 8º. 7854. d. 31. (6.)

—— Catalogue d'une jolie collection de dessins provenant du cabinet de M***, dont la vente aura lieu . . . 18 et . . . 19 mars [1833], *etc.* pp. 25. 1833. 8º. *See* M***. 7854. d. 31. (3.)

—— Catalogue de dessins anglais, du premier ordre, dont la vente aura lieu . . . 10 mai 1833, *etc.* pp. 15. [*Paris,* 1833.] 8º. 7854. e. 26. (2.)

—— Catalogue d'objets de haute curiosité, en ivoires sculptés, bronzes . . . tableaux, dessins . . . provenant du cabinet de Madame L. K *** , dont la vente aura lieu . . . 20 mai 1833, *etc.* pp. 67. [1833.] 8º. *See* K *** , L., *Madame.* 7854. d. 31. (2.)

CATALOGUES.

—— Catalogue d'une belle et nombreuse collection de tableaux, anciens et modernes, et de quelques objets d'art . . . dont la vente . . . aura lieu . . . 29 et . . . 30 novembre 1833, *etc.* pp. 14. [*Paris*, 1833.] 8°. **7854. d. 31. (5.)**

—— Catalogue d'une agréable collection de tableaux des diverses écoles anciennes et modernes dont la vente aura lieu . . . 2 et . . . 3 décembre 1833, *etc.* pp. 26. *Paris*, 1833. 8°. **7854. d. 31. (4.)**

—— A Supplement to the London Catalogue of Books published in February 1831 ; containing all the new works published in London, from that period to December 1832, inclusive, *etc.* [Compiled by Robert Bent.] pp. 43. *Robert Bent: London*, 1833. 8°. Circ. **90. a.**

—— [Another copy.] **618. f. 22. (2.)**

—— Catalogue d'une très-belle collection de tableaux anciens et modernes, objets d'art . . . dont la vente aura lieu . . . 30 et . . . 31 janvier 1834, *etc.* pp. 46. [*Paris*,] 1834. 8°. **7854. d. 31. (14.)**

—— Catalogue d'une bonne collection de tableaux des différentes écoles, tant anciennes que modernes . . . dont la vente se fera . . . 14 et . . . 15 avril 1834, *etc.* pp. 23. *Paris*, 1834. 8°. **7854. d. 31. (13.)**

—— Catalogue d'une précieuse collection de tableaux des trois écoles et par de grands maîtres . . . le tout provenant du cabinet de M. A . . . ., dont la vente se fera . . . 14 et . . . 15 avril [1834], *etc.* pp. 34. 1834. 8°. *See* A . . . ., M. **7854. d. 31. (8.)**

—— Catalogue de dessins, aquarelles . . . et tableaux, provenant du cabinet de M. le duc de R * * *, dont la vente aura lieu . . . 18 et 19 . . . avril 1834, *etc.* pp. 18. 1834. 8°. *See* R * * *, *M. le duc de.* **7854. d. 31. (12.)**

—— Catalogue des livres de la bibliothèque de feu M T * * * * * * *, dont la vente se fera . . . 22 mai, 1834, *etc.* pp. viii. 124. 1834. 8°. *See* T * * * * * * *, M. **T. 2401. (1.)**

—— Catalogue d'une collection de tableaux des trois écoles, et composant le cabinet formé . . . par Mr J. A. L. B. dont la vente aura lieu . . . 25 et . . . 26 novembre [1834], *etc.* pp. 23. 1834. 8°. *See* B., J. A. L., Mr. **7854. d. 31. (9.)**

—— Catalogo della biblioteca di un amatore bibliofilo [i.e. Marquis G. F. Durazzo]. pp. 251. *Italia* [*Genoa*], [1834-35]. 4°. **11904. l. 11.**

—— Catalogue de raretés bibliographiques en livres et manuscrits de théologie, la plupart d'une haute antiquité . . . provenant de la bibliothèque d'un amateur. pp. ii. 96. *Paris*, 1834. 8°. **S.C. 845/4.**

—— Хронологической списокъ ста сочиненій . . . на арабскомъ, персидскомъ и турецкомъ языкахъ, недостающихъ большею частію въ Европейскихъ библіотекахъ, коихъ отысканіемъ . . . слѣдовало бы заняться для пользы наукъ особамъ имѣющимъ свое пребываніе на Востокѣ. Notice chronologique d'une centaine d'ouvrages . . . tant arabes que persans et turcs, qui manquent en grande partie aux différentes bibliothèques de l'Europe, *etc.* pp. 24. *С.-Петербургъ*, 1834. 4°. **825. kk. 24. (2.)**

—— Catalogue d'une précieuse collection de tableaux des écoles anciennes et modernes, formant le cabinet de M. F. ; dont la vente se fera . . . 22 avril 1835, *etc.* pp. 23. 1835. 8°. *See* F., M. **7854. d. 32. (1.)**

CATALOGUES.

—— Catalogue d'une jolie collection de tableaux anciens et modernes, objets d'arts [*sic*] et de haute curiosités [*sic*] . . . dont la vente aura lieu les 27, 28 et 29 avril 1835, *etc.* pp. 31. *Paris*, 1835. 8°. **7854. e. 26. (3.)**

—— Catalogue de tableaux des diverses écoles, qui seront vendus . . . 11 et . . . 12 mai 1835, *etc.* (Ces tableaux ont été rassemblées par Mr M.) pp. 22. 1835. 8°. *See* M., Mr. **7854. d. 32. (3.)**

—— Vente pour cause de départ, d'une jolie collection d'objets d'art, meubles anciens . . . 25 et . . . 26 mai 1835, *etc.* pp. 16. [*Paris*, 1835.] 8°. **562. e. 77. (2.)**

—— Catalogue d'une belle et riche collection de tableaux, anciens et modernes, meubles précieux . . . provenant du cabinet de feu M. l'abbé B * * *, dont la vente . . . aura lieu . . . 20 et . . . 21 novembre, *etc.* pp. 32. [1835 ?] 8°. *See* B * * *, *M. l'abbé.* **7854. cc. 33. (1.)**

—— London Catalogue of Books, with their sizes, prices, and publishers. Containing the books published in London . . . since the year 1814 to December 1834. [Compiled by Robert Bent.] pp. 350. *Robert Bent: London*, 1835. 8°. Circ. **90. a.**

—— [Another copy.] **11900. c. 43. (1.)**

—— Catalogue de tableaux, composant la belle collection de M. N * * *, amateur de province, dont la vente aura lieu . . . 25 et . . . 26 avril 1836, *etc.* pp. 36. *See* N * * *, M., *Amateur de province.* 1836. 8°. **7854. e. 26. (4.)**

—— Catalogue d'une collection précieuse d'anciens livres, dont la vente se fera le 16. novbr. 1836 à Hamm, *etc.* pp. 12. *Hamm*, 1836. 8°. **S.C. 231. (5.)**

—— Bibliotheca Piscatoria. A catalogue of books upon angling. [By William Pickering.] [*William Pickering :*] *London*, 1836. 12°. **7905. a. 13.**

—— Catalogue of a Select Law Library. [By Simon Greenleaf.] pp. 16. MS. NOTES. [*Cambridge, Mass.*, 1836.] 8°. **6005. f. 15.**

—— A Chronological List of Books and Single Papers, relating to the subject of the rate of mortality, annuities, and life-assurance. With the titles of the several Parliamentary reports and tables connected with friendly societies, *etc.* pp. 32. *Privately printed: London*, 1836. 8°. **1027. l. 8.** *One of an edition of* 100 *copies.*

—— Catalogue de tableaux et objets de curiosité, provenant de la collection de M. D * *, amateur, dont la vente aura lieu . . . 3 avril [1837], *etc.* pp. 22. 1837. 8°. *See* D * *, M., *Amateur.* **7854. cc. 36. (6.)**

—— Catalogue de tableaux italiens, espagnols . . . dont la vente aura lieu . . . 21 et . . . 22 avril 1837, *etc.* [Compiled by — George.] pp. 28. *Paris*, 1837. 8°. **7854. cc. 33. (3.)**

—— Catalogo di edizioni Aldine e Cominiane, che si vendono . . . all'asta pubblica dal 30 maggio al 3 giugno 1837 in Firenze, *etc.* pp. 12. *Firenze*, 1837. 8°. **822. b. 33.**

—— Catalog einer ausgewählten Bibliothek anerkannt werthvoller, meistens neuer Bücher aus allen Wissenschaften . . . welche vom 17. Juli 1837 an gegen baare Zahlung in Heidelberg versteigert werden sollen, *etc.* pp. 26. *Heidelberg*, 1837. **S.C. 845. (6.)**

—— Catalogo di una scelta collezione di libri attualmente in vendita ai prezzi notati a ciascun articolo. pp. 96. *Pisa*, 1837. 8°. **S.C. 543. (9.)**

CATALOGUES.

—— Supplement to the London Catalogue of Books, with their sizes, prices, and publishers. Containing the books published in London, from December 1834 to December 1836. [Compiled by Robert Bent.] pp. 48.
Robert Bent: London, 1837. 8º.   Circ. **90**. a.

—— [Another copy.]   **11900**. c. **43**. (2.)

—— Catalogue d'une belle collection de tableaux des différentes écoles, dont la vente aura lieu . . . 22 et . . . 23 janvier 1838, *etc.* pp. 19. [*Paris*,] 1838. 8º.
7854. cc. **36**. (9.)

—— Catalogue de tableaux capitaux des écoles italienne, hollandaise . . . dont la vente aura lieu . . . 26 mars 1838, *etc.* pp. 23. [*Paris*,] 1838. 8º. **7854**. cc. **38**. (3.)

—— Notice de tableaux, dont quelques-uns proviennent de la galerie des ducs d'Albe ; avec supplément de 37 études de Casati, dont la vente aura lieu . . . 14 . . . 15 et . . . 16 mai 1838, *etc.* pp. 10. *Paris*, 1838. 8º.
7854. cc. **36**. (11.)

—— A Catalogue of Books published in London, September 1837 to December 1838 (during the year 1839[-1844]). *See* PERIODICAL PUBLICATIONS.—*London.* The Publishers' Circular. 1837, *etc.* 8º.   P.P. **6481**.

—— Primo elenco degli oggetti che si propongono per la lotteria da eseguirsi in beneficio dei poveri rimasti orfani pel cholera, *etc.* pp. 12. *Roma*, 1838. 12º. **8228**. aaaa. **6**.

—— Elenco degli oggetti che si propongono per la lotteria da eseguirsi in beneficio dei poveri rimasti orfani pel cholera, *etc.* pp. 36. [*Rome*, 1838.] 12º. **8228**. aaaa. **5**.

—— Notice de livres dont la vente se fera . . . 8 janvier 1840, *etc.* pp. 24. MS. NOTES AND PRICES. [*Paris*, 1840.] 8º.   **821**. h. **24**. (4.)

—— Catalogue de livres provenant de la bibliothèque de M * * * [i.e. J. J. Techener], dont la vente se fera . . . 13 janvier, *etc.* pp. 38. MS. NOTES AND PRICES. 1840. 8º. *See* M * * *.   **821**. h. **24**. (6.)

—— Catalogue de tableaux anciens et modernes, provenant de la collection formée par M. le comte de * * *, et de quelques objets de curiosité dont la vente sera faite . . . 8 . . . 9 et . . . 10 avril 1840, *etc.* pp. 66. *Paris*, 1840. 8º.   **7854**. d. **33**. (3.)

—— Bibliotheca Americana, being a choice collection of books, relating to North and South America and the West Indies, including voyages to the Southern Hemisphere, maps, engravings and medals. [By David B. Warden.] pp. 124. *Fain & Thunot: Paris*, 1840. 8º. **619**. d. **38**.
Previous edition 1831.

—— Desiderata. [An Italian bookseller's list.] pp. 32. [1840 ?] 16º.   **616**. a. **37**. (2.)

—— Oriental Manuscripts purchased in Turkey. [A catalogue of the collection of John Lee.] pp. 71.
Richard Watts: [London, 1840.] 4º.   **11907**. g. **31**.
Previous edition 1831.

—— Vollständiges Verzeichniss der Literatur der allgemeinen Anatomie des Menschen und der Haussäugethiere in systematischer Eintheilung. pp. 35. *Bern*, 1840. 4º.
7420. c. **4**.

—— Catalogue of 160 Lots of Land, and 5 Wharves in the South Cove, to be sold at auction on Tuesday, April 20, 1841 . . . The right of choice, among said lots, will be sold by auction, *etc.* pp. 16.   *Crocker & Brewster: Boston*, 1841. 8º.   **10409**. w. **4**. (1.)

CATALOGUES.

—— Catalogue d'une belle collection de tableaux des écoles flamande, hollandaise et française, réunis par un amateur ; dont la vente : . . aura lieu à Gand . . . 26 avril 1841, *etc.* pp. 46. *Gand*, [1841.] 8º.   **7854**. cc. **33**. (5.)

—— Almindeligt dansk-norsk Forlagscatalog. Udgivet af Forlagsforeningen i Kjøbenhavn, *etc.* 1841. 8º. *See* COPENHAGEN.—*Forlagsforeningen.*   **11899**. f. **38**. (1.)

—— Polytechnische Bücher-Kunde, oder beurtheilendes Verzeichniss der vorzüglichsten Bücher über Chemie, Technologie, Fabrikwissenschaft . . . Dritte ganz umgearbeitete Ausgabe. [By J. C. Leuchs.] pp. viii. 224. *Nürnberg*, 1841. 8º.   **011901**. h. **24**.

—— Catalogue de curiosités bibliographiques . . . recueillis par le Bibliophile voyageur. Cinquième année. [The " avertissement " signed : P. L., i.e. P. Lacroix.] 1842. 8º. *See* L., P.   **11900**. bbb. **1**. (1.)

—— Catalogue de livres et manuscrits, la plupart d'une haute antiquité . . . suivis d'une collection considérable d'Elzevirs . . . et d'autographes. Dont la vente se fera . . . 2 mars 1843 et jours suivants . . . Les adjudications seront faites par Me Regnard, *etc.* pp. 213. *Paris*, 1842. 8º.
S.C. **676**. (6.)

—— [Another copy.]   **11902**. bbb. **40**. (3.)
Imperfect ; wanting all except the title-page, Avertissement, and Table des divisions.

—— Catalogue d'une bibliothèque choisie. Pour faire suite à l'ouvrage intitulé Les Mauvais livres, les mauvais journaux, et les romans. [By J. B. Boone.] pp. 146–261. *Bruxelles*, 1843. 16º.   **616**. a. **36**.
The pagination is apparently continuous with that of " Les Mauvais livres."

—— Catalogus peccatorum in usum confessariorum. pp. 77. *Ratisbonae*, 1843. 12º.   **1359**. a. **46**. (2.)

—— Selected Centuries of Books from the library of a Priest in the Diocese of Salisbury [i.e. William Maskell]. pp. 153. [*William Pickering: London*,] 1843. 8º.   **11900**. c. **23**.
One of an edition of fifty copies privately printed by C. Whittingham.

—— [Another copy.] MS. NOTES [by W. Maskell].
11900. d. **29**.
Interleaved.

—— Catalogue of Books received [by the Bodleian Library] from Stationers' Hall in the year 1843. pp. 88. [*Oxford*, 1844.] 8º.   **11912**. aa. **56**.

—— Supplement to the London Catalogue of Books, edition dated 1839. Containing the new works and new editions published in London from January 1839 to January 1844, *etc.* [Compiled by Thomas Hodgson.] pp. iv. 156. *Thomas Hodgson: London*, 1844. 8º.   **618**. f. **32**.

—— Bibliografia del Estudiante, o Guia de la lectura y del estudio para los niños y jóvenes aplicados. pp. 109. *Madrid*, 1845. 16º.   **11901**. a. **19**.

—— A List of Early English Printers and Books. pp. 32. *T. C. Savill: [London*, 1845 ?] 4º.   **11917.gg.4.**

—— Catalogue de livres rares et précieux . . . provenant de la bibliothèque de M. le P. d' E * * * * * * [i.e. André Masséna, Prince of Essling], dont la vente se fera . . . 16 février 1846, *etc.* pp. 94. 1845. 8º. *See* E * * * * * *, M. le P. d'.   **11901**. b. **44**. (3.)

CATALOGUES.

—— Catalogue d'une collection précieuse de livres . . . qui seront adjugés au plus offrant à Halle le 16. mars 1846, *etc.* pp. 402. [*Halle*, 1846.]   **11914. e. 30.**

—— A Catalogue (Sampson Low's Catalogue) of Book published in the United Kingdom during the year 1845 –(1856). [1846–57.] *See* PERIODICAL PUBLICATIONS.— *London.* The Publishers' Circular. 1837, *etc.* 8°.   **P.P. 6481.**

—— The London Catalogue of Books published in Great Britain. With their sizes, prices, and publishers' Names. From 1814 to 1846. [Compiled by Thomas Hodgson.] pp. viii. 542. *Thomas Hodgson: London*, 1846. 8°.   **11900. f. 24.**

—— Svensk bokhandels-katalog utgifven år 1845. (Til-lägg till Svensk bokhandels-katalog 1848.—Tillägg till Svensk bokhandels-katalog 1851.) 3 pt.   *Stockholm*, 1846–52. 8°.   **618. f. 30.**

—— Catalogue de beaux livres anciens, manuscrits et auto-graphes, provenant du cabinet de M. J. L. B., dont la vente aura lieu . . . 6 avril 1847, *etc.* pp. 16. 1847. 8°. *See* B., M. J. L.   **11900. bbb. 1. (7.)**

—— Catalogue des livres de médecine, d'art militaire . . . composant la bibliothèque de M. G. B., dont la vente aura lieu le 3 mai 1847, *etc.* pp. 68. 1847. 8°. *See* B., M. G.   **822. e. 18. (4.)**

—— Catalogue de livres en partie, rares et précieux, prove-nant de la bibliothèque de M. Eug. P. dont la vente se fera . . . 18 mai 1847, *etc.* pp. 42. 1847. 8°. *See* P. (Eug.)   **822. e. 18. (8.)**

—— Catalogue de curiosités bibliographiques, livres rares . . . recueillis par le Bibliophile voyageur. Dixième année. [The " avertissement " signed: P. L., i.e. P. Lacroix.] pp. 56. 1847. 8°. *See* L., P. **822. e. 17. (8.)**

—— Catalogue des livres anciens . . . des dessins, des vieilles estampes . . . et d'un choix de livres précieux imprimés en Chine, composant le cabinet de M. K. L. A * * P. de M., dont la vente se fera . . . 17 février. 1848, *etc.* pp. 115. 1848. 8°. *See* M., M. K. L. A * * P. DE.   **822. b. 27.**

—— Catalogue de beaux livres français, italiens, espagnols, etc. . . . . provenant de la bibliothèque de M. de L * * * * * *, dont la vente aura lieu . . . 7 décembre 1848, *etc.* pp. 92. 1848. 8°. *See* L * * * * * *, DE, *M.*   **822. d. 32.**

—— Bibliotheca Londinensis : a classified index to the literature of Great Britain during thirty years. Arranged from and serving as a key to the London Catalogue of Books, 1814–46, *etc.* [Compiled by Thomas Hodgson.] pp. vii. 283. *Thomas Hodgson: London*, 1848. 8°.   **Circ. 91. a.**

—— [Another copy.]   **11900. f. 26.**

—— Deutscher Zeitungs-Katalog. Verzeichniss der in deutscher Sprache erscheinenden periodischen Schriften, *etc.* 1848–65. 8°.   *See* PERIODICAL PUBLICATIONS.— *Leipsic.*   **P.P. 6523.**

—— Wegweiser auf dem Gebiete der sozial-demokratischen Literatur Deutschlands. Dritte vermehrte Auflage, bis Dez. 1848. pp. 10. *Leipzig*, [1848.] 8°.   **823. a. 14. (3.)**

CATALOGUES.

—— Catalogue des livres rares et curieux composant la bibliothèque de M. G. B * * * *, dont la vente aura lieu . . . 30 avril 1849, *etc.* pp. 136. 1849. 8°. *See* B * * * *, M. G.   **11914. e. 39.**

—— Catalogue d'une précieuse collection de livres . . . provenant du cabinet de M. Ch. B * * * de V. (Dont la vente aura lieu le 9 juillet [1849].) pp. ii. 260. 1849. 8°. *See* V., M. CH. B * * * DE.   **823. b. 36.**

—— Catalogue d'un choix rare de médailles antiques grecques et romaines . . . de divers objets d'antiquités . . . et de livres sur la numismatique et l'histoire naturelle, la vente . . . aura lieu, par suite du décès de M. M * * *, touriste étranger . . . 26 novembre 1849, *etc.* pp. 24. 1849. 8°. *See* M * * *, M., *Touriste étranger*.   **7757. c. 10. (1.)**

—— Beurtheilende Übersicht derjenigen durch den Druck verfielfältigten Karten, Situations- und Festungs-Pläne von Europa, welche für deutsche Militairs von praktischem Interesse sind. Tl. 1. Central Europa. 1849. 4°. *See* PRUSSIA.—*Army.*—*Staff.*—*Topographische Abteilung.*   **10105. f. 9.**

—— A Bibliographical Catalogue of Books, Translations of the Scriptures, and other Publications in the Indian Tongues of the United States, *etc.* [The foreword signed : H. R. S., i.e. Henry R. Schoolcraft.] 1849. 8°. *See* S., H. R.   **4999. d. 32.**

—— Bibliotheca scatologica, ou Catalogue raisonné des livres traitant des vertus faits et gestes de très noble et très ingénieux Messire Luc—à rebours—Seigneur de la Chaise et autres lieux . . . Traduit du prussien et enrichi de notes très congruantes au sujet par trois savants en us. [By P. Jannet, J. F. Payen, and A. A. Veinant.] pp. 143. *Scatopolis* [*Paris*], 5850 [1849]. 8°. [*Journal de l'ama-teur de livres.* tom. 2. Complément.]   **011904. aaa. 48.**

—— [Another issue.] *Scatopolis* [*Paris*], 5850 [1849]. 8°.   **011900. aaa. 26.**

—— Supplement to the London Catalogue of Books published in Great Britain, with their sizes, prices, and publishers' names, from 1846 to 1849. Including a classified index, *etc.* [Compiled by Thomas Hodgson.] pp. 56. *Thomas Hodgson: London*, 1849. 8°.   **11900. f. 25.**

—— Catalogue des livres rares et précieux de la bibliothèque de M. E. B * * *, dont la vente se fera le 10 avril 1850, *etc.* pp. iv. 376. 1850. 8°. *See* B * * *, M. E.   **822. b. 15.**

—— Catalogue des livres rares et précieux de la bibliothèque de M. M * * *, dont la vente aura lieu . . . 11 novembre [1850], *etc.* pp. 476. 1850. 8°. *See* M * * *, M.   **822. b. 34.**

—— Catalogue d'une collection. Poissons et reptiles de Amboina, Ceram et Boero. pp. 48. [1850 ?] 8°.   **7290. b. 32. (4.)**

—— Catalogue des écrits, gravures et dessins condamnés depuis 1814 jusqu'au 1er janvier 1850. Suivi de la liste des individus condamnés pour délits de presse. pp. 202. *Paris*, 1850. 12°.   **011902. e. 14.**

—— [Another issue.]   *Paris*, 1850. 12°.   **823. a. 29.**

—— [Another copy.]   **011904. eee. 10.**

—— Catalogue des livres proposés aux bibliothèques parois-siales de la province ecclésiastique d'Avignon. pp. 54. 1850. 8°. *See* AVIGNON, *Province of.—Comité Central pour l'Établissement des Bibliothèques Paroissiales dans la Pro-vince d'Avignon.*   **011903. k. 9. (1.)**

CATALOGUES.

—— Grande collection de camées. pp. 7. [1850?] 8º.
787. g. 37.

—— The London Catalogue of British Plants . . . Third edition. [Compiled by H. C. Watson and G. E. Dennes.] pp. 16. iv. 1850. 8º. *See* LONDON.—III. *Botanical Society of London.* **7055. e. 2.**

—— Thesaurus librorum rei catholicae. Handbuch der Bücherkunde der gesammten Literatur des Katholicismus und zunächst der katholischen Theologie, *etc.* (Ergänzungsheft. Theologisches Fach- und Sachregister, oder übersichtliche Zusammenstellungen des Inhalts des Thesaurus, *etc.*) 2 Bd. *Würzburg,* 1850. 8º.
4999. bbb. 48.

—— Catalogue de lettres autographes . . . provenant du cabinet de M. de C*** [i.e. Pierre Capelle] . . . dont la vente aura lieu . . . 20 mars 1851 et jours suivants, *etc.* 1851. 8º. *See* C***, M. de. **S.C. 673. (4.)**

—— The London Catalogue of Books published in Great Britain. With their sizes, prices, and publishers' names. 1816 to 1851. pp. 644. *Thomas Hodgson : London,* 1851. 8º. **Circ. 90. a.**

—— Catalogue d'une jolie collection de lettres autographes de personnages célèbres en tous genres, dépendant de la succession de feu M. J. L***, dont la vente aura lieu . . . 24 mai 1852, *etc.* pp. 86. 1852. 8º. *See* L***, M. J. **823. b. 26.**

—— Katalog ogólny książek polskich drukowanych od roku 1830. do 1850. . . . Z oznaczeniem formatu . . . ceny pierwotnej oraz z dodaniem podziału naukowego książek niniejszym spisem objętych. Zebrał i wydał W. R. [i.e. W. Rafalski.] pp. 268. 56. 1852. 8º. *See* R., W.
824. d. 14.

—— Catalogue d'une petite collection de livres rares et précieux . . . provenant du cabinet de M. A. C., dont la vente se fera . . . 4 mai 1853, *etc.* pp. iii. 48. MS. PRICES. *See* C., M. A. **11902. f. 27.**

—— Catalogue d'une précieuse collection de livres, manuscrits, autographes, dessins et gravures composant actuellement la bibliothèque de M. A. A. R. [i.e. A. A. Renouard.] pp. iv. 420. 1853. 8º. *See* R., M. A. A. **824. c. 24**

—— Catalogue historique des médailles et pièces de monnaie depuis la fondation de la dynastie ottomane, l'an 699 de l'Hégire, par Sultan Osman-Kan jusqu'à Sultan Abdul-Medjid-Kan [in the collection of M. Bilazikji], *etc.* pp. 12. *Paris,* 1853. 4º. **Dept. of Coins & Medals.**

—— The Classified Index to the London Catalogue of Books published in Great Britain, 1816 to 1851. Arranged throughout in regular alphabet, *etc.* pp. xiv. 285. *Thomas Hodgson : London,* 1853. 8º. **Circ. 90. a.**

—— The London Catalogue of British Plants . . . Fourth edition. [Compiled by H. C. Watson and J. T. Syme.] pp. 16. 1853. 8º. *See* LONDON.—III. *Botanical Society of London.* **7055. e. 3.**

—— Catalogue des livres rares et précieux composant la bibliothèque de M. Ch. G***** [i.e. C. J. B. Giraud], dont la vente aura lieu . . . 26 mars 1855, *etc.* pp. xix. 464. 1855. 8º. *See* G*****, M. Ch.
11900. f. 22.

—— Библіографическій указатель книгъ, вышедшихъ въ Россіи въ первой (второй) половинѣ 1854 года и статей, помѣщенныхъ въ журналахъ и газетахъ того же полугодія. [By V. E. Mezhov.] 2 част. *Санктпетербургъ,* 1855. 8º. **11904. k. 13.**

CATALOGUES.

—— Catalogue général des ouvrages de propriété française publiés antérieurement au 12 mai 1854 et déposés en exécution de l'art. 2, § 5 de la Convention littéraire du 22 août 1852 ; avec tables alphabétiques, *etc.* [Edited by L. Gonne.] pp. ix. 124. 338. 31. *Bruxelles,* 1855. 8º.
11904. dd. 21.

—— The London Catalogue of Books published in Great Britain. With their sizes, prices, and publisher's names. 1831 to 1855. pp. vi. 583. *Thomas Hodgson : London,* 1855. 8º. **Circ. 90. a.**

—— [Another copy.] **011904. a. 49.**

—— Catalogue de livres relatifs à l'histoire de France, à l'histoire de Paris, aux beaux-arts et à la bibliographie, provenant de la bibliothèque de M. de N*** . . . dont la vente se fera . . . 28 mai 1856, *etc.* pp. 144. 1856. 8º. *See* N***, M. de. **823. g. 66.**

—— Catalogue d'un choix remarquable de livres rares et curieux provenant du cabinet de M. le comte P. de M . . . . Dont la vente aura lieu . . . 8 décembre 1856, *etc.* 1856. 8º. *See* M . . ., P. de, *M. le comte.* **823. g. 65.**

—— Catalogue des livres . . . composant la bibliothèque de feu M. Pierre-Joseph D***, ancien notaire à Cambrai, dont la vente aura lieu . . . 8 décembre 1856, *etc.* pp. vii. 183. 1856. 8º. *See* D*** (Pierre J.) *Ancien notaire à Cambrai.* **824. g. 34.**

—— The American Catalogue of Books : or, English guide to American literature, giving the full title of original works published in the United States since the year 1800. With especial reference to works of interest to Great Britain, *etc.* pp. vii. 190. *Sampson Low, Son & Co. : London,* 1856. 8º. **11902. bb. 42.**

—— A Catalogue of Books, the property of the author of the Commercial Dictionary [i.e. J. R. MacCulloch]. [With a portrait.] pp. 175. *G. E. Eyre & W. Spottiswoode : London,* 1856. 8º. **011903. f. 17.** *Privately printed.*

—— A Catalogue of the British Phænogamous Plants and Ferns, arranged according to the natural and Linnean systems, showing the months of flowering. pp. 48. *G. Booth : Hyde,* 1856. 12º. **7030. aa. 18.**

—— Förteckning öfver svenska bokhandelns under år 1855(–1859) utkomne böcker, lithografiska arbeten, kartor, *etc.* 5 pt. *Stockholm,* 1856–60. 8º. **11900. c. 25.**

—— The Religious Literature of the Past Year. A summary, partly reprinted from the table of contents to the " Literary Churchman," *etc.* *J. H. & J. Parker : Oxford & London,* 1856. 16º. **1882. d. 1. (147.)** *Imperfect ; wanting all except the titlepage and the last leaf.*

—— Catalogue des livres rares et précieux, manuscrits et imprimés, composant la bibliothèque de M. C. R*** de Milan [i.e. C. Riva], dont la vente aura lieu . . . 8 janvier 1857, *etc.* pp. xii. 256. MS. PRICES. 1856. 8º. *See* R***, M. C., *de Milan.* **11904. f. 38.**

—— Catalogue de lettres autographes. [A sale catalogue issued by J. Charavay, 26, 27 Nov. 1857.] pp. 25. MS. PRICES. [*Paris,* 1857.] 8º. **11900. bbb. 5. (11.)** *Imperfect ; wanting the titlepage.*

—— Catalogue of Illustrated Works, Reward Cards, etc. suitable for prizes in the public schools of Upper Canada, *etc.* pp. 32. 1857. 8º. *See* ONTARIO.—*Department of Public Instruction.* **8304. b. 2. (2.)**

CATALOGUES.

—— Catalogue of the Universal Circulating Musical Library, including the Supplements of 1855 & 1856. pp. viii. 1072. *Gustav Scheurmann & Co.: London*, [1857.] 8°.
7900. ee. 9.

—— Supplement III. pp. xx [x]. 1074–1341. *Augener & Co.: London ; Darmstadt* printed, 1861. 8°.
7900. ee. 9. a.

—— A General Catalogue of Books in Every Department of Literature, for public school libraries in Upper Canada, *etc.* pp. 263. 1857. 8°. *See* ONTARIO.—*Department of Public Instruction.*
11904. bb. 3.

—— Répertoire des ouvrages de législation, de droit et de jurisprudence en matière civile, administrative, commerciale et criminelle publiés . . . en France depuis 1789 jusqu'à la fin de décembre 1856, *etc.* pp. 122. *Paris*, 1857. 8°.
5425. f. 8.

—— Catalog einer bedeutenden Sammlung von Antiquitäten welche am 4. Januar 1858 . . . versteigert werden soll, *etc.* pp. 48. *Leipzig*, 1857. 8°.
7707. b. 40. (6.)

—— Catalogue d'autographes. [A sale catalogue issued by J. Charavay, 1–3 May 1858.] pp. 23. MS. PRICES. *Paris*, [1858.] 8°.
11900. bbb. 5. (14.)
Imperfect ; wanting the titlepage.

—— The British Catalogue of Books published during the year 1857(–1860). [1858–61.] *See* PERIODICAL PUBLICATIONS.—*London.* The Publishers' Circular. 1837, *etc.* 8°.
P.P. 6481.

—— Catalogue d'autographes. pp. 16. MS. PRICES. *Strasbourg*, [1858?] 8°.
11900. bbb. 5. (19.)
Imperfect ; wanting the titlepage.

—— Katalog der geschichtlichen, geographischen und militärischen Literatur des Grossherzogthums Baden. Ein Handbuch für Historiker, Geographen und Militär. pp. 57. *Freiburg*, 1858. 4°.
11901. b. 46.
Lithographed.

—— Catalogue d'une jolie collection de livres relatifs à l'Orient, particulièrement à l'Empire Ottoman, provenant du cabinet d'un membre du corps diplomatique étranger. La vente aura lieu . . . 17 et . . . 18 mars. 1859, *etc.* pp. 40. *Paris*, 1859. 8°.
11900. c. 29.

—— Библіографія за 1856 и 1857 гг. или указатель книгъ, составленный . . . В. Н. М. [i.e. by V. I. Mezhov], *etc.* pp. 424. 1859. 8°. *See* PERIODICAL PUBLICATIONS.— *Moscow.*—*Русская Бесѣда.*
11904. h. 25.

—— Catalogue d'une magnifique collection de livres . . . d'une collection superbe de portraits ; de deux dessins originaux de Crabeth etc. ayant formé en grande partie la bibliothèque d'un amateur, et dont la vente aura lieu . . . 21 mai 1860, *etc.* pp. 94. *Rotterdam*, [1860.] 8°.
11914. aa. 36.

—— Catalogue de livres rares provenant des bibliothèques de feu son Exc. M. le baron de W. et de quelques autres amateurs, dont la vente aura lieu le 30 octobre 1860 et jour [*sic*] suivants (15 février 1861 et jours suivants], *etc.* 1860, 61. 8°. *See* W., *M. le baron de.* **11917. aa. 15.**

—— List of Bengali Books, useful either for educational purposes or for libraries. pp. 5. [1860?] 8°.
11900. dd. 13.

—— Förteckning öfver en samling svenska, norska och danska mynt, hufvudsakligen från medeltiden, äfvensom böcker i numismatik . . . som försäljas på Stockholms Bok-auktionskammare . . . den ellofte, 11, december . . . 1861. pp. 75. *Stockholm*, 1861. 8°.
7756. bbb. 40. (4.)

CATALOGUES.

—— The English Catalogue of Books for 1860 [*etc.*] 1861– . *See* PERIODICAL PUBLICATIONS.—*London.* The Publishers' Circular. 1837, *etc.* 8°.
P.P. 6481.

—— Bibliographie des principaux ouvrages relatifs à l'amour, aux femmes, au mariage . . . Par M. le C. d'I * * * [i.e. Jules Gay]. 1861. 8°. *See* I * * *, *M. le C. d'.*
11900. cc. 2.

—— Библіографическій указатель книгъ и журнальныхъ статей, относящихся до южно-русскаго края, съ 1858–1860 гг. [By V. I. Mezhov.] pp. 27. [*Saint Petersburg*, 1861.] 8°.
11904. h. 1. (3.)

—— [Another copy.]
11903. g. 33.

—— Trente années de la littérature belge. Bibliotheca belgica. Catalogue général des principales publications belges depuis 1830 jusqu'à 1860. 1861. 8°. *See* SCHNÉE (A.)
011908. de. 13.

—— Verzeichniss einer höchst werthvollen Sammlung antiker Jagdwaffen aus allen Jahrhunderten, welche am 25. und 26. April 1862 in Dresden . . . versteigert werden soll. *Dresden*, [1862.] 8°.
7907. bbb. 38. (6.)

—— Catalogue de la bibliothèque de M. le Vicomte d'O · · · . . . dont la vente aura lieu le 15 décembre 1862. pp. viii. 192. 1862. 8°. *See* O · · · (d') *Viscount.*
11927. b. 12.

—— A Catalogue of Books, the Property of a Political Economist [i.e. J. R. M'Culloch]; with critical and bibliographical notices. [By M'Culloch.] pp. viii. 394. *London*, 1862. 8°.
Cup.400.d.6.

—— Catalogue des livres en partie rares et précieux composant la bibliothèque de M. H. D. L. [i.e. H. de Lasize?] dont la vente aura lieu le mercredi 7 janvier 1863 et les six jours suivants, *etc.* pp. viii. 171. 1862. 8°. *See* L., H. D.
11915. bb. 23.

—— Catalogue des livres rares et précieux de la bibliothèque de M. le Comte H. de Ch***, *etc.* (La vente aura lieu le 26 janvier 1863.) pp. x. 147. 1863. 8°. *See* CH*** (H. de) *M. le Comte.*
11915. bb. 24.

—— Catalogue d'une collection de livres rares sur l'orient et les Indes Occidentales dont la vente se fera . . . 13 mai 1863, *etc.* pp. 19. *Paris*, 1863. 8°.
11914. e. 35.

—— Catalogue d'une magnifique collection de livres . . . formant la troisième partie d'une riche bibliothèque dont la vente aura lieu . . . 30 novembre 1863, *etc.* pp. 118. *Rotterdam*, [1863.] 8°.
11914. e. 32.

—— Библіографическій указатель вышедшихъ въ 1860, 1861 и 1862 гг. въ Россіи книгъ и статей по части языкознанія. [By V. I. Mezhov.] (Перепечатано изъ VI. выпуска "Филологическихъ Записокъ" 1863.) pp. 24. [*Saint Petersburg*, 1863.] 8°. **11904. h. 1. (5.)**

—— Catalogue of Postage Stamps, American and Foreign, and U.S. Revenue Stamps. [By George Dexter.] pp. 78. *Sever & Francis: Cambridge* [*Mass.*], 1863. 8°.
8247. aa. 13.

—— Bibliographie des ouvrages relatifs à l'amour, aux femmes, au mariage . . . Par M. le C. d'I * * * [i.e. Jules Gay]. Seconde édition, revue, corrigée et considérablement augmentée, *etc.* 1864. 8°. *See* I * * *, *M. le C. d'.*
11901. bbb. 16.

CATALOGUES.

—— Guida-manuale per far collezione di francobolli. Descrizione dettagliata delle emissioni di 1475 varietà di francobolli di ogni stato del mondo dal 1840 al 1863. [By U. Franchi.] pp. 26. MS. ADDITIONS [by the author]. *Firenze*, 1864. 8°. Crawford **805. (2.)**

—— [Another copy.] [Guida-manuale per far collezione dei francobolli, *etc.*] [By U. Franchi.] MS. ADDITIONS [by the author]. [*Florence*, 1864.] 8°. Crawford **769. (2.)** *Wanting the wrapper.*

—— Musica theatralis d. i. vollständiges Verzeichniss sämmtlicher, seit dem Jahre 1750 bis zu Ende des Jahres 1863 im deutschen und auswärtigen Handel gedruckt erschienenen, Opern-Clavier-Auszüge mit Text, und sonstiger, für die Bühne bestimmter Musikwerke, *etc.* pp. 56. *Erfurt*, 1864. 8°. **7898. g. 36. (3.)**

—— Catalogue d'une collection iconographique polonaise, composée des dessins originaux, gravures, xylographies . . . illustrant l'histoire, la géographie . . . de l'ancienne Pologne, de ses provinces et pays limitrophes. [A sale catalogue. By J. I. Kraszewski.] pp. 292. *Dresde*, [1865.] 8°. **7855. bb. 4.**

—— A New Catalogue of Errors, Latin text with English translation. Syllabus novus errorum, e lingua Latina in Anglicanam translatus. By a Man of the World. [A parody of the Syllabus of 8 Dec. 1864.] *Lat. & Eng.* pp. 15. *Charles Cull: London*, 1865. 8°. **3940. aa. 72.**

—— Catalogue of Roman Catholic Relics. [A reprint of " A Catalogue of the Most Eminently Venerable Relics of the Roman Catholic Church," published in 1818.] pp. 9. [*Privately printed: Middle Hill*, 1866.] fol. Tab. **436. b. 3. (5.)**

—— קרית ספר Ausführlicher bibliographischer Catalog der . . . Sammlungen hebräischer und jüdischer Bücher und Handschriften, nachgelassen vom Rabbiner Jakob Emden . . . und anderen. [By M. Roest.] Lfg. 1. pp. 224. *Amsterdam*, 1867. 8°. **11902. c. 37.**

—— Bibliotheca juridica. Handbuch der gesammten neueren juristischen und staatswissenschaftlichen Literatur, *etc.* 1867, 77. 8°. *See* WUTTIG (G. W.) **011907. ee. 20.**

—— Catalogue des journaux publiés à Paris en 1867 . . . Cinquième édition. 1867. 8°. *See* SCHULZ ET THUILLIÉ. **11899. ff. 42.**

—— Catalogue of Official Reports upon Geological Surveys of the United States and British Provinces. (From the American Journ. of Science and Arts.) pp. 14. [*New York*, 1867.] 8°. **11902. d. 28.**

—— Literatur über das Finanzwesen des Preussischen Staates. Beiheft des Königlich Preussischen Staats-Anzeigers, November 1867. Zweite Auflage. pp. 50. *Berlin*, 1867. fol. **8225. g. 20.**

—— The London Catalogue of British Plants . . . Sixth edition. [Compiled by H. C. Watson.] pp. 32. 1867. 8°. *See* LONDON.—III. *Botanical Society of the British Isles.* **7030. cc. 39.**

—— Musica sacra, *etc.* 3 Abt.
  Abt. 1. Vollständiges Verzeichniss aller seit dem Jahre 1750–1867 gedruckt erschienener Compositionen für die Orgel, Lehrbücher für die Orgel, Schriften über Orgelbaukunst, *etc.* pp. 56. 1867.
    Nachtrag zu Abtheilung 1. Vollständiges Verzeichniss aller seit dem Jahre 1867 bis Ende 1871 gedruckt erschienener Compositionen, *etc.* pp. 16. 1872.

CATALOGUES.

—— Abt. 2. Vollständiges Verzeichniss aller seit dem Jahre 1750–1871 gedruckt erschienener Choralbücher, Liturgieen, Schriften über Liturgie, Choral- und Gemeindegesang . . . Im Anhange: Abhandlung über den Choral und die ältere Literatur desselben, von J. A. P. Schulz. pp. 47. 1872.
  Abt. 3. Oratorien, Messen, Cantaten und andere Werke der Kirchenmusik im Clavier-Auszuge oder mit Begleitung der Orgel, *etc.* pp. 26. 1872.
Erfurt, 1867–72. 8°. **7897. c. 24.**

—— [Another copy of Abt. 1.] **7896. bb. 31. (8.)**

—— Verzeichniss der bis Ende Februar 1867 im Buchhandel erschienenen Werke und Schriften, welche sich auf den Krieg von 1866 beziehen . . . 2. Auflage. pp. 23. *Berlin*, [1867.] 8°. **11902. bb. 50. (10.)**

—— Verzeichniss einer Brandenburg-Preussischen Münzsammlung, welche am 27. April [1868] . . . zu Berlin öffentlich versteigert soll, *etc.* [The preface signed : V . . . .] 1868. 8°. *See* V . . . . **7756. cc. 29.**

—— Catalogue d'un marchand libraire du XVe siècle tenant boutique à Tours, publié par le Dr Achille Chereau. Avec notes explicatives. pp. 66. 1868. 12°. *See* PARIS.— *Académie des Bibliophiles.* **11900. a. 28. (5.)**

—— Die deutsche Literatur von 1854–1867 über öffentliche Gesundheitspflege, zunächst in technischer Beziehung. Nebst einigen Mittheilungen aus der englischen und französischen Literatur, *etc.* pp. iv. 53. *München*, 1868. 8°. **11902. c. 41. (3.)**

—— Literatur über das Hypothekenwesen des Preussischen Staates. Beiheft des Königl. Preussischen Staats-Anzeigers. pp. iv. 112. 63. *Berlin*, 1868. 8°. **5656. cc. 15.**

—— Catalogue des livres rares et précieux, manuscrits et imprimés, de la bibliothèque de M. le baron J. P * * * * *. (Table alphabétique des noms d'auteurs et des ouvrages anonymes . . . suivie de la liste des prix d'adjudication.) [A sale catalogue, dated : 19 April 1869. The preface signed: L. P., i.e. L. Potier.] 2 pt. 1869. 8°. *See* P * * * * *, J., M. le Baron. S.C. **1071. (2.)**

— — Catalogue des journaux publiés à Paris en 1869 . . . Sixième édition, augmentée et corrigée, *etc.* 1869. 8°. *See* SCHULZ ET THUILLIÉ. **011901. f. 26.**

—— Catalogus de theologia aliisque disciplinis librorum: qui quondam ad Religiosos Ordines Conimbricenses pertinuerunt ; et nunc quasdam in collectiones distributi, brevi tempore, Conimbricae, auctione constituta, sunt vendendi. 12 pt. *Conimbricae*, 1869. 8°. **11912. a. 3.** *This set contains two copies of each part.*

—— Catalogue of Books relating to China and the East. pp. 29. [1870 ?] 8°. **11903. bb. 50. (3.)**

—— Catalogue détaillé, raisonné et anecdotique d'une jolie collection de livres rares et curieux dont la plus grande partie provient de la bibliothèque et dont la vente aura lieu . . . 30 novembre . . . 1er et . . . 2 décembre 1871, *etc.* [A sale catalogue of the collection of P. C. Monselet.] pp. x. 125. *Paris*, 1871. 8°. **011904. g. 19.**

—— Bibliographie des ouvrages relatifs à l'amour, aux femmes, au mariage . . . Par M. le C. d'I * * * [i.e. Jules Gay]. 3me édition, entièrement refondue et considérablement augmentée, *etc.* 1871, *etc.* 8°. *See* I * * *, M. le C. d'. **11903. b. 35.**

CATALOGUES.

-- — Katalog aller seit dem Jahre 1840 bis auf die neueste Zeit ausgegebenen Brief- und Couvert-Marken. Nach der Alfred Moschkau'schen Sammlung bearbeitet. [By Gustav Bauschke.] pp. 96. *Leipzig*, 1871. 8º.
Crawford **521**. (2.)
Another issue is entered under SCHAUBEK (G.) pseud. [i.e. Gustav Bauschke.]

—— Montanistische Bibliothek. Verzeichniss der in Deutschland und im Auslande in den Jahren 1866-1870 auf den Gebieten des Berg-, Hütten- und Salinenwesens, der Mineralogie, Geognosie . . . erschienenen Bücher, Zeitschriften und Karten, *etc.* pp. xvi. 71. *Leipzig*, 1871. 8º. **820**. d. **9**. (2.)

—— Catalogue des journaux publiés à Paris en 1872 . . . Septième édition. 1873. 8º. *See* SCHULZ (L.) ET FILS. **11905**. a. **18**.

—— Catalogue des ouvrages condamnés comme contraires à 'a morale publique et aux bonnes mœurs du 1er janvier 1814 au 31 décembre 1873, *etc.* pp. 112. *Paris*, 1874. 8º. **11900**. aaa. **32**. (3.)

—— A Catalogue of Sanskrit Manuscripts in Private Libraries of the North-West Provinces, *etc.* 1874. 8º. *See* INDIA. —*North-Western Provinces*. **14096**. d. **11**.

—— List of English Books printed not later than the year 1600. Part II. History. [A catalogue of the library of Henry Pyne.] *Chiswick Press:* [*London*,] 1874. 8º. **011904**. h. **45**.
Privately printed. Later edition 1878.

—— List of Plates of Skeletons of Birds that have been published. pp. 15. *R. Hobson: Wellington, Salop.*, 1874. 16º. **7284**. aa. **16**.

—— The London Catalogue of British Plants . . . Seventh edition. [1874.] 8º. *See* LONDON.—III.*Botanical Society of the British Isles.* **7055**. cc. **17**. (4.)

—— Списокъ русскихъ анонимныхъ книгъ съ именами ихъ авторовъ и переводчиковъ. Дополненіе къ каталогамъ русскихъ книгъ Сопикова, Шторха . . . Глазунова и Базунова Г.Г. [i.e. by G. N. Gennadi.] pp. iii. 47. 1874. 8º. *See* G., G. **11905**. k. **21**. (3.)

—— Catalogue des tableaux et objets d'art provenant de collections célèbres dont la vente aura lieu à Rome les 1., 15 et 16 janvier 1875, *etc.* pp. 87. *Florence*, 1874. 4º. **7806**. de. **1**.

—— A Reference Catalogue of Current Literature. Containing the full titles of books now in print and on sale, *etc.*
Editions of the following years: 1874, 1875, 1877, 1880, 1885, 1889, 1894, 1898, 1902, 1906, 1910, 1913, 1920, 1921, 1924, 1928, 1932.
Joseph Whitaker: London, 1875-1932. 8º.
[Continued as :]
The Reference Catalogue of Current Literature. A national inclusive book-reference index of all books in print and on sale in the British Isles, *etc.*
J. Whitaker & Sons: London, 1936-. 4º.
L.R.266.a.& Circ.91.aa.

—— Bibliographie des ouvrages relatifs aux pélerinages, aux miracles, au spiritisme et à la prestidigitation, imprimés en France et en Italie, l'an du jubilé 1875. pp. 70. *Turin*, 1876. 8º. **11904**. e. **14**.

—— [Another copy.] **11904**. e. **16**.

—— Catalogue des tableaux, livres, dessins . . . composant le cabinet de M. L. C. [i.e. L. Constantin.] 1876. 8º. *See* C., M. L. **11899**. cc. **24**.

CATALOGUES.

—— A Catalogue of Modern Works on Science and Technology . . . Fifth (seventh–fourteenth, sixteenth–nineteenth, twenty-third–twenty-fifth, twenty-seventh–forty-second) edition. *Chapman & Hall: London*, 1876-1914. 8º. **011904.g.26.**& BB. E. b. **3**.
Imperfect; wanting the first–fourth, sixth, fifteenth, twenty-first, twenty-second and twenty-sixth editions.

—— A Classified Catalogue of School, College . . . and General Educational Works in use in the United Kingdom and its dependencies in 1876, *etc.* pp. vi. 154. *London*, 1876. 8º. **8306**. e. **4**.

—— Katalog von Werken über den Zeichenunterricht, *etc.* [With " Supplement."] 2 pt. *Neuwied*, 1876. 8º. **011908**. f. **34**.

—— Notes on the Pictures, Plate, Antiquities, etc., at Carton, Kilkea Castle, 13 Dominick Street, Dublin, and 6, Carlton-House-Terrace, London, 1876 [in the possession of Charles William FitzGerald, Duke of Leinster]. pp. 48. [*London*, 1876.] 16º. **7858**. aaa. **2**.

—— Catalogue de la bibliothèque de M. de X*** . . . Dont la vente aura lieu Rue des Bons-Enfants, nº 28 . . . le lundi 16 avril et les cinq jours suivants, *etc.* pp. 168. 1877. 8º. *See* X***, M. de. **11916**. e. **15**.

—— Katalog von kartographischen Werken: Atlanten, Karten, Plänen, etc. und Veranschaulichungsmitteln für den Unterricht in der astronomischen Geographie, *etc.* pp. xxxvi. 283. *Neuwied & Leipzig*, 1877. 8º. **11905**. f. **4**.

—— Catalogo collettivo della libreria italiana. 1878 [*etc.*]. 8º. *See* MILAN.—*Associazione Tipografico-Libraria Italiana.* **11906**. i. **4**.

—— List of English Books printed not later than the year 1600. [A catalogue of the library of H. Pyne.] pp. 141. *Privately printed:* [*London*,] 1878. 8º. **011904**. h. **24**.
Pp. 58–97, containing " Part 2. History," are a reissue of pp. 58–97 of the edition of Pt. 2 published in 1874.

—— A List of Serial Publications now taken in the Principal Libraries of Boston and Cambridge . . . December, 1878 pp. 30. *J. Wilson & Son: Cambridge* [*Mass.*], 1878. 8º. **11905**. k. **24**.

—— Svensk bok-katalog för åren 1866-1875 [*etc.*]. *Stockholm*, 1878-. 8º. **2115.e-f.**& 2330. g.

—— Catalogue de manuscrits précieux des XIIIe, XVe et XVIe siècles [including the library of Anne de Polignac] . . . dont la vente aura lieu le . . . 18 mars 1879, *etc.* pp. 31. *Paris*, 1879. 8º. **11906**. f. **16**.

—— Bibliographie clérico-galante. Ouvrages galants ou singuliers sur l'amour, les femmes, le mariage, le théâtre, etc., écrits par des abbés, prêtres, chanoines, religieux, religieuses, évêques, archevêques, cardinaux et papes. Par l'Apôtre bibliographe [i.e. Antoine Laporte]. pp. xxviii. 178. *Paris*, 1879. 8º. **11908**. bb. **17**. (2.)

—— —— Histoire d'une Bibliographie clérico-galante. Sa naissance d'un chanoine et d'un journaliste. Le Pourquoi—le comment. Par l'Apôtre bibliographe [i.e. Antoine Laporte]. pp. 28. *Paris*, 1879. 8º. **11905**. h. **17**.

—— —— [Another copy.] **11908**. bb. **17**. (1.)

—— Preis-Verzeichniss der in der Österreichisch-Ungarischen Monarchie und im Auslande erscheinenden Zeitungen und periodischen Druckschriften für das Jahr 1879, *etc.* (Erster—dritter Nachtrag.) 4 pt. 1879. 4º. *See* AUSTRIA.—*Postamt.—Zeitungs-Expedition.* **11905**. l. **24**.

CATALOGUES.

—— [A collection of sale-catalogues of works by and relating to Camões.] 10 pt. *Lisboa, Porto, etc.*, 1880–1904. 8°.
11912. b. 33.

—— Bibliotheca juridica. Verzeichniss der vorzüglichsten Werke aus allen Zweigen der Rechts- und Staatswissenschaften. Siebente, sehr vermehrte . . . Ausgabe, *etc.* pp. 181. *Wien*, 1880. 8°. **011899. l. 33.**

—— General English Book Catalogue for the retail trade, comprising a selection of works in the various departments of literature. pp. xii. 107. *W. H. Kühl: Berlin*, 1880. 8°. **11904. bb. 37.**

—— Hagiologia. Verzeichniss von Lebensbeschreibungen einzelner Heiligen, Seligen, hervorragender Ordensleute, etc., sowie Leben der Heiligen in Sammelausgaben. Erschienen 1840–1880. pp. 63. *Freiburg i. B.*, 1880. 12°.
4999. bbb. 15.

—— Inventaire des biens d'un serrurier lyonnais en 1372. Publié d'après le titre original par V. de V. pp. 7. *Lyon*, 1880. 8°. **7708. de. 14. (4.)**

—— Catalogue des ouvrages périodiques que reçoivent les principales bibliothèques de Belgique. pp. vii. 100. 1881. 8°. *See* BELGIUM.—*Ministère de l'Intérieur.— Bureau de Traduction.* **11905. a. 26.**

—— The Furniture Trade Catalogue, containing designs for every description of modern furniture . . . With . . . index and price list, *etc.* pp. 27. viii. ff. clxv. *Wyman & Sons: London*, 1881. fol. **1810. a. 19.**

—— Hand-Catalog für Juristen. Eine Auswahl der vorzüglichsten Werke u. Zeitschriften aus der Rechts- u. Staatswissenschaft mit besonderer Berücksichtigung der Gesetze für die Markgrafschaft Mähren, *etc.* pp. 66. *Brünn*, 1881. 8°. **11904. a. 16. (3.)**

—— The London Catalogue of British Mosses and Hepatics . . . Second edition [of the work by C. P. Hobkirk and Henry Boswell]. [Edited by F. A. Lees.] pp. 32. 1881. 8°. *See* LONDON.—III. *Botanical Record Club.*
07075. e. 6. (6.)

—— Bibliographie des ouvrages de poésie et de théâtre français, faisant partie de la bibliothèque de feu M. le baron de ***, membre de plusieurs sociétés savantes. (La vente aux enchères . . . aura lieu . . . 8 septembre 1882, *etc.*) pp. 96. *Stockholm*, 1882. 8°. **11902. aa. 32.**

—— Catalogue of Books on Angling, including ichthyology, pisciculture, fisheries and fishing laws. From the library of a practitioner of more than fifty years' experience in the art of angling [i.e. John Bartlett]. pp. 77. *J. Wilson & Son: Cambridge [Mass.]*, 1882. 4°.
11905. aa. 31.

—— Catalogue de livres rares et curieux sur l'amour, les femmes et le mariage, faisant partie du cabinet d'un bibliophile suédois. 2 pt. MS. PRICES. *Stockholm*, 1883 [i.e. K. R. L. Manderström]. **011904. bb. 37.**

—— Lijst der boekwerken geregistreerd op het Departement van Justitie volgens artt. 24–26 der wet van 28 juni 1881 tot regeling van het auteursrecht, *etc.* 1883. 8°. *See* AMSTERDAM.—*Vereeniging ter Bevordering van de Belangen des Boekhandels.* **011903. k. 14.**

—— Bibliothèque cynégétique d'un amateur, avec notes bibliographiques, *etc.* pp. 228. *Paris*, 1884. 8°.
7945. bb. 43.

CATALOGUES.

—— Pattern Book & Price List of Surgical Needles & Pins. ff. 10. *White & Pike: Birmingham*, [1884.] 8°.
7482. c. 2.

Printed on one side of the leaf only.

—— Bibliotheca arcana, seu Catalogus librorum penetralium . . . By Speculator morum [i.e. Henry S. Ashbee]. pp. xxii. 141. xxv. *G. Redway: London* 1885. 4°.
2745. m. 6.

—— [Another copy.] **C. 134. d. 7.**

—— Bibliotheca juridica. Systematisches Verzeichniss der neueren und gebräuchlicheren auf dem Gebiete der Staats- u. Rechtswissenschaft erschienenen Lehrbücher, *etc.* pp. xii. 67. *Leipzig*, 1885. 8°. **11901. a. 20.**

—— Catalogue général des manuscrits des bibliothèques publiques de France. 1885– . 8°. *See* FRANCE.— *Ministère de l'Instruction Publique.* **Bar. T. 3. a.**

—— Catalogo alfabetico di libri di scacchi e altri giuochi. pp. 22. *Firenze*, 1886. 8°. **11900. b. 39. (3.)**

—— The London Catalogue of British Plants. Part I . . . Eighth edition. [Edited by F. J. Hanbury.] pp. 39. *G. Bell & Sons: London*, [1886.] 8°. **7031. bb. 35.**
Previous editions, published under the direction of the London Botanical Exchange Club, are entered under LONDON. —III. *London Botanical Exchange Club. Later edition* 1890.

—— Répertoire des ouvrages pédagogiques du XVIe siècle. Bibliothèques de Paris et des Départements. pp. xvi. 733. 1886. 8°. [*Mémoires et documents scolaires, publiés par le Musée Pédagogique.* fasc. 3.] *See* PARIS.—*Centre Nationale de Documentation Pédagogique.—Musée Pédagogique.* **S.E. 124/52.**

—— Verzeichnis von Werken und Aufsätzen, welche in älterer und neuerer Zeit über die Geschichte und Sprache der Zigeuner veröffentlicht worden sind. pp. 15. *Leipzig*, 1886. 8°. **11904. a. 31. (8.)**

—— A Classified Catalogue of Educational Works in use in the United Kingdom and its dependencies in 1887, *etc.* pp. iv. 248. *Sampson Low & Co.: London*, 1887. 8°.
011900. ee. 34.

—— Catalogo della collezione d'un distinto numismatico . . . Bellissima serie di monete bizantine . . . monete della Bulgaria, Moldavia . . . di cui la vendita . . . avrà luogo in Milano . . . il 1° novembre 1888, *etc.* pp. 86. *Firenze*, 1888. 8°. **7756. de. 20. (3.)**

—— Catalogue de beaux livres anciens et modernes . . . provenant de la bibliothèque de M. P. de R . . . . . (La vente aura lieu du mercredi 19 au samedi 22 décembre 1888.) 1888. 8°. *See* R . . . ., M. P. de. **011902. k. 14.**

—— Catalogue des timbres-poste, cartes, etc. de Turquie. [Compiled by Alfred Glavany.] pp. 48. *Constantinople*, 1889. 16°. **Crawford 784. (10.)**

—— "Service" Periodicals of the World, with rates of annual subscription to all parts of the globe, *etc.* *W. H. Everett & Son: London*, [1889.] 8°.
011902. g. 28.

—— Catalogue de livres rares et précieux, manuscrits et imprimés, composant la bibliothèque de feu M. le baron Ach. S ****** [i.e. Baron A. Seillière]. (La vente aura lieu . . . 5 mai 1890, *etc.*) 1890. 8°. *See* S ****** (Ach.) *Baron.* **011908. k. 3.**

—— Catalogue d'un joli choix de livres rares et précieux reliés en maroquin ancien et moderne, *etc.* (La vente aura lieu le 2 Juin 1890.) pp. viii. 89. *Paris*, 1890. 8°.
11908. s. 25.

CATALOGUES.

—— Catalogue de timbres-poste orientaux—usés—en detaille [*sic*], en gros et par séries. [By G. Sotiroff.] pp. 5. *Varna*, 1890. 8°.   Crawford **690**. (**3**.)

—— The London Catalogue of British Plants. Part I . . . Eighth edition. With corrections. [Edited by F. J. Hanbury.] pp. 39.   *George Bell & Sons: London*, [1890.] 8°.   **7031**. h. **11**. (**1**.)
   Previous edition 1886 ; *later edition* 1895.

—— [A list of works by or relating to English classical scholars. By J. E. B. Mayor.] 2 sheets. [1891.] fol.   **1865**. c. **1**. (**23**.)

—— Catalogue des thèses et écrits académiques . . . Années scolaires 1884–89 [*etc.*]. 1892 [1885]– . 8°. *See* FRANCE. —*Ministère de l'Instruction Publique, etc.*
     11913.bb.83.

—— Catalogue of Works performed at The Monday Popular Concerts . . . commencing February 14, 1859 and finishing April 11, 1892. [1892 ?] 8°. *See* LONDON.—III. *Saint James's Hall.*   M. d. **480**. b.

—— Catalogue of Books selected from the Library of an English Amateur. [The preface signed : C., i.e. G. E. S. M. Herbert, Earl of Carnarvon.] 1893, 97. fol. *See* C.   **667.k.3.**

—— Bibliographie des ouvrages relatifs à l'amour, aux femmes, au mariage . . . par M. le Cte d'I * * * [i.e. Jules Gay]. 4e édition, *etc.* 1894, *etc.* 8°. *See* I * * *, M. le C. d'.   **2745.m.1.**

—— Catalogue des monuments et inscriptions de l'Égypte antique. sér. 1 tom. 1–3. 1894–1909. fol. *See* EGYPT. —*Service des Antiquités de l'Égypte.*   **7710**. t. **2**.

—— Reproduction—traduction. Catalogue spécial pour les reproductions de romans-feuilletons, nouvelles, variétés . . . dans les journaux de France et de l'étranger. Quatrième édition. pp. iii. 259. *Paris*, 1894. 12°.   **11902**. aaa. **14**.

—— The London Catalogue of British Plants. Part I . . . Ninth edition. [Edited by F. J. Hanbury.] pp. 50. *G. Bell & Sons: London*, 1895. 8°.   **07076**. f. **37**. (**3**.)
   Previous edition 1890 ; *later edition* 1908.

—— Prix-courant des timbres-postes, cartes-postales, cartelettre, etc. d'Orient. [By G. C. Genov.] pp. 10. *Philippople*, 1895. 8°.   Crawford **795**. (**15**.)

—— [Lists of books published by the American Printing House for the Blind and by other American firms.] [1896.] 4°.   **13007**. a. **69**.
   Embossed.

—— A Catalogue of the . . . Contents of Hengrave Hall, Bury St. Edmunds . . . For sale by auction on Thursday, the 5th of August, 1897, *etc.* pp. 134. 1897. 8°. *See* HENGRAVE HALL.   S.C. **1108**.

—— Catalogue des livres rares composant la bibliothèque musicale d'un amateur [i.e. Joaquim de Vasconcellos]. pp. 193. *Porto*, 1898. 8°.   Hirsch **482**.

—— Catalogue of all the Books, printed in the United States, with the prices, and places where published, annexed. Published by the Booksellers in Boston. [A reprint of the edition of 1804.] pp. 79. *See* GROWOLL (A.) Book-Trade Bibliography in the United States, *etc.* 1898. 8°.   Ac. **9728**/2.

CATALOGUES.

—— The Bibliography of Progressive Literature. Descriptive catalogue comprising a complete and classified list of works relating to science, philosophy, religion, *etc.* pp. 96. *New Epoch Publishing Co.: New York*, [1899.] 8°.   **11905**. aa. **33**.

—— Catalogue d'une bibliothèque de droit international et sciences auxiliaires. Brouillon de la table systématique des fiches. pp. xxiv. 406.   *Paris ; Leipzig ; Barcelone* [printed], 1899. 4°.   **11901**. e. **30**.

—— The Pocket Standard Catalogue of the Revenue Stamps of Canada. pp. 23. 1899. 12°.   Crawford **786**. (**4**.)

—— Catalogo generale della libreria italiana dall'anno 1847 a tutto il 1899, *etc.* [With supplements.] 1900– . 8°. *See* MILAN.—*Associazione Tipografico-Libraria Italiana.*
     2111.b–c.

—— Catalogue général de médailles françaises. [With Supplements 1–11.] 23 pt. [1900–02.] 8°. *See* BOUDEAU (E.)   **7755**. aaa. **54**.

—— Preis-Verzeichniss der in der österreichisch-ungarischen Monarchie und im Auslande erscheinenden Zeitungen und periodischen Druckschriften für das Jahr 1901 . . . Bearbeitet von dem K. K. Post-Zeitungs-Amte I in Wien. 1901. 4°. *See* AUSTRIA.—*Postamt.*—*Zeitungs-Expedition.*
     11908.k.1.

—— International Catalogue of Scientific Literature. 1902– . 8°. *See* LONDON.—III. *Royal Society.*
     11908. t. **1**, *etc.*

—— Указатель литературы о Сіонизмѣ. pp. x. 212. *С.-Петербургъ*, 1903. 8°.   **011907**. f. **13**.

—— Списокъ книгъ, вышедшихъ въ Россіи въ 1903 (1905) году, *etc.* 1904–[06]. 8°. *See* RUSSIA.—*Министерство Внутреннихъ Дѣлъ.*—*Главное Управленіе по дѣламъ печати.*   **011902**. l. **50**.

—— Catalogue des objets d'art et d'ameublement . . . composant la collection de M. H.-J. M***, et dont la vente aura lieu . . . 9 février 1905, *etc.* 1905. 4°. *See* M * * *, H. J.   **7808**. d. **16**.

—— Catalogue of a unique and extremely important collection of autograph letters and manuscripts of the world's greatest composers. [With eight facsimile reproductions.] *Chiswick Press: London*, [1905 ?] fol.   L.R. **261**. c. **9**.

—— The Colonial Catalogue of Publishing, Printing, Stationery, & Allied Trades, 1905(–1907). [1905–07.] 4°. *See* PERIODICAL PUBLICATIONS.—*London.* **11909**. v. **20**.

—— Библіографическій каталогъ. Профили редакторовъ и сотрудниковъ. [A bibliography of Russian revolutionary periodicals.] pp. 28. 202. *Genève*, 1906. 8°.   **11902**. aaa. **69**.

—— Bibliografía Zaragozana del siglo xv. Por un Bibliofilo aragonés (X. X. [i.e. Juan Manuel Sánches]). 1907. 4°. *See* X., X.   **11907**. s. **4**.

—— The London Catalogue of British Plants . . . Tenth edition. [Edited by F. J. Hanbury.] pp. 48. *G. Bell & Sons: London*, 1908. 8°.   **07031**. df. **52**. (**6**.)
   Previous edition 1895; *later edition* 1925.

—— Costumes militaires français et étrangers. Recueils, suites, estampes détachées, livres, états et annuaires, aquarelles, composant la collection de feu M. A. B***. [A sale catalogue.] 1909. 8°. *See* B***, A.
     S.C. **1151**.

—— Elenchus librorum vetustiorum apud * * [i.e. Ingram Bywater] hospitantium. pp. 142. [1911.] 8°.
     011904. aaa. **18**.

CATALOGUES.

—— Inventario de una Colección de Libros de Arte que reune A. C. 1911. 12º. *See* C., A. **011899. e. 12.**

—— Catalogo de Camilliana. Obras originaes, traduzidas, prefaciadas, annotadas, com extractos, referentes ou dedicadas a Camillo Castello Branco . . . Collecção que será vendida em leilão no dia 2 de março de 1917, *etc.* pp. 28. *Lisboa*, [1917.] 8º. **11912. a. 2.**

—— Catalogue des objets d'art et d'ameublement . . . provenant de la collection de M. le Duc de G***, et dont la vente aura lieu . . . le vendredi 22 mai 1925, *etc.* [1925.] 4º. *See* G***, *M. le Duc de.* **S.C. 1114.**

—— Catalogus van academische geschriften in Nederland en Nederlandsch Indië verschenen. [1925– .] 8º. *See* UTRECHT.—*Nederlandsche Vereeniging van Bibliothecarissen en Bibliotheekambtenaren.* **Ac. 9626.**

—— The London Catalogue of British Plants . . .' Eleventh edition. [Edited by F. J. Hanbury.] pp. 55. *G. Bell & Sons: London*, 1925. 8º. **07075. e. 33.** *Previous edition* 1908. *Interleaved. Subsequently incorporated in "List of British Vascular Plants", which is entered under* LONDON.—*III. British Museum.—Department of Botany.*

—— Some Explanatory Notes on the Eleventh Edition of the London Catalogue of British Plants. Reprinted from the 'Journal of Botany.' pp. 23. *G. Bell & Sons and Taylor & Francis: London*, [1926.] 8º. **07028. h. 62.**

—— Bibliographie du chômage. Bibliography of Unemployment. Bibliographie der Arbeitslosigkeit. pp. 155. *Genève*, 1926. 8º. [*International Labour Office. Studies and Reports.* ser. C. no. 12.] **U.N.H.6.** *Later edition* 1930.

—— Catalogue des porcelaines . . . tapisseries, objets d'art . . . composant la collection de Madame J***, dont la première vente aura lieu . . . les jeudi 17 et vendredi 18 mars 1927 et le samedi 19 mars 1927, *etc.* [1927.] 4º. *See* J . . . , *Madame.* **S.C. 1112.**

—— A Seventeenth-Century German Mock Catalogue. (Catalogus etlicher sehr alten Bücher welche neulich in Irrland auff einem alten eroberten Schlosse in einer Bibliothec gefunden worden, Anno 1650.) Edited by H. Gordon Ward. pp. 16. *Kegan Paul & Co.: London*, 1928. 8º. **011899. aaa. 23.**

—— Bibliographie du chômage. Bibliography of Unemployment. Bibliographie der Arbeitslosigkeit. 2e édition, *etc.* pp. viii. 217. *Genève*, 1930. 8º. [*International Labour Office. Studies and Reports.* ser. C. no. 14.] **U.N.H.6.** *Previous edition* 1926.

—— Catalogue of Rare and Modern Books on History of Music. A family of violin experts since A.D. 1849 [i.e. R. S. Williams and Sons, Company]. pp. 24. [*Toronto*, 1930?] 8º. **11925. g. 24.**

—— Biblioteca scientifico-politecnica internazionale. Bibliografia delle più importanti opere italiane e straniere sulle scienze esatte ed dell'ingegnere, arti applicate, tecnologie, scienze agrarie ed economiche pubblicate dal 1926 al 1931, *etc.* pp. 528. *Milano*, 1932. 8º. **011903. e. 68.**

—— Catálogo General de la Librería Española e Hispanoamericana. Años 1901–1930. 1932– . fol. *See* SPAIN. —*Cámaras Oficiales del Libro.* **2111.e.–f.**

CATALOGUES.

—— Catalogue des sièges et meubles . . . tableaux . . . dessins anciens . . . tableaux anciens . . . objets d'art et d'ameublement . . . tapisseries appartenant à M. A*** G***, et dont la vente . . . aura lieu . . . les mardi 8 et mercredi 9 mai 1934, *etc.* 1934. 4º. *See* G***, A***, *M.* **S.C. 1115.**

—— Catalogue général des manuscrits des bibliothèques de Belgique. *Gembloux*, 1934– . 8º. **2701.bm.3.**

—— Une Bibliothèque scolaire du XIe siècle d'après le catalogue provenant de l'abbaye d'Anchin. Introduit, réédité et commenté par Jean Gessler, *etc.* [A catalogue of an unidentified library, from the MSS. of the Abbey of Anchin.] pp. 78. *Bruxelles; Paris*, 1935. 8º. **11900. ee. 79.**

—— Répertoire de bibliographie française. Contenant tous les ouvrages imprimés en France et aux colonies et les ouvrages français publiés à l'étranger, 1501–1930. fasc. 1–10. A-ACKER—ARMIEUX-ARTHAUD. *Paris, Paris*, 1935–41. fol. **11908. s. 33.** *No more published.*

—— [Another copy.] **11917.d.10.**

—— Catalogue. Day of sale: Monday, June 29th, 1936 . . . A special collection of Mauritius [postage-stamps]. [The sale described in a MS. note as "2nd Hind sale, balance of collection," i.e. the collection of Arthur Hind.] pp. 18. pl. IV. MS. PRICES. [*H. R. Harmer: London*, 1936.] 8º. **S.C. Sta. 8.** *Imperfect; wanting all before p. 5. With 4 leaves from unidentified sale catalogues of Mauritius stamps tipped in. Catalogues of the sales of the Hind collection, 30 April— 4 July 1934, are entered under* HIND (*Arthur*)

—— Catalogue of Selected Color Reproductions. Prepared for the Carnegie Corporation of New York. [Compiled by A. Van R. Hovey.] 1936. 4º. *See* HOVEY (Angelica Van R.) **7864. ppp. 24.**

—— The Architects' Standard Catalogue . . . *Eleventh* edition, 1950–51–52 *etc.* *Standard Catalogue Co.: London*, 1950– .4º. **P.P. 2505. sfg.**

—— The Municipal & Public Works Standard Catalogue. Seventh [*etc.*] edition—1951–1953 [*etc.*]. *Standard Catalogue Co.: London*, [1951– .] 4º. **P.P. 2505. sfi.**

—— The Overseas Architects' Standard Catalogue, 1951–52–53 [*etc.*] *Standard Catalogue Co.: London*, [1951– .]4º. **P.P. 2505. sfh.**

—— A Catalogue of the Contents of Hengrave Hall, Hengrave, near Bury St. Edmunds . . . to be sold by auction by Messrs. Knight, Frank & Rutley in conjunction with Arthur Rutter, Sons & Co. . . . on . . . September 15th, *etc.* [With plates.] pp. 156. *Northwood*, [1952.] 8º. **S.C. 1107.**

—— The Building Trades Standard Catalogues.
> pt. 1. The Builders' Standard Catalogue . . . Ninth [*etc.*] edition—1953–1955 [*etc.*].
> pt. 2. The Builders' Merchants' Standard Catalogue . . . Fifth [*etc.*] edition—1953–1955 [*etc.*].

Standard Catalogue Co.: London, 1952– . 4º. **P.P. 2505. sff.**

—— A Catalogue of Cylinder Flaws on King George VI Great Britain Commemoratives. (Second edition.) pp. 20. *Crabtree Press: Brighton*, 1954. 8º. **08247. p. 31.**

CATALOGUES.

Select Index of Titles.

CATALOGUES. [Select Index of Titles.]

CATALOGUES. [Select Index of Titles.]

CATALOGUES. [Select Index of Titles.]

CATALOGUES. [Select Index of Titles.]

CATALOGUS. See also Catalogues.

—— Catalogus Almae Dioecesis Transsilvanicae Latini et Armeni Ritus Catholicae, etc. See Transylvania, Diocese of.

—— Catalogus Canonicorum Regularium . . . Ordinis Praemonstratensis in Caes. Reg. ditionibus Austriacis. See Praemonstratensians.

—— Catalogus codicum manuscriptorum Bibliothecae palatinae Vindobonensis. See Vienna.—Kaiserlich-königliche Hofbibliothek.

—— Catalogus observantis Minorum provinciae S. Joannis a Capistrano. See Franciscans.

—— Catalogus patrum et fratrum Ordinis Minorum S. P. Francisci Provinciae Hungariae. See Franciscans.

—— Catalogus uniuersalis pro nundinis Francofurtensibus. See Frankfort Fair.

—— Catalogus venerabilis cleri Almæ Dioecesis Rosnaviensis. See Rosenau, Diocese of.

—— Catalogus venerabilis cleri Almae Dioecesis Szathmariensis. See Szatmar, Diocese of. Calendarium Dioecesanum, etc.

—— Catalogus venerabilis cleri Almæ Dioecesis Vaciensis. See Waitzen, Diocese of. Calendarium Dioecesanum v. cleri Vaciensis.

—— Catalogus venerabilis cleri Dioecesis Latini ritus M. Varadinensis. See Grosswardein, Diocese of.

CATALON (Pierre) La Discipline ecclésiastique des églises reformées de France, etc. [With a preface by J. de Labadie.] pp. 229. E. Raban: Orange, 1658. 4º.
491. e. 35.

CATALONI (Filippo) Bellissima istoria della vita, conversione e morte di Pietro Barliario, nobile Salernitano e famoso mago. [By F. Cataloni. In verse.] [1800 ?] 12º. See Barliario (P.) **1071. c. 24. (7.)**

—— [Another edition.] Vita, conversione, e morte di Pietro Barliario, nobile Salernitano e famosissimo mago, composta in ottava rima, etc. pp. 24. Todi, [1800 ?] 12º.
11426. b. 74. (17.)

—— [Another edition.] pp. 24. Todi, [1812 ?] 12º.
11426. aaa. 37. (7.)

—— [Another edition.] pp. 24. Lucca, [1820 ?] 12º.
1071. c. 23. (6.)

CATALONIA.

LAWS.

i. Collections.

i. General.

—— Begin. [fol. 1 recto :] Com per ordinacio deles Corts generals del principat de Cathalunya, celebrades enla Ciutat de Barçalona, per lo Serenissimo, Rey don Ferrando p̄mer de gloriosa memoria a .xxxi. de agost any mil quatrecents tretze, fos ordonat: que los vsatges de Barçalona e cōstitucions de Cathalūya, fossen collocats en

CATALONIA. [Laws.—i. Collections.—i. General.]

propris titols, e en lenga vulgar, etc. [fol. 4 recto :] Taula e sumari molt vtil dels titols en general e en special de tots los vsatges de Barcelona constitucions e capitols de cort e consuetuts scrites de Cathalūya e comemoracions de Pere albert contēgudes enlos deu libres dela presēt compilacio, etc. [fol. 38 recto :] De la sancta fe catholica, etc. [fol. 293 recto :] Pragmatica del Rey en Marti disposant dela forma e manera que sa seruar enla occupacio delas temporalitats. G.𝔏. [Pedro Michael : Barcelona, 20 Feb. 1495.] fol. **IB. 52538.**
394 leaves, ff. 3 (1st A1), 34 (1st D8), 37 (a1). 291, 292 (1st G5, 6) blank. ff. 38–394 numbered i–ccclxii, with errors. Sig. [*2] A–C⁸ D⁸ [**]²; a⁸ b⁸ c¹⁰ d¹⁰ e⁶ f–[⁸ 8⁸ t⁸ u¹⁰ v⁶ x–z⁸ A–F⁸ G⁶ A–L⁸ M⁶ N⁸. Double columns, 39, 40 lines to a column. Imperfect; wanting two leaves of the second of the quires signed C and leaves 4 and 5 of the third of the quires signed B. The imprint is supplied from a copy recorded as having a colophon. Sheets [*]² and [**]² are bound between leaves A1 and 2 and D7 and 8 respectively.

—— Capitols e ordinacions per los Drets d'l General de les entrades E exides del Principat de Cathalunya. G.𝔏. Stampat per P. Monpezat : Barçelona, 1557. 4º.
1375. g. 10.

—— Constitutions y altres Drets de Cathalunya (Pragmaticas y altres drets de Cathalunya.—Constitutions y altres drets de Cathalunya superfluos contraris, y corregits) compilats en virtut del Cap. de Cort xxiiii de las Corts per la S. C. y Reyal Maiestat del Rey Don Philip . . . celebradas en la vila de Montso any m.d.lxxxv. ms. notes. 3 vol. Estampadas en casa de H. Gotart : Barcelona, 1588, 89. fol. **709. k. 16.**

—— Capitols dels Drets, y altres coses del General del Principat de Cathalunya, y Comtats de Rossello, y Cerdanya fets en Corts generals del Any m.cccc.lxxxi. fins en lo Any m.d.lxiiii. inclusiue . . . Nouament manats imprimir, etc. ff. 171. Estampats en casa de L. Deu & H. Margarit : Barcelona, 1620. 4º. **1239. a. 4.**
A second titlepage follows the table of contents.

—— [Another copy.] **177. a. 23.**

—— Libre dels quatre Senyals, del General de Cathalunya. Contenint diuersos Capitols de Cort, Ordinations, declarations, priuilegis, y cartas reals fahents per lo dit General, etc. pp. 340. H. Margarit : Barcelona, 1634. 4º.
C. 68. h. 9.

—— [Another edition.] Capitols dels Drets y altres coses del General del Principat de Cathalunya, y Comtats de Rossello, y Cerdanya fets en Corts generals del Any m.cccc.lxxxi. fins en lo any m.d.lxiii., etc. (Capitols sobre lo redres del General de Cathalunya fets per la S. C. R. Magestat del Rey don Philip any m.d.lxxxv.) 2 pt. ms. notes. G. Nogues : Barcelona, 1635. 4º.
1239. a. 1. (1.)
Previous edition 1620.

—— [Another edition.] 2 pt. Estampat en casa Matheuat : Barcelona, 1671. 4º. **1239. a. 2.**

—— [Another edition.] Libre dels Quatre Senyals del General de Catalunya. Contenint diversos Capitols de Cort, Ordinacions, declaracions, Privilegis, y cartas Reals fahents per lo dit General, etc. pp. 340. R. Figueró : Barc., 1698. 4º. **1239. a. 9.**
Previous edition 1634.

—— Traduccion al Castellano de los Usages y demás Derechos de Cataluña que no están derogados ó no son notoriamente inútiles, con indicacion del contenido de estos y de las disposiciones por las que han uenido á serlo, ilustrada con notas sacadas de los mas clásicos autores del principado por . . . P. N. Vives y Cebriá. (Indice general.) 5 tom. Barcelona, 1832–38. 4º. **711. f. 21, 22.**

CATALONIA. [Laws.—i. Collections.—i. *General.*]

—— Traducción al castellano de los usages y demás derechos de Cataluña que no están derogados ó no son notoriamente inútiles, con indicación del contenido de estos y de las disposiciones por las que han venido á serlo, ilustrada con notas sacadas de los mas clásicos autores del Principado por el Doctor D. Pedro Nolasco Vives y Cebriá . . . Segunda edición corregida y aumentada. 5 tom. *Madrid, Barcelona*, 1861–67. 8º. **5384. c. 18.**

—— Constitutions y altres drets de Cathalunya, *etc.* [A facsimile of the edition of 1704.] 3 vol. *Barcelona*, 1909. fol. **5384. h. 7.**

—— Els Diplomes carolingis a Catalunya. Per Ramon d'Abadal i de Vinyals, *etc.* [A collection of documents covering the period 780–1025.] 2 pt. *Barcelona*, 1926–50, 52. 4º. [*Institut d'Estudis Catalans. Memòries de la Secció Històrico-arqueològica.* no. 2. *Catalunya carolíngia.* vol. 2.] **Ac. 138. dc.**

ii. *Chronological Series.*

—— Constitutions de Cathalunya. [fol. 2 *recto:*] Constitucions fetes per lo illustrissimo e serenissimo senyor Rey don Ferrando . . . En la segona cort de cathalunya Celebrada en Barcelona en lany Mil. cccc. lxxxxiij. 𝕲.𝔏. *per Iohannē Rosenbach: Barchinone, die* xxx. Mēsis May, 1494. fol. **IB. 52544.**
28 *leaves. Sig.* a–d⁸·⁶. *The title is on the verso of the first leaf, which is either a cancel or a facsimile on old paper. It bears a woodcut of the arms of Spain, and the second leaf is surrounded by a metal-cut border with N. Spindeler's device, being the border used in the Tirant lo Blanch, Valencia, 1490, cut down.*

—— Constitucions fetes per la Sacra Cessarea catholica y real magestat ď dõ Carles . . . y dela . . . Senyora dona Joanna mare sua . . . en la primera cort de Barcelona celebrada . . . en lany Mil.D.xx. 𝕲.𝔏. *C. amoros; a despeses de mestre L. Milla: Barcelona*, 1520. fol. **T. 97*. (4.)**

—— [Another copy.] **C. 62. f. 22. (3.)**

—— Costitucions fetis p. la Sacra Caesarea Catholica y Real Magestat del Emperador Don Carles; y per la . . . Senyora dona Johanna mare sua . . . en la tercera Cort de Cathalunya . . . en lany M.D.xxx.iiij. 𝕲.𝔏. *C. Amoros; a despeses d' Mestre I. milla: Barcelona*, 1534. fol. **T. 97*. (6.)**

—— [Another copy.] **C. 62. f. 22. (7.)**

—— Ordinacions sobre los redres del general e casa dela Deputacio del Principat de Catalunya. Fetes enla cort general celebrada . . . Enla vila de Monço: en lany .M.D.xxxvij. 𝕲.𝔏. *Ç. Amoros: [Barcelona*, 1537.] 4º. **C. 62. c. 24.**

—— Ordinations sobre les Generalitats y casa dela Deputatio ďl Principat de Cathalunya. Fetes enles Corts generals: celebrades . . . Enla vila de Mõço en lany .M.D.xl.ij. 𝕲.𝔏. *Estampat en casa d'I. Cortey: [Barcelona,]* 1554. 4º. **C. 62. c. 23.**

—— Constitutions fetes per la Sacra Catholica Real Magestat del Rey Don Phelip . . . en la segona Cort de Cathalunya . . . en lany MDLXXXVI [or rather, 1585]. ff. lvi. *I. Cendrat; a despeses de D. Bages: Barcelona*, 1586. fol. **503. g. 22.**

—— Constitutions fetes per la S. C. R. Magestat del Rey Don Phelip Segon . . . en la primera cort, celebra als Cathalans . . . en lo any 1599. (Capitols y actes de Cort.) ff. lxvii. *G. Graels & G. Dotil: Barcelona*, 1603. fol. **5383. g. 3.**

—— [Another edition.] ff. lxviii. *G. Nogues: Barcelona*, 1635. fol. **503. g. 25.**

CATALONIA. [Laws.—i. Collections.—ii. *Chronological Series.*]

—— Ordinacions, y Cridas fetas per lo . . . Consistori dels Senyors Deputats, y Oydors de Comptes del General del Principat de Cathalunya . . . en lo trienni de 1698, novament impressas ab summaris, numeros, y repertoris, *etc.* pp. 250. *R. Figueró: Barcelona*, 1698. 4º. **5383. f. 15.**

—— Ordinacions, y Cridas fetas per lo molt illustre Concistori, dels Senyors Deputats y Oydors de Comptes del General del Principat de Cathalunya . . . en lo trienni de 1701. pp. 248. *Barcelona*, 1701. 4º. **1239. a. 5.**

—— Constitucions, Capitols, y Actes de Cort, fetas, y atorgats per la S.C.R. Magestat del Rey . . . Don Felip iv. de Aragò, y v. de Castella . . . en la primera Cort, celebrada als Cathalans, en la ciutat de Barcelona . . . en los anys 1701. y 1702. pp. 100. *Barcelona*, 1702. fol. **503. g. 30.**

—— Constitucions, Capitols, y Actes de Cort fetas, y atorgats per la S.C.R. magestat del Rey Nostre Senyor Don Carlos iii . . . en la cort celebrà als Cathalans en la ciutat de Barcelona . . . en lo any de 1706. pp. 196. *Barcelona*, 1706. fol. **1238. h. 16.**

LAWS.—IV. SEPARATE LAWS.

—— [A decree forbidding criticism of the doctrine of the Immaculate Conception of the Blessed Virgin Mary. 1451.] *Cat. & Span. See* ARAGON.—[*Separate Laws, etc.*]—John i., *King.* Aduertencias, *etc.* 1617. 4º. **477. a. 15. (3.)**

—— *Begin.* Carolus impator Romanorum. In Dei nomine Nouerint vniuersi, *etc.* [An act of the Cortes of Catalonia, 1528, granting supplies for the war with France, etc. Written partly in Latin and partly in Catalan.] 𝕲.𝔏. [*Barcelona?* 1528?] fol. **T. 97*. (5.)**

—— [Another copy.] **C. 62. f. 22. (5.)**

—— Estatuto de Cataluña. Ley de 15 de septiembre de 1932. pp. 28. 1932. 8º. *See* SPAIN.—[*Laws, etc.*]—iv. Alcalá-Zamora y Torres (Niceto) *President.* [1931–36.] **5384. de. 20.**

—— La Venda i la Distribució del Blat. Text del decret que regula la venda i la distribucio del blat de la present collita, la distribució de la farina i de les despulles de la mòlta i el consum de pa al territori de Catalunya, durant el període comprès entre el 1er d'agost del 1937 i el 31 de juliol del 1938. [30 July 1937.] pp. 12. *Barcelona*, 1937. 8º. **5384. ee. 10.**

TREATIES.

—— Tratado de alianza entre la Ser.ma Reyna Anna de Inglaterra y el Principado de Catalunña . . . concluido en Genova . . . 1705. *See* GEORGE ii., *King of Great Britain and Ireland.* [*Appendix.*] Recort de la aliança fet al Serenissim Jordi-August Rey de la Gran-Bretanya, *etc.* 1898. 8º. **09077. ee. 71.**

MISCELLANEOUS OFFICIAL PUBLICATIONS.

—— Anuari de les biblioteques populars 1922(–35). 13 pt. *Barcelona*, [1923–36.] 8º. **P.P. 6477. baa.**
The issues for the years 1924/25–1930, bearing the title "Anuario de las bibliotecas populares", were issued by the Diputacion Provincial of the Province of Barcelona.

—— Censo de Cataluña, ordenado en tiempo del Rey Don Pedro el Ceremonioso [1359], *etc.* pp. 376. *Barcelona*, 1856. 8º. [*Coleccion de documentos ineditos del Archivo General del la Corona de Aragon.* tom. 12.] **9181. d.**

CATALONIA. [MISCELLANEOUS OFFICIAL PUBLICATIONS.]

—— Diari oficial de la Generalitat de Catalunya. any 5. vol. 4. 30 nov. 1937. [*Barcelona,*] 1937. fol.
O.G. c. **75.**

—— Don Francisco Antonio de Lacy, conde de Lacy . . . gobernador y capitan general del exército, y principado de Cataluña . . . concedemos libre, y seguro pasaporte, *etc.* [A passport, made out to H. Giraudy.] [*Barcelona,* 1791.] *s. sh.* fol.
S. o. **244.**

—— Mancomunitat de Catalunya. Escola del Treball. Deu anys d'acció escolar. [With plates.] pp. 46. *Barcelona,* 1923. 8°.
8355. de. **60.**

—— Mancomunitat de Catalunya. Laboratori general d'assaigs i condicionament. pp. 96. *Barcelona,* 1923. 8°.
07943. bb. **19.**

—— Mancomunitat de Catalunya. L'Obra realitzada, anys 1914–1923. 3 vol. *Barcelona,* 1923. 8°. 010160. f. **3.**

—— Political and Social Changes in Catalonia during the Revolution, July 19th—December 31st 1936. [Edited by J. G. Martin.] pp. 42. [*Barcelona,* 1937.] 8°.
08026. ee. **16.**

—— Tarifa dels Prens de les Teles y altres sorts de robes, y mercaderies, que entren en lo Principat de Cathalunya, *etc.* (Tarifa del corrent trienni de M.DC.LXXXXVIII.) pp. 155. *R. Figueró: Barcelona,* 1698. 4°.
5383. f. **16.**

Imperfect; wanting pp. 41–48.

LEGISLATIVE BODIES.

CORTS.

—— Procesos de las antiguas Cortes y Parlamentos de Cataluña, Aragon y Valencia, *etc.* 8 tom. *Barcelona,* 1847–51. 8°. [*Coleccion de documentos ineditos del Archivo General de la Corona de Aragon.* tom. 1–8.]
9181. d.

—— Parlaments a les Corts Catalanes. Text, introducció, notes i glossari per Ricard Albert i Joan Gassiot. pp. 307. *Barcelona,* 1928. 8°. [*Els Nostres Clàssics.* no. 19, 20.]
W.P. **4906/11.**

—— Capitols de Cort fets sobre lo redres del general y casa dela diputacio del principat de Cathalunya enla Setena Cort general . . . enla sglesia d' sancta Maria d'la vila d' Móço: En lany. M.D.L.iij. **G. L.** ff. xiij. *Stampats en casa d' I. Cortey: Barcelona,* 1553. 4°. **1375.** d. **26.**

—— Capitols del General del Principat de Cathalunya, Comtats de Rossello, y Cerdanya, fets en les Corts celebrades en lo monestir de Sant Francesch de Barcelona, per la S.C.R.M. del Rey Don Phelip . . . en lo any M.D.XCIX. pp. 198. *H. Margarit: Barcelona,* 1630. 4°.
1239. a. 1. (2.)

—— Capitols del General del Principat de Cathalunya . . . fets en les Corts celebrades . . . per la S. C. R. M. del Rey . . . don Phelip IV. de Aragò, y v. de Castella . . . en los anys M.DCC.I. y M.DCC.II., *etc.* pp. 136. *Barcelona,* 1702. 4°. **1239.** a. **8.**

Diputació.

—— Capitols resultants de las Sententias fetas per los . . . Visitadors del General de Cathalunya, acerca dels carrechs dels Officials de la casa de la Deputatio, y General de Barcelona y altres publicadas en lo any M.DC.XXI. ff. 114. *H. Margarit: Barcelona,* 1621. 4°.   5383. f. **13.**

CATALONIA. [LEGISLATIVE BODIES.]

—— Capitols, y Desliberations resultants de las sententias fetas per los . . . Visitadors del General de Cathalunya, acerca dels carrechs dels Officials de la Squadra de las Galeras de Cathalunya, y altras subjectes à la present Visita, publicadas en lo any M.DC.XXI. pp. 38. *H. Margarit: Barcelona,* 1621. 4°.   5383. f. **14.**

—— Summari compendios y substancial dels procehiments, sentencias, y prouisions de la visita del General de Cathalunya, feta contra los Deputats, Oydors, y Officials del dit General, que son estats en lo-trienni del any 1623 fins en lo del any 1626, *etc.* ff. 65.   *G. Margarit: Barcelona,* 1628. 4°.   5383. aaa. **1.**

—— Directori de la Visita del General de Catalunya, y brev sumari de sentencias de las visitas fetas desde lo any 1599. fins la ultima feta en lo any 1635, *etc.* MS. NOTES. *G. Nogues: Barcelona,* 1636. 4°.   5384. aaa. **38.**

—— [Another edition.] Directori de la Visita del General del Principat de Catalunya, y Comptats de Rossellò, y Cerdanya: y Capitols resultants acerca dels Carrechs, y Obligacions dels Senyors Diputats, y Oydors, y Oficials de la Casa de la Deputaciò, y General de Catalunya, y altres. pp. 240. *A. Lacavalleria: Barcelona,* 1672. 4°.
1239. a. 3.

—— [Another edition.] Van anyadits en esta vltima impressiò las Ciutats, Vilas, y Llochs del present principat, *etc. R. Figueró: Barcelona,* 1698. 4°.   1239. a. 6.

—— Recopilacio de diferents vots, y altres documents, en justificacio dels Drets de la Generalitat de Cathalunya . . . Traduhits alguns dells, de idioma Llati, en llengua Cathalana, *etc.* pp. 301. *R. Figueró: Barcelona,* [1689.] 4°.
1239. a. 7.

JUNTA SUPERIOR.

—— Manifiesto de la Junta Superior de Cataluña, sobre la pérdida de Tarragona, y sus resultas en el primer exército. pp. xx. 102. *Solsona,* 1811. 4°.   8042. g. **11.** (1.)

DIPUTACIÓN PROVINCIAL.

—— Apéndice al Procurador General de la Nacion y del Rey. (Representacion de la Diputacion Provincial de Cataluña contra el abuso de la libertad de la imprenta, y en favor de la Inquisicion.) pp. 8. *Palma,* 1813. 4°.
636. g. 16. (12.)

DEPARTMENTS OF STATE AND OFFICIAL BODIES.

COMISSARIAT DE PROPAGANDA.

—— The Cultural Work of Liberal Governments in the Generalitat of Catalonia. pp. 19. *Barcelona,* [1937.] 8°.
8355. bb. **34.**

—— Economic Transformation in Catalonia. Seen through the eyes of a foreigner. By André Jean. pp. 31. *Barcelona,* [1936.] 8°.   08042. bb. **28.**

—— L'Esdevenidor d'Espanya. La meva fe en la victòria— raons. Text de la conferència pronunciada a París, pel senyor Angel Ossorio i Gallardo. pp. 19. *Barcelona,* 1937. 8°.   12302. aaa. **6.**

—— Infants. [Reproductions of drawings.] [*Barcelona,* 1937.] fol.   L.R. **22.** c. **17.**

—— " Nova Iberia " Magazine. no. 2, 3/4. *Barcelona,* 1937. fol.   P.P. **4092.** bbf.

—— Set mesos i set dies a l'Espanya de Franco. [By I. de Aberrigoyen.] pp. 102. *Barcelona,* 1938. 8°.
08026. df. **18.**

—— Troisième anniversaire de la mort de Francesc Macia. Allocution de S. E. le Président Lluis Companys. pp. 15. [*Barcelona,* 1936.] 8°.   08042. a. **84.**

CATALONIA. [DEPARTMENTS OF STATE AND OFFICIAL BODIES.]

—— Les Veus de la Intel·ligència i la Lluita del Poble Espanyol. Pròleg de Carles Pi i Sunyer. (Antecedents y Documents.) pp. 78. *Barcelona*, 1937. 8°.
08042. a. 90.

DEPARTAMENT DE CULTURA.

—— Catàleg dels Llibres. Llista primera. [Compiled by the Servei de Biblioteques del Front of the Direcció Tècnica de Biblioteques Populars.] pp. 63. *Barcelona*, 1937. 8°. **011899. e. 17.**

—— Presència · de Catalunya. 1. La terra. El paisatge català a través dels seus poetes, *etc.* pp. 219. *Barcelona*, 1938. 8°. **10162. aa. 24.**

DIRECCIÓ GENERAL D'AGRICULTURA.

—— [Miscellaneous publications.] 5 pt. *Barcelona*, 1937. 8°. **07078. g. 20.**

—— Apunts d'Economia Agrícola. Conferències donades els dies 10 i 11 de desembre del 1936 [by J. Llovet Mont-ros] . . . Extret . . . del " Butlletí del Departament d'Agricultura." pp. 43. *Barcelona*, 1937. 8°. **8276. r. 40.**

—— El Decret de sindicació obligatòria dels conreadors de la terra i l'experiència cooperativa. Conferències donades els dies 7 i 8 de desembre del 1936 [by G. Fauquet] . . . Extret . . . del " Butlletí del Departament d'Agricultura." pp. 18. *Barcelona*, 1937. 8°. **08285. g. 89.**

DIRECCIÓ TÈCNICA DE BIBLIOTEQUES POPULARS.

Servei de Biblioteques del Front.

—— Catàleg dels Llibres. Llista primera. [Compiled by the Servei de Biblioteques del Front.] pp. 63. 1937. 8°. *See* supra : DEPARTAMENT DE CULTURA. **011899. e. 17.**

PROPAGANDA COMISSARIAT.

—— *See* supra : COMISSARIAT DE PROPAGANDA.

REAL AUDIENCIA.

—— Ordenanzas de la Real Audiencia de el Principado de Cathaluña, *etc.* pp. 144. *Barcelona*, 1742. fol. **5385. ee. 11.**

SERVEI DE BIBLIOTEQUES DEL FRONT.

—— *See* supra : DIRECCIÓ TÈCNICA DE BIBLIOTEQUES POPULARS.

MISCELLANEOUS INSTITUTIONS AND SOCIETIES.

COMISION PARA LA CONSERVACIÓN DEL DERECHO DE CATALUÑA.

—— Adhesiones recibidas de los Revdos. Prelados . . . y Provisores eclesiásticos del Principado de Cataluña á la solicitud que elevó á las Córtes en súplica de que se conserve al Principado su Derecho civil especial la Comision . . . y publicadas por la propia comision. pp. 46. *Barcelona*, 1885. fol. **4625. e. 14.**

MANCOMUNITAT.

—— Petició d'autonomia, presentada al govern d'Espanya per la Mancomunitat de Catalunya. *Enq.* pp. 22. *Barcelona*, 1919. 8°. **08042. c. 44.**

PARTIT SOCIALISTA UNIFICAT DE CATALUNYA.

—— Davant la 1ª Conferencia Nacional del Partit Socialista Unificat de Catalunya—Internacional Comunista. 6 articles a propòsit del Projecte de Resolució Política. Per Pere Ardiaca. [*Barcelona*, 1937.] 8°. **08042. cc. 22.**

CATALONIA.

—— Informe presentado al pleno ampliado del comité central del Partido Socialista Unificado de Cataluña . . . por el secretario general, camarada J. Comorera, 30 de enero de 1937. pp. 39. [*Barcelona*, 1937.] 8°. **8042. f. 40.**

Comité Militar P.S.U.—U.G.T.

—— Como Luchar para Vencer. Regles militars per · les milicies antifeixistes de Catalunya. *Span.* no. 1–7. [*Barcelona*, 1937.] 8°. **08042. c. 13.** *Imperfect ; wanting no.* 8.

Primera Conferència Nacional.

—— [Addresses delivered at the conference. With portraits.] 6 pt. [*Barcelona*, 1937.] 8°. **08042. bb. 35.**

APPENDIX.

—— Als mals efectes de tota Cathalunya. [Verses.] *1. Matevat: Barcelona*, 1643. 4°. **9180. e. 2. (48.)**

—— L'Architecture gothique civile en Catalogne. [Lectures delivered at the Institut d'Art et d'Archéologie de l'Université de Paris.] Par Filangiere [*sic*] di Candida Gonzaga [and others], *etc.* [Edited by Pierre Lavedan.] pp. 144. pl. LII. 1935. 4°. *See* PARIS.—*Université de Paris.—Institut d'Art et d'Archéologie.* **07815. d. 52.**

—— La Catalogne à l'époque romane. Conférences faites . . . en 1930 par MM. Anglès, Folch i Torrès, Ph. Lauer, Nicolau d'Olwer, Puig i Cadafalch, *etc.* pp. viii. 268. pl. VIII. *Paris*, 1932. 4°. [*Bibliothèque d'Art Catalan. Publications.* no. 2.] **Ac. 442. f.**

—— La Catalogne rebelle. (" Estat Català.") Tout le procès des conjurés catalans, précédé d'une notice sur la Catalogne et son mouvement national et suivi de quelques documents officiels. pp. 269. *Paris*, 1927. 8°. **8042. k. 21.**

—— Catalonia, a poem ; with notes illustrative of the present state of affairs in the Peninsula. pp. 48. *J. Ballantyne & Co.: Edinburgh*, 1811. 8°. **80. i. 12.**

—— Catalonia Monastica. Recull de documents i estudis referents a monestirs catalans. 1927, *etc.* 4°. *See* MARY, *the Blessed Virgin.—Churches, etc.*—Montserrat.—*Nuestra Señora de Montserrat.* **4786. i. 5.**

—— Cataluña ante España. [By various authors. With portraits.] pp. 302. *Madrid*, 1930. 8°. **10161. dd. 31.** *No. 4 of the " Cuadernos de la Gaceta Literaria."*

—— Cataluña invencible sin fortalezas, é inconquistable con ellas. [Signed : D. A. V.] 1811. 4°. *See* V., D. A. **8042. f. 29.**

—— Catalunya. (Revista mensual.) *See* PERIODICAL PUBLICATIONS.—*Barcelona.*

—— Catalunya carolíngia . . . Per R. d'Abadal i de Vingals.
2. Els diplomes carolingis a Catalunya. 2 pt. 1926–50, 52.
3. Els Comtats de Pallars i Ribagorça. [With maps.] 1955– .

Barcelona, 1950– . 4°. [*Institut d'Estudis Catalans. Memòries de la Secció Històrico-arqueològica.* no. 2, *etc.*] **Ac. 138. dc.**

—— Ce qu'est le Catalogne. [With an account of the Foyer antefasciste français in Barcelona.] pp. 30. *Barcelona*, [1938 ?] 8°. **08042. a. 88.**

—— Comedia nueva. La ciencia, afecto y valor forman magia por amor, y el Magico en Cataluña. Primera parte. (Comedia nueva. Vencen impulsos de amor los afectos del honor y el Mágico en Cataluña. Segunda parte.—Comedia nueva. Entre venganza y amor, hallar la dicha mayor, y el Mágico en Cataluña. Tercera parte.) [In verse.] 3 pt. *Barcelona*, [1765 ?] 4°. **1342. e. 1. (41–43.)**

CATALONIA. [Appendix.]

—— Desmayo de Cataluña, desconfianza de Inglaterra, desaliento de Portugal, flaqueza de Alemania; y valeroso animo de España: en versos comicos, *etc.* *Madrid,* 1707. 4°. **1323. g. 1. (4.)**

—— Diccionari Nomenclàtor de Pobles i Poblats de Catalunya. pp. xii. 660. 1931. 8°. *See* Barcelona.—*Centre Excursionista de Catalunya.*—*Club Alpí Català.*
010160. ee. 7.

—— Documents per la història cultural de Catalunya en el segle XVIII. *See* Casanovas (I.)

—— A Geographical and Historical Account of the Principality of Catalonia, and Earldom of Barcelona, *etc.* pp. 63. *J. Nutt: London,* 1705. 4°. **577. h. 27. (2.)**

—— Histoire de tout ce qui s'est passé en la Catalogne, depuis qu'elle a secoüé le joug de l'Espagnol. Contenant le progrez de la guerre de Catalogne és années 1640. & 1641. auec la signalée victoire de Monjuique. [By G. Sala.] Les Secrets publics de la Catalogne, ou la Pierre de touche des intentions de l'Ennemy . . . et L'Appuy de la verité Catalane, oppugnée par vn libelle, qui commence, La Iustification Royalle. 3 pt. *I. Berthelin: Rouen,* 1642. 4°. **1060. i. 28.**

—— Kort en bondigh verhael van alles wat sich notabels heeft toe ghedragen in de provintie van Catalonien, en daer omtrent. Beginnende van den oorspronck, waeruyt dese oproeren ontstaen, *etc.* *C. van de Pas: Amsterdam,* [1641?] 4°. **1060. h. 18. (4.)**

—— Levantamiento y Guerra de Cataluña en tiempo de Don Juan II. Documentos relativos á aquellos sucesos, *etc.* 13 tom. *Barcelona,* 1858–64. 8°. [*Coleccion de documentos ineditos del Archivo General de la Corona de Aragon.* tom. 14–26.] **9181. d.**

—— Luz de la Verdad. Preguntas, y respuestas en favor de Cataluña, y sus hijos. Originadas de una disputa avida entre cinco soldados de acavallo de las tropas de España. Dispuestas en la forma siguiente por uno de los mesmos propugnantes. [1670?] 8°. **8042. a. 35.**

—— Monumenta Cataloniæ. Materials per a la historia de l'art a Catalunya. vol. 1–3. *Barcelona,* [1932–36.] 4°. **L.R. 276. c. 16.**

—— Noticia universal de Cataluña, en amor, servicios, y finezas, admirable, en agravios, opressiones, y desprecios, sufrida, en constituciones, privilegios, y libertades, valerosa . . . Por el B. D. A. V. Y. M. F. D. P. D. N. 1641. 4°. *See* N., B. D. A. V. Y. M. F. D. P. D.
795. e. 20.

—— [Another edition.] [1641?] 8°. *See* N., B. D. A. V. Y. M. F. D. P. D. **9180. e. 1. (2.)**

—— Le Parlement de la Catalogne. *Paris,* [1939.] 8°.
9180. ee. 25.

—— Les Plans et profils des principales villes et lieux considérables de la Principauté de Catalogne. Avec la carte générale, et les particulières de chaque gouvernement. [Plates engraved by A. Perelle.] *Paris,* [1660?] *obl.* 8°. **1256.kk.8.(1.)**

—— El Problema Comarcal de Catalunya. [Essays by Francesc Glanadell and others. With a map.] pp. 142. *Barcelona,* 1931. 8°. **8042. k. 23.**

—— Proyecto de apéndice del Código Civil para Cataluña. [Edited by M. Trias y Domenech.] 1896. 8°. *See* Barcelona.—*Academia de Derecho.* **5384. b. 11.**

CATALONIA. [Appendix.]

—— Recort de la aliança fet al Serenissim Jordi-August, Rey de la Gran-Bretanya . . . ab una carta del Principat de Catalunya y Ciutat de Barcelona, any 1736. (Cum adnotationibus Alani Albionis.) Ara novament publicat per un redactor de la Veu de Catalunya (N. Font y Sagué). 1898. 8°. *See* George II., *King of Great Britain and Ireland.* [*Appendix.*] **09077. ee. 71.**

—— Relacion diaria de todo lo sucedido en el principado de Cataluña desde 15 de Julio hasta 8 de Septiembre deste presente año de 1650. *I. Gomez de Blas: Sevilla,* 1650. 4°. **1445. f. 17. (31.)**

—— Relation de ce qui s'est passé en Catalogne. (Suite de la relation, *etc.*) [The dedicatory letter signed: D. C., i.e. — de Caissel.] 1678, *etc.* 12°. *See* C., D. **9078. aaa. 15.**

—— [A reissue of pt. 1.] 1679. 12°. *See* C., D. **1196. a. 20.**

—— Segredos publicos, pedra de toque dos intentos do Inimiguo, & luz da verdade que manifesta os enganos, e cautelas de huns papeis volantes que vai espalhando o inimigo por o Principado de Catalunha . . . Traduzido de Catalão em Portugues. ff. 35. *L. de Queiros: Lisboa,* 1641. 4°. **1060. c. 29. (8.)**

—— Secretos publicos, piedra de toque, de las intenciones del Enemigo, y luz de la verdad. Que manifesta los engaños y cautelas de unos papeles volantes, que và distribuyendo el enemigo por el Principado de Cataluña. Traduzidos fielmente de Catalan en Castellano, *etc.* [*Barcelona?* 1641.] 8°. **9180. e. 1. (6.)**

—— Sucessos de la Guerra en el Principado de Cataluña, sobre el sitio que el Frances tiene puesto a las plaças de Perpiñan y Salzes, *etc.* *I. Gomez de Blas: Seuilla,* 1639. 4°. **1445. f. 22. (42.)**

—— The Viceroy of Catalonia, or the Double Cuckold. Made English by James Morgan, Gent. [A translation of "Le Double-Cocu" by Sébastien Brémond.] pp. 155. *J. B. for J. Magnes & R. Bentley: London,* 1678. 12°. **12512. aa. 1. (2.)**

CATALONIAN MEDICAL TEXT. A Brief Catalonian Medical Text. Edited by John Burnam, *etc.* [ff. 122 recto–125 verso of Codex Matritensis A. 113.] [1913.] 8°. *See* Madrid Codex A 113.
Dept. of Manuscripts.

CATALONIEN. *See* Catalonia.

CATALUCCIO (Francesco) Antonio di San Giuliano e la politica estera italiana dal 1900 al 1914. pp. 173. 1935. 8°. *See* Florence.—*Regio Istituto di Scienze Sociali "Cesare Alfieri."* **9150. ppp. 7.**

—— Storia del nazionalismo arabo. [With maps.] pp. 333. *Milano,* 1939. 8°. [*Manuali di politica internazionale.* no. 17.] **8012.pp.1/17.**

CATALUÑA. *See* Catalonia.

CATALUNHA. *See* Catalonia.

CATALUNYA. *See* Catalonia.

CATAMARANS.

—— Catamarans, *etc.* (Edited by J. Morwood.) 1955. 8°. *See* Morwood (John M. B.) **8808. l. 56.**

CATAMARCA.—*Instituto Nacional del Profesorado Secundario.*—*Centro de Estudiantes.*

—— Ariadna. año 1, no. 3, 4/5. set., dic., 1947. *Catamarca,* 1947. 8°. **P.P. 4126. ieb.**

CATAN (CHRISTOPHE DE) *See* CATTAN.

CATANAEUS (BALDUS) *See* CATANI.

CATANAEUS (JOANNES MARIA) *See* APHTHONIUS, *Sophista*. Aphthonii . . . Præexercitamenta, I. M. Catanæo interprete. *Gr. & Lat.* 1524. 8°. [*Contenta in hocce libello. Eloquentiæ encomium autore Philippo Melanchthone, etc.*] **1089. g. 2. (1.)**

—— —— 1689. 8°. **1385. c. 15.**

—— *See* APHTHONIUS, *Sophista*. Aphthonii Progymnasmata, Partim à Rodolpho Agricola, partim a Ioanne Maria Catanæo, latinitate donata, *etc.* 1596. 8°. **1481. ddd. 50.**

—— *See* APHTHONIUS, *Sophista*. Aphthonii Progymnasmata, partim à Rodolpho Agricola, partim à J. M. Catanæo, latinitate donata, *etc.* 1635. 8°. Mic. A. **586. (5.)**

—— *See* APHTHONIUS, *Sophista*. Aphthonii . . . Rhetorica progymnasmata I. M. Catanæo tralatore. 1523. fol. [*Continentur hoc uolumine. Georgii Trapezuntii Rhetoricorum libri v, etc.*] **11340. k 1.**

—— *See* APHTHONIUS, *Sophista*. Aphthonii declamatoris præexercitamenta, I. M. Catanæo interprete. [1534?] 8°. **527. d. 1.**

—— —— 1539. 8°. **519. a. 18. (4.)**

—— —— 1543. 8°. **11391. aa. 13. (3.)**

—— —— 1572. 8°. Voyn. **42.**

—— —— 1583. 8°. **11825. aa. 2.**

—— —— 1642. 12°. **527. a. 13.**

—— —— 1644. 8°. [*Operum Græcorum, Latinorum & Italorum rhetorum tomus primus, etc.* tom. 8.] **836. e. 3.**

—— —— 1645. 12°. **11391. a. 3.**

—— —— 1649. 12°. **C. 29. a. 4.**

—— —— 1650. 8°. **1089. e. 11.**

—— —— 1665. 12°. **11805. aa. 5.**

—— —— 1670. 12°. **8460. aa. 12.**

—— *See* ISOCRATES. [*Panegyricus.—Latin.*] Isocratis . . . Oratio panegyrica . . . per J. M. Catanæum in latium [*sic*] . . . translata. 1509. 4°. **834. g. 30. (2.)**

—— *See* PLINIUS CAECILIUS SECUNDUS (C.) [*Works.—Latin.*] *Begin.* Clarissimo Præsidi Gratianopolis: Iafredo Carolo . . . Ioannes Maria Catanæus felicitatem. *End.* In hoc uolumine continentur. C. Plinii Cecilii Secundi epistolarum libri nouem. Eiusdem . . . libellus epistolarum ad Traianum . . . Eiusdē panagyricus . . . cum enarrationibus I. M. Catanæi. 1506. fol. **10902. i. 10.**

—— —— 1510. fol. **10902. h. 15.**

—— —— 1519. fol. **10902. i. 9.**

—— —— 1530. 8°. **1082. f. 10.**

—— —— 1533. fol. **C. 82. i. 5.**

—— —— 1600. 4°. **10902. g. 7.**

—— —— 1625. 4°. **10905. h. 8.**

—— —— 1650. 8°. **1082. b. 8.**

—— *See* PLINIUS CAECILIUS SECUNDUS (C.) [*Epistolae.— Latin.*] Caii Plinii Caecilii Secundi Epistolarum libri x, notis . . . J. M. Catanæi . . . illustrati, *etc.* 1669. 8°. **57. l. 20.**

—— —— 1734. 4°. **636. k. 2.**

CATANAEUS (JOANNES MARIA)

—— *See* SUIDAS. [Lexicon Graecum.] *Begin.* [fol. 1 *recto:*] διαλογος στεφανου του μελανος, *etc.* [fol. 3 *recto:*] To μεν παρον βιβλιον Σουιδα, *etc.* [With a prefatory epistle by J. M. Catanaeus.] 1499. fol. IC. **26913.**

—— Io: Mariæ Catanæi Genua. [A poem.] *Lat. Impressum apud I. Mazochium: Romæ,* [1514.] 4°. **837. h. 1. (3.)**

—— [Another edition.] Con introduzione e appendice storica a cura del socio Girolamo Bertolotto. 1894. *See* GENOA. —*Società Ligure di Storia Patria, etc.* Atti, *etc.* vol. 24. 1858, *etc.* 8°. Ac. **6510.**

CATANEA PARASOLE (ELISABETTA) Pretiosa gemma delle virtuose donne. Doue si vedono . . . lauori di punto . . . disegnati da Isabella Catanea Parasole. E di nuouo dati in luce da Lucchino Gargano, con alcuni altri . . . lauori nuouamente inuentati. (Fac-simile eliotipico della stampa originale del 1600–01.) *Venice,* 1879. obl. 8°. **7742. df. 2.**
No. 12 of the " Raccolta di opere antiche sui disegni dei merletti di Venezia."

—— Studio delle virtuose dame; Roma, Antonio Facchetti, 1597. [*London,*] 1884. obl. 4°. [*Quaritch's Reprints of Rare Books.* Quarto series. no. 2.] **12204. h. 4.**

—— Teatro delle nobili et virtuose donne doue si rappresentano varij disegni di lauori nouamente inuentati, e disegnati da Elisabetta Catanea Parasole. (Fac-simile eliotipico della stampa originale del 1616.) ff. 52. *Venezia,* 1891. obl. 4°. **7742. dg. 1.**
Part of "Raccolta di opere antiche sui disegni dei merletti."

—— [Another edition.] Musterbuch für Stickereien und Spitzen von Elisabetta Parasole. 1616. ff. 46. *Berlin,* 1891. obl. fol. **1810. a. 25.**

CATANEA PARASOLE (ISABELLA) *See* CATANEA PARASOLE (Elisabetta)

CATANEIS (HENRICUS DE) *See* CICERO (M. T.) [*Supposititious Works.—Rhetorica ad C. Herennium.—Latin.*] *Begin.* [fol. 2 *recto:*] M. T. Ciceronis Ad C. Hærenniū Rhætoricoǝ Liber primus. *End.* [fol. 48 *verso:*] Marci Tullii C. Rhetoricoǝ opus p . . . henricum đ cataneis . . . emendatū, *etc.* 1479. 4°. **C. 1. b. 16.**

CATANEO, *il Danese.* Dell'Amor di Marfisa, tredici canti. pp. 106. *Appresso F. de Franceschi: Venetia,* 1562. 4°. **81. i. 29.**

CATANEO (GIACOMO) *See* VALTELLINA. Li Statuti di Valtellina . . . per M. G. Trauerso con l'aiuto di M. G. Cataneo . . . in questo ordine ridotti, *etc.* 1668. fol. **5326. f. 3. (1.)**

—— —— 1737. 4°. **1376. d. 16.**

CATANEO (GIOVANNI DE) *Count. See* CATANEO (T.) Opere postume, *etc.* [Edited by Count G. de Cataneo and P. Cataneo.] 1736. 4°. **94. h. 13.**

—— La Fisica, e l'amore. Prose sdrucciole . . . S'aggiungono quattro epistole dello stesso autore su i medesimi soggetti; e tre epistole sopra i drammi antichi, e moderni. pp. 321. *Lucca,* 1756. 8°. **1063. e. 7.**

CATANEO (GIOVANNI MARIA) *See* CATANAEUS (Joannes M.)

CATANEO (GIROLAMO) *Jesuit.* Le Sagge difficoltà del principato di Genova. Discorso, *etc.* pp. 55. *A. G. Francelli: Cesena, Genova,* [1651.] 8°. **1301. a. 22.**

CATANEO (GIROLAMO) *Military Engineer.* Dell'arte militare libri tre, ne' quali si tratta il modo di fortificare, offendere, diffendere, & fare gli'allogiamenti campali; con l'essamini de' bombardieri, & formare le battaglie . . . in questa terza impressione ampliati, & corretti. [Consisting of " Opera nuoua di fortificare " forming pt. 1 and 2, and " Tauole bruissime."] [With plates.] 3 pt. *Appresso T. Bozzola: Brescia,* 1571. 4°.
534. g. 25. (3.)
The titlepage is mutilated. The colophon reads " Appresso V. Sabbio. Ad instanza di T. Bozola."

—— [Another edition.] Dell'arte militare, libri cinque, *etc.* [With the addition of " Nuouo ragionamento del fabricare le fortezze " and " Modo di formare . . . le moderne battaglie."] [With plates.] MS. NOTES. 5 pt. *Appresso P. M. Marchetti: Brescia,* 1584. 4°.
52. f. 23. (1.)
The colophon reads " Appresso T. Bozzola."

—— Dell'arte del misurare, libri due, nel primo de' quali s'insegna a misurare, et partir i campi. Nel secondo a misurar le muraglie, imbottar grani, vini, fieni, e strami; col liuellar dell'acque, *etc.* 2 pt. *Appresso P. M. Marchetti: Brescia,* 1584. 4°. 52. f. 23. (2.)

—— Modo di formare con prestezza le moderne battaglie di picche, archibugieri, et cavalleria; con tre auisi del modo del marchiare; in modo di dialogo. Di nuouo dato in luce. [With a plate.] ff. 30. *Appresso F. & P. M. de' Marchetti: Brescia,* 1571. 4°. 1397. g. 26. (2.)
The colophon reads " Appresso V. Sabbo [sic], a instanza di F., & P. M. de' Marchetti."

—— Nuouo ragionamento del fabricare le fortezze; si per prattica, come per theorica; oue diffusamente si mostra tutto quello ch'à tal scientia si appartiene. [With plates.] ff. 35. *Appresso G. F. et P. M. fratelli de' Marchetti: Brescia,* 1571. 4°. 1397. g. 26. (1.)

—— Opera nuoua di fortificare, offendere et difendere; et far gli alloggiamenti campali, secondo l'uso di guerra. Aggiontoui nel fine, vn trattato de gl'essamini de' bombardieri, *etc.* ff. 93. *Appresso G. B. Bozola: Brescia,* 1564. 4°. 8825. b. 16.
The colophon reads " Appresso L. di Sabbio."

—— Le Capitaine . . . contenant la maniere de fortifier places, assaillir, & defendre. Auec l'ordre qu'on doit tenir pour asseoir vn camp, & mespartir les logis d'iceluy. Le tout reueu, corrigé, & augmenté en plusieurs lieux par l'auteur, & depuis mis en François. [Translated by Jean de Tournes. With plates.] pp. 150. *J. de Tournes: Lyon,* 1574. 4°. 534. i. 4. (1.)

—— [Another edition.] pp. 150. *I. Roussin: Lyon,* 1593. 4°. 8827. eee. 29.

—— Rote perpetue, per le quali si puo con qual numero di due dadi si voglia, ouero con due dadi secondo l'horologio d'Italia ritrouar quando si fà la luna; le feste mobili . . . Et in che giorno entra il principio d'ogni mese. ff. 29. *Appresso F. Marchetti: Brescia,* [1562.] 4°. 8767. k. 31.

—— Tauole breuissime per sapere con prestezza quante file uanno à formare una giustissima battaglia. Con li suoi armati di corsaletti, *etc.* ff. iv. 38. *À instantia di G. B. Bozola; appresso L. di Sabbio: Brescia,* 1563. 8°. 534. c. 2. (2.)

—— Most Briefe Tables to knowe redily howe manye ranckes of footemen armed with Corslettes, as vnarmed, go to the making of a iust battayle . . . Tourned out of Italion into English by H. G. 1574. *See* MACCHIAVELLI (N.) [*Libro dell'Arte della Guerra.*] The Arte of Warre, *etc.* 1573, *etc.* 4°. 8825. bb. 19.

—— [Another edition.] *See* MACCHIAVELLI (N.) [*Libro dell'Arte della Guerra.*] The Arte of Warre, *etc.* 1588. 4°. 1140. h. 2.

CATANEO (JEROSME) *See* CATANEO (Girolamo) *Military Engineer.*

CATANEO (LORENZO)
—— Il Geloso, *etc.* [A poem.] pp. 48. *Bartolomeo Fontana: Venetia,* 1626. 12°. 1481. ddd. 36. (2.)

—— Le Tre gelose. Canzoni . . . Per Costante, caualiere senza core. pp. 40. *G. Pauoni: Genoua,* 1612. 4°. 82. i. 32. (1.)

CATANEO (PIETRO) *Senese. See* FRÉART DE CHAMBRAY (R.) Parallèle de l'architecture antique et de la moderne, auec vn recueil des dix principaux autheurs . . . sçauoir, Palladio et Scamozzi . . . D. Barbaro et Cataneo, *etc.* 1650. fol. 560*. e. 1.

—— —— 1702. fol. 60. g. 3. (2.)

—— —— 1766. 4°. 7820. cc. 7.

—— *See* FRÉART DE CHAMBRAY (R.) A Parallel of the Antient Architecture with the Modern . . . in a collection of ten principal authors . . . viz. Palladio and Scamozzi . . . D. Barbaro and Cataneo, *etc.* 1664. fol. 60. h. 6.

—— I quattro primi libri di Architettura di P. Cataneo, *etc.* ff. 54. *In casa de' figliuoli di Aldo: Vinegia,* 1554. fol.
C.80.g.12.

—— [Another copy.] 50. f. 12. (2.)

—— L'Architettura di Pietro Cataneo Senese. Alla quale oltre all'essere stati . . . riuisti . . . i primi quattro libri per l'adietro stampati, sono aggiunti di piu il quinto, sesto, settimo, e ottauo libro, *etc.* pp. 196. [*P. Manutius:*] *Venetia,* 1567. fol. L.R.294.b.25.

—— Le Pratiche delle due prime matematiche . . . Con la aggionta, Libro d'albaco e geometria con il pratico e uero modo di misurar la terra. ff. 79 [83]. *Appresso G. Griffio, ad instantia di P. Cataneo: Venetia,* 1559. 4°. 529. d. 2.

—— [Another edition.] Ricorrette, & meglio ordinate, con alcune aggiontioni de lo stesso autore. Diuise in libri quattro. ff. 88. *Appresso G. Griffio, ad instantia di P. Cataneo: Venetia,* 1567. 4°. 529. g. 8. (4.)

CATANEO (PIETRO) *Son of Tommaso Cataneo. See* CATANEO (T.) Opere postume, *etc.* [Edited by Count G. de Cataneo and P. Cataneo.] 1736. 4°. 94. h. 13.

CATANEO (ROCCO) *See* CICERO (M. T.) [*De Partitione Oratoria.—Italian.*] Dialogo . . . dintorno alle partitioni oratorie: con la spositione di M. R. Cataneo. 1545. 8°. 525. c. 24. (3.)

CATANEO (TOMMASO) Opere postumi, *etc.* [Edited by Count G. de Cataneo and P. Cataneo.] pp. 280. *Venezia,* 1736. 4°. 94. h. 13.

—— Vita di S. Giovanni da Capistrano, *etc.* pp. 176. *Ad istanza dell'Autore: Parma,* 1691. 4°. 4867. e. 23.

CATANEO DE LACOMARINO (GIACOMO) *See* CATANEUS (J.)

CATANEUS (BALDUS) *See* CATANI (Baldo)

CATANEUS (EUGENIUS) *Bishop of Telese. See* DEIS (J. de) Successores S. Barnabæ Apostoli in ecclesia Mediolanensi . . . per I. de Deis collecti . . . deinde a R.P. D. E. Cataneo aucti, *etc.* 1589. 8°. 698. c. 6. (2.)

—— —— 1628. fol. 4605. h. 10.

CATANEUS (Jacobus) De morbo Gallico tractatus. *See* Luisini (L.) De morbo Gallico omnia quae extant, *etc.* tom. 1. 1566, *etc.* fol. **1167. eee. 23.**

—— [Another edition.] *See* Luisini (L.) Aphrodisiacus, *etc.* tom. 1. 1728, *etc.* fol. **774. n. 6.**

CATANEUS (Joannes Baptista) *See* Cathaneis (J. B. de)

CATANEUS (Joannes Lucidus) *Begin.* [fol. 2 *recto:*] Illustrissimo atœ excel. D. D. Fran. Gonzaga Marchioni Mantuae quarto. Io. Lucidus Cataneus iurisconsul. Mantuanus salutem. [fol. 3 *recto:*] Io. Lucidi Catanei . . . oratio in funere Illustrissimæ Barbaræ Marchionissæ Mantuæ. M.cccclxxxii. [fol. 14 *verso:*] Io. Lucidi Catanei . . . Oratio funebris pro . . . Francisco Gonzaga . . . Cardinale Mantuano. [fol. 25 *verso:*] Illustrissimi . . . Frederici Gonzagae III. Marchionis Mantuani Epicedion per eundem Ioannem Lucidum Cataneum. [fol. 36 *recto:*] Oratiuncula eiusdem ad populum responsiua pro . . . D. Francisco Gŏzaga IIII, *etc.* [fol. 38 *verso:*] Extemporarium responsum eiusdem oratori . . . Marchionis Montisferati, *etc.* [fol. 41 *recto:*] Io. Lucidi Catanei . . . ad Alexandrum VI. Pon. Maximum oratio. *per Angelum Vgoletum: Parmę, die prima Martii, 1493. 4°.* **IA. 30348.**
50 leaves, the first and last blank. Sig. a–e⁸ A¹⁰. 24 lines to a page. Without the blank leaves.

—— [Another copy of quire A.] **IA. 30348a.**

—— *Begin.* [fol. 1 *recto:*] Io. Lucidi Catanei .v. iu. doctoris archidiaconi ac Cōsiliarii Marchionalis Mātuani & oratoris ad Alexādrū .vi. Pont. Max. Oratio. *End.* [fol. 7 *verso:*] Habita Romæ . . . Die quinta Nouēbris. M.cccc.xcii. [*Stephan Plannck: Rome,* 1492?] 4°. **IA. 18514.**
8 leaves, the last blank. Sig. a⁸. 27 lines to a page.

—— [Another copy.] **IA. 18515.**
Imperfect; wanting ff. 3–6, which are replaced by four leaves of an oration by Jason de Maino.

—— Iº Lucidi Catanei .v. iu. doctoris Archidiaconi ac Consiliarii Marchionalis Mantuani & oratoris ad Alexandrum .vi. Ponti. maxi. Oratio. [*Andreas Freitag: Rome,* 1492?] 4°. **IA. 18950.**
6 leaves. Sig. a⁶. 34 lines to a page.

—— [Another copy.] **IA. 18951.**

—— [Another copy.] **IA. 18952.**

CATANEUS (Joannes Maria) *See* Catanaeus.

CATANEUS (Laurus) Lauri Catanei . . . oratio, a Laurentio filio, decem annorum puero, Rocchæ habita, in aduentu . . . Francisci Mariæ Henrici Senogalliensis Episcopi, *etc.* [Followed by "Capitolo cantato da Laura Catanea, sorella del sudetto putto . . . alla prima entrata di Monsignor Ḥenrico."] *Apud S. Martellinum: Maceratæ,* 1581. 4°. **1074. g. 18. (6.)**

CATANEUS (Nicolaus Antonius) Rarioris hydropis uteri historia. 1752. *See* Calogierà (A.) Raccolta d'opuscoli scientifici e filologici, *etc.* tom. 47. 1728, *etc.* 12°. **247. c. 16.**

CATANEUS DIACETIUS (Franciscus) *See* Cattani da Diacceto (Francesco)

CATANI (　　　) *See* Minar (J.) Principis da Grammatica nel linguaig Todaisc, *etc.* [The preface signed: Minar, Catani, Paoli.] 1778. 8°. **885. e. 22.**

CATANI (Baldo) Oratio . . . in funere Sixti v., *etc.*— Oratio post obitum Urbani VII. de subrogando nouo pontifice. *See* Muret (M. A.) M. Antonij Mureti . . . orationum volumina duo, *etc.* vol. 1. 1603. 12°. **1090. b. 2.**

CATANI (Baldo)

—— La Pompa Funerale fatta dall'Illmo & R^mo Sr Cardinale Montalto nella traportazione dell'ossa di Papa Sisto il quinto, scritta, & dichiarata da B. Catani. [Followed by "Lælij Peregrini . . . oratio funebris de Sixto v.," *etc.* With illustrations.] pp. 111 [101]. *Nella stamperia Vaticana: Roma,* 1591. 4°. **702. k. 13.**

CATANI (Francesco) *Bishop of Fiesole. See* Cattani da Diacceto.

CATANI (Francesco Saverio) Il Papa, o siano Ricerche sul primato di questo sacerdote. [By F. S. Catani.] pp. 167. ms. note. 1783. 8°. *See* Pope. **1356. b. 11. (4.)**

—— La Reale Medicide, esponente la morte di Francesco Primo Gran-Duca di Toscana e della Bianca Capello . . . Tragica festa teatrale, illustrata di rami, e d'istoriche annotazioni. [By F. S. Catani. In verse. With portraits.] pp. 167. 1778. 8°. *See* Francis I. [de' Medici], *Grand Duke of Tuscany.* **11715. h. 28.**

—— La Reale Medicide, esponente nella morte di Don Garzia i fatti più speciali di Cosimo Duca II. di Firenze . . . Tragica festa teatrale. Illustrata di rami, e d'istoriche annotazione. [By F. S. Catani. In verse.] pp. 140. 1777. 4°. *See* Cosmo I [De' Medici], *Grand Duke of Tuscany.* **841. i. 36.**

CATANI (Tommaso) In cerca di Cavallette. Gita nelle alpi apuane raccontata a' miei scolari. pp. 56. *Firenze,* 1884. 8°. **10107. d. 4. (1.)**

CATANIA. Catania e sue vicinanze. Manuale pel viaggiatore. pp. 127. *Catania,* 1867. 8°. **10151. aa. 13.**
The date on the wrapper is 1868.

—— Descrizione di Catania, *etc.* [By F. Paternò Castello, Duke di Carcaci.] pp. 284. *Catania,* 1841. 8°. **10136. f. 18.**

—— Le Femmine di Catania. [An eulogy of the women of Catania for their conduct in the political struggle of 1820.] [1820.] *s. sh.* fol. **8032. m. 7. (9.)**

—— [Another edition.] [1820.] *s. sh.* fol. **8032. m. 7. (11.)**

—— Guida letteraria, scientifica, artistica, amministrativa e commerciale di Catania. pp. 349. *Catania,* 1881. 8°. **10151. bbb. 9.**

—— Istoria dove s'intende come un giuocatore in Catania per causa di giuoco diede l'anima sua e di sua moglie al demonio, *etc.* [In verse.] pp. 8. *Lucca,* 1800. 12°. **11429. b. 57. (32.)**

—— Le Tremblement de terre, arriué dans la ville de Catania. *See* France. [*Appendix.—History and Politics.—Miscellaneous.*] La Relation véritable, de ce qui a esté proposé par l'Ambassadeur de France au grand Seigneur devant l'Isle de Candie, *etc.* [1669?] 16°. **9210. aaa. 7.**

ACCADEMIA DEGLI ETNEI.

—— Varj componimenti degli Etnei per la morte di Ignazio Vincenzo Paternò Castello principe v. di Biscari, *etc.* [With a portrait.] pp. 218. *Catania,* 1787. 4°. **662. c. 37.**

ACCADEMIA GIOENIA DI SCIENZI NATURALI.

—— Atti (Acta), *etc.* 20 vol. *Catania,* 1825–43. 4°.

—— Serie seconda. 20 vol. *Catania,* 1844–66. 4°.

—— Serie terza. 20 vol. *Catania,* 1867–88. 4°.

CATANIA.

—— Serie quarta. 20 vol. *Catania*, 1889–1907. fol.

—— Serie quinta. 20 vol. *Catania*, 1908–35. fol.

—— Serie sesta. *Catania*, 1936– . fol.   Ac. **2805.**

BENEDICTINE ABBEY.

—— [For catalogues of the Library of the Benedictine Abbey at Catania issued subsequent to its acquisition by the Commune:] *See* infra : BIBLIOTECA COMUNALE AI BENEDETTINI.

BIBLIOTECA COMUNALE AI BENEDETTINI.

—— Catalogo ragionato delle edizioni del secolo xv. e de' manoscritti che si conservano nella biblioteca de' Benedettini casinesi in Catania, compilato dal bibliotecario . . . Francesco Tornabene. pp. ix. 202. *Catania*, 1846. 8º.
011902. i. 25. (1.)

—— I Diplomi esistenti nella Biblioteca Comunale ai Benedettini. Regesto. [Compiled by Carmelo Ardizzone. With facsimiles.] pp. 400. 37. *Catania*, 1927. fol.
11909. v. 16.

BIBLIOTECA UNIVERSITARIA.

—— *See* infra :   UNIVERSITÀ DEGLI STUDI DI CATANIA.

CIRCOLO BELLINI.

—— Omaggio a Bellini nel primo centenario dalla sua nascita, *etc.* (Bibliografia belliniana.) pp. 388. *Catania*, 1901. 4º.   **10629. i. 10.**

DEPUTAZIONE DI STORIA PATRIA PER LA SICILIA, SEZIONE DI CATANIA.

—— *See* infra : SOCIETÀ DI STORIA PATRIA PER LA SICILIA ORIENTALE.

MUSEO BISCARI.

—— Inventario del Museo Biscari in Catania. pp. 62. *Catania*, 1871. 8º.
Dept. of Greek & Roman Antiquities.

—— Il Museo Biscari. [A catalogue, with a historical introduction. Compiled by Guido Libertini.] vol. 1. pp. xxvii. 327. pl. cxxv. *Milano, Roma*, 1930. fol.
L.R. 273. b. 11.
No more published.

REGIA UNIVERSITÀ DEGLI STUDI DI CATANIA.

—— *See* infra : UNIVERSITÀ DEGLI STUDI DI CATANIA.

SOCIETÀ DI STORIA PATRIA PER LA SICILIA ORIENTALE.

Società di Storia Patria per la Sicilia Orientale, 1904–35.
R. Deputazione di Storia Patria per la Sicilia, Sezione di Catania, 1936–45.
Deputazione di Storia Patria per la Sicilia, Sezione di Catania, 1946–48.   •
Società di Storia Patria per la Sicilia Orientale, 1949– .

—— Archivio storico per la Sicilia orientale. anno 2. fasc. 1 ; anno 5. fasc. 1. *Catania*, 1905, 08. 8º.   Ac. **6504.**

—— Seconda serie. anno 1–11. *Catania*, 1925–35. 8º.
Ac. **6504. (2.)**

CATANIA.

—— Miscellanea di studi sicelioti ed italioti in onore di Paolo Orsi, *etc.* [With plates.] pp. v. 432.   *Catania*, [1921.] 4º.   **7702. t. 6.**

—— Ottanta lettere inedite del Panormità tratte dai codici milanesi . . . [Edited by Remigio Sabbadini.] Nuovi documenti sul Panormità tratti dagli archivi palermitani. [Edited by M. Catalano-Tirrito.] pp. 209.   *Catania*, 1910. 8º.   Ac. **6504/2.**
Vol. 1 of the " Biblioteca della Società di Storia Patria per la Sicilia Orientale."

UNIVERSITÀ DEGLI STUDI DI CATANIA.

Regia Università degli Studi di Catania, 1444–1946.
Università degli Studi di Catania, 1946– .

Works by individual authors published by the university are entered under the authors' names.

—— Storia della Università di Catania, dalle origini ai giorni noªtri. Scritta da Michele Catalano, Matteo Gaudioso, Giuseppe Paladino, Guido Libertini, Gaetano Curcio, Carmelina Naselli. pp. 493. *Catania*, 1934. 8º.
Ac. **2600/2.**

—— *Biblioteca Universitaria.* La Biblioteca Universitaria di Catania. Cenni storici e statistici. (Estratto dalla Relazione sull'Università di Catania.) pp. 10. *Catania*, 1872. 8º.   Ac. **2600.**

Biblioteca Universitaria e Ventimilliana.

—— Catania. R. Biblioteca Universitaria. (R. Biblioteca Ventimiliana.) [By G. Tamburini.] *In:* Inventari dei manoscritti delle biblioteche d'Italia. vol. 20. pp. 133–164. 1913. 8º.   **011900. dd. 20.**

Facoltà di Lettere e Filosofia.

—— Siculorum gymnasium. Rassegna semestrale della Facoltà di Lettere e Filosofia dell'Università di Catania. N.S. *Catania*, 1948– . 8º.   Ac. **2600. b.**

CATANIA, ALESSANDRO, *Bishop of.* [1725–1726.] *See* BURGOS.

——, GIUSEPPE BENEDETTO, *Archbishop of.* [1867–1894.] *See* DUSMET (G. B.) *Cardinal.*

——, INNOCENZO, *Bishop of.* [1624–1633.] *See* MASSIMO (I.) successively *Bishop of Bertinoro* and *of Catania.*

——, OCTAVIUS, *Bishop of.* [1638–1646.] *See* BRANCIFORTIUS (O.) successively *Bishop of Cefala* and *of Catania.*

——, SALVATOR, *Bishop of.* [1818–1820.] *See* FERRO (S. de)

CATANIA (FRANCISCUS) Francisci Catania . . . Quæstio de medicamento purgante. pp. 24. 291.   *P. de Isola: Panormi*, 1648. 4º.   **1188. i. 5. (2.)**
The titlepage is engraved.

CATANIA (GIOVANNI TOMMASO DI) Croniche antiquissime dall'anno DCCCCLXXXVI sino al MDLII. *See* PELLICCIA (A. A.) Raccolta di varie croniche . . . appartenenti alla storia del regno di Napoli. tom. 1. 1780, *etc.* 4º.
1318. h. 1.

CATANIA (GIUSEPPE ROMANO) *See* ROMANO-CATANIA.

CATANIA (JOANNES THOMAS DE) *See* CATANIA (Giovanni T. di)

CATANIA (PAOLO) Teatro oue si rappresentano le miserie humane. E le mentite apparenze di questo fallace mondo. In canzoni siciliane . . . date in luce per Giachino Ferreri. Con gionta d'altre canzoni sopra la sequenza del Sanctissimo Sacramento, e di morti, con la Ninna della Madonna. pp. [451.] *A. Colicchia: Palermo*, 1665. 8º.
1071. c. 15.
Cropped.

CATANIO (GIROLAMO) *See* CATANEO.

CATAÑO.

—— Fundación del pueblo de Cataño. (Fundación y supresión del pueblo de la Trinidad de Paloseco.) Documentos y comentarios. Por G. E. Morales Muñoz. [With illustrations.] pp. 286. *San Juan de Puerto Rico*, 1946. 8°.
10482. aa. 45?

CATAÑO (IGNACIO) Lamentos de Ferrer y Cataño. [Signed: S. I. L.] 1821. 4°. *See* L., S. I.
9770. bb. 7. (58.)

CATANUSI (PLACIDE) *See* PETRARCA (F.) [*Canzoniere.— Italian and French.*] Les Œuvres amoureuses de Petrarque, traduites . . . par le Sieur P. Catanusi. 1669. 12°.
11422. bbb. 8.

CATANUTUS (NICOLAUS) Isagogicon, siue Facilis introductio ad vniuersam pharmaceuticæ artis praxim, *etc.* pp. 197. *In ædibus Senatus, apud I. Rossi: Catanæ,* 1650. 4°.
546. f. 9.

CATANZARO.—*Biblioteca Comunale.* Notazione bibliografica degli incunabuli conservati nella Biblioteca comunale di Catanzaro. pp. 8. *Reggio d'Emilia,* 1936. 8°. [*Pubblicazioni della Scuola di Bibliografia Italiana.* no. 37.]
Ac.9530.

—— *Museo Provinciale.* Museo provinciale di Catanzaro. Catalogo della collezione numismatica. Monete medioevali e moderne, medaglie, ecc., descritte per cura del Dᵣ Solone Ambrosoli. pp. 226. *Catanzaro,* 1894. 8°.
7757. c. 46.

CATANZARO, LUCAS, *Bishop of.* [1629–1631.] *See* CASTELLINUS.

—— MICHELE BASILIO, *Bishop of.* [1818–1823.] *See* CLARI.

CATANZARO (ANGELA)

—— Mama [*sic*] mia Italian Cookbook. The home book of Italian cooking. pp. 286. *Liveright Publishing Corporation : New York,* [1954.] 8°.
7950. bb. 55.

CATANZARO (CARLO) *See* CHIARI (C.) Profili di artisti. Con prefazione biografica di C. Catanzaro. 1883. 8°.
10629. aaa. 46. (1.)

—— *See* GHERARDI DEL TESTA (T.) L'Egoista e l'uomo di cuore. Commedia . . . Con prefazione biografica di C. Catanzaro. 1876. 8°.
11715. bbb. 57.

—— *See* GIACOMETTI (P.) Lotta crudele . . . Dramma . . . di P. Giacometti. Con una biografia sull'autore scritta . . . dal cav. C. Catanzaro. 1876. 8°.
11715. ee. 52.

—— *See* MURATORI (L.) Un Segreto. Dramma, *etc.* (Con prefazione biografica di C. Catanzaro.) 1876. 8°.
11715. bbb. 57.

—— Giuseppe Rovani. Profilo critico-biografico, con prefazione di Pietro Fanfani. pp. 35. *Firenze,* 1875. 8°.
10602. e. 3. (4.)

—— Il Progresso femminile in Italia. Manuale illustrato biografico delle scrittrici ed artiste viventi. 4 fasc. pp. 185. *Firenze,* 1894–97. 8°.
10632. bb. 55.

—— Vignette in penna di alcuni scrittori contemporanei. pp. 166. *Siena,* 1876. 8°.
11840. cc. 8.

CATANZARO (FRANCESCO ALBERTINO DA) Trattato dell'Angelo custode . . . con l'officio dell'Angelo custode . . . Et vn altro trattato vtilissimo della deuotione uerso la Beatissima Vergine. Fatto da vn Sacerdote Napolitano, Dottore in Teologia. 2 pt. *G. Facciotti: Roma,* 1612. 16°.
1019. a. 15.

CATANZARO (GIACINTO) *See* SENECA (L. A.) [*Supposititious Works.—Octavia.—Italian.*] Ottavia. Tragedia . . . Tradotta . . . da G. Catanzaro. 1897. 8°.
11707. de. 22.

CATAPULT, *pseud.* A Few Remarks on the Ordnance Committees, and the great Gun Controversy. By Catapult. pp. 15. *W. Mitchell: London,* 1863. 8°.
8822. bb. 8. (9.)

CATARA-LETTIERI (ANTONIO) *See* ANGELIS (S. de) Sull' uomo. Pensieri del prof. A. Catara-Lettieri. Rivista bibliografica, *etc.* 1870. 8°.
8485. bbb. 29. (3.)

CATARDI (VICENZU) Na Frazzata de canzuni gaddipuline. pp. 44. *Gallipoli,* 1891. 8°.
11429. ee. 35. (6.)

CATARGIU (LASCAR) Lascar Catargiu. [A biographical sketch.] pp. 48. *Bucureşti,* 1907. 8°. **10600. s. 8. (3.)**

CATARINA. [For Saints, Sovereigns and Princesses of Sovereign Houses of this name :] *See* CATHARINE.

CATARINA DE SAN JUAN.

—— *See* CARRASCO PUENTE (R.) Bibliografía de Catarina de San Juan y de la china poblana, *etc.* 1950. 4°.
2717.dd.1.(a.)/3.

CATARINETA. Cansó nova de la Catarineta. pp. 4. *Barcelona,* [1850 ?] 4°.
11450. f. 26. (68.)

CATARINEU (ESTÉBAN AZAÑA Y) *See* AZAÑA Y CATARINEU.

CATARINO (AMBROGIO) successively *Bishop of Minori* and *Archbishop of Conza. See* POLITI (Lancelotto)

CATASTINI (ALESSANDRO) Formula del contratto per il far de censi di misericordia. 1608. 4°.
8275. bb. 16. (2.)

—— Modo del' far' censi in qual si voglia luogo da potersi estinguere in tredici anni ed' in piu ed' in manco tempo, à voluntà de contraenti. pp. 13. *H. Gazeau: Lione,* 1608.
8275. bb. 16. (1.)

CATASTROPHE.

—— Awful Catastrophe ! From " Pope's Weekly News." [A political skit in the form of a poster. By J. H. Deeble.] [c. 1845.] *s. sh. obl.* fol.
1876. f. 26. (8.)

CATASTROPHES. Les Catastrophes amoureuses, ou le Retour à la vertu ; histoire vraisemblable. Par J. C. M. P. [i.e. J. C. M. Pichenot.] 1796. 8°. *See* P., J. C. M.
1094. cc. 20.

CATASÚS (TRINITAT)

—— Trinitat Catasús. [Selected poems.] Tria i pròleg de Tomàs Garcés. pp. 58. *Barcelona,* 1924. 8°. [*Els poetes d'ara.*]
11453. e. 1/16.

CATAT (LOUIS) Voyage à Madagascar. 1889–1890. [With illustrations.] pp. 436. *Paris,* 1895. 4°.
1787. aaa. 13.

CATAUDELLA (QUINTINO) La Poesia di Aristofane. pp. vii. 201. *Bari,* 1934. 8°.
20002. a. 37.

CATAVENTO.

—— O Catavento. Dialogo entre um corcunda e dous liberaes sobre a constituição de Portugal feita pelas Cortes de 1821 e 1822. [By J. J. Ferreira de Moura.] pp. 54. *Paris,* 1826. 8°.
8042. aa. 35.

CATCALL (Sir CRITICK) *pseud. See* WIT. Wit for Money ; or, Poet Stutter, *etc.* [The dedication signed : Sir Critick Catcall.] 1691. 4°.
641. h. 1. (5.)

CATCH-BIZ TIME TABLE. *See* PERIODICAL PUBLICATIONS.—*London.*

CATCH CLUB. *See also* LONDON.—III. *Noblemen's and Gentlemen's Catch Club.*

—— The Catch Club: a collection of all the songs, catches, glees, duets, &c. as sung by Mr. Bannister, Mr. Arrowsmith [and others] . . . at the Royalty Theatre . . . To which is added, Hippesley's Drunken-Man, as altered and spoken by Mr. Lee Lewes. (Third edition: with additions.) pp. 30. *J. Griffith: London*, [1787 ?] 8°.
11779. c. **88.** (**1.**)

CATCH (HOLNEY) *pseud.* [i.e. G. A. HIGLETT.] *See also* HIGLETT (G. A.)

—— The Harrogate Philatelic Congress . . . Unauthorised report. [A skit.] pp. 14. *Wood & Son: Perth*, [1921.] 8°.
08247. ff. **69.**

CATCH (JACK) A Bill and Answer, betwixt Jack Catch plaintiff, and Slingsby Bethel & al. defendents, of the year, 1681, *etc.* [Signed: J. B. In verse.] 1686. fol. *See* B., J.
1347. l. **42.**

—— An Hue and Cry after the Pretender. By Jack Catch, Esq; Executioner-General, *etc.* pp. 4. [*Edinburgh ?* 1716.] fol.
C. 115. i. **3.** (**36.**)

—— A Hue and Cry after the Pretender, by Jack Catch, &c. [1716 ?] *s. sh.* fol.
807. g. **5.** (**66.**)

—— A Seasonable Hue and Cry after the Pretender. By Jack Catch . . . A new edition. To which is added, An excellent Song on Young Perkin, *etc.* pp. 15. *Richard Single-ten: London*, 1745. 8°.
111. c. **65.**

CATCHES. Great Catches; or, Grand matches. [By Eleanor F. Blakiston.] 2 vol. *Saunders, Otley & Co.: London*, 1861. 12°.
12635. g. **7.**

CATCHESIDE (DAVID GUTHRIE)
—— The Genetics of Micro-Organisms. pp. vii. 223. *Sir Isaac Pitman & Sons: London*, 1951. 8°.
7008. ddd. **34.**

CATCHESIDE (F. L.) Life of S. Cuthbert, Bishop of Lindisfarne. (Second edition.) [With plates.] pp. xii. 57. *E. W. Allen: London; Poulton & Co.: Aylesbury*, [1879.] 8°.
4827. bbb. **23.**

CATCHINGS (THOMAS CLENDENIN) *See* MISSISSIPPI, *State of.* The Mississippi Code of 1906 . . . Prepared and annotated by A. H. Whitfield. T. C. Catchings, *etc.* 1906. 8°.
A.S.M.236/2.

CATCHINGS (WADDILL) *See* FOSTER (William T.) and CATCHINGS (W.) Money, *etc.* [1924.] 8°. **8207.** t. **20.**

—— *See* FOSTER (William T.) and CATCHINGS (W.) Old King Cole in Trouble. [1926.] 8°. **08286.** aa. **51.**

—— *See* FOSTER (William T.) and CATCHINGS (W.) Profits. [1926.] 8°. **08206.** ee. **1.**

—— *See* FOSTER (William T.) and CATCHINGS (W.) The Road to Plenty, *etc.* [1929.] 8°. **012706.** i. **25.**

—— *See* GOTTSCHALK (H.) Die Kaufkraftlehre. Eine Kritik der Unterverbrauchslehren von J. A. Hobson . . . W. Catchings. 1932. 8°. **8228.** s. **18.**

—— Our Common Enterprise. A way out for labor and capital. pp. 27. *Ryerson Press: Toronto*, 1922. 8°.
08285. e. **77.**

CATCHOURINE (C.) *See* KACHURIN (S. P.)

CATCHPENNY (CHRISTOPHER) *pseud. See* SMOKE'EM (Simon) *pseud.* The Campaign; or, the Birmingham theatrical war . . . By S. Smoke'em . . . C. Catchpenny. 1775. 12°. **11795.** aa. **12.**

CATCHPOLE (GEORGE) George Catchpole; or, Jack, the Donkey that stole apples, *etc.* pp. 46. *S.P.C.K.: London*, [1864.] 16°. **4416.** a. **79.** (**6.**)

CATCHPOLE (GEORGE G.) The Silver Fox. (A text book for breeders.) [With plates.] pp. 145. *Metropolitan Press Agency: London*, 1930. 8°. **7209.** b. **17.**

CATCHPOLE (H.)
—— Elementary Urdu, general and military. Roman script. pp. vi. 146. *W. S. Cowell: Ipswich*, 1946. 8°.
12908. a. **10.**

CATCHPOLE (HUBERT R.)
—— Regnier de Graaf, 1641–1673 . . . Reprinted from Bulletin of the History of Medicine, *etc.* [With plates, including portraits.] [1940.] 8°. **10759.** l. **25.**

CATCHPOLE (LESLIE THOMAS) The Lynton and Barnstaple Railway, 1895–1935. [With plates, including maps.] pp. 62. *Oakwood Press: Sidcup*, 1936. 8°.
20020. cc. **38.**

—— (Second edition, revised.) pp. 67. *Oakwood Press: Sidcup*, 1936. 8°. **20029.** eee. **22.**

—— The Lynton & Barnstaple Railway. (Fourth edition.) pp. 35. pl. XII. *Oakwood Press: South Godstone*, 1949. 8°. **08235.** aaa. **67.**

CATCHPOLE (MARGARET) The History of Margaret Catchpole, a Suffolk girl. [By Richard Cobbold.] Author's complete edition, *etc.* pp. 189. *G. Routledge & Sons: London*, 1887. 8°. **12620.** g. **36.**
Other editions are entered under the author's name.

CATCHPOLE (NAT)
—— Flowering Shrubs and Small Trees. [With plates.] pp. 234. *W. H. & L. Collingridge: London*, 1948. 8°.
7035. bb. **14.**

—— Simple Pruning, *etc.* pp. ix. 129. *W. H. & L. Collingridge: London*, [1930.] 8°. [" *Amateur Gardening* " *Simple Handbooks.*] **07032.p.35/4.**

—— (Second edition, enlarged.) Edited by A. J. Macself. pp. x. 132. *W. H. & L. Collingridge: London*, [1934.] 8°.
07028. a. **43.**

CATCHPOOL (CORDER) *See* CATCHPOOL (Thomas C. P.)

CATCHPOOL (EDMUND) A Text-Book of Sound, *etc.* pp. vii. 203. *W. B. Clive: London*, [1895.] 8°. [*University Tutorial Series.*] **12205.** c. **292.**

—— Second edition, *etc.* pp. vii. 203. *W. B. Clive: London*, [1896.] 8°. [*University Tutorial Series.*] **12205.** c. **267.**

—— Fourth edition. pp. viii. 216. *W. B. Clive: London*, 1903. 8°. [*University Tutorial Series.*] **12205.** c. **543.**

—— (Sixth impression, fifth edition.) Revised and enlarged by John Satterly. pp. viii. 380. *W. B. Clive: London*, 1909. 8°. [*University Tutorial Series.*] **12205.** e. **131.**

—— Textbook of Sound. By E. Catchpool . . . and John Satterly . . . Revised by C. T. Archer. (Sixth edition.) pp. 360. *University Tutorial Press: London*, 1944. 8°.
8716. k. **16.**

—— Textbook of Sound. By Edmund Catchpool . . . and John Satterly . . . Revised by H. N. V. Temperley. (Seventh edition.) pp. 379. *University Tutorial Press: London*, 1949. 8°. **8716.** m. **6.**

CATCHPOOL (THOMAS CORDER PETTIFOR)
—— *See* GREAVES (Jean C.) Corder Catchpool. [With a portrait.] 1953. 8°. **4909.** a. **25.**

CATCHPOOL (THOMAS CORDER PETTIFOR)

——   Corder Catchpool's Statement at his Court Martial. *Ward: Croydon*, [1917.] 8º.
                                    1879. cc. 5. (18.)

—— The Fifth Year. Corder Catchpool as an " observer " looks at the past year's work of the Central Board for Conscientious Objectors. 1944. 8º. *See* LONDON.—III. *Central Board for Conscientious Objectors.* **08425. f. 96.**

—— Letters of a Prisoner for Conscience Sake, *etc.* pp. xvi. 163. *G. Allen & Unwin: London*, 1941. 8º.
                                      10922. de. 13.

—— " The Life which takes away the Occasion of all Wars," *etc.* pp. 14. *Friends' Bookshop: London*, [1920.] 8º.
                                      8425. tt. 7.

—— On Two Fronts. By T. C. Catchpool. Edited by his sister, with a foreword by J. Rendel Harris. pp. 176. *Headley Bros.: London*, 1918. 12º.   **9083. aa. 18**

—— Third edition. pp. 160. *G. Allen & Unwin: London*, 1940. 8º.   **10922. a. 40.**

—— Peace Aims and War Methods. pp. 10. *Friends' Peace Committee: London*, [1940.] 8º.   **8426. aa. 9.**

—— Quakerism. pp. 15. *Friends' Council for International Service: London*, [1920.] 8º.   **4152. ff. 7.**

—— La Kvakerismo. pp. 14. *Friends' Council for International Service: London*, [1920.] 8º.   **4152. ff. 6.**

—— Kväkarna, *etc.* pp. 23. *Friends' Council for International Service: London; Stockholm* [printed], 1923. 8º.   **4152. ee. 52.**

CATCHPOOL (WILLIAM) International Arbitration. pp. 17. *H. K. Lewis: London*, 1894. 16º. **8425. a. 87.**

—— Joseph Sturge, the Champion of Peace, Freedom & Reform. pp. 14. *Dyer Bros.: London*, [1877.] 8º.
                                  10803. b. 1. (10.)

—— [A reissue.] *See* MEN. Six Men of the People, *etc.* [1882.] 8º.   **10803. aa. 6. (2.)**

CATCOT (ALEXANDER STOPFORD) *See* CATCOTT.

CATCOTT (ALEXANDER) *the Elder. See* CATCOTT (Alexander S.)

CATCOTT (ALEXANDER) *the Younger. See* CATCOTT (Alexander S.) Sermons. [Edited by A. Catcott.] 1752. 8º.   **4460. aaa. 4.**

—— *See* CHATTERTON (Thomas) *Poet.* [*Single Works.*] Thomas Chatterton and the Vicar of Temple Church, Bristol [i.e. A. Catcott], A.D. 1768–1770, *etc.* 1888. 8º.
                                10804. c. 20. (3.)

—— Remarks on the Second Part of the Lord Bishop of Clogher's Vindication of the Histories of the Old and New Testament; chiefly, with respect to his Lordship's interpretation of the Mosaic account of the Creation and Deluge. (A Treatise on the Deluge, *etc.*) [With plates.] 2 pt. *E. Withers: London*, 1756, 61. 8º.
                            4378. cc. 13. (1, 2.)

—— [Another copy of pt. 2.] pp. 296. *M. Withers: London*, 1761. 8º.   **987. i. 8.**

—— The second edition, considerably enlarged. pp. viii. 423. *Printed for the Author: London*, 1768. 8º.
                              4373. e. 13.

—— [Another copy.]   **4373. e. 12.**

—— A Supplement to a Book, entituled, A Treatise on the Deluge. Illustrated by a copper-plate, *etc.* pp. 65. *Farley & Cocking: Bristol*, 1768. 8º. **4378. cc. 13. (3.)**

—— [Another copy.]   **4373. b. 48. (2.)**
Imperfect; wanting pp. 33–48. Pp. 49–64 appear in duplicate.

CATCOTT (ALEXANDER STOPFORD) *See* MUSAEUS, *the Grammarian.* [*English.*] The Poem of Musæus, on the Loves of Hero and Leander. Paraphras'd in English, heroick verse. [By A. S. Catcott.] [With a poem in MS. by A. S. Catcott.] 1715. 8º.   **11335. c. 48. (1.)**

—— An Answer to the Observations on a Sermon preached before the Corporation of Bristol . . . on Sunday the 16th day of August 1735 . . . By A. S. Catcott. As also an Appendix, being a reply to some objections made to the sermon . . . in the Bibliothèque Britannique for the months of July, August and September, 1736 . . . By the author of the sermon. pp. 106. *S. & F. Farley: Bristoll*, 1737. 8º.   **4108. de. 12. (3.)**

—— *See infra :* [The Supreme and Inferiour Elahim.] The Examiner Examined, or the Examination of the Remarks upon, and Mr. Catcott's Answer to, the Observations upon his sermon considered, *etc.* 1739. 8º.   **4108. de. 12. (3.)**

—— *See* GITTINS (Daniel) An Answer to a Pamphlet entitled, An Examination of Mr. Hutchinson's Remarks, and Mr. Catcott's Answer to the Observations on his sermon preach'd at Bristol, *etc.* 1739. 8º.
                              4109. aa. 22. (6.)

—— *See* HUTCHINSON (John) *Theological Writer.* An Examination of Mr. Hutchinson's Remarks and Mr. Catcott's Answer to the Observations on his Sermon preached before the Corporation of Bristol . . . By the author of the Observations. 1738. 8º.
                              03149. e. 6.

—— The Antiquity and Honourableness of the Practice of Merchandize. A sermon preached before the Worshipful Society of Merchants of the City of Bristol . . . November the 10th, 1744. pp. 21. *Bristol*, 1744. 4º.
                              694. h. 1. (16.)

—— [Another copy.]   **226. f. 11. (19.)**

—— The Court of Love, a vision, from Chaucer. pp. 32. *Anthony Peisley: Oxford*, 1717. 8º.   **11631. d. 10.**

—— The Exercises Performed at a Visitation of the Grammar-School of Bristol on Thursday the 7th of April, MDCCXXXVII. To which are added, verses on the Grammar-School [by Francis Woodward] . . . Publish'd by A. S. Catcott. *Felix Farley: Bristoll*, [1737 ?] 8º.
                              11335. c. 48. (2.)

—— Sermons. [Edited by Alexander Catcott.] pp. v. 270. *Felix Farley: Bristol*, 1752. 8º.   **4460. aaa. 4.**

—— [Another edition.] pp. 491. *E. Withers: London*, 1753. 8º.   **4453. cc. 7.**

—— The second edition. pp. 491. *Robinson & Roberts: London*, 1767. 8º.   **4453. d. 9.**

—— The Supreme and Inferiour Elahim. A sermon preached before the Corporation of Bristol . . . on Sunday the 16th of August, 1735, *etc.* pp. 38. *H. Woodfall: London*, 1736. 4º.   **693. f. 6. (10.)**

—— [Another copy.]   **91. h. 20.**

—— The second edition. pp. 40. *John Oswald: London*, 1742. 8º.   **4473. e. 22. (4.)**

—— *See* BRISTOL.—*Corporation.* Obsevations [*sic*] on a Sermon preach'd [by A. S. Catcott] before the Corporation of Bristol, *etc.* [By Arthur Bedford.] 1736. 8º.   **4374. bb. 28. (1.)**

—— *See* HUTCHINSON (John) *Theological Writer.* An Examination of Mr. Hutchinson's Remarks and Mr. Catcott's Answer to the Observations on his Sermon preached before the Corporation of Bristol . . . By the author of the Observations. 1738. 8º.
                              03149. e. 6.

CATCOTT (ALEXANDER STOPFORD)

—— *See* SHARP (Thomas) *Archdeacon of Northumberland.* Two Dissertations concerning the Etymology and Scripture-meaning of the Hebrew words Elohim and Berith. Occasioned by some notions lately advanced in relation to them. [With reference to A. S. Catcott's " The Supreme and Inferiour Elahim."] 1751. 8°. **1016. f. 15. (4.)**

—— The Examiner Examined, or, the Examination of the Remarks upon, and Mr. Calcott's Answer to, the Observations upon his sermon considered. With some observations upon the Hebrew Grammar. [The whole by Julius Bate. A reply to John Hutchinson's " Remarks upon the Observations on a Sermon preach'd . . . by A. S. Catcott " and to Arthur Bedford's " Observations on a Sermon preach'd before the Corporation of Bristol."] pp. 113. *G. Strahan: London,* 1739. 8°. **4224. e. 42. (1.)**

—— Remarks upon the Observations on a Sermon preach'd before the Corporation of Bristol . . . By A. S. Catcott . . . With a continuation of the evidence, till the predictions were complete. [By John Hutchinson.] pp. 172. *A. Dodd: London,* 1737. 8°. **4374. bb. 28. (2.)**

—— Tractatus, in quo tentatur conamen recuperandi notitiam principiorum veteris & veræ philosophiæ, prout eadem, in usum humani generis, primum protulerunt Sacræ Literæ, nuper explicuit . . . Joannes Hutchinsonus; unde deducuntur modus & ratio formandi cœlos & orbes iisdem insitas, *etc.* pp. 56. pl. 3. *G. Strahan: Londini; J. Willson: Bristolliæ,* 1738. 4°. **3149. i. 12.**

—— The Antient Principles of the True and Sacred Philosophy, as lately explained by John Hutchinson . . . Translated, with additional notes and a preliminary dissertation on the character and writings of Moses, by Alexander Maxwell. pp. 236. pl. 3. MS. NOTES. *A. Maxwell: London,* 1822. 8°. **8485. d. 3.**

CATCOTT (GEORGE SYMES) *See* WHITSON (John) *Alderman.* The Aged Christian's Final Farewell to the World . . . To which is prefixed, some account of the author . . . by G. S. Catcott [the editor]. 1789. 8°. **T. 1025. (1.)**

—— —— 1829. 8°. **697. l. 18.**

—— Memoir of Alderman Whitson, *etc.* [By G. S. Catcott.] pp. 8. [1850?] 8°. *See* WHITSON (John) *Alderman.* **C. 55. k. 1.**

—— A Descriptive Account of a Descent made into Penpark-Hole . . . in the year 1775, now first published: to which is added, a copper-plate engraving of that remarkable cavern. Also, the narratives of Captains Sturmey and Collins . . . in the years 1669 and 1682. pp. 51. *J. Rudhall: Bristol,* 1792. 8°. **577. e. 26. (7.)**

—— [Another copy.] **290. f. 31.**

CATE (TEN) *See* BIK (P. V.) Open brief betreffende den vrijen arbeid op Java, naar anleiding der brochures van de oud-residenten. Bik en Bekking en een artikel van den adsistent-resident met verlof ten Cate, *etc.* 1859. 8°. **8022. dd. 37. (1.)**

—— *See* BIK (P. V.) Vervolg op den open brief betreffende den vrijen arbeid op Java, *etc.* 1859. 8°. **8155. b. 86. (11.)**

CATE (A. W. NAUDIN TEN)

—— Deli in woord en beeld. *Amsterdam,* 1905. obl. fol. **1790. a. 9.**

CATE (ADAM HENDRIK TEN)

—— Eenige toepassingen van de ultra-kortegolftherapie in de gynaecologie. Academisch proefschrift, *etc.* [With a summary in English.] pp. 90. *Meppel,* 1946. 8°. **7583. c. 4.**

CATE (ALICE E.) Henry Hudson. The romantic story of an unromantic man. pp. 121. *R. G. Badger: Boston,* [1932.] 8°. **10881. p. 22.**

CATE (E. JANE) A Year with the Franklins; or, To suffer and be strong. pp. 276. *Harper & Bros.: New-York,* 1846. 12°. **12805. f. 16.**

CATE (B. TEN BRUGGEN) *See* BRUGGENCATE.

CATE (GERARDUS TEN) Epistola . . . in qua dubiorum & difficilium quorundam e prophetis locorum explicatio evangelicæ historiæ congruens traditur. *See* OFFERHAUS (L.) Leonardi Offerhausii Spicilegiorum historico-chronologicorum libri tres, *etc.* 1739. 4°. **222. i. 21.**

CATE (HENDRIK POPKO TEN)

—— Een Onderzoek naar het vitamine C gehalte van het bloed in oorlogstijd uit de algemeene praktijk. Academisch proefschrift, *etc.* [With summaries in English and German.] pp. viii. 105. *Zutphen,* 1941. 8°. **7621. ff. 1.**

CATE (ISAAC TEN) *See* PÉRIGNON (P.) *Baron.* Mémoire à l'Assemblée nationale de France, pour MM. Ten Cate et Vollenhoven, *etc.* 1790. 4°. **936. f. 2. (12.)**

CATE (J. TEN) Een Bezoek, gebragt aan den Directeur en de Leeraren, werkzaam aan de Hoogere Burgerschool te Sneek. pp. 25. *Sneek,* [1867.] 8°. **8306. ee. 48. (8.)**

—— Een Woord over het middelbaar onderwijs. pp. 27. *Sneek,* 1867. 8°. **8306. df. 22. (5.)**

—— Een Wederwoord, naar aanleiding van " Een Woord over het middelbaar onderwijs " door J. ten Cate, aan het publiek gericht door Directeur en Leeraren . . . aan de Hoogere Burgerschool te Sneek. pp. 30. *Sneek,* 1867. 8°. **8306. ee. 46. (3.)**

CATE (J. J. BLAUPOT TEN) De Regering en de armwet. pp. 66. *Groningen,* 1861. 8°. **5684. bb. 12.**

CATE (JAMES LEA)

—— *See* CRAVEN (Wesley F.) and CATE (J. L.) The Army Air Forces in World War II . . . Prepared under the editorship of W. F. Craven . . . J. L. Cate, *etc.* 1948, *etc.* 8°. **9104.dd.3.**

—— *See* THOMPSON (James W.) Medieval and Historiographical Essays in honor of James Westfall Thompson. Edited by J. L. Cate and E. N. Anderson. 1938. 8°. **09010. c. 1.**

CATE (M. WEIMAR TEN) 1444–1485. Schetsen uit de middeleeuwen. De roode en de witte roos, of de twist der huizen van York en Lancaster. pp. 135. *Arnhem,* 1861. 8°. **9007. cc. 30.**

CATE (NAHUM) *See* TATE (N.)

CATE (S. H. TEN) *See* DIJK (J. van) *Character in Fiction.* Jan van Dijk, lotgevallen van een Nederlandschen Kolonist . . . Op nieuw bewerkt . . . door S. H. ten Cate, *etc.* 1881. 8°. **12580. n. 28.**

CATE (STEVEN TEN) 1869–1870. Wereldgeschiedenis der laatste twee jaren, *etc.* [With a map.] pp. vii. 765. *Zwolle,* 1872 [1871, 72]. 8°. **9073. e. 23.** *Published in parts. The title on the wrapper reads:* " *Geschiedenis van de Jaren 1869 en 1870.*"

—— Geschiedenis van Nederlandsch Oost-Indië van de vroegste tijden tot onze dagen. Geschetst in tafereelen. pp. xv. 1–160. *Zwolle,* 1874. 8°. **9056. dd. 6.** *No more published.*

CATE (Steven ten)

—— Neêrland's glorie. De geschiedenis der Nederlandsche Republiek van 1648–1713 . . . Met illustratiën van J. C. Leich. 2 dl. *Amsterdam*, 1875, 76. 8º.   **9406. g. 4.**
Published in parts.

—— Neêrland's rampen. Geschiedenis der Nederlandsche Republiek van 1702–1806 (1702–1795). [With plates.] 2 dl. *Amsterdam*, 1876, 78. 8º.   **9406. dd. 3.**
Published in parts.

—— Neêrland's roem ter zee. De geschiedenis van ons zeewezen, van zijn ontstaan tot den vrede van Utrecht, 1713. Geschetst in tafereelen. 2 dl. *Amsterdam*, 1877. 8º.   **9414. g. 25.**

—— Het Vaticaansche Concilie in de jaren 1869 en 1870. pp. viii. 362. *Zwolle*, 1872. 8º.   **5017. aaa. 8.**

CATE (Steven Blaupot ten) *See* Huizinga (D.) Nieuwe uitstapjes in het rijk der natuur . . . Met eene aanbeveling van S. Blaupot ten Cate, *etc.* 1891. 8º.
7001. aa. 25.

—— *See* Periodical Publications.—*Groningen.* Tijdscrift voor het armwesen; onder redactie van S. Blaupot ten Cate en Mr. W. de Sitter. 1852, *etc.* 8º. P.P. **1134.** d.

—— Gedachten over de getals-vermindering bij de Doopsgezinden in Nederland; naar aanleiding der schets van J. H. Halbertsma: Over de herkomst der Doopsgezinden. pp. 38. *Amsterdam*, 1844. 8º.   **4685. e. 8.**

—— Geschiedenis der Doopsgezinden in Friesland. Van derzelver ontstaan tot dezen tijd, uit oorspronkelijke stukken en echte berigten opgemaakt. [With a map.] pp. xii. 394. *Leeuwarden*, 1839. 8º.   **4685. d. 27.**
The titlepage is engraved.

—— Geschiedenis der Doopgezinden in Groningen, Overijssel, en Oost-Friesland . . . Met bijlagen en kaarten. 2 dl. *Leeuwarden & Groningen*, 1842. 8º.   **4685. cc. 12.**

—— Geschiedenis der Doopsgezinden in Holland, Zeeland, Utrecht en Gelderland. Van derzelver ontstaan tot op dezen tijd, *etc.* [With plates and a map.] 2 dl. *Amsterdam*, 1847. 8º.   **4685. e. 26.**

—— Geschiedenis van Nederlands zeevaart en handel, *etc.* pp. x. 144. *Amsterdam*, 1836. 8º.   **8246. g. 20.**

—— Geschiedkundig onderzoek naar den Waldenzischen oorsprong van de Nederlandsche Doopsgezinden. pp. xii. 146. *Amsterdam*, 1844. 8º.   **4685. e. 22.**

—— Handleiding tet de kennis der wet op't lager onderwijs, met eene geschiedkundige schets der wetgeving op't lager onderwijs in Nederland, *etc.* pp. 111. *Groningen*, 1871. 8º.   **8305. bbb. 5.**

—— De Wet, Regering, en Tweede Kamer in betrekking tot den hoogleerar Dr P. Hofstede de Groot, als schoolopziener. pp. 56. *Groningen*, 1862. 8º.   **8309.cc.40.(6.)**

CATE (Steven Hermanszoon ten) *See* Cate (Steven ten)

CATE (Wilhelmus Jacobus ten) *Resp. See* Scheidius (E.) Observationes etymologicae, *etc.* pt. 4. 1772. 4º.
12904. e. 9.

CATE (Wirt Armistead) Lucius Q. C. Lamar. Secession and reunion. [A biography. With plates, including portraits.] pp. xiii. 594. *University of North Carolina Press: Chapel Hill*, [1935.] 8º.   **010886. g. 13.**

CATE (Yo ten)

—— *See* Alphonso xi., *King of Castile and Leon.* [*Appendix.*] Poema de Alfonso xi. Estudio preliminar y vocabulario, *etc.* 1942. 8º.   **11450. h. 41.**

CÂTEAU CAMBRÉSIS, *Le.*

—— Ville du Câteau. Inventaire sommaire des archives communales antérieures à 1790. pp. xxxiv. 83. *Lille*, 1887. 4º. [*Collection des inventaires-sommaires des archives communales antérieures à* 1790.] S. **148.** b. **20.**

CATEAUX (Albert) *See* Janssens (E.) and Cateaux (A.) Les Belges au Congo, *etc.* 1906, *etc.* 8º. [*Bulletin de la Société Royale de Géographie d'Anvers.* tom. 30, *etc.*] Ac. **6096.**

CATECHESIMO. *See* Catechismo.

CATECHESIS. Catechesis Heidelbergensis. *See* Heidelberg Catechism.

—— Catechesis Racoviensis. *See* Poland.—*Socinian Churches.*

—— Catechesis Theotisca. *See* Theotisc Catechism.

CATECHISATIE-BOEK. Catechisatie-boek over de leer der zaligheid . . . Bewerkt door een leeraar der Gereformeerde Kerk in Zuid-Afrika [i.e. John Murray]. Veertiende uitgave. pp. x. 224. *Capetown, Johannesburg; Londen* [printed], 1891. 8º.   **3504. ccc. 33.**

CATECHISE. A Ministerial Catechise, suitable to be learnt by all Modern Provincial Governors, Pensioners, Placemen, &c. Dedicated to T —————— H——————, Esq. pp. 8. *Isaiah Thomas: Boston*, 1771. 8º.
8175. c. 24.

CATECHISM. [For the Catechism of the Church of England:] *See* Liturgies.—*Church of England.—Common Prayer.—Catechism.*

—— [For the Catechism of the Church of Geneva:] *See* Geneva, *Church of.—Catechism.*

—— [For the Catechism of the Church of Scotland, issued in 1552, 1637, 1641 and 1644:] *See* Scotland.—*Church of Scotland.* [*Catechism.*]

—— [For the Catechism of the Episcopal Church of Scotland:] *See* Scotland.—*Episcopal Church.—Catechism.*

—— [For the Longer and the Shorter Catechism of the Assembly of Divines, approved by the General Assembly of the Church of Scotland in 1648:] *See* England.—*Assembly of Divines.—Confession of Faith with Catechisms.*

—— [For the Roman Catholic Catechism approved by the Cardinal Archbishop and Bishops of England and Wales and entitled "Catechism of Christian Doctrine":] *See* Christian Doctrine.

—— [For the First and Second Catechism of the Wesleyan Methodists:] *See* Wesleyan Methodists.—*Conference.*

—— [For "A Catechism of Agriculture" and other catechisms bearing the series-title "Pinnock's Catechisms":] *See* Pinnock (William)

—— The Annotated Catechism, 1884: being the Reformed Catechism, 1883, with annotations by the author. Second edition. pp. vi. 72. *Williams & Norgate: London*, 1889. 8º.   **8410. ccc. 24.**

—— An Apostolical Catechism, or a Brief summary of the arguments in support of the Established Church . . . By a Lay Member of Magdalen College, Cambridge. 1830. 12º. *See* England.—*Church of England.* [*Appendix.*]   T. **1308.** (**3.**)

—— An Astronomical Catechism . . . By a Minister in the Country (J. D.). 1792. 12º. *See* D., J. **8562. aaa. 18.**

—— A Biblical Catechism, introductory to . . . the Church Catechism, *etc.* 1841. 12º. *See* Bible.—*Appendix.* [*Miscellaneous.*]   **3505.** b. **37.**

CATECHISM.

—— A bryefe and necessary Catechisme or Instruction. Very needefull to be knowne of al Housholders, wherby they may the better teache and instructe theyr families, in such pointes of Christian Religion as is most meete, etc. 𝔅.𝔏. *John Charlewood: London,* 1577. 8°. **3932. a. 1. (2.)**

—— A breefe Catechisme so necessary and easie to be learned euen of the simple sort, that whosoeuer can not, or will not attaine to the same, is not to be counted a good Christian . . . It standeth of three parts. *Imprinted by Hugh Singleton: London,* 1582. 8°. **3505. c. 50. (4.)**

—— A Catechism, containing an explanation of words and phrases generally employed in the religious instruction of the young. pp. 40. *Francis Humble: Durham,* 1825. 16°. T. **861. (6.)**

—— A Catechism. For use in the Church of the Province of South Africa where sanctioned by the Bishop. [1937.] 16°. *See* AFRICA, *South, Province of.* **03504. de. 34.**

—— A Catechism. The Answers are selected from the Bible, the Liturgy, Homilies and Articles of the Church of England, with Scripture proofs. pp. 8. *Edwards: Oswestry,* [1825 ?] 12°. **908. c. 5. (4.)**

—— A Catechism, to be learnt before the Church Catechism. pp. 16. *J. Masters: London,* [1846 ?] 16°. **1354. a. 43. (4.)**

—— A Catechism and Confession of Faith . . . By R. B. [i.e. Robert Barclay.] 1740. 12°. *See* B., R. **4152. a. 45.**

—— Catechism and Instructions for Confession. pp. 32. *Burns & Oates: London,* [1885 ?] 24°. **03504. de. 5. (4.)**

—— Catechism ar ffyddlondeb fel deiliaid, etc. 1814. 8°. *See* CATECISM. **872. e. 31. (8.)**

—— A Catechism explanatory of the Church and its various Denominations. pp. 102. *Hamilton, Adams & Co.: London,* 1864. 8°. **3505. aaa. 12.**

—— A Catechism for Candidates for Confirmation. Second edition. pp. 24. *Wertheim, Macintosh & Hunt: London,* 1859. 12°. **4327. a. 74. (4.)**

—— A Catechisme for Children, that they may come to learn of Christ, etc. [Signed: G. F., i.e. George Fox.] 1657. 8°. *See* F., G. E. **1667. (3.)**

—— A Catechisme for Children in yeeres and Children in Understanding. Chiefly intended for their instruction in the family. [By John Stalham.] pp. 19. *I. L. for Christopher Meredith: London,* 1644. 8°. E. **1186. (2.)**

—— A Catechism for Children under eight years of age. pp. 15. *John Snow: London,* [1844.] 32°. **1354. a. 43. (3.)**

—— A Catechism for Every-body. [On total abstinence.] pp. 4. [1845 ?] 12°. **4139. bbb. 25. (18.)**

—— Catechism for First Communicants. Or, Instructions for the worthy making and preserving the fruits of the first communion . . . With permission of Superiors. The second edition, to which is added Instructions for Indulgences (by the R.R. Charles Bp. of Ramaten). pp. 22. *J. P. Coghlan: London,* 1781. 12ᶜ. **3504. de. 3. (1.)**

—— Catechism for First Confession. [By] S. D. L. [1849.] 32°. *See* L., S. D. **3505. a. 70.**

CATECHISM.

—— A Catechism for Infants. pp. 18. *H. & C. Treacher: Brighton,* 1871. 12°. **3504. df. 1. (13.)**

—— A Catechisme for Souldiers; to save soules and prevent blood. Shewing the termes upon which the profession of a souldier may be undertaken, etc. pp. 13. *T. M. for Edward Thomas: London,* 1659. 8°. E. **2124. (2.)**

—— A Catechisme for the Times. [The postscript signed: I. K.] 1645. 12°. *See* K., I. **874. c. 16.**

—— Catechism for Young Children. (Sawal o jawab larkon ke liye.) *Eng. & Hindustani.* pp. 61. *Presbyterian Mission Press: Allahabad,* 1846. 16°. **3504. a. 86.**

—— Second edition. pp. 61. *Presbyterian Mission Press: Allahabad,* 1852. 16°. **14104. a. 23.**

—— Catechism for Young Children; preparatory to the Church Catechism. pp. 30. *G. R. Wright: London,* 1856. 32°. **4416. b. 58. (5.)**

—— A Catechism founded upon Experience and Reason . . . The second edition, corrected. To which is prefixed, An Introductory Epistle to a friend, concerning natural religion. [By William Dudgeon.] pp. 32. *T. Cooper: London,* 1739. 8°. **1018. l. 21.**

—— Catechism made Practical. The Christian instructed, I. In the principles of Christian religion ; positively, in the Shorter Catechism. II. In what he is to refuse, and what to hold fast, in the greatest points of controversie . . . III. In the practice of several duties, etc. 2 pt. *For Jonathan Robinson: London,* 1688. 12°. **1018. i. 8.**

—— A Catechism of Arithmetic . . . By a Friend to Youth. pp. 71. *W. Pinnock: Newbury,* [1815 ?] 12°. **8506. aa. 35.**

—— A Catechism of Botany . . . By a Friend to Youth. pp. 70. *Pinnock & Maunder: London,* [1820 ?] 12°. T. **2086. (2.)**

—— A Catechism of Chronology . . . By a Friend to Youth. pp. 69. *W. Pinnock: Newbury,* [1815 ?] 24°. T. **967*. (5.)**

—— Eighth edition. pp. 70. *Pinnock & Maunder: London,* [1820 ?] 12°. **12201. aa. 6. (8.)**

—— A Catechism of Citizenship. [By T. Sylvan Jones.] [1915.] 8°. **1879. c. 4. (184.)**

—— Catechism of Confirmation . . . Translated and adapted from the French. By a Priest of the Diocese of Oxford. [The introduction signed: E. M. C.] pp. 36. *A. R. Mowbray & Co.: Oxford, London,* [1879.] 16°. **3456. c. 55. (6.)**

—— A Catechism of Drawing; in which the rules for attaining a knowledge of that accomplished art are given in language adapted to the comprehension of the youthful student. Third edition. pp. 65. *Pinnock & Maunder: London,* [1820 ?] 12°. **12835. aa. 89. (1.)**

—— Catechism of Elementary Hygiene. [Edited by P. de Maria.] pp. 122. *St. Lewis Industrial School: Hongkong,* [1911.] 8°. **7404. e. 61.**

—— A Catechism of General Knowledge . . . By a Friend to Youth. Second edition. pp. 70. *W. Pinnock: Newbury,* [1815 ?] 24°. T. **967*. (3.)**

—— A Catechism of Geography . . . By a Friend to Youth. pp. 70. *Philip Rose: Bristol,* [1815 ?] 12°. **9504. aaa. 8. (2.)**

—— A Catechism of Geography and Astronomy. *Eng. & Canarese.* pp. 60. *Wesleyan Mission Press: Bangalore,* 1842. 12°. **14176. h. 5. (1.)**

CATECHISM.

—— A Catechism of Geometry . . . By a Friend to Youth. pp. 72. *Pinnock & Maunder: London,* [1820?] 12º.
T. 2086. (4.)

—— A Catechism of Geometry . . . By a friend to youth. Second edition. pp..72. *Pinnock & Maunder: London,* [1820?] 12º.
12835.aa.89.(3.)

—— Catechism of Health, or "the Mens sana in corpore sano," *etc.* (Second edition.) pp. 15. *Job Caudwell: London,* [1865.] 32º.
7405. a. 13.

—— The Catechism of Humbug, by a Fellow of the University of London . . . Second edition. pp. 92. *Hodges & Smith: Dublin,* 1835. 12º.
12352. c. 13.

—— [Another copy.] The Catechism of Humbug, *etc.* *Dublin,* 1835. 12º.
8565. a. 30. (4.)

—— The Catechism of Man. Pointing out from sound principles, and acknowledged facts, the rights and duties of every rational being. pp. vii. 21. *D. I. Eaton: London,* [1794?] 8º.
E. 2161. (3.)

—— [Another copy.]
8135. b. 5. (1.)

—— [Another edition.] pp. vi. 17. *R. Carlile: London,* 1818. 8º.
1103. e. 40. (19.)

—— A Catechism of Mineralogy . . . By a Friend to Youth. pp. 72. *Pinnock & Maunder: London,* [1820?] 12º.
T. 2086. (6.)

—— A Catechism of Modern History . . . By a Friend to Youth. pp. 70. *Pinnock & Co.: [Newbury,]* 1812. 24º.
T. 967*. (8.)

—— A Catechism of Natural History . . . For the use and instruction of youth. pp. 70. *Pinnock & Maunder: London,* [1820?] 12º.
T. 967*. (1.)

—— [Another edition.] A Catechism of Natural History . . . By a Friend to Youth. pp. 67. *Philip Rose: Bristol,* [1825?] 16º.
7207. aa. 12.

—— A Catechism of Navigation . . . By a Friend to Youth. pp. 70. *W. Pinnock: Newbury,* [1815?] 12º.
8805. a. 14.

—— [A reissue.] *Pinnock & Maunder: London,* [1820?] 12º.
T. 967*. (2.)

—— Catechism of Outpost Duty. [The introduction signed: E. A. C.] 1881. 16º. *See* C., E. A.
8831. a. 47.

—— A Catechism of Perspective; intended as a companion to the Catechisms of Drawing & Architecture . . . By a friend to youth. [With plates.] pp. 34. *Pinnock & Maunder: London,* [1820?] 12º.
12835.aa.89.(2.)

—— A Catechism of Photography . . . Reprinted from the "Photographic News." pp. vi. 97. *Cassell, Petter & Galpin: London,* 1859. 8º.
787. c. 56.

—— A Catechism of Phrenology . . . By a Member of the Phrenological Society of Edinburgh. Second edition. pp. 71. *W. P. McPhun: Glasgow,* 1831. 12º.
T. 1366. (5.)

—— A Catechism of Religious Controversy. 3 pt. *J. P. Garneau: Quebec,* 1919, 18. 16º.
3940. aa. 62.

—— Catechism of Short-hand. By a Newspaper Editor and Reporter. pp. 24. *Houlston & Stoneman: London,* 1855. 12º.
1043. b. 42. (5.)

—— A Catechism of the Criminal Procedure Code, *etc.* [The preface signed: K. S. R.] 1893. 8º. *See* R., K. S.
5319. b. 22.

CATECHISM.

—— A Catechism of the Incarnation. pp. 67. *Joseph Masters: London,* 1851. 12º.
4225. a. 13.

—— Catechism of the Outlines of Masonry Works. [The preface signed: C. H. D. S.] [1886.] 12º. *See* S., C. H. D.
7808. aa. 42. (2.)

—— A Catechism of the Sacrament of Baptism, compiled from the formularies, and other authorized publications of the United Church of England and Ireland. pp. 54. *J. Hatchard & Son: London,* 1849. 12º.
4325. a. 7.

—— A Catechism of Theology. pp. xii. 120. *Joseph Masters: London,* 1866. 12º.
3505. aa. 69.

—— A Catechism of Trade and Commerce . . . By a Friend to Youth. pp. 72. *Pinnock & Maunder: London,* 1817. 12º.
T. 2086. (7.)

—— A Catechism of Universal History . . . By a Friend to Youth. pp. 72. *W. Pinnock: Newbury,* [1815?] 24º.
T. 967*. (6.)

—— A Catechism of Useful Knowledge, adapted for schools. Fifth edition. pp. 53. *W. R. M'Phun: Glasgow,* 1835. 12º.
T. 1592. (20.)

—— A Catechism on Baptism, founded chiefly on the Thirty-nine Articles and Holy Scripture. (Fourth edition.) pp. 8. *Henry Batty: London,* [1850.] 8º. 4326. d. 20.

—— Fifth edition, revised. pp. 16. *J. H. Batty: London,* 1854. 16º.
4326. b. 19.

—— A Catechism on Church Property. By the author of "Parishioners in Council," &c. Third edition. pp. 14. *Church Defence Institution: London,* [1873.] 16º.
4109. a. 87. (4.)

—— A Catechism on Confirmation. pp. 15. *Printed for the Author: [Colombo,]* 1834. 16º.
3504. de. 44. (1.)

—— A Catechism on Confirmation: its meaning, and the preparation required. (5th ed.) pp. 8. *Heard & Sons: Truro,* 1880. 8º.
3505. df. 39. (3.)

—— Catechism on Field Training . . . Revised and edited by Lieut.-Col. W. Plomer . . . Fourth edition [of the work originally compiled by F. A. L. Davidson]. pp. xi. 260. *Gale & Polden: London,* [1909.] 8º. *[Gale & Polden's Military Series.]*
8821. eee. 28.

—— Catechism on Field Training—Infantry . . . Revised and brought up to date by Colonel H. O'Donnell . . . Fifth edition. pp. xv. 215. pl. xxx. *Gale & Polden: London,* 1912. 8º. *[Gale & Polden's Military Series.]*
8821. f. 2.

—— Catechism on Field Training—Infantry . . . Revised and brought up to date by Colonel H. O'Donnell . . . Sixth edition. pp. xv. 219. pl. xxx. *Gale & Polden: London,* 1914. 8º. *[Gale & Polden's Military Series.]*
8821. f. 10.

—— [A reissue.] 1916. 8º. *[Gale & Polden's Military Series.]*
8821. f. 19.

—— A Catechism on the Church. [The introduction signed: J. R. W., i.e. J. R. West.] 1848. 8º. *See* W., J. R.
3504. de. 10. (2.)

—— A Catechism on the Church. pp. 22. *J. Watson: Wakefield,* 1849. 12º.
3504. a. 60.
Printed for private use. A different work from the preceding.

—— A Catechism on the Corn Laws; with a list of fallacies and the answers. Third edition. [By Thomas P. Thompson.] *In:* The Pamphleteer. vol. 27. pp. 363–413. .1826. 8º.
P.P. 3557. w.

CATECHISM.

—— A Catechism on the Creed, the Lord's Prayer, and the Ten Commandments. Compiled and in parts written by a Priest of the Diocese of St. Edmundsbury and Ipswich. pp. 23. *H. R. Allenson: London*, [1928.] 16º.
03504. e. 42.

—— A Catechism on the Duty of Prayer, and of Publick Worship. pp. 14. [1800?] 16º. **4409. ee. 43. (3.)**

—— Catechism on the General Train and Interlocking Rules. The complete questions and answers for employees' promotion examination. pp. 61. *T. Eaton Co.: Toronto & Winnipeg*, [1916.] 12º. **8767. a. 66.**

—— A Catechism on the Holy Catholick and Apostolick Church. *See* CATHOLIC CHURCH.

—— Catechism on the Laying-on of Apostles' Hands. pp. 12. *H. Williams & Co.: Liverpool*, 1879. 12º.
764. m. 5. (4.)

—— [Another edition.] pp. 12. [1880.] 12º.
764. i. 1. (21.)

—— Catechism on the Standard Code of Train Rules [in Canada]. 225 questions and answers. pp. 49. [*Toronto*,] 1905. 8º. **8235. a. 106.**

—— A Catechism on the "Voluntary Principle." pp. 16. *Church Defence Institution: London*, [1873.] 8º.
4108. a. 77. (8.)

—— [Another edition.] A Catechism on the "Voluntary Principle"; or, In which is the voluntary principle better worked, in the Church, or in Dissent? By the author of "Parishioners in Council" . . . Third thousand. pp. 14. *Church Defence Institution: London*, [1873.] 16º.
4103. aa. 56. (6.)

—— A Catechism treating of the Unity of the Church, its ministry, liturgy, offices, and articles: with more especial reference to the objections of non-conformists, and the question of liturgical revision. By a Country Curate. pp. vi. 100. *Joseph Masters: London*, 1861. 24º.
4108. a. 89.

—— A Catholick Catechism, in an explanation of the Creed, the Ten Commandments, the Lord's Prayer, and the Two Sacraments, in the express words of Scripture only . . . By a British Protestant Divine. The third edition, corrected. pp. xii. 48. *J. Clark & R. Hett: London*, 1724. 12º. **3505. aa. 89,**

—— Companion to the Catechism [of the Catholic Apostolic Church]. pp. 48. *Kemp & Boyce: Melbourne*, 1885. 12º.
764. m. 5. (11.)

—— A Compendious Chatechisme [*sic*], newly set forth for the benefit of such as intend the Sacrament of Christ's Body and Blood, *etc.* [The preface signed: J. F.] 1645. 8º. *See* F., J. **E. 1185. (3.)**

—— A Curious Catechism, found in an odd corner, giving a detail of the cause of the present distresses and their probable remedies, *etc.* [A chap-book.] pp. 7. *G. Caldwell: Paisley*, [1830?] 8º. **11621. aaa. 1. (5.)**

—— An Easy Catechism, originally compiled for the instruction of Negroes, by a Clergyman of the Established Church of Jamaica . . . and now reprinted, with a collection of hymns, for general use . . . Second edition. pp. 131. *James Nisbet: London*, 1832. 12º.
4422. e. 18. (5.)

—— Easy Catechism for Little Children, *etc.* pp. 23. *T. Laurie: Edinburgh; T. Bosworth: London*, [1870?] 12º.
764. m. 5. (5.)

CATECHISM.

—— An Easy Catechism for the Younger Classes of Sunday Schools. Revised by several clergy. pp. 40. *J. Parker & Co.: Oxford & London*, 1875. 16º.
4422. aaa. 6.

—— An Easy Catechism of the Old Testament History. 1855. 16º. *See* BIBLE.—*Appendix.—Old Testament.* [*Miscellaneous.*] **3128. a. 70. (5.)**

—— Ethnographical and Folklore Catechism. [By William Crooke.] *Eng., Hindi & Hindustani.* pp. 28. *Khichri Samachar Press: Mirzapur*, [1892.] fol.
14156. k. 19.

—— A Family Catechism . . . By J. W. Minister of the Gospel at Haddingtoun [i.e. John Wilson]. 1712. 8º. *See* W., J., *Minister of the Gospel at Haddingtoun.*
3506. df. 5.

—— Financial Catechism for Electors; giving "chapter and verse" for the statements made. By a voter for South-West Lancashire. Fourth edition. pp. 8. *James Greenway: Southport*, 1880. 8º. Dept. of Manuscripts.

—— The First Catechism. [By Isaac Watts.] pp. 14. *Philanthropic Press: London*, 1792. 24º. **3505. a. 63.**

—— A First (Second) Catechism for the Children of the Church, *etc.* (A Catechism for the Children of the Church on Confirmation.) 3 pt. *Church Sunday School Union: London*, [1882.] 16º. **3505. de. 20.**

—— A First Catechism for the Children of the Church. In English and Hindi. [Edited and translated by E. B. Trotter.] ff. iv. 55. *S.P.C.K.: London*, 1923. 16º.
03504. e. 41.
The title on the cover reads: " A First Catechism and Short Confirmation Catechism."

—— First Catechism in Thompson Language. pp. 32. [*St. Louis' Mission: Kamloops, B.C.*, 1892?] 8º.
884. g. 15. (2.)

—— The Gradual Catechism. Introductory to the Church Catechism. pp. 71. *J. T. Hayes: London*, [1877.] 16º. [*Evangelist Library.* Catechetical Series.] **4193. aa. 47.**

—— The Historical Catechism, containing ingenious answers to many notable questions of several wonderful matters in antient history. pp. 16. *Printed in the Pye-Corner: London*, [1750?] 8º. **9009. aa. 3.**

—— [Another edition.] pp. 24. *W. & C. Dicey: London*, [1760?] 12º. **T. 851. (5.)**

—— [Another edition.] pp. 8. *J. & J. Robertson: Glasgow*, 1778. 12º. **1078. k. 23. (3.)**

—— [Another edition.] pp. 24. *Robert Turner: London*, 1778. 12º. **9005. aaa. 8.**

—— [Another edition.] pp. 24. *Robert Turner: London*, 1782. 12º. **9005. aa. 15.**

—— [Another edition.] pp. 8. *J. & M. Robertson: Glasgow*, 1784. 12º. **12804. f. 36. (2.)**

—— Illustrated Catechism for Little Children. [Translated from "Catéchisme illustré des petits enfants."] pp. 28. *Montreal*, [1912.] 8º. **03504. ee. 18.**

—— An Instructive Catechism; being a preservative for young and old to avoid schism. By R. C., Philo-Presbyter, *etc.* [1785?] 12º. *See* C., R., *Philo-Presbyter.*
12331. b. 34. (19.)

—— A Little Catechism, with little verses, and little sayings, for little children. [By John Mason.] pp. 14. *For John Lawrence: London*, 1692. 8º. **1018. i. 10. (4.)**

CATECHISM.

—— A Metaphysical Catechism. Containing a sum of the doctrines of materialism and necessity, as at present professed. pp. 38. *J. Johnson: London*, 1782. 8°.
8463. c. 1. (1.)

—— Musical Catechism, in three parts . . . New edition, with alterations and corrections by the author. pp. 58. *D. Hogan: Philadelphia*, 1823. 16°. **7895. a. 35.**

—— Musical Catechism, with tunes, for the use of the blind. *Institution Press: Glasgow*, 1838. obl. 8°. **13008. a. 11.** *Embossed.*

—— Third edition, enlarged, *etc. Institution Press: Glasgow*, 1838. obl. 8°. **13008. a. 10.** *Embossed.*

—— A New Catechism, with Dr. Hickes's Thirty Nine Articles. [By Daniel Defoe?] pp. x. 7–38. *Ben. Bragg: London*, 1710. 8°. **E. 1989. (5.)**

—— [Another copy.] **T. 1761. (7.)**

—— [Another copy.] **116. f. 15.**

—— The second edition corrected. pp. x. 8–28. *Ben. Bragg: London*, 1710. 8°. **3506. bb. 34.**

—— The third edition enlarg'd. pp. 35. *Ben. Bragg: London*, 1710. 8°. **1019. l. 13. (1.)**

—— A New Catechism for the Fine Ladies. [A parody, by Uvedale Price, of the Catechism of the Church of England.] pp. 32. *Paris*, 1733. 8°. **12315. g. 39.** *The imprint is fictitious. With two MS. letters by the author inserted.*

—— A New Historical Catechism, containing witty answers to several questions of many wonderful matters . . . By a Doctor of Divinity in the Church. pp. 24. *Newry*, 1776. 12°. **4375. df. 9. (2.)**

—— [Another edition.] A New Historical Catechism . . . The Captivities of Jerusalem lamented, *etc.* [With " Publius Lentulus' Epistle to Rome, concerning Christ."] pp. 39. *T. Martin: London*, [1800?] 8°. **4532. aaa. 2.**

—— [Another edition.] pp. 24. *W. Macnie: Stirling*, [1820?] 12°. **4532. aaa. 1.**

—— [Another edition.] pp. 24. *Printed for the Booksellers: Glasgow*, 1829. 12°. **11621. b. 18. (4.)**

—— [Another copy.] **12331. e. 43. (4.)**

—— A New Historical Catechism, *etc.* pp. 24. *Printed for the Booksellers: [Glasgow?]* 1839. 12°. **4431. c. 13. (8.)**

—— A New Political Catechism for the Present Times. Very proper to be learned by every British subject, *etc.* 1740. 8°. *See* BRITISH SUBJECT. **8132. a. 10.**

—— A Poetical Catechism, intended for the use of young persons attending Sabbath Schools for religious instruction. pp. 63. *Printed for the Author: Glasgow*, 1806. 12°. **3505. b. 4.**

—— A Political Catechism. [The advertisement signed: R. R., i.e. Robert Robinson.] 1782. 8°. *See* R., R. **1389. e. 47.**

—— A Political Catechism. pp. 79. *Field & Tuer: London*, [1889.] 8°. **8139. aa. 39.**

—— Political Catechism: a treatise, in four parts, on Organic Reform. Part I. Administrative Reform. Part II. Parliamentary Reform. pp. 33. *T. Richards: London*, 1858. 8°. **8133. bb. 42. (19.)**

—— [Another copy.] **C. T. 357. (18.)**

CATECHISM.

—— A Political Catechism; serving to instruct those that have made the protestation concerning the power and priviledges of parliament; taken out of His Majesties Answer to the 19 proposition. *See* STATE TRACTS. State Tracts, *etc.* pt. 1. 1693, *etc.* fol. **L. R. 41. d. 12.**

—— A Practical Catechisme. [By Henry Hammond.] pp. 354. *[John Hall:] Oxford*, 1645. 8°. **1018. h. 5.**

—— A Practical Catechism, in fifty-two lessons: one for every Sunday in the year. With an appendix for particular states. [By John Gother.] pp. 442. *T. Meighan: [London,]* 1735. 12°. **4404. d. 19.**

—— A Practical Catechism on the Sundays, Feasts and Fasts, of the whole year . . . [By William Crathorne.] Fifth edition. pp. 260. FEW MS. NOTES. *Keating & Co.: London*, 1819. 12°. **3505. a. 30.**

—— A Practicall Catechisme; or, a View of those principall truths of the word, which most directly tend to Life and Godlinesse . . . Second edition. By D. R. B. in Divin. [i.e. Daniel Rogers.] 1633. 4°. *See* R., D., *B. in Divin.* **3506. c. 54.**

—— A Primitive Catechism; by way of question and answer. In two parts . . . With the texts of Scripture proper for the proof of the several answers. By a Presbyter of the Church of England [i.e. Daniel Whiston]. [Edited by William Whiston.] 2 pt. *J. Senex; W. Taylor: London*, 1718. 8°. **873. l. 20.**

—— [Another copy.] **873. l. 2. (6.)** *Imperfect; wanting pp. 87–90.*

—— Second edition, enlarged. pp. 80. MS. NOTES [by William Whiston]. *John Whiston: London*, 1751. 8°. **873. l. 21.**

—— [Another copy.] MS. NOTES [by William Whiston]. **873. l. 22.**

—— A Rational Catechism: or, an Instructive conference between a father and a son. (Advice to a son [in verse].) [By William Popple.] pp. 143. *Andrew Sowle: London*, 1687. 8°. **4377. aa. 10.** *With an additional titlepage reading " Two Treatises of Rational Religion," and bearing the date 1692.*

—— [Another edition.] pp. 106. *Widow of J. J. Schipper: Amsterdam*, 1712. 12°. **844. a. 20.**

—— [A reissue.] *Amsterdam*, 1722. 12°. **3505. a. 13.**

—— Entretien instructif d'un père avec son fils, sur les premiers principes de la religion & de la morale. Ou catéchisme raisonné. Traduit de l'anglois. [A translation of " A Rational Catechism."] Par Milord * * *. pp. xxxii. 136. *Amsterdam*, 1732. 12°. **3505. c. 61.**

—— A Reformed Catechism. 1883. pp. 15. *C. Green & Son: London*, 1883. 16°. **3505. de. 30. (3.)**

—— A Sacramental Catechism: in which the nature of the Covenant of Grace, and the visible seals thereof, Baptism, and the Lord's-Supper . . . are plainly open'd, by way of question, and answer, *etc.* pp. 96. *Samuel Terry & L. Bixou, alias Tabb: Limerick*, [1724?] 12°. **3506. a. 61.**

—— The Second Initiatory Catechism with Exercises, *etc.* (Second edition.) pp. 38. *James Gall: Edinburgh*, [1820?] 12°. **3505. aa. 76.**

—— A Key to the Second Initiatory Catechism, and Scripture Statements. With an introduction explanatory of the lesson system of teaching . . . Revised and greatly enlarged. pp. 210. *James Gall: Edinburgh*, [1830?] 12°. **3504. aa. 59.**

—— A Short Catechism [on religion]. pp. 8. *A. M. for Tho. Underhill: London*, 1659. 8°. **E. 1845. (3.)**

CATECHISM.

—— A shorte Catechisme. A briefe and godly bringinge vp of youth in the knowledge and comaundements of God in fayth, prayer and other articles, necessary to be knowen of all those that wilbe partakers of the kyngdom of Jesus Christ: set forth in maner of a Dialogue. [By Edmond Allen.] 𝕲.𝕷. *[C. Froschauer: Zurich,]* 1550. 16º. **C. 53. gg. 22.**
Imperfect; wanting sig. D 3, E 4, 5, G 3–6.

—— [Another copy.] **C. 53. gg. 21.**
Imperfect; wanting the titlepage, and all before sig. C. *The titlepage has been supplied in facsimile.*

—— The Short Catechism. Proposed new version of the Shorter Catechism, for use in schools, *etc.* [1891.] 8º. *See* ENGLAND.—*Assembly of Divines.* [*Shorter Catechism.*]
03504. ff. 5. (5.)

—— A Short Catechism, and New Looking-Glass, *etc.* [Songs.] *L. Deming: Boston,* [1835?] *s. sh.* 4º. **11630. f. 7. (88.)**

—— A Short Catechism, compiled for the use of schools. [By Michael Longridge.] pp. 8. *"Courant" Office: Newcastle,* 1838. 12º. **4136. c. 7. (17.)**

—— [For editions of " A Short Catechism, contayning the principles of religion, *etc.*" :] *See* BALL (John) *a Puritan Divine.*

—— A Short Catechisme, holding forth and explaining the first Principles of the Oracles of God. pp. 21. *T. F. for Iohn Rothwell: London,* 1646. 8º. **E. 1186. (10.)**

—— A Short Catechisme, or Playne instruction, conteynynge the summe of Christian learning, sett fourth by the Kings Maiesties Authoritie . . . 1553. 1812. 8º. [*RANDOLPH (John) successively Bishop of Oxford, of Bangor and of London. Enchiridion theologicum, etc.* vol. 1.] *See* CHRISTIAN LEARNING. **495. f. 12.**

—— A Short Catechisme, or the Examination of Communicants concerning their knowledge before they be admitted to the Sacrament of the Lords Supper, being according to the Rules in the Ordinance of Parliament, Octob. 20, 1645 . . . With an appendix containing some questions and answers for the further unfolding the doctrine of the sacraments. The third edition corrected and much inlarged. pp. 14. *For William Ley: London,* 1647. 8º.
E. 1185. (10.)

—— A Short Catechism, with the A, B, C, the Ten Commandments, the Lord's Prayer, and the Belief. pp. 30. *James Chalmers: Aberdeen,* 1753. 12º. **3505. aa. 73.**

—— [A Short Catechism against all Sectaries.] A Dialogue betwixt Two Protestants, in answer to a Popish Catechism, called A Short Catechism against all Sectaries [translated, by C. M., from an unidentified work], *etc.* [By John Rawlet.] pp. 262. *For Samuel Tidmarsh: London,* 1685. 8º. **3936. bb. 30.**
A MS. *copy of " A Short Catechism against all Sectaries" is contained in the volume of tracts bearing the press-mark* T. 1850.

—— A Dialogue betwixt Two Protestants . . . [By John Rawlet.] The second edition corrected. pp. 247. *Samuell Tidmarsh: London,* 1686. 8º. **3942. eee. 85.**

—— The third edition corrected. pp. 247. *For Samuel Tidmarsh: London,* 1686. 8º. **702. c. 17.**

—— [Another copy.] **3938. b. 76.**

—— [Another copy.] **T. 1850. (3.)**

—— The fourth edition corrected. pp. 247. *For Samuel Manship: London,* 1691. 8º. **3938. cc. 40.**

—— [Another copy.] **222. e. 18. (1.)**

CATECHISM.

—— A Short Catechism for Children. [Signed: F. W.] [1800?] 8º. *See* W., F. **3505. df. 39. (2.)**

—— A Shorte Catechisme for Householders. With prayers to the same adioyning. [By Edward Dering.] *Imprinted by Iohn Charlewood: London,* 1582. 8º. **C. 36. a. 12.**

—— [Another edition.] *Printed by James Roberts: London,* 1597. 8º. **3506. de. 2.**

—— [Another edition.] *Printed by W. Iaggard: [London,]* 1611. 8º. **3505. b. 27. (3.)**

—— A Short Catechisme for Householders. with Prayers to the same adioyning. [By Edward Dering.] Heervnto are added vnder the Aunswer vnto euerie Question, the prooues of the Scripture, for euerie poynt of the sayd Catechisme. Gathered by Iohn Stockwood, *etc.* 𝕭.𝕷. *Iohn Charlewood: London,* 1582. 8º. **3504. aaa. 12.**

—— A Short Catechisme for Housholders. With prayers to the same adioygning. [By Edward Dering.] Heervnto are added . . . the prooues of the Scripture . . . Gathered by Iohn Stockwood . . . Newlie corrected and abridged. 𝕭.𝕷. *John Charlewood: London,* 1583. 8º.
3505. c. 49. (5.)

—— A short Catechisme for the instruction of the inhabitants of S. M. for the better preparation of the sacrament of the Lords-Supper. The first part. *I. F. for Ralph Smith: London,* 1645. 8º. **E. 1185. (4.)**

—— A Short Catechism for very young children. [The advertisement signed: C. M., i.e. Charles Marriott.] 1852. 8º. *See* M., C. **3504. b. 15.**

—— A Short Catechism of Faith and Practice. [The preface signed: H. H., i.e. Henry Humble.] pp. 31. *G. J. Palmer: London,* 1869. 16º. **876. a. 22.**

—— A Short Catechism on the Baptismal Vow and Confirmation. pp. 16. *J. H. & J. Parker: Oxford & London,* 1863. 8º. **4323. aa. 8.**

—— A Short Catechism: composed . . . by J. B., Minister at Bradford in Somerset [i.e. John Buckley]. 1646. 8º. *See* B., J., *Minister at Bradford in Somerset.*
E. 1185. (2.)

—— A Simple Catechism, for the use of Charity Children. pp. 24. *J. Belcher & Son: Birmingham,* 1822. 12º. **3504. c. 26.**

—— A Simple Catechism on the Seasons of the Church, explained by the history of the New Testament, *etc.* pp. 36. *J. H. & J. Parker: Oxford,* 1865. 12º. **3477. aa. 14.**

—— A Small Catechism, selected chiefly from the Scriptures, *etc.* 1803. 8º. *See* BIBLE.—*Appendix.* [*Miscellaneous.*] **3504. df. 5.**

—— A Theistic Catechism. pp. 20. *G. J. Cross: London,* [1870.] 16º. **3504. de. 2. (4.)**

—— A Useful Catechism for the Present Times. By a Clergyman of the Church of England. Second edition. pp. 12. *Weston, Simons & Sydenham: Dorchester,* 1833. 12º. **4108. de. 19. (3.)**

—— The Wid. Catechism: or, a Dialogue between an old gentleman that kill'd two wives with kindness in one month, and an eminent widow that mourn'd three months for one husband. 1709. 8º. *See* WIDOW. **1076. l. 22. (29.)**

CATECHISM NOTES. *See* IRELAND.—*Roman Catholic Church.*

CATECHISM SERIES. Catechism Series. [Medical works.] *E. & S. Livingstone: Edinburgh,* 1889– . 8º.
[Latest edition of each part:] **07306. e. 1/1,** *etc.*
[Earlier editions:] **07306. ee. 1/1,** *etc.*

CATÉCHISME.

—— Après le Catéchisme. Cours d'instruction religieuse, *etc.* [The "déclaration de l'auteur" signed : S.] 1887. 8º. *See* S. **3505. de. 35.**

——   Catechisme.
Vien & voy, ⎱ {Apocalypse} VI. I.
Prend & devore, ⎰   X. IX.
Medite & Pratique.
Nouvelle édition, reveuë & augmentée. pp. 194.
O. de Varennes: Charenton, 1671. 12º. **3506. aaa. 30.**

—— Catéchisme à l'usage de toutes les églises de l'Empire français . . . Troisième édition, augmentée d'une table des matières, *etc.* pp. viii. 126. *Bayeux,* [1807.] 12º. **3506. de. 65.**

—— Catéchisme à l'usage des grandes filles, pour estre mariées. Ensemble la manière d'attirer les amans, *etc.* pp. 12. *P. Seyer: Rouen,* [1700?] 12º. **T. 2074. (8.)**

—— [Another edition.] pp. 12. *Beauvais,* [1810?] 12º. **08416. e. 29.**

—— [Another edition.] pp. 11. *Épinal,* [1850?] 24º. **12430. aa. 14. (4.)**

—— Catéchisme abregé en la langue de Madagascar pour instruire sommairement ces peuples, *etc.* [1785.] 8º. *See* MADAGASCAR. [*Appendix.*] **3505. df. 33.**

—— Catéchisme anticonstitutionnel, à l'usage . . . des départemens, *etc.* [The prefatory letter signed : M. G. N.] 1790. 8º. *See* N., M. G. **F.R. 79. (14.)**

—— Catéchisme avec les passages. A l'usage des pauvres. [By Daniel de Superville.] pp. 92. *Berlin,* 1756. 8º. **3505. ccc. 26.**

—— Catéchisme avec les passages. A l'usage de l'École de Charité. Nouvelle édition en françois et en allemand. (Catechismus mit Sprüchen, *etc.*) [By Daniel de Superville.] pp. 175. 1794. 8º. *See* BERLIN.—*Armen-Schule.* **1223. c. 37.**

—— Catéchisme Bambara. *See* BAMBARA CATECHISM.

—— Catéchisme catholique. *See* CATHOLIC CATECHISM.

—— Catéchisme créole. *See* CREOLE CATECHISM.

—— Catéchisme de controverse. [By Lionel Saint-George Lindsay.] 3 pt. *Québec,* 1902, 03. 8º. **03504. ff. 11.**

—— Catéchisme de droit pénal, par M. J. E. B. 1855. 8º. *See* B., M. J. E. **5425. a. 3.**

—— Catéchisme de l'honnête-homme, ou Dialogue entre un caloyer & un homme de bien ; traduit du grec vulgaire, par D. L. F. R. C. D. C. D. G. [or rather, written by Voltaire.] *See* RECUEIL. Recueil nécessaire. 1765. 8º. **1350. b. 12. (1.)**

—— [Another edition.] *See* M . . . . . Y (M. D.) L'Evangile de la raison. [1766.] 8º. **1350. b. 12. (2.)**

—— Catéchisme de l'université, ou un Écolier catholique et des professeurs universitaires ; par un Montagnard vivarois [i.e. N. Deschamps]. Deuxième édition, revue et augmentée. [A satire against the philosophic and religious views of the professors of the University of Paris.] pp. xix. 304. *Paris; Lyon,* 1843. 12º. **1356. a. 12.**

—— [Catechisme de la grace.]

—— *See* JANSENISTS. Les Iansenistes reconnus Caluinistes, par Samuel Des-mares . . . Dans sa version latine du Catechisme de la grace des Iansenistes, imprimée à Groningue 1651. [By Jean Brisacier. With the Latin text, and a translation into French, of Desmarets's preface to," Synopsis veræ catholicæque doctrinæ de gratia," translated by him from an anonymous work by Mathieu Feydeau entitled " Catechisme de la grace."] 1652. 12º. **855. a. 8.**

CATÉCHISME.

—— [Le Catéchisme de la médecine physiologique.] Conversations on the Theory and Practice of Physiological Medicine ; or, Dialogues between a savant and a young physician, a disciple of Professor Broussais . . . Translated from the French [of F. J. V. Broussais]. 1825. 8º. *See* CONVERSATIONS. **784. k. 25.**

—— Le Catéchisme de la religion naturelle commenté par trois amis, *etc.* pp. 36. *Paris,* 1866. 18º. **8465. aaa. 33. (5.)**

—— Catéchisme des bons prêtres et de la paix. pp. 8. *Paris,* 1791. 8º. **F. 157. (12.)**

—— Catéchisme des courtisans, ou les Questions de la cour, et autres galanteries. [A reprint of " Catéchisme des courtisans de la cour de Mazarin," with the addition of " Autre catéchisme à l'usage de la Cour Ecclésiastique de France contre le jansénisme " and " La passion de Mr. Fouquet."] pp. 32. *Cologne* [*Holland?*], 1668. 12º. **12316. eee. 10.**

—— [Another edition.] pp. 48. *Cologne* [*Holland?*], 1680. 12º. **8405. aa. 20.**

—— [Another edition.] [With notes.] 1856. *See* FOURNIER (E.) Variétés historiques et littéraires, *etc.* tom. 5. 1855, *etc.* 16º. **12234. aa. 8.**

—— Catéchisme des électeurs. pp. 16. [1791.] 8º. **F.R. 99. (14.)**

—— Catéchisme des maltôtiers, par demandes & par réponses. Suivi de la chanson, & du dialogue de Bourvalais avec le Diable d'argent. pp. 12. *Rouen,* [1715?] 12º. **12331. aa. 50. (7.)**

—— Catechisme des partisans, ou Resolutions théologiques, touchant l'imposition, leuées & employ des finances . . . Par le R.P.D. P. D. S. J. [i.e. P. de Saint Joseph.] 1649. 4º. *See* I., D. P. D. S., *Le R.P.* **1199. g. 22. (3.)**

—— Catéchisme des petits enfants. Par un Frère de Sainte-Croix. pp. 38. *Montréal,* 1917. 16º. **03504. e. 34.**

—— Catéchisme dogmatique et pratique, sur l'obéissance due à l'église ; à l'usage de ceux qui veulent conserver la foi dans les circonstances présentes : rédigé d'après les Brefs authentiques de N.S.P. le Pape Pie VI., *etc.* pp. 96. *Paris,* 1792. 8º. **F.R. 160. (5.)**

—— Catéchisme du citoyen, ou Élémens du droit public français . . . suivi de fragmens politiques par le même auteur. [By J. Saige.] pp. 220. *En France,* 1788. 8º. **R. 665. (1.)**

—— Catéchisme du citoyen, ou Élemens du droit public françois, par demandes & réponses ; suivi de fragmens politiques par le même auteur [i.e. J. Saige]. pp. 140. *En France,* 1788. 8º. **R. 186. (16.)**

—— [Another copy.] Catéchisme du citoyen, *etc.* *En France,* 1788. 8º. **R. 186. (15.)** *Imperfect ; wanting the Avertissement, pp.* iii–iv.

—— Le Catéchisme du curé intrus. Seconde édition. pp. 36. *Paris,* 1791. 8º. **F. 94. (7.)**

—— Le Catéchisme du genre humain, *etc.* [By F. Boissel.] pp. 132. 1789. 8º. **F. 513. (3.)**

—— [Another edition.] pp. 206. 1789. 8º. **899. d. 22. (5.)**

—— Catéchisme, en langue Kibemba, par J. D., Missionnaire des Pères Blancs. 1900. 12º. *See* D., J., *Missionnaire,* *etc.* **3505. df. 60.**

—— Le Catéchisme en vers. Avec plusieurs airs de piété. Par ✱ ✱ ✱ ✱ ✱ ✱. pp. 42. *F. le Cointe: Paris,* 1680. 8º. **1073. d. 39.**

—— Catéchisme évangélique. [By Émile Demole.] pp. 344. *Genève,* 1841. 12º. **3506. f. 4.**

CATÉCHISME.

—— Après le Catéchisme. Cours d'instruction religieuse, etc. [The " déclaration de l'auteur " signed : S.] 1887. 8°. See S. **3505. de. 35**

—— Catéchisme historique. Édition revisée et augmentee. pp. 128. *Montréal*, 1920. 8°. **03504. ff. 38**.

—— Catéchisme historique de la papauté. Ouvrage destiné à l'instruction des enfans de tout âge. Par M. l'abbé de * * * * *, ci-devant comte de Lyon. pp. 95. *Paris*, 1791. 8°. **F. 102. (9.)**

—— Catéchisme historique et dogmatique, sur les contestations qui divisent maintenant l'Église, etc. [By J. B. R. Pavie de Fourquevaux.] 2 tom. *La Haye*, 1729, 30. 12°. **3559. aa. 21.**

—— Catéchisme illustré des petits enfants. pp. 28. *Montréal*, [1912.] 8°. **03504. ee. 17.**

—— Illustrated Catechism for Little Children. [Translated from " Catéchisme illustré des petits enfants."] [1912.] 8°. *See* CATECHISM. **03504. ee. 18.**

—— Catéchisme national. pp. 139. *En France*, 1789. 8°. **910. b. 10. (1.)**

—— Catéchisme patriotique à l'usage des mères de famille. pp. 56. 1789. 8°. **R. 190. (3.)**

—— Catéchisme politique, monarchique et françois. pp. 68. [*Paris*, 1789.] 8°. **F. 870. (6.)**

—— [Another copy.] Catéchisme politique, monarchique et françois. 1789. 8°. **R. 190. (4.)**

—— Catéchisme populaire républicain. [By C. M. R. Leconte de Lisle.] pp. 31. *Paris*, 1871. 16°. **8005. de. 19.**

—— Catéchisme pour le peuple sur l'Église. pp. 23. [*Paris*, 1791 ?] 8°. **F. 94. (11.)**

—— Catéchisme pour les vieux enfants. [A reprint of " Catéchisme des christicoles " published in 1799/1800.] pp. 28. *Bruxelles*, [1900.] 8°. **4016. h. 29.**

—— Catéchisme pratique, ou Instructions familières, à l'usage du peuple, propres à régler sa foi et sa conduite envers l'autorité de l'Église, etc. pp. 52. *Paris*, [1791.] 8°. **F.R. 151. (4.)**

—— Petit catéchisme à l'usage des enfants pour les disposer à la confession . . . Publié par ordre de Monseigneur l'Évêque de Nice. pp. 72. *Nice*, 1872. 8°. **03504. e. 3. (1.)**

—— Petit catéchisme, à l'usage du clergé, de la noblesse, & du tiers-état de France ; publié par ordre de Monseigneur le Bon-Sens . . . & redigé par un citoyen du tiers-état. pp. 26. [1789.] 8°. **F. 140. (8.)**

—— [Another copy.] **910. c. 13. (7.)**

—— [Another copy.] Petit catéchisme, à l'usage du Clergé, de la Noblesse & du Tiers-État . . . rédigé par un citoyen du Tiers-État. [*Paris*, 1789.] 8°. **R. 54. (4.)**

—— Petit catéchisme en patois créole. pp. vi. 21. [*Port Louis*,] 1949. 32°. **3506. de. 67.**

—— Le Petit catéchisme national. [1791 ?] 8°. *See* PERIODICAL PUBLICATIONS.—Paris.—*Journal de la Cour et de la Ville.* Supplément du no. 1. **R. 199. (17.)**

—— Petit catéchisme patriotique à l'usage des pauvres d'esprit. pp. 14. [1790 ?] 8°. **R. 199. (16.)**

—— Petit catéchisme sur le ixe article du Symbole. Credo Sanctam Ecclesiam Catholicam, etc. pp. 15. [*Paris*, 1791 ?] 8°. **F. 140. (9.)**

CATECHISMO. [For the Spanish word occasionally spelt thus :] *See* CATECISMO.

—— Il Catechesimo. Translatato della lingua Todescha in la lingua Italiana per Salomon Sueigger. [A translation of the " Kleiner Catechismus " of Martin Luther.] pp. 21. *G. Gruppenbach : in Tubinga*, 1585. 8°. **C. 62. a. 16.**

—— Catechismo algonquino. *See* ALGONQUIN CATECHISM.

CATECHISMO.

—— Cathecismo [*sic*] das principaes verdades tocantes ao scisma. Que ao clero e povo dos Reinos de Portugal e Algarves offerece hum Sacerdote Portuguez. pp. 20. [1835.] 24°. **3900. a. 61.**

—— [For editions of " Catechismo maggiore. Seconda parte del Compendio della Dottrina Cristiana " :] *See* CHRISTIAN DOCTRINE.

—— Catechismo nazionale. Dialogo. [A political satire.] [1848.] *s. sh.* 4°. **804. k. 13. (190.)** *Lithographed.*

—— Catechismo repubblicano. pt. 1. pp. 55. *Bologna*, 1796. 12°. **1317. l. 2/1. (13.)**

—— Nuovo catechismo pel 1831. [A political satire. By — Tadini.] [1831.] 16°. **1196. c. 4. (4.)** *Imperfect ; wanting all after p. 4.*

CATECHISMS. [For the Catechisms of the Wesleyan Methodists :] *See* WESLEYAN MATHODISTS.—*Conference.*

—— Catechisms for the Instruction of Youth ; and adapted for the use of Sunday Schools in general, with Scriptural proofs, etc. pp. 86. *W. Booth : Selby*, [1830 ?] 12°. **T. 2293. (1.)**

—— Catechisms for the Young. In accordance with the teachings of the Church of England. [1879–82.] 32°. *See* ENGLAND.—*Church of England.—Church of England Sunday School Institute.* **3506. de. 46.**

—— The Elementary Catechisms. 11 pt. *Groombridge & Sons : London*, 1850–58. 32°. **12203. a. 47.** *Imperfect ; wanting no. 9, entitled " Physical Geography."*

—— [For the series of catechisms known as " Pinnock's Catechisms " :] *See* PINNOCK (William)

CATECHISMUS. Catechismus. Dat is : De groote Kinderleere. Vergadert wt de oude Doctoren der heyliger Kercken, etc. *N. van Oldenborch : [Antwerp ?]*, 1538. 8°. **3504. de. 24. (2.)**

—— Catechismus, oder Kinder-Bericht. Das ist : Kurze . . . Ausslegung, der Sechs Fürnembsten Hauptstuck, vnserer wahren Religion, so einem jeden Christen . . . zu wissen, von nöthen, etc. *Gedruckt inn Verlegung C. Reysers : [Ulm ?]* 1586. 8°. **3505. b. 43.**

—— Catechismus. To jest nauka barzo pożyteczna każdemu wiernemu krześcijaninowi, jako sie [*sic*] ma w zakonie Bożym a w wierze i w dobrych uczynkach sprawować. 1543r. Wydał Franciszek Pułaski. pp. vi. 176. *Kraków*, 1910. 8°. [*Biblioteka pisarzów polskich.* no. 56.] **Ac. 750/45.**

—— Catechismus ad ordinandos, juxta doctrinam Catechismi Concilii Tridentini . . . Quinta editio recognita, plurimisque aucta instructionibus, etc. [By S. Sulpitius a Sancta Pelagia.] pp. 451. *Antverpiæ*, 1721. 12°. **1224. d. 9.**

—— Catechismus Calvinisticus. *See* CALVINISTIC CATECHISM.

—— Catechismus Heidelbergensis. *See* HEIDELBERG CATECHISM.

—— Catechismus jn preüssnischer sprach, vnd dagegen das deüdsche. *H. Weinreich : Königssberg*, 1545. 4°. **C. 40. e. 52.**

—— [For editions of " Catechismus latino-gallicus. Le Catechisme latin-francois . . . Auquel est adioustee la maniere d'administrer les Sacremens et de celebrer le Mariage : auec les prieres ecclesiastiques, etc." :] *See* LITURGIES.—*Calvinistic and Zwinglian Churches.* [*Liturgy of Calvin.—French and Latin.*]

—— Un cuort Catechismus par quels 'ls quals nun saun Scrittüra. *Scuol*, 1763. 12°. **885. e. 5.**

CATECHISMUS

—— Paruus catechismus pro pueris in schola. Katechysmus, to gest, kratičké obsaženij a Weyklad přednjch Cžlankův Wijry a Náboženstwij Křestianského čemuž se Dijtky w Sskolách počátečne wyvčugi. [A translation of the " Kleiner Catechismus " of Martin Luther.] *Lat. & Boh.* *v G. Dačického: w Starém Městě Pražském,* [1580?] 8°.
628. d. 11. (4.)

CATECHISMUS-SCHULE. Catechismus-Schule zur nothwendig- und erbaulichen Belehrung uñ Unterricht der Catechumenorum oder derjenigen Kinder welche der Christlichen Confirmation und des heiligen Abendmahls sich nützlich . . . gebrauchen wollen aus und neben dem Catechismo [i.e. Luther's Catechismus] eröffnet. pp. 62. *Weimar,* 1726. 8°. **1225. a. 28. (2.)**

—— Kleine Catechismus-Schule. Das ist: Kurtzer Vnterricht, wie die Catechismus-Lehren bey der Jugend vnd den Vnwissenden zutreiben . . . [By Justus Gesenius.] Sampt einer Vorred Johannis Schmidt . . . dess Kirchen-Convents Præsidenten in Strassburg. pp. 436. *Gedruckt bey C. Dietzeln: [Strasburg,]* 1632. 12°.
3505. a. 2.

CATECHIST. The Catechist. *See* PERIODICAL PUBLICATIONS.—*Stalybridge.*

—— The Catechist; a fragment. Parts first and second. By the author of " Lily Douglas," *etc.* [i.e. Miss — Grierson.] 2 pt. pp. 138. *William Oliphant: Edinburgh,* 1823. 12°. **3505. aaa. 35.**
The titlepage of pt. 2 bears the date 1822 *and the words " Third edition."*

—— Fourth edition. pp. 156. *William Oliphant: Edinburgh,* 1827. 12°. **4417. aa. 22.**

—— [Another edition of pt. 1.] The Catechist . . . Lesson first, *etc.* pp. 36. *American Sunday School Union: Philadelphia,* 1827. 12°. **864. g. 11.**

—— The Catechist; or, Light from a cloud of witnesses; being extracts from the writing of the Reformers and Martyrs. 2 no. *R. B. Lusk: Greenock,* 1830. 12°.
764. b. 3. (7.)

—— The Catechist's Manual. [By Edward Molloy Holmes.] With an introduction by Samuel, Lord Bishop of Oxford. pp. xi. 270. *J. H. & J. Parker: Oxford, London,* 1865. 8°. **3506. aaa. 35.**

CATÉCHISTE. Notes d'un Catéchiste, ou Court commentaire littéral sur le Catéchisme des provinces ecclésiastiques de Québec, Montréal, Ottawa, par un prêtre du diocèse de Montréal. [With the text.] pp. xvi. 708. 1897. 8°. *See* QUEBEC, *R.C. Ecclesiastical Province of.* **3506. ee. 27.**

CATECHIZER. The Catechizer's Assistant, designed for the use of parents, masters, and teachers. pp. 20. *R.T.S.: London,* [1830?] 12°. *[First Series Tracts, etc.* no. 74.] **863. k. 4.**

CATECHUMEN. The Catechumen. By the author of " The True Baptism." pp. iv. 35. *J. Nisbet & Co.: London,* 1853. 8°. **3506. c. 19.**

—— The Catechumen, or an Account given by the young person to the Minister, of his knowledge in religion, upon his first admission to the Lord's Table . . . The second edition. pp. 87. *For W. Crooke: London,* 1690. 12°.
3505. bb. 16. (1.)

CATECHUMEN REPORTER. The Catechumen Reporter and Sabbath School Teacher's Guide. *See* PERIODICAL PUBLICATIONS.—*London.* The Reporter, *etc.*

CATÉCHUMÈNE. Le Cathécumène. [By Charles Borde.] (Relation de la mort du Chevalier de la Barre par Mr. Cass * * [Cassen, i.e. Voltaire].—Relation du bannissement des Jésuites de la Chine. [By Voltaire.] —Sermon prêché à Basle . . . par Josias Rossette. [By Voltaire.]) pp. 76. [1768?] 8°. **831. d. 25. (3.)**

CATECHUMINI. Cathecuminorum et Benedictionis salis, & aquæ libellus iuxta ritum Cenetensis Ecclesiæ. *See* LITURGIES.—*Latin Rite.—Rituals.—*II. *Ceneda.*

CATECISM. Catechism ar ffyddlondeb fel deiliaid, llywodraeth esgobawl, a chonffirmasiun, neu fedydd esgob. pp. 8. *Thomas Gee: Dinbych,* 1814. 8°.
872. e. 31. (8.)

—— Catecism byrr a buddiol. Yr ail waith yn argraphedig, wedi ci gymmeryd gyntaf gan mwyaf o'r Saesonaeg. pp. 48. *Morgan Jones, etc.: Aberhonddu,* 1774. 12°.
04411. de. 14. (4.)

CATECISMO.

—— Catecismo castellano-indio. *See* CASTILIAN-INDIAN CATECHISM.

—— Catecismo de Agricultura. (Segunda edicion.) pp. iv. 100. *R. Ackermann: Londres,* [1824?] 12°.
7077. b. 30.

—— Catecismo de Astronomia. pp. iv. 102. *R. Ackermann: Londres,* [1826?] 12°. **T. 129*. (4.)**

—— Catecismo de Geografía, *etc.* pp. vii. 93. *R. Ackermann: Londres,* [1823.] 12°. **10003. aaaa. 12.**

—— Catecismo de Historia de los Imperios Antiguos. pp. v. 223. *R. Ackermann: Londres,* [1825.] 12°. **T. 130*. (1.)**

—— Catecismo de Historia Moderna desde Carlo Magno hasta Carlos V. (Desde Carlo V. hasta la Independencia de America). 2 pt. *R. Ackermann: Londres,* [1826.] 12°. **T. 130*. (4, 5.)**

—— Catecismo de Industria, Rural y Doméstica. (Segunda edicion.) pp. iv. 100. *R. Ackermann: Londres,* [1825?] 12°. **7942. aa. 54.**

—— Catecismo de la doctrina social . . . Escrito en forma de diálogo, entre un Cura y un Alcalde, por un miembro de la Sociedad, hijo del distrito federal. pp. 56. *México,* 1833. 12°. **8403. a. 41. (2.)**

—— Catecismo de Quimica. pp. 113. *R. Ackermann: Londres,* [1827.] 12°. **8908. a. 24.**

—— Catecismo Patriótico. pp. 8. *Cádiz,* 1809. 4°.
9180. ccc. 2. (4.)

—— Catecismo pequeño en español. pp. 7. *S. Paulo,* 1924. 8°. **12912. d. 23. (3.)**

CATECISMOS.

—— Catecismos vários. [Facsimiles of a MS., dated 1716, entitled " Catecismos varios y Exposiciones de la Doctrina Christiana . . . por algunos Padres de la Compañia de Iesus." Edited by P. Ayrosa.]

1. El Tesoro de la Doctrina Christiana en lengua Guarani. ff. 39. 1952. 8°. W.P. c. 202/1.

3. Catecismo y exposición breve de la doctrina christiana por el P. M. G. de Ripalda, emendado y traducido en guarani por Francisco Martínez. ff. 95. 1954. 8°.
W.P. c. 202/3.
4. Catecismo maior o Doctrina christiana clarissima, *etc.* 1955. 8°. W.P. c. 202/4.
5. Varias doctrinas en lengua guarani. Por el P. Simon Bandini. 1956. 8°. W.P. c. 202/5.
6. Compendio de la doctrina christiana para niños, compuesto en lengua francesa por el R.P. Francisco Pomeij. Traducido en lengua guarani, por el P. Christoval Altamirando. 1955. 8°. W.P. c. 202/6.

São Paulo, 1952– . 8°. W.P. c. 202.
Universidade de São Paulo. Faculdade de Filosofia, Ciências e Letras. Boletim no. 155, *etc.*

CATECUMENO. *See* N., N. Lettere dedicate a Monsignor . . . J. Monico, *etc.* (Lettere di un Anonimo [i.e. I. Reggio] ad un Catecumeno [i.e. S. D. Luzzatto] e risposte del Catecumeno all'Anonimo.) 1823. 8º.
4372. f. 10. (4.)

CATE HOEDEMAKER (HERMAN TEN) *See* HOEDE-MAKER.

CATEL (A. F.) *of Saint-Dizier*. Thèse pour le doctorat en médecine, *etc.* (Questions sur diverses branches des sciences médicales.) pp. 39. *Paris*, 1842. 4º. [*Collection des thèses soutenues à la Faculté de Médecine de Paris.* An 1842. tom. 3.] **7371. c. 17.**

CATEL (ALBERT)
—— *See* PREUILLY.—*Abbaye Cistercienne*. Chartes & documents . . . publiés et mis en ordre avec introduction, notes et tables par A. Catel et M. Lecomte. 1927. 8º.
9232. cc. 4.

CATEL (ALPHONSE FRANÇOIS) Des fièvres intermittentes en général. pp. 27. *Paris*, 1847. 4º. [*Collection des thèses soutenues à la Faculté de Médecine de Paris.* An 1847. tom. 3.]
7372. a. 11.

CATEL (BLAISE JEAN LOUIS) Dissertation sur la topographie médicale des prisons flottantes, dites Pontons, suivie de quelques considérations sur les maladies qui y régnaient, *etc.* pp. 22. *Paris*, 1816. 4º.
1183. e. 6. (11.)

CATEL (CHARLES DE) *See* CATEL (G. de) Memoires de l'histoire du Languedoc, *etc.* [Edited by C. de Catel.] 1633. fol. **C. 74. h. 8.**

CATEL (CHARLES SIMON)
—— *See* HELLOUIN (F.) and PICARD (J.) *of Laigle*. Un Musicien oublié. Catel, *etc.* [With a portrait.] 1910. 8º. **Hirsch 2848.**

—— *See* MONTAN BERTON (H.) Discours de M. Berton . . . prononcé aux funérailles de M. Catel, *etc.* [1830.] 4º. **733. g. 17. (121.)**

—— Traité d'harmonie, *etc.* pp. iii. 70. *Paris*, an x [1802]. fol. **M.H. 2188.** *Engraved.*

—— Traité d'harmonie . . . Abhandlung über die Harmonie, Generalbasslehre. *Fr. & Ger.* pp. iv. 60. *Leipzig*, [1802.] fol. **Hirsch 5240.** *The titlepage is engraved.*

—— A Treatise on Harmony . . . Translated . . . with some additional notes & explanations. pp. 64. *Chappell & Co.: [London*, 1820?] fol. **M.H. 2878. (1.)** *Engraved.*

—— A Treatise on Harmony . . . Translated by Mrs. Cowden Clarke . . . The musical portion . . . revised by . . . Josiah Pittman. pp. 44. *J. Alfred Novello: London, New York*, 1854. 8º. **M.E. 330. b. (3.)**

—— A Treatise on Harmony . . . Translated . . . and carefully edited by Speranza and T. Westrop. pp. 65. *C. Sheard: London*, [1876.] 8º. **M.E. 768.**

—— Trattato di armonia . . . Tradotto . . . dall'abate Pietro Alfieri, *etc.* pp. 83. *Roma*, 1840. fol. **M.H. 2188. a.** *Lithographed.*

CATEL (FRANZ) *See* FROMMEL (C.) Europa's Eden in Bildern . . . Ansichten und Costüm-Bilder von Italien . . . Nach Original-Gemälden in Stahl gestochen von C. Frommel, Catel, *etc.* [1858.] 8º. **10132. d. 4.**

—— *See* LUEDEMANN (W. von) Carl Frommel's pittoreskes Italien . . . Die Scenen aus dem Volksleben nach Zeichnungen von Catel, *etc.* 1840. 8º. **10129. d. 13.**

CATEL (FRANZ)
—— *See* SICKLER (F. C. L.) 30 Bilder zu Horazens Werken . . . nach Zeichnungen v. Catel, *etc.* 1829. 4º.
1782. c. 29.

—— Drei Schreiben aus Rom gegen Kunstschreiberei in Deutschland. Erlassen und unterzeichnet von F. Catel, Jos. Koch, Friedr. Riepenhausen, Joh. Riepenhausen, von Rohden, Alb. Thorwaldsen, Ph. Veit, Joh. Chr. Reinhart, Friedr. Rud. Meyer, *etc.* pp. 67. *Dessau*, 1833. 8º.
1401. i. 22.

CATEL (GUILLAUME DE) Histoire des Comtes de Tolose. [710–1271.] Auec quelques traitez & chroniques anciennes, concernans la mesme histoire. (Les Comtes de Tolose. Auec leurs portraits tirez d'vn vieux liure manuscrit Gascon.—Comites Tolosani fratris Bernardi Guidonis.—Chronicon Magistri Guillelmi de Podio-Laurentii.—Præclara Francorum facinora . . . incerto autore.—Aliud Chronicon autoris anonymi.—Chronicon Ecclesiæ Sancti Pauli Narbonensis.) 2 pt. *P. Bosc: Tolose*, 1623. fol.
805. i. 8.

—— [Another copy.] **137. f. 4.**

—— [Another copy.] **G. 930.**

—— Memoires de l'histoire du Languedoc, *etc.* (Éloge de Catel.) [Edited by Charles de Catel.] pp. 1038. *P. Bosc: Tolose*, 1633. fol. **C. 74. h. 8.**

—— *See* PONSAN (G. de) Histoire de l'Académie des Jeux Floraux, *etc.* (pt. 5. Examen général de tout ce que Catel a dit dans ses Mémoires du Corps des Sept Trobadors ou Poëtes de Toulouse, & des Jeux Floraux institués par la Dame Clémence d'Isaure.) 1764, *etc.* 8º. **617. c. 22.**

CATEL (JEAN) Walt Whitman: la naissance du poète. [With a portrait.] pp. 483. *Paris*, 1929. 8º. [*Bibliothèque de littérature comparée.*] **W.P. 8051/5.**

CATEL (LOUIS) Vorschläge zu einigen wesentlichen Verbesserungen der Fabrikation der Ziegel . . . Nebst einer Kupfertafel. pp. vi. 68. *Berlin*, 1806. 8º. **T. 984. (9.)**

CATEL (P.) L'Examinateur français. Sixteen hundred questions on French grammar, translation, and literature, *etc.* pp. vii. 86. *A. G. Dennant: London, Dublin*, [1870.] 8º. **12952. de. 1. (5.)**

CATEL (P. F.) Dissertation sur la péripneumonie, *etc.* pp. 21. *Paris*, 1811. 4º. **1182. h. 12. (21.)**

CATEL (SAMUEL HENRI) *See* GEORGI (J. G.) Description de la ville de St. Pétersbourg . . . traduit de l'allemand [by S. H. Catel], *etc.* 1793. 8º. **281. i. 22.**

—— *See* PARIS.—*Académie Française*. Dictionnaire de l'Académie Françoise . . . Nouvelle édition, enrichie de la traduction allemande des mots, par S. H. Catel. 1800, *etc.* 4º. **626. k. 12–13.**

CATEL (V.) De l'urine dans quelques affections fébriles chirurgicales. pp. 62. *Paris*, 1874. 4º. [*Collection des thèses soutenues à la Faculté de Médecine de Paris.* An 1874. tom. 3.] **7374. a. 8.**

CÂTELAIN. *See* CHÂTELAIN.

CATELAIN (E. J.) *pseud.* [i.e. ÉMILE and G. CATELAIN.] Rimes d'amour. pp. 169. *Paris*, 1890. 8º. **11483. cc. 35.**

CATELAIN (ÉMILE) *See* CATELAIN (E. J.) *pseud.* [i.e. E. and G. Catelain.]

CATELAIN (G.) *See* CATELAIN (E. J.) *pseud.* [i.e. E. and G. CATELAIN.]

CATELAN (DE)
—— Catalogue d'une collection précieuse de tableaux, des trois écoles, composant le cabinet de M.*** [identified in a MS. note as — de Catelan] dont la vente aura lieu le 16 janvier 1816, *etc.* (Par M. Laneuville.) pp. 19. 1816. 8º. *See* LANEUVILLE (J. L.) **562. e. 33. (3.)**

CATELAN (DE)

—— [Another copy.] MS. PRICES.   **562. e. 26. (11.)**

—— [Another copy.] MS. PRICES.   **562. e. 27. (1.)**

CATELAN (ANTONIN) *See* CATELAN (Jules A. A.)

CATELAN (JEAN DE) *Bishop of Valence. See* CATELLAN.

CATELAN (JULES AIMÉ ANTONIN) De l'albuminurie dans ses rapports avec d'autres manifestations morbides. pp. 32. *Paris*, 1872. 4º. [*Collection des thèses soutenues à la Faculté de Médecine de Paris.* An 1872. tom. 3.]
    7373. n. 9.

CATELAN (LAURENS) *See* GAY (François) *Professeur.* Une Lignée d'apothicaires montpelliérains [L. Catelan and his family] . . . Discours, *etc.* 1896. 8º. **9906. bb. 16.**

—— Discours et demonstration des ingrediens de la confection d'Alkermes reformee . . . contre les discours faicts par le Sr Jaques Fontaine. pp. 316. *I. Mallet: Lyon*, 1614. 12º.   **1038. b. 40.**

—— Confectionis Alchermes genuina descriptio. [Abridged and translated by J. S. Strobelberger from the "Discours et demonstration des ingrediens de la confection d'Alkermes reformee."] *See* STROBELBERGER (J. S.) Joan. Stephani Strobelbergeri . . . Tractatus nouus . . . de cocco baphica, *etc.* 1620. 4º.   **959. a. 5. (1.)**

—— [Histoire de la nature . . . de la lycorne.] Ein schöner newer historischer Discurs, von der Natur, Tugenden, Eigenschafften, vnd Gebrauch dess Einhorns . . . Beneben vielen andern denckwürdigen Historien . . . von Georgio Fabro . . . in Hochteutsch . . . vbergesetzt, vnd mit schönen . . . Figuren gezieret. pp. 149. *In Verlegung L. Jennisii: Franckfurt*, 1625. 8º.
    778. a. 37. (1.)

—— [Another copy.]   **B. 642. (1.)**

—— Rare et curieux discours de la plante appellée Mandragore, *etc.* pp. 53.   *Aux despens de l'autheur: Paris*, 1639. 12º.   **780. a. 35. (5.)**

—— Rare et curieux discours sur les vertus et proprietez de la Theriaque, *etc.* pp. 11 [5–]54.   *I. Pech: Montpelier*, 1629. 12º.   **780. a. 11. (1.)**

—— [Traicté de l'origine, vertus . . . de la pierre bezoar.] Ein newer historischer vnd medicinischer Tractat, vom Bezoar Stein . . . ins Teutsch vbergesetzt.   *In Verlegung L. Jennisii: Franckfurt*, 1627. 8º.
    778. a. 37. (2.)

—— Traicté des eaux distillées qu'un apothicaire doit tenir en sa boutique, *etc.* pp. 31. *See* BAUDERON (B.) Paraphrase sur la pharmacopée, *etc.* 1623. 8º.   **547. d. 11.**

—— [Another edition.] *See* BAUDERON (B.) Pharmacopée, *etc.* liv. 2. 1644. 8º.   **547. d. 13.**

—— [Another edition.] *See* BAUDERON (B.) Pharmacopée, *etc.* liv. 2. [1650.] 8º.   **547. d. 14.**

—— [Another edition.] *See* BAUDERON (B.) La Pharmacopée, *etc.* liv. 2. 1681. 4º.   **546. k. 12.**

—— Tractatus de aquis destillatis, *etc. See* BAUDERON (B.) Pharmacopoea, *etc.* lib. 2. 1639. fol.   **547. k. 21. (1.)**

CATELANI (ALBERTO) Sopra un attentato alla vita del Conte M. M. Boiardo. Documenti, *etc.* pp. 27. *Reggio nell'Emilia*, 1891. 8º.   **10601. d. 35. (5.)**

CATELANI (ANACLETO) *See* KIEFFER (J. G.) Ristretto dell'origine, e progresso dell'Imperio Romano . . . Compilato dal libro intitolato Dissertatio de S. R. I. Electorum origine dal padre D. A. Catelani, *etc.* 1711. 8º.
    8073. aaa. 26.

—— Il Principato sinonimo di servitú e' la servitù gloria del Principato. Discorso sacro politico, *etc.* pp. 24. *I. Paci: Lucca*, 1691. 4º.   **4424. dd. 3. (3.)**

CATELANI (ANGELO) *See* VALDRIGHI (L. F.) *Count.* Musurgiana. N. 10. Ricordi e documenti sulle scuole di musica progettate per Modena dal fu maestro A. Catelani. 1882. 8º.   **7900.p.28/8.**

—— *See* VALDRIGHI (L. F.) *Count.* Musurgiana. Serie II. no. 1. Cataloghi della musica di composizione e proprietà del Mº Angelo Catelani, preceduti dalle sue Memorie auto-biografiche, *etc.* 1893. 8º.   **7900.p.28/10.**

—— Delle opere di Alessandro Stradella esistenti nell'archivio musicale della R. Biblioteca Palatina di Modena elenco, con prefazione e note. pp. 42. *Modena*, 1866. 8º.
    7896. g. 13

—— [Another copy.]   Hirsch **5203.**

—— Memorie della vita e delle opere di Claudio Merulo. Note e aggiunte di Giacomo Benvenuti. [With a portrait.] pp. 95. *Milano*, 1931. 8º.   Hirsch **3696.**

—— La Vecchia Cappella della Corte Estense e la Commissione incaricata ad organizzare una nuova scuola di musica in Modena. (Estratto dalla Gazzetta di Modena.) pp. 8. [*Modena*, 1860.] 8º.   **7806. aaa. 1. (12.)**

CATELANI (BERNARDINO) La Bella figlia del sole nella Divina Comedia. [Paradiso. XXVII. 136–138.] Lettera. pp. 15. *Faenza*, 1878. 8º.   **11421. aa. 18. (6.)**

CATELANI (CARLO BONAVENTURA) *Begin.* Illustrissimus . . . princeps D. Annibal Albanus meritam in utroq; iure sumit lauream . . . Epigramma.   *Urbini*, 1703. *s. sh.* fol.   **838. m. 22. (16.)**

CATELANI (VIRGINIA) Sonetti. *See* CIPARISSIANO (Teleste) *Pastore Arcade, pseud.* Poesie italiane. 1716. 8º.   **1062. f. 13.**

CATELANO (FRANCESCO) *See* ORIO (Cidalmo) *pseud.* [i.e. F. Catelano.]

CATELANUS (CAROLUS BONAVENTURA) *See* CATELANI (Carlo B.)

CATELANUS (LAURENTIUS) *See* CATELAN (Laurens)

CATELEY, afterwards **LASCELLES** (ANNE) *See* CATLEY.

CATELIANUS (DIONYSIUS) *Bishop of Cythera. See* DIONUSIOS [Katelianos], *Bishop of Cythera.*

CATELIN (ADOLPHE)

—— F. Halévy. Notice biographique. pp. 16. *In:* HALÉVY (J. F. F. E.) Le Dilettante d'Avignon. *Paris*, 1863. 4º.
    M.F. 85. j.

CATELIN (CAMILLE DE) *Viscount. See* ARVE (Stéphen d') *pseud.* [i.e. C. de Catelin.]

CATELIN (CHARLES) Fleurs du printemps. [Poems.] pp. 288. *Paris*, [1875.] 12º.   **11482. b. 1.**

CATELIN (ED. DE) Code des actionnaires, droits et devoirs des rentiers de l'état, *etc.* pp. 144. *Paris*, 1857. 16º.
    5425. a. 8.

CATELIN (JEAN ANTOINE FIRMIN) Discours. *See* LAGET (B. P. de) Discours prononcés sur la tombe de Monsieur B. P. de Laget. [1857.] 8º.   **10662. g. 33. (9.)**

CATELINE (JEREMY) The Rules and Directions of the Ordinance of Parliament, concerning Suspension from the Lords Supper in case of Ignorance, resolved into a short catechisme. pp. 25. 1647. 8º. *See* ENGLAND.—*Parliament.—Parliamentary Proceedings.*—II.   E. **1185. (11.)**

—— [Another edition.] pp. 25. 1648. 8º. *See* ENGLAND.—*Parliament.—Parliamentary Proceedings.*—II.
    03504. e. 18.

CATELINI DA CASTIGLIONE, *Family of. See* CANTINI (L.) Memorie appartenente alla vita di Sant'Appiano e notizie istoriche dei signori Catelini da Castiglione, *etc.* 1829. 8º.   **4865. bbb. 21. (3.)**

CATELLA. Catella ægrotans. Fabula. [By Jean Commire.] pp. 4. *E typographia G. Martin: Parisiis*, 1689. 8º.
    T. 1775. (6.)

CATELLA (IRIS)

—— See GIBBONS (Stella D.) [Cold Comfort Farm.] La Ferme de froid accueil . . . Traduit . . . par I. Catella et Marie-Thérèse Baudron. 1946. 8º. **12650. a. 120**.

CATELLACCI (ANTONIO) See DANTE ALIGHIERI. [*Divina Commedia.—Italian and Latin.—Inferno*.] L'Inferno . . . tradotto . . . in versi eroici latini corrispondenti dal dottore A. Catellacci. 1819. 8º. **1463. f. 7**.

CATELLAN (ANTOINE) and CATELLAN (CHARLES) Almanach homœopathique . . . par MM. Catellan frères, *etc.* pp. xvii. 537. 1860, *etc.* 8º. *See* PERIODICAL PUBLICATIONS.—*Paris.* **P.P. 3292. fa.**

CATELLAN (CHARLES) *See* PERIODICAL PUBLICATIONS.—*Paris.* Almanach homœopathique . . . par MM. Catellan frères, *etc.* 1860. 8º. **P.P. 3292. fa.**

CATELLAN (DOMINIQUE) Considérations sur quelques points de la doctrine de l'irritation. Tribut académique, *etc.* pp. 36. *Montpellier*, 1824. 4º. **1181. c. 16. (12.)**

CATELLAN (JEAN DE) *Bishop of Valence.* Les Antiquités de l'eglise de Valence. Avec des réflexions sur ce qu'il y a de plus remarquable dans ces antiquités, *etc.* pp. 366. *Valence*, 1724. 4º. **706. i. 17.**

—— Discours sur les vertus de tres-haut . . . Prince Louis XIV. Roy de France et de Navarre. *See* LOUIS XIV., *King of France.* [*Panegyrics, Elegies, etc.*] Recueil de plusieurs oraisons funèbres de Louis XIV, *etc.* tom. 2. 1716. 12º. **236. b. 31**.

CATELLAN (JEAN ANTOINE DE) *Marquis. See* CATELLAN DE CAUMONT.

CATELLAN DE CAUMONT (JEAN ANTOINE DE) *Marquis. See* BORDEAUX.—*Parlement.* Remontrances du Parlement de Bordeaux . . . sur l'enlévement de M. de Catellan. [1788.] 8º. **F. 4. (4.)**

—— *See* BRITTANY.—*Parlement.* Très-humbles et très-respectueuses rémontrances . . . pour l'usage des lettres de cachet, la détention de M. de Cathelan, *etc.* [1788.] 8º. **R. 24. (11.)**

—— *See* TOULOUSE.—*Parlement.* Lettre . . . au Roi, au sujet de M. de Catellan, avocat-général. Du vingt-septième mars 1788. [1788.] 8º. **R. 26. (38.)**

—— *See* TOULOUSE.—*Parlement.* Remontrances . . . du 21 avril 1788, concernant les lettres de cachet : et la détention de M. de Catellan . . . au château de Lourde. 1788. 8º. **R. 26. (42.)**

—— *See* TOULOUSE.—*Parlement.* Seconde lettre . . . au Roi, au sujet de la détention de M. de Catellan . . . Du 3 mai 1788. [1788.] 8º. **R. 26. (44.)**

CATELLANI (ENRICO LEVI) *See* LEVI CATELLANI.

CATELLANI (VINCENZO) Discorso sopra gl'influssi delle stelle. [By V. Catellani.] pp. 23. 1778. 12º. *See* DISCORSO. **8562. aa. 19.**

CATELLANUS (LAURENTIUS) *See* CATELAN (Laurens)

CATELLEW (ORAN) The Book without a Name. Chiefly on naturism, or the religion of science. pp. xv. 173. [*C. W. Daniel: London*, 1913.] 8º. **3558. c. 38.**

CATELLI (ATTILIO) Le Ultime ore di Giuseppe Mazzini. Scena drammatica in versi. pp. 12. *Firenze*, 1876. 16º. **11715. bbb. 63.**

CATELLUCCIO, *de Campania. See* CATENACCIO, *of Anagni.*

CATENA. Catena classicorum. *See* HOLMES (Arthur) *Fellow of Clare College, Cambridge,* and BIGG (C.)

—— A Chronological Catena of Ancient Fathers and Councils, together with the teaching of the reformers and more recent divines of our Church, on the doctrine of spiritual regeneration in Holy Baptism. pp. vii. 150. *J. H. Parker: Oxford & London*, 1850. 8º. **4325. d. 14.**

CATENA (BARTOLOMMEO) Chiesa e riti.—Biblioteca Ambrosiana. *See* CANTÙ (C.) Milano e il suo territorio. [1844.] 8º. **10129. e. 6.**

CATENA (GIOVANNI BATTISTA) *See* GIGLI (G.) Lezioni di lingua toscana . . . Coll' aggiunta . . . di varie poesie . . . raccolte dall'abate G. Catena, *etc.* 1736. 8º. **72. a. 20.**

—— —— 1744. 8º. **72. a. 21.**

—— *See* MEDICI (G. de') *Cardinal, etc.* Lettere del Cardinale G. de Medici . . . estratte da un codice MS. da G. B. Catena. 1752. 4º. **661. h. 20.**

CATENA (GIOVANNI GIROLAMO) Della Beretta Rossa da darsi a Cardinali religiosi. Discorso. (Lettera del R.P.M. Tomaso Gratiani all'illustrissimo Cardinale Alessandrino.) pp. 41. *Presso à G. Ferrari: Roma*, 1592. 4º. **Legg. 273. (2.)**

—— Discorso . . . sopra la traduttione delle scienze, & d'altre facultà. pp. 95. *Appresso F. Ziletti: Venetia*, 1581. 8º. **627. d. 13. (4.)**

—— [Another copy.] **74. b. 17.**

—— I. Hieronymi Catenæ Latina monumenta. [Poems.] ff. 66 [166]. *Apud H. Bartolum: Papiæ*, 1577. 8º. **1070. e. 12.**

—— [Select poems.] 1719. *See* ITALIAN POETS. Carmina illustrium poetarum italorum. tom. 3. 1719, *etc.* 8º. **657. a. 18.**

—— Vita del gloriosissimo Papa Pio Quinto . . . Con una raccolta di lettere di Pio V. à diuersi principi, & le risposte, con altre particolari. Et i nomi delle galee e de' capitani, cosi Christiani, come Turchi, che si trouarono alla battaglia nauale. pp. 246. *Per F. Osanna: Mantoua*, 1587. 4º. **484. b. 14.**

—— [Another edition.] Dall'istesso autore riueduta & ampliata. pp. 367. *Per A. Gardano & F. Coattino: Roma*, 1587. 8º. **484. a. 26.**

CATENA (HIERONYMUS) *See* CATENA (Giovanni G.)

CATENA (JOANNES HIERONYMUS) *See* CATENA (Giovanni G.)

CATENA (PETRUS) Petri Catena Oratio pro idea methodi. ff. 8. *Apud G. Perchacinum: Patauii*, 1563. 4º. **835. f. 14. (2.)**

—— [Another copy.] **113. b. 9.**

—— Petrus Cathena . . . super loca mathematica contenta in Topicis & Elenchis Aristotelis, nunc . . . in lucem ædita. ff. 16. *C. de Tridinum Montisferrati: Venetiis*, 1561. 4º. **716. e. 30.**

—— [Universa loca in logicam Aristotelis in mathematicas disciplinas hoc novum opus declarat.] pp. 110. [*F. Marcolini: Venice*, 1556.] 4º. **519. e. 32. (3.)** *Imperfect; wanting the titlepage.*

CATENA (VINCENZO)

—— *See* ROBERTSON (Giles) Vincenzo Catena. [With reproductions and a catalogue of Catena's works.] 1954. 4º. **7868. ff. 53.**

CATENAC (F. H.) Juges et tribunaux agricoles. La juridiction consulaire étendue à l'agriculture. [With a bibliography.] pp. viii. 160. *Toulouse*, 1899. 8º. **05402. g. 24.**

CATENACCI (HERCULE) *See* JACQUEMART (A.) History of the Ceramic Art . . . Containing . . . woodcuts by H. Catenacci, *etc.* 1873. 8º. **2268. d. 11.**

—— *See* LACOMBE (J. P.) Les Armes et les armures . . . Ouvrage illustré . . . par H. Catenacci. 1868. 12º. **8826. bbb. 17.**

CATENACCI (Hercule)

—— *See* Paris. [*Appendix.—Topography, etc.*] Paris dans sa splendeur . . . Vignettes de F. Benoist, Catenacci, *etc.* 1861. fol. **1782. d. 1.**

CATENACCIIS (Onuphrius Geraldinus de) *See* Geraldinus de Catenacciis.

CATENACCIO, *of Anagni.*

—— *See* Cato (M. P.) *the Censor.* [*Supposititious Works.— Disticha de Moribus.—Italian.*] Duecento meridionale. Il " Libro de Cato " di Catenaccio. 1941. 8º. [*Archivum romanicum.* vol. 25.] **P.P. 4884. db.**

CATENACIO, *de Campania. See* Catenaccio, *of Anagni.*

CATENHUSEN (Carl Friedrich Wilhelm) *See* Moraht (A.) C. F. W. Catenhusen . . . Ein Denkmal. 1861. 8º. **4885. cc. 35.**

—— Sechs Predigten. pp. 69. *Schönberg,* 1839. 8º. **4427. e. 17. (8.)**

CATENI (Cammillo) *See also* Alisio (Cammillo) *pseud.* [i.e. C. Cateni.]

—— Cicalata . . . in lode dei maccheroni.—Cicalata . . . in lode del bue. 1808. *See* Florentine Authors. Cicalate d'autori fiorentini, *etc.* 1809. 8º. **12330. g. 14.**

CATENIUS (H. A. N.) *See also* Melantjong, *pseud.* [i.e. H. A. N. Catenius?]

—— Poeĕ gata Basa Atjeh?—Spreekt gij Atjehsch?—Samenspraken, gezegden en spreekwijzen in de Hollandsche, Maleische en Atjehsche taal. pp. xxxv. 182. *Breda,* 1888. 4º. **14623. c. 9.**

CATENIUS-VAN DER MEIJDEN (J. M. J.)

—— Groot nieuw volledig Oost-Indisch kookboek. 1381 recepten voor de volledige Indische rijsttafel met een belangrijk aanhangsel voor de bereiding dier tafel in Holland . . . Vierde druk. pp. 484. *Semarang,* 1942. 8º. **7948. c. 11.**

CATER (Donald Brian)

—— Basic Pathology and Morbid Histology. pp. 330. *John Wright & Sons: Bristol,* 1953. 8º. **7443. d. 4.**

CATER (Douglass)

—— *See* Childs (Marquis W.) and Cater (D.) Ethics in a Business Society. [1954.] 8º. **8413. bb. 4.**

CATER (Fred W.)

—— Geological Investigations of Chromite in California. *San Francisco,* 1948– . 8º. [*California. Department of Natural Resources. Division of Mines. Bulletin.* no. 134, pt. 3, *etc.*] **A.S. c. 35/12.**

CATER (Frederick Ives) Northamptonshire Nonconformity 250 years ago. pp. 32. *Archer & Goodman: Northampton,* 1912. 8º. **4715. de. 7.**

CATER (Harold Dean)

—— *See* Adams (Henry B.) Henry Adams and his Friends. A collection of his unpublished letters. Compiled, with a biographical introduction, by H. D. Cater, *etc.* 1947. 8º. **10922. c. 27.**

CATER (*Sir* John James)

—— Paper on Ancient Currency, Monetary Systems, and Ancient Banking, *etc.* pp. 73. *Blades & Co.: London,* 1899. 8º. **7756. bbb. 43.**

CATER (Joseph) Bisley Bits; or, Records of a Surrey corner. pp. 127. *Simpkin, Marshall & Co.: London,* 1892. 8º. **10360. e. 25.**

—— Gens Caterorum: being a collection of material . . . relating to the Cater family. *Simpkin, Marshall & Co.: London,* 1894. 4º. **9902. h. 39.** *Imperfect; wanting all after p. 94.*

CATER (Philip) *See* Taylor (John) calling himself *One of the Twelve Apostles of the Church of Latter Day Saints.* Three Nights' Public Discussion between the Revds C. W. Cleeve, James Robertson, and P. Cater, and Elder John Taylor, *etc.* 1850. 8º. **4139. e. 62.**

—— The Clerical Gewgaw, called Apostolic Succession. Broken to Pieces, in letters to Rev. T. Hugo . . . Second edition. pp. 48. *London,* [1875?] 8º. **4109. aaa. 46.**

—— The Great Fiction of the times, or Apostolic succession, with other doctrines of Puseyism, proved to be unscriptural and absurd, *etc.* pp. 128. *S. Prentice: Canterbury; Strange: London,* [1844.] 8º. **4109. bb. 3.**

—— The Great St. Derby Day; or, Evenings with my Lords Spiritual and Temporal about the horses and asses of the English Race Course, *etc.* pp. 64. *Stoke Newington,* [1870?] 8º. **7905. aa. 55.**

—— Memoirs of the Life and Character of the late Rev. John Paul Porter. pp. 204. *The Author: Bath,* 1834. 12º. **1124. d. 24.**

—— Punch in the Pulpit . . . Second edition. pp. 240. *William Freeman: London,* 1862. 8º. **4498. aa. 8.**

—— Third edition. pp. 240. *William Freeman: London,* 1863. 8º. **4498. bb. 9.**

—— Spiritual Despotism: or, the Pig and the Lord Mayor, the Dean of Canterbury, the Bishop and the Sheriff of London. A poem, *etc.* pp. vi. 48. *Houlston & Wright: London,* 1858. 12º. **11650. a. 32.**

CATER (Samuel) *See* Barnardiston (Giles) The Life of Christ magnified in his Minister. Or, certain testimonies thereof, relating to . . . G. Barnardiston . . . which were given forth severally by S. Cater [and others], *etc.* 1681. 8º. **1415. a. 33.**

—— *See* Green (Joseph J.) Biography of Samuel Cater . . . 1627–1711. 1914. 4º. **10855. g. 15. (1.)**

—— *See* Harrison (Joseph) *of Fakenham, Norfolk.* The Lamentable Cry of Oppression, *etc.* [With a postscript signed: S. Cater.] 1679. 4º. **C.110.f.36.**

—— *See* W., G., and C., S. Innocency against Envy . . . By G. W. and S. C. [i.e. S. Cater?] 1691. 4º. **4152. ee. 46. (8.)**

—— Another Epistle to Friends. *See* Woolrich (Humphrey) A General Epistle to Friends of Truth, *etc.* [1665.] 4º. **4151. c. 144.**

—— The Innocent Cleared and the Guilty Made Manifest. Being a reply to a printed paper . . . titled, Apostacy of the people called Quakers from the faith once delivered to the saints; subscribed by Francis Houlcroft and Joseph Oddey, *etc.* pp. 30. 1676. 4º. **4151. b. 29.**

—— The Liberty of an Apostate Conscience Discovered: being a plain narrative of the controversie . . . between Francis Bugg . . . and S. Cater and George Smith, *etc.* pp. 80. *John Bringhurst: London,* 1683. 8º. **856. f. 18. (4.)**

—— *See* Bugg (Francis) The Painted-Harlot both stript and whipt . . . Being . . . a brief answer to . . . S. Caters narrative . . . entituled, The Lib. of an Apost. Cons. [The Liberty of an Apostate Conscience], *etc.* 1683. 4º. **4152. cc. 43.**

CATER (SAMUEL)

—— A Relation of some of the most material matters that passed in a public dispute at Thriploe in Cambridgeshire the 15th day of the 2d month 1676. between Francis Holdcraft, and Joseph Odde . . . on the one party, and S. Cater, with some others of the Friends of Truth called Quakers. [Signed: S. Cater, J. Webb, J. B., i.e. Jacob Baker.] pp. 8. [1676.] 4°.   **4152. ee. 18. (7.)**

—— A Salutation in the Love of God . . . unto all the faithful brethren and sisters in Christ Jesus our Lord . . . With a word of exhortation . . . unto all whose faces are set Sionward, *etc.* pp. 14. 1672. 4°.
4152. aa. 4.

—— Samuel Cater's Testimony concerning James Parnell. *See* PARNELL (James) A Collection of the Several Writings given forth . . . through J. Parnell. 1675. 4°.
874. k. 2.

CATER (WILLIAM) *Bookseller.* A Catalogue of Valuable and Elegant Books . . . Which will begin to be sold . . . the 21st of March, 1768 . . . by William Cater, *etc.* pp. 118. [*London*, 1768.] 8°.   **128. i. 17. (3.)**

—— A Catalogue of a Valuable and Elegant Collection of Books, consisting of several libraries, lately purchased . . . which will begin to be sold . . . 21st of November, 1768 . . . by William Cater, *etc.* pp. 110. [*London*, 1768.] 8°.   **128. i. 18. (4.)**

—— A Catalogue of several thousand Valuable and Elegant Books . . . which will begin to be sold . . . the 18th of December, 1769 . . . by William Cater, *etc.* pp. 94. [*London*, 1769.] 8°.   **128. k. 1. (5.)**

—— A Catalogue of many thousand Valuable and Elegant Books . . . which will begin to be sold . . . the 3d of December, 1770 . . . by W. Cater, *etc.* pp. 168. [*London*, 1770.] 8°.   **128. k. 3. (4.)**

—— A Catalogue of Several Valuable Libraries and Collections of Books . . . which will begin to be sold . . . on . . . May 1, 1780 . . . by William Cater, *etc.* pp. ii. 160. [*London*, 1780.] 8°.   **11917. e. 40. (1.)**

—— A Catalogue of Several Valuable Libraries and Collections of Books . . . which will be selling . . . on Monday, Jan. 7th, 1782 . . . by Willam Cater, *etc.* pp. 140. [*London*, 1782.] 8°.   **128. k. 11. (2.)**

—— A Catalogue of Several Valuable Libraries and Collections of Books . . . which will be selling . . . June 9th, 1783 . . . by William Cater, *etc.* pp. 152. [*London*, 1783.] 8°.   **128. k. 13. (1.)**

—— A Catalogue of Several Valuable Libraries and Collections of Books . . . which will be selling . . . July 7th, 1783 . . . By William Cater, *etc.* pp. 152. [*London*, 1783.] 8°.   **S.C. 715. (3.)**

CATER (WILLIAM) *Churchwarden of Ware.* *See* ALSTON (Rowland G.) An Expostulatory Letter . . . to the Churchwardens of Ware [i.e. James Hudson and W. Cater], *etc.* 1843. 8°.   **1353. g. 35.**

—— *See* HUDSON (James) and CATER (W.) A Letter to R. G. Alston, Esq., in reply to his . . . letter to the Churchwardens of Ware, *etc.* 1843. 8°.   **1353. g. 39.**

CATER (WILLIAM ALEXANDER) The Mediæval Church and Crypt of St. Mary of the Arches, otherwise St. Mary-le-Bow. *See* MASTERMAN (John H. B.) *Bishop of Plymouth.* Three Papers on the Church of Saint Mary-le-Bow, *etc.* [1916.] 8°.   **7817. c. 22.**

—— The Priory of Austin Friars, London, 1253–1538 . . . Reprinted from the "Journal of the British Archæological Association," *etc.* [With plates.] pp. 46. [*London*, 1912.] 8°.   **4535. de. 14. (6.)**

CATER (WILLIAM EDMUND) Jephthah, and other poems. pp. 80.   *A. Shortrede & Co.: Hongkong*, 1860. 12°.
11641. de. 24.

CATERAS (SPYROS) *See* KATERAS (Spuros)

CATERBI (GIUSEPPE) *See* BIBLE.—*Matthew.* [*Italian.—Italian dialects.—Rome.*] Il Vangelo di S. Matteo, volgarizzato in dialetto Romano dal Sig. G. Caterbi, *etc.* 1861. 16°.   **3022. b. 26.**

—— La Chiesa di S. Onofrio e le sue tradizioni religiose storiche artistiche e letterarie. pp. 224.   *Roma*, 1858. 8°.   **10130. dd. 18.**

CATERERS.

—— The Caterers' Record. *See* ENGLAND.—*National Caterers' Federation.*

CATERERS EMPLOYEES UNION. *See* LONDON.—III.

CATERGIAN (JOSEPHUS) *See* GAT'ĔRČEAN (Yôsep')

CATERGIAN (SAMUEL) *See* GAT'ĔRČEAN (Samouel)

CATERHAM. The Parish Registers of Caterham, Surrey. Transcribed by Capt. R. R. Bruce Bannerman . . . Edited by W. Bruce Bannerman. pp. 139.   *Croydon*, 1917, 18. 8°. [*Publications of the Surrey Parish Register Society.* vol. 14, 15.]   **Ac. 8125.**

—— *Congregational School.* The Magazine of the Congregational School, Caterham Valley, *etc.* (Caterham School Magazine.) *London*, 1887– . 8°.   **P.P. 6152. lg.** *Imperfect; wanting vol. 6. no. 1, vol. 21. no. 62, vol. 22. no. 63, 64.*

Urban District Council.
—— The "Borough" Guide to Caterham (Official Guide to Caterham—Official Guide to Caterham & Warlingham). *E. J. Burrow & Co.: Cheltenham*, [1912?– .] 8°.
10354. a. 199. *Various editions.*

CATERHAM AND WARLINGHAM.—*Urban District Council.*
—— [For publications of the Caterham Urban District Council continued by the Caterham and Warlingham Urban District Council:] *See* CATERHAM.—*Urban District Council.*

CATERHAM DISTRICT DIRECTORY. *See* DIRECTORIES.—*Caterham.*

CATERINA. [For Saints, Sovereigns and Princesses of Sovereign Houses of this name:] *See* CATHARINE.

CATERINA. Caterina. By the author of "Lauterdale" [i.e. J. Fogerty]. 3 vol.   *Hurst & Blackett: London*, 1887. 8°.   **012639. l. 12.**

—— Caterina dannata per aver condotta una vita libertina. [A chap-book, in verse.] pp. 14.   *Firenze*, 1878. 16°.
12350. aa. 42. (6.)

—— Caterina, ossia l'Assedio di Belgrado. *See* BELGRADE. [*Appendix.*] L'Assedio di Belgrado.

CATERINA, *Palantina.* *See* MORIGGI (Caterina)

CATERINA, *pseud.* The Fortune-telling Birthday Book. By Caterina. pp. 252.   *H. J. Drane: London; printed in Holland*, [1901.] 16°.   **8632. aa. 39.**

CATERINE. [For Saints, Sovereigns and Princesses of Sovereign Houses of this name:] *See* CATHARINE.

CATERINETTA [Fieschi-Adorno], *Saint. See* Catharine [Adorni], *Saint.*

CATERING. Economical Catering for Home and Communal Use. pp. 128. *Good Housekeeping Magazine: London*, [1939.] 8⁰. **07941. pp. 11.**

CATERING EQUIPMENT DIGEST.

—— Catering Equipment Digest. *See* Periodical Publications.—*London.*

CATERING MANAGEMENT. Catering Management: a comprehensive guide . . . Written by experts and authorities . . . Illustrated, *etc.* 4 vol. *Waverley Book Co.: London*, 1920. 8⁰. **7953. i. 18.**

CATERING PRIMERS.

—— Universal Catering Primers. [General editor: A. C. Marshall.] [1947– .] 8⁰. *See* England.—*National Council for Hotel and Catering Education.* **W.P. 2372.**

CATERING QUARTERLY. *See* London.—III. *Industrial Catering Association.*

CATERING TRADE.

—— Catering Trade Working Party. *See* England.— *Ministry of Food.* [1939– .]

CATERING TRADES SERIES. *See* Long (John N.)

CATERING WAGES COMMISSION. *See* England. —*Ministry of Labour and National Service.*

CATERING WAGES GUIDE.

—— Catering Wages Guide and Ready Reckoner. With 5400 calculations. Specially compiled for caterers operating within the Unlicensed Place of Refreshment Catering Wages Regulation. pp. 32. *Ronald Coleman: Ryde,* [1949.] 8⁰. **08548. k. 8.**

CATERINI (Angiolo) *See* Horatius Flaccus (Q.) [*Ars Poetica.—Italian.*] La Poetica . . . in 476 endecasillabi, preceduta da un discorso giustificativo sù questa, ed altre maniere di versioni, per A. Caterini. 1875. 8⁰. **11386. b. 2.**

—— *See* Meneghini (G.) Mitra Caterinii. Nuova specie di conchiglia, *etc.* [Edited by A. Caterini.] 1873. 4⁰. **7298. c. 34.**

—— Breve istoria delle collezioni Cateriniane. [By A. Caterini.] pp. 28. 1873. 8⁰. *See* Caterini (G. B. C.) **7204. aaa. 5. (5.)**

—— Epigrafi sepolcrali, commemorative ed altre. pp. 47. *Pisa*, 1875. 8⁰. **4865. bbb. 19. (3.)**

CATERINI (Francesco) and **UGOLINI** (Luigi)

—— Il Libro degli uccelli italiani. Manuale di ornitologia italiana . . . II edizione riveduta ed ampliata, *etc.* [With illustrations.] pp. xl. 679. *Firenze*, 1943. 8⁰. **7286. p. 80.**

CATERINI (Giovanni Battista Caterino) *See* Meneghini (G.) Mitra Caterinii. Nuova specie di conchiglia scoperta dal compianto G. B. Caterino Caterini, *etc.* 1868. 8⁰. **7298. d. 37. (9.)**

—— *See* Meneghini (G.) Mitra Caterinii . . . Coll'aggiunta della descrizione . . . di alcune nuove conchiglie scoperte dal detto G. B. Caterini. 1873. 4⁰. **7298. c. 34.**

—— Breve istoria delle collezioni Cateriniane. [By Angiolo Caterini.] pp. 28. *Livorno*, 1873. 8⁰. **7204. aaa. 5. (5.)**

CATERINI (Prospero) *See* States of the Church.— *Congregazione degli Studi.* Collectio legum et ordinationum de recta studiorum ratione . . . cura P. Caterini . . . denuo edita et aucta. 1841, *etc.* 4⁰. **1240. e. 1.**

CATERINI MICHELANGELI (Amilcare) Alle falde dell'Etna. Scene selvaggi. [With a preface by R. P. Vassallo.] pp. 129. *Catania*, 1885. 8⁰. **12470. ee. 18.**

CATERINO (Cirillo) Storia della minoritica provincia napoletana di S. Pietro ad Aram. 3 vol. *Napoli,* 1926, 27. 8⁰. **04784. i. 2.**

CATERINUS (Ambrosius) *Senensis. See* Politi (L.) successively *Bishop of Minori* and *Archbishop of Conza.*

CATERINUS (Prosper) *See* Caterini (Prospero)

CATERLY (James) Les Roumains. [With plates and maps.] tom. 1. pp. 306. *Paris*, 1908. 8⁰. **9136. a. 14.**

No more published.

CATERNAULT (Stanislas)

—— Essai sur la gastrotomie dans les cas de tumeurs fibreuses péri-utérines, *etc.* pp. 135. *Strasbourg*, 1866. 4⁰. [*Collection générale des dissertations de la Faculté de Médecine de Strasbourg.* sér. 2. tom. 40.] **7381.* e.**

CATERPILLAR TRACTOR COMPANY.

—— [Advertising booklets.] *Peoria*, [1953– .] 4⁰ & 8⁰. **W.P. c. 837.**

CATERPILLARS. The Catterpillers of this Nation Anatomized, in a brief . . . discovery of house-breakers, pick-pockets, &c. Together with the life of a penitent high-way-man . . . To which is added, the manner of hectoring & trapanning as it is acted in and about the City of London. pp. iv. 38. *For M. H.: London,* 1659. 4⁰. **518. h. 2.**

CATERS (Christian de) Visages du Japon. [With plates and a map.] pp. 225. *Paris*, 1936. 8⁰. **010056. a. 50.**

CATERS (Louis de) Le Lion de Camors. Épisode des guerres de la Chouannerie, 1795–1804. Illustrations de Jules Girardet. pp. 300. *Paris*, 1894. 4⁰. **012547. m. 58.**

—— Revanche d'amour. pp. 339. *Paris*, [1893.] 12⁰. **012550. ee. 41.**

CATES (Adolphus H.) *See* Lockwood (Henry F.) and Cates (A. H.) The History and Antiquities of the Fortifications to the City of York. 1834. fol. **747. f. 5.**

CATES (Harry Arthur)

—— *See* Grant (John C. B.) and Cates (H. A.) A Handbook for Dissectors, *etc.* 1953. 8⁰. **7422. a. 14.**

—— Primary Anatomy . . . Second edition. pp. ix. 344. *Baillière, Tindall & Cox: London; Baltimore* printed, 1951 [1952]. 8⁰. **7422. s. 25.**

—— Primary Anatomy. By H. A. Cates . . . and J. V. Basmajian . . . Third edition. pp. xii. 339. pl. iv. *Baillière, Tindall & Cox: London; printed in U.S.A.,* 1955. 8⁰. **7423. c. 21.**

CATES (Henry Joseph) The Welfare of the School Child, *etc.* pp. ix. 153. pl. vi. *Cassell & Co.: London,* 1919. 8⁰. [*English Public Health Series.*] **W.P. 6109/6.**

CATES (John M.)

—— U.N. Maritime Conference: Geneva, 1948. *See* MacDonald (Eula) Toward a World Health Organization. 1948. 8⁰. [*International Organization and Conference Series.* ser. 4. Intergovernmental Maritime Consultative Organization. no. 1.] **A.S. 408/23. (4c.)**

CATES (JOSEPH) *See* CATES (Henry J.)

CATES (THOMAS) *See* BIGGES (Walter) [A Summarie and True Discourse of Sir Frances Drakes West Indian Voyage, *etc.*] [Edited by T. Cates.] [1589.] 4°.
G. 6510.

—— —— 1589. 4°. C. 32. f. 25.

—— *See* DRAKE (*Sir* Francis) Descriptio secundi itineris sive navigationis . . . à Francisco Draken . . . in Indiam Occidentalem susceptæ, *etc.* [Based on the account edited by T. Cates.] 1599. fol. [BRY (*T. de*) *America.*— *Part* VIII.—*Latin.*] C.115.h.3.(3.)

—— —— 1625. fol. [BRY (*T. de*) *America.*—*Part* VIII.— *Latin.*] 579. k. 15. (4.)

—— *See* DRAKE (*Sir* Francis) A Summarie and True Discourse of Sir Francis Drakes West-Indian Voyage, *etc.* [Based on the account edited by T. Cates.] 1652. 4°. 1045. e. 22.

—— *See* DRAKE (*Sir* Francis) Beschreibung der andern Reyss vnnd Kriegssrüstung oder Schiffahrt dess Francisci Draken, *etc.* [Based on the account edited by T. Cates.] 1600. fol. [BRY (*T. de*) *America.*—*Part* VIII.—*Appendix.* —*German.*] 10003. e. 32. (2.)

CATES (WILLIAM LEIST REDWIN) *See* MAUNDER (Samuel) The Biographical Treasury . . . Thirteenth edition . . . revised, and partly rewritten . . . by W. L. R. Cates, *etc.* 1866. 8°. 10603. aaa. 22.

—— —— 1873. 8°. 012215. de. 7.

—— *See* MERLE D'AUBIGNÉ (J. H.) History of the Reformation in Europe in the time of Calvin. (vol. 6-8. Translated by W. L. R. Cates.) 1863, *etc.* 8°. 4571. cc. 10.

—— *See* WOODWARD (Bernard B.) and CATES (W. L. R.) Encyclopædia of Chronology, *etc.* 1872. 8°. 2070.b.

—— A Dictionary of General Biography: with a classified and chronological index of the principal names. Edited by W. L. R. Cates. Second edition, with a supplement completing the work to the present time. pp. i [ix]. 161. *Longmans & Co.: London*, 1867. 8°. 10603. f. 3.

—— Third edition revised throughout and completed to the present time. [With supplement.] pp. viii. 1552. *Longmans & Co.: London*, 1881, 85. 8°. 2092.c.
The supplement, published in 1885, has a cancel titlepage bearing the words " Fourth edition, with supplement . . . down to the end of 1884."

—— History of England from the death of Edward the Confessor to the death of King John . . . With an introductory sketch of the previous history by the Rev. G. W. Cox. pp. xxi. 200. *Longmans & Co.: London*, 1874. 8°. 9510. de. 3.

—— The Pocket Date Book, or Classified tables of dates of the principal facts, historical, biographical, and scientific, from the beginning of the world to the present time. pp. vi. 248. *Chapman & Hall: London*, 1863. 8°. 9008. c. 21.

CATESBY AND SONS. Catesby & Sons' Art Exhibition. May, MDCCCCXIV. (Catalogue.) pp. 15. *Spottiswoode & Co.: London*, [1914.] 12°. 7855. c. 57.

CATESBY (CLIFTON) *See* ENGLAND.—*Parliament.*—*Parliamentary Proceedings.*—II. A Declaration of the Lords and Commons . . . with their Resolution. That if Captaine Catesby . . . or any others, which are or shall be taken prisoners, by his Majesties Army, shall be put to death . . . the like punishment shall be inflicted . . . upon such prisoners, as have bin or shall bee taken by the forces . . . of . . . Parliament, *etc.* 1642. 4°. 100. b. 70.

CATESBY (JULIETTE) *Lady.* Lettres de Milady Juliette Catesby, à Milady Henriette Campley, son amie. [A novel. By Marie J. Riccoboni.] Seconde édition. pp. 172. *Amsterdam*, 1759. 12°. 1208. b. 24.

—— Troisieme édition. pp. 216. *Amsterdam*, 1759. 12°. 12511. de. 17.

—— Quatrième édition. pp. 227. *Amsterdam*, 1760. 12°. 12510. ee. 10.

—— Letters from Juliet Lady Catesby to her friend Lady Henrietta Campley. Translated from the French [of M. J. Riccoboni, by Frances Brooke]. The fourth edition. pp. 251. *R. & J. Dodsley: London*, 1764. 8°. 12612. c. 6.

—— The fifth edition. pp. 249. *J. Dodsley: London*, 1769. 12°. 12614. b. 16.

—— The sixth edition. pp. 249. *J. Dodsley: London*, 1780. 12°. 12510. c. 19.

—— Письма Іюліи Леди Катесбей къ Генріеттѣ Леди Камплей. [By M. J. Riccoboni.] Переводъ съ аглинскаго [*sic*]. [The dedication by the translator is signed: Василій Куличкинъ.] pp. 268. въ Санктпетербургѣ, 1797. 12°. 867. i. 30. (2.)

CATESBY (MARGARET) *See* BISSET (William) *Elder Brother of St. Catherine's Collegiate Church.* A Funeral Sermon preach'd at Whiston . . . for Mrs. Margaret Catesby, *etc.* 1727. 8°. 1416. b. 4.

CATESBY (MARK) Hortus Europæ Americanus: or, a Collection of 85 curious trees and shrubs, the produce of North America . . . Together with . . . observations on their culture . . . Adorn'd with 63 figures on 17 copperplates, *etc.* pp. vi. 41. *J. Millan: London*, 1767. 4°. 452. f. 14.

—— The Natural History of Carolina, Florida and the Bahama Islands . . . Histoire naturelle de la Caroline, la Floride, & les Isles Bahama, *etc.* (An Account of Carolina, and the Bahama Islands.—Appendix.) *Eng. & Fr.* 2 vol. 3 pt. *The Author: London*, 1731–43 [48]. fol. C.113.i.1.
The Appendix, the " Account " and the Index in English, French and Latin were published in 1748. *A slip bearing the syllable " Pre " is pasted over the " Per " of " Perfixed " on the titlepage. In this copy are bound up a second copy of the preface; and the Linnæan indices to vol.* 1. & 2., *taken from the 3rd edition of* 1771. *The last line of the French text to pl.* 9 *reads " ver."*

—— [Another copy.] 687. l. 3.
Imperfect; wanting the map, the list of encouragers of the work, the " Account," the Appendix, and the Index in English, French and Latin. In this copy the last line of the French text to pl. 9 *reads " l'hiver."*

—— [Another copy.] 44. k. 7, 8.
Imperfect; wanting the Appendix. In this copy the last line of the French text to pl. 9 *begins: " d'un grand usage."*

—— Sammlung verschiedener ausländischer und seltener Vögel, worinnen ein jeder dererselben . . . in einer richtigen und sauber illuminirten Abbildung vorgestellet wird von Johann Michael Seligmann. [Portions of the text and copies of the illustrations of Mark Catesby's " Natural History of Carolina," *etc.* and of George Edwards' " A Natural History of Uncommon Birds." Translated by J. M. Seligmann and G. L. Huth.] Tl. 1–7. *Nürnberg*, 1749–70. fol. 41. i. 14–16.
Imperfect; wanting Tl. 8, 9.

CATESBY (MARK)

—— Piscium, serpentum, insectorum aliorumque nonnullorum animalium nec non plantarum . . . imagines quas Marcus Catesby in posteriore parte splendidi illius operis quo Carolinae, Floridae et Bahamensium insularum tradidit historiam naturalem . . . descripsit vivis coloribus pictas edere coeperunt Nicolaus Fredericus Eisenberger et Georgius Lichtensteger et ad finem perduxerunt beati Georgii Wolfgangi Knorrii heredes. (Die Abbildungen verschiedener Fische, Schlangen, *etc.*) *Lat. & Ger.* pp. 100. 9. *Norimbergae*, 1777. fol. **1819. d. 3.**

CATESBY (ROBERT) *See* ENGLAND.—*Proclamations.*—II. James I. [1603–1625.] By the King. [A proclamation for the apprehension of Thomas Percy, R. Catesby and others in connection with the Gunpowder Plot.] 1605. fol. **C.112.h.1.(58.)**

—— *See* JONES (Mary W.) The Gunpowder Plot and Life of Robert Catesby, *etc.* 1909. 8°. **010352. e. 6.**

—— Catesby. A tragedy of the 'Gunpowder Plot,' *etc.* pp. viii. 88. *Billing & Sons: Guildford*, 1897. 4°. **11781. h. 25.**

CATET (S.) *See* CATTET.

CATEYSSON (J.) Indicador Geral da Viação do Brazil, *etc.* pp. 185. *Paris, Lisboa*, 1901. 8°. **P.P. 2596. fa.**

CATEZ (ELIZABETH) *See* ÉLISABETH [Catez], de la Trinité, Carmelite Nun.

CATFORD. [Institutions, societies, etc. situated in the district of Catford are entered alphabetically under LONDON.—III.]

CATFORD AND HITHER GREEN GUIDE. *See* PERIODICAL PUBLICATIONS.—*London.*

CATFORD (BARBARA) Ernest the Elephant . . . Illustrated by Nancy Catford. pp. 69. *Frederick Muller: London*, 1935. 16°. **012807. de. 103.**

—— Jolly Steps for Tiny Folks. 12 pt. *Oxford University Press: London*, [1939.] 8°. **12822. a. 12.**

CATFORD (J.)

—— *See* BENTWICH (Joseph S.) and·MENDILOW (A. A.) How the English Live. By J. S. Bentwich and A. A. Mendilow, assisted by J. Catford. 1949. 8°. **010368. k. 13.**

CATFORD (JAMES S.) Catford's Eclipse Album of Ilfracombe and North Devon views. *Edwin Oborne: London; "made in Germany,"* [1892.] 8°. **10352. l. 27.**

CATFORD (JOHN CUNNISON)

—— *See* OGDEN (Charles K.) Word-stress and Sentence Stress, *etc.* [Edited, and partly written by J. C. Catford.] 1950. 8°. **P.P. 4977. bab. (5.)**

CATFORD (NANCY) *See* CATFORD (Barbara) Ernest the Elephant . . . Illustrated by N. Catford. 1935. 16°. **012807. de. 103.**

—— Dan the Duckling. Written and illustrated by N. Catford. pp. 69. *Frederick Muller: London*, 1938. 16°. **12821. a. 9.**

—— Derek the Dragon. Written and illustrated by N. Catford. pp. 69. *Frederick Muller: London*, 1939. 16°. **12822. a. 16.**

—— Making and Modelling. Written and illustrated by N. Catford. Edited by Susan French. pp. 20. *Daily Mail School-Aid Department: London*, [1946.] 8°. [*Young Britain Series for Schools.*] **W.P. 1352/4.**

CATFORD (NANCY)

—— Making Nursery Toys. Written and illustrated by N. Catford. pp. 128. *Frederick Muller: London*, 1944. 8°. **7948. a. 5.**

—— Making your own Party Decorations. Written and illustrated by N. Catford. [With plates.] pp. 96. *Frederick Muller: London*, 1951. 8°. **7947. bb. 35.**

—— Maurice the Mouse. Written and illustrated by N. Catford. pp. 69. *Frederick Muller: London*, 1937. 16°. **12810. a·. 89.**

—— Modelling with Plastics. [With illustrations.] pp. 34. *" Daily Mail " Publications: London*, [1951.] 8°. **W.P.57.**

—— [Another copy.] Modelling with Plastics. *London*, [1951.] 8°. **7949. f. 54.**

—— Percy the Penguin . . . Written and illustrated by N. Catford. pp. 69. *Frederick Muller: London*, 1936. 16°. **20055. e. 61.**

—— Robert the Rabbit. Written and illustrated by N. Catford. pp. 69. *Frederick Muller: London*, 1934. 16°. **012804. c. 38.**

—— Ronnie the Robin. Written and illustrated by N. Catford. pp. 69. *Frederick Muller: London*, 1937. 16°. **12805. d. 92.**

—— Sammy the Squirrel. Written and illustrated by N. Catford. pp. 69. *Frederick Muller: London*, 1937. 16°. **12805. d. 91.**

CATHABAPTISTAE. *See* ANABAPTISTS.

CATHAL. The Limit. Being a collection of rhymes concerning a pig-boat and other matters. By Cathal. pp. 17. *Brewer & Co.: Hongkong*, 1917. 8°. **011648. e. 11.**

CATHAL (J.) L'Occupation de Lunéville par les Allemands, 1870–1873. Préface de M. le général Farny . . . Avec 14 photographies documentaires. pp. xii. 221. *Paris, Nancy*, 1913. 8°. **09076. a. 41.**

CATHALA (ADOLPHE) De la version, et de son emploi dans la pratique des accouchements. Tribut académique, *etc.* pp. 60. *Montpellier*, 1837. 4°. **1181. h. 6. (9.)**

CATHALA (ARNAUD BONNET) *See* BONNET CATHALA.

CATHALA (CHARLES) Étude sur le procédé d'Esmarch, ses avantages et ses inconvénients. Thèse, *etc.* pp. 54. *Montpellier*, 1875. 4°. **7379. k. 8. (1.)**

CATHALA (J.) *of Siran.* Des fractures du crâne et en particulier du rocher. pp. 34. *Paris*, 1875. 4°. [*Collection des thèses soutenues à la Faculté de Médecine de Paris. An 1875. tom. 4.*] **7374. b.**

CATHALA (J. PIERRE FULCRAND) Considérations générales sur la menstruation et sur les maladies des filles, *etc.* pp. 22. *Montpellier*, 1809. 4°. **1180. f. 15. (20.)**

CATHALA (JEAN) *of Avène.* Des eaux minérales d'Avène au point de vue thérapeutique. Thèse, *etc.* pp. 56. *Montpellier*, 1855. 4°. **7379. c. 14. (8.)**

CATHALA (JEAN) *Writer of Travel Books.* Portrait de l'Estonie. [With plates and a map.] pp. ii. 209. *Paris*, 1937. 8°. **010281. de. 33.**

CATHALA (PIERRE) Barreau de Paris. Éloge d'Henri Barboux. Discours, *etc.* pp. 40. *Mesnil-sur-l'Estrée*, 1921. 8°. **10657. cc. 21.**

CATHALA (PIERRE)

—— Face aux réalités. La direction des finances françaises sous l'occupation, *etc.* [With a portrait.] pp. xxv. 302. *Paris*, 1948. 8º.   **8230. a. 76.**

CATHALA-COTURE (ANTOINE DE) Histoire politique, ecclésiastique et littéraire du Querci . . . Continuée par M*** membre de plusieurs académies [i.e. — de Teulières?]. (Histoire du siége de Montauban.) 3 tom. *Montauban, Paris*, 1785. 8º.   **576. g. 2–4.**

CATHALAN (ANTOINE) *See* CATHELAIN.

CATHALAN (BLASCO PELEGRÍN) *See* PELEGRÍN CATALAN.

CATHALAN (M. A. DENIS) Essai sur la médecine symptomatique, *etc.* [A thesis.] pp. 29. *Montpellier*, [1807.] 4º.   **1180. f. 8. (17.)**

CATHALINA. [For Saints, Sovereigns and Princesses of Sovereign Houses of this name:] *See* CATHARINE.

CATHALUÑA. *See* CATALONIA.

CATHALUNYA. *See* CATALONIA.

CATHANEIS (BAPTISTA DE) *See* CATHANEIS (Joannes B. de)

CATHANEIS (JOANNES BAPTISTA DE) *See* CARMELITES. Speculum ordinis Fratrū Carmelitarum, *etc.* (Per baptistā uenetū de Cathaneis emendatum, *etc.*) [1507?] fol.   **C. 53. d. 14.**

CATHARARINA. Amor, omnia, vincit, vidi, vici, veni. My little book to all mankind by the triune imperial crown and government of all nations, Her Royal Majesty Zion Holy Ghost, Empress Regina, Zion Cathararina, beloved Bride of Heaven. pp. 12.   [*Printed for the Author: Lowestoft*, 1858.] 8º.   [MISSING.]
Imperfect; wanting pp. 3, 4, 9, 10. *Pp.* 5, 6, 7, 8 *are in duplicate.*

CATHARI.

—— Summa in Catharos auctore anonymo. *In:* KARSAVIN (L. P.) Очерки религіозной жизни въ Италіи XII–XIII вѣковъ. pp. 675–815. 1912. 8º. [*Записки Историко-филологическаго факультета Императорскаго С.-Петербургскаго Университета.* част. 112.]   **Ac. 1123. i/3. (16.)**

CATHARINA. [For Saints, Sovereigns and Princesses of Sovereign Houses of this name:] *See* CATHARINE.

—— Schoone Catharina, beeld der beelden. Liedeken of samenspraeke tusschen eenen jongman en eene jonge dogter. (Liedeken of herders-klagt van Philander en zyne liefste Dorinde.—Een over oud liedeken van de wonderlyke kragt der minne.) *Gent*, [1840?] *s. sh. obl.* fol.   **1871. c. 1. (58.)**

CATHARINA, *de Gebweiler*. Ven. Catharinæ de Gewesweiler, Priorissæ Subtiliensis . . . De vitis primarum sororum monasterii sui liber, ex Ms. cod. Tiliensi. Accessit Appendix de vitis aliquot aliarum . . . ejusdem ordinis virginum e diversis Mss. Codd. collecta [by Matthias Thanner]. 1725. *See* PEZ (B.) R. P. Bernardi Pezii . . . Bibliotheca ascetica, *etc.* tom. 8. 1723, *etc.* 8º.   **3705. aaa. 8.**

—— Lebensbeschreibungen der ersten Schwestern des Klosters der Dominikanerinnen zu Unterlinden von deren Priorin, C. von Gebsweiler. Aus dem Lateinischen übersetzt und eingeleitet von Ludwig Clarus. Mit einem Anhange vom "Leben mehrerer Mönche" im Kloster zu Waldsassen. [By Joannes de Ellenbogen.] Nebst einem Stahlstiche. pp. 488. *Regensburg*, 1863. 8º. [*Reliquien aus dem Mittelalter.* Bd. 4.]   **3622. aa. 3.**

CATHARINA, *de Gewesweiler. See* CATHARINA, *de Gebweiler.*

CATHARINA, *pseud.* [i.e. J. C. JOLLES?] Juf. [A tale.] *See* BERMAN (A. J.) Landjuweel, *etc.* bundel 2. 1878. 8º.   **12356. g. 7.**

CATHARINA WILLEMINA. Aanmerkelyke levens beschryving of lotgevallen van eeu [*sic*] Rotterdammer Juffrouw Cattrina Willemina (Catharina Willemina), *etc.* [1790?] 8º. *See* CATTRINA WILLEMINA.   **12580. bb. 39.**

CATHARINE. *See also* CATHERINE.

—— A Bridal Ode on the Marriage of Catherine and Petruchio. [A satire on Catharine Macaulay's marriage with William Graham.] pp. 19.   *J. Bew: London*, 1779. 4º.   **643. k. 21.**

—— Catharine. By the author of "Agnes and the Little Key" [i.e. Nehemiah Adams]. pp. 160. *Knight & Son: London*, [1859.] 8º.   **4407. b. 95.**

—— Catharine and Petruchio. [A comedy. Altered from Shakespeare's "Taming of the Shrew," by David Garrick.] pp. 8. [*J. Harrison & J. Wenman: London*, 1780.] 8º.   **11770. g. 4. (30.)**

—— A Remarkable Moving Letter! [The advertisement signed: Catharine. A satire, in verse, on Catharine Macaulay's marriage with William Graham.] pp. 10. *Robert Faulder: London*, 1779. 4º.   **840. k. 13. (1.)**

CATHARINE [OF ARAGON], *Consort of Arthur, Prince of Wales. See* CATHARINE, *Queen Consort of Henry VIII., King of England.*

CATHARINE, *Consort of Charles Anthony Frederick Meinrad Fidelis, Prince of Hohenzollern-Sigmaringen. See* ZINGELER (C. T.) Katharina, Fürstin von Hohenzollern . . . die Stifterin von Beuron. [1912.] 8º.   **010706. i. 43.**

CATHARINE [OF AUSTRIA], *Consort of Charles Emmanuel I., Duke of Savoy. See* CACCIA (F.) Oratione . . . fatta nella morte della serenissima Infante Donna Caterina d'Austria, Duchessa di Sauoia. [1598.] 4º.   **835. f. 16. (8.)**

—— *See* MOLINO (C.) Nozze illustri. (Naratione delle nozze di Sua Altezza il Duca di Savoia con la Serenissima Donna Caterina, Infante di Spagna.) [1882.] 8º.   **10601. d. 11. (6.)**

—— *See* PELUSIUS (J.) De nuptiis Caroli Emanuelis . . . Sabaudiæ ducis . . . et augustissimæ Catherinæ Austriacæ, *etc.* 1585. 8º.   **1213. e. 43.**

—— *See* ROFREDUS (P. M.) Ad Sereniss. . . . Carolum Eman. Sabaudie Ducem de auspicato cum Catharina Austriaca . . . conjugio . . . oratio. 1585. 4º.   **10631. d. 13.**

—— *See* SILVA (G. A.) Relazione dell'ingresso della Infanta Caterina d'Austria in Torino nel x giorno di agosto MDLXXXV, *etc.* 1876. 8º.   **9930. g. 14.**

CATHARINE, *Consort of Charles Philip, Margrave of Brandenburg. See* FRIEDLAENDER (Julius) Markgraf Karl Philipp von Brandenburg und die Gräfin Salmour, *etc.* 1881. 8º.   **10704. c. 12. (3.)**

—— *See* NEIGEBAUR (J. D. F.) Die Heirath des Markgrafen Carl von Brandenburg mit der Markgräfin Catharina von Balbiano, *etc.* 1856. 8º.   **9384. b. 10.**

CATHARINE [DE' MEDICI], *Consort of Ferdinand, Duke of Mantua. See* CASATO (G.) Il Matrimonio di Ferdinando Gonzaga con Caterina de Medici, *etc.* 1882. 8º.   **10630. ee. 5. (1.)**

CATHARINE [DE' MEDICI], *Consort of Ferdinand, Duke of Mantua.*

—— *See* GEMMA (F.) Ritratto della . . . Principessa Caterina di Toscana, *etc.* 1737. 4°. **1371. i. 7.**

CATHARINE [OF HENNEBERG], *Consort of Frederick, Margrave of Meissen and Langrave of Thüringen. See* MUELLER (August W.) Die erlauchten Stammmütter des Hauses Sachsen Ernestinischer Linie, *etc.* [Including a biography of the Margravine Catharine.] 1862. 4°.
10703. g. 38. (3.)

CATHARINE [OF BRANDENBURG], *Consort of Gabriel Bethlen, Prince of Transylvania. See* GABRIEL [Bethlen], *Prince of Transylvania.* Le Triomphe admirable observé en l'aliance de Betheleem Gabor, prince de Transilvanie avec la princesse Catherine de Brandebourg, *etc.* 1855. 16°. [*FOURNIER* (E.) *Variétés historiques et littéraires.* tom. 1.] **12234. aa. 8.**

—— *See* KŐVÁRI (L.) Brandenburgi Katalin. [A biographical notice.] 1852. 8°. [*VAHOT* (I.) *Losonczi Phönix.* köt. 3.] **12264. g. 8.**

—— *See* SZABÓ (Gy.) Bethlen Gábor házassága brandenburgi Katalinnal. 1888. 8°. **Ac.825/27.**

CATHARINE, *Consort of George, Duke of Holstein-Oldenburg. See* CATHARINE, *Queen Consort of William, King of Wurtemburg.*

CATHARINE [DE BOURBON], *Consort of Henry, Duke of Lorraine and of Bar. See* BENOIST (P.) [Epistre consolatoire, a Monseigneur le Duc de Lorraine, touchant la bonne esperance de la Conuersion de Madame . . . Duchesse de Bar, à l'Eglise Catholique Apostolique & Romaine.] [1601.] 12°. **12235. aaa. 1. (8.)**

—— *See* DAVY DU PERRON (J.) *Cardinal, etc.* Articles des ministres et autres appellez par Madame [i.e. Catharine de Bourbon] pour la Conference entre eux & Monsieur l'Euesque d'Evreux, *etc.* 1601. 4°. **850. a. 2. (2.)**

—— *See* DAVY DU PERRON (J.) *Cardinal, etc.* Discours veritable, du pour-parler de la Conférence, proposée entre le Sieur Euesque d'Evreux, & les ministres de Madame [Catharine de Bourbon], *etc.* 1602. 8°. **1193. e. 31.**

—— *See* HURTREL (Alice) Les Amours de Catherine de Bourbon . . . et du comte de Soissons. 1882. 8°.
012548. ee. 54.

—— *See* LA FOREST D'ARMAILLÉ (M. C. A. de) *Countess.* Catherine de Bourbon, *etc.* 1865. 12°. **10660. aaa. 20.**

—— *See* MACDOWALL (H. C.) Henry of Guise and other portraits. (Catherine of Navarre.) 1898. 8°.
010663. h. 28.

—— *See* OVEREND (George C.) The Persecuted Princess [i.e. Catharine de Bourbon], *etc.* 1875. 16°. **10663. aa. 30.**

—— Lettres et poésies . . . 1570–1603. Publiées par Raymond Ritter. pp. xiv. 233. pl. II. *Paris,* 1927. 8°.
10906. h. 32.

CATHARINE [SFORZA], *Consort of Jerome, Lord of Imola and of Forlì. See* AMADORI (C.) La Caterina Sforza del Conte Pier Desiderio Pasolini. 1894. 8°.
10629. f. 43.

—— *See* BURRIEL (Antonio) *Jesuit.* Vita di Caterina Sforza Riario Contessa d'Imola e Signora di Forli, *etc.* [With a portrait.] 1795. 4°. **1448. k. 18.**

—— *See* CERATO (M.) Caterina Sforza. Conferenza, *etc.* 1903. 4°. **10629. g. 22.**

CATHARINE [SFORZA], *Consort of Jerome, Lord of Imola and of Forlì.*

—— *See* GOTTSCHEWSKI (A.) Über die Porträts der Caterina Sforza und über den Bildhauer Vincenzo Onofri, *etc.* 1908. 8°. [*Zur Kunstgeschichte des Auslandes.* Hft. 58.]
7803. t. 27. (1.)

—— *See* GRILLI (A.) Dieci lettere inedite di Caterina Sforza, *etc.* 1912. 8°. **010902. i. 10. (4.)**

—— *See* OLIVA (F.) A sua Eccellenza Donna T. Chiaramonti Gaddi . . . La vita di C. Sforza Visconti. 1821. 8°.
10630. c. 29.

—— *See* PASOLINI DALL'ONDA (P. D.) *Count.* Caterina Sforza. 1893. 8°. **10633. dd. 2.**

—— —— 1913. 8°. **10633. aa. 38.**

—— *See* PASOLINI DALL'ONDA (P. D.) *Count.* Catherine Sforza . . . Translated . . . bỳ Paul Sylvester. 1898. 8°. **10629. df. 19.**

—— *See* PASOLINI DALL'ONDA (P. D.) *Count.* Caterina Sforza. Nuovi documenti, *etc.* 1897. 8°. **10630. d. 52.**

—— *See* RANDI (A.) Caterina Sforza. 1951. 8°.
010632. cc. 23

—— *See* RODOCANACHI (E.) Une Ancêtre des Bourbons, Catharine Sforza. 1904. 8°. **10600. g. 19. (10.)**

—— *See* ROMANA (A.) Le Tre Caterine. (Caterina Sforza Riario . . . Caterina de Medici . . . Caterina II di Russia.) 1921. 8°. **010603. b. 8.**

—— Experimenti de la Exma Sra Caterina da Furlj, *etc.* [Edited by P. D. Pasolini.] pp. 249. *Imola,* 1894. 8°.
07305. m. 1.

CATHARINE [DE ROHAN-SOUBISE], *Consort of John II., called the Younger, Count Palatine of the Rhine. See* MARCHEGAY (P.) Recherches sur les poésies de Mlles de Rohan-Soubise. 1874. 8°. **11826. i. 3.**

CATHARINE [OF AUSTRIA], *Consort of John III., King of Portugal.* Letters of the Queen [i.e. Catharine of Austria]. *See* FORD (Jeremiah D. M.) and MOFFATT (Lucius G.) Letters of the Court of John III., King of Portugal, *etc.* 1933. 8°. **9180. tt. 1.**

CATHARINE [OF BURGUNDY], *Consort of Leopold, called the Glorious, Duke of Austria. See* STOUFF (L.) Catherine de Bourgogne et la féodalité de l'Alsace autrichienne, *etc.* 1913. 8°. **9902. a. 11.**

—— *See* STOUFF (L.) Comptes du domaine de Catherine de Bourgogne, duchesse d'Autriche, dans la Haute-Alsace, *etc.* 1907. 8°. **07707. k. 26.**

CATHARINE, *Consort of Peter Theodorovich, Grand Duke of Russia, afterwards Peter III., Emperor of Russia. See* CATHARINE II., *Empress of Russia.*

CATHARINE [OF CLEVES] *Duchess de Guise.* Le Chant Douloureux de Madame la Duchesse de Guyse sur la mort & trespas de feu Monseigneur le Duc De Guyse, son espoux . . . et sur celle de feu Monseigneur le Cardinal son frère, *etc.* De l'imprimerie de H. Velu: [Paris, 1589?] 8°.
1193. h. 27. (4.)

—— Pleurs et Souspirs lamentables, de Madame de Guyse: sur la mort & assasinat fait à son espoux, Monseigneur le Duc De Guyse, *etc.* pp. 14. *F. Le Jeune: Paris,* [1589.] 8°. **1193. h. 27. (3.)**

CATHARINE [OF AVIZ], *Duchess of Braganza. See* COIMBRA.—*Universidade de Coimbra.* Allegações de Direito, que se offereceram ao muito alto, & muito poderoso Rei Dom Henrique . . . na causa da soccessaõ destes Reinos por parte da Senhora Dona Catherina, *etc.* 1580. fol. **1322. k. 9.**

CATHARINE [OF AVIZ], *Duchess of Braganza.*

—— *See* COIMBRA.—*Universidade de Coimbra.* Jus succedendi in Lusitaniæ regnum Dominæ Catharinæ regis Emmanuelis ex Eduardo filio neptis, *etc.* 1641. fol.
1321. h. 4.

—— *See* TH., M. P. Be. Iv. Declaration du droit de legitime succession, sur le royaume de Portugal, apartenant à la Royne mere du Roy Treschrestien. Auec la responce aux consultations sur ce faites . . . pour Catherine Duchesse de Bragance, *etc.* 1582. 8°. **1195. a. 2. (1.)**

CATHARINE I., *Empress of Russia.*

WORKS.

—— Respuesta de la Czarina. [Signed: Cathalina. Dated: 15 June 1716.] *See* GEORGE I., *King of Great Britain and Ireland.* Traduccion de vna carta que el Rey de Inglaterra escrivio (à 11 de april de 1726.) a la Czarina de Moscovia, y Russia, *etc.* [1726.] 4°. **1323. d. 22. (1.)**

—— Testament Ihro Käyserl. Majestät Catharina Alexiejowna Selbsthalterin von Russland . . . Welche den 17. May 1727. zu Petersburg hochseelig verschieden ist . . . Nach dem Petersburgischen Exemplar. *Stockholm*, [1727.] 4°. **8094. g. 16. (1.)**

APPENDIX.

BIOGRAPHY.

I. *General Biography.*

—— *See* ANDREEV (V. V.) Екатерина первая. [1869.] 8°.
10795. e. 1. (10.)

—— *See* GROT (Ya. K.) Библіографическія и историческія замѣтки . . . Происхожденіе Екатерины I., *etc.* 1877. 8°. [*Записки Императорской Академіи Наукъ.* том. 31. прил. но. 3.] Ac. **1125/48.**

—— —— 1877 [1878]. 8°. [*Сборникъ Отдѣленія Русскаго Языка и Словесности Императорской Академіи Наукъ.* том. 18. но. 4.] Ac. **1125/39.**

—— *See* LA MARCHE (C. F. S. de) *pseud.* Russische Anekdoten von der Regierung und Tod Peters des Dritten . . . welchen zum Anhange beygefüget die Lebensgeschichte Catharinen der Ersten. 1764. 8°.
8094. aa. 6.

—— *See* LE BOVIER DE FONTENELLE (B.) The Northern Worthies: or, the lives of Peter the Great . . . and of his Illustrious Empress Catharine, the late Czarina, *etc.* [With a portrait.] 1730, *etc.* 12°. **611. a. 10.**

—— *See* MOTTLEY (John) The History of the Life and Reign of the Empress Catharine, *etc.* [With a portrait.] 1744. 8°. **1056. g. 11, 12.**

—— *See* PETER I., called *the Great, Emperor of Russia.* The History of the Life of Peter the First . . . Also, the birth and rise of the Empress Catharine, *etc.* [By John Mottley.] 1739. fol. **1200. cc. 15.**

—— *See* PETER I., called *the Great, Emperor of Russia.* Походные и путевые журналы императора Петра 1-го 1695 [*etc.*] года. [Containing in the journals for 1711–1726 materials relating to Catharine I.] [1853, *etc.*] 8°.
10795. g. 18–33.

—— *See* SEMEVSKY (M. I.) Царица Катерина Алексѣевна, Анна и Виллимъ Монсъ, 1692–1724, *etc.* (Очерки и разсказы изъ русской исторіи XVIII. в.) [With a portrait.] 1884. 8°. **010795. g. 11.**

—— Mémoires du règne de Catherine Impératrice & Souveraine de toute la Russie &c &c &c. [By J. Rousset de Missy.] [With a portrait and maps.] pp. 613. *La Haye*, 1728. 12°. **1200. b. 27.**

CATHARINE I.. *Empress of Russia.* [APPENDIX.]

—— The Northern Heroine. Being authentick memoirs of the late Czarina, Empress of Russia. Containing I. An account of her extraction, birth, education, deportment, and deserving advancement to that throne. II. An exact pedigree of the Czar's family, and issue; with his own character of the Czarina. III. Verses on her death, by Aaron Hill, Esq. pp. 28. *H. Curll: London*, 1727. 8°.
113. b. 62.

II. *Separate Events.*

1724.

—— Beskrifning om Hennes Keyserliga Majestets Catharinæ Alexievnæ Cröning, som . . . firades uti . . . Muscou på den 7:de dag i Maji Månad Åhr 1724. Öfuersatt på Swenska, effter det Ryska originalet, *etc.* pp. 30. *Stockholm*, 1725. 4°. **9004. k. 13. (4.)**

—— Проектъ церемоніала коронаціи Государыни Императрицы Екатерины Алексѣевны. 1855. *See* PETER I., called *the Great, Emperor of Russia.* Походные и путевые журналы императора Петра 1-го 1695 [*etc.*] года. 1724. [1853, *etc.*] 8°. **10795. g. 31.**

1726.

—— *See* RUSSIA.—*Камерфурьеры.* Журналъ Камеръ-Фурьерскій 1726 [*etc.*] года. [Containing in the journal for 1726 material relating to Catharine I.] [1853, *etc.*] 8°. **10795. g. 34.**

1727.

—— Записка о кончинѣ Государыни Императрицы Екатерины Алексѣевны, и о вступленіи на престолъ . . . императора Петра II. Алексѣевича. pp. 4. *See* RUSSIA.—*Камерфурьеры.* ЖурналъКамеръ-Фурьерскій 1726 [*etc.*] года. pt. 1, 1726. [1853, *etc.*] 8°.
10795. g. 34.

MISCELLANEOUS.

—— *See* BRI KNER (A. G.) Peter's des Grossen Briefwechsel mit Katharina. 1880. 8°. [*Historisches Taschenbuch.* Folge 5. Jahrg. 10.] **P.P. 3625.**

—— *See* GEORGE MIKHAILOVICH, *Grand Duke of Russia.* Монеты царствованій Императрицы Екатерины I. и Императора Петра II. 1904. fol. **7756. i. 4.**

—— Catharine of Russia: or, The Child of the Storm. An historical drama founded on an incident in the life of Peter the Great . . . As performed at the London Theatres, *etc.* [By D. W. Osbaldiston?] pp. 16. *D. W. Osbaldiston: London*, [1850.] 12°.
11777. b. 7. (3.)

—— [Descriptions of documents by or relating to the Empress Catharine I.] *See* PETER I., called *the Great, Emperor of Russia.* Письма Петра Великаго хранящіяся въ Императорской Публичной Библіотекѣ, *etc.* 1872. 8°. **10795. ee. 11.**

CATHARINE II., *Empress of Russia.*

WORKS.

—— Сочиненія . . . Изданіе Александра Смирдина. 3 том. *Санктпетербургъ*, 1849, 50. 18°. [*Полное собраніе сочиненій русскихъ авторовъ.*] **12206. c. 9–11.**

—— Сочиненія . . . съ объяснительными примѣчаніями А. Н. Пыпина. [With portraits.] том. 1–5, 7–12. 1901–07. 8°. *See* RUSSIA.—*Академія Наукъ СССР.*
Ac. **1125/77.**

TWO OR MORE WORKS.

—— Théâtre de l'Hermitage de Cathérine II, Impératrice de Russie; composé par cette princesse, par plusieurs personnes de sa société, et par quelques ministres étrangers, *etc.* [With a portrait. Edited by J. H. Castéra.] 2 tom. *Paris*, an VII [1799]. 8°. **86. d. 13, 14.**

CATHARINE II., *Empress of Russia.* [Two or More Works.]

—— Письма и бумаги Императрицы Екатерины II. хранящіяся въ Императорской Публичной Библіотекѣ, *etc.* pp. 160. 11. 1873. 4⁰. *See* infra : LETTERS.
10921. l. 6.

—— Сочиненія Императрицы Екатерины II. Произведенія литературныя. Подъ редакціей Арс. И. Введенскаго. Съ портретомъ автора, гравированнымъ И. Ф. Деинингеромъ, и очеркомъ ея литературной дѣятельности. pp. 448. С.-Петербургъ, 1893. 8⁰.
012265. b. 11.

—— Drey Lustspiele wider Schwärmerey und Aberglauben. 1) Der Betrüger. 2) Der Verblendete. 3) Der sibirische Schaman. Von I. K. M. d. K. a. R. [i.e. von Ihrer Kaiserlichen Majestät der Kaiserin aller Reussen.] [With a preface by the publisher, Friedrich Nicolai.] pp. xvi. 347. *Berlin & Stettin*, 1788. 8⁰.
11746. e. 20.

LETTERS.

Original languages.

—— [For collections of official despatches and rescripts :] *See* RUSSIA. [*Laws, etc.*—B. ii.]

—— Anhang, welcher einen Theil der Correspondenz der Kayserin mit dem Ritter von Zimmermann enthält, als Belege. [Thirty letters, including some from Zimmermann.] *Fr. See* MARCARD (H. M.) Zimmermanns Verhältnisse mit der Kayserin Catharina II., *etc.* 1803. 8⁰.
010920. e. 10.

—— Переписка Императрицы Екатерины II, съ графомъ Румянцовымъ-Задунайскимъ. *Russ.* pp. 86. *Москва*, 1805. 8⁰.
10920. f. 27.

—— Переписка Императрицы Екатерины II. съ разными особами. *Russ.* pp. 156. *Санктпетербургъ*, 1807. 8⁰.
10920. f. 28.

—— Высочайшія собственноручныя письма и повелѣнія . . . Императрицы Екатерины Великія къ покойному генералу Петру Дмитріевичу Ерапкину и всеподаннѣйшія его донесенія . . . собранныя и . . . изданныя . . . Яковомъ Ростомъ. *Russ.* pp. 343. *Москва*, 1808. 8⁰.
10920. f. 3.

—— Переписка Императрицы Екатерины II. съ графомъ П. И. Панинымъ. *Russ.* pp. 37. 1863. *See* GROT (Ya. K.) Матеріалы для исторіи Пугачевскаго бунта, *etc.* pt. 2. 1862, *etc.* 8⁰. [*Записки Императорской Академіи Наукъ.* том. 3. прил. но. 4.] Ac. **1125/48.**

—— Письма Екатерины II. къ Адаму Васильевичу Олсуфьеву 1762–1783. Съ примѣчаніями М. Н. Лонгинова. [Edited by P. I. Bartenev.] (Изъ Русскаго Архива 1863 года.) *Russ.* pp. 114. *Москва*, 1863. 8⁰.
10920. ccc. 2.

One of an edition of sixty copies.

—— Бумаги Императрицы Екатерины II, хранящіяся въ Государственномъ Архивѣ Министерства Иностранныхъ Дѣлъ. [The majority in Russian, with Russian translations of the rest. Edited by P. P. Pekarsky, Ya. K. Grot and G. Th. Shtendman.] 5 том. *С.-Петербургъ*, 1871–85. 8⁰. [*Сборникъ Русскаго Историческаго Общества.* том. 7, 10, 13, 27, 42.] Ac. **7886.**

—— Письма и бумаги Императрицы Екатерины II. хранящіяся въ Императорской Публичной Библіотекѣ. Изданы А. Ф. Бычковымъ. (Памяти Екатерины Второй своей великой основательницы Императорская Публичная Библіотека.) [With facsimiles.] *Russ.* pp. 169. 10. 1873. 8⁰. *See* LENINGRAD.—*Императорская,* afterwards *Государственная, Публичная Библіотека.*
10921. l. 6.

CATHARINE II., *Empress of Russia.* [LETTERS.—*Original languages.*]

—— Briefwechsel zwischen Leopold II., Franz II. und Catharina II. *Fr. See* LEOPOLD II., *Emperor of Germany.* Leopold II., Franz II und Catharina. Ihre Correspondenz, *etc.* 1874. 8⁰.
10920. i. 1.

—— [Correspondence with Gustavus III., King of Sweden.] *See* GROT (Ya. K.) Екатерина II. и Густавъ III. 1877. 8⁰. [*Сборникъ Отдѣленія русскаго языка и словесности Императорской Академіи Наукъ.* том. 18. no. 1.]
Ac. **1125/39.**

—— Письма Императрицы Екатерины II. къ Гримму, 1774–1796. Изданныя съ поясните́льными примѣчаніями Я. Грота. *Fr.* pp. viii. 734. *С.-Петербургъ*, 1878. 8⁰. [*Сборникъ Императорскаго Русскаго Историческаго Общества.* том. 23.] Ac. **7886.**

—— *See* GRIMM (F. M. von) *Baron.* Письма Гримма къ Императрицы Екатерины II, *etc.* (Préface du tome XXIII. Lettres de Catherine II à Grimm.—Notes du tome XXIII pour le texte des lettres de Catherine II à Grimm.) 1885. 8⁰. [*Сборникъ Императорскаго Русскаго Историческаго Общества.* том. 44.]
Ac. **7886.**

—— Политическая переписка Императрицы Екатерины II. (Изданъ барономъ Ф. А. Бюллеромъ, при содѣйствіи магистра Ульяницкаго.) [The majority in Russian, with Russian translations of the rest.] част. 1–9. *Москва, С.-Петербургъ*, 1885–1914. 8⁰. [*Сборникъ Императорскаго Русскаго Историческаго Общества.* том. 48, 51, 57, 67, 87, 97, 118, 135, 145.] Ac. **7886.**
No more published.

—— Письма Государыни Императрицы Екатерины Великой къ Фельдмаршалу Графу П. С. Салтыкову. 1762–1771. (Записка Императрицы Екатерины Великой о Рославльскомъ конномъ полку или Рязанскихъ драгунахъ. *Fr. & Russ.*) [With notes signed : П. Б., i.e. P. I. Bartenev.] pp. 110. *Москва*, 1886. 8⁰.
10921. l. 17.

—— Briefwechsel zwischen Heinrich Prinz von Preussen und Katharina II. von Russland. Von Dr. R. Krauel. *Fr.* pp. viii. 178. 1903. 8⁰. [*Quellen und Untersuchungen zur Geschichte des Hauses Hohenzollern.* Reihe 1. Bd. 2.] *See* FREDERICK HENRY LOUIS, *Prince of Prussia.*
9917. dd. 27.

—— Der Briefwechsel zwischen der Kaiserin Katharina II. von Russland und Joh. Georg Zimmermann (1785–1791). Herausgegeben von Dr. E. Bodemann. *Fr.* pp. xxv. 157. *Hannover & Leipzig*, 1906. 8⁰. **010910. c. 37.**

—— [Letters of Catharine II. to Stanislaus Augustus, King of Poland, 2 Aug. 1762—5 Jan. 1764.] *Fr.* 1914. *See* STANISLAUS AUGUSTUS [Poniatowski], *King of Poland.* Mémoires du roi Stanislas-Auguste Poniatowski. tom. 1. pt. 3. 1914, *etc.* 8⁰. **20010. cc. 37.**

—— Correspondance de Falconet avec Catherine II, 1767–1778. Publiée avec une introduction et des notes par L. Réau. *Fr.* pp. xliv. 274. 1921. 8⁰. [*Bibliothèque de l'Institut Français de Petrograd.* tom. 7.] *See* FALCONET (E. M.)
Ac. **1117.**

—— Les Lettres de Catherine II au prince de Ligne, 1780–1796. Publiées avec quelques notes par la princesse Charles de Ligne. [With a portrait.] *Fr.* pp. 236. *Bruxelles & Paris*, 1924. 8⁰. **10906. eee. 11.**

—— Documents of Catherine the Great. The Correspondence with Voltaire, and the " Instruction " of 1767 in the English text of 1768. Edited by W. F. Reddaway. pp. xxxii. 349. *University Press: Cambridge*, 1931. 8⁰.
010920. bb. 10.

CATHARINE II., *Empress of Russia.* [LETTERS.—*Original languages.*]

—— Correspondance artistique de Grimm avec Catherine II. Publiée par M. Louis Réau. [With plates, including portraits.] *Fr.* 1932. 8°. [*Archives de l'Art français. Nouvelle période.* tom. 17.] *See* GRIMM (F. M. von) *Baron.*   Ac. 4550/3.

—— Grande lettre de l'Impératrice envoyée le 2 août [1762], *etc. Fr. See* STANISLAUS AUGUSTUS [Poniatowski], *King of Poland.* Mémoires secrets et inédits de Stanislas Auguste . . . relatifs à ses rapports intimes avec l'impératrice Catherine II et à son avènement au trône, *etc.* 1862. 8°.   10790. aa. 28. (2.)

—— Письмо Императрицы Екатерины II-й къ графу П. И. Панину, главноначальствующему надъ войсками противу самозванца, Пугачова, въ отвѣтъ на доношенія его послѣ поимки послѣдняго. (20-го ноября. 1774 г.) *Russ. See* PUGACHEV (E. I.) Допросы Емельяну Пугачову, *etc.* 1858. 8°.   9455. de. 29. (1.)

Polyglot.

—— [Correspondence with Stanislaus Augustus, King of Poland, 2 Aug. 1762—5 Jan. 1764.] *Fr. & Pol. See* STANISLAUS AUGUSTUS [Poniatowski], *King of Poland.* Pamiętniki Stanisława Augusta Poniatowskiego, króla Polskiego, *etc.* 1862. 8°.   10795. bb. 36. (9.)

—— Письма Императрицы Екатерины II. къ Г-жѣ Жоффрень. [1763–1768.] Сообщено А. Ф. Гамбургеромъ. *Fr. & Russ.* 1867.   *See* LENINGRAD.—*Императорское Русское Историческое Общество.* Сборникъ, *etc.* том. I. 1867, *etc.* 8°.   Ac. 7886.

—— [Correspondence with the Grand Duke Paul Petrovich and the Grand Duchess Mary Theodorovna, 1783–90.] *Fr. & Russ.* 1875. *See* PAVLOVSK.—*Архивъ Дворца.* Бумаги изъ архива, *etc.* pt. 2. 1872, *etc.* 8°. [*Сборникъ Русскаго Историческаго Общества.* том. 15.] Ac. 7886.

—— Переписка Императрицы Екатерины II съ Фальконетомъ. [Edited with notes and appendices by A. A. Polovtsov.] *Fr. & Russ.* pp. xliv. 450. *С.-Петербургъ,* 1876. 8°. [*Сборникъ Русскаго Историческаго Общества.* том. 17.]   Ac. 7886.

—— Переписка Императрицы Екатерины II съ Королемъ Фридрихомъ II., *etc. Fr. & Russ.* 1877. *See* SAINT PETERSBURG.—*Императорское Русское Историческое Общество.* Сборникъ, *etc.* том. 20. 1867, *etc.* 8°.   Ac. 7886.

—— Письма Императрицы Екатерины II къ датской королевѣ Юліанѣ Маріи. (Священникъ I. Я. Щелкуновъ.) . . . Kejserinde Catharina II's breve til Enkedronning Juliane Marie. [With one from the latter and a résumé of the preface and introduction in Danish.] *Fr. & Russ.* pp. 147. *København,* 1914. 8°.   010902. f. 20.

Translations.

—— Letters and Notes of the Empress Catherine to the Princess Daschkaw, with four letters to Mlle. Leoffschin. *Eng. See* DASHKOVA (E. R.) *Princess.* Memoirs of the Princess Daschkaw, Lady of honour to Catherine II., *etc.* vol. 2. 1840. 8°.   1202. h. 20.

—— Correspondence of Catherine the Great, when Grand-Duchess, with Sir Charles Hanbury-Williams, and Letters from Count Poniatowski. Edited and translated by the Earl of Ilchester and Mrs. Langford-Brooke. (Introduction. By M. Serge Goriaïnov . . . Written in 1909.) [With portraits.] pp. 288. *Thornton Butterworth : London,* 1928. 8°.   10906. h. 29.

CATHARINE II., *Empress of Russia.* [LETTERS.—*Translations.*]

—— Lettres d'amour de Catherine II à Potemkine. Correspondance inédite. Publiée avec une introduction et des notes par Georges Oudard. [The translation of the Russian and standardizing of the French texts by A. Kashina.] [With portraits.] pp. 213. *Paris,* 1934. 8°.   010910. aa. 16.

—— [Letters, 1744–1745.] *Ger. See* SIEBIGK (F.) Katharina der Zweiten Brautreise nach Russland, *etc.* 1873. 8°.   10795. aaa. 15.

—— [Letters to Caroline, Landgravine of Hesse-Darmstadt, translated from the French.] *See* KEYSERLING (A. T. B.) *Countess.* Um eine deutsche Prinzessin. Ein Briefwechsel Friedrichs des Grossen, der Landgräfin Karoline von Hessen-Darmstadt und Katharinas II. von Russland, 1772–1774, *etc.* [1935.] 8°.   010910. aa. 43.

—— Письма Императрицы Екатерины II и четыре письма къ дѣвицѣ Левшиной. *Russ. See* DASHKOVA (E. R.) *Princess.* Записки . . . Переводъ съ англійскаго языка. 1859. 8°.   10790. cc. 30.

—— [Another edition.] *See* DASHKOVA (E. R.) *Princess.* Матеріалы для біографіи Княгини Е. Р. Дашковой, *etc.* [1875.] 8°. [*Собраніе матеріаловъ для исторіи возрожденія Россіи.* vol. 6.]   9455. aaa. 4.

—— [Selected letters to Baron Grimm translated into Russian.] *See* GROT (Ya. K.) Екатерина II. въ перепискѣ съ Гриммомъ. 1879, *etc.* 8°. [*Сборникъ Отдѣленія русскаго языка и словесности Императорской Академіи Наукъ.* том. 20. но. 1 ; том. 21. но. 4 ; том. 33. но. 4.]   Ac. 1125/39.

SINGLE WORKS.

—— Антидотъ—Противоядіе, *etc. See infra :* Antidote.

—— Были и небылицы. 7 pt. 1783. 8°. [*Собесѣдникъ любителей российскаго слова.* част. 2–8.] *See* BUILI. 011824. g. 48.

—— Вольное но слабое переложеніе изъ Шакеспира, комедія Вотъ каково имѣть корзину и бѣлье. [By Catharine II. Based on the "Merry Wives of Windsor."] pp. 106. 1787. 8°. [*Россійскій Өеатръ.* част. 14.] *See* SHAKESPEARE (W.) [*Merry Wives of Windsor.—Russian.*]   1343. h. 7.

—— *See* LIRONDELLE (A.) Catherine II., élève de Shakespeare. [A criticism of her adaptation of the "Merry Wives of Windsor."] [1908.] 8°.   11764. г. 2

—— Вопроситель. *See infra :* Невѣста невидимка.

—— Вотъ каково имѣть корзину и бѣлье. *See supra :* Вольное но слабое переложеніе изъ Шекспира, *etc.*

—— Госпожа Вѣстникова съ семьею. Комедія въ одномъ дѣйствіи. Сочинена въ Ярославлѣ. [By Catharine II.] 1786. 8°. [*Россійскій Өеатръ.* част. 11.] *See* VYESTNIKOVA, *Gospozha.*   1343. h. 6.

—— *See* GROT (Ya. K.) Екатерина II. и Густавъ III. (Приложенія:—I. "Горе-Богатырь" Екатерины II. [Maintaining that this work is a satire on Gustavus III.]) 1877. 8°. [*Сборникъ Отдѣленія русскаго языка и словесности Императорской Академіи Наукъ.* том. 18. no. 1.]   Ac. 1125/39.

—— [Гражданское и начальное ученіе.—III. Разговоры и сказки.] Erzählungen und Gespräche. Von I.K.M.d.K.a.R. [i.e. Ihrer Kaiserlichen Majestät der Kaiserin aller Reussen.] [Edited by C. F. Nicolai.] Tl. 1–8. 1783–88. 8°. *See* R., I. K. M. d. K. a.   1313. d. 32–35.

—— [Гражданское и начальное учение.—III. Разговоры и сказки.] [Another copy of Tl. 1–7.] Erzählungen und Gespräche. Von I. K. M. d. K. a. R. [i.e. Ihrer Kaiserlichen Majestät der Kaiserin aller Reussen.] 1783–86. 8°. *See* R., I. K. M. d. K. a. **243. h. 14–16.**

—— Опера комическая Февей, составлена изъ словъ сказки, пѣсней рускихъ и иныхъ сочиненій. [Based on " Сказка о царевичѣ Февеѣ " by Catharine II. published in " Гражданское и начальное ученіе."] pp. 54. 1788. 8°. [*Россійскій Театръ.* част. 20.] *See* FEVEI. **1343. h. 10.**

—— Ivan Czarowitz ; or, the Rose without prickles that stings not. A tale . . . Translated from the Russian language. [A translation of " Сказка о царевичѣ Хлорѣ " from " Гражданское и начальное ученіе."] pp. 29. *Robinson & Sons : London,* 1793. 8°. **N. 2048. (1.)**

—— Хлоръ Царевичь или роза безъ шиповъ, которая не колется, иносказательное зрѣлище въ трехъ дѣйствіяхъ. 1786 года. [An opera, adapted from the story by Catharine II., " Сказка о Царевичѣ Хлорѣ," published in " Гражданское и начальное ученіе."] 1788. 8°. [*Россійскій Театръ.* част. 23.] *See* CHLORUS, *Tsarevich.* **1343. h. 12.**

—— Дѣтскіе разговоры. [Enclosed in a letter from Catharine II., who was probably the author.] 1872. 8°. [*Сборникъ Русскаго Историческаго Общества.* том. 9.] *See* RAZGOVORUI. **Ac. 7886.**

—— Записка Императрицы Екатерины Великой о Рославльскомъ Конномъ Полку или Рязанскихъ Драгунахъ. *Fr. & Russ.* 1886. *See supra :* LETTERS.—*Original languages.* Письма . . . Императрицы Екатерины Великой къ Фельдмаршалу Графу П. С. Салтыкову, *etc.* 1886. 8°. **10921. l. 17.**

—— Записки Императрицы Екатерины II. *See infra :* Mémoires de l'Impératrice Catherine II., écrits par elle-même.

—— Записки касательно россійской исторіи. [By Catharine II. The publication was continued in част. 13–15.] Эпоха 1, 2. 1783, 84. 8°. [*Собесѣдникъ любителей россійскаго слова.* част. 1–12.] *See* RUSSIA. [*Appendix.—History and Politics.*] **011824. g. 48.**

—— Записки касательно россійской исторіи. [By Catharine II.] 6 част. 1787–94. 8°. *See* RUSSIA. [*Appendix.—History and Politics.*] **1312. f. 7–11.**

—— [Another copy.] Записки касательно Россійской Исторіи. Сочиненіе Государыни Императрицы Екатерины II. 6 част. *Въ Санктпетербургѣ,* 1801, 1793. 8°. **9457. bb. 18.**
Част. 1–4 have only the cancel titlepages, dated 1801. *Част. 5 has the original titlepage, dated* 1793. *Част. 6 has no titlepage.*

—— Aufsätze betreffend die russische Geschichte. Von I.K.M.d.K.a.R. [i.e. Ihrer Kaiserlichen Majestät der Kaiserin aller Reussen.] [Translated from the Russian by C. G. Arndt.] 7 Bd. 1786–88. 8°. *See* R., I. K. M. d. K. a. **9454. aaaa. 2.**

—— [Another edition.] 2 Tl. 1787. 8°. *See* RUSSIA. [*Appendix.—History and Politics.*] **9454. bb. 8.**

—— Имянины Госпожи Ворчалкиной. Комедія . . . въ пяти дѣйствіяхъ, сочинена въ Ярославлѣ. [By Catharine II.] 1786. 8°. [*Россійскій Театръ.* част. 11.] *See* VORCHALKINA, *Gospozha.* **1343. h. 6.**

—— Комедія Обманщикъ. *See infra :* Обманщикъ.

—— Комедія Обольщенный. *See infra :* Обольщенный.

—— Комедія Разстроенная семья осторожками и подозрѣніями. *See infra :* Разстроенная семья, *etc.*

—— Комедія Шаманъ Сибирской. *See infra :* Шаманъ Сибирской.

—— [For editions of " Матеріалы Екатерининской Законодательной Комиссіи ":] *See* RUSSIA.—*Коммиссія о сочиненіи проекта Новаго Уложенія.*

—— [For editions of " Наказъ, данный Коммиссіи о сочиненіи проэкта новаго Уложенія " :] *See* RUSSIA. [*Laws, etc.*—D. ii. *Instruction on the New Code.*]

—— Начальное управленіе Олега. Подражаніе Шакеспиру, *etc.* [By Catharine II.] 1787. 8°. [*Россійскій Театръ.* част. 14.] *See* OLEG, *Grand Duke of Russia.* **1343. h. 7.**

—— Невѣста невидимка. Комедія въ одномъ дѣйствіи. Сочинена въ Ярославлѣ. [By Catharine II. Originally entitled " Вопроситель."] 1786. 8°. [*Россійскій Театръ.* част. 12.] *See* NEVYESTA. **1343. h. 6.**

—— Недоразумѣнія, комедія, въ пяти дѣйствіяхъ, *etc.* [By Catharine II.] 1789. 8°. [*Россійскій Театръ.* част. 31.] *See* NEDORAZUMYENIYA. **1343. h. 16.**

—— Новогородской Богатырь Боеславичь, опера комическая, составлена изъ сказки, пѣсней рускихъ, и иныхъ сочиненій. [By Catharine II.] 1788. 8°. [*Россійскій Театръ.* част. 20.] *See* BOESLAVICH'. **1343. h. 10.**

—— О время ! Комедія въ трехъ дѣйствіяхъ. Сочинена въ Ярославлѣ во время чумы 1772 года. [By Catharine II.] 1786. 8°. [*Россійскій Театръ.* част. 11.] *See* VREMYA. **1343. h. 6.**

—— O temps ! O mœurs ! Comédie en trois actes, composée . . . en 1772, par l'Impératrice Catherine II. et traduite du russe en français, par M. Leclerc. Imprimée pour la Société des Bibliophiles Français. Année 1826. pp. 78. 1827. *See* PARIS.—*Société des Bibliophiles Français.* Mélanges, *etc.* tom. 5. 1820, *etc.* 8°. **Ac. 8933/5. (5.)**

—— Комедія Обманщикъ. Вторымъ тисненіемъ. [An attack on Cagliostro. By Catharine II.] pp. 70. 1786. 8°. *See* OBMANSHCHIK. **G. 18502. (2.)**

—— Обманщикъ. Комедія въ пяти дѣйствіяхъ. [By Catharine II.] pp. 80. 1787. 8°. [*Россійскій Театръ.* част. 13.] *See* OBMANSHCHIK. **1343. h. 7.**

—— Der Betrüger, ein Lustspiel. Aus dem Russischen übersezt. pp. 64. 1786. 8°. *See* BETRUEGER. **11758. bbb. 54.**

—— Комедія Обольщенный. [By Catharine II.] pp. 88. [1786.] 8°. *See* OBOL'SHCHENNUY. **G. 18502. (3.)**

—— Обольщенный, комедія въ пяти дѣйствіяхъ. 1787. 8°. [*Россійскій Театръ.* част. 13.] *See* OBOL'SHCHENNUY. **1343. h. 7.**

—— Опера комическая Февей, *etc. See supra :* Гражданское и начальное ученіе.

—— Опера комическая, Храброй и смѣлой витязь Ахридѣичь. *See infra :* Храброй и смѣлой витязь Ахридѣичь.

—— Передняя знатнаго боярина. Комедія въ одномъ дѣйствіи, сочинена въ городѣ Ярославлѣ, *etc.* [By Catharine II.] 1786. 8°. [*Россійскій Театръ.* част. 11.] *See* PEREDNYAYA. **1343. h. 6.**

—— Подражаніе Шакеспиру, историческое представленіе безъ сохраненія ѳеатральныхъ обыкновенныхъ правилъ, изъ жизни Рюрика. [By Catharine ii.] 1787. 8⁰. [*Россійскій Ѳеатръ.* част. 14.] *See* Rurik, *Grand Duke of Russia.* **1343. h. 7.**

—— [Another edition.] Вновь изданное съ примѣчаніями Генералъ Маіора И. Болтина. pp. xlvi. 59. 1792. 8⁰. *See* Rurik, *Grand Duke of Russia.* **1343. i. 2.**

—— Imitation de Schakespear, scène historique, sans observation d'aucune règle du théâtre, tirée de la vie de Rurick, *etc.* [Extracted from a copy of tom. 2 of "Théâtre de l'Hermitage de Cathérine ii."] [1799.] 8⁰. **11738. bbb. 33. (6.)**

—— Проектъ Императрицы Екатерины ii. объ устройствѣ свободныхъ сельскихъ обывателей. Сообщено В. И. Вешняковымъ. 1877. *See* Leningrad. —*Императорское Русское Историческое Общество.* Сборникъ, *etc.* том. 20. 1867, *etc.* 8⁰. **Ac. 7886.**

—— Комедія Разстроенная семья осторожками и подозрѣніями. [By Catharine ii.] 1788. 8⁰. [*Россійскій Ѳеатръ.* част. 20.] *See* Sem'ya. **1343. h. 10.**

—— Der Familienzwist, durch falsche Warnung und Argwohn. Ein Lustspiel in fünf Aufzügen. [An adaptation of Разстроенная семья.] Von I. K. M. d. K. a. R. [i.e. Ihrer Kaiserlichen Majestät der Kaiserin aller Reussen.] 1789. 8⁰. [*Deutsche Schaubühne.* Bd. 9.] *See* R., I. K. M. d.K. a. **752. a. 1/9.**

—— Родословникъ князей великихъ и удѣльныхъ рода Рюрика. (Родословникъ, служащій такъ же пятою частію Записокъ касательно россійской Исторіи, продается у Іоанна Вейтбрехта.) [By Catharine ii.] pp. 277. 1793. 8⁰. *See* Rurik, *House of.* **9915. a. 16.**

—— Хлоръ Царевичь, *etc. See* supra: Гражданское и начальное ученіе.

—— Опера комическая, Храброй и смѣлой витязь Ахридѣичь. [By Catharine ii.] 1788. 8⁰. [*Россійскій Ѳеатръ.* част. 20.] *See* Ivan Akhridyeich, *Tsarevich.* **1343. h. 10.**

—— Комедія: Шаманъ Сибирской. [By Catharine ii.] pp. 108. 1786. 8⁰. *See* Siberian Wizard. **G. 18502. (1).**

—— Шаманъ Сибирской. Комедія въ пяти дѣйствіяхъ. 1787. 8⁰. [*Россійскій Ѳеатръ.* част. 13.] *See* Siberian Wizard. **1343. h. 7.**

—— Antidote 1770. (Antidote, ou Examen du mauvais livre . . . intitulé: "Voyage en Siberie . . . Par M. l'Abbé Chappe d'Auteroche . . . mdcclxviii.") [By Catharine ii.] pt. 1, 2. 1770. 8⁰. *See* Chappe d'Auteroche (J.) **10292. b. 8.**

—— The Antidote; or, an Enquiry into the merits of a book, entitled "A Journey into Siberia" . . . In which many essential errors . . . are pointed out . . . By a Lover of Truth [i.e. Catharine ii.]. Translated . . . by a Lady. pp. iv. 202. 1772. 8⁰. *See* Chappe d'Auteroche (J.) **979. i. 1.**

—— Антидотъ — Противоядіе — Полемическое сочиненіе Государыни Императрицы Екатерины Второй. Переводъ съ французскаго подлинника. 1869. *See* Bartenev (P. I.) Осмнадцатый вѣкъ, *etc.* кн. 4. 1868, *etc.* 8⁰. **9455. e. 26.**

—— Aufsätze betreffend die russische Geschichte. *See* supra: Записки касательно россійской исторіи.

—— Der Betrüger. *See* supra: Обманщикъ.

—— Description d'une mascarade donnée à St.-Pétersbourg au Palais d'Hiver, lors du séjour du Prince Henry de Prusse en cette capitale, *etc.* [By Catharine ii. From the Empress's autograph.] pp. 24. [1856.] 8⁰. [*Журналъ Камеръ-Фурьерскій.* pt. 40.] *See* Frederick Henry Louis, *Prince of Prussia.* **10795. g. 72.**

—— Der Familienzwist durch falsche Warnung und Argwohn. *See* supra: Разстроенная семья осторожками и подозрѣніями.

—— Le Flatteur et les flattés, proverbe, *etc.* [Extracted from a copy of tom. 1 of "Théâtre de l'Hermitage de Catherine ii."] [*Paris*, 1799.] 8⁰. **11738. bbb. 33. (3.)**

—— Il n'y a point de mal sans bien, *etc.* [Extracted from a copy of tom. 2 of "Théâtre de l'Hermitage de Catherine ii."] [*Paris*, 1799.] 8⁰. **11738. bbb. 33. (5.)**

—— Imitation de Schakespear, scène historique . . . tirée de la vie de Rurick. *See* supra: Подражаніе Шакеспиру.

—— Ivan Czarowitz. *See* supra: Гражданское и начальное ученіе.

—— Mémoire de Catherine ii sur la Révolution en 1792. *See* Larivière (Charles de) Catherine le grand d'après sa correspondance, *etc.* 1895. 8⁰. **010795. de. 83.**

—— Mémoires de l'Impératrice Catherine ii., écrits par elle-même, et précédés d'une préface par A. Herzen, *etc.* pp. xvi. 352. *Trübner & Cⁱᵉ.: Londres*, 1859 [1858]. 8⁰. **10790. c. 22.**

—— Seconde édition, revue et augmentée de huit lettres de Pierre iii, et d'une lettre de Catherine ii. au Comte Poniatowsky. pp. xvi. 370. *Trübner & Cⁱᵉ: Londres*, 1859. 8⁰. **10790. c. 11.**

—— Memoirs of the Empress Catherine ii., written by Herself. With a preface by A. Herzen. Translated from the French [of the second edition]. pp. xvi. 352. *Trübner & Co.: London*, 1859. 8⁰. **10790. a. 32.**

—— Memoirs of Catherine the Great. Translated by Katharine Anthony. (Based on the German edition by Erich Boehme.) [With plates, including portraits and a facsimile of a letter from Lafayette.] pp. ix. 337. *A. A. Knopf: New York & London*, 1927. 8⁰. **010795. dd. 29.**

—— The Memoirs of Catherine the Great. Edited by Dominique Maroger. With an introduction by Dr. G. P. Gooch, C.H. Translated from the French by Moura Budberg. [With plates, including a portrait.] pp. 400. *Hamish Hamilton: London*, 1955. 8⁰. **10798. ee. 10.**

—— Memoiren der Kaiserin Katharina ii. Nach den von der Kaiserlich Russischen Akademie der Wissenschaften veröffentlichten Manuskripten übersetzt und herausgegeben von Erich Boehme. [With portraits.] 2 Bd. *Leipzig*, 1913. 8⁰. **010790. df. 69.**

—— Записки Императрицы Екатерины ii. Изданіе Искандера. Переводъ съ французскаго. [Translated from Herzen's second edition, with an altered and abbreviated preface.] pp. viii. 277. *Trübner & Co.: London*, 1859. 8⁰. **10790. c. 10.**

—— Erinnerungen Katharina der Zweiten nach ihren eigenen Memoiren. [An abridged translation of the edition of 1859.] Deutsch von K. von Alvensleben. pp. 162. *Berlin*, [1900.] 8⁰. [*Das Weiberregiment an den Höfen Europas, etc.* Bd. 3.] **09078. aa. 54.**

CATHARINE II., *Empress of Russia.* [SINGLE WORKS.]

—— Katharina II. in ihren Memoiren. Aus dem Französischen und Russischen übersetzt und herausgegeben von Erich Boehme. Mit 16 Bildnissen. [An abridgment.] pp. xx. 467. *Leipzig,* 1923. 8°. 010795. aaa. 33.

—— O temps ! O mœurs ! *See* supra : О время !

—— La Rage aux proverbes. [Extracted from a copy of tom. 1 of " Théâtre de l'Hermitage de Catherine II."] [*Paris,* 1799.] 8°. 11738. bbb. 33. (2.)

—— Le Tracassier, proverbe. [Extracted from a copy of tom. 1 of " Théâtre de l'Hermitage de Catherine II."] [*Paris,* 1799.] 8°. 11738. bbb. 33. (1.)

—— Les Voyages de M. Bontems, proverbe. [Extracted from a copy of tom. 2 of " Théâtre de l'Hermitage de Catherine II."] [*Paris,* 1799.] 8°. 11738. bbb. 33. (4.)

WORKS EDITED, TRANSLATED OR WITH PREFACES BY CATHARINE II.

—— *See* MARMONTEL (J. F.) Велизеръ . . . Переведенъ на Волгѣ, *etc.* [Translated by the suite of Catharine II., under her supervision. The ninth chapter translated by Catharine herself.] 1785. 8°. G. 17602.

—— *See* PERIODICAL PUBLICATIONS.— *Leningrad,* Библіографическая рѣдкость " Всякая Всячина " 1769 г., *etc.* [Edited by G. V. Kozitsky for Catharine II.] 1893. 4°. 1866. c. 2.

—— *See* RUSSIAN LITERATURE. Собесѣдникъ любителей россійскаго слова, *etc.* [Edited by Catharine II. and Princess E. R. Dashkova.] 1783, *etc.* 8°. 011824. g. 48.

APPENDIX.

BIOGRAPHY.

I. *General.*

—— *See* ALEXEI, *Prince de* G . . . . . Catherine II de Russie et ses favoris, *etc.* [1874.] 16°. 10790. a. 1.

—— *See* ANDREESCU (C. I.) La France et la politique orientale de Catherine II, *etc.* 1927, *etc.* 8°. [*Mélanges de l'École roumaine en France.* 1927 ; 1929. pt. 1.] Ac. 743. g.

—— *See* ANTHONY (Katharine S.) Catherine the Great. 1926. 8°. 10790. h. 4.

—— —— 1930. 8°. 010795. aaa. 88.

—— *See* ARKHANGEL'SKY (A. S.) Императрица Екатерина II. въ исторіи русской литературы и образованія. 1897. 8°. 9456. ee. 15.

—— *See* ARETZ (G.) [Eine Frau regiert.] The Empress Catherine. [With portraits.] 1947. 8°. 10797. ee. 69.

—— *See* ARETZ (G.) Kaiserin Katharina II. [With portraits.] 1946. 8°. 10797. f. 34.

—— *See* BIL'BASOV (V. A.) Исторія Екатерины Второй. 1895. 8°. 010795. ee. 18.

—— —— 1900. 8°. 010795. k. 30.

—— *See* BIL'BASOV (V. A.) Geschichte Katharina II. . . . Bd. XII: Katharina im Urtheile der Weltliteratur, *etc.* [A bibliography.] 1897. 8°. 010795. e. 2.

—— *See* BRIKNER (A. G.) Katharina die Zweite . . . Mit Portraits, *etc.* 1883. 8°. [*ONCKEN* (N.) *Allgemeine Geschichte in Einzeldarstellungen.* Hauptabt. 3. Tl. 10.] 9012. de. 1/26.

CATHARINE II., *Empress of Russia.* [APPENDIX.—BIOGRAPHY.—I. *General.*]

—— *See* BRIKNER (A. G.) Исторія Екатерины Второй, *etc.* [With portraits.] 1885. 8°. 10790. ee. 18.

—— *See* BRYANCHANINOV (N. V.) Catherine II, impératrice de Russie, *etc.* [With portraits.] 1932. 8°. 010795. g. 51.

—— *See* CAPEFIGUE (J. B. H. R.) La Grande Cathérine, impératrice de Russie. [With a portrait.] 1862. 12°. 10790. aa. 8.

—— *See* CARO (J.) Katharina II. von Russland, *etc.* 1876. 8°. 10602. i. 6. (8.)

—— *See* CASTÉRA (J. H.) Histoire de Catherine II, Impératrice de Russie. Avec seize portraits, *etc.* [1800.] 8°. 151. c. 9–11.

—— *See* CASTÉRA (J. H.) History of Catharine II, *etc.* 1800. 8°. 1200. f. 27.

—— *See* CHULA, *Prince.* The Education of the Enlightened Despots. A review of the youth of . . . Catherine II of Russia. 1948. 8°. 010604. cc. 12.

—— *See* DASHKOVA (E. R.) *Princess.* Memoiren der Fürstin Daschkoff. Zur Geschichte der Kaiserin Katharina II., *etc.* 1857. 8°. 10790. a. 11.

—— *See* DIRIN (P. P.) Великая Княгиня Екатерина Алексѣевна, 1729–1761 г., *etc.* [With a portrait.] 1884. 8°. 10795. ee. 32.

—— *See* DREIFUSS (J.) The Romance of Catherine and Potemkin. [With portraits.] [1938.] 8°. 010795. m. 3.

—— *See* DU BOUZET (C.) La Jeunesse de Catherine II. 1860. 8°. 10790. b. 21. (6.)

—— *See* ELMÉN (C.) Kejsarinnan Catarina II:s Lefverne. 1809. 8°. 1200. f. 15.

—— *See* GLINKA (S. N.) Русское чтеніе, *etc.* (част. 2. Духъ вѣка Екатерины Второй. [A biographical study.]) 1845. 8°. 9455. d. 18.

—— *See* GOLDSMITH (Margaret L.) Studies in Aggression. (Catherine the Great, 1729–1796. [With a portrait.]) 1948. 8°. 09078. c. 65.

—— *See* GRIBBLE (Francis H.) The Comedy of Catherine the Great. [With portraits.] 1912. 8°. 10795. df. 3.

—— *See* GRIBOVSKY (A. M.) Записки о Екатеринѣ Великой, состоявшаго при ея особѣ Статсъ-Секретаря . . . А. М. Грибовскаго, *etc.* 1847. 8°. 10790. dd. 19.

—— —— 1864. 8°. 10790. e. 30. (5.)

—— *See* GRIMM (F. M. von) *Baron.* Историческая записка о происхожденіи . . . моей . . . преданности Императрицѣ Екатеринѣ II., *etc.* *Fr. & Russ.* 1868. 8°. [*Сборникъ Русскаго Историческаго Общества.* том. 2.] Ac. 7886.

—— *See* HAIGOLD (J. J.) *pseud.* Neuverändertes Russland oder Leben Catharinä der zweyten Kayserinn von Russland, *etc.* [With a portrait.] 1767. 8°. 10795. aa. 8.

—— —— 1771, 72. 8°. 150. d. 2, 3.

—— *See* HAIGOLD (J. J.) *pseud.* M. Johann Joseph Haigold's Beylagen zum Neuveränderten Russland. 1769, 70. 8°. 150. a. 1, 2.

—— *See* HODGETTS (E. A. B.) The Life of Catherine the Great, *etc.* [With portraits.] [1914.] 8°. 010790. h. 27.

CATHARINE II., *Empress of Russia*. [APPENDIX.—BIO-
GRAPHY.—I. *General*.]

—— *See* HOFFMANN-HARNISCH (W.) Die grosse Katharina.
Geschichte einer Karriere. [With portraits.] [1936.] 8º.
20012. f. 17.

—— *See* HYDE (Harford M.) The Empress Catherine and
Princess Dashkov. [With an appendix containing
" Unpublished Fragments of Conversations between
Catherine II and Princess Dashkov ". With portraits.]
1935. 8º. **10796. cc. 2.**

—— *See* JAUFFRET (E.) Catherine II et son règne. 1860. 8º.
9455. bb. 2.

—— *See* JUSTE (T.) La Grande Catherine, *etc.* 1889. 8º.
10790. bbb. 38.

—— *See* KAUS (G.) Katharina die Grosse, *etc.* [With portraits.] [1935.] 8º. **20003. f. 56.**

—— *See* KAUS (G.) Catherine the Great, *etc.* [With portraits.] 1935. 8º. **20020. aaa. 5.**

—— *See* KOLOTOV (P. S.) Дѣянія Екатерины II, Императрицы . . . Всероссійскія. [With a portrait.] 1811. 8º.
611. e. 32.

—— *See* KOROVINA (D. F.) *Countess*. Katharina II. als
Grossfürstin und Kaiserin von Russland . . . Mit . . .
Porträtbeilagen. 1912. 8º. **10795. de. 28.**

—— *See* KOTZEBUE (A. F. F. von) [*Miscellaneous Writings*.]
Das merkwürdigste Jahr meines Lebens, *etc.* (Anhang.
[By A. T. J. A. M. M. de Fortia de Piles.] Ueber die
Mémoires secrets sur la Russie [i.e. " Mémoires secrets
sur la Russie, et particulièrement sur la fin du règne de
Catherine II." by C. F. P. Masson].) 1801. 8º.
10707. bb. 5.

—— *See* KOTZEBUE (A. F. F. von) [*Miscellaneous Writings*.]
The Most Remarkable Year in the Life of Augustus von
Kotzebue, *etc.* (Appendix. An examination of a work
entitled " Secret Memoirs of the Court of Russia.")
1802. 12º. **10707. aaa. 25.**

—— *See* KOTZEBUE (A. F. F. von) [*Miscellaneous Writings*.]
Une Année mémorable de la vie d'Auguste de Kotzebue,
etc. (Appendice. Examen de l'ouvrage intitulé Mémoires
secrets sur la Russie.) 1802. 12º. **614. d. 31.**

—— *See* KOTZEBUE (A. F. F. von) [*Miscellaneous Writings*.]
Kurze und gelassene Antwort des Herrn von Kotzebue
auf eine lange und heftige Schmähschrift des Herrn von
Masson [entitled : "Lettres d'un Français à un Allemand,"
in reply to criticisms of his "Mémoires secrets sur la
Russie."] 1802. 8º. **011824. ee. 37.**

—— *See* KOTZEBUE (A. F. F. von) [*Miscellaneous Writings*.]
Nöthige Erläuterungen zu der Schrift des Herrn von
Kotzebue : Das merkwürdigste Jahr meines Lebens. Von
einem Freunde der Wahrheit [i.e. J. C. Kaffka]. [Re-
lating to Catharine II.] 1802. 8º. **614. c. 31.**

—— *See* LAPPO-DANILEVSKY (A. S.) Очеркъ внутренней
политики Императрицы Екатерины II. 1898. 8º.
9004. m. 13. (5.)

—— *See* LAVATER-SLOMAN (M.) Catherine II et son temps,
etc. [With portraits.] 1952. 8º. **10798. aa. 52.**

—— *See* LEFORT (A. A.) Исторія царствованія Государыни
Императрицы Екатерины II. 1837, *etc.* 8º. **9454. e. 3.**

—— *See* MAKAROVA (S.) Царствованіе Екатерины II.
Историческій очеркъ разсказанный для юношества, *etc.*
1875. 8º. **9454. g. 5.**

—— *See* MARCARD (H. M.) Zimmermanns Verhältnisse mit
der Kayserin Catharina II. und mit dem Herrn Weikard,
etc. 1803. 8º. **010920. e. 10.**

CATHARINE II., *Empress of Russia*. [APPENDIX.—BIO-
GRAPHY.—I. *General*.]

—— *See* MASSON (C. F. P.) Mémoires secrets sur la Russie
et particulièrement sur la fin du règne de Catherine II
et le commencement de celui de Paul Ier, ou Lettres en
réponse à M. de Kotzebue, auteur d'Une Année la plus
remarquable de ma vie . . . Tome quatrième. 1803. 8º.
282. k. 20.

—— *See* MASSON (C. F. P.) Mémoires secrets sur la Russie
. . . Tome quatrième, *etc.* (Un Mot à l'auteur de
l'Examen de trois ouvrages sur la Russie [i.e. A. T. J. A.
M. M. de Fortia de Piles].) 1804. 8º. **1056. g. 15. (2.)**

—— *See* MASSON (C. F. P.) Major Masson's geheime Denkwürdigkeiten über Russland, *etc.* [Chiefly relating to
Catharine II.] 1844. 8º. [*Bibliothek auserwählter
Memoiren des XVIII. und XIX. Jahrhunderts*. Bd. 2.]
1426. h. 17.

—— *See* MASSON (C. F. P.) Mémoires secrets sur la Russie
pendant les règnes de Catherine II et de Paul Ier, *etc.* [An
abridgment.] 1859. 12º. [*BARRIÈRE (J. F.) Bibliothèque des mémoires*. tom. 22.] **10662. bb. 17.**

—— *See* MAZZUCCHELLI (M.) La Semiramide del Nord,
Caterina II di Russia, *etc.* [With portraits.] 1931. 8º.
010795. ee. 61.

—— *See* MILYUKOV (P. N.) Catherine II. [With a portrait.]
1936. 8º. [*Hommes d'état*. vol. 3.] **010604.b.2.**

—— *See* MURAT (M.) *Princess Lucien Murat*. La Grande
Catherine, *etc.* [With portraits.] 1932. 8º.
010795. i. 78.

—— *See* MURAT (M.) *Princess Lucien Murat*. The Private
Life of Catherine the Great, *etc.* [With a portrait.]
1928. 8º. **010795. aaa. 73.**

—— *See* PEKARSKY (P. P.) Матеріалы для исторіи
журнальной и литературной дѣятельности Екатерины II.
[With specimens of her literary works.] 1863. 8º.
[*Записки Императорской Академіи Наукъ*. том. 3.
прил. no. 6.] **Ac. 1125/48.**

—— *See* PETER III., *Emperor of Russia*. [*Appendix.—Biography.—I*.] The History of the Reigns of Peter III. and
Catharine II. of Russia. Translated from the French
[i.e. from J. H. Castéra's " Vie de Cathérine II "], *etc.*
1798. 8º. **9455. c. 23.**

—— *See* POKROVSKY (V. I.) Екатерина II. Ея жизнь и
сочиненія. Сборникъ историко-литературныхъ статей,
etc. 1905. 8º. **010790. g. 35.**

—— *See* POLOVTSOV (A.) Les Favoris de Catherine la Grande,
etc. 1939. 8º. **10797. b. 16.**

—— *See* POLOVTSOV (A.) The Favourites of Catherine the
Great. [With a portrait.] 1940. 8º. **10797. b. 37.**

—— *See* QUIBERON (P.) Catherine the Great . . . With presentation portrait of E. Bergner (as Catharine the Great),
etc. [1934.] 8º. **10795. p. 7.** & **Cup. 649. d. 11. (2.)**

—— *See* RÉAU (L.) Catherine la Grande, inspiratrice d'art
et Mécène. [With portraits.] 1930. 4º.
10790. pp. 13.

—— *See* ROMANA (A.) Le Tre Caterine. (Caterina II di
Russia.) 1921. 8º. **010603. b. 8.**

—— *See* RUSSIA. [*Appendix.—History and Politics*.] Mémoires secrets sur la Russie, et particulièrement sur la
fin du règne de Catherine II. et le commencement de celui
de Paul I, *etc.* [By C. F. P. Masson. With portraits.]
1800. 8º. **282. k. 17, 18.**

—— —— 1800, *etc.* 8º. **10292. cc. 1.** & **282. k. 19.**

CATHARINE II., *Empress of Russia.* [APPENDIX.—BIO-GRAPHY.—I. *General.*]

—— *See* RUSSIA. [*Appendix.—History and Politics.*] Mémoires secrets sur la Russie, et particulièrement sur la fin du règne de Catherine II et sur celui de Paul I . . . Tome troisième. [By C. F. P. Masson. With a portrait.] 1802. 8º.　　　　　　　　　　　　　**1056. g. 15. (1.)**

—— *See* RUSSIA. [*Appendix.—History and Politics.*] Mémoires secrets sur la Russie, et particulièrement sur la fin du règne de Catherine II et sur celui de Paul I, *etc.* [By C. F. P. Masson.] 1804. 8º.　　　　　　**1056. g. 14.**

—— *See* SAINT PETERSBURG, *Court of.* Secret Memoirs of the Court of Petersburg : particularly towards the end of the reign of Catharine II. and the commencement of that of Paul I. . . . Translated from the French [i.e. from " Mémoires secrets sur la Russie " by C. F. P. Masson]. 1800. 8º.　　　　　　　　　　　**10290. cc. 35.**

—— —— 1895. 8º.　　　　　　　　　　**10290. cc. 1.**

—— *See* SAINT-JEAN (　　) *Sekretär des Fürsten Potemkin, pseud.* Lebensbeschreibung des Gregor Alexandrowitsch Potemkin . . . Als Beitrag zu der Lebensgeschichte der Kaiserin Catharina II. . . . Herausgegeben von [or probably written by] F. Rothermel. 1888. 8º.
　　　　　　　　　　　　　　10790. bbb. 36.

—— *See* SCHLEGELBERGER (G.) Die Fürstin Daschkowa. Eine biographische Studie zur Geschichte Katharinas II. 1935. 8º.　　　　　　**012213.y.1/24.**

—— *See* SCHLOEZER (K. von) Friedrich der Grosse und Katharina die Zweite. (Eine Darstellung der Beziehungen Friedrichs des Zweiten zum russischen Hofe vom Jahre 1740 bis 1772.) 1859. 8º.　**9385.b.21.**

—— *See* SCHNITZLER (J. H.) Catherine II ,Impératrice de Russie et sa cour, *etc.* 1864. 8º. [*Société Littéraire de Strasbourg. Lectures publiques.* Avril, mai et juin 1864.]
　　　　　　　　　　　　　　Ac. 8940/2.

—— *See* SERGEANT (Philip W.) The Courtships of Catherine the Great. [With portraits.] 1905. 8º.
　　　　　　　　　　　　　　010795. ee. 29.

—— —— [1910.] 8º.　　　　　　　**010790. df. 60.**

—— —— 1925. 8º.　　　　　　　　**010795. b. 42.**

—— *See* STANISLAUS AUGUSTUS [Poniatowski], *King of Poland.* Mémoires secrets et inédits de Stanislas Auguste, Comte Poniatowski, dernier roi de Pologne, rélatifs à ses relations intimes avec l'impératrice Catherine II, *etc.* 1862. 8º.　　　　　　**10790. aa. 28. (2.)**

—— —— 1914, *etc.* 8º.　　　　　　**20010.cc. 37.**

—— *See* STANISLAUS AUGUSTUS [Poniatowski], *King of Poland.* Pamiętniki Stanisława Augusta Poniatowskiego, króla Polskiego, *etc.* [On his relations with Catharine II.] 1862. 8º.　　　　　　**10795. bb. 36. (9.)**

—— *See* STEPANOV (A. V.) Екатерина II. Ея . . . интимная жизнь, *etc.* 1895. 8º.　　**10790. b. 23.**

—— *See* SUMAROKOV (P. I.) Обозрѣніе царствованія и свойствъ Екатерины Великія. 1832. 8º.
　　　　　　　　　　　　　　10790. dd. 31.

—— *See* SUMAROKOV (P. I.) Черты Екатерины Великія. 1819. 8º.　　　　　　　**10790. c. 23.**

—— *See* TANNENBERG (G. von) *Baron.* Leben Catharina II. Kaiserin . . . aller Reussen, *etc.* [With a portrait.] 1797. 8º.　　　　　　　　**1449. f. 18.**

—— *See* TOURNEUX (M.) Diderot et Catherine II. 1899. 8º.　　　　　　　　**10661. p. 8.**

CATHARINE II., *Empress of Russia.* [APPENDIX.—BIO-GRAPHY.—I. *General.*]

—— *See* VINOGRADOV (A. A.) Императрица Екатерина II. и западный край. Значеніе царствованія императрицы для края и памятникъ ей въ г. Вильнѣ, *etc.* [With a portrait.] 1904. 4º.　　　**09456. h. 2.**

—— *See* WALISZEWSKI (K.) Autour d'un Trône. Catherine II. de Russie, ses collaborateurs, ses amis, ses favoris. Avec un portrait, *etc.* 1894. 8º.　**010795. g. 30.**

—— *See* WALISZEWSKI (K.) The Story of a Throne, Catherine II. of Russia, *etc.* [With a portrait.] 1895. [1894.] 8º.　　　　　　**010795. h. 2.**

—— *See* WALISZEWSKI (K.) Le Roman d'une Impératrice. Catherine II de Russie d'après ses mémoires, sa correspondance et les documents inédits des Archives d'État. Portrait, *etc.* 1893. 8º.　　　**010795. g. 24.**

—— *See* WALISZEWSKI (K.) The Romance of an Empress, Catherine II. of Russia, *etc.* [With a portrait.] 1894 [1893]. 8º.　　　　　**010795. g. 28.**

—— Anekdoten aus dem Privatleben der Kaiserin Catharina, Pauls des Ersten und seiner Familie. (Aus den Papieren eines jungen Pohlen gezogen, der unter dem, von dem Grossfürsten, Paul Petrowitsch, selbst kommandirten Corps, als Inspektionsadjutant diente.) pp. 167. *Hamburg,* 1797. 12º.　　　**010790. de. 46.**

—— Annalen der Regierung Katharina der Zweiten, Kaiserinn von Russland. [By H. F. von Storch.] Bd. 1. Gesetzgebung. Tl. 1. pp. viii. 252. *Leipzig [Riga],* 1798. 8º.
　　　　　　　　　　　　　　10790. e. 16.

　　No more published.

—— Authentic Memoirs of the Life and Reign of Catherine II. Empress of all the Russias. Collected from authentic MS's, translations, &c. of the King of Sweden, Right Hon. Lord Mountmorres, Lord Malmesbury, M. De Volney, and other indisputable authorities. Embellished with an elegant frontispiece. pp. vi. 291. *B. Crosby : London,* 1797. 12º.　　　　　　　　**611. c. 8.**
　　Printed for the Author.

—— Духъ Екатерины Великія . . . премудрыя Матери отечества, или черты и анекдоты, изображающіе характеръ . . . . сея . . . Монархини, съ присовокупленіемъ краткаго описанія Ея жизни И. С. [i.e. by Ivan Sreznevsky.] [With a portrait.] 1814. 8º. *See* S., I.　**10790. c. 13.**

—— Geheime Nachrichten über Russland unter der Regierung Catharinens II. und Pauls I. Ein Gemälde der Sitten des Petersburger Hofes gegen das Ende des achtzehnten Jahrhunderts. [Translated from " Mémoires secrets sur la Russie " by C. F. P. Masson.] 3 Tl.　　*Paris,* 1800-02. 8º.　　　　　　**10290. aa. 23.**
　　Tl. 3 is in two Abt.

—— Histoire secrète des amours et des principaux amans de Catherine II. . . . Avec figures. pp. 312. *See* PETER III., *Emperor of Russia.* [*Appendix.—Biography.—I.*] Histoire de Pierre III., *etc.* [By J. C. Thiébault de Laveaux.] tom. 3. [1799.] 8º.　　　　**1200. f. 10.**

—— [Another edition.] Par un Ambassadeur de l'époque [i.e. J. C. Thiébault de Laveaux]. Avec gravure. (Nouvelle édition, réimprimée textuellement sur l'édition originale.) pp. 293. *Paris,* [1873.] 12º.
　　　　　　　　　　　　　　10790. aaa. 1.

—— Katharine II. Kaiserin von Russland. [By Friedrich Samuel Mursinna ? With two genealogical tables and a portrait.] pp. 78. *Chemnitz,* 1804. 8º.
　　　　　　　　　　　　　　10602. d. 21. (2.)

CATHARINE II., *Empress of Russia.* [APPENDIX.—BIO-
GRAPHY.—I. *General.*]

—— Memoirs of Catherine II. and the Court of St. Petersburg during her reign and that of Paul I., by one of her
courtiers. [A translation of "Mémoires secrets sur la
Russie" by C. F. P. Masson. With portraits.] (Édition
de luxe.) pp. 353.　　　*Printed for the Grolier Society:*
London, [1904.]　8°.　[*Secret Court Memoirs.* no. 20.]
010661. c. 1/12.

—— La Messaline du Nord, ou Histoire secrète et véridique
des amours cyniques de Catherine II., Impératrice de
Russie. Par une dame de qualité. [The preface signed:
V. P.]　1834.　8°.　*See* P., V.　　　**1449. a. 23.**

—— Über das Leben und den Karakter der Kaiserin von
Russland Katharina II. Mit Freymuthigkeit und Un-
parteylichkeit. [By J. G. Seume.] pp. 160.
Altona [*Leipzig*], 1797.　8°.　　　　**10790. bbb. 5.**
Imperfect; wanting pp. 141–2 and pp. 155–6.

—— Vie de Catherine II, Impératrice de Russie. [By J. H.
Castéra.] Avec six portraits gravés en taille-douce.
2 tom.　*Paris,* 1797.　8°.　　　　**151. c. 12, 13.**

—— The Life of Catharine II. Empress of Russia. An enlarged translation [by W. Tooke] from the French [i.e.
from J. H. Castéra's "Histoire de Catherine II," the
revised version of his "Vie de Catherine II"]. With seven
portraits . . . and a correct map of the Russian empire.
3 vol.　*T. N. Longman; J. Debrett: London,* 1798.　8°.
10790. cc. 28.

—— The third edition, with considerable improvements.
3 vol.　　*T. N. Longman & O. Rees; J. Debrett: London,*
1799.　8°.　　　　　　　**989. b. 18–20.**

—— The fourth edition, with great additions and a copious
index. 3 vol.　　*T. N. Longman & O. Rees: London,*
1800.　8°.　　　　　　　**1200. f. 12–14.**

—— The fifth edition, with great additions and a copious
index. By W. Tooke. 3 vol.　　*J. Moore: Dublin,*
1800.　8°.　　　　　　　　**610. h. 24.**

—— Geheime Lebens- und Regierungsgeschichte Katharinens
der Zweiten, Kaiserin von Russland . . . Aus dem
Französischen . . . Mit sechs Portraits. [A translation
of "Vie de Catherine II" by J. H. Castéra.] 2 Bd.
Paris, 1798.　8°.　　　　　　**10790. c. 21.**

—— Zweyte, verbesserte Ausgabe. 2 Bd.　　　*Paris,*
1798.　8°.　　　　　　　**10790. bb. 11.**

—— Leben Katharinens der Zweiten Kaiserin von Russland.
Aus dem Französischen. [A translation of "Vie de
Catherine II." by J. H. Castéra.] Bd. 1, 2.　　*Paris*
[*Altenburg*], 1798.　8°.　　　　**1200. b. 6.**
Imperfect; wanting Bd. 3, 4.

II. *Separate Events.*

1744–1745.

—— *See* SIEBIGK (F.) Katharina der Zweiten Brautreise
nach Russland 1744–1745, *etc.* [With some of Catharine's
letters.]　1873.　8°.　　　　**10795. aaa. 15.**

1745.

—— *See* HOXA (J.) Kurze Beschreibung der auf das . . .
Vermählungsfest Jhro beyderseits Kaiserl. Hoheiten des
. . . Fürstens . . . Peters Feodorowitz . . . wie auch der
. . . Fürstin . . . Catharina Alexiewna . . . an dem An-
halt-Zerbstischem Hofe . . . vorgestellten Illumination,
etc.　1758.　fol.　[*Samuelis Lentzii Becmannus enucleatus,*
etc.]　　　　　　　　**9905. h. 4.**

CATHARINE II., *Empress of Russia.* [APPENDIX.—BIO-
GRAPHY.—II. *Separate Events.*]

1758–1761.

—— *See* CHECHULIN (N. D.) Екатерина II. в борьбе за
престол, *etc.* [With portraits.]　1924.　8°.
010795. bbb. 55.

1762.

—— *See* ANICHKOV (D. S.) Слово о превратныхъ понятіяхъ
человѣческихъ . . . На . . . день восшествія на
всероссійскій престолъ Ея императорскаго величества
. . . императрицы Екатерины Алексѣевны . . . тор-
жественно праздднованный . . . іюня 30 дня 1779 году
говоренное . . . Д. Аничковымъ. [1779.]　4°.
691. f. 12. (7.)

—— *See* LA MARCHE (C. F. S. de) *pseud.* Anecdotes russes;
ou Lettres . . . écrites de Petersbourg en 1762, tems du
règne et du détrônement de Pierre III, Empereur de Russie;
[Relating to the succession of Catharine II.]　1764.　8°.
etc.　　　　　　　　　　**150. a. 26.**

—— —— 1765.　8°.　　　　　　　**9475. aaa. 5.**

—— —— 1766.　12°.　　　　　　**10795. aa. 29.**

—— —— 1769, *etc.*　8°.　　　　　**1436. c. 35. (1.)**

—— *See* LA MARCHE (C. F. S. de) *pseud.* Russische Anekdoten von der Regierung und Tod Peters des Dritten;
imgleichen von der Erhebung und Regierung Catharinen
der Andern. Ferner von dem Tode des Kaysers Iwan, *etc.*
1764.　8°.　　　　　　　**8094. aa. 6.**

1764.

—— Журналъ путешествію Ея Императорскаго Величества въ Эстляндію и Лифляндію. (1764 года Іюня 20
дня.) pp. 52.　*въ Санктпетербургѣ,* 1769.　8°.
1427. b. 32. (1.)

—— *See* KUPRIYANOV (I.) Гофъ-Фурьеръ. Журналъ высочайшаго путешествія императрицы Екатерины Второй
въ Нарву, Ревель, Ригу, Митаву и обратно въ Санктпетербургъ, съ 20-го Іюня по 25-е Іюля 1764 года.
[1855.]　8°.　　[*Камеръ-Фурьерскій Журналъ.* 1764.
дополненіе.]　　　　　　**10795. g. 65.**

1772.

—— *See* SABATHIER DE CABRES (　　) Catherine II, sa
cour et la Russie en 1772. [With a preface signed:
S. S., i.e. S. A. Sobolevsky.]　1862.　8°.　**9455. d. 35.**

1773.

—— *See* NEJIN.—Γραικον Ἀδελφατον. Begin. *Πανευ-*
σπλαχνικωτατη Κυρια! *etc.* [Loyal addresses, the first presented to Catharine II.]　[1773.]　4°.　**870. h. 18. (6.)**

1773–1774.

—— *See* BIL'BASOV (V. A.) Дидро въ Петербургѣ (1773–74).
[An account of the intercourse of Diderot with Catharine
II. With some letters.]　1884.　8°.　**10795. cc. 22.**

1780.

—— Топографическія примѣчанія на знатнѣйшія мѣста
путешествія Ея Императорскаго Величества въ бѣлорус-
скія намѣстничества. 1780. pp. 133. [*Saint Petersburg,*
1780.]　12°.　　　　　　**1427. c. 2.**

1786.

—— Дневная записка путешествія Ея Императорскаго
Величества чрезъ Псковъ и Полоцкъ въ Могилевъ а
оттуда обратно чрезъ Смоленскъ и Новгородъ. 1867.
　　　See LENINGRAD.—*Императорское Русское*
Историческое Общество. Сборникъ, *etc.* том. 1.
1867, *etc.*　8°.　　　　　　**Ac. 7886.**

CATHARINE II., *Empress of Russia.* [Appendix.—Bio-graphy.—ii. *Separate Events.*]

1787.

—— *See* Psalidas (A. P.) Αἰκατερινα [*sic*] ἡ Β΄, ἤτοι Ἱστορια συντομος της ἐν τῃ ὁδοιπορια αὐτης προς τους ἐν Νιζνῃ και Ταυρια Γραικους ὑπ᾽ αὐτης δειχθεισης εὐνοιας, *etc.* 1792. 8°. **868. b. 19.**

—— Журналъ высочайшаго путешествія . . . Императрицы Экатерины II. . . . въ полуденныя страны Россіи въ 1787 году. pp. 137. *Москва*, 1787. 8°. **1426. g. 4.**

—— Путешествіе Ея Императорскаго Величества въ полуденный край Россіи, предпріемлемое въ 1787 году. [With a map.] pp. 149. [*Saint Petersburg,*] 1786. 8°. **1426. h. 1.**

—— [Another copy.] **L.P.** **1427. i. 2.**

1788.

—— *See* Zastrow (C.) Aus dem Leben der nordischen Semiramis [Catharine II.] und andere historische Skizzen. Von K. Zastrow, Neumann-Strela u. A. [1896.] 8°. **012552. b. 5.**

1791.

—— Αἰκατερινῃ εἰρηνοποιῳ. [A Pindaric ode by Frederick North, 5th Earl of Guilford, on occasion of the Peace of Galatz.] (All'esimio autore della Ode Greca Pindarica alla gran Caterina Pacificatrice canzone. [By D. Komoutos.]) [*Leipzig*, 1791.] 4°. **870. h. 17.**

1796.

—— *See* Ghika (S.) Πονημα στιχουργικον . . . εἰς τον θανατον της ἀοιδιμου μητρος Κυριας Δομνης Αἰκατερινης, *etc.* 1808. 4°. **871. f. 17.**

—— Кончина Императрицы Екатерины Вторыя. Историческое и статистическое [или] краткое начертаніе о Ней, и о Россіи въ Ея царствованіе. [From G. Glinka's edition of H. F. Storch's Annalen.] pp. 34. *Москва*, 1801. 8°. **10790. a. 30. (3.)**

Miscellaneous.

—— *See* Amburger (Erik) Russland und Schweden 1762–1772. Katharina II., die schwedische Verfassung und die Ruhe des Nordens. 1934. 8°. **09010. d. 1/251.**

—— *See* Berling (Carl) *Direktorial-Assistent, etc.* Die Meissner Porzellangruppen der Kaiserin Katharina II. in Oranienbaum, *etc.* 1914. 8°. **7808. t. 2.**

—— *See* Bourrée (M. D.) *Baron de Corberon.* Un Diplomate français à la cour de Catherine II, 1775–1780. Journal intime du chevalier de Corberon, *etc.* 1901. 8°. **010795. e. 47.**

—— *See* Europe. Du péril de la balance politique de l'Europe. [An attack on the northern policy of Catharine II. Variously attributed to Gustavus III., King of Sweden, and others.] 1789. 8°. **F. 937. (1.)**

—— —— 1789. 8°. **714. b. 26.**

—— *See* Ferrão (António) Gomes Freire na Russia. Cartas . . . e outros documentos . . . precedidos dum estudo sobre a política externa de Catarina II. Por A. Ferrão. 1917. 8°. **10634. ee. 11.**

—— *See* George Mikhailovich, *Grand Duke of Russia.* Монеты царствованія Императрицы Екатерины II. 1894. fol. **7756. v. 3.**

—— *See* Gooch (George P.) Catherine the Great, and other studies. [With a portrait.] 1954. 8°. **10797. g. 78.**

CATHARINE II., *Empress of Russia.* [Appendix.—Miscellaneous.]

—— *See* Goudar (A. de) Considérations sur les causes de l'ancienne foiblesse de l'Empire de Russie et de sa nouvelle puissance. Avec . . . l'Éloge de Catherine II., *etc.* 1772. 8°. **712. h. 42.**

—— *See* Grismondi (P.) *Countess.* A Caterina II Imperatrice di tutte le Russie. [An ode.] [1788.] fol. **L.R. 233. c. 9.**

—— *See* Grot (Ya. K.) Екатерина II и Густавъ III. 1877 [1878]. 8°. [*Сборникъ Отдѣленія русскаго языка и словесности Императорской Академіи Наукъ.* том. 18. no. 1.] **Ac. 1125/39.**

—— *See* Gustavus III., *King of Sweden.* The Danger of the Political Balance, *etc.* [An attack on the northern policy of Catharine II.] 1791. 8°. **153. a. 8.**

—— *See* Karamzin (N. M.) [Историческое похвальное слово Екатеринѣ II.] Lobrede auf Catharina die Zweyte . . . übersetzt von J. Richter. 1802. 8°. **10790. aa. 1.**

—— *See* Kleinschmidt (A.) Katharina II. als Civilisatorin. 1891. 8°. [*Deutsche Zeit- und Streit-Fragen.* Neue Folge. no. 80.] **12209. f.**

—— *See* Larivière (Charles de) Catherine le Grand d'après sa correspondance. Catherine II. et la Révolution Française d'après de nouveaux documents, *etc.* 1895, *etc.* 8°. **010795. de. 83.**

—— *See* Lavrovsky (N. A.) О педагогическомъ значеніи сочиненій Екатерины Великой. 1856. 8°. **8308. e. 2.**

—— *See* Le Normand (M. A. A.) L'Ombre immortelle de Catherine II au tombeau d'Alexandre Ier. 1826. 8°. **8051. de. 40. (4.)**

—— *See* Loret (M.) Kościół Katolicki a Katarzyna II., 1772–1784. 1910. 8°. [*Monografie w zakresie dziejów nowożytnych.* tom 12.] **9476. ddd. 21.**

—— *See* Molé Gentilhomme (P. H. J.) and Saint-Germain Leduc (P. E. D.) Catherine II. ou la Russie au dix-huitième siècle, *etc.* 1854. 12°. **12514. bbbb. 39.**

—— *See* Odhner (C. T.) Gustaf III och Katarina II efter Freden i Värälä. 1895. 8°. [*Svenska Akademiens Handlingar ifrån år* 1886. del. 9.] **Ac. 1071.**

—— *See* Shumigorsky (E. S.) Очерки изъ русской Исторіи. I. Императрица-Публицистъ. Эпизодъ изъ исторіи литературной дѣятельности Екатерины II. 1887. 8°. **9454. c. 15.**

—— *See* Smitt (F. von) Frédéric II, Catherine et le Partage de la Pologne, *etc.* 1861. 8°. **9476. e. 9.**

—— *See* Suireishchikov (E. B.) Слово на . . . день Рожденія Императрицы . . . Всероссійскія Екатерины Вторыя . . . Апрѣля 24 дня, 1780 года, говоренное. 1780. 8°. **691. f. 12. (10.)**

—— *See* Tengberg (N. A.) Om Kejsarinnan Catharina IIs åsyftade stora Nordiska Alliance. 1863. 8°. **9455. bb. 26.**

—— *See* Thomson (Gladys S.) Catherine the Great and the Expansion of Russia. [With a portrait.] 1947. 8°. **W.P. 1030/10.**

—— *See* Trachevsky (A. S.) Союзъ Князей и нѣмецкая политика Екатерины II., Фридриха II., Іосифа II. 1783-1790 г., *etc.* 1877. 8°. **9327. e. 4.**

—— *See* Turbandus (Turbans) Turbans Turbandus der grossen Miranda kleiner Sohn. Von einer diplomatischen Feder. [A comment on the reigns of Catharine II. and Paul I. By J. F. E. Albrecht.] 1802. 8°. **.8081. a. 19.**

CATHARINE II., *Empress of Russia.* [APPENDIX.—MIS-
CELLANEOUS.]

—— *See* VARKLOV ( ) Hynme à Cathérine II. Impératrice de Russie. Traduit du russe de M. de Varclow. Par
M. Chalumeau, *etc.* [1777.] 8º. **934. g. 2. (7.)**

—— *See* WUERST (F. G. von) Rede am Namenstage der
Kayserinn [Catharine II. of Russia], den 24sten November
1788, *etc.* [1788.] 8º. **10703. aa. 40.**

—— *See* ZENOGLE (Z.) *Yeoman of the Bulse, pseud.* Semiramis : or, the Shuttle. A cantata. From the Chronicles
for 1792. [A satire on Catharine II.] 1792. 4º.
644. k. 23. (9.)

—— A Catherine Seconde, Impératrice et Autocratrice de
toutes les Russies. Ode. (Àprès la Paix conclue près de
Silistrie en 1774. entre la Russie & la Porte Ottomane.)
pp. 13. [*Berlin ?*] 1775. 8º. **11481. e. 45. (1.)**

—— Catharina II. Dargestellt in ihren Werken zur Beherzi-
gung der Völker Europens. Vom Verfasser der ökono-
misch-politischen Hefte für den Norden [i.e. Carl Ernst
Christian Mueller]. pp. 199. *Berlin,* 1794. 8º.
10790. bb. 21.

—— Catherine II, Impératrice de Russie. Tragédie en cinq
actes. Par M. G.***. [i.e. — Godineau.] 1807. 8º.
See G.***, M. **11738. n. 7. (5.)**

—— Componimenti poetici di varj autori in lode di Caterina II., *etc.* pp. 135. *Napoli,* 1771. 4º. **11431. g. 2.**

—— Дворъ Императрицы Екатерины II., ея сотрудники и
приближенные. Сто восемьдесятъ девять силуэтовъ.
(La Cour de l'Impératrice Catherine II., ses collaborateurs,
etc.) [Edited by A. Krugly. With a silhouette of
Catharine II.] *Russ. & Fr.* 2 том. *С.-Петербургъ,*
1899. 8º. **010790. i. 17.**

—— Elogio di Catterina Seconda, Imperadrice delle Russie.
Scritto da celebre autore Francese [viz. Ange de Goudar]
in occasione dei gloriosi trionfi riportati dalle Armi di
questa sovrana nella presente Guerra. Traduzione . . .
nella Toscana favella [by F. Griselini], *etc.* [With plans.]
pp. 64. *Venezia,* 1773. 4º. **010795. f. 9.**

—— Katharine II. vor dem Richterstuhle der Menschheit.
Grösstentheils Geschichte. pp. 8. 59.
St. Petersburg [*Leipsic*], 1797. 8º. **10790. c. 2.**

—— O niebespieczeństwie Wagi politczney albo Wykład
przyczyn które zepsuły równowáżność na Północy od
wstąpienia na Tron Rossyiski Katarzyny II. [Translated
by — Bieńkowski from " Du péril de la balance politique
de l'Europe " variously attributed to Gustavus III, King
of Sweden, and others.] pp. 150. *w Brzegu,* 1790. 8º.
900. e. 9.

—— Ode to Her Imperial Majesty Catherine the Great,
presented by the Chief National School at St. Peters-
burgh, on the day of her . . . . visit January the 21st,
1785, *etc.* [Translated by S. Weston. With a frontispiece.] pp. 27. *Baldwin, Cradock & Joy: London,*
1815. 8º. **B. 690. (3.)**

—— [Another copy.] **11585. d. 10.**
*In this copy the words " Smirnow " and " Secretary "
in the dedication have been covered by printed slips reading
" Smirnove " and " Chaplain."*

—— L'Ombre de Catherine II. aux Champs Élysées. pp. 118.
Au Kamschatca, 1797. 8º. **114. i. 58.**

—— [Another edition.] Conférences de Cathérine II avec
Louis XVI, le grand-Frédéric et Piérre-le-grand, aux
Champs-Élysées. pp. 140. *Moscow; Paris,* 1797. 8º.
F. 928. (11.)

CATHARINE II., *Empress of Russia.* [APPENDIX.—MIS-
CELLANEOUS.]

—— A Set of Prints engraved after the most Capital Paintings
in the collection of Her Imperial Majesty, the Empress of
Russia, lately in the possession of the Earl of Orford
[i.e. George Walpole, 3rd Earl] at Houghton in Norfolk ;
with plans, elevations, sections, chimney pieces & ceilings.
[With descriptions taken from the " Ædes Walpoliana "
of Horace Walpole, Earl of Orford, with a French translation by J. N. Jouin de Sauseuil. With portraits of
Catharine II. and of Sir Robert Walpole, afterwards Earl
of Orford, as frontispieces.] 2 vol. FEW MS .NOTES.
J. & J. Boydell: London, 1788 [1787, 88]. fol.
Tab. 1226. a.
*Some of the plates are proofs and there are also proofs
additional to some plates. There are some plates not
recorded in the descriptions, and an additional copy of the
dedication to the Empress. The titlepages are engraved and
the individual plates bear dates ranging from 1774–1788.*

SELECT INDEX OF TITLES.

CATHARINE II., *Empress of Russia.*

CATHARINE II., *Empress of Russia.*

CATHARINE [OF BRAGANZA], *Queen Consort of Charles II.,
King of Great Britain and Ireland.*

—— *See* BLUTEAU (R.) Oraçoens gratulatorias na feliz
vinda da muito alta . . . Rainha da Gram Bretanha, *etc.*
1693. 4º.   C. **125. c. 2. (2.)**

—— *See* CADENEDUS (Jacobus) Pallas Pronuba in faustis-
simis nuptiis Caroli Secundi & Catharinæ, *etc.* 1662. 4º.
       E. **1957. (10.)**

—— *See* CAMBRIDGE.—*University of Cambridge.* [*Academic
Addresses.*] Epithalamia Cantabrigiensia in nuptias . . .
Caroli II . . . et Catharinæ, *etc.* 1662. 4º. **161. b. 35.**

—— *See* CARDONNEL (P. de) *Poet.* Tagus sive epithalamium
Caroli II . . . et Catharinæ, *etc.* 1662. 8º. **1070. e. 6.**

—— *See* CROUCH (John) *Poet.* Flowers strowed by the Muses
against the coming of the . . . Infanta of Portugal
Catharina Queen of England. 1662. 4º. **11623. e. 4.**

—— *See* D., J. An Hymenæan Essay . . . upon the royall
match of his . . . majesty Charles the Second, with . . .
Katharine, Infanta of Portugall. 1662. 1662. 4º.
       994. l. 40.

—— *See* DAVIDSON (Lillias C.) Catherine of Bragança, *etc.*
[With portraits.] 1908. 8º.   **2404. d. 10.**

—— *See* FONSECA (S. de) Relaçam dedicada as magestades
de Carlos, Catherin[a], *etc.* [An account in verse of Queen
Catharine's arrival at Portsmouth and journey to London.]
1662. 4º.   **011451. g. 38.**

—— *See* FONSECA (F. de) Relaçam das festas de Palacio,
egrandesas de Londres, dedicada amagestade da serenissima
Rainha da Gran Bretanha. 1663. 4º.
       C. **125. c. 2. (3.)**

—— *See* GAYTON (Edmund) To the most illustrious Prince
his Highnesse James Duke of York. A votive song for
her sacred Majesties happy arrivall. [1661 ?] fol.
       C. **40. m. 11. (30.)**

—— *See* H., S., *a Cosmopolite.* Iter Lusitanicum ; or, the
Portugal voyage. With what memorable passages inter-
ven'd at the shipping . . . of Katherine Queen of Great
Britain from Lisbon to England, *etc.* 1662. 4º.
       11626. d. 20.

—— *See* IZANDRO, *Toureiro de Forcado.* Festas reays na
corte de Lisboa ao feliz cazamento dos Reys da graõ
Bretanha Carlos, & Catherina, *etc.* 1661. 4º.
       C. **125. c. 2. (5.)**

—— *See* L., J. A Poem Royal to . . . Charles II . . . and
. . . Catharina, *etc.* 1662. fol.   C. **20. f. 2. (51.)**

—— *See* MACKAY (Janet) Catherine of Braganza. [With
portraits.] 1937. 8º.   **10807. ff. 28.**

—— *See* MELLO E TORRES (F. de) *Marquis de Sande.* Relaçam da forma com que a Magestade del Rey da Graõ
Bretanha manifestou a seus reynos, tinha ajustado seu
casamento com a Serenissima Infante . . . Catherina,
etc. 1661. 4º.   **1444. g. 8. (8.)**

—— *See* OXFORD.—*University of Oxford.* [*Academic Addresses, Poems, etc.*] Domiduca Oxoniensis, sive Musæ
academicæ gratulatio ob auspicatissimum . . . Catharinæ
Lusitanæ, regi suo desponsatæ in Angliam appulsum.
1662. 4º.   **1213. l. 38.**

—— *See* PORTUGUESE. t'Samen-spraeck, tusschen een Por-
tugees ende een Spanjaert over het besloten houwelijk
van den herstelden Koninck van Engelant, met de
Dochter van den Hertogh van Bragance, *etc.* 1661. 4º.
       8122. ee. 7. (2.)

CATHARINE [OF BRAGANZA], *Queen Consort of Charles II.,
King of Great Britain and Ireland.*

——— *See* REYNOLDS (Lancelot) A Panegyrick on . . .
Katherine Queen of England, *etc.* [1661.] 4º.
       1077. i. 25.

—— *See* STOOP (Dirk) [A set of seven large plates by
D. Stoop of the visit of Edward Montagu, Earl of Sand-
wich, to Lisbon . . . to escort Catharine of Braganza to
England, and of her voyage and arrival in England.]
1662. fol.   G. **8187.**

—— *See* WENLOCK (John) *of Langham.* Upon our Royall
Queens Majesties most happy arrivall. 1661. fol.
       Lutt. I. **18.**

—— An Exact and True Relation of the Landing of Her
Majestie at Portsmouth . . . together with a perfect
account of her . . . mariage, *etc.* [In verse.] *London,*
1662. *s. sh.* fol.   C. **20. f. 2. (50.)**
Mutilated.

—— An Heroick Poem, most humbly dedicated to the Sacred
Majesty of Catharine, Queen Dowager. [On the death
of King Charles II.] pp. 6.   *Nathaniel Thompson :*
London, 1685. 4º.   **11630. c. 5. (6.)**

—— Inventário dos bens da rainha da Grã-Bretanha D.
Catarina de Bragança. [The text of a document of 1706.
with an introduction by Virgínia Rau and a facsimile.]
1948. *See* COIMBRA.—*Universidade de Coimbra.—Bibliotheca.* Boletim bibliográfico. (Boletim da biblioteca.
vol. 18.) 1914, *etc.* 8º.   Ac. **2699. ba.**

—— Relaçam diaria, da jornada, que . . . D. Catherina fez
de Lisboa á Lóndres, indo já desposada com Cárlos II.,
etc.   *H. Valente de Oliveira : Lisboa,* 1662. 4º.
       9195. c. 26. (6.)

—— [Another copy.] Relaçam diaria, da jornada, que . . .
D. Catherina fez de Lisboa a Londres, *etc. Lisboa,*
1662. 4º.   C. **125. c. 2. (1.)**

—— Relacion de las fiestas que se hizieron en Lisboa, con la
nueua del casamiento de la Serenissima Infanta de Portugal
Doña Catalina, ya Reyna de la Gran Bretaña, con el
Serenissimo Rey de la Gran Bretaña Carlos segundo deste
nombre. Y todo lo que sucedió hasta embarcarse para
Inglaterra.   *En la officina de Henrique Valente de*
Oliueira : Lisboa, 1662. 4º.   C. **125. c. 2. (9.)**

—— To the Queen, upon Her Majesties Birthday. By E. W.,
Esq. [i.e. Edmund Waller.] [1663.] *s. sh.* fol. *See* W.,
E., *Esq.*   C.**121.g.9.(11.)**

CATHARINE, *Queen Consort of Eric XIV., King of Sweden.*
See AHLQVIST (A. G.) Karin Månsdotter, *etc.*
1874. 8º.   **10761. bbb. 3.**

—— *See* ARNELL (S. A.) Karin Månsdotter, *etc.* [With portraits.] 1951. 8º.   **10763. n. 13.**

CATHARINE, *Queen Consort of Henry V., King of England.*
See BAUDOT DE JUILLY (N.) Caterine de France, reine
d'Angleterre. 1749. 12º. [*Bibliothèque de campagne.*
tom. 2.]   **244. f. 2.**

—— Histoire de Caterine de France, reine d'Angleterre. [By
N. Baudot de Juilly.] pp. 349.   *Chez la veuve Chavance*
& M. Chavance : Lyon, 1696. 12º.   C. **67. b. 7.**
The arms of a member of the House of Bavaria are stamped
on the covers.

—— [Another copy, with a different titlepage.]   *Chez*
G. de Luyne : Paris, 1696. 12º.   **836. b. 16.**

CATHARINE [OF ARAGON], *Queen Consort of Henry VIII.,
King of England. See* CLAREMONT (Francesca) Catherine
of Aragon. [With portraits.] 1939. 8°. **010807. h. 5.**

—— *See* DEANS (Richard S.) The Trials of Five Queens:
Katherine of Aragon, *etc.* 1909. 8°. **10600. v. 17.**

—— *See* DIXON (William H.) History of Two Queens.
I. Catharine of Aragon, *etc.* 1873. 8°. [*Collection of
British Authors.* vol. 1320–1322.] **12267.a.1/129.**

—— —— 1873, *etc.* 8°. **10805. cc. 24.**

—— *See* DU BOYS (A.) Catherine d'Aragon et les origines
du schisme anglicain. 1880. 8°. **10806. f. 7.**

—— *See* DU BOYS (A.) Catharine of Aragon and the Sources
of the English Reformation, *etc.* 1881. 8°.
 4705. aaa. 8.

—— [For works having special reference to the divorce of
Henry VIII. from Catharine of Aragon:] *See* HENRY VIII.,
King of England. [*Biography.—Divorce.*]

—— *See* MATTINGLY (Garrett) Catherine of Aragon. [With
a portrait.] 1942. 8°. **010807. h. 19.**

—— *See* NAUSEA (F.) *Bishop of Vienna.* Friderici Nauseæ
. . . in diuam Catharinam . . . Angliæ . . . reginā funebris
oratio. 1536. 8°. **G. 1489.**

—— Four Curious Documents. I. A Letter from Katherine
of Arragon, to Mary, her Daughter. II. Anne Boleyn's
last Letter to Henry VIII. III. The Proclamation of Lady
Jane Grey's Title to the Crown. IV. A Letter from the
Princess . . . Mary, to her Father, Henry VIII. 1536.
pp. 19. *Privately printed: Edinburgh,* 1886. 8°. [*Historical Reprints.* no. 14.] **9525. e. 10.**

—— The Traduction ỻ Mariage of the Princesse (Kateryne
daughter to . . . the kinge and quene of Spayne).
[Being a programme of ceremonies appointed to be
observed at the landing of the Princess, her entry into
London, and her marriage with Arthur, Prince of
Wales.] 𝔅.𝔏. MS. NOTES. *Richard Pynson:* [*London,*
1501.] 4°. **C. 21. b. 29.**
*Imperfect; wanting sig. a. 3 & 4 and b. 3 & 4. The
titlepage is mutilated.*

—— [Another edition.] 1751. *See* SOMERS (John) *Baron
Somers.* A Fourth Collection of scarce . . . Tracts, *etc.*
vol. 2. 1752, *etc.* 4°. **184. a. 14.**

—— [Another edition.] *See* SOMERS (John) *Baron Somers.*
A Collection of scarce . . . Tracts, *etc.* vol. 1.
1809, *etc.* 4°. **750. g. 1.**

—— View of the Wardrobe Stuff of Katharine of Arragon.
1854. *See* LONDON.—III. *Camden Society.* The Camden
Miscellany. vol. 3. 1847, *etc.* 4°. . Ac. **8113/39.**

CATHARINE [HOWARD], *Queen Consort of Henry VIII.,
King of England.*

—— *See* GLENNE (Michael) Catharine Howard, *etc.* [With
a portrait.] [1948.] 8°. **010807. f. 25.**

—— Cancion nueva de Catalina Howar en
el último dia de su vida. Primera (Segunda) parte.
pp. 4. *Barcelona,* 1859. 4°. **11450. f. 27. (81.)**

CATHARINE [PARR], *Queen Consort of Henry VIII., King
of England. See* GARNETT (Frederick B.) *C.B.* Queen
Katherine Parr and Sudeley Castle, *etc.* 1894. 8°.
 10803. g. 15. (8.)

CATHARINE [PARR], *Queen Consort of Henry VIII., King
of England.*

—— *See* GORDON (Marian A.) Life of Queen Katharine Parr.
[With portraits.] [1951.] 8°. **10807. ff. 43.**

—— *See* SUDELEY. A Brief Historical Account of the Castle
. . . of Sudeley . . . including . . . particulars relative
to Queen Katherine Parr. 1844. 8°. **10360. cc. 8.**

—— Prayers and Meditations.—The Lamentation . . . of a
Sinner. *See* EDWARD VI., *King of England.* Writings of
Edward the Sixth . . . Queen Catherine Parr, *etc.*
1831. 12°. **865.b.3.**

—— The Lamentacion of a synner, made by the moste
vertuous Lady quene Caterine, bewailyng the ignoraunce
of her blind life : set foorth ỻ put in print at the instant
desire of the right gracious lady Caterine duchesse of
Suffolke, and the ernest request of the right honourable
Lord William Parre, Marquesse of Northampton. [With
a preface by William Cecil, afterwards Lord Burghley.]
𝔅.𝔏. *Edwarde Whitchurche: London,* 1548. 8°.
 G. 12003.

—— [Another edition.] 𝔅.𝔏. *John Alde: Lonon* [sic],
1563. 8°. **C. 12. c. 10.**

—— [Another edition.] 1810. *See* HARLEIAN MISCELLANY.
The Harleian Miscellany, *etc.* vol. 5. 1808, *etc.* 4°.
 2072.g.

—— Meditations of Queen Catherine Parr . . . being extracts from a work written by her about the year 1540
[i.e. the "Lamentation"], *etc.* pp. 16. *R.T.S.:*
London, [1840 ?] 8°. [*First Series Tracts.* no. 153.]
 863. k. 11.

—— Prayers or meditacions, wherin the mind is stirred
paciently to suffre all afflictions here, to sette at naught
the vaine prosperitee of this worlde, and alwaie to long
for the eveclastyng [sic] felicitee : collected out of certayne holy woorkes by the moste vertuous and gracious
Princes Catharine, Quene of Englande, France and Irelande. 𝔅.𝔏. *Thomas Berthelette: London,*
1545 [1550 ?]. 16°. **G. 11660.**
Interleaved.

—— Prayers or Medytacions, wherein the mynd is stirred,
paciently to suffre all afflictions here : to set at nought the
vayneprosperitee of this worlde, and alwaie to longe for
the euerlastynge felicitee : Collected out of holy woorkes
by the most vertuous and graciouse Princesse Katherine
quene of Englande Fraunce, and Irelande. 𝔅.𝔏. *Thomas
Berthelet: London,* 1545 [c. 1550]. 8°. **C. 132. h. 13.**

—— [Another edition.] 𝔅.𝔏. *Thomas Berthelet: London,*
1545 [1550 ?]. 8°. **C. 25. b. 28.**

—— [Another edition.] 𝔅.𝔏. [*London,*] 1546. 16°.
 C. 18. a. 16. (1.)
Imperfect; wanting sig. c. 5.

—— [Another edition.] 𝔅.𝔏. *Thomas Barthelet: London,*
1547. 8°. **G. 12134.**

—— [Another edition.] 𝔅.𝔏. *Wylliam Copland, for
John Waley, and Wylliam Seres: London,* 1559. 16°.
 C. 53. gg. 5.

—— [Another edition.] 𝔅.𝔏. [*Henry Wykes ? London ?*
1562 ?] 8°. **1350. a. 16. (4.)**

—— [Another edition.] *See* BIBLE.—*Selections.* [*English.*]
[The Psalmes, or Prayers, *etc.*] [1566 ?] 16°.
 C. 17. a. 20.

CATHARINE [Parr], *Queen Consort of Henry VIII., King of England.*

—— [Another edition.] *See* Bible.—*Selections.* [*English.*] The Psalmes, *etc.* 1568. 16º.   C. **36**. a. **39**.

—— [Another edition.] *See* Bible.—*Selections.* [*English.*] The Psalmes, *etc.* 1571. 16º.   C. **18**. a. **9**.

—— [Another edition.] 𝕭.𝕷. [*H. Middelton for C. Barker ? London ?* 1574 ?] 32º.
    Dept. of British & Medieval Antiquities.
    Imperfect; wanting all after sig. F 4. Bound, with two other tracts, in a gold binding with enamelled reliefs, representing on one side the lifting up of the serpent by Moses in the wilderness, and on the other the judgment of Solomon. Formerly in the possession of Queen Elizabeth.

—— [Another copy.]   C. **39**. k. **14**. (4.)
    A fragment, consisting of sheets C and D only.

—— [Another edition.] *See* Bible.—*Selections.* [*English.*] The Psalmes, *etc.* 1585. 12º.   C. **18**. a. **7**.

—— [Another edition.] *See* Bible.—*Selections.* [*English.*] The Psalmes, *etc.* 1595. 32º.   C. **18**. a. **22**.

—— [Another edition.] pp. 96. *R.T.S.: London,* 1831. 32º.
                C. **0**. d. **15**.

—— Queen Catharine Parr. (A pious prayer of Queen Catharine Parr.) *See* Lady. The Lady's Monitor: selected from the writings of Lady Jane Grey, Queen Catharine Parr, *etc.* 1828. 8º.   **1116**. a. **5**. (2.)

—— Prayers or medytacions, *etc.* [Being reprinted titlepages only, with a collation by J. Taylor appended to each, of various copies and editions, 1545–63.] [*Northampton,* 1870.] 8º.   **4999**. g. **5**.

CATHARINE [de' Medici], *Queen Consort of Henry II., King of France.*

LETTERS.

—— [Two letters, dated 4 and 20 March 1579 respectively, addressed to François de Tersac.] *See* Carsalade Du Pont (J. de) François de Tersac, baron de Montberaud, *etc.* 1871. 8º.   **10602**. i. **6**. (2.)

—— Correspondance et négociations de la reine Catherine de Médicis. [Edited by Count H. de Laferrière-Percy.] tom. 1. pp. 680. [*Paris,* 1873.] 4º.   **10909**. m. **11**.
    The work was intended to form part of the "Collection des documents inédits sur l'histoire de France." No more published.

—— Lettres de Catherine de Médicis. Publiées par M. le Cᵗᵉ Hector de la Ferrière (tom. 1–5; par M. le Cᵗᵉ Baguenault de Puchesse, tom. 6–9). *10* tom.   *Paris,* 1880–1909. 4º. [*Collection de documents inédits sur l'histoire de France.*]   **1885**. c. **26**.

—— Lettres inédites de Charles IX, de Catherine de Médicis et du duc d'Anjou, *etc.* pp. 38. 1893. 8º. [*Curiosités bourbonnaises.* no. 4.] *See* Charles IX., *King of France.*   **010171**. l. **26**.

—— Lettre de Catherine de Médicis au cardinal de Chastillon. 1835. *See* Cimber (M. L.) *pseud.* Archives curieuses de l'histoire de France, *etc.* sér. 1. tom. 4. 1834, *etc.* 8º.   **805**. b. **2**.

—— [A letter, dated 30 December 1561, addressed to the Parlement of Paris.] *See* Charles IX., *King of France.* Lettres du roy et de la reine-mère au Parlement de Paris, au sujet du tumulte arrivé à la porte Sainct-Anthoine, *etc.* 1835. 8º. [*Archives curieuses de l'histoire de France, etc.* sér. 1. tom. 4.]   **805**. b. **2**.

CATHARINE [de' Medici], *Queen Consort of Henry II., King of France.*

—— Avis donnez par Catherine de Médicis à Charles IX pour la police de sa cour et pour le gouvernement de son estat. [A letter, written in 1563.] 1835. *See* Cimber (M. L.) *pseud.* Archives curieuses de l'histoire de France, *etc.* sér. 1. tom. 5. 1834, *etc.* 8º.   **805**. b. **2**.

—— [A letter, dated 4 August 1582, to the Mayor and magistrates of Orleans, on the encouragement of manufactures.] *See* Laffémas (B. de) *Sieur de Bauthor.* Lettres et exemples de la feu royne mère, *etc.* 1836. 8º. [*Cimber (M. L.) Archives curieuses de l'histoire de France, etc.* sér. 1. tom. 9.]   **805**. b. **3**.

SINGLE WORKS.

—— Canticque de la Royne mere, louant Dieu & les vaillans Capitaines de France, qui ont chassé l'Angloys hors du Haure de Grace. *Par B. Rigaud: Lyon,* 1563. 8º.
                1073. c. **14**. (2.)

APPENDIX.

Biography.

—— *See* A., V. M. V. Li gran trionphi, et fbste [*sic*] fatte alla corte de la Cesarea Maesta . . . La solenne intrata in Burcelles de la Regina di Francia, *etc.* [1544.] 4º.
                1318. c. **7**. (7.)

—— *See* Barthélemy (E. M. de) *Count.* Catherine de Médicis à Épernay pour la négociation de la paix de Nemours conclue avec les Guises en 1585, *etc.* 1884. 8º.
                9079. aa. **24**. (2.)

—— *See* Baschet (A.) La Diplomatie vénitienne. Les princes de l'Europe au XVI. siècle. François 1ᵉʳ— Philippe II.—Catherine de Médicis . . . d'après les rapports des ambassadeurs vénitiens, *etc.* 1862. 8º.
                9150. g. **20**.

—— *See* Beaune (R. de) successively *Bishop of Mende, Archbishop of Bourges, etc.* Oraison funebre faicte aux obseques de la Royne mere du roy, *etc.* 1589. 8º.
                1058. a. **33**.

—— *See* Bouchot (H.) Catherine de Médicis. 1899. 4º.
                L.R. **271**. b. **6**.

—— *See* Boulé (A.) Catherine de Médicis et Coligny. (Étude historique.) 1913. 8º.   **09008**. bb. **17**. (5.)

—— *See* Broes (W.) Filip van Marnix, heer van St. Aldegonde . . . Ter inleiding Margareta van Parma en Katharina van Medicis, *etc.* 1838, *etc.* 8º.   **10760**. dd. **12**.

—— *See* Camilucci (E.) Caterina de' Medici, *etc.* 1935. 8º.
                010665. df. **28**.

—— *See* Capefigue (J. B. H. R.) Catherine de Médicis, mère des rois François II, Charles IX, et Henri III. 1856. 12º.   **10659**. b. **10**.

—— *See* Cartault (E.) Entrée du Roy Charles IX et de la Reyne-Mère Catherine de Médicis en la ville de Sens le 15 mars, 1565, *etc.* 1882. 8º.   **9930**. gg. **16**.

—— *See* Castelnau (M. de) *Seigneur de Mauvissière.* Les Memoires de Messire Michel de Castelnau . . . illustrez et augmentez de plusieurs commentaires & manuscrits . . . servans à donner la verité de l'histoire des regnes de François II, Charles IX, & Henry III, et de la regence du gouvernement de Catherine de Medicis, *etc.* 1731. fol.
                187. f. **5**.

CATHARINE [DE' MEDICI], *Queen Consort of Henry II.,
King of France.* [APPENDIX.—BIOGRAPHY.]

—— *See* CHAMPION (P. H. A. J. B.) Catherine de Médicis présente à Charles IX son royaume, 1564–1566. [With a portrait.] 1937. 8°.   **010665. e. 61.**

—— *See* CHARLES IX., *King of France.* Recueil des choses notables, qui ont esté faites à Bayonne, à l'entreueuë du Roy Treschrestien Charles neufieme . . . & la Royne sa treshonoree mere, auec la Royne Catholique sa sœur. 1566. 4°.   **286. i. 2.**

—— *See* CHÉRUEL (P. A.) Marie Stuart et Catherine de Médicis. Étude historique sur les relations de la France et de l'Écosse, *etc.* 1858. 8°.   **1325. e. 22.**

—— *See* GALZY (J.) Catherine de Médicis. [With a portrait.] 1936. 8°.   **010665. e. 52.**

—— *See* HENRY II., *King of France.* C'est l'ordre qui a esté tenu à la nouuelle et ioyeuse entrée, que . . . le Roy . . . Henry deuxiesme . . . a faicte en . . . Paris . . . 1549. (S'ensuit l'ordre de l'entrée de la Royne.) [1549.] 4°.   **9930. f. 48. (1.)**

—— *See* HENRY II., *King of France.* C'est la deduction du somptueux ordre, plaisantz spectacles et magnifiques theatres dressés et exhibés par les citoiens de Roüen . . . à . . . Henry secõd . . . et à . . . ma Dame Katharine de Medicis, la Royne son espouze, &c. 1551. 4°.   **811. d. 26.**

—— *See* HENRY II., *King of France.* Entrée à Rouen du roi Henri II et de la reine Catherine de Médicis en 1550. (C'est la deduction du somptueux ordre plaisantz spectacles . . . dressés et exhibés par les citoiens de Rouen, *etc.*) 1885. 4°.   **Ac. 8939/26.**

—— *See* HENRY II., *King of France.* L'Entrée à Rouen du roi et de la reine Henri II et Catherine de Médicis, d'après la relation imprimée en 1550, *etc.* (L'entrée du Roy nostre Sire faicte en sa ville de Rouen, *etc.*) 1882. 4°.   **Ac. 8938/42.**

—— *See* HENRY II., *King of France.* La Magnificence de la superbe et triumphante entree de la . . . cité de Lyon faicte au Treschrestien Roy de France Henry deuxiesme . . . et à la Royne Catherine son espouse le XXIII. de Septembre M.D.XLVIII. 1549. 4°.   **811. g. 33.**

—— —— 1937. 4°.   **Ac. 8921/18.**

—— *See* HENRY II., *King of France.* La Magnifica et triumphale entrata del Christianiss. Re di Francia Henrico secondo . . . fatta nella . . . città di Lyone à luy & à la sua serenissima consorte Chaterina alli 21. di Septemb. 1548, *etc.* 1549. 4°.   **605. c. 19.**

—— *See* HERBILLON (E. E.) Les Deux Médicis (Catherine de Médicis, Marie de Médicis). 1932. 8°.   **10632. s. 28.**

—— *See* HÉRITIER (J.) Les Premières années de Catherine de Médicis, *etc.* 1939. 8°. [*Les Œuvres libres.* no. 218.]   **12208. ee. 218.**

—— *See* HILLIGER (B.) Katharina von Medici und die Zusammenkunft in Bayonne (1565). 1892. 8°. [*Historisches Taschenbuch.* Sechste Folge. Jhrg. 11.]   **P.P. 3625.**

—— *See* LACOMBE (B. de) Catherine de Médicis entre Guise et Condé. 1899. 8°.   **010661. i. 45.**

—— *See* LUZZATTI (I.) Caterina de' Medici, 1519–1589, *etc.* [With portraits.] 1939. 8°.   **10635. b. 31.**

CATHARINE [DE' MEDICI], *Queen Consort of Henry II.,
King of France.* [APPENDIX.—BIOGRAPHY.]

—— *See* MARCKS (E.) Die Zusammenkunft von Bayonne, *etc.* [On the meeting of Catharine with Elizabeth, Queen of Spain.] 1889. 8°.   **9079. h. 8.**

—— *See* MARIÉJOL (Jean H.) Catherine de Médicis, *etc.* 1920. 8°.   **10657. dd. 9.**

—— *See* MAZZONI (J.) Iacobi Mazonii oratio . . . in exequiis Catherinæ Medices Francorum Reginæ. 1589. 4°.   **12301. c. 34. (13.)**

—— *See* PALANDRI (E.) Les Négociations politiques et religieuses entre la Toscane et la France à l'époque de Cosme Ier et de Catherine de Médicis, *etc.* 1908. 8°. [*Université de Louvain. Recueil de travaux publiés par les membres des conférences d'histoire et de philologie.* fasc. 22.]   **Ac. 2646/4.**

—— *See* REUMONT (A. von) Die Jugend Caterina's de' Medici, *etc.* 1856. 16°.   **10631. a. 35.**

—— *See* REUMONT (A. de) La Jeunesse de Catherine de Médicis, *etc.* 1866. 8°.   **10630. bb. 10.**

—— *See* ROEDER (Ralph) Catherine de' Medici and the Lost Revolution. [With portraits.] 1937. 8°.   **010663. l. 63.**

—— *See* ROMANA (A.) Le Tre Caterine. (Caterina Sforza. Caterina de Medici. Caterina II di Russia.) 1921. 8°.   **010603. b. 8.**

—— *See* RONDINELLI (G.) Orazione . . . delle lodi della Reina di Francia Caterina de Medici, *etc.* 1661. 8°. [*DATI (C. R.) Prose fiorentine, etc.* vol. 1.]   **630. d. 31.**

—— —— 1716. 8°. [*DATI (C. R.) Prose fiorentine, etc.* pt. 1. vol. 1.]   **659. b. 18.**

—— —— 1735. 4°. [*DATI (C. R.) Prose fiorentine, etc.* tom. 1.]   **629. i. 14.**

—— *See* ROSE (John B.) A Treatise on the Reign and Times of Queen Catherine de Medici. 1871. 8°.   **10631. aaa. 34.**

—— *See* SAUZÉ (C.) Les Conférences de La Mothe-Saint-Héray entre Henri de Navarre et Catherine de Médicis, 1582. 1895. 8°.   **9226. l. 25.**

—— *See* SICHEL (Edith) Catherine de' Medici and the French Reformation, *etc.* 1905. 8°.   **09225. h. 17.**

—— *See* SICHEL (Edith) The Later Years of Catherine de' Medici. 1908. 8°.   **10633. g. 37.**

—— *See* THOMPSON (James Westfall) The Wars of Religion in France, 1559–1576. The Huguenots, Catherine de Medici and Philip II. 1909. 8°.   **4629. dd. 16.**

—— *See* TROLLOPE (Thomas A.) The Girlhood of Catherine de' Medici. 1856. 8°.   **10633. aa. 2.**

—— *See* VAN DYKE (Paul) Cathérine de Médicis. [With portraits.] 1923. 8°.   **10657. c. 19.**

—— *See* WALDMAN (Milton) Biography of a Family. Catherine de Medici and her children, *etc.* [With portraits.] 1936. 8°.   **20030. b. 22.**

—— *See* WATSON (Francis L.) The Life and Times of Catherine de' Medici, *etc.* [With portraits.] 1934. 8°.   **10655. i. 35.**

—— Catherine de Médicis 1519–1589. Par l'auteur de " La Vérité sur Marie Stuart " [i.e. Louis F. E. de Meneval]. pp. xvii. 300. *Paris*, 1880. 12°.   **10658. bb. 27.**

CATHARINE [DE' MEDICI], *Queen Consort of Henry II.,*
King of France. [APPENDIX.—BIOGRAPHY.]

—— Discours merueilleux de la vie, actions & deportemens
de Catherine de Medicis, Royne mere. Auquel sont
recitez les moyens qu'elle a tenu pour vsurper le gouuerne-
ment du Royaume de France, & ruiner l'estat d'iceluy.
[Attributed variously to H. Estienne, T. de Bèze, J. de
Serres and P. Pithou.] pp. 164. 1575. 8°.
1058. a. 12. (1.)

—— [Another edition.] pp. 95. 1575. 8°.
1059. b. 18. (2.)

—— Troisieme edition plus correcte, mieux disposée que la
premiere & seconde, & augmentée de quelques par-
ticularitez. pp. cxviii. 1578. 8°. **1193. d. 20.**

—— [Another edition.] pp. 138. *Selon la copie imprimée*
à Paris, 1649. 8°. **610. a. 25.**

—— [Another edition.] pp. 180. *A. Vlacq: La Haye,*
1660. 12°. **611. a. 12. (1.)**

—— [Another edition.] *See* HENRY III., *King of France.*
[*Biography.*—I.] Recueil de diverses pieces servans à
l'histoire de Henry III, *etc.* 1663. 4°. **286. c. 27.**

—— [Another edition.] pp. 168. *See* HENRY III., *King of*
France. [*Biography.*—I.] Recueil de diverses pieces,
servant à l'histoire de Henry III., *etc.* 1663. 12°.
594. a. 26. (1.)

—— [Another edition.] pp. 113. *Iouxte la copie imprimée*
à Paris, 1663. 12°. **611. a. 12. (2.)**

—— [Another edition.] pp. 156. *Suivant la copie imprimée*
à la Haie, 1663. 12°. **1199. a. 14.**

—— [Another copy.] **G. 15204. (2.)**

—— [Another edition.] *See* HENRY III., *King of France.*
[*Biography.*—I.] [Recueil de diverses pieces servant à
l'histoire de Henry III., *etc.*] 1666. 12°.
611. a. 12. (3.)

—— Discours merveilleux de la vie, actions & déportemens de
la reyne Catherine de Médicis . . . Suivant la copie imprimée
à la Haië, MDCLXIII. [Attributed variously to H. Estienne,
T. de Bèze, J. de Serres and P. Pithou.] *In:* Recueil de
diverses pièces servant à l'histoire de Henry III., *etc.*
1666. 12°. **1471. c. 40.**

—— [Another edition.] *See* JOURNAL. Journal des choses
memorables advenues durant le regne de Henry III, *etc.*
tom. 1. pt. 2. 1720. 8°. **1443. c. 3.**

—— [Another edition.] *See* L'ESTOILE (P. de) Journal de
Henri III., *etc.* tom. II. 1744. 8°. **680. b. 14.**

—— [Another edition.] 1836. *See* CIMBER (M. L.) *pseud.*
Archives curieuses de l'histoire de France, *etc.* sér. 1.
tom. 9. 1834, *etc.* 8°. **805. b. 3.**

—— A Meruaylous discourse vpon the lyfe, deedes and
behauiours of Katherine de Medicis, Queene mother, *etc.*
[Translated from the French.] pp. 196. *Heydelberge;*
[*H. Middleton? London,*] 1575. 8°. **610. a. 24.**

—— [Another copy.] **285. a. 21.**

—— [Another edition.] Ane Mervellous discours vpon the
lyfe, deides and behauiours of Katherine de Medicis,
Quene Mother, *etc.* pp. 138. *Cracow* [*Edinburgh?*],
1576. 8°. **285. a. 9.**
The titlepage is mounted.

CATHARINE [DE' MEDICI], *Queen Consort of Henry II.,*
King of France. [APPENDIX.—BIOGRAPHY.]

—— Ane Meruellous discours Vpon the lyfe, deides, and
behauiours of Katherine de Medicis, *etc.* [Attributed
variously to H. Estienne, T. de Bèze, J. de Serres, and
P. Pithou.] pp. [138.] *Paris,* 1576. 4°.
Mic. A. 605. (7.)
MICROFILM (*negative*) *of a copy, cropped, of another issue*
of the preceding in the Folger Shakespeare Library. Made
by the Folger Shakespeare Library, 1955.

—— The History of the Life of Katharine de Medicis, Queen
Mother and Regent of France, or, The Exact Pattern of
the present French King's policy. [Translated in part
from the " Discours merveilleux de la vie . . . de Catherine de Médicis."] pp. 96. *For John Wyat: London,*
1693. 8°. **610. c. 17.**

—— [Another copy.] **1481. a. 28.**

—— Offentlichs vnd inn warheit wolgegründts Aussschreiben
der vbelbefridigte Ständ in Frankreich, die sich Mal
Content nennen: Inhaltend: Die Wunderlich Beschreibung des Lebens . . . der Catherine von Medicis . . .
Auss dem Frantzösischen ins Teutsch gebracht durch
Emericum Lebusium [i.e. J. Fischart]. [1575?] 8°.
1058. a. 34.

—— [Another edition.] [1580?] 8°. **1059. a. 31.**

—— Catharinæ Mediceæ Reginæ Matris, vitæ, actorum, &
consiliorum, quibus vniuersum regni Gallici statum
turbare conata est, stupenda eaque vera enarratio.
[Translated from the French.] pp. 116. 1575. 8°.
610. c. 16.

—— [Another copy.] FEW MS. NOTES. **285. e. 13.**

—— [Another copy.] **G. 2223. (1.)**

—— [Another copy.] pp. 116. **G. 14757. (2.)**

—— [Another edition.] Legenda. S. Catharinæ Mediceæ
Reginæ matris, vitæ, actorum, & consiliorum, quibus
vniuersum regni Gallici statum turbare conata est,
stupenda eaque vera enarratio. pp. 103. 1575. 8°.
G. 15440.

—— The History of the Life of Katharine de Medicis . . . or,
the Exact Pattern of the present French King's policy.
See supra: Discours merveilleux de la vie . . . de
Catherine de Médicis.

—— C'est l'ordre et forme qui a este tenue au Sacre &
Couronnemēt de treshaulte & tresillustre Dame, Madame
Catharine de Medicis, Royne de France faict en l'Eglise
Monseigneur sainct Denys, en France, le x iour de Iuin
M.D.XLIX. ff. 11. *On les vend par I. Dallier: Paris,*
[1549.] 4°. **813. f. 54.**

—— [Another edition.] ff. 10. *Par I. Dallier: Paris,*
[1549.] 4°. **9930. f. 48. (2.)**

—— [Another edition.] L'Ordre tenu au sacre et couronne-
ment de la royne Catherine de Medicis, femme du roy
Henry II. l'an 1549. *See* GODEFROY (T.) Le Ceremonial
de France, *etc.* 1619. 4°. **605. c. 21.**

—— L'Ordre tenu à l'entrée de la royne Catherine de Medicis,
femme du roy Henry II, à Paris, l'an 1549. *See* GODEFROY
(T.) Le Ceremonial de France, *etc.* 1619. 4°.
605. c. 21.

—— The verye trueth of the conference betwixt the Queene
mother, and the Prince of Conde. ꝫ.ꝫ. [*W. Seres? or*
R. Hall?: London?] 1562. 8°. **C. 123. a. 3.**

CATHARINE [DE' MEDICI], *Queen Consort of Henry II.,*
King of France.

Miscellaneous.

—— *See* CHEVALIER (C.) Archives royales de Chenonceau.
Debtes et créanciers de la Royne mère Catherine de
Médicis, 1589–1606. Documents publiés pour la première fois d'après les archives de Chenonceau, *etc.*
1862. 8°.   **09210. e. 10.**

—— *See* DEFRANCE (E.) Catherine de Médicis. Ses astro-
logues et ses magiciens-envoûteurs, *etc.* 1911. 8°.
              10633. e. 23.

—— *See* FRANCE.—Henry III, *King.* [1574–1589.] Articles
resolus et accordez à Nerac, en la conference de la Royne
mere du Roy . . . auec le Roy de Nauarre, *etc.*
1579. 8°.   **1193. g. 22. (10.)**

—— *See* FRANCE.—Henry III., *King.* [1574–1589.] Missiue à
la Reine Mere, sur le fait de l'edict du Roy, fait en Iuillet
dernier, 1585. pour reunir tous ses suiets à la Religion
Romaine. 1586. 8°.   **901. b. 19.**

—— *See* HUILLARD-BRÉHOLLES (J. L. A.) [Essai sur le
caractère et l'influence de Catherine de Médicis.] Sul
carattere e l'influenza di Caterina de' Medici, *etc.* 1847. 8°.
             010665. p. 1.

—— *See* LAFFÉMAS (B. de) *Sieur de Bauthor.* Lettres et
exemples de la feu royne mère, comme elle faisoit trauailler
aux manufactures, et fournissoit aux ouuriers de ses
propres deniers, *etc.* 1836. 8°.   [CIMBER (*M. L.*)
Archives curieuses de l'histoire de France, etc. sér. 1.
tom. 9.]   **805. b. 3.**

—— *See* LUZIO (A.) Leonardo Arrivabene alla corte di
Caterina de' Medici, 1549–1559, *etc.* 1902. 4°.
             10632. g. 26.

—— *See* TH. (M. P. Be. Iu.) Declaration du droit de legitime
succession sur le royaume de Portugal, apartenant à la
Royne mere du Roy Treschrestien, *etc.* 1582. 8°.
            1195. a. 2. (1.)

—— [Articles reprinted from periodicals.] *See* WEBER
(Bernerd C.) (Catherine de' Medici: a royal bibliophile.
[1949.]) [1939, *etc.*] 8°.   **W.P. 4256.**

—— Ad augustissimam Galliarum Reginam, de natiuitate
filiæ catholici Hispaniarum Regis carmen N.S. 1566. 4°.
See S., N.   **1477. aaa. 14. (8.)**

—— Catherine de Médicis dans le cabinet de Marie-Antoinette
à St Cloud. Premier dialogue. pp. 8. [*Paris,* 1790 ?] 8°.
             F.R. 124. (2.)

—— Catherine de Medicis, or the Rival Faiths. pp. 380.
Smith, Elder & Co.: London, 1834. 12°.   **N. 1227.**

—— Compte de dépenses de Catherine de Médicis. 1836.
See CIMBER (M. L.) *pseud.* Archives curieuses de l'histoire de France, *etc.* sér. 1. tom. 9. 1834, *etc.* 8°.
             805. b. 3.

—— Discours fait à la Royne Mere du Roy, par un sien
fidelle subiet pour le bien de la paix de se royaume auãt
qu'elle partist pour aller la traicter auec le Roy de Nauarre
pp. 23. 1586. 8°.   **1192. e. 37.**

—— Festin donné à la royne Catherine au logis épiscopal
de l'évesché de Paris, le dix-neuviesme jour de juing
1549. (Fragment inédit . . . extrait d'un compte original.) 1835. *See* CIMBER (M. L.) *pseud.* Archives
curieuses de l'histoire de France, *etc.* sér. 1. tom. 3.
1834, *etc.* 8°.   **805. b. 1.**

CATHARINE [DE' MEDICI], *Queen Consort of Henry II.,*
King of France. [APPENDIX.—MISCELLANEOUS.]

—— Inventaire des meubles de Catherine de Médicis en 1589.
Mobilier, tableaux, objets d'art, manuscrits. Par Edmond
Bonnaffé. pp. 219. *Paris,* 1874. 8°.   **10630. b. 7.**

—— *Begin.* Talisman magique et superstitieux de Catherine
de Medicis, Reine de France, *etc.* (L'original est . . .
conservé au cabinet de l'abbé Fauvel qui la fait ainsi
graver, *etc.*) [*Paris,* 1770 ?] *s. sh.* 8°.   **1103. c. 6. (8.)**
Engraved.

CATHARINE, *Queen Consort of Jerome Napoleon, King of*
Westphalia. *See* FREDERICA CATHARINE SOPHIA
DOROTHEA.

CATHARINE, *Queen Consort of John III., King of Sweden.*

—— *See* HAHR (August) *Professor at the University of Uppsala.*
Drottning Katarina Jagellonica och Vasarenässansen, *etc.*
1940. 8°. [*Skrifter utgivna av K. Humanistiska Veten-*
skaps-Samfundet i Uppsala. bd. 34. no. 1.] Ac. **1078.**

—— Testamentum Catharinæ Jagellonicæ, Reginæ Sveciæ, ex
schedis Bibliothecæ Acad. Upsal. editum . . . Præside
mag. Joh. Henr. Schröder . . . P.p. Carolus Wilhelmus
Pålman, *etc.* pp. iv. 10. *Upsaliæ,* [1831.] 4°.
            10760. b. 25. (1.)

—— Historya prawdziwa o przygodzie żałosnej książęcia
Finlandzkiego Jana i Królewny Katarzyny. 1570.
Wydał A. Kraushar. 1892. 8°. [*Bibljoteka pisarzów*
polskich. no. 22.] *See* JOHN III., *King of Sweden.*
            Ac. 750/45.

CATHARINE [OF PODIEBRAD], *Queen Consort of Matthias I.*
[*Corvinus*], *King of Hungary.* Budán felfedezett gazdag
sírbolt, mellyben hihetöleg Katalin, Mátyás Király első
hitvessének, és Podiebrad György leányának teteme
találtatott. [By M. Jankovich.] pp. 22.   *Pesten,*
1827. 8°.   **7709. b. 50.**

CATHARINE [OPALIŃSKA], *Queen Consort of Stanislaus I.*
Leszczyński, King of Poland. *See* CUNY (L. A.) Oraison
funèbre de très-haute . . . princesse Catherine Opalinska,
Reine de Pologne, *etc.* 1747. 4°.   **113. e. 8.**

CATHARINE, *Queen Consort of William, King of*
Wurtemberg. *See* AUTEL (A. H. d') Rede bei der
Beisetzung des Leichnames Ihrer Majestät der Königin
von Württemberg, Catharina Paulowna, *etc.* [1819.] 8°.
           4426. df. 11. (9.)

—— *See* BOZHERYANOV (I. N.) Великая княгиня Екатерина Павловна . . . королева Виртембергская . . .
Біографическій очеркъ, съ приложеніемъ портрета и
автографа. 1888. 8°.   **10704. i. 17.**

—— *See* ELENEV (N. A.) Путешествіе Вел. Кн. Екатерины
Павловны въ Богемію въ 1813 году. [With portraits
and extracts from her letters.] 1936. 8°. **10215. p. 4.**

—— *See* MERKLE (J.) Katharina Pawlowna Königin von
Württemberg, *etc.* [With a portrait.] 1889. 8°.
           10704. e. 36.

—— *See* MERKLE (J.) Segensreiche Wirksamkeit durch vier
Generationen, *etc.* (III. Katharina Pawlowna, Grossfürstin
von Russland, Königin von Württemberg.) 1893. 8°.
           10703. ff. 10.

—— *See* VRIES (I. de) *Baroness de Günzburg.* Catherine
Pavlovna, grande-duchesse russe, 1788–1819, *etc.* [With a
portrait.] 1941. 8°.   **010709. i. 78.**

—— Correspondance de l'empereur Alexandre Ier avec sa
sœur la grande-duchesse Catherine, princesse d'Alden-
bourg, puis reine de Wurtemberg, 1805–1818. [Edited by
the Grand Duke Nicholas Mikhaïlovich.] Orné de
8 planches et de 2 fac-simile d'autographes. pp. xxvi. 287.
1910. 8°. *See* ALEXANDER I., *Emperor of Russia.*
[*Works.*]   **10902. g. 24.**

CATHARINE, *Queen Consort of William, King of Wurtemberg.*

—— Scenes of Russian Court Life. Being the correspondence of Alexander I. with his sister Catherine. Translated by Henry Havelock. Edited with an introduction by the Grand Duke Nicholas. pp. 331. [1917.] 8°. *See* ALEXANDER I., *Emperor of Russia.* [*Works.*]
010902. h. 18.

CATHARINE [CORNARO], *Queen of Cyprus. See* CENTELLI (A.) Caterina Cornaro e il suo regno. Con tre ritratti, *etc.* 1892. 8°. **10632. df. 21.**

—— *See* FORRER (L.) Caterina Cornaro, regina di Cipro, et le sue monete, *etc.* 1906. 8°. **7756. bb. 21. (8.)**

—— *See* LOREDANA, *pseud.* Caterina Cornaro, patrizia veneta, regina di Cypro, *etc.* [With portraits.] 1938. 8°. **10635. e. 15.**

—— *See* PLANIUS (J. B.) Ioānis Baptistae planii Brixiani: Iureconsulti celeberrimi ad Augustissimam Cyprorum Reginā Oratio, *etc.* [On the occasion of Catharine's entry into Brescia.] [1497.] 4°. **IA. 31161.**

CATHARINE, *Queen of Kandy. See* SENAVIRATNE (J. M.) Great Sinhalese Men of History. (vol. 2. Life and Times of Dona Catherina, the first Catholic Queen of Kandy.) [1931, *etc.*] 8°. **10607.ee.85/2.**

CATHARINE, *Queen of Navarre.*

—— Testament de Catherine de Foix, reine ae Navarre, Pampelune, 25 juin 1504. *See* ANTHONY (R.) *Historian,* and COURTEAULT (H.) Les Testaments des derniers rois de Navarre . . . Catherine de Foix, 1504, *etc.* 1940. 8°. **12238. dd. 1/30.**

CATHARINE [LABOURÉ], *Saint. See* CASSINARI (E.) [La Beata Caterina Labouré.] Life of Blessed Catherine Labouré, *etc.* [With portraits.] 1934. 8°. **20018. e. 12.**

—— *See* CRAPEZ (E.) Venerable Sister Catherine Labouré . . . Taken chiefly from " La vénerable Catherine Labouré " by the Rev. E. Crapez. 1920. 8°. **4864. dg. 28.**

—— *See* DAYDÍ (L.) La Bienaventurada Sor Catalina Labouré . . . y la Medalla Milagrosa. [With a portrait.] 1933. 8°. **4869.a.10.**

—— *See* EGAN (M. J.) The Story of the Miraculous Medal. [On the visions of Catherine Labouré.] 1948. 8°. **4869. a. 7.**

—— *See* FULLERTON (*Lady* Georgina C.) The Miraculous Medal. Life and visions of Catherine Labouré, *etc.* 1880. 8°. **4865. bbb. 25.**

—— *See* LOUIS-LEFEBVRE (M. T.) The Silence of St. Catherine Labouré, *etc.* 1953. 8°. **4832. a. 12.**

—— *See* MULVEY (James) Saint Catherine Labouré and the Miraculous Medal. [With a portrait.] [1952.] 8°. **4831. cc. 6.**

—— *See* ROME, *Church of.—Congregatio Rituum.* Parisien. Beatificationis et canonizationis . . . C. Labouré . . . Nova positio super virtutibus. 1928. fol. **5052. f. 66.**

CATHARINE, *Saint, of Alexandria. See* BOBBE (H.) Mittelhochdeutsche Katharinen-Legenden in Reimen. Eine Quellenuntersuchung. 1922. 8°. **011824. c. 13/19.**

—— *See* BRÉMOND (M. J. F. R. I. H.) Sainte Catherine d'Alexandrie, *etc.* 1917. 8°. [*L'Art et les Saints.*] **W.P. 6017/4.**

CATHARINE, *Saint, of Alexandria.*

—— *See* CALYBS (P.) Diue Catharine virginis . . . heroica vitæ descriptio, *etc.* 1515. 4°. **11403. bb. 53.**

—— *See* CAPGRAVE (John) The Life of St. Katharine of Alexandria, *etc.* 1893. 8°. **Ac. 9925/75.**

—— *See* CASTIGLIONE (G. A.) Gli Honori de gli antichi Disciplinati, *etc.* (Gli Honori del sacro tempio di S. Catherina al Ponte de' Fabbri di Porta Ticinese di Milano . . . Con la vita . . . di S. Gottardo . . . e'l martirio di S. Catherina vergine.) 1622. 8°. **4785. cc. 18.**

—— *See* DORLANDUS (P.) Deuotissimi Patris Petri Dorlandi . . . De Natiuitate Conuersione & vita inuictissimæ martiris beatissimæᶜǥ virginis Katherinæ . . . Libellus. 1513. 8°. **4827. a. 21.**

—— *See* ETIRO (P.) *pseud.* Vita di S. Caterina vergine e martire, *etc.* 1630. 12°. **1121. d. 7.**

—— —— 1636. 12°. **4824. a. 21.**

—— *See* FILIPPI (M.) Vita di santa Caterina, vergine e martire, *etc.* 1592. 8°. **1063. b. 16.**

—— *See* HARDWICK (Charles) *Archdeacon of Ely.* An Historical Inquiry touching Saint Catharine of Alexandria: to which is added a Semi-Saxon legend. 1849. 4°. [*Publications of the Cambridge Antiquarian Society.* vol. 2. no. 15.] **Ac. 5624/6.**

—— *See* HARRIS (James R.) A New Christian Apology, *etc.* [With reference to the " Μαρτυριον της ἁγιας Αἰκατερινης " of Simeon Metaphrastes.] 1923. 8°. **3624. bb. 9.**

—— *See* HARTMANN (Gulielmus) *Jesuit.* Illustris philosophiæ Christianæ defensio adversus Maximini ferociam propugnante ad usque magisterii, martyriiq; gloriosi lauream Catharina, *etc.* [1731.] 4°. **T. 1857. (14.)**

—— *See* KNUST (H.) Geschichte der Legenden der h. Katharina von Alexandrien, *etc.* 1890. 8°. **4824. df. 5.**

—— [For editions of the office of St. Catharine :] *See* LITURGIES.—*Greek Rite.—Separate Offices of Saints.*

—— *See* MIELOT (J.) Vie de sᵗᵉ Catherine d'Alexandrie, *etc.* 1881. 4°. **1232. h. 15.**

—— *See* MIELOT (J.) Leben der heiligen Katharina von Alexandrien, *etc.* 1886, *etc.* 4°. **4827. h. 1.**

—— *See* OPALIŃSKI (S. M.) Lilium candidissimum . . . divinissima virgo & martyr, Catharina, in Basilica Casimiriensi, floridissimi Ordinis Cracoviensis S. Augustini, odoratum, *etc.* [1718 ?] fol. **4828. f. 19.**

—— *See* PETRUS, *Frater.* Hec est noua . . . legenda . . . tractans de origine. et vite. ordine. de conuersione. ac magistrali disputatione. ast de passione. morte. ꝛ miraculis . . . virginis et martiris sancte Katherine. Ciuis . . . vrbis Alexandrine. 1500. 4°. **IA. 1492.**

—— *See* PETRUS, *Frater.* Dis ist ein nüwe . . . legend von dem vrsprung vnnd leben. marter vnd sterben. vnd ouch von den wunderzeichē der . . . Iunckfrawen vnd marterin sant Katherinen. 1500. 4°. **IA. 1496.**

—— *See* PIETRO, *Aretino.* La Vita di Catherina vergine. [1540 ?] 8°. **1370. a. 5.**

—— —— 1541. 8°. **218. b. 11. (2.)**

—— *See* POLANSKY (T.) Janua virtutis et scientiæ sancta partheno-martyr Catharina . . . panegyricè celebrata, *etc.* [1730.] 4°. **T. 1857. (12.)**

CATHARINE, *Saint, of Alexandria.*

—— *See* RABBANUS, *Abbas.* Diue v̇ginis scē Katherine historia seu eiusdē passionis series Rabbani abbatꝫ. [1476?] fol. [*Insignis duarum passionum domini Iesu Christi . . . collectio.*]   IB. **3501.**

—— —— [1490?] 4°. [*KANNEMANN (J.) Passio Christi,* etc.]   IA. **8027.**

—— *See* RICHIEDEI (P.) Delle lodi di S. Caterina vergine e martire . . . Oratione, *etc.* [1680?] 4°. **4828. d. 26.**

—— *See* RINALDI (B. di) Leggenda di S. Caterina d'Alessandria, *etc.* 1885. 8°. [*PERCOPO (E.) IV. Poemetti sacri dei secoli XIV° e XV°, etc.*]   **12226. de. 3. (1.)**

—— [For editions of the Parthenice secunda, vitam et martyrium sanctae Catharinae virginis martyrisque complectens, by Baptista Spagnuoli:] *See* SPAGNUOLI (B.) *Mantuanus.*

—— *See* VARNHAGEN (H.) Zur Geschichte der Legende der Katharina von Alexandrien. Nebst lateinischen Texten, *etc.* 1891. 8°.   **4829. f. 18. (4.)**

—— *See* ZONCA (G.) Il Pomogranato. Panegirico, ouero discorso in lode della vergine e martire Santa Caterina d'Alessandria, *etc.* 1631. 4°.   **4829. aaa. 8.**

—— Alexandriai Szent Katalin verses legendája, ugyanazon szentnek két kisebb prózai életével együtt. Régi codexekből, nyelvjegyzetekkel kiadta Toldy Ferenc. pp. xxxix. 287. *Pest*, 1855. 8°.   **11586. ee. 19.**

—— Die altčechische Katherinenlegende der Stockholm-Brünner Handschrift. Einleitung. Text mit Quellen. Wörterbuch. Von Dr. Franz Spina. pp. xxxiv. 115. *Prag*, 1913. 8°.   **4828. d. 33.**

—— Andächtiger Rueff von dem H. Leben vnd Marterkampff der glorwürdigen Jungkfrawen S. Catharina . . . Nebst siben bewerthen vnd warhafften Miraclen . . . Sampt angehängter erschröcklicher Historia von einer vnbuessfertigen Indianischen Catharina, so verworffen vnd verdambt worden. pp. 34. *A. Aperger: Augsburg,* 1631. 8°.   **11517. bbb. 24.**

—— Buched Seint y Katrin. *See* TATHAN, *Saint.* Vita Sancti Tathei und Buched Seint y Katrin. Re-edited, after Rees, from the MSS. in the British Museum, by H. Idris Bell. 1909. 4°. [*Bangor Welsh MSS. Society. Publications.* no. 2.]   Ac. **8217.**

—— La Deuota Rapresentatione di Santa Catherina Vergine & Martire. Di nuouo stampata. [In verse. With woodcuts.] *Dirimpeto a Badia: Firenze,* 1554. 4°.   **11426. cc. 24.**

—— [Another edition.] Nuouamente ristampata. *Ad istantia di P. Bigio: Firenze,* 1561. 4°. **11426. f. 27.**

—— [Another edition.] Di nuouo ristampata, e corretta. [With woodcuts.] *Siena,* [1565?] 4°. C. **34. h. 5. (23.)**

—— [Another edition.] Di nuouo ricorretta, & aggiuntoui nel fine il suo Martirio. [With a woodcut.] *Alla Loggia del Papa: Siena,* 1606. 4°.   **11426. f. 28.**

—— Dvě verse starofrancouzské legendy o Sv. Kateřině Alexandrinské. Vydal Jan Urban Jarník, *etc. Lat. & Fr.* pp. li. 349. 1894. 4°. *See* PRAGUE.—*Česká Akademie Císaře Františka Josefa, etc.*   Ac. **799. b/2.**

—— Fragmentum vitæ Sanctæ Catharinæ Alexandrinensis metricum. E libro MS. edidit Johannes Paulson. pp. xxxi. 72. *Lundæ*, 1891. 8°.   **11409. f. 53.**

—— [Another copy.]   **4827. aaa. 4.**

CATHARINE, *Saint, of Alexandria.*

—— Eine gereimte altfranzösisch-veronesische Fassung der Legende der heiligen Katharina von Alexandrien. Mit Einleitung . . . kritisch herausgegeben von Hermann Breuer. *Fr. See* THIERRY, *de Vaucouleur.* Ein altfranzösische Fassung der Johanneslegende, *etc.* 1919. 8°. [*Zeitschrift für romanische Philologie.* Beihft. 53.] [MISSING.]

—— Historia, vita, miracoli, e morte di santa Caterina vergine et martire, *etc.* [In verse. With two woodcuts.] *Appresso alle scalee di Badia: Fiorenza,* [1550?] 4°.   **11426. c. 14.**

—— Ein hübsch new geistlich Lied von der H. Jungkfrauwen vnd Märterin S. Catharina.   *S. Philot: Fryburg inn Vchtlandt,* 1607. 8°.   **11515. a. 52. (11.)**

—— Die Katharinenlegende der H.S. 11, 143. der Kgl. Bibliothek zu Brüssel. Herausgegeben von Dr. William Edward Collinson. pp. xii. 178.   *Heidelberg,* 1915. 8°. [*Germanische Bibliothek.* Abt. 2. Bd. 10.]   **2276. e. 2/10.**

—— Die Katharinen-Passie. Ein Druck von Ulrich Zell. In Nachbildung herausgegeben und untersucht von Hermann Degering und Max Joseph Husung.   *Berlin,* 1928. 8°. [*Seltene Drucke der Preussischen Staatsbibliothek zu Berlin.* no. 2.]   **11914. d. 47/2.**

—— Eine lateinische Bearbeitung der Legende der Katharina von Alexandrien in Distichen, *etc. See infra:* Passio Sanctae Catherinae Alexandrinae metrica.

—— The Legend of St. Katherine of Alexandria. Edited, from a manuscript in the Cottonian Library, by James Morton. [The Early English text with a modern English translation.] pp. xv. 143. 1841. 4°. *See* EDINBURGH. —*Abbotsford Club.*   R. Ac. **8247/20.**

—— Die Legende der hl. Katharina von Alexandrien. Untersuchungen und Texte unter Zugrundelegung der Bielefelder Handschrift. Inaugural-Dissertation . . . von Siegfried Sudhof. ff. 200. [1951.] fol.   **4830. i. 11.** *Typewritten.*

—— La Leggenda di S. Caterina d'Alessandria in decima rima. [Edited by Pasquale Papa.] *See* ROSSI (V.) Miscellanea nuziale Rossi-Teiss. 1897. 8°.   **12352. h. 21.**

—— Liedeken op het leven en Martelie van de H. Catharina, *etc. See* JEW. Liedeken van eenen Jode, *etc.* [1850?] *s. sh.* fol.   **1871. c. 1. (33.)**

—— The Life and Martyrdom of Saint Katherine, of Alexandria, virgin and martyr. Now first printed from a manuscript of the early part of the fifteenth century in the possession of Henry Hucks Gibbs, with preface, notes, glossary [by H. H. Gibbs] and appendix. (The Life of Saint Katherine. From the Royal MS. . . . With its Latin original from the Cotton MS. . . . Edited . . . by Dr. E. Einenkel.) 2 pt. 1884. 4°. *See* LONDON. —III. *Roxburghe Club.*   C. **101. d. 17.**

—— The Lif of saincte Katheryne. B.L.   [*R. Pynson? London,* 1510?] 4°.   Cup. **645. e. 1. (9.)** *A fragment consisting of a single sheet of four leaves, of which the first has the signature a ii, and bears a woodcut which is repeated on the verso.*

—— [Another edition.] The life of the glorious and blessed virgin and martyr Saincte Katheryne. B.L. *Ihon Waley: London,* [1555?] 4°.   C. **53. bb. 3.**

CATHARINE, *Saint, of Alexandria.*

—— The Life of St. Katharine [in verse]: The Tale of the Knight and his Wife [in verse]: and An Account of the Magical Manuscript of Dr. Caius. Edited by James Orchard Halliwell. pp. iv. 32. *For private circulation: Brixton Hill,* 1848. 4°. **11631. h. 25.**
One of an edition of seventy-five copies.

—— [Another issue.] **F.P.** [*Contributions to Early English Literature, etc.*] **741. k. 15.**

—— The Life of Saint Katherine. From the Royal MS. 17A. xxvii., &c., with its Latin original from the Cotton MS. Caligula, A. viii, &c. Edited, with introduction, notes, and glossary, by Dr. Eugen Einenkel. pp. lxii. 188. 1884. 8°. *See* LONDON.—III. *Early English Text Society.*
. Ac. **9925/58.**

—— [Another copy.] . Ac. **9927/59.**

—— *See* VICTOR (O. E.) Zur Textkritik und Metrik der frühmittelenglischen Katharinenlegende (E. E. T. S. 80), *etc.* 1912. 8°. **012902. h. 32. (4.)**

—— Μαρτυριον της ἁγιας Αἰκατερινας, *etc.* [Three Greek texts, with Latin versions of the first and third.] *See* VITEAU (J.) Passions des saints Écaterine et Pierre d'Alexandrie, *etc.* 1897. 8°. **4829. f. 24.**

—— Passio Sanctae Catherinae Alexandrinae metrica . . . Edidit H. Varnhagen. pp. 25. *Erlangae,* 1891. 4°. **11405. h. 12.**

—— [A reissue, with supplement.] Eine lateinische Bearbeitung der Legende der Katharina von Alexandrien in Distichen . . . Herausgegeben von Hermann Varnhagen. Nebst dem lateinischen Texte des Mombritius. pp. 32. *Erlangen,* 1892. 4°. **4828. e. 10. (1.)**

—— Seynt Katerine. [From the Auchinleck MS. In verse.] *See* CATHOLIC LEGENDS. Legendæ Catholicæ, *etc.* 1840. 16°. . **1346. c. 11.**

—— Sainte Catherine, tragédie. [In verse. By —— Saint Germain.] pp. 83. [*Paris?* 1650?] 12°. **163. d. 67.**
Part of a larger work.

—— Sanctae Catherinae virginis et martyris translatio et miracula Rotomagensia saec. XI. [With an introduction by Albert Poncelet.] *See* PONCELET (A.) La Vie de S. Willibrord, *etc.* 1903. 8°. **4830. e. 2. (2.)**

—— Житїє й страдачество стыл . . . єкатєрїны ново превєдєно [by Arsenios the Greek], *etc.* *See* ARSENIOS, *the Greek.* Анѳолоґїон сїєстъ цвѣтослȯвїє, *etc.* [1660.] 8°. **C. 110. b. 1. (2.)**

—— Sinte Katherinen Legende gheboertē eñ der bekeringhe. eñ passye der heyligher maghet. beghint hier seer deuotelick. [With a woodcut.] *bij mij Gouaert Bac: antwerpen,* [1495?] 4°. **IA. 49965.**
36 leaves. Sig. a–f⁶. 31 lines to a page.

—— Une Version arabe de la Passion de Sᵗᵉ Catherine d'Alexandrie. [Edited by Paul Peeters.] Extrait des Analecta Bollandiana, *etc.* *Arab. & Lat.* pp. 32. *Bruxelles,* 1907. 8°. **4804. dd. 15. (3.)**

—— Жизнь и страданія Св. . . . Екатерины, *etc.* pp. 35. *Москва,* 1887. 12°. **4827. de. 38.**

—— Život Svaté Kateřiny. Legenda. V Královské Bibliotéce v Stokholmě objevil a vydal Josef Pečírka . . . K tisku zredigoval a vysvětlením temnějších slov opatřil K. J. Erben. pp. xxix. 221. *v Praze,* 1860. 12°.
11586. aa. 17.

CHURCHES AND INSTITUTIONS.

—— AARDENBURG.—*Sante Katelijnen-Begijnhof.* Eenige oorkonden over het Begijnhof van Aardenburg. [Edited by L. Ceyssens.] 1935. *See* BRUGES.—*Société d'Émulation.* Annales, *etc.* tom. 78. 1839, *etc.* 8°. Ac. **5517.**

CATHARINE, *Saint, of Alexandria.* [CHURCHES AND INSTITUTIONS.]

—— BAMBERG.—*St. Katharina-Spital.* Das Copialbuch des St. Katharina-Spitals zu Bamberg in vollständigen Auszügen der Urkunden von 1265–1502 mitgetheilt von C. A. Schweitzer. 1847. *See* BAMBERG.—*Historischer Verein.* Bericht, *etc.* no. 10. 1834, *etc.* 8°. Ac. **7014.**

—— BLAIRGOWRIE.—*St. Catherine's Church.* St. Catherine's Church, Blairgowrie. Resignation of the Rev. Mr. Marshall . . . Letters for the use of the Congregation. pp. 7. [1843.] 8°. **908. d. 5. (8.)**

—— FIERBOIS.—*Chapelle de Sainte Catherine.* Les Miracles de Madame sainte Katherine, de Fierboys en Touraine, 1375–1446. Publiés . . . d'apres un manuscrit de la Bibliothèque impériale par M. l'abbé J.-J. Bourassé. *Tours,* 1858. 12°. **4824. c. 14.**

—— The Miracles of Madame Saint Katherine of Fierbois. Translated from the edition of the abbé J. J. Bourassé . . . by Andrew Lang. pp. 151. *Way & Williams: Chicago; David Nutt: London,* 1897. 8°.
K.T.C. 26. a. 14.

—— MÜNSTER, *Westphalia.—Minoritenkloster bei St. Catharinen.*
—— Votum gratulatorium in adventu serenissimi, et reverendissimi domini, D. Clementis Augusti episcopi Monasteriensis, et Paderbornensis . . . humillimè oblatum, & dicatum â Fratribus Minoribus S. Francisci Conventualibus Monasterij ad S. Catharinam. [*Münster,*] 1719. fol.
12301. m. 7.

—— NOTTINGHAM.—*Church of Saint Catharine.* "Dear S. Catharine's." Being a suggested method of visiting a church, and also a history of the parish and church of S. Catharine, Nottingham, by the Vicar (J. M. F. Lester). [1929.] 8°. *See* LESTER (John M. F.) **04705. d. 23.**

—— ROME.—*Chiesa di Santa Caterina.—Compagnia delle Vergini Miserabili di Santa Caterina della Rosa di Roma.* Constitutioni della Compagna delle Vergini Miserabili di Santa Catherina della Rosa di Roma. pp. 32. *Per F. Zanetti: Roma,* 1582. 8°. **4071. a. 16.**

—— SAINT PETERSBURG.—*Rzymsko-Katolickie Towarzystwo Dobroczynności Kościoła św. Katarzyny.* "Charitas." Księga zbiorowa wydana na rzecz R.-K. Towarzystwa Dobroczynności przy Kościele Sw. Katarzyny w Petersburgu. pp. 585. *Petersburg,* 1894. 8°. **12352. g. 38.**

—— SARAGOSSA.—*Convento di Santa Catalina.* Festivas Aclamaciones, Metricos Aplausos, a la solemne Canonizacion de la esclarecida virgen Santa Catalina de Bolonia . . . Celebrados en el . . . Convento de Santa Catalina de Zaragoça . . . dia 24. de Octubre de 1713. *Zaragoça,* [1713.] 4°. **1073. k. 22. (4.)**

—— SOISSONS.—*Collège de Sainte-Catherine.* Texte de chartes concernant l'ancien Collège Sainte-Catherine à Soissons. 1891. *See* SOISSONS.—*Société historique et archéologique.* Bulletin, *etc.* sér. 2. tom. 19. 1847, *etc.* 8°.
Ac. **6893.**

CATHARINE [DE' VIGRI], *Saint, of Bologna. See* CATHARINE, *Saint, of Alexandria.—Churches and Institutions.—Saragossa.—Convento di Santa Catalina.* Festivas Aclamaciones, Metricos Aplausos, a la solemne Canonizacion de . . . Santa Catalina de Bolonia . . . Celebrados en el . . . Convento de Santa Catalina de Zaragoça, *etc.* [1713.] 4°. **1073. k. 22. (4.)**

—— *See* GRASSETTI (G.) Vita della B. Caterina di Bologna 1620. 4°. **4828. c. 23.**

—— —— 1639. 4°. **485. b. 12.**

—— —— 1652. 4°. **485. d. 21.**

CATHARINE [DE' VIGRI], *Saint, of Bologna.*

—— *See* MARIANO, *di Cadore.* Vita della serafica vergine Caterina da Bologna, *etc.* 1707. 8°.   **1225. a. 12.**

—— *See* MARY, *the Blessed Virgin.—Churches and Institutions.—Saragossa.—Convento de Nuestra Señora de Jerusalen.* Sagrados Plausibles Himnos, que à la Canonizacion de la serafica virgen boloñesa Santa Catalina consagra el religiosissimo Convento de Nuestra Señora de Jerusalen de la Orden de Santa Clara, *etc.* [1713.] 4°.
1073. k. 22. (5.)

—— *See* NANNETTI (E.) Vita di S. Catterina Vigri detta da Bologna, *etc.* 1841. 16°.   **4412. b. 51. (5.)**

—— *See* ROME, *Church of.—Congregatio Rituum.* Acta canonizationis Sanctorum Pii v. Pont. Max., Andreæ Avellini, Felicis à Cantalicio, & Catharinæ de Bononia, *etc.* 1720. fol.   **487. l. 13.**

—— *See* ROME, *Church of.—Popes.*—Clement XI. [1700–1721.] Clemens Papa XI. Ad perpetuam rei memoriam, *etc.* [A brief announcing the canonization of St. Catharine of Bologna. 21 March 1714.] 1714. *s. sh.* fol.
1896. d. 15. (44.)

—— [Le Armi necessarie alla battaglia spirituale.] *Begin.* [fol. 1 *recto :*] Incomenza uno libretto cōposto da una beata religiòsa del corpo dē cristo Sore Caterina da bologna. [fol. 68, *recto :*] ¶Incomēzão alcune ,cose dʼ ʾla uita dʼ la sopranominata beata Caterina [in verse].
[*Balthasar Azoguidus : Bologna,* 1475 ?] 8°.   **G. 967.**
72 leaves, without signatures. 21 lines to a page.

—— [Another edition.] Libro deuoto de la beata Chaterina Bolognese del ordine del Seraphico Sācto Frācesco elqual essa lascio scripto de sua propria mano. [With a woodcut.] *Per H. P. de Benedictis : Bologna,* 1511. 4°.
3677. b. 16. (1.)

—— [Another edition.] Il Libro della Beata Caterina Bolognese, dell'Ordine del Seraphico Santo Francesco, quale essa lasciò scritta di sua mano. [With a woodcut.] [1550 ?] 8°.   **3834. a. 10.**

—— [Another edition.] Le Armi necessarie alla battaglia spirituale, *etc. See* GRASSETTI (G.) Vita della B. Caterina di Bologna, *etc.* 1639. 4°.   **485. b. 12.**

—— [Another edition.] *See* GRASSETTI (G.) Vita della B. Caterina di Bologna, *etc.* 1652. 4°.   **485. d. 21.**

—— The Spiritual Armour. By St. Catharine of Bologna. Together with The Way of the Cross, by Blessed Angela of Foligno. Translated . . . by Alan G. McDougall. pp. xiii, 39. *Burns, Oates & Co. : London,* 1926. 12°.
04402. ff. 52.

—— Diuinum .B. Catharinae Bononiensis Opusculum in latinum a Io. Ant. Flaminio Forocorneliensi, ex uernaculo cŏuersum, cũ eiusdem Sanctæ Virginis uita ab eodē Flaminio contexta.   *Per Hieronymũ de Benedictis : Bononiæ,* 1522. 4°.   Hirsch I. 1. (2.)

—— *Begin.* [fol. 1 *recto :*] Incomēcia la tabula de li capituli del libro de la uita de la btā Catherina da Bologna, *etc.* [fol. 2 *recto :*] Incomentia la uita de la beata Catherina da Bologna, *etc.* [By Dionisio Paleotti.] [fol. 25 *recto :*] Incomencia una deuota laude de la uita de la sopranominata beata Catherina, *etc. per Z. A. de li benedicti : Bologna,* 1502. 4°.   **3677. b. 16. (2.)**

—— *Church of, at Ferrara.* La Nuova chiesa di S. Catterina dei Vegri aperta in Ferrara li XXIV ottobre MDCCCLVIII. (Estratto dalla Gazzetta di Ferrara.) pp. 8. [*Ferrara,* 1858.] 8°.   **10129. bb. 31.**

CATHARINE [DE' RICCI], *Saint, of Florence. See* BAYONNE (H.) Vie de sainte Catherine de Ricci de Florence, *etc.* 1873. 12°.   **4826. aaaa. 6.**

—— *See* BAYONNE (H.) La Vita di santa Caterina de' Ricci, *etc.* 1874. 8°.   **4827. bbb. 2.**

—— *See* CAPES (Florence M.) St. Catherine de' Ricci. Her life, her letters, her community, *etc.* [1905.] 8°.
4827. dg. 10.

—— *See* CATTANI DA DIACCETO (F. de) *Bishop of Fiesole.* Breue raccolto della vita et costumi di suor Caterina de Ricci, *etc.* 1592. 4°.   **1232. c. 3.**

—— *See* FABER (Frederick W.) The Saints and Servants of God, *etc.* (The Life of St. Catherine of Ricci.) 1847, *etc.* 8°.   **4826. c. 7.**

—— *See* FIDELIS, *of Siegmaringen, Saint.* Distinta relazione della seguita solenne canonizazione de cinque santi, Fedele da Sigmaringa . . . Caterina Ricci, *etc.* [1746.] 4°.   **1230. d. 20. (19.)**

——, *See* GUIDI (Filippo) *Dominican.* Vita della venerabile madre suor Caterina de Ricci, *etc.* 1617. 4°.
1231. c. 11.

—— —— 1622. 4°.   **1231. c. 12.**

—— *See* MARCHESE (D. M.) *Bishop of Pozzuoli.* Vita della venerabile serva di Dio suor Catarina de' Ricci, *etc.* 1683. 4°.   **1231. c. 16.**

—— —— 1746. 4°.   **1231. c. 19.**

—— *See* RAZZI (S.) La Vita della reuerenda serua di Dio, la madre suor Caterina de Ricci, *etc.* 1594. 4°.
1232. c. 13.

—— *See* ROME, *Church of.—Congregatio Rituum.* Florentina beatificationis & canonizationis vener. servæ Dei sororis Catharinæ Ricciæ . . . Positio super dubio : An constet de virtutibus theologalibus . . . & cardinalibus, *etc.* 1713. fol.   **1229. g. 2.**

—— *See* ROME,—*Church of.—Congregatio Rituum.* Florentina beatificationis & canonizationis ven. servæ Dei Catharinæ de Ricciis . . . Positio super dubio, An, & de quibus miraculis constet in casu, *etc.* 1729. fol.   **1229. g. 3.**

—— *See* ROME, *Church of.—Congregatio Rituum.* Florentina beatificationis & canonizationis ven. servæ Dei Catharinæ de Ricciis . . . Positio additionalis super dubio, An, & de quibus miraculis constet in casu, *etc.* 1731. fol.
1229. g. 4.

—— *See* ROME, *Church of.—Congregatio Rituum.* Florentina canonizationis B. Catharinæ de Ricciis . . . Positio super dubio An, & de quibus miraculis constet post indultam eidem Beatæ venerationem, *etc.* 1742. fol. **1229. g. 6.**

—— *See* ROME, *Church of.—Congregatio Rituum.* Acta canonizationis Sanctorum Fidelis a Sigmaringa . . . Catharinæ de Ricciis, *etc.* 1749. 4°.   **4827. h. 5.**

—— *See* SANDRINI (D. M.) Vita di santa Caterina de' Ricci *etc.* 1747. 4°.   **1231. d. 8.**

—— *See* VALSECCHI (V.) Compendio della vita della beata Caterina de' Ricci, *etc.* 1733. 4°.   **4827. e. 6.**

—— Le Lettere spirituali e familiari di S. Caterina de' Ricci . . . Raccolte e illustrate da Cesare Guasti. pp. cxxiv. 480. *Prato,* 1861. 8°.   **3677. aaa. 8.**

—— Vita di S. Caterina de' Ricci . . . Cavata da' Sommarij de' Processi fatti per la sua beatificazione e canonizazione, *etc.* pp. xv. 199. *Roma,* 1746. 4°.   **1231. d. 6.**

CATHARINE [Adorni], *Saint, of Genoa. See* Huegel (F. von) *Baron.* The Mystical Element of Religion as studied in Saint Catherine of Genoa and her friends. 1908. 8°.   **03558. g. 4.**

—— —— 1923. 8°.   **03558. h. 12.**

—— *See* Marcone (A.) Delle relazioni fra Cristoforo Colombo e S. Caterina da Genova, *etc.* 1895. 8°. **10631. de. 35.**

—— *See* Serianni (G.) De B. Catharina Flisca Adurna. Oratio, seu expositio illius vitæ, virtutum & miraculorum, *etc.* 1737. 4°.   **T. 78*. (39.)**

—— *See* Smith (Sheila Kaye) Quartet in Heaven. [Biographical studies of St. Catherine of Genoa and others.] 1952. 8°.   **4831. ee. 4.**

—— *See* Upham (Thomas C.) Life of Madame Catharine Adorna, *etc.* 1855. 8°.   **4829. c. 7.**

—— Libro de la vita mirabile & dottrina santa, de la beata Caterinetta da Genoa, Nel quale si contiene vna vtile & catholica dimostratione & dechiaratione del purgatorio. [The "Vita" by C. Marabotto and E. Vernazza. The "Trattato del purgatorio" by Saint Catharine, followed by "Dialogo della detta Madonna Caterinetta tra l'anima & il corpo." With a woodcut.] ff. 271. *Per A. Bellono: Genoua,* 1551. 8°.   **1371. b. 2.**

—— [Another edition.] Vita della beata Caterina Adorni da Genoua. Nel quale si contiene vna santa & vtile dottrina & vna catholica dichiaratione del Purgatorio. Con vn dialogo . . . tra l'Anima, il Corpo, l'humanità, l'Amor proprio, & il Signore, composto dalla medesima. Nuouamente . . . ricorretta e ristampata. pp. 331. *F. Giunti: Fiorenza,* 1589. 8°.   **1224. c. 13.**

—— [Another edition.] Vita mirabile e dottrina santa della B. Caterina da Genoua Fiesca Adorna, scritta dal suo confessore e ristampata in tutto conforme al suo originale. Coll' aggionta d'vna vtile e cattolica dichiaratione del Purgatorio, e d'vn Dialogo distinto in tre libri composti dalla medema, *etc.* pp. 399. *Genova,* 1712. 4°.   **4829. c. 1.**

—— [Another edition.] Vita mirabile e dottrina celeste di santa Caterina Fiesca Adorna da Genova; scritta già da Cattaneo Marabotto . . . e da Ettore Vernazza . . . insieme col Trattato del Purgatorio, e col Dialogo della Santa. Il tutto . . . ricorretto, e alla moderna ortografia ridotto. (Altre notizie intorno a santa Caterina . . . principalmente circa la sua canonizzazione tratte dalla Vita che ne scrisse il padre Alessandro Maineri.) pp. xvi. 514. 1743. 8°. *See MARABOTTO.*   **662. b. 21.**

—— La Vie et les oeuures spirituelles de S. Catherine d'Adorny de Gennes, reueuës et corrigeez. [A translation of the "Vita" of C. Marabotto and E. Vernazza. Followed by "Le Dialogue de la bienheureuse et ser. Catherine Adorny" and "Traicté du purgatoire."] (Le tout . . . nouuellement traduict d'italien en françois, par les Venerables Peres Religieux de la Chartreuse de Bourg-Fontaine.) pp. 717. *P. Rigaud: Lyon,* 1616. 12°.   **862. e. 22.**

The titlepage is engraved.

—— Nouuelle édition, plus nette & plus correcte, par Jean Desmarets. 2 pt. *F. Lambert: Paris,* 1667, 66. 12°.   **862. e. 23.**

—— Les Œuvres de sainte Catherine de Gênes, précédées de sa vie par M. le Vᵗᵉ Marie-Théodore de Bussierre. pp. ix. 511. *Paris,* 1860. 8°.   **3677. b. 6.**

CATHARINE [Adorni], *Saint, of Genoa.*

—— Vita della beata Catherina Adorni da Genoua. [By C. Marabotto and E. Vernazza.] Con vn Dialogo . . . tra l'anima, il corpo, l'humanità, l'amor proprio & il Signore, composto da essa Beata. Nuouamente corretta & ristampata. pp. 395. *G. Sarzina: Venetia,* 1615. 8°.   **862. e. 21.**

—— Dialogo di S. Caterina da Genova . . . fra l'anima, il corpo, l'amor proprio, lo spirito, l'umanità ed il Signore Iddio, *etc.* pp. 182. *Milano,* 1882. 8°.   **3832. aa. 3.**

—— The Treatise on Purgatory by St. Catherine of Genoa. Translated from the original Italian. With a preface by the Very Rev. H. E. Manning. pp. viii. 28. *Burns & Lambert: London,* 1858. 8°.   **4373. a. 15.**

—— The Treatise of S. Catherine of Genoa on Purgatory, newly translated by J. M. A. [i.e. John Marks Ashley.] Edited with an introductory essay on Hell and the intermediate state, by a Priest Associate of the Guild of All Souls. pp. 56. *John Hodges: London,* 1878. 8°.   **4372. bb. 24.**

—— Treatise on Purgatory. [With "Introductory Sketch" signed: W. F. P.] pp. 64. *Catholic Truth Society of Ireland: Dublin,* 1909. 16°.   **4256. eee. 6.**

—— Saint Catherine of Genoa. Treatise on Purgatory. The Dialogue. Translated by Charlotte Balfour and Helen Douglas Irvine. With a portrait.] pp. 142. *Sheed & Ward: London,* 1946. 8°.   **4257. pp. 9.**

—— Katharina von Genua. Lebensbild und geistige Gestalt. Ihre Werke. [By Lili Sertorius.] pp. 269. *München,* 1939. 8°.   **20014. aa. 3.**

—— [Trattato del purgatorio.] Traktat o czyśćcu . . . przetłumaczyła S. Leonja—Niepokalanka. pp. 78. *Warszawa,* 1938. 8°.   **4257. bbb. 54.**

—— Scelta de' Panegirici recitati in lode di Santa Caterina da Genova in occasione della prima solennis. novena e festa . . . celebrata dopo la sua Canonizzazione nella chiesa della Santissima Annunziata . . . Con la raccolta di varj componimenti poetici degli Arcadi di Genova, *etc.* pp. 272. *Genova,* 1739. 4°.   **1224. g. 16.**

—— Vita di Santa Caterina Fieschi-Adorno da Genova. [By Alessandro Maineri.] (Ricavata dai Processi fatti per la canonizzazione della Santa e stampata in Roma nel 1737.) Con un compendio delle sue opere, cioè del Trattato del Purgatorio e del Dialogo fra l'anima ed il corpo. pp. 160. *Genova,* 1887. 16°. **4824. aa. 20. (3.)**

CATHARINE [Audley], *Saint, of Ledbury. See* Audley (Catherine) called Saint Catharine of Ledbury.

CATHARINE [Benincasa], *Saint, of Sienna.* L'Opere della Serafica Santa Caterina da Siena nuovamente pubblicate da Girolamo Gigli. 4 tom.

    1. La Vita della Serafica S. Caterina da Siena. Tradotta . . . dalla Leggenda Latina che ne compilò il B. Raimondo da Capua . . . pel signor Bernardino Pecci, *etc.* pp. xlvi. 513. 1707.

    2, 3. L'Epistole della Serafica . . . S. Caterina da Siena . . . aggiuntevi nuovamente le annotazioni del padre Federigo Burlamacchi, *etc.* 2 pt. 1721, 13.

    4. Il Dialogo della Serafica Santa Caterina da Siena . . . diviso in quattro trattati . . . Aggiuntovi un quinto trattato (della consumata perfettione) . . . e orazioni della Santa . . . ed una Scrittura apologetica di monsig. Raffaelle M. Filamondo . . . contro alcuni detrattori della Santa. pp. xxxx. 392. 1707.

Siena, Lucca, 1707-21. 4°.   **663. c. 9-12.**
  Tom. 2 is imperfect; wanting pp. i-xxviii. Vol. 1, 3 & 4 were published at Siena; vol. 2 at Lucca.

CATHARINE [Benincasa], *Saint, of Sienna.*

—— Supplimento alla vulgata Leggenda di S. Caterina . . . Scritto già in lingua latina dal B. Tommaso Nacci Caffarini, ed ora ridotta nella italiana dal p. Amb. A. Tantucci, *etc.* pp. xv. 280. *Lucca,* 1754. 4°. **663. c. 13.**

—— [Another copy of tom. 1.] **205. b. 2.**

—— [Another copy of tom. 2, with a different titlepage.] **223. k. 8.**

—— [Another copy of tom. 3.] **223. k. 9.**

—— [Another edition of tom. 4.] Il Dialogo della Serafica Santa Caterina da Siena . . . Tomo quarto. Edizione seconda. pp. xxxx. 392. *Lucca,* 1726. 4°. **10. a. 13.**

—— [Another copy of the Supplimento.] **4825. f. 21.**

—— *Begin.* [fol. 2 *recto:*] Epistole utile e diuote de la beata e seraphica Vergine. Sancta Chaterina da Siena . . . Et sono in tutto .xxxi. ne lequale se contene mirabel doctrina, *etc. End.* [fol. 47 *verso:*] Finisse quelle Epistole de la beata e seraphicha [*sic*] ṽgine sancta Chaterina da Siena: che se contiene nel presente libro. correcte diligentemente ꝛ emendate per vno Frate del ordine di frati p̄dicatori, *etc.* 𝕲.𝕷. *per Iohāne Iacomo di Fontanesi: Bologna,* A di .xviij. de Aprile, 1492. 4°. **IA. 29003.**
48 leaves, the first and last blank. Sig. a–f⁸. *34, 35 lines to a page. Without the blank leaves.*

—— Epistole deuotissime de Sancta Catharina da Siena. [fol. 2 *recto:*] La Epistola del beato Stephano Certosino. [fol. 8 *recto:*] Inuentario de le Epistole del presente Volume. [fol. 11 *recto:*] Epistole Vtile & deuote de la Beata e Seraphica Vergine Sancta Catharina da Siena, *etc.* [Edited by Bartolommeo da Alzano. With a woodcut.] *in Casa de Aldo Manutio: Venetia,* a di xv. Septembrio, 1500. fol. **IB. 24504.**
422 leaves, 11–421 numbered i–ccccxiiii *with errors. Sig.* ∗¹⁰ a–y⁸ A–G⁸ H¹⁰ I–N⁸ O¹⁰ P–Z⁸ AA–FF⁸. *40 lines to a page.*

—— [Another copy.] **9. c. 2.**

—— [Another copy.] **G. 19904.**

—— Epistole et orationi della seraphica vergine Santa Catharina da Siena . . . Vi e aggionta le vita & canonizatione della detta Santa, con alcuni capitoli in sua laude, *etc.* [Edited by Aldo Manuzio.] ff. 350. *Appresso F. Toresano; per P. Nicolini: Vinetia,* 1548. 4°. **3834. aa. 40.**

—— Lettere deuotissime della beata vergine santa Caterina da Siena. Nuouamente . . . ristampate. [Edited by A. Manuzio.] ff. 373. *Al segno della Speranza: Venetia,* 1562. 4°. **3836. b. 43.**

—— Epistole della serafica vergine S. Caterina da Siena scritte da lei a pontefici, cardinali, prelati ed altre persone ecclesiastiche . . . purgate dagli errori dell'altre impressioni colle annotazioni del P. Federico Burlamacchi. 2 tom. *Milano,* 1842, 43. 8°. **1223. g. 6.**

—— Le Lettere di S. Caterina da Siena ridotte a miglior lezione . . . con proemio e note di Niccolò Tommaseo. 4 vol. *Firenze,* 1860. 8°. **10909. c. 3.**

—— A cura di Piero Misciattelli . . . Terza edizione. 6 vol. *Siena,* 1913, 21. 8°. **010920. bbb. 3.**

—— Epistolario di Santa Caterina da Siena. A cura di Eugenio Dupré Theseider. *Roma,* 1940– . 8°. [*Fonti per la storia d'Italia.* no. 82, *etc.*] **Ac. 6543. (49.)**

CATHARINE [Benincasa], *Saint, of Sienna.*

—— Saint Catherine of Siena as seen in her Letters. Translated & edited with introduction by Vida D. Scudder. pp. x. 352. *J. M. Dent & Co.: London,* 1905. 8°. **3836. de. 2.**

—— Lettres . . . Traduites de l'italien par E. Cartier. 3 tom. *Paris,* 1858. 8°. **4827. d. 11.**

—— Obra delas epistolas y oraciones de la bien auenturada virgen sancta catherina de sena . . . Las quales fueron traduzidas d'l toscano en nuestra lengua castellana por mandado del . . . Cardenal despaña Arcobispo . . . de Toledo, ⁊c. (Epistola de fray esteuan d'sena, *etc.*) 𝕲.𝕷. ff. cccxviii. *Por A. G. d'Brocar: Alcala de Henares,* 1512. fol. **C. 63. i. 4.**

—— [Another edition.] Ramillete de Epistolas y Oraciones celestiales . . . de . . . Santa Cathalina de Sena . . . que mandò traducir a la lengua Castellana, de la Toscana . . . Don Fr. Francisco Ximenez de Cisneros, *etc.* (Epistola de Fr. Estevan de Sena.) pp. 476. *A costa de I. Cassañes y I. Surià: Barcelona,* 1698. fol. **489. i. 16. (1.)**

—— La Cella interna di S. Caterina da Siena delineata . . . con la penna serafica della medesima Santa, per opera di D. Carlo Tomasi, *etc.* [Selections from the letters.] 2 pt. *A spese del Tinassi: Roma,* 1668. 8°. **846. b. 26.**

—— [Eight letters.] *Fr. See* Labande-Jeanroy (T.) Les Mystiques italiens, *etc.* 1918. 8°. **3670. df. 19.**

—— *Begin.* [fol. 2 *recto:*] Al Nome de Iesu christo crucifixo & d̄ maria dolze & del glorioso patriarcha Dominico. Libro de la diuina prouidētia cōposto in ul'gare de la Seraphica uergene sācta Chaterina da siena, *etc.* [fol. 137 *recto:*] Finisse el libro d̄ la ꝑuidentia diuina d̄ la spoxa d̄ xp̄o. Sācta Chaterina da siena . . . Finis. Questa lettera ne laquale se cōtene el transito de la beata chatarina da siena scripse Barducio de pero canigani, *etc.* [*Balthasar Azoguidus: Bologna,* 1475?] fol. **IB. 28535.**
147 leaves, the first blank. Without signatures. Double columns, 40 lines to a column. Without the blank leaf.

—— [Another copy.] **IB. 28536.**
Without the blank leaf.

—— [Another copy.] **G. 11762.**
Without the blank leaf.

—— *Begin.* [fol. 1 *recto:*] In comencia el prolago Inn̄el libro dela diuina doctrina reuellata a q̄lla gloriosa & sanctissima vergene sancta Caterina de siena sorella del terczo abito de San⸳ dominico fundatore & patre dellordine de fra predicatoꝛ, *etc.* ꝑ *Conradum Bonebach: [Naples,]* Die vicesima octaua Mensis Aprilis, 1478. fol. **IB. 29513.**
120 leaves, the last blank. Without signatures. Double columns, 40–42 lines to a column. Without the blank leaf.

—— Dialogo de la seraphica uirgine sancta Catherina da siena de la diuina prouidentia. [fol. 2 *recto:*] Epistola prohemiale . . . Alle illustrissime . . . duchesse. Madonna isabella cōsorte dello illustrissimo signore zuā Galeazo sforza potētissimo duca di Milano: & madōna beatrice cōsorte dello illustrissimo signore Ludouico sforza dignissimo duca di Barri singularissime del ordīe de frati p̄dicatori . . . protetrice & benefatrice. frate. N. del p̄dicto ordīe de obseruātia & del cōuento di sancta Maria da le gratie de Milano professo . . . Salute, *etc.* [fol. 9 *recto:*] Libro della diuina prouidentia, *etc.* [fol. 171 *recto:*] Pii secūdi pontificīs maximi ī uitā & canonizationem beatæ catherīæ senenensis [*sic*] epistola. [fol. 176 *recto:*] Vno capitulo in rima fato ꝑ nastagio da monte altīo ī laude & reuerentia di sancta catherina da siena, *etc.* [With woodcuts.] *per mathio di codeca ad instantia de lucantonio de zōta: uenetia,* adi xvii de mazo, 1494. 4°. **IA. 22761.**
180 leaves. Sig. AA⁸; a–x⁸ y⁴. *Double columns, 38 lines to a column.*

CATHARINE [BENINCASA], *Saint, of Sienna.*

—— [Another copy.] IA. **22762.**
Imperfect : wanting the titlepage.

—— [Another edition.] Con la sua uita : & canonizatiōe & alcuni . . . capitoli composti in sua gloria & laude. Nouamente reuisto : & . . . castigato. ff. clxvii. *C. Arriuabeno : Venetia,* 1517. 8°. **1350. a. 14.**
The foliation is irregular.

—— [Another edition.] Et un breue compendio della sua vita et canonizatione . . . Di nuouo . . . corretto e ristampato. pp. 652. *G. Sarzina : Venetia,* 1611. 8°. **1019. h. 25.**

—— Libro della divina dottrina, volgarmente detto Dialogo della divina provvidenza. Nuova edizione secondo un inedito codice senese. A cura di Matilde Fiorilli. pp. 474. *Bari,* 1912. 8°. [*Scrittori d'Italia.*] **12227. eee. 1/23.**

—— The Dialogue of the Seraphic Virgin Catherine of Siena, dictated by her . . . Translated from the original Italian with an introduction on the study of mysticism by Algar Thorold. pp. vii. 360. *Kegan Paul & Co. : London,* 1896. 8°. **3836. df. 7.**

—— A new and abridged edition. pp. 344. *Kegan Paul & Co. : London,* 1907. 8°. **3836. de. 3.**

—— [Another edition.] pp. xxv. 353. *Burns, Oates & Co. : London,* 1925. 8°. **3835. a. 83.**

—— Dialogus Seraphice ac Diue Catharine de Senis cum nōnullis aliis orationibus. [fol. 2 *recto :*] Marcus Ciuilis Brixian⁹ Fratri Paulo sancheo . . . S. P. d. [fol. 4 *recto :*] Epistola Diui Stephani Carthusiensis. [fol. 9 *verso :*] Incipit liber diuine doctrine, *etc.* [fol. 181 *verso :*] Pij secundi pontificis maximi in vitam canonizatione₃ [*sic*] beate Catherine Senensis Epistola. [Edited by Marco Civile. The translation attributed to Raimundus de Vineis de Capua.] ⅭⅬ. *per Bernardinum de misintis : Brixie,* die quintodecimo mensis Aprilis, 1496. 8°.
IA. **31244.**
192 leaves, the last blank. Sig. a–z⁸ ₸⁸. Double columns, 40 lines to a column. Without the blank leaf.

—— Dialogos de S. Catalina de Sena. Traduzidos de lengua latina en castellana, por el R. P.P. Fr. Lucas Loarte. pp. 483. *Andres Garcia de la Iglesia : Madrid,* 1668. 4°. **1471. aa. 47.**

—— Libro de la Divina Doctrina, vulgarmente llamado " El Diálogo " . . . Esta obra fué traducida . . . por los Padres Dominicos del Convento de Atocha, en Madrid . . . Nuevamente la reedita la Redacción de Misiones Dominicanas, *etc.* [With an introduction by Raimundo Gutiérrez.] pp. lv. 616. *Avila,* 1925. 8°. **3835. aaa. 13.**

—— Fioreti Utilissimi Extracti dal diuoto Dyalogo vulgare de la Seraphica Sposa di Christo sancta Catharina da Siena, *etc. L. de Rubei : Ferrara,* 1511. 8°. G. **9900.**

—— [Trattato della consumata perfettione.] On Consummated Perfection. pp. 42. *Catholic Truth Society : London,* 1895. 24°. **3943. a. 51. (3.)**

—— [Trattato della consumata perfettione.] On Consummated Perfection. *See* DRANE (Augusta T.) The History of St. Catherine of Siena, *etc.* 1899. 8°. **4829. b. 28.**

—— [Another edition.] *See* DRANE (Augusta T.) The History of St. Catherine of Siena, *etc.* 1915. 8°. **4829. dg. 16.**

—— Le più belle pagine di Caterina da Siena. Scelte da Tommaso Gallarati-Scotti. [With a portrait.] pp. xvi. 279. *Milano,* 1922. 12°. [*Le più belle pagine degli scrittori italiani.* vol. 10.] **012226. a. 1/10.**

CATHARINE [BENINCASA], *Saint, of Sienna.*

—— Sayings of the Seraphic Virgin, S. Catherine of Siena, arranged for every day in the year by a gleaner mid God's saints. With an introductory essay by Abbot Ford. pp. xxi. 126. *Burnes, Oates & Co. : London,* 1924. 16°. **3833. a. 65.**

—— The Little Flowers of Saint Catherine of Siena. Culled from old manuscripts by Innocenzo Taurisano . . . Translated . . . by Charlotte Dease. [With a portrait.] pp. 153. *Harding & More : London,* [1930.] 8°. **4830. de. 21.**

APPENDIX.

—— *See* ANTONY (Catherine M.) *pseud.* Saint Catherine of Siena, her life and times, *etc.* 1915. 8°. **4830. ee. 15.**

—— *See* BORGHESI (N.) Vita Sanctae Catharinae Senensis. 1501. 4°. **4829. b. 1.**

—— *See* BUONINSEGNI (F.) Il Trionfo delle stimmate di santa Caterina da Siena, *etc.* 1640. 4°. **1231. c. 5.**

—— *See* BUTLER (Alban) La Vita di santa Caterina da Siena, *etc.* 1875. 16°. **4827. de. 13.**

—— *See* BUTLER (Josephine E.) Catharine of Siena, *etc.* 1878. 8°. **4829. a. 6.**

—— *See* BUTLER (Josephine E.) Catharine of Siena, *etc.* 1879. 8°. **4828. de. 4.**

—— *See* BUTLER (Josephine E.) Catharine of Siena, *etc.* 1881. 8°. **4823. a. 77.**

—— *See* BUTLER (Josephine E.) Catharine of Siena, *etc.* 1894. 8°. **4831. aa. 40.**

—— *See* CALISSE (C.) S. Caterina da Siena. 1895. 8°. [*Commissione Senese di Storia Patria. Conferenze . . . tenute* 1895.] Ac. **6521/5.**

—— *See* CAPECELATRO (A.) *Cardinal.* Storia di S. Caterina da Siena, *etc.* 1856. 8°. **4827. b. 11.**

—— —— 1858. 8°. **4827. b. 12.**

—— —— 1878. 8°. **4826. aaa. 31.**

—— *See* CARMI (M.) Pier Jacopo Martelli. Studi. (No. 1. P. J. Martelli, A. Zeno e G. Gigli. Una pagina della storia del Vocabolario Cateriniano.) 1906. 8°. **11853. c. 25.**

—— *See* CHAVIN DE MALAN (J. E.) Histoire de sainte Catherine de Sienne, *etc.* 1846. 8°. **1232. c. 9.**

—— *See* CHIRAT (A. H.) Sainte Catherine de Sienne, *etc.* 1888. 8°. **4829. e. 25.**

—— *See* CURTAYNE (Alice) Saint Catherine of Siena. [1929.] 8°. **4830. bbb. 35.**

—— *See* CURTAYNE (Alice) St. Catherine of Siena. 1951. 8°. **3943. f. 5.**

—— *See* DEROSSI DI SANTA ROSA (P.) Storia del tumulto dei Ciompi avvenuto in Firenze l'anno 1378, coll'aggiunto di un compendio della vita di S. Caterina da Siena. 1843. 8°. **9150. c. 23.**

—— *See* DRANE (Augusta) The History of St. Catherine of Siena, *etc.* 1887. 8°. **4828. eee. 4.**

—— —— 1899. 8°. **4829. b. 28.**

—— —— 1915. 8°. **4829. dg. 16.**

—— *See* EATON (Jeanette) The Flame. Saint Catherine of Siena. 1931. 8°. **4830. g. 22.**

CATHARINE [BENINCASA], *Saint, of Sienna.* [APPENDIX.]

—— *See* FAURE, afterwards GOYAU (Lucie F.) Vers la joie. Ames païennes. Ames chrétiennes . . . Sainte Catherine de Sienne. 1906. 8º. **012355. f. 18.**

—— *See* FAWTIER (R.) Sainte Catherine de Sienne. Essai de critique des sources. 1921, *etc.* 8º. [*Bibliothèque des Écoles françaises d'Athènes et de Rome.* fasc. 121, 135.] **Ac. 5206/2.**

—— *See* FAWTIER (R.) La Double expérience de Catherine Benincasa . . . par Robert Fawtier . . . et Louis Canet. 1948. 8º. **4831. de. 1.**

—— *See* FLAVIGNY (L. M. de) *Countess.* Sainte Catherine de Sienne. 1880. 12º. **4827.bbb.36.**

—— *See* FORBES (Frances A. M.) St. Catherine of Siena, *etc.* [1914.] 8º. [*Standard-Bearers of the Faith.*] **4830.h.46/2.**

—— *See* FRIGERIO (P.) Vita di S. Caterina da Siena raccolta . . . dalle opere della Santa, *etc.* 1656. 4º. **1231. c. 7.**

—— *See* GARDNER (John E. G.) Saint Catherine of Siena, *etc.* 1907. 8º. **4827. dg. 4.**

—— *See* GAUTHIEZ (P.) Sainte Catherine de Sienne, *etc.* 1916. 8º. **4830. aaa. 12.**

—— *See* GIGLI (G.) [Vocabolario Cateriniano.] [1717.] 4º. **12942. g. 12.**

—— —— [1760?] 4º. **12942. g. 16.**

—— —— 1866. 8º. **12942. aaa. 7.**

—— *See* GILLET (Martin) *name in religion of* STANISLAS GILLET. The Mission of St. Catherine, *etc.* [1955.] 8º. **W.P. c. 507/4.**

—— *See* GRANERUS (D.) *Begin.* Illmo y Rmo Señor, Fray Antonio Mexia, Procurador general de la Orden de Santo Domingo, dize, *etc.* [A refutation of certain statements made by some of the Franciscans concerning the merits of St. Catharine of Sienna.] [1580?] fol. **9181. e. 10. (7.)**

—— *See* HASE (C. A. von) Caterina von Siena, *etc.* 1864. 8º. **4824. bb. 32.**

—— *See* JORDAN (Édouard) La Date de naissance de sainte Catherine de Sienne. [1922.] 8º. **4829. g. 39.**

—— *See* JØRGENSEN (J.) [Den hellige Katharina af Siena.] Saint Catherine of Siena, *etc.* [With a portrait.] 1938. 8º. **20031. d. 39.**

—— *See* KAFTAL (George) St. Catherine in Tuscan Painting. [With illustrations.] 1949. 8º. **7868. f. 15.**

—— *See* LAURENT (Hyacinthus) Fontes vitae S. Catharinae Senensis historici, *etc.* 1936, *etc.* 8º. **4626.g.4.**

—— *See* LEMONNYER (A.) Sainte Catherine de Sienne, *etc.* 1934. 8º. **20003. e. 11.**

—— *See* LEONROD (O. von) *Baroness.* Die heilige Catarina von Siena, *etc.* 1880. 8º. **4827. bbb. 32.**

—— *See* LEVASTI (A.) S. Caterina da Siena, *etc.* [With a portrait.] 1947. 8º. **4824. m. 15.**

—— *See* LEVASTI (A.) [S. Caterina da Siena.] My Servant, Catherine, *etc.* 1954. 8º. **4831. ee. 10.**

—— *See* LOMBARDELLI (G.) Sommario della disputa a difese delle sacre stimate di santa Caterina da Siena, *etc.* 1601. 4º. **1231. b. 21. (2.)**

—— *See* MAFFEI (G. M.) Della vita di Caterina vergine, *etc.* 1628. 8º. **1224. c. 14.**

CATHARINE [BENINCASA], *Saint, of Sienna.* [APPENDIX.]

—— *See* MARINELLA (L.) De' gesti . . . e della vita maravigliosa della serafica S. Caterina, da Siena . . . libri sei. 1624. 4º. **1231. c. 20.**

—— *See* MASETTI (P. T.) Memorie istoriche della chiesa di Santa Maria sopra Minerva . . . Aggiuntevi alcune notizie sul corpo di S. Caterina da Siena, e sulle varie sue traslazioni. 1855. 8º. **4380. bbb. 46. (6.)**

—— *See* MAURICE-DENIS, afterwards DENIS-BOULET (N.) La Carrière politique de Sainte Catherine de Sienne, *etc.* [1939.] 8º. **4824. n. 1.**

—— *See* NARDI (F.) Saint Bernard, sainte Catherine de Sienne . . . sur le pouvoir temporel du Pape, *etc.* 1862. 8º. **8033. bb. 36. (6.)**

—— *See* OLMI (G.) La Vergine Benincasa, ossia Vita illustrata di S. Caterina da Siena. 1890. 8º. **4795. aa. 3.**

—— *See* OPHOVIUS (M.) D. Catharinæ Senensis . . . vita ac miracula, *etc.* 1603. 4º. **4828. aa. 34.**

—— *See* ORIGONI (A.) Divote meditazioni sopra la vita della . . . vergine Sr. Caterina da Siena, *etc.* 1732. 8º. **4827. bbb. 19.**

—— *See* PERITO (M.) Santa Caterina da Siena. Il pensiero e l'insegnamento, *etc.* 1921. 8º. **4830. de. 14.**

—— *See* PIERSON (Arthur T.) Catharine of Siena, *etc.* 1898. 8º. **4829. cc. 18.**

—— *See* PINUS (J.) *Bishop of Rieux.* Divæ Catherinæ Senensis . . . vita, *etc.* 1505. 4º. **4827. bb. 30.**

—— —— 1521. fol. [*RAVISIUS (J.)* *De memorabilibus mulieribus.*] **1329. l. 8.**

—— *See* POLITI (L.) *successively Bishop of Minori and Archbishop of Conza.* The Life of the Blessed Virgin, Sainct Catharine of Siena, *etc.* 1609. 8º. **1482. a. 32.**

—— *See* POLLARD (Alfred W.) *C.B., Keeper of Printed Books, British Museum.* St. Catherine of Siena. 1919. 16º. **4869.a.20/3.**

—— *See* POLLIO LAPPOLI (G.) *called il Pollastrino.* Opera della Diva & Seraphica Catharina da Siena. 1505. 4º. **11426. d. 57.**

—— *See* RICHARDSON (Jerusha D.) The Mystic Bride. A study of the life-story of Catherine of Siena, *etc.* [1911.] 8º. **4826. eee. 19.**

—— *See* SAVI-LOPEZ (M.) Santa Caterina da Siena. 1924. 8º. **4830. bbb. 20.**

—— *See* SECKENDORFF (E. von) *Baroness.* Die kirchenpolitische Tätigkeit der heiligen Katharina von Siena unter Papst Gregor XI, 1371–1378, *etc.* 1917. 8º. **9072. c. 1/64.**

—— *See* SOUCY (V. de) Couronne des saintes femmes . . . Sainte Catherine de Sienne, *etc.* 1842. 8º. **4826. bb. 3.**

—— *See* SYRETT (Netta) The Story of Saint Catherine of Siena, *etc.* 1910. 8º. **4828. eee. 7.**

—— *See* TANTUCCI (A. A.) Dissertazione . . . in cui si risponde . . . a cio, che si legge nella storia ecclesiastica dell' Abate di Fleuri spettante alla serafica santa Caterina da Siena, *etc.* 1749. 8º. **1231. c. 30.**

—— [For editions of the Legenda Minor of St. Catharine, condensed by Tommaso Caffarini from the Legenda Major of Raimundus de Vineis de Capua:] *See* THOMAS [Nacci Caffarini], *de Senis.*

—— *See* TOMMASEO (N.) Lo Spirito, il cuore, la parola di Caterina da Siena, *etc.* 1922. 8º. **4829. d. 39.**

CATHARINE [BENINCASA], *Saint, of Sienna.* [APPENDIX.]

—— *See* TOURON (A.) Vita della serafica vergine S. Caterina da Siena, *etc.* 1764. 4°. **1231. d. 23.**

—— *See* UNDSET (S.) Caterina av Siena. [With portraits.] 1951. 8°. **4831. e. 3.**

—— *See* UNDSET (S.) Catherine of Siena, *etc.* 1954. 8°. **4832. aa. 15.**

—— *See* VANNI (F.) D. Catharinæ Senensis . . . vita ac miracula selectiora, *etc.* 1608. 4°. **4828. cc. 7.**

—— *See* VINEIS (R. de) *de Capua.* Vita [sanctae Catharinae Senensis] auctore Fr. Raimundo Capuano, *etc.* 1675. fol. [*BOLLANDUS* (*J.*) *and* HENSCHENIUS (*G.*) *Acta Sanctorum, etc.* Aprilis. tom. 3.] **485. e. 11.**

—— —— 1738. fol. [*BOLLANDUS* (*J.*) *and* HENSCHENIUS (*G.*) *Acta Sanctorum, etc.* Aprilis. tom. 3.] **1227. f.**

—— —— 1866. fol. [*BOLLANDUS* (*J.*) *and* HENSCHENIUS (*G.*) *Acta Sanctorum, etc.* Aprilis. tom. 3.] **L. 23. a. 1.**

—— *See* VINEIS (R. de) *de Capua. Begin.* [fol. 1 *recto :*] Here begynneth the lyf of saint katherin of senis the blessid. virgin, *etc.* [1493 ?] fol. **C. 10. b. 14.**

—— *See* VINEIS (R. de) *de Capua. Begin.* [fol. 1 *recto :*] Alnome digesu cristo crucifixo edimaria dolce. Comincia el prolago della infrascripta legenda dell amirabile uergine. Beata chaterina da siena, *etc.* [A translation begun by Neri di Landoccio Pagliaresi and finished by an anonymous translator.] 1477. 8°. **IA. 27023.**

—— *See* VINEIS (R. de) *de Capua. Begin.* [fol. 2 *recto :*] Incomencia il prologo de la perfecta et cōsummata hystoria e uita de sancta Catherina Senese, *etc.* [An anonymous translation.] 1489. 4° **IA. 26368.**

—— *See* VINEIS (R. de) *de Capua. Begin.* [fol. 1 *recto :*] Incomincia il prohemio ne ladmirabile legēda de la seraphica uergine . . . sancta Catherina da Siena, *etc.* [An abridged translation.] [1490 ?] 4° **IA. 26387.**

—— *See* VINEIS (R. de) *de Capua.* Vita miracolosa della serafica S. Catherina da Siena, *etc.* 1587. 8°. **1478. e. 16.**

—— *See* VINEIS (R. de) *de Capua.* Vita di S. Caterina da Siena . . . Tradotta dal cav. B. Pecci. 1839. 8°. **1231. d. 17.**

—— —— 1842. 8°. **1223. g. 5.**

—— *See* WARD (Maisie) The Saints in Pictures. (Saint Catherine of Siena.) 1950, *etc.* 8°. **W.P. 898.**

—— *See* VINEIS (R. de) *de Capua.* La vida de la seraphica sča catherina [de] Zena, *etc.* 1511. 4°. **C. 63. c. 18.**

—— *See* WITTS (Florence) The Story of Catherine of Siena. [1901.] 8°. **4829. cc. 38.**

—— *See* ZUCCHELLI (N.) and LAZZARESCHI (E.) S. Caterina da Siena ed i Pisani. 1916. 8°. **4830. e. 11.**

—— Breve ristretto della vita della serafica vergine Santa Caterina da Siena . . . dato in luce da un Religioso del medesimo Ordine, *etc.* pp. 84. *Firenze,* 1728. 12°. **1370. a. 43. (2.)**

—— D. Catharinæ Senensis . . . vita ac miracula selectiora formis æneis expressa. [Plates with descriptions in Latin and Italian.] [*Rome ?* 1650 ?] 4°. **554. b. 44.**

CATHARINE [BENINCASA], *Saint, of Sienna.* [APPENDIX.]

—— Hystori vnd wunderbarlich legend Katharine von Senis, der hailigen junckfrawen, mit sampt zwayen predigen, die ain von diser hailigen Katarina, die ander von sant Vincentio prediger ordens. [A translation of the "Vita Sanctae Catharinae" of Raimundus de Vineis de Capua. With woodcuts.] ff. lxxxix. *Gedruckt durch H. Otmar ; Verlegung des J. Rynman : Augspurg,* 1515. fol. **C. 53. g. 7.**

—— Here foloweth dyuers doctrynes deuoute 7 fruytfull, taken out of the lyfe of . . . Saynt Katheryn of Seenes, *etc.* *See* RICHARDUS, *Prior S. Victoris Parisiensis.* Here foloweth a veray deuoute treatyse . . . of the mightes and vertues of mannes soule, *etc.* 1521. 4°. **C. 37. f. 19.**

—— [Another edition.] *See* GARDNER (John E. G.) The Cell of Self-Knowledge, *etc.* 1910. 8°. **012202. e. 13/9.**

—— I Miracoli di Caterina di Iacopo da Siena di anonimo fiorentino. A cura di Francesco Valli. pp. xxii. 32. *Firenze,* 1936. 8°. *Fontes vitae S. Catharinae Senensis historici.* vol. 4 **4626. g. 5.**

—— Obres fetes en lahor de la seraphica senta catherina d' sena en lo seu sagrat monestir de les monges de la insigne ciutat de valencia per diuersos trobadors narrades lo dia de sent miquel del any mdxi., *etc.* [A facsimile of the edition published at Valencia, c. 1530.] *G. L.* [1880 ?] 8°. **11450. h. 30.**

—— *Begin.* Here begynneth the Orcharde of Syon, in the whiche is conteyned the reuelacyons of seynt Katheryne of Sene, with ghostly fruytes 7 precyous plantes for the helthe of mannes soule, *etc.* [Translated from the "Vita Sanctae Catharinae" of Raimundus de Vineis de Capua by Dane James.] *B. L.* *Wynkyn de Worde : London,* 1519. fol. **C. 11. b. 6.**

—— La Rappresentatione di Santa Caterina da Siena, *etc.* [In verse.] *Siena,* [1550 ?] 4°. **11426. f. 26.**

—— [Another edition.] Nuouamente ricorretta, e ristampata. *Firenze,* 1556. 4°. **C. 34. h. 30.**

—— [Another edition.] *Appresso G. Baleni : Firenze,* 1588. 4°. **11426. dd. 86.**

—— St. Catharine of Siena. pp. 32. *Catholic Truth Society : London,* [1891.] 8°. **3943. aa. 4.**

—— St. Catherine of Siena. By a sister of the Community of St. Mary the Virgin. pp. v. 57. *Church Literature Association : London,* 1939. 8°. **20033. e. 17.**

—— Saint Catherine of Siena and her Times. By the author of "Mademoiselle Mori" [i.e. Margaret Roberts]. With twenty-eight illustrations. pp. viii. 300. *Methuen & Co. : London,* 1906. 8°. **2214. d. 8.**

—— La vida dela seraphica sča catherina de Sena. [A facsimile of the woodcuts contained in the Valencian edition of 1511 of the work by Raimundus de Vineis de Capua bearing this title.] [1880 ?] 8°. **899. f. 16. (7.)**

—— La Vie de madame Saincte Katherine de Seine. [An abridged translation of the "Vita Sanctae Catharinae" of Raimundus de Vineis de Capua.] *G. L.* ff. lxii. *Iehan Petit : [Paris,]* 1503. 4°. **C. 97. b. 12.**

CATHARINE [ULFSDOTTER], *Saint, of Sweden.*

—— *See* COLLIJN (I. G. A.) Iconographia Birgittina Typographica . . . Katherina i medeltida bildtryck, *etc.* 1915, *etc.* fol. **11906. l. 16.**

CATHARINE [Ulfsdotter], *Saint, of Sweden.*

—— *See* Kylander (P.) Berättelse om S. Birgitta och S. Catharina, *etc.* 1806. 8°. [*Gjörwell* (*C. C.*) *Brefväxling.* bd. 4.] **1455. a. 21.**

—— *See* Silfverstolpe (C.) Förhandlingarna rörande Katarina Ulfsdotters kanonisation. 1876. 8°. [*Historiskt Bibliotek.* dl. 2.] **9431. i. 6.**

—— *Begin.* [fol. 1 *recto*:] Faciem tuam illumina super seruū tuum domine. Beatissime pater Circa canonizationem Beate Catherine de suetie, *etc. End.* [fol. 18 *recto*:] Per dñm nostrū ihesum xp̄m 7c̄. [A report on the claims of Catharine of Sweden to canonisation, by Joannes Franciscus de Pavinis.] **G.⅊. few ms. notes.** [*Eucharius Silber: Rome,* 1480?] 8°. **IA. 18802.** 18 *leaves, without signatures.* 41 *lines to a page.*

—— Legenda S. Catharinæ, filiæ S. Birgittæ. E codice Aboensi nunc primum edita. Venia ampl. Fac. Phil. Lund. p.p. Dr. Ernestus Rietz et C. A. Skottsberg. (Laur. Pettersson, Gustavus Adolph. Collin, Fredericus W. C. Areschoug, Ernestus Lud. Ödmansson, Gustavus Fredericus Carlberg, Paulus Joh. Hallbäck.) 7 pt. *Lundæ,* 1847–50. 8°. **4825. c. 7.**

—— Incipit Vita siue legenda cum miraculis diuæ Chaterinæ filiæ S. Birgittæ, *etc.* [By Ulpho, monk of Vadstena.] 1557. *See* Bridget, *Saint, of Sweden.* [*Revelationes.*] Memoriale effigiatum librorum prophetiarum seu visionum B. Brigidæ alias Birgittæ. pt. 2. 1556, *etc.* fol. **489. i. 4.**

—— [Another edition.] *See* Bridget, *Saint, of Sweden.* [*Revelationes.*] Revelationes cœlestes seraphicæ matris S. Birgittæ Suecæ, *etc.* 1680. fol. **3845. aaa. 4.**

—— *Begin.* [fol. 2 *recto*:] Incipit vita siue legēda cū miraculis dñe Katherine . . . filie sc̄te Birgitte de regno Suecie. [By Ulpho.] [A facsimile of the Stockholm edition of 1487.] [*Stockholm,* 1869.] 8°. **4829. aaa. 15.**

—— Processus seu negocium canonizacionis B. Katerine de Vadstenis. Codex A 93 Bibl. Reg. Holm. Suecice et britannice praefatus edidit Isak Collijn. [A facsimile.] pp. xxxiii. fol. clxij. *Hafniae,* 1943. fol. [*Corpus codicum Suecicorum medii aevi.* vol. 2.] MS. Facs. **464. (2.)**

CATHARINE [Thomás], *Saint, of Valldemossa. See* Despuig y Dameto (A.) *Cardinal.* Vida de la Beata Catalina Tomás, *etc.* 1930. 8°. **4831.cc.16.**

—— *See* Magraner (P. A.) Vida de Santa Catalina Thomás, verge mallorquina. 1931. 8°. **20002. aa. 27.**

—— *See* Planas (S.) Panegírico pronunciado . . . en honra de la beata Catalina Tomas, *etc.* 1862. 8°. **4866. bb. 45. (3.)**

—— *See* Rome, *Church of.—Congregatio Rituum.* Maioricen. Canonizationis beatae Catharinae Thomasiae . . . Iudicium medicum-legale [on the miraculous healing of Ana Monleón y Beltrán] . . . doctoris Philippi Pelagallo. [1901.] fol. **5035. aa. 26.**

—— *See* Rome, *Church of.—Congregatio Rituum.* Majoricen. Canonizationis beatæ Catharinae Thomasiae . . . Novissima positio super miraculis. [1922.] fol. **5035. aa. 37.**

—— *See* Rome, *Church of.—Congregatio Rituum.* Compendium vitae virtutum et miraculorum necnon actorum in causa canonizationis beatae Catharinae Thomasiae, *etc.* 1930. fol. **5035. aa. 25.**

—— *See* Rome, *Church of.—Congregatio Rituum.* Maioricen. Canonizationis beatæ Catharinæ Thomasiae . . . Positio super tuto. [1930.] fol. **5035. aa. 36.**

CATHARINE [Thomás], *Saint, of Valldemossa.*

—— *See* Rome, *Church of.—*[*Popes.*]—Pius vi. [1775–1799.] [A collection of 10 decrees of beatification of Catharine Thomás and others.] 1786, *etc.* fol. & 4°. **1897. c. 4. (4.)**

—— *See* Tomas (M.) Certamen poetico en honor de la venerable madre Sor Catharina Thomasa Mallorquina, *etc.* 1636. 4°. **C. 63. b. 37.**

—— Ristretto della vita della beata Caterina Thomàs, canonichessa regolare dell' Ordine di S. Agostino. pp. xvi. 91. *Roma,* 1792. 4°. **4868. g. 5.**

CATHARINE ALEXIEVNA, *Consort of Peter 1., called the Great, Emperor of Russia. See* Catharine i., *Empress of Russia.*

CATHARINE ALEXIEVNA, *Consort of Peter Thedorovich, Grand Duke of Russia, afterwards Peter iii., Emperor of Russia. See* Catharine ii., *Empress of Russia.*

CATHARINE CHARLOTTE [de la Trémoille], *Consort of Henry 1., Prince of Condé. See* Charlotte Catharine.

CATHARINE CHARLOTTE [de Gramont], *Consort of Louis 1., Prince of Monaco. See* Asseline (A.) Madame de Monaco, 1639–1678, *etc.* [1884.] 18°. **010663. ee. 4.**

CATHARINE FRANCES, *of the Sisters of Saint Joseph.* The Convent School of French Origin in the United States, 1727 to 1843. A dissertation, *etc.* pp. 246. *Philadelphia,* 1936. 8°. **08385. a. 2.**

CATHARINE FRANCIS, *Abbess of the English Monastery of Franciscan Nuns in Brussels. See* Paludanus (J.) A Short Relation of the Life, virtues and miracles of S. Elizabeth, called the Peace-maker, Queen of Portugal . . . Translated out of Dutch by Sister Catharine Francis, *etc.* 1628. 8°. **701. a. 5. (2.)**

CATHARINE HENRIETTA, *Duchess d'Elbeuf.* Les Amours de Madame d'Elbeuf. Nouvelle historique. Contenant plusieurs anecdotes du Cardinal de Richelieu. pp. 220. *Amsterdam,* 1739. 12°. **12511. e. 7.**

CATHARINE MARGARET, *Princess of Nassau-Saarbrücken. See* Usener-Klipstein (H.) Gänse-Gretl. Das Leben der Fürstin Katharina von Nassau-Saarbrücken, *etc.* [With a portrait.] 1937. 8°. **010703. h. 64.**

CATHARINE PAVLOVNA, *Queen Consort of William, King of Wurtemberg. See* Catharine, *Queen Consort, etc.*

CATHARINE SUSAN'S CALENDAR. *See* Ephemerides.

CATHARINO CARDOSO (Nuno)

—— Cintra. Noticia histórico-arqueológica e artística do Paço da Vila, do Palacio da Pena e do Castelo dos Monros. [With abridgments in French and English, and plates.] pp. 95. *Porto,* 1930. 8°. **10163. de. 19.** *Monumentos de Portugal.* no. 7.

CATHARINUS (Ambrosius) *Dominican* [Lancelotto Politi]. *See* Politi (L.) successively *Bishop of Minori* and *Archbishop of Conza.*

CATHARINUS (Johann) Klag vnd Traurpredigt, gehalten zu Felssberg am 3. Maji . . . 1632. (In obitum Mauritii Senioris H. L., *etc.*) *See* Maurice, *Landgrave of Hesse-Cassel.* Monumentum sepulcrale, *etc.* 1641. fol. **143. f. 17.**

CATHARINUS (Nicolaus) *See* Catherinot (Nicolas)

CATHARO (Hosanna de) *See* Hosanna, *of Cattaro.*

CATHAROS. Catharos. Diogenes in his singularitie . . . By T. L. [i.e. Thomas Lodge], of Lincoln's Inne, Gent. 1591. 4°. *See* L., T., *of Lincoln's Inne, Gent.*

C. 27. b. 12.

CATHARSIS. The Catharsis of Husbandry. By a Virginia Farmer [i.e. Fairfax Harrison] . . . A paper read at the Farmers' Dinner at the University Club of New York, January 11, 1912. pp. 14. [1912.] 8°.

07076. h. 68. (6.)

CATHARUS (ARETIUS) *pseud.* [i.e. MARTIN LUTHER.] Aretii Cathari de magistratu seculari, secunda pars, in qua ostenditur, quàm longè lateǵ pateat magistratus secularis. [Pt. 2 of J. Lonicer's Latin translation of Luther's " Von weltlichen Obrigkeit."] *See* BELLIUS (Martin) *pseud.* De hæreticis, *etc.* 1554. 8°.

1114. a. 1.

CATHARY (CLÉMENT) *See* DAURIGNAC (J. M. S.) *pseud.* Vie du révérend père Clément Cathary, *etc.* 1865. 12°.

4865. aaa. 22.

CATHAY ANNUAL. *See* SINGAPORE.—*Cathay Cinema.*

CATHAY CINEMA, *Singapore. See* SINGAPORE.

CATHAY ORGANISATION.

—— Cathay Organisation Film News. (Cathay Organisation Film Review.) Nov. 1951, *etc. Penang*, 1951– . 8°.

P.P. **1912.** fkm.

CATHAY ORGANISATION FILM NEWS. *See* CATHAY ORGANISATION.

CATHAY ORGANISATION FILM REVIEW. *See* CATHAY ORGANISATION. Cathay Organisation Film News.

CATHCART, *Family of, of Schaw.*

—— *See* OLIPHANT (Margaret E. B.) afterwards GRAHAM (M. E. M.) The Beautiful Mrs. Graham and the Cathcart Circle. [With portraits.] 1927. 8°.

010855. h. 11.

CATHCART ( ) *Miss.* Adelaide; a story of modern life. [By Miss Cathcart.] 3 vol. 1833. 12°. *See* ADELAIDE.

N. 1001–03.

—— The Heir of Mordaunt. By the author of " Adelaide " [i.e. Miss Cathcart]. 3 vol. 1835. 12°. *See* MORDAUNT.

N. 1155.

CATHCART (CHARLES SCHAW) *Lord Cathcart.*

—— *See* STEWART (*Sir* John S. N. S.) *Bart.* [Documents connected with the law suit between Sir John Schaw-Stewart, Bart., and Lord Cathcart.] [1753, *etc.*] fol. & 4°.

6356. h. 1.

CATHCART (CHARLES WALKER) [For editions of " A Surgical Handbook for the use of Students, Practitioners, *etc.*," by F. M. Caird and C. W. Cathcart:] *See* CAIRD (Francis M.) and CATHCART (C. W.)

—— *See* GIBSON (George Alexander) *M.D.* Edinburgh Hospital Reports . . . Edited by . . . G. A. Gibson . . . C. W. Cathcart, *etc.* 1893, *etc.* 8°.

07686. h.

—— *See* HENLE (A.) [Die Behandlung der tuberkulösen Gelenkerkrankungen und der kalten Abscesse.] The Conservative Treatment of Tubercular Joint Disease and Cold Abscess . . . Translated . . . by C. W. Cathcart. 1900. 8°.

7616. dd. 11.

—— *See* PERIODICAL PUBLICATIONS.—*Edinburgh.* The Edinburgh Clinical and Pathological Journal. Edited by J. Graham Brown . . . C. W. Cathcart, *etc.* 1884. 8°.

P.P. 2856.

CATHCART (CHARLES WALKER)

—— Descriptive Catalogue of the Anatomical and Pathological Specimens in the Museum of the Royal College of Surgeons . . . By C. W. Cathcart (vol. 1, 2 ; by Theodore Shennan, vol. 3). 3 vol. 1898–1903. 8°. *See* EDINBURGH.—*Royal College of Surgeons.* Ac. **3850.** c/2.

—— The Essential Similarity of Innocent and Malignant Tumours. A study of tumour growth, *etc.* pp. xii. 79. xxxviii. *J. Wright & Co.: Bristol,* 1907. 8°.

7630. k. 18.

—— Training, and how to Keep always Fit. pp. 52. *E. & S. Livingstone: Edinburgh,* 1921. 4°.

7383. dd. 21.

CATHCART (CHARLES WALKER) and **CAIRD** (FRANCIS MITCHELL)

—— Johnston's Students' Atlas of Bones and Ligaments. pl. xxx. *W. & A. K. Johnston: Edinburgh,* 1885. 4°. **1832.** c. 16.

CATHCART (CHARLES WALKER) and **HARTLEY** (JAMES NORMAN JACKSON)

—— Requisites and Methods in Surgery, *etc.* pp. viii. 476. *Oliver & Boyd: Edinburgh, London,* 1928. 8°. **07481.** ee. 24.

CATHCART (CLARINDA) The History of Miss Clarinda Cathcart, and Miss Fanny Renton. [The dedication signed : J. M., i.e. Jean Marishall.] 1766. 12°. *See* M., J.

12614. ff. 2.

—— The third edition. 1767. 12°. *See* M., J.

12612. bbb. 3.

CATHCART (EDWARD PROVAN) *See* BENEDICT (Francis G.) and CATHCART (E. P.) Muscular Work. A metabolic study, *etc.* 1913. 8°. [*Publications of the Carnegie Institution of Washington.* no. 187.] Ac. **1866.**

—— *See* FINLAYSON (James) *M.D.* Finlayson's Clinical Manual . . . Edited by . . . E. P. Cathcart, *etc.* 1926. 8°.

07306. f. 47.

—— *See* GLASGOW.—*University of Glasgow.—Institute of Physiology.* Collected Papers. N.s. I [*etc.*]. Edited by E. P. Cathcart . . . and A. Hunter. 1934, *etc.* 4°. [*Glasgow University Publications.* no. 34, *etc.*] Ac. **1487.**

—— *See* PATON (Diarmid N.) A Practical Course of Chemical Physiology . . . By D. N. Paton . . . E. P. Cathcart, *etc.* 1918. 8°.

7407. pp. 9.

—— *See* PHYSIOLOGY. Practical Physiology, *etc.* (Chemical Physiology. By E. P. Cathcart.) 1922. 8°.

7405. t. 13.

—— —— 1925. 8°.

7405. h. 26.

—— —— 1929. 8°.

7406. ppp. 8.

—— Communal Health. pp. 48. *Craig Wilson: Glasgow,* 1944. 8°. [*The British Way.* no. 10.] W.P. **12132**/10.

—— Elementary Physiology in its relation to Hygiene. pp. 23. 1919. 8°. *See* ENGLAND.—*Army.—Medical Services, etc.* [*Miscellaneous Official Publications.*]

7404. e. 63.

—— The Human Factor in Industry. pp. vi. 105. *Oxford University Press: London,* 1928. 8°. **08286.** cc. 21.

—— Nutrition and Dietetics, *etc.* pp. 79. *London,* 1928. 8°. [*Benn's Sixpenny Library.* no. 7.] **12199.** c. 1/7.

CATHCART (Edward Provan)

—— The Physiology of Protein Metabolism. [With a bibliography.] pp. viii. 142. *Longmans & Co.: London,* 1912. 8°. [*Monographs on Biochemistry.*] **8910. ee. 1/10.**

—— New edition. pp. viii. 176. *Longmans & Co.: London,* 1921. 8°. [*Monographs on Biochemistry.*]
8910. ee. 1/26.

—— The Physique of Man in Industry. By E. P. Cathcart, D. E. R. Hughes and J. G. Chalmers. pp. iv. 52. *London,* 1935. 8°. [*Industrial Health Research Board. Report.* no. 71.] **B.S. 25/7.**

—— The Physique of Women in Industry. A contribution towards the determination of the optimum load. By E. P. Cathcart . . . and E. M. Bedale [and others], *etc.* [With plates.] pp. vi. 142. *London,* 1927. 8°. [*Industrial Fatigue Research Board. Report.* no. 44.]
B.S. 25/7.

—— Studies in Nutrition. An inquiry into the diet of families in the Highlands and Islands of Scotland. By E. P. Cathcart, A. M. T. Murray and J. B. Beveridge. pp. 37. *London,* 1940. 8°. [*Medical Research Council. Special Reports Series.* no. 242.] **B.S. 25/8.**

CATHCART (Edward Provan) and **MURRAY** (Annabel Mary Tough)

—— A Dietary Survey in Terms of the actual Foodstuffs consumed. pp. 56. *London,* 1936. 8°. [*Medical Research Council. Special Report Series.* no. 218.] **B.S. 25/8.**

—— Studies in Nutrition. An inquiry into the diet of families in Cardiff and Reading. By E. P. Cathcart and A. M. T. Murray, assisted by M. Shanks. pp. 28. *London,* 1932. 8°. [*Medical Research Council. Special Report Series.* no. 165.] **B.S. 25/8.**

—— A Study in Nutrition. An inquiry into the diet of 154 families of St. Andrews. By E. P. Cathcart and A. M. T. Murray, assisted by M. Shanks. pp. 60. *London,* 1931. 8°. [*Medical Research Council. Special Report Series.* no. 151.] **B.S. 25/8.**

CATHCART (Edward Provan) and **ORR** (John Boyd) *Baron Boyd-Orr.*

—— The Energy Expenditure of the Infantry Recruit in Training. pp. 69. 1919. 8°. *See* England.—*Army.*—*Medical Services, etc.* [*Miscellaneous Official Publications.*] **8831. d. 45.**

CATHCART (*Hon.* Eleonora) *See* Houstoune (E.) *Lady.*

CATHCART (Elias) *See* Savigny (F. C. von) The History of the Roman Law during the Middle Ages. Translated . . . by E. Cathcart. 1829. 8°.
1127. e. 13.

—— Disputatio juridica, ad tit. v. lib. xxxiii. Digest. De Optione vel, etc. pp. 18. *A. Smellie: Edinburgh,* 1817. 4°. [missing.]

CATHCART (Elizabeth) *Baroness. See* Ford (Edward) Justice of the Peace. Tewin-Water, or the Story of Lady Cathcart, *etc.* 1876. 8°. **010856. g. 22.**

CATHCART (Frederick Henry) *See* England.—*Trotting Union of Great Britain.* Racing Calendar of the Alexandra Park Trotting Club . . . Compiled by F. Cathcart. [1889, *etc.*] 8°. **P.P. 2489. sg.**

CATHCART (*Hon. Sir* George) Correspondence of Lieut.-General the Hon. Sir George Cathcart, K.C.B., relative to his military operations in Kaffraria . . . and to his measures for the future maintenance of peace on that frontier, *etc.* [With maps.] pp. xiii. 401. *John Murray: London,* 1856. 8°. **10096. g. 21.**

—— Commentaries on the War in Russia and Germany in 1812 and 1813 . . . With plans and diagrams. pp. xv. 383. *John Murray: London,* 1850. 8°. **1311. e. 10.**

CATHCART (George Clark) *See* Tod (Hunter F.) Hunter Tod's Diseases of the Ear. Revised and largely re-written by G. C. Cathcart, *etc.* 1926. 8°.
20036. a. 1/263.

—— The Treatment of Chronic Deafness by the Electrophonoïde Method of Zünd-Burguet. pp. viii. 88. *Oxford University Press: London,* 1926. 8°. [*Oxford Medical Publications.*] **20036. a. 1/265.**

—— Second edition. pp. xiii. 111. *Oxford University Press: London,* 1931. 8°. [*Oxford Medical Publications.*]
20036. a. 1/199.

CATHCART (George Lambert) *See* Harnack (Axel) An Introduction to the Study of the Elements of the Differential and Integral Calculus. From the German, *etc.* [Translated by G. L. Cathcart.] 1891. 8°.
8535. f. 37.

CATHCART (George R.) *See* Periodical Publications. —*New York.* The American Publisher and Bookseller, *etc.* (G. R. Cathcart, editor.) 1867, *etc.* 4° & 8°.
P.P. 6491. fa.

—— *See* Swinton (William) and Cathcart (G. R.) Golden Book of Tales, *etc.* 1882. 8°. **12411. f. 13.**

CATHCART (Gertrude Dorman) First Book of Physiology and Hygiene, *etc.* pp. vi. 158. *Macmillan & Co.: London,* 1914. 8°. [*First Books of Science.*]
8707. de. 1/12.

CATHCART (James Leander)

—— The Diplomatic Journal and Letter Book of James Leander Cathcart, 1788–1796. *In:* Proceedings of the American Antiquarian Society. vol. 64. pt. 2. pp. 303–436. 1954. 8°. **Ac. 5798/2.**

—— Tripoli. First war with the United States. Inner history. Letter book by J. L. Cathcart, first consul to Tripoli, and last letters from Tunis, compiled by his daughter J. B. Cathcart Newkirk. pp. viii. 355. *Herald Print: La Porte, Ind.,* [1902.] 8°.
09061. bb. 24.

CATHCART (John) *Director of the Hospital in the late Expedition to the West Indies.*

—— A Letter to the Honourable Edward Vernon . . . concerning some gross misrepresentations in a pamphlet, lately published, and intitled, Original Papers relating to the Expedition to the Island of Cuba. pp. 55. *M. Cooper: London,* 1744. 8°. **1061. h. 4. (2.)**

CATHCART (John) *Novelist.*

—— The Unknown Mr. Alias. pp. 128. *T. A. & E. Pemberton: Manchester,* [1946.] 8°. **012646. b. 90.**

CATHCART (JOHN FERGUSSON) *See* HOOKER (*Sir* Joseph D.) *G.C.S.I.* Illustrations of Himalayan Plants, chiefly selected from drawings made for the late J. F. Cathcart, *etc.* 1855. fol. **762. h. 11.**

CATHCART (MARY ANNE) *afterwards* **NAPIER** (MARY ANNE) *Baroness Napier.* *See* HOUSTOUNE (Eleonora) *Lady.* Petition of Dame Eleonora Cathcart, Lady Houstoune . . . Containing . . . also a vindication of Miss Cathcart . . . from the malicious reflections . . . against her in a . . . Petition . . . published . . . for Sir John [Houstoune]. [1749.] 4°. [MISSING.]

CATHCART (R. N.)

—— *See* PERIODICAL PUBLICATIONS.—*Whiteabbey.* Whiteabbey and District Year Book, 1942 [*etc.*]. (Assistant editor, R. N. Cathcart.) 1942, *etc.* 8°. P.P. **2513. p.m.**

CATHCART (ROBERT)

—— Memoir of Robert Cathcart, Esq. [By John George Wood, Writer to the Signet.] [With a portrait.] pp. 105. *T. Constable: Edinburgh,* 1838. 8°. **10860. aa. 59. (4.)**

—— Memoir and Correspondence of the late Robert Cathcart . . . Second edition. [By John George Wood, *Writer to the Signet.*] [With a portrait.] pp. 171. *W. Oliphant & Son: Edinburgh,* 1839. 12°. **1126. b. 33.**

CATHCART (VERA) *Countess.* It Came to pass. pp. 318. *John Long: London,* 1926. 8°. NN. **12469.**

—— Men for Pieces. pp. 285. *John Long: London,* 1927. 8°. NN. **12638.**

—— The Sign. pp. 286. *John Long: London,* 1927. 8°. NN. **13308.**

—— The Woman Tempted. pp. 318. *John Long: London,* 1924. 8°. NN. **10268.**

—— Popular edition. pp. 318. *John Long: London,* 1925. 8°. NN. **11431.**

CATHCART (WILLIAM) *D.D.* The Ancient British and Irish Churches, including the life and labors of St. Patrick . . . With maps, illustrations, *etc.* pp. 347. *Baptist Tract & Book Society: London; Philadelphia* printed, 1894. 8°. **4705. cc. 13.**

CATHCART (WILLIAM) *Earl Cathcart.* *See* CULLEN (William) *M.D.* A Letter to Lord Cathcart . . . concerning the recovery of persons drowned, and seemingly dead . . . To which is added, An Extract from the Journals of the Board of Police, containing a paper presented by Lord Cathcart . . . on the same subject. 1784. 8°. **T. 297. (10.)**

CATHCART (WILLIAM) *Printer.* *See* EPHEMERIDES. The Jamaica Almanack, *etc.* (1842 compiled by W. Cathcart.) [1840, *etc.*] 12°. P.P. **2586. f.**

CATHCART (WILLIAM HUTTON)

—— The Barrel; or, the Deil's dilemma. [A poem.] pp. 15. *J. Smith & Son: Glasgow,* 1941. 8°. **11657. aaa. 33.**

—— The Value of Science in the Smithy and Forge . . . Edited by John Edward Stead, *etc.* pp. xiv. 163. *C. Griffin & Co.: London,* 1916. 8°. **08709. aa. 17.**

CATHCART (WILLIAM LEDYARD) and **CHAFFEE** (JONATHAN IRVIN) The Elements of Graphic Statics and of General Graphic Methods, *etc.* pp. viii. 312. *Constable & Co.: London,* 1911. 8°. **08766. d. 46.**

CATHCART-JONES (OWEN) *See* JONES.

CATHÉCUMÈNE. *See* CATÉCHUMÈNE.

CATHEDRA. Cathedra Apostolica. *See* ROME, *Church of.*

—— Cathedra Rotomagensis. *See* ROUEN.—*Cathedral Church.*

CATHEDRAL. The Cathedral, or the Catholic and Apostolic Church in England. [In verse. By Isaac Williams. With plates.] pp. xvi. 307. *J. H. Parker: Oxford,* 1838. 8°. **994. a. 42.**

—— The Cathedral . . . Second edition. [By Isaac Williams.] pp. xvi. 307. *John Henry Parker: Oxford; J. G. & F. Rivington: London,* 1839. 8°. **11658. e. 19.**

—— The Cathedral . . . Third edition. [By Isaac Williams.] pp. xvi. 311. *J. H. Parker: Oxford,* 1841. 8°. **11657. e. 23.**

—— Seventh edition. pp. xvi. 296. *J. H. & J. Parker: Oxford,* 1857. 16°. **11630. aa. 42.**

CATHEDRAL ANTHEMS.

—— Cathedral Anthems. (New edition.) pp. lxxv. 272. 1895. 8°. *See* DUBLIN.—*Association for Promoting Christian Knowledge.* **3130. e. 64.**

CATHEDRAL BOOKS. *See* WENGRAF (Paul)

CATHEDRAL BUILDERS QUARTERLY BULLETIN. *See* LIVERPOOL.—*Cathedral Church.*

CATHEDRAL CHRONICLE.

——*See* WESTMINSTER, *Archdiocese of.* Westminster Cathedral Chronicle.

CATHEDRAL CHURCH OF S. MARY MONTHLY PAPER. *See* MARY, *the Blessed Virgin.* [*Churches and Institutions.*]—*Edinburgh.*—*Cathedral Church of Saint Mary.*

CATHEDRAL COMMISSION. *See* ENGLAND.—*Commission for Inquiring into the State of the Cathedral and Collegiate Churches.*

CATHEDRAL COMMISSIONERS. Cathedral Commissioners for England. *See* ENGLAND.—*Church of England.*

CATHEDRAL COURIER.

—— The Cathedral Courier. *See* SINGAPORE.—*St. Andrew's Cathedral.* The Cathedral Monthly Paper.

CATHEDRAL ORGANIST. The Cathedral Organist. By the author of " Madeleine's Forgiveness," *etc.* pp. 128. *S.P.C.K.: London; Pott, Young & Co.: New York,* [1873.] 16°. **4413. ccc. 11.**

CATHEDRAL ORGANISTS' ASSOCIATION. *See* ENGLAND.

CATHEDRAL PRIORY CHURCH.

—— Cathedral Priory Church of Norwich. *See* NORWICH.—*Cathedral Church.*

CATHEDRAL QUARTERLY.

—— The Cathedral Quarterly. A record of the work at, and in connection with the cathedral churches in communion with the See of Canterbury. *See* PERIODICAL PUBLICATIONS.—*Leighton Buzzard.*

CATHEDRAL RECORD. *See* LIVERPOOL, *Archdiocese of.*

CATHEDRAL RHYMES. Cathedral Rhymes, suggested by passages in the Liturgy and Lessons. By the author of " Recollections of Childhood," " A Sister's Record," &c. pp. vii. 151. *E. Churton: London,* 1847. 12º.
11645. c. 9.

CATHEDRAL TRUSTS. Cathedral Trusts and their Fulfilment. Revised, reprinted, and enlarged from the April number, 1854, of the Church of England Quarterly Review. pp. 29. *Sampson Low & Son: London,* 1854. 8º.
4108. b. 17.

CATHEDRAL WEALTH. Cathedral Wealth and Cathedral Work. pp. 30. *Society for the Liberation of Religion from State-Patronage and Control: London,* 1861. 8º.
4107. bb. 21.

CATHEDRALS.

—— Cathedrals, *etc.* [The compiler's note to the reader signed: G. E. B.] 1926. 4º. *See* B., G. E. 7822. cc. 3.

—— Our Cathedrals. A collection of sixteen permanent photographs, with descriptive letterpress. pp. 16. *S. Bagster & Sons: London,* [1905.] *obl.* 8º.
7817. aaa. 8.

CATHELAN (ANTOINE)

—— Passevent Parisien respondent a Pasquin Rommain. De la vie de ceux qui sont allez demourer, & se disent viure selon la reformation de l'Euangile, au pais iadis de Sauoye . . . faict en forme de Dialogue. [Variously attributed to A. Cathelan and Artus Désiré.] ff. 48. MS. NOTE. 1556. 16º. *See* PASSEVENT, *Parisien, pseud.*
11736. a. 37.

CATHELAN (JEAN ANTOINE DE) *See* CATELLAN.

CATHELIN (FERNAND) Les Migrations des oiseaux, *etc.* pp. 168. *Paris,* 1920. 8º.
7286. eee. 25.

CATHELIN (RENÉ GÉRALD) French Practice for General School Examinations. [With " Exercises in French Composition."] 2 pt. *Blackie & Son: London & Glasgow,* 1926, 28. 8º.
12951. ee. 10.

CATHELINEAU (ALEXANDRE) Voyage à la lune d'après un manuscrit authentique projété d'un volcan lunaire. pp. 310. *Paris,* 1865. 12º.
12515. ee. 10.

CATHELINEAU (EMMANUEL DE) La Grèce douloureuse: ou les Rythmes d'amitié . . . [Sonnets.] Avec un portrait de l'auteur et des illustrations par Raoul Trémolières. pp. 190. *Angers,* 1938. 8º.
11484. aa. 31.

CATHELINEAU (HENRI DE) *See* FONTENAY (L. de) *Baron.* Souvenirs d'un volontaire de Cathelineau, *etc.* 1899. 8º.
09076. a. 13.

—— Le Corps Cathelineau pendant la guerre, 1870–1871 . . . 2me édition. 2 pt. *Paris,* 1871. 12º.
9077. bb. 18.

—— —— *See* BAULMONT (L.) Alsace et Bretagne. Légion Bretonne . . . Réponse au général de Cathelineau [i.e. to his " Le Corps Cathelineau pendant la guerre 1870–1871 "]. 1871. 8º.
9078. gg. 9. (3.)

—— L'Heure à Dieu. Dernières paroles du manifeste de Mgr le comte de Chambord 8 mai 1871. pp. 41. *Paris,* 1873. 8º.
8051. dd. 5.

CATHELINEAU (JACQUES)

—— *See* CANTITEAU (J.) Le Premier généralissime de la grande armée catholique et royale de la Vendée, *etc.* [" Éloge funèbre de M. Cathelineau," together with a letter concerning Cathelineau, both by J. Cantiteau.] [1925 ?] 8º.
10655. i. 49.

CATHELINEAU (JACQUES)

—— *See* OLLIVIER (Gustave) L'Armée du général Cathelineau. 1870. 8º.
9077. bb. 42.

—— *See* PORT (C.) La Légende de Cathelineau, *etc.* 1893. 8º.
010662. h. 36.

CATHELINEAU (LÉONCE) *See* CIVRAY, *Sénéchaussée de.* Cahiers de doléances de la sénéchaussée de Civray . . . Publiés par P. Boissonnade, L. Cathelineau. 1925. 8º.
9231. s. 38.

—— *See* DEUX-SÈVRES, *Department of the.* Cahiers de doléances des sénéchaussées de Niort et de Saint-Maixent . . . 1789. Publiés par L. Cathelineau. 1912. 8º.
9231. s. 28.

CATHELL (DANIEL WEBSTER) The Physician Himself, and what he should add to his scientific acquirements . . . *Third* edition. pp. 208. *Cushings & Bailey: Baltimore,* 1882. 8º.
7679. f. 10.

—— The Physician Himself, and what he should add to the strictly scientific. pp. 194. *Cushings & Bailey: Baltimore,* 1882. 8º.
7682. b. 19.

—— Tenth edition, *etc.* pp. 343. *F. A. Davis Co.: Philadelphia & London,* 1892. 8º.
7679. e. 19.

CATHELOTTE (ADRIEN JEAN JOSEPH) Contribution à l'étude des abcès urineux du périnée. pp. 52. *Paris,* 1872. 4º. [*Collection des thèses soutenues à la Faculté de Médecine de Paris.* An 1872. tom. 3.]
7373. n. 9.

CATHELOTTE (ADRIEN JOSEPH) Du cancer du sein et de ses diverses méthodes de traitement. pp. 32. *Paris,* 1848. 4º. [*Collection des thèses soutenues à la Faculté de Médecine de Paris.* An 1848. tom. 3.]
7372. b. 6.

CATHENA (PETRUS) *See* CATENA.

CATHER (JOHN) *Archdeacon of Tuam.* A Voice for Disestablishment ; being letters on the Irish Church. pp. 18. *Longmans & Co.: London,* 1869. 8º.
4165. aaa. 26.

CATHER (JOHN) *of London. See* KATHER.

CATHER (KATHERINE DUNLAP) *See* JORDAN (David S.) and CATHER (K. D.) High Lights of Geography. 1925, *etc.* 8º.
010005. e. 58.

—— Boyhood Stories of Famous Men, *etc.* pp. x. 278. *Century Co.: New York,* 1916. 8º.
10600. eee. 8.

—— [Another edition.] Illustrated by M. L. Bower. pp. 253. *G. G. Harrap & Co.: London,* 1920. 8º.
010603. e. 3.

—— [A reissue.] *London,* 1924. 8º. [*Told through the Ages.*]
12411. p. 1/7.

—— Boyhood Stories of Master Painters & Musicians . . . Illustrated, *etc.* (First published with other stories in " Boyhood Stories of Famous Men " . . . New edition.) pp. 123. *G. G. Harrap & Co.: London,* 1922. 8º. [*All Time Tales.* no. 20.]
012804. d. 1/34.

—— [Another edition.] [With a questionnaire.] pp. 131. *G. G. Harrap & Co.: London,* 1927. 8º. [*All Time Tales.* no. 20.]
012804. d. 1/42.

—— The Castle of the Hawk, etc. pp. vii. 228. *Century Co.: New York & London,* [1927.] 8º.
12712. aa. 28.

—— Educating by Story-Telling, *etc.* pp. xviii. 396. *World Book Co.: Yonkers-on-Hudson,* 1918. 8º. [*Play School Series.*]
W.P. 6052/1.

CATHER (KATHERINE DUNLAP)

—— [Another edition.] pp. 442. *G. G. Harrap & Co.: London*, 1919. 8°. **08311. e. 7.**

—— Girlhood Stories of Famous Women . . . Illustrated. pp. xiv. 336. *Century Co.: New York & London*, [1924.] 8°. **08415. f. 75.**

—— Religious Education through Story-Telling. pp. 219. *Abingdon Press: New York, Cincinnati*, [1925.] 8°. [*Abingdon Religious Education Texts.*] **04192. d. 1/46.**

—— Younger Days of Famous Writers . . . Illustrated. pp. xiii. 326. *Century Co.: New York & London*, [1925.] 8°. **010603. de. 22.**

CATHER (THOMAS)

—— Thomas Cather's Journal of a Voyage to America in 1836. pp. 48. *Rodale Press: London*, 1955. 8°. [*Miniature Books.*] **W.P. c. 299/17.**

CATHER (WILLA SIBERT)

—— *See* DAICHES (David) Willa Cather. A critical introduction. [1951.] 8°. **11868. m. 32.**

—— *See* SERGEANT (Elizabeth S.) Willa Cather. A memoir. [With a portrait.] [1953.] 8°. **10887. g. 32.**

—— April Twilights, and other poems. pp. 66. *William Heinemann: London; printed in U.S.A.*, 1924. 8°. **011686. g. 57.**

—— Alexander's Bridge. [A tale.] pp. 174. *Constable & Co.: London; Houghton Mifflin Co.: Boston & New York; Cambridge Mass.* [printed], 1912. 8°. **012704. aa. 25.**

—— [Another edition.] Alexander's Bridges . . . Illustrated. pp. 182. *William Heinemann: London*, 1912. 8°. **NN. 421.**

—— Death Comes for the Archbishop. pp. viii. 298. *William Heinemann: London*, 1927. 8°. **12713. a. 1.**

—— [Another edition.] With drawings and designs by Harold Von Schmidt. pp. 343. *William Heinemann: London; printed in U.S.A.*, [1930.] 4°. **012603. bb. 19.**

—— Death Comes for the Archbishop. pp. 299. *William Heinemann: London*, 1933. 8°. [*Windmill Library.*] **W.P. 8860/9.** *A reissue of the edition of 1927.*

—— [A reissue.] *London & Toronto*, 1936. 8°. **012601. aa. 14.**

—— A Lost Lady. pp. 166. *William Heinemann: London*, 1924. 8°. **012631. d. 50.**

—— (New edition.) pp. 173. *William Heinemann: London*, 1928. 8°. [*Windmill Library.*] **W.P. 8860/3.**

—— Lucy Gayheart. pp. 254. *Cassell & Co.: London*, 1935. 8°. **A.N. 2537.**

—— My Antonia, *etc.* pp. xiii. 418. *William Heinemann: London; Cambridge, Mass.* printed, 1919. 8°. **NN. 5641.**

—— My Mortal Enemy. pp. 122. *A. A. Knopf: New York*, 1926. 8°. **012640. b. 112.**

—— [Another edition.] pp. 122. *William Heinemann: London; printed in U.S.A.*, 1928. 8°. **012603. i. 55.**

—— Mon ennemi mortel. Grande nouvelle inédite. (Traduit par J. Balay et J. E. Burton.) 1935. *See* PERIODICAL PUBLICATIONS.—*Paris.* Les Œuvres libres, *etc.* no. 173. 1921, *etc.* 8°. **12208. ee. 173.**

CATHER (WILLA SIBERT)

—— Not Under Forty. pp. v. 165. *Cassell & Co.: London*, 1936. 8°. **12357. ss. 27.**

—— O Pioneers ! [A novel.] pp. 309. *William Heinemann: London; Cambridge, Mass.* printed, 1913. 8°. **012704. cc. 43.**

—— Obscure Destinies. [Three tales.] pp. 223. *Cassell & Co.: London*, 1932. 8°. **A.N. 1237.**

—— One of Ours. pp. 459. *A. A. Knopf: New York*, 1922. 8°. **012703. eee. 13.**

—— [Another edition.] pp. 372. *William Heinemann: London*, 1923. 8°. **NN. 9141.**

—— The Professor's House. pp. 283. *A. A. Knopf: New York*, 1925. 8°. **012705. h. 69.**

—— [Another edition.] pp. 275. *William Heinemann: London*, 1925. 8°. **12709. aa. 28.**

—— Sapphira and the Slave Girl. pp. vi. 295. *Cassell & Co.: London*, 1941. 8°. **12724. c. 16.**

—— Shadows on the Rock. pp. 277. *Cassell & Co.: London*, 1932. 8°. **NN. 19500.**

—— The Song of the Lark. pp. 489. *Houghton Mifflin Co.: Boston & New York*, 1915. 8°. **NN. 3117.**

—— [Another edition.] pp. 489. *John Murray: London; Cambridge, Mass.* [printed], 1916. 8°. **12625. r. 1.**

—— [Another edition.] pp. viii. 580. *Cassell & Co.: London*, 1938. 8°. **12646. g. 7.**

—— Youth and the Bright Medusa. [Tales.] pp. 303. *William Heinemann: London; printed in U.S.A.*, 1921. 8°. **NN. 7412.**

CATHERALL (ARTHUR) *See also* CHANNEL (A. R.) *pseud.* [i.e. A. Catherall.]

—— *See* BLOW (Geor. W.) The Steam and Steel Omnibus . . . Stories by A. Catherall. 1950. 4°. **8773. c. 19.**

—— *See* SCOUT STORY OMNIBUS. The Scout Story Omnibus. (Stories written by A. Catherall.) [1954.] 4°. **12830. h. 35.**

—— Adventurers Ltd. [Tales reprinted from " The Scout."] pp. vii. 248. *London*, 1938. 8°. [*Black's Boys' and Girls' Library.*] **12813. g. 1/61.**

—— Adventurers, Ltd. pp. 127. *Lutterworth Press: London*, 1954. 8°. **12836. h. 11.** *Part of the " Crown Library."*

—— Black Gold. A novel, *etc.* pp. 216. *C. A. Pearson: London*, 1939. 8°. **12824. a. 4.**

—— The Bull Patrol. pp. 95. *Lutterworth Press: London*, [1941.] 8°. [*Junior Wren Books.*] **12837.ee.2/6.**

—— Camp-Fire Stories, and how to tell them, *etc.* pp. 160. *Herbert Jenkins: London*, 1935. 8°. **20055. ee. 25.**

—— Cock o' the Town. Illustrated by Kenneth Brookes. pp. 140. *Boy Scouts Association: London*, 1950. 8°. **12810. aaa. 75.**

—— Jackals of the Sea . . . With . . . drawings . . . by Geoffrey Whittam. pp. v. 184. *J. M. Dent & Sons: London*, 1955. 8°. **12837. h. 27.**

CATHERALL (Arthur)

—— Keepers of the Khyber, *etc.* pp. 208. *T. Nelson & Sons: London*, 1940. 8°. [*Coronet Library.* no. 13.]
W.P. **6191/13**.

—— Lost with all Hands, *etc.* pp. 199. *T. Nelson & Sons: London*, [1940.] 8°. [*Coronet Library.* no. 17.]
W.P. **6191/17**.

—— Lost with all Hands . . . Illustrated by S. Drigin. pp. 199. *Thomas Nelson & Sons: London*, [1955.] 8°. [*Apex Series.*]
W.P. **3297/9**.

—— Pirate Sealer. pp. 188. *Children's Press: London & Glasgow*, 1953. 8°. [*Collins Schoolboys' Library.* no. 2.]
W.P. B. **153/2**.

—— Raid on Heligoland. pp. 253. *Collins: London & Glasgow*, 1940. 8°. **12825. dd. 8**.

—— Raid on Heligoland. pp. 253. *See* OMNIBUS. Omnibus of War Adventures, *etc.* [1941.] 8°. **012826. b. 6**.

—— Raid on Heligoland. pp. 190. *Collins: [Glasgow,]* 1942. 8°. [*Laurel and Gold Series.* vol. 130.]
012208. ccc. 1/111.

—— Riders of the Black Camel. pp. 172. *Venturebooks: Bath*, 1949. 8°. **12832. f. 17**.

—— The Rival Tugboats. pp. v. 248. *S. W. Partridge & Co.: London*, 1937. 8°. **20059. d. 33**.

—— The River of Burning Sand. pp. 240. *Collins: London & Glasgow*, 1947. 8°. **12830. bb. 38**.

—— [A reissue.] The River of Burning Sand. *London & Glasgow*, 1953. 8°. [*Collins Schoolboys' Library.* no. 5.]
W.P. B. **153/5**.

—— Rod o' the Rail. pp. 64. *C. A. Pearson: London*, [1936.] 8°. [*Boy's Ace Library.* no. 13.]
W.P. **11287/13**.

—— The Scuttlers . . . Illustrated by A. Bruce Cornwell and Drake Brookshaw. pp. v. 202. *Thomas Nelson & Sons: London*, 1955. 8°. **12833. aa. 39**.

—— Sea Wraith. pp. 167. *Lutterworth Press: London*, 1955. 8°. **12816. b. 78**.

—— Shanghaied ! pp. 188. *Children's Press: London & Glasgow*, [1954.] 8°. **12827. ccc. 66**.

—— Ten Fathoms Deep . . . With . . . line drawings . . . by Geoffrey Whittam. pp. v. 180. *J. M. Dent & Sons: London*, 1954. 8°. **12836. h. 35**.

—— Tomorrow's Hunter. pp. 256. *Herbert Jenkins: London*, 1950. 8°. NNN. **1057**.

—— Vanished Whaler . . . Illustrated by S. Drigin. pp. 191. *T. Nelson & Sons: London*, [1939.] 8°. [*Coronet Library.* no. 1.]
W.P. **6191/1**.

—— Vanished Whaler, *etc.* (Reprinted.) pp. 188. *Thomas Nelson & Sons: London*, 1953. 8°. [*Apex Series.*]
W.P. **3297/5**

—— Vibrant Brass, *etc.* pp. 272. *J. M. Dent & Sons: London*, 1954. 8°. NNN. **5444**.

CATHERALL (Arthur)

—— Wild Goose Saboteur . . . With drawings by Kenneth Brookes. pp. 191. *J. M. Dent & Sons: London*, 1955. 8°. **12838. ee. 29**.

—— Wings for a Gull. pp. 248. *Frederick Warne & Co.: London & New York*, [1950.] 8°. **12826. m. 1**.

CATHERALL (Samuel)

—— Cato Major. A Poem. Upon the model of Tully's Essay of Old Age. In four books. pp. xvi. 88. *J. Roberts: London*, 1725. 8°. **1465. f. 47**.

—— [Another edition.] Cato Major ; a Poem upon the model of Tully's Essay, *etc.* pp. 96. *J. Sadler: Liverpool*, 1755. 8°. **11633. c. 13**.

—— Εἰκὼν Σωκρατικὴ. Or, a Portraiture of Socrates, extracted out of Plato [chiefly from the Apology, Crito and Phaedo]: in blank verse. pp. 53. *A. Peisley: Oxford*, 1717. 8°. **11631.c.9**.

—— An Essay on the Conflagration, in blank verse. [With a portrait of Thomas Burnet.] pp. 66. *Anthony Peisley: Oxford*, 1720. 8°. **1465. f. 3**.

—— [Another copy.] **161. k. 9**.

—— [Another copy.] **1465. f. 27**.
Imperfect ; wanting the portrait.

—— A Sermon Preach'd at the Funeral of . . . the Lady Viscountess, Dowager, Cholmondeley, *etc.* pp. 26. *Robert Clavell: London*, 1692. 4°. **1416. e. 2**.

—— [Another copy.] **226. h. 11. (21.)**

—— [Another copy.] **1416. e. 1**.
Cropped.

CATHERALL (Thomas) Catherall's Hand Book. The Stranger's best guide to Llandudno and the Great Orme's Head . . . With illustrations. pp. 64. *T. Catherall: Bangor*, [1855 ?] 8°. **10369. bbb. 21**.

—— [Another edition.] pp. 64. *T. Catherall: Bangor*, [1860 ?] 8°. **10369. c. 15. (4.)**

—— The Handbook to Llandudno . . . Edited by Richard Greene . . . New edition, with considerable additions . . . and a map of the district. pp. vii. 132. *Catherall & Prichard: Chester*, [1873.] 8°. **10347. h. 4. (2.)**
The title on the cover reads: "Catherall's Guide to Llandudno."

CATHERIN (Philibert) *See* BART-LOI (L.) Au service du pape et de la France. Catherin, 1861–1870. 1901. 8°. **10660. k. 13**.

CATHERINA, *da Palanza.* *See* MORIGGI (Caterina)

CATHERINE. *See also* CATHARINE.

—— [For Saints, Sovereigns and Princesses of Sovereign Houses of this name :] *See* CATHARINE.

—— Catherine, or the Austrian Captive. *See* BELGRADE. [*Appendix.*] The Siege of Belgrade, a comic opera, *etc.*

—— Deux histoires. Catherine. M. Alexandre. Par C. G ****. 1871. 12°. *See* G ****, C. **12517. ee. 2**.

—— Catherine Grown Older : a sequel to Catherine Hamilton. By M. F. S. [i.e. M. Seamer, afterwards Seymour.] 1875. 8°. *See* S., M. F. **12804. df. 4**.

CATHERINE [Burke], *de Saint-Thomas, Ursuline.*

—— *See* QUEBEC.—*Ursulines.* Les Ursulines de Québec, *etc.* [By Mère Adèle de Sainte-Marie, assisted by Mère Catherine de Saint-Thomas.] 1863, *etc.* 8°. **04785. k. 37**.

CATHERINE [D'ORNELLAS], *de Jésus-Christ.* [Au chevet de la souffrance.] At the Bedside of the Sick. Precepts and counsels for hospital nurses . . . Translated by E. F. Peeler. pp. xii. 151. *Burns, Oates & Co.: London,* 1938. 8°. **07687. e. 93.**

—— At the Bedside of the Sick . . . Translated by E. F. Peeler. (Second impression.) pp. x. 150. *Burns Oates & Washbourne: London,* 1951. 8°. **7689. a. 77**

CATHERINE [SIMON], *de Saint Augustin.* See RAGUENEAU (P.) La Vie de la mère Catherine de Saint Augustin, *etc.* 1671. 8°. **4866. de. 12.**

CATHERINE, *Mademoiselle, pseud.* Manuel complet de la cuisinière bourgeoise . . . Nouvelle edition. Ornée de . . . gravures. pp. 336. *Paris,* 1860 8°. **7953. e. 23.**

CATHERINE, *Sister.* The Personality and Characteristics of the Devil. By Sister Catherine. pp. 48. *Martin & Son: London,* 1906. 8°. **4373. df. 6. (4.)**

—— Self-Sacrifice: what is it? By Sister Catherine. pp. 45. *A. H. Stockwell: London,* 1903. 8°. **4404. g. 30.**

CATHERINE AURELIA, *Foundress of the Institute of the Precious Blood* [AURELIA CAOUETTE].

—— Life of Mother Catherine Aurelia of the Precious Blood, foundress of the Institute of the Precious Blood, 1833–1905. By a member of the Institute . . . Second edition. [With plates, including a portrait.] pp. xxii. 205. *B. Herder Book Co.: St. Louis & London,* 1930. 8°. **4987. dd. 28.**

CATHERINE CALICO, *pseud.* See CALICO (C.)

CATHERINE FREDERIC, *Sister.*

—— . . . and spare me not in the making. Pages from a novice's diary. pp. 93. *Clonmore & Reynolds: [Dublin,]* 1955. 8°. **4987. ee. 10.**

CATHERINE REEF UNITED CLAIMHOLDERS GOLD MINING COMPANY. Rules of the Catherine Reef . . . Company . . . Peg Leg Gully, Eaglehawk, Bendigo. pp. 12. *H. Ashley: Sandhurst [Victoria],* 1861. 8°. **8225. bbb. 38. (3.)**

CATHERINE THOMAS, *Carmelite Nun.*

—— My Beloved. The story of a Carmelite nun. [With plates.] pp. 252. *McGraw-Hill Book Co.: New York,* [1955.] 8°. **4787. aa. 12.**

CATHERINE (ROBERT)

—— Le Style administratif. pp. 158. *Paris,* 1947. 8°. **12956. aa. 12.**

CATHERINEAU (J. EUGÈNE) Dissertation sur les scrophules; thèse, *etc.* pp. 30. *Paris,* 1833. 4°. **1184. f. 3. (33.)**

CATHÉRINEAU (JEAN) Épître à Alexandre Dumas sur le volume des bouts-rimés et sur son séjour à Bordeaux. [In verse.] pp. 7. *Bordeaux,* 1865. 8°. **11482. g. 32. (3.)**

—— Julien, ou l'Amour d'un marin; drame en cinq actes. [In verse.] pp. 70. *Bordeaux,* 1863. 8°. **11737. ff. 36. (1.)**

CATHERINET DE VILLEMAREST (CHARLES MAXIME)

—— *See* also AVRILLION ( ) *Mademoiselle, pseud.* [i.e. C.M. Catherinet de Villemarest.]

—— *See* BLANGINI (J. M. M. F.) Souvenirs . . . publiés par . . . M. de Villemarest. 1834. 8°. **932. f. 3.**

CATHERINET DE VILLEMAREST (CHARLES MAXIME)

—— *See* ITALY. [*Appendix.—Miscellaneous.*] L'Hermite en Italie, *etc.* [Edited by M. Catherinet de Villemarest.] 1825. 12°. **932. b. 5.**

—— *See* JONGHE (E. van A.) calling herself IDA SAINT-ELME. Mémoires d'une contemporaine, *etc.* [With contributions by M. Catherinet de Villemarest.] 1827, *etc.* 8°. **10659. p. 6.**

—— —— 1828. 8°. **1441. e. 6–9.**

—— *See* WAIRY (L. C.) Mémoires de Constant, *etc.* [tom. 5, 6 by M. Catherinet de Villemarest.] 1830. 8°. **1450. g. 3.**

—— Monsieur de Talleyrand. [A biography, by C.M. Catherinet de Villemarest.] tom. 1, 2. 1834. 8°. *See* TALLEYRAND-PÉRIGORD (C. M. de) *Prince of Benevento.* **1201. e. 16.**

—— Life of Prince Talleyrand, *etc.* [Translated from the French of M. Catherinet de Villemarest.] 4 vol. 1834–36. 8°. *See* TALLEYRAND-PÉRIGORD (C. M. de) *Prince of Benevento.* **612. i. 24.**

—— Napoléon. 1769–1821. pp. 14. *Paris,* 1848. 8°. **10660. d. 40. (11.)**

—— Maxime de Villemarest, chroniqueur et nouvelliste, 1785–1852. Documents inédits recueillis et publiés par Roger Bedel. pp. 186. *Mayenne,* 1918. 8°. **012238. c. 1.**

CATHERINOT (NICOLAS) Les Axiomes du droit français . . . Avec une notice sur la vie et les écrits de l'auteur par Édouard Laboulaye . . . et une bibliographie raisonnée des écrits de Catherinot par Jacques Flach. pp. 64. *Paris,* 1883. 8°. **5423. bb. 16.**

—— An Integral Facsimile of Annales typographiques de Bourges . . . printed and published at Bourges, France, July 23, 1683. With an introductory note by Douglas C. McMurtrie. pp. 7. 8. *Privately printed: Chicago,* 1942. 8°. **11907. c. 43.**

—— An Integral Facsimile of L'Art d'imprimer . . . printed and published at Bourges, France, March 10, 1685. With an introductory note by Douglas C. McMurtrie. pp. 6. 12. *Privately printed: Chicago,* 1942. 8°. **011903. h. 54.**

—— Nicolai Catharini Observationum et conjecturarum liber. *See* OTTO (E.) Thesaurus juris Romani, *etc.* tom. 1. 1725, *etc.* fol. **499. d. 2.**

—— [Another edition.] *See* OTTO (E.) Thesaurus juris Romani, *etc.* tom. 1. 1733, *etc.* fol. **5206. h. 1.**

—— [Another edition.] *See* OTTO (E.) Thesaurus juris Romani, *etc.* tom. 1. 1741, *etc.* fol. **5254. f. 8.**

—— Nicolai Catharini Observationum et conjecturarum libri quatuor. Ejusdem Gratianus recensitus. 1753. *See* MEERMAN (G.) Novus thesaurus juris civilis, *etc.* tom. 6. 1751, *etc.* fol. **18. h. 11.**

—— Les Parallèles de la Noblesse. 1838. *See* LEBER (J. M. C.) Collection des meilleurs dissertations, *etc.* tom. 20. 1826, *etc.* 8°. **910. d. 23.**

CATHERWOOD (ALFRED) A Concise and Practical Treatise on the Principal Diseases of the Air-passages, Lungs, and Pleura. pp. xii. 208. *Duncan & Malcolm: London,* 1841. 8°. **1187. k. 10.**

—— Second edition. pp. xii. 208. *Aylott & Jones: London,* 1847. 8°. **7616. aa. 7.**

CATHERWOOD (BENJAMIN F.) *See* GANNETT (Frank E.) and CATHERWOOD (B. F.) Industrial and Labour Relations in Great Britain, *etc.* 1939. 8°.   **8288. g. 1.**

—— Basic Theories of Distribution. [With portraits.] pp. ix. 262.   *P. S. King & Son: London,* 1939. 8°.
8204. cc. 15.

CATHERWOOD (FREDERICK) *See* STEPHENS (John L.) Incidents of Travel in Central America . . . Revised . . . with additions, by F. Catherwood. 1854. 8°.
808. ff. 2.

—— *See* VON HAGEN (Victor W.) Frederick Catherwood, Arch^t, *etc.* [With plates.] 1950. 8°.   **7711. dd. 12.**

—— Engineer's Report. [A report addressed to the Committee of Management of the Demerara Railway Company, October 30th., 1846. Followed by "Estimate of the cost of constructing the railway as proposed between Georgetown and Mahaica Creek, on the East coast of Demerara," "Estimate of Passenger and Goods Traffic," and two appendices, each signed: F. Catherwood.] *In:* Report of the London Committee Management of the Demerara Railway Company, *etc.* pp. 15–[51]. 1847. 8°.
10470. f. 30. (6.)

—— Views of Ancient Monuments in Central America, Chiapas, and Yucatan. pp. 24. pl. 25.   *F. Catherwood: London,* 1844. fol.   **Cup. 652. m. 38.**

CATHERWOOD (GRACE ADELE) *See* RADZIWILL (C.) *Princess,* afterwards KOBB, afterwards DANVIN (C.) Child of Pity . . . By the Princess Radziwill, with the collaboration of G. A. Catherwood. 1930. 8°.
A.N. 594.

—— The Faith of the Little Shepherd, *etc.* pp. 92. *J. H. Sears & Co.: New York,* 1926. 8°.   [MISSING.]

—— [Another edition.] pp. 95. *Skeffington & Son: London,* [1927.] 8°.   [MISSING.]

CATHERWOOD (JOHN) Disputatio medica inauguralis, de apoplexia, *etc.* Praes. J. Munniks. pp. 8. *Trajecti ad Rhenum,* 1710. 4°.   **1185. k. 17. (24.)**

—— A New Method of Curing the Apoplexy. With an appendix, containing some observations upon the use and abuse of physick. pp. viii. 77.   *W. Taylor: London,* 1715. 8°.   **1190. h. 6.**

CATHERWOOD (JOHN JAMES) *See* SMITH (Charles) *Writer on the Corn Laws.* Tracts on the Corn-Trade & Corn-Laws . . . A new edition with additions from the marginal manuscripts of Mr. Catherwood, *etc.* 1804. 8°.
960. f. 5.

—— An Account of the Quantities of Corn and Grain exported from, and imported into, England & Scotland . . . from . . . 1771 to . . . 1784, with the bounties and drawbacks paid and the duties received thereon ; together with the average price of corn in England under each year. *W. Brown; R. Turner: [London,* 1784 ?] *s. sh.* fol.
1880. b. 42. (2.)

CATHERWOOD (MARY HARTWELL) The Chase of Saint-Castin, and other stories of the French in the New World. pp. 266.   *Houghton & Co.: Boston,* 1894. 8°.
012706. ee. 42.

—— Craque-o'-Doom. A story . . . Illustrated. pp. 238. *J. B. Lippincott & Co.: Philadelphia,* 1881. 12°.
12642. i. 12.

—— The Days of Jeanne d'Arc. [A tale.] pp. ix. 278. *Century Co.: New York,* 1897. 8°.   **012704. f. 1.**

—— [Another copy, with a different titlepage.]   *Gay & Bird: London,* 1898. 8°.   **012706. m. 60.**

CATHERWOOD (MARY HARTWELL)

—— The Lady of Fort St. John.   *Sampson Low & Co.: London,* [1893.] 8°.   **012706. h. 42.**

—— Lazarre. pp. 436.   *B. F. Stevens & Brown: London,* [1901.] 8°.   **012707. m. 30.**

—— [Another edition.] With illustrations by André Castaigne. pp. 436.   *Grant Richards: London,* 1902. 8°.
012639. ccc. 46.

—— Old Kaskaskia. pp. 200.   *Houghton & Mifflin: Boston & New York,* 1893. 8°.   **012706. k. 12.**

—— The Romance of Dollard . . . Illustrated. pp. 206. *Century Co.: New York,* [1889.] 8°.   **012705. k. 4.**

—— The Story of Tonty. pp. viii. 225.   *Grant Richards: London,* 1904. 8°.   **012628. d. 20.**

—— The White Islander. [With illustrations.] pp. viii. 164. *T. Fisher Unwin: London,* 1893. 8°.   **012706. m. 4.**

CATHEU (FRANÇOISE DE)

—— La Collégiale de Saint-Junien. Le tombeau, les peintures murales. [With illustrations, including plans.] pp. 90. *Paris,* 1948. 8°.   **7813. d. 2.**

CATHEUX (   ) *Sieur de.* Une Ambassade russe [headed by Prince P. I. Potemkin] à la cour de Louis XIV. pp. vi. 32. *Paris,* 1860. 4°. [*Bibliothèque russe et polonaise. Bibliothèque russe.* Nouvelle sér. vol. 3.]
12264. a.

CATHEY (JAMES H.) Truth is Stranger than Fiction ; or, the True genesis of a wonderful man. [An inquiry into the parentage of Abraham Lincoln. With portraits.] pp. 185. [*H. T. Rogers: Asheville, N.C.,* 1899.] 8°.
010882. e. 40.

—— [Another copy.] Truth is Stranger than Fiction, *etc.* [1899.] 8°.   **C. 121. a. 4.**

CATHIE (CAMERON) Nostalgia for No Known Place. [Poems.] pp. 46.   *Roger Ingram: [London ?]* 1938. 8°.
11657. aa. 5.

CATHIE (DIARMID CAMERON)

—— She's Right. [A novel.] pp. 191.   *Collins: London,* 1953. 8°.   **NNN. 4086.**

CATHKIN (JAMES)

—— A Relation of James Cathkin, his imprisonment and examination about printing of the nullitie of Perth Assemblie. By himself. *In:* The Bannatyne Miscellany, *etc.* vol. 1. pp. 197–215. 1827. 4°.   **R. Ac. 8248/19.**

CATHLEEN. *See* KATHLEEN.

CATHLES (ALBERT) Dumping and Costing. pp. 11. *Gee & Co.: London,* 1933. 8°. ["*Accountant*" *Lecture Series.* no. 17.]   **8233. dd. 4/17.**

—— The Principles of Costing. pp. 64.   *London,* 1921. 8°. [*Accountant Students' Library.* vol. 2.]
08230. ee. 65/2.

—— Second edition. pp. 108. *Gee & Co.: London,* 1924. 8°. [*Accountant Students' Library.* vol. 2.]
08230. ee. 65/2a.

CATHLIN (LÉON) Les Treize paroles du pauvre Job . . . et autres proses de ténèbres et de guerre. Préface par Étienne Lamy. pp. liii. 200. *Paris,* 1920. 8°.
12547. ppp. 34.

CATHO. *See* CATO.

CATHODE RAY, *pseud.* [i.e. MARCUS GRAHAM SCROGGIE.]

—— Second Thoughts on Radio Theory. By "Cathode Ray" of Wireless World. pp. 409.   *Iliffe & Sons: London,* 1955. 8°.   **8762. bb. 53.**

CATHOLIC. *See* BERTHOLDI (H.) Das Schneidemühler Glaubensbekenntniss . . . Kritik der Schrift: Offenes Glaubensbekenntniss der sich nennenden: christlich-apostolisch-katholische Gemeinde zu Schneidemühl [by Jan Czerski], beleuchtet von einem Katholiken. 1845. 8°.
3910. b. 11.

—— *See* BIBLE.—*Gospels.* [*English.*] A New Version of the Four Gospels; with notes . . . by a Catholic [i.e. John Lingard]. 1836. 8°.
1005. d. 7.

—— *See* HASE (T.) Notitia libri cui titulus Der so wahrhaffte, als gantz auffrichtige . . . Catholicus [by Ernest, Landgrave of Hesse-Cassel]. 1730. 8°. [*Museum historico-philologico-theologicum.* vol. 2. pt. 3.]
4372. d. 25.

—— *See* OBSERVER. Answer to a pamphlet signed "A Catholic," and entitled "A Reply to Remarks" [on a handbill signed: W. O. Woolfrey], *etc.* 1839. 12°.
3939. aaa. 68.

—— *See* VOX POPULI. Intrichi del nostro tempo . . . auttore Vox Populi, *etc.* [An answer to a pamphlet entitled: "Il Cattolico di Stato."] [1635?] 4°.
3901. e. 1.

—— A tre quesiti d'un apostata divenuto ministro evangelico metodista [i.e. G. B. Corica], risposta d'un cattolico. pp. 11. *Siracusa*, 1880. 4°.
3900. g. 6. (7.)

—— Advice from a Catholick to his Protestant Friend, touching the doctrine of Purgatory. By way of letter. pp. 18 [16]. [*Douai?*] 1687. 12°.
698. b. 50.

—— L'Affaire Dreyfus et la révision. Par un Catholique. pp. 14. *Bordeaux*, 1898. 8°.
05402. eee. 29. (3.)

—— Der alte Rock und die neue Kirche. Eine kurze Darstellung der neuesten katholischen Zustände. Zur Belehrung des Volkes. Von einem Katholiken. pp. 114. *Lahr*, 1845. 12°.
1368. a. 30.

—— L'Amour. Par un Catholique [i.e. Léon Gautier]. pp. 166. *Paris*, 1860. 12°.
8415. aa. 7.

—— An den Verfasser der Schrift: Zweites offenes Bedenken die Kniebeugungs-Frage . . . betreffend [i.e. Count C. von Giech]. Offenes Sendschreiben von einem Katholiken. [Signed: Ihr ehemaliger katholischer Correferent.] pp. 16. *München*, 1845. 8°.
3910. eee. 16.

—— *See* GIECH (C. von) *Count.* Antwort an den Verfasser der Schrift: "Offenes Sendschreiben von einem Katholiken an den Verfasser der Schrift: "Zweites offenes Bedenken, *etc.*" 1845. 8°.
3910. d. 34.

—— Une Année à Rome. Impressions d'un Catholique. pp. 410. *Paris*, 1866. 8°.
10131. bb. 22.

—— Gli Atti pontificii di Pio IX. Pensieri di un cattolico, scritti nel 1865. pp. 158. *Palermo*, 1869. 8°.
3902. bb. 24.

—— Beleuchtung der "Rechtfertigung" des apostolisch-katholischen Priesters Czerski in Schneidemühl hinsichtlich seines Abfalles von der römischen Hofkirche. Von einem Katholiken. pp. 52. *Gnesen*, 1845. 8°.
3910. a. 12.

—— Le Bon catholique; contenant des preuves claires et simples de l'illégitimité des nouveaux pasteurs, une instruction sur le schisme, des prières et des lectures tirées de l'Écriture Sainte et des Saints Pères, relatives au tems présent . . . Par une société de catholiques. Nouvelle édition . . . avec plusieurs augmentations, et notamment des brefs des 13 avril 1791, et 19 mars 1792. 3 pt. FEW MS. NOTES. [*Paris*, 1792?] 8°. **F. 128. (1.)**

—— The British Lion and the Papal Bull; a poem. By a Catholic. pp. 12. *S. B. Oldham: Dublin*, 1851. 12°.
11648. a. 27.

CATHOLIC.

—— The Case of Ordination Consider'd . . . By a Catholick. pp. 92. *John Baker: London*, 1712. 8°. **T. 1805. (8.)**

—— The Catholic. *See* PERIODICAL PUBLICATIONS.—*London.*

—— The Catholic. [Attacking the Church of Rome.] *See* PERIODICAL PUBLICATIONS.—*Manchester.*

—— The Catholic. Edited by Rev. T. Connellan. *See* PERIODICAL PUBLICATIONS.—*Dublin.*

—— The Catholic. A tale of contemporary society. pp. iv. 363. *John Lane: London & New York; New York* [printed], 1902. 8°.
012637. aa. 33.

—— Catholic and Protestant. pp. 40. *Joseph Masters: London*, 1853. 4°. [*Churchman's Library.*]
4431. a. 12. (23.)

—— The Catholic at Nine P.M., *etc.* pp. 7. *Burns, Oates & Co.: London*, [1942.] 8°.
4398. de. 16.

—— A Catholic at the Front. pt. 1, 4. 1915, 18. 8°. *See* HOWARD (Alfred) *Catholic Soldier.* **3943. aa. 110.**

—— Catholic because Roman Catholic. A statement and the reply. pp. 20. *Catholic Truth Society: London*, 1917. 8°.
3943. aa. 21.

—— The Catholic Controversy. [Correspondence between "Catholic," i.e. Valentine T. Sellers and "Barney Flanagan," arising out of a review of Gladstone's "Vatican Decrees." Reprinted from the Lawrence "Journal and Citizen."] pp. 27. [*Lawrence, Mass.*, 1874.] 8°.
3938. cc. 54.

—— The Catholic's Manual of Instructions and Devotions. pp. x. 489. *Rockliff Bros.: Liverpool*, 1867. 12°.
3455. aaa. 4.

—— The Catholic's Plea. An appeal to the Bible. [In verse.] pp. 16. *Burns, Oates & Co.: London*, [1870.] 8°.
3938. dd. 1.

—— The Catholic's Pocket Prayer Book. Compiled from approved sources. pp. 192. *R. & T. Washbourne: London*, [1915.] 32°.
944. aa. 15.

—— The Catholic's Temperance Library. [Tracts by various authors. With a preface by Cardinal Manning.] vol. 1. *Catholic Truth Society: London*, 1891. 8°. **3939. ee. 7.**
No more published.

—— The Catholic's Vade Mecum: a select manual of prayers for daily use. pp. xvi. 371. *Burns & Lambert: London*, 1851. 16°.
3455. a. 50.

—— Le Catholique christianizé. [A letter on the troubles of France during the minority of Louis XIII.] pp. 15. [*Paris?*] 1615. 8°.
1058. b. 30. (4.)

—— Les Catholiques et la République. [Signed: Un Catholique.] pp. 70. *Paris*, 1891. 12°.
8051. ccc. 35. (3.)

—— The Christianity of Catholicism, being an appeal to the Society of Evangelical Friends, and to Dissenters generally, on the tendency and effects of their rule of faith, by a Catholic. pp. 28. *T. Jones: London; Lynch: Manchester*, [1839.] 8°. **T. 2441. (4.)**

—— Conservatives and Liberals judged by their conduct to the Catholics of England and Ireland. By a Catholic [i.e. Myles W. P. O'Reilly]. pp. 18. *Browne & Nolan: Dublin*, 1867. 8°.
8146. cc. 14. (3.)

—— Crímenes de la Demagojia. El Colegio Apostólico de Guadalupe en Zacatecas. [Signed: Un Católico.] pp. 80. *Guadalajara* [*Mexico*], 1859. 4°. **8180. bb. 40.**

CATHOLIC.

—— De la crise religieuse. Méditations et fantasies. Par un Catholique. pp. 31. *Paris*, 1865. 8°.
3901. dd. 44. (6.)

—— Denkschrift über die Auflehnung des rheinischen Episcopats gegen die Staatsgewalt. Von einem Katholiken. pp. 16. *Leipzig*, 1853. 8°. **3914. d. 78. (2.)**

—— Le Dernier mot du socialisme, par un Catholique [i.e. C. F. Chevé]. pp. v. 192. *Paris*, 1848. 12°.
8275. bb. 45.

—— Das deutsche Collegium in Rom. Entstehung, geschichtlicher Verlauf, Wirksamkeit, gegenwärtiger Zustand und Bedeutsamkeit desselben; unter Beifügung betreffender Urkunden und Belege dargestellt von einem Katholiken [i.e. Heinrich Bode]. pp. iv. 202. *Leipzig*, 1843. 8°. **702. h. 31.**

—— Disputa fra un Cattolico ed un Ebreo che si converte alla S. fede di Gesù Cristo per l'autorità stessa della Sinagoga e del Sommo Pontefice di lei, *etc.* [The dedicatory letter signed: G. S. R.] 1876. 8°. *See* R., G. S.
4034. bbb. 1.

—— Disputatio inter Catholicum et Paterinum hæreticum. *See* MARTÈNE (E.) and DURAND (U.) Thesaurus novus anecdotorum, *etc.* tom. 5. 1717. fol. **10. f. 6.**

—— Doctrina moralis Jesuitarum. Die Moral der Jesuiten, quellenmässig nachgewiesen aus ihren Schriften von einem Katholiken. Zweite erweiterte Ausgabe der "Flores theologiae moralis Jesuitarum"—"Blüthen der Jesuiten-Moral." pp. xvi. 340. *Celle*, 1874. 8°. **4091. bbb. 5.**

—— Du mouvement religieux en Angleterre, ou les Progrès du catholicisme et le retour de l'Église anglicane à l'unité; par un Catholique [i.e. Jules Gandon]. pp. xx. 466. *Paris*, 1844. 8°. **1367. d. 11.**

—— [Another edition.] pp. xi. 321. *Louvain*, 1844. 8°.
4705. c. 2.

—— Entretien d'un Catholique & d'un Protestant calviniste, sur le sujet des reliques. pp. 110. *See* GROSTESTE-DES-MAHIS (M.) Deux lettres, *etc.* 1685. 12°. **3901. a. 25.**

—— Épître d'un Catholique, publiée par un Républicain. [A satire, in verse.] pp. 8. [*Paris*, 1797.] 8°.
F. 546. (22.)

—— Der Erzbischof von Cöln und die preussische Staatsregierung. Von einem Katholiken [Johann Otto Ellendorf?]. pp. viii. 39. *Rudolstadt*, 1838. 8°. **699. e. 16.**

—— Faisons-nous Protestants! Par un Catholique. pp. 30. *Paris*, 1860. 8°. **3901. ff. 2. (4.)**

—— I. Question: Why are you a Catholic? . . . Written by the Reverend Father S. C., Monk of the Holy Order of St. Benedict [i.e. Serenus Cressy], *etc.* 1686. 4°. *See* C., S., *Reverend Father, Monk, etc.* **T. 1866. (1.)**

—— [Another edition.] I. Question. Why are you a Catholique? The answer, enlarged in this second edition, follows. II. Question. But why are you a Protestant? An answer attempted—in vain. [By Serenus Cressy.] pp. 133. [*Douay?* 1690?] 8°. **3932. aa. 14.**
Cropped.

—— Gegen die ultramontane jesuitische Richtung im Katholicismus. Von einem Katholiken. Zwanglose Blätter. I. pp. 12. *Wien*, 1869. 8°. **3913. bb. 92.**
No more published.

—— Der heilige Rock . . . Von einem Katholiken [signing himself: N. S., S.L.]. 1868. 8°. *See* S., N., *S.L.*
3911. a. 5.

CATHOLIC.

—— Histoire de la communauté des biens dans l'antiquité et dans l'ère chrétienne, ou Tradition universelle du catholicisme et de l'humanité. Par un Catholique [i.e. C. F. Chevé]. 2 tom. *Nancy*, 1866. 8°. **8205. g. 27.**

—— Is Germany anti-Catholic? By a Catholic. pp. 30. *Burns & Oates: London*, [1916.] 8°. **3911. cc. 60.**

—— Ist Deutschland anti-katholisch? Von einem Katholiken. pp. 48. *Burns & Oates: London*, [1916?] 8°.
3907. b. 40.

—— Ist das Band der Ehe sogar ohne Ausnahm unauflöslich als es die Kanonisten vorgeben? Eine Frage, die ein Katholick beantwortet. pp. 36. 1773. 8°.
1250. b. 30. (4.)

—— Der jetzige Religionskrieg in der Schweiz, seine Ursachen, Freunde und Feinde, die Jesuiten daselbst, Lage und Stärke der Katholiken—Sonderbündler—*x.* Ein klarer, gedrängter Ueberblick von einem Katholiken. pp. 20. *Düsseldorf*, 1847. 12°. **8072. a. 13.**

—— Jubilé séculaire de Toulouse. Réponse à divers écrits touchant les événements qui se sont passés à Toulouse en 1562, par un Catholique. pp. 15. *Toulouse*, 1862. 8°. **4632. e. 7.**

—— Katholisch ist gut Sterben! Katholisches Volkslied mit Notendruck. Nebst katholischen Fürbitten und dem Hirten-Gebete des . . . Bischofs Wilhelm Arnoldi zu Trier. 6te vermehrte und verbesserte Auflage. *Bonn*, 1846. 32°. **11522. aa. 53. (2.)**

—— Katholisch und Ultramontan. Zur Orientirung. Von einem entschiedenen Katholiken und eifrigen Patrioten. Juli 1868. pp. 81. *München*, 1868. 8°.
3911. bb. 58. (8.)

—— Leone XIII e padre Tosti. La Conciliazione. [Remarks on the work of that name by Luigi Tosti.] L'Italia ed il Papato. [Signed: Un Cattolico.] pp. 22. *Roma*, 1887. 8°. **4050. h. 11. (2.)**

—— Letters between a Catholic and a Protestant on the Doctrines of the Church of Rome; originally published . . . under the signatures of W. L. and Horace Bentley. 1827. 8°. *See* L., W. **T. 1192. (20.)**

—— Lettre d'un Catholique [signed: Un simple enfant de l'Église] à M. l'abbé Blanchard [in reference to his pamphlet entitled "Deuxième suite à la controverse pacifique"]. (Première suite à la Lettre d'un Catholique à M. l'abbé Blanchard.) pp. 20. *Jos. Booker: Londres*, [1806.] 8°. **3901. cc. 10.**

—— Lettres à un Protestant sur l'autorité de l'Église et le schisme, par un Catholique. (Lettre de M. l'abbé Mermillod à l'auteur.) pp. xxx. 292. *Paris*, 1859. 12°.
3901. aa. 18.

—— Lettres très importantes et très curieuses d'un Catholique à Mgr Cart, évêque de Nîmes. pp. 139. *Paris*, 1844. 8°. **1356. e. 33.**

—— Der Lügengeist der heutigen katholischen Journalistik oder der Mainzer "Katholik" in seiner wahren Gestalt enthüllt von einem Katholiken. pp. 39. *Siegen & Wiesbaden*, 1845. 8°. **3910. b. 19.**

—— Mahnung eines Katholiken an seine christlichen Mitbrüder. I. Die Trierer Rockschau und was damit zusammenhängt. II. Wichtige Aktenstücke über die Umtriebe der Jesuiten und Jesuitenpartei in Frankreich und Belgien, *etc.* pp. 56. *Minden*, 1845. 16°.
3910. a. 11.

—— Memoriale di un Cattolico [i.e. Alessio A. Pelliccia] alla Santità di Papa Pio VI. [In favour of the court of Naples, on the question of the homage claimed by the Pope.] pp. 94. [*Naples*, 1788?] 4º. **663.** f. **25.** (4.)

—— Modest Reflections on the Right Reverend the Bishop of Norwich [Charles Trimnell] his late charge to the Reverend Clergy of his Diocess. By a Catholick. pp. 13–80. *Printed for the Author*, 1710. 4º. **698.** g. **25.** (4.)

—— Mᵍʳ Maret et le Concile du Vatican, ou Simple coup d'œil d'un Catholique sur le livre intitulé : Du Concile général et de la paix religieuse par un ancien Professeur de Théologie [i.e. H. L. C. Maret]. (Pièces justificatives.) pp. 103. *Lyon; Paris*, [1869.] 8º. **5016.** bb. **11.**

—— Un Mot aux quarante-cinq brochures [upon the pamphlet entitled: "Le Pape et le Congrès"]. Opinion individuelle d'un Catholique. pp. 8. *Paris*, 1860. 8º. **8033.** d. **18.** (3.)

—— Muss der Katholik an die päpstliche Unfehlbarkeit glauben? Verdeutschung der Denkschrift eines Concilsvaters über die Nothwendigkeit der Einstimmigkeit bei dogmatischen Concilsbeschlüssen, nebst Vorwort, Einleitung und Abhang, betreffend die Freiheit des Vatikanischen Concils, vom Uebersetzer. [A translation of Bishop F. A. P. Dupanloup's " De l'unanimité moral nécessaire dans les conciles pour les définitions dogmatiques. Mémoire presenté aux Pères du Concile du Vatican."] 1870. 8º. *See* DUPANLOUP (F. A. P.) *Bishop of Orleans*. **3911.** ee. **46.** (7.)

—— Offenes Glaubensbekenntniss der sich christlich-apostolisch-katholisch nennenden Gemeinde zu Schneidemühl, beleuchtet von einem Katholiken. pp. 23. *Posen*, 1844. 8º. **3910.** d. **12.**

—— Oui ou non? Par un Catholique. [Urging the Bishops and Clergy to declare themselves as to the doctrines of Father Hyacinthe, the Abbé Gratry and others on the Vatican Council.] pp. 16. *Paris*, 1870. 8º. **3902.** g. **44.** (4.)

—— Padre Agostino da Montefeltro e le sue prediche. [Signed : Un Cattolico.] pp. 16. *Firenze*, 1893. 8º. **4864.** cc. **32.** (3.)

—— Le Pape devant la révolution. Par un Catholique. pp. 28. *Paris*, 1860. 8º. **8033.** d. **18.** (2.)

—— Pape et Roi. [On the temporal power of Pius IX.] Par un Catholique. pp. 32. *Paris*, 1861. 8º. **8033.** d. **22.** (5.)

—— Pensées d'un Catholique sur les affaires de Rome en vue du Congrès de Paris de 1860. pp. 15. *Paris*, 1860. 8º. **8033.** c. **33.** (7.)

—— Pensieri politico-razionali di un Cattolico. pp. 14. *Roma*, 1871. 8º. **4375.** b. **52.**

—— ¿ Puede un Católico colaborar con el Nazismo? pp. 19. *Paris*, [1937.] 8º. **08073.** d. **34.**

—— The Queen or the Pope? A tract for the times; by a Catholic, M.A., LL.M. (Third edition.) pp. 12. *William Macintosh: London; John Ferguson: Manchester*, 1868. 8º. **3940.** bb. **52.** (11.)

—— Rationaler und historischer Standpunkt zur Beurtheilung des Verhältnisses zwischen Staats-Regierungen und dem römischen Stuhle in Beziehung auf gemischte Ehen; mit einem Rückblicke auf die Kölner Angelegenheit. Von einem Katholiken. pp. vi. 154. *Köln*, 1838. 8º. **699.** e. **30.**

—— Le Rationalisme étudié dans la vie de Jésus de M. Ernest Renan. Par un Catholique. pp. xxxviii. 440. *Besançon, Vesoul*, 1869. 8º. **4808.** h. **25.**

—— Reasons for being a Catholic. By E. H. 1899. 16º. *See* H., E. **3939.** a. **11.** (3.)

—— Recherches sur les causes de l'athéisme, en réponse à la brochure de Mᵍʳ Dupanloup [entitled " L'Athéisme et le péril social,"] par une Catholique. pp. 56. *Paris*, 1867. 8º. **4014.** f. **46.**

—— Réflexions d'un Catholique à l'occasion de l'affaire Guibord. [Concerning the refusal of the rites of the Roman Catholic Church at his burial.] pp. 16. *Montréal*, 1870. 8º. **3902.** g. **42.** (6.)

—— Supplément aux Réflexions d'un Catholique à l'occasion de l'affaire Guibord, *etc.* pp. 18. *Montréal*, 1891. 8º. **3902.** g. **41.** (11.)

—— Das Reformationsjahr 1556 nach Schenkel und Holtzmann beleuchtet von einem Katholiken. [On D. Schenkel's " Die Reformatoren und die Reformation " and J. Holtzmann's " Das Jahr 1856."] pp. 13. *Heidelberg*, 1856. 8º. **3910.** ee. **40.** (6.)

—— The Reformed Catholique : or, the True Protestant . . . [By Sir Roger Lestrange.] The second edition corrected. pp. 35. *For Henry Brome: London*, 1679. 4º. **108.** d. **65.**

—— Rome et les Gallicans. Par un Catholique. pp. 64. *Paris*, 1870. 8º. **3902.** g. **41.** (9.)

—— A Safeguard from Shipwracke to a prudent Catholike, *etc. See* VIRTUMNUS, *Romanus*. Virtumnus Romanus, or, a Discourse penned by a Romish Priest, *etc.*

—— La Situation en France, par un Catholique, ou Lettre au cardinal Lavigerie. pp. 16. *Toulouse*, 1891. 8º. **8051.** de. **24.** (7.)

—— The Spirit and Truth of the Gospel : in a dialogue between a Catholic and a Sandemanian, *etc.* pp. xx. 52. *G. Keith: London*, 1777. 8º. **3940.** bbb. **29.** (1.)

—— To the Readers of Religious Tracts. (The True Principles of Catholics.) [The preface signed : A Catholic.] pp. 12. *J. Whittaker: Wirksworth*, 1838. 12º. **908.** c. **5.** (6.)

—— A Treatise of Equivocation : wherein is largely discussed the question whether a Catholike or any other person before a magistrate beyng demaunded uppon his oath whether a Preiste were in such a place, may—notwᵗʰstanding his perfect knowledge to the contrary—wᵗʰout Periury . . . answere, No, wᵗʰ this secreat meaning reserued in his mynde, That he was not there so that any man is bounde to detect it. Edited by David Jardine. pp. xxxii. 107. *Longmans & Co.: London*, 1851. 8º. **3935.** b. **1.**

—— The True Catholic. pp. 12. *R.T.S.: London*, [1830?] 12º. [*First Series Tracts*. no. 211.] **863.** k. **14.**

—— Über den Cölibats-Zwang . . . bei der römisch-katholischen Geistlichkeit. Von einem Katholiken. pp. 19. *Karlsruhe*, 1874. 8º. **3913.** e. **4.** (7.)

—— Ultimatum d'un Catholique au Décret qui exige le serment relatif à la Constitution prétendue civile du clergé. pp. 8. [*Paris?* 1790.] 8º. **F.R. 161.** (3.)

—— Unterredungen über das katholische Kirchenjahr zwischen einem Katholiken und Protestanten. Von einem Priester in Köln . . . Zweite Auflage. pp. 350. *Aschaffenburg*, 1846. 16º. **3910.** a. **54.**

CATHOLIC.

—— Vérités hardies, qui, heureusement, n'empêchent pas d'être bon Catholique. pp. 32. [*Paris*, 1791.] 8º.
F.R. 151. (5.)

—— La Voix du Peuple est la voix de Dieu. Plus d'abus dans la religion catholique. Plus de Jésuites . . . Par un Catholique. pp. 115. *Carouge*, 1862. 8º.
3900. g. 22

—— Waarom werd Ds. A. H. H. Bechger van Roomsch priester Protestantsch leeraar? Door een Katholiek. Antwoord op de brochure [by H. Wenva] "Van Roomsch priester tot Protestantsch leeraar" enz. pp. 29. *Amersfoort*, 1895. 8º.
3925. i. 51. (4.)

—— Die Wahlen zum Hause der Abgeordneten in Preussen. Von einem Katholiken [i.e. Peter Franz Reichensperger]. pp. 40. *Paderborn*, 1858. 8º.
8073. g. 19.

—— Extract dess veri, sinceri, & discreti Catholici; oder, eines gewissen in wenig gedruckten Exemplarien alleine bestehenden Buchs, Der warhaffte, auffrichtige, und discrete Catholische genannt [by Ernest, Landgrave of Hesse-Cassel] . . . vom Authore selbsten dergestalt nunmehro zusammen gesetzt. pp. 215. 1673. 4º.
477. a. 19.

—— Why are you a Catholic? [By Serenus Cressy.] *See* supra: I. Question. Why are you a Catholic? The answer follows, *etc.*

—— Why I am and why I am not a Catholic. [By various authors.] pp. 255. *Cassell & Co.: London*, 1931. 8º.
3939. i. 48.

—— Zur Kenntniss der Gesellschaft Jesu. Von einem Katholiken [i.e. Franz Ernst Pipitz]. pp. 78. *Zürich & Winterthur*, 1843. 8º.
1367. k. 20.

CATHOLIC ACCOMPLISHMENT. Katholische Leistung in der Weltliteratur der Gegenwart. Dargestellt von führenden Schriftstellern und Gelehrten des In- und Auslandes. [With a bibliography.] pp. 387. *Freiburg i. B.*, 1934. 8º.
11857. b. 67.

CATHOLIC ACTION. A Call to Catholic Action. A series of conferences on the principles which should guide Catholics in the social-economic crisis of today. [By various authors.] 2 vol. *J. F. Wagner: New York*, [1935.] 8º.
20029. h. 21.

—— A Manual of Catholic Action. Its nature and requirements. By an Irish Priest. pp. viii. 150. *M. H. Gill & Son: Dublin*, 1933. 8º.
3939. de. 55.

CATHOLIC ACTION SOCIETY. *See* ENGLAND.

CATHOLIC ADVICE. The Catholic Advice. [A poem.] *Pitts: [London*, 1800?] *s. sh. fol.*
1872. a. 1. (87.)

CATHOLIC ADVISORY COUNCIL. *See* ENGLAND.— *Church of England.*

CATHOLIC AFRICAN TEACHERS' FEDERATION. *See* AFRICA, *South.*

CATHOLIC ALMANAC.

—— The Catholic Almanack for 1886, *etc.* (The Catholic Almanack and Register.—The Catholic Almanac and Year Book.—The Catholic Almanac.) *See* EPHEMERIDES.

——   The Catholick Almanack for . . . 1687. *See* EPHEMERIDES.

CATHOLIC ALMANAC.

—— The Catholic Almanac and Directory for Divine Service in the Archdiocese of Sydney, *etc. See* EPHEMERIDES.

—— The Catholick Almanack, and Guide to the Services of the Church, *etc. See* EPHEMERIDES.

—— The Catholic Almanack and Kalendar, *etc. See* EPHEMERIDES.

—— Catholic Almanac of Ontario. *See* EPHEMERIDES.

CATHOLIC ALPHABET. The Catholic Alphabet of Sacred Subjects. *R. Washbourne: London*, [1870.] *s. sh. fol.*
1880. d. 2. (47.)

CATHOLIC ANNUAL.

—— *See* PERIODICAL PUBLICATIONS.—*London.*

CATHOLIC ANNUAL REGISTER. *See* PERIODICAL PUBLICATIONS.—*London.*

CATHOLIC APOLOGY. The Catholique Apology, with a reply to the Answer [of William Lloyd, Bishop of St. Asaph]. Together with a clear refutation of the Seasonable Discourse, its Reasonable Defence & Dr Du Moulin's Answer to Philanax [i.e. Philanax Anglicus]; as also Dr Stillingfleet's last Gun-powder Treason Sermon, his attaque about the Treaty of Munster, & all matter of fact charg'd on the English Catholiques by their Enemies. By a Person of honour [Roger Palmer, Earl of Castlemaine]. The third edition much augmented. pp. 600. [*Antwerp?*] 1674. 8º.
699. b. 28.

—— A Reply to the Answer [by William Lloyd, Bishop of St. Asaph] of the Catholique Apology; or a cleere vindication of the Catholiques of England from all matter of fact charg'd against them by their enemyes. [By Roger Palmer, Earl of Castlemaine.] pp. 288. [*Antwerp?*] 1668. 8º.
3935. aa. 5.

—— [Another copy.]
G. 4336.

CATHOLIC APOSTOLIC CHURCH. [For individual Irvingite Churches, see under the name of the place where they are situated.]

—— [For Liturgies, etc. used by the Catholic Apostolic Church:] *See* LITURGIES.—*Irvingites.*

—— [Miscellaneous articles, tracts, etc., relating to the Catholic Apostolic Church. Collected by Clement Boase.] fol.
764. n. 14.

—— [Extracts from various periodicals, relating to the Catholic Apostolic Church. Collected by Clement Boase.] 1830–77. 8º.
764. h. 11.

—— [A collection of documents relating to the Catholic Apostolic Church; the binding lettered: "The Shorter Testimonies."] [1836–67.] 8º & fol.
4136. f. 14.

—— [A Tract on the restoration of the Ministry of Apostles.] pp. 4. *Strangeways & Walden: London,* [1861.] 8º.
764. m. 6. (12.)

—— Answers to Inquiries in regard to the Catholic Apostolic Church. [By John Sidney Davenport.] pp. 8. [1860?] 12º.
764. k. 5. (10.)

—— Apostles and Prophets. Substance of a letter to the "Standard of the Cross," January 8th, 1885, with additions. [By — Dubois, Elder?] pp. 8. [1885.] 8º.
764. i. 1. (25.)

—— Apostles and the Sealing through their Ministry. [By Robert Bruce Kennard.] pp. 16. *Thomas Bosworth: London,* [1871.] 12º.
4402. b. 34.

—— [Another copy.]
764. k. 17. (11.)

CATHOLIC APOSTOLIC CHURCH.

—— Apostles Given, Lost, and Restored. [By Thomas Carlyle, of the Scottish Bar.] pp. 48. *C. Goodall & Son: London*, 1853. 12°.　　　　　　　**4139. e. 5.**

—— [Another copy.]　　　　　　　**764. i. 21. (5.)**

—— Apostles' Doctrine and Fellowship, *etc.* [The preface signed: R. H., i.e. Richard Hughes.] 1871. 8°. *See* H., R.　　　　　　　**764. l. 5. (5.)**

—— Apostolic Lordship and the Interior Life. A narrative of five years' communion with Catholic Apostolic Angels. By the author of "The Communion of Saints" [i.e. William Grant], *etc.* pp. 120. 1873. 8°.
764. h. 13. (4.)

—— Catholic Apostolic Church. [An explanation of its tenets. By William Fettes Pitcairn.] pp. 4. *Printed for private circulation*, [1874?] 8°.　　**764. l. 15. (3.)**

—— [Another copy.]　　　　　　　**764. l. 15. (11.)**

—— The Catholic Apostolic Church—Irvingism: its pretensions and claims, considered in connection with the facts of its history, and the teaching of the New Testament and early Christian antiquity. By a late Member [James Harrison], *etc.* pp. vi. 104.　　*G. J. Stevenson: London; Blake: Newcastle-on-Tyne*, 1872. 8°.　　**4139. f. 10.**

—— [Another copy.]　　　　　　　**764. h. 3. (1.)**

—— [Another copy.]　　　　　　　**764. f. 13.**

—— The Census and the Catholic Apostolic Church. [By Francis V. Woodhouse.] pp. 16. *Thomas Bosworth: London*, 1854. 8°.　　　　**764. m. 8. (3.)**

—— [Another copy.]　　　　　　　**4108. b. 29.**

—— The Church of Christ, A.D. 1834. [By Henry Drummond, M.P.] no. 1–4. *W. Johnston & Son: Greenock; Robson & Co.: London*, [1834.] 12°.　**764. k. 11. (9.)**
No. 4 was published in London.

—— [Another copy of no. 3.]　　　　**764. d. 13. (2.)**

—— L'Église de N. S. Jésus-Christ, A.D. 1836. [An adaptation of no. 2 of "The Church of Christ, A.D. 1834" by Henry Drummond, M.P.] pp. 16. *J. Fraser: Londres*, 1836. 12°.　　　　　**764. k. 11. (10.)**

—— Extract of Letter, written to a member of the flock, on the Work of God through Apostles. [By William Fettes Pitcairn.] pp. 3. [1874.] 8°.　**764. l. 15. (2.)**

—— A Few Words about "Irvingism." [By William Flewker.] pp. 14. *Simpkin, Marshall & Co.: London*, [1848.] 16°.　　　　　　**4135. a. 45.**

—— [Another copy.]　　　　　　　**764. m. 9. (13.)**

—— [Another edition.] A Few Words on the Restoration of the Ministry of Apostles in the Church Catholic . . . Second thousand. pp. 15.　*Simpkin, Marshall & Co.: London*, 1849. 16°.　　　　**764. m. 9. (14.)**

—— [Another copy.]　　　　　　　**4139. e. 4.**

—— Irvingism. A parochial address. [With a reply beginning: "A Pamphlet under the title of 'Irvingism.'"] 2 pt. *R. S. Cheek: Witham*, [1830?] 8°.
4136. b. 26. (3.)

—— Irvingism; or, the Apostolic Catholic Church. (By a Member.) pp. 8. *See* ENCYCLOPAEDIAS. Cyclopædia of Religious Denominations, *etc.* 1853. 8°.
4503. aa. 19.

CATHOLIC APOSTOLIC CHURCH.

—— The Last Days of Irvingism; or Ritualism, Romanism, and the Catholic Apostolic Church . . . By the author of The Catholic Apostolic Church, "Irvingism," and Medieval Christianity [i.e. James Harrison]. pp. vi. 26. *G. J. Stephenson: London*, 1873. 8°.　**764. h. 13. (2.)**

—— The Ministries & Sacraments of the Catholic Apostolic Church: the former compared with Holy Scripture, and the latter with the standards of the Reformed Churches as exhibited in the works of the late Principal Cunningham . . . In letters by Two Presbyterians. pp. 24. *Geo. Gallie: Glasgow*, 1869. 8°.　**764. k. 18. (7.)**

—— The New Apostles; or, Irvingism, its history, doctrines, and practices. [By John Dix, afterwards Ross.] pp. iv. 175. *J. Blackwood: London*, [1859.] 8°.
4139. c. 65.

—— [Another copy.]　　　　　　　**764. d. 9. (1.)**

—— A Reply to "New Apostles, or Irvingism, &c." By one who has been twenty-five years a Minister in the Catholic Apostolic Church [John George Francis]. pp. 32. *Bosworth & Harrison: London*, 1861. 8°.
4139. d. 49.

—— [Another copy.]　　　　　　　**764. l. 2. (12.)**

—— The True Revival of the Church of Christ, and her hope in the last days. A letter, addressed to a Clergyman, with reference to a book entitled "The New Apostles." [By Edward Wilton Eddis.] pp. 42. *Bosworth & Harrison: London*, 1860. 8°.
4139. c. 9.

—— [Another copy.]　　　　　　　**764. k. 16. (5.)**

—— Notes addressed to Lay-Assistants engaged in Evangelist work. pp. 4. [1880?] 8°.　　**764. g. 11. (5.)**

—— Notes of a Ministry to the Deacons of the Churches, 29th May, 1854. [By William Henry Place.] pp. 16. *George Barclay: London*, 1854. 8°.　**764. l. 13. (13.)**

—— On the Office of Angel in the Church of Christ. Two sermons addressed to the congregation in Albury, by a minister of the universal church [Isaac Capadose]. pp. 12. [1889.] 8°.　　　　　**764. i. 19. (3.)**

—— Our Present Position. An address delivered February, 1901. pp. 15. *Printed for private circulation: [London, 1901.]* 8°.　　　　　　**764. h. 1. (10.)**

—— The Permanency of the Apostolic Office, as distinct from that of Bishops, with reasons for believing that it is now revived, in the Church. By a Presbyter of the Protestant Episcopal Church [John Sidney Davenport]. 1853. 8°. *See* APOSTOLIC OFFICE.　　**764. k. 5. (1.)**

—— Regulations as to the Building and Repairing of Churches. pp. 11. *Strangeways & Walden: London*, [1863.] 8°.　　　　　　**764. g. 11. (4.)**

—— La Restauration et le perfectionnement de l'Église aux derniers jours. pp. viii. 136. *Paris*, 1858. 8°.
764. g. 4.

—— The Restoration of Apostles. A homily, *etc.* [By Nicholas Armstrong.] pp. 8. *Strangeways & Walden: London*, [1868.] 8°.　　　　**764. i. 6. (6.)**

—— Sixty Signs in Confirmation of the Belief that the work wrought in "the One Holy Catholic Church," and falsely called Irvingism, is the true spiritual work of God, *etc.* [By William J. B. Moore.] pp. 4. *Printed for private circulation: [London*, 1878.] 8°.　**764. l. 7. (3.)**

CATHOLIC APOSTOLIC CHURCH.

—— Some Popular Objections to the Claims of the, so called, "Catholic Apostolical Churches," considered, *etc.* [Signed: A. B., i.e. Robert B. Kennard.] 1876. 8°. *See* B., A.   **4107. f. 2. (8.)**

—— The Testimony of the XII Apostles, 1835, to the Bishops of England, King William IV., Chief Rulers in Church and State. *Eng., Lat., Dan., Fr., & Ger.* 7 pt. [1835.] 4°.
764. n. 15.

—— The True Apostleship not Modern; or, a Refutation of the claims of the churches called "Irvingite" to an apostleship and to spiritual gifts. By a Member of the Church under the care of the late Rev. Edward Irving. pp. ii. 72. *J. Nisbet & Co.: London*, 1838. 12°.
764. b. 2. (2.)

—— Was sind die sogenannten Irvingianer für Leute? Eine Frage, beantwortet für Alle die über diese Sache etwas Zuverlässiges zu wissen wünschen. [By C. J. T. Boehm.] pp. 44. *Berlin*, 1851. 8°.   **4136. df. 22.**

—— "Who are the Irvingites?" An answer to serious and candid inquirers. Translated from the German [of C. J. T. Boehm]. pp. 24. *Goodall & Son: London*, 1851. 8°.
764. i. 15. (2.)

—— What are the Specialties of the so-called Catholic Apostolic Church? pp. 4.   *J. W. N. Keys & Son: Plymouth*, [1875.] 8°.   **764. k. 17. (3.)**

—— What is the Catholic Apostolic Church? pp. 16. *Wesleyan Conference Office: London*, [1834.] 8°.
764. d. 9. (3.)

—— "What meaneth this?" . . . "Catholic Apostolic Church." (A statement for candid inquirers.) 3 pt. *University Works: London*, [1870.] 8°.
764. k. 18. (18.)

—— Winke zur Orientierung in der sogenannten Irvingianer-Litteratur. pp. 48. *Augsburg*, 1887. 8°.
4136. aa. 28. (3.)

CATHOLIC APOSTOLIC CHURCH. [1944– .]

—— [For the church formed in 1944 by the amalgamation of the Old Catholic Orthodox Church, the Ancient British Church, the Independent Catholic Church, and the British Orthodox Catholic Church, and known as the Western Orthodox Catholic Church:] *See* WESTERN ORTHODOX CATHOLIC CHURCH.

CATHOLIC ASSOCIATION [DUBLIN]. *See* DUBLIN.

CATHOLIC ASSOCIATION [LONDON]. *See* LONDON. —III.

CATHOLIC ASSOCIATION FOR INTERNATIONAL PEACE. *See* WASHINGTON, D.C.

CATHOLIC ASSOCIATIONS. Die katholischen Vereine und Wohlthätigkeits-Anstalten, deren Geschichte, Zweck, Regeln, Privilegien und Ablässe dargestellt von einem Priester der Königgrätzer Diöcese . . . Zweite vermehrte Auflage. pp. 631.   *Leipzig & Meissen*, 1856. 8°.   **4784. d. 44.**

CATHOLIC AUTHORS. Ktyb yl Qari fuq bosta ḥuejjeg maḥtura myn kotba Kattolici. (Reading-Book on different subjects selected from Catholic authors.) *Eng. & Maltese.* pp. 155. *Malta*, 1832. 12°. **621. a. 9.**

CATHOLIC BALANCE. The Catholic Balance: or, a Discourse determining the controversies concerning I. the Tradition of Catholic doctrines. II. the Primacy of S. Peter and the Bishop of Rome. III. the Subjection and Authority of the Church in a Christian State: according to the suffrages of the primest antiquity. Written . . . at the request of a private gentleman. [By Samuel Hill.] pp. 136. *For Robert Clavell: London*, 1687. 4°.
T. 1841. (3.)

—— [Another copy.]   **222. d. 21. (1.)**

CATHOLIC BALLAD. The Catholick Ballad: or an Invitation to Popery, upon considerable grounds and reasons. To the tune of 88. [By Walter Pope. With musical notes.] 𝕭.𝕷.   *For Henry Brome: London*, 1674. *s. sh.* fol.   **C.121.g.9.(56.)**

—— [Another edition.] 𝕭.𝕷.   [*London*, 1674?]   *s. sh.* fol.
Rox. I. 26.

—— [Another edition.] 𝕭.𝕷.   *For Henry Brome: London*, 1675. *s. sh.* fol.   **Lutt. III. 106.**

—— [Another edition.] 𝕭.𝕷.   *For Henry Brome: London*, 1678. *s. sh.* fol.   **1872. a. 1. (149.)**

—— [Another edition.] 𝕭.𝕷.   *London*, 1689. *s. sh.* fol.
82. l. 8. (63.)

—— Canticum Catholicum, sive invitatio ad religionem Romanam. Fundata rationibus ponderosis. Latine reddita [from the English of Walter Pope], *etc.*   *Pro Johanne Leigh: Londini*, 1675. *s. sh.* fol.   **Lutt. I. 169.**

—— Reflections upon the Catholick Ballad [of Walter Pope]. [In verse.] *For E. T.: London*, 1675. *s. sh.* fol.
Lutt. III. 107.

CATHOLIC BAPTISM. The Catholic Baptism of Bells Defended, on the same ground which supports the ceremonies, forms, and modes of worship adopted by many Protestants; with an exhibition of the unscriptural religion of Protestants in general . . . With . . . strictures on "A Father's Reasons for not having his children baptized." In twelve letters . . . By a member of the Universal Church. pp. 67.   *The Author: London*, 1826. 8°.   **4325. bb. 23.**

CATHOLIC BEDSIDE BOOK.

—— The Catholic Bedside Book. *See* KEELAN (Bernard C. L.)

CATHOLIC BIBLE CONGRESS. *See* CAMBRIDGE.

CATHOLIC BIBLICAL ASSOCIATION. *See* ENGLAND.

CATHOLIC BILL. An Inquiry into the effects which will be produced by the passing of the Catholic Bill, *etc.* 1829. 8°.   *See* ENGLAND.—*Parliament.* [*Bill.*—II.] [1829. March 10.]   **T. 1259. (14.)**

CATHOLIC BIOGRAPHICAL LIBRARY. Catholic Biographical Library. no. 1–3.   *Robert Washbourne: London*, 1867–70. 8°.   **4823. b. 14.** *No more published.*

CATHOLIC BIOGRAPHIES.

—— Catholic Biographies. vol. 21, 24.   *Catholic Truth Society: London*, 1912, 14. 8°.   **3943. aa. 383.**

CATHOLIC BIRTHDAY BOOK. The Catholic Birthday Book. By a Lady. [The preface signed: M. T. F.] [1880.] 16°. *See* F., M. T.   **4401. aaaa. 25.**

CATHOLIC BISHOPS. Pro caussa Italica ad Episcopos Catholicos, actore Presbytero Catholico [Carlo Passaglia]. pp. 85. *Florentiæ*, 1861. 8°.   **8033. c. 40. (6.)**

—— Per la causa Italiana ai Vescovi Cattolici apologia di un Prete Cattolico [Carlo Passaglia]. Versione dal Latino di Alessandro Ferranti, *etc.* pp. 93. *Firenze*, 1861. 8°.
8033. a. 44. (5.)

CATHOLIC BISHOPS AND VICARS APOSTOLIC IN GREAT BRITAIN. *See* ENGLAND.—*Catholic Church.—Bishops.*

CATHOLIC BISHOPS OF ENGLAND. *See* ENGLAND.—*Catholic Church.—Bishops.*

CATHOLIC BOOK BULLETIN. *See* PERIODICAL PUBLICATIONS.—*Dublin.*

CATHOLIC BOOK NOTES. *See* PERIODICAL PUBLICATIONS.—*London.*

CATHOLIC BOUQUET. The Catholic Bouquet. By a Lady, a Convert. S. M. S., *etc.* [Hymns.] 1845. 24º. *See* S., S. M. **1066. a. 52.**

CATHOLIC BOY SCOUTS OF IRELAND. *See* DUBLIN.

CATHOLIC BOYS' BRIGADE. *See* ENGLAND.

CATHOLIC BROADSHEETS.
—— Catholic Broadsheets. *Michael White: London,* [1951– .] fol. **W.P. 8423.**

CATHOLIC BULLETIN. The Catholic Bulletin and Book Review. *See* PERIODICAL PUBLICATIONS.—*Dublin.* The Catholic Book Bulletin.

—— Catholic Bulletin of Foreign News. *See* ENGLAND.— *Ministry of Information.* [1939–46.]—*Religions Division.* Foreign Catholic Bulletin.

CATHOLIC BURGOMASTER. Ein katholischer Bürgermeister als konfessionsloser Pfarrer. Eine harmlose Zeitbetrachtung von einem Wiener Bürger in einsamen Stunden. [Consisting of a dialogue, followed by two letters signed: N. N.] pp. 44. *Graz,* 1871. 16º. **3913. a. 76. (2.)**

CATHOLIC C.O.
—— The Catholic C.O. *See* NEW YORK.—*Association of Catholic Conscientious Objectors.*

CATHOLIC CALENDAR. Catholic Calendar and Almanack for 1863. *See* EPHEMERIDES.

—— The Catholic Calendar, and Church Guide for Great Britain for . . . 1868. *See* EPHEMERIDES.

—— The Catholic Calendar, and Laity's Directory for . . . 1857. *See* EPHEMERIDES.

—— Catholic Calendar for the Archdiocese of St. Andrews and Edinburgh. *See* EPHEMERIDES.

CATHOLIC CATECHISM. Catéchisme catholique. pp. 139. *Berne,* 1876. 8º. **3506. aaaa. 6.**

—— A Katekismo Katolik. Gazelle-Halbinsel, Neu-Pommern. pp. 137. *Hongkong,* 1914. 8º. **03504. g. 16.**

—— Ui Katorika—Pope—o te Vikario-raa Apotoro i Tahiti, *etc.* [Catholic Catechism for the use of the Apostolic Vicariate of Tahiti, by Florentin Étienne Jaussen, R.C. Bishop of Tahiti.] *Tahitian.* pp. 99. *Tahiti,* 1851. 16º. **3505. de. 41.**

—— Ui Katorika o te Vikario-raa Apotoro i Tahiti, *etc.* (Catéchisme catholique du Vicariat apostolique de Tahiti.) [By Florentin Étienne Jaussen, R.C. Bishop of Tahiti.] *Tahitian & Fr.* pp. 90. *Saint-Cloud,* [1860.] 16º. **3505. de. 42.**

—— Kleyne Catholyke Catechismus, bequaam om de eerste beginselen van het Christelijk Geloof de kinderen in te planten. pp. 48. *Antwerpen,* 1736. 12º. **3504. aa. 61. (1.)**

—— Kleiner katholischer Katechismus von der Unfehlbarkeit. Ein Büchlein zur Unterweisung von einem Vereine katholischer Geistlichen. Achte . . . Auflage. pp. 14. *Köln & Leipzig,* 1872. 8º. **3910. aaa. 2.**

CATHOLIC CATECHISM QUESTION. Ein Votum über die katholische Katechismusfrage in der oberrheinischen Kirchenprovinz. Oder: Welchem der neuesten Katechismen, dem Mainzer, Hirscher' oder Schuster'schen gebührt der Vorrang? Von einem practischen Katecheten der Diöcese Rottenburg. pp. 53. *Regensburg,* 1846. 8º. **3911. a. 27.**

CATHOLIC CAUSE. A Defence of the Catholyke Cause . . . Written by T. F. [Thomas Fitz-Herbert], *etc.* 1602. 4º. *See* F., T. **3936. bb. 49.**

CATHOLIC CELEBRITIES. Célébrités catholiques. [By E. Veuillot, L. Veuillot and others. With portraits.] 17 pt. *Paris,* [1861–66.] 8º. **4863. dd. 26.** *Imperfect; wanting the lives of Pitra, Pie and Plantier.*

—— [Another edition.] Célébrités catholiques contemporaines. Par MM. Louis Veuillot, Eugène Veuillot, Henry de Riancey & Léopold Giraud, *etc.* [With portraits.] pp. 364. *Paris,* 1870. 8º. **4805. h. 28.**

CATHOLIC CENTRAL BUREAU. *See* SHANGHAI.

CATHOLIC CHAMPION. The Catholic Champion. [A tract in favour of Catholic emancipation.] pp. 16. *J. Clements: [London,* 1829.] 8º. **8145. d. 10.**

CATHOLIC CHARITABLE ORGANIZATIONS.
—— A Handbook of Catholic Charitable Organizations. Second edition. pp. 81. *Catholic Social Guild: Oxford,* 1935. 8º. **08285. a. 148.** *The first edition was compiled by the Superior Council of the Society of Saint Vincent de Paul and published as the " Catholic Social Year Book " for 1927.*

CATHOLIC CHARITABLE WORKS. Handbook of Catholic Charitable and Social Works. *See* CATHOLIC CHARITIES. Handbook of Catholic Charities, *etc.*

CATHOLIC CHARITIES. Handbook of Catholic Charities, Associations, etc., in Great Britain. pp. viii. 103. *Catholic Truth Society: London,* 1894. 8º. **4192. b. 42.**

—— [Another edition.] Handbook of Catholic Charitable and Social Works, *etc.* pp. viii. 144. *Catholic Truth Society: London,* 1905. 8º. **4192. de. 16.**

—— Third edition, revised, *etc.* pp. viii. 158. *Catholic Truth Society: London,* 1909. 8º. **4192. de. 17.**

—— Third edition, entirely revised. pp. viii. 111. *Catholic Truth Society: London,* 1912. 8º. **4192. de. 32.**

CATHOLIC CHILD. The Catholic Child's Magazine of Religious and Entertaining Instruction. *See* PERIODICAL PUBLICATIONS.—*London.*

—— The Catholic Child's Prayer Book. pp. 32. *T. Richardson & Son: London & Derby,* [1848.] 32º. **1221. a. 35. (5.)**

CATHOLIC CHILD WELFARE COUNCIL. *See* ENGLAND.

CATHOLIC CHILDREN.
—— The Catholic Children's Gem. *See* PERIODICAL PUBLICATIONS.—*Osgodby.*

—— A Collection of Prayers for the use of Catholic Children. pp. 18. *St. Benedict's Institute: Colombo,* [1893.] 16º. **3455. df. 4. (3.)**

CATHOLIC CHILDREN.

—— Legalised Perversion of Catholic Children in the English Workhouses, with a special reference to its practice in the Cuckoo-Farm School at Hanwell. Being the substance of a lecture delivered at Hanwell . . . Oct. 10. 1864. In a letter to the Editor of the Times, inadmissible in that paper. By a Catholic Englishman. pp. 28. *Burns, Lambert & Oates: London,* [1864.] 8°. **3939. aaa. 55.**

—— The Sacramental Register for Catholic Children and Young People, and for the use of Confraternities. *T. Richardson & Sons: London,* [1877.] 8°.
4326. cc. 4.

CATHOLIC CHILDREN'S REALM. *See* PERIODICAL PUBLICATIONS.—*Hinckley.*

CATHOLIC CHIMNEY CORNER. *See* PERIODICAL PUBLICATIONS.—*London.* The Children's Corner, *etc.*

CATHOLIC CHRISTIAN. The Catholic Christian. A magazine of the Catholic Christian Church. *See* ENGLAND. —*Churches and Religious Bodies.—Catholic Christian Church.*

—— The Catholic Christian instructed in the Sacraments . . . of the Church . . . By R . . . . . C . . . . [i.e. Richard Challoner]. 1737. 12°. *See* C . . . . . . , R . . . . . .
3504. b. 53.

—— *See* MIDDLETON (Conyers) A Letter from Rome . . . To which are added, A Prefatory Discourse, containing an answer to all the objections of the writer [Richard Challoner, Bishop of Debra] of a Popish book, intituled, The Catholic Christian instructed . . . and a Postscript, *etc.* 1741. 8°. **700. e. 8.**

—— —— 1742. 8°. **3936. bbb. 23.**

—— —— 1812. 8°. **3936. g. 7.**

—— *See* MIDDLETON (Conyers) Lettre écrite de Rome . . . Avec un discours préliminaire, où en répondant à toutes les objections d'un livre papiste [by Richard Challoner, Bishop of Debra] intitulé "Le Chrétien catholique instruit," on a rassemblé de nouveaux faits . . . pour constater la vérité qu'on a dessein d'établir dans cette lettre, *etc.* 1744. 12°.
3938. aa. 51.

—— *See* MIDDLETON (Conyers) Popery Unmask'd. Being the substance of Dr. Middleton's celebrated Letter from Rome . . . With an abstract of the Doctor's reply to the objections of the writer of a Popish book [Richard Challoner, Bishop of Debra], intituled, The Catholic Christian instructed, *etc.* 1744. 12°. **3936. bb. 16.**

—— —— 1759. 12°. **3938. aa. 48.**

—— A Conference between Two Gentlemen, a Papist and Protestant, concerning Religion: in which the principal arguments of a late book [by Richard Challoner, Bishop of Debra], entitled, The Catholick Christian instructed, are answered. pp. 61. *M. Cooper: London,* 1749. 8°. **3936. c. 10.**

—— Handbüchlein eines katholischen Christen, worin die nothwendigsten Früh-, Abend-, Mess-, Beicht-, Kommunion- und Vespergebete, samt andern auserlesenen Andachtsübungen enthalten sind. [1820?] 12°. *See* LITURGIES.—*Latin Rite.—Combined Offices.—v. Paroissiens, etc.—General.* **4407. aa. 38.**

—— Was hat der katholische Christ von der Ehe und gemischten Ehe zu halten? Von einem katholischen Geistlichen. pp. 44. *Regensburg,* 1862. 8°.
5175. aaa. 53. (5.)

CATHOLIC CHRISTIAN CHURCH. *See* ENGLAND. —*Churches and Religious Bodies.*

CATHOLIC CHRISTIAN DOCTRINES. Influence of Catholic Christian Doctrines on the Emancipation of Slaves. By a Member of the Sodality of the B.V. Mary, Church of the Most Holy Redeemer. East Boston. pp. 35. *Patrick Donahoe: Boston,* 1863. 12°. **8156. a. 70. (4.)**

CATHOLIC CHRISTIANS. Anrede an einen kleinen Kreis katholischer Christen, welche die römische Kirche verlassen wollen, *etc.* pp. 16. *Danzig,* [1845.] 8°.
3910. d. 13.

—— Catholic-Christians: or, Rome and England. A letter, *etc.* [Signed: H. M. J.] 1869. 12°. *See* J., H. M.
3940. aa. 34.

CATHOLIC CHURCH. *See also* ROME, *Church of.* [*Appendix.*]

—— Avis charitable aux fidelles sincérement attachés à la communion de l'Église catholique. Où l'on fait voir . . . que les simples fidelles ne courent aucun risque pour leur salut, quelque parti qu'ils prennent dans les circonstances présentes, *etc.* pp. 16. *Chartres,* [1791.] 8°.
F.R. 151. (6.)

—— Seconde édition. pp. 16. *Paris,* 1791. 8°.
F.R. 151. (7.)

—— A Catechism on the Holy Catholick and Apostolick Church. I. On the unity of the Church. II. On the ministry and discipline of the Church. III. On the communion of Saints in the Church, *etc.* pp. 22. *J. H. Parker: Oxford,* 1838. 8°. **3504. df. 2. (4.)**

—— [Another copy.] A Catechism on the Holy Catholick and Apostolick Church, *etc. Oxford,* 1838. 8°.
4431. a. 41. (5.)

—— [Another copy.] **T. 2301. (17.)**

—— Third edition. pp. 23. *J. H. Parker: Oxford,* 1838. 12°. **908. c. 5. (5.)**

—— Fifth edition. pp. 35. *J. H. Parker: Oxford,* 1841. 12°. **908. b. 7. (3.)**

—— The Catholic Church. A compendious statement of the scripture doctrine regarding the nature and chief attributes of the Kingdom of Christ. By C. F. A. 1867. 8°. *See* A., C. F. **3554. b. 1.**

—— The Catholic Church and the Bible. pp. 20. *Catholic Truth Society: London,* [1903.] 8°. **3943. aa. 395.**

—— Catholic Church of England. *See* ENGLAND.—*Churches and Religious Bodies.*

—— The Contrast. The Catholic Church and the Papacy. *John Kensit: London,* 1889. 4°. **3940. m. 13.**

—— A Defence of the Holy Catholick Church's Notion of Transubstantiation against all Hereticks and Scismaticks. [An attack on the doctrine of transubstantiation.] pp. 20. *Sylvanus Pepyat: Dublin,* 1731. 8°. **3940. d. 69.**

—— A Discourse of the true and visible Markes of the Catholique Church. By T. B. [i.e. T. de Bèze.] 1622. 8°. *See* B., T. **702. a. 43.**

—— Envoy de l'Eglise Catholique, au Roy. Par Monsieur de M. Ar. de B. 1588. 8°. *See* M., *Monsieur de, Ar. de B.* **1192. e. 38.**

CATHOLIC CHURCH.

—— An Explanation of the Construction, Furniture & Ornaments of a Catholic Church, of the vestments of the clergy, and of the nature and ceremonies of the Holy Sacrifice of the Mass. pp. iv. 90. *Prior Park Press: [Bath,]* 1844. 12°. **3477. bb. 62. (1.)**

—— [Another copy.] **908. c. 5. (7.)**

—— An Explanation of the Parts of a Catholic Church . . . With a descriptive chart. By a Catholic Priest. Second edition. pp. 36. *G. J. Palmer: London,* 1867. 16°. **3477. aa. 12.**

—— First Catechism on the Holy Catholic Church. pp. 4. *James Burns: London,* [1841.] 8°. [*Tracts on Christian Doctrine.* vol. 1. no. 10.] **1353. a. 10.**

—— Begin. [fol. 1 recto:] Hic continent̄ om̄s Patriarchatus Archiepiscopatus et Episcopatus totius ecclesie katholice siue omnium puinciarū tā Orientalium ᵹ Occidentalium nationum. **G.L.** *p Iohannē Schaur: Auguste,* [14]94. 4°. **IA. 6824.**
8 leaves, without signatures. 30 lines to a page.

—— [Another edition.] **G.L.** FEW MS. NOTES. *J. Otmar: Vindelice Auguste,* 1505. 4°. **1365. c. 1.**

—— I Believe in ' the Holy Catholic Church.' Reprinted from ' Thoughts on the Church Catechism.' pp. 43. *J. & C. Mozley; Masters & Son: London,* 1864. 12°. **4108. aa. 88. (3.)**

—— " I Believe One Catholic and Apostolic Church." pp. 8. *J. T. Hayes: London,* [1884.] 8°. **4109. e. 9. (1.)**

—— Illustria Ecclesiæ Catholiæ trophoea, ex recentibus Anglicorum martyrum, Scoticæ proditionis, Gallicorumᵹ furorum rebus gestis . . . erecta. [Edited by E. Vendius] 1573. 8°. *See* VENDIUS (E.) **1368. a. 4.**

—— Nature's Voice in the Holy Catholic Church. A series of designs for church decoration, *etc.* [The preface signed: F. F., i.e. Frederic Fysh.] 1864. *obl.* 16°. *See* F., F. **3477. a. 54.**

—— One Catholic and Apostolic Church. Six broadcast talks. pp. 63. *Epworth Press: London,* 1949. 8°. **4382. b. 11.**

—— La Perpetuité de la foy de l'Église Catholique touchant l'Eucharistie. Avec la refutation de l'écrit d'un ministre contre ce traité . . . Quatrième édition. [By Antoine Arnauld and Pierre Nicole.] pp. 475. *Paris,* 1666. 12°. **1472. aa. 19.**
Later editions are entered under ARNAULD (A.) *Doctor of the Sorbonne.*

—— Projet proposé pour la restauration de l'Église catholique primitive. pp. 8. *Paris,* 1856. 8°. **3901. f. 40. (1.)**

—— Sacramentarium Ecclesiæ Catholicæ. A Sacramentary designed to incorporate the contents of all the Sacramentaries anywhere used in the Church, previous to the sixteenth century. Part I. Advent and Christmas. *Lat. & Eng.* pp. v. 219. *For the Author, by Joseph Masters: London,* 1857. 16°. **3475. a. 35.**

—— A Short Catechism for the Instruction of the Young in the Doctrine of the Holy Catholic Church. By a Clergyman of the Church of England. pp. 24. *Skeffington & Southwell: London,* 1850. 12°. **3505. a. 74.**

—— Some Account of the Reasons of my Conversion to the Catholic Church. By a late clergyman of the Anglican Communion. In letters to a friend. Third edition. pp. 63. *James Burns: London,* 1847. 8°. **4110. cc. 5. (5.)**

CATHOLIC CHURCH.

—— Two Lectures on the Holy Catholic Church, with reference to the position of different sects. By a Member of the Church. pp. viii. 71. *J. H. Parker: Oxford,* 1852. 16°. **3938. a. 12.**

—— Worin besteht die wahre apostolisch-katholische Kirche und kann sie durch eine deutsch-katholische vermittelt werden ? pp. 88. *Leipzig,* 1845. 8°. **3910. e. 20.**

CATHOLIC CHURCH EXTENSION SOCIETY OF CANADA. *See* TORONTO.

CATHOLIC CHURCH-LAW. Abriss des katholischen Kirchenrechts für Geistliche und Studirende von einem Schüler des † Herrn v. Möhler. pp. iv. 297. *Stuttgart,* 1853. 8°. **5125. a. 24.**

CATHOLIC CHURCHES.

—— Die Orgel, ihre Aufgabe und Lage in den katholischen Kirchen. Mit besonderer Rücksicht auf die Lage der Orgel im Dom zu Osnabrück. pp. 38. *Münster,* 1868. 8°. **[MISSING.]**

CATHOLIC CITIZEN. The Catholic Citizen. *See* LONDON.—III. *Catholic Women's Suffrage Society.* The Catholic Suffragist.

CATHOLIC CLAIMS. The Catholic Claims Rejected: being an answer to the letters of " An English Catholic," " The Revd. Sydney Smith," and " Mr. Charles Butler," and " thirty-two thousand " other popish productions . . . By an English Protestant. [A reply to " A Letter to the Freeholders of the County of York. By an English Catholic," i.e. the Hon. Edward R. Petre, and to other works.] pp. 64. *J. Wolstenholme & Son: York,* 1826. 8°. **T. 1004. (10.)**

—— Extracts from the Speeches and Writings of Eminent Public Characters, respecting the Catholic Claims: with a few prefatory remarks. pp. viii. 108. *Booker: London,* 1813. 8°. **8145. b. 21.**

CATHOLIC CLERGY. *See also* ROME, *Church of.*— *Clergy.*

—— Le Budget du presbytère, ou Considérations sur la condition temporelle du clergé catholique; par un curé-desservant [i.e. J. L. P. Fèvre]. 1858. 8°. *See* FRANCE.—*Church of France.*—*Clergy.* [*Appendix.*] **3901. f. 7.**

—— Dell'origine delle immunità del clero cattolico e d'ogni altro sacerdozio creduto dagli uomini legittimo e santo. [By C. Adorno Hinojosa.] pp. xvi. 425. *Cesena,* 1791. 4°. **5061. bb. 8.**

—— Ehrentempel der katholischen Geistlichen . . . nebst einer poetischen Zugabe, Kirchliches, hohe Kirchenhirten und Priester betreffend, *etc.* 2 pt. *Wien,* 1846. 8°. **1372. e. 15.**

CATHOLIC CLUB. Catholic Club of the City of New York. *See* NEW YORK.

CATHOLIC COMMISSION.

—— Catholic Commission on Intellectual and Cultural Affairs. *See* WASHINGTON, *D.C.*

CATHOLIC COMMITTEE. *See* DUBLIN.

—— *See also* ENGLAND.

CATHOLIC COMMUNION. An Essay towards a Proposal for Catholick Communion. Wherein above sixty of the principal controverted points . . . being call'd over, 'tis examined, how many of them may, and ought to be laid aside . . . for the effecting a general peace. By a Minister of the Church of England [i.e. Joshua Basset]. pp. 248. *John Nutt: London,* 1704. 8°. **699. b. 4. (2.)**

CATHOLIC COMMUNION.

—— An Essay towards a Proposal for Catholick Communion . . . By a Minister of the Church of England [i.e. Joshua Basset]. Fairly and impartially consider'd, the whole mystery and artifice detected, and the secret design expos'd and defeated [by Edward Stephens], *etc.* [With the text.] pp. xiv. 202. MS. NOTES. *John Hartley: London*, 1705. 8°. **3935. cc. 15.**

—— [Another copy.] **3936. c. 50.**

—— The Essay towards a Proposal for Catholick Communion, &c. lately publish'd by a—pretended—Minister of the Church of England [i.e. Joshua Basset], printed at large, and answered chapter by chapter . . . By N. Spinckes. pp. 320. *Richard Sare: London*, 1705. 8°. **3938. bb. 75.**

—— An Essay towards a Proposal for Catholick Communion . . . By a Minister of the Church of England [i.e. Joshua Basset]. pp. xii. 198. *R. Faulder: London*, 1801. 8°. **3940. e. 19.**

—— An Eirenicon of the Eighteenth Century. Proposal for Catholic Communion by a Minister of the Church of England [i.e. Joshua Basset]. New edition, with introduction, notes and appendices. Edited by Henry Nutcombe Oxenham. pp. x. 327. *Rivingtons: London*, 1879 [1878]. 8°. **3938. f. 1.**

—— Concordia Discors: or, Some animadversions upon a late treatise; entituled, An Essay for Catholick Communion [by Joshua Basset]. In a letter to a friend at Westminster [by a Pre]sbyter of the Church of England [i.e. Samuel Grascome]. pp. 86. *[Ge]orge Sawbridge: London*, 1705. 8°. **3943.a.74.**
The titlepage is slightly mutilated.

—— [Another copy.] Concordia Discors, *etc.* [By Samuel Grascome.] *London*, 1705. 8°. **3938. aa. 54.**
The titlepage is slightly mutilated.

—— Les Intrus dévoilés, ou Adresse à tous les fidèles qui veulent persévérer dans la communion catholique apostolique & romaine. Imprimée particuliérement pour ceux du diocèse du Mans. pp. 32. [1791.] 8°. **F. 106. (3.)**

CATHOLIC COMPANION. *See* PERIODICAL PUBLICATIONS.—*Hinckley.*

CATHOLIC CONFEDERACY OF KILKENNY. *See* IRELAND.—*General Assembly at Kilkenny.*

CATHOLIC CONFESSION. Ane schort catholik confession of the heades of the religion now controuerted in Scotland answering against the heretical negative confession set furth be Ihone Craig in his catechise. From a manuscript . . . in the Barberini Library, Rome. *See* LAW (Thomas G.) Catholic Tractates of the Sixteenth Century, *etc.* 1901. 8°. **Ac. 9943/20.**

CATHOLIC CONFESSION OF FAITH. Wahres Catholisches Glaubens-Bekänntnüss, so ein grosser Fürst, zu Steur der heiligen Warheit, und seinen lieben getreuen Untersassen zur Nach- und Unterricht auffsetzen lassen, *etc.* 1698. 8°. **3910. eee. 1. (7.)**

CATHOLIC CONGREGATIONS. Können katholische Gemeinden nach dem Abgange ihrer Geistlichen sich andere selbst wählen und setzen oder vom Patron setzen lassen? Beantwortet nach Wahrheit und Recht. [With reference to the German ecclesiastical legislation of May 1873 and May 1874.] pp. 48. *Paderborn*, 1876. 8°. **3913. de. 3. (8.)**

CATHOLIC CONGRESS.

—— Catholic Congress for International Peace. *See* CATHOLIC CONGRESS FOR INTERNATIONAL PEACE.

CATHOLIC CONGRESS FOR INTERNATIONAL PEACE.

—— [The Hague, 1938.] The Foundations of International Order. Reports presented and conclusions adopted at a Catholic Congress on International Peace held at the Hague . . . 1938. pp. 128. *Oxford*, 1938. 8°. [*Catholic Social Year Book.* 1938.] **P.P. 2484. daa.**

CATHOLIC CONTROVERSY. The Catholic Controversy. [Correspondence between "Catholic" and "Barney Flanagan," *etc.*] *See* CATHOLIC.

CATHOLIC CONVERT. A Dialogue between a New Catholick Convert and a Protestant, shewing the doctrin of transubstantiation to be as reasonable to be believ'd as the great mystery of the Trinity by all good Catholicks. pp. 6. *By Henry Hills: London*, 1686. 4°. **T. 1879. (1.)**

—— [Another copy.] **222. d. 14. (2.)**

—— An Answer to a late Dialogue between a New Catholick Convert and a Protestant, to prove the mystery of the Trinity to be as absurd a doctrine as transubstantiation. By way of short notes on the said dialogue. [By William Sherlock.] pp. 14. *For Thomas Bassett: London*, 1687. 4°. **474. a. 21. (4.)**
Cropped.

—— [Another copy.] **T. 1879. (2.)**
Cropped.

—— [Another copy.] **222. d. 14. (3.)**

—— [Another copy.] **222. d. 14. (4.)**

—— A Second Dialogue between a New Catholick Convert and a Protestant. Shewing why he cannot believe the doctrine of transubstantiation, though he do firmly believe the doctrine of the Trinity. [By Richard Kidder.] pp. 8. *For B. Aylmer: London*, 1687. 4°. **222. d. 14. (5.)**

—— [Another copy.] **T. 1879. (3.)**

—— [Another copy.] **3935. c. 1.**
The third leaf is mutilated.

CATHOLIC COUNCIL. Catholic Council for International Relations. *See* ENGLAND.

CATHOLIC CRITIC. The Catholic Critic: a journal of education and letters. *See* PERIODICAL PUBLICATIONS.—*Galway.*

CATHOLIC CRUSADE. *See* ENGLAND.—*Church of England.—Church Societies.*

—— The Catholic Crusade against Intemperance. pp. 31. *Burns & Oates: London*, [1911.] 8°. **8436. f. 61.**

CATHOLIC CUSTOMS.

—— Catholic Customs. A guide for the laity in England. pp. 92. *Catholic Truth Society: London*, 1900. 16°. **3943. a. 10.**

CATHOLIC DESIRE. A Catholic Desire. [A tract on the words "That I may win Christ."] pp. 24. 1860. 12°. [MISSING.]

CATHOLIC DEVOTION. Le Dévouement catholique pendant le choléra de 1832 et 1849. [By L. F. Guérin.] Deuxième édition. pp. 214. *Lille*, 1860. 16°. **4863. b. 10.**

CATHOLIC DIARY.

—— Catholic Diary. [1897.] *See* EPHEMERIDES.

CATHOLIC DIGEST. *See* PERIODICAL PUBLICATIONS.—
Dublin.

CATHOLIC DIRECTORY. The Catholic Directory,
Almanack and Ecclesiastical Register. *See* DIRECTORIES.
—*Clerical.* The Catholic Directory and Annual Register,
etc.

—— Catholic Directory, Almanack and Registry of Ireland,
England, and Scotland. *See* DIRECTORIES.—*Clerical.* A
Complete Catholic Directory, Almanack, and Registry, *etc.*

—— The Catholic Directory and Annual Register. *See*
DIRECTORIES.—*Clerical.*

—— Catholic Directory for the Clergy & Laity of Scotland.
See DIRECTORIES.—*Clerical.* The Directory to the Service
of the Catholic Church, *etc.*

—— The Catholic Directory of British South Africa. *See*
DIRECTORIES.—*Clerical.*

—— Catholic Directory of India. *See* DIRECTORIES.—
Clerical.

—— Prudence True Patriotism; or, an Exposure of the arts,
views, and characters of the Catholic Directory. (Second
edition, with additions.) pp. 41. *John Barlow: Dublin,*
1815. 8°. **8135. b. 35.**

CATHOLIC DISCOURSE. Discours Catholique, sur
les causes & remedes des Malheurs intentés au Roi, &
escheus à son peuple, par les rebelles Caluinistes. (Vœu
à Dieu du peuple de France pour son Roy.—Cantique
d'oraison pour le peuple de Lyon.—Le Tombeau du
Caluinisme, *etc.* [In verse.]) [By G. de Saconay?] pp. 94.
Par M. Ioue: Lyon, 1568. 8°. **3900. b. 62.**

CATHOLIC DISILLUSIONMENT. Desengaño
Catholico. Por D. J. D. F. [1706?] 4°. *See* F.,
D. J. D. **1445. f. 21. (44.)**

—— [Another edition.] Desengaño Catholico. Por D. I.
D. F. [1710.] 4°. *See* F., D. I. D. T. **1302. (15.)**

—— [Another edition.] [1710?] 4°. *See* F., D. I. D.
12330. l. 16. (10.)

CATHOLIC DISSENTERS.
—— Heads of a Bill for the Relief of Protesting Catholic
Dissenters. pp. 6. MS. NOTES. [1789.] fol.
Dept. of MSS. Add. MS. **5416. B. 6.**
The title is taken from the endorsement.

CATHOLIC DIVINE SERVICE. Musterblätter nebst
Anleitung zur Anfertigung des für den katholischen
Gottesdienst vorgeschriebenen und gebräuchlichen Weiss-
zeuges als Altartücher, Communiontücher . . . heraus-
gegeben von einem Freunde der christlichen Kunst.
(Cyclus 1–3; Cyclus 4 von B. Zehe.) *Münster,*
[1854–]1864. 8°. **7742. w. 20, 21.**
Only Cyclus 4 contains the author's name.

CATHOLIC DOCTRINE. Breve esposizione di cattolica dottrina ad uso degl' Italiani, Inglesi, Francesi,
Spagnuoli, Latini, e Tedeschi. Con un appendice per
l'abjura de' protestanti compilata da un sacerdote de'
chierici regolari detti volgarmente Teatini.
Ital., Eng., Fr., Span., Lat. & Ger. pp. 146. *Roma,*
1815. 8°. **1351. f. 12.**

—— A Brief Outline of Catholic Doctrine. pp. 12.
Nazareth Press: Hongkong, 1940. 8°. **20046. b. 13.**

—— A Catechism of Catholic Doctrine. pp. 44. *Clifton
Press: Colombo,* 1894. 16°. **03504. e. 3. (6.)**

CATHOLIC DOCTRINE.
—— A Catechism of Catholic Doctrine. Approved by the
Archbishops and Bishops of Ireland. [With illustrations.]
pp. 108. *M. H. Gill & Son: Dublin,* [1951.] 8°.
3507. aa. 26.

—— The Catholic Doctrine of Eucharistic Sacrifice: what is
it? pp. 47. *E. Marlborough & Co.: London,* [1879.] 8°.
4372. f. 1. (16.)

—— A Conference of the Catholike and Protestante Doctrine
with the expresse words of Holie Scripture. Which is
the second parte of the Prudentiall Balance of Religion.
Wherein is . . . shewed, that in more then 260. points
of controuersie, Catholiks agree with the holie Scripture,
both in words and sense: and Protestants disagree in both
. . . Written first in Latin, but now augmented and
translated into English. [A translation of "Collatio
doctrinæ Catholicorum ac Protestantium, *etc.*" by Richard
Smith, Bishop of Chalcedon.] pp. 798. 1631. 4°. *See*
CATHOLICS. **3935. dd. 4.**

—— Cudisch della doctrina catholica, *etc.* pp. iv. 160.
Cuera, 1891. 8°. **3506. df. 45.**

—— La Dottrina cattolica delle indulgenze difesa contro
alcuni libri ultimamente pubblicati a danno della verità
e a pregiudizio de' buoni fedeli. [By A. Siatich.] pp. 219.
Fuligno, 1789. 8°. **1356. b. 15. (1.)**

—— Les Principes de 89 et la doctrine catholique. Par un
professeur de grand séminaire [i.e. Léon Godard]. pp. 155.
Paris, 1861. 8°. **8007. e. 13.**

—— Sommaire de la doctrine catholique en tableaux synoptiques . . . par l'auteur des Paillettes d'or. Troisième
partie, *etc.* [The "Déclaration de l'auteur" signed: S.]
1886. 16°. *See* S. **3559. bb. 2.**

—— Sommario della dottrina cattolica in tavole sinottiche
. . . Opera dell'autore delle Pagliuole d'oro, *etc.* [The
preface signed: S.] 1890. 8°. *See* S. **3559. aa. 40.**

CATHOLIC DOCUMENTS. *See* LONDON.—III. *Pontifical Court Club.*

CATHOLIC DOGMA. Essai sur la formation du dogme
catholique. [By Princess Cristina Triulzi-Belgiojoso.]
4 tom. *Paris,* 1842, 43. 8°. **1351. g. 11, 12.**

CATHOLIC EDUCATION. An Essay on Education,
Catholic and mixed. A poem . . . By a Catholic Priest
[i.e. James Casey]. pp. 64. *James Duffy: Dublin,*
1868. 16°. **11652. a. 70. (1.)**

CATHOLIC EDUCATION COUNCIL. *See* ENGLAND.

CATHOLIC EDUCATION OFFICE. *See* MELBOURNE.

CATHOLIC EDUCATIONAL YEAR-BOOK. *See*
PERIODICAL PUBLICATIONS.—*Liverpool.*

CATHOLIC EDUCATORS. Lebensbilder katholischer
Erzieher. *See* HUBERT (W. E.)

CATHOLIC EMANCIPATION. *See* MACCOY (Mary)
A Poem in answer to an anonymous pamphlet; in three
letters, called Friendly Hints to Catholic Emancipation.
1813. 12°. **4136. a. 65.**

—— Arguments for and against Catholic Emancipation.
pp. 92. *J. J. Stockdale: London,* 1813. 8°.
3943. de. 10. (5.)

—— A Brief Warning against the Measure commonly called
"Catholic Emancipation," *etc.* pp. 72. *C. J. G. &
F. Rivington: London,* 1829. 8°. **T. 1252. (4.)**

CATHOLIC EMANCIPATION.

—— The Case of Conscience Solved; or, Catholic Emancipation proved to be compatible with the Coronation Oath. In a letter from a Casuist in the country, to his friend in town . . . With a supplement in answer to considerations on the said oath, by John Reeves, Esq. pp. 89. *R. Faulder: London*, 1801. 8°. **08139.ccc.48.(6.)**

—— [Another copy.] **108. f. 52.**

—— Catholic Emancipation. [By — Corneille.] pp. 59. *John Stockdale: London*, 1805. 8°. **1103. k. 20.**

—— Catholic Emancipation, calmly considered. pp. 22. *C. & J. Rivington & Richard Nichols: London*, 1825. 8°. **T. 1002. (6.)**

—— Catholic Emancipation, 1829 to 1929. Essays by various writers, *etc.* pp. ix. 280. *Longmans & Co.: London*, 1929. 8°. **04705. d. 6.**

—— An Essay on Toleration: in which the subject of Catholic Emancipation is considered. By a Presbyter of a Church in England. pp. 36. *T. Williams: [London,]* 1805. 8°. **3938. bb. 78. (2.)**

—— Restriction No Persecution; or, Catholic Emancipation incompatible with Protestant security. pp. 27. *J. Hatchard: London*, 1813. 8°. **3940. cc. 1. (6.)**

CATHOLIC EMANCIPATION CENTENARY COMMITTEE. *See* IRELAND.—*Irish Free State.*

CATHOLIC ENGLISHMEN. Have Catholic Englishmen a Mission? pp. 12. *Burns & Oates: London,* [1885.] 8°. **3940. h. 12. (2.)**

CATHOLIC EVIDENCE GUILD. *See* LONDON.—III.

CATHOLIC EXCHANGE AND INFORMATION BUREAU. *See* SINGAPORE.

CATHOLIC EXPOSITION. Exposicion Católica, ó Principios i reglas de conducta de los católicos en la situacion actual de la Iglesia granadina. [Drawn up by R. Cuervo.] pp. 6. *Bogotá*, 1853. 8°. **8179. b. 63. (3.)**

CATHOLIC FAITH. [For the translation of the "Catechismo maggiore" entitled "The Catholic Faith":] *See* CHRISTIAN DOCTRINE.

—— A Briefe Historie of the Glorious Martyrdom of XII. Reuerend Priests, executed within these twelue monethes for confession and defence of the Catholike Faith. But vnder the false pretence of Treason, *etc.* [By William Allen.] 1582. 8°. **C.110.b.11.**

—— Historia del glorioso martirio di sedici sacerdoti martirizati in Inghilterra per la confessione . . . della fede Catolica l'anno 1581, 1582 & 1583 . . . [By William Allen.] Tradotta di lingua Inglese in Italiana da vno del Collegio Inglese di Roma. S'è aggiunto il martirio di due altri sacerdoti & vno secolare Inglese, martirizati l'anno 1577 & 1578. [With six copper-plate engravings, with explanatory Latin verses, illustrating the apprehension, examination and execution of a priest.] pp. 210. 1583. 8°. *See* ENGLAND. [*Appendix.—Religion.*] **4705. a. 8.**

—— [Another copy.] **701. a. 2. (1.)**

—— [Another edition.] pp. 205. 1584. 8°. *See* ENGLAND. [*Appendix.—Religion.*] **701. a. 43.**

—— [Another edition.] Historia del glorioso martirio di diciotto sacerdoti, et vn secolare . . . s'è aggiunto al presente il martirio di cinque altri sacerdoti, *etc.* pp. 222. 1585. 8°. *See* ENGLAND. [*Appendix.—Religion.*] **698. c. 7. (2.)**

—— [Another copy.] **G. 935.**

CATHOLIC FAITH.

—— A Catalogue of diuers Visible Professors of the Catholike Faith . . . Taken out of the Appendix to the Reply of A. D. [i.e. John Piercy] vnto M. Ant. Wotton, and M. Ioh. White Ministers. 1614. 8°. *See* D., A. **C. 26. k. 4. (2.)**

—— Catholic Faith and Practice: being considerations of present use and importance in point of religion and liberty, formed upon the Catholic principles of the learned Jeremy Taylor, and other judicious writers of the Church of England; and addressed to the ingenious author of the Life of Cardinal Pole [i.e. Thomas Phillips]. [By John Jones, Vicar of Shephall.] pp. xv. 56. *Robert Horsfield: London*, 1765. 8°. **480. a. 20. (9.)**

—— [Another issue.] Catholic Faith and Practice; being considerations . . . in behalf of the Protestant religion, and of religious liberty, against the artful attempts of the emissaries of Rome, to undermine both in these Kingdoms. Wherein the character of . . . Bishop Taylor is fully vindicated from the unfair representations of Mr. Phillips in his life of Cardinal Pole, *etc.* pp. xv. 58. *Robert Horsfield: London*, 1765. 8°. **3936. c. 11.**

—— Catholic Faith in the Holy Eucharist. Papers . . . Edited by the Rev. C. Lattey. pp. x. 215. *W. Heffer & Sons: Cambridge*, 1923. 8°. [*Papers from the Summer School of Catholic Studies.* 1922.] **4382.aa.13/1.**

—— Second edition, revised and enlarged. pp. xii. 225. *W. Heffer & Sons: Cambridge*, 1923. 8°. [*Papers from the Summer School of Catholic Studies.* 1922.] **4382.aa.13/3.**

—— Third edition, revised and enlarged. pp. xvi. 248. *W. Heffer & Sons: Cambridge*, 1928. 8°. [*Papers from the Summer School of Catholic Studies.* 1922.] **4382.aa.13/6.**

—— An Epistle of Comfort, to the Reuerend Priestes, & to . . . other of the Laye sort restreyned in Durance for the Catholicke Fayth. [By Robert Southwell.] ff. 214. *Paris*, [1604?] 8°. **699. b. 10.**

—— [Another edition.] pp. 419. 1605. 8°. **3935. a. 26.**

—— [Another copy.] **3935. aaa. 12.**

—— Of the one, onely and singular onely one Catholick, and Roman Faith, *etc.* [By "Mr. K."] 1672. 4°. [*M., S. A Defence of the Protestant Religion against Popery, etc.*] *See* K., *Mr.* **3936. bbb. 16.**

—— [For the work entitled: "Pharetra fidei catholicæ sive idonea disputatio inter Christianos et Judæos."] *See* CHRISTIANS.

—— A Plain and Rational Account of the Catholick Faith, with a preface and appendix in vindication of Catholick morals from old calomnies revived . . . in a scurrilous libel, entituled A Protestant's Resolution, &c. [By Robert Manning.] Second edition, revised and corrected. pp. xxiii. 217. *Rouen*, 1721. 8°. **3938. aaa. 26.**

The first edition, entitled "Modern Controversy," is entered under CONTROVERSY.

—— [Another edition.] To which is annext, The Reform'd Churches prov'd destitute of a Lawful Ministry. The third edition, revised and corrected. 2 pt. *Rouen*, 1721, 22. 8°. **698. d. 25.**

—— The Power of the Catholic Faith, *etc.* (In loving remembrance of Maria Charlotte B. [i.e. M. C. Brett.]) [1864.] 8°. *See* B. (Maria C.) **4920. aa. 8.**

CATHOLIC FAITH.

—— Eine Predigt. Der katholische Glaube wird von aller Welt angenommen werden. Für das katholische Volk. pp. 17. *Ulm*, 1845. 8º. **3910. b. 22.**

—— Protexta de la Santa Fee Católica, Apostólica, Romana, con todo lo demás que contiene para la toma de posesiones de beneficios eclesiásticos, *etc. Lat.* pp. 8. *México*, 1807. 4º. **4182. b. 52. (1.)**

—— Stepping Stones to the Catholic Faith. Sacramental teaching for children. By a Religious of St. Peter's Community, Kilburn. pp. 124. *Society of SS. Peter & Paul: London*, [1923.] 8º. **4324. ff. 7.**

—— [Another edition.] By the author of ' Audrey and John.' (New edition.) pp. 124. *A. R. Mowbray & Co.: London & Oxford*, 1939. 8º. **4018. ee. 16.**

—— [A reissue.] Stepping Stones to the Catholic Faith, *etc.* [With plates.] *A. R. Mowbray & Co.: London & Oxford*, 1948. 8º. **4327. e. 17.**

—— A Treatise of the Nature of Catholick Faith and Heresie . . . By N. N. [i.e. Peter Talbot, R.C. Archbishop of Dublin.] 1657. 8º. *See* N., N. **3935. a. 21.**

—— Tumelo e Katholike. Katekisima ea bana le bakatekumena. pp. 40. *Mazenod*, [1952.] 8º. **3507. aa. 41.**

—— Der uralte katholische Glaube. [By I. Lindl.] pp. 62. *Nürnberg*, 1845. 8º. **3910. a. 13.**

CATHOLIC FAMILIES. Morning Prayers; the Litanies, and other evening prayers, which are usually said in Catholic families. With the daily examination of conscience. pp. 96. *C. Croshaw: York*, [1850?] 32º. **3456. aa. 6.**

CATHOLIC FAMILY ANNUAL. The Catholic Family Annual. *See* PERIODICAL PUBLICATIONS.—*London.* The Illustrated Catholic Family Annual.

—— Catholic Family Annual and Almanac for the Diocese of Liverpool. *See* LIVERPOOL, *Archdiocese of.*

CATHOLIC FAMILY REVIEW. *See* PERIODICAL PUBLICATIONS.—*Saint Helens.*

CATHOLIC FEDERATION.

—— Catholic Federation of Students. *See* AFRICA, *South.* [Union of South Africa.]

CATHOLIC FELLOW-CHRISTIANS. Die Mutterkirche. Ein Friedenswort an unsere katholischen Mitchristen. Mit zwei offenen Briefen als Beilage. pp. 56. *Frankfurt*, 1854. 12º. **3913. a. 67.**

CATHOLIC FILM INSTITUTE. *See* LONDON.—III.

CATHOLIC FILM NEWS. *See* LONDON.—III. *Catholic Film Institute.*

CATHOLIC FILM SOCIETY. *See* LONDON.—III. *Catholic Film Institute.*

CATHOLIC FLORIST. The Catholic Florist: a guide to the cultivation of flowers for the Altar . . . Illustrated by historical notices and fragments of ecclesiastical poetry. [By William H. J. Weale.] With a preface by the Rev. Frederick Oakeley. pp. xxii. 327. xxix. *Richardson & Son: London*, 1851. 12º. **7055. b. 11.**

CATHOLIC FREETHINKER. The Catholic Freethinker. (An occasional publication.) [Edited by Francis H. Laing.] no. 1. pp. 8. *R. Washbourne: London*, 1882. 4º. **3940. b. 4. (1.)**
Other publications of F. H. Laing with this title are entered under his name.

—— The Catholic Freethinker's Fly Sheet. Edited by Dr. Laing, *etc. See* LAING (Francis H.)

CATHOLIC GAMESTERS. The Catholick Gamesters, or a Dubble Match of Bowleing . . . To the tune of, The Plot in the Meal-Tub . . . Published by a By-stander, *etc.* [With an engraving representing incidents in the Popish Plot.] [1680?] *s. sh.* fol. *See* BYSTANDER. **1865. c. 19. (50.)**

CATHOLIC GAZETTE. *See* LONDON.—III. *Catholic Missionary Society.* The Missionary Gazette.

CATHOLIC GEM.

—— The Catholic Gem. *See* PERIODICAL PUBLICATIONS.—*Osgodby.* The Catholic Children's Gem.

CATHOLIC GENTLEMAN'S MAGAZINE. *See* PERIODICAL PUBLICATIONS.—*London.*

CATHOLIC GIRLS' MAGAZINE. *See* PERIODICAL PUBLICATIONS.—*London.* The Children's Corner, *etc.*

CATHOLIC GREGORIAN ASSOCIATION. *See* LONDON.—III.

CATHOLIC GUARDIAN. The Catholic Guardian; or, the Christian Family Library. *See* PERIODICAL PUBLICATIONS.—*Dublin.*

CATHOLIC GUILD. Catholic Guild of Israel. *See* LONDON.—III.

CATHOLIC HERALD YEAR BOOK. *See* PERIODICAL PUBLICATIONS.—London.—*Catholic Herald.*

CATHOLIC HIERARCHY. The Catholick Hierarchie: or, the Divine right of a sacred dominion in Church and conscience, truly stated, asserted, and pleaded. [By Isaac Chauncy. With a preface signed: Catholicus Verus.] pp. 152. *For Sam Crouch & Tho. Fox: London*, 1681. 4º. **4105. df. 3. (2.)**

CATHOLIC HISTORICAL REVIEW. *See* WASHINGTON, D.C.—*Catholic University of America.*

CATHOLIC HOLIDAY GUIDE.

—— The Catholic Holiday Guide. *See* PERIODICAL PUBLICATIONS.—*Ormskirk.*

CATHOLIC HOME ALMANAC. *See* EPHEMERIDES.

CATHOLIC HOME ANNUAL. *See* PERIODICAL PUBLICATIONS.—*Hamilton, Ontario.*

—— *See also* PERIODICAL PUBLICATIONS.—*London.*

CATHOLIC HOME JOURNAL. *See* PERIODICAL PUBLICATIONS.—*London.*

CATHOLIC INDUSTRIALISTS' CONFERENCE. *See* ENGLAND.

CATHOLIC INSTITUTE. Catholic Institute [Liverpool]. *See* LIVERPOOL.

—— Catholic Institute for Deaf-Mute Boys, Montreal. *See* MONTREAL.

—— Catholic Institute of Great Britain. *See* ENGLAND.

CATHOLIC INSTITUTE MAGAZINE. *See* LIVER-POOL.—*Catholic Institute.*

CATHOLIC INSTRUCTION. Enseñanza Catolica. pp. 4. [*Bogotá*, 1863.] 8º.   **8179. e. 34.** (30.)

CATHOLIC INSTRUCTION BOOK. Katholisches Lehr-Gebeth-Gesang- und Schulbuch gesammelt und verfasset von einem Pfarrh. des Metzer Bistums, *etc.* pp. 54. 630. *Strassburg*, 1789. 12º.   **765. a. 2.**

CATHOLIC INTEMPERANCE. An Anodyne to soothe Catholic Intemperance . . . By a Political Apothecary. [The introductory statements signed: W. P. R., i. e. William P. Russel.] 1812. 8º. *See* R., W. P.   **701. e. 22.** (2.)

CATHOLIC INTERESTS. Les Intérêts catholiques en 1891. pp. 259. *Paris*, 1891. 18º.   **3900. bb. 37.**

CATHOLIC INTERNATIONAL OUTLOOK.

—— Catholic International Outlook. *See* ENGLAND.—*Sword of the Spirit.* "The Sword of the Spirit," *etc.*

CATHOLIC IRELAND. *See* PERIODICAL PUBLICATIONS.—*Dublin.*

CATHOLIC JOURNALISTS. Les Journaux religieux et les journalistes catholiques. pp. 32.   *Paris*, 1860. 8º.   **8052. f. 57.** (9.)

CATHOLIC JUNIOR. *See* PERIODICAL PUBLICATIONS.—*London.*

CATHOLIC KEEPSAKE. *See* PERIODICAL PUBLICATIONS.—*London.*

CATHOLIC LADY. The Catholic Lady's Pocket-Book and Almanack. *See* EPHEMERIDES.

CATHOLIC LAITY. The Catholic Laity. *See* PERIODICAL PUBLICATIONS.—*Dublin.*

—— Why are the Catholic Laity poor? By an Irish Catholic. pp. 16. *Elliot Stock: London*, 1896. 8º.   **3939. h. 9.** (2.)

CATHOLIC LAND FEDERATION. Catholic Land Federation of England and Wales. *See* ENGLAND.

CATHOLIC LAYMAN. *See* PERIODICAL PUBLICATIONS.—*Dublin.*

CATHOLIC LAYMEN. The Catholic Laymen's Directory of India. *See* DIRECTORIES.—*India.*

CATHOLIC LEAGUE. Nueva relacion, y curioso romamce [*sic*] in que se da cuenta de las dos armadas que ay en la mar, y de la gente q̃ tiene en tierra la Liga Catolica, y el Gran Sultan, *etc.* [1716.] 4º.   **1312. c. 77.** (8.)

CATHOLIC LEAGUE APOSTLESHIP.
—— Catholic League Apostleship of Prayer. *See* ENGLAND.

CATHOLIC LECTURE. Prove All Things, Hold Fast that which is Good. A dialogue in which are considered some of the arguments used at the Catholic Lecture delivered at Banbury . . . August 12, 1828. pp. 12. *J. L. Wheeler: Oxford*, [1828.] 12º.   **3942. aa. 24.**

CATHOLIC LEGENDS. Catholic Legends: a new collection, selected, translated, and arranged from the best sources. pp. x. 258. *Burns & Lambert: London*, 1855. 8º.   [MISSING.]

—— [A reissue of pp. 1–122.] Catholic Legends and Traditions. A new selection. *London*, [1859.] 8º.   **4827. a. 13.**

A reissue of pp. 123–241 of the 1855 edition of " Catholic Legends," entitled " The Monks of Lerins, and other tales of old time," is entered under LERINS.

CATHOLIC LEGENDS.

—— Legendae Catholicae. A lytle boke of seyntlie gestes. [In verse. Edited by William B. D. D. Turnbull from the Auchinleck MS.] pp. xvi. 257. *Edinburgh Printing Co.: Edinburgh*, 1840. 16º.   **1346. c. 11.** *One of an edition of forty copies.*

—— [Another copy.]   **991. a. 38.**

—— [Another copy.]   **G. 18816.**

CATHOLIC LETTER. The Catholick Letter to the Seeker : or, a Reply to the Protestant Answer [i.e. to " Transubstantiation contrary to Scripture : or, the Protestant's Answer to the Seeker's Request," by Robert Nelson]. Shewing that Catholicks have express Scriptures, for believing the Real Presence ; and that Protestants have none at all, for denying it. [Signed: N. N.] 1688. 4º. *See* N., N.   **222. d. 14.** (11.)

—— *See* PROTESTANT. The Protestant's Answer to the Catholick Letter to the Seeker: or, a Vindication of the Protestant's Answer to the Seeker's Request. 1688. 4º.   **108. e. 59.**

CATHOLIC LIBERAL EDUCATION. The New Departure in Catholic Liberal Education. By a Catholic Barrister. pp. 40. *Burns & Oates: London*, 1878. 8º.   **8304. b. 4.** (14.)

—— Second edition. With additions and appendix. pp. 81. *M. H. Gill & Son: Dublin*, 1878. 8º.   **8306. df. 9.** (3.)

—— The Problem of Catholic Liberal Education. By the author of " Remarks on the Present Condition of Catholic Liberal Education " [i.e. William J. Petre, Baron Petre]. pp. 40. *Burns & Oates: London*, 1877. 8º.   **8365. ee. 13.**

CATHOLIC LIBRARY. The Catholic Library. [Edited successively by Alban Goodier and Cuthbert Lattey.] 18 vol. *Manresa Press; B. Herder: London*, 1914–24. 8º.   **3605. l. 1.**

—— Catholic Library of Religious Knowledge. [Translated from a French series entitled " Bibliothèque catholique des sciences religieuses."] 25 vol. *Sands & Co.: London*, [1929–35.] 8º.   **03605. g. 4.** *No more published in this series.*

CATHOLIC LIFE. Familiar Sketches of Catholic Life: in a series of letters from a foreign Catholic to an English Protestant. pp. 330. *Burns & Lambert: London*, 1851. 16º.   **4061. b. 14.**

CATHOLIC LITANY BOOK. Vollständigstes katholisches Litaneienbuch, enthaltend zweihundert Litaneien, mit passenden Kirchen- und Ablassgebeten, und einem Anhang allgemeiner Andachtsübungen . . . nach den ältesten lateinischen und bewährtesten neuern Werken bearbeitet von einem katholischen Priester. [With plates.] pp. 668. *Einsiedeln & New York*, 1859. 12º.   **3395. aa. 5.**

CATHOLIC LITERARY CIRCULAR. *See* PERIODICAL PUBLICATIONS.—*London.*

CATHOLIC LITERARY MAGAZINE. *See* BOLTON.—*Bolton Catholic Literary Society.*

CATHOLIC LITERATURE.

—— The Guide to Catholic Literature, 1888–1940. An author-subject-title index . . . of books and booklets, in all languages, on all subjects, by Catholics or of particular Catholic interest, *etc.* *W. Romig & Co.: Detroit*, [1940–] 8º.   **11924. d. 36.**

CATHOLIC LITERATURE ASSOCIATION. *See* ENGLAND.—*Church of England.—Anglo-Catholic Congress.*

CATHOLIC LUMINARY. The Catholic Luminary and Ecclesiastical Repertory. *See* PERIODICAL PUBLICATIONS. —*Dublin.*

CATHOLIC LUTHERAN. Der Katholische Lutheraner, das ist handgreiflicher Beweis aus den Schriften Luthers, dass ein Lutheraner den wahren Römisch-Katholischen Glauben annehmen . . . kann, ohne einen Nagelbreit von der Lehre Luthers abzuweichen. In einer Unterredung zwischen zwei Lutheranern Bonifacius und Fidelis dargestellt. [A reprint of Georg Kauffmann's anonymous tract. Edited by A. Biermann.] [1868.] 16º. *See* BONIFACIUS. **3906. a. 18.**

—— Bogumił i Wilhelm, czyli rozmowa przyjacielska dwóch protestantów o religii katolickiéj. Z niemieckiego [of "Der Catholische Lutheraner" by G. Kauffmann]. pp. 94. 1844. 8º. *See* BOGUMIŁ. **3910. b. 15.**

—— *See* BONIFACIUS. Wer hätt es gemeint! O mein Gott wer hätt es gemeint! Verwundert sich ein Pohlnischer Edelmann, mit Nahmen Bonifacius, welcher neulich in Erwegung eines gewissen Controvers-Büchels, so durch einen Jesuiten in Druck gegangen, auss dem Lutherthumb zum Römisch-Katholischen Glauben bekehrt worden, *etc.* [Relating to G. Kauffmann's anonymous tract "Der Catholische Lutheraner."] 1721. 12º. **3925. a. 10.**

—— Besser unterwiesener Catholischer Lutheraner, das ist: ein vertrauliches Gespräch, darinnen von Fideli und Bonifacio, zweyen Catholischen, aus denen Schrifften Lutheri, die Frage beantwortet . . . wird, ob ein Lutheraner den wahren Catholisch-Römischen Glauben annehmen, und öffentlich profitiren könne, ohne einen Nagelbreit von der reinen Lehre . . . Lutheri nicht abzuweichen? [Relating to G. Kauffmann's anonymous tract, "Der Catholische Lutheraner."] 1737. 8º. *See* FIDELIS. **3906. aa. 47.**

CATHOLIC MAGAZINE. The Catholic Magazine. *See* PERIODICAL PUBLICATIONS.—*London.*

—— *See also* PERIODICAL PUBLICATIONS.—*London.* The Edinburgh Catholic Magazine.

—— The Catholic Magazine and Register. *See* PERIODICAL PUBLICATIONS.—*London.* Dolman's Magazine.

—— The Catholic Magazine and Review. *See* PERIODICAL PUBLICATIONS.—*Birmingham.*

CATHOLIC MANNERS. Mores Catholici: or, Ages of Faith. [By Kenelm H. Digby.] 11 bk. *Joseph Booker: London,* 1831–42. 8º. **1352. b. 9.**

—— [Another edition.] 3 vol. *C. Dolman: London,* 1845–47. 8º. **1352. k. 2–4.**

CATHOLIC MANUAL. Catholic Manual for Children. Compiled and translated from approved sources. [With Hymns.] 2 pt. *Richardson & Son: London,* 1869. 16º. **876. a. 18.**

—— Catholisch Manual oder Handbuch, dariñe begriffen seynd: Die Evangelia mit den Episteln dess gantzen Jahrs. Cantuale oder Psalmbüchlein teutscher vnd lateinischer meistentheils alter Gesäng . . . Klein Catechismus D. Petri Canisij . . . jetzt von newem vbersehen, vermehret, *etc.* 3 pt. *H. Eychen: Hildessheim,* 1647. 12º. **765. aa. 17.**

CATHOLIC MANUALS. Catholic Manuals for Social Students. 3 pt. *Catholic Social Guild: Oxford,* [1920, 21.] 8º. **8287. a. 52.**

CATHOLIC MANUALS.

—— Catholic Manuals of Philosophy. *See* CATHOLIC PHILOSOPHY. Manuals of Catholic Philosophy.

CATHOLIC MARGINAL NOTES. Katholische Randbemerkungen zu einigen Erscheinungen der neuesten antikatholischen Literatur. Eine Beleuchtung der Angriffe auf kathol. Lehren, Einrichtungen und Institute, auch den Jesuiten-Orden. pp. xiii. 93. *Mainz,* 1853. 16º. **3911. a. 56. (1.)**

CATHOLIC MASS-FOUNDATIONS.

—— Ueber Nutzlosigkeit katholischer Messfundationen oder auch Fundationsmessen. Von Dr. H . . . . ., aus Preussen. 1865. 8º. *See* H . . . . ., *Dr., aus Preussen.* **3911. aa. 54. (6.)**

CATHOLIC MEDICAL GUARDIAN. *See* ENGLAND.— *Guild of St. Luke, St. Cosmas, and St. Damian.*

CATHOLIC MEDICAL QUARTERLY.

—— *See* ENGLAND.—*Guild of St. Luke, St. Cosmas & St. Damian.* The Catholic Medical Guardian.

CATHOLIC MEMORIAL. Katholische Denkschrift, Seiner Heiligkeit [i.e. to Pope Pius VI.] zu überreichen. Ein nach dem Tode des Verfassers herausgegebenes Werk. Aus dem Wälschen. [A translation of the "Memoria cattolica" of Carlo Borgo, criticising Pope Clement XIV's Brief for the suppression of the Jesuits.] pp. 264. *Frankfurt & Leipzig,* 1784. 8º. **853. c. 32.**

CATHOLIC MEN OF SCIENCE SERIES. *See* WINDLE (*Sir* Bertram C. A.)

CATHOLIC MEN'S JOURNAL. *See* ENGLAND.— *Catholic Young Men's Society.—Birmingham Branch.*

CATHOLIC MIND. *See* PERIODICAL PUBLICATIONS.— *Dublin.*

CATHOLIC MIRACLES.

—— Catholic Miracles [mainly extracted from the Legenda Aurea]; illustrated with seven designs, including a characteristic portrait of Prince Hohenlohe, by George Cruikshank. To which is added, a reply to Cobbett's Defence of Catholicism, and his libel on the Reformation. pp. 102. *Knight & Lacey: London,* 1825. 8º. **T. 1001. (9.)**

CATHOLIC MIRROR. The Catholick Mirrour, or, a Looking-Glasse for Protestants. Wherein they may plainly see the errours of their Church, and the truth of the Roman Catholick, *etc.* pp. 147. *Paris,* 1662. 8º. **3939. a. 3.**

—— Freymüthiger Bescheid ertheilet dem ungenandten Concipienten der so betitulten Speculi Veritatis Catholici [by B. K.], *etc.* 1720. 4º. *See* K., B. **3908. d. 58. (12.)**

CATHOLIC MISCELLANY. The Catholic Miscellany and Monthly Repository of Information. *See* PERIODICAL PUBLICATIONS.—*London.*

CATHOLIC MISSION SERIES. *See* DUBLIN.— *Catholic Truth Society of Ireland.*

CATHOLIC MISSIONARIES. Die Missionsgeschichte späterer Zeiten, oder gesammelte Briefe der katholischen Missionare, *etc.* 1795–98. 8º. *See* JESUITS. [*Letters from Missions.*] **4767. bb. 1.**

—— The Plain Man's Reply to the [Catholick] Missionaries. [By William Assheton.] pp. 35. *For Ric. Chiswell: London,* 1686. 24º. **1019. a. 12.** *The titlepage is mutilated.*

CATHOLIC MISSIONARY SOCIETY. *See* LONDON. —III.

CATHOLIC MISSIONS. The Catholic Missions. *See* ASSOCIATION DE LA PROPAGATION DE LA FOI.

—— Catholic Missions. *See also* ASSOCIATION DE LA PROPAGATION DE LA FOI. Illustrated Catholic Missions.

—— Die katholischen Missionen. Geschildert aus der Neuzeit. Mit einem Anhange: Zwei Missionen in den Jahren 1716 und 1718. pp. 259. *Regensburg*, 1852. 8°.
4765. d. 8.

CATHOLIC MODERATOR. The Catholike Moderator: or a Moderate Examination of the Doctrine of the Protestants . . . First written in French by a Catholike gentleman (H. C. [i.e. Cardinal Jacques Davy Du Perron]), *etc.* [A translation of "Examen pacifique de la doctrine des Huguenots."] 1623. 4°. *See* C., H.
3939. aaa. 38. (1.)

CATHOLIC MONTHLY LETTERS. *See* ENGLAND. —*British Catholic Information Society.*

CATHOLIC MONTHLY MAGAZINE. *See* PERIODICAL PUBLICATIONS.—*Birmingham.*

CATHOLIC MORAL TEACHING. Handbuch der katholischen Sittenlehre. *See* TILLMANN (F.)

CATHOLIC MYSTICS. Lichtstrahlen aus den Schriften katholischer Mystiker. *See* JOCHAM (M.)

CATHOLIC NATIONAL SCHOOL. Die katholische Volksschule, ihre Aufgabe, ihre gegenwärtige Leistung und ihre nothwendige Umgestaltung. Von einem badischen Ortsschulinspector [i.e. H. Rolfus]. pp. iv. 88. *Mainz*, 1859. 8°.
8309. ee. 26. (7.)

CATHOLIC NEW-YEARS-GIFT. Strena Catholica, seu Explicatio . . . noui Fidelitatis Iuramenti. Ab E. I. Sacræ Theologiæ studioso [i.e. Thomas Preston] composita, *etc.* 1620. 8°. *See* I., E., *Student in Divinitie.*
G. 20033.

CATHOLIC NEWS YEAR BOOK. *See* PERIODICAL PUBLICATIONS.—Birmingham.—*Catholic News.*

CATHOLIC NURSE.

—— The Catholic Nurse. Journal of the Catholic Nurses Guild. *See* ENGLAND.—*Catholic Nurses Guild.*

CATHOLIC NURSES' GUILD.

—— *See* ENGLAND.

—— Catholic Nurses' Guild of Malaya. *See* MALAYA.

CATHOLIC OFFERING. The Catholic Offering; counsels to the young on their leaving school and entering into the world. By a member of the Ursuline Community, Black Rock, Cork, authoress of "The Spirit of Prayer," *etc.* pp. viii. 293. *James Duffy: Dublin*, 1859. 12°.
4407. bb. 40.

CATHOLIC OUTLOOK. The Catholic Outlook: the bulletin of the League of Knowledge. *See* LONDON.—III. *League of Knowledge.*

CATHOLIC PACIFISTS' ASSOCIATION. *See* CANADA.

CATHOLIC PARDON.

—— The Catholike Pardon: given first in Paradise, and sithence newly confirmed by our Almightie Father, with many large Priuileges, Graunts, and Bulles graunted for euer . . . Drawne out of French into English, by William Hayward: and now reuised and enlarged, by Henoch Clapham. 𝔅.𝔏. *T. Este for George Vincent: London*, 1602. 8°.
C. 132. h. 12. (2.)

CATHOLIC PARENTS' AND ELECTORS' ASSOCIATION. *See* ENGLAND.

CATHOLIC PARISH MAGAZINE. *See* PERIODICAL PUBLICATIONS.—*Glasgow.*

CATHOLIC PARISH PRIEST. Doveri del parroco cattolico in questi tempi. [The preface signed: Un Parroco.] 1850. 8°. *See* PARROCO.
4071. c. 13.

CATHOLIC PENNY PRAYER BOOK. The Catholic Penny Prayer Book, designed for the use of schools. pp. 32. *T. Richardson & Son: London*, [1873.] 32°.
[MISSING.]

CATHOLIC PEOPLE. Aviso Importante al Pueblo Católico, ó sea Centinela alerta para defensa de la religion. pp. 4. *Puebla*, 1821. 4°.
9770. bb. 28. (14.)

—— *See* SAGELI JEREZ (M.) Reflecciones sobre el papel titulado: Aviso Importante al Pueblo Católico, *etc.* 1821. 4°.
9770. bb. 9. (12.)

—— Belehrungen über die gemischten Ehen in fünf Gesprächen für das katholische Volk. Von katholischen Geistlichen. pp. 47. *Crefeld*, 1846. 12°.
5175. a. 41. (3.)

CATHOLIC PHARMACEUTICAL GUILD. *See* LONDON.—III.

CATHOLIC PHARMACIST. *See* LONDON.—III. *Catholic Pharmaceutical Guild.*

CATHOLIC PHILOSOPHY.

—— Études de philosophie catholique sur l'art. De la souffrance et du sentiment religieux dans la tragédie: Oedipe-Roi, Polyeucte, Athalie. [By Jean Baptiste Charles Riobé.] pp. 107. *Le Mans*, 1860. 8°.
7805. c. 8.

—— Manuals of Catholic Philosophy. (Catholic Manuals of Philosophy.) [Edited by Richard F. Clarke.] 8 vol. *Longmans & Co.: London*, 1888–92. 8°.
8470. a. 1–8.
Continued as "Stonyhurst Philosophical Series."

CATHOLIC PICTORIAL. *See* PERIODICAL PUBLICATIONS.—*Dublin.*

CATHOLIC PILL. A Catholick Pill to Purge Popery. With a preparatory preface, obviating the growing malignity of Popery against Catholick Christianity. By a true Son of the Catholick Apostolick Church, *etc.* pp. 91. *For J. Coles & Will. Miller: London*, 1677. 8°.
3936. aaa. 29.

CATHOLIC POLITICIAN. Gewissensangst, eines fürnehmen Catholischen Politici, welcher bey diesem wandelbaren Glück fast Lutherisch werden wil. Entdecket einem fürnehmen Catholischen Geistlichen zu Stade. *P. Langen: Halberstadt*, 1631. 4°.
1315. d. 10. (26.)

CATHOLIC POLITICS. Some First Lines of Catholic Politics, traced from the human sovereignty of Christ on earth . . . By a Catholic Englishman. pp. vii. 16. *W. H. Allen & Co.: London*, 1881. 8°. **3940. h. 8. (9.)**

CATHOLIC POPULAR WRITINGS. Bibliothek katholischer Volksschriften. 8 Bd. *Zürich*, 1868, 69. 12°.
[MISSING.]

CATHOLIC PRAYER BOOK. A Catholic Prayer Book. For the use of Catholics serving in the Defence Forces of the Crown in time of war. pp. 96. *Burns, Oates & Co.: London*, [1940.] 24°.
03456. de. 169.

CATHOLIC PRAYER BOOK CALENDAR. *See* EPHEMERIDES.

CATHOLIC PRAYERS. Catholic Prayers for Church of England People, *etc.* [The preface signed : A. H. S., i.e. Arthur H. Stanton.] 1895. 16⁰. *See* S., A. H.
3456. df. 65.

—— An Octave of Catholic Prayers for the eventful year 1851. By a Protestant Catholic . . . Edited by the Rev. Edward Phillips. pp. vii. 32. *Seeleys : London,* 1851. 8⁰.
3455. b. 72. (4.)

CATHOLIC PREACHERS. Catholic Preachers of To-day. Seventeen sermons. With an introduction by . . . Cardinal Bourne. pp. xvi. 265. *Longmans & Co.: London,* 1928. 8⁰.
04478. ee. 62.

CATHOLIC PRESBYTERIAN. *See* PERIODICAL PUB-LICATIONS.—*London.*

CATHOLIC PRESS ASSOCIATION. *See* BEBING-TON.

CATHOLIC PRIESTS. Du mariage des prêtres catho-liques. pp. 198. *Rennes,* 1868. 8⁰.
3901. dd. 3.

CATHOLIC PRINCES. Ad Principes Catholicos, de præsenti reipublicæ statu. *See* MERCURY. Le Mercure d'Estat, *etc.* 1634. 8⁰.
596. a. 24.

—— Aux Princes Catholiques, sur l'estat present des affaires publiques en response du discours pour induire les Princes Chrestiens à se liberer de la tyrannie de la Maison d'Austriche. [Translated from the Latin.] *See* MERCURY. Le Mercure d'Estat, *etc.* 1634. 8⁰.
596. a. 24.

    —— *See* LIBERTÉ. A ceux qui veulent conseruer leur liberté, ou l'acquerir. [A reply to the pamphlet entitled " Ad principes Catholicos."] 1634. 8⁰. [*Le Mercure d'Estat, etc.*]
596. a. 24.

—— De par les Princes Catholiques vnis auec le clergé, la noblesse, & le peuple, pour la religion & bien de l'estat. Auec le reglement de Monseigneur le Duc Daumalle. pp. 8. [*J. Hulpeau:*] *Paris,* 1589. 8⁰. **3900. a. 60. (3.)**

—— La Ligue et puissance association des Princes Catho-liques côtre les Protestans d'Allemagne. Auec ce qui s'est passé fraischement en Boheme entre le comte de Buquoy & le comte de Mansfeld. pp. 14. *S. Moreau: Paris,* 1620. 8⁰.
1367. b. 4.

CATHOLIC PROGRESS. *See* LONDON.—III. *Young Men's Catholic Association.*

CATHOLIC PULPIT. The Catholic Pulpit. *See* PERIODICAL PUBLICATIONS.—*London.*

—— *See also* PERIODICAL PUBLICATIONS.—*Birmingham.*

—— The Catholic Pulpit, Educator and Expositor. *See* PERIODICAL PUBLICATIONS.—*London.*

CATHOLIC QUESTION. An Abstract of the Argu-ments on the Catholic Question. [By Theobald Mac-kenna.] pp. 37. *J. Budd: London,* 1805. 8⁰.
8145. bbb. 13.

—— A Calm Statement of the Catholic Question . . . By a Clergyman of the establish'd Church. pp. 35. *T. Cadell: London,* 1826. 8⁰. **T. 1192. (18.)**

—— The Catholic Question. A warning to the British Nation. Sixth edition. pp. 16. *R. Clay: London,* [1828 ?] 12⁰.
3938. aaa. 2. (16.)

—— Catholic Question. Evidence of the British Constitu-tion, established at the Glorious Revolution, 1688 ; with a view to the principles of the House of Brunswick, as identified with the inheritance of the throne, and to a consideration whether the removal of the disabilities of Roman Catholics, can be effected consistently with those principles . . . By a Devonshire Freeholder. pp. 72. *Septimus Prowett: London,* [1829 ?] 8⁰. **T. 1252. (6.)**

CATHOLIC QUESTION.

—— The Catholic Question Argued, upon the principles of those who support it on the ground of expediency : in two letters from a gentleman in Ireland to his friend in London. 2 pt. *F. C. & J. Rivington: London,* 1821. 8⁰.
701. e. 23. (7.)

—— The Catholic Question considered in its various relations religious and political. pp. 61. *J. Didot, Senior: Paris,* 1828. 8⁰.
3940. e. 71. (1.)

—— The Catholic Question discussed and decided, par-ticularly as it regards the admission of Catholics into Parliament. With a preface in refutation of Mr. M'Cul-loch's opinion on Absenteeism, *etc.* pp. 35. *J. Hatchard & Son: London,* 1828. 8⁰. **T. 1230. (9.)**

—— The Catholic Question in 1828. By an elector of the University of Oxford. pp. 35. *Hurst, Chance & Co.: London,* 1828. 8⁰. **T. 1230. (7.)**

—— The Catholic Question, viewed in connection with the approaching county election.—From the Sheffield Inde-pendent. [Signed : A Protestant Freeholder.] pp. 8. [1826.] 8⁰.
8145. d. 11.

—— An Historical Essay on the Origin of Religious Persecu-tion ; auxiliary to the consideration of what is called the Catholic Question. pp. 49. *Ridgway: London,* 1827. 8⁰.
T. 2007. (5.)

—— Letters, &c. [by the Duke of Newcastle and others] on the Catholic Question and the Establishment of Bruns-wick Clubs, *etc.* pp. 41. 1828. *See* PERIODICAL PUB-LICATIONS.—*London.* The Pamphleteer, *etc.* vol. 29. 1813, *etc.* 8⁰.
P.P. 3557. w.

—— On the Catholic Question, properly Roman-Catholic Question. pp. 32. *William Ballintine: London,* 1807. 4⁰.
108. f. 50.

—— Pros and Cons ; or, a Brief analysis of the late debate and division on the Catholic question . . . With a short commentary. pp. 24. *James Ridgway: London,* 1827. 8⁰.
T. 1191. (3.)

—— A Short View of the Catholic Question. [By Charles W. Martin.] pp. 33. *J. Hatchard & Son: London,* 1829. 8⁰.
T. 1252. 8.

—— [Another copy.] MS. NOTE.
3943. h. 6.

—— Thoughts on the Catholic Question. pp. 49. *J. Hatchard: London,* 1807. 8⁰. **3942. c. 2. (1.)**

—— Thoughts upon the Catholic Question, by an Irish Roman Catholic [i.e. Anthony R. Blake]. pp. 85. *R. Milliken & Son: Dublin,* 1828. 8⁰.
8275. ee. 24. (4.)

—— The True, and Only True Description and View of the Catholic Question, *etc.* pp. 11. *J. Hatchard & Son: London,* 1829. 8⁰. **T. 1252. (9.)**

CATHOLIC QUESTIONS. Katholikus kérdések. [A series of tracts.] évf. 1. füz. 1–12. *Pesten,* 1871–72. 16⁰.
3913. aa. 65.
No more published after évf. 3. The wrapper of füz. 1 is dated 1872. *Those of füz.* 11 *and* 12 *are dated* 1873.

CATHOLIC READERS. The Ideal Catholic Readers . . . By a Sister of St. Joseph [i.e. Sister Mary Domitilla]. [With a " Manual for Teachers."] 8 pt. *Macmillan Co.: New York,* 1915, 16. 8⁰. **12980. c. 6.**

CATHOLIC RECORD SOCIETY. The Catholic Record Society. *See* LONDON.—III.

CATHOLIC RECORD SOCIETY.

—— Catholic Record Society of Ireland. *See* MAYNOOTH.—
St. Patrick's College.

CATHOLIC REFORM. Gedanken eines evangelischen
Laien über die katholische Reform. pp. 23. 1845. 8°.
3910. e. 21.

CATHOLIC REGULARS. Ueber die Kleidertracht der
katholischen Ordensgeistlichen, *etc.* [A skit. By
M. Plein.] pp. 26. *Frankfurt & Leipzig*, 1782. 8°.
12314. de. 37.

CATHOLIC RELIGION. Auisi notabili intorno al
progresso della religione Catholica, estratta parte dalle
Lettere annali del Seminario Inglese di Sua Santità in
Fiandra per l'anno 1578, parte da lettere . . . riceuute
da i Catholici d'Inghilterra.   *Per A. Benacci: Bologna,*
1579. 4°.   **G. 6185.**

—— [Another edition.] [*A. Colaldi ?*] *Oruieto*, 1588. 4°.
4767. f. 5.

—— A Catalogue of the Lords, Knights and Gentlemen, of
the Catholick Religion, that were slain in the late warr,
in defence of their King and Countrey. As also of those
whose estates were sold by the Rump, *etc.*   [*London ?*
1660 ?] *s. sh.* fol.   **1865. c. 9. (56.)**

—— Conjuration contre la religion catholique, et les souverains ; dont le projet, conçu en France, doit s'exécuter
dans l'univers entier, *etc.* [By J. F. Le Franc.] pp. 375.
Paris, 1792. 8°.   **F. 966. (1.)**

—— Entwurf einer in Sachen der katholischen Religion an
das königl. Preussische Staats-ministerium zu richtenden
Denkschrift. pp. 39. *Münster*, 1871. 12°.
3911. aa. 55. (15.)

—— An Essay upon the Reasonableness and Usefulness of
the Catholick Religion, *etc.* pp. 60. *J. Roberts: London,*
1722. 8°.   **108. f. 28.**

—— Handwörterbuch zur Erklärung und Verdeutschung der
in der katholischen Religion und Kirche, so wie bei dem
Cultus . . . vorkommenden Ausdrücke und Fremdwörter.
pp. 123. *Augsburg*, 1846. 16°.   **4520. a. 10.**

—— The Prudentiall Ballance of Religion, wherin the
Catholike and Protestant religion are weighed together
with the weights of Prudence, and right Reason. [By
Richard Smith, Bishop of Chalcedon.] The first part.
pp. 1–352. 343–598. [*F. Bellet ? Saint Omer ?*] 1609. 8°.
3936. b. 42.

Pt. 2, entitled " Collatio doctrinæ Catholicorum ac Pro-
testantium cum . . . sacræ scripturæ verbis," was published
under the author's name.

—— [Another copy.]   **3936. aa. 34.**
The titlepage is slightly mutilated.

—— Réclamation de la nation, de la loi et de la raison en
faveur de la religion catholique. pp. 34. *Paris*, 1792. 8°.
F. 171. (2.)

—— La Religion en action, ou la Religion catholique considérée dans un grand nombre d'exemples puisés à des
sources respectables . . . Quatrième édition. pp. 204.
Metz, [1855 ?] 12°.   **4805. bb. 17.**

—— A Short and Easy Guide to the Truths of the Catholic
Religion. Taken from the writings of Bossuet, Fénélon,
Pascal and Bullet, by the Superior of a College. Trans-
lated from the French by L. C. Wynn. pp. 126.
T. Richardson & Son: London, 1847. 8°.   **1360. d. 11.**

CATHOLIC RELIGION.

—— The Theatre of Catholique and Protestant Religion . . .
Written by I. C., Student in diuinitie [i.e. John Colleton].
1620. 8°. *See* C., I., *Student in Divinity.*
3936. aa. 42.

—— Troisième lettre au rédacteur du Courier de Londres,
sur cette question : La religion catholique est-elle à
rétablir en France ? [By Marquis T. G. de Lally
Tollendal.] pp. 60. *J. de Boffe: Londres*, 1801. 8°.
3901. d. 40. (5.)

—— Unterweisungen über die Glaubens-Wahrheiten der
katholischen Religion. Blüthenlese aus den besten und
neuesten Religions-Schriften. pp. 202. 17. 8.   *Bonn,*
1846. 8°.   **3911. a. 9.**

CATHOLIC RELIGIOUS INSTRUCTION. Catholic Religious Instruction, suitable for standard 1 (2).
(Second edition.) 2 pt. *T. Richardson & Sons: London,*
[1877.] 16°.   **3506. de. 47.**

—— [Another edition.] Catholic Religious Instruction, suitable for standard 1(–3). 3 pt.   *T. Richardson & Son:*
London & Derby, [1879, 80.] 12°.   **3506. de. 50.**

—— Revised edition of 1883. 3 pt. *T. Richardson & Son:*
London, [1884.] 12°.   **3940. a. 50.**

CATHOLIC REMEMBRANCER. *See* EPHEMERIDES.

CATHOLIC RENAISSANCE. Della rinascenza cattolica. Narrazione d'un alunno di Propaganda Fide.
[By Count T. Mamiani della Rovere.] pp. 188. *Firenze,*
1862. 8°.   **3901. bbb. 13.**

CATHOLIC REPRESENTER.

—— The Catholic Representer. Or the Papist Misrepre-
sented and Represented. Second part. [By John Gother.]
1687 [1686, 87]. 4°. *See* PAPIST.   **222. d. 7. (15.)**

CATHOLIC REVIEW. *See* PERIODICAL PUBLICATIONS.
—*London.*

CATHOLIC REVIVAL. Heroes of the Catholic Revival.
Catholic Literature Association: London, [1932– .] 12°.
W.P. 10015.

CATHOLIC RITUAL. The Form of Godliness : being
some remarks on Catholic ritual, by a Priest of the Church
of England. pp. 37. *J. Masters: London*, 1867. 8°.
3477. cc. 66. (9.)

CATHOLIC SAILORS. Polyglot Dialogues for Workers
among Catholic Sailors. (Dialogues polyglottes, etc.)
Eng. Fr., It. Span. Port., Dutch. pp. 15. [1898.] *obl.* 8°.
12901. a. 39.

CATHOLIC SCHOOLS. Elementary Books for Catholic
Schools. 2 no.   *Burns, Lambert & Co.: London,*
1860. 12°.   **12202. b. 47.**

—— First Book of Lessons for the use of Catholic Schools.
Eng., Sinhal. & Tamil. pp. 21.   *Catholic Orphanage*
Press: Colombo, 1876. 8°.   **14165. l. 4. (1.)**

—— Lehrbuch der allgemeinen Weltgeschichte für katholische Schulen. Ein frei bearbeiteter Auszug vom Verfasser des " Handbuchs der allgem. Weltgeschichte für
Schule und Haus " . . . und der " Allgemeinen Weltgeschichte &c. für alle Stände." pp. xviii. 395.
Stuttgart, 1845. 8°.   **1309. c. 14.**

CATHOLIC SCOUT. *See* DUBLIN.—*Catholic Boy Scouts*
of Ireland.

CATHOLIC SCOUT.

—— The Catholic Scout's Prayer Book. pp. 56. *Catholic Truth Society: London,* 1912. 16°. **3943. a. 9.**

CATHOLIC SCOUT LEADERS' BULLETIN. *See* DUBLIN.—*Catholic Boy Scouts of Ireland.*

CATHOLIC SCRIPTURE MANUALS. Catholic Scripture Manuals, *etc.* 1904, *etc.* 8°. *See* BIBLE. [*Polyglott.*] **03051. k.**

CATHOLIC SCRIPTURIST. The Catholike Scripturist, or the Plea of the Roman Catholikes, shewing the Scriptures to hold forth the Roman faith in above forty of the cheife controversies now under debate. By I. M. [i.e. James Mumford.] 1662. 8°. *See* M., I. **3936. aaa. 27.**

CATHOLIC SERIES. The Catholic Series. 37 pt. *John Chapman: London,* 1844–54. 12°. **3605. b. 9–35.**

CATHOLIC SERMONS. Catholic Sermons. (Select discourses by eminent ministers of all denominations.) vol. 1. no. 1–9. vol. 2. no. 13–24. *E. Curtice: London,* 1873, 74. 8°. **4479. bbb. 46.** *Imperfect; wanting vol. 1. no. 10–12. no. 1 and 2 are of the 3rd edition. Continued as "Pulpit Echoes."*

—— [Another edition.] 2 vol. *F. E. Longley: London,* 1874, 75. 8°. **4465. aaa. 14.**

—— A Select Collection of Catholick Sermons, preach'd before . . . King James II., *etc.* 2 vol. *London,* 1741. 8°. **G. 20111, 12.**

CATHOLIC SHEET ALMANACK. *See* EPHEMERIDES.

CATHOLIC SLAVES. Noticia do glorioso successo que tiveraõ os Escravos Catholicos, que estavaõ em poder do Graõ Turco : e o feliz levantamento, com que recuperaraõ a sua liberdade, levando comsigo hum grande navio de guerra Turco . . . e com felicidade se refugiáraõ á Ilha de Malta. pp. 8. *Lisboa,* 1761. 4°. **9004. gg. 33. (34.)**

CATHOLIC SOCIAL CATECHISM.

—— A Catholic Social Catechism. pp. 24. *Catholic Truth Society: London,* [1911.] 8°. [*Catholic Social Guild Pamphlets.* no. 9.] **3943. aa. 54/9.**

—— [A reissue.] *London,* 1912. 8°. [*Catholic Social Guild Pamphlets.* ser. 2.] **3943. aa. 55/2.**

CATHOLIC SOCIAL GUILD. *See* ENGLAND.

CATHOLIC SOCIAL GUILD PAMPHLETS. *See* ENGLAND.—*Catholic Social Guild.*

CATHOLIC SOCIAL GUILD SERIES.

—— *See* ENGLAND.—*Catholic Social Guild.* Catholic Social Guild Pamphlets.

CATHOLIC SOCIAL SERVICE CONFERENCE. *See* DUBLIN.

CATHOLIC SOCIAL STUDY GUILD. *See* MONTREAL.

CATHOLIC SOCIAL UNION. *See* LONDON.—III.

CATHOLIC SOCIAL YEAR BOOK. *See* ENGLAND. —*Catholic Social Guild.*

CATHOLIC SOCIETIES VOCATIONAL ORGANISATION CONFERENCE. *See* IRELAND.—*Irish Free State.*

CATHOLIC SOVEREIGNS. Diritti dei sovrani e dei vescovi cattolici per opporsi alle massime giurisdizionali della Corte di Roma. [By V. Besozzi.] pp. 80. *Amsterdam* [*Florence ?*], 1783. 8°. **1356. b. 8. (2.)** *Originally published at Pavia in 1782, with the title: "Riflessioni sopra l'autorità de' vescovi e de' principi nella chiesa. Di V. B."*

CATHOLIC SPECTATOR. The Catholic Spectator, Selector and Monitor. *See* PERIODICAL PUBLICATIONS.— *London.* Catholicon, *etc.*

CATHOLIC STANDPOINT. Der katholische Standpunkt in Bezug auf den Entwurf des Volksschulgesetzes wahrheitsgetreu dargelegt von Dr. H. 1892. 8°. *See* H., *Dr.* **8304. aa. 17. (8.)**

CATHOLIC STATE WAGGON. Catholic State Waggon . . . From the Westminster Review, *etc.* [An allegory, followed by arguments for Catholic emancipation. By Thomas Perronet Thompson. With a woodcut by Robert Seymour.] pp. 16. *Cowie & Strange: London,* 1829. 8°. **8138. e. 26.**

CATHOLIC STUDENT CORPORATIONS. Die katholischen Studentenkorporationen. Bedeutung und Aufgaben derselben in der Gegenwart. Von einem deutschen Katholiken. 1897. *See* HAFFNER (P. L.) *Bishop of Mainz.* Frankfurter zeitgemässe Broschüren. Neue Folge. Bd. 18. 1880, *etc.* 8°. **12209. g.**

CATHOLIC STUDENTS.

—— Catholic Students' Society. *See* SINGAPORE—*University of Malaya.*

CATHOLIC STUDIES. Catholic Studies in Social Reform. *See* ENGLAND.—*Catholic Social Guild.*

CATHOLIC SUFFRAGIST. *See* LONDON.—III. *Catholic Women's Suffrage Society.*

CATHOLIC SUMMER SCHOOL. Catholic Summer School on Russia. *See* CAMBRIDGE.—*Cambridge Summer School on Russian Studies.*

CATHOLIC SUPREMACY. The One Catholic Supremacy, the Divine Salvation of the Church. [By Thomas Carlyle, of the Scottish Bar.] Second edition, enlarged. pp. 24. *John Ollivier: London,* 1851. 12°. **3938. a. 13.**

—— [Another copy.] **764. i. 21. (1.)**

CATHOLIC TABLE-TALK. Ein Catholisch Tisch-Gespräch . . . von der disputirlichen Frage : ob man schuldig, einem jeden, Trew . . . zu halten . . . A. I. F. 1617. 4°. *See* F., A. I. **3910. aaa. 43. (2.)**

CATHOLIC TALES. Catholic Tales for the Young. 13 pt. *T. Richardson & Son: London,* 1875–86. 12°. [MISSING.]

CATHOLIC TEACHERS.

—— Catholic Teachers' Federation. *See* ENGLAND.

CATHOLIC THESES. Catholick Theses on several Chief Heads of Controversy. [By Abraham Woodhead.] [*Obadiah Walker? Oxford,* 1689.] 4°. **3935. cc. 12.** *A fragment consisting of pp. 1–100, preceded by two leaves, containing the Preface. No more published.*

—— [Another copy.] **4325. bb. 67. (3.)**

CATHOLIC THOUGHT AND THINKERS SERIES.
See O'Dowd (William B.) and Martindale (C. C.)

CATHOLIC THOUGHTS. Catholic Thoughts on the Church of Christ and the Church of England (on the Bible and Theology). [By Frederick Myers.] 2 pt. *For private distribution: Cambridge*, [1841 ?] 8°. **4109. aaa. 37.**

—— [Another edition of pt. 2.] pp. viii. 310. xii. *For private distribution: Keswick*, [1848 ?] 8°. **3939. h. 4.**

CATHOLIC TOTAL ABSTINENCE LEAGUE. See England.—*League of the Cross and Crusade against Intemperance.*

CATHOLIC TRACT SOCIETY. Catholic Tract Society. (Tract, no. I., IV., V.) 3 pt. *W. E. Andrews: London*, [1835 ?] 12°. **908. c. 5. (8.)**

CATHOLIC TRACTS. Fifty Catholic Tracts on Various Subjects. ser. 1. 50 no. *Catholic Publication Society: New York*, [1870.] 8°. **3939. bb. 43.**

—— A Selection of Catholic Tracts. Reprinted for the St. Austin's Society. pp. iv. 202. *Commercial Press: Bombay*, 1867. 8°. **4017. i. 6.**

CATHOLIC TRADITION. Tradition catholiq.; ou, Traicté de la croyance des Chrestiens . . . Par Th. A. I. C. [i.e. Morton Eudes.] 1609. 8°. *See* C., Th. A. I. **701. d. 31.**

—— Catholique Traditions. Or, a Treatise of the belief of the Christians . . . Written . . . by Th. A. I. C. [i.e. Morton Eudes], *etc.* 1609. 4°. *See* C., Th. A. I. **3901. cc. 8.**

CATHOLIC TRUTH. Catholic Truth. *See* London.—III. *Catholic Truth Society.*

—— Katholische Wahrheit und protestantischer Irrthum in fünfzig Fragen und Antworten: Ein Controverskatechismus für's katholische Volk. pp. 168. *Regensburg*, 1846. 16°. **3911. a. 28.**

—— An Outline of the Catholic Truth. With meditations thereon. pp. xv. 118. *Joseph Masters: London*, 1873. 16°. **3504. aa. 56.**

CATHOLIC TRUTH QUARTERLY. *See* Dublin.— *Catholic Truth Society of Ireland.*

CATHOLIC TRUTH SOCIETY. Catholic Truth Society. *See* London.—III.

—— Catholic Truth Society of Hongkong. *See* Hongkong.

—— Catholic Truth Society of Ireland. *See* Dublin.

—— Catholic Truth Society of Scotland. *See* Edinburgh.

CATHOLIC UNION GAZETTE. *See* England.— *Catholic Union of Great Britain.*

CATHOLIC UNION OF GREAT BRITAIN. *See* England.

CATHOLIC UNION OF INTERNATIONAL STUDIES. [La Société internationale.] International Relations from a Catholic standpoint. [Edited by Eugène Beaupin.] Translated from the French. Edited [i.e. the translation edited] . . . by Stephen J. Brown. pp. xv. 199. *Browne & Nolan: Dublin*, 1932. 8°. **08425. de. 114.**

CATHOLIC UNITY. El Libro de la Unidad Católica. Año de 1876. [Papal and episcopal documents and speeches made in the Spanish Congress and Senate on the article of the proposed constitution concerning religious toleration.] (Apéndice. Noticia histórica de la unidad católica y de la libertad de cultos en España. [By F. de A. Aguilar.]) pp. clxxxii. 755. *Madrid*, 1877. 8°. **3900. h. 1.**

CATHOLIC UNITY.

—— Towards Catholic Unity. [1939– .] 8°. *S.P.C.K.: London*, **W.P. 5704.**

—— Tracts on Catholic Unity. By Members of the Church of England. no. 1–9. [1852, 53.] 8°. *James Darling: London*, **4107. d. 99.** *No more published.*

—— La Unidad Católica.—Dia de San Pedro Apóstol. pp. 4. [*Bogotá*, 1863.] 8°. **8179. e. 34. (28.)**

—— [Another copy.] **8179. e. 34. (49.)**

CATHOLIC UNIVERSITY. Catholic University of America. *See* Washington, D.C.

—— Catholic University of Ireland. *See* Dublin.

—— Catholic University of Peking. *See* Peking.

CATHOLIC UNIVERSITY GAZETTE. *See* Dublin. —*Catholic University of Ireland.*

CATHOLIC UNIVERSITY OF AMERICA STUDIES.

—— Catholic University of America Studies in Economics. *See* Washington, D.C.—*Catholic University of America.— School of Social Science.*

—— Catholic University of America Studies in Sociology. *See* Washington, D.C.—*Catholic University of America.— School of Social Science.*

CATHOLIC VETO. The Catholic Veto and the Irish Bishops. A reply to a lecture delivered [by Joseph V. Butler] at the Mansion House. Edited by Rev. Richard Fleming. pp. iv. 71. *M. H. Gill & Son: Dublin*, 1911. 8°. **4136. df. 11. (4.)**

CATHOLIC VINDICATOR. The Catholic Vindicator. (A weekly penny publication.) *See* Periodical Publications.—*London.*

—— The Catholic Vindicator, a weekly paper in reply to "The Protestant," *etc. See* Periodical Publications.— *London.*

CATHOLIC WEEKLY INSTRUCTOR. *See* Periodical Publications.—*Derby.*

CATHOLIC WHIT-FRIDAY PROCESSION. *See* Manchester.

CATHOLIC WHO'S WHO. Catholic Who's Who and Year-Book. *See* Periodical Publications.—*London.*

CATHOLIC WOMAN. The Catholic Woman's Outlook. *See* London.—III. *Catholic Women's League.*

CATHOLIC WOMEN. Catholic Women's League. [London] *See* London.—III.

—— Catholic Women's Missionary League. *See* London. —III.

—— Catholic Women's Suffrage Society. *See* London.—III.

CATHOLIC WOMEN'S LEAGUE MAGAZINE.

—— The Catholic Women's League Magazine. *See* London. —III. *Catholic Women's League.*

CATHOLIC WORKER.

—— The Catholic Worker. [New York.] *See* Periodical Publications.—*New York.*

CATHOLIC WORKER.

—— Catholic Worker. [Wigan.] [For the " Catholic Worker " newspaper, see the Catalogue of Newspapers.]

—— [For works published by the " Catholic Worker " :] *See* PERIODICAL PUBLICATIONS.—*Wigan.—Catholic Worker.*

CATHOLIC WORKER BULLETIN.

—— " Catholic Worker " Bulletin. *See* PERIODICAL PUBLICATIONS.—*Wigan.—Catholic Worker.*

CATHOLIC WORKER PAMPHLETS. *See* PERIODICAL PUBLICATIONS.—*Wigan.—Catholic Worker.*

CATHOLIC WORKERS' COLLEGE. *See* OXFORD.

CATHOLIC WORKERS MOVEMENT. Die katholische Arbeiterbewegung. *See* GERMANY.—*Verbandszentrale der katholischen Arbeitervereine Westdeutschlands.*

CATHOLIC WORLD. *See* PERIODICAL PUBLICATIONS.—*New York.*

CATHOLIC WORSHIP. Papers on Catholic Worship. no. 1. Vespers and Benediction of the Most Holy Sacrament. pp. 4. *Richardson & Son: Derby,* [1851.] 8°.
3475. c. 6.

No more published.

CATHOLIC YEAR.

—— The Catholic Year. *See* UNITED STATES OF AMERICA.—*National Council of Catholic Men.*

CATHOLIC YEAR BOOK. The Catholic Year Book and Clergy List. *See* PERIODICAL PUBLICATIONS.—*London.*

—— The Catholic Year Book for 1951 [*etc.*]. *See* PERIODICAL PUBLICATIONS.—*London.*

CATHOLIC YOUNG MEN. Catholic Young Men's Association. *See* SINGAPORE.

—— Catholic Young Men's Society. *See* ENGLAND.

CATHOLIC YOUTH.

—— Catholic Youth. Archdiocese of Birmingham. *See* BIRMINGHAM, *Archdiocese of.—Catholic Youth Council.*

—— Catholic Youth and Family. *See* PERIODICAL PUBLICATIONS.—*Durban.*

—— Manual of Prayers for the use of Catholic Youth, *etc.* [Translated by the Daughters of the Cross, with additions and alterations, from "Die heilige Messe" of the Rev. Dickmans, P. P.] [1892.] 8°. *See* DICKMANS ( ) *Rev., P.P.* 3456. dd. 19.

CATHOLICA, *Vera, pseud.* The Supremacy of the Holy Ghost; or, the Apostasies of the Church. [Signed: Vera Catholica.] pp. 4. [1880.] 8°. 764. m. 5. (19.)

CATHOLICA UNIVERSITAS OTTAWIENSIS. *See* OTTAWA.—*University of Ottawa.*

CATHOLICI. Catholici. *See* CATHOLICS.

—— Catholici angli. *See* ENGLISH CATHOLICS; ENGLAND.—*Catholics.*

—— Catholici anglicani. *See* ENGLISH CATHOLICS.

CATHOLICISM. Catholicism. [By John G. Francis.] pp. 15. *C. Goodall & Son: London,* 1851. 8°.
764. l. 17. (6.)

CATHOLICISM.

—— Catholicism or Ritualism ? A letter to ' A Ritualist ' in answer to that addressed by him to Monsignor Capel. By two Catholics. 1872. 8°. *See* RITUALIST.
3939. cc. 38.

—— Catholicism: or, several enquiries touching visible church-membership . . . By W. A. [i.e. William Allen.] 1683. 8°. *See* A., W. 4103. c. 52. (1.)

—— Catholicism versus the War, 1914–1918. [By G. Lanes.] *H. Slack & Co.: Lincoln,* [1940 ?] 8°. 1856. g. 3. (44.)

—— Catholicism without Popery; an essay to render the Church of England a means and a pattern of union to the Christian world. pp. 94. *For J. Lawrence: London,* 1699. 8°. 698. h. 12. (1.)

—— Le Catholicisme et le Protestantisme considérés sous le point de vue politique. pp. viii. 117. *Strasbourg,* 1823. 8°. 859. c. 26. (1.)

—— Il Cattolicismo e la demagogia italiana. pp. 69. *Roma,* [1850.] 8°. 4051. e. 8.

—— Il Cattolicismo vive ? ! . . . od è morto ? ! . . . Morirà ? ! . . . è abbattuto il Papato ? ! Pensieri di un vescovo italiano. pp. 175. *Roma,* 1877. 8°. 4050. aaa. 2.

—— The Coming Catholicism. By Six Anglican Priests, *etc.* pp. 79. *Robert Scott: London,* 1920. 8°. 4106. e. 65.

—— Historical Outlines of Political Catholicism : its papacy—prelacy—priesthood—people. [By William Bullen.] pp. xii. 220. *Chapman & Hall: London,* 1853. 8°.
3940. f. 59.

—— Katholicismus, Protestantismus und eine deutsche Nationalkirche. Den Katholiken und Protestanten Deutschlands gewidmet von B. v. H. [i.e. Bernhard Spiegel.] 1861. 8°. *See* H., B. v. 3914. aa. 28. (4.)

—— Der Katholicismus und der moderne Staat. Andeutungen zur richtigern Würdigung ihres gegenseitigen Verhältnisses, namentlich in Deutschland und Italien. pp. 123. *Berlin,* 1873. 8°. 3913. bb. 8.

—— Katholicismus und Protestantismus. Ein Wort zur Abwehr und Verständigung veranlasst durch neuere Vorgänge. Von einem evangelischen Geistlichen. pp. 24. *Darmstadt,* 1868. 8°. 3913. e. 1. (3.)

—— Kritische Geschichte der kirchlichen Unfehlbarkeit zur Beförderung einer freiern Prüfung des Katholizismus. [By F. A. Blau.] pp. xviii. 598. *Frankfurt,* 1791. 8°.
3911. aa. 30.

—— [Another copy.] 3911. a. 65.

—— La Morale indépendante et le Catholicisme. pp. 31. *Metz,* [1867.] 8°. 8467. g. 34. (3.)

—— On Modern Catholicism. [A sermon. By T. F. Dibdin.] pp. 14. *Edward Brewster: London,* [1840.] 8°.
C. 28. i. 13. (6.)

—— [Another copy.] G. 19798. (1.)
Privately printed.

—— Panorama des Katholicismus. Fassliche Darstellung des Inneren und Aeusseren der katholischen Kirche . . . Ein katholisches Conversations-Lexicon. Bd. 1. 2 pt. *Bonn,* 1846. 8°. 4530. a. 14. (1.)
No more published.

—— Studien über Katholizismus, Protestantismus und Gewissensfreiheit in Deutschland. [By Onno Klopp.] pp. vi. 472. *Schaffhausen,* 1857. 8°. 4650. b. 31.

CATHOLICISM.

—— Ueber die Perfectibilität des Katholicismus. Streitschriften zweier katholischer Theologen, zugleich ein Beitrag zur Aufhellung einiger wichtigen Begriffe aus Bolzano's Religionswissenschaft. pp. vii. 399. *Leipzig*, 1845. 8°.   **3910. dd. 36.**

CATHOLICISME. *See* CATHOLICISM.

—— Catholicisme romain. *See* ROMAN CATHOLICISM.

CATHOLICISME FRANÇAIS. *See* FRENCH CATHOLICISM.

CATHOLICITÉ.

—— Catholicité. Revue d'information et d'action, *etc. See* PERIODICAL PUBLICATIONS.—*Lille.*

CATHOLICITY. Catholicity: an aid thereto for those who already believe the truth of Holy Scripture. Compiled by a Catholic Priest. pp. 14.   *Burns & Oates: London*, [1877.] 12°.   **3940. de. 1. (9.)**

—— The Catholicity of the Church's Love, and the humility of her ceremonial. Four letters in reply to a devout layman. By an English Priest [i.e. Samuel B. Harper]. pp. 35. *Joseph Masters: London*, 1850. 12°.   **4107. a. 22.**

—— What is Catholicity? Articles and letters . . . Collected by W. W. 1916. 8°. *See* W., W. **3942. de. 45.**

CATHOLICK. *See* CATHOLIC.

CATHOLICK INTELLIGENCE. *See* PERIODICAL PUBLICATIONS.—*London.*

CATHOLICKE. *See* CATHOLIC.

CATHOLICKES. *See* CATHOLICS.

CATHOLICKS. *See* CATHOLICS.

CATHOLICON. The Catholicon. *See* PERIODICAL PUBLICATIONS.—*Birmingham.*

—— Catholicon; or, the Christian philosopher, *etc. See* PERIODICAL PUBLICATIONS.—*London.*

—— Catholicon abbreviatum. [A vocabulary in Latin and French.] 𝕲.𝔏. [*per martinum morin: Rothomagi*, ultima die Iunii, 1492.] 4°.   G. **7500.** 120 *leaves. Sig.* a–p⁸. *Double columns, 41 lines to a column. Imperfect, wanting the last eight leaves.*

—— Catholicon Anglicum, an English-Latin wordbook, dated 1483. Edited, from the Ms. No. 168 in the Library of Lord Monson, collated with the Additional Ms. 15, 562, British Museum, with introduction and notes, by Sidney J. H. Herrtage . . . With a preface by Henry B. Wheatley. pp. lii. 432.   *Published for the Early English Text Society, by N. Trübner & Co.: London*, 1881. 8°.   Ac. **9925/55.**

—— [Another copy.]   Ac. **9927/54.**

—— [A reissue.] Catholicon Anglicum, *etc.*   *Camden Society:* [*London,*] 1882. 8°.   Ac. **8113/121.**

—— Le Catholicon de Lille, glossaire latin-français, *etc.* 1886. 8°.   [*Académie Royale de Belgique. Mémoires couronnés, etc.* Collection in-8°. tom. 37.] *See* LILLE.   Ac. **985/4.**

CATHOLICOS, *pseud.* A Short Address to the Roman-Catholic Addressers. By Catholicos. pp. 16. *Dublin*, [1806.] 8°.   **3936. aa. 8.**

CATHOLICS. *See also* ENGLAND.—*Catholics.*

CATHOLICS.

—— The Admission of the Catholics into the Legislature inconsistent with constitutional principles, and of advantage to none but the priesthood. pp. 55.   *J. Hatchard & Son: London*, 1827. 8°.   T. **1190. (5.)**

—— Aduis, sur ce qui est a faire, tant contre les Catholiques simulez, que les ennemis ouuerts de l'Eglise Catholique Apostolique & Romaine. pp. 32.   *Chez N. Niuelle: Paris*, 1589. 8°.   **3900. aa. 47. (5.)**

—— Appel aux catholiques. Exposé des droits de la papauté. [By A. S. Rastoul de Mongeot.] pp. 45. *Bruxelles & Leipzig*, 1860. 8°.   **8033. c. 37. (7.)**

—— Aux catholiques. Jubilé du Concile 1869. Par l'abbé G. M. J. D. . . . Cinquième édition. 1869. 12°.   *See* D., G. M. J., *l'Abbé.*   **5017. a. 9.**

—— Aux catholiques. La grande question du jour, ou l'Église Catholique ou la Révolution. Par l'abbé G. M. J. D. . . . Deuxième édition. 1870. 12°.   *See* D., G. M. J., *l'Abbé.*   **3902. a. 64. (3.)**

—— L'Ave Maria des catholiques; avec sa suitte. [A satire in verse.] pp. 8. 1611. 8°.   **11475. d. 12.**

—— Avis aux catholiques et aux protestants. Petites confidences. pp. 16. *Paris*, 1858. 8°.   **3901. e. 48. (5.)**

—— Avis aux vrais catholiques, ou Conduite à tenir dans les circonstances actuelles, *etc.* (Seconde édition . . . augmentée par l'auteur.) pp. 26. *Paris*, 1791. 8°.   F.R. **151. (8.)**

—— Troisième édition, *etc.* pp. 29. *Paris*, 1791. 8°.   F. **144. (5.)**

—— A Brief Discours contayning certayne Reasons why Catholiques refuse to goe to Church. Written by a learned and vertuous man, to a frend of his in England. And dedicated by I. H. (John Howlet) [i.e. R. Parsons, the author] to the Queenes most excellent Maiestie. 𝔅.𝔏. ff. 70. *John Lyon: Doway*, 1580. 8°.   **698. b. 38.** *The running title of the volume is " The 1 Parte Contayning Reasons Of Refusal."*

—— [Another edition.] *Doway*, 1599. 16°.   **846. a. 31. (1.)**

—— [Another edition.] *Doway*, 1601. 12°.   **3932. a. 7·**

—— A Briefe Treatise in which is made playne, that Catholics living and dying in their profession, may be saued. Agaⁱnst a minister, N. E., who in his Epistle exhorteth an honourable person to forsake her ancient Catholike Roman religion, *etc.* [By William Wright.] 1623. 4°. *See* E., N.   C. **26. h. 19.**

—— The Case of the Catholics Considered; and an expedient proposed for the final settlement of it. With an appendix, containing remarks upon Mr. Reeves's pamphlet [entitled " Considerations upon the Coronation Oath "]. pp. 24. *H. D. Symonds: London*, 1801. 8°.   **108. f. 47.**

—— Catechismus Catholicorum, per imagines pro ignorantibus, qui litteras nesciunt, expressus. Catholischer Catechismus, *etc.* [By J. C. Haffner.] *Lat. & Ger. Augspurg*, 1709. 12°.   **555. a. 12.** *Engraved throughout.*

—— Catholics and Roman Catholics. *E. Longhurst: London*, [1872.] *s. sh.* 8°.   **4405. k. 1. (75.)**

—— Catholics and the Bible. pp. 12. *Catholic Truth Society: London*, 1921. 8°.   **3943. aa. 11.**

CATHOLICS.

—— The Catholicks Defence for their Adoration of the Body and Blood of our Lord . . . in the holy sacrament of the Eucharist. [By Abraham Woodhead.] pp. 38.
[*Obadiah Walker:*] *Oxford*, 1687. 4°. [*Two Discourses concerning the adoration of our B. Saviour, etc.*] T. **1973**. (1.)

—— Catholics face the World Crisis. (An international Catholic manifesto.) [Translated from the French.] pp. 13. [1943.] 8°. *See* ENGLAND.—*Sword of the Spirit.*
3942. aa. **64.**

—— Catholics in Singapore. [c. 1950.] 8°. *See* GOH (Charles S.)
4716. aa. **64.**

—— Católicos y Conservadores. pp. 228.
Madrid, 1885. 8°. **8042**. aaa. **8.**

—— Los Católicos y los judíos . . . Escritos de Dr. Mariano Alcour, Rev. Gregory Feige, Padre Pierre Charles. 11ª edición. pp. 47. *México*, 1952. 8°. **4035**. aa. **89.**

—— Cattolici e Italiani. [A political pamphlet.] pp. 30.
Roma, 1879. 8°. **8032**. cc. **10.** (8.)

—— A Conference of the Catholike and Protestante Doctrine with the expresse words of Holie Scripture. Which is the second parte of the Prudentiall Balance of Religion. Wherein is . . . shewed, that in more then 260. points of controuersie, Catholiks agree with the holie Scripture, both in words and sense: and Protestants disagree in both . . . Written first in Latin, but now augmented and translated into English. [A translation of " Collatio doctrinæ Catholicorum ac Protestantium, *etc.*," by Richard Smith, Bishop of Chalcedon.] pp. 798. *By the widdowe of Marke Wyon: Doway*, 1631. 4°. **3935**. dd. **4.**
Part I is entered under CATHOLIC RELIGION.

—— Le Confiteor des catholiques. [A satire, in verse.] pp. 8. 1611. 8°. **11475**. d. **13.**

—— La Consolation des catholiques, dans les maux causés par le schisme à l'Église & à la France. Lettre d'un curé déplacé du diocèse de Meaux, à ses paroissiens fidèles. pp. 15. *Paris*, 1792. 8°. F.R. **158.** (7.)

—— A Consolatory Letter to all the afflicted Catholikes in England. [Signed: H. B.] [1590?] 8°. *See* B., H.
3939. aa. **17.**

—— Corpus Catholicorum. Werke katholischer Schriftsteller im Zeitalter der Glaubensspaltung. *Münster i. W.*, 1919– . 8°. W.P. **5182.**

—— Le Credo des catholiques, en suite du Pater Noster. [A satire, in verse.] pp. 7. 1611. 8°. **901.** a. **17.** (6.)

—— [Another edition.] pp. 7. [1611?] 8°. **11475**. d. **14.**

—— De la liberté de l'Église et des droits des Catholiques. Troisièmes documents. 1848. 8°. *See* SWITZERLAND.—*Roman Catholic Church.* **3901**. f. **34.**

—— Einladung an alle Katholiken, durch vereintes Gebet von Gott die Wiedervereinigung Deutschlands im wahren Glauben zu erflehen. pp. 32. *Regensburg*, 1844. 12°.
1219. e. **33.**

—— Entretiens pacifiques de deux nouveaux catholiques. [By D. A. de Brueys.] pp. 134. *P. Roeland: Straesbourg*, 1686. 12°. **3900**. a. **25.**
P. 119 is slightly mutilated.

—— Épître aux vrais catholiques. [On the civil constitution of the clergy.] pp. 23. [1791.] 8°. F.R. **151.** (9.)

CATHOLICS

—— Exhortation aux vrais catholiques, pour passer saintement le Carême, et se disposer à la Pâque. [By A. F. X. Mainaud de Pancemont, Bishop of Vannes.] pp. 15.
Paris, 1792. 8°. F. **165.** (9.)

—— Five Letters on the Grievances of Catholics. By a Student of Lincoln's Inn. pp. 24. *Thomas Davison: London*, 1819. 8°. T. **2009.** (3.)

—— Der göttliche Glaubensweg für Katholiken und Nichtkatholiken . . . Von einem wahren Altkatholiken. Achte Auflage. pp. 111. *Wien*, 1874. 16°. **4372**. b. **17.** (11.)

—— Holy Readings, giving the cream of many books in one, hopeful and good for all Catholics everywhere. By the author of " Catholic Hours." Fourth edition.
pp. viii. 396. *R. Washbourne: London*, [1868.] 32°.
4411. aa. **8.**

—— Instructions and Advice to Catholicks upon occasion of the late earthquakes. pp. 8. [*London?*] 1750. 8°.
4405. dd. **5.**

—— Katholiken ! Was hat man aus Eurer Religion gemacht ? pp. 16. *Bonn*, [1874?] 16°. **3913**. de. **1.** (1.)

—— Die Katholiken als Verehrer der Heiligen, ihrer Reliquien und Bilder vor dem Richterstuhl der Vernunft und des Christenthums . . . Von einem kathol. Geistlichen der Diözese Trier [i.e. J. H. Schmitz]. pp. 23. *Trier*, 1845. 8°. **3910**. c. **23.**

—— Katholiken, lasst euch nicht in die Irre führen ! Ein kurzes Wort zur Belehrung und Aufklärung über das unfehlbare Lehramt der Kirche. pp. 20. *Soest*, 1870. 8°. **3913**. a. **64.** (10.)

—— Katolicy a nowy ustrój świata. pp. 15. *London*, [1942.] 8°. [*Wydawnictwa Polskiej Misji Katolickiej.* no. 1.] W.P. **424/1.**

—— A Little Catechism for Little Catholics. pp. 35.
Griffith & Farran: London, 1893. 8°. **3504**. dg. **25.** (3.)

—— Manuel des catholiques pour les dangers du schisme actuel. pp. 31. [*Paris*, 1791.] 8°. F.R. **151.** (10.)

—— Moyens pour les catholiques persécutés, contre les torts et les rigueurs de la persécution. pp. 29. *Paris*, [1791.] 8°. F. **172.** (5.)

—— Le Pater Noster des catholiques. [A satire, in verse.] pp. 8. 1611. 8°. **11475**. d. **15.**

—— [Another edition.] pp. 8. [1612?] 8°.
11452. aaa. **9.**

—— Principia juris publici ecclesiastici Catholicorum, ad statum Germaniæ accommodata, *etc.* [By G. C. Neller.] pp. 286. *Francofurti & Lipsiæ*, 1768. 8°. **877**. g. **9.**

—— The Progenie of Catholicks and Protestants. Whereby on the one side is proved the lineal descent of Catholicks . . . from the holie Fathers of the Primitive Church . . . And on the other, the never-being of Protestants, *etc.* [By Lawrence Anderton.] 5 pt. *Widow of N. Courant: Rouen*, 1633. 4°. **3936**. g. **9.**

—— The Real Principles of Catholicks: or, a Catechism for the adult . . . By J— H—, C. A - D. S. [i.e. John Hornihold.] 1749. 8°. *See* H—, J—, C. A - D. S.
1353. c. **5.**

—— [Another edition.] 1773. 8°. *See* H—, J—, C. A - D. S.
3504. b. **51.**

CATHOLICS.

—— Rechtfertigung der gemischten Ehen zwischen Katholiken und Protestanten . . . Von einem Katholischen Geistlichen [i.e. Johann Christian Müller]; mit einer Vorrede von . . . Leander van Ess. pp. 221.   *Köln,* 1821. 8°.   **5175. c. 54.**

—— Religious Union; being a sketch of a Plan for uniting the Catholics and Presbyterians with the Established Church. pp. 24.   *J. Mawman: London,* 1801. 8°.   **695 g. 20. (3.)**

—— [Another copy.]   **B. 694. (8.)**

—— Remonstrance à tous bons et vrais catholiques, lesquels veulent sonstenir [*sic*] et maintenir nostre mere saincte Eglise, contre les faulx Heretiques de ce temps. De Vailly le 7. Feburier 1589. pp. 19.   *D. Binet: [Paris,]* 1589. 8°.   **1192. e. 92. (3.)**

—— Réponse à deux questions importants, relatives à la conduite que les catholiques doivent tenir dans les circonstances présentes . . . Par un prêtre catholique. pp. 56. [1791.] 8°.   **F. 125. (6.)**

—— Responce aux calomnies proposez contre les catholiques. pp. 59. [1588?] 8°.   **1192. e. 40.**

—— Lo Scisma non è una minaccia dei rivoluzionari ma un timore giustissimo dei cattolici. Avvertenze di un prete cattolico [i.e. Carlo Passaglia]. pp. 51.   *Torino,* 1861. 8°.   **3901. bb. 51. (3.)**

—— Stimmen zur Orientirung der Katholiken in Kirche und Staat. 2 Bd.   *Wien,* 1863. 8°.   **3911. a. 18.**

—— Tales for Young Catholics. (Tales for the Young.) 9 pt.   *T. Richardson & Sons: London,* [1877–85.] 8°.   **4413. ee. 59.**

—— Die tweede Gazette van Blyschap des Maents Mey, over verscheyden Victorien der catholijcken, *etc.* pp. 6.   *A. Verhoeuen: t'Hantwerpen,* 1621. 4°.   [*Gazette of Antwerp,* 1621, no. 81.]   **P.P.3444.af.(237.)**

—— Die Vereinigung der Katholiken und Protestanten. Eine Bibelschrift für die ganze Christenheit, *etc.* pp. 15.   *Stuttgart,* 1845. 8°.   **3910. e. 22.**

—— La Vérité sur la confession auriculaire. Aux catholiques et aux protestants. pp. 79.   *Lyon,* 1861. 8°.   **3901. bb. 51. (2.)**

—— We Catholics! I. Critical Catholics. II. Concerning the Clergy. III. Concerning the Laity. IV. Pull Together. pp. 32.   *Burns & Oates: London,* [1885.] 8°.   **3940. h. 12. (3.)**

—— We Catholics, Bishops, Priests & People. By one of them. pp. 12.   *Kegan Paul & Co.: London,* [1904.] 8°.   **3942. de. 5. (7.)**

—— Why do Catholics Believe? pp. 24.   *Catholic Truth Society of Ireland: Dublin,* [1944.] 8°.   **3942. eee. 77.**

—— Wo soll das hinaus? Ein freies Wort zur Warnung für besonnene Katholiken von einem deutschen Theologen [i.e. Gerhard Schneemann]. pp. 16.   *Paderborn,* 1870. 8°.   **3911. aa. 39.**

CATHOLICUM.

—— [Catholicum paruum.] [fol. 2 *recto:* A la premiere lettre de abc, *etc.*]   *pour maistre Loijs garbin: genue,* le .xv. jour de Iuin, 1487. 4°.   **IA. 38439.**
   120 *leaves, the last blank, the first perhaps bearing a title. Sig.* a–p⁸. *Double columns,* 39 *lines to a column. Imperfect; wanting quires* a–c *and* e, *and sig.* d1, d8, f1, f8, p1 *and* p8.

CATHOLICUM.

—— Catholicum paruum.   [*Engelhart Schultis? : Lyons?* c. 1490?] 4°.   **IA. 42021.**
   126 *leaves, the last blank. Sig.* a–o⁸ p⁶ q⁸. *Double columns,* 36 *lines to a column.*

CATHOLICUS, *pseud.*   *See also* CATHOLICOS, *pseud.*

—— A Caution against the Educational Writings of Edward Clodd . . . By Catholicus. pp. 51.   *J. F. Shaw & Co.: London,* 1880. 8°.   **4372. df. 10. (3.)**

—— The Claims of Liberal Anglicanism. By Catholicus. pp. 96.   *Burns, Oates & Co.: London,* 1922. 8°.   **4106. f. 50.**

—— Comments on "Christian Unitarianism . . . The third edition." By Catholicus. pp. 42.   *G. W. Fulcher: Sudbury,* 1836. 12°.   **4226. e. 8.**

—— The Doctrine of Justification and the Harmony of the Apostles Paul and James considered, with particular reference to the treatise of Bishop O'Brien entitled " An attempt to explain and establish the doctrine of justification by faith only." In three letters [signed: Catholicus] reprinted from the British Magazine, *etc.* pp. 40.   *Rivingtons: London,* 1862. 8°.   **4256. aa. 12.**

—— The Irish University Question: its history and its solution. By "Catholicus." pp. iv. 56.   *Simpkin, Marshall & Co.: London,* 1905. 8°.   **8308. f. 48.**

—— L'Irlanda nella sua condizione attuale. [Signed: Catholicus.] pp. 12.   *Roma,* 1887. 8°.   **8139. ff. 6. (2.)**

—— The Jews' Disability Bill considered. [Signed: Catholicus.] [1848.] 4°.   **764. n. 12. (4.)**

—— A Letter to the Rev. Lord Charles Thynne, in answer to his " Letter to his late parishioners." By Catholicus. pp. 73.   *F. & J. Rivington: London,* 1853. 8°.   **3940. f. 44.**

—— Letters between Catholicus and Anglo-Catholicus, upon the innovations at Keswick . . . Reprinted from the " Kendal Mercury." pp. 67.   *Kendal,* 1855. 12°.   **4108. a. 21.**

CATHOLICUS, *pseud.* [i.e. HENRY COTTON.] Notes on the Preface to the Rhemish Testament, printed in Dublin, 1813. [By Catholicus.] pp. v. 154.   *Printed for the Author: Dublin,* 1817. 8°.   **1117. g. 8.**

CATHOLICUS, *pseud.* [i.e. Cardinal HENRY EDWARD MANNING.] Dr. Nicholson's Accusation of the Archbishop of Westminster. (Reprinted from the "Tablet.") [In reference to his sermon on the Devotion of the Sacred Heart.] By Catholicus. pp. ii. 81.   *Burns & Oates: London,* [1873.] 8°.   **4136. aa. 46.**

CATHOLICUS, *pseud.* [i.e. HENRY PORTSMOUTH.] An Essay on the Simplicity of Truth; being an attempt to ascertain the use and extent of discipline, in the Church of Christ; to which is added, a postscript on tithes. Particularly addressed to the people called Quakers; by Catholicus. pp. viii. 81.   *E. & C. Dilly: London,* 1779. 8°.   **T. 354. (6.)**

—— *See* PHIPPS (Joseph) Cursory Observations on a late Publication, intitled, " An Essay on the Simplicity of Truth," signed Catholicus. 1779. 8°.   **855. g. 13. (4.)**

CATHOLICUS, *pseud.* [i.e. Cardinal JOHN HENRY NEWMAN.] The Tamworth Reading Room. Letters on an address delivered by Sir Robert Peel, Bart., on the establishment of a reading room at Tamworth. By Catholicus. Originally published in the Times, and since revised . . . by the author. pp. 42.   *John Mortimer: London,* 1841. 8°.   **722. g. 17.**

CATHOLICUS, *pseud.* [i.e. JOSEPH MENDHAM.] The Episcopal Oath of Allegiance to the Pope in the Church of Rome . . . in its original and in its latest form; the latter translated into English: with some remarks in particular upon what is called the persecuting clause. By Catholicus. pp. 38. *F. C. & J. Rivington: London,* [1822.] 8º. **701. e. 19. (14.)**

CATHOLICUS, *pseud.* [i.e. WILLIAM MATTHEWS.] A New and Seasonable Address to the Disciplinarians of the people called Quakers, relative to tithes and taxes. By Catholicus. Second edition. pp. 32. [*London ?*] 1798. 8º. **5155. aa. 55.**

—— *See* CRYPTONYMUS, *pseud.* A Brief Reply to Catholicus's Seasonable Address to Disciplinarians. 1798. 12º. **T. 457. (4.)**

CATHOLICUS, *Verus, pseud.* The Apostolic " Eirenicon "; or Papal " Primacy " a Figment. [In reply to E. B. Pusey.] . . . By Catholicus Verus. pp. 62. *W. H. Kelly & Bro.: New York,* 1866. 16º. **4051. aa. 6.**

CATHOLICUS, *Verus, pseud.* [i.e. ANDREW CARMICHAEL.] A Letter to the Roman Catholic Clergy of Ireland, on the primary doctrine of revealed religion, and the purity of the early Irish Church. By Catholicus Verus. pp. 68. xxiv. *R. Hunter: London,* 1824. 8º. **3938. e. 28.**

CATHOLICUS ECCLESIASTES. *See* CATHOLIC CLERGYMAN.

CATHOLICUS (CHRISTIANUS) *pseud.* [A letter beginning: " Monsieur, voyant dans votre avant dernière qu'un chanoine de votre Cathédrale étoit occupé à mettre les canonistes à contribution en faveur du triumvirat de Gand," *etc.* and signed: " Christianus mihi nomen, Catholicus cognomen."] [1813?] 8º. **1356. d. 10. (3.)** *Cropped.*

CATHOLICUS (MERCURIUS) *pseud. See* MERCURIUS, *Catholicus.*

CATHOLICUS (NICOCLES) *pseud. See* NICOCLES, *Catholicus.*

CATHOLICUS (PETER) *pseud.* The Virgin Mary: her pedigree and relations. By Peter Catholicus. Reprinted from the " Theological Quarterly Magazine," *etc.* pp. 32. *Darling & Son: London,* 1877. 8º. **4829. b. 24. (1.)**

CATHOLICUS (PHILALETHES) *pseud. See* PHILALETHES, *Catholicus.*

CATHOLICUS (PRESBYTER) *pseud.* [i.e. WILLIAM HARNESS.] *See* PRESBYTER, *Catholicus.*

CATHOLICUS (TESTIS-MUNDUS) *pseud.* [i.e. EDMUND HALL.] *See* TESTIS-MUNDUS, *Catholicus.*

CATHOLIJCKEN. *See* CATHOLICS.

CATHOLIKE. *See* CATHOLIC.

CATHOLIKES. *See* CATHOLICS.

CATHOLIQUE. *See also* CATHOLIC.

—— Le Catholique. *See* PERIODICAL PUBLICATIONS.—*Paris,*

—— Le Catholique français. Organe de l'Église catholique gallicane. *See* FRANCE.—*Église Catholique Gallicane.*

—— Catholique néerlandais. *See* DUTCH CATHOLIC.

—— Catholique romain. *See* ROMAN CATHOLIC.

CATHOLIQUES. *See* CATHOLICS.

—— Catholiques anglais. *See* ENGLISH CATHOLICS; ENGLAND.—*Catholics.*

CATHOLISCHE ANLEITUNG. *See* CATHOLIC GUIDE.

CATHOLISCHE EYDGENOSSEN. *See* CATHOLIC CONFEDERATES.

CATHOLISCHER. *See* CATHOLIC.

CATHOLISCHER LUTHERANER. *See* CATHOLIC LUTHERAN.

CATHOLISCHES GLAUBENS-BEKENNTNISS. *See* CATHOLIC CONFESSION OF FAITH.

CATHOLISCHES TISCH-GESPRAECH. *See* CATHOLIC TABLE-TALK.

CATHOLONGNE. *See* CATALONIA.

CATHOMEN (JOSEPH)

—— Familienschutz im schweizerischen Strafgesetzbuch. Dissertation, *etc.* pp. ix. 190. *Disentis,* 1944. 8º. **5549. g. 60.**

CATHON (DIONYSIUS) *See* CATO.

CATHOYS (JULES DE) *See* ARIA (d') Contes merveilleux traduits du russe par M. d'Aria, *etc.* [With an introduction by J. de Cathoys.] 1887. 8º. **12806. s. 17.**

CATHRALL (WILLIAM) *See* DIRECTORIES.—*Municipal.* The Municipal Corporations Directory, 1866. [Edited by W. Cathrall.] 1866. 8º. **P.P.2486.bed.**

—— A Guide through North Wales, including Anglesey, Caernarvonshire, Denbighshire, Flintshire . . . with the adjacent borders . . . Designed to accompany the Ordnance maps . . . With a notice of the geology of the country, by A. C. Ramsay. pp. xii. 334. *Edward Stanford: London,* 1860. 8º. **10369. b. 27.**

—— The History of North Wales, comprising a topographical description of the several counties . . . To which is prefixed a review of the history of Britain, from the Roman period to the Saxon Heptarchy, *etc.* [With plates.] 2 vol. *J. Gleave & Sons: Manchester,* 1828. 4º. **578. h. 6.**

—— The History of Oswestry . . . with notices of botany, geology, statistics, angling and biography . . . Illustrated with wood-engravings . . . after sketches by Mr. R. Cruikshank. pp. 294. *George Lewis: Oswestry,* [1855.] 8º. **10368. f. 3.**

—— The Illustrated Hand-book to North Wales . . . Edited by W. F. Peacock, *etc.* [With a map.] pp. xlviii. 184. *Catherall & Prichard: Chester,* [1868.] 8º. **10369. b. 19.**

—— Wanderings in North Wales; a road and railway guide-book, *etc.* [With maps and plates.] pp. xxx. 264. *W. S. Orr & Co.: London,* [1851.] 8º. **10370. a. 40.**

CATHREIN (VICTOR) The Champions of Agrarian Socialism. A refutation of E. de Laveleye and Henry George . . . Translated, revised, and enlarged by . . . J. U. Heinzle [from " Ein Vorkämpfer des Agrarsocialismus " and " Das Privatgrundeigenthum im Lichte des Naturrechts," contributed by V. Cathrein to " Stimmen aus Maria-Laach," Bd. 22 and 23 respectively]. pp. 125. *P. Paul & Bro.: Buffalo,* 1889. 8º. **8275. aa. 50.**

—— Die Aufgaben der Staatsgewalt und ihre Grenzen, *etc.* pp. iv. 147. *Freiburg i B.,* 1882. 8º. [*Stimmen aus Maria-Laach.* Ergänzungshefte. no. 21.] **P.P. 86. k.**

—— Die Einheit des sittlichen Bewusstseins der Menschheit. Eine ethnographische Untersuchung. 3 Bd. *Freiburg i. B.,* 1914. 8º. **10006. s. 8.**

—— Die englische Verfassung. Eine rechtsgeschichtliche Skizze. pp. 123. *Freiburg i. B.,* 1881. 8º. [*Stimmen aus Maria-Laach.* Ergänzungshefte. no. 15.] **P.P. 86. k.**

CATHREIN (VICTOR)

—— Glauben und Wissen. Eine Orientierung in mehreren religiösen Grundproblemen der Gegenwart für alle Gebildeten . . . Zweite und dritte, unveränderte Auflage. pp. vi. 245. *Freiburg i. B.*, 1903. 8°. **4380. h. 16.**

—— Vierte und fünfte, bedeutend vermehrte Auflage. pp. ix. 305. *Freiburg i. B.*, 1911. 8°. **4374. b. 3.**

—— Die Grundlage des Völkerrechts. pp. 108. *Freiburg i. B.*, 1918. 8°. [*Stimmen der Zeit.* Ergänzungshefte. Reihe 1. Hft. 5.] **P.P. 86. k.**

—— Die katholische Moral in ihren Voraussetzungen und ihren Grundlinien. Ein Wegweiser in den Grundfragen des sittlichen Lebens für alle Gebildeten. pp. xiv. 545. *Freiburg i. B.*, 1907. 8°. **4403. gg. 1.**

—— Moralphilosophie. Eine wissenschaftliche Darlegung der sittlichen, einschliesslich der rechtlichen, Ordnung. 2 Bd. *Freiburg i. B.*, 1890, 91. 8°. **8467. h. 15.**

—— Fünfte, neu durchgearbeitete Auflage. 2 Bd. *Freiburg i. B.*, 1911. 8°. **8409. m. 19.**

—— Socialism Exposed and Refuted . . . A chapter from the author's Moral Philosophy. From the German by Rev. J. Conway. pp. 164. *Benziger Bros.: New York*, 1892. 8°. **08275. e. 25.**

—— Philosophia Moralis. In usum scholarum. [An abridgment of " Moralphilosophie."] pp. x. 396. *Friburgi Brisgoviae*, 1893. 8°. **8409. h. 20.**

—— Recht, Naturrecht und positives Recht. Eine kritische Untersuchung der Grundbegriffe der Rechtsordnung. Zweite . . . Auflage. pp. vii. 327. *Freiburg i. B*, 1909. 8°. **06005. ee. 18.**

—— Religion und Moral, oder Gibt es eine Moral ohne Gott? Eine Untersuchung des Verhältnisses der Moral zur Religion. pp. v. 142. *Freiburg i. B.*, 1900. 8°. [*Stimmen aus Maria-Laach.* Ergänzungshefte. no. 75.] **P.P. 86. k.**

—— Die Sittenlehre des Darwinismus. Eine Kritik der Ethik Herbert Spencers. pp. x. 146. *Freiburg i. B.*, 1885. 8°. [*Stimmen aus Maria-Laach.* Ergänzungshefte. no. 29.] **P.P. 86. k.**

—— Sozialdemokratie und Christentum, oder Darf ein Katholik Sozialdemokrat sein? pp. 29. *Freiburg i. B.*, 1919. 8°. **08276. g. 66.**

—— Der Socialismus. Eine Untersuchung seiner Grundlagen und seiner Durchführbarkeit . . . Fünfte . . . vermehrte Auflage, *etc.* pp. xvi. 198. *Freiburg i. B.*, 1892. 12°. **08276. f. 34.**

—— Neunte, bedeutend vermehrte Auflage. pp. xvi. 438. *Freiburg i. B.*, 1906. 8°. **08275. aaa. 71.**

—— Vierzehnte bis sechzehnte Auflage. pp. xii. 358. *Freiburg i. B.*, 1923. 8°. **08286. cc. 64.**

—— Het Socialisme. [Translated by P. J. M. Aalberse.] pp. xii. 338. *Leiden*, 1905. 8°. **08275. aaa. 56.**

CATHREW (GRAVES) *See* IRELAND.—*Courts of Law and Equity.* Irish Common Law Reports . . . By J. S. Armstrong . . . G. Cathrew, *etc.* [1852, *etc.*] 8°. [MISSING.]

CATHREY (THOMAS CHARLES) Rosabel: and Helvetia: poems in two cantos each. pp. 71. *W. J. Cleaver: London*, 1840. 12°. **1164. l. 44.**

CATI (HERCOLE) *See* LIPSIUS (Justus) Della politica . . . libri sei . . . tradotti . . . dal . . . Sig. Cavalier H. Cati, *etc.* 1618. 4°. **8009. f. 18.**

CATI (LODOVICO) *See* LIPSIUS (Justus) Della politica . . . libri sei, *etc.* [Edited by L. Cati.] 1618. 4°. **8009. f. 18.**

CATIA (JOANNES FRANCISCUS) *Count.* *See* CACCIA (Giovanni F.) *Count.*

CATIANUS (GABRIEL) De eo quod interest syntagma. *See* TRACTATUS. Primum [*etc.*] volumen tractatuum, *etc* vol. 8. 1549. fol. **5305. i.**

—— [Another edition.] 1753. *See* MEERMAN (G.) Novus thesaurus juris civilis, *etc.* tom. 7. 1751, *etc.* fol. **18. h. 12.**

ĆATIB-ČELEBIJA. *See* MUŚŢAFĀ IBN 'ABD ALLĀH, called KATIB CHELEBĪ, *etc.*

CATICHIMA. Catichima edo Fedea laburzki, Paul-Thérèse-David d'Astros, Bayonaco Jaun Aphezpicuaren manuz imprimatua; hau bakharric irakhatsia içaiteco Diocesa gucian. pp. x. 132. *Bayonan,* [1842.] 12°. **872. d. 4.**

—— [Another edition.] pp. x. 132. *Bayonan,* [1842 ?] 12°. **872. e. 40.**

—— [Another edition.] pp. x. 132. *Bayonan,* [1855.] 12°. **3505. bbb. 44.**

—— Catichima edo Fedea laburzki François-Antoine Jauffret Baionaco Jaun Aphezpicuac publicatua bere diocesan bakharric iracatsia izaiteco. pp. vii. 135. *Baionan,* 1902. 16°. **3506. aa. 59.**

CATIFORIS (S. J.) *See* KATEPHORES (S. I.)

CATIFORO (ANTONIO) *See* KATEPHOROS (Antonios)

CATIGNANO (GIOVANNI) *See* GIOVANNI, *dalle Celle.*

CATILINA (LUCIUS SERGIUS) *See* BANG (Jens G.) Catilina, *etc.* 1902. 8°. **09039. dd. 9.**

—— *See* BEESLY (Edward S.) Catiline, Clodius and Tiberius. 1878. 8°. **10606. bb. 51.**

—— *See* BLONDEL (J. E.) Histoire économique de la conjuration de Catilina. 1893. 8°. **9041. g. 16.**

—— *See* BOISSIER (M. L. A. G.) La Conjuration de Catilina. 1905. 8°. **09039. bb. 10.**

—— *See* BRUECKNER (C. A. F.) Cicero num Catilinam repetundarum reum defendit? 1844. 4°. **9004. l. 1. (1.)**

—— *See* CAMPANACIUS (J. M.) Genuensis Reip. motus a J. A. Flisco excitatus, eiusdem et L. Sergii Catilinæ comparatio. 1588. 4°. **661. b. 9.**

—— [For editions of Cicero's Orations against Catiline :] *See* CICERO (M. T.) [*Orations.—In L. Sergium Catilinam.*]

—— *See* FELICIUS (C.) *Durantinus.* C. Felicii Durantini . . . ad Leonem x præfatio. Ejusdem . . . de coniuratione L. Catilinæ liber vnus. 1518. 4°. **803. e. 1.**

—— *See* FELICIUS (C.) *Durantinus.* The Conspiracie of Catiline . . . Translated bi T. Paynell, *etc.* 1557. 4°. **C. 13. a. 3.**

—— *See* FRISCH (H.) Den første catilinariske Sammensværgelse. En Studie i historiske Gisninger. 1947. 8°. [*Studier fra Sprog- og Oldtidsforskning.* no. 202.] **Ac. 9877/2.**

—— *See* HAGEN (E.) *Professor, etc.* Untersuchungen über römische Geschichte . . . Erster Theil. Catilina. 1854. 8°. **9039. h. 9.**

CATILINA (Lucius Sergius)

—— See HARDY (Ernest G.) The Catilinarian Conspiracy in its Context: a re-study of the evidence. 1924. 8°.
9042. b. 8.

—— See PARETI (L.) La Congiura di Catilina, etc. 1934. 8°.
9042. aaa. 16.

—— See ROMAN HISTORIES. Le Summaire et Recueil des histoires Rommaines . . . et de la tres cruelle coniuration de Luce Cathilin, etc. 1532. fol.
1308. l. 10.

—— [For editions of Sallust's account of the Conspiracy of Catiline:] See SALLUSTIUS CRISPUS (C.)

—— See SCHOENBRUNN (W.) Erziehung zum kritischen Denken bei der Lektüre lateinischer Klassiker. (Ciceros I. Catilinarische Rede.) 1921. 8°.
8313. aa. 27/2.

—— See SPECK (H. B. G.) Katilina im Drama der Weltliteratur, etc. 1906. 8°.
011853. bb. 1/4.

—— See STERN (Ernst von) Catilina und die Parteikämpfe in Rom der Jahre 66–63, etc. 1883. 8°.
9041. bb. 22.

—— See WIRZ (H.) Catilina's und Cicero's Bewerbung um das Konsulat, etc. 1864. 8°.
9039. c. 2.

—— [For editions of the spurious speeches of Catiline issued with editions of Cicero's Catiline Orations:] See CICERO (M. T.) [Orations.—In L. Sergium Catilinam.]

—— [For editions issued with the works of Sallust:] See SALLUSTIUS CRISPUS (C.)

—— Lucij Sergij Catilinæ in M. Tullium Ciceronem responsiuæ inuectiuæ duæ. See CICERO (M. T.) [Supposititious Works.—In L. Sergium Catilinam Oratio Quinta.] M. Tul. Ciceronis in L. Catilinam inuectiua oratio, etc. 1551. 4°.
G. 9325. (2.)

—— Catiline. An historical tragedy in three acts. [In verse.] By the author of the Indian Merchant. pp. 39. Moore: London, 1833. 8°.
11779. f. 21.

—— Catiline his Conspiracy. A tragœdie. The author B. J. [i.e. Ben Jonson.] 1669. 4°. See J., B.
1346. d. 8.

—— [Another edition.] 1674. 4°. See J., B.
640. k. 30.

—— The Conspiracie of Lucius Catiline. [By C. Felicius, Durantinus.] Translated into englishe by Thomas Paynell, etc. ℬ.𝔏. ff. 74. In officina Thomae Bertheleti: Londini, 1541. 4°.
Huth 152.

—— [For editions of " The Conspirators; or, the Case of Catiline, etc.," a satire on the directors of the South Sea Company:] See BRITANNICUS, pseud. [i.e. Thomas Gordon.]

—— [For editions of " The Conspirators; or the Case of Catiline. Part II. By the author of the first part," i.e. Thomas Gordon:] See CONSPIRATORS.

—— [For editions of the anonymous " Declamatio contra L. Ser. Catilinam," formerly ascribed to M. Porcius Latro, included in editions of the works of Sallust:] See SALLUSTIUS CRISPUS (C.)

—— Declamatio in Lucium Sergium Catilinam, eine Schuldeklamation aus der römischen Kaiserzeit. Nach einer Münchener Handschrift des XV. Jahrhunderts herausgegeben von Dr. Heinrich Zimmerer. Tl. 1. pp. 80. München, 1888. 8°.
11396. bb. 2.
No more published.

—— Histoire de la conjuration de Catilina, où l'on a inséré les Catilinaires de Cicéron. [By Isaac Bellet.] pp. xiv. 285 [385]. Paris, 1752. 8°.
9041. a. 24.

CATILINA (Lucius Sergius)

—— The History of Catiline's Conspiracy : faithfully related out of the classical authors. With some general observations for assisting the interests of peace and virtue. pp. 183. Hen. Hills Jun. for Robert Boulter : London, 1683. 8°.
1482. aaa. 7.

—— The History of Catiline's Conspiracy [by Sallust], with the four [Catilinarian] Orations of Cicero; to which are added notes and illustrations . . . by G. F. Sydney. pp. xv. 283. T. N. Longman: London, 1795. 8°.
9039. ccc. 12.

—— Réflexions sur Catilina et sa conjuration. [Against the establishment of a republic in France.] pp. [143]–151. [1792.] 8°.
R. 211. (3.)
Imperfect ; wanting all before p. 143.

CATILINARIAE PRODITIONES. See CATILINARIAN TREASONS.

CATILINARIAN TREASONS. In. Catilinarias proditiones, ac proditores domesticos odæ 6. Ex officina Iosephi Barnesii: Oxoniæ, 1586. 12°.
C. 59. fff. 10.

CATILINE. See CATILINA (L. S.)

CATILLO, Mount. Brevi cenni sul traforo del Monte Catillo eseguito in Tivoli per la diversione dell'Aniene. (Petit essai sur le percement du Mont Catille.) Ital. & Fr. [Rome, 1835.] 8°.
3902. e. 1. (8.)

CATIN (Jean Baptiste) Nouveau manuel pratique de la mouture anglaise perfectionnée par la meunerie des environs de Paris. pp. viii. 327. Liége, 1864. 8°.
8766. ee. 19.

CATINA. See CATANIA.

CATINAT. Catinat. Histoire d'un vieux cheval de fiacre. pp. 69. Poitiers, [1888.] 12°.
12315. ccc. 41. (4.)

CATINAT (E.) Éléments de stratégie. pp. 160. Paris, 1895. 8°.
8829. aa. 23.

CATINAT (Maurice)

—— Les Bords de la Seine avec Renoir et Maupassant. " L'École de Chatou." [With illustrations.] pp. 119. Chatou, 1952. 8°.
10175. d. 25.

CATINAT (Nicolas de) Marshal of France. See CATINAT DE LA FAUCONNERIE.

CATINAT DE LA FAUCONNERIE (Nicolas de) Marshal of France. See BROGLIE (César P. E. de) Prince. Catinat. L'homme et la vie, 1637–1712. 1902. 8°.
010661. a. 3.

—— See LA HARPE (J. F. de) Éloge de Nicolas de Catinat, Maréchal de France. 1775. 8°.
611. f. 20. (5.)

—— —— 1812. 8°. [Choix d'éloges couronnés par l'Académie française. tom. 2.]
1329. d. 8.

—— See MOREAU DE BRASEY (J.) Journal de la campagne de Piemont, sous le commandement de Mr de Catinat, etc. 1691. 8°.
9078. bb. 7.

—— —— 1692. 8°.
9077. aaa. 4.

—— See SAHUGUET D'ESPAGNAC (M. R.) Éloge de Nicolas de Catinat, etc. 1775. 8°.
10663. dd. 21. (1.)

—— Mémoires et correspondance du Maréchal de Catinat, mis en ordre et publiés d'après les manuscrits autographes . . . Par M. Bernard Le Bouyer de St Gervais [and P. R. Auguis]. Avec gravures, portrait, facsimilé, cartes, etc. 3 tom. Paris, 1819. 8°.
10663. ee. 11.

—— [Another copy.]
286. f. 13.

CATINAT DE LA FAUCONNERIE (Nicolas de)
Marshal of France.

—— Analyse et extraits d'une partie du volume 1170 du
Dépôt de la Guerre contenant la correspondance de Catinat
et des officiers sous ses ordres pendant la campagne de
1692. *See* Rochas d'Aiglun (É. A. A. de) Documents
inédits relatifs à l'histoire et à la topographie militaires
des Alpes. La campagne de 1692 dans le Haut Dauphiné,
etc. 1874. 8°. **9220. eee. 17.**

—— Éloge du Maréchal de Catinat. [By Count J. A. H.
de Guibert.] pp. 88. *Edimbourg [Paris]*, 1775. 8°.
611. f. 20. (7.)

—— Mémoires pour servir à la vie de Nicolas de Catinat,
Maréchal de France. [Variously attributed to Marquis
C. M. de Créquy and Marquis L. M. de Créquy.] pp. 302.
Paris, 1775. 8°. **10660. aa. 31.**

—— Vie de Nicolas de Catinat. pp. 40. [*Paris?* 1770?] 8°.
611. f. 20. (8.)

CATINAUD (Jean Baptiste Anatole Paul) De l'examen
des malades. pp. 50. *Paris*, 1857. 4°. [*Collection des
thèses soutenues à la Faculté de Médecine de Paris.* An 1857.
tom. 3.] **7373. a. 3.**

CATINAUD (René) *See* Magnane (Georges) *pseud.* [i.e.
R. Catinaud.]

CATINEAU LA ROCHE (Pierre Marie Sebastien)
See Bonnet de Treyches (J. B.) and Catineau La
Roche (P. M. S.) Observations . . . sur la librairie
. . . adressés à Sa Majesté. 1808. 4°. **T. 951. (5.)**

—— La France et l'Angleterre comparées sous le rapport des
industries agricole, manufacturière et commerciale, *etc.*
pp. 298. *Paris*, 1844. 8°. **1302. e. 2.**

CATINELLI (Carlo) *Count.* Eine Erwiederung in Eisen-
bahn-Angelegenheiten. pp. 50. *Görz*, 1850. 4°.
8235. i. 9.

—— Sopra la questione italiana. Studj. pp. 491. *Gorizia*,
1858. 8°. **8032. h. 9.**

—— La Question italienne: études . . . Édition originale
française par le Dr. Henri Schiel. pp. 226. *Bruxelles
& Leipzig*, 1859. 8°. **8032. g. 8.**

—— Sulla identità dell'antico coll'odierno Timavo, memoria.
1829. *See* Trieste.—*Società del Gabinetto di Minerva.*
L'Archeografo triestino, *etc.* vol. 2. 1829, *etc.* 8°.
P.P. 3964.

CATINI (Étienne) *See* Mugnier (F.) Antoine Govéan,
professeur de droit. Sa famille—son biographe Étienne
Catini. 1901. 8°. [*Mémoires et documents de la Société
savoisienne d'histoire et d'archéologie.* tom. 40.]
Ac. 5240.

CATIUS, *Junior*, *pseud.* [i.e. Elizabeth R. Torrey.]
Theognis: a lamp in the cavern of evil. By Catius
Junior. pp. 346. *Wentworth & Co.: Boston*, 1856. 8°.
4373. c. 10.

CATIUS (Franciscus) *See* Caccia (Francesco)

CATIZZANI (Policarpo)

—— *See* Gatto (A.) Διηγησις της τρομερας πολιορκιας και
αλωσεως της Ἀμμοχωστου . . . δημοσιευθεισα ὑπο του
ἱερεως Πολυκαρπου Κατιτξανη, *etc.* 1897. 8°.
9136. de. 9.

CATLEDGE (Turner) *See* Alsop (Joseph W.) and Catledge (T.) The 168 days. 1938. 8°. **20032. a. 21.**

CATLETT (James M.) *See* Warder (J. B.) and Catlett
(J. M.) Battle of Young's Branch; or, Manassas Plain,
etc. 1862. 16°. **9605. aa. 16.**

CATLETT (John) A Perpetual and Vniversal Almanack,
etc. pp. 89. *L. Lloyd: London*, [1656.] 8°.
531. a. 40.

CATLEY, afterwards **LASCELLES** (Anne) *See* Ambross
( ) *Miss.* The Life and Memoirs of the late Miss Ann
Catley, *etc.* [1790?] 8°. **10825. bb. 35.**

—— A Brief Narrative of the Life of . . . Miss C * tl * y,
etc. pp. 56. [1780?] 12°. *See* C * tl * y, *Miss.*
1414.b.65.(4.)

—— The Life of Miss Anne Catley, *etc.* [With a portrait.]
pp. 78. *London*, 1888. 8°. **10825. cc. 26.**

CATLIN (Albertus Wright) "With the Help of God and
a few Marines." [A history of the U.S. Marine Corps
during the European War. With plates.] By Brigadier
General A. W. Catlin and Walter A. Dyer. pp. xvi. 425.
Curtis Brown: London; Garden City, N.Y. printed,
1919. 8°. **9082. b. 11.**

CATLIN (George) *See* Reichenbach (A. B.) Die Völker
der Erde nach ihrer Eigenthümlichkeit in Regierungs-
form . . . durch Wort und Bild geschildert nach den
Werken eines Barrow . . . Catlin, *etc.* 1859, *etc.* 8°.
10003. d. 13.

—— [For publications of the George Catlin Indian Gallery,
Washington:] *See* Washington, *D.C.—Smithsonian
Institution.—United States National Museum.*

—— The Breath of Life; or Mal-respiration and its effects
upon the enjoyments & life of man. pp. 75.
Trübner & Co.: London, 1861. 8°. **7615.b.14.**
Lithographed throughout.

—— [Another edition.] Shut your Mouth . . . With 26
illustrations from drawings by the author. pp. 92.
N. Trübner & Co.: London, 1869. 8°. [MISSING.]

—— Fourth edition, considerably enlarged. pp. 102.
N. Trübner & Co.: London, 1870. 8°. **7615.aaa.11.**

—— A Descriptive Catalogue of Catlin's Indian Gallery.
Containing portraits, landscapes, costumes, &c. and
representations of the manners and customs of the North
American Indians . . . exhibiting at the Egyptian Hall,
Piccadilly. pp. 47. *C. Adlard: London*, [1840.] 4°.
792. g. 3.

—— Last Rambles amongst the Indians of the Rocky
Mountains and the Andes. [With plates.] pp. x. 361.
Sampson Low & Co.: London, 1868. 8°.
10408. aaa. 31.

—— [Another edition.] pp. 351. *Gall & Inglis: Edinburgh, London*, [1877.] 8°. **10413. bb. 4.**

—— Letters and Notes on the Manners, Customs, and
Condition of the North American Indians. [With
plates.] 2 vol. *The Author: London*, 1841. 8°.
792. k. 16.

—— [Another copy.] **G. 16050, 51.**

—— Letters and Notes on the Manners, Customs and Condition of the North American Indians . . . Second edition.
2 vol. *The Author: London*, 1842. 8°. **10009. t. 16.**

—— Illustrations of the Manners, Customs and Condition of
the North American Indians . . . Ninth edition [of
"Letters and Notes," *etc.*]. 2 vol. pl. 180.
H. G. Bohn: London, 1857. 8°. **10008. r. 11.**

—— [Another edition.] 2 vol. pl. 180. *Chatto &
Windus: London*, 1876. 8°. **2374. g. 7.**

CATLIN (George)

—— Life amongst the Indians. A book for youth. [With plates.] pp. viii. 366.   *Sampson Low & Co.: London,* 1861. 8°.   **10412. a. 6.**

—— [Another edition.] pp. xii. 339.   *Sampson Low & Co.: London,* 1867. 8°.   **10408. aaa. 30.**

—— [Another edition.] pp. xiv. 352. pl. VII.   *Gall & Inglis: London, Edinburgh,* [1874.] 8°.   **10413. b. 28.**

—— La Vie chez les Indiens. Scènes et aventures de voyage parmi les tribus des deux Amériques. Ouvrage . . . traduit et annoté par F. de Lanoye, et illustré de 25 gravures sur bois. pp. 394. *Paris,* 1863. 8°.
                                          12206. i. 16. (2.)

—— The Lifted and Subsided Rocks of America with their influences on the oceanic, atmospheric, and land currents, and the distribution of races. pp. xii. 228.   *Trübner & Co.: London,* 1870. 8°.   **7108. aaa. 15.**

—— Museum of Mankind. [Proposals by G. Catlin for the construction of a floating museum.] pp. 16.   *W. J. Golbourn: London,* 1851. 8°.   **7959. b. 11.**

—— [Another edition.] pp. 16.   *T. Brettell: London,* 1852. 8°.   **7959. b. 12.**

—— Catlin's North American Indian Portfolio. Hunting scenes and amusements of the Rocky Mountains and Prairies of America. [Plates, with an introduction.] *Geo. Catlin: London,* 1844. fol.   **651. b. 8.**

—— [Another issue.] *London,* 1844. fol.   **1788. c. 7.**
In this issue the plates are coloured, and there are six additional plates. Without the introduction.

—— Catlin's Notes for the Emigrant to America. pp. 15.   *The Author: London,* 1848. 8°.   **8007. e. 43. (6.)**

—— Catlin's Notes of Eight Years' Travels and Residence in Europe, with the North American Indian Collection. With anecdotes and incidents of the travels and adventures of three different parties of American Indians, whom he introduced to the Courts of England, France and Belgium. 2 vol. pl. 24. *The Author: London,* 1848. 8°.
                                            10105. e. 15.

—— O-kee-pa: a religious ceremony; and other customs of the Mandans . . . With thirteen coloured illustrations. pp. vi. 52. *Trübner & Co.: London,* 1867. 8°.
                                              4505. dd. 12.

—— Steam Raft, suggested as a means of security to human life. [Edited by Joseph Adshead. With plates.] pp. 16. *George Falkner: Manchester,* 1860. 8°. **8806. d. 51. (4.)**

—— Unparalleled Exhibition. The fourteen Ioway Indians and their interpreter, just arrived from the Upper Missouri, *etc.* pp. 28. MS. NOTES. *W. S. Johnson: London,* 1844. 12°.   **10412. a. 4.**

—— [Another edition.] pp. 28.   *W. S. Johnson: London,* 1844. 12°.   **10412. a. 5.**

—— Opinions of the English and United States Press on Catlin's North American Indian Museum; exhibiting in the Egyptian Hall, Piccadilly. pp. 24.   *C. Adlard: London,* [1841.] 12°.   **792. c. 32. (2.)**

CATLIN (George B.) The Story of Detroit. pp. xix. 764. *Detroit News: Detroit,* 1926. 8°.   **010410. g. 19.**

CATLIN (George Edward Gordon) *See* DURBIN (Evan F. M.) and CATLIN (G. E. G.) War and Democracy, *etc.* 1938. 8°.   **08425. h. 35.**

CATLIN (George Edward Gordon)

—— *See* DURKHEIM (E.) The Rules of Sociological Method . . . Edited by G. E. G. Catlin. 1938. 8°.
                                          Ac. 2691. d/37. (19.)

—— *See* WOLLSTONECRAFT, afterwards GODWIN (Mary) The Rights of Women, by M. Wollstonecraft, & The Subjection of Women, by J. S. Mill. [With an introduction by G. E. C. Catlin.] 1929. 8°.
                                            12206. p. 1/622.

—— Above all Nations. An anthology [of extracts from books and newspapers recording acts of kindness done to enemies in the second World War]. Compiled by G. Catlin, Vera Brittain & Sheila Hodges, *etc.* pp. 87. *Victor Gollancz: London,* 1945. 8°.   **9101. ee. 35.**

—— America's Aims. Extracts from recent speeches by American statesmen; together with the text of the Atlantic Charter. (2nd impression.) [Compiled by G. E. G. Catlin.] pp. 16.   *American & British-Commonwealth Association: London,* [1944.] 8°. [*ABC Series.* no. 3.]
                                            12213. g. 6/3.

—— Anglo-American Union as a Nucleus of World Federation. pp. 40.   *Macmillan & Co.: London,* 1942. 8°. [*Federal Tracts.* no. 8.]   **W.P. 5371/8.**

—— The Anglo-Saxon Tradition. pp. xii. 286.   *Kegan Paul & Co.: London,* 1939. 8°.   **08004. f. 5.**

—— A History of the Political Philosophers. [With portraits.] pp. xvii. 802.   *George Allen & Unwin: London,* 1950 [1951]. 8°.   **8012. b. 10.**

—— In the Path of Mahatma Gandhi. [With plates, including portraits.] pp. 332.   *Macdonald & Co.: London,* 1948. 8°.   **10608. ccc. 44.**

—— Liquor Control. pp. 256.   *Thornton Butterworth: London,* 1931. 8°. [*Home University Library.* vol. 151.]
                                            12199. p. 1/165.

—— New Trends in Socialism. Edited by G. E. G. Catlin, *etc.* pp. xiv. 293.   *L. Dickson & Thompson: London,* 1935. 8°.   **8287. a. 22.**

—— One Anglo-American Nation. The foundation of Anglo-Saxony as basis of world federation. A British response to Streit, *etc.* pp. 155.   *Andrew Dakers: London,* [1941] 8°.   **8011. aa. 7.**

—— [A reissue.] One Anglo-American Nation, *etc. London,* 1941. 8°.   **8011. a. 10.**

—— Preface to Action. pp. 319.   *G. Allen & Unwin: London,* 1934. 8°.   **8286. b. 2.**

—— The Science and Method of Politics. pp. xii. 360. *Kegan Paul & Co.: London; A. A. Knopf: New York,* 1927 [1926]. 8°.   **08007. g. 33.**

—— A Study of the Principles of Politics: being an essay towards political rationalization. pp. 469.   *G. Allen & Unwin: London,* 1930. 8°.   **08007. i. 27.**

—— Thomas Hobbes as Philosopher, Publicist and Man of Letters: an introduction. pp. 63.   *Basil Blackwell: Oxford,* 1922. 8°.   **08486. ff. 3.**

—— The Unity of Europe. pp. 31.   *C. & J. Temple: London,* [1944.] 8°.   **8029. e. 35.**

CATLIN (George Henry) Speech . . . on the Right of Members to their Seats in the House of Representatives, *etc.* pp. 8. *Globe Office: Washington,* 1844. 8°.
                                            8177. cc. 51. (32.)

CATLIN (George L.) The Postillion of Nagold, and other poems. pp. 128. *Conrad Wittwer: Stuttgart*, 1884. 16°.
11688. e. 7.

—— Switzerland. The St. Gothard Railway. pp. 48. *Art Institute Orell Fussli: Zurich*, 1893. 8°. **10108. aa. 39.**

—— Suisse. À travers les Alpes par le chemin de fer du Saint-Gothard . . . Traduit de l'anglais. pp. 51. *Zurich*, 1895. 8°. **10108. aa. 40.**

CATLIN (Jacob) The Doctrine of Divine Sovereignty a Motive to Morality.—The Character and claims of Christ vindicated.—The Wicked . . . openly reject and despise the Almighty. *See* Sermons. Sermons on Important Subjects, *etc.* 1797. 8°. **4460. bb. 23.**

CATLIN (Lucy Cornelia) The Hospital as a Social Agent in the Community . . . Illustrated. pp. 113. *W. B. Saunders Co.: Philadelphia & London*, 1918. 8°. **08285. b. 43.**

CATLIN (Ralph) *pseud.* [i.e. David Sievert Lavender.] *See also* Lavender (David S.)

CATLIN (W. Wilkins) *See* Chicago.—*Sunset Club.* Echoes of the Sunset Club . . . Compiled by W. W. Catlin, *etc.* [1891.] 8°. **12350. i. 27.**

CATLIN (Warren Benjamin) The Labor Problem in the United States and Great Britain. pp. x. 659. *Harper & Bros.: New York & London*, 1926. 8°. **08248. eee. 48.**

—— [Another copy.] **8286. ff. 3.**
With a slip pasted on the titlepage stating that the work is submitted as a thesis for the degree of D.Phil. at Columbia University, and another on the last leaf bearing the author's Vita.

—— Revised edition. pp. xii. 765. *Harper & Bros.: New York & London*, 1935. 8°. **8287. c. 7.**

CATLIN (Zachary) *See* Ovidius Naso (P.) [*Tristia.— English.*] Publ. Ovid. de Tristibus . . . Translated into English verse by Z. Catlin. 1639. 8°. **1068. g. 20. (6.)**

—— The Hidden Treasure: opened in two sermons, *etc.* pp. 43. *M. Flesher, for Robert Dawlman: London*, 1633. 4°. **4474. aaa. 11.**

CATLINA. La Catlina da Budri, ouero il Furto amoroso, comedia onesta e spaseuole. [By Adriano Banchieri.] pp. 94. *Per lo Sarti: Bologna*, [1628.] 12°. **162. b. 25.**

CATLING (A. H.) The Kaiser under the Searchlight. pp. 138. *T. Fisher Unwin: London*, 1914. 8°. **010705. de. 26.**

CATLING (A. W. E.) *See* Marvello (Harry) *pseud.* [i.e. A. W. E. Catling.]

CATLING (C. T.) and **DOYLE** (T. J.) Origin of the Royal Antediluvian Order of Buffaloes, *etc.* pp. 7. *Porter: London*, [1923.] 8°. **04785. g. 19.**

CATLING (Gordon)

—— All about building your own Enlarger. [With illustrations.] pp. 56. *Focal Press: London & New York*, 1953. 8°. [*Photo Guides.*] **W.P. 13581/44.**

—— All about photographing Great Occasions with your Camera. [With illustrations.] pp. 56. *Focal Press: London & New York*, [1953.] 8°. [*Photo Guides.* no. 52.] **W.P. 13581/52.**

—— All about taking Parties and Groups with your Camera. pp. 56. *Focal Press: London & New York*, 1953. 8°. [*Focal Photo Guide.* no. 47.] **W.P. 13581/47.**

CATLING (Gordon)

—— All about taking Weddings with your Camera. [With illustrations.] pp. 56. *Focal Press: London & New York*, [1952.] 8°. [*Focal Photo Guide.* no. 37.] **W.P. 13581/37.**

—— The Beauty of Kent. [With illustrations.] *Jarrold & Sons: Norwich*, [1953.] 8°. [*Magna-Crome Books.*] **W.P. 3517/22.**

—— The Beauty of Sussex. [Photographs.] *Jarrold & Sons: Norwich*, [1954.] 8°. [*Magna-Crome Books.*] **W.P. 3517/20.**

—— Brighton & Hove in Pictures. *Jarrold & Sons: Norwich*, [1954.] 8°. [*Magna-Crome Books.*] **W.P. 3517/21.**

—— Crusing and Sailing for Everyone . . . Illustrated by Winston Megoran. [With a portrait.] pp. 119. *Nicholas Kaye: London*, 1952. 8°. **8803. aa. 12.**

—— Group Photography, *etc.* [With illustrations.] pp. 112. *Focal Press: London, New York*, 1948. 8°. [*Fotojob Books.*] **W.P. 721/3.**

—— Wedding Photography. pp. 96. *Focal Press: London & New York*, 1945. 8°. [*Fotojob Books.*] **W.P. 721/1.**

—— Wedding Photography . . . Second edition. pp. 96. *Focal Press: London, New York*, 1946. 8°. [*Fotojob Books.*] **W.P. 721/2.**

—— The Young Cameraman. [With illustrations.] pp. 128. *Nicholas Kaye: London*, 1949. 8°. **8913. c. 10.**

CATLING (Harry Debron) *See* Cambridge.—*University of Cambridge.*—*Cambridge Antiquarian Society.* Catalogue of the First Exhibition of Portraits in the Cambridge Antiquarian Society's Collection, *etc.* [By F. G. Walker and H. D. Catling.] 1908. 8°. **07806. g. 47. (5.)**

CATLING (Muriel)

—— Topsy. The autobiography of a winter lamb. pp. 39. *A. H. Stockwell: London*, [1941.] 4°. **12823. c. 8.**

—— Ugly Puppling. pp. 45. *Arthur H. Stockwell: Ilfracombe*, 1949. 8°. **12832. g. 24.**

CATLING (Robert Mason) and **ROGERS** (J. P.)

—— G. H. Doble. A memoir and a bibliography. pp. 28. *Sidney Lee: Exeter*, [1949.] 8°. **11925. e. 19.**

CATLING (Skene) Fever Heat. pp. 246. *Methuen & Co.: London*, 1931. 8°. **NN. 17577.**

—— Vanguard to Victory. An account of the British Expeditionary Force during its first months in France in the Second Great War, *etc.* [With plates.] pp. xv. 235. *Methuen & Co.: London*, 1940. 8°. **9100. aa. 23.**

CATLING (Thomas) My Life's Pilgrimage . . . Introduction by the Right Honourable Lord Burnham, *etc.* pp. xviii. 384. *John Murray: London*, 1911. 8°. **010854. g. 10.**

—— The Press Album. Published in aid of the Journalists' Orphan Fund. Edited by T. Catling. pp. xv. 224. *John Murray: London*, 1909. 8°. **12271. s. 5.**

—— A Savage Club Souvenir. [A miscellany presented to Thomas Catling. With plates.] pp. xv. 244. 1916. 8°. *See* London.—iii. *Savage Club.* **010349. d. 47.**

CATLING (Winifred) "Narcissus," and other poems. pp. 29. *F. H. Morland: Amersham*, [1913.] 16°. **11607. aaaa. 11. (3.)**

CATLOW (AGNES) The Conchologist's Nomenclator. A catalogue of all the recent species of shells included under the subkingdom "Mollusca" . . . By A. Catlow . . . assisted by Lovell Reeve. pp. viii. 326. *Reeve Bros.: London,* 1845. 8º. **7299. c. 10.** *Interleaved.*

—— Drops of Water; their marvellous and beautiful inhabitants displayed by the microscope. pp. xviii. 194. pl. IV. *Reeve & Benham: London,* 1851. 12º. **1258. b. 11.**

—— Popular Conchology; or, the Shell cabinet arranged: being an introduction to the modern system of conchology. With a sketch of the natural history of the animals, an account of the formation of the shells, and a complete descriptive list of the families and genera. pp. xx. 300. *Longman & Co.: London,* 1843. 8º. **729. a. 22.**

—— Second edition. pp. xxiv. 370. *Longman & Co.: London,* 1854. 8º. **1258. c. 15.**

—— Popular Field Botany; containing a familiar and technical description of the plants most common to the various localities of the British Isles, adapted to the study of either the artificial or natural systems. pp. xxxii. 380. pl. 20. *Reeve, Benham & Reeve: London,* 1848. 16º. **1251 b. 13.**

—— Popular Garden Botany: containing a familiar and scientific description of most of the hardy and half-hardy plants introduced into the flower garden. pp. xii. 320. pl. xx. *Lovell Reeve: London,* 1855. 8º. **7030. b. 13.**

—— Popular Greenhouse Botany; containing a familiar and technical description of a selection of the exotic plants introduced into the greenhouse. pp. xii. 311. pl. xx. *Lovell Reeve: London,* 1857. 8º. **7030. b. 14.**

CATLOW (AGNES) and **CATLOW** (MARIA E.)

—— The Children's Garden and what they made of it . . . Illustrated by Mrs. Harry Criddle. pp. 126. *Cassell & Co.: London,* 1865. 8º. **12804. cc. 31.**

—— Sketching Rambles; or, Nature in the Alps and Apennines . . . Illustrated, *etc.* 2 vol. *J. Hogg & Sons: London,* [1861.] 8º. **10196. d. 20.**

CATLOW (JOANNA)

—— Sisters to Simon. [A novel.] pp. 239. *Hutchinson: London,* 1955. 8º. **NNN. 6030.**

CATLOW (JOSEPH PEEL) On the Principles of Æsthetic Medicine, or the natural use of sensation and desire in the maintenance of health and the treatment of disease, as demonstrated by induction from the common facts of life. pp. 325. *J. Churchill & Sons: London,* 1867. 8º. **7320. cc. 8.**

CATLOW (LESLIE) The Documents of Death. [A novel.] pp. 270. *A. H. Stockwell: London,* [1934.] 8º. **NN. 22439.**

CATLOW (MARIA E.) *See* CATLOW (Agnes) and (M. E.) The Children's Garden and what they made of it, *etc.* 1865. 8º. **12804. cc. 31**

—— *See* CATLOW (Agnes) and (M. E.) Sketching Rambles; or, Nature in the Alps and Apennines, *etc.* [1861.] 8º. **10196. d. 20.**

—— Popular British Entomology; containing a familiar description of the insects most common in the various localities of the British Isles. pp. xx. 269. pl. xv. *Reeve, Benham & Reeve: London,* 1848. 8º. **729. b. 26.**

CATLOW (MARIA E.)

—— Popular Geography of Plants; or, a Botanical excursion round the world: by E. M. C. [i.e. M. E. Catlow.] Edited by Charles Daubeny. pp. xl. 370. pl. 20. 1855. 8º. *See* C., E. M. **7030. b. 12.**

—— [A reissue.] Plants of the World and where they grow, *etc.* 1865. 8º. *See* C., E. M. **7030. bb. 14.**

—— Popular Scripture Zoology, containing a familar history of the animals mentioned in the Bible. pp. xvi. 360. pl. xvi. *Reeve & Co.: London,* 1852. 8º. **3126. cc. 10.**

—— The Star of Poland, with other scenes and sketches from history. pp. 208. *William Freeman: London,* 1865. 8º. **12620. bb. 24.**

CATLOW (SAMUEL) *See* COLLINS (Joshua) *pseud.* A Guide in the selection and use of elementary School-Books . . . A new edition, revised and enlarged by the Rev. S. Catlow. 1818. 12º. **1212. l. 4. (2.)**

—— Observations on a Course of Instruction, for young persons in the middle classes of life. pp. 93. *J. Gales: Sheffield,* 1793. 8º. **C.T. 451. (6.)**

CATMOS VALE. Catmos Vale, *etc.* [Poems.] pp. 16. *W. Wileman: London,* [1880.] 16º. **11652. a. 71. (9.)**

CATNACH (AGNES) A New Grammar Book. pp. viii. 199. *Blackie & Son: London,* 1919. 8º. **12980. a. 31.**

CATNACH (JAMES) *See* HINDLEY (Charles) *of Bookseller's Row, Strand.* The Life and Times of James Catnach, *etc.* 1878. 8º. **11899. f. 9.**

—— "The Catnach Press." A collection of the books and woodcuts of James Catnach, late of Seven Dials, printer. [With an account of his Life. Compiled by Charles Hindley.] pp. 48. *Reeves & Turner: London,* [1869.] 8º. **11899. bb. 37.**

—— An Attempt to Exhibit the Leading Events of the Queens Life, in cuts and verse. [Signed: Jas. C - tn - - h, i.e. James Catnach.] 1821. *s. sh.* fol. *See* C - TN - - H (Jas.) **Tab. 597. a. 1. (67.)**

—— [Another copy.] **1852. b. 9. (85.)**

—— The Charlie's Holiday; or, the Tears of London at the funeral of Tom and Jerry: also, the Death and Last Will of Poor "Black Billy Waters." [Signed: J. C., i.e. J. Catnach. Founded on Pierce Egan's "Life in London."] (Second edition.) [1823?] *s. sh.* fol. *See* C., J. **1875. d. 8. (99.)**

—— The Death, Last Will, and Funeral of "Black Billy" (Billy Waters): also, the Tears of London for the Death of Tom and Jerry. [Signed: J. C., i.e. J. Catnach. Founded on Pierce Egan's "Life in London."] (Tenth edition.) [1823?] *s. sh.* fol. *See* C., J. **1875. d. 7. (15.)**

—— [Another copy.] **1875. d. 8. (100.)**

—— An Elegy on the Queen . . . A Lament for Caroline, the Rose of England. [Signed: J. C., i.e. J. Catnach?] [1821.] *s. sh.* fol. *See* C., J. **1852. c. 9. (81.)**

—— Green in France: or, Tom and Jerry's rambles through Paris. Attempted in cuts and verse. *J. Catnach: [London,* 1822?] *s. sh.* fol. **1875. d. 8. (101.)**

—— Life in London: or, the Sprees of Tom and Jerry; attempted in cuts and verse. (Founded on Pierce Egan's "Life in London.") (Fifth edition.) *Jas. Catnach: London,* [1822?] *s. sh.* fol. **1875. d. 7. (11.)**

CATNACH (James)

—— Life in London ; or, the Sprees of Tom and Jerry, *etc.* (Twenty-first edition.)   *Jas. Catnach: London,* [1822 ?] *s. sh.* fol.   **1875. d. 8. (98.)**

—— Life in London : or, the Sprees of Tom and Jerry, *etc.* [Founded on Pierce Egan's " Life in London."] (Thirty-fifth edition.) *Jas. Catnach: London,* [1822 ?] *s. sh.* fol.   **1875. d. 8. (97.)**

—— The New Marriage Act displayed in cuts and verse. (Third edition.) *J. Catnach:* [*London,* 1822.] *s. sh.* fol.   **1875. d. 7. (12.)**

—— The New Marriage Act, *etc.* (Seventh edition.) *J. Catnach:* [*London,* 1822 ?] *s. sh.* fol. **1875. d. 8. (102.)**

—— (Eleventh edition.)   *J. Catnach:* [*London,* 1822 ?] *s. sh.* fol.   **1875. d. 8. (103.)**

—— (Twentieth edition:)   *J. Catnach:* [*London,* 1822 ?] *s. sh.* fol.   **1875. d. 8. (104.)**

—— The Woes of Caroline. [Signed: J. C., i.e. J. Catnach ?] (Bow thy Head thou Lily Pale.—The Poor Royal Stranger without any Home.) [Verses on Queen Caroline.] [1820.] *s. sh.* 4°. *See* C., J.   **1152. b. 9. (6.)**

CATO, *the Censor, pseud.* Caird's High Farming harrowed. By Cato the Censor. Reprinted from Blackwood's Magazine, with an Appendix. pp. 38. *W. Blackwood & Sons: Edinburgh & London,* 1850. 8°.   **8246. d. 13.**

—— Intimidation ; a political satire. [In verse.] By Cato' the Censor. pp. 41. *W. Eden: London,* 1842. 8°.   **1466. g. 41.**

CATO, *Chemicus.* Cato Chemicus. Tractatus quo veræ ac genuinæ philosophiæ hermeticæ, & fucatæ ac sophisticæ pseudo chemiæ & utriusque magistrorum characterismi accurate delineantur.   *G. Liebernickel: Hamburgi,* 1690. 12°.   **1036. a. 5. (3.)**

—— [Another edition.] *See* MANGET (J. J.) Jo. Jacobi Mangeti . . . Bibliotheca chemica, *etc.* tom. 1. 1702. fol.   **44. i. 11.**

CATO, *der Frantzösische. See* FRENCH CATO.

CATO, *Junr., pseud.* The Monthly London Journal : containing, the most material occurences . . . By Cato Junr. no. 2. Nov. 1722. 1722. 8°.   *See* PERIODICAL PUBLICATIONS.—*London.*   [MISSING.]

CATO, *Parvus, pseud. See* MERCURIUS, *Rusticus, pseud.* Bibliophobia. Remarks on the present languid and depressed state of literature and the book trade . . . With notes by Cato Parvus. 1832. 8°.   **C. 28. i. 13. (1.)**

CATO, *pseud.* Cato Redivivus. A satirical review. 1881. [In verse. Signed: Cato.] pp. 32.   *W. P. Dolby: Stamford ; Hamilton & Adams: London,* [1881.] 8°.   **11602. e. 18. (12.)**

—— Cato's Dream. [Concerning the speech of F. Atterbury, Bishop of Rochester, at his trial by the House of Lords.] *Thomas Hume: Dublin,* 1723. *s. sh.* fol.

C.133.g.7.(7.)

—— Cato's Letter to the People of England. [A political pamphlet. Reprinted from the New Times.] pp. 11. *F. Humble & Co.: Durham,* [1821.] 8°.   **8135. aaa. 18. (12.)**

—— Cato's Letter to the Right Hon. the Earl of Harewood, *etc. A. Mitchell:* [*London,* 1820.] *s. sh.* fol. **8135. e. 4. (44.)**

CATO, *pseud.*

—— Cato's Letters ; to the Earl of Harewood, and the Earl of Liverpool ; with a letter to the Queen, by a widowed wife. pp. 66. *Rouse, Kirkby, & Lawrence: Canterbury,* 1821. 8°.   **08139. b. 50. (1.)**

—— The Tendencies of the Foundling Hospital in its present extent considered . . . in several letters to a Senator [signed: Cato]. 2 pt. *Printed for private use: London,* 1760. 4°.   **1144. k. 22. (1.)**

—— [Another edition.] 2 pt.   *R. & J. Dodsley: London,* 1760. 4°.   **191. a. 18.**

—— Thoughts on a Question of Importance proposed to the public, whether it is probable that the immense extent of territory acquired by this nation at the late Peace, will operate towards the prosperity, or the ruin of the island of Great Britain ? [The author's dedicatory letter signed: Cato.] pp. 48. *J. Dixwell: London,* 1765. 8°.   **1093. e. 74.**

—— [Another copy.]   **102. e. 19.**

CATO, *pseud.* [i.e. FRANK OWEN, MICHAEL MACKINTOSH FOOT and PETER HOWARD.] Guilty Men. By " Cato." pp. 125. *Victor Gollancz: London,* 1940. 8°. [*Victory Books.* no. 1.]   **8140.df.9/1.**

CATO, *pseud.* [i.e. GEORGE BURGES.] *See also* BURGES (George) *Vicar of Halvergate.*

—— Cato to Lord Byron on the Immorality of his Writings. pp. 128. *W. Wetton: London,* 1824. 8°.   **11826. dd. 33. (1.)**

—— Cato to Lord Byron on the Immorality of his Writings . . . Second edition. pp. 128.   *W. Wetton: London,* 1824. 8°.   **11861. b. 50.**

—— Third edition. pp. 128. *W. Wetton: London,* 1824. 8°.   **T. 1167. (2.)**

—— [Cato to Lord Byron on the Immorality of his Writings.] pp. 128. MS. NOTES. [*W. Wetton: London,* 1824.] 8°.   Ashley **2727.** *Imperfect ; wanting the title leaf which is replaced by a leaf reading " Cato to Lord Byron on the Immoral & Dangerous Tendency of his Writings."*

CATO, *pseud.* [i.e. JOHN TRENCHARD.] *See also* TRENCHARD (John) *Political Writer.*

—— A Discourse of Standing Armies ; shewing the folly, uselessness, and danger of standing armies in Great Britain. By Cato [i.e. J. Trenchard, assisted by Walter Moyle]. pp. 36. *T. Warner: London,* 1722. 8°.   **T. 1617. (1.)**

—— The second edition. pp. 36.   *T. Warner: London,* 1722. 8°.   **8133. c. 14.**

CATO, *pseud.* [i.e. JOHN TRENCHARD and THOMAS GORDON.] *See also* TRENCHARD (John) *Political Writer,* and GORDON (Thomas) *of Kirkcudbright.*

—— A Collection of Cato's Political Letters in the London Journal, to December 17, inclusive, 1720. The second edition, with a new preface. (The Second collection, continued to the end of January, 1720.—The Political Letters in the London Journal, continued to the end of March, 1721.) 3 pt. *J. Roberts: London,* 1721. 8°.   **10921. bbb. 7. (1.)**

—— Cato's Letters. 4 vol.   *W. Wilkins: London,* 1724, 23. 12°.   **292. a. 38-41.** *Subsequent editions are entered under the authors.*

CATO, *pseud.* [i.e. JOHN TRENCHARD and THOMAS GORDON.]

—— *See* DICEPHILUS, *pseud.* Cato's Letter to the Bishop of Rochester. 1723. *s. sh.* fol. **C.133.g.7.(8.)**

—— *See* JACKSON (John) *Rector of Rossington.* A Defense of Human Liberty, in answer to the principal arguments which have been alledged against it, and particularly to Cato's Letters on that subject. 1725. 8°. **226. a. 13.**

—— —— 1730. 8°. **T. 1960. (8.)**

—— *See* POPLICOLA, *pseud.* Poplicola's Supplement to Cato's Letter, concerning Popularity, *etc.* 1722. 8°. **1474. b. 5.**

—— Cato's Principles of Self-Preservation, and Publick Liberty; truly stated and fairly examined . . . By a Subject of Cæsar [i.e. John Gaynam], *etc.* pp. 36. *T. Warner: London,* 1722. 8°. **101. f. 22.**

—— The Censor censur'd: or, Cato turned Catiline . . . With a word or two of a standing force, and a hint of ingratitude. In a letter [on "Cato's Letters" by J. Trenchard and T. Gordon] from a Gentleman in the country to his friend in London. pp. 29. *J. Roberts: London,* 1722. 8°. **8132. df. 10. (1.)**

CATO, *Redivivus.* Cato Redivivus. A satirical review. 1881. [In verse. Signed: Cato.] [1881.] 8°. *See* CATO, *pseud.* **11602. e. 18. (12.)**

CATO, *Uticensis, Lucensis, pseud.* [i.e. F. Maurello.] *See* CATONE, *l' Uticense, Lucchese, pseud.*

CATO (A. C.)

—— A Survey of Native Education in Fiji, Tonga, and Western Samoa, with special attention to Fiji. (Thesis.— University of Melbourne.) [With a bibliography. Typescript, with diagrams and photographs added.] pp. xv. iv. 598. ii. v. xxv. [*Melbourne,* 1951.] Mic. A. **6.** MICROFILM.

CATO (ALEXANDER MCLEAN) " First Aid " to Sailors, *etc.* pp. 36. *Pewtress & Co.: London,* 1895. 8°. [*Papers read before the Shipmasters' Society.* no. 36.] **08805. bb. 1/36.**

CATO (ANGELUS) *Archbishop of Vienne. See* GUAINERIUS (A.) *Begin.* [fol. 2 *verso:*] Angelus cato supinas de Beneuento . . . Antonello Bolumbrello Regio medico S.P.D. [fol. 3 *recto:*] Tractatus de febribus . . . feliciter incipit. [Edited by A. Cato.] 1474. fol. **IB. 29383.**

—— *See* SILVATICUS (M.) *Begin.* [fol. 1 *recto:*] [Tabula Pandecte, *etc.*] [fol. 8 *recto:*] Inclyto. atque. gloriosissimo. Ferdinando. Siciliae. Regi. Angelus. Cato. Supinas. De. Benevento. philosophus. et. medicus. foelicitatem. *End.* [fol. 341 *verso:*] Explicit. liber Pandectarum. Quem Angelus Cato Supinas de Beneuēto Philosophus & medicus magna cū diligētia ʒ emēdate imprimendū curauit, *etc.* 1474. fol. **IC. 29360.**

CATO (CONRAD) The Navy Everywhere. [With maps.] pp. ix. 297. *Constable & Co.: London,* 1919. 8°. **9082. cc. 20.**

—— The Navy in Mesopotamia, 1914 to 1917. pp. xi. 211. *Constable & Co.: London,* 1917. 8°. **9082. a. 19.**

CATO (DIONYSIUS) [For editions of the " Disticha de moribus " attributed to Dionysius Cato:] *See* CATO (M. P.) *the Censor.* [*Supposititious Works.*]

CATO (ERCOLE) *See also* ZAGO, *di Santa Rentua, pseud.* [i.e. E. Cato.]

—— *See* BODIN (Jean) *Political Writer.* Demonomania degli stregoni . . . tradotta dal Kᵣ H. Cato, *etc.* 1592. 4°. **30. b. 11.**

CATO (ERCOLE)

—— *See* ESTIENNE (C.) L'Agricoltura et casa di villa . . . tradotta dal Cavaliere H. Cato. 1581. 4°. **235. f. 14.**

—— —— 1623. 4°. **441. b. 9.**

—— *See* LE ROY (Louis) *Professor of Greek at the Collège Royal, Paris.* La Vicissitudine ò mutabile varietà delle cose . . . Tradotta dal Sig. . . . H. Cato. 1585. 4°. **73. c. 8.**

—— —— 1592. 4°. **721. i. 22.**

—— Discorso . . . recitata [*sic*] nell' Accademia degl' Intrepidi. pp. 16. *V. Baldini: Ferrara,* 1603. 4°. **835. f. 8.**

—— Oratione fatta . . . nelle essequie dell'Illustriss. . . . Sig. D. Hippolito d'Este Card. di Ferrara, celebrate nella Città di Tiuoli. pp. 13. *V. Baldini: Ferrara,* 1587. 4°. **10631. c. 46. (9.)**

—— Del caualier Hercole Cato Sopra il bello, & amenissimo luogo del mag. sig. Giulio Benalio. [A poem.] *Per V. Baldini: Ferrara,* 1584. 4°. **161. n. 48. (1.)**

CATO (HERCOLE) *See* CATO (Ercole)

CATO (LYDIO) *Ravennate, pseud.* [i.e. BERNARDINO GATTI.] Egloge de Lydio Cato Rauennate. ff. 59. *S. de Luere: Venetia,* 1512. 8°. **241. c. 32.**

—— [Another copy.] **C. 20. a. 31. (1.)**

CATO (MARCUS PORCIUS) *the Censor.*

ARRANGEMENT							COL.
Works	.	.	.	.	.	.	502
Fragments	.	.	.	.	.	.	502
De Re Rustica	.	.	.	.	.	.	503
Supposititious Works—							
Disticha de Moribus	.	.	.	.			507
Fragmenta ex libris Originum			.	.	.		524
Appendix	.	.	.	.	.	.	525

WORKS.

—— M. Porcii Catonis quæ exstant, ab Ausonio Popma Frisio collecta et restituta. Eiusdem Ausonii ad eadem notæ. pp. 165. *Ex Officina Plantiniana, apud F. Raphelengium: Lugduni Batauorum,* 1590. 8°. **967. a. 19.**

—— M. Porcii Catonis de agricultura, siue, de re rustica, liber: post vltimam A. Popmæ editionem centum amplius locis auctus correctusque, studio atque opera Ioannis Meursii. Item Fragmenta eiusdem scribtoris, ab A. Popma diligenter collecta, restituta. pp. 165 [175]. 79. *Ex Officina Plantiniana, apud C. Raphelengium: [Leyden,]* 1598. 8°. **1254. b. 22.**

—— [Another copy.] **967. a. 21. (2.)** *Imperfect; wanting the first six leaves and the notes of Meursius.*

—— M. Porcii Catonis de re rustica liber. Fragmenta quæ supersunt. Ausonius Popma Frisius iterum recensuit & notas addidit. Accesserunt Ioannis Meursi ad librum de re rustica, notæ, Ausonii Popmæ de instrumento fundi liber. 2 pt. *Sumptibus I. Commelini Viduæ: Franekeræ,* 1620. 8°. **246. c. 9. (2.)**

FRAGMENTS.

—— [Fragments. With a commentary by A. Riccoboni.] *See* RICCOBONI (A.) Antonii Riccoboni Rhodigini de historia commentarius, *etc.* 1568. 8°. **580. a. 3.**

—— [Fragments.] *See* SALLUSTIUS CRISPUS (C.) [*Works.— Latin.*] C. Crispi Sallustii quæ extant, *etc.* 1710. 4°. **53. c. 3.**

CATO (Marcus Porcius) *the Censor.* [Fragments.]

—— [Another edition.] *See* Sallustius Crispus (C.) [*Works. —Latin.*] Caii Crispi Sallustii quæ exstant, *etc.* 1724. 4°.
588. g. 19.

—— [Another edition.] *See* Sallustius Crispus (C.) [*Works. —Latin.*] Caii Crispi Sallustii quae exstant, *etc.* 1737. 4°.
686. i. 7.

—— [Another edition.] *See* Sallustius Crispus (C.) [*Works. —Latin.*] C. Crispi Sallustii quae exstant, *etc.* tom. 2. 1742. 4°.
587. h. 2, 3.

—— Catoniana, sive M. Porcii Catonis Censorii quae supersunt operum fragmenta. Nunc primum seorsum auctius edidit H. Albertus Lion, *etc.*. pp. 109. *Gottingae,* 1826. 8°.
8460. c. 19.

—— Catonianae poesis reliquiae ex recensione Alfredi Fleckeiseni. pp. 19. *Lipsiae,* [1854.] 8°. **11385. d. 4.**

—— M. Porcii Catonis Originum libri septem. Reliquias disposuit et de instituto operis disputavit Dr. Albertus Bormann. pp. 48. *Brandenburgii,* 1858. 4°. **11352. e. 5.**

—— M. Catonis praeter librum de re rustica quae extant. Henricus Jordan recensuit et prolegomena scripsit. pp. cix. 135. *Lipsiae,* 1860. 8°. **11352. e. 6.**

—— M. Porcii Catonis Origines. *See* Peter (Hermann) Historicorum Romanorum relliquiae, *etc.* vol. 1. 1870, *etc.* 8°.
9039. e. 23.

—— Fragmenta Originum. *See* Peter (Hermann) Historicorum Romanorum fragmenta, *etc.* 1883. 8°.
2048. f. 23.

Appendix.

—— *See* Janzer (B.) Historische Untersuchungen zu den Redenfragmenten des M. Porcius Cato, *etc.* 1937. 8°.
11311. g. 22.

DE RE RUSTICA.

Latin.

—— *Begin.* [fol. 1 *verso:*] gEorgius Alexandrinus Petro Priolo .M. filio .S. Priscas dictiões de tribus rei rusticæ scriptoribus ānotatas, *etc.* [fol. 2 *recto:*] Enarrationes breuissimae priscarum vocum Marci Catonis. [fol. 16 *recto:*] Epistola. gEorgius Alexandrinus Bernardo Iustiniano equiti & senatori facundissimo salutem. [fol. 17 *verso:*] Marci Catonis prisci de re rustica libri capita. [fol. 20 *recto:*] Marci Catonis prisci de re rustica liber. [fol. 41 *verso:*] M. T. Varronis rei rusticae capita libri .i. [fol. 43 *recto:*] Marci Terentii Varronis rerum rusticarum ad Fundaniam uxorem liber .i. [fol. 88 *recto:*] Lucii Iunii Moderati Columellae rei rusticae capitula libri primi. [fol. 92 *recto:*] Lutii Iunii Moderati Columellae rei rusticae liber primus. [fol. 240 *recto:*] Epistola. gEorgius Alexandrinus Dominico Georgio insigni patritio .S., *etc.* [fol. 243 *recto:*] Palladii Rutilii Tauri Aemiliani viri illustris de re rustica liber primus. [De re rustica of Cato, Varro and Columella. Edited by Georgius Merula. De re rustica of Palladius. Edited by Franciscus Colucia.] *Opera et impensa Nicolai Ienson: Venetiis,* 1472. fol.
C. 5. c. 7.

302 *leaves, ff.* 15, 86, 87 *and* 242 *blank. Without signatures.* 40 *lines to a page. Without the blank leaves. Fol.* 240 *is bound after fol.* 91.

—— [Another copy.]
G. 9023.
Without the blank leaves 15, 86, 87.

—— [Another copy.]
IB. 19658.
Imperfect; wanting ff. 1–14, 240, 241, 266, 269 *and the blank leaves* 15, 86, 87.

CATO (Marcus Porcius) *the Censor.* [De re rustica.— *Latin.*]

—— [Another edition.] *Begin.* [fol. 1 *verso:*] gEorgius Alexandrinus Petro Priolo .M. filio .S., *etc.* [fol. 20 *recto:*] Marci Catonis prisci de re rustica liber. [fol. 43 *recto:*] Marci Terentii Varronis rerum rusticarum ad Fundaniam uxorem liber .i. [fol. 92 *recto:*] Lutii Iunii Moderati Columellae rei rusticae liber primus. [fol. 243 *recto:*] Palladii Rutilii Tauri Aemiliani viri illustris de re rustica liber primus. [fol. 303 *recto:*] Registrum. *Opera et impensis Bartholomei Bruschi al' Botoni:* [*Reggio Emilia,*] Nonis Iunii [5 June], 1482. fol. **169. k. 4.**
Reprinted, mostly with the same page-contents, from the edition printed at Venice 1472. 303 *leaves, ff.* 15, 86, 87 *and* 242 *blank. Sig.* A⁶ a⁸; b¹⁰ c¹⁰ d⁸; e–g¹⁰ h⁸ i⁶; k¹⁰ l¹⁰ m–z⁸ &⁸ ꝑ⁸ ꝗ⁸ aa⁸ bb¹² cc⁸ dd⁸ ee–gg¹⁰ hh¹⁰⁺¹. 40 *lines to a page. Without the blanks.*

—— [Another copy.]
G. 9024.
Sheets c 1–4 *are of a different setting up. Imperfect; wanting sheet cc* 3, *the place of which is taken by a duplicate of sheet ee* 3. *Without the blanks.*

—— [Another edition.] Marci Catonis prisci de re rustica liber. *See* Columella (L. J. M.) Opera Agricolationum: Columellæ: Varronis: Catonisꝗ, *etc.* 1494. fol.
IB. 29054.

—— [Another edition.] *See* Columella (L. J. M.) Opera Agricolationum: Columellæ: Varronis: Catonisꝗ, *etc.* 1496. fol.
IB. 34061.

—— [Another edition.] *See* Columella (L. J. M.) Opera Agricolationum: Columellæ: Varronis: Catonisꝗ, *etc.* 1499. fol.
IB. 34043.

—— [Another edition.] *See* Columella (L. J. M.) Opera Agricolationum: Columellæ: Varronis: Catonisꝗ, *etc.* 1504. fol.
441. h. 13.

—— Libri de re rustica. M. Catonis lib. i. M. Terentii Varronis lib. iii. L. Iunii Moderati Columellae lib. xii. Eiusdem de arboribus liber . . . Palladii lib. xiiii. De duobus dierum generibus: simulq; de umbris, & horis, quæ apud Palladium, in alia epistola ad lectorem [by A. P. Manutius]. Georgij Alexandrini enarrationes priscarum dictionum, quæ in his libris Catonis: Varronis: Columellæ. [Edited by J. Jucundus.] ff. 308. *In aedibus Aldi, & Andreae soceri: Venetijs,* 1514. 4°.
451. g. 13.

—— [Another copy.] **685. g. 6.**

—— [Another copy.] **160. n. 3.**

—— [Another copy.] **G. 8965.**

—— M. Cato de re rustica. *See* Angelius (N.) *Bucinensis.* Libri de re rustica, *etc.* 1515. 4°.
235. g. 12.

—— [Another edition.] *See* Angelius (N.) *Bucinensis.* Libri de re rustica, *etc.* 1521. 4°.
35. a. 20.

—— Libri de re rustica. M. Catonis lib. i. M. Terentii Varronis lib. iii. L. Iunii Moderati Columellæ lib. xii . . . Palladii lib. xiiii, *etc.* ff. 391. *Per I. Mazochiū: Tiguri,* 1528. 8°.
970. a. 6.
The contents are those of the edition of 1514.

—— [Another issue.] [*Zurich,*] 1528. 8°. **971. a. 31.**
In this issue the printer's name and place of printing are not given in the colophon.

—— Libri de re rustica, M. Catonis, M. Terentii Varronis, L. Iunii Moderati Columellę, Palladii Rutilii, *etc.* [With the notes of G. Merula and P. Beroaldus.] pp. 311. *Vęnundantur I. Badio Ascensio:* [*Paris,*] 1529. fol.
724. k. 16.

CATO (MARCUS PORCIUS) *the Censor.* [DE RE RUSTICA.—*Latin.*]

—— [Another edition.] pp. 506. FEW MS. NOTES. *Prælo A. Augerelli, impensis I. Parui & G. à Prato: Lutetiæ,* 1533. fol. **456. c. 16.**

—— Libri de re rustica. M. Catonis lib. I. M. Terentii Varronis lib. III. L. Iunii Moderati Columellæ lib. XII. Eiusdem de arboribus liber separatus ab aliis. Palladii lib. XIIII, *etc.* ff. 295. *Ex officina I. Hervag.: Basileæ,* 1535. 4°. **441. b. 1.** *The contents are those of the edition of* 1514.

—— De re rustica. M. Catonis Liber I. M. Terentij Varronis Lib. III. Palladij Lib. XIIII. L. Iunij Moderati Columellæ Lib. XIII. Priscarum uocum in libris de re rustica enarrationes, per Georgium Alexandrinum. Philippi Beroal. in lib. XIII. Columellæ annotationes. Aldus de dierum generibus, *etc.* pp. 814. *I. Gymnicus excudebat: Coloniæ,* 1536. 8°. **7074. aaa. 11.**

—— Libri de re rustica, M. Catonis lib. I. M. Terentii Varronis lib. III. Per Petrum Victoriū, ad ueterum exemplarium fidem, suæ integritati restituti. ff. 113. *Ex officina R. Stephani: Parisiis,* 1543. 8°. **988. b. 2.**

—— [Another copy.] **967. a. 5. (1.)**

—— [Another copy.] **234. c. 25.**

—— [Another copy.] **G. 8919. (1.)**

—— Marci Catonis ac M. Teren. Varronis de re rustica libri. Per Petrum Victorium, ad ueterum exemplarium fidem, suæ integritati restituti. pp. 226. MS. NOTES. *Apud S. Gryphium: Lugduni,* 1549. 8°. **450. d. 1. (1.)**

—— [Another copy.] **967. a. 6. (1.)**

—— Methodus rustica Catonis atq. Varronis præceptis aphoristicis per locos communes digestis a Theodoro Zuingero typice delineata & illustrata. [With the text.] pp. 494. *P. Pernæ opera atque impensa: Basileæ,* [1576.] 8°. **967. c. 2.** *Imperfect; wanting pp.* 273–288.

—— Rei rusticae auctores latini veteres, M. Cato, M. Varro, L. Columella, Palladius: priores tres, e vetustiss. editionibus; quartus, e veteribus membranis aliquammultis in locis emendatiores: cum tribus indicibus, *etc.* pp. 775. *Ex H. Commelini typographio:* [*Heidelberg,*] 1595. 8°. **967. a. 9.**

—— [Another copy.] **687. a. 12.**

—— [Another copy.] COPIOUS MS. NOTES [by A. Askew]. **723. c. 3.** *Interleaved. Imperfect; wanting all after p.* 155.

—— M. Porcius Cato. De re rustica. *See* GESNER (J. M.) Scriptores rei rusticae veteres latini, *etc.* 1735. 4°. **681. e. 1.**

—— [Another edition.] *See* GESNER (J. M.) Scriptores rei rusticae veteres latini, *etc.* tom. 1. 1773, *etc.* 4°. **441. e. 14, 15.**

—— [Another edition.] *See* GESNER (J. M.) Scriptores rei rusticae veteres latini, &c. tom. 1. 1787, *etc.* 8°. **159. g. 6.**

—— [Another edition.] *See* SCHNEIDER (J. G.) Scriptorum rei rusticae veterum latinorum tomus primus [*etc.*]. tom. 1. 1794, *etc.* 8°. **966. i. 1.**

—— M. Porci Catonis de agri cultura liber. M. Terenti Varronis rerum rusticarum libri tres. Ex recensione Henrici Keilii. (Index verborum . . . Composuit Richardus Krumbiegel.) 3 vol. *Lipsiae,* 1882–1902. 8°. **07077. i. 64.**

CATO (MARCUS PORCIUS) *the Censor.* [DE RE RUSTICA.—*Latin.*]

—— M. Porci Catonis de agri cultura liber. Recognovit Henricus Keil. pp. v. 88. *Lipsiae,* 1895. 8°. *Part of the* " *Bibliotheca scriptorum graecorum et romanorum Teubneriana.*" **7087.a.15.**

Latin and English.

—— Marcus Porcius Cato on Agriculture. Marcus Terentius Varro on Agriculture. With an English translation by William Davis Hooper . . . Revised by Harrison Boyd Ash. pp. xxv. 542. *William Heinemann: London; Harvard University Press: Cambridge, Mass.,* 1934. 8°. [*Loeb Classical Library.*] **2282. d. 134.**

Latin and Catalan.

—— D'Agricolia. Text revisat i traducció de Mn. Salvador Galmés. pp. xxvi. 84. 86. *Barcelona,* 1927. 8°. [*Escriptors Llatins.*] **Ac. 137. (17.)**

—— [Another copy.] **07075. f. 34.**

Latin and French.

—— M. Porcius Caton. Économie rurale.—M. Porcius Cato. De re rustica. (Traduction de feu Antoine.) 1851. *See* NISARD (J. M. N. D.) Collection des auteurs latins, *etc.* (Les agronomes latins, *etc.*) 1850, *etc.* 8°. **11306. m. 14.**

Latin and Italian.

—— Marco Porcio Catone. De re rustica. Con note. [With an Italian translation by Giuseppe Compagnoni.] 3 tom. *Venezia,* 1792–94. 8°. [*Rustici latini volgarizzati.*] **235. f. 21–23.**

English.

—— Roman Farm Management. The Treatises of Cato (De agricultura) and Varro (Rerum rusticarum libri tres). Done into English, with notes of modern instances, by a Virginia Farmer. [The preface signed: F. H., i.e. Fairfax Harrison.] pp. xii. 365. *Macmillan Co.: New York,* 1913. 8°. **07073. f. 11.**

—— Cato the Censor on Farming. Translated by Ernest Brehaut. [With plates.] pp. xlv. 156. *Columbia University Press: New York,* 1933. 8°. [*Records of Civilization.* no. 17.] **Ac.2688/45.(17.)**

French.

—— L'Économie rurale de Marcus Porcius Caton. [Translated by C. F. Saboureux de la Bonneterie.] *See* SABOUREUX DE LA BONNETERIE (C. F.) Traduction d'anciens ouvrages latins relatifs à l'agriculture, *etc.* tom. 1. 1773. 8°. **7077. d. 40.**

Italian.

—— Delle cose rustiche, opera . . . volgarizzata dal cavaliere Giuseppe Compagnoni. pp. viii. 199. *Milano,* 1851. 8°. **7075. b. 10.**

—— Il Libro dell'agricoltura. [Translated by G. G. Curcio.] *See* CURCIO (G. G.) La Primitiva civiltà latina agricola, *etc.* 1929. 8°. **07704. df. 23.**

Selections.

—— Catonis De agri cultura c. VII et VIII cum adnotationibus Henrici Keilii. pp. xii. [1881.] *See* HALLE, *on the Saale.—Academia Fridericiana.* Index scholarum in Universitate Litteraria Fridericiana Halensi . . . per aestatem anni MDCCCLXXXI(–MDCCCLXXXXV) . . . habendarum. Summer 1881. [1881, *etc.*] 4°. **Ac. 2320/13.**

CATO (Marcus Porcius) *the Censor.* [De re rustica.]

—— Cato's Farm Management. Eclogues from the De Re Rustica of M. Porcius Cato, done into English, with notes of other excursions in the pleasant paths of agronomic literature, by a Virginia Farmer. [The preface signed: F. H., i.e. Fairfax Harrison.] pp. 60. *Privately printed: Chicago,* 1910. 8°.   **7074. f. 35.**

Appendix.

—— *See* Bradley (Richard) *F.R.S.* A Survey of the Ancient Husbandry and Gardening collected from Cato, Varro, *etc.* 1725. 8°.   **453. c. 29.**

—— *See* Gummerus (H.) Der Römische Gutsbetrieb als wirtschaftlicher Organismus nach den Werken des Cato, Varro und Columella. 1906. 8°. [*Klio.* Beihft. 5.]   **P.P. 3548. ha.**

—— *See* Hoerle (J.) Catos Hausbücher. Analyse seiner Schrift De Agricultura, nebst Wiederherstellung seines Kelterhauses und Gutshofes, *etc.* 1929. 8°. [*Studien zur Geschichte und Kultur des Altertums.* Bd. 15. Hft. 3, 4.]   **Ac. 2026/9.**

—— *See* Keil (H.) Henrici Keilii De libris manu scriptis Catonis de agri cultura disputatio. [1882.] 4°. [*Index scholarum in universitate litteraria Fridericiana Halensi . . . per aestatem anni* MDCCCLXXXI(–MDCCCLXXXV) *. . . habendarum.* Summer 1882.]   **Ac. 2320/13.**

—— *See* Meister (A. L. F.) Alberti Ludov. Frieder. Meisteri De torculario Catonis vasis quadrinis libellus ad locum difficillimum de re rustica capp. xviii. xviiii. xx. xxi. xxii. illustrandum. 1764. 4°.   **235. f. 13.**

—— *See* Rottböll (C. F.) Anmærkninger og Oplysninger til M. Porcius Cato de re rustica, *etc.* 1790. 4°.   **448. f. 15.**

—— *See* Ursinus (Fulvius) Notæ ad M. Catonem, M. Varronem, L. Columellam de re rustica, *etc.* 1587. 8°.   **724. a. 3.**

—— *See* Vettori (Pietro) *the Elder.* Petri Victorii Explicationes suarum in Catonem, Varronem, Columellam castigationum. 1542. 8°.   **7074. b. 41. (2.)**

Origines.

—— [For editions of the genuine fragments of the Origines:] *See supra:* Fragments.

—— [For editions of the supposititious fragments of the Origines:] *See infra:* Supposititious Works.

SUPPOSITITIOUS WORKS.

Disticha de Moribus.

Latin.

Editions without commentary.

—— *Begin.* Meretrices fuge. Patere lege₃ ꝙ tu iꝑe tuleris, *etc.* G.A. on vellum. [*Italy* 1480?] fol.   **IB. 50.**
A fragment, consisting of a single leaf of text only, of an edition printed from wood blocks or metal plates. **34** *lines to a page.*

—— *Begin.* [fol. 1 *recto:*] Cato ad filiū suū. quum aīaduerterē ꝙ plurimos hoīes ꝗuiter errare ī via moꝗ, *etc. End.* [fol. 6 *verso:*] Finiūt disticha Catonis ad filiū suū Rcā hortographia Ꝉ emendate impressa, *etc.* G.A. ꝑ Iacobū de Breda: [*Deventer,*] 1485. 4°.   **IA. 47560.**
6 leaves. Sig. a⁶. **29** *lines to a page.*

—— Moralia Catonis ad filium ei⁹ carissimum. [fol. 2 *recto:*] Cato ad filium suum. [C]Vm animaduerterem ꝙ plurimos homines grauiter errare in via morum, *etc.* [With a woodcut.] G.A.   [*Richard Paffraet:*] *Dauētrie In platea episcopi,* 1491. 4°.   **IA. 47661.**
8 leaves. Sig. a⁸. **28** *lines to a page.*

CATO (Marcus Porcius) *the Censor.* [Supposititious Works.—Disticha de Moribus.—*Latin.—Editions without commentary.*]

—— *Begin.* [fol. 1 *recto:*] Cum anīaduerterē ꝙm prīmos homines grauiter errare in via morū, *etc. End.* [fol. 6 *verso:*] Explicit hic chato dans castigamiua [*sic*] nato. G.A. [*Christian Snellaert: Delft,* 1495?] 4°.   **IA. 47216.**
6 leaves, without signatures. **30** *lines to a page. With the device of the printer on the verso of fol. 6.*

—— *Begin.* [fol. 1 *recto:*] Cato ad Filium suum. CVm animaaduerterem [*sic*] ꝙ plurimos homines grauiter errare in via morum, *etc. End.* [fol. 6 *verso:*] Finiunt disticha Catonis ad filium suū. G.A.   [*Arnold Kempen: Zwoll,* 1505?] 4°.   **C.56.e.7.**
With the device of the printer on the verso of fol. 6.

—— Libellus catonis de moribus. G.A.   [*G. Philippe: Paris,* 1505?] 4°.   **11375. c. 11.**
The name of the printer is contained in the device on the titlepage.

—— Liber Catonis. *See* Libri. [*Libri minores, etc.*] [1507?] 4°.   **C. 63. c. 8.**

—— Disticha moralia titulo Catonis inscripta. *In officina Petri Gromorsi: Parisiis,* 1523. 8°.   **1482. aa. 29.**

—— Precepta ad bene beateꝗ viuendū emendata per diligenter. *See* Donatus (A.) [*Ars Minor.*] Aelij Donati . . . . grāmatices rudimēta, *etc.* 1526. 4°.   **C. 47. d. 7.**

—— Socratici Catonis de præceptis ad vitæ humanæ institutionem maxime facentibus [*sic*] . . . opusculum. *See* Forestus (H.) Hortensiae Ioannis Foresti Brixiani filiæ Compendium, *etc.* 1558. 4°.   **12932. bbb. 12. (1.)**

—— Disticha moralia, titulo Catonis inscripta. *Ex officina R. Stephani: Lutetiæ,* 1566. 8°.   **680. a. 28. (4.)**

—— Catonis disticha, siue Carmen de moribus. D. Laberij, P. Syri, & aliorum veterum sententiæ, Iambicis versibus singulis comprehensæ. Et alia, *etc.* ff. 22. ms. addition and signature [of E. Baluze]. *Ex officina R. Stephani: Lutetiæ,* 1577. 8°.   **1067. g. 15. (1.)**
In this copy two leaves, pp. 49–52, are inserted from a later edition.

—— Dionysii Catonis Disticha de moribus ad filium. Recognita de novo ad metaphrasin & castigationes Iosephi Scaligeri a I.R. in usum scholarum. *Excudebat Andreas Hart: Edinburgi,* 1620. 8°. **11409. ccc. 13. (3.)**

—— Disticha moralia, sive Cato. Item M. Antonii Mureti Institutio puerilis . . . Nec non disticha sententiosa variorum authorum. [Edited by J. Gezelius, Bishop of Åbo.] *Literis & impensis I. G. D. Ep. Ab.* [*J. Gezelius, Bishop of Åbo*]: *Aboæ,* 1669. 8°. **11409. ccc. 12. (5.)**

—— Catonis Disticha moralia, et Lilii Monita pædagogica; or, Cato's Moral Distichs, and Lily's Pædagogical Admonitions . . . in a method entirely new; viz. The words of the author placed according to their grammatical construction, in the lower part of the page. An alphabetical vocabulary of all the words, shewing their parts of speech and signification. The themes of the verbs with their government. A table of scanning . . . By John Stirling . . . The second edition. pp. 39. *Printed for the Author: London,* 1734. 8°.   **11385. b. 15.**

—— Catonis Disticha. *See* Amati (P.) Collectio Pisaurensis omnium poematum, carminum, fragmentorum latinorum, *etc.* tom. 4. 1766. fol.   **653. d. 14.**

—— Dionysii Catonis Disticha moralia, *etc. See* Renouard (A. A.) Carmina ethica, *etc.* 1795. 12°.   **1213. l. 31.**

CATO (MARCUS PORCIUS) *the Censor.* [SUPPOSITITIOUS WORKS.—DISTICHA DE MORIBUS.—*Latin.—Editions without commentary.*]

—— Dionysii Catonis Disticha de moribus, *etc. See* PHAEDRUS, *the Fabulist.* Phædri, Aviani, aliorumque veterum Fabulæ, *etc.* 1823. 12º. **11312. a. 29.**

—— Dionysii Catonis Distichorum de moribus ad filium liber primus(—quartus). *See* WEBER (Wilhelm E.) Corpus poetarum Latinorum, *etc.* 1833. 4º. **11352. e. 15.**

—— Catonis Philosophi liber. Post Ios. Scaligerum vulgo dictus Dionysii Catonis Disticha de moribus ad filium. Ad fidem vetustissimorum librorum manuscriptorum atque inpressorum recensuit Ferdinandus Hauthal. pp. xxxviii. 80. *Berolini,* 1869. 8º. **11355. ff. 22.**

—— Catonis Disticha. 1881. *See* BAEHRENS (E.) Poetae Latini minores, *etc.* vol. 3. 1879, *etc.* 8º.
2049. b. 11.

—— Dicta Catonis quae vulgo inscribuntur Catonis Disticha de moribus. Iterum edidit Geyza Némethy. pp. 82. 1895. 8º. *See* PEST.—*Magyar Tudományos Akadémia.*
8407. dd. 33.

—— [Another copy.] **11375. d. 28. (7.)**

—— Catonis Disticha. Facsimilés, notes, liste des éditions du xvᵉ siècle. [Edited with an introduction by Joseph Nève.] pp. 125. *Liége,* 1926. 8º. **11375. dd. 12.**

Editions with the commentary of Philippus de Bergamo.

—— *Begin.* [fol. 1 *recto:*] [O]Mnia quecunꝗ facitis in verbo aut in ope omnia in nomine dñi nostri hiesu xp̄i facite, *etc.* [fol. 56 *verso:*] Explicit. Registrum. [fol. 57 *recto:*] [A]D gloriam ꝛ laudem domini et saluatoris nostri hiesu xp̄i, *etc. End.* [fol. 484 *recto:*] Ob prime omnium rerum cause preconia. militantisꝗ ecclesie eruditõeꝫ, Cathonis magni autoris moralissimi ethica pregnantissima, torquēdo Auguste imposita, *etc.* [The Disticha de moribus, with the commentary of Philippus de Bergamo entitled Speculum regiminis.] 𝕲.𝕷. [*Anton Sorg:*] *Auguste,* die crastina festi omnium sanctorum [2 Nov.], 1475. fol.
167. c. 25.
484 *leaves, without signatures.* 40 *lines to a page.*

—— [Another copy.] **G. 9745.**
Imperfect; wanting ff. 341, 342.

—— *Begin.* [fol 2 *recto:*] [O]Mne qd̄cunꝗ facitis in verbo aut opere omnia in nomine dñi nostri ihesu xp̄i facite, *etc. End.* [fol. 376 *recto:*] Explicit catho moralizatus Deo gratias. [With the commentary of Philippus de Bergamo.] 𝕲.𝕷. [*Martin Huss and Johann Siber: Lyons,* 1480?] fol.
IB. 41608.
376 *leaves, ff.* 1 *and* 180 *blank,* 44–375 *numbered* i–cccxxx. *The unnumbered leaves are signed* A–D⁸ E⁶ F⁶; *the numbered leaves are without signatures. Double columns,* 48 *lines to a column. Without the blank leaves.*

—— Philippi de Pergamo Speculum regiminis alias Catho moralisatus. 𝕲.𝕷. [*Michael Wenssler: Basle,* 1485?] fol. **IB. 37123a.**
342 *leaves,* 43–166 *numbered* i–cxxiiii, *with errors. Sig.* A–D⁸ E¹⁰; G–K⁸ L¹⁰ M–V⁸ X¹⁰; aa–yy⁸. *Double columns,* 47–48 *lines to a column.*

Editions with the commentary of Erasmus.

—— Libellus elegãtissimus qui inscribitur Cato de p̄ceptis vite cõis Erasmo Roterodamo Castigatore ꝛ interprete. *See* ERASMUS (D.) [*Works translated, etc., by Erasmus.*] Opuscula aliquot Erasmo Roterodamo castigatore et interprete, *etc.* [1514?] 4º. **11312. bb. 10.**

CATO (MARCUS PORCIUS) *the Censor.* [SUPPOSITITIOUS WORKS.—DISTICHA DE MORIBUS.—*Latin.*]

—— Contenta in hoc opere sunt hæc. Catonis p̄cepta moralia recognita atꝗ interpretata ab Erasmo Roterodamo. Mimi Publiani. Septem sapientū illustres sententię. Institutio homīs christiani uersib. hexametris. per Erasm. Roterodamum. Isocratis Paręnesis ad Demonicum Rudolpho Agricola interprete, recognita per Martinum Dorpium. (Ausonii ecloga de Vita humana.) [*M. Schürer: Strasburg,* 1515.] 4º. **8406. ee. 32.**

—— [Another edition.] [With "Epicteti Stoici Enchiridion."] *Apud M. Schurerium: Argentorati,* 1516. 4º
8406. ee. 33.

—— Hæc nunc damus lector, partim locupletiora castigatioraꝗ, partim noua. Disticha moralia, titulo Catonis, cum scholiis auctis Erasmi Roterodami. Mimi Publiani, cum eiusdem scholiis auctis recogniti. Institutum hominis Christiani carmine per eūdem Erasmum Roterodamum. Isocratis paraenesis ad Demonicum (p . . . Rodolphū Agricolā e Græco ī Latinū Sermonem traducta), denuo cū Græcis collata per Erasmum. Erudita . . . Epistola . . . Eucherii, episcopi Lugdunensis . . . de philosophia Christiana, recognita et scholiis illustrata per Erasmū Roterodamū. (Dicta sapientum e Græcis . . . Erasmo interprete.) [*T. Martin: Louvain,* 1517.] 4º. **697. d. 5. (6.)**
The name of the printer is contained in the device on the verso of the last leaf.

—— Contenta in hoc opere sunt hæc. Catonis præcepta moralia recognita atꝗ interpretata ab Erasmo Roterodamo. Mimi Publiani. Septē sapientum illustres sententiæ. Institutio hominis Christiani uersi. hexametris per Erasmū Roterodamū. Isocratis Paręnesis ad Demonicū Rudolpho Agricola interprete, recognita per Martinum Dorpium. (Epicteti Stoici Enchiridion.) *Apud L. Shurerium: Selestadij,* 1520. 4º. **721. f. 1.**

—— Ioan. Frobenius, studiosæ iuuentuti S. Accipite nūc opuscula quædā moralia, *etc.* pp. 171. *Per I. Frobenium: Basileæ,* 1520. 4º. **720. f. 27. (1.)**
The contents are those of the edition printed at Louvain by T. Martin, 1517.

—— Catonis Disticha moralia, cum scholijs auctis Erasmi Roteroda. Apothegmata Græciæ sapientum interprete Erasmo. Eadem per Ausonium cum scholijs Erasmi. Mimi Publiani, cum eiusdem scholijs auctis, recogniti. Institutum hominis Christiani carmine per eundem Erasmum Roterod. Isocratis Paraenesis ad Demonicum (per . . . Rodolphum Agricolam . . . traducta) denuo cum Græcis collata per Eras. Rot. *I. Cnoblochus excudebat: Argentorati,* 1523. 8º. **11375. b. 8.**

—— [Another edition.] *In officina typographica N. Fabri: Lipsiæ,* [1525?] 8º. **874. h. 23. (5.)**

—— [Another edition.] MS. NOTES. *Excudebat N. Faber: Lipsiæ,* 1532. 8º. **232. k. 10.**

—— [Another edition.] *Per Winandum de worde: Londini,* 1532. 8º. **Huth 82.**

—— [Another edition.] ff. 63. *Apud S. Colinæum: Parisiis,* 1533. 8º. **11352. aaa. 31. (3.)**

—— Cato's Distichs de Moribus Improved . . . Containing not only a correct numerical clavis, with a construing and parsing index, but also a literal translation of Erasmus's Comment on each distich . . . By J. Roberts . . . The second edition. pp. vi. 114. *C. Hitch; J. Hodges: London,* 1745. 12º. **1211. e. 29.**

Editions with the commentary of Robertus de Euremodio.

—— *Begin.* [fol. 1 *recto:*] Prelocucio Remigii in Exposicionem Cathonis. [fol. 2 *verso:*] Ethica siue distigium Cathonis. [With the commentary of Robertus de Euremodio.] [*Constance?* 1475?] 4º. **IA. 38316.**
58 *leaves, the last blank. Without signatures.* 23 *lines to a page.*

CATO (MARCUS PORCIUS) *the Censor.* [SUPPOSITITIOUS WORKS.—DISTICHA DE MORIBUS.—*Latin.*]

—— Moralissimus Catho. cū elegantissimo cōmento. *End.* [fol. 47 *verso:*] Hic finē aspice Cathonis viri moralissimi . . . Cum cōmento fratris Roberti de euromodio, *etc.* [With a woodcut.] **G.L.** *p Gerardū Leeu: In oppido Antwerpiēsi*, prima die Marcij, 1485. 4°. G. **9494**.
48 *leaves, the last blank. Sig.* a–f⁸. *The number of lines to a page varies.*

—— [Moralissimus Cato cū elegantissimo cōmento.] [fol. 2 *recto:*] Incipit liber de doctrina Catonis ampliatus per sermones rhetoricos ᴢ morales. per fratrem Robertū de Euremodio, *etc. End.* [fol. 47 *verso:*] Hic finem aspice Catonis viri moralissimi . . . Cum commento fratris Roberti de euromodio, *etc.* **G.L.** [*Johann Amerbach:*] *Basilee*, decimaquarta die Iunij, 1486. 4°. IA. **37291**.
48 *leaves, the last blank. Sig.* a–f⁸. *The number of lines to a page varies. Imperfect; wanting the titlepage.*

—— Moralissimus Cato cū elegantissimo cōmento. *End.* [fol. 41 *verso:*] Hic finem aspice Catonis viri moralissimi . . . Cum cōmento fratris Roberti de Euromodio, *etc.* **G.L.** [*Martin Flach:*] *Argētine*, vigesimo die Septēbris, 1487. 4°. IA. **2106**.
42 *leaves, the last blank. Sig.* a–d⁸ e¹⁰. *The number of lines to a page varies. Without the blank leaf.*

—— Catho moralissimus cum elegantissimo commento. *End.* [fol. 40 *verso:*] Hic finē aspice Cathonis viri moralissimi . . . Cum ǫmento fratris Roberti de euremodio, *etc.* [With a woodcut.] **G.L.** *p Gerardū leeu: in oppido antwerpiēsi*, tercio kalēdas nouēbris [30 Oct.], 1487. 4°. IA. **49766**.
40 *leaves. Sig.* a⁸ b⁸ c–f⁶. *The number of lines to a page varies.*

—— Cato moralissimus cum elegantissimo Cōmento. *End.* [fol. 47 *verso:*] Hic finem aspice Catonis viri moralissimi . . . Cum commento fratris Roberti d' euromodio, *etc.* **G.L.** *p Nicolaū kesler: Basilee*, iij. die mensis Marcij, 1488. 4°. IA. **37597**.
48 *leaves, the last blank. Sig.* a–f⁸. *The number of lines to a page varies. Without the blank leaf.*

—— *Begin.* [fol. 2 *recto:*] Incipit liber de doctrina Catonis ampliatus per sermones rhetoricos & morales per fratrem Robertū de Euremodio monachū Clareuallis. *per Mathiam morauum: Neapoli*, die .xvj. Julij, 1488. 4°. IA. **29435**.
The text in roman type, the commentary in gothic. 40 *leaves, the first blank. Sig.* a–e⁸. *Without the blank leaf. Ff.* 2 *and* 40 *are mounted.*

—— Cato moralissimus cum elegantissimo commento. *End.* [fol. 31 *recto:*] Hic finem aspice Catonis viri moralissimi . . . cum Cōmento fratris Roberti de euromodio, *etc.* **G.L.** *per Wolfgangnum* [sic] *hopyl: Parisij*, xiiij. kalēdas Ianuarias [19 Dec.], 1494. 4°. IA. **40132**.
32 *leaves, the last blank. Sig.* a–d⁸. *The number of lines to a page varies. Without the blank leaf.*

—— Cato moralissim⁹ cū elegantissimo cōmento. *End.* [fol. 35 *verso:*] Hic finem aspice Catonis viri moralissimi . . . Cum commento fratris Roberti de Euromodio, *etc.* **G.L.** *p Iacobum de Breda: Dauentrie*, xvi mēsis Iulij, 1496. 4°. IA. **47884**.
36 *leaves, the last blank. Sig.* a–f⁸·⁴. *The number of lines to a page varies.*

—— Cato moralissim⁹ cū elegātissiō commento (per fratrem Robertum de Euremodio). [With a woodcut.] **G.L.** *Per henricū eckert: Antwerpie*, 1504. 4°. **8409. f. 18**.

CATO (MARCUS PORCIUS) *the Censor.* [SUPPOSITITIOUS WORKS.—DISTICHA DE MORIBUS.—*Latin.*]

Editions with the anonymous commentary beginning: " *Summi deus largitor premii.*"

—— *Begin.* [fol. 2 *recto:*] sVmmi deus largitor premij, *etc. End.* [fol. 48 *recto:*] Expliciunt glosule cathonis et declinatur explicit expliciunt. non plus inuenitur et est verbum defectiuum. [The Disticha de moribus, with the anonymous commentary.] **G.L.** [*Guillaume Le Roy: Lyons*, 1485 ?] fol. IB. **41529**.
48 *leaves, the first blank. Sig.* a–f⁸. 43 *lines of commentary to a page. Without the blank leaf.*

—— Cathonem glosatū et moralisatum. [fol. 2 *recto:*] [S]ummi deus largitor premij, *etc.* **G.L.** [*Johann Grüninger: Strasburg*, 1490 ?] 4°. IA. **1513**.
70 *leaves, the last blank. Sig.* a–h⁸ i⁶. 43 *lines of commentary to a page.*

—— [The "Disticha de moribus," with the anonymous commentary.] *See* AUCTORES. Auctores octo opusculorū, *etc.* 1494. 4°. IB. **42036**.

—— Catho cum glosa et moralisatione. [fol. 1 *verso:*] [S]Vmmi deus largitor premij, *etc.* [With a woodcut.] **G.L.** FEW MS. NOTES. *p Henricum Quentell: Colonia*, 1494. 4°. IA. **4628**.
48 *leaves. Sig.* A–H⁶. 47 *lines of commentary to a page.*

—— [The "Disticha de moribus," with the anonymous commentary.] *See* AUCTORES. Auctores octo opusculorum, *etc.* 1495. 4°. IB. **42056**.

—— [Catho cum commento.] [fol. 2 *recto:*] [S]Vmmi deus largitor premii, *etc.* [*André Bocard: Paris*, 1495 ?] 4°. IA. **40242**.
46 *leaves. Sig.* a–e⁸ f⁶. 46 *lines of commentary to a page. Imperfect; wanting the titlepage and fol.* 8.

—— Chato cū glosa et moralisatione. [fol. 1 *verso:*] [S]Vmmi deus largitor premij, *etc.* [With a woodcut.] **G.L.** *p Henricum Quentell: Colonia*, 1496. 4°. IA. **4657**.
48 *leaves. Sig.* A–H⁶. 47 *lines of commentary to a page.*

—— Catho cum glosa et moralisatione. [fol. 1 *verso:*] [S]Vmme [*sic*] deus largitor p̄mij, *etc.* [With a woodcut.] **G.L.** *per Iohannem Schensperger: in Imperiali Ciuitate Augusta*, 1497. 4°. IA. **6379**.
48 *leaves. Sig.* a–h⁶. 46 *lines of commentary to a page.*

—— [The "Disticha de moribus," with the anonymous commentary] *See* AUCTORES. Auctores octo opusculoᴚ, *etc.* 1498. 4°. IB. **41981**.

—— [Catho cum commento.] [fol. 2 *recto:*] Prohemium. [S]Vmmi deus largitor premii, *etc. End.* [fol. 44 *recto:*] Liber Cathonis cum glosa finit feliciter, *etc.* **G.L.** *per Georgium mittelhuβ* [*for Michel Le Noir*]: *parisius*, Mensis Augusti, die vicesima, 1500. 4°. IA. 40097. (1.)
44 *leaves. Sig.* a⁸ b–g⁶. 48 *lines of commentary to a page. Imperfect; wanting the titlepage bearing the device of M. Le Noir.*

—— Catho cum commento. [fol. 2 *recto:*] SVmmi deus largitor premii, *etc.* **G.L.** *Venundantur in officina Michaelis angier: Cadomi; in domo Iohannis mace: Redonis*, [1510.] 4°. C. **56. e. 5**.
With the device of Jean Mace on the titlepage. The colophon reads: Impressus Cadomi per Laurentium hostingue pro Michaele angier vniuersitatis eiusdē loci librario . . . ᴢ Iohāne mace librario Redonis cōmorante, etc.

—— *Begin.* [fol. 2 *recto:*] SVmmi deus largitor premii, *etc.* [fol. 3 *verso:*] CVm animaduerterem ǭplurimos homines errare grauiter in via morum, *etc. End.* [fol. 36 *verso:*] Liber Cathonis finit feliciter, *etc.* **B.L.** *Per wynandū de worde: Lōdoñ.*, 1514. 4°. C. **21. c. 10**.
Imperfect; wanting the first leaf.

CATO (MARCUS PORCIUS) *the Censor.* [SUPPOSITITIOUS WORKS.—DISTICHA DE MORIBUS.—*Latin.*]

—— *Begin.* [fol. 2 *recto:*] SVmmi deus largitor premii, *etc.* *End.* [fol. 36 *verso:*] Liber Cathonis finit feliciter, *etc.* 𝔅.𝔏. *Lōdōn.*, 1514. 4°.   Mic. A. **125.** (**23.**) MICROFILM *of British Museum imperfect copy* C. 21. c. 10. *Made by the British Museum Microfilm Service.*

—— [The " Disticha de moribus," with the anonymous commentary.] *See* AUCTORES. Authores cum commento, *etc.* 1519. 4°.   **11352.** e. **4.**

Editions with miscellaneous commentaries.

—— [Documenta moralia Catonis.] *Begin.* [fol. 2 *recto:*] Regist꜕ in p̄cepto꜕ numero. vna cum titulis eorundē, *etc.* [fol. 26 *recto:*] Remissorium supra thematū tam euangelio꜕ q̄ epl̄a꜕ dominicalium, *etc.* [fol. 63 *recto:*] Prologus Kathonis de omni cecitate homīs erranti in via mo꜕. & hoc in genere Incipit feliciter. Cum animaduerterem q̄ p̄rimos homines, *etc. End.* [fol. 381 *recto:*] Docūmta moralia cathonis In oīm xp̄iano꜕ morū & erro꜕ correctiōem etcꜗ [*sic*] extirpacōem disserte exarata. atqui [*sic*] & auspicato In l̄moes tp̄m videlicet dn̄icalium feria꜕cꜗ vna cum euāgelio꜕ ac epl̄a꜕ introductiōibus seu thematibus. p anni circulū. iux̄ materia꜕ predicanda꜕ p̄gruentium venustissime moralizata sunt, *etc.* [Containing the prefatory epistle and the prose precepts of Cato with a voluminous commentary.] 𝔊.𝔏. [*Johann Zainer: Ulm,* 1475 ?] fol.   **IB. 9134.** 382 *leaves, ff.* 1, 62 *and* 382 *blank,* 63–381 *numbered* I–CCCXIX. *Without signatures.* 34 *lines to a page. Without the blank leaves* 62 *and* 382.

—— Io. Ba. Ascensii. in librum quem Catoni ascribunt, cōmentarii. [With the text.] *See* BADIUS (J.) *Ascensius.* [*Works, including compilations by Badius.*] Siluæ Morales, *etc.* 1492. 4°.   **IB. 41900.**

—— Sequit̃ Catonis carmen de moribus per Anto. Mancinellū correctum. [With a commentary by Jodocus Badius Ascensius.] *See* MANCINELLUS (A.) Opera, *etc.* 1511. 4°.   **827.** g. **12.**

—— M. Io. Policarpi Seueritani . . . In quatuor ethycorum libros : Senece Junioris Catonis Cordubensis Cōmentarius. [With the text.] *See* DONATUS (A.) [*Ars minor.*] Dionisii: appollonii: donati: de octo orationis partibus libri, *etc.* 1517. 4°.   **12933.** g. **4.**

—— Liber Catonis. (Cū additionib⁹ recēter. in margine additis.) 1525. 8°. *See* AUCTORES. Octo Autores, *etc.* 1525. 8°.   **1070.** d. **7.**

—— Catonis Disticha Moralia ex cᷝ castigatione D. Erasmi Roterodami una cum annotationib⁹ & scholijs Richardi Tauerneri anglico idiomate conscriptis in usum Anglicæ inuentutis. ff. xlvii.   *Excusus in aedibus M. Richardi Tauerneri per Richardum Bankes: Londini,* 1540. 8°.   **1460.** a. **32.**

—— Catonis Disticha Moralia ex castigatione D. Erasmi Roterodami una cum annotationib' & scholijs Richardi Tauerneri, *etc. Londini,* 1540. 8°.   Mic. A. **125.** (**24.**) MICROFILM *of British Museum copy* 1460. a. 32. *Made by the British Museum Microfilm Service.*

—— Catonis Disticha Moralia ex castigatione D. Erasmi Roterodami vna cum annotationibus et scholijs Richarde [*sic*] Tauerneri Anglico idiomata [*sic*] conscriptis . . . Aliquot sentenciæ insignes ex varijs collectæ scriptoribus per eundem Erasmum. Mimi publiani, cum Anglicis eiusdem Richarde [*sic*] scholijs, recogniti. *Imprinted by Ihon Waley: London,* 1562. 8°.   **11643.** a. **59.**

CATO (MARCUS PORCIUS) *the Censor.* [SUPPOSITITIOUS WORKS.—DISTICHA DE MORIBUS.—*Latin.*]

—— Disticha Catonis. Recensuit et apparatu critico instruxit Marcus Boas. Opus post mortem Marci Boas edendum curavit Henricus Johannes Botschuyver. [With plates.] pp. lxxxiv. 303. *Amstelodami,* 1952. 8°.   **011388.** c. **34.**

Polyglot.

—— Disticha moralia nomine Catonis inscripta : cum Gallica interpretatione, &, vbi opus fuit, declaratione Latina. Hæc editio præter præcedētes non solum authoris Maturini Corderij recognitiōe, sed & Græcā Maximi Planudæ interpretationem habet. Dicta septem Sapientum Græciæ ad finē adiecta sunt, cum sua quoque interpretatiuncula. pp. 128. *Ex officina R. Stephani : Lutetiæ,* 1580. 8°.   **G. 8356.** (**2.**)

—— [Another edition.] pp. 128.   *Ex officina R. Stephani : Lutetiæ,* 1585. 8°.   **8460.** b. **6.**

—— Dionysii Catonis Disticha de moribus ad filium, Græce a Max. Planude, Jos. Scaligero, Matth. Zubero, & Joh. Mylio : Germanice ex mente Jos. Scaligeri potissimum & Casp. Barthii a Martino Opitio expressa. Cum excerptis ac notis ex altera ejusdem recensione brevioribus ; hac editione passim denuo interpolatis & noviter auctis, additis insuper Johanis Sturmi lemmatibus a Christiano Daumio. Qui et addidit incerti veteris poetæ monosticha ; anonymi Salutaris titulo inscripti disticha selectiora ; ut & S. Columbani eique tributa carmina cum notis brevibus. [Edited by C. Daumius.] pp. 268.   *Impensis J. L. Stumpfeldii: Cygneæ,* 1672. 8°.   **237.** c. **39.** (**1.**)

—— Dionysii Catonis Disticha de moribus ad filium . . . lectissimis etiam adornata flosculis poëticis. Unà cum . . . interpretatione quincuplice. [The Greek version by Joseph J. Scaliger ; the English by Charles Hoole ; the German by M. Opitz von Boberfeld.] Adjecta sunt Lemmata Catoniana, suis quaeque restituta distichis. *Lat., Gr., Eng., Dutch, Fr., Ger.* pp. xvi. 347. pl. 6. *Amstelaedami,* 1759. 8°.   **29.** b. **23.**

—— [Another copy.]   **G. 17820.**

—— [Another copy.] Dionysii Catonis Disticha de moribus, *etc. Amstelaedami,* 1759. 8°.   **11386.** cc. **9.** (**1.**) *Imperfect ; wanting the plates.*

—— Historia critica Catoniana, per singulorum seriem consuetam Dionysii Catonis Distichorum ex ordine deducta. Cui praemittuntur Maximi Planudis metaphrasis graeca, cum castigationibus Josephi Scaligeri in eandem perpetuis : itemque Desiderii Erasmi concinna expositio. Adnexae sunt . . . Barthii, Opitii, Daumii, Wachii, Boxhornii, Cannegieteri, Withofii, & Arntzeniorum fratrum, animadversiones selectae. Addita quoque ad calcem Distichorum cuique nova paraphrasis [and the French metrical version of the abbé — Salmon]. pp. viii. 640. *Amstelaedami,* 1759. 8°.   **1001.** k. **1.**

—— [Another copy.]   **11375.** f. **9.**

—— [Another copy.]   **G. 17821.**

—— [Another copy.]   **30.** i. **16.** *Imperfect ; wanting the frontispiece.*

—— [Another copy.] Historia critica Catoniana, *etc. Amstelaedami,* 1759. 8°.   **11386.** cc. **9.** (**2.**) *Imperfect ; wanting the frontispiece and pp.* vii, viii.

—— Distiques de Caton, en hollandais, en latin et en français. *See* BOULARD (A. M. H.) Essai de traduction interlinéaire, des cinq langues, hollandaise, allemande, danoise, suédoise, et hébraïque, *etc.* 1802. 8°.   **11474.** g. **10.**

CATO (MARCUS PORCIUS) *the Censor.* [SUPPOSITITIOUS
WORKS.—DISTICHA DE MORIBUS.]

Latin and Greek.

—— Κατωνος 'Ρωμαιου γνωμαι παραινετικαι διστιχοι ἀς
μετηνεγκεν . . . εἰς την ἑλλαδα διαλεκτον Μαξιμω [*sic*]
'Οπλανοιδης. (Catonis Romani sententiæ morales distichæ,
uersæ . . . in Græcum a Maximo planude.) *See* HESIOD.
[*Opera et Dies.—Greek and Latin.*] In hoc opere continentur Hesiodi ascræi duo libri, *etc.* [1515?] 4°.
11335. c. 49. (1.)

—— [Another edition.] *See* NACHTIGALL (O.) Græce et
Latine. Moralia quædam instituta, *etc.* 1523. 8°.
525. b. 1.

—— Catonis Disticha moralia, cum scholijs Des. Eras. Rot.
Eadem Disticha Græce, a Maximo Planude e Latino uersa.
Apophthegmata Græciæ sapientū interprete Erasmo.
Eadem per Ausonium cum Scholijs Eras. Mimi Publiani,
cum eiusdem scholijs, recogniti. Institutū hominis
Christiani carmine per eundem Eras. Roterod. Isocratis
parænesis ad Demonicum (per . . . Rodolphum Agri-
colam e Græco in Latinum sermonem traducta). Additis
aliquot sapientum dictis. *Apud I. Frob.* [*i.e. Froben*]:
Basileæ, 1526. 8°. 524. d. 16. (3.)

—— Catonis Disticha moralia, Latine et Græce, cum scholijs
D. Erasmi Roterod. De ciuilitate morum per Erasmum
Rot. Reliqua quæ adiuncta sunt æque ad mores perti-
nentia, uersa pagina indicabit. pp. 141.
COPIOUS MS. NOTES. *In officina Frobeniana: Basileæ,*
1534. 8°. 11375. b. 9.
*The contents are those of the edition of 1526, and the " De
civilitate morum " of Erasmus is not contained in the volume.*

—— Catonis Disticha de moribus, cum scholiis D. Eras. Roter.
Eadem græcè à Maximo Planude è Latinis versa . . .
Reliqua sequens pagina indicabit. *Apud hæredes
A. Birckmanni: Coloniæ,* 1571. 8°. 524. d. 16. (1.)
The contents are those of the edition of 1526.

—— [Another edition.] *In ædibus Henrici Middletoni:
Londini,* 1572. 8°. 524. d. 17.

—— Dionysii Catonis Disticha de Moribus, *etc.* (Κατωνος
γνωμαι παραινετικαι διστιχοι, ἀς μετηνεγκεν . . . εἰς
την 'Ελλαδα διαλεκτον Μαξιμος ὁ Πλανουδης.) *See*
PUBLIUS, *Syrus.* Publii Syri Mimi Selectæ Sententiæ, *etc.*
1598. 8°. 524. d. 16. (2.)

—— Dionysii Catonis Disticha de moribus ad filium. Eadem
græce reddita per Ios. Scaligerum. *See* SCALIGER (J. J.)
Iosephi Scaligeri . . . Opuscula diuersa Græca & Latina,
etc. 1605. 8°. 1088. k. 19.

—— Matthæi Zuberi . . . Cato Græcus. [With the Latin
text.] Ad . . . Iosephi Scaligeri notas iterata hac editione
accomodatus & emendatus. Adcesserunt Michaelis
Verini . . . Sententiæ CCCXXIIX. pp. 75. *Apud Danielem
ac Dauidem Aubrios, & C. Schleichium: Hanouiæ,*
1619. 8°. 11408. aaa. 24.

—— Dionysii Catonis Disticha de moribus ad filium: cum
D. Erasmi Roterodami brevi expositione. Eadem græce
reddita per Ios. Scaligerum . . . cum eiusdem notis . . .
Syri item Mimiambi ab eodem Græce redditi. pp. 152.
Apud A. Cloucquium: Lugduni Batavorum, 1626. 8°.
8410. ccc. 37.

—— Dionysii Catonis Disticha, de moribus ad filium. Cum
notis integris Scaligeri, Barthii, Daumii; scholiis atque
animadversionibus selectis Erasmi, Opitii, Wachii; et
metaphrasi graeca Planudis et Scaligeri. Quibus accedunt Boxhornii dissertatio, et Henrici Cannegieteri

CATO (MARCUS PORCIUS) *the Censor.* [SUPPOSITITIOUS
WORKS.—DISTICHA DE MORIBUS.]

rescripta Boxhornio de Catone; nec non Joan. Hild.
Withofii dissertationes binae de Distichorum auctore et
vera illorum lectione. Recensuit, suasque adnotationes
addidit Otto Arntzenius. Editio altera auctior & emendatior. pp. lxxvi. 578. *Amstelaedami,* 1754. 8°.
672. d. 20.

—— [Another copy.] G. 17822.

Latin and English.

—— *Begin.* [fol. 2 *recto:*] Hic incipit paruus Chato. [C]Vm
aīa aduerterē quam hoīes grauiter errare, *etc.* [fol. 3
verso:] Hic incipit magnus Chato. sI deus est animus
nobis vt carmina dicunt, *etc.* *End.* [fol. 28 *recto,* line 22:]
Explicit Chato. [The text with an English translation in
verse by Benedict Burgh. With woodcuts.] 𝕲.𝕷.
[*William Caxton: Westminster,* 1481 ?] fol. IB. 55034.
28 leaves, the first blank. Sig. a–c⁸ d⁴. *29 lines to a page.*

—— *Begin.* [fol. 2 *recto:*] Hic incipit paruus Chato. [C]Um
aīa aduerterē quam hoīes grauiter errare, *etc.* *End.*
[fol. 28 *recto,* line 22:] Explicit Chato. [The text with an
English translation in verse by Benedict Burgh.] 𝕲.𝕷.
[*Westminster,* 1481 ?] fol. Mic. A. 125. (22.)
MICROFILM *of British Museum copy* I.B. 55034. *Made
by the British Museum Microfilm Service.*

—— *Begin.* [fol. 2 *recto:*] Here begynneth the prologue or
prohemye of the book callid Caton, *etc.* [fol. 8 *recto:*]
cVm animaduerterem quam plurimos homines errare in
via morū, *etc.* [*ibid.,* l. 8:] wHan I remembre ₸ consydere
in my corage that moche peple erre greuously in the waye
of maners, *etc.* *End.* [fol. 79 *recto:*] Here fynyssheth
this present book whiche is sayd or called Cathon translated oute of Frensshe in to Englysshe by William Caxton
in thabbay of westmynstre the yere of oure lord
MCCCCLXXXIII . . . the xxiij day of decembre. 𝕭.𝕷.
FEW MS. NOTES. [*William Caxton: Westminster,*
1483 ?] fol. C. 10. b. 8.
80 leaves, ff. 1, 6, 7 *and* 80 *blank. Sig.* (ij, iij)⁶ a–h⁸ i¹⁰.
*38 lines to a page. Without the blank leaves. An edition
of the French original of Caxton's translation₂is entered below
under the sub-heading: Latin and French.*
⅄printed at Lyons, 15₂⅄.

—— *Begin.* [fol. 2 *recto:*] Here begynneth the prologue or
prohemye of the book callid Caton, *etc.* *End.* [fol. 79
recto:] Here fynyssheth this present book whiche is sayd
or called Cathon translated oute of Frensshe in to Englysshe by William Caxton, *etc.* [*William Caxton:
Westminster,* 1483 ?] fol. Mic. A. 120. (1.)
MICROFILM *of the copy of the preceding in Cambridge
University Library. Made by the British Museum Microfilm Service.*

—— Here begynneth the boke of Cato both in Latyn and
Englyshe. [The English translation in verse by Benedict
Burgh.] *See* ISOCRATES. [*Orationes singulae.—Ad Demonicum.—English.*] [The Godly aduertisement or good
counsell of the famous orator Isocrates, intitled Parænesis
to Demonicus, *etc.*] [1557.] 8°. G. 9792.

—— Cato construed, or A familiar and easie interpretation
vpon Catos morall Verses. First doen in Laten and
Frenche by Maturinus Corderius, and now newly englished, *etc.* (Dicta insignia septem sapientum Græciæ, cum
interpretatione.) 𝕭.𝕷. *For Andrewe Maunsell: London,*
1584. 8°. 11375. a. 9.
Cropped.

—— Cato Variegatus, or Catoes Morall Distichs: translated
and paraphras'd, with variations of expressing, in English
verse. By Sʳ Richard Baker, *etc.* [With the Latin text.]
pp. 102. *Printed by Anne Griffin, and are to be sold by
Anne Bowler: London,* 1636. 4°. C. 34. f. 25.

—— [Another copy.] C. 95. c. 24.

CATO (Marcus Porcius) *the Censor.* [Supposititious Works.—Disticha de Moribus.]

—— 1. Catonis disticha de Moribus ; 2. Dicta insignia septem Sapientum Græciæ. 3. Mimi Publiani, sive, Senecæ Proverbia, Anglo-Latina. Cato item grammaticè interpretatus, Latinis & vernaculis vocibus, pari ordine, sed diversis lineis alternatis . . . A Carolo Hoolo . . . 1. Cato's Distichs concerning Manners, etc. pp. 70.
W. Wilson for the Company of Stationers: London, 1659. 8º.
12934. a. 6. (2.)

—— Cato's Disticks of Manners. (Catonis Disticha de moribus.) *See* Wright (James) *M.A.* Sales Epigrammatum . . . Made English by J. Wright. 1663. 8º. **833. c. 4.**

—— [A reissue.] *See* Wright (James) *M.A.* Sales Epigrammatum, etc. 1664. 8º. **11388. a. 44.**

—— 1. Catonis disticha de Moribus ; 2. Dicta insignia septem Sapientum Græciæ. 3. Mimi Publiani, sive, Senecæ Proverbia, Anglo-Latina. Cato item grammaticè interpretatus Latinis & vernaculis vocibus pari ordine sed diversis lineis alternatis . . . A Carolo Hoolo, *etc.* pp. 70.
B. G. for the Company of Stationers: London, 1688. 8º.
12935. de. 21. (1.)
Previous edition 1659.

—— [Another edition.] pp. 70. *Company of Stationers: London,* 1704. 8º. **722. d. 11. (1.)**

—— [Another edition.] pp. 70. *Company of Stationers: London,* 1722. 8º. **11385. b. 14.**

—— Parvus Cato. Magnus Cato. Translated by Benet Burgh. Printed at Westminster by William Caxton about the year 1477. *University Press: Cambridge,* 1906. 8º. [Jenkinson (Francis J. H.) *A series of photogravure facsimiles.*] **12207. n. 35/6.**

—— The Distichs of Cato . . . Translated . . . with introductory sketch, by Wayland Johnson Chase. pp. 43. *Madison,* 1922. 8º. [*University of Wisconsin Studies in the Social Sciences and History.* no. 7.] **Ac. 1792/6.**

—— Dicta Catonis. *See* Duff (John W.) and (A. M.) Minor Latin Poets, *etc.* 1934. 8º. **2282. d. 135.**

Latin and Czech.

—— Catonis disticha moralia, cum scholijs D. Erasmi Roterodami. Et enarratione Boiemica Pauli Aquilinatis Hradeceni. *Excudebat G. Nigrinus: Pragæ,* 1578. 8º. **12975. e. 5. (3.)**

—— Dionysii Catonis Disticha moralia Latino & Bohemico metro edita a I. A. Comenio . . . 1662. *See* Doležal (P.) Grammatica Slavico-Bohemica, *etc.* 1746. 8º. **236. d. 25.**

—— Der Böhmische Cato, *etc.* (Vollständige Ausgabe in vier Büchern.) *See* Dobrovský (J.) Dobrowsky's Slavin, *etc.* 1834. 8º. **829. c. 5.**

—— Dionysia Katona Mrawopisy . . . Dionysii Catonis sententiæ morales distichæ de moribus ad filium . . . Z Dobrowského Slawjna 2ho wydánj zwláště tištěny. pp. 62. *w Praze,* 1834. 8º. **1001. b. 8.**

—— Dionysia Katóna Mravná naučení. Z latiny časoměrně přeložil Jan Amos Komenský. S textem latinským. *See* Rozum (J. V.) Staročeská Biblioteka, *etc.* dil 1. 1853, *etc.* 16º. **12204. a. 1.**

Latin and Danish.

—— Cato De moribus ; Latino-Danicus. *Literis P. Morsingii: Hafniæ,* 1657. 8º. **829. a. 17. (1.)**

CATO (Marcus Porcius) *the Censor.* [Supposititious Works.—Disticha de Moribus.]

Latin and Dutch.

—— Dē grootē Cathoon vol vruchtbarigher leeringhen historiē eñ exempelē also hi sinē sone ond'wees eñ leerde in duechdē eñ goedē manieren datmen hetē mach Tregement der sielē eñ des lichaēs wten walschen in duytschen n v ierst [*sic*] ghetranslateert, *etc.* [With the Latin text. With woodcuts.] ff. xcii. *Gheprent bi C. de Graue: Tantwerpē,* 1519. fol. **11385. k. 21.**

—— De Boec van Catone, een Dietsch leerdicht, uit het Latyn, naer een handschrift van het einde der xiii eeuw. [With the Latin text, and an introduction by D. J. van der Meersch.] pp. 94. *Gent,* [1846 ?] 8º. [*Maetschappy der Vlaemsche Bibliophilen.* ser. 2. no. 8.] **Ac. 9035/2.**

Latin and French.

—— Le Cathon en francoys nouuellement ĩprime. [With the Latin text.] Auecques plusieurs beaulx exemples tres vtilles et proufittables a toutes personnes desirant le salut de son ame. [With a woodcut.] **G.L.** *p O. Arnoullet: Lyon,* 1527. 4º. **11375. d. 6.**

—— [Les Mots dorés de Cathon, en françois et en latin.] [With a woodcut.] **G.L.** [*Paris,* 1530 ?] 8º. **1072. a. 12. (3.)**
Imperfect; wanting all before sig D 4 and after sig. P 4.

—— Les Motz et sentences dorees du maistre de saigesse Caton en Frãcoys et Latin. Auecques bons Enseignemens, Prouerbes . . . & ditz moraulx de Saiges . . . Ensemble plusieurs quæstions enigmatiques. Adiouste de nouueau plusieurs Epitaphes, *etc.* [The French translation in verse.] *On les vend par I. mousnier: Lyō,* 1538. 16º. **C. 19. a. 5.**

—— Disticha de moribus, nomine Catonis inscripta, cum Latina & Gallica interpretatione [by M. Cordier]. Epitome in singula ferè disticha. Dicta sapiētum cum sua quoque interpretatiuncula. Omnia recognita, *etc.* pp. 138. *Ex officina R. Stephani: Parisiis,* 1541. 8º. **827. c. 45. (4.)**

—— Catonis Disticha de moribus. Adiecta . . . Latina & Gallica interpretatione . . . Epitome. D. Erasmi Rot. in singula disticha. Dicta Sapientum Græciæ, aliis sententiis, explicata & vulgaribus versibus reddita, *etc.* [Translated and edited by Charles Estienne.] ff. 52. *Apud F. Stephanum: Parisiis,* 1547. 8º. **1485.a.26.**
Without "Dicta Sapientum Graeciae."

—— Disticha de moribus, nomine Catonis inscripta, cum Latina & Gallica interpretatione, *etc.* pp. 119. *Excudebat R. Stephanus: Lutetiæ,* 1561. 8º. **1001. b. 7.**
Previous edition 1541.

—— Disticha Moralia, nomine Catonis inscripta, Gallicaque interpretatione locupletata, & . . . Latina declaratione illustrata. Huic postremæ editioni, præter Dicta septem sapientum Græciæ, olim Gallicè reddita, & Maturini Corderij castigationes, accesserunt non paucæ grauissimorum virorum sententiæ . . . hactenus in lucem non editæ. Omnia ab innumeris mendis . . . vindicata, & Indice . . . aucta. pp. 123. *Apud I. Gazaud: Lugduni,* 1588. 8º. **11388. aa. 9.**

—— Dionysii Catonis Distichorum de moribus ad filium liber primus(—quartus).—Les Distiques moraux de Denys Caton, *etc.* (Traduction nouvelle par Jules Chenu.) *See* Avianus (F.) Les Fables d'Avianus, *etc.* 1843. 8º. **11306. k. 25. (2.)**

CATO (MARCUS PORCIUS) *the Censor*. [SUPPOSITITIOUS WORKS.—DISTICHA DE MORIBUS.]

Latin and German.

—— Katho. [fol. 1 *verso*:] Hye lert der weyss Catho seynen sun. [fol. 2 *recto*:] [C]Vm animaduerterē quam plurimos Hōies grauiter errare in via morum, *etc.* [*ibid.*, l. 6:] Süsslich hub er auff vnd sprach do er genuck leute sah, *etc.* [The Disticha, with a German translation in verse. With a woodcut.] G.L. [*Heinrich Knoblochtzer: Heidelberg ?* 1490?] 4°. IA. 12987. 18 *leaves*. *Sig.* a–c⁶. 31 *lines to a page*.

—— [Another edition.] [Katho.] [fol. 2 *recto*:] [C]Vm animaduerterem quemplurimos homines grauiter errare in via morum, *etc.* [*ibid.*, l. 7:] Süsslichen hub er auff vnd sprach do er nun genug leute sach, *etc.* G.L. *von Johanne Zainer*: *Vlm*, [1490?] 4°. IA. 9287. 20 *leaves*. *Sig.* [a⁸ b⁶] c⁶. 28 *lines to a page*. *Imperfect; wanting the title-leaf.*

—— [Another edition. With an interlinear gloss.] Catho teutonice expositus. [fol. 2 *recto*:] Incipit doctrina viri moralissimi Marci Cathonis, *etc.* [*ibid.*, l. 6:] so ich catho hab gedacht, *etc.* [l. 8:] OVm [*sic*] animaduerterem ꝗ plurimos, *etc.* [l. 20:] wann ich gedacht han in mynem muot, *etc.* [With a woodcut.] G.L. *A Iohanne Otmar: Reutlingen*, Circa festum Dionisij [9 Oct.], 1491. 4°. IA. 10730. 26 *leaves, the last blank*. *Sig.* a⁸ b–d⁶. 38 *lines to a page*. *Without the blank leaf*.

—— [Another edition.] Catho in latin vnd tutsch. [fol. 1 *verso*:] Cum animaduerterem ꝗ plurimos homines grauiter errare in via morū, *etc.* [*ibid.*, l. 7:] Suſlich hub er vff vñ sprach do er genug leute sach, *etc.* [With a woodcut.] G.L. [*Michael Furter: Basle*, 1495?] 4°. IA. 37830. 16 *leaves*. *Sig.* A⁶ B⁴ C⁶. 34 *lines to a page*.

—— [Another edition.] Katho moralissimus. [fol. 2 *recto*:] CVm animiaduerterez [*sic*] quāplurimos hoīes grauiter errare ī via morū, *etc.* [*ibid.*, l. 6:] Sues hueb er auff vnd sprach Da er genueg leut sach, *etc.* [With a woodcut.] G.L. [*Johann Winterburg: Vienna*, 1495?] 4°. IA. 51535. 18 *leaves*. *Sig.* a⁸ b⁶ c⁴. 30 *lines to a page*.

—— [Another edition. With an interlinear gloss.] Katho. Marci cathonis libri morales cum expositione alemanica. [fol. 2 *recto*:] Prologus. Incipit doctrina viri Moralissimi Marci Cathonis, *etc.* [*ibid.*, l. 4:] so ich katho hab gedacht in mynē gemut, *etc.* [l. 5:] cVm animaduerterē ꝗ plurimos homines, *etc.* [l. 14:] wā ich hab gedacht in minē mut, *etc.* [With a woodcut.] G.L. *per Iohānem Pruβ.*: [*Strasburg*,] Sexto nonas Marcij [2 March], 1499. 4°. IA. 1688. 18 *leaves*. *Sig.* A–C⁶. *The number of lines to a page varies*.

—— [Another edition.] Cathonis carmen de moribus p Anthonium Mancinellum correctum. [With 2 woodcuts.] G.L. *p H. Hölczel conciuem Nurmbegēsem:* [*Nuremburg*,] 1503. 4°. 524. g. 26.

—— Catho in latin: durch Sebastianū Brant geteütschet· [In verse.] G.L. *I. Knoblouch imprimebat: Argentiñ.*, 1508. 4°. 11403. bb. 22

—— [Another edition.] G.L. FEW MS. NOTES. *p I. Knoblouch: Argentine*, 1509. 4°. 11517. cc. 8. (2.)

—— Cathonis viri in moribus grauissimi Codicillus de doctrinis moralibus latino sermone metrice conscriptus. Teutonicis quoꝗ alterationibus. Ac rhicmaticis [*sic*] sententijs denuo interpretatus [by S. Brant]. G.L. [*W. Huber: Nuremburg*, 1510?] 4°. 1001. k. 2.

CATO (MARCUS PORCIUS) *the Censor*. [SUPPOSITITIOUS WORKS.—DISTICHA DE MORIBUS.]

—— Disticha de moribus, nomine Catonis inscripta, cum Latina & Germanica interpretatione, Germanis hactenus non uisa. Epitome in singula fere disticha. Dicta Sapientum cum sua quoꝗ interpretatiuncula. Omnia recognita, nonnulla adiecta, quædam immutata. Maturino Corderio autore. Adiecimus ad finem libellum utilissimum De disciplina et institutione puerorum. [*J. Knoblouch: Strassburg*, 1540.] 8°. 827. d. 36. (6.) *Imperfect; wanting the 85 leaves after sig.* B 3.

—— Dionysii Catonis Disticha de moribus ad filium. Ex mente Ios. Scaligeri potissimùm & Casp. Barthii Germanicè expressa à Martino Opitio. Cum ejusdem excerptis ac notis breuioribus. [With the Latin text.] *See* OPITZ VON BOBELFELD (M.) Martini Opitij . . . Weltliche Poemata, *etc.* Tl. 1. 1644. 8°. 1064. f. 33. (2.)

—— [Another edition.] Adduntur & S. Columbani Carmina, Incerti monosticha de moribus, & anonymi veteris, Salutaris titulo inscripti, disticha selectiora, curante Christiano Daumio. pp. 175. *Typis M. Göpneri; impensis J. Scheibii Bibliopolæ Lipsiensis: Cygneæ*, 1656. 8°. 12935. aa. 11. (3.)

—— Der deutsche Cato. Geschichte der deutschen Übersetzungen der im Mittelalter unter dem Namen Cato bekannten Distichen . . . Von Dr Fr. Zarncke. [With the text in Latin and German.] pp. vi. 198. *Leipzig*, 1852. 8°. 11851. f. 10.

—— Der Neusohler Cato. Ein kritischer Beitrag zur Entwicklungsgeschichte der deutschen Catobearbeitungen von Leopold Zatočil. [With the text in Latin and German.] pp. 118. *Berlin*, 1935. 8°. 11858. c. 4.

Latin and Icelandic.

—— Festschrift der Universität Kiel zur Feier des Geburtsfestes seiner Majestät des Kaisers und Königs Wilhelm II. Hugsvinnsmál. Eine altisländische Übersetzung der Disticha Catonis. Herausgegeben von Hugo Gering. pp. xiii. 39. 1907. 8°. *See* KIEL.—*Academia Christiana Albertina*. Ac. 1030/7.

Latin and Italian.

—— Begin. [fol. 1, *recto*:] Incomenza una breue et utile expositione con la sententia et consructione [*sic*] del sapientissimo Catone. [The Disticha with an Italian translation and an Italian paraphrase.] *per Andreā fritag: Rome*, A di .viii. de Zenaro [1493?] 4°. IA. 19348. 30 *leaves*. *Sig.* a⁸ b⁸ c⁶ d⁸. 35 *lines of commentary to a page*.

Latin and Provençal.

—— Die altprovenzalische Version der Disticha Catonis. Von Rudolf Tobler [i.e. edited by him]. [With the Latin text.] pp. 104. *Berlin*, 1897. 8°. [*Romanische Studien*. Hft. 3.] 12952. ppp. 1/3.

Latin and Spanish.

—— Disticha de moribus, nomine Catonis inscripta, cum Latina & Hispanica interpretatione. Epitome in singula ferè disticha. Dicta sapientum cum sua quoque interpretatiuncula. Omnia recognita, nonnulla adiecta, quædam immutata. pp. 144. *Apud I. & F. Frellonios: Lugduni*, 1543. 8°. 1067. e. 31.

—— Traslación del Doctor Chatón. 1940. [A facsimile of the edition, generally regarded as having been printed in 1490, of the work entitled " La traslation del muy excellente doctor Chaton llamado fecha por vn egregio maestro Martin garcia." The translation in verse.] [*Valencia*,] 1954. 8°. 11453. f. 13. *Incunables poéticos castellanos*. no. 3.

CATO (MARCUS PORCIUS) *the Censor*. [SUPPOSITITIOUS
WORKS.—DISTICHA DE MORIBUS.]

Dutch and French.

—— Die Dietsce Catoen, een middelnederlandsch leerdicht.
Kritisch uitgegeven door Dr. W. T. A. Jonckbloet.
[With "Les Distiques de Caton par Jehan Lefèvre."]
pp. 78. *Leiden*, 1845. 8°. **11555. f. 37. (4.)**

English.

—— *Begin.* [fol. 1 *recto :*] Hic Incipit paruus Catho.
  Cũ aĩadůterẽ quã plurimos hoĩes g̃uiter errare
  Whan I aduerte to my remembrance
  And see how fele folkes erren greuously, *etc.*
[fol. 3 *recto*, l. 15 :] Hic finis parui cathonis. [fol. 3 *verso :*]
Hic Incipit magnus Catho.
End. [fol. 34 *verso :*]
  Here haue I fonde that shal you guyde ꝛ lede
  Streight to gode fame ꝛ leue you in hir hous.
  Explicit Catho.
[A translation in English verse by Benedict Burgh.]
[*William Caxton : Westminster*, 1477 ?] 4°.
  Mic. A. 125. (34.)
*34 leaves, the first blank. Without signatures. 23 lines
to a page. Without the blank leaf. Duff 76.*
MICROFILM *of the copy in Cambridge University Library.
Made by the British Museum Microfilm Service.*

—— *Begin.* [fol. 2 *recto :*]
  Hic Incipit paruus Catho
  [C]Vm aĩduerterem quã hoĩes grauiter errare
  Whanne I aduerte to my remembrance
  And see how fele folkes erren greuously
  In the wey of vertuous gouernance, *etc.*
[fol. 3 *recto*, l. 15 :] Hic finis parui cathonis. [fol. 3 *verso :*]
Hic Incipit magnus Catho.
[fol. 34 *verso*, l. 15 :]
  Here haue I fonde that shal you guyde ꝛ lede
  Streight to gode fame ꝛ leue you in his hous
  Explicit Catho. [Caxton's second edition, Duff 77.]
[*William Caxton : Westminster*, c. 1477.] 4°.
  Mic. A. 423.
*34 leaves, the first blank. Without signatures. 23 lines
to a page.*
MICROFILM (*negative*) *of the copy in the Henry E.
Huntington Library, wanting the blank leaf. Made by the
Henry E. Huntington Library.*

—— Preceptes of Cato, with annotacions of D. Erasmus, *etc.*
[With " The sage and prudent saiynges of the seuen wise-
men " and " The saiynges of Publius." Translated by
Robert Burrant.] 𝕭.𝕷. *In officina Richardi Graftoni :
Londini*, 1553. 16°. **C. 59. aa. 2.**

—— [Another edition.] Newelye imprinted. 𝕭.𝕷. MS. NOTE.
Imprinted by John Tysdale : London, 1560. 16°.
  C. 17. a. 3.

—— The short Sentencez of the wýȝ Cato : Transláted
out-of Latin intoo English by W. Bullokar, imprinted with
tru Ortŏgraphy, and Grammar-nŏtȝ. *See* AESOP. [*English.—Collections.*] Æȝopȝ Fablȝ in tru Ortŏgraphy, *etc.*
1585. 8°. **C. 58. c. 23.**

—— Cato translated grammatically . . . Done for the good
of schools, *etc.* [With " Sayings of wise men among the
Grecians," " Sayings of Mimus Publianus " and " Isocrates admonition to Demonicus." The translator's
epistle dedicatory signed : I. B., i.e. John Brinsley.]
ff. 84. *H. L.* [*i.e. H. Lownes*] *for Thomas Man : London*,
1622. 8°. **11388. a. 10.**

—— Cato in English Verse. With a three-fold table directing
to varietie. 1. Of lessons for all sorts of persons. 2. Of
copies for writing-schollers. 3. Of poesies for the house
and schoole. The second edition . . . By Iohn Penketh-
man. [*A. Mathews*] *for Richard Hawkins : London*,
1624. 8°. **C. 71. a. 20.**

CATO (MARCUS PORCIUS) *the Censor*. [SUPPOSITITIOUS
WORKS.—DISTICHA DE MORIBUS.]

—— Dionysius Cato his four books of Moral Precepts. Translated . . . into English meeter : by J. M. [With MS.
additions of short Latin poems and an English version of
' Qui mihi discipulus.'] pp. 22. *Edinburgh*, 1700. 12°.
  11388. a. 11.

—— Cato's Moral Distichs Englished in couplets [by James
Logan]. pp. 23. *B. Franklin : Philadelphia*, 1735. 4°.
  C. 118. c. 2. (5.)

—— [Another copy.] **230. l. 13.**

—— [A Middle-English verse translation of the " Disticha
de moribus."] *See* GOLDBERG (M. O.) Die Catonischen
Distichen während des Mittelalters in der englischen und
französischen Literatur, *etc.* Tl. 1. 1883. 8°.
  11388. bbb. 15.

Catalan.

—— Libre de Cato. *See* BONSENYOR (J.) Jahuda Bonsenyor. Llibre de paraules, *etc.* 1889. 8°.
  12305. k. 3.

Dutch.

—— Catoos koppel-dichten van de seden, vertaeld ende
berijmd door Samuel Ampzing. pp. 31. *A. Roman :
Haerlem*, 1632. 4°. **11556. cc. 65. (5.)**

—— [Another copy.] **11557. bbb. 66. (7.)**

—— [Another edition.] *See* AMPSING (S.) De Christelycke
Catechismus, *etc.* 1658. 8°. **12352. a. 23. (2.)**

—— Zedevaarzen van Dionys Cato, aan zyn zoon. *See*
HORATIUS FLACCUS (Q.) [*Selections.—Dutch.*] Byge-
dichten uit Horatius, *etc.* 1721. 8°. **11557. de. 68. (4.)**

—— De " Disticha Catonis " in het Middelnederlandsch door
Dr. A. Beets. pp. 107. *Groningen*, 1885. 8°. [*Bibliotheek van Middelnederlandsche letterkunde.* afl. 37.]
  11557. dd. 9. (1.)

French.

—— L'afaitement Catun translaté par Elye de Wincestre
nebst den Überarbeitungen Everarts und eines Anonymus.
(Herausgegeben von E. Stengel.) *See* OVIDIUS NASO (P.)
[*Ars Amatoria.—French.*] Maître Elie's Überarbeitung
der ältesten französischen Übertragung von Ovid's Ars
Amatoria, *etc.* 1886. 8°. **11498. i. 18/47.**

German.

—— Ein deutscher kathon mit ainem Register. [fol. 2
recto :] OElicher mensch nun welle gar eben, *etc.* [*ibid.*,
l. 13 :] Nu vachet des weisen meisters gedichte an also,
etc. [In verse. With woodcuts.] [*Conrad Dinckmut :
Ulm*,] 1492. 4°. **IA. 9375.**
*20 leaves. 2 to 11 numbered i–x, with errors, 15 and 16
numbered x and ix. Without signatures. 26 lines to a
page. A different translation from those in editions containing the Latin and German texts.*

—— Catho Teutsch. Von gemeinem Leben dieser Zeit, *etc.*
[In verse. With a woodcut.] *Gedruckt durch
Arnoldt Keiser : Cölln*, [1570 ?] 8°. **524. b. 35.**
A different translation from the preceding.

Greek.

—— Κατωνος ῾Ρωμαιου Γνωμαι παραινετικαι διστιχοι ἀς
μετηνεγκεν ἐκ τῆς Λατινων φωνης εἰς την ἑλλαδα
διαλεκτον Μαξιμως ὁ Πλανουδης. *See* THEOCRITUS.
[*Greek.*] Ταδε ἐνεστι ἐν τηδε τη βιβλω. Θεοκριτου
εἰδυλλια, *etc.* 1495. fol. **IB. 24405a.**

CATO (MARCUS PORCIUS) *the Censor.* [SUPPOSITITIOUS WORKS.—DISTICHA DE MORIBUS.]

—— [Another edition.] *See* ALEANDRO (Girolamo) *the Elder, Cardinal.* Γνωμολογια, *etc.* 1512. 4°. **832. h. 1.**

—— [Another edition.] *See* BONINI (E.) Ἐγχειριδιον γραμματικης εἰσαγωγης, *etc.* 1514. 8°. **C. 66. d. 9.**

—— [Another edition.] *See* BONINI (E.) Ἐγχειριδιον γραμματικης, *etc.* 1516. 8°. **622. c. 4.**

—— [Another edition.] *See* CHRYSOLORAS (E.) Ἐρωτηματα, *etc.* 1517. 8°. **679. a. 14.**

—— [Another edition.] *See* CHRYSOLORAS (E.) Ἐρωτηματα, *etc.* 1540. 8°. **827. a. 14.**

—— [Another edition.] *See* CHRYSOLORAS (E.) Ἐρωτηματα, *etc.* 1544. 8°. **622. c. 7.**

—— [Another edition.] *Apud I. Bogardum:* [*Paris,*] 1544. 8°. **8463. bbb. 29. (2.)**

—— [Another edition.] *See* CHRYSOLORAS (E.) Ἐρωτηματα, *etc.* 1548. 8°. **622. c. 8.**

Hungarian.

—— Az Cátónak jó erkölcsre tanító parancsolati. *See* TOLDY (F.) Régi Magyar mesék, *etc.* köt. 1. 1858. 12°. **12305. bbb. 4.**

Italian.

—— Cato tradutto de versi Latini in vulgari cō diligentia per Nocturno Neapolitano. *See* NOTTURNO, *Napolitano, pseud.* Le opere Artificiose de Nocturno Neapolitano, *etc.* 1526. 8°. **240. c. 4.**

—— Libro di Cato. (Volgarizzamento antico toscano.) *See* ARISTOTLE. [*Ethica Nicomachea.—Summaries and Paraphrases.—Italian.*] L'Etica d'Aristotle, *etc.* 1734. 4°. **31. h. 14.**

—— Libro de' Costumi di Dionisio Catone. *See* TÉOLI (C.) Gli Ammaestramenti degli antichi, *etc.* 1872. 8°. **8460. aaa. 13.**

—— Duecento meridionale. Il " Libro de Cato " di Catenaccio [i.e. Catenaccio's paraphrase in Italian verse of the " Disticha de Moribus "]. [Edited with an introduction and notes by Antonio Altamura.] *In:* Archivum romanicum. vol. 25. pp. 231–268. 1941. 8°. **P.P. 4884. db.**

Serbo-Croatian.

—— Slate rieci navkaa Katouieh iskora, istomacene i sloxene ù pyesni, yesikom Dubrouackiem, po Marinu Buresicchiu . . . i ktomuy oduecchie Psalam Pokorni Dauidou, s'yednom ispouiesti Gospodinu Bogu, *etc.* *Venetia,* 1562. 8°. **C. 38. c. 42.**

Spanish.

—— Castigos y exemplos de Catō. Nueuamente ympresso. [In verse.] 𝕲.𝕷. *por P. de castro: Medina del cāpo,* 1542. 4°. **C. 39. f. 28. (9.)**

—— Exemplos de Caton, Sacados a luz agora de nueuo por el licenciado Miguel de Cervantes. *Sebastián de Cormellas: Barcelona,* 1609. 8°. **L.R. 263. b. 9.** *A photocopy.*

Appendix.

—— *See* AVIANUS (F.) Flavii Aviani Fabulae . . . Accedunt variae lectiones in . . . Catonis Disticha, curante J. A. Nodell, *etc.* 1787. 8°. **637. g. 3.**

CATO (MARCUS PORCIUS) *the Censor.* [SUPPOSITITIOUS WORKS.—DISTICHA DE MORIBUS.]

—— *See* BIBLE.—*Appendix.*—*Proverbs.* [*Miscellaneous.*] *Begin.* [fol. 2 recto: Hie nach volget das Register, etc.] [fol. 3 recto:] [H]ie nach volgēt gůt nüczlich lere vñ underweÿsung in teütsch beschribē auss den parabolen . . . Auch auss Kathone . . . gezogen, *etc.* [14]72. fol. **IB. 5647.**

—— *See* BISCHOFF (O. E.) Prolegomena zum sogenannten Dionysius Cato, *etc.* 1893. 8°. **11312. o. 14. (4.)**

—— *See* BOAS (M.) Alcuin und Cato. [With the text of the " Praecepta vivendi per singulos versos quae monastica dicuntur," and a discussion of their relation to the Disticha of Cato.] 1937. 8°. **3851. df. 17.**

—— *See* BOAS (M.) De Cato van Adam de Suel. 1935. 8°. **11312. t. 47.**

—— *See* BOAS (M.) Die Epistola Catonis. [On the dedicatory letter accompanying the " Disticha Catonis."] 1934. 8°. [*Verhandelingen der Koninklijke Akademie van Wetenschappen te Amsterdam.* Afd. Letterkunde. Nieuwe reeks. dl. 33. no. 1.] **Ac. 944/3.**

FRAGMENTA EX LIBRIS ORIGINUM.

—— *Begin.* Greci tam impudēti iactantia iam effundūt⁻, *etc.* [Spurious fragments of Cato's " Origines." With a commentary by Joannes Annius.] *See* ANNIUS (J.) *Viterbiensis. Begin.* [fol. 2 recto:] Fratris Ioannis Annii Viterbensis . . . de comentariis Antiquitatū . . . Epistola incipit. 1498. fol. **IB. 19034.**

—— [Another edition.] M. Porcii Catonis De Origine gentium & Vrbiū Italicarum fragmenta. *See* AUCTORES. Auctores Vetustissimi, *etc.* 1498. 4°. **IA. 24330.**

—— [Another edition.] Fragmenta Catonis. *See* BEROSUS, *the Chaldean.* [*Suppositicious Fragments.*] Berosus babylonicus. De his quæ præcesserunt inundationem terrarum, *etc.* [1510.] 4°. **804. a. 39.**

—— [Another edition.] [With a commentary by Joannes Annius.] *See* ANNIUS (J.) *Viterbiensis.* Antiquitatū variarū volumina XVII, *etc.* 1512. fol. **588. i. 11.**

—— Catonis fragmentum ex originibus. *See* ANTONIO, *de Lebrixa, the Elder.* [*Works edited or with commentaries by Antonio de Lebrixa.*] Opuscula in hoc uolumine cōtenta. Archilochus de tēporum antiquitate, *etc.* 1512. 4°. **C. 55. c. 19.**

—— [Another edition.] [With a commentary by Joannes Annius.] *See* ANNIUS (J.) *Viterbiensis.* Antiquitatū variarū volumina XVII, *etc.* 1515. fol. **201. e. 15.**

—— M. Portii Catonis ex libris Originum fragmenta. *See* FRAGMENTA. Fragmenta vetustissimorum autorū, *etc.* 1530. 4°. **803. f. 16.**

—— [Another edition.] *See* VARRO (M. T.) [*De Lingua Latina.*] M. Terentii Varronis de lingua Latina libri tres, *etc.* 1535. 8°. **623. b. 2. (1.)**

—— [Another edition.] *See* VARRO (M. T.) [*De Lingua Latina.*] M. Terentii Varronis de lingua Latina libri tres, *etc.* 1536. 8°. **623. b. 3.**

—— [Another edition.] *See* ANTIQUITATES. Antiquitatum uariarum autores, *etc.* 1552. 16°. **803. a. 1.**

—— M. Catonis fragmenta de originibus, cum commentariis Annii. *See* BEROSUS, *the Chaldean.* [*Suppositicious Fragments.*] Berosi sacerdotis Chaldaici, antiquitatum Italiae ac totius orbis libri quinque, *etc.* 1552. 8°. **804. a. 38.**

CATO (MARCUS PORCIUS) *the Censor*. [SUPPOSITITIOUS
WORKS.—FRAGMENTA EX LIBRIS ORIGINUM.]

—— [Another edition.] *See* BEROSUS, *the Chaldean*. [*Supposititious Fragments*.] Berosi Chaldæi sacerdotis Reliquorumque consimilis argumenti autorum . . . tomus prior [*etc*.]. tom. 2. 1554. 16°.　　**802. a. 23, 24.**

—— M. Porcii Catonis Ex libris Originum fragmenta. *See* ANTIQUITATES. Antiquitatum uariarum autores, *etc*. 1560. 16°.　　**9007. aa. 6.**

—— [Another edition.] *See* BONUTIUS (J.) Historia antiqua, *etc*. pt. 1. 1599, *etc*. 8°.　　**802. d. 31.**

—— M. Catonis fragmenta de originibus, cum commentariis Annij. *See* BEROSUS, *the Chaldean*. [*Supposititious Fragments*.] Berosi sacerdotis chaldaici, antiquitatum libri quinque, *etc*. 1612. 8°.　　**803. d. 35.**

—— The Contrast: Duty and Pleasure, Right and Wrong. [Versions in various languages of a moral maxim occurring in a speech of Cato the Censor. Collected and arranged in chronological order by W. A. G.] Fifth edition. *Kegan Paul, Trench, Trübner, & Co.: London*, 1890. 16°.　　**011652. h. 32.**

—— Sixth edition. pp. 35.　*Kegan Paul, Trench, Trübner & Co.: London*, 1893. 16°.　　**11604. a. 54. (2.)**

—— Fragmenti di M. Catone de le origini con il commento di Annio. *See* BEROSUS, *the Chaldean*. [*Supposititious Fragments*.] I Cinque libri de le antichità de Beroso, *etc*. 1550. 8°.　　**583. a. 1.**

—— —— *See* BARREIROS (G.) Chorographia, *etc*. (Censura . . . sobre hūs fragmentos intitulados em. M. Portio Catam de Originibus, os quaes Ioannes Annio Viterbiense tirou á luz & interpretou.) 1561. 4°.　　**C. 62. b. 35.**

APPENDIX.

—— *See* CORTE (F. della) Catone censore. La vita e la fortuna. 1949. 8°.　　**10608. c. 18.**

—— *See* CORTESE (J.) De M. Porcii Catonis vita, operibus et lingua. 1882. 8°.　　**11840. k. 39. (2.)**

—— *See* CORTESE (J.) Grammatica Catoniana. 1882. 8°.　　**12934. h. 9.**

—— *See* DELTOUR (N. F.) De Sallustio Catonis imitatore seu quid in scriptis C. Crispi Sallustii, ad imitationem M. Porcii Catonis Censorii referri possit, *etc*. 1859. 8°.　　**11352. c. 5.**

—— *See* DIETZE (L.) De sermone Catoniano. 1871. 8°.　　**11312. c. 44. (9.)**

—— *See* ELMER (Herbert C.) The Copulative Conjunctions Que, Et, Atque in the Inscriptions of the Republic, in Terence, and in Cato, *etc*. 1887. 8°.　　**12902. dd. 26. (3.)**

—— *See* FABIUS MAXIMUS (Q.) called *Cunctator*. Fabius und Cato, ein Stück der römischen Geschichte. [By Baron A. von Haller.] 1774. 8°.　　**243. e. 9.**

—— *See* GNAUK (R.) Die Bedeutung des Marius und Cato maior für Cicero. 1936. 8°.　　**20010. g. 44.**

—— *See* HALLER (A. von) *Baron*. Fabio e Catone. Squarcio di storia romana, *etc*. 1783. 8°.　　**9039. c. 5. (1.)**

—— *See* JAEGER (O.) Darstellungen aus der römischen Geschichte, *etc*. (Bdchn. 3. Marcus Porcius Cato.) 1869, *etc*. 8°.　　**9039. c. 18.**

CATO (MARCUS PORCIUS) *the Censor*. [APPENDIX.]

—— *See* JORDAN (Heinrich) Quæstionum Catonianarum capita duo, *etc*. [1856.] 8°.　　**8363. a. 6. (3.)**

—— *See* LIVIUS (T.) *Patavinus*. M. Catonis Cos. et L. Valerij Tr. Pl. legis Oppiæ suasio et dissuasio, ex T. Liuij libro XXXIV. 1604. 4°.　　**686. g. 19. (2.)**

—— *See* MARCUCCI (F.) Studio critico sulle opere di Catone il maggiore. 1902. 8°.　　**11313. d. 33.**

—— [For editions of the Life of Cato by Cornelius Nepos:] *See* NEPOS (C.)

—— *See* PADBERG (F.) Cicero und Cato Censorius. Ein Beitrag zu Ciceros Bildungsgang, *etc*. 1933. 8°.　　**10607. e. 39.**

—— [For editions of Plutarch's life of Cato:] *See* PLUTARCH. [*Vitae Parallelae*.]

—— *See* SKOG (J.) De Marco P. Catone Censorio dissertatio, *etc*. [1695.] 12°.　　**113. a. 7.**

—— *See* TILL (R.) Die Sprache Catos. 1935. 8°. [*Philologus*. Supplementbd. 28. Hft. 2.]　　[MISSING.]

—— *See* VOLLERTSEN (G. H.) Quaestionum Catonianarum capita duo, sive de vita Catonis ejusque fontibus atque de Originibus, *etc*. 1880. 4°. [*Schriften der Universität zu Kiel*. Bd. 26.]　　**Ac. 1030.**

—— *See* ZEDERGOL'M (K.) О жизни и сочиненіяхъ Катона Старшаго. Разсужденіе, *etc*. 1857. 8°.　　**10790. ee. 16. (3.)**

—— Catone convertito. Avvertimenti ad un giovine di belle speranze. [By Count Domenico Gnoli.] pp. 23. *Imola*, 1872. 8°.　　**8409 b. 3.**

—— Orationes aduersariae M. Portij Catonis, & L. Valerij de lege Oppia. Item duæ Persei atq; Demetrii, fratrum, apud Philippum. (Philippi patris querela ad filios.) [The whole extracted from Books 34 and 40 of Livy.] pp. 32. *Excudebat C. Wechelus: Parisiis*, 1531. 8°.　　**5255. a. 31.**
The headtitles of the last three orations are transposed by mistake in printing.

CATO (MARCUS PORCIUS) *of Utica*.

—— *See* AFZELIUS (Adam) *of Copenhagen*. Die politische Bedeutung des jüngeren Cato. 1941. 8°. [*Classica et mediaevalia*. vol. 4.]　　**Ac. 9876.**

—— 　　　　　　　　　　　　*See* BUTENSCHOEN (J. F.) Caesar, Cato und Friedrich von Preussen, *etc*. 1789. 8°.　　**9004. bb. 8.**

—— *See* CIPOLLA (C.) M. Porcio Catone Uticense, custode del Purgatorio. [On Dante's view of Cato.] 1900. 8°.　　**11422. dd. 5. (1.)**

—— *See* GERLACH (F. D.) Marcus Porcius Cato der jüngere, *etc*. 1866. 8°.　　**10605. c. 39. (4.)**

—— *See* HORTENSIUS (Q.) Le Vite di quattro illustri Senatori Romani, Ortensi, M. P. Catone Uticense, *etc*. 1748. 8°.　　**277. i. 37.**

—— *See* LANCKOROŃSKI (S.) Cato Stanislai Lanczkoronsky . . . Declamatio . . . in laudem M. Portii Catonis, *etc*. 1602. 4°.　　**7942. h. 21. (3.)**

—— *See* OMAN (*Sir* Charles W. C.) *K.B.E.* Seven Roman Statesmen of the Later Republic . . . Cato, *etc*. 1902. 8°.　　**2402. b. 2.**

—— [For editions of Plutarch's life of Cato:] *See* PLUTARCH. [*Vitae Parallelae*.]

CATO (MARCUS PORCIUS) *of Utica.*

—— *See* THEOBALD (Lewis) The Life and Character of Marcus Portius Cato, *etc.* 1713. 4°.   **81. c. 1. (1.)**

—— *See* WARTMANN (H.) Leben des Cato von Utica, *etc.* 1859. 8°.   **10604. bb. 14.**

—— Cato Redivivus ; or, New wine in old bottles. A tragedy born again. [In verse.] pp. 150.   *S. Tinsley & Co.:* *London*, 1879. 8°.   **11781. bbb. 36.**

—— Catone. Drama . . . [By P. A. D. B. Metastasio.] Done into English by Mr. Humphreys.   *Ital. & Eng.* pp. 63.   *T. Wood: London*, 1732. 8°.   **639. d. 19. (6.)** *The last leaf is mutilated.*

—— Parody on Cato's Soliloquy [in Act v., Scene 1 of Addison's " Cato "].   [*Fowler: Salisbury*, 1785 ?] *s. sh.* 12°.   **11621. i. 11. (24.)**

—— The Unfortunate General : or the History of the life and character of Cato. Together with a key, and explanation, of the new-play [by J. Addison], call'd Cato, a tragedy. pp. 24.   *Edw. Midwinter: London*, [1713 ?] 8°.   **641. f. 38.**

CATO (PUBLIUS VALERIUS) [For editions of the poems known as " Diræ," variously attributed to Virgil and to P. Valerius Cato, included in editions of the works or minor poems of Virgil :] *See* VIRGILIUS MARO (P.)

—— Valerii Catonis Diræ. *See* EPIGRAMMATA. Epigrammata et Poematia vetera, *etc.* 1590. 12°.   **1001. e. 1.**

—— [Another edition.] *See* EPIGRAMMATA. Epigrammata, *etc.* 1596. 12°.   **1002. a. 1.**

—— [Another edition.] *See* BOXHORN (M. Z.) Poetæ satyric minores, *etc.* 1633. 12°.   **1213. c. 6. (2.)**

—— [Another edition.] Christophorus Arnoldus ex editionibus & emendationibus variorum expressit, & repræsentavit. Accedit ejusdem ad omnia poëtæ commentarius liber. pp. 287.   *E typographeo F. Hackii: Lugd. Bat.*, 1652. 12°.   **1089. c. 20.**

—— [Another edition.] *See* AMATI (P.) Collectio Pisaurensis omnium poematum . . . latinorum, *etc.* tom. 4. 1766. fol.   **653. d. 14.**

—— [Another edition.] 1782. *See* WERNSDORF (J. C.) Poetæ latini minores, *etc.* tom. 3. 1780, *etc.* 8°.   **160. k. 12.**

—— [Another edition.] *See* PETRONIUS ARBITER (T.) [*Latin.*] T. Petronii Arbitri Satiricon, *etc.* 1790. 8°.   **1489. aa. 14.**

—— [Another edition.] Ex recensione Wernsdorfiana. 1824. *See* LEMAIRE (N. E.) Bibliotheca classica latina, *etc.* vol. 135. 1819, *etc.* 8°.   **11305. m. 5.**

—— [Another edition.] Carmina Valerii Catonis cum Augusti Ferdinandi Naekii annotationibus. Accedunt eiusdem Naekii de Virgilii libello Iuvenalis ludi, de Valerio Catone eiusque vita et poesi, de libris tam scriptis quam editis, qui carmina Catonis continent, dissertationes IV. Cura Ludovici Schopeni. pp. x. 437.   *Bonnæ*, 1847. 8°.   **11385. g. 39.**

—— [Another edition.] Ueber die strophische Composition der Diræ des Valerius Cato. Mit einigen kritischen Bemerkungen von Dr. Franz Caspar Goebbel. [With the text.] pp. 52.   *Warendorf*, 1861. 8°.   **11312. cc. 48. (5.)**

—— [Another edition.] Valeri Catonis quae feruntur Carmina. Recensuit . . . Franc. Caspar Goebbel, *etc.* pp. 32.   *Warendorpii*, 1865. 8°.   **11388. bb. 35.**

CATO (PUBLIUS VALERIUS)

—— Valerius Caton. Traduction nouvelle par M. Cabaret-Dupaty.   *Lat. & Fr.   See* CABARET-DUPATY (J. R. T.) Poetæ minores, *etc.* 1842. 8°.   [*Bibliothèque latine-française, etc.* sér. 2.]   **11306. k. 31.**

CATO (VALERIUS)   *See* CATO (Publius Valerius)

CATO-BATAVUS, *pseud.* [i.e. A. TINNE.] Brief van Cato-Batavus, aan zyn vriend, den Gryzen Hollander, over de onlangs voorgevallene rencontre, tusschen het Esquader van den Schout by Nagt Grave van Byland, en dat van den Commodore Fielding. pp. 16.   *'s Hertogenbosch*, [1780.] 8°.   **934. f. 9. (6.)**

CATOEN (DIONYSIUS)   *See* CATO.

CATOIR (EUGENIUS AUGUSTUS) Dissertatio inauguralis juridica, de collatione, secundum jus civile hodiernum, *etc.* pp. 38.   *Leodii*, 1825. 4°.   **498. f. 9. (12.)**

CATOIR (JOHANNES NICOLAUS) Disputatio theologica de arca Noachi et diluvio, *etc.   Praes.* J. Braunius.   *Groningæ*, 1704. 4°.   **T. 2196. (10.)**

—— [Another copy.]   **T. 2172. (27.)**

CATOIRA (GOMEZ HERNANDEZ) An Account of the Voyage and Discovery which was made in the South Sea . . . under the command of Alvaro de Mendaña, *etc.   See* AMHERST (William A. T.) *Baron Amherst of Hackney*, and THOMSON (*Sir* B. H.) *K.C.B.* The Discovery of the Solomon Islands by Alvaro de Mendaña, *etc.* vol. 2. 1901. 4°.   **K.T.C. 102. b. 6.**

CATOIRE (   )   *See* DEZALLIER D'ARGENVILLE (A. J.) [La Conchyliologie.] COPIOUS MS. NOTES [by — Catoire]. [1780.] 4°.   **443. f. 9.**

CATOIRE (PIERRE)

—— André Vésale. Mystique et expériences. pp. 159.   *Bruxelles*, 1947. 8°.   **010760. g. 95.**

CATOIS (PIERRE ÉMILE) Étude sur le panaris et son traitement. pp. 39.   *Paris*, 1875. 4°. [*Collection des thèses soutenues à la Faculté de Médecine de Paris.* An 1875. tom. 4.]   **7374. b.**

CATOLICISMO.   *See also* CATHOLICISM.

—— El Catolicismo neto. *See* PERIODICAL PUBLICATIONS.— *London.* Pure Catholicism.

CATÓLICO.   *See also* CATHOLIC.

—— El Católico. Periodico religioso, filosófico, histórico y literario. *See* PERIODICAL PUBLICATIONS.—*Lima.*

—— El Católico. Periodico religioso, político-cristiano, científico, y literario. *See* PERIODICAL PUBLICATIONS.— *Mexico.*

CATÓLICOS.   *See* CATHOLICS.

—— Católicos Españoles. *See* SPANISH CATHOLICS.

CATOLOGUE.   *See* CATALOGUE.

CATON. The Registers of Caton, 1585–1718. Indexed by Henry Brierley. pp. 121.   *Preston*, 1922. 8°. [*Lancashire Parish Register Society.* vol. 59.]   **Ac. 8088/50. (1.)**

CATON, *le Censeur, pseud.* Harangue & Remonstrance presentées au Roy par le Censeur Caton : sur les affaires de ce temps. pp. 24.   [*Paris,*] 1619. 12°.   **8052. bb. 20.**

CATON, *le Censeur, pseud.* [i.e. FRANCISQUE TAPON FOUGAS.] Le Baron de Saint-Ignace, ou Tartufe en 1850. Comédie-drame, en cinq actes et en vers, avec prologue et épilogue. Par Caton le Censeur. pp. 104.   *Paris*, 1850. 12°.   **11739. b. 32. (4.)**

CATON, *pseud.* Advis de Caton en l'assemblée des Chambres, ce 11. de mars 1615. Sur le sujet de la Paulete. pp. 15. 1615. 8°.   **8052. bbb. 16. (9.)**

—— " El Monitor," o la Guerra de relijion. [Signed: Caton.] pp. 25. *Bogotá*, 1861. 8°.   **8179. e. 34. (18.)**

CATON, *pseud.* [i.e. CHARLES CATON DE COURT.] La Campagne de L'Ille, contenant un journal fidéle de ce qui s'est passé au siége de cette importante place & à l'occasion de Wynendael; comme aussi le fameux passage de l'Escaut. [With tables and plans. The dedicatory epistle signed: Caton.] pp. 204. *La Haye*, 1709. 12°.   **292. c. 30. (1.)**

CATON CHRESTIEN, *pseud.* [i.e. MATTHIEU DE MORGUES, *Sieur de Saint Germain.*] *See* CHRESTIEN (C.) *pseud.*

CATON FRANÇOIS. *See* FRENCH CATO.

CATON, *Family of. See* KEIDEL (George C.) [Essays on Catonsville and the Caton family.] 1919, *etc.* 8°.   **09917. ccc. 26.**

CATON (ALETHEIA C.) *See* ERNST (Otto) *pseud.* Asmus Semper . . . Translated by A. Caton. 1909. 8°.   **12552. w. 25.**

—— *See* ERNST (Otto) *pseud.* Dolls—Dead and Alive . . . Translated by A. C. Caton. 1911. 16°. **012199. de. 3/3.**

—— *See* ERNST (Otto) *pseud.* Roswitha . . . Translated by A. C. Caton. 1913. 8°.   **12555. tt. 32.**

—— —— 1913, *etc.* 8°.   **012555. a. 12.**

—— *See* SALUS (H.) Children : a Märchen. [Translated by A. C. Caton.] 1910. 16°. **012199. de. 3/1.**

—— —— 1912. 16°.   **012199. de. 3/2.**

CATON (ALICE GERTRUDE) *See* BECK (William E.) and CATON (A. G.) " Adventurers for God." [1922.] 8°.   **04192. a. 12.**

—— Old Time Stories and Old World Customs . . . Illustrated. 3 pt. *Macmillan & Co.: London*, 1913. 8°.   **09009. aaa. 26.**

—— The Romance of Wirral. [With illustrations and a map.] pp. 81. *Philip, Son & Nephew: Liverpool*, 1913. 8°.   **010352. g. 52.**

—— The Romance of Wirral . . . Second edition. pp. 81. *Philip, Son & Nephew: Liverpool*, 1946. 8°.   **10359. aa. 19.**

—— Soldiers of the Cross. pp. viii. 101. *Longmans & Co.: London*, 1917. 8°. [*London Diocesan Sunday School Manuals.*]   **04419.i.35/13.**

—— Stories from History and Literature. 3 ser. *Macmillan & Co.: London*, 1912. 8°. **12200. bb. 21.**

CATON (ANNIE ROSE) Activity and Rest. The life and work of Mrs. William Archer, *etc.* [With a portrait.] pp. xv. 149. *P. Allan & Co.: London*, 1936. 8°.   **010821. e. 14.**

—— Gond Neighbours of the Jamai Village Ashram, Central Provinces. [With plates.] pp. 19. [1937.] 8°.   **010056. aa. 17.**

—— The Key of Progress. A survey of the status and conditions of women in India. By several contributors . . . Edited by A. R. Caton. [With a bibliography.] pp. ix. 250. *Oxford University Press: London*, 1930. 8°.   **08416. bb. 28.**

CATON (ANNIE ROSE) and BERRY (MARIAN)

——   A Signpost to Civic Health and Welfare, *etc.* pp. v. 138.   *P. S. King & Son: London*, 1927. 8°. [*Signpost Series.* no. 1.]   **W.P. 8876/1.**

CATON (DENNIS)

—— Advertising explained. pp. 111.   *George Allen & Unwin: London*, 1949. 8°.   **8230. a. 77.**

CATON (JOHN DEAN) The Antelope and Deer of America. A comprehensive scientific treatise, *etc.* [With a portrait.] pp. 426.   *Hurd & Houghton: New York*, 1877. 8°.   **7206. dd. 1.**

—— Miscellanies. [With a portrait.] pp. vii. 360. *Houghton, Osgood & Co.: Boston*, 1880. 8°. **12296. f. 4.**

—— A Summer in Norway . . . Also, an account of the red-deer, reindeer and elk. [With plates, including a portrait.] pp. 401.   *Jansen, McClurg & Co.: Chicago*, 1875. 8°.   **10281. dd. 1.**

CATON (R.) *Maître de Poste de Nantes.* Réflexions d'un maître de poste, sur le projet de réglement concernant les postes aux chevaux, présenté au Couseil [*sic*] des Cinq-Cents, le 7 germinal, par le représentant Brion, au nom des commissions des Transports, Postes et Messageries et des Finances. pp. 8. [*Paris*, 1794 ?] 8°.   **F. 472. (3.)**

CATON (RICHARD) *See* ARGONAUTS. A Narrative of the Voyage of the Argonauts . . . illustrated by the photographer [i.e. R. Caton], *etc.* 1881. 8°.   **10281. f. 10.**

—— *See* HOWARD (Theodore A.) Vivisection. A reply to a letter written by Dr. Caton, *etc.* 1897. 8°.   **8425. e. 26. (10.)**

—— Description of the Model of the Central Part of Ancient Rome as it existed at the close of the reign of the Emperor Constantine, about A.D. 335 . . . Second edition. [With a plate.] pp. 16. 1899. 8°.   *See* LIVERPOOL.—*Free Public Library, Museum, etc.*   **010136. f. 57.**

—— How to Live. A short account, in simple words, of the laws of health, with brief references to habits and conduct, *etc.* pp. 42. *Williams & Norgate: London*, 1905. 8°.   **7306. aa. 32. (1.)**

—— I. I-em-hotep and Ancient Egyptian Medicine. II. Prevention of Valvular Disease. The Harveian Oration delivered before the Royal College of Physicians on June 21, 1904, *etc.* pp. 34. pl. v.   *C. J. Clay & Sons: London*, 1904. 8°.   **7680. df. 22.**

—— The Prevention of Valvular Disease of the Heart. A proposal to check rheumatic endocarditis in its early stage and thus prevent the development of permanent organic disease of the valves, *etc.* pp. x. 92. *C. J. Clay: London*, 1900. 8°.   **7616. dd. 12.**

—— Two Lectures on the Temples and Ritual of Asklepios at Epidaurus and Athens . . . Reprinted from " Ötia Merseiana."   pp. 42. *S. Austin & Sons: Hertford*, 1899. 8°.   **4506. f. 17.**

—— Second edition. pp. ii. 49. *C. J. Clay & Sons: London*, 1900. 8°.   **4503. g. 23.**

CATON (T. MOTTE) Popular Remarks, medical and literary, on nervous, hypochondriac, and hysterical diseases : to which are prefixed, observations on suicide, with an attempt to delineate the soul and its character. pp. 74. *W. Neely: London*, [1815 ?] 8°.   **7660. b. 10.**

CATON (T. Motte)

—— Practical Observations on the Debilities, natural and contracted, of the Generative Organs of both sexes . . . Eleventh edition. pp. 90. *J. Martin: London*, 1814. 8°. [MISSING.]

CATON (William) *See* Eusebius, *Pamphili, Bishop of Caesarea in Palestine.* [*Historia Ecclesiastica.—English.*] An Abridgement . . . of the . . . Chronologies . . . contained in that famous Ecclesiasticall History of Eusebius . . . by W. Caton. 1661. 12°.   **4530. aa. 22.**

—— —— 1698. 8°.   **4532. a. 9.**

—— *See* Fell, afterwards Fox (Margaret) An Evident Demonstration to God's Elect, *etc.* [With a postscript signed: W. C., i.e. W. Caton.] 1660. 4°.   **4152. f. 19. (13.)**

—— *See* Friends, *Society of.* Three General Epistles for the Whole Body of Friends.   1)   W. Caton.   2) from R. Greenway: 3) C. Bacon. 1662. 4°.   **4151. b. 30.**

—— *See* Hendricks (P.) The Backslider Bewailed . . . Translated . . . by W. C. [i.e. W. Caton.] 1665. 4°.   **4152. b. 42.**

—— *See* Moore (William) *of the Society of Friends.* Newes out of the East, *etc.* [Edited by W. Caton.] 1664. 4°.   **4152. f. 20. (5.)**

—— *See* Stubs (John) *of Bishoprick.* A True Declaration of the Bloody Proceedings of the Men in Maidstone . . . against J. Stubs [and] W. Caton, *etc.* 1655. 4°.   **E. 843. (2.)**

—— *See* Zins-Penninck (J.) Some Worthy Proverbs . . . Translated by . . . W. C. [i.e. W. Caton.] 1663. 4°.   **4152. c. 34.**

—— [Two letters, the first dated 4 August 1663, the second 14 November 1663.] *See* Jackson (Henry) *Quaker.* A Visitation of Love, *etc.* 1663. 4°.   **4151. c. 71.**

—— Eine Beschirmung d' Unschüldigen wider die Lästermäuler. Oder eine kurtze Antwort auf fünff schändliche Bücher, aussgegeben wider das Volck Quäker genant. Das 1. durch Christianum Pauli . . . genant Augensalbe. Das 2. durch Johann Berckenthal . . . genant Der Quäker Hertzen-grund. Das 3. . . . genant Der Quaker Quackeley. Das 4. . . . genant Der Quaker Natur und Eigenschafft. Das 5. . . . durch Benedict Figken . . . genant Der Alte Anabaptist, und der Newe Quaker . . . Zuletzt ist auch beygefüget ein Klarer Beweiss [by B. Furly], dass Hermes Trismegistus, Socrates, Plato und viel andere Heydnische Philosophi von Christo dem Sohne . . . Gottes gewust, geschrieben und gezeuget haben ; wider die falsche Stellung Christiani Pauli, *etc.* pp. 78. *Amsterdam*, 1664. 4°.   **4152. g. 2.**

—— *See* Figk (B.) Doctrina Fanaticorum, oder eine vollkommene Relation und Wissenschafft von der neuen Quäcker eigentlichen Lehr und Opinion . . . und wider . . . William Caton und denn noch andere . . . gerichtet, *etc.* 1679. 8°.   **1368. c. 4. (2.)**

—— *See* Pauli (C.) Hellklingender Wiederschall, oder eine Beschirmung der Unschuldigen . . . darin dargethan wird wie übel . . . W. Caton auff sich genommen, seiner Brüder Sache . . . gegen C. P. [i.e. C. Pauli] Augensalbe auszuführen, *etc.* 1665. 8°.   **4139. bb. 63. (5.)**

—— An Epistle to King Charles the II. sent from Amsterdam . . . the 28. of the 10. month, 1660, *etc.* pp. 15. *For Thomas Simmons: London*, 1660. 4°.   **100. g. 44.**

CATON (William)

—— A Journal of the Life of . . . Will. Caton. Written by his own hand. pp. 83. *For Thomas Northcott: London*, 1689. 4°.   **855. f. 9. (2.)**

—— [Another edition.] To which are now added . . . some of his letters. 1845. *See* Evans (William) *Publisher, of Philadelphia*, and Evans (Thomas) *Publisher, etc.* The Friends' Library, *etc.* vol. 9. 1837, *etc.* 8°.   **4152. gg. 4.**

—— [Another edition.] Journals of the Lives and Gospel Labours of William Caton and John Burnyeat. Second edition. Also, a brief memoir concerning John Croker, of Plymouth, *etc.* pp. xviii. 330.   *Harvey & Darton: London*, 1839. 12°. [Barclay (John) *A Select Series . . . Chiefly the productions of early members of the Society of Friends.* vol. 6.]   **1372. b. 3.**

—— The Moderate Enquirer resolved in a plain description of several objections . . . concerning the contemned people, commonly called Quakers . . . Written . . . by W. C. [i.e. W. Caton.] pp. 36. 1671. 4°. *See* C., W.   **4152. ee. 18. (4.)**

—— Moderatus Inquisitor resolutus: in aparta [*sic*] descriptione objectionum multarum . . . De populo illo contempto, vulgariter appellato Trementes, Anglice Quakers, *etc.* (The Moderate Enquirer resolved, *etc.*) *Lat. & Eng.* pp. 121. *Pro Roberto Wilson: Londini*, 1660. 8°.   **856. f. 30. (1.)**

—— Den Matelijcken ondersoeker voldaen, *etc.* (De derde mael in het Nederduyts herdruckt.) pp. 27. *S. Swart: Amsterdam*, 1669. 4°.   **855. i. 1. (15.)**

—— De Oorsaeck van de pest, en andere oordeelen uytgevonden ; met een goede remedie . . . Oock yets aen de Doops-gesinde—soo genaemt—soo in de Geunieerde Provintien als elders, *etc.* pp. 24.   *C. Cunradus: Amsterdam*, 1665. 4°.   **855. i. 1. (36.)**

—— William Caton's Salutation and Advise unto Gods Elect, *etc.* *For Thomas Simmons: London*, 1660. *s. sh. fol.*   **T. 377. (12.)**

—— The Sea-mens Invitation, with a passenger's observation in some particular things which concern them that practise navigation, *etc.* pp. 15. *For Thomas Simmons: London*, 1659. 4°.   **T. 377. (13.)**

—— The Testimony of a Cloud of Witnesses, who . . . have testified against that horrible evil of forcing of conscience, and persecution about matters of religion . . . Composed together and translated into English by . . . W. Caton. pp. 51. 1662. 4°.   **4152. f. 4. (13.)**

—— Truths Caracter of Professors and their Teachers, *etc.* pp. 56. *For Thomas Simmons: London*, 1660. 4°.   **4106. b. 35.**

—— Een Woort ter rechter tijt, tegens dat gemeene spreeckwoort, van mijn geest-getuygt, 't welck spottelijck en lasterlijck veelsins ghebruyckt werdt, door god'loose en ydele menschen, *etc.* pp. 8. *Amsterdam*, 1669. 4°.   **855. i. 1. (23.)**

—— Een Woort tot de Doopsgesinde. *See* Keith (George) *Rector of Edburton.* Het Decksel gescheurt, ende een deure geopent tot de eenvoudige, *etc.* 1670. 4°.   **855. i. 1. (47.)**

CATON (William) and **ROELOFFZ** (Jan)

——   Een Rechtvaerdighe verdedginge der waerheyt onses Godts ; ofte een antwoordt op een boek—genaemt Antwoordt op seker geschrift— uytgegeven door Pieter Joosten de Volder, *etc.* pp. 31. *A. J. van der Beeck: Hoorn*, 1662. 4°.   **855. i. 1. (32.)**

CATON (William Charles) Die Rolle des Obersten House im Rahmen der Friedensaktion Wilsons im Jahre 1916/17. Inaugural-Dissertation, *etc.* pp. 71. *Heidelberg,* 1937. 8º. **20010. c. 61.**

CATON DE COURT (Charles)
—— *See also* Caton, *pseud.* [i.e. C. Caton de Court.]

—— *See* Genest (C. C.) Portrait de M. de Court. 1696. 8º. **612. b. 25. (5.)**

CATONE, *l'Uticense, Lucchese, pseud.* [i.e. Francesco Maurello.] Enimmi di Catone l'Uticense Lucchese. (Ænigmatum Catonis Uticensis latina æmulatio.) *Ital. & Lat.* pp. 142. 142. *Parma,* 1760. 8º. **90. i. 16.**

CATONE (Dionysius) *See* Cato.

CATONE (Marco Porcio) *See* Cato (M. P.) *the Censor.*

CATONE (Marco Porzio) *Uticense. See* Cato (M. P.) *of Utica.*

CATONI (Julius) De pubertate constituenda per potentiam generativam quæ in quæstionibus medicinæ legalis dirimendis apprime inservit. Dissertatio, *etc.* pp. 19. *Ticini Regii,* 1819. 8º. **7383*. d. 13. (10.)**

CATONI (Michael) Animadversiones in argumenta, e quibus epidemico-constitutionalem vel contagiosam cholerae orientalis indolem auctores eruere nituntur, *etc.* pp. 32. *Ticini Regii,* [1832.] 8º. **7383*. b. 4. (8.)**

CATONIUS (Alexander) Exercitium academicum de pluvia, *etc.* Praes. H. Vallerius. pp. 44. *Upsaliæ,* [1708.] 8º. **1090. e. 9. (4.)**

CATONIUS (Ericus) Specimen academicum de arce Calmariensi, *etc.* Praes. A. Grönwall. pp. 38. *Upsaliæ,* [1735.] 4º. **1056. d. 18. (5.)**

—— [Another copy.] **150. b. 16. (3.)**

CATON-THOMPSON (Gertrude) *See* Thompson.

CATOPTRICON. Catoptricon. A scrapbook. *R. Henseler: London,* [1865.] 4º. **8225. bbb. 33.**

CATOR (Ambrose) *See* Baudot (Jules) *Bénédictin de Farnborough.* The Lectionary: its sources and history . . . Translated . . . by A. Cator. 1910. 8º. **3477. df. 5.**

—— *See* Rego (S. de) The Apostle of Ceylon, Fr. Joseph Vaz . . . Translated [and abridged] . . . by A. Cator. 1913. 8º. **4864. dg. 3.**

CATOR (Charles) Address to the Throne read at a General Meeting of the Clergy of the Archdeaconry of York, *etc.* pp. 13. *Baldwin & Cradock: London,* 1829. 8º. **1225. h. 10. (22.)**

—— An Affectionate Address and Caution to the Parishioners of Stokesley, *etc.* pp. 6. *W. Braithwaite: Stokesley,* 1837. 8º. **1225. h. 10. (3.)**

—— The Cholera Morbus, a Visitation of Divine Providence. A sermon . . . Second edition. pp. 30. *Baldwin & Cradock: London,* 1832. 8º. **T. 1345. (16.)**

—— Third edition. pp. 32. *Baldwin & Cradock: London,* 1832. 8º. **1225. h. 10. (11.)**

—— The Church Rate Question. A letter addressed to the Right Hon. Lord Palmerston, *etc.* pp. 16. *Rivingtons: London,* 1856. 8º. **4108. d. 17.**

—— The Church Rate Question. A second letter addressed to the Right Hon. Lord Palmerston, *etc.* pp. 8. *Rivingtons: London,* 1857. 8º. **4108. d. 18.**

CATOR (Charles)

—— " A Citizen of No Mean City." A sermon, *etc.* pp. 39. *J. G. F. & J. Rivington: London,* 1839. 8º. **T. 2456. (5.)**

—— [Another edition.] To this sermon is prefixed an advertisement, containing a reply to the Wesleyan Methodist Magazine, for December 1839; and to the appendix is added the correspondence between the late Lord Mayor's Chaplain [C. Cator] and Sir Peter Laurie, Kt upon the Minutes of the Court of Common Council pp. 38. 8. 15. *J. G. F. & J. Rivington: London* [1839.] 8º. **1225. h. 10. (20.**

—— The Claim of the Christian Minister to Attention from the People. A sermon, *etc.* pp. 31. *Baldwin & Cradock: London,* 1832. 8º. **T. 1345. (21.)**

—— Second edition. pp. 32. *Baldwin & Cradock: London,* 1832. 8º. **1225. h. 10. (12.)**

—— Continuing in the Apostles' Doctrine and Practice. 1834. *See* Family Sermons. Original Family Sermons. vol. 4. no. 21. 1833, *etc.* 8º. **694. b. 4.**

—— Coronation Sermon preached at Stokesley . . . June 28th, 1838. pp. 15. *J. G. & F. Rivington: London,* 1838. 12º. **T. 2297. (12.)**

—— Second edition, *etc.* pp. 15. *J. G. & F. Rivington: London,* 1838. 12º. **1225. h. 10. (17.)**

—— The Doctrine and Ritual of the Church of England. Designed as a second series of letters on the necessity of a national Church, addressed to His Grace the Archbishop of Canterbury, *etc* pp. 167. *Baldwin & Cradock: London,* 1836. 8º. **4106. g. 9.**

—— [Another copy. **1225. h. 10. (24.)**

—— The Efficacy of Prayer; being an address delivered in the Parish Church of Stokesley on Tuesday, February 27th, 1872, *etc.* pp. 8. *Tweddell & Sons: Stokesley,* 1872. 12º. **4473. a. 28. (8.)**

—— A Farewell Sermon, preached at the Parish Church of Carshalton . . . on Sunday, the 9th of August 1835. pp. 29. *Baldwin & Cradock: London,* 1835. 8º. **T. 1910. (10.)**

—— [Another copy.] **1225. h. 10. (14.)**

—— A Farewell Sermon, preached at the Parish Church of Kirk-Smeaton . . . on Sunday the 13th of September 1829. pp. 24. *Baldwin & Cradock; Simpkin & Marshall: London,* 1829. 8º. **1225. h. 10. (10.)**

—— Influence of the Visible Church upon the World. A sermon, *etc.* pp. 19. *Baldwin & Cradock: London,* 1836. 8º. **1225. h. 10. (16.)**

—— Instruction in the " Principles of the Doctrine of Christ " necessary to render effectual Baptismal Regeneration. A sermon, *etc.* pp. 32. *Baldwin, Cradock & Joy: London,* 1826. 8º. **1225. h. 10. (6.)**

—— The King's Position as Temporal Head of the Church of England vindicated, in a sermon, *etc.* pp. 20. *Baldwin & Cradock: London,* 1836. 8º. **4476. f. 20.**

—— [Another copy.] **1225. h. 10. (15.)**

—— A Letter to the Archdeacon of Cleveland. [On " the recent Acts of the Legislature as they affect the Church and her Clergy."] pp. 11. *Printed for the Author: Stokesley,* 1838. 12º. **1225. h. 10. (5.)**

CATOR (CHARLES)

—— The Necessity of a National Church considered in a series of letters to the Right Honourable Sir Robert Peel . . . (Letter v. Ireland. Addressed to the Right Honourable the Lords Spiritual and Temporal, and the Commons, in Parliament assembled.) Second edition. pp. 93. *Baldwin & Cradock: London*, 1835. 8º. T. **1570.** (1.) *Five letters, each with a separate titlepage.*

—— Third edition. pp. 76. *Baldwin & Cradock: London,* 1836. 8º. **1225.** h. **10.** (23.)

—— On the Necessity of a National Church. A third series of letters to the Right Honorable Wm. E. Gladstone, *etc.* pp. 35. *Rivingtons: London,* 1866. 8º. **4108.** cc. **5.**

—— " Our Father." A sermon, *etc.* pp. 43. *J. G. & F. Rivington: London,* 1839. 8º. T. **2456.** (3.)

—— Second edition. pp. 43. *J. G. & F. Rivington: London,* 1839. 8º. **4476.** f. **21.**

—— [Another copy.] **1225.** h. **10.** (19.)

—— The Practical Benefit of Public Worship. A sermon, *etc.* pp. 20. *J. G. F. & J. Rivington: London,* [1840.] 8º. **1225.** h. **10.** (21.)

—— Protest against the Commutation of Tithes, and correspondence with the Tithe Commissioners. pp. 11. *Rivington & Co.: London,* 1838. 12º. T. **2379.** (10.)

—— [Another copy.] **1225.** h. **10.** (7.)

—— Reply to the Circular for the Abolition of Pluralities, *etc.* pp. 11. *Rivington & Co.: London,* 1838. 12º. T. **2295.** (7.)

—— [Another copy.] **1225.** h. **10.** (4.)

—— Sermon preached . . . at Stokesley Church, Yorkshire, on Friday, April 26, 1861. pp. 8. *Rivingtons: London,* 1861. 8º. **4477.** e. **16.**

—— A Sermon preached at the Visitation of the Archdeacon of York, holden at Doncaster, on the 9th of June, 1826, *etc.* pp. 40. *Baldwin, Cradock & Joy: London,* 1826. 8º. **1225.** h. **10.** (2.)

—— A Sermon (" This is My Body ") preached in The Cathedral Church of St. Paul . . . on Sunday, the twenty-first day of April, 1839, *etc.* pp. 36. *J. G. & F. Rivington: London,* [1839.] 8º. T. **2412.** (21.)

—— " This is My Body." A sermon . . . Second edition. pp. 41. *J. G. & F. Rivington: London,* 1839. 8º. **4476.** f. **22.**

—— Third edition. pp. 43. *J. G. & F. Rivington: London,* 1839. 8º. **4476.** f. **23.**

—— [Another copy.] **1225.** h. **10.** (18.)

—— [Another edition.] A Sermon preached in the Cathedral Church of St. Paul, *etc.* pp. 40. *J. Rider: London,* 1839. 4º. **4475.** f. **45.** (18.)

—— Spiritual State of England and Ireland contrasted. A sermon, *etc.* pp. 28. *Baldwin & Cradock: London,* 1829. 8º. T. **1280.** (8.)

—— [Another copy.] **1225.** h. **10.** (9.)

—— The Stewardship of the Christian Mysteries. *See* DUGARD (George) and WATSON (A.) Sermons by XXXIX Living Divines of the Church of England, *etc.* 1840. 8º. **1113.** k. **16.**

—— Three Sermons preached in the Parish Church of Stokesley, in Yorkshire, *etc.* pp. 43. *R. Hastings: London,* [1847.] 8º. **4460.** c. **6.**

CATOR (CHARLES)

—— The Work of an Evangelist, a sermon, *etc.* pp. 44. *Baldwin & Cradock: London,* 1833. 8º. T. **1465.** (5.)

—— [Another copy.] **1225.** h. **10.** (13.)

—— " The Writing of a Man's Hand," to the reformed British Parliament, in defence of the union of the Church and State. pp. 119. *Baldwin & Cradock: London,* 1833. 8º. T. **1444.** (8.)

—— [Another copy.] **1225.** h. **10.** (25.)

CATOR (CHARLES OLIVER FREDERICK) Meteorological Diagram shewing the Daily Elements throughout the year 1865. *Edward Stanford: London,* [1866.] *s. sh. obl.* fol. **1880.** d. **1.** (17*.)

CATOR (DOROTHY) Everyday Life among the Head-Hunters, and other experiences from East to West . . . With 34 illustrations from photographs. pp. xiv. 212. *Longmans & Co.: London,* 1905. 8º. **010055.** g. **31.**

—— In a French Military Hospital. pp. vii. 99. *Longmans & Co.: London,* 1915. fol. **9082.** gg. **35.**

CATOR (GEORGE) Trust Companies in the United States . . . A dissertation, *etc.* pp. 113. *Lord Baltimore Press: Baltimore,* 1902. 8º. **8223.** b. **72.**

—— [Another issue, without the author's " Vita."] *Baltimore,* 1902. 8º. [*Johns Hopkins University Studies in Historical and Political Science.* ser. 20. no. 5, 6.] Ac. **2689.**

CATOR (HENRY WILLIAM) Oratorian Biographies. [Edited by H. W. Cator.] 8 pt. *Catholic Truth Society: London,* 1913. 8º. **4805.** aaaa. **20.**

CATOR (MURRAY) Station Stories. pp. 303. *J. W. Arrowsmith: Bristol,* [1895.] 8º. **012629.** gg. **9.**

CATOR (PETER) Christian Education in India. Why should English be excluded? A letter to the Hon. Arthur Kinnaird, M.P. pp. 44. *Seeley, Jackson & Halliday: London,* 1858. 8º. **8023.** c. **11.**

CATOR (WRITSER JANS) The Economic Position of the Chinese in the Netherlands Indies. pp. xi. 264. *University of Chicago Press: Chicago; Oxford printed,* 1936. 8º. **8234.** b. **5.**

CATOR (WRITSER L.) *See* CATOR (W. J.)

CATOURZE, JEAN BERTRAND, *Sieur de. See* BERTRAND (J.) *Sieur de Catourze, etc.*

CATOYRA (FÉLIX ESTRADA) *See* ESTRADA CATOYRA.

CATOYRA (IGNACIO) Opusculo o Compendiosa obra que demuestra la venida, y predicacion evangelica de . . . Sant-Iago el Mayor en nuestro Hispanico Emisferio. Dirigido . . . contra la Dissertacion historica [entitled " Voz da Verdade "] que impugna dicha . . . venida de Sant Iago á España que novissimamente suscitó en Lisboa . . . Miguel de Santa Maria, *etc.* pp. 161. *Sevilla,* [1735.] 4º. **4824.** cc. **48.**

CATRAMI (NICHOLAS) *See* NIKOLAOS, *Archbishop of Zante* [Nikolaos Katrames].

CATRANI (O. D.) Nella fausta circostanza del maritaggio di Alessandro Maria Frattini di Roma e Giuseppa Catrani di Tiferno a dimostrazione di vero gradimento ai novelli sposi uno de' più prossimi agnati O. D. C. [i.e. O. D. Catrani.] [Verses by various authors.] pp. 27. 1827. 8º. *See* C., O. D. **899.** d. **12.** (10.)

CATRANO, BENINCASA, *Count di. See* BENINCASIUS (B.) *Count di Catrano.*

CATRARES (JOHANNES) Στιχοι του Κατραρη. Εἰς τον ἐν φιλοσοφοις φιλοσοφον και ῥητορικωτατον Νεοφυτον ἀνακρεοντειοι. *See* MATRANGA (P.) Anecdota græca, etc. 1850. 8°.　**832. g. 35.**

CATREVAS (CHRISTINA) That Freshman . . . Illustrated. pp. vii. 322.　*D. Appleton & Co.: New York & London,* 1910. 8°.　**012705. bb. 41.**

CATRICE (C. E. ÉDOUARD) De la fièvre intermittente. pp. 36. *Paris,* 1849. 4°. [*Collection des thèses soutenues à la Faculté de Médecine de Paris.* An 1849. tom. 2.]　**7372. c. 2.**

CATRICE (PAUL)

—— *See* EUROPE, *Central.* L'Avenir de l'Europe Centrale. (Conclusion par P. Catrice.) 1945. 8°.　**08028. ddd. 13.**

CATRIK (JOHN) *Bishop of Exeter. See* LACY (Edmund) successively *Bishop of Hereford* and *of Exeter.* The Register of Edmund Lacy, Bishop of Exeter, *etc.* (pt. 1. The Register of Institutions. With some account of the Episcopate of John Catrik, A.D. 1419.) 1909, *etc.* 8°.　**2210. e. 5.**

CATRIN (LOUIS) *See* DU CAZAL (L. J.) and CATRIN (L.) Médecine légale militaire. [1893.] 8°.　**08709. f. 23.**

—— Quelques considérations sur les hémorrhagies et la rachialgie dans la dothiénentérie. pp. 46.　*Paris,* 1874. 4°. [*Collection des thèses soutenues à la Faculté de Médecine de Paris.* An 1874. tom. 3.]　**7374. a. 8.**

CATRIN (LOUIS HIPPOLYTE) Études historiques et statistiques sur Le Nouvion-en-Thiérache, son canton et les communes limitrophes . . . suivies de notices monographiques sur chacune des localités du canton. Ouvrage orné de cartes, de dessins d'églises et d'une vue du Nouvion en 1870. 3 pt. *Vervins; Le Nouvion,* 1870, 71. 8°.　**10168. g. 11.**

CATRIONA, *pseud.* [i.e. CATHERINE MORISON.] *See also* MORISON (Catherine)

—— Dod ! That beats a' ; or, Jining the " Co." A humorous Scottish sketch . . . By Catriona. pp. 11.　*Scottish Co-operative Wholesale Society: Glasgow,* 1927. 8°.　**011779. f. 105.**

CATRON (FRANCIS) *See* CATROU (François)

CATROU (FRANÇOIS) *See* ANABAPTISTS. Histoire des Anabatistes [*sic*], ou relation curieuse de leur doctrine, *etc.* [Translated, by F. Catrou ?, from L. Hortensius's " Tumultuum Anabaptistarum liber unus," with additions by the translator.] 1695. 12°.　**4650. a. 13.**

—— *See* MANUCCI (N.) Histoire générale de l'Empire du Mogol . . . Sur les mémoires portugais de M. Manouchi . . . Par le père F. Catrou. 1705. 4°.　**581. h. 19.**

—— —— 1705. 12°.　**800. c. 13.**

—— —— 1708. 12°.　**800. c. 14.**

—— —— 1715. 4°.　**150. g. 17.**

—— —— 1715. 12°.　**583. a. 10–13.**

—— *See* MANUCCI (N.) The General History of the Mogol Empire . . . Extracted from the Memoirs of M. Manouchi . . . by F. F. Catrou. 1709. 12°.　**9055. b. 9.**

—— —— 1826. 8°.　**802. k. 18.**

—— —— 1907. 8°.　**09057. a. 18.**

—— —— 1908. 8°.　**9055. bbb. 39.**

CATROU (FRANÇOIS)

—— *See* PERIODICAL PUBLICATIONS.—*Trévoux.* Mémoires pour l'histoire des sciences et des beaux arts. [Edited by F. Catrou and others.] 1701, *etc.* 12°.　**261. c. 1,** *etc.*

—— *See* VIRGILIUS MARO (P.) [*Works.—Polyglott.*] Les Poësies de Virgile ; avec des notes critiques & historiques. Nouvelle édition, revuë, corrigée, & augmentée. Par le P. F. Catrou, *etc.* Lat. & Fr. 1729. 12°.　**237. f. 19–22.**

CATROU (FRANÇOIS) and ROUILLÉ (PIERRE JULIEN)

—— 　　　　　　　　　　 Histoire romaine, depuis la fondation de Rome. Avec des notes historiques, géographiques & critiques, *etc.* 20 tom.　*Paris,* 1725–37. 4°.　**197. b. 1–20.**

—— The Roman History : with notes historical, geographical, and critical. [The translator's dedication signed : R. Bundy.] 6 vol.　*T. Woodward ; J. Peele: London,* 1728–37. fol.　**1855. f. 16.**

—— [Another copy.] **L.P.**　**204. i. 1–6.**

—— [A reissue.] The Roman History, *etc.*　*London,* 1728. fol.　**L.R. 301. c. 1.** *With a different dedication.*

　　—— *See* ALITOFILO, *pseud.* Copia di lettera . . . nella quale si contengono varie osservazioni critiche pertinenti all'istoria Romana scritta da padri Catrou e Rouille, *etc.* [1726 ?] 4°.　**196. b. 13.**

　　—— *See* OZELL (John) [A printed letter, respecting J. Ozell's intended translation of Catrou and Rouillé's Roman History.] [1729.] *s. sh.* fol.　**1087. c. 28. (1*.)**

　　—— *See* OZELL (John) No. 1. of the Herculean Labour . . . Being serious and facetious remarks on . . . defects in the folio translation of the Roman History [of F. Catrou and P. J. Rouillé] by the Rev. Mr. Bundy, *etc.* 1729. 8°.　**1087. c. 28. (2, 3.)**

　　—— *See* OZELL (John) Mr. Ozell's Defence against the Remarks [by R. Bundy ?] publish'd by Peele and Woodward . . . on his Translation of the Roman History [of F. Catrou and P. J. Rouillé]. 1725. 8°.　**1087. c. 27. (1.)**

CATROUX (　　　　)
—— *See* FÉRAL (J.) Catalogue des objets d'art anciens . . . dont la vente . . . aura lieu . . . le . . . 24 juin 1937 . . . Commissaire-priseur : Mᵉ E. Ader . . . assisté de MM. Féral et Catroux, *etc.* 1937. 4°.　**07812. w. 13.**

CATROUX (GEORGES ALBERT JULIEN)
—— Dans la bataille de Méditerranée. Égypte-Levant-Afrique du Nord, 1940–1944. Avec 4 cartes. pp. 446. *Paris,* 1949. 8°.　**9102. e. 5.**

—— J'ai vu tomber le rideau de fer.　Moscou, 1945–1948. pp. 317. [*Paris,*] 1952. 8°.　**8032. m. 45.**

—— The French Union. [Translated by Stuart R. Schram.] *New York,* 1953. 8°. [*International Conciliation.* no. 495.]　**Ac. 2297. f.**

CATS. ' Cats.' Not by Louis Wain. [Aphorisms on women.] pp. 122. *Duckworth & Co.: London,* 1916. 8°.　**012305. k. 21.**

—— Cats & Kittens. *See* PERIODICAL PUBLICATIONS.—*Horsham.*

CATS.

—— Cats and Kittens. The magazine for every cat-lover. *See* PERIODICAL PUBLICATIONS.—*Derby*.

—— Cats at School and Cats at Home. Companion plates for wall decoration, *etc.* *Ernest Nister : London*, [1892.] fol. **1757. b. 13. (7.)**

—— Cats let out of a Scarlet Bag ; or, Catholic Pusses caught in a Protestant Priest-Trap ; or, what Protestants will have to believe, if they become Catholics. pp. 16. *Printed for the Author : Norwich*, 1824. 8°. **3940. b. 83.**

—— Cats' Tales. [By] M. F. S. [i.e. Mrs. F. Seamer, afterwards Seymour.] 1873. 16°. *See* S., M. F. **12803. aa. 4.**

—— Comical Cats and Dogs. 2 companion plates for wall decoration, *etc. Ernest Nister : London*, [1892.] 4°. **1757. b. 13. (5.)**

—— Seventeen Cats ; a true story, *etc.* [The preface signed : H. H., i.e. Helen Hunt, afterwards Jackson.] [1884.] 8°. *See* H., H. **12805. u. 7.**

CATS AND KITTENS YEAR BOOK. *See* PERIODICAL PUBLICATIONS.—*Derby*.—*Cats and Kittens*.

CATS (   ) *Prêtre. See* HENNEPIN (L.) La Morale pratique du Jansenisme, ou Appel . . . contre les oppressions & vexations du Sieur Cats, Prestre, *etc.* 1698. 12°. **861. a. 11.**

CATS (CAREL) *See* BIBLE.—*New Testament.* [*Dutch.*] Het Nieuwe Testament of Verbond van onsen Heere Iesus Christus. Op nieuws uyt het Grieks vertaalt, *etc.* [Translated by C. Cats.] 1701. 8°. **3041. aa. 13. (1.)**

—— *See* BIBLE.—*Appendix.*—*New Testament.* [*Miscellaneous.*] Sleutel of Reden-geving, dienende tot bewijs van de vertaling des Nieuwen Testaments of Verbonds van onsen Heere Iesus Christus. Op nieuws uyt het Grieks overgeset door C. Catz. 1701. 8°. **3041. aaa. 13. (2.)**

CATS (HENRICUS) *See* BIBLE. [*Dutch.*] Bijbel, *etc.* [The version of 1636, 37, revised by H. Cats.] 1834. 4°. **3041. g. 8. (1, 2.)**

CATS (ILSE) *See* JOBST (G.) Kleinwohnungsbau in Holland. Unter Mitarbeit von . . . I. Cats . . . verfasst, *etc.* 1922. 8°. **07815. h. 6.**

CATS (JACOB)

WORKS.

—— Alle de wercken, so ouden als nieuwe, van de Heer Iacob Cats. [With engravings.] 2 vol. 13 pt. *I. I. Schipper : Amsterdam*, 1655. fol. **11565. k. 4.** *With an additional titlepage, engraved, bearing the portrait of the author. The " Ouderdom, buyten-leven, en hofgedachten op Sorghvliet " and the " Koningklyke herderinne Aspasia " also have engraved titlepages.*

—— Alle de wercken, so ouden als nieuwen van de Heer Jacob Cats . . . op nieus vermeerdert met des autheurs Tachtigh-jarigh leven, Huyshoudinge en Bedenckingen op Zorgh-vliet. [With engravings.] 14 pt. *J. J. Schipper : Amsterdam*, 1658 [1657–59]. fol. **11555. h. 1.** *With an additional titlepage, engraved, bearing the portrait of the author. Eight of the parts have engraved titlepages.*

—— Alle de wercken van de Heer Jacob Cats, *etc.* 3 vol. *Jacobus Savry : Dordrecht*, 1659, 58. 4°. **11555. eee. 1** *With an additional titlepage, engraved, bearing the portrait of the author. Four of the works have engraved titlepages.*

CATS (JACOB) [WORKS.]

—— Alle de wercken, zoo oude als nieuwe, van de Heer Jacob Cats . . . vermeerdert met des autheurs Tachtigjarigh Leven, en bedenckingen op Zorgvliet. [With engravings.] 12 pt. *I. I. Schipper : Amsterdam*, 1665. 4°. **11555. f. 11.** *With an additional titlepage, engraved. Four of the parts have engraved titlepages.*

—— Alle de wercken . . . van den Heer Jacob Cats . . . Hier komen noch by des dichters Gedachten op slapeloose nachten, nevens zijn gansche Twee en tachtig-jarig leven, door hemzelf in dichtmaat beschreven, en nooit voor deezen gedrukt. 2 dl. *Amsterdam ; Utrecht*, 1700. fol. **11555. h. 2.** *Each dl. has an additional titlepage, engraved, bearing the portrait of the author.*

—— Alle de werken van Jakob Cats, uitgegeven door Mr. R. Feith. [With a portrait.] 19 dl. *Amsterdam*, 1790–99. 12°. **633. a. 1–9.**

—— Alle de wercken van den Heere Jacob Cats. 9 dl. *Schiedam*, 1852–60. 16°. [*Klassiek, letterkundig Panthéon.* no. 1, 7, 11, 16, 24, 39, 45–46, 58, 69.] **12258. aa.**

—— Vader Cats uitgegeven voor het Nederlandsche volk. Met eene voorrede van W. I. Hofdijk. pp. vii. 706. *Tiel*, [1861.] 4°. **11555. h. 3.** *The titlepage is engraved and bears a portrait of the author.*

—— Al de werken van Jacob Cats. Met eene levensbeschrijving van den dichter, *etc.* pp. iv. 759. *Schiedam*, [1869.] 8°. **11557. e. 26.**

—— Al de werken van Jacob Cats. Met eene levensbeschryving van den dichter. Oorspronkelijke spelling. pp. viii. 846. *Schiedam*, [1879.] 8°. **11555. g. 3.**

—— Alle de werken van Jacob Cats. Bezorgd, en met ophelderingen voorzien door W. N. Wolterink. Versierd met . . . gravures. 2 dl. *Dordrecht*, 1880 [1878–83]. fol. **11565. k. 2.** *Published in parts.*

TWO OR MORE WORKS.

—— Zinne- en minnebeelden ; Selfstryd ; Tooneel der mannelyke agtbaarheidt ; Galathea, of Hardersklagt ; Klagende maegden ; en andere mengelrymen, *etc.* 4 pt. *Leyden*, 1736. 8°. **12305. bb. 39.** *With an additional titlepage, engraved. " Galathea " has an engraved titlepage.*

—— Bie-boek, hoofdzaekelyk behelzende hoe eenen voorzigtigen biënhouder zich zal schikken om 't meeste voordeel daer uyt te trekken . . . Waer by gevoegd is J. Cats Tachtig-jarig leven, en huyshouding, of kort begryp van het buyten-leven op Zorgvlied, *etc.* 2 pt. *Gent*, [1820 ?] 8°. **11555. d. 11.**

SPEECHES.

—— Oratio, in Parlamento Reipublicæ Anglicanæ, viva . . . voce, ab . . . I. Cats . . . Ordinum Generalium Belgii . . . Legato Extraordinario, habita die 29. Decem. 1651. [*Amsterdam ?*] 1652. 4°. **8122. ee. 4. (8.)**

—— Oratie van . . . J. Cats, Extraordinaris Ambassadeur vande . . . Staten Generael . . . mondelingh ghedaen in 't Parlament van de Republijcke van Engelandt, den 29. Decemb. M.D.C.LI. Wt het Latijn overgheset. *I. Iacobsz. den Abt : Rotterdam*, 1652. 4°. **8079. c. 37.**

—— [Another edition.] [*Amsterdam ?*] 1652. 4°. **8122. ee. 4. (9.)**

CATS (Jacob) [Speeches.]

—— Propositie van zijn Excell. de Heer Ambassadeur Cats gedaen in den Raedt van Staten van de Republijcque van Engelant den 1 Ianuarij 1652. Wt 't Latyn in 't Neder-duyts vertaelt. *J. Jacobsz. den Abt: Rotterdam*, 1652. 4°. **1309. l. 14. (77.)**
Imperfect; wanting all but the first two leaves.

—— De Derde oratie van de Heeren Extraordinari Ambassa-deurs der . . . Staten Generael (J. Cats, G. Schaep, Van der Perre), ghedaen voor den Raedt van Staten tot Londen, ende over gelevert aen 't Parlement den 13 Iuny 1652. Als mede het antwoordt des Parlements van de Republycke van Engelandt gegeven so op dese en de twee voorgaende oratien . . . den 3. en 6. Juny gedaen. *P. Pietersz.: Rotterdam*, 1652. 4°. **8079. c. 36.**

—— [Another edition.] *P. Pietersz.: Rotterdam*, 1652. 4°. **8122. ee. 4. (14.)**

—— Oratie van . . . den Ambassadeur I. Catz, ter occasie van dese laetste zee-ghevecht tusschen den Engelschen Admirael ende den Admirael Tromp voorghevallen, voor de Heere Ghedeputeerde van 't Parlement, ghedaen tot Londen. (Excellentissimi Domini D. Jacobi Catz Oratio occasione pugnæ navalis recenter commissæ.) *Dutch & Lat.* *I. Iansz.: [Amsterdam,]* 1652. 4°. **8079. c. 38.**

—— Oratie . . . ter occasie van dese laetste zee-ghevecht tusschen den Engelschen admirael ende den Admirael Tromp voorghevallen, voor de Heere Ghedeputeerde van 't Parlement, ghedaen tot Londen. [The Dutch ver-sion only.] *I. Iansz.: [Amsterdam,]* 1652. 4°. **8122. ee. 4. (13.)**

SINGLE WORKS.

—— Afbeeldinge van 't Huwelyck en 't geen daer omtrent is onder de gedaente van een fuyck. *See infra*: Ouder-dom, buyten-leven, en Hof-gedachten, op Sorgh-Vliet.

—— Doot-kiste voor de levendige, of Sinne-beelden uyt Godes Woordt, *etc. See infra*: Ouderdom, buyten-leven, en Hof-gedachten, op Sorgh-Vliet.

—— Faces Augustæ, *etc. See infra*: 's Werelts begin, midden, eynde, *etc.*

—— Galathee, ofte Harder. Minne-klachte. [In verse.] pp. 62. *A. vander Venne & I. Ockerss.: 's Gravenhage*, 1629. 8°. **11555. c. 38. (2.)**

—— Ghedachten op slapeloose nachten, waer-inne de deughden van herberghsaemheyt ende mededeelsaemheyt aende noodtdruftighe; wijt-lustigh vertoont, ende de vruchten der selver naer 't leven afghemaelt werden . . . Nu . . . eerst ghedruckt, naer het eyghen gheschrifte van den Heere Cats, *etc.* [In verse.] pp. 29. *P. van Pee: Brugghe*, 1689. 4°. **11557. g. 2.**

—— [Another edition.] Mitsgaders het Twee-en-tachtigh-jarig leven van den selven heere, van zyn geboorte tot zyn dood toe; door hem zelf in vaerzen beschreven. Den sevenden Druk. Met vernieuwde figuueren. pp. 235. *Amsteldam*, 1725. 8°. **11555. aaa. 59. (1.)**
With an additional titlepage, engraved, bearing the date 1715.

—— Den achsten druk. Met vernieuwde figuuren. pp. 235. *Leyden*, 1732. 4°. **11556. g. 36. (2.)**
With an additional titlepage, engraved.

—— Houwelyck, dat is de gantsche gelegentheyt des echten-staets. [With engravings.] 6 dl. *I. P. van de Venne: Middelburgh*, 1625. 4°. **11556. k. 18.**
With an additional titlepage, engraved.

CATS (Jacob) [Single Works.]

—— [Another edition.] pp. 881. *A. vande Venne: 's Graven-Hage*, 1628. 8°. **1064. c. 27.**
With an additional titlepage, engraved.

—— [Another edition.] 6 dl. *J. Ockers.: s' Gravenhage*, 1630. 4°. **11556. g. 33.**
With an additional titlepage, engraved.

—— [Another edition.] 6 dl. *B. A. Berentsma:* [Middelburg ?] 1633. 4°. **638. g. 3. (1.)**
With an additional titlepage, engraved.

—— [Another edition.] pp. 671. *M. Havius: Dordrecht*, 1634. 12°. **1461. a. 27.**
With an additional titlepage, engraved.

—— [Another edition.] pp. 387. *F. Pels: Amstelredam*, 1642. 8°. **1064. c. 28.**
With an additional titlepage, engraved.

—— [Another edition.] 6 dl. *H. Passchiers van Wesbusch: Haerlem*, 1642. 4°. **638. i. 31.**
With an additional titlepage, engraved.

—— [Another edition.] pp. 538. *Amsterdam*, 1720. 8°. **11555. aaa. 11.**
With an additional titlepage, engraved.

—— Klagende maagden [*sic*] en raat voor de selve: alle maagden van Holland door de Maagt van Dordregt gunstelijk toege-eygent. (Liefdes granaat-appel.) [Edi-ted by M. Havius. With woodcuts.] 2 pt. *Amsterdam*, 1722. obl. 16°. **11555. a. 16.**
Imperfect; wanting the last leaf of pt. 2.

—— [Another copy.] **11556. a. 8.**
Imperfect; wanting the first woodcut and the last three leaves.

—— [Another edition.] 2 pt. *Amsterdam*, 1754. obl. 16°. **11555. a. 17.**

—— [Another edition.] 2 pt. *Dordrecht*, 1781. obl. 16°. **11555. a. 18.**

—— Koningklyke herderin Aspasia. Blyeyndig-spel, *etc. See infra*: Ouderdom, buyten-leven, en Hof-gedachten, op Sorgh-Vliet.

—— Liedeken van Cats. Tot divertissement der jonge minnaren. (Vermaekelyk liedeken van het klepper-mantjen.—Vermaekelyk liedeken van den lierman.) *Gent*, [1840?] *s. sh. fol.* **1871. c. 1. (10.)**

—— Monita amoris virginei, sive officium puellarum in castis amoribus, emblemate expressum. pp. 23. *Hamburgi*, 1786. *8°. **11409. l. 50.**

—— Iacobi Catzii I. C. Monita amoris virginei, sive Officium puellarum in castis amoribus, emblemate expressum. Maechden-plicht, ofte Ampt der ionckvrouwen, in eerbaer liefde aenghewesen door sinne-beelden. [Poems.] *Lat. & Dutch.* pp. 123. *W. I. Blaeu: Amstelredam*, [1618?] 4°. **11408. g. 21. (2.)**

—— [Another edition.] pp. 124. *W. I. Blaeuw: Amstelredam*, 1622. 4°. **11556. g. 32. (2.)**

—— Magden-plicht ofte Ampt der Iongvrouwē. *Dutch*. [Amsterdam ? 1633 ?] 8°. **11555. aaa. 61. (3.)**
The titlepage is engraved.

—— An Emblematicall Dialogue, interpreted from . . . I. Catzius; which sheweth how Virgins in their chaste loves ought to beare themselves. [In verse.] *See* HEYWOOD (Thomas) *Dramatist.* Pleasant Dialogues and Dramma's, *etc.* 1637. 8°. **1076. i. 29.**

—— [Another edition.] *See* Heywood (Thomas) *Dramatist.* Pleasant Dialogues and Dramma's, *etc.* 1903. 8º.
11853. v. 1/3.

—— L'Amour virginal; ou, le Devoir des jeunes filles dans leurs chastes amours . . . Traduit du latin en français par Auguste Abadie . . . Avec commentaires, citations et notes bibliographiques. pp. xiii. 63. *Paris*, 1886. 8º.
8416. f. 41.

—— Des . . . Herrn . . . Jacob Cats Jungfern-Pflicht, oder Amt der Jungfrauen in erbarer Liebe, angewiesen durch vier und viertzig Siñ-Bilder. Aus dem Holländischen ins Teutsch übersetzt, durch Cosmus Conrad Cuno. [In verse.] pp. 110. *Augspurg*, 1707. 8º. **11556. bbb. 3.**

—— A' férjhez vágyó Fillis és oktató Anna, lakodalmi-versben Lydi Jakób-ból. [A Hungarian version of the Dutch poem by J. Lydius based upon "Monita amoris virginei . . . Magden-plicht, *etc.*" of J. Cats. The translator's introduction signed: A' vers-író F. J., i.e. József Fábchich?] pp. 48. *Pesten*, 1787. 8º. **897. a. 12. (4.)**

—— Ouderdom, buyten-leven, en Hof-gedachten, op Sorgh-Vliet. (Invallende gedachten op voorvallende gelegentheden.—Koninklyke herderin Aspasia, blyeyndig-spel.—Afbeeldinge van 't huwelyck, en 't geen daer omtrent is, onder de gedaente van een Fuyck.—Doot-kiste voor de levendige, of Sinnebeelden uyt Godes Woordt.) 5 pt.
J. J. Schipper: Amsterdam, 1656, 55. 4º. **11556. g. 35.**
Each work, except the "Hof-gedachten," has an additional titlepage, engraved. The titlepage of the "Hof-gedachten" bears the date 1655.

—— [Another edition.] [With "Tachtig-jarigh leven, Huys-houdinge, en Bedenckingen, op Sorgh-Vliet."] 7 pt.
I. I. Schipper: Amsterdam, 1655 [1658]. 8º.
11557. aa. 25.

—— [Another edition.] Op nieuws vermeerderd met des auteurs Tachtig jarig leven, en Bedenkingen op Zorg-vliet. 7 pt. *Amsterdam*, [1741?] 8º. **11555. aaa. 12.**
With an additional titlepage, engraved.

—— Self-Stryt, dat is crachtighe beweginghe van vlees en gheest, poëtischer wijse verthoont in den persoon . . . van Joseph, ten tijde hy by Potiphars huys-vrouwe wiert versocht tot overspel. Mitsgaders schriftmatighe beschrijvinghe van de heymenisse ende eygenschap des Christelijcken self-strijts, *etc.* pp. 119. *J. P. van de Venne: Middelburgh*, 1620. 4º. **11556. g. 8.**
With an additional titlepage, engraved.

—— [Another edition.] pp. 119. *J. P. van de Venne: Middelburgh*, 1620. 4º. **11556. g. 32. (3.)**
With an additional titlepage, engraved.

—— Tweede druck, *etc.* pp. 119. *I. P. van de Venne: Middelburgh*, 1621. 4º. **11556. g. 9.**
With an additional titlepage, engraved.

—— [Another edition.] Tweede druk. pp. 119.
I. Pietersz.: Middelburgh, 1621. 4º. **11556. h. 28. (1.)**
With an additional titlepage, engraved. The titlepage of the "Sinne-beeld, de heymenisse ende eyghenschap des christelijcken self-stryts aen-wijsende" bears the date 1624.

—— Derde druk, *etc.* pp. 119. *Weduwe van J. P. vande Venne: Middelburgh*, 1625. 4º. **638. g. 3. (2.)**
With an additional titlepage, engraved.

—— [Another edition.] pp. 251. [*Middelburgh*, 1625?] *obl.* 16º. **11555. a. 14.**
With an additional titlepage, engraved.

—— [Another edition.] Op nieuws vermeerdert ende verbetert vanden autheur, ende met nieuwe, aerdige afbeeldingen van kopere platen verçiert. pp. 43. 95.
A. vander Venne & I. Ockerss.: 's Gravenhaghe, 1628. 8º.
11555. b. 6.

—— [Another edition.] pp. 251. [*Middelburgh ?* 1630?] *obl.* 16º. **11557. eee. 39.**
With an additional titlepage, engraved.

—— [Another edition.] Self-srydt [*sic*], *etc.* 2 pt. [*Amsterdam ?*] 1633. 8º. **11555. aaa. 61. (4.)**

—— Selbststreit, das ist, kräfftige Bewegung dess Fleisches wider den Geist. Poetischer Weise abgebildet in der Person Josephs . . . Auss dem Holländischen . . . übersetzet durch Ernst Christoph Homburg. [With engravings, including a portrait of the translator.] pp. 294. *In Verlegung W. Endters: Nürnberg*, [1647.] *obl.* 8º. **1160. b. 14.**
With an additional titlepage, engraved.

—— [Selsam trougeval tusschen een Spaens edelman en een heydinne.] Tim. Ritzschens verteutschte Spanische Ziegeunerin. Aus dem Holländischen J. C. [i.e. Jacob Cats.] [1656.] 4º. *See* C., J. *Hirsch* III. 874.

—— Silenus Alcibiadis, sive Proteus, vitæ humanæ ideam, emblemate trifariam variato, oculis subijciens [*sic*]. [The text of the poems in Dutch, Latin and French. With engravings.] 3 pt. *Ex officina I. Hellenij: Middelburgi*, 1618. 4º. **831. i. 17.**
Each pt. has an additional titlepage, engraved.

—— [Another edition.] 3 pt. [*Amsterdam*, 1620?] 4º. **11556. g. 32. (1.)**
Each pt. has an engraved titlepage. Imperfect; wanting the general titlepage.

—— [Another edition.] Proteus, ofte Minne-beelden verandert in sinne-beelden, *etc.* (Sinne-rijcke ende stichtelijcke, leersame redenen: tot verklaringe van de voorgaende sinne-beelden.) 2 pt. [*The Hague*,] 1628. 8º.
11555. c. 38. (1.)

—— [Another edition.] Iacobi Catzii I. C. Silenus Alcibiadis, *etc.* pp. 244. *W. Blaeu: Amsterdam*, [1630?] 4º.
11408. g. 21. (1.)
With an additional titlepage, engraved.

—— Iacobi Catzii I. C. Silenus Alcibiadis, *etc.* [Containing the Dutch and French portions of the original only.] pp. 64. 51. 51. 51. [*Amsterdam ?*] 1624. *obl.* 16º. **1160. a. 1.**
With an additional titlepage, engraved.

—— Iac. Catz minnelijcke, zedelijcke, en stichtelijcke Sinne-Beelden, *etc.* [Containing the Dutch portions of the original only.] [*Amsterdam ?* 1633?] 8º.
11555. aaa. 61. (1.)
The titlepage is engraved.

—— Moral Emblems, with aphorisms, adages, and proverbs, of all ages and nations, from Jacob Cats and Robert Farlie. With illustrations . . . from designs found in their works, by John Leighton, F.S.A. The whole translated and edited, with additions, by Richard Pigot. pp. xvi. 239. *Longman & Co.: London*, 1860. 4º.
1347. i. 14.

—— Second edition. pp. xvi. 241. *Longman & Co.: London*, 1862. 4º. **1347. i. 21.**

—— Moral Emblems . . . from J. Cats and Robert Farlie . . . Translated and edited, with additions, by Richard Pigot . . . Third edition. pp. xvi. 241. *Longmans, Green, Reader, & Dyer: London*, 1865. 4º.
12305. m. 18.

—— Iac. Catzii Silenus Alcibiadis sive Proteus, dit zijn sedelijcke verclaerīgē over sijne Sīne Beeldē. [*Amsterdam ?* 1680?] 8º. **11555. aaa. 61. (2.)**
The titlepage is engraved.

CATS (JACOB) [SINGLE WORKS.]

—— Spiegel van den ouden ende nieuwen tijdt, bestaende uyt spreeck-woorden ende sin-spreucken, *etc.* [With engravings.] 3 dl.   *I. Burchoorn: s' Graven-Hage,* 1632. 4°.   **11556. g. 36. (1.)**
With an additional titlepage, engraved.

—— Tweeden druck, vermeerdert, *etc.* 3 dl.   *H. van Esch: Dordrecht,* 1633. 8°.   **1070. l. 14.**

—— [Another edition.]   Den lesten druck, van nieus oversien en gecorrigeert, *etc.* pp. 320.   *J. Braat: Dordrecht,* 1647. 8°.   **1064. c. 29.**

—— [Another edition.]   pp. 416.   *M. Feermans: Briel,* 1652. 8°.   **11556. b. 9.**
With an additional titlepage, engraved.

—— [Another edition.]   Den lesten druck, van niews oversien en gecorrigeert, *etc.* pp. 320.   *Amsterdam,* 1722. 8°.
                          11555. aaa. 59. (2.)
With an additional titlepage, engraved.

—— Tooneel van de mannelicke achtbaerheyt, aen-gewesen in de voor-sprake, teghen-sprake, ende uyt-sprake, gedaen over de weygheringhe van de Koninginne Vasthi, aen de Ghesaenten des Konincx Assuerus, *etc.* [In verse. With engravings.] pp. 60.   *I. P. van de Venne: Middelburgh,* 1622. 4°.   **11556. g. 32. (4.)**

—— [Another edition.]   pp. 60.   *I. P. van de Venne: Middelburgh,* 1622. 4°.   **11556. h. 28. (2.)**

—— Derde druck, vermeerdert en verbetert.   pp. 68 [78]. *A. vande Venne: 's Graven-Hage,* 1632. 4°.
                          638. g. 3. (3.)

—— [Another edition.]   [*Amsterdam?*] 1633. 8°.
                          11555. aaa. 61. (5.)

—— [Another edition.]   pp. 122.   [*Amsterdam?*] 1641. *obl.* 16°.   **11555. a. 15.**

—— Uytbreydinge over den achtsten Psalm Davids.   Door I. C. [i.e. J. Cats.] [In verse.] pp. 56.   1642. 4°.   *See* BIBLE.—*Psalms.—Selections.* [*Dutch.—Single Psalms.*]
                          1473. bb. 6.

—— 's Werelts begin, midden, eynde, besloten in den trou-ringh, met den proef-steen van den selven. (I. Cats Lof-sangh op het gheestelyck houwelick van Godes Sone.) [In verse. With engravings.] pp. 772. 136. *M. Havius: Dordrecht,* 1637. 4°.   **11556. g. 34.**
With an additional titlepage, engraved.

—— [Another edition.]   pp. 639.   *M. Havius: Dordrecht,* 1638. 8°.   **11555. b. 7.**
With an additional titlepage, engraved.

—— [Another edition.]   pp. 679.   *C. Loots-Man: Amsterdam,* 1699. 8°.   **11557. aa. 26.**
With an additional titlepage, engraved.

—— [Another issue.]   *Amsterdam,* 1699. 8°.
                          011556. df. 11.
With the illustrations from woodcuts instead of engravings.

—— [Another edition.]   [With a portrait.]   pp. 673. *Amsterdam,* 1719. 8°.   **11557. e. 11.**
With an additional titlepage, engraved.

—— [Another edition.]   pp. 673.   *Amsterdam,* [1730?] 8°.
                          11555. aaa. 10.
With an additional titlepage, engraved.

CATS (JACOB) [SINGLE WORKS.]

—— Faces Augustæ, sive poematia, quibus illustriores nuptiæ, à I. Catsio . . . antehac Belgicis versibus conscriptæ, iam à Caspare Barlæo & Cornelio Boyo Latino carmine celebrantur, *etc.* (Casparis Barlæi Dialogi aliquot nuptiales, quibus quæstiones quædam de nuptiis & conjugio, à I. Catsio, nuper Belgico idiomate pertractatæ, jam Latino latius explicantur.—Casparis Barlæi Nuptiæ peripateticæ, sive universæ philosophiæ ad statum conjugalem festiva applicatio.—Casparis Barlæi Faces sacræ, sive Hymnus Salomonis, quo, sub typo nuptiarum Salomonis & filiæ Pharaonis, nuptiæ Christi & ecclesiæ adumbrantur. —Iacobi Lydii Sermonum convivalium libri duo.) 4 pt. *Sumptibus M. Havii: Dordraci,* 1643. 4°.   G. **17560.**

—— [Another edition.] [With engravings.] 4 pt. *Sumptibus M. Havii: Dordraci,* 1643. 8°.   **11409. ee. 2.**

—— [Another copy.]   **11409. b. 6.**
Imperfect; wanting the portrait of Elizabeth, daughter of Frederick V., Elector Palatine and King of Bohemia.

—— [Another edition.]   4 pt.   *Apud J. Elsevirium: Lugduni Batavorum,* 1656. 4°.   **11556. dd. 17.**

—— J. Katsens Aeltern-Spiegel (Masanissa und Sofonisba, Holländischer Ehe-Betrug), aus desselben Holländischem gehoochdeutschet, durch C. Chr. Dedekinden. [Extracts from " 's Werelts begin, midden, eynde, besloten in den trou-ringh."]   *A. Löfflers Verlag: Dresden,* 1654. 8°.
                          11522. df. 3. (2.)

—— Trauungs-Betrug, unlängsten in Holland geschehen . . . In die Hochädle Teutsche Helden-Sprache übersetzt, und . . . zum andernmahl hervorgegeben von J. S. [i.e. J. Schwieger.] (Folget die Vertheidigung des Trauungs-Betruges.—Jungfern-Markt. In die Hoch-ädle-Teutsche Heldensprache versetzet von Jacob Schwiegern.) [Extracts from " 's Werelts begin, midden, eynde, besloten in den trou-ringh."] 3 pt.   *Melchior Koch: Glükstadt,* 1659. 12°.   **11840. a. 11. (4.)**

—— Paradisus: sive, Primorum humani generis parentum nuptiæ, *etc.* [Extracted from " Faces Augustae."] *See* MASENIUS (J.) Sarcotis, *etc.* 1753. 8°.   **1461. d. 12.**

—— Iac. Catsii Patriarcha bigamos [extracted from " Faces Augustae "], cui Hugonis Grotii Historiam Ionae junxit Car. Poppo Froebel. pp. iv. 91.   *Rudolphopoli,* 1821. 32°.
                          11408. a. 5.

SELECTIONS.

—— Nuttelyck Huys-boeck. Behelsende eene bespiegeling des's mensche . . . benevens alle de overgebleven gedichten die in geen van zyn andere werken gevonden worden. Als mede de lof en rouw-gedichten en graftschriften op den Heere J. Cats. Tweede druk. pp. 321. *Leyden,* 1769. 8°.   **11556. b. 10.**
With an additional titlepage, engraved.

—— [Selected poems.] pp. 71.   *Amsterdam,* [1827.] 16°. [*Keur van Nederlandsche letteren.* dl. 5. stk. 25.]
                          11556. aaa. 31.

—— Dichterlijke vertellingen uit den Trouwring en het Huwelijk van Jacob Cats. pp. 319.   *'s Gravenhage,* 1851. 16°.   **11555. a. 19.**
With an additional titlepage, engraved.

—— Zedekundige grondregels, getrokken uit de werken van Jacob Cats. pp. 24. *See* PRINS (J. J.) De Christelijke zedeleer, *etc.* [1868.] 8°.   **3128. ccc. 7.**

APPENDIX.

—— *See* CAREW (George) *Esq.* An Appeal from the Supream Court of Judicature of Holland, Zealand, and West Friesland, to the King of Great Brittain, or, the Case briefly stated between G. Carew . . . and the Heirs of Sir J. Cats. 1674. 4°.   **712. g. 52. (4.)**

CATS (Jacob) [Appendix.]

—— *See* Derudder (G.) Un Poète néerlandais. Cats, sa vie et ses œuvres. 1898. 8º.   **10705. ee. 42.**

—— *See* Ellemeet (W. C. M. de J. van) Museum Catsianum. Verzameling van W. C. M. de J. van Ellemeet. 1839–1870. 1870. 4º.   **7855. i. 10.**

—— —— 1887. 8º.   **7855. h. 34.**

—— *See* Ellemeet (W. C. M. de J. van) Uittreksel uit het Museum Catsianum, of de verzameling der verschillende uitgaven van J. Cats's werken. 1873. 4º. **11903. m. 3.**

—— *See* Geysbeek (P. G. W.) Het Leven en de verdiensten van Jakob Cats, in gesprekken. 1829. 8º.   **633. a. 10.**

—— *See* Huet (C. B.) Portretten van Nederlanders. (Jacob Cats.) 1940. 8º.   Ac. **9017/15. (8.)**

—— *See* Smilde (H.) Jacob Cats in Dordrecht. Leven en werken gedurende de jaren 1623–1636. 1938. 8º. **10761. h. 42.**

—— *See* Stoppelaar (J. H. de) Jacob Cats te Middelburg 1603–1623, *etc.* 1860. 8º.   **10760. dd. 16. (3.)**

—— De Geest van den Ridder Jacob Cats, de Nederlanders aanmoedigende ter bescherming van de duurgekochte vryheid. pp. 8. [*Amsterdam ?* 1780 ?] 4º.
                    934. g. 12. (14.)

—— De Ridder Jacob Cats ontwaakt door eenen Schoot op 't Scheveningse Strand, verreezen uit den dood ; rymt op zyn Zorgvlied weer met nieuwherstelde kragten, of 't allereerst gevolg zyns slapeloose nachten. pp. 12. *Amsterdam*, [1780 ?] 8º.   **934. g. 12. (13.)**

     —— Welmeenende en openhartige vaderlands-gezinde zang, in beantwoording van die, van den door een Schoot op't Scheeveninge Strand ontwaakten, en uit den dood verreezenen . . . Ridder J. Cats. [Signed : E. C.] [1782 ?] 8º. *See* C., E.   **934. g. 12. (13*.)**

CATS (Matthias) *See* Felisius (M.)

CATS BUSSEMAKER (Ulco) *See* Bussemaker.

CATSBY (Dorinda) The History of Miss Dorinda Catsby, and Miss Emilia Faulkner : in a series of letters. 2 vol. *S. Bladon : London*, 1772. 12º.   **12611. aa. 6.**

CATSIUS (Jacobus) *See* Cats (Jacob)

CATSKILL.—*Catskill Association.* Catskill Association, formed for the purpose of improving the Town of Catskill, *etc.* (Deed of Conveyance in Trust. Articles, *etc.*) [With maps.] pp. 47. *Mitchell & Turner : New-York*, 1837. 12º.
                    10408. b. 34.

CATSKILL MOUNTAIN GUIDE. Catskill Mountain Guide . . . Illustrated. [The preface signed : W. V. L., i.e. Walton Van Loan.] [1876.] 8º. *See* L., W. V.
                    10408. ee. 7. (4.)

CATSKIN. [For editions of " The Catskin's Garland," under the title of " The Wandering Young Gentlewoman ; or, Cat-Skin " :] *See* Gentlewoman.

—— The Catskin's Garland, *etc.* [A ballad.] pp. 8. *J. Kendrew : York*, [1800 ?] 12º.   **11621. c. 3. (48.)**

—— [Another edition.] Catskin's Garland, or, the Wandering Young Gentlewoman, *etc.* pp. 8.   *T. Cheney : Banbury*, [1800 ?] 12º.   **1078. i. 28. (21.)**

CATSKIN.

—— Cat-Skin's or, the Wandering Young Lady's Garland, *etc.* pp. 8. [1815 ?] 16º.   **11601. aaa. 47. (2.)**

—— Cat-Skin's Garland, *etc.* pp. 8.   *Swindells : Manchester*, [1820 ?] 16º.   **11601. aa. 55. (5.)**

CATS SMALLENBURG (F. van) *See* Smallenburg.

CATT (Carrie Chapman) *See* Asylum. Asylum for Refugees under our Immigration Laws . . . Prepared for Committee of Ten. Mrs. C. Chapman Catt, Chairman. [1934.] 4º.   **8286. d. 31.**

—— *See* Peck (Mary G.) Carrie Chapman Catt, *etc.* [With portraits.] 1944. 8º.   **10890. d. 22.**

—— Address of the President at the Seventh Congress of the International Woman Suffrage Alliance, Budapest, Hungary . . . 1913. pp. 15.   *International Woman Suffrage Alliance : London*, [1913.] 8º.   **08415. i. 9. (2.)**

—— The World Movement for Woman Suffrage, 1904 to 1911. Being the presidential address delivered at Stockholm to the sixth convention of the International Woman Suffrage Alliance, *etc.* pp. 14.   *International Woman Suffrage Alliance : London*, 1911. 8º.   **08415. k. 3. (1.)**

CATT (Charles H.)
—— The Budding Gardener. [With illustrations.] pp. x. 126.   *Pilot Press : London*, 1948 [1949]. 8º.
                    7035. bb. 27.

——   Growing Pains. The story of the first year of a school young farmers' club, *etc.* pp. 42.
[*National Federation of Young Farmers' Clubs : Radlett*, 1940. 8º.   **07078. e. 32.**

CATT (David) *the Elder.* *See* Dawson (Herbert) The Footsteps of Providence . . . Some remarkable incidents . . . in the life of D. Catt, *etc.* [1914.] 8º.   **4920. eee. 19.**

CATT (David) *the Younger.* *See* Martin (W. Stanley) and Catt (D.) Pictures & Portraits from The Pilgrim's Progress. [1922.] 8º.   **4421. c. 38**

—— *See* Martin (W. S.) and Catt (D.) Pictures & Portraits from the Pilgrim's Progress. 1922. 8º.   **04414. b. 3.**

—— Scenes from the Microscope . . . Illustrated. pp. 80. *Protestant Times Publishing Co. : London*, 1905. 8º.
                    7002. de. 31.

CATT (Edith Francis)
—— The Joys and Troubles of Life. [Verses.] pp. 16. *Arthur H. Stockwell : Ilfracombe*, 1953. 8º.
                    11658. aaa. 232.

CATT (Elizabeth Willett) Journal of Journey to Scotland in 1836. [Edited by Edgar W. Willett and Percy A. Willett. With a portrait.] pp. 46.   [*Printed for private circulation*, 1909.] 8º.   K.T.C. **36. a. 4.** *One of an edition of fifty copies.*

CATT (George R.)
—— The Pictorial History of Manchester . . . Reprinted from " The Pictorial Times : " with additions and corrections. pp. 40.   [*Pictorial Times*] *Office : [London*, 1845 ?] 8º.   **10358. l. 55.** *Mutilated.*

CATT (Heinrich de) *See* Catt (Henri A. de)

CATT (Henri Alexandre de) Unterhaltungen mit Friedrich dem Grossen. Memoiren und Tagebücher von Heinrich de Catt. Herausgegeben von Reinhold Koser. Mit einer facsimilirten Tafel. *Fr.* pp. xxxii. 504. *Leipzig,* 1884. 8°. [*Publicationen aus den k. preussischen Staatsarchiven.* Bd. 22.] **9386. ee. 1/22.**

—— Gespräche Friedrichs des Grossen mit Henri de Catt. [Selected and translated from " Unterhaltungen mit Friedrich dem Grossen."] pp. x. 353. *Leipzig,* 1885. 8°. **10708. bb. 33.**

—— Gespräche Friedrichs des Grossen mit Henri de Catt. Herausgegeben von Friedrich von Oppeln-Bronikowski. pp. 111. *Leipzig,* [1933.] 8°. [*Insel-Bücherei.* no. 435.] **012213. de. 1/435.**

—— Gespräche Friedrich's des Grossen mit H. de Catt und dem Marchese Lucchesini. Kritisch festgestellte Auswahl, in deutscher Uebersetzung herausgegeben von Dr. Fritz Bischoff. pp. viii. 276. *Leipzig,* 1885. 8°. **10704. cc. 21.**

—— Frederick the Great: the memoirs of his reader, Henri de Catt, 1758–1760. Translated by F. S. Flint. With an introduction by Lord Rosebery. 2 vol. *Constable & Co.: London,* 1916. 8°. **010706. k. 27.**

CATT (James)
—— House Repairs. pp. 95. *W. & G. Foyle : London,* 1953. 8°. [*Foyles Handbooks.*] **W.P. 2940/74.**

CATT (Richard) And Afterwards the Judgment. pp. 299. *Chapman & Hall: London,* 1914. 8°. **NN. 1615.**

—— Nature's Cry. [A novel.] pp. 238. *Bohemian Publishing Co.: London,* [1913.] 8°. **12624. ee. 10.**

CATTA (J. D.) Essai sur quelques crustacés erratiques. pp. 33. pl. 2. *Paris,* 1876. 8°. [*Bibliothèque de l'École des Hautes Études.* Section des sciences naturelles. tom. 14. no. 4.] **Ac. 8929/5.**

CATTA (Tony) *See* Crouzil (L.) and Catta (T.) Guide juridique du clergé, *etc.* 1914. 8°. **5408. g. 12.**

—— Un Romancier de vraie France : René Bazin. pp. iv. 215. *Paris,* 1936. 8°. **010665. g. 12.**

—— Yves de Joannis, élève au Séminaire français, brigadier au 51e d'artillerie, 1893–1914 . . . Avec un portrait. pp. iv. 302. *Paris,* [1919.] 8°. **10657. aa. 10.**

CATTABENI (Guglielmo)
—— *See* Dante Alighieri. [*Divina Commedia.—Inferno.—Selections and Extracts.—Volapük.*] Canto primo della Divina Commedia . . . tradotto in volapük da G. Cattabeni, *etc.* 1889. 8°. **11420. d. 3. (4.)**

CATTALA (J. E.) Considérations sur la pneumonie catarrhale et ses variétés. Thèse, *etc.* pp. 46. *Montpellier,* 1856. 4°. **7379. d. 2. (13.)**

CATTALDI (Pietro Antonio) *See* Cataldi.

CATTALINICH (Giovanni) Storia della Dalmazia. 3 tom. *Zara,* 1834, 35. 8°. **1056. l. 5.**

CATTAN (Christophe de) La Geomance du seigneur Christofe de Cattan . . . Auec la Roüe de Pythagoras. Le tout corrigé, augmenté, & mis en lumiere par Gabriel du Preau, *etc.* ff. 178. *Par G. Gilles : Paris,* 1558. 4°. **1141. c. 5. (1.)**

—— [Another edition.] ff. 145. *Pour G. Gilles : Paris,* 1567. 4°. **719. f. 3.** *The titlepage is engraved.*

CATTAN (Christophe de)
—— [Another edition.] ff. 145. *Pour G. Gilles : Paris,* 1571. 4°. **719. h. 17.**

—— [Another edition.] ff. 145. *Par G. Gilles : Paris,* 1577. 4°. **1141. c. 5. (2.)**

—— The Geomancie of Maister Christopher Cattan . . . Whereunto is annexed the wheele of Pythagoras. Translated out of French into our English tongue (by Francis Sparry). 𝔅.𝔏. pp. 240. ms. notes. *Printed by John Wolfe, and are to be sold at Edward White's shop: London,* 1591. 4°. **8631. bb. 26.**

—— [Another copy.] **1141. c. 6.** *Imperfect ; wanting the titlepage, the whole of sig. A and the table of contents.*

—— [Another edition.] 𝔅.𝔏. pp. 265. *E. A. for Edward White : London,* 1608. 4°. **719. e. 44.** *Badly cropped.*

CATTAN (Jéhouda) *See* Ḳaṭṭān (Judah)

CATTAN (Lucien) Essai sur Walter Pater. pp. 212. *Paris,* 1936. 8°. **11858. aa. 46.**

CATTANEI DI MOMO (Filibert) *Baron.* Die Bildung eines österreichisch-deutschen Vereines für orientalische und transatlantische Verkehrsanstalten . . . Mit 2 Karten. [With " Beilagen."] pp. 103. *Wien,* 1865. 8°. **8246. h. 23. (5.)**

CATTANEIS DE MOMO (Aloysius Ferdinandus de) De calore animali, dissertatio physiologica inauguralis, *etc.* pp. 47. *Ticini Regii,* 1820. 8°. **7383*. c. 17. (4.)**

CATTANEO (Achille)
—— *See* Pavia.—*Università di Pavia.—Istituto Botanico dell' Università e Laboratorio Crittogamico.* Archivio triennale del Laboratorio di Botanica Crittogamica, *etc.* (Archivio del Laboratorio Crittogamico Garovaglio. Vol. 4 redatto dal Dr A. Cattaneo.) 1874, *etc.* 8°. **Ac. 107.**

CATTANEO (Achille) and **OLIVA** (L.)
—— Dei miceti trovati sul corpo umano. (Estratto dal vol. v dell'Archivio del Laboratorio di Botanica crittogamica di Pavia.) [With plates.] *Milano,* 1883. 8°. **7306. cc. 10. (1.)**

CATTANEO (Andreas) De physiologiæ ad medicinam practicam utilitate, dissertatio inauguralis, *etc.* pp. 19. *Ticini Regii,* [1827.] 8°. **7383*. c. 3. (7.)**

CATTANEO (Angelo) Gli Uomini d'ordine richiesti e reclamati dalla nazione. pp. 115. *Crema,* 1898. 8°. **08275. ee. 55.**

CATTANEO (Antonio) *Chimico-farmacista.* *See* Mīkhā'īl, al-Ṣabbāgh. La Colomba messaggiera ratta più del lampo, più pronta delle nube . . . Nel volgare italiano trasportata, e di note . . . accresciuta da A. Cattaneo. 1822. 12°. **14533. a. 10.**

—— *See* Periodical Publications.—*Milan.* Giornale di farmacia-chimica . . . Compilato da A. Cattaneo. 1824, *etc.* 8°. **P.P. 3180.**

—— Il Latte e i suoi prodotti. [With a plate.] pp. xvi. 483. *Milano,* 1839. 8°. **7077. e. 11.**

CATTANEO (Antonio) *Chirurg. Doct.* De lupulo et lupulina, dissertatio inauguralis, *etc.* pp. 16. *Ticini Regii,* [1830.] 8°. **7383*. c. 10. (10.)**

CATTANEO (ANTONIO) *Professore di fisica.* Macedonio Melloni. Discorso. pp. 24. [*Milan,* 1869.] 8°.
10631. bb. 54. (10.)

CATTANEO (BALDO) Harangue . . . prononcee a Rome le huictiesme d'Octobre 1590. deuant les . . . Cardinaux, entrans au conclaue pour l'eslection d'vn Pape: traduicte de Latin en François, par B. D. T. pp. 17.   *Par R. Colomiez: Tolose,* 1590. 8°.   3900. a. 66. (2.)

CATTANEO (CAJETAN) *See* CATTANEO (Gaetano) *Jesuit*

CATTANEO (CARLO) *Giureconsulto.*
—— *See* BORSA (M.) Carlo Cattaneo, *etc.* [With portraits.] 1945. 8°.   10633. s. 69.

——   *See* CHIESA (E.) L'idea politica di Carlo Cattaneo, *etc.* 1893. 8°.
8033. h. 27. (9.)

—— *See* CONTI (Giovanni) *of Rome.* Il Pensiero politico sociale di Carlo Cattaneo. 1946. 16°.   8012. a. 46.

—— *See* LEVI (Alessandro) Il Positivismo politico di Carlo Cattaneo, *etc.* [With a bibliography.] 1928. 8°.
08007. ee. 44.

—— *See* MARIO (A.) and MARIO (J. W.) Carlo Cattaneo. Cenni e reminiscenze. 1884. 8°.   10629. aaa. 43.

—— *See* MILANI (Giovanni) *Engineer.* Risposta . . . all'opuscolo del dottore C. Cattaneo intitolato Rivista di varii scritti intorno alla strada ferrata da Milano a Venezia, *etc.* 1841. 4°.   8235. l. 18.

—— *See* NOLLI (G.) La Filosofia di Carlo Cattaneo. 1901. 8°.   08464. f. 32.

—— *See* TOMMASINI-MATTIUCCI (P.) Il Pensiero di C. Cattaneo e di G. Mazzini nelle poesie di Giosue Carducci, *etc.* 1909. 8°.   11851. w. 18.

—— *See* ZANONI (E.) Carlo Cattaneo. 1878. 8°.
10629. aaa. 7.

—— Opere edite ed inedite . . . raccolte e ordinate per cura di A. Bertani. (Per la parte filosofica ne assunse la publicazione A. Mario.) 7 vol. *Firenze,* 1881–92. 8°.
12225. aaa. 15.

—— Alcuni scritti. 3 vol. *Milano,* 1846. 8°.
12225. d. 6.

—— Scritti politici ed Epistolario, pubblicati da G. Rosa e J. W. Mario, 1836–1848. [With a portrait.] vol. 1. *Firenze,* 1892. 8°.   012357. h. 34.
Imperfect; wanting vol. 2, 3.

—— Scritti storici-letterarî-linguistici-economici . . . Ordinati per cura di C. Romussi. pp. 349. *Milano,* 1898. 8°.
12227. b. 14.

—— Epistolario di Carlo Cattaneo. Raccolto e annotato da Rinaldo Caddeo. Con appendice di scritti e documenti inediti e rari. *Firenze.* 1949–56. 8°.   10923.k.3.

—— Considerazioni sulle cose d'Italia nel 1848. A cura di Cesare Spellanzon. Seconda edizione riveduta e accresciuta. [With a map.] pp. lxxxix. 175.   *Chieri,* 1946. 8°.   9168. cc. 33.
Saggi. no. 32.

—— D'alcune instituzioni agrarie dell'alta Italia applicabili a sollievo dell'Irlanda. Lettere del dottor C. Cattaneo a Roberto Campbell, *etc.* pp. 85. *Milano,* 1847. 8°.
7075. f. 8.

—— L'Insurrection de Milan en 1848. pp. vii. 216. *Paris,* 1848. 8°.   1317. c. 26.

CATTANEO (CARLO) *Giureconsulto.*

—— Dell'insurrezione di Milano nel 1848 e della successiva guerra. Memorie, *etc.* [A translation, with additions, of "L'Insurrection de Milan."] pp. 272.   *Brusselle,* 1849. 12°.   1316. d. 29.

—— [Another edition.] pp. viii. 256. *Milano,* 1884. 8°.
9150. bb. 7.

—— Memorie di economia publica dàl 1833 al 1860. vol. 1. pp. xix. 534. *Milano,* 1860. 8°.   8205. f. 18.
No more published.

—— Notizie naturali e civili su la Lombardia. [With maps and plans.] vol. 1. pp. cxii. 491. *Milano,* 1844. 8°.
1300. g. 4.
No more published.

—— Osservazioni sui prezzi attuali delle sete. Articolo . . . estratto dagli Annali di statistica, economia pubblica, *etc.* pp. 16. *Rimini,* [1836.] 8°.   899. d. 15. (10.)

—— Ricerche economiche sulle interdizioni imposte dalla legge civile agli Israeliti . . . Estratto dal vol. XXIII. degli Annali di giurisprudenza pratica, *etc.* pp. 143. *Milano,* 1836. 8°.   1122. i. 26.

—— Stati uniti d'Italia. A cura di Norberto Bobbio. pp. 337. *Torino,* 1945. 8°.   8032. aa. 46.

—— Sulla ferrovia dalle Alpi Elvetiche all'Europa Centrale. Lettera ai cittadini genovesi. (Dal Politecnico di Milano.) pp. 15. *Lugano,* 1865. 8°.   08235. bb. 34. (3.)

—— Sulle interdizioni israelitiche. A cura di G. A. Belloni. pp. 219. *Roma,* 1944. 8°.   4517. aa. 2.

—— La Vita nell'Universo. [A review of Lioy's work of that name.] *See* LIOY (P.) Conferenze scientifiche, *etc.* 1872. 8°.   8706. aaaa. 11.

—— Le più belle pagine di Carlo Cattaneo. Scelte da Gaetano Salvemini. [With a portrait.] pp. xxxi. 268. *Milano,* 1922. 12°. [*Le più belle pagine degli scrittori italiani.* vol. 5.]   012226. a. 1/5.

—— A Carlo Cattaneo nel primo centenario della sua nascita. [Short articles by various writers, with a bibliography of Cattaneo by A. Vismara.] pp. 32. *Milano,* 1901. fol.
1764. a. 27.

CATTANEO. (CARLO) *Physicist.*
—— *See* SOMIGLIANA (C.) La Meccanica razionale e la fisica matematica nell'Italia settentrionale e in Svizzera . . . A cura di C. Somigliana, B. Finzi, C. Cattaneo. 1947. 8°. [*Relationes de auctis scientiis tempore belli.* no. 18.]
Ac. 101. b/6. (18.)

—— Attrazione Newtoniana ritardata. *In Civitate Vaticana,* 1942. 8°. [*Pontificia Academia Scientiarum. Acta.* vol. 6. no. 28.]   Ac. 101. b/3.

CATTANEO (CARLO) *Professore nel Regio Liceo di Catania.* Dinamica elementare. pp. viii. 145. *Milano,* 1884. 8°.
012200. h. 55.
One of the "Manuali Hoepli."

CATTANEO (CARLO AMBROGIO) *See* CHINA. Difesa del giudizio formato dalla S. Sede Apostolica . . . intorno a' riti e ceremonie cinesi. Contro un libello sedizioso intitolato "Alcune riflessioni intorno alle cose presenti della Cina" [variously attributed to C. A. Cattaneo, Tommaso Cattaneo and Tommaso Ceva], *etc.* 1709. 4°.
1120. g. 2.

—— Opere . . . Nuova edizione . . . Aggiuntevi le opere postume. 5 tom. *Venezia,* 1821. 4°.   3678. cc. 3.

—— Alcune riflessioni intorno alle cose presenti della Cina. [Variously attributed to C. A. Cattaneo, T. Cattaneo and T. Ceva.] [1709.] fol. *See* CHINA. [*Appendix.*]
1316. m. 7. (4.)

CATTANEO (CARLO GIULIO) *See* ISOCRATES. [*Orationes Selectae.—Italian.*] Isocrate. Studii—versione [of the Έλενης Έγκωμιον, Πλαταικος and Κατα των Σοφιστων] —commenti. Saggio del professore Dr. C. G. Cattaneo. 1879. 8°. **11312. c. 38.**

CATTANEO (CORNELIO) *See* DORMI, *Il, pseud.* [i.e. C. Cattaneo.]

CATTANEO (FRANCESCO) Tributo de amicizia con epigrammi di maniera greca al sig. marchese D. Carlo Emmanuele Cacciapiatti . . . nelle sue nozze colla signora . . . Donna Giuseppa Cacciapiatti. pp. 6. xii. [*G. B. Bodoni: Parma,*] 1791. 16°. **L.R. 233. a. 8.**

—— [Another copy.] **L.R. 233. a. 6.**

CATTANEO (GAETANO) *Jesuit.* Lettera prima (seconda, terza) del padre G. Cattaneo . . . al sig. Giuseppe suo fratello [on his mission to Paraguay], *etc. See* MURATORI (L. A.) Il Christianesimo felice nelle missioni de' padri della Compagnia di Gesù nel Paraguai, *etc.* 1743. 4°. **209. c. 17.**

—— The First (—Third) Letter of Father Cajetan Cattaneo. [On his voyage from Cadiz to Paraguay.] *In:* MURATORI (L. A.) A Relation of the Missions of Paraguay, *etc.* pp. 205–280. 1759. 8°. **4768. de. 14.**

CATTANEO (GAETANO) *of Milan. See* BOSSI (G.) Un Ricordo a Giuseppe Bossi. Sue poesie . . . colla vita scritta da G. Cattaneo sino all'ieri sconosciuta, *etc.* 1885. 8°. **11436. ee. 30.**

—— *See* ITALIANS. Vite e ritratti di illustri Italiani. (Descrizione delle medaglie [i.e. those of Napoleon I. relating to Italy] dettata da G. Cattaneo.) 1812, *etc.* fol. **1321. m. 2.**

—— —— 1820. fol. **10631. i. 11.**

—— *See* MILAN.—*Imperiale Reale Museo di Milano.* Monete cufiche dell' I. R. Museo di Milano. [By Count C. O. Castiglioni. Edited by G. Cattaneo.] 1819. 4°. **603. k. 2.**

—— Equejade. Monumento antico di bronzo del Museo nazionale Ungherese, considerato ne' suoi rapporti coll'antichità figurata. pp. xxiv. 128. pl. IV. **L.P.** *Milano,* 1819. 4°. **819. l. 9.**

—— [Another copy.] **L.P.** **7707. f. 9.**

—— Osservazioni sopra un frammento antico di bronzo di greco lavoro rappresentante Venere. Pubblicate in occasione delle nozze fausstissime della marchesa Cristina Trivulzio col conte Giuseppe Archinti. [With plates.] pp. 48. *Milano,* 1819. 4°. **7707. f. 1. (2.)**

CATTANEO (GIACOMO)

—— *See* GENOA.—*Accademia Ligure di Scienze e Lettere.* La Società . . . nel primo decennio dalla sua fondazione, 1889–99. (Relazione del presidente prof. G. Cattaneo.) 1900. 8°. **08709. bb. 7. (3.)**

—— Gli Amebociti dei cefalopodi e loro confronto con quelli d'altri invertebrati . . . Con 4 tavole. *See* GENOA.— *Università di Genova.* Quarto Centenario Colombiano. Atti, *etc.* 1892. 8°. **Ac. 2602/2.**

—— Le Colonie lineari e la morfologia dei molluschi. Studio, *etc.* pp. xxiv. 420. *Milano,* 1882. 8°. **8708. dd. 6.**

—— Darwinismo. Saggio sulla evoluzione degli organismi. pp. vii. 111. *Milano,* 1880. 8°. **7006. b. 24.**

—— Passatempi lariani. [In verse.] pp. viii. 100. *Milano,* 1884. 8°. **11429. cc. 21.**

CATTANEO (GIOVANNI) *Author of* "*Le Petit Hérodote.*" *See* BERYBER, *Mr., pseud.* [i.e. G. Cattaneo.]

CATTANEO (GIOVANNI) *Capitano Aiutante Maggiore.* Il Nuovo regolamento d'esercizio e di manovra spiegato diffusamente alla Guardia Nazionale d'Italia. 4 vol. *Venezia,* 1869. 8°. **8829. a. 28.**

CATTANEO (GIOVANNI DE) *See* D., A. M. T. F. *Begin.* All' ottimo genitore Francesco de Cattaneo questi sensi di . . . lutto per l'immatura morte dell'egregio filio G. de Cattaneo . . . A. M. T. F. D. . . . consecra. 1808. 8°. **T. 2358. (5.)**

CATTANEO (GIOVANNI MARIA) *See* CATANAEUS (Joannes M.)

CATTANEO (GIOVANNO PIETRO) *See* GRACIAN (L.) *pseud.* Il Criticon . . . Traduzione dallo spagnuolo in italiano di G. P. Cattaneo. 1730. 8°. **1458. c. 8.**

CATTANEO (GOTTARDO) *See* CORBELLINI (A.) Risposta di un malpratico [A. Corbellini] ad alcune ricerche di un altro malpratico [G. Cattaneo], sul progetto di un monte delle sete in Milano, *etc.* 1838. 8°. **8227. aaa. 61. (3.)**

—— Dei vantaggi della foglia primitiva nell'allevamento dei bachi da seta. pp. 16. *Milano,* 1866. 8°. **1145. d. 29.**

—— Della riacclimazione del gelso . . . Quinta edizione, con aggiunte, *etc.* pp. 32. *Milano,* 1865. 8°. **1145. d. 28.**

—— IX. edizione . . . cui fanno seguito autorevoli giudizj di agricoltori italiani, *etc.* pp. 52. *Milano,* [1871?] 8°. **7293. g. 49. (7.)**

CATTANEO (IRENE) *See* ANCONA (P. d') L'Arte italiana del Rinascimento . . . A cura di P. d'Ancona . . . I. Cattaneo, *etc.* 1932. fol. **7803. s. 21.**

—— Salvator Rosa. Con 32 riproduzioni in fototipo. pp. 242. *Milano,* 1929. 8°. **10633. pp. 37.**

CATTANEO (LUIGI) Intorno al concetto di costituzione. Saggio, *etc.* pp. 112. *Roma,* 1887. 8°. **8006. bbb. 2.**

—— L'Ordinamento dei ministeri. pp. 83. *Roma,* 1886. 8°. **8074. f. 11. (3.)**

CATTANEO (MARCELLO) *See* FOA (Moyse Benjamino) afterwards CATTANEO (Marcello)

CATTANEO (MARCUS ANTONIUS) Laudatio in funere Ludovici I. Hetruriæ regis, *etc.* [With a plate.] pp. 25. *Romae,* 1803. 4°. **1356. k. 4. (22.)** *The titlepage is engraved.*

CATTANEO (NICOLÒ EUSTACHIO) Frusta musicale, ossia Lettere sugli abusi introdotti nella musica. pp. xxiv. 189. *Milano,* 1836. 8°. **785. c. 41.**

—— Gramatica della musica, ossia Elementi teorici di questa bell'arte. pp. 62. *Milano,* 1828. 8°. **7807. f. 7. (1.)**

CATTANEO (PETRUS) De notaeomyelitide, dissertatio inauguralis, *etc.* pp. 24. *Ticini Regii,* [1827.] 8°. **7383*. b. 3. (3.)**

CATTANEO (RAFFAELE) L'Architettura in Italia dal secolo VI al mille circa. Ricerche storico-critiche, *etc.* pp. 306. *Venezia,* 1888. 8°. **7814. f. 12.**

—— Architecture in Italy from the Sixth to the Eleventh Century . . . Translated by the Contessa Isabel Curtis-Cholmeley in Bermani. Illustrated. pp. 363. *T. Fisher Unwin: London,* 1896. 8°. **7817. d. 13.**

CATTANEO (RICCARDO GAUDENZIO) Le Basi dell'elezione politica nel governo rappresentativo. Studio, *etc.* pp. 211. *Torino,* 1878. 8°. **8009. i. 7.**

CATTANEO (SILVAN) Novelle. [Selected from the "Dodici giornate" by Bartolommeo Gamba. With illustrations.] ON VELLUM. *Venezia*, 1813. 8°.
C. 41. c. 22.
One of an edition of eight copies, all printed on vellum.

CATTANEO (TOMMASO) *See* CHINA. Difesa del giudizio formato dalla S. Sede Apostolica . . . intorno a' riti e ceremonie cinesi. Contro un libello sedizioso intitolato "Alcune riflessioni intorno alle cose presenti della Cina" [variously attributed to C. A. Cattaneo, T. Cattaneo and T. Ceva], *etc.* 1709. 4°.
1120. g. 2.

—— Alcune riflessioni alle cose presenti della Cina. [Variously attributed to C. A. Cattaneo, T. Cattaneo and T. Ceva.] [1709] fol. *See* CHINA. [*Appendix.*] 1316. m. 7. (4.)

CATTANEO (VINCENZO) *See* ITALY. [*Codes.—Civil Code.*] Il Codice civile italiano annotato dall'avvocato V. Cattaneo, *etc.* 1865, *etc.* 8°.
5326. cc. 14.

CATTANEO (WENCESLAO) Rudimenti teorici di musica. pp. 31. *Milano*, 1842. 8°.
785. g. 37.

CATTANEO LEONARDI (NICCOLÒ GRILLO) *Marquis*. *See* GRILLO CATTANEO LEONARDI.

CATTANÈS (HÉLÈNE) Les "Fastnachtspiele" de Hans Sachs, *etc.* pp. 172. *Strasbourg*, 1923. 8°. [*Smith College Studies in Modern Languages.* vol. 4. no. 2, 3.]
Ac. 1877/2.

CATTANEUS (EUGENIUS) *Bishop of Telese.* *See* CATANEUS

CATTANEUS (FRANCISCUS MARIA) *See* LODI (J. T.) Ianuen. restitutionis dotium pro M. et R. Laurentio Spinola . . . contra MM. Hieronymum et F. M. Cattaneos, *etc.* 1713. fol.
501. g. 19. (13.)

CATTANEUS (HIERONYMUS) *See* LODI (J. T.) Ianuen. restitutionis dotium pro M. et R. Laurentio Spinola . . . contra MM. H. et Franciscum Mariam Cattaneos, *etc.* 1713. fol.
501. g. 19. (13.)

CATTANEUS (JOSEPH JOANNES ANTONIUS) *Count.* De juribus Mediolanensis Ducatus in flumine Oleo plenissimum votum Advocati Fiscalis Comitis Don J. J. A. Cattanei. [*Milan?* 1719.] fol.
5326. i. 1. (5.)

CATTANI (ALFRED)
—— Zürich 600 Jahre im Bund der Eidgenossen 1351–1951 . . . Mit Beiträgen von Prof. Dr. Leonhard von Muralt. [With illustrations.] pp. 324. *Zürich*, 1951. fol.
10196. t. 5.

CATTANI (ANDREA LUIGI) *Bishop of Samminiato.* Ne' funerali dell' eminentissimo principe Giuseppe Ulisse Cardinal Gozzadini Vescovo d'Imola, celebrati . . . da Monsignore A. L. Cattani, *etc.* (Orazione funerale di Plasone Ecatombeo [i.e. G. G. Cremona].) [With poems on the same subject by various authors. The whole edited by A. L. Cattani. With a portrait of Gozzodini.] pp. 79. *Firenze*, 1729. 4°.
610. k. 17. (7.)

CATTANI (ANNETTA) *See* CATTANI (G.) Quattro canti e due frammenti della Pigmeide o Farsa, *etc.* [Edited by A. Cattani.] 1878. 8°.
11436. ee. 13. (22.)

CATTANI (C.) Das Alpenthal Engelberg und seine Berg-, Wasser-, Milch- und Molkenkuren. Mit mehrern Lithographien und dem Titlis-Panorama. [With a preface by C. G. Imhof.] pp. vi. 29. *Luzern*, 1852. 8°.
7470. f. 52. (4.)

—— Engelberg, ses environs et ses cures de lait et de petit-lait . . . Traduit de l'allemand, *etc.* pp. 39. *Lucerne*, 1854. 8°.
7470. d. 73. (3.)

CATTANI (DANTE) Alessandro VI. Dramma. pp. 210. *Bologna*, 1887. 8°.
11715. bbb. 41.

CATTANI (GIOVANNI) Quattro canti e due frammenti della Pigmeide o Farsa. Poema inedito civile e religioso, *etc.* [Edited by Annetta Cattani.] pp. 32. *Parma*, 1878. 8°.
11436. ee. 13. (22.)

CATTANI (GIUSEPPINA) *See* TIZZONI (G.) Bakteriologische Untersuchungen über den Tetanus. Von . . . G. Tizzoni . . . J. Cattani, *etc.* 1890. 8°. [*Beiträge zur pathologischen Anatomie.* Bd. 7. Hft. 2.]
P.P. 3206. aa.

—— Ueber die Reaction der Gewebe auf specifische Reize . . . Hierzu Tafel, *etc.* 1890. *See* ZIEGLER (E.) and NAUWERCK (C.) Beiträge zur pathologischen Anatomie, *etc.* Bd. 7. Hft. 2. 1886, *etc.* 8°.
P.P. 3206. aa.

CATTANI (HEINZ) Entwicklung des Talgerichts von Engelberg unter der Klosterherrschaft. 1935. *See* EINSIEDELN.—*Historischer Verein der fünf Orte Lucern, Uri, Schwyz, Unterwalden und Zug.* Der Geschichtsfreund, *etc.* Bd. 90. 1843, *etc.* 8°.
Ac. 6940.

CATTANI (IDA MARIE)
—— Studien zum deutschen Tassobild des 17. und 18. Jahrhunderts. Untersuchungen über die Uebersetzungen des Befreiten Jerusalems von D. von Werder, J. F. Kopp und W. Heinse. Inaugural Dissertation, *etc.* pp. 108. *Willisau*, 1941. 8°.
11868. m. 33.

CATTANI (JOSEPHINE) *See* CATTANI (Giuseppina)

CATTANI (L.)
—— Geltungsbereich der Steuervereinbarungen nach schweizerischem Recht. Dissertation, *etc.* pp. vi. 73. *Zürich*, 1955. 8°.
05551. g. 11.

CATTANI (NICCOLÒ ANTONIO) Opuscoli o dissertazioni fisico-mediche d'intorno alle qualità . . . dell'aere in genere di ciascun paese, ed in ispecie di quello di Bevagna nell'Umbria. E sopra le virtù medicinali dell'acqua commune in genere, ed in ispecie di alcune acque minerali dell'Umbria medesima, *etc.* pp. 195. *Assisi*, 1745. 4°.
234. k. 1.

CATTANI (PAUL) Gesundheitspolitik. pp. 101. *Zürich*, 1918. 8°. [*Schriften für Schweizer Art und Kunst.* Hft. 71–73.]
12216. d. 1/47.

CATTANI (PIETRO ANTONIO) *See* CATALDI.

CATTANI DA DIACCETO (FRANCESCO DE') *Bishop of Fiesole.* *See* AMBROSE, *Saint, Bishop of Milan.* [*Single Works.*] Gli Uffici di S. Ambruogio . . . tradotti in volgar Fiorentino. Per . . . F. Cattani da Diacceto, *etc.* 1558. 8°.
3623. a. 33.

—— *See* PASSAVANTI (J.) Lo Specchio di vera penitenza. [With a prefatory letter by F. de' Cattani da Diacceto.] 1580. 12°.
4399. a. 3.

—— Breue raccolto della vita et costumi di suor Caterina de Ricci, dell'ordine di S. Domenico. *G. Marescotti: Fiorenza*, 1592. 4°.
1232. c. 3.

—— Discorso . . . sopra la Superstizzione dell'Arte Magica. ff. 36. *V. Panizzi & M. Peri: Fiorenza*, 1567. 4°.
8630. dd. 19.

—— [Another copy.]
8630. cc. 27.
Slightly cropped.

—— L'Essamerone del Reuerendo M. F. Cattani da Diacceto, *etc.* ff. 180. *L. Torrentino: Fiorenza*, 1563. 4°.
222. k. 23.

CATTANI DA DIACCETO (Francesco de') *Bishop of Fiesole.*

— La Vita dell'immaculata . . . vergine Santa Maria madre di Dio et Signor nostro Giesu Christo. pp. 260. *B. Sermartelli: Fiorenza*, 1570. 4º. **1218. f. 6.**

— Vita dell'inclito et santissimo Domenico, Patriarca del sagro ordine de predicatori. pp. 207. *B. Sermartelli: Fiorenza*, 1572. 4º. **4825. d. 1.**

— Vite dello inuittissimo martire Santo Romolo, primo vescouo di Fiesole. Et di piu altri santi vescovi suoi successori. (Esortazione del Reuerendissimo . . . F. de Cattani da Diacceto . . . fatta al clero, nel suo sinodo diocesano a di 14. di Maggio 1578.) pp. 206. *B. Sermartelli: Fiorenza*, 1578. 8º. **662. e. 11.**

— [Another copy.] **485. a. 10.**

— Vita di S. Andrea Corsini, vescovo di Fiesole, scritta de Francesco suo successore e da altri. *See* Maffei (G. P.) Vite di diciassette confessori di Cristo, *etc.* 1746. 4º. **4805. cc. 9.**

— The Life of B. Andrew, Bishop of Fesula. Written by Francis his successour and others. *See* Maffei (G. P.) Fuga sæculi, *etc.* 1632. 4º. **C. 26. h. 2.**

CATTANI DA DIACCETO (Francesco de') *Philosopher.* Opera omnia F. Cattanei Diacetii . . . nunc primum in lucem edita . . . Accessit index rerum & verborum memorabilium copiosissimus. (T. Zuinggeri . . . præfatio. —Vita Diacetii per E. Lapinium.) pp. 371. *Per H. Petri, & P. Pernam: Basileæ*, 1563. fol. **526. m. 8. (1.)**
Imperfect; wanting sig. a of the index.

— Panegirico di Francesco da Diacceto [i.e. the "Panegirico allo Amore"]. *L. Vicentino: Roma*, 1526. 4º. **84. b. 17. (2.)**

— I tre libri d'amore di M. F. Cattani da Diacceto . . . Con un Panegerico [*sic*] all' Amore ; et con la vita del detto autore, fatta da M. Benedetto Varchi. pp. 207. *G. Giolito de' Ferrari: Vinegia*, 1561. 8º. **721. b. 13. (2.)**

— [Another copy.] **232. a. 17.**

CATTANIO (Ascanio) Umilissime riflessioni delli Notaj del collegio di Mantova all' Eccelso Arciducale Maestrato nella causa di relazione pendente sopra l'affare del Registro. [Signed by A. Cattanio and others.] 1730. fol. *See* Mantua.—*Collegio dei Notai.* **5322. ee. 20. (3.)**

CATTANIO (Francesco) Riflessioni sopra il sistema di G. Brown [i.e. John Brown, M.D., author of "Elements of Medicine"]. pp. 36. *Milano*, 1795. 8º. **7383*. c. 6. (1.)**

CATTANIUS (Andreas) Andreae Cattanii Imolensis opus de intellectu et de causis mirabilium effectuum. [On the Metaphysica or Al-Shifā of Avicenna.] [*Florence*, 1505?] 4º. **1478. aa. 21.**

CATTANT (D.)

— *See* Aristophanes. [*Plutus.—Greek and French.*] Aristophane. Plutus. (Comédie . . . expliquée, traduite et annotée par M. Cattant.) 1843. 8º. **11304.c.6/1.**

CATTAPANI (Henrietta Gardner) Songs of Sentiment. pp. 154. 1909. 8º. **11687. ee. 46.**

CATTARAN MONUMENTS.

— Monumenta catarensia. *See* Barada (M.)

CATTARO.

— Kotor i Boka Kotorska . . . Preštampano iz "Nove Evrope," *etc.* [Articles by various writers, with plates, and a map.] pp. 95. *Zagreb*, 1934. 8º. **10127. g. 10.**

CATTARO.

—— Newe Zeittung, Bericht, so geschehen von dem fürnemen Obersten Hauptman des Venedischen Kriegs Zeugs auff dem Meer, an den . . . Herzogen von Venedig, antreffende die . . . Zerstörung der Stat Cattaro, welche durch einen Erdbidem den 6. tag Brachmonats des 1564. Jars zerstört . . . Andere warhaffte Newezeitung, Wie im Ungerlandt in einer Stat Cassauia genant, ein Burger sampt seiner Haussfrawen . . . gestorben, *etc.* [1564?] 4º. **9165. c. 22.**

—— Newe Zeyttung, Kurtzer Bericht, so geschehen dem fürnemen Obersten Hauptmañ dess Venedischen Kriegszugs auff dem Meer, an den . . . Hertzogen von Venedig, antreffende die . . . Zerstörung der Statt Cattaro . . . durch einen Erdbidem, *etc.* [*Nürmberg*, [1564.] 4º. **1312. c. 49.**
Valentin Geyssler:

—— Prva knjiga kotorskih notara od god. 1326–1335. Uredio i dodao uvod, regeste i kazala Antun Mayer. [With facsimiles and a map.] pp. 645. *Zagreb*, 1951. 8º. [*Monumenta catarensia.* vol. 1.] **Ac. 741. bb.**

—— *C.K. Realni i Veliki Gimnazij.* Drugi godišnji program C.K. Realnog i Velikog Gimnazija u Kotoru za godinu školsku 1873–74, *etc.* pp. 67. *u Dubrovniku*, 1874. 8º. **8358. c. 139.**

Поморски Музеj.
—— Годишњак. 1952 [*etc.*]. *Котор*, 1952– . 8º. **P.P. 2459. xe.**

CATTARO, Francesco, *Bishop of.* [1894–1895.] *See* Ucellini.

——, Marco Antonio, *Bishop of.* [1801–1818.] *See* Gregorina.

——, Petrus, *Bishop of.* [1471–1493.] *See* Bruti (P. dei Conti)

CATTARUZZI (Humbert) How to Out-think your Opponent; or, T. N. tactics for close-in fighting, *etc.* pl. 36. *J. J. Newbegin: San Francisco*, 1918. 8º. **7911. cc. 15.**

CATTAUI (Adolphe) *See* Cairo.—*Société de Géographie d'Égypte.* Publications speciales . . . Sous la direction de M. A. Cattaui Bey. 1923, *etc.* 8º. **Ac. 6042. d/2.**

—— *See* Foucart (George) *Egyptologist*, and Cattaui (A.) La Société Sultanieh de Géographie du Caire, son œuvre, 1875–1921. 1921. 8º. [*Société Royale de Géographie d'Égypte. Publications spéciales.*] **Ac. 6042. d/2. (9.)**

—— *See* International Geographical Congress. [Cairo, 1925.] Congrès international de géographie . . . Compte rendu publié par le secrétaire général du Congrès (A. Cattaui). 1925, *etc.* 8º. **Ac. 5996/14.**

—— Causeries sur les hiéroglyphes et deux étapes de l'histoire ancienne de l'Égypte. [With plates.] pp. 134. *Le Caire*, 1925. 4º. **12902. eee. 16.**

—— Les Mystères égyptiens et les associations secrètes. pp. 15. *Paris*, 1889. 8º. **4503. bb. 23. (3.)**

CATTAUI (Georges)

—— *See* Cattaui (R.) and Cattaui (G.) Mohamed-Aly et l'Europe, *etc.* 1950. 8º. **09062. aa. 34.**

—— L'Amitié de Proust. Avec . . . une lettre inédite de Marcel Proust, *etc.* pp. 228. *Paris*, 1935. 8º. [*Les Cahiers Marcel Proust.* no. 8.] **W.P. 2209/8.**

CATTAUI (Georges)

—— Charles de Gaulle. [With a portrait.] pp. 205. *Thonon-les-Bains*, 1945. 8º.   **010665. d. 48.**

—— Instances d'Israël. *See* Jews. Les Juifs, *etc.* 1937. 8º.   **4034. c. 65.**

—— Marcel Proust. Proust et son temps—Proust et le temps, *etc.* [With portraits and a facsimile.] pp. xvi. 286. *Paris*, 1952. 8º.   **10666. a. 40.**

—— Symbole de la France. Le Mistère français—Saint Louis et l'ordre temporel chrétien. pp. 140. *Neuchâtel*, 1944. 8º. [*Collection des cahiers du Rhône.* no. 18.]   **W.P. 2920/18.**

—— Trois poëtes. Hopkins, Yeats, Eliot. [With portraits.] pp. 168. *Paris*, [1947.] 8º.   **11854. s. 45.**

CATTAUI (Joseph)

—— L'Égypte. Aperçu historique et géographique, gouvernement et institutions, vie économique et sociale. (Publié sous la direction de J. Cattaui.) [With plates, including a portrait, plans, and a map.] pp. xii. 456. 1926. 8º. *See* Compagnie Universelle du Canal Maritime de Suez.   **09062. bb. 20.**

CATTAUI (René) Le Règne de Mohamed Aly d'après les archives russes en Égypte. *Le Caire*, 1931– . 8º. [*Société Royale de Géographie d'Égypte. Publications spéciales.*]   **Ac. 6042. d/2. (32.)**

CATTAUI (René) and **CATTAUI** (Georges)

—— Mohamed-Aly et l'Europe, *etc.* [With plates, including portraits.] pp. xvi. 300. *Paris; Geneva* printed, 1950. 8º.   **09062. aa. 34.**
The date in the colophon is 1949.

CATTE, *Donna*. I Chiassi di Donna Catte in altanella, che vede la regatta de' 3. giugno 1767, fatta per onorar . . . el Duca regnante di Wirtemberga: canzonetta su l'aria: " Putte care ve saludo." *Venezia*, 1767. 8º.   **805. d. 22. (13.)**

CATTE (de) *See* Katte (J. H. von)

CATTEAU-CALLEVILLE (Jean Pierre Guillaume) Histoire de Christine, reine de Suède, avec un précis historique de la Suède depuis les anciens tems jusqu'à la mort de Gustave-Adolphe-le-Grand, *etc.* (Pièces relatives à l'histoire de Christine.) 2 tom. *Paris*, 1815. 8º.   **610. e. 2.**

—— [Another copy.]   **1199. f. 20, 21.**

—— Histoire des Révolutions de Norwège, suivie du tableau de l'état actuel de ce pays et de ses rapports avec la Suède. 2 tom. *Paris*, 1818. 8º.   **152. c. 16, 17.**

—— Tableau de la mer Baltique, considérée sous les rapports physiques, géographiques, historiques et commerciaux, avec une carte, *etc.* 2 tom. *Paris*, 1812. 8º.   **152. c. 14, 15.**

—— Tableau des états danois, envisagés sous les rapports du mécanisme social. 3 tom. *Paris*, 1802. 8º.   **572. c. 26.**

—— Tableau général de la Suède. 2 tom. *Lausanne*, 1790. 8º.   **153. c. 16.**

—— A General View of Sweden . . . Together with the manners and customs of its inhabitants . . . Translated from the French, *etc.* pp. xx. 410. *G. G. J. & J. Robinson: London*, 1790. 8º.   **10280. d. 31.**

CATTEAU-CALLEVILLE (Jean Pierre Guillaume)

—— La Vie de Renée, duchesse de Ferrare. pp. 36. *Berlin*, [1781.] 8º.   **10631. bbb. 41. (1.)**

—— Voyage en Allemagne et en Suède, contenant des observations . . . et le tableau de la dernière révolution de Suède. 3 tom. *Paris*, 1810. 8º.   **1047. ee. 10.**

CATTECHISTA. Il Cattechista in cattedra, che istruisce d'ogni lor dovere . . . secondo la scorta ed indrizzo del Catechismo romano, *etc.* 6 pt. *Roma*, 1750. 12º.   **3506. a. 46.**

CATTEDRA. Cattedra Ambulante d'Agricoltura per la Provincia di Milano. *See* Milan, *Province of.*

CATTEGAT. Directions for Sailing from the Cattegat into the Sound, and through the Grounds for Falsterborn and into the East Sea ; as also, for running into Copenhagen, and through the King's-Channel . . . and likewise, on coming from the Baltic back. pp. 24. *R. Wilkinson: London*, 1801. 8º.   **533. f. 36.**

—— Sailing Directions for the Cattegat, Sound, and the Great and Little Belts, to the Baltic Sea. Compiled from the Danish and Swedish surveys. pp. 75. *Charles Wilson: London*, 1871. 8º.   **10496. aa. 44.**

CATTELA (J. E. Spinosa)

—— Efficient Business Management through Budgeting and Budgetary Control. pp. vi. 145. *Macdonald & Evans: London*, 1948. 8º.   **8218. e. 36.**

CATTELAIN (E.)

—— L'Ypérite, ou gaz moutarde, *etc.* pp. 111. *Paris*, 1940. 8º.   **8899. f. 42.**

CATTELAIN (Philippe) *See* Beschi (C. G.) Aventures du gourou Paramarta. Conte drôlatique indien. Orné de nombreuses eaux-fortes par Bernay & Cattelain. 1877. 8º.   **12315. h. 3.**

—— Mémoires inédits du Chef de la Sûreté sous la Commune. [With a preface by P. Peltier.] pp. 294. *Paris*, [1900.] 8º.   **9231. f. 16.**

CATTELL (Alexander Gilmore) Complimentary Banquet given by the Presidents of the National Banks of the City of Philadelphia to the Hon. A. G. Cattell, upon the eve of his departure to Europe, as the fiscal agent of the United States Government, *etc.* pp. 48. *West Bros.: Philadelphia*, 1873. 8º.   **8228. h. 35.**

CATTELL (Charles Cockbill) *See also* Charles (Christopher) *pseud.* [i.e. C. C. Cattell.]

—— *See* Dawson (George) *Minister of the Church of the Saviour, Birmingham.* The Speeches of George Dawson, M.A., on "Shakespeare." Selected by C. C. Cattell. [1878.] 8º.   **12301. bb. 57.**

—— Against Christianity. Shewing its theory incredible and its practice impossible. pp. 32. *Freethought Publishing Co.: London*, 1888. 8º.   **04376. e. 92. (7.)**

—— The Age of the Earth and of Animal and Vegetal Life, with special reference to the views of Sir J. W. Dawson [in " Fossil Men and their Modern Representatives "]. pp. 16. *G. & J. H. Shipway: Birmingham*, 1886. 8º.   **07105. i. 28.**

—— Co-operative Production. pp. 16. *G. H. Reddalls: Birmingham*, 1874. 8º.   **8277. a. 61. (1.)**

—— The Dark Side of Christianity, showing it unreasonable and impractical. (Second edition.) pp. 16. *C. Watts: London*, [1870?] 8º.   **4016. eee. 29. (1.)**

CATTELL (Charles Cockbill)

—— Did Bacon write Shakespeare? A reply to Ignatius Donnelly. pp. 32. *Simpkin, Marshall & Co. London,* 1888. 8°. **11763. bb. 9. (2.)**

—— The Downfall of the English Land System. [By C. C. Cattell.] pp. 23. [1871?] 8°. *See* ENGLISH LAND SYSTEM. **8138. ee. 27. (1.)**

—— Gems from the Ocean of Truth. Selected by C. Cattell. pp. 94. *Simpkin, Marshall & Co.: London,* 1896. 8°. **8409. d. 21.**

—— In Search of a Religion, and notes by the way. pp. 16. *C. Watts: London,* [1880?] 8°. **4016. eee. 29. (3.)**

—— Is Darwinism Atheistic? *Freethought Publishing Co.: London,* 1884. 8°. [*Atheistic Platform.* no. 8.] **4018. b. 45.**

—— Laconics for Free Inquirers: extracted from the works of the best authors. pp. 88. *J. A. Langford: Birmingham,* 1855. 8°. **12298. a. 4.**

—— The Land: how to make it feed its people, *etc.* (Second edition.) pp. 14. *Beacon & Nutt: Birmingham,* [1879.] 8°. **8138. ee. 27. (3.)**

—— Lord Bacon: did he write Shakespeare's Plays? A reply to Judge Holmes, Miss D. Bacon, *etc.* pp. 16. *G. & J. H. Shipway: Birmingham,* 1879. 8°. **11763. aaa. 29.**

—— The Man of the Past, the evidence of his natural origin & great antiquity. pp. 50. *Simpkin, Marshall & Co.: London,* [1891.] 8°. **7004. de. 23. (4.)**

—— The Martyrs of Progress: being historical sketches of the perils & persecutions of discoverers and teachers of all ages and nations. pp. iv. 59. *C. Watts: London,* 1878. 8°. **10600. aaa. 9.**

—— Mr. John Bright and Labour Representation. pp. 4. *Willet: Birmingham,* [1875?] 8°. **8138. ee. 27. (2.)**

—— Radicalism & Imperialism: a funeral sermon on departed Tory power, *etc.* pp. 16. *Beacon & Nutt: Birmingham,* [1880.] 8°. **8138. ee. 27. (4.)**

—— Ralph Waldo Emerson . . . Description and estimate of his writings. pp. 14. *Watts & Co.: London,* [1880?] 8°. **11825. bbb. 46.**

—— A Search for the First Man, and what I found on the way. pp. 68. *Cornish Bros.: Birmingham,* 1883. 8°. **7007. a. 13.**

—— Shakespeare: did he write the works attributed to him? Third edition, with notes on " What Shakespeare Learnt at School " [three articles with that title by T. S. Baynes, published in " Fraser's Magazine," 1879–80]. pp. 15. *H. Cattell & Co.: London,* [1885?] 8°. **11764. c. 21.**

—— A String of Pearls from the Masters of Thought & Language. pp. viii. 140. *Cornish Bros.: Birmingham,* [1876.] 8°. **12270. de. 4.**

—— Thoughts for Thinking. From the literature of all ages. Selected by C. C. Cattell. pp. 32. *Simpkin, Marshall & Co.: London,* 1889. 8°. **12305. dd. 8.**

—— What is a Freethinker? with a special reference to Mr. R. W. Dale, M.A., on " Atheism and the House of Commons." pp. 16. *Watts & Co.: London,* [1880.] 8°. **4016. eee. 29. (4.)**

CATTELL (David Tredwell)

—— Communism and the Spanish Civil War. [With a bibliography.] pp. xii. 290. *University of California Press: Berkeley & Los Angeles,* 1955. 8°. [*University of California Publications in International Relations.* vol. 4.] **Ac. 2689. g/35.**

CATTELL (David Tredwell)

—— [Another copy.] Communism and the Spanish Civil War. *Berkeley & Los Angeles,* 1955. 8°. **9196. d. 16.**

CATTELL (George Trew)

—— Crowmarsh, Culham & Goring Rural Sanitary Districts. Report to the Rural District Councils of Crowmarsh, Culham & Goring for the year ending December 31st, 1911. By G. T. Cattell . . . Medical Officer of Health. pp. 24. [1912.] 8°. *See* CROWMARSH.—*Rural District Council.* **A.R. 920.**

—— ⎯⎯⎯⎯⎯ Sewage Disposal in Berkshire. pp. 24. *Phillimore & Co.: London,* 1904. 8°. **08708. b. 20. (15.)**

CATTELL (Henry Ware) *See* ZIEGLER (Ernst) *Professor der Pathologie in Freiburg i. B.* A Text-book of Special Pathological Anatomy . . . Translated and edited . . . by . . . H. W. Cattell. 1896, *etc.* 8°. **2255. e. 19.**

—— Lippincott's New Medical Dictionary. A vocabulary of the terms used in medicine and the allied sciences, with their pronunciation, etymology, and signification . . . Freely illustrated with figures in the text. pp. xviii. 1108. *J. B. Lippincott Co.: Philadelphia,* 1910. 8°. **7307. b. 11.**

—— Post-Mortem Pathology. A manual of post-mortem examinations and the interpretations to be drawn therefrom . . . With 162 illustrations. pp. xii. 372. *J. B. Lippincott Co.: Philadelphia & London,* 1903. 8°. **7481. k. 13.**

CATTELL (James McKeen) *See* BEDDARD (Frank E.) The Progressive Science Series . . . American editor— Professor J. M. Cattell. 1898, *etc.* 8°. **2244. e. 1,** *etc.*

—— *See* DIRECTORIES.—*Education.* [*United States of America.*] Leaders in Education. A biographical directory. Edited by J. M. Cattell. 1932. 8°. **010885. g. 1.**

—— *See* DIRECTORIES.—*Education.* [*United States of America.*] Leaders in Education . . . Edited by J. M. Cattell, J. Cattell and E. E. Ross, *etc.* 1941. 8°. **Ref. 416.**

—— *See* DIRECTORIES.—*Science.* [*United States of America.*] American Men of Science. Edited by J. M. Cattell and J. Cattell. 1933. 4°. **010883. i. 24.**

—— *See* DIRECTORIES.—*Science.* [*United States of America.*] American Men of Science . . . Edited by J. M. Cattell and J. Cattell, *etc.* 1938. 8°. **10890. d. 7.**

—— *See* DOLLEY (Charles S.) and CATTELL (J. M.) On Reaction-Times and the Velocity of the Nervous Impulse. [1894.] 8°. **7305. f. 6. (14.)**

—— *See* FULLERTON (George S.) and CATTELL (J. M.) On the Perception of Small Differences, *etc.* 1892. 8°. [*Publications of the University of Pennsylvania. Philosophical Series.* no. 2.] **Ac. 2692. p/3.**

—— *See* PERIODICAL PUBLICATIONS.—*New York.* Archives of Philosophy, Psychology and Scientific Methods. Edited by J. M. Cattell and Frederick J. E. Woodbridge. 1905, *etc.* 8°. **P.P. 1247. ga.**

—— *See* PERIODICAL PUBLICATIONS.—*New York.* The Popular Science Monthly, *etc.* [vol. 57–vol. 87. no. 3 edited by J. M. Cattell.] 1872, *etc.* 8°. **P.P. 1449. c.**

—— *See* PERIODICAL PUBLICATIONS.—*New York.* The Psychological Review. Edited by J. M. Cattell, *etc.* [1894, *etc.*] 8°. **P.P. 1247. e.**

CATTELL (James McKeen)

—— *See* Periodical Publications.—*New York.* The Scientific Monthly. Edited by J. M. Cattell.
1915, *etc.* 8°.   **P.P.1449.ca.**

—— *See* Philadelphia.—*University of Pennsylvania.* Publications of the University . . . Philosophical Series. Edited by G. S. Fullerton . . . and J. M. Cattell.
[1890, *etc.*] 8°.   -   **Ac. 2692. p/3.**

—— Scientific Societies and Associations. *See* United States of America.—*Commission to the Paris Universal Exposition,* 1900. Monographs on Education in the United States, *etc.* vol. 2. 1900. 8°.   **8385. f. 13.**

—— University Control . . . Together with a series of . . . letters . . . and articles by J. Jastrow . . . G. T. Ladd, *etc.* pp. viii. 484.   *Science Press: New York & Garrison, N.Y.,* 1913. 8°.   **8385. f. 21.**
Vol. 3 of a series entitled " Science and Education."

—— The Psychological Researches of James McKeen Cattell. A review by some of his pupils. pp. v. 101.   *New York,* 1914. 8°. [*Archives of Psychology.* no. 30.]
P.P. 1247. gb.

CATTELL (Jaques)

—— *See* Directories. — *Education.* [*United States of America.*] Directory of American Scholars . . . Edited by J. Cattell. 1942. 4°.   **10890.g.12.**

—— *See* Directories.—*Education.* [*United States of America.*] Directory of American Scholars . . . Edited by J. Cattell, *etc.* 1951. 8°.   **10800.bb.22.**

—— *See* Directories.—*Education.* [*United States of America.*] Leaders in Education . . . Edited by J. M. Cattell, J. Cattell and E. E. Ross, *etc.* 1941. 8°.
Ref.416.

—— ——   *See* Directories.—*Science.* [*United States of America.*] American Men of Science . . . Edited by J. M. Cattell and J. Cattell, *etc.* 1933. 4°.
010883. i. 24.

—— *See* Directories.—*Science.* [*United States of America.*] American Men of Science . . . Edited by J. M. Cattell and J. Cattell, *etc.* 1938. 8°.   **10890.d.7.**

—— *See* Directories.—*Science.* [*United States of America.*] American Men of Science . . . Edited by J. Cattell, *etc.* 1944. 8°.   **10890.g.14.**

—— *See* Directories.—*Science.* [*United States of America.*] American Men of Science . . . Edited by J. Cattell, *etc.* 1949. 8°.   **10890.g.18.**

—— *See* Directories.—*Science.* [*United States of America.*] Men of Science . . . Edited by J. Cattell, *etc.* 1955, *etc.* 4°.   **10865.i.16.&.Ref.610.**

CATTELL (Joseph) The Destroying Angel Recalled. A sermon preach'd in the parish-church of Rothwell, *etc.* pp. 22.   *London; C. Ratten: Harborough; W. Ratten: Coventry,* 1716. 8°.   **4474. d. 32.**

CATTELL (Mary) A Caution to Evil Reporters, and Unfaithful Advisers, continued in a series of letters, showing the deception . . . practised to betray . . . the ignorant . . . man, with other . . . particulars, addressed to the Society of Friends, commonly called Quakers. pp. 48.
J. B. & John Courthope & Bayly: Rotherhithe, [1837.] 12°.
T. 2301. (2.)

CATTELL (Mary)

—— A Caution to Unfaithful Advisers, in a series of letters, showing the deception practised to betray and ruin the inexperienced man. [Relating to the case of Such v. Cattell at the Northampton Assizes.] pp. 27.   *J. B. & John Courthope: Rotherhithe,* [1837.] 12°.
T. 2062. (2.)

—— A Caution to Unfaithful Advisers, in a series of letters, showing the deception practised to betray and ruin the inexperienced man. [Relating to the case of Cattell v. Corrall at the Warwick Assizes.] pp. 28.   *J. B. & John Courthope & Bayly: Rotherhithe,* [1837.] 12°.
T. 2301. (3.)

CATTELL (Milly) Behind the Purdah, or, the Lives and legends of our Hindu sisters. [With illustrations.] pp. iv. 92.   *Thacker, Spink & Co.: Calcutta & Simla,* 1916. 8°.   **08415. h. 61.**

CATTELL (Psyche) Dentition as a Measure of Maturity. pp. viii. 91. *Cambridge, Mass.,* 1928. 8°.   [*Harvard Monographs in Education.* no. 9.]   **Ac. 2692/29.**

CATTELL (Raymond Bernard) *See* Kretschmer (E.) [Geniale Menschen.] The Psychology of Men of Genius . . . Translated, with an introduction, by R. B. Cattell, *etc.* 1931. 8°.   **08458. c. 1/4.**

—— Cattell Group Intelligence Scale . . . Tables of norms, *etc. G. G. Harrap & Co.: London,* [1930.] 8°.
08311.k.20.

—— Cattell Intelligence Tests, Group & Individual, *etc.* [With twelve demonstration cards and two examiner's keys. *10* pt. *and Handbooks.*]*G. G. Harrap & Co.: London,* 1933-*52.* 8° & fol.   **1878. f. 60.**

—— Crooked Personalities in Childhood and After. An introduction to psychotherapy. pp. xi. 215.
Nisbet & Co.: London; University Press: Cambridge, 1938. 8°. [*Contemporary Library of Psychology.*]
8459.ppp.23/7.

—— Description and Measurement of Personality. pp. xx. 602. *World Book Co.: Yonkers-on-Hudson, N.Y.,* [1946.] 8°. [*Measurement and Adjustment Series.*]
8313.de.1/19.

—— " F " Test. For use as a group or individual test. pp. 19. *University of London Press: London,* [1938.] 4°.
8312. c. 4.

—— Factor Analysis. An introduction and manual for the psychologist and social scientist. (Under the editorship of Gardner Murphy.) pp. xiii. 462.   *Harper & Bros.: New York,* [1952.] 8°.   **08466. i. 25.**

—— The Fight for our National Intelligence. pp. xx. 166. *P. S. King & Son: London,* 1937. 8°.   **08459. g. 77.**

—— A Guide to Mental Testing for psychological clinics, schools and industrial psychologists, *etc.* pp. xvi. 312. *University of London Press: London,* 1936. 8°.
08459. f. 9.

—— A Guide to Mental Testing . . . New edition. pp. xvi. 411.   *University of London Press: London,* 1948. 8°.   **8473. aa. 30.**

—— A Guide to Mental Testing . . . New edition. pp. xv. 446. *University of London Press: London,* 1953. 8°.
8475. c. 12.

—— Human Affairs. [Essays on the application of science to the study of society.] Planned and edited by R. B. Cattell . . . J. Cohen . . . R. M. W. Travers. [With portraits of the editors and contributors.] pp. xi. 359. *Macmillan & Co.: London,* 1937. 8°.   **12357. tt. 9.**

CATTELL (Raymond Bernard)

—— An Introduction to Personality Study. pp. 235. *Hutchinson's University Library: London,* 1950. 8°. [*Hutchinson's University Library.* no. 47.]
W.P. 1413/47.

—— The Midland Attainment Tests. 6 no.
Arithmetic Test Papers. no. 1, 2.
English Test Papers. no. 1, 2. 4, 5.
University of London Press: London, [1938.] 4°.
8312. c. 19.

—— Personality. A systematic theoretical and factual study. pp. xii. 689. *McGraw-Hill Book Co.: New York,* 1950. 8°. [*McGraw-Hill Publications in Psychology.*]
W.P. 10156/44.

—— Psychology and Social Progress. Mankind and destiny from the standpoint of a scientist. pp. 418. *C. W. Daniel Co.: London,* 1933. 8°.
8277. r. 17.

—— Psychology and the Religious Quest. An account of the psychology of religion and a defence of individualism. pp. 195. *T. Nelson & Sons: London,* 1938. 8°. [*Discussion Books.* no. 23.]
012209. d. 3/23.

—— The Subjective Character of Cognition and the pre-sensational development of perception . . . A thesis, *etc.* pp. viii. 166. *University Press: Cambridge,* 1930. 8°. [*British Journal of Psychology.* Monograph Supplements. no. 14.]
Ac. 3833. ba. (3.)

—— Under Sail through Red Devon, being the log of the voyage of 'Sandpiper.' [With plates.] pp. xiv. 366. *A. Maclehose & Co.: London,* 1937. 8°. **010352. c. 46.**

—— Your Mind and Mine. An account of psychology for the inquiring layman and the prospective student, *etc.* pp. 314. *G. G. Harrap & Co.: London,* 1934. 8°.
08466. ee. 10.

CATTELL (Richard Bernard) and **WARREN** (Kenneth W.)

—— Surgery of the Pancreas. pp. xviii. 374. *W. B. Saunders Co.: Philadelphia & London,* 1953. 8°.
7484. f. 39.

CATTELL (Thomas) Human Laws Obligatory upon the Conscience. A sermon preach'd at the Assizes held at Lancaster, *etc.* pp. 32. *C. Rivington: London,* 1734. 8°.
225. h. 11. (10.)

CATTELL (Thomas Ware) Search the Scriptures. [A sermon.] *See* Duffield (John T.) The Princeton Pulpit, *etc.* 1852. 8°. **4485. e. 95.**

CATTELL (William Cassady) Joseph Addison Alexander, D.D. [An address. With a portrait.] *See* Alexander (Archibald) *D.D.* The Alexander Memorial. 1879. 8°.
4986. ee. 29.

—— Memoir of William C. Cattell, D.D., LL.D. 1827–1898. [With a portrait.] pp. 86. *J. B. Lippincott Co.: Philadelphia,* 1899. 8°. **4986. dd. 34.**

CATTELLANI (Giorgio) L'Avvenire coloniale d'Italia nel Benadir, Somalia. Manuale . . . corredato di carte geographiche, *etc.* pp. 183. *Napoli,* 1897. 8°.
10097. a. 46.

—— D'Arme et amori. Historie. pp. 56. *Napoli,* 1888. 8°. **12315. d. 28. (3.)**

CATTELLE (Wallis Richard) The Diamond. [With illustrations.] pp. 433. *John Lane: London, New York,* 1911. 8°. **07106. g. 3.**

CATTELLE (Wallis Richard)

—— The Pearl: its story, its charm, and its value . . . With sixteen illustrations. pp. 376. *J. B. Lippincott Co.: Philadelphia & London,* 1907. 8°.
7299. cc. 10.

—— Precious Stones. A book of reference for jewellers . . . Illustrated. pp. 224. *J. B. Lippincott Co.: Philadelphia & London,* 1903. 8°. **07107. h. 20.**

CATTELOUP (Bon Auguste) De la cachexie paludéenne en Algérie. pp. 82. *Paris,* 1852. 8°.
7560. aaa. 53. (1.)

—— De la pneumonie d'Afrique. pp. 68. *Paris,* 1853. 8°. **7560. bb. 47. (2.)**

—— Quelques considérations sur le service sanitaire en campagne, et principalement sur l'importance des évacuations des malades et des blessés au moyen des chemins de fer. pp. ii. 42. *Versailles,* 1862. 8°. **7686. bb. 54. (2.)**

—— Recherches sur la dyssenterie du nord d'Afrique. pp. 145. *Paris,* 1851. 8°. **7560. aaa. 18.**

—— Thèse pour le doctorat en médecine, *etc.* (Questions sur diverses branches des sciences médicales.) pp. 23. *Paris,* 1839. 4°. [*Collection des thèses soutenues à la Faculté de Médecine de Paris.* An 1839. tom. 3.]
7371. a. 3.

CATTENBAERT (Jasper) Hollands op-komst, oft Bedenkingen, op de schaadelijke schriften, genaamt Graafelyke regeeringe, en Interest van Holland, uitgegeven door V. D. H. [van den Hoven, i.e. P. ♰. de la Court] . . . vergadert door J. C. [i.e. J. Cattenbaert.] Dezen tweeden druk by den autheur vermeerdert. 2 pt. 1662. 8°. *See* C., J. **157. b. 6. (1.)**

CATTENBURCH (A. L. van) 1304. Intogt der Hollanders binnen Zierikzee onder Jonker Willem, Grave van Oostervant: geschiedkundige aanteekeningen . . . Met een portret, 3 wapenkaarten en eene kart van Zeeland. pp. 113. *Leiden,* 1865. 8°. **9405. dd. 11.**

CATTENBURGH (Adriaan van) Adriani à Cattenburgh Bibliotheca scriptorum Remonstrantium, cui subjunctum est Specimen controversiarum inter Remonstrantes et Socinum ejusque asseclas, exhibitum ipsissimis scriptorum verbis. 2 pt. *Amstelædami,* 1728. 8°.
1126. a. 15.

The titlepage is engraved.

—— Adriani à Cattenburch . . . Dissertatio de multiplici sapientia Noachi; adjecta altera . . . de Turris Babelis exstructione item de confusione linguarum et gentium dispersione. pp. 37. *Harlemi,* 1742. 4°.
3165. bb. 23.

—— Adriani à Cattenburch . . . Syntagma sapientiæ Mosaicæ: in quo multa ex Mosis libris eruuntur contra Atheos, Deistas et Libertinos, variaque illustrantur de antiquitate multarum artium et scientiarum. pp. 349. *Amstelædami,* 1737. 4°. **690. c. 18.**

—— Adriani à Cattenburch . . . Spicilegium Theologiæ Christianæ Philippi à Limborch . . . variis dissertationibus . . . refertum. [Intended as a supplement to Limborch's work. With a portrait.] pp. 1129. *Amstelædami,* 1726. fol. **473. d. 5.**

—— Vervolg der historie van het leven des Heeren Huig de Groot . . . door A. van Cattenburgh. pp. 454. *See* Brandt (Caspar) Historie van het leven des Heeren H. de Groot, *etc.* 1727. fol. **10760. g. 12.**

CATTENOZ (Léon) Nouvel appareil pour la lithotritie. pp. 42. *Paris*, 1863. 4°. [*Collection des thèses soutenues à la Faculté de Médecine de Paris.* An 1863. tom. 2.]
7373. e. 6.

CATTERALL (George Crook) A New Testament Church and the Church of England. pp. iv. 54. *Hall, Virtue & Co.: London; T. S. Turner: Boroughbridge*, 1853. 8°.
4105. a. 12.

CATTERALL (Helen Honor Tunnicliff) Judicial Cases concerning American Slavery and the Negro. Edited by H. T. Catterall. (With additions by James J. Hayden.) 5 vol. *Washington*, 1926–37. 8°. [*Carnegie Institution of Washington.* Publication no. 374.]
Ac. 1866.

CATTERALL (J. B.) The Hebrew Servant. Addresses, etc. pp. 56. *G. Morrish: London*, [1925.] 8°.
04478. de. 53.

—— Memorials of J. B. Catterall's Ministry. [Addresses. Edited by H. F. Nunnerley.] pp. 242. *G. Morrish: London*, [1929.] 8°.
04478. de. 78.

CATTERALL (Ralph Charles Henry) The Second Bank of the United States. pp. xiv. 538. *Chicago*, 1903. 8°. [*Decennial Publications of the University of Chicago.* ser. 2. vol. 2.]
Ac. 2691. d/11.

CATTERALL (Robert) Gospel Messages for the Times, etc. pp. 225. *Jarrold & Sons: London*, 1915. 8°.
4476. k. 11.

CATTERICK CAMP. *See* England.—*Army.*

CATTERICK (Jack) *See* Catterick (John James)

CATTERICK (John) Black Out, and other verses. *Olivers Printing Works: Battle*, [1939.] 4°.
11656. b. 23.

CATTERICK (John James)

—— Doing as we Like. pp. 8. *Industrial Christian Fellowship: Westminster*, [1945.] 8°. **4398. bb. 27.**

CATTERINA. [For Saints, Sovereigns and Princesses of Sovereign Houses of this name:] *See* Catharine.

CATTERINA (Attilio) *See* Fasiani (G. M.) and Catterina (A.) Scritti di chirurgia erniaria, etc. 1937. 8°.
Ac. 100. b/2.

—— Bassini's Operation for the Radical Treatment of Inguinal Hernia, etc. pp. 57. pl. 16. *H. K. Lewis & Co.: London; Bolzano* printed, 1934. obl. fol. **7481. r. 1.**

CATTERINETTI FRANCO (Giuseppe) Della forza morale e materiale di un popolo. Discorso. pp. 24. *Roma*, 1847. 16°.
8032. a. 23.

—— L'Età presente. Riflessioni sopra la scienza moderna e le arti. pp. 150. *Verona*, 1880. 8°. **8703. de. 16.**

CATTERMOLE'S HISTORICAL ANNUAL. *See* Periodical Publications.—*London.*

CATTERMOLE (Charles) *See* L., E. M. Records and Traditions of Upton-on-Severn . . . With . . . illustrative sketches by C. Cattermole, etc. 1869. 8°.
10368. ccc. 24.

—— *See* Lawson (Emily M.) The Nation in the Parish . . . With . . . illustrations by C. Cattermole, etc. 1884. 8°.
10352. bb. 39.

CATTERMOLE (George) *See* Art Album. The Art Album. Sixteen facsimiles of water-colour drawings by G. Cattermole, T. S. Cooper, etc. 1861. 4°.
7855. f. 21.

—— *See* Beauties. Beauties of Poetry and Art. Embellished with . . . illustrations by G. Cattermole, T. S. Cooper, etc. [1865.] 4°. **C.109.d.11.**

—— *See* Calabrella (E. C. de) *Baroness.* Evenings at Haddon Hall . . . With illustrations . . . by G. Cattermole. 1846. 8°. **1457. k. 5.**

—— *See* Calabrella (E. C. de) *Baroness.* Evenings at Haddon Hall . . . With illustrations . . . by G. Cattermole. 1848. 8°. **12643. s. 16.**

—— —— [1849.] 8°. [*Bohn's Illustrated Library.*]
2502. b. 9.

—— *See* Cattermole (Richard) The Great Civil War, or the Times of Charles I. and Cromwell . . . With . . . engravings, from drawings by G. Cattermole. [1846.] 4°.
789. d. 19.

—— *See* Dickens (Charles) [*Barnaby Rudge.*] Barnaby Rudge . . . With illustrations by G. Cattermole and H. K. Browne. 1841. 8°. **G. 18070.**

—— *See* Dickens (Charles) [*Old Curiosity Shop.*] The Old Curiosity Shop . . . With illustrations by G. Cattermole and H. K. Browne. 1841. 8°. **G. 18069.**

—— *See* Haddon Hall. The History and Antiquities of Haddon Hall: illustrated by lithographs from drawings by G. Cattermole, etc. 1869. 4°. **10358. h. 10.**

—— *See* Hall (Samuel C.) The Baronial Halls, and Picturesque Edifices of England. From drawings by J. D. Harding, G. Cattermole, etc. 1848. fol. **557*. g. 9.**

—— *See* Lawson (John P.) Scotland, delineated in a series of views by . . . C. Stanfield . . . G. Cattermole, etc. 1847, etc. fol. **Tab.819.c.2.**

—— *See* M. The Calendar of Nature . . . With designs by G. Cattermole. 1834. 12°. **972. b. 27.**

—— *See* Periodical Publications.—*London.* Cattermole's Historical Annual . . . Illustrated by G. Cattermole. 1841, etc. 8°. **P.P. 6920.**

—— *See* Periodical Publications.—*London.* Heath's Picturesque Annual. (With engravings from drawings by C. Stanfield, G. Cattermole, etc.) 1832, etc. 8°.
P.P. 6910.

—— *See* Roscoe (Thomas) Wanderings and Excursions in North Wales . . . With . . . engravings . . . from drawings, by Cattermole, Cox, etc. 1836. 8°.
563. c. 21.

—— *See* Tillotson (John) *Miscellaneous Writer.* The New Waverley Album. Illustrated with . . . engravings . . . after designs by C. Stanfield . . . G. Cattermole, etc. [1859.] 4°. **1259. a. 15.**

CATTERMOLE (George Moyse) Cattermole's Conversion Tables, etc. 75 pt. *G. M. Cattermole: London*, [1921–33.] fol. **1887. c. 31.**

—— Cattermole's Income Tax Table at 4/6 [etc.] in the £. *G. M. Cattermole: London*, [1923– .] 8°.
8505. h. 36.

—— Cattermole's Interest Tables. 61 pt. [*G. M. Cattermole: London*, 1915–20.] fol. & 8°.
1887. c. 29.

CATTERMOLE (LEONARDO) Odds and Ends. [In prose and verse.] pp. 200. *J. E. Adlard: London*, 1886. 8°.
12330. bbb. 46.

CATTERMOLE (MAURICE A.) *See* PERIODICAL PUBLICATIONS.—*London.* The "Oliver" Magazine. Edited by M. A. Cattermole. 1903, *etc.* 8°. **P.P. 5793. d.**

CATTERMOLE (RICHARD) *See* BUTLER (Joseph) successively *Bishop of Bristol* and *of Durham.* Fifteen Sermons . . . With an introductory essay, by the Rev. R. Cattermole, *etc.* 1841. 8°. **4477. de. 30.**

—— *See* PONS (Jacques S.) The Doctrine of the Church of Geneva illustrated, *etc.* [ser. 2 edited by J. S. Pons and R. Cattermole.] 1825, *etc.* 8°. **1005. dd. 6.**

—— Becket, an historical tragedy : The Men of England, an ode : and other poems. [By R. Cattermole.] pp. viii. 206. 1832. 8°. *See* THOMAS [Becket], *Saint, Archbishop of Canterbury.* **T. 1414. (3.)**

—— The Book of the Cartoons [i.e. Raphael's] . . . The engravings by Warren. pp. 185. *Joseph Rickerby : London*, 1837. 8°. **564. e. 23.**

—— Cattermole's Historical Annual. *See* PERIODICAL PUBLICATIONS.—*London.*

—— The Council of Constance and the War in Bohemia. [By R. Cattermole.] pp. 304. 1855. 16°. *See* CONSTANCE.—*Council of Constance*, 1414–18. [*Appendix.*] **5015. a. 16.**

—— Forty Sermons ; with an introductory essay, on the origin, rights, and duties of the National Church. pp. xxxi. 460. *John W. Parker : London*, 1839. 8°. **1113. k. 14.**

—— Gems of Sacred Literature. [The preface signed : R. C., i.e. R. Cattermole.] 2 vol. 1841. 8°. *See* C., R. **1110. b. 33.**

—— Gems of Sacred Poetry. [Edited by R. Cattermole?] 2 vol. 1841. 8°. *See* GEMS. **1110. b. 34.**

—— [Another copy.] Gems of Sacred Poetry. 1841. 8°. *See* GEMS. **03440. cc. 35.**

—— The Great Civil War of Charles I. and the Parliament . . . With . . . engravings, from drawings by George Cattermole. 2 vol. *London*, 1841, 44. 8°. [*Cattermole's Historical Annual.*] **P.P. 6920. & 6910.** *With additional titlepages, engraved. Vol.* 2 *was issued as Heath's Picturesque Annual for* 1845.

—— [Another edition.] pp. 279. *Fisher, Son & Co. : London*, [1846.] 4°. **789. d. 19.** *With an additional titlepage, engraved.*

—— The Literature of the Church of England, indicated in selections from the writings of eminent divines : with memoirs of their lives and historical sketches of the times in which they lived. 2 vol. *J. W. Parker : London*, 1844. 8°. **3755. h. 3.**

—— The Moral Causes and Remedy of the Public Distress. A sermon, *etc.* pp. 40. *J. Hatchard & Son : London*, 1831. 8°. **T. 1375. (3.)**

—— [Another copy.] The Moral Causes and Remedy of the Public Distress, *etc. London*, 1831. 8°. **C. 126. h. 2. (2.)** *Author's presentation copy to S. T. Coleridge.*

—— Sermons, *etc.* pp. xii. 289. *B. Fellowes : London*, 1832. 12°. **1023. d. 23. (2.)**

CATTERMOLE (RICHARD) and **STEBBING** (HENRY)

—— The Sacred Classics : or, Cabinet library of divinity. Edited by the Rev. R. Cattermole . . . and the Rev. H. Stebbing. 30 vol. *J. Hatchard & Son : London*, 1834–36. 8°. **496. ee. 1–14.** *Vol.* 2 *is of the second edition.*

CATTERMOLE (WILLIAM) Emigration. The advantages of emigration to Canada, being the substance of two lectures delivered at . . . Colchester, and at . . . Ipswich . . . May, 1831. [With a map.] pp. x. 211. *Simpkin & Marshall : London*, [1831 ?] 12°. **T. 1578. (1.)**

CATTERMOLE MANCINI (EVELINA) *See* LARA, *Contessa, pseud.* [i.e. E. Cattermole Mancini.]

CATTERPILLERS. *See* CATERPILLARS.

CATTERSON-SMITH (ROBERT) *See* SMITH.

CATTERUCCIA (LUIGI M.)

—— Pitture vascolari italiote di soggetto teatrale comico. pp. 99. pl. xvi. *Roma*, 1951. 8°. **07813. bb. 25.**

CATTET (JEAN FRANÇOIS) *See* CATTET (S.) La Fausseté du protestantisme . . . Ouvrage . . . achevé par . . . J. F. Cattet. 1864. 8°. **3901. ff. 8.**

CATTET (JEAN JOACHIM FRANÇOIS) Essai sur la contagion, thèse par . . . J. J. F. Cattet, et Jean-Baptiste-Joseph Gardet . . . les trois premières parties par le cit. Gardet et les deux dernières par le cit. Cattet. pp. xxx. 523. *Paris*, 1802. 8°. **1182. b. 15. (3.)**

CATTET (S.) La Fausseté du protestantisme, suivie d'un appendice sur le méthodisme . . . Ouvrage commencé par l'auteur de La Vérité de l'Église catholique démontrée (S. Cattet) et achevé par . . . J. F. Cattet. 2 tom. *Lyon*, 1864. 8°. **3901. ff. 8.**

—— Notice sur la vie du R. P. Cholleton. pp. 77. *Lyon*, 1852. 12°. **4865. aaa. 14.**

—— La Vérité de l'Église catholique démontrée. 2 tom. *Lyon, Paris*, 1854. 8°. **4061. g. 8.**

CATTEY (AMÉDÉE) Manuel formulaire social militaire universel pour les militaires et les travailleurs en vue de faire obtenir l'union . . . franco-américaine-russophile. [With a chart of badges.] pp. 252. *Paris*, 1893. 8°. **08275. f. 12.**

CATTHALANUS (HIERONYMUS PAULUS) De Donatione Const. *See* ROME.—[*Emperors.*]—Constantine I., surnamed *the Great.* [324–337.] Donationis, quæ Constantini dicitur, priuilegium, *etc.* [1530 ?] 8°. **1020. d. 4.**

CATTHO (ANGELO) *Archbishop of Vienna. See* CATO.

CATTIAUX (JEAN BAPTISTE) Thèse pour le doctorat en médecine, *etc.* (Questions sur diverses branches des sciences médicales.) pp. 28. *Paris*, 1841. 4°. [*Collection des thèses soutenues à la Faculté de Médecine de Paris. An* 1841. tom. 3.] **7371. c. 3.**

CATTICICH (MATTEO) *See* MATTIOLI (G. B.) Commemorazione del socio onorario M. Catticich, *etc.* 1878. 8°. **10604. g. 3. (1.)**

CATTIE (JOSEPH THÉODORE) Gemeenzame brieven van een vriend der natuur, door Max van Edijck. [Purporting to be edited by J. T. Cattie, but in fact written by him.] pp. 294. [1877.] 8°. *See* EDIJCK (Max van) **8704. bb. 17.**

CATTIE (Joseph Théodore)

—— Göthe ein Gegner der Descendenztheorie. Eine Streitschrift gegen Ernst Haeckel. pp. 31. *Utrecht,* 1877. 8°. **7006. ee. 7. (7.)**

CATTIER (Edmond) *See* Errera (L.) Recueil d'œuvres de Léo Errera. [Edited by E. Cattier.] 1908, *etc.* 8°. **12236. cc. 17.**

—— Cinquantenaire des chemins de fer belges. Cortège historique des moyens de transport. Dessins et aquarelles de A. Heins. Texte par E. Cattier. pp. iv. 82. pl. 36. *Bruxelles,* 1886. *obl.* fol. **L.R.406.d.1.**

—— Idées d'un bourgeois sur l'architecture. Recueillies par E. Cattier [or rather, written by him]. pp. 242. *Bruxelles,* [1891.] 8°. **7817. g. 20.**

CATTIER (Félicien) Droit et administration de l'État indépendant du Congo. pp. xix. 504. *Bruxelles,* 1898. 8°. **8155. eee. 8.**

—— Étude sur la situation de l'État indépendant du Congo. Seconde édition. [With a map.] pp. ix. 362. *Bruxelles, Paris,* 1906. 8°. **8027. e. 40.**

—— *See* Rolin (H.) La Question coloniale. A propos d'un livre récent (Étude sur la situation de l'État indépendant du Congo, par M. F. Cattier). 1906. 8°. [*Revue de l'Université de Bruxelles.* année 11. no. 6.] **P.P. 4479. d.**

—— Évolution du droit pénal germanique en Hainaut jusqu'au xve siècle, *etc.* 1894. *See* Mons.—*Société des Sciences, des Arts et des Lettres de Hainaut.* Mémoires et publications, *etc.* sér. 5. tom. 7. 1840, *etc.* 8°. **Ac. 1013.**

CATTIER (Fernand) La Vie vertueuse et dangereuse de Jules Ferry. [With a portrait.] pp. 332. *Épinal,* 1931. 8°. **10655. de. 3.**

CATTIER (Isaac) *See also* Teladonianus Magnus, *pseud.* [i.e. I. Cattier.]

—— *See* Papin (N.) La Poudre de sympathie, deffendue contre les objections de Mr Cattier. 1651. 8°. **1171. f. 34. (5.)**

—— Diuers traictez, à sçavoir, De la nature des bains de Bourbon, & des abus qui se commettent à present en la boisson de ces eaux; auec vne instruction pour s'en seruir vtilement. De la macreuse. De la poudre de sympathie.—Response à Monsieur Papin . . . touchant la poudre de sympathie, en laquelle est traicté de l'Esprit vniuersel, & des proprietez de l'Ayman. 3 pt. *P. David; Paris,* 1651. 8°. **1171. f. 34. (2, 4.)** *The titlepage of pt. 3 bears the imprint of E. Martin. Imperfect; wanting the titlepage of pt. 2.*

—— [Letters to P. Le Givre.] *See* Le Givre (P.) Le Secret des eaux minérales acides . . . Avec les lettres . . . de M. Cattier . . . qui combattent l'opinion de l'autheur, *etc.* 1667. 12°. **1171. a. 30.**

—— Diffibulatoris μωρολογια. [By I. Cattier. In reply to the "Centonis κακορραφιας diffibulatio" of René Moreau.] pp. 24. 1646. 4°. *See* Diffibulator. **551. b. 8. (5.)**

—— I. Cattieri . . . Dissertatio de rheumatismo. pp. 153. *Apud viduam Petit: Parisiis,* 1653. 8°. **1188. b. 24. (1.)**

—— Isaaci Cattierii . . . Observationes medicinales, *etc.* pp. 77. *See* Borel (P.) Petri Borelli . . . Historiarum et observationum medicophysicarum centuriæ iv., *etc.* 1656. 8°. **957. l. 3.**

CATTIER (Isaac)

—— [Another edition.] pp. 86. *See* Borel (P.) Petri Borelli . . . Historiarum et observationum medicophysicarum centuriæ iv., *etc.* 1670. 8°. **1169. f. 1.**

—— [Another edition.] pp. 86. *See* Borel (P.) Petri Borelli . . . Historiarum et observationum medicophysicarum centuriæ iv., *etc.* 1676. 8°. **957. b. 5.**

—— Obseruations chirurgiques. Tirées des obseruations médicinales d'Isaac Cattier. *See* Bonnet (T.) Bibliothèque de médecine et de chirurgie, *etc.* tom. 4. 1708. 4°. **549. h. 13.**

—— Seconde apologie de l'vniuersité en Medecine de Montpellier. Répondant aux Curieuses recherches des vniuersitez de Paris & de Montpellier, faites par vn vieil docteur medecin de Paris [i.e. Jean Riolan]. Énuoyée à Monsieur Riolan, professeur anatomique par vn ieune docteur en medecine de Montpellier [i.e. I. Cattier]. pp. 248. 1653. 4°. *See* Montpellier.—*Université de Montpellier.* **551. b. 8. (8.)**

—— *See* Guillemean (C.) Cani miuro. Sive Curto fustis, *etc.* [In reply to the "Seconde apologie de l'Université en Medecine de Montpellier" of I. Cattier.] 1654. 4°. **1179. f. 12. (4.)**

CATTIER (Philippe) Gazophylacium Græcorum, hoc est, methodus admirabilis, secundum quam intra horæ spatium possit quis addiscere innumera vocabula Græca deriuata, *etc.* pp. 44. ms. notes. *Apud Authorem: Parisiis,* 1651. 4°. **12924. bb. 23.**

—— [Another edition.] Cum auctario Frid. Ludov. Abresch. pp. 14. 114. *Trajecti ad Rhenum,* 1757. 8°. **622. b. 25.**

—— [Another edition.] Ex editione altera, multis partibus locupletiori. pp. 16. 132. *Lugduni Batavorum,* 1809. 8°. **624. e. 5.**

—— [Another edition.] pp. vii. 61. *Typis ac sumptibus Academicis: Cantabrigiæ,* 1810. 4°. **623 l. 13. (1.)**

CATTIERUS (Isaacus) *See* Cattier.

CATTIEUCHLAN, *pseud.* Jack Verschoyle's Wife. An antiquated novel. By Cattieuchlan. pp. 510. *Gay & Bird: London,* 1905. 8°. **012631. bb. 26.**

CATTILIO (Assio) Lingua universale commerciale. Corso pratico-veloce di Volapük, *etc.* pp. xvi. 116. *Milano,* 1888. 8°. **12902. aa. 34. (3.)**

CATTIN (Dominique Hubert Joseph Dubois) *See* Dubois-Cattin.

CATTIN (Étienne)

—— Ceux du rail. Récits. pp. 238. *Paris,* 1955. 8°. **12517. cc. 39.**

CATTIN (François) La Religieuse éclairée sur les devoirs de son état, *etc.* pp. viii [xii]. 304. *Lyon, Paris,* 1857. 12°. **4071. a. 17.**

CATTIN (L.) *See* Morellet (C. V.) La Vérité actuelle sur le Canal de Suez . . . Compte rendu par M. Morellet . . . et M. l'abbé Cattin. 1868. 8°. **8235. g. 40. (5.)**

CATTIN (N. D. A.) Des signes de la mort du foetus pendant la grossesse et pendant l'accouchement. Dissertation, *etc.* pp. 27. *Strasbourg,* 1836. 4°. [*Collection générale des dissertations de la Faculté de Médecine de Strasbourg.* vol. 52.] **7381. d.**

CATTIN (Reine Joseph) De la galvano-caustie, ou application de la chaleur électrique dans les opérations chirurgicales. pp. 62. *Paris,* 1858. 4°. [*Collection des thèses soutenues à la Faculté de Médecine de Paris.* An 1858. tom. 4.] **7373. b. 2.**

CATTIN (Y. M.) Dissertation sur l'amaurose ; thèse, *etc.* pp. 20. *Paris*, 1832. 4°.   **1184. e. 8. (16.)**

CATTISTOCK. The Parish Register of Cattistock, Co. Dorset, vol. i., 1558–1711. Transcribed in index form by : the Rev. Richard Grosvenor Bartelot, *etc.* ff. 64. [*London*,] 1938. 4°. [*Society of Genealogists. Transcripts of Parish Registers.*]   **Ac. 5962. b/17.** *Typewritten.*

CATTLE. Cattle : a practical handbook. With chapter on management and feeding. pp. 108.   *London*, [1909.] 8°. [*Vinton's Country Series.*]   **07293. ee. 50/3.**

—— Cattle ; their breeds, management . . . New edition, revised by James Sinclair . . . Veterinary section revised by A. H. Archer . . . With illustrations. pp. 192. *G. Routledge & Sons : London*, 1893. 8°.   **07293. g. 8.**

—— [A reissue.] *Vinton & Co. : London*, 1896. 8°. [*Popular Live Stock Series.*]   **07291. f. 70/1.**

—— Cattle ; their varieties and management in health and disease . . . With illustrations. [By George Armatage.] pp. vii. 120.   *F. Warne & Co. : London* ; *Scribner, Welford & Armstrong : New York*, [1873.] 8°.   **7294. aaa. 29.** *Part of " Warne's Country Library."*

—— Cattle at the Crossroads. Broadcast discussions [between W. S. Mansfield and others] . . . from the series " Farming Today," *etc.* [The editorial note signed. J. G.] [1944.] 8°. *See* G., J.   **07295. b. 49.**

CATTLE, BANANA, COCONUT AND CITRUS INVESTIGATION COMMITTEE. *See* JAMAICA.

CATTLE BREEDERS' ASSOCIATION, CEYLON. *See* CEYLON.

CATTLE COMMITTEE. *See* ENGLAND.—*Board of Agriculture and Fisheries.*

CATTLE DISEASES. Shall we prevent Cattle Diseases ? . . . A few words on the Cattle Disease and Importation Bills, *etc.* 1864. 8°. *See* ENGLAND.— *Parliament.* [*Bills.*—II.] [1864. Feb. 19.]   **7294. dd. 8.**

CATTLE PLAGUE. The Cattle Plague of 1865, and its cure. By E. H. 1865. 8°. *See* H., E.   **7295. bbb. 79. (2.)**

—— The Cattle Plague. A plain sermon preached in a village church . . . Jan. 28. 1866 . . . Second edition. pp. 14. *Parker & Co. : Oxford* ; *John Hodges : Frome Selwood*, 1866. 8°.   **4478. cc. 13.**

CATTLE PLAGUE COMMISSION. *See* ENGLAND.— *Commissioners appointed to inquire into the Origin and Nature of the Cattle Plague.*

CATTLE SHOW WEEK AMUSEMENT GUIDE. The Cattle Show Week Amusement Guide for 1861 ; containing a descriptive account of every theatre and music hall, the Crystal Palace, and all places of public entertainment in the Metropolis. pp. 18. *Edwin Owen : London*, [1861.] 8°.   **10350. bbb. 26. (2.)**

CATTLE (CHARLES HENRY) British Medical Association. Nottingham Meeting, 1892. Guide to Nottingham and the neighbourhood. Edited by C. H. Cattle, *etc.* [With illustrations and map.] pp. 116. 1892. 8°. *See* ENGLAND.— *British Medical Association.*   **10368. cc. 44.**

—— [Another copy.]   **10368. cc. 52.**

CATTLE (EDWARD) *See* ELWENSPOEK (C.) Jew Süss Oppenheimer . . . Translated by E. Cattle. 1931. 8°.   **010703. df. 47.**

—— *See* KLOERSS (S.) — and Sons . . . Translated . . . by E. Cattle. 1930. 8°.   **12556. pp. 30.**

CATTLE (ROBERT) *See* BAYNTUN (Samuel A.) Yorkshire Spring Assizes. 1833. Report of the cause Bayntun versus Cattle, *etc.* [1833.] 16°.   [MISSING.]

CATTLE (WILLIAM) Justification by Faith. A sermon. [1851.] *See* WESLEYAN-METHODIST MINISTERS. Sermons by Wesleyan-Methodist Ministers. vol. 2. 1850, *etc.* 12°.   **4461. f. 24.**

CATTLEY (ALEX. R.)

—— Set of 20 Post Cards of British Regiments, Ticonderoga, 1758–1777. [1945 ?] 8°.   *See* TICONDEROGA.—*Fort Ticonderoga Museum.*   **1865. c. 4. (151.)**

CATTLEY (H.) *See* MICKIEWICZ (A.) Konrad Valenrod . . . Translated . . . by H. Cattley. 1841. 8°.   **1161. h. 32.**

CATTLEY (STEPHEN) The Speech of S. Cattley, Esq. at the Bank of England . . . shewing that the present high price of bullion is owing to the indiscriminate grant of licences to foreign ships. To which is added an Appendix. pp. 39.   *J. M. Richardson ; J. Hatchard : London*, 1811. 8°.   **1028. e. 2. (7.)**

CATTLEY (STEPHEN REED) *See* FOX (John) *the Martyrologist.* The Acts and Monuments of John Foxe . . . Edited by the Rev. S. R. Cattley. 1841, *etc.* 8°.   **1123. k. 7–14.**

—— *See* MAITLAND (Samuel R.) *D.D.* Remarks on the Rev. S. R. Cattley's Defence of his Edition of Fox's Martyrology. 1842. 8°.   **702. h. 20. (2.)**

—— The First Stone of a New Building : together with some account of the proceedings of the Committee organized to further the establishment of a refuge for persons discharged from custody. pp. 23.   *Arthur Taylor : London*, 1846. 8°.   [MISSING.]

—— A Sermon preached . . . before the Right Honourable Lord Mayor, the Worshipful the Aldermen . . . previous to the election of a Lord Mayor for the ensuing year. pp. 23. *J. Rider : London*, 1849. 8°.   **4475. f. 44. (17.)**

CATTLEY (T. F.)

—— Anonyma. [Poems.] pp. 36.   *Spottiswoode, Ballantyne & Co. : Eton College*, 1941. 8°.   **11657. c. 53.**

CATTLIN (FREDERICK FISHER) Rural Economy ; practical observations on the relative position of landlord and tenant. pp. 28.   *Longmans & Co. : London* ; *Thomas Medhurst : Windsor*, 1866. 8°.   **7075. bb. 15.**

CATTLIN (THOMAS MAGNUS) Observations on the Administration of Justice in the Equity, Common Law, Bankruptcy, Insolvency, County, and Criminal Courts : with suggestions for a more efficient remedy in prosecuting the proceedings in those courts. pp. 32.   *Wildy & Sons : London*, 1856. 8°.   [MISSING.]

—— Statement relative to the Ejectment, Smyth v. Smyth. Tried at Gloucester August 10, 11, 12, 1853. [With a genealogical table.] pp. 52. *E. Cox : London*, 1854. 8°.   [MISSING.]

CATTO (ALEXANDER) With the Scottish Troops in France, *etc.* pp. 83. *Aberdeen Daily Journal : Aberdeen*, 1918. 4°.   **9083. g. 47.**

CATTÒ (ANGELO) Tenebre e luce nella Divina Commedia. Conferenza tenuta al circolo "La Famiglia piemontese" la sera del XXVI. marzo MCMVIII. pp. 35. *Milano*, [1908.] 8°. **11851. t. 24. (8.)**

CATTÒ (FORTUNATO) Influenza fisico-morale della ginnastica. pp. 90. *Milano*, 1869. 8°. **7907. g. 23.**

CATTO (GAVIN J.) A Synopsis of the Law of Bankruptcy in Scotland as affected by the Bankruptcy Scotland Act, 1913. For the use of bankers. pp. 37. *William Dunlop: Edinburgh*, 1914. 8°. [MISSING.]

CATTO (MAX) *See* CATTO (Maxwell J.)

CATTO (MAXWELL JEFFREY)

—— *See also* KENT (Simon) *pseud.* [i.e. M. J. Catto.]

—— Décor. A modern comedy in three acts. ff. 96. *Max Finkell: London*, [1933.] 4°. **11778. h. 49.** *Typewritten.*

—— The Flanagan Boy. pp. 225. *George G. Harrap & Co.: London*, 1949. 8°. **NN. 39610.**

—— French Salad. A comedy in three acts. ff. 85. *Max Finkell: London*, 1934. 4°. **011779. l. 2.** *Typewritten.*

—— Ginger Charley. [A novel.] pp. 316. *Martin Secker: London*, 1939. 8°. **NN. 31233.**

—— Green Waters. A play in three acts. pp. 116. *London*, [1937.] 8°. [*French's Acting Edition.* no. 35.] **11791. t. 1/476.**

—— The Hairy Man. [A novel.] pp. 400. *Martin Secker: London*, 1939. 8°. **012634. p. 5.**

—— The Killing Frost. pp. 299. *William Heinemann: London*, 1950. 8°. **NNN. 1187.**

—— The Mummers. pp. 268. *William Heinemann: London*, 1953. 8°. **NNN. 4555.**

—— Polka. A play in three acts. ff. 91. *Max Finkell: London*, [1933.] 4°. **11778. h. 53.** *Typewritten.*

—— A Prize of Gold. pp. 234. *William Heinemann: London*, 1953. 8°. **NNN. 3954.**

—— Procession in Purple. A play in three acts. ff. 85. *Max Finkell: London*, [1933.] 4°. **11778. h. 51.** *Typewritten.*

—— Punch without Judy. A play in three acts. pp. 111. *G. Allen & Unwin: London*, 1940. 8°. **11782. c. 35.**

—— River Junk. [A novel.] pp. 311. *Arthur Barker: London*, 1937. 8°. **NN. 28168.**

—— The Sickle. pp. 273. *William Heinemann: London*, 1952. 8°. **NNN. 2603.**

—— They Walk Alone. A play in three acts. pp. 133. *Martin Secker: London*, 1939. 8°. **11782. a. 6.**

—— Venetian Summer. A comedy in three acts. ff. 103. *Max Finkell: London*, [1933.] 4°. **11778. h. 52.** *Typewritten.*

CATTO (THOMAS SIVEWRIGHT) *Baron.*

—— *See* ENGLAND.—*Scottish Home Department.—Committee on Scottish Financial and Trade Statistics.* Report of the Committee, *etc.* [Chairman, Lord Catto.] 1952. 8°. **B.S. 155/7. (16.)**

CATTO (WILLIAM STEPHEN) and **WILLIAMS** (FREDERICK JAMES HORSLEY) An Introduction to Co-ordinate Geometry. The straight line and circle. pp. 212. *G. G. Harrap & Co.: London*, 1939 [1938]. 8°. **2242. aa. 30.**

—— A Modern Elementary Trigonometry. pp. 263. *G. G. Harrap & Co.: London*, 1936. 8°. **08535. df. 12.**

CATTO (WILLIAM T.) A Semi-centenary Discourse delivered in the first African Presbyterian Church, Philadelphia . . . 1857: with a history of the church from its first organization: including a brief notice of Rev. John Gloucester, its first pastor, *etc.* pp. 111. *J. M. Wilson: Philadelphia*, 1857. 8°. **4475. g. 35.**

CATTOI (N.)

—— *See* FERNÁNDEZ BORDAS (A.) and CATTOI (N.) Archivos del suelo argentino, *etc.* 1946. 8°. **7079. a. 63.**

CATTOIR (FRANÇOIS) Les Débuts de la mission du général de Lamoricière dans les États romains en 1860. Souvenirs de son sécrétaire F. Cattoir. Publiés par le Vte Ch. Terlinden. 1935. *See* ROME.—*The City.—Institut Historique Belge de Rome.* Bulletin, *etc.* fasc. 15. 1919, *etc.* 8°. **Ac. 104. ff.**

CATTOIS (FRANÇOIS PIERRE) *See* VERDIER (A.) and CATTOIS (F. P.) Architecture civile et domestique au moyen âge . . . Dessinée et publiée par A. Verdier et par le Dr. F. Cattois, *etc.* 1852, *etc.* 4°. **1264. f. 15.**

—— Quelques vues sur l'hérédité physiologique et pathologique; thèse, *etc.* pp. 29. *Paris*, 1834. 4°. **1184. f. 5. (27.)**

CATTOLICA DOTTRINA. *See* CATHOLIC DOCTRINE.

CATTOLICA (PASQUALE LEONARDI) III. Congresso Geografico Italiano. Conferenza. (Dei metodi seguiti dal R. Ufficio Idrografico nel disegno e nella riproduzione delle carte idrografiche.) pp. 33. *Genova*, 1898. 8°. **10136. h. 29.**

—— Trattato di navigazione, *etc.* pp. xii. 699. pl. IV. *Livorno*, 1893. 8°. **8805. cc. 44.**

CATTOLICA (PASQUALE LEONARDI) and **LURIA** (ARISTIDE)

—— Fari e segnali marittimi. Nozioni sulla costruzione e funzione dei segnali, con un cenno sull'amministrazione dei fari in Italia ed all'estero. [With plates.] 2 pt. *Torino*, 1916. 8°. **8808. cc. 9.**

CATTOLICI. *See* CATHOLICS.

—— Cattolici Liberali. *See* LIBERAL CATHOLICS.

CATTOLICISMO. *See* CATHOLICISM.

CATTOLICO. *See* CATHOLIC.

CATTOLICO-ROMANO. *See* ROMAN CATHOLIC.

CATTOLICO (ERASMO) *pseud. See* ERASMO, *Cattolico, pseud.*

CATTON (CHARLES) Animals drawn from Nature and engraved in aqua-tinta, by C. Catton, jun. With a description of each animal. [Thirty-six plates.] *The Author; sold by I. & J. Taylor: London*, 1788. obl. 4°. **460. a. 5.**

CATTON (G. A.)

—— The A.B.C. of Bookcraft. [With illustrations.] pp. 96. *Evans Bros.: London*, 1950. 4°. **7948. c. 37.**

CATTON (James) Eden, a theological poem. pp. 65.
S. Barlow: Darlington, 1837. 8°.   **011648**. df. **83**.

—— An Essay on the Pastoral Office, containing a defence of Wesleyan Methodism, especially the rights and exercises of her pastors. pp. viii. 143.   *J. Mason: London*, 1840. 8°.   **1120**. g. **24**.

—— The History and Description of the Shetland Islands, *etc.* pp. iv. 126. *P. I. Tuxford: Wainfleet*, 1838. 8°.   **10370**. ee. **32**.

CATTON (James Alfred Henry) The Real Football. A sketch of the development of the Association game. pp. 215. *Sands & Co.: London*, 1900. 8°.   **7912**. c. **17**.

—— Wickets and Goals. Stories of play. [With plates.] pp. ix. 303. *Chapman & Hall: London*, 1926. 8°.   **07911**. gg. **23**.

CATTON (John Leslie)
—— Combustion and Modern Coal-burning Equipment. pp. vi. 121. *Sir Isaac Pitman & Sons: London*, 1946. 8°.   **8768**. ccc. **21**.

CATTON (John Morris) Civil Service Appointments. The " ABC " guide to the English Civil Service at home and abroad. pp. vii. 160.   *Swan Sonnenschein & Co.: London*, 1887. 8°.   **8008**. bbb. **17**.

CATTON (Josiah) Catton's Triplex Shorthand Practice Book. no. 1. pp. 32.   *J. A. Catton: St. Albans*, [1896?] obl. 8°.   **12991**. a. **10**.

—— Es00persteno : an adaptation of Pitman's Shorthand to Esperanto . . . English text. pp. 16.   *The Author: St. Albans*, [1909.] 8°.   **12991**. g. **75**.
Typewritten.

—— [Another edition, considerably altered.] pp. 24. *The Author: St. Albans*, [1910.] 8°.   **12991**. bbb. **21**. (1.)

—— Espersteno . . . Text in Esperanto, *etc.* pp. 23. *J. Catton: St. Albans*, [1912.] 8°.   **12991**. g. **83**.
Lithographed.

CATTON (Samuel) A Short Sketch of a Long Life, of S. Catton, once a Suffolk plough-boy, showing what prayer and perseverance may do. [By himself.] pp. 26. *Arpthorpe; Caudwell: London; Rees & Gupper: Ipswich*, [1863.] 8°.   **4903**. df. **34**. (2.)

—— Fourth edition. pp. 29.   *Harpthorpe* [sic] ; *Caudwell: London*, [1865.] 8°.   **10804**. aaa. **2**. (6.)

CATTON (Thomas) Astronomical Observations made by the Rev. T. Catton . . . Reduced and printed under the superintendence of George Biddell Airy, *etc.* pp. 30. *Taylor & Francis: London*, 1853. 4°.   **8561**. m. **11**.

CATTON (William) A Poem on the Taking of Cape Breton and Cherbourg, also the destroying their Fleet at St. Maloe's, by . . . the late Duke of Marlborough. (An Encomium on . . . Ferdinand, Prince of Brunswick . . . Lord George Sackville, and the . . . Marquiss of Granby.—An Encomium on Eaton School.—A short Touch on the Number of Lines in this Poem.) [1758?] *s. sh.* fol.   **C.121.g.9.(207.)**

—— Sacred to the Memory of . . . Major General Wolfe, *etc.* [With other verses.] [1760?] *s. sh.* fol.   **C.121.g.9.(208.)**

CATTONARI (Carlotta) Storia di C. Cattonari e sua famiglia al tempo del bombardamento di Venezia. Scritta da lei medesima. pp. 12. *Venezia*, 1850. 8°.   **10631**. cc. **44**. (2.)

CATTORINI (Pier Emilio)
—— *See* Hegi (G.) [Alpenflora.] Flora alpina, *etc.* (Ha riveduto e corretto P. E. Cattorini.) 1953. 8°.   **7035**. e. **28**.

CATTRHINUS (Joannes Georgius) *Resp.* Partis secundæ metaphysicæ disputatio quinta de accidentibus in genere, *etc. See* Scheiblerus (C.) C. Scheibleri . . . epitome metaphysicæ specialis, *etc.* 1617. 4°.   **525**. d. **7**. (6.)

CATTRINA WILLEMINA. Aanmerkelyke levens beschryving of lotgevallen van een Rotterdammer Juffrouw Cattrina Willemina . . . Benevens het gevangen nemen bei de Turk, het afsterven van haar minnen . . . Door haar zelven beschreven. pp. 295.   *Amsteldam*, [1790?] 8°.   **12580**. bb. **39**.

CATTS (Dorothy Marguerite)
—— Dawn to Destiny. [A novel.] pp. 223.   *Consolidated Press: Sydney*, 1946. 8°.   **NN. 38622**.

—— James Howard Catts, M.H.R. . . . Compiled by D. M. Catts. [A biography. With plates, including portraits.] pp. xvii. 241. *Ure Smith: Sydney*, [1954.] 8°.   **10864**. d. **2**.

—— Those Golden Years. pp. 240.   *Hutchinson: London*, 1955. 8°.   **NNN. 7076**.

CATTS (James Howard)
—— *See* Catts (Dorothy M.) James Howard Catts, M.H.R., *etc.* [A biography. With portraits.] [1954.] 8°.   **10864**. d. **2**.

CATTUFFIO PANCHIANIO, *Bubulco Arcade, pseud.* [i.e. Zaccaria Valaresso.] *See* Panchianio (C.) *Bubulco Arcade, pseud.*

CATTUS (Franciscus Antonius) Isagogae Anatomicae. pp. 185 [189].   *Excudebat R. Amatus: Neapoli*, 1557. 8°.   **548**. e. **5**.

CATTY (C. M.) *See* Ernst (Paul) *Oberstabsarzt.* English Version of Dr. Ernst's German text of the pageant by C. M. Catty. 1913. 8°.   [Heidelberg.—*Historical Pageant*, 1913. *Grand Historical Pageant, etc.*]   **11747**. i. **16**. (3.)

CATTY (Charles Stratford) Poems and Legends. pp. ix. 385. *Smith, Elder & Co.: London*, 1914. 8°.   **011649**. e. **77**.

—— Poems of the Past and Present. pp. viii. 266. *Watts & Co.: London*, 1937. 8°.   **2292**. f. **32**.

CATTY (Frederick Adam) *See* Archenholz (J. W. von) The History of the Seven Years War . . . Translated . . . by F. A. Catty. 1843. 18°.   **1439**. a. **11**.

—— Handbook for Ems and its Environs. With observations on the use of its mineral waters and an account of the geology of the neighbourhood. [With a map.] pp. vii. 193. *L. J. Kirchberger: Bad Ems*, 1844. 16°.   **1170**. e. **34**.

CATTY (Lewis) *See* Voltaire (F. M. A. de) [*Histoire de Charles XII.*] Histoire de Charles XII . . . Nouvelle édition . . . revue et corrigée . . . par M. Catty, *etc.* 1832. 8°.   **590**. c. **28**.

—— Exercises on French Grammar . . . for the use of . . . the Royal Military Academy at Woolwich. pp. xviii. 312. *G. & S. Robinson: London*, 1814. 12°.   **12954**. b. **4**.

CATTY (NANCY) *See* O'GRADY (Hardress M.) and CATTY (N.) The Early Stages of Spoken and Written English. 1920. 8°. **8306.cc.39/9.**

—— The Child at Home. His occupations and first lessons. pp. vi. 190. *Sidgwick & Jackson: London,* 1932. 8°. **08311. b. 46.**

—— A First Book on Teaching. pp. xvi. 189. *Methuen & Co.: London,* 1929. 8°. **08311. bb. 59.**

—— Second edition, revised. pp. xvi. 191. *Methuen & Co.: London,* 1931. 8°. **08308. a. 22.**

—— A First Book on Teaching. (Sixth edition, revised.) pp. xvi. 191. *Methuen & Co.: London,* 1949. 8°. **08311. aaa. 75.**

—— A First Book on Teaching. (Sixth edition, revised, reprinted with minor corrections.) pp. xvi. 191. *Methuen & Co.: London,* 1955. 8°. **8313. cc. 69.**

—— Jane's First Term, *etc.* pp. 94. *G. G. Harrap & Co.: London,* 1936. 8°. **20055. e. 50.**

—— Learning and Teaching in the Junior School. pp. ix. 123. *Methuen & Co.: London,* 1941. 8°. **8312. a. 33.**

—— Learning and Teaching in the Junior School . . . Second edition. pp. ix. 123. *Methuen & Co.: London,* 1947. 8°. **08311. c. 74.**

—— Learning and Teaching in the Junior School. (Third edition, reprinted, with minor corrections.) pp. ix. 124. *Methuen & Co.: London,* 1954. 8°. **8313. cc. 58.**

—— Modern Education of Young Children . . . [By various authors.] Edited with an introduction by N. Catty. pp. xiv. 128. *Methuen & Co.: London,* 1933. 8°. **08311. c. 40.**

—— Nursery Schools for Blind Children. A report on the development of the Sunshine Home Nursery Schools from 1932 to 1943. pp. 23. *National Institute for the Blind: London,* [1944.] 8°. [*N.I.B. Bulletins.* no. 14.] **P.P. 1108. cbe.**

—— Primary Schools for Blind Children, *etc.* pp. 15. *National Institute for the Blind: London,* [1948.] 8°. [*N.I.B. Bulletins.* no. 16.] **P.P. 1108. cbe.**

—— Social Training from Childhood to Maturity. pp. viii. 103. *Methuen & Co.: London,* 1951. 8°. **08408. g. 73.**

—— The Story of Jane, *etc.* pp. 55. *G. G. Harrap & Co.: London,* 1931. 8°. **012803. e. 81.**

—— A Study of Modern Educational Theory and its Applications. pp. xii. 132. *Sidgwick & Jackson: London,* 1921. 8°. **08311. ff. 67.**

—— The Theory and Practice of Education. pp. xii. 257. *Methuen & Co.: London,* 1934. 8°. **08311. a. 30.**

—— The Theory and Practice of Education. (Fourth edition, reprinted with minor corrections.) pp. xii. 253. *Methuen & Co.: London,* 1954 [1955]. 8°. **8312. a. 56.**

—— Training in Appreciation. Art : literature : music. Edited by N. Catty. pp. vii. 104. *Sidgwick & Jackson: London,* 1921. 8°. **08311. g. 36.**

CATTY (TWM JOHN) *See* TWM SHON CATTI.

CATUELAN (DE) *Count. See* SHAKESPEARE (W.) [*Dramatic Works.—French.*] Shakespeare traduit de l'Anglois. [By P. Le Tourneur, the Count de Catuelan and J. Fontaine-Malherbe.] 1776, *etc.* 4°. **80. g. 1-10.**

CATUFFE ( ) *See* PERIODICAL PUBLICATIONS.—*The Hague.* Journal littéraire. [1729–32 edited by — Catuffe and others.] 1715, *etc.* 8°. **262. d. 12–28. & 263. d. 1-5.**

CATUL (G. VALERI) *See* CATULLUS (Caius Valerius)

CATULLE-MENDÈS (JANE) *See* MENDÈS (Jane)

CATULLIUS (ANDREAS) Andreæ Catullij . . . Septuplex Triumphus, siue Deiparæ Virginis septem Gaudia. (A. Catullij . . . Septuplex Gladius : siue Deiparæ Virginis septem Dolores.—A. Catullij Lachrymæ, siue amores casti.) [Poems.] 3 pt. *Ex officinâ C. Martini: Tornaci,* 1614. 8°. **11408. aaa. 12.**

—— Andreæ Catullii . . . Tornacum, civitas metropolis, et cathedra episcopalis Nerviorum. pp. 252. xlvii. *Ex typographiâ I. Mommartii: Bruxellæ,* 1652. 4°. **572. c. 19.**

—— [Another copy.] **154. f. 3.**

CATULLO, *Cieco Muranese,* called IL MARETTINO. Comedia di Messer Latantio vecchio, e de la sua innamorata madonna Isabella, con vn Bulo, ilquale ha nome Gieci, fauorito de la ditta madonna Isabella, *etc.* [In verse.] *Per M. Pagan: Venetia,* 1558. 8°. **11725. aa. 7.**

—— El glorioso trionfo della santissima Vitoria ch'ebbero gli christiani contra i nemici di Jesu Christo, *etc.* [*Venice?* 1572?] 12°. **1071. g. 7. (79.)** *The titlepage is cropped.*

CATULLO (CAIO VALERIO) *Dottore in medicina.* Reclami ed osservazioni concernenti la geognosia delle Alpi Venete. pp. 21. *Padova,* 1842. 8°. **7105. d. 33. (2.)**

CATULLO (CAIO VALERIO) *the Poet. See* CATULLUS.

CATULLO (GIOVANNI) Memoria mineralogico-chimica sopra l'acqua minerale di Civillina, scoperta dal sig. G. Catullo. A cui s'aggiungono le storie delle malattie sanate con la medesima. pp. 72. *Verona,* 1819. 8°. **1170. l. 27.**

CATULLO (MARÍA ELENA) *See* BURGOS (F.) and CATULLO (M. E.) Tejidos Incaicos y Criollos, *etc.* 1927. fol. **7742. r. 19.**

CATULLO (TOMMASO ANTONIO) *See* KELLER (A.) T. Catullo. Parole pronunciate da Keller in Padova. [A funeral oration.] 1869. 8°. **10631. e. 42. (8.)**

—— Cenni biografici del cavaliere Pier Luigi Mabil, giuntovi il prospetto ragionato delle sue opere edite ed inedite. pp. 80. *Padova,* 1836. 8°. **T. 2116. (2.)**

—— Dei terreni di sedimento superiore delle Venezie e dei fossili bryozoari, antozoari e spongiari ai quali danno recetto, memoria. pp. 88. viii. pl. XIX. *Monaco,* 1857. fol. **7107. f. 3.** *The date in the colophon is* 1856.

—— Elementi di mineralogia, applicati alla medicina e alla farmacia. [With plates.] 2 vol. *Padova,* 1833. 8°. **726. h. 21.**

—— Memoria geognostico-paleozoica sulle Alpi Venete . . . Inserita nella parte prima del tomo XXIV delle Memorie della Società Italiana delle Scienze residente in Modena. pp. 158. 16. pl. XIII. *Modena,* 1846. 4°. **7105. f. 8.**

—— Osservazioni sopra i monti che circoscrivono il distretto di Belluno. pp. 147. *Verona,* 1818. 8°. **1254. f. 29.**

—— Osservazioni sopra i terreni postdiluviani delle provincie austro-venete. pp. 95. *Padova,* 1834. 8°. **T. 1572. (14.)**

—— Saggio di zoologia fossile. pp. 348. pl. VIII. **L.P.** *Padova,* 1827. fol. **443. g. 22.**

CATULLO (Tommaso Antonio)

—— Trattato sopra la costituzione geognostico-fisica dei terreni alluviali o postdiluviani delle province Venete . . . Edizione notevolmente accresciuta. pp. 464. *Padova*, 1844. 8°. **7108. c. 12.**

—— Prospetto degli scritti publicati da T. A. Catullo, professore emerito di storia naturale . . . Compilato da un suo amico e discepolo. pp. 284. *Padova*, 1857. 4°. **7006. dd. 4.**

CATULLUS (Caius) Caninius, *pseud*. [i.e. Henricus Harderus.] *See* Harderus (H.)

CATULLUS (Caius Valerius)

WORKS.

Latin.

—— [fol. 92 *verso:*] uAler⁹ Catull⁹ scriptor lyric⁹ Veronę nascitur, *etc*. [fol. 93 *recto:*] Hextichum Guarini Veronensis Oratoris Clarissimi In libellum Valerii Catulli eius conciuis. [*ibid.:*] Val. Catulli Veronensis Poetę Cl. Liber Ad Cornelium Gallum. [fol. 126 *recto:*] Catulli Veronensis Epigrammaton Libellus Explicitus est. *See* Tibullus (A.) [*Latin*.] *Begin*. [fol. 1 *verso:*] a Vrelius Propertius elegię Scriptor egregius Patria Beuania fuit, *etc*. [fol. 2 *recto:*] Albii Tibulli .eq. Ro. Poetę .Cl. Liber primus, *etc*. 1472. 4°. **C. 19. d. 8.**

—— *Begin*. [fol. 1 *recto:*] Val. Catulli Veronensis poetae doctissimi liber. ad Cornelium Gallum incipit. [fol. 36 *recto:*] P. Papini Statii Surculi Siluarum liber primus, *etc*. *End*. [fol. 96 *recto:*] Correctū p. d. frāciscū puteolanū : & uere ultra impressionē uenetiis factā ī. iii. milib⁹ locis emēdatū, *etc*. *Per me Stephanū Corallū : Parmæ*, ' secūdo caľ. septembris,' 1473. 4°. **G. 9542.** 96 *leaves, without signatures*. 34 *lines to a page*.

—— [Another copy.] FEW MS. NOTES. **IB. 30215.** *Imperfect ; wanting all after fol. 35*.

—— *Begin*. [fol. 1 *verso:*] uAlerius Catull⁹ scriptor lyricus Veronæ nascitur, *etc*. [fol. 2 *recto:*] Hextichum Guarini Veronensis Oratoris Clarissimi In libellum Valerii Catulli eius conciuis. [*ibid*. l. 9:] Val. Catulli Veronensis Poetæ. Cl. Liber Ad Cornelium Gallum. [fol. 37 *verso:*] Tibulli Vita. [fol. 38 *recto:*] Albii Tibulli. eq. Ro. Poetæ. Cl. Liber primus quod spretis diuitiis & militia Deliā amet & amori seruiat. [fol. 69 *verso:*] Vita Propertii. [fol. 70 *recto:*] Propertii Aurelii nautæ poetæ clarissimi Elegiaᵦ liber primus. ad Tullum. [fol. 128 *verso:*] Catulli. Tibulli. Proptii. & liber Siluaᵦ Statii papinii ī isto uolumine cōtinet̃ etc. [fol. 129 *recto:*] P. Papini Statii Surculi Siluarum liber primus. [*Philippus de Lavagnia : Milan ,*] *opere & impensa Iohannis de colonia & Iohannis* manthē : *Veneciis*, 1475. 4°. **C. 19. d. 9.** 188 *leaves, ff*. 36, 68 *and* 188 *blank*. *Sig*. a–c⁸ d⁶ e⁶ ; [a–d⁸] ; A–F⁸ G⁶ H⁶ ; A–F⁸ G⁶ H⁶. 35, 36 *lines to a page*. *The colophon occurs on fol*. 128 *verso at the end of the works of Propertius*. *The signatures mostly cut away*.

—— [Another copy.] **C. 3. b. 19.** *Without the blanks ff*. 36 *and* 188. *The signatures mostly cut away*.

—— [Another copy.] MS. NOTES. **G. 9543.** *Without the blank leaf, fol*. 68. *The signatures cut away*.

—— *Begin*. [fol. 1 *verso:*] [V]Alerius Catullus scriptor liricus Verone nascitur, *etc*. [fol. 2 *recto:*] Hextichū Guarini Veronēsis Oratoris Clarissimi in libellū Valerii Catulli eius ꝯciuis. [*ibid*. l. 9:] Val. Catulli. Veronēsis Poete Cl. Liber Ad Cornelium Gallum. *End*. [fol. 41 *verso:*] Catulli Veronensis Epigrammaton Libellus Explicitus est. [*Ulrich Han ? : Rome*, 1475 ?] 4°. **G. 9475.** 42 *leaves, the last blank*. *Without signatures*. 30 *lines to a page*.

CATULLUS (Caius Valerius) [Works.—*Latin*.]

—— *Begin*. [fol. 1 *verso:*] iOannes Calphurnius Hermolao iuris utriusque doctori peritissimo . . . S.P., *etc*. [fol. 2 *recto:*] Val. Cat. Vero. poetae cl. ad Cornelium Galum. [fol. 29 *recto:*] Albii Tibulli. eq. Ro. Poetæ. Cl. Liber primus, *etc*. [fol. 51 *recto:*] Propertii poetae elegiographi clarissimi. liber primus. [fol. 97 *verso:*] Papinii Statii Neapolitani Syluarum liber primus ad Stellam. [fol. 146 *recto:*] Carmen Ioannis Calphurnii . . . ad Ioannē Inderbachiū Pontificē Tridētinū de laudibus eius & de interitu Beati Simonis infantis a Iudeis mactati. [The whole edited by J. Calphurnius.] *Actum per Iouannnem* [sic] *renensem & Dionysium Bertochum : Vincentiæ*, 1481. fol. **C. 3. c. 10.** 149 *leaves, ff*. 145 *and* 149 *blank*. *Sig*. a⁸ b⁸ c–e⁶ f–h⁸ i–l⁶ m⁸ n⁶ o⁶ p⁸ q⁷ r–t⁶ u⁸ x⁸ y⁴. 45, 46 *lines to a page*. *Without the last blank leaf*.

—— [Another copy.] **G. 9538.** *Without the blank leaves*.

—— *See* Albertini (A.) Calfurnio bresciano. La sua edizione di Catullo, 1481. 1954. 8°. [*Commentari dell' Ateneo di Brescia*. anno 1953.] **Ac. 28.**

—— [fol. 27 *recto :*] uAlerius Catullus scriptor lyricus Veronæ nascitur, *etc*. [*ibid*. l. 13 :] Hextichum [*sic*] Guarini Veronensis Oratoris Clarissimi In bellum [*sic*] Valerii Catulli eius conciuis. [*ibid*. l. 21 :] Val. Catulli Veronensis Poetæ. Cl. Liber Ad Cornelium Gallum. [fol. 55 *verso:*] Catulli ueronēsis epigrāmaton libellus explicit. *See* Tibullus (A.) [*Latin*.] *Begin*. [fol. 1 *verso:*] Tibulli Vita, *etc*. 1481. fol. **IB. 34021.**

—— *Begin*. [fol. 2 *recto:*] Iacobus Comes iuliarius Veronensis suo Parthenio salutem. [fol. 2 *verso:*] Antonius Parthenius Lacisius Veronēsis Iulio Pōponio salutē. [fol. 4 *recto:*] Val. Cat. Vero. poetae cl. ad Cornelium Nepotem. [With the commentary of Antonius Parthenius Lacisius.] *per Boninum de Boninis : Brixiæ*, viii. Idus Apriles [6 April], 1485. fol. **IB. 31083.** 56 *leaves, the first and last blank*. *Sig*. a–h⁶ i⁸. 57 *and* 58 *lines of commentary to a page*.

—— [fol. 45 *verso:*] [Iacobus Comes iulianus Veronensis suo Parthenio salutem.] [fol. 47 *recto:*] Val. Cat. Vero. poetae cla. ad Cornelium nepotem. [With the commentary of Antonius Parthenius Lacisius.] *See* Tibullus (A.) [*Latin*.] *Begin*. [fol. 2 *recto:*] Bernardinus Veronensis clarissimo uiro Baptistæ Vrsino, *etc*. [fol. 3 *verso:*] Albii Tibulli . . . Liber primus, *etc*. 1487. fol. **167. c. 7.**

—— [fol. 37 *recto:*] Antonius Parthēius Lacisius Veronēsis Iulio Pōpōio salutē. [fol. 38 *recto:*] Valerii catulli Veronēsis poetæ clarissimi ad Cornelium nepotem, *etc*. [With the commentary of Antonius Parthenius Lacisius.] *See* Tibullus (A.) [*Latin*.] Tibullus Catullus & Propertius cū commento. 1491. fol. **IB. 22858.**

—— [fol. 37 *recto:*] aNtonius Parthenius Lacisius Veronēsis Iulio Pōponio salutem. [fol. 38 *recto:*] Valerii Catulli Veronēsis poetę clarissimi ad Cornelium nepotem, *etc*. [With the commentary of Antonius Parthenius Lacisius.] *See* Tibullus (A.) [*Latin*.] Tibullus Catullus & Proptius ꝯū comento. 1493. fol. **IB. 23928.**

—— Catullus una cū commentariis Eruditi Viri Palladii Tusci [*sic*] Patauini. *per Ioannem tacuinum : Venetiis*, die .xxviii. Aprilis, 1496. fol. **IB. 24056.** 36 *leaves*. *Sig*. a–f⁶. 61 *lines of commentary to a page*.

—— [fol. 37 *recto:*] Antoni⁹ Parthenius Lacisius Veronensis Iulio Pōponio salutē. [fol. 39 *recto:*] Valerii catulli Veronēsis poetæ clarissimi ad Cornelium nepotem. [With the commentaries of Antonius Parthenius Lacisius

CATULLUS (Caius Valerius) [Works.—*Latin.*]

and Palladius Fuscus.] [fol. 97 *recto:*] Emendatıonū
Hieronymi Auācii Veronēsis . . . in Catullū . . . Editio
Secunda. *See* TIBULLUS (A.) [*Latin.*] Tibullus cum
commentariis Cyllænii Veronensis, *etc.* 1500. fol.
IB. 24101.

—— Catullus. Tibullus. Propertius. [Catullus edited by
Hieronymus Avantius, and followed by an epistle from
him to M. Sanuto, containing emendations to Lucretius.]
3 pt. *In aedibus Aldi: Venetiis,* 1502. 8°.
678. a. 18.

*In this and the following copy the introductory epistle of
Aldus Manutius is addressed " Marino Sannuto . . .
Leonardi filio."*

—— [Another copy.] C. 4. e. 8.

—— [Another copy.] 1068. h. 3. (1.)
*In this copy and in the following three copies the intro-
ductory epistle of Aldus Manutius is addressed " Marino
Sannuto . . . Benedicti filio."*

—— [Another copy.] G. 9619.

—— [Another copy.] C.128.e.25.
*In this copy, in which the initial capitals have been il-
luminated, " Propertius " is misprinted " Propetius " on
the titlepage.*

—— [Another copy.] ON VELLUM. C. 19. f. 11.
With the initial capitals illuminated.

—— Catullus. Tibullus. Propetius [*sic*]. FEW MS. NOTES.
[*B. de Gabiano: Lyons,* 1502.] 8°. 1068. h. 16.
*A counterfeit of the Aldine edition of 1502, including the
epistle of Aldus, but omitting that of Avantius.*

—— Catullus. Propertius. Tibullus. (Olim magna ex parte
emendati per Aldū Manutiū . . . Nūc recogniti per
Benedictum Philologū Florentinum.) *Opera & impensa
P. bibliopolæ giūtæ f.: Florentiæ,* 1503. 8°. 1068. h. 14.

—— Catullus. Tibullus. Propertius. [*B. de Gabiano:
Lyons,* 1505 ?] 8°. 1068. h. 18.
*A counterfeit of the Aldine edition of 1502, including
the epistles of Aldus and Avantius.*

—— Catullus. Tibullus. Propertius. 3 pt. ff. 148.
In ædibus Aldi, et Andreæ soceri: Venetiis, 1515. 8°.
1068. h. 4.

—— [Another copy.] C. 4. e. 9.

—— Catullus, Tibullus, Propertius. Cn. Cornelii galli poetæ
. . . aut ut quidam uolūt Maximiani quæ recolligi
potuere fragmenta. [Edited by Hieronymus Avantius.]
Impressum sumptu B. Trot: Lugduni, 1518. 8°.
1000. b. 20.

—— Val. Catulli Epigrammata. [Edited by Antonius Parthenius Lacisius.] *See* TIBULLUS (A.) [*Latin.*] Al.
Tibulli elegiaruȝ libri quatuor, *etc.* 1520. fol.
656. c. 14.

—— Alexandri Guarini Ferrariensis in C. V. Catullum Vero-
nensem per Baptistam patrem emendatum expositiones
cum indice, *etc.* pp. 115. MS. NOTES. *Per Georgium
de Rusconibus: Venetiis,* 1521. 4°. C. 128. c. 1.
In a contemporary blind-tooled binding.

—— Catullus. Tibullus. Propertius. ff. 167. *Apud
S. Colinæum: Parisiis,* 1529. 8°. 237. a. 26.

—— C. Valerii Catulli Veronensis liber I. Alb. Tibulli . . .
libri IIII. Sex. Aurelii Propertij Vmbri libri IIII. Cn.
Cornelii Galli fragmenta. ff. 192. *Excudebat H. Petrus:
Basileæ,* 1530. 8°. 1068. i. 22.

CATULLUS (Caius Valerius) [Works.—*Latin.*]

—— Catullus. Tibullus. Propertius. ff. 142. *Per
M. Sessam: Venetiis,* 1531. 8°. 11388. aa. 6.
The titlepage is engraved.

—— Catullus. Tibullus. Propertius. Multis in locis restituti.
ff. 168. *Apud S. Colinæum: Parisiis,* 1534. 8°.
238. k. 11.
Previous edition 1529.

—— Catullus. Tibullus. Propertius. His accesserunt Corn.
Galli fragmenta. pp. 319. *Apud S. Gryphium: Lugduni,*
1542. 8°. 237. f. 25.

—— Catullus. Tibullus. Propertius. ff. 160. *Ex officina
S. Colinæi: Parisiis,* 1543. 16°. 683. a. 9.
Including the " Priapea." Previous edition 1534.

—— [Another copy.] Catullus. Tibullus. Propertius.
Parisiis, 1543. 16°. C. 128. e. 5. (2.)

—— [Another copy.] COPIOUS MS. NOTES. 1068. m. 2.
*Imperfect; wanting the titlepage and sig. a ii, iii.
Mounted in 4°.*

—— Catullus. Tibullus. Propertius. His accesserunt Corn.
Galli fragmenta. pp. 336. *Apud S. Gryphium: Lugduni,*
1548. 16°. 11340. a. 4.
Previous edition 1542.

—— Catullus. Tibullus. Propertius. His accesserunt Corn.
Galli fragmenta. pp. 335. *Excudebat I. Gryphius:
Venetiis,* 1553. 8°. 238. k. 7.

—— Catullus, et in eum commentarius M. Antonii Mureti.
ff. 134. *Apud P. Manutium, Aldi filium: Venetiis,*
1554. 8°. 1001. b. 29.
Including the " Priapea."

—— [Another copy.] C. 4. e. 10.

—— [Another copy.] G. 9476.

—— Catullus, et in eum commentarius M. Antonii Mureti.
Ab eodem correcti, & scholiis illustrati, Tibullus, et
Propertius. 3 pt. *Apud P. Manutium, Aldi f.: Venetiis,*
1558. 8°. 11375. a. 10.
*Including the " Priapea." The imprint is taken from
pt. 2.*

—— [Another copy.] G. 9791. (1.)
Imperfect; wanting pt. 2 and 3.

—— Catullus, et in eum commentarius M. Antonii Mureti.
Ab eodem correcti, & scholiis illustrati. pp. 263. *Apud
G. Rouillium: Lugduni,* 1559. 8°. 1068. h. 6.
Including the " Priapea."

—— Catullus, Tibullus, Propertius, Cor. Galli fragmenta.
Omnia ex vetust. exempl. multo, quam antea, emenda-
tiora, additis annot. ff. 134 [144]. *Ex officina
C. Plantini: Antuerpiæ,* 1560. 16°. 683. a. 10.
Including the " Priapea."

—— Catullus, et in eum commentarius M. Antonii Mureti.
Ab eodem correcti, & scholiis illustrati, Tibullus, et
Propertius. 3 pt. [*P. Manutius:*] *Venetiis,* 1562. 8°.
11375. b. 10.
Including the " Priapea." Previous edition 1558.

—— Catullus. Cum commentario Achillis Statii, *etc.* pp. 415.
In aedibus Manutianis: Venetiis, 1566. 8°.
C. 4. e. 11.

—— Catullus. Tibullus. Propertius. Item, Corn. Galli fragmenta. [Catullus and Tibullus edited by Victor Giselinus
and Theodorus Pulmannus; Propertius with the notes of
G. Canterus; Gallus edited by T. Pulmannus.] pp. 348.
Apud A. Gryphium: Lugduni, 1573. 16°.
1001. a. 13. (2.)
*In this edition of Catullus the numbering does not allow
for the omitted " Priapea," but runs consecutively to 63;
the following poem is also numbered 63. The final poem is
numbered 115. The numbering has been corrected in MS.*

CATULLUS (Caius Valerius) [Works.—*Latin.*]

—— Catulli, Tibulli, Propertii noua editio. Iosephus Scaliger . . . recensuit. Eiusdem in eosdem Castigationum liber, *etc.* 2 pt. MS. NOTES. *Apud M. Patissonium, in officina R. Stephani: Lutetiæ*, 1577. 8°.
1002. b. **5.**

—— [Another copy.] MS. NOTES. C. **19.** b. **8. (1.)**

—— [Another copy of the "Castigationes."] **827.** c. **2. (2.)**

—— Catulli, Tibulli, Propertii, noua editio. Iosephus Scaliger recensuit. Ejusdem in eosdem Castigationum liber, *etc.* (M. Antonii Mureti Commentarius in Catullum. Eiusdem Scholia in Tibullum, & Propertium.) 3 pt. *Apud A. Radæum: Antuerpiæ*, 1582. 8°.
1002. b. **6. (1, 2.)**

—— Catullus, Tibullus, Propertius: seriò castigati. (Peruigilium Veneris, quod quidam Catullo tribuunt.) pp. 223. MS. NOTES. *Ex officina Plantiniana; apud F. Raphelengium: Lugd. Batauorum*, 1591. 16°.
1002. a. **7. (1.)**
Including the " Priapea."

—— Catullus, Tibullus, Propertius . . . nunc denuo recogniti ac variis lectionibus & notis illustrati a Iano Dousa, filio. Accessit Peruigilium Veneris. (Item Iani Dousæ patris in Propertium Paralipomena.) 2 pt. *Ex officina Plantiniana; apud F. Raphelengium: Lugduni Bat.*, 1592. 16°. **165.** k. **24.**
Including the " Priapea."

—— [Another copy.] **1002.** a. **8.**
Badly worm-eaten.

—— Catulli, Tibulli, Propertii, et Cornelii Galli, Opera, Horatii Tuscanellæ . . . laboribus . . . in indicis ordinem . . . adducta . . . His etiam Scholia . . . accesserunt. pp. 342. 173. *S. Henricpetri: Basileæ*, 1592. 8°.
237. a. **28. (1.)**
Slightly cropped. This edition contains the " Pervigilium Veneris," and the " Priapea " separately.

—— Catulli, Tibulli, Propertii noua editio. Iosephus Scaliger . . . recensuit. Eiusdem in eosdem castigationum liber auctus et recognitus ab ipso auctore. 2 pt. *In Bibliopolio Commeliniano:* [*Heidelberg,*] 1600. 8°.
1068. h. **5.**

—— [Another copy.] **1002.** b. **7.**

—— [Another copy.] MS. NOTE. C. **47.** c. **17.**
With the arms and initial of Henri de La Tour, Duke de Bouillon, stamped on the binding.

—— Catullus, Tibullus, Propertius: seriò castigati. pp. 213. *Ex officina Plantiniana Raphelengii:* [*Leyden,*] 1603. 16°.
C. **66.** a. **8.**
Including the " Priapea." Previous edition 1591.

—— [Another copy.] **835.** a. **23.**

—— C. Val. Catulli, Albii Tibulli, Sex. Aur. Propertii, opera omnia quæ extant. Cum variorum doctorum virorum commentariis, notis, *etc.* (Theodori Marcilii . . . In C. Valerium Catullum Asterismi.—Q. Val. Catulli, Albii Tibulli, Sext. Aur. Propertii, noua editio. Iosephus Scaliger . . . recensuit.) pp. 936. 19. L.P. *M. Orry: Lutetiæ*, 1604. fol. **72.** l. **4.**
Including the " Priapea."

—— [A reissue.] *Lutetiæ*, 1608. fol. **655.** d. **3.**

—— Opera Catulli, Tibulli, Propertii, et Corn. Galli, siue Maximiani potius. Cum indice . . . vocum singularum, labore . . . Horatii Tuscanellae . . . confecto . . . Editio auctior insuper poëmatis aliquot, quae verè Corn. Galli. pp. 342. 191. FEW MS. NOTES. *Typis Wechelianis; apud Cl. Marnium & her. J. Aubrii: Hanouiae*, 1608. 8°.
11385. aa. **13.**

CATULLUS (Caius Valerius) [Works.—*Latin.*]

—— Ioannis Passerati . . . Commentarii in C. Val. Catullum, Albium Tibullum, et Sex. Aur. Propertium. Cum tribus . . . indicibus. [With the text.] pp. 712. [*C. Morellus:*] *Parisiis*, 1608. fol. Cup. **652.** cc. **11.**
Including the " Priapea." The text is without pagination. The titlepage contains an engraving of Paris.

—— [Another copy.] **72.** l. **5.**

—— [Another copy.] G. **8865.**

—— C. Valerii Catulli Veronensis ad Cornelium Nepotem liber. *See* G., A. P. B. P. Corpus omnium veterum poetarum Latinorum, *etc.* pt. 1. 1611. 4°.
11352. e. **8.**

—— Catullus, Tibullus, Propertius: seriò castigati. (Pervigilium Veneris quod quidam Catullo tribuunt.) pp. 213. *Ex officina Plantiniana Raphelengii:* [*Antwerp,*] 1613. 16°.
C. **20.** f. **47.**
Including the " Priapea." Previous edition 1603.

—— Caii Valerii Catulli, Albii Tibulli, Sexti Aurelii Propertii, quæ extant. Accesserunt vberiores animaduersiones, in quibus . . . loca vitiosa corriguntur . . . obscura illustrantur . . . opera & studio Iani Gebhardi. Editio auctior insuper poëmatis quæ Maximiano, & Corn. Gallo tribuuntur. Additus est . . . Index vocum singularum labore Horatii Tuscanellæ . . . confectus. (Iani Gebhardi . . . animadversiones, cum Iani Meleagri in C. Valerium Catullum Spicilegio.) 2 pt. *Sumptibus Danielis & Dauidis Aubriorum, nec non C. Schleichii: Hanouiæ*, 1618. 8°. **1002.** b. **8.**

—— [A reissue.] Caii Valerii Catulli, Albii Tibulli, Sexti Aurelii Propertii, quæ exstant. Cum . . . Joannis Livineii notis nunquam antehac editis, qui & Propertium ad exemplar Vaticanum & membranas Joan. Sambuci contulit. Nec non . . . Jani Gebhardi animaduersionibus, *etc.* 3 pt. *In officina Wecheliana, apud Danielem & Dauidem Aubrios & C. Schleichium: Francofurti*, 1621, 18. 8°. **1002.** b. **9.**
With a new titlepage, new preliminaries, and the addition of Livineius's notes.

—— C. Valerii Catulli Veronensis ad Cornelium Nepotem liber. *See* LATIN POETS. Corpus omnium veterum poetarum Latinorum, *etc.* 1627. 4°. **833.** i. **1.**

—— Catullus, Tibullus, Propertius cum C. Galli (vel potius Maximiani) fragmentis quæ extant. pp. 240. *Apud Ioann. Ianssonium: Amsterodami*, 1640. 16°.
1471. a. **2.**

—— Catullus, Tibullus, Propertius, cum C. Galli (vel potius Maximiani) fragmentis quæ extant. pp. 260. *Typis L. Elzevirii: Amstelodami*, 1651. 16°. **1067.** a. **2.**
Including the " Priapea." The titlepage is engraved.

—— Catullus, Tibullus, et Propertius, et quae sub Galli nomine circumferuntur; cum selectis variorum commentariis accurante Simone Abbes Gabbema. [With the " Lives " by Petrus Crinitus, and an additional " Schediasma " on Tibullus by Janus Dousa the elder.] pp. 886. *Typis G. à Zijll, & T. ab Ackersdijck: Trajecti ad Rhenum*, 1659. 8°. **11388.** bb. **25.**
Including the " Priapea," here printed in a different type. With an additional titlepage, engraved.

—— Catullus, Tibullus, et Propertius, ex recensione Joannis Georgii Grævii, cum notis integris Jos. Scaligeri, M. Ant. Mureti, Achill. Statii, Roberti Titii, Hieronymi Avantii, Jani Dousæ patris, & filii, Theodori Marcilii, nec non selectis aliorum. 2 pt. *Ex officina R. à Zyll: Trajecti ad Rhenum*, 1680. 8°. **160.** n. **16, 17.**
Including the " Priapea." With an additional titlepage, engraved.

CATULLUS (Caius Valerius) [Works.—*Latin.*]

—— Cajus Valerius Catullus et in eum Isaaci Vossii observationes. pp. 327 [343]. **L.P.** *D. à Gaesbeeck: Lugduni Batavorum,* 1684. 4º. **672. d. 21**

—— [Another copy.] **78. b. 21.**

—— [Another copy, with a different titlepage.] *Prostant apud Isaacum Littleburii Bibliopolam Londinensem,* 1684. 4º. **653. a. 14.**

—— [Another copy.] **L.P.** **G. 9505.**

—— C. Valerii Catulli opera. Interpretatione et notis illustravit Philippus Silvius . . . in usum Serenissimi Delphini. (Albii Tibulli . . . Elegiarum libri quatuor. Interpretatione et notis illustravit P. Silvius, *etc.*—Sexti Aurelii Propertii . . . Elegiarum libri quatuor. Interpretatione et notis illustravit P. Silvius, *etc.*) 2 tom. pp. 794. *F. Leonard: Parisiis,* 1685. 4º. **55. d. 7, 8.**
Including the " Priapea," here printed in italics. With an additional general titlepage, engraved.

—— Catullus, Tibullus, Propertius, cum C. Galli (vel potius Maximiani) fragmentis. Serio castigati. pp. 239. *I. Haring: Amstaeledami,* 1686. 8º. **11355. a. 3.**
Including the " Priapea," here printed in italics. The titlepage is engraved.

—— C. Valerii Catulli opera, ex recensione Isaaci Vossii, cum ejusdem notis ac observationibus. Editio secunda, *etc.* pp. 327 [343]. few ms. notes [by Richard Bentley]. *C. Boutesteyn; D. à Gaesbeeck; J. de Vivie; P. van der Aa; Lugduni Batavorum,* 1691. 4º. **679. d. 6.**
Previous edition 1684.

—— Catulli, Tibulli, et Propertii opera ad optimorum exemplarium fidem recensita. Accesserunt variæ lectiones quæ in libris . . . notatu digniores occurrunt. pp. 520. *Typis Academicis; impensis Jacobi Tonson Bibliopolæ Londin.: Cantabrigiæ,* 1702. 4º. **53. e. 1.**
With an additional titlepage, engraved. Catullus's poems are numbered I–CXIII.

—— C. Valerii Catulli Veronensis ad Cornelium Nepotem liber. [The poems numbered I–CXIII.] *See* Maittaire (Michael) Opera et fragmenta veterum poetarum Latinorum, *etc.* vol. 1. 1713. fol. **655. d. 1.**

—— Catulli, Tibulli, et Propertii opera. [Edited by Michael Maittaire.] pp. 243. *J. Tonson & J. Watts: Londini,* 1715. 12º. **11375. aa. 11.**
Catullus's poems are numbered I–CXIII.

—— [Another copy.] **L.P.** **159. l. 23.**

—— [Another copy.] **L.P.** **G. 17804.**

—— C. Valerii Catulli Veronensis ad C. Nepotem liber. [A reprint of Maittaire's edition of 1713.] *See* Latin Poets. Corpus omnium veterum poetarum Latinorum, *etc.* tom. 1. 1721. fol. **679. g. 1.**

—— Catullus, Tibullus, Propertius, ad optimorum exemplarium fidem recensiti [by M. Brochard], cum . . . variis lectionibus margini appositis. pp. xi. 312. *Lutetiæ Parisiorum,* 1723. 4º. **77. e. 1.**
Catullus's poems are numbered I–CX.

—— [Another copy.] ms. notes [by Jeremiah Markland]. **834. k. 1.**
Imperfect; wanting the works of Propertius.

—— [Another copy.] **L.P.** **G. 17803.**

CATULLUS (Caius Valerius) [Works.—*Latin.*]

—— C. Valerius Catullus Veronensis; et in eum Jo. Antonii Vulpii . . . novus commentarius locupletissimus. pp. xl. 608. *Patavii,* 1737. 4º. **654. d. 18.**
Including the " Priapea."

—— [Another copy.] **53. e. 2.**

—— [Another copy.] **L.P.** **G. 9554.**

—— Cajus Valerius Catullus in integrum restitutus ex manuscripto nuper Romæ reperto, & ex Gallicano . . . & Vossii & aliorum . . . Critice Joannis Francisci Corradini de Allio in interpretes veteres, recentioresque . . . cum vita poetæ nondum edita. pp. 182. ms. notes. *Venetiis,* 1738. fol. **653. d. 3.**

—— [Another copy.] **56. c. 6.**

—— Catullus, Tibullus, et Propertius, pristino nitori restituti, & ad optima exemplaria emendati [by N. Lenglet du Fresnoy]. (Pervigilium Veneris, quod male quidam tribuunt Catullo.) Accedunt fragmenta Cornelio Gallo inscripta. [The life of Catullus by G. F. Corradino dall'Aglio; those of Tibullus and Propertius by P. Crinitus. With plates.] pp. xvi. 344. *Lugduni Batavorum,* 1743. 12º. **673. a. 15.**
Catullus's poems are numbered consecutively I–CXI, the " Priapea" forming the last three numbers.

—— [Another copy.] **166. b. 20.**

—— [Another copy.] **G. 9620, 21.**

—— [Another issue.] 3 vol. on vellum. *Lutetiæ Parisiorum,* 1743. 12º. **C. 19. f. 14–16.**
In this issue the work is divided into three volumes and the matter has been slightly rearranged. Each volume has a separate pagination.

—— Catulli, Tibulli, Propertii Opera. [Edited by Usher Gahagan.] 2 vol. *J. Brindley: Londini,* 1749. 18º. **989. a. 34.**
With an additional titlepage, engraved.

—— [Another copy.] **165. b. 17.**

—— C. Valerius Catullus (Tibullus, Propertius), pristino nitori restitutus, & ad optima exemplaria emendatus. Cum fragmentis C. Gallo inscriptis. [With plates.] pp. xvi. 344. *Lutetiæ Parisiorum,* 1754. 12º. **1002. b. 11.**
A reprint of the Leyden edition of 1743. *This copy is without the separate titlepages to Tibullus and Propertius.*

—— [Another copy, with a different titlepage.] *Parisiis,* 1754. 12º. **159. c. 1.**
With separate titlepages to Tibullus and Propertius.

—— C. Valerii Catulli Veronensis ad Cornelium Nepotem liber. *See* Amati (P.) Collectio Pisaurensis omnium poematum . . . Latinorum, *etc.* tom. 1. 1766. fol. **653. d. 11.**

—— Catulli, Tibulli, et Propertii opera. pp. 372 [352]. *Typis Johannis Baskerville: Birminghamiæ,* 1772. 4º. **53. e. 3.**
Pp. 201–352 *are mis-numbered* 221–372.

—— [Another copy.] Catulli, Tibulli, et Propertii opera. *Birminghamiæ,* 1772. 12º. **011388. a. 8.**

—— Catulli, Tibulli, et Propertii opera. pp. 276. *Typis Johannis Baskerville: Birminghamiæ,* 1772. 12º. **165. m. 19.**

—— Catulli, Tibulli, et Propertii opera. [With the dedicatory epistle of M. Maittaire.] pp. 243. *J. F. & C. Rivington; T. Longman; T. Cadell: London,* 1776. 12º. **11385. a. 2.**
A reissue of Maittaire's edition of 1715.

589

CATULLUS (Caius Valerius) [Works.—*Latin.*]

—— Catullus, Tibullus, Propertius, cum Galli (vel potius Maximiani) fragmentis et Pervigilio Veneris. Præmittitur notitia literaria studiis Societatis Bipontinæ. Editio accurata. pp. lviii. 455 [355]. 1783. 8°. *See* Zweibruecken.—*Societas Bipontina.* 1002. i. 2.
Including the "Priapea".

—— Caius Valerius Catullus. Recensuit Iohannes Wilkes, Anglus. pp. 124. *Typis Iohannis Nichols: Londini,* 1788. 4°. **431**. a. **26**.
Including the "Priapea."

—— [Another copy.] T. **150**. (3.)

—— [Another copy.] **672**. d. **22**.

—— [Another copy.] **165**. m. **17**.

—— [Another copy.] G. **9477**.

—— C. Valerii Catulli Carmina varietate lectionis et perpetua adnotatione illustrata a Frid. Guil. Doering . . . Accedit index, *etc.* 2 tom. *Lipsiæ,* 1788, 92. 8°. **1002**. i. **3**.
Including the "Priapea."

—— [Another copy.] **1002**. i. **4, 5**.

—— Catulli, Tibulli, Propertii opera. [With a preface by the Abate Visconti.] pp. xvi. 409. *Typis Bodonianis: Parmæ,* 1794. fol. C. **5**. e. **1**.
Including the "Priapea," here printed at the end of Catullus's poems.

—— Catullus, Tibullus, Propertius, cum Galli (vel potius Maximiani) fragmentis et Pervigilio Veneris. Præmittitur notitia literaria studiis Societatis Bipontinæ. Editio secunda. *x* pp. lvi. 310. *Biponti,* 1794. 8°. **160**. f. **12**.
[Previous edition 1783.*]*
See Zweibruecken.—Societas Bipontina.

—— Catullus, Tibullus et Propertius. (Cn. Cornelii Galli, vel potius Maximiani elegiarum libellus.—Asinii Cornelii Galli elegia, *etc.*—Pervigilium Veneris.) pp. 303. *Rotterodami,* 1805. 12°. **1002**. a. **9**.
Including the "Priapea." The titlepage is engraved.

—— Catulli Carmina. Poems of Catullus, with some explanatory and philosophical notes, and several odes [chiefly in Latin] written in imitation of this author in more modern times. [Edited by Abraham John Valpy?] pp. vii. 111. *A. J. Valpy: London,* [1816?] 12°. **1000**. g. **23**.
Including the "Priapea."

—— Catulli, Tibulli et Propertii opera, ex optimis editionibus sedulo accurata. (C. V. Catulli carmina, ex editione F. G. Doering, sedula recensione accurata.—Albii Tibulli carminum libri tres, cum quarto Sulpiciae et aliorum, ex editione C. G. Heyne, sedula recensione accurati.—Sex. Aurelii Propertii carmina, ex editione C. T. Kuinoel, sedula recensione accurata.) 3 pt. *Sumptibus Rodwell & Martin, etc.: Londini,* 1816. 12°. **11385**. de. **9**.

—— C. Valerii Catulli carmina quae exstant omnia, ex recensione F. G. Doering. pp. lx. 486. *Augustæ Taurinorum,* 1820. 8°. G. **17805**.
Including the "Priapea."

—— Catulli, Tibulli, et Propertii, opera, ex optimis editionibus sedulâ recensione accurata. [Edited by John Carey; Catullus from the text of F. G. Doering, Tibullus from that of C. G. Heyne, Propertius from that of C. T. Kuinoel.] 3 pt. *Excudit T. Davison; sumptibus Rodwell & Martin: Londini,* 1822. 12°. **11312**. a. **2**.
Including the "Priapea."

—— C. Valerii Catulli opera omnia ex editione F. G. Doeringij cum notis et interpretatione in usum Delphini, variis lectionibus, notis variorum . . . et indice . . . recensita. 2 vol. pp. vii. 837. lxvi. *A. J. Valpy: Londini,* 1822. 8°. [*Delphin and Variorum Classics.*] **11388**. d. **4**.

590

CATULLUS (Caius Valerius) [Works.—*Latin.*]

—— C. Valerii Catulli carmina . . . recognovit, varietatem lectionis indicesque adjécit Carolus Julius Sillig. pp. xlvi. 378. *Gottingæ,* 1823. 8°. **11385**. cc. **14**.
Including the "Priapea," the last two printed in italics.

—— Caii Valerii Catulli carmina, e recensione Frid. Guil. Doeringii . . . edidit J. A. Amar. (Albii Tibulli carmina. Ex . . . Chr. Gott. Heyne castigatione edidit J. A. Amar.) pp. 278. *Parisiis,* 1821. 16°. [*Amar du Rivier (J. A.) Scriptores Latini principes.* vol. 4.] **834**. a. **6**.
Including the "Priapea."

—— Catullus, Tibullus et Propertius. pp. 64, 66, 93. *G. Pickering: Londini,* 1824. 32°. C. **0**. g. **3**. (2.)
With an additional titlepage, engraved.

—— Catulli, Tibulli, et Propertii opera, in usum tironum proborum recognita et castigata. pp. 243. MS. NOTES. *E. Williams: Etonæ,* 1825. 8°. **11388**. b. **13**.
Including the "Priapea."

—— C. Valerius Catullus ex editione Frid. Guil. Doeringii, cui suas et aliorum annotationes adjecit Josephus Naudet. (Sur Catulle. [Translated by F. Arnaud from the Italian of A. S. Conti.]—Dissertatio de Manlii et Juliæ epithalamio, et versio Gallica eiusdem carminis. [By J. Naudet.]—De Coma Berenices, dissertatio Italica, auctore Ugo Foscolo.) pp. xxiv. 627. *Parisiis,* 1826. 8°. [*Bibliotheca classica Latina.* vol. 5.] **11305**. f. **19**.
Including the "Priapea."

—— C. Valerius Catullus. (Carmina [including the "Priapea"].) *See* Walker (William S.) Corpus poetarum Latinorum. 1828. 8°. **1461**. h. **8**.

—— C. Valerii Catulli Veronensis ad Cornelium Nepotem liber. *See* Weber (W. E.) Corpus poetarum Latinorum, *etc.* 1833. 4°. **11352**. e. **15**.

—— C. Valerii Catulli Veronensis carmina annotatione perpetua illustravit Frid. Guil. Doering. pp. ix. 255. *Altonae,* 1834. 8°. **1001**. k. **22**.
Previous edition 1788, 92.

—— Catullus, Juvenalis, Persius, expurgati. In usum Scholæ Harroviensis. pp. 195. *Apud Longman & Socios: Londini,* 1839. 8°. **833**. d. **1**.

—— Carmina [including the "Priapea"]. *See* Walker (William S.) Corpus poetarum Latinorum. 1849. 8°. **11386**. cc. **7**.

—— Catullus, Tibullus, Propertius. [Edited by Moriz Haupt.] pp. 372. *Lipsiae,* 1853. 16°. **11355.a.41.**

—— [Another copy.] Catullus, Tibullus, [P]ropertius. *Lipsiae,* 1853. 16°. **11355**. a. **7**.
The titlepage is mutilated.

—— Q. Valerii Catulli Veronensis liber. Recognovit Augustus Rossbach. Editio secunda. pp. xxiii. 76. *Lipsiæ,* 1860. 8°. **11340**. d. **41**.
Part of the "Bibliotheca scriptorum græcorum et romanorum Teubneriana."

—— Q. Valerii Catulli Veronensis liber, ex recensione Caroli Lachmanni. Editio altera. pp. 87. *Berolini,* 1861. 8°. **11385**. d. **5**.

—— G. Valeri Catulli liber. Ludovicus Schwabius recognovit et enarravit.

    vol. 1. pt. 1. Quaestionum Catullianarum pars 1.
    vol. 2. pt. 2. Catulli liber, etc.

Gissae, 1862, 66. 8°. **11355**. bb. **21**.
No more published.

CATULLUS (Caius Valerius) [Works.—*Latin.*]

—— Catulli Veronensis liber. Recognovit R. Ellis. pp. xxiv. 87. *Macmillan & Soc.: Londini,* 1866. 16°.
11375. aa. 12.

—— Catulli Veronensis liber. Recognovit, apparatum criticum, prolegomena, appendices addidit R. Ellis. (Editio maior.) [With facsimiles.] pp. lx. 354. *E Typographeo Clarendoniano: Oxonii,* 1867. 8°. **11375. dd. 8.**

—— Catulli, Tibulli, Propertii carmina. Accedunt Laevii, Calvi, Cinnae, aliorum, reliquiae et Priapea. Recensuit et praefatus est Lucianus Mueller. 3 pt. *Lipsiae,* 1870. 8°. **11340. ccc. 37.**
Imperfect; wanting pp. 35–46, of Catullus, pp. 103–106 of the Priapea, and pp. 35–46 of Propertius. Part of the " Bibliotheca scriptorum graecorum et romanorum Teubneriana." Previous edition in the series, 1860.

—— Catulli Veronensis liber. Recensuit et interpretatus est Aemilius Baehrens. 2 vol. *Lipsiae,* 1876, 85. 8°.
11355. g. 3.
Each vol. has a special, as well as a general, titlepage.

—— Catulli Veronensis liber. Iterum recognovit, apparatum criticum, prolegomena, appendices addidit R. Ellis. pp. lxxvii. 410. *E Typographeo Clarendoniano: Oxonii,* 1878. 8°. **011388.c.1.**
Previous edition 1867.

—— Die Gedichte des Catullus. Herausgegeben und erklärt von Alexander Riese. pp. xliii. 288. *Leipzig,* 1884. 8°. **11388. cc. 7.**

—— Catulli Veronensis liber. Ad optimos codices denuo collatos Ludovicus Schwabius recognovit. Indices . . . adiecti sunt. pp. xxiiii. 156. *Berolini,* 1886. 8°.
11388. bb. 29.
Previous edition 1862, 66.

—— C. Valeri Catulli Veronensis carmina. Bernhardus Schmidt recognovit. Editio major. pp. cxxxvi. 88. *Lipsiae,* 1887. 8°. **11388. bbb. 6.**

—— Gai Valeri Catulli carmina. Recognovit Ioh. P. Postgate. pp. xii. 89. *Sumptibus G. Bell et filiorum: Londini,* 1889. 16°. **11355. b. 5.**

—— Catulle. Manuscrit de St.-Germain-des-Prés—Bibliothèque Nationale, n° 14137—précédé d'une étude de M. Émile Chatelain. Photolithographie, *etc.* pp. vii. ff. 36. *Paris,* 1890. 8°. [*Collection de reproductions de manuscrits, etc.* Classiques latins. no. 1.]
MS. Facs. 27.

—— C. Valeri Catulli carmina, recognita a Ioh. P. Postgate. 1893. *See* Postgate (John P.) Corpus poetarum Latinorum, *etc.* 1893, *etc.* 4°. **2045. h.**

—— Catulli Veronensis liber. Recensuit Aemilius Baehrens. Nova editio a K. P. Schulze curata. pp. lxxvi. 127. *Lipsiae,* 1893. 8°. **11385. f. 6.**
Previous edition 1876, 85.

—— Catullus. Edited by Elmer Truesdell Merrill. [With a facsimile.] pp. l. 273. *Ginn & Co.: Boston & London,* 1893. 8°. [*College Series of Latin Authors.*] **11305. ee.**

—— Catullus: with the Pervigilium Veneris. Edited by S. G. Owen. Illustrated by J. R. Weguelin. pp. xx. 211. **F.P.** *Lawrence & Bullen: London,* 1893. 8°.
K.T.C. 15. a. 4.
With an additional titlepage, engraved.

—— Liber Catulli Bibliothecae Marcianae Venetiarum (Cod. Lat. lxxx. classis xii). [A facsimile. Prepared by Constantino Nigra.] **L.P.** [*Venice,* 1893.] 8°.
11385. i. 4.
No. 19 of an edition of thirty copies.

CATULLUS (Caius Valerius) [Works.—*Latin.*]

—— Catulli Veronensis liber. Edited by Arthur Palmer. pp. lv. 97. *Macmillan & Co.: London & New York,* 1896. 8°. [*Parnassus Library of Greek and Latin Texts.*]
012207. h. 1.

—— Catulli carmina recognovit brevique adnotatione critica instruxit Robinson Ellis. *E Typographeo Clarendoniano: Oxonii; H. Frowde: Londini & Novi Eboraci,* [1904.] 8°. [*Scriptorum Classicorum Bibliotheca Oxoniensis.*]
11305.dd
Previous edition 1878.

—— Catulli Veronensis liber. Erklärt von Gustav Friedrich. pp. 560. *Leipzig & Berlin,* 1908. 8°. **11375. ff. 18.**
Part of a series entitled: " Sammlung wissenschaftlicher Kommentare zu griechischen und römischen Schriftstellern."

—— Catulli carmina. Edited, with introduction and notes, by Charles Stuttaford. pp. xxvii. 231. *G. Bell & Sons: London,* 1909. 8°. **11375. de. 13.**

—— Catulli, Tibulli, Properti carmina quae extant omnia, cura Robinson Ellis, Joannis P. Postgate, Joannis S. Phillimore. pp. 318. *Apud P. H. Lee Warner, Mediceæ Societatis Librarium: Londini,* 1911. 4°. [*Scriptorum Classicorum Bibliotheca Riccardiana.* no. 2.]
C. 98. i. 3/2.

—— Catulli, Tibulli, Propertii carmina, a Mauricio Hauptio recognita. Editio septima ab Johanne Vahleno curata et a Rudolfo Helmio edita. pp. 371. *Lipsiae,* 1912. 8°.
11385. de. 6.
With an additional titlepage, engraved. Previous edition 1853.

—— Q. Valerii Catulli carmina. Recensuit, praefatus est, appendicem criticam addidit Carolus Pascal. pp. xv. 122. *Aug. Taurinorum,* 1916. 8°. [*Corpus scriptorum latinorum Paravianum.* no. 1.] **011306.aa.2/1.**

—— Catulli Veronensis liber. Recensuit Elmer Truesdell Merrill. pp. vi. 92. *Lipsiae & Berolini,* 1923. 8°.
11355.b.48.
Part of the " Bibliotheca scriptorum graecorum et romanorum Teubneriana." Previous edition in the series, 1870.

—— Il Libro di Catullo. Introduzione, testo e commento di M. Lenchantin de Gubernatis. pp. xci. 286. *Torino,* 1933. 8°. [*Biblioteca di filologia classica.*]
011306.bb.2/3.

—— Catulli veronensis liber. Recensuit Mauritius Schuster. pp. xiv. 153. *Lipsiae,* 1949. 8°. **2049. d. 41.**
Part of the " Bibliotheca scriptorum graecorum et romanorum Teubneriana." Previous edition in the series, 1923.

—— Catulli codex brixianus A vii 7. Prolegomenis instruxit typis edendum curavit Verginius Cremona, *etc.* [With facsimiles.] pp. cx. 85. *Bononiae,* 1954. 8°.
11388. l. 6.
Biblioteca Civica Queriniana, Brescia. Studi queriniani. no. 2.

Latin and English.

—— The Carmina of Caius Valerius Catullus, now first completely Englished into verse and prose; the metrical part by Capt. Sir Richard F. Burton . . . and the prose portion, introduction and notes . . . by Leonard C. Smithers. [With a prefatory letter by Isabel Lady Burton.] pp. xxiii. 313. *Printed for the Translators: London,* 1894. 8°. **11385. g. 31.**

—— [Another copy.] **K.T.C. 11. a. 9.**

—— Catullus, Tibullus and Pervigilium Veneris. (The Poems of G. Valerius Catullus. Translated by F. W. Cornish.—Tibullus. Translated by J. P. Postgate.—Pervigilium Veneris. Translated by J. W. Mackail.) pp. xi. 375. *William Heinemann: London; Macmillan Co.: New York,* 1912. 8°. [*Loeb Classical Library.*] **2282. d. 13.**

CATULLUS (Caius Valerius) [Works]

—— The Poems of Gaius Valerius Catullus. [With omissions.] With an English translation by Francis Warre Cornish. pp. x. 160. *University Press: Cambridge*, 1904. 4°.
11375. cc. 13.

—— The Poems of Gaius Valerius Catullus. With notes and a translation [with omissions] by Charles Stuttaford. pp. xxxii. 286. *G. Bell & Sons: London*, 1912. 8°.
11386. e. 7.

—— Catullus. Translated [into verse] by Sir William Marris. [With omissions.] pp. 169. *Clarendon Press: Oxford*, 1924. 16°.
11375. eee. 18.

—— The Poems of Catullus. Done into English verse by Hugh Macnaghten. [With omissions.] pp. viii. 157. *University Press: Cambridge*, 1925. 8°. **011779. h. 53.**

—— Catulli Carmina. The Poems of Catullus. With complete verse translations and notes by F. C. W. Hiley . . . Illustrations by Véra Willoughby. pp. xvi. 215. *Piazza Press: London*, 1929. 8°. **11355. d. 31.**

Latin and Catalan.

—— Poesies. Text revisat i traducció de Joan Petit . . . i Josef Vergés. pp. xxvi. 91. 99. *Barcelona*, 1928. 8°. [*Escriptors Llatins.*] **Ac. 137. (19.)**

Latin and French.

—— Les Poesies de Catulle de Verone. En Latin & en François, de la traduction de M. D. M. [i.e. Michel de Marolles.] pp. 388. *G. de Luyne: Paris*, 1653. 8°.
11355. aaa. 22.
Including the " Priapea."

—— Traduction en prose de Catulle, Tibulle et Gallus. [With a preliminary discourse, notes, etc.] Par l'auteur des Soirées helvétiennes, & des Tableaux [i.e. A. F. J. Masson, Marquis de Pezay; or rather, by J. B. F. C. David ?]. 2 tom. *Amsterdam, et se trouve à Paris*, 1771. 8°. **77. b. 12.**
With an engraved frontispiece. The poems of Catullus include the Pervigilium Veneris, and are not arranged in the traditional order.

—— [Another edition.] 2 tom. *Amsterdam, et se trouve à Paris*, 1771. 12°. **1002. b. 13, 14.**

—— Traduction complète des poésies de Catulle, suivie des poésies de Gallus et de la Veillée des Fêtes de Vénus ; avec des notes . . . les parodies des poëtes latins modernes, et les meilleures imitations des poëtes français ; par François Noel. [With a frontispiece, and a plan of Catullus's villa at Sirmio.] 2 tom. *Paris*, 1803. 8°.
77. a. 20.
Including the " Priapea."

—— Poésies de Catulle, traduction de C. L. Mollevaut. pp. vi. 193. *Paris*, 1816. 12°. **11355. aaa. 5.**
Part of a collected edition of the works of Mollevaut. The poems are not in the traditional order.

—— Poésies de C. V. Catulle. Traduction nouvelle [in prose] par Ch. Héguin de Guerle. pp. xvi. 278. *Paris*, 1837. 8°. [*Panckoucke (C. L. F.) Bibliothèque latine-française.*] **11306. f. 19.**
Including the " Priapea."

—— Catulle. (Traduction nouvelle, par M.M. Collet . . . et Joguet. [In prose.]) 1850. *See* Nisard (J. M. N. D.) Collection des auteurs latins, *etc.* 1850, *etc.* 8°.
11306. m. 4.

—— Poésies complètes de Catulle. Nouvelle traduction en vers français, par A. Canel. pp. xxviii. 287. *Rouen*, 1860. 12°. **11385. bb. 15.**
Including the " Priapea."

CATULLUS (Caius Valerius) [Works]

—— C. Valerii Catulli liber. Les Poésies de Catulle. Traduction en vers français par Eugène Rostand. Texte revu . . . avec un commentaire . . . par E. Benoist. 2 tom. pp. lxxix. xiv. 561. *Paris*, 1879, 82. 8°. **11388. bb. 8.**

—— Poésies de C. V. Catulle. Traduction nouvelle par A.-E. Billault de Gérainville . . . Première partie. Notice, texte latin et traduction. pp. 412. *Paris*, 1882. 12°.
11386. bbb. 10.
No more published. Including the " Priapea."

—— C. Valeri Catulli liber. Les poésies de Catulle. Traduction en vers français par Eugène Rostand . . . Avec un commentaire critique & explicatif par E. Benoist (et E. Thomas). 2 tom. pp. lxxix. xiv. 836. *Paris*, 1882, 90. 8°. **11386. f. 16.**

—— Catulle et Tibulle, œuvres. Traduction nouvelle. Introduction et notes de Maurice Rat. pp. 326. *Paris*, 1931. 8°. **11352. df. 33.**

—— Catulle. Poésies. Texte établi et traduit par Georges Lafaye . . . Deuxième édition revue et corrigée. pp. xxxviii. pp. 127. *Paris*, 1949. 8°. [*Collection des Universités de France.*] **2319. c. 62.**

Latin and German.

—— Catulli liber carminum recognitus et emendatus a Theodoro Heyse. (Catull's Buch der Lieder in deutscher Nachbildung von T. Heyse.) pp. xii. 299. *Berolini*, 1855. 16°. **11355. c. 2.**

—— Catull. Sämtliche Gedichte. Urtext und deutsche Übertragung. Bearbeitet und nach den Übersetzungen von Theodor Heyse u. a. herausgegeben von Wilhelm Schöne. (3. Auflage.) pp. 89. 108. *München*, 1941. 8°.
011388. a. 15.

Latin and Italian.

—— Carmina C. Valerii Catulli Veronensis. (Versi di C. Valerio Catullo, *etc.*) [With a translation by " Parmindo Ibichense," i.e. F. M. Biaccha, and a life of Catullus by Filippo Argelati.] 1740. *See* Malatesta (G. R.) Corpus omnium veterum poetarum Latinorum, *etc.* tom. 21. 1731, *etc.* 4°. **77. c. 21.**

—— Catullo, Tibullo, e Properzio d'espurgata lezione, tradotti dall' ab. Raffaele Pastore. pp. 549. *Vinegia*, 1776. 12°. **1002. b. 10.**
Including the " Priapea," here printed at the end.

—— Quarta edizione . . . accresciuta . . . Colla giunta degli argomenti ed osservazioni e note, *etc.* 2 tom. *Bassano*, 1805. 12°. **1001. b. 25, 26.**
Previous edition 1776.

—— Libro di C. Valerio Catullo . . . tradotto in versi italiani a rincontro del testo latino da Luigi Subleyras, nell' anno MDCCLXX. (Seconda edizione.) pp. 159. *Roma*, 1812. 12°. **11388. b. 30.**
Including the " Priapea."

—— I Carmi di Caio Valerio Catullo, tradotti ed annotati dal prof. Luigi Toldo, con alcuni cenni di biografia e di bibliografia, *etc.* pp. lxix. 350. *Imola*, 1883. 8°.
11386. h. 19.
Including the " Priapea."

Latin and Polish.

—— Q. Valerii Catulli Veronensis liber ad editionem Caroli Lachmanni. (Q. Waleryusza Katulla Weroneńczyka poezye przełożone . . . przez Szymona Baranowskiego.) 1839. *See* Raczyński (E.) *Count.* Biblioteka klassyków łacińskich, *etc.* tom 4. 1837, *etc.* 8°. **11304. dd. 1/2.**

CATULLUS (CAIUS VALERIUS) [WORKS]

English.

—— The Poems of Caius Valerius Catullus translated. [With omissions.] With a preface and notes. By the Hon. George Lamb. 2 vol. *John Murray: London,* 1821. 8º.
1002. b. 12.

—— Erotica. The Poems of Catullus and Tibullus, and the Vigil of Venus. A literal prose translation with notes, by Walter K. Kelly. To which are added the metrical versions of Lamb and Grainger, and a selection of versions by other writers. pp. viii. 400. *London,* 1854. 8º.
[*Bohn's Classical Library.*] 2500. e. 16.
Imperfect; wanting pp. 47–50, 53–54.

—— The Poems of Catullus. [With omissions.] Translated into English verse, with an introduction and notes by Theodore Martin. pp. xxxi. 199. *Parker, Son & Bourn: London,* 1861. 8º. 11385. c. 8.

—— The Poems of Valerius Catullus, translated into English verse. With life of the poet, excursûs, and illustrative notes. By James Cranstoun. pp. xii. 291.
W. P. Nimmo: Edinburgh, 1867. 8º. 11375. e. 23.

—— The Poems and Fragments of Catullus, translated in the metres of the original by Robinson Ellis. pp. xx. 116.
John Murray: London, 1871. 8º. 11388. aa. 10.

—— The Poems of Catullus. Translated into English verse by Theodore Martin. Second edition, revised and corrected. pp. lvi. 252. *W. Blackwood & Sons: Edinburgh & London,* 1875. 8º. 2280. a. 25.
Previous edition 1861.

—— Catullus. Translated [with omissions] into English verse by T. Hart-Davies. pp. xlii. 167.
C. Kegan Paul & Co.: London, 1879. 8º. 11388. b. 6.

—— Catullus. The complete poems. Translated and edited by F. A. Wright . . . With an introduction. [Including some versions by other translators.] pp. viii. 249.
G. Routledge & Sons: London; E. P. Dutton & Co.: New York, [1926.] 8º. [*Broadway Translations.*]
L.R. 34. a. 1/39.
The poems are re-arranged, but with the traditional numbering.

—— The Complete Poetry of Gaius Catullus, translated by Jack Lindsay, with decorations engraved on wood by Lionel Ellis, and an essay by the translator, *etc.*
Fanfrolico Press: London, [1929.] 8º. C. 98. f. 20.

—— Catullus and Tibullus in English Verse. By Arthur S. Way. pp. 123. *Macmillan & Co.: London,* 1936. 8º.
20030. bb. 28.

—— Catullus. The Complete Poems. A new translation with introduction and commentary by Jack Lindsay. pp. xxii. 124. *Sylvan Press: London,* 1948. 8º.
011388. a. 19.
Previous edition 1929.

French.

—— Poésies de Catulle, traduites en vers français par Eugène Yvert. pp. iiii. 202. *Amiens,* 1873. 8º.
11385. e. 9.
No. 97, 98 are wrongly numbered 107, 108.

German.

—— Joachim Meiers von Perleberg, Durchl. Römerin Lesbia. Das ist, Alle Gedichte des berühm[t]en Lateinischen Poeten Catullus, nebst [E]inführung fast aller Geschichten damahliger [Z]eit . . . In einer anmuthigen Liebes-Geschicht [*sic*] vorgestellet, und mit . . . Kupffern gezieret. pp. 1276. *M. G. Weidmann: Leipzig,* 1690. 8º.
11355. bbb. 8.
Slightly cropped.

CATULLUS (CAIUS VALERIUS) [WORKS]

—— Catullus übersetzt von Konrad Schwenck. [With omissions.] Anhang. Sechster Gesang der Odyssee. pp. xii. 212. *Frankfurt,* 1829. 12º. 11352. aaa. 6.

—— Katull's Gedichte. Im Versmasse der Urschrift übersetzt von Karl Uschner. [With omissions.] pp. xii. 130.
Berlin, 1866. 16º. 11388. a. 12.

—— Des Quintus Valerius Catullus Dichtungen in rein deutschem Gewande von J. H. E. Delagrise. [With omissions.] Nebst Einleitung und sachlichen Erläuterungen, hauptsächlich von M. Haupt, aus dessen Leipziger Vorlesungen über Catull. [With a translation of Horace's " Carmen Saeculare " annexed.] pp. xxxv. 173.
Helmstedt, 1870. 8º. 11388. aaa. 13.

—— Catull's Buch der Lieder [with omissions], in deutscher Nachbildung von Theodor Heyse. Zweite völlig umgearbeitete Auflage aus des Verfassers Nachlasse herausgegeben von A. Herzog. pp. xvii. 163. *Berlin,* 1889. 8º.
11386. aaa. 19.
Previous edition, with the Latin text, 1855.

—— Catulls Gedichte [with omissions] in neuen Übersetzungen von Franz Frese. pp. 66. *Salzwedel,* 1891. 8º.
11385. c. 48. (4.)

—— Valerius Catullus' sämtliche Dichtungen in deutscher Übertragung nebst ausführlichen Erläuterungen von Dr. Mauriz Schuster. pp. viii. 276. *Wien,* 1906. 8º.
11355. d. 15.

Hungarian.

—— Gaius Valerius Catullus versei. Irodalom-történeti tanulmánynyal bevezetve és jegyzetekkel kisérve forditotta Csengeri János. pp. 152. *Budapest,* 1880. 16º.
[*Olcsó könyvtar.* sz. 105.] 12215.a.1/105.

Italian.

—— I Carmi di Caio Valerio Catullo, tradotti in italiano dal professore Donato Bocci. pp. xxxiv. 208. *Torino,* 1874. 8º. 11388. b. 1.

—— Catullo (versione di G. Rigutini ed altri), Tibullo e Properzio. Tradotti da varj. [Edited by G. Rigutini.] pp. ix. 533. *Firenze,* 1896. 24º. 11386. de. 3.
Catullus is given with omissions, and the order of the poems is changed. Imperfect; wanting pp. 225–240, *forming part of the version of Tibullus.*

Russian.

—— Стихотворенія Катулла. Въ переводѣ и съ объясненіями А. Фета. pp. xxxi. 140. iv. *Москва,* 1886. 8º.
011306. b. 1. (2.)

SMALLER COLLECTIONS.

Latin.

—— C. Valeri Catulli Veronensis, ad Cornelium Nepotem liber. [Omitting several poems, some of which have been partially supplied in MS. by Ben Jonson, the former owner of the book.] *See* CHORUS. [Chor]us poetarum classicorum duplex, *etc.* pt. 1. 1616. 8º.
C. 45. f. 15, 16.

—— Orationes ex Catullo collectæ. [The speech of Attis from Carm. LXIII, and that of Ariadne and Aegeus from Carm. LXIV.] *See* ROGERS (Franciscus) Orationes ex poetis Latinis excerptæ, *etc.* 1711. 8º. 1001. b. 3.

—— C. Valerii Catulli, Albii Tibulli, et Sexti Aurelii Propertii selecta et casta carmina, notis illustrata. pp. 164.
Venetiis, 1755. 12º. 011388. aa. 9.

CATULLUS (Caius Valerius) [Smaller Collections.
—*Latin*.]

—— C. Valerii Catulli, Albii Tibulli, et Sexti Aurelii Propertii
casta carmina, ad scholasticorum usum selecta, notisque
. . . illustrata. Editio altera locupletior, *etc.* pp. 226.
Venetiis, 1762. 12º. **11385. aa. 14.**

—— Selecta veterum poetarum epigrammata. C. Val. Catulli
(C. Valerii Martialis). *See* Plautus (T. M.) [*Captivi.—
Latin.*] M. Acci Plauti Capteivei, *etc.* [1770?] 8º.
11707. a. 22.

—— C. Valerii Catulli, Albii Tibulli, et Sexti Aurelii Propertii selecta carmina notis illustrata. pp. 204. *Parmæ*,
1791. 12º. **11375. e. 10.**

—— C. Valerii Catulli carmina sex priora, cum commentariis
Ian. Broukhusii, Isaac Verburgii et editoris. *See* Huschke
(I. G.) Analecta litteraria, *etc.* 1826. 8º.
11312. d. 12.

—— The Poems of Catullus: selected and prepared for the
use of schools and colleges. By F. M. Hubbard.
pp. xii. 146. *Perkins & Marvin: Boston*, 1836. 12º.
11375. b. 11.

—— Selecta e Catullo, in usum juventutis: notas quasdam
Anglice scriptas, adjecit Gulielmus Gifford Cookesley.
pp. vi. 89. *E. P. Williams: Etonæ*, 1845. 12º.
1002. m. 5.

—— Excerpta e carminibus Catulli, Tibulli, Propertii, et
Ovidii. Selections from the poems of Catullus, Tibullus,
Propertius and Ovid. With notes by William Bodham
Donne. pp. 229. *John Weale: London*, 1860. 12º.
11306. b. 12.
Part of " Weale's Classical Series."

—— [Another edition.] pp. 229. *Virtue Bros. & Co.:
London*, 1864. 12º. **11306. bbb. 8.**
Part of " Weale's Classical Series."

—— Catulli, Tibulli, Propertii poemata selecta. Selections
from Catullus, Tibullus, and Propertius. With English
notes. By A. H. Wratislaw . . . and F. N. Sutton.
pp. xv. 160. *Whittaker & Co.; George Bell: London*,
1869. 8º. [*Grammar School Classics.*] **11305. b. 13.**

—— C. Valerius Catullus. [Selected poems. With notes by
N. Pinder.] *See* Pinder (North) Selections from the
Less-Known Latin Poets, *etc.* 1869. 8º. **2320. f. 22.**

—— Catulli Veronensis carmina selecta, secundum recogni-
tionem R. Ellis. [Selected by Edwin Palmer.] pp. 61.
E Typographeo Clarendoniano: Oxonii, 1872. 8º.
11388. aa. 11.

—— [Selected poems.] *See* Munro (Hugh A. J.) *Fellow of
Trinity College, Cambridge.* Criticisms and Elucidations
of Catullus. 1878. 8º. **11312. dd. 1.**

—— Select Poems of Catullus. Edited, with introduction,
notes and appendices by Francis P. Simpson, *etc.*
pp. xlv. 205. *London*, 1879. 8º. **11388. b. 7.**
One of " Macmillan's School Class Books."

—— New edition, *etc.* pp. xlv. 207. *London*, 1880. 8º.
11375. bbb. 15.

—— Poems of Catullus. Selected and edited by H. V. Macnaghten . . . and A. B. Ramsay. pp. viii. 147.
Duckworth & Co.: London, 1899. 8º. **11355. bbb. 23.**

—— [Selections.] *See* Schulze (C. P.) Römische Elegiker,
etc. 1900. 8º. **11355. c. 13.**

—— [Selected poems. Previous edition 1878.] *See* Munro
(Hugh A. J.) *Fellow of Trinity College, Cambridge.* Criticisms and Eludications of Catullus, *etc.* 1905. 8º.
011313.ccc.7.

CATULLUS (Caius Valerius) [Smaller Collections.
—*Latin*.]

—— Catulli Veronensis carmina selecta. Recensuit S. G.
Owen. Tabulis ornavit J. R. Weguelin. pp. 112.
A. H. Bullen: London, 1906. 8º. **11355. bb. 6.**
*The illustrations are those of the complete edition published
in 1893.*

—— Poems of Catullus. Selected and edited by H. V. Macnaghten . . . and A. B. Ramsay . . . Second edition.
pp. viii. 147. *Duckworth & Co.: London*, 1908. 8º.
11386. e. 27.
Previous edition 1899.

—— Selections from Catullus. Edited with introduction,
notes and vocabulary, by Michael Macmillan. pp. 121.
Clarendon Press: Oxford, 1920. 8º. [*Oxford Junior
Latin Series.*] **W.P. 4602/5.**

—— [A reissue, with the addition of illustrations.] *Oxford
University Press: London*, 1929. 8º. **11375. de. 31.**

—— Catullus. Selections from the poems, together with
translations of three poems by F. L. Lucas. Edited by
F. Kinchin Smith . . . and T. W. Melluish. pp. 126.
G. Allen & Unwin: London, 1942. 8º. [*The Roman
World Series.*] **W.P. 12743/2.**

Latin and English.

—— [Selected epigrams, with a translation into English verse
by Thomas Tooly.] *See* Basia. Basia ; or, the Charms of
kissing, *etc.* 1719. 8º. **11633. bb. 1. (7.)**

—— Catulli quædam carmina. [With a translation by John
Hanway.] *See* Horatius Flaccus (Q.) [*Carmina,
Satirae, and Epistolae.—Selections.—Latin and English.*]
Translations of several Odes, Satyrs, and Epistles of
Horace, *etc.* 1730. 8º. **1000. g. 21. (2.)**

—— [Selected poems.] *See* Harman (Edward G.) Poems
from Horace, Catullus, *etc.* 1897. 8º. **11355. e. 31.**

—— Translations from Catullus, with an introduction, by
R. Kennard Davies. pp. 125. *G. Bell & Sons: London*,
1913. 8º. **11386. e. 31.**

—— From Catullus, chiefly concerning Lesbia. By Arthur
Symons. pp. 73. *Martin Secker: London*, 1924. 4º.
11375. g. 23.

—— Catullus in English Poetry. By Eleanor Shipley
Duckett. [A selection of translations and adaptations.]
pp. 199. *Northampton, Mass.*, 1925. 8º. [*Smith College
Classical Studies.* no. 6.] **Ac. 1877.**

—— Imitation of Twenty-Six Lyrics. [With the text.] *See*
Havelock (Eric A.) The Lyric Genius of Catullus.
1939. 8º. **11311. e. 27.**

Latin and French.

—— Les Amours de Catulle. [A romance by J. de La
Chapelle, containing many of the poems of Catullus, with
French translations.] 4 pt. *See* La Chapelle (J. de)
Œuvres, *etc.* tom. 1. 1700. 12º. **95. k. 15.**

—— Choix de quelques poésies de Catulle. [With a verse
translation by A. E. X. Poisson de Lachabeaussière.]
See Poisson de Lachabeaussière (A. E. X.) Poésies
galantes, *etc.* 1803. 8º. **1065. l. 26.**

—— Poésies choisies de Catulle traduites en vers français
par L. Cœuret . . . Suivies de la traduction en vers
français des vers de Catulle à Lesbie par l'un des plus
célèbres prosateurs de notre époque. [With the Latin
text.] pp. iv. 127. *Paris*, 1872. 12º. **12237.a.15.**

CATULLUS (Caius Valerius) [Smaller Collections.]

Latin and German.

—— [Selected poems. With a German translation by Carl Wilhelm Ramler.] 1791. *See* MARTIALIS (M. V.) [*Latin and German.*] Marcus Valerius Martialis, *etc.* Tl. 5. 1787, *etc.* 12°.   **11386. aa. 25.**

—— Catulls Gedichte in ihrem geschichtlichen Zusammenhange übersetzt und erläutert von Rudolf Westphal. pp. xii. 282. *Breslau*, 1867. 8°.   **11375. f. 10.**

Latin and Greek.

—— Οὐαλεριου Κατουλλου ᾳσματα δυο, το ξδ′ (’Επιθαλαμιον Πηλεως και Θετιδος) και ξστ′ (Περι της Κομης της Βερενικης) μεθηρμηνευμενα ἐμμετρως εἰς την Ἑλληνιδα φωνην [by Philippos Ioannou]. *See* ΙΟΑΝΝΟΥ (Ph.) Φιλολογικα παρεργα, *etc.* 1874. 8°.   **11355. cc. 1.**

Latin and Italian.

—— Poemetto di Catullo intorno alle nozze di Peleo e di Teti ed un epitalamio dello stesso. Tradotti in versi italiani [by Giuseppe Torelli]. (Inno di Cleante a Giove.—Versi premessi dal Volpi all’ edizion di Properzio.) pp. 80. *Verona*, 1781. 8°.   **11386. b. 52.**

—— Le Oneste poesie di C. Valerio Catullo. [With a verse translation by Luigi Lanzi.] *See* LANZI (L. A.) Opere postume. tom. 2. 1817. 4°.   **831. bb. 5.**

—— Catullo e Lesbia. Studi di Mario Rapisardi, *etc.* [With the “Lesbia” poems, and an Italian verse translation.] pp. 321. *Firenze*, 1875. 12°.   **11312. b. 2.**

—— La Poesia di Catullo, *etc.* [Edited, with introduction, verse translation and commentary, by Vincenzo Errante.] 2 vol. *Milano*, 1945. 8°.   **011388. b. 11.**

Latin and Swedish.

—— Catullus och Lesbia. Akademisk afhandling . . . af Georg Evald Westergrèen, *etc.* [Consisting chiefly of translations of selected poems. With the Latin text.] pp. 30. *Helsingborg*, 1856. 8°.   **11375. bb. 12.**

English.

—— The Adventures of Catullus, and History of his Amours with Lesbia. Intermixt with translations of his choicest poems. By several hands. Done from the French [of Jean de la Chapelle’s “ Les Amours de Catulle ”]. pp. 400. *J. Chantry: London*, 1707. 12°.   **12510. bbb. 25.**

—— Translations out of Catullus, Tibullus, Propertius, Pindar and Anacreon. By several hands. *See* PETRONIUS ARBITER (T.) The Works of Petronius Arbiter, translated, *etc.* 1713. 8°.   **1080. m. 7.**

—— Specimens of Translations from Catullus and Virgil into English prose, for the use of University students, by Herbert A. Strong, *etc.* pp. 84. *James Maclehose: Glasgow*, 1870. 8°.   **11386. aaa. 22.**

—— [Selections, by various translators.] *See* BANKS, afterwards DAVIES (James) *Prebendary of Hereford Cathedral.* Catullus, Tibullus, and Propertius. 1876. 8°. [*Ancient Classics for English Readers.* Supplementary series.]   **11306. bbb. 30.**

—— [Selected poems.] *See* JUVENALIS (D. J.) [*Satirae Selectae.—English.*] Juvenal, Persius, Martial, and Catullus. An experiment in translation, by W. F. Shaw. 1882. 8°.   **11375. bbb. 24.**

—— The Lesbia of Catullus. Arranged and translated by J. H. A. Tremenheere. pp. 173. *T. Fisher Unwin: London*, 1897. 8°.   **11375. bbb. 46.**

CATULLUS (Caius Valerius) [Smaller Collections.]

—— [Selected poems, translated by Hugh V. Macnaghten.] *See* MACNAGHTEN (Hugh V.) The Story of Catullus. 1899. 8°.   **10606. bbb. 24.**

—— Lyrics from Catullus. *See* LINGHAM (Henry C. J.) The Living Pillars of the Colosseum, *etc.* [1901.] 8°.   **011649. eee. 22.**

—— Valerius Catullus . . . Selected poems. Rendered into English rhymed verse by L. R. Levett. pp. 70. *Heffer & Sons: Cambridge; Simpkin, Marshall & Co.: London*, 1905. 8°.   **11375. de. 8.**

—— Verse Translations from Catullus and Horace. By F. C. W. Hiley. pp. 20. *W. Heffer & Sons: Cambridge*, 1919. 8°.   **11375. b. 45.**

—— Some Poems of Catullus. Translated [in verse], with an introduction, by J. F. Symons-Jeune. [With a facsimile.] pp. xxvi. 115. *William Heinemann: London*, 1923. 8°.   **11352. df. 20.**

—— Catullus Versions. By F. C. W. Hiley. pp. 21. *F. C. W. Hiley: London*, 1935. 4°.   **20020. d. 2.** *Reproduced from typewriting.*

—— Selected Poems of Valerius Catullus. A literal prose translation. (Based on the “ Selections from Catullus ” edited by Michael Macmillan.) pp. 45. *James Brodie: London*, [1951.] 8°. [*Brodie’s Interleaved Classical Translations.*]   **W.P. 11526/40.**

Afrikaans.

—— Die Liefde van Catullus. Deur T. J. Haarhoff. pp. 80. *Bloemfontein & Kaapstad*, 1933. 8°.   **11352. c. 32.**

Czech.

—— Láska a svět. (Výbor.) Překlady V. Klepla. pp. 88. *Praha*, 1928. 8°.   **11375. aa. 39.**

Danish.

—— Catul’s Kærlighed og Had, *etc.* [Selected poems, translated by Axel Juel.] pp. 108. *København*, 1937. 16°.   **11385. df. 6.**

French.

—— Catulle. [Translations from Catullus by various hands.] 1788. *See* BIBLIOTHÈQUE. Bibliothèque universelle des dames. (Mélanges. tom. 11.) 1785, *etc.* 12°.   **12206. d. 24.**

—— Morceaux choisis de Catulle, Gallus, Properce, Tibulle, Ovide, Maximien, Pétrarque et Jean Second; précédés d’une notice biographique sur chacun de ces poètes, et traduits en vers, par Louis Langlois. pp. 313. *Paris*, 1852. 8°.   **11355. cc. 9.**

—— Traduction en vers français. Poésies de Catulle. [A selection.] Moretum de Virgile. [Translated by P. de Constantin.] pp. viii. 77. *Paris*, 1859. 12°.   **11385. b. 16.**

—— Catulle. Odes à Lesbie et Épithalame de Thétis et Pélée. Notices par A.-J. Pons. Illustrations de Poirson. pp. x. 85. *Paris*, 1889. 12°.   **11388. c. 2.**

German.

—— Catull. [Selected poems, translated by Heinrich Stadelmann.] *See* STADELMANN (H.) Aus Tibur und Teos, *etc.* 1868. 8°.   **11335. a. 39.**

—— Catulls Buch der Lieder. Deutsch von Rudolf Westphal. [Selections.] pp. viii. 167. *Leipzig*, 1884. 8°.   **11375. aaa. 6.**

CATULLUS (Caius Valerius) [Smaller Collections.]

—— Catulls ausgewählte Gedichte. Verdeutscht von Dr. Friedrich Pressel. Dritte Auflage. [With a separate titlepage.] pp. viii. 116. *In:* Langenscheidtsche Bibliothek sämtlicher griechischen und römischen Klassiker, *etc.* Bd. 62. [1888.] 8°.   **012213. g. 1/62.**

—— [Selections, translated by F. Frese.] *See* FRESE (Franz) *Translator*. C. Valerius Catullus, eine biographische Skizze, *etc.* 1890. 4°.   **11312. ee. 1. (5.)**

Italian.

—— [Selected poems, translated into Italian prose by Z. Carini.] *See* CARINI (Z.) Poesie scelte di Catullo, Tibullo, e Properzio voltate in lingua italiana, *etc.* 1874. 8°.   **11388. aaa. 11.**

—— [Another edition.] *See* CARINI (Z.) Poesie scelte di Catullo, Tibullo e Properzio, voltate in lingua italiana, *etc.* 1880. 8°.   **11355. bb. 4.**

—— Alcune versioni da Catullo. [By Giacinto Casella. *See* CASELLA (G.) Opere edite e postume. vol. 2. 1884. 8°.   **12225. b. 1.**

—— [Selected poems, translated into Italian verse by Domenico Menghini.] *See* MENGHINI (D.) Gli Amori e i carmi di Albio Tibullo. 1901. 8°.   **11340. d. 23.**

—— [Selected poems, translated into Italian verse by G. Puccianti.] *See* PUCCIANTI (G.) Saggio di traduzioni da Catullo, Orazio, *etc.* 1903. 16°.   **11375. eee. 7.**

Russian.

—— Книга лирики. Перевод, вступительная статья и примечания А. И. Пиотровского. (2-ое дополненное и исправленное издание.) pp. 147.   *Ленинград*, 1929. 8°.   **11352. df. 35.**

Serbo-Croatian.

—— [Selected poems.] *In:* ŠOP (N.) Katul, Propercije, Tibul, *etc.* pp. 9–32. 1950. 8°.   **W.P. D. 294/4.**

Swedish.

—— Sånger af Catullus från Verona. Öfversättningsförsök af Elias Janzon. 2 pt. *Upsala*, 1889, 91. 8°. [*Upsala Universitets årsskrift.* 1889, 1891.]   **Ac. 1075/6.**

Ukrainian.

—— Пісні, *etc. See* FRANKO (T.) Старе вино в новім місці. Вибір веселих віршів, *etc.* 1913. 8°.   **20003. aa. 18.**

SINGLE POEMS.

AD CAMERIUM.

—— Q. Valerii Catulli carmen LV in antiquam formam restituere conatus est Ferdinandus Handius. *See* JENA.— *Academia Jenensis.* Novi prorectoratus auspicia die v. m. Augusti a. MDCCCXLVIII rite capienda civibus indicit Academia Ienensis, *etc.* [1848.] 4°.   **11352. f. 28. (2.)**

AD LESBIAM CARMEN SAPPHICUM.

—— Sapphus carmen Catullo interprete. [With Sappho's final stanza translated, presumably by Florent Chrestien, and Sappho's original.] *See infra:* CARMEN NUPTIALE. Κ. Οὐαλέριου Κατούλλου ἐπιθαλάμιον, *etc.* 1587. 4°.   **77. a. 11. (2.)**

—— *See* IMMISCH (O.) Catulls Sappho. [On Catullus's translation of verses by Sappho. With the Greek and Latin text.] 1933. 8°. [*Sitzungsberichte der Heidelberger Akademie der Wissenschaften.* Phil-hist. Klasse. Jahrg. 1933/34. Abh. 2.]   **Ac. 892/2.**

CATULLUS (Caius Valerius) [Single Poems.]

—— *See* RUKŠA (A.) De Catulli carmine LI eiusque exemplari Graeco. [On Catullus's " Ad Lesbiam carmen Sapphicum " and Fragment no. 2 of Sappho.] 1946. 8°. [*Contributions of Baltic University.* no. 10.]   **Ac. 2631.**

AD MALLIUM.

—— C. Valerii Catulli Elegia ad Manlium. Lectionem constituit Laur. Santenius. [With notes.] *Lat.* pp. 67. *Lugduni Batavorum*, 1788. 4°.   **834. k. 2.**

—— *See* HOERSCHELMANN (W.) De Catulli carmine duodeseptuagesimo commentatio. [1889.] 4°.   **11312. ee. 4. (1.)**

—— *See* SURINGAR (G. T.) Gerardi Tiaard Suringar . . . prolusio exhibens criticas in Catulli Epithalamium Pelei et Thetidos, nec non in ejusdem carmen ad Manlium observationes. 1803. 4°   **833. d. 21. (1.)**

ATTIS.

—— Attis . . . Studio introduttivo, testo critico e commento. Con una nota bibliografica e metrica. A cura di Vincenzo Bongi, *etc.* pp. vii. 67. *Firenze*, 1944. 8°.   **011388. b. 10.**

—— C. Valeri Catulli Attin annotavit, illustravit, anglicè reddidit Carolus Grant Allen. (The Attis of Caius Valerius Catullus. Translated into English verse, with dissertations on the myth of Attis, on the origin of tree-worship, and on the galliambic metre, *etc.*) *Lat. & Eng.* pp. xvi. 154. *Apud Davidem Nutt: Londini*, 1892. 8°. [*Bibliothèque de Carabas.* vol. 6.]   **12202. ff. 1.**

—— Catulo. Atis. *Span. See* JIMÉNEZ AQUINO (M.) Rapto de Helena . . . Versos, *etc.* 1922. 8°.   **11305. ee. 3.**

CARMEN NUPTIALE.

—— Q. Valerii Catulli Epithalamium. *See infra:* IN NUPTIAS JUNIAE ET MALLII. Des Qu. Valerius Catullus Hochzeitsgesänge, *etc.* 1858. 4°.   **11355. k. 2.**

—— Κ. Οὐαλέριου Κατούλλου ἐπιθαλάμιον. Q. Valerii Catulli . . . epithalamium, seu Carmen nuptiale. A Q. Sept. Florente Christiano Graecis versibus expressum. (Sapphus carmen Catullo interprete.—Σαπφους μελος.) *Lat. & Gr.* pp. 7.   *Apud F. Morellum: Lutetiæ*, 1587. 4°.   **77. a. 11. (2.)**

—— [Another copy.]   **G. 8580. (3.)**

—— [Another copy.] L.P.   **G. 8825.**

—— Traduzione dell' Epitalamio di Catullo, Vesper adest, fattasi da tre Parmigiani, *etc.* [Translations into Italian verse by Giuseppe Adorni and Gaspare Ortalli, and a paraphrase in verse by Tommaso Gasparotti. With the Latin text.] pp. 52. FEW MS. NOTES. *Co' Tipi Bodoniani: Parma*, 1827. 4°.   **11375. ee. 40.**

—— *See* ROBORTELLO (F.) Francisci Robortelli . . . De historica facultate disputatio . . . Eiusdem explicatio in Catulli Epithalamium, *etc.* 1548. 8°.   **1088. k. 16.**

COMA BERENICES.

—— Callimachi poematium de Coma Berenices, à Catullo Latinis versibus redditum. (C. V. Catulli Epistolium ad Ortalum, in quo Callimachi carmina à se expressa mittere se ad eum dicit.) [With a commentary by Marc Antoine Muret.] *See* CALLIMACHUS. [*Collections.*] Callimachi Cyrenæi hymni, *etc.* 1577. 4°.   **74. f. 15. (2.)**

—— Callimachi poëmatium de Coma Berenices, a Catullo Latinis versibus redditum. [With notes by Anne Dacier.] *See* CALLIMACHUS. [*Collections.*] Καλλιμαχου Κυρηναιου ὑμνοι, *etc.* 1675. 4°.   **1475.bb.8.**

CATULLUS (Caius Valerius) [Single Poems.—Coma Berenices.]

—— Callimachi Elegia a Catullo expressa. (In Elegiam Catulli Callimacheam adnotationes.) *See* Callimachus. [*Fragments.*] Callimachi elegiarum fragmenta . . . collecta atque illustrata a L.-C. Valckenaer, *etc.* 1799. 8°.
1002. i. 1.

—— Callimachi Elegia de Coma Berenicis a C. Valerio Catullo Latinis versibus reddita ac deinde ab Ant. Mar. Salvinio totidem Graecis versibus expressa. [With the Italian version of Francesco Maria Biacca, and the Greek version of Joseph Scaliger.] *See* Callimachus. [*Collections.*] Καλλιμαχου Κυρηναιου ὑμνοι, *etc.* 1764. 8°.
997. h. 13.

—— La Chioma di Berenice, poema di Callimaco tradotto da Valerio Catullo, volgarizzato ed illustrato da Ugo Foscolo. [With Catullus's prefatory poem to Ortalus.] *Lat. & Ital.* pp. 228. *Milano,* 1803. 8°. 832. k. 28.

—— La Chioma di Berenice, poema di Callimaco tradotto da C. Valerio Catullo, volgarizzato e dedicato da Tommaso Puccini, *etc. Lat. & Ital.* pp. xxix. *Firenze,* 1807. 8°.
11335. h. 11.

—— La Chioma di Berenice, poema di Callimaco, tradotto da Valerio Catullo, volgarizzato ed illustrato da Ugo Foscolo. [Including Catullus's prefatory poem to Ortalus.] Con l'aggiunta delle vite di Berenice e Tolomeo Evergete di E. Q. Visconti, e delle lettere filologiche sul cavallo alato d'Arsinoe di V. Monti. [With a portrait of Foscolo.] *Lat. & Ital.* pp. xii. 291. L.P. *Milano,* 1833. 8°.
11386. e. 6.

Printed on blue paper.

—— La Chioma di Berenice, poema di Callimaco tradotto da Valerio Catullo, volgarizzato ed illustrato [by Ugo Foscolo]. *Lat. & Ital.* 1850. *See* Foscolo (N. U.) Opere edite e postume, *etc.* vol. 1. 1850, *etc.* 8°.
12227.df.16/1.

—— La Chioma di Berenice. Traduzione e commento di Costantino Nigra. Col testo latino di Catullo riscontrato sui codici. [Together with the Italian translation of Ugo Foscolo.] pp. 179. *Milano,* 1891. 8°. 11312. i. 18.

—— La Chioma di Berenice dichiarata del Dr. Pier Marco Rossi. [With the Latin text and a translation into Italian verse by Mattia Zuzzi.] pp. 54. *Lanciano,* 1894. 8°.
11385. bb. 33. (9.)

—— Coma Berenices : or, the Lock of Berenice. [Translated into English verse by William Dodd.] *See* Callimachus. [*Collections.*] The Hymns of Callimachus, translated, *etc.* 1755. 4°. 74. g. 7.

—— The Locks of Berenice. Translated from the Latin of Catullus (by H. W. Tytler). *See* Callimachus. [*Collections.*] The Works of Callimachus, translated into English verse, *etc.* 1793. 4°. 75. g. 23.

—— [Another edition.] *See* Hesiod. [*Works.—English.*] The Works of Hesiod, Callimachus, and Theognis, *etc.* 1856. 8°. [*Bohn's Classical Library.*] 2500. f. 9.

—— Berenices Locke, nach der lateinischen Uebertragung des C. Valerius Catullus. [Translated into German verse by Wilhelm Ernst Weber.] *See* Callimachus. [*Selections.*] Bruckstücke, *etc.* 1826. 8°. [*Weber (W. E.) Die elegischen Dichter der Hellenen.*] 11335. bb. 16.

—— Γ. Οὐαλεριου Κατουλλου. Ἡ περι του πλοκαμου της Βερενικης ἐλεγεια συν τῳ προτεταγμενῳ αὐτης ἐπιστολιῳ ἡρωελεγειοις ἐκφρασθεισα ἑλληνικοις και μετα σημειωσεων συνοδευθεισα τινων ὑπο Χ. Φιλητα. pp. 24. Ἀθηνησιν, 1865. 8°. 11375. c. 9.

CATULLUS (Caius Valerius) [Single Poems.—Coma Berenices.]

—— Elegia di Catullo che la trasporto da Callimacho sopra la Chioma di Berenice. [Translated into Italian verse by Antonio Lavagnoli.] *See* Callimachus. [*Selections.*] Inno di Callimacho sopra i Lavacri di Pallade, *etc.* 1788. 8°. [*La Batracomiomachia d'Omero, etc.*]
11335. bbb. 37.

—— Poema di Catullo sulla Chioma di Berenice tradotto dal signor abate Antonio Conti. Di nuovo pubblicato. (Per le nozze di . . . Maria Vendramin . . . e Francesco Ricci.) pp. 31. *Co' Tipi Bodoniani : Crisopoli [Parma],* 1793. 8°. L.R. 233. a. 16.

—— Per le fauste nozze degl' illustrissimi signori Francesco Fontana . . . e Flaminia Rossi. La Chioma di Berenice. [Translated into Italian verse by Giulio Trento.] pp. 8. *Treviso,* 1801. 8°. T. 2278. (8.)

—— Chioma di Berenice. [Translated into Italian verse, with notes, by Dionigi Strocchi.] *See* Callimachus. [*Hymns.*] Inni di Callimacho, *etc.* 1816. 8°.
11335. g. 19.

—— La Chioma di Berenice. Elegia di Catullo. [Translated into Italian verse by Angelo Dalmistro.] *See* Dalmistro (A.) All'egregio signor Jacopo Crescini, *etc.* 1826. 8°.
11436. bb. 50. (1.)

De Phaselo.

—— Phaselus Catulli, et ad eam, quotquot exstant, parodiæ. Cum annotationibus . . . Accesserunt alia quædam eiusdem generis, edita à Sixto Octaviano. pp. 68. *Apud Ioannem Marcantium : Eboraci* [*Antwerp ?*], 1579. 8°.
C. 56. b. 17.

—— Phaselus Catulli, & ad eundem Parodiarum à diversis auctoribus scriptorum decades quinq;. Quibus accesserunt in eum ipsum Phaselum notæ philologicæ Andreæ Senftlebi. Ex bibliotheca Nicolai Henelii [and edited by him]. 2 pt. *Typis G. Ritzschens ; impensis J. Lischkii : Lipsiæ,* 1642. 8°. 1213. k. 4. (3.)

—— The Pinnace of Catullus. Carminum iv. [Translated into English verse by W. J. Blew.] *See* Blew (William J.) Medea, *etc.* 1887. 8°. 11705. a. 28.

Epithalamium Juniae et Manlii.

—— Des Kaius Valerius Katullus Brautlied auf die Vermaehlung des Manlius Torquatus und der Iulia Aurunculeia. Lateinisch und Deutsch mit Anmerkungen von D. Ioh. Phil. Krebs. pp. vi. 82. *Giessen,* 1813. 4°.
11355. c. 1.

—— Des Qu. Valerius Catullus Hochzeitgesänge [carm. 61, 62] kritisch behandelt von Karl Pleitner. [With the Latin text of both, and a verse translation of carm. 61.] Mit einer Tabelle und einer lithographirten Abbildung. *Lat. & Ger.* pp. 100. *Dillingen,* 1858. 4°.
11355. k. 2.

—— Carme nuziale di C. V. Catullo per le nozze di Manlio Torquato con Vinia Arunculea, tradotto in altrettanti versi italiani e collo stesso metro da G. V. [i.e. Giuliano Vanzolini.] *Lat. & Ital.* pp. 23. *Pesaro,* 1879. 8°.
11355. aaa. 6.

—— Dissertatio de Manlii et Juliæ Epithalamio, et versio Gallica ejusdem carminis. [By Joseph Naudet.] *See supra* : Works.—Latin. C. V. Catullus ex editione F. G. Doeringii, *etc.* 1826. 8°. 11305. f. 19.

Fletus Passeris Lesbiae.

—— Auf den Tod eines Sperlings. *Ger. See* Horatius Flaccus (Q.) [*Carmina and Epodi.—Selections.—German.*] Karl Wilhelm Ramlers Oden aus dem Horaz. (Anhang aus dem Katull.) 1769. 8°. 11526. de. 5. (4.)

CATULLUS (CAIUS VALERIUS) [SINGLE POEMS.]

NULLI SE DICIT.

—— In Dispraise of a Woman. Catullus, with variations. [Verses in imitation of Catullus, carm. 70. With the Latin text.] *Appledore Private Press*, 1886. 8°.
11649. f. 21.
One of an edition of twenty-five copies.

NUPTIAE PELEI ET THETIDOS.

—— C. Valerii Catulli Epithalamium Pelei ac Thetidis. *See* REICHARD (H. G.) Sylloge opusculorum veterum poeticorum, *etc.* 1793. 8°.
1001. e. 12.

—— The Marriage of Peleus and Thetis. A poem. Translated from the Latin of Catullus. With some notes, and the original annexed. By the Rev. George Francis Ottey. pp. xi. 50. *J. Hatchard & Son: London*, 1827. 8°.
11375. d. 7.

—— [Another copy.]
T. 1248. (14.)

—— The Marriage of Peleus and Thetis. Partly taken from Catullus. [By Tankerville Chamberlayne.] *See* CHAMBERLAYNE (Tankerville) The Marriage of Peleus and Thetis, and other poems. 1870. 8°.
11648. bb. 29.

—— Les Noces de Thétis et de Pélée, de Catulle, traduites en vers français [by Georges Adrien Crapelet], avec le Latin en regard. (Notes.) pp. 56. *Paris*, 1809. 8°.
1001. g. 1. (3.)

—— Les Noces de Thétis et de Pélée, poème de Catulle, traduit en vers français, par M. P. L. Ginguené. [With preface, variant readings, notes, and the Latin text.] pp. 251. *Paris*, 1812. 12°.
1002. b. 17.

—— C. Valerii Catulli carmen de Nuptiis Pelei et Thetidis, cum versione Germanica Christiani Friderici Eisenschmidt. In usum tironum illustravit Carl Gotthold Lenz. pp. 193. *Altenburgi*, 1787. 8°.
1002. b. 15.

—— L'Epitalamio di Catullo nelle nozze di Peleo e di Teti. Tradotto in ottava rima dal Signor Giovambatista Parisotti. *Lat. & Ital.* pp. 69. *Padova*, 1731. 8°.
76. e. 27. (1.)

—— Epitalamio nelle nozze di Peleo e di Teti di Cajo Valerio Catullo. Tradotto in verso Toscano [by Ottavio Nerucci], *etc. Lat. & Ital.* pp. 47. *Siena*, 1751. 8°.
76. e. 27. (2.)

—— Epitalamio di Teti e Peleo. Saggio di traduzione di Attilio Tambellini. *Lat. & Ital.* pp. 40. *Bologna*, 1884. 8°.
11409. f. 21. (4.)

—— Ariadne Forsaken. A poem. [Translated from Catullus's " Nuptiae Pelei et Thetidos."] pp. iv. 14. *William Griffin: London*, 1772. 4°.
11385. k. 33.

—— C. Valerii Catulli Carmen LXIV. A Prothalamion for Peleus and Thetis. Translated by C. P. L. Dennis. pp. 18. *Burns, Oates & Co.: London*, 1925. 8°.
11352. c. 21.

—— Digtet om Peleus' og Thetis' Bryllup.—Q. Valerii Catulli carm. LXIV. Oversat af Thor Lange. [In hexameters.] *Dan. See* MADVIG (J. N.) Opuscula philologica ad J. N. Madvigium . . . a discipulis missa, *etc.* 1876. 8°.
12902. d. 15.

—— Les Noces de Thetis et de Pelée. Poëme de Catulle, traduit en vers françois, avec des remarques. Par M. L. G. (Le Gendre fils.) *Lyon*, 1701. 12°. **1002. b. 16.**
Imperfect; wanting all after p. 112.

CATULLUS (CAIUS VALERIUS) [SINGLE POEMS.—NUPTIAE PELEI ET THETIDOS.]

—— Epithalamio di Catullo nelle nozze di Peleo et di Theti. [Translated into Italian verse by Lodovico Dolce.] *See* JUVENALIS (D. J.) [*Satirae Singulae.*] Paraphrasi nella sesta Satira di Giuvenale, *etc.* 1538. 8°. **237. b. 34.**

—— Le Nozze di Teti e di Pelèo, poema di Catullo, in italiani versi recato dal conte Saverio Broglio d'Ajano. pp. 48. *Parma*, 1784. 8°.
1002. i. 6.

—— Epitalamio (Le Nozze de Peleo e di Teti) di C. Valerio Catullo . . . volgarizzato per le . . . nozze del Nob. Sig. March. Luigi Sale di Vicenza e di Sua Eccellenza Fiorenza Vendramin [by Girolamo Trevisan]. pp. 33. *Padova*, 1792. 8°.
11409. f. 21. (1.)

—— Peleo e Teti: poemetto di Catullo. Traduzione. *Ital. See* ITALIAN POEMS. Poemetti italiani. vol. 9. 1797. 12°.
1062. f. 9.

—— Poemetto di Catullo intorno alle Nozze di Pèleo e di Teti . . . tradotto in versi sciolti italiani dal signor Benedetto del Bene. pp. 27. [*Verona?* 1800?] 4°.
T. 58*. (5.)

—— Le Nozze di Teti e di Pelèo : poema di Catullo in italiani versi recato dal conte Saverio Broglio d'Ajano. [Previous edition 1784.] *See* ITALIAN METRICAL VERSIONS. Poemetti, ed altri versioni metriche italiane, *etc.* 1801. 12°.
11420. aaa. 8.

—— Le Nozze di Peleo e Teti, carme de Q. V. Catullo fatto italiano da Ugo Antonio Amico. pp. 37. *Pistoia*, 1867. 8°.
11375. aaa. 12.

—— Le Nozze di Teti e Peléo di C. Valerio Catullo. Traduzione di Giuseppe Biadego. pp. 26. *Verona*, 1873. 8°.
11388. bb. 2.

—— Le Nozze di Peleo e Teti, poemetto di Q. Valerio Catullo. Traduzione di Donato Bocci. pp. 32. *Casale Monferrato*, 1874. 8°.
11375. h. 6.

—— Le Nozze di Peleo e di Teti. Epitalamio di Q. V. Catullo recato in versi italiani da Pacifico Levi, pubblicato da Alessandro Bonacini, *etc.* pp. 20. *Modena*, 1882. 8°.
11386. g. 9.

—— Le Nozze di Peleo e Teti. Poema di C. Valerio Catullo. Tradotto da Raffaelle Belli. pp. 30. *Viterbo*, 1888. 8°.
11385. bb. 33. (3.)

—— Quando Egle Modena dava fede di sposa a Isacco Rosselli-Tedesco Luigi Rasi questa sua traduzione dell'aureo poema di C. V. Catullo per le Nozze di Peleo e Teti pubblicava come augurio di felicità. pp. 30. L.P. [*Florence,*] 1894. 8°.
11422. h. 13.

—— *See* BERNARDINE [Realini], *of Lecce, Saint.* Bernardini Realini . . . in Nuptias Pelei et Thetidis Catullianas commentarius, *etc.* 1551. 4°.
1482. c. 32.

—— *See* LEMERCIER (A. P.) *Docteur ès lettres.* Étude sur les sources du poème LXIV. de Catulle. 1893. 8°.
11312. p. 18. (4.)

—— *See* SELL (Lewis L.) De Catulli carmine sexagesimo quarto questiones diversae, *etc.* 1918. 8°.
11313. aaa. 9.

—— *See* SURINGAR (G. T.) Gerardi Tiaard Suringar . . . prolusio exhibens criticas in Catulli Epithalamium Pelei et Thetidos, nec non in ejusdem carmen ad Manlium observationes. 1803. 4°.
833. d. 21. (1.)

CATULLUS (Caius Valerius)

APPENDIX.

—— *See* Anastasi (A.) Catullo e l'umanesimo. 1919. 8°.
20009. h. 19.

—— *See* Ardizzone (M.) Studi sopra Catullo, *etc.* 1876. 8°.
11312. e. 4.

—— *See* Avantius (H.) Hieronymi auancii Veronensis . . .
in Val. Catullum, & in Priapeias Emendationes, *etc.*
1495. fol. **IB. 24046.**

—— *See* Baehrens (E.) Analecta Catulliana, *etc.* 1874. 8°.
11824. h. 1. (8.)

—— *See* Barth (C. von) Casp. Barthii Observationes ad
D. Junii Juvenalis scholia vetera et ad aliquot Catulli
. . . aliorumque locos, *etc.* 1827. 8°. **11312. e. 1.**

—— *See* Belli (Marco) Magia e pregiudizi in Catullo, *etc.*
1898. 8°. **11312. n. 25.**

—— *See* Birt (T.) Commentariolus Catullianus tertius.
1895. 4°. **11312. m. 50. (4.)**

—— *See* Birt (T.) De amorum in arte antiqua simulacris
et de pueris minutis apud antiquos in deliciis habitis
commentariolus Catullianus alter, *etc.* 1892. 4°.
7808. f. 21. (6.)

—— *See* Boehme (P.) Quaestiones Catullianae. 1862. 8°.
11312. d. 44. (5.)

—— *See* Braga (D.) Catullo. 1938–1948. (Rassegna degli
studi relativi a Catullo.) 1950. 8°. [*Doxa.* anno 3.
fasc. 2/3.] **P.P. 4188. id.**

—— *See* Buedinger (M.) Catull und der Patriciat, *etc.*
1890. 8°. [*Sitzungsberichte der Kaiserlichen Akademie
der Wissenschaften.* Phil.-hist. Classe. Bd. 121.]
Ac. 810/6.

—— *See* Camozzi (G. B.) Polemica Catulliana. 1888. 8°.
11312. f. 34. (1.)

—— *See* Cartault (Augustin) Catulle, l'homme et l'écri-
vain, *etc.* 1889. 8°. **10602. dd. 14. (8.)**

—— *See* Conington (John) The Style of Lucretius and
Catullus as compared with that of the Augustan poets.
1867. 8°. **11312. f. 22. (6.)**

—— *See* Connely (Willard) Imprints of Sappho on Catullus.
[1925.] 8°. **20017. k. 4. (2.)**

—— *See* Corte (F. della) Due studi catulliani. 1951. 8°.
011313. aa. 39.

—— *See* Couat (A.) Étude sur Catulle, *etc.* 1875. 8°.
11312. f. 3.

—— *See* Dousa (J.) *the Elder.* J. Dousæ . . . Præcidanea
pro Q. V. Catullo. 1582. 16°. **1088. b. 1. (1.)**

—— *See* Drachmann (A. B.) Catuls Digtning, *etc.*
1887. 8°. **11312. m. 18.**

—— *See* Ellis (Robinson) Catullus in the xivth Century.
1905. 8°. **11312. e. 16.**

—— *See* Ellis (Robinson) A Commentary on Catullus.
1876. 8°. **12205. r. 19.**

—— —— 1889. 8°. **2320. f. 19.**

—— *See* Emperor (John B.) The Catullian Influence in
English Lyric Poetry, circa 1600–1650. 1928. 8°. [*Uni-
versity of Missouri Studies.* vol. 3. no. 3.]
Ac. 2691. m/15.

CATULLUS (Caius Valerius) [Appendix.]

—— *See* Ferrero (L.) Interpretazione di Catullo.
1955. 8°. **11313. s. 61.**

—— *See* Frank (Tenney) Catullus and Horace, *etc.*
1928. 8°. **10607. e. 30.**

—— *See* Franke (O. von) De artificiosa carminum Catul-
lianorum compositione . . . Adjectum est H. Useneri de
Catulli carmine lxviii. epimetrum. 1866. 8°.
11312. c. 44. (5.)

—— *See* Frese (Franz) *Translator.* C. Valerius Catullus,
eine biographische Skizze mit neuen Übersetzungsproben.
1890. 4°. **11312. ee. 1. (5.)**

—— *See* Giri (G.) De locis qui sunt aut habentur corrupti
in Catulli carminibus. 1894. 8°. **11312. o. 19.**

—— *See* Grebe (F. W.) Studia Catulliana. 1912. 8°.
11313. g. 45.

—— *See* Harrington (Karl P.) Catullus and his Influence.
[1924.] 8°. **012207. ee. 12/12.**

—— *See* Havelock (Eric A.) The Lyric Genius of Catullus.
1939. 8°. **11311. e. 27.**

—— *See* Heinsius (Nicolaas) *the Elder.* Nicolai Heinsii . . .
Adversariorum libri iv. Subjiciuntur ejusdem notæ ad
Catullum et Propertium, *etc.* 1742. 4°. **631. k. 15.**

—— *See* Hénin de Cuvillers (E. F. d') *Baron.* Journal
historique des opérations militaires du siège de Peschiera
. . . suivi d'une note sur la maison de campagne de
Catulle, située à l'extrêmité de la presqu'île de Sermione.
[1801.] 4°. **9150. d. 10.**

—— *See* Hermes (Franz) *of the Königl. Friedrichs-
Gymnasium, Frankfort on the Oder.* Neue Beiträge zur
Kritik und Erklärung des Catull. 1889. 4°.
11312. m. 24. (4.)

—— *See* Heussner (F.) Observationes grammaticae in
Catulli Veronensis librum. 1870. 8°. **11312. cc. 46. (2.)**

—— *See* Howe (George) *of the University of North Carolina.*
Nature Similes in Catullus. 1911. 8°. [*Studies in Philo-
logy of the University of North Carolina.* vol. 7.]
Ac. 2685. k/2.

—— *See* Huschke (I. G.) Epistola critica in Propertium
. . . Accedunt nonnulla in Catullum, *etc.* 1792. 8°.
1002. i. 15.

—— *See* Jungclaussen (W. T.) Zur Chronologie der
Gedichte des Quintus Valerius Catullus. 1857. 4°.
11355. i. 9.

—— *See* Klotz (R.) J. L. G. Beckio . . . gratulatur R.
Klotz. Insunt emendationes Catullianae. 1859. 4°.
836. i. 21. (3.)

—— *See* Lafaye (G.) Catulle et ses modèles, *etc.* 1894. 8°.
11312. o. 10.

—— *See* Macnaghten (Hugh V.) The Story of Catullus.
1899. 8°. **10606. bbb. 24.**

—— *See* MacPeek (James A. S.) Catullus in Strange and
Distant Britain. [On the influence of Catullus on English
literature.] 1939. 8°. [*Harvard Studies in Comparative
Literature.* vol. 15.] **Ac. 2692/14.**

—— *See* Martini (Felice) Caio Valerio Catullo. Monografia. 1880. 8°. **11312. bbbb. 3.**

—— *See* Menozzi (E.) De Catulli carm. xlix. et lxxxxv.
commentationes scripsit E. Menozzi. 1895. 8°.
11312. ee. 16. (3.)

CATULLUS (Caius Valerius) [Appendix.]

—— *See* Mitscherlich (C. W.) Epistola critica in Apollodorum . . . Accedunt nonnulla in . . . Catullum. 1782. 12°.   **243. d. 34.**

—— *See* Mitscherlich (C. W.) C. G. Mitscherlichii . . . Lectiones in Catullum, *etc.* 1786. 8°.   **1002. b. 18.**

—— *See* Monti (Arnaldo) Note filologiche intorno alle edizioni di Catullo, di Virgilio . . . curate dal prof. Carlo Pascal, *etc.* 1921. 8°.   **11313. b. 14.**

—— *See* Morgenstern (O.) Curae Catullianae. 1894. 4°.   **11312. ee. 7. (8.)**

—— *See* Munno (G.) Levia, *etc.* (La Lirica di Catullo.) 1931. 8°.   **11313. aa. 32.**

—— *See* Munro (Hugh A. J.) *Fellow of Trinity College, Cambridge.* Criticisms and Elucidations of Catullus. 1878. 8°.   **11312. dd. 1.**

—— —— 1905. 8°.   **011313.ccc.7.**

—— *See* Muscogiuri (F.) Catulliane, *etc.* 1889. 8°.   **11312. p. 3. (2.)**

—— *See* Orioli (F.) Francisci Oriolii . . . Epistolæ in C. Valerium Catullum. 1822. 8°.   **T. 1234. (1.)**

—— *See* Pascal (Carlo) Poeti e personaggi catulliani. 1916. 8°. [*Biblioteca di filologia classica.* no. 12.]   **011313.de.1/12.**

—— *See* Peiper (L. R. S.) Q. Valerius Catullus. Beiträge zur Kritik seiner Gedichte. 1875. 8°. **11825. i. 21. (6.)**

—— *See* Pohl (Josephus) Lectionum Catullianarum specimen. 1860. 8°.   **11312. cc. 30.**

—— *See* Ramminger (A.) Motivgeschichtliche Studien zu Catulls Basiagedichten. Mit einem Anhang: Aus dem Nachleben der Catullischen Basiagedichte. 1937. 8°.   **11311. e. 15.**

—— *See* Ribbeck (O.) C. Valerius Catullus, eine literarhistorische Skizze, *etc.* 1863. 8°. **10605. cc. 43. (1.)**

—— *See* Schnelle (I.) Untersuchungen zu Catulls dichterischer Form. 1933. 8°. [*Philologus.* Supplementbd. 25. Hft. 3.]   [Missing.]

—— *See* Sciascia (P.) L'Arte in Catullo, *etc.* 1896. 8°.   **11312. bb. 19.**

—— *See* Stenersen (L. B.) Catul's Digtning oplyst i dens Sammenhæng med den tidligere græske og latinske Literatur. 1887. 8°.   **11312. m. 23. (1.)**

—— *See* Stocchi (G.) Vita e carmi di C. Valerio Catullo. Indagini storico-critiche. 1875. 8°.   **11388. aaa. 4.**

—— *See* Suess (J.) Catulliana. 1877. 8°.   **11312. h. 40. (7.)**

—— *See* Svennung (J.) Catulls Bildersprache. Vergleichende Stilstudien. 1945, *etc.* 8°. [*Uppsala Universitets årsskrift.* 1945. no. 3, *etc.*]   **Ac. 1075/6.**

—— *See* Tartara (A.) Alexandri Tartara Animadversiones in locos nonnullos Valerii Catulli et Titi Livi, *etc.* 1882. 8°.   **11312. h. 43. (11.)**

—— *See* Ullman (B. L.) The Identification of the Manuscripts of Catullus cited in Statius' edition of 1566, *etc.* 1908. 8°.   **11313. g. 24. (2.)**

—— *See* Ulmann (J.) Führer durch die Halbinsel Sermione, nebst einer biographischen Skizze des römischen Dichters Catullus. [1897.] 12°.   **10136. bb. 10.**

CATULLUS (Caius Valerius) [Appendix.]

—— *See* Vorlaender (G.) De Catulli ad Lesbiam carminibus. Dissertatio philologica, *etc.* [1864.] 8°.   **8363. b. 3. (20.)**

—— *See* Weber (H. E. B.) Quaestiones Catullianæ. 1890. 8°.   **11312. d. 49.**

—— *See* Weise (August) Zum Kritik des Catull, *etc.* 1863. 4°.   **11312. i. 40. (2.)**

—— *See* Wetmore (Monroe N.) Index verborum Catullianus. 1912. 8°.   **2049.h.**

—— *See* Wheeler (Arthur L.) Catullus and the Traditions of Ancient Poetry. 1934. 8°. [*Sather Classical Lectures.* vol. 9.]   **Ac. 2689. g/17.**

—— *See* Withof (J. H.) J. H. Withofii Oratio de Telchinibus . . . Accedunt emendationes quorundam deploratissimorum Callimachi et Catulli locorum, quæ huic orationi ansam dederunt, *etc.* 1737. 4°. **898. d. 16. (2.)**

—— *See* Wright (Frederic A.) Three Roman Poets: Plautus, Catullus, Ovid, *etc.* 1938. 8°. **011388. b. 1.**

—— *See* Ziwsa (C.) Das eurhythmische Technik des Catullus, *etc.* 1879. 8°. **11312. k. 30. (1.)**

—— The Adventures of Catullus, and History of his Amours with Lesbia. Intermixt with translations of his choicest poems. By several hands. Done from the French [of Jean de la Chapelle's " Les Amours de Catulle "]. pp. 400. 1707. 12°. *See supra* : [*Smaller Collections.—English.*]   **12510. bb. 12.**

CATULLUS (Gaius Valerius) *See* Catullus (Caius V.)

CATULLUS (Quintus Valerius) *See* Catullus (Caius V.)

CATULUS (Quintus Lutatius) *See* Buettner (R.) *Oberlehrer im Fürstl. Gymnasium zu Gera.* Porcius Licinus und der litterarischer Kreis des Q. Lutatius Catulus, *etc.* 1893. 8°.   **11312. f. 55.**

—— Q. Lutatii Catuli de consulatu et de rebus gestis suis liber. *See* Peter (Hermann) Historicorum romanorum relliquiae, *etc.* vol. 1. 1870, *etc.* 8°. **9039. e. 23.**

CATUR (Samuel) *See* Cater.

CATUREGLI (Natale)   *See* Pisa, *Archbishopric of.* Regesto della chiesa di Pisa. A cura di N. Caturegli. 1938. 8°.   **9150. p. 1/14.**

CATUREGLIUS (Petrus) *See* Ephemerides. Ephemerides motuum cœlestium . . . ad meridianum Bononiæ supputatæ, *etc.* [1817–36 by P. Catureglius.] 1819, *etc.* 4°.   **8564. f. 6.**

CATURELLI (Alberto)

—— El Pensamiento español en la obra de Félix Frías. pp. viii. 79. *Córdoba, R.A.,* 1951. 8°.   [*Universidad Nacional de Córdoba. Instituto de Estudios Americanistas.* Serie histórica. no. 20.]   **Ac. 2694. gb/4.**

CATURLA (María Luisa)

—— Un Pintor gallego en la corte de Felipe iv. Antonio Puga . . . Seguido del apéndice, Los libros que poseía el pintor, por F. J. Sánchez Cantón. pp. 98. pl. v. *Santiago de Compostela,* 1952. 8°.   **10635. l. 46.** *Cuadernos de estudios gallegos.* anejo 6.

CATUS, *Iratus, pseud.* [i.e. Andreas Strempfel.] Dirae saeculares, sive satira in aevum Josephinum. Composuit Catus Iratus. pp. 19. *Graecii,* 1877. 8°.   **11409. gg. 5.**

—— Editio altera, castigata, uberior. pp. 27. *Græcii,* 1878. 8°.   **11409. f. 1.**

CATUS, *pseud.* [i.e. ANDREAS STREMPFEL.] Der Teufel auf dem Kirchenchor. Ein musikalisches Lebensbild aus der Gegenwart in 3 Akten von "Catus," *etc.* pp. 15. *Graz*, 1870. 16°. **11528. aa. 12.**

CATUS (CHARLES IGNACE PONS BOUTIER DE) *See* BOUTIER DE CATUS.

CATUS (PETRUS ANTONIUS) Ecloga . . . Meliboeus. *I. Fabrianus excudebat: Patauij*, 1550. 4°. **162. e. 61.**

CATUS (VALENTINUS) *See* PROBUS (M. V.) *Begin.* Hoc in volumine cōtinentur. Probi instituta artium, *etc.* [Edited by A. J. Parrhasius, and re-edited by V. Catus.] 1504. fol. **624. i. 12.**

CATUṢPARIṢATSŪTRA. *See* CHATUSH-PARISHAT-SŪTRA.

CATWG, *Ddoeth.* *See* CADOC, *Saint.*

CATZ (CAREL) *See* CATS.

CATZ (ELSA)

—— *See* PUSHKIN (A. S.) Jewgenij Onegin . . . In Nederlandse verzen overgezet door E. Catz, *etc.* [1949.] 8°. **011565. dd. 4.**

CATZELU (DOMINICO DI) *See* GAZTELU (Domingo de)

CATZIUS (JACOBUS) *See* CATS (Jacob)

CATZIUS (JOSIAS) The Gathering together of the Jews in great bodies under J. Catzius . . . for the conquering of the Holy Land. *See* DOOMSDAY. Doomes-day: or, the Great day of the Lords judgement, *etc.* 1647. 4°. **E. 383. (23.)**

CATZIUS (L. N.) Specimen medicinæ practicæ: Arthritis communis vulgo podagra, non minus facile curatur quam quartana, proponebat L. N. Catzius. pp. 29. *P. vander Slaart: Rotterodami*, 1695. 4°. **781. c. 28. (3.)**

CATZSCHIUS (JOACHIMUS) *Resp.* De partibus humani corporis, earumque actionibus. 1606. *See* HORST (G.) *M.D., the Elder.* Disputationum medicarum prima [*etc.*]. disp. 3. 1606, *etc.* 4°. **1179. c. 3. (16.)**

—— De urinis. 1607. *See* HORST (G.) *M.D., the Elder.* *Praes.* Disputationum medicarum prima [*etc.*]. disp. 14. 1606, *etc.* 4°. **1179. c. 3. (27.)**

—— [Another edition.] *See* HORST (G.) *M.D., the Elder.* G. Horstii Disputationum medicarum viginti, *etc.* disp. 14. 1609. 8°. **1184. a. 1.**

CATZ SMALLENBURG (F. VAN) *See* SMALLENBURG (F. van Cats)

CAU, *of Pritdin.*

—— *See* KERSHAW, *afterwards* CHADWICK (Norah) The Lost Literature of Celtic Scotland. Caw of Pritdin and Arthur of Britain. 1953. 8°. [*Scottish Gaelic Studies.* vol. 7. pt. 2.] **Ac. 1482. e.**

CAU (CORNELIS) *See* NETHERLANDS.—*United Provinces.*—*Staten Generaal.* Groot Placaet-Boeck, *etc.* [Edited successively by C. Cau, S. van Leeuwen and others.] 1658, *etc.* fol. **5696.h.1.**

CAU (GIOVANNI) Alessandro Volta, *etc.* [With plates.] pp. 215. *Milano*, 1927. 8°. **10634. bbb. 18.**

CAU (IMAN) Disputatio iuridica inauguralis de usufructu, *etc.* pp. 12. *Lugduni Batavorum*, 1703. 4°. **501. e. 19. (21.)**

CAU (JANUS PAULUS THEODORUS) Dissertatio historico-politica inauguralis continens historiam marchionatus Verae et Vlissingae, *etc.* pp. 91. *Lugduni-Batavorum*, 1838. 8°. **9406. d. 4.**

CAU (JEAN)

—— Le Tour d'un monde. Roman. pp. 207. [*Paris,*] 1952. 8°. **12519. f. 4.**

CAU (JEAN BAPTISTE ANTOINE) Essai sur la fièvre inflammatoire, *etc.* pp. 22. *Montpellier*, 1821. 4°. **1180. i. 14. (15.)**

CAU (JOHAN CONSTANTINUS) Disputatio medica inauguralis continens quasdam positiones medicas, theoreticas, practicas, chemicas, et physicas, *etc.* *Praes.* J. Wittichius. pp. 8. *Lugduni Batavorum*, 1727. 4°. **1185. i. 3. (17.)**

CAUB (RITTER VON) *pseud.* [i.e. CURT RITTER.] Heil Hitler Dir ! Das Volksliederbuch des neuen Deutschland. Bearbeitet von Ritter von Caub. [With musical notes.] pp. 64. *Leipzig*, [1933.] 8°. **20001. b. 11.**

CAUBÈRE (JOSEPH) Hypertrophie générale des ganglions lymphatiques. pp. 36. *Paris*, 1859. 4°. [*Collection des thèses soutenues à la Faculté de Médecine de Paris.* An 1859. tom. 3.] **7373. b. 15.**

CAUBÈRE (MATHIEU) *See* TERTULLIANUS (Q. S. F.) [*Two or more Works.—French.*] Tertullien. Vingt-trois traités. [Translated by Louis Géry, M. Caubère, and others.] 1837. 8°. **12200. p. 1/12.**

CAUBERGH (O. C. VAN) Dissertatio inauguralis juridica de causis ob quas debitor de eo tenetur quod creditoris interest, *etc.* pp. 27. *Leodii*, 1826. 4°. **498. f. 10. (20.)**

CAUBERT (JEAN) *See* FROGIER DE PONLEVOY (A.) Actes de la captivité et de la mort des RR. PP. P. Olivaint . . . J. Caubert, *etc.* 1871. 12°. **4867. aaa. 34.**

—— *See* FROGIER DE PONLEVOY (A.) Acts of the Captivity and Death of the Fathers P. Olivaint . . . J. Caubert, *etc.* 1871. 8°. **4867. aaa. 35.**

—— *See* ROME, *Church of.—Congregatio Rituum.* Parisien. beatificationis seu declarationis martyrii servorum Dei. P. Olivaint . . . I. Caubert . . . Positio super introductione causae. 1893. fol. **5051. f. 46.**

CAUBERT (LÉON) *See* BRENTANO (L.) [Die gewerbliche Arbeiterfrage.] La Question ouvrière. Traduit . . . par L. Caubert. 1885. 18°. **8275. bbb. 32.**

—— Souvenirs chinois. Avec dix-sept planches, *etc.* pp. 180. *Paris*, 1891. 4°. **010057. ee. 16.**

CAUBET (ARMAND) Contribution à l'histoire de l'hématémèse comsidérée [*sic*] au point de vue étiologique. pp. 66. *Paris*, 1870. 4°. [*Collection des thèses soutenues à la Faculté de Médecine de Paris.* An 1870. tom. 2.] **7373. l. 10.**

CAUBET (CYRILLE) Des affections ulcéreuses du cœur dans les maladies graves. pp. 120. *Paris*, 1872. 4°. [*Collection des thèses soutenues à la Faculté de Médecine de Paris.* An 1872. tom. 3.] **7373. n. 9.**

CAUBET (EDMOND) *See* AUVARD (A.) and CAUBET (E.) Anesthésie chirurgicale et obstétricale. [1892.] 8°. **7482. aa. 6.**

CAUBET (F.) Liquéfaction des mélanges gazeux. [With six plans.] pp. 174. *Paris*, 1901. 8°. **8904. d. 19.**

CAUBET (Henri) De la fistule vésico-vaginale. Proposition d'une sonde double-airigne. Thèse, *etc.* pp. 51. *Montpellier*, 1838. 4°.   **1181.** i. **2.** (7.)

CAUBET (J. A. Durand) *See* Durand-Caubet.

CAUBET (Jean Marie Lazare) La Francmaçonnerie. Lettre à Mgr l'Évêque d'Orléans [in reply to his " Étude sur la francmaçonnerie "]. pp. 48. *Paris*, 1875. 8°.   **4784.** ff. **11.** (6.)

—— Souvenirs, 1860–1889. Avec une préface de G. Wyrouboff. pp. xi. 276. *Paris*, 1893. 12°.   **010662.** ff. **31.**

CAUBET (Joseph Léon) Essai sur le service médical de l'armée en campagne. pp. 62. *Paris*, 1871. 4°. [*Collection des thèses soutenues à la Faculté de Médecine de Paris.* An 1871. tom. 2.]   **7373.** m. **16.**

CAUBET (Léo) *See* Caubet (Marie P. V. C. L.)

CAUBET (Marie Pierre Victor Camille Léopold) Les Conditions du travail dans le Royaume-Uni de Grande-Bretagne et d'Irlande, *etc.* pp. 133. *Paris, Nancy*, 1891. 8°. [*Recueil de rapports sur les conditions du travail dans les pays étrangers.*]   **08276.** k. **36/10.**

CAUBET (P.) *Chirurgien externe de l'Hôpital Saint-Éloi de Montpellier.* Essai sur l'emploi du forceps. Tribut académique, *etc.* pp. 23. *Montpellier*, 1833. 4°.   **1181.** f. **16.** (1.)

CAUBET (Paul) Thèses présentées à la Faculté des Sciences de Paris . . . 1re . . . Étude des principales inegalités du mouvement de la lune qui dépendent de l'inclinaison. 2e . . . Propositions données par la Faculté. pp. 91. *Toulouse*, 1910. 4°.   **8561.** m. **35.**

CAUBET (Richard) Die Königl. Preuss. Seehandlung. pp. 42. *Leipzig*, 1851. 8°.   **8807.** d. **5.** (2.)

CAUBOUE (Achille) *See* Cauboue (Noel G.)

CAUBOUE (Noel Guillaume) Considérations éclectiques sur les maladies vénériennes. Tribut académique, *etc.* pp. 16. *Montpellier*, 1837. 4°.   **1181.** h. **7.** (5.)

—— Dissertation sur la scarlatine, *etc.* pp. 16. *Nismes*, 1837. 4°.   **1181.** h. **9.** (25.)

CAUBRAITH (Robert) Quadrupertitū in oppositiones: conuersiones: hypotheticas: et Modales . . . omnem ferme difficultatem dialecticam enodans. G.L. ff. cxli. *In ędibus Acensianis et Ioannis Grandisiunci:* [*Paris,*] 1510. fol.   **722.** l. **20.** (1.)

CAUBRIÈRE (Joseph Marie) Synthesis Decretalium Sinarum, e Decretis Regionalium Synodorum, ab anno 1803, ad annum 1910 habitarum in Sinis, necnon aliquibus documentis, ab anno 1784, ad annum 1884 a S. C. de P. Fide editis seu approbatis. pp. xi. 368. *Hongkong*, 1914. 8°.   **5051.** b. **25.**

CAUBUL. *See* Kabul.

CAUBULEE, *pseud.* The Crisis in India : its causes and proposed remedies. By a Military Officer of thirty-two years' experience in India. [Originally published in a London daily newspaper. Signed : " Caubulee."] pp. 69. *Richard Bentley : London*, 1857. 8°.   **8022.** b. **20.**

—— Second edition, with six additional letters. pp. vii. 7–111. *Richard Bentley : London*, 1857. 8°.   **8022.** b. **21.**

CAUCA, *Province of.* Memoria del Gobernador de Cauca (J. J. Hoyos) a la Camara Provincial en sus sesiones de 1843. pp. 24. [1843.] 4°.   **L.A.S.387/2.(6.)**

CAUCAL (Eugène) Monroe, président aux États-Unis. *See* Comettant (J. P. O.) Trois ans aux États-Unis. tom. 2. 1856. 8°.   **10412.** b. **6.**

CAUCAL (Eusèbe Marie Léon) Dissertation sur les fièvres intermittentes, *etc.* pp. 29. *Paris*, 1816. 4°.   **1183.** c. **15.** (17.)

CAUCAL (Jules) De l'hémorrhagie utérine ; thèse, *etc.* pp. 25. *Paris*, 1831. 4°.   **1184.** e. **1.** (21.)

CAUCAL (P. A.) Propositions de médecine et de chirurgie. pp. 31. *Paris*, 1848. 4°. [*Collection des thèses soutenues à la Faculté de Médecine de Paris.* An 1848. tom. 3.]   **7372.** b. **6.**

CAUCANAS (Hippolyte) Réflexions sur les qualités indispensables pour l'étude et l'exercice de l'art de guérir ; thèse, *etc.* pp. 23. *Paris*, 1817. 4°.   **1183.** d. **9.** (13.)

CAUCANAS (Joseph) Essai sur la pathogénie & le diagnostic de l'ascite. Thèse, *etc.* pp. 68. *Montpellier*, 1875. 4°.   **7379.** k. **11.** (6.)

CAUCANAS (Pierre Léopold Auguste) Quelques considérations sur les causes générales de maladie, ou Essai sur l'aitiologie, *etc.* pp. 39. *Montpellier*, 1810. 4°.   **1180.** g. **2.** (18.)

CAUCASE. *See* Caucasus.

—— Le Caucase. *See* Periodical Publications.—*Paris.*

—— Le Caucase du Nord. *See* Caucasus.—*Народная Партія Горцевъ Кавказа.* Şimalî-Kafkasya, *etc.*

CAUCASIA. Caucasia, Georgia & Europe. pp. 24. *Imp. Sigma : Paris*, [1922.] 8°.   **08027.** de. **44.**

CAUCASIAN. Anthropology for the People : a refutation of the theory of the Adamic origin of all races. By Caucasian. pp. 334. *Everett Waddey Co.: Richmond, Va.*, 1891. 8°.   **10007.** bb. **15.**

CAUCASIAN MINERAL WATERS. Кавказскія Минеральныя Воды . . . Къ столѣтнему юбилею. 1803–1903 г. [With portraits and illustrations.] pp. 296. 1904. 4°. *See* Russia.—*Министерство Земледѣлія, etc.*   **7470.** i. **24.**

—— Кавказскія Минеральныя Воды, въ Ставропольской Губерніи, Пятигорскаго уѣзда, *etc.* 1860. 8°. *See* Pyatigorsk, *District of.*   **7470.** cc. **8.**

CAUCASIAN PHILOLOGY.

—— Тексты и разыскания по кавказской филологии. 1925. 8° *See* Russia.—*Академия Наук СССР.*   Ac. **1125/228.**

CAUCASIAN QUARTERLY. *See* Periodical Publications.—*Paris.*

CAUCASIAN SPHERE. Mémoire explicatif sur la sphère caucasienne et spécialement sur le Zodiaque . . . Par C. G. S. [i.e. C. G. Schwartz.] 1813. 4°. *See* S., C. G.   **8562.** e. **24.** (1.)

CAUCASICA. *See* Periodical Publications.—*Leipsic.*

CAUCASUS. *See also* Russia.—*Transcaucasian Provinces.*

—— The Caucasus. Der Kaukasus. Organ of independent national thought. *See* Periodical Publications.—*Munich.*

—— Contes et légendes du Caucase. (Contes géorgiens. D'après le texte géorgien du Prince Saba Soulkan Orbéliani.—Sagesse et mensonge, contes . . . des xvIIe et XVIIIᵉ siècles, traduits en langue russe par M. Tsagarelli.—Contes mingréliens, d'après le texte en langue géorgienne et russe de M. Tsagarelli.—Contes arméniens.) Traduits par J. Mourier. pp. 112. *Paris,* 1888. 8°. [*Collection orientale.* no. 1.]

14003.aa.6/1.

—— Геологическія изслѣдованія въ области перевальной желѣзной дороги черезъ главный Кавказскій хребетъ. Д. С. Бѣлянкинъ, И. М. Каркъ, Ф. Ю. Левинсонъ-Лессингъ, В. П. Ренгартенъ, А. Н. Рябининъ, Г. М. Смирновъ . . . Recherches géologiques dans la région du Transcaucasien projeté . . . Avec une carte géologique, 33 planches, 10 feuilles de cartes, *etc.* *С.-Петербургъ,* 1914. 4°.

7106. de. 7.

—— Der Kaukasus, seine Völkerschaften, deren Kämpfe *rc.,* nebst einer Charakteristik Schamils. Mit einer genauen Karte. [By Ludwig Moser.] pp. 88. *Wien,* 1854. 8°.

10057. d. 10.

—— Lettres sur le Caucase et la Géorgie, suivies d'une rélation d'un voyage en Perse en 1812. [By Wilhelm and Frederika von Freygang.] pp. 353. *Hambourg,* 1816. 8°.

151. c. 2.

—— Матеріалы по археологіи Кавказа. *See* MOSCOW.—*Московское Археологическое Общество.*

—— Матеріалы для геологіи Кавказа. *See* CAUCASUS, *Viceroyalty of.*—*Кавказское Горное Управленіе.*

—— Матеріалы по исторіи Грузіи и Кавказа. *See* RUSSIA.—*Академія Наукъ СССР. Грузинскій Филіалъ.*—*Институтъ Языка, Исторіи и Матеріальной Культуры, etc.*

—— Природные условія северо-западного Кавказа и пути рационального использованія их в сельскохозяйственном производстве. 1950, 52. 8°. *See* RUSSIA.—*Академія Наукъ СССР.*—*Комиссія по Изученію Естественныхъ Производительныхъ Силъ Россіи.*

7080. h. 42.

—— Les Prisonniers du Caucase. La Jeune Libérienne. Par l'auteur du Lépreux de la cité d'Aoste [i.e. Xavier de Maistre], *etc.* pp. vi. 305. *Paris,* 1825. 24°.

12549. l. 7.

—— Сборникъ статистическихъ свѣдѣній о Кавказѣ, издаваемый Кавказскимъ Отдѣломъ Императорскаго Русскаго Географическаго Общества. том. 1. 1869. 8°. *See* LENINGRAD .—*Императорское,* afterwards *Государственное, Русское Географическое Общество.*—*Кавказскій Отдѣлъ.*

Ac. 6130/22.

—— Учрежденіе управленія Кавказскаго и Закавказскаго края. Изданіе 1869 года. pp. 60. [*Saint Petersburg,* 1869.] 8°.

10281. h. 11.

—— Le Voyage au Caucase. Comedy in three acts. [By E. Blavet and M. Carré.] Translated with the sanction of the author, *etc.* pp. 69. *Farquharson Roberts & Phillips: London,* 1886. 8°. **11739. de. 20. (6.)** *Printed for private circulation.*

Народная Партія Горцевъ Кавказа.

—— Şimalî - Kafkasya. Северный-Кавказ . . . Орган Народной Партии Горцев Кавказа. (Ежемесячный журнал.) nos. *1*-40, 42-52, 55-56, 60-62. eytul—1-ci teşrin ; сент.-окт. 1934—mayis-haziran ; май-июнь 1939. *Paris,* 1934-39. 4°. **P.P. 4842. dhc.**

—— *Сѣверо-Кавказскій Научно-Изслѣдовательскій Историко-Лингвистическій Институтъ имени С. М. Кирова.* Языки северного Кавказа и Дагестана. Сборникъ лингвистическихъ изслѣдованій. Под редакціей Г. П. Сердюченко. (Les Langues du Caucase septentrional & du Daghestan, *etc.*) [The introduction in Russian and German. With summaries in German.] *Москва, Ленинград,* 1935— 8°. **Ac. 9890.**

CAUCASUS, *North.*—*Сѣверо-Кавказское Краевое Земельное Управленіе.*

—— Извѣстія по опытному дѣлу Северного Кавказа. (Journal of Agricultural Research, North Caucasus.) вып. 11-12, 14, 17. *Ростовъ на Дону,* 1928, 29. 8°.

P.P. 2346. e.

CAUCASUS, *Viceroyalty of the.*

MISCELLANEOUS OFFICIAL PUBLICATIONS.

—— Кавказскій Сборникъ, издаваемый по указанію . . . главнокомандующаго Кавказскою Арміею. (Подъ редакціею . . . Полковника Чернявскаго—генералъ-лейтенанта Потто.) том. 1.—том. 32. част. 1. *Тифлисъ,* 1876-1912. 8°.

010291. k. 1.

DEPARTMENTS OF STATE AND PUBLIC INSTITUTIONS.

—— *Кавказскій Военный Округъ. See* RUSSIA.—*Army.*—*Кавказскій Военный Округъ.*

Кавказскій Статистическій Комитетъ.

—— Сводъ статистическихъ данныхъ, извлеченныхъ изъ посемейныхъ списковъ населенія Кавказа. 5 pt.

1. Закатальскій округъ.
2. Ахалкалакскій уѣздъ Тифлисской губерніи.
3. Черноморскій округъ.
4. Даргинскій округъ Дагестанской области.
5. Сигнахскій уѣздъ Тифлисской губерніи.

Тифлисъ, 1887, 88. 8°. [*Статистическій временникъ Кавказскаго Края.* том. 1. вып. 1-5.] S. NF. **10.**

—— Статистическій Временникъ Кавказскаго Края. том. 1. вып. 1-5. *Тифлисъ,* 1887, 88. 8°. S. NF. **10.**

—— Карсская Область. Сводъ статистическихъ данныхъ извлеченныхъ изъ посемейныхъ списковъ населенія Кавказа. вып. 1. pp. 283. *Тифлисъ,* 1889. 8°. **8223. df. 23.**

—— Сборникъ свѣдѣній о Кавказѣ . . . Изданный подъ редакціею . . . Н. Зейдлица. том. 1-9. *Тифлисъ,* 1871-85. 8°. **10291. k. 4.**

Кавказское Горное Управленіе.

—— Матеріалы для геологіи Кавказа. сер. [1], 2, кн. 1. *Тифлисъ,* 1886, 87. 8°. S. NS. **15.**

—— Отчетъ Кавказскаго Горнаго Управленія за 1908 (-1915) годъ. 8 pt. *Тифлисъ,* 1909-16. 8°. S. NS. **4.**

—— *Кавказскій Учебный Округъ.* Программа преподаванія русскаго языка и словесности (Латинскаго языка, греческаго языка, черченія, рисованія и чистописанія, математики, физики и космографіи, естественной исторіи, географіи, исторіи) въ гимназіяхъ и прогимназіяхъ Кавказскаго Учебнаго Округа, *etc.* 9 pt. MS. NOTES. *Тифлисъ,* 1868, 67-71. 8°.

8358. e. 10.

—— *Кавказское Горское Управленіе.* Сборникъ свѣдѣній о Кавказскихъ горцахъ, *etc.* вып. 1-9. *Тифлисъ,* 1868-76. 8°. **10291. i. 21.**

CAUCASUS. *Viceroyalty of the.*

—— Управление Горною Частью на Кавказе и за Кавказом. *See* supra : Кавказское Горное Управление.

CAUCASUS AND BLACK SEA, IGNATY, *Bishop of.* [1857–1861.] *See* IGNATY.

CAUCCI (FILIPPO GIOSIA) [For official documents issued by F. G. Caucci as Reggente della Cancellaria Apostolica:] *See* ROME, *Church of.—Cancellaria Apostolica.*

CAUCCIUS (PHILIPPUS JOSIAS) *See* CAUCCI (Filippo G.)

CAUCH (JOHN) The Funeral Guide; or, a correct list of the burial fees, &c. of the various . . . grounds . . . in the metropolis, & five miles round. Also, the cemeteries near London . . . names and residences of sextons or parish clerks . . . registrars of births and deaths, *etc.* pp. 80. *The Author: London,* 1840. 12°.　　**796. c. 9.**

CAUCHARD (　　) *Vicaire de Notre-Dame à St.-Lo.*

—— *See* PEZERIL (　　) *Fils, garde nationale.* Réponse de l'auteur de l'adresse aux citoyens du district de St-Lo, à quelques tirades d'un mémoire à consulter pour M. Cauchard. [1791.] 8°.　　**R. 171. (9.)**

CAUCHE (FRANÇOIS) Relation du voyage que François Cauche a fait à Madagascar, isles adjacentes, & coste d'Afrique . . . Avec des notes en marge. *See* MORISOT (C. B.) Relations véritables, *etc.* 1651. 4°.
982. f. 24

—— A Voyage to Madagascar, the Adjacent Islands, and Coast of Africk. pp. 77. 1710. *See* COLLECTION. A New Collection of Voyages and Travels, *etc.* pt. 5. 1708, *etc.* 4°.　　**566. d. 2.**

CAUCHEMAR (IAIN) *pseud.* Tentative Poems. pp. 32. *Shakespeare Head Press: Oxford,* 1937. 8°.
11655. bb. 80.

CAUCHEMÉ (VICTOR) Description des fouilles archéologiques exécutées dans la Forêt de Compiègne sous la direction de M. Albert de Roucy. [With plates.] livr. 1–4. pp. 1–144. 1900–12. 4°. *See* COMPIÈGNE.—*Société Historique de Compiègne.*　　[MISSING.]

CAUCHI (PAUL)

—— Chopin. Centennial memory, 1849–1949, *etc.* [A lecture.] pp. 11. *Roberts Press: Gzira,* [1949.] 8°.
7898. t. 31.

CAUCHIE (ALFRED HENRI JOSEPH) *See* ESSEN (L. van der) Alfred Cauchie, *etc.* [With a portrait.] 1922. 8°.
10658. h. 27.

—— *See* LOUVAIN.—*Academia Lovaniensis.* Revue d'histoire ecclésiastique, *etc.* [1900–22 edited by A. Cauchie and others.] 1900, *etc.* 8°.　　**Ac. 2646/3.**

—— *See* STATES OF THE CHURCH. [*Nuncios.*] Recueil des instructions générales aux nonces de Flandre, 1596–1635, publié par A. Cauchie et R. Maere. 1904. 8°.
Ac. 987/39.

—— Le Comte L. C. M. de Barbiano di Belgiojoso et ses papiers d'État conservés à Milan. 1912. *See* BELGIUM.—*Commission Royale d'Histoire.* Compte rendu des séances, *etc.* (Bulletin, *etc.*) tom. 81. 1902, *etc.* 8°.　　**Ac. 986.**

—— Un Demi-siècle d'enseignement historique à l'Université de Louvain. *See* MOELLER (C.) Mélanges d'histoire offerts à C. Moeller, *etc.* vol. 1. 1914. 8°. **Ac. 2646/4.**

CAUCHIE (ALFRED HENRI JOSEPH)

—— Godefroid Kurth, 1847–1916. Le patriote, le chrétien, l'historien. [With a portrait.] pp. viii. 142. *Bruxelles,* 1922. 8°.　　**010761. i. 20.**

—— [Another copy, with a different titlepage.] **F.P.**
010761. i. 19.

—— La Grande Procession de Tournai . . . Notice historique publiée à l'occasion du huitième centenaire de la procession. pp. 127. *Louvain,* 1892. 8°. **9930. f. 77.**

—— Notes sur quelques sources manuscrites de l'histoire belge à Rome. 1893. *See* BELGIUM.—*Commission Royale d'Histoire.* Compte rendu, *etc.* sér. 5. tom. 2. 1851, *etc.* 8°.　　**Ac. 986.**

—— La Querelle des investitures dans les diocèses de Liège et de Cambrai. pt. 1, 2. *Louvain,* 1890, 91. 8°. [*Université de Louvain. Recueil de travaux publiés par les membres de la conférence d'histoire.* fasc. 2, 4.]
Ac. 2646/4.

No more published.

CAUCHIE (ALFRED HENRI JOSEPH) and **ESSEN** (LÉON VAN DEN)

—— Inventaire des archives farnésiennes de Naples au point de vue de l'histoire des Pays-Bas catholiques. Publié par A. Cauchie . . . et L. van der Essen. pp. ccxxvi. 557. 1911. 8°. *See* BELGIUM.—*Commission Royale d'Histoire.*　　**Ac. 987/7.**

CAUCHIE (ALFRED HENRI JOSEPH) and **HOVE** (ALPHONSE VAN)

—— Documents sur la Principauté de Liège, 1230–1532, spécialement au début du XVIe siècle. Extraits des papiers du cardinal Jérome Aléandre—Manuscrit vatican latin 3881 et manuscrit de l'Université de Bologne, 954, t. III.—Publiés par A. Cauchie et A. Van Hove. 2 tom. 1908, 20. 8°. *See* BELGIUM.—*Commission Royale d'Histoire.*　　**Ac. 987/32.**

CAUCHIE (AMÉDÉE) *See* LESUEUR (F.) and CAUCHIE (A.) Département de Loir-et-Cher. Cahiers de doléances du bailliage de Blois et du bailliage secondaire de Romorantin pour les États généraux de 1789. Publiés par . . . . F. Lesueur . . . A. Cauchie. 1907, *etc.* 8°. **9231. s. 10.**

CAUCHIE (MAURICE) *See* LE METEL DE BOISROBERT (F.) Épistres en vers. Édition critique, avec un commentaire . . . par M. Cauchie. 1921, *etc.* 8°. **Ac. 9812/31.**

—— *See* SCARRON (Paul) Poésies diverses. Textes originaux, publiés avec notes et variantes par M. Cauchie. 1947, *etc.* 8°.　　**Ac. 9812/58.**

—— Thematic Index of the Works of François Couperin. pp. 133. *Lyrebird Press: Monaco; Paris* [printed], [1949.] 8°.　　**M.e.1.77.**

CAUCHOIS (CHARLES AUGUSTIN SYLVAIN) Sur la pathogénie des hémorrhagies traumatiques secondaires. pp. 164. *Versailles,* 1873. 4°. [*Collection des thèses soutenues à la Faculté de Médecine de Paris.* An 1873. tom. 5.]
7373. o.

—— [Another edition.] pp. ii. 160. *Paris,* 1873. 8°.
7441. aaa. 13.

CAUCHOIS (HENRI) *See* FRANCE.—*Constitutions.—Constitution of 1852.* La Constitution de l'Empire français avec les sénatus-consultes, lois . . . lettres patentes et messages qui s'y rattachent annotés par H. Cauchois, *etc.* 1869. 8°.　　**5423. cc. 11.**

—— *See* GOUJET (C.) and MERGER (C. B.) Dictionnaire de droit commercial, *etc.* [Compiled with the assistance of H. Cauchois and — Portier.] 1845, *etc.* 8°.
882. d. 4–6.

CAUCHOIS (HENRI)

—— Cours oral de franc-maçonnerie symbolique en douze séances. pp. xi. 207. *Paris*, 1863. 8°. **4784. cc. 24.**

CAUCHOIS-LEMAIRE (LOUIS AUGUSTIN FRANÇOIS)

See BIBLE.—*Gospels.* [*French.*] Les Quatre Évangiles, précédés . . . d'un avant-propos par Cauchois-Lemaire. 1823. 12°. **1409. b. 25.**

—— *See* GUYET (A. M. I.) Pétitions présentées . . . à MM. les Membres des États-généraux par MM. Guyet et Cauchois-Lemaire, exilés . . . des Pays-bas au mépris de l'art. IV de la loi fondamentale; suivies de leur protestation. 1817. 8°. **934. c. 13. (14.)**

—— *See* NETHERLANDS. [Kingdom of the Netherlands.] *Staten-Generaal.—Tweede Kammer.* Discours et opinions de MM. les membres . . . relative aux pétitions de . . . Guyet et Cauchois-Lemaire, *etc.* 1818. 8°. **5696. e. 9. (3.)**

—— *See* PERIODICAL PUBLICATIONS.—*Paris.* Bibliothèque historique, *etc.* [By L. A. F. Cauchois-Lemaire and others.] 1818, *etc.* 8°. **P.P. 3485.**

—— Histoire de la révolution de 1830. Précédée d'un résumé historique de la restauration et d'une esquisse préliminaire sur le mouvement démocratique. tom. 1. pp. 535. *Paris*, 1842. 8°. **1442. i. 11.** *No more published.*

—— Lettres sur les Cent-Jours, publiées par . . . Cauchois-Lemaire, avec notes et pièces justificatives. pp. xvi. 170. *Paris*, 1822. 8°. **9220. c. 18.**

—— Sur la crise actuelle. Lettre à S. A. R. le duc d'Orléans. pp. 69. *Paris, Leipzig*, 1827. 8°. **523. e. 13. (13.)**

CAUCHON (JOSEPH) L'Union des provinces de l'Amérique britannique du Nord . . . Extrait du " Journal de Québec." pp. 152. *Québec*, 1865. 8°. **8154. bbb. 35.**

—— The Union of the Provinces of British North America . . . Translated by George Henry Macaulay. pp. iv. 154. *Hunter, Rose & Co.: Quebec*, 1865. 8°. **8154. aaa. 27.**

CAUCHON (PIERRE) successively *Bishop of Beauvais* and *of Lisieux.*

—— *See* JOAN [d'Arc], *Saint.* [*Biography.*—II. *Special.*] Instrument public des sentences portées les 24 et 30 mai 1431 par Pierre Cauchon et Jean Le Maître, *etc.* 1954. 8°. **4384.m.23/2.**

—— *See* RIGNÉ (R. de) La Clef de l'erreur judiciaire de Mgr. Pierre Cauchon. 1928. 8°. **4829. e. 36.**

—— *See* SARRAZIN (Albert) *Avocat.* Pierre Cauchon, juge de Jeanne d'Arc, *etc.* 1901. 8°. **4864. g. 3.**

CAUCHON DE MAUPAS DU TOUR (HENRI) successively *Bishop of Puy* and *of Évreux.* Ordonnance de Monseigneur l'Évesque d'Évreux portant défense de lire, vendre, & débiter une traduction du Nouveau Testament imprimée à Mons 1667. Nov. 27. 1667. [1667.] *s. sh.* fol. *See* ÉVREUX, *Diocese of.* **1897. c. 8. (48.)**

—— La Vie de la vénérable mère Ieanne Françoise Fremiot, fondatrice . . . de l'Ordre de la Visitation de Saincte Marie . . . Septième édition, reueuë & corrigée. pp. 799. *S. Piget: Paris*, 1658. 8°. **862. f. 25.**

CAUCHY (AUGUSTIN LOUIS) *Baron.* *See* BONCOMPAGNI (B.) *Prince.* La Vie et les travaux du Baron Cauchy . . . par C. A. Valson. [A review.] (Indicazione degli scritti di A. Cauchy contenuti in otto raccolte scientifiche. [By E. Narducci.]) 1869. 4°. [*Bulletino di bibliografia e di storia delle scienze matematiche e fisiche, etc.* tom. 2.] **P.P. 1574.**

CAUCHY (AUGUSTIN LOUIS) *Baron.*

—— *See* C., M. Estratto dalla Gazzetta piemontese n° 113. [An appreciation of a work on the calculus by Baron A. L. Cauchy published in Sept. 1832.] [1832.] *s. sh.* 4°. **T. 27*. (6.)**

—— *See* FALK (M.) Sur la méthode d'élimination de Bezout et Cauchy. 1879. 4°. [*Nova Acta Regiæ Societatis Scientiarum Upsaliensis.* ser. 3. vol. 10.] **Ac 1076.**

—— *See* MANNING (Henry P.) Developments obtained by Cauchy's Theorem, *etc.* 1891. 8°. **8531. cc. 28. (4.)**

—— *See* MELLIN (R. H.) Über die fundamentale Wichtigkeit des Satzes von Cauchy für die Theorien der Gamma- und der hypergeometrischen Functionen. 1896. 4°. [*Acta Societatis Scientiarum Fennicæ.* tom. 21. no. 1.] **Ac. 1094/2.**

—— *See* MOIGNO (F. N. M.) Leçons de calcul différentiel et de calcul intégral, rédigées d'après les méthodes et les ouvrages . . . de M. A. L. Cauchy. 1840, *etc.* 8°. **1394. e. 27.**

—— *See* MOIGNO (F. N. M.) Leçons de mécanique analytique . . . redigées . . . d'après les méthodes d'A. Cauchy, *etc.* 1868, *etc.* 8°. **8765. bbb. 38.**

—— *See* MOIGNO (F. N. M.) Note sur la détermination du nombre des racines réelles ou imaginaires d'une équation numérique, comprises entre des limites données. Théorèmes de Rolle . . . de Cauchy, *etc.* [1840.] 4°. **8504. f. 33. (3.)**

—— *See* MOIGNO (F. N. M.) Vorlesungen über die Integralrechnung. Vorzüglich nach den Methoden von A. L. Cauchy bearbeitet, *etc.* 1846. 8°. **8533. bb. 14.**

—— *See* VALSON (C. A.) La Vie et les travaux du Baron Cauchy, *etc.* 1868. 8°. **10660. cc. 7.**

—— Œuvres complètes d'Augustin Cauchy, *etc.* 1882– . 4°. *See* PARIS.—*Académie des Sciences.* **Ac. 424/6.**

—— Considérations sur les ordres religieux, adressées aux amis des sciences. pp. 76. *Paris*, 1844. 8°. **1367. i. 29. (1.)**

—— [Another edition.] 1850. *See* MIGNE (J. P.) Encyclopédie théologique, *etc.* tom. 22. 1844, *etc.* 4°. **L.R. 272. a. 1.**

—— Cours d'analyse de l'École Royale Polytechnique . . . 1re partie. Analyse algébrique. (Notes.) pp. xiv. 576. *Paris*, 1821. 8°. **1137. i. 14.** *No more published.*

—— Exercices d'analyse et de physique mathématique. 4 tom. *Paris*, 1840–47. 4°. **530. l. 11–14.**

—— Exercices de mathématiques. pt. 1–4; pt. 5. pp. 1–72. *Paris*, 1826–30. **530. l. 9.** *No more published.*

—— Démonstration du parallélogramme des forces. (Extraite de l'ouvrage Exercices de mathématiques.) *See* MONGE (G.) *Count de Péluse.* Traité élémentaire de statique, *etc.* 1846. 8°. **8530. d. 28.**

—— Mémoire sur la résolution des équations numériques et sur la théorie de l'élimination. [Extracted from the " Exercices de mathématiques."] pp. 64. *Paris*, 1829. 4°. **8532. ff. 35. (1.)**

—— Extrait du Mémoire [entitled " Mémoire sur la mécanique céleste "] présenté à l'Académie de Turin, le 11 octobre 1831. pp. [1]–56. [1831.] 4°. **530. l. 7. (7.)** *Reproduced by lithography from the author's MS. Imperfect; wanting pp. 57–204.*

CAUCHY (Augustin Louis) *Baron.*

—— Leçons sur le calcul différentiel. pp. ii. 289. *Paris,* 1829. 4°. **530. l. 7. (5.)**

—— A. L. Cauchy's Vorlesungen über die Differenzialrechnung, mit Fourier's Auflösungsmethode der bestimmten Gleichungen verbunden. Aus dem Französischen übersetzt von Dr. C. H. Schnuse, *etc.* (Zusätze.) 2 pt. *Braunschweig,* 1836, 46. 8°. **8533. bb. 5.**

—— Leçons sur les applications du calcul infinitésimal à la géometrie. 2 tom. *Paris,* 1826, 28. 4°. **530. l. 8. (2.)**

—— Vorlesungen über die Anwendungen der Infinitesimalrechnung auf die Geometrie . . . Deutsch bearbeitet von Dr. C. H. Schnuse. pp. xiii. 428. *Braunschweig,* 1840. 8°. **8533. bbb. 14.**

—— Mémoire à consulter adressé aux membres des deux Chambres. pp. 15. *Paris,* 1844. 8°. **1356. e. 51. (5.)**

—— Mémoire sur l'analogie des puissances et des différences et sur l'intégration des équations linéaires. pp. 12. [1825.] 4°. **530. l. 7. (2.)**
Reproduced by lithography from the author's MS.

—— Mémoire sur l'application du calcul des résidus à la solution des problèmes de physique mathématique. pp. 56. *Paris,* 1827. 4°. **530. l. 7. (4.)**

—— [Another copy.] **8532. e. 36. (9.)**

—— Mémoire sur la dispersion de la lumière. pp. 24. *Paris,* 1830. 4°. **8532. e. 41. (1.)**

—— Mémoire sur la rectification des courbes et la quadrature des surfaces courbées. pp. 9 [11]. *Paris,* 1832. 4°. **530. l. 7. (10.)**
Reproduced by lithography from the author's MS.

—— Mémoire sur la résolution des équations numériques et sur la théorie de l'élimination. *See* supra : Exercices de mathématiques.

—— Mémoire sur la résolution générale des équations d'un degré quelconque, *etc.* pp. 44. [*Paris,* 1837.] 4°. **8532. ff. 35. (2.)**

—— Mémoire sur le système de valeurs qu'il faut attribuer à divers élémens déterminés par un grand nombre d'observations, pour que la plus grande de toutes les erreurs, abstraction faite du signe, devienne un minimum. Extrait du Journal de l'École Polytechnique. pp. 49. *Paris,* 1830. 4°. **530. l. 7. (6.)**

—— Mémoire sur les intégrales définies, lu à l'Institut le 22 août 1814. *See* PARIS.—*Académie des Sciences.* Extrait du Procès-verbal de la séance . . . du lundi 7 novembre 1814. [1814.] 4°. **530. l. 7. (1.)**

—— Mémoire sur les intégrales définies, prises entre des limites imaginaires. pp. 68. *Paris,* 1825. 4°. **530. l. 7. (3.)**

—— Abhandlung über bestimmte Integrale zwischen imaginären Grenzen . . . Herausgegeben von P. Stäckel. pp. 80. *Leipzig,* 1900. 8°. [*Ostwald's Klassiker der exakten Wissenschaften.* no. 112.] **8706. eee. 1/112.**

—— Mémoire sur les rapports qui existent entre le calcul des résidus et le calcul des limites, et sur les avantages qu'offrent ces deux nouveaux calculs dans la résolution des équations algébriques ou transcendantes. pp. 80. [1831.] 4°. **530. l. 7. (9.)**
Reproduced by lithography from the author's MS.

—— Mémoire sur une méthode générale pour la détermination des racines réelles des équations algébriques ou même transcendantes, *etc.* pp. 32. [*Paris,* 1837.] 4°. **8532. ff. 35. (3.)**

CAUCHY (Augustin Louis) *Baron.*

—— Nouveaux exercices de mathématiques. (Mémoire sur la dispersion de la lumière.) pp. 236. *Prague,* 1835, 36. 4°. **8532. ff. 14.**
Published in parts.

—— Quelques réflexions sur la liberté d'enseignement. pp. 44. *Paris,* 1844. 8°. **1356. e. 49. (5.)**

—— Rapports à l'Academie des Sciences [on " Mémoires " contributed by A. Bravais]. *See* BRAVAIS (A.) Études cristallographiques, *etc.* 1866. 4°. **8715. f. 21.**

—— [Recherches sur les polyèdres.] Untersuchungen über die Vielflache. [Translated by R. Haussner.] *See* HAUSSNER (R.) Abhandlungen über die regelmässigen Sternkörper, *etc.* 1906. 8°. **8706. eee. 1/151.**

—— Résumé d'un Mémoire sur la mécanique céleste, et sur un nouveau calcul, appellé calcul des limites. *Turin,* 1831. 4°. **530. l. 7. (8.)**
Reproduced by lithography from the author's MS.

—— Résumé des leçons données à l'École Royale Polytechnique, sur le calcul infinitésimal. tom. 1. pp. xii. 172. *Paris,* 1823. 4°. **530. l. 8. (1.)**
No more published. Continued by: " Leçons sur les applications du calcul infinitésimal à la géometrie."

—— Sept leçons de physique générale . . . Avec appendices . . . par M. l'abbé Moigno. pp. xii. 108. *Paris,* 1868. 12°. **8704. aaa. 33. (4.)**

—— [Sur l'intégration des équations aux différences partielles du premier ordre, *etc.*] Ueber die Integration der partiellen Differentialgleichungen erster Ordnung in einer beliebigen Zahl von Veränderlichen. *See* LAGRANGE (J. L.) *Count.* Zwei Abhandlungen zur Theorie der partiellen Differentialgleichungen erster Ordnung. Von Lagrange und Cauchy, *etc.* 1900. 8°. **8706. eee. 1/113.**

—— [Sur la théorie de la lumière.] Über die Theorie des Lichtes. Nach einem lithographirten Memoire des Freih. A. L. Cauchy . . . frei bearbeitet von Franz Xaver Moth. pp. viii. 120. *Wien,* 1842. 8°. **1395. e. 29.**

CAUCHY (Charles Arthur) Considérations sur le système artériel de la main. pp. 32. *Paris,* 1875. 4°. [*Collection des thèses soutenues à la Faculté de Médecine de Paris. An 1875. tom. 4.*] **7374. b.**

CAUCHY (Clément Adolphe Octave) Considérations sur quelques diarrhées des enfants. pp. 48. *Paris,* 1871. 4°. [*Collection des thèses soutenues à la Faculté de Médecine de Paris. An 1871. tom. 2.*] **7373. m. 16.**

CAUCHY (Eugène François) De la propriété communale, et de la mise en culture des communaux, à l'occasion du projet de décret proposé à l'Assemblée nationale par son Comité de l'administration départementale et communale. pp. 155. *Paris,* 1848. 8°. **8275. e. 10.**

—— Le Droit maritime international considéré dans ses origines, et dans ses rapports avec les progrès de la civilisation, *etc.* 2 tom. *Paris,* 1862. 8°. **6835. bb. 22.**

—— Du duel considéré dans ses origines et dans l'état actuel des mœurs. 2 tom. *Paris,* 1863. 8°. **6875. e. 16.**

—— *See* PARIS.—*Institut de France.* Institut Royal . . . Rapport par le comte Portalis . . . sur un ouvrage de E. Cauchy intitulé : Du duel, *etc.* [1846.] 8°. **[MISSING.]**

—— Les Précédents de la Cour des Pairs, recueillis et mis en ordre . . . par E. Cauchy. pp. xvi. 660. *Paris,* 1839. 8°. **1128. h. 9.**

—— Les Précédents de la Cour des Pairs, recueillis et mis en ordre, *etc.* pp. xvi. 710. *Paris,* 1839. 8°. **5425. k. 14.**

CAUCHY (EUGÈNE FRANÇOIS)

—— Ode latine adressée au Premier Consul de la République française, Napoléon Bonaparte . . . Avec une traduction française. pp. 23. *Paris*, 1802. 8°.   **934. c. 18. (2.)**

—— *See* HUILLARD (A.) Ode au premier consul, imitée d'une ode latine de M. Cauchy. [1804.] 8°.
935. e. 21. (1.)

CAUCHY (PHILIPPE FRANÇOIS) Mémoire couronné en réponse à la question proposée par l'Académie . . . "Décrire la constitution géologique de la province de Namur, les espèces minérales et les fossiles accidentels que les divers terrains renferment," *etc.* pp. 148.   *Bruxelles,* 1825. 4°. [*Mémoires sur les questions proposées par l'Académie Royale des Sciences et Belles Lettres de Bruxelles.* tom. 5.]   **Ac. 985/6.**

—— Principes généraux de chimie inorganique, avec un tableau synoptique des corps inorganisés d'origine inorganique. pp. 297. vii. *Bruxelles,* 1838. 8°.
1141. k. 5.

CAUCICH (A. R.) *See* PERIODICAL PUBLICATIONS.— *Florence.* Bullettino di numismatica italiana, diretto da A. R. Caucich. 1867, *etc.* 4°.   **P.P. 1952. ba.**

—— *See* RAMELLI (C.) Della zecca fabrianese . . . Opera ristampata con giunte e correzioni per A. R. Caucich. 1867. 8°.   **7756. f. 28. (5.)**

CAUCICH (GUIDO) Notizie storiche intorno alla istituzione delle officine monetarie italiane dalla caduta dell'Impero romano d'Occidente fino ai nostri giorni. fasc. 1. pp. x. 41. *Firenze, Roma,* 1895. 8°.
7757. f. 37.
No more published.

CAUCINO (ANTONIO) *See* BOGGIO (P. C.) and CAUCINO (A.) Legge provinciale e comunale commentata, *etc.* 1860. 8°.   **5326. cc. 4.**

—— Le Fabbricerie. Un delitto di leso buon senso. [Signed: C., i.e. A. Caucino?] pp. 12. 1868. 8°. *See* C.
8246. cc. 41. (7.)

—— Le Fabbricerie e le leggi 7 luglio 1866, N° 3036, e 15 agosto 1867, N° 3848—soppressione degli ordini religiosi e liquidazione dell'Asse ecclesiastico— . . . ed in appendice le sentenze 31 dicembre 1867 del Tribunale civile di Firenze e 15 febbraio 1868 della Corte d'Appello di Torino. pp. 104. *Torino,* 1868. 8°.   **5326. c. 16.**

CAUCUS, *King.* King-Caucus, or " Secrets Worth Knowing." Disclosed in official communications between the Prime Minister at Washington, and the Ambassador at Albany. pp. 20. [1824.] 12°.   **8176. aaa. 12. (8.)**

CAUCUS PARLIAMENT. The Caucus Parliament. May, 1880. [A political satire.] pp. 32.   *George Gale: Lincoln,* [1880.] 8°.   **8139. b. 6. (3.)**

CAUD (LUCILE DE) *Countess. See* CHATEAUBRIAND (L. de) afterwards CAUD (L. de) *Countess.*

CAUDA (DOMENICO LUIGI) *See* SAVOY. Raccolta . . . delle leggi . . . manifesti ecc. pubblicati . . . sotto il felicissimo dominio della Real Casa di Savoia, *etc.* [tom.] edited by D. L. Cauda.] 1818, *etc.* fol. **S.H.588/4.**

CAUDA (ERNESTO) Dizionario poliglotta della cinematografia . . . Tedesco, inglese, francese, italiano, *etc.* pp. 467. *Città di Castello,* 1936. 8°.   **11794. i. 56.**

CAUDA (GIUSEPPE) A velario aperto e chiuso. Figure, tipi, impressioni, *etc.* [Sketches from Italian theatrical history.] pp. 210. *Chieri,* 1920. 8°.   **011795. b. 51.**

CAUDA (GIUSEPPE ANTONIO) Cantata drammatica per le fortunatissime nozze de' nobilissimi signori il signor marchese Tommaso Scarampi di Villanova, conte di Camino, e la damigella Vittoria, Costa di Carrù. [Signed: T. G. A. C., Accademico Fossanese, i.e. Teologo G. A. Cauda.] 1782. 8°. *See* C., T. G. A., *Accademico Fossanese.*   **11715. cc. 7. (1.)**

CAUDAL. Saynete intitulado El Caudal del Estudiante, *etc.* pp. 8. *Madrid,* 1799. 4°.   **1342. f. 5. (33.)**

CAUDAL (EMMANUEL)

—— *See* TURRECREMATA (J. de) *Cardinal.* Apparatus super decretum florentinum unionis graecorum . . . Edidit, introductione, notis, indicibus ornavit E. Caudal. 1942. 4°. [*Pontificium Institutum Orientalium Studiorum. Concilium florentinum. Documenta et scriptores.* vol. 2. fasc. 1.]   **Ac. 2002. bb/3.**

CAUDEBEC.—*Notre Dame de Caudebec. See* MARY, *the Blessed Virgin.—Churches and Institutions.*—Caudebec.— *Notre Dame de Caudebec.*

CAUDEL (LÉON) *See* CAIX DE SAINT-AYMOUR (A. de) *Count.* La Grande voie romaine de Senlis à Beauvais . . . Études de M. l'abbé Caudel, *etc.* 1873. 8°. [MISSING.]

CAUDEL (MAURICE) *See* TUNISIA—[*Laws.*—I.] Législation de la Tunisie, *etc.* (Supplément. Recueil des lois, décrets et règlements promulgués dans la Régence de Tunis du 1er janvier 1888 au 1er janvier 1896, par M. Caudel.) 1888, *etc.*   **5408. d. 2.**

—— Angleterre et Empire Britannique. 1908. *See* PERIODICAL PUBLICATIONS.—*Paris.* La Vie politique dans les deux mondes, *etc.* année 1. 1908, *etc.* 8°.
P.P. 3612. caa.

—— Nos libertés politiques. Origines — évolution — état actuel. pp. vii. 462. *Paris,* 1910. 8°.   **8050. ee. 22.**

—— Pour les étudiants étrangers en France. Notes, conseils, lectures. pp. x. 251. *Paris,* 1934. 8°.
8357. d. 45.

—— Les Premières invasions arabes dans l'Afrique du Nord. 21–78 H.—641–697 J.-C. pp. vi. 201. *Paris,* 1900. 8°. [*Bibliothèque d'archéologie africaine.* no. 3.]
07703. h. 56.

CAUDELL (ANDREW NELSON) Orthoptera of the Expedition [the Harriman Alaska Expedition]. 1904. *See* HARRIMAN (Edward H.) Harriman Alaska Series. vol. 8. 1901, *etc.* 8°.   **Ac. 1875/8.**

CAUDEMBERG (SCAEVOLA CHARLES GIRARD DE) *See* GIRARD DE CAUDEMBERG.

CAUDÉRAN (HIPPOLYTE) *See* NERSES, *Patriarch of Armenia, at Constantinople,* 1876. Promenade sur les bords de l'Euphrate, *etc.* [Edited by H. Caudéran.] 1891. 8°.   **10077. h. 26. (5.)**

—— Dialecte bordelais, essai grammatical. (Extrait des Actes de l'Académie impériale des Sciences, Belles-Lettres et Arts de Bordeaux.) pp. 64. *Paris,* 1861. 8°.
12953. df. 2. (10.)

—— Histoire de la sainte église de Bordeaux, sixième siècle, *etc.* pp. 249. *Toulouse,* 1878. 12°.   **4829. aa. 2.**

CAUDERLIER (ÉMILE) L'Alcoolisme en Belgique, *etc.* pp. 163. *Bruxelles,* 1893. 8°.   **8435. ee. 10.**

—— L'Évolution économique du xixe siècle. Angleterre, Belgique, France, États-Unis. pp. 246.   *Bruxelles,* 1903. 8°.   **8205. cc. 36.**

CAUDERLIER (Émile)

—— Une Excursion en Sicile. pp. 108. *Verviers*, [1884.] 8°.
10129. b. 4.

—— Petit dialogue dédié aux membres de la Ligue patriotique contre l'Alcoolisme. Le gin et le Congo. pp. xvi. 20. *Bruxelles*, 1895. 8°. **8436. g. 10.**

CAUDERLIER (Gustave) Les Lois de la population en France . . . Avec une préface par E. Levasseur. Avec Atlas de démographie statique et dynamique de 72 planches. pp. xix. 184. *Paris*, 1902. 8° & *obl.* fol.
1883. a. 4.

—— Les Lois de la population et leur application à la Belgique. pp. 572. *Bruxelles*, 1899. 8°. **8285. f. 41.**

—— *See* COSTE (A.) Les Lois de la population d'après M. G. Cauderlier, *etc.* 1901. 8°. **8226. t. 4.**

—— La Vérité sur l'émigration des travailleurs, et des capitaux belges dans la République Argentine . . . Deuxième édition, *etc.* pp. 64. *Bruxelles*, 1889. 8°.
8154. b. 12. (4.)

CAUDERLIER (Philippe)

—— Le Livre de la grosse et de la fine charcuterie française, belge, italienne, allemande et suisse. pp. 253. *Paris ; Bruxelles* [printed], [1878.] 8°. **7950. aa. 36.**

CAUDESAIGUES (Léopold) De la maladie de Basedow ou goître exophthalmique. pp. 42. *Paris*, 1872. 4°. [*Collection des thèses soutenues à la Faculté de Médecine de Paris.* An 1872. tom. 3.] **7373. n. 9.**

CAUDEVELLE (E. J.) L'Enseignement à Boulogne. *See* BOULOGNE-SUR-MER. Boulogne-sur-Mer et la région boulonnaise, *etc.* 1899. 8°. **10172. k. 9.**

CAUDIBILLA Y PERPIÑAN (   ) La Historia de Thobias, sacada de la Sagrada Escritura, y compuesta en octaua rima, *etc.* ff. 205. *S. Matevad : Barcelona*, 1615. 8°. **011451. e. 29.**

CAUDIER (Joseph) *See* FRANCE.—*Convention Nationale.* Observations sur un décret de la Convention . . . du 3 février 1793, qui a accordé des lettres de représailles au capitaine Caudier . . . contre les sieurs Pozzo, Boggiano, et autres habitans de Gênes. [1793.] 8°. **F. 808. (17.)**

CAUDILL (Rebecca)

—— Happy Little Family . . . Pictures by Decie Merwin. pp. 116. *John C. Winston Co.: Philadelphia, Toronto*, [1947.] 8°. **12827. h. 22.**

—— The House of the Fifers, *etc.* pp. 184. *Longmans, Green & Co.: New York*, 1954. 8°. **012826. k. 77.**

—— Saturday Cousins . . . Pictures by Nancy Woltemate. pp. vii. 120. *John C. Winston Co.: Philadelphia, Toronto*. [1953.] 8°. **12844. n. 13.**

—— Schoolhouse in the Woods . . . Pictures by Decie Merwin. pp. 120. *John C. Winston Co.: Philadelphia, Toronto*, [1949.] 8°. **12828. bbb. 93.**

—— Up and down the River . . . Pictures by Decie Merwin. pp. 115. *John C. Winston Co.: Philadelphia, Toronto*, [1951.] 8°. **12834. b. 13.**

CAUDILL (Watson G.) and **PERROS** (George P.)

—— Preliminary Inventory of the Records of the Joint Congressional Aviation Policy Board, 1947–48 . . . Compiled by W. G. Caudill and G. P. Perros. pp. v. 26. 1954. 4°. [*U.S. National Archives. Preliminary Inventories.* no. 74.] *See* UNITED STATES OF AMERICA.—*Congress.*—*Joint Congressional Aviation Policy Board.* **A.S. 288/9.**

CAUDINE FORKS. Le Forche Caudine illustrate. [Signed : F. D., i.e. Francisco Daniele.] 1778. fol. *See* D., F. **188. g. 5.**

—— Relation véritable et intéressante du Combat des Fourches Caudines livré à la place Maubert au sujet des Bouffons. pp. 15. [*Paris*,] 1753. 8°. **1103. b. 21. (22.)**

—— [Another copy.] Relation véritable et intéressante du Combat des Fourches Caudines, *etc.* [*Paris*,] 1753. 8°.
Hirsch 1. 498.

CAUDIVILLA SANTAREN DE ASTORGA (   ) *See* CAUDIBILLA Y PERPIÑAN (   )

CAUDLE, *Mrs.* Mrs. Caudle in Crinoline. [A folding brochure of coloured. plates by Thomas Onwhyn.] *W. H. J. Carter: London*, [1860 ?] 4°. **12316. aaa. 53.** *The plates bear the imprint : Rock & Co.: London.*

—— Mrs. Caudle's Changeable Faces. [A coloured lithograph, with a rotating card affixed.] *Mackenzie: London*, [1845.] *s. sh. obl.* fol. **1881. a. 3. (58.)**

CAUDLE DUET. The Caudle Duet . . . Versified from " Punch " [i.e. from Douglas Jerrold's " Mrs. Caudle's Curtain Lectures," contributed to " Punch "], expreslsy [*sic*] for the Rosherville Gardens, by Mr. Baron Nathan. *Office of the " Kentish Independent ": Gravesend*, [1845.] *s. sh.* fol. **1881. a. 3. (57.)**

CAUDLE (Frederick L.)

—— *See* FINCH (Vernor C.) Elementary Meteorology. By V. C. Finch . . . F. L. Caudle. [1942.] 8°. **8753. g. 5.**

—— *See* KNIGHT (Austin M.) Modern Seamanship . . . Chapters on weather prepared by F. L. Caudle. 1945. 8°.
08805. b. 28.

—— Workbook in Elementary Meteorology. pp. viii. 191. *McGraw-Hill Book Co.: New York, London*, [1945.] 8°.
8754. b. 41.

CAUDLE (Phoebe) *Widow, pseud.* The Precious Secret of Taming Husbands, discovered . . . By Phœbe Caudle, widow. Being an answer to the impertinent . . . pamphlet, entitled, " The Grand Secret of Wife-Taming," *etc.* pp. 16. *George Vickers: London*, [1858.] 8°.
8415. g. 10.

CAUDLE (Robert) Our Trip to the Great Exhibition. [A religious tract.] pp. 12. *George Herbert: Dublin*, 1863. 12°. [MISSING.]

CAUDLE (Rodney Duane) and **CLARK** (George Bromley)

—— Stresses around Mine Openings in some Simple Geologic Structures. pp. 41. *Urbana*, 1955. 4°. [*University of Illinois Engineering Experiment Station. Bulletin.* no. 430.]
Ac. 2692. u/4.

CAUDMONT (Oscar Philippe) Sur les engorgements de la prostate. pp. 64. *Paris*, 1847. 4°. [*Collection des thèses soutenues à la Faculté de Médecine de Paris.* An 1847. tom. 3.] **7372. a. 11.**

CAUDRI (C. M. Bramine)

—— The Larger Foraminifera from San Juan de Los Morros, State of Guarico, Venezuela. pp. 54. pl. 5. *Ithaca*, 1944. 8°. [*Bulletins of American Paleontology.* vol. 28. no. 114.] Ac. 2692. g/12.

CAUDRILLIER (G.) *See* MARION (M.) Département de la Gironde. Documents relatifs à la vente des biens nationaux. Publiés par M. Marion . . . J. Benzacar . . . Caudrillier. 1911, *etc.* 8°. [*Collection de documents inédits sur l'histoire économique de la Révolution française.*] **9231. s. 23.**

—— La Trahison de Pichegru et les intrigues royalistes dans l'Est avant Fructidor. pp. lxii. 402. *Paris*, 1908. 8°.
09231. l. 13.

CAUDRON (C. A. D. F.) Tableau historique et description générale de la maladie décrite sous le nom d'anémie, et qui a attaqué tous les ouvriers d'une galerie d'une mine de charbon de terre en exploitation à Fresnes, département du Nord. Thèse, *etc.* pp. 21. *Paris*, 1818. 4°.
1183. e. 3. (22.)

CAUDRON (Eugène) Des adénomes de l'utérus et de leur traitement. pp. 62. *Paris*, 1873. 4°. [*Collection des thèses soutenues à la Faculté de Médecine de Paris.* An 1873. tom. 5.] 7373. o.

CAUDRON (P. Aug.) Dissertation sur la péripneumonie inflammatoire, *etc.* pp. 32. *Paris*, 1815. 4°.
1183. c. 8. (14.)

CAUDULLO (Antonino) La Musica nei poemi omerici in rapporto alla quistione omerica. pp. 104. *Catania*, 1905. 8°. 11315. p. 6.

CAU-DURBAN (David) *See* Toulouse.—*Basoche du Sénéchal.* Statuts de la Basoche du Sénéchal de Toulouse, par M. l'abbé Cau-Durban. 1903. 4°. [MISSING.]

—— Abbaye du Mas-d'Azil, monographie et cartulaire 817–1774. pp. 210. *Foix*, 1896. 8°. 4630. dd. 7.

—— La Période révolutionnaire à Castelnau-Durban. pp. 56. *Foix*, 1892. 8°. 9008. g. 11. (7.)

CAUDWELL'S TEMPERANCE AND ALLIANCE ALMANAC. *See* Ephemerides.

CAUDWELL (Christopher) *pseud.* [i.e. Christopher Saint John Sprigg.] *See also* Sprigg (C. St. J.)

—— The Crisis in Physics . . . Edited with an introduction by Professor H. Levy. pp. xvi. 245. *John Lane: London*, 1939. 8°. 2244. c. 5.

—— Further Studies in a Dying Culture . . . Edited and with a preface by Edgell Rickword. pp. 256. *Bodley Head: London*, 1949. 8°. 012357. f. 75.

—— Illusion and Reality. A study of the sources of poetry. pp. xiv. 351. *Macmillan & Co.: London*, 1937. 8°. 08459. f. 69.

—— Illusion and Reality. A study of the sources of poetry. (New edition.) pp. 342. *Lawrence & Wishart: London*, 1946. 8°. 11867. c. 7.

—— This my Hand. [A novel.] pp. 319. *Hamish Hamilton: London*, 1936. 8°. NN. 25300.

—— Studies in a Dying Culture, *etc.* pp. xxv. 228. *John Lane: London*, 1938. 8°. 12358. e. 24.

CAUDWELL (Francis) The Cross in Dark Places and among all Sorts and Conditions. Recollections of thirty years work in North and East London. pp. vii. 144. *Wells Gardner & Co.: London*, 1903. 8°. 4192. b. 54.

—— Handbook for Mission Workers, *etc.* pp. 32. *E. Longhurst: London*, [1874.] 16°. 4136. a. 53.

—— [Another copy.] 4192. a. 55.

CAUDWELL (Francis William Hugh)

—— *See* Duguid (Charles) *City Editor of " The Morning Post."* How to Read the Money Article . . . Revised by F. W. H. Caudwell, *etc.* 1931. 8°. 8224. ee. 30.

—— A Practical Guide to Investment. A review of the comparative merits of all types of British stock exchange securities. pp. 165. *Effingham Wilson: London*, 1930. 8°. 8224. ee. 11.

CAUDWELL (Francis William Hugh)

—— A Preface to Mining Investment. pp. 57. *Effingham Wilson: London*, 1929. 8°. 8224. aaa. 22.

CAUDWELL (Francis William Hugh) and **GRIFFITH** (*Sir* Elis Arundell Ellis) *Bart.*

—— Stock Market Forces. A preface to speculative investment, *etc.* pp. x. 132. *Methuen & Co.: London*, 1932. 8°. 8224. p. 41.

CAUDWELL (Hugo)

—— The Creative Impulse in Writing and Painting. pp. x. 162. pl. XII. *Macmillan & Co.: London*, 1951. 8°. 7813. de. 38.

—— Introduction to French Classicism. pp. ix. 255. *Macmillan & Co.: London*, 1931. 8°. 11822. s. 11.

CAUDWELL (Irene) All about Ceremonies. A description of some ceremonies of the Church. pp. 85. *Society of SS. Peter & Paul: London*, 1923. 8°. 3478. aa. 51.

—— Bethlehem Tableaux. pp. viii. 24. *Faith Press: London*, 1938. 8°. 11782. bb. 35.

—— " By Thy Cross and Passion." A sacred drama. pp. 44. *Faith Press: London*, 1927. 8°. 011779. ff. 111.

—— " By Thy Glorious Resurrection." A sacred drama. pp. viii. 63. *Faith Press: London*, 1939. 8°. 11782. bb. 72.

—— " By Thy Holy Nativity." A sacred drama. pp. ix. 53. *Faith Press: London*, 1932. 8°. 011781. h. 92.

—— The Care of God's House. Cleaning and preparing the church for worship. pp. 76. *Faith Press: London*, 1943. 8°. 3477. bbb. 63.

—— Ceremonies of Holy Church. Simple explanations. pp. 137. *Faith Press: London*, 1948. 8°. 3479. aa. 44.

—— The Christ Child. A children's nativity play. pp. 20. *Faith Press: London*, 1946. 8°. 11783. a. 36.

—— " Come Ye to Bethlehem." A Nativity play. pp. viii. 47. *Faith Press: London*, 1936. 8°. 011779. k. 120.

—— Come Ye to Calvary. A sacred drama. pp. xi. 59. *Faith Press: London*, 1937. 8°. 011779. k. 137.

—— Damien, the Leper Saint, 1840–1889. pp. xi. 187. *Philip Allan: London*, 1931. 8°. 4865. f. 38.

—— Down Our Way. A comedy in one act. pp. 16. *Mothers' Union:* [*London*, 1937.] 8°. 11783. aa. 57.

—— Flowers in Church. A practical handbook for church decorators. pp. vii. 95. *A. R. Mowbray & Co.: London & Oxford*, [1932.] 8°. 3474. a. 27.

—— Golgotha. A passion play in the words of Holy Scripture. pp. xii. 59. *Faith Press: London*, 1938. 8°. 011781. f. 60.

—— Helps by the Way. Aids to public and private devotion. pp. 88. *Faith Press: London*, 1935. 12°. 4403. de. 51.

—— In the Morning. Thoughts for the sick & wounded. [An anthology in verse and prose.] Compiled by I. Caudwell. *Society of SS. Peter & Paul: London*, 1915. 16°. 11603. de. 34.

CAUDWELL (IRENE)

—— The Iscariot. A sacred drama. pp. viii. 56.   *Faith Press: London*, 1944. 8°.   **11783**. aaa. **38**.

—— Lord of the Ages. A sacred play illustrating the Church's teaching on the Blessed Sacrament. pp. 48. *Universities' Mission to Central Africa: London*, [1930.] 8°.
          011781. eee. **101**.

—— The Mystic Tree. A mystery play. pp. 31.   *G.F.S. Central Office: London*, 1921. 8°.   **011779**. ff. **112**.
With a typewritten sheet of " Suggested Additions."

—— The Passion in Daily Life. pp. 79.   *Faith Press: London*, 1938. 8°.   **4225**. df. **62**.

—— Passiontide Tableaux. pp. 30.   *Faith Press: London*, 1936. 8°.   **11780**. c. **3**.

—— The Pepper-Pot Church: St. Anne's, Wandsworth. [With plates.] pp. 60.   *Faith Press: Leighton Buzzard*, [1947.] 8°.   **07816**. i. **69**.

—— Simon Peter. A sacred drama on the Passion. pp. x. 61. *Faith Press: London*, 1934. 8°.
          011779. k. **6**.

—— Twenty Questions on Flowers in Church. Answered by I. Caudwell. pp. 24.   *A. R. Mowbray & Co.: London & Oxford*, 1950. 8°. [*Twenty Questions Series.* no. 8.]
          W.P. **3885/8**.

CAUDWELL (JOB) Caudwell's Temperance & Alliance Almanac. *See* EPHEMERIDES.

—— Job Caudwell's Threepenny Pledge Book for the Pocket, *etc.* [Ruled blank leaves for signatures, etc.] *Job Caudwell: London*, [1865.] obl. 16°.   **8435**. a. **1**.

—— Vegetarian Cookery for the Million, *etc.* pp. 16. *Job Caudwell: London*, [1864.] 16°.   **7953**. aa. **16**.

—— (Second edition.) pp. 16.   *Job Caudwell: London*, [1865.] 16°.   **7955**. a. **46**. (**11**.)

—— (Third edition.) pp. 16.   *Job Caudwell: London*, [1865.] 16°.   **7955**. a. **46**. (**12**.)

—— (Fourth edition.) pp. 16.   *Job Caudwell: London*, [1865.] 16°.   **7954**. aa. **22**.

—— (Fifth edition.) pp. 16.   *Job Caudwell: London*, [1865.] 16°.   **7954**. aa. **23**.

—— (Sixth edition.) pp. 16.   *Job Caudwell: London*, [1865.] 16°.   **7954**. aa. **24**.

CAUDWELL (LEONARD VERNON) *See* FORD (Herbert G.) and CAUDWELL (L. V.) An Elementary Latin Exercise Book. 1911. 8°.   **12934**. dd. **31**.

CAUDWELL (O.) Aero Engines. For pilots and ground engineers. pp. vii. 112. *Sir I. Pitman & Sons: London*, 1940. 8°.   **08770**. aaa. **21**.

—— [A reissue.] Aero Engines, *etc. London*, 1941. 8°.
          8772. a. **12**.

—— Aero Engines. Overhaul, testing and installation for ground engineers. pp. vii. 111. *Sir I. Pitman & Sons: London*, 1942. 8°.   **8772**. a. **18**.

CAUDWELL (VERA) The Sole Condition. pp. 318. *John Long: London*, 1926. 8°.   NN. **11959**

CAUDWELL (W.) La Politique générale européenne en Afrique. [With a map.] pp. 186. *Paris*, 1912. 8°.
          08026. b. **2**.

CAUÉ (ANTONIO RENIU Y)   *See* RENIU Y CAUÉ.

CAUER (CARL) *See* CAUER (E.) Cauer-Album. [Eight photographs of statues by Emil, Carl and Robert Cauer.] [1870.] 4°.   **7875**. dd. **4**.

CAUER (EDUARD) *See* CAUER (Paul E.)

CAUER (EMIL) Cauer-Album. [Eight photographs of statues by Emil, Carl and Robert Cauer.]   *Cassel*, [1870.] 4°.   **7875**. dd. **4**.
Wanting the wrapper.

CAUER (FRIEDRICH) De fabulis græcis ad Romam conditam pertinentibus. pp. 34. *Berolini*, 1884. 8°.
          11840. k. **41**. (**4**.)

—— Ciceros politisches Denken. Ein Versuch. pp. vi. 148. *Berlin*, 1903. 8°.   **8009**. e. **35**.

—— Hat Aristoteles die Schrift vom Staate der Athener geschrieben? *etc.* pp. 78. *Stuttgart*, 1891. 8°.
          11312. bbbb. **19**.

—— Parteien und Politiker in Megara und Athen. Studien zur Geschichte Griechenlands im Zeitalter der Tyrannis. pp. 97. *Stuttgart*, 1890. 8°.   **9004**. l. **34**. (**9**.)

—— Philotas, Kleitos, Kallisthenes. Beiträge zur Geschichte Alexanders des Grossen. 1893. *See* PERIODICAL PUBLICATIONS.—*Leipsic.* Jahrbücher für Philologie und Pädagogik, *etc.* Neue Folge der Supplemente. Bd. 20. Hft. 1. 1855, *etc.* 8°.   [MISSING.]

—— Die römische Aeneassage von Naevius bis Vergilius. 1886. *See* PERIODICAL PUBLICATIONS.—*Leipsic.* Jahrbücher für Philologie und Pädagogik, *etc.* Neue Folge der Supplemente. Bd. 15. Hft. 1. 1855, *etc.* 8°.
          [MISSING.]

CAUER (LUDWIG) [For reports, etc., of the school directed by L. Cauer:] *See* BERLIN.—*Cauersche Erziehungs-Anstalt zu Charlottenburg.*

CAUER (MINNA) *See* ERZIEHUNG. Nationale und humanistische Erziehung! von K. v. Kalckstein, M. Cauer und A. Eulenburg. 1891. [*Deutsche Schriften für nationales Leben.* Reihe 1.]   **12250**. l. **1**.

CAUER (PAUL) *See also* LOGANDER (L.) *pseud.* [i.e. P. Cauer.]

—— *See* HOMER. [*Odyssey.—Greek.*]   Homeri Odyssea scholarum in usum edidit P. Cauer. 1886, *etc.* 8°.
          11305. bbb. **17**. (**1**.)

—— *See* HOMER. [*Odyssey.—Greek.*]   Ὁμήρου Ὀδύσσεια . . . Edidit P. Cauer. 1890. 8°.   **11315**. c. **41**.

—— Anmerkungen zur Odyssee. Für den Gebrauch der Schüler. 4 Hft. *Berlin*, 1894–97. 8°.   **11335**. bb. **67**.

—— Aus Beruf und Leben. Heimgebrachtes. pp. xii. 352. *Berlin*, 1912. 8°.   **012354**. ff. **22**.

—— De dialecto attica vetustiore quaestionum epigraphicarum pars prior. 1875. *See* CURTIUS (G.) Studien zur griechischen und lateinischen Grammatik, *etc.* Bd. 8. Hft. 1, *etc.* 1868, *etc.* 8°.   **2274**. d. **14**.

—— Delectus inscriptionum graecarum propter dialectum memorabilium. pp. xxiv. 176. *Lipsiae*, 1877. 8°.
          7704. c. **25**.

—— [Another edition.] Iterum composuit P. Cauer. pp. xvi. 365. *Lipsiae*, 1883. 8°.   **7704**. c. **33**.

—— [Another edition.] pp. xvi. 373. *Lipsiae*, 1883. 8°.
          7706.aaa.49.

CAUER (Paul)

—— [Another edition.] Dialectorum graecarum exempla epigraphica potiora. 'Delectus inscriptionum graecarum propter dialectum memorabilium' . . . editio tertia reno- vata. Edidit Eduardus Schwyzer. pp. xvi. 463. *Lipsiae*, 1923. 8º. [Missing.]

—— Die dorischen Futur- und Aoristbildungen der abge- leiteten Verba auf -ζω. *See* Leipsic.—*Grammatische Ge- sellschaft.* Sprachwissenschaftliche Abhandlungen, *etc.* 1874. 8º. Ac. 9828.

—— Grammatica militans. Erfahrungen und Wünsche im Gebiete des lateinischen und griechischen Unterrichtes. pp. 168. *Berlin*, 1898. 8º. 12924. m. 6.

—— Grundfragen der Homerkritik. pp. 321. *Leipzig,* 1895. 8º. 11315. h. 34.

—— Zweite, stark erweiterte und zum Teil umgearbeitete Auflage. pp. viii. 552. *Leipzig*, 1909. 8º. 11315. n. 16.

—— Dritte umgearbeitete und erweiterte Auflage. pp. viii. 709. *Leipzig*, 1923. 8º. 11313. r. 36.

—— Die Kunst des Übersetzens. Ein Hilfsbuch für den lateinischen und griechischen Unterricht . . . Fünfte, vermehrte und verbesserte Auflage, *etc.* pp. viii. 178. *Berlin*, 1914. 8º. 011824. aaa. 3.

—— *See* Tolman (Herbert C.) The Art of Translating. With special reference to Cauer's Die Kunst des Uebersetzens. 1901. 8º. 012901. ff. 58.

—— Palaestra vitae. Eine neue Aufgabe des altklassischen Unterrichtes. pp. viii. 156. *Berlin*, 1902. 8º. 11312. t. 8.

—— Dritte, vielfach verbesserte Auflage. pp. x. 181. *Berlin*, 1913. 8º. 11313. bb. 31.

—— Quaestiones de pronominum personalium formis et usu homerico. 1875. *See* Curtius (G.) Studien zur griechischen und lateinischen Grammatik, *etc.* Bd. 7. Hft. 1. 1868, *etc.* 8º. 2274. d. 14.

—— Walther Rathenaus staatsbürgerliches Programm. Dar- stellung und Kritik. pp. 72. *Berlin*, 1918. 8º. 08072. b. 25.

—— Wort- und Gedankenspiele in den Oden des Horaz. pp. 59. *Kiel & Leipzig*, 1892. 8º. 11312. p. 4. (14.)

CAUER (Paul Eduard) De Karolo Martello. Dissertatio inauguralis, *etc.* pp. 75. *Berolini*, [1846.] 8º. 10660. b. 18.

—— Friedrich der Grosse und das classische Alterthum. *See* Breslau.—*Wissenschaftlicher Verein.* Herrn Professor Dr. Friedrich Haase wünschen Glück . . . die Mitglieder des Wissenschaftlichen Vereins in Breslau, *etc.* 1863. 4º. 8356. h. 3. (2.)

—— Friedrichs des Grossen Gedanken über die fürstliche Gewalt. pp. 31. *Berlin*, 1863. 8º. 8006. cc. 15.

—— Friedrich des Grossen Grundsätze über Erziehung und Unterricht. pp. 26. *Danzig*, 1873. 4º. 787. h. 62. (4.)

—— Quaestionum de fontibus ad Agesilai historiam perti- nentibus pars prior. pp. 93. *Vratislaviae*, 1847. 8º. 11312. f. 27. (1.)

—— Ueber die Cæsares des Kaisers Julianus Apostata. pp. 48. *Breslau*, 1856. 4º. 10605. g. 15.

CAUER (Paul Eduard)

—— Über die Flugschriften Friedrichs des Grossen aus der Zeit des siebenjährigen Krieges. pp. 64. *Potsdam,* 1865. 8º. 8073. dd. 36. (4.)

—— Über die Urform einiger Rhapsodien der Ilias. pp. 55. *Berlin*, 1850. 8º. 11315. f. 30. (2.)

—— Zum Andenken an Gotthold Ephraim Lessing, *etc.* pp. 26. *Berlin*, 1881. 8º. 10708. d. 4. (1.)

—— Zur Geschichte und Charakteristik Friedrichs des Grossen. Vermischte Aufsätze . . . Mit einer Lebens- beschreibung des Verfassers von Ernst Hermann. pp. vi. 392. *Breslau*, 1883. 8º. 10704. g. 17.

CAUER (Robert) *See* Cauer (E.) Cauer-Album. [Eight photographs of statues by Emil, Carl and Robert Cauer.] [1870.] 4º. 7875. dd. 4.

CAUERSCHE ERZIEHUNGS-ANSTALT ZU CHARLOTTENBURG. *See* Berlin.

CAUËT (Fernand) *See* Barrès (A. M.) L'Esprit de Barrès. Pages choisies avec une introduction par F. Cauët. 1938. 8º. 12238. bbb. 3.

—— *See* Bornecque (H.) and Cauët (F.) Le Dictionnaire latin-français du baccalauréat. 1936. 4º. 012933. bbb. 25.

—— "Le Beffroi," 1900. Revues et régionalisme. (Discours de réception de M. le docteur M.-N. Secret à l'Académie d'Amiens et réponse de M. Fernand Cauët.) pp. 87. *Paris*, 1932. 8º. 11878.de.7.

—— Les Poésies de Paul Bourget. Discours, *etc.* pp. 36. *Amiens*, 1926. 8º. 11825. aa. 41.

CAUËT (S.) Notes sur le dernier duc de Bouillon et les manuscrits qu'il a laissés. pp. 56. *Évreux,* 1900. 8º. 010663. h. 55.

CAUFAPÉ (Anicet) Nouvelle explication de la gangrène, proposée et demandée par Messieurs de l'Académie de Paris dans leur Journal du mois de février de l'année présente. pp. 112. *J. Boude: Toulouse*, 1681. 12º. 783. c. 19.

—— Nouvelle explication des fièvres ; avec des observations singulières sur les matières les plus importantes pour bien exercer la médecine. Seconde édition. Reveuë, corrigée & augmentée, *etc.* pp. 492. *D. Desclassan: Toulouse,* 1696. 12º. 1166. d. 14. *Imperfect; wanting tom. 2, which was published under the title "Réflexions singulières sur le fréquent usage de la saignée, etc."*

CAUFEYNON ( ) *Docteur, pseud.* [i.e. Jean Fauconney.] L'Eunuchisme. Histoire générale de la castration, *etc.* pp. 226. *Paris*, [1903.] 8º. *The titlepage is mutilated.* 7641. aaa. 46.

CAUFLEY ( ) *Lady, Wife of Sir Hugh Caulveley. See* Caulveley.

CAUFUNGERUS (Georgius) *See* Melanchthon (P.) [*Separate Works.*] Ioannis Magiri . . . Anthropologia, hoc est: Commentarius . . . in Philippi Melanchthonis libellum de anima completus & locupletatus operâ G. Caufungeri. 1603. 8º. 784. b. 9.

CAUGHEY (James) *See* Baxter (Richard) [*Selections.*] A Sinner's Prayer. By S. Stevenson. [Extracts from the works of R. Baxter and J. Caughey.] [1905.] 12º. 3457. k. 7.

—— Arrows from my Quiver . . . Selected from the private papers of Rev. J. Caughey. With an introduction by Rev. Daniel Wise. pp. 477. *W. C. Palmer, Jr.: New York*, 1868. 8º. 3755. aaa. 4.

CAUGHEY (JAMES)

—— Earnest Christianity illustrated; or, Selections from the journal of the Rev. J. Caughey . . . With a brief sketch of Mr. Caughey's life, by John Unwin. pp. 406. *Partridge & Co.: London*, 1857. 8°. **4985. b. 28.**

—— Glimpses of Life in Soul-saving; or, Selections from the journal and other writings of the Rev. J. Caughey. With an introduction by Rev. Daniel Wise. pp. 477. *W. C. Palmer, Jr.: New York*, 1868. 8°. **3755. aaa. 5.**

—— Letters on various subjects. [With a portrait.] 5 vol. *Simpkin, Marshall & Co.: London*, 1844–47. 8°. **1369. a. 16.**

—— Report of a Farewell Sermon delivered in the Methodist New Connexion Chapel . . . Nottingham, by the Rev. J. Caughey . . . To which is added, an epitome of his farewell address at Sheffield, and an account of his embarkation at Liverpool. pp. 20. *R. Sutton: Nottingham*, 1847. 12°. **4485. b. 33. (4.)**

—— Revival Miscellanies; containing twelve revival sermons, and thoughts on entire sanctification, revival preaching . . . Twenty-fourth thousand. pp. 420. *J. Ainsworth: Manchester; Houlston & Stoneman: London*, [1854.] 12°. **4407. e. 53.**

Published in parts.

—— (Fifteenth edition.) Edited by the Rev. Ralph W. Allen & the Rev. Daniel Wise. pp. 177. *W. B. King: London; E. Squire: Louth*, 1854. 8°. [*The Revivalist.* vol. 2.] **P.P. 718. c.**

—— Revival Sermons and Addresses. pp. iv. 332. *R. D. Dickinson: London*, 1891. 8°. **4478. dd. 17.**

—— A Voice from America; or, Four sermons . . . Reported by a Manchester Minister. Second edition, *etc.* [The editor's preface signed: A. W.] pp. 48. *James Ainsworth: Manchester*, 1847. 12°. **4485. a. 13. (1.)**

—— A Second Voice from America; or Four sermons . . . Second edition. [The editor's preface signed: A. W.] pp. 56. *J. Ainsworth: Manchester*, 1848. 12°. **4485. a. 13. (2.)**

—— The Third Voice from America, *etc.* pp. 60. *J. Ainsworth: Manchester*, 1849. 12°. **4485. a. 13. (3.)**

—— A Brief Memoir of the Labours, and a Vindication of the Character and Call of the Rev. J. Caughey: including a critical examination of the resolution of the Wesleyan Conference, and of the President's declaration prohibitory of his labours. By "A Wesleyan Methodist." pp. 81. *Simpkin Marshall & Co.: London*, 1847. 8°. **1373. e. 14.**

CAUGHEY (JOHN) Aspirations and Achievements, *etc.* pp. 87. *Elliot Stock: London*, 1934. 8°. **04402. h. 94.**

CAUGHEY (JOHN WALTON)

—— *See* BOLTON (Herbert E.) and CAUGHEY (J. W.) Chronicles of California. [General editors: H. E. Bolton and J. W. Caughey.] 1948, *etc.* 8°, *etc.* **W.P. 14208.**

—— *See* HARVEY (Rowland H.) Robert Owen: social idealist . . . Edited, with a foreword by J. W. Caughey. 1949. 8°. [*University of California Publications in History.* vol. 38.] **Ac. 2689. g/11.**

—— *See* RICE (William B.) The Los Angeles Star, 1851–1864 . . . Edited by J. W. Caughey. 1947. 8°. **11867. ff. 18.**

CAUGHEY (JOHN WALTON)

—— *See* WARE (Joseph E.) The Emigrants' Guide to California . . . With introduction and notes by J. Caughey. 1932. 8°. **10413. n. 14/4.**

—— Bernardo de Gálvez in Louisiana, 1776–1783. [With a portrait and a bibliography.] pp. xii. 290. *Berkeley*, 1934. 8°. [*Publications of the University of California at Los Angeles in Social Sciences.* vol. 4.] **Ac. 2689. g/42.**

—— [Another copy.] **08355. f. 16.** *One of twenty-five copies printed on rag paper.*

—— California. [With plates.] pp. xiv. 680. *Prentice-Hall: New York*, 1940. 8°. **10413. p. 22.**

—— California . . . Second edition. (Second printing.) pp. xii. 666. *Prentice-Hall: New York*, 1954. 8°. **9617. ee. 16.** *Part of the " Prentice-Hall History Series."*

—— Gold is the Cornerstone . . . With vignettes by W. R. Cameron. [On the discovery of gold in California, 1848, and its consequences.] pp. xvi. 321. *University of California Press: Berkeley & Los Angeles*, 1948. 8°. [*Chronicles of California.*] **W.P. 14208/1.**

—— Hubert Howe Bancroft, Historian of the West. [With plates, including portraits.] pp. ix. 422. *University of California Press: Berkeley & Los Angeles*, 1946. 8°. **10890. c. 3.**

—— Rushing for Gold. Edited by J. W. Caughey. [Papers by various authors.] pp. 111. *University of California Press: Berkeley & Los Angeles*, 1949. 8°. [*Pacific Coast Branch of the American Historical Association. Special Publication.* no. 1.] **Ac. 8504. c/2.**

CAUGHEY (ROBERT ANDREW) Reinforced Concrete. pp. viii. 292. *Chapman & Hall: London; printed in U.S.A.*, 1937. 8°. **08770. d. 26.**

CAUGHIE (DAVID) *See* PERIODICAL PUBLICATIONS.— *London.* The Glasgow Infant School Magazine. Compiled by D. Caughie, *etc.* 1869. 24°. **P.P. 1163. df.**

CAUGHT. Caught Napping. [A satire on the ritual of the Church of England.] pp. 31. *G. J. Palmer: London*, 1866. 8°. [MISSING.]

—— Fourth edition. pp. 32. *G. J. Palmer: London*, 1875. 16°. [MISSING.]

CAUJOLE (PAUL) Les Tribulations d'une ambulance française en Perse. Ouvrage illustré de 48 photographies. pp. 180. *Paris*, 1922. 8°. **09084. b. 53.**

CAUJOLLE (JEAN BAPTISTE) Quelques considérations sur la sympathie qui règne entre le système cutané et les autres systèmes de l'économie vivante. Essai, *etc.* pp. 23. *Toulouse*, [1802.] 4°. **1180. d. 14. (11.)**

CAUKERCKEN (LOUIS VAN) *See* DILIS (E.) Louis van Caukercken, chroniquer anversois, et son livre de raison. 1911. 8°. [*Annales de l'Académie Royale d'Archéologie de Belgique.* sér. 6. tom. 3.] **Ac. 5513.**

CAULAINCOURT (ARMAND AUGUSTIN LOUIS DE) *Duke of Vicenza. See* BERVILLE (Saint-Albin) and BARRIÈRE (J. F.) Collection des mémoires relatifs à la Révolution française. (Examen impartial des calomnies répandues sur M. de Caulaincourt à l'occasion de la catastrophe de Monseigneur le duc d'Enghien.) 1821, *etc.* 8°. **910. f. 16.**

CAULAINCOURT (ARMAND AUGUSTIN LOUIS DE) *Duke of Vicenza.*

—— *See* LOUIS ANTONY HENRY [de Bourbon Condé], *Duke d'Enghien.* De l'assassinat de Monseigneur le duc d'Enghien et de la justification de Monsieur de Caulaincourt, *etc.* [With the text of the article defending Caulaincourt, published in the Journal des Débats, 26 April 1814.] 1814. 8º. R. 16*. (21.)

—— —— 1814. 8º. 8052. k. 11. (2.)

—— —— 1814. 8º. R. 16*. (22.)

—— *See* NICHOLAS MIKHAILOVICH, *Grand Duke of Russia.* Les Relations diplomatiques de la Russie et de la France, d'après les rapports des ambassadeurs d'Alexandre [Prince A. B. Kurakin] et de Napoléon [A. A. L. de Caulaincourt, and John Law of Lauriston], *etc.* 1905, *etc.* 8º. 9075. i. 3.

—— Mémoires du général de Caulaincourt, duc de Vicence, Grand Écuyer de l'Empereur. Introduction et notes de Jean Hanoteau. [With portraits.] 3 tom. *Paris,* 1933. 8º. 10655. r. 5.

—— Memoirs of General de Caulaincourt, Duke of Vicenza, 1812–1813. Edited by Jean Hanoteau. Translated by Hamish Miles. (Memoirs of General de Caulaincourt, 1814. Translated by George Libaire.) [With a portrait.] 2 vol. *Cassell & Co.: London,* 1935. 8º. 010665. ff. 28.

—— Memoirs of General de Caulaincourt, Duke of Vicenza . . . Edited by Jean Hanoteau. (Vol. 1, 2, translated by Hamish Miles. Vol. 3 translated by George Libair.) 3 vol. *Cassell & Co.: London,* 1950. 8º. [*Cassell's Pocket Library.*] **012213.n.2/4.**

—— Souvenirs du duc de Vicence recueillis et publiés [or rather, written] par Charlotte de Sor . . . Deuxième édition. 2 tom. *Paris,* 1837. 8º. 1201. h. 23.

—— Recollections of Caulaincourt, Duke of Vicenza. [A translation of " Souvenirs du duc de Vicence recueillis et publiés par Charlotte de Sor."] 2 vol. *Henry Colburn: London,* 1838. 12º. 1201. h. 24.

—— [Another copy.] 20098. c. 6.

CAULAIS (JACQUES) Couleur du temps. [Verses.] pp. 175. *Paris,* 1938. 8º. 11484. a. 34.

CAULDRON. The Cauldron. *See* PARSONS (C. H.) and BROTHER.

CAULDWELL (JAMES)

—— Priscilla's Birthday. [A tale for children.] *Brockhampton Press: Leicester,* 1953. 16º. 12830. a. 155.

—— Two Little Chums. *Brockhampton Press: Leicester,* 1953. 16º. 12830. a. 154.

CAULERY (JEAN)

—— *See* BECKER (G.) Jean Caulery et ses chansons spirituelles . . . Avec la musique d'une chanson. 1880. 12º. Hirsch 2244. (2.)

CAULÈS (JEAN BAPTISTE) Dissertation sur la pleurésie, *etc.* pp. 22. *Paris,* 1809. 4º. 1182. h. 4. (3.)

CAULET (ÉTIENNE FRANÇOIS DE) *Bishop of Pamiers. See* CAULET (François E. de)

CAULET (EUGÈNE ERNEST JULIEN) Remarques sur un cas de péri-oesophagite. pp. 34. *Paris,* 1864. 4º. [*Collection des thèses soutenues à la Faculté de Médecine de Paris.* An 1864. tom. 2.] 7373. e. 13.

CAULET (FRANÇOIS ÉTIENNE DE) *Bishop of Pamiers. See* DOUBLET (G.) François de Caulet . . . et la vie ecclésiastique dans un diocèse ariégeois, *etc.* 1896. 8º. 4864. ff. 12.

—— *See* DOUBLET (G.) Un Prélat janséniste, F. de Caulet, *etc.* 1895. 8º. 4864. ee. 6.

—— *See* PAVILLON (N.) *Bishop of Alet.* Lettre circulaire écrite en 1668, par Messeigneurs les Évêques d'Alet, de Pamiez, de Beauvais et d'Angers à Messeigneurs les Archevêques et Évêques de France. Sur le dessein que la Cour de Rome avoit de leur faire faire leur procès contre la disposition des SS. Canons, *etc.* 1704. 12º. [*INQUISITION, Tribunal of.—States of the Church.* Avis sincères aux Catholiques des Provinces-Unies sur le decret d'Inquisition de Rome contre M. l'Archevêque de Sebaste, *etc.* pt. 2.] 1016. l. 27.

—— *See* PORT ROYAL, *Abbey of.* Vie des quatres évesques engagés dans la cause de Port-Royal, M. d'Alet . . . M. de Pamiers, *etc.* 1756. 12º. 4864. bb. 16.

—— *See* VIDAL (J. M.) Documents sur M. de Caulet, évêque de Pamiers, *etc.* 1936. 8º. 20009. d. 16.

—— *See* VIDAL (J. M.) Histoire des évêques de Pamiers. (5. F.-E. de Caulet.) 1926, *etc.* 8º. 20011. d. 30.

CAULET (JEAN DE) *Bishop of Grenoble.*

—— *See* BASSETTE (L.) Jean de Caulet, Évêque et Prince de Grenoble, 1693–1771, *etc.* [With a portrait.] 1946. 4º. 4869. c. 2.

CAULEY (MARY WINIFRED) The Science and Art of Home-making. pp. viii. 312. *American Book Co.: New York,* [1935.] 8º. 7943. t. 41.

CAULFEILD (ALFRED HANS WARING) Tuberculosis. *See* FITZGERALD (John G.) An Introduction to the Practice of Preventive Medicine, *etc.* 1927. 8º. 07305. m. 38.

CAULFEILD (ALGERNON SAINT GEORGE) The Temple of the Kings at Abydos. Sety I. . . . With drawings by H. L. Christie and a chapter by W. M. Flinders Petrie. pp. iv. 23. pl. xxvi. *London,* 1902. 4º. [*Egyptian Research Account.* Eighth year, 1902.] **7700.d.8.**

CAULFEILD (*Mrs.* C. T.) *See* EDGE, afterwards CAULFEILD (Kathleen M.)

CAULFEILD (CHARLES) *Bishop of Nassau. See* FREKE (James) A Sermon preached . . . at the Consecration of . . . C. Caulfeild . . . as first Bishop of Nassau. 1861. 8º. 4477. e. 29.

—— Apostolic Doctrine and Fellowship: a sermon. pp. 16. *W. E. Painter: London,* [1843.] 8º. 1355. d. 10. (3.)

—— The Fall of Babylon, as exhibited in prophecy. pp. xii. 244. *John Robertson: Dublin,* 1839. 8º. 1113. b. 29.

CAULFEILD (EDWARD WARREN) The Genius of Christianity according to Scripture, applied by way of test to professing Churches. pp. viii. 209. *Noyes & Son: Bath,* 1864. 12º. 4375. bb. 11.

CAULFEILD (EDWIN TOBY) The Advent, Kingdom, and Divinity of the Messiah, demonstrated in a plain and scriptural exposition of the Sacred Text. pp. xvi. 202. *J. Hatchard & Son: London,* 1825. 12º. 862. k. 25.

—— Church Reform: a letter to . . . Lord John Russell. pp. 30. *J. Nisbet & Co.: London,* 1851. 8º. 4107. d. 18.

CAULFEILD (Edwin Toby)

—— " Peter." A " Stone." " This Rock "; " The Keys." Matt. xvi. 18, 19. A commentary . . . A second edition, revised and enlarged. pp. xii. 306. *Hamilton, Adams & Co.: London,* 1877. 8°. **3939. de. 1.**

—— Some Remarks in Defence of the Doctrine of an Imputed Righteousness. pp. xvi. 154. *Longman & Co.: London,* 1833. 12°. **1118. c. 9.**

CAULFEILD (*Mrs.* Edwin Toby) *See* Caulfeild (Frances S.)

CAULFEILD (Edwin Vivian Stuart) How to Ski and how not to . . . Photographs by K. Delap. pp. viii. 244. *J. Nisbet & Co.: London,* 1911. 8°. **7912. cc. 29.**

—— How to ski and how not to, *etc.* (Revised edition.) [With plates.] pp. viii. 286. *Nisbet & Co.: London,* [1921.] 8°. **7917. f. 36.**

—— (Sixth impression.) pp. vii. 286. *J. Nisbet & Co.: London,* 1924. 8°. **7907. bbb. 47.**

—— Ski-ing Turns. [With eight illustrative cards.] pp. 279. *Nisbet & Co.: London,* 1922. 8°. **07911. ee. 10.**

CAULFEILD (Frances Sally) The Deluge. A poem. pp. 170. *Baldwin & Cradock: London,* 1837. 8°. **T. 2095. (7.)**

—— The Innocents; a sacred drama. Ocean; and the Earthquake at Aleppo; poems. [By F. S. Caulfeild.] pp. 63. 1824. 8°. *See* Innocents. **11644. cc. 13.**

CAULFEILD (Francis) *See* Homer. [*Odyssey.—English.*] The Odyssey, translated . . . by F. Caulfeild, *etc.* 1921. 8°. **11315. m. 10.**

—— —— 1923. 8°. **20031. a. 14/13.**

CAULFEILD (J.) *Cornet.* The Manners of Paphos, or Triumph of Love. [A poem.] pp. iv. 63. *E. & C. Dilly: London,* 1777. 4°. **643. k. 6. (6.)**

—— [Another copy.] **161. l. 21.**

—— [Another edition.] pp. 89. *D. Chamberlaine, etc.: Dublin,* 1777. 8°. **992. g. 1. (6.)**

—— [Another copy.] **12330. aaa. 8. (3.)**

CAULFEILD (James) *Earl of Charlemont.*

—— *See* Craig (Maurice J.) The Volunteer Earl. Being the life and times of J. Caulfeild, First Earl of Charlemont. [With portraits.] 1948. 8°. **10862. ee. 21.**

—— *See* Hardy (Francis) Memoirs of the Political and Private Life of James Caulfeild, Earl of Charlemont. 1810. 4°. **614. l. 29.**

—— —— 1812. 8°. **615. g. 10, 11.**

—— *See* Petrarca (F.) [*Canzoniere.—Sonetti.—Italian and English.*] Select Sonnets . . . With translation and illustrative notes by James, late Earl of Charlemont. 1822. 8°. **11421. g. 26.**

—— *See* R., T. Original Letters, principally from Lord Charlemont . . . and other distinguished noblemen . . . to the Right Hon. H. Flood, *etc.* 1820. 4°. **831. k. 23.**

—— The Manuscripts and Correspondence of James, First Earl of Charlemont. [Containing " Lord Charlemont's Memoirs of his political life, 1755–1783," and a catalogue of, and extracts from his correspondence, 1747–1799. Edited by Sir John T. Gilbert.] 2 vol. *London,* 1891, 94. 8°. [*Historical Manuscripts Commission.* 12th Report. Appendix. pt. 10; 13th Report. Appendix. pt. 8.] **Bar.T.1.(28.)**

CAULFEILD (James) *Major General, Bengal Army.* A Letter to the Right Honourable the President of the Board of Control. pp. 15. *Smith, Elder & Co.: London,* 1838. 8°. **908. d. 5. (9.)**

—— Memoranda respecting Proposed Reforms in the Government of India. pp. 7. *Smith, Elder & Co.: London,* 1853. 8°. **8023. bbb. 38.**

—— The Punjaub and the Indian Army. pp. 16. *Smith, Elder & Co.: London,* 1846. 8°. **1398. d. 16.**

CAULFEILD (John) *Curate of St. Anne's Church, Dublin.* A Sermon upon Faith, preached in St. Anne's Church, Dublin, *etc.* pp. 23. *William Watson: Dublin,* 1773. 4°. **4473. g. 11. (4.)**

CAULFEILD (John) *Lieutenant-Colonel.* The Case of Lieutenant-Colonel John Caulfeild, and the rest of the officers of the regiment of foot, late under the command of Colonel Robert Whyte, humbly submitted to the Honourable the commons assembled in Parliament. [1701 ?] *s. sh.* fol. **816. m. 17. (54.)**

CAULFEILD (John Trevor) A Book of Lancing Verse. [Compiled by J. T. Caulfeild.] 1928. 8°. *See* Lancing College. **11601. l. 2.**

CAULFEILD (Kathleen Mary) *See* Edge, afterwards Caulfeild (K. M.)

CAULFEILD (Montgomerie) *See* Flood (Arthur E.) Correspondence between Captn. and Adjutant Caulfeild, Lt. A. E. Flood, and Col. the Rt. Hon. the Earl of Meath, Co. Dublin Regiment of Militia. 1866. 8°. **1417. f. 58. (6.)**

—— Decision of his Excellency the Earl of Kimberley, Lord Lieutenant of Ireland, on the late fracas in the Co. Dublin Regiment of Militia, together with a letter on the subject from the Right Honourable the Earl of Meath, Colonel of the Co. Dublin Regiment (in reply to a pamphlet published by Mr. Flood, entitled " Correspondance [*sic*] between Captain and Adjutant Caulfeild, Lieutenant A. E. Flood, and Col. the Rt. Hon. the Earl of Meath, co. Dublin Regiment of Militia "). pp. 8. *P. J. Carroll: Dublin,* 1866. 16°. **8827. aaa. 53.**

CAULFEILD (Ruby van Allen) The French Literature of Louisiana, *etc.* [A thesis. With a bibliography.] pp. xv. 282. *New York; Bordeaux* [printed], 1929. 8°. [*Publications of the Institute of French Studies.*] **Ac. 2688. k. (13.)**

—— [Another issue.] **11856. aaa. 21.** *Without the leaf bearing the author's vita.*

CAULFEILD (Sophia Frances Anne) *See* Directories.— *Girls' Clubs.* A Directory of Girls' Societies . . . By S. F. A. Caulfeild. 1886. 8°. **8365. aaa. 31.**

—— Avenele, and other poems. pp. ix. 220. *Longmans & Co.: London,* [1870.] 8°. **11650. bbb. 7.**

—— [Another copy.] **11646. c. 60.**

—— By Land and Sea; by S. F. A. Caulfield; and, Ben, " a Rough Diamond." (By the author of " Honour and Glory " [i.e. Jeanie Hering].) [Reprinted from " Little Folks."] pp. 160. *Cassell & Co.: London,* [1880.] 8°. **12809. k. 26.**

—— The Dawn of Christianity in Continental Europe, and the planting of the Order of Knights of the Hospital of St. John of Jerusalem in England. pp. 132. *Elliot Stock: London,* [1909.] 8°. **4532. df. 1.**

CAULFEILD (SOPHIA FRANCES ANNE)

—— Desmond, and other poems. pp. viii. 243.
Longmans & Co.: London, [1870.] 8º.   **11650. ee. 6.**

—— The Home Nurse. A handbook for sickness and emergencies, formerly known as "Sick Nursing at Home" . . . Third edition, much enlarged. pp. xii. 171.
Elliot Stock: London, 1903. 8º.   **07687.g.16.**

—— House Mottoes and Inscriptions : old and new. [With illustrations.] pp. viii. 146.   *Elliot Stock: London*, 1902. 8º.   [MISSING.]

—— New and revised edition, illustrated. pp. vii. 150.
Elliot Stock: London, 1908. 8º.   **012305. g. 28.**

—— The Lives of the Apostles, their contemporaries and successors . . . With an introduction by the Rev. S. Baring-Gould. pp. xxvii. 287.   *Hatchards: London*, [1887.] 8º.
4823. cc. 8.

—— "The Prisoners of Hope" : a series of twenty-six lectures. pt. 1. pp. 87.   *Marshall Bros.: London*, [1909.] 8º.   **4465. l. 2.**
No more published.

—— Restful Work for Youthful Hands, *etc.* pp. 224.
Griffith, Farran & Co.: London, 1888. 8º.
12806. r. 17.

—— True Philosophy : a reply to certain statements made in "Scientific Religion," by . . . Mr. Laurence Oliphant. pp. xii. 187.   *Hatchards: London*, 1888. 8º.
4017. bbb. 27.

—— The Voice of the Fathers : their erudition and unanimity . . . The introduction by . . . Viscount Halifax. pp. xv. 198.   *S. C. Brown & Co.: London*, 1905. 8º.
3622. aa. 10.

CAULFEILD (SOPHIA FRANCES ANNE) and **SAWARD** (BLANCE C.)

—— The Dictionary of Needlework, an encyclopædia of plain and fancy needlework . . . Illustrated with upwards of 800 wood engravings. Plain sewing, textiles, dressmaking, appliances, and terms, by S. F. A. Caulfeild . . . Church embroidery, lace and ornamental needlework, by B. C. Saward. pp. 528.   *L. Upcott Gill: London*, 1882 [1881, 82]. 4º.
2268. e. 4.

CAULFEILD (VIVIAN) *See* CAULFEILD (Edwin V. S.)

CAULFIELD (HANS) The Carnal Mind Enmity against God. 1831. *See* IRISH PULPIT. The Irish Pulpit, *etc.* ser. 2. no. 14. 1827, *etc.* 8º.   **1025. k. 14*.**

—— The Nineteenth of July ! Being an answer to the famous declaration of the Roman Catholics . . . disclaiming certain admitted doctrines of their holy mother Church . . . The second edition . . . By a Patriotic Loyalist [i.e. H. Caulfield.] pp. 23. 1826. 8º.   *See* IRELAND.—*Roman Catholics.*   **8275. ee. 24. (1.)**

CAULFIELD (J. BENJAMIN) Mathematical & Physical Geography . . . To which are annexed a copious appendix and geographical tables, *etc.* pp. vi. 200.   *Edwards & Hughes: London*, 1850. 8º.   **1295. b. 14.**

CAULFIELD (J. P. T.) Mr. Thomas Walker and "Fairplay." Reply of the "Boy-Politician" (J. P. T. Caulfield) to the "Boy-Lecturer." pp. 7.   *R. P. Hurren: Melbourne*, [1883.] 8º.   **1414. f. 83. (6.)**

CAULFIELD (JAMES) *Bishop of Ferns.* The Reply of the Right Rev. Doctor Caulfield . . . and of the Roman Catholic Clergy of Wexford, to the misrepresentations of Sir R. Musgrave, Bart. [in "Memoirs of the different rebellions in Ireland, from the arrival of the English "], *etc.* (Fourth edition.) pp. vii. 60.   *H. Fitzpatrick: Dublin*, 1801. 8º.   **8133. bb. 42. (4.)**
The letter from Edward Cooke, dated Dec. 12. 1798, which concludes the text, is printed on a separate slip pasted on p. 60.

—— *See* MUSGRAVE (*Sir* Richard) Observations on the Reply of the Right Reverend Doctor Caulfield . . . to the misrepresentations of Sir Richard Musgrave, *etc.* 1802. 4º.   **3939. e. 3. (1.)**

CAULFIELD (JAMES) *Bookseller. See* AUBREY (John) [*Lives.*] The Oxford Cabinet, *etc.* [Edited by J. Caulfield.] 1797. 4º.   **134. c. 14.**

—— *See* BURTON (Richard) *pseud.* Admirable Curiosities, Rarieties, and Wonders in England, *etc.* [Edited by J. Caulfield.] 1811. 4º.   **190. b. 4.**

—— *See* BURTON (Richard) *pseud.* Historical Remarks on the Ancient and Present States of the Cities of London and Westminster, *etc.* [Edited by J. Caulfield.] 1810. 4º.
10349. cc. 14.

—— *See* BURTON (Richard) *pseud.* The History of the House of Orange, *etc.* [Edited by J. Caulfield.] 1814. 4º.
9918.bbb.39.

—— *See* BURTON (Richard) *pseud.* The History of the Kingdom of Ireland, *etc.* [Edited by J. Caulfield.] 1811. 4º.
186. c. 3.

—— *See* BURTON (Richard) *pseud.* The Wars in England, Scotland, and Ireland, *etc.* [Edited by J. Caulfield.] 1810. 4º.   **193. d. 17.**

—— *See* CROUCH (*Nathaniel.*) The History of the Kingdom of Scotland, *etc.* [Edited by J. Caulfield.] 1813. 4º.
9512. h. 5.

—— *See* GRANGER (James) *Vicar of Shiplake.* A Biographical History of England . . . Fifth edition, with upwards of four hundred additional lives. [Edited by J. Caulfield.] 1824. 8º.   **2094. f.**

—— *See* GRANGER (William) *Compiler.* The New Wonderful Museum . . . by W. Granger, assisted by . . . J. Caulfield, and others. 1802, *etc.* 8º.   **G. 13546-48.**

—— *See* LEMOINE (Henry) *Bookseller.* The Eccentric Magazine ; or Lives and portraits of remarkable characters. [Compiled and edited successively by H. Lemoine and J. Caulfield.] 1812, *etc.* 8º.   **P.P. 5734.**

—— —— 1814. 4º.   **132. c. 7, 8.**

—— *See* NAUNTON (*Sir* Robert) The Court of Queen Elizabeth . . . With considerable biographical additions by J. Caulfield. 1814. fol.   **196. g. 14.**

—— *See* SCULPTOR (Satiricus) *Esq., pseud.* Chalcographimania ; or, the Portrait-collector and printseller's chronicle, *etc.* [With contributions by J. Caulfield ?] 1814. 8º.   **79. e. 21.**

—— *See* WILSON (Henry) *Author of* "*Wonderful Characters.*" The Book of Wonderful Characters . . . Chiefly from the text of H. Wilson and J. Caulfield, *etc.* [1869.] 8º.
2407. bb. 2.

—— Blackguardiana : or, a Dictionary of rogues . . . illustrated with eighteen portraits of the most remarkable professors in every species of villainy. Interspersed with . . . curious anecdotes, cant terms, flash songs, *etc.* [By J. Caulfield.] [1795.] 8º. *See* BLACKGUARDIANA.
12983. ff. 24.

CAULFIELD (James) *Bookseller.*

—— Calcographiana. The printseller's chronicle and collector's guide to the knowledge and value of engraved British portraits. [With a portrait of the author.] pp. viii. 163. *J. Caulfield: London,* 1814. 8°.
58. g. 18.

—— [Another copy.] Calcographiana, *etc. London* 1814. 8°. **7868. b. 14.**
With additional illustrations and cuttings inserted.

—— A Catalogue of Portraits of Foreigners who have visited England, as noticed by Lord Clarendon, Heath in his Civil Wars, Thurloe in his State Papers, *etc.* [By J. Caulfield.] pp. 57. 1814. 12°. *See* HYDE (Edward) *1st Earl of Clarendon.* **52. b. 24.**

—— Cromwelliana. A chronological detail of events in which Oliver Cromwell was engaged; from the year 1642 to his death, in 1658. With a continuation of other transactions to the Restoration. [Compiled by J. Caulfield.] pp. 6. 196. **L.P.** 1810. fol. *See* CROMWELL (O.) *Lord Protector of the Commonwealth of England, Scotland and Ireland.* [*Biography.*—I.] **196. g. 9.**

—— [Another copy.] **G. 5308.**

—— An Enquiry into the Conduct of Edmond Malone, Esq. concerning the manuscript papers of John Aubrey, F.R.S., in the Ashmolean Museum, Oxford. [By J. Caulfield.] pp. 19. 1797. 8°. *See* MALONE (Edmond) **81. d. 1.**

—— A Gallery of British Portraits, containing those of distinguished and noble personages during the reigns of James I and Charles I, and under the Commonwealth, from original pictures and drawings not before engraven, with biographical notices collected from the best authorities by J. Caulfield. pp. viii. 40. **L.P.** *G. Smeeton & J. Caulfield: London,* 1814. fol. **133. i. 4.**
There are three impressions of each plate; one plain, one partially coloured, and one on a tinted ground.

—— [Another copy.] **L.P.** **G. 10887.**

—— The High Court of Justice; comprising memoirs of the principal persons who sat in judgment on King Charles the First . . . Illustrated with their portraits, autographs, and seals, *etc.* pp. xi. 112. *John Caulfield: London,* 1820. 4°. **G. 4960.**
The plates are in duplicate; one impression of each being on India paper.

—— The History of the Gun-Powder Plot: with several historical circumstances prior to that event, connecting the plots of the Roman Catholics to re-establish Popery in this kingdom. Digested and arranged from authentic materials by J. Caulfield. pp. 94. *Vernor & Hood: London,* 1804. 8°. **G. 3271.**

—— Londina Illustrata. Graphic and historic memorials of monasteries, churches . . . charitable foundations, palaces, halls, courts, processions, places of early amusement and modern & present theatres, in the cities and suburbs of London & Westminster. [The text by J. Caulfield.] 2 vol. 1819. fol. *See* LONDON.—IV. *Appendix.—History and Topography.* **Map.24.b.4,5.**

—— [Another copy of vol. 1.] **190. f. 9.**

—— [Another copy of vol. 1.] Londina illustrata, *etc.* 1819. fol. *See* LONDON.—IV. [*Appendix.—History and Topography.*] **G. 10301.**

—— Memoirs of Sir Robert Naunton . . . With some of his posthumous writings, *etc.* [Compiled by J. Caulfield.] pp. 50. 1814. fol. *See* NAUNTON (Sir Robert) **133. g. 1.**

CAULFIELD (James) *Bookseller.*

—— Memoirs of the Celebrated Persons composing the Kit-Cat Club; with a prefatory account of the origin of the association: illustrated with forty-eight portraits, from the original paintings by Sir Godfrey Kneller. [By J. Caulfield.] pp. x. 261. 1821. 4°. *See* LONDON.—III. *Kit Cat Club.* **562*. e. 26.**

—— Portraits, Memoirs, and Characters of Remarkable Persons, from the reign of King Edward the Third, to the Revolution, *etc.* 2 vol. pp. iv. 214. *J. Caulfield & I. Herbert: London,* 1794, 95. 8°. **131. b. 23.**

—— [Another copy.] **G. 1427.**

—— A new edition, completing the twelfth class of Granger's Biographical History of England, *etc.* 3 vol. *R. S. Kirby: London,* 1813. 8°. **1329. f. 13.**

—— Portraits, Memoirs, and Characters, of Remarkable Persons, from the Revolution in 1688 to the end of the reign of George II., *etc.* [Including portraits by George Cruikshank.] 4 vol. *H. R. Young & T. H. Whitely: London,* 1819, 20. 8°. **10803. f. 9.**

—— [Another copy.] **L.P.** **562*. d. 9–12.**
Vol. 1 is a remounted copy of another edition.

CAULFIELD (James) *Earl of Charlemont. See* CAULFEILD.

CAULFIELD (James) *Major General, Bengal Army. See* CAULFEILD.

CAULFIELD (John) *Song Writer.* Canterbury-Hall Comic Songs, *etc.* 3 no. [1855.] 8°. *See* LONDON.—III. *Canterbury Hall, etc.* **1342. k. 12. (1.)**

CAULFIELD (Malachy Francis)

—— The Black City. [A novel.] pp. 239. *Jonathan Cape: London,* 1952. 8°. **NNN. 3271.**

CAULFIELD (Montgomerie) *See* CAULFEILD.

CAULFIELD (Richard) *See* CLOYNE, *Diocese of.* Rotulus Pipæ Clonensis, ex originali . . . nunc primum editus . . . opera et studio R. Caulfield. 1859. 4°. **9510. h. 11.**

—— *See* CORK.—*Corporation.* The Council Book of the Corporation of the City of Cork . . . Edited . . . by R. Caulfield. 1876. 4°. **10390. e. 1.**

—— *See* CORK.—*Cork Historical and Archaeological Society.* The Ancient and Present State of the County and City of Cork . . . With the addition of numerous original notes, etc., from the MSS. of the late Thomas Crofton Croker, F.S.A. and R. Caulfield, *etc.* 1893, *etc.* 8°. **Ac.8323/2.**

—— *See* COX (Sir Richard) *1st Bart., Lord Chancellor of Ireland.* Autobiography of the Rt. Hon. Sir Richard Cox . . . Edited by R. Caulfield. 1860. 12°. **10817. bbb. 23. (4.)**

—— *See* DAVIES (Rowland) Journal of the Very Rev. Rowland Davies . . . Edited, with notes, and an appendix, and some account of the author and his family, by R. Caulfield. 1857. 4°. [*Camden Society.* vol. 68.] **Ac. 8113/64.**

—— *See* FINBARR, *Saint, Bishop of Cork.* The Life of Saint Fin Barre . . . Edited, with notes . . . by R. Caulfield. 1864. 4°. **4827. bb. 5.**

CAULFIELD (Richard)

—— See Kinsale.—Corporation. The Council Book of the Corporation of Kinsale . . . 1652 to 1800 . . . Edited . . . by R. Caulfield. 1879. 4°. **10390. f. 22.**

—— See Trinity.—Parish of the Holy Trinity, Cork. The Register of the Parish of the Holy Trinity, Cork . . . With extracts from the parish books . . . Edited by R. Caulfield. 1877. 8°. **4534. e. 2. (5.)**

—— See Youghal.—Corporation. The Council Book of the Corporation of Youghal . . . Edited . . . by R. Caulfield. 1878. 4°. **10390. e. 3.**

—— Annals of St. Fin Barre's Cathedral, Cork, etc. pp. vi. 127. Purcell & Co.: Cork, 1871. 8°. **4735. aa. 15.**

—— Annals of the Cathedral of St. Coleman, Cloyne . . . Illustrated. pp. vii. 59. pl. vi. Purcell & Co.: Cork, 1882. 8°. **04735. f. 10.**

—— Handbook to the Cathedral Church of St. Fin Barre, Cork. With engravings and ground plan. pp. 32. Purcell & Co.: Cork, 1881. 8°. **10347. c. 7. (8.)**

—— A Lecture on the History of the Bishops of Cork, and Cathedral of St. Fin Barre, etc. pp. 40. Purcell & Co.: Cork, 1864. 8°. **4735. b. 23.**

—— Sigilla ecclesiæ hibernicæ illustrata. The episcopal and capitular seals of the Irish cathedral churches illustrated. pt. 1–4. pp. 48. pl. viii. H. Ridings: Cork; J. M'Glashan: Dublin, 1853[–56]. 8°. **4735. e. 9.** No more published.

CAULFIELD (Sophia Frances Anne) See Caulfeild.

CAULFIELD (William)

—— A Sermon preached at the Funeral of Edward Drury, Esq: on the 30th day of January, 1722–3, etc. pp. 19. Edwin Sandys: Dublin, 1723. 4°. **4480. ee. 104.**

CAULFIELD-GILES (Henry Robert) See Giles.

CAULIACO (Giudo de) See Guido, de Cauliaco.

CAULIER (Petrus) Disputatio medica inauguralis de calculo renum, & vesicæ, etc. Ex officina F. Hackii: Lugduni Batavorum, 1654. 4°. **1185. g. 4. (11.)**

CAULIN (Antonio) Historia coro-graphica, natural y evangelica de la Nueva Andalucia, provincias de Cumaná, Guayana y Vertientes del Rio Orinoco. [With a map.] pp. 482. Madrid, 1779. fol. **601. l. 19.** The titlepage is engraved.

—— [Another edition.] pp. iii. 448. Caracas, 1841. 8°. **9772. c. 17.**

—— [Another edition.] See Parra (C.) Analectas de Historia Patria, etc. 1935. fol. **20087. b. 16.**

CAULIN (Louis Alexandre Eudoxe) Quelques seigneuries au Vallage et en Champagne propre, précédées de notions sur le régime féodal, etc. pp. iii. 531. Troyes, 1867. 8°. **9904. h. 24.**

CAULINCOURT (Armand Augustin Louis de) Duke of Vicenza. See Caulaincourt.

CAULIUS (Joannes) Pausiae Pictoris et Stephanionis Mimi Dialogus, vna cum quibusdam epistolis. Apud P. Turræum: Lugduni, 1547. 8°. **12314. e. 39.**

CAULKINS (Frances Manwaring) Bride Brook. A legend of New London, Connecticut. [In verse.] pp. 11. Colfax & Holt: New London, 1852. 12°. **11686. aa. 47. (4.)**

CAULKINS (Frances Manwaring)

—— Colporteur Songs written for the American Messenger. pp. 12. [New London ? 1847 ?] 12°. **11645. b. 7.**

—— History of New London, Connecticut, from the first survey of the coast in 1612 to 1852. pp. 679. The Author: New London, 1852. 8°. **10412. d. 5.**

—— [Another edition.] With memoir of the author. pp. xviii. 696. H. D. Utley: New London, 1895. 8°. **10413. i. 23.**

—— History of Norwich, Connecticut, from its settlement in 1660, to January 1845. pp. 359. Thomas Robinson: Norwich [Conn.], 1845. 12°. **10410. c. 17.**

—— History of Norwich, Connecticut: from its possession by the Indians, to the year 1866. (Entirely re-written.) [With portraits.] pp. 704. The Author: Hartford, 1866. 8°. **10410. dd. 1.**

CAULKINS (Nehemiah) Narrative of Nehemiah Caulkins, an extract from "American Slavery, as it is." pp. 22. American & Foreign Anti-Slavery Society: New York, 1849. 8°. **8156. aa. 18.**

CAULLE (Joseph) Saint Germain l'Écossais, apôtre de la vallée de la Bresle. (Société Havraise d'Études Diverses. Extrait du recueil de ses publications.) pp. 18. 8°. Le Havre, 1934. 8°. **20010. d. 9.**

CAULLERY (Maurice Jules Gaston Corneille)

—— See Ferchault de Réaumur (R. A.) Histoire des fourmis, etc. (Les papiers laissés par de Réaumur. Introduction du tome vii des Mémoires pour servir à l'histoire des insectes. Par M. Caullery.) 1928, etc. 8°. [Encyclopédie entomologique. sér. A. tom. 32. suppl.] **7297. p. 4/32a.**

——

Conceptions modernes de l'hérédité, etc. pp. 312. Paris, 1935. 8°. **7002. pp. 31.**

—— Glanures biologiques, publiées à l'occasion du cinquantenaire de la fondation de la station, 1874–1924. [Edited by M. Caullery.] pp. xv. 283. pl. xiv. Paris, 1925. 4°. [Travaux de la Station zoologique de Wimereux. tom. 9.] **Ac. 3554.**

—— Histoire des sciences biologiques. 1935. See Hanotaux (G. A. A.) Histoire de la nation française. tom. 15. [1920, etc.] 4°. **9210. ff. 3/15.**

—— [Le Parasitisme et la symbiose.] Parasitism and Symbiosis . . . Translated by Averil M. Lysaght. [With a bibliography.] pp. xii. 340. Sidgwick & Jackson: London, 1952. 8°. [Text-books of Animal Biology.] **W.P. 4414/9.**

—— Present Theories of Evolution and the Problems of Adaptation. (The Joseph Leidy Memorial Lecture in Science.) pp. 18. University of Pennsylvania: Philadelphia, 1933. 8°. **7002. ppp. 24.**

—— Le Problème de l'évolution, etc. pp. 447. Paris, 1931. 8°. **07001. k. 39.**

—— La Science française depuis le xviie siècle . . . 2e édition revue et corrigée. pp. 214. Paris, 1948. 8°. **08709. aa. 63.**

Collection Armand Colin. no. 165.

—— Les Universités et la vie scientifique aux États-Unis. pp. xii. 302. Paris, 1917. 8°. **8385. aa. 7.**

—— Universities and Scientific Life in the United States . . . Translated by James Houghton Woods and Emmet Russell. pp. xvii. 269. Harvard University Press: Cambridge [Mass.], 1922. 8°. **8385. ee. 12.**

CAULLERY (MAURICE JULES GASTON CORNEILLE)

—— Volume jubilaire dédié à Maurice Caullery. [With a portrait.] pp. 851. xxxiv. *Paris*, 1938. 4°. [*Travaux de la Station zoologique de Wimereux.* tom. 13.]
Ac. 3554.

CAULLERY (MAURICE JULES GASTON CORNEILLE) and **MESNIL** (FÉLIX)

—— Les Formes épitoques et l'évolution des cirratuliens, *etc.* pp. 200. pl. VI. *Paris, Lyon*, 1898. 8°. [*Annales de l' Université de Lyon.* fasc. 39.]
Ac. 365.

CAULLET (GUSTAVE) Catalogue [of the Musée de Peinture et de Sculpture, Courtray] . . . Édition illustrée de 33 reproductions. pp. xxx. 186. 1912. 8°. *See* COURTRAY.—*Musée de Peinture et de Sculpture.*
7856. a. 25.

—— "La Deffense de Monseigneur le Duc et Madame la Duchesse d'Austriche et de Bourgongne." Description de cet incunable, précédée d'un aperçu critique sur la carrière et l'œuvre de Jean Brito . . . extrait du Bulletin du Cercle historique et archéologique de Courtrai, *etc.* pp. 26. *Courtrai*, 1906. 8°.
011904. bb. 40.

—— Les Manuscrits de Gilles Le Muisit et l'art de la miniature au XIVe siècle. Le relieur tournaisien Janvier. (Extrait du Bulletin du Cercle historique et archéologique de Courtrai.) [With plates.] pp. 26. *Courtrai*, 1908. 8°.
7857. g. 59.

CAULLET DE VEAUMOREL (L.) *See* MESMER (F. A.) Aphorismes de M. Mesmer . . . Ouvrage mis au jour par M. Caullet de Veaumorel, *etc.* 1785. 8°.
7410. dg. 25.

—— Neue Beiträge zur praktischen Anwendung des thierischen Magnetismus . . . Ein Nachtrag zu den Lehrsäzzen des Hrn. Mesmers. [Consisting of "Beobachtungen über den thierischen Magnetismus," signed: Ritter von C., with notes by L. Caullet de Veaumorel, together with "Herrn Del . . ."—i.e. D'Eslon's—"Verfahrungsart, um zu magnetisiren" by L. Caullet de Veaumorel] . . . Aus Hrn Caullet de Veaumorel dritter Ausgabe . . . übersetzt. [The translator's preface signed: T. F. E., i.e. Theophil F. Ehrmann.] Nebst einem Anhange [entitled "Wunderbare Geschichte der Kuren Valentin Greatrakes . . . aus J. Nic. Pechlini . . . Observationibus physico-medicis," *etc.*]. pp. 112. *Strasburg*, 1786. 8°.
775. f. 27.

CAULTON (ISABELLA) The Domestic Hearth, and other poems. pp. vii. 181. *Bradshaw & Blacklock: Manchester*, 1843. 8°.
11646. bb. 15.

—— Second edition. pp. vii. 192. *Bradshaw & Blacklock: Manchester*, 1844. 8°.
11646. bb. 46.

—— Poems for Home. pp. 96. *Richard Russell: Leamington Spa*, 1851. 12°.
11645. aa. 21.

CAULTON (J. STEWART) Christmas Rhymes and Woodcuts for children & others. pp. 30. *Society of SS. Peter & Paul: London*, 1923. 8°.
011644. de. 9.

CAULUS (BENJAMIN) Quelques considérations cliniques sur la pneumonie du vieillard. pp. 58. *Paris*, 1874. 4°. [*Collection des thèses soutenues à la Faculté de Médecine de Paris.* An 1874. tom. 3.]
7374. a. 8.

CAULVELEY ( ) *Lady. See* JONES (George) *of Chester.* A Letter of a Sad Tragedy by Prince Griffin at Sayton, neere Chester: and his severall attempts against the Lady Caufely, *etc.* 1648. 4°.
E. 431. (12.)

CAULVELEY (*Sir* HUGH) *See* GRIFFITH (John) *of Llyne.* A Vindication or Iustification of J. Griffith, Esq. against the horrid . . . verdict of the Coroners Iury in Cheshire: which was packt by the means of that pocky . . . Knave, Sir Hugh Caulveley Knight, *etc.* 1648. 4°.
E. 435. (44.)

CAULX. *See* CAUX.

CAULY (EUGÈNE ERNEST) Cours d'instruction religieuse à l'usage des catéchismes de persévérance et des maisons d'éducation, *etc.* pp. 568. *Paris*, 1884. 12°.
03504. f. 93.

—— Cours d'instruction religieuse à l'usage des catéchismes de persévérance, *etc.* (Recherche de la vraie religion.—Apologétique chrétienne.) 2 pt. *Paris*, 1885. 8°.
03504. f. 93.

—— Histoire du Collège des Bons-Enfants de l'Université de Reims depuis son origine jusqu'à ses récentes transformations . . . Édition ornée de plans, gravures et vignettes, *etc.* pp. xiii. 776. *Reims*, 1885. 8°.
010170. h. 15.

CAUMARTIN (CHARLES MARIE) Faculté de Droit de Paris. Thèse pour la licence. (Jus romanum. Collatio bonorum.—Collatio dotis.—Droit français. Rapport des donations et des legs.) pp. 90. *Paris*, 1858. 8°.
5406. aaa. 5. (8.)

CAUMARTIN (JEAN) Les Principales sources de documentation statistique, *etc.* pp. 38. *Paris*, 1935. 8°.
11911. dd. 12.

CAUMARTIN (LOUIS FRANÇOIS LEFÈVRE DE) *See* LEFÈVRE DE CAUMARTIN.

CAUMEL-DECAZIS (ROSELINE) Les Revendications de l'Irlande: poème. pp. 22. *Paris*, 1888. 12°.
11483. cc. 29. (2.)

CAUMELS (DE) *Marquis. See* ROJAS CLEMENTE Y RUBIO (S. de) Essai sur les variétés de la vigne qui végètent en Andalousie . . . Traduit par M. le Mls de Caumels, *etc.* 1814. 8°.
451. c. 29.

—— *See* ROJAS CLEMENTE Y RUBIO (S. de) Tables synoptiques des caractères distinctifs de la vigne. Extraites de l'essai sur les vignes d'Andalousie . . . par M. le Mls de Caumels. 1816. 8°.
B. 675. (7.)

CAUMETTE (CH.) Eclaircissemens des antiquités de la ville de Nismes, par Monsieur * * * Avocat de la même ville [i.e. C. Caumette]. pp. 64. pl. IV. 1766. 8°. *See* NÎMES.
665. b. 11.

—— Dernière édition, *etc.* pp. 56. pl. IV. 1781. 8°. *See* NÎMES.
7705. a. 25.

CAUMO (GIUSEPPE) Sulla condizione dei Romani vinti dai Longobardi. Dissertazione. pp. 34. *Firenze*, 1870. 8°.
9039. h. 4.

CAUMOND (THOMAS) De l'influence des météores et des saisons sur la production des maladies. Tribut académique, *etc.* pp. 23. *Montpellier*, an X [1802]. 4°.
1180. d. 12. (17.)

CAUMONT, JOSEPH DE SEYTRES, *Marquis de. See* SEYTRES.

——, NOMPAR II, *Seigneur de. See* NOMPAR.

CAUMONT, *Family of. See* JAURGAIN (J. B. E. de) La Maison de Caumont-La Force, *etc.* 1912. 4°.
9904. v. 17.

CAUMONT (ALDRICK ISIDORE FERDINAND) Cours public de droit maritime . . . ou Amendement des lois nautiques. Discours de clôture, *etc.* pp. 62. *Paris, Bruxelles*, 1866. 8°.
[MISSING.]

CAUMONT (ALDRICK ISIDORE FERDINAND)

—— Dictionnaire universel de droit maritime au point de vue commercial, administratif et pénal, *etc.* pp. 896. *Paris, Bruxelles*, 1867. 8°. **6835.ee.1.**

—— Discours de clôture du cours public de droit économique, ou Moralité dans le droit. pp. 24. 1864. 8°. *See* HAVRE-DE-GRÂCE.—*Société Havraise d'études diverses.* **5425. ff. 10.**

—— Étude sur la vie et les travaux de Grotius, ou le Droit naturel et le droit international. [With a portrait of the author.] pp. 316. *Paris*, 1862. 8°. [MISSING.]

—— Langue universelle de l'humanité, ou Télégraphie parlée par le nombre agissant . . . au moyen de phrases [from the Psalms] en huit langues : français, anglais, allemand, italien, espagnol, latin, grec, hébreu, *etc.* pp. iii. 23. *Paris, Bruxelles*, 1867. fol. **1890. b. 15.**

—— Législation, doctrine et jurisprudence sur l'abordage maritime. Avec une table, *etc.* (Application des warrants à la propriété maritime.) 2 pt. *Paris*, 1865. 8°. **6835. d. 12.**

—— Nantissement et vente des navires. Application des warrants à la propriété maritime. pp. 31. *Paris*, 1863. 8°. **6825. b. 10.**

—— Plan de Dieu, ou physiologie du travail. pp. 26. *Paris*, 1862. 8°. **8282. f. 20. (6.)**

CAUMONT (ANNE DE) *Countess de Saint-Paul. See* ARTAUD DE LA FERRIÈRE, *afterwards* LA FERRIÈRE-PERCY (C. C. M. H.) *Count.* Deux romans d'aventure au xvie siècle, Arabella Stuart—Anne de Caumont, *etc.* 1898. 8°. **10603. cc. 19.**

CAUMONT (ANTONIN NOMPAR DE) *Duke de Lauzun. See* ANNE MARY LOUISA [d'Orléans], *Duchess de Montpensier.* Les Amours de Mademoiselle, avec Mr le Comte de Lauzun, *etc.* [1672.] 12°. **12511. aaaa. 12.**

—— —— [1675 ?] 8°. **901. a. 26.**

—— —— 1676, *etc.* 12°. **1080. b. 27.**

—— *See* BRULART DE GENLIS (S. F.) *Marchioness de Silléry.* Le Duc de Lauzun, *etc.* 1808. 12°. **10667. aa. 3.**

—— *See* CAUMONT (A. A. G. M. J. N. de) *Duke de la Force.* Lauzun, *etc.* [With a portrait.] 1919. 8°. **10655.h.55/5.**

—— *See* CORYN (M. S.) Knave of Hearts. Being the romantic adventures of Count de Lauzun, *etc.* [With a portrait.] 1937. 8°. **10655. h. 33.**

—— *See* DELORT (J.) Histoire de la détention des philosophes . . . à la Bastille et à Vincennes : précédée de celle de Fourcquet . . . et de Lauzun. 1829. 8°. **1195. e. 8.**

—— *See* SANDARS (Mary F.) Lauzun : courtier and adventurer, *etc.* 1908. 8°. **10660. p. 13.**

CAUMONT (ARCISSE DE) *See* CAEN.—*Société Linnéenne, etc.* Mémoires . . . publiés par M. de Caumont . . . Seconde série, *etc.* 1829. 4°. **7107. e. 5.**

—— *See* DAUDIN (J. A.) Essai sur les poteries romaines . . . publié par M. de Caumont. 1829. 4°. **7703.b.26.**

—— *See* FRANCE.—*Société Française d'Archéologie.* Bulletin monumental . . . dirigé par M. de Caumont. 1834, *etc.* 8°. **Ac. 5296.**

—— *See* KNIGHT (Henry G.) Relation d'une excursion monumentale en Sicile et en Calabre . . . Traduction (par M. A. Campion) communiquée à la Société française pour la conservation des monuments, par M. de Caumont. 1839. 8°. **1049. g. 29.**

CAUMONT (ARCISSE DE)

—— *See* KNIGHT (Henry G.) Voyage archéologique fait en Normandie en 1831 . . . communiqué à la Société pour la conservation des monuments par M. de Caumont. 1838. 8°. **1049. g. 28.**

—— *See* PERIODICAL PUBLICATIONS.—*Caen.* Revue normande, rédigée . . . sous la direction de M. de Caumont. 1830, *etc.* 8°. **P.P. 4340.**

—— Abécédaire ou rudiment d'archéologie, *etc.* [On ecclesiastical architecture.] pp. iv. 416. *Paris*, 1850. 8°. **7705. bb. 7.**

—— 3e édition. [Edited by A. Hardel.] pp. xvi. 614. *Paris*, 1854. 8°. **7705. bb. 10.**

—— Cinquième édition. [Edited by A. Hardel.] pp. x. 800. *Caen*, 1868. 8°. **X. 410/110.**

—— Abécédaire ou rudiment d'archéologie—Architectures civile et militaire, *etc.* pp. ii. 494. *Paris*, 1853. 8°. **7705. bb. 8.**

—— Troisième édition. [Edited by A. Hardel.] pp. vii. 100. *Paris*, 1869. 8°. **07702. c. 2.**

—— Abécédaire ou rudiment d'archéologie, ère gallo-romaine, *etc.* pp. vii. 498. *Paris*, 1862. 8°. [MISSING.]

—— [Another copy.] **7705. bb. 9.**

—— Abécédaire ou rudiment d'archéologie . . . Ère gallo-romaine . . . Deuxième édition. [With illustrations and a portrait.] pp. lvi. 656. *Caen*, 1870. 8°. **07705. b. 29.**

—— Archéologie des écoles primaires. pp. 428. *Caen*, 1868. 12°. **7707. a. 6.**

—— Cours d'antiquités monumentales . . . Histoire de l'art dans l'ouest de la France depuis les temps les plus reculés jusqu'au xviie siècle, *etc.* [With an atlas.] 7 pt. *Paris*, 1830–41. 8° & obl. 8°. **L.R. 110. b. 11.**

—— Histoire sommaire de l'architecture . . . au moyen âge . . . Extrait des 4e et 5e parties du Cours d'antiquités monumentales professé, en 1830, par le même auteur, *etc.* pp. 427. pl. xxx. *Caen*, 1838. 8°. [*Bulletin monumental.* tom. 2.] **Ac. 5296.**

—— *See* DUCHESNE DE LA SICOTIÈRE (P. F. L.) Cours d'antiquités monumentales par M. de Caumont. [A review.] [1842 ?] 8°. **7708. c. 32. (3.)**

—— *See* LAMOTHE (L. de) Examen de la sixième partie du cours d'antiquités monumentales professé . . . par M. de Caumont. 1844. 8°. **811. h. 9. (1.)**

—— Définition élémentaire de quelques termes d'architecture. pp. 168. MS. NOTES [by Edward Cresy]. *Paris*, 1846. 8°. **1401. g. 34. (4.)**

—— Essai sur la topographie géognostique du département du Calvados. pp. 312. *Caen*, 1828. 8°. **871.h.86.**

—— Atlas. *Paris*, 1828. obl. fol. **871.h.86.**

—— Feuille de route de Caen à Cherbourg, à l'usage des membres de la 27e session du Congrès scientifique de France, qui s'ouvrira à Cherbourg, le 2 septembre 1860. pp. vi. [3]–111. *Caen*, 1860. 8°. **10172. ee. 27.**

—— Mémoire géologique sur quelques terrains de la Normandie occidentale. (Extrait des Mémoires de la Société Linnéenne du Calvados.) [With plates.] pp. 15 [151]. *Paris*, 1825. 8°. **725. f. 20. (1.)**

CAUMONT (Arcisse de)

—— Extrait du premier Mémoire de M. de Caumont, sur la géologie de l'arrondissement de Bayeux, *etc.* pp. 6. [1824?] 8º.   **725. f. 20. (3.)**

—— Second Mémoire sur la géologie de l'arrondissement de Bayeux, *etc.* pp. 31. [1824?] 8º.   **725. f. 20. (4.)**

—— Première course géologique dans le département de la Manche. Observations, *etc.* pp. 8. [1823?] 8º.
                                                     725. f. 20. (2.)

—— Promenades archéologiques dans les communes du littoral de l'arrondissement de Caen, *etc.* pp. 88. *Luc,* [1846.] 8º.   [MISSING.]

—— Rapport verbal sur une excursion archéologique en Lorraine, en Alsace, à Fribourg en Brisgaw et dans quelques localités de la Champagne, fait à la Société française pour la conservation des monuments, *etc.* (Extrait du Bulletin monumental.) pp. 86. *Paris,* 1851. 8º.
                                                     [MISSING.]

—— Statistique monumentale du Calvados. 5 tom. *Paris,* 1846, 67. 8º.   **10170. d. 33.**

—— Statistiques routières de la Basse-Normandie. [Edited by A. Hardel.] pp. iv. [3]–474. *Paris,* 1855. 8º.
                                                     10173. cc. 8.

CAUMONT (Armand) Fleurs d'automne. Sonnets. pp. 56. *Francfort,* 1896. 8º.   **11482. i. 36.**

—— Goethe et la littérature française. pp. 37. *Frankfurt,* 1885. 4º.   **11764. i. 17. (10.)**

CAUMONT (Armand de) *Marquis de Montpouillan.* Ode pour la caualcade qui s'est faite à Genève le XXVII. Auril 1665. Commandée par Monsieur le Marquis de Monpouillan. [*Geneva,* 1665.] 4º.   **11408. e. 68. (7.)**

CAUMONT (Armand Nompar de) *Duke de la Force.* *See* HENRY [de Lorraine], *Duke de Mayenne.* La Prise du ieune marquis de la Force et de son frère le sieur de Montpouillan, *etc.* 1621. 8º.   **1193. h. 13. (19.)**

CAUMONT (Auguste Armand Ghislain Marie Joseph Nompar de) *Duke de la Force.* *See* GRENTE (G. F. X. M.) *Bishop of Le Mans.* Pierre de Nolhac. (Discours prononcé par Mgr Grente et réponse de M. le duc de la Force.) 1938. 8º.   **010655. ee. 5.**

—— *See* HANOTAUX (G. A. A.) Histoire du cardinal de Richelieu. [tom. 3, etc. by G. Hanotaux and the Duke de La Force.] 1893, *etc.* 8º.   **4857. d. 1.**

—— L'Architrésorier Lebrun, gouverneur de la Hollande, 1810–1813. pp. v. 378. *Paris,* 1907. 8º.
                                                     10660. s. 6.

—— Au temps de Louis XIV. (Récits.) [With plates.] pp. 34. *Paris,* 1938. 8º. [*La Petite Illustration.* Roman. no. 423.]   **P.P. 4283. m. (1.)**

—— Comédies sanglantes, drames intimes. pp. 224. *Paris,* 1930. 8º.   **010603. df. 25.**

—— Curiosités historiques. pp. 258. *Paris,* 1923. 8º.
                                                     9210. e. 6.

—— Dames d'autrefois. [Biographical essays. With portraits.] pp. 259. *Paris,* 1933. 8º.   **10655. pp. 9.**

—— Femmes fortes. [Biographical essays. With portraits.] pp. 206. *Paris,* 1936. 8º.   **010665. df. 65.**

—— Le Grand Conti. [With a portrait and a bibliography.] pp. 342. *Paris,* 1922. 8º.   **10657. bb. 19.**

CAUMONT (Auguste Armand Ghislain Marie Joseph Nompar de) *Duke de la Force.*

—— Histoire et portraits. [With plates.] 2 *sér.* *Paris,* 1937–39. 8º.   **012356. ee. 86.**

—— Lauzun, un courtisan du Grand Roi. [With plates, including portraits.] pp. 254. *Paris,* 1919. 8º. [*Figures du passé.*]   **10655. h. 55/5.**

—— Le Maréchal de la Force, 1558–1652. [With a portrait.] *Paris,* 1924, 28. 2 Vol. 8º.   **10656. gg. 50.**

—— Le Maréchal de La Force, *etc.* pp. 373. *Paris,* 1950. 8º.   **010665. t. 35.**

CAUMONT (Charlotte de) afterwards **LA TOUR D'AUVERGNE** (Charlotte de) *Viscountess de Turenne.* *See* LA TOUR D'AUVERGNE.

CAUMONT (Charlotte Rose de) *See* HURTREL (A.) Les Amours de Catherine de Bourbon . . . et du comte de Soissons. Souvenirs du règne de Henri IV. [Founded on C. R. de Caumont's " Histoire secrète de Catherine de Bourbon."] 1882. 8º.   **012548. ee. 54.**

—— Die geheime Geschichte von Burgund, nebst den Begebenheiten der Königinn von Navarra Margaretha von Valois. [A translation of " Histoire secrète de Bourgogne " and of pt. 1 of " Histoire de Marguerite de Valois " by C. R. de Caumont.] pp. 534. 1745. 8º. *See* BURGUNDY. [*Appendix.*]   **1319. c. 24.**

—— Les Fées. Contes des contes. Par Mademoiselle de * * * [i.e. C. R. de Caumont.] pp. 240. 1708. 12º. *See* FÉES.   **12314. b. 49.**

—— [Another edition.] 1785. *See* CABINET. Le Cabinet des fées, *etc.* tom. 6. 1785, *etc.* 8º.   **89. c. 20.**

—— La Bonne femme. [A tale, extracted from " Les Fées."] *See* LESCURE (M. F. A. de) Le Monde enchanté, *etc.* 1883. 8º.   **12411. g. 6.**

—— Fairer than a Fairy. [Translated from " Plus belle que fée."]—The Good Woman. [Translated from " La Bonne femme."] [Tales from " Les Fées."] *See* PLANCHÉ (James R.) Four and Twenty Fairy Tales, *etc.* 1858. 8º.
                                                     12431. d. 27.

—— Gustave Vasa, histoire de Suède. [By C. R. de Caumont.] 1749. 12º. [*Bibliothèque de campagne, etc.* tom. 1.] *See* GUSTAVUS I. [Vasa], *King of Sweden.*
                                                     244. f. 1.

—— Histoire de Marguerite de Valois, Reine de Navarre, soeur de François I. [By C. R. de Caumont.] 2 tom. 1696. 12º. *See* MARGARET [d'Angoulême], *Queen Consort of Henry II., King of Navarre.*   **1472. a. 10.**

—— Histoire de Marguerite de Valois, reine de Navarre, *etc.* [By C. R. de Caumont.] 2 vol. 1749. 12º. *See* MARGARET [d'Angoulême], *Queen Consort of Henry II., King of Navarre.*   **244 f. 14, 15.**

—— Histoire de Marguerite de Valois, reine de Navarre. (tom. 5. Notices sur les personnages de l'histoire de la reine de Navarre—tom. 6. Notice sur la vie de François Premier.—Recueil de quelques poésies de François Ier.—Remarques et éclaircissements pour rétablir la vérité des événements de l'histoire de la reine de Navarre. [By the editor, J. B. de La Borde.]) 6 tom. *Paris,* 1783. 12º.   **244. e. 20–25.**

—— Histoire secrète de Bourgogne. [By C. R. de Caumont.] 2 tom. pp. 536. 1694. 12º. *See* BURGUNDY. [*Appendix.*]   **9210. b. 1.**

—— [Another edition.] 2 tom. 1710. 12º. *See* BURGUNDY. [*Appendix.*]   **596. c. 30.**

CAUMONT (Charlotte Rose de)

—— [Another edition.] pp. iv. 288. *Londres [Paris],* 1747. 12º. [*Recueil de romans historiques.* tom. 7.]
244. b. 23.

—— [Another edition.] pp. 463. *See* Bibliothèque. Bibliothèque de campagne, *etc.* tom. 13. 1749. 12º.
244. f. 13.

—— [Another edition.] Notices sur les personnages de l'histoire secrète de Bourgogne. [By the editor, J. B. de la Borde.] 3 tom. *Paris,* 1782. 12º. **244. e. 17–19.**

—— The Secret History of Burgundy : or, the amorous and political intrigues of Charles Duke of Burgundy, and Louis XI. of France . . . Faithfully collected by a person of quality of the French Court [i.e. C. R. de Caumont], and now first done into English [by Gabriel Roussillon]. pp. xii. 396. 1723. 12º. *See* Burgundy. [*Appendix.*]
12512. ccc. 24.

—— Histoire secrète des amours de Henry IV, Roi de Castille, surnommé l'Impuissant. [By C. R. de Caumont.] pp. 260. 1695. 12º. *See* Henry IV., *King of Castile and of Leon.*
12513. cc. 41. (2.)

—— Nouvelle édition. pp. xxiii. 260. 1734. 16º. *See* Henry IV., *King of Castile and Leon.* **1444. a. 8.**

—— [Another edition.] 1746. 12º. [*Recueil de romans historiques.* tom. 2.] *See* Henry IV., *King of Castile and Leon.* **244. b. 18.**

—— [Another edition.] 1749. 12º. [*Bibliothèque de campagne, etc.* tom. 4.] *See* Henry IV., *King of Castile and Leon.* **244. f. 4.**

—— Les Jeux d'esprit ou la promenade de la Princesse de Conti à Eu . . . Publiés . . . avec une introduction par M. le Marquis de la Grange, *etc.* pp. 152. *Paris,* 1862. 8º. [*Trésor des pièces rares ou inédites.*]
12235. b. 14.

CAUMONT (F. G.) Essai sur le traitement des maladies de la moelle et de ses méninges. pp. 44. *Paris,* 1869. 4º. [*Collection des thèses soutenues à la Faculté de Médecine de Paris.* An 1869. tom. 3.] **7373. k. 9.**

CAUMONT (Franz Caze de) *See* Caze de Caumont.

CAUMONT (Georges) Jugements d'un mourant sur la vie. Conversations humoristiques et familières d'un malade avec la Divinité. [Edited by Benjamin Buisson.] pp. vi. 307. *Paris,* 1876. 8º. **12352. bb. 1.**

—— Notes morales sur l'homme et sur la société. pp. 301. *Paris,* 1872. 12º. **8405. ee. 3.**

CAUMONT (Henri) Jean-Jacques Rousseau et l'Isle de Saint-Pierre. [A poem.] pp. 23. *Zurich,* 1859. 8º.
11481. d. 51. (5.)

CAUMONT (Henri Nompar de) *Duke de la Force.* Mémoires du Marquis de Montpouillan. (Écrits par le Marquis de Castelnaut [i.e. H. N. de Caumont], d'après les confidences que ce dernier reçut de son frère, M. de Montpouillan.)—Mémoires du Marquis de Castelnaut, *etc. See* Caumont (J. N. de) *Duke de la Force.* Mémoires authentiques de Jacques Nompar de Caumont, duc de la Force, *etc.* tom. 4. 1843. 8º. **1450. h. 5.**

CAUMONT (Jacques Nompar de) *Duke de la Force.* *See* Casale Monferrato. La Leuee du siege de Cazal . . . par l'armée . . . conduite par Monseigueur le Mareschal de Schomberg, & Monseigneur le Mareschal de la Force. 1630. 8º. **1192. h. 5. (1.)**

—— *See* Caumont (A. A. G. M. J. N. de) *Duke de la Force.* Le Maréchal de la Force, 1558–1652. [With a portrait.] 1924, *etc.* 8º. **10656.gg.50.**

CAUMONT (Jacques Nompar de) *Duke de la Force.*

—— *See* Caumont (A. A. G. M. J. N. de) *Duke de La Force.* Le Maréchal de La Force, *etc.* 1950. 8º. **010665. t. 35.**

—— *See* Henry [de Lorraine], *Duke de Mayenne.* Deffaite des trouppes du Marquis de la Force, *etc.* 1621. 8º.
1193. h. 13. (21.)

—— Mémoires authentiques de Jacques Nompar de Caumont, duc de la Force, et de ses deux fils, les marquis de Montpouillan et de Castelnaut, suivis de documents curieux et de correspondances inédites de Jeanne d'Albret, Henri III, Henry IV, Catherine de Bourbon . . . et autres personnages marquants . . . Recueillis, mis en ordre et précédés d'une introduction par le marquis de la Grange. 4 tom. *Paris,* 1843. 8º. **1450. h. 4, 5.**

—— [Another copy.] **10661. e. 12.**

—— Récit véritable de la diuision & tumulte arriué de nouueau en la Ville de Clerac, entre les habitans & les garnisons du Marquis de la Force, sur le bruict du siège qu'on y va dresser, *etc.* pp. 14. *N. Letho: Paris,* 1622. 8º. **9210. aaa. 30.**

CAUMONT (Jean) Considerations sur l'hygiène des nouveau nés, *etc.* pp. 20. *Strasbourg,* 1831. 4º. [*Collection générale des dissertations de la Faculté de Médecine de Strasbourg.* vol. 44.] **7381*. b.**

CAUMONT (Jean de) *Champenois.* Aduertissement des aduertissemens, au peuple tres-chrestien. [A sermon against the Protestants.] ff. 23. 1587. 8º. **3900. b. 63.**

—— De l'Union des Catholiques avec Dieu et entre eux mesmes. pp. 73. *Chez N. Niuelle: Paris,* 1587. 8º.
3900. a. 60. (1.)

—— The Firme Foundation of Catholike Religion against the bottomlles pitt of heresies, wherein is shewed that onlye Catholikes shalbe saued, and that all heretikes of what sect soeuer are excluded frõ the knigdome [*sic*] of heauen. Compiled by Iohn Caumont of Champanye, and translated out of Frenche into Englishe by Iohn Paunchfoot the elder, *etc.* pp. 120. [*Charles de Boscard: Douai,* 1605 ?] 8º.
C. 110. a. 28.

CAUMONT (Jean de) *Seigneur de Montpouillan. See* Caumont (H. N. de) *Duke de la Force.* Mémoires du marquis de Montpouillan. (Écrits par le marquis de Castelnaut, d'après les confidences que ce dernier reçut de son frère, M. de Montpouillan.) 1843. 8º. [*Mémoires authentiques de Jacques Nompar de Caumont, duc de la Force, etc.* tom. 4.] **1450. h. 5.**

—— *See* Henry [de Lorraine], *Duke de Mayenne.* La Prise du ieune marquis de la Force, et de son frère le sieur de Montpouillan, *etc.* 1621. 8º. **1193. h. 13. (19.)**

CAUMONT (Joseph Marie Combette de) *Viscount. See* Combette de Caumont.

CAUMONT (L. A.) A Key to A. I. Calais' Wellington College French Exercise Book, *etc.* pp. 128. *David Nutt: London,* 1894. 8º. **12953. de. 33.**

CAUMONT (Louis Joseph Nompar de) *Duke de la Force.* Lettre à M. le maire de Montauban. (Note envoyé . . . . . . à MM. les rédacteurs du Journal de Paris, *etc.*) [Concerning a libel against the Duke.] [1790.] 8º.
F. 587. (4.)

CAUMONT (Louise Victoire de) afterwards **GRI-MOARD DE BEAUVOIR DE MONTLAUR** (L. V. de) *Countess du Roure. See* Grimoard de Beauvoir de Montlaur.

CAUMONT (Mary) A Dish of Matrimony. pp. 239. *Elliot Stock: London,* 1894. 8º. **012630. g. 49.**

CAUMONT (MARY)

—— The Hanleys; or, Wheels within wheels. pp. iv. 391. *Elliot Stock: London*, 1888. 8º. **012633. h. 25.**

—— Uncle Antony's Note-Book. [Tales for children.] pp. iv. 152. *F. V. White & Co.: London*, 1881. 8º. **12803. h. 23.**

—— Wilbourne Hall. [A novel.] 2 vol. *T. Fisher Unwin: London*, 1885. 8º. **12619. u. 6.**

CAUMONT (Ox.) *Princess de Turenne.* See LA TOUR D'AUVERGNE (Anne de) *Viscountess de Turenne.*

CAUMONT (PIERRE HENRI DE) *See* PERROT (P. E.) M. de Caumont. Notice biographique, *etc.* [1857?] 8º. **10662. d. 15.**

CAUMONT-BRÉON (P. J.) *See* NOELLAT (H.) Excursion dans le royaume de Tanjore . . . Première partie, précédée d'une notice biographique par M. Caumont-Bréon. 1884. 8º. [*Mémoires de la Société bourguignonne de Géographie et d'Histoire.* tom. 1.] Ac. **6024.**

—— Notice historique sur le village de Meuilley, *etc.* [With illustrations.] pp. x. 91. *Dijon*, 1858. 8º. **10169. aaa. 10.**

CAUMONT DE LA FORCE (CHARLOTTE ROSE DE) *See* CAUMONT (C. R. de)

CAUMONT DE SEYTRES (JOSEPH) *See* SEYTRES (J. de) *Marquis de Caumont.*

CAUMONT-FORCE (WILLIAM DE LA) *See* FORCE.

CAUMONT-LA FORCE, *Family of. See* JAURGAIN (Jean de) La Maison de Caumont-La Force, *etc.* 1912. 4º. **9904. v. 17.**

CAUMONT-LA FORCE (ANNE JACOBÉ DE) *Countess de Balbi. See* CAUMONT (A. A. G. M. J. N. de) *Duke de la Force.* Dames d'autrefois. (La Comtesse de Balbi.—Lettres de Louis XVIII à la comtesse de Balbi.) [With portraits.] 1933. 8º. **10655. pp. 9.**

—— *See* REISET (M. A. de) *Viscount.* Les Reines de l'émigration. Anne de Caumont-La Force, Comtesse de Balbi, *etc.* 1909. 8º. **10661. pp. 21.**

CAUMPEDENE. *See* CHIPPING CAMPDEN.

CAUMPEDENE (HUGO DE) *See* HUGO, *of Caumpedene.*

CAUNA. *See* KAUNAS.

CAUNA, BERNARD AUGUSTIN DE CABANNES, *Baron de. See* CABANNES.

ÇÂUNAKA. *See* ŚAUNAKA.

CAUNDISHE (RICHARD) *See* CAVENDISH.

CAUNDLE BISHOP. *See* BISHOP'S CAUNDLE.

CAUNE (VOLDEMARS)

—— *See* RIGA.—*Latvijas Valsts Bibliotēka.* Bibliografija 1 [*etc.*]. Latveešu zinatne un literatura, *etc.* (1921–23. A. Ģintera un V. Caunes sakārtojumā.—1924–27. Rediǵ. V. Caune.—1928, 29. V. Caune sakārtojumā.) 1920, *etc.* 8º. Ac. **9645.**

—— *See* RIGA.—*Latvijas Valsts Bibliotēka.* Valsts bibliotēkas biļetens . . . Rediǵējuši (1927–34): M. Stumbergs, V. Caune, *etc.* 1927, *etc.* 8º. Ac. **9645/3.**

—— Bibliotēkas iekārta. pp. 127. *Rīgā*, 1929. 8º. **11900. m. 1.**

CAUNEDO (NICOLÁS CASTOR DE) *See* CAUNEDO Y SUÁREZ DE MOSCOSO (N. C.)

CAUNEDO Y SUÁREZ DE MOSCOSO (NICOLÁS CASTOR) Album de un Viage por Asturias . . . Segunda edicion. pp. 52. *Oviedo*, 1858. fol. **10161. f. 19.**

CAUNES (AUGUSTE) Du gouvernement de tous, ou De la république sans anarchie, sans déchirements et sans factions; dédié au peuple souverain. pp. 35. *Paris*, [1848.] 12º. **8052. d. 10.**

—— Le Massacre de juin, ou le Tombeau de la liberté . . . 3e lampion républicain. pp. 40. *Paris*, [1848.] 8º. **8052. e. 17.**

CAUNES (JEAN PIERRE) *See* BARTHEZ (L.) Mémoire pour les citoyens Barthez, Caunes, *etc.* 1798. 8º. **F. 983. (8.)**

CAUNES (LUDOVIC) Hémorrhagies supplémentaires de la menstruation. Thèse, *etc.* pp. 74. *Montpellier*, 1863. 4º. **7379. e. 18. (8.)**

CAUNIÈRE (FERDINAND) De la médecine naturelle chez les anciens et les modernes, *etc.* pp. 424. *Paris*, 1865. 8º. **7321. g. 4.**

—— De la médecine naturelle indo-malgache considérée surtout au point de vue de la thérapeutique. pp. iii. 147. *Paris*, 1862. 12º. **7461. aaa. 31.**

—— La Médecine naturelle devant ses juges et devant l'opinion. pp. 61. *Paris*, 1858. 8º. **7391. c. 5.**

—— Requête de la médecine naturelle à l'Académie des Sciences lue dans sa séance ordinaire du 24 juin, 1861. pp. 15. *Paris*, 1861. 8º. [MISSING.]

CAUNT (BENJAMIN) Copy of Verses on the Awful Fire at Benjamin Caunt's in Saint Martin's Lane, *etc.* [*London*, 1855?] *s. sh.* 4º. **C. 116. i. 1. (141.)**

CAUNT (GEORGE WILLIAM) *See* JESSOP (Charles M.) and CAUNT (G. W.) The Elements of Hydrostatics. 1910. 8º. **8506. i. 1/30.**

—— *See* LOUIS (Henry) and CAUNT (G. W.) Tacheometer Tables. 1919. 8º. **08548. ee. 22.**

—— *See* LOUIS (Henry) and CAUNT (G. W.) Traverse Tables, *etc.* 1901. 8º. **08548. de. 4.**

—— Elementary Calculus. pp. 388. *Clarendon Press: Oxford*, 1939. 8º. **08535. aa. 49.**

—— An Introduction to the Infinitesimal Calculus, with applications to mechanics and physics. pp. xx. 568. *Clarendon Press: Oxford*, 1914. 8º. **8503. g. 5.**

CAUNT (GEORGE WILLIAM) and **JESSOP** (CHARLES MINSHALL)

—— Geometrical Conics. pp. 80. *London*, [1905.] 8º. [*Arnold's Mathematical Series.*] **012200. gg. 1/31.**

CAUNTER'S AND DANIELL'S ORIENTAL ANNUAL. *See* PERIODICAL PUBLICATIONS.—*London.* The Oriental Annual.

CAUNTER, *Family of. See* CAUNTER (Frederic L.) Caunter Family Records, *etc.* 1930. 8º. **09915. e. 25.**

CAUNTER (C. H.) Ornamental Lathework for Amateurs . . . By C. H. C. [i.e. C. H. Caunter.] pp. 121. [1914.] 8º. *See* C., C. H. **07816. a. 2.**

CAUNTER (CYRIL FRANCIS) Death to the Killer. pp. 280. *Eldon Press: London*, 1935. 8º. **A.N. 2284.**

CAUNTER (Cyril Francis)

—— Ex-Gangster. pp. 313. *Eldon Press: London*, 1933. 8º.
NN. **21376.**

—— Light Aero Engines. A practical manual, *etc.*
pp. xiii. 288. *Sir I. Pitman & Sons: London*, 1930. 8º.
8769. de. 17.

—— Madness Opens the Door. pp. 319.
Thornton Butterworth: London, [1932.] 8º. NN. **21034.**

—— Model Petrol Engines, *etc.* pp. 68. *London*,
[1922.] 8º. [*Model Engineer Series.* no. 44.]
08756. aaa. 1/46.

—— Small Electric Lighting Sets. pp. 264. *J. Munro & Co.:*
Glasgow, [1923.] 8º. **8759. a. 38.**

—— Small Four-Stroke Aero Engines. pp. viii. 87. *Sir*
I. Pitman & Sons: London, 1936. 8º. [*Aeronautical*
Engineering Series.] **08773.ee.1/5.**

—— Small Two-Stroke Aero Engines. pp. viii. 79.
Sir I. Pitman & Sons: London, 1936. 8º. [*Aeronautical*
Engineering Series.] **08773.ee.1/4.**

—— The Two-Cycle Engine, *etc.* pp. xiii. 277. *Sir*
I. Pitman & Sons: London, 1932. 8º. **08769. aaa. 66.**

CAUNTER (Frederic Lyde) Caunter Family Records.
[With plates and genealogical tables.] pp. 81.
Solicitors' Law Stationery Society: London, 1930. 8º.
09915. e. 25.

—— Lyde Records. [With a pedigree.] pp. 72. *Solicitors'*
Law Stationery Society: London, 1933. 8º. **9902. b. 40.**

CAUNTER (George Henry) *See* Ney (M.) *Prince de la*
Moskowa. Military Studies by Marshal Ney . . . trans-
lated from the . . . original manuscripts by G. H.
Caunter, etc. 1833. 8º. **1140. h. 9.**

—— The Hand-Book of Chemistry, *etc.* pp. xiv. 279.
W. S. Orr & Co.: London, 1839. 8º. **8905. de. 2.**

CAUNTER (Hobart) *See* Caunter (John H.)

CAUNTER (John Alan Lyde) 13 Days. The chronicle
of an escape from a German prison . . . Illustrated by the
author. pp. xv. 224. *G. Bell & Sons: London*, 1918. 8º.
9083. aa. 33.

CAUNTER (John Eales) The Campaign in the Free
State, to the 13th March 1900, and its lessons. pp. 38.
Gale & Polden: London, [1901.] 8º. **09061. a. 10.**

—— The Officer's Field Book. [With "refills."] 2 pt.
Hugh Rees: London, 1909. *obl.* 16º. **8825. a. 62.**

CAUNTER (John Hobart) *See* Bible. [*English.*] The
Holy Bible . . . With notes by the Rev. J. H. Caunter.
1840. 8º. **689. d. 1.**

—— *See* Lectures. Familiar Lectures to Children . . .
Edited by the Rev. H. Caunter. 1835. 8º. **863. c. 43.**

—— *See* Westall (Richard) Illustrations of the Bible.
By Westall and Martin. With descriptions by the Rev.
H. Caunter. 1835, *etc.* 4º. **3125. h. 6.**

—— —— [1877.] 12º. **3128. df. 12.**

—— The Cadet; a poem . . . containing remarks on British
India. To which is added, Egbert and Amelia . . . with
other poems. By a late resident in the East [i.e. J. H.
Caunter]. 2 vol. 1814. 12º. *See* Cadet. **993. d. 46.**

—— Caunter's and Daniell's Oriental Annual, 1839. Eastern
Legends by the Rev. H. Caunter . . . With twenty-two
engravings, from drawings by . . . W. Daniell.
pp. vi. 268. 1838. 12º. *See* Periodical Publications.
—*London.* **P.P. 6891.**

CAUNTER (John Hobart)

—— The Fellow Commoner. [A novel. By J. H. Caunter.]
3 vol. 1836. 12º. *See* Fellow-Commoner. N. **1344.**

—— India. [Historical Tales.] 3 vol. *Edward Churton:*
London, 1836. 12º. [*The Romance of History.*]
N. **1352.**

—— [Another edition.] With illustrations. pp. vi. 514.
F. Warne & Co.: London, [1872.] 8º.
[*The Romance of History.*] **012619.a.1/3.**

—— An Inquiry into the History and Character of Rahab.
pp. 379. *Longman & Co.: London*, 1850. 8º.
4805. g. 10.

—— The Island Bride, in six cantos. pp. 243.
Edward Bull: London, 1830. 8º. **993. h. 13.**

—— The Oriental Annual, or Sciences in India; comprising
. . . engravings from original drawings by William Daniell
. . . and a descriptive account by . . . H. Caunter. (1837.
Lives of the Moghul Emperors.—1838. The Oriental
Annual, or Scenes in India.—By H. Caunter, with drawings
by W. Daniell.) 5 vol. *London*, 1834–38. 8º. [*Oriental*
Annual, 1834–1838.] 8º. **P.P. 6890. b.**
Each volume has an additional titlepage, engraved.

—— [Another copy.] The Oriental Annual, *etc.* **L.P.**
London, 1834–38. 8º. **P.P. 6890.**
Wanting the issue for 1837.

—— The Poetry of the Pentateuch. 2 vol. *E. Churton:*
London, 1839. 8º. **1110. e. 25.**

—— St. Leon: a drama, *etc.* [By J. H. Caunter.] pp. 131.
1835. 8º. *See* Saint Leon. T. **1604. (11.)**

—— A Sermon preached at Saint Peter's, Cornhill, *etc.*
pp. 32. *J. Madden & Co.: London*, 1839. 8º.
908. d. 5. (10.)

—— Sermons. (Sermons preached in St. Paul's Chapel
. . . St. Marylebone.) 3 vol. *E. Bull; J. G. &*
F. Rivington: London, 1832–42. 8º. **1021. i. 12, 13.**

CAUNTER (Julien)

—— How to do Tricks in Amateur Films. pp. 176. *Focal*
Press: London & New York, 1955. 8º. [*Focal Cine-*
books.] **W.P. 2671/21.**

—— How to produce Effects in Amateur Films. pp. 184.
Focal Press: London & New York, 1955. 8º. [*Focal*
Cinebooks.] **W.P. 2671/22.**

CAUNTER (Lilian Jane)

—— *See* Bunyan (John) [*Single Works.—Pilgrim's Progress.*
—Abridgments, Extracts and Adaptations.] The Children's
Pilgrim's Progress. Adapted . . . by L. J. Caunter, *etc.*
[1950.] 8º. **04413. k. 33.**

CAUNTER (Macdonald) *See* Caunter (Richard M.)

CAUNTER (Mary) The Stories of Genesis for the Little
Ones. pp. 124. *J. Masters & Co.: London*, 1876. 12º.
3149. de. 2.

CAUNTER (Richard Macdonald) Attila, a tragedy;
and other poems. pp. 316. *T. & W. Boone: London*,
1832. 8º. **11781. df. 1.**

—— Sermon, preached on the opening of Trinity Chapel,
Forest Row, East Grinstead, *etc.* pp. 18. *T. &*
W. Boone: London, 1836. 8º. **4475. cc. 112. (13.)**
With a ms. *letter of the author inserted.*

—— Two Sermons to Seamen, preached . . . in March, 1829.
pp. 18. *Sealy, Bryers & Walker: Dublin*, 1895. 8º.
4475. i. 3. (7.)

CAUNTER (Violet Sibyl) Uncle Godfrey, or the Christmas Gift, *etc.* pp. 63. *S.P.C.K.: London,* [1869.] 16⁰.
[Missing.]

CAUNTINO (Estrio) *pseud.* [i.e. Giovanni Battista Cotta.] *See also* Cotta (G. B.)

—— Rime. 2 pt. 1717, 20. *See* Rome.—*Arcadia.* Rime degli Arcadi, *etc.* tom. 4, 8. 1716, *etc.* 8⁰.
240. k. 7, 11.

CAUPAIN (Henri) Le desert ď deuotion q̇ est vng traicte plaisãt, vtile ꝛ ꝓffitable a toutes manieres ď gẽs deuotz . . . Nouuellemẽt ꝓpose pour inciter les cueurs a feruentement aimer dieu ꝛ apeter les biẽs eternelz, *etc.* (Compose par vng frere mineur du couuent dabbeuille.) **G. ℥.** *Imprime a Paris,* [1530?] 8⁰. **695. a. 2.**
The author's name is given, as he himself indicates, in an acrostic at the end of the book, and below the acrostic occur the initials F. H. C., i.e. Frère Henri Caupain.

CAUPENNE (Alfred de Cès) *See* Cès-Caupenne.

CAUPERT (Johann Georg Carl) Einige Worte zum Andenken des heute vor hundert Jahren in Eyrichshof geborenen Johann Georg Meusel, *etc. See* Meusel (J. G.) Eine kleine Gabe, am hundertjährigen Geburtstage des Herrn Joh. Georg Meusel, *etc.* 1843. 8⁰.
10705. aa. 30. (2.)

CAUPERT (Maximilien) La Théorie des relations considérée comme base de la science et du progrès actuel. pp. 440. *Paris,* 1852. 8⁰. **4376. d. 6.**

CAUPIS (Thomas) Alphabetnm [*sic*] Religiosorum. *See* Richardinus (R.) Exegesis in Canonem diui Augustini, *etc.* 1530. 8⁰. **3670. de. 4.**

CAUQUIL ( ) *Docteur, Chevalier de l'Ordre Impérial de la Légion-d'Honneur.* Études économiques sur l'Algérie. Administration, colonisation, cantonnement des indigènes. pp. 98. *Oran,* 1860. 8⁰. **8155. ee. 25.**

CAUQUIL (Alexandre Stanislas) Questions tirées au sort . . . Thèse pour obtenir le grade de docteur en médecine. pp. 36. *Montpellier,* [1843.] 4⁰. **1182. c. 17. (6.)**

CAUQUIL (Augustin) Faculté de Droit d'Aix. Thèse pour le doctorat. Droit romain. De l'hypothèque conventionnelle. Droit français. De l'hypothèque maritime. Commentaire de la loi du 10 juillet 1885. pp. 286. *Oran,* 1887. 8⁰. **5403. f. 5.**

CAUQUIL (C.) Les Remèdes nouveaux. Exposé succint des principaux éléments médicamenteux introduits dans la thérapeutique de 1878 à 1888. pp. 141. *Montpellier; Paris,* 1888. 8⁰. **7510. c. 3.**

CAUQUIL (Gabriel) Étude sur la coxalgie et son traitement. Thèse, *etc.* pp. 58. *Montpellier,* 1877. 4⁰.
7379. l. 1. (2.)

CAURANT (Eugène Louis Ernest) Relation médicale d'un voyage de France à la Nouvelle-Calédonie à bord de la frégate Iphygénie. pp. 88. *Paris,* 1869. 4⁰. [*Collection des thèses soutenues à la Faculté de Médecine de Paris. An* 1869. *tom* 3.] **7373. k. 9.**

CAURIA. *See* Coria.

CAURIANA (Philippe) *See* Cavriana (Filippo A.)

CAURIANI (Federico) *See* Cavriani.

CAURIUOLO (Alfonso) *See* Cavriuolo.

CAURO (A.) Exposition du moyen curatif des accidens produits par la morsure de l'araignée 13-guttata ou Théridion malmignatte du département de la Corse . . . Thèse, *etc.* pp. 17. *Paris,* 1833. 4⁰. **1184. e. 14. (17.)**

CAURO (J.) La Liquéfaction des gaz. Méthodes nouvelles. —Applications. pp. 83. *Paris,* 1899. 8⁰. **8909. d. 12.**

CAURO (Pierre) De l'ablation de l'utérus dans les cas d'inversion de cet organe . . . Thèse, *etc.* pp. 40. *Montpellier,* 1876. 4⁰. **7379. k. 18. (3.)**

—— Du chancre phagédénique et de son traitement. Thèse, *etc.* pp. 56. *Montpellier,* 1877. 4⁰. **7379. l. 1. (4.)**

CAURO (Victor) *See* Aḥmad ibn Khālid, al-Nāṣirī. Récits sur la vie de Mohammed . . . Traduction et notes de V. Cauro. 1916. 12⁰. **14555. b. 29.**

CAUS (Isaac de) Nouuelle inuention de leuer l'eau plus hault que sa source auec quelques machines mouantes par le moyen de l'eau, et vn discours de la conduite d'icelle. pp. 32. pl. xxvi. *Londre,* 1644. fol.
536. m. 8. (1.)
With an additional titlepage, engraved.

—— New and Rare Inventions of Water-Works, shewing the easiest waies to raise water higher then [*sic*] the spring. By which invention perpetual motion is proposed . . . First written in French . . . And now translated into Engiish by John Leak. pp. 34. pl. xxvi. *Joseph Moxon: London,* 1659. fol. **8776. g. 36.**
The titlepage is engraved.

—— [Another edition.] A New and Rare Invention of Water-Works . . . As also, a Description of Capt. Savory's Engine for Raising of vast Quantities of water by Fire. [With plates.] pp. 47. *J. Moxon: London,* 1704. 4⁰. **C. 54. c. 12. (1.)**

—— Wilton Garden. [Engravings.] pl. 26. *Sould by Thomas Rowlett:* [*London,* 1645?] obl. fol. **441. g. 19.**

CAUS (Salomon de) Hortus Palatinus a Friderico Rege Boemiæ Electore Palatino Heidelbergæ extructus, Salamone de Caus Architecto. [The dedication and the description of the plates are in French.] pl. 30. *I. T. de Bry: Francofurti,* 1620. fol. **535. l. 10. (1*.)**
The titlepage is engraved.

—— [Another copy.] **441. k. 4.**
Imperfect; wanting the dedication, the folding-plate headed " Scenographia. Hortus Palatinus" and pl. 25, 26. Pl. 1 is partially mutilated.

—— [Another issue.] [The dedication and the description of the plates are in German.] pl. 30. *I. T. de Bry: Francofurti,* 1620. fol. **731. m. 17. (2.)**
The titlepage is engraved.

—— [Another copy.] **G. 6636.**
Imperfect; wanting the folding plate headed " Scenographia. Hortus Palatinus."

—— Institution harmonique, *etc.* 2 pt [*Jan Norton: Francfort,* 1615.] fol. **Hirsch i. 107.**
The imprint has been supplied in manuscript.

—— [Another copy.] **558. f. 21.**

Imperfect; wanting the titlepage, which is supplied in MS.

—— La Perspective, auec la raison des ombres et miroirs. [With diagrams.] *Jan Norton: Londres,* 1612. fol.
561*. f. 15.
The titlepage is engraved.

—— [Another issue.] *Londres,* 1612. fol. **747. d. 26. (1.)**
The titlepage is engraved. Imperfect; wanting the address to the reader and six leaves numbered 36–41.

—— La Pratique et demonstration des horloges solaires. Auec vn discours sur les proportions, tiré de la raison de la 35 proposition du premier livre d'Euclide, *etc.* [With diagrams.] pp. 80. *H. Droüart: Paris,* 1624. fol.
533. l. 13.

CAUS (Salomon de)

—— [Another copy.] La Pratique et demonstration des horloges solaires, etc. Paris, 1624. fol.
Hirsch I. **108.** (2.)

—— Les Raisons des forces mouuantes. Auec diuerses machines tant vtilles que plaisantes. Aus quelles sont adioints plusieurs desseings de grotes et fontaines. [With illustrations.] 3 pt. *J. Norton: Francfort*, 1615. fol.
535. l. 23.
The titlepages of pt. 1 and 2 are engraved.

—— Les Raisons des forces mouuantes . . . Augmentées de plusieurs figures, auec le discours sur chacune. 3 pt.
Hierosme Drouüart: Paris, 1624. fol.
Hirsch I. **108.** (1.)
The titlepages of pt. 1 and 2 are engraved.

—— [Another issue.] Les Raisons des forces mouuantes, etc.
C. Serestre: Paris, 1624. fol. **535.** l. **10.** (1.)
Imperfect: wanting ff. 22. 23, 25. 26, 29. 31 of pt. 1. and f. 17 of pt. 2.

—— Von Gewaltsamen bewegungen. Beschreibung etlicher so wol nützlichen alss lustigen Maschiner, beneben Vnderschiedlichen abriessen etliher Höllen od' Grotten vnd lust Brunnē . . . Erstlich in Franszösischer Jetzundt aber in vnsser Deutsche Sprach an tag geben. [With illustrations.] 3 pt.
A. Pacquart: Franckfurt, [1615.] fol. **1811. b. 12.** (1.)
The titlepages of pt. 1 and 2 are engraved. The titlepage of pt. 3, by a printer's error, bears the date 1515.

CAUSA. *See* WILSON (Samuel) *Baptist Minister*. The Deity and Satisfaction of Christ asserted. Being an answer to the second part of an anonymous pamphlet [by Hopton Haynes?], intitled, Causa Dei contra Novatores; or, God ever propitious to his people, etc. 1747. 8°.
4372. cc. 21. (2.)

—— Causa Dei asserta per justitiam ejus, cum cæteris ejus perfectionibus, cunctisque actionibus conciliatam. pp. 48.
Amstælodami, 1710. 8°. **1019. m. 5.**

—— Causa Dei contra Novatores: or, the Religion of the Bible and the Religion of the Pulpit compared, etc. [Signed A. B., i.e. Hopton Haynes.] 1747. 8°. *See* B., A.
4327. d. 63. (2.)

—— Causa Helvetica. *See* SWISS CAUSE.

—— Causæ veteris epitaphium, in antecessum ab anonymo autore scriptum. pp. 4. *Prostant venales in officinâ G. Abington: Paganopoli* [London, 1681?] fol.
1872. a. 1. (155.)

—— Editio altera. Accedit Causa vetus conclamata. pp. 19.
Prostant in officinâ B. Tooke: Neapoli sive Augustæ Trinobantûm [London], 1685. 4°. **8122. bb. 36.**

—— The Old Cause's Epitaph by Anticipation. Since rendred in English. [In verse.] pp. 20. 1683. 4°. *See* CAUSE.
11623. e. 12. (6.)

CAUSA (Cesare) *See* GIUSTI (G.) Poesie . . . con note ed illustrazioni storiche di C. Causa, etc. 1882. 8°.
2284. c. 10.

—— *See* MAINARDI (A.) *Piovano*. Il Piovano Arlotto. Satire, celie ed arguzie del celebre burlone fiorentino, raccolte e compilate da C. Causa. 1879. 8°.
12314. e. 40.

—— —— 1885. 8°. **12330. bbb. 45.**

—— Gino Capponi. Ricordi storico-biografici raccolti e ordinati per cura di C. Causa. [With a portrait.] pp. 64.
Firenze, 1876. 8°. **10602. h. 5.** (8.)

CAUSA (Cesare)

—— Giordano Bruno, bruciato vivo in Roma il 16 febbraio 1600. pp. 15. *Firenze*, 1889. 8°. **10602. c. 27.** (2.)

—— Giovanni Passanante condannato a morte per avere attentato alla vita di S. M. Umberto I. Re d'Italia. Dalla nascita, alla grazia sovrana. pp. 127. *Firenze*, 1879. 8°.
10629. aa. 17.

—— [A reissue.] *Firenze*, 1886. 8°. **10629. a. 23.**

—— La Guerra italo-turca e la conquista della Tripolitania e della Cirenaica. Narrazione storica . . . Nuova edizione con oltre cento fotografie . . . numerosi disegni e due carte geografiche, etc. pp. 805. *Firenze*, 1912. 8°.
9061. eee. 4.

—— Segreti amori della Giulia fioraja. Racconto sociale. pp. 63. *Firenze*, 1872. 8°. **12471. aa. 40.** (6.)

—— Vita dei fratelli Bandiera fucilati a Cosenza il 25 luglio 1844. Narrazione storica. pp. 128. *Firenze*, 1888. 8°.
10629. a. 33.

—— [Another edition.] pp. 128. *Firenze*, 1895. 8°.
10629. de. 1.

—— [Another edition.] pp. 128. *Firenze*, 1904. 8°.
10629. de. 5.

—— Vita di Ciro Menotti, impiccato a Modena il 26 maggio 1831. Narrazione storica. pp. 128. *Firenze*, 1888. 8°.
10629. a. 34.

—— Vita e viaggi di Cristoforo Colombo. Narrazione storica. [With illustrations.] pp. 524. *Firenze*, 1892. 8°.
10630. cc. 32.

—— Vita galante e scandalosa di Antonietta la ballerina. pp. 64. *Firenze*, 1872. 8°. **12471. aa. 40.** (5.)

CAUSA (Mario Gorino) *See* GORINO CAUSA.

CAUSAE.

—— P. B. D. [i.e. Philip B. Duncan] de causis belli quibusdam, de anglico, non ad verbum convertit Pacis Defensor [i.e. Richard Walker]. MS. NOTES [by the translator].
1853. 8°. *See* D., P. B. **8425. c. 59.** (4.)

CAUSALITY. Causality. Lectures delivered before the Philosophical Union, University of California, 1932. pp. 231. *Berkeley, Cal.*, 1932. 8°. [*University of California Publications in Philosophy*. vol. 15.]
Ac. 2689. g/18.

—— [Another copy.] **08458. dd. 20.**

CAUSANS, JACQUES DE VINCENS, *Marquis de*. *See* VINCENS.

CAUSANS (JOSEPH LOUIS VINCENT DE MAULÉON DE) *See* MAULÉON DE CAUSANS.

CAUSARD (AUGUSTE) Bourbonne et ses eaux minérales . . . Avec une carte. pp. 324. *Paris*, 1870. 12°.
7470. de. 15.

CAUSARD (DIDIER THÉODORE) Considérations sur les scrophules; thèse, etc. pp. 33. *Paris*, 1833. 4°.
1184. f. 3. (1.)

CAUSARD (MARCEL) Thèses presentées à la Faculté des Sciences de Paris . . . 1re thèse.—Recherches sur l'appareil circulatoire des aranéides. 2e thèse.—Propositions données par la Faculté, etc. pp. 109. pl. VI. *Lille*, 1896. 8°. **7297. cc. 3.**
Containing only the " Recherches."

CAUSARD (Victor Auguste) Essai sur la paralysie suite de contusion des nerfs. pp. 74. *Paris*, 1861. 4º. [*Collection des thèses soutenues à la Faculté de Médecine de Paris. An 1861. tom. 2.*] **7373. d. 3.**

CAUSARD D'ARCÉMONT (Henry Léopold) Dissertation sur l'emploi de la belladona en médecine, *etc.* pp. 24. *Paris*, 1824. 4º. **1183. h. 4. (25.)**

CAUSATION.

—— Is Causation or Power in Nature a Reality, or a Mere Anthropomorphic Fancy? [By Richard H. Hutton. A paper read before the Metaphysical Society.] pp. 6. [*London*, 1879.] 8º. **Cup. 400. c. 2. (44.)**

CAUSE. The Cause. *See* Periodical Publications.— *Philadelphia.*

—— The Cause and Cure of Railway Labor Disputes . . . By an experienced Railway Man. pp. 16. *Simpkin, Marshall & Co.: London*, 1902. 8º. **8285. de. 34. (8.)**

—— Cause and Effect: or, Has God forsaken the earth? A question for the times, by a Student of Nature. pp. 26. *Hamilton, Adams & Co.; W. Brown & Co.: London*, 1875. 8º. **4017. g. 41. (3.)**

—— The Cause and Prevention of Great Calamities, *etc.* [Signed: G. W.] 1705. *s. sh. fol. See* W., G. **L. 7. a. 3. (35.)**

—— La Cause des proscrits, ou Notice critique et raisonnée sur les lois relatives à l'émigration, *etc.* pp. 95. *Paris*, [1800.] 8º. **F. 734. (1.)**

—— La Cause du peuple. *See* Periodical Publications.— *Paris.*

—— Cause ed effetti. 1898–1900. [An anarchist publication.] *A. Galassini: London*, 1900. fol. **1880. d. 16. (34.)**

—— La Cause générale. *See* Periodical Publications.— *Paris.* Общее Дѣло.

—— The Cause of a Crisis . . . By A. J. O. [i.e. A. J. Ogilvy.] 1894. 8º. *See* O., A. J. **08226. h. 14. (17.)**

—— The Cause of Death from what is called Death from Old Age is now revealed to man, *etc.* pp. viii. 63. *George Hamilton: London*, [1883.] 8º. **7306. de. 24. (3.)**

—— The Cause of God, and of these nations, sought out and drawn forth from the rubbish of the lusts and interests of men, *etc.* pp. 33 [34]. *London*, 1659. 4º. **100. f. 47.**

—— The Cause of our Present Distresses; and the remedies that have been suggested for their relief, shortly considered. pp. 34. *J. M. Richardson: London*, 1826. 8º. **T. 1131. (3.)**

—— The Cause of the Poor [and other poems]. [By Ed. Harper Wade?] *Desbarats & Co.: Montreal*, [1891?] 8º. **11688. df. 36.**

—— The Cause of World Unrest. With an introduction by the editor of "The Morning Post" (H. A. Gwynne). pp. 269. *Grant Richards: London*, 1920. 8º. **08282. aa. 82.**

—— Cause première de toutes les crises sociales, financières, alimentaires, industrielles, etc. pp. 34. *Paris*, 1858. 8º. **8205. e. 36. (7.)**

—— The Good Old Cause briefly demonstrated, *etc.* [Signed: R. H., i.e. Richard Hubberthorn.] 1659. 4º. *See* H., R. **4152. f. 22. (14.)**

CAUSE.

—— The Good Old Cause Revived. [A satire on the Whigs.] [*London*, 1680.] *s. sh. fol.* **C. 20. f. 4. (93.)**

—— [Another copy.] **C. 20. f. 2. (342.)**

—— [A photographic facsimile.] [1937.] *s. sh. fol.* **C. 20. f. 4. (93*.)**

—— The Great Cause of the Present Distress, and the Remedy. By a Friend to the Home Trade. pp. 15. *H. Guy: Chelmsford*, 1843. 8º. **1390. g. 54.**

—— Is there not a Cause? By the author of "Is it never too late to mend?", "Absent from the Body, *etc.*" pp. 24. *J. F. Shaw & Co.: London*, [1889.] 12º. **8630. cc. 37. (5.)**

—— The Just Cause; or, the Claims of the Dissenters expounded, *etc.* 1835. 12º. *See* Dissenters. **908. c. 7. (15.)**

—— The Old Cause's Epitaph by Anticipation. Since rendred in English. [A translation of the anonymous work "Causæ veteris epitaphium." In verse.] pp. 20. *H. H. for William Abington: London*, 1683. 4º. **11623. e. 12. (6.)**

—— The Real Cause of Strikes and how to prevent them. pp. 7. *The Field & Queen: London*, [1919.] 8º. **08285. b. 51.**

—— The Real Cause of the Depreciation of the National Currency Explained; and the means of remedy suggested. [By Peter Carey.] pp. 45. *J. M. Richardson: London*, 1810. 8º. **1027. l. 17. (3.)**

—— [Another copy.] The Real Cause of the Depreciation of the National Currency explained, *etc.* [By P. Carey.] *London*, 1810. 8º. **8220. aa. 3. (3.)**

—— The Real Cause of the High Price of Gold Bullion. [By Edward Cooke.] pp. 39. *J. J. Stockdale: London*, 1819. 8º. **8225. d. 16.**

—— The Real Cause of the Present Depression in the Cotton Trade . . . In twenty-four letters. By a retired manufacturer. pp. 32. *J. Heywood: Manchester*, 1886. 8º. **8229. i. 18. (7.)**

—— This Cause We Serve. [On religion and the war.] pp. 63. *Covenant Publishing Co.: London*, [1943.] 8º. **4398. bb. 13.**

—— The True Cause of all our Miseries, discovered in their visible effects, *etc. See* Somers (John) *Baron Somers.* A Scarce . . . Collection of Tracts, *etc.* vol. 3. 1748. 4º. **184. a. 3.**

—— [Another edition.] 1813. *See* Somers (John) *Baron Somers.* A Collection of Scarce . . . Tracts, *etc.* vol. 9. 1809, *etc.* 4º. **750. g. 9.**

—— The True Cause of Depreciation traced to the state of our Silver Currency. [By A. W. Rutherford.] pp. 32. *Galabin & Marchant: London*, [1819?] 8º. **B. 497. (16.)**

—— The True Good Old Cause Rightly Stated, and the false uncased. [By William Prynne.] pp. 8. [*London*, 1659.] 4º. **E. 983. (6*.)**

—— [Another copy.] **287. g. 25. (6.)**

CAUSE (Hendrik) De Koninglycke Hovenier, aanwyzende de middelen om boomen, bloemen en kruyden, te zaayen, planten, aen queeken en voort teelen. Met . . . platen verciert. pp. 224. *M. Doornik: Amsterdam*, [1676.] fol. **450. i. 3. (1.)**

The titlepage is engraved.

CAUSEBROOKE (Arthur)

—— College Chapel Echoes. [On College Chapel, Stepney Green. With plates.] pp. 125.　　*A. H. Stockwell: Ilfracombe*, [1942.]　8º.　　**20047. aaa. 13.**

CAUSEI DE LA CHAUSSE (Michelangelo) *See* La Chausse (Michel A. de)

CAUSER (Edward) A Treatise on the Morbid Respiration of Domestic Animals, *etc.* pp. xii. 214.　*J. Smith & Son: Glasgow*, 1822.　8º.　　**779. d. 17.**

CAUSERET (Charles) *See* Castaigne (E. J.) Trois fabulistes . . . Étude bibliographique, *etc.* [With reference to C. Causeret's " Trois fabulistes "]. 1889. 12º.　　**11850. aaaa. 38. (6.)**

—— Étude sur la langue de la rhétorique et de la critique littéraire dans Cicéron. pp. 245.　*Paris*, 1886.　8º.　　**11312. o. 25.**

CAUSERIE. Causerie. The intimate magazine.　*See* Periodical Publications.—*London*.

—— Eene Causerie over schutterij en leger, door een officier van de armée. [Signed: *Δ*.]　1864.　8º.　*See* D.　　**8824. d. 53. (4.)**

CAUSERIES.　Causeries cartésiennes.　*See* Cartesian Talks.

—— Causeries en vers d'une jeune personne du monde. [By Baroness V. Bartakovics. With musical notes.] pp. 74.　*Vienne*, 1870.　12º.　　**11482. bb. 47. (7.)**

—— Causeries familières. Dédiées aux jeunes filles, *etc. See* Periodical Publications.—*Paris*.

—— Causeries familières sur les sciences, les arts et la littérature.　*See* Periodical Publications.—*Paris*.

—— Causeries maternelles sur les premiers dons de Dieu . . . Petites leçons historiques . . . par Mme . . . . . ., Inspectrice. [The dedication signed : L.]　1852.　8º.　*See* L.　　**12202. ff. 2.**

—— Causeries scientifiques.　*See* Periodical Publications.—*Paris*.

—— Causeries sur les affaires du tems, entre les deux premiers jongleurs d'Europe [i.e. King Louis Philippe and Talleyrand]. pp. 39.　*J. Teuten: Londres*, [1835.]　8º.　　**T. 1918. (3.)**

—— Causeries typographiques. [Edited by Marius Audin.] Troisième (—12e) opuscule, *etc. Lyon*, 1921–26.　8º & 4º.　　**11900. t. 20.**
No more published.

CAUSES. A Book for the Public. New discovery. The Causes of the Circulation of the Blood; and the true nature of the planetary system, *etc.* [By Alfred Mead?] pp. 61.　*A. Mead: London*, 1848.　8º.　　**7405. e. 10.**

—— Causes amusantes et connues. [Edited by Robert Estienne, libraire de Paris.] 2 tom.　*Berlin* [*Paris*], 1769, 70.　12º.　　**230. f. 16, 17.**

—— [Another copy.]　　**G. 16500, 01.**

—— Causes and Cure of the Present Distress. pp. 30.　*James Ridgway: London*, 1830.　8º.　　**T. 1282. (1.)**

—— The Causes and Prevention of Consumption, and tuberculous and scrofulous diseases generally. Extracted from " A Treatise on Pulmonary Consumption, &c." pp. 75.　*Marchant:* [*London*,] 1835.　8º.　　**7630. e. 45. (1.)**

CAUSES.

—— Causes célèbres étrangères publiées en France pour la première fois et traduites de l'anglais, de l'espagnol, de l'italien, de l'allemand . . . Par une société de jurisconsultes et de gens de lettres. 5 tom.　*Paris*, 1827, 28.　8º.　　**1131. d. 29, 30.**

—— Causes criminelles célèbres du xixe siècle, rédigées par une société d'avocats. 4 tom.　*Paris*, 1827, 28.　8º.　　**5425. k. 7.**
Tom. 4 is wrongly designated " Tome huitième " on the titlepage.

—— Causes de la décadence du goût sur le théâtre, *etc.* [By Louis Charpentier.] 2 pt.　*Paris*, 1768.　12º.　**241. h. 32.**

—— Les Causes de nos désastres. Projet de réorganisation de l'armée, faisant suite à La Campagne de 1870 jusqu'au 1er septembre. Par un officier d'état-major de l'armée du Rhin. pp. 239.　1871.　*See* Campagne. La Campagne de 1870, *etc.* [1870, *etc.*]　8º.　　**9078. g. 7.**

—— [Another copy.]　　**9080. f. 3.**

—— Les Causes et les effets. [A political tract.] pp. 15.　[*Paris*, 1789.]　8º.　　**F. 9. (3.)**

—— [Another copy.]　　**F. 53. (11.)**

—— [Another copy.]　　**F. 69**. (10.)**

—— The Causes of the Contempt of the Clergy considered in a sermon intended to have been preached at a Visitation. pp. 16.　*C. Dilly: London*, 1796.　12º.　　**T. 1046. (14.)**

—— The Causes of the Discontents, in relation to the Plague, and the provisions against it, fairly stated and consider'd. [By Edmund Gibson, Bishop of London.]　pp. 14.　*J. Roberts: London*, 1721.　4º.　　**551. b. 9. (7.)**

—— [Another copy.]　　**1167. e. 32.**

—— The Causes of the Present Complaints, fairly stated and fully refuted. [By John Almon.] pp. 24.　*J. Sewell: London*, 1793.　8º.　　**8135. b. 24. (4.)**

—— Causes of the Present National Distress, with suggestions for their equitable removal. [By John Warner.] pp. 16.　*Fisher, Son & Co.; Simpkin & Marshall: London*, [1845?]　8º.　　**8227. c. 12.**

—— Causes of the War and the Road to Victory. By G. D.　[1914.]　8º.　*See* D., G.　　**04403. e. 82.**

—— Des causes de la Révolution et de ses résultats. [By Count A. de Lezay-Marnezia.] pp. 32.　*Paris*, 1797.　8º.　　**F. 573. (1.)**

—— Des causes des désordres, et de la misère publique. pp. 59.　*Paris*, 1792.　8º.　　**F. 14. (5.)**

—— [Another edition.] pp. 59.　*Paris*, 1792.　8º.　　**F. 504. (6.)**

—— Des causes qui ont opéré la Révolution. pp. 32.　[*Paris*, 1790?]　8º.　　**F. 573. (2.)**

—— Des causes qui retardent la conversion du monde. On the Causes which retard the Conversion of the World. Translated from the French by a clergyman of the Church of England. pp. 66.　*L. & G. Seeley: London*, 1842.　8º.　　**4372. bbb. 18.**

—— The Immediate Causes, and Remote Consequences of the Peace, considered. pp. iv. 66.　*R. Thurgood: London*, 1801.　8º.　　**E. 2179. (3.)**

—— On the Causes and Consequences of the Present Monetary Crisis : or, the First Principles of political economy applied to the gold supplies. pp. v. 62.　*Groombridge & Sons: London*, 1857.　8º. **8227.b.37.**

CAUSES.

—— On the Causes of the Present Discontents; with strictures on the politics of the last number of the Edinburgh Review. [Reprinted from Blackwood's Magazine.] pp. 62. *William Blackwood: Edinburgh,* 1820. 8⁰.
8135. e. 25.

—— [Another copy.] **1102. f. 3. (6.)**

—— One of the Causes of Agricultural Depression. pp. 3. *" Bradford Observer ": Bradford,* [1885?] 8⁰.
C.T. 305. (4.)

—— Possible Causes of Inaccurate Shooting—Rifle. *Gale & Polden: Aldershot,* [1935.] 12⁰. **8821. ee. 48.** *A folding card.*

—— The True Causes of the Present Scarcity of Mill'd Money, discovered; with some proposals humbly offered to prevent abuses in exporting of bullion. [*London?* 1690?] *s. sh.* fol. **8223. d. 38. (10.)**

—— The True Causes of the Present Scarcity of Money; and the proper remedies for it. pp. 8. *London,* [1700?] 4⁰. **104. f. 44.** *A reprint of a pamphlet published in* 1690. *Cropped.*

—— What are the Causes of the Prolonged Depression in Trade? By a Scotch Banker [George D. Charles]. Reprinted from " The Edinburgh Property Review." pp. 22. *Edinburgh Publishing Co.: Edinburgh; Simpkin, Marshall & Co.: London,* 1879. 8⁰. **8229. cc. 18. (9.)**

CAUSETTE (JEAN BAPTISTE) *See* CAUSSETTE.

CAUSEY (DAVID) Uninvited Guests, *etc.* (A short account of the animals living on or in us.) pp. 120. ix. *A. A. Knopf: New York,* 1932. 8⁰. **07299. e. 30.**

CAUSEY (ELIZABETH)

—— Told to the Toddlers. Stories of Jesus for his very little children. pp. xiii. 62. *Lutterworth Press: London & Redhill,* 1945. 8⁰. **4786. df. 10.**

CAUSID (SIMON) Verzeichniss der Hochfürstlich-Hessischen Gemählde-Sammlung in Cassel. pp. 258. 1783. 8⁰. *See* CASSEL.—*Königliche, afterwards Staatliche, Gemälde-Galerie.* **1402. c. 21.**

CAUSIDICADE. The Causidicade; a panegyri-satyri-serio-comic-dramatical poem on the strange resignation, and stranger—promotion. [A political satire, on the appointment of William Murray as Solicitor-General. By Macnamara Morgan.] pp. 29. *M. Cooper: London,* 1743. 4⁰. **11630. c. 14. (15.)** *Later editions are entered under* PELAGIUS (*Porcupinus*) *pseud.*

—— *See* FLAP-BUGG (F.) *pseud.* Causticks applied to the Causidicade, *etc.* 1743. 4⁰. **11795. e. 29.**

CAUSIDICUS. Causidicus, a poetic lash: in three parts. Containing: a real Picture of the Times; the Study at the Temple; with a Visit to a certain Judge; and a most extraordinary Trial. pp. 50. *J. Bowen: London,* 1779. 4⁰. **163. l. 17.**

Slightly cropped.

CAUSIDICUS, *pseud.* [Letters to the Committee for Conducting the Free Press.] *See* GUATIMOZIN, *pseud.* The Letters of Guatimozin on the Affairs of Ireland . . . To which are added, the Letters of Causidicus, *etc.* 1779. 8⁰. **8145. cc. 37.**

—— The Last of the Vestals. A tale of Rome, in the fourth century. By Causidicus. *F. Gleason: Boston,* 1846. 8⁰. **12706. g. 34.**

CAUSIDICUS. *pseud.*

—— A Letter to Charles Purton Cooper, Esq. . . . on the appointment of a permanent judge in the Court of Chancery in the place of the Lord Chancellor, and a change in the appellate jurisdiction of the Court of Chancery and the House of Lords. By Causidicus. pp. 29. *Henry Lindsell: London,* 1835. 8⁰. T. **2020. (3.)**

—— [Another copy.] **1382. d. 5. (1.)**

—— A Second Letter to Charles Purton Cooper, Esq. . . . on the appointment of a permanent judge in the Court of Chancery in the place of the Lord Chancellor . . . By Causidicus. pp. 31. *Henry Lindsell: London,* 1835. 8⁰. T. **2020. (4.)**

—— [Another copy.] **1382. d. 5. (2.)**

—— Novum " Antidotum Lincolniense."—The Law not " Public Opinion." Some remarks on the Bishop of Lincoln's reply to the one hundred and forty [of the clergy of his diocese, respecting the proposed alteration of the Ornaments Rubric]. Addressed to a layman. By Causidicus. *W. Drewett: London; John Morton: Boston* [*Lincs.*], 1866. 8⁰. **3475. aa. 12.**

CAUSIDICUS, *pseud.* [i.e. SAMUEL WHITCOMBE.] A Refutation of the Chief Doctrines of Parliamentary Reformers. [Signed: Causidicus.] pp. 22. *R. Cantwell: London,* [1806?] 8⁰. **8135. cc. 14.**

CAUSIDICUS (BAVIUS) *pseud.* [i.e. MACNAMARA MORGAN.] *See also* MORGAN (M.)

—— *See* FLAP-BUGG (F.) *pseud.* Causticks applied to the Causidicade . . . With remarks upon the poetry of B. Causidicus. 1743. 4⁰. **11795. e. 29.**

CAUSIN (NICOLAS) *See* CAUSSIN.

CAUSINO (NICOLO) *See* CAUSSIN (Nicolas)

CAUSIT (ADOLPHE) *de Montbazens.* De l'allaitement—galactopaitrophie. pp. 62. *Paris,* 1848. 4⁰. [*Collection des thèses soutenues à la Faculté de Médecine de Paris.* An 1848. tom. 3.] **7372. b. 6.**

CAUSIT (ADOLPHE) *Membre de la Société Anatomique.* Étude sur les polypes du larynx chez les enfants, et en particulier sur les polypes congénitaux. [With plates.] pp. 146. *Paris,* 1867. 4⁰. [*Collection des thèses soutenues à la Faculté de Médecine de Paris.* An 1867. tom. 3.] **7373. h. 6.**

CAUSIT (G. F. VALENTIN) Dissertation sur le rhumatisme articulaire aigu; thèse, *etc.* pp. 27. *Paris,* 1826. 4⁰. **1183. i. 2. (20.)**

CAUSLEY (CHARLES) Benedict, *etc.* *Frederick Muller: London,* 1938. 8⁰. [*One-Act Plays.* no. 24.] **W.P. 11251/24.** *A reissue of pp. 101–124 of " Six One-Act Plays for Festivals."*

—— The Conquering Hero . . . A comedy in one act, *etc.* pp. 12. *J. Curwen & Sons: London; G. Schirmer: New York,* [1937.] 8⁰. **11791. g. 40.**

—— Farewell, Aggie Weston. [Poems.] pp. 32. *Hand & Flower Press: Aldington,* [1951.] 8⁰. [*Poems in Pamphlet.* 1951. no. 1.] **P.P. 5126. bbt.**

—— Hands to dance. pp. 222. *Carroll & Nicholson: London,* 1951. 8⁰. **012642. r. 96.**

CAUSLEY (CHARLES)

—— How Pleasant to Know Mrs. Lear. A Victorian comedy in one act. *Frederick Muller: London, 1948.* 8°. [*One-Act Plays.* no. 44.] W.P. **11251/44**.

—— Runaway . . . A comedy in one act, *etc.* pp. 15. *J. Curwen & Sons: London,* [*1936.*] 8°. **11780. b. 51**.

—— Survivor's Leave. pp. 46. *Hand & Flower Press: Aldington, 1953.* 8°. **11658. aaa. 242**.

CAUSOCALYBITES (NEOPHYTUS) *See* NEOPHUTOS, *of Kausokalubia.*

CAUSSADE, MARIN JOSEPH EMMANUEL AUGUSTE DIEU-DONNÉ DE LAS CASES, *Marquis de la. See* LAS CASES.

CAUSSADE (A.) L'Accord parfait, ou le Trio ministériel. [On the Villèle Ministry.] pp. 16. *Paris, 1824.* 8°. **8006. ee. 3. (9.)**

CAUSSADE (BERTRAND) Quelques considérations sur l'ischurie, causée par l'état pathologique de la membrane muqueuse du canal de l'urètre. Thèse, *etc.* pp. 46. *Montpellier, 1821.* 4°. **1180. i. 15. (5.)**

CAUSSADE (CLÉMENT) Aperçu critique de la valeur de certains moyens médicamenteux réputés spécifiques de la phthisie pulmonaire. Thèse, *etc.* pp. 71. *Montpellier, 1866.* 4°. **7379. g. 4. (3.)**

CAUSSADE (FRANÇOIS DE) *See* AUBIGNÉ (T. A. d') Œuvres complètes . . . Accompagnées de notices biographique, littéraire & bibliographique . . . par E. Réaume & F. de Caussade. *1873, etc.* 8°. **12236. df. 3**.

—— *See* COURIER DE MÉRÉ (P. L.) [*Complete Works.*] Oeuvres . . . Avec notice et notes par F. de Caussade. *1880, etc.* 12°. **12239. aaa. 19**.

CAUSSADE (J.) *of Rouffignac.* Recherches pour servir à l'histoire pathologique de la cataracte et de son traitement par l'aiguille. Thèse, *etc.* pp. 55. *Montpellier, 1859.* 4°. **7379. d. 18. (5.)**

CAUSSADE (JEAN GÉRÔME LOUIS BECHON DE) *See* BECHON DE CAUSSADE.

CAUSSADE (JEAN PIERRE DE) [L'Abandon à la providence divine.] Abandonment to Divine Providence . . . Edited by the Rev. J. [or rather H.] Ramière . . . Second English edition [including the " Spiritual Counsels "] from the tenth complete French edition by E. J. Strickland. pp. xiii. 377. *Catholic Records Press: Exeter,* [*1925.*] 8°. **04402. g. 26**.

—— Self-Abandonment to Divine Providence . . . Revised and edited by Father P. H. Ramière, S. J. A new translation by Algar Thorold. With an introduction by Dom David Knowles. pp. xxv. 148. *Burns, Oates & Co.: London, 1933.* 8°. **04402. g. 40**.

—— The Spiritual Letters of Father P. J. de Caussade, S.J., on the practice of self-abandonment to Divine Providence. A new translation by Algar Thorold, *etc.* [Being bks. 1–3 of pt. 2 of the " Spiritual Counsels."] pp. xiii. 152. *Burns, Oates & Co.: London, 1934.* 8°. **04400. de. 21**.

—— Ordeals of Souls. A continuation [i.e. bks. 4 and 5] of his spiritual letters on the practice of self-abandonment to Divine Providence . . . A new translation by Algar Thorold. pp. vi. 117. *Burns, Oates & Co.: London, 1936.* 8°. **04400. e. 65**.

CAUSSADE (JEAN PIERRE DE)

—— Comfort in Ordeals. A continuation [i.e. bks. 6 and 7] of the Spiritual Letters . . . Translated by Algar Thorold. pp. vii. 129. *Burns, Oates & Co.: London, 1937.* 8°. **04400. f. 59**.

—— [Instructions spirituelles en forme de dialogues sur les divers états d'oraison suivant la doctrine de M. Bossuet, *etc.*] On Prayer. Spiritual instructions on the various states of prayer according to the doctrine of Bossuet, Bishop of Meaux. Translated . . . by Algar Thorold. With an introduction by Dom John Chapman, *etc.* pp. xli. 286. *Burns, Oates & Co.: London, 1931.* 8°. **03456. eee. 61**.

—— On Prayer . . . Translated . . . by Algar Thorold. With an introduction by Dom J. Chapman. (Second revised edition.) pp. xxxvii. 273. *Burns Oates & Washbourne: London, 1949.* 8°. **3458. b. 38**.

—— The Workings of the Divine Will. Gleanings from Père Caussade, S.J. From the French. Revised by a Father of the Society of Jesus. pp. 62. *Burns & Oates: London, 1879.* 16°. **4402. h. 4**.

—— Second edition. pp. 109. *Burns & Oates: London, 1881.* 16°. **4400. e. 6**.

—— Thirteenth edition. pp. vii. 86. *Burns, Oates & Co.: London, 1935.* 12°. **4403. de. 74**.

CAUSSADE (JULES) Diagnostic différentiel des tumeurs du scrotum. Thèse, *etc.* pp. 118. 29. *Montpellier, 1849.* 4°. **7379. a. 12. (13.)**

CAUSSADE (LÉO) Notes & causeries sur le dressage des chevaux en liberté. pp. 94. *Bruxelles, 1885.* 8°. **12806. m. 23**.

CAUSSADE (LOUIS) *See* PARISOT (Jacques) *Professeur agrégé à la Faculté de Médecine de Nancy,* and CAUSSADE (L.) Traitement des gangrènes pulmonaires. [1925.] 8°. [*Congrès Français de Médecine. Reports, etc.* session 18.] **Ac.3712.b/18**.

CAUSSADE (PIERRE JEAN DE) *See* CAUSSADE (Jean P. de)

CAUSSANEL (LOUIS) Considération générales sur la kératite. pp. 30. *Paris, 1869.* 4°. [*Collection des thèses soutenues à la Faculté de Médecine de Paris.* An 1869. tom. 3.] **7373. k. 9**.

CAUSSE ( ) Réponse pour Jacques Guillaume Pascal Causse [by his son] . . . aux réflexions de A. M. . . . sur l'article VII du titre II de la résolution du 23 brumaire an VI, au Conseil des Anciens. pp. 13. [*Paris, 1798 ?*] 8°. **F. 990. (15.)**

CAUSSE (ADOLPHE) La Bible de Reuss et la renaissance des études d'histoire religieuse en France. pp. 41. *Paris, 1929.* 8°. [*Cahiers de la Revue d'histoire et de philosophie religieuses.* no. 19.] **Ac. 2633. b/3**.

—— Les Dispersés d'Israël. Les origines de la diaspora et son rôle dans la formation du judaïsme. pp. 166. *Paris, 1929.* 8°. [*Études d'histoire et de philosophie religieuses.* fasc. 19.] **Ac. 2633. b/2**.

—— Du groupe ethnique à la communauté religieuse. Le problème sociologique de la religion d'Israël. pp. 343. *Paris, 1937.* 8°. [*Études d'histoire et de philosophie religieuses.* fasc. 33.] **Ac. 2633. b/2**.

—— L'Église réformée de Valence . . . Du Concordat à nos jours. Impressions et souvenirs. *See* DRAUSSIN (H.) L'Église réformée de Valence, *etc.* 1924. 8°. **4630. dg. 20**.

CAUSSE (ADOLPHE)

—— Essai sur le conflit du christianisme primitif et de la civilisation. pp. 76. *Paris*, 1920. 8°. **4398.c.17.**

—— Israël et la vision de l'humanité. pp. 152. *Strasbourg, Paris*, 1924. 8°. [*Études d'histoire et de philosophie religieuses.* fasc. 8.] Ac. **2633**. b/2.

—— Les " Pauvres " d'Israël. Prophètes, psalmistes, messianistes. pp. 172. *Strasbourg, Paris*, 1922. 8°. [*Études d'histoire et de philosophie religieuses.* fasc. 3.] Ac. **2633**. b/2.

—— Les Plus vieux chants de la Bible. pp. 175. *Paris*, 1926. 8°. [*Études d'histoire et de philosophie religieuses.* fasc. 14.] Ac. **2633**. b/2.

CAUSSÉ (AUGUSTE) De l'opium considéré comme agent thérapeutique dans le traitement des maladies, mais surtout dans le choléra-morbus. Thèse, *etc.* pp. 16. *Montpellier*, 1830. 4°. **1181**. f. **1.** (**9.**)

CAUSSÉ (BARTHÉLEMY) Le Vray Bouclier de la Foy Chrestienne, mis par dialogues. Demonstrant par la saincte Escriture, les erreurs & fausses allegations d'vn liure intitulé, Le Bouclier de la foi : iadis fait par vn moine de sainct Victor à Paris [i.e. Nicole Grenier] . . . Reueu & amplement augmenté, *etc.* pp. 565. *Z. Durant : Genève*, 1563. 12°. **854**. a. **4.**
Slightly mutilated.

CAUSSE (CHARLES) *See* MAËL (Pierre) *pseud.* [i.e. C. Causse and Charles Vincent.]

CAUSSE (ÉMILE) Un Drame ignoré, ou Histoire de la famille Begon. [With " Le Roi et la lessiveuse."] pp. 63. *Nîmes*, 1866. 8°. **12513**. dd. **5.**

—— Nouvelles locales. pp. 94. *Nîmes*, 1863. 8°. **12513**. dd. **4.**

CAUSSE (ÉTIENNE) Madame Necker de Saussure et l'éducation progressive. [With portraits.] 2 vol. *Paris*, 1930. 4°. **10657**. i. **8.**

—— Les Nouveaux Logia de Jésus. Thèse, *etc.* pp. 66. *Paris*, [1899.] 8°. [MISSING.]

CAUSSE (GEORGES) L'Affaire Casério. Étude de médecine légale et de psychopathologie historique. pp. 86. *Paris*, [1937.] 8°. **5408**. cc. **20.**

CAUSSE (H.) *of Ahrensburg.* Mittheilungen über künstlichen Anzug der Arundo phragmites—das gemeine Rohr. pp. 24. *Oldesloe*, 1855. 8°. **7077**. d. **50.** (**3.**)

CAUSSE (HENRI) De la constitution des alcaloïdes végétaux. Par X. [or rather, H.] Causse. pp. 87. *Paris, Lyon*, 1899. 8°. [*Annales de l'Université de Lyon.* Nouvelle série. I. Sciences, *etc.* fasc. 2.]
Ac.**365**.(a.)

CAUSSE (J. P.) Dissertation sur les larmes. pp. 24. *Paris*, 1812. 4°. **1182**. i. **4.** (**11.**)

CAUSSE (JACQUES GUILLAUME PASCAL) *See* CAUSSE ( ) Réponse pour J. G. P. Causse, *etc.* [1798 ?] 8°. F. **990.** (**15.**)

CAUSSE (JOANNES ISAACUS LUDOVICUS) I. I. L. Causse . . . Commentatio sacra ad Luc. XIII. 1-5. 1780. *See* BARKEY (N.) Museum Haganum, *etc.* tom. 4. pt. 2. 1774, *etc.* 8°. **1013**. a. **6.**

—— An sobrium proselytos faciendi studium Judaicae religionis indoli repugnet ? disquisitio. 1777. *See* BARKEY (N.) Museum Haganum, *etc.* tom. 1. pt. 2. 1774, *etc.* 8°. **1013**. a. **5.**

CAUSSE (PAUL PIERRE XAVIER) De la cachexie paludéenne en Afrique. Thèse, *etc.* pp. 36. *Montpellier*, 1851. 4°. **7379**. b. **6.** (**8.**)

CAUSSÉ (SÉVERIN) *See* CHEVALLIER (J. B. A.) Mémoire sur l'empoisonnement par les allumettes chimiques. Par M. le Dr. S. Caussé . . . Rapport [by J. B. A. Chevallier on the facts supplied in S. Caussé's " Mémoire "], *etc.* 1854. 8°. **7510**. aaa. **29.** (**32.**)

—— Dissertation sur les hémorrhagies traumatiques, et les moyens proposés pour les arrêter. pp. 59. *Montpellier*, 1828. 4°. **1181**. e. **5.** (**17.**)

—— Mémoire médico-légal sur la luxation des vertèbres cervicales, *etc.* pp. 92. *Albi*, [1853.] 8°. [MISSING.]

CAUSSE (X.) *See* CAUSSE (Henri)

CAUSSE-MAËL (FRED) La Croisière de l'Homme rouge. Roman de la révolution irlandaise, 1915. pp. 268. *Paris*, 1918. 8°. **12547**. v. **28.**

CAUSSENIUS (JOHAN CONRADUS) Disputatio, de mandatis cum vel sine clausula, ad methodum Glaumianam ante hàc conscripta. *See* HOLSTENIUS (G.) *Bishop of Arðs.* Clärliche Anzeig . . . wieviel ein Jedweder in divina methodo Glaumiana . . . aussrichten . . . könne, *etc.* 1628. 4°. **5505**. cc. **26.**

CAUSSETTE (JEAN BAPTISTE) Le Bon sens de la foi exposé en réponse aux objections philosophiques & scientifiques du jour. 2 vol. *Paris*, 1870. 8°. **4017**. h. **17.**

—— Entretiens avec Marthe ; conférences prêchées aux dames du monde. pp. 461. *Paris, Bruxelles*, 1882. 18°. [MISSING.]

—— Oraison funèbre de . . . Monseigneur Jean-François-Anne-Thomas Landriot, archevêque de Reims. pp. 40. *Reims*, 1874. 8°. **4865**. bbb. **20.** (**5.**)

—— Vie du Cardinal D'Astros . . . suivie de pièces justificatives et de documents inédits. [With a portrait.] pp. xxiv. 666. xc. *Paris*, 1853. 8°. **4863**. e. **26.**

—— St. Bernard and his Work. A discourse . . . Translated from the French by the Right Rev. Abbot Burder. pp. 54. *T. Richardson & Son : London*, 1874. 16°. **4823**. aa. **28.**

CAUSSEUS (MICHAEL ANGELUS) *See* LA CHAUSSE (M. A. de)

CAUSSEUS DE LA CHAUSSE (MICHAELANGELUS) *See* LA CHAUSSE (M. A. de)

CAUSSIDIÈRE (MARC) *See* CHENU (J. E. A.) Les Montagnards de 1848, encore quatre nouveaux chapitres, précédés d'une réponse à Caussidière, *etc.* 1850. 12°. **1320**. a. **15.**

—— *See* MIOT (J.) Réponse aux deux libelles . . . de Chenu et de Delahodde, d'après les . . . documens fournis et publiés par Caussidière, *etc.* 1850. 12°. **1320**. a. **31.**

—— *See* MIRECOURT (E. de) *pseud.* Histoire contemporaine, *etc.* (no. 86. Le Prince Napoléon. Caussidière. [With portraits.]) 1867, *etc.* 8°. **10661**. aaa. **33.**

—— Mémoires . . . Troisième édition. 2 tom. *Paris*, 1849. 8°. **1320**. d. **34.**

—— Secret History of the Revolutions of 1848. Memoirs of Citizen Caussidière. 2 vol. *Richard Bentley : London*, 1848. 12°. **1320**. d. **15, 16.**

CAUSSIDOU ( ) See PERIODICAL PUBLICATIONS.— *Algiers.* Manuel du cultivateur africain, par M. Caussidou. 1839. 8º. **7073. aaa. 53. (1.)**

CAUSSIDOU (CHARLES JULES JACQUES) Étude sur la fracture de l'extrémité inférieure du radius. Thèse, *etc.* pp. 43. *Montpellier*, 1867. 4º. **7379. g. 10. (8.)**

CAUSSIN (ED.) *Capitaine.* Vers Taza. Souvenirs de deux ans de campagne au Maroc, 1913–1914, *etc.* [With plates and maps.] pp. ix. 293 [296]. *Paris*, 1922. 8º. **09061. h. 4.**

CAUSSIN (EDMOND THÉOPHILE) Des hémorrhagies utérines qui peuvent survenir avant et pendant le travail de l'accouchement. pp. 32. *Paris*, 1854. 4º. [*Collection des thèses soutenues à la Faculté de Médecine de Paris.* An 1854. tom. 4.] **7372. g. 4.**

CAUSSIN (JEAN JACQUES ANTOINE) *See* CAUSSIN DE PERCEVAL.

CAUSSIN (NICOLAS) *See* HORAPOLLO. Horapollinis Hieroglyphica Græce & Latine, cum integris observationibus & notis J. Merceri . . . et selectis N. Caussini, *etc.* 1727. 4º. **704. f. 5.**

—— *See* PARIS.—*Université de Paris.* III. Requeste de l'Université de Paris . . . contre les libelles que les Jésuites ont publiez sous les tiltres d'Apologie par le P. Caussin, *etc.* 1644. 8º. **860. d. 15. (1–3.)**

—— *See* RICHEOME (L.) Iusta anniversaria Henrico Magno seu Consolatio ad Reginam Galliæ . . . In funestam mortem Henrici IV . . . Francorum Regis . . . Ex Gallico R. P. Richeomij. [Translated by N. Caussin.] 1613. 4º. **10660. ff. 23.**

—— *See* ROCHEMONTEIX (C. de) Nicolas Caussin, confesseur de Louis XIII, et le cardinal de Richelieu, *etc.* 1911. 8º. **4864. df. 18.**

—— Une Vocation et une disgrace à la cour de Louis XIII. Lettre inédite du P. Caussin à Mˡˡᵉ de La Fayette sur les faits qui les concernent l'un et l'autre, précédée d'une introduction par le P. Ch. Daniel. pp. 110. *Paris*, 1861. 12º. **4865. aa. 16.**

—— Regnum Dei, seu Dissertationes in libros Regum, in quibus quæ ad institutionem principum, illustriumque virorum, totamque politicen sacram attinent, insigni methodo tractantur. (Domus Dei. In qua de mirabilibus coeli, totaque astrologia, et vita coelesti luculente . . . disseritur. Addita quoque ad calcem, Ephemeris astrologica, et historica, *etc.* [With the "Angelus Pacis ad Principes Christianos."]) 4 pt. *D. Bechet: Parisiis*, 1650. fol. **3125. f. 14. (1, 2.)**

—— Angelus Pacis. Ad Principes Christianos. pp. 106. *D. Bechet: Parisiis*, 1650. 12º. **8425. aaa. 21.**

—— [Another edition.] pp. 106. *Apud I. Kinchium: Coloniæ*, 1651. 12º. **864. b. 10. (4.)** *The titlepage is engraved.*

—— [Another edition.] pp. 47. *See* CELLOT (L.) R.P. L. Cellotii . . . Orationes panegyricæ, *etc.* 1674. 12º. **1090. d. 3.**

—— The Angel of Peace to all Christian Princes. Written in French by N. Caussin, S.J. pp. 114. [*Roger Daniel. London?*] 1650. 12º. **E. 1401. (1.)** *Other editions of this work were attached to "The Holy Court," the English version of "La Cour Sainte."*

—— Apologie pour les religieux de la Compagnie de Iesus. A la Reyne Régente . . . Troisiesme édition, reueuë et augmentée. pp. 141. *Paris*, 1644. 8º. **4091. b. 38. (2.)**

CAUSSIN (NICOLAS)

—— [Another edition.] pp. 219. *I. Tournay: Liège*, 1644. 12º. **4091. a. 11.**

—— Le Buisson ardent. *See* MIGNE (J. P.) Collection intégrale et universelle des orateurs sacrés, *etc.* tom. 1. 1844, *etc.* 4º. **3676. a. 1.**

—— La Cour sainte . . . Première partie . . . Tome I. De l'Institution chrestienne. (Tome II. Des maximes de la Foy.—Tome III. De l'empire de la raison sur les passions.—Seconde partie . . . Tome I. Les Monarques. —Tome II. Les Reynes, dames, & caualiers.—Tome III. Les Hommes d'Estat & de Dieu.) 6 tom. *C. Sonnius & D. Bechet: Paris*, 1645. 8º. **4400. b. 2.**

—— The Holy Court. Or, the Christian Institution of Men of Quality. With examples of those, who in Court have flourished in Sanctity . . . Written in French, & translated into English by T. H. [i.e. Thomas Hawkins.] 2 vol. *Paris*; [*St. Omer*, printed,] 1626, 31. 4º. **4400. aa. 40.** *Vol. 2 is without a titlepage.*

—— The Holy Court in three tomes . . . The third tome now first published in English: the first and second newly reuiewed, and much augmented, according to the last edition of the authour. 3 tom. *Printed by Iohn Cousturier:* [*Rouen*], 1634. fol. **694. l. 16.** *With an additional titlepage, engraved.*

—— [Another copy.] **694. m. 18. (1.)** *Imperfect; wanting the engraved titlepage, the engraving of the Arch of Constantine, the dedication of tom 2 to the Countess of Portland, and the whole of tom. 3.*

—— The Holy Court, fourth tome. The Commaund of Reason, ouer the Passions . . . Translated . . . by Sʳ T. H. (Thomas Hawkins.) pp. 330. *Printed by Iohn Cousturier:* [*Rouen*,[1638. **694. l. 17.** *With an additional titlepage, engraved.*

—— [Another copy, with a different titlepage.] **694. m. 18. (2.)** *Imperfect; wanting the engraved titlepage.*

—— [Another copy, with a different titlepage.] **8408. i. 2.** *Imperfect; wanting the engraved titlepage.*

—— The Holy Court, in five tomes . . . (The Angel of Peace to all Christian Princes.) Translated into English by Sʳ T. H. [Thomas Hawkins] and others. 3 pt. *Printed by William Bentley; sold by John Williams: London*, 1650. fol. **4375. h. 5.** *Pt. 1 contains tom. 1–3; pt. 2, tom. 4 and 5; pt. 3 "The Angel of Peace." There is an additional general titlepage, engraved.*

[La Cour sainte.]

—— The Holy Court . . . The third edition. pp. 855. **L.P.** *Printed for John Williams: London*, 1663. fol. **L. 20. p. 2.** *With an additional titlepage, engraved.*

—— [A reissue.] The third edition. *Printed for J. W.* [*John Williams*]; *sold by Thomas Rookes: London*, 1664. fol. **4375. h. 6.**

—— The fourth edition. pp. 855. *For John Williams: London*, 1678. fol. **1232. i. 15.** *With an additional titlepage, engraved.*

—— Heilige Hoffhaltung, das ist: Christliche Vnderweisung für alle . . . weltliche Standts-Personen, forderst aber die jenige, welche an Fürstlichen Höfen bedient . . . Erstlich . . . in Frantzösischer Sprach beschrieben; anjetzo durch R.P. Udalricum Groschan . . . in die Teutsche Sprach vbersetzt, *etc.* 3 Tl. *J. W. Friessem: Cöllen*, 1677, 76. 4º. **1224. h. 15.**

CAUSSIN (Nicolas)

—— Corte Divina, o Palacio Celestial. Primero y segundo tomo, que son diez, y onze de la Corte Santa. Escriviola en lengua latina . . . N. Causino . . . y en la Española, el Doct. D. E. de Aguilar y Zuñiga. pp. 368.
I. Fernandez de Buendia : Madrid, 1675. 8º.
1395. h. 54.

—— L'Histoire de l'incomparable Reyne Marie Stuart. [Extracted from " La Cour sainte."] *See* Jebb (Samuel) De vita & rebus gestis . . . Mariæ Scotorum Reginæ, *etc.* vol. 2. 1725. fol.
1321. l. 2.

—— The Unfortunate Politique (or the Life of Herod). First written in French by C. N. (the judicious and eloquent Causinus.) Englished by G. P. [Extracted from " La Cour sainte."] pp. 218. *L. Lichfield for Ioseph Godwin : Oxford*, 1638. 8º. **1448. a. 19.**

—— [A reissue.] *Oxford*, 1639. 8º. **12512. a. 13.**

—— A Voice from the Dead : or the Speech of an Old Noble Peer : being the excellent oration of the learned and famous Boetius to the Emperor Theodoricus. [A fictitious work extracted from Sir Thomas Hawkin's translation of " La Cour sainte " by N. Caussin.] pp. 8. 1681. 4º. *See* Boethius (A. M. T. S.) [*Doubtful or Supposititious Works.—Oration to the Emperor Theodoric.*] **12301. bbb. 9.**

—— [Another edition.] 1746. 4º. [*Harleian Miscellany.* vol. 7.] *See* Boethius (A. M. T. S.) [*Doubtful or Supposititious Works.—Oration to the Emperor Theodoric.*] **185. a. 11.**

—— [Another edition.] 1810. 8º. [*Harleian Miscellany.* vol. 8.] *See* Boethius (A. M. T. S.) [*Doubtful or Supposititious Works.—Oration to the Emperor Theodoric.*] **1326. g. 8.**

—— [Another edition.] 1811. 4º. [*Harleian Miscellany.* vol. 7.] *See* Boethius (A. M. T. S.) [*Doubtful or Supposititious Works.—Oration to the Emperor Theodoric.*] **2072.g.**

—— The Spirit of the Holy Court . . . [Selections from " The Holy Court."] Translated into English by Sir T. Hawkins and reprinted from the edition of 1634 by C. T. Gatty. pp. 170. *Simpkin, Marshall & Co. : London*, 1898. 12º. **4399. b. 14.**

—— Historia di Maria Stuarda, Regina di Francia, e di Scotia . . . Portata dal Francese nell'Italiano dal Padre Carlo Antonio Berardi. pp. 120. *D. Lovisa : Venetia*, [1650 ?] 12º. **600. b. 43.**

—— [Another edition.] pp. 120. *G. A. Remondinj : Bologna, Bassano*, [1690 ?] 12º. **600. b. 49.**

—— N. Caussini . . . De eloquentia sacra et humana libri xvi. Editio tertia . . . locupletata, cum . . . indicibus, *etc.* pp. 1010. *Sumptibus M. Henault, N. de la Vigne, P. Gaultier, N. de la Coste : Lutetiæ Parisiorum*, 1630. 4º. **836. k. 12.**

—— Editio ultima . . . locupletata, *etc.* pp. 1011. *Ex typographia M. Henault ; apud I. Libert : Parisiis*, 1643. 4º. **4498. dd. 4.**

—— N. Caussini De figuris. [Extracted from Book vii of " De eloquentia sacra et humana."] *See* Autori. Degli autori del ben parlare, *etc.* pt. 2. 1643. 4º. **836. e. 10.**

—— [Another edition.] *See* Greek Rhetoricians. Operum Græcorum, Latinorum & Italorum rhetorum tomus primus, *etc.* tom. 1. 1644. 4º. **836. e. 1.**

CAUSSIN (Nicolas)

—— De symbolica Ægyptiorum sapientia. (Polyhistor symbolicus, electorum symbolorum, & parabolarum historicarum stromata, *etc.*) 2 pt. *R. de Beauvais : Paris*, 1618. 4º. **1480. bb. 3.**
With an additional titlepage, engraved, reading : " Electorum symbolorum et parabolarum historicarum syntagmata, etc."

—— [Another copy of pt. 1.] **7704. d. 16.**

—— [Another edition.] 2 pt. *Apud I. Kinckium : Coloniæ Agrippinæ*, 1631. 8º. **787. a. 85.**
The titlepage of pt. 1 is engraved.

—— [Another edition.] Symbolica Ægyptiorum sapientia . . . nunc post varias editiones denuo edita. (Polyhistor symbolicus, *etc.*) 2 pt. *I. Iost : Parisiis*, 1634. 8º. **705. b. 23.**

—— Excerptum Nic. Caussini . . . de Hierogliphicis cum notis et supplementis. (Accedit Specimen bibliothecae demoticae et hieraticae Aegyptiae, *etc.*) [The " Excerptum " taken from the 1634 edition of the " De symbolica Aegyptiorum sapientia."] *See* Martinetti (G. G.) Opuscula quinque, *etc.* 1828. 8º. **7704. e. 15.**

—— [Ephemeris astrologica et historica.] Effemeride astrologica et historica . . . Tradotta dalla lingua Latina nell'Italiana. pp. 477. *C. Zenero : Bologna*, 1652. 12º. **580. a. 29.**

—— [Epistola . . . ad R.P. Mutium Vitelescium.] Apologia del Padre Niccolò Caussino . . . scritta per difesa di sestesso al P. Muzio Vitteleschi . . . Tradotta dalla lingua Latina. pp. 77. *Lugano*, 1762. 8º. **4092. b. 1. (1.)**

—— L'Impiété domptée sous les Fleurs de Lys. pp. 135. *S. Rigaud : Lyon*, 1636. 8º. **3901. bb. 48. (1.)**

—— [La Journée chrestienne.] The Christian Diary. pp. 134. [*Cambridge*,] 1648. 12º. **E. 1207. (2.)**

—— [Another copy.] **4401. aa. 46. (2.)**
Imperfect ; wanting pp. 35–38.

—— [Another edition.] pp. 134. *For John Williams : London*, 1649. 12º. **4409. aa. 1. (1.)**

—— [La Sagesse évangelique pour les sacrez entretiens du Caresme.] The Penitent ; or, Entertainments for Lent . . . Translated into English by S. B. B. [i.e. Sir Basil Brook.] pp. 230. [*Roger Daniel ? : London ? 1643 ?*] 12º. **4409. aa. 1. (2.)**
The titlepage is mutilated.

—— [Another edition.] pp. 264. *For John Williams : London*, 1672. 12º. **4408. b. 49.**

—— [Another edition.] pp. 244. *T. Meighan : London*, 1741. 12º. **4401. aa. 35.**

—— [Another edition.] pp. 248. *John Sadler : Liverpool*, 1755. 18º. **1412. a. 37.**

—— [Another edition.] pp. viii. 279. *W. Bancks : Wigan*, 1785. 12º. **1481. d. 9.**

—— Thesaurus Græcæ poeseos, ex omnibus Graecis poëtis collectus. Liber primus (secundus). 2 pt. *R. de Beauuais : Parisiis*, 1612. 8º. **C. 47. d. 5.**
This copy was presented as a prize to Paul Scarron. It has the arms of Charles de Gonzague-Clèves, Duke of Nevers, afterwards Duke of Mantua, stamped on the binding.

—— [Another edition.] 2 pt. pp. 603. *Sumptibus B. Gaultheri : Moguntiæ*, 1614. 8º. **622. b. 3.**

CAUSSIN (Nicolas)

—— Tragoediæ sacræ. 5 pt.   *S. Cramoisy: Parisiis,*
1620. 8°.   **11712. aaa. 8. (2.)**

—— [Another issue.] 5 pt.   *S. Chappelet: Parisiis,*
1620. 8°.   **11712. b. 25.**

—— [Another edition.] pp. 383.   *S. Chappelet:*
Parisiis, 1629 [1620]. 16°.   **840. a. 3.**
The titlepage is engraved.

—— Le Triomphe de la Piété. A la gloire des armes du roy,
& l'amiable reduction des âmes errantes. pp. 168.
S. Rigaud: Lyon, 1636. 8°.   **3901. bb. 48. (2.**

CAUSSIN DE PERCEVAL (Armand Pierre)

—— *See* Aḥmad Klićan Wāṣif, *Efendi.* Précis historique de
la guerre des Turcs contre les Russes . . . tiré des annales
de . . . Vassif-Éfendi, par P. A. Caussin de Perceval.
1822. 8°.   **09077. ee. 70.**

——   *See*
Bocthor (E.) Dictionnaire français-arabe, revu et augmenté par A. Caussin de Perceval. 1828, *etc.* 4°.
                                 622. i. 9.

—— —— 1848. 8°.   **12904. h. 4.**

—— —— 1882. 8°.   **12904. h. 5.**

—— *See* Muḥammad Asʿad Ṣafvat. Précis historique de la
destruction du corps des Janissaires par le Sultan Mahmoud
en 1826. Traduit par A. P. Caussin de Perceval.
1833. 8°.   **14456. c. 17.**

—— *See* Wallon (H. A.) Éloges académiques. (Notice sur
la vie et les travaux de M. A. P. Caussin de Perceval.)
1882. 8°.   **10664. c. 19.**

—— Essai sur l'histoire des Arabes avant l'Islamisme,
pendant l'époque de Mahomet, et jusqu'à la réduction de
toutes les tribus sous la loi musulmane. 3 tom. *Paris,*
1847, 48. 8°.   **09057. bb. 21.**

—— Grammaire arabe-vulgaire, suivie de dialogues, lettres,
actes, *etc.* pp. viii. 118. 43. 16. *Paris,* 1824. 4°.
                                 12907. eee. 3.

—— [Another edition.] pp. xv. 172. 12. *Paris,* 1833. 4°.
                                 622. h. 17.

—— Troisième édition. pp. xv. 172. 12.   *Paris,*
1843. 8°.   **12906. d. 1.**

—— Quatrième édition. pp. xv. 167. 12.   *Paris,*
1858. 8°.   **12906. c. 8.**

CAUSSIN DE PERCEVAL (Jean Jacques Antoine)
See ʿAlī ibn ʿAbd al-Raḥmān, *called* Ibn Yūnus. Le
Livre de la Grande Table Hakémite . . . Traduit par le
Cᵉⁿ Caussin. 1804. 4°.   **14544. e. 6.**

—— *See* Apollonius, *Rhodius.* [*French.*] L'Expédition des
Argonautes . . . Poème . . . traduit par J. J. A. Caussin.
[1797.] 8°.   **997. i. 14.**

—— *See* Apollonius, *Rhodius.* Jason et Médée, ou la Con-
quête de la toison d'or. (Traduit . . . par J.-J.-A.
Coussin de Perceval.) 1930. 8°.   **11340. aaa. 29.**

—— *See* Arabian Nights. [*French.*] Les Mille et une nuits,
contes arabes, traduits . . . par M. Galland, continués
par M. Caussin de Perceval, *etc.* 1806. 12°.
                                14582. a. 1-9.

—— *See* Daunou (P. C. F.) Institut Royal de France . . .
Funérailles de M. Caussin de Perceval. Discours, *etc.*
[1835.] 4°.   **733. h. 1. (14.)**

CAUSSIN DE PERCEVAL (Jean Jacques Antoine)

—— *See* Riedesel (J. H. von) *Baron.* Voyages en Sicile
. . . Suivis de l'Histoire de la Sicile par le Novairi (traduite de l'arabe par J. J. A. Caussin). 1802. 8°.
                                212. a. 19.

—— *See* Valerius Flaccus (C.) L'Argonautique . . .
poëme traduit . . . en prose par J. J. A. Caussin de
Perceval. 1835. 8°. [*Panckoucke (C. L. F.) Biblio-*
thèque latine-française.]   **11306. i. 32.**

—— Catalogue des livres et manuscrits arabes, des ouvrages
de littérature et d'histoire, composant la bibliothèque de
feu M. Caussin de Perceval . . . dont la vente aura lieu le
jeudi 30 novembre 1871, *etc.* pp. vi. 47.   *Paris,*
1871. 8°.   **S.C. 1221.**

—— Institut Royal de France . . . Funérailles de M.
Langlès. Le 30 janvier 1824, *etc.* [The funeral orations
by J. J. A. Caussin de Perceval, and J. B. Gail.] pp. 5.
[*Paris,* 1824.] 4°.   **733. g. 17. (82.)**

CAUSSINUS (Nicolaus) *See* Caussin (Nicolas)

CAUSSONEL (Benoît) *See* Toulouse.—*Parlement.* Arrest . . . du 6 mars 1765 (qui condamne une brochure
intitulée: Lettre d'un Écolier des Soi-disans [i.e. the
Jesuits], &c. à être lacérée & brûlée). [Condemning an
anti-Dominican letter by the said scholar to P. J. Dufour
on the thesis by B. Caussonel, a Dominican, entitled:
"Ad venerandas Sancti Doctoris exuvias."] [1765.] 12°.
                               4091. bb. 42. (21.)

CAUSSY (F.) *Writer on Opera.*

—— *See* Wagner (W. R.) [*Tristan und Isolde.*] Tristan
und Isolde . . . Texte allemand avec introduction et
traduction française de F. Caussy, *etc.* 1944. 8°.
                               11749. aa. 1.

CAUSSY (Fernand) *See* Frederick II., *called the Great,*
King of Prussia. [*Correspondence.*] Nachträge zu dem
Briefwechsel Friedrichs des Grossen mit Maupertuis und
Voltaire . . . Herausgegeben von . . . F. Caussy, *etc.*
1917. 8°. [*Publikationen aus den K. Preussischen Staats-*
archiven. Bd. 90.]   **9386. ee. 1/90**

—— *See* Ligne (C. J. de) *Prince.* Mes écarts . . . Réflexions
. . . accompagnées d'une notice et d'une bibliographie
par F. Caussy. 1906. 8°.   **012355. f. 27.**

—— *See* Sénac de Meilhan (G.) Considérations sur
l'esprit et les mœurs. Choisies, introduites et com-
mentées par F. Caussy. 1905. 8°.   **8411. e. 37.**

—— *See* Voltaire (F. M. A. de) [*Collections.—Prose and*
Verse.] Œuvres inédites. Publiées par F. Caussy.
1914. 8°.   **12238. i. 9.**

—— Laclos, 1741-1803, d'après des documents originaux,
suivi d'un mémoire inédit de Laclos. pp. 365.   *Paris,*
1905. 8°.   **010664. i. 17.**

—— Voltaire, seigneur de village. Ouvrage illustré de trois
portraits de Voltaire et de quatre cartes. pp. xi. 355.
Paris, 1912. 8°.   **010664. h. 41.**

CAUST (Arnold) *See* Caust (Charles A.)

CAUST (Charles Arnold) *See* Caust (E. W.) Heroism
in Daily Life. A memoir of Arnold and Ray Caust, *etc.*
[With portraits.] 1915. 8°.   **4920. h. 19.**

CAUST (Edgar W.) Heroism in Daily Life. A memoir of
Arnold and Ray Caust, *etc.* [With portraits.] pp. 191.
C. H. Kelly: London, 1915. 8°.   **4920. h. 19.**

CAUST (Ray) *See* Caust (Thomas R.)

CAUST (Thomas Ray) *See* Caust (E. W.) Heroism in Daily Life: a memoir of Arnold and Ray Caust, *etc.* [With portraits.] 1915. 8°. **4920. h. 19**.

CAUSTEN (James H.) Review of the Veto Message of President Pierce of February 17, 1855, on the Bill relating to French spoliations. pp. 46. [*Washington*, 1855.] 8°. **8175. cc. 84. (10.)**

—— A Sketch of the Claims of Sundry American Citizens on the Government of the United States, for indemnity, for depredations committed on their property by the French . . . By a Citizen of Baltimore [i.e. J. H. Causten]. pp. 145. 1826. 8°. *See* American Citizens. **1414. f. 76. (1.)**

CAUSTIC, Mrs., *pseud.* [i.e. Ann Tuttle Jones Bullard.] *See also* Bullard (A. T. J.)

—— Matrimony: or, Love affairs in our village twenty years ago. By Mrs. Caustic. Second edition. pp. viii. 316. *M. W. Dodd: New York*, 1853. 12°. **12706. e. 7**.

—— [Another edition.] Love Affairs; or, How a flirt was caught in his own trap. pp. viii. 120. *James Blackwood: London*, 1854. 8°. **12631. e. 3**.

CAUSTIC, *pseud.* The Newcastle Critic, or a poetic epistle to the Dramatic Draco of the Tyne Mercury . . . By Caustic. pp. 8. *Printed for the Author: Newcastle*, 1814. 8°. **11602. ff. 10. (3.)**

—— Strictures on a Sermon entitled "Apostacy" . . . preached . . . by the Rev. William J. E. Bennett. [On occasion of the Rev. Alexander Chirol's secession to the Church of Rome.] By Caustic. pp. 18. *T. W. Saunders: London*, 1847. 8°. **4475. c. 30**.

CAUSTIC (Christopher) *M.D., LL.D., pseud.* [i.e. Thomas Green Fessenden.] Democracy Unveiled, or, Tyranny stripped of the garb of patriotism. By Christopher Caustic, LL.D., &c. &c. [In verse.] Third edition, *etc.* 2 vol. *I. Riley & Co.: New York*, 1806, 05. 12°. **1164. i. 4**.

—— A Poetical Petition against Tractorising Trumpery, and the Perkinistic Institution, in four cantos . . . addressed to the Royal College of Physicians, by Christopher Caustic, M.D., LL.D., *etc.* [With reference to the "Metallic Tractors" invented by Elisha Perkins and popularized by B. D. Perkins.] pp. 92. *T. Hurst; J. Ginger: London*, 1803. 8°. **11641. f. 71. (1.)**

—— Terrible Tractoration!! A poetical petition against galvanising trumpery, and the Perkinistic Institution . . . Second edition, with great additions. pp. xxxi. 186. *T. Hurst: J. Ginger: London*, 1803. 12°. **11633. aa. 8**.

—— First American, from the second London edition, revised and corrected by the author, with additional notes. pp. xxxv. 192. *Samuel Stansbury: New-York*, 1804. 12°. **11687. aa. 21**.

—— The Modern Philosopher; or, Terrible Tractoration! . . . Second American edition, revised, corrected and much enlarged by the author. pp. xxxii. 271. *Samuel Stansbury: Philadelphia*, 1806. 8°. **11687. cc. 31**.

CAUSTIC (Cosmo) *Gent., pseud.* [i.e. Christopher Reid.] *See* Trimstave (Tyro) *M.D., pseud.* [i.e. C. Reid.] Killvillain . . . With a preface and notes by C. Caustic. 1835. 8°. **11650. cc. 26. (1.)**

CAUSTICK (Christopher) *M.D., LL.D., pseud.* [i.e. Thomas Green Fessenden.] *See* Caustic.

CAUSTIER (Eugène) Le Monde malgache. *See* Madagascar. Ce qu'il faut connaître de Madagascar, *etc.* [1896.] fol. **10094. ee. 1**.

CAUSTON (Abraham W.) *See* Cawston (Abraham)

CAUSTON (Bernard)

—— The Moral Blitz. War propaganda and Christianity. pp. 126. *Secker & Warburg: London*, 1941. 8°. [*Searchlight Books.* no. 15.] **W.P. 10146/15**.

CAUSTON (Bernard) and **YOUNG** (George Gordon) Keeping it Dark; or, the Censor's handbook, *etc.* pp. 83. *Mandrake Press: London*, [1930.] 8°. **11823. pp. 12**.

CAUSTON (Eric Edward Nicholson) Militarism and Foreign Policy in Japan. pp. 207. *G. Allen & Unwin: London*, 1936. 8°. **20030. b. 13**.

CAUSTON (Hon. Frances Hesther) *See* Harding (John) *Bishop of Bombay.* "Occupy Till I Come": a sermon . . . on the death of the Hon. F. H. Causton. 1840. 8°. **T. 2457. (18.)**

CAUSTON (Henry Kent Staple) *See* Mildmay (Sir William) *Bart.* The Method and Rule of Proceeding upon all Elections . . . within the City of London . . . With additional notes on Wardmote Elections; an historical review of the City electoral franchises; and of the Incorporated Mysteries with their Liverymen, Electors of London. By H. K. S. Causton. 1841. 12°. **1130. c. 39**.

—— *See* Walton (Isaak) *the Angler.* The Complete Angler . . . With a new introduction and notes [by H. K. S. C., i.e. H. K. S. Causton]. 1851. 8°. **7905. a. 6**.

—— *See* Walton (Isaak) *the Angler.* Walton's Lives . . . (Part 1.) The Life of Dr. Donne, *etc.* [Edited by H. K. S. Causton.] [1852.] 8°. **10815. b. 55**.

—— An Essay on Mr. Singer's "Wormwood"; embracing a restoration of the author's reply, mutilated in "Notes and Queries," No 72; with a note on the Monk of Bury; and a reading of Shakspere's Sonnet, CXI. "supplementary to all the commentators." pp. 52. *H. K. Causton: London*, [1851.] 12°. **11762. e. 22**.

—— The Howard Papers: with a biographical pedigree and criticism. [Founded on the manuscripts of Walter Howard.] pp. xvi. 690. *H. K. Causton & Son: London*, [1862.] 8°. **9914. aa. 21**.

—— The Howard Papers, *etc.* [A prospectus.] *Henry Kent Causton & Son: London.* [1862.] 8°. **9918. cc. 45. (1.)**

—— The Rights of Heirship; or, the Doctrine of descents and consanguinity, as applied by the laws of England to the succession of real property and hereditaments; and as affected by the new statutes of inheritance and limitation: including the descent of titular honours and coat armour: and the respective rights of participation in the personal estate of an intestate, *etc.* [With tables.] pp. xxi. 306. *H. K. Causton & Co.: London*, 1842. 12°. **1380. d. 23**.

—— *Begin.* To the Parishioners of the Parish of St. Edmund the King and Martyr, Lombard Street. [A reply by H. K. S. Causton to a statement impugning his father's conduct.] pp. 16. [*H. K. Causton: London*, 1847.] 8°. **1302. c. 15. (1.)**

CAUSTON (J. D.) Christian Sonnets: or, Stanzas on the various names, titles, and characters of Christ. pp. x. 60. *D. Cox: London*, 1817. 12°.   **11641. df. 4.**

—— The Day of Christ; a poem. Ruth; a pastoral. Sonnets to the Months, and several minor pieces, sacred and moral. pp. viii. 141. *The Author: London*, 1842. 8°.
11645. f. 34.

CAUSTON (JOHN FERRISS) The Comedy of a Suburban Chapel. pp. 337. *Hutchinson & Co.: London*, 1901. 8°.
012639. cc. 39.

—— A Modern Judas. pp. 373.   *Digby & Long: London*, [1897.] 8°.   **012626. m. 16.**

—— The Philanthropist. A novel. pp. 314.   *John Lane: London & New York; Cambridge, U.S.A.* [printed], 1904. 8°.   **012707. c. 3.**

CAUSTON (*Sir* JOSEPH) **AND SONS.** Sir J. Causton & Sons . . . Brewery Books, *etc. See* WESTCOTT (William)

—— Sir J. Causton & Sons' Registered Manufacturers' "Prime Cost" Books, *etc.* [Blank forms.] *Causton & Sons: London*, [1884.] fol.   **1887. c. 5.**

CAUSTON (MARY ISABEL MARGARET)

—— For the Healing of the Nations. The story of British Baptist medical missions, 1792–1951. [With plates.] pp. 183.   *Carey Kingsgate Press: London*, 1951. 8°.
4768. bbb. 22.

CAUSTON (PETER) Carmina Tria . . . 1. De conflagratione Londini.   2. In laudem Holandiæ . . . 3. Tunbrigialia, editio tertia. pp. 12. 10.   *Typis J. Richardson; prostant venalia apud Thomam Mercer: Londini*, 1689. 4°.   **161. n. 16.**

—— Tunbrigialia.   P. C. Merc. Lond. ad G. F.   (Editio altera priori longe auctior.) pp. 10. *Typis J. Richardson: Londini*, 1686. 8°.   **1213. f. 42.**
The first twelve lines of the poem form an acrostic, indicating the author's name.

—— [Another edition.] pp. 12.   *Londini*, 1709. 8°.
11408. aaa. 25.

—— Tonbridgialia: or, the Pleasures of Tunbridge. A poem. In Latin and English heroic verse. pp. 17.   *Mount Sion, Tunbridge Wells*, 1705. 4°.   **11602. f. 24. (4.)**
Cropped.

CAUSTON (*Mrs.* RICHARD KNIGHT) *See* CAUSTON (Selina M.) *Baroness Southwark.*

CAUSTON (SELINA MARY) *Baroness Southwark.* Claudius. [A historical romance of the time of Domitian.] pp. 556. *Hatchards: London*, 1879 [1878]. 8°.   **4422. k. 1.**

—— Social & Political Reminiscences . . . With reproductions of a number of portraits from pencil sketches by the author, and also of sketches by the late Sir Frank Lockwood and A. S. Cope. pp. vi. 312.   *Williams & Norgate: London*, 1913. 8°.   **010826. i. 5.**

—— 'Twixt Two Eternities. pp. 315.   *Routledge & Sons: London*, 1893. 8°.   **012641. m. 33.**

CAUTER (THEODORE) and **DOWNHAM** (JOHN STANLEY)

—— The Communication of Ideas. A study of contemporary influences on urban life. [With plates.] pp. xviii. 324. *Published for The Reader's Digest Association by Chatto & Windus: London*, 1954. 8°.   **8289. t. 8.**

CAUSTON (THOMAS) and **HIGBED** (THOMAS) A Confession of Faith . . . by J. Causton and T. Higbed, *etc.* 1809. *See* RICHMOND (Legh) The Fathers of the English Church, *etc.* vol. 4. 1807, *etc.* 8°.   **478. b. 8.**

CAUSTON (THOMAS HENRY) *See* RYAN (Vincent W.) *Bishop of the Island of Mauritius.* A Sermon preached on occasion of the death of the . . . Rev. T. H. Causton. 1854. 8°.   **4906. d. 30.**

—— A Sermon preached in the Cathedral Church of St. Paul before the Right Honourable the Lord Mayor, the Judges . . . and the City Officers . . . the twenty-first of April, 1833, *etc.* pp. 24.   *J. Rider: London*, 1833. 4°.
4475. e. 114. (16.)

—— A Sermon preached in the Cathedral Church of St. Paul, before the Right Honourable the Lord Mayor, the Judges . . . and the City Officers . . . the second day of June, 1833. pp. 26.   *J. Rider: London*, 1833. 4°.
4475. e. 114. (17.)

—— A Sermon preached in the Parish Church of St. Lawrence Jewry, before the Right Honourable the Lord Mayor . . . and the City Officers . . . the twenty-eighth day of September, 1833, before the Election of a Lord Mayor. pp. 24.   *J. Rider: London*, 1833. 4°. **4475. f. 45. (14.)**

CAUSTON (WILLIAM) *See* BOETHIUS (A. M. T. S.) [*De Consolatione Philosophiae.—English.*] Anicius Manlius Torquatus Severinus Boethius, his Consolation of Philosophy, in five books. Translated into English [by W. Causton]. 1730. 8°.   **524. h. 23.**

—— *See* BOETHIUS (A. M. T. S.) [*De Consolatione Philosophiae.—English.*] The Comforts of Philosophy . . . from the Latin . . . by W. Causton . . . and Mr. Bellamy. 1768. 4°. [BELLAMY (D.) *Ethic Amusements.*]
90. e. 10.

CAUTEREN (PH. VAN) *See* MILL (John S.) Over vrijheid . . . Uit het Engelsch vertaald door P. van Cauteren. 1870. 8°.   **Ac. 9038/4.**

CAUTEREN (W. VAN) Vers le Katanga de Banana à Pweto. [With illustrations.] pp. 43.   *Bruxelles*, 1904. 8°. [*Publications de la Société d'Études Coloniales de Belgique.*]   **Ac. 2348/3.**

CAUTES, *pseud.* [i.e. KÁROLY BOROVSZKY.] *See also* BOROVSZKY (K.)

—— Die Lage der ungarischen Landwirthschaft. Von Cautes. pp. 115. *Budapest*, 1895. 8°.   **8276. ff. 42.**

CAUTHEN (CHARLES EDWARD)

—— South Carolina goes to War, 1860–1865. pp. vii. 256. *University of North Carolina Press: Chapel Hill*, 1950. 8°. [*James Sprunt Studies in History and Political Science.* vol. 32.]   **Ac. 2685. k.**

CAUTHERLEY (CHARLES) Costs in the County Court . . . Being a guide to their allowance by the Judge and taxation by the Registrar. pp. xii. 178. *W. Clowes & Sons: London*, 1886. 8°.   **6405. aaa. 43.**

CAUTILLO (FRANCESCO) Dissertazione sulla staurita di S. Pietro a Fusariello delle sei nobili famiglie Aquarie, *etc.* pp. cclxviii. *Napoli*, 1791. 4°.   **810. k. 21.**

CAUTIO. Cautio criminalis seu de processibus contra sagas liber. Ad magistratus Germaniæ hoc tempore necessarius . . . Auctore incerto theologo orthod. [i.e. Friedrich von Spee.] pp. 938 [398].   *P. Lucius: Rinthelii*, 1631. 8°.   **8632. aaa. 57.**

—— Editio secunda. pp. 459.   *Sumptibus I. Gronaei: Francofurti*, 1632. 8°.   **719. b. 23.**

—— [Another edition.] pp. 407.   *Sumpt. M. Endteri: Solisbaci*, 1695. 12°.   **8631. a. 2.**

—— [Another edition.] pp. 407.   *Solisbaci*, 1718. 12°.
879. a. 23.

CAUTION. Caution. (A grocery bill has just been issued, of which every sensible man ought to be ashamed, and regret that such Cannibals should be found in our decent little parish [i.e. Diss, in Norfolk].) [In verse.] [*Diss*, 1860?] *s. sh.* fol.   **1871. e. 1. (249.)**

—— A Caution against Convents, of vital importance to ladies who dread a gloomy . . . life. By a Graduate of Oxford . . . With a letter to . . . the Queen. Seventh edition. *Eng., Fr. & Lat.* pp. 15.   *The Author: London; Binns & Goodwin: Bath*, [1851.] 8º.
3939. c. 50.

—— A Caution against Inconsistency. Or, the connexion between praying and swearing; in relation to the civil powers. [By Jeremy Collier.] *See* COLLECTION. A Choice Collection of Papers relating to State Affairs, *etc.* vol. 1. 1703. 8º.   **1103. f. 1.**

—— A Caution against Mistakes in Religion. In a letter to a religious family. pp. 31.   *Printed for the Author: Coventry*, 1760. 8º.   **1476. b. 21. (2.)**

—— A Caution against Sacriledge: or, Sundry queries concerning tithes. Collected and composed by one that hath no propriety in tithes, and humbly tendred to this present Parliament. pp. 6. *Abraham Miller for Thomas Underhill: London*, 1659. 4º.   **E. 989. (18.)**
An earlier edition, entitled " An Item against Sacriledge," is entered under ITEM.

—— A Caution against Tumultuous Petitions: from a Gentleman in the Countrey, to his friend in London, Decemb. 30. 1679. pp. 2. *For W. C.: London*, 1680. fol.
1850. c. 5. (31.)

—— A Caution for Scolds: or, a True way of taming a shrew To the tune of, Why are my eyes still flowing. [A ballad.] 𝔅.𝔏. [*London*, 1685?] *s. sh.* fol.   **Rox. II. 51.**

—— The Caution of Miss R——, a young lady, to all young women, *etc.* [1780?] fol. *See* R——, *Miss.*
C. 116. i. 1. (41.)

—— A Caution to Bankers, Merchants, and Manufacturers, against a Series of Commercial Frauds prevalent throughout Great Britain and Ireland, *etc.* 1831. 8º. *See* ENGLAND. [*Appendix.—Trade and Commerce.*] **8220. aa. 10.**

—— A Caution to keepe Money; shewing the Miserie of the Want thereof, *etc.* pp. 8.   *For G. Lindsey; sold by F. Coules, I. Wright, & T. Bates: London*, 1642. 4º.
E. 146. (21.)

—— Caution to Love Letter Writers. Copy of a letter, picked up by a gentleman on the road in the neighbourhood of Newcastle-upon-Tyne. (Letter 2d.—Reply to the two letters.) 3 pt.   *W. Fordyce: Newcastle*, [1820?] *s. sh.* 4º.   **L.R. 38. c. 18. (8.)**

—— A Caution to Married Couples: being a true relation how a man in Nightingale-lane having beat and abused his wife, murthered a tub-man that endeavoured to stop him from killing her with a half-pike, *etc.* pp. 8.   *For D. M.: London*, 1677. 4º.   **10803. aa. 16. (5.)**

—— A Friendly Caution. Take care of your soul. *T. Combe: Leicester*, [1820?] *s. sh.* 4º.
1897. c. 8. (66.)

—— An humble Caution concerning the danger of removing godly and approved ministers out of Sequestrations. pp. 8. *Printed by Thomas Ratcliffe: London*, 1660. 4º.
E. 1030. (7.)

—— A Kind Caution to Prophane Swearers. By a Minister of the Church of England [i.e. Josiah Woodward]. pp. 3. *Joseph Downing: London*, 1704. 4º.   **T. 680. (17.)**

—— [Another edition.] pp. 3.   *Joseph Downing: London*, 1705. 4º.   **4418. c. 34.**

CAUTION.

—— A Kind Caution to Prophane Swearers, *etc.* [By Josiah Woodward.] pp. 12. *J. Downing: London*, [1705?] 12º.
4372. aa. 17. (2.)

—— [Another edition.] pp. 12.   *Joseph Downing: London*, 1707. 12º.   [MISSING.]

—— [Another edition.] pp. 12.   *M. Downing: London*, 1739. 12º.   [MISSING.]

—— A Kind Caution to Watermen, and such as go upon the River. pp. 12. *Joseph Downing: London*, 1707. 12º.
4403. bb. 48. (13.)

—— A Necessary and Seasonable Caution, concerning Elections. [*London*, 1660.] *s. sh.* fol.   **669. f. 24. (32.)**

—— A Serious Caution to the Poor. December 8, 1792. [Signed: The Poor Man's Friend.]   [*London?* 1792.] *s. sh.* fol.   **648. c. 26. (14.)**

CAUTION (CALEB) *pseud.* Ten Minutes' Advice on the Choice and Employment of an Attorney . . . By Caleb Caution. pp. 36. *Robert Tyas; John Nicholls: London*, 1841. 12º.   [MISSING.]

CAUTIONS. Cautions against the Fair. pp. 8. *R.T.S.:* [*London*, 1830?] 12º.   [MISSING.]

—— Cautions for the Times. Addressed to the parishioners of a parish in England by their former Rector. [Edited by Richard Whately. Largely written by William Fitzgerald, successively Bishop of Cork, Cloyne and Ross, and of Killaloe.] no. 1–7. pp. 4–124. *J. W. Parker: London*, 1851. 8º.   **3939. c. 16. (1.)**

—— Cautions to Young Sportsmen. pp. 24. *James Robson: London*, 1800. 8º.   **7907. cc. 28. (1.)**

—— Seasonable Cautions for Juries, Solicitors and Witnesses; to deterre from man-catching. pp. 2.   *For Francis Smith: London*, 1681. *s. sh.* fol.
1879. c. 4. (106.)

CAUTIOUS, *a Country-man, pseud.* The Wishing Commonwealths-men: or, a queint Dialogue betwixt Cautious a Country-man, and Wish-well a Citizen, *etc.* pp. 6. [*London*,] 1642. 4º.   **100. b. 39.**

—— [Another copy.]   **E. 114. (11.)**

CAUTIOUS CLARA, *Ship.* Inquiry into the Wreck of the Ship " Cautious Clara." [A satire.] [1879.] 8º.
12350. g. 20. (19.)

CAUTIUS (CAMILLUS) *See* CAUZIO (Camillo)

CAUTLEY (A. E.) Talks on Victories of Love in Many Lands, *etc.* [A tract on Missions.] pp. 27. *United Council for Missionary Education: London*, [1915.] 4º. [" *Talks* " Series.]   **4763. h. 13. (5.)**

—— Pictures illustrating " Talks on Victories of Love." [Two sheets.] [*London*, 1915.] fol.   **1865. c. 11. (110.)**

CAUTLEY (CAUTLEY HOLMES) The Millmaster. pp. iv. 396. *Edward Arnold: London*, 1906. 8º.
012633. cc. 9.

—— Paul Malsis. pp. 285.   *Selwyn & Blount: London*, 1924. 8º.   **NN. 10627.**

—— The Weaving of the Shuttle. pp. 302. *Duckworth & Co.: London*, 1912. 8º.   **NN. 181.**

CAUTLEY (EDMUND) The Diseases of Infants and Children. pp. xvi. 1042. *Shaw & Sons: London*, 1910. 8º.
07580. k. 8.

CAUTLEY (EDMUND)

—— The Natural and Artificial Methods of Feeding Infants and Young Children. pp. viii. 376. *J. & A. Churchill: London*, 1897. 8º.   **07581. de. 50.**

—— Second edition. pp. xii. 418.   *J. & A. Churchill: London*, 1903. 8º.   **07581. f. 69.**

CAUTLEY (FRANCIS) *See* CAUTLEY (Proby F. L.)

CAUTLEY (GEORGE SPENCER) The Afterglow: songs and sonnets for my friends. [By G. S. Cautley.] pp. 265. 1867. 8º. *See* AFTERGLOW.   **11648. bbb. 49.**

—— Second edition. pp. x. 246. 1869. 8º. *See* AFTERGLOW.   **11648. bbb. 50.**

—— A Century of Emblems . . . With illustrations, *etc.* pp. xviii. 135. *Macmillan & Co.: London*, 1878. 8º.   **11650. cc. 3.**

—— The Three Fountains: a faery epic of Euboea. With other verses. By the author of "The Afterglow" [i.e. G. S. Cautley]. pp. viii. 136. 1869. 8º. *See* FOUNTAINS.   **11648. bbb. 48.**

CAUTLEY (HENRY MUNRO)

—— Norfolk Churches . . . With 274 original photographs [and a map], *etc.* pp. xiii. 272. *Norman Adlard & Co.: Ipswich*, 1949 [1950]. 8º.   **07822. h. 2.**

——   Royal Arms and Commandments in our Churches . . . With 60 illustrations, *etc.* pp. vii. 137. *N. Adlard & Co.: Ipswich*, 1934. 8º.   **9906. a. 34.**

—— Suffolk Churches and their Treasures . . . With three colour and 415 other photographs by the author. pp. ix. 363. *B. T. Batsford: London*, 1937. 8º.   **7820. r. 41.**

CAUTLEY (*Sir* HENRY STROTHER) *Bart. See* STUTFIELD (George H.) The Law relating to Betting, Time-Bargains and Gaming . . . Third edition. By G. H. Stutfield and H. S. Cautley. 1892. 8º.   [MISSING.]

—— *See* STUTFIELD (George H.) The Rules and Usages of the Stock Exchange . . . Second edition, by the author and H. S. Cautley. 1893. 8º.   **08227. e. 52.**

—— —— 1901. 8º.   **08228. g. 69.**

CAUTLEY (PROBY FRANCIS LISTER) The Cube-City: twenty sermons, *etc.* pp. 92.   *Skeffington & Son: London*, [1919.] 8º.   **4461. ee. 23.**

CAUTLEY (*Sir* PROBY J.) *See* CAUTLEY (*Sir* P. T.)

CAUTLEY (*Sir* PROBY THOMAS) *See* FALCONER (Hugh) *M.D., F.R.S.*, and CAUTLEY (*Sir* P. T.) Fauna Antiqua Sivalensis, *etc.* 1846. 8º & fol.   **1255. l. 4.**

—— Ganges Canal, *etc.* [By Sir P. T. Cautley. With a lithographed view and a map.] *Eng., Hindi & Hindustani.* pp. 24. [12.] [28.] 1854. 4º. *See* GANGES CANAL.   **14109. e. 31.**

—— Ganges Canal. A disquisition on the heads of the Ganges and Jumna Canals . . . In reply to strictures by Major-General Sir Arthur Cotton. [With maps.] pp. vi. 104.   *Printed for private circulation: London*, 1864. 8º.   **8776. b. 50.**

—— The Ganges Canal. A reply to the statements made by Major-General Sir Arthur Cotton, on the projection of the Ganges Canal Works.   *Printed for private circulation: London*, 1863. 8º.   **8235. bb. 23.**

CAUTLEY (*Sir* PROBY THOMAS)

—— Ganges Canal. A valedictory note to Major-General Sir Arthur Cotton, respecting the Ganges Canal, with a postscript touching certain misrepresentations of a writer in the "Times" on the same subject. pp. 19. *Printed for private circulation: London*, 1863. 8º.   **8776. aaa. 21.**

—— Notes and Memoranda on the Eastern Jumna, or Doab Canal, and on the Water Courses in the Deyra Doon. [With maps and tables.] pp. 275. *Roorkee*, 1853. 8º. [*Professional Papers Printed at the Civil Engineering College, Roorkee.* no. 1.]   **Ac. 4323.**

—— Notes and Memoranda on the Water Courses in the Deyra Doon, North Western Provinces, *etc.* pp. 40. *G. H. Huttmann: Calcutta*, 1845. fol.   **8777. k. 46.**

—— On the Use of Wells, &c. in Foundations. *See* ABBOTT (*Sir* Frederick) Practical Treatise on Permanent Bridges for Indian Rivers, *etc.* 1850. 8º.   **8768. bbb. 23. (1.)**

—— [Another edition.] *See* ABBOTT (*Sir* Frederick) Practical Treatise on Permanent Bridges for Indian Rivers, *etc.* 1860. 8º.   **8775. bb. 52. (7.)**

—— Report on the Ganges Canal, from Hurdwar to Cawnpore and Allahabad. [By Sir P. T. Cautley. With plates and maps.] pp. xiii. 125. 86. 1845. fol. *See* INDIA. [*Miscellaneous Official Publications.*]   **I.S. 110.**

—— Report on the Ganges Canal Works: from their commencement until the opening of the Canal in 1854. 3 vol. *Smith, Elder & Co.: London*, 1860. 4º & 8º.   **8776. d. 1. & f. 7.**

—— Plans. pl. 66.   *Smith, Elder & Co.: London*, 1860. fol.   **14001. i. 23.**

CAUTLEY (RICHARD WILLIAM) Descriptions of Land. A text-book for survey students. pp. ix. 89. *Macmillan Co.: New York*, 1913. 8º.   **6306. aaaa. 14.**

CAUTLEY (SPENCER) *See* GOSSIP. Woodland Gossip . . . Illustrated by Frederick Leighton . . . and the Rev. S. Cautley. 1864. 8º.   **12804. cc. 22.**

CAUTUS. A Letter to the Right Reverend . . . William Skinner, D.D., Bishop of Aberdeen, and Primus of the Church in Scotland, on the subject of the Right Hon. W. E. Gladstone's proposal to admit the laity into the Synods of that Church. By Cautus. pp. 16. *R. Lendrum & Co.: Edinburgh*, 1852. 8º.   **4175. d. 19.**

—— A Second Letter to Sir Robert Peel, Bart., M.P., on Railway Legislation. By Cautus. pp. 23. *James Fraser: London*, 1837. 8º.   **T. 2134. (7.)**

—— Some Words on Railway Legislation, in a letter addressed to Sir R. Peel, Bart. By Cautus. pp. 16. *James Fraser: London*, 1837. 8º.   **8229. ff. 47. (1.)**

CAUTY (HENRY EVANS) Diseases of the Skin, in twenty-four letters on the principles and practice of cutaneous medicine. pp. x. 365.   *J. & A. Churchill: London; Adam Holden: Liverpool*, 1874. 8º.   **7641. c. 27.**

CAUTY (WILLIAM) Natura, Philosophia & Ars in Concordia. Or, Nature, philosophy, and art in friendship, an essay. In four parts. I. Demonstrating the necessity and practicability of building all manner of houses proof against fire and vermin . . . II. An entirely new plan of constructing chimnies, so as the smoke cannot reverberate. III. Plain methods pointed out, by which smoky chimnies may be effectually cured. IV. Certain and easy directions to all mechanics in wood, how to finish houshold furniture, and the wainscotting of rooms, so as no vermin can exist

CAUTY (William)
therein . . . With drawings and references. To which is added, six letters on interesting subjects. pp. xvi. 110. *The Author: London*, 1772. 8°. **56. b. 1.**

CAUVAIN (Henri) *the Elder*. De la colonisation de l'Algérie. pp. 72. *Paris*, 1857. 12°. **8155. a. 18.**

—— De la situation et de l'avenir des offices ministériels. pp. 16. *Paris*, 1848. 8°. **8052. g. 15.**

CAUVAIN (Henri) *the Younger*. L'Aiguille qui tue. Edited by P. W. Packer . . . Édition autorisée. pp. 64. *Oxford University Press: London*, 1933. 8°. [*Oxford Rapid-Reading French Texts.* ser. 2. no. 4.] **W.P. 488/8.**

—— Un Cas de folie. pp. 347. *Paris*, 1882. 12°. **12518. c. 19.**

—— [Un Cas de folie.] The Original Story of A Village Priest. As performed at the Haymarket Theatre . . . Translated . . . by Albert D. Vandam. pp. 205. *Trischler & Co.: London*, 1890. 8°. **012547. g. 57.**

—— [Another edition.] pp. 205. *F. Warne & Co.: London & New York*, [1893?] 8°. [*Library of Continental Authors.* no. 9.] **012208. f. 16.**

—— Le Grand vaincu. Dernière campagne du Marquis de Montcalm au Canada. [A novel.] Dessins de Maillart, *etc.* pp. 295. *Paris*, [1884.] 8°. **12513. m. 15.**

—— [Another edition.] pp. 336. *Paris*, 1885. 18°. **12511. k. 4.**

—— Madame Gobert, *etc.* [Tales.] pp. 366. *Paris*, 1884. 12°. **12510. p. 15.**

—— La Main sanglante. pp. 345. *Paris*, 1885. 12°. **12511. u. 16.**

—— La Mort d'Éva. pp. 314. *Paris*, 1881. 12°. **12518. k. 25.**

—— Rosa Valentin, l'espion. pp. 360. *Paris*, 1882. 18°. **12518. b. 25.**

CAUVAIN (Jules) *See* DESLYS (C.) and CAUVAIN (J.) La Revanche de Marguerite. 1879. 12°. **12517. i. 26.**

—— *See* FERÉ (O.) *pseud.*, and CAUVAIN (J.) Les Buveurs d'absinthe, *etc.* 1865. 12°. **12515. ee. 20.**

—— *See* ROBERT (Adrien) *pseud.*, and CAUVAIN (J.) Les Proscrits de 93. 1866. 12°. **12515. e. 29.**

—— Contes & chroniques des eaux et des bains de mer. pp. 212. *Paris*, 1865. 12°. **12516. bbb. 7.**

—— Histoire de l'Inquisition, 382–1820. pp. 128. *Paris*, 1872. 32°. **4071. aa. 19.**

CAUVAL (Edmond) *See* CHASSIN (C. L.) and CAUVAL (E.) Société universelle de la littérature, des sciences et des arts. Statuts proposés. 1857. 8°. **011840. g. 38. (1.)**

CAUVARD ( ) *Abbé*. Vie de Saint Agnan, évêque d'Orléans. pp. vii. 91. *Dijon*, 1863. 8°. **4826. aaa. 6.**

CAUVET (Alfred) La Vraie prononciation française. pp. 70. *Paris*, 1869. 12°. **12953. de. 1. (9.)**

—— [Another edition.] La Prononciation française et la diction . . . Nouvelle édition. pp. 105. *Paris*, 1881. 12°. **12950. bb. 43.**

CAUVET (Désiré) Cours élémentaire de botanique. 2 vol. *Paris*, 1885. 18°. **7033. cc. 1.**

—— Nouveaux éléments d'histoire naturelle médicale, *etc.* 2 tom. *Paris*, 1869. 12°. **7509. aaa. 12.**

—— Nouveaux éléments de matière médicale, comprenant l'histoire des drogues simples, *etc.* 2 tom. *Paris*, 1886, 87. 8°. **7560. aa. 12.**

CAUVET (Émile) Du mariage des serfs ; explication de deux traités de parcours passés l'un entre le Vicomte de Narbonne et ses feudataires, l'autre entre le Chapitre de Saint-Just et celui de Saint-Paul. 1877. *See* NARBONNE.—*Commission Archéologique et Littéraire de l'Arrondissement de Narbonne.* Bulletin, *etc.* tom. 1. 1877, *etc.* 8°. **Ac. 5323.**

—— Étude historique sur Fonfroide, abbaye de l'Ordre de Citeaux, située dans le diocèse & la vicomté de Narbonne, de 1093 à 1790. pp. xvi. 608. *Montpellier, Paris*, 1875. 8°. **4785. dd. 3.**

—— Étude historique sur l'établissement des Espagnols dans la Septimanie aux VIIIe et IXe siècles, et sur la fondation de Fontjoncouse par l'Espagnol Jean, au VIIIe siècle. 1877. *See* NARBONNE.—*Commission Archéologique et Littéraire de l'Arrondissement de Narbonne.* Bulletin, *etc.* tom. 1. 1877, *etc.* 8°. **Ac. 5323.**

—— [Another edition.] pp. 188. *Montpellier*, 1898. 8°. **09210. df. 12.**

—— Traité des assurances maritimes. 2 tom. *Paris*, 1879, 81. 8°. [MISSING.]

CAUVET (G.) Les Berbères en Amérique. Essai d'ethnocinésie préhistorique, *etc.* pp. 455. *Alger*, 1930. 8°. **010006. i. 18.**

—— Le Chameau. Anatomie, physiologie, races, *etc.* [With illustrations.] 2 vol. *Paris*, 1925, 26. 8°. **7209. c. 19.**

CAUVET (J. V.) Traité sur les assurances maritimes, comprenant la matière des assurances, du contrat à la grosse et des avaries. 2 tom. *Paris*, 1862. 8°. **6836.b.2.**

CAUVET (Jules) Le Droit pontifical chez les anciens Romains dans ses rapports avec le droit civil. Étude sur les antiquités juridiques de Rome. pp. 91. *Caen*, 1869. 8°. **5205. aa. 4. (2.)**

—— L'Empereur Justinien et son œuvre législative. Étude historique et juridique. pp. 105. *Caen*, 1880. 8°. **5254. bb. 22.**

CAUVET DUHAMEL (B.) *See* TOLSTOI (A. N.) Count Ibicus, ou les Aventures de Nevzorov. Traduit . . . par B. Cauvet Duhamel, *etc.* 1926. 8°. **12591. b. 54.**

—— *See* ZAMYATIN (E. I.) Nous autres. Traduit . . . par B. Cauvet-Duhamel, *etc.* 1929. 8°. **012591. k. 41.**

CAUVIER (Jean Camille) Dissertation sur le goître, *etc.* pp. 31. *Strasbourg*, 1822. 4°. [*Collection générale des dissertations de la Faculté de Médecine de Strasbourg.* vol. 29.] **7381.*b.**

CAUVIÈRE (André Léger F.) *See* CHAPPLAIN (J. J. A.) Notice nécrologique sur Cauvière, *etc.* 1860. 8°. **10660. cc. 53. (7.)**

—— *See* GIRARD (Jules J. A.) Notice historique sur le Dr. Cauvière, *etc.* 1861. 8°. **10662. dd. 29. (6.)**

—— Dissertation sur l'extraction des calculs vésicaux par l'appareil latéral, *etc.* pp. 24. *Paris*, 1803. 8°. **1183. b. 2. (7.)**

CAUVIÈRE (André Léger F.)

—— Observations sur quelques maladies scrofuleuses des articulations, et sur les abcès par congestion, *etc.* [A thesis.] pp. 16. *Montpellier*, 1807. 4°.
1180. f. 7. (19.)

CAUVIÈRE (Jules) Berryer, sa vie judiciaire . . . Deuxième édition. pp. 80. *Marseille*, 1871. 8°.
10660. gg. 18.

CAUVIGNY (François) *Sieur de Colomby.* See Trogus Pompeius. [*French.*] L'Histoire universelle de Trogue Pompée . . . traduite . . . par le Sieur de Collomby Cauvigny, *etc.* 1682. 12°. **584. a. 21.**

—— Lettres de Monsieur de Coulomby. *See* Faret (N.) Recueil de lettres nouuelles. 1627. 8°. **1085. g. 3.**

—— [Another edition.] *See* Faret (N.) Recueil de lettres nouuelles. tom. 1. 1634. 8°. **1085. d. 2.**

—— Les Plaintes de la captiue Caliston, a l'inuincible Aristarque. [In verse.] pp. 15. 1605. 8°.
11474. bb. 20.

CAUVIN ( ) *Anti-Jesuit Writer.* Arrest de la Cour du Parnasse pour les Jésuites. Poëme. Avec notes et figures. [By — Cauvin.] pp. 6. 55. 1762. 12°. *See* Parnassus. **11498. cc. 4. (3.)**

CAUVIN ( ) *Revolutionary Satirist.* L'Arrière-petit-fils du père Duchesne en rimes burlesques et libres à ses frères d'armes des armées du Rhin et de la Moselle, réunies, *etc.* no. 1, 2. *Paris*, [1793?] 8°. F. **1037. (5.)**

—— Confession du père Duchesne, marchand de fourneaux. [In verse. Signed : — Cauvin.] pp. 4. [*Paris*, 1793?] 8°.
R. 218. (65.)

CAUVIN (Alphonse) De la fièvre intermittente pernicieuse. Thèse, *etc.* pp. 56. *Montpellier*, 1844. 4°.
1182. d. 9. (4.)

CAUVIN (André)

—— *See* Latouche (John T.) Congo . . . Photographed by A. Cauvin. 1945. 4°. **10095. t. 7.**

CAUVIN (Antoine) *See* Ephemerides. Almanach de la Principauté de Monaco . . . Par A. C. [i.e. A. Cauvin.] [1833.] 8°. **P.P. 2386. e.**

—— Mémoires pour servir à l'histoire . . . de la commune de Contes et du hameau de Sclos, *etc.* pp. 424. *Nice*, 1885. 8°. **10169. de. 19.**

CAUVIN (C.) Le Retour de l'île d'Elbe et les cent jours dans les Basses-Alpes. 2 vol. *Digne*, 1916, 22. 8°.
9210. dd. 17.

Vol. 1 *bears the date* 1920 *on the wrapper.*

CAUVIN (E. C.) and **ROBERTS** (Harry) *A.S.C.* Souvenir of Deelfontein Hospital. [Fourteen pages of photographs with letterpress.] [1901.] obl. 8°. **9060. a. 8.**

CAUVIN (Jean) *See* Calvin.

CAUVIN (Jean François) Des bienfaits de l'insolation; thèse, *etc.* *Paris*, 1815. 4°. **1183. c. 13. (9.)**

CAUVIN (Joseph) *of Algiers.* Les Anglais réformateurs de Notre Saint Père le Pape. Satire politique. [In verse.] pp. 16. *Alger, Paris*, 1860. 8°. **11481. d. 50. (14.)**

—— Le Jésuitisme devant le sens commun. pp. 134. *Paris*, 1865. 12°. **4091. aa. 20.**

—— Notre-Dame d'Afrique, poésie, *etc.* pp. 8. *Alger*, 1860. 8°. **11475. f. 24. (6.)**

CAUVIN (Joseph) *Secretary to Lord Brougham. See* Brande (William T.) A Dictionary of Science, Literature, and Art . . . Edited by W. T. Brande, assisted by J. Cauvin. 1842. 8°. **740. g. 12.**

—— —— 1847. 4°. **815. h. 1.**

—— —— 1852. 8°. **740. g. 11.**

—— —— 1853. 8°. **7953. i. 19.**

—— *See* Ephemerides. 1872. Almanack for Time and Eternity. By Dr. Alban Stolz . . . Translated . . . by J. Cauvin. 1871. 16°. **P.P. 2483. q.**

—— *See* Lemprière (John) *D.D.* Lemprière's Classical Dictionary, abridged . . . by E. H. Barker. A new edition, revised . . . by J. Cauvin. 1843. 12°.
609*. b. 20.

—— *See* Scott (*Sir* Walter) *Bart.* [*Waverley Novels.—Selections.*] Diamonds from the Waverley Mines; or, Maxims . . . selected from the novels of Sir W. Scott. By J. Cauvin. 1872. 8°. **12602. aaa. 20.**

—— *See* Stolz (A.) Diamond or Glass . . . Translated by J. Cauvin. 1871. 16°. **3913. a. 3.**

—— *See* Stolz (A.) The Everlasting Salutation . . . Translated . . . by J. Cauvin. 1872. 16°. **4402. e. 28.**

—— A Treasury of the English & German Languages, founded upon the best authors and lexicographers in both languages, *etc.* pp. vii. 640. *W. Blackwood & Sons: Edinburgh & London*, 1870. 8°. **12962. n. 14.**

CAUVIN (Pierre) Guide du commerce. Indicateur niçois, suivi d'un Cicerone de l'étranger pour Nice et ses environs, *etc.* 2 pt. *Nice*, 1855. 8°. **10174. aaa. 3.**

CAUVIN (S. C. Victorin) Essai sur l'éclampsie des femmes enceintes. Thèse, *etc.* pp. 26. *Montpellier*, [1837.] 4°. **1181. h. 11. (16.)**

CAUVIN (Tanneguy Joseph) *Sieur d'Argences.* Harangue (par T. J. Cauvin, Sr d'Argences) faite en la présence du Roy de la Grande-Bretagne [James II., 21 June 1692] à Pontaudemer. Publiée avec une introduction par G. A. Prévost. pp. vi. 9. 1892. *See* Rouen.—*Société des Bibliophiles Normands.* Miscellanées. Pièces historiques, *etc.* sér. 3. 1877, *etc.* 4°. **Ac. 8938/30.**

CAUVIN (Thomas) Documents relatifs à l'histoire des corporations d'arts et métiers du diocèse du Mans, rassemblés par T. Cauvin, et publiés par M. l'abbé Lochet. pp. viii. 504 [496]. *Le Mans*, 1860. 12°. **5425. aa. 7.**

—— Essai sur la statistique du département de la Sarthe. pp. 377. *Au Mans*, 1834. 12°. **10168. b. 27.**

—— Géographie ancienne du diocèse du Mans, par M. Th. Cauvin, suivie d'un Essai sur les monnaies du Maine, par M. E. Hucher, *etc.* [With plates and a map.] pp. 43. xcvi. 735. *Paris*, 1845. 4°. [*Institut des Provinces de France.* Mémoires. sér. 2. tom. 1.] **732. l. 14.**

CAUVY (Benjamin) Le Salut des vignes. Véritable point de vue sous lequel il convient de considérer la maladie . . . de la vigne causée par le phylloxera pour le combattre, *etc.* pp. 24. *Montpellier*, 1874. 8°. **7078. f. 8. (2.)**

CAUVY (F.) Des fractures du crâne. Thèse, *etc.* [With plates.] pp. xv. 207. *Montpellier*, 1868. 4°.
7379. h. 4. (1.)

—— [Another edition.] pp. xv. 204. pl. III. *Montpellier, Paris*, 1868. 8°. **7481. cc. 10.**

CAUVY (Jean Baptiste) De la non-existence de la fièvre typhoïde envisagée comme fait morbide distinct. Thèse, *etc.* pp. 109. *Montpellier*, 1856. 4°. **7379. c. 22. (6.)**

CAUVY (LAURENT BARTHÉLEMI) Dissertation sur les hémorrhagies ou pertes utérines qui surviennent après l'accouchement, *etc.* pp. 20. *Montpellier, 1824.* 4°.
1181. c. 16. (7.)

CAUVY (PAUL) Des appareils employés dans les fractures de la jambe. pp. 42. *Paris, 1869.* 4°. [*Collection des thèses soutenues à la Faculté de Médecine de Paris.* An 1869. tom. 3.]
7373. k. 9.

CAUVY (VICTOR) Quelques observations pratiques médicochirurgicales, *etc.* [A thesis.] pp. 28. *Montpellier, 1810.* 4°.
1180. g. 1. (10.)

CAUWELAERT (AUGUSTINUS JUSTINUS VAN)

—— Harry. [A novel.] pp. 315. *Amsterdam,* [1934.] 8°.
012584. e. 20.

—— Het Individualisme van " Van nu en straks." *In:* Koninklijke Vlaamse Academie voor Taal- en Letterkunde. Publicaties. reeks 10. no. 1. pp. 53–72. 1944. 8°.
Ac. **7556/10.**

—— Liederen van droom en daad . . . Vierde druk. pp. 110. *Antwerpen, Bussum, 1927.* 8°.
011556. f. 84.

—— De Romancier en zijn jeugd. [With plates.] pp. 68. *Antwerpen, 1944.* 8°.
11867. ee. 11.

—— Vertellen in Toga. pp. 138. *Amsterdam, Antwerpen, 1935.* 8°.
012584. bb. 23.

—— De Vlaamsche jongeren van gisteren en heden, 1910–1927. [An anthology of verse.] pp. 158. *Antwerpen, Eindhoven, 1927.* 8°.
11557. c. 29.

CAUWELAERT (FRANS VAN) Losse bladen over staatkunde. 1e reeks. Vrij België. pp. vii. 143. *Leiden,* [1918.] 8°.
8081. de. 13.

—— Naar de toekomst. 1913. *See* ROOSES (M.) Vlaanderen door de eeuwen heen, *etc.* dl. 2. 1912, *etc.* 4°.
10270. ff. 20.

—— Verhandelingen en voordrachten . . . Een keur. [With a portrait.] pp. 94. *Brussel, 1927.* 8°. **012352. d. 47.**

CAUWELAERT (K. A. VAN)

—— *See* DAWSON (Christopher H.) [The Judgement of the Nations.] Het Oordeel van de volken. (Vertaald door K. A. van Cauwelaert.) 1947. 8°.
8012. d. 20.

CAUWENBERG (WINFRED JOSEPH) Methyl Isopropyl Indigoid Dyes from Cymene. Dissertation, *etc.* pp. 43. *New York, 1930.* 8°.
8900. ff. 9.

CAUWENBERGH (ÉTIENNE VAN) Les Pélerinages expiatoires et judiciaires dans le droit communal de la Belgique au moyen âge. pp. viii. 244. *Louvain, 1922.* 8°. [*Université de Louvain. Recueil de travaux publiées par les membres des conférences d'histoire, etc.* fasc. 48.]
Ac. **2646/4.**

CAUWENBERGH (JOZEF) Eine Mutter. *See* FLEMISH LIFE. Vlämisches Leben. Geschichten, *etc.* 1867. 8°.
12581. df. 22.

CAUWENBERGH (PAUL VAN) Étude sur les moines d'Égypte depuis le concile de Chalcédoine, 451, jusqu'à l'invasion arabe, 640. pp. viii. 195. *Paris, Louvain, 1914.* 8°.
04782. f. 22.

CAUWENBERGHE (EDUARD F. VAN) L'Église de Notre-Dame de Pamele à Audendarde et ses restaurateurs. [Including A. Vanassche's " Rapport fait à la Commission Royale des Monuments," and E. F. van Cauwenberghe's criticisms on it.] pp. xiv. 132. *Audendarde, 1880.* 8°.
7814. ee. 7.

CAUWENBERGHE (PETRUS VAN) *Resp. See* BUKENTOP (H. de) Pædagogus ad Sancta Sanctorum, *etc.* 1696. 8°.
1112. b. 3. (4.)

CAUWENBERGHS (CLÉMENT VAN) La Corporation des Quatre Couronnés d'Anvers, ou les Architectes anversois du moyen âge, 1324–1542. pp. 53. *Anvers, 1889.* 8°.
7817. e. 31.

—— Notice historique sur les peintres-verriers d'Anvers du XVe au XVIIIe siècle. pp. 82. *Anvers, 1891.* 8°.
07812.ppp.8.

CAUWÈS (ALBERT) Des rapports du mariage avec la nationalité. pp. xvii. 294. *Paris, 1901.* 8°.
5176. e. 14.

CAUWÈS (GEORGES) L'Extension des principes de la Convention de Genève aux guerres maritimes. pp. 253. *Paris, 1899.* 8°.
06955.h.8.

CAUWÈS (PAUL LOUIS) Précis du cours d'économie politique professé à la Faculté de Droit à Paris, *etc.* 2 tom. *Paris, 1878, 79.* 8°.
8207. cc. 4.

—— Deuxième édition, revue, *etc.* 2 tom. *Paris, 1881, 82.* 8°.
8205. ff. 4.

—— Cours d'économie politique . . . Troisième édition. 4 tom. *Paris, 1893.* 8°.
8205. h. 15.

CAUWET (ALFRED) Rose et Papillon, comédie de salon en un acte, en vers. pp. 24. *Paris, 1864.* 12°.
11739. aa. 59. (3.)

CAUX. Les Bâtards de Caulx, farce nouuelle et fort ioyeuse à v. personnages. 1837. *See* LE ROUX DE LINCY (A. J. V.) and MICHEL (F.) Recueil de farces, *etc.* tom. 3. 1837, *etc.* 8°.
1343. e. 19.

—— Cahiers de Caux. *See* MORAL REARMAMENT.

—— Le Monde ouvrier et Caux. Déclarations de syndicalistes et de socialistes faites à Caux, *etc.* pp. xiii. 93. *Caux,* [1950.] 8°.
4194. bb. 36.

CAUX, *Bailliage de.* Registre des fiefs et arrière-fiefs du bailliage de Caux en 1503. Publié pour la première fois avec une introduction et des notes par A. Beaucousin. pp. xxii. 326. 1891. 8°. *See* ROUEN.—*Société de l'Histoire de Normandie.*
Ac. **6890/26.**

—— *Noblesse.* Mandat, pouvoirs et instructions que la noblesse du bailliage de Caux . . . donne à ses députés aux États-Généraux, convoqués à Versailles le 27 avril 1789. pp. 18. *Caudebec, et se trouve à Paris,* [1789.] 8°.
F.R. 25. (28.)

CAUX-HEFTE.

—— Caux-Hefte. *See* MORAL REARMAMENT. Cahiers de Caux.

CAUX INFORMATION SERVICE. *See* MORAL REARMAMENT.—*World Assembly for Moral Re-Armament.*

CAUX (DAVID DE) Varia philosophica et medica, *etc.* pp. 239. *J. Lucas: Rothomagi, 1674.* 12°. **784. d. 22.**

CAUX (FRANCIS PERCIVAL DE) *See* DE CAUX.

CAUX (FRANÇOIS LE PICARD DE) *See* LE PICARD (F.) de Caux.

CAUX (GABRIEL GRIMAUD DE) *See* GRIMAUD DE CAUX.

CAUX (GILLES DE) Sieur de Montlebert.

—— *See* SANADON (N. E.) [Villartio, liberata victoria . . . ode.] A Monseigneur le Maréchal Duc de Villars. Ode. Traduite . . . par M. de Caux. 1712. 12°.
11409. l. 42. (8.)

CAUX (Gilles de) *Sieur de Montlebert.*

—— *See* Sanadon (N. E.) [Villartio, liberata victoria . . . ode.] Ode. A M. le Maréchal Duc de Villars. [Translated by G. de Caux.] 1745. 4º.   [*Bibliothèque poëtique.* tom. 4.]   **84. h. 4.**

—— ·L'Horloge de sable figure du monde, poëme. *See* Bibliothèque. Bibliothèque poëtique, *etc.* tom. 4. 1745. 4º. **84. h. 4.**

——   Lysimachus. Tragédie, *etc.* [In verse.] pp. 64. *Paris,* 1738. 8º.   **11738. aaa. 22. (4.)**

—— Marius, tragédie. [In verse.] pp. xii. 64.   *Paris,* 1716. 12º.   **164. a. 22.**

—— [Another edition.] *See* French Theatre. Théâtre françois, *etc.* tom. 11. 1737. 12º.   **640. d. 40.**

—— [Another edition.] 1803. *See* Petitot (C. B.) Répertoire du théâtre françois, *etc.* tom. 2. 1803, *etc.* 8º.   **86. e. 2.**

—— [Another edition.] 1808. *See* Théâtre. Théâtre des auteurs du second ordre, *etc.* Tragédies. tom. 2. 1808, *etc.* 12º.   **242. d. 9.**

—— [Another edition.] *See* French Theatre. Répertoire général du théâtre français, *etc.* tom. 25. 1813. 12º.   **11735. c. 9. (3.)**

—— Marius. Treurspel. Gevolgd naar het Fransche, *etc.* *See* Feitama (S.) Tooneelpoëzy, *etc.* dl. 1. 1735. 4º.   **11754. d. 4.**

—— [Another edition.] Verbeterd in dezen tweeden druk. pp. 56. *Amsteldam,* 1757. 8º.   **636. c. 14. (5.)**

CAUX (Henri de) Catalogue général des gentils-hommes de la Province de Languedoc. Dont les titres de noblesse ont esté remis devant Monsieur de Bezons . . . lesquels titres ont esté confirmez par jugement souverain dudit Sr. de Bezons . . . En vertu de la Commission de sa Majesté pour la recherche de la Noblesse, du mois de mars 1668, *etc.* 2 pt. *I. Martel: Pezenas,* 1676. fol.   **1327. l. 3.**

CAUX (Louis Victor de) *Viscount. See* Decaux de Blacquetot.

CAUX (N. de) *See* Caux (Gilles de) *Sieur de Montlebert.*

CAUX (Paul de) *See* Periodical Publications.—*Paris.* Le Foyer des familles . . . M. P. de Caux, directeur. 1859, *etc.* 4º.   **P.P. 4267.**

CAUX (Salomon de) *See* Caus.

CAUX (Sébastien Charles Philibert Cahuzac de) *See* Cahuzac de Caux.

CAUX DE CAPPEVAL (N. de) *See* Voltaire (F. M. A. de) [*La Henriade.*] Voltarii Henriados libri decem, Latinis versibus et Gallicis ; adposito duplici poemate . . . Auctore Calcio Cappavalle. 1775. 8º.   **1161. e. 12.**

—— L'Anti-Scurra, ou Préservatif contre les Bouffons italiens. [By N. de caux de Cappeval. In verse.] pp. 7. [1753.] 8º. *See* Anti-Scurra.   **1103. b. 21. (14.)**

—— Apologie du goût françois relativement à l'opéra. Poeme, avec un discours apologetique, *etc.* [By N. de Caux de Cappeval.] pp. 80. [1754.] 8º. *See* French Taste.   Hirsch 1. **109.**

—— Épître aux Bouffonnistes. [In verse. Signed: L'Anti-Scurra. Sometimes attributed to N. de Caux de Cappeval.] pp. 8. [1753.] 8º. *See* Anti-Scurra.   **557*. d. 30. (7*.)**

—— Another copy.]   **1103. b. 21. (10.)**

CAUX DE CAPPEVAL (N. de)

—— |Another copy.] Épître aux Bouffonnistes. [1753.] 8º. *See* Anti-Scurra.   Hirsch 1. **159.**

—— Réflexions liriques. [In verse, on French and Italian Opera. Sometimes attributed to N. de Caux de Cappeval.] pp. 8. [1753.] 8º. *See* Réflexions. **1103. b. 21. (11.)**

—— |Another copy.] Réflexions liriques. [1753.] 8º. *See* Réflexions.   Hirsch 1. **492.**

—— La Reforme de l'Opéra [In verse. Sometimes attributed to N. de Caux de Cappeval.] pp. 8. [1753.] 8º. *See* Réforme.   **557*. d. 30. (7.)**

—— [Another copy.]   **1103. b. 21. (16.)**

—— [Another copy.] La Réforme de l'Opéra. [1753.] 8º. *See* Réforme.]   Hirsch 1. **493.**

CAUZ (Constantin Franz Florian Anton von) *See* Kauz.

CAUZAR, *pseud.* The True Crusaders : a missionary poem. With some smaller pieces, some of which have been revised by James Montgomery. Stories of the Poor-House. By Cauzar. pp. 246. *George Herbert: Dublin,* 1872. 8º.   **11649. de. 5.**

CAUZIO (Camillo) *See* Ovidius Naso (P.) [*Metamorphoses.—Italian.*] Libro nono del Metamorphosis, *etc.* [Translated into Italian verse by C. Cauzio.] [1545 ?] 8º.   **238. k. 22.**

—— Camilli Cautii . . . Tractatus de pensionibus episcopalibus. *See* Tractatus. Tractatus vniversi iuris, *etc.* tom. 15. pt. 2. 1584. fol.   **499. g. 11.**

—— Camilli Cautii . . . Scholia pro religione. In quibus agitur, de imagine Dei, de homine, & angelis, de lege Dei, de natura humana, de pietate hominis, de persona Christi. ff. 77.   *Apud F. Laurentinum: Venetiis,* 1559. 8º.   **1413. c. 9.**
The running title is " Scholion pro religione in Lutherani Catechismi Art. primum(–sextum)."

—— Camilli Cautii . . . Scholia pro religione. Quibus præcipue omnis accidentium, & adorationis Eucharistiæ difficultas ; atque Catholicæ doctrinæ ratio . . . explicantur. His adiectæ sunt eiusdem epistolæ quinque, ad rem facientes. pp. 223. *Venetiis,* 1559. 8º.   **847. i. 10.**
A different work from the preceding.

CAUZIQUE (Adèle) Sous le ciel basque. [Essays. With plates.] pp. 111. *Paris,* 1936. 8º.   **12357. s. 39.**

CAUZIUS (Constantinus Franciscus Florianus Antonius de) *See* Kauz.

CAUZONS (Thomas de) *pseud.* Histoire de l'Inquisition en France. 2 tom. *Paris,* 1909, 12. 8º.   **4630. dg. 29.**

—— La Magie et la sorcellerie en France, *etc.* 4 vol. *Paris,* [1910, 11.] 8º.   **08631. l. 54.**

CAVA. La Cava ; or, Recollections of the Neapolitans. pp. 338. *Saunders, Otley & Co.: London,* 1860. 8º.   **10151. d. 9.**

CAVA, *Monastery of.* Chronicon Cavense ab anno 569 usque ad 1318 nunc primum editum, *etc.* 1725. *See* Muratori (L. A.) Rerum italicarum scriptores, *etc.* tom. 7. 1723, *etc.* fol.   **L.1.h.1/7.**

—— [Another edition.] 1782. *See* Pelliccia (A. A.) Raccolta di varie croniche . . . appartenenti alla storia del regno di Napoli. tom. 4. 1780, *etc.* 4º.   **1318. h. 4.**

CAVA, *Monastery of.*

—— Codex diplomaticus Cavensis, nunc primum in lucem editus curantibus DD. Michaele Morcaldi, Mauro Schiani, Sylvano de Stephano, O.S.B. Accedit Appendix qua praecipua Bibliothecae MS. membranacea describuntur per D. Bernardum Caietano de Aragonia. 8 tom. *Neapoli*, 1873–93. 4°.　　　**9150. i. 2.**

—— Poche parole sulla Badia Cavense. pp. 24. *Napoli*, 1861. 8°.　　　**8033. f. 33. (1.)**

—— Vitæ quatuor priorum Abbatum Cavensium, Alpherii, Leonis, Petri, atque Constabilis: auctore anonymo Abbate Venusino, fere æquali. 1725. *See* MURATORI (L. A.) Rerum italicarum scriptores, *etc.* tom. 6. 1723, *etc.* fol.　　　**L.1.h.1/6.**

CAVA, SILVESTER, *Bishop of.* [1818–1832.] *See* GRANITO.

CAVA (FABIO) *See* SANTORELLI (A.)　Il Protomedico Napolitano . . . Dialogo raccolto da vn discepolo del Dottor A. Santorello e dato in luce dal Signor F. Cava. 1652. 4°.　　　**775. i. 13. (1.)**

CAVACCI (JACOPO) *See* CAVACIUS (Jacobus)

CAVACCIA (GIOVANNI BATTISTA)　L'Anello matrimoniale; trattato. pp. 144.　*Per F. Paganello: Milano*, 1599. 8°.　　　**604. a. 17. (4.)**

CAVACCIA (JOANNES)　Aula Zabarella, siue Elogia illustrium Patauinorum, conditorisq; vrbis. ex historijs chronicisque collecta a I. Cauaccia . . . et a comite Iacobo Zabarella . . . aucta & illustrata . . . Vbi insuper omnis Romana historia dignoscitur, pulcrioresque res, & antiquitates Vrbis Patauinæ, Prouinciæque & Reipublicæ Venetæ . . . in lucem perferuntur. pp. 286. *I. de Cadorinis: Patauij*, 1670. 4°.　**661. b. 17. (1.)**

CAVACEPPI (BARTOLOMEO)　Raccolta d'antiche statue, busti, bassirilievi ed altre sculture, restaurate da B. Cavaceppi. [Plates, with introductory text.] 3 vol. *Roma*, 1768–72. fol.　　　**1265. h. 26–28.** *Imperfect; wanting the text of vol.* 1.

—— Reise von Rom nach Wien und Potsdam, im Jahre 1768, *etc.* [Extracted and translated from " Raccolta d'antiche statue."] *See* BERNOULLI (Johann) *the Younger.* Sammlung kurzer Reisebeschreibungen, *etc.* Bd. 1. 1781, *etc.* 8°.　　　**1045. b. 1.**

CAVACIA (FRANCISCUS) *See* VIVALDUS (J. L.) Aureum opus de veritate contritionis, *etc.* [With commendatory notices by F. Cavacia and others.] 1503. fol.　　　**C. 26. m. 3.**

CAVACIOCCHI (ALBERTO)　Relazioni e rapporti finali sulla campagna del 1849 nell'Alta Italia. [Edited by A. Cavaciocchi. With maps.] pp. xii. 842. 1911. 8°. *See* ITALY.—*Army.*—*Corpo di Stato Maggiore.*　　**9168. bb. 10.**

CAVACIOCCHI (GIUSEPPE)　La Compagnia della Morte. Ricordi di un volontario della Legione Cipriani. [With a preface by A. Labriola.] pp. xix. 142.　*Napoli*, 1898. 8°.　　　**9136. bbb. 38.**

CAVACIUS (JACOBUS)　Historiarum Cœnobij D. Iustinæ Patauinæ, libri sex. pp. 306.　*Ex typographia A. Muschij: Venetiis*, 1606. 4°.　　**859. k. 4.**

—— [Another copy.]　　　**205. a. 8.**

—— Secunda impressio. pp. 306.　*Ex typographia Seminarii: Patavii*, 1696. 4°.　　**490. h. 2.**

—— Illustrium anachoretarum elogia, siue religiosi viri musæum. [Edited by L. Pignoria. With plates.] pp. 157. *In Typographia Pinelliana: Venetiis*, 1625. 4°.　　　**C. 78. b. 19.** *The titlepage is engraved.*

CAVACIUS (JACOBUS)

—— [Another copy.]　　　**204. d. 13.**

—— [Another edition.] pp. 157.　*Typis I. Dragondelli: Romæ*, 1661. 4°.　　　**695. h. 1.**

CAVADA (FREDERICK F.)　Libby Life. Experiences of a prisoner of war in Richmond, Va., 1863–64. [With plates.] pp. 221.　*King & Baird: Philadelphia*, 1864. 8°.　　　**9604. aaa. 11.**

CAVADA MENDEZ DE VIGO (AUGUSTIN DE LA) Historia geográfica, geológica y estadística de Filipinas. 2 tom. *Manila*, 1876. 4°.　　**010055. f. 4.**

CAVADAS (JUAN JOSÉ)　Proposición que el ciudadano regidor Juan José Cavadas hizo en cabildo ordinario el dia 11 del corriente [July], y fué . . . aprobada por el M. Y. A. de esta capital. [Petitioning the Congress of the State of Durango to hold the elections for the second congress.] *Durango*, 1826. *s. sh.* fol.　**9770. k. 9. (19.)**

CAVA DE GUEVA (TOMMASO)　Comitato di Vigilanza in Napoli contro gli attentati in danno delle proprietà. pp. 8.　*Napoli*, 1871. 8°.　　**5373. d. 5.**

CAVADINI (ADA)

—— This was the A.T.S. pp. 108.　*Dorothy Crisp & Co.: London*, [1946.] 8°.　　**12332. eee. 53.**

CAVAFIS (COSTANTINO) *See* KABAPHES (K. P.)

CAVAFY (CONSTANTINE P.) *See* KABAPHES (K. P.)

CAVAGLIÀ (ENRICO) *See* MURRI, *afterwards* BONMARTINI (T.) *Countess.* Perchè Linda Murri è innocente. Arringhe pronunciate avanti la Corte d'Assise di Torino [by G. Gottardi, E. Cavaglià, and others]. [1906.] 8°.　　　**6055. eee. 6.**

CAVAGLIERI (ARRIGO)　Règles générales du droit de la paix. [With a portrait.] *See* HAGUE.—*Académie de Droit International.* Recueil des Cours, *etc.* 1929, vol. 1. 1930, *etc.* 8°.　　　**Ac. 2099/2.**

CAVAGLIERI (DOMENICO)　Puro, e distinto ragguaglio del gran pesce chiamato balenotto buffalino, detto anco capo d'olio, preso in vicinanza del porto di Pesaro il giorno delli 18. aprile 1715. *Venezia*, 1715. *s. sh.* fol.　　　**Cup. 651. e. (88.)**

CAVAGLIERI (GUIDO) *See* FLORIAN (E.) and CAVAGLIERI (G.) I Vagabondi, *etc.* 1897, *etc.* 8°.　**6057. h. 23.**

—— Cooperazione e questioni pratiche di scienza dell'amministrazione e di diritto amministrativo. pp. 115. *Roma*, 1897. 8°.　　　**08282. i. 11.**

CAVAGNA (GAUDENZIO)　Zootecnia. Pregi e difetti degli animali domestici, col modo di conoscerne l'etá. pp. 279. *Milano*, 1871. 8°.　　　**7294. bb. 18.**

CAVAGNARI (ALFONSO)　Corte d'Appello di Parma. Intorno alla capacità di succedere dei religiosi professi dopo la pubblicazione del Codice civile italiano.　Per la signora Clotilde [or rather, Elisa] Longhi—monaca—contro la signora Rosa Longhi in Bervitius. pp. 36. *Parma*, 1869. 8°.　　　**5322. e. 13.**

—— Del reato di lenocinio. Necessità di modificazioni al progetto del codice penale presentato dal ministro Vigliani. Studi. pp. 80. *Parma*, 1874. 8°.　**5325. bb. 11.**

—— Giovanni Giscala. Melodramma tragico in quattro parti . . . da rappresentarsi sulle scene dell'I. R. Teatro alla Scala la quaresima 1856. [In verse.] pp. 30. *Milano*, 1856. 8°.　　　**906. h. 4. (3.)**

CAVAGNARI (Alfonso)

—— Il Libro primo del progetto del codice penale italiano. Note. pp. xvi. 189. *Parma*, 1876. 8°.　　**5361. d. 3**.

—— Proposta di legge per la soppressione dell'ordine di San Giovanni di Gerusalemme. pp. 22.　*Parma*, 1863. 8°.
　　　　　　　　　　　　　　　　4784. c. 35. (8.)

CAVAGNARI (Antonio)

—— Corso moderno di filosofia del diritto. vol. 2. *Padova*, 1892. 8°.　　　　　　　　　**5427. b. 6**.
　Imperfect ; wanting vol. 1.

—— Il Nuovo diritto degli individui e dei popoli, *etc.* pp. viii. 458. *Padova*, 1869. i°.　　**5326. a. 9**.

CAVAGNARI (Camillo) Nuovi orizzonti del diritto civile in rapporto colle istituzioni pupillari. Saggio di critica e riforma legislativa con appendice, *etc.* pp. xx. 451. *Milano*, 1891. 8°.　　　　　**5359. ee. 27**.

CAVAGNARI (Giuseppe) Il Re dei paesani. [With other tales.] pp. 275. *Como*, 1886. 8°. **12470. aaa. 31**.

CAVAGNARI (*Sir* Louis) *See* Cavagnari (*Sir* Pierre L. N.)

CAVAGNARI (*Sir* Pierre Louis Napoleon) *See* Kālī-prasanna De. The Life and Career of Major Sir Louis Cavagnari, *etc.* 1881. 8°.　　**10817. i. 23**.

CAVAGNARI (Pietro) Alcune particolarità storiche della vita di Pietro Cavagnari. [By himself. With a portrait.] 2 pt. *Parma*, 1837. 4°.　　**1449. k. 18**.

CAVAGNARI (Vittorio Wautrain) *See* Wautrain Cavagnari.

CAVAGNARO (Carlo) Gli Ebrei in Egitto. pp. 436. *Genova*, 1890[–92]. 8°.　　　　**4516. e. 33**.
　Published in parts.

CAVAGNA SANGIULIANI (Antonio) L'Agro voghe-rese. Memorie sparse di storia patria. [With a biblio-graphy of the author's works.] vol. 1. pp. xi. 416. 24. *Casorate Primo*, 1890. 8°.　　　**10132. h. 9**.
　No more published.

—— Le Chiese e il chiostro di Piona. [With plates.] 1905. *See* Como, *Province of.*—*Commissione Provinciale per la Conservazione dei Monumenti.* Rivista archeologica della provincia di Como. fasc. 50. 1872, *etc.* 8°.　Ac. **5218**.

—— Dell'Abazia di S. Alberto di Butrio e del Monasterio di S. Maria della Pietà detto Il Rosario, in Voghera, provincia di Pavia. Illustrazioni Storiche. pp. 312. *Milano*, 1865. fol.　　　　　**4605. ff. 19**.

—— Documenti vogheresi dell'Archivio di Stato di Milano. [Edited by A. Cavagna Sangiuliani.] pp. xv. 400. *Pinerolo*, 1910. 8°.　　[*Biblioteca della Società Storica Subalpina.* no. 47.]　　　　Ac. **6536**.

—— Studi storici. vol. 1. pp. 200. *Milano*, 1870. 8°.
　　　　　　　　　　　　　　　9166. g. 9.
　No more published.

CAVAGNINI (Gieronimo) *See* Kavanjin (Jerolim)

CAVAGNIS (Felice) *Cardinal. See* Rome, *Church of.* [*Corpus Juris Canonici.*] Institutiones juris publici ecclesiastici quas in scholis Pontificii Seminarii Romani tradidit Can. F. Cavagnis. 1883. 8°.　**5107. aaa. 11**.

—— *See* Vistalli (F.) Il Cardinal Cavagnis, *etc.* 1913. 8°.
　　　　　　　　　　　　　　4867. gg. 20.

CAVAGNIS (Felice) *Cardinal.*

—— Nozioni di diritto publico naturale ed ecclesiastico. pp. 372. *Roma*, 1886. 8°.　　　**5107. aaa. 13**.

CAVAIGNAC, *Family of. See* Républicain. Les Cavai-gnac et les Carnot. 1892. 8°.　　**8051. ccc. 36. (4.)**

CAVAIGNAC (Éléonore Louis Godefroy) *See* Ambert (J.) *Baron.* Portraits républicains. Armand Carrel—Godefroy Cavaignac. 1870. 12°.　　**10662. bbb. 1**.

—— *See* Cavaignac (L. E.) Deux déclarations solennelles de M. E. Cavaignac. [Biographies of his father and brother.] [1848.] fol.　　　**1851. d. 1. (4.)**

—— Dubois Cardinal, proverbe historique.—Une Tuerie de Cosaques, scènes d'invasion. (Publié par Charles Lemesle.) pp. 250. *Paris*, 1831. 8°.　**12237. b. 1**.

—— Romans militaires . . . Avec une préface par Emmanuel Gonzalès. pp. xxiii. 244. *Paris*, 1866. 8°.
　　　　　　　　　　　　　　12515. f. 9.

—— La Force révolutionnaire. *See* Paris. [*Appendix.—History.*] Paris révolutionnaire. tom. 1. 1838. 8°.
　　　　　　　　　　　　　　10170. ccc. 23.

—— [Another edition.] *See* Paris. [*Appendix.—History.*] Paris révolutionnaire. 1848. 8°.　　**1321. a. 15**.

CAVAIGNAC (Eugène) *General. See* Cavaignac (Louis E.)

CAVAIGNAC (Eugène) *Historian.* Chronologie de l'his-toire mondiale. Deuxième édition revue et augmentée. pp. 231. *Paris*, 1934. 8°.　　　**9011. bb. 5**.

—— Études sur l'histoire financière d'Athènes au vᵉ siècle. [With plates.] pp. lxxv. 192. *Paris*, 1908. 8°. [*Biblio-thèque des Écoles Françaises d'Athènes et de Rome.* fasc. 100.]
　　　　　　　　　　　　　　　Ac. **5206/2**.

—— Histoire de l'antiquité. [With " Index général."] 4 tom. *Paris*, 1917, 1913–20. 8°.　　**09004. d. 23**.

—— Histoire du monde. Publiée sous la direction de E. Cavaignac.

　tom. 1.　Prolégomènes. [By E. Cavaignac. With a map.] pp. ix. 373. 1922.
　tom. 2.　Le Monde méditerranéen jusqu'au ivᵉ siècle avant J.-C. Par E. Cavaignac. [With maps.] pp. viii. 708. 1929.
　tom. 3.　Indo-européens et Indo-iraniens. L'Inde jusque vers 300 av. J.-C. Par Louis de La Vallée Poussin. Nouvelle édition. pp. 407. 1936.
　tom. 5.　no. 1.　La Paix romaine. Par E. Cavaignac. pp. 492. 1928.
　　　　no. 2.　L'Empire romain et l'église. Par Jacques Zeiller. pp. 360. 1928.
　tom. 6.　no. 1.　L'Inde aux temps des Mauryas et des Barbares, Grecs, Scythes, Parthes et Yue-Tehi. Par Louis de La Vallée Poussin. [With a map.] pp. 376. 1930.
　　　　no. 2.　Dynasties et histoire de l'Inde depuis Kanishka jusqu'aux invasions musulmanes. Par Louis de la Vallée Poussin. pp. 396. 1935.
　tom. 7.　no. 1.　Le Monde musulman et byzantin jusqu'aux Croisades. [pt. 1. Le Monde musulman. By M. Gaudefroy-Demombynes. pt. 3. La Russie chrétienne. By S. T. Platonov. Translated from the Russian. A continuation, " La Russie moscovite " forms tom. 8. no. 4.] pp. 591. 1931.
　　　　no. 2.　La Chrétienté médiévale, 395–1254. pp. xviii. 501. 1929.
　tom. 8.　no. 1.　L'Inde du viiᵉ au xviᵉ siècle. Par Ishwari Prasad . . . Traduit sur la 2e édition par H. de Saugy. pp. xxiii. 619. 1930.
　　　　no. 2.　Les États hindouisés d'Indochine et d'Indo-nésie. Par G. Cœdes. pp. xi. 466. 1948.
　　　　no. 3.　L'Empire mongol. 1re phrase. Par René Grousset. (2ème phrase. Par Lucien Bouvat.) 2 vol. 1941.

CAVAIGNAC (Eugène) *Historian.*

> tom. 8. no. 4. La Russie moscovite. Par S. F. Platonov. [A continuation of tom. 7. no. 1. pt. 3 of " La Russie chrétienne."] pp. xii. 149. 1932.
> tom. 9. L'Amérique pré-colombienne et la conquête européenne. Par M. le Colonel Langlois. pp. liv. 522. 1928.
> Politique mondiale, 1492–1757. Par E. Cavaignac. [Introduction to volumes 10 & 11.] pp. viii. 163. 1934.
> tom. 10. L'Hégémonie européenne. Période italo-espagnole. Par Herman vander Linden. pp. xi. 470. 1936.
>
> tom. 12. no. 1. Le Monde anglo-saxon au xixe siècle. Par P. Vaucher. pp. 243. 1926.
> no. 2. L'Empire allemand, 1871–1900. Par E. Vermeil. pp. xxiii. 262. 1926.
> tom. 13. La Civilisation européenne moderne.
> pt. 1. Les Arts plastiques. Par Samuel Rocheblave. pp. 257. 1928.
> pt. 2. La Musique. Par Lucien Chevaillier. pp. 107. 1928.
> pt. 3. Les Sciences exactes. Par J. Pérès. pp. 196. 1930.
> pt. 4. La Chimie. Par H. Metzger. pp. 169. 1930.
> pt. 5. La Biologie. Par L. Ambard. pp. 113. 1930.

Paris, 1922–48. 8°.　　　　**9137. i. 1.**
No more published.

—— Histoire générale de l'antiquité. pp. 579.　*Paris*, 1946. 8°.　[*Publications de la Faculté des Lettres de l'Université de Strasbourg.* fasc. 102.]　Ac. **2633.** e.

—— Le Monde méditerranéen jusqu'au ive siècle avant J.-C. *See* supra : Histoire du monde.

—— La Paix romaine. *See* supra : Histoire du monde. tom. 5. no. 1.

—— Politique mondiale, 1492–1757. *See* supra : Histoire du monde.

—— Population et capital dans le monde méditerranéen antique. pp. viii. 163.　*Strasbourg, Paris*, 1923. 8°. [*Publications de la Faculté des Lettres de l'Université de Strasbourg.* fasc. 18.]　Ac. **2633.** e.

—— Le Problème hittite. pp. xviii. 200. pl. viii.　*Paris*, 1936. 8°. [*Études d'archéologie et d'histoire.*]
07707.f.49/2.

—— Subbiluliuma et son temps. pp. 108.　*Paris*, 1932. 8°. [*Publications de la Faculté des Lettres de l'Université de Strasbourg.* fasc. 58.]　Ac. **2633.** e.

CAVAIGNAC (Godefroy) *Politician. See* Cavaignac (Jacques M. E. G.)

CAVAIGNAC (Godefroy) *Republican Writer. See* Cavaignac (Éléonore L. G.)

CAVAIGNAC (Hippolyte Gaston) Le Mouvement syndical dans la typographie française. pp. 176.　*Paris*, 1932. 8°.　**8231.** d. 4.

CAVAIGNAC (Jacques Marie) Les Deux généraux Cavaignac. Souvenirs et correspondance [of J. M. and L. E. Cavaignac]. 1808–1848. pp. 272. *Paris*, [1899.] 8°.　**010661. i. 39.**

CAVAIGNAC (Jacques Marie Eugène Godefroy) *See* Lemaître (Jules) La Campagne nationaliste. Conférences de Jules Lemaître & G. Cavaignac en province, 1900–1902. 1902. 8°.　**8050. bbb. 45.**

—— Conseil de Guerre de Rennes. Affaire Dreyfus. Dépositions de M. Cavaignac et de M. le général Roget. Audiences des 14, 16 & 17 août 1899. pp. 86.　*Rennes*, 1899. 8°.　**05402. ff. 39. (3.)**

CAVAIGNAC (Jacques Marie Eugène Godefroy)

—— La Formation de la Prusse contemporaine. Les origines—Le ministère de Stein, *etc.* 2 tom.　*Paris*, 1891, 98. 8°.　**9386. g. 2.**

—— République Française . . . Chambre des Députés. Extrait du procès-verbal de la séance du mercredi 8 février 1893. Discours de M. G. Cavaignac, *etc.*　*Paris*, [1893.] *s. sh.* fol.　**1889. d. 3. (296.)**

CAVAIGNAC (Jean Baptiste) *Conventionnel. See* Bayonne. Exposé succinct de la conduite de Bayonne depuis le commencement de la Révolution et de quelques faits relatifs au gouvernement de Pinet et Cavaignac, *etc.* [1795.] 8°.　**F. 991. (12.)**

—— *See* Cavaignac (L. E.) Deux déclarations solennelles de M. E. Cavaignac. [Biographies of his father and brother.] [1848.] fol.　**1851. d. 1. (4.)**

—— Cavaignac à ses collègues. [Exculpating himself from some imputations in the " Messager du soir."] pp. 6. [*Paris*, 1795.] 8°.　**F. 1021. (12.)**

—— Convention nationale. Compte rendu . . . par Cavaignac . . . des recettes et dépenses qu'il a faites durant ses missions à l'armée des Côtes de Brest . . . à Auch pour une levée extraordinaire de chevaux et à l'armée des Pyrénées-occidentales pour le complément des troupes à cheval, *etc.* pp. 4. *Paris*, an iii [1795.] 8°.　**F. 1552. (25.)**

—— Convention nationale. Rapport fait au nom du Comité de Sureté générale . . . sur la reddition de Verdun. pp. 40. [*Paris*, 1792.] 8°.　**F. 1232. (4.)**

—— Opinion . . . sur la question de savoir : Si Louis xvi peut être jugé ? pp. 4. [*Paris*, 1793.] 8°.　**F. 914. (7.)**

CAVAIGNAC (Jean Baptiste) *of Montbazens.* Dissertation sur la coqueluche. Tribut académique, *etc.* pp. 23. *Montpellier*, 1824. 4°.　**1181. c. 16. (3.)**

CAVAIGNAC (Louis Eugène) *See* Boullenot (B. A.) *Count de Bligny.* Procès entre le général Cavaignac et l'ancienne commission exécutive, *etc.* [1848.] *s. sh.* fol.　**1850. b. 7. (5.)**

—— *See* Castille (H.) Portraits politiques, *etc.* (no. 3. Le général Cavaignac.) 1856, *etc.* 16°.　**10603. a. 18.**

—— *See* Cavaignac (J. M.) Les Deux généraux Cavaignac. Souvenirs et correspondance [of J. M. and L. E. Cavaignac], *etc.* [1899.] 8°.　**010661. i. 39.**

—— *See* Chantelauze (A. de) Des candidats à la présidence : Cavaignac ou Bonaparte ? [1848.] *s. sh.* fol.　**1850. c. 1. (2.)**

—— *See* Chernuishevsky (N. G.) Кавеньякъ, *etc.* 1874. 8°.　**10602. d. 22. (3.)**

—— *See* Garon (　　) *Chirurgien-Major.* Émile Girardin et Cavaignac, *etc.* [1848.] 8°.　**8052. g. 41.**

—— *See* Ibos (P. E. M.) Le Général Cavaignac, *etc.* [With a portrait.] 1930. 8°.　**10655.h.55/16.**

—— *See* Jacquot (T. F.) Expédition du général Cavaignac dans le Sahara algérien, *etc.* 1849. 8°.　**9061. f. 33.**

—— *See* La Guéronnière (L. E. A. de) *Viscount.* Études et portraits contemporains . . . Le général Cavaignac. 1856. 8°.　**10604. d. 3.**

—— *See* Mirecourt (E. de) *pseud.* Les Contemporains. (pt. 86. E. Cavaignac.) 1855, *etc.* 16°.　**10662. a. 35.**

CAVAIGNAC (Louis Eugène)

—— *See* Mirecourt (E. de) *pseud.* Histoire contemporaine, *etc.* (no. 96. E. Cavaignac.) 1867, *etc.* 8°.
10661. aaa. **34**.

—— *See* Montfort (H.) Biographie politique et militaire du général Cavaignac, *etc.* 1848. 8°. **10660**. e. **29**. (**1**.)

—— *See* Pius ix., *Pope.* Lettre du Pape au général Cavaignac. [A fictitious work, satirizing the foreign policy of Cavaignac.] [1848.] *s. sh.* fol. **1850**. c. **1**. (**47**.)

—— *See* Saint Piève ( ) Napoléon au peuple Français. [Advocating General Cavaignac's claims to the Presidency.] [1848.] fol. **1850**. c. **1**. (**27**.)

—— *See* States of the Church.—*Consiglio de' Ministri.* Dichiarazione del Governo Romano intorno alla deliberazione del generale Cavaignac annunziata all'Assemblea Nazionale il giorno 28 novembre 1848. [1848.] 4°.
4863. f. **1**. (**57**.)

—— De la régence d'Alger. Notes sur l'occupation. pp. 245. *Paris*, 1839. 8°. **1321**. c. **15**.

—— Deux déclarations solennelles de M. E. Cavaignac. [Biographies of his father and brother.] [*Paris*, 1848.] *s. sh.* fol. **Hendon.**

—— Observations présentées au citoyen Cavaignac . . . chef du pouvoir exécutif, sur les effets de la création d'une banque hypothécaire foncière. pp. 20. *Lyon*, 1848. 8°.
8225. e. **12**.

CAVAIGNAC (Marie Julie)
—— Les Mémoires d'une inconnue [i.e. M. J. Cavaignac]. Publiés sur le manuscrit original. 1780–1816. pp. xi. 419. 1894. 8°. *See* Mémoires. **010663**. g. **11**.

CAVAILHÈS (Jean Raymond Marie Olivier) Essai sur les abcès par congestion provenant de la carie vertébrale. Thèse, *etc.* pp. 37. *Paris*, 1835. 4°. [*Collection des thèses soutenues à la Faculté de Médecine de Paris.* An 1835.]
1184. g. **3**. (**17**.)

CAVAILHON (Édouard) La France Ferrycide. pp. 240. *Paris*, 1888. 16°. **8052**. aaa. **14**.

—— Les Haras de la France. 2 tom.
    tom. 1. Les Haines contre les courses. pp. xcvi. 272.
    tom. 2. Historique des diverses familles de pur sang en Angleterre et en France. pp. x. 401.
Paris, 1886, 89. 18°. **7908**. df. **2**.

—— Les Sportsmen pendant la guerre. Épisodes de 1870–1871. Avec une préface d'Armand Silvestre. pp. v. 326. *Paris*, 1881. 8°. **12357**. aaa. **4**.

CAVAILHON (François Edmond) Pétition à la Convention nationale . . . sur une invention télégraphique. pp. 4. [*Paris*, 1795.] 8°. **F. 1201**. (**19**.)

CAVAILLÉ (Augustin) Les Filouteries du jeu. Révélations, *etc.* pp. vii. 353. *Paris*, 1875. 12°.
7906. de. **32**.

CAVAILLÉ (J.) Les Intoxications professionnelles. Le charbon professionnel . . . Avec une préface de M. le Dr. J. P. Langlois . . . Avec 4 gravures dans le texte et une planche en couleurs. pp. x. 362. *Paris, Nancy*, 1911. 8°. **07640**. ee. **41**.

—— La Journée de huit heures. La loi du 23 avril 1919, *etc.* pp. 146. *Paris*, 1919. 8°. **5408**. de. **18**.

CAVAILLÉ (Jean Pierre) *See* Raugel (F.) Recherches sur quelques maîtres de l'ancienne facture d'orgues française. Les Épine, J. P. Cavaillé, *etc.* [1931.] 8°.
7897. s. **12**.

CAVAILLÉ-COLL (Aristide) *See* Carlez (J.) Le Grand orgue de l'église Saint-Pierre de Caen reconstruit par . . . A. Cavaillé-Coll, *etc.* 1881. 8°. [MISSING.]

—— *See* Mary, *the Blessed Virgin.*—*Churches and Institutions.*—Paris.—*Notre Dame de Paris.* Grand orgue de . . . Notre-Dame de Paris, reconstruit par . . . A. Cavaillé-Coll, *etc.* 1868. 8°. [MSSSING.]

—— *See* Philbert (C. M.) Causerie sur le grand orgue de la maison A. Cavaillé-Coll à Saint-Ouen de Rouen. 1890. 8°. **7899**. k. **5**.

—— *See* Sheffield.—*Albert Hall.* Le Grand orgue de la nouvelle salle de concert de Sheffield . . . construit par A. Cavaillé-Coll. 1874. 8°. **7899**. k. **2**.

—— De l'orgue et de son architecture . . . Deuxième tirage, revu et augmenté. pp. 34. *Paris*, 1872. 8°.
7899. k. **4**.

CAVAILLER ( ) Observation [*sic*] à la suite de la pétition présentée à la Convention nationale par le citoyen Cavailler . . . pour Cavailler [or rather, Vaillé] son beau frère. pp. 6. [*Paris*, 1794?] 8°.
F. 1020. (**17**.)

—— [Another copy.] **F. 809**. (**6**.)

—— [Another copy.] **F. 739**. (**6**.)
With a different titlepage, on which the misprints " Observation," for " Observations," and " Cavailler," for " Vaillé," have been corrected.

CAVAILLÈS (Ernest)
—— *See* Fletcher (Charles R. L.) and Kipling (R.) Une Histoire d'Angleterre pour la jeunesse . . . Texte en prose traduit par L. Fabulet et le Lt-Colonel E. Cavaillès, *etc.* 1932. 4°. **File 784**.

CAVAILLÈS (Henri)
—— La Route française, son histoire, sa fonction. Étude de géographie humaine. pp. 399. *Paris*, 1946. 8°.
8218. bb. **29**.

—— La Transhumance pyrénéenne et la circulation des troupeaux dans les plaines de Gascogne. pp. 132. *Paris*, 1931. 8°. **8282**. t. **33**.

—— La Vie pastorale et agricole dans les Pyrenées des Gaves, de l'Adour et des Nestes. Étude de géographie humaine. pp. 413. pl. xiii. *Paris*, 1931. 8°. **8282**. t. **32**.

CAVAILLÈS (Jean) *See* Cantor (G.) Briefwechsel Cantor-Dedekind. Herausgegeben von † E. Noether . . . und J. Cavaillès. 1937. 8°. **010921**. l. **15**.

—— *See* Ferrières (G.) Jean Cavaillès, philosophe et combattant, 1903–1944, *etc.* [With a portrait.] 1950. 8°.
010665. s. **28**.

—— Essais philosophiques. Publiés par J. Cavaillès. no. 1, 2, 4. *Paris*, 1939–48. 8°. **8477**. h. **10**.
No. 3 was not published. Actualités scientifiques et industrielles. no. 804, 838, 1020.

—— Méthode axiomatique et formalisme. 3 pt.
    i. Le Problème du fondement des mathématiques.
    ii. Axiomatique et système formel.
    iii. La Non-contradiction de l'arithmétique.
Paris, 1938. 8°. [*Le Progrès de l'esprit.* no. 9–11.]
W.P. 13033/9–11.

—— Remarques sur la formation de la théorie abstraite des ensembles. 2 pt. pp.145.
    i. Préhistoire. La création de Cantor.
    ii. Dedekind. Les axiomatisations. Zermelo, Fraenkel, Von Neumann.
Paris, 1938. 8°. [*Le Progrès de l'esprit.* no. 7, 8.]
W.P. 13033/7, 8.

CAVAILLON.—*Monastère des Religieuses Carmélites.* Fondation du Monastère des Religieuses Carmélites de Cavaillon en l'année 1668. pp. 48. *Avignon,* 1862. 12°. **4632. aa. 23.**

CAVAILLON, DOMENICO, *Bishop of.* [1585.] *See* GRIMALDI.

——, FRANCESCO MARIA, *Bishop of.* [1742–1757.] *See* MANZI.

——, FRANÇOIS, *Bishop of.* [1657–1659.] *See* HALLIER.

CAVAILLON (**)** Exposition de l'histoire de France, depuis le commencement de la monarchie, jusqu'à la paix d'Aix la Chapelle . . . en 1748. pp. 514. *Paris,* 1775. 12°. **284. b. 5.**

—— [Another copy.] **G. 15433.**

CAVAILLON (ADOLPHE**)** De l'emploi de l'ergot de seigle pendant le travail de l'accouchement . . . Thèse, *etc.* pp. 52. *Montpellier,* 1865. 4°. **7379. f. 13. (9.)**

CAVAL (MAURICE**)**

—— The Burning Passion. (Translated from the French.) pp. 130. *Kaye Publications: London,* [1953.] 8°. **Cup. 367. c. 103.**

—— Desire me. (Translated from the French.) pp. 132. *Kaye Publications: London,* [1953.] 8°. **Cup. 367. c. 77.**

—— My Lovers. (Translated from the French.) pp. 132. *Kaye Publications: London,* [1953.] 8°. **Cup. 367. c. 102.**

—— The Nude in the Mirror. (Translated from the French.) pp. 132. *Kaye Publications: London,* [1953.] 8°. **Cup. 367. c. 80.**

CAVALAIRE.—*Syndicat d'Initiative de Cavalaire.* Cavalaire pittoresque : la mer, les bois, la montagne, *etc.* [A guide, with maps.] pp. 31. [*Cavalaire,* 1930 ?] 8°. **010169. ff. 48.**

CAVALCA (ALESSANDRO**)** Essamine militare nel quale si contengono le risposte fatte dal Capitano A. Cavalca . . . La seconda volta dato alla stampa, *etc.* pp. 187. [*Sessa :*] *Venetia,* 1620. 4°. **8825. b. 15.**

CAVALCA (DOMENICO**)** *See* BIBLE.—*Acts.* [*Italian.*] Volgarizzamento degli Atti Apostolici di D. Cavalca, *etc.* 1769. 8°. **[MISSING.]**

—— —— 1837. 8°. **[MISSING.]**

—— —— 1871. 8°. **3022. bbb. 9.**

—— *See* FRANCESCHINI (L.) Fra Simone da Cascia e il Cavalca, *etc.* 1897. 8°. **011824. k. 48.**

—— *See* FRANCESCHINI (L.) Tradizionalisti e concordisti in una questione letteraria del secolo XIV. [A critique of the work by N. Mattioli entitled : " Fra Giovanni Salerno . . . e le sue opere volgari inedite, con uno s . . . di altre attribuite al P. Cavalca."] 1902. 8°. **4864. ee. 38.**

—— *See* GREGORY I., *Saint,* surnamed *the Great, Pope. Begin.* [fol. 1 *recto :*] In comenza . . . il dialogo de sam Gregorio tratto delatino . . . per maistro lunardo da udene [or rather, by D. Cavalca], *etc.* 1475. fol. **167. d. 17.**

—— *See* GREGORY I., *Saint,* surnamed *the Great, Pope. Begin.* [fol. 2 *recto :*] Incomincia il prologo del vulgarizatore [D. Cavalca] del Dyalogo de miser sancto Gregorio papa, *etc.* 1487. 4°. **IA. 21641.**

CAVALCA (DOMENICO**)**

—— *See* GREGORY I., *Saint,* surnamed *the Great, Pope.* Volgarizzamento del Dialogo di San Gregorio e dell' Epistola di S. Girolamo ad Eustochio, opera del P. D. Cavalca, *etc.* 1764. 8°. **3832. bb. 44.**

—— *See* NASELLI (C.) Domenico Cavalca. 1925. 8°. **20013. b. 32.**

—— Opere edite ed inedite del P. D. Cavalca. 1846. *See* GIGLI (O.) Biblioteca classica sacra, *etc.* secolo xiv. tom. 4. 1844, *etc.* 4°. **3622. d. 1.**

—— Disciplina degli spirituali col Trattato delle trenta stoltizie, *etc.* [Edited by G. G. Bottari.] pp. xxxi. 299. *Roma,* 1757. 8°. **3832. bb. 43.**

—— [Poems.] 1820. *See* ITALIAN PARNASSUS. Parnaso italiano. vol. 8. 1819, *etc.* 12°. **11421. b. 27.**

—— Ammaestramento alla orazione. Testo attribuito al Cavalca pubblicato e annotato per cura di Camillo Belli. pp. 33. *Novi-Ligure,* 1869. 8°. **11805. ccc. 26. (3.)**

—— [Disciplina degli spirituali.] *Begin.* [fol. 1 *recto :*] Iesus. Maria. Prolago [*sic*] sopra el deuotissimo & utile libro che si chiama la disciplina degli spirituali, *etc.* [fol. 91 *recto :*] Conpiuta e la predecta opera laquale sic hiama [*sic*] illibro della diciplina [*sic*] degli spirituali, *etc.* [*Antonio Miscomini: Florence,* 1485 ?] 4°. **IA. 27231.** 92 *leaves, the last blank. Sig.* a–l⁸ m⁴. 25 *lines to a page. Without the blank leaf.*

—— *Begin.* [fol. 1 *recto :*] Sermone e tractato ꝑtra li deffecti de molti ch' hano appariētia de spirituali. De la īfrascripta epistola de sancto paulo ad galathas, *etc. End.* [fol. 44 *recto :*] Finito lo libro de la disciplina de li spirituali, *etc.* [By D. Cavalca.] G.𝔏. 1490. 8°. *See* SERMONE. **IA. 26644.**

—— La Disciplina de gli spirituali, *etc.* [Edited by S. Razzi.] pp. 154. *Apresso B. Sermartelli: Fiorenza,* 1569. 8°. **4378. aaa. 13.**

—— [Esposizione del Credo.] *Begin.* [fol. 2 *recto :*] Incomincia la tabula del primo libro del : Credo in dio. [fol. 4 *recto :*] Iucomincia [*sic*] la expositione del credo in Dio in uulgare, *etc.* [By D. Cavalca.] 1489. 4°. *See* APOSTLES' CREED. [*Appendix.*] **IA. 22266.**

—— [Another edition.] Esposizione del Simbolo degli Apostoli. [Edited by G. G. Bottari.] 2 pt. *Roma,* 1763. 8°. **3832. c. 25.**

—— [Frutti della lingua.] Libro molto deuoto ꝛ spirituale de fructi della lingua. [With a woodcut.] *per Lorenzo morgiani & Giouāni di Piero: firēze,* Adi quatro di septembre, 1493. fol. **IB. 27795.** 90 *leaves. Sig.* a–f⁸·⁶ g–i⁶ k⁶ l–o⁶. *Double columns,* 38, 39 *lines to a column.*

—— Libro deuotissimo et spirituale de fructi della lingua. [fol. 142 *verso :*] Impresso . . . con soṁa diligētia emēdato & correcto, excepto alcuni fogli del prīcipio di decto tractato: & tale defecto nō da nostra inaduertentia, ma da una copia o uero exēplo tutto corrotto & falsificato impresso per lo adrieto i firēze ꝑ unaltro nō diligēte impressore ꝑcedette, *etc.* [With a woodcut.] [*Bartolommeo di Libri :*] *Firenze,* [1494 ?] 4°. **C. 4. h. 10.** 142 *leaves. Sig.* [*2] a–r⁸ s⁴. 33 *lines to a page.*

—— Libro molto deuoto ꝛ spirituale de fructi della lingua. ꝛ galante ꝛ vtillissime cose dentro nouamente stampato. [With a woodcut.] ff. 148. [*C. de Pensis :*] *Venetia,* 1503. 4°. **C. 48. e. 12.**

CAVALCA (Domenico)

—— Frutti della lingua . . . ridotti alla sua vera lezione. [Edited by G. G. Bottari.] pp. 375. *Roma*, 1754. 8°.
3832. bb. 41.

—— [Pungi lingua.] *Begin.* [fol. 1 *recto:*] Iohannes Philippus de lignamine Messanēsis siculus. S. D. N. Sixti IIII. familiaris Reuerendo patri domino Mattheo de Marcho Abbati Monasterii Sancti Placidi Salutem. [fol. 3 *recto:*] [I]N comēza la tauola de lo īfrascripto tractato chiamato Pongie lingua, *etc.* [fol. 4 *recto:*] In cōmenza el tractato dicto pongie lingua, *etc.* [*Joannes Philippus de Lignamine: Rome,*] 1472. fol. **G. 10540. (1.)**
132 *leaves, without signatures.* 30 *lines to a page.*

—— *Begin.* [fol. 1 *recto:*] In Nomine Patris et Filii et Spiritus sancti amen. Incomincia ilbellissimo et utile tractato contra il peccato della lingua Prologo sopra decta opera, *etc.* *Per Nicholaum* [*i.e. Nicolaus Laurentii*]: *Florentie,* [1477 ?] 4°. **IB. 27109.**
118 *leaves, the last blank. Sig.* a¹⁰ b–i⁸ l–p⁸ q⁴. 31 *lines to a page. Without the blank leaf.*

—— *Begin.* [fol. 1 *verso:*] Al nome del Saluatore nostro misier yhesu xp̄o: Incomēcia il tractato dicto pongi lingua, *etc.* [*Philippus de Lavagnia ? Milan,* 1477 ?] fol. **C. 9. b. 3.**
96 *leaves, without signatures. Double columns,* 34 *lines to a column.*

—— [fol. 2 *recto:*] In nomine Patris et filii et spiritus sancti amen. Incomincia ilbellissimo ed utile tractato cōtra el peccato della lingua Prologo sopra decta opera, *etc.* *p Lorenzo di Mathio chericho & p Giouāni di Piero: firenze,* Adi octo doctobre, 1490. fol. **IB. 27773.**
72 *leaves. Sig.* a–f⁸ g–k⁶. *Double columns,* 39 *lines to a column. Imperfect ; wanting the first and the last leaves.*

—— Pungi Lingua. [With a woodcut.] 𝕲.𝕷. *per mi Hercules de nani: Bologna,* a di .xxiii di Marzo, 1493. 4°. **IA. 29015.**
80 *leaves. Sig.* a–m⁸·⁴ n⁸. *Double columns.* 39 *lines to a column.*

—— Tractato ouero libro chiamato Pungi lingua. [With a woodcut.] [*Bartolommeo di Libri :*] *Firenze,* adi dieci di Giugnio, 1494. 4°. **IA. 27302.**
112 *leaves. Sig.* a–o⁸. 33 *lines to a page.*

—— Pungi Lingua. [With a woodcut.] 𝕲.𝕷. [*Baptista de Tortis :*] *Venexia,* Adi .viiii. de Octubrio, 1494. 4°. **G. 19832. (1.)**
80 *leaves. Sig.* a–k⁸. *Double columns,* 38, 39 *lines to a column.*

—— Pungilingua . . . ridotto alla sua vera lezione. [Edited by G. G. Bottari.] pp. 294. *Roma,* 1751. 8°.
3832. bb. 40.

—— Spechio de peccati: composto per . . . Dominico da Pisa . . . Nouamente impresso. *B. de Zanis da Porteso: Venetia,* 1503. 4°. **3832. bb. 29.**

—— [Another edition.] Ridotto a miglior lezione . . . per opera di Francesco del Furia. pp. xxxii. 130. *Firenze,* 1828. 8°. **1360. l. 6.**

—— [Specchio di croce.] *Begin.* [fol. 1 *recto:*] Incomincia il prologo nel deuoto e morale libro intitulato Spechio de croce. [By D. Cavalca.] [fol. 141 *recto:*] Incomīcia la Tabula sopra il libro deuoto: e morale: intitulato Spechio di croce. [1477 ?] 4°. *See* SPECCHIO. **IA. 20152.**

—— *Begin.* [fol. 1 *recto:*] In commincia il prologo nel d'uoto e morale libro ītitulato Spechio d' croce. [fol. 75 *verso:*] In comīcia la Tabḽa sopra il libro deuoto e morale: intitulato Spechio di croce. 𝕲.𝕷. [1480 ?] 4°. *See* SPECCHIO. **IA. 25085.**

CAVALCA (Domenico)

—— *Begin.* [fol. 2 *recto:*] In nomine Ihesu christi crucifixi amen. Questo libro se chiama il spechio della croce, *etc.* 𝕲.𝕷. 1481. 4°. *See* SPECCHIO. **IA. 26577.**

—— *Begin.* [fol. 1 *recto:*] Incomincia il prologo del deuoto e morale libro ītitulato Spechio de croce. [fol. 75 *verso:*] Incomincia la tabula sopra il libro deuoto: e marale [*sic*]: intitulato Spechio di croce. 𝕲.𝕷. [1482 ?] 4°. *See* SPECCHIO. **IA. 20670.**

—— *Begin.* [fol. 1 *recto:*] Incomencia il prologo nel diuoto e morale libro intitulato Spechio de croce. [fol. 63 *verso:*] In comincia la Tabula sopra il libro deuoto e morale intitulato Spechio di Croce. 𝕲.𝕷. [1490 ?] 4°. *See* SPECCHIO. **IA. 22687.**

—— [Spechio di Croce.] 1490. 4°. *See* SPECCHIO. **IA. 27705.**

—— *Begin.* [fol. 2 *recto:*] In Nome Del padre & del figliuolo & dello spirito sancto Amen. Questo libro sichiama lo specchio della croce, *etc.* [With a woodcut.] *Per Christoforo de Pensa : Venetia,* adi .xi. Zenaro, 1497. 4°. **IA. 23489.**
66 *leaves. Sig.* a–g⁸ h⁶ i⁴. 39 *lines to a page.*

—— [Another edition.] Libro titulato Spechio di croce nouamente impresso 𝓏 con debita diligentia corretto. Et in lingua fiorentina ridutto, *etc.* *p Maestro Māfrino bon de Monfera: Venetia,* 1515. 4°. **3832. bb. 3.**

—— [Another edition.] *V. Roffinello : Vinegia,* 1545. 8°. **1350. a. 22.**

—— [Another edition.] Ridotto alla sua vera lezione. [The editor's preface signed : G. B., i.e. G. G. Bottari.] pp. 248. *Roma,* 1738. 8°. **3832. bb. 39.**

—— [Another edition.] Secondo un testo della Biblioteca Quiriniana di Brescia . . . con un ragionamento sopra la sua eccellenza di Giuseppe Taverna. pp. lxxiv. 222. *Brescia,* 1822. 8°. **3832. c. 26.**

—— [Another edition.] Ora ridotto alla sua vera lezione per cura di Bartolommeo Sorio. [With the preface of G. G. Bottari.] pp. xli. 332. *Venezia,* 1840. 8°. **3833. aa. 44.**

—— El espejo dela cruz. [Translated from the ' Specchio della croce ' of D. Cavalca. With a woodcut.] 𝕲.𝕷. 1492. 4°. *See* ESPEJO. **IA. 52361.**

—— [Trattato della pazienza.] *Begin.* [fol. 1 *recto:*] Nel nome del nostro saluatore messer iesu christo e de la gloriosissima uerzene Maria incomincia el nobile tractato de la pacientia utilissimo ad ogni stato : compilato dal conpositore [*sic*] del Spechio de croce [i.e. D. Cavalca]. 𝕲.𝕷. [1480 ?] 4°. *See* TRATTATO. **IA. 26456.**

—— *Begin.* [fol. 1 *recto:*] Nel nome del nostro saluatore messer iesu christo & de la gloriosissima uerzene Maria incomincia el nobile tractato de la patiētia utilissimo ad ogni stato compilato dal compositore Spechio de croce. 1488. 4°. *See* TRATTATO. **IA. 23452.**

—— *Begin.* [fol. 1 *recto:*] Nel nome del nostro saluatore misser iesu chrysto : 𝓏 dela gloriosissima vergene Maria Incomincia il nobil tractato de la Patiētia . . . vtilissimo ad ogni stato compilato dal cōpositore Spechio di croce. 1490. 4°. *See* TRATTATO. **IA. 23588.**

—— *Begin.* [fol. 2 *recto:*] Incomincia lutile & diuoto tractato dellibro della patientia. Loquale sichiama medicina dicuore, *etc.* *p Francesco Bonacorsi: Firenze,* Adi dodici di maggio, 1490. 4°. **IA. 27607.**
132 *leaves. Sig.* a–q⁸, r⁴. 28 *lines to a page. Imperfect ; wanting the first leaf, bearing the title.*

CAVALCA (Domenico)

—— *Begin.* [fol. 1 *recto:*] Nel nome del nostro saluatore misser iesu christo & de la gloriosissima uerzene Maria incomincia el nobile tractato de la patientia utilissimo ad ogni stato compilato dal compositore Spechio de croce. 1494. 4°. *See* Trattato. IA. **23469**.

—— Medicina del cuore ovvero Trattato della pazienza . . . ridotto alla sua vera lezione. [Edited by G. G. Bottari.] pp. xv. 326. *Roma*, 1756. 4°. **3832. bb. 42**.

—— [Another edition.] pp. xii. 276. *Milano*, 1838. 12°. **4410. g. 21**.

—— Volgarizzamento delle vite de' SS. Padri, di Fra D. Cavalca. tom. 1(–3). (tom. 4–6. Vite di alcuni Santi scritte nel buon secolo della lingua Toscana.) [With dedications and prefaces by D. M. Manni.] 6 tom. *Milano*, 1830. 12°. **1370. c. 33–38**.
With the autograph of Robert Southey.

—— [Another edition.] Vite de' Santi Padri . . . colle vite di alcuni altri santi, postillate e recate a miglior lezione . . . per cura di B. Sorio . . . e di A. Racheli. pp. xi. 655. *Trieste*, 1858. 8°. **3678. f. 3**.

CAVALCABO ( ) L'Escrime encore et toujours à Lyon. Par Cavalcabo, Aimé Vingtrinier, Ernest Gayet. pp. 36. *Lyon*, 1889. 8°. **7908. bbb. 45. (3.)**

CAVALCABÒ (Agostino)

—— *See* Bonetti (C.) Antonio Stradivari. Notizie e documenti, *etc.* [Compiled by C. Bonetti, A. Cavalcabò and U. Gualazzini.] 1937. 8°. Hirsch **1519**.

—— *See* Cremona. Gli Statuti di Cremona del mcccxxxix e di Viadana del secolo xiv. [Edited by G. Solazzi, A. Cavalcabò.] 1946, *etc.* 8°. [*Bollettino storico cremonese.* ser. 2. anni 11/12. vol. 15, *etc.*] P.P. **3556**. ni.

—— Cremona dal 19 marzo al 31 luglio, 1848. *In :* Bollettino storico cremonese. ser. 3. anni. 1/2. pp. 5–71. 1949. 8°. P.P. **3556**. ni.

—— Le Ultime lotte del comune di Cremona per l autononia, 1310–1322. 1936. *See* Periodical Publications.—*Cremona.* Bollettino storico cremonese. ser. 2. anno 1. 1931, *etc.* 8°. P.P. **3556**. ni.

—— Le Vicende storiche di Viadana. Secoli xii–xv. *In :* Bollettino storico cremonese. vol. 18. pp. 159–216. 1954. 8°. P.P. **3556**. ni.

CAVALCABÒ (Clemente Baroni) *See* Baroni Cavalcabò.

CAVALCABO (Girolamo) Neues kunstliches Fechtbuch . . . aus dem geschrieben Welschen Exemplar durch Monsieur de Villamont . . . in Französische Sprach transferirt. Nun aber . . . verdeutscht durch Conrad von Einsidell. [With plates.] pp. 59. *Impensis H. Grossii : Leipzig*, 1612. obl. 4°. **7905. aaa. 3**.
The titlepage is engraved. The date in the colophon is 1611.

CAVALCABO (Hieronymus) *See* Cavalcabo (Girolamo)

CAVALCABÒ (Maria) *See* Pizzi (B.) Compendio della vita virtuosamente condotta dalla nobil donna Marietta Villani Cavalcabò. 1803. 12°. **4864. aaa. 9**.

CAVALCABÒ (Zacharia) *See* Vizani (A.) Trattato dello schermo, *etc.* [Edited by Z. Cavalcabò.] 1588. 4°. C. **31. e. 41**.

CAVALCADE.

—— Cavalcade. *See* Periodical Publications.—*Sydney.*

CAVALCANTE (Ippolito) *Duke di Buonvicino. See* Cavalcanti.

CAVALCANTE BERNARDES (Lísia Maria)

—— *See* Gourou (P.) Observações geográficas na Amazônia. (Tradução do francês de L. M. Cavalcante Bernardes.) [1949.] 8°. [*Revista brasileira de geografia.* ano 11. no. 3, ano 12. no. 2.] Ac. **6198**.

CAVALCANTE DE FREITAS (Lafayette)

—— Faculdade de Medicina do Rio de Janeiro. These apresentada . . . pelo doutor L. Cavalcante de Freitas . . . Dos dispensarios no tratamento das molestias da infancia, *etc.* pp. x. 76. *Rio de Janeiro*, 1903. 4°. **7379**. n. 3. (6.)

CAVALCANTI (Nabor Carneiro Becerra) *See* Nabor Carneiro Becerra Cavalcanti ( )

CAVALCANTI (Adolpho Barbalho Uchõa) *See* Barbalho Uchõa Cavalcanti.

CAVALCANTI (Amaro) The Brasilian Language and its Agglutination. pp. 179. iii. *Typographia Nacional : Rio Janeiro*, 1883. 8°. **12910. e. 19**.

CAVALCANTI (Andrea) *See* Ruspoli (F.) Sonetti . . . Col commento di A. Cavalcanti. 1876. 8°. **12226. c. 17. (1.)**

—— La Carità da Frati, novella inedita. [Edited by Giovanni Dotti.] pp. 27. *Firenze*, 1871. 8°. **12471. g. 23**.
One of an edition of twenty-five copies.

—— Esequie del serenissimo Principe Francesco, celebrate in Fiorenza dal serenissimo Ferdinando II. Granduca di Toscana . . . il dì 30. d'Agosto 1634. pp. 52. *G. B. Landini : Fiorenza*, 1634. 4°. **605. d. 29. (1.)**

—— Notizie intorno alla vita di Bernardo Segni. *See* Segni (B.) Storie fiorentine, *etc.* tom. 1. 1778. 4°. **1440. k. 8**.

—— [Another edition.] 1805. *See* Italian Classics. Collezione de' classici italiani. vol. 96. 1804, *etc.* 8°. **12201.p.1/96.**

—— [Another edition.] *See* Segni (B.) Storie fiorentine, *etc.* vol. 1. 1830. 8°. **9150. bbb. 10**

—— Novella inedita. *See* Papanti (G.) Catalogo dei novellieri italiani, *etc.* vol. 2. 1871. 8°. **11904. g. 17**.

—— Novellette intorno a Curzio Marignoli, poeta fiorentino . . . per cura di Giulio Piccini. pp. 100. *Bologna*, 1870. 8°. **12226. c. 3. (2.)**

—— [Another edition.] Notizie intorno alla vita e costumi di Curzio da Marignolle. 1600. *See* Marignolli (C.) Rime varie, *etc.* 1885. 8°. **12226. de. 3. (3.)**

—— Il Vicario burlato. Novella. pp. 15. *Firenze*, 1870. 16°. **12471. bb. 42. (6.)**
One of an edition of forty-six copies.

CAVALCANTI (Angelo) Per l'arrendamento della Neve colla fedelissima città di Napoli. [*Napoli*, 1732.] fol. **5326. f. 1. (2.)**

CAVALCANTI (Bartolommeo) Lettere . . . tratte dagli originali che si conservano nell' Archivio Governativo di Parma. [Edited by Amadio Ronchini.] pp. xliii. 229. *Bologna*, 1869. 8°. **12226. bbb. 20. (2.)**

—— Calculo della castrametatione. *See* Polybius, *the Historian.* Polibio del modo dell'accampare, *etc.* 1552. 8°. **54. a. 20**.

CAVALCANTI (Bartolommeo)

—— Delle Republiche et delle spetie di esse, discorsi xv. *See* Contarini (G.) *Cardinal.* Della Republica . . . di Venetia libri v., *etc.* 1591. 8°.   **1057. b. 15.**

—— [Another copy.] Delle republiche & delle spetie di esse, *etc. See* Contarini (G.) *Cardinal, etc.* Della republica et magistrati di Venetia, *etc.* 1591. 8°.   **1482. aa. 37.**

—— Giuditio sopra la tragedia di Canace e Macareo. [By B. Cavalcanti.] *See* Speroni degli Alvarotti (S.) Giuditio, *etc.* 1550. 8°.   **11715. aa. 51.**

—— [Another edition.] *See* Speroni degli Alvarotti (S.) Giuditio, *etc.* 1566. 12°.   **638. c. 23. (1.)**

—— Oratione alla militia Fiorentina. *See* Sansovino (F.) Delle orationi volgarmente scritte . . . parte prima [*etc.*]. pt. 1. 1562. 4°.   **835. f. 6. (1.)**

—— [Another edition.] *See* Sansovino (F.) Diuerse orationi, *etc.* pt. 1. 1569. 4°.   **835. f. 5.**

—— [Another edition.] *See* Sansovino (F.) Delle orationi volgarmente scritte . . . parte prima [*etc.*]. pt. 1. 1575. 4°.   **835. f. 7.**

—— [Another edition.] 1731. *See* Dati (C. R.) Prose fiorentine, *etc.* pt. 1. vol. 6. 1716, *etc.* 8°.   **659. b. 20.**

—— [Another edition.] *See* Dati (C. R.) Prose fiorentine, *etc.* tom. 4. 1735. 4°.   **629. i. 17.**

—— La Retorica di M. B. Cavalcanti . . . diuisa in sette libri : doue si contiene tutto quello, che appartiene all'arte oratoria, *etc.* pp. 563.   *Appresso G. Giolito de' Ferrari : Vinegia*, 1559. fol.   **C. 83. e. 14.**

—— [Another edition.] Con le postille di M. Pio Portinaio, *etc.* pp. 563. *Per B. Cesano : Pesaro*, 1559. 4°.   **836. f. 3.**

—— [Another edition.] In questa seconda editione . . . dall' istesso autore reuista & . . . accresciuta, *etc.* pp. 563. *Appresso G. Giolito de' Ferrari : Vinegia*, 1559. fol.   **C. 108. h. 1.**

—— [Another edition.] In questa terza editione . . . dall' istesso autore reuista. pp. 563.   *Appresso G. Giolito de' Ferrari : Vinegia*, 1560. fol.   **74. h. 1.**

—— [Another edition.] pp. 563.   *Appresso B. Robini : Venetia*, 1569. 4°.   **819. g. 4.**

—— [Another edition.] pp. 571.   *Appresso C. & F. Franceschini : Venetia*, 1574. 4°.   **C. 81. b. 10.**

—— Trattati ouero discorsi . . . sopra gli ottimi reggimenti delle Republiche antiche et moderne, con un discorso di M. Sebastiano Erizo de' Gouerni ciuili, *etc.* 2 pt. *Appresso I. Sansouino il Giouane : Venetia*, 1571. 4°.   **232. h. 28.**

   The date in the colophon is 1570.

—— [Another copy.]   **521. d. 10. (1.)**
   Imperfect ; wanting pt. 2.

—— [Another edition.] (Vita di M. B. Cavalcanti tratta dalla Storia della letteratura Italiana del cavaliere Girolamo Tiraboschi.) 1805. *See* Italian Classics. Collezione de' classici italiani. vol. 161. 1804, *etc.* 8°.
                    12201.p.1/161.

—— [Another edition.] Con le tre lettere sopra la riforma di un repubblica . . . Trattato del reggimento degli stati di G. Savonarola. Gli avvertimenti civili di F. Guicciardini. L'Apologia di L. de' Medici. pp. 260. *Torino*, 1852. 8°.   **8006. b. 9.**

CAVALCANTI (Borgninus) *See* Cavalcanus.

CAVALCANTI (Domenico Andrea) *See* Cavalcanti (F. A.) *Archbishop of Cosenza.* Vindiciae Romanorum Pontificum, *etc.* [Edited by D. A. Cavalcanti.] 1749. fol.   **1228. i. 6.**

—— Vita del Cardinale Egidio Carrillo de Albornoz, Legato Apostolico in Italia. [With a portrait.] pp. xxvi. iv. 128. *Firenze*, 1736. 4°.   **1371. e. 9.**

CAVALCANTI (Domenico Gaetano) La Sacra Liturgia della Chiesa nel santo Sacrificio augustissimo esposta a fedeli, *etc.* [With plates.] 5 tom.   *Napoli*, 1763–66. 12°.   **1016. c. 28.**

CAVALCANTI (Domingos Olympio Braga) *See* Olympio Braga Cavalcanti.

CAVALCANTI (Elena) *See* Elena, *da Udine, etc.*

CAVALCANTI (Estevão) *See* Carneiro da Cunha (M. F.) Processo monstro urdido por E. Cavalcanti e F. Cavalcanti, *etc.* 1852. 8°.   **1414. h. 10. (5.)**

CAVALCANTI (Francisco) *See* Carneiro da Cunha (M. F.) Processo monstro urdido por E. Cavalcanti e F. Cavalcanti, *etc.* 1852. 8°.   **1414. h. 10. (5.)**

CAVALCANTI (Franciscus Antonius) *Archbishop of Cosenza.* Vindiciae Romanorum Pontificum . . . Opus posthumum. [Edited by D. A. Cavalcanti.] pp. 384. *Romae*, 1749. fol.   **1228. i. 6.**

CAVALCANTI (Giovanni) Istorie fiorentine . . . Con illustrazioni. [The editor's preface signed : F. P., i.e. F. L. Polidori.] 2 vol. *Firenze*, 1838, 39. 8°.   **804. f. 19.**

—— Istorie fiorentine. A cura di Guido di Pino. pp. xxxii. 444. *Milano*, 1944. 8°.   **9170. ee. 3.**
   Orfeo. no. 1.

—— Della carcere, dell'ingiusto esilio e del trionfal ritorno di Cosimo Padre della Patria, narrazione genuina, tratta dall'Istoria fior. ms. di G. Cavalcanti. Con illustrazioni. [Edited by Domenico Moreni.] pp. xxx. 304. **L.P.** *Firenze*, 1821. 4°.   **10630. h. 20.**

CAVALCANTI (Guido)

—— *See* Agresta (Giuseppe) Studio dantesco. [On Inferno x, 61–63, with special reference to G. Cavalcanti.] 1899. 8°.   **11420. dd. 34. (1.)**

——   *See* Ferrai (Maria) La Poesia amorosa nei migliori poeti del dolce stil nuovo . . . Guido Cavalcanti, *etc.* 1900. 8°.   **11853. g. 13.**

—— *See* Gatta (L.) Guido Cavalcanti negli albori del " dolce stil nuovo." 1907. 8°.   **11826. q. 49.**

—— *See* Morello (V.) Dante, Farinata, Cavalcanti, *etc.* 1927. 8°.   **011420. dd. 29.**

—— *See* Ovidio (F. d') Nota sul verso del x canto dell'Inferno : " Forse cui Guido vostro ebbe a disdegno." [1870.] 8°.   **11420. g. 20. (5.)**

—— *See* Robertis (D. de) Cino e Cavalcanti o le due rive della poesia. 1952. 8°. [*Studi medievali.* vol. 18. fasc. 1.]   **P.P. 4184. da.**

—— *See* Salvadore (G.) La Poesia giovanile e la Canzone d'amore di Guido Cavalcanti, *etc.* 1895. 8°.
                    011851. k. 1.

—— *See* Shaw (James E.) Guido Cavalcanti's Theory of Love. The Canzone d'amore and other related problems, *etc.* 1949. 8°.   **Ac. 2702/26. (1.)**

CAVALCANTI (GUIDO)

—— *See* VOSSLER (C.) Die philosophischen Grundlagen zum " Süssen neuen Stil " des . . . Guido Cavalcanti, *etc.* 1904. 8°.   **11421. ccc. 36.**

—— Sonetti e canzoni. *See* TUSCAN AUTHORS. Sonetti e canzoni di diuersi antichi autori toscani, *etc.* 1527. 8°.
                                  11422. b. 17. (1.)

—— Sonetti e ballate. *See* TUSCAN AUTHORS. Rime di diuersi autori toscani, *etc.* 1532. 8°.   **241. e. 21.**

—— [Another edition.] *See* TUSCAN AUTHORS. Sonetti, e canzoni di diversi antichi autori toscani, *etc.* 1727. 12°.
                                  11422. bb. 11.

—— [Another edition.] *See* TUSCAN AUTHORS. Rime di diversi antichi autori toscani, *etc.* 1740. 8°.
                                  1062. f. 14.

—— Poesie. *See* SERASSI (P. A.) Poesie d'alcuni antichi rimatori toscani, *etc.* 1774. 8°.   **1062. i. 34. (2.)**

—— Rime . . . edite ed inedite. Aggiuntovi un volgarizzamento antico [by J. Mangiatroja] . . . del comento di Dino del Garbo sulla canzone : " Donna mi prega," ec. per opera di Antonio Cicciaporci. pp. xxxiii. 152. *Firenze*, 1813. 8°.   **11426. i. 19.**

—— Rime antiche. *See* ITALIAN LANGUAGE. Poeti del primo secolo della lingua italiana, *etc.* vol. 2. 1816. 8°.   **11421. f. 23.**

—— [Poems.] 1820. *See* ITALIAN PARNASSUS. Parnaso italiano, *etc.* vol. 6. 1819, *etc.* 16°.   **11421. b. 26.**

—— Rime. *See* DANTE ALIGHIERI. [*Canzoniere.—Italian.*] Rime di Dante Alighieri, *etc.* 1828. 16°.   **11421. a. 9.**

—— Rime. *In :* DANTE ALIGHIERI. [*Canzoniere.—Italian.*] Rime di Dante Alighieri, *etc.* pp. 128–151. 1828. 16°.
                                  11421. a. 10.

—— Rime. *See* RIME. Rime inedite d'ogni secolo, *etc.* 1870. 8°.   **11422. d. 27. (10.)**

—— Le Rime di Guido Cavalcanti. Testo critico pubblicato dal prof. Nicola Arnone. [With a table.] pp. cxli. 99. *Firenze*, 1881. 8°.   **2284. f. 5.**

—— Rime. *See* ERCOLE (P.) Guido Cavalcanti e le sue rime. Studio storico-letterario seguito dal testo critico delle rime con commento. 1885. 8°.   **11840. b. 58.**

—— Le Rime di Guido Cavalcanti. A cura di Ercole Rivalta. pp. 205. *Bologna*, 1902. 8°.   **11427. k. 6.**

—— Rime. Con introduzione e appendice bibliografica di E. C. [i.e. Emilio Cecchi.] pp. 166.   *Lanciano,* 1910. 8°.   **11436. h. 24.**

—— Rime. [Three ballate and three sonetti.] *See* BENEDETTO (L. di) Studi sulle rime di Cino da Pistoia, *etc.* 1923. 8°.   **011850. d. 9.**

—— Tre canzoni di Guido Cavalcanti con i facsimili dei manoscritti senesi e la vita del poeta di Celso Cittadini. [The editor's introduction signed : O. R., i.e. Olga Rudge ?] pp. 32. *Siena*, 1949. 8°.   **11436. i. 45.** *Quaderni dell' Accademia Chigiana.* no. 19.

—— Sonnets and Ballate of Guido Cavalcanti. With translations of them and an introduction by Ezra Pound. *Ital. & Eng.* pp. vii. 135.   *S. Swift & Co.: London,* 1912. 8°.   **11436. h. 26.**

CAVALCANTI (GUIDO)

—— Al gran Cosmo Medici . . . Comento sopra la canzone di Guido Caualcanti. Di F. Paolo del Rosso. [With the text.] pp. 167.   *Appresso B. Sermartelli : Fiorenza,* 1568. 8°.   **1062. d. 30.**

—— L'Espositione del M^ro Egidio Colonna sopra la Canzone d'amore di Guido Cavalcanti. [With the text.] Con alcune breui annotationi intorno ad essa di Celso Cittadini. Insieme con vna sua succinta descrittion della vita e con le rime di esso Caualcanti. pp. 100.   *Appresso S. Marchetti : Siena*, 1602. 8°.   **1161. d. 14. (1.)**

—— [Another copy.]   **G. 10627.**

—— La Spositione di Girolamo Frachetta, sopra la canzone di Guido Caualcanti, Donna mi prega, &c. [With the text.] pp. 96. *Appresso i Gioliti : Venetia*, 1585. 4°.
                                  240. l. 3.

—— La Canzone . . . ' Donna mi prega,' ridotta a miglior lezione e comentata massimamente con Dante. [By Francesco Pasqualigo.] Estratto dall'Alighieri, anno II. pp. 129. *Venezia*, 1890. 8°.   **11420. gg. 7.**

—— La Canzone d'amore di Guido Cavalcanti. [The text of the poem " Donna me prega," with commentary by M. Casella.] 1944. *See* FLORENCE.—*Accademia della Crusca.* Studi di filologia italiana, *etc.* vol. 7. 1927, *etc.* 8°.   **Ac. 80/5.**

—— The Canzone d'amore of Cavalcanti according to the commentary of Dino del Garbo. Text and commentary. [Edited, with an historical analysis of the commentary, by Otto Bird. With an English translation of the canzone.] 1940, 41. *See* TORONTO.—*University of Toronto.* —*Saint Michael's College.*— *Pontifical Institute of Mediaeval Studies.* Mediaeval Studies. vol. 2, 3. 1939, *etc.* 8°.
                                  Ac. 2702. d/2.

CAVALCANTI (IPPOLITO) *Duke di Buonvicino.*

—— La Cucina teorico-pratica, ovvero il Pranzo periodico di otto piatti al giorno . . . Finalmente quattro settimane secondo le stagioni della cucina casareccia in dialetto napolitano . . . Quarto edizione. pp. 702. *Napoli*, 1844. 8°.   **7947. aa. 20.**

—— Cucina teorica-pratica comulativamente [*sic*] col suo corrispondente riposto . . . Con la practica di scalcare, e come servirsi dei pranzi e cene . . . Finalmente quattro settimane secondo le stagioni della vera cucina casareccia in dialetto napolitano . . . Settima ediz. migliorata del tutto, *etc.* [With a folding plate.] pp. 471.   *Napoli,* 1852. 8°.   **7947. b. 28.**

CAVALCANTI (LUCRETIA) *See* TROIANO (G.) Lettera consolatoria . . . con alcune rime di diuersi . . . autori nella morte della Signora L. Caualcanti. 1568. 4°.
                                  1062. l. 36. (1.)

CAVALCANTI DE ALBUQUERQUE (LUIZ RODOLPHO) *See* BRAZIL.—*Ministerio dos Negocios da Fazenda.* Estados da Amazonia. Commercio e navegação de transito internacional . . . Revogação dos tratados por L. R. Cavalcanti de Albuquerque. 1902. 8°.
                                  L.A.S. 178/6.

CAVALCANTINI (GUGLIELMO) Vita, e Miracoli di San Guglielmo Confessore, dell'Ordine Eremitano di S. Agostino, Duca d'Aquitania . . . Di nuoue aggiuntaui la vita di San Galgano e del Beato Andrea da Mon Reale dell'istesso Ordine . . . per F. Angelo Carezani. (Breue relatione del Beato Ghese.) [Edited by F. Carezani.] pp. 155. *G. Fontani : Pisa*, 1614. 4°.
                                  1231. b. 12.
The work does not contain the life of Andrea.

CAVALCANTINI (Guglielmo)

—— [Another edition.] Ristampata, corretta, e di varie annotazioni arricchita da Agostino Salvini. pp. xvi. 215. *V. Vangelitti: Firenze*, 1693. 8º.   **1231. a. 10.**

CAVALCANUS (Borgninus) Tractatus . . . de tutore & curatore. *See* Tractatus. Tractatus vniuersi iuris, *etc.* tom. 8. pt. 2. 1584. fol.   **499. f. 11.**

—— [Another edition.] Tractatus . . . de tutore, et curatore et de vsufructu mulieri relicto . . . Nunc secundo in lucem editus & . . . repurgatus, *etc.* pp. 460. *L. Spinedani: Venetiis*, 1606. 8º.   **877. g. 17.**

—— [Another edition.] *See* Montanus (Paulus) Tractatus de tutore, curatore, et usufructu mulieri relicto, *etc.* 1675. fol.   **499. c. 14.**

CAVALCANUS (Hortensius) Practica et theorica de testibus, in qua de qualitate, numero, probatione, et reprobatione testium . . . pertractatur, *etc.* pp. 313. *F. Osanna: Mantuæ*, 1603. 4º.   **5305. a. 26.**

CAVALCASELLE (Giovanni Battista) [For works written by G. B. Cavalcaselle in collaboration with Sir J. A. Crowe:] *See* Crowe (*Sir* Joseph A.) *K.C.M.G.*, and Cavalcaselle (G. B.)

—— *See* Foresi (A.) Capriole del cavaliere Gaetano Milanesi . . . e suicidio del cavaliere G. B. Cavalcaselle. [A satire.] 1874. 8º.   **12331. h. 4.**

—— Sulla conservazione dei monumenti e oggetti di belle arti e sulla riforma dell'insegnamento accademico. [Edited by F. dall'Ongaro.] pp. 33. *Firenze*, 1870. 8º.
7811.p.33.

CAVALCHA (Domenico) *See* Cavalca.

CAVALCHINI (Carolus Albertus) *Cardinal. See* Rome, *Church of.—[Popes.]*—Benedict xiv. [1740–1758.] S.D.N. Benedicti xiv. Declaratio super matrimoniis inter Protestantes et Catholicos, nec non super eadem materia . . . dissertationes . . . Cavalchini, *etc.* 1746. 8º.
1376. c. 9.

CAVALEER. *See* Cavalier.

CAVALEERS. *See* Cavaliers.

CAVALEIRS. *See* Cavaliers.

CAVALERI (Aloysius) De natura phthisis pulmonalis minime contagiosa, dissertatio inauguralis, *etc.* pp. 28. *Ticini Regii*, 1819. 8º.   **7383. b. 2. (9.)**

CAVALERI (Girolamo) I Giouedi estiui. Componimenti accademici di diuersi, publicati dal . . . sig. G. Caualeri. pp. 262. *M. A. Rossi: Bergamo*, 1645. 12º.
1402. a. 10.

CAVALERI (Michele) Il Museo Cavaleri e il Municipio di Milano. pp. viii. 655. *Milano*, 1875. 8º.
5322. f. 1.

CAVALERIE.

—— [La Cavalerie au combat et dans les guerres de l'avenir. Par P. S.] Cavalry in Action in the Wars of the Future. Studies in applied tactics by P. S. [i.e. Paul Joseph Silvestre?] Translated from the French by John Formby, *etc.* [With maps.] 1905. 8º. *See* S., P.   **8832. d. 7.**

—— Die Cavalerie der Jetztzeit; ihre Bedeutung, ihr Gebrauch und Stärkeverhältniss zu den anderen Waffen . . . Von Mr., Oberstlieutenant i. P. des Generalquartiermeisterstabes. 1860. 8º. *See* Mr., *Oberstlieutenant, etc.*   **8827. bbb. 3.**

CAVALERIE.

—— Cavalerie en campagne. Études d'après la carte. pp. 327. *Paris*, 1888. 8º.   **8833. f. 28.**

CAVALERIIS (Joannes Baptista de) *See* Cavalieri (Giovanni B.)

CAVALERIIS (Marcellus de) Statera sacra Missam iuxta ritum Ordinis Prædicatorum practicè, historicè, & mysticè expendens, *etc.* pp. 537. *Typis hæredum L. A. de Fusco: Neap.*, 1686. 8º.   **Legg 7.**

CAVALERI PAZOS (José de) *See* Cervantes Saavedra (M. de) [*Ocho Comedias y Ocho Entremeses.*] Ocho Entremeses, *etc.* [With an introduction by J. de Cavaleri Pazos.] 1816. 8º.   **1342. d. 1.**

CAVALERISM. *See* Cavalierism.

CAVALERIUS (Bonaventura) *See* Cavalieri.

CAVALERIUS (Jacobus) *Cardinal. See* Cavalieri (Jacopo dei)

CAVALERO (Claudio) Racconto istorico della celebre vittoria ottenuta da Luchino Visconti, principe di Milano, per la miracolosa apparizione di Santo Ambrogio, seguita il di xxi febbrajo, l'anno mccxxxix in Parabiago, raccolto da gravi scrittori, ed accresciuto di varie notizie spettanti al medesimo luogo dal P. C. Cavalero. pp. 100. *Milano*, 1745. 4º.   **1232. d. 13.**

CAVALÉRY (Thimoléon Reboul de) *See* Reboul de Cavaléry.

CAVALESIO (Benedictus à) *See* Bonelli (B.)

CAVALETTA (Orsina) Rime. *See* Licino (G. B.) Rime di diuersi celebri poeti dell'età nostra, *etc.* 1587. 8º.
84. b. 4.

CAVALETTO (Ercole) Rime. *See* Licino (G. B.) Rime di diuersi celebri poeti dell'età nostra, *etc.* 1587. 8º.
84. b. 4.

CAVALETTO (Hercole) *See* Cavaletto (Ercole)

CAVALHEIRO. Comedia nova intitulada: O Cavalheiro da Virtude, e a Mulher Estravagante. pp. 40. *Lisboa*, 1784. 4º.   **11728. g. 44. (7.)**

—— [Another copy.]   **11728. g. 45. (15.)**

CAVALHEIRO (António Rodrigues) *See* Rodrigues Cavalheiro.

CAVALHEIRO (David de Vaegas) *See* Vaegas Cavalheiro.

CAVALI VENKAT RÁMASSWÁMI. *See* Veṇkaṭa Rāmasvāmi, *Kāvali.*

CAVALIÉ (Charles) Faculté de Droit de Paris. Thèse pour la licence, *etc.* (Jus romanum: De negotiis gestis. —Droit français: Des engagements qui se forment sans conventions.) pp. 57. *Paris*, 1858. 8º.
5406. aaa. 5. (9.)

CAVALIÉ (Firmin) Quelques principes d'hygiène à l'usage des femmes enceintes. pp. 40. *Paris*, 1867. 4º. [*Collection des thèses soutenues à la Faculté de Médecine de Paris.* An 1867. tom. 3.]   **7373. h. 6.**

CAVALIÉ (Ludovic) Faculté de Droit de Paris. Thèse pour la licence, *etc.* (Jus romanum. De acquirenda vel omittenda hereditate.—Droit français. Des successions.) pp. 93. *Paris*, 1859. 8º.   **5406. b. 11. (7.)**

CAVALIER.

—— Cavalier. [London.] *See* Periodical Publications.— *London.*

—— The Cavalier. [New York.] *See* Periodical Publications.—*New York.*

—— The Cavalier. [By W. H. Bellamy.]—Shamrock Shore. [Songs.] [*London*, 1850?] *s. sh.* 4°. C. 116. i. 1. (40.)

—— Answer to the Cavalier [i.e. to W. H. Bellamy's song].—Thou art gone from my gaze.—I'm a Flirt. [Songs.] [*London*, 1850?] *s. sh.* 4°. C. 116. i. 1. (235.)

—— Der Cavalier auf Reisen im Jahr 1837. Vom Verfasser der "Ansichten aus der Cavalierperspective im Jahr 1835" [i.e. J. D. F. Neigebaur]. pp. vi. 384. *Leipzig,* 1838. 12°. 1049. f. 23.

—— Cavalier françois. *See* French Cavalier.

—— The Cavalier's Catechisme, and Confession of his Faith . . . All familiarly explained . . . betweene a zealous minister of the gospell, and a gentleman who had serv'd His Majesty in the late unhappy warre, very usefull for all sorts of people to practise. pp. 16. *For Richard Burton: London,* 1647. 8°. E. 1186. (7.)

—— [Another edition.] *For N. Butter: London,* 1660. *s. sh.* fol. C. 40. m. 11. (23.)

—— The Cavaleers Complaint. (An Eccho to the Cavaleers complaint.) [In verse.] *For Robert Crofts: London,* 1661. *s. sh.* fol. 669. f. 26. (69.)

—— [Another copy.] Lutt. ii. 33.

—— The Cavaliers Diurnall, written by adventure, *etc.* [A satire.] pp. 8. [*London,* 1647.] 4°. E. 383. (4.)

—— The Cavalier's Genius: being a proper new ballad. [*London,* 1663?] *s. sh.* fol. Lutt. ii. 32.

—— The Cavaliers Letanie. Lately compos'd by a well-willer to His Majesties person, and all his most loyall subjects, *etc.* [A satire, in verse.] pp. 7. [*London,*] 1648. 4°. E. 425. (21.)

—— [Another copy.] 164. k. 7.

—— The Cavaleers Letany. [In verse.] *For Robert Crofts: London,* 1661. *s. sh.* fol. 669. f. 27. (1.) *A different work from the preceding.*

—— [Another copy.] Lutt. ii. 34.

—— The Cavalier's Litany. [In verse.] *For Charles Brome: London,* 1682. 1682. *s. sh.* fol. 112. f. 44. (16.) *A different work from both the preceding.*

—— The Character of a Cavaliere with his brother Seperatist; both striving which shall bee most active in dividing the two nations, now so happily, by the blessing of God, united. pp. 6. *For W. H.: London,* 1647. 4°. E. 383. (5.)

—— The Debauched Cavalleer; or the English Midianite . . . Penned by G. L. and C. L. [i.e. George Lawrence and Christopher Love], *etc.* 1642. 4°. *See* L., G. and L., C. E. 240. (43.)

—— Five Love-Letters from a Cavalier (the Chevalier Del.), in answer to the Five Love-Letters written to him by a Nun. 1683. 12°. *See* Del., *Chevalier.* 1102. b. 9.

—— The Melancholy Cavalier . . . A poëm, by J. C. 1654. 8°. *See* C., J. E. 1493. (3.)

CAVALIER.

—— Memoirs of a Cavalier: or a Military journal of the wars in Germany, and the wars in England; from the year 1632 to the year 1648, *etc.* [By Daniel Defoe.] pp. 338. *A. Bell: London,* [1720.] 8°. 195. a. 5.

—— [Another copy.] G. 13279.

—— (Second edition.) pp. v. 338. *John Scolfield: Leedes,* [1750?] 8°. 838. c. 2.

—— Moderate Caualier; or, the Soldiers description of Ireland and of the country disease, with receipts for the same. [By William Mercer. In verse.] pp. 36. [*Cork,*] 1675. 4°. 11631. bb. 44.

—— [Another copy.] G. 5577.

—— The Old Cavalier. [A ballad. With the music.] *For C. Bates: [London,* 1710?] *s. sh.* fol. C. 39. k. 6. (21.)

—— Une Révolution dans la tactique de la cavalerie. Par un Cavalier. pp. 23. *Paris,* 1890. 8°. 8831. l. 9. (5.)

—— The Young Cavalier. [By W. H. Bellamy.]—England Europe's glory. [Songs.] [*London,* 1850?] *s. sh.* 4°. 11621. k. 4. (81.)

CAVALIER LYRICS.

—— Cavalier Lyrics, and other 17th century love poems. pp. 44. *Chatto & Windus: London,* 1941. 8°. [*Zodiac Books.* no. 27.] W.P. 1004/27.

CAVALIER (Anthony Ramsden) In Northern India. A story of mission work . . . With an introduction by the Right Hon. the Lord Kinnaird. [With illustrations.] pp. xiv. 174. *S. W. Partridge & Co.: London,* [1899.] 8°. 4765. d. 35.

CAVALIER (Caliste) *See* Cavalier (Henri L. A. C.)

CAVALIER (César Juste) Essai d'une classification naturelle des maladies dites catarrhales. Thèse, *etc.* pp. 133. *Montpellier,* 1822. 4°. 1181. c. 6. (20.)

CAVALIER (Édouard) Histoire de la France depuis Louis xiv jusqu'à nos jours. Questions et réponses . . . Première partie, histoire moderne, 1643–1815. pp. iv. 1018. *Paris,* 1869. 12°. 09225. f. 24. *No more published.*

CAVALIER (Edward Frederic) The Preacher's Dictionary. A biblical conspectus, and compendium of religious and secular thought, past and present, topically arranged. pp. vii. 641. *Hodder & Stoughton: London,* 1900. 8°. 4371. f. 23.

—— Second edition. pp. vii. 641. *Hodder & Stoughton: London,* 1904. 8°. 4377. ff. 28.

CAVALIER (Étienne) Considérations générales sur l'amputation, et les principaux accidens qui peuvent se manifester à sa suite. Thèse, *etc.* pp. 24. *Paris,* 1827. 4°. 1183. i. 9. (19.)

CAVALIER (François Louis) *See* Clément (Jules) Le Vétérinaire . . . Sous les auspices de M. Cavalier, *etc.* [1860?] 12°. 7294. d. 7.

—— Dissertation sur l'asthme, *etc.* pp. 33. *Paris,* 1817. 4°. 1183. d. 10. (14.)

CAVALIER (Gaston) *See* Bauquier (H.) and Cavalier (G.) Histoire numismatique du comte de Chambord, *etc.* 1911, *etc.* 4°. 7757.cc.38.

CAVALIER (GEORGES) La Filleule du maréchal, parodie satirique de La Filleule du roi, *etc.* pp. 31. *Bruxelles,* 1875. 8°. **11740. f. 17. (3.)**

CAVALIER (HENRI LOUIS ANTOINE CALISTE) *See* MONT-PELLIER.—*Bibliothèque de la Ville de Montpellier.* Catalogue des livres, médailles et objets d'art ou de curiosité légués par le Dr. C. Cavalier. 1898. 8°. **011900. f. 45.**

—— *See* PERIODICAL PUBLICATIONS.—*Montpellier.* Année médicale et scientifique . . . Par MM. Moutet . . . et Cavalier. 1864, *etc.* 8°. **P.P. 1424. o.**

—— Coup d'œil sur l'hygiène, considérée dans son passé, son présent et son avenir. pp. 97. *Montpellier,* 1864. 8°. **7390. bb. 8.**

—— Essai sur la fureur épileptique. Thèse, *etc.* pp. 127. *Montpellier,* 1850. 4°. **7379. b. 2. (17.)**

—— Fragments de critique médicale. 1863–1868. pp. 387. *Montpellier,* 1868. 8°. [MISSING.]

CAVALIER (JEAN) *Colonel. See* CAMISARDS. Nouveaux mémoires pour servir à l'histoire des trois Camisars, où l'on voit les déclarations de Monsieur le colonel Cavallier, *etc.* 1708. 8°. **700. e. 21. (7.)**

—— *See* GRUBB (Arthur P.) Jean Cavalier, *etc.* [With portrait.] 1931. 8°. **10655. bb. 10.**

—— *See* PUAUX (N. A. F.) Vie de Jean Cavalier, *etc.* 1868. 8°. **010664. g. 8.**

—— Memoirs of the Wars of the Cevennes, *etc.* pp. xxiv. 348. *Printed for the Author: Dublin,* 1726. 8°. **488. c. 11.**

—— The second edition. pp. xiv. 348. *J. Clarke: London,* 1727. 8°. **1123. e. 25.**

—— Mémoires sur la guerre des Cévennes. Traduction et notes par Frank Puaux. Avec une carte. pp. xxi. 330. *Paris,* 1918. 8°. **9226. cc. 14.**

CAVALIER (JEAN) *the French Prophet.*

—— *See* N., N. An Account of the Lives and Behaviour of the three French Prophets [E. Marion, J. Cavalier, and D. Fage], *etc.* 1708. 8°. **695. c. 5. (9.)**

CAVALIER (JEAN) *Sculptor. See* JULIUS (A.) Jean Cavalier och några andra elfenbenssnidare, *etc.* [With plates.] 1926. 8°. **7876. f. 5.**

CAVALIER (L. J.) Observations sur quelques lésions du diaphragme, et en particulier sur sa rupture, *etc.* pp. 26. *Paris,* 1804. 4°. **1182. f. 14. (2.)**

CAVALIER (LOUIS) Considérations sur l'entérite. Dissertation, *etc.* pp. 27. *Strasbourg,* 1818. 4°. [*Collection générale des dissertations de la Faculté de Médecine de Strasbourg.* vol. 25.] **7381.* b.**

CAVALIER (VICTOR CHARLES) Essai sur la marche à suivre dans la rédaction des rapports de médecine nautique. Tribut académique, *etc.* pp. 51. *Montpellier,* 1835. 4°. **1181. g. 10. (23.)**

CAVALIER (Z. LANGRANA) An Astrological Birthday Book. pp. 132. *Pite & Thynne: [London,* 1912.] 8°. **8610. dg. 5.**

—— A Colour Scheme in a Chaplet of Gems. pp. 28. *Pite & Thynne: Chelsea,* [1912.] 16°. **012356. g. 27. (3.)**

—— The Soul of the Orient. [A novel.] pp. 280. *Murray & Evenden: London,* [1913.] 8°. **NN. 785.**

CAVALIERE (ALFREDO) *See* RAIMON (Pierre) *de Toulouse.* Le Poesie di Piere Raimon de Tolosa, *etc.* [Edited and translated by A. Cavaliere.] 1935. 8°. [*Biblioteca dell' " Archivum romanicum."* ser. 1. vol. 22.] **P.P. 4884. dba.**

CAVALIERE (ALFREDO)

—— Cento liriche provenzali. Testi, versioni, note, glossario. Introduzione di Giulio Bertoni: " La Lirica dei trovatori." pp. xxv. 639. pl. XIII. *Bologna,* 1938. 8°. **11498. dd. 64.**

CAVALIERI.

—— Cavalieri Costantiniani. *See* GEORGE, *Saint and Martyr.* —*Ordine Costantiniano di S. Giorgio.*

—— Cavalieri gierosolimitani. *See* JOHN, *the Baptist, Saint.*—*Knights Hospitallers of the Order of St. John of Jerusalem.*

CAVALIERI (ADOLFO) Carlo Mayr. (Biografia.) pp. 37. *Ferrara,* 1882. 8°. **10629. a. 15. (3.)**

CAVALIERI (ANGELO) Del volgare eloquio di Dante Alighieri in relazione al secentesimo anniversario della sua nascita. Cenni. 1866. *See* DANTE ALIGHIERI. [*Appendix.—Miscellaneous.*] Dante e il suo secolo. vol. 2. 1865, *etc.* 4°. **1871. d. 9. (32.)**

CAVALIERI (BUONAVENTURA) *See also* FILOMANTIO (Silvio) *pseud.* [i.e. B. Cavalieri.]

—— *See* AVISO (U. d') Trattato della sfera, *etc.* (Vita del Padre Bonauentura Caualieri.) 1682. 12°. **533. a. 23. (2.)**

—— *See* FERRIA (T.) Elogio di Bonaventura Cavalieri, *etc.* 1873. 8°. **10631. e. 42. (15.)**

—— *See* FRISI (P.) Elogj de Galileo Galilei e di Bonaventura Cavalieri. 1778. 8°. **1450. e. 20. (1.)**

—— *See* FRISI (P.) Elogio di Bonaventura Cavalieri. 1829. 8°. [*Collezione de' classici italiani.* vol. 350.]

12202.p.1/350.

—— *See* MASOTTI (A.) Commemorazione di B. Cavalieri, *etc.* [With a bibliography of his works.] 1949. 8°. **010632. bbb. 24.**

—— *See* PIOLA (G.) Elogio di Bonaventura Cavalieri, *etc.* 1844. 4°. **814. l. 32.**

—— *See* PREDARI (F.) Della vita e delle opere di Bonaventura Cavalieri . . . Cenni. [1843.] 8°. **10630. dd. 2. (7.)**

—— Compendio delle regole de triangoli, con le loro dimostratoni. (Tauola prima logaritmica.) 2 pt. *G. Monti: Bologna,* 1638. 12°. **530. a. 5.**

—— Directorium generale vranometricum, in quo trigonometriæ logarithmicæ fundamenta, ac regulæ demonstrantur, astronomicæq; supputationes ad solam ferè vulgarem additionem reducuntur, *etc.* (Tabula trigonomᶜᵃ logarithmica.) 2 pt. *Typis N. Tebaldini: Bononiæ,* 1632. 4°. **532. f. 4.**

—— Exercitationes geometricæ sex. pp. 543. *Typis I. Montij: Bononiæ,* 1647. 4°. **530. i. 24.**

—— Geometria indiuisibilibus continuorum noua quadam ratione promota . . . In hac postuma editione ab erroribus expurgata. pp. 543. *Ex typographia de Ducijs: Bononiæ,* 1653. 4°. **530. i. 25.**

—— Nuoua prattica astrologica di fare le direttione secondo la via rationale, e conforme ancora al fondamento del Kepplero per via di logaritmi. Con vna centuria di varii problemi, e con il compendio delle regole de triangoli. 2 pt. *Per il Ferroni: Bologna,* 1639. 12°. **718. c. 24.** *The titlepage is engraved.*

CAVALIERI (Buonaventura)

—— Sfera astronomica del Padre B. Caualieri . . . Con l'vso della figura, e prattiche di essa. Cauate da i manoscritti dell'autore da Vrbano d'Aviso . . . E dato in luce, con la vita di detto autore, *etc.* [A reissue of the "Trattato della sfera" published by U. d'Aviso in 1682.] pp. xxiv. 231 [331]. *A. Manari: Roma,* 1690. 12°.
1395. a. 41.

—— Lo Specchio vstorio, ouero Trattato delle settioni coniche et alcuni loro mirabili effetti intorno al lume, caldo, freddo, suono, e moto ancora. pp. 224. pl. 10.
C. Ferroni: Bologna, 1632. 4°. **716. e. 2.**

—— [Another edition.] [Edited by U. d'Aviso.] pp. 136. pl. 10. *G. B. Ferroni: Bologna,* 1650. 4°.
529. h. 34.

—— De echeis, hoc est, de vasis theatralibus . . . diatriba. Quae est caput XXXVI operis . . . cujus titulus est Lo Specchio vstorio. Nunc primum de italica in latinam linguam conversa. Interprete A. A. F. S. T. D. 1741. *See* Poleni (G.) *Marquis.* Exercitationes Vitruvianae primæ [*etc.*]. (Exercitationes tertiae.) 1739, *etc.* 4°.
1261. c. 20.

—— [Another edition.] *See* Vitruvius Pollio (M.) M. Vitruvii Pollionis architectura, *etc.* vol. 1. 1825, *etc.* 4°.
560. d. 2.

—— Trigonometria plana et sphærica, linearis et logarithmica, *etc.* (Canon duplex trigonometricus.) [With a dedication by Sigismundus Pellegrius.] 2 pt. MS. NOTES. *Typis hæredis V. Benatij: Bononiæ,* 1643. 4°.
8534. d. 3.

CAVALIERI (Domenico) Teorie fondamentali della filosofia del diritto. pp. 169. *Messina,* 1896. 8°.
[MISSING.]

CAVALIERI (Emilio de')

—— *See* Gandolfi (Riccardo) Appunti di storia musicale . . . Emilio de' Cavalieri. 1893. 8°. Hirsch **1171.** (4.)

—— *See* Rolandi (U.) Emilio de' Cavalieri, il Granduca Ferdinando e l'Inferigno. [1928?] 8°. Hirsch **2849.**

CAVALIERI (Enea) *See* Franchetti (L.) La Sicilia. Con prefazione di E. Cavalieri. 1925. 8°.
010151. e. 17.

CAVALIERI (Florio Giuseppe) Poesie. *See* Italian Poems. Poesie italiane di rimatori viventi, *etc.* 1717. 8°.
240. l. 21.

CAVALIERI (Fortunato) Scirocco e Levante. Ricerche meteorologiche, raccolte sull'osservatorio di S. Giovanni di Gerace, *etc.* pp. 53. *Reggio-Calabria,* 1880. 8°.
8755. h. 34. (2.)

CAVALIERI (Giovanni Battista) *See* Ciccarelli (A.) Le Vite de pontefici di Antonio Ciccarelli . . . Con l'effigie di G. B. de Cauallieri. 1588. 4°. **4855. e. 5.**

—— *See* Ciccarelli (A.) Le Vite degli imperatori Romani con le figure intagliate in rame da G. B. de Caualieri. 1590. 4°. **C. 65. gg. 12.**

—— *See* Circignano (N.) Ecclesiæ Anglicanæ trophæa; siue sanctor. Martyrum . . . passiones . . . Romæ in Collegio Anglico per N. Circinianum depictæ; nuper autem per I. B. de Cauallerijs æneis typis repræsentatæ. 1584. fol. **551. e. 35.**

—— *See* Circignano (N.) Ecclesiæ militantis triumphi; siue . . . Martyrum . . . certamina . . . in ecclesia S. Stephani Rotundi Romæ N. Circiniani pictoris manu . . . depicta . . . a I. B. de Cauallerijs æneis typis . . . expressa. [1583.] fol. **551. e. 36.**

CAVALIERI (Giovanni Battista)

—— *See* Dosio (G. A.) Cosmo Medici Duci Florentinor. et Senens. Vrbis Romæ aedificiorum illustrium quæ supersunt reliquiæ summa cum diligentia . . . stilo ferreo descriptæ, et a I. B. de Caualerijs æneis tabulis incisis repræsentatæ. 1569. 4°. **574. i. 26.**

—— *See* Rome.—*The City.* [*Appendix.—Antiquities.*] Antiquarum statuarum Vrbis Romæ, quæ in publicis priuatisque locis visuntur, icones. Parte terza. [Sixty-one plates without letterpress, mostly engraved by G. B. Cavalieri.] 1584. 4°. **786. k. 48.**

—— *See* Rome.—*The City.* [*Appendix.—Antiquities.*] Antiquarum statuarum Vrbis Romæ . . . icones. [A collection of 157 plates, some engraved by G. B. Cavalieri.] 1621. fol. **C. 74. d. 5. (1.)**

—— *See* Treterus (T.) Romanorum imperatorum effigies. Elogiis, ex diuersis scriptoribus, per T. Treterū . . . collectis, illustratæ opera et studio I. B. de Cauallerijs, *etc.* 1590. 8°. **10605. de. 7.**

—— Antiquarum statuarum vrbis Romæ primus et secundus liber. pl. 100. [*Rome,* 1569.] 4°. **C. 80, c. 14. (1, 2.)**

—— Illustriores effigies L. Pontificum Rom. [*Rome,* 1589.] fol. **562*. e. 16.**
Imperfect; with plates by other artists inserted.

—— Opera nela quale ui e molti Mostri de tutte le parti del mondo antichi et moderni con le dechiarationi a ciascheduno fina al presēte anno 1585 . . . I. B. de Cauallerijs . . . incisore. *Roma,* 1585. fol. **C. 51. i. 10.**

—— Pontificum romanorum effigies . . . opera et studio I. B. de Caualerijs collectæ ac typis æneis incisæ. (Adiecta est in singulos pontifices breuis elucidatio ex diuersis autoribus collecta.) pl. 230. *Ex typographia D. Basæ: Romæ,* 1580. 8°. **861. b. 2.**

CAVALIERI (Giovanni Michele) In authentica Sacræ Rituum Congregationis decreta commentariorum tomus primus(—tertius). 4 vol. *Brixiæ; Bergomi,* 1743-51. 4°.
1237. e. 6-9.
Tom. 1 *is in two volumes.*

—— [Another edition.] R.P. Ioannis Michaelis Cavalieri . . . opera omnia liturgica, seu Commentaria in authentica Sacræ Rituum Congregationis decreta ad romanum præsertim Breviarium, Missale & Rituale quomodolibet attinentia . . . Opus . . . in hac novissima editione ab auctore curis postumis auctum . . . atque integro tomo ex manuscriptis ejus schedis . . . locupletatum. [With a portrait.] 5 tom. *Venetiis,* 1758. fol. **1222. k. 3, 4.**

—— [Another edition.] 5 tom. *Augustæ Vindelicorum,* 1764. fol. **L. 18. h. 8.**

—— [Another copy.] **L. 18. h. 5.**

—— *See* Bauldry (M.) Manuale sacrarum cæremoniarum . . . Accedit collectio omnium S.R.C. decretorum tam ad Breviarium quam ad Missale pertinentium, ex . . . Cavalieri atque aliis concinnata. 1778. 4°. **692. e. 6.**

CAVALIERI (Giuseppe) Catalogue des livres composant la bibliothèque de M. G. Cavalieri à Ferrara. [With plates.] pp. 524. *Florence,* 1908. 8°. **011903. cc. 35.**

CAVALIERI (Giuseppe Antonio) Il Domestico esempio, poemetto. *See* Graziani (I. G.) Notizie istoriche della chiesa arcipretale di S. Pietro in sylvis, *etc.* 1772. 4°.
4605. ff. 26.

—— Istoria della chiesa della Madonna del popolo detta S. Maria in Aula Regia della città di Comacchio. pp. vii. 159. *Comacchio,* 1782. 4°. **4605. c. 18.**

CAVALIERI (JACOPO DEI) *Cardinal.* *See* ROME, *Church of.*—*Rota.* Decisiones Sacræ Rotæ Romanæ coram J. Caualerio, *etc.* 1629. fol. **705. i. 2.**

CAVALIERI (JOANNES MICHAEL) *See* CAVALIERI (Giovanni M.)

CAVALIERI (MARIA FRANCHI DE') *See* FRANCHI DE' CAVALIERI.

CAVALIERI (PIO FRANCHI DE') *See* FRANCHI DE' CAVALIERI.

CAVALIERI (PROSPERO) Memorie sulle vite ed opere de' PP. abati G.-L. Mingarelli e M.-A. Monsagrati. pp. ix. 142. *Ferrara,* 1817. 8°. **4867. ee. 32.**

—— Notizie della Pubblica Biblioteca di Ferrara. pp. xiii. 159. *Ferrara,* 1818. 8°. **820. g. 21.**

CAVALIERI SAN-BERTOLO (NICOLA) Istituzioni di architettura statica e idraulica. [With plates.] 2 vol. *Bologna,* 1826, 27. 4°. **7815. cc. 7.**
The dates on the wrappers read 1828, 1829.
—— [Another edition.] 2 vol. *Mantova,* 1831. 4°. **1261. b. 2.**

CAVALIERISM. The Primitive Cavalerism revived: or, a Recognition of the principles of the old Cavaleers . . . By an Old Loyal Cavaleer. pp. 10. *Printed by George Croom: London,* 1684. fol. **8133. h. 8. (7.)**

—— [Another copy.] **8133. i. 1. (5.)**

CAVALIERS. An Apology vindicating the Cavaleers from a partiall, or rather a passionate aspersion too rigorously put upon them, for making churches prisons and stables: wherein is discussed . . . the unavoydable necessity of it. pp. 20. *London,* 1643. 4°. **E. 102. (18.)**

—— The Cavaliers Bible, *etc. See infra :* XXXIII Religions, Sects, *etc.*

—— The Cavaliers Catechisme; or, the Reformed Protestant catechising the Antichristian Papists, Malignants, Incendiaries, and other ill-affected persons under the name of Cavaliers. With their distinct answer thereunto. [A satire.] *For Thomas Watson: London,* 1643. 4°. **E. 100. (22.)**

—— The Cavaliers New Common-prayer Booke unclasp't . . . A collection of prayers and thanksgivings, used in His Majesties chappell, and in his armies, *etc.* 1644. 4°. *See* CHARLES I., *King of Great Britain and Ireland.* [*Appendix.*] **E. 8. (18.)**

—— The Cavalliers Advice to His Majesty; with his Majestie's answer . . . Together with his intentions for the avoyding of my Lord of Essex his approach neere his person, *etc.* pp. 6 [8]. *For Thomas Banks: London,* 1642. 4°. **E. 117. (15.)**

—— A Caveat for the Cavaliers. *See* RICH (Robert) *Earl of Warwick.* A Most Worthy Speech, spoken by the . . . Earle of Warwicke, *etc.* 1642. 4°. **E. 128. (30.)**

—— A Caveat to the Cavaliers: or an antidote against mistaken cordials, *etc.* [By R. L., i.e. Sir Roger L'Estrange. 1661. 4°. *See* L., R. **523. c. 33.**

—— A Copy of a list of all the Cavalliers, and brave Commanders of his Majesties marching army, with the number of captaines, in each severall regiment, *etc.* *For Francis Wright: London,* 1642. *s. sh.* fol. **669. f. 6. (91.)**

—— An Exact and True Relation of a most cruell . . . murther committed by one of the Cavaliers on a woman in Leicester; billeted in her house, *etc.* pp. 7. *For E. Husbands & I. Franck: London,* 1642. 4°. **E. 117. (20.)**

CAVALIERS.

—— The Insolency and Cruelty of the Cavaliers. Being a true and exact relation of the plundering and pillaging of Winslow and Swanborne, and diverse other townes in the counties of Buckingham, and Hartford, *etc.* pp. 6. *For Robert Wood: London,* 1643. 4°. **E. 102. (16.)**

—— The Last of the Cavaliers. [By Rose Piddington.] 3 vol. *Richard Bentley: London,* 1859. 8°. **12635. d. 4.**

—— New edition. pp. 434. *Richard Bentley: London,* 1863. 8°. **12618. bb. 3.**

—— [Another edition.] 2 vol. *Bernard Tauchnitz: Leipzig,* 1862. 16°. [*Collection of British Authors.* vol. 593, 594.] **12267. a. 1/55.**

—— A New Discovery of a great and bloody Plot intended by 2500 Cavaliers, to murther 120 Parliament-men on . . . the second of November 1648, *etc.* pp. 6. *For R. Smithurst: London,* 1648. 4°. **E. 469. (8.)**

—— Nocturnall Occurences, or Deeds of darknesse committed by the Cavaleers in their rendevous . . . Answering a booke . . . to which is annexed, the exercise of souldiers; beginning with these words, Round-heads stand to your armes. *For E. Christopher: London,* 1642. 4°. **E. 117. (16.)**

—— One Argument more against the Cavaliers; taken from their violation of Churches, *etc.* pp. 20. [*London,* 1643.] 4°. **E. 101. (20.)**

—— A Shrill Cry in the Eares of Cavaliers, Apostates, and Presbyters, for the resolve of XIII queries, touching the primitive state of this nation, since the Conquest: the late proceedings of the army, the covenant, and other weighty matters . . . By a Well-willer to peace and truth. pp. 14. *By Robert Ibbitson: London,* 1648. 4°. **E. 541. (10.)**

—— [Another copy.] **103. b. 18.**

—— XXXIII Religions, Sects, Societies and Factions of the Cavaliers now in armes against the Parliament . . . Their chiefe tenents exactly observed; their actions traced, *etc.* By Andrew Coe: [*London,* 1644.] 4°. **E. 35. (26.)**

—— The Cavaliers Bible, or a Squadron of XXXVI several religions by them held and maintained . . . The second edition, corrected and enlarged. *By Jane Coe: London,* 1644. 4°. **E. 4. (24.)**

—— XXXVI. severall Religions held and maintained by the Cavaliers: with a list of the names of the chief commanders in the squadron. The third edition, corrected and enlarged. *By Jane Coe: London,* 1645. 4°. **E. 288. (13.)**

—— A True and Perfect Relation of the manner of the apprehension and taking of 46 rebellious Cavalliers at Brackly in Northamptonshire under the command of Sir J. Byron . . . Whereunto is annexed the true coppy of a letter from Sir J. Byron, *etc.* pp. 8. *For Thomas Bates: London,* 1642. 4°. **E. 117. (11.)**

—— True Intelligence from the West; or, a True relation of the desperate proceedings of the Rebels and Cavaliers gathered together at Angry-Fisherton in Wiltsheire, *etc.* pp. 6. *For Thomas Tempest: London,* 1647. 4°. **E. 404. (14.)**

—— A True Narration of the Surprizall of sundry Cavaliers being sent from Nottingham to Oxford, as they were lodged at Brackley: and also of a cabinet and packet of writings, *etc.* [*London,* 1642.] *s. sh.* fol. **669. f. 6. (76.)**

CAVALIERS.

—— A True Relation of the Barbarous Crueltie of divers of the bloudy Cavaleers, as in all parts, so more especially . . . in the County of Northampton . . . as may be seene by the examinations of diverse persons, *etc.* *For Ioseph Hunscot: London*, 1642. 4°. **E. 110.** (6.)

—— The Unfaithfulnesse of the Cavaliers and Commissioners of Array in keeping their Covenants . . . fully discovered in a true narration of the inhumaine carriages of the Earle of Rivers, Lord Cholmondely . . . and their partie, during the treatie of pacification in Cheshire, and after it was concluded, *etc.* *For Thomas Vnderhill: London*, 1643. 4°. **E. 84.** (37.)

—— The Wicked Resolution of the Cavaliers, declaring their malice and hatred to the Parliament, the Commonwealth, and especially the city of London : necessary in these times, that all true hearted souldiers and well affected persons may arme themselves with resolution against their cruell intentions, *etc.* pp. 6. *For Jo. Smith: London*, 1642. 4°. **E. 127.** (42.)

CAVALLARI (ALBERTO)

—— *See* HOGBEN (Lancelot T.) [From Cave Painting to Comic Strip.] Dalla pittura delle caverne ai fumetti. (Traduzione di A. Cavallari.) 1952. 8°. **7950. bb. 66.**

CAVALLARI (CRISTOFORO) *See* CAVALLARI (F. S.) Topografia archeologica di Siracusa. Eseguita . . . dai professori Dr F. S. Cavallari e Dr A. Holm e dall' ingegnere C. Cavallari. 1883, *etc.* fol. **7705. h. 23.**

—— *See* CAVALLARI (F. S.) Die Stadt Syrakus im Alterthum . . . Deutsche Bearbeitung der Cavallari-Holm'schen Topografia archeologica di Siracusa, *etc.* 1887. 8°. **7706. bb. 38.**

CAVALLARI (ELISABETTA) La Fortuna di Dante nel trecento. pp. 462. *Firenze*, 1921. 8°. **011420. dd. 5.**

CAVALLARI (FRANCESCO SAVERIO) *See* SARTORIUS VON WALTERSHAUSEN (W.) *Baron.* Carta topografica dell'Etna. Per il barone Sartorius di Waltershausen, coll'assistenza di S. Cavallari, *etc.* 1845, *etc.* *obl.* fol. **648. b. 26.**

—— La Cappella del Real Palazzo di Palermo, disegnata e dipinta da Andrea Terzi ; illustrata dai professori Dr S. Cavallari, G. Meli ed I. Carini. pp. lxviii. *Palermo*, 1872 [1872–90]. fol. **Tab. 1282. aa.** *Published in parts.*

—— Euryalos e le opere di difesa di Siracusa, con taluni annotazioni sulla popolazione della Sicilia, *etc.* pp. 66. *Palermo*, 1895. 4°. [*Atti della Reale Accademia di Scienze, Lettere e Belle Arti di Palermo.* ser. 3. vol. 3.] **Ac. 99.**

—— Su alcuni vasi orientali con figure umane rinvenuti in Siracusa e Megara-Iblea, *etc.* pp. 42. pl. v. *Palermo*, 1887. 4°. [*Atti della Reale Accademia di Scienze, Lettere e Belle Arti di Palermo.* Nuova serie. vol. 9.] **Ac. 99.**

—— Topografia archeologica di Siracusa. Eseguita . . . dai professori Dr F. S. Cavallari e Dr Adolfo Holm e dall' ingegnere Cristoforo Cavallari. (Appendice.) 2 pt. *Palermo*, 1883, 91. fol. **7705. h. 23.**

—— Atlante. 1883. fol. **1703. d. 19.**

—— Die Stadt Syrakus im Alterthum. Autorisierte deutsche Bearbeitung der Cavallari-Holm'schen Topografia archeologica di Siracusa von B. Lupus. pp. xii. 343. *Strassburg*, 1887. 8°. **7706. bb. 38.**

CAVALLARI (FRANCESCO SAVERIO)

—— Zur historischen Entwickelung der Künste nach der Theilung des römischen Reichs. 1847. *See* GOTTINGEN STUDIES. Göttinger Studien. [1845, *etc.*] 8°. **8706. d. 23.**

—— Zur Topographie von Syrakus. 1845. *See* GOTTINGEN STUDIES. Göttinger Studien. [1845, *etc.*] 8°. **8706. d. 23.**

—— [Another edition.] Abgedruckt aus den Göttinger Studien, 1845. pp. 26. *Göttingen*, 1845. 8°. **10130. c. 7.**

CAVALLARI (GIUSTO)

—— La Campagna granaria in Sicilia nell'epoca romana. pp. 42. *Catania*, 1951. 8°. **7082. b. 24.**

CAVALLARI (LUIGI) *See* WIKOFF (H.) Trial of Wikoff, Vannoud, and Cavallari, for a conspiracy to effect a forced marriage between Miss Gamble and one of the accused, *etc.* 1852. 8°. **1132. f. 22.**

CAVALLARI (SAVERIO) *See* CAVALLARI (Francesco S.)

CAVALLARI (UGO) Un Metodo geometrico per la risoluzione del triangolo sferico di posizione. [With a summary in English.] *Milano*, 1933. 8°. **08535. h. 1.**

CAVALLARI (VITTORIO)

—— La Costituzione tribunizia istriana. *In:* Rivista di storia del diritto italiano. vol. 23. pp. 37–96. 1950. 8°. **P.P. 1379. k.**

—— Raterio e Verona. Qualche aspetto di vita cittadina nel x secolo. *In:* Studi storici veronesi Luigi Simeoni. vol. 5. pp. 11–67. 1954. 8°. **P.P. 4234. bc.**

CAVALLARI CANTALAMESSA (GIULIA) L'Ottavo centenario dello Studio Bolognese. Memoria. pp. 18. *Rocca S. Casciano*, 1888. 8°. **8304. b. 18.** (5.)

CAVALLARIO (DOMINGO) *See* CAVALLARIUS (Dominicus)

CAVALLARIUS (DOMINICUS) Institutiones juris canonici quibus vetus & nova Ecclesiæ disciplina & mutationum caussæ enarrantur. 6 tom. *Bassani*, 1796. 8°. **1375. c. 3.**

—— Editio prima Hispana, ad ipsum auctoris opus ex amussim aptata. 2 tom. *Valentiae Edetanorum*, 1834. 8°. **706. a. 11.**

—— Instituciones del Derecho Canónico . . . Traduccion nuevamente corregida por un profesor de jurisprudencia de la universidad de esta corte, y con notas . . . por . . . Jorge Gisbert . . . Tercera edicion, adicionada, *etc.* 2 tom. *Madrid & Santiago*, 1849, 50. 8°. **5051. b. 24.**

CAVALLARIUS (JOANNES BAPTISTA) Io. Baptistæ Cauallarii . . . De morbo epidemiali qui Nolam, & Campaniam vniuersam vexauit curatiuus, & præseruatiuus discursus. [With a plate.] pp. 92. *Apud I. I. Carlinū: Neapoli*, 1602. 4°. **1167. e. 19.** (2.)

CAVALLARO (G.)

—— Panormos pre-romana. [With plates.] *In:* Archivio storico siciliano. ser. 3. vol. 4. pp. 7–182. 1951. 8°. **P.P. 3556. u.**

CAVALLARO (ROSARIO) Sul nuovo sistema di studii secondo i programmi governativi adottato nel Collegio Cutelli in Catania, orazione inaugurale, *etc.* pp. 26. *Catania*, 1869. 4°. **8356. f. 14.** (4.)

CAVALLAZZI (ANTONIO) La Sorpresa della epigrafia celto-etrusco-pelasgica. Decifrazione di oltre cento iscrizioni, etc. pp. 367. pl. XIV. *Milano*, 1927. 8°.
07704. f. 44.

CAVALLER (A. MESQUIDA) *See* MESQUIDA CAVALLER (A.)

CAVALLERA (FERDINAND) *See* ATHANASIUS, *Saint, Patriarch of Alexandria.* [*Selections.*] Saint Athanase, 295–373. Par F. Cavallera. [Extracts from his works, translated into French, with connecting notes.] 1908. 8°. 3622. aa. 19.

—— *See* BACKER (A. de) Bibliothèque de la Compagnie de Jésus, *etc.* (Corrections et additions. Cinquième fascicule mis en ordre et publié avec la table alphabétique des noms d'auteurs par F. Cavallera.) 1890, *etc.* 4°.
B.B.A.h.2.

—— *See* JOHN, *Chrysostom, Saint, Patriarch of Constantinople.* [*Homilies.—Collections.—Greek and French.*] Sur l'incompréhensibilité de Dieu. Introduction de F. Cavallera. 1951. 8°. W.P. A. 481/28.

—— *See* MIGNE (J. P.) Patrologiæ cursus completus . . . Series græca, *etc.* (Indices digessit F. Cavallera.) 1857. 4°. 2001. b.–2002. b.

—— *See* VILLER (M.) Dictionnaire de spiritualité . . . Publié sous la direction de M. Viller . . . assisté de F. Cavallera et J. de Guibert, *etc.* 1932, *etc.* 4°.
2009.g.

—— Mélanges offerts au R.P. Ferdinand Cavallera . . . à l'occasion de la quarantième année de son professorat à l'Institut Catholique. [With a portrait and a bibliography.] pp. xvii. 524. 1948. 8°. *See* TOULOUSE.—*Institut Catholique.—Bibliothèque.* 4381. ff. 4.

—— Saint Jérôme, sa vie et son œuvre. pt. 1. tom. 1, 2. *Louvain, Paris*, 1922. 8°. [*Spicilegium sacrum Lovaniense.* fasc. 1, 2.] W.P. 7396/1.

—— Le Schisme d'Antioche, IVe–Ve siècle. [With a bibliography.] pp. xix. 342. *Paris*, 1905. 8°. 04530. h. 3.

CAVALLERI (DANZIO) Diritto giudiziario civile. Ordinamento giudiziario. Principi generali della proc. civ. [Edited by E. Noseda.] pp. xv. 606. *Milano*, 1906. 8°.
5359. c. 6.

—— La Legislazione sulle acque. Parte 1ᵃ. Le acque pubbliche. Parte 2ᵃ. Le acque private. pp. xiii. 274. *Milano*, 1902. 8°. 012200. hh. 39.
One of the " Manuali Hoepli."

CAVALLERI (FERDINANDO) *See* BIONDI (L.) *Marquis.* Intorno al ritratto della N. D. Sig. Marchesa Maria Maddalena Crosa di Vergagni dipinto dal Cav. F. Cavalleri. 1832. 8°. 898. d. 3. (10.)

—— Sopra un'antica greca pittura esistente nel Museo dell'Accademia Etrusca di Cortona riconosciuta per la Musa Polinnia, osservazioni. [With a plate.] pp. 25. *Cortona*, 1852. 4°. 7869.d.5.

CAVALLERI (FRANCESCO) Istruzione ed educazione femminile. Monografia e discorsi. pp. 236. *Torino*, 1875. 8°. 8306. bbb. 3.

CAVALLERI (GIOVANNI BATTISTA DEI) *See* CAVALIERI.

CAVALLERI (GIOVANNI MARIA) Sulla luce problematica che manifestasi in tutto il cielo nel passaggio delle stelle cadenti in agosto e novembre, *etc.* (Estratto dai Rendeconti del Reale Istituto Lombardo, *etc.*) pp. 10. *Milano*, 1867. 8°. 8560. dd. 18. (6.)

CAVALLERIA. Della Caualleria. Grundtlicher Bericht von allem was zu der Reutterei gehörig und einem Cavallier davon zuwissen geburt. (Grundtlicher Bericht vom Zeumen, *etc.*) [By G. E. von Löhneisen. With plates.] 2 Tl. *Remling*, 1609, 10. fol. C. 46. l. 4.
The titlepage is engraved.

CAVALLERÍA (FRANCISCO DE LA) *See* CAVALLERÍA Y PORTILLO.

CAVALLERÍA (FRANCISCO DIEGO ROMERO DE LA) *See* ROMERO DE LA CAVALLERÍA.

CAVALLERÍA (PETRUS DE LA) Tractatus Zelus Christi contra Iudæos, & Sarracenos, infideles. Ab illust. Doct. P. de la Cauallería . . . anno 1450. compositus, nec vnquam impressus. Quem . . . Martinus Alfonsus Viualdus . . . quàm maximè expurgatum, cumque exemplari studiosissimè collatum, & glossis . . . à se conscriptis illustratum, indice præterea locupletissimo, & numeris marginalibus auctum, exornatumque edit . . . Ad hæc . . . tractatus accessit, à Samuele Rabbi ad Isaach Rabbi conscriptus, *etc.* 2 pt. *Apud B. de Baretiis: Venetijs*, 1592. 4°. 3835. b. 25.

CAVALLERÍA Y PORTILLO (FRANCISCO DE LA) Historia de la . . . villa de Villa-Robledo, en la Provincia de la Mancha Alta, en el Reyno de Toledo, con algunos elogios, y vidas de sus varones ilustres. pp. 313. *Madrid*, 1751. 4°. 10161. c. 34.

—— Vida de la V. Virgen, y sierva de Dios la Madre Agueda de la Natividad . . . fundadora del Beaterio . . . de Carmelitas Descalzas . . . de Villa-Robledo, *etc.* pp. 416. *Madrid*, 1750. 4°. 4826. aaa. 5.

CAVALLERIIS (JOANNES BAPTISTA DE) *See* CAVALIERI (Giovanni B.)

CAVALLERINO (ANTONIO) Il Conte di Modona. Tragedia. [In verse.] ff. 51. *P. Gadaldino: Modona*, 1582. 4°. 11714. b. 7. (1.)

—— Ino. Tragedia. [In verse.] ff. 55. *P. Gadaldino: Modona*, [1583.] 4°. 11714. b. 7. (3.)

—— Rosimonda Regina. Tragedia. [In verse.] ff. 47. *P. Gadaldino: Modona*, [1582.] 4°. 11714. b. 7. (2.)

—— Telefonte. Tragedia. [In verse.] ff. 46. *P. Gadaldino: Modona*, [1582.] 4°. 11715. bb. 20.

CAVALLERIO (GIOVANNI BATTISTA DE) *See* CAVALIERI (G. B.)

CAVALLERO (AGOSTINO) Le Macchine a vapore. Il materiale e l'esercizio tecnico della strade ferrate, *etc.* vol. 1. pp. xxiii. 705. pl. xxxv. *Torino*, 1882. 8°. 08767. dd. 2.
No more published.

CAVALLERO (IÑIGO DE OYANGUREN) *See* OYANGUREN CAVALLERO.

CAVALLERO (ISIDORO) *See* GOMEZ DE QUEVEDO VILLEGAS (F.) [*Collections.—Prose.*] Parte primera de las obras de . . . F. de Quevedo Villegas, *etc.* [With a preface by I. Cavallero.] 1687. 4°. 635. g. 1.

CAVALLERO (JOSEPH GARCÍA) *See* GARCÍA CAVALLERO.

CAVALLERO (LUYS) Los que seruis á los Reyes [and six other romances on the Constable Alvaro de Luna]. 1607. *See* PEREZ (Diego) *Native of Alcalá de Henares.* Comienzan seys Romances, *etc.* quaderno 2. 1606, *etc.* 4°.
C. 63. g. 22.

CAVALLERO (MANUEL) Défense de Saragosse, ou Relation des deux siéges soutenus par cette ville en 1808 et 1809 . . . Traduit par M. L. V. Angliviel de la Beaumelle. pp. 153. *Paris*, 1815. 8°. 281. f. 25.

CAVALLERO (PEDRO) *See* AGUILA (A. de) Por Andres de Azeytuna . . . con el Fiscal desta Corte, y P. Cauallero, *etc.* [1630?] fol. 1322. l. 10. (25.)

CAVALLERO (PEDRO RENDON) *See* RENDON CAVALLERO.

CAVALLERO (UGO) *Count.*

—— *See* CANEVARI (E.) La Fine del maresciallo Cavallero, *etc.* [1950.] 8º. **10634. l. 19.**

—— *See* CAVALLERO (C.) *Count.* Il Dramma del maresciallo Cavallero, *etc.* [With portraits.] 1952. 8º. **10634. k. 40.**

—— Comando supremo. Diario 1940–43 del Capo di S.M.G. [With plates, including portraits.] pp. xxviii. 463. [*Bologna,*] 1948. 8º. **9102. bb. 22.**
Testimoni per la storia del " nostro tempo." no. 2.

—— Il Dramma del maresciallo Cavallero. Rivelazioni e memorie. [With portraits.] pp. 173. pl. 12. [*Milan,*] 1952. 8º. **10634. k. 40.**
Il libro del giorno. no. 7.

CAVALLERO DE LOS OLIVOS, afterwards **PRIETO DE BONILLA** (GERTRUDIS) *See* PRIETO DE BONILLA.

CAVALLERO DE LOS OLIVOS (JOSEPH) *See* ARAMBURU (M. de) Por Doña Gertrudis Prieto de Bonilla . . . en el pleyto que le ha movido D. J. Cavallero de los Olivos . . . sobre la successión del mayorazgo que fundaron D. Alvaro Alonso, y D. Alonso Prieto de Bonilla, *etc.* 1770. fol. **5385. ee. 2.**

CAVALLEROS. *See* CABALLEROS.

CAVALLERO Y GÓNGORA (ANTONIO) *Archbishop of Santa Fé. See* CABALLERO Y GÓNGORA.

CAVALLER PIRIS (JOSÉ) Iglesia y Ex-convento de Ntra. Sra. del Socorro—El Socós, *etc.* [With plates.] pp. 129. *Ciudadela, Baleares,* 1929. 8º. **4625. b. 48.**

CAVALLERY (ANTOINE) Dissertation sur la cause de la chaleur et de la froideur des eaux minérales, *etc.* pp. 47. 1739. *See* BORDEAUX.—*Académie Royale des Sciences, etc.* Recueil des dissertations qui ont remporté le prix, *etc.* tom. 5. 1715, *etc.* 12º. **273. a. 9.**

—— Dissertation sur la cause de la diaphanéité et de l'opacité des corps, *etc.* pp. 52. 1738. *See* BORDEAUX.—*Académie Royale des Sciences, etc.* Recueil des dissertations qui ont remporté le prix, *etc.* tom. 5. 1715, *etc.* 12º. **273. a. 9.**

CAVALLETTI (GIACOMO HAMILTON) Forza, materia e ragione. Osservazioni sul materialismo. pp. 205. *Firenze,* 1870. 8º. **8464. aaa. 22.**

—— In occasione del IX Congresso Pedagogico Italiano. Pensieri. pp. 57. *Bologna,* 1874. 8º. **8309. df. 36. (13.)**

—— La Rivoluzione conservatrice. pp. 160. *Firenze,* 1879. 8º. **8033. e. 4.**

CAVALLETTO (ALBERTO) *See* SPERI (T.) Le Ultime lettere di T. Speri . . . con prefazione dell'on. deputato A. Cavalletto. 1887. 8º. **10920. c. 32.**

—— Lettere inedite. *See* PELLINI (S.) I Deputati di Casalmaggiore, *etc.* 1899. 8º. **010910. c. 22. (4.)**

CAVALLI. I Cavalli. *See* PERIODICAL PUBLICATIONS.—*Milan.*

CAVALLI (AGAMENNONE) Rime de diuersi autori Rauennati. Nella elettione di Monsig. . . . Cardinal Cesi, in protettore della Città di Rauenna. (Diuersorum autorum Rauennatum carmina.) [Edited by A. Cavalli.] pp. 35. 43–61. *Appresso G. Minzocchio, & L. Zanotti: Ravenna,* 1584. 4º. **11422. d. 6.**

CAVALLI (ANTONIO) *Marquis. See* PETRARCA (F.) [*Two or more Works.—Latin and Italian.*] Francisci Petrarchae Poemata minora, *etc.* (Poesie minori volgarizzate da poeti viventi o da poco defunti [A. Cavalli and others].) 1829, *etc.* 12º. **11421. dd. 20.**

—— Elogio del canonico Gaspare Saporetti, *etc.* pp. 19. *Forlì,* [1819.] 8º. **10602. h. 14. (1.)**

CAVALLI (ATANAGIO) Il Vesuvio. Poemetto storico-fisico. Con annotazioni. pp. clvii. pl. II. *Milano,* 1769. 8º. **1063. l. 28.**

CAVALLI (CARLO) *Dottore.* Cenni statistico-storici della Valle Vigezzo. 3 tom. *Torino,* 1845. 8º. **1300. g. 19.**

—— Dissertatio inauguralis medica de tetano ejusque speciatim nosogenia, *etc.* pp. 64. *Ticini Regii,* [1824.] 8º. **7383*. b. 11. (15.)**

—— Storia ragionata di straordinaria malattia che dura da vent'otto anni. pp. 261. *Milano,* 1834. 8º. **1169. g. 30.**

CAVALLI (CARLO) *Marquis. See* PEREIRA (Gregorio P.) Dissertazione sopra la giusta valuta della moneta, *etc.* [Edited by C. Cavalli.] 1757. 8º. **8207. b. 1. (4.)**

—— All'eminentissimo . . . Cardinale Gaetano Fantuzzi, solennemente acclamato Protettore . . . di Ravenna, orazione. pp. xvii. *Ravenna,* 1771. fol. **T. 38*. (21.)**

CAVALLI (EMMANUELE) Riflessioni storiche-legali-canoniche al seguito di un grave errore dottrinale e di una pericolosa teorica a danno del real capitolo cattedrale di Lucera. pp. 50. *Lucera,* 1888. 4º. **4532. g. 11. (2.)**

CAVALLI (FRANCESCO) *See* CAVALLI (Pier F.)

CAVALLI (GIAN GIACOMO) A ro serenissimo Gian Battista Durasso Duxe de Zena, in ra sò elettion. Panegirico boscareccio. *G. Pauon: Zena,* 1640. 4º. **240. k. 25.**

—— Ra Cittara zeneize. Poexie, *etc.* pp. 267. *G. Pauoni: Genoua,* 1636. 12º. **11431. a. 14.**
The titlepage is engraved.

—— [Another edition.] La Cetra genouese, *etc.* pp. 274. *G. Bottari: Genoua,* [1650?] 12º. **11429. aa. 13.**

—— [Another edition.] Ra Cittara zeneize . . . In questa nuoeua restampa de chiù poemi accrescioua. pp. 298. *G. Marin: Zena,* 1665. 12º. **11431. df. 1.**

—— [Another edition.] Ricorretta, accresciuta . . . colla giunta di alcune rime de' più antichi rimatori genovesi [Paolo Foglietta, Barnaba Cicala Casero and a writer using the initials B. S.]. [Edited by " Drusino Cisseo," i.e. G. M. Priani.] pp. 404 [304]. *Genova,* 1745. 8º. **240. i. 43.**

—— [Another edition.] Ricorretta ed accresciuta di note da un dilettante genovese. pp. xviii. 315. *Genova,* 1823. 8º. **11431. a. 15.**

CAVALLI (GIOVANNI) *See* ALLASON (U.) La Vita e le opere di Giovanni Cavalli. 1880. 8º. **10629. ee. 37.**

—— *See* DUCASTEL (C.) Aperçu sur les canons rayés se chargeant par la bouche et par la culasse, et sur les perfectionnements apporté à l'art de la guerre, par Jean Cavalli. Compte-rendu. 1863. 8º. **8828. cc. 44. (2.)**

—— Mémoire sur divers perfectionnements militaires . . . lu dans la séance de l'Académie des Sciences de Turin, du 25 mars, 1855 . . . Traduit de l'italien. [With diagrams.] pp. 135. pl. IV. *Paris,* 1856. 8º. **8827. g. 8.**

—— Mémoire sur les canons se chargeant par la culasse, sur les canons rayés, et sur leur application à la défense des places et des côtes. pp. 88. *Paris,* 1849. 8º. **1262. d. 9.**

CAVALLI (GIOVANNI)

—— Atlas. pl. VII. *Paris*, 1849. fol.　　**1261**. d. **24**.

—— *See* MAURICE DE SELLON (P. E.) Examen du Mémoire sur les canons se chargeant par la culasse . . . par J. Cavalli. 1849. 8°.　　**8825**. d. **34**. (9.)

—— Mémoire sur les équipages de ponts militaires. pp. vi. 118. pl. x. *Paris*, 1843. 8°.　　**1397**. h. **14**.

CAVALLI (GIUSEPPE) *See* BARBERI (G.) All'Illmo . . . Signore Monsignor Governatore di Roma e sua Congregazione Criminale . . . Romana homicidii. Per . . . G. Cavalli . . . Ristretto di fatto, e di raggione con sommario. [1761.] fol.　　**T. 81***. (6.)

—— *See* BARBERI (G.) All'Illmo . . . Signore Monsignor Governatore di Roma e sua Congregazione Criminale . . . Romana homicidii. Per . . . G. Cavalli . . . Memoriale addizionale. [1761 ?] fol.　　**T. 81***. (8.)

CAVALLI (GIUSEPPE) *Photographer.*

—— [A collection of photographs. Edited, with an introduction, by Mario Finazzi.] *Ital., Fr. & Eng.* pl. 20. *Bergamo*, [1946.] fol.　　**L.R. 298**. c. **17**. *Immagini.* no. 1.

CAVALLI (GUSTAF) Kort öfversigt öfver Gustaf Cavallis samling af svenska plåtmynt. pp. 18.　　*Stockholm*, 1890. 4°.　　Dept. of Coins & Medals.

CAVALLI (HERCULE) Monnaies et cours des changes de tous les États du monde, *etc.* pp. 57. *Paris*, 1874. 8°.　　**8227**. g. **45**. (14.)

CAVALLI (IGNAZIO) Nuovo regolamento per gli esercizi ad uso della Guardia Nazionale . . . Con modificazioni al servizio di piazza. pp. 86. *Milano*, 1868. 8°.　　**8829**. h. **35**. (3.)

CAVALLI (JACOPO) Commercio e vita privata di Trieste nel 1400. (Ragguaglio delle monete in corso a Trieste nel 1400. [By A. Puschi.]) pp. xxiii. 421.　　*Trieste*, 1910. 8°.　　**10132**. h. **24**.

CAVALLI (JEAN) *See* CAVALLI (Giovanni)

CAVALLI (LUDOVICUS) *See* DUNS (J.) *Scotus.* R.P.F. Ioannis Duns . . . opera, *etc.* [Edited by L. Wadding, with the assistance of L. Cavalli.] 1639. fol.　　**472**. h **2–13**.

CAVALLI (MARINO) *the Elder.*

—— Informatione dell'offitio dell'ambasciatore . . . Manoscritto edito a cura di Tommaso Bertelè. [With a portrait.] pp. 108. pl. 3. *Firenze, Roma*, 1935. 8°.　　**8410**. g. **37**.

—— Relation de Marino Cavalli, 1546. *Ital. & Fr. See* VENICE.—*Ambassadors.* Relations des Ambassadeurs vénitiens, *etc.* tom. 1. 1838. 4°. [*Collection de documents inédits sur l'histoire de France.* sér. 1.]　　**1885**. c. **7**.

—— Eine unbekannte venezianische Relazion über die Türkei 1567. (Relatione de le cose di Costantinopoli del 1567, di Messer Marin di Cavalli.) Von [i.e. edited by] W. Andreas. *Ital.* pp. 13. *Heidelberg*, 1914. 8°. [*Sitzungsberichte der Heidelberger Akademie der Wissenschaften. Phil.-hist. Klasse.* Jahrg. 1914. Abh. 5.]　　Ac. **892/2**.

CAVALLI (MARINO) *the Younger.*

—— *See* DELFINO (Giovanni) *Cardinal, Bishop of Vicenza.* Compendio dei dispacci di Francia di Giovanni Dolfin e di Antonio Priuli, ambasciatori straordinarii ad Enrico IV in occasione del suo matrimonio con Maria de Medici nell'anno 1600. [Signed: Gio. Dolfin, Antonio Priuli, Marin Cavalli.] 1857. 8°. [*Relazioni degli stati europei lette al Senato dagli ambasciatori veneti nel secolo decimosettimo, etc.* ser. 2. vol. 1.]　　**9073**. e.

CAVALLI (MARINO) *the Younger.*

—— Compendio dei dispacci di Francia di Marino Cavalli, ambasciatore ad Enrico IV, dall'anno 1599 al 1603. 1857. *See* VENICE.—Senato. Relazioni degli stati europei, *etc.* ser. 2. vol. 1. 1856. *etc.* 8°.　　**9073**. e.

CAVALLI (MARIO) Degli scrittori politici italiani nella seconda metà del sec. XVII. Alcune considerazioni. pp. 121. *Bologna*, 1903. 8°.　　**011853**. gg. **46**.

CAVALLI (OTTAVIO) Il Padre del Figliuol Prodigo proposto a' Governanti della Repubblica per esemplare del lor governo. Orazione detta nella sala del Senato della . . . Repubblica di Lucca, *etc.* pp. 24. *Lucca*, [1735.] 4°.　　[MISSING.]

CAVALLI (PIER FRANCESCO) *See* PRUNIÈRES (H.) Cavalli et l'opéra vénitien au XVIIe siècle. [With the text of unpublished works of Cavalli, and with facsimiles.] 1931. 8°.　　**W.P. 8974/8a**.

CAVALLI (SERAFINO) *See* CABALLUS (Seraphinus)

CAVALLI (SIGISMONDO) *See* MICHIEL (G.) La Saint-Barthélemy devant le Sénat de Venise. Relations des ambassadeurs G. Michiel et S. Cavalli. 1872. 8°.　　**9210**. cc. **7**.

CAVALLI (STEFANO) A True Relation of the Ceremonies perform'd at the Solemn Coronation of his Holiness Pope Clement the IX. [Translated by Philip Ayres.] *See* A., P., *Gent.* A Short Account of the Life and Death of Pope Alexander the VII., *etc.* 1667. 4°.　　**C.121.b.5.(7.)**

—— [Another edition.] *See* A., P., *Gent.* A Short Account of the Life . . . of Pope Alexander the VII., *etc.* 1750. 4°. [SOMERS (J.) *Baron Somers.* A Second Collection of Tracts. vol. 3.]　　**184**. a. **7**.

—— [Another edition.] *See* A., P., *Gent.* A Short Account of the Life . . . of Pope Alexander the VII., *etc.* 1812. 4°. [SOMERS (J.) *Baron Somers.* A Collection of Tracts. vol. 8.]　　**750**. g. **8**.

CAVALLI (TEOFILO)

—— Papa Sarto. [With plates, including portraits.] pp. 153. *Bologna*, 1954. 8°.　　**4857**. b. **4**.

CAVALLI (VENTURA) Odi amorose, *etc.* pp. 51. *G. B. Ciotti: Venetia*, 1602. 12°.　　**11427**. de. **11**. (2.)

—— Odi heroiche. pp. 48. *G. B. Ciotti: Venetia*, 1602. 12°.　　**11427**. de. **11**. (1.)

CAVALLIER. *See* CAVALIER.

CAVALLIER, BROTHER, AND COMPANY. Economy and Cleanliness, Certainty and Dispatch combined in the Petrisseur, or dough-kneading machine. A patent apparatus, which was invented and is herein described by Cavallier, Brother, and Company of Paris, *etc.* pp. 15. *W. Foat: London*, 1830. 8°.　　**T. 1313**. (8.)

CAVALLIER DEL SOLE. *See* CABALLERO DEL FEBO.

CAVALLIER (CHARLES) Étude sur les travaux hagiologiques, littéraires et archéologiques de . . . Paul Terris, *etc.* pp. 31. *Montpellier*, 1878. 8°.　　**3900**. f. **2**. (7.) *One of an edition of* 100 *copies.*

—— Mougères. Fragments recueillis et publiés sous la direction de Mgr l'évêque de Montpellier. Étude bibliographique. pp. 23. *Montpellier*, 1878. 8°.　　**11905**. h. **21**. (6.) *One of an edition of* 100 *copies.*

—— Saint Vincent de Paul et sa mission sociale, par A. Loth . . . Étude bibliographique et iconographique par C. Cavallier. pp. 27. *Montpellier*, 1885. 8°.　　**4867**. cc. **24**. (8.)

CAVALLIER (FRANÇOIS) Essai nosographique sur la vaccine, *etc.* pp. 23. *Montpellier*, [1807.] 4º.
1180. f. 7. (20.)

CAVALLIER (GABRIEL) Faculté de Droit de Paris. Thèse pour la licence. (Jus romanum. De bonorum possessione contra tabulas.—Droit français. De la révocation des testaments et de leur caducité.) pp. 55. *Paris*, 1860. 8º.
5406. c. 6. (6.)

CAVALLIER (JEAN) *See* CAVALIER.

CAVALLIER (VINCENT) Considérations médicales sur les voyages; thèse, *etc.* pp. 27. *Paris*, 1833. 4º.
1184. e. 11. (17.)

CAVALLIERI (GIOVANNI BATTISTA DE') *See* CAVALIERI (G. B.)

CAVALLIERS. *See* CAVALIERS.

CAVALLI-HOLMGREN (A. F.) *See* SWEDEN.— *Bohusläns Gille.* Roskildefredens 250-årsdag. Ett minnesblad utgifvet af Bohusläns Gille. (Redaktionskommitté: A. F. Cavalli-Holmgren. O. Hellkvist. H. Leander.) 1908. fol.
9435. i. 19.

CAVALLI-MOLINELLI (PIETRO ACHILLE) *See* LOUIS AMADEUS JOSEPH MARIA FERDINAND FRANCIS [of Savoy], *Duke degli Abruzzi.* Osservazioni scientifiche eseguite durante la spedizione polare di S. A. R. Luigi Amedeo, *etc.* (Parte seconda. Materiale scientifico di zoologia, botanica e mineralogia raccolto dal medico . . . P. A. Cavalli-Molinelli.) 1903. 4º.
8706. h. 10.

—— Relazione sul ritorno colle slitte dal parallelo di 83º 16' alla Baia di Teplitz. (Relazione sulle condizioni sanitarie durante la spedizione.) *See* LOUIS AMADEUS JOSEPH MARIA FERDINAND FRANCIS [of Savoy], *Duke degli Abruzzi.* La " Stella Polare " nel mare artico, *etc.* 1903. 8º.
10460. df. 2.

—— Report of Dr. A. Cavalli Molinelli on his journey with sledges while returning from the latitude of 83º 16' to Teplitz Bay. *See* LOUIS AMADEUS JOSEPH MARIA FERDINAND FRANCIS [of Savoy], *Duke degli Abruzzi.* On the " Polar Star " in the Arctic Sea, *etc.* 1903. 8º.
2370. g. 6.

CAVALLIN (ANDERS)

—— Studien zu den Briefen des hl. Basilius. [Translated from the Swedish manuscript by Ernst Blauert.] pp. xii. 126. *Lund*, 1944. 8º.
3671. c. 1.

CAVALLIN (CARL BERNHARD SEBASTIAN) Om konvergenter till bestämda integraler, *etc.* pp. 13. *Stockholm*, 1887. 8º. [*Bihang till Kongl. Svenska Vetenskaps-Akademiens handlingar.* bd. 13. afd. 1. no. 3.]
Ac. 1070/7.

—— Om maximi- och minimikonvergenter till en viss klass bestämda integraler, *etc.* pp. 17. *Stockholm*, 1889. 8º. [*Bihang till Kongl. Svenska Vetenskaps-Akademiens handlingar.* bd. 15. afd. 1. no. 3.]
Ac. 1070/7.

CAVALLIN (CHRISTIAN) *See* SOPHOCLES. [*Philoctetes.*— *Greek.*] Sophoclis Philocteta. Recensuit . . . C. Cavallin. 1875. 8º.
11705. ff. 6.

—— Chr. Cavallin och A. Th. Lysander. Smärre skrifter i urval, samlade och utgifna [by Hans Cavallin and Sven Lysander] . . . Med inledning och lefnadsteckningar Martin Weibull. pp. x. x. 98. xv. 512. *Stockholm*, 1891. 8º.
012357. i. 25.

—— De L. Apulejo, scriptore latino, adversaria, *etc.* pp. 54. *Lundae*, 1857. 8º.
10605. c. 40. (6.)

CAVALLIN (CHRISTIAN)

—— Latinskt lexicon . . . i etymologisk uppställning utarbetadt . . . Stereotyperad upplaga. 2 dl. *Stockholm*, 1871. 8º.
12934. h. 18.

CAVALLIN (HANS) *See* CAVALLIN (C.) Chr. Cavallin och A. Th. Lysander. Smärre skrifter i urval, samlade och utgifna [by H. Cavallin and S. Lysander], *etc.* 1891. 8º.
012357. i. 25.

—— *See* KIPLING (Rudyard) [*Single Works.*] [The Story of the Gadsbys.] Herrskapet Gadsbys historia, och andra berättelser från Indien . . . Öfversättning af H. Cavallin. 1897. 8º.
File 590.

—— *See* KIPLING (Rudyard) [*Selections.*] Mannen, som ville bli kung, och andra berättelser från Indien . . . Öfversättning . . . af H. Cavallin. 1897. 8º.
File 588.

—— *See* KIPLING (Rudyard) [*Selections.*] Wi Willi Winki, och andra berättelser från Indien . . . Öfversättning . . . af H. Cavallin. 1897. 8º.
File 589.

—— *See* KIPLING (Rudyard) [*Selections.*] Emirens predikan, och andra berättelser från Indien . . . Öfversättning . . . af H. Cavallin. 1898. 8º.
File 591.

—— *See* KIPLING (Rudyard) [*Selections.*] Berättelser från Indien. [Translated by H. Cavallin.] 1917. 8º.
12654. d. 27.

CAVALLIN (PAUL BERNHARD SEVERIN) Identiska og syntetiska satser . . . Akademisk avhandling. pp. iv. 79. *Lund*, 1894. 8º.
08464. i. 25. (3.)

CAVALLIN (SAMUEL) Literarhistorische und textkritische Studien zur Vita S. Caesarii Arelatensis [of Cyprianus, Bishop of Toulon, and others]. pp. ix. 136. *Lund*, 1934. 8º. [*Lunds Universitets årsskrift.* Ny följd. avd. 1. bd. 30. no. 7.]
Ac. 1067.

—— Vitae sanctorum Honorati et Hilarii episcoporum Arelatensium. Recensuit S. Cavallin. (Sermo Hilarii de vita S. Honorati. Vita S. Hilarii. Epitaphium Hilarii.) pp. 199. *Lund*, 1952. 8º. [*Skrifter utgivna av Vetenskaps-Societeten i Lund.* vol. 40.]
Ac. 1069/2.

CAVALLIN (SAMUEL GUSTAF) Loci illius Livii (lib. i. cap. xxxii): " Quarum rerum, litium, causarum condixit pater patratus populi Romani Quiritium patri patrato priscorum Latinorum, hominibusque priscis Latinis, quæ res dari, fieri, solvi oportuit, quas res nec dederunt, nec fecerunt, nec solverunt, dic, quid censes? " explicatio, quam . . . præside Joh. Gust. Ek . . . publice defendet . . . S. G. Cavallin . . . in Academia Carolina, *etc.* pp. 16. *Lundæ*, 1850. 8º.
9039. bbb. 31. (2.)

—— Trenne föredrag. pp. 58. *Christianstad*, 1865. 8º.
9435. dd. 29. (7.)

CAVALLIN (SAMUEL JOHAN) *See* CLARUS. Clarus saga. Clari fabella. Islandice et Latine edidit G. Cederschiöld. [The Latin translation by S. J. Cavallin.] 1879. 4º.
12431. v. 14.

CAVALLIN (SEVERIN) *See* LUND.—*Regia Academia Carolina.* Lunds universitets matrikel 1846, *etc.* [With a historical list of the professorate, etc., edited by S. Cavallin.] 1846. 8º.
8355 c. 49. (3.)

—— Lunds stifts herdaminne, efter mestadels otryckta källor utarbetadt. 5 dl. *Lund*, 1854–58. 8º.
4685. e. 14.

—— Principii Schleiermacheri dogmatici expositio critica, *etc.* pp. 70. *Lundæ*, 1849. 8º.
3559. b. 11.

CAVALLIN (Severin)

—— Ur skånska presthusens häfder. pp. 126. *Lund,* 1878. 8°. **4695. b. 2.**

CAVALLINI ( ) *See* Leocadia. Leocadia. Melodramma, *etc.* [Adapted by — Cavallini from ' Léocadie ' by A. E. Scribe and — Mélesville.] 1835. 8°.
906. g. 7. (6.)

CAVALLINI (Alessandro) Le Vite di alcuni uomini illustri, che . . . negli anni 1848 e 1849 . . . sollevarono alla maggiore altezza di gloria il nome di Roma. vol. 1, 2. *Roma,* 1873. 8°. **10631. df. 14.**

CAVALLINI (Gaetano) *Dottore di gius-canonico.* Allocuzione seconda recitata nella chiesa di S. Teresa di Mantova . . . nella festa della B. V. del Carmine fatta . . . il giorno 1 settembre MDCCIC. in cui si cantò solenne Te-Deum in ringraziamento della liberazione di detta città. pp. 15. *Mantova,* 1799. 4°. **4423. b. 14.**

CAVALLINI (Gaetano) *of Ferrara.* Monumenti storici. Omaggio al sangue miracoloso che si venera nella basilica parrocchiale di Santa Maria del Vado, in Ferrara. pp. xiv. 823. *Ferrara,* 1878. 8°. **4571. dd. 1.**

CAVALLINI (Philippus) *See* Buonamici (G. F.) *Maltese.* Melita liberata a peste, seu Consilia quædam . . . aduersus luem quæ anno 1676. in Melita grassabatur . . . recognita, & vindicata per Fr. P. Cavallini. 1690. 12°.
1167. d. 47.

—— Breuis enumeratio plantarum præsenti anno a Publico Sapientiæ Romanæ Medicinalium Simplicium Professore ostensarum ; & quæ in Hortum Hyemalem reddactę asseruantur, *etc.* (Pugillus Meliteus, seu omnium herbarum in insula Melita . . . enascentium perbreuis enarratio.) pp. 144. *Typis I. B. Molo: Romæ,* 1689. 12°.
434. a. 27. (1.)

—— [Another copy.] **972. b. 3. (3.)**

CAVALLINI (Pietro)

—— *See* Horb (F.) Cavallinis Haus der Madonna, *etc.* 1945. 8°. [*Göteborgs Kungl. Vetenskaps- och Vitterhets-Samhälles handlingar.* följd 6. ser. A. bd. 3. no. 1.]
Ac. **1063.**

—— *See* Lothrop (Stanley B.) A Bibliographical Guide to Cavallini and the Florentine painters before 1450, *etc.* 1917. 8°. **011903. b. 19.**

CAVALLINO (Bernardo) *See* Rinaldis (A. de) Bernardo Cavallino. Ventisei riproduzioni, *etc.* 1921. 8°.
7811. ppp. 24/3.

CAVALLIUS (Carl Erik Hyltén) *See* Hyltén-Cavallius (C. E.)

CAVALLIUS (Carl Fredrik)

—— *See* Sahlgren (J.) and Liljeblad (S. S.) Sagor från Småland. Upptecknade av prosten C. F. Cavallius och andra, *etc.* 1939. 8°. [*Svenska sagor och sägner.* no. 3.]
Ac. **6251/5.**

CAVALLIUS (Gunnar Olof Hyltén) *See* Hyltén-Cavallius.

CAVALLO (Buonaventura) Vita del B. Nicolò Albergati Card. di Santa Croce. [With a portrait.] pp. 290. *V. Mascardi: Roma,* 1654. 4°. **485. c. 20.**
The titlepage is engraved.

—— Vita Beati Nicolai Albergati . . . ex ea quam Italicè edidit F. B. Cauallus . . . conuersa à reuerendo P. Lud. I. è Societate Iesu [i.e. Louis Janin]. pp. 158. *I. Dupuis: Parisiis,* 1659. 4°. **4868. f. 7.**
With an additional titlepage, engraved.

CAVALLO (Francesco) *See* Caballus (Franciscus)

CAVALLO (Gian Giacomo) *See* Cavalli.

CAVALLO (Marco) Rinaldo Furioso . . . Nouamente stampato ı . . . corretto. G.ıl. ff. 95. *F. Bindoni & M. Pasini: Vinegia,* 1526. 8°. G. **10993.**

CAVALLO (Sebastiano) *See* Cicero (M. T.) [*Orations.— Italian.*] Orationi di M. T. Cicerone di Latine fatte Italiane [by S. Fausto, S. Cavallo and others]. 1556. 8°.
835. c. 6–8.

CAVALLO (Tiberius) *See* Magalhaes (J. J. de) Description of a Glass-Apparatus for making . . . the best mineral waters . . . Together with the description of two new eudiometers . . . with an examination of the strictures of Mr. T. Cavallo . . . upon these eudiometers. 1783. 8°. **1034. h. 26. (8.)**

—— A Complete Treatise of Electricity in Theory and Practice ; with original experiments. pp. xvi. viii. 412. pl. III. *E. & C. Dilly: London,* 1777. 8°. **538. f. 15.**

—— The second edition, with . . . additions and alterations. pp. xxiv. 495. pl. IV. *C. Dilly & J. Bowen: London,* 1782. 8°. **8756. ccc. 5.**

—— The third edition, in two volumes, containing the practice of medical electricity, besides other additions and alterations. (Volume III. Containing the discoveries and improvements made since the third edition.) 3 vol. *C. Dilly: London,* 1786–95. 8°. **32. h. 13–15.**

—— [Another copy of vol. 3.] **538. f. 17.**

—— The fourth edition. 3 vol. *C. Dilly: London,* 1795. 8°.
8756. bbb. 45.

—— Trattato completo d'elettricità teorica e pratica . . . Tradotto . . . Con addizioni e cangiamenti fatti dall' autore. pp. xx. 511. pl. III. MS. NOTES. *Firenze,* 1779. 8°. **8755. bb. 49.**

—— Description, and Use, of the Telescopical Mother-of-Pearl Micrometer. pp. 41. *C. Dilly: London,* 1793. 8°.
117. d. 52.

—— The Elements of Natural or Experimental Philosophy. [With plates.] 4 vol. *T. Cadell & W. Davies: London,* 1803. 8°. **32. i. 11–14.**

—— An Essay on the Medicinal Properties of Factitious Airs. With an appendix on the nature of blood. pp. viii. 256. *C. Dilly: London,* 1798. 8°. **546. d. 25. (2.)**

—— [Another copy.] **41. e. 9.**

—— An Essay on the Theory and Practice of Medical Electricity. pp. xvi. 112. *Printed for the Author: London,* 1780. 8°. **778. e. 14.**

—— The second edition, corrected, *etc.* pp. xii. 124. *P. Elmsly: London,* 1781. 8°. **543. d. 29.**

—— Evolution. To Correspondents on the Subject of the Eversion. [Signed: T. C., i.e. Tiberius Cavallo?] pp. 87. [1803?] 8°. *See* C., T. **716. c. 34.**

—— Explanation and Index of Two Mineralogical Tables. pp. 44. *Charles Dilly: London,* 1786. 8°.
B. 548. (3.)
Without the tables.

—— Tiberius Cavallo . . . Mineralogische Tafeln . . . nebst einem Register und der Anweisung, wie man dasselbe gebrauchen solle ; übersetzt von Johann Reinhold Forster. *Halle,* 1786. fol. **441. k. 1.**

CAVALLO (Tiberius)

—— The History and Practice of Aerostation.
pp. viii. 326. pl. II. *C. Dilly: London*, 1785. 8°.
977. b. 31.

—— Histoire et pratique de l'aérostation . . . Traduit de
l'anglois. pp. iii. 243. pl. II. *Paris*, 1786. 8°.
8755. c. 22.

—— A Treatise on Magnetism, in Theory and Practice, with
original experiments. pp. xii. 343. pl. II. *C. Dilly:
London*, 1787. 8°. **958. i. 20.**

—— [Another copy.] **34. a. 10.**

—— The third edition, with a supplement. pp. xi. 335. pl. III.
W. & S. Jones: London, 1800. 8°. **716. d. 37.**

—— A Treatise on the Nature and Properties of Air, and other
permanently elastic fluids. To which is prefixed, An
Introduction to Chymistry. pp. xii. 835. pl. III.
Printed for the Author: London, 1781. 4°. **456. b. 20.**

—— [Another copy.] **32. e. 19.**

CAVALLON (Teodoro) *See* Serino (F. da) Croniche
ovvero annali di Terra Santa . . . Pubblicate per la
prima volta dal P. T. Cavallon. 1939. 8°. [*Biblioteca
bio-bibliografica della Terra Santa e dell'Oriente francescano.*
Nuova serie. tom. 11, 12.] **04784. i.**

CAVALLOS (Agustin de) New Light from Spanish
Archives on the Voyage of Olivier van Noort: the Vice-
Admiral Ship, the Hendrik Frederick, on the west coast
of the Americas, 1600. [A letter of Fray Agustin de
Cavallos to the Audiencia de Guatemala.] Introduction,
editing, and footnotes by Engel Sluiter, Dutch transla-
tion of the Spanish document by . . . Dr. C. F. A. van
Dam and Dr. H. C. Barrau. Reprinted from Bijdragen
voor Vaderlandsche Geschiedenis en Oudheidkunde, *etc.*
Span. & Dutch. The Hague, 1937. 8°. **9551. m. 13.**

CAVALLOTTI (Anna Maria) *See* Carbonari. Memorie
sulle società segrete dell'Italia Meridionale e specialmente
sui Carbonari. Traduzione dall'inglese de A. M. Cavallotti. 1904. 8°. [*Biblioteca storica del Risorgimento
italiano.* ser. 4. no. 2.] **9169.de.1/28.**

CAVALLOTTI (Felice) *See* Matarazzo Casini (L.) Nel
x° anniversario della morte di F. Cavallotti, *etc.* 1908. 8°.
10632. aaa. 61.

—— *See* Mohr (A. de) Felice Cavallotti. La vita e le opere.
[With portraits.] 1899. fol. **1764. a. 25.**

—— *See* Tyrtaeus. [*Works.—Greek and Italian.*] Canti e
frammenti di Tirteo. Versione letterale e poetica [by
F. Cavallotti], con testo e note, *etc.* 1878. 8°.
11335. bb. 10.

—— —— 1898. 8°. **11340. b. 40.**

—— Opere. 10 vol. *Milano*, [1895.] 8°. **12227. aaa. 25.**

—— Opere. [With a preface by Guido Marangoni.] 3 vol.
Milano, 1909, 10. 8°. **12227. df. 12.**

—— Alcibiade, la critica e il secolo di Pericle. Lettera . . .
a Yorick, figlio di Yorick. pp. 133. *Milano*, 1874. 8°.
10602. i. 1. (13.)

—— Alcibiade. Scene greche in dieci quadri. Con note.
pp. xxviii. 390 [332]. *Milano*, 1875. 8°.
11715. bbb. 5.

—— Ἀλκιβιάδης. Ἑλληνικαὶ σκηναι . . . Ἐκ τῆς Ἰταλικῆς
ὑπὸ Γ. Ι. Δουρουτη καὶ Κ. Χ. Βαμβα. pp. 184.
Ἐν Ἀθηναις, [1890.] 16°. **11715. c. 10.**

CAVALLOTTI (Felice)

—— Anticaglie. [Poems, with an essay entitled: "Del
verismo e della nova metrica." With a portrait.] pp. 316.
Roma, 1879. 8°. **12357. m. 3.**

—— Il Cantica dei Cantici, scherzo poetico in un atto in
martelliani. Nuova edizione, *etc.* pp. 69. *Milano*,
1891. 8°. **11715. df. 4.**

—— Collana dei martiri italiani. Storia della insurrezione di
Roma nel 1867. [With illustrations.] pp. 670. *Milano*,
1869. 8°. **9166. h. 17.**

—— Cura radicale. Scherzo comico in un atto, in versi
martelliani. Quinta edizione. pp. 63. *Milano*,
1898. 8°. **11714. c. 2. (1.)**

—— Della proprietà letteraria ed artistica e sua perpetuità.
Lettera al deputato Antonio Billia. pp. 80. *Milano*,
1871. 8°. **5326. c. 15.**

—— Italia e Grecia. pp. xviii. 168. *Catania*, 1898. 8°.
9136. bb. 22.

—— Lettre de M. F. Cavallotti à M. E. Sonzogno. *See*
Musset (E. St. B.) Union helléno-latine. F. Cavallotti
à la France, *etc.* 1890. 8°. **8026. ee. 24. (10.)**

—— Il Libro dei versi. pp. 369. *Milano*, [1898.] 8°.
11429. dd. 5.

—— Luna di miele. Dramma . . . Dodicesima edizione.
pp. 63. *Milano*, 1898. 8°. **11714. c. 2. (2.)**

—— Nicarete, ovvero la Festa degli albi. Commedia greca
in un atto. Quinta edizione. pp. 62. *Milano*,
1898. 8°. **11714. c. 2. (3.)**

—— I Pezzenti. Dramma storico in cinque atti [in verse],
con note storiche. pp. 158. *Sesto S. Giovanni*, 1917. 8°.
11714. cc. 18.

—— Il Povero Piero. Dramma in tre atti. Sesta edizione.
pp. 80. *Milano*, 1898. 8°. **11714. c. 2. (4.)**

—— Sic vos non vobis. Proverbio in un atto. Quarta
edizione. pp. 62. *Milano*, 1898. 8°. **11714. c. 2. (5.)**

—— La Sposa di Mènecle. Comedia in un prologo e tre
atti, con note. pp. xv. 307. *Roma*, 1882. 8°.
11715. ee. 11.

—— Felice Cavallotti nella vita e nelle opere. [By A. Bizzoni,
G. Bovio, and others.] pp. 293. *Milano*, [1898.] 8°.
10631. df. 53.

CAVALLOTTI (G. B.) La Poesia del dolore in Silvio
Pellico e Giacomo Leopardi. Commemorazione, *etc.*
pp. 43. *Saluzzo*, 1902. 8°. **011853. g. 59. (2.)**

CAVALLOTTI (Giuseppe) Notizie istoriche relative a
Francesco Sforza, che fu il primo fondatore del Grande
Ospitale di Milano, con altre notizie particolari intorno le
vicende di si interessante luogo pio. [The dedication
signed: G. C., i.e. G. Cavallotti.] pp. 73. 1829. 8°.
See C., G. **10630. dd. 2. (3.)**

CAVALLOTTI (Joseph) De arsenico. Diatriba inauguralis, *etc.* pp. 28. *Ticini Regii*, [1828.] 8°.
7383*. c. 9. (16.)

CAVALLOTTO (Giandomenico) Saggio di osservazioni
particolari sopra lo stato in cui attrovasi presentemente la
naval costruzione in Venezia, in quella parte, che ris-
guarda li vascelli da cavico per uso del commercio, con
alcune osservazioni . . . sopra la costruzione de' vascelli
da guerra. pp. xvi. 160. pl. II. *Venezia*, 1766. 4°.
8806. ccc. 5.

CAVALLUCCI (ANTONIO) *See* FEDELI (C.) La Vestizione di S. Bona, quadro di A. Cavallucci. 1917. 8º.
[MISSING.]

—— *See* ROSSI (G. G. di) Vita di Antonio Cavallucci da Sermoneta, pittore. [With a portrait.] 1796. 8º.
10635. i. 20.

CAVALLUCCI (CAMILLO JACOPO) *See* ITALY. [*Appendix.* —*Miscellaneous.*] Les Grands maîtres de la Renaissance. Les arts en Italie . . . Par . . . le Marquis de Baldassini, C. J. Cavallucci [and others], *etc.* 1888. fol.
1759. c. 8.

—— Manuale di storia dell'arte. vol. 1-3. *Firenze*, 1895-1908. 8º.
7814. aa. **21**.
Vol. 3 is of the second edition and is in 2 pt. Imperfect ; wanting vol. 4.

—— Manuale di storia dell'arte italiana. ⌊Adapted ′by Eugenio Duprè from "Manuale di storia dell'arte." With illustrations.] 3 vol. *Firenze*, 1925-30. 8º.
07815.cc.5.

—— Notizia storica intorno alle gallerie di quadri antichi e moderni della R. Accademia delle Arti del Disegno in Firenze. pp. 23. 1873. 8º. *See* FLORENCE.—*Accademia delle Arti del Disegno.*
7875. c. **39**. (2.)

—— [Another edition.] pp. 119. MS. NOTES AND ADDITIONS. *See* FLORENCE.—*Accademia delle Arti del Disegno.*
7875. c. **39**. (1.)

—— [Ánother copy.]
[MISSING.]

—— S. Maria del Fiore e la sua facciata. Narrazione storica. pp. x. 173. *Firenze*, 1887. 8º.
4605. c. **10**.

—— Vita ed opere del Donatello . . . Tavole . . . con testo. pp. 39. *Milano*, 1886. fol.
[MISSING.]

CAVALLUCCI (CAMILLO JACOPO) and **MOLINIER** (ÉMILE)

—— Les Della Robbia, leur vie et leur œuvre, d'après des documents inédits. Suivi d'un catalogue de l'œuvre des Della Robbia en Italie et dans les principaux musées de l'Europe. pp. 289. *Paris*, 1884. 4º.
1763. b. **12**.

CAVALLUCCI (GIACOMO) La France vue par un Italien d'aujourd'hui. pp. 183. *Naples ; Paris*, 1935. 8º.
010168. f. **77**.

—— Salvator Viale et la littérature corse. Thèse, *etc.* [With a bibliography.] pp. 132. *Besançon*, 1930. 8º.
10655. h. 6.

—— Vauvenargues dégagé de la légende. pp. xxvii. 418. *Naples, Paris*, 1939. 8º.
10655. l. 6.

CAVALLUCCI (VINCENZO) *See* BECCUTI (F.) called IL COPPETTA. Rime . . . corrette e di copiose note corredate da V. Cavallucci. 1751. 4º.
839. g. **17**.

—— *See* MAFFEI (F. S.) *Marquis.* La Merope, tragedia . . . con alcune operette [by V. Cavallucci and others], colle quali si critica, si difende, e s'illustra la detta tragedia, compilate, e raccolte per D. V. Cavallucci. 1747. 4º.
839. i. **27**.

—— Del modo di tinger la porpora degli antichi. Discorso, *etc. Perugia*, 1786. 8º.
665. c. **15**. (4.)

—— Istoria critica del sagro anello col quale fu da San Gioseffo sposata Maria Vergine, e che religiosamente si conserva nel duomo di Perugia. pp. xii. 163. *Perugia*, 1783. 8º.
1365. b. 5.

CAVALLUS (BONAVENTURA) *See* CAVALLO.

CAVALLUS (FRANCISCUS) *See* CABALLUS.

CAVALLUZZI (C.) La Poesia del Prati e dell'Aleardi nel secondo romanticismo. pp. 104. *Città di Castello*, 1898. 8º.
011852. de. **11**.

CAVALRY. Cavalry: remarks on its organization, equipment, and instruction ; compiled from various authorities. By an Officer of Hussars. pp. viii. 75. *T. Egerton : London*, 1819. 12º.
8826. b. **12**.

—— [La Cavalerie au combat et dans les guerres de l'avenir. Par P. S.] Cavalry in Action in the Wars of the Future. Studies in applied tactics by P. S. [i.e. Paul Joseph Silvestre ?] Translated from the French by John Formby, *etc.* [With maps.] 1905. 8º. *See* S., P.
8832. d. **7**.

CAVALRY CLUB. *See* LONDON.—III.

CAVALRY JOURNAL. *See* LONDON.—III. *Royal United Service Institution.*

CAVALRY STUDIES. Cavalry Studies from Two Great Wars. Comprising The French Cavalry in 1870, by Lieutenant-Colonel Bonie. The German Cavalry in the Battle of Vionville—Mars-la-Tour, by Major Kaehler. The Operations of the Cavalry in the Gettysburg Campaign, by Lieutenant-Colonel George B. Davis. pp. 267. *Hudson-Kimberly Publishing Co. : Kansas City*, 1896. 8º. [*International Series.* no. 2.]
8822. c. **28**.

CAVALRY TACTICS. Cavalry Tactics. By a Cavalry Officer. pp. 143. *Edward Stanford : London*, 1897. 16º.
8825. aa. **43**.

CAVALUTTI (NICOLAUS) De animi pathematum in animalium œconomiam efficacia atque effectibus disceptatio inauguralis, *etc.* pp. 12. *Patavii*, 1831. 8º.
7306. b. 9. (30.)

CAVAN.

—— Cavan, Past and Present. By Bridie M. Smith. The official guide, *etc.* pp. 40. *E. J. Burrow & Co. : Cheltenham*, [1927.] 8º.
10354. a. **200**.

—— A New Song ball'd [*sic*] the Barrack Hill, Cavan. *P. Brereton : Dublin*, [1865 ?] *s. sh.* fol.
C. **116**. h. 3. (66.)

—— A New Song on the Sporting Races of Cavan. *P. Brereton : Dublin*, [1865 ?] *s. sh.* fol. C. **116**. h. 3. (20.)

—— [Another edition.] The Whole Humours of the Sporting Races. *B. Brereton : Dublin*, [1865 ?] *s. sh.* fol.
C. **116**. h. 3. (19.)

—— *Breifny Antiquarian Society.* The Breifny Antiquarian Society's Journal, 1921 [*etc.*]. *Cavan*, 1921- 8º.
Ac. **5781**.

CAVAN, FREDERICK EDWARD GOULD, *Earl of.* [1839-1900.] *See* LAMBART.

——, RICHARD, 4*th Earl of.* [1666-1742.] *See* LAMBART.

CAVAN (GEORGE) *See* GEORGE, *pseud.* [i.e. G. Cavan.]

CAVAN (JORDAN TRUE) *See* CAVAN (Ruth S.) and CAVAN (J. T.) Building a Girl's Personality, *etc.* [1932.] 8º.
04192. d. **1/77**.

CAVAN (ROMILLY) Beneath the Visiting Moon. A novel. pp. 378. *William Heinemann : London, Toronto*, 1940. 8º.
NN. **31804**.

—— Characters in Order of Appearance. A novel. pp. vii. 438. *Constable & Co. : London*, 1938. 8º.
NN. **28730**.

CAVAN (ROMILLY)

—— Heron. [A novel.] pp. vi. 345.　*J. M. Dent & Sons:*
London, 1934. 8°.　　　　　　　NN. **22700.**

—— I'll see you again. A comedy in three acts. pp. 84.
Charles H. Fox: London, [1946.] 8°.　**11782. cc. 61.**

—— Mary Cloud. A novel. pp. 558.　*William Heinemann:*
London, Toronto, 1939. 8°.　　**12631. ppp. 5.**

—— The Splendour Falls. pp. 352.　*J. M. Dent & Sons:*
London, 1936. 8°.　　　　　　　NN. **26287.**

—— To-morrow is also a Day. pp. 416.　*J. M. Dent & Sons:*
London, 1935. 8°.　　　　　　　NN. **24769.**

CAVAN (RUTH SHONLE) Suicide. pp. xxvii. 359.
Chicago, 1928. 8°.　[*University of Chicago Sociological*
Series.]　　　　　　　　　Ac. **2691. d/37. (3.)**

CAVAN (RUTH SHONLE) and **CAVAN** (JORDAN TRUE)

——　　　　　　　　　Building a Girl's Per-
sonality. A social psychology of later girlhood. pp. 175.
Abingdon Press: New York, [1932.] 8°. [*Abingdon*
Religious Education Monographs.]　**04192. d. 1/77.**

CAVAN (RUTH SHONLE) and **RANCK** (KATHERINE HOW-
LAND)

——　　　　　　　　　　The Family
and the Depression. A study of one hundred Chicago
families. pp. xvii. 208.　*Chicago*, 1938. 8°. [*Social*
Science Studies. no. 35.]　　Ac. **2691. d/36. (36.)**

CAVAN (SAMUEL) Confession, Absolution, Baptismal Regeneration. Together with Archbishop Cranmer's . . .
doctrine concerning Christ's presence in the Sacrament of
the Lord's Supper, *etc.* pp. 30.　*Simpkin, Marshall & Co.:*
London; G. Langley & Son: Mansfield, 1867. 8°.
　　　　　　　　　　　　4326. aaa. 10.

—— Some Forcible Quotations and Plain Remarks about the
Lord's Supper, *etc.* pp. 44.　*Simpkin, Marshall & Co.:*
London; G. Langley & Son: Mansfield, 1866. 8°.
　　　　　　　　　　　　4327. bbb. 12.

—— The True Church Doctrine of the Lord's Supper. pp. 19.
Simpkin, Marshall & Co.: London; Bontoft & Co.:
Alford, 1873. 8°.　　　　　**4402. d. 3. (4.)**

CAVAÑA (AGUSTIN MORETO Y) *See* MORETO Y CABAÑA.

CAVANA (GIOVANNI NICOLÒ) *See* SOPRANI (R.) Le Vite
de' pittori . . . che in Genoua operarono . . . Aggion-
taui la vita dell'autore per opera di G. N. Cavana, *etc.*
1674. 4°.　　　　　　　　**133. d. 13.**

CAVANAGH (　　　) Exploits glorieux du célèbre
Cavanagh. pp. 15. [*Paris*, 1789.] 8°.　**F. 470. (2.)**

CAVANAGH (AGNES BERNARD)

—— Pope Gregory VII and the Theocratic State. A dissertation, *etc.* pp. xiv. 143.　*Catholic University of America:*
Washington, 1934. 8°.　　　**4572. d. 22.**

CAVANAGH (ANGUS L.) Physics Laboratory Manual.
Containing experiments and exercises designed especially
for a first course in physics in secondary schools. By
A. L. Cavanagh . . . Clyde M. Westcott . . . Harry
La V. Twining. ff. v. 60. *Ginn & Co.: Boston*, [1912.] 4°.
　　　　　　　　　　　　8709. d. 6.

Printed on one side of the leaf only.

CAVANAGH (CHRISTOPHER) *See* WEBSTER (Edward) Parliamentary Costs . . . Fourth edition by C. Cavanagh.
1881. 8°.　　　　　　　　[MISSING.]

CAVANAGH (CHRISTOPHER)

—— The Great Land Question: being a verbatim transcript
of the correspondence in Doe versus Roe. pp. iv. 207.
Stevens & Haynes: London, 1875. 8°.　**6305.aaa.7.**

—— The Law and Procedure of Summary Judgment on
specially endorsed writ under Order XIV. pp. xxx. 229.
Waterlow & Sons: London, 1887. 8°　**6281.c.30.**

—— The Law of Money Securities, *etc.* pp. xlviii. 664.
Stevens & Sons: London, 1879. 8°.　**6375.f.13.**

—— Second edition. pp. lxvii. 805.　*W. Clowes & Sons:*
London, 1885. 8°.　　　　　**6376.r.27.**

—— Principles and Precedents of Modern Conveyancing, 1882.
pp. xxxi. 794. *Waterlow & Sons: London*, 1882. 8°.
　　　　　　　　　　　　6306.k.16.

CAVANAGH (FRANCIS) *See* CAVANAGH (Thomas F.)

CAVANAGH (FRANCIS JOSEPH L.) Head Troubles and
their causes, *etc.* pp. 72. [*Toronto*, 1898.] 8°.
　　　　　　　　　　　　7410. eee. 7.

—— Head Troubles, etc., and some of their causes, *etc.*
(Second edition.) pp. 104. [*Toronto*,] 1914. 8°.
　　　　　　　　　　　　7410. ccc. 33.

—— The New Science of the Thumbs and Finger Nails.
pp. 106. [*Toronto*,] 1916. 8°.　　**7404. tt. 14.**

—— Cavanagh's Phrenological Chart, *etc.* pp. 165. [*Toronto*,
1903.] fol.　　　　　　　　**7409. g. 3.**

—— [Another edition.] [*Toronto*, 1911.] fol.　**7409. h. 5.**

CAVANAGH (J. C.)

—— A Study of the Pulping Properties of Three Trees of E.
sieberiana, using the Sulphate Process . . . By J. C.
Cavanagh . . . H. E. Dadswell . . . A. W. Mackney . . .
T. M. Reynolds. pp. 32. *Melbourne*, 1938. 8°. [*Council*
for Scientific and Industrial Research. Pamphlet. no. 86.]
　　　　　　　　　C.S.G.548/3.(2.)

CAVANAGH (JAMES A.) Adventures of an Insurance
Agent. [With plates, including portraits.] pp. 145.
Juta & Co.: Cape Town & Johannesburg, [1924.] 8°.
　　　　　　　　　　　　010094. ee. 48.

CAVANAGH (JOHN RICHARD) and **MAC GOLDRICK**
(JAMES BARTHOLOMEW)

—— Fundamental Psychiatry. (Second printing.)
pp. x. 590. *Bruce Publishing Co.: Milwaukee*, 1954. 8°.
　　　　　　　　　　　　7661. h. 47.

CAVANAGH (KIT) *pseud.* A Dunleary Legend, and other
tales . . . Illustrated by Alfred E. Kerr. pp. 90.
Quota Press: Belfast, [1934.] 4°.　**20053. i. 26.**

CAVANAGH (MAEVE) *pseud.* [i.e. MAEVE CAVANAGH
MACDOWELL.] *See* MACDOWELL (M. C.)

CAVANAGH (MICHAEL) Memoirs of Gen. T. F. Meagher,
comprising the leading events of his career, *etc.*
pp. 496. 38. *Messenger Press: Worcester, Mass.*, 1892. 8°.
　　　　　　　　　　　　10882. g. 1.

CAVANAGH (MORGAN PETER) *See* KAVANAGH.

CAVANAGH (NICHOLAS)

—— Night Cargoes. A smuggling story . . . Drawings by
William Stobbs. pp. 224.　*Peter Lunn: London*,
1946. 8°.　　　　　　　　**12821. dd. 89.**

—— Night Cargoes . . . Illustrated by Alma K. Lee.
pp. vii. 180. *Longmans, Green & Co.: London*, 1952. 8°.
[*Heritage of Literature Series.* Section A. no. 48.]
　　　　　　　　　　　　012208. cc. 1/90.

CAVANAGH (Nicholas)

—— Sister to the Mermaid. [A tale for children.] Drawings by William Stobbs. pp. 217. *Peter Lunn: London*, 1946. 8°. **12830. bb. 31.**

CAVANAGH (Pius) *See* Thomas, *Aquinas, Saint.* [*Selections.—English.*] The Maxims of St. Thomas Aquinas . . . Edited by Fr. P. Cavanagh. [1890.] 32°. **3455. aaaa. 7. (3.)**

—— Gleanings for Saints and Sinners about St. Mary Magdalen. pp. 116. *Catholic Truth Society: London*, 1888. 8°. **4823. b. 9.**

—— Good and Bad Confessions. pp. 24. *Catholic Truth Society: London*, 1904. 32° **3943.a.51.(2.)**

—— The Life of St. Thomas Aquinas, the Angelic Doctor. Edited by . . . P. Cavanagh. pp. viii. 254. *Burns & Oates: London*, [1890.] 8°. **4829. de. 6.**

CAVANAGH (Thomas Francis) The Care of the Body. pp. xvi. 292. *Methuen & Co.: London*, 1907. 8°. [*New Library of Medicine.*] **2256. d.**

—— The Care of the Body. [Abridged.] pp. viii. 151. *Methuen & Co.: London*, 1916. 8°. [*Methuen's Health Series.*] **07305. aa. 3/5.**

CAVANAGH (Timothy) Scotland Yard Past and Present. Experiences of thirty-seven years. pp. vii. 229. *Chatto & Windus: London*, 1893. 8°. **12331. ee. 30.**

CAVANAGH (William Francis)

—— Our Supernatural Destiny. Events in the Christian Church. [In verse.] pp. 84. *Arthur H. Stockwell: Ilfracombe*, [1954.] 8°. **11660. b. 49.**

CAVANAGH (William Henry) Colonial Expansion. Including the rise and fall of historic settlements. pp. 263. *R. G. Badger: Boston*, [1924.] 8°. **9555. t. 6.**

CAVANAH (Frances) Boyhood Adventures of Our Presidents . . . Illustrated, *etc.* pp. 256. *Rand, McNally & Co.: Chicago*, [1938.] 8°. **010886. g. 44.**

—— Children of the White House, *etc.* pp. 35. *Rand, McNally & Co.: New York*, [1936.] 4°. **20052. h. 41.**

CAVANAH (Lucretia) and **MYERS** (Alonzo Franklin) Handwriting for Expression. (Teachers' first book.—Pupils' first[—sixth] book.—Teachers' manual.—Pupils' second book, manuscript edition.) 9 pt. *American Book Co.: New York*, [1937.] obl. 8°. **7941. tt. 26.**

—— Handwriting for Expression . . . Manuscript edition. *American Book Co.: New York*, [1937- .] obl. 8° & 8°. **W.P. 12626.**

CAVANAS (Jean Baptiste) called Dalainval.

—— *See* Waltron, *Le Comte de.* Le Comte de Waltron . . . Pièce en trois actes [by H. F. Möller], arrangée pour le théâtre de Monsieur, frère du Roi, par M. Dalainval, *etc.* 1789. 8°. **11738. aa. 13. (3.)**

CAVAÑAS (Manuel German Toral) *See* Toral Cabañas.

CAVANAUGH (John) *See* Rockne (Knute K.) The Autobiography of Knute K. Rockne . . . With introduction and postscript by Father J. Cavanaugh. [1931.] 8°. **10880. v. 6.**

CAVANAUGH (M. Jean Carmel)

—— *See* Holyday (Barten) Technogamia, by Barten Holyday. A critical edition. A dissertation . . . by Sister M. J. C. Cavanaugh. 1942. 8°. **11773. g. 27.**

CAVANÇO (Francisco de) Informe en que se ponen de manifiesto las proposiciones, y materias que se tratan en el libro, cuyo titulo es: Regla de la Tercera Orden elucidada. Y los motiuos que tiene la Orden . . . para suplicar en el Real Consejo de Castilla, mande recoger . . . la licencia que tiene dada para que se imprima dicho libro. ff. 22. *Madrid*, 1673. fol. **4783. e. 3. (43.)**

CAVANDER (Carolus Plantin) Dissertatio chemica de sulphate barytæ, *etc.* *Praes.* J. Gadolin. pp. 14. *Aboæ*, [1805.] 4°. **B. 378. (4.)**

CAVANDER (Christian) Historisk och oeconomisk beskrifning öfwer Sagu sochn i Åbo lähn, *etc.* pp. 26. *Åbo*, [1753.] 4°. **B. 669. (13.)**

CAVANDINI (Ada) *See* Cavadini.

CAVANHAC (Henri Alexandre) Thèse présentée . . . à la Faculté de Médecine de Montpellier, *etc.* (Questions tirées au sort.) pp. 43. *Montpellier*, 1840. 4°. **1182. c. 2. (1.)**

CAVANI (Jacques) De la fistule vésico-vaginale. Thèse, *etc.* pp. 46. *Montpellier*, 1834. 4°. **1181. g. 2. (10.)**

CAVANILLAS (Julián Cortés) *See* Cortés Cavanillas.

CAVANILLES (Antonio) Diálogos políticos y literarios y discursos académicos . . . Segunda edición. [With a preface by Fernan Caballero.] pp. xxi. 300. *Madrid*, 1859. 8°. **12230. c. 3.**

—— Discurso contestando al anterior [i.e. to the reception-address of Vicente Vazquez Queipo]. *See* Vazquez Queipo (V.) Discursos leidos ante la Real Academia de Historia en la recepción pública del Excmo. sr. D. V. Vazquez Queipo. 1861. 8°. **8355. ee. 11. (7.)**

—— Historia de España. 5 tom. *Madrid*, 1860–63. 8°. **9180. g. 4.**

—— Lequeitio en 1857. pp. 162. 51. *Madrid*, 1858. 8°. **10160. b. 17.**

—— Memoria sobre el Fuero de Madrid, del año de 1202. pp. 71. 1852. *See* Madrid.—*Real Academia de la Historia.* Memorias, *etc.* tom. 8. 1796, *etc.* 4°. Ac. **6630/3.**

—— Poesías inéditas . . . leidas en la Academia del Mirto 1823–1826. Publícalas precedida de un prólogo Santiago Montoto. pp. 66. *Sevilla*, 1934. 8°. **20002. e. 32.**

CAVANILLES (Antonio Josef) *See* Cavanilles y Centi (A.) and Lagasca (M.) Dos Noticias históricas del inmortal botánico . . . Don Antonio José Cavanilles, *etc.* [With a portrait.] 1917. 4°. **10634. i. 1.**

—— *See* Periodical Publications.—*Madrid.* Anales de Historia Natural. [Edited by A. J. Cavanilles and others.] 1799, *etc.* 8°. **P.P. 2005.**

—— Colección de papeles sobre controversias botánicas de D. A. J. Cavanilles con algunas notas del mismo á los escritos de sus antagonistas. pp. 274. *Madrid*, 1796. 8°. **236. i. 32.**

—— Descripción de las plantas que D. A. J. Cavanilles demostró en las lecciones públicas del año 1801 (1802), precedida de los principios elementales de la botanica. pp. cxxxvi. 625. *Madrid*, 1802. 8°. **451. c. 17, 18.**

—— Ant. Iosephi Cavanilles Icones et descriptiones plantarum, quæ aut sponte in Hispania crescunt, aut in hortis hospitantur. 6 vol. *Matriti*, 1791–1801. fol. **450. h. 12, 17.**

—— [Another copy.] **36. g. 4–9.**

CAVANILLES (Antonio Josef)

—— [Another copy of vol. 1.] **456. f. 6.**

—— *See* Ruiz (H.) Respuesta . . . á la impugnación que ha divulgado . . . Don Josef Antonio Cavanilles [in his " Icones et descriptiones plantarum "], contra el Pródromo de la flora del Perú, *etc.* 1796. 4°.
B. 92. (1.)

—— Monadelphiæ classis dissertationes decem. 3 vol. pp. x. 463. pl. ccxcvi. *Matriti,* 1790. 4°.
447. e. 14–16.

—— [Another copy.] **36. c. 6–8.**

—— Observaciones sobre la historia natural, geografia, agricultura, población y frutos del Reyno de Valencia; con estampas, *etc.* 2 vol. **L.P.** *Madrid,* 1795, 97. fol.
183. e. 6.

—— Antonii Josephi Cavanilles Observationes in quintum fasciculum D. L'Héritier [i.e. of his " Stirpes novæ "]. pp. 18. [1790?] 4°. **B. 14. (10.)**

—— Observations . . . sur le cinquième fascicule de M. L'Héritier. (Extrait du Journal de physique de mars 1789.) pp. 10. [1790?] 4°. **B. 14. (11.)**

—— Observations . . . sur l'article Espagne de la nouvelle Encyclopédie [by N. Masson de Morvilliers]. pp. 155. *Paris,* 1784. 8°. **B. 746. (9.)**

—— [Another copy.] **281. f. 37.**

—— Observaciones sobre el artículo España de la nueva . . . Encyclopedia. Traducidas al Castellano por Don M. Rivera. pp. 115. *Madrid,* 1784. 8°. **804. a. 6. (2.)**

CAVANILLES (Josef Antonio) *See* Cavanilles (A. J.)

CAVANILLES Y CENTI (Antonio) and LAGASCA (Mariano) Dos Noticias históricas del inmortal botánico y sacerdote hispano-valentino Don Antonio José Cavanilles . . . Con anotaciones y los estudios bio-bibliográficos de Cavanilles y Centi y de La Gasca por el Dr. Eduardo Reyes Prósper. [With portraits.] pp. 265. *Madrid,* 1917. 4°. **10634. i. 1.**

CAVANIOL (Henri) Une Année à Chaumont. Juillet 1830—juillet 1831. pp. iii. 370. *Chaumont,* 1898. 12°.
010168. e. 17.

—— Aux temps lointains. [Archaeological essays.] pp. iv. 270. *Chaumont,* 1899. 12°. **[MISSING.]**

—— Chaumont. Les origines. La vieille cité. [With illustrations.] 2 tom. *Chaumont,* 1905. 8°.
010169. ee. 3.

—— Chaumont, 1831–1835. 2 tom. *Chaumont,* 1900, 01. 8°. **010168. e. 18.**

—— Chaumont, 1835–1848. 2 tom. *Chaumont,* 1903, 04. 8°. **010168. i. 28.**

—— Daniel. [A tale.] pp. 155. *Chaumont,* 1864. 8°.
12515. bb. 14.

—— L'Invasion de 1870–71 dans la Haute-Marne. [With a preface by H. Soret.] pp. xv. 469. *Chaumont,* 1873. fol. **9073. ff. 4.**

—— Les Monuments en Chaldée, en Assyrie et à Babylone d'après les récentes découvertes archéologiques. Avec neuf planches lithographiées, *etc.* pp. ii. 368. *Paris,* 1870. fol. **7702. f. 5.**

—— Nidintabel. La Perse ancienne. [A novel.] pp. ii. 342. *Paris,* 1868. 8°. **12516. i. 3.**

CAVANIS (Marc' Antonio) La Zuca. Ditirambo. *See* Gamba (B.) Collezione delle migliori opere scritte in dialetto Veneziano. Poeti moderni. vol. 5. 1817. 8°.
11431. a. 23.

CAVANNA (Agustin Moreto y) *See* Moreto y Caba

CAVANNA (Betty) *pseud.* [i.e. Elizabeth Cavanna Headley.]
—— Secret Passage . . . A tale. Illustrations by Jean MacLaughlin. pp. 216. *John C. Winston Co.: Philadelphia, Toronto,* [1946.] 8°. **12830. ff. 6.**

—— Spring comes riding. pp. 192. *Lutterworth Press: London,* 1952. 8°. **12834. ee. 19.**

—— Spurs for Suzanna . . . Illustrated by Stanley Lloyd. pp. 229. *Lutterworth Press: London & Redhill,* 1948. 8°.
12829. bb. 18.

CAVANNA (Francesco) *See* Cleomenes iii., *King of Sparta.* Il Cleomene. Drama per musica, *etc.* [With a dedication by F. Cavanna.] [1731.] 12°.
905. k. 3. (3.)

CAVANNA (Guelfo) *See* Periodical Publications.— *Florence.* Rassegna semestrale delle scienze fisico-naturali in Italia, diretta e pubblicata dai dottori G. Cavanna e G. Papasogli. 1875, *etc.* 8°. **P.P. 1449. g.**

—— Ancora sulla polimelia nei batraci anuri. Sopra alcuni visceri del gallo cedrone, *etc.* pp. 21. pl. ii. 1879. *See* Florence.—*Università di Firenze.* Pubblicazioni . . . Sezione di scienze fisiche e naturali. 1877, *etc.* 8°. **Ac. 8848/3.**

—— Il Canto xxv del Purgatorio letto da G. Cavanna nella Sala di Dante in Orsanmichele. pp. 39. *Firenze,* 1908. 8°. [*Lectura Dantis.*] **2284. h. 3/19.**

—— Elementi per una bibliografia italiana intorno all'idrofauna, agli allevamenti degli animali acquatici e alla pesca. pp. viii. 170. *Firenze,* 1880. 8°. **011908. de. 10.**

—— [Another copy.] **11904. cc. 14.**

—— Studi e ricerche sui picnogonidi. Parte prima. Anatomia e biologia. Descrizione di alcuni batraci anuri polimeliani e considerazioni intorno alla polimelia. pp. 38. 1877. *See* Florence.—*Università di Firenze.* Pubblicazioni . . . Sezione di scienze fisiche e naturali. 1877, *etc.* 8°. **Ac. 8848/3.**

CAVANNA (Nicola) *See* Oddi (G.) La Franceschina Testo . . . edito per la prima volta nella sua integrità dal P. N. Cavanna. 1933. 4°. **20001. dd. 28.**

—— Assisi e dintorni. Edizione terza . . . corretta ed ampliata dal P. Michelangelo Bacheca. [With illustrations.] pp. 186. *Assisi,* 1953. 8°. **010151. df. 92.**

—— L'Umbria francescana illustrata. Con 127 fotoincisioni. [With a map.] pp. xv. 415. *Perugia,* 1910. 8°.
10136. aaa. 49.

CAVANNA (Stefano) La Sardegna e le sue ferrovie complementari. Loro storia. Considerazioni e proposte. pp. 104. *Sassari,* 1885. 8°. **8235. e. 3.**

CAVANUS (Ludovicus) [Epigrams.] *Lat.* 1719. *See* Italian Poets. Carmina illustrium poetarum italorum. tom. 3. 1719, *etc.* 8°. **657. a. 18.**

CAVARA (Cesare) *See* Lazarus, *Saint, of Bethany.* Leggenda di Lazzaro, Marta, e Maddalena . . . data nuovamente in luce sopra una rara edizione del secolo xv per cura di C. Cavara. 1853. 8°. **[MISSING.]**

—— *See* Phaedrus, *the Fabulist.* Le Favole di Fedro . . . Tradotte in vario metro da C. Cavara. 1870. 8°.
12305. cc. 40.

CAVARA (Cesare)

—— *See* Pyramus. La Istoria di Piramo e Tisbe, pubblicata per cura di C. Cavara. 1861. 8°. [*Reale Commissione pe'testi di lingua nelle Provincie dell'Emilia. Collezione di opere inedite o rare, etc.* vol. 1.] Ac. **6500**.

—— Armonie popolari . . . scelte dalla edizione bolognese del 1863. pp. 46. *Brescia*, 1878. 4°. **11436**. g. **2**.

—— Poesie popolari erotiche e morali. pp. 116. [*Bologna,*] 1852. 8°. **11436**. e. **56**.

CAVARA (Fridiano)

—— Contribuzione alla micologia lombarda. 1892. *See* Pavia.—*Università di Pavia.—Istituto Botanico dell'Università e Laboratorio Crittogamico.* Atti dell'Istituto Botanico, *etc.* ser. 2. vol. 2. 1888, *etc.* fol. Ac. **107**.

—— Funghi mangerecci e funghi velenosi . . . Seconda edizione riveduta ed ampliata, *etc.* pp. xxiv. 230. pl. LVI. *Milano*, 1919. 16°. **12199**. i. **20**. *One of the " Manuali Hoepli."*

CAVARD (André) Mémoires du Comte de Vordac, Général des Armées de l'Empereur, *etc.* [By A. Cavard.] pp. 326. 1703. 12°. *See* Vordac (de) *Count, pseud.* **168**. a. **14**.

—— [Another edition.] pp. 327. 1711. 12°. *See* Vordac (de) *Count, pseud.* **613**. b. **24**.

CAVARD (Eugène Joseph) Victor de Musset et Henri Beyle Stendhal à l'Armée de réserve, 1800. pp. 23. *Paris*, 1912. 8°. **10600**. c. **14**. (4.)

CAVARD (Pierre) La Cathédrale St. Maurice de Vienne pendant la Révolution. [With illustrations.] pp. 205. *Vienne*, 1935. 8°. **20009**. bb. **23**. *The date in the colophon and on the wrapper is* 1936.

CAVARÉ (Frédéric) De la menstruation envisagée aux trois périodes de la vie utérine. Thèse, *etc.* pp. 35. *Paris*, 1837. 4°. **1184**. h. **16**. (15.)

CAVARÉ (Jean Paul) Dissertation médico-chirurgicale sur les cas qui nécessitent l'opération de l'empyème, *etc.* pp. 16. *Montpellier*, 1804. 4°. **1180**. e. **12**. (23.)

CAVARÉ (Louis) *of Verdun.*

—— Dissertation sur le vomissement des enfans, *etc.* pp. 23. *Strasbourg*, 1815. 4°. [*Collection générale des dissertations de l'École Spéciale de Médecine de Strasbourg.* vol. 21.] **7381***b.

CAVARÉ (Louis) *Professeur à la Faculté de Droit de l'Université de Rennes.*

—— Le Droit international public positif. 2 tom. *Paris*, 1951. 8°. **6956**. dd. **22**.

CAVARÉ (Marie Paul) Faculté de Droit de Paris. Du contrat de société en droit romain. Du contrat de société civile, et spécialement des associations coopératives. Thèse pour le doctorat. pp. iv. 367. *Paris*, 1867. 8°. **5206**. dd. **16**.

CAVARI (Stefano) Relazione delli due mortari fabbricati per servizio della fortezza Urbana da S. Cavari, *etc.* [With folding plates.] pp. 26. *Eredi del Sarti : Bologna*, 1696. 4°. **1140**. h. **32**.

CAVARLAY (Henri Auguste Marie Édouard Aubusson de) *See* Aubusson de Cavarlay.

CAVARNOS (Johannes P.)

—— *See* Gregory, *Saint, Bishop of Nyssa.* Gregorii Nysseni Opera, *etc.* (vol. 8. pt. 1. Opera ascetica. Ediderunt W. Jaeger, J. P. Cavarnos.) 1952, *etc.* 8°. W.P. c. **114/8**.

CAVAROC (Antoine) Dissertation sur la délivrance après l'accouchement ; thèse, *etc.* pp. 28. *Paris*, 1829. 4°. **1184**. c. **15**. (5.)

CAVAROC (F.) Essai sur la poche des eaux. pp. 78. *Paris*, 1869. 4°. [*Collection des thèses soutenues à la Faculté de Médecine de Paris.* An 1869. tom. 3.] **7373**. k. **9**.

CAVAROZ (Narcisse) Quelques mots sur l'emploi des réfrigérants en chirurgie. Thèse, *etc.* pp. 39. *Montpellier*, 1853. 4°. **7379**. b. **14**. (12.)

CAVARRETTA (Giuseppe) Verdi. Il genio, la vita, le opere. pp. 141. *Palermo*, 1899. 8°. **10632**. df. **10**.

CAVASELICE (Giuseppe Maria) La Novena, e i sette venerdì precedenti alla festività del grand'appostolo delle Spagne S. Vincenzo Ferrerio cioè discorsi morali su l'eroiche sue virtù, e . . . miracoli, *etc.* pp. 218. *Napoli*, 1741. 4°. **4828**. e. **15**.

CAVASSE (Auguste) *See* Periodical Publications.—*Paris.* Annuaire général des sciences médicales, par A. Cavasse. 1858, *etc.* 8°. P.P. **3012**. b.

—— De la pneumonie interstitielle du sommet des poumons chez les vieillards. pp. 56. *Paris*, 1868. 4°. [*Collection des thèses soutenues à la Faculté de Médecine de Paris.* An 1868. tom. 3.] **7373**. i. **7**.

—— [Another edition.] pp. 51. *Paris*, 1868. 8°. **7615**. e. **1**. (7.)

CAVASSE (Joseph Auguste) Essai sur les fractures traumatiques des cartilages du larynx. pp. 40. *Paris*, 1859. 4°. [*Collection des thèses soutenues à la Faculté de Médecine de Paris.* An 1859. tom. 3.] **7373**. b. **15**.

CAVASSI (Antonio) Dell'origine ed antica dignità del notariato. Dissertazione. pp. 52. *Udine*, 1814. 8°. [missing.]

CAVASSICO (Bartolomeo) Le Rime di B. Cavassico . . . con introduzione e note di V. Cian, e con illustrazioni linguistiche e lèssico a cura di C. Salvioni. 2 vol. *Bologna*, 1893, 94. 8°. **12226**. de. **17**. (3.) & **18**.

CAVASSI TRACANELLI (Elena Maria) [Sonnets.] *See* Ciparissiano (Teleste) *Pastore Arcade, pseud.* Poesie italiane di rimatrici viventi. 1716. 8°. **1062**. f. **13**.

CAVATIO (Carlo Girolamo) Alleggiamento dello Stato di Milano per le imposte, e loro ripartimenti, *etc.* pp. 792. *G. B. & G. C. Malatesta : Milano*, 1653. fol. **8228**. k. **1**.

CAVATIUS (Jacobus) *See* Cavacius.

CAVATORE. Il Cavatore di tesori. Farsa di autore anonimo. Libera traduzione inedita dal tedesco di Giuseppe Foppa. pp. 37. 1808. *See* Teatro. Il Teatro moderno, *etc.* Terza raccolta. tom. 8. 1796, *etc.* 8°. **639**. d. **12**.

CAVATTONI (Cesare) *See* Castelnovo (G. da) Composizioni latine di Girolamo da Castelnovo, Vicentino, le quali, copiate sopra un manoscritto della Communale di Verona, son poste a luce nelle nozze Da Schio-Marcello. [Edited by C. Cavattoni.] 1864. 8°. **010910**. dd. **44**. (1.)

—— *See* Manzoni (A.) *Count.* L'Inno . . . sulla Pentecoste, *etc.* [Edited by C. Cavattoni.] 1870. 8°. **11436**. b. **61**. (5.)

—— Dante e il Benaco, *etc.* pp. 11. *Verona*, 1866. 8°. **11420**. g. **21**. (5.)

CAVATTONI (Cesare)

—— Documenti fin qua rimasti inediti che risguardano alcuni de' posteri di Dante Alighieri. Pubblicazione del sacerdote C. Cavattoni con alcune sue osservazioni. *See* SMANIA (M. A.) Albo dantesco veronese. 1865. 8°.
11421. h. 29.

—— Memorie intorno alla vita, agli scritti, al culto ed al corpo di S. Zenone . . . S'aggiunge la descrizione della sua basilica. pp. xvi. 280. *Verona,* 1839. 8°.
4828. c. 12.

—— Nell'inaugurazione fatta a' xv di aprile MDCCCLXIX della Biblioteca Comunale e degli Antichi Archivj Veronesi. Discorsi dell'ab. C. Cavattoni e del dott. cav. Giulio Camuzzoni. pp. 19. *Verona,* 1869. fol.
11902. i. 21. (2.)

—— Osservazioni . . . sopra l'operetta intitolata Ritratto di Dante Alighieri, scoperto nuovamente in Verona e illustrato per cura del sacerdote professore Giovanni Sauro. pp. 52. *Verona,* 1843. 8°. **11421. i. 8. (1.)**

—— Storia della Biblioteca Comunale di Verona che dinanzi il corpo municipale . . . lesse C. Cavattoni . . . xv. dicembre M.DCCC.LVII. pp. 23. *Verona,* 1858. 8°.
11900. ee. 11.

—— La Vita della venerabile Maria Clotilde Adelaide, Principessa di Francia e Regina di Sardegna. pp. xi. 249. *Verona,* 1858. fol. **10630. f. 3.**

CAVAYÉ (Célestin) Essai sur la force médicatrice. Thèse, *etc.* pp. 104. *Montpellier,* 1844. 4°.
1182. d. 7. (24.)

CAVAYE (George Ross) *See* DIRECTORIES.—*Military.* [*Scotland.*] The Scottish Military Directory. Compiled by . . . G. R. Cavaye, *etc.* 1890, *etc.* 8°.
P.P.2511.fl.

CAVAYÉ (Henri) Essai sur le tabac. Thèse, *etc.* pp. 47. *Montpellier,* 1856. 4°. **7379. d. 2. (2.)**

CAVAYÉ (Jean Pierre Fortuné Benjamin) Considérations générales sur l'homme dans son enfance. Dissertation, *etc.* pp. 31. *Montpellier,* 1817. 4°.
1180. h. 10. (4.)

CAVAYÉ (P.) Épreuves ou prémières feuilles d'impression [of a tragedy in verse entitled: " Ulysse à Ithaque," by P. Cavayé]. pp. 59. 1806. 8°. *See* ULYSSES, *the Hero.*
11738. aaa. 27. (4.)

CAVAZZA (E.) *See* MEREDITH (George) Modern Love . . . With foreword by E. Cavazza. 1891. 8°.
11649. f. 25.

CAVAZZA (Filippo)

—— Intorno alla origine della umana sociabilità. 1941. *See* ROME.—*The City.*—*Pontificio Museo Missionario Etnologico.* Annali Lateranensi. vol. 5. 1937, *etc.* 8°.
Ac. 2002. i.

CAVAZZA (Francesco G.) *See* MAZZETTI (S.) Alcune aggiunte . . . alle opere dell'Alidosi, del Cavazza, *etc.* 1848. 8°. **20003. c. 53.**

—— Della statua di Gregorio XIII sopra la porta del Palazzo Pubblico in Bologna. Memoria. pp. 47. *Bologna,* 1888. 8°. **7807. k. 11. (7.)**

—— Le Scuole dell'antico Studio di Bologna. 4 pt. 1893-95. *See* BOLOGNA.—~~Regia~~ *Deputazione di Storia Patria per le Provincie di Romagna.* Atti e memorie, *etc.* ser. 3. vol. 11, 12. 1862, *etc.* 8°. **Ac. 6495.**

—— [Another edition.] pp. xiv. 314. lxviii. *Milano,* 1896. 8°. **07807.1.2.**

CAVAZZA (Franco)

—— Le Agitazioni agrarie in provincia di Bologna dal 1910 al 1920, *etc.* pp. xii. 196. *Bologna,* 1940. 8°.
8287. f. 73.

CAVAZZA (Gabriele) Viaggio a Costantinopoli di Sier Lorenzo Bernardo per l'arresto del Bailo Sier Girolamo Lippomano Cav., 1591 Aprile. [Here attributed to G. Cavazza. Edited by Federico Stefani.] pp. 47. 1886. *See* VENICE.—*Deputazione Veneta di Storia Patria.* Monumenti storici. ser. 4. Miscellanea. vol. 4. 1876, *etc.* 4°. **Ac. 6580/2.**

CAVAZZA (Giovanni Antonio) *See* CAVAZZI.

CAVAZZA (Pietro) *See* LYSIAS, *the Orator.* [*In Eratosthenem.*] Orazione contro Eratostene, commentata da P. Cavazza. 1885. 8°. **11391. aaa. 11.**

—— Aristotele e la Costituzione di Atene. Discorso, *etc.* pp. 30. *Firenze,* 1891. 8°. **8009. i. 32.**

—— *See* COSTANZI (V.) Quaestiuncula Aristotelea. [A criticism of P. Cavazza's " Aristotele e la Costituzione di Atene."] [1893.] 8°.
8465. ee. 25. (9.)

CAVAZZANA (Giuseppe)

—— Il Borgo di Casteggio. Note di storia locale. pp. 95. *Casteggio,* 1944. 8°. **010151. ee. 36.**

—— Itinerario gastronomico ed enologico d'Italia. Con ventun tavole, *etc.* pp. 149. *Milano,* 1949. 8°.
7949. l. 49.

CAVAZZANI (Aloysius) De gastrica irritatione a phthiseos speciebus mentita dissertatio inauguralis, *etc.* pp. 13. *Patavii,* 1830. 8°. **7306. b. 7. (4.)**

CAVAZZANI (Giovanni Antonio) *See* BIANCOLINI (G. B. G.) Notizie delle chiese di Verona. [Edited by A. Oliveti, G. A. Cavazzani, and others.] 1749, *etc.* 4°.
661. d. 5–13. (1.)

CAVAZZANI SENTIERI (Aida) Carmelita Manara nell'Italia eroica dell'unità. Con appendice e documenti inediti, *etc.* [With plates, including a portrait.] pp. 326. *Milano,* 1937. 8°. **10634. i. 29.**

—— Ugo Foscolo e i primordi del Risorgimento nazionale. pp. ix. 182. *Modena,* 1934. 8°. [*Collezione storica del Risorgimento italiano.* ser. 1. vol. 9.] **W.P. 1538/9.**

CAVAZZI ( ) *See* LABAT (Eugène) *pseud.* [i.e. — Cavazzi.]

CAVAZZI (Alfonso) *See also* PERRASIO (Orieno) *pseud.* [i.e. A. Cavazzi.]

—— Adelaide. Tragedia. pp. 94. *Modena,* 1711. 8°.
638. d. 21. (3.)

—— [Another copy.] **85. b. 27. (3.)**

—— Motezuma, Imperadore del Messico. Tragedia. pp. 135. *Modena,* 1709. 8°. **638. d. 21. (1.)**

—— [Another copy.] **85. b. 27. (1.)**

—— Niso ed Eurialo. Tragedia. pp. 126. *Modena,* 1710. 8°. **638. d. 21. (2.)**

—— [Another copy.] **85. b. 27. (2.)**

—— Pertinace. Tragedia. pp. 108. *Modena,* 1712. 8°.
85. b. 28. (1.)

CAVAZZI (Francesco) Vie et rajeunissement. Une nouvelle méthode générale de traitement et mes expériences de rajeunissement de Bologne et de Paris . . . Mémoires lus à la Société de Médecine de Paris par les Drs Louis Dartigues et Léopold-Lévi, avec la discussion relative, notes et réponses de l'auteur, *etc.* pp. 72. pl. XVII. *Paris; Bologne* [printed], 1934. 8°.
7580. r. 11.

CAVAZZI (GIOVANNI ANTONIO) Istorica descrizione de'tre regni, Congo, Matamba, et Angola, situati nell'Etiopia inferiore occidentale e delle missioni apostoliche esercitateui da Religiosi Capuccini . . . compilata dal P. G. A. Cauazzi . . . e nel presente stile ridotta dal P. Fortunato Alamandini. [With plates.] pp. 933.   *G. Monti:*
Bologna, 1687. fol.   **569. i. 9.**

—— [Another copy.]   **G. 7210.**

—— [Another edition.] [With plates.] pp. 785.   *Nelle*
stampe dell'Agnelli: Milano, 1690. 4°.   **4767. ff. 15.**

—— [Another copy.]   **G. 7153.**

—— Relation historique de l'Éthiopie occidentale : contenant la description des royaumes de Congo, Angolle, & Matamba, traduite de l'Italien . . . & augmentée de plusieurs relations portugaises des meilleurs auteurs . . . par . . . J. B. Labat. [With folding plates.] 5 tom.   *Paris,*
1732. 12°.   **279. a. 15-19.**

—— [Another copy.]   **G. 12395-99.**

—— Historische Beschreibung der . . . drey Königreichen, Congo, Matamba, vnd Angola, vnd der jenigen Apostolischen Missionen, so von denen P.P. Capucinern daselbst verrichtet worden. Von P. J. A. Cavazzi . . . zusammen getragen, vnd nachmals durch P. Fortunatum Alamandini . . . in gegenwärtigen Form gerichtet, anietzo aber auss dem Welschen in die Teutsche Sprach übersetzet. [With plates.] pp. 1030. *J. Jäcklin: München*, 1694. 4°.
                                                      4765. b. 16.

CAVAZZI (JOANNES ANTONIUS) *See* CAVAZZI (Giovanni A.)

CAVAZZI (LUIGI) La Diaconia di S. Maria in Via Lata e il monastero di S. Ciriaco. Memorie storiche. [With illustrations.] pp. xviii. 446. *Roma*, 1908. 8°.
                                                      4606. g. 1.

CAVAZZO (GIOVANNI LUCA) *Count della Somaglia.* Compendio della storia di Milano. [With portraits.] pp. 108. pl. III. **L.P.** *Milano*, 1834. 4°.   **574. l. 15.**

—— Monaco di Baviera. Lettere. pp. 128. **L.P.**
Milano, 1838. 8°.   **573. h. 28.**

CAVAZZOCCA (FRANCESCO) *See* GRAY (Thomas) *the Poet.* [*Elegy written in a Country Churchyard.—Translations.*] Elegia di Tommaso Gray sopra un cimitero di campagna, tradotta . . . in più lingue [by F. Cavazzocca and others], *etc.* 1843. fol.   **1465. k. 23.**

CAVAZZOLI (GALASSO DE') Galassii Vicentini Theseidos libri tres. Praemisso Carmine ad posteros de laudibus et commodis urbis et agri Vicentini. pp. 102.   *Vicetiae,*
1874. 8°.   **11403. aaa. 4.**
One of an edition of 100 *copies.*

CAVAZZONI (MARCO ANTONIO)

—— *See* JEPPESEN (K.) Die italienische Orgelmusik am Anfang des Cinquecento. Die "Recerchari, motetti, canzoni, libro primo" des Marco Antonio—Cavazzoni—da Bologna, *etc.* [With facsimiles and transcriptions of the music.] 1943. fol.   **M. F. 1831.**

CAVAZZONI (VIRGINIA BAZANI) *See* BAZZANI CAVAZZONI.

CAVAZZONI PEDERZINI (ANDREA) *See* CALORI CESIS (F.) Commemorazione [of A. Cavazzoni Pederzini]. [1864.] *s. sh.* 8°.   **10630. dd. 2. (10.)**

CAVAZZONI PEDERZINI (FORTUNATO) *See* DANTE ALIGHIERI.[Single Works-Convito.-Italian]Il Convito . . . con note . . . di F. Cavazzoni Pederzini . . . e d'altri. 1831. 8°.   **1062. g. 19.**

CAVAZZONI PEDERZINI (FORTUNATO)

—— *See* THOMAS, *de Aquileia.* La Guerra d'Atila. [Edited by F. Cavazzoni Pederzini.] 1843. 16°.   **1440. a. 13.**

—— Dialoghi filosofici, con altre prose minori. pp. 345.
Modena, 1842. 8°.   **12225. d. 7.**

CAVAZZONI PEDERZINI (LUIGI) Memoria storica sul governo che della Badia di Nonantola ebbe S. Carlo Borromeo, *etc.* pp. 36. *Modena*, 1836. 8°.
                                                    4520. bbb. 1. (6.)

CAVAZZONI ZANOTTI (FRANCESCO MARIA) *See also* PILIACO (Orito) *pseud.* [i.e. F. M. Cavazzoni Zanotti.]

—— *See* ANSALDI (C. I.) Casti Innocentis Ansaldi . . . Vindiciæ Maupertuisianæ ab animadversionibus F. M. Zanotti [in his "Ragionamento . . . sopra un libro franzese del Signore di Maupertuis intitolato: Essai de philosophie morale"], *etc.* 1754. 4°.   **90. i. 33.**

—— *See* BARBIERI (L.) *Count.* Dissertazione, e parere . . . su la controversia tra li signori Clemente Baroni de Cavalcabò, e F. M. Zanotti intorno la natura della felicità. 1763. 8°.   **T. 2362. (2.)**

—— *See* BERTOLDO.   Bertoldo, con Bertoldino e Cacasenno, in ottava rima, *etc.* [Canto VI by F. M. Cavazzoni Zanotti.] 1736. 4°.   **639. l. 17.**

—— —— 1737. 8°.   **11431. bb. 19**

—— —— [1737.] 12°.   **1063. f. 3.**

—— —— 1739. 8°.   **1063. f. 4.**

—— *See* BERTOLDO. Bertoldo, Bertoldino e Cacasenno. [Canto VI by F. M. Cavazzoni Zanotti.] 1791. 8°. [*Parnaso italiano.* tom. 55.]   **240. h. 15.**

—— —— 1802. 8°.   **11431. bb. 14.**

—— —— 1842. 8°.   **1464. k. 16.**

—— *See* BERTOLDO. Traduzion dal Toscan in lengua Veneziana de Bertoldo, Bertoldin e Cacasseno, *etc.* [With the text of the Tuscan original, canto VI of which was written by F. M. Cavazzoni Zanotti.] 1747. 8°.
                                                      84. b. 33.

—— *See* BOLOGNA.—*Instituto delle Scienze ed Arti Liberali.* De Bononiensi scientiarum et artium instituto . . . commentarii. [Edited by F. M. Cavazzoni Zanotti.] 1731, *etc.* 4°.   **659. g. 6-15.**

—— *See* EPHEMERIDES. Ephemeridum coelestium motuum Manfredii errata insigniora . . . accedente præfatione F. M. Zanotti. 1730. 8°.   **532. b. 19. (3.)**

—— *See* FANTUZZI (G.) Notizie della vita e degli scritti di F. M. Zanotti, *etc.* 1778. 8°.   **10631. c. 27.**

—— *See* MAGNANI (A.) Orationes habitae in publico Archigymnasio Bononiensi, *etc.* (De laudibus F. M. Zanotti.) 1794. fol.   **1876. f. 3.**

—— *See* MONTI (Antonio) *Canonico.* Orazione . . . all'occasione de' solenni funerali del chiarissimo uomo Francesco Maria Zanotti. 1779. 4°.   **10630. ff. 50.**

—— *See* MORGAGNI (G. B.) Carteggio tra Giambattista Morgagni e F. M. Zanotti. 1875. 8°.   **10909. i. 3.**

—— *See* PROVENZAL (D.) I Riformatori della bella letteratura italiana . . . F. M. Zanotti, *etc.* 1900. 8°.
                                                      11853. aaa. 1.

CAVAZZONI ZANOTTI (Francesco Maria)

—— *See* Salani (P.) Il Canzoniere . . . Raccolto da F. M. Zanotti, *etc.* 1801. 4°.   **11431. ee. 45.**

—— Opere. [With a dedication by G. Lucchesini, and a portrait.] 8 tom. *Bologna*, 1779–99. 4°. **12225. ee. 7.**

—— Opere scelte. [With a portrait.] 2 vol.   *Milano*, 1818. 8°. [*Collezione de' classici italiani.* vol. 273, 274.]
12201.p.1/273,274.

—— Francisci Mariae Zanotti Carmina. Editio altera . . . auctior. pp. viii. 56. *Bononiae*, 1757. 8°.
1062. e. 33. (2.)

—— [Another copy.]   **1213. m. 29.**

—— Della forza de' corpi che chiamano viva libri tre, *etc.* pp. xx. 311. *Bologna*, 1752. 4°.   **233. i. 3.**

—— Dell'arte poetica ragionamenti cinque, *etc.* pp. xii. 401. *Bologna*, 1768. 8°.   **1062. k. 32.**

—— Lettere del Sig. F. M. Zanotti, del Pad. Giambatista Martini . . . del Pad. Giovenale Sacchi . . . nelle quali si propongono, e risolvono alcuni dubbj appartenenti al trattato : Della divisione del tempo nella musica, nel ballo, e nella poesia . . . e all'altro : Delle quinte successive nel contrappunto, e delle regole degli accompagnamenti [both works by G. Sacchi], *etc.* pp. 59. *Milano*, 1782. 4°.   **557*. e. 6. (3.)**

—— [Selected letters.] 1830. *See* Italian Classics. Collezione de' classici italiani. vol. 351. 1804, *etc.* 8°.
12201.p.1/351.

—— Orazione . . . in lode della pittura, della scoltura, e dell'architettura . . . con due altre orazioni d'incerti autori [or rather by F. M. Cavazzoni Zanotti] nell'una delle quali si impugnano la proposizione, e le ragioni dell'orazione sopra detta, nell'altra si defendono. pp. 82. MS. NOTE. *Bologna*, [1750.] 8°.   **T. 2286. (2.)**

—— [Another copy.]   **75. a. 31.**

—— [Another edition.] *See* Albèri (E.) Tesoro della prosa italiana, *etc.* 1841. 4°.   **12226. g. 13.**

—— Poesie volgari, e latine. [Edited by Francesco Algarotti.] pp. xvi. 112. *Firenze*, 1734. 8°.
1085. m. 25. (2.)

—— [Another copy.]   **83. d. 7.**

—— Poesie . . . Italiane e latine colla traduzione di queste in endecasillabi fatta dal P. Pier Maria Brocchieri. 2 pt. *Nizza*, 1785. 8°.   **1062. b. 34.**

—— Poesie volgari . . . accresciute di gran numero in questa seconda edizione. (Sermone del Signor Conte Francesco Algarotti al Signor Eustachio Manfredi.) [With a preface by Count Gregorio Casali and a portrait.] pp. xxxxiv. 134. *Bologna*, 1757. 8°.   **1062. e. 33. (1.)**

—— Raccolta di alcune poesie volgari e latine, *etc.* pp. 118. *Milano*, 1759. 12°.   **11427. aaa. 28.**

—— Rime. 1791. *See* Rubbi (A.) Parnaso italiano. *etc.* tom. 51. 1784, *etc.* 8°.   **240. h. 11.**

—— Sopra le figure circoscritte al circolo ed alla sfera, *etc.* 1753. *See* Gori (A. F.) Symbolae litterariae, *etc.* vol. 10. 1748, *etc.* 8°.   **787. g. 22.**

—— [Fourteen sonnets.] 1711. *See* Gobbi (A.) Scelta di sonetti, *etc.* pt. 3. 1709, *etc.* 8°.   **240. k. 16.**

—— [Four Latin elegies.] 1756. *See* Morei (M. G.) Arcadum carmina, *etc.* pt. 2. 1757, *etc.* 8°.   **78. c. 34.**

CAVAZZONI ZANOTTI (Giovanni Pietro) *See also* Larisseate (Trisalgo) *pseud.* [i.e. G. P. Cavazzoni Zanotti.]

—— *See* Barotti (G. A.) Del dominio delle donne, *etc.* [Edited by G. P. Cavazzoni Zanotti.] 1745. 8°.
8415. ee. 27. (1.)

—— *See* Bertoldo. Bertoldo, Bertoldino e Cacasenno. [Canto III by G. P. Cavazzoni Zanotti.] 1791. 8°. [*Parnaso italiano.* tom. 55.]   **240. h. 15, 16.**

—— —— 1802. 8°.   **11431. bb. 14.**

—— *See* Bertoldo. Traduzion dal Toscan in lengua Veneziana de Bertoldo, Bertoldin e Cacasseno, *etc.* [With the text of the Tuscan original, canto III of which was written by G. P. Cavazzoni Zanotti.] 1747. 8°.
84. b. 33.

—— *See* Bertoldo. Bertoldo, con Bertoldino e Cacasenno in ottava rima, *etc.* [Canto III by G. P. Cavazzoni Zanotti.] 1736. 4°.   **639. l. 17.**

—— —— 1737. 8°.   **11431. bb. 19.**

—— —— [1737.] 12°.   **1063. f. 3.**

—— —— 1739. 8°.   **1063. f. 4.**

—— —— 1842. 8°.   **1464. k. 16.**

—— *See* Guidalotti Franchini (G.) Vita di D. M. Viani pittor bolognese, *etc.* [Edited by G. P. Cavazzoni Zanotti.] 1716. 8°.   **117. a. 56.**

—— *See* Malvasia (C. C.) *Count.* Le Pitture di Bologna . . . Con nuova e copiosa aggiunta [by G. P. Cavazzoni Zanotti]. 1706. 12°.   **673. a. 26.**

—— —— 1732. 12°.   **171. b. 21.**

—— —— 1766. 12°.   **52. b. 31.**

—— *See* Manfredi (E.) Opere idrauliche. (Vita di Eustachio Manfredi scritta da G. Cavazzoni Zanotti.) 1822. 4°.   **537. l. 6.**

—— *See* Manfredi (E.) Rime, *etc.* [Edited by G. P. Cavazzoni Zanotti.] 1748. 8°.   **240. i. 42.**

—— *See* Provenzal (D.) I Riformatori della bella letteratura italiana . . . G. Zanotti, *etc.* 1900. 8°.
11853. aaa. 1.

—— *See* Salani (P.) Il Canzoniere . . . colla vita dell'autore [by G. P. Cavazzoni Zanotti], *etc.* 1801. 4°.
11431. ee. 45.

—— *See* Salani (P.) Poesie diverse. (Brevi memorie intorno alla vita del padre abate D. P. Salani descritta da G. Zanotti.) 1761. 4°.   **11431. cc. 50.**

—— [Selected letters.] *See* Fabri (D.) Delle lettere familiari d'alcuni Bolognesi del secolo decimottavo, *etc.* vol. 1. 1820. 8°.   **1454. c. 2.**

—— [Selected letters.] 1830. *See* Italian Classics. Collezione de' classici italiani. vol. 351. 1804, *etc.* 8°.
12201.p.1/351.

—— Lettere familiari scritte ad un amico in difesa del conte Carlo Cesare Malvasia, autore della Felsina Pittrice. *See* Malvasia (C. C.) *Count.* Felsina pittrice, *etc.* tom. 2. 1841. 8°.   **1402. k. 36.**

—— Avvertimenti . . . per lo incamminamento di un giovane alla pittura. (In laude della pittura e della poesia : Sermone al . . . signor G. Zanotti. [In verse.]) pp. 135. *Bologna*, 1756. 8°.   **7868.a.38.**

CAVAZZONI ZANOTTI (GIOVANNI PIETRO)

—— Alcuni avvertimenti per lo incamminamento di un giovane alla pittura. *See* PIAZZETTA (G. B.) Studj di pittura, *etc.* 1760. *obl.* fol.   59. c. 15.

—— [Another edition.] *See* CARRER (L.) Ammaestramenti per la pittura, *etc.* 1839. 12°.   1422. a. 12.

—— Il Claustro di San Michele in Bosco di Bologna de' Monaci Olivetani dipinto dal famoso Lodovico Carracci e da altri eccellenti maestri usciti dalla sua scuola descritto ed illustrato da G. Cavazzoni Zanotti. Con la compiuta serie delle dipinture diligentemente disegnate, *etc.* [With a portrait of the author.] pp. 117. pl. 47.   *Bologna*, 1776. fol.   650. a. 6.

—— Dialogo di G. P. Cavazzoni Zanotti . . . in difesa di Guido Reni. *See* BARUFFALDI (G.) *the Elder.* Osservazioni critiche . . . nelle quali esaminandosi la Lettera toccante le Considerazioni del marchese G. G. Orsi sopra la Manièra di ben pensare ne' componimenti [by D. Bouhours], scritta da un Accademico *₊* [i.e. Count F. Montani], *etc.* 1735. 4°. [*Considerazioni del marchese G. G. Orsi, etc.* tom. 2.]   89. g. 14.

—— [Another edition.] *See* MALVASIA (C. C.) *Count.* Felsina pittrice, *etc.* tom. 2. 1841. 8°.   1402. k. 36.

—— Didone. [A tragedy. In verse.] 1825. *See* ITALIAN CLASSICS. Collezione de' classici italiani. vol. 341. 1804, *etc.* 8°.   12201.p.1/341.

—— Nuovo fregio di gloria a Felsina sempre pittrice, nella vita di Lorenzo Pasinelli pittor bolognese, *etc.* pp. 120. *Bologna*, 1703. 8°.   1422. a. 2.

—— [Another copy.]   276. a. 20.
Cropped.

—— Le Pitture di Pellegrino Tibaldi e di Niccolò Abbati esistenti nell'Instituto di Bologna descritte ed illustrate da G. Zanotti. pp. 45. pl. XXXXI. *Venezia*, 1756. fol.   688. l. 9.

—— [Another copy.]   3 Tab. 25.

—— Poesie. [With a portrait.] 3 pt.   *Bologna*, 1741–45. 8°.   240. l. 16–18.

—— [Another copy.]   1062. e. 30–32.
Imperfect; wanting leaves Ff 1 and 2 of pt. 1.

—— Prendendo l'abito religioso nel venerabil monastero di S. Chiara d'Apiro la Signora Geltrude Maria Virginia Amadesi . . . co i nomi di Suor Maria Geltrude Maddalena Catarina. [A collection of complimentary verses by various authors, edited by G. P. Cavazzoni Zanotti.] *Bologna*, 1719. 8°.   11431. aaa. 55. (1.)

—— Storia dell'Accademia Clementina di Bologna aggregata all'Instituto delle Scienze e dell'Arti. [With portraits.] 2 vol. *Bologna*, 1739. 4°.
Dept.of Prints & Drawings.
—— [Another copy.]   658. h. 6, 7.

—— [Another copy.]   129. f. 6, 7.

—— Vita di Eustachio Manfredi. [With a portrait.] pp. 74. *Bologna*, 1745. 4°.   10633. k. 50.

—— [Selected sonnets.] 1711. *See* GOBBI (A.) Scelta di sonetti, *etc.* pt. 3. 1709, *etc.* 8°.   240. k. 16.

—— [Selected poems.] *See* ITALIAN POEMS. Poesie italiane di rimatori viventi, *etc.* 1717. 8°.   240. l. 21.

CAVAZZONUS ZANOTTUS (FRANCISCUS MARIA) *See* CAVAZZONI ZANOTTI (Francesco M.)

CAVAZZUTI (GIUSEPPE) *See* TIRABOSCHI (G.) Carteggio fra Girolamo Tiraboschi e Clementino Vannetti, 1776–1793. Per cura di G. Cavazzuti, *etc.* 1912. 8°.   10902. g. 30.

—— Di Alfonso III. d'Este. 1907. *See* MODENA.— *Deputazioni di Storia Patria per le Provincie Modenesi, etc.* Atti e memorie, *etc.* ser. 5. vol. 5. 1892, *etc.* 8°.   ∫ Antiche   Ac. 6520.

—— Esposizione del canto XIII. dell'Inferno di Dante. pp. 45. *Modena*, 1906. 4°.   11421. dd. 17.

—— Federico Carandini e i suoi scritti storico-militari. pp. 76. lvii. *Modena*, 1906. 8°.   011853. i. 76.

—— Lodovico Antonio Muratori, 1672–1750. [With a portrait.] pp. 118. *Modena*, 1950. 8°.   010632. cc. 15.

—— Lodovico Castelvetro. pp. xvi. 220. 61.   *Modena*, 1903. 8°.   10633. g. 5.

—— Monaldo Leopardi e i redattori della "Voce della verità." 1937. 8°. *See* MODENA.—Reale Accademia di Scienze, Lettere ed Arti. Memorie, *etc.* ser. 5. vol. 2. 1833, *etc.* 4°, *etc.*   Ac. 92.

—— Studi sulla letteratura politico-militare dall'assedio di Firenze alla guerra dei trent'anni. pp. xiii. 231. *Modena*, 1905. 8°.   011852. g. 71.

CAVAZZUTI (PIETRO)

—— Bellini a Londra. pp. 77. pl. 2. *Firenze*, 1945. 8°.   10630. k. 19.

ČAVČIĆ (MAURO VETRANIĆ) *See* VETRANIĆ ČAVČIĆ.

CAVE. The Cave of Death. A romance of Lake Superior. pp. 40. *Cameron & Ferguson: Glasgow*, [1871.] 8°.   12704. bbb. 33.

—— The Cave of Death. An elegy. Inscribed to the memory of the deceased relations of the author. [By Thomas Tournay.] pp. 24. *Printed for the Author: Canterbury*, 1776. 4°.   11656. e. 85.

—— [Another copy.] The Cave of Death, *etc.* *Canterbury*, [1776.] 4°.   T. 919. (9.)
Cropped.

—— Hid in a Cave; and The Selfish Little Girl, *etc.* pp. 126. *Cassell & Co.: London*, [1869.] 8°.   12808. ff. 12.

CAVE.

—— Cave sérieux & intéressant: ou Avis salutaire adressé à la Grande Bretagne: où la Monarchie universelle envahie par la Fr**** se voit tout à découvert, *etc.* [By Jean Baptiste Denis.] pp. 160. *Gibraltar*, 1738. 8°.   8132. b. 8.
The imprint is fictitious. Printed in London.

CAVE AND COMPANY. Cave's New London. The History of London; or, the Stranger's guide through the British metropolis and its environs, *etc.* no. 1. pp. 1–24. *Cave & Co.: London*, 1822. 8°.   10351. f. 36.
No more published.

CAVE HOUSE SCHOOLS. *See* UXBRIDGE.

CAVE RESEARCH GROUP. *See* ENGLAND.

CAVE SCIENCE. *See* ENGLAND.—*British Speleological Association.*

CAVE, *Family of, of Yateley.*

—— *See* CAVE (Thomas S.) A Family Record, 1500–1729. [On the Cave family of Yateley.] [1933.] 8°.   9918. a. 49.

CAVE, *Family of, of York.*

—— *See* COOPER (Thomas P.) The Caves of York : topographical draughtsmen, artists, engravers and copper-plate printers, *etc.* 1934. 8°. **9917. bb. 44.**

CAVE ( ) *Dr.* Dr. Cave's Advanced Tables, *etc.* no. 1. [*London ?* 1877.] 16°. **1801. d. 1. (93.)**

CAVE (ALEXANDER JAMES EDWARD) On the Human Crania from New Guinea collected by Lord Moyne's expedition. *See* GUINNESS (Walter E.) *Baron Moyne.* Walkabout, *etc.* 1936. 8°. **010028. h. 24.**

CAVE (ALFRED) *See* DORNER (J. A.) A System of Christian Doctrine . . . Translated by . . . A. Cave . . . and . . . J. S. Banks. 1880, *etc.* 8°. [*Clark's Foreign Theological Library.* ser. 5. vol. 4, 5, 9, 10.] **3625. dd.**

—— *See* SPENCE (Henry D. M.) *Dean of Gloucester,* and EXELL (J. S.) The Pulpit Commentary, *etc.* (Leviticus. Introductions [by] R. Collins . . . A. Cave, *etc.*) 1880, *etc.* 8°. **3131. d. 1/3.**

—— The Battle of the Standpoints. The Old Testament and the Higher Criticism. pp. 58. *Eyre & Spottiswoode : London,* 1890. 8°. **3155. de. 16.**

—— The Bible View of Sin. *See* FAITH. The Ancient Faith in Modern Light, *etc.* 1897. 8°. **4372. cc. 27.**

—— The Church as a Means of Grace. An address, *etc.* pp. 28. *Hodder & Stoughton : London,* [1886.] 16°. **4479. a. 29. (2.)**

—— The Inspiration of the Old Testament inductively considered, *etc.* pp. xii. 468. *London,* 1888. 8°. [*Congregational Lectures.* New series. no. 7.] **4462. i. 15.**

—— An Introduction to Theology : its principles, its branches, its results, and its literature. pp. xv. 576. *T. & T. Clark : Edinburgh,* 1885. 8°. **03560 .g.5.**

—— Second edition, largely rewritten. pp. xiii. 610. *T. & T. Clark : Edinburgh,* 1896. 8°. **3554. gg. 16.**

—— The Scriptural Doctrine of Sacrifice. pp. 524. *T. & T. Clark : Edinburgh,* 1877. 8°. **4257. d. 1.**

—— New edition, *etc.* pp. 550. *T. & T. Clark : Edinburgh,* 1890. 8°. **4256. f. 4.**

—— The Spiritual World. pp. viii. 254. *Hodder & Stoughton : London,* 1894. 8°. **4371. e. 21.**

—— The Story of the Founding of Hackney College, *etc.* pp. 64. *Printed for private circulation : London,* [1898.] 8°. **8366. bbb. 28.**

CAVE (ALFRED THOMAS TOWNSHEND VERNEY) *Baron Braye.*

—— *See* EDGELL (A. T. T. W.) afterwards CAVE (A. T. T. V.) *Baron Braye.*

CAVE (AMBROSE) *See* WALTERS (R.) The Tryal of Rowland Walters . . . and Ambrose Cave, Gent., for murthering of Sir Charles Pymm, Bart., *etc.* 1688. fol. **L.R.404.n.5.(17.)**

CAVE (ANGELA) The Mermaid Tavern. The Newdigate prize poem, 1928. pp. 10. *Basil Blackwell : Oxford,* 1928. 8°. **011644. eee. 71.**

CAVE (ANN ESTELLA SARAH PENFOLD) *Countess Cave. See* MALLET (*Sir* Charles E.) Lord Cave . . . With an introductory chapter by Countess Cave, *etc.* [With portraits.] 1931. 8°. **10823. d. 16.**

CAVE (ANN ESTELLA SARAH PENFOLD) *Countess Cave.*

—— Ant Antics. Presented and illustrated by Estella Cave. With accompaniments by Stanley Baldwin, Jack Spratt, Tom, Dick & Harry, *etc.* pp. 115. *John Murray : London,* 1933. 4°. **12331. dd. 29.**

—— Memories of Old Richmond, with some sidelights on English history . . . With sketches and a plan by George A. Brandram, *etc.* pp. xiii. 326. *John Murray : London,* 1922. 8°. **010368. ee. 54.**

—— Odds and Ends of My Life. [With plates.] pp. xi. 215. *John Murray : London,* 1929. 8°. **10824. df. 11.**

—— Three Journeys, *etc.* [With plates, including portraits.] pp. 286. *Thornton Butterworth : London,* 1928. 8°. **010028. g. 5.**

CAVE (ARTHUR)

—— Government and you, *etc.* pp. xi. 178. *Methuen & Co. : London,* 1952. 8°. **8140. df. 18.**

CAVE (ARTHUR CHARLES)

—— The Quartermaster's Handbook. pp. 31. *Gale & Polden : Aldershot,* [1943.] 8°. **8837. g. 50.**

—— The Quartermaster's Handbook . . . Second edition. pp. 47. *Gale & Polden : Aldershot,* [1944.] 8°. **8839. b. 10.**

CAVE (B.) *of Birmingham.* Bunyan's Pilgrim's Progress . . . explained in easy verse. In which is attempted to shew . . . the spiritual meaning of that celebrated work, *etc.* pp. 32. *The Author : Birmingham,* 1812. 12°. **4410. bb. 3.**

CAVE (BRIAN) *See* CAVUS.

CAVE (BRYAN WILLIAM CAVE-BROWNE)

—— 'To-Night is on the Mountain.' Poems 1941–1946. pp. vii. 30. *Oxford University Press : London,* 1948. 8°. **11658. aaa. 212.**

CAVE (C. P. HADDON)

—— *See* HOCKING (Douglas M.) and CAVE (C. P. H.) Air Transport in Australia. 1951. 8°. **8236. e. 72.**

CAVE (CHARLES) Poems. pp. 50. *A. L. Humphreys : London,* 1917. 16°. **011651. h. 152.**

CAVE (CHARLES HENRY) A History of Banking in Bristol. From 1750 to 1899. Containing numerous portraits, *etc.* pp. xvii. 292. **L.P.** *Privately printed : Bristol,* 1899. 4°. **8248. k. 6.**

CAVE (CHARLES JOHN PHILIP) Clouds & Weather Phenomena, for artists and other lovers of nature. [With plates.] pp. vi. 29. *University Press : Cambridge,* 1926. 8°. **8753. de. 12.**

—— Clouds & Weather Phenomena . . . A new edition. Revised and with many new photographs. pp. viii. 22. *University Press : Cambridge,* 1943. 8°. **8753. b. 30.**

—— Medieval Carvings in Exeter Cathedral . . . With A Note on the Art of the Exeter Carvers by Nikolaus Pevsner. pp. 43. pl. 64. *Penguin Books : London,* 1953. 8°. [*King Penguin Books.* no. 62.] **12208. a. 4/62.** *The number on the flyleaf is given in error as* 41.

—— Roof Bosses in Medieval Churches. An aspect of Gothic sculpture . . . Illustrated with telephotographs. pp. viii. 235. *University Press : Cambridge,* 1948. 4°. **7877. f. 2.**

CAVE (CHARLES JOHN PHILIP)

—— The Roof Bosses of Lincoln Minster. [With plates.] pp. 12. *Friends of Lincoln Cathedral: Lincoln,* 1949. 8°. [*Lincoln Minster Pamphlets.* no. 3.] W.P. **3495.**

—— The Roof Bosses of the Cathedral Church of Christ, Canterbury. [With plates.] pp. 22. [*Canterbury,*] 1934. 8°. [*Canterbury Papers.* no. 4.] W.P. **9780/4.**

—— The Roof Bosses of Winchester Cathedral. [With plates.] pp. 22. *Friends of Winchester Cathedral: Winchester,* 1935. 8°. **07815. eee. 67.**

—— The Roof Bosses of Winchester Cathedral. [With plates.] pp. 20. *Friends of Winchester Cathedral: Winchester,* 1953. 8°. **7823. e. 40.**

—— The Structure of the Atmosphere in clear weather. A study of soundings with pilot balloons. pp. xii. 144. *University Press: Cambridge,* 1912. 4°. **8754. d. 2.**

CAVE (CHARLES JOHN PHILIP) and DINES (JOHN SOMERS)

—— Soundings with Pilot Balloons in the Isles of Scilly, November and December 1911. *Meteorological Office: London,* 1920. 4°. [*Geophysical Memoirs.* no. 14.] B.S. **26/9. (14.)**

CAVE (EASTWOOD) Poems from Dreary Court. pp. 170. *J. C. Hotten: London,* 1873. 8°. **11652. bb. 32.**

CAVÉ (EDMOND LUDOVIC AUGUSTE) *See* CORALLI (J.) La Tentation, ballet-opéra . . . par MM. * * * [i.e. E. L. A. Cavé and A. Dittmer] et Coraly, *etc.* 1832. 8°. **11738. bbb. 34. (2.)**

—— *See* HURTADO ( ) Le Diable à Séville, opéra-comique . . . par M. Hurtado [and E. L. A. Cavé]. 1831. 8°. **11738. bbb. 34. (1.)**

—— *See* L . . . . (Adolphe de) Un Tableau de famille . . . comédie en un acte, par A. de L . . . [i.e. A. de Leuven] et * * * [i.e. E. L. A. Cavé and A. Dittmer]. 1829. 8°. **11738. h. 29. (2.)**

—— *See* LANGLÉ (J. A. F.) Les Biographes, comédie . . . par M. F. Langlé et * * * [i.e. E. L. A. Cavé and A. Dittmer]. 1826. 8°. **11738. bbb. 34. (3.)**

—— *See* LANGLÉ (J. A. F.) Les Deux élèves . . . Comédie vaudeville . . . par Langlé, Rochefort et * * * [i.e. E. L. A. Cavé and A. Dittmer]. 1827. 8°. **11738. g. 37. (2.)**

—— *See* LUC ( ) le *Sieur, pseud.* Une Commission de censure, scènes non historiques . . . Seconde édition publiée . . . par E. C . . . . [i.e. E. Cavé] et G. F. D. 1827. 8°. **11738. bbb. 34. (7.)**

CAVE (EDMUND) *See* RUSSELL (Francis) *M.A., Barrister-at-Law.* Russell on the Power and Duty of an Arbitrator . . . Thirteenth edition. By E. Cave . . . and E. Wetton. 1935. 8°. **6327.c.9.**

CAVE (EDNA SELENA)

—— Craft Work, *etc.* [With plates.] pp. xix. 272. *D. Appleton-Century Co.: New York, London,* 1940. 8°. **07945. h. 65.**

CAVE (EDWARD) *Printer. See* NICHOLS (John) *F.S.A., Printer.* A Prefatory Introduction descriptive of the Rise and Progress of the (Gentleman's) Magazine, with anecdotes of the projector [E. Cave], *etc.* 1821. 8°. [*Gentleman's Magazine.* General Index, 1787–1818.] **2121.h.**

CAVE (EDWARD) *Printer.*

—— *See* PERIODICAL PUBLICATIONS.—*London.* The Gentleman's Magazine, *etc.* [1731–54 edited by E. Cave.] 1731, *etc.* 8°. **2120.f.–2121.h.**

CAVE (EDWARD) *Sporting Journalist. See* ATKINS (Charles) Game Bird Shooting . . . Edited by E. Cave. 1931. 8°. **20016. c. 12.**

—— *See* DUFF (James) *Writer on Archery.* Bows and Arrows . . . Edited by E. Cave, *etc.* 1927. 8°. [MISSING.]

—— *See* WHITFORD (Caleb B.) Training the Bird Dog . . . New edition . . . by E. Cave, *etc.* 1928. 8°. **07295. ee. 38.**

CAVE (EDWARD HENRY PAUL) *See* KOHNSTAM (Geoffrey L. S.) and CAVE (E. H. P.) The Radiological Examination of the Male Urethra, *etc.* 1925. 8°. **7470. i. 30.**

CAVE (ELSIE) Poems for Children. pp. 53. *Morland: Amersham,* 1920. 8°. **011648. f. 140.**

CAVÉ (ÉMILE) *See* LE SAGE D'HAUTEROCHE (M.) *Count d'Hulst.* Mgr. d'Hulst, Député. (Discours parlementaires.) [Edited by E. Cavé.] 1898. 8°. **4866. de. 27.**

CAVE (ESTELLA PENFOLD) *Countess. See* CAVE (Ann Estella Sarah Penfold) *Countess.*

CAVE (FITZHERBERT ASTLEY CAVE BROWNE) *See* EPHEMERIDES. The Clergyman and Church Worker's Visiting List . . . Edited by F. A. C. B. Cave, *etc.* [1885, *etc.*] 8°. P.P. **2482. fi.**

CAVE (FLOYD AUGUSTINE)

—— *See* WALKER (Robert A.) and CAVE (F. A.) How California is governed. 1954. 8°. **8177. n. 16.**

—— The Origin and Consequences of World War II, *etc.* (Edited by F. A. Cave.) pp. xv. 820. *Dryden Press: New York,* 1948. 8°. **9102. p. 3.**

CAVE (FRANCIS OSWIN) and MACDONALD (JAMES DAVID)

—— Birds of the Sudan : their identification and distribution . . . Illustrated by D. M. Reid Henry. [With plates and maps.] pp. xxvii. 444. *Oliver & Boyd: Edinburgh, London,* 1955. 8°. **7288. e. 9.**

CAVE (G. H.) *See* SMITH (William Wright) and CAVE (G. H.) The Vegetation of the Zemu and Llonakh Valleys of Sikkim. 1911. 8°. [*Records of the Botanical Survey of India.* vol. 4. no. 5.] **7028. r.**

CAVE (*Sir* GENILLE CAVE-BROWNE) *Bart.* From Cowboy to Pulpit. [With plates.] pp. 312. *Herbert Jenkins: London,* 1926. 8°. **4920. k. 7.**

—— Why I Preach . . . Being a short biographical sketch and an introduction to Adventures in Many Lands, *etc.* pp. 8. *London,* 1919. 8°. **4908. de. 22.**

CAVE (GEORGE) *of Taunton.* Historical Notices of the Church of St. Mary Magdalene, Taunton. *See* COTTLE (James) *Rev., M.A., LL.D.* Some Account of the Church of St. Mary Magdalene, *etc.* 1845. 8°. **4705. f. 15.**

CAVE (GEORGE) *Viscount Cave. See* GALE (Charles J.) A Treatise on the Law of Easements . . . Sixth edition, by G. Cave. 1888. 8°. **6306.l.6.**

—— —— 1899. 8°. [MISSING.]

—— *See* MALLET (*Sir* Charles E.) Lord Cave, *etc.* [With portraits.] 1931. 8°. **10823. d. 16.**

CAVE (George) *Viscount Cave.*

—— *See* Sweet (George) Concise Precedents in Conveyancing . . . Third edition by C. C. Tucker . . . and G. Cave. 1884. 8º. **6305.h.4.**

—— —— 1886. 8º. [Missing.]

—— The Licensing Bill, 1908. The case against the Bill, *etc.* pp. 16. *National Union of Conservative and Constitutional Associations: Westminster,* [1908.] 8º. [*N.U.* no. 711.] **8139. dd.**

CAVE (Gillian)

—— The Opening of " Regent House," Royal Terrace, Barrack Road, Northampton. Brochure, *etc.* [By G. Cave.] pp. 19. [c. 1950.] 8º. *See* Northampton.—*Regent House.* **7960. ff. 30.**

CAVE (Goffe) How to Control the Sex of Calves, *etc.* [By G. Cave.] pp. 9. [1924.] 16º. *See* Sex. **7294. a. 16.**

CAVE (Haddon) *See* Horn (G. M.) The History of Group II, City of London R.A.S.C., M.T. (V.) . . . Edited . . . by Capt. P. Linden . . . and Lieut. H. Cave. [1919.] 8º. **9082. c. 4.**

CAVE, afterwards **MORTON** (Harriet) Brought to Jesus. A Bible picture book for little readers. pp. 46. *S. W. Partridge & Co.: London,* [1895.] 4º. **3226. h. 13.**

—— Eighty Years Ago. pp. 347. *Hatchards: London,* 1874 [1873]. 8º. **4413. d. 22.**

—— Foreshadowed; or, the Foster brothers. A life story. pp. 264. *S. W. Partridge & Co.: London,* [1890.] 8º. **4410. p. 38.**

—— The Foster Brothers; or, Foreshadowed . . . New edition. pp. 264. *S. W. Partridge & Co.: London,* [1904.] 8º. [Missing.]

—— From Egypt to Canaan. For little children, *etc.* pp. ix. 250. *Hatchards: London,* 1882. 8º. **4516. aaa. 10.**

—— [Another edition.] pp. 247. *T. Nelson & Sons: London,* 1891 [1890]. 8º. **3128. h. 11.**

—— From the Beginning, or Stories from Genesis for little children. pp. xii. 230. *Hatchards: London,* 1881. 8º. **3128. df. 40.**

—— [Another edition.] pp. 268. *T. Nelson & Sons: London,* 1891. 8º. **3128. h. 16.**

—— Granny's Tale: a ballad for little children. pp. 44. *Hamilton, Adams & Co.: London,* [1869.] 8º. **11648. a. 86. (14.)**

—— Jubilee Echoes. A poem in celebration of the fifty years reign of Queen Victoria. 1837–1887. *James E. Hawkins: London,* [1887.] 4º. **11651. i. 36.**

—— Mary of Garway Farm; or, the Despised warning. [In verse.] pp. 30. *S. W. Partridge & Co.: London,* [1868.] 8º. **11649. aa. 46.**

—— May Blossoms; lines on the jubilee of Her Majesty the Queen. pp. 32. *W. Kent & Co.: London,* [1869.] 8º. **11650. bbb. 37.**

—— Milly's Mission; or, Harry and his mother. A ballad. pp. 30. *S. W. Partridge & Co.:* [*London,* 1869.] 8º. **11649. df. 45. (9.)**

—— Short Chapters on Genesis. Adapted for use at family prayer. pp. 232. *S. W. Partridge & Co.: London,* [1898.] 8º. **3165. de. 24.**

CAVE, afterwards **MORTON** (Harriet)

—— Stories of Christ the Lord in simple verse for little children. pp. 62. *Hamilton, Adams & Co.: London,* [1870.] 16º. **11650. a. 55.**

—— The Story of Jesus for little children, *etc.* pp. x. 298. *Hatchards: London,* 1880. 8º. **4808. b. 11.**

—— Fourth edition. pp. 316. *S. W. Partridge & Co.: London,* [1889.] 8º. **4808. bbb. 27.**

—— A Trio of Cousins. A tale of 1791. pp. 256. *S. W. Partridge & Co.: London,* [1891.] 8º. [Missing.]

CAVE, afterwards **MORTON** (Harriet) and **HANKEY** (Anne)

—— Addresses and Stories for Mothers' Meetings. pp. viii. 276. *Hamilton, Adams & Co.: London,* [1883.] 8º. [Missing.]

CAVE (Helen) The Musical Four-in-hand. A . . . card game. [Cards and book of rules in a case.] *Ewald & Co.: London,* [1880.] 32º. [Missing.]

CAVE (Henry) Antiquities of York, drawn and etched by Henry Cave. [With descriptive letterpress.] pp. 21. pl. 40. *R. Ackermann: London,* 1813. 4º. **191. e. 12.**

—— [Another copy.] **G. 3510.**

CAVE (Henry William) Picturesque Ceylon and Its Ruined Cities . . . A new edition [of " Picturesque Ceylon " and " The Ruined Cities of Ceylon "]. [With plates.] 4 pt. *Sampson Low & Co.: London,* 1903. 4º. **Tab. 538. b. 10.**

—— The Book of Ceylon: being a guide to its railway system and an account of its varied attractions for the visitor and tourist . . . Illustrated from photographs by the author. pp. xii. 664. *Cassell & Co.: London,* 1908. 8º. **010057. i. 43.**

—— The Ceylon Government Railway. A descriptive and illustrated guide, mainly extracted from the author's larger work " The Book of Ceylon." [With a map.] pp. 240. *Cassell & Co.: London,* 1910. 8º. **10056. p. 6.**

—— Golden Tips. A description of Ceylon and its great tea industry . . . Illustrated from photographs by the author, *etc.* pp. xii. 474. *Sampson Low & Co.: London,* 1900. 8º. **010057. h. 40.**

—— Third edition. pp. xii. 476. *Cassell & Co.: London,* 1904. 8º. **010057. h. 60.**

—— Picturesque Ceylon. [With plates.] 3 vol.
    vol. 1. Colombo and the Kelani Valley. 1893.
    vol. 2. Kandy and Peradeniya. 1894.
    vol. 3. Nuwara Eliya and Adam's Peak. 1895.
Sampson Low & Co.: London, 1893–95. 4º. **10058. l. 12.**

—— The Ruined Cities of Ceylon . . . Illustrated with photographs taken by the author. pp. 126. *Sampson Low & Co.: London,* 1897. 4º. **7705. ee. 43.**

—— A new edition. pp. 15. 165. 6. *Sampson Low & Co.: London,* 1900. 8º. **7706. g. 21.**

—— Third edition. pp. 15. 165. 6. *Hutchinson & Co.: London,* 1904. 8º. **07708. e. 16.**

CAVE (Herbert) Fertilizers: their sources, manufacture and uses. pp. xi. 116. *London,* [1926.] 8º. [*Pitman's Common Commodities, etc.*] **07077. f. 1/105.**

CAVE (HERBERT) *B.A.* Practical Exercises in Spoken English. pp. 63. *G. G. Harrap & Co.: London*, 1930. 8°.
12981. aaa. 75.

—— New edition. pp. 96. *G. G. Harrap & Co.: London*, 1934. 8°.
12984. df. 46.

CAVE (HUGH BARNETT)

—— Long Were the Nights. The saga of PT Squadron " X " in the Solomons. By H. B. Cave, with the cooperation of Lieutenant Commander Alan R. Montgomery . . . Lieutenant Robert L. Searles . . . and Lieutenant (jg) Leonard A. Nikolovic, *etc.* (Fourth printing.) pp. xi. 220. *Dodd, Mead & Co.: New York*, 1944. 8°.
09059. aaa. 12.

CAVE (J. M.)

—— *See* HALCROW (M.) and CAVE (J. M.) Peasant Agriculture in Barbados. 1947. 8°. [*Barbados. Department of Science and Agriculture. Bulletin.* New series. no. 11.]
C.S. F. 43/4.

CAVE, afterwards **WINSCOM** (JANE) Poems on Various Subjects, entertaining, elegiac, and religious. [With a portrait.] pp. 26. iv. 50. *Printed for the Author: Winchester*, 1783. 12°.
11632. aaa. 10.

—— [Another edition.] pp. 172. *Printed for the Author: Bristol*, 1786. 12°.
993. c. 43. (1.)

—— The second edition. pp. 190. *Printed for the Author: Shrewsbury*, 1789. 12°.
11632. c. 6.

—— The fourth edition, corrected and improved, *etc.* pp. 204. *N. Biggs: Bristol*, 1794. 12°.
11633. aaa. 7.

—— [A reissue.] *Bristol*, 1795. 12°.
11633. aaa. 8.

—— The Author's Plea, and other verses. (Selected from " Poems on Various Subjects.") ff. 8. *Privately printed for Bache Matthews: Birmingham*, 1927. 8°.
11656. a. 30.

No. 20 of an edition of 100 copies.

CAVE (JOHN) *Glover.* An Epistle to the Inhabitants of Gillingham . . . Wherein is a looking-glass for the faithful, to shew them their names were written in the Lamb's Book of Life, before the foundation of the world, *etc.* pp. ii. 148. *Printed for the Author: Brecon*, 1781. 8°.
4377. e. 10.

—— The second edition. pp. 200. *Printed for the Author: Brecknock*, 1787. 8°.
4378. d. 13.

CAVE (JOHN) *of Brentry House, Clifton.* Catalogue of the Collection of Pictures . . . the property of John Cave, Esq., deceased, *etc.* pp. 11. [*London*, 1843.] 8°.
[MISSING.]

CAVE (JOHN) *pseud.* [i.e. JOHN CAVE WINSCOMBE.] Poems. pp. vi. 105. *Gay & Bird: London*, 1908. 8°.
11649. gg. 36.

—— The Queen of the Fiord, and other poems. pp. xiii. 201. *Kegan Paul & Co.: London*, 1910. 8°. **011650. i. 4.**

—— Who shall Have Her? pp. 319. *John Long: London*, [1909.] 8°.
012625. aaa. 20.

—— The Wiles of a Wife. pp. 315. *John Long: London*, 1908. 8°.
012627. aaa. 34.

CAVE (JOHN) *Rector of Cold-Orton.* The Duty and Benefit of Submission to the Will of God in Afflictions. Discovered in two sermons. pp. 39. *For Richard Chiswell: London*, 1682. 4°.
1418. g. 18.

—— [Another copy.] **226. h. 11. (18.)**

CAVE (JOHN) *Rector of Cold-Orton.*

—— King David's Deliverance and Thanksgiving, applied to the case of our King and nation, in two sermons, *etc.* pp. 63. *For Richard Chiswell: London*, 1683. 4°.
696. f. 10. (8.)

—— A Sermon preached in a country audience . . . by a Priest of the Church of England [i.e. J. Cave]. pp. 30. 1679. 4°. *See* SERMON.
226. f. 18. (6.)

CAVE (JOHN OTWAY) The Business Transfer Agent and Trade Valuer. pp. xii. 171. *Sir I. Pitman & Sons: London*, 1934. 8°.
08206. ee. 42.

—— The Practice of an Auctioneer, Valuer and Estate Agent. [With a supplement.] pp. viii. 376. viii. *Estates Gazette: London*, 1944. 8°.
8234. eee. 54.

—— The Practice of Dilapidations and Specifications for Repairs. pp. 191. *Estates Gazette: London*, 1936. 8°.
7941. r. 17.

—— Property Surveys, Reports and Correspondence, *etc.* [A new edition of " Report Writing for Auctioneers, Surveyors, Valuers and Estate Agents."] pp. v. 141. *Estates Gazette: London*, 1946. 8°.
8231. c. 108.

—— Report Writing for Auctioneers, Surveyors, Valuers and Estate Agents. pp. 79. *Estates Gazette: London*, 1915. 8°.
8223. dg. 2.

—— Second edition. pp. 93. xvi. *Estates Gazette: London*, [1930.] 8°.
8224. cc. 5.

—— The Students' Handbook. For candidates taking the professional examinations, intermediate stage, of the Chartered Surveyors' Institution, valuation sub-division, the Auctioneers' and Estate Agents' Institute and the Incorporated Society of Auctioneers and Land Property Agents. 2 vol. *Estates Gazette: London*, 1938. 8°.
8232. ee. 1.

CAVE (JOHN OTWAY) and **KEVAN** (HERBERT JOHN)

—— Auctioneering and Estate Agency Outlined. Being a practical guide to the training of an auctioneer, valuer, & estate agent. pp. 324. *Estates Gazette: London*, [1933.] 8°. **8244. cc. 44.**

—— Book-keeping and Estate Accounts. pp. 236. *Estates Gazette: London*, [1935.] 8°.
8230. f. 36.

—— Book-Keeping Estate and Farm Accounts, *etc.* [A revised edition of " Book-Keeping and Estate Accounts."] pp. 221. *F. P. Wilson: London*, [1948.] 8°.
8218. a. 20.

—— Book-keeping: up-to-date. A practical treatise for the use of auctioneers, surveyors, *etc.* pp. 143. *Estates Gazette: London*, 1908. 8°.
8533. dd. 35.

—— [Another edition.] pp. xlviii. 3–144. *Estates Gazette: London*, 1908. 8°.
8533. dd. 37.

—— (Second edition.) pp. x. 184. *Estates Gazette: London*, 1922. 8°.
08531. ee. 5.

CAVE (JOSEPH A.) A Jubilee of Dramatic Life and Incident . . . Edited by Robert Soutar, *etc.* [With a portrait.] pp. 218. *Thomas Vernon: London*, [1894.] 8°.
10826. aaa. 47.

CAVE (JULIA MARY STURMY)

—— *See* HALE (Marie C.) Yours in the Fight, Wilson Carlile . . . By M. C. Hale. With the co-operation of J. M. S. Cave. 1945. 8°.
4910. a. 6.

CAVE (LAURENCE TRENT) The French in Africa. [With maps.] pp. xi. 243. *C. J. Skeet: London,* 1859. 8°.
10095. f. 25.

CAVE (LAWRENCE) Scenes in the Life of a Sailor. pp. 162. *Digby & Long: London,* [1890.] 8°. **4905. de. 37.**

CAVE (Sir LEWIS WILLIAM) *Judge of the High Court of Justice.* See ADDISON (Charles G.) Addison on the Law of Contracts . . . By L. W. Cave. 1869. 8°.
[MISSING.]

—— —— 1875. 8°. [MISSING.]

—— *See* ADDISON (Charles G.) Wrongs and their Remedies . . . Fifth edition. By L. W. Cave. 1879. 8°.
[MISSING.]

—— *See* BURN (Richard) *LL.D.* Burn's Justice of the Peace . . . Thirtieth edition. (vol. 3 by L. W. Cave.) 1869. 8°. **6281.i.1.**

—— *See* ENGLAND.—*Court for Crown Cases Reserved.* Crown Cases Reserved for Consideration, and decided by the Judges of England . . . By the Hon. E. C. Leigh, and L. W. Cave. 1866. 8°. **6120.cc.2.**

—— *See* ENGLAND.—*Court for Crown Cases Reserved.* The Law Reports. Cases determined by the Court for Crown Cases Reserved. Reported by Hon. E. C. Leigh, L. W. Cave, *etc.* 1872, *etc.* 8°. **5807.a.14.**

—— *See* SMITH (Horace) *Metropolitan Magistrate,* and SODEN (T. S.) A Manual of the Law of Landlord and Tenant . . . Edited by L. W. Cave. 1871. 8°. [MISSING.]

—— *See* STONE (John) *Barrister-at-Law.* Stone's Practice of Petty Sessions . . . Seventh edition. By Thomas Bell, and L. W. Cave. 1861. 12°. [MISSING.]

—— A Supplement to the seventh edition of Stone's Practice of Petty Sessions. pp. xx. 192. *V. & R. Stevens: London,* 1863. 12°. **6281.aaa.4.**

CAVE (MABEL H.) First Steps to Nursing. A manual for would-be probationers . . . With a preface by Sir John Wolfe Barry. pp. 128. *S. W. Partridge & Co.: London,* [1913.] 8°. [MISSING.]

CAVÉ (MADELEINE)

—— L'Œuvre paradoxale de Freud. Essai sur la théorie des névroses. (2e édition.) pp. 159. *Paris,* 1948. 8°.
08464. df. 10.
Part of the " Bibliothèque de philosophie contemporaine."

CAVE (MARGARET) The Christian, and other poems, *etc.* pp. 43. *A. R. Mowbray & Co.: Oxford, London,* 1905. 8°.
011651. g. 66.

CAVÉ (MARIE ÉLISABETH) Le Dessin sans maître. Méthode pour apprendre à dessiner de mémoire . . . 2e édition. pp. 95. pl. 6. *Paris,* 1851. 8°. [MISSING.]

—— 3e édition. pp. 110. *Paris,* 1852. 8°. [MISSING.]

—— Drawing without a Master. The Cavé method for learning to draw from memory . . . Translated from the fourth Paris edition, revised . . . by the author. [Preceded by an article by Eugène Delacroix, translated from the " Revue des deux mondes " and entitled " Drawing without a master, by Madame Elisabeth Cavé."] pp. 134. *G. P. Putnam & Son: New York,* 1868. 8°.
[MISSING.]

—— Abrégé de la méthode Cavé pour apprendre à dessiner juste et de mémoire, *etc.* pp. 71. *Paris,* [1862.] 12°.
[MISSING.]

—— La Femme aujourd'hui, la femme autrefois. [With a portrait.] pp. vi. 288. *Paris,* 1863. 8°. **8415. h. 19.**

CAVE (MARION STILWELL) and CONSTANCE (LINCOLN)

—— Chromosome Numbers in the Hydrophyllaceae. 5 pt. *Berkeley and Los Angeles,* 1942–59. 8°. [*University of California Publications in Botany.* vol. 18. no. 9, 13, 20. vol. 23. no. 7 ; vol. 30. no. 3.] **Ac. 2689. g/32.**
One of thirty copies printed on 100% rag paper.

CAVE (NORMAN LESLIE)

—— The Iris. [With plates.] pp. 216. *Faber & Faber: London,* 1950. 8°. **7035. cc. 22.**

CAVE (OLIVER) On the Principle of the Union between Church and States : a sermon. pp. 23. *J. G. & F. Rivington: London,* 1834. 8°. **T. 1465. (15.)**

CAVE (PAUL) *Lieutenant.*

—— Patagonie. Détroit de Magellan et canaux latéraux. Instruction rédigée . . . par M. P. Cave. pp. ix. 231. *Paris,* 1879. 8°. [*France. Ministère de la Marine et des Colonies. Dépôt des Cartes et Plans de la Marine.* Publication 606.] **S. 323/606.**

CAVE (PHYLOLAURO DI) *pseud.*

—— Dialogo amoroso. [In verse.] [*p Calistro Dubbioso di Simeone di Nicolo: Siena,* 1533.] 8°. **G. 10342.**
Imperfect ; wanting the last 24 leaves, comprising sig. V–Y.

CAVE (RENÉE) *See* BRUCKNER (Ferdinand) *pseud.* Les Races . . . Adaptation . . . de R. Cave. 1934. fol. [*La Petite Illustration.* Théâtre. no. 345.]
P.P. 4283. m. (2.)

CAVE (RICHARD) *Printer.* *See* PERIODICAL PUBLICATIONS.—*London.* The Gentleman's Magazine, *etc.* [1754–66 edited by D. Henry and R. Cave.] 1731, *etc.* 8°.
2120.f.–2121.h.

CAVE (Sir RICHARD) The Judgement of the Court of Warre upon the charge laid against Sir Richard Cave for the delivery up of Hereford. Oxford, 26 Junij, 1643. *Printed by Leonard Lichfield: Oxford,* 1643. *s. sh.* fol.
669. f. 7. (26.)

CAVE (RICHARD PHILIP)

—— Elementary Map Reading, *etc.* pp. 48. *Methuen & Co.: London,* [1943.] 8°. **010004. e. 78.**

—— Elementary Map Reading, *etc.* (Third edition, revised and reset.) pp. 48. *Methuen & Co.: London,* 1953. 8°.
010005. d. 33.

CAVE (ROBERT HAYNES) Christianity and Modern Thought. Four Advent sermons, *etc.* pp. 82. *J. Parker & Co.: Oxford & London,* 1872. 8°. **4465. aa. 29.**

—— The Church and the Prayer Book. Short studies in English church history. pp. 46. *J. Hodges: London,* 1898. 8°. **4707. cc. 20.**

—— The Foundations : a course of short sermons to farm labourers. pp. 104. *J. H. & J. Parker: London,* 1861. 8°. **4464. b. 7.**

—— In the Days of Good Queen Bess, *etc.* [A tale.] pp. xi. 203. *Burns & Oates: London,* [1897.] 8°.
04410. k. 8.

CAVE (ROBERT OTWAY) *See* LEICESTER. Leicester Election. The Corporation and Mr. Otway Cave. Statement (in reference to the agreement entered into at the last Leicester Election between the friends of Sir C. A. Hastings and the friends of Mr. O. Cave), *etc.* 1828. 8°.
T. 1241. (8).

CAVE (ROY CLINTON) and COULSON (HERBERT HENRY) A Source Book for Medieval Economic History. pp. xx. 467. *Bruce Publishing Co.: Milwaukee,* [1936.] 8°.
8234. f. 10.

CAVE (STANLEY REGINALD)

—— Budgetary Control, Standard Costing and Factory Administration. pp. 152. *Gee & Co.: London*, 1955. 8°.
8231. c. 119.

CAVE (*Right Hon. Sir* STEPHEN) *See* HARDWICK (Charles) *of Preston*. The Present Insurance Crisis: the Government action, and Mr. Cave's Bill. [1870.] 12°.
8226. aa. 25. (7.)

—— A Few Words on the Encouragement given to Slavery and the Slave Trade, by recent measures and chiefly by the Sugar Bill of 1846. pp. 34. *John Murray: London*, 1849. 8°.
8155. c. 15.

—— On the Distinctive Principles of Punishment and Reformation. A paper, *etc.* pp. viii. 20. *James Ridgway: London*, 1857. 8°. [MISSING.]

—— Papers relating to Free Labour and the Slave Trade; with a corrected report of the debate in the House of Commons . . . upon the resolutions proposed by Mr. Cave . . . for more effectual suppression of the African slave-trade. pp. 64. *Robert Barclay: London*, 1861. 8°.
8156. c. 74. (9.)

—— Prevention and Reformation: the duty of the state, or of individuals? With some account of a reformatory institution. pp. 26. *James Ridgway: London*, 1856. 8°.
[MISSING.]

CAVE (SYDNEY) *See* STIRLING (John) The Study Bible, *etc.* (The Acts of the Apostles . . . By S. Cave.) 1926, *etc.* 8°.
03126. h. 2/12.

—— *See* STORR (Vernon F.) and CAVE (S.) The Westminster Books. Edited by Archdeacon Storr and Principal S. Cave. 1932, *etc.* 8°.
W.P. 6908.

—— The Christian Estimate of Man. pp. 235. *Duckworth: London*, 1944. 8°. [*Studies in Theology.*]
12207. d. 1/44.

—— The Christian Way. A study of New Testament ethics in relation to present problems. pp. 280. *Nisbet & Co.: London*, 1949. 8°.
3228. b. 24.

—— Christianity and some Living Religions of the East. pp. 221. *Duckworth: London*, 1929. 8°. [*Studies in Theology.*]
12207. d. 1/29.

—— The Doctrine of the Person of Christ. pp. 259. *Duckworth: London*, 1925. 8°. [*Studies in Theology.*]
12207. d. 1/28.

—— The Doctrine of the Work of Christ. pp. vii. 277. *University of London Press; Hodder & Stoughton: London*, 1937. 8°. [*London Theological Library.*]
3606. ff. 1/3.

—— The Doctrines of the Christian Faith. pp. 307. *Hodder & Stoughton: London*, 1931. 8°. **04018. g. 44.**

—— [A reissue.] The Doctrines of the Christian Faith. (Third impression.) *Independent Press: London*, 1952. 8°.
04018. m. 4.

—— The Gospel of St. Paul . . . A reinterpretation in the light of the religion of his age and modern missionary experience. pp. 283. *Hodder & Stoughton: London*, 1928. 8°.
04808. df. 31.

—— Hinduism or Christianity? A study in the distinctiveness of the Christian message. The Haskell Lectures given in the Graduate School of Theology, Oberlin College, 1939. pp. 240. *Hodder & Stoughton: London*, 1939. 8°.
04373. e. 14.

CAVE (SYDNEY)

—— An Introduction to the Study of Living Religions of the East. pp. 255. *Duckworth & Co.: London*, 1921. 8°. [*Studies in Theology.*]
12207. d. 1/26.

—— Redemption Hindu and Christian. pp. x. 263. *Oxford University Press: London*, 1919. 8°. [*Religious Quest of India.*]
4506. i. 28/4.

—— What Shall We Say of Christ? pp. 241. *Hodder & Stoughton: London*, 1932. 8°. [*Westminster Books.*]
W.P. 6908/3.

CAVE (THOMAS) *See* ENGLAND.—*Trustees appointed for the Survey and Administration of the Property of Deans and Chapters*, 1649. The Parliamentary Survey of the Lands and Possessions of the Dean and Chapter of Worcester, made in or about the year 1649 . . . Edited . . . by T. Cave and R. A. Wilson. 1924. 4°.
Ac. 8166/39.

—— John Baskerville, 1706–1775, the printer, his ancestry. Richard Baxter, 1615–1691, and Kidderminster Parish Church. A retrospect. pp. 31. 13. *G. T. Cheshire & Sons: Kidderminster*, 1923. 4°. **9907. f. 30.**
One of an edition of eighteen copies printed for private circulation.

—— [Another edition.] pp. 41. *City of Birmingham School of Printing:* [*Birmingham*,] 1936. fol. **9907. pp. 13.**

CAVE (*Sir* THOMAS) *3rd Bart. See* LEICESTER, *County of.* A True State of the Proceedings at the Leicestershire Election . . . Candidates: Sir T. Cave, Sir J. Palmer, *etc.* [1715.] 4°. **T. 1700. (11.)**

CAVE (*Sir* THOMAS) *5th Bart.* A Diary of a Journey from Stanford Hall to the North of Scotland and back in the year 1763. *See* HOLME (Christopher) A History of the Midland Counties, *etc.* 1891. 8°. **10360. d. 24.**

CAVE (*Sir* THOMAS) *7th Bart. See* NICHOLS (John) *F.S.A., Printer*. The History and Antiquities of the County of Leicester . . . including . . . the later collections of Mr. Stavely . . . Sir T. Cave, *etc.* 1795, *etc.* fol. **2065. e.**

CAVE (THOMAS STURMY)

—— A Family Record, 1500–1729. [On the Cave family of Yateley.] [1933.] 8°. **9918. a. 49.**

—— History of the First Volunteer Battalion Hampshire Regiment, 1859 to 1889. With appendix containing notes and illustrations in reference to the Corps from 1890 to 1903. [With plates.] pp. xi. 434. 1905. 8°. *See* ENGLAND.—*Army.—Infantry.—Royal Hampshire Regiment, First Volunteer Battalion.*
8822. a. 35.

CAVE (THOMAS STURMY) and **TEBBUTT** (LOUIS)

—— The British Army and the Business of War. 1896. pp. 40. *Gale & Polden: London*, 1896. 8°. **8827. ee. 44. (8.)**

—— [Another edition.] Mobilization for War. The South African field force and home defence. pp. vi. 40. *Gale & Polden: London*, 1900. 8°. **8822. e. 1. (4.)**

CAVE (VERNEY CAVE-BROWNE) The Rest of the Righteous. A sermon preached . . . on . . . the first Sunday after the funeral of T. B. T. Dickins, *etc.* pp. 26. *Joseph Masters: London*, [1868.] 8°. **4906. dd. 29. (7.)**

—— Signs of the Times. A sermon, *etc.* pp. 16. *Burns & Oates: London*, 1879. 8°. **4479. d. 3. (12.)**

CAVE (Verney Cave-Browne)

—— The Soul's Life through Death. A sermon preached . . . after the funeral of the Hon. and Rev. C. B. Wykeham-Fiennes. pp. 18. *Joseph Masters: London,* 1870. 8°. **4906. dd. 29. (12.)**

CAVE (William) *D.D.* *See* Justin, *Martyr, Saint.* [*Dialogus cum Tryphone.—Greek and Latin.*] Sancti Justini . . . cum Tryphone Judæo dialogus . . . Subjunctis emendationibus & notis R. Stephani . . . Cavii, *etc.* 1719. 8°. **674. f. 3.**

—— Lives of the Christian Fathers and Martyrs . . . Abridged from Cave.—Primitive Christianity . . . By W. Cave. *See* Fleetwood (John) *D.D.* The Life of our Lord, *etc.* 1854. 8°. **1217. g. 1.**

—— Antiquitates Apostolicæ: or, the Lives, acts and martyrdoms of the Holy Apostles . . . To which are added, the lives of the two Evangelists, SS. Mark and Luke. pp. xiii. 176. *See* Taylor (Jeremy) *Bishop of Down and Connor, and of Dromore.* Antiquitates Christianæ: or, the History of the life and death of the Holy Jesus . . . The first part, containing the Life of Christ, written by Jer. Taylor . . . The second, containing the Lives of the Apostles . . . by W. Cave . . . by whom also is added an Apparatus, or Discourse introductory to the whole work, concerning the three great dispensations of the Church, *etc.* 1675. fol. **4807. h. 1.**

—— The third edition. pp. lxviii. 234. *R. Norton, for R. Royston: London,* 1677. fol. **480. d. 12. (1.)**

—— [Another copy.] Antiquitates apostolicae . . . Third edition. *London,* 1677. fol. **1471. cc. 16. (1.)** *Imperfect; wanting the plate following the table of contents. In this copy the address "To the Reader," and the table of contents precede "An Apparatus or discourse introductory."*

—— [Another edition.] pp. 188. *See* Taylor (Jeremy) *Bishop of Down and Connor, and of Dromore.* Antiquitates Christianæ, *etc.* 1684. fol. **4807. h. 4.**

—— The fifth edition revised, with some additions. pp. lxviii. xviii. 238. *M. Flesher, for R. Royston: London,* 1684. fol. **483. f. 17. (1.)**

—— Antiquitates Apostolicæ, *etc.* pp. xiv. 188. *J. H. for L. Meredith: London,* 1694. fol. [*Taylor (Jeremy) Bishop, etc.* Antiquitates Christianæ. pt. 2.] **1471. d. 4.**

—— [Another edition.] pp. 188. 1702. *See* Taylor (Jeremy) *Bishop of Down and Connor, and of Dromore.* Antiquitates Christianæ, *etc.* 1703, *etc.* fol. **676. g. 16.**

—— [Another edition.] *See* Taylor (Jeremy) *Bishop of Down and Connor, and of Dromore.* Antiquitates Christianæ, *etc.* 1742. fol. **4807. h. 5.**

—— [Another edition.] With an introductory essay by the Rev. Henry Stebbing. 2 vol. *J. Hatchard & Son: London,* 1834. 8°. [*Cattermole (R.) and Stebbing (H.) The Sacred Classics, etc.* vol. 2, 3.] **496. ee. 1.**

—— [Another edition.] The Lives, Acts, and Martyrdoms of the Holy Apostles . . . With an introductory essay, by the Rev. Henry Stebbing. pp. 156. *Thomas George: New York,* 1836. 8°. [*Christian Library.* vol. 2.] **3624. bb. 3.**

—— The Lives of the Holy Evangelists and Apostles. [Abridged from W. Cave's "Antiquitates Apostolicæ."] *See* Taylor (Jeremy) *Bishop of Down and Connor, and of Dromore.* The Life of . . . Jesus Christ, *etc.* 1758. 12°. **4824. aa. 61.**

CAVE (William) *D.D.*

—— [Another edition.] *See* Taylor (Jeremy) *Bishop of Down and Connor, and of Dromore.* The Life of . . . Jesus Christ, *etc.* 1796. 12°. **4806. b. 41.**

—— The Lives of the Apostles, and the two evangelists Saint Mark and Saint Luke . . . A new edition, carefully revised, by Henry Cary. pp. xii. 460. *Printed by J. Vincent for Thomas Tegg: Oxford & London,* 1840. 8°. **4805. i. 20.**

—— Apostolici: or, the History of the lives, acts, death and martyrdoms of those who were contemporary with or immediately succeeded the Apostles. As also the most eminent of the Primitive Fathers for the first three hundred years. To which is added a Chronology of the three first ages of the Church. (vol. 2. Ecclesiastici: or, the History of the lives, acts, death and writings of the most eminent Fathers of the Church; that flourisht in the fourth century . . . Together with an introduction containing an historical account of the state of paganism under the first Christian Emperors.—An Appendix containing a brief account of some other eminent Fathers that flourish'd in this fourth century.) 2 vol. *A. C. for Richard Chiswell: London,* 1677, 83. fol.– *The Chronology at the end of vol. 1 bears the date 1676. The special titlepage to the Appendix to vol. 2 bears the date 1682. The half-title reads "The Lives of the Primitive Fathers." With an additional titlepage, engraved.* **480. d. 12. (2.). 13.**

—— [Another copy of vol. 1.] Apostolici, *etc.* *London,* 1677. fol. **1471. cc. 16. (2.)**

—— The second edition, corrected. 2 vol. *J. R. for Richard Chiswel: London,* 1682, 83. fol. **480. d. 14. & 483. f. 17. (2.)**

—— [Another copy of vol. 2.] **205. e. 5.**

—— [Another edition of vol. 1.] pp. xxxii. 335. *B. W. for Richard Chiswell: London,* 1687. fol. **205. e. 4.**

—— [Ecclesiastici.] Lives of the most eminent Fathers of the Church . . . A new edition, carefully revised, by Henry Cary. 3 vol. *Printed by J. Vincent for Thomas Tegg: Oxford & London,* 1840. 8°. **4805. i. 21.**

—— The Life of St Ignatius, Bishop of Antioch. [Extracted from Cave's "Lives of the Primitive Fathers."] pp. 36. *James Burns: London,* [1843.] 12°. **1372. a. 29. (1.)**

—— The Life of St. Polycarp, Bishop of Smyrna. [Extracted from Cave's "Lives of the Primitive Fathers."] pp. 37. *James Burns: London,* [1843.] 12°. **1372. a. 29. (2.)**

—— Chartophylax Ecclesiasticus: quo prope 1500 scriptores ecclesiastici . . . eorumq; patria, ordo, secta, munera, ætas & obitus: editiones operum præstantiores; opuscula quin & ipsa fragmenta breviter indicantur . . . A Chr. nato ad annum usq; MDXVII. Accedunt scriptores gentiles Christianæ religionis oppugnatores; & brevis cujusvis sæculi conspectus, *etc.* pp. 336. *Impensis Richardi Chiswell: Londini,* 1685. 8°. **487. e. 21. (1.)**

—— [Another copy.] **270. f. 37.**

—— *See* Colomiès (P.) Ad Gulielmi Cave . . . Chartophylacem Ecclesiasticum paralipomena. 1686. 8°. **701. b. 31.**

—— A Discourse concerning the Unity of the Catholick Church maintained in the Church of England. [Variously attributed to W. Cave and to George Thorp.] pp. 57. 1684. 4°. *See* England.—*Church of England.* [*Appendix.*] **T. 1869. (1.)**

CAVE (WILLIAM) *D.D.*

—— [Another edition.] *See* POPERY. A Preservative against Popery, *etc.* vol. 1. 1738. fol. **478. f. 11.**

—— [Another edition.] *See* GIBSON (Edmund) successively *Bishop of Lincoln* and *of London.* A Preservative against Popery, *etc.* vol. 1. 1848, *etc.* 8°. **3940. k. 6/1.**

—— A Dissertation concerning the Government of the Ancient Church, by Bishops, Metropolitans and Patriarchs. More particularly, concerning the ancient power and jurisdiction of the Bishops of Rome, *etc.* p. 334. *For R. Chiswel: London,* 1683. 8°. **854. e. 38.**

—— Wilhelmi Cave . . . Epistola apologetica adversus iniquas Joannis Clerici criminationes in Epistolis criticis & ecclesiasticis nuper editis. Qua argumenta ejus pro Eusebij Arianismo ad examen revocantur . . . multa de usu & auctoritate sanctorum Patrum, de quibusdam Clementis Alexandrini dogmatibus, de Concilio Nicæno I & II aliisque nonnullis disseruntur. pp. 119. *Impensis Sam. Smith & Benj. Walford: Londini,* 1700. 8°. **4531. a. 9.**

—— The Lives of the Primitive Fathers. *See* supra: Apostolici.

—— Primitive Christianity: or, the Religion of the ancient Christians in the first ages of the Gospel. 2 vol. *J. M. for Richard Chiswell: London,* 1673. 8°. **852. b. 20.**
With an additional titlepage, engraved.

—— The second edition. 2 pt. *J. M. for Richard Chiswell: London,* 1675. 8°. **478. a. 1.**

—— Primitive Christianity . . . The third edition. 2 pt. *J. G. for R. Chiswell: London,* 1676. 8°. **4536. a. 12.**
With an additional titlepage, engraved.

—— The sixth edition. pp. 468. *R. Chiswel: London,* 1702. 8°. **4530. aaa. 15.**

—— The seventh edition corrected. pp. 468. *Daniel Midwinter & Benjamin Cowse: London,* 1714. 8°. **1113. d. 3.**

—— [Another edition.] The seventh edition. pp. 468. *J. Walthoe: London,* 1728. 8°. **4532. aaa. 3.**

—— [Another edition.] With an introductory essay, and notes, by the Rev. Wm. Trollope. 2 vol. *J. Hatchard & Son: London,* 1834. 8°. [CATTERMOLE *(R.)* and STEBBING *(H.)* *The Sacred Classics, etc.* vol. 12, 13.] **496. ee. 6.**

—— Erstes Christenthum, oder Gottesdienst der alten Christen in den ersten Zeiten des evangelii; aus dem englischen anitzo übersetzet. pp. 778. *J. T. Fritsch: Leipzig,* 1694. 8°. **4533. a. 4.**

—— [Another edition.] pp. 778. *J. T. Fritsch: Leipzig,* 1696. 8°. **4533. e. 4. (1)**

—— Primitive Christianity . . . Abridged and adapted to modern use, with additional reflections, by John Brewster. pp. xx. 172. *C. & J. Rivington: London,* 1825. 12°. **864. d. 16.**

—— Primitive Christianity. [An extract.] 1825. *See* WESLEY (John) A Christian Library, *etc.* vol. 19. 1819, *etc.* 8°. **495. e. 10.**

—— *See* ARNOLD (Gottfried) Die erste Liebe, das ist Wahre-Abbildung der ersten Christen . . . Worinnen zugleich des Hn. W. Cave erstes Christenthum . . . erläutert wird, *etc.* 1712. fol. **4534. h. 2.**

CAVE (WILLIAM) *D.D.*

—— Scriptorum Ecclesiasticorum historia literaria a Christo nato usque ad sæculum XIV. facili methodo digesta . . . Accedunt scriptores gentiles, Christianæ religionis oppugnatores; & cujusvis sæculi breviarium . . . Præmissa denique prolegomena, quibus plurima ad antiquitatis ecclesiasticæ studium spectantia traduntur . . . Accedit ab alia manu [i.e. by Henry Wharton] appendix ab ineunte sæculo XIV. ad annum usque M.DXVII. (Scriptorum Ecclesiasticorum historia literaria . . . pars altera: qua plusquam DC. scriptores novi . . . recensentur . . . Accedit ad finem cujusvis sæculi Conciliorum omnium . . . historica notitia. Ad calcem verò operis dissertationes tres. I. De scriptoribus ecclesiasticis incertæ ætatis. II. De libris & officiis ecclesiasticis Græcorum. III. De Eusebii Cæsariensis Arianismo adversùs Joannem Clericum.—Appendix . . . in qua scriptores ecclesiastici et concilia sæculorum XIV. & XV. recensentur. R. G. [i.e. Robert Gery] auctore.) 2 vol. *Typis T. H. & impensis Richardi Chiswell: Londini,* 1688, 98. fol. **480. d. 15, 16.**

—— Editio novissima, valde accuratior, *etc.* pp. xxxxviii. 668. 241. *Coloniæ Allobrogum,* 1720. fol. **480. i. 2.**

—— Editio novissima, ab auctore ipsomet ante obitum recognita & auctior facta. 2 vol. *È Theatro Sheldoniano: Oxonii,* 1740, 43. fol. **L. 1. h. 7/1.**

—— [Another copy.] **120. g. 12, 13.**

—— *See* DAWSON (Thomas) *D.D.* Disceptatio epistolaris de coelestibus testimoniis I. Joh. v. 7. in qua . . . evincitur αὐθεντια istius versiculi . . . Ex dissertatione singulari . . . G. Cavei . . . Luciani Samosat. testimonio innixa; ab ἀνεκδοτοις ejus Historiæ liter. jam publici juris facta. 1734. 8°. [MISSING.]

—— *See* MARCK (J. à) Johannis Marckii Textuales exercitationes ad . . . selecta loca Veteris & Novi Testamenti, *etc.* (De sibyllinis carminibus additamentum, quo ad Historiam literariam G. Cave . . . respondetur.) 1694. 4°. **3109. a. 8.**

—— *See* POTE (J.) A Letter to A . . . . B . . . . Esq. concerning subscriptions and the compleat edition of Dr. Cave's Historia literaria, now printing, *etc.* 1737. 4°. **698. l. 9. (14.)**

—— *See* POTE (J.) A Second Letter concerning the compleat edition of Dr. Cave's Historia literaria, now printing, *etc.* 1739. 4°. **698. l. 9. (15.)**

—— *See* SEELEN (J. H. a) Ad saeculorum N. T. characteres Caveo-Whartono-Gerianos observationes. [1747.] 4°. **4531. b. 32.**

—— Éclaircissemens littéraires sur un projet de bibliothèque alphabétique, sur l'Histoire littéraire de Cave, et sur quelques autres ouvrages semblables: avec des règles pour étudier et pour bien écrire. Ouvrage périodique. [By Jacques Martin.] Lettre 1, 2. *Paris,* 1736. 4°. **823. h. 9. (6.)**
No more published.

—— [Another copy of Lettre 1.] **698. l. 9. (16.)**

—— A Serious Exhortation, with some important advices, relating to the late Cases about Conformity, recommended to the present Dissenters from the Church of England. [By W. Cave.] pp. 44. 1683. 4°. *See* DISSENTERS. **701. g. 14. (8.)**

—— [Another copy.] **110. f. 12.**

—— [Another edition.] pp. 44. 1685. 4°. [*A Collection of Cases and other discourses, etc.* vol. 2.] *See* DISSENTERS. **4106. h. 1.**

CAVE (William) *D.D.*

—— [Another edition.] *See* Dissenters. A Collection of Cases . . . written to recover Dissenters, *etc.* 1694. fol.
700. m. 13.

—— [Another edition.] *See* Dissenters. A Collection of Cases . . . written to recover Dissenters, *etc.* vol. 3. 1718. 8°.
226. b. 20.

—— A Sermon preached before the King at Whitehall January xxiii. 167⅔. pp. 27. *W. Godbid, for Richard Chiswell: London,* 1676. 4°.
694. g. 13. (8.)

—— A Sermon preached before the King at White-Hall . . . January 18th. 168⅘. pp. 34. *For Richard Chiswel: London,* 1685. 4°.
226. i. 2. (12.)

—— [Another copy.]
226. g. 22. (5.)

—— A Sermon preached before the Right Honourable the Lord Mayor, Aldermen, and Citizens of London . . . the fifth of November, MDCLXXX. pp. 35. *M. White, for R. Chiswel: London,* 1680. 4°.
694. g. 25. (4.)

—— [Another copy.]
226. i. 4. (13.)

—— Tabulæ Ecclesiasticæ quibus scriptores ecclesiastici, eorumq; patria, ordo, ætas, & obitus breviter exhibentur, à Christo nato ad annum usq; MDXVII. *Typis J. D., impensis Richardi Chiswell: Londini,* 1674. fol.
699. k. 8.

CAVEAT. A Caveat against Discord, or, a Word for union and peace addressed to all parties. By a Constitutional Briton. pp. 4. *Simmons, Kirkby & Jones: Canterbury,* [1792.] 12°.
8138. h. 1. (12.)

—— A Caveat against Flattery, and Profanation of Sacred Things to Secular Ends : upon sight of the order of the Convention for the thanksgiving, and consideration of the misgovernment and misfortunes of the last race of Kings of this nation. [By Edward Stephens.] *See* English Government. The True English Government, *etc.* 1689. 4°.
8122. d. 46.

—— A Caveat against Seditious Malcontents: or, a Dis-swasive from encouraging or fomenting popular discontents and disorders, in the Kingdom. In a serious and earnest address to the subjects of Great Britain. By a Country Clergyman. pp. 31. *Rest Fenner: London,* 1734. 8°.
8133. c. 15.

—— Caveat emptor. *See* England.—*National Association of Local Government Officers.—West Kent Branch.*

—— A Caveat for Cut-purses ; with a warning to all purse-carriers, *etc.* [A ballad.] 𝔅.𝔏. *For W. Gilbertson: [London,* 1663 ?] *s. sh.* fol.
Rox. II. 46.

—— A Caveat for Knaves. [A satire upon Parliament and the Army.] pp. 8 [6]. [*London,*] 1648. 4°.
E. 451. (45.)

—— A Caveat on the part of Public Credit, previous to the opening of the Budget, for the present year, 1768. pp. 14. *London,* 1768. 4°.
11642. g. 27. (3.)

—— The second edition. pp. 20. *J. Almon: London,* 1768. 4°.
T. 920. (14.)

—— A Caveat to the Treaters ; or, the Modern schemes of partition examin'd. With relation to the safety of Europe in general and of Great Britain and Ireland in particular, *etc.* 1711. 8°. *See* Europe.
101. c. 70.

—— A Caveat to the Will of a certain Northern Vicar. Addressed to the Reverend W. C * * * * *, Rector of K * * * * W * * * *. 1766. 4°. *See* C * * * * *, W., *Rector of K * * * * W * * * *.*
11642. h. 23.

CAVEAT EMPTOR, *pseud.* [i.e. *Sir* George Stephen.]

—— The Adventures of a Gentleman in Search of a Horse. By Caveat Emptor, Gent., One, &c. [With illustrations by R. Cruikshank.] pp. xi. 336. *Longman, Rees, Orme, Brown, Green, & Longman: London,* 1835. 8°.
7920. aa. 31.

—— Adventures of a Gentleman in Search of a Horse. [The preface signed : Caveat Emptor.] pp. xxi. 216. *Saunders, Otley & Co.: London,* 1861. 8°ᵒ **7905.c.15**

CAVEAU. Câveau Lîgeois. *See* Liége, *City of.—Câveau Lîgeois.*

—— Le Caveau moderne, ou le Rocher de Cancalle. Chansonnier de table, composé des meilleurs chansons de l'ancien Caveau . . . Seconde édition corrigée et augmentée. pp. 307. *Paris,* 1807. 12°.
1094. b. 8.

CAVE-BROWNE (John) *See* Browne.

CAVE-BROWNE-CAVE (*Sir* Genille) *Bart. See* Cave.

CAVE-BROWNE CAVE (Verney) *See* Cave.

CAVEDA (José) Ensayo histórico sobre los diversos géneros de arquitectura empleados en España desde la dominacion Romana hasta nuestros dias. pp. 544. *Madrid,* 1848. 8°.
1264. d. 6.

—— Geschichte der Baukunst in Spanien . . . Übersetzt von Paul Heyse, herausgegeben von Franz Kugler, *etc.* pp. x. 294. *Stuttgart,* 1858. 8°.
[Missing.]

—— Examen crítico de la restauracion de la monarquia visigoda en el siglo VIII. 1879. *See* Madrid.—*Real Academia de la Historia.* Memorias, *etc.* tom. 9. 1796, *etc.* 4°.
Ac. 6630/3.

—— Memorias para la historia de la Real Academia de San Fernando y de las Bellas Artes en España, desde el advenimiento al trono de Felipe V, hasta nuestros dias. 2 tom. *Madrid,* 1867. 8°.
7806.cc.7.

—— La Poesia considerada como Elemento de la Historia : discurso leido por Don J. Caveda en el acto de su recepcion en la Real Academia Española, *etc.* (Contestacion al anterior discurso por el Excmo. Sr. Marqués de Pidal.) pp. 45. *Madrid,* 1852. 8°.
11825. h. 25. (1.)

—— Poesías selectas en dialecto asturiano de D. Antonio González Reguera . . . y otros, publicadas por . . . J. Caveda. Nueva edicion anotada y aumentada . . . de D Fermin Canella Secades. pp. 317. *Oviedo,* 1887. 8°.
11450. de. 44.

CAVEDALIS (Antonius) De febribus intermittentibus animadversiones, *etc.* pp. 18. *Patavii,* 1831. 8°.
7306. b. 9. (48.)

CAVEDALIS (Giovanni Battista) I Commentari. Con introduzione e note di Vincenzo Marchesi. [With a portrait and maps.] 2 vol. 1928, 29. 8°. *See* Udine.—*Accademia di Udine.*
9165. p. 11.

CAVEDA Y NAVA (José) Memoria de Varones Célebres Asturianos, *etc. See* Álvarez de la Rivera M. (S.) Biblioteca Histórico-Genealogica Asturiana, *etc.* vol. 1. 1924, *etc.* 4°.
9915.t.38.

CAVEDONE (Giovanni) Due novelle [entitled " Giovanni Cavedone " and " Bonaccorso di Lapo Giovanni "] aggiunte in un codice del MCCCCXXXVII contenente Il Decamerone di Giovanni Boccaccio. [The editor's preface signed : A. C., i.e. Antonio Cappelli.] pp. xii. 71. *Bologna,* 1866. 8°.
12226. bbb. 12. (5.)

CAVEDONI (Celestino) See Bortolotti (P.) Notizie intorno alla vita ed alle opere di Monsignor C. Cavedoni, con appendice di sue lettere, etc. 1866. 8°.
10631. e. 7.

—— See Bortolotti (P.) Spicilegio epigrafico modenese, o sia Supplimento alle sillogi epigrafiche Cavedoniane. 1875. fol.   Dept. of Greek & Roman Antiquities.

—— See Cappelli (A.) Necrologia di Mons. Celestino Cavedoni, etc. 1866. 4°.   4867. h. 11.

—— See Carellius (F.) Francisci Carellii numorum Italiae veteris tabulas ccii edidit C. Cavedonius. 1850. fol.
7756. h. 16.

—— See Cicero (M. T.) [De Fato.—Latin.] Nuovi frammenti del libro di Cicerone: de Fato, etc. [With notes by C. Cavedoni.] 1853. 16°.   7704. f. 43. (21.)

—— See Crespellani (A.) and Vandelli (G.) Corrispondenza archeologica fra Celestino Cavedoni, Arcangelo Crespellani e Gaetano Vandelli. 1895. 8°. [Atti e memorie della R. Deputazione di Storia Patria. ser. 4. vol. 7.]   Ac. 6520.

—— See Galvani (G.) Count. Saggio di alcune postille alla Divina Commedia con una lettera in fine all'autore [by C. Cavedoni]. 1828. 8°.   011421. b. 5.

—— See Galvani (G.) Count. Saggio di alcune postille alla Divina Commedia, con una lettera di C. Cavedoni, etc. 1894. 8°.   011420. a. 1/6.

—— See Modena.—Reale Biblioteca Estense. Cenni storici del Museo annesso alla R. Biblioteca Estense in Modena. [Based on C. Cavedoni's "Tributo alla memoria di Francesco iv. Duca."] 1873. 8°.   11904. dd. 27. (4.)

—— See Rosini (G.) Risposta all'articolo del Sig. Don C. Cavedoni [on Tasso] che trovasi nel num. 2 del tomo i delle Nuove Memorie di religione, di morale e di letteratura, etc. [1832.] 8°.   11426. g. 1.

—— See Witte (J. J. A. M. de) Baron. Notice sur Celestino Cavedoni. 1866. 8°.   12236. i. 8. (9.)

—— L'Aes grave del Museo Kircheriano, ovvero le Monete primitive de' popoli dell'Italia media ordinate e descritte . . . Roma . . . 1839, etc. (Notizia bibliografica.) [A review of the work by Giuseppe Marchi and Pietro Tessieri.] pp. 23. [Rome, 1840?] 8°. 7755. d. 26. (4.)

—— Annotazioni al Corpus inscriptionum graecarum che si pubblica dalla R. Accademia di Berlino. (Estratto delle Memorie di religione, di morale e di letteratura.) pp. 168. Modena, 1848. 8°.   [MISSING.]

—— Biografia del cavaliere Ab. Giambatista Zannoni inserita nel tomo iv della continuazione delle Memorie di religione, morale e letteratura. pp. 96. Modena, 1835. 8°.
10631. e. 23.

—— Biografia del professore Ippolito Rosellini. Con alcune osservazioni intorno alla consonanza de' monumenti dell'Egitto con le Sante Scritture. (Estratto delle Memorie di religione, di morale e di letteratura.) pp. 75. Modena, 1845. 8°.
Dept. of Egyptian & Assyrian Antiquities.

—— Cenni archeologici intorno alle Terremare nostrane. (Estratto dal vol. ii degli Atti e Memorie delle RR. Deputazioni di Storia patria per le provincie Modenesi e Parmensi.) pp. 12. Modena, 1865. fol. 7707. f. 1. (9.)

—— Cenni storici . . . intorno al culto della miracolosa imagine della B. Vergine Maria ausiliatrice del popolo Modenese, ristampati nel secondo centenario della incoronazione della medesima. pp. 32. Modena, 1873. 16°.   4605. a. 15.

CAVEDONI (Celestino)

—— Cenni storici intorno alla vita, ai miracoli ed al culto del glorioso San Geminiano, etc. pp. 169. Modena, 1856. 8°.   4827. aa. 17.

—— Congetture sopra alcuni specchi etruschi. (Estratto dal fasc. 17° del Giornale letterario scientifico modenese.) pp. 24. Modena, 1841. 8°.   07708. b. 7.

—— Decade di antiche gemme intagliate scopertesi a questi ultimi anni nell'agro Modenese e nel Reggiano. (Estratto dal Indicatore modenese.) pp. 19. [1855?] 8°.
[MISSING.]

—— Dell'antica Via Romana che da Modena metteva ad Ostiglia passando per Colicaria nelle vicinanze di Mirandola. Lettera, etc. (Estratto dall'Indicatore modenese.) pp. 11. [1852?] 12°.   [MISSING.]

—— Dell'origine ed incrementi dell'odierno R. Museo Estense delle medaglie e della dispersione dell'altro ad esso anteriore. pp. 30. Modena, 1846. 4°. 7704. k. 4. (9.)

—— Delle monete antiche in oro, un tempo del Museo Estense, descritte da Celio Calcagnini intorno all'anno 1560, memoria. [Extracted from the "Memorie della R. Accademia di Scienze . . . di Modena."] pp. 38. Modena, 1825. 4°.   7755. e. 2. (3.)

—— Di alcune monete antiche degli ultimi re della Tracia. (Estratto delle Memorie di religione, di morale e di letteratura.) pp. 15. Modena, 1846. 8°.
Dept. of Coins & Medals.

—— Dichiarazione degli antichi marmi modenesi; con le notizie di Modena al tempo dei Romani. pp. xi. 316. pl. ii. Modena, 1828. 8°.   787. h. 16.

—— Dichiarazione di due antiche gemme incise provenienti dalle parti di Reggio, l'una ortodossa e l'altra gnostica. pp. 11. Modena, 1852. 8°.   7706. c. 31. (1.)

—— Dichiarazione di un bassorilievo mitriaco della R. Galleria Palatina di Modena. (Estratta dal vol. i degli Atti e Memorie delle Deputazioni di Storia patria per le provincie di Modena e Parma.) [With a plate.] pp. 4. [Modena, 1863.] fol.   7703. h. 2.

—— Elenco dell'opere del Cav. Zannoni. See Zannoni (G. B.) Storia della Accademia della Crusca, etc. 1848. 8°.   8356. cc. 16.

—— Indicazione dei principali monumenti antichi del Reale Museo Estense del Catajo, etc. pp. 127. Modena, 1842. 8°.   7707. d. 40. (4.)

—— Indicazione di alcuni oggetti antichi scopertisi nell'Agro Modenese e Reggiano nel decorso dell'anno m.dccc.xlvi. e ne' primi mesi del corrente m.dccc.xlvii. (Estratto dal vol. i., Memorie e documenti per servire alla storia degli Stati Estensi.) pp. 22. [1847.] 8°.   [MISSING.]

—— Lettera archeologica sopra alcune iscrizioni romane scopertesi di recente negli Stati Estensi. pp. 15. Modena, 1846. 8°.   [MISSING.]

—— Notizia letteraria dell'antica vita di S. Geminiano scritta circa l'anno 910. Descrizione del codice dell'Archivio capitolare contenente la relazione della edificazione della nuova basilica, etc. 1886. See Modena.—Deputazione di Storia Patria per le Antiche Provincie Modenesi. Monumenti di storia patria delle provincie modenesi. vol. 14. 1861, etc. 4°.   9167. m. 1/1.

—— Notizie inedite di un pittore italiano (Maestro Ardimento) che operava in Reggio di Lombardia in sul principio del secolo xii, e di alcuni antichi vescovi di quella città. (Estratto dal tomo viii. degli Opuscoli religiosi letterarj e morali che si stampano in Modena, etc.) pp. 8. [1861.] 8°.   [MISSING.]

CAVEDONI (Celestino)

—— Notizie sopra gl'interrimenti che hanno alzato il suolo di Modena. (Articolo estratto dai Nuovi annali delle scienze naturali di Bologna.) pp. 12. [1846.] 8º.

[Missing.]

—— Nuovi studi sopra le antiche monete consolari e di famiglie romane. (Estratto dal tomo x. degli Opuscoli religiosi, letterarj e morali che si stampano in Modena, etc.) pp. 28. [1861.] 8º. **7756. de. 10. (1.)**

—— Numismatica Biblica, o sia Dichiarazione delle monete antiche memorate nelle Sante Scritture. [With a plate.] pp. 158. *Modena*, 1850. 8º. **3128. g. 17.**

—— Biblische Numismatik . . . übersetzt und mit Zusätzen versehen von A. von Werlhof, etc. 2 Tl. *Hannover*, 1855, 56. 8º. **3129. e. 16.**

—— L'Orazione dominicale parafrasata da Dante Allighieri . . . esposta co' riscontri delle divine Scritture e de' santi padri della Chiesa. *See* DANTE ALIGHIERI. [*Appendix.— Sixth Centenary.*] Omaggio a Dante Alighieri, etc. 1865. 8º. **11421. h. 23.**

—— Osservazioni sopra le antiche monete di Atene. pp. 36. *Modena*, 1836. 8º. **7755. d. 26. (3.)**

—— Osservazioni sopra le monete antiche della Cirenaica. Estratte dal tomo XVI della Continuazione delle Memorie di religione, di morale e di letteratura. pp. 84. *Modena*, 1843. 8º. Dept. of Coins & Medals.

—— Osservazioni sopra un sepolcreto etrusco scoperto nella collina modenese, estratte dal tomo XIII della Continuazione delle Memorie di religione, di morale e di letteratura. pp. 49. *Modena*, 1842. 8º. **7801. b. 24.**

—— Raffronti tra gli autori biblici e sacri e la Divina Commedia. Con prefazione e per cura di R. Murari. pp. 168. *Città di Castello*, 1896. 8º. [*Collezione di opuscoli danteschi.* vol. 29, 30.] **011420. a. 1/23.**

—— Ragguaglio critico del discorso sopra le iscrizioni cristiane antiche del Piemonte del . . . cavaliere Costanzo Gazzera. pp. 30. *Modena*, 1851. 8º. **7704. c. 39. (14.)**

—— Ragguaglio storico archeologico de' precipui ripostigli antichi di medaglie consolari e di famiglie romane d'argento, etc. pp. 291. *Modena*, 1854. 8º. **813. c. 18.**

—— Saggio di osservazioni sulle medaglie di famiglie romane ritrovate in tre antichi ripostigli dell'Agro Modenese negli anni MDCCCXII, MDCCCXV e MDCCCXXVIII. (Estratto dalle Memorie di religione, morale e letteratura, che si stampano in Modena.) pp. 199. *Modena*, 1829. 8º. **602. c. 7.**

—— Scavi di Modena. (Estratto dalla Gazzetta di Modena.) *Modena*, 1862. 8º. [Missing.]

CAVEDONI (Pietro) *See* MASINELLI (A.) Elogio funebre di Mons. Can. D. Pietro Cavedoni, etc. 1862. 8º. **4867. ee. 14. (3.)**

—— D'un altare dedicato nel duomo di Modena alla Risurrezione del Salvatore. pp. 19. *Modena*, 1856. 12º. **10151. aa. 19. (2.)**

—— Dell'altare di San Giuseppe nel duomo di Modena. pp. 16. *Modena*, 1857. 12º. **10151. aa. 19. (5.)**

—— Dell'altare di San Sebastiano nel duomo di Modena. pp. 24. *Modena*, 1858. 12º. **10151. aa. 19. (6.)**

—— Dell'altare di Sant'Antonio di Padova nel duomo di Modena. pp. 28. *Modena*, 1857. 12º. **10151. aa. 19. (4.)**

—— Dell'ancona di Serafino de' Serafini nel duomo di Modena all'altare di Santa Lucia. pp. 22. *Modena*, 1856. 12ᶜ. **10151. aa. 19. (3.)**

CAVEDONI (Pietro)

—— Descrizione del pulpito del duomo di Modena. pp. 19. *Modena*, 1855. 12º. **10151. aa. 19. (1.)**

—— Sventure del duomo di Modena. pp. 18. *Modena*, 1859. 12º. **10151. aa. 19. (7.)**

CAVEESHAR (Sardul Singh) *President of the Indian National Congress. See* ṢĀRDŪL SINGH, Kaviṣvara.

CAVEESSIEUR (Sardul Singh) *President of the Indian National Congress. See* ṢĀRDŪL SINGH, Kaviṣvara.

CAVELA (Foto) *See* TSABELAS (Photos)

CAVELER (William) Architectural Illustrations of Warmington Church, Northamptonshire. pp. 16. pl. 18. *J. H. Parker: Oxford & London*, 1850. fol. **1261. d. 16.**

—— Buckinghamshire. 1848. *See* ENGLAND. [*Appendix. —Descriptions, Travels and Topography.*] The Ecclesiastical and Architectural Topography of England, etc. 1848, etc. 8º. **2261. e. 10.**

—— Huntingdonshire. 1851. *See* ENGLAND. [*Appendix.— Descriptions, Travels and Topography.*] The Ecclesiastical and Architectural Topography of England, etc. 1848, etc. 8º. **2261. e. 10.**

—— Select Specimens of Gothic Architecture . . . from the earliest to the latest date, etc. [Plates, with descriptive letterpress.] *The Author: London*, 1835. 4º. **560*. d. 28.**

CAVELI, Venkata Ramasswami. *See* VEṄKAṬA RAMASVĀMI, Kāvali.

CAVELIER (Adrien Louis Marie) *See* PRUD'HON (P. P.) Description de la toilette présentée à . . . l'Impératrice-Reine, et du berceau offert à S. M. le Roi de Rome . . . Dessinés et gravés par A. L. Cavelier et A. Pierron. 1811. fol. **788. h. 12.**

CAVELIER (Jean) Relation du voyage entrepris par feu M. Robert Cavelier, Sieur de La Salle, pour découvrir dans le Golfe du Mexique l'embouchure du fleuve de Missisipy. Par son frère. pp. 54. *Manate*, 1858. 8º. **10411. e. 28. (1.)**

—— [Another copy.] **10411. b. 5.**

—— Account of La Salle's Voyage to the Mouth of the Mississipi. *See* SHEA (John G.) Early Voyages up and down the Mississippi, etc. 1861. 4º. **10410. f. 14.**

—— Cavelier's account of La Salle's Voyage to the Mouth of the Mississippi, his landing in Texas and march to the Mississippi. *See* COX (Isaac J.) The Journeys of René Robert Cavelier, Sieur de La Salle, etc. 1905. 8º. **9551. b. 15/6.**

CAVELIER (René Robert) *Sieur de la Salle. See* ABBOTT (John S. C.) Through Prairie and Forest; or, the Adventures of La Salle, discoverer of the Mississippi, etc. [1879.] 8º. **12707. ff. 13.**

—— *See* BARTLETT (Charles H.) and LYON (R. H.) La Salle in the Valley of the St. Joseph, etc. 1899. 8º. **9551. bb. 34.**

—— *See* BURTON (Clarence M.) Historical Paper, etc. (La Salle and the Griffon.) 1903. 8º. **9551. i. 27.**

—— [For the account of La Salle's last voyage written by his brother Jean Cavelier:] *See* CAVELIER (J.)

—— *See* CHESNEL (P.) Histoire de Cavelier de la Salle, etc. 1901. 8º. **09055. d. 4.**

CAVELIER (RENÉ ROBERT) *Sieur de la Salle.*

—— *See* COLT (N.) The Devil's Hole. With an account of a visit made to it in 1679 by R. Cavelier de la Salle. To which is added a memoir of the life of La Salle, *etc.* 1859. 8º. **10411. aa. 50. (1.)**

—— *See* COX (Isaac J.) The Journeys of René Robert Cavelier, Sieur de La Salle, as related by his faithful lieutenant H. de Tonty; his missionary colleagues, Fathers Z. Membré, L. Hennepin and A. Douay, *etc.* 1905. 8º. **9551. b. 15/6.**

—— *See* FRASER (John) *of Montreal.* Historic Canadian Ground. The La Salle homestead of 1666, *etc.* 1892. 8º. **10411. f. 38. (4.)**

—— *See* GAITHER (Frances) The Fatal River. The life and death of La Salle. [With a bibliography.] [1931.] 8º. **10655. s. 15.**

—— *See* GIROUARD (D.) Les Anciens forts de Lachine et Cavelier de la Salle. 1891. 8º. **9555. ee. 15.**

—— *See* GIROUARD (D.) Lake St. Louis . . . and Cavelier de La Salle, *etc.* 1893. 4º. **10470. i. 18.**

—— *See* GRAVIER (G.) Cavelier de la Salle, *etc.* 1871. 8º. **10408. g. 5.**

—— *See* GRAVIER (G.) Découvertes et établissements de Cavelier de La Salle . . . dans l'Amérique du Nord, *etc.* 1870. 8º. **10408. g. 18.**

—— *See* HASBROUCK (L. S.) La Salle. 1916. 8º. **10884. a. 17/16.**

—— [For editions and translations of Louis Hennepin's " Nouveau voyage d'un pais plus grand que l'Europe, avec les réflections des entreprises du Sieur de la Salle, sur les mines de St. Barbe " :] *See* HENNEPIN (L.)

—— *See* HOGEBOOM (Amy) The Mysterious Valley : Adventures of Robert la Salle, *etc.* [1941.] 8º. **12826. b. 1.**

—— *See* JACKS (Leo V.) La Salle. 1931. 8º. **10655. bb. 13.**

—— *See* JARAY (G. L.) Cavelier de la Salle, Founder of the French Empire in America, *etc.* 1939. 8º. [*Rice Institute Pamphlet.* vol. 26. no. 1.] **Ac. 1720/2.**

—— [For editions and translations of H. Joutel's " Journal historique du dernier voyage que feu M. de la Sale fit dans le Golfe de Mexique, *etc.*" :] *See* JOUTEL (H.)

—— *See* LA RONCIÈRE (C.G.B.de) Le Père de la Louisiane : Cavelier de la Salle. [1936.] 8º. **010665. e. 59.**

—— *See* LECLERCQ (C.) Account of La Salle's attempt to reach the Mississippi by sea, *etc.* 1852. 8º. [*Historical Collections of Louisiana.* pt. 4.] **1444. i. 4.**

—— *See* LOCKRIDGE (Ross F.) La Salle, *etc.* 1931. 8º. **10655. b. 19.**

—— *See* MEMBRÉ (Z.) Narrative of the first Attempt of M. Cavelier de la Salle to explore the Mississippi . . . Narrative of the adventures of La Salle's party at Fort Crevecoeur . . . from February 1680 to June 1681. 1852. 8º. [*Historical Collections of Louisiana.* pt. 4.] **1444. i. 4.**

—— *See* PARKMAN (Francis) *the Younger.* La Salle and the Discovery of the Great West, *etc.* 1879. 8º. **2398. d. 8.**

—— —— 1885. 8º. **9555. bbb. 14.**

—— —— 1901. 8º. **9555. df. 8.**

CAVELIER (RENÉ ROBERT) *Sieur de la Salle.*

—— *See* REMINGTON (Cyrus K.) The Ship-yard of the Griffon, a brigantine built by René Robert Sieur de la Salle, *etc.* 1891. 8º. **10410. eee. 29.**

—— *See* SEYMOUR (Flora W.) La Salle, Explorer of our Midland Empire. 1939. 8º. **010655. h. 2.**

—— *See* SMYTH (Clifford) Builders of America. (vol. 8. La Salle and the Pioneers of France.) 1931. 8º. **10880. p. 9/8.**

—— *See* SPARKS (Jared) Life of Robert Cavelier de la Salle. 1844. 8º. [*Library of American Biography.* vol. 11.] **10883. df. 8.**

—— [For editions and translations of H. de Tonti's " Dernières découvertes dans l'Amérique septentrionale de M. de la Sale " :] *See* TONTI (H. de)

—— *See* VILLIERS (Marc de) *Baron.* L'Expédition de Cavelier de la Salle dans le golfe de Mexique, 1684–1687. 1931. 4º. **10482. h. 16.**

—— Memoirs, etc. relating to the Discovery of the Mississippi, *etc. See* FALCONER (T.) *County Court Judge.* On the Discovery of the Mississippi, *etc.* 1844. 12º. **1447. g. 22.**

—— [Another edition.] *See* FRENCH (Benjamin F.) Historical Collections of Louisiana, *etc.* pt. 1. 1846, *etc.* 8º. **1444. i. 1.**

CAVELIER DE CUVERVILLE (JULES MARIE ARMAND) *See* CARAYOL (J.) Au Tonkin et en Chine . . . Préface de M. le vice-amiral de Cuverville. 1902. 8º. **09055. aa. 2.**

—— *See* ÉTIENNE (A.) Le R.P. Dorgère, ancien missionnaire au Dahomey. Récits & souvenirs . . . Préface du vice-amiral de Cuverville. 1909. 8º. **4864. de. 24.**

—— *See* SALINIS (A. de) Le Protectorat français sur la Côte des Esclaves . . . Préface du vice-amiral de Cuverville. 1908. 8º. **09061. aa. 37.**

—— *See* UNITED STATES OF AMERICA.—*Navy.* L'Artillerie navale aux États-Unis. Traduit . . . par M. Cavelier de Cuverville. 1865. 8º. **8805. bbb. 31. (4.)**

—— Les Bâtiments cuirassés. pp. 41. *Paris*, 1865. 8º. **8806. c. 4.**

—— Le Canada et les intérêts français. pp. 79. *Paris*, 1898. 12º. **8154. aa. 37.**

—— Cours de tir. Études théoriques et pratiques sur les armes portatives, *etc.* pp. xl. 754. pl. 15. *Paris*, 1864. 8º. **8826. ee. 31.**

—— Les Leçons de la Guerre. Port-Arthur—Tsoushima. Ce qu'il faut à la marine. pp. vii. 198. *Paris, Nancy*, 1906. 8º. **09055. aa. 39.**

CAVELIER DE CUVERVILLE (LOUIS HIPPOLYTE HENRI) Du rectocèle vaginal. pp. 35. *Paris*, 1868. 4º. [*Collection des thèses soutenues à la Faculté de Médecine de Paris.* An 1868. tom. 3.] **7373. i. 7.**

CAVELIER DE CUVERVILLE (LOUIS PAUL MARIE) —— Lettre à nos commettants par MM. de Cuverville . . . Keller . . . Vicomte Anatole Lemercier. pp. 8. *Paris*, 1860. 8º. **8052. e. 22.**

CAVELIER DE CUVERVILLE (PAUL DE) Faculté de Droit de Paris. Thèse pour la licence. (Jus romanum. De usufructu, *etc.*—Droit français. Des conventions matrimoniales, *etc.*) pp. 48. *Paris*, 1860. 8º. **5406. c. 6. (7.)**

CAVELL (Alexander Corry)

—— [For editions of " Intermediate Chemistry " written by A. C. Cavell in collaboration with Thomas M. Lowry :] *See* Lowry (Thomas M.) and Cavell (A. C.)

—— Chemistry for Junior Forms. pp. viii. 295. *Macmillan & Co.: London,* 1946. 8°.　　**08900. aa. 23**.

—— An Introduction to Chemistry. 2 vol. pp. xiii. xi. 711. *Macmillan & Co.: London,* 1940. 8°.　　**8902. ff. 34**.

—— An Introduction to Chemistry . . . Second edition. *Macmillan & Co.: London,* 1946– . 8°.　　**W.P. 1552**.

—— New Style Tests in Chemistry. pp. 47. *E. Arnold & Co.: London,* 1941. 8°.　**8903.h.23.**

CAVELL (Edith Louisa) *See* Baucq (P.) Face à la mort. Journal de Philippe Baucq, fusillé par les Allemands avec Miss Cavell. 1924. 8°.　　**10656. bb. 15**.

—— *See* Baumann (F.) Der Fall Edith Cavell. [With portraits and a facsimile.] [1933.] 8°.　　**09081. bbb. 28**.

—— *See* Beck (James M.) The Case of Edith Cavell, *etc.* [1915.] 8°.　　　　　　　　[Missing.]

—— *See* Blackburn (Douglas) *Novelist.* The Martyr Nurse. The death and achievement of Edith Cavell. [1915.] 8°.　　　　　　　　**010854. de. 55**.

—— *See* England.—*Foreign Office.* Correspondence with the United States Ambassador respecting the execution of Miss Cavell at Brussels. 1915. 8°.　　**09083. dd. 6**.

—— *See* Felstead (Sidney T.) Edith Cavell. The crime that shook the world, *etc.* [1940.] 8°.　　**10859. f. 11**.

—— *See* Giglioli (I.) Edith Cavell. 1915. 8°.　　　　　　　　**10855. f. 31**.

—— *See* Got (A.) L'Affaire Miss Cavell, *etc.* 1921. 8°.　　　　　　　　[Missing.]

—— *See* Got (A.) The Case of Miss Cavell, *etc.* [1920.] 8°.　　　　　　　　[Missing.]

—— *See* Hill (William T.) The Martyrdom of Nurse Cavell, *etc.* 1915. 8°.　　　**10827. aa. 63**.

—— *See* Jesus Christ. [*De Imitatione Christi.—English.*] Of the Imitation of Christ . . . The ' Edith Cavell ' edition. With an introduction by . . . Bishop H. E. Ryle. [1920.] 8°.　　**012209. df. 129**.

—— *See* Judson (Helen) Edith Cavell. [With a portrait.] 1941. 8°.　　　　　**10859. b. 31**.

—— *See* Leeds (Herbert) Edith Cavell, *etc.* [1915.] 8°.　　　　　　　　**010826. de. 27**.

—— *See* Libiez (A.) L'Affaire Cavell, *etc.* 1922. 8°.　　　　　　　　[Missing.]

—— *See* Protheroe (Ernest) A Noble Woman. The life story of Edith Cavell. 1916. 8°.　　**010826. de. 31**.

—— —— 1928. 8°.　　　　**010856. aaa. 31**.

—— *See* Sarolea (Charles) The Murder of Nurse Cavell. 1915. 8°.　　　　　**9082. df. 30**.

—— Nurse Cavell, Dog Lover. Edited with an introduction by Rowland Johns, *etc.* [A facsimile reproduction of MS. notes by Nurse Cavell on the care of dogs. With a portrait.] pp. v. 25. *Methuen & Co.: London,* 1934. 8°.　　**010825. g. 13**.

CAVELL (Edith Louisa)

—— [A Design for a Memorial to Edith Cavell.] [1918.] *s. sh.* fol.　　**1820.h.8.(104.)**

—— The Death of Edith Cavell. pp. 64. *Daily News & Leader: London & Manchester,* [1915.] 12°.　　**09083. a. 55**.

—— Nurse Cavell: the story of her life and martyrdom. pp. 64. *C. A. Pearson: London,* 1915. 8°.　　**010854. de. 53**.

—— Programme of Ceremony of the Unveiling of the Cavell Memorial, St. Martin's Place, on Wednesday, March 17th, at noon, by Her Majesty Queen Alexandra. [*London,* 1920.] 4°.　　**10825. g. 25**.

—— La Vie et la mort de Miss Edith Cavell, d'après des documents inédits, récits de témoins, communiqués officiels et comptes rendus de la presse. Préface de M. Paul Painlevé . . . Avec deux portraits hors-texte de Miss Cavell. pp. xix. 230. *Paris,* 1915. 8°. **010854. de. 57**.

CAVELL (F. M. Strutt) Lady Doctors. *See* Turner (Percival) Guide to the Medical and Dental Professions, *etc.* [1895.] 8°.　　　　[Missing.]

CAVELL (Harold John)

—— Exercises in Chemistry. pp. 55. *William Heinemann: London,* 1951. 8°.　　**08909. a. 67**.

CAVELLATUS (Ivo) *See* Galfridus, *Monumetensis, Bishop of St. Asaph.* Britānie vtriusc̗ regū ⁊ pr̄icipū origo et gesta insignia ab Galfrido Monemutensi . . . in latinū sermonē traducta : & . . . cura . . . I. Cauellati . . . edita. 1508. 4°.　　**598. d. 1. (1.)**

—— —— 1517. 4°.　　　　**598. d. 1. (2.)**

CAVELLET (M.) Dissertation inaugurale sur la carie des vertèbres cervicales, *etc.* pp. 24. *Paris,* 1822. 4°.　　**1183. g. 5. (9.)**

CAVELLI, Giovanni Pietro Campana, *Marquis di. See* Campana.

CAVELLI (Campana de) *Marchioness. See* Campana.

CAVELLI (O.) *See* Bliemchen (Fritze) *Particularist, pseud.* Memoiren des Particularisten Bliemchen aus Dresden. Mit Federzeichnungen von O. Cavelli. 1879. 8°.　　**12316. h. 30**.

CAVELLIER (Blaise) Rapport et projet de décret, présentés à l'Assemblée nationale au nom du Comité de la marine sur les approvisionnemens, fournitures & ouvrages de la marine. pp. 15. [*Paris,* 1792.] 8°.　**F. 1175. (5.)**

—— Supplément à l'opinion de M. Cavellier sur les dénonciations dirigées contre M. Bertrand, & la prétendue justification de ce ministre. pp. 7. *Paris,* [1792.] 8°.　　**F.R. 98. (20.)**

CAVELLUS (Hugo) *R.C. Archbishop of Armagh. See* Mac Caghwell.

CAVELLY VENKATA RAMASWAMY. *See* Veṅkaṭa Ramasvāmi, *Kāvali.*

CAVE-MOYLE (Thomas Henry) *See* Moyle.

CAVEN (John) Post-Mortem Examinations. Methods and technique, *etc.* pp. 40. *J. A. Carveth & Co.: Toronto,* [1900.] 8°.　　**07481. h. 17**.

CAVEN (Robert Martin) Carbon and its Allies, *etc.* pp. xxi. 468.   *C. Griffin & Co.: London,* 1917. 8°. [*Text-book of Inorganic Chemistry.* vol. 5.]   W.P. **2754.**

—— The Foundations of Chemical Theory. An introductory textbook. pp. viii. 266.   *Blackie & Son: London,* 1920. 8°.   **8903. b. 25.**

—— Atoms and Molecules : being part I and chapter XII of "The Foundations of Chemical Theory." pp. viii. 141. *Blackie & Son: London & Glasgow,* 1927. 8°.   **8710. aa. 26.**

—— Gas and Gases. pp. 256.   *Williams & Norgate: London,* 1926. 8°. [*Home University Library.* vol. 122.]   **12199. p. 1/131.**

—— Joseph Priestley, 1733–1804. pp. 25. 1933. 8°. *See* London.—III. *Royal Institute of Chemistry.*   Ac. **3921/7.**

—— Manuals of Pure and Applied Chemistry. General editor : R. M. Caven. 4 pt.   *Blackie & Son: London,* 1924–28. 8°.   **8897. ee. 34.**

—— Quantitative Chemical Analysis and Inorganic Preparations. 2 pt.   *Blackie & Son: London,* 1923, 25. 8°.   **8902. a. 26.**

—— [Another edition.] 2 pt.   *Blackie & Son: London & Glasgow,* 1927. 8°.   **8902. a. 42.**

—— A Short System of Qualitative Analysis for Students of Inorganic Chemistry. pp. viii. 162.   *Blackie & Son: London,* 1917. 8°.   **8907. d. 9.**

—— Systematic Qualitative Analysis for Students of Inorganic Chemistry. pp. xii. 240.   *Blackie & Son: London,* 1909. 8°.   **08909. h. 51.**

CAVEN (Robert Martin) and **CRANSTON** (John Arnold)

——   Symbols and Formulæ in Chemistry. An historical study. pp. ix. 220. *Blackie & Son: London & Glasgow,* 1928. 8°. [*Manuals of Pure and Applied Chemistry.*]   **8897. ee. 34/4.**

CAVEN (Robert Martin) and **LANDER** (George Druce)

——   Systematic Inorganic Chemistry from the standpoint of the Periodic Law. A text-book for advanced students. pp. xix. 374. *Blackie & Son: London,* 1906. 8°.   **8904. a. 3.**

—— (New and enlarged edition.) pp. xviii. 460. *Blackie & Son: London,* 1922. 8°.   **8903. ff. 20.**

—— [Another edition.] pp. xviii. 510.   *Blackie & Son: London & Glasgow,* 1930. 8°.   **8902. c. 33.**

—— Fifth edition. Revised by A. B. Crawford. pp. xxv. 546.   *Blackie & Son: London & Glasgow,* 1936. 8°.   **8901. df. 31.**

CAVEN (Stewart) The Green Enigma. pp. 353. *Howard Latimer: London,* [1913.] 8°.   NN. **1428.**

—— A Pair of Idols. pp. 231.   *Chapman & Hall: London,* 1919. 8°.   NN. **5693.**

—— Palmers Green. [A novel.] pp. iii. 375. *G. P. Putnam's Sons: New York & London,* 1912. 8°.   NN. **422.**

—— Wit's End. pp. 288.   *Wishart & Co.: London,* 1927. 8°.   NN. **13282.**

CAVEN (William) Christ's Teaching concerning the Last Things, and other papers. [With a biographical sketch of the author by James A. Macdonald.] pp. xxxii. 328. *Hodder & Stoughton: London; Westminster Co.: Toronto,* 1908. 8°.   **4223. ee. 6.**

CAVENAGH (Bernard) The Very Extraordinary Life and Singular Characteristics of Mr. Cavanagh the celebrated Fasting Man, *etc.* pp. 12.   *C. Lowe: London,* 1841. 8°.   [MISSING.]

CAVENAGH (Francis Alexander) *See* Blackwood (Frederick T. H. T.) *Marquis of Dufferin and Ava.* Letters from High Latitudes . . . With . . . notes by F. A. Cavenagh. 1915. 8°.   **10470. ss. 1.**

—— *See* Borrow (George A.) Wanderings in Spain . . . With introduction, notes, etc., by F. A. Cavenagh. 1914. 8°.   **012273. de. 49.**

—— *See* Landor (Walter S.) Imaginary Conversations. Selected and edited, with introduction and notes, by F. A. Cavenagh. 1914. 8°.   **12316. pp. 17.**

—— *See* Landor (Walter S.) Imaginary Conversations . . . With . . . notes by F. A. Cavenagh and A. C. Ward. 1934. 8°.   **12356. ppp. 10.**

—— *See* Lowell (James R.) Lowell's Fireside Travels. With . . . notes by F. A. Cavenagh. 1915. 12°.   **12354. ppp. 7.**

—— *See* Mill (James) *Economist.* James & John Stuart Mill on Education. Edited by F. A. Cavenagh. 1931. 8°.   **8312.a.25/1.**

—— *See* Peacock (Thomas L.) Maid Marian . . . With introduction, notes, etc., by F. A. Cavenagh. 1912. 8°.   **012273. de. 47.**

—— *See* Scott (*Sir* Walter) *Bart.* [*Waverley Novels.*] New Annotated Editions of the Waverley Novels, *etc.* (The Antiquary. Edited by F. A. Cavenagh.) 1914, *etc.* 8°.   **12643.aa.66/1.**

—— *See* Scott (*Sir* Walter) *Bart.* [*Waverley Novels.*] New Annotated Editions of the Waverley Novels, *etc.* (Ivanhoe. Edited by F. A. Cavenagh.) 1914, *etc.* 8°.   **12643.aa.66/4.**

—— *See* Scott (*Sir* Walter) *Bart.* [*Waverley Novels.*] New Annotated Editions of the Waverley Novels, *etc.* (A Legend of Montrose. Edited by F. A. Cavenagh.) 1914, *etc.* 8°.   **12643.aa.66/5.**

—— *See* Smith (Alexander) *Poet.* Dreamthorp . . . With . . . notes by F. A. Cavenagh. 1914. 8°.   **12357. de. 33.**

—— *See* Spencer (Herbert) [*Miscellaneous Writings.*] Herbert Spencer on Education. Edited by F. A. Cavenagh. 1932. 8°.   **8312.a.25/4.**

—— *See* Tennyson (Alfred) *Baron Tennyson.* [*Selections and Extracts.*] Oenone and Lotos-Eaters. Edited with introduction and notes by F. A. Cavenagh. [1915.] 8°.   **11646. g. 66.**

—— *See* Tennyson (Alfred) *Baron Tennyson.* [*Selections and Extracts.*] Selected Poems . . . Edited by . . . F. A. Cavenagh. 1916. 8°.   **11611. i. 22.**

—— *See* Wilson (John D.) and Cavenagh (F. A.) Landmarks in the History of Education. General editors : J. Dover Wilson . . . F. A. Cavenagh. 1931, *etc.* 8°.   **8312.a.25.**

—— The Development of Educational Thought in the United Kingdom, 1920–35. *See* London.—III. *University of London.—Institute of Education.* A Review of Educational Thought, *etc.* [1936.] 8°.   Ac. **2666. e/2.**

—— The Ethical End of Plato's Theory of Ideas. A thesis, *etc.* pp. 89.   *Henry Frowde: Oxford,* 1909. 8°.   **8459. h. 6.**

CAVENAGH (Francis Alexander)

—— The Life and Work of Griffith Jones of Llanddowror. pp. 72. *University of Wales Press Board: Cardiff,* 1930. 8º. **4908. i. 10.**

CAVENAGH (Sir Orfeur) The Native Army in India. A paper, *etc.* pp. 22. 1879. 8º. *See* London.—III. *East India Association.* **8022. de. 39. (7.)**

—— Reminiscences of an Indian Official. pp. xi. 372. *W. H. Allen & Co.: London,* 1884. 8º. **10816. c. 27.**

—— Rough Notes on the State of Nepal, its government, army and resources. [With a map.] pp. iv. 264. xix. *Printed for private circulation: Calcutta,* 1851. 12º. **8023. bbb. 4.**

CAVENAGHI (Luigi) Relazione . . . sul restauro del Cenacolo Vinciano. *See* Beltrami (L.) Il Cenacolo di Leonardo, *etc.* 1908. 8º. [Missing.]

CAVENAGH-MAINWARING (James G.) *See* Mainwaring.

CAVENDER (Curtis H.) *See* Decanver (H. C.) *pseud.* [i.e. C. H. Cavender.]

CAVENDISH. The Registers of Cavendish Church. Copied . . . by O. G. Knapp, *etc.* ff. 294. [*London,*] 1939. 4º. [*Society of Genealogists. Transcripts of Parish Registers.*] **Ac. 5962. b/24.**

Typewritten.

CAVENDISH. Cavendish; or, the Patrician at sea. [By William J. Neale.] 3 vol. *H. Colburn & R. Bentley: London,* 1831. 12º. **N. 810.**

CAVENDISH, *pseud.* [i.e. Henry Jones.] *See* Bennett (Joseph) *Billiard-Player.* Billiards . . . Edited by Cavendish. 1873. 8º. **7915.cc.6.**

—— —— 1881. 8º. [Missing.]

—— —— 1884. 8º. [Missing.]

—— —— 1889. 8º. [Missing.]

—— —— 1894. 8º. [Missing.]

—— —— 1899. 8º. **2270. cc. 10.**

—— *See* Bennett (Joseph) *Billiard-Player.* The Spot-Stroke . . . Edited by "Cavendish," *etc.* 1872. 16º. [Missing.]

—— *See* D., B. W., and Cavendish, *pseud.* Whist with and without Perception, *etc.* 1889. 8º. **7913.bb.79.**

—— *See* Merry Andrew. Whist. The American Lead Controversy. By "Merry Andrew." With a letter by "Cavendish." 1885. 8º. [Missing.]

—— *See* Portland, *pseud.* The Whist Table. A treasury of notes . . . by "Cavendish" . . . and other . . . players, *etc.* [1895.] 8º. [Missing.]

—— *See* Trumps, *pseud.* Modern Whist . . . Compiled from the latest works by "Cavendish," *etc.* 1892. 8º. [Missing.]

—— American Leads Simplified. Reprinted, with additions, from the nineteenth edition of "The Laws and Principles of Whist." pp. 14. *T. De La Rue & Co.: London,* 1891. 8º. [Missing.]

—— Second edition. pp. 14. *T. De La Rue & Co.: London,* 1891. 8º. [Missing.]

—— Third edition. pp. 15. *T. De La Rue & Co.: London,* 1892. 8º. [Missing.]

CAVENDISH, *pseud.* [i.e. Henry Jones.]

—— Fourth edition. pp. 15. *T. De La Rue & Co.: London,* 1894. 8º. [Missing.]

—— Card Essays, Clay's Decisions, and Card-table Talk. pp. x. 260. *T. De La Rue & Co.: London,* 1879. 8º. **7913.ee.4.**

—— Card Essays, Clay's Decisions, and Card-table Talk . . American edition, with an index. [With a portrait.] pp. vi. 290. *Henry Holt & Co.: New York,* 1880. 8º. **7921. dd. 94.**

Leisure Hour Series. no. 109.

—— Casse-Tête . . . With a hundred and fifty diagrams and solutions. pp. 53. *T. De La Rue & Co.: London,* 1881. 8º. [Missing.]

—— "Cavendish's" Improved Table Croquet. Directions and rules. pp. 14. *Parkins & Gotto: London,* [1866.] 12º. [Missing.]

—— The Game of Bézique. pp. 34. *T. De La Rue & Co.: London,* 1870. 8º. **7913.b.20.**

—— The Game of Drôle. Rules and directions for playing. pp. 10. *T. De La Rue & Co.: London,* 1869. 32º. [Missing.]

—— The Games of Lawn Tennis, with the authorised laws, and Badminton. pp. 29. *T. De La Rue & Co.: London,* 1876. 8º. [Missing.]

—— Second edition. pp. 30. *T. De La Rue & Co.: London,* 1878. 8º. [Missing.]

—— Third edition. pp. 30. *T. De La Rue & Co.: London,* 1880. 8º. [Missing.]

—— Fifth edition. pp. 30. *T. De La Rue & Co.: London,* 1883. 8º. [Missing.]

—— Sixth edition. pp. 55. *T. De La Rue & Co.: London,* 1885. 8º. [Missing.]

—— Seventh edition. pp. 60. *T. De La Rue & Co.: London,* 1886. 8º. [Missing.]

—— Eighth edition. pp. 62. *T. De La Rue & Co.: London,* 1888. 8º. [Missing.]

—— Ninth edition. pp. 77. *T. De La Rue & Co.: London,* 1890. 8º. [Missing.]

—— The Laws and Principles of Whist. *See infra:* The Principles of Whist.

—— The Laws of Écarté adopted by the Turf Club, *etc.* pp. 62. *T. De La Rue & Co.: London,* 1878. 8º. [Missing.]

—— Second edition. pp. 62. *T. De La Rue & Co.: London,* 1878. 8º. [Missing.]

—— Third edition. pp. 72. *T. De La Rue & Co.: London,* 1886. 8º. **7915.aa.46.**

—— Fourth edition, revised and greatly enlarged. pp. x. 148. *T. De La Rue & Co.: London,* 1897. 8º. **7913.df.29.**

—— The Laws of Piquet, edited by "Cavendish" . . . with a treatise on the game. pp. xix. 118. *T. De La Rue & Co.: London,* 1873. 16º. **7913.b.19.**

—— Second edition. pp. xix. 118. *T. De La Rue & Co.: London,* 1881. 8º. **7913.bb.53.**

—— Fifth edition. pp. iv. 131. *T. De La Rue & Co.: London,* 1887. 8º. **7908.aa.60.**

—— Sixth edition. pp. iv. 138. *T. De La Rue & Co.: London,* 1889. 8º. **7915.b.46.**

CAVENDISH, *pseud.* [i.e. HENRY JONES.]

—— Seventh edition. pp. viii. 204. *T. De La Rue & Co.: London,* 1890. 8°. [MISSING.]

—— Eighth edition. pp. viii. 208. *T. De La Rue & Co.: London,* 1892. 8°. **7913.ccc.35.**

—— Ninth edition. pp. viii. 208. *T. De La Rue & Co.: London,* 1896. 8°. **7913.df.24.**

—— [A reissue.] *London,* 1913. 8°. [MISSING.]

—— The Laws of Rubicon Bézique adopted by the Portland Club, with a guide to the game. pp. iv. 49. *T. De La Rue & Co.: London,* 1887. 8°. **7913.bb.78.**

—— Second edition. pp. iv. 50. *T. De La Rue & Co.: London,* 1892. 8°. **7912.aa.17.**

—— Third edition. pp. iv. 51. *T. De La Rue & Co.: London,* 1895. 8°. **7913.df.19.**

—— The Laws of Rubicon Piquet adopted by the Portland Club; edited by " Cavendish." pp. 18. *Printed for private circulation: London,* 1882. 8°. [MISSING.]

—— The Laws of Vingt-et-un agreed to by the editors of " The Field " and " Bell's Life," and the laws of Loo of the Blenheim Club. Edited by Cavendish. pp. 7. *Printed for private circulation: London,* 1874. 8°. [MISSING.]

—— Musical Whist with Living Cards. Introduction, historical & descriptive notes. pp. 42. *T. De La Rue & Co.: London,* 1892. 4°. [MISSING.]

—— On the Card to lead at Whist, from suits of five, or more . . . Reprinted from " The Field." pp. 15. *Printed for private circulation: London,* 1873. 8°. [MISSING.]

—— On the Laws of Croquet. pp. 15. *Printed for private circulation:* [*London,*] 1868. 8°. [MISSING.]

—— Patience Games, with examples played through, *etc.* pp. 216. *T. De La Rue & Co.: London,* 1890 [1889]. *obl.* 4°. **Cup.1246.c.37.**

—— The Pocket Guide to Backgammon and Russian Backgammon. pp. 21. *T. De La Rue & Co.: London,* 1878. 32°. [MISSING.]

—— Third edition. pp. 21. *T. De La Rue & Co.: London,* 1910. 32°. [MISSING.]

—— [A reissue.] *London,* 1913. 32°. [MISSING.]

—— The Pocket Guide to Bézique. By Cavendish . . . Sixth edition. pp. 18. *Thos. De la Rue & Co.: London,* 1872. 32°. **7911.a.15.**

—— A Pocket Guide to Calabrasella, *etc.* pp. 14. *T. De La Rue & Co.: London,* 1870. 32°. [MISSING.]

—— The Pocket Guide to Chess. 9 pt. *London,* 1878–1922. 32°. **7911.a.16.** *Various editions.*

—— The Pocket Guide to Cribbage. 7 pt. *London,* 1873–1924. 32°. [MISSING.] *Various editions.*

—— The Pocket Guide to Croquet. pp. 18. *T. De La Rue & Co.: London,* 1869. 32°. **7919.d.34.**

—— The Pocket Guide to Dominoes. pp. 22. *T. De La Rue & Co.: London,* 1886. 32°. [MISSING.]

CAVENDISH, *pseud.* [i.e. HENRY JONES.]

—— The Pocket Guide to Draughts and Polish Draughts. 6 pt. *T. De La Rue & Co.: London,* 1878–1918. 32°. [MISSING.] *Various editions.*

—— The Pocket Guide to Écarté, *etc.* 5 pt. *T. De La Rue & Co.: London,* 1870–1909. 32°. [MISSING.] *Various editions.*

—— The Pocket Guide to Euchre, *etc.* pp. 18. *T. De La Rue & Co.: London,* 1870. 32°. [MISSING.]

—— Fourth edition. pp. 22. *T. De La Rue & Co.: London,* 1890. 16°. [MISSING.]

—— The Pocket Guide to Fifteen and Thirty-four Puzzles. pp. 12. *T. De La Rue & Co.: London,* 1880. 32°. [MISSING.]

—— Second edition. pp. 14. *T. De La Rue & Co.: London,* 1880. 32°. [MISSING.]

—— The Pocket Guide to Go-Bang. pp. 12. *T. De La Rue & Co.: London,* 1876. 32°. [MISSING.]

—— Second edition. pp. 13. *T. De La Rue & Co.: London,* 1877. 32°. [MISSING.]

—— Third edition. pp. 13. *T. De La Rue & Co.: London,* 1877. 32°. [MISSING.]

—— The Pocket Guide to Imperial. pp. 22. *T. De La Rue & Co.: London,* 1881. 32°. [MISSING.]

—— The Pocket Guide to Piquet. 10 pt. *T. De La Rue & Co.: London,* 1890–1919. 32°. [MISSING.] *Various editions.*

—— The Pocket Guide to Polish Bézique, *etc.* pp. 18. *T. De La Rue & Co.: London,* 1873. 32°. [MISSING.]

—— The Pocket Guide to Rubicon Bézique. 3 pt. *T. De La Rue & Co.: London,* 1893–1910. 32°. [MISSING.] *Various editions.*

—— The Pocket Guide to Sixty-Six. pp. 15. *T. De La Rue & Co.: London,* 1875. 32°. [MISSING.]

—— The Pocket Guide to Spoil-Five, Twenty-Five & Forty-Five, *etc.* pp. 18. *T. De La Rue: London,* 1870. 32°. [MISSING.]

—— The Pocket Guide to Whist. 7 pt. *T. De La Rue & Co.: London,* [1864]–1924. 32°. [MISSING.] *Various editions.*

—— The Pocket Laws of Écarté, *etc.* pp. 14. *T. De La Rue & Co.: London,* 1870. 32°. **Cup.550.aa.48.**

—— The Pocket Laws of Whist. In accordance with the code adopted by the London Clubs, compiled . . . by " Cavendish." pp. 18. *T. De La Rue & Co.: London,* 1864. 32°. [MISSING.]

—— [Another edition.] pp. 18. *T. De La Rue & Co.: London,* 1865. 16°. [MISSING.]

—— Eighth edition. pp. 18. *T. De La Rue & Co.: London,* 1897. 32°. [MISSING.]

—— Pocket Rules for leading at Whist. With a table of leads and practical hints for whist players. pp. 18. *T. De La Rue & Co.: London,* [1865.] 16°. [MISSING.]

CAVENDISH, *pseud.* [i.e. HENRY JONES.]

—— Third edition. pp. 18. *T. De La Rue & Co.: London,* 1875. 32º. [MISSING.]

—— Ninth edition. pp. 22. *T. De La Rue Co.: London,* 1889. 32º. [MISSING.]

—— Eleventh edition. pp. 18. *T. De La Rue & Co.: London,* 1897. 32º. [MISSING.]

—— The Principles of Whist stated and explained, and its practice illustrated on an original system, by means of hands played completely through. pp. 80. *Bancks Bros.: London,* [1862.] 8º. **7913.b.21.**

—— The Laws and Principles of Whist stated and explained . . . Fifth edition [of " The Principles of Whist "]. pp. 96. *Bancks Bros.: London,* 1863. 8º. **7913.aaa.2.**

—— Seventh edition. pp. 107. *Bancks Bros.: London,* 1864. 8º. **7913.aaa.22.**

—— Eighth edition, with numerous additions. pp. 120. *T. De La Rue & Co.: London,* 1868. 8º. [MISSING.]

—— Ninth edition, with numerous additions. pp. 120. *T. De La Rue & Co.: London,* 1871. 8º. **7913.bb.22.**

—— Tenth edition, revised and . . . enlarged. pp. xi. 268. *T. De La Rue & Co.: London,* 1874. 8º. **7913.bbb.29.**

—— Eleventh edition, revised and . . . enlarged. pp. xi. 268. *T. De La Rue & Co.: London,* 1876. 8º. **7913.b.7.**

—— Thirteenth edition . . . enlarged. pp. xi. 268. *T. De La Rue & Co.: London,* 1879. 8º. **7915.bbb.7.**

—— Fourteenth edition. pp. xii. 276. *T. De La Rue & Co.: London,* 1884. 8º. **7913.b.77.**

—— The Laws and Principles of Whist . . . Sixteenth edition. pp. xii. 288. *In:* The Whist Triad, *etc.* 1884. 8º. **7921. a. 7. (2.)**
The date on the titlepage is 1886.

—— Fifteenth edition. pp. xii. 272. *T. De La Rue & Co.: London,* 1885. 8º. **7913.b.78.**

—— [A reissue.] The Laws and Principles of Whist, *etc.* London, 1886. 8º. **7915. aaa. 61.**

—— Seventeenth edition. pp. xii. 291. *T. De La Rue & Co.: London,* 1888. 8º. **7915.bbb.51.**

—— Eighteenth edition. pp. xii. 294. *T. De La Rue & Co.: London,* 1889. 8º. **7915.df.54.**

—— Nineteenth edition. pp. xii. 294. *T. De La Rue & Co.: London,* 1891. 8º. **7913.ccc.26.**

—— Twentieth edition, *etc.* pp. xii. 305. *T. De La Rue & Co.: London,* 1892. 8º. **7913.ccc.34.**

—— Twenty-first edition. pp. xiv. 320. *T. De La Rue & Co.: London,* 1893. 8º. **7913.df.10.**

—— Twenty-second edition. pp. xii. 306. *T. De La Rue & Co.: London,* 1895. 8º. **7913.df.16.**

—— American edition. pp. x. 318. *C. Scribner's Sons: New York,* 1895. 8º. **7912.b.2.**

—— Twenty-third edition, *etc.* pp. xii. 306. *T. De La Rue & Co.: London,* 1898. 8º. **7913.df.34.**

—— Twenty-fourth edition. Containing the New Code of Laws, revised in 1900. pp. xi. 306. *T. De La Rue & Co.: London,* 1901. 8º. **7912.b.15.**

CAVENDISH, *pseud.* [i.e. HENRY JONES.]

—— Whist Studies : being hands of whist played through according to the system of Cavendish, and in illustration of the principles laid down in that work [i.e. in his " Principles of Whist stated and explained "]. By A. C. [i.e. James Innes Minchin] and B. D. [i.e. F. Arbuthnot]. 1863. 8º. *See* C., A., and D., B. [MISSING.]

—— Recreations with Magic Squares, the Eight Queens' Problem solved by Magic Squares and Domino Squares. pp. 84. *T. De La Rue & Co.: London,* 1894. 8º. [MISSING.]

—— Round Games at Cards, *etc.* pp. iv. 55. *T. De La Rue & Co.: London,* 1875 [1874]. 8º. **7913.b.22.**

—— Second edition. pp. iv. 61. *T. De La Rue & Co.: London,* 1887. 8º. **7913.bb.7.**

—— Second Sight for Amateurs. ff. iv. 99. *Printed for private circulation:* [London,] 1888. 4º. **7913.f.34.**
One of an edition of twenty-five copies.

—— Whist Developments. American leads and the plain-suit echo. pp. xiv. 172. *T. De La Rue & Co.: London,* 1885. 8º. **7913.bb.67.**

—— Second edition. pp. xiv. 172. *T. De La Rue & Co.: London,* 1885. 8º. [MISSING.]

—— Third edition. pp. xiv. 172. *T. De la Rue: London,* 1887. 8º. **7908.aa.59.**

—— Fourth edition. pp. xiv. 181. *T. De La Rue & Co.: London,* 1891. 8º. [MISSING.]

CAVENDISH, *pseud.* [i.e. SAMUEL BEVAN.] *See also* BEVAN (Samuel)

—— To All Who Smoke. A few words in defence of tobacco ; or, a plea for the pipe . . . By " Cavendish." pp. 96. *Baily Bros.: London,* 1857. 8º. **8435. aaa. 65. (2.)**

CAVENDISH ASSOCIATION. *See* ENGLAND.

CAVENDISH INSTITUTE. Complete Guide to the Mail Order Business [and other pamphlets]. *Cavendish Institute: London,* [1924– .] 8º. **W.P. 7996.**

CAVENDISH LABORATORY. *See* CAMBRIDGE.—*University of Cambridge.*

CAVENDISH LIBRARY. The " Cavendish Library." 9 vol. *T. Warne & Co.: London,* [1887–90.] 8º. **12295. ccc. 10.**

CAVENDISH SOCIETY. *See* LONDON.—III.

CAVENDISH SOCIETY, *Cambridge. See* CAMBRIDGE. —*University of Cambridge.—Cavendish Laboratory.— Physics Research Society.*

CAVENDISH, *Family of. See* BICKLEY (Francis L.) The Cavendish Family, *etc.* 1911. 8º. **9914. tt. 1.**

—— *See* COLLINS (Arthur) Historical Collections of the Noble Families of Cavendish, Holles, *etc.* 1752. fol. **133. g. 14.**

—— *See* HEAPE (Robert G.) Buxton under the Dukes of Devonshire. 1948. 8º. **10359. d. 36.**

—— *See* KENNET (White) *Bishop of Peterborough.* Memoirs of the Family of Cavendish. 1708. 8º. **1328. a. 17**

—— —— 1737. 12º. **11602. bb. 33. (10.)**

CAVENDISH, *Family of, Earls and Dukes of Devonshire.*

—— *See* GROVE (Joseph) *of Richmond.* The Lives of all the Earls and Dukes of Devonshire, *etc.* 1764. 8⁰.
1202. d. 10.

CAVENDISH (A. C.) *See* IKHWĀN AL-ŠAFĀ. Studies in Hindustanee. Ikhwan us safa . . . Translated by A. C. Cavendish. 1885. 8⁰.
14112. aaa. 32.

CAVENDISH (ALFRED EDWARD JOHN) An Reisimeid Chataich. The 93rd Sutherland Highlanders, now 2nd Bn. The Argyll and Sutherland Highlanders, Princess Louise's, 1799–1927. [With plates, including portraits.] pp. xxvi. 446. 1928. 4⁰. *See* ENGLAND.—*Army.—Infantry.—Princess Louise's (Argyll and Sutherland Highlanders), 2nd Battalion.*
8820. d. 2.

—— Korea and the Sacred White Mountain . . . with an account of an ascent of the White Mountain by Captain H. E. Goold-Adams. With . . . illustrations and . . . maps. pp. 224. *G. Philip & Son: London,* 1894. 8⁰.
10057. d. 3.

CAVENDISH (CAROLINE G.) *See* PEABODY (Helen) At Rest Among the Laos . . . Edited by C. G. Cavendish. [1882.] 8⁰.
4766. bb. 23.

—— Lilies; or, Letters to school-girls. By popular writers. Edited by C. G. Cavendish. pp. 87. *S. W. Partridge & Co.: London,* [1885.] 16⁰.
4401. i. 28.

—— Polished Corner-Stones; or, Letters to school-girls. By popular writers. Edited by C. G. Cavendish. pp. 107. *S. W. Partridge & Co.: London,* [1883.] 16⁰.
4401. i. 10.

CAVENDISH (CHARLES) The Lure. A story of crime . . . The story of the film adapted from the stage play . . . by Major J. S. Clair. pp. 253. *W. Collins Sons & Co.: [London,* 1930.] 8⁰.
012600. h. 15.

CAVENDISH (*Hon.* CHARLES) *See* NAILOUR (William) A Commemoration Sermon preached at Darby, Feb. 18. 1674, for the Honourable Colonel C. Cavendish, slain in the service of King Charles I., in 1643. 1675. 8⁰.
C. 121. b. 5. (8.)

CAVENDISH (*Lord* CHARLES) *See* LOWTHER (James) *Earl of Lonsdale.* The Rt. Hon. C. Cavendish Esq. . . . Appellant; Sir J. Lowther, Respondent. The Respondents case. [1759.] *s. sh.* fol. **816. m. 5. (35.)**

—— The Right Honourable Charles Cavendish, Esquire, commonly called Lord Charles Cavendish, sole executor and residuary legatee of Sir William Lowther . . . Appellant. Sir James Lowther, Baronet, Respondent. The case of the Appellant. pp. 3. [*London,* 1759.] fol.
816. m. 5. (34.)

CAVENDISH (*Sir* CHARLES) *Bart. See* BROCKDORFF (C. L. G. C. von) *Baron.* Des Sir Charles Cavendish Bericht für Joachim Jungius über die Grundzüge der Hobbes'schen Naturphilosophie. 1934. 8⁰. [*Veröffentlichungen der Hobbes-Gesellschaft, Ortsgruppe Kiel.* no. 3.] Ac. **634.**

CAVENDISH (CHARLES WILLIAM) Plain Directions for Private Devotion, drawn from the writings of the Saints. Two sermons. pp. 32. *Joseph Masters: London,* 1850. 8⁰.
3475. d. 41. (5.)

—— *See* SMITH (William G. P.) A Letter in reply to " the Preface " to two Sermons by C. W. Cavendish. 1850. 8⁰.
4108. bb. 80. (2.)

CAVENDISH (CHARLOTTE) *pseud.* [i.e. NETLEY LUCAS.] The Biography of H.M. Queen Mary. [With portraits.] pp. 251. *A. E. Marriott: London,* 1930. 8⁰.
10807. ee. 11.

CAVENDISH (CHRISTIAN) *Countess of Devonshire. See* POMFRET (Thomas) The Life of . . . Christian, late Countess Dowager of Devonshire. 1685. 8⁰. **1112. c. 3.**

—— An Elegy on the Truly Honourable . . . Lady, Countesse of Devonshire, *etc.* [*London,* 1675.] *s. sh.* fol.
Lutt. I. **38.**

CAVENDISH (*Lady* CLARA) *pseud.* A Marriage of Mystery; or, the Lost bride. pp. 188. *F. A. Brady: New York,* [1868 ?] 8⁰.
12706. h. 22.

—— The Woman of the World. A drama in two acts. Adapted from the popular tale of that name, published in " Reynolds's Miscellany." pp. 52. *London,* [1859.] 8⁰. [*Lacy's Acting Edition of Plays.* vol. 38.] **2304. e. 12.**

CAVENDISH (EDWARD WILLIAM SPENCER) *Duke of Devonshire.*

—— Old Master Drawings from Chatsworth. [An exhibition catalogue.] pp. 32. *Arts Council: [London,]* 1949. 8⁰.
W.P. **12368/119.**

CAVENDISH (ELIZABETH) *afterwards* **MONK** (ELIZABETH) *Duchess of Albemarle, afterwards* **MONTAGU** (ELIZABETH) *Duchess of Montagu. See* MONK.

CAVENDISH (ELIZABETH CHRISTIANA) *Duchess of Devonshire.*

—— *See* FOSTER (Vere H. L.) The Two Duchesses, Georgiana, Duchess of Devonshire, Elizabeth, Duchess of Devonshire. Family correspondence, *etc.* 1898. 8⁰. **010920. k. 14.**

—— *See* STUART (Dorothy M.) Dearest Bess. The life and times of Lady Elizabeth Foster, afterwards Duchess of Devonshire, from her unpublished journals and correspondence. [With portraits.] 1955. 8⁰. **10864. cc. 35.**

—— Anecdotes and Biographical Sketches. [With a portrait.] pp. xxi. 137. *Privately printed: London,* 1863. 8⁰.
12360. ff. 34.

CAVENDISH (FRANCIS WILLIAM HENRY) *See* PERIODICAL PUBLICATIONS.—*London.* The Foreign-Office List. [1852–54 compiled by F. W. H. Cauendish; 1855–63 compiled by F. W. H. Cavendish and E. Hertslet.] [1852, *etc.*] 8⁰. **B.S. 14/143. & Ref. 102.**

—— Society, Politics, and Diplomacy, 1820–1864. Passages from the journal of F. W. H. Cavendish. With four illustrations. pp. 416. *T. Fisher Unwin: London, Leipsic,* 1913. 8⁰.
010826. e. 19.

CAVENDISH (*Hon.* FREDERICK) A Full Report, with notes, of the Trial of an Action wherein the Hon. Frederick Cavendish was plaintiff and the Hope Assurance Company of London were defendants . . . To which is added a copy of the reports of the inspectors appointed to view the premises immediately subsequent to the fire. pp. 249. *H. Fitzpatrick: Dublin,* 1813. 8⁰. **1131. e. 30.**

—— Report of the Trial of an Action wherein the Hon. F. Cavendish was Plaintiff and the Hope Insurance Company of London Defendants. pp. 73. *John Cumming: Dublin,* 1813. 8⁰. **1132. k. 17. (1.)**

CAVENDISH (*Lady* FREDERICK) *See* CAVENDISH (*Hon.* Lucy C.) *Lady Frederick Cavendish.*

CAVENDISH (*Lord* FREDERICK CHARLES) *See* AINSLIE (Henry) Man's Wrath no Instrument of God's Righteous Retribution. A sermon preached . . . on receiving intelligence of the assassinations [of Lord F. Cavendish and T. H. Burke] in Dublin, *etc.* [1882.] 8⁰.
4473. g. 14. (5.)

CAVENDISH (*Lord* FREDERICK CHARLES)

—— *See* GLADSTONE (Stephen E.) A Life given for Ireland. A sermon preached at the dedication of a memorial window . . . to the late Lord F. Cavendish, *etc.* 1883. 12º. **4907. aa. 1. (6.)**

—— *See* IRELAND.—Spencer (John Poyntz) *Earl Spencer, Lieutenant-General.* A Proclamation, *etc.* [Offering a reward for information leading to the arrest of persons harbouring the murderers of Lord Frederick Cavendish and T. H. Burke.] [1882.] fol. **C.S. A. 26/15. (1.)**

—— *See* LLOYD (Samuel) *Primitive Methodist Minister, Bradford.* Memorials of Lord Frederick Cavendish . . . A sermon, *etc.* 1883. 8º. **4477. i. 37. (13.)**

—— *See* WICKHAM (Edward C.) *Dean of Lincoln.* Suffering and Hope. A sermon . . . in memory of Lord F. C. Cavendish, *etc.* 1883. 8º. **4473. g. 19. (14.)**

CAVENDISH (GEORGE) The Negotiations of Thomas Woolsey, the Great Cardinall of England, containing his life and death. Composed by one of his owne servants, being his gentleman-usher [i.e. George Cavendish]. pp. 118. 1641. 4º. *See* WOLSEY (Thomas) *Cardinal.* **4863. c. 48.**

—— [Another edition.] The Life and Death of Thomas Woolsey, *etc.* pp. 157. 1667. 8º. *See* WOLSEY (Thomas) *Cardinal.* **1124. c. 2.**

—— [Another edition.] The Memoirs of that great favourite, Cardinal Woolsey, *etc.* pp. 230. 1706. 8º. *See* WOLSEY (Thomas) *Cardinal.* **1124. d. 3.**

—— [Another edition.] The Secret History of the Cardinal [Wolsey]. *See* GROVE (Joseph) *of Richmond.* The History of the Life and Times of Cardinal Wolsey, *etc.* vol. 1. 1742, *etc.* 8º. **614. g. 1, 2.**

—— [Another edition.] The Negotiations of Thomas Wolsey, *etc.* 1745. *See* HARLEIAN MISCELLANY. The Harleian Miscellany, *etc.* vol. 5. 1744, *etc.* 4º. **185. a. 9.**

—— [Another edition.] The Secret History of the Cardinal. *See* GROVE (Joseph) *of Richmond.* The History of the Life and Times of Cardinal Wolsey, *etc.* vol. 1. 1748. 8º. **G. 14164.**

—— [Another edition.] The Negotiations of Thomas Wolsey, *etc.* 1810. *See* HARLEIAN MISCELLANY. The Harleian Miscellany, *etc.* vol. 5. 1808, *etc.* 4º. **2072. g.**

—— [Another edition.] Cardinal Wolsey. *See* WORDSWORTH (Christopher) *Master of Trinity College, Cambridge.* Ecclesiastical Biography, *etc.* vol. 1. 1818. 8º. **204. c. 12.**

—— The Life of Cardinal Wolsey, and Metrical Visions; from the original autograph manuscript. With notes and other illustrations, by Samuel Weller Singer. (Who wrote Cavendish's life of Wolsey? A dissertation by Joseph Hunter.) 2 vol. *Harding, Triphook & Lepard: London,* 1825. 8º. **2406. h. 1.**

—— [Another copy.] **G. 1437.**

—— Cardinal Wolsey. *See* WORDSWORTH (Christopher) *Master of Trinity College, Cambridge.* Ecclesiastical Biography, *etc.* vol. 1. 1839. 8º. **1126. g. 11.**

—— The Life of Cardinal Wolsey . . . A new edition. [Edited by John Holmes. With a portrait.] pp. xi. 285. *Rivingtons: London,* 1852. 4º. **614. g. 30.**

—— Cardinal Wolsey; his rise and life, as related by Cavendish. [Slightly altered, and edited by E. H.] pp. iv. 100. *Chapman & Hall: London,* 1855. 8º. **1155. g. 9.**

CAVENDISH (GEORGE)

—— The Life of Cardinal Wolsey . . . To which is added Thomas Churchyard's tragedy of Wolsey, *etc.* pp. 284. *G. Routledge & Sons: London,* 1885. 8º. [*Morley's Universal Library.* vol. 24.] **12204. gg. 1/24.**

—— The Life of Thomas Wolsey, Cardinal, *etc.* [Transcribed from the original manuscript by F. S. Ellis.] pp. iv. 287. *William Morris: Kelmscott Press, Hammersmith,* 1893. 8º. **C. 43. e. 11.**

—— [The Life and Death of Thomas Wolsey. (Edited by F. S. Ellis.) (The Tragedy of Cardinal Wolsey. By T. Churchyard.) pp. 283. *J. M. Dent & Co.: London,* 1899. 8º. [*Temple Classics.*] **012200. de. 8/17.**

—— The Life and Death of Thomas Wolsey . . . Edited by Grace H. M. Simpson. pp. 196. *R. & T. Washbourne: London,* 1901. 8º. **4863. bbb. 9.**

—— [Another edition.] Illustrated with portraits by Holbein. pp. vi. 192. *Houghton Mifflin & Co.: Boston & New York,* 1905. 4º. **C. 100. k. 6.**

—— [Another edition.] Edited, with notes and an introtion, by Mary Tout. pp. xv. 114. *Macmillan & Co.: London,* 1908. 8º. [*English Literature for Secondary Schools.* Historical section.] **012273. de. 20.**

—— [Another edition.] To which is added Thomas Churchyard's 'Tragedy of Wolsey.' With an introduction by Henry Morley. pp. xii. 250. *G. Routledge & Sons: London,* [1907.] 8º. [*New Universal Library.*] **12204. p. 2/115.**

—— The Life and Death of Thomas Wolsey, *etc.* pp. 192. *Alcuin Press: Chipping Campden,* 1930. 4º. **4863. f. 24.**

—— Who Wrote Cavendish's Life of Wolsey? [By the Rev. Joseph Hunter.] pp. 56. *Richard Rees: London,* 1814. 4º. **131. b. 8.**

—— [Another copy.] **G. 18496. (2.)**

CAVENDISH (GEORGIANA) *Duchess of Devonshire. See* FOSTER (Vere H. L.) The Two Duchesses, Georgiana, Duchess of Devonshire, Elizabeth, Duchess of Devonshire. Family correspondence, *etc.* 1898. 8º. **010920. k. 14.**

—— *See* GOWER (Iris I. Leveson) *afterwards* PALMER (I. I.) The Face without a Frown. Georgiana, Duchess of Devonshire. [With portraits.] 1944. 8º. **10860. b. 33.**

—— *See* PAPHIAD. The Paphiad . . . Humbly dedicated to . . . the Duchess of Dev-n—re [i.e. Devonshire]. 1785. 4º. **11660. c. 11.**

—— Georgiana. Extracts from the correspondence of Georgiana, Duchess of Devonshire. Edited by the Earl of Bessborough. [With plates, including portraits.] pp. x. 307. *John Murray: London,* 1955. 8º. **10923. c. 7.**

—— Georgiana Duchess of Devonshire's Diary. November 20, 1788—January 12, 1789. *See* SICHEL (Walter S.) Sheridan, *etc.* vol. 2. 1909. 8º. **2407. f. 2.**

—— The Passage of the Saint Gothard. *See* SWITZERLAND. Sketch of a Descriptive Journey through Switzerland, *etc.* 1816. 8º. **1429. d. 3.**

—— Passage du mont Saint-Gothard, poëme . . . traduit . . . par l'abbé de Lille. (The Passage of the Mountain of Saint Gothard, a poem.) *Fr. & Eng.* pp. v. 44. *Prosper & Co.: London,* 1802. 4º. **1346. i. 8.**

CAVENDISH (GEORGIANA) *Duchess of Devonshire.*

—— The Passage of Saint-Gothard. Passage du Saint-Gothard. (Traduit par Jacques Delille.) *Eng. & Fr. In:* DELILLE (J.) Dithyrambe sur l'immortalité de l'âme, *etc.* pp. 36–115. 1082 [1802]—an 10. 8°.
11484. bb. 20. (1.)

—— [Another edition.] pp. 52. *Prosper & Co.: London,* 1802. 8°. **1161.g.40.**

—— [Another edition.] *See* LILLE (J. de) Dithyrambe sur l'immortalité de l'âme, *etc.* 1802. 12°. **1164. l. 6.**

—— [Another edition.] *See* LILLE (J. de) Dithyrambe sur l'immortalité de l'âme, *etc.* 1082 [1802]. 8°.
11474. g. 7.

—— The Passage of the Saint Gothard . . . with an Italian translation by G. Polidori. pp. viii. 41. *Gameau & Co.: London,* 1803. fol. **C. 5. e. 7.**

—— [Another copy.] **G. 8191.**

—— Die Reise über den Gotthard. Ein Gedicht. *See* SWITZERLAND. Scizze einer mahlerischen Reise durch die Schweiz, *etc.* 1816. 8°. **10195. cc. 9.**

—— Il Tragitto di San Gotardo. *See* MILTON (J.) [*L'Allegro.—Italian.*] L'Allegro di Milton, *etc.* 1805. 12°.
11626. b. 38.

—— [Another edition.] *See* POLIDORI (G.) La Magion del terrore, *etc.* 1843. 16°. **1463. b. 26.**

—— The Sylph. A novel. [By Georgiana Cavendish, Duchess of Devonshire.] pp. 262. 1779. 12°. *See* SYLPH. **12613. a. 34.**

—— [Another edition.] 2 vol. 1783. 8°. *See* SYLPH.
1154. i. 9.

—— The Duchess of Devonshire's Cow ; a poem. [By William Combe.] pp. 11. *J. Bew: London,* 1777. 4°.
163. l. 52.

—— An Heroic Epistle to the Noble Author of the Duchess of Devonshire's Cow. A poem. [By William Combe.] pp. 11. *J. Bew: London,* 1777. 4°. **163. l. 54.**

—— An Interesting Letter to the Duchess of Devonshire. [By William Combe.] pp. 113. *J. Bew: London,* 1778. 8°. **117. a. 59.**

—— A Letter to Her Grace the Duchess of Devonshire. [By William Combe.] *Fielding & Walker: London,* 1777. 4°. **112. c. 14.**

—— A Second Letter to Her Grace the Duchess of Devonshire. [By William Combe.] A new edition. pp. 15. *Fielding & Walker: London,* 1777. 4°. **112. c. 15.**

—— On the Death of the Duchess of Devonshire. [A poem.] *W. Bulmer & Co.: [London,* 1806.] *s. sh.* 4°.
11647. e. 1. (66.)

CAVENDISH (GILBERT) Horæ Subsecivæ. Observations and discourses. [Variously attributed to Grey Brydges, Lord Chandos, and to Gilbert Cavendish.] pp. 542. 1620. 8°. *See* HORAE. **722. c. 4.**

CAVENDISH (GUILLAUME) *Marquis de Newcastle. See* CAVENDISH (William) 1*st Duke of Newcastle.*

CAVENDISH (HARRIE) *See* CAVENDISH (Henry) *M.P. for Derbyshire.*

CAVENDISH (*Lady* HARRIET) *See* GOWER (Henrietta E. L.) *Countess Granville.*

CAVENDISH (*Mrs.* HARRY) *See* MACKIE, afterwards HOPKINS, afterwards CAVENDISH (Pauline B.)

CAVENDISH (HENRY) *M.P. for Derbyshire. See* FOX ( ) *Servant of Henry Cavendish.* Mr. Harrie Cavendish His Journey to and from Constantinople, 1589, *etc.* [With a portrait.] 1940. 8°. [*Camden Miscellany.* vol. 17.] **A. 8113/39.**

CAVENDISH (*Hon.* HENRY) *See* AYKROYD (Wallace R.) Three Philosophers. Lavoisier, Priestley and Cavendish. [With a portrait.] 1935. 8°. **10602. ppp. 5.**

—— *See* CUVIER (G. L. C. F. D. de) *Baron.* Éloges historiques, *etc.* (Éloge historique de Henri Cavendish.) 1860. 8°. **10663. ee. 14.**

—— *See* CUVIER (G. L. C. F. D. de) *Baron.* Recueil des éloges historiques, *etc.* (Éloge historique de Henri Cavendish.) tom. 2. 1819, *etc.* 8°. **611. f. 25.**

—— *See* DISCOVERY. The Discovery of Oxygen . . . A concise account of the labours of . . . Cavendish, *etc.* 1895. 8°. **8907. aaa. 36.**

—— *See* STEINER (Lewis H.) Henry Cavendish and the Discovery of the Chemical Constitution of Water, *etc.* 1855. 8°. **8907. bb. 8.**

—— *See* THORPE (*Sir* Thomas E.) Cavendish and his Discoveries. A lecture. [1876.] 8°. **8708. h. 29. (21.)**

—— *See* WILSON (George) *M.D., F.R.S.E.* The Life of the Honble Henry Cavendish, including abstracts of his more important scientific papers and a critical inquiry into the claims of all the alleged discoverers of the composition of water. 1851. 8°. **Ac. 3922/3.**

—— The Scientific Papers of the Honourable Henry Cavendish, F.R.S. [With plates and illustrations.] 2 vol.

> vol. 1. The Electrical Researches. Edited . . . by James Clerk Maxwell . . . Revised by Sir Joseph Larmor.
> vol. 2. Chemical and Dynamical. Edited . . . by Sir Edward Thorpe . . . With contributions by Dr. Charles Chree . . . Sir Joseph Larmor.

University Press: Cambridge, 1921. 8°. **8704. g. 13.**

—— The Electrical Researches of the Honourable Henry Cavendish, F.R.S., written between 1771 and 1781, edited from the original manuscripts . . . by J. C. Maxwell. pp. lxvi. 454. *University Press: Cambridge,* 1879. 8°. **8757. d. 5.**

—— Experiments on Air. Papers published in the Philosophical Transactions. pp. 52. *W. F. Clay: Edinburgh,* 1893. 8°. [*Alembic Club Reprints.* no. 3.] **8909. g. 38.**

—— Tables for Clearing the Apparent Distances of the Moon from the Sun or a Star, from the effects of Parallax and Refraction. *See* MENDOZA Y RIOS (J. de) Tables for Facilitating the Calculations of Nautical Astronomy, *etc.* pt. 2. 1801. 4°. **435. g. 25.**

—— [Extracts from the Cavendish papers.] *See* HARRIS (*Sir* William S.) Rudimentary Electricity, *etc.* 1854. 12°.
08756. a. 75.

CAVENDISH (*Right Hon. Sir* HENRY) *Bart. See* ENGLAND. —*Parliament.—House of Commons.—Proceedings.*—II. Sir Henry Cavendish's Debates of the House of Commons during the thirteenth Parliament of Great Britain, commonly called the Unreported Parliament. 1841, *etc.* 8°.
807. f. 20, 21.

—— *See* ENGLAND.—*Parliament.—House of Commons.—Proceedings.*—II. Government of Canada. Debates of the House of Commons in . . . 1774 . . . Drawn up from the notes of . . . Sir H. Cavendish, *etc.* 1839. 8°.
809. e. 9.

CAVENDISH (*Right Hon. Sir* HENRY) *Bart.*

—— Statement of the Public Accounts of Ireland. pp. 240.
John Stockdale: London, 1791. 8º. **1102. h. 15. (4.)**

CAVENDISH (HENRY FREDERICK COMPTON) *See* B., J.
The Cruise round the World of the Flying Squadron,
1869–1870. (Compiled by J. B., with the assistance
of H. Cavendish.) 1871. 8º. **10028. e. 10.**

CAVENDISH (IANTHE) Dr. Brown's Partner. pp. 312.
W. J. Ham-Smith: London, 1912. 8º. **NN. 96.**

CAVENDISH (JACK) *pseud.* A Sapphick Epistle from Jack
Cavendish to the Honourable and most beautiful Mrs.
D****. [A satire.] pp. 23. *M. Smith:* [*London,*
1771 ?] 4º. **11630. e. 9. (4.)**
The pagination is slightly irregular.

—— [Another copy, with a different titlepage.] *T. Southern:*
London, [1771 ?] 4º. **11631. g. 31. (10.)**
Imperfect; wanting pp. 15, 16, 15*, 16*.

CAVENDISH (JEAN) *See* MALLESON (Miles) Young
Heaven, & three other plays. (Young Heaven: a play in
one act by J. Cavendish & M. Malleson.) 1918. 8º.
011779. e. 26.

CAVENDISH (LUCY CAROLINE) *Lady Frederick Cavendish.*
See LYTTELTON (*Hon.* William H.) *Canon of Gloucester.*
The Life of Man after Death . . . With . . . In Memo-
riam, by Lady F. Cavendish. 1893. 8º. **4372. c. 46.**

—— The Diary of Lady Frederick Cavendish. Edited by
John Bailey, *etc.* [With plates, including portraits.] 2 vol.
John Murray: London, 1927. 8º. **010855. eee. 3.**

—— The Secret of Miss Yonge's Influence. *See* ROMANES
(Ethel) Charlotte Mary Yonge, *etc.* 1908. 8º.
010854. df. 9.

CAVENDISH (MARGARET) *Duchess of Newcastle. See*
CAVENDISH (William) *1st Duke of Newcastle.* The
First Duke and Duchess of Newcastle-upon-Tyne, *etc.*
1910. 8º. **010827. ee. 30.**

—— *See* GOULDING (Richard W.) Margaret—Lucas—
Duchess of Newcastle. [With a portrait.] 1925. 8º.
010855. e. 5.

—— *See* J., H., *of Gray's Inne, Gent.* To the most excellent
princesse the . . . Duchesse of Newcastle. [Verses.]
1667. fol. **Lutt. 1. 105.**

—— *See* MONTÉGUT (E.) Le Maréchal Davout . . . La
Duchesse et le Duc de Newcastle. 1895. 8º.
010663. f. 61.

—— *See* PERRY (Henry T. E.) The First Duchess of Newcastle and her Husband as Figures in Literary History.
1918. 8º. [*Harvard Studies in English.* vol. 4.]
Ac. 2692/16.

—— The Life of the 1st Duke of Newcastle, & other writings.
[With an introduction by Ernest Rhys.] pp. xxvii. 299.
J. M. Dent & Sons: London & Toronto, [1915.] 8º.
[*Everyman's Library.*] **12206.p.1/535.**

—— Letters of Margaret Lucas to her future husband,
William Cavendish, Marquis, afterwards Duke, of New-
castle, 1645. [Edited by R. W. Goulding.] *See* LONDON.
—III. *Roxburghe Club.* Letters written by Charles
Lamb's " princely woman, the thrice noble Margaret
Newcastle " to her husband ; by . . . William Plumer
to the third Duke of Portland and Lord William Bentinck,
etc. 1909. 4º. **C. 101. f. 7.**

CAVENDISH (MARGARET) *Duchess of Newcastle.*

—— The Life of the thrice Noble . . . Prince, William
Cavendishe, Duke, Marquess, and Earl of Newcastle, *etc.*
(Some few notes of the authoresse.) pp. 199. *Printed by*
A. Maxwell: London, 1667. fol. **614. l. 37.**

—— [Another copy.] **194. c. 15.**

—— [Another copy.] **G. 1712.**

—— [Another edition.] pp. 259. *Printed by A. Maxwell:*
London, 1675. 4º. **614. g. 24.**

—— [Another copy.] **G. 14136.**

—— [Another edition.] The Lives of William Cavendishe,
Duke of Newcastle, and of his wife . . . Edited with a
preface and occasional notes by Mark Antony Lower.
pp. xliv. 310. *J. R. Smith: London,* 1872. 8º. [*Library*
of Old Authors.] **2340. b. 4.**

—— [Another edition.] The Life of William Cavendish,
Duke of Newcastle . . . Edited by C. H. Firth . . . With
. . . portraits. pp. lxviii. 388. *J. C. Nimmo: London,*
1886. 8º. **10817. d. 12.**

—— [Another edition.] The Cavalier in Exile : being the
lives of the first Duke & Dutchess [*sic*] of Newcastle.
pp. xxxv. 242. *London,* 1903. 8º. [*Newnes' Pocket*
Classics.] **12269. ee. 33/1.**

—— [Another edition.] The Life of William Cavendish,
Duke of Newcastle . . . Edited by C. H. Firth . . .
Second edition, revised, with additional notes. With
twelve appendices and an index. pp. xlvii. 232.
G. Routledge & Sons: London, [1906.] 8º. [*London*
Library.] **12207. pp. 2/10.**

—— De vita et rebus gestis nobilissimi illustrissimique
Principis Guilielmi Ducis Novo-castrensis commentarii
. . . ex Anglico in Latinum conversi. (Appendicula con-
tinens paucula Auctoris observata.) [Translated by
Walter Charleton.] pp. 235. MS. NOTES. *Excudebat*
T. M.: Londini, 1668. fol. **611. l. 16.**

—— Natures Pictures drawn by Fancies Pencil to the Life
. . . In this volume there are several feigned stories of
natural descriptions, as comical, tragical, *etc.*
pp. 390 [404]. MS. NOTES. *For J. Martin & J. Allestrye:*
London, 1656. fol. **G. 11599.**

—— [Another copy.] MS. NOTES. **841. m. 25.**
Imperfect; wanting the frontispiece, titlepage, pp. 399–402
and the last leaf.

—— Second edition. pp. 718. *Printed by A. Maxwell:*
London, 1671. fol. **8407. h. 12.**

—— A Treasure of Knowledge ; or, the Female oracle :
wherein is delineated the experienced traveller ; likewise
the she anchoret, *etc.* [Extracted from " Nature's
Pictures."] *See* NICOL (Alexander) *Schoolmaster.* Poems,
etc. 1766. 12º. **11632. b. 40.**

—— Observations upon Experimental Philosophy. To which
is added, The Description of a New Blazing World. 4 pt.
Printed by A. Maxwell: London, 1666. fol. **31. f. 4.**

—— [Another edition of pt. 4.] The Description of a New
World, called the Blazing-World. pp. 158. *Printed by*
A. Maxwell: London, 1668. fol. **8407. h. 10.**
Imperfect ; wanting the portrait, for which another,
published in 1799, *is substituted.*

—— Orations of Divers Sorts, accommodated to divers places.
pp. 309. *London,* 1662. fol. **72. g. 14.**

CAVENDISH (MARGARET) *Duchess of Newcastle.*

—— The Philosophical and Physical Opinions, written by her Excellency the Lady Marchioness of Newcastle. pp. 174. *For J. Martin & J. Allestrye: London,* 1655. fol. **31. e. 8.**

—— [Another copy.] **722. l. 1.**

—— [Another copy.] **C. 39. h. 27. (2.)**
Imperfect ; wanting the titlepage.

—— [Another edition.] pp. 458. MS. NOTES.
Printed by William Wilson: London, 1663. fol.
8407. h. 9.

—— Grounds of Natural Philosophy . . . Second edition, much altered from the first, which went under the name of Philosophical and Physical Opinions. pp. 311.
Printed by A. Maxwell: London, 1668. fol. **536. l. 14.**

—— [Another copy.] **31. f. 5.**

—— Philosophicall Fancies, *etc.* pp. 94. *Printed by J. Martin & J. Allestrye: London,* 1653. 8°.
E. 1474. (1.)

—— Philosophical Letters ; or, Modest Reflections upon some opinions in natural philosophy maintained by several learned authors of this age expressed by way of letters. pp. 542. *London,* 1664. fol. **31. f. 3.**

—— Playes written by . . . the Lady Marchioness of Newcastle. pp. 679. *A. Warren for J. Martyn, J. Allestry & T. Dicas: London,* 1662. fol. **644. k. 2.**

—— [Another copy.] **79. l. 14.**

—— [Another copy.] **G. 19053. (1.)**

—— Plays, never before printed. [With a portrait.] 5 pt.
Printed by A. Maxwell: London, 1668. fol. **644. l. 17.**

—— [Another copy.] **G. 19053. (2.)**

—— [Another copy.] FEW MS. NOTES. **79. l. 15.**
Imperfect ; wanting the portrait.

—— Poems, and Fancies. pp. 214. *T. R. for J. Martin & J. Allestrye: London,* 1653. fol. **79. h. 10.**

—— [Another copy, with a different titlepage.]
FEW MS. NOTES [by the author]. **C. 39. h. 27. (1.)**
With an additional leaf, containing verses by the Duke of Newcastle.

—— The second impression . . . corrected. pp. 299.
By William Wilson: London, 1664. fol. **11626. h. 1.**

—— [Another copy.] **G. 19054.**

—— [Select poems.] *See* POEMS. Poems by Eminent Ladies, *etc.* 1755. 12°. **994. g. 1, 2.**

—— Select Poems of Margaret Cavendish . . . Edited by Sir Egerton Brydges. pp. 20. *Privately printed: Lee Priory, Kent,* 1813. 8°. **1087. k. 13. (1.)**
One of an edition of twenty-five copies. With an additional titlepage, engraved.

—— Selected Poetry. *See* ENGLISH POETESSES. Four Early English Poetesses, *etc.* [1908.] 8°. [*Hull Booklets.* no. 7.] **12204. d. 13/7.**

—— A True Relation of the Birth, Breeding, and Life of Margaret Cavendish, Duchess of Newcastle. Written by herself. With a critical preface, &c, by Sir Egerton Brydges. pp. 9. 36. *Privately printed: Lee Priory, Kent,* 1814. 8°. **131. c. 18.**

—— [Another copy.] **G. 14279. (1.)**

CAVENDISH (MARGARET) *Duchess of Newcastle.*

—— CCXI Sociable Letters. pp. 453. *Printed by William Wilson: London,* 1664. fol. **88. h. 17.**

—— The World's Olio. pp. 216. *Printed for J. Martin & J. Allestrye: London,* 1655. fol. **90. e. 19.**

—— [Another copy, with a different titlepage.]
FEW MS. NOTES. **841. m. 22.**

—— Second edition. [With a portrait.] pp. 424. *Printed by A. Maxwell: London,* 1671. fol. **8407. h. 11.**

—— —— *See* DU VERGER ( ) *of Douai.* Du Verger's Humble Reflections upon some passages of the . . . Marchionesse of Newcastles Olio, *etc.* 1657. 8°.
699. b. 35.

—— [Selections.] *See* CAVENDISH (William) 1st *Duke of Newcastle.* A Collection of Letters and Poems written . . . to the late Duke and Dutchess of Newcastle. 1678. fol. **10921. l. 8.**

—— [Selections.] *See* CAVENDISH (William) 1st *Duke of Newcastle.* The Cavalier and his Lady. Selections from the works of the first Duke and Duchess of Newcastle, *etc.* 1872. 8°. **11650. de. 13.**

—— Letters and Poems in honour of the incomparable Princess, Margaret, Duchess of Newcastle. pp. 182.
Printed by Thomas Newcombe: [*London,*] 1676. fol.
841. m. 23.

CAVENDISH (MARY) *Duchess of Devonshire. See* WILLIAMSON (Joseph) *Chaplain to the Duchess of Devonshire.* A Modest Essay upon the Character of . . . the Duchess-Dowager of Devonshire. 1710. 4°. **1416. f. 22.**

CAVENDISH (PATRICIA)
—— *See* CARRINGTON (Noel) and CAVENDISH (P.) Camping by Water. Edited by N. Carrington and P. Cavendish. 1950. 8°. **010368. r. 71.**

CAVENDISH (PETER) *pseud.* [i.e. SYDNEY HORLER.] *See also* HORLER (S.)

—— Romeo and Julia. pp. 311. *Hodder & Stoughton: London,* 1928. 8°. **NN. 14306.**

CAVENDISH (REGINALD) Daphne. A novel. pp. 249.
Bickers & Son: London, 1906. 8°. **012633. d. 14.**

CAVENDISH (RICHARD) *M.A.*

—— *See* ARCHIMEDES. [*Two or more Works.*] Archimedis opera nonnulla, *etc.* [With MS. notes and a poem by R. Cavendish beginning "Draw nye ye Muses all of myghty Jove the lyne."] 1558. fol.
C. 71. ff. 3.

—— The Image of Nature and Grace, conteyning the whole course and condition of mans estate. B.L. ff. 125.
Iohn Daye: London, [1574.] 8°. **C. 53. i. 4.**
With the author's autograph, and a copy of his epitaph inserted.

CAVENDISH (Hon. RICHARD) *See* LAICUS. Laicus ad Laicum . . . A Letter to the Hon. Mr. Cavendish, on occasion of his address to the Bishop of London, impugning the decision of the Judicial Committee, *etc.* 1850. 8°. **4107. c. 6.**

—— A Letter to Archdeacon Hare on the Judgment in the Gorham Case . . . Third edition, with remarks on the Archdeacon's postscript. pp. 46. *John Ollivier: London,* 1850. 8°. **4325. e. 18.**

CAVENDISH (Hon. RICHARD)

—— A Letter to the Lord Archbishop of Canterbury on the actual relations between Church and State . . . Suggested by Baptist Noel's Essay. pp. 40. *John Ollivier: London,* 1849. 8°. **4105. d. 9.**

CAVENDISH (SOPHIA MATILDA) Tales of My Aunt . . . Edited by Mr. Taylor. pp. 161. *W. Darton: Uxbridge,* [1829.] 12°. **012807. de. 63.**

CAVENDISH (SPENCER COMPTON) Duke of Devonshire.
See BOISSEVAIN (C.) Open Letter to the Duke of Devonshire. [A reply to a speech by the Duke of Devonshire on the attitude of the foreign press during the South African War. [1900.] 8°. **8156. d. 2. (3.)**

—— *See* ENGLAND.—*Parliament.*—*Bills.* - [L.] [1886. April 13.] Speeches by the Phantom Member, on the Second Reading of the Bill for the Government of Ireland, in reply to Lord Hartington, *etc.* [1886?] 8°. **8146. f. 23. (3.)**

—— *See* GOSCHEN (George J.) *Viscount Goschen.* The Disruption Bill. Speeches of the Right Hon. G. J. Goschen . . . and . . . the Marquis of Hartington, *etc.* [1886.] 8°. **8146. c. 6. (11.)**

—— *See* HOLLAND (Bernard H.) The Life of Spencer Compton, eighth Duke of Devonshire . . . With portraits. 1911. 8°. **2406. b. 11.**

—— *See* JONES (Morris R.) The Education Act, 1902. Together with . . . the principal explanatory remarks of . . . the Duke of Devonshire, *etc.*— [1903.] 8°. **[MISSING.]**

—— *See* LEACH (Henry) *Biographer.* The Duke of Devonshire. A personal and political biography, *etc.* [With portraits.] 1904. 8°. **010817. ee. 31.**

—— *See* LIBERALS. Speeches of Leading Liberals [Sir W. Harcourt, Lord Hartington and others] on current politics, *etc.* 1880. 16°. **8139. b. 6. (12.)**

—— *See* LONDON.—III. *Liberal Unionist Association.* The Case for the Union explained and set forth by Lord Hartington . . . and others. [1886, *etc.*] 8°. **8146. bb. 32.**

—— An Address delivered before the University of Edinburgh, on his inauguration as Lord Rector, by the Marquis of Hartington, *etc.* pp. 24. *William Ridgway: London,* 1879. 8°. **8306. df. 9. (8.)**

—— The Approaching General Election. Speeches of the Marquis of Hartington . . . and . . . John Bright . . . at Manchester . . . October . . . 1879. Revised by the speakers. pp. 59. *H. J. Infield: London,* 1879. 8°. **8139. b. 3. (11.)**

—— Election Speeches in 1879 and 1880. With address to the Electors of North-East Lancashire. pp. 256. *C. Kegan Paul & Co.: London,* 1880. 8°. **8138. de. 23.**

—— The Government of Ireland Bill. Speech . . . delivered . . . May 18th, 1886. pp. 22. *Liberal Committee for the maintenance of Legislative Union between Great Britain and Ireland: London,* [1886.] 8°. **8146. c. 6. (4.)**

—— Indian Criminal Procedure Bill. Speech . . . in the House of Commons on August 23rd, *etc.* pp. 10. *National Press Agency: [London,* 1883.] 8°. **8023. ee. 17. (11.)**

—— The Irish Question. Speech. (March 5th, 1886.) 1887. *See* LONDON.—III. *Eighty Club.* The "Eighty" Club. Objects. Rules. Report, *etc.* 1887. [1887, *etc.*] 8°. **P.P. 2505. aze.**

CAVENDISH (SPENCER COMPTON) Duke of Devonshire.

—— The Liberal Reason Why, explained in a letter to the Marquis of Hartington, M.P., by a Church Dignitary. pp. 29. *Longmans & Co.: London,* 1880. 8°. **8138. df. 7. (7.)**

—— The Masterpieces in the Duke of Devonshire's Collection of Pictures. Sixty photogravures. With a preface by S. A. Strong. pp. 22. pl. 60. *Franz Hanfstaengl: London,* 1901. fol. **L.R. 27. b. 5.**

—— Reproductions of Drawings by Old Masters in the Collection of the Duke of Devonshire at Chatsworth. With an introduction by S. A. Strong. pp. 16. ff. 70. *Duckworth & Co.: London,* 1902. fol. **1899. f. 13.** *No. 92 of ninety-eight copies printed on vellum.*

CAVENDISH (THOMAS)

—— *See* DRAKE (Sir Francis) Early English Voyagers; or, the Adventures and discoveries of Drake, Cavendish and Dampier. 1886. 8°. **10803. bb. 5.**
See DRAKE (Sir Francis) The Famous Voyage of Sir Francis Drake . . . To which is added, The prosperous Voyage of Mr. T. Candish round the world, *etc.* 1742. 8°. **978. k. 1.**

—— *See* DRAKE (Sir Francis) Lives and Voyages of Drake, Cavendish, and Dampier, *etc.* 1831. 12°. **12203. t. 1/5.**

—— —— 1846. 12°. **12205. b. 54.**

—— *See* DRAKE (Sir Francis) Lives and Voyages of the Famous Navigators Drake and Cavendish. 1895. 8°. **012200. g. 4/15.**

—— *See* ENGLISH NAVIGATORS. An Historical Account of all the Voyages round the World, performed by English Navigators . . . extracted from the journals of . . . Drake, Cavendish, *etc.* 1774, *etc.* 8°. **1045. e. 1.**

—— [For editions of "The Worthy and Famous Voyage of Master Thomas Cavendish, made round about the Globe of the Earth . . . Begun in the year 1586," by N. H. :] *See* H., N.

—— [For editions of "The Last Voyage of the worshipfull M. Thomas Candish . . . intended for the South Sea . . . Written by M. Iohn Iane ":] *See* JANE (John)

—— [For editions of "Aanmerkelyke reys, en verwonderlijk-seldsame voorvallen op de selve van Antony Knivet, gedaan uyt Engelland na de Zuyd-zee, met Thomas Candish ":] *See* KNIVET (A.)

—— *See* MOORE (John H.) A New and Complete Collection of Voyages, *etc.* (vol. 1. The Voyages of Captain T. Cavendish.) [1780?] fol. **10003. f. 2.**

—— [For editions of "The Admirable and prosperous Voyage of the Worshipfull Master Thomas Candish . . . into the South sea . . . begun in the yeere of our Lord 1586 . . . Written by Master Francis Pretty ":] *See* PRETTY (Francis)

—— Master Thomas Candish his discourse of his fatall and disastrous voyage towards the South Sea, *etc. See* PURCHAS (Samuel) Purchas his Pilgrimes, *etc.* pt. 4. 1625. fol. **679. h. 14.**

—— Copye, Ouergeset wt de Engelsche taele . . . Geschreuen aen milore Tresorier. Van Mr. T. Candische, *etc.* [A translation of Cavendish's letter to Lord Hounsdon, 9 Sept. 1588, published by Hakluyt with Pretty's account of the first voyage.] *C. Claesz: Amstelredam,* [1589.] 4°. **T. 1716. (36.)**

—— Schiffart Herrn Thomæ Candischen . . . vmb den gantzen Erdboden, Anno 1586. vorgenommen, vnd Anno 1588. vollbracht. [By F. Pretty.] *See* BRY (T. de) [America.—Part XIV.—German.] Vierzehender Theil Americanischer Historien, *etc.* 1630. fol. **G. 6626. (7.)**

CAVENDISH (Thomas)

—— [A reissue.] *See* Bry (T. de) [*America.—Abridgments. —Gottfried.*] Newe Welt und Americanische Historien, *etc.* 1631. fol. **G. 6635.**

—— [Another edition.] *See* Bry (T. de) [*America.— Abridgments.—Gottfried.*] Newe Welt und Americanische Historien, *etc.* 1655. fol. **566. k. 12.**

—— Twee vermaarde scheeps-togten van Thomas Candisch . . . de eerste rond-om den geheelen aard-kloot, gedaan in het jaar 1586. en vervolgens . . . [By F. Pretty.] De tweede behelst een ongelukkige . . . reys na de Zuyd-zee . . . met des Admiraals eygen hand geschreeven, *etc.* [With maps.] pp. 64. *Leyden,* 1706. 8º. [*Aa (Pieter van der) Bookseller. Naaukeurige Versameling der gedenkwaardigste zee en land reysen, etc.* vol. 68.] **979. e. 20. (1.)**

—— [Another edition.] coll. 38. *Leyden,* [1727.] fol. [*Aa (Pieter van der) Bookseller. De Aanmerkenswaardigste . . . Zee- en Landreizen der Portugeezen, etc.* dl. 5.] **566. l. 7.**

CAVENDISH (William) 1*st Duke of Devonshire.*

—— *See* Danger. The Danger of Living in a Known Sin, and the Hazard of a death-bed repentance, *etc.* 1738. 8º. **1415. f. 62.**

—— *See* Griffith (John) *Curate of Edensor.* A Sermon occasioned by the Death of the late Duke of Devonshire. 1707. 8º. **1417. b. 5.**

—— *See* Grove (Joseph) *of Richmond.* The Lives of all the Earls and Dukes of Devonshire, *etc.* [Including " The Life of William, the First Duke of Devonshire."] 1764. 8º. **1202. d. 10.**

—— *See* Hazard. The Hazard of a Death-Bed-Repentance, fairly argued from the late Remorse of W— late D— of D— [William Cavendish, Duke of Devonshire], *etc.* [By J. Dunton.] 1708. 8º. **696. d. 28.**

—— *See* Hazard. The Hazard of a Death-Bed Repentance, fairly argued from the late remorse of W., late D—— of D—— [i.e. William Cavendish, 1st Duke of Devonshire], *etc.* 1708. 8º. **276. i. 35.**

—— —— 1728. 8º. **4401. p. 1.**

—— —— [Another edition of pt. 1.] The Danger of Living in a Known Sin, *etc.* 1738. 8º. **1415. f. 62.**

—— *See* Kennet (White) *Bishop of Peterborough.* A Sermon preached at the Funeral of . . . William, Duke of Devonshire, *etc.* 1707. 8º. **1417. b. 7.**

—— —— 1708. 8º. **696. d. 29.**

—— —— 1797. 8º. **276. l. 20.**

—— *See* Wilmot (John) *Earl of Rochester.* The Works of the Earls of Rochester, Roscommon, Dorset, the Duke of Devonshire, *etc.* 1721, *etc.* 12º. **C.123.c.3.**

—— —— 1731. 12º. **C.123.c.6.**

—— —— 1735. 12º. **C. 117. a. 66.**

—— —— 1739. 12º. **C.123.c.7.**

—— —— 1739. 12º. **C.123.c.5.**

—— —— 1752. 12º. **C.123.c.9.**

—— —— [c. 1800.] 12º. **Cup.800.i.6.**

—— —— [c. 1810.] 12º. **Cup.800.i.5.**

CAVENDISH (William) 1*st Duke of Devonshire.*

—— The Charms of Liberty: a poem, in allusion to the Archbishop of Cambray's Telemachus. By the late Duke of D—— [i.e. W. Cavendish, 1st Duke of Devonshire]. 1708. 8º. [*The Satyrical Works of Titus Petronius Arbiter, in prose and verse.*] *See* D——, *Duke of.* **11306. d. 4.**

—— [Another edition.] To which is added, Epigrams, poems and satyrs. Written by several hands. pp. 16. 1709. 8º. [*A Collection of the Best English Poetry, by several hands.* vol. 2.] *See* D——, *Duke of.* **C.124.b.7.(42.)**

—— [Another edition.] pp. 16. 1709. 8º. *See* D——, *Duke of.* **12331. ee. 31. (9.)**

—— [Another edition.] *See* Petronius Arbiter (T.) [*English.*] The Works of Petronius Arbiter, *etc.* 1713. 8º. **1080. m. 7.**

—— [Another edition.] An Allusion to the Bishop of Cambray's Telemachus, *etc. See* Gent (Thomas) *of York.* Pater patriæ, *etc.* [1738.] 12º. **1162. f. 18. (1.)**

—— Reasons for His Majesties Passing the Bill of Exclusion. In a letter to a friend. [By W. Cavendish, 1st Duke of Devonshire?] pp. 6. 1681. fol. *See* Charles II., *King of Great Britain and Ireland.* [*Appendix.*] **102. i. 27.**

—— The True Copy of a paper delivered by the Lord De - - - - - - - - - - - [i.e. W. Cavendish, 1st Duke of Devonshire] to the Mayor of Darby, where he quarter'd the one and twentieth of November 1688. [A proclamation, justifying the rising against James II.] 1688. *s. sh.* fol. *See* De - - - - - - - - - - -, *Lord.* **T. 98*. (16.)**

—— [Another copy.] **816. m. 3. (32.)**

—— [Another copy.] **T. 100*. (193*.)**

—— [Another issue.] **T. 100*. (186.)**

—— The Court in Tears: or, a Narrative of the life of the late William, Duke of Devonshire, *etc.* [With a woodcut.] pp. 8. *T. Robinson: London,* 1707. 8º. **G. 1874. (1.)**

CAVENDISH (William) 2*nd Duke of Devonshire.* *See* Fane (*Hon.* John) The Hon. John Fane, Esq; and Mary his wife . . . Appell^ts . . . William Duke of Devonshire [and others] . . . Respond^ts. The Appellant's case. [1718.] fol. **19. h. 1. (77.)**

—— *See* Fane (*Hon.* John) The Honourable John Fane, Esq; and Mary his wife, Appell^ts . . . William Duke of Devonshire and . . . the Lord James Cavendish Respond^ts. The Respondents case. [1718.] fol. **19. h. 1. (78.)**

—— *See* Grove (Joseph) *of Richmond.* The Lives of all the Earls and Dukes of Devonshire, *etc.* [Including " The Life of William, the Second Duke of Devonshire."] 1764. 8º. **1202. d. 10.**

CAVENDISH (William) 3*rd Duke of Devonshire.*

—— *See* Grove (Joseph) *of Richmond.* The Lives of all the Earls and Dukes of Devonshire, *etc.* [Including " The Life of William, Third Duke of Devonshire."] 1764. 8º. **1202. d. 10.**

—— *See* Kennet (White) *Bishop of Peterborough.* Memoirs of the Family of Cavendish, Dukes of Devonshire . . . To which are added some particulars relating to the present Duke. 1737. 12º. **11602. bb. 33. (10.)**

CAVENDISH (WILLIAM) *3rd Duke of Devonshire.*

—— An Address humbly inscribed to his Grace, the Duke of Devonshire, Lord Lieutenant of Ireland . . . By the author of Happiness [i.e. John Ward]. [In verse.] pp. 20. *William Smith: Dublin,* 1737. fol. **11633. h. 24.**

—— [Collectio figuraria gemmarum antiquarum ex dactyliotheca Ducis Devoniæ.] [Drawn by A. Gosmond de Vernon and engraved by C. Du Bosc.] pl. 101. [*London,* 1730?] fol. **C. 20. c. 2.**
Privately printed. Imperfect; wanting the titlepage.

CAVENDISH (WILLIAM) *4th Duke of Devonshire.* [For documents issued by the Duke of Devonshire as Lord Lieutenant of Ireland:] *See* IRELAND.—Cavendish (W.) *4th Duke of Devonshire, Lord Lieutenant.*

—— Catalogues of the Collections of Pictures of the Duke of Devonshire, General Guise, and the late Sir Paul Methuen. [By Horace Walpole, Earl of Orford.] ff. 44. *Strawberry-Hill,* 1760. 8°. **688. c. 28. (1.)**
Printed on one side of the leaf only.

—— His Majesty's Attorney General, at the relation of . . . William Duke of Devonshire, and the said William Duke of Devonshire, Appellants. John Wall, Henry Thornhill . . . Respondents. The Appellants case. pp. 7. [*London,* 1760.] fol. **516. m. 19. (3.)**

—— His Majesty's Attorney General, at the relation of . . . William Duke of Devonshire, and the said Duke of Devonshire, Appellants. John Wall, Henry Thornhill . . . Respondents. The case of the Respondents, *etc.* pp. 6. [*London,* 1760.] fol. **516. m. 19. (4.)**

—— *Begin.* To the Right Honble ******. [A letter to W. Cavendish, 4th Duke of Devonshire, on the political dissensions in Ireland and his administration as Lord-Lieutenant.] [1755.] 8°. *See* To. **8145. bb. 55.**

CAVENDISH (WILLIAM) *5th Duke of Devonshire. See* ADAIR (*Right Hon. Sir* Robert) [Sketch of the Character of the late Duke of Devonshire. With an appendix, containing copies of his verses, *etc.*] 1811. 4°. **131. a. 12.**

—— Letters which passed in Great Britain [between the Duke of Devonshire and others and Lord North] relative to the Absentee Tax. pp. 14. *Dublin,* 1773. 8°. **8145. aaa. 17.**

CAVENDISH (WILLIAM) *7th Duke of Devonshire.* Opening Address [at Owens College, Manchester]. *See* STEWART (Balfour) *and* WARD (A. W.) Essays and Addresses, by Professors and Lecturers of the Owens College, Manchester, *etc.* 1874. 8°. **8364. ee. 19.**

—— Catalogue of the Library at Chatsworth [in the possession of the Duke of Devonshire]. [With an historical notice by Sir G. F. Lacaita.] 4 vol. *Chiswick Press: London,* 1879. 8°. **11908. f. 1.**

—— [Another copy.] **L.P.** **11901. l. 2.**

—— A Letter to his Grace the Duke of Devonshire, Chancellor of the University of Cambridge. [On the offer to the University of the collections of ancient Greek art formed by Colonel Leake.] [Signed: A Member of the Senate, i.e. John H. Marsden.] pp. 15. *For private circulation: London,* [1863.] 8°. [MISSING.]

CAVENDISH (WILLIAM) *Duke of Newcastle. See* CAVENDISH (Margaret) *Duchess of Newcastle.* The Life of the thrice Noble . . . Prince, William Cavendishe, Duke, Marquess, and Earl of Newcastle, *etc.* 1667. fol. **614. l. 37.**

CAVENDISH (WILLIAM) *Duke of Newcastle.*

—— —— 1675. 4°. **614. g. 24.**

—— —— 1870. 8°. **2340. b. 4.**

—— —— 1886. 8°. **10817. d. 12.**

—— —— 1903. 8°. **12269.ee.33/1.**

—— —— [1906.] 8°. **12207. pp. 2/10.**

—— —— [1915.] 8°. **12206.p.1/535.**

—— *See* CAVENDISH (Margaret) *Duchess of Newcastle.* De vita et rebus gestis . . . Gulielmi Ducis Novo-castrensis, *etc.* 1668. fol. **611. l. 16.**

—— *See* CHARLES II., *King of Great Britain and Ireland.* [*Biography.*—II.] A Declaration of the Proceedings of his highnesse the Prince of Wales and the Marquis of Newcastle . . . for the defence . . . of the King's Majestie's royall person . . . Sent in a letter . . . June 29, 1648. 1648. 4°. **E. 450. (6.)**

—— *See* ENGLAND.—*Parliament.*—*Parliamentary Proceedings.* —II. The Parliaments Determination, concerning the Levies . . . Also a remarkable Passage concerning the Earle of New-castle (that the said Earle hath put in about 500. Men in Garrison, and . . . is about to raise a Troope of Horse), *etc.* [4 July 1641.] 1641. 4°. **1103. d. 78. (1.)**

—— *See* ENGLAND.—*Army.*—*Regulations and Orders.*—I. Orders and Institutions of War made . . . by His Majesty, and by Him delivered to . . . the Earle of Newcastle . . . With the Earles Speech to the Army at the . . . publishing the said Orders prefixt. 1642. 4°. **E. 127. (23.)**

—— *See* ENGLAND. [*Appendix.*—*History and Politics.*—II.] Another Miraculous Victory obtained by the Lord Fairfax against the Earl of Newcastle, at Barnham Moore, *etc.* 1643. 4°. **E. 106. (3.)**

—— *See* FAIRFAX (Ferdinando) *Baron Fairfax.* The Good and Prosperous Success of the Parliament's Forces, in Yorkshire, against the Earl of Newcastle . . . in a letter from . . . Lord Fairfax, *etc.* 1642. 4°. **E. 87. (1.)**

—— —— 1642. 4°. **523. c. 36. (7.)**

—— *See* FAIRFAX (Ferdinando) *Baron Fairfax.* A Happy Victory obtained by the Lord Fairefax, and Captaine Hotham, over the Earle of New-Castle . . . in Yorkshire . . . as it was sent in a letter from the said Lord Fairfax, *etc.* 1642. 4°. **G. 3581. (7.)**

—— *See* FAIRFAX (Ferdinando) *Baron Fairfax.* A Second Letter from the Rt. Hon. the Lord Fairfax, of his proceedings against the Earl of Newcastle . . . in Yorkeshire, *etc.* 1642. 4°. **E. 84. (15.)**

—— *See* HOTHAM (John) *Captain.* A Most true Relation of the great and bloody battell fought by Capt. Hotham . . . against the Earl of New-castle, *etc.* 1642. 4°. **E. 129. (9.)**

—— *See* LINCOLN, *County of.* The Protestation and Declaration of Divers Knights, Esquires and Freeholders of the Counties of Lincolne and Nottingham: against the unjust oppressions . . . of William Earle of Newcastle and his Cavaleers, *etc.* 1643. 4°. **E. 84. (17.)**

—— *See* MONTAGU (Edward) *Earl of Manchester.* A True Relation of the late Fight betweene the . . . Earle of Manchesters Forces, and the Marquesse of Newcastle's Forces, *etc.* 1643. 4°. **E. 71. (5.)**

CAVENDISH (WILLIAM) *Duke of Newcastle.*

—— *See* MONTÉGUT (E.) Le Maréchal Davout . . . La Duchesse et le Duc de Newcastle. 1895. 8°.
010663. f. 61.

—— *See* PERRY (Henry T. E.) The First Duchess of Newcastle and her Husband as Figures in Literary History. 1918. 8°. [*Harvard Studies in English.* vol. 4.]
Ac. 2692/16.

—— *See* TURBERVILLE (Arthur S.) A History of Welbeck Abbey and its Owners. (vol. 1. William Cavendish, First Duke of Newcastle.) 1938, *etc.* 8°. **09915. a. 36.**

—— *See* WIDRINGTON (*Sir* William) A True . . . Relation of the great Victories obtained by the Earl of Manchester and the Lord Fairfax; against the Earl of Newcastle's army in the North, *etc.* 1643. 4°. **E. 71. (22.)**

—— *See* WILLOUGHBY (Francis) *Baron Willoughby of Parham.* A True Relation of a great Victory obtained by . . . the Lord Willoughby . . . against divers forces of the Earle of New-castle, *etc.* 1643. 4°. **E. 84. (23.)**

—— The Country Captaine, and the Varietie. Two comedies. Written by a Person of Honor [i.e. W. Cavendish, Duke of Newcastle]. 2 pt. 1649. 12°. *See* COUNTRY CAPTAIN.
643. a. 19.

—— [Another issue.] The Country Captaine, *etc.* 1649. 12°. *See* COUNTRY CAPTAIN. **83. a. 38.**

—— [Another copy.] The Country Captaine, *etc.* 1649. 12°. *See* COUNTRY CAPTAIN. **G. 11162.**

—— A Declaration and Summons sent by the Earl of New-castle to the town of Manchester to lay down their arms; with the resolute answer of the commanders in chief and souldiers in Manchester, *etc.* pp. 8. *For Peter Cole: London,* 1643. 4°. **E. 60. (14.)**

—— Some Notable Observations upon the late Summons by the Earl of Newcastle of the Town of Manchester. Written by a worthy member of the House of Commons, and appointed to be printed. [With the summons.] pp. 8. *For Edward Husbands: London,* 1643. 4°. **E. 63. (18.)**

—— A Declaration made by the Earl of New-castle . . . for his resolution of Marching into Yorkshire. As also a just vindication of himself from that . . . aspersion laid upon him, for entertaining some Popish recusants in his forces. pp. 8. *London,* 1642. 4°. **E. 83. (1.)**

—— [Another edition.] pp. 19. *M. A. Richardson: Newcastle,* 1843. 8°. [*Reprints of Rare Tracts, etc. Historical.* vol. 1.] **1077. f. 86.**

—— *See* ENGLAND. [*Appendix.—History and Politics.—* II. 1642.] Equitable and Necessary Considerations and Resolutions for Association of Arms . . . against the now professed combination of Papists, *etc.* [Occasioned by " A Declaration made by the Earl of Newcastle, *etc.*"] 1642. 4°. **E. 83. (20.)**

—— A Confutation of the Earl of New Castles reasons for taking under his command and conduct divers Popish recusants in the northerne parts; wherein is shewed both the unlawfulnesse and danger of arming of papists, *etc.* [A reply to " A Declaration made by the Earl of Newcastle, *etc.*"] pp. 13. *For Henry Overton: London,* 1643. 4°. **E. 86. (13.)**

—— A Declaration of . . . the Earle of Newcastle . . . in answer of six groundlesse aspersions cast upon him by the Lord Fairfax, in his late warrant bearing date, Feb. 1642. pp. 10. *Printed by Stephen Bulkley: York,* 1642. 4°. **E. 92. (17.)**

CAVENDISH (WILLIAM) *Duke of Newcastle.*

—— [Another edition.] An Answer of the . . . Earle of New-castle . . . to the six groundlesse aspersions cast upon him by the Lord Fairefax, *etc.* pp. 13. *H. H.* [*Henry Hall*]: *Oxford,* 1642. 4°. **100. b. 50.**

—— *See* FAIRFAX (Ferdinando) *Baron Fairfax.* The Answer of Ferdinando Lord Fairfax to a Declaration of William, Earle of Newcastle, touching a late warrant issued by the Lo: Fairfax, dated Feb. 2, 1642, *etc.* 1642. 4°. **E. 91. (28.)**

—— Observations upon the Earle of New-Castles Declaration. pp. 16. *London,* 1643. 4°. **E. 91. (10.)**

—— The Humorous Lovers. A comedy. pp. 59. *J. M. for H. Herringman: London,* 1677. 4°.
644. g. 30.

—— [Another copy.] **83. a. 39. (2.)**
Imperfect; wanting the licence-leaf.

—— Methode et inuention nouuelle de dresser les cheuaux . . . Oeuure . . . traduit de l'anglois de l'auteur, par son commandement [by J. de Solleysel], enrichy de plusieures belles figures en taille douce. pp. 271. *I. van Meurs: Anuers,* 1658. fol. **64. i. 14.**
With an additional titlepage, engraved.

—— [Another copy.] **C. 43. i. 19.**

—— [Another copy.] **G. 6054.**

—— Seconde édition. pp. 236. *Jean Brindley: Londres,* 1737. fol. **64. i. 6.**
With the copper-plates and engraved titlepage of the Antwerp edition.

—— A General System of Horsemanship in all it's branches: containing a faithful translation of that most noble . . . work of his Grace William Cavendish entitled, The Manner of feeding, dressing and training of horses . . . With all the original copper plates. (vol. 2. containing I. Directions for the choice of stallions and mares . . . II. The manner of keeping . . . race-horses . . . III. The perfect knowlege of horses. Translated from the French edition published . . . by Gaspar de Saunier . . . The Osteology and myology of a horse, *etc.*) 2 vol. *J. Brindley: London,* 1743. fol. **788. i. 19, 20.**

—— [Another copy.] **64. i. 4, 5.**

—— A New Method and Extraordinary Invention to Dress Horses, *etc.* pp. 352. *Printed by Tho. Milbourn: London,* 1667. fol. **558*. f. 24.**
A different work from the preceding.

—— [Another edition.] pp. xii. 343. *James Kelburn: Dublin,* 1740. 12°. **7294. b. 13.**

—— A Pleasante & Merrye Humor off a Roge. [Edited by Francis Needham.] pp. viii. 38. *R. Clay & Sons: Bungay,* 1933. 8°. [*Welbeck Miscellany.* no. 1.]
W.P. 10493/1.

—— The Triumphant Widow, or the Medley of humours. A comedy. pp. 98. *J. M. for H. Herringman: London,* 1677. 4°. **644. g. 31.**

—— [Another copy.] **83. a. 39. (1.)**

—— *Begin.* Vicesimo tertio Novembris, 1643. At a Councell of Warre held at Chesterfield. [The decision of a Council of War acquitting Sir John Hinderson of charges of negligence. Signed by the Duke of Newcastle and others.] [1643.] *s. sh.* fol. **1851. b. 21. (7.)**

CAVENDISH (WILLIAM) *Duke of Newcastle.*

—— The Cavalier and his Lady. Selections from the works of the first Duke and Duchess of Newcastle. Edited, with an introductory essay, by Edward Jenkins. pp. 284. *Macmillan & Co.: London,* 1872. 8°. **11650. de. 13.**

—— A Collection of Letters and Poems written by several persons of honour and learning, upon divers important subjects, to the late Duke and Dutchess of Newcastle. pp. 182. MS. NOTE [by R. Farmer]. *For Langly Curtis: London,* 1678. fol. **10921. l. 8.**

—— The First Duke and Duchess of Newcastle-upon-Tyne. By the author of "A Life of Sir Kenelm Digby" [i.e. Thomas Longueville] . . . With illustrations. pp. xiii. 287. *Longmans & Co.: London,* 1910. 8°. **010827. ee. 30.**

—— A New-Come Guest to the Towne. That is, the Descriminant Oath which the Earle of Newcastle imposeth upon the Countie and Citie of Yorke . . . Written by a Yorke-Shire Gentleman . . . with a particular List of the names of the most violent Papists . . . that bare armes, or are ayding . . . the Earle of Newcastle. pp. 8. *For Matthew Walbancke: London,* 1644. 4°. **C. 59. g. 20. (14.)**

—— A New Discovery of Hidden Secrets; in several letters, propositions, articles and other writings concerning the Earle of Newcastle, Captaine John Hotham, and many other malignant gentry of the Northerne counties: all lately found in Pomfract castle . . . With a declaration of the Committee of Yorkshire, and some observations thereupon, *etc.* pp. 6. *For John Wright: London,* 1645. 4°. **E. 267. (2.)**

—— Le Nouueau Newcastle, ou Nouueau traité de cavalerie géometrique, théorique et pratique. [By C. Bourgelat.] pp. xiv. 190. *Lausanne & Genève,* 1744. 8°. **1040. c. 28.**

—— El Nuevo Newkastle . . . Traducido del Frances [of C. Bourgelat] . . . y aumentado con un diccionario de equitacion . . . por Don Francisco de Layglesia. pp. xxx. 347. *Madrid,* 1801. 12°. **1040. a. 26.**

CAVENDISH (WILLIAM) *3rd Earl of Devonshire. See* HOLLES (Denzil) *Baron Holles.* The Speech of Denzell Holles . . . upon the impeachment of the Earles of North-hampton, Devon-shire, *etc.* 1642. 4°. **E. 200. (48.)**

CAVENDISH (*Sir* WILLIAM) [For the Life of Cardinal Wolsey," written by George Cavendish, but often attributed to Sir W. Cavendish:] *See* CAVENDISH (George)

CAVENDISH (WILLIAM GEORGE SPENCER) *6th Duke of Devonshire. See* CLIFFORD (*Sir* Augustus W.) A Sketch of the Life of the Sixth Duke of Devonshire. 1870. 4°. **10817. k. 16.**

—— *See* MARKHAM (Violet R.) Paxton and the Bachelor Duke [i.e. W. G. S. Cavendish, 6th Duke of Devonshire]. [With portraits.] 1935. 8°. **010825. ff. 17.**

—— A Catalogue of the Duplicates of the Library of . . . the Duke of Devonshire . . . which will be sold by auction, by R. H. Evans . . . November 24 [1815], *etc.* pp. 42. *W. Bulmer & Co.: London,* [1815.] 8°. **822. b. 28.**

—— Handbook of Chatsworth and Hardwick. [By W. G. S. Cavendish, 6th Duke of Devonshire.] pp. 242. *Privately Printed: London,* [1845.] 4°. **C. 114. d. 6.**

—— *See* THOMPSON (Francis) *M.A.* A History of Chatsworth. Being a supplement to the sixth Duke of Devonshire's Handbook. 1949. fol. **L.R. 294. c. 13.**

CAVENDISH BENTINCK (*Lord* CHARLES) *See* BENTINCK.

CAVENDISH BENTINCK (*Right Hon.* GEORGE AUGUSTUS FREDERICK) *See* BENTINCK.

CAVENDISH BENTINCK (*Lord* HENRY) *See* BENTINCK.

CAVENDISH BENTINCK (MARGARET) *Duchess of Portland. See* BENTINCK.

CAVENDISH BENTINCK (RUTH) *See* BENTINCK.

CAVENDISH BENTINCK (*Lord* WILLIAM CHARLES) *See* BENTINCK.

CAVENDISH BENTINCK (*Lord* WILLIAM GEORGE FREDERICK) *See* BENTINCK.

CAVENDISH BENTINCK (WILLIAM HENRY) *3rd Duke of Portland. See* BENTINCK.

CAVENDISH BENTINCK (WILLIAM JOHN ARTHUR CHARLES JAMES) *6th Duke of Portland. See* BENTINCK.

CAVENDISH-BENTINCK-SCOTT (WILLIAM HENRY CAVENDISH) *4th Duke of Portland. See* BENTINCK, afterwards BENTINCK-SCOTT.

CAVENDISHIANA. Cavendishiana, a treatise on the head dress. By One of the Hairy Club, author of "Neck-clothitania." Embellished with coloured engravings. pp. 20. *J. J. Stockdale: London,* 1821. 12°. **7743. a. 13.**

CAVENDISH-MAY (E. W.) *See* MAY.

CAVÈNE (LÉON) Le Célèbre miracle de Saint Janvier à Naples et à Pouzzoles examiné au double point de vue historique et scientifique, avec une introduction sur le miracle en général. Ouvrage honoré d'une lettre d'approbation de S. G. Mgr. de Cabrières, évêque de Montpellier. Illustré de 35 gravures, *etc.* pp. xvi. 356. *Paris,* 1909. 8°. **3900. g. 18.**

CAVENNE (CHARLES) Quelques réflexions sur l'hypocondrie. Dissertation inaugurale, *etc.* pp. 12. *Montpellier,* 1822. 4°. **1181. c. 7. (4.)**

CAVENNE (CONSTANT) Études sur les hernies abdominales et leur cure radicale. pp. 80. *Paris,* 1844. 8°. **1188. k. 27.**

CAVENNE (FERDINAND) Un Mot sur l'administration. pp. 16. *Paris,* 1863. 8°. **5425. ff. 9.**

—— Notes sur Volvic et les carrières. pp. 30. *Thiers,* 1861. 8°. **10169. dd. 27. (3.)**

CAVENNE (L. E.) Propositions sur les soins généraux qu'il convient d'administrer aux femmes pendant le travail de l'enfantement; thèse, *etc.* pp. 13. *Paris,* 1820. 4°. **1183. f. 2. (30.)**

CAVENS (LOUIS) *Count. See* RIVIÈRE (C.) Bruxelles. La médaille d'honneur de la ville. [With special reference to the presentation of the medal to Count Louis Cavens.] 1927. 8°. **010271. g. 21.**

—— Le Canal de Willebroeck, *etc.* (A la mémoire de Jean de Locquenghien et de ses compagnons.) [With illustrations, including a portrait.] pp. 40. [*Brussels,* 1921.] 8°. **010271. g. 8.**

—— 1830. Le centenaire, sa célébration à Bruxelles et dans les chefs-lieux de province. pp. 4. [*Brussels,* 1923.] fol. **1865. c. 9. (76.)**

—— Napoléon 1er . . . Apollon II. pp. viii. 193. *Bruxelles,* 1909. 8°. **10656. dd. 10.**

CAVENS (Louis) _Count._

—— La Préservation de Waterloo, _etc._ pp. 22. _Bruxelles_, [1914.] 8°.   **010271. l. 17.**

CAVENTOU (Eugène) _See_ Wurtz (C. A.) Dictionnaire de chimie . . . Par A. Wurtz . . . avec la collaboration de MM. J. Bouis, E. Caventou, _etc._ 1868, _etc._ 8°.   **08909. dd.**

CAVENTOU (Joseph Bienaimé) _See_ Bayle (A. L. J.) Encyclopédie des sciences médicales. Par MM. Alibert . . . Caventou, _etc._ 1834, _etc._ 8°.   **07305. cc. 3.**

—— _See_ Paris.—_Académie Royale de Médecine, etc._ Sicherste Methode, die Anwesenheit des Arseniks bei Arsenikvergiftungen zu ermitteln . . . bekannt gemacht von Husson, Adelon . . . und Caventou, _etc._ 1842. 8°.   [MISSING.]

—— Nouvelle nomenclature chimique, d'après la classification adoptée par M. Thenard. pp. xvi. 298. _Paris_, 1816. 8°.   **44. e. 12.**

—— Traité élémentaire de pharmacie théorique, d'après l'état actuel de la chimie, _etc._ pp. xxiv. 718. pl. 2. _Paris_, 1819. 8°.   **547. g. 5.**

CAVERHILL (Jerdon) _See_ Rutherford (Helen) Proof in the Process . . . against J. Caverhill . . . and others, _etc._ [1786?] 4°.   [MISSING.]

CAVERHILL (John) Experiments on the Cause of Heat in Living Animals and Velocity of the Nervous Fluid. pp. 67. _G. Scott: London_, 1770. 8°.   **784. l. 17. (1.)**

—— An Explanation of the Seventy Weeks of Daniel, and of the several sections of these seventy weeks . . . To which is added an exposition of the chronology of the Jewish Judges, _etc._ pp. 219. _T. Evans: London_, 1777. 8°.   **1016. f. 16. (1.)**

—— A Treatise on the Cause and Cure of the Gout. pp. xi. 187. pl. II. _G. Scott: London_, 1769. 8°.   **1188. d. 12.**

CAVERHILL (P. Z.) _See_ Edgecombe (G. H.) Rocky Mountains Forest Reserve. Report . . . By G. H. Edgecombe . . . and P. Z. Caverhill. 1911. 8°. [_Department of the Interior, Canada. Forestry Service. Bulletin._ no. 18.]   **C.S. E. 15.**

CAVERHILL (W. Melville) _See_ Melville (Alan) _pseud._ [i.e. W. M. Caverhill.]

CAVERI (Nicolò)

—— _See_ Revelli (P.) Un Cartografo genovese amico a Cristoforo Colombo: Nicolò Caveri, " Nicolaus de Cauerio." 1948. 8°.   **10634. h. 34.**

CAVERIBERT (Raoul) La Vie et l'œuvre de Rayer. [With a portrait.] pp. 61. _Paris_, 1931. 8°. **10655. i. 20.**

CAVERLEY (Walter) _See_ Calverley.

CAVERLY FAMILY. The Caverly Family; or, Mrs. Linden's teachings. By H. H. H. 1860. 12°. _See_ H., H. H.   **12806. bb. 36.**

CAVERLY (Don Philip)

—— A Primer of Electronics. pp. xi. 235. _McGraw-Hill Book Co.: New York & London_, 1943. 8°.   **08755. aaa. 48.**

—— Primer of Electronics and Radiant Energy . . . Second edition. pp. ix. 343. _McGraw-Hill Book Co.: New York_, 1952. 8°.   **8761. d. 27.**

CAVERLY (R. B.) and **BANKES** (George Nugent) Leading Insurance Men of the British Empire. pp. xii. 565. _Index Publishing Co.: London_, [1892.] 4°. **10804. ee. 17.**

CAVERLY (Robert Boodey) Heroism of Hannah Duston, together with the Indian wars of New England. pp. 408. _B. B. Russell & Co.: Boston_, 1875. 12°.   **9603. bb. 4.**

—— History of the Indian Wars of New England, with Eliot the Apostle fifty years in the midst of them. 2 vol. _J. H. Earle: Boston_, 1882. 8°.   **9603. bb. 23.** _Vol._ 1 _is another edition of_ " _Heroism of Hannah Duston, etc._"

CAVERN. The Cavern of Death. A moral tale. Second edition. pp. 141. _J. Bell: London_, 1794. 12°.   **12614. eee. 8.**

With an engraved frontispiece.

—— La Caverne de la mort, traduit de l'anglais [i.e. from " The Cavern of Death "], sur la troisième édition, par L. F. Bertin. pp. 201. an VII [1798/99]. 12°. _See_ Caverne.   **12808. u. 2.**

CAVERNE. La Caverne de la mort, traduit de l'anglais [i.e. from " The Cavern of Death "], sur la troisième édition, par L. F. Bertin. pp. 201.   _Paris_, an VII [1798/99]. 12°.   **12808. u. 2.**

—— La Caverne des brigands; ou Recueil des assassinats, des vols, des brigandages des scélérats qui ont expié leurs crimes dans leurs entreprises et sur l'échafaud. pp. 143. _Paris_, [c. 1815.] 12°.   **10711. a. 21. (2.)** _The titlepage is engraved._

CAVERNI (Raffaello) _See_ Galilei (G.) Problemi naturali di G. Galilei e di altri autori della sua scuola raccolti . . . e annotati da R. Caverni. 1874. 8°.   **8705. aaa. 2.**

—— Storia del metodo sperimentale in Italia. 5 tom. _Firenze_, 1891–98. 8°.   **8705. dd. 14.**

CAVERNO, _Family of._ _See_ Caverno (Arthur) Record of the Caverno Family. 1874. 8°.   **9916. aaa. 6. (2.)**

CAVERNO (Arthur) Record of the Caverno Family. pp. 36. _Morning Star Steam Job Printing Establishment: Dover, N.H._, 1874. 8°.   **9916. aaa. 6. (2.)**

CAVERNO (Julia Harwood) _See_ Northampton, _Mass._—_Smith College._ Smith College Classical Studies. (Editors, no. 1–5. J. E. Brady, J. H. Caverno; no. 6–11. J. H. Caverno, F. A. Gragg.) 1920, _etc._ 8°.   **Ac. 1877.**

CAVERO (Francisco Cavero y) _See_ Cavero y Cavero.

CAVERO (Juan Francisco Calvo y) _See_ Calvo y Cavero.

CAVERO (Margarita) Sagradas Aclamaciones poeticas à la profesion de . . . Doña M. Cavero . . . en el Real Convento de Sta Lucia, _etc._ [_Saragossa_, 1693.] 4°.   **1073. k. 22. (26.)**

CAVERO (Pedro Arnal) _See_ Arnal Cavero.

CAVERO EGÚZQUIZA (Justiniano) _See_ Martínez Izquierdo (S.) and Cavero Egúzquiza (J.) Geografía de los Estados Unidos Perú-Bolivianos, _etc._ 1880. 8°.   **10408. ee. 28. (1.)**

CAVERO MARTINEZ (Juan Clemente) El Huerfano de Mompeller, o Vida de San Roque. Opúsculo en verso. pp. 24. _Cuenca_, 1857. 8°.   **11452. c. 29.**

CAVEROT (Louis Joseph Eusèbe) _Cardinal._ _See_ Déchelette (J.) Vie du cardinal Caverot, _etc._ 1890. 8°.   **4856. cc. 7.**

CAVERO Y CAVERO (Francisco) Con la Segunda Bandera en el Frente de Aragón. Memorias de un alférez provisional. pp. 158. *Zaragoza*, 1938. 8°. **9180.** r. **34.**

CAVERO Y SALAZAR (José) Elogio del Excmo. Señor Don Joaquin de la Pezuela y Sanchez, Virey del Perú, *etc.* pp. 68. *Lima*, 1816. 4°. [*Coleccion de las composiciones de eloquencia y poesía con que la Real Universidad de San Márcos de Lima celebró . . . el recibimiento de . . . Señor Don J. de la Pezuela y Sanchez, etc.*] Ac. **2698/2.**

CAVERS (Charles) Hades ! The Ladies ! Being extracts from the diary of a draper, Charles Cavers, Esquire, late of Bond Street, London, West. Foreword by Sacheverell Smith. [By William Y. Darling.] pp. xv. 363. *Gurney & Jackson: London, Edinburgh*, 1933. 8°. **12349.** s. **21.**

CAVERS (Francis) *See* London.—III. *British Ecological Society.* The Journal of Ecology. Edited . . . by F. Cavers. 1913, *etc.* 8°. Ac. **3297.**

—— Botany for Matriculation. pp. viii. 568. *London*, 1909. 8°. [*University Tutorial Series.*] **12205.** e. **141.**

—— Second edition. (Revised by L. C. Fox.) pp. viii. 509. *University Tutorial Press: London*, 1931. 8°. **12205.** e. **158.**

—— (Third edition.) Revised by L. C. Fox. pp. viii. 516. *University Tutorial Press: London*, 1934. 8°. **12205.** e. **163.**

—— Junior Botany. pp. xii. 288. *University Tutorial Press: London*, 1915. 8°. **07029.** g. **30.**

—— Life Histories of Common Plants. pp. xi. 363. *London*, 1908. 8°. [*University Tutorial Series.*] **12205.** e. **120.**

—— Plant Biology. A text-book of elementary botany arranged for modern methods of teaching. pp. xvi. 460. *London*, 1907. 8°. [*University Tutorial Series.*] **12205.** e. **94.**

—— Practical Botany. pp. xvi. 408. *London*, 1911. 8°. [*University Tutorial Series.*] **12205.** c. **379.**

—— Second edition. pp. xvi. 420. *University Tutorial Press: London*, 1915. 8°. **07029.** g. **32.**

—— Third edition. pp. xvi. 426. *University Tutorial Press: London*, 1928. 8°. **07030.** de. **67.**

—— Fourth edition. pp. xvi. 429. *University Tutorial Press: London*, 1933. 8°. **12205.** c. **602.**

—— The Senior Botany. pp. vi. 464. *London*, 1910. 8°. [*University Tutorial Series.*] **12205.** c. **5.**

—— Second edition. pp. vi. 500. *University Tutorial Press: London*, 1918. 8°. **12205.** e. **150.**

CAVERSAZZI (Ciro)

—— *See* Carnovali (G.) called Il Piccio. Giovanni Carnovali, il Piccio. Terza edizione, *etc.* [Reproductions. With an introduction by C. Caversazzi.] 1946. 4°. **7868.** dd. **43.**

—— *See* Mascheroni (L.) Poesie e prose italiane e latine edite ed inedite . . . Testo critico preceduto da una introduzione per cura di C. Caversazzi. 1903. 8°. [*Contributi alla biografia di Lorenzo Mascheroni.* vol. 1.] Ac. **29.**

—— *See* Tallone (C.) Cesare Tallone, *etc.* [With an introduction by C. Caversazzi.] [1921.] 4°. [missing.]

CAVERSHAM.

—— A Guide to Caversham-on-Thames. (The official guide.) Specially compiled by Robert Martin. Containing a map of the district, *etc.* pp. 56. *E. J. Burrow: Cheltenham*, [1910?] 8°. **10354.** a. **201.**

—— *Oratory School.* The Oratory School, Caversham, Reading. Its history, development and present-day activities. pp. 28. *British Publishing Co.: Gloucester*, [1938.] *obl.* 8°. **08366.** o. **12.**

Queen Anne's School.

—— Queen Anne's School Chronicle. vol. **56,** *etc.* [*Caversham*,] 1950 —. 8°. P.P. **6152.** nab.

CAVERSINUS (Bartholomæus) *See* Erasmus (D.) [*Colloquia.—Epicureus.*] Epicureus . . . scholijs illustratus et e Latino sermone in Græcum conuersus per B. Cauersinum. 1567. 8°. **527.** e. **3.** (5.)

CAVERT (Samuel McCrea) *See* Brown (William A.) *the Elder.* The Church through Half a Century. Essays in honor of William Adams Brown . . . Editors: S. McC. Cavert, H. P. Van Dusen. 1936. 8°. **20029.** c. **29.**

CAVERT (Walter Dudley) Story Sermons from Literature and Art. pp. xi. 151. *Harper & Bros.: New York, London*, [1939.] 8°. **04400.** ee. **56.**

CAVES. Caves and Caving. *See* England.—*British Speleological Association.*

—— The Caves of the Earth : their natural history, features and incidents. pp. 192. *R.T.S: London*. [1847.] 16°. **4420.f.10.**

CAVES (William Thomas)

—— Wholesale Textile Distribution, *etc.* pp. xi. 172. *Mirror Printing Co.: Eastbourne*, 1951. 8°. **8219.** l. **20.**

CAVESTANY (Genaro) Memorias de un Sesentón Sevillano . . . Colección de artículos publicados en " El Liberal " de Sevilla. [With a portrait.] tom. 1. pp. 152. *Sevilla*, 1917. 8°. **10163.** a. **5.** *Imperfect; wanting tom. 2.*

CAVESTANY (Juan Antonio) *See* Cortezo (C. M.), Discursos leídos ante la Real Academia Española en la recepción pública del Excmo. Sr. D. C. M. Cortezo. (Discurso del Excmo. Señor D. J. A. Cavestany.) 1918. 4°. [missing.]

—— Al Pie de la Giralda. Poesías. pp. 234. *Madrid*, [1929.] 8°. **11452.** h. **19.**

CAVESTANY (Juan Antonio) and **VELARDE** (José P.)

—— Pedro el Bastardo. Drama en tres actos y en verso. pp. 85. *Madrid*, 1888. 8°. **11726.** e. **8.** (3.)

CAVET (Estienne) Pourtraict racourcy du b. heureux François de Sales, euesque de Geneue, tiré par E. Cavet chanoine en 1632. Nouuellement réimprimé par les soins de Léon Galle. pp. xxxix. 180. *Moûtiers*, 1899. 8°. **4823.** de. **11.** *No. 75 of an edition of 100 copies.*

CAVEUS (Guilielmus) *See* Cave (William) *D.D.*

CAVEYRAC (Jean Novi de) *See* Novi de Caveirac.

CAVEZZALI (Alberto) Sunti di pedagogia, compilati in conformità dei vigenti programmi delle scuole normali. pp. 191. *Norara*, 1882. 8°. **8310.** c. **7.**

CAVI (SCIPIONE) *See* FEA (C.) Risposta antiquario-legale alla scrittura del sig. avvocato S. Cavi. [A refutation of the Giorgi family's claim to antiquities found in the ruins of Veii.] 1822. 8º.   **5357. d. 17.**

CAVIA (DOMINGO S.) La Impotencia y el error en la persona en el matrimonio. Estudio médico-legal y réplica al dictamen fiscal del doctor Ernesto Quesada en un juicio sobre nulidad del matrimonio. pp. 188. *Buenos Aires*, 1915. 8º.   [MISSING.]

CÁVIA (FIDEL ABAD Y) *See* ABAD Y CÁVIA.

CÁVIA (MARIANO DE) *See* BÁIG BAÑOS (A.) Cávia como Cervantista. 1928. 8º.   **11824. w. 12.**

—— *See* LUGILDE Y HUERTA (M.) Figuras anarquistas vistas a través del Quijote. Con asimilaciones de M. de Cavia. 1918. 8º.   **011853. a. 46.**

—— Cuentos en Guerilla. pp. 174. *Barcelona*, [1897.] 16º.   **12489. aa. 30.**

CAVIA (PEDRO FELICIANO SÁENZ DE) *See* SÁENZ DE CAVIA.

CAVIARE, *pseud.* [i.e. JOHN FRANCIS O'DONNELL.] The Emerald Wreath: a fireside treasury of legends, stories, &c. By Caviare. With numerous illustrations engraved by the Brothers Dalziel. pp. 240. *James Duffy: Dublin*, [1864.] 16º.   **12631. aa. 18.**
With an additional titlepage, engraved.

CAVICAEO (JACOBO) *See* CAVICEO (Jacopo)

CAVICCHIOLI (A.) La Rotta dei Ronchi nell'ottobre 1872. Relazione, *etc.* pp. 48. *Revere*, 1873. 8º.   **8776. e. 1. (2.)**

CAVICCHIONI (A. C.) Vocabolario italiano-swahili. pp. 216. 1923. 8º. *See* ITALY.—*Ministero delle Colonie*.   **12911. b. 2.**

CAVICE (JACQUES) *See* CAVICEO (Jacopo)

CAVICEO (GIACOMO) *See* CAVICEO (Jacopo)

CAVICEO (JACOPO) *Begin.* [fol. 2 *recto:*] Beltrando de Rubeis Parmensi Guidonis legionis uenetæ Ducis Filio: Iacobus Cauiceus Parmensis. [In praise of a lady named Lupa.] [*Venice*, 1491 ?] 4º.   **IA. 25001.**
12 leaves, the first and last blank. Sig. a⁸ b⁴. *37 lines to a page. Without the last blank leaf.*

—— Confessionale vtilissimuȝ . . . nuper castigatum, *etc.* G.ℒ. ff. 79.   *Per F. Bindonum ꝛ M. Pasinum socios: Venetijs*, 1529. 8º.   **4061. aa. 47.**

—— Libro del Peregrino nouamente impresso e redutto alla sua syncerita, *etc.* (Vita de Iacobo Cauicæo per Georgio Anselmo.) [*O. Salado & F. Ugoleto: Parma*,] 1513. 4º.   **12410. bb. 31.**

—— [Another edition.] ff. cccxlvi. *In officina Minutiana: Mediolani*, 1515. 8º.   **1481. aa. 30.**
With the device of Nicolaus Gorgonzola on the titlepage.

—— [Another edition.]   *Per M. Bonum de Montis* [sic] *Ferrato: Venetiis*, 1516. 4º.   **1074. k. 26.**

—— [Another edition.]   *Per Bernardino de Lisona: Venetia*, 1520. 4º.   **1481. c. 20.**

—— [Another edition.] Diligentemente in lingua toscha correcto, et nouamente stampato, & historiato. *G. di Rusconi* [*for*] *N. Zoppino & V. cõpagni: Venetia*, 1520. 8º.   **12315. aaa. 12.**

—— [Another edition.]   *G. F. & G. A. di Rusconi* [*for*] *N. Zoppino e V. cõpagni: Venetia*, 1524. 8º. **4411. b. 16.**

CAVICEO (JACOPO)

—— [Another edition.]   *H. di Rusconi* [*for*] *N. Zoppino: Venetia*, 1526. 8º.   **1074. e. 10.**

—— [Another edition.] Nouamente impresso e redutto alla sua syncerita, *etc.* ff. cccxii.   *I. M. de Pelipariis: Vercelli*, 1531. 8º.   **1074. e. 12.**

—— [Another edition.] ff. 279. [*Venice*,] 1533. 8º.   **245. f. 27.**

—— [Another edition.] ff. 271.   *P. di Nicolini da Sabbio: Vinegia*, 1538. 8º.   **243. e. 30.**

—— [Another edition.] ff. 271.   *P. di Nicolini da Sabbio: Vinegia*, 1547. 8º.   **8406. aaa. 4.**

—— Dialogue treselegant intitule le Peregrin, traictant de lhonneste et pudique amour concilie par pure et sincere vertu, traduict de vulgaire Italien en langue Frācoyse, par maistre Francoys dassy, *etc.* [With woodcuts.] G.ℒ. ff. clxix.   *N. couteau, pour G. du Pre: Paris*, 1527. 4º.   **C. 38. g. 6.**
With the arms of Louis Alexandre de Bourbon, Count of Toulouse, stamped in gold on the binding.

—— [Another edition.] G.ℒ. ff. cxlviij.   *C. nourry: Lyon*, 1528. fol.   **12470. h. 5.**

—— [Another edition.] Dialogue très elegāt intitulé, le Peregrin . . . traduict . . . par maistre francoys dassy . . . Reueu . . . par Jehan martin, *etc.* G.ℒ. ff. ccxxiiii. 1531. 4º. *See* PEREGRINO.   **243. k. 25.**

—— [Another edition.] G.ℒ. ff. ccxxiiii. 1535. 4º. *See* PEREGRINO.   **12403. f. 24.**

—— [Another edition.] ff. cccxxvii. 1540. 8º. *See* PEREGRINO.   **G. 17363.**

—— Peregrino. Libro de los honesto[s] Amores de Peregrino y Ginebra. [Translated by H. Diaz.] G.ℒ. 1527. fol. *See* PEREGRINO.   **G. 10284.**

—— Novella. (Tratta dal libro terzo del romanzo intitolato Il Peregrino.) pp. 11. *Lucca*, 1855. 8º.   **12470. f. 27. (4.)**
One of an edition of fifty copies.

—— *Begin.* [fol. 2 *recto:*] Maximo humanæ imbecilitatis Simulachro fortunæ bifronti Vita Petrimariæ de rubeis Viri illustris, *etc.* [*Venice*, 1491 ?] 4º.   **IA. 25003.**
6 leaves, the first blank. Sig. a⁶. *37 lines to a page. Without the blank leaf.*

—— *Begin.* [fol. 1 *recto:*] Vrbium dicta ad Maximilianū Federici Tertii cœsaris [sic] filiū romanoꝛ Regem triumphantissimū, *etc.* [*Venice*, 1491 ?] 4º.
6 leaves, the last blank. Sig. a⁶. *38 lines to a page. Without the blank leaf.*   **IA. 25002.**

CAVICEUS (JACOBUS) *See* CAVICEO (Jacopo)

CAVIEDES (JUAN) *See* VALLE Y CAVIEDES (J. del)

CAVIER (LOUP) *See* FLACH (S.) Excellente et notable profession catholique de M. S. Flach . . . Nouuellement traduict de Latin . . . par F. L. Cauier. 1576. 8º.   **3900. a. 46.**

CAVIEZEL (GIAN) Metoda prattica e ligera per imprender il Linguach Tudasch seguond Dr. F. Ahn. [An adaptation of Ahn's "A New . . . Method of learning the German Language."] pp. iv. 68. *Coira*, 1863. 8º.   **12941. aa. 19.**

CAVIEZEL (HARTMANN) *See* FUERSTENAU. Ils Statuts ner Urdens a Tschentaments dad amadus Cumins, numnadameng da Fürstenau ad Ortenstein . . . Publicau tras Major H. Caviezel. 1896. 8º. [*Annalas della Sociedad Rhaeto-romanscha.* annada 10.]   **Ac. 9817.**

CAVIEZEL (HARTMANN)

—— General-Lieutenant Johann Peter Stoppa und seine Zeit. Vortrag, *etc.* pp. 60. *Chur*, 1893. 8°.
10601. ff. 10. (8.)

—— [Another issue.] [1893.] *See* COIRE.—*Geschicht-forschende, afterwards Historisch-Antiquarische, Gesell-schaft von Graubünden.* Achter [*etc.*] Jahresbericht, *etc.* Jahrg. 1892. [1879, *etc.*] 8°. **Ac. 6930/3.**

—— Litteratura veglia. [A collection of Romansch verse, compiled by H. Caviezel.] 1893. *See* COIRE.—*Societad Rhaeto-Romanscha.* Annalas, *etc.* annada 8. 1886, *etc.* 8°. **Ac. 9817.**

CAVIEZEL (LUZIUS) Dus Priedis p' ilg gi fœderal, *etc.* pp. 16. *Cuera*, 1857. 8°. **885. f. 33. (2.)**

CAVIEZEL (M.) Das Engadin in Wort und Bild. [With maps.] pp. 394. *Samaden*, 1896. obl. 8°. **10196. df. 1.**

—— Das Oberengadin. Ein Führer auf Spaziergängen, kleinen und grossen Touren. pp. viii. 204. *Chur*, 1876. 8°. **10196. aaaa. 12.**

—— Tourist's Guide to the Upper Engadine. Translated . . . by A. M. H. With map. pp. v. 204. *Edward Stanford: London*, 1877. 8°. **10196. aaaa. 25.**

CAVIGIOLI (RICCARDO) L'Aviazione austro-ungarica sulla fronte italiana, 1915–1918. [With illustrations.] pp. 353. *Milano*, 1934. 8°. **9086. aa. 2.**

CAVIGIOLIS (JOANNES BAPTISTA EX) I. Baptistæ ex Cauigiolis de Massaria . . . de morbis nouis interpola, cum aliquot paradoxis, *etc.* pp. 152. MS. NOTES. *Ex officina Marnesiorum fratrum: Pictauii*, 1541. 8°. **1172. f. 15.**

CAVIGLIA (ALBERTO) Claudio di Seyssel, 1450–1520. La vita nella storia de' suoi tempi. [With the text of several of his letters.] pp. xx. 656. *Torino*, 1928. 8°. [*Miscel-lanea di storia italiana.* tom. 54.] **Ac. 6550.**

—— Un Piccolo santo, Giovanni Moraschi da Alessandria, alunno del Collegio Salesiano S. Giovanni Evangelista. pp. 213. *Torino*, 1919. 8°. **4865. de. 25.**

CAVIGLIA (ENRICO)

—— Il Conflitto di Fiume, *etc.* [With maps.] pp. 305. [*Milan*,] 1948. 8°. **9168. p. 21.**
Part of a series entitled " Memorie e documenti."

—— Diario, aprile 1925—marzo 1945. [With plates, in-cluding portraits.] pp. xii. 589. *Roma*, 1953. 8°. **10635. n. 7.**

La Nave d'Ulisse. vol. 4.

—— La Dodicesima battaglia—Caporetto. II. edizione. [With maps.] pp. xi. 309. *Verona*, 1934. 8°. **09080. cc. 30.**

—— Le Tre battaglie del Piave. Con dieci carte e grafici. pp. 317. *Milano*, 1934. 8°. **09079. c. 13.**

CAVIGLIA (H. BUENAVENTURA) *See* BUENAVENTURA CAVIGLIA.

CAVIGLIA (OSCAR R. SUÁREZ) *See* SUÁREZ CAVIGLIA.

CAVIGLIONE (CARLO) Bibliografia delle opere di Antonio Rosmini disposte in ordine cronologico. [With a portrait.] pp. iv. 122. *Torino*, [1925.] 8°. **11908. a. 35.**

CAVIGNE (PIERRE GONTIER SAINT-MARTIN) *See* GONTIER-SAINT-MARTIN-CAVIGNE.

CAVILEERS. *See* CAVALIERS.

CAVILL (   ) [For editions of " A Myrroure for Magistrates," to which — Cavill contributed :] *See* BALDWIN (William) *Poet.*

CAVILLE (J. B.) Les Périgordinismes corrigés. Par I. B. C . . . . . . [i.e. J. B. Caville]. pp. iv. 68. 1818. 8°. *See* C., I. B. **12950. f. 10.**

CAVILLIER (FRANÇOIS)

—— *See* BRIQUET (J.) Biographies des botanistes à Genève . . . Rédaction : Fr. Cavillier. 1940. 8°. [*Berichte der Schweizerischen Botanischen Gesellschaft.* vol. 50a.] **Ac. 3256.**

—— *See* BURNAT (E.) Autobio-graphie, publiée avec une étude . . . par J. Briquet et F. Cavillier. 1922. 8°. **10656. cc. 1.**

CAVILLON (A.) L'Hôpital de Senlis pendant l'occupation allemande, du 2 au 10 septembre 1914. (Deuxième édition.) pp. 21. *Senlis*, 1915. 8°. **09083. b. 19**

CAVILLONUS (CELSUS HUGO DISSUTUS) *See* DESCOUSU (Celse H.)

CAVILLY (GEORGES DE) *pseud.* [i.e. GEORGES VIBERT.] La Séparation de corps et le divorce . . . Manuel des époux mal assortis, *etc.* pp. iv. 236. *Paris*, 1882. 8°. **5176 bb. 10.**

CAVIN (BERTHE) *See* DHANA-GOPĀLA MUKHOPĀDHYĀYA. Joli-Cou . . . Traduction de B. Cavin, *etc.* [1933 ?] 8°. **12828.a.93.**

—— *See* SCHEURMANN (E.) [Die Lichtbringer.] Messagers de lumière . . . Traduit . . . par B. Medici-Cavin. [1934.] 8°. **10493. aaa. 23.**

—— *See* SCHEURMANN (E.) Le Papalagui, *etc.* (Traduit par B. Cavin.) 1932. 8°. **12208. ee. 136.**

—— *See* SIEBERER (A.) [Katalonien gegen Kastilien.] Espagne contre Espagne. Traduit . . . par B. Medici-Cavin. 1937. 8°. **08042. a. 75.**

CAVINA (PIETRO MARIA) Commercio de due mari, Adriatico, e Mediterraneo per la più breue, e spedita strada dell'Italia occidentale considerato nell'antichissima strada per l'Apen-nino, e sopra il pensiero di vn nouo canale nauigabile dà Faenza all'Adriatico. [With a map.] pp. 35. *G. A. Zarafogli: Faenza*, 1682. 4°. **T. 30*. (11.)**

—— De legitimo tempore paschatis Hebraeorum, & Chris-tianorum dissertatio historico-astronomico-legalis, *etc.* pp. 127. *I. I. Hertz: Venetiis*, 1667. 4°. **4034. dd. 29.**

—— Fauentia antiquissima regio rediuiua conatu historico-geographico Petri M. Kauinæ. [With a map.] pp. 143. *Ex calcographis I. Zarafallij: Fauentiæ*, 1670. 4°. **658. d. 17. (1.)**
With an engraved frontispiece.

—— [Another edition.] Petri Mariæ Kavinæ . . . Faventia rediviva ; seu Descriptio historico-geographica regionis ac civitatis Faventiæ, *etc.* [With a map.] coll. 54. *Lugduni-Batavorum*, [1722.] fol. [*GRAEVIUS* (J. G.) *Thesaurus antiquitatum et historiarum Italiae, etc.* tom. 7. pt. 2.] **L.R.302.a.2/7.**

—— *See* RICCEPUTI (B.) La Verità rediuiua à fauore della città di Forli, ouero Difesa delle antiche ragioni dell'istessa città, già offuscate dalla Rediuiua Faenza del Sig. P. M. Cauina, *etc.* 1673. 4°. **174. c. 5.**

CAVINA (Pietro Maria)

—— Fax, seu Lampas volans, magnum meteoron visum post occasum solis diei 31 martij 1676. Epistolica dissertatio . . . iterum edita. Adiectis cl. virorum dubitationibus, auctorisq; responsis. 2 pt. *Ex typographia I. Zarafallij: Fauentiæ,* [1676.] fol. **717. k. 14. (1.)**

CAVING.

—— Caving. The Journal of the Westminster Spelæological Group. *See* LONDON.—III. *Westminster Spelæological Group.*

CAVINO (Giovanni dal) *See* LAWRENCE (Richard H.) Medals by Giovanni Cavino, the " Paduan." 1883. 8°. [MISSING.]

—— *See* RIZZOLI (L.) Due bassorilievi in bronzo di Giovanni dal Cavino. 1902. fol. **Dept. of Coins & Medals.**

CAVINS (Lorimer Victor) Standardization of American Poetry for School Purposes. pp. x. 134. *University of Chicago Press: Chicago,* 1928. 8°. **011824. dd. 27.**

CAVIOLE (Charles) Essai sur les principales applications de l'iode, *etc.* pp. 30. *Paris,* 1853. 4°. [*Collection des thèses soutenues à la Faculté de Médecine de Paris.* An 1853. tom. 4.] **7372. f. 6.**

CAVIOLE (Jean François) Dissertation sur l'hygiène des femmes enceintes, *etc.* pp. 21. *Paris,* 1815. 4°. **1183. c. 5. (39.)**

CAVIS-BROWN (John) *See* BROWN.

CAVITELLIUS (Ludovicus) Lodouici Cauitellii Patritii Cremonen. Annales quibus res vbicȝ gestas memorabiles a patriæ suæ origine vscȝ ad annum salutis 1583. breuiter ille complexus est. ff. 431. *Apud C. Draconium: Cremonæ,* 1588. 4°. **659. d. 5.**

—— [Another copy.] **795. g. 1.**

—— [Another edition.] [With plates.] 1704. *See* GRAEVIUS (J. G.) Thesaurus antiquitatum et historiarum Italiae, *etc.* tom. 3. pt. 2. 1725, 04, *etc.* fol. **L.R.302.a.2/3.**

CAVIUS (Gulielmus) *See* CAVE (William) *D.D.*

CAVLING (Henrik) Det danske Vestindien . . . Med Vignetten . . . samt to Kort. pp. 155. *København,* 1894. 8°. **10480. e. 35.**

—— Dänisch-Westindien . . . Deutsch von Dr. Burmeister-Norburg. pp. 162. *Berlin,* 1902. 8°. [*Kreuz und Quer durchs Leben.* no. 2.] **010708. ee. 86.**

—— Fra de dybe Dale. Roman. pp. 284. *København,* 1894. 8°. **012581. l. 36.**

CAVLING (Viggo) [Fællesaanden.] The Collective Spirit. An idealistic theory of evolution. Translated . . . by W. Worster. pp. 237. *Methuen & Co.: London,* 1925. 8°. **07001. de. 47.**

CAVO (Andres)

—— *See* RICO GONZÁLEZ (V.) Historiadores mexicanos del siglo XVIII. Estudios historiográficos sobre . . . Cavo, *etc.* 1949. 8°. **11867. l. 11.**

—— De vita Josephi Juliani Parrenni Havanensis. [With a portrait.] pp. lxix. *Romae,* 1792. 4°. **4986. g. 13.**

—— Los Tres siglos de Mexico durante el gobierno Español hasta la entrada del Ejército Trigarante, obra escrita . . . por el padre A. Cavo . . . Publicala con notas y suplemento el lic. Carlos María de Bustamante, *etc.* 4 tom. *Mexico,* 1836, 38. 8°. **9771. b. 4.**

CAVOLEAU (Jean Alexandre) Description du département de la Vendée, et considérations générales sur la guerre civile de 1793, 1794 et 1795. pp. 385. *Nantes,* 1818. 4°. **179. a. 18.**

—— Œnologie française, ou Statistique de tous les vignobles et de toutes les boissons vineuses et spiritueuses de la France, suivie de considérations générales sur la culture de la vigne, *etc.* [With tables.] pp. 436. *Paris,* 1827. 8°. **7075. de. 13.**

—— Statistique ou description générale du département de la Vendée . . . Annotée et considérablement augmentée par A.-D. de la Fontenelle de Vaudoré. [With a map.] pp. xvi. 944. *Fontenay-le-Comte,* 1844. 8°. **1302. h. 25.**

CAVOLINI (Filippo) Memoria per servire alla storia compiuta del fico, e della proficazione relativamente al regno di Napoli. 1782. *See* AMORETTI (C.) and SOAVE (F.) Opuscoli scelti sulle scienze, *etc.* tom. 5. 1778, *etc.* 4°. **981. h. 5.**

—— Memoria sulla generazione dei pesci e dei granchi. pp. 127. *Napoli,* 1787. 4°. **432. l. 21. (2.)**

—— Memorie per servire alla storia de' polipi marini. pp. 279. pl. IX. *Napoli,* 1785. 8°. **432. l. 21. (1.)**

—— [Another copy.] **41. g. 12.** *Imperfect; wanting the " Memoria terza."*

—— Memorie postume sceverate dalle schede autografe di Filippo Cavolini per cura ed a spese di S. D.-Chiaie. pp. xxxiv. 344. *Benevento,* 1853. 4°. **7004. d. 2.**

—— Riflessioni sulla generazione dei funghi. *See* AMORETTI (C.) and SOAVE (F.) Opuscoli scelti sulle scienze, *etc.* tom. 1. 1778, *etc.* 4°. **981. h. 1.**

—— Riflessioni sulla memoria del sig. abate Raimondo Maria de Termeyer sopra il pulce acquajolo, *etc. See* AMORETTI (C.) and SOAVE (F.) Opuscoli scelti sulle scienze, *etc.* tom. 1. 1778, *etc.* 4°. **981. h. 1.**

—— Onoranze e festeggiamenti nel 1° centenario dalla morte di Filippo Cavolini promosse . . . dalla Società di Naturalisti in Napoli, 12–13 settembre 1910. pp. 110. *Napoli,* 1911. 8°. [*Bollettino della Società di Naturalisti in Napoli.* vol. 24. Suppl.] **Ac. 2811. b.**

CAVONIUS (Gösta Edvin)

—— Folkskollärarnas föregångare i Finland. Klockare och sockenskolmästare under frihetstiden, *etc.* pp. 384. *Helsingfors; Leipzig,* 1943. 8°. [*Bidrag till kännedom af Finlands natur och folk.* H. 90.] **Ac. 1094/4.**

CAVOS (Albert) Traité de la construction des théâtres, *etc.* pp. xv. 112. *Paris; Saint-Pétersbourg,* 1847. 4°. [MISSING.]

—— Atlas. pl. 25. fol. [MISSING.]

—— Ueber die architectonische Einrichtung von Theater-Gebäuden . . . Nach der französischen Urschrift in's Deutsche übertragen. pp. 28. pl. 21. *Leipzig,* 1849. fol. [MISSING.]

CAVOUR, *Abbey of. See* MARY, *the Blessed Virgin.— Churches and Institutions.—*Cavour.—*Monasterium Sanctae Mariae.*

CAVOUR (Camillo Benso di) *Count.*

LETTERS.

—— Lettere inedite del conte Camillo di Cavour. [Correspondence with U. Rattazzi. Edited by D. Berti.] 1862. *See* PERIODICAL PUBLICATIONS.—*Tyrin.* Rivista contemporanea, *etc.* vol. 28. fasc. 98. 1854, *etc.* 8°. **P.P. 4202. b.**

CAVOUR (CAMILLO BENSO DI) *Count.* [LETTERS.]

◄── Lettres inédites du comte de Cavour au commandeur Urbain Rattazzi. Traduites en français et précédées d'une étude sur le Piémont, depuis 1848, et M. Rattazzi, par M. Charles De la Varenne. Avec un portrait de M. Rattazzi, *etc.* [A translation of "Lettere inedite del conte Camillo di Cavour," edited by D. Berti.] pp. xv. 271. *Paris,* 1862. 12º.   **10910. aaa. 14.**

──── Count Cavour's Inedited Letters, and British Diplomacy in 1856. [A review of "Lettere inedite del conte Camillo di Cavour," edited by D. Berti.] pp. 20. *W. Jeffs: London,* 1862. 8º.
8033. c. 33. (12.)

──── Lettere edite ed inedite di Camillo Cavour. Raccolte ed illustrate da Luigi Chiala. 7 vol. *Torino,* 1883–87. 8º.
10905. f. 1.

──── Seconda edizione riveduta ed accresciuta. vol. 1. *Torino,* 1884. 8º.   **10910. h. 1.**
Imperfect; wanting vol. 2–7.

──── La Politique du comte Camille de Cavour de 1852 à 1861. Lettres inédites, avec notes. [Correspondence with Emmanuel d'Azeglio. Edited by N. Bianchi.] pp. viii. 419. *Turin,* 1885. 8º.   **8032. bb. 28.**

──── Lettere edite ed inedite di Camillo Cavour a Michelangelo Castelli, 1847–1861. *See* CASTELLI (M.) Il Conte di Cavour, *etc.* 1886. 8º.   **10629. df. 12.**

──── C. Cavour. Nouvelles lettres inédites, recueillies et publiées avec notes historiques par Amédée Bert. pp. x. 573. *Turin,* 1889. 8º.   **010920. g. 7.**

──── Le Comte de Cavour et la comtesse de Circourt. Lettres inédites publiées par le comte Nigra. [With a portrait of the Countess de Circourt.] pp. 193.   *Turin, Rome,* 1894. 8º.   **010920. i. 2.**

──── Count Cavour and Madame de Circourt. Some unpublished correspondence. Edited by Count Nigra. Translated by Arthur John Butler. [With a portrait of the Countess de Circourt.] pp. 157.   *Cassell & Co.: London,* 1894. 8º.   **010920. k. 1.**

──── *See* BERTI (D.) Sulla correspondenza del conte Camillo di Cavour colla contessa di Circourt. 1895. 8º.
10920. k. 22.

──── Nuove lettere inedite del conte Camillo di Cavour. Con prefazione e note di Edmondo Mayor. pp. xxiii. 634. *Torino,* 1895. 8º.   **010920. i. 3.**

──── Cavour agricoltore. Lettere inedite di Camillo Cavour a Giacinto Corio. Precedute da un saggio di Ezio Visconti. pp. iv. 390. *Firenze,* 1913. 8º.   **010905. e. 5.**

──── Lettere edite ed inedite di Camillo Cavour. Raccolte ed illustrate da Luigi Chiala . . . Terza edizione sulla scorta della II edizione riveduta e accresciuta a cura del dott. Marco Rossi. vol. 1. pp. xv. 594.   *Torino,* 1913. 8º.   **010920. b. 30.**
No more published. Previous edition 1884.

──── Il Carteggio Cavour-Nigra dal 1858 al 1861. A cura della R. Commissione Editrice. 4 vol.   *Bologna,* 1926–29. 8º. [*Pubblicazioni della R. Commissione Editrice de' Carteggi Cavouriani.*]   **9104.1.5/1.**

──── La Questione Romana negli anni 1860–1861. Carteggio del conte di Cavour con D. Pantaleoni, C. Passaglia, O. Vimercati. A cura della Commissione Reale Editrice. [With facsimiles.] 2 tom. *Bologna,* 1929. 8º. [*Pubblicazioni della R. Commissione Editrice de' Carteggi Cavouriani.*]   **9104.1.5/3.**

CAVOUR (CAMILLO BENSO DI) *Count.* [LETTERS.]

──── Cavour e l'Inghilterra. Carteggio con V. E. d'Azeglio. A cura della Commissione Reale Editrice. 3 vol. *Bologna,* 1933. 8º. [*Pubblicazioni della R. Commissione Editrice de' Carteggi Cavouriani.*]   **9104.1.5/2.**

──── Carteggio Cavour-Salmour. A cura della R. Commissione Editrice. [Including the third chapter of Salmour's unfinished work, "La Vérité sur quelques événements de ma vie," and the unpublished "Correspondance particulière de Camille de Cavour avec son ami Roger de Salmour." Collected and annotated by the latter. With facsimiles.] pp. xxiv. 316.   *Bologna,* 1936. 8º. [*Pubblicazioni della R. Commissione Editrice de' Carteggi Cavouriani.*]   **9104.1.5/4.**

──── La Liberazione del Mezzogiorno e la formazione del Regno d'Italia. Carteggi di Camillo Cavour con Villamarina, Scialoja, Cordova, Farini, ecc. A cura della Commissione Editrice. *Bologna,* 1949–54. 8º. [*Commissione per la Pubblicazzione dei Carteggi di Camillo Cavour. Pubblicazioni.*] 5 Vol.   **9104.1.5/5.**

SPEECHES.

──── Discorsi parlamentari . . . Raccolti e pubblicati per ordine della Camera dei Deputati. [Edited by G. Massari.] 12 vol. *Torino,* 1863–85. 8º.   **12301. i. 20.**

──── Il Conte di Cavour in Parlamento. Discorsi raccolti e pubblicati per cura di I. Artom e A. Blanc, *etc.* pp. xlvi. 684. *Firenze,* 1868. 8º.   **12302. aa. 44.**

──── Five Parliamentary Speeches. Edited by Peter Warren. *Ital.* pp. xxiii. 99. *Clarendon Press: Oxford,* 1923. 8º.
8033. de. 19.

──── Discorsi parlamentari. Nuova edizione a cura di A. Omodeo e L. Russo. *Firenze,* [1932–] 8º. [*Documenti di storia italiana.* Nuova serie.] **W.P.6842.a/3.**

──── Œuvre parlementaire du comte de Cavour. Traduite et annotée par I. Artom et Albert Blanc. pp. vii. 648. *Paris,* 1862. 8º.   **8005. dd. 6.**

──── A Speech on the Treaty of Navigation and Commerce between Sardinia and France, delivered in the House of Deputies at Turin . . . on the 8th and 9th of April, 1852. Translated from the French by R. H. Major. pp. x. 55. *William Pickering: London,* 1852. 8º.
8246. c. 47. (8.)

──── The Speech of Count Camillo Cavour . . . at the sitting of the 16th April, 1858, on the proposed law relative to conspiracy against foreign sovereigns, political assassination, and the composition of the jury upon the press. pp. 44. *C. Whittingham: London,* 1858. 8º.
8032. bb. 48.

──── Discorso pronunziato alla Camera dei Deputati nelle tornate del 19 e del 20 maggio 1858 . . . sul progetto di legge per concedere facoltà al governo di contrarre un prestito di 40 milioni di lire. pp. 74. *Torino,* 1858. 8º.
8033. de. 46.
The author's presentation copy to W. E. Gladstone.

──── [Speech on the Roman Question, 25 March 1861.] *Fr. See* ITALY.—*Camera dei Deputati.* La Question romaine devant le Parlement italien, *etc.* [1861.] 8º.
[1861–1939] **8032. h. 19**

──── Die Politische Weisheit des Fürsten von Bismarck und des Grafen Camillo von Cavour. Dargelegt von Filippo Mariotti . . . Autorisierte Uebersetzung von M. Bernardi. [Extracts from speeches.] 2 Bd. 1888. 8º. *See* BISMARCK-SCHOENHAUSEN (O. E. L. von) *Prince.* [*Speeches. —Extracts.*]   **8026. ee. 15.**

CAVOUR (CAMILLO BENSO DI) *Count.*

WRITINGS.

—— Opere politico-economiche. [Edited, with a biography, by Luigi Chiali. With a portrait.] pp. c. 165. 707. *Cuneo*, 1855. 8°. **8206. f. 21.**

—— [Another issue.] Ouvrages politiques-économiques (Opere politico-economiche.) 5 pt. *Coni*, 1855–57. 8°. **8205. c. 46**

—— Gli Scritti del conte di Cavour, nuovamente raccolti e pubblicati da Domenico Zanichelli. 2 vol. *Bologna*, 1892. 8°. **12226. d. 5.**

—— [Another copy.] **12225. aaa. 17.**

—— Scritti politici. Nuovamente raccolti e pubblicati da Giovanni Gentile. pp. xix. 324. *Roma*, 1925. 8°. **8033. i. 15.**

—— [Considérations sur l'état actuel de l'Irlande et sur son avenir.] Considerations on the Present State and Future Prospects of Ireland . . . Translated from the French by a Friend to Ireland. pp. iv. 138. *Longman & Co.: London*, 1845. 8°. **1390. h. 33.**

—— Thoughts on Ireland: its present and its future . . . Translated by W. B. Hodgson. pp. xi. 110. *Trübner & Co.: London; A. Ireland & Co.: Manchester*, 1868. 8°. **8145. aaa. 8.**

—— Diario inedito, con note autobiografiche, del conte di Cavour. Pubblicato per cura e con introduzione di Domenico Berti. pp. lxx. 356. *Roma*, 1888. 8°. **10630. g. 21.**

—— —— *See* RODOCANACHI (E. P.) Le Comte de Cavour de 1833 à 1835, *etc.* [A review of " Diario inedito, con note autobiografiche, del conte di Cavour."] 1891. 8°. **10601. ff. 4. (9.)**

—— Idee economiche del conte di Cavour, tolte dai suoi scritti e discorsi parlamentari, raccolte e pubblicate da Arturo Perrone. pp. 159. *Torino*, 1887. 8°. **8226. bb. 4.**

APPENDIX.

—— *See* ÂNE. L'Âne et les trois voleurs, *etc.* [A political satire on Garibaldi, Cavour and Mazzini.] 1860. 8°. **11739. d. 14. (6.)**

—— *See* ARCO (Ciro d') *pseud.* Camille de Cavour. Commémoration, *etc.* 1861. 8°. **10631. e. 43. (2.)**

—— *See* ARESE (Franco) Cavour e le strade ferrate, 1839–1850, *etc.* 1953. 8°. **10636. dd. 15.**

—— *See* BAVIERA (I.) Il Conte di Cavour e l'Italia. 1874. 8°. **8033. aa. 1.**

—— *See* BERNARDI (M.) *Translator.* Cavour. [A biographical sketch.] 1888. 8°. **12249. m. 3.**

—— *See* BERTI (D.) Il Conte di Cavour avanti il 1848. 1886. 8°. **10629. g. 2.**

—— *See* BIANCHI (N.) Il Conte Camillo di Cavour, *etc.* [With a portrait.] 1863. 8°. **10631. f. 27.**

—— *See* BONDILH (H.) L'Unité italienne. Victor Emmanuel et Cavour devant l'Europe, *etc.* 1864. 8°. **8033. bb. 33. (4.)**

—— *See* BONGHI (R.) Camillo Benso di Cavour, *etc.* 1861. 16°. **10631. a. 49. (4.)**

CAVOUR (CAMILLO BENSO DI) *Count.* [APPENDIX.]

—— *See* BONGHI (R.) Ritratti contemporanei. Cavour-Bismarck-Thiers. 1879. 8°. **10601. b. 1.**

—— *See* BORGHETTI (G.) L'Ambasciatrice di Cavour [i.e. Virginia Verasis, Countess di Castiglione]. 1930. 8°. **10633. tt. 3.**

—— *See* BOTTA (V.) A Discourse on the Life, Character, and Policy of Count Cavour, *etc.* 1862. 8°. **10631. f. 17.**

—— *See* BOURGIN (N. G. M.) Cavour. [With a portrait.] 1936. 8°. [*Hommes d'État.* vol. 3.] **010604. b. 2.**

—— *See* BRIANO (G.) Apparecchio alle elezioni generali. (pt. 4. Camillo Cavour.) 1856, *etc.* 8°. **8032. d. 13.**

—— *See* BROFFERIO (A.) *the Elder.* Career and Policy of Count Cavour. Political memoirs extracted from " The History of my own Times," *etc.* [1861.] 8°. **10631. b. 10.**

—— *See* BUZZICONI (G.) La Bibliografia di Cavour. 1898. 8°. **11905. aa. 46**

—— *See* CADOGAN (Hon. Sir Edward C.G.) K.B.E.) Makers of Modern History. Three types: Louis Napoleon—Cavour—Bismarck. 1905. 8°. **10603. f. 4.**

—— *See* CADOGAN (Hon. Sir Edward C.G.) K.B.E. The Life of Cavour . . . With a portrait. 1907. 8°. **10633. cc. 7.**

—— *See* CAMPO FREGOSO (L.) *Count.* Il Monumento Cavour considerato in rapporto coll'arte, colla storia e col pensiero italiano, *etc.* 1873. 8°. [MISSING.]

—— *See* CAPPA (A.) Cavour. 1932. 8°. **10632. ppp. 31.**

—— *See* CARRÉ (Eugène) Protestation à propos de M. de Cavour. [Reasons for not subscribing to his monument.] 1861. 8°. **8033. c. 36. (5.)**

—— *See* CASTELLI (M.) Il Conte di Cavour, *etc.* [With a selection of Cavour's letters to Castelli, 1847–1861.] 1886. 8°. **10629. df. 12.**

—— *See* CASTILLE (H.) Portraits politiques au dix-neuvième siècle. (sér. 2. no. 10. Le Comte de Cavour.) 1856, *etc.* 16°. **10603. a. 19.**

—— *See* CERNUSCHI (H.) Réponse à une accusation portée par M. de Cavour, *etc.* 1861. 8°. **8033. c. 35. (8.)**

—— *See* CHIALA (L.) Politica segreta di Napoleone III. e di Cavour in Italia e in Ungheria, 1858–1861, *etc.* 1895. 8°. **9080. ee. 16.**

—— *See* CODIGNOLA (A.) Anna Giustiniani. Un dramma intimo di Cavour, *etc.* [With a portrait.] 1940. 8°. **010632. aa. 35.**

—— *See* COOPER (Basil H.) Count Cavour: his life and career. 1860. 8°. **10630. a. 10.**

—— *See* CURÀTULO (G. E.) Garibaldi, Vittorio Emanuele. Cavour nei fasti della patria. Documenti inediti, *etc.* 1911. 4°. **Tab. 535. b. 7.**

—— *See* DICEY (*Sir* Edward) Cavour. A memoir. 1861. 8°. **10631. c. 12.**

—— *See* DRESLER (A.) Cavour und die Presse. [With a portrait.] 1939. 8°. **10634. i. 38.**

—— *See* FONTANÈS (E.) Cavour. Conférence, *etc.* 1875. 12°. **10630. aaa. 2.**

—— *See* FOSSATI (Antonio) *Political Economist.* Il Pensiero e la politica sociale di Camillo Cavour. 1932. 4°. **8004. h. 17.**

CAVOUR (CAMILLO BENSO DI) *Count.* [APPENDIX.]

—— *See* FREDERIKSEN (N. C.) Cavour. [A review of Countess E. Martinengo Cesaresco's " Cavour."] [1899.] 8°.   **10601. g. 16. (7.)**

—— *See* FRIEDENSBURG (W.) Cavour. 1911. 8°.
                                               10634. e. 22.

—— *See* GAY (Harry N.) Cavour und die Tausend. [1910.] 8°.   **9168. c. 12. (3.)**

—— *See* GAY (Harry N.) Vittorio Emanuele e Cavour a Parigi e a Londra, 1855. 1912. 8°.   **9168. t. 7.**

—— *See* GHIRON (S.) Aneddoti sulla vita di Cavour, *etc.* 1910. 8°.   **10631. aaa. 36.**

—— *See* GIACOMETTI (Z.) Die Genesis von Cavours Formel " libera Chiesa in libero Stato." 1919. 8°.   **4606. f. 6.**

—— *See* GONNI (G.) Cavour, Ministro della Marina, *etc.* 1926. 8°.   **9150. bb. 26.**

—— *See* GRAMEGNA (L.) Il Piemonte nel Risorgimento italiano. Cavour e i Torinesi nel 1859. 1910. 8°.
                                               9167. bb. 27.

—— *See* IDEVILLE (H. d') *Count.* Cavour. 1883. 8°.
                                               12206. c. 37.

—— *See* INGRATO. Cavour avvelenato da Napoleone III, *etc.* 1872. 8°.   **12471. aa. 41. (8.)**

—— *See* ISAIA (A.) Negoziato tra il conte di Cavour e il cardinale Antonelli conchiuso per la cessione del poter temporale del Papa. 1862. 8°.   **8033. b. 69. (7.)**

—— *See* JUSTE (T.) Le Comte de Cavour. [1883.] 8°.
                                               10629. aa. 52.

—— *See* KRAUS (F. X.) Die Erhebung Italiens im neunzehnten Jahrhundert. Cavour, *etc.* 1902. 8°.
                                               10600. w. 2/2.

—— *See* LA RIVE (W. de) Le Comte de Cavour. Récits et souvenirs. 1862. 8°.   **010632. bb. 37.**

—— *See* LA RIVE (W. de) Le Comte de Cavour, récits et souvenirs. 1863. 12°.   **10631. aa. 23.**

—— *See* LA RIVE (W. de) Reminiscences of the Life and Character of Count Cavour, *etc.* 1862. 8°. **10631. f. 19.**

—— *See* LA RIVE (W. de) Il Conte di Cavour. Racconti e memorie. Con tre lettere inedite del Conte di Cavour, *etc.* 1911. 8°.   **9168. a. 1/3.**

—— *See* LAW DE LAURISTON (N.) *Count.* Garibaldi et Cavour. 1861. 8°.   **8033. d. 26. (9.)**

—— —— 1861. 8°.   **8033. c. 34. (11.)**

—— *See* LUZIO (A.) Garibaldi, Cavour, Verdi. Nuova serie di studi e ricerche sulla storia del Risorgimento. 1924. 8°.   **9168. aa. 24.**

—— *See* MACNAUGHT (John) Cavour. A lecture, *etc.* 1869. 12°.   **10630. a. 49.**

—— *See* MARCHETTI (L.) Cavour e la Banca di Torino, 1847–1850, *etc.* 1952. 8°.   **10636. dd. 14.**

—— *See* MARRIOTT (*Sir* John A. R.) The Makers of Modern Italy. Mazzini—Cavour—Garibaldi. 1889. 8°.
                                               9166. b. 41.

—— —— 1931. 8°.   **9168. c. 34.**

—— *See* MARTINENGO-CESARESCO (Evelyn) *Countess.* Cavour. 1898. 8°.   **10600. ee. 12/1.**

CAVOUR (CAMILLO BENSO DI) *Count.* [APPENDIX.]

—— *See* MARTINENGO-CESARESCO (Evelyn) *Countess.* Cavour. [Translated into Italian.] 1901. 8°.
                                               10632. de. 24.

—— *See* MASI (E.) Cavour and the Kingdom of Italy, 1849–61. 1909. 8°.   [*Cambridge Modern History.* vol. 11.]   **2070.g.**

—— *See* MASSARI (G.) Il Conte di Cavour. Ricordi biografici, *etc.* [With a portrait.] 1873. 8°. **10631. g. 32.**

—— —— 1935. 8°.   **20010. e. 39.**

—— *See* MASSARI (G.) Cavour. Biographische Aufzeichnungen . . . Mit Cavour's Portrait. 1874. 8°.
                                               10631. e. 17.

—— *See* MASSARI (G.) Diario 1858–60 sull'azione politica di Cavour, *etc.* [With a portrait.] 1931. 8°.
                                               9165.v.7.

—— *See* MATTER (P.) Cavour et l'unité italienne. 1922, *etc.* 8°.   **2404. e. 8.**

—— *See* MAZADE (C. de) Le Comte de Cavour. 1877. 8°.
                                               10631. ee. 27.

—— *See* MAZADE (C. de) The Life of Count Cavour, *etc.* 1877. 8°.   **10631. ee. 28.**

—— *See* MAZZIOTTI (M.) Il Conte di Cavour e il suo confessore. Studio storico con documenti e carteggi inediti. [1915.] 8°.   **10634. aa. 11.**

—— *See* MAZZIOTTI (M.) Le Comte de Cavour et son confesseur, *etc.* 1919. 8°.   **10634. aa. 9.**

—— *See* MIRANDE (M.) Le Comte de Cavour et la houille blanche. 1927. 8°.   **10633. c. 33.**

—— *See* MIRECOURT (Eugène de) *pseud.* Histoire contemporaine. (no. 34. Cavour.) 1867, *etc.* 8°.
                                               10661. aaa. 25.

—— *See* MISTRALI (F.) *Baron.* Il Conte di Cavour, *etc.* [With a portrait.] 1859. 4°.   **932. e. 8.**

—— *See* MONTALEMBERT (C. F. R. de) *Count.* Lettre à M. le comte de Cavour. [On the Roman question.] 1860. 8°.   **8032. h. 35. (11.)**

—— *See* MONTALEMBERT (C. F. R. de) *Count.* Deuxième lettre à M. le comte de Cavour. 1861. 8°.
                                               8033. c. 33. (11.)

—— *See* NAZARI-MICHELI (I.) Cavour e Garibaldi nel 1860, *etc.* 1911. 8°.   **9168. v. 4.**

—— *See* NOLAN (Edward Henry) *Ph.D.* The Liberators of Italy : or the Lives of Garibaldi . . . Count Cavour, *etc.* [1864.] 4°.   **9165. i. 10.**

—— *See* ORSI (Pietro) *Count.* Cavour, *etc.* [With portraits.] [1910.] 8°.   **10633. aaa. 20.**

—— *See* ORSI (Pietro) *Count.* Cavour e la formazione del Regno d'Italia. 1913. 8°.   **10633. aa. 28.**

—— *See* ORSI (Pietro) *Count.* Cavour and the Making of Modern Italy, *etc.* [With portraits.] 1914. 8°.
                                               10602. pp. 1.

—— —— 1926. 8°.   **10602. pp. 7.**

—— *See* OSIKA-OSTROVERKHA (M.) Кавур. Від Піемонту до Італії. [With a portrait.] 1939. 8°. [*Квартальник Вістника.* 1939. ч. 1.]   **P.P. 4842. dmi.**

CAVOUR (Camillo Benso di) *Count.* [Appendix.]

—— *See* Ottosen (J.) Camillo Cavour. 1887. 8º.
012210. b. 3/7.

—— *See* Paléologue (G. M.) Cavour . . . Avec un portrait, *etc.* [1926.] 8º. 10634. df. 18.

—— *See* Paléologue (G. M.) Cavour, *etc.* [With portraits.] 1927. 8º. 10632. t. 35.

—— *See* Paléologue (G. M.) Cavour. Ein grosser Realist. [With a portrait.] 1928. 8º. 010632. d. 6.

—— *See* Panzini (A.) Il Conte di Cavour, *etc.* [With portraits.] 1931. 8º. 10633. tt. 6.

—— *See* Pingel (M.) Camillo Cavour, Kongeriget Italiens Grundlægger. 1878. 8º. [*Kulturhistoriske Personligheder.* no. 7.] 10601. cc. 24.

—— *See* Prato (Giuseppe) Fatti e dottrine economiche alla vigilia del 1848. L'Associazione agraria subalpina e C. Cavour. 1921. 8º. [*Biblioteca di storia italiana recente.* vol. 9.] Ac. 6550/3.

—— *See* Reyntiens (H. N.) Bismarck & Cavour. L'unité de l'Allemagne & l'unité de l'Italie, *etc.* 1875. 8º.
8026. f. 37.

—— *See* Ruffini (F.) Camillo di Cavour e Mélanie Waldor. Secondo lettere e documenti inediti, *etc.* 1914. 8º.
9168. a. 1/8.

—— *See* Ruffini (F.) La Giovinezza del conte di Cavour, *etc.* [With a portrait.] 1912. 8º. 9168. a. 1/5.

—— *See* Ruffini (F.) L'Insegnamento di Cavour. 1916. 8º.
8032. c. 51.

—— *See* Ruffini (F.) Ultimi studi sul conte di Cavour. 1936. 8º. 20012. eee. 7.

—— *See* Sassi (D.) Il Conte Camillo Benso di Cavour. [With a portrait.] 1873. 4º. 10630. h. 1.

—— *See* Scherillo (M.) Dante, simbolo della patria. Cavour e la marina italiana, *etc.* 1916. 8º. 12354. w. 5.

—— *See* Sforza (Giovanni) *of Massa di Lunigiana.* Nel primo centenario della nascita di Camillo Cavour. [On some events in Cavour's career in the years 1858 to 1861.] 1910. fol. 1765. b. 27.

—— *See* Silvestri (M. A.) Couza e Cavour, *etc.* 1920. 8º.
9134. bb. 8.

—— *See* Smith (Denis Mack) Cavour and Garibaldi, 1860. A study in political conflict. [With a portrait.] 1954. 8º
8033. n. 3

—— *See* Stefani (G.) Cavour e la Venezia Giulia, *etc.* 1955. 8º. W.P. 545/33.

—— *See* Strachey (Marjorie) Mazzini, Garibaldi & Cavour. 1937. 8º. W.P. 12079/4.

—— *See* Tamborra (A.) Questione italiana e questione rumena nella politica di Cavour. 1950. 8º. [*Archivio storico italiano.* no. 396.] P.P. 3557.

—— *See* Tessitore (S.) Il Conte di Cavour e le corporazioni religiose. 1911. 8º. 4782. g. 13.

—— *See* Thayer (William R.) The Life and Times of Cavour, *etc.* 1911. 8º. 10632. tt. 1.

—— —— 1915. 8º. 10633. f. 41.

—— *See* Treitschke (G. H. von) Cavour, *etc.* [With a portrait.] 1939. 8º. 10635. c. 36.

CAVOUR (Camillo Benso di) *Count.* [Appendix.]

—— *See* Turotti (F.) Biografia del conte Camillo Benso di Cavour, *etc.* 1861. 8º. 10629. aa. 16.

—— *See* Vera (A.) Il Cavour e libera Chiesa in libero Stato. 1871. 8º. 3902. g. 39.

—— —— 1887. 8º. [*Mariano* (R.) *Augusto Vera. Saggio biografico, etc.*] 10629. g. 5.

—— *See* Vera (A.) Cavour et l'Église libre dans l'État libre, *etc.* 1874. 8º. 3902. g. 4.

—— *See* Verasis (F.) Le Piémont et le ministère du comte de Cavour. 1857. 8º. 8032. g. 39. (2.)

—— *See* Vilbort (J.) Cavour. 1861. 8º.
10631. f. 39. (8.)

—— *See* Watripon (A.) La Vie et la mort du comte de Cavour. Édition illustrée des portraits de Cavour, *etc.* 1861. 8º. 10662. i. 3.

—— *See* White (Andrew D.) Seven Great Statesmen in the Warfare of Humanity with Unreason. (Cavour.) 1910. 8º. 10601. w. 9.

—— *See* Whyte (Arthur J. B.) The Early Life and Letters of Cavour, 1810–1848. [With portraits.] 1925. 8º.
10634. bbb. 7.

—— *See* Whyte (Arthur J. B.) The Political Life and Letters of Cavour, 1848–1861. [With a portrait.] 1930. 8º.
10634. cc. 33.

—— *See* Zanichelli (D.) Cavour. 1905. 8º.
10633. e. 12.

—— *See* Zanichelli (D.) Cavour, *etc.* [A reissue with a preface by F. Ruffini and with a portrait.] 1926. 8º.
10633. b. 32.

—— Biographie du comte Camille-Benso de Cavour, mort le 6 juin 1861. Traduit de l'Italien. pp. 8. *Gand,* [1861.] 8º. 10601. aa. 7. (6.)

—— Brevi cenni biografici sulla vita dell'illustre statista conte Camillo Benso di Cavour. Editi per cura di due operai. [The introduction signed: C. C. ed A. B.] 1873. 8º. *See* C., C. and B., A. 10630. ee. 1. (6.)

—— Cavour jugé par trois hommes d'état. pp. 15. *Paris,* 1861. 8º. 10631. f. 39. (4.)

—— Le Comte de Cavour. Notice biographique par l'auteur de " Pétrarque et son siècle " [i.e. A. S. Rastoul de Mongeot]. pp. 42. *Bruxelles,* 1859. 8º.
10631. f. 39. (3.)

—— Il Conte C. B. di Cavour e il suo monumento in Torino, novembre 1873. Monografia storico-biografico-descrittiva del Prof. A. F. 1873. 8º. *See* F., A., *Prof.*
10631. d. 10.

—— Il Conte di Cavour e l'Italia. pp. 31. *Torino,* 1859. 8º.
8033. h. 30. (6.)

—— La Mort du comte de Cavour et la politique européenne. pp. 15. *Paris,* 1861. 8º. 8032. h. 36. (7.)

—— [Another edition.] pp. 15. *Paris,* 1861. 8º.
8033. c. 38. (3.)

—— Storia e vita politica del conte Camillo B. di Cavour avvelenato da Napoleone III. pp. 64. *Torino,* 1873. 8º.
10631. de. 1. (10.)

CAVOUR (Christodoulos) Τὸ Ἀτέλεστον μνημόσυννον ἢ Δίκη νεκρων κατα ζωντων. [By C. Cavour.] pp. 123. 1863. 8º. *See* Mnemosunon. 8028. bb. 47.

CAVOUR (GUSTAVO BENSO DI) *Marquis.* Fragmens philosophiques. pp. 398. *Turin,* 1841. 8º. **1386. e. 9.**

CAVOUR (GUSTAVO BENSO DI) *Marquis,* and **DEVINCENZI BERNARDI** (GIUSEPPE)

—— Relazione al Ministro d'Agricoltura, Industria, e Commercio . . . dei Regii Commissarii Generali del Regno d'Italia presso l'Esposizione Internazionale del 1862, Marchese G. B. di Cavour e Comm. G. Devincenzi. pp. 29. 1862. 8º. *See* ITALY.—*Ministero di Agricultura, Industria e Commercio.*
[MISSING.]

—— [Another copy.] [MISSING.]

CAVOYE (EUSTACHE DAUGER DE) *See* OGIER DE CAVOYE (E.)

CAVOYE (EUSTACHE OGIER DE) *See* OGIER DE CAVOYE (E.)

CAVOYE (LOUIS OGIER DE) *Marquis. See* OGIER DE CAVOYE.

CAVRIANA. Dialoghi agrarj tenuti in Cavriana l'anno 1786. [By A. Gualandris.] pp. viii. 286. *Mantova,* 1788. 8º. **07077. i. 6.**

CAVRIANA (FILIPPO ANTONIO) Philippi Caurianæ De obsidione Rupellæ commentarius. Histoire du siège de la Rochelle en 1573, traduite du latin de Philippe Cauriana. [Translated and edited by L. Delayant. With plans.] *Lat. & Fr.* pp. xliii. 160. 1856. 8º. *See* ROCHELLE.—*Société Littéraire.* **9210. dd. 12.**

—— Discorsi . . . sopra i primi cinque libri di Cornelio Tacito, *etc.* [With the text in Latin and Italian.] pp. 664. 1600. 4º. *See* TACITUS (C. C.) [*Annales.*] **587. g. 16.**

—— Orazione del cavalier Filippo Cauriana recitata da lui al Capitolo Generale, de l'anno 1599. in Pisa, *etc. Nella Stamperia di M. Sermartelli: Firenze,* 1599. 4º.
12301.c.5.(3.)

CAVRIANI (FEDERICO) *Marquis. See* OVIDIUS NASO (P.) [*Amores.—Italian.*] Amori ovidiani. Traduzione anacreontica di F. Cavriani, *etc.* 1802. 8º. **654. c. 16.**

—— De' vantaggi dell'orologio oltramontano sopra l'italiano. Osservazioni, *etc.* [Extracted from the " Giornale fisicomedico, *etc.*" edited by L. V. Brugnatelli.] [*Pavia,* 1792.] 8º. **7383*. d. 19. (3.)**

—— Delle scienze, lettere ed arti dei Romani della fondazione di Roma sino ad Augusto. [With a portrait.] 2 vol. *Mantova,* 1822, 23. 8º. **820. h. 24.**

—— Poesie varie. pp. viii. 134. *Parma,* 1802. 8º.
639. k. 24.

—— Vita di Francesco Petrarca. pp. 93. *Mantova,* 1816. 8º. **10630. aa. 17.**

CAVRIANI (IPPOLITO) *See* ALPHONSO I. [d'Este], *Duke of Ferrara.* Lettera . . . ad Isabella Estense Gonzaga. Descrizione d'un torneo dato a Bologna nel 1490. [Edited by I. Cavriani.] 1882. 8º. **10905. g. 13. (3.)**

CAVRINES (E. H. F. DE) *pseud.* Esquisses historiques des troubles des Pays-Bas au XVIᵉ siècle. 2 vol. *Bruxelles,* 1865. 8º. **9414. f. 8.**

—— Seconde édition. 2 vol. *Bruxelles,* 1865. 8º.
9414. f. 11.

CAVRIOLO (HELIA) *See* CAPREOLUS (Elias)

CAVRIUOLO (ALFONSO) *See* FONTANA (M. P.) Il Sontuoso apparato fatto dalla magnifica Città di Brescia, *etc.* [Edited by A. Cavriuolo.] [1591.] fol. **9930. i. 20.**

CAVRIUOLO (PAOLO) Sette libri de' cathologi à varie cose appartenenti, non solo antiche, ma anche moderne: opera utile molto alla historia, *etc.* pp. 567. *Appresso G. Giolito de' Ferrari & Fratelli: Vinegia,* 1552. 8º.
1448. a. 7.

CAVRO (LUCIEN) *See* THUREAU-DANGIN (F.) and DUNAND (M.) Til-Barsib. Par F. Thureau-Dangin et M. Dunand, avec le concours de L. Cavro, *etc.* 1936. 4º.
L.R. 56. a. 1/23.

CAVROIS (ALEXANDRE) *Baron.* Les Sociétés houillères du Nord et du Pas-de-Calais. Étude historique et juridique. [A thesis.] pp. 411. *Paris,* 1896. 8º. **08228. i. 18.**

CAVROIS (JULES) and **DUHEM** (HENRI) En canot de Douai au Helder . . . 30 eaux-fortes par R. Bureau d'après les croquis de M. Henri Duhem, *etc.* pp. xv. 192. *Paris,* 1881. 8º. **10271. bbb. 4.**

CAVROIS (LOUIS) Cartulaire de Nôtre-Dame-des-Ardents à Arras. [Miscellaneous documents, edited by L. Cavrois.] pp. 260. *Arras,* 1876. 8º. **4629. c. 3.**

—— O'Connell et le Collége anglais à Saint-Omer . . . Seconde édition, *etc.* pp. 112. *Arras; Saint-Omer,* 1867. 8º. **8356. bb. 54. (6.)**

—— Origine de l'Académie d'Arras . . . Dissertation historique, lue à l'Académie d'Arras, *etc.* pp. 28. *Paris; Arras,* 1866. 8º. **8355. df. 4. (4.)**

CAVUS (ANDREAS) *See* CAVO (Andres)

CAVUS (BRIANUS) *See* SMITH (Henry) *Minister of St. Clement Danes.* Jurisprudentiæ, Medicinæ et Theologiæ Dialogus, *etc.* [Edited by B. Cavus.] 1592. 12º.
1213. k. 16. (3.)

CAVVADIAS (PANAGIOTIS) *See* KABBADIAS.

CAVYLL ( ) *See* CAVILL.

CAW, *of Pritdin. See* CAU, *of Pritdin.*

CAW CAW. Caw Caw . . . A tale of the spring-time by R. M., *etc.* 1882. 8º. *See* M., R. **12806. u. 15.**

CAW (GEORGE) The Poetical Museum. Containing songs and poems on almost every subject. Mostly from periodical publications. [The preface signed: G. C., i.e. G. Caw.] pp. viii. 392. 1784. 8º. *See* C., G.
11621. b. 34.

CAW (*Sir* JAMES LEWIS) *See* ARMSTRONG (*Sir* Walter) Sir Henry Raeburn . . . With . . . a bibliographical and descriptive catalogue by J. L. Caw. 1901. fol.
L.R. 22. b. 1.

—— *See* BARRETT (James A. S.) The Principal Portraits and Statues of Thomas Carlyle. A list compiled by J. A. S. Barrett, with the assistance of J. L. Caw and S. Cursiter . . . With a commentary by J. L. Caw, *etc.* [1928.] 8º.
10823. h. 13.

—— *See* CROCKETT (William S.) and CAW (*Sir* J. L.) Sir Walter Scott, *etc.* 1903. 8º. [*Bookman Biographies.* no. 5.] **10600. ff. 29.**

—— *See* EDINBURGH.—*National Gallery of Scotland.* The National Gallery of Scotland. Fifty-six photogravures of the chief pictures, with a descriptive and historical account of the collection by J. L. Caw. [1912.] 4º.
[MISSING.]

—— *See* EDINBURGH.—*Scottish National Portrait Gallery.* Catalogue of the Scottish National Portrait Gallery . . . Continued and revised by J. L. Caw, *etc.* 1895. 8º.
7861. r. 58.

CAW (Sir James Lewis)

—— See Edinburgh.—*Scottish National Portrait Gallery*. Catalogue . . . Compiled by . . . J. M. Gray. Rearranged, revised and continued by J. L. Caw, *etc*. 1899. 8°.   [Missing.]

—— —— 1905. 8°.   **7856. h. 1.**

—— See Raeburn (Sir Henry) Portraits by Sir H. Raeburn. With an introductory essay by J. L. Caw. 1909. 4°.
                                                                [Missing.]

—— See Reid (Andrew T.) The Collection of Pictures formed by Andrew T. Reid of Auchterarder. With notes by Sir J. L. Caw. 1933. 4°.   **L.R. 259. a. 8.**

—— See Reid (John) *of Glasgow, of the North British Locomotive Co.* Catalogue of the Collection of Pictures of the British, French & Dutch Schools belonging to John Reid. With notes by J. L. Caw. 1913. fol.   **556*. b. 2.**

—— Hours in the Scottish National Gallery . . . With 16 illustrations. pp. 143. *Duckworth: London*, 1927. 8°.
                                            7855.c.65.

—— Notes Historical and Descriptive on the Mural Decorations painted by William Hole, R.S.A. in the Hall of the Scottish National Portrait Gallery, Edinburgh. pp. 24. 1902. 8°. See Edinburgh.—*Scottish National Portrait Gallery*.   [Missing.]

—— The Pictures, and how to enjoy them. A popular guide to the National Gallery of Scotland. pp. 51. 1926. 8°. See Edinburgh.—*National Gallery of Scotland*.
                                                                [Missing.]

—— The Portraits of the Cecils. [With plates.] See Cecil (William) *Baron Burghley*. William Cecil, *etc*. pt. 3. 1904. fol. [*Historical Monograph Series*.]
                                            L.R. 31. b. 9.

—— Raeburn . . . Illustrated with eight reproductions in colour. pp. 80.   *T. C. & E. C. Jack: London; F. A. Stokes Co.: New York*, [1909.] 8°. [*Masterpieces in Colour*.]   **07805.a.29.**

—— The Scott Gallery. [Portraits of Sir Walter Scott, his family, friends, etc., and scenes associated with his life.] A series of one hundred and forty-six photogravures together with descriptive letterpress. 2 pt.   *T. C. & E. C. Jack: Edinburgh*, 1903. fol.   **L.R. 21. a. 1.**

—— Scottish History told by Portraits. A popular guide to the Scottish National Portrait Gallery, *etc*. [By J. L. Caw. With plates.] pp. 20. 1924. 8°.   See Edinburgh.—*Scottish National Portrait Gallery*.   [Missing.]

—— Second edition. pp. 23. 1934. 8°. See Edinburgh.—*Scottish National Portrait Gallery*.   **7860. s. 46.**

—— Scottish Painting past and present, 1620–1908. [With plates.] pp. xiii. 503.   *T. C. & E. C. Jack: Edinburgh & London*, 1908. 4°.   **7863. r. 24.**

—— Scottish Portraits. With an historical and critical introduction and notes by J. L. Caw. 2 vol.   *T. C. & E. C. Jack: Edinburgh*, 1902, 03. fol.
                                            K.T.C. 125. b. 6.
One of twenty-five copies with the plates printed on Japanese vellum.

—— Sir James Guthrie, P.R.S.A., LL.D. A biography . . . Guthrie as Interpreter, by Frank Rinder. Personal Memories, by John Warrack. [With portraits and a catalogue of the artist's works.] pp. xv. 243. pl. xlvi. *Macmillan & Co.: London*, 1932. 4°.   **L.R. 259. c. 15.**

CAW (Sir James Lewis)

—— William McTaggart, R.S.A. . . . A biography and an appreciation. pp. xiv. 302. pl. 51.   *J. Maclehose & Sons: Glasgow*, 1917. 4°.   **L.R. 26. c. 8.**

CAW (Nanny) Nanny Caw: a story of God's Providence. By the author of "Sabbath-School Fruit," *etc*. pp. 11. *Johnstone & Hunter: Edinburgh*, 1852. 32°. [Missing.]

—— [Another edition.] pp. 11. See Christian Experience. Christian Experience, *etc*. pt. 2. 1859. 16°.
                                            4986. a. 17.

CAW (Thomas) Disputatio medica inauguralis, de hæmoptoe, *etc*. pp. 45.   *Balfour, Auld & Smellie: Edinburgi*, 1769. 8°.   **T. 267. (2.)**

—— [Another copy.]   **T. 231. (4.)**

CAWADIAS (Alexander Panagis)

—— See Pulay (E.) Constitutional Medicine and Endocrinology. Edited by E. Pulay . . . A. P. Cawadias . . . P. Lansel. 1944, *etc*. 8°.   **W.P. 614.**

—— Clinical Endocrinology and Constitutional Medicine. pp. iv. 362. pl. 10. *Frederick Muller: London*, 1947. 4°.
                                            7443. bbb. 18.

——   Diseases of the Intestines. [With a bibliography.] pp. xiv. 299. *Baillière & Co.: London*, 1927. 8°.   **07630. ee. 1.**

—— Hermaphroditos. The human intersex. pp. 78. pl. ix. *William Heinemann, Medical Books: London*, 1943. 8°.
                                            Cup.366.aa.27.

—— Hermaphroditos . . . Second edition. pp. x. 81. pl. x. *William Heinemann—Medical Books: London*, 1946. 8°.
                                            Cup.366.aa.28.

—— The Modern Therapeutics of Internal Diseases. An introduction to medical practice. pp. xi. 147. *Baillière & Co.: London*, 1931. 8°.   **7440. p. 3.**

CAWALLIN (Carl Bernhard Sebastian) See Cavallin.

CAWAS N. DAJI. The Coronation Souvenir. (Editor: Cawas N. Daji.) [A collection of articles published to commemorate the coronation of King George vi. With plates, including portraits.] pp. 152.   *D. D. Kanga: Bombay*, [1937.] 4°.   **9930. k. 39.**

CAWCUTT (Thomas) See Allen (John) *Pastor of a Baptist Church in Petticoat Lane, etc.* The Christian Pilgrim . . . Revived by T. Cawcutt. 1809. 12°.   **4405. ff. 3.**

—— See Christian Pilgrim. The Christian Pilgrim, *etc*. [By J. Allen. With the preface of the 1809 edition by T. Cawcutt.] [1857.] 12°.   **4405. d. 6.**

—— The Dream; or, a Flaming torch in an Arminian fog. pp. 38. *E. Justins: London*, 1804. 8°.   **4375. cc. 14.**

CAWDELL (James) The Miscellaneous Poems of J. Cawdell, Comedian . . . To which is annexed an Answer to a late libellous compilation, called the Stockton Jubilee. [With a plate representing an actor on the stage, presumably the author.] pp. 194.   *The Author: Sunderland*, 1785. 8°.   **1162. k. 12.**

CAWDELL (William) A Short Account of the English Concertina, its uses and capabilities, facility of acquirement, and other advantages. By an Amateur. [The preface signed: W. C., i.e. W. Cawdell.] pp. 23. 1866. 8°. See C., W.   **7868.a.18.**

CAWDLE (ALFRED) Rabies. Its course and symptoms: preventative and curative measures. pp. 8.
W. Ridgway: London, 1889. 8°. **07305. i. 5. (5.)**

CAWDOR, *Thanes of*. The Book of the Thanes of Cawdor. A series of papers selected from the Charter Room at Cawdor, 1236–1742. [Edited by C. Innes. With plates.] pp. lxxvii. 471. 1859. 4°. *See* ABERDEEN, *City of.—Spalding Club*. **Ac. 8244/19.**

CAWDOR, ELIZABETH, *Countess of*. *See* CAMPBELL.

——, JOHN DUNCAN VAUGHAN, *Earl*. [1900– .] *See* CAMPBELL.

——, JOHN FREDERICK, *Earl*. [1790–1860.] *See* CAMPBELL.

——, JOHN FREDERICK VAUGHAN, *Earl*. [1817–1898.] *See* CAMPBELL.

——, SARAH MARY, *Countess of*. *See* CAMPBELL.

CAWDOR (WILMA)

—— *See* VICKERS (Vincent C.) Economic Tribulation. [Edited by W. Cawdor.] 1941. 8°. **8222. aa. 21.**

CAWDRAY (ROBERT) *See* CAWDREY.

CAWDREY (DANIEL) *See* BARLEE (William) Prædestination . . . defended against Post-destination . . . To which are prefixed the epistles of Dr. E. Reynolds, and Mr. D. Cawdrey. 1656. 4°. **E. 904. (1.)**

—— *See* COTTON (John) *of Boston, Mass*. A Defence of Mr. John Cotton. From the imputation of Selfe Contradiction, charged on him by Mr. Dan: Cawdrey [in "The Inconsistencie of the Independent way with Scripture and it self"], *etc.* 1658. 8°. **4103. b. 47.**

—— The Account Audited and Discounted; or, a Vindication of the Diatribe against Doctor Hammonds Paradiatribees. By D. C. [i.e. D. Cawdrey.] pp. 438. 1658. 8°. *See* C., D. **E. 1850.**

—— Bowing towards the Altar, upon Religious Reasons, impleaded as grossely superstitious. Being an answer to Dr Duncons Determination, lately reprinted. pp. 31. *For J. Rothwel: London*, 1661. 4°. **4103. e. 13.**

—— Church-Reformation promoted: in a sermon on Matth. 18. vers. 15, 16, 17. Preached at Northampton . . . As also. 1. Some Animadversions upon Mr. Humphry's second Vindication, for promiscuous admission to the Sacrament. 2. Some Animadversions upon Mr. Sanders his Antidiatribe, tending to the same end of Church-Reformation. pp. 192. *W. Wilson, for John Wright: London*, 1657. 8°. **853. d. 8.**

—— Diatribe triplex: or a Threefold Exercitation, concerning 1, superstition; 2, will-worship; 3, Christmas festivall; with . . . Dr. Hammond. pp. 204. *For John Wright: London*, 1654. 8°. **4375. a. 10.**

—— —— *See* HAMMOND (Henry) *D.D.* An Account of Mr. Cawdry's Triplex Diatribe concerning Superstition, *etc.* 1655. 4°. **1482. aaa. 21. (3.)**

—— The Goodman, a publick good; 1, passively; 2, actively, as it was manifested in a sermon preached to the Honourable House of Commons, at the late solemne fast, Jan. 31. 1643. pp. 43. *T. Harper, for C. Greene & P. W.: London*, 1643. 4°. **E. 34. (1.)**

—— Humilitie, the Saints Liuerie; or, the Habit of humilitie, the grace of graces: fetched out of the wardrobe of Saint Paul. As it was deliuered . . . in two sermons at Blacke-Fryers in London, *etc.* pp. 51. *John Haviland, for Edward Brewster: London*, 1624. 4°. **4473. aaa. 13.**

CAWDREY (DANIEL)

—— The Inconsistencie of the Independent way with Scripture and it self; manifested in a threefold discourse: 1, Vindiciæ Vindiciarum with M. Cotton; 2, a review of M. Hookers Survey of Church-discipline: the first part; 3, a diatribe with the same M. Hooker, concerning baptism of infants, *etc.* pp. 219. *A. Miller, for C. Meredith: London*, 1651. 4°. **E. 629. (1.)**

—— *See* STONE (Samuel) *Teacher of the Church of Christ, etc.* A Congregational Church is a Catholike Visible Church . . . Wherein satisfaction is given to what M. Cawdrey writes touching that subject, in his review of Mr. Hooker's survey of church discipline. 1652. 4°. **873. e. 5.**

—— Independencie a great Schism: proved against Dr. Owen his Apology in his tract of schism; as also an appendix to the former discourse, shewing the inconstancy of the Dr., *etc.* pp. 229 [249]. *J. S. for John Wright: London*, 1657. 8°. **4135. a. 23.**

—— Independency further proved to be a Schism. Or, a Survey of Dr. Owens Review of his Tract of Schism; with a Vindication of the Authour from his unjust clamours and false aspersions. pp. 158. *For John Wright: London*, 1658. 8°. **856. a. 13.**

—— *See* OWEN (John) *D.D.* Of Schisme. [A reply to "Independency further proved to be a Schism" by D. Cawdrey.] 1658. 8°. [*A Defence of Mr. John Cotton. From the imputation of Selfe Contradiction, etc.*] **4103. b. 47.**

—— A Sober Answer to a Serious Question propounded by Mr. G. Firmin . . . viz. Whether the Ministers of England are bound by the Word of God to baptise the children of all such parents which say they believe in Jesus Christ; but are grossly ignorant, scandalous in their conversation, scoffers at godliness, and refuse to submit to church-discipline . . . Which may serve also as an appendix to the diatribe with Mr. Hooker, lately published, concerning the baptisme of infants, *etc.* pp. 31. *For Christopher Meredith: London*, 1652. 4°. **E. 683. (23.)**

—— *See* FIRMIN (Giles) A Sober Reply to the Sober Answer of . . . Mr. Cawdrey, *etc.* 1653. 4°. **4323. b. 30.**

—— Vindiciæ Clavium: or, A Vindication of the Keyes of the Kingdome of Heaven, into the hands of the right Owners. Being some Animadversions upon a Tract of Mr. I. C. (Mr. Cotton) called, The Keyes of the Kingdome of Heaven. As also upon another Tract of his, called, The Way of the Churches of New-England . . . By an earnest well-wisher to the Truth [i.e. D. Cawdrey]. pp. 90. 1645. 4°. *See* COTTON (John) *of Boston, Mass*. **E. 299. (4.)**

—— [Another copy.] **105. b. 55.**

—— [Another copy, imperfect.] **4103. bbb. 10.**

CAWDREY (DANIEL) and **PALMER** (HERBERT)

—— Sabbatum Redivivum: or, the Christian Sabbath vindicated; in a full discourse concerning the Sabbath and the Lord's Day: wherein, whatsoever hath been written of late, for, or against the Christian Sabbath is exactly, but modestly, examined: and the perpetuity of a Sabbath deduced, from grounds of nature, and religious reason . . . Divided into foure parts. Part I. Of the Decalogue in generall, and other laws of God, together with the relation of time to religion. pp. 368. *Robert White, for Thomas Underhill: London*, 1645. 4°. **E. 280. (3.)**

CAWDREY (Daniel) and **PALMER** (Herbert)

—— Sabbatum Redivivum . . . The second part. Of the fourth commandment of the Decalogue in speciall. (The third part. In three questions concerning the old Sabbath.—The fourth part. In three questions concerning the Lords day.) pp. 682. *Thomas Maxey, for Samuel Gellibrand & Thomas Underhill: London*, 1652. 4°.
E. **648**.

CAWDREY (Robert) A Short and Fruitfull Treatise, of the profit and necessitie of Catechising . . . Hereunto is added . . . a briefe Method for Catechising &c. . . . Now once againe augmented by R. C. (R. Cawdrey.) *Adam Islip, for Thomas Man: London*, 1604. 8°.
843. g. **25**.

—— A Table Alphabeticall, containing and teaching the true writing and vnderstanding of hard vsuall English words, borrowed from the Hebrew, Greeke, Latine, or French, &c. . . . Set forth by R. C. [i.e. R. Cawdrey] and newly corrected, and much inlarged . . . The 3. edition. 1613. 12°. *See* C., R. **12981**. aa. **32**.

—— The fourth edition. 1617. 12°. *See* C., R.
828. a. **31**.

—— A Treasurie or Store-House of Similies . . . Newly collected into heades and common places. pp. 860. *Printed by Tho. Creede: London*, 1600. 4°. **12304**. d. **16**.

—— [Another edition.] pp. 860. *Printed by Thomas Creede: London*, 1609. 4°. **4410**. n. **15**.

—— [A reprint of the 1609 edition.] pp. 416. *See* Spencer (John) *Librarian of Sion College.* Καινα και Παλαια. Things New and Old, *etc.* 1868. 8°. **4405**. i. **22**.

CAWDREY (Zachary) The Certainty of Salvation to them who dye in the Lord. A sermon preached at the funeral of the Right Honourable George Lord Delamer, *etc.* pp. 32. *London printed; for P. Gillworth: New-Castle, Staffordshire; and J. Thurston: Nantwich*, 1684. 4°.
4902. cc. **2**.

—— A Discourse of Patronage, being a modest enquiry into the original of it, and a further prosecution of the history of it. With an humble supplication to the pious nobility and gentry, to endeavour the prevention of the abuses of that honorary trust . . . By Z. C. Rector of Barthomly in Cheshire [i.e. Z. Cawdrey]. pp. 45. *Printed for John Leigh, and Thomas Cockerel: London*, 1675. 4°. *See* C., Z., *Rector of Barthomly in Cheshire.* **1490**. m. **33**.

—— [A reissue.]

A Discourse of Patronage, being a modest enquiry into the original of it, and a further prosecution of the history of it. With a true account of the original and rise of vicaridges, *etc.* pp. 45. *For J. Leigh & T. Cockerel: London*, 1675. 4°. **517**. g. **19**. (2.)

—— A Preparation for Martyrdom . . . In a dialogue. betwixt a Minister, and a Gentleman his Parishioner. [By Z. Cawdrey.] pp. 46. 1681. 4°. *See* Minister.
873. e. **108**.

CAWDRY (Daniel) *See* Cawdrey.

CAWDWELL (Thomas) A Defence of an Ordained Ministry, against the democratical Principles of the Brownists, and others, *etc.* pp. viii. 95. *John Clark & Richard Hett: London*, 1724. 8°. **701**. g. **19**. (5.)

—— The Origin of Churches: or, a Discourse shewing 1. The different acceptations of the word Church, in Scripture. *etc.* pp. 64. *J. & B. Clark: London*, 1723. 8°.
4535. b. **14**. (2.)

CAWDWELL (Thomas)

—— The Power of Synods discuss'd, in an enquiry whether Christ appointed them, *etc.* pp. vii. 36. *J. Clarke: London*, 1724. 8°. **4109**. a. **15**. (5.)

CAWEIN (Daniel) Offener Brief und Bericht des protestantischen Presbyteriums zu Ingenheim und Appenhofen, im Namen der Gemeinden an die protestantischen Glaubensgenossen in der ganzen Pfalz. [Signed by D. Cawein, J. J. Nussloch and others.] pp. 8. *Landau*, 1846. 8°. **3911**. e. **23**.

CAWEIN (Madison Julius) *See* Rothert (Otto A.) The Story of a Poet: Madison Cawein, *etc.* [With portraits.] 1921. 8°. [*Filson Club Publications.* no. 30.]
Ac. **8423**.

—— Accolon of Gaul, with other poems. pp. 164. *J. P. Morton: Louisville*, 1889. 8°. **11688**. k. **1**.

—— Blooms of the Berry. pp. 202. *J. P. Morton: Louisville*, 1887. 8°. **11688**. h. **9**.

—— The Cup of Comus: fact and fancy. pp. 96. *Cameo Press: New York*, 1915. 8°. **011686**. g. **14**.

—— Days and Dreams. Poems. pp. vi. 173. *G. P. Putnam's Sons: New York & London*, 1891. 12°.
11688. e. **30**.

—— Intimations of the Beautiful, and Poems. pp. vii. 208. *G. P. Putnam's Sons: New York*, 1894. 8°.
11688. ee. **13**.

—— Kentucky Poems ·. . With an introduction by Edmund Gosse. pp. xxii. 264. *Grant Richards: London*, 1902. 8°. **11687**. de. **45**.

—— Moods and Memories. Poems. [Selected from the author's " Blooms of the Berry " and " The Triumph of Music." With additional pieces.] pp. xii. 310. *G. P. Putnam's Sons: New York & London*, 1892. 8°.
11688. de. **9**.

—— Myth and Romance. Being a book of verses. pp. vi. 85. *G. P. Putnam's Sons: New York & London*, 1899. 8°. **11687**. de. **44**.

—— New Poems. pp. vii. 247. *Grant Richards: London*, 1909. 8°. **011650**. eee. **26**.

—— The Poet and Nature, and The Morning Road. pp. xiv. 241. *J. P. Morton & Co.: Louisville, Kentucky*, 1914. 8°. **011686**. eee. **28**.

—— The Poet, the Fool, and the Faeries. pp. xii. 259. *Small, Maynard & Co.: Boston*, [1912.] 8°.
011686. de. **18**.

—— Red Leaves and Roses. Poems. pp. vi. 205. *G. P. Putnam's Sons: New York*, 1893. 8°.
11688. df. **37**.

—— The Shadow Garden—a phantasy—and other plays. [In verse.] pp. v. 259. *G. P. Putnam's Sons: New York & London*, 1910. 8°. **11778**. k. **23**.

—— The Triumph of Music, and other lyrics. pp. vi. 171. *J. P. Morton & Co.: [Louisville,]* 1888. 8°.
11688. de. **8**.

—— The White Snake, and other poems. Translated from the German [of various authors] into the original meters by M. Cawein. [With a portrait.] pp. 79. *J. P. Morton & Co.: Louisville*, 1895. 4°. **11688**. k. **2**.

CAWEIN (MADISON JULIUS)

—— Poems of Nature and Love. [Selections from " Accolon of Gaul," and " Lyrics and Idyls."] pp. viii. 211.
G. P. Putnam's Sons: New York, 1893. 12⁰.
11688. aaa. 27.

—— Poems . . . selected by the author. With a foreword by William Dean Howells. pp. xix. 298.
Macmillan Co.: New York, 1911. 8⁰. **011686. e. 1.**

CAWLEY (A.)

—— *See* JACOBSON (R. R. E.) The Occurrence of Columbite in Nigeria. By R. R. E. Jacobson . . . A. Cawley, *etc.*
1951. 8⁰. **W.P. 9473/9.**

CAWLEY (CHARLES MILLS) *See* KING (James G.) and CAWLEY (C. M.) The Hydrogenation-Cracking of Tars. 1935, *etc.* 8⁰. [*Department of Scientific and Industrial Research. Fuel Research Board. Technical Paper.* no. 40, 41, 45, 48, *etc.*] **B.S. 38. f/2.**

CAWLEY (CHARLES MILLS) and **KING** (JAMES GRIEVE)

—— The Extraction of Ester Waxes from British Lignite and Peat. pp. iv. 29. *London*, 1946. 8⁰. [*Department of Scientific and Industrial Research. Fuel Research Board. Technical Paper.* no. 52.] **B.S. 38. f/2.**

CAWLEY (ELIZABETH HOON)

—— *See* COBDEN (Richard) [*Diaries.*] The American Diaries of Richard Cobden. Edited . . . by E. H. Cawley.
1952. 8⁰. **10861. d. 41.**

CAWLEY (FRANK) The Banker's Office Diary . . . Arranged by F. Cawley. 20 pt. [1909–31.] fol. *See* EPHEMERIDES. **P.P. 2505. hch.**

—— The Banker's Private Diary . . . Arranged by F. Cawley. 22 pt. [1909–31.] fol. *See* EPHEMERIDES. **P.P. 2505. hci.**

CAWLEY (FRANK STANTON) *See* HRAFNKELL, *Freysgoði.* Hrafnkels Saga Freysgoða. Edited with introduction and glossary by F. S. Cawley. 1932. 8⁰. **12973. c. 14.**

CAWLEY (FREDERICK) The Transcendence of Jesus Christ. A study of the unique features of His person. With special reference to the Fourth Gospel, *etc.* pp. xv. 308.
T. & T. Clark: Edinburgh, 1936. 8⁰. **4223. dd. 16.**

CAWLEY (GEORGE) *See* COLE (Sanford D.) Commander George Cawley . . . ' the Pilot's Friend,' *etc.*
1910. 8⁰. **010854. de. 13.**

CAWLEY (JOHN) *Archdeacon of Lincoln.* The Case of Founders Kinsmen: with relation to the Statutes of ---------- [All Souls] College in the University of ---------- [Oxford] humbly proposed and submitted to better judgments. [By J. Cawley.] pp. 23.
[1700?] 4⁰. *See* CASE. **517. e. 8.**

—— The Nature and Kinds of Simony discussed. Wherein it is argued, Whether letting an Ecclesiastical Jurisdiction to a Lay Surrogate, under a yearly pension reserved out of the profits, be reducible to that head, *etc.* pp. 32.
For R. Baldwin: London, 1689. 4⁰. **517. g. 19. (4.)**

—— [Another copy.] **T. 750. (1.)**

CAWLEY (ROBERT RALSTON)

—— *See* MILTON (John) [*Prose Works.—Brief History of Moscovia.*] Milton's Literary Craftsmanship. A study of A Brief History of Moscovia. With an edition of the text. By R. R. Cawley. 1941. 8⁰. [*Princeton Studies in English.* vol. 24.] **Ac. 1833/5.**

CAWLEY (ROBERT RALSTON)

—— *See* PEACHAM (Henry) *the Younger.* The Truth of Our Times . . . With an introduction by R. R. Cawley.
1942. 12⁰. [*Facsimile Text Society. Publication.* no. 55.] **Ac. 9730.**

—— A Brief History of the First Presbyterian Church, Princeton, New Jersey, *etc.* *Princeton Printing Co.: Princeton*, 1954. 8⁰. **04735. i. 15.**

——   Drayton and the Voyagers . . . Reprinted from the " Publications of the Modern Language Association of America." 1923. 8⁰.
011850. e. 86.

—— Drayton's Use of Welsh History . . . Reprinted from " Studies in Philology," *etc.* [1925.] 8⁰. **011850. e. 84.**

—— Milton and the Literature of Travel. pp. vii. 158.
Princeton University Press: Princeton, 1951. 8⁰. [*Princeton Studies in English.* no. 32.] **Ac. 1833/5.**

—— Shakespere's Use of the Voyagers in " The Tempest " . . . Reprinted from the " Publications of the Modern Language Association of America." 1926. 8⁰.
11764. h. 35.

—— Sir Thomas Browne and his Reading. [Reprinted from the Publications of the Modern Language Association of America.] 1933. 8⁰. **11824. s. 13.**

—— Unpathed Waters. Studies in the influence of the voyages on Elizabethan literature. pp. viii. 285.
Princeton University Press: Princeton, 1940. 8⁰.
11864. cc. 22.

—— The Voyagers and Elizabethan Drama. pp. xiv. 428.
D. C. Heath & Co.: Boston; Oxford University Press: London, 1938. 8⁰. [*Modern Language Association of America. Monograph Series.* no. 8.] **Ac. 2683/3.**

—— Warner and the Voyagers. (Reprinted for private circulation from " Modern Philology.") 1922. 8⁰.
011850. e. 85.

CAWLEY (THOMAS) *See* CHURCH (Thomas) *D.D.* A Sermon preached in the Parish Church of Wandsworth . . . May 16, 1748, at the funeral of the Reverend T. Cawley.
1768. 4⁰. **4905. e. 13.**

CAWLEY (WILLIAM) The Laws of Q. Elizabeth, K. James, and K. Charles the First. concerning Jesuites, Seminary Priests, Recusants, &c. and concerning the Oaths of Supremacy and Allegiance, explained by divers judgments and resolutions of the . . . Judges. Together with other observations . . . To which is added the Statute xxv. Car. II. cap. 2. for preventing dangers which may happen from Popish Recusants, *etc.* pp. 267. 1680. fol. *See* ENGLAND. [*Laws and Statutes.—*IV. *Recusants.*]
17. d. 14.

CAWNPORE.—*Medical Relief Society. See* LUCKNOW.— *Medical Relief Society.*

—— *Native Female Orphan Asylum.* 1843. Second Report (1845. Fourth Report) of the Native Female Orphan Asylum at Cawnpore. 2 pt. *Mission Press; Cawnpore Press: Allahabad*, 1843, 45. 8⁰. **8285. de. 10.**

—— *Society of Textile Technologists.* Textile Annual, 1936 [*etc.*]. *Cawnpore*, 1936– . 8⁰. **P.P. 2548. v.**

Sugar Technologists' Association of India.

—— Proceedings of the Eighth [*etc.*] Annual Convention of the Sugar Technologists' Association of India. *Cawnpore*, [1939– .] 8⁰. **Ac. 3958.**

CAWNPORE.

—— Year-Book, 1940–41. pp. 241. 22. *Cawnpore*, [1942.] 8º.
8234. d. 65.

—— Indian Sugar Manual, 1942 [*etc.*]. [With maps.]
[*Cawnpore*, 1942– .] 4º. **P.P. 2548. vb.**

—— A Manual for the Manufacturing Control. Bulletin no. 11, fifth edition, 1931, of de Vereeniging het Proefstation voor de Java, Suikerindustrie, Pasoeroean. Translated for the Sugar Technologists' Association of India (by C. W. P. Van der Meyden), *etc.* pp. ii. 86.
[*Cawnpore*, 1939.] 4º. **8898. g. 26.**

—— A Manual for the Milling Control in Sugar Factories. [A translation, by A. Schouten, of Bulletin no. 4 of the Experimental Station for the Java Sugar Industry, Technical Department. With folding charts.] pp. iii. 90. *Cawnpore*, 1942. 4º. **7947. b. 25.**

—— Methods of Chemical Control for Cane Sugar Factories and Gur Refineries. [By Noël Deerr.] pp. xiii. 387. *Cawnpore*, 1936. 8º. [MISSING.]

CAWNPORE CURRENCY DEPARTMENT. *See* AGRA AND OUDH, *United Provinces of*.

CAWNPORE OUTBREAK. The Cawnpore Outbreak and Massacre. pp. 37. *J. F. Bellamy: Calcutta*, 1857. 8º. **9004. l. 3. (1.)**

CAWOD (JOHN) *of Louth, Lincolnshire*. *See* GOULDING (Richard W.) John Cawod, and the first volume of the Louth Churchwardens' Accounts, *etc.* 1911. 8º.
4535. de. 14. (1.)

—— *See* JAMES, *Saint, Church of, at Louth, Lincolnshire*. The First Churchwardens' Book of Louth, *etc.* [Compiled by J. Cawod.] 1941. 8º. **20040. c. 17.**

CAWOOD, *the Rook*. *See* CAWWOOD.

CAWOOD (ADAM)

—— This Historic Town of Mansfield. [An autobiographical note. With a portrait.] ff. 10. *The Author: Mansfield*, 1951. *obl.* 8º. **010368. k. 149.**
Typewritten.

CAWOOD (CHARLES) A Poetical Account of the Opening of the Ganges Canal, *etc.* pp. 52. *The Author: Agra*, 1854. 8º. **11645. aaa. 42.**

CAWOOD (FRANCIS) An Essay: or Scheme: towards establishing and improving the fishery, and other manufactures of Great-Britain, *etc.* 2 pt. pp. 150. *The Author: London*, 1721, 17. 8º. **1028. h. 16. (6.)**
Pt. 2 is entitled "Britain's Honour, and True Way to obtain Wealth."

CAWOOD (JOHN) *Perpetual Curate of Bewdley*. The Christian Watchman: a sermon on occasion of the death of the Reverend Thomas Best . . . The second edition. pp. 45. *L. B. Seeley & Son: London*, 1823. 8º.
4905. bb. 19.

—— The Church of England and Dissent. An article . . . enlarged from the 48th no. of the British Review . . . Second edition, with additions. pp. iv. 67.
L. B. Seeley & Sons: London, 1831. 12º. **4106. aa. 14.**

—— A new edition, enlarged. pp. 48. 1834. 8º. *See* ENGLAND.—*Church of England*. [*Appendix*.]
4135. a. 32.

CAWOOD (JOHN) *Perpetual Curate of Bewdley*.

—— The Prayer of the Humble for the Favour of the Lord. *See* ENGLAND.—*Church of England*. [*Appendix*.] Sermons contributed by Clergymen of the Church of England, *etc.* vol. 1. 1834. 8º. **1025. k. 15.**

—— Sermons. 2 vol. *Hamilton, Adams & Co.; J. Hatchard & Son: London*, 1842. 8º. **1357. e. 7.**

CAWOOD (JOHN) *Vicar of Pensax*. Is a Revision of the Prayer-Book desirable at the present time? Being the substance of a paper read before the Ludlow, Leominster, and Tenbury Lay and Clerical Church Association, at Ludlow, *etc.* pp. 20. *Seeley, Jackson & Halliday: London*, 1869. 8º. **3475. aaa. 62. (13.)**

CAWOOD (S.) Charity Yorke; or, Jottings from a woman's life. A story. pp. 207. *Newman & Co.: London*, 1881. 8º. **12642. a. 18.**

CAWPRA JOURNAL. *See* CHEAM.—*Cheam and Worcester Park Ratepayers' Association*.

CAWRDAF (GWILYM) *Bardic Name of William Ellis Jones*. *See* JONES (William E.) *called* GWILYM CAWRDAF.

CAWS (ALLAN GEORGE) and **SMITH** (DOUGLAS HECTOR)

—— Vocational Aptitude Tests for Shorthand Students. pp. 15. *Sir I. Pitman & Sons: London*, [1943.] 8º.
012991. e. 13.

CAWS (JOHN) *See* GROSSE (Alexander) Christ the Christians Choice; or, a Sermon preached at the funerall of J. Caws, *etc.* 1645. 4º. **E. 286. (19.)**

CAWS (LUTHER WINTHER) The Unfolding Dawn. pp. vii. 224. *H. R. Allenson: London*, [1906.] 8º.
04402. e. 65.

—— The Unrecognised Stranger, and other sermons. pp. 201. *H. R. Allenson: London*, 1898. 8º. **4464. d. 5.**

—— The Unveiled Glory; or, Sidelights on the higher evolution. pp. 205. *J. Clarke & Co.: London*, 1912. 8º.
7002. de. 29.

CAWS (R. BROOKE)

—— Notes on the Origin and History of Coutts & Company. pp. 8. [1946.] 8º. *See* COUTTS AND Co. **8219. df. 14.**

CAWS (SAINT JOHN) Diary of the Voyage of the "Loch Sloy." pp. 158. *Empire Printing & Publishing Co.: London*, 1886. 8º. **010025. de. 16.**

CAWSE (GEORGE ANDREWS) Modbury. [Topography and antiquities of the town.] pp. 32. *The Author: London*, 1860. 8º. **10368. aaa. 53. (3.)**

CAWSE (JOHN) The Art of Painting Portraits, Landscapes, Animals, Draperies, Satins, &c., in Oil Colours: practically explained by coloured palettes. pp. 47. pl. XI. *Rudolph Ackermann: London*, 1840. 8º. **786. i. 29.**

—— Introduction to the Art of Painting in Oil Colours . . . Second edition. pp. 22. pl. 7. *R. Ackermann & Co.: London*, 1829. 8º. [MISSING.]

CAWSEY (H. S.) Diseases: Horses and Cattle. pp. 143. *Dr. Cawsey's Veterinary Remedies: Regina*, [1921.] 8º.
07295. b. 18.

CAWSON (FRANK HOTCHKISS)

—— Consumer's Co-operation in Britain, *etc.* (Editing and narration by F. H. Cawson.) [With illustrations.] pp. 26. *British Council: London*, 1952. 8º. [*Study Box*.]
W.P. B. 872/1.

CAWSON (Frank Hotchkiss)

—— The Education of the Adult. (Reprinted.) pp. 32. *British Council:* [London,] 1952. 8°. [*Study Box.*]
W.P. B. **872/13.**

CAWSTON (Abraham) *See* Addleshaw (William P.) A Salopian Worthy (Abraham Causton), *etc.* 1909. 16°. [*Sette of Odd Volumes. Privately printed Opuscula.* no. 60.]
Ac. **9128.**

—— The Fortunate Youth; or, Chippenham Croesus: containing the commencement, action, and denouement of the Newmarket Hoax, *etc.* pp. 42. *J. Johnston: London,* 1818. 8°.
1132. g. 81.

—— Interesting Memoirs of Abraham W. Causton, called the Fortunate Youth; containing a series of the most astonishing impositions ever practised, *etc.* pp. 28. *G. Smeeton: London,* [1818.] 8°. **10602. h. 1. (4.)**

—— Newmarket Hoax! Interesting memoirs . . . Second edition. pp. 28. *G. Smeeton: London,* [1818.] 8°.
G. **14793. (2.)**

CAWSTON (Arthur) The Advantages of adopting a general scheme in making improvements to the London streets, *etc.* pp. 21. *J. Truscott & Son:* [London, 1893.] 8°. [MISSING.]

—— A Comprehensive Scheme for Street Improvements in London, accompanied by maps and sketches. pp. x. 136. *Edward Stanford: London,* 1893. 4°. **10349. h. 33.**

CAWSTON (Cecil Faulkner) *See* Liturgies.—*Church of England.—Occasional Offices.—Dedication of Church Furniture, etc.—Norwich.* Norwich Cathedral. Order of Service to be used . . . at the Dedication and Unveiling of Memorial Windows erected . . . in memory of . . . Lieut. C. F. Cawston, *etc.* [1904.] 8°. **3406. df. 33.**

CAWSTON (E. P.) *Solicitor of the Supreme Court.*

—— The Temple Bureau of Emergency Legislation . . . By a Solicitor of the Supreme Court [i.e. E. P. Cawston]. [1944– .] 8°. *See* Temple Bureau. W.P. **15349.**

CAWSTON (E. W. L.) Jeanne de Rentaille. Ketchen. [Two tales.] By E. W. L. C. [i.e. E. W. L. Cawston.] pp. 122. 1896. 8°. *See* C., E. W. L. **012807. e. 68.**

CAWSTON (Edward P.)

—— *See* Earp (R. W.) and Cawston (E. P.) Eight Men and a Woman, *etc.* [1944.] 8°. **11783. aa. 71.**

CAWSTON (Edward Percy)

—— Mobile Spigot-Mortar Tactics. *Practical Press: London,* [1944.] 8°. **8837. h. 23.**

—— Practical Notes on Field Entrenchments for use in the Cambridge University Cadet Battalions. pp. 28. *J. Hall & Son: Cambridge,* 1916. 8°. **8826. bbb. 58.**

—— A Realistic Forecast solving a score of Home Guard Problems. pp. 47. *Caxton's Modern Press: Walton-on-Thames,* [1944.] 8°. **8839. b. 15.**

CAWSTON (Frederick Gordon) "Bilharzia," a paper for the practitioner . . . Reprinted from "The Journal of Tropical Medicine and Hygiene." pp. 20. *J. Bale & Co.: London,* 1925. 8°. [MISSING.]

—— Lessons from the Life of Jesus. pp. 71. *Marshall & Co.: London & Edinburgh,* [1930.] 8°. **04808. de. 82.**

CAWSTON (Frederick Gordon)

—— The Normal Sexual Life. pp. 12. *J. L. van Schaik: Pretoria,* [1929.] 12°. **08416. e. 86.**

—— Talks to Men in Gaol. pp. 45. *J. L. Van Schaik: Pretoria,* [1930.] 8°. **4452. d. 31.**

CAWSTON (George) and **KEANE** (Augustus Henry) The Early Chartered Companies, A.D. 1296–1858. pp. xi. 329. *Edward Arnold: London & New York,* 1896. 8°. **8248. ee. 4.**

CAWSTON (Sir John Westerman) K.C.B. *See* B., B. C. The Princess Inja, *etc.* (Illustrated by J. W. Cawston.] 1889. obl. 4°. **12807. t. 18.**

CAWTHORN AND HUTT.

—— Catalogue of the British Library, 24 Cockspur Street, *etc.* pp. 293. *London,* [1881.] 8°. **11917. aa. 53.**

CAWTHORN (Alice M.) Lessons on the Gospels for Sundays and Holy-days . . . With critical and explanatory notes by Laura Soames, *etc.* pp. viii. 182. *Church of England Sunday School Institute: London,* [1878.] 8°. [MISSING.]

CAWTHORN (James) Benevolence, the Source and Ornament of Civil Distinctions. A sermon, preached . . . before the Worshipful Company of Skinners, *etc.* pp. 30. [*London,* 1748.] 4°. **225. i. 19. (18.)**

—— Poems. pp. iii. 226. *W. Woodfall: London,* 1771. 4°. **11630. f. 10.**

—— The Poems of Mr. Cawthorn. 1790. *See* Johnson (Samuel) *LL.D.* The Works of the English Poets, *etc.* vol. 65. 1790, *etc.* 8°. **238. d. 26.**

—— Poetical Works. To which is prefixed the life of the author. 1794. *See* Anderson (Robert) *M.D.* A Complete Edition of the Poets of Great Britain. vol. 10. 1793, *etc.* 8°. **11607. ff. 1/10.**

—— The Poems of J. Cawthorn. [With a life.] *See* Chalmers (Alexander) *F.S.A.* The Works of the English Poets, *etc.* vol. 14. 1810. 8°. **11613.c.1.**

—— The Poems of J. Cawthorn. (The life of J. Cawthorn. By R. A. Davenport.) 1822. *See* British Poets. The British Poets, *etc.* vol. 60. 1822. 12°. **11603. aa. 4.**

—— Abelard to Heloise. [Selected from the "Poems."] *See* Abaelardus (P.) [*Letters.*] Letters, *etc.* 1805. 12°. **12611. a. 14.**

—— Abelard to Eloisa.—The Regulation of the Passions.—Lady Jane Grey to Lord Guilford Dudley. [Selected from the "Poems."] *See* Pratt (Samuel J.) The Cabinet of Poetry, *etc.* vol. 5. 1808. 12°. **11604. f. 19.**

—— Select Poems. 1809. *See* Park (Thomas) *F.S.A.* The Works of the British Poets, *etc.* (Supplement. vol. 4.) 1808, *etc.* 16°. **1066. d. 14.**

—— Abelard to Heloise. *See* Abaelardus (P.) [*Letters.*] Letters of Abelard and Heloise, *etc.* 1818. 12°. **10909. aaa. 1.**

—— Select Poems . . . With a Life of the author, by E. Sanford. 1819. *See* Sanford (Ezekiel) The Works of the British Poets, *etc.* vol. 24. 1819, *etc.* 12°. **11602. a. 12.**

—— A Sermon, preach'd before the Worshipful Burgesses of Westminster . . . April the 18th, 1745. Being the day appointed . . . for the election of the two chief Burgesses, *etc.* pp. 23. *C. Hitch: London,* 1745. 8°. **4474. bb. 13.**

—— [Another copy.] **225. f. 12. (15.)**

CAWTHORN (JOHN) A Catalogue of . . . Books . . . on sale . . . by J. Cawthorn, *etc.* pp. 2. 161. *W. Pople: London,* 1815. 8°. **S.C.765.(4.)**

—— Cawthorn's Minor British Theatre. Consisting of the most esteemed farces and operas. 6 vol. **L.P.** *John Cawthorn: London,* 1806, 05–07. 8°. **11770. e. 1.**

CAWTHORN (LAURENCE) The Most Lamentable and Deplorable Accident which . . . befell L. Cawthorn, a Butcher in St. Nicholas Shambles in Newgate Market, who being suspected to be dead, by the two [*sic*] hasty covetousness and cruelty of his land-lady Mrs. Cook . . . was suddenly and inhumanely buried. pp. 15. *For W. Gilbertson: London,* 1661. 8°. **1197. b. 33. (3.)**

CAWTHORN (MARY) and **CURTIS** (HENRY JONES) Collections for a History of Pirbright. [With plates.] ser. 1. pp. 197. [*Pirbright,*] 1931. 4°. **L.R. 177. d. 7.** *Reproduced from typewriting. No more published.*

CAWTHORNE (ELSIE M.) A Year without a Chaperon. pp. 320. *John Long: London,* 1912. 8°. **NN. 378.**

CAWTHORNE (GEORGE JAMES) The Insurer's Handbook . . . Compiled and edited by G. J. Cawthorne. pp. 76. *Oldham & Co.: London,* [1899.] 8°. **8228. aa. 76.**

CAWTHORN (GEORGE JAMES) and **HEROD** (RICHARD S.)

—— Royal Ascot, its History and its Associations . . . With . . . illustrations, *etc.* pp. xvi. 335. *Longmans & Co.: London,* 1900. 8°. **7905.f.5.**

—— [Another edition.] Revised and enlarged, *etc.* pp. xiii. 386. *A. Treherne & Co.: London,* 1902. 8°. **7907.dd.31.**

CAWTHORNE (GRAHAM)

—— Mr. Speaker, Sir. pp. 164. *Cleaver-Hume Press: London,* 1952. 8°. **8140. aaa. 42.**

CAWTHORNE (HENRY HOWARTH) Science in Education: its aims and methods. pp. vi. 110. *Oxford University Press: London,* 1930. 8°. **08311. aa. 62.**

CAWTHORNE (JAMES) *Murderer.* A Particular Account of J. Cawthorne, who was executed . . . 1821, for the murder of his wife. *W. Brooke: Lincoln,* [1821.] *s. sh.* fol. **1889. d. 3. (180.)**

CAWTHORNE (JAMES) *Poet.* See CAWTHORN.

CAWTHORNE (JOHN FENTON) A Copy of the Proceedings of a Court Martial holden for the trial of J. F. Cawthorne, Esq; Colonel of the Westminster Regiment of Middlesex Militia. pp. 435. [*London,* 1796.] fol. **20. d. 14.**

CAWTHORNE (JOSEPH) See also CINCINNATUS, *pseud.* [i.e. J. Cawthorne.]

—— See also CORIOLANUS, *pseud.* [i.e. J. Cawthorne.]

—— See WALPOLE (Robert) *Earl of Orford.* The Celebrated Speech of Sir R. Walpole against short Parliaments . . . With a preface on the times [by J. Cawthorne?], *etc.* 1793. 8°. **8135. d. 77.**

—— The Immediate Necessity of Building a Lazzaretto for a Regular Quarantine, after the Italian manner, to avoid the Plague, and to preserve private property from the plunderers of wrecks upon the British coast: a practice as dangerous in its consequences, as it is barbarous in the execution. [By J. Cawthorne?] pp. 38. 1768. 4°. *See* NECESSITY. **T. 42. (12.)**

CAWTHORNE (JOSEPH)

—— A Letter to the King in justification of a Pamphlet [by John Reeves], entitled, "Thoughts on the English Government": with an Appendix in answer to Mr. Fox's Declaration of the Whig Club. 2 pt. *The Author: London,* 1796. 8°. **103. e. 61.**

—— A Plan of Reconciliation with America; consistent with the dignity and interests of both countries, *etc.* [By J. Cawthorne.] pp. 48. 1782. 8°. *See* UNITED STATES OF AMERICA. [*Appendix.—History and Politics.*—II.] **103. d. 61.**

CAWTHORNE (WILLIAM ANDERSON)

—— Who Killed Cockatoo. [A nursery rhyme.] By W. A. C. [i.e. W. A. Cawthorne.] pp. 19. [1860?] 8°. *See* C., W. A. **11643. bbb. 14. (8.)**

CAWTHORPE (MARGARET A.) Lyrics from the Westland. pp. 90. *William Briggs: Toronto,* 1912. 8°. **011686. de. 22.**

CAWTHRA, *Family of.* See BROCK (Anna M.) Past and Present. Notes [on the Cawthra family], *etc.* 1924. 4°. **9907. h. 15.**

CAWTHRA (HENRY) See BROCK (Anna M.) Past and Present. Notes by H. Cawthra and others, *etc.* 1924. 4°. **9907. h. 15.**

CAWTHRON INSTITUTE OF SCIENTIFIC RESEARCH. See NELSON, *New Zealand.*

CAWTHRON (THOMAS) See EASTERFIELD (*Sir* Thomas H.) *K.B.E.* The Aims and Ideals of the Cawthron Institute, *etc.* [With a portrait.] 1921. 8°. **8709. m. 12.**

CAWTON (THOMAS) *the Elder.* The Life and Death of that Holy . . . Man of God Mr Thomas Cawton . . . With severall of his speeches and letters, while in exile . . . To which is annexed, a Sermon [entitled "God's Rule for a Godly Life"] preach'd by him at Mercers Chappel, Febr. 25. 1648 . . . for which he was committed prisoner to the Gate-house in Westminster, *etc.* 2 pt. pp. 120. 1662. 8°. *See* CAWTON (Thomas) *the Younger.* **1416. a. 32.**

CAWTON (THOMAS) *the Younger.* See HURST (Henry) The Faithful and Diligent Servant of the Lord, blessed at the Coming of his Lord. As it was lately unfolded in a funeral discourse on the death of Mr. T. Cawton, *etc.* 1677. 4°. **1415. e. 26.**

—— *See* VINCENT (Nathaniel) Israel's Lamentation . . . In a sermon preached at the funeral of . . . T. Cawton, *etc.* 1677. 4°. **1415. e. 27.**

—— The Life and Death of that Holy . . . Man of God Mr Thomas Cawton . . . With severall of his speeches and letters, while in exile . . . To which is annexed, a Sermon preach'd by him at Mercers Chappel, Feb. 25. 1648, not long after the inhumane beheading of His Majesty; for which he was committed prisoner to the Gate-house in Westminster, *etc.* [With a commendatory preface by A. Jackson, E. Calamy and others.] 2 pt. pp. 120. *For T. Basset & R. Hall: London,* 1662. 8°. **1416. a. 32.**

—— [Another copy.] **G. 1326.** *With a portrait of Thomas Cawton the elder inserted.*

CAWWOOD, the Rooke. The Pleasant History of Cawwood the Rooke. Or, The Assembly of Birds, with the severall Speeches which the Birds made to the Eagle, in hope to have the Government in his Absence : And lastly, how the Rooke was banished ; with the Reason why crafty Fellowes are called Rookes. As also fit Morralls and Expositions added to every Chapter. [With woodcuts.] *T. C. [Thomas Cotes] for F. Grove : London,* 1640. 4º.
Huth 83.

—— [Another edition.] 𝖡.𝖫. *R. I. for Francis Grove : London,* 1656. 4º.
1080. i. 62.

—— [Another edition.] 𝖡.𝖫. *For I. Wright, I. Clarke, W. Thackeray & T. Passinger : [London],* 1683. 4º.
12403. aaa. 3.

—— [Another edition.] *See* REYNARD THE FOX. [*English.— Miscellaneous Versions.*] The most Pleasing and Delightful History of Reynard the Fox, *etc.* 1723. 12º.
1164. a. 23.

—— [Another edition.] *See* REYNARD THE FOX. [*English.*] The most Pleasing . . . History of Reynard the Fox, *etc.* 1735. 12º.
11511. a. 24.

CAXA (JUAN) *See* PEREZ DE LARA (J.) Por parte de Enrique Nuñez padre de doña Polonia muger que fue de don Iuan Caxa. Con el mesmo D. Iuan Caxa sobre auerla muerto. [1625 ?] fol.
1322. l. 10. (34.)

CAXA (QUIRITIUS) Noch ein anderer Sendtbrieff H. Quiritij Caxa . . . auss dem Collegio auff jener seydt dess Meers, in Brasilien gelegen, an seinen . . . Herren Prouincialem [*sic*] im Jahr 1575 zu Latein aussgangen. Darinnen begriffen die fürnembste Geschichten, den Christlichen Glauben daselbst, neuw angenommen, belangende. Jetzundt aber in die gemeine teutsche Sprach verdolmetschet, *etc.* 1586. 8º. [*CYSAT (R.) Warhafftiger Bericht, von den neuw-erfundnen Japponischen Inseln und Königreichen, etc.*] *See* JESUITS. [*Letters from Missions.*]
10055. aa. 25.

CAXA DE LERUELA (MIGUEL) Restauracion de la Antigua Abundãcia de España, o Prestantissimo, vnico, y facil reparo de su carestia presente. pp. 288. *L. Scorigio : Napoles,* 1631. 4º.
1029. k. 6.

— [Another copy.]
281. f. 32.

—— Segunda reimpression. [Edited by J. de Buytrago.] pp. 247. *Madrid,* 1732. 4º.
08227. de. 24.

CAXAL (DIEGO BOLERO Y) *See* BOLERO Y CAXAL.

CAXANES (BERNARDUS) Aduersus Valentinos et quosdam alios nostri temporis Medicos, de ratione mittendi sanguinem in febribus putridis, libri III. pp. 189. *Ex officina P. Mali : Barcinone,* 1592. 8º.
783. b. 6. (1.)

CAXÉS (JUAN DE) Œuvres dramatiques. [Four autos.] (Publiées par Léo Rouanet.) *Span.* 1901. *See* PERIODICAL PUBLICATIONS.—*Paris.* Revue hispanique, *etc.* tom. 8. 1894, *etc.* 8º.
P.P. 4331. aea.

—— Los Trabajos de Josef, auto. (Publicado por A. Restori.) 1902. *See* PERIODICAL PUBLICATIONS.—*Paris.* Revue hispanique, *etc.* tom. 9. 1894, *etc.* 8º. P.P. 4331. aea.

CAXIAS, LUIZ ALVES DE LIMA E SILVA, *Duke de. See* ALVES DE LIMA E SILVA.

CAXTILIAN, *pseud.*

—— Maiden Over ; or, Casual cracks for cricketers. [By] Caxtilian. [With illustrations.] pp. 60. *G. T. Bagguley : Newcastle, Staffs.,* 1948. 8º.
7919. de. 46.

CAXTON, *pseud.* [i.e. WILLIAM HENRY RHODES.] The Political Letters of " Caxton." pp. 18. *Alta California Power Presses : San Francisco,* 1855. 8º.
8176. bb. 43. (7.)

CAXTON CLUB. *See* CHICAGO.

CAXTON CONVALESCENT HOME. *See* LIMPSFIELD.

CAXTON HISTORICAL READERS. The Caxton Historical Readers. Book v. The Tudor Period, with biographies of leading persons. pp. vi. 233. *A. M. Holden : London,* 1900. 8º. [*Professor Meiklejohn's Series.*]
12201. ee. 19. (16.)
No more published.

CAXTON HOUSE PRINTING OFFICE. *See* DUNDEE.

CAXTON LITERARY JOURNAL. The Caxton Literary Journal and Amateur's Scrap-book. *See* PERIODICAL PUBLICATIONS.—*London.*

CAXTON MAGAZINE. *See* LONDON.—III. *Institute of Printers and Kindred Trades of the British Empire.*

CAXTON POETS.

—— The Caxton Poets. *Caxton Press : Christchurch,* 1948– . 8º.
W.P. a. 600.

CAXTON PRESS.

—— A Catalogue of Publications from the Caxton Press, Christchurch, up to February 1941. pp. 42. [*Caxton Press : Christchurch, N.Z.,* 1941.] 8º.
11900. a. 83.

—— Printing Types. A second specimen book of faces commonly in use at the Caxton Press, Christchurch, New Zealand. pp. 75. [*Caxton Press : Christchurch,*] 1948. 8º.
Cup.510.ve.3.

—— A Specimen Book of Printing Types. *Christchurch, N.Z.,* 1940. 8º.
11900. aaa. 99.

CAXTON PUBLISHING COMPANY. " The Caxton " Engineering Workshop Chart. [*London,* 1938.] s. sh. fol.
1811. a. 1. (126.)

CAXTON SERIES. The Caxton Series. 11 vol. *George Newnes : London,* 1901, 02. 8º. K.T.C. 36. a. 11. *Printed on Japanese vellum.*

CAXTON (GULIELMUS) *See* CAXTON (William)

CAXTON (PISISTRATUS) *pseud.* [i.e. EDWARD GEORGE EARLE LYTTON BULWER, afterwards BULWER LYTTON, Baron Lytton.] *See also* BULWER, afterwards BULWER LYTTON.

—— The Boatman. By Pisistratus Caxton. [A poem.] (Originally published in Blackwood's Magazine.) pp. 16. *W. Blackwood & Sons : Edinburgh & London,* 1864. 8º.
11651. d. 29. (17.)

—— " My Novel " . . . New edition. 2 vol. *G. Routledge & Co. : London,* 1855. 8º.
12651. f. 92.

—— What will he do with it ? By Pisistratus Caxton, *etc.* 4 vol. *W. Blackwood & Sons : Edinburgh & London,* 1859. 8º.
12635. c. 5.

CAXTON (TIMOTHY) *pseud.* [i.e. JOHN CLOSE.] Adventures of an Author ; or, the Westmoreland novelist. Edited [or rather, written] by Timothy Caxton . . . With illustrations, *etc.* 4 no. pp. 104. *William Strange : London,* 1846, 47. 8º.
12623. f. 25.

—— [Another copy of no. 1.]
12619. g. 21.

CAXTON (WILLIAM)

ADVERTISEMENT.

—— Caxton's Advertisement. Photolithograph of the copy preserved in the Bodleian Library, Oxford . . . Issued, with an introductory note, by Edward W. B. Nicholson. pp. 7. *Bernard Quaritch: London,* [1892.] 8°.

011902. m. 21. (11.)

PROLOGUES AND EPILOGUES.

—— The Prologues and Epilogues of William Caxton. [Edited, with a biographical introduction.] By W. J. B. Crotch. pp. clxiii. 115. *London,* 1928. 8°. [*Early English Text Society.* Original series. 176.]

Ac. 9925/132.

—— [Another copy.] **Ac. 9927/130.**

—— Certain Prefaces and Epilogues by W. Caxton, 1475–1490. 1903. *See* ARBER (Edward) An English Garner. (Fifteenth Century Prose and Verse.) 1903, *etc.* 8°.

[MISSING.]

—— Wm: Caxton's Prologues and Epilogues. [A selection.] pp. 45. *Vyvyan Richards: London,* 1927. 8°.

011904. a. 56.

—— Aus Caxtons Vorreden und Nachworten. [The text of Caxton's prefaces and postscripts to " The Recuyell of the Historyes of Troy," " The History of Jason " and " The Aeneid," with a commentary.] Von Rudolf Hittmair. pp. 124. *Leipzig,* 1934. 8°. [*Aus Schrifttum und Sprache der Angelsachsen.* Bd. 1.] **W.P. 11560/1.**

WORKS TRANSLATED, EDITED, ETC., BY CAXTON.

—— [*Aeneis.*]

See LEISI (E.) Die tautologischen Wortpaare in Caxton's " Eneydos." Zur synchronischen Bedeutungs- und Ursachenforschung, *etc.* 1947. 8°. **11865. cc. 32.**

—— *See* VIRGILIUS MARO (P.) [*Aeneis.—English.*] *Begin.* [fol. 1 *recto:*] After dyuerse werkes made, translated and achieued, *etc. End.* [fol. 85 *recto:*] Here fynyssheth the boke yf [*sic*] Eneydos, compyled by Vyrgyle, whiche hathe be translated oute of latyne into frenshe, And oute of frenshe reduced in to Englysshe by me wyllm̄ Caxton, *etc.* [1490.] fol. **IB. 55135.**

—— *See* VIRGILIUS MARO (P.) [*Aeneis.—English.*] Caxton's Eneydos 1490 englisht from the French Liure des Eneydes, 1483. Edited by the late W. T. Culley . . . and F. J. Furnivall, *etc.* 1890. 8°. **Ac. 9926/31.**

—— —— 1913. 8°. **Ac. 9927. b/30**

—— [*Ars moriendi.*] *See* ARS. [*Ars moriendi.—English.*] Ars moriendi ; printed by William Caxton. [Translated from the Latin by W. Caxton ? A facsimile.] [1869.] 4°. **11899. bb. 33.**

—— *See* ARS. [*Ars moriendi.—English.*] Ars moriendi . . . Photolithograph of the unique and perfect copy, printed about 1491 by William Caxton or Wynken de Worde, preserved in the Bodleian library, Oxford. Issued, with an introductory note, by Edward W. B. Nicholson. [1891.] 8°. **4403. i. 8.**

—— [*Art and Craft to know well to Die.*] *See* ARS. [*De arte bene moriendi.—English.*] *Begin.* [fol. 1 *recto:*] Here begynneth a lityll treatise shorte and abredged spekynge of the arte ẑ crafte to knowe well to dye. *End.* [fol. 13 *recto:*] Thus endeth the trayttye abredged of the arte to lerne well to deye, translated oute of frenshe [i.e. from a French version of the " De arte et scientia bene moriendi "] in to englysshe. by willm Caxton, *etc.* [1490 ?] fol. **C. 11. c. 8.**

CAXTON (WILLIAM) [WORKS TRANSLATED, EDITED, ETC., BY CAXTON.]

—— *See* ARS. [*De arte bene moriendi.—English.*] A Reprint in facsimile of a treatise spekynge of the arte & crafte to knowe well to dye, translated oute of frenshe in to englysshe by W. Caxton. 1875. fol. **550. e. 26.**

—— *See* ARS. [*De arte bene moriendi.—English.*] The Book of the Craft of Dying (De arte moriendi). [Followed by " The Art and Craft to know well to Die," translated by W. Caxton.] 1917. 8°. [*COMPER* (*F. M. M.*) *The Book of the Craft of Dying, and other early English tracts, etc.*] **04403. ff. 34.**

[*Blanchardyn and Eglantine.*]

—— *See* BLANCANDIN. *Begin.* [fol. 2 *recto:*] VNto the right noble puyssaūt ẑ excellēt pryncesse my redoubted lady my lady Margarete duchesse of Somercete . . . I wyllyam caxton . . . presente this lytyl book . . . whiche boke I late receyued in frenshe from her good grace and her cōmaundement wyth alle For to reduce ẑ translate it in to our maternal ẑ englysh tonge, *etc.* [fol. 7 *recto:*] The first chapitre of this present boke conteyneth how Blanchardyn departed out of the court of his fader kynge of fryse, *etc.* [1489.] fol. **Mic. A. 600.**

—— *See* BLANCANDIN. Caxton's Blanchardyn and Eglantine, c. 1489 . . . [Translated by W. Caxton.] Edited by Dr. Leon Kellner. 1890. 8°. **Ac. 9926/32.**

—— —— 1906. 8°. **Ac. 9927. b/31.**

—— [*Book of Fame.*] *See* CHAUCER (Geoffrey) [*The House of Fame.*] *Begin.* [fol. 2 *recto:*] The book of Fame made by Gefferey Chaucer. [Edited by W. Caxton.] [1486 ?] fol. **C. 10. b. 13.**

—— [*Book of Good Manners.*] *See* LE GRAND (Jacques) Augustinian Friar. *Begin.* [fol. 1 *recto:*] [Whan I consydere the condycions ẑ maners of the comyn people, *etc.*] [fol. 1 *verso:*] [Here begynneth the table of a book named ẑ Intytuled the book of good maners the which was made ẑ composed by the venerable & dyscrete persone Frere Jacques le graunt, *etc.*] [Translated by W. Caxton.] [1487.] fol. **IB. 55125.**

—— —— 1494. fol. **IB. 55494.**

—— *See* MANNERS. *Begin.* [fol. 1 *recto:*] The fyrste partye of this boke wherof the fyrste chapytre speketh of pryde, *etc. End.* [fol. 76 *verso:*] Here endeth and fynysshed the boke named and Intytled good maners. [By Jacques Le Grand. Translated by W. Caxton.] 1507. 4°. **C. 40. d. 6.**

—— [*Book of the Knight of the Tower.*] *See* LA TOUR LANDRY (G. de) *Begin.* [fol. 1 *recto:*] aLle vertuouse doctryne ẑ techynge had ẑ lerned of suche as haue endeuoured them to leue for a remembraunce, *etc.* [fol. 5 *recto:*] Here begynneth the book whiche the knyght of the toure made, *etc. End.* [fol. 104 *verso:*] Here fynysshed the booke whiche the knyght of the Toure made . . . translated oute of Frenssh in to our maternall Englysshe tongue by me William Caxton, *etc.* 1484. fol. **IB. 55085.**

—— *See* LA TOUR LANDRY (G. de) The Booke of Thenseygnmentes and Techynge that the Knyght of the Towre made to his Doughters . . . [Translated by W. Caxton.] Edited with notes and a glossary by Gertrude Burford Rawlings. 1902. 4°. **8416. e. 37.**

—— [*Canterbury Tales.*] *See* CHAUCER (Geoffrey) [*Canterbury Tales.*] *Begin.* [fol. 2 *recto:*] wHan that Apprill with his shouris sote, *etc.* [Edited by W. Caxton.] [1478 ?] fol. **167. c. 26.**

CAXTON (WILLIAM) [WORKS TRANSLATED, EDITED, ETC., BY CAXTON.]

—— See CHAUCER (Geoffrey) [Canterbury Tales.] Begin. [fol. 2 recto:] Prohemye. gRete thankes lawde and honour ought to be gyuen vnto the clerkes poetes and historiographs, etc. [Edited with a proem by W. Caxton.] [1484?] fol.   G. 11586.

—— —— [1492?] fol.   C. 11. c. 15.

—— —— 1498. fol.   G. 11587. (1.)

—— [Cato.] See CATO (M. P.) the Censor. [Supposititious Works.—Disticha de moribus.—Latin and English.] Begin. [fol. 2 recto:] Here begynneth the prologue or prohemye of the book callid Caton, etc. End. [fol. 79 recto:] Here fynyssheth this present book whiche is sayd or called Cathon translated oute of Frensshe in to Englysshe by William Caxton, etc. [1483?] fol.   C. 10. b. 8.

—— [Chronicles of England.] See ENGLAND. [Appendix.— History and Politics.—I.] Begin. [fol. 2 recto:] In the yere of thyncarnacion of our lord Ihū crist M.CCC.lxxx . . . I haue endeuourd me to enprinte the cronicles of Englond as in this booke shall by the suffraunce of god folowe, etc. [With a continuation sometimes attributed to W. Caxton.] [1480.] fol.   IA. 55026.

—— —— 1482. fol.   IB. 55062.

—— —— [1485?] fol.   G. 5991.

—— —— 1493. fol.   G. 5993.

—— [Confessio Amantis.] See GOWER (John) the Poet. Begin. [fol. 2 recto:] tHis book is intituled confessio amantis, that is to saye in englysshe the confessyon of the louer, etc. [Edited by W. Caxton.] 1493 [1483]. fol.   IB. 55077.

—— [Cordiale.] See CORDIALE. Begin. [fol. 2 recto:] aL Ingratitude vtterly settyng apart, etc. [fol. 4 recto:] mEmorare nouissima et ineternum non peccabis, etc. [fol. 4 verso:] Thus endeth the prologue of this book named. Cordyal, etc. [fol. 76 verso:] tHis book is thus translated out of frenshe into our maternal tongue by . . . Anthoine Erle Ryuiers, etc. [Edited, with an epilogue, by W. Caxton.] [1479.] fol.   C. 11. c. 2.

—— [Curial.] See CHARTIER (A.) Begin. [fol. 1 recto:] Here foloweth the copye of a lettre whyche maistre Alayn Charetier wrote to hys brother, etc. End. [fol. 6 recto:] Thus endeth the Curial made by maystre Alain Charretier. Translated thus in Englyssh by Wylliam Caxton. [1484?] fol.   C. 10. b. 17.

—— See CHARTIER (A.) The Curial made by maystere Alain Charretier. Translated . . . by W. Caxton. 1484. Collated with the French original by Prof. Paul Meyer, and edited by Frederick J. Furnivall. 1888. 8°.   Ac. 9926/30.

—— —— 1935. 8°.   Ac. 9927. b/29.

—— [Description of Britain.] See ENGLAND. [Appendix.— Descriptions, Travels and Topography.] [The Description of Britain.] Begin. [fol. 1 verso:] Hit is so that in many and diuerse places the comyn cronicles of englond ben had, etc. End. [fol. 29 recto:] Here endeth het [sic] discripcion of Britayne . . . which I haue taken oute of Policronicon [by Ranulphus Higden], etc. [Edited by W. Caxton.] 1480. fol.   C. 10. b. 24.

—— —— 1498. fol.   C. 11. b. 1. (2.)

—— [Dialogues in French and English.] See LIVRE. Dialogues in French and English. By W. Caxton. Adapted from a fourteenth-century book of dialogues (Le Livre des mestiers) in French and Flemish. Edited from Caxton's printed text, about 1483, with introduction, notes, and word-lists, by Henry Bradley. 1900. 8°.   Ac. 9926/49.

CAXTON (WILLIAM) [WORKS TRANSLATED, EDITED, ETC., BY CAXTON.]

—— See LIVRE. Caxton's Dialogues. Tres bonne doctrine pour aprendre briefment fransoys et engloys Ryght good lernyng for to lerne shortly frenssh and englyssh. 1931. 4°. [Le Livre des Mestiers de Bruges et ses dérivés, etc.]   11901. pp. 24.

—— [Dicts or Sayings of the Philosophers.] See DICTS. Begin. [fol. 2 recto:] wHere it is so that euery humayn Creature, etc. [fol. 74 recto:] [hEre endeth the book named the dictes or sayengis of the philosophres . . . Whiche book is late translated out of Frenshe . . . by . . . Antone Erle of Ryuyers, etc.] [Edited, with additional matter, by W. Caxton.] 1477. fol.   IB. 55005.

—— —— 1477 [1480?]. fol.   C. 10. b. 2.

—— —— [1490?] fol.   IB. 55143.

—— —— 1528. 4°.   C. 12. e. 22.

—— See DICTS. The Diches and Sayings of the Philosophers. A facsimile reproduction of the first book printed in England by W. Caxton, etc. 1877. fol.   11899. k. 2.

—— See LEGMAN (Gershon) A Word on Caxton's Dictes. 1948. 8°.   11867. ccc. 13.

—— [Doctrinal of Sapience.] See DOCTRINAL. Begin. [fol. 1 recto:] [This that is written in this lytyl boke ought the prestres to lerne, etc.] End. [fol. 92 recto:] [Thus endeth the doctrinal of sapyence . . . whyche is translated out of Frenshe in to englysshe by wyllyam Caxton, etc.] [1489.] fol.   IB. 55129.

—— [Fables of Aesop.] See AESOP. [English.—Collections.] Begin. [fol. 2 recto:] Here begynneth the book of the subtyl historyes and Fables of Esope whiche were translated out of Frensshe in to Englysshe by W. Caxton, etc. 1484. fol.   C. 11. c. 17.

—— —— [1500?] fol.   IB. 55523.

—— See AESOP. [English.—Collections.] The Fables of Esope in Englishe, etc. [1570?] 8°.   12304. aaa. 32.

—— —— 1634. 8°.   636. b. 38.

—— —— 1647. 8°.   12305. bb. 14.

—— —— 1658. 12°.   E. 1889.

—— See AESOP. [English.—Collections.] The Fables of Aesop, as first printed by W. Caxton in 1484 . . . edited and induced by Joseph Jacobs. 1889. 8°. [Bibliothèque de Carabas Series. vol. 4, 5.]   12202. ff. 1.

—— See AESOP. [English.—Collections.] The Fables of Esope. Translated out of Frensshe in to Englysshe by: W. Caxton, etc. 1931. 4°.   C. 102. h. 11.

—— [Feats of Arms and of Chivalry.] See PISAN (Christine de) Begin. [fol. 1 recto:] Here begynneth the table of the rubryshys of the boke of the fayt of armes and of Chyualrye, etc. [fol. 3 recto:] Here begynneth the book of fayttes of armes ı of Chyualrye, etc. [Translated by W. Caxton.] 1489. fol.   IB. 55131.

—— See PISAN (Christine de) The Book of Fayttes of Armes and of Chyualrye. Translated and printed by W. Caxton . . . Edited by A. T. P. Byles. 1932. 8°.   Ac. 9925/144.

—— —— 1937. 8°.   Ac. 9925/157.

[Four Sons of Aymon.]

—— See AYMON. [Les Quatre fils Aymon.—Prose Versions.— English.] [sig. B 3 recto:] Reynawde one of the sones of Aymon, wherof specyally treateth now this historye. Thenne marched fourthe Lohier ı wente in the firste of alle and after hym his folke by goode conduytte, etc. [Translated by W. Caxton.] [1489.] fol.   Mic. A. 504. (3.)

CAXTON (WILLIAM) [WORKS TRANSLATED, EDITED, ETC., BY CAXTON.]

—— *See* AYMON. [*Les Quatre fils Aymon.—Prose Versions.—English.*] The right plesaunt and goodly historie of the foure sonnes of Aimon, *etc.* [Translated by W. Caxton.] 1554. fol.   C. **12**. i. **7**.

—— *See* AYMON. [*Les Quatre fils Aymon.—Prose Versions. —English.*] The Right Plesaunt and Goodly Historie of the Foure Sonnes of Aymon. Englisht from the French by W. Caxton, and printed by him about 1489. Edited from the unique copy, now in the possession of Earl Spencer, by Octavia Richardson. 1884, *etc.* 8°.   Ac. **9926/23**.

—— [*Game and Play of the Chess.*] *See* GAME. *Begin.* [fol. 2 *recto:*] [T]O the right noble, right excellent 7 vertuous prince George duc of Clarence . . . William Caxton . . . sendes vnto yow peas, *etc.* [A translation by W. Caxton, from Jean de Vignay's and Jean Ferron's French versions, of the " De ludo scaccorum " of J. de Cessolis.] [1476?] fol.   C. **10**. b. **23**.

—— *See* GAME. *Begin.* [fol. 2 *recto:*] [tHe holy appostle and doctour of the peple saynt Poule sayth in his epystle, *etc.*] [A translation by W. Caxton, from J. de Vignay's and J. Ferron's French versions, of the " De ludo scaccorum " of J. de Cessolis.] [1483?] fol. C. **10**. b. **1**.

—— *See* GAME. The Game of the Chesse, by W. Caxton. [A facsimile reprint of Caxton's second edition.] [1855.] fol.   **7915**. i. **11**.

—— *See* GAME. The Game of the Chesse . . . Reprinted in phonetic spelling, *etc.* [1857.] 8°.   **12991**. h. **11**.

—— *See* CESSOLIS (J. de) Caxton's Game and Playe of the Chesse . . . A verbatim reprint of the first edition. With an introduction by William E. A. Axon. 1883. 8°.   **12204**. hh. **6**.

—— [*Godfrey of Boloyne.*] *See* HERACLIUS, *Emperor of the East. Begin.* [fol. 2 *recto:*] tHe hye couragyous faytes, And valyaunt actes of noble Illustrous and vertuous personnes ben digne to be recounted, *etc.* [fol. 12 *recto:*] Here begynneth the boke Intituled Eracles, and also of Godefrey of Boloyne, *etc. End.* [fol. 143 *verso:*] Thns [*sic*] endeth this book . . . translated 7 reduced out of freusshe [*sic*] in to englysshe by me . . . Wylliam Caxton, *etc.* [Translated from a French version of the " Historia rerum in partibus transmarinis gestarum " of Gulielmus, Archbishop of Tyre.] 1481. fol.
C. **11**. c. **4**.

—— *See* GODFREY [de Bouillon], *King of Jerusalem.* The History of Godefrey of Boloyne and of the Conquest of Jerusalem. [Translated by W. Caxton from a French version of the " Historia rerum in partibus transmarinis gestarum " of Gulielmus, Archbishop of Tyre.] 1893. 4°.
C. **43**. f. **4***.

—— *See* GULIELMUS, *Archbishop of Tyre.* Godeffroy of Boloyne, or, the Siege and Conqueste of Jerusalem . . . Translated from the French by W. Caxton . . . Edited . . . with introduction, notes, vocabulary. and indexes, by Mary Noyes Colvin. 1893. 8°.   Ac. **9926/37**.

—— [*Golden Legend.*] *See* LEGENDA AUREA. *Begin.* [fol. 2 *recto:*] tHe holy 7 blessed doctour saynt Ierom sayth thys auctoryte do alweye somme good werke, *etc. End.* [fol. 448 *recto:*] Thus endeth the legende named in latyn legenda aurea, *etc.* [Translated by W. Caxton from the " Legenda Aurea " of Jacobus de Voragine, with the aid of the French translation of Jean de Vignay and a previous English version of that translation.] [1483?] fol.
C. **11**. d. **8**.

—— —— [1493.] fol.   IB. **55161**.

—— —— [1498.] fol.   C. **11**. c. **16**.

CAXTON (WILLIAM) [WORKS TRANSLATED, EDITED, ETC., BY CAXTON.]

—— —— 1503. fol.   C. **15**. c. **7**.

—— —— [1510?] 4°.   C. **53**. b. **22**.

—— —— [1512?] fol.   G. **11924**.

—— —— 1527. fol.   ◆ C.**122**.h.**7**.

—— *See* JACOBUS, *de Voragine, Archbishop of Genoa.* The Golden Legend. A reproduction from a copy [of the first edition of W. Caxton's translation] in the Manchester Free Library. With an introduction by Alfred Aspland, editor. 1878. fol.   Ac. **4660**. (13.)

—— *See* JACOBUS, *de Voragine, Archbishop of Genoa.* The Golden Legend of master William Caxton done anew. 1892. 4°.   C. **43**. f. **1**.

—— *See* JACOBUS, *de Voragine, Archbishop of Genoa.* The Golden Legend . . . As Englished by William Caxton. 1900, *etc.* 8°.   **012200**. de. **8/58**.

—— *See* JACOBUS, *de Voragine, Archbishop of Genoa.* The Golden Legend . . . Translated by William Caxton . . . Selected and edited by George V. O'Neill. 1914. 8°.
4830. aaa. **9**.

—— *See* THOMAS [Becket], *Saint, Archbishop of Canterbury. Begin.* Here begynneth the lyfe of the blessed martyr saynte Thomas. [Extracted from Caxton's translation of the " Legenda Aurea " of Jacobus de Voragine.] [1510?] 4°.   G. **1344**.

—— *See* LEGENDA AUREA. The Life of St. George from Caxton's translation of the Golden Legend. [1920.] 8°.
W.P. **5827/3**.

—— [*History of Charles the Great.*] *See* CHARLES I., *Emperor of the West.* CHARLEMAGNE. [*Romances.*] *Begin.* [fol. 2 *recto:*] SAynt Poul doctour of veryte sayth to vs, *etc.* [fol. 2 *verso:*] Somme persones of noble estate . . . haue desyred me to reduce thystorye and lyf of the noble and crysten prynce Charles the grete kynge of frauuce [*sic*] 7 emperour of Rome, *etc.* [Translated by W. Caxton from " La Conqueste du grand Roy Charlemaigne des Espaignes " of Jean Baignon.] 1485. fol.   C. **10**. b. **9**.

—— *See* CHARLES I., *Emperor of the West.* CHARLEMAGNE. [*Romances.*] The Lyf of the Noble and Crysten Prynce, Charles the Grete. Translated . . . by William Caxton . . . Edited . . . with introduction, notes. and glossary, by Sidney J. H. Herrtage. 1881. 8°.   Ac. **9926/23**.

—— —— 1934. 8°.   Ac. **9927**. b/**23**.

—— [*History of Jason.*] *See* JASON, *the Argonaut. Begin.* [fol. 2 *recto:*] fOr asmoche as late . . . I translated aboke out of frensshe . . . Therefor . . . I entende to translate the . . . boke of thistories of Iason, *etc.* [Translated from the French of R. Le Fevre by W. Caxton.] [1477?] fol.   C. **10**. b. **3**.

—— *See* JASON, *the Argonaut.* The veray trew history of the valiaūt knight Iaso How he conqueryd or wan the golden fles. by the Counsel of Medea, *etc.* [Translated from the French of Raoul le Fèvre by W. Caxton.] 1492. fol.
I.B.49847.

—— *See* LE FEVRE (R.) The History of Jason. Translated from the French . . . by W. Caxton, c. 1477. Edited by John Munro. 1913. 8°.   Ac. **9926/75**.

—— [*House of Fame.*] *See supra :* [*Book of Fame.*]

CAXTON (WILLIAM) [WORKS TRANSLATED, EDITED, ETC.,
BY CAXTON.]

—— [*Life of Our Lady.*] *See* LYDGATE (John) *Begin.*
[fol. 1 *recto :*] tHis book was compyled by dan Iohn
Lydgate . . . in thonoure . . . of the byrthe of our moste
blessyd lady, &c. [Edited, and with three stanzas at the
end added, by W. Caxton.] [1484?] fol. C. 10. b. 18.

—— *See* LYDGATE (John) *Begin.* [fol. 1 *recto :*] tHis book
was compyled by dan Iohn lydgate . . . in thonoure glorye
ꝼ reuerence of the byrthe of our moste blessyd lady, *etc.*
[Edited, and three stanzas added at the end, by W.
Caxton.] [1484?] fol. Mic. A. 125. (13.)

—— [*Life of Saint Winifred.*] *See* WINIFRED, *Saint. Begin.*
[fol. 2 *recto :*] Here begynneth the lyf of the holy ꝼ blessid
vyrgyn saynt Wenefryde, *etc.* [fol. 14 *recto :*] Thus
endeth the decollacion, the lyf after, and the translacion
of saynte Wenefrede . . . reduced in to Englysshe by
me William Caxton [from the Latin of Robertus, Prior
of Shrewsbury]. [1485.] fol. C. 10. b. 19.

—— [*Lives of the Holy Fathers.*] *See* JEROME, *Saint.* [*Vitae
Patrum.*] Vitas patrum. *End.* [fol. 355 *verso :*] Thus
endyth the moost vertuouse hystorye of the . . . lyues
of holy faders . . . whiche hath be translated out of
Frensshe in to Englysshe by Wyllyam Caxton, *etc.*
1495. fol. C. 11. b. 3.

—— [*Metamorphoses.*] *See* OVIDIUS NASO (P.) [*Metamorphoses.—English.*] Six Books of Metamorphoseos [x–xv]
in whyche ben conteyned the Fables of Ovyde. Translated out of Frensshe into Englysshe by William Caxton.
Printed from a manuscript in the library of Mr. Secretary
Pepys, *etc.* [Edited by George Hibbert.] 1819. 4°.
C. 101. a. 24.

—— *See* OVIDIUS NASO (P.) [*Metamorphoses.—English.*]
Ovyde hys Booke of Methamorphose. Books x–xv.
Translated by W. Caxton, *etc.* 1924. 4°. 11352. g. 7.

—— [*Mirror of the World.*] *See* MIRROR. *Begin.* [fol. 2
recto :] Here begynneth the table of the rubrices of this
presente volume named the Mirrour of the world, *etc.*
[Translated by W. Caxton from the prose " Image du
monde."] [1481.] fol. IB. 55040.

—— *See* MIRROR. The myrrour: ꝼ dyscrypcyon of the
worlde, *etc.* [W. Caxton's translation, revised.]
[1527?] fol. C. 11. b. 13.

—— *See* IMAGE. Caxton's Mirrour of the World. Edited by
O. H. Prior. 1912. 8°. Ac. 9926/74.

—— [*Morte darthur.*] [For editions of Sir Thomas Malory's
" Morte darthur " edited and with a prologue by W.
Caxton :] *See* ARTHUR, *King of Britain.* [*Sir Thomas
Malory's Morte darthur.*]

—— [*Order of Chivalry.*] *See* ORDER. *Begin.* [fol. 2 *recto :*]
Here begynneth the Table of this present booke Intytled
the Book of the ordre of chyualry, *etc.* [fol. 49 *recto :*]
Here endeth the book of thordre of chyualry, whiche book
is translated oute of Frensshe in to Englysshe . . . by me
William Caxton, *etc.* [A translation of Ramón Lull's
" Libre del Orde de Cauayleria."] [1484?] 4°.
IA. 55071.

—— *See* ORDER. The Order of Chivalry. (Translated from
the French by William Caxton, edited by F. S. Ellis.)
1892, *etc.* 8°. C. 43. e. 10.

—— *See* LULL (R.) The Book of the Ordre of Chyualry.
Translated . . . by W. Caxton from a French version
of Ramon Lull's " Le Libre del Orde de Cauayleria."
Together with Adam Loutfut's Scottish transcript . . .
Edited by Alfred T. P. Byles. 1926. 8°
Ac. 9925/124.

CAXTON (WILLIAM) [WORKS TRANSLATED, EDITED, ETC.,
BY CAXTON.]

—— [*Paris and Vienne.*] *See* PARIS, *le Chevalier. Begin.*
[fol. 1 *recto :*] Here begynneth thystorye of the noble . . .
knyght Parys, and of the fayr Vyēne, *etc. End.* [fol. 35
verso :] Thus endeth thystorye of the noble and valyaunt
knyght parys and the fayr vyenne translated out of
frensshe . . . in to englysshe by wylliam Caxton, *etc.*
1485. fol. C. 10. b. 10.

—— —— [1510?] 4°. C. 116. bb. 8.

—— *See* PARIS, *le Chevalier.* Paris and Vienne (translated
by W. Caxton) . . . With a preface, glossary, and notes.
[Edited by William C. Hazlitt.] 1868. 4°. 12205. l. 11.

—— [*Pilgrimage of the Soul.*] *See* PILGRIMAGE. *Begin.*
[fol. 2 *recto :*] This book is intytled the pylgremage of the
sowle, *etc.* [fol. 6 *recto :*] Incipit Liber primus. Here
begynneth the book of the pylgremage of the sowle, late
translated oute of Frensshe in to Englysshe, *etc.* [Edited
by W. Caxton.] 1483. fol. IB. 55069.

—— [*Polychronicon.*] *See* HIGDEN (R.) *Begin.* [fol. 2 *recto :*]
Prohemye. gRete thankynges lawde ꝼ honoure we
merytoryously ben bounde to yelde and offre vnto
wryters of hystoryes, *etc.* [fol. 31 *recto :*] Cronica Ranulphi
Cistrencis Monachi, *etc.* [The " Polychronicon " translated into English by John Trevisa. Edited and continued from 1357 to 1460 by W. Caxton.] 1482. fol.
G. 6011, 12.

—— —— 1495. fol. C. 11. b. 2.

—— —— 1527. fol. C. 15. b. 3.

—— [*Recuyell of the Histories of Troy.*] *See* LE FEVRE (R.)
Begin. [fol. 2 *recto :*] hEre begynneth the volume intituled . . . the recuyell of the historyes of Troye . . .
translated . . . out of frenshe . . . by W. Caxton, *etc.*
[1475?] fol. C. 11. c. 1.

—— —— [1503.] fol. G. 10509.

—— —— 1553. fol. C. 21. d. 15.

—— *See* TROY. The Ancient Historie of the Destruction of
Troy . . . Translated . . . by W. Caxton, *etc.* 1607. 4°.
C. 117. bb. 3.

—— —— 1617. 4°. C. 117. bb. 2.

—— *See* TROY. The Destruction of Troy, *etc.* [Translated
by W. Caxton.] 1663. 4°. 1077. i. 47.

—— —— 1670. 4°. 12403. aa. 27.

—— —— [1676.] 4°. 1077. e. 15.

—— —— 1680. 4°. 1077. f. 12.

—— —— 1684. 4°. G. 17515.

—— —— 1702. 4°. 1077. g. 29.

—— —— 1708. 4°. 12612. e. 19.

—— —— 1738. 4°. 12510. e. 6.

—— *See* LE FEVRE (R.) The Recuyell of the Historyes of
Troye. [Translated by W. Caxton.] 1892. fol.
C. 43. f. 2.

—— *See* LE FEVRE (R.) The Recuyell of the Historyes of
Troye . . . Translated . . . by W. Caxton . . . With a
critical introduction, index and glossary . . . by H.
Oskar Sommer. 1894. 8°. 12403. f. 25.

CAXTON (WILLIAM) [WORKS TRANSLATED, EDITED, ETC., BY CAXTON.]

—— [*Reynard the Fox.*] *See* REYNARD THE FOX. [*English.— Caxton's Translation.*] *Begin.* [fol. 2 *recto :*] This is the table of the historye of reynart the foxe, *etc. End.* [fol. 84 *verso :*] For I haue . . . folowed as nyghe as I can my copye whiche was in dutche, and by me willm Caxton translated in to . . . englyssh, *etc.* [1481.] fol.
C. **11**. c. **3**.

—— —— 1550. 8⁰. 686. d. **15**.

—— *See* REYNARD THE FOX. [*English.—Caxton's Translation.*] The History of Reynard the Fox, from the edition printed by W. Caxton . . . With notes, and an introductory sketch of the literary history of the romance, by William J. Thoms. 1844. 8⁰. Ac. **9480**/12.

—— *See* REYNARD THE FOX. [*English.—Caxton's Translation.*] The History of Reynard the Fox. Translated . . . by William Caxton . . . Edited by Edward Arber. 1878. 8⁰. [*English Scholar's Library.* no. 1.] **12205.ee.1/1.**

—— —— 1880. 4⁰. [MISSING.]

—— *See* REYNARD THE FOX. [*English.—Caxton's Translation.*] The History of Reynard the Fox. Translated . . . by William Caxton, 1481. Edited by Edmund Goldsmid. 1884. 8⁰. **012202**. de. **11**.

—— *See* REYNARD THE FOX. [*English.—Caxton's Translation.*] The History of Reynard the Fox. [Edited by H. Morley.] 1889. 8⁰. [*MORLEY* (*Henry*) *Early Prose Romances.*] **012207**. i. **6**.

—— *See* REYNARD THE FOX. [*English.—Caxton's Translation.*] The History of Reynard the Fox, by W. Caxton. [Edited by H. Halliday Sparling.] 1892. fol. C. **43**. f. **3**.

—— *See* REYNARD THE FOX. [*English.—Caxton's Translation.*] The History of Reynard the Fox . . . A free rendering into verse of the translation . . . by William Caxton . . . By F. S. Ellis, *etc.* 1894. 4⁰. K.T.C. **20**. a. **1**.

—— *See* REYNARD THE FOX. [*English.—Caxton's Translation.*] The History of Reynard the Fox . . . A metrical version of the old English translation [by W. Caxton] . . . By F. S. Ellis, *etc.* 1897. 8⁰. **11517**. e. **29**.

—— *See* REYNARD THE FOX. [*English.—Caxton's Translation.*] Reynard the Fox. Edited by Thos. Cartwright. [Retold for children from W. Caxton's translation.] 1908. 8⁰. **012202**. e. **7/8**.

—— *See* REYNARD THE FOX. [*English.—Caxton's Translation.*] The Epic of the Beast . . . English translations of the History of Reynard the Fox (Caxton's text : modernized), *etc.* [1924.] 8⁰. L.R. **34**. a. **1/24**.

—— *See* REYNARD THE FOX. [*English.—Caxton's Translation.*] Reynard the Fox. Adapted from Caxton by E. L. and F. J. H. Darton. [1928.] 8⁰. **012403**. de. **75**.

—— [*Royal Book.*] *See* BOOK. *Begin.* [fol. 2 *recto :*] [When I remember and take hede of the conuersacion of vs that lyue in this wretched lyf, *etc.*] [fol. 3 *recto :*] HEre foloweth the table of the rubriches of thys presente book entytled ɔ named Ryal, *etc. End.* [fol. 161 *recto :*] THis book was . . . translated or reduced out of frensshe [i.e. the " Somme du roi " of Laurent, a Dominican] . . . by me wyllyam Caxtou [*sic*], *etc.* [1488 ?] fol.
C. **10**. b. **22**.

—— —— [1507.] 4⁰. C. **11**. a. **23**.

—— [*Troilus and Cressida.*] *See* TROILUS. *Begin.* [fol. 2 *recto :*] tThe [*sic*] double sorow of Troylus to telle, *etc.* [By Geoffrey Chaucer. Edited by W. Caxton.] [1485 ?] fol. C. **11**. c. **10**.

CAXTON (WILLIAM) [WORKS TRANSLATED, EDITED, ETC., BY CAXTON.]

—— [*Tullius of Old Age and of Friendship.*] *See* CICERO (M. T.) [*Two or more Works.—English.*] *Begin.* [fol. 2 *recto :*] hEre begynneth the prohemye vpon the reducynge . . . of the . . . book named Tullius de senectute, *etc.* [fol. 73 *recto :*] Here foloweth the said Tullius de Amicicia translated . . . by . . . The Erle of wurcestre, *etc.* [Revised and edited by W. Caxton.] 1481. fol. IB. **55045**.

APPENDIX.

—— *See* AURNER (Nellie S.) Caxton . . . A study of the literature of the first English press. 1926. 8⁰. **010856**. d. **25**.

—— *See* BEEDHAM (Brailsford H.) A List of the Reproductions, both imitation and in fac-simile, of the productions of the press of William Caxton, *etc.* 1879. 4⁰. **11899**. ff. **10**.

—— *See* BLADES (William) The Biography and Typography of William Caxton, *etc.* 1877. 8⁰. **011899**. i. **30**.

—— —— 1882. 8⁰. **2308**. c. **3**.

—— *See* BLADES (William) Here after follows a few words on William Caxton . . . being an abridgment of the Biography by W. Blades, *etc.* 1926. fol. **10825**. k. **41**.

—— *See* BLADES (William) A Catalogue of Books printed by—or ascribed to the press of—William Caxton, *etc.* 1865. 8⁰. **11899**. c. **4**.

—— *See* BLADES (William) How to tell a Caxton, with some hints where and how the same might be found. 1870. 8⁰. **11899**. aaa. **17**.

—— *See* BLADES (William) The Life and Typography of William Caxton, *etc.* 1861, *etc.* 4⁰. N.L.**3**.c.

—— *See* BUTLER (Pierce) *of Tulane University.* Legenda Aurea . . . A study of Caxton's Golden Legend, with special reference to its relations to the earlier English prose translation, *etc.* 1899. 8⁰. **011852**. i. **19**.

—— *See* BUTT (Arthur N.) William Caxton, mercer & courtier, author & printer, *etc.* 1878. 8⁰. **11899**. f. **12**. (8.)

—— *See* CICERO (M. T.) [*Cato Major.—English.*] Caxton : Tulle of Olde Age. Textuntersuchung mit literarischer Einführung von Heinz Susebach. 1933. 8⁰. **12981**. f. **75**.

—— *See* CLARK (Richard) Monument to Caxton. Five letters printed in the ' Sunday Times ' newspaper, relative to William Caxton and subjects connected therewith. 1847. 8⁰. **823**. e. **58**. (1.)

—— *See* CUNNINGTON (Susan) The Story of William Caxton, *etc.* 1917. 8⁰. **010603**. c. **1/21**.

—— *See* DE RICCI (Seymour) A Census of Caxtons. 1909. 4⁰. [*Illustrated Monographs issued by the Bibliographical Society.* no. 15.] Ac. **9670**/2.

—— *See* D'ISRAELI (Isaac) The First English Printer : being an essay from ' Amenities of Literature ' [on W. Caxton]. [1933.] 4⁰. **11902**. v. **26**.

—— *See* D'ISRAELI (Isaac) The First English Printer. [1949.] 4⁰. **11912**. dd. **64**.

—— *See* DUFF (Edward G.) Caxton's Tully of Old Age and Friendship, 1481, now for the first time collated . . . With an exact description of all the extant copies. 1912. 8⁰. **11900**. cc. **8**.

CAXTON (WILLIAM) [APPENDIX.]

—— *See* DUFF (Edward G.) Horae beate Virginis Marie secundum Usum Sarum. The unique copy printed at Westminster by William Caxton circa 1477. A monograph. 1908. 8°.　　**011907. de. 24.**

—— *See* DUFF (Edward G.) William Caxton. 1905. 4°.
　　Ac. 4711/2.

—— *See* FERRES (John) William Caxton: a contribution in commemoration of the festival held in Melbourne, 1871, to celebrate the fourth centenary of the first printing in the English language, *etc.* 1871. 8°.　　**11911. aa. 35.**

—— *See* GOVERNAL. The Gouernayle of Helthe: with The Medecyne of yᵉ Stomacke. Reprinted from Caxton's edition . . . with introductory remarks and notes, by W. Blades. 1858. 8°.　　**C. 31. e. 22.**

—— *See* HAMMERSCHLAG (J.) Dialekteinflüsse im früh-neuenglischen Wortschatz. Nachgewiesen an Caxton und Fabyan. 1937. 8°.　　**12984. t. 1/31.**

—— *See* HITTMAIR (R.) William Caxton, Englands erster Drucker und Verleger. 1931. 8°.　　**011899. aaa. 40.**

—— *See* JACKSON (Holbrook) William Caxton. An essay. 1933. fol.　　**11900. t. 17.**

—— *See* KNIGHT (Charles) *Publisher.* William Caxton, the first English printer. A biography. 1844. 12°.
　　1156. b. 1. (1.)

—— *See* KOENNECKE (G.) Ein unbekannter Druck von William Caxton aus dem Jahre 1483 [Sixtus IV., Sex epistolae], *etc.* 1874. 8°.　　**11899. c. 19. (4.)**

—— *See* LEWIS (John) *Vicar of Minster.* The Life of Mayster Wyllyam Caxton, *etc.* 1737. 8°.　　**674. f. 18.**

—— *See* LONDON.—III. *Church of Saint Margaret, Westminster.* A History and Description of the Caxton Memorial Window, *etc.* [1882.] 8°.　　**11899. bb. 31. (5.)**

—— *See* LONDON.—III. *South Kensington Museum, etc.* Caxton Celebration, 1877. Catalogue of the loan collection of antiquities, curiosities, and appliances connected with the art of printing, South Kensington. Edited by G. Bullen. [1877.] 8°.　　**11899. b. 12.**

—— [Another copy.]　　**C. 61. e. 8.**
Inlaid and interleaved in eight quarto volumes with special titlepages, containing the collection of correspondence, prospectuses, circulars, portraits, photographs, facsimiles, newspaper cuttings, and other articles relating to the exhibition, formed by William Blades.

—— *See* MAGNIEN (C.) Une Page d'histoire anglo-belge, 1441–1472? Caxton à la cour de Charles-le-Téméraire, à Bruges; introduction de l'imprimerie en Angleterre, 1472–1474. 1912. 8°. [*Annuaire de la Société d'Archéologie de Bruxelles.* tom. 23.]　　**Ac. 5519/4.**

—— *See* MIDDLETON (Conyers) A Dissertation concerning the Origin of Printing in England. Shewing, that it was first introduced and practised by . . . William Caxton, *etc.* 1735. 4°.　　**819. k. 33.**

—— *See* PLOMER (Henry R.) William Caxton, 1424–1491. 1925. 8°.　　**010803. eee. 1/9.**

—— *See* PRICE (Francis C.) Fac-similes illustrating the labours of William Caxton at Westminster . . . With a memoir of our first printer, *etc.* 1877. 4°. **11899. i. 11.**

—— *See* REUL (P. de) The Language of Caxton's Reynard the Fox, *etc.* 1901. 8°. [*Université de Gand. Recueil de travaux publiés par la Faculté de philosophie et lettres.* fasc. 26.]　　**Ac. 2647/3.**

CAXTON (WILLIAM) [APPENDIX.]

—— *See* ROBERTS (William W.) William Caxton, Writer and Critic, *etc.* 1930. 8°.　　**10824. k. 29.**

—— *See* ROEMSTEDT (H.) Die englische Schriftsprache bei Caxton, *etc.* 1891. 4°.　　**12903. h. 27. (6.)**

—— *See* ROME, *Church of.*—[*Popes.*]—Sixtus IV. [1471–1484.] Earliest Printing in England: an Indulgence of 1476 [printed by Caxton]. By [i.e. edited and translated by] A. W. Pollard. [With a facsimile.] 1929. 8°.
　　11905. l. 36.

—— *See* SHACKFORD (Martha H.) Caxton's Esope, *etc.* 1953. 8°.　　**11871. ee. 19.**

—— *See* THOMAS (*Sir* Henry) *Principal Keeper of Printed Books, British Museum.* Wilh. Caxton uyss Engelant. Evidence that the first English printer learned his craft at Cologne. [With facsimiles.] 1928. 4°. **11901. r. 3.**

—— *See* WIENCKE (H.) Die Sprache Caxtons. 1930. 8°.
　　W.P. 4979/11.

—— *See* WINKLER (G.) Das Relativum bei Caxton und seine Entwicklung von Chaucer bis Spenser, *etc.* [1933.] 8°.
　　11856. a. 2.

—— *See* WINSHIP (George P.) ⟨*the Elder.* William Caxton. A paper read at a meeting of the Club of Odd Volumes in Boston, *etc.* 1909. 4°.　　**C. 99. g. 8.**

—— —— 1937. 8°.　　**Ac. 2689. gm.**

—— —— 1939. fol.　　**11900. k. 52.**

—— *See* WINSHIP (George P.) ⟨*the Elder.* William Caxton and the First English Press . . . A bio-bibliographical essay . . . Together with an original leaf of the Polychronicon. 1938. fol.　　**C.122.h.6.**

—— Caxton and the Art of Printing. pp. 192.　　*R.T.S.:* London, [1852.] 12°.　　**4420.g.25.**

—— Caxton Celebration. Opening Festival . . . June 30, 1877. (Toasts.—Menu.) [1877.] 8°. **1882. c. 2. (84.)**

—— A Caxton Memorial; extracts from the churchwarden's accounts of the parish of St. Margaret, Westminster, illustrating the life and times of William Caxton . . . [By Theophilus C. Noble.] Reprinted . . . from The Builder, *etc.* pp. 32. *Wyman & Sons: London,* [1880.] 12°.
　　10347. aa. 8. (8.)
For private circulation only.

—— A Dialogue in the Shades, between William Caxton, Fodius, a bibliomaniac, and William Wynken, Clerk, a descendant of Wynken de Worde: to which is added, the Story of Dean Honywood's Grubs. [In verse.] With explanatory notes, by W. W. [With "A Ballad entitled Rare Doings at Roxburghe-Hall."] [By William Clarke.] *W. Clarke: London,* 1817. 8°.　　**1466. i. 22. (2.)**

—— Life of William Caxton, with an account of the invention of printing, *etc.* [By W. Stevenson.] pp. 32. *See* LIVES. Lives of Eminent Persons, *etc.* 1833. 8°.　　**737. d. 9.**

—— La Vie et les ouvrages de William Caxton, premier imprimeur anglais. [By A. J. V. Le Roux de Lincy.] Extrait de la Revue britannique, *etc.* pp. 47. [*Paris,* 1844.] 8°.　　**10854. cc. 13. (1.)**

—— Who was Caxton? . . . A monograph. [Signed: R. H. B., i.e. Rowland Hill Blades.] 1877. 8°. *See* B., R. H.　　**11899. b. 11.**

—— William Caxton. An excerpt from the General Catalogue of Printed Books of the British Museum. pp. 8. 1926. fol. *See* LONDON.—III. *British Museum.—Department of Printed Books.*　　**11909. w. 21.**

CAXTONIAN.

—— The Caxtonian. *See* MARDON, SON AND HALL, LIMITED.

CAY (A. M.) War Cartoons . . . With an introduction and commentary by R. L. Orchelle. ff. 23. *Continental Times Co.: Berlin*, 1916. fol. **12316. w. 2.**
Printed on one side of the leaf only.

CAY (ALFRED) Balaam's Wish : the death of the righteous. A sermon preached . . . on occasion of the death of Mrs. W. C. Moore . . . and also of the decease of J. Soper, Esq., of Newington. Second edition. pp. 14.
A. M. Pigott: London, [1862.] 8º. **4955. bb. 2.**

—— Voices of the Battle Field. The great Captain of sufferers a suffering army's hope. [A sermon.] pp. 35.
A. M. Pigott: [London,] 1857. 12º. **4406. c. 22.**

—— Revised edition. pp. 35. *A. M. Pigott: [London,]* 1857. 12º. **4407. b. 41.**

CAY (ARMISTEAD) *See* PERIODICAL PUBLICATIONS.—*London.* New Catalogue of British Literature, 1896 (1897) . . . Compiled by C. Chivers (and A. Cay). 1897, *etc.* 8º. **P.P. 6484. aca.**

—— Accentia. A system of accented and abbreviated shorthand. pp. 73. *E. R. Blackett: Bath*, [1899.] 8º. **12991. g. 48.**

CAY (GEORGE) *See* HELPS. Helps & Hindrances to Home Happiness, *etc.* (Essay I. By G. Cay.) 1860. 8º. **8407. c. 37. (5.)**

CAY (HENRY BOULT) *See* ENGLAND. [*Laws and Statutes.* —II.] The Statutes at Large, from Magna Charta to the thirtieth year of King George II. [vol. 1–6.] By . . . J. Cay, *etc.* [Edited by H. B. Cay.] 1758, *etc.* fol. **18.f.2–7.**

—— *See* ENGLAND. [*Laws and Statutes.*—VI.] An Abridgment of the Publick Statutes now in force . . . From Magna Charta . . . to the first year of . . . King George III. inclusive. By J. Cay, and continued from the eleventh year of his late Majesty, by H. B. Cay, *etc.* 1762. fol. **505. i. 4, 5.**

—— *See* ENGLAND. [*Laws and Statutes.*—VI.] An Abridgment of the Publick Statutes, now in force . . . from the eleventh year of King George II. to the first year of . . . King George III. inclusive : being a supplement to the Abridgment of . . . J. Cay. By H. B. Cay. 1766. fol. **505. i. 3.**

CAY (JOHN) *Bencher of Gray's Inn. See* ENGLAND. [*Laws and Statutes.*—II.] The Statutes at Large, from Magna Charta to the thirtieth year of King George II. [vol. 1–6.] By . . . J. Cay, *etc.* [Edited by H. B. Cay]. 1758, *etc.* fol. **18.f.2–7.**

—— *See* ENGLAND. [*Laws and Statutes.*—VI.] An Abridgment of the Publick Statutes in force and use from Magna Charta . . . to the eleventh year . . . of King George II, inclusive. By J. Cay. 1739. fol. **505. i. 1, 2.**

—— *See* ENGLAND. [*Laws and Statutes.*—VI.] An Abridgment of the Publick Statutes now in force . . . From Magna Charta . . . to the first year of . . . King George III. inclusive. By . . . J. Cay, and continued . . . by H. B. Cay, *etc.* 1762. fol. **505. i. 4, 5.**

—— *See* ENGLAND. [*Laws and Statutes.*—VI.] An Abridgment of the Publick Statutes now in force . . . from the eleventh year of King George II., to the first year of . . . King George III. inclusive : being a supplement to the Abridgment of . . . J. Cay. By H. B. Cay. 1766. fol. **505. i. 3.**

CAY (JOHN) *Bencher of Gray's Inn.*

—— *See* ROLLE (Henry) *Chief Justice of the Court of King's Bench.* Un Abridgment des plusieurs cases . . . del Common Ley, *etc.* COPIOUS MS. NOTES [by H. Boult and J. Cay]. 1668. fol. **506. g. 11, 12.**

CAY (JOHN) *Founder of Caius College, Cambridge. See* CAIUS.

CAY (JOHN) *Sheriff of Linlithgow.*

—— An Analysis of the Scottish Reform Act, with the decisions of the Courts of Appeal. [With the text of the Act.] 2 pt. pp. xii. iv. 391. 1837, 40. 8º. *See* ENGLAND. [*Laws and Statutes.*—VIII. William IV.] [2 & 3 Will. IV. c. 65.] **1130. g. 26.**

—— An Analysis of the Scottish Reform Act . . . With the decisions of the Courts of Appeal. [With the text of the Act.] pp. viii. x. 782. 1850. 8º. *See* ENGLAND. [*Laws and Statutes.*—VIII. William IV.] [2 & 3 Will. IV. c. 65.] **6584. c. 25.**

CAY (NOWELL) A Foe in the Family. pp. 294. *Digby, Long & Co.: London*, 1905. 8º. **012631. bbb. 6.**

—— In Hot Pursuit. pp. 318. *Digby, Long & Co.: London*, 1906. 8º. **012632. d. 22.**

—— [Another edition.] *Aldine Publishing Co.: London*, [1920.] 8º. [*Mascot Novels.* no. 125.] **12644. a. 1/125.**

—— The Presumption of Stanley Hay, M.P., *etc.* pp. 286. *F. Warne & Co.: London & New York*, 1901. 8º. **012639. a. 3.**

CAY (OSYTH) Wisdom Teeth. [A novel.] pp. 251. *Collins: London*, 1933. 8º. **NN. 19960.**

CAY (ROBERT HODSHON) *Judge of the High Court of Admiralty in Scotland.* Report . . . to the . . . Commissioners for inquiring into the administration of justice in Scotland. pp. 45. *Mundell, Doig & Stevenson: Edinburgh*, 1809. 8º. [MISSING.]

CAY (THOMAS) *See* CAIUS.

CAYADO (HENRIQUE) *See* CAIADUS (Henricus)

CAYADO (HERMICUS) *See* CAIADUS (Henricus)

CAYCEDO (BERNARDO J.)

—— Grandezas y miserias de dos victorias. [On the foundation of the Colombian Republic, with special reference to Antonio Nariño.] pp. 226. *Bogotá*, 1951. 8º. **9774. de. 23.**

CAYCEDO (FRANCISCO DE FIGUEROA Y) *See* FIGUEROA Y CAYCEDO.

CAYCEDO Y FLÓREZ (FERNANDO) *Archbishop of Santa Fé de Bogota. See* GONZÁLEZ QUIJANO (A.) El Arzobispo Prócer. Lectura . . . con ocasión del centenario de la muerte del Ilustrísimo señor doctor F. Caicedo y Flórez, *etc.* [With a portrait.] 1932. 8º. **4865. f. 43.**

—— Memorias para la Historia de la Santa Iglesia Metropolitana de Santafe de Bogota, *etc.* pp. 112. [*Bogotá,*] 1824. 4º. **4745. cc. 9.**

—— Oración . . . en alabanza del Ilustrísimo señor . . . Christoval de Torres, *etc.* pp. 20. 52. *Santafe de Bogota*, 1793. 4º. **4866. bb. 12.**

CAYCI (M. A.)

—— *See* WILSON (Wilbur M.) A Study of the Practical Efficiency under Static Loading of Riveted Joints connecting Plates. [By] W. M. Wilson . . . M. A. Cayci. 1952. 8º. [*University of Illinois Engineering Experiment Station. Bulletin Series.* no. 402.] **Ac. 2692. u/4.**

CAYCO (FLORENTINO) *See* POBLADOR (H.) Philippine Arithmetics, *etc.* (Sixth and seventh grades. By H. Poblador and F. Cayco.) [1924, *etc.*] 8°.
08534. df. 53.

—— *See* POBLADOR (H.) Philippine Arithmetics. Third (fourth) grade. [Revised edition.] By H. Poblador, F. Cayco, and C. Osias. [1932.] 8°. 08534. df. 62.

CAYÉ (AUGUST) Ueber die Entwicklung der elastischen Fasern des Nackenbandes. Inauguraldissertation, *etc.* pp. 10. *Kiel*, 1869. 4°. [*Schriften der Universität zu Kiel.* Bd. 16. VII. Medic. 5.] Ac. 1030.

CAYE (GEORGES) and **SAILLARD** (AUGUSTE) Traité pratique de mécanique et d'électricité industrielles . . . Illustré, *etc.* 2 tom. *Paris*, 1901, 05. 8°. 08766. b. 46.

CAYENNE. Cayenne. [Letters from French Republicans sentenced to transportation.] pp. 22. *Manchester*, 1855. 8°. 10408. aa. 33. (2.)

—— Lettre escrite de Cayenne contenant ce qui s'est passé en la descente des François, & leur establissement en l'Amerique. pp. 14. *G. de Luyne : Paris*, 1653. 4°.
523. k. 8. (1.)

—— Tableau de Cayenne, ou de la Guiane Française, contenant des renseignemens exacts sur son climat, ses productions, *etc.* [By Viscount L. A. M. V. de Galard Terraube.] (Observations sur un livre qui vient de paraître, sous le titre de Voyage à la Guiane et à Cayenne [by L . . . . M . . . . B . . . ., published by L. M. Prudhomme, and compiled by him ?].) pp. 230. *Paris*, an VII [1799]. 8°. 798. f. 7.

—— Neue Reise nach Cayenne. Oder zuverlässige Nachrichten von der französischen Guiana . . . Aus den [*sic*] Tagebuche eines französischen Bürgers [i.e. Viscount L. A. M. V. de Galard Terraube] mit Anmerkungen von M. G * *. Mit einer Charte von Guiana. pp. viii. 212. *Leipzig*, 1799. 8°.
1431. f. 17.

—— Neue Auflage. pp. viii. 212. *Leipzig*, 1802. 8°.
1424. e. 13.
Imperfect ; wanting the map.

CAYENNE, NICOLAS, *Bishop of. See* JACQUEMIN.

CAYER. *See* CAHIER.

CAYES. Extrait des registres du greffe de l'administration de la commune des Cayes. [Respecting the investiture of General Rigaud with plenary powers to restore order in the Island of St. Domingo ; with a letter from the General surrendering those powers.] pp. 23. [*Cayes*, 1796.] 8°. F. 717. (14.)

CAYET (FRANÇOIS JOSEPH BARTHÉLEMY AUGUSTE CÉSAR LEFEBVRE) *See* LEFEBVRE-CAYET.

CAYET (PIERRE VICTOR PALMA) *See* PALMA CAYET.

CAYETANO, *Saint. See* GAETAN.

CAYETANO ( ) *Padre.* Explicación de la Doctrina cristiana, según el método con que la enseñan los padres de las Escuelas Pias . . . dispuesta en forma de diálogo entre maestro y discípulo. pp. 300. *Paris*, 1860. 12°.
3505. a. 14.

CAYETANO LUCBAN (F. D.) *See* BIBLE.—*Luke.* [*Bicol.*] An Mahal na Evangelio . . . cuyog qui San Lucas, *etc.* [Translated by F. D. Cayetano Lucban.] 1898. 8°. 3068. df. 49.

CAYEUX. The Lost Statue of Cayeux [and other sketches]. By a Religious of the Community [of the Convent of the Holy Name]. pp. 47. *Convent of the Holy Name : Malvern Link*, [1930.] 8°. [MISSING.]

CAYEUX (AIMÉ JULIEN) Dissertation sur la phthisie pulmonaire, *etc.* pp. 19. *Paris*, 1811. 4°.
1182. h. 14. (21.)

CAYEUX (E.) Côte est de Madagascar au point de vue du colon : ses produits, ses terres, ses forêts, ses ports, sa main d'œuvre de 1890 à 1895. pp. 126. [*Port Louis*,] 1898. 8°. 010095. h. 7.

CAYEUX (LOUIS) Le Dahlia, *etc.* pp. 184. *Paris*, 1934. 8°. 07028. a. 60.

CAYEUX (LUCIEN) *See* POIDEBARD (Antoine) Un Grand port disparu, Tyr. Recherches aériennes et sous-marines, 1934–1936. Conclusion par L. Cayeux, *etc.* 1939. 4°.
L.R. 56. a. 1/29.

—— Contribution à l'étude micrographique des terrains sédimentaires, *etc.* pp. 589. pl. x. *Lille*, 1897. 4°. [*Mémoires de la Société Géologique du Nord.* tom. 4. no. 2.] Ac. 3119.

—— Description physique de l'île de Délos. pt. 1. pp. 216. pl. v. *Paris*, 1911. 4°. [*Exploration archéologique de Délos faite par l'École Française d'Athènes.* fasc. 4.] Ac. 5206. b/2.

—— Études des gîtes minéraux de la France . . . Les minerais de fer oolithique, *etc.* 2 fasc. 1909, 22. 4°. *See* FRANCE.—*Ministère des Travaux Publics.*
1829. h. 1.

—— Introduction à l'étude pétrographique des roches sédimentaires . . . Texte. (Atlas.) 2 tom. pp. viii. x. 524. pl. LVI. *Paris*, 1916. 4°. [*Mémoires pour servir à l'explication de la carte géologique détaillée de la France.*] 7109.1.1/12.

—— Les Roches sédimentaires de France. Roches carbonatées —calcaires et dolomies. pp. 463. pl. XXVI. *Paris*, 1935. 4°. 7109. m. 1.

CAYEUX (PHILIPPE) De l'hermétisme à la médecine, *etc.* pp. 128. *Paris*, 1938. 8°. 7409. bb. 38.

CAYLA. Une Visite au Cayla. Par Madame * * *. pp. 21. *Paris*, 1865. 12°. 10172. c. 30. (2.)

CAYLA (CH.) Observations d'anatomie microscopique sur le rein des mammifères, *etc.* pp. 47. *Paris*, 1839. 4°. [*Collection des thèses soutenues à la Faculté de Médecine de Paris.* An 1839. tom. 3.] 7371. a. 3.

CAYLA (FRANÇOIS ALEXIS) De l'hydropsie des villosités choriales, *etc.* pp. 39. *Paris*, 1839. 4°. [*Collection des thèses soutenues à la Faculté de Médecine de Paris.* An 1849. tom. 2.] 7372. c. 2.

CAYLA (JEAN) Thèse pour le doctorat en médecine, *etc.* (Questions sur diverses branches des sciences médicales.) pp. 26. *Paris*, 1839. 4°. [*Collection des thèses soutenues à la Faculté de Médecine de Paris.* An 1839. tom. 3.] 7371. a. 3.

CAYLA (JEAN MAMERT) *See* ALEMBERT (J. Le R. d') Sur la destruction des Jésuites en France, précédé d'une introduction et suivi d'un épilogue par J.-M. Cayla. 1865. 16°. 4092. a. 8.

—— *See* ALISON (Alexander) La Nouvelle Réforme et ses principes. Premier essai . . . Traduit de l'anglais par M. J.-M. Cayla. 1861. 8°. 8007. dd. 5.

CAYLA (Jean Mamert)

—— *See* Goudelin (P.) Œuvres complettes . . . Avec traduction en regard, nôtes historiques et littéraires [*sic*]. Par J. M. Cayla, *etc.* 1843. 8°.　　　**1464. k. 2.**

—— *See* Rome, *Church of.*—*Cancellaria Apostolica.* La Boutique des Papes, ou Taxes casuelles de la Chancellerie romaine . . . Ouvrage annoté et continué jusqu'à nos jours par J.-M. Cayla. 1872. 12°.　　**4051. df. 7.**

—— Boïeldieu. [An extract from the author's " Célébrités européennes."] [*Paris*, 1855.] 8°.　　Hirsch **2684.**

—— Ces bons messieurs de St Vincent-de-Paul. Deuxième édition. pp. 320. *Paris*, 1863. 12°.　　**4784. aaa. 31.**

—— César Pontife. Réponse à l'Encyclique du 8 décembre. pp. 31. *Paris*, 1865. 8°.　　**8032. i. 18. (4.)**

—— Les Congrès de Malines, ou la Conspiration jésuitique. pp. 36. *Paris*, 1864. 12°.　　**3901. bb. 50. (3.)**

—— La Conspiration cléricale. pp. 32. *Paris*, 1862. 8°.　　**8033. d. 24. (9.)**

—— Les Curés mariés par le Concile. pp. 144. *Paris*, 1869. 12°.　　**3902. b. 18.**

—— Le Diable, sa grandeur et sa décadence. pp. viii. 402. *Paris*, 1864. 12°.　　**8631. bb. 10.**

—— L'Enfer démoli. pp. 327. *Paris*, 1865. 12°.　　**8631. bb. 11.**

—— L'Expulsion des Jésuites. pp. 213. *Paris*, [1876.] 12°.　　**4091. bb. 1.**

—— La Fin du papisme. pp. 191. *Paris*, 1873. 16°.　　**3902. aaa. 15.**

—— La France sans le pape. pp. 32. *Paris*, 1861. 8°.　　**8033. d. 22. (6.)**

—— Guerre aux couvents . . . Avec l'histoire de la nonne de Cracovie (Barbara Ubrick) et autres séquestrations. pp. 139. *Paris*, 1870. 12°.　　**3902. bbb. 29.**

—— Histoire des capitales. Constantinople ancienne et moderne. pp. 100. *Paris*, 1855. 8°.　　**9135. f. 12.**

—— Histoire des Invalides . . . Illustrée par Eugène Charpentier. pp. 112. *Paris*, [1852.] 8°.　　**9220. h. 3.**

—— Histoire des vaisseaux. Le Vengeur et la Belle-Poule. pp. 32. *Paris*, 1855. 8°.　　**8806. k. 8.**

—— Les Jésuites hors la loi. pp. iv. 171. *Paris*, 1869. 12°.　　**4092. c. 14.**

—— Le Milliard des couvents. pp. 32. *Paris*, 1865. 8°.　　**3901. g. 39. (1.)**

—— Le Nouveau pape. pp. 31. *Paris*, 1862. 8°.　　**8033. bb. 37. (6.)**

—— Pape et empereur. pp. 32. *Paris*, 1860. 8°.　　**8033. d. 18. (4.)**

—— —— *See* Bénézet (E.) La Question religieuse. Réponse à la brochure Pape et empereur. 1860. 8°.　　**8033. c. 37. (5.)**

—— —— *See* Maffre (C.) Séparation de l'Église et de l'État. Réponse à la brochure Pape et empereur. 1860. 12°.　　**4051. aaa. 23.**

—— —— *See* Mathieu (J. M. A. C.) *Cardinal.* Un Mot du cardinal Mathieu, sur la brochure : Pape et empereur, de M. Cayla. 1860. 8°.　　**8032. h. 35. (10.)**

CAYLA (Jean Mamert)

—— Pape et Pologne. pp. 31. *Paris*, 1863. 8°.　　**8093. g. 15.**

—— Plus de couvents ! pp. 32. *Paris*, 1861. 8°.　　**8033. c. 35. (3.)**

—— Plus de pape-roi. pp. 31. *Paris*, 1862. 8°.　　**8032. h. 38. (9.)**

—— Plus de question romaine. Appel au concile national. pp. 32. *Paris*, 1861. 8°.　　**8033. c. 31. (1.)**

—— Les Prêtres à marier. pp. 31. *Paris*, 1861. 8°.　　**3901. g. 37. (9.)**

—— Le 89 du clergé. pp. 32. *Paris*, 1861. 8°.　　**3901. g. 37. (10.)**

—— Si j'étais pape. Solution et conclusion. pp. 32. *Paris*, 1861. 8°.　　**8033. c. 35. (7.)**

—— Quelques mots de réponse aux brochures de M. Cayla. pp. 36. *Nîmes*, 1861. 8°.　　**8033. bb. 34. (3.)**

CAYLA (Jean Mament) and **PERRIN-PAVIOT** (　　)

—— 　　　　　　　　　　　　　　Histoire de la ville de Toulouse depuis sa fondation jusqu'à nos jours, publiée sous la direction de M. J. M. Cayla et Perrin-Paviot. Ornée de douze gravures, *etc.* pp. 555. *Toulouse*, 1839. 8°.　　**1301. k. 11.**

CAYLA (Paul) Les Théories de Law. pp. 147. *Paris*, 1909. 8°.　　**08207. k. 28.**

CAYLA (Robert) *See* Pavil (J.) Par le trou du souffleur. (Croquis présentés par R. Cayla.) [1925.] 8°.　　**012316. i. 8.**

CAYLA (Simon) Du traitement de la fièvre typhoïde chez les enfants par les bains froids, méthode de Brand. Relation d'une épidémie observée à l'hospice de la Charité de Lyon. Thèse, *etc.* pp. 130. *Montpellier*, 1874. 4°.　　**7379. k. 4. (14.)**

CAYLAC DE CEYLAN (Agathe Pauline) *Countess de Bradi.* Du savoir-vivre en France au dix-neuvième siècle, ou Instruction d'un père à ses enfants . . . 6e édition. pp. 227. *Paris, Strasbourg*, 1858. 12°.　　**8407. a. 15.**

—— Réfutation de quelques opinions avancées dans le Mémoire à consulter de M. le Comte de Montlosier. pp. 31. *Paris*, 1826. 8°.　　**R. 140. (2.)**

CAYLET (J. L.) Essai sur la nephritis, *etc.* [A thesis.] pp. 19. *Montpellier*, 1815. 4°.　　**1180. h. 5. (3.)**

CAYLEY (Arthur) *Historical Writer.* The Life of Sir Walter Ralegh, Knt. [With a portrait.] 2 vol. *Cadell & Davies : London*, 1805. 4°.　　**10816. f. 25.**

—— [Another copy.]　　**G. 1948.**

—— The second edition. 2 vol. *Cadell & Davies : London*, 1806. 8°.　　**294. k. 11, 12.**

—— Memoirs of Sir Thomas More, with a new translation of his Utopia, his History of King Richard III, and his Latin poems. 2 vol. *Cadell & Davis : London*, 1808. 4°.　　**133. e. 17, 18.**

CAYLEY (Arthur) *Sadlerian Professor of Mathematics, University of Cambridge. See* Carver (Walter B.) On the Cayley-Veronese Class of Configurations, *etc.* 1905. 8°.　　**8532. dd. 30. (2.)**

CAYLEY (ARTHUR) *Sadlerian Professor of Mathematics. University of Cambridge.*

—— *See* LA GOURNERIE (J. de) Recherches sur les surfaces réglées tétraédrales symétriques . . . avec des notes par A. Cayley. 1867. 8°.　　**8531. bbb. 10.**

—— *See* PERIODICAL PUBLICATIONS.—*London.* The Quarterly Journal of Pure and Applied Mathematics. Edited by J. J. Sylvester . . . assisted by . . . A. Cayley, *etc.* 1855, *etc.* 8°.　　**P.P. 1566.**

—— The Collected Mathematical Papers of Arthur Cayley. (Supplementary volume, containing Titles of Papers and Index.) 14 vol. *University Press : Cambridge,* 1889–98. 4°.　　**8534. g. 2.**

—— An Elementary Treatise on Elliptic Functions. pp. x. 384. *Deighton, Bell & Co. : Cambridge,* 1876. 8°.　　**8530. h. 1.**

—— Second edition. pp. xii. 386. *G. Bell & Sons : London,* 1895. 8°.　　**8530. cc. 44.**

—— [On Poinsot's four new Regular Solids.] Über Poinsots vier neue regelmässige Körper. [Reprinted from the Philosophical Magazine.] *See* HAUSSNER (R.) Abhandlungen über die regelmässigen Sternkörper, *etc.* 1906. 8°. [*Ostwald's Klassiker der exakten Wissenschaften.* no. 151.]　　**8706. eee. 1/151.**

—— The Principles of Book-keeping by Double Entry. pp. 20. *University Press : Cambridge,* 1894. 8°.　　**8533. d. 27. (11.)**

—— Sur un cas particulier de la surface du quatrième ordre avec seize points singuliers . . . Extrait du Journal des mathématiques pures et appliquées, *etc.* pp. 7. [*Paris,* 1865.] 4°.　　**8532. h. 3. (2.)**

—— Tables des formes quadratiques binaires pour les déterminants négatifs depuis D = − 1 jusqu'à D = −100, pour les déterminants positifs non carrés depuis D = 2 jusqu'à D = 99 et pour les treize déterminants négatifs irréguliers qui se trouvent dans le premier millier . . . Extrait du Journal des mathématiques pures et appliquées, *etc.* pp. 16. *Paris,* [1860?] 4°.　　**8532. h. 3. (1.)**

CAYLEY (CHARLES BAGOT) *See* AESCHYLUS. [*Prometheus Vinctus.—English.*] The Prometheus Bound . . . Translated in the original metres. By C. B. Cayley. 1867. 8°.　　**11705. aaa. 6.**

—— *See* BIBLE.—*Psalms.* [*English.—Miscellaneous Metrical Versions.*] The Psalms in Metre. [With notes.] By C. B. Cayley. 1860. 8°.　　**3089. d. 35.**

—— *See* BIBLE.—*Psalms.—Selections.* [*English.*] Specimens of a Metrical Version of the Psalms, by C. B. Cayley. [1860.] fol.　　**1879. cc. 15. (43.)**

—— *See* DANTE ALIGHIERI. [*Divina Commedia.—English.*] Dante's Divine Comedy . . . Translated in the original ternary rhyme by C. B. Cayley. 1851, *etc.* 8°.　　**11422. bbb. 16.**

—— *See* DIEZ (F. C.) Introduction to the Grammar of the Romance Languages . . . Translated by C. B. Cayley. 1863. 8°.　　**12943. e. 13.**

—— *See* GARRIDO (F.) and CAYLEY (C. B.) The History of Political and Religious Persecutions, *etc.* [1876, *etc.*] 8°.　　**4534. f. 1.**

—— *See* HOMER. [*Iliad.—English.*] The Iliad . . . Homometrically translated. By C. B. Cayley. 1877. 8°.　　**11315. dd. 1.**

CAYLEY (CHARLES BAGOT)

—— *See* MALINCONTRI (F.) Filippo Malincontri, or Student-life in Venetia. An autobiography . . . Translated . . . by C. B. Cayley. 1861. 8°.　　**12634. cc. 9.**

—— *See* PETRARCA (F.) [*Canzoniere.—English.*] Qui comincian le rime di M. F. Petrarca. The Sonnets and Stanzas of Petrarch. Translated by C. B. Cayley, *etc.* 1879. 8°.　　**2284. c. 15.**

—— Psyche's Interludes. [In verse.] pp. viii. 110. *Longman & Co. : London,* 1857. 8°.　　**11650. b. 30.**

CAYLEY (CORNELIUS) *See* CHRISTIANITY. Letters and Queries [by J. Priestley] addressed to the Anonymous Answerer of an Appeal to the serious and candid Professors of Christianity ; to the Rev. Mr. T. Morgan, and to Mr. C. Caley. 1771. 12°.　　**4015. a. 13.**

—— *See* COPPIN (Richard) The Advancement of all things in Christ and of Christ in all things, *etc.* [Edited, with a preface, by C. Cayley.] [1763.] 8°.　**4139. bbb. 52. (2.)**

—— *See* PHILAGATHUS, *pseud.* A Practical Improvement of the Divinity and Atonement of Jesus . . . humbly offered as a supplement to the tracts lately published by Mr. Cayley, *etc.* 1772. 12°.　　**11632. aaa. 64.**

—— *See* SHEPHERD. The Seraphical Young Shepherd . . . Now translated from the French, and enlarged with notes. To which are added, a few fragments. By C. Cayley. [1762.] 12°.　　**4409. ee. 33.**

—— *See* SHEPHERD. The Seraphical Young Shepherd . . . To which is added . . . a Small Bunch of Violets, *etc.* 1762. 12°.　　**4412. k. 19.**

—— —— 1779. 12°.　　**1126. a. 20**

—— —— 1793. 12°.　　**4408. bb. 47.**

—— *See* SHEPHERD. The Seraphical Shepherd on the Day of Judgment, *etc.* [Conversation no. 5 extracted from " The Seraphical Young Shepherd." Translated by C. Cayley.] 1852. 12°.　　**4406. e. 45. (5.)**

—— An Evangelical Dialogue between Cornelius Cayley and Echo : setting forth the great mercy . . . of God towards Man, *etc.* [In verse.] pp. 8. *Printed for the Author : London,* [1780.] 8°.　　**1162. l. 26. (2.)**

—— [Another edition.] *See* PIECES. Pious Pieces in Verse, *etc.* 1821. 12°.　　**11641. aaa. 42.**

—— A Letter to the Rev. Mr. Potter. In answer to his sermon, preach'd at Reymerston in Norfolk, against the people call'd Methodists. pp. 31. *R. Davy : Norwich,* 1758. 8°.　　**4139. c. 25.**

—— *See* POTTER (Robert) *Prebendary of Norwich.* An Appendix to the Sermon on the pretended inspiration of the Methodists. Occasioned by Mr. Cayley's Letter. 1758. 8°.　　**4473. c. 6. (10.**

—— The Olive-branch of Peace. With the Shulamite : a poem. pp. 40. *Printed for the Author : Leeds,* 1771. 8°.　　**1162. l. 26. (1.)**

—— The Riches of God's Free Grace, display'd in the Conversion of Cornelius Cayley, *etc.* pp. 143. *Norwich,* 1757. 8°.　　**4902. aaa. 59.**

—— The third edition, with some interesting enlargements. [With a portrait.] pp. 124. *J. Bowling : Leeds,* 1778. 12°.　　**1416. a. 33.**

—— The fifth edition. With enlargements. pp. 96. *J. Capes : Leeds,* 1813. 12°.　　**899. d. 16. (8.)**

CAYLEY (CORNELIUS)

—— The Riches of God's Free Grace displayed in the Life and Conversion of Cornelius Cayley . . . A new edition. pp. 48. 1819. *See* HISTORICS. Sacred Historics, *etc.* 1819. 8°. **04422. c. 3.**

—— The Riches of God's Free Grace displayed in the Life and Conversion of Cornelius Cayley, *etc.* pp. 48. 1820. *See* HISTORICS. Sacred Historics, *etc.* 1814. 8°. **1474. bb. 28. (4.)**

—— The seventh edition, with a portrait. pp. 160. *Ebenezer Fowler: London*, 1837. 8°. **4905. aaa. 41.**

—— The fifth edition. With enlargements. [A reprint with extracts from " A Small Bunch of Violets " and " A Tour through Holland." Edited by J. P. Wilson.] pp. xvi. 228. *Spottiswoode & Co.: London*, [1862.] 8°. **4903. bbb. 18.**

—— A new edition, edited by the editor of the " Little Gleaner " [i.e. S. Sears]. pp. 102. *Houlston & Wright: London*, 1863. 12°. **4903. cc. 15.**

—— A Tour through Holland, Flanders, and part of France . . . The second edition, with emendations and several enlargements. pp. vii. 97. *G. Wright: Leeds*, 1777. 12°. **010107. ee. 5.**

CAYLEY (EDWARD STILLINGFLEET) *the Elder.* Agricultural Committee of 1836. A letter to H. Handley . . . a member of the late Committee on Agricultural Distress in the House of Commons, on the proceedings of that Committee, and in answer to Mr. Shaw Lefevre's pamphlet. pp. 22. *Joseph Moxon: York; J. Ridgway & Sons: London*, 1836. 8°. **7077. d. 16.**

—— Corn Laws. Speech . . . on the motion of Mr. Villiers, for " A Committee of the whole House to consider Act 9 Geo. IV. c. 60, relating to Foreign Corn," *etc.* pp. 63. *Ridgway: London*, 1839. 8°. **8135. dd. 9. (8.)**

—— Corn, Trade, Wages, and Rent; or, Observations on the circumstances of the present financial crisis, *etc.* pp. 47. *James Ridgway: London*, 1826. 8°. **T. 1174. (2.)**

—— Letters to the Right Honourable Lord John Russell, M.P., on the Corn Laws. pp. 31. *John Ollivier: London*, 1846. 8°. **8245. d. 23.**

—— *See* MOORSOM (Richard) A Letter to the Earl of Mulgrave . . . with some remarks on Mr. Cayley's Letter to Lord John Russell. [1847.] 12°. **8225. b. 79.**

—— On Commercial Economy, in six essays, *etc.* pp. vii. 260. *James Ridgway: London*, 1830. 8°. **08207. e. 91. (2.)**

—— Reasons for the Formation of the Agricultural Protection Society, addressed to the industrious classes of the United Kingdom. pp. 24. 1844. 8°. *See* ENGLAND.—*Agricultural Protection Society.* **1391. g. 21. (6.)**

CAYLEY (EDWARD STILLINGFLEET) *the Younger.* The European Revolutions of 1848. 2 vol. *Smith, Elder & Co.: London*, 1856. 8°. **9077. e. 25.**

—— Fair Trade and Free Trade . . . Reprinted from the " St. James' Gazette." pp. 16. " *Chronicle and Mail* ": *Bradford*, 1881. 8°. **8229. de. 31. (3.)**

—— The War of 1870 and the Peace of 1871. pp. 172. *John Sampson: York; Whittaker & Co.: London*, 1871. 8°. **8026. a. 32.**

CAYLEY (ETHEL B.) Poems. pp. 78. *B. H. Blackwell: Oxford*, 1911. 8°. **011650. e. 109.**

CAYLEY (GEORGE) Synoptical Tables, shewing the component parts of the principal mineral waters, collected from the works of Doctor Saunders, Doctor Garnett, Mr. Peacock of Darlington, and the late Mr. William Brunton . . . With some observations . . . by G. Cayley. pp. 34. *W. Farrer: Ripon; Longman & Co.: London*, 1809. 8°. **7470. d. 12.**

CAYLEY (Sir GEORGE) *Bart.* Aerial Navigation. [First published in " Nicholson's Journal."] pp. x. 40. *London*, 1910. 8°. [*Aeronautical Classics.* no. 1.] **08767. b. 1/1.**

—— Aeronautical and Miscellaneous Note-Book, ca. 1799-1826, of Sir George Cayley. [Edited by J. E. Hodgson.] With an appendix comprising a list of the Cayley Papers. pp. xx. 93. *Cambridge*, 1933. 8°. [*Newcomen Society. Extra publication.* no. 3.] **Ac. 4313. e /2. (3.)**

—— A Letter on the subject of Parliamentary Reform, addressed to Major Cartwright. pp. 29. *T. Sotheran: York*, 1818. 8°. **1102. f. 1. (2.)**

—— Five Letters on the Present State of the Country, addressed to Sir George Cayley, Bart. By a Yorkshire Freeholder. pp. 24. *T. Sotheran: York*, 1818. 8°. **1102. g. 23. (1.)**

CAYLEY (GEORGE JOHN) [Ode.] *See* ANDERSON (George) *of Glasgow*, and FINLAY (J.) The Burns Centenary Poems, *etc.* 1859. 8°. **11648. f. 7.**

—— Las Alforjas (or, the Bridle-Roads of Spain). 2 vol. *Richard Bentley: London*, 1853. 12°. **10160. b. 11.**

—— The Bridle Roads of Spain . . . Second edition, with illustrations. pp. xi. 372. *G. Routledge & Co.: London*, 1856. 8°. **10162. b. 16.** *With an additional titlepage.*

—— (Third edition.) With an introduction by Martin Hume, M.A., and recollections of the author by Lady Ritchie and Mrs. Cobden Sickert. [With a portrait.] pp. 397. *T. Fisher Unwin: London*, 1908. 8°. **10162. d. 5.**

—— The Death of Baldur. *See* CAMBRIDGE.—*University of Cambridge.* [*Official Documents.—Publications.—Prize Poems and Essays.*] A Complete Collection of the English Poems which have obtained the Chancellor's Gold Medal, *etc.* vol. 1. 1859, *etc.* 8°. **011650. f. 14.**

—— Indignant Rhymes, addressed to the electoral body at large. By an Illused Candidate [i.e. G. J. Cayley]. pp. 23. 1859. 12°. *See* RHYMES. **11647. bbb. 37.**

—— [Another edition.] pp. 16. [1860.] 8°. *See* RHYMES. **11649. d. 42. (14.)**

—— The Service and the Reward. A memoir of the late Robert Wilson Roberts, R.N. pp. vii. 44. *D. F. Oakey: London*, 1858. 8°. **10804. a. 42. (2.)**

—— Some Account of the Life and Adventures of Sir Reg^d Mohun, Bt. Done in verse . . . Canto first (second, third). pp. 179. *William Pickering: London*, 1849, 50. 8°. **11645. e. 40.**

—— The Working Classes; their interest in administrative, financial and electoral reform. pp. 38. *D. F. Oakey: London*, 1858. 8°. **8138. d. 15.**

—— The Working Classes, *etc.* pp. 38. *Daniel F. Oakey: London*, 1858. 8°. **C.T. 357. (19.)**

CAYLEY (HENRY) Guide to Travellers on the maintenance of health in unhealthy countries. pp. 20. *H. Cox: London*, 1896. 16°. **[MISSING.]**

—— Tropical Diseases of the Liver. *See* DAVIDSON (Andrew) Hygiene & Diseases of Warm Climates, *etc.* 1893. 8°. **[MISSING.]**

CAYLEY (HUGH) A Matter of Morals. An incident. pp. 224. *Grant Richards: London*, 1903. 8°.
012628. a. 1.

CAYLEY (J.) *Translator.*

——   *See* HOYLAND (Francis) Poems and Translations. [With verse translations of Psalms 1, 8 and 150 by J. Cayley.] 1763. 4°.   **1346. i. 55.**

CAYLEY (NEVILLE WILLIAM)

—— *See* TROUGHTON (Ellis Le G.) Furred Animals of Australia . . . With . . . plates . . . by N. W. Cayley. 1941. 8°.   **07209. c. 4.**

——   *See* WATERHOUSE (Gustavus A.) What Butterfly is that? . . . Illustrations by N. W. Cayley. 1932. 8°.   **7299. f. 43.**

—— Australian Parrots. Their habits in the field and aviary . . . Illustrated by the author. pp. xxviii. 332. *Angus & Robertson: Sydney & London*, 1938. 8°.
7286. r. 28.

—— Budgerigars in Bush and Aviary. [With plates.] pp. xii. 148. *Angus & Robertson: Sydney*, 1933. 8°.
7286. ppp. 12.

—— The Fairy Wrens of Australia. Blue birds of happiness. [With plates.] pp. 88. *Angus & Robertson: Sydney, London*, 1949. 4°.   **7287. ppp. 27.**

—— Feathered Friends. A Gould League Annual . . [Essays by various authors.] Edited by N. W. Cayley. [With plates.] pp. 55. 1935. 8°. *See* NEW SOUTH WALES.—*New South Wales Gould League of Bird Lovers.*
7286. r. 13.

—— What Bird is that? A guide to the birds of Australia . . . Illustrated by the author. pp. xix. 319. pl. xxxvi. *Angus & Robertson: Sydney*, 1931. 8°. **7286. ppp. 6.**

—— What Bird is that? *etc.*   pp. xix. 319. *Angus & Robertson: Sydney*, 1935. 8°. **7286. ppp. 56.**

CAYLEY (REGINALD ARTHUR)

—— An Architectural Memoir of Old Basing Church, Hants. By the Rev. R. A. Cayley . . . The Armorials and Monuments of the Paulet Family, Dukes of Bolton and Marquesses of Winchester. By S. James A. Salter. pp. 24. *Charles J. Jacob: Basingstoke*, 1891. 8°.
08230. b. 50. (13.)

CAYLEY (WILLIAM) *See* MURCHISON (Charles) A Treatise on the Continued Fevers of Great Britain . . . Third edition, edited by W. Cayley. 1884. 8°. **7561. k. 6.**

—— *See* STEWART (Alexander P.) Some Considerations on the Nature and Pathology of Typhus and Typhoid Fever . . . Edited by W. Cayley. 1884. 8°. **Ac. 3838/46.**

—— Croonian Lectures on some points in the Pathology and Treatment of Typhoid Fever, *etc.* pp. 126. *J. & A. Churchill: London*, 1880. 8°. **7560. de. 8.**

CAYLEY-ROBINSON (FREDERIC) *See* ROBINSON.

CAYLEY-ROBINSON (WINIFRED) *See* ROBINSON.

CAYLEY-WEBSTER (HERBERT) *See* WEBSTER.

CAYLOR (ROSE) The Woman on the Balcony. pp. 288. *John Long: London*, [1928.] 8°. **NN. 13715.**

CAYLUS, ANNE CLAUDE PHILIPPE DE TUBIÈRES DE GRIMOARD DE PESTELS DE LEVIS, *Count de. See* TUBIÈRES DE GRIMOARD DE PESTELS DE LEVIS.

——, ARTHUR ROUGÉ, *Duke de. See* ROUGÉ.

CAYLUS, CHARLES, *Marquis of. See* TUBIÈRES DE GRIMOARD DE PESTELS DE LEVIS.

——, JOSEPH LOUIS ROBERT DE LIGNERAC, *Duke de. See* ROBERT DE LIGNERAC.

——, MARTHE MARGUERITE HIPPOLYTE DE TUBIÈRES DE GRIMOARD DE PESTELS DE LEVIS, *Marchioness de. See* TUBIÈRES DE GRIMOARD DE PESTELS DE LEVIS.

CAYLUS (CHARLES M. J. PONS) *See* PONS-CAYLUS.

CAYLUS (DANIEL CHARLES GABRIEL DE TUBIÈRES DE GRIMOARD DE PESTELS DE LEVIS DE) *Bishop of Auxerre. See* TUBIÈRES DE GRIMOARD DE PESTELS DE LEVIS DE CAYLUS.

CAYLUS (ERNEST) Politique extérieure des États-Unis. Doctrine Monroe. [A series of letters, edited by C. Montagut.] pp. 31. *Paris*, 1865. 8°.
8177. cc. 53. (4.)

CAYMAN ISLANDS.

LAWS.—I. GENERAL COLLECTIONS.

—— Law 1 of 1907 [*etc.*].   [*Kingston, Jamaica?* 1907– .] 4° & fol.   C.S. F. **168.**

MISCELLANEOUS OFFICIAL PUBLICATIONS.

—— Annual Report on the Cayman Islands, *etc. See infra* : Cayman Islands, Jamaica. Report, *etc.*

—— Annual Report on the Cayman Islands, Dependency of Jamaica, for the year 1946 [*etc.*]. *London*, 1948– . 8°. [*Colonial Annual Reports.*]   B.S. **7/51. (10.)**

—— Cayman Islands, Jamaica. Report for 1918-19(–1931. 1933). (Annual Report on the Social and Economic Progress of the People of the Cayman Islands . . . 1934[–1937].) 16 pt. *London*, 1921–38. 8°. [*Colonial Reports—Annual.* no. 1092, 1205, 1231, 1262, 1298, 1337, 1382, 1431, 1481, 1540, 1575, 1702, 1745, 1794, 1839, 1872.]
B.S. **7/51.**
Previous Reports were published as Parliamentary Papers. No Report was issued for 1932.

—— Estimates of the Revenue and Expenditure of the Cayman Islands, 1946–47, *etc.* ff. 34. [*Kingston, Jamaica*, 1946?] *obl.* fol.   C.S. F. **163.**
Reproduced from typewriting.

—— Report on the General State of Health of the Cayman Islands during 1938. (Report on Health Conditions in the Cayman Islands during 1949.)   *Grand Cayman*, 1939, [50.] fol.   C.S. F. **165.**
Reproduced from typewriting.

CAYMARI (ONOFRE GONZÁLEZ Y) *See* GONZÁLEZ Y CAYMARI.

CAYME PRESS PAMPHLETS. Cayme Press Pamphlets. no. 1–10. *Cayme Press: London*, 1926–[31.] 8°.
12207. dd. 1.

CAYMI (NORBERTO) *See* CAIMO.

CAYMO (NORBERTO) *See* CAIMO.

CAYMUS (BERNARDINUS) *See* CAIMI (Bernardino)

CAYMUS (FRANCISCUS) *See* PETRARCA (F.) [*De Vita Solitaria.—Latin.*] De uita solitaria. [fol. 60 *recto:*] Francisci Petrarce Poete Laureati Epistola de dispositione uite sue ad Gubernatorem patriæ. [Edited by F. Caymus.] 1498. fol.   IB. **26782.**

CAYNE (John) A Letter sent from the Queenes Court in Holland, sent from Mr. Cayn her Maiesties servant, to Mr. Sanders neere Cheering-Crosse (concerning fourteene messengers which are gone from the States in Holland to his Majesty at Yorke). *See* England. [*Miscellaneous Public Documents, etc.*—III.] The Kings Maiesties Speech to the Lords for the raising of forces, *etc.* 1642. 4º.
8138. b. 97. (1.)

CAYOL (Jean Bruno) *See* Bayle (A. L. J.) Encyclopédie des sciences médicales. Par MM. Alibert . . . Cayol [and others], *etc.* 1834, *etc.* 8º.
07305. cc. 3.

—— *See* Periodical Publications.—*Paris*. Revue médicale historique et philosophique, *etc.* (Revue médicale française et étrangère. [Subsequently edited by J. B. Cayol and others.]—Nouvelle série par J. B. Cayol.) 1820, *etc.* 8º.
P.P. 2904.

—— Clinique médicale, suivi d'un Traité des maladies cancéreuses. pp. l. 624. *Paris*, 1833. 8º. **775. k. 11.**

—— De la fièvre typhoïde et du typhoïdisme. pp. 68. *Paris*, 1853. 8º.
7560. cc. 41. (1.)

—— Du ver rongeur de la tradition hippocratique. Défense de l'hippocratisme moderne contre les attaques d'un certain parti néo-catholique. pp. 68. *Paris*, 1854. 8º.
7680.cc.9.

—— Recherches sur la phthisie trachéale. pp. 81. *Paris*, 1810. 4º.
1182. h. 10. (10.)

CAYOL (Jean Jacques) La Divinité du catholicisme démontrée par la nécessité d'une religion révélée. pp. 376. *Marseille*, 1862. 12º.
3901. bbb. 14.

CAYOL (Joseph Amédée) Manuel de l'administration des corps de troupes en campagne. pp. 260. *Paris*, 1862. 8º.
8828. ff. 5.

CAYOLLA (Lourenço) O Despertar d'um sonho . . . Romance historico, *etc.* pp. 178. *Lisboa*, 1898. 8º.
12491. e. 34.

CAYON (Jean) *See* Bournon (J.) Chroniques, lois, mœurs et usages de la Lorraine . . . publiés . . . par J. Cayon. 1838. 4º.
805. h. 8.

—— *See* Champé (A. de) *Dame de Vendières*. Trois lettres . . . au duc de Lorraine *etc.* [Edited by J. Cayon.] 1838. 4º.
1454. k. 7.

—— *See* Héraudel (J.) Élégie de ce que la Lorraine a souffert depuis quelques années, *etc.* [Edited by J. Cayon.] 1839. 4º.
1461. i. 4.

—— *See* Richerius, *Senoniensis*. Chronique de Richer . . . publiée . . . par J. Cayon. 1842. 4º. **805. h. 9.**

—— *See* Uzier (A.) Triomphe du corbeau. [Edited by J. Cayon.] 1839. 8º. **1081. h. 28.**

—— Ancienne chevalerie de Lorraine, ou Armorial historique et généalogique des maisons qui ont formé ce corps souverain, eu [*sic*] droit de siéger aux assises ; avec un discours préliminaire, *etc.* pp. xxxv. 234. *Nancy*, 1850. 4º.
9915. f. 27.

—— Chroniques et description du lieu de la naissance à Lay-Saint-Christophe de Saint Arnou, évêque de Metz . . . Notices sur les comtes du Chaumontois . . . Par J. Cayon . . . en collaboration de L.-E. Ancelon. [With plates.] pp. 44. *Nancy*, 1856. 4º. **4824. e. 3.**

—— Les Ducs de Lorraine 1048–1757. Costumes et notices historiques. Le tout recueilli, dessiné, décrit et gravé sur cuivre, *etc.* [With plates.] pp. vi. 62. *Nancy*, 1854. 4º.
9915. bb. 17.

CAYON (Jean)

—— Église des Cordeliers, la Chapelle-ronde, sépultures de la maison de Lorraine, à Nancy. Histoire et description de ces édifices. Avec gravures et plans. pp. 100. *Nancy*, 1842. 8º. **1263. e. 19.**
With an additional titlepage, engraved.

—— Famille de Carpentier, seigneurs de Juvigny, *etc.* pp. iii. 16. *Nancy*, 1860. 4º. **9917. h. 8.**

—— Histoire physique, civile, morale et politique de Nancy, ancienne capitale de la Lorraine, *etc.* [With plates.] pp. vii. 440. *Nancy*, 1846. 8º. **10172. d. 16.**

—— Maison de Landrian en Lorraine. Ancienne chevalerie. pp. 15. xxxvi. *Nancy*, 1863. 4º. **9915. f. 32.**

—— Maison de Lignières, *etc.* pp. 32. *Nancy*, 1862. 4º.
9917. h. 10.

—— Notre-Dame de Bonsecours-lès-Nancy, autrefois Notre-Dame de la Victoire et des Rois. (Inscriptions monumentales de l'église Notre-Dame de Bonsecours lès Nancy, avec la traduction.) pp. 36. 8. *Nancy*, 1843. 8º.
703. i. 25.

—— Souvenirs et monumens de la bataille de Nancy. v janvier 1477. [Documents. Edited by J. Cayon.] *Saint-Nicolas-de-Port*, 1837. fol. **1319. k. 3.**

CAYO-PUTO. El Gran Hospital de Cayo-Puto, dedicado al autor del periódico titulado : La Canoa. [A skit. Signed : El Tocayo de Clarita.] pp. 7. *México*, 1820. 4º. **9770. bb. 3. (42.)**

CAYOT-DÉLANDRE (François Marie)

—— Le Morbihan ; son histoire et ses monuments. pp. 560. *Vannes*, 1847. 8º. **010171. g. 2.**

CAYOTTE (Louis) Dictionnaire des rimes classées d'après l'ordre alphabétique inversé et précédé d'un traité de versification française. pp. xxxviii. 269. *Paris*, 1906. 8º.
2276. d. 22.

CAYRADE (Jules) Recherches critiques et expérimentales sur les mouvements réflexes. pp. 182. *Paris*, 1864. 4º. [*Collection des thèses soutenues à la Faculté de Médecine de Paris*. An 1864. tom. 2.] **7373. e. 14.**

CAYRADE (Paul Joseph Hypolite) Dissertation sur les abcès du foie, *etc.* pp. 19. *Strasbourg*, 1828. 4º. [*Collection générale des dissertations de la Faculté de Médecine de Strasbourg*. vol. 39.] **7381.*b.**

CAYRASCO DE FIGUEROA (Bartolomé) *See* Cairasco de Figueroa.

CAYRÉ (Fulbert) La Méditation selon l'esprit de saint Augustin. pp. 94. *Paris ; Bruges* [printed], [1934.] 8º.
3670. df. 36.

—— Les Sources de l'amour divin. La Divine Présence d'après saint Augustin, *etc.* pp. viii. 271. *Paris ; Bruges* [printed], [1933.] 8º. **3670. df. 32.**

—— [La Spiritualité des Religieux de l'Assomption.] Assumptionist Spirituality. A synthesis of the teaching of Fr. Emmanuel d'Alzon. Translated and adapted . . . by . . . Andrew Beck. [With a portrait.] pp. 63. *Washbourne & Bogan : London*, [1934.] 8º.
4400. d. 56.

CAYRE (G.) Histoire des évêques et archevêques de Toulouse, depuis la fondation du siége jusqu'à nos jours. pp. 646. *Toulouse*, 1873. 8º. **4632. df. 6.**

CAYRE (J. B. M.) Dissertation sur l'idiotisme, *etc.* pp. 21. *Paris*, 1819. 4º. **1183. e. 13. (21.)**

CAYRÉ (MARCELLUS) Considérations cliniques sur les névropathies goutteuses primitives. Thèse, *etc.* pp. 65. *Montpellier*, 1868. 4º.   7379. h. **6.** (**8.**)

CAYREL (JEAN BAPTISTE FRANÇOIS) Dissertation sur la gastrite aiguë ; thèse, *etc.* pp. 28. *Paris*, 1831. 4º.
1184. d. **15.** (**16.**)

CAYREL (LOUIS CLAUDE) Essai sur quelques méthodes métasyncritiques employées dans le traitement de la syphilis, *etc.* pp. 36. *Strasbourg*, 1830. 4º. [*Collection générale des dissertations de la Faculté de Médecine de Strasbourg.* vol. 42.]   7381.* b.

CAYRENCOURT (MARGUERITE DE) *See* YOURCENAR (M. de) *pseud.* [i.e. M. DE CAYRENCOURT.]

CAYRO (PASQUALE) Dissertazione istorica in cui dimostransi li primi popoli d'Italia, non che l'esistenza, antichità, e sito della città un tempo Lirio chiamata, quindi Fregelli ed altresi sue notizie storiche. pp. xlii. 126. *Napoli*, 1795. 4º.   9166. f. **12.**

—— Storia sacra, e profana d'Aquino, e sua diocesi. 2 vol. *Napoli*, 1808, 11. 4º.   10151. e. **7.**

CAYRO (PIUS) De Christi Domini resurgentis gloria oratio, *etc.* pp. xvii. *Romae*, [1816.] 4º.   898. g. **1.** (**15.**)

CAYROCHE (J. P. F. V.) Dissertation sur la luxation consécutive de l'articulation coxo-fémorale, *etc.* pp. 21. *Paris*, 1814. 4º.   1183. c. **4.** (**7.**)

CAYROL (JEAN)
—— L'Espace d'une nuit. Roman. pp. 172. *Paris*, 1954. 8º. [*Cahiers du Rhône.* no. 66.] **W.P.2920/43.**

—— Je vivrai l'amour des autres.
On vous parle. pp. 179. 1947.
Les premiers jours. pp. 309. 1947.
Le feu qui prend. pp. 254. 1950.
Neuchâtel, Paris ; printed in *France*, 1947-50. 8º. [*Collection des cahiers du Rhône.*]   W.P. **2920/28.**

—— Lazare parmi nous. [On experiences in a concentration camp.] pp. 106. *Neuchâtel* ; *Paris* ; [printed in *France*,] 1950. 8º. [*Collection des cahiers du Rhône.*]   W.P. **2920/36.**

—— Miroir de la rédemption. Précédé de Et nunc. pp. 83. *Neuchâtel*, 1944. 8º. [*Les Poètes des cahiers du Rhône.* no. 14.]   W.P. **1412/14.**

—— Les Mots sont aussi des demeures. [Poems.] pp. 140. *Neuchâtel* ; *Paris*, 1952. 8º. [*Les Poètes des cahiers du Rhône.* no. 22.]   **W.P.1412/22.**

—— La Noire, *etc.* pp. 222. *Paris*, 1949. 8º. [*Collection des Cahiers du Rhône.*]   W.P. **2920/32.**

—— Passe-temps de l'homme et des oiseaux. Suivi de Dans le meilleur des mondes, *etc.* pp. 107. *Neuchâtel, Paris*, 1947. 8º. [*Les Poètes des cahiers du Rhône.* no. 20.]   W.P. **1412/20.**

—— Le Vent de la mémoire. Roman. pp. 221. *Neuchâtel* ; *Paris* ; *Abbeville* [printed], 1952. 8º. [*Collection des Cahiers du Rhône*].   **W.P.2920/42.**

CAYROL (L.) Quelques considérations sur l'albuminurie, *etc.* pp. 22. *Strasbourg*, 1859. 4º. [*Collection générale des dissertations de la Faculté de Médecine de Strasbourg.* sér. 2. tom. 23.]   7381.* d.

CAYROL (LOUIS NICHOLAS JEAN JOACHIM DE) *See* VOLTAIRE (F. M. A. de) [*Letters.*] Lettres inédites . . . recueillies par M. de Cayrol, *etc.* 1856. 8º.
10910. f. **3.**

CAYROL (LOUIS NICHOLAS JEAN JOACHIM DE)
—— Dissertation sur l'emplacement du champ de bataille où César défit l'armée des Nervii et de leurs alliés, par M. de C . . . . ., Membre de l'Académie d'Amiens [i.e. L. N. J. J. de Cayrol]. pp. 62. 1832. 8º. *See* C . . . . ., M. de, *Membre de l'Académie d'Amiens.*   803. f. **14.**

—— Essai historique sur la vie et les ouvrages de Gresset. [With a portrait.] 2 tom. *Amiens* ; *Paris*, 1844. 8º.
10660. d. **15.**

—— Observations sur les positions occupées successivement par l'armée romaine que commandait César, depuis Durocortorum jusqu'à Bratuspantium, pendant sa campagne contre les Belges. pp. 15. *Beauvais*, 1849. 8º.
1319. h. **12.**

CAYROU (ALCIDE) *See* SHAKESPEARE (William) [*Smaller Collections of Plays.—French.*] Chefs-d'œuvre de Shakespeare. Traduction en vers par M. A. Cayrou, *etc.* 1876. 8º.   11765. ff. **2.**

CAYROU (FRÉDÉRIC) Moun Gabèlat. Recueil de poésies en langue d'oc, *etc.* pp. xi. 117. *Montauban*, 1922. 8º.
11483. dd. **44.**

CAYROU (GASTON) Le Français classique. Lexique de la langue du dix-septième siècle . . . 69 illustrations documentaires. pp. xxviii. 888. *Paris*, 1923. 8º.
12951. aa. **52.**

CAYRÚ, BENTO DA SILVA LISBOA, *Baron de. See* SILVA LISBOA.

——, JOSÉ DA SILVA LISBOA, *Viscount de. See* SILVA LISBOA.

CAYSAC (GEORGES) Introduction à l'étude du dialecte cantonais. pp. iii. 229. *Hongkong*, 1926. 8º.
012903. f. **10.**

CAYSSAC (F.) Dissertation sur la coxalgie ; thèse, *etc.* pp. 20. *Paris*, 1831. 4º.   1184. d. **17.** (**17.**)

CAYTON (HORACE R.) and **DRAKE** (SAINT CLAIR)
—— Black Metropolis. pp. xxxiv. 809. *Jonathan Cape : London* ; printed in *U.S.A.*, 1946. 8º.   010410. a. **40.**

CAYTON (HORACE R.) and **MITCHELL** (GEORGE SINCLAIR) Black Workers and the New Unions. pp. xviii. 473. *University of North Carolina Press : Chapel Hill*, 1939. 8º.   8289. dd. **7.**

CAYUELA (ARTURO MARÍA) *See* MENÉNDEZ Y PELAYO (M.) Menéndez y Pelayo, orientador de la cultura . . . Con preliminares, notas e índices. Por A. M. Cayuela. 1939. 8º.   10630. l. **9.**

CAYUGA COUNTY HISTORICAL SOCIETY. *See* AUBURN, *New York.*

CAYWOOD (JOHN) *See* CAWOD (John) *of Louth, Lincolnshire.*

CAYWOOD (LOUIS RICHARD)
—— Excavations at Green Spring Plantation. pp. v. 29. pl. XVII. 1955. 4º. *See* UNITED STATES OF AMERICA.— *National Park Service.*   A.S. **197/22.**

CAYWOOD (MARK) Paradise Island. pp. 278. *Geoffrey Bles : London*, [1927.] 8º.   NN. **13283.**

—— Virginia's Quest. pp. 254. *Arthur Gray : London*, [1934.] 8º.   NN. **21895.**

CAYX (REMY JEAN BAPTISTE CHARLES) *See* PETITOT (C. B.) Collection complète des mémoires relatifs à l'histoire de France . . . avec des notices sur chaque auteur . . . par M. Petitot. [With the collaboration of R. J. B. C. Cayx and others.] 1819, *etc.* 8º.   909. e. 3–k. **12.**

CAYX (Remy Jean Baptiste Charles)

—— *See* Poirson (A.) and Cayx (R. J. B. C.) Précis de l'histoire ancienne, *etc.* 1843. 8°. **9008. c. 3.**

CAYZAC (Joseph) The Mission Boy. A romance of new Africa. pp. vii. 120.   *Burns, Oates & Co.: London,* 1927 [1926]. 8°.   **4764. h. 2.**

CAYZER, IRVINE AND CO.

—— The Clansman. vol. 1. no. 2, 4—vol. 8. no. 5. Winter 1948; Summer 1949—Autumn 1956.   *London,* 1948–56. 8°.   **P.P. 5793. ngc.**
Subsequently incorporated in " Seaview."

CAYZER (Charles William) *See also* Wynne (Charles Whitworth) *pseud.* [i.e. C. W. Cayzer.]

—— Amy Robsart and other poems. pp. x. 54. *J. Parker & Co.: Oxford,* [1893.] 8°.   **11653. e. 51.**

—— By the Way of the Gate. Poems and dramas. 2 vol. *Kegan Paul & Co.: London,* 1911. 8°.   **011650. i. 94.**

—— Poems on Love and Nature. pp. ix. 117. *Elliot Stock: London,* 1896. 8°.   **011652. l. 55.**

CAYZER (Thomas) Carburetted Water Gas and Carbon Monoxide Poisoning. Reprinted from " The Public Health Engineer," with additions. pp. 15.   *Eyre & Spottiswoode: London,* 1897. 8°.   **7306. df. 28. (5.)**

CAYZER (Thomas S.) Britannia : a collection of the principal passages in Latin authors that refer to this island. With vocabulary and notes . . . Illustrated with a map and 29 woodcuts. pp. xxiii. 165.   *Griffith & Farran: London,* 1878 [1877]. 8°.   **10347. aaa. 1.**

—— Horæ Latinæ ; a new Latin reading book. pp. 160. *Educational Trading Co.: Birmingham ; Simpkin, Marshall & Co.: London,* [1868.] 8°.   **12933. aaa. 40.**

—— One Thousand Algebraical Tests . . . Fourth edition, revised and stereotyped. [With answers.] 2 pt. *Griffith, Farran & Co.: London,* [1887.] 8°.   **8535. f. 2.**

—— One Thousand Arithmetical Tests ; or, the Examiner's assistant ; specially adapted . . . for examination purposes, *etc.* [With answers.] 2 pt.   *Griffith & Farran: London,* 1861. 12°.   **8504. b. 12, 13.**

—— One Thousand Geometrical Tests ; comprising exercises in mensuration, Euclid, practical geometry, and trigonometry, *etc.* pp. 82.   *Simpkin, Marshall & Co.: London ; Educational Trading Co.: Birmingham,* 1868. 8°.   **8530. ee. 17.**

CAZA. La Caza. Revista de los cazadores. *See* Periodical Publications.—*Madrid.*

—— Entremez, intitulado : A Caza de Dança, ou Theatro da mocidade ocioza. pp. 16. *Lisboa,* 1783. 8°.   **11726. bb. 45. (31.)**

CAZA (Francesco)

—— *Begin.* [fol. 2 *recto :*] Tractato vulgare de canto figurato de francesco caza. [Based on the second part of the " Practica musicae " of Franchinus Gaforns. With a prefatory epistle, in Latin, by Gaforns, addressed to Philipinus Fliscus.] **G.ℑ.** *Opera magistri iohanis petri de lomacio Leonardus pachel Impressit: Mediolani,* die quinto Iunij, 1492. 4°.   Hirsch I. **110.**
12 *leaves. Sig.* a⁸ b⁴. 26 *lines to a page.*

—— Tractato vulgare de canto figurato, Mailand 1492, in Faksimile mit Übersetzung herausgegeben von Johannes Wolf. Mit einem Verzeichnis der nachweisbaren musiktheoretischen Inkunabeln. pp. 92. *Berlin,* 1922. 8°. [*Veröffentlichungen der Musik-Bibliothek Paul Hirsch.* Reihe I, vol. I.]   **M.G.1401.**

CAZABAN (Pierre Prosper) Recherches et observations sur la pellagre, dans l'arrondissement de Saint-Sever, Landes. pp. 52. *Paris,* 1848. 4°. [*Collection des thèses soutenues à la Faculté de Médecine de Paris.* An 1848. tom. 3.]   **7372. b. 6.**

CAZABAT (Jean) Essai sur la dysenterie, *etc.* [A thesis.] pp. 24. *Montpellier,* 1813. 4°.   **1180. g. 10. (11.)**

CAZABONNE (A.) Les Églises de Tarbes. Première notice, l'église Ste Thérèse, Carmes. pp. 28.   *Tarbes,* 1864. 8°.   **4632. aa. 20.**

—— Notes sur l'organisation des Conseils de Préfecture. pp. 56. *Tarbes,* 1861. 8°.   **5424. cc. 9.**

CAZAC (Henry Pierre) Polémique d'Aristote contre la théorie platonicienne des idées. Essai philosophique suivi d'éclaircissements sur quelques points du péripatétisme. (Extrait du Bulletin de la Société académique des Hautes Pyrénées.) pp. 93. *Tarbes,* 1889. 8°.   **8469. h. 15. (5.)**

CAZADOR.

—— El Cazador mas sabio del Catholico bosque, demuestrase en este romance las experiencias de la caza politica, â su amado Rey, y Señor Don Fernando sexto, *etc.* [*Madrid ?* c. 1760.] 4°.   **1481. c. 41. (34.)**

CAZADOR (Juan)

—— Estampas Cinegéticas Españolas. pp. 108. *Barcelona,* 1943. 8°.   **07209. aaa. 4.**

CAZADORI. Cazadori al fogher che se la conta. [In verse. With illustrations.] pp. 106. *Padova,* 1856. 8°.   **11431.f.25.**

CAZAINTRE (François Marie Fortuné) Quelques réflexions sur l'hygiène qui convient aux gens de lettres. Tribut académique, *etc.* pp. 16. *Montpellier,* 1817. 4°.   **1180. h. 10. (23.)**

CAZAINTRE (Jean) Nouès dé J. C., R. dé S.-P. [i.e. J. Cazaintre, Ritou dé Sant-Papoul], dioucéso dé Carcassouno. pp. 32. 1810. 12°. *See* C., J., R. *dé S.-P.*   **11498. b. 8.**

CAZAL. *See* Casale Monferrato.

CAZAL (   ) Commandant. La Guerre ! La guerre ! Roman de demain. pp. 218. *Paris,* [1939.] 8°.   **12549. ee. 22.**

—— La Guerre ! La guerre ! Maginot Siegfried. Roman de demain. pp. 222. *Paris,* [1939.] 8°.   **12549. f. 9.**
A different work from the preceding.

CAZAL (Edmond) Histoire anecdotique de l'Inquisition d'Espagne, *etc.* [With plates.] pp. x. 237.   *Paris,* 1932. 8°.   **4625. cc. 10.**

—— Histoire anecdotique de l'Inquisition en Italie et en France, *etc.* [With plates.] pp. v. 244. *Paris,* 1924. 8°.   **4606. f. 9.**

—— L'Inféconde. Roman. (La vie après la guerre.) pp. 246. *Paris,* [1920.] 8°.   **012547. aa. 66.**

—— Sainte Thérèse. [With a bibliography.] pp. 313. *Paris,* [1921.] 8°.   **4830. eee. 2.**

CAZAL (Gustave) Essai sur la pneumonie aiguë simple. Thèse, *etc.* pp. 36. *Montpellier,* 1839. 4°.   **1181. i. 7. (3.)**

CAZAL (H.) Quelques considérations sur le diagnostic de la phthisie pulmonaire. Thèse, *etc.* pp. 32. *Montpellier,* 1849. 4°.   **7379. a. 11. (17.)**

CAZAL (Joseph de Malvin) *See* Malvin-Cazal.

CAZAL (René Marie) Essai historique, anecdotique sur le parapluie, l'ombrelle et la canne et sur leur fabrication. [With plates.] pp. 106. *Paris*, 1844. 12º.
7742. aaa. 20.

CAZAL (U.) Études sur le moyen-âge. Le Mal des Ardents. [By U. Cazal and G. and R. Mortier.] 1908. *See* Bourges.—*Commission Historique du Cher.* Mémoires. sér. 4. vol. 22. 1857, *etc.* 8º.
Ac. 6780.

CAZALAS (Eutrope) *See* Cazalas (Jean J. A. M. E.)

CAZALAS (Jean Jules André Marie Eutrope) *See* Bennigsen (L. A. G. von) *Count.* Mémoires . . . Avec une introduction, des annexes et des notes du capitaine du génie breveté E. Cazalas. [1907, *etc.*] 8º.
9078. a. 9.

—— *See* Lebedev (V. T.) Russes et Anglais en Asie Centrale. Vers l'Inde . . . Traduit . . . par le capitaine . . . Cazalas, *etc.* 1900. 12º.
8028. aaa. 13.

—— *See* Martuinov (E. I.) Le Blocus de Plevna . . . Traduit . . . par E. Cazalas. [1904.] 8º.
9136. h. 17.

—— *See* Stern (Erich) Nouvelle méthode pour construire et dénombrer certains carrés magiques . . . Traduit . . . par le général E. Cazalas. 1937. 8º.
08535. gg. 17.

—— De Stralsund à Lunebourg. Épisode de la campagne de 1813. [On the retreat of the troops commanded by Baron Joseph Morand. With maps.] pp. 67. pl. II. *Paris*, 1911. 8º.
09008. cc. 14. (6.)

CAZALAS (Laurent) Du diabète. Thèse, *etc.* pp. 110. *Montpellier*, 1875. 4º.
7379. k. 11. (15.)

CAZALAS (Louis) Considérations générales et pratiques sur le traitement de la dyssenterie ; suivies d'un résumé sur la dyssenterie épidémique . . . observée à l'hôpital militaire de Metz . . . Mémoire présenté à la Société des Sciences médicales de la Moselle. pp. 81. *Metz*, 1845. 8º.
1169. l. 30.

—— Recherches pour servir à l'histoire médicale de l'eau minérale sulfureuse de Labassère, *etc.* pp. 96. *Paris*, 1851. 8º.
7470. cc. 9.

—— Thèse pour le doctorat en médecine. (Questions sur diverses branches des sciences médicales.) pp. 36. *Paris*, 1838. 4º.
1184. i. 2. (28.)

CAZALAT (Antoine Galy) *See* Galy-Cazalat.

CAZALÈS (Edmond de) *See* Periodical Publications.—*Paris.* L'Université catholique, *etc.* (tom. 5–20 rédigé par . . . MM. A. Bonnetty . . . E. de Cazalès [and others].) 1836, *etc.* 8º.
P.P. 99.

—— Études historiques et politiques sur l'Allemagne contemporaine. pp. vii. 446. *Paris*, 1853. 12º.
8073. c. 20.

—— Nos maux et leurs remèdes. pp. x. 327. *Paris*, 1876. 12º.
3902. bbb. 5.

CAZALÈS (Jacques Antoine Marie de) *See* Barnave (A. P. J. M.) Duel et funeste combat . . . entre MM. Barnave et Cazalès. [1791 ?] 8º.
F. 415. (10.)

—— *See* Barnave (A. P. J. M.) Lettre à Messieurs Barnave et Cazalès . . . sur leur duel du 10 août 1790. [1790.] 8º.
F.R. 52. (1.)

—— *See* Député. Observations d'un député sur la motion de M. de Cazalés [of 17 February 1790] (d'inviter les assemblées de département à nommer d'autres députés, en fixant le terme où doit finir la présente législature). [1790.] 8º.
F.R. 52. (19.)

CAZALÈS (Jacques Antoine Marie de)

—— *See* Gérard (Michel) Le Chien et le chat, ou MM. Gérard et Cazalès. 1790. 8º.
F. 1036. (14.)

—— *See* Grossin de Bouville (L. J.) *Count.* Opinion . . . sur cette question proposée par M. de Cazalès dans la séance de l'Assemblée nationale, du 17 février. L'Assemblée nationale doit-elle décréter que les départements, aussitôt qu'ils seront assemblés, nommeront de nouveaux députés à l'Assemblée nationale ? [1790.] 8º.
F.R. 53. (3.)

—— *See* Riquetti (A. B. L.) *Viscount de Mirabeau.* Cazalez et le vicomte de Mirabeau, insultés en sortant de l'Assemblée nationale le 13 avril 1790, croient devoir au public, le récit de cet événement, *etc.* [1790.] 8º. **F. 362. (18.)**

—— *See* Schumm (A.) Frankreichs letzter Ritter (J. A. M. von Cazalès), *etc.* 1903. 8º. [*Frankfurter zeitgemässe Broschüren.* Neue Folge. Bd. 22. Hft. 9.] **12209. g.**

—— Discours . . . à la séance du mardi 29 mars 1791. pp. 7. *Paris*, 1791.] 8º.
8050. d. 61. (19.)

—— Discours . . . sur le renvoi des ministres, prononcé dans l'Assemblée nationale le 19 octobre 1790. (Supplément à l'Ami du Roi.) pp. 16. [*Paris*, 1790.] 8º.
F. 1267. (12.)

—— [Another copy.] **F. 1006. (3.)**

—— [Another copy.] **F.R. 97. (15.)**

—— Lettre adressée . . . au Roi. (Lettre au président de la Convention nationale.—A M. Pétion, maire provisoire.) [Dated : South Wold, Nov. 1792.] pp. 4. [1792.] 8º.
R. 9. (9.)

—— Lettres . . . au Roi, au président de la Convention nationale, à M. Péthion, & suivies d'une lettre de M. Budaut, sur le procès de Louis XVI. pp. 8. *Paris*, 1792. 8º.
F. 899. (9.)

—— Opinion . . . dans l'affaire de Nancy. pp. 22. [*Paris*, 1790.] 8º.
F. 326. (6.)

—— [Another copy.] **F. 328. (13.)**

—— Opinion . . . sur le serment éxigé des officiers de l'armée. pp. 14. *Paris*, 1791. 8º. **F. 1267. (13.)**

—— [Another edition.] pp. 7. *Paris*, 1791. 8º.
8050. d. 61. (18.)

—— Opinion . . . sur les successions. pp. 37. *Paris*, 1791. 8º. **F. 541. (26.)**

—— [Another edition.] pp. 26. [*Paris*, 1791.] 8º.
8050. d. 61. (17.)

—— Confession testamentaire de M. Cazalès à l'abbé Maury. [A political squib.] pp. 7. [*Paris*, 1790 ?] 8º.
F. 778. (14.)

—— Détail du combat qui a eu lieu au Bois de Boulogne entre M. de Cazalès et M. Barnave. pp. 8. [1790.] 8º.
F.R. 53. (4.)

—— Grand duel arrivé . . . au Bois de Boulogne ; entre Messieurs Cazalès et Barnave, députés de l'Assemblée nationale. pp. 4. [*Paris*, 1790.] 8º. **F. 381. (15.)**

—— Grand récit de l'événement tragique arrivé à M. Cazalès . . . blessé mortellement par M. Barnave. pp. 8. [*Paris*, 1790 ?] 8º. **F. 837. (1.)**

—— Vœu, repentir et conversion de M. de Cazalès à l'article de la mort. [A political satire occasioned by the duel between Cazalès and Barnave.] pp. 4. [1790.] 8º.
F.R. 53. (5.)

CAZALÈS (JAKOB ANTON MARIA VON) *See* CAZALÈS (Jacques A. M. de)

CAZALET (ADOLPHE) Esquisses littéraires et morales. pp. 262. *Paris,* 1853. 12°.   **12236. aaa. 4.**

CAZALET (EDWARD) The Berlin Congress and the Anglo-Turkish Convention . . . With map, *etc.* pp. 32. *Edward Stanford: London,* 1878. 8°. **8028. de. 12. (6.)**

—— Bimetallism and its Connection with Commerce. pp. 31. *Effingham Wilson: London,* 1879. 8°. **8229. cc. 16. (5.)**

—— *See* GIBBS (Henry H.) *Baron Alderham.* Silver and Gold. [A letter to E. Cazalet, referring to his pamphlet on bimetallism.] 1879. 8°.   **8229. cc. 18. (10.)**

—— *See* HANKEY (Thomas) On Bi-Metallism . . . A reply to Mr. Cazalet and Mr. Gibbs. 1879. 8°.   **8229. cc. 18. (12.)**

—— The Eastern Question : an address to working men . . . With map showing the projected line of the Euphrates Valley Railway. pp. 42.   *Edward Stanford: London,* 1878. 8°.   **8028. de. 7. (11.)**

—— [Another copy.]   **8028. de. 8. (12.)**

—— England's Policy in the East : our relations with Russia and the future of Syria . . . Second edition. pp. 32. *Edward Stanford: London,* 1879. 8°.   **8028. ee. 10. (11.)**

CAZALET (EDWARD ALEXANDER) О значенiи Джона Говарда въ исторiи тюремной реформы. pp. iv. 91. *Москва,* 1892. 8°.   **6057. e. 34.**

CAZALET (F. A.) *See* GRUBER (O. von) [Ferienkurs in Photogrammetrie.] Photogrammetry . . . Translated . . . by G. T. McCaw . . . and F. A. Cazalet. 1932. 8°.   **8909. ccc. 39.**

CAZALET (LUCY) A Short History of Russia. pp. 88. *Clarendon Press: Oxford,* 1915. 8°.   **9455. b. 32.**

CAZALET (NICOLAS SUBERBIE) *See* SUBERBIE-CAZALET.

CAZALET (PHILÉMON J.) Quelques mots adressés aux membres de l'Église évangélique de Lyon. pp. 12. *Lyon,* 1861. 12°.   **3925. c. 80. (11.)**

CAZELET (THEODORA)

—— *See* JESUS CHRIST.—*Mother Church of Christ, Scientist, etc.* The Central Sign . . . Edited by A. C. Bill and T. Cazelet. 1917. 8°.   **4182. g. 5.**

CAZALET (VICTOR ALEXANDER) *See* BAILLIE (*Sir* Adrian W. M.) India from a Back Bench. By Sir A. Baillie . . . V. Cazalet, *etc.* 1934. 8°.   **20017. i. 41.**

—— With Sikorski to Russia. pp. 55.   MS. CORRECTIONS. *Curwen Press: London,* 1942. 8°.   **09101. de. 27.** *Printed for private circulation.*

CAZALET (WILLIAM WAHAB) The History of the Royal Academy of Music, compiled from authentic sources. pp. xxiv. 356. *T. Bosworth: London,* 1854. 8°.   **7895.c.37.**

—— [Another copy.] The History of the Royal Academy of Music, *etc. London,* 1854. 8°.   Hirsch **1294.**

—— On the Musical Department of the late Exhibition, *etc.* pp. 16. *Rudall, Rose & Carte: London,* 1852. 8°.   [MISSING.]

—— On the Reading of the Church Liturgy. pp. 72. *John Crockford: London,* 1862. 8°.   **3477. bb. 15.**

CAZALET (WILLIAM WAHAB)

—— On the Right Management of the Voice in Speaking and Reading ; with some remarks on phrasing and accentuation. pp. 41. *T. Bosworth: London,* 1855. 8°.   **11805. e. 36. (7.)**

—— Third edition, enlarged. pp. 106. *Bosworth & Harrison: London,* 1860. 8°.   **7610.a.9.**

—— Stammering : the cause and cure. pp. 28. *Bosworth & Harrison: London,* 1857. 12°.   **1186. b. 27. (5.)**

—— Fifth edition. pp. 46.   *Henry Renshaw: London,* [1873.] 8°.   [MISSING.]

—— The Voice ; or, the Art of singing. pp. 70. *Addison, Hollier & Lucas: London,* 1861. 12°.   **7896.b.10.**

CAZALIS (ADOLPHE) Essai sur le froid, et son emploi thérapeutique dans quelques maladies. Tribut académique, *etc.* pp. 42. *Montpellier,* 1826. 4°.   **1181. d. 9. (9.)**

CAZALIS (ÉMILE) Les Positions sociales du syndicalisme ouvrier en France. pp. xx. 243. *Paris,* 1923. 8°.   **08285. g. 50.**

CAZALIS (EUGÈNE E.) Propositions de médecine. Thèse, *etc.* pp. 29. *Paris,* 1837. 4°.   **1184. h. 10. (8.)**

CAZALIS (FRÉDÉRIC) *Directeur du Messager agricole.* *See* CAZALIS-ALLUT (L. C.) Œuvres agricoles de Cazalis-Allut . . . Recueillies et publiées par son fils le Dr F. Cazalis, *etc.* 1865. 8°.   **7075. ff. 6.**

—— *See* ROVASENDA (G. DI) *Count.* Essai d'une ampélographie universelle . . . Traduit de l'italien, annoté et augmenté . . . par . . . F. Cazalis . . . G. Foëx, *etc.* 1881. 4°.   **7075. k. 3.**

—— Traité pratique de l'art de faire le vin . . . Avec 68 figures, *etc.* pp. viii. 413. *Montpellier, Paris,* 1900. 8°.   **07945.f.20.**

CAZALIS (FRÉDÉRIC) *of Montpellier.* Quelques aperçus sur le role du médecin légiste dans les procès criminels. Thèse, *etc.* pp. 106. *Montpellier,* 1844. 4°.   **1182. d. 10. (7.)**

CAZALIS (HENRI) *See also* CASELLI (Jean) *pseud.* [i.e. H. Cazalis.]

——   *See also* LAHOR (Jean) *pseud.* [i.e. H. Cazalis.]

—— *See* SZTANKAY-POGÁNY (I.) Jean Lahor [i.e. H. Cazalis], l'homme et l'œuvre. [With a portrait and a bibliography.] 1935. 8°.   **Ac. 829/2.**

—— De la dégénérescence amyloïde, et de la stéatose du foie et des reins dans les longues suppurations et dans la septicémie chirurgicale. pp. 44. *Paris,* 1875. 4°. [*Collection des thèses soutenues à la Faculté de Médecine de Paris.* An 1875. tom. 4.]   **7374. b.**

—— L'Eau de Challes, Savoie . . . et ses principales indications. pp. 41. *Paris,* 1876. 8°.   **7462. ee. 3. (6.)**

—— Henri Regnault, sa vie et son œuvre. [With a portrait.] pp. 210. *Paris,* 1872. 8°.   **10662. df. 12.**

—— L'Illusion. [Poems.] pp. 200. *Paris,* 1875. 12°.   **11482. ccc. 3.**

CAZALIS (JOSEPH) De la valeur de quelques phénomènes congestifs dans la dothiénentérie. pp. 121. *Paris,* 1874. 4°. [*Collection des thèses soutenues à la Faculté de Médecine de Paris.* An 1874. tom. 3.]   **7374. a. 8.**

CAZALIS (Stanislas) De l'asthme. pp. 43. *Paris*, 1850. 4º. [*Collection des thèses soutenues à la Faculté de Médecine de Paris.* An 1850. tom. 3.] **7372. c. 15.**

CAZALIS-ALLUT (Louis César) Œuvres agricoles de Cazalis-Allut . . . Recueillies et publiées par son fils le Dr. Frédéric Cazalis et précédées d'une notice biographique sur l'auteur par M. H. Marès. [With a portrait.] pp. xxvi. 474. *Paris*, 1865. 8º. **7075. ff. 6.**

—— Mélanges de viticulture, d'œnologie et d'agriculture. pp. 45. *Montpellier*, 1859. 8º. **1253. c. 40.**

CAZALIS DE FONDOUCE (Paul) *See* Periodical Publications—*Paris*. Matériaux pour l'histoire positive et philosophique de l'homme, *etc.* (Matériaux pour l'histoire primitive et naturelle de l'homme [année 9, *etc.*] . . . par E. Cartailhac avec le concours de MM. P. Cazalis de Fondouce et Chantre.) 1865, *etc.* 8º. **P.P. 3862. ea.**

—— Derniers temps de l'âge de la pierre polie dans l'Aveyron. La grotte sépulcrale de Saint-Jean d'Alcas, *etc.* pp. 90. pl. iv. *Paris*, 1867. 8º. **7705. cc. 19. (12.)**

—— L'Homme fossile dans l'Aveyron sur une caverne de l'âge de la pierre, *etc. See* Lyell (*Sir* Charles) *Bart.* L'Ancienneté de l'homme, *etc.* 1864. 8º. **7108. bb. 28.**

—— Les Parpaillots. Recherches sur l'origine de ce sobriquet donné aux réformés de France aux xviᵉ et xviiᵉ siècles. pp. 19. *Montpellier*, 1860. 8º. **4632. bb. 9.**

—— Recherches sur la géologie de l'Egypte d'après les travaux les plus récents, notamment ceux de M. Figari-Bey, et le canal maritime de Suez. pp. 93. *Montpellier, Paris*, 1868. 8º. **7107. cc. 4.**

—— Les Temps préhistoriques dans le Sud-Est de la France. L'homme dans la vallée inférieure du Gardon. pt. 1. pp. 56. pl. xiv. *Montpellier, Paris*, 1872. 4º. **1707. a. 2.**

—— Les Temps préhistoriques dans le Sud-Est de la France. Allées couvertes de la Provence. Second mémoire . . . Suivi d'une étude sur les mollusques trouvés dans les Allées du Castellet par H. Nicolas. pp. 64. pl. vii. *Montpellier, Paris*, 1878. 4º. **7708. g. 8.**

CAZALLA (   ) *See* Chamberlain (John) *Writer on Spain.* El Atraso de España. Traducción de Cazalla. [1919.] 8º. **10162. b. 23.**

CAZALLA (Costanza) *See* Cazalla (D.) The Martyrs of Spain and the Liberators of Holland. Memoirs of the sisters Dolores and Costanza Cazalla. 1862. 8º. **4414. e. 19.**

—— —— 1870. 8º. **4806. bb. 17.**

CAZALLA (Dolores) The Martyrs of Spain and the Liberators of Holland. Memoirs of the sisters Dolores and Costanza Cazalla. By the author of " Tales and Sketches of Christian Life " [i.e. Elizabeth Charles], *etc.* pp. viii. 357. *J. Nisbet & Co.: London*, 1862 [1861]. 8º. **4414. e. 19.**

—— [Another edition.] pp. 456. *T. Nelson & Sons: London*, 1870. 8º. **4806. bb. 17.**

CAZALLA DEL RÍO, Felipe López-Valdemoro de Aranda, *Count de. See* López-Valdemoro de Aranda.

CAZALS (Antoine Lucien) Une Page de l'histoire du Lauragais, ou Histoire de la ville et de la communauté de Montesquieu-sur-Canal depuis les temps les plus anciens jusqu'à nos jours. pp. 302. *Toulouse*, 1883. 8º. **10168. aa. 19.**

CAZALS (Frédéric Auguste)

—— *See* Bayard (J. E.) The Latin Quarter, Past and Present . . . Illustrated by . . . F.-A. Cazals. 1926. 8º. **10167. g. 25.**

CAZALS (Frédéric Auguste)

—— *See* Verlaine (P.) Confessions. Illustrations de F. A. Cazals. 1899. 18º. **010664. g. 19.**

—— Iconographies de certains poëtes présents. Album no. 1 (2). *Paris*, 1894, 96. 4º. **12315. i. 94.** *No more published.*

—— Le Jardin des Ronces, 1889–1899. [Poems illustrated by the author. Preceded by a poem by Albert Mérat and a preface by Rachilde.] pp. xvi. 180. *Paris*, 1902. 8º. **011483. k. 22.**

CAZALS (Frédéric Auguste) and **LE ROUGE** (Gustave)

——   Les Derniers jours de Paul Verlaine. Nombreux documents et dessins, avec une préface de Maurice Barrès . . . Deuxième édition. pp. x. 270. *Paris*, 1911. 8º. **10661. ppp. 30.**

—— Nouvelle édition revue, *etc.* pp. x. 277. *Paris*, 1923. 8º. **10656. b. 14.**

CAZALS (Guilhem Peire de)

—— Guilhem Peire de Cazals, le troubadour et ses poèmes. Édition critique. [By Jean Mouzat.] *In:* Annales de l'Institut d'Études Occitanes. no. 14–16. avr.–oct. 1953. 1953. 8º. **Ac. 560.**

CAZALS (P.) *See* Dechepare (B.) Poésies basques, *etc.* [Edited by P. Cazals.] 1874. 8º. **11451. bbb. 26.**

CAZALS DE FABEL (G.) Le Poète Raymond de la Tailhède. Étude précédée de deux poèmes de Raymond de la Tailhède. pp. 35. *Albi*, 1938. 8º. **11858. e. 19.**

CAZALUPUS (Joannes Baptista) *See* Caccialupus.

CAZALY (Sarah) *See* Lebaudy (*Mme* Jules) Christine Myriane . . . Translated by Miss S. Cazaly. [1898.] 8º. **012643. c. 7.**

CAZALY (William Henry) *Major, I.M.S.*

——   The Common Snakes of India and Burma and how to recognise them. pp. ii. 60. iv. *Pioneer Press: Allahabad*, 1914. 8º. **7290. e. 58.**

CAZALY (William Henry) *Writer on Wireless.*

—— A.C./D.C. Test Meters. Principles, design and construction of instruments of workshop grade for testing low-power apparatus. By W. H. Cazaly . . . and Thomas Roddam. pp. viii. 180. *Sir Isaac Pitman & Sons: London*, 1951. 8º. **8761. bb. 24.**

—— Radio Service Test Gear. An outline of the principles upon which radio receiver test and measuring instruments operate. pp. v. 89. *Sir I. Pitman & Sons: London*, 1945. 8º. **8760. a. 34.**

CAZAMIAN (F.) *See* Azéma (P. E. M.) Œuvres poétiques . . . Avec une notice biographique et littéraire par F. Cazamian. 1877. 12º. **11482. e. 14.**

CAZAMIAN (Louis) *See* Browning (Robert) [*Smaller Collections.*] Hommes et femmes—Men and Women . . . Traduit avec une introduction par L. Cazamian. 1938. 8º. **11657. a. 42.**

—— *See* Chaucer (Geoffrey) [*Canterbury Tales.—Two or more Tales.*] Les Contes de Canterbury . . . Traduction: Prologue, par L. Cazamian, *etc.* 1942. 8º. **11626. l. 10.** ↑ *French.*

—— *See* Legouis (E.) Histoire de la littérature anglaise. (Époques moderne et contemporaine. Par L. Cazamian.) 1933. 8º. **011840. a. 32.**

CAZAMIAN (Louis)

—— *See* LEGOUIS (E.) A History of English Literature. (Modern Times. By L. Cazamian.) 1926, *etc.* 8°.
20017. d. 7.

—— —— 1930. 8°. 20017. c. 19.

—— —— 1933. 8°. 20017. e. 13.

—— *See* LEGOUIS (E.) A History of English Literature. The Middle Ages and the Renascence . . . By E. Legouis . . . Modern Times . . . By L. Cazamian. Translated . . . by . . . the author, *etc.* 1947. 8°. 11867. ee. 39.

—— *See* LEGOUIS (E.) A History of English Literature . . . Modern times . . . By L. Cazamian, *etc.* 1954. 8°.
11869. pp. 41.

—— *See* MICHELET (J.) L'Oiseau . . . Edited by L. Cazamian. 1907. 8°. 12239. f. 27.

—— The Aims and Method of Higher Literary Studies. (Three lectures.) *Houston*, 1929. 8°. [*Rice Institute Pamphlet.* vol. 16. no. 1.] Ac. 1720/2.

—— Andrew Lang and the Maid of France, *etc.* pp. 30. *Oxford University Press: London*, 1931. 8°. [*Andrew Lang Lecture.* 1931.] W.P. 9198/5.

—— L'Angleterre moderne. Son évolution. pp. 329. *Paris*, 1911. 8°. 12350. v. 35.

—— Modern England. pp. xi. 291. *J. M. Dent & Sons: London*, 1911. 8°. 12355. w. 8.

—— Carlyle. pp. 264. *Paris*, 1913. 8°. 010827. e. 45.

—— Carlyle . . . Translated by E. K. Brown. pp. ix. 289. *Macmillan Co.: New York*, 1932. 8°. 10823. aaa. 24.

—— Ce qu'il faut connaître de l'âme anglaise. pp. 160. *Paris*, 1927. 8°. 010348. ff. 10.

—— Criticism in the Making. pp. xi. 196. *Macmillan Co.: New York*, 1929. 8°. 11823. p. 8.

—— The Development of English Humour. Part I. From the early times to the Renascence. pp. vii. 160. *Macmillan Co.: New York*, 1930. 8°. 11865. aa. 10.

—— The Development of English Humor. Parts I and II. pp. viii. 421. *Duke University Press: Durham, N.C.*, 1952. 8°. 11869. cc. 38.

—— Essais en deux langues. pp. xv. 318. *Paris*, 1938. 8°. 12358. e. 29.

—— Études de psychologie littéraire. pp. 250. *Paris*, 1913. 8°. 011853. aa. 45.

—— L'Évolution psychologique et la littérature en Angleterre, 1660–1914. pp. viii. 268. *Paris*, 1920. 8°.
011851. a. 42.

—— Les Forces britanniques. Lettre à tous les français. pp. 14. *J. Truscott & Son: Londres*, 1916. 8°.
09083. a. 62.

—— La Grande Bretagne. [With illustrations and maps.] pp. 540. *Paris*, 1934. 8°. 010360. cc. 36.

—— La Grande-Bretagne et la guerre. Esquisse d'une évolution sociale. pp. 331. *Paris*, 1917. 8°.
08027. df. 69.

—— A History of French Literature. pp. xiii. 464. *Clarendon Press: Oxford*, 1955. 8°. 11871. p. 19.

—— L'Humour de Shakespeare. pp. 233. *Paris*, 1945. 8°.
11768. a. 26.

CAZAMIAN (Louis)

—— La Poésie romantique anglaise. pp. 87. *Paris*, 1939. 8°.
11858. e. 40.

—— Richardson. 1913. *See* WARD (*Sir* Adolphus W.) and WALLER (A. R.) The Cambridge History of English Literature, *etc.* vol. 10. 1907, *etc.* 8°. 11870.g.1.

—— Retour d'un anglicisant à la poésie française . . . The Zaharoff Lecture for 1937. pp. 21. *Clarendon Press: Oxford*, 1938. 8°. 11858. d. 98.

—— Le Roman social en Angleterre, 1830–1850. Dickens—Disraeli—Mrs. Gaskell—Kingsley. pp. 575. *Paris*, 1904. 8°. [*Bibliothèque de la Fondation Thiers.* fasc. 3.]
Ac. 443.

—— Nouvelle édition. 2 vol. *Paris*, 1935. 8°.
11856. eee. 26.

—— Symbolisme et poésie. L'exemple anglais. pp. 252. *Neuchâtel*, [1947.] 8°. 11867. aa. 30.

—— Three Studies in Criticism : three lectures, *etc. Houston*, 1924. 8°. [*Rice Institute Pamphlet.* vol. 11. no. 2.]
Ac. 1720/2.

CAZAMIAN (MADELEINE L.) L'Autre Amérique. pp. 328. *Paris*, 1931. 8°. 010410. e. 23.

—— Le Roman et les idées en Angleterre. *Strasbourg*, 1923– . 8°. [*Publications de la Faculté des Lettres de l'Université de Strasbourg.* fasc. 15, 73,125,etc.] Ac. 2633. e.

CAZAMOLLETTA (ZAN) Nuoua scelta di villanelle di diuersi autori . . . raccolte da Z. Cazamolletta. *Appresso C. Giolita: Trino*, [1590 ?] 8°. 11426. a. 26.

CAZANGA TERRASA Y REJON INANA Y TORRE DE IRISARRI (DIEGO DIONISIO ISIDRO ANTONIO JOSÉ) *Obispo de Brujulia, pseud.* La Pajarotada . . . Carta jocoseria, o agri-dulce, o sub-acida, *etc.* 6 pt. *Chuquisaca*, [1832.] 4°. 12314. bbb. 46.

CAZANOBES (JEAN JULES) Faculté de Droit de Paris. Thèse pour la licence. (Jus romanum. Qui potiores in pignore vel hypotheca habeantur et de his qui in priorum creditorum locum succedunt.—Droit français. Dispositions générales.) pp. 52. *Paris*, 1859. 8°.
5406. b. 11. (8.)

CAZANOU (EUGÈNE) Tumeurs blanches des synoviales tendineuses ou tumeurs fongueuses de ces synoviales. pp. 42. *Paris*, 1866. 4°. [*Collection des thèses soutenues à la Faculté de Médecine de Paris.* An 1866. tom. 3.]
7373. g. 6.

CAZANOVA (J.) *pseud.*

—— *See* CARRÉ (E.) La Ceinture de chasteté en police correctionnelle. Plaidoirie, *etc.* [With special reference to " La Ceinture de chasteté " by J. Cazanova, pseud.]
1884. 8°. 5425. k. 11. (2.)

CAZANOVE (ADOLPHE) Considérations générales sur la goutte. Thèse, *etc.* pp. 48. *Montpellier*, 1864. 4°.
7379. f. 7. (11.)

CAZANOVE (AMAURY DE) Les Chevaleresques. [Poems.] pp. 288. *Paris, Pau*, 1879. 8°. 11483. c. 22.

CAZARD (PAUL) Aux quatre coins des océans. Souvenirs d'un consul. [With illustrations, including a portrait.] pp. 228. *Aurillac*, 1938. 8°. 10028. p. 4.

CAZARIIS (MARTINUS DE) *See* GARATIS.

CAZASSA (GIOVANNI) Oh che scemmaje ! ! [Political verses.] [*Genoa*, 1848.] *s. sh.* fol. 804. k. 13. (350.)

CAZAUBON (A. C.) Des signes fournis par l'auscultation dans les maladies du cœur ; thèse, *etc.* pp. 25. *Paris,* 1833. 4º. **1184. f. 1. (25.)**

CAZAUBON (D. AUGUSTE) De l'hydrocèle accidentelle de la tunique vaginale ; thèse, *etc.* pp. 24. *Paris,* 1834. 4º. **1184. f. 10. (13.)**

CAZAUBON (J. B.) Questions d'hygiène et d'économie rurales. pp. 40. *Paris,* 1856. 4º. [*Collection des thèses soutenues à la Faculté de Médecine de Paris. An 1856 tom. 4.*] **7372. i. 4.**

CAZAUBON (LÉONCE) *See* CAMÕES (L. de) [*Rimas.—Selections.*] Sonnets choisis . . . traduits . . . par L. Cazaubon. 1879. 8º. **11452. cc. 2.**

CAZAUD (CHARLES DE) *Marquis. See* CASAUX.

CAZAUD (M.) De la pneumonie aiguë ; thèse, *etc.* pp. 18. *Paris,* 1826. 4º. **1183. i. 3. (2.)**

CAZAUD (ROGER)

—— [La Fatigue des métaux.] Fatigue of Metals . . . Translated by A. J. Fenner, *etc.* [With plates.] pp. xiv. 334. *Chapman & Hall : London,* 1953. 8º. **8763. ccc. 46.**

—— Recherches sur la fatigue des aciers. pp. 158. 1934. 8º. *See* FRANCE.—*Ministère de l'Air.* **7109. dd. 20.**

CAZAUGRAN (B.) Quelques considérations sur les épanchements pleurétiques. Thèse, *etc.* pp. 60. *Montpellier,* 1854. 4º. **7379. c. 9. (8.)**

CAZAUGRAN (P. LÉONARD) De l'air, considéré sous le triple point de vue chimique, physique et médical. Tribut académique, *etc.* pp. 52. *Montpellier,* 1817. 4º. **1180. h. 9. (30.)**

CAZAURAN (A. R.) *See* MACFARLAND (Daniel) The Trial of Daniel McFarland for the shooting of A. D. Richardson . . . Compiled by A. R. Cazauran, *etc.* [1870.] 8º. **[MISSING.]**

CAZAURAN (JEAN MARIE) *See* BERDOUES. Cartulaire de Berdoues, publié et annoté par l'abbé Cazauran. 1905. 8º. **4633. cc. 8.**

—— Comté de Panjas. Son passé, son église et ses peintures romanes. pp. 43. *Paris,* 1892. 8º. **10107. ff. 28. (6.)**

—— Diocèse d'Auch. Histoire paroissiale. Baronnie de Bourrouillan. Histoire seigneuriale et paroissiale. pp. xviii. 603. *Paris,* 1887. 8º. **10171. f. 5.**

—— Diocèse d'Auch. Histoire paroissiale. Monguilhem et Toujouse. pp. 403. *Paris,* 1890. 8º. **010171. h. 40.**

CAZAUVIEILH (EUGÈNE) De la pneumonie lobulaire des enfants à la mamelle. pp. 64. *Paris,* 1854. 4º. [*Collection des thèses soutenues à la Faculté de Médecine de Paris. An 1854. tom. 4.*] **7372. g. 4.**

CAZAUVIEILH (JEAN BAPTISTE) Du suicide, de l'aliénation mentale et des crimes contre les personnes, comparés dans leurs rapports réciproques. Recherches sur ce premier penchant chez les habitans des campagnes. pp. vi. 332. *Paris,* 1840. 8º. **722. g. 30.**

—— Recherches anatomico-physiologiques sur l'encéphale . . . Thèse, *etc.* pp. 34. *Paris,* 1827. 4º. **1183. i. 9. (23.)**

CAZAUX (   ) *Maire de Rabastens.* A Nosseigneurs de l'Assemblée nationale. Des commissaires, *etc.* [A petition respecting the formation of the municipality of Rabastens.] pp. 8. MS. NOTES. [1790.] 8º. **R. 648. (10.)**

CAZAUX (   ) *Maire de Rabastens.*

—— A Nosseigneurs de l'Assemblée nationale. Le sieur Cazaux, *etc.* [A petition respecting the formation of the municipality of Rabastens.] pp. 4. [1790.] 8º. **R. 648. (9.)**

CAZAUX (CHARLES DE) *Marquis. See* CASAUX.

CAZAUX (DOMINIQUE BARON) *See* BARON CAZAUX.

CAZAUX (F. LÉON) De l'amputation sus-malléolaire. Thèse, *etc.* pp. 41. *Montpellier,* 1859. 4º. **7379. e. 2. (3.)**

CAZAUX (G.) *See* LARRAÑAGA (V.) L'Ascension de Notre-Seigneur dans le Nouveau Testament . . . Traduit . . . par G. Cazaux. 1938. 8º. **Ac. 2002. d. (48.)**

—— Atourgal et Cyprien. Suite romancée. pp. 221. *Bordeaux,* 1939. 8º. **12549. f. 30.**

—— Autres pages d'idéologie. pp. 130. *Bordeaux,* 1935. 8º. **08466. de. 60.**

—— En glanant de loin en loin. pp. 105. *Bordeaux,* 1930. 8º. **12357. p. 15.**

—— En marge des arcanes. (La personnalité.—Préexistence et survivance.) pp. 86. *Bordeaux,* 1937. 8º. **8634. ccc. 23.**

—— Escale en Portugal. Notes de voyage. pp. 158. *Bordeaux,* 1930. 8º. **010160. de. 47.**

—— [Another issue.] *Bordeaux,* 1930. 8º. **010160. de. 72.**

—— Études et variétés. pp. 86. *Bordeaux,* 1932. 8º. **12357. r. 5.**

—— Feuilles nouvelles et compléments. pp. 95. *Bordeaux,* 1933. 8º. **12357. ppp. 1.**

—— Pages retrouvées. pp. 106. *Bordeaux,* 1948. 8º. **12361. e. 20.**

—— Parenthèses. pp. 146. *Bordeaux,* 1949. 8º. **12361. e. 21.**

—— Paroles d'un ilote. (Parenthèses. [Political notes.]—Âme et matière.) pp. 79. *Bordeaux,* 1936. 8º. **08052. b. 51.**

—— Paysages d'Arcachon. Notes de voyage. pp. 103. *Bergerac,* 1929. 8º. **010168. f. 68.**

—— Quelques vues de Marseille. Notes de voyage, avec deux cartes. pp. 75. *Bordeaux,* 1929. 8º. **10167. de. 40.**

—— Voyage dans les Landes et sur le littoral de Gascogne. Notes de voyage. pp. 177. *Bordeaux,* 1932. 8º. **010167. de. 9.**

CAZAUX (J.) *of Lüe.* Quelques réflexions sur l'emploi de l'acide arsénieux dans le traitement des fièvres intermittentes paludéennes. Thèse, *etc.* pp. 42. *Montpellier,* 1853. 4º. **7379. b. 12. (11.)**

CAZAUX (J. M.) Révoltons-nous Populo ! A bas les privilèges de la juiverie moderne ! Place à la justice universelle ! Préparation des cahiers électoraux de 1889. pp. 16. *Tarbes, Pau,* 1889. 8º. **8051. f. 24. (3.)**

CAZAUX (JEAN) Surréalisme et psychologie. Endophasie et écriture automatique. pp. 61. *Paris,* 1938. 8º. **8471. df. 15.**

CAZAUX (Joseph de) Faculté de Droit de Paris. Thèse pour le doctorat. (Des réserves.—De la quotité indisponible de droit exceptionnel.) pp. 55. *Paris*, 1851. 8º.
5406. a. 1. (3.)

CAZAUX (L. F. G. de) La Balance du commerce est-elle un vain mot, comme le disent les économistes? pp. 8. *Paris*, 1829. 8º.
712. g. 27. (4.)

—— Économie politique. Défense des principes de gouvernement de Sully et de Colbert. pp. 8. *Toulouse*, [1831?] 8º.
712. g. 27. (5.)

—— Économie politique. La France doit-elle proclamer la liberté du commerce avec l'extérieur? *etc.* pp. 16. *Paris*, 1828. 8º.
712. g. 27. (7.)

—— Économie politique. Réfutation d'un nouveau raisonnement de J.-B. S. (J.-B. Say) tendant à prouver que les lois restrictives de la liberté d'importer les produits étrangers sont sans but utile. pp. 4. *Toulouse* [1830?] 8º.
712. g. 27. (6.)

CAZAUX (Marcellin) De la toux, sa valeur séméiotique ses indications thérapeutiques. pp. 32. *Paris*, 1867. 4º. [*Collection des thèses soutenues à la Faculté de Médecine de Paris.* An 1867. tom. 3.]
7373. h. 6.

—— Lettres médicales sur les Eaux-Bonnes. pp. xii. 80. *Paris*, 1875. 8º.
7470. ff. 7.

CAZAUX (Michel) Des lésions traumatiques de l'urèthre chez l'homme dans la contusion du périnée. [With a plate.] pp. 56. *Paris*, 1872. 4º. [*Collection des thèses soutenues à la Faculté de Médecine de Paris.* An 1872. tom. 3.]
7373. n. 9.

CAZAUX (P.) Essai sur le ramolissement de la membrane muqueuse de l'estomac; thèse, *etc.* pp. 43. *Paris*, 1829. 4º.
1184. c. 13. (13.)

CAZAUX (Raymond) Propositions sur la médecine et la chirurgie; thèse, *etc.* pp. 15. *Paris*, 1828. 4º.
1184. c. 3. (31.)

CAZAVIEILLE (E. Henri) Dissertation médico-chirurgicale sur le tétanos traumatique. Tribut académique, *etc.* pp. 19. *Montpellier*, 1817. 4º.
1180. h. 11. (10.)

CAZAZIS (N.) *See* Kazazes.

CAZE (Alphonse) Considérations médicales sur les passions. Thèse, *etc.* pp. 54. *Montpellier*, 1857. 4º.
7379. d. 9. (7.)

CAZE (Jean François) *See* De Lacroix (O.) and Caze (J. F.) Mémoire pour les Français créanciers de l'Espagne. [1818?] 8º.
1141. h. 20. (15.)

—— Les Agraviados d'Espagne suivi de notices sur les hommes qui ont joué un rôle dans les affaires d'Espagne depuis . . . 1823. Par F. C. [i.e. J. F. Caze.] pp. 92. 1827. 8º. *See* C., F.
8042. cc. 25. (3.)

—— Notice sur Alger. pp. 38. *Paris*, 1831. 8º.
1389. i. 56. (3.)

CAZE (Paul)
—— Jean de Coras. Notice historique lue le 16 décembre 1866, à l'ouverture de la conférence des avocats. pp. 36. *Toulouse*, 1867. 8º.
11806. bb. 26. (2.)

CAZE (Pierre) Comparaison des constitutions de la Grande Bretagne et de la France. pp. xiv. 344. *Paris*, 1792. 8º.
F.R. 83. (2.)

CAZE (Pierre)
—— Supplément aux considérations de Mallet-Dupan sur la révolution. pp. 44. [*Paris*,] an 3 [1794]. 8º.
R. 212. (5.)

CAZE (Pierre Jacques) Considérations physiologiques et pathologiques sur l'ostéomalaxie, *etc.* [A thesis.] pp. 24. *Montpellier*, 1819. 4º.
1180. i. 7. (5.)

CAZE (Robert) Les Enfants. L'élève Gendrevin. pp. 336. *Paris*, 1884. 12º.
12510. s. 6.

—— Les Femmes. Grand'mère. pp. 347. *Paris*, 1886. 8º.
12491. n. 22.

—— Les Femmes. La semaine d'Ursule . . . Deuxième édition. pp. 304. *Paris*, 1885. 12º.
12511. s. 6.

—— Les Filles. Femmes à soldats. pp. 284. *Bruxelles*, 1884. 8º.
012550. ccc. 52.

—— Les Filles. Le martyre d'Annil. pp. 288. *Bruxelles*, 1883. 8º.
012550. ccc. 50.

—— Paris vivant. pp. 291. *Paris*, 1885. 8º. **12357. f. 41.**

CAZEAU (René) Les Associations étrangères en France. pp. 196. *Paris*, 1920. 8º.
8228. r. 13.

CAZEAUX (Euryale) *See* Cazeaux (Pierre E.)

CAZEAUX (Jean Paul) Aperçu sur la leucorrhée, *etc.* [A thesis.] pp. 48. *Montpellier*, 1822. 4º. **1181. c. 5. (1.)**

CAZEAUX (Louis) Biographie de l'abbé Ferdinand Muhe . . . Accompagnée de quelques faits relatifs à l'histoire contemporaine de l'église d'Alsace. [With a portrait.] pp. 86. *Strasbourg*, 1865. 8º. **4885. cc. 6.**

—— Essai sur la conservation de la langue allemande en Alsace. pp. 44. *Strasbourg*, 1867. 8º.
12963. cc. 19. (11.)

—— Examen critique du Non possumus de M. A. Schæffer, *etc.* pp. 20. *Strasbourg*, 1870. 8º. **3902. f. 10. (2.)**

CAZEAUX (Pierre) *See* Le Saulnier de Vauhello (H. L. M.) Mémoire sur les attérages des côtes occidentales de France . . . Par M. Le Saulnier de Vauhello . . . assisté de MM. Wissocq, Cazeaux, *etc.* 1833. 4º.
S.323/37.

—— De l'hémorrhagie tocique . . . Thèse, *etc.* pp. 50. *Paris*, 1835. 4º. **1184. f. 18. (1.)**

—— Traité théorique et pratique de l'art des accouchements, comprenant l'histoire des maladies qui peuvent se manifester pendant la grossesse et le travail, et l'indication des soins à donner à l'enfant nouveau-né . . . Deuxième édition. pp. xv. 847. *Paris*, 1845. 8º. **1176. h. 24.**

—— Huitième édition, revue et annotée par S. Tarnier. pp. x [xii]. 1162. *Paris*, 1870. 8º. **7581. e. 17.**

—— Dixième édition, revue et annotée par S. Tarnier. pp. xii. 1178. *Paris*, 1883. 8º. **7580. ee. 13.**

—— A Theoretical and Practical Treatise on Midwifery, including the diseases of pregnancy and parturition . . . Translated from the second French edition, with occasional notes and a copious index, by R. P. Thomas, *etc.* pp. 765. *Lindsay & Blakiston: Philadelphia*, 1850. 8º.
07580. c. 21.

—— Fifth American from the seventh French edition. By W. R. Bullock, *etc.* pp. 1124. *Lindsay & Blakiston: Philadelphia*, 1871. 8º.
07580. i. 29.

—— [Obstetrics: the theory and practice. . . . Seventh edition. Edited and revised . . . with additions . . . by R. J. Hess, *etc.*] pp. 1081. pl. xii. [*H. K. Lewis: London*; [printed in *U.S.A.*,] 1885 [1884].] 8º.
7580. h. 1.

Imperfect; wanting the titlepage.

CAZEAUX (PIERRE EURYALE) *See* PERIODICAL PUBLI-
CATIONS.—*Paris*. Le Magasin pittoresque, publié sous la
direction de MM. E. Cazeaux et E. Charton.
1833, *etc.* 4°.   P.P. **4270.**

—— Du rôle des femmes dans l'agriculture. Esquisse d'un
institut rural féminin, par P. E. C. [i.e. P. E. Cazeaux.]
pp. 196. 1869. 12°. *See* C., P. E.   **1145. b. 12.**

CAZE DE CAUMONT (   ) *Writer on Sport.*
—— Le Sport il y a cinquante ans. pp. 49.   *Paris,*
1905. 8°.   **7922. aa. 65.**

CAZE DE CAUMONT (FRANZ) *See* FRANCE. [*Laws,
etc.*—I.] Bulletin des lois de la République, *etc.* (Table
décennale . . . Rédacteur, M. Franz Caze de Caumont.
Du 1er janvier 1884 au 31 décembre 1893.) [1794, *etc.*] 8°.
                                                 P.P. **1362.**

CAZE DE LA BOVE (ANGÉLIQUE) *See* DUCOS (A.)

CAZEGAS (LUIS) *See* CACEGAS.

CAZELLES (MASARS DE) *See* MASARS DE CAZELLES.

CAZELLES (ÉMILE HONORÉ) *See* BENTHAM (Jeremy)
[*Single Works.*] La Religion naturelle, son influence sur le
bonheur du genre humain, d'après les papiers de J.
Bentham . . . Traduit . . . par M. E. Cazelles.
1875. 12°.   **8469. aaa. 9.**

—— *See* MILL (John S.) L'Assujettisement des femmes. . . .
Traduit . . . par M. E. Cazelles. 1869. 8°.
                                              8415. ccc. 34.

—— *See* SPENCER (Herbert) [*First Principles.*] Les Premiers
principes . . . Traduit . . . par M. E. Cazelles, *etc.*
1883. 8°.   **8462. dd. 10.**

—— *See* SPENCER (Herbert) [*Principles of Biology.*] Principes
de biologie . . . Traduit . . . par M. E. Cazelles, *etc.*
1893, *etc.* 8°.   **8468. l. 11.**

—— *See* SPENCER (Herbert) [*Principles of Sociology.*]
Principes de sociologie . . . Traduit . . . par M. E.
Cazelles. 1896, *etc.* 8°.   **08277. i. 32.**

—— Du traitement de l'ectropion cicatriciel. pp. 100. *Paris,*
1860. 4°. [*Collection des thèses soutenues à la Faculté de
Médecine de Paris.* An 1860. tom. 2.]   **7373. c. 10.**

—— Outline of the Evolution-Philosophy . . . Translated
from the French by the Rev. O. B. Frothingham. With
an appendix by E. L. Youmans. pp. 167.
D. Appleton & Co.: New York, 1890. 8°.   **7006. e. 19.**

CAZELLES (HENRI) Église et état en Allemagne de
Weimar aux premières années du IIIe Reich. pp. 283.
Paris, 1936. 8°.   **20010. cc. 41.**

CAZEMIER (LUKAS JAN) Oud-Egyptiese voorstellingen
aangaande de ziel. Proefschrift, *etc.* pp. 134.
Wageningen, 1930. 8°.
             Dept. of Egyptian & Assyrian Antiquities.

CAZENAVE (ALPHÉE) *See* CAZENAVE (Pierre L. A.)

CAZENAVE (J.) *de Gers.* Réflexions sur quelques maladies
des yeux. Thèse, *etc.* pp. 19. *Paris,* 1837. 4°.
                                              1184. h. 14. (25.)

CAZENAVE (J.) *de Villane d'Ornon.* Considérations
anatomiques, physiologiques, et pathologiques rélatives
à la médecine des enfans; thèse, *etc.* pp. 92.   *Paris,*
1817. 4°.   **1183. d. 11. (18.)**

CAZENAVE (J. B.) Dissertation sur la fièvre adynamique
continue; thèse, *etc.* pp. 33. *Paris,* 1819. 4°.
                                              1183. e. 11. (30.)

CAZENAVE (JULES JACQUES) De quelques infirmités de
la main droite qui s'opposent à ce que les malades puissent
écrire, et du moyen de remédier à ces infirmités, *etc.*
[With a plate.] pp. 37. *Paris,* 1846. 8°.   **782. i. 25.**

—— Ébauche médicale rétrospective sur un nom [that of
Broussais] qui est et qui demeurera célèbre, *etc.* pp. 22.
Paris, 1868. 8°.   [MISSING.]

—— Éloge du docteur de Grateloup de Bordeaux. pp. 35.
Paris, 1862. 8°.   **10663. c. 3.**

—— Histoire abrégée des sondes et des bougies uréthro-
vésicales employées jusqu'à ce jour; description et
appréciation pratique de celles qui ont été inventées, *etc.*
[With a plate.] pp. 51. *Paris,* 1875. 8°.
                                              7306. c. 3. (10.)

—— Histoire de trois lithotrities et de trois tailles bilatérales
exceptionelles. pp. vii. 44. *Paris,* 1856. 8°.
                                              7480. c. 30. (7.)

—— Réflexions générales sur l'emploi du chloroforme dans
les opérations, *etc.* pp. 18. *Paris,* 1861. 8°.
                                              7480. b. 29. (8.)

CAZENAVE (P. J. R.) Essai sur la délivrance, *etc.* [A
thesis.] pp. 16. *Paris,* 1805. 4°.   **1182. g. 4. (22.)**

CAZENAVE (PIERRE LOUIS ALPHÉE) *See* ADELON (N. P.)
Dictionnaire de médecine . . . par Adelon, Béclard . . .
Cazenave, *etc.* 1832, *etc.* 8°.   **773. f. 1–16.**

—— *See* CHAUSIT (J. M.) Traité élémentaire des maladies de
la peau . . . d'après l'enseignement de . . . A. Cazenave,
etc. 1853. 8°.   [MISSING.]

—— Appendice thérapeutique du Codex . . . Édité par
Béchet jeune. pp. 218. *Paris,* 1841. 8°.   **777. d. 32.**

—— Bibliothèque médicale . . . Les gourmes. pp. 58.
Paris, 1873. 8°.   [MISSING.]

—— Compendium des maladies de la peau et de la syphilis.
livr. 1. *Paris,* 1869. 8°.   **7640. h. 29.**
Imperfect; wanting livr. 2.

—— De la décoration humaine; hygiène de la beauté.
pp. iv. 324. *Paris,* 1867. 12°.   **7383. aaa. 10.**

—— [Another edition.] Hygiène de la beauté. De la
décoration humaine. pp. iv. 324. *Paris,* [1884.] 12°.
                                              7404. bbb. 16.

—— Leçons sur les maladies de la peau professées à l'École
de Médecine de Paris, *etc.* pp. 233. pl. 59.   *Paris,*
1845–[56.] fol.   **788. i. 27.**
Published in parts.

—— Maladies de la peau. (Thèse.) pp. 16.   *Paris,*
1827. 4°.   **1183. i. 12. (4.)**

—— Pathologie générale des maladies de la peau. pp. 386.
Paris, 1868. 8°.   **7640. bbb. 12.**

—— Traité des maladies du cuir chevelu, suivi de conseils
hygiéniques sur les soins à donner à la chevelure, *etc.*
pp. viii. 400. pl. VIII. *Paris,* 1850. 8°.   **1187. i. 34.**

—— Diseases of the Human Hair . . . With a description
of an apparatus for fumigating the scalp by T. H. Burgess.
pp. viii. 110. *Henry Renshaw: London,* 1851. 16°.
                                              1186. a. 68.

—— Traité des syphilides ou maladies vénériennes de la
peau, *etc.* pp. 630. *Paris,* 1843. 8°.   **779. h. 51.**

—— Atlas. pl. XII. fol.   **779. l. 16.**

CAZENAVE (PIERRE LOUIS ALPHÉE) and **SCHEDEL** (HENRY EDWARD)

—— Abrégé pratique des maladies de la peau, d'après les auteurs les plus estimés et surtout d'après les documens puisés dans les leçons cliniques de M. le docteur Biett . . . Troisième édition . . . augmentée. pp. lxii. 595. *Paris*, 1838. 8º.
7641. g. 19.

—— Manual of Diseases of the Skin . . . With notes and additions, by Thomas H. Burgess. pp. viii. 320. *Henry Renshaw: London*, 1842. 8º. **1187. a. 34.**

—— Second edition, considerably enlarged and improved. pp. vii. 432. *Henry Renshaw: London*, 1854. 8º.
1188. a. 21.

CAZENAVE DE LACAUSSADE (JULES JEAN JACQUES) De la phlébite en général. pp. 46. *Paris*, 1846. 4º. [*Collection des thèses soutenues à la Faculté de Médecine de Paris*. An 1846. tom. 2.] **7371. f. 16.**

CAZENAVE DE LA ROCHE (ANNE MARIE ÉDOUARD SIMON STYLITE YVON) Louis XVII, ou l'Ôtage de la Révolution, *etc*. pp. 326. *Paris*, 1929. 8º.
10655. a. 12.

CAZENAVE DE LA ROCHE (ÉDOUARD) Coup d'œil sur la paralysie générale des aliénés. pp. 28. *Paris*, 1848. 4º. [*Collection des thèses soutenues à la Faculté de Médecine de Paris*. An 1848. tom. 3.] **7372. b. 6.**

—— Dix-sept années de pratique aux Eaux-Bonnes. pp. 231. *Paris*, 1867. 8º. **7470. dd. 16.**

—— Du climat de l'Espagne sous le rapport médical. pp. 278. *Paris*, 1863. 8º. [MISSING.]

—— Recherches cliniques sur les Eaux-Bonnes. pp. 105. *Paris*, 1854. 8º. **7470. cc. 10.**

—— Recherches sur les offuscations du soleil et les météores cosmiques. (Extrait des Mémoires de l'Académie des Sciences et Lettres de Montpellier.) pp. viii. 80. *Paris*, 1868. 4º. **8560. g. 5. (1.)**

—— Résumé des observations météorologiques faites à la Faculté des Sciences de Montpellier pendant l'année 1867. pp. 11. *Montpellier*, 1868. 8º. **8752. a. 8.**

—— Venise et son climat. pp. 58. *Paris*, 1865. 8º.
[MISSING.]

CAZENEUVE (ALBERT) Les Chemins de fer à l'Exposition Universelle. 4 sér. *Paris*, 1878–81. 8º. **8767. bb. 12.**

—— L'Empire et les partis. Lettres à un ami. pp. ix. 125. *Paris*, 1875. 8º. **8033. e. 1.**

—— La France et les partis. Lettres à un ami. pp. 24. *Toulouse*, 1888. 8º. **8051. e. 38. (4.)**

CAZENEUVE (AUGUSTE) Des fractures de l'extrémité supérieure du tibia par arrachement et de la lenteur de leur consolidation. pp. 52. *Paris*, 1875. 4º. [*Collection des thèses soutenues à la Faculté de Médecine de Paris*. An 1875. tom. 4.] **7374. b.**

CAZENEUVE (B. VALENTIN) Essai sur l'endocardite aiguë; thèse, *etc*. pp. 54. *Paris*, 1836. 4º.
1184. g. 11. (14.)

—— Ulcère simple de l'estomac, *etc*. pp. 24. *Lille*, 1862. 8º. **7440. aa. 40. (5.)**

CAZENEUVE (H. J.) *See* BARUIKIN (V. A.) and CAZENEUVE (H. J.) Le Foyer endémique de choléra de Rostov-sur-le-Don, *etc*. 1925. 8º. **U.N.o.84.(3.)**

CAZENEUVE (H. J.)

—— Organisation of the Public Health Services in Latvia. pp. 72. 1925. 8º. *See* LEAGUE OF NATIONS.—*Health Organisation*. **U.N.o.84.(5.)**

CAZENEUVE (HENRI) Quelques considérations sur le traitement des rétrécissements organiques de l'urètre et sur la périnéotomie plus particulièrement. Thèse, *etc*. pp. 46. *Montpellier*, 1857. 4º. **7379. d. 8. (10.)**

CAZENEUVE (J. E.) De l'hydrocèle de la tunique vaginale. Thèse, *etc*. pp. 47. *Montpellier*, 1857. 4º.
7379. d. 7. (6.)

CAZENEUVE (JEAN MICHEL) Mémoire justificatif de l'innocence du frère Léotade . . . condamné aux travaux forcés à perpétuité . . . comme auteur du viol et du meurtre de Cécile Combettes, *etc*. [With plans.] pp. xii. 440. *Toulouse*, 1859. 8º. **5405. c. 9.**

—— Plaidoyer prononcé . . . devant la Cour royale d'Agen, pour Dame Bernarde Émilie Lecomte . . . contre le sieur de Sainte-Colombe . . . appelant d'un jugement qui le condamne à des dommages-intérêts pour rapt de séduction. pp. 160. *Toulouse*, 1844. 8º. **1131. f. 27.**

—— Relation historique de la procédure et des débats de la Cour d'assises de la Haute-Garonne, dans la cause de Louis Bonafous . . . condamné pour viol et assassinat sur la personne de Cécile Combettes, aux travaux forcés à perpétuité, *etc*. [With plans.] pp. 692. 104. *Toulouse*, 1848. 8º. **5423. b. 1.**

—— [Another copy.] **5423. cc. 12.**

—— Démonstration de l'innocence de Louis Bonafous frère Léotade . . . condamné, pour viol et assassinat sur la personne de Cécile Combettes, aux travaux forcés à perpétuité . . . faisant suite à la Relation et l'abrégé historique de la procédure et des débats aux fins d'une demande en réhabilitation de sa mémoire, *etc*. [With plans.] pp. xi. 354. *Toulouse*, 1855. 8º. **5424. d. 10.**

CAZENEUVE (JEAN PIERRE) Procès des Congrégations [represented by J. P. Cazeneuve and others] contre Léo Taxil. ⸖ Le célibat ecclésiastique et l'enseignement religieux. Plaidoyer pour Léo Taxil par Eugène Delattre . . . Compte rendu complet du procès. pp. 79. *Paris*, [1880.] 8º. ⸖ [*i.e.* G. Jogand-Pagès.] **5424. aaa. 21.**

CAZENEUVE (JOHN) and **WITHERIDGE** (WILLIAM) A True State of the Case, relative to the dispute about the Parish Register Book, of Chatham in Kent. To which is added, an answer to a . . . . charge made against the late churchwardens of that parish, in a pamphlet lately published by the minister (Walter Frank), intituled, "Letters and instruments relative to the dispute, &c." pp. 36. *John Townson: Chatham*, 1766. 8º.
10368. e. 5. (2.)

CAZENEUVE (JOSEPH) Dissertation sur l'hystérie. Tribut académique, *etc*. pp. 24. *Montpellier*, 1818. 4º.
1180. i. 2. (6.)

CAZENEUVE (MARIUS) A la cour de Madagascar. Magie et diplomatie. pp. 342. *Paris*, 1896. 8º. **010097. f. 10.**

CAZENEUVE (PAUL) Les Colorants de la houille au point de vue toxicologique et hygiénique . . . Affaire de la succursale de la B. Anilin & Soda Fabrik à Neuville-sur-Saône. pp. 169. *Lyon*, 1887. 8º. **7391. g. 9.**

—— La Coloration des vins par les couleurs de la houille. Méthodes analytiques, *etc*. pp. viii. 318. *Paris*, 1886. 12º.
[MISSING.]

CAZENEUVE (PAUL)

—— La Génération spontanée, d'après les livres d'Henri Baker et de Joblot, *etc.* pp. 24. *Lyon*, 1893. 8°.
8709. c. 12. (5.)

CAZENEUVE (PAUL DE) and **HARAINE** (FRANÇOIS) Les États-Unis de Vénézuéla. pp. xv. 300. *Paris*, 1888. 8°.
10481. b. 40.

CAZENOVE AND CO.

—— Cazenove & Co., 1785–1955. [For the most part by Albert A. Martin. With plates.] pp. 16. [*London*, 1954.] 8°.
8290. ff. 20.

CAZENOVE (ANNIE) Aunt Dorothy's Story. pp. 60. *S.P.C.K.: London*, [1881.] 16°.
[MISSING.]

—— Fragments in Prose and Verse. Collected and arranged by A. Cazenove. pp. 48. *Griffith & Farran: London*, 1883. 16°.
4400. e. 28.

—— Madge Allerton. A story. pp. viii. 320. *Walter Smith: London*, 1882. 8°.
12643. aaa. 13.

—— Thoughts and Verses, collected and arranged by A. Cazenove. pp. 64. *Griffith, Farran & Co.: London*, 1884. 32°.
12357. a. 25.

—— Whispers of Love and Wisdom. Collected and arranged by A. Cazenove. With a preface by C. M. Yonge. pp. 68. *Griffith & Farran: London*, 1882. 16°.
4400. e. 25.

CAZENOVE (ARTHUR) The Beloved Disciple. [A sermon.] *See* FOWLE (Edmund) Plain Preaching for a Year, *etc.* vol. 3. 1873. 12°.
4463. de. 2.

—— The Duty of Trusting. [A sermon.] *See* FOWLE (Edmund) Plain Preaching for a Year, *etc.* vol. 2. 1873. 12°.
4463. de. 2.

—— Life and Death of S. Stephen. [A sermon.] *See* FOWLE (Edmund) Plain Preaching for a Year, *etc.* vol. 1. 1873. 12°.
4463. de. 2.

—— Lord Strafford. A lecture, *etc.* pp. 32. *David Batten: London*, 1860. 8°.
10816. de. 18. (2.)

CAZENOVE (ARTHUR QUIRIN MAURICE DE) *See* CAZENOVE D'ARLENS (Constance de) Deux mois à Paris et à Lyon sous le Consulat. Journal de Mᵐᵉ de Cazenove d'Arlens . . . Publié . . . par A. de Cazenove. 1903. 8°.
Ac. 6885. c/25.

—— Jean Dumas, conseiller et chambellan du Roi. 1897. *See* NÎMES.—*Académie de Nîmes.* Mémoires, *etc.* sér. 7 tom. 20. 1832, *etc.* 8°.
Ac. 330/2.

CAZENOVE (BERNARD DE LERISSON)

—— Grouse Shooting and Moor Management . . . Illustrated from photographs. pp. 144. *Country Life: London*, 1936. 8°.
07908.f.33.

CAZENOVE (FLORA) Just a Simple Gardening Book. pp. xiv. 142. *Hodder & Stoughton: London*, [1913.] 8°.
07029. eee. 47.

CAZENOVE (HENRY)

—— A Narrative in two parts: written in 1812. [On a journey mainly through France, Switzerland and Greece in the years 1803–11. By H. Cazenove. With a map.] pp. 238. 1813. 8°. *See* NARRATIVE.
10105. d. 1.

CAZENOVE (JOHN) *See* MALTHUS (Thomas R.) Definitions in Political Economy . . . A new edition, with a preface, notes, and supplementary remarks by J. Cazenove. 1853. 8°.
8205. a. 11.

—— Considerations on the Accumulation of Capital, *etc.* [By J. Cazenove.] pp. vii. 64. 1822. 8°. *See* CONSIDERATIONS.
8229. aaaa. 21. (1.)

—— An Elementary Treatise on Political Economy, *etc.* pp. viii. 150. *A. H. Baily & Co.: London*, 1840. 8°.
8207. f. 5. (6.)

—— The Evidence that would have been given by Mʳ —— [i.e. J. Cazenove] . . . before the Committee of Secrecy appointed to inquire into the expediency of renewing the Bank Charter. pp. 22. 1832. 8°. *See* ENGLAND.—*Bank of England.* [*Appendix.*]
8229. aaaa. 21. (4.)

—— The Money Crisis. [By J. Cazenove.] pp. 16. 1847. 8°. *See* MONEY CRISIS.
8229. aaaa. 21. (12.)

—— Outlines of Political Economy ; being a plain and short view of the laws relating to the production, distribution and consumption of wealth, *etc.* [By J. Cazenove.] pp. 161. 1832. 8°. *See* OUTLINES.
T. 1410. (4.)

—— Questions respecting the National Debt and Taxation stated and answered. pp. 44. *J. M. Richardson: London*, 1829. 8°.
T. 1275. (4.)

—— [Another copy.] MS. NOTES.
8229. aaaa. 22. (5.)

—— A Selection of curious and entertaining Games at Chess, *etc.* [By J. Cazenove.] ff. 87. 1817. 8°. *See* SELECTION.
[MISSING.]

—— Thoughts on a few Subjects of Political Economy pp. 102. *Simpkin, Marshall & Co.: London*, 1859. 8°.
8205. c. 54.

—— Supplement to Thoughts on a few Subjects of Political Economy. pp. 54. *Simpkin, Marshall & Co.: London*, 1861. 8°.
8205. c. 55.

CAZENOVE (JOHN GIBSON) *See* PART. "Part of the Price." With a preface by the Rev. Chancellor Cazenove. 1883. 8°.
[MISSING.]

—— Historic Aspects of the à priori Argument concerning the Being and Attributes of God. Being four lectures . . . with appendices, *etc.* pp. x. 150. *Macmillan & Co.: London*, 1886. 8°.
4373. h. 25.

—— Inconsistency: real and apparent. A sermon preached before the University of Oxford, *etc.* pp. 36. *Rivingtons: London*, 1866. 8°.
4477. bb. 73. (7.)

—— Mahometanism. An article reprinted from "The Christian Remembrancer," *etc.* pp. 128. *J. & C. Mozley: London*, 1856. 8°.
4505. a. 8.

—— Modern Theism. Being brief notes upon a recent publication ("Christian Theology and Modern Scepticism"), by the Duke of Somerset K.G. Reprinted from the Guardian. pp. 21. *William Ridgway: London*, 1872. 8°.
4017. ff. 3.

—— On Certain Characteristics of Holy Scripture, with special reference to an essay on the interpretation of Scripture [by Benjamin Jowett] contained in "Essays and Reviews." Reprinted, with additions, from "The Christian Remembrancer," *etc.* pp. 71. *J. & C. Mozley: London*, 1861. 8°.
4373. cc. 51. (2.)

—— Possibilities of Union. A sermon, *etc.* pp. 27. *J. & C. Mozley: London*, 1865. 8°.
4478. cc. 67. (11.)

CAZENOVE (JOHN GIBSON)

—— St. Hilary of Poitiers and St. Martin of Tours. pp. viii. 269. *S.P.C.K.: London*, 1883. 8º. [*The Fathers for English Readers.*] **4421.a.46.**

—— Some Aspects of the Reformation. An essay suggested by Dr. Littledale's lecture on "Innovations." pp. 198. *William Ridgway: London*, 1869. 8º. **4570. bb. 7.**

—— Universalism and Eternal Punishment. A theological essay . . . Reprinted, with additions, from the Christian Remembrancer, *etc.* pp. 72. *J. & C. Mozley: London*, 1863. 8º. **4373. bb. 48. (6.)**

—— Versatility. A sermon preached before the University of Oxford, *etc.* pp. 30. *J. H. & J. Parker: Oxford & London*, 1859. 8º. **4477. c. 16.**

CAZENOVE (LÉONCE DE) Considérations sur les sociétés protectrices des animaux, *etc.* pp. 203. *Lyon*, 1865. 8º. **8425. c. 3.**

—— La Guerre et l'humanité au 19e siècle. pp. 412. *Paris,* [1876.] 8º. **7686.dd.5.**

CAZENOVE (QUIRIN JULES RAOUL DE) *See* GENEVA. Les Criées faites en la citée de Genève l'an mil cinq cent soixante . . . Réimpression . . . accompagnée d'une notice par R. de Cazenove. 1879. 4º. **12330. i. 16.**

—— Généalogie de la maison de Rapin de la Chaudane, en Maurienne, en France & en Prusse, 1250–1864, suivie de la postérité par alliances de P. de Rapin Sgr de Thoyras, dressée au 1er janvier 1792, continuée jusqu'au 1er janvier 1864. pp. cclix. *Lyon*, 1865. 4º. **9904. l. 18.** *One of an edition of fifty copies.*

—— Le Peintre Adrien van der Kabel et ses contemporains. Discours de réception, *etc.* 1889. *See* LYONS.—*Académie des Sciences, Belles-Lettres et Arts.* Mémoires, *etc.* Classe des lettres. tom. 26. 1845, *etc.* 8º. **Ac. 364.**

—— Le Peintre Van der Kabel et ses contemporains, avec le catalogue de son œuvre peinte et gravée, 1631–1705 [With a portrait.] pp. 64. 64. *Lyon*, 1888. 8º. [MISSING.]

—— Rapin-Thoyras, sa famille, sa vie et ses oeuvres. Étude historique suivie de généalogies. [With a portrait.] *Paris*, 1866. 4º. **10660. i. 8.**

CAZENOVE (RAOUL DE) *See* CAZENOVE (Quirin J. R. de)

CAZENOVE D'ARLENS (CONSTANCE DE) Alfrede, ou le Manoir de Warwick. [By C. de Cazenove d'Arlens.] 2 vol. 1794. 12º. *See* ALFREDE. **12517. a. 11.**

—— Le Château de Bothwell, ou l'Héritier. Par l'auteur du Manoir de Warwick [i.e. C. de Cazenove d'Arlens]. 3 tom. 1819. 12º. *See* BOTHWELL, *Château de.* **12808. pp. 6.**

—— Deux mois à Paris et à Lyon sous le Consulat. Journal de Mme de Cazenove d'Arlens (février-avril, 1803). Publié . . . par A. de Cazenove. pp. xxxvi. 176. 1903. 8º. *See* PARIS.—*Société d'Histoire Contemporaine.* **Ac. 6885. c/25.**

CAZENTRE (J. ÉMILE) Considérations sur la nature, le siége et le traitement du choléra-morbus épidémique; thèse, *etc.* pp. 27. *Paris*, 1833. 4º. **1184. e. 14. (2.)**

CAZERES (FRANCISCO DE) *See* CACERES.

CAZERES (RODRIGO DE) *See* ALTAMIRANO Y LOAYSA (P.) *Begin.* Don P. Altamirano y Loaisa suplica a V. M., *etc.* [A petition on the claims of R. de Cazeres to the inheritance of his father.] [1630?] fol. **1324. i. 2. (74.)**

CAZERES E FARIA (LEANDRO DOREA) *See* DOREA CACERES E FARIA.

CAZERES PACHECO (ANTONIO) *See* CACERES PATIECUS (Antonius).

CAZES (ALBERT) *See* DU TROUSSET DE VALINCOUR (J. B. H.) Lettres à Madame la marquise * * * sur le sujet de la Princesse de Clèves. Introduction et notes d'A. Cazes, *etc.* 1925. 8º. **012201. c. 1/27.**

—— *See* MOTIER (M. M.) *Countess de La Fayette.* Œuvres complètes de Madame de Lafayette. (La Princesse de Clèves. Texte établi et présenté par A. Cazes.) 1934, *etc.* 8º. **W.P. 10689/2.**

—— Pierre Bayle. Sa vie, ses idées, son influence, son œuvre, *etc.* pp. xxii. 264. *Paris*, 1905. 8º. **010662. g. 65.**

CAZES (ANDRÉ) *See* GRIMM (F. M. von) *Baron.* Correspondance inédite, 1794–1801, du baron Grimm au comte de Findlater. [Edited by A. Cazes.] 1934. 8º. **010920. b. 19.**

—— Grimm et les Encyclopédistes. pp. 407. *Paris,* 1933. 8º. **10709. h. 3.**

CAZES (B. A. JOSEPH) Du bubon vénérien de la région inguinale envisagé surtout au point de vue du traitement local. Thèse, *etc.* pp. 82. *Montpellier*, 1874. 4º. **7379. k. 2. (10.)**

CAZÈS (D.) Essai sur l'histoire des Israélites de Tunisie depuis les temps les plus reculés jusqu'à l'établissement du protectorat de la France en Tunisie. pp. 211. *Paris,* 1888. 12º. **4033. de. 43.**

CAZES (E. BRIVES) *See* BRIVES CAZES.

CAZES (ÉLIE DE) *Ancien Sous-Préfet.* Le XXIV février et l'ouvrage de M. Capefigue, avec un mot sur l'histoire de la Révolution de 1848 de M. A. Lamartine. pp. 42. *Paris, Toulouse*, 1849. 8º. **9077. g. 10.**

CAZES (ÉLIE DE) *Duke. See* DECAZES.

CAZES (ÉMILIEN NOËL LAURENT) Le Château de Versailles et ses dépendances. L'histoire et l'art. [With illustrations and plans.] pp. xii. 735. *Versailles*, 1910. 8º. **010171. l. 7.**

CAZES (FÉLIX) Essai sur la paralysie . . . Thèse, *etc.* pp. 33. *Paris*, 1824. 4º. **1183. h. 2. (3.)**

CAZES (FRANÇOIS ISIDORE) Essai sur la phthisie pulmonaire; thèse, *etc.* pp. 28. *Paris*, 1824. 4º. **1183. h. 8. (7.)**

CAZES (FRANÇOIS JOSEPH MARIE FRÉDÉRIC) Généralités de l'hérédité des maladies. pp. 38. *Paris*, 1857. 4º. [*Collection des thèses soutenues à la Faculté de Médecine de Paris. An 1857. tom. 3.*] **7373. a. 3.**

CAZES (FRANÇOIS XAVIER OVIDE) Considérations générales sur le cancer, suivie, d'un essai sur le squirrhe du foie. Tribut académique, *etc.* pp. 44. *Montpellier*, 1841. 4º. **1182. c. 10. (3.)**

CAZES (FRIX) Essai sur le panaris et ses différentes espèces, *etc.* pp. 27. *Montpellier*, 1815. 8º. **1180. h. 2. (14.)**

CAZES (J. FRIX) Quelques réflexions sur le scorbut; Tribut académique, *etc.* pp. 17. *Montpellier*, 1821. 4º. **1181. c. 2. (13.)**

CAZES (JEAN) Versailles et ses fantômes. Conférence. *etc.* pp. 58. *Hanoi*, 1939. 8º. **010171. s. 8.**

CAZÈS (JEAN BARTHÉLEMY) Projet de décret présenté à l'Assemblée nationale, au nom du Comité de division, sur la circonscription des paroisses de l'entier département des Basses-Pyrénées, *etc.* (Amendemens proposés au projet de décret sur la circonscription des paroisses du département des Basses-Pyrénées.) 2 pt. *Paris*, 1792. 8º. **F.R. 157. (25.)**

CAZÈS (Jean Barthélemy)

—— Projet de décret présenté au nom du Comité de division . . . sur la circonscription des paroisses de la ville d'Amboise, le 24 juillet 1792, *etc.* pp. 3. [*Paris,* 1792.] 8°. F.R. **157. (23.)**

—— Projet de décret sur la circonscription des cures de la ville de Vatan, présenté au nom du Comité de division . . . le 29 mai 1792. [*Paris,* 1792.] *s. sh.* 8°. F.R. **157. (21.)**

—— Projet de décret sur la circonscription des paroisses de Chaumont, présenté . . . au nom du Comité de division . . . le 15 janvier 1792. pp. 2. *Paris,* [1792.] *s. sh.* 8°. F.R. **157. (18.)**

—— Projet de décret sur la circonscription des paroisses de la ville de Lagni . . . présenté à la séance du premier mai 1792 . . . au nom du Comité de division, *etc.* pp. 2. [*Paris,* 1792.] *s. sh.* 8°. F.R. **157. (20.)**

—— Projets de décrets sur la distraction des municipalités de Sainte-Eulalie, Loupiac, Saint-Christophe, Saint-Martin-Cantalès, Saint-Projet et Saint Chamand, du district d'Aurillac, pour être réunies à celui de Mauriac, département du Cantal, présentés le 30 janvier 1792 . . . au nom du Comité de division, *etc.* pp. 10. *Paris,* [1792.] 8°. F.R. **109. (13.)**

—— Rapport et projet de décret . . . présentés au nom de la Commission extraordinaire des douze et du Comité de division . . . sur la translation provisoire de l'administration du district de la ville de Montmédi en celle de Stenai. Le 27 juillet 1792. pp. 4. *Paris,* [1792.] 8°. F.R. **111. (13.)**

—— Rapport et projet de décret, présentés . . . au nom du Comité de division, sur le nombre et le placement des notaires publics du département du Haut-Rhin ; le 20 juillet 1792, *etc.* pp. 6. [*Paris,* 1792.] 8°. F.R. **189. (28.)**

—— Rapport et projet de décret présentés . . . au nom du Comité de division, sur les communes de Chaume et de Jours, département de la Côte-d'Or, le 31 mai, 1792. pp. 3. *Paris,* [1792.] 8°. F.R. **110. (14.)**

—— Rapport et projet de décret, présentés . . . sur le nombre & le placement des notaires dans le département du Calvados au nom du Comité de division, le 22 juillet 1792, *etc.* pp. 7. [*Paris,* 1792.] 8°. F.R. **189. (20.)**

—— Rapport et projet de décret, sur l'église & l'oratoire de la paroisse de Saint-Pierre de Toulouse, fait et présenté . . . au nom du Comité de division . . . mars 1792. pp. 4. [*Paris,* 1792.] 8°. F.R. **157. (19.)**

—— Rapport et projet de décret, sur l'établissement d'un second juge-de-paix à Bergerac, présentés . . . le 20 juillet 1792, *etc.* pp. 4. [*Paris,* 1792.] 8°. F.R. **185. (5.)**

—— Rapport et projet de décret, sur l'établissement d'un second juge-de-paix dans la ville de Bayonne . . . du 4 juillet 1792, *etc.* pp. 4. [*Paris,* 1792.] 8°. F.R. **185. (4.)**

—— Rapport et projet de décret sur la contestation élevée entre les départemens de Rhône-&-Loire & de la Haute-Loire, à raison de la réunion définitive des deux communes de Riotord et de Saint-Ferréol, à l'un ou à l'autre de ces deux départemens, fait et présenté . . . au nom du Comité de division . . . le 8 mars 1792. pp. 31. *Paris,* 1792. 8°. F.R. **109. (40.)**

—— [Another copy.] F. **1217. (11.)**

CAZÈS (Jean Barthélemy)

—— Rapport et projet de décret sur la pétition de la ville de Brioude, relative à l'emplacement du cimetière de sa paroisse, *etc.* pp. 3. [*Paris,* 1792.] 8°. F.R. **157. (24.)**

—— Rapport et projet de décret sur la réunion des communes de Segrois et Saint-Vivant à celle de Vergy . . . présentés . . . le 20 juillet 1792, *etc.* pp. 6. [*Paris,* 1792.] 8°. F.R. **111. (30.)**

—— Rapport et projet de décret, sur le nombre & le placement des notaires publics du département des Basses-Pyrénées ; présentés . . . au nom du Comité de division . . . juin 1792. pp. 8. [*Paris,* 1792.] 8°. F.R. **189. (18.)**

—— Rapport présenté à l'Assemblée nationale, au nom du Comité de division, sur le nombre & le placement des notaires publics, établis dans le département de la Loire-inférieure . . . le 29 mai 1792. pp. 8. *Paris,* 1792. 8°. F.R. **189. (31.)**

—— Rapport sur la démarcation des limites du département de Paris, & de celui de Seine & Oise, du côté de Saint-Cloud, fait au nom du Comité de division . . . le 24 juin 1792, *etc.* pp. 11. *Paris,* 1792. 8°. F. **626. (19.)**

—— Rapport sur le traitement des vicaires desservans et des curés ou vicaires qui font, par le Bis-in-die, un double service dans deux églises, *etc.* pp. 7. [*Paris,* 1792.] 8°. F.R. **157. (22.)**

CAZES (Jules) Quelques mots sur la cataracte. Thèse, *etc.* pp. 38. *Montpellier,* 1840. 4°. **1181. i. 21. (15.)**

CAZES (Julien) Dissertation sur la néphrite, *etc.* pp. 19. *Paris,* 1822. 4°. **1183. g. 6. (8.)**

CAZES (L. E.) Essai sur le rhumatisme aigu, *etc.* [A thesis.] pp. 25. *Montpellier,* 1815. 4°. **1180. h. 5. (1.)**

CAZES (Léon) De la trachéotomie dans le croup chez les enfants. pp. 36. *Paris,* 1860. 4°. [*Collection des thèses soutenues à la Faculté de Médecine de Paris.* An 1860. tom. 2.] **7373. c. 10.**

CAZES (Noël) De l'otorrhée. Thèse, *etc.* pp. 44. *Montpellier,* 1869. 4°. **7379. h. 11. (9.)**

CAZES (Paul de) *See* Quebec, *Province of.* Code scolaire de la province de Québec . . . Préparé par P. de Cazes. 1899. 8°. [missing.]

—— Manuel de l'instituteur catholique de la province de Québec . . . Édition nouvelle contenant le programme d'études, les règlements concernant l'examen pour les brevets de capacités et la loi de pension de retraite. pp. 156. *Montréal,* 1905. 8°. **8385. e. 13.**

—— Manuel des commissaires et syndics d'écoles de la province de Québec. pp. viii. 156. *Québec,* 1908. 8°. **8385. e. 14.**

—— Notes sur le Canada . . . Nouvelle édition. pp. 235. *Québec,* 1880. 12°. **10470. aa. 34.**

—— Le Petit manuel canadien. "Notes sur le Canada" augmentées. pp. 294. *Québec,* 1884. 8°. **10470. aa. 28.**

CAZES (Romain) Étude sur les adhérences du cœur. pp. 36. *Paris,* 1875. 4°. [*Collection des thèses soutenues à la Faculté de Médecine de Paris.* An 1875. tom. 4.] **7374. b.**

CAZES D'AIX (J. A.) and **BÉRARD** (J.) Histoire de l'art. Peinture. École française. pp. 203. *Paris,* 1892. 8°. [missing.]

CAZET (Cl.) Du mode de filiation des racines sémitiques et de l'inversion. pp. 107. *Paris,* 1882. 8°. **12902. f. 4.**

—— Généalogies des racines sémitiques. pp. xi. 243. *Paris,* 1886. 8°. **12903. f. 27.**

CAZIMIR, *Duke de.* *See* JOHN CASIMIR, *Count Palatine of the Rhine.*

CAZIMIR (OTILIA) Fluturi de noapte. Poezii. pp. 120. *Bucureşti*, [1926.] 8°.   **011586. bbb. 22.**

CAZIN (ACHILLE) La Chaleur, *etc.* pp. iii. 375.   *Paris*, 1867. 12°.   **8715. aaa. 42.**

—— The Phenomena and Laws of Heat . . . Translated and edited by Elihu Rich, *etc.* pp. xi. 265. *Sampson Low & Co.: London*, 1868. 8°.   **8715. aa. 40.**

—— Die Wärme . . . Deutsch bearbeitet. Herausgegeben durch Prof. Dr. Phil. Carl. pp. vi. 295.   *München*, 1870. 8°. [*Naturkräfte.* Bd. 3.]   **8707. ccc.**

—— L'Étincelle électrique, *etc.* pp. 315. *Paris*, 1876. 8°.   **8756. de. 8.**

—— Les Forces physiques, *etc.* pp. iv. 292. *Paris*, 1869. 8°.   **8705. bbb. 5.**

—— Traité théorique et pratique des piles électriques . . . Annoté et publié par M. Alfred Angot. pp. vi. 311. *Paris*, 1881. 8°.   **8756. de. 18.**

CAZIN (BERTHE) *See* MALO (H.) Critique sentimentale. Souvenirs sur les Cazins, *etc.* [With portraits.] 1922. 8°.   **10656. aaa. 14.**

CAZIN (CHARLES) *See* CAZIN (Jean C.)

CAZIN (FRANÇOIS JOSEPH) Monographie médico-pratique et bibliographique de la belladone. [With a plate.] pp. 62. *Paris*, 1856. 8°.   **7509. e. 8.**

—— Traité pratique et raisonné des plantes médicinales indigènes . . . Deuxième édition considérablement augmentée, *etc.* pp. xiv. 1076. *Paris*, 1858. 8°.

   —— Atlas. pl. XL. *Paris*, 1858. 8°.   **7030. h. 13.**

CAZIN (FRANÇOIS SIMON) Les Mémoires d'un médecin. pp. 251. *Vire*, 1864. 12°.   **12515. bbb. 7.**

CAZIN (FRIEDRICH) Offener Brief an die deutschen Eisenbahn-Verwaltungen in Angelegenheit einiger Verbesserungen im Güter-Verkehr. pp. 16.   *Leipzig*, 1865. 8°.   **8235. h. 50. (8.)**

CAZIN (HENRY) Étude anatomique et pathologique . . . sur les diverticules de l'intestin. [With a plate.] pp. 114. *Paris*, 1862. 4°. [*Collection des thèses soutenues à la Faculté de Médecine de Paris.* An 1862. tom. 2.]   **7373. d. 13.**

CAZIN (HUBERT MARTIN) *See* CAZINOPHILE. Cazin, sa vie et ses éditions. 1863. 12°.   **11900. a. 9.**

   —— —— 1876. 16°.   **11900. a. 2.**

—— *See* LIVRES-BIJOUX. Livres-Bijoux, précurseurs des Cazins, *etc.* [1885.] 12°.   **11899. aa. 8.**

—— *See* PERIODICAL PUBLICATIONS.—*Paris.* Bulletin du cazinophile, *etc.* 1880. 18°.   **011903. g. 9.**

—— Bibliographie du petit-format dit Cazin. pp. 72. *Paris*, 1877. 12°.   **11899. bb. 6.**

—— Manuel du Cazinophile. Le petit-format à figures, collection parisienne in-18—vraie collection de Cazin. pp. 178. *Paris*, 1878. 12°.   **11902. aaa. 2.**

CAZIN (J. M. MICHEL) *See* MALO (H.) Critique sentimentale. Souvenirs sur les Cazin, *etc.* [With a portrait.] 1922. 8°.   **10656. aaa. 14.**

CAZIN (JEAN BAPTISTE LOUIS) A l'Assemblée électorale de 1792. (La nécessité d'appeler des artistes &c. à la Convention nationale.) [*Paris*, 1792.] *s. sh.* 8°.   **F. 1208. (24.)**

CAZIN (JEAN BAPTISTE LOUIS)

—— Notice d'une jolie collection de tableaux et dessins, la plupart modernes, et provenant de la succession de feu M. Cazin . . . qui seront . . . vendus . . . les . . . 22 et . . . 23 (mars 1824), *etc.* pp. 12. MS. PRICES. *Paris*, 1824. 8°.   **562. e. 55. (23.)**

CAZIN (JEAN CHARLES) *See* MALO (H.) Critique sentimentale. Souvenirs sur les Cazin, *etc.* [With a portrait.] 1922. 8°.   **10656. aaa. 14.**

CAZIN (JEANNE) Un Drame dans la montagne . . . Ouvrage illustré . . . par G. Vuillier. pp. 273. *Paris*, 1882. 8°.   **12206. m. 12.**

—— L'Enfant des Alpes . . . Ouvrage illustré . . . par Tofani. pp. 273. *Paris*, 1886 [1885]. 8°. **12206. m. 11.**

—— Histoire d'un pauvre petit . . . Ouvrage illustré . . . par Tofani. pp. 278. *Paris*, 1884. 8°.   **12206. m. 13.**

—— Les Orphelins bernois. Ouvrage illustré . . . par J. Girardet. pp. 263. *Paris*, 1894. 8°.   **012550. ee. 18.**

—— Perlette . . . Ouvrage illustré de 56 gravures d'après les dessins de Myrbach. pp. 331. *Paris*, 1887. 8°.   **12206. m. 10.**

—— Les Petits montagnards . . . Ouvrage illustré . . . par G. Vuillier. pp. 303. *Paris*, 1881. 8°.   **12810. bb. 1.**

—— Les Saltimbanques ; scènes de la montagne . . . Ouvrage illustré . . . par Eug. Girardet. pp. 320. *Paris*, 1888. 8°.   **12206. m. 9.**

CAZIN (MARIE) *See* MALO (H.) Critique sentimentale. Souvenirs sur les Cazin, *etc.* [With a portrait.] 1922. 8°.   **10656. aaa. 14.**

CAZIN (MAURICE) La Cure solaire des blessures de guerre (Méthode Rollier). 9 figures originales. pp. 86. *Paris*, 1917. 8°.   [MISSING.]

—— Notes cliniques et thérapeutiques de chirurgie de guerre. pp. 95. *Paris*, 1916. 8°.   **07482. l. 16.**

—— Deuxième édition. 57 figures originales. pp. 172. *Paris*, 1917. 8°.   **07481. f. 40.**

CAZIN (MICHEL) *See* CAZIN (J. M. M.)

CAZIN (PAUL) *See* PADEREWSKI (I. J.) *Prime Minister of Poland.* A la mémoire de Frédéric Chopin. Discours, *etc.* (Traduction P. Cazin.) 1911. 8°.   **7895. s. 5. (3.)**

—— *See* PASEK (Jan C.) Les Mémoires de J.-C. Pasek . . . Traduits et commentés par P. Cazin. [1922.] 8°.   **010795. aaa. 24.**

—— *See* REYMONT (W. S.) L'Apostolat du knout en Pologne. Notes de voyage . . . Traduites . . . par P. Cazin. 1912. 8°.   **010291. e. 2.**

—— *See* TUWIM (J.) La Locomotive. Le navet. La radio des oiseaux . . . Adapté . . . par P. Cazin, *etc.* [1939.] 8°.   **12815. aa. 34.**

—— L'Alouette de Pâques. [Tales and sketches.] pp. 254. *Paris*, 1924. 8°.   **012547. ccc. 62.**

—— Le Bestiaire des deux Testaments. pp. 207.   *Paris*, 1928. 8°.   **012305. k. 42.**

—— Décadi, ou la Pieuse enfance. pp. 279. *Paris*, 1921. 8°.   **012547. b. 41.**

—— L'Hôtellerie du Bacchus sans tête. pp. 236.   *Paris*, 1925. 8°.   **012551. ee. 80.**

CAZIN (Paul)

—— L'Humaniste à la guerre. Hauts de Meuse, 1915. pp. 249. *Paris*, 1920. 8°.   **9081. b. 3.**

—— Lubies. pp. iv. 260. *Paris*, 1927. 8°.   **12515. r. 11.**

—— La Tapisserie des jours. (Histoire de ma vie au courant de toute une année.) pp. ix. 240. *Paris*, 1934. 8°.
10655. ppp. 22.

CAZINOPHILE. Cazin, sa vie et ses éditions, par un Cazinophile [i.e. C. A. Brissart-Binet]. pp. 245. *Cazinopolis* [*Rheims*], 1863. 18°.   **11900. a. 9.**

—— Réimpression de l'édition de 1863. pp. 266. *Cazinopolis* [*Châlons-sur-Marne*], 1876. 16°.
11900. a. 2.

—— Manuel du Cazinophile. Le petit-format à figures, collection parisienne in-18—vraie collection de Cazin. 1878. 12°. *See* CAZIN (H. M.)   **11902. aaa. 2.**

CAZIOT (Eugène) *See* LOCARD (E. A. A.) and CAZIOT (E.) Conchyliologie française. Les coquilles marines des côtes de Corse. 1900. 8°.   **7299. dd. 3.**

—— Étude sur la faune des mollusques vivants terrestres et fluviatiles de l'île de Corse. pp. 354. 14. pl. II. *Bastia*, 1902. 8°. [*Bulletin de la Société des Sciences Historiques & Naturelles de la Corse.* fasc. 266–269.]   **Ac. 2861.**
The date on the wrapper is 1903.

—— Historique du 1er Régiment de Pontonniers . . . d'après les archives du Corps, *etc.* pp. 303. 1890. 8°. *See* FRANCE.—*Army.—Pontonniers, 1er Régiment.*   **8833. g. 3.**

CAZIRE, *pseud.* [i.e. ELIZABETH SHELLEY.] *See* VICTOR, *pseud.* [i.e. P. B. Shelley], and CAZIRE, *pseud.* Original Poetry by Victor and Cazire. 1810. 8°.   Ashley **4030.**

CAZIS (Jules Paul Victor de) *See* DECAZIS.

CAZIS (Roseline de) Mehemed-Mourad v, ou le Réveil de la Turquie. [In verse.] pp. 31. *Paris*, 1876. 8°.
11482. i. 16. (10.)

CAZIS DE LAPEYROUSE (Paul de) De la thoracentèse. pp. 50. *Paris*, 1865. 4°. [*Collection des thèses soutenues à la Faculté de Médecine de Paris.* An 1865. tom. 2.]   **7373. f. 8.**

CAZIUS (Unico Guillelmus Elisa) Dissertatio inauguralis juridica de his quæ ad succedendum requiruntur, *etc.* pp. 31. *Leodii*, 1829. 4°.   **498. f. 14. (21.)**

CAZO. Cazo acontecido nos banhos do mar . . . Por M. M. S. 1861. 16°. *See* S., M. M.
11452. aaaa. 1. (56.)

CAZOBONUS (Isaacus) *See* CASAUBON (Isaac)

CAZOLLA (Joannes Franciscus) *See* TARTAGNI (A.) de *Imola.* Consiliorum . . . liber primus (—septimus), *etc.* [Edited by J. F. Cazolla.] 1585. fol.   **502. k. 7.**

CAZONE. *See* CANZONE.

CAZORLA (Eduardo) *See* SPENCER (Herbert) [*Principles of Sociology.*] Principios de sociología . . . traducidos por E. Cazorla. 1883. 8°.   **8469. bb. 28.**

CAZORLA (Emilio Camps) *See* CAMPS CAZORLA.

CAZOTTE (Jacques) *See* ARABIAN NIGHTS. [*English.*] The Arabian Nights' Entertainments, *etc.* (Arabian Tales; or, a continuation of the Arabian Nights' Entertainments . . . Newly translated from the original Arabic into French, by Dom Chaves . . . and M. Cazotte.) [1813.] 8°.   **12410. ee. 14.**

CAZOTTE (Jacques)

—— *See* ARABIAN NIGHTS. [*French.*] Les Veillées du sultan Schahriar, avec la sultane Scheherazade; histoires . . . traduites de l'arabe par M. Cazotte et D. Chavis, *etc.* 1793. 8°. [*Le Cabinet des fées.* tom. 38–41.]
89. d. 25–28.

—— *See* ARABIAN NIGHTS. [*German.*] Arabische Mährchen. Fortsetzung der ächten Tausend und einen Nacht. [Translated from the French of J. Cazotte and D. Chavis.] 1790, *etc.* 8°. [*Die blaue Bibliothek aller Nationen.* Bd. 5–8.]   **12410. b. 2.**

—— *See* BOURGEOIS (Armand) Pages inédites ou ignorées sur Cazotte et son séjour à Pierry, 1760–1792, *etc.* 1911. 8°.   **10661. p. 14.**

—— *See* CHARMANT (E.) Monsieur Cazotte, homme de mystère. [1939.] 8°.   **010655. g. 27.**

—— *See* LAVALETTE (A. de) Mémoire (pour le sieur Cazotte et pour la demoiselle Fouque) sur les demandes formées contre le général et la société des Jésuites, *etc.* 1761. 12°.   **4092. bb. 15. (1.)**

—— *See* ROUHETTE ( ) and TARGET (G. J. B.) Mémoire (pour le Sieur Cazotte et la Demoiselle Fouqué) . . . contre le Général et la Société des Jésuites, *etc.* 1761. 12°.
860. d. 22. (4.)

—— *See* ROUHETTE ( ) and TARGET (G. J. B.) Second mémoire pour le Sieur Cazotte et la Demoiselle Fouqué contre le Général et la Société des Jésuites. [1761.] 12°.
860. d. 22. (5.)

—— *See* SHAW (Edward P.) Jacques Cazotte, *etc.* [With a bibliography.] 1942. 8°. [*Harvard Studies in Romance Languages.* vol. 19.]   **Ac. 2692/21.**

—— *See* TRINTZIUS (R.) Jacques Cazotte ou le XVIIIe siècle inconnu. [With a portrait.] 1944. 8°.   **10661. w. 13.**

—— Œuvres badines et morales de M *******. [The dedication signed: " Gazotte " [*sic*].] tom. 1, 2. *Amsterdam*, 1776. 8°.   **12236. de. 7.**
No more of this edition published.

—— Œuvres badines et morales de M. C*** (Cazotte). III volume, 1 partie. (Fables et contes allégoriques.) pp. viii. 182. *Lausanne & Paris*, 1788. 8°.
637. h. 26.
Imperfect; wanting vol. 1 and 2, and pt. 2 of this third vol.

—— Œuvres badines et morales . . . Nouvelle édition. 3 tom. **L.P.** *Londres* [*Paris*], 1798. 12°. G. **12414–16.**

—— Œuvres badines et morales, historiques et philosophiques . . . Première édition complète. 3 tom. *Paris*, 1816. 8°.
98. d. 19–21.

—— Le Diable amoureux. Préface de A. J. Pons. Eaux-fortes de F. Buhot. Variantes et bibliographie. (L'Honneur perdu et recouvré en partie.—La Prophétie de Cazotte inventée par La Harpe.) pp. 320. *Paris*, 1878. 8°.
12239. d. 4.

—— Contes de J. Cazotte : Mille et une fadaises. La patte du chat. Contes divers. Avec une notice bio-bibliographique par Octave Uzanne. [With a portrait.] pp. xxx. 218. *Paris*, 1880. 8°.   **12517. k. 15.**

—— A Thousand and One Follies (Les mille et une fadaises) and His Most Unlooked-for Lordship (Le Lord Impromptu). Translated . . . by Eric Sutton. With an introduction by Storm Jameson. pp. xvii. 189. *Chapman & Hall: London*, 1927. 8°. [*XVIII Century French Romances.* vol. 11.]   **012511. bb. 5/10.**

CAZOTTE (Jacques)

—— Le Diable amoureux. Nouvelle espagnole. [By J. Cazotte. With illustrations by C. P. Marillier.] pp. vii. 144. 1772. 8°. *See* Diable. **1073. i. 15.**

—— [Another edition.] 1788. *See* Voyages. Voyages imaginaires, songes, *etc.* tom. 35. 1787, *etc.* 8°. **303. g. 24.**

—— [Another edition.] Le Diable amoureux. Roman fantastique par J. Cazotte. Précédé de sa vie . . . par Gérard de Nerval. Illustré . . . par Édouard de Beaumont. pp. 292. *Paris*, 1871. 8°. **12516. h. 7.**

—— [Another edition.] Avec une introduction par Alexandre Piedagnel. pp. xi. 119. *Paris*, 1877. 8°. **12238. a. 20.**

—— [Another edition.] pp. 136. *Paris*, [1880.] 12°. **12514. bbb. 1.**

—— [Another edition.] Avec la préface de Gérard de Nerval. Sept eaux-fortes par Ad. Lalauze. pp. lxxvii. 126. *Paris*, 1883. 8°. **12510. p. 3.**

—— The Devil in Love, translated from the French. pp. vii. 170. 1793. 12°. *See* Devil. **12516. aaa. 22.**

—— Biondetta, or the Enamoured spirit : a romance. Translated from "Le Diable amoureux," *etc.* pp. xiii. 220. *John Miller : London*, 1810. 12°. **1458. d. 16.**

—— The Devil in Love . . . With six engravings on copper by J. E. Laboureur. pp. x. 87. *William Heinemann : London*, 1925. 8°. **012547. d. 20.**
One of an edition of seventy-five copies. With a duplicate set of plates.

—— A szerelmes ördög. Fordította Angyal Géza. Fáy Dezső rajzaival. pp. 132. *Budapesten*, 1924. 16°. **012590. c. 96.**

—— La Guerre de l'Opéra. Lettre écrite à une dame de province, par quelqu'un qui n'est d'un coin, ni de l'autre [i.e. J. Cazotte]. pp. 24. [1752.] 8°. *See* Paris.— *Théâtre National de l'Opéra.* **1103. b. 21. (15.)**

—— [Another copy.] La Guerre de l'Opera, *etc.* [By J. Cazotte.] [1752.] 8°. *See* Paris—*Académie Royale de Musique.* Hirsch i. 111.

—— Le Lord Impromptu ; nouvelle romanesque, traduite de l'anglois [or rather, written by J. Cazotte]. 2 pt. 1768. 12°. *See* Lord. **12614. a. 5.**

—— [Le Lord Impromptu.] La Magia bianca, ovvero la Mirabile e curiosa istoria di Ricardo Oberthon, novella inglese. [The dedication signed : Fassdown. In fact a translation of "Le Lord Impromptu," written in French by J. Cazotte.] 2 pt. 1785. 8°. *See* Fassdown ( ) *pseud.* **12519. aa. 30.**

—— Observations sur la lettre de Rousseau au sujet de la musique françoise. [By J. Cazotte.] pp. 19. 1753. 8°. *See* Rousseau (J. J.) [*Lettre sur la Musique Françoise.*] **640. e. 22. (4.)**

—— [Another copy.] Observations sur la lettre de J. J. Rousseau, *etc.* [By J. Cazotte.] 1753. 8°. *See* Rousseau (J. J.) [*Lettre sur la Musique Françoise.*] Hirsch i. 111a.

—— Ollivier, poème. [In prose. By J. Cazotte.] 2 tom. 1763. 8°. *See* Ollivier. **1478. c. 37.**

—— [Another edition.] 2 tom. on vellum. *Paris*, 1780. 18°. **C. 26. c. 12–15.**
Part of the "Collection d'ouvrages français" printed by order of the Count d'Artois. One of three copies printed on vellum.

CAZOTTE (Jacques)

—— La Patte du chat. Conte zinzimois. [By J. Cazotte.] pp. 126. 1741. 8°. *See* Patte. **1093. f. 9.**

—— Les Posthumes ; lettres reçues après la mort du mari, par sa femme, qui le croit à Florence. Par feu Cazotte [or rather by N. A. E. Restif de la Bretonne]. 4 pt. *Paris*, 1802. 12°. **Tab. 604. c. 3.**
The half-title reads : "Lettres du tombeau, ou les Posthumes."

—— [Another copy.] **Tab. 604. c. 6.**

CAZOTTE (Jacques) and **SÉDAINE** (Michel Jean)

—— Les Sabots, opéra-comique en un acte, mêlé d'ariettes ; par Mrs. C . . . . [i.e. J. Cazotte] & Sédaine, *etc.* pp. 24. 1777. 8°. [*Recueil général des opéra bouffons, etc.* tom. 1.] *See* C . . . . and Sédaine (M. J.) **11735. b. 2.**

CAZRAEUS (Petrus) *See* Gassend (P.) Petri Gassendi De proportione qua gravia decidentia accelerantur, epistolæ tres. Quibus ad totidem epistolas . . . P. Cazraei . . . respondetur. 1646. 4°. **8707. f. 1. (3.)**

CAZTELU (Dominico de) *See* Gaztelu.

CAZULLI CASABIANCA (Pier Alessandro) Il Feudalesimo e la Sardegna nel medio-evo. pp. 153. *Napoli*, 1880. 8°. **5306. c. 11.**

CAZURRO (Manuel) *See* Cazurro y Ruiz.

CAZURRO (Mariano Zacarias) *See* Vila (F. P.) El Hombre propone y Dios dispone. Leyenda original. [Edited by M. Z. Cazurro.] 1850. 8°. **11451. f. 41.**

—— Los Dos Doctores. Comedia en dos actos y en verso. pp. 88. *Madrid*, 1846. 8°. [*Galería Dramática.* vol. 70.] **1342. g. 11. (5.)**

—— Las Jorobas. Capricho comico original en un acto y en verso. pp. 35. *Madrid*, 1850. 8°. **11726. d. 3. (10.)**

—— La Pension de Venturita. Comedia en tres actos y en verso. pp. 93. *Madrid*, 1850. 8°. **11726. d. 3. (11.)**

—— Trabajar por Cuenta Ajena, comedia en tres actos y en verso. 1864. *See* Museo. Museo Dramático ilustrado. tom. 2. 1863, *etc.* 4°. **2298. i. 2.**

CAZURRO Y RUIZ (Manuel) *See* Lo Bianco (S.) Métodos usados en la estación zoológica de Nápoles para la conservación de los animales marinos . . . Traducidos por Don M. Cazurro. 1891. 8°. **Ac. 2826.**

—— Enumeración de los ortópteros de España y Portugal. 1888. *See* Madrid.—*Sociedad Española de Historia Natural.* Anales, *etc.* tom. 17. 1872, *etc.* 8°. **Ac. 2826.**

—— Los Monumentos megalíticos de la provincia de Gerona. pp. 84. pl. xxxvi. 1912. 8°. *See* Madrid.—*Junta para Ampliación de Estudios e Investigaciones Científicas.—Centro de Estudios Históricos.* **Ac. 145. b/4.**

—— Terra Sigillata.—Los vasos aretinos y sus imitaciones galo-romanas en Ampurias. [With illustrations.] 1911. *See* Barcelona.—*Institut d'Estudis Catalans.* Anuari. any 3. [1907, *etc.*] 4°. **Ac. 138.**

CAZWINI. *See* Zakarīyā ibn Muḥammad, al-Kazwīnī.

CAZZA (Giovanni Agostino) Rime. ff. 94. *Appresso G. Giolito : Vinegia*, 1546. 8°. **1071. e. 16.**

—— Le Rime spirituali di M. G. A. Cazza. ff. 104. *Appresso F. & G. Sesalli : Nouara*, 1552. 8°. **11427. b. 24.**

CAZZA (Giovanni Agostino)

—— Rime. 1587. *See* Dolce (L.) Il primo [*etc.*] volume delle rime scelte, *etc.* vol. 2. 1565, *etc.* 12°.
11422. a. 12.

—— Le Rime di G. A. Cazza . . . date in luce la seconda volta da Giuseppe Albetti. (Vita di G. A. Cazza . . . compilata dell'editore.) pp. 19. 152. *Torino*, 1770. 8°.
T. 2364. (1.)

—— Le Satire, et Capitoli piaceuoli di M. G. A. Cazza. ff. 107. 1549. 8°.
241. d. 14.

CAZZAGO (Baldassar) Rime. *See* Ruscelli (G.) Rime di diuersi eccelenti autori Bresciani, *etc.* 1553. 8°.
1062. d. 1. (1.)

CAZZAGO (Francesco Bettoni) *Count. See* Bettoni-Cazzago.

CAZZALUPUS (Joannes Baptista) *See* Caccialupus.

CAZZAMALI (Luigi) L'Arte dello scrivere nei Promessi Sposi [of Manzoni], *etc.* pp. 43. *Lodi*, 1892. 8°.
011850. h. 13. (7.)

CAZZAMINI MUSSI (Francesco) *See* Rovani (G.) Le Più belle pagine di Giuseppe Rovani. Scelte da F. Cazzamini-Mussi. 1935. 8°.
012226. a. 1/62.

—— I Canti dell'adolescenza—1904–1907. pp. 166. *Torino*, 1908. 8°.
11429. d. 31.

—— Il Giornalismo a Milano, dalle origini alla prima guerra d'indipendenza. [With plates and facsimiles.] pp. 467. *Milano*, 1934. 8°.
11856. aaa. 10.

—— Il Giornalismo a Milano dal quarantotto al novecento. pp. 370. pl. XIII. *Como*, 1935. 8°.
11856. de. 48.

—— Milano durante la dominazione spagnola, 1525–1706. pp. 875. *Milano*, 1947. 8°.
010136. ff. 21.

CAZZANI (Pietro)

—— *See* Alfieri (V.) *Count.* [*Works.*] Opere, *etc.* (Vol. 3, *etc.* Scritti politici e morali. A cura di P. Cazzani.) 1951, *etc.* 8°.
Ac. 91.

CAZZANIGA (Antonio)

—— I Problemi cronologici della medicina legale. [With a bibliography.] *In:* Archivio di antropologia criminale, psichiatria e medicina legale. vol. 60. pp. 187–404. 1940. 8°.
P.P. 3237. e.

CAZZANIGA (Fulvio) L'Eguaglianza studiata nella storia e nella scienza. 2 vol. *Cremona*, 1885. 8°.
8012.r.43.

CAZZANIGA (Ignazio)

—— Saggio critico ed esegetico sul Pervigilium Veneris. *In:* Studi classici e orientali. vol. 3. pp. 47–101. 1955. 8°.
Ac. 2599.

CAZZATI (Mauritio) Risposta alle oppositioni fatte dal Signor Giulio Cesare Arresti nella lettera al lettore posta nell'opera sua musicale. pp. 72. *Per gli hh. del Dozza: Bologna*, 1663. 4°.
557*. c. 26.

CAZZIALUPIS (Joannes Baptista de) *See* Caccialupus.

CAZZOLA (Clementina) *See* Ongaro (F. dall') Clementina Cazzola. Ricordi. 1868. 8°.
10630. ee. 34. (4.)

CAZZULI (Agostino) *See* Agostino, *da Crema, Augustinian* [A. Cazzuli.]

CAZZULI (Giovanni Antonio) *See* Leuwis (D. de) *de Rickel.* Trattato della vita militare . . . tradotto . . . dal R. M. G. A. Cazzuli, *etc.* 1563. 8°.
1360. c. 4.

CAZZUOLA (Ferdinando) Le Piante utili e nocive agli uomini e agli animali che crescono spontanee e coltivate in Italia, con brevi cenni sopra la coltura, sopra i prodotti, e sugli usi che se ne fanno, *etc.* pp. viii. 217. *Torino & Roma*, 1880. 8°.
7030. f. 8.

C - - BB - - R (C - - lly)

—— On Miss B - - ks and Miss H —. [A poem.] By C - - lly C - - bb - - r, Esqr. [i.e. Colley Cibber.] *In:* Poems on several occasions, from genuine manuscripts of Dean Swift . . . Mr. C — r, *etc.* pp. 17–19. 1749. 8°.
1346. g. 2. (2.)

C—B—R, *Mr.*

—— The Difference between Verbal and Practical Virtue. [A Satire in Verse on A. Pope.] With a prefatory epistle from Mr. C—b—r [i.e. Colley Cibber] to Mr. P. [Pope.] [The whole by John Lord Hervey.] pp. 7. *J. Roberts: London*, 1742. fol.
840. m. 1. (15.)

C - - - B - - - R, *Mr.* A Letter to Mr. C - - - b - - - r [i.e. Colley Cibber], on his Letter to Mr. P - - -. [By John Lord Hervey.] pp. 26. *J. Roberts: London*, 1742. 8°.
641. g. 30. (1.)

—— [Another copy.]
641. h. 5. (3.)

CC. Contributions of CC., now declared in full as Criticus Criticorum. [Remarks on the reviews and critical notices of Dr. Horace Bushnell's "God in Christ."] pp. 60. *Brown & Parsons: Hartford*, 1849. 8°.
4183. aaa. 87. (4.)

CC. (A.) *Avv.* Il progetto del dazio sul macino considerato . . . Brevi riflessi dell Avv. A. CC. pp. 13. *Firenze*, 1868. 8°.
8226. ff. 29. (10.)

CC * * A., *Grenadier patriote.* Un Centenaire bibliographique, *etc.* [A reprint of "Le Premier cri de la Savoie vers la liberté. Par CC * * A. Grenadier Patriote," i.e. B. Voiron.] 1891. 16°. *See* Voiron (B.)
8032. a. 4.

C—D, *D. of.* A Full and Complete History of His R——l H—— the D—— of C——d [i.e. Henry Frederick, Duke of Cumberland] and Lady G——r [i.e. Henrietta, Lady Grosvenor], the fair Adultress, *etc.* 2 vol. MS. NOTES. *J. Brough: London*, 1770. 8°.
1452. c. 30.

C—D, *Earl of. See* H——ND, *Mr.* Love Elegies. By Mr. H——d [i.e. James Hammond]. With a preface by the Earl of C——d [Chesterfield]. 1743. 8°. 11631. d. 25.

—— A Dialogue between the Earl of C——d [Chesterfield] and Mr. Garrick, in the Elysian shades. [In verse.] pp. 36. *T. Cadell: London*, 1785. 4°. T. 25. (2.)

—— [Another copy.]
644. k. 18. (20.)

C - - - - - - - - D, *Mr.*

—— A Late Epistle to Mr C - - - - - - - - d. [Signed: B — g.] [1756.] *s. sh.* fol. *See* B — g.
1865. c. 4. (153.)

C—D, *Mr.* A Lenten Litany, by Mr. C—d [i.e. William Coward?], *etc. See* Pecunia. Pecuniæ obediunt omnia, *etc.* 1698. 8°.
1078. l. 24.

C—D, *Mr.* The Twins: or, the Female traveller. A novel. Written by Mr. C—d, author of Faulconer's, Boyle's and Vaughen's Voyages, &c. [i.e. William Rufus Chetwood.] pp. 48. *London*, 1742–3. 8°.
012618. df. 6.

C＊＊＊＊＊D, *Rabbi.* A Dissertation upon II. Kings, x. 22. Translated from the Latin of Rabbi C＊＊＊＊＊d [i.e. George Costard]. With a dedication, preface, and post-script critical and explanatory. By the translator. pp. 44. *M. Cooper: London,* [1753?] 8º.　　　**1107. e. 2.**

C＊＊＊＊＊＊＊D (S＊＊＊＊＊) A Tour to Paris in the Summer of 1816. By S＊＊＊＊＊ C＊＊＊＊＊＊＊d. pp. 35. *Printed for the Author: London,* 1816. 8º.　**10169. aa. 5.**

C——D (W. R.) *See* Ch——D.

C . . . D'A . . . (François de) *Marquis. See* Fabre (B.) Un Initié des sociétés secrètes supérieures. "Franciscus, Eques a capite galeato" (le marquis François de C . . . d'A . . .), *etc.* 1913. 8º.　**04785. i. 53.**

CE. C'est lui. [An attack on Chrétien F. Lamoignon.] pp. 7. [1788?] 8º.　　　　　　　**R. 20. (7.)**

—— Ce qu'on a dit, ce qu'on a voulu dire, Lettre à Madame Folio. [By F. L. C. Marin.] pp. 16. [*Paris,* 1763?] 8º.　　　　　　　　　　**1103. b. 21. (20.)**

—— [Another copy.] Ce qu'on a dit, ce qu'on a voulu dire, *etc.* [*Paris,* 1763?] 8º.　　**Hirsch I. 345.**

—— Ce qu'on a surement oublié. [On the course proper to be taken by the States General.] pp. 14.　[*Paris,* 1789?] 8º.　　　　　　　**F. 425. (7.)**

—— Ce que vous ne savez pas. no. 1. [A political pamphlet.] pp. 8. [*Paris?* 1790.] 8º.　　**F.R. 126. (13.)**

—— Ce que vous ne voyez pas. no. 1. pp. 8.　[*Paris,* 1789?] 8º.　　　　　　**R. 190. (5.)** *No more published.*

—— Cé qu'é lainô. Chanson sur l'escalade de Genève en lengage savoyard. Éditée par André Burger . . . avec le concours de Maria Brun et André Duckert. *Savoyard & Fr.* pp. 51. *Genève; Lille,* 1952. 8º. [*Société de Publications Romanes et Françaises.* no. 37.]　　**Ac. 9807.**

C——E. Ueber die Schminke, ihre Bereitung, ihren Ge-brauch, und ihren schädlichen und nützlichen Einfluss auf den menschlichen Körper. Bearbeitet für die Toilette von einem Freund der Schönen. [The dedication signed: C——e.] pp. xvi. 92. *Frankfurt,* 1796. 8º.　　　　　　　　　　**1175. f. 4. (7.)**

C--------E, *Bishop of.* A Modest Enquiry address'd to the Bishop of C--------e [Robert Clayton, Bishop of Cork and Ross]. [In verse.] pp. 8. [*Dublin?*] 1738. 8º.　　　　　　　　　**11643. bbb. 24. (1.)**

—— [Another copy.]　　**C. 71. bb. 15. (12.)**

CE FASTU? *See* Udine.—*Società Filologica Friulana.*

C——E (A——R) Poems on Several Occasions. By A——r C——e. pp. 16. *Glasgow,* 1784. 8º.　**1465. e. 26. (1.)**

CÉ (Alain de)

—— L'Évasion d'un Saint Cyrien. (Roman vécu.) *See* Oeuvres. Les Oeuvres nouvelles. no. 1. [1942, *etc.*] 8º.　　　　　　　　　　**W.P. 10531/1.**

CÉ (Camille) *pseud.* [i.e. Camille Chemin.] [For works written in collaboration by J. Gaument and C. Cé :] *See* Gaument (Jean) *pseud.,* and Cé (C.) *pseud.*

—— *See* Tourneur (C.) La Tragédie de la vengeance . . . Traduit . . . par C. Cé, *etc.* [1925.] 8º. **11771. c. 8.**

CÉ (Camille) *pseud.* [i.e. Camille Chemin.]

—— *See* Webster (John) *Dramatist.* Le Démon blanc . . . suivi de La Duchesse d'Amalfi. Traduction de C. Cé. [1922.] 8º.　　　　　**11778. dd. 39.**

—— Le Livre des résignations. Poème. pp. 285.　*Paris,* 1908. 8º.　　　　**011483. bbb. 34.**

—— Regards sur l'œuvre d'Édouard Estaunié. pp. 357. *Paris,* 1935. 8º.　　　　**11856. eee. 15.**

—— Le Squelette dans le placard. Roman, *etc.* pp. 314. *Rouen,* [1941?] 8º.　　**012548. eeee. 73.**

CEA (Didacus de) Didaci de Cea . . . Archielogia sacra principum Apostolorum Petri et Pauli. 1697. *See* Roca-berti (J. T. de) *Archbishop of Valencia.* Bibliotheca maxima pontificia, *etc.* tom. 8. 1698, *etc.* fol.　　　　　　　　　　**484. e. 7.**

—— Thesaurus Terrae Sanctae, quem seraphica minorum religio de obseruantia inter infideles, per trecentos et amplius annos religiose custodit, fideliterque administrat. pp. 355. *Typis S. Congreg. de Fide Propaganda: Romæ,* 1639. 4º.　　　　　　**490. e. 32.**

CEA (Genaro Rus de) *See* Rus de Cea.

CEADEL (Eric Bertrand)

—— *See* Honda (Minobu) and Ceadel (E. B.) Post-War Japanese Research on the Far East, *etc.* 1954. 8º. [*Asia Major.* New series. vol. 4. pt. 1.]　**P.P. 3803. eb.**

—— *See* Honda (Minobu) and Ceadel (E. B.) A Survey of Japanese Contributions to Manchurian Studies. 1955. 8º. [*Asia Major.* New series. vol. 5. pt. 1.]　　　　　　　　　　**P.P. 3803. eb.**

—— Literatures of the East. An appreciation. Edited by E. B. Ceadel, *etc.* pp. xiii. 194. *John Murray: London,* 1953. 8º. [*Wisdom of the East Series.*]　**14003. a. 108.**

CEAD-LEABHAR. Ceaꝺ-leaꝺap ᵹaoiꝺilᵹe-Sasp-ꝺeapla. *See* Irish-English Primer.

CEAGH (F. Jay) The Passing of the Dragon. pp. 62. *Cassell & Co.: London,* 1900. 8º.　**04410. h. 56.**

CÉALIS (Édouard) De Sousse à Gafsa. Lettres sur la campagne de Tunisie, 1881–1884. Préface de G. Lar-roumet. pp. xi. 279. *Paris,* [1897.] 18º.　　　　　　　　　　**10097. ccc. 26.**

CEANAIDEACH (Iain) *See* Kennedy (John) *Minister of the Gospel.*

CEAN-BERMUDEZ (Juan Agustin) *See* Milizia (F.) Arte de Ver en las Bellas Artes del Diseño . . . traducido . . . por D. J. A. Cean-Bermudez, *etc.* 1827. 8º.　　　　　　　　　　**1402. f. 44.**

—— Cartas. *See* Serrano y Sanz (M.) Cartas de D. Martín Fernández de Navarrete, D. Agustín Ceán Bermúdez, y D. Diego Clemencín, á D. Tomás González, *etc.* 1899. 8º. [*Revue hispanique.* tom. 6.]　　　　　　　　　　**P.P. 4331. aea.**

—— Coleccion lithographica de cuadros del Rey de España . . . Fernando VII . . . lithographiada por hábiles artistas, bajo la direccion de José de Madrazo. [With descriptive text by J. A. Cean-Bermudez and José Musso.] 3 tom. *Madrid,* 1826–32. fol.　　　**1899.e.19.** *The titlepage is engraved.*

—— Descripcion artística de la catedral de Sevilla. [With appendix.] pp. xxii. 200. xlvii. *Sevilla,* 1804, 05. 8º.　　　　　　　　　　**4625. a. 13.**

CEAN-BERMUDEZ (JUAN AGUSTIN)

—— [Another edition.] Enriquecida con notas y adornada con cuatro láminas de las vistas de este templo. pp. 118. *Sevilla*, 1863. 4°. **7816. aaa. 3.**

—— Diccionario historico de los mas ilustres profesores de las bellas artes en España. 6 tom. *Madrid*, 1800. 8°. **10604. l. 23.**

—— [Another copy.] **786. a. 31.**

—— *See* MUÑOZ Y MANZANO (C.) *Count de la Viñaza*. Adiciones al Diccionario histórico de los más ilustres profesores de las bellas artes en España de don J. A. Cean Bermudez. 1889, *etc.* 8°. **10632. de. 36.**

—— Memorias para la Vida del Excmo. Señor D. Gaspar Melchor de Jove Llanos, y noticias analiticas de sus obras. (Apéndice. Algunas Poesias del Señor Don Gaspar de Jove Llanos.) pp. 395. *Madrid*, 1814. 8°. **830. d. 17.**

—— Sumario de las Antigüedades Romanas que hay en España, en especial las pertenecientes á las bellas artes. pp. xxviii. 538. *Madrid*, 1832. fol. **573. l. 10.**

CEAPRANO (S.) Amate con giudizio ! [A physiological treatise.] pt. 1. vol. 1. pp. 200. *Torino*, 1886. 8°. **1093. a. 2.**

No more published.

CEARÁ, *Province of.*

MISCELLANEOUS PUBLIC DOCUMENTS.

—— Confederação do Equador. A Provincia do Ceará em 1824. Dos volumes 5.° e 6.° da collecção "Presidentes do Ceará—correspondencia com os Ministerios do Imperio e da Guerra." pp. 346. *Rio de Janeiro*, 1929. 8°. [*Archivo Publico Nacional. Publicações.* vol. 24.] **11915. i. 1/24.**

APPENDIX.

—— Relatorio e contas da subscripção promovida em favor das victimas da secca do Ceará pela Commissão Central Cearense organisada n'esta Côrte em 7 de Maio de 1877. pp. 128. *Rio de Janeiro*, 1879. 8°. **8277. g. 30.**

CÉARD (CH. ODIER) *See* ODIER-CÉARD.

CÉARD (HENRY)

—— *See* BURNS (C. A.) Henry Céard and his Relations with Flaubert and Zola. [1953.] 8°. **11870. g. 2.**

—— *See* DAUDET (Alphonse) Œuvres complètes. Édition définitive . . . précédée d'un essai de biographie littéraire par H. Céard. 1899, *etc.* 8°. [MISSING.]

—— *See* GAVAULT (P.) Snob. Préface de H. Céard. 1895. 8°. **012550. i. 43.**

—— *See* GONCOURT (E. L. A. de) Madame Saint-Huberty . . . Postface de H. Céard, *etc.* [1925.] 8°. **010662. a. 52.**

—— *See* GONCOURT (J. A. de) Lettres, *etc.* [With a preface by H. Céard.] 1885. 18°. **10910. bbb. 39.**

—— *See* GONCOURT (J. A. de) Lettres. Introduction d'H. Céard, *etc.* [1930.] 8°. **010905. de. 64.**

—— *See* ZAVIE (E.) Prisonniers en Allemagne . . . Avec une préface de M. H. Céard. 1917. 8°. **09081. aa. 3.**

—— Une Belle journée. pp. 346. *Paris*, 1881. 12°. **12518. g. 31.**

CÉARD (HENRY)

—— A Lovely Day . . . Translated by Ernest Boyd. pp. 197. *A. A. Knopf: London; printed in U.S.A.*, 1926. 8°. **12515. p. 7.**

—— Le Mauvais livre, et quelques autres comédies. (Théâtre sans acteurs.) pp. 212. *Paris*, [1923.] 8°. **11735. dd. 36.**

—— La Saignée. [A tale.] *See* MÉDAN. Les Soirées de Médan, *etc.* 1880. 12°. **12518. g. 4.**

—— [Another edition.] *See* MÉDAN. Les Soirées de Médan. *etc.* 1890. 8°. **012548. f. 54.**

—— Sonnets de guerre, 1914–1918. pp. 71. *Paris*, 1919. 4°. **11483. i. 25.**

—— Terrains à vendre au bord de la mer. pp. 775. *Paris*, 1918. 8°. **12547. tt. 27.**

—— Tout pour l'honneur. Drame en un acte, en prose, tiré de la nouvelle de M. Émile Zola, Le Capitaine Burle. pp. 43. *Paris*, 1890. 8°. **11740. cc. 1. (9.)**

CÉARD (HENRY) and **CROZE** (J. L.)

—— Laurent. Comédie en un acte, en vers, *etc.* pp. 36. *Paris*, 1909. 8°. **11736. e. 33. (3.)**

CÉARD (ROBERT) Souvenirs des travaux du Simplon. [With plates.] pp. ix. 82. *Genève*, 1837. fol. **647. b. 4.**

CEARENSE (CATULLO DA PAIXÁO)

—— Fábulas e alegorias. Sexta edição. [Poems.] pp. 252. *Rio de Janeiro*, [1953.] 8°. **11454. b. 15.**

—— Oração á Bandeira. [In verse.] pp. 63. 1938. obl. 12°. *See* RIO DE JANEIRO, *Federal District of.—Serviço de Divulgação.* **11452. de. 17.**

CEARNACH (CONALL) *pseud.* [i.e. FREDERICK WILLIAM O'CONNELL.] *See* CONALL, *Cearnach, pseud.*

CEATHARLACH. *See* CARLOW.

CEAWLIN, *Bretwalda*. *See* GODSAL (Philip T.) The Conquests of Ceawlin, *etc.* 1924. 8°. **9510. dd. 15.**

CEBÀ (ANSALDO) *See* RIO (A. F.) The Four Martyrs, *etc.* (Philip Howard, A. Cebà, *etc.*) 1856. 8°. **4825. b. 18.**

—— *See* THEOPHRASTUS. [*Characteres.—Italian.*] I Charatteri morali di Theofrasto interpretati per A. Cebà. 1620. 4°. **231. f. 24.**

—— Alcippo, Spartano. Tragedia. [In verse.] 1725. *See* ITALIAN THEATRE. Teatro italiano, *etc.* tom. 3. 1723, *etc.* 8°. **638. c. 11.**

—— [Another edition.] *See* ITALIAN THEATRE. Teatro italiano, *etc.* tom. 3. 1746. 8°. **687. f. 28.**

—— Il Cittadino di republica, *etc.* pp. 239. *Giuseppe Pauoni: Genoua*, 1617. fol. **1475. c. 13.**

—— Le Gemelle Capovane: tragedia. [In verse.] 1723. *See* ITALIAN THEATRE. Teatro italiano, *etc.* tom. 2. 1723, *etc.* 8°. **638. c. 10.**

—— [Another edition.] *See* ITALIAN THEATRE. Teatro italiano, *etc.* tom. 2. 1746. 8°. **687. f. 27.**

—— Lettere . . . ad Agostino Pallauicino di Stefano. [With a portrait.] pp. 364. *G. Pauoni: Genoua*, 1623. 4°. **93. c. 2.**

CEBÀ (ANSALDO)

—— Oratione nell'incoronatione del Serenissimo Agostino Doria, Duce della Republica di Genoua . . . Col sermone del molto R. P. D. Girolamo Coleta. (Componimenti d'alcuni signori, in lode di Sua Serenita.) [Edited by Antonio Prato.] pp. 88. *G. Pauoni: Genoua,* 1601. 4º. **74. d. 19.**

—— La Principessa Silandra. Tragedia. [In verse.] pp. 133. *G. Pauoni: Genoua,* 1620. 8º. **11714. b. 2.**

—— La·Reina Esther. [A poem.] pp. 327. *G. Pauoni: Genoua,* 1615. 4º. **82. f. 1.**

—— Rime, *etc.* ff. 78. *Appresso M. Nutio: Anuersa,* 1596. 8º. **11427. df. 10.**

—— Rime. pp. 713. *B. Zannetti: Roma,* 1611. 4º. **839. k. 14.**

CEBADA (EMILIO MORENO) *See* MORENO CEBADA.

CEBADAL. Entremes del Cebadal. pp. 8. *Salamanca,* [1780?] 16º. **11726. aa. 1. (7.)**

CEBADERA (PRIMITIVO) *See* SERVAT (C.) and CEBADERA (P.) Los Anarquistas, *etc.* 1893. 8º. **11726. b. 15. (5.)**

CEBALLOS (BLAS ANTONIO DE) *See* CEVALLOS.

CEBALLOS (CIRO B.) "Aurora y Ocaso." Por los "cuistres." Ensayo histórico de política contemporánea, 1867–1906. 2 tom. *México,* 1907, 12. 8º. **9772. s. 4.**

CEBALLOS (FERNANDO DE) Insania ó las Demencias de los filósofos confundidas por la sabiduría de la Cruz. Obra inédita . . . la publica D. Leon Carbonero y Sol. pp. xlvi. 321. *Madrid,* 1878. 8º. **8466. ff. 17.**

—— Juicio final de Voltaire, con su historia civil y literaria y el resultado de su filosofia en la funesta revolucion de Europa ; escrita por el Viagero de Lemnos (el R. P. Fr. F. Ceballos), segun la oyó y copió de los filósofos infernales en los abismos de Antiparos. La da a luz Don Leon Carbonero y Sol. 2 tom. *Sevilla,* 1856. 8º. **12491. g. 26.**

—— Observaciones sobre reforma eclesiástica. Obra pósthuma . . . aumentada. pp. 167. *Puebla,* 1820. 4º. **4182. bb. 31.**

—— La Sidonia Bética, ó Disertaciones acerca del sitio de la Colonia Asido y Cátedra Episcopal Asidoniense, *etc.* pp. xxxv. 194. *Sevilla,* 1864. 8º. **10161. c. 5.**

CEBALLOS (FERNANDO JOSÉ DE VELASCO Y) *See* VELASCO Y CEBALLOS.

CEBALLOS (GERONIMO DE) *See* CEVALLOS.

CEBALLOS (GONZALO) Estudios sobre icneumónidos de España, *etc. Madrid,* 1924– . 8º. [*Trabajos del Museo Nacional de Ciencias Naturales.* Serie zoológica. no. 50.] **Ac. 2828/2.**

CEBALLOS (GREGORIO VASQUEZ ARCE I)

—— *See* VÁZQUEZ DE ARCE Y CEBALLOS (G.)

CEBALLOS (IGNACIO ORTIZ DE) *See* ORTIZ DE ZEVALLOS.

CEBALLOS (JOSÉ J.) Derecho Criminal. Reincidencia. Estudio sobre el art. 5º Lib. 2º del Proyecto de Cod. Pen. Disertacion, *etc.* pp. 31. *Buenos Aires,* 1872. 8º. [MISSING.]

CEBALLOS (JUAN) Consejos higiénicos, preservativos del Cólera-morbo. Discusion sobre su contagio. pp. 88. *Cadiz,* 1855. 8º. **7561. e. 62. (5.)**

CEBALLOS (JUAN DE LA PEZUELA Y) *Marquis de la Pezuela, Count de Cheste. See* PEZUELA Y CEBALLOS.

CEBALLOS (LUIS) and **MARTÍN BOLAÑOS** (MANUEL) Estudio sobre la Vegetación Forestal de la Provincia de Cádiz. Trabajo que se publica como complemento al Mapa forestal de la misma, *etc.* pp. xviii. 353. *Madrid,* 1930. 8º. **07073. l. 25.**

—— Mapa Forestal de la Provincia de Cádiz. 4 sh. *Madrid,* 1931. fol. **Maps 18392. (2.)**

CEBALLOS (LUIS G.) Documentos Inéditos relativos a Hernán Cortés y su Familia. (Arreglados por D. L. G. Ceballos.) pp. ix. 465. *México,* 1935. 4º. [*Publicaciones del Archivo General de la Nación.* vol. 27.] **L.A.S.F.17/2.**

CEBALLOS (MARÍA ISABEL VILLA) *of the Convent of Our Lady of Guadalupe, of Mexico. See* MARÍA ISABEL.

CEBALLOS (PEDRO DE) *See* CEVALLOS.

CEBALLOS (PEDRO ANTONIO DE) *See* CEVALLOS.

CEBALLOS (RÓMULO VELASCO) *See* VELASCO CEBALLOS.

CEBALLOS NIETO (DANIEL)

—— San Agustín, filósofo del Cristianismo . . . Conferencia, *etc.* pp. 25. [*Popayán ?* 1954.] 8º. **4831. a. 55.**

CEBALLOS QUINTANA (ENRIQUE) La Camisa de Adan. Novela, *etc.* pp. 239. *Madrid,* [1889.] 8º. **12489. cc. 50.**

—— La Gloria de Once Reinados. [In verse.] pp. 64. *Madrid,* 1875. 8º. **11450. ee. 14.**

—— El Libro de Juan Soldado. (Nueva edicion corregida y aumentada.) pp. 126. *Madrid,* 1876. 16º. **11450. b. 4.**

—— Lo Mejor de la Mujer. Novela, *etc.* pp. 239. *Madrid,* 1877. 8º. **12491. cc. 10.**

—— Las Mujeres de la Noche, novela de costumbres. pp. 271. *Madrid,* 1876. 8º. **12491. aaaa. 28.**

—— El Quijote de los Siglos, novela, *etc.* pp. 256. *Madrid,* 1876. 8º. **12491. aaaa. 27.**

CEBALLOS TERESÍ (JOSÉ G.) La Realidad económica y financiera de España en los treinta años del presente siglo. (Historia económica, financiera y política de España en el siglo xx.) 8 tom. *Madrid,* 1931–33. 8º. **8230. bb. 11.**

CEBALLOS Y CRUZADA (CARLOS G. DE) El Imperio del Jesuitismo, ó Revelaciones acerca de la Asociación de Padres de familia. pp. 205. *Madrid,* 1896. 8º. **4092. cc. 10.**

—— El 1.º de Mayo en España, ó las Causas del socialismo en nuestra patria y sus remedios. pp. 128. *Madrid,* 1892. 8º. **8277. ee. 40.**

CEBALLOS Y DEL CONDE (RAMÓN DE) De Méjico. pp. 126. *Madrid,* 1858. 4º. **8179. bb. 53. (4.)**

—— XXIV Capitulos en vindicacion de Méjico. pp. 197. *Madrid,* 1856. 4º. **8179. e. 5.**

CEBE (LOUIS ANTOINE) De l'influence des causes essentielles internes sur les maladies externes. Essai, *etc.* pp. 38. *Montpellier,* an x [1802]. 4º. **1180. d. 14. (1.)**

CEBE-HABERSKÝ (JAROSLAV)

—— Dum mrtvých. Věznice Moabit a Plötzensee 1940–1942. pp. 147. *v Praze*, 1946. 8°. **6058.** pp. 31.

CEBERIO (ALFREDO O.)

—— Cuba y sus Tributos. Apuntes para la reforma de nuestra sistema tributario. pp. 28. *Habana*, 1931. 8°. **8231. f. 86.**

CEBES.

GREEK.

—— *Begin.* [fol. 2 *recto :*] Κεβητος Πιναξ. [᾽Ε]τυγχανομεν περιπατουντες ἐν τῳ του κρονου ἱερῳ, *etc.* [fol. 17 *recto :*] Βασιλειου του μεγαλου λογος παραινετικος προς τους νεους πως ἀν ἐξ ῾Ελληνικων ὠφελοιντο λογων. [fol. 31 *recto :*] Πλουταρχου χαιρωνεως περι παιδων ἀγωγης. [fol. 55 *recto :*] Ξενοφωντος. ῾Ιερων. ἡ Τυραννικος. [*Laurentius de Alopa: Florence*, 1496 ?] 8°. **IA. 28035.** *74 leaves, the first blank. Sig. a–ι⁸ κ². 22 lines to a page.*

—— [Another copy.] **G. 7898.** *Without the blank leaf.*

—— Κεβητος Θηβαιου Πιναξ. Cebetis Thebani Tabula. Τα του Πυθαγορου χρυσα ἐπη. Aurea carmina Pythagoræ. pp. 36. *Ex officina C. Wecheli : Parisiis*, 1548. 8°. **C. 97. aa. 10. (1.)**

—— [Another edition.] ff. 15. *Apud M. Iuuenem : Parisiis*, 1549. 8°. **8461. aaa. 9.**

— — Cebetis Thebani Tabula. *Apud V. Sabbium : Brixiæ*, 1589. 8°. **1385. a. 24.**

—— Κεβητος Θηβαιου Πιναξ. *See* LASCARIS (C.) Γραμματικη, *etc.* [1645.] 8°. **622. c. 26.**

—— [Another edition.] *See* LASCARIS (C.) Γραμματικη, *etc.* 1808. 8°. **868. d. 34.**

—— Κεβητος Πιναξ. Des Cebes Gemälde. Mit einer Einleitung . . . Anmerkungen und einem vollständigen Wörterbuche. Für Schulen herausgegeben von Johann David Büchling. Von Neuem bearbeitet von Georg Friedrich Wilhelm GIOSSE. pp. xlii. 181. *Meissen*, 1813. 8°. **8461. bb. 14.**

—— Tableau de Cébès . . . avec des notes, par M. Fleury Lécluse . . . Texte grec revu par l'éditeur. pp. 31. *Paris*, 1833. 12°. **8461. a. 38.**

—— Κεβητος Θηβαιου Πιναξ. *See* THEOPHRASTUS. [*Characteres.—Greek.*] Theophrasti Characteres, *etc.* 1844. 8°. **11304. aaa. 29.**

—— Κεβητος Πιναξ. Cebetis Tabula. Recognovit, praefatus est, apparatu critico et verborum indice instruxit Fridericus Drosihn. pp. xiv. 39. *Lipsiae*, 1871. 12°. **11340. bb. 40.** *Part of the " Bibliotheca scriptorum graecorum et romanorum Teubneriana."*

—— Κεβητος Πιναξ. Cebetis Tabula. With introduction and notes by C. S. Jerram. pp. xxxix. 55. *Oxford*, 1878. 8°. [*Clarendon Press Series.*] **2320. b. 7.**

—— Κεβητος Πιναξ. La Tavola di Cebete, con prefazione e note ad uso delle scuole e con un saggio bibliografico. Per cura di Giuseppe Barone. pp. xxiii. 70. *Napoli*, 1883. 8°. **8470. cc. 6. (3.)**

—— Κεβητος Πιναξ. Cebes' Tablet, with introduction, notes, vocabulary, and grammatical questions. By Richard Parsons. pp. 94. *Ginn & Co.: Boston*, 1887. 8°. **8462. b. 14.**

CEBES. [GREEK.]

—— Κεβητος Πιναξ. Cebetis Tabula. Recensuit Carolus Praechter. pp. xi. 40. *Lipsiae*, 1893. 8°. **2048. a. 8.** *Part of the " Bibliotheca scriptorum graecorum et romanorum Teubneriana."*

—— Κεβητος Πιναξ. Cebetis Tabula. With introduction and notes by C. S. Jerram . . . Abridged school edition. pp. xxiv. 44. *Oxford*, 1898. 8°. [*Clarendon Press Series.*] **2319. aa. 25.**

GREEK, LATIN AND ARABIC.

—— Tabula Cebetis Græce, Arabice [according to the translation by Ibn Miskawaih], Latine. Itcm Aurea Carmina Pythagoræ, cum paraphrasi Arabica, auctore Iohanne Elichmanno . . . Cum præfatione Cl. Salmasii. (Cebetis Thebani Tabula e Græco in Latinum conversa per Ludovicum Odaxium Patavinum.) 2 pt. *Typis I. Maire: Lugduni Batavorum*, 1640. 4°. **14540. a. 31.**

—— [Another issue.] *See* EPICTETUS. Simplicii Commentarius in Enchiridion Epicteti . . . Cum versione Hieronymi Wolfii, *etc.* 1640. 4°. **C. 81. b. 14.**

GREEK AND LATIN.

—— Κεβητος Θηβαιου Πιναξ. (Cebetis Thebani Tabula.) *See* LASCARIS (C.) Constantini Lascaris . . . De octo partibus orationis liber primus, *etc.* [1502 ?] 4°. **681. c. 15.**

—— [Another edition.] *See* LASCARIS (C.) Constantini Lascaris Institutiones uniuersæ, *etc.* 1510. 4°. **624. c. 11.**

—— [Another edition.] *See* LASCARIS (C.) *Begin.* In hoc libro hæc habentur. Constantini Lascaris . . . de octo partibus oronis Lib. I, *etc.* 1512. 4°. **C. 16. h. 4.**

—— Κεβητος . . . Πιναξ. (Cebetis . . . Tabula.) *See* HESIOD. [*Opera et Dies.—Greek and Latin.*] *Begin.* In hoc opere continentur, Hesiodi . . . duo libri, *etc.* [1515.] 4°. **11335. c. 49. (1.)**

—— Κεβητος . . . Πιναξ. (Dfbftes [*sic*] . . . Tabula.) *See* LASCARIS (C.) *Begin.* In hoc libro hæc continentur. Constantini Lascaris . . . de octo partibus oronis Lib. I, *etc.* 1515. 4°. **624. c. 12.**

—— Cebetis tabula ϗ greca ϗ latina, opus morale, & vtile oïbus & præcipue adolescētibus. Carmina Aurea Pythagoræ. Phocylidis Poema ad bene, beatecȝ viuendum. *T. Martini: [Louvain*, 1520 ?] 4°. **624. c. 6. (5.)**

—— [Another copy.] FEW MS. NOTES. **G. 17114**

—— Κεβητος . . . Πιναξ. (Cebetis . . . Tabula.) *See* LASCARIS (C.) *Begin.* In hoc libro haec continentur. Constantini Lascaris . . . de octo partibus orationis Lib. I, *etc.* 1521. 4°. **624. c. 13.**

—— Κεβητος . . . Πιναξ. (Cebetis . . . Tabula.) *See* NACHTIGALL (O.) Graece et Latine. Moralia quædam instituta, ex uarijs authoribus, *etc.* 1523. 8°. **525. b. 1.**

—— Κεβητος . . . Πιναξ. (Cebetis . . . Tabula.) *See* LASCARIS (C.) Constantini Lascaris . . . de octo orationis partibus, *etc.* 1533. 8°. **622. c. 24.**

—— [Another edition.] *See* LASCARIS (C.) Constantini Lascaris . . . de octo orationis partibus, *etc.* 1540. 8°. **12924. a. 7.**

—— [Another edition.] *See* LASCARIS (C.) Constantini Lascaris . . . Græcæ institutiones, *etc.* 1542. 4°. **624. c. 15.**

CEBES. [Greek and Latin.]

—— Κεβητος . . . Πιναξ. Cebetis . . . Tabula. Theodorico Adamæo interprete. pp. 51. *Apud I. Lodoicum: Parisiis*, 1545. 8º. C. 97. aa. 10. (2.)

—— Cebetis . . . Tabula. (Κεβητος . . . Πιναξ.) *See* Lascaris (C.) Constantini Lascaris . . . Grammaticæ compendium, *etc.* 1546. 8º. 622. c. 25.

—— [Another edition.] *See* Colloquia. Familiarium colloquiorum formulæ, *etc.* 1547. 8º. G. 7899.

—— [Another edition.] *See* Lascaris (C.) Constantini Lascaris . . . Grammaticæ compendium, *etc.* 1547. 8º. C. 16. c. 13.

—— [Another edition.] *See* Lascaris (C.) Constantini Lascaris . . . Grammaticæ compendium, *etc.* 1557. 8º. C. 16. c. 9.

—— Κεβητος . . . Πιναξ. (Cebetis . . . Tabula, qua uitæ humanæ prudenter instituendæ ratio continetur: Hieronymo Wolfio . . . interprete.—Hieronymi Wolfij in Tabulam Cebetis Annotationes.) *See* Epictetus. Epicteti Enchiridion, *etc.* 1561. 8º. 526. h. 1.

—— [Another edition.] *See* Epictetus. Epicteti Enchiridion, *etc.* 1563. 8º. C. 19. c. 18.

—— Κεβητου . . . Πιναξ. (Cebetis . . . Tabula, *etc.*) [The Latin translation by H. Wolfius.] *See* Epictetus. Epicteti Enchiridion, *etc.* 1585. 16º. 165. k. 3.

—— Κεβητος . . . Πιναξ. Cebetis . . . Tabula, *etc.* [The Latin translation by H. Wolfius.] *See* Thesaurus. Thesaurus philosophiæ moralis, *etc.* 1589. 16º. 526. a. 9.

—— Κεβητος . . . Πιναξ. (Cebetis . . . Tabula . . . Hieronymo Wolfio . . . interprete.—Hieronymi Wolfij in Tabulam Cebetis Annotationes.) *See* Epictetus. Epicteti . . . Encheiridion, *etc.* 1595. 8º. 526. h. 3.

—— Κεβητος . . . Πιναξ. (Cebetis . . . Tabula, *etc.*) [The Latin translation by H. Wolfius.] *See* Plutarch. [*Selections.—Greek and Latin.*] Apophthegmata philosophorum, *etc.* 1595. 12º. 12305. a. 1.

—— Κεβητος . . . Πιναξ. (Cebetis . . . Tabula . . . Hieronymo Wolfio . . . interprete.—Hieronymi Wolfij in Tabulam Cebetis Annotationes.) *See* Epictetus. Epicteti . . . Encheiridion, *etc.* 1596, *etc.* 8º. C. 78. a. 25.

—— Κεβητος . . . Πιναξ. (Cebetis . . . Tabula.) [The Latin translation by H. Wolfius.] *See* Epictetus. Epicteti Enchiridion, *etc.* 1616. 32º. C. 20. f. 26.

—— Κεβητος . . . Πιναξ. Cebetis . . . Tabula. Cum versione & notis V. C. Ioannis Caselii . . . Ex bibliotheca Geverharti Elmenhorstii nunc primum edita. pp. 126. *I. Marci: Lugduni Batauorum*, 1618. 4º. C. 74. b. 6.

—— Cebetis . . . Tabula, *etc.* [With the Latin translation of H. Wolfius.] (Breves in Tabulam Cebetis notae. [By J. D. Snecanus.]) *See* Epictetus. Epicteti Enchiridion, *etc.* 1634. 32º. 8460. a. 1.

—— [Another edition.] *See* Epictetus. Epicteti Enchiridion, *etc.* 1646. 32º. 524. a. 1.

—— Cebetis . . . Tabula, *etc.* (Κεβητος . . . Πιναξ.) *See* Epictetus. Epicteti Enchiridion, *etc.* 1653. 12º. 528. a. 1.

—— Cebetis . . . Tabula, *etc.* [With the Latin translation by H. Wolfius, and with notes by J. D. Snecanus.] *See* Epictetus. Epicteti Enchiridion, *etc.* 1654. 32º. 8405. aa. 2.

CEBES. [Greek and Latin.]

—— Κεβητος . . . Πιναξ. Cebetis . . . Tabula . . . Hieronymo Wolfio . . . interprete. (Hieronymi Wolfii . . . Annotationes.) *See* Epictetus. Epicteti . . . Enchiridion, *etc.* pt. 1. 1655. 8º. 526. h. 7.

—— Cebetis . . . Tabula, *etc.* [With the Latin translation by H. Wolfius, and with notes by J. D. Snecanus.] *See* Epictetus. Epicteti Enchiridion, *etc.* 1657. 32º. 8410. a. 29.

—— Cebetis . . . Tabula, *etc.* (Notæ in Cebetis Tabulam.) [The Latin translation by H. Wulfius.] *See* Epictetus. Epicteti Enchiridion, *etc.* 1659. 8º. E. 1800. (2.)

—— Κεβητος . . . Πιναξ. Cebetis . . . Tabula . . . Hieronymo Wolfio . . . interprete. *See* Epictetus. Epicteti . . . Enchiridion, *etc.* pt. 1. 1670. 8º. 525. g. 10.

—— Cebetis . . . Tabula, *etc.* [With the Latin translation by H. Wolfius, and with notes by J. D. Snecanus.] *See* Epictetus. Epicteti Enchiridion, *etc.* 1670. 32º. 526. a. 10.

—— [Another edition.] *See* Epictetus. Epicteti Enchiridion, *etc.* 1670. 32º. C. 12. a. 5.

—— Cebetis . . . Tabula, *etc.* (Ex recensione Abrahami Berkelii.) [With the Latin translation of H. Wolfius and notes by H. Wolfius and others.] *See* Epictetus. Epicteti Enchiridium, *etc.* 1670. 8º. 8406. bbb. 17.

—— Κεβητος . . . Πιναξ. Cebetis . . . Tabula. [The Latin translation by H. Wolfius.] *See* Epictetus. 'Επικτητου 'Εγχειριδιον, *etc.* 1670. 8º. 1475. a. 43.

—— [Another edition.] *See* Epictetus. 'Επικτητου 'Εγχειριδιον, *etc.* 1680. 12º. 715. b. 4.

—— Cebetis . . . Tabula, *etc.* [With the Latin translation by H. Wolfius and notes by H. Wolfius and others.] *See* Epictetus. Epicteti Enchiridium, *etc.* 1683. 8º. 165. l. 19.

—— Κεβητος . . . Πιναξ. Cebetis . . . Tabula (ex interpretatione Hieronymi Wolfii) . . . Multis in locis restituta ex mss. codicibus . . . ab Jacobo Gronovio, cujus accedunt notæ & emendationes. pp. 199. *Apud H. Wetstenium: Amstelædami*, 1689. 8º. 526. f. 1.

—— Cebetis . . . Tabula, *etc.* [With the Latin translation by H. Wolfius, and with notes by J. D. Snecanus.] *See* Epictetus. Epicteti Enchiridion, *etc.* 1701. 12º. 524. a. 2.

—— Κεβητος . . . Πιναξ. (Cebetis . . . Tabula.) [The Latin translation by H. Wolfius.] *See* Epictetus. 'Επικτητου 'Εγχειριδιον, *etc.* 1702. 12º. 715. a. 32.

—— Κεβητος . . . Πιναξ.—Cebetis . . . Tabula. [Based on the edition of J. Gronovius. With the Latin translation of H. Wolfius.] *See* Lucian, *of Samosata.* [*Dialogues.—Collections.—Greek and Latin.*] Luciani Samosatensis Colloquia selecta, *etc.* 1708. 12º. 720. a. 2.

—— Κεβητος . . . Πιναξ. Cebetis . . . Tabula, *etc.* [The Latin translation by M. Meibomius.] *See* Epictetus. Epicteti Manuale et Sententiae, *etc.* pt. 2. 1711. 4º. 525. g. 11.

—— Κεβητου . . . Πιναξ. Cebetis . . . Tabula. Novâ versione, in puerorum usus, donata, et selectioribus criticorum notis illustrata. Accedit quoque . . . Ludovici Odaxii versio; necnon notæ, & index verborum . . . Operâ Thomæ Johnson. pp. ii. 179. *Impensis Authoris: Londini*, 1720. 8º. 678. b. 2.

—— [Another copy.] 165. d. 8.

CEBES. [GREEK AND LATIN.]

—— Cebetis . . . Tabula, *etc.* [With the Latin translation of H. Wolfius and notes by H. Wolfius and others.] *See* EPICTETUS. Epicteti Enchiridium, *etc.* 1723. 8°.
525. g. 12.

—— Κεβητος . . . Πιναξ. Cebetis . . . Tabula. [The Latin translation by H. Wolfius.] *See* LUCIAN, *of Samosata.* [*Dialogues.—Collections.—Greek and Latin.*] Luciani . . . Colloquia selecta, *etc.* 1732. 12°.
8460. aa. 11.

—— Κεβητος . . . Πιναξ. Cebetis . . . Tabula, *etc. See* EPICTETUS. Ἐπικτητου Ἐγχειριδιον, *etc.* 1744. 12°.
165. k. 2.

—— Κεβητος . . . Πιναξ. Cebetis . . . Tabula . . . Adjecto indice trilingui copiosissimo. Studio atque opera Thomæ Nugent. In usum scholarum. pp. xi. 56 [57]. *Impensis Josephi Davidson: Londini,* 1745. 8°.
715. c. 1.
Interleaved. With a few MS. notes by Charles Burney on inserted leaves.

—— [Another copy.]
165. l. 2.

—— Ὁ του Κεβητος Πιναξ. Accedit interpretatio Latina [by H. Wolfius] ex editione Jacobi Gronovii. pp. 76. 19. *Robertus Foulis: Glasguae,* 1747. 12°. 1385. a. 8. (2.)

—— [Another copy.] ON VELLUM. C. 8. b. 2.
Imperfect; wanting all after p. 72.

—— Cebetis . . . Tabula, Græce & Latine, *etc.* [The Latin translation by H. Wolfius.] *See* EPICTETUS. Epicteti Enchiridium, *etc.* 1750. 16°.
524. b. 6.

—— Ὁ του Κεβητος Πιναξ. Accedit interpretatio Latina [by H. Wolfius] ex editione Jacobi Gronovii. pp. 91. *R. & A. Foulis: Glasguæ,* 1757. 8°.
165. l. 3.

—— Κεβητος . . . Πιναξ. Cebetis . . . Tabula. Edidit Josephus Simpson. pp. 58. *See* EPICTETUS. Epicteti Manuale, *etc.* pt. 2. 1758. 8°.
525. g. 13.

—— Κεβητος Θηβαιου Πιναξ. (Cebetis Thebani Tabula [translated by H. Wolfius].) *In: Πλατωνος Ἀπολογια Σωκρατους. Κριτων, etc.* 1759. 12°. 8473. de. 36.

—— Ὁ του Κεβητος Πιναξ. Accedit interpretatio Latina [by H. Wolfius], ex editione Jacobi Gronovii. pp. 91. *R. & A. Foulis: Glasguae,* 1771. 8°.
525. a. 8.

—— Κεβητος . . . Πιναξ.—Cebetis . . . Tabula. *See* LUCIAN, *of Samosata.* [*Dialogues.—Collections.—Greek and Latin.*] Luciani . . . Colloquia selecta, *etc.* 1771. 12°.
720. c. 10.

—— Κεβητος . . . Πιναξ. [Wanting the Latin translation.] *See* LUCIAN, *of Samosata.* [*Dialogues.—Collections.—Greek and Latin.*] Luciani . . . Colloquia selecta, *etc.* 1777. 12°.
8468. a. 36.

—— Κεβητος . . . Πιναξ.—Cebetis . . . Tabula. Latine. *See* EPICTETUS. Ἐπικτητου Ἐγχειριδιον, *etc.* 1796. 12°.
8408. a. 18.

—— Κεβητος . . . Πιναξ.—Cebetis . . . Tabula (in Latinum conversa per Ludovicum Odaxium). *See* EPICTETUS. Epicteti Manuale, *etc.* 1798. 8°.
674. c. 16.

—— Κεβητος . . . Πιναξ.—Cebetis . . . Tabula. [Edited by Joseph Simpson.] *See* EPICTETUS. Epicteti Enchiridion, *etc.* 1804. 8°.
166. i. 8.

—— Κεβητος . . . Πιναξ. (Cebetis . . . Tabula.) [The Latin translation by L. Odassi.] pp. 15. *See* THEOPHRASTUS. [*Characteres.—Greek and Latin.*] Theophrasti Characteres, *etc.* 1840. 8°.
011306.cc.2.

CEBES.

GREEK AND FRENCH.

—— Κεβητος . . . Πιναξ. (Γαλλιστι μεθερμηνευσαντος του F. Th. [i.e. J. F. Thurot.]) *See* EPICTETUS. Ἐπικτητου Ἐγχειριδιον, *etc.* 1826. 8°. [Προδρομος Ἑλληνικης Βιβλιοθηκης. Παρεργα. tom. 7.]
160. d. 12.

GREEK AND ITALIAN.

—— La Tavola di Cebete Tebano. (Κεβητος . . . Πιναξ.) 2 pt. L.P. *Co' tipi Bodoniani: Parma,* 1793. 4°.
714. f. 4.
One of an edition of 100 copies.

—— [Another copy.]
G. 7974.

LATIN AND ITALIAN.

—— Traduzione della Tavola di Cebete, in versi sciolti [with the Latin text], ed alcune rime profane, morali, e sagre del N. H. Co: Cornelio Pepoli. pp. 128. *Venezia,* 1763. 8°.
8461. c. 14.

—— La Tavola di Cebete, poemetto anonimo latino [in part original, in part based on the Tabula], trasportato in ottava rima da Pietro Guadagnoli. pp. xi. 190. *Arezzo,* 1782. 8°.
T. 2284. (1.)

ARABIC AND SPANISH.

—— Paráfrasis árabe [by Ibn Miskawaih] de la Tabla de Cebes, traducida en castellano é ilustrada con notas por D. Pablo Lozano y Casela. (Version libre castellana de la paráfrasis árabe.—Tres centurias de sentencias árabes, traducidas por primera vez. Texto árabe de la paráfrasis, sin mociones ni version, para exercicio de los principiantes.) pp. xl. 219. 29. *Madrid,* 1793. 4°.
14540. c. 33.

—— [Another copy.]
29. c. 1.

LATIN.

—— Cebetis . . . Tabula e Græco in Latinum conuersa per Ludouicum Odaxium. *See* CENSORINUS. Index librorum: qui in hoc uolumine continentur. Censorinus de die natali, *etc.* 1497. fol. Maps C. 7. b. 12. (4–9.)

—— [Another edition.] *See* CENSORINUS. Index librorum: qui in hoc volumine continentur. Censorinus de die natali, *etc.* [1500?] 4°.
IA. 24363.

—— [Another edition.] *See* CENSORINUS. Index operum quæ in hoc volumine continentur. Censorini de die natali liber, *etc.* [1503?] 4°.
IA. 24356. (1.)

—— Tabula Cebetis philosophi socratici, cū Iohānis Aesti-cāpiani Epistola. [With a woodcut.] *Per . . . N. Lamperter & B. Murrer: Erancphordio* [sic], 1507. 4°.
C. 57. c. 45.
The lower part of the woodcut is missing.

—— Cebetis . . . Tabula (in latinū cōuersa per Ludouicū Odaxium), in qua . . . totius uitæ humanæ ratio, hoc est ingressus, medium, & exitus . . . describunt̄, cum scholiis per Huldrichum Fabri . . . marginibus adiectis. *Per I. Singreniū: Viennæ,* 1519. 4°. 520. c. 18. (3.)

—— Cebetis Thebani . . . tabula (in Latinum conuersa per Lodouicum Odaxium), uitæ totius humanæ cursum graphice continens. Addito Ioannis Camertis . . . Commētariolo, *etc.* *In officina H. Vietoris: Cracouia,* 1524. 4°.
715. b. 3.

—— Cebetis . . . Tabula, quæ humanæ uitæ imaginem repræsentat, in Latinam linguam conuersa, per Theodoricum Adamæum . . . Aurea carmina Pythagoræ. pp. 30. *Ex officina C. Wecheli: Parisijs,* 1547. 8°.
527. e. 3. (4.)

—— Iusti Velsij . . . In Cebetis . . . Tabulam commentariorum libri sex, *etc.* [With a Latin version of the text.] pp. 441. *Lugduni,* 1551. 4°.
525. g. 28.

CEBES. [Latin.]

—— Cebetis . . . Tabula e Græco in Latinum conuersa per Lodouicum Odaxium. (Ioannis Camertis in tabulam Cebetis Commentariolum.) *See* Solinus (C. J.) Commentaria in C. Iulii Solini Polyhistora, *etc.* 1557. fol.
586. i. 20.

—— Cebetis Tabula. A Caspare Barthio Latine versa. *See* Barth (C. von) Casp. Barthii opuscula varia, *etc.* 1612. 8°. **1213. i. 27. (1.)**

—— Cebetis . . . Tabula, *etc.* [Translated into Latin by H. Wolfius.] *See* Epictetus. Epicteti . . . Enchiridion, *etc.* [1660.] 24°. **718. a. 6.**

English.

—— The Table of Cebes the Philosopher. (Translated out of latine into english by sir Frances Poyngz.) How one may take profite of his ennemies, translated out of Plutarche. A treatise perswadying a man paciently to suffer the death of his freend (by Erasmus Roterodamus). 𝕭.𝕷. *Imprinted by Thomas Berthelet: London,* [1530?] 16°. **231. a. 45.**

—— The Table of Cebes . . . containing a prescript method for the well ordering of the life of man. [Translated by John Healey.] *See* Epictetus. Epictetus his Manuall, *etc.* 1610. 12°. **8407. a. 50. (2.)**

—— [A reissue.] The table of Cebes, *etc. In:* Epictetus his Manuall, *etc.* 1610. 12°. **Mic. A. 577. (2.)**

—— [Another edition.] *See* Epictetus. Epictetus Manuall, *etc.* 1616. 12°. **1385. a. 12.**

—— The Tablet of Cebes, or, the Embleme of humane life. (Rendered into English by John Davies [from the French of G. Boileau].) *See* Epictetus. The Life, and Philosophy, of Epictetus, *etc.* 1670. 8°. **232. k. 6.**

—— The Tablet of Cebes . . . or a True emblem of human life: done out of Greek into English. With an additional treatise concerning tranquillity of mind, written by Hipparchus. And translated by Robert Warren. (Apelles his Table, being a picture of humane life.) pp. 124. *For John Pindar: Cambridge,* 1699. 12°. **8403. a. 25.**

—— The Mythological Picture of Cebes, *etc.* (Translated by Jeremy Collier.) *See* Aurelius Antoninus (M.) called *the Philosopher, Emperor of Rome.* [*Meditations.—English.*] The Emperor Marcus Antoninus his Conversation with himself, *etc.* 1701. 8°. **524. h. 20.**

—— Cebes's Table, in verse. (By a Lady [addressed as " Selina " in complimentary verses].) *See* Epictetus. The Porch and Academy opened, or, Epictetus's Manual newly turn'd into English verse, *etc.* 1707. 8°. **11633. bbb. 13.**

—— The Mythological Picture of Cebes. (Translated by Jeremy Collier.) *See* Aurelius Antoninus (M.) called *the Philosopher, Emperor of Rome.* [*Meditations.—English.*] The Emperor Marcus Antoninus his Conversation with himself, *etc.* 1726. 8°. **[Missing.]**

—— The Tablature of Cebes . . . Translated . . . by Samuel Boyse . . . The third edition. pp. 50. *R. & A. Foulis: Glasgow,* 1750. 8°. **1481. aa. 10. (2.)**

—— The Table of Cebes, or, the Picture of human life. In English verse. With notes. By Thomas Scott. pp. 44. *R. & J. Dodsley: London,* 1754. 4°. **11630. e. 1. (10.)**

—— [Another copy.] **834. k. 11. (3.)**

—— [Another copy.] **840. k. 6. (14.)**

—— The Circuit of Human Life: a vision in which are allegorically described, the virtues and vices. Taken from the Tablature of Cebes, *etc.* pp. 115. *T. Carnan: London,* 1774. 12°. **700. b. 27. (1.)**

CEBES. [English.]

—— The Picture of Human Life, containing some excellent rules for a virtuous and prudent conduct. Translated from the Greek of Cebes . . . With an essay on allegorical mode of writing. The second edition. By a Gentleman of the University. pp. 56. *J. Nicholson: Cambridge,* 1777. 12°. **112. a. 28.**

—— The Picture of Human Life, translated from the Greek, *etc.* [The translation variously attributed to Samuel Johnson and Joseph Spence.] *See* Lobo (J.) A Voyage to Abyssinia, *etc.* 1789. 8°. **10097. d. 2.**

—— The Emblem of Human Life . . . Rendered into English by John Davies, *etc.* pp. 36. *Thomson & Co.: Glasgow,* 1901. 8°. **8460. dd. 1.** *Lithographed.*

—— Κεβητος . . . Πιναξ. The Picture of Kebes the Theban, *etc.* (Translated by Hugh E. Seebohm.) pp. 52. *Essex House Press: Chipping Campden,* 1906. 8°. **C. 99. a. 9.**

—— The Tablet of Kebes. (Translated by R. Thomson Clark.) *See* Clark (R. T.) *Translator of Classical Authors.* The Characters of Theophrastos, *etc.* [1909.] 8°. **8464. aa. 28.**

Dutch.

—— Cebetis . . . Tafereel, *etc.* (Kebes Tavereels kort begrip door H. L. Spieghel. [In verse.]) *See* Epictetus. Epictetus Handt-boexken, *etc.* 1615. 8°. **11555. c. 37. (2.)**

French.

—— Le Tableau de Cebes . . . maintenant exposé en ryme Françoyse [by G. Corrozet]. (La Volupté vaïcue. Emblemes. [In verse.]) ff. xlix. *Imprimé par D. Ionot* [sic] ; *on les uend . . . en la boutique de G. Corrozet: Paris,* 1543. 8°. **232. k. 14.**

—— Le Tableau de Cebés thebain. [Translated by R. Estienne.] ff. 29. [*R. Estienne: Paris,* 1611.] 8°. **11826. bbb. 3. (5.)** *Imperfect; wanting the titlepage.*

—— Le Tableau de Cebes, ou il est traité de la maniere de paruenir à la felicité naturelle. [Translated by G. Boileau.] (Remarques sur le Tableau de Cebes.—La Belle melancholie. A Philandre. [By G. Boileau.]) pp. 88. *L. Chamhoudry: Paris,* 1653. 8°. **11335. a. 6.**

—— Troisiéme edition. *See* Epictetus. ʻLa Vie d'Epictete, *etc.* 1657. 12°. **276. a. 19.**

—— [Another edition.] *See* Epictetus. La Vie d'Epictete, *etc.* 1667. 12°. **C. 65. h. 11.**

—— [Another edition.] *See* Le Roy (Marin) *Sieur de Gomberville.* Le Theatre moral de la vie humaine, *etc.* [1678?] fol. **8406. h. 22.**

—— Le Tableau de Cebès. [Translated by J. B. Morvan de Bellegarde.] (Remarques sur le Tableau de Cebès.) *See* Epictetus. Les Caracteres d'Epictete, *etc.* 1709. 12°. **8461. a. 14.**

—— [Another edition.] *See* Epictetus. Les Caracteres d'Epictete, *etc.* 1721. 12°. **232. k. 38.**

—— [Another edition.] *See* Epictetus. Les Caracteres d'Epictete, *etc.* 1741. 12°. **526. e. 20.**

—— Tableau de Cébès, traduit du grec [by J. N. Belin de Ballu]. *See* Epictetus. Manuel d'Épictete, *etc.* 1790. 8°. **1385. e. 17.**

—— Le Tableau de Cébès . . . Imitation du grec, en vers libres, par Desforges. *See* Epictetus. Le Manuel d'Épictète, *etc.* [1797.] 4°. **525. k. 30.**

CEBES. [FRENCH.]

—— Tableau de la vie humaine. [Translated by M. Meunier.] *See* AURELIUS ANTONINUS (M.) called *the Philosopher, Emperor of Rome.* [*Meditations.—French.*] Marc-Aurèle. Pensées pour moi-même, *etc.* 1933. 8°. **08466. de. 5.**

GERMAN.

—— Tabula Cebetis. Eine . . . Tafel, dariñ das gantze menschliche Leben . . . abgemahlet wirdt . . . Auss Griechischer Sprach verdeutschet [by B. Pirckheimer]. *See* PIRCKHEIMER (B.) Theatrum Virtutis & Honoris, *etc.* 1606. 8°. **12331. aa. 58.**

—— Teutsche und gebundene Uebersetzung des Sinnbildes Cebetis. [By J. F. A. von Uffenbach.] *See* UFFENBACH (J. F. A. von) Des Herrn Joh. Fried. von Uffenbach gesammelte Neben-Arbeit, *etc.* 1733. 8°. **11517. aa. 55.**

—— Das Gemälde des Kebes. Aus einer alten griechischen Handschrifft. pp. xxxx. 78. *Moskau,* 1785. 8°. **1387. h. 6. (2.)**

—— Das Gemälde von Kebes. Deutsch von Dʳ Friedrich S. Krauss. Der Schluss aus dem Arabischen des Ibni Muskveïh, von Prof. Dʳ Friedrich Müller. pp. 33. *Wien,* 1882. 8°. **14540. a. 34. (2.)**

ITALIAN.

—— Cebete Thebano, che in vna tauola dipinta philosophica-mente mostra le qualita de la vita humana. Dialogo ridotto di Greco in volgare [by F. A. Coccio]. ff. 11. *Impresso per F. Marcolini: Venetia,* 1538. 8°. **11715. b. 14.**

—— Discorsi morali di Agostino Mascardi su la Tavola di Cebete. (La Tavola . . . vulgarizata da A. Mascardi.) vol. 1. pp. 403. *G. Pellagallo: Venetia,* 1627. 4°. **29. d. 7.**

The titlepage is engraved. No more published.

—— [Another edition.] vol. 1. pp. 358. *G. P. Pinelli: Venetia,* 1638. 4°. **524. g. 25.** *The titlepage is engraved.*

—— [Another edition.] vol. 1. pp. 303. *G. P. Pinelli: Venetia,* 1642. 4°. **525. l. 17.** *The titlepage is engraved.*

—— [Another edition.] In questa nuoua impressione cor-retti e migliorati. pp. 491. *N. Pezzana: Venetia,* 1674. 12°. **526. e. 5.**

—— Quadro di Cebete . . . trasportato in lingua italiana [by A. Pimbiolo degli Engelfreddi]. pp. xxxvii. *Padova,* 1761. 4°. **231. l. 7.**

POLISH.

—— Obraz Cebesa i Doręcznik Epikteta. Z greckiego przełożył i uwagami objaśnił x. Hołowiński. pp. 160. *Wilno,* 1845. 8°. **8405. ee. 9.**

SPANISH.

—— Tabla de Cebetes philosopho thebano sacada de grieco en castellano por el doctor poblacion, *etc.* *Apud S. Colinæum: Parisiis,* 1532. 8°. **C. 97. aa. 10. (3.)**

—— Comienca la tabla de Cebetes. *See* ERASMUS (D.) [*Apophthegmata.*] Libro de vidas y dichos graciosos, *etc.* 1549. 8°. **1075. k. 8.**

—— Tabla de Cebes . . . trasladada de Griego en Castellano por Ambrosio de Morales. (Argumento y Breue Declara-cion de la Tabla. [By A. de Morales.]) *See* PEREZ DE OLIVA (F.) Las Obas [*sic*] del Maestro Fernan Perez de Oliua, *etc.* 1586. 4°. **248. g. 14.**

CEBES.

—— La Tabla de Kebes en Romanze por el M. Gonzalo Korreas. *See* CORREAS (G.) Ortografia Kastellana, *etc.* 1630. 8°. **8460. aaa. 22.**

—— La Tabla de Cebes, *etc.* [Translated by A. de Morales.] (Argumento y Breve Declaracion de la Tabla. [By A. de Morales.]) pp. 27. 1672 [1673]. *See* TEATRO. Theatro moral de toda la philosophia, *etc.* pt. 3. 1669, *etc.* fol. **28. g. 11.**

—— [Another edition.] *See* PEREZ DE OLIVA (F.) Las Obras del Maestro Fernan Perez de Oliva, *etc.* tom. 2. 1787. 8°. **12230. a. 22.**

APPENDIX.

—— *See* MUELLER (Carl C.) De arte critica Cebetis Tabulae adhibenda. 1877. 8°. **11312. h. 42. (3.)**

—— *See* SCHLEGEL (Johann H.) Animadversorum ad Cebetis Tabulam primitias . . . proferunt respondens J. H. Schlegelius . . . et opponens C. A. Schildenbergerus. [1744.] 4°. **T. 2216. (5.)**

CEBETE. *See* CEBES.

CEBETES. *See* CEBES.

ČEBOTAREV (BORIS V.) *See* CHEBOTAREV.

CEBREIRO BLANCO (LUIS)

—— *See* MADRID.

~~ficas.~~—*Instituto Histórico de Marina.* Colección de diarios y relaciones para la historia de los viajes y descubrimientos. (Textos revisados, confrontados e interpretados gráfica-mente por L. Cebreiro Blanco.) 1943, *etc.* 8°. **Ac. 4378.**

CEBREIROS (NAZARIO) Las Reformas Militares. Estudio crítico. pp. 288. *Santander,* 1931. 8°. **8820. df. 18.**

CEBREROS (DIEGO) Seuilla Festiua. Aplauso celebre, y panegirico que se celebro en el Colegio del Angel de la Guarda . . . á la beatificacion de San Juan de la Cruz . . . Sacala á luz el licenciado Don D. Cebreros. pp. 271. *J. Cabezas: Seuilla,* 1676. 4°. **486. c. 4. (2.)**

CEBREROS Y BUENO (RAFAEL) Pensamientos. pp. 157. *Madrid,* 1877. 8°. **8042. b. 9.**

CEBRIÀ, Saint. *See* CYPRIAN, Saint, Bishop of Carthage.

CEBRIÁ (PEDRO NOLASCO VIVES Y) *See* VIVES Y CEBRIÁ.

CEBRIÁN Y AUGUSTÍN (PEDRO) *Count de Fuenclara·* [For official documents issued by the Count de Fuenclara as Viceroy of Mexico:] *See* MEXICO.—[*Laws, etc.—*II.]— Cebrián y Augustín (P.) *Count de Fuenclara, Viceroy.* [1742–1746.]

CEBRIÁN YUSTI (PRÍAMO) and **LOS ARCOS Y MIRANDA** (ANTONIO)

—— Teoría general de las proyecciones geográficas y su aplicación á la formación de un mapa de España. [With a map.] pp. 270. pl. II. 1895. 8°. *See* SPAIN.—*Insti-tuto Nacional de Estadística.* **10162. f. 3.**

CEBROOKE (ELIZABETH) *See* ABBOT (E.)

CEBUSKÝ (ANTONÍN) Kurzgefasste Grammatik der böhmi-schen Sprache . . . Fünfte Auflage. pp. viii. 216. *Wien,* 1870. 8°. **12976. g. 6.**

CEBY (   ) Opuscules lyriques, *etc.* (Airs notés des opuscules lyriques.) 2 pt. *E. Booker: Londres,* 1801. 8°. **11475. c. 6.**

CECAUMENUS. *See* KEKAUMENOS.

CECCALDI (A. F.) Considérations et réflexions sur la cataracte. Thèse, *etc.* pp. 78. *Montpellier,* 1870. 4°.
7379. h. 16. (6.)

CECCALDI (ALI) Faculté de Droit de Paris. Thèse pour la licence, *etc.* (Jus romanum. Quando ex facto tutoris . . . minores agere vel conveniri possunt, *etc.*—Droit français. De l'émancipation, *etc.*) pp. 70. *Paris,* 1858. 8°. **5406. aaa. 5. (10.)**

CECCALDI (CHARLES LÉON COLONNA) *See* COLONNA CECCALDI.

CECCALDI (DOMINIQUE ALBERT ÉDOUARD) Faculté de Droit de Paris. Thèse pour la licence, *etc.* (Jus romanum. Communi dividundo, *etc.*—Droit français. Des sociétés civiles, *etc.*) pp. 33. *Paris,* 1857. 8°.
5406. aa. 3. (19.)

CECCALDI (F.) *Writer on Cartography.*

—— *See* BERTHELOT (A. M.) and CECCALDI (F.) Les Cartes de la Corse de Ptolémée au XIXe siècle. 1939. 8°.
10005. s. 19.

CECCALDI (FERDINAND) Essai sur l'habitude ; thèse, *etc.* pp. 33. *Paris,* 1830. 4°. **1184. d. 2. (30.)**

CECCALDI (GABRIEL FERDINAND) Au pays de la poudre. En campagne avec les "Joyeux," Maroc Occidental, 1911-1912. [With a map.] pp. iv. 230. *Paris,* 1914. 8°. **09061. ff. 33.**

CECCALDI (GEORGES COLONNA) *See* COLONNA CECCALDI.

CECCALDI (JEAN) Contributions directes en ce qui concerne les militaires des armées de terre et de mer. Recueil annoté des dispositions constitutionnelles, législatives et réglementaires sur les contributions directes, *etc.* pp. xi. 334. *Paris,* 1869. 8°. **5423. d. 8.**

CECCALDI (MARCO ANTONIO) *See* GROSSA (G. della) Historia di Corsica . . . diuisa in tredici libri, de' quali i primi noue hebbero principio da G. della Grossa, proseguendo anchora à quello P. A. Monteggiani, e doppo M. A. Ceccaldi, *etc.* 1594. 4°. **178. h. 20.**

—— Chronique de Marc' Antonio Ceccaldi. 1889. *See* LETTERON (L. A.) Histoire de la Corse, *etc.* tom. 2. 1888, *etc.* 8°. [*Bulletin de la Société des Sciences Historiques & Naturelles de la Corse.* fasc. 97–99.]
Ac. 2861/17.

CECCALDI (T. COLONNA) *See* COLONNA CECCALDI.

CECCANO (JOANNES DE) *See* JOANNES, *de Ceccano.*

CECCAREL (MATTEO) Della vita e degli scritti di Paolo Marzolo. pp. 360. *Treviso,* 1870. 8°. **10631. bb. 30.**

CECCARELLI (ALFONSO) *See* ALLACCI (L.) [*Single Works.*] Leonis Allatii Animadversiones in antiquitatum etruscarum fragmenta . . . Additur ejusdem animadversio in libros A. Ciccarelli, *etc.* 1642. 8°. **604. b. 6.**

—— Alphonsi Ciccarelli . . . De Clitumno, Umbriæ flumine celeberrimo, opusculum. Editio novissima, auctior & emendatior. 1723. *See* GRAEVIUS (J. G.) Thesaurus antiquitatum et historiarum Italiæ, *etc.* tom. 9. pt. 8. 1729, *etc.* fol. **L.R.302.a.2/9.**

—— Alphonsi Cicarelli De origine, antiquitate et nobilitate illustrissimae domus Sanctacruciae. *See* ADRIANI (G. B.) *Professore di Storia.* Della vita e delle varie nunziature del cardinale P. Santa Croce, *etc.* 1869. 8°.
4863. e. 23.

CECCARELLI (ALFONSO)

—— Dell'historia di Casa Monaldesca . . . libri cinque, nella quale si ha notitia di molte altre cose accadute in Toscana, & in Italia. (Dell' origine di Oruieto.) pp. 222. *Appresso G. de gl' Angeli: Ascoli,* 1580. 4°. **606. c. 34.**

—— [Another copy.] **663. c. 2.**

—— [Another copy.] **137. b. 7.**

—— Opusculum de tuberibus . . . Adiecimus etiam opusculum de Clitumno flumine, *etc.* ff. 34. *Ad instantiam L. Bozetti: Patauii,* 1564. 8°. **966. b. 40.**

CECCARELLI (AMATO)

—— Note di pedagogia sulla Regola di S. Benedetto. *In:* Benedictina. anno 4. fasc. 3/4—anno 5. fasc. 3/4. 1950, 51. 8°. **P.P. 4188. ic.**

CECCARELLI (ANNA) L'Idea pedagogica di Leonardo da Vinci. pp. 176. *Roma,* 1914. 8°. **8305. e. 105.**

CECCARELLI (ANTONIO) *See* CICARELLI.

CECCARELLI (GALENO) La Tubercolosi delle ghiandole linfatiche. *See* DONATI (M.) La Tubercolosi extrapolmonare, *etc.* vol. 1. 1936, *etc.* 8°. **7439. v. 1.**

CECCARELLI (GIOACCHINO)

—— Farinata degli Uberti nel canto decimo dell'Inferno. pp. 25. *Roma,* 1906. 8°. **11420. c. 10. (2.)**

CECCARELLI (GIUSEPPE) *See* also CECCARIUS, *pseud.* [i.e. G. Ceccarelli.]

—— I Braschi. [With special reference to Giovanni Angelo Braschi, Pope Pius VI.] pp. 49. pl. x. 1949. 8°. *See* ROME.—*The City.*—*Istituto di Studi Romani.*
9918. a. 45.

CECCARELLI (IPPOLITO) *See* ROME.—*The City.*—*Collegium Medicorum.* Antidotario Romano Latino, et volgare. Tradotto da H. Cesarelli, *etc.* 1635, *etc.* 4°.
546. k. 11. (1, 2.)

—— —— 1639. 4°. **777. c. 4.**

CECCARELLI (JACOPO) Feo Belcari e le sue opere. 3 pt. *Siena,* 1907. 8°. **11852. s. 21.**

CECCARELLO. Dialogo di Ceccarello, e Matarello alla villanesca, *etc.* *Per V. Benacci: Bologna,* [1590 ?] 8°.
1071. c. 63. (13.)

—— [Another edition.] *V. Benacci: Bologna,* [1620 ?] 8°.
11426. b. 73. (10.)

CECCARELLUS (CAROLUS FRANCISCUS) Lingua ignea : sive de S. Ivone, pauperum patrono, oratio habita in eiusdem templo, *etc.* pp. 15. *Typis hæredum F. Corbelletti: Romæ,* 1638. 4°. **4829. d. 19. (2.)**

CECCARINI (GIOVANNI) Lettera . . . relativa al granito dell'isola del Giglio. pp. 13. *Roma,* 1828. 8°.
[MISSING.]

CECCARIUS, *pseud.* [i.e. GIUSEPPE CECCARELLI.] *See* also CECCARELLI (G.)

—— *See* MUÑOZ (A.) *Writer on Art.* Giuseppe Gioacchino Belli. [Edited by A. Muñoz, Ceccarius and L. de Gregori.] 1942. fol. **11861.h.11.**

CECCARIUS, *pseud.* [i.e. GIUSEPPE CECCARELLI.]

—— Saggio di bibliografia romana. (Bibliografia romana.) III, *etc.* 1947/1948, *etc.* *Roma*, 1948– . 8°. **2772. b. 1.**
Part of the " Collana dei romanisti."

CECCARONI (AGOSTINO) Il Conclave. Storia, costituzioni, cerimonie. [Edited by Giacinto Marietti.] pp. xvi. 195. *Torino, Roma*, 1901. 8°. **5015. b. 6.**

CECCARONI (FABRIZIO) Per la celebrazione della prima messa del conte Girolamo Fantaguzzi . . . Sonetto. *Roma*, 1827. *s. sh.* fol. **898. i. 10. (12.)**

CECCHELLI (CARLO)

—— *See* ARMELLINI (Mariano) *of Rome.* Le Chiese di Roma . . . Nuova edizione . . . a cura di C. Cecchelli, *etc.* 1942. 4°. **7816. g. 30.**

—— *See* MARK, *Saint and Evangelist.* Note storiche ed archeologiche sul testo della " Translatio Sancti Marci." [By N. McCleary. Translated from the English by C. Cecchelli.] 1935. 8°. **20003. k. 27.**

—— *See* MILAN.—*Basilica di S. Lorenzo Maggiore.* La Basilica di S. Lorenzo Maggiore in Milano. [By A. Calderini, G. Chierici and C. Cecchelli.] [1951.] 4°. **07822. v. 3.**

—— Archeologia ed arte cristiana dell'antichità e dell'alto medioevo, 1940–1950. [A bibliography.] *In:* Doxa. anno 3. fasc. 2/3. pp. 97–160. 1950. 8°. **P.P. 4188. id.**

—— Bibliografia del mondo " barbarico." [With plates.] *Roma*, 1954– . 8°. **BB.L. a. 1.**

—— Il Campidoglio. LXIV tavole, con introduzione e note illustrative di C. Cecchelli, *etc.* pp. 37. pl. 64. 1925. fol. *See* ROME.—*The City.—Municipio.* [MISSING.]

—— I Margani, i Capocci, i Sanguigni, i Mellini. pp. 55. pl. IV. 1946. 8°. *See* ROME.—*The City.—Istituto di Studi Romani.* **10633. s. 67.**

—— Monumenti cristiano-eretici di Roma. [With plates.] pp. viii. 274. *Roma*, [1945 ?] fol. **L.R. 262. c. 15.**

—— Sguardo generale all'architettura bizantina in Italia. [With plates.] 1935. *See* ROME.—*The City.—Istituto per l'Europa Orientale.* Studî bizantini. vol. 4. 1924, *etc.* 8°. **Ac. 8805. e.**

—— Studi e documenti sulla Roma sacra. *Roma*, 1938– . 8°. [*Miscellanea della R. Deputazione Romana di Storia Patria.* no. 10, 18, etc.] **Ac. 6540/3.**

—— Il Vaticano. La basilica, i palazzi, i giardini, le mura. pp. 105. pl. 444. *Milano, Roma*, [1928.] 4°. **L.R. 21. b. 3.**

—— La Vita di Roma nel medio evo. [With plates.]
1. Le arti minori e il costume. 1951-1952– .

Roma, 1951-1952– . 8°. **W.P. A. 536.**

—— Zara. [With illustrations.] pp. 218. *Roma*, 1932. fol. [*Catalogo delle cose d'arte e di antichità d'Italia.* fasc. 4.] **7812. t. 1/3.**

CECCHEREGLI (ALESSANDRO) Delle attioni, et sentenze del S. Alessandro de' Medici, primo Duca di Fiorenza, ragionamento, *etc.* ff. 59. *Appresso G. Giolito de' Ferrari: Vinegia*, 1564. 4°. **1199. c. 5. (1.)**
An additional titlepage, taken from a copy of the 1565 *reissue, has been inserted in this copy.*

CECCHEREGLI (ALESSANDRO)

—— [A reissue.] *Vinegia*, 1565. 4°. **1199. e. 6. (1.)**

—— [Another copy.] **277. e. 44.**

—— [Another copy.] **G. 6200.**

—— [Another edition.] pp. 112. *Nella stamperia de' Giunti: Firenze*, 1580. 8°. **171. d. 2.**
The date in the colophon is 1579.

—— [Another edition.] Nuouamente ricorretto, e ristampato. pp. 111. *Appresso A. Padouani: Firenze*, 1587. 12°. **611. a. 33.**

—— [Another edition.] Nuouamente corretto & ristampato. pp. 112. *Nella stamperia del Sermartelli: Firenze*, 1602. 8°. **611. c. 24.**

—— [Another edition.] pp. 200. *Bologna*, 1865. 8°. **12226. bbb. 11. (3.)**

—— Quattro novelle di M. Alessandro Ceccherelli [extracted from " Delle azioni e sentenze del S. Alessandro de' Medici "] e due di M. Giuseppe Betussi, con molta diligenza ristampate. pp. 36. *F.P. Lucca*, 1854. 8°. **12470. g. 3.**
One of an edition of sixty copies.

CECCHERELLI (ALESSANDRO) *See* CECCHEREGLI.

CECCHERELLI (ALFONSO) *See* CECCARELLI.

CECCHERELLI (CLAUDIO)

—— El Bautismo y los franciscanos en México, 1524–1539. *In:* Missionalia hispanica. año 12. no. 35. pp. 209–289. 1955. 8°. **Ac. 132. cba.**

CECCHERELLI (EMILIA) Giovan Battista Zannoni, con speciale riguardo ai suoi Scherzi comici e al teatro vernacolo fiorentino. Saggio. pp. 216. *Firenze*, 1915. 8°. **11851. ee. 32.**

CECCHERINI (RICCARDO VITTORIO) *See* ROME.—*The City.—Società Italiana per il Progresso delle Scienze.* Atti, *etc.* (Indice della seconda serie. Riun. 11–20—1921–1931. Publicato per cura del vice-segretario aggiunto Ing. R. V. Ceccherini.) 1927, *etc.* 4°. **Ac. 2804/2.**

CECCHERINI (UGO)

—— Bibliografia della Libia, in continuazione alla " Bibliografia della Libia " di F. Minutilli. pp. ix. 204. 1915. 8°. *See* ITALY.—*Ministero delle Colonie.* **11925. bb. 6.**

—— Pubblicazioni in morte di S.A.R. il principe Amedeo di Savoia, duca d'Aosta. Bibliografia compilata da U. Ceccherini. pp. 39. *Firenze*, 1890. 8°. **011903. e. 27. (4.)**

—— Pubblicazioni in morte di Umberto i., rè d'Italia. Bibliografia compilata da U. Ceccherini. pp. 95. *Firenze*, 1902. 8°. **11899. h. 23. (5.)**

CECCHETTI (ANNA MANDER) *See* MANDER CECCHETTI.

CECCHETTI (ARTURO) *See* FUSCO (A. de) Dalla libertà all'oppressione austriaca . . . Con prefazione di A. Cecchetti, *etc.* 1911. 8°. **9168. aaa. 3.**

CECCHETTI (BARTOLOMEO) *See* KOL'TSOVA MASAL'SKAYA (E. M.) *Princess.* Gli Albanesi in Rumenia . . . Traduzione . . . di B. Cecchetti, *etc.* 1873. 8°. **9135. ee. 25.**

—— *See* PADOVAN (V.) and CECCHETTI (B.) Sommario della nummografia veneziana, *etc.* 1866. 8°. [MISSING.]

—— Gli Archivii della Repubblica Veneta dal secolo XIII al XIX. Memoria. pp. 65. *Venezia*, 1865. 8°. **9150. ee. 11.**

CECCHETTI (Bartolomeo)

—— Di alcune opere della principessa Dora d'Istria [pseudonym of Princess E. M. Kol'tsova-Masal'skaya]. Cenni. pp. 55. *Venezia*, 1868. 8°.　　　**11850**. d. **19**. (3.)

—— Il Doge di Venezia. pp. xix. 322. *Venezia*, 1864. 8°.
8032. cc. **21**.

—— Dora d'Istria [i.e. Princess E. M. Kol'tsova Masal'skaya] e la poesia albanese. [With a bibliography.] pp. 31. *Venezia*, 1869. 8°.　　　**11436**. aaa. **50**.

—— Programma dell' I. R. Scuola di Paleografia in Venezia, *etc.* [With facsimiles.] pp. 64. *Venezia*, 1862. fol.
1701. a. **18**.

—— La Republica di Venezia e la corte di Roma nei rapporti della religione. 2 vol. *Venezia*, 1874. 8°.
4606. d. **1**.

—— La Vita dei Veneziani fino al 1200. Saggio. pp. 74. *Venezia*, 1870. 8°.　　　**9150**. ee. **12**.

CECCHETTI (Enrico) *See* Beaumont (Cyril W.) Enrico Cecchetti, *etc.* [With portraits.] 1929. 8°.
10634. b. **16**.

—— *See* Beaumont (Cyril W.) and Idzikowski (S.) A Manual of the Theory and Practice of Classical Theatrical Dancing—méthode Cecchetti, *etc.* 1922. 8°. [Missing.]

—— *See* Racster (O.) The Master of the Russian Ballet. The memoirs of Cav. E. Cecchetti, *etc.* [With a portrait.] [1923.] 8°.　　　**10634**. d. **23**.

CECCHETTI (Joannes Clemens) Dissertationes, quibus Judæorum errores, falsaque de promisso sibi Messia præjudicia refelluntur. pp. viii. 231. *Vicetiæ*, 1750. 4°.
855. k. **8**.

CECCHETTI (Raimondo) Degli asili libri tre. pp. 127. *Padova*, 1751. 8°.　　　**1127**. b. **35**.

—— [Another copy.]　　　T. **2286**. (3.)

—— Raymundi Cecchetti Oratio in funere Jo. Ernesti Harrachii Episcopi Nittriensis. [Edited by J. D. Cribellus.] pp. xx. *Romæ*, 1740. 4°.　　　T. **40***. (5.)

CECCHI (Alberto) Cuore d'una volta. [Essays reprinted from various periodicals.] A cura di Antonio Baldini e Orio Vergani. pp. 302. *Milano*, 1935. 8°.
12356. ss. **5**.

CECCHI (Andrea) *See* Molino (Astianatte) *pseud*. Le Minchiate ; enimmi. [Edited by A. Cecchi.] [1643.] 24°.　　　**11427**. a. **25**.

CECCHI (Antonio) *See* Gray (Ezio M.) Aurore. Antonio Cecchi, *etc.* [With a portrait.] 1939. 8°.
10635. b. **26**.

—— *See* Ribera (A.) Vita di Antonio Cecchi. [With portraits.] 1940. 8°.　　　**010632**. bb. **18**.

—— L'Abissinia settentrionale e le strade che vi conducono da Massaua. Notizie a corredo di due grandi carte geografiche redatte in base alle più recenti scoperte. pp. vi. 48. *Milano*, 1887. 8°.　　　**10097**. df. **19**.

—— Da Zeila alle frontiere del Caffa. Viaggi di A. Cecchi. 3 vol. 1886, 85, 87. 8°. *See* Florence.—*Società Geografica Italiana*.　　　Ac. **6010/11**.

—— Relazione intorno alle ultime vicende della spedizione italiana in Africa attraverso i regni di Ghera-Gomma-Gimma-Guma. Esposta alla Società Geografica in Roma. pp. 46. *Pesaro*, 1882. 8°.　　　**10097**. df. **10**. (4.)

CECCHI (Baccio) Descrizione dell' apparato e de gl'intermedi fatti per la storia dell'esaltazione della Croce. *See* Cecchi (G. M.) L'Esaltazione della Croce, *etc.* 1592. 8°.
1071. h. **35**.

CECCHI (Basilio) In caserma. Ricordi della vita militare. pp. 58. *Napoli*, 1888. 8°.　　　**8830**. aaa. **37**. (2.)

CECCHI (Domenico) *Architect. See* Lucimetro. Lucimetro, o sia la Misura della luce. [By François Marie, Capuchin.] Opera d'invenzione tradotta dal francese . . . da D. Cecchi. 1707. 4°.　　　**537**. f. **45**.

CECCHI (Domenico) *of Florence*. Iesu. Riforma. Sancta. et Pretiosa. Hafatta Domenico di Ruberto di Ser Mainardo Cecchi. p chōseruatione della citta di Firenze & pel bē comūe eqāto elbuono eluero lume eltesoro dognuno. et della citta et fara hoseruare la giustitia el buon gouerno et notate bene hogni chosa. Che questa e lauera et buona uia auenire presto ī granfilicita ogniūo etcĒ. Et dipoi inbrieue tempo tutta italia. et tutto luniuerso mondo pche īparerãno da questa etcĒ.　　*Per Francescho di Dino di Iacopo:* [*Florence*,] 1496. 4°.　　IA. **27713**. 28 *leaves*. Sig. a–c⁸ d⁴. 26 *lines to a page*.

CECCHI (Emilio) *See* Cavalcanti (G.) Rime. Con introduzione e appendice bibliografica di E. C. [i.e. E. Cecchi.] 1910. 8°.　　　**11436**. h. **24**.

—— *See* Gojorani (C.) Opere scelte . . . Prefazione di E. Cecchi. 1914. 8°.　　　**12227**. bb. **16**.

—— *See* Leibnitz (G. W. von) *Baron*. [*Separate Works*.] Nuovi saggi sull'intelletto umano. Tradotti da E. Cecchi. 1909, *etc.* 8°. [*Classici della filosofia moderna*. vol. 8.]　　　**08461**. de. **1/8**.

—— [America amara.] Bitteres Amerika, *etc.* (Berechtigte Übersetzung von A. Graf Alegiani.) [Impressions of travels in the United States and in Mexico. With plates.] pp. 394. *Oldenburg, Berlin*, 1942. 8°.　　**010410**. c. **38**.

—— Corse al trotto, e altre cose, *etc.* [Essays.] pp. 575. pl. xxxvi. *Firenze*, 1952. 8°.**12361.cc.2.**

—— Di giorno in giorno. Note di letteratura italiana contemporanea, 1945–1954. pp. 404. *Milano*, 1954. 8°.
11872. b. **22**.

—— Giotto, *etc.* pp. 175. pl. 200. *Milano*, 1937. 8°.
7864. pp. **34**.

—— Lorenzo il Magnifico. Commemorazione tenuta nel v anniversario della nascita. pp. 12. *Roma*, 1949. 8°. [*Problemi attuali di scienza e di cultura*. quad. 12.]
Ac. **102/22**.

—— Messico. Nuova edizione accresciuta. pp. 205. *Firenze*, 1948. 8°.　　　**010481**. d. **8**.

—— L'Osteria del cattivo tempo. (iv edizione.) [Essays.] pp. 220. [*Milan*,] 1950. 8°.　　　**12361**. aa. **29**. *Part of the series "Lo Specchio."*

—— Pittura italiana dell'ottocento. Centoventi tavole, *etc.* pp. ix. 108. *Milano*, 1938. 8°.　　　**7859**. t. **24**.

—— La Poesia di Giovanni Pascoli. Saggio critico. pp. 151. *Napoli*, 1912. 8°.　　　**011852**. bb. **29**.

—— Scrittori inglesi e americani, *etc.* pp. 304. [*Lanciano*,] 1935. 8°.　　　**11856**. de. **51**.

—— Scrittori inglesi e americani. [With additional essays.] pp. 442. [*Milan*,] 1947. 8°.　　　**11861**. c. **28**. *Il Pensiero critico.* no. 1.

CECCHI (Emilio)

—— Storia della letteratura inglese nel secolo xix. vol. 1. pp. viii. 392. *Milano*, 1915. 8°. **011852. e. 36.**
No more published.

—— Studi critici. pp. 354. *Ancona*, 1912. 8°.
011853. c. 7.

—— [Trecentisti senesi.] The Sienese Painters of the Trecento . . . Translated . . . by Leonard Penlock, *etc.* pp. 178. pl. cclvi. *F. Warne & Co.: London & New York; Rome* printed, 1931. fol. **7852. t. 14.**

—— L'Uva acerba. [Poems.] pp. 61. *Milano*, 1947. 8°.
11436. p. 4.
Part of the series " Opera prima."

CECCHI (Filippo) Nuovo apparato per dimostrare l'eguaglianza della rapidità di caduta dei corpi gravi e leggieri. pp. 7. *Firenze*, 1872. 8°. **8704. e. 25. (7.)**

CECCHI (Giovanni Maria) *See also* Canto de' Bischeri (B. dal) *pseud.* [i.e. G. M. Cecchi.]

—— *See* Berni (F.) the Poet. [*Single Works.*] Lezione o vero Cicalamento di Maestro Bartolino dal Canto de' Bischeri [i.e. G. M. Cecchi] sopra 'l sonetto Passere [by F. Berni], *etc.* 1863. 8°. **12226. bbb. 1. (2.)**

—— *See* Fiacchi (L.) Dei proverbi toscani . . . Con la dichiarazione de' proverbi di G. M. Cecchi . . . Aumentata di molti pezzi tratti dalle commedie inedite del medesimo Cecchi. 1820. 8°. **12330. dd. 14. (2.)**

—— *See* Fiacchi (L.) Lettera . . . intorno alla vita e alle opere di G. M. Cecchi, *etc.* 1812. 8°. **10631. de. 20.**

—— *See* Rizzi (F.) Le Commedie osservate di Giovan Maria Cecchi, *etc.* 1904. 8°. [*Indagini di storia letteraria e artistica.* no. 3.] **11851. aaa. 11.**

—— *See* Rizzi (F.) Delle farse e commedie morali di G. M. Cecchi, *etc.* 1907. 8°. [*Indagini di storia letteraria e artistica.* no. 10.] **11851. aaa. 11.**

—— *See* Scoti-Bertinelli (U.) Sullo stile delle commedie di G. M. Cecchi, *etc.* 1906. 8°. **11850. t. 3.**

—— Comedie . . . Libro primo. Nel quale si contengono La Dote, la Moglie, il Corredo, la Stiaua, il Donzelo, gl'Incantesimi, lo Spirito. 7 pt. *Appresso B. Giunti: Venetia*, 1585. 8°. **241. g. 38.**
No more published.

—— [Another copy.] **G. 10384.**

—— [Seven comedies.] 7 pt.
    1. La Dote.
    2. La Moglie.
    3. Gl' Incantesimi.
    4. La Stiava.
    5. I Dissimili.
    6. L'Assiuolo.
    7. Il Servigiale.
Firenze, 1750. 8°. [*Teatro comico fiorentino.* tom. 1, 2.]
639. f. 5.

—— Commedie di Giovan Maria Cecchi, premessavi una lettera intorno alla vita ed alle opere dell' autore di Luigi Fiacchi, *etc.* 2 vol. *Milano*, 1850. 8°. **11715. ee. 24.**

—— Commedie inedite . . . pubblicate per cura di Giovanni Tortoli, con note. pp. xvi. 453. *Firenze*, 1855. 8°.
11715. e. 18.

—— Commedie . . . pubblicate per cura di Gaetano Milanesi. 2 vol. *Firenze*, 1856. 12°. **2298. f. 6.**

—— L'Assiuolo, commedia e saggio di proverbj . . . coll'aggiunta di uno studio sulle commedie dell'autore e di una lezione sui proverbj toscani per Luigi Fiacchi. pp. viii. 145. *Milano*, 1863. 8°. [*Biblioteca rara.* vol. 8.]
12225. aa.

35–30

CECCHI (Giovanni Maria)

—— Commedie . . . pubblicate per cura di Michele dello Russo. 2 vol. *Napoli*, 1864, 69. 8°. **11715. ee. 48.**

—— Commedie . . . La Dote.—La Moglie.—Gl'Incantesimi. —La Stiava.—I Dissimili.—L'Assiuolo. Con prefazione di Olindo Guerrini. pp. 318. *Milano*, 1883. 8°.
11714. c. 19.

—— Drammi spirituali inediti . . . Con prefazione e note di Raffaello Rocchi. [With a portrait.] 2 vol. *Firenze* 1895, 1900. 8°. **11715. g. 32.**

—— [Another copy.] Drammi spirituali, *etc.* *Firenze*, 1895, 1900. 8°. Hirsch **871.**

—— L'Assiuolo, comedia. ff. 45. *Appresso G. Giolito de Ferrari: Vinegia*, 1550. 12°. **162. a. 37.**
The date in the colophon is 1551.

—— [Another copy.] **G. 10339. (3.)**

—— [Another copy.] **839. a. 5. (1.)**
Imperfect; wanting all after fol. 24. *Ff.* 25–36 *of a different work have been bound in error.*

—— Compendio di più ritratti, *etc.* [The editor's preface signed: F. di V.] pp. 95. *Bologna*, 1867. 8°.
12226. bbb. 14. (5.)

—— I Dissimili, comedia. pp. 45. *Appresso G. Giolito de Ferrari e fratelli: Vinegia*, 1550. 12°. **1071. l. 11. (3.)**

—— [Another copy.] **1071. a. 2. (3.)**

—— [Another copy.] **G. 10339. (5.)**

—— Il Donzello, comedia. ff. 43. *Appresso B. Giunti: Venetia*, 1585. 8°. **638. c. 25. (1.)**
Also issued as part of the edition of the " Comedie" published in 1585.

—— La Dote, comedia. ff. 47. *Appresso G. Giolito de Ferrari: Vinegia*, 1550. 12°. **G. 10339. (4.)**

—— [Another edition.] ff. 47. *Appresso G. Giolito de Ferrari, et fratelli: Vinegia*, 1556. 12°.
1071. l. 6. (9.)

—— [Another copy.] **162. a. 38.**

—— L'Esaltazione della Croce con i suoi intermedi, *etc.* [In verse.] (Descrizione dell'apparato, e de gl'intermedi fatti per la storia dell'esaltazione della Croce. [By B. Cecchi.]) 2 pt. *Appresso M. di B. Sermartelli: Firenze*, 1592. 8°. **1071. h. 35.**
The date in the colophon of pt. 1 *is* 1586.

—— [Another copy.] **162. f. 21.**
Imperfect; wanting pt. 2.

—— Il Figliuol prodigo. Commedia. *See* Pacini (S.) Commedie del teatro antico fiorentino, *etc.* 1877. 8°.
11715. bbb. 13.

—— Gl'Incantesimi, comedia. ff. 42. *Appresso G. Giolito de Ferrari e fratelli: Vinegia*, 1550. 12°.
1071. a. 2. (2.)

—— [Another copy.] **162. a. 39.**

—— [Another copy.] **G. 10339. (1.)**

—— Le Maschere e il Samaritano, commedie . . . ora per la prima volta pubblicate, *etc.* (Lettera del sig. abate Luigi Fiacchi intorno alla vita e all'opere di Gianmaria Cecchi.) pp. xxix. 127. *Firenze*, 1818. 8°. **1343. n. 3.**

—— La Moglie, comedia. ff. 36. *Appresso G. Giolito de Ferrari: Vinegia*, 1550. 12°. **G. 10339. (6.)**

CECCHI (GIOVANNI MARIA)

—— [Another edition.] ff. 36 [43]. *Appresso G. Giolito de' Ferrari, et fratelli: Vinegia*, 1556. 12°.
1071. l. 6. (8.)

—— [Another copy.] **162. a. 40.**

—— [Another edition.] ff. 40. [*Appresso B. Giunti: Venetia*, 1585.] 8°. **638. c. 25. (2.)**
Imperfect; wanting the titlepage. Also issued as part of the edition of the " Comedie " published in 1585.

—— La Pittura. Farsa inedita. *See* SCOTI-BERTINELLI (U.) Sullo stile delle commedie di G. M. Cecchi, *etc.* 1906. 8°.
11850. t. 3.

—— Li Sbarbati. Commedia. [With a portrait.] pp. 201. *Firenze*, 1880. 8°. **11715. f. 7.**

—— Il Servigiale, comedia . . . Nuouamente stampata con gli intermedii. [In verse.] pp. 99. *Appresso i Giunti: Fiorenza*, 1561. 8°. **1071. k. 7. (6.)**

—— [Another copy.] **1071. h. 19. (1.)**

—— [Another copy.] **162. f. 22.**

—— La Stiava, comedia. pp. 36. *Appresso G. Giolito de Ferrari e fratelli: Vinegia*, 1550. 12°. **1071. a. 2. (1.)**

—— [Another copy.] **G. 10339. (2.)**

—— Le Più belle pagine di G. M. Cecchi. Scelte da Ettore Allodoli. [With a portrait.] pp. xvi. 267. *Milano*, 1928. 12°. [*Le più belle pagine degli scrittori italiani.* vol. 46.] **012226. a. 1/46.**

CECCHI (PERFETTO) Verbale di adunanza dei sindaci della valle Bormida di Cairo Dego Spigno e relazione letta alla medesima dal dottor P. Cecchi. pp. 15. *Savona*, 1861. 8°. **8235. f. 46.**

CECCHI (PIER LEOPOLDO) Studi sull'arte contemporanea. Il Vela e Duprè. Il monumento a Cavour. Estratto dalla Rivista europea. pp. 29. *Firenze*, 1873. 8°.
[MISSING.]

—— Torquato Tasso, il pensiero e le belle lettere italiane nel secolo XVI. pp. 433. *Firenze*, 1877. 8°. **11840. cc. 18.**

CECCHI (SILVIO) La Sapienza del popolo intorno al matrimonio. Proverbi, illustrati dal prof. S. Cecchi. pp. 98. *Siena*, 1878. 8°. **12304. ee. 33.**

CECCHINI (ALESSANDRO) Due discorsi sopra la cupola di S. Maria del Fiore. *See* NELLI (G. B.) Discorsi di architettura, *etc.* 1753. 4°. **61. b. 7.**

CECCHINI (FRANCESCO) " Ferroviaria " res ac negotia. Nuova istoria delle rane che vogliono il re. Narrata agl'impiegati di ferrovia. pp. 78. *Pistoia*, 1886. 8°.
8235. f. 42. (2.)

CECCHINI (G.) *Writer on Astronomy*, and **GRATTON** (L.)

—— Le Stelle nuove, *etc.* [With plates.] 1943. *See* ROME. —*The City.—Reale Accademia d'Italia.* Atti, *etc.* (Memorie della Classe di scienze fisiche, matematiche e naturali. vol. 13.) 1939, *etc.* 8°. **Ac. 104. fc/12.**

CECCHINI (GIOVANNI) *See* AZZI VITELLESCHI (G. degli) and CECCHINI (G.) Codice nobiliare araldico, *etc.* 1933. 8°. **5373. de. 8.**

—— *See* SIENA. [REPUBLIC OF SIENA, 1147-1557.] Il Caleffo vecchio del Comune di Siena. Pubblicato da G. Cecchini. 1931, *etc.* fol. **L.R. 252. b. 2.**

CECCHINI (GIOVANNI)

—— La Galleria Nazionale dell'Umbria in Perugia. [With plates.] pp. 255. 1932. 8°. *See* PERUGIA.—*Galleria Nazionale dell'Umbria.* **W.P. 5133/8.**

—— Mostra dell'arte della stampa umbra. Catalogo a cura di Giovanni Cecchini. Palazzo Trinci, Foligno, 12 settembre—4 ottobre XX. [With facsimiles.] pp. xvi. 217. pl. 31. 1943. 8°. *See* FOLIGNO.—*Palazzo Trinci.* **11898. cc. 38.**

—— Saggio sulla cultura artistica e letteraria in Perugia nel secolo XIX. pp. xvi. 261. *Foligno*, [1922.] 8°.
010151. eee. 5.

CECCHINI (LAUDOMIA) La Ballata romantica in Italia. pp. 74. *Firenze*, 1901. 8°. **11805. i. 36.**

CECCHINI (MARIO) Bilancio fatto in Roma . . . frà li due modi di curare le ferite, comunale, e del celebre Magati. *See* SANCASSANI (D. A.) Dilucidazioni fisico-mediche, *etc.* tom. 1. 1731. fol. **543. i. 5.**

CECCHINI (PIETRO MARIA) Discorsi intorno alle commedie, commedianti, & spettatori . . . Doue si comprende quali rappresentationi si possino ascoltare, & permettere. pp. 37. *D. Amadio: Vicenza*, 1614. 4°.
11795. c. 47.

—— La Flaminia schiaua; comedia. ff. 64. *G. A. Somascho: Venetia*, 1612. 12°. **1071. k. 14. (2.)**

—— Frutti delle moderne comedie, et auisi a chi le recita. pp. 42. *G. Guareschi: Padoua*, 1628. 4°.
11795. d. 23.

CECCHINI (TOMASO)

—— *See* PLAMENAC (D.) Toma Cecchini, kapelnik stolnih crkava u Splitu i Hvaru u prvoj polovini XVII stoljeća. Biobibliografijska studija. [With a list of his musical works.] 1938. 8°. [*Rad Jugoslavenske Akademije Znanosti i Umjetnosti.* knj. 262.] **Ac. 741/2.**

CECCHINO. Canzonetta nuova sopra di Cecchino che chiede per sposa Terresina. *Roma*, 1811. *s. sh.* 4°.
1071. m. 14. (45.)

—— [Another copy.] **1071. m. 14. (48.)**

CECCHINO (TOMASO) *See* CECCHINI.

CECCHI TOLDI (ANTONIO) *See* BARBACCIANI-FEDELI (R.) Decisione dell'illustrissimo sig. avvocato Ranieri Barbacciani Fedeli . . . nella Piscien. nullit. contract. tra il . . . cavaliere A. Cecchi Toldi i signori alienatari. 1829. 8°. **898. h. 2. (6.)**

CECCHUS, *Asculanus.* *See* STABILI (F. degli) called CECCO D'ASCOLI.

CECCO, *d'Ascoli.* *See* STABILI (F. degli) called CECCO D'ASCOLI.

CECCO, *Family of.* *See* RENZETTI (L.) Memorie di casa nostra [i.e. of the family De Cecco], *etc.* 1894. 8°.
9904. dd. 42. (7.)

CECCO (LEONARDO DE) De cordis palpitatione dissertatio inauguralis medico-chirurgica, *etc.* pp. 15. *Patavii*, 1830. 8°. **7306. b. 7. (13.)**

CECCODÈA. *See* RICCIARDI (F.) *da Pistoja*, called CECCODÈA.

CECCON (ANTONIO) Di Niccola Villani e delle sue opere. pp. xiii. 158. *Cesena*, 1900. 8°. **11853. aaa. 39.**

CECCONI (ANGELO) Studi di letteratura e d'arte.
pp. xiv. 252. *Firenze*, 1898. 8°.   **011850. f. 86.**

CECCONI (BENEDICTUS ANTONIUS) De originis aortae
aneurismate dictio, *etc.* pp. 19. *Patavii*, 1830. 8°.
                                              7306. b. 8. (40.)

CECCONI (COSIMO) *See* BERNABEI (A. N.) Dissertazione
delle morti improvise, *etc.* [Edited by C. Cecconi.]
1708. 4°.   **1038. l. 26.**

CECCONI (EMANUELE) Balbiche rime. (Sonetti arramaz-
zati a la Siciliana.) *Caltanissetta*, 1911. 8°.
                                              11431. ccc. 39. (5.)

—— Fiori in fascio. pp. 19. *Palermo*, 1911. 8°.
                                              11431. ccc. 39. (4.)

—— La Veglia dei ricordi. (Terzine.) pp. xiv.
Caltanissetta, 1912. 8°.   **11431. e. 45. (1.)**

CECCONI (EUGENIO) *Archbishop of Florence.* Laudi di
una compagnia fiorentina del secolo XIV. fin qui inedite.
(Ricordo delle nozze di Enrico Cecconi con Luisa Ricasoli,
XXIV maggio MDCCCLXX.) pp. xii. 72. *Firenze*, 1870. 8°.
                                              11421. h. 16.

—— Storia del Concilio ecumenico vaticano scritta sui documenti originali. Parte prima. Antecedenti del Concilio.
4 vol. *Roma*, 1873, 79. 8°.   **5016. dd. 1.**
No more published.

—— Histoire du Concile du Vatican d'après les documents
originaux . . . Préliminaires du Concile. Ouvrage traduit . . . par M. Jules Bonhomme . . . et M. D. Duvil-
lard. 4 tom. *Paris*, 1887. 8°.   **2208. d. 3.**

—— Studi storici sul Concilio di Firenze, con documenti
inediti o nuovamente dati alla luce sui manoscritti di
Firenze e di Roma. pt. 1. pp. 55. 224. dcviii. *Firenze*,
1869. 8°.   **5015. ee. 14.**
No more published.

CECCONI (EUGENIO) *Translator.*

—— *See* KIPLING (Rudyard) [*Single Works.*] Racconti della
Jungla . . . [Seven tales from "The Jungle Book" and
"The Second Jungle Book."] Versi tradotti da Y. [i.e.
E. Cecconi.] 1903. 8°.   File **677.**

CECCONI (GIACOMO) Contributo alla fauna vallom-
brosana. 1898. *See* FLORENCE.—*Società Entomologica
Italiana.* Bullettino, *etc.* anno 29. 1869, *etc.* 8°.
                                              Ac. **3603.**

—— Ricordi zoologici di un viaggio all'isola di Candia.
1896. *See* FLORENCE.—*Società Entomologica Italiana.*
Bullettino, *etc.* anno 27. 1869, *etc.* 8°.   Ac. **3603.**

CECCONI (GIOSUÈ) La Storia di Castelfidardo dalla prima
origine del castello a tutta la prima metà del secolo XVI.
Aggiunta un'appendice di documenti inediti ed editi
rarissimi. pp. 165. xciii. *Osimo*, 1879. 8°. **10136. h. 4.**

—— Vita e fatti di Boccolino Guzzoni da Osimo, capitano
de ventura del secolo XV, narrati con documenti inediti
ed editi rarissimi. pp. xv. 204. *Osimo*, 1889. 8°.
                                              10630. ff. 34.

CECCONI (GIOVANNI) Delle condizioni e dei bisogni presenti dell' esercito italiano studiato nella sua vita pratica
in pace ed in guerra. Pensieri. pp. 86.   *Firenze*,
1867. 8°.   **8826. cc. 37. (6.)**

—— La Genesi dell'Italia. pp. 296. *Firenze*, 1887. 8°.
                                              10129. bbb. 22.

—— Il Principe Napoleone in Toscana. (Estratto dalla Rivista
moderna.) pp. 11. *Roma*, 1891. 8°. **10601. f. 9. (10.)**

CECCONI (GIOVANNI)

—— Torino è in pericolo—si salvi Torino. Storia di diciotto
giorni dal 27 aprile al 15 maggio 1859. Conferenza, *etc.*
pp. 32. *Torino*, 1882. 8°.   **9166. bb. 20.**

—— Il 27 aprile 1859. Narrazione. pp. 63.   *Firenze*,
1892. 8°.   **9004. dd. 3. (8.)**

CECCONI (GIOVANNI FRANCESCO) Il Sacro rito di con-
sacrare le chiese, *etc.* pp. 178. *Roma*, 1728. 4°.
                                              3477. dg. 16.

—— Scala genealogica, e cronologica di tutti i principati,
e regni della terra dal principio del mondo fino all'anno
. . . 1721, *etc.* [With engravings.] 2 pt.   *Roma*,
1721. fol.   **1855. e. 3.**

CECCONI (LEONARDO) *Bishop of Montalto.* Dissertazione
sopra l'origine, significati, uso, e morali ammaestramenti
per la divota recita dell'Alleluja. pp. viii. 76. *Velletri*,
1769. 8°.   **1222. h. 23. (1.)**

—— Storia di Palestrina, città del prisco Lazio . . . Illustrata
con antiche iscrizioni e notizie finora inedite. [With a
map.] pp. xvi. 431. *Ascoli*, 1756. 4°.   **177. b. 9.**

—— [Another copy.]   **660. a. 22.**
Imperfect; wanting the map.

CECCONI (LUIGI)
—— Di Pier Luigi da Palestrina. Memoria, *etc.* pp. viii. 26.
Roma, 1826. 8°.   Hirsch **4189.**
The date in the colophon is 1825.

——   Sopra la Basilica Emilia e Fulvia
prenestina. Dissertazione, *etc.* pp. 9. *Roma*, [1840.] 4°.
                                              898. i. 3. (2.)
One of an edition of fifty copies.

—— Sopra una statua presso Preneste rinvenuta. Dissertazione, *etc.* pp. 8. *Roma*, 1839. 4°.   **898. i. 3. (3.)**
One of an edition of fifty copies.

—— [Another copy.]   **898. i. 4. (12.)**

CECCONI (MARIO ROSELLI) *See* ROSELLI CECCONI.

CECCONI FANTONI CASTRUCCI (PIETRO) Tra-
gedie, altre poesie e prose del Pastore Arcade Chelingo
Didimeo (P. Cecconi Fantoni Castrucci). pp. vi. 329.
Parigi, 1840. 8°.   **1342. l. 12.**

CECCOPERIUS (FELIX) De Christi Domini reviviscentis
gloria, oratio, *etc.* pp. xv. *Romæ*, [1817.] 4°.
                                              T. **78*. (19.)**

CECCOPERIUS (FRANCISCUS) Lucubrationum Canonica-
lium Bibliotessera, hoc est, libri quatuor. In quibus
agitur de canonicorum præcedentia, de eorum officio in
choro, ministerio in missæ sacrificio, ac potestate maxime
in capitulo, *etc.* pp. 319. *Apud H. Pacium, etc.: Lucæ*,
1662. 4°.   Legg **76.**

—— [Another edition.] Joannis Jacobi Scarfantoni . . .
Animadversiones ad Lucubrationes Canonicales Francisci
Ceccoperii de canonicorum præcedentia . . . novo ordine
. . . digestas decisionibus sacræ Rotæ Romanæ, &
clarissimorum jurisconsultorum votis ad materiam editis,
ejusdem Scarfantoni opera ac studio auctas, atque
illustratas. 3 vol. *Viterbii; Venetiis*, 1751. fol.
                                              5035. k. 1.

CECCOTTI (GIROLAMO) Replica all'autore dei Riflessi
sopra l'inclinazione della gran torre di Pisa, pubblicati
nel Giornale di commercio di Firenze . . . Confutazione
alle Miscellanee artistiche dell'architetto sig. Alessandro
Gherardesca sulla pendenza della torre della Primaziale
pisana, ed al opuscolo del sig. Bartolommeo Polloni.
pp. 41. *Pisa*, 1838. 8°.   **1401. h. 16.**

CECCUCCI (EGISTO) Histoire des Conciles œcuméniques . . . Traduite par J. B. Jaugey. [With plates.] pp. 466. *Paris*, [1871.] fol. [*Actes et histoire du Concile œcuménique de Rome, etc.* tom. 4.] Cup. **652. b. 1.**

ČEČETKA (FRANTIŠEK JAROSLAV) Mistr Jan Hus. Historický roman. Ilustroval V. Černý. pp. 400. *v Praze*, [1927.] 8°. **20013. d. 18.**
Pages 217 to 264 are numbered 199 to 246 in error.

—— F. J. Čečetka: Od Kolébky do hrobu. Lidopisné obrázky z Poděbradska. Se 42 vyobrazeními. pp. 246. *v Praze*, 1900. 8°. **12450. i. 6.**

ČEČETKA (JURAJ)
—— Učitel' l'udu Samuel Tešedík. pp. 101. *Matica Slovenská: Martin*, 1952. 8°. **10798. c. 3.**
Knižnica Osvety. sv. 9.

CECH. Cech Rzeźnikow i Masarzy " na Kotłowem." *See* CRACOW.

ČECH. *See also* BOHEMIAN.

—— Čěch. List volný, *etc. See* PERIODICAL PUBLICATIONS.—*Geneva.* La Voix libre de Bohème.

ČECH (A.) *Prosektor Nemocnice v Plzni.*
—— O zádním Schmorlově uzlu. [With plates.] pp. 58. 1940. 8°. *See* PRAGUE.—*Česká Akademie Císaře Františka Josefa pro Vědy, Slovesnost a Umění, etc.* **7423. dd. 13.**

ČECH (ADOLF) Z mých divadelních pamětí. pp. 124. *v Praze*, [1904.] 8°. **011795. aa. 2.**

ČECH (CARL OTAKAR) *See* ČECH (Karel O.)

ČECH (EDUARD) *See* FUBINI (G.) Úvahy z teorie kongruencí a komplexů přímek, *etc.* (Překlad obstaral . . . E. Čech.) 1924. 8°. [*Spisy vydávané přírodovědeckou fakultou Masarykovy University.* čís. 39.] Ac. **747.**

—— Courbes tracées sur une surface dans l'espace projectif, *etc.* Brno, 1924– . 8°. [*Spisy vydávané přírodovědeckou fakultou Masarykovy University.* čís. 46, *etc.*] Ac. **747.**

—— Propriétés projectives du contact. *Brno*, 1928– . 8°. [*Spisy vydávané přírodovědeckou fakultou Masarykovy University.* čís. 91, *etc.*] Ac. **747.**

—— Sur les surfaces qui admettent ∞^1 déformations projectives en elles mêmes. pp. 47. *Brno*, 1924. 8°. [*Spisy vydávané přírodovědeckou fakultou Masarykovy University* čís. 40.] Ac. **747.**

ČECH (EMERICH) *See* CZECHOSLOVAKIA.—*Ministerstvo Železnic.* Railways of the Czechoslovak State. A series of photographic views . . . Text by E. Čech, *etc.* [1925?] *obl.* 4°. **S.R.40.**

ČECH (JAN) *pseud.* [i.e. J. B. HEISLER.] *See also* HEISLER (J. B.)

—— Death Stalks the Forest, *etc.* [An account of the resistance of the Carpatho-Russian guerrillas to the Hungarian occupation. With plates.] pp. 75. *Lindsay Drummond: London*, 1943. 8°. **9100. h. 92.**

—— Death Stalks the Forest, *etc.* (New enlarged and up-to-date edition.) pp. 95. *Trinity Press: London*, 1944. 8°. **9100. a. 74.**

—— The Third Front. A play . . . Translated by Kevin Browne. pp. 75. *New Europe Publishing Co.: London*, 1943. 8°. **11758. n. 13.**

ČECH (JAN) *pseud.* [i.e. J. B. HEISLER], and **MELLON** (J. E.)
—— Czechoslovakia, land of dream and enterprise, *etc.* [With illustrations and a map.] pp. 184. 1944. 8°. *See* CZECHOSLOVAKIA.—*Ministerstvo Zahraničnich Věci.—Informační Oddělení.* **10215. l. 21.**

—— Czechoslovakia . . . (New revised impression [of the work by J. Čech and J. E. Mellon].) By J. B. Heisler and J. E. Mellon, *etc.* pp. 180. 1945. 8°. *See* HEISLER (J. B.) and MELLON (J. E.) **10215. l. 25.**

ČECH (KAREL OTAKAR) Phenol, Thymol und Salicylsäure als Heilmittel der Brutpest der Bienen, *etc.* pp. 26. *Heidelberg*, 1877. 8°. **7297. bb. 11.**

—— Russlands Industrie auf der nationalen Ausstellung in Moskau 1882. Kritische Betrachtungen über die wichtigsten Industriezweige Russlands. pp. x. 382. *Moskau; Altenburg* [printed], 1885. 8°. **8246. eee. 13.**
With an additional titlepage, engraved.

—— Studien über quantitative Bestimmungen der Gerbsäuren in Gerbematerialien. (Inaugural-Dissertation.) [With a plate.] pp. 86. *Heidelberg*, 1867. 8°. **8908. aaa. 42. (4.)**

ČECH (LEANDER) *See* BOHEMIAN LITERATURE. Literatura česká devatenáctého století, *etc.* (díl. 3. část 2. Napsali: L. Čech, J. Jakubec and others].) 1911, *etc.* 8°. **11865.f.12.**

—— *See* PALACKÝ (F.) Spisy drobné. (díl 3. Spisy aesthetické a literární. Uspořádal . . . L. Čech.) 1898, *etc.* 8°. **012265. i. 9.**

—— Karolina Světlá. Kritická studie . . . Doplněný otisk z časopisu " Hlídka literárni." pp. 220. *v Brně*, 1891. 8°. **011824. h. 81.**

—— Karolina Světlá. Obraz literárně-historický. pp. 198. *v Telči*, [1907.] 8°. **011852. de. 1.**
A different work from the preceding.

ČECH (SVATOPLUK) *See* BĚLÍK (J.) Za Svatoplukem Čechem. Životopisný a literární nástin, *etc.* [1908.] 8°. **010790. de. 65.**

—— *See* BORECKÝ (J.) Svatopluku Čechovi. Památník Jednoty Svatopluka Čecha, *etc.* [With a " Bibliografie literatury o životě a díle S. Čecha," by V. Bitnar, and portraits.] 1946. 8°. **11867. g. 6.**

—— *See* NOVÁK (A.) Svatopluk Čech. Dílo a osobnost. [With a portrait.] 1921. 8°. **11870. bb. 9.**

—— *See* NOVOTNÝ (K.) Básník mezi lidmi. Život . . . S. Čecha na vsi. S korespondencí z let 1895–1908. [1912.] 8°. **10795. b. 38.**

—— *See* PRAGUE.—*Universita Carolina.—Akademický Čtenářský Spolek.* Almanah Českého Studentstva . . . Uspořádali: O. Hostinský, S. Čech, *etc.* 1869. 8°. **8356. aaa. 11.**

—— *See* STREJČEK (F.) O Svatopluku Čechovi. 1908. 8°. **010790. e. 50.**

—— *See* SUTNAR (J.) Svatopluk Čech zrcadlem Češství. 1909. 8°. **11850. bb. 46. (3.)**

—— *See* SUTNAR (J.) Sv. Čech a F. X. Šalda. Staťobranná [of Sutnar's book " Sv. Čech zrcadlem Češství " against Šalda's criticism]. 1909. 8°. **11850. bb. 46. (2.)**

—— *See* SVOBODA (E.) Alšovo přátelství se Svatoplukem Čechem. [With plates, including portraits.] 1946. 8°. **10797. f. 38.**

ČECH (Svatopluk)

—— Sebrané spisy. 30 díly.

   díl 1. Druhý květ. Odlesky přítomnosti a minulosti.
     pp. 236. 1899.
   díl 2. Lešetínský kovář, a menší básně. pp. 288. 1899.
   díl 3, 11, 15, 18, 29. První (—poslední) kniha povídek a
     črt. 5 vol. 1899–1909.
   díl 4. Báchorky veršem. pp. 341. 1899.
   díl 5, 7, 23. Vzpomínky z cest a života. 3 vol. 1900–09.
   díl 6. Václav z Michalovic. Evropa. Čerkes. Anděl.
     pp. 267. 1900.
   díl 8. Václav Živsa. Slavie. pp. 296. 1901.
   díl 9. Výlety Pana Broučka. pp. 337. 1901.
   díl 10. Čtyři cykly básní. pp. 286. 1902.
   díl 12, 14, 17. Větší prósa. 3 vol. 1902–05.
   díl 13. Dagmar. Adamité. pp. 325. 1903.
   díl 16. Tři cykly básní a Sníh. pp. 315. 1904.
   díl 19. Doplněk veršů. pp. 287. 1905.
   díl 20. Doplněk prósy. pp. 291. 1905.
   díl 21. Ikaros. Román. pp. 238. 1908.
   díl 22. Povídky a humoresky. pp. 306. 1909.
   díl 24. Menší básně. II. pp. 286. 1909.
   díl 25. Satiry a různé črty. pp. 381. 1909.
   díl 26. Pestré cesty po Čechách. pp. 287. 1909.
   díl 27. Roháč na Sioně, a jiné zlomky. pp. 398. 1909.
   díl 28. Prósa poučná a příležitostná. pp. 420. 1909.
   díl 30. Poslední verše. pp. 216. 1910.

   v Praze. 1899–1910. 8°.   **012265. g. 8.**

—— [Supplement.] Svatopluk Čech. Dílo a člověk. Napsal V. Flajšhans. Bibliografii sestavila J. Flajšhansová. [With a portrait.] pp. 296. *v Praze.* 1906. 8°.   **012265. g. 8.**

—— Novellen . . . Aus dem Böhmischen übersetzt von F. Bauer. pp. 110. *Leipzig,* [1884.] 16°.
     012207. f. 18. (9.)

—— Приповетке . . . Превео с чешког С. А. Поповић. pp. 63. *Панчево,* [1880.] 16°. [*Народна Библиотека Браће Јовановића.* св. 126.]   **012265. e. 5/61.**

—— Adamité. [A poem.] Illustroval Alfons Mucha. pp. 124. *v Praze,* 1897. 8°.   **011586. m. 12.**

—— Cesta na Kavkaz. (Vyňato z III. svazku Vzpomínek z cest a života. Text upravil a doslov napsal Miloslav Novotný.) pp. 86. *v Praze,* 1952. 8°. **010058. pp. 5.** *Milé knížky.* sv. 6.

—— Cestovní poznámky Svatopluka Čecha z roku 1889. Upravil a vydal F. S. [i.e. F. Strejček], *etc.* [With a portrait.] pp. 37. *v Ml. Boleslavi,* 1910. 8°.
     10230. cc. 25.

—— Hanuman. Bajka. pp. 95. *v Praze,* 1884. 16°. [*Poetické Besedy.* čís. 17.]   **11586. cc. 49/17.**

—— Two Mock Epics. Hanuman, by Svatopluk Czech—translated from the 17th edition; and, Tantum Religio, or, Sir Blasius, by W. W. Strickland. pp. 118. *Robert Forder: London,* 1894. 8°. **11602. ccc. 35. (1.)**

—— Jitřní písní. pp. 68. *v Praze,* 1887. 16°. [*Poetické Besedy.* čís. 35.]   **11586. cc. 49/35.**

—— Kratochvilná historie o ptáku Velikánu Velikánoviči. Veršem napsal Svatopluk Čech. Illustroval Viktor Oliva. pp. 87. *v Praze,* 1890. 8°.   **20002. e. 62.**

—— [Mezi knihami a lidmi.] Unter Büchern und Menschen. Erzählung . . . Aus dem Böhmischen übersetzt von F. Bauer. pp. 80. *Leipzig,* [1882.] 16°.
     012207. f. 16. (5.)

—— Modlitby k Neznámému. Druhé, nezměněné vydání. pp. 119. *v Praze,* 1897. 8°.   **011586. e. 100.**

—— Na Valdštýně. Ze čtyř cyklů básní, s původními dřevoryty K. Vika. pp. 12. *Praha,* 1924. 4°. [*Hollar.* roč. 2. sv. 1. příl.]   **Ac. 4583.**

—— [Another copy.]   **C. 98. e. 25.**

—— Nová sbírka veršovaných prací od S. Čecha. pp. 243. *v Praze,* 1880. 8°.   **11586. ee. 47.**

ČECH (Svatopluk)

—— Třetí vydání. no. 1–3. *v Praze,* 1886. 16°. [*Poetické Besedy.* čís. 28–30.]   **11586. cc. 49/28–30.**

—— Vydání čtvrté. pp. 243. *v Praze,* 1894. 16°.
     011586. df. 11.

—— Nové písně, *etc.* pp. 118. *v Praze,* 1923. 8°.
     011586. bb. 113.

—— Petrklíče. Báchorka . . . Druhé vydání. pp. 59. *v Praze,* 1884. 16°. [*Poetické Besedy.* čís. 3.]
     11586. cc. 49/3.

—— [Písně otroka.] Lieder des Sklaven . . . Aus dem Tschechischen übersetzt von Eduard Neumann. pp. 47. *Karlsbad,* 1933. 8°.   **20001. f. 33.**

—— Povídky, arabesky a humoresky . . . Druhé vydání. 4 pt. *v Praze,* 1885, 79–83. 8°.   **12208. d. 12.** *Čis. 6, 10, 12, 26 of "Salonní Bibliotéka." Pt. 1 only is of the second edition.*

—— Prvotiny Svatopluka Čecha. Vydal a úvody napsal Ferdinand Strejček. (1. Epika a lyrika. [With a portrait.]) pp. 300. *v Praze,* 1913. 8°.
     11587. b. 23.

—— Zpěvník Jana Buriana. Druhé vydání. pp. 111. *v Praze,* 1895. 8°.   **011586. h. 16.**

—— Vzpomínky na Svatopluka Čecha sestavila Redakce Máje. S podobiznou básníka z let osmdesátých. pp. 86. [1908.] 8°. *See* PERIODICAL PUBLICATIONS.—Prague.— *Máj.*   [MISSING.]

ČECH (Vladimir S.) *See* ČECH (S.) Sebrané spisy. (Pokračování posmrtné. Pořádá V. S. Čech.) 1899, *etc.* 8°.
     012265. g. 8.

CECHI (Giovanni Maria) *See* CECCHI.

CECHINI (Gio. Paulo)

—— Sentenza di Paride, ad' uso di foro. Con la contesa delle tre dee. Idilio morale, *etc.* *Gio. Antonio Giuliani: Venetia,* 1644. 12°.   **1481. ddd. 11. (3.)**

CECHINO (Tomaso) *See* CECCHINI.

CECHNER (Antonín) Soupis památek historických a uměleckých v politickém okresu Broumovském . . . Se 404 illustracemi v textu. [With a summary in French.] pp. xiii. 352. *v Praze,* 1930. 8°. [*Soupis památek historických a uměleckých v Republice Československé. A.* Země Česká. no. 45.]   **Ac. 799. c.**

—— Soupis památek historických a uměleckých v politickém okresu Kaplickém . . . S 482 vyobrazeními, *etc.* [With a summary in French.] pp. xi. 457. *v Praze,* 1921. 8°. [*Soupis památek historických a uměleckých v Čechach.* no. 42.]   **Ac. 799. c.**

—— Soupis památek historických a uměleckých v politickém okresu Rakovnickém . . . Se . . . vyobrazeními, *etc.* 2 díl. *v Praze,* 1911, 13. 8°. [*Soupis památek historických a uměleckých v Království Českém.* no. 36, 39.]
     Ac. 799. c.

CECHO, *Asculano. See* STABILI (F. degli) called CECCO D'ASCOLI.

ČECHOR (Václav) Macedonie a Válka Slovansko-Turecká. S mapkou poloostrova Balkánského. pp. 68. *v Třebíči,* 1903. 8°.   **8027. bb. 34.**

ČECHOSLOVÁK. *See* PERIODICAL PUBLICATIONS.— *London.*

CECHOSLOVAKISCH-UNGARISCHER GE-
MISCHTER SCHIEDSGERICHTSHOF. *See*
HAGUE.—*Tribunal Arbitral Mixte Hungaro-Tchécoslovaque.*

CECHOWICIUS (MARTINUS) *See* CZECHOWICZ.

ČECHY. *See* BOHEMIA.

CECI. Ceci tuera cela. [A political tract.] pp. 16. *Paris,*
1861. 8°. **8010. c. 39. (10.)**

CECI (CARLO) Piccoli bronzi del Real Museo Borbonico
distinti per categorie in dieci tavole, descritti e desegnati
da C. Ceci. pl. x. *Napoli,* 1854. *obl.* fol. **558*. e. 30.**

CECI (CONSALVO)
—— Libertà ideale e libertà storica, *etc.* [With a portrait.]
pp. xi. 195. *Bari,* 1950. 8°. **8470. a. 28.**
Biblioteca di cultura moderna. no. 471.

CECI (GETULIO) Alla ricerca di Fra Jacopone. Notizie
biografiche inedite e saggio di edizione critica.
pp. viii. 269. *Todi,* 1932. 8°. **4517.s.10.**

—— Todi nel medio evo. vol. 1. pp. xxxix. 370. *Todi,*
1897. 4°. **10136. h. 34.**
No more published.

CECI (GIUSEPPE) *See* BERARDUCCI (G. C.) Cronache dei
fatti del 1799 . . . a cura di G. Ceci. 1900. 8°.
1827. g. 2/1.

—— *See* CROCE (B.) La Rivoluzione napoletana del 1799
. . . Albo pubblicato . . . a cura di B. Croce, G. Ceci,
etc. 1899. fol. **1855. dd. 11.**

—— *See* PERIODICAL PUBLICATIONS.—*Naples.* Il Vesuvio,
etc. [Edited by G. Ceci.] 1869. 8°. **12331. c. 17.**

—— Bibliografia per la storia delle arti figurative nell'Italia
meridionale, *etc.* 2 vol. pp. vii. 763. 1937. 8°. *See*
NAPLES.—*Reale Deputazione Napoletana di Storia Patria.*
Ac. 6533/2.

—— Le Chiese e le cappelle abbattute o da abbattersi nel
risanamento edilizio di Napoli. 3 pt. 1890–92. *See*
NAPLES.—*Società di Storia Patria.* Archivio storico, *etc.*
anno 15–17. 1876, *etc.* 8°. **Ac. 6534.**

—— Maestri organari a Napoli dal xv al xviii secolo. *See*
SCRITTI. Scritti storici, *etc.* 1931. 4°. **9150. g. 37.**

—— Saggio di una bibliografia per la storia delle arti figurative nell'Italia meridionale. Memoria, *etc.* pp. 76.
1909. *See* NAPLES.—*Società Pontaniana, etc.* Atti. vol. 39.
1832, *etc.* 4°. **Ac. 94/2.**

CECI (LUIGI)
—— *See* ITALY.—*Ministero della Pubblica Istruzione.—Com-
missione Reale per il Riordinamento degli Studi Superiori.*
Relazioni e proposte. (pt. 1. Relazione generale—rel.
prof. L. Ceci—e schema delle proposte.) 1914. 8°.
S. 61. d.

—— *See* PERIODICAL PUBLICATIONS.—*Milan.* Giornale
italiano di filologia e linguistica classica. Diretto dai
dottori L. Ceci e G. Cortese. 1886. 8°. **P.P. 4884. f.**

—— La Riforma universitaria e le note dell'on. Odoardo
Luchini. pp. 118. *Roma,* 1883. 8°. **8357. cc. 28.**

—— Scritti glottologici. fasc. 1. pp. 40. *Firenze,*
1882. 8°. **12904. h. 3.**
No more published.

CECIAL (TOMÉ) *Ex-Escudero del Bachiller Sanson Carrasco,*
pseud. [i.e. JUAN PABLO FORNER.] *See also* FORNER
(J. P.)

CECIAL (TOMÉ) *Ex-Escudero del Bachiller Sanson Carrasco,*
pseud. [i.e. JUAN PABLO FORNER.]

—— *See* DANZA. Que Preciosa va la Danza, *etc.* [A reply
to a pamphlet, here attributed to Tomé Cecial, entitled:
"Prision y trabajos del pobresillo Pensador mexicano."]
1822. 4°. **9770. bb. 13. (8.)**

—— Reflexiones sobre la Leccion Crítica que ha publicado
D. Vicente Garcia de la Huerta; las escribia en vindicacion de la buena memoria de Miguel de Cervantes Saavedra
Tomé Cecial . . . Las publica Don Juan Pablo Forner.
pp. 146. *Madrid,* 1786. 8°. **899. aa. 2. (4.)**

—— [Another copy.] **Cerv. 508.**

CECIL. Cecil; or, the Adventures of a coxcomb. A novel.
[By Catherine G. F. Gore.] 3 vol. *Richard Bentley:*
London, 1841. 12°. **N. 2120.**

—— [Another edition.] pp. 398. *Richard Bentley: London,*
1845. 8°. [*Standard Novels.* no. 97.] **1153. d. 15.**

—— Cecil, a Peer, a sequel to Cecil, or, the Adventures of a
coxcomb. By the same author [i.e. Catherine G. F.
Gore]. 3 vol. *T. & W. Boone: London,* 1841. 12°.
N. 2127.

—— Cecil's Tryst. A novel. By the author of 'Lost Sir
Massingberd' [i.e. James Payn], *etc.* 3 vol.
Tinsley Bros.: London, 1872. 8°. **12629. h. 2.**

—— New edition. pp. 364. *Chapman & Hall: London,*
1874. 8°. **12600. f. 4.**

CECIL, *Aunt.* Aunt Cecil's Christmas Story for the Little
Ones. pp. 87. *Protestant Episcopal Society for the*
Promotion of Evangelical Knowledge: New York,
[1866.] 12°. **12803. de. 44.**

CECIL, *Brother.* *See* LITURGIES.—*Church of England.*
[*Adaptations of Latin Liturgical Books.*] Manual for the
Unction of the Sick . . . Translated and arranged by
Brother Cecil. 1868. 8°. **3475. aaa. 2.**

CECIL, *Cousin.* Cousin Cecil; or, the Wheel of fortune. A
domestic romance. By the author of "Dorinda; or, the
Miser's will," *etc.* pp. 157. *E. Lloyd: London,* [1852.] 8°.
12624. f. 11.

CECIL, *pseud.* [i.e. CHARLES EDWARD FISHER.] The Homestead, embracing observations and reflections on America
and Ireland, on the writer's return from the United
States: with occasional poems. By Cecil. pp. iv. 116.
H. E. Tresidder: London, 1862. 8°. **11649. bb. 20.**

—— Kanzas and the Constitution. By "Cecil." pp. 16.
Damrell & Moore: Boston, 1856. 8°. **8177. f. 30.**

—— The Law of the Territories. [Two essays, the second
signed: Cecil.] pp. 127. *C. Sherman & Son:*
Philadelphia, 1859. 8°. **6625.aa.1.**

CECIL, *pseud.* [i.e. CORNELIUS TONGUE.] *See* YOUATT
(William) The Horse . . . A new edition, re-edited and
revised with observations on breeding cavalry horses, by
Cecil. 1855. 8°. **7295. d. 40.**

—— Hints on Agriculture, relative to profitable draining
and manuring; also, the comparative merits of the pure
breeds of cattle and sheep. By Cecil, *etc.* pp. iv. 180.
T. C. Newby: London, 1858. 12°. **7075. b. 11.**

—— Hunting Tours: descriptive of various fashionable
countries and establishments, with anecdotes of masters
of hounds . . . By "Cecil." pp. xiii. 439. *Saunders,*
Otley & Co.: London, 1864. 8°. **7906.bb.4.**

—— The second edition, with four illustrations. pp. 304.
F.P. *P. Allan & Co.: London,* 1924. 8°.
07911. eee. 54.

CECIL, *pseud.* [i.e. CORNELIUS TONGUE.]

—— Records of the Chase, and Memoirs of Celebrated Sportsmen; illustrating some of the usages of olden times . . . By Cecil. [With plates.] pp. xx. 435. *Longman & Co.: London*, 1854. 8°. **7905. c. 5.**

—— A new edition thoroughly revised. pp. xxiv. 355. *G. Routledge & Sons: London*, 1877. 8°. **7907. ff. 42.**

—— The third edition, with four illustrations. pp. xi. 291. **F.P.** *P. Allan & Co.: London*, 1922. 8°. **7911. bb. 22**. *No. 42 of fifty copies on Fine Paper.*

—— Stable Practice; or, Hints on training for the turf, the chase, and the road . . . By Cecil, author of "The Stud Farm." pp. xv. 240. *Longman, Brown, Green & Longmans: London*, 1852. 8°. **7905. c. 4.**

—— The Stud Farm; or, Hints on breeding for the turf, the chase, and the road . . . By Cecil. pp. xiii. 202. *Longman & Co.: London*, 1851. 8°. **7295. d. 5.**

—— Second edition. pp. xiii. 213. *Longman & Co.: London*, 1856. 8°. **7295. d. 6.**

—— A new edition—thoroughly revised. pp. xii. 244. *G. Routledge & Sons: London*, 1873. 8°. **7293. aaa. 36.**

CECIL PAPERS.

—— [For the calendar of the collection of manuscripts of the Cecil family, known as the Cecil Papers, published by the Historical Manuscripts Commission:] *See* CECIL (Robert A. T. G.) *Marquis of Salisbury.*

CECIL, *Family of.* *See* DENNIS (George R.) The House of Cecil. [With portraits.] 1914. 8°. **9903. bbb. 6.**

—— *See* STANLEY (Matilda L.) The "Hatfield Business." The Cecil plot, *etc.* 1904. 4°. **1418. k. 45. (3.)**

CECIL (*Lord* ADELBERT PERCY) Eternal Life and the Holy Ghost. By A. P. C. (Lord A. P. Cecil.) pp. 30. *G. Morrish: London*, [1890?] 32°. [MISSING.]

—— A Short Summary of the Epistle to the Ephesians. By A. P. C. [i.e. Lord A. P. Cecil.] pp. 62. [1882?] 8°. *See* C., A. P. [MISSING.]

CECIL (ALBINIA) *afterwards* WRAY (ALBINIA) *Lady. See* WRAY.

CECIL (ALGERNON) British Foreign Secretaries, 1807–1916. Studies in personality and policy. [With portraits.] pp. xii. 378. *G. Bell & Sons: London*, 1927. 8°. **09525. i. 1.**

—— A Dreamer in Christendom; or, What you will. [Essays.] pp. 308. *G. Bell & Sons: London*, 1925. 8°. **04503. e. 34.**

—— Essays in Imitation. pp. ix. 153. *John Murray: London*, 1910. 8°. **12355. r. 16.**

—— Facing the Facts in Foreign Policy. A retrospect and a prospect. pp. 129. *Eyre & Spottiswoode: London*, 1941. 8°. **8029. b. 1.**

—— The Foreign Office. 1923. *See* WARD (*Sir* Adolphus W.) and GOOCH (G. P.) The Cambridge History of British Foreign Policy, *etc.* vol. 3. 1922, *etc.* 8°. **2084. g.**

—— A House in Bryanston Square. pp. 360. *Eyre & Spottiswoode: London*, 1944. 8°. **12359. g. 35.**

CECIL (ALGERNON)

—— A House in Bryanston Square. (Second edition.) pp. 360. *Eyre & Spottiswoode: London*, 1945. 8°. **012359. cc. 2.**

—— A Life of Robert Cecil, First Earl of Salisbury . . . With illustrations [including portraits]. pp. xii. 406. *John Murray: London*, 1915. 8°. **010826. k. 27.**

—— Metternich, 1773–1859. A study of his period and personality. [With portraits.] pp. ix. 344. *Eyre & Spottiswoode: London*, 1933. 8°. **10709. f. 25.**

—— Metternich, *etc.* (Revised edition.) pp. 324. *Eyre & Spottiswoode: London*, 1943. 8°. **010703. h. 87.**

—— Metternich, *etc.* (Third edition.) pp. x. 7–324. *Eyre & Spottiswoode: London*, 1947. 8°. **10709. df. 34.**

—— A Portrait of Thomas More, scholar, statesman, saint. [With plates, including a portrait.] pp. xiii. 442. *Eyre & Spottiswoode: London*, 1937. 8°. **20030. c. 19.**

—— Queen Victoria and her Prime Ministers. [With portraits.] pp. vii. 356. *Eyre & Spottiswoode: London*, 1953 [1952]. 8°. **09525. k. 22.**

—— Six Oxford Thinkers. Edward Gibbon. John Henry Newman. R. W. Church. James Anthony Froude. Walter Pater. Lord Morley of Blackburn. pp. x. 301. *John Murray: London*, 1909. 8°. **10804. d. 11.**

—— The World We Live in. [A novel.] pp. 288. *Hutchinson & Co.: London*, [1925.] 8°. **NN. 10755.**

CECIL (ALICIA MARGARET) *Baroness Rockley. See* AMHERST (*Hon.* A. M. Tyssen) *afterwards* CECIL (A. M.) *Baroness Rockley.*

CECIL (ALLAN)

—— Turquoise Clues. [A novel.] pp. 208. *Rich & Cowan: London*, [1949.] 8°. **NN. 40032.**

CECIL (ANNE) *afterwards* DE VERE (ANNE) *Countess of Oxford. See* DE VERE.

CECIL (ARTHUR) *See* BELL (Florence E. E.) *Lady,* and CECIL (A.) Time is Money, *etc.* [1905.] 12°. **2304. h. 44.**

CECIL (BRIAN) Messrs. Brian Cecil and John Bull, at the Meeting held in Trafalgar Square, upon the Eastern Question. December 29th, 1877. [In verse.] (Second edition.) pp. iv. 27. *Simpkin & Marshall: London; W. Sharland: Southampton*, [1878.] 8°. **11653. de. 18. (3.)**

CECIL (BROWNLOW) *Earl of Exeter.* Letters on Love, Marriage, and Adultery; addressed to the Right Honourable the Earl of Exeter. pp. 98. *J. Ridgway: London*, 1789. 8°. **12354. h. 26. (2.)**

CECIL (CATHARINE) *See* CECIL (Richard) *Minister of St. John's Chapel, Bedford Row.* Original Thoughts on Various Passages of Scripture . . . Edited by C. Cecil. 1848. 8°. **3125. d. 17.**

—— *See* CECIL (Richard) *Minister of St. John's Chapel, Bedford Row.* The Remains of the Rev. Richard Cecil . . . With an introduction by his daughter (C. Cecil), *etc.* 1876. 8°. **3752. aaa. 5.**

—— *See* HAWKES (Sarah) *Mrs.* Memoirs of Mrs. Hawkes . . . By [or rather, edited by] C. Cecil, *etc.* 1838. 8°. **1124. e. 8.**

CECIL (CHARLES) The Magnet of Literary Attractions. Edited by Charles Cecil. Illustrated with . . . plates. pp. xii. 312. *Renshaw & Kirkman: London,* [1840?] 12°.
12314. f. 29.

—— The Poetic Keepsake. A selection of . . . poems from " The Drawing-Room Album." Edited by Charles Cecil. pp. iv. 124. *R. A. Charlton: London,* [1845?] 16°.
11601. a. 35.

CECIL (*Mrs.* CHARLES) New Juvenile Scrap Book; a collection of most interesting tales and narratives, for the entertainment and instruction of young people. Edited by Mrs. Charles Cecil. With fine steel engravings. pp. viii. 144. *Renshaw & Kirkman: London,* [1835?] 4°.
12350. f. 9.

—— [A reissue.] New Juvenile Annual . . . By Mrs. Charles Cecil, *etc.* 1849. 4°. *See* PERIODICAL PUBLICATIONS.— *London.*
12815. aaa. 52.

—— Sacred Melodies: a Christian and literary remembrancer. Edited by Mrs. Charles Cecil. [With plates.] pp. viii. 136. *Edward Lacey: London,* [1835?] 12°.
11601. aa. 4.

—— The Seraph: or, Gems of poetry, for the serious and contemplative mind . . . Edited by Mrs. Charles Cecil. pp. v. 140. *Edward Lacey: London,* [1835?] 12°.
11601. aa. 5.

CECIL (CHARLES R.) The Business Letter-Writer. pp. 61 *W. Foulsham & Co.: London,* [1920.] 8°. **08228. a. 46.**

—— The Business Letter Writer, *etc.* pp. 63. *W. Foulsham & Co.: London,* [1952.] 8°. [*Foulsham's " New " Popular Handbooks.*]
W.P. 9687/23.

—— The Popular Reciter. Compiled and edited by C. R. Cecil. pp. 64. *W. Foulsham & Co.: London,* [1920.] 8°.
012273. aaa. 16.

—— [A reissue.] The Popular Reciter, *etc.* *London,* [1952.] 8°. [*Foulsham's " New " Popular Handbooks.* no. 1.]
W.P. 9687/22.

—— Toasts and Speeches: how to prepare and deliver them. pp. 61. *W. Foulsham & Co.: London,* [1920.] 8°.
011805. e. 64.

—— Toasts and Speeches . . . Revised edition. pp. 61. *W. Foulsham & Co.: London,* 1949. 8°. [*Foulsham's " New " Popular Handbooks.*]
W.P. 9687/18.

CECIL (*Lord* DAVID) *See* CECIL (*Lord* Edward C. D. G.)

CECIL (DOROTHY) The Conflict, and other poems. pp. 28. *A. H. Stockwell: London,* [1927.] 8°. **011644. ee. 55.**

CECIL (E.) *pseud.*

—— Life of Lafayette. Written for children . . . With six illustrations. pp. 218. *Crosby & Nichols: Boston,* 1863. 8°.
10663. aa. 37.

CECIL (EDGAR ALGERNON ROBERT GASCOYNE) *Viscount Cecil of Chelwood. See* GORE (William G. A. O.) *Baron Harlech.* Welsh Disestablishment and Disendowment . . . With a preface by Lord Robert Cecil. 1912. 8°.
4106. c. 61.

—— *See* HURST (Joseph) *Barrister-at-Law,* and CECIL (E. A. R. G.) *Viscount Cecil of Chelwood.* The Principles of Commercial Law, *etc.* 1891. 8°. [MISSING.]

—— —— 1906. 8°. [MISSING.]

CECIL (EDGAR ALGERNON ROBERT GASCOYNE) *Viscount Cecil of Chelwood.*

—— The Way of Peace. Essays and addresses. [With a portrait.] pp. 256. *P. Allan & Co.: London,* 1928. 8°.
08425. ff. 9.

—— All the Way. [An autobiography. With plates, including portraits.] pp. 262. *Hodder & Stoughton: London,* 1949. 8°.
10861. h. 36.

—— The Achievement of World Order, *etc.* pp. 30. *London,* [1936.] 8°. [*University College Union Society. Foundation Week Orations.*]
Ac. 2666. f/4. (21.)

—— Black List and Blockade. Interview with the Rt. Hon. Lord Robert Cecil . . . in reply to the Swedish Minister. (Oct. 5th, 1916.) pp. 10. *Eyre & Spottiswoode: London,* 1916. 8°.
08028. h. 22.

—— Conservative and Unionist Women's Franchise Association. Address delivered by Lord Robert Cecil on December 8th, 1908. pp. 12. *Conservative & Unionist Women's Franchise Association: London,* [1909.] 8°.
08415. f. 13. (1.)

—— The Co-operation of Nations, *etc.* pp. 32. *University of London Press: London,* [1928.] 8°. [*Rickman Godlee Lecture.* no. 1.]
Ac.2666.f/7.(1.)

—— Disarmament. Being a speech delivered . . . at the Special Meeting of the General Council of the League of Nations Union . . . October 21st, 1927. pp. 21. *League of Nations Union: London,* 1927. 12°. **8425. tt. 62.**

—— An Emergency Policy. [A proposal for a treaty of mutual assistance by the United Nations.] pp. 30. *Hutchinson & Co.: London,* [1948.] 8°. **8010. h. 21.**

—— Great Experiment. An autobiography. [With plates, including portraits.] pp. 390. *Jonathan Cape: London,* 1941. 8°.
9100.k.53.

—— International Arbitration, *etc.* pp. 26. *Clarendon Press: Oxford,* 1928. 8°. [*Burge Memorial Lecture.* 1928.]
W.P. 4556/2.

—— The League as a Road to Peace. *See* WOOLF (Leonard S.) The Intelligent Man's Way to Prevent War, *etc.* 1933. 8°.
08425. e. 65.

—— A League of Nations. An address delivered by the Rt. Hon. Lord Robert Cecil . . . on the occasion of his installation as Chancellor of the University of Birmingham. 12th November, 1918. pp. 16. *Cornish Bros.: Birmingham,* 1918. 8°.
8425. ppp. 46.

—— A League of Nations Policy. (A speech in explanation of Resolutions passed on 20th January, 1922, by the General Council of the League of Nations Union.) pp. 15. *League of Nations Union:* [*London,*] 1922. 8°.
012301. eee. 78.

—— A Letter to an M.P. on Disarmament. pp. 40. *L. & V. Woolf: London,* 1931. 8°. [*Hogarth Letters.* no. 2.]
012201. aaa. 4/2.

—— The Lords Question . . . With historical notes and extracts from speeches by Mr. Balfour . . . and others, on the Unionist reform proposals and the Parliament Bill. pp. 64. *West Strand Publishing Co.: London,* [1910.] 8°.
8138. b. 98.

—— The Machinery of Government, *etc.* pp. 23. *Oxford University Press: London,* 1932. 8°. [*Barnett House Papers.* no. 16.]
8295.f.23/16.

CECIL (EDGAR ALGERNON ROBERT GASCOYNE) *Viscount Cecil of Chelwood*.

—— Minorities and Peace, *etc.* [With a portrait.] pp. 31. *London*, 1934. 4°. [*Lucien Wolf Memorial Lecture.* no. 1.]
Ac. 8106/15.

—— The Moral Basis of the League of Nations. The Essex Hall Lecture, 1923, *etc.* pp. 63. *Lindsey Press: London,* 1923. 8°.
8425. bb. 75.

—— [Another edition.] The League of Nations : its moral basis, *etc.* pp. 31. *G. H. Doran Co.: New York,* [1924.] 8°. [*Christianity and World Problems.* no. 4.]
8287.i.23/4.

—— The New Outlook. pp. 43. *G. Allen & Unwin: London*, 1919. 8°.
8138. f. 64.

—— Peace and Pacifism . . . The Romanes Lecture . . . 1938. pp. 33. *Clarendon Press: Oxford*, 1938. 8°.
8425. ppp. 71.

—— Queen Alexandra. *See* ALEXANDRA, *Queen Consort of Edward VII., King of Great Britain and Ireland.* [*Biography.—General.*] Queen Alexandra, *etc.* 1925. 4°.
10806. i. 16.

—— A Real Peace. pp. v. 34. *Hamish Hamilton: London,* 1941. 8°.
8029. a. 17.

—— Report of the Foundation Oration [on the future of the League of Nations], *etc.* pp. 16. *London*, [1925.] 8°. [*University College Union Society. Foundation Week Orations.*]
Ac. 2666. f/4. (13.)

—— Why Mail Censorship is Vital to Britain. An interview with the Rt. Hon. Lord Robert Cecil, Minister of Blockade, *etc.* pp. 10. *J. Truscott & Son: London*, 1916. 8°.
08028. h. 23.

CECIL (EDGAR ALGERNON ROBERT GASCOYNE) *Viscount Cecil of Chelwood*, and CLAYTON (HENRY JAMES)

—— Our National Church. pp. vi. 236. *F. Warne & Co.: London & New York*, 1913. 8°. [*Imperial Library.*]
012210.bb.2/1.

CECIL (EDWARD) *Dramatist. See* PHILIPS (Austin) and CECIL (E.) The Fourth Man, *etc.* [1916.] 8°. [*French's Acting Edition.* vol. 165.]
2304. h. 56.

CECIL (EDWARD) *Viscount Wimbledon. See* DALTON (Charles) *F.R.G.S.* Life and Times of General Sir Edward Cecil, Viscount Wimbledon, *etc.* [With a portrait.] 1885. 8°.
10817. i. 5.

—— The Gouernment of Ireland vnder the Honorable . . . Gouernour Sir Iohn Perrot . . . beginning 1584. and ending 1588. Being the first booke of the continuation of the historie of that kingdome, *etc.* [The dedication signed : E. C. S., i.e. E. Cecil.] pp. 136. 1626. 4°. *See* S., E. C.
287. a. 12.

—— [Another copy.]
G. 5526.

—— [Another copy.]
C. 21. b. 30.

—— A Iournall, and Relation of the action, which by his Maiesties commandement Edward Lord Cecyl, Baron of Putney, and Viscount of Wimbledon . . . Admirall, and Lieutenant Generall of his Maiestyes forces, did vndertake vpon the coast of Spaine, 1625. pp. 33. [*London ?*] 1626. 4°.
E. 1943. (3.)

—— [Another copy.]
G. 2488.

—— [Another edition.] pp. 30. [*London ?*] 1627. 4°.
808. d. 15.

Cropped.

CECIL (EDWARD) *Viscount Wimbledon.*

—— Beschreibung der Reiss, oder Relation der Expedition Heerrn Edoardi Cecil . . . gegen Hispanien aussgeloffen 1625. *See* BRY (J. T. de) and BRY (J. I. de) [India Orientalis. Abridgment.] Orientalische Indien, *etc.* 1628. fol.
10003. e. 14.

—— A Speech made in the Lower House of Parliament. Anno 1621. by Sir Edward Cicill, colonell. [A spurious work, written by Thomas Scott, B.D., Minister at Utrecht. pp. 5. [*London,*] 1621. 4°.
1093. b. 81.

—— [Another edition.] pp. 5. [*London,*] 1624. 4°.
1104. b. 32

CECIL (*Lord* EDWARD CHRISTIAN DAVID GASCOYNE) *See* ASQUITH (*Lady* Cynthia M. E.) and CECIL (*Lord* E. C. D. G.) Cans and Can'ts. [1927.] 4°. [MISSING.]

—— *See* AUSTEN (Jane) [*Works.*] The Works of Jane Austen. (Sense and Sensibility . . . With an introduction by Lord David Cecil.) 1907, *etc.* 8°.
012209. df. 67.

—— *See* COWPER (William) *the Poet.* [*Selections.*] Selections from Cowper . . . Edited with an introduction by Lord David Cecil. 1933. 8°.
012272. a. 13.

—— *See* WILLIAMS (Charles W. S.) The New Book of English Verse . . . Associate editors: Lord David Cecil, E. de Selincourt, *etc.* 1935. 8°.
11655. b. 13.

—— An Anthology of Modern Biography. Edited by Lord David Cecil. pp. xvi. 229. *T. Nelson & Sons: London,* 1936. 8°. [*Modern Anthologies.* no. 2.]   W.P. 9063/2.

—— [Another edition.] Modern Biography . . . With notes and questions by A. J. J. Ratcliff. pp. xvi. 256. *T. Nelson & Sons: London & Edinburgh,* 1937. 8°. [*Teaching of English Series.* no. 205.]
012207. aa. 1/176.

—— Antony and Cleopatra. The Fourth W. P. Ker Memorial Lecture delivered in the University of Glasgow, 4th May, 1943. pp. 30. *Glasgow*, 1944. 8°. [*Glasgow University Publications.* no. 58.]
Ac. 1487.

—— Early Victorian Novelists. Essays in revaluation. pp. 332. *Constable & Co.: London*, 1934. 8°.
11856. a. 6.

—— Early Victorian Novelists, *etc.* pp. 253. *Penguin Books: Harmondsworth*, 1948. 8°. [*Pelican Books.* no. 190.]
012209. d. 4/190.

—— The English Poets . . . With 12 plates . . . and 13 illustrations, *etc.* pp. 47. *William Collins: London,* 1941. 8°. [*Britain in Pictures.*]   W.P. 10933/1(1)

—— The English Poets. *See* TURNER (Walter J.) Impressions of English Literature, *etc.* 1943. 8°.
W.P. 10933/1. (61.)

—— Hardy the Novelist. An essay in criticism . . . The Clark Lectures . . . 1942. pp. 157. *Constable & Co.: London*, 1943. 8°.
11865. c. 6.

—— Hatfield House. An illustrated survey of the Hertfordshire home of the Cecil family. History written by Lord David Cecil. Contents described by the Marquess of Salisbury, K.G., P.C. pl. 30. *English Life Publications: Derby*, [1951.] obl. 8°.
7823. de. 7.

—— Jane Austen . . . The Leslie Stephen Lecture . . . 1935. pp. 42. *University Press: Cambridge*, 1935. 8°.
11856. e. 2.

CECIL (*Lord* EDWARD CHRISTIAN DAVID GASCOYNE)

—— Lord M.; or, the Later life of Lord Melbourne. [With plates, including portraits.] pp. xiii. 347. *Constable: London*, 1954. 8°. **10864. b. 42.**

—— The Oxford Book of Christian Verse. Chosen and edited by Lord David Cecil. pp. xxxiii. 560. *Clarendon Press: Oxford*, 1940. 8°. **2292. b. 34.**

—— Poets and Story-Tellers. pp. 201. *Constable: London*, 1949. 8°. **11864. a. 42.**

—— The Poetry of Thomas Gray . . . From the Proceedings of the British Academy, *etc.* pp. 20. *Geoffrey Cumberlege: London*, [1945.] 8°. [*Warton Lecture on English Poetry.* 1945.] **Ac. 1186/7.**

—— The R.A.F.: a layman's glimpse. *See* ROTHENSTEIN (*Sir* William) Men of the R.A.F. 1942. 8°. **8829. k. 43.**

—— Reading as one of the Fine Arts. An inaugural lecture, *etc.* pp. 16. *Clarendon Press: Oxford*, 1949. 8°. **11868. bb. 41.**

—— Sir Walter Scott. [With a portrait.] pp. 59. *Constable & Co.: London*, 1933. 8°. [*Raven Miscellany.*] **C. 100. g. 38/2.**

—— The Stricken Deer; or, the Life of Cowper. [With plates, including portraits.] pp. xi. 303. *Constable & Co.: London*, 1929. 8°. **10824. b. 4.**

—— [Another edition.] pp. ix. 303. *Constable & Co.: London*, 1933. 8°. [*Crown Constables.*] **12213.f.2/1.** A reduced photographic facsimile of the preceding.

—— Two Quiet Lives. Dorothy Osborne, Thomas Gray. [With plates.] pp. 256. *The Bobbs-Merrill Co.: Indianapolis, New York*, [1948.] 8°. **10862. b. 9.**

—— Two Quiet Lives. (Dorothy Osborne. Thomas Gray.) [With portraits.] pp. xi. 194. *Constable: London*, 1948. 8°. **10861. h. 28.**

—— Walter Pater, the Scholar-Artist . . . The Rede Lecture, delivered in the University of Cambridge, 19 May 1955. pp. 29. *University Press: Cambridge*, 1955. 8°. **11871. p. 21.**

—— William Cowper. pp. 19. *London*, 1932. 8°. [*English Association. Pamphlet.* no. 81.] **Ac. 2664.**

—— The Young Melbourne, and the story of his marriage with Caroline Lamb. [With plates, including portraits.] pp. xiii. 277. *Constable & Co.: London*, 1939. 8°. **10858. f. 18.**

—— The Young Melbourne and the Story of his Marriage with Caroline Lamb, *etc.* [With plates, including portraits.] pp. 286. *Pan Books: London*, 1948. 8°. **10862. a. 37.**

CECIL (*Lord* EDWARD HERBERT GASCOYNE) The Leisure of an Egyptian Official. [With a portrait.] pp. ix. 336. *Hodder & Stoughton: London*, [1921.] 8°. **010855. d. 32.**

CECIL (ELIZABETH) *Countess of Salisbury. See* BOWLES (Charles E. B.) Settlement of Lands . . . with a view to the marriage of Robert Cecil . . . with Elizabeth Brooke, *etc.* 1889. 4°. **9915. f. 15.**

CECIL (*Lady* ELIZABETH) *afterwards* **BOYLE** (ELIZABETH) *Countess of Orrery. See* BOYLE.

CECIL (ERNEST) Flames Unquelled. pp. 284. *Henry Walker: London*, [1927.] 8°. **NN. 12901.**

CECIL (ERNEST) and **KERR** (NORAH)

—— Human. pp. 263. *Heath Cranton: London*, [1921.] 8°. **NN. 6896.**

CECIL (*Lord* EUSTACE BROWNLOW HENRY GASCOYNE) Dates, Battles, and Events of Modern History. pp. viii. 45. *C. J. Stewart: London*, 1857. 16°. **9007. a. 9.**

—— Impressions of Life at Home and Abroad. [Reprinted from the "St. James's Medley."] pp. viii. 277. *Hurst & Blackett: London*, 1865. 8°. **12355. g. 6.**

—— Seven Short Essays on Social and Political Subjects. pp. 71. *John Murray: London*, 1910. 8°. **12361. f. 22.** Printed for private circulation.

—— Speeches on Army Reform by G. O. Trevelyan . . . examined and considered. pp. 22. *Edward Stanford: London*, 1871. 8°. **8826. dd. 19.**

CECIL (EVELYN) The Incomparable Chrichtoun. An historical sketch, *etc.* ff. 16. [*London*, 1933.] 4°. **11781. i. 59.** *Typewritten.*

—— The Phantom Leader . . . Lyrics by George Tootell. ff. 60. [*London*, 1934.] 4°. **11778. h. 58.** *Typewritten.*

—— "S.S. Romantic" . . . Lyrics by Leigh Kelway, *etc.* [*London*, 1933.] 4°. **11778. h. 66.** *Typewritten.*

CECIL (EVELYN) *Baron Rockley.* Notes of my Journey round the World . . . With fifteen . . . illustrations. pp. vi. 207. *Longmans & Co.: London*, 1889. 8°. **10028. ee. 17.**

—— On the Eve of the War. A narrative of impressions during a journey in Cape Colony, the Free State, the Transvaal, Natal, and Rhodesia. September, 1899, to January, 1900 . . . With map and illustrations. pp. viii. 147. *John Murray: London*, 1900. 8°. **9060. c. 10.**

—— Primogeniture. A short history of its development in various countries and its practical effects. pp. 16. 231. *John Murray: London*, 1895. 8°. **6005.e.10.**

CECIL (*Hon. Mrs.* EVELYN) *See* AMHERST (*Hon.* Alicia M. Tyssen) *afterwards* CECIL (A. M.) *Baroness Rockley.*

CECIL (*Lady* FLORENCE MARY GASCOYNE) *See* CECIL (*Lord* Rupert W. E. G.) Changing China. By the Rev. Lord William Gascoyne-Cecil, assisted by Lady Florence Cecil. 1910. 8°. **10057. dd. 54.**

CECIL (*Lady* FRANCES H.) *pseud.* [i.e. FRANCES H. SAYERS.] Paradise Found, and other poems. pp. vi. 68. *J. Nisbet & Co.: London*, 1882. 8°. **11653. ee. 19.**

CECIL (GEORGE) The History of Opera in England. pp. 80. *Barnicott & Pearce: Taunton*, 1930. 8°. **7899. ppp. 30.**

CECIL (*Lady* GWENDOLEN GASCOYNE) Life of Robert, Marquis of Salisbury. [With a portrait.] 4 vol. *Hodder & Stoughton: London*, 1921–32. 8°. **10814. d. 1.**

CECIL (HENRY) *Marquis of Exeter.*

—— The Remarkable Trial of the Rev. William Sneyd, for seducing, debauching, and carrying off, the wife of Henry Cecil . . . June 26th, 1790. pp. 12. [1790?] 8°. **6497. b. 73.**

CECIL (HENRY) *Marquis of Exeter.*

—— Two Actions for Criminal Conversation with the whole of the evidence . . . the first between Henry Cecil . . . plaintiff, and the Rev. William Sneyd, defendant, for cohabiting with Mrs. Cecil . . . The second between Hooker Barttelot . . . plaintiff and Samuel Hawker . . . defendant, for cohabiting with Mrs. Barttelot, *etc.* pp. 67. *M. Smith: London*, 1790. 4°. **518. l. 12. (5.)**

CECIL (HENRY) *of Sheffield.* See SHEFFIELD.—*Sheffield Regional Copec Conference.* The Fourfold Challenge of To-day . . . Edited . . . by H. Cecil, *etc.* 1925. 8°. **08282. ee. 44.**

—— Brightest England and the Way in. By Henry Cecil, Henry Davies, Fred E. Dodson, Arnold Freeman, Eben. Lewis, and J. S. Pinner. pp. viii. 47. *G. Allen & Unwin: London*, [1919.] 8°. **08285. b. 58.**

CECIL (HENRY) *pseud.* [i.e. HENRY CECIL LEON.]

—— According to the Evidence. pp. 224. *Chapman & Hall: London*, 1954. 8°. **NNN. 5126.**

—— Brothers in Law. pp. 222. *Michael Joseph: London*, 1955. 8°. **NNN. 6370.**

—— Brothers in Law [i.e. An extract from " Brothers in Law."] pp. 32. *Michael Joseph: London*, 1955. 8°. **12846. g. 54.**
The cover title reads " 'Trailer' for Brothers in Law ".

—— Full Circle. pp. 235. *Chapman & Hall: London*, 1948. 8°. **NN. 39004.**

—— Natural Causes. pp. 251. *Chapman & Hall: London*, 1953. 8°. **NNN. 4376.**

—— No Bail for the Judge. pp. 227. *Chapman & Hall: London*, 1942. 8°. **NNN. 3119.**

—— The Painswick Line. pp. 270. *Chapman & Hall: London*, 1951. 8°. **NNN. 1929.**

—— Ways and Means. pp. 272. *Chapman & Hall: London*, 1952. 8°. **NNN. 3596.**

CECIL (HENRY) *Writer of Verse.* Poems. pp. viii. 225. *Smith, Elder & Co.: London*, 1858. 8°. **11651. c. 19.**

—— The Two Thousand of Two Hundred Years Ago. [In verse.] pp. 15. *Ward & Co.: London*, 1862. 8°. **11650. bb. 48.**

CECIL (HENRY L.) and HEAPS (WILLARD ALLISON)

—— School Library Srrvice in the United States. An interpretative survey. pp. 334. *H. W. Wilson Co.: New York*, 1940. 8°. **011900. b. 68.**

CECIL (HUGH) A Book of Beauty. [Photographs of women by H. Cecil, with accompanying poems selected by him.] pp. 73. *P. Allan & Co.: London*, [1926.] 4°. **11609. k. 15.**

CECIL (HUGH MORTIMER) *pseud.* [i.e. ERNEST NEWMAN.]

—— Pseudo-philosophy at the End of the Nineteenth Century . . . I. An irrationalist trio: Kidd—Drummond—Balfour. pp. xvi. 308. *University Press: London*, 1897. 8°. **08464. h. 14.**

CECIL (HUGH RICHARD HEATHCOTE GASCOYNE) *Baron Quickswood.* See ANGLO-CATHOLICISM. Anglo-Catholicism of To-day . . . [By] Lord Hugh Cecil, the Dean of Exeter, *etc.* 1934. 8°. **4106. cc. 27.**

CECIL (HUGH RICHARD HEATHCOTE GASCOYNE) *Baron Quickswood.*

—— See LITURGIES.—*Church of England.—Common Prayer. —Communion Office.* [*English.*] The Communion Service as it might be. Together with an introduction and notes by H. Cecil. 1935. 8°. **3407. b. 24.**

—— See RAVEN (Charles E.) and DWELLY (F. W.) *Dean of Liverpool.* Two Letters . . . concerning the action of Lord Hugh Cecil against Liverpool Cathedral. 1934. 8°. **010920. l. 36.**

—— See ROBERTSON (*Right Hon.* John M.) The Common Sense of Home Rule. A reply to Lord Hugh Cecil. 1911. 8°. **8138. eee. 17. (5.)**

—— Christ's Presence in the Eucharist according to the Prayer Book and Articles. pp. 8. *S.P.C.K.: London*, [1932.] 8°. [*Theology Reprints.* no. 11.] **W.P. 4555/11.**

—— The Church and the Realm. pp. 40. *Press & Publications Board of the Church Assembly: London*, 1932. 8°. **4106. i. 16.**

—— Conservatism. pp. 255. *Williams & Norgate: London*, [1912.] 8°. [*Home University Library of Modern Knowledge.*] **12199. p. 1/50.**

—— Conservative Ideals. An address. pp. 16. *National Unionist Association: Westminster*, [1923.] 16°. [*National Unionist Association.* no. 2184.] **8139. dd.**

—— [Another copy.] Conservative Ideals, *etc. Westminster*, [1923.] 16°. **8139. eee. 23.**

—— Liberty and Authority. [An address.] pp. 69. *Edward Arnold: London*, 1910. 8°. **08407. k. 16.**

—— The Ministry of Women in Statutory Services. pp. 15. *S.P.C.K.: London*, 1951. 8°. **08416. k. 119.**

—— Nationalism and Catholicism. pp. 64. *Macmillan & Co.: London*, 1919. 8°. **8425. pp. 15.**

—— Natural Instinct the Basis of Social Institutions, *etc.* pp. 15. *Oxford University Press: London*, 1926. 8°. [*Barnett House Papers.* no. 9.] **8295. f. 23/9.**

—— Presidential Address to the British Constitution Association . . . March 4th, 1907. See ENGLAND.—*British Constitution Association.* Political Socialism: a remonstrance, *etc.* 1908. 8°. **8139. de. 52/2.**

—— Second Chambers in the British Dominions and in Foreign Countries. See RIGHTS. Rights of Citizenship, *etc.* 1912. 8°. **8005. ccc. 36.**

CECIL (HUGH RICHARD HEATHCOTE GASCOYNE) *Baron Quickswood*, and EVANS (OWEN)

—— Royal Commission on the Church in Wales. Digest of the memorandum of Lord Hugh Cecil . . . and the Ven. Archdeacon Evans. In supplement to the Report signed by them as members of the Commission. [By Frank Morgan.] pp. 56. [1911.] 8°. See ENGLAND.—*Royal Commission on the Church of England and other Religious Bodies in Wales and Monmouthshire.* **4165. a. 112. (2.)**

CECIL (J.) *Mrs.* See CECIL (Richard) *Minister of St. John's Chapel, Bedford Row.* Remains of the Rev. R. Cecil . . . To which is prefixed . . . a memoir of his life by Mrs. Cecil. [1854.] 8°. **3755. a. 28.**

CECIL (JAMES) *3rd Earl of Salisbury.* An Elegy in Commemoration of the Right Honourable James Earl of Salisbury, *etc. For Langly Curtis: London*, 1683. *s. sh.* fol. **Lutt. I. 135.**

CECIL (JAMES) 1st *Marquis of Salisbury.* [Official correspondence of James Cecil, Marquis of Salisbury, Lord Chamberlain with Earl Cholmondeley and William Taylor concerning the King's Theatre, Haymarket.] *See* TAYLOR (William) *Manager of the King's Theatre, Haymarket.* A Concise Statement, *etc.* 1791. 8°.
641. d. 31. (21.)

—— Aldborough, Suffolk. Catalogue of elegant household furniture . . . which will be sold by auction . . . the 3rd. of August, 1824 . . . by order of the executors of the late . . . Marquis of Salisbury. pp. 26. *Staughton: Hartford,* [1824.] 8°.
824. i. 49. (1.)

—— A Letter to the Right Honorable Lord Viscount Cranborne, Lord Lieutenant . . . of the County of Hertford. [On his having signed a protest against a county petition for economic reform.] pp. 22 [23]. *J. Almon: London,* 1780. 8°.
8135. cc. 15.

CECIL (JAMES EDWARD HUBERT GASCOYNE) *Marquis of Salisbury.*

—— [For the Calendar of the Manuscripts of the Most Honourable the Marquess of Salisbury, published by the Historical Manuscripts Commission:] *See* CECIL (Robert A. T. G.) *Marquis of Salisbury.*

—— Conservative Policy. I.—A moral unrest in industry. II.—Attitude to trade unions . . . Reprinted . . . from " The Times." pp. 18. *National Unionist Association: Westminster,* [1924.] 8°. [*National Unionist Association.* no. 2313.]
8139. dd.

—— Joint Committee on Indian Constitutional Reform. Statement representing the Minority Recommendations of the Marquis of Salisbury . . . Lord Middleton . . . Lord Rankeillour, . . . Sir Reginald Craddock . . . Sir Joseph Nall . . . being Conservative members of the Indian Committee opposed to the White Paper and the Majority Report. pp. 51. *St. Catherine Press: London,* 1934. 8°. **20018. g. 10.**

—— Post-War Conservative Policy. pp. 14. *John Murray: London,* [1942.] 8°.
08139. aa. 83.

CECIL (JAMES EMILIUS WILLIAM EVELYN GASCOYNE) *Viscount Cranborne.* Biographical Sketches of Great Monarchs for Young People. pp. ii. 136. *J. Whitaker: London,* 1853. 16°.
10604. a. 24.

—— Historical Sketches and Reviews. Reprinted from the " St. James's Medley." ser. 1. 21 pt. *John Mitchell: London,* [1862.] 8°.
9007. f. 9.

—— History of France for Children. In letters to his nieces. By Viscount Cranborne. pp. 188. *Joseph Masters: London,* 1853. 12°.
1319. c. 11.

CECIL (JOHN) D.D. *See* CREITTON (W.) An Apologie and Defence of the K. of Scotlande against the infamous libell forged by John Cecill [in his memorial to the King of Spain], *etc.* 1893. 8°. [*Publications of the Scottish History Society.* vol. 15.]
Ac. 8256.

—— *See* OGILVIE (John) *Jesuit.* Summary of Memorials presented to the King of Spain by J. Ogilvy of Poury and Dr. J. Cecil, 1596. 1893. 8°. [*Publications of the Scottish History Society.* vol. 15.]
Ac. 8256.

—— A Discoverye of the errors committed, and injuryes don to his Ma: off Scotlande, the Nobilitye off the same realme, and John Cecyll . . . by a malitious Mythologie titled an Apologie, and cōpiled by William Criton Pryest, *etc.* ff. 39. [1599.] 8°.
C. 55. b. 4.

CECIL (JOHN) *Earl of Exeter.* Begin. The Earl of Exeter with divers other Lords and Gentlemen are proprietors and owners . . . of 36000 acres of fenn, *etc.* [The case of the Earl of Exeter and others, in relation to the level known as the Lindsey Level in the county of Lincoln.] [1661 ?] *s. sh.* fol.
816. m. 8. (26.)

—— [Another edition.] *Begin.* The Earl of Exeter with divers other Lords and Gentlemen, *etc.* [1661 ?] *s. sh.* fol.
Cup. 645. b. 11. (43.)

CECIL (JOHN) *pseud.* [i.e. WILLIAM HONE.] Sixty Curious and Authentic Narratives and Anecdotes, *etc.* pp. vi. 288. *William Hone: London,* 1819. 12°.
G. 13696.

—— [Another edition.] pp. vi. 288. *Joel Smith: Boston,* 1825. 12°.
10603. a. 5.

CECIL (K. H. D.)

—— Coronation Poem and Love-Songs. pp. 63. *Elkin Mathews: London,* 1911. 16°. [*Vigo Cabinet Series.* no. 85.]
12205. w. 3/85.

—— The Historical Tragedy of Nero. [In verse.] pp. 159. *Kegan Paul & Co.: London,* 1904. 8°. **11779. ff. 28.**

—— Poems. By K. H. D. [i.e. K. H. D. Cecil.] pp. xv. 270. 1902. 8°. *See* D., K. H. **11652. dd. 17.**

—— The Poet and his Soul. [A poem.] pp. 62. *Kegan Paul & Co.: London,* [1909.] 8°. **011650. ee. 11.**

CECIL (LANGFORD) Fenacre Grange. A novel. 3 vol. *Tinsley Bros.: London,* 1870. 8°. **12627. dd. 2.**

CECIL (LOUIS) S. Giles, Cripplegate. pp. 46. *The Vicar of S. Giles, Cripplegate Without: London,* [1903.] 8°.
07816. e. 4.

CECIL (LOUIS) *Novelist.* Erpingham. [A novel.] pp. 145. *Provost & Co.: London,* 1879. 8°. **12619. ccc. 6.**

CECIL (MARY) Breezy Episodes. Thirty-one original monologues, *etc.* pp. xii. 134. *Samuel French: New York,* 1932. 8°. **012316. g. 65.**

CECIL (MARY CATHERINE) *Marchioness of Salisbury,* afterwards **STANLEY** (MARY CATHERINE) *Countess of Derby.* See GARDNER (Winifred A. H. C.) *Baroness Burghclere.* A Great Lady's Friendships. Letters to Mary, Marchioness of Salisbury, Countess of Derby, 1862–1890, *etc.* [With a portrait.] 1933. 8°.
2410. f. 12.

—— *See* WELLESLEY (Arthur) *Duke of Wellington.* [*Works.*] A Great Man's Friendship. Letters of the Duke of Wellington to Mary, Marchioness of Salisbury, 1850–1852 . . . With a biographical sketch of Lady Salisbury. With portraits. 1927. 8°. **10906. b. 22.**

CECIL (MARY ROTHES MARGARET) *Baroness Amherst of Hackney.* Bird Notes from the Nile. pp. xii. 113. *A. Constable & Co.: Westminster,* 1904. 8°.
7285. cc. 14.

CECIL (OLIVE) Behold the Body ! pp. 286. *John Long: London,* [1932.] 8°. **NN. 21112.**

—— Four Women Went. pp. 286. *John Long: London,* [1931.] 8°. **NN. 18596.**

—— Lighter of Candles. pp. 283. *E. Nash & Grayson: London,* 1930. 8°. **NN. 16628.**

—— The Pepper-Pot Problem. pp. 287. *John Long: London,* [1933.] 8°. **NN. 19897.**

CECIL (Patricia)

—— Kata, Son of Red Fang, Wolf Dog of the North . . . Illustrated by Henry C. Pitz. pp. vii. 181. *John C. Winston Co.: Philadelphia, Toronto,* [1954.] 8º.
12838. cc. 10.

CECIL (R.) The Secret of the Water Trough. pp. 96. *Hornsey Journal: London,* 1931. 8º. [*F.P. Racing Novels.* no. 90.]
012614. aaa. 1/90.

CECIL (Richard) *Minister of St. John's Chapel, Bedford Row.* See BIBLE.—*Psalms.* [*English.—Miscellaneous Metrical Versions.*] The Psalms of David selected from various versions, *etc.* [By R. Cecil.] 1785. 12º.
3433. bb. 17.

—— —— 1786. 18º.
1017. c. 4.

—— *See* BIBLE.—*Psalms.* [*English.—Miscellaneous Metrical Versions.*] The Psalms of David, selected from various versions, and adapted to public worship, *etc.* [By R. Cecil.] 1788. 12º.
03440. df. 51.

—— —— 1794. 18º.
851. h. 1.

—— —— 1799. 12º.
3435. cc. 25.

—— —— 1802. 12º.
3433. bb. 23.

—— —— 1816. 12º.
3435. d. 33.

—— —— 1822. 12º.
3436. bb. 49.

—— —— 1825. 12º.
3434. b. 31.

—— —— 1829. 12º.
3435. ccc. 16.

—— —— [1830?] 16º.
3437. b. 8.

—— *See* LOANE (Marcus L.) Oxford and the Evangelical Succession. [Biographical studies of R. Cecil and others. With a portrait.] 1950. 8º.
4909. b. 16.

—— *See* NEWTON (John) *Rector of St. Mary Woolnoth.* The Works of the Reverend John Newton . . . With a life of the author by the Rev. Richard Cecil, *etc.* [1839.] 4º.
3757. dd. 1.

—— *See* NEWTON (John) *Rector of St. Mary Woolnoth.* The Life of John Newton, written by himself; with continuation by the Rev. R. Cecil. [1854.] 8º.
3605. aaa. 11.

—— *See* WILSON (Daniel) *Bishop of Calcutta.* The Blessedness of the Christian in Death. Two sermons occasioned by the death of the Rev. R. Cecil. 1810. 8º.
4905. cc. 18.

—— The Works of the Rev. Richard Cecil . . . with a memoir of his life. Arranged and revised, with a view of the author's character, by Josiah Pratt, *etc.* [With a portrait.] 4 vol. *Whittingham & Rowland: London,* 1811. 8º.
493. d. 22–25.

—— Memoirs of John Bacon, Esq. R.A. . . . Also, of the Hon. and Rev. Wm. Bromley Cadogan . . . A new edition. pp. iv. 186. *L. B. Seeley: London,* 1822. 8º.
4920. aaaa. 43.

—— The Character and Commendation of a Faithful Minister. A sermon preached . . . on the death of . . . the Rev. John Newton. pp. 43. *J. Hatchard: London,* 1808. 12º.
4906. aa. 20.

—— Early Piety Recommended, in a discourse addressed to the Schools for Religious Instruction at St. John's Chapel, Bedford Row . . . Second edition. pp. 36. *T. Williams: London,* 1802. 12º. 4372. aa. 30. (3.)

—— [Another edition.] pp. 32. *R.T.S.: London,* [1805?] 16º.
864. a. 25. (2.)

CECIL (Richard) *Minister of St. John's Chapel, Bedford Row.*

—— Elementary Religious Truths gathered from the five Books of Moses . . . in a course of sermons compiled from the original sermon notes of the Reverend R. Cecil and by him committed . . . to the present editor . . . the Reverend William Cecil. 2 vol. *Deighton, Bell & Co.: Cambridge,* 1881. 8º.
4465. k. 14.

—— A Fragment, written in illness. pp. 32. *Algar Bros.: Sheffield,* 1853. 24º.
04403. g. 53.

—— Fragments and Abstracts of Sermons. *See* HAWKES (Sarah) *Mrs.* Memoirs of Mrs. Hawkes, *etc.* 1838. 8º.
1124. e. 8.

—— Friendly Advice from a Minister to the Servants of his Parish. [By R. Cecil.] pp. 91. 1793. 12º. *See* MINISTER.
694. c. 35. (2.)

—— Second edition. pp. 96. 1794. 12º. *See* MINISTER.
8285. aa. 26. (4.)

—— [Another edition.] pp. 44. *London,* [1830?] 12º. [*First Series Tracts.* no. 456.]
863. k. 23.

—— A Friendly Visit to the House of Mourning. [By R. Cecil.] pp. 72. 1792. 12º. *See* VISIT. 694. c. 35. (1.)

—— The third edition. pp. 72. 1793. 12º. *See* VISIT.
4409. aa. 60.

—— The sixth edition. pp. 72. 1799. 12º. *See* VISIT.
4411. df. 43. (3.)

—— [Another edition.] pp. 56. 1802. 8º. *See* VISIT.
4403. bb. 7.

—— The eighth edition. pp. 91. 1806. 8º. *See* VISIT.
4402. cc. 43.

—— A new edition. pp. 60. *W. Simpkin & R. Marshall: London,* 1820. 12º.
4406. aa. 41.

—— [Another edition.] *See* GORDON (Robert) *D.D., of the Free High Church, Edinburgh.* The Mourner's Companion, *etc.* 1825. 12º.
4404. k. 8.

—— [Another edition.] pp. 52. *R.T.S.: London,* [1825?] 12º.
863. f. 31. (3.)

—— [Another edition.] pp. 32. *R.T.S.: London,* [1830?] 12º. [*First Series Tracts.* no. 100.]
863. k. 6.

—— [Another edition.] *See* IVES (Levi S.) *Bishop of the Protestant Episcopal Church in North Carolina.* New Manual of Private Devotions, *etc.* 1831. 12º.
3456. cc. 46.

—— New edition. pp. 36. *S.P.C.K.: London,* 1836. 12º. [*Religious Tracts.* vol. 6.]
863. i. 19.

—— A new edition. pp. 54. *S.P.C.K.: London,* 1842. 12º.
4410. aa. 45. (2.)

—— A Friendly Visit to the House of Mourning. pp. 103. *Hamilton, Adams & Co.: London,* 1844. 32º.
4409. n. 30.

—— [Another edition.] pp. 72. *S.P.C.K.: London,* [1861.] 12º.
4406. cc. 9.

—— Ymweliad cyfeillgar a thy galar. pp. 152. *D. U. Lewis: Rhyl,* 1855. 24º.
4377. a. 15.

—— The Great Teacher; or, the True source of spiritual influences to the Church. A sermon. pp. 15. *Seeleys: London,* 1853. 12º.
4475. aa. 22.

CECIL (RICHARD) *Minister of St. John's Chapel, Bedford Row.*

—— Memoirs of John Bacon, Esq. R.A. with reflections drawn from a review of his moral and religious character. [With a portrait.] pp. 118. *F. & C. Rivington: London,* 1801. 8º. **1373. e. 16.**

—— [Another copy.] **276. i. 6.**

—— [Another copy.] **G. 14502.**

—— [Another copy.] **G. 14503.**

—— Memoirs of the Honourable and Reverend William Bromley Cadogan. *See* CADOGAN (*Hon.* William B.) Discourses, *etc.* 1798. 8º. **1021. i. 5.**

—— Life of the Honourable and Reverend William Bromley Cadogan . . . Abridged. pp. 72. *R.T.S.: London,* [1832.] 12º. [*Christian Biography.*] **864. f. 11/24.**

—— Memoirs of the Revᵈ John Newton . . . with general remarks on his life, connexions and character. pp. vii. 322. *J. Hatchard: London,* 1808. 12º. **1112. c. 5.**

—— The third edition. pp. viii. 322. *J. Hatchard: London,* 1808. 12º. **4902. bbb. 17.**

—— A new edition. pp. vi. 204. *L. B. Seeley: London,* 1820. 8º. **4903. bb. 6.**

—— [Another edition.] pp. 127. *W. Baynes & Son: London,* 1824. 12º. **10825. bbb. 19. (3.)**

—— New edition. pp. v. 186. *L. B. Seeley: London,* 1824. 12º. **4905. aa. 9.**

—— [Another edition.] pp. v. 132. *W. Baynes & Son: London,* 1825. 24º. **4903. b. 56.** *With an additional titlepage, engraved.*

—— [Another edition.] *See* NEWTON (John) *Rector of St. Mary Woolnoth.* The Works of the Rev. John Newton, *etc.* 1827. 8º. **493. d. 26.**

—— [Another edition.] pp. 46. *H. T. Warren: London,* [1839?] 8º. **1126. k. 7.**

—— Original Thoughts on Various Passages of Scripture; being the substance of sermons preached by the late Rev. Richard Cecil never before published . . . Edited by Catharine Cecil. [With a portrait.] pp. xxviii. 691. *Seeleys: London,* 1848. 8º. **3125. d. 17.**

—— The Pageant is Over! Two sermons: I. The Fashion of the world: on the funeral of Lord Nelson. II. Thanksgiving: on the death of Lord Nelson and the victory of Trafalgar. pp. 16. *Seeleys: London,* 1852. 8º. **10815. b. 11.**

—— Reasons for Repose, addressed to a Christian, *etc.* [Signed: R. C., i.e. R. Cecil.] [1804.] 12º. *See* C., R. **4372. aa. 30. (4.)**

—— [Another edition.] pp. 64. *R.T.S.: London,* 1838. 16º. **1121. a. 56.**

—— [Remains.] The Life, Character, and Remains of the Rev. Richard Cecil . . . Collected and revised by Josiah Pratt . . . A new edition. [With a portrait.] pp. clxxix. 435. *Whittingham & Rowland: London,* 1811. 8º. **4902. g. 17.**

—— Remains of the Rev. Richard Cecil . . . Sixth edition. pp. viii. 323. *L. B. Seeley: London,* 1816. 12º. **4407. e. 49.**

—— Seventh edition. pp. viii. 323. *L. B. Seeley: London,* 1821. 12º. **4903. df. 12.**

CECIL (RICHARD) *Minister of St. John's Chapel, Bedford Row.*

—— [Another edition.] pp. 84. *See* CHRISTIAN LIBRARY. The Christian Library, *etc.* vol. 2. 1836. 8º. **3624. bb. 3.**

—— [Another edition.] pp. 180. *A. Simpson: London,* [1840?] 12º. **3752. b. 1.**

—— [Another edition.] pp. vi. 297. *Johnstone & Hunter: Edinburgh,* 1854. 8º. [*Christian's Fireside Library.* vol. 14.] **3605. aaa. 14.**

—— [Another edition.] To which is prefixed the author's letters, and a memoir of his life by Mrs. Cecil. A new edition. pp. cxxvii. 224. *Knight & Son: London,* [1854.] 8º. **3755. a. 28.**

—— Complete edition. pp. iv. 224. *Knight & Son: London,* [1854.] 8º. **3755. a. 27.**

—— A new edition, with an introduction by his daughter (Catharine Cecil), *etc.* pp. xvi. 240. *Elliot Stock: London,* 1876. 8º. **3752. aaa. 5.**

—— A Sermon preached . . . before the Society for Missions, *etc. See* ENGLAND.—*Church of England.—Church Missionary Society.* Proceedings, *etc.* vol. 1. 1801, *etc.* 8º. **P.P. 935.**

—— Short Hints to a Soldier, in a letter from his friend. pp. 16. *Religious Tract Society: London,* [1810?] 12º. [*First Series Tracts.* no. 103.] **4431. bbb. 17. (15.)**

—— Short Hints to a Soldier, in a letter from his friend. pp. 12. *R.T.S.: London,* [1830?] 12º. [*First Series Tracts.* no. 103.] **863. k. 7.**

—— The Sword of the Lord. A sermon preached on the general fast . . . Feb. 25, 1805, *etc.* pp. 32. *F. C. & J. Rivington: London,* 1805. 8º. **4476. h. 15.**

—— To Children. [A tract.] pp. 16. *American Tract Society: New York,* [1820?] 32º. [MISSING.]

—— The True Patriot. A sermon, *etc.* pp. vii. xxxv. *F. & C. Rivington: London,* 1798. 8º. **695. g. 19. (13.)**

—— [Another copy.] **4476. ee. 16. (4.)**

CECIL (RICHARD) *of Turvey, Bedfordshire.* Faith and Purity. Two charges addressed to missionaries proceeding to the South Seas. To which is added, a letter relative to the preservation of health. pp. 71. *T. Ward & Co.: London,* 1838. 12º. **694. a. 27.**

CECIL (ROBERT) *Earl of Salisbury. See* BOWLES (Charles E. B.) Settlement of Lands . . . with a view to the marriage of Robert Cecil . . . with Elizabeth Brooke, *etc.* 1889. 4º. **9915. f. 15.**

—— *See* BRITISH STATESMEN. Lives of Eminent British Statesmen. (vol. 5. Robert Cecil, Earl of Salisbury.—Thomas Osborne, Earl of Danby. By Thomas P. Courtenay.) [1838.] 8º. **12203. tt. 1/29.**

—— *See* CECIL (Algernon) A Life of Robert Cecil, First Earl of Salisbury, *etc.* [With portraits.] 1915. 8º. **010826. k. 27.**

—— *See* CECIL (Robert A. T. G.) *Marquis of Salisbury.* Calendar of the Manuscripts of the Most Hon. the Marquis of Salisbury, *etc.* [Comprising State correspondence during the administration of Robert, Earl of Salisbury.] 1883, *etc.* 8º. [*Historical Manuscripts Commission.* no. 9.] **Bar.T.1.(9.)**

—— *See* HICKS (Leo) Sir Robert Cecil, Father Persons and the Succession, *etc.* 1955. 8º. [*Archivum historicum Societatis Jesu.* anno 24. fasc. 47.] **Ac. 2002. f.**

CECIL (ROBERT) *Earl of Salisbury.*

—— *See* JOHNSON (Richard) *Romance Writer.* A Remembrance of the Honors due to the Life and Death of Robert Earle of Salisbury, *etc.* 1612. 4⁰. C. **33.** g. **19.**

—— *See* THEOBALD (Lewis) Memoirs of Sir Walter Raleigh . . . In which are inserted, the private intrigues between the Count of Gondamore . . . and the Lord Salisbury. 1719. 4⁰. **613.** k. **12.** (5.)

—— The Secret Correspondence of Sir Robert Cecil with James VI. King of Scotland. [Edited by Sir David Dalrymple, Lord Hailes.] pp. xi. 235. *Edinburgh; for A. Millar: London,* 1766. 12⁰. **600.** d. **27.**

—— [Another copy.] **292.** b. **14.**

—— [Another edition.] *See* JAMES I., *King of Great Britain and Ireland.* [*Letters.*—I.] Correspondence of King James VI. of Scotland with Sir Richard Cecil and others in England, *etc.* 1861. 4⁰. Ac. **8113/73.**

—— Letters . . . to Sir George Carew . . . Edited by John Maclean. pp. vii. 167. 1864. 4⁰. *See* LONDON.—III. *Camden Society.* Ac. **8113/82.**

—— The Secret Correspondence of Sir Robert Cecil with James VI. King of Scotland . . . Edited by Edmund Goldsmid. 3 vol. *Privately printed: Edinburgh,* 1887. 8⁰. [*Collectanea Adamantæa.* vol. 19.] **012202.** ee. **7.**

—— The Copie of a Letter [signed: R. C., i.e. R. *Cecil.*], to the Right Honourable the Earle of Leycester, Lieutenant generall of all her Maiesties forces in the vnited Prouinces of the lowe Countreys . . . With a report of certeine petitions and declarations [praying for the execution of the sentence on Mary Queen of Scotland] made to the Queenes Maiestie at two seuerall times, from all the Lordes and Commons lately assembled in Parliament. And her Maiesties answeres thereunto by her selfe deliuered, *etc.* pp. 32. 1586. 4⁰. *See* C., R. **292.** f. **28.**

—— [Another copy.] C. **33.** b. **3.**

—— [Another copy.] G. **6144.**

—— Copye van eenen brief [signed: R. C., i.e. R. *Cecil.*], aen den E. den Graue van Leycester . . . Met een verhael, van seker begeerten ende verthooningen aen de Con. Majesteyt . . . Noch is hier bygevoecht, eē warachtige copye vande proclamatie onlancx gepubliceert by de Co. Ma. tot verclaringhe vande sententie onlancx ghegheuen tegen de Coninginne vā Scotlant. Mitsgaders eeinghe brieuen gheschreuen by de Schotsche Coninginne, aen den verrader Anthony Babington, *etc.* 1587. 4⁰. *See* C., R. T. **1716.** (10.)

—— [Another copy.] C. **33.** b. **24.** (12.)

—— La Copie d'vne lettre inscrite à . . . Monseigneur le Comte de Lecestre [signed: R. C., i.e. R. Cecil] . . . Auec vn recit de certaines requestes . . . faictes . . . à la Maiesté de la Royne, de la part de tous les Seigneurs & de la communauté dernierement assemblez aux Estats. Ensemble, les responces sus cela donées [*sic*] par sa Maiesté mesme, *etc.* pp. 28. 1587. 4⁰. *See* C., R. C. **55.** d. **19.**

—— The State and Dignitie of a Secretarie of Estates Place, with the care and perill thereof, written by the Right Honourable Robert late Earle of Salisbury. With his excellent Instructions to the late Earle of Bedford, for the Government of Barwick. pp. 17. *London,* 1642. 4⁰. T. **773.** (6.)

—— [Another copy.] G. **3828.**

—— [Another copy.] E. **128.** (31.)

CECIL (ROBERT) *Earl of Salisbury.*

—— [Another edition.] *See* JAMES I., *King of Great Britain and Ireland.* [*Extracts.*] The Prince's Cabala, *etc.* 1715. 12⁰. **522.** a. **34.**

—— [Another edition.] 1744. *See* HARLEIAN MISCELLANY. The Harleian Miscellany, *etc.* vol. 2. 1744, *etc.* 4⁰. **185.** a. **6.**

—— [Another edition.] *See* SOMERS (John) *Baron Somers.* A Fourth Collection of Scarce and Valuable Tracts, *etc.* vol. 1. 1752, *etc.* 4⁰. **184.** a. **13.**

—— [Another edition.] 1809. *See* HARLEIAN MISCELLANY. The Harleian Miscellany, *etc.* vol. 2. 1808, *etc.* 4⁰. **2072.g.**

—— [Another edition.] 1811. *See* SOMERS (John) *Baron Somers.* A Collection of Scarce and Valuable Tracts, *etc.* vol. 5. 1809, *etc.* 4⁰. **750.** g. **5.**

—— An Answere to certaine scandalous Papers, scattered abroad under colour of a Catholicke Admonition. [With the text of a letter addressed "To the Earle of Salisbury" and signed: A. B. C., &c.] *Imprinted by Robert Barker: London,* 1606. 4⁰. **3935.** b. **8.**

—— [Another edition.] *See* TONGE (Ezerel) Jesuits Assassins, *etc.* 1680. fol. **193.** d. **12.** (6.)

—— A Remembrance of the Honors due to the Life and Death of Robert Earle of Salisbury, *etc.* [The address " to the world " signed: R. I., i.e. Richard Johnson.] [1819?] 8⁰. *See* I., R. **1077.** f. **22.** (1.)

—— [Another edition.] [1820?] 8⁰. [*BROCKETT* (*John T.*) *Three Biographical Tracts.*] *See* I., R. G. **13865.**

—— A true coppy of a bold and most peremptory Letter sent to the Honorable Earle of Salisbury, by A. B. C. &c. To mittigate his prosecuting of Recusants. 1641. 4⁰. *See* A. B. C., *etc.* E. **172.** (12.)

CECIL (ROBERT) *Writer of Verse.* Levant, and other poems. pp. 39. *Fortune Press: London,* [1940.] 8⁰. **11656.** l. **11.**

—— Time, and other poems. pp. 30. *Putnam: London,* 1955. 8⁰. **11659.** cc. **37.**

CECIL (*Lord* ROBERT) *See* CECIL (Edgar A. R. G.) *Viscount Cecil of Chelwood.*

CECIL (ROBERT ARTHUR JAMES GASCOYNE) *Marquis of Salisbury.*

—— *See* CECIL (*Lord* Edward C. D. G.) Hatfield House. An illustrated survey . . . History written by Lord David Cecil. Contents described by the Marquess of Salisbury, K.G., P.C. [1951.] *obl.* 8⁰. **7823.** de. **7.**

—— *See* HITLER (Adolf) *Leader and Chancellor of the German Reich.* The Redistribution of the World . . . With a foreword by Viscount Cranborne. [1939.] 8⁰. W.P. **11492/70.**

—— Commonwealth and Empire. (An address to the Primrose League.) pp. 16. *Conservative Political Centre:* [*London,* 1953.] 16⁰. [*Commonwealth Series.* no. 1.] W.P. B. **411/1.**

—— Parliamentary Government . . . Presidential address delivered to the British Group of the Inter-Parliamentary Union . . . on . . . February 19th, 1942. pp. 6. *British Group, Inter-Parliamentary Union: London,* [1942.] 8⁰. **8140.** ff. **13.**

—— A Time for Wisdom . . . From a speech delivered . . . January 8th, 1945. [With a portrait.] pp. 7. *National Union of Conservative & Unionist Associations:* [*London,* 1945.] 8⁰. **08139.** c. **94.**

CECIL (ROBERT ARTHUR JAMES GASCOYNE) *Marquis of Salisbury.*

—— Why we are at War. pp. 8. *Deverell, Gibson & Hoare: London,* [1939?] 8°. [*National Union of Conservative and Unionist Associations.* no. 3745.] **8139. dd.**

CECIL (ROBERT ARTHUR TALBOT GASCOYNE) *Marquis of Salisbury.* See AITKEN (William F.) The Marquess of Salisbury, K.G., *etc.* [With a portrait.] 1901. 8°.
10601. e. 22/2.

—— *See* BAGENAL (Philip H. D.) The Tory Policy of the Marquis of Salisbury, *etc.* 1885. 8°. **8139. aa. 21.**

—— *See* BUTLER (*Sir* George G. G.) *K.B.E.* The Tory Tradition . . . Salisbury. 1914. 8°. **8139. c. 26.**

—— *See* C., F. M. Which shall we have? Mrs G. O. M. (The Grand Old Madam [i.e. W. E. Gladstone]) or The Hertfordshire Man [i.e. the Marquis of Salisbury], *etc.* [1887.] 8°.
11778. c. 1. (4.)

—— *See* CECIL (*Lady* Gwendolen G.) Life of Robert, Marquis of Salisbury. [With a portrait.] 1921, *etc.* 8°.
10814. d. 1.

—— *See* COTTON (*Sir* Arthur T.) *K.C.S.I.* Irrigation in India. An address . . . In reply to the Marquis of Salisbury [i.e. to his speech at Manchester, 23 Jan. 1875], *etc.* [1875.] 8°. **8768. l. 16. (3.)**

—— *See* DĀDĀBHĀĪ NAUROZJĪ. Lord Salisbury's "Blackman." [A collection of newspaper comments on Lord Salisbury's speech on the candidature of Dādābhāī Naurozjī for Holborn in 1886.] 1889. 8°.
10601. f. 9. (4.)

—— *See* DOLMAN (Frederick) Lord Salisbury and Reform, *etc.* [1884.] 8°. [*Junior Liberal Association. Association Pamphlets.* no. 1.] **8139. a. 59.**

—— *See* ELLIS (James J.) The Marquis of Salisbury. [With a portrait.] 1892. 8°. **4907. e. 10.**

—— *See* ENGLAND.—*Parliament.*—*Bills.*—*II.* [1886. *April* 13] Speeches by the Phantom Member, on the Second Reading of the Bill for the Government of Ireland, in reply to . . . Lord Salisbury. [1886?] 8°. **8146. f. 23. (3.)**

—— *See* EWING (Thomas J.) Mr. Gladstone & Ireland; or, Lord Salisbury and the Orange faction. 1886. 8°.
8146. aaa. 16. (2.)

—— *See* FALCON (Charles H.) The Marquis of Salisbury, K.G. [1898.] 8°. **10815. df. 15.**

—— *See* FORSHAW (Charles F.) Poetical Tributes to the memory of the late . . . Marquis of Salisbury, *etc.* 1904. 8°. **11652. dd. 43.**

—— *See* HOW (Frederick D.) The Marquis of Salisbury, *etc.* 1902. 8°. **010817. e. 31.**

—— *See* JEYES (Samuel H.) Life and Times of . . . the Marquis of Salisbury. [1895, *etc.*] 8°. **10816. h. 13.**

—— *See* JUNIUS, *Secundus, pseud.* Salisburism and Coercion v. Parnelism and Crime, *etc.* 1887. 8°.
8146. ff. 37. (5.)

—— *See* KENNEDY (Aubrey L.) Old Diplomacy and New . . . From Salisbury to Lloyd-George, *etc.* [With portraits.] 1922. 8°. **09504. i. 19.**

—— *See* KENNEDY (Aubrey L.) Salisbury, 1830–1903 : portrait of a statesman. [With portraits.] 1953. 8°.
10863. ee. 21.

—— *See* MEE (Arthur) *Editor of "The Children's Newspaper."* Lord Salisbury. The record premiership of modern times. 1901. 8°. **10816. aa. 29.**

CECIL (ROBERT ARTHUR TALBOT GASCOYNE) *Marquis of Salisbury.*

—— *See* MONTAGU (*Lord* Robert) Scylla or Charybdis; which? Gladstone or Salisbury? 1887. 8°.
8139. aa. 34.

—— *See* OSBORNE (*Lord* Sidney G.) Letter to the Marquis of Salisbury on a late article [by the latter] in the "National Review," respecting "Labourers' and Artisans' Dwellings," *etc.* 1883. 8°. **8277. ee. 30. (3.)**

—— *See* OXFORD.—*University of Oxford.*—*University Museum.* The Unveiling of the Statue of Sydenham . . . by the Marquess of Salisbury . . . With an address by Sir H. W. Acland [and Lord Salisbury's reply]. 1894. 8°.
10855. dd. 1.

—— *See* PALADINI (C.) Interviste. Gladstone . . . Salisbury. 1902. 8°. **10600. de. 29.**

—— *See* POTTER (George) *Publisher.* The People's Edition of the Life of the . . . Marquess of Salisbury. 1888. 8°.
010603. g. 4. (9.)

—— *See* PRELLER (H.) Salisbury und die türkische Frage im Jahre 1895, *etc.* 1930. 8°. **9386. h. 13/9.**

—— *See* PULLING (Frederic S.) The Life and Speeches of the Marquis of Salisbury. 1885. 8°. **10817. de. 7.**

—— *See* REID (Andrew) *Political Writer.* Gladstone or Salisbury? 1886. 8°. **8139. aa. 27.**

—— *See* RODGERS (Edward) and MOYLE (E. J.) The Right Hon. Lord Salisbury, *etc.* 1902. 8°. [*Men of the Moment.* no. 3.] **10803. i.**

—— *See* SALMON (Edward) *O.B.E.* The Marquis of Salisbury, K.G. 1901. 32°. **10803. a. 24/6.**

—— *See* SCOTT (John L.) Lord Salisbury and Popery, *etc.* 1886. 8°. **3942. c. 3. (1.)**

—— *See* SCRUGGS (William L.) Lord Salisbury's Mistakes, *etc.* [1896.] 8°. **8180. f. 43. (11.)**

—— —— [1896.] 8°. **8179. cc. 13. (9.)**

—— *See* SMITH (W. Brooke) Lord Salisbury. [1902.] 16°. [*Miniature Series. Biography.* no. 3.] **10803. a. 17.**

—— *See* TRAILL (Henry D.) The Marquis of Salisbury, *etc.* 1892. 8°. **10803. cc. 17/7.**

—— *See* VENEZUELA.—*Ministerio de Relaciones Exteriores.* Memorandum del Ministerio . . . acerca de la Nota de Lord Salisbury al Señor Olney, fechada á 26 de Noviembre de 1895, *etc.* 1896. 8°. **8179. aa. 85.**

—— Speeches of the Marquis of Salisbury, with a sketch of his life. Edited by H. W. Lucy. pp. 256. *G. Routledge & Sons: London,* 1885. 8°. **12301. bbb. 28.**

—— Conservative Demonstration at Glasgow. Speech of the Marquess of Salisbury . . . October 1st, 1884. pp. 16. *National Union of Conservative & Constitutional Associations: Westminster,* [1884.] 8°.
8138. cc. 8. (12.)

—— The Conservative Demonstrations at Plymouth. Speeches by the Marquess of Salisbury, on June 4th and 5th 1884. pp. 24. 1884. *See* ENGLAND.—*National Union of Conservative and Constitutional Associations. Publications.* 1872, *etc.* 8°. **8138. aaa. 56.**

—— The Conservative Party and the Franchise Bill. Speeches of the Marquis of Salisbury . . . and . . . Sir Stafford Northcote . . . at the Cannon Street Hotel, London, July 28, 1884. pp. 19. *Conservative Central Office: Westminster,* [1884.] 8°. **08139. c. 140.**

CECIL (ROBERT ARTHUR TALBOT GASCOYNE) *Marquis of Salisbury.*

—— Conservative Policy. A speech . . . to the South London Conservative Associations . . . November 4th 1885. Revised, *etc.* pp. 16. *Simson & Co.: Hertford,* [1885.] 8°. **8139. bb. 41. (2.)**

—— Conservative Policy. Speech . . . at Brighton . . October 15th 1885. Revised, *etc.* pp. 19. *Simson & Co.: Hertford,* [1885.] 8°. **8139. bb. 41. (3.)**

—— Conservative Policy. Speech . . . at Newport, Monmouthshire, Oct. 7th 1885. Revised, *etc.* pp. 24. *Simson & Co.: Hertford,* [1885.] 8°. **8139. bb. 40. (4.)**

—— [The Danish Duchies.] Question des duchés danois. Quarterly Review de janvier 1864. Traduction par le Bon D. [i.e. Théodore Decazes.] [A translation of an article contributed to the Quarterly Review for January, 1864, by R. A. T. G. Cecil, Marquis of Salisbury.] pp. 48. 1864. 8°. *See* DANISH DUCHIES. **8092. bb. 29.**

—— Essays . . . Biographical. (Foreign Politics.) [Reprinted from the Quarterly Review, 1861–1864.] 2 vol. *John Murray: London,* 1905. 8°. **12352. df. 2.**

—— Evolution. A retrospect. The revised address delivered before the British Association for the Advancement of Science, Oxford, 1894. pp. 58. *Roxburghe Press: London,* 1894. 8°. **7006. aaa. 28.**

—— [Evolution, *etc.*] Actualités scientifiques . . . Les limites actuelles de notre science. Discours présidentiel . . . traduit par . . . W. de Fonvielle. pp. xviii. 54. *Paris,* 1895. 8°. **8708. g. 34.**

—— Foreign Affairs. Speech at the Free Trade Hall, Manchester, October 17th, 1879. pp. 22. [1879.] *See* ENGLAND.—*National Union of Conservative and Constitutional Associations.* Publications, *etc.* 1872, *etc.* 8°. **8138. aaa. 56.**

—— Lord Robert Cecil's Gold Fields Diary. With introduction and notes by Ernest Scott. [With plates, including a portrait.] pp. 44. *Melbourne University Press; Oxford University Press: Melbourne,* 1935. 8°. **10493. aa. 18.**

—— Lord Robert Cecil's Gold Fields Diary. With introduction and notes by Sir Ernest Scott. (Second edition.) pp. 32. *Melbourne University Press: [Melbourne,]* 1945. 8°. **010097. g. 80.**

—— The House of Lords; a speech . . . Printed in the reporting style of phonography. *I. Pitman & Sons: London,* [1890.] 8°. [*The Reporter's Reader.* no. 4.] **12991. bb. 49.**

—— Mr. Parnell and the Irish Question. A speech . . . in Rossendale, on December 3rd, 1890, *etc.* pp. 15. *Conservative Central Office: [London,]* 1890. 8°. **8146. cc. 6. (7.)**

—— Speech . . . on the Established Church—Ireland—Bill, in the House of Lords, 26th June 1868. From the "Standard," *etc.* pp. 8. *National Union of Conservative and Constitutional Associations: London,* 1868. 8°. **4165. b. 19.**

—— The Theories of Parliamentary Reform. 1858. *See* OXFORD ESSAYS. Oxford Essays, *etc.* [1855, *etc.*] 8°. **12356.t.16.**

—— Wozzle. By a Wozzleite [i.e. the Marquis of Salisbury]. Reprinted from "The Globe," *etc.* pp. vi. 136. [1903.] 8°. *See* WOZZLEITE. **012314. i. 68.**

CECIL (ROBERT ARTHUR TALBOT GASCOYNE) *Marquis of Salisbury.*

—— The Beaconsfield Administration. Lord Salisbury. (Echo, April 14.) pp. 3. *A. Ireland & Co.: Manchester,* [1880.] 8°. **8139. df. 22. (13.)**

—— The Kidnapping of Bulgarians during the Russo-Turkish war. Correspondence [of Edmund Sturge, F. W. Chesson, and others] with the Marquis of Salisbury, K.G. pp. 31. *P. S. King: London,* 1879. 8°. **8027. de. 17. (2.)**

—— The Manuscripts of the Most Honourable the Marquis of Salisbury, at Hatfield House. [A catalogue. By J. S. Brewer.] 5 pt. 1872–79. *See* ENGLAND.—*Royal Commission on Historical Manuscripts.* First [*etc.*] Report. 3rd–7th Report. Appendix. 1870, *etc.* fol. **Bar.T.1.(2–6.)**

—— [Another copy.] **B.S. 33/1. (1.)**

—— Calendar of the Manuscripts of the Most Hon. the Marquis of Salisbury, K.G. . . . preserved at Hatfield House, Hertfordshire. (Calendar of the Cecil Manuscripts.) [Vol. 1–3 edited by S. R. Scargill-Bird, vol. 4–12 by R. A. Roberts, vol. 13, 14 by E. Salisbury, vol. 15, *etc.* by M. S. Giuseppi.] *London,* 1883– . 8°. [*Historical Manuscripts Commission.* no. 9.] **Bar.T.1.(9.)**

—— The Marquis of Salisbury. A personal and political sketch, *etc.* [By Sir Alfred F. Robbins.] pp. 24. *National Press Agency: [London,]* 1882. 8°. **8139. aa. 53. (3.)**

—— New . . . edition. pp. 24. *National Press Agency: [London,]* 1882. 8°. **8139. aa. 53. (4.)**

CECIL (ROBERT ARTHUR TALBOT GASCOYNE) *Marquis of Salisbury,* and CAIRNS (HUGH MACCALMONT) *Baron Cairns.*

—— London Chatham and Dover Railway Arbitration. First Award. [Dated: 18 Aug. 1870.] pp. 56. *C. Roworth & Sons: London,* 1870. 8°. **8235. i. 45. (7.)**

—— London Chatham and Dover Railway Arbitration. Second and Final Award. [Dated: 24 Feb. 1871.] pp. 23. *C. Roworth & Sons: London,* [1871.] 8°. **[MISSING.]**

CECIL (ROBERT GASCOYNE) *Viscount Cranborne. See* CECIL (R. A. T. G.) *Marquis of Salisbury.*

CECIL (ROSE) Rose Cecil. A novel. 3 vol. *William Lane: London,* 1797. 8°. **N. 2356.**

CECIL (*Lord* RUPERT WILLIAM ERNEST GASCOYNE) *Bishop of Exeter. See* SAEKI (P. Y.) The Nestorian Monument in China . . . With an introductory note by Lord William Gascoyne-Cecil, *etc.* 1916. 8°. **11094. d. 18.**

—— Changing China. By the Rev. Lord William Gascoyne-Cecil, assisted by Lady Florence Cecil. [With illustrations.] pp. xvi. 342. *J. Nisbet & Co.: London,* 1910. 8°. **10057. dd. 54.**

—— The Church Army. What it is and what it does. (Appendix, containing short details of the work of the Church Army. Compiled by H. C. Crosfield.) [With illustrations.] pp. 62. *Church Army Press: Oxford,* 1908. 8°. **4193. aa. 49.**

—— Difficulties and Duties. Being the substance of a charge given on his primary visitation by the Right Rev. Lord William Cecil. pp. vii. 139. *Nisbet & Co.: London,* [1920.] 8°. **4445. de. 18.**

CECIL (*Lord* RUPERT WILLIAM ERNEST GASCOYNE) *Bishop of Exeter.*

—— The Possibilities of Doing Good in a Country Parish. pp. 15. *S.P.C.K.: London*, [1937.] 8º. **4498. p. 6.**

—— Science and Religion. pp. 105. *Hodder & Stoughton: London*, 1906. 8º. **4018. d. 7.**

—— " They Shall be Comforted." [A sermon.] pp. 15. *S.P.C.K.: London*, [1915.] 16º. **4473. a. 68.**

—— Lord Rupert Ernest William Gascoyne Cecil, 63rd Bishop of Exeter, *etc.* [A memoir, with appreciations by various writers. With a portrait.] [1936.] 8º.
20029. h. 10.

CECIL (RUSSELL LAFAYETTE) Colds. Cause, treatment and prevention. pp. viii. 111. *D. Appleton & Co.: New York & London*, 1925. 8º. [MISSING.]

—— The Diagnosis and Treatment of Arthritis . . . Reprinted from Oxford Monographs on Diagnosis and Treatment. pp. viii. 263. pl. 17. *Oxford University Press: New York*, [1936.] 8º. [*Oxford Medical Publications.*]
20036.a 1/590.

—— The Specialities in General Practice. Edited by R. L. Cecil, *etc.* pp. xvi. 818. *W. B. Saunders Co.: Philadelphia, London*, 1951. 8º. **7321. k. 4.**

—— A Text Book of Medicine. By American authors. Edited by Russell L. Cecil . . . Associate editor for diseases of the nervous system, Foster Kennedy . . . Third edition, revised and entirely reset. pp. xix. 1664. *W. B. Saunders Co.: Philadelphia & London*, 1933. 8º.
07306. cc. 25.

—— Fourth edition, revised and entirely reset. pp. xx. 1614. *W. B. Saunders Co.: Philadelphia & London*, 1937. 8º.
7320. r. 8.

—— Fifth edition, revised and entirely reset, *etc.* pp. xx. 1744. *W. B. Saunders Co.: Philadelphia & London*, 1940. 8º. **7320. r. 12.**

—— A Textbook of Medicine by American Authors. Edited by R. L. Cecil . . . Associate editor for diseases of the nervous system Foster Kennedy . . . Sixth edition, revised and entirely reset, *etc.* pp. xxv. 1566. *W. B. Saunders Co.: Philadelphia & London*, 1943. 8º.
07305. l. 37.

—— A Textbook of Medicine. Edited by R. L. Cecil . . . with the assistance of Walsh McDermott . . . Associate editor for diseases of the nervous system : Harold G. Wolff . . . Seventh edition, illustrated. pp. xxxiii. 1730. *W. B. Saunders Co.: Philadelphia & London*, 1947. 4º.
7320. v. 2.

The eighth edition is entered under CECIL (R. L.) *and* LOEB (*Robert F.*)

CECIL (RUSSELL LAFAYETTE) and **LOEB** (ROBERT FREDERICK)

—— A Textbook of Medicine. Edited by R. L. Cecil . . . R. F. Loeb . . . Associate editors, Alexander B. Gutman . . . Walsh McDermott . . . Harold G. Wolff . . . Eighth edition. pp. xxxi. 1627. *W. B. Saunders Co.: Philadelphia & London*, 1951. 8º. **7321. k. 3.**
The seventh edition is entered under CECIL (R. L.)

—— A Textbook of Medicine. Edited by R. L. Cecil . . . R. F. Loeb . . . Associate editors : Alexander B. Gutman . . . Walsh McDermott . . . Harold G. Wolff . . . Ninth edition, *etc.* pp. xxxiv. 1786. *W. B. Saunders Co.: Philadelphia, London*, 1955. 8º. **7321. l. 4.**

CECIL (SABINA) Little Ann ; or, the Picture-book. pp. 15. *John Marshall: London*, [1814 ?] 16º.
012806. de. 15. (11.)

—— Little Edward ; or, the Picture book. pp. 14. *E. Marshall: London*, [1825 ?] 16º. **012806. de. 15. (8.)**

—— Little Eliza ; or, the Picture-Book. pp. 11. *John Marshall: London*, 1819. 16º. **12809. de. 23.**

—— [Another edition.] *E. Marshall: London*, [1825 ?] 16º.
012806. de. 15. (2.)

—— Little Henry ; or, the Picture-book. pp. 11. *John Marshall: London*, 1817. 16º.
012806. de. 15. (9.)

—— Little James ; or, the Picture-book. pp. 16. *John Marshall: London*, 1822. 16º. **012806. de. 15. (3.)**

—— Little Jane ; or, the Picture-book. pp. 16. *John Marshall: London*, 1822. 16º.
012806. de. 15. (4.)

—— Little John ; or, the Picture-book. pp. 15. *John Marshall: London*, 1815. 16º.
012806. de. 15. (6.)

—— Little Mary ; or, the Picture-book. pp. 15. *John Marshall: London*, [1815 ?] 16º.
012806. de. 15. (7.)

—— Little Sally ; or, the Picture-book. pp. 12. *John Marshall: London*, 1817. 16º.
012806. de. 15. (10.)

—— Little Thomas ; or, the Picture-book. pp. 16. *John Marshall: London*, 1822. 16º.
012806. de. 15. (5.)

CECIL (*Lord* THOMAS) Circumstances connected with the Stamford Petition against the return of Lord T. Cecil and Colonel Chaplin, as members for that Borough. Extracted from the Stamford News, *etc.* pp. 23. *J. Drakard: Stamford*, [1830.] 8º. **900. g. 27. (13.)**

CECIL (TOM) Massage Séche. pp. 90. *Simpkin, Marshall & Co.: London; Whittaker & Williams: St. Leonards-on-Sea*, 1888. 8º. **7461. aaa. 8.**

CECIL (WILLIAM) *Baron Burghley.* See CABALA. Cabala. Scrinia Ceciliana. Mysteries of state & government. In letters of the late famous Lord Burghley, *etc.* 1663. 4º.
595. f. 8.

—— *See* CATHARINE [Parr], *Queen Consort of Henry* VIII., *King of England.* The Lamentacion of a synner, *etc.* [With a preface by W. Cecil.] 1548. 8º. **G. 12003.**

—— —— 1563. 8º. **C. 12. c. 10.**

—— *See* CECIL (Robert A. T. G.) *Marquis of Salisbury.* Calendar of the Manuscripts of the Most Hon. the Marquis of Salisbury, *etc.* [Comprising State correspondence during the administration of Sir William Cecil, afterwards Lord Burghley.] 1883, *etc.* 8º. [*Historical Manuscripts Commission.* no. 9.]
Bar.T.1.(9.)

—— *See* CHARLTON (William H.) Burghley. The life of William Cecil, Lord Burghley, *etc.* 1847. 8º.
1303. k. 3.

—— *See* DEVEREUX (Robert) 2nd *Earl of Essex.* Opinions delivered by the Earl of Essex, Lord Burleigh [and others] . . . on the alarm of an invasion from Spain, in . . . 1596. [1794 ?] 8º. **8135. c. 18.**

CECIL (William) *Baron. Burghley.*

—— *See* DIGGES (*Sir* D.) The Compleat Ambassador: or two treaties of the intended marriage of Qu: Elizabeth . . . comprised in letters of negotiation of Sir Francis Walsingham . . . Together with the answers of the Lord Burleigh . . . and others, *etc.* 1655. fol.
594. f. 17. (1.)

—— *See* GILLOW (Joseph) Lord Burghley's Map of Lancashire in 1590, *etc.* [With a facsimile.] 1907. 8°.
Maps.198.c.1.

—— *See* HAYNES (Samuel) A Collection of State Papers . . . Transcribed from original letters and other authentick memorials . . . left by William Cecill Lord Burghley, *etc.* 1740. fol.
2082.e.

—— *See* HUME (Martin A. S.) The Great Lord Burghley, *etc.* 1898. 8°.
10815. dd. 7.

—— —— 1906. 8°.
2406. c. 7.

—— *See* MACAULAY (Thomas B.) *Baron Macaulay.* [*Essays.*] Burleigh and his Times, *etc.* 1904. 8°. **012209. ff. 1/50.**

—— *See* MURDIN (William) A Collection of State Papers . . . Transcribed from original papers and other authentic memorials . . . left by William Cecill Lord Burghley, *etc.* 1759. fol.
2082.e.

—— *See* NARES (Edward) Memoirs of the Life and Administration of William Cecil, Lord Burghley, *etc.* 1828, *etc.* 4°.
614. l. 2.

—— *See* PAZ SALAS (P. de) La felicissima Armada, *etc.* MS. NOTES [by Lord Burghley]. 1588. fol.
192. f. 17. (1.)

—— *See* PHILLIPS (Gerald W.) Lord Burghley in Shakespeare. Falstaff, Sly and others. [Maintaining that certain characters are portraits of Lord Burghley.] 1936. 8°.
11767. c. 12.

—— *See* PHILOPATRIS (John) *pseud.* An Advertisement written to a Secretarie of my L. Treasurers of Ingland [Lord Burghley] . . . Also of a letter written by the L. Treasurer in defence of his gentrie . . . intercepted, published & answered by the papistes. 1592. 12°.
G. 6095.

—— *See* READ (Conyers) Mr. Secretary Cecil and Queen. Elizabeth. [With a portrait.] 1955. 8°. **9512. f. 31.**

—— *See* ROME, *Church of.*—Paul III., *Pope.* [1534–1549.] Consilium delectorum Cardinalium, *etc.* MS. NOTES [by W. Cecil]. 1538. 4°.
C. 60. g. 13.

—— *See* SMITH (Alan G. C. G.) William Cecil, *etc.* [With a portrait.] 1934. 8°.
010825. g. 1.

—— *See* THEODORET, *Bishop of Cyrus.* Theodoriti . . . De evangelicæ veritatis . . . cognitione, *etc.* [With the autograph of W. Cecil.] 1540. 8°.
C.107.a.16.

—— Iustitia Britannica. Per quam liquet perspicue aliquot in eo regno perditos ciues, seditionis & armorum ciuilium authores, regniꝗ hostium propugnatores acerrimos, vt communi Ecclesiæ Reiꝗ publicæ paci, cautius prospiceretur, morte mulctatos esse: propter religionem vero, aut cæremonias Romanas, neminem in capitis discrimen vocatum: licet ab aduersarijs secus multo, & admodum malitiose publicetur. Perscriptum primum in nostrate lingua, deinde versum in Latinam. [Followed by " De summa eorum clementia, qui habendis quæstionibus præfuerant, contra proditores quosdam, deꝗ; tormentis quæ in eosdem, ob proditionem, non ob religionem, exprompta sunt." Translations of "The Execution of Iustice in England " and " A Declaration of the fauourable dealing of her Maiesties Commissioners appointed for the Examination of certaine Traitours," both by W. Cecil.] 2 pt. 1584. 8°. *See* BRITISH JUSTICE.
598. a. 30.

CECIL (William) *Baron Burghley.*

—— The Lord Treasurer Burleigh's Advice to Queen Elizabeth in matters of religion and state.—A Declaration of the favourable Dealing of her Maiesties Commissioners appointed for the examination of certaine traytours. 1583. *See* SOMERS (John) *Baron Somers.* A Fourth Collection of Scarce . . . Tracts, *etc.* vol. 1. 1752, *etc.* 4°.
184. a. 13.

—— [Another edition.] *See* SOMERS (John) *Baron Somers.* A Collection of Scarce . . . Tracts, *etc.* vol. 1. 1809, *etc.* 4°.
750. g. 1.

—— [Letters.] *See* WRIGHT (Thomas) *M.A., F.S.A.* Queen Elizabeth & her Times. A series of original letters, selected from the inedited private correspondence of the Lord Treasurer Burghley [and others], *etc.* 1838. 8°.
610. h. 9.

—— The Lord Treasurer Burleigh his Advice to Queen Elizabeth in matters of religion and state. *See* BACON (Francis) *Viscount St. Albans.* [*Two or more Works.*] The Felicity of Queen Elizabeth, *etc.* 1651. 12°.
E. 1398. (2.)

—— [Another edition.] 1746. *See* HARLEIAN MISCELLANY. The Harleian Miscellany, *etc.* vol. 7. 1744, *etc.* 4°.
185. a. 11.

—— [Another edition.] [1811.] *See* HARLEIAN MISCELLANY. The Harleian Miscellany, *etc.* vol. 7. 1808, *etc.* 4°.
2072.g.

—— Certaine Precepts, or directions, for the well ordering and carriage of a mans life . . . [By W. Cecil.] With some other precepts and sentences of the same nature added: taken from a person of a like place and qualitie. pp. 41. 1617. 8°. *See* PRECEPTS.
8405. a. 51.

—— [Another edition.] pp. 16. 1618. 8°. *See* PRECEPTS.
8404. aa. 47.

—— [Another edition.] Precepts, or Directions for the well ordering and carriage of a mans life . . . left by William, Lord Burghly, to. his sonne at his death . . . Also some other Precepts and Advertisements added, which sometimes was the Iewell and delight of the right Honourable Lord . . . Francis, Earle of Bedford, *etc.* (A glasse wherein those enormities and foule abuses may most evidently be seen, which are the destruction and overthrow of every Christian commonwealth.) pp. 144. *Thomas Harper for Thomas Jones: London,* 1636. 8°.
721. a. 41.

—— [Another edition.] Also some other precepts . . . added, *etc.* [With a portrait.] pp. 138. [*Thomas Harper*] *for Thomas Jones: London,* 1637. 8°. **8405. a. 8.**

—— [Another edition.] The Lord-Treasurer Burleigh's Advice to his Son. *See* INSTRUCTIONS. Instructions for Youth, *etc.* 1722. 12°.
1031. d. 7.

—— [A reissue.] *See* INSTRUCTIONS. Walsingham's Manual, *etc.* 1728. 12°.
8005. b. 32.

—— [Another edition.] Ten Precepts which William Lord Burleigh gave to his second son Robert, *etc. See* STANHOPE (Philip D.) *4th Earl of Chesterfield.* [*Letters to his Godson.*] The Art of Pleasing, *etc.* 1783. 8°.
1210. h. 2. (2.)

—— [Another edition.] *See* STANHOPE (Philip D.) *4th Earl of Chesterfield.* [*Letters to his Godson.*] The Art of Pleasing, *etc.* 1783. 8°.
1081. d. 30. (2.)

—— [Another edition.] *See* STANHOPE (Philip D.) *4th Earl of Chesterfield.* [*Letters to his Son.—Abridgments, Extracts, etc.*] Lord Chesterfield's Advice to his Son, *etc.* 1784. 8°.
1478. d. 14.

CECIL (WILLIAM) *Baron Burghley.*

—— [Another edition.] pp. 15. *T. Appleby: North Shields,* 1811. 8°.   **8410. d. 29. (1.)**

—— [Another edition.] Lord Burleigh's Advices to his Son. *See* WISDOM. Practical Wisdom, *etc.* 1824. 12°.   **1031. d. 22.**

—— Heylsame Lehren, so da dienen zur Richtschnur des gantzen menschlichen Lebens, durch . . . W. Cecill . . . seinem geliebten Sohne zum besten entworffen, und durch C. G. v. Bessel . . . ins Teutsche versetzet. *See* LIMBURG (H. zu) Thesaurus paternus, *etc.* 1681. 12°.   **8403. a. 15. (2.)**

—— [Another edition.] *See* B., Ch. G. Schmiede des politischen Glücks. 1667, *etc.* 12°.   **1094. b. 40.**

—— [Another edition.] *See* BESSEL (C. G. von) Schmiede dess politischen Glüks, *etc.* 1673. 8°.   **1192. cc. 2. (1.)**

—— [Another edition.] *See* BESSEL (C. G. von) Neuvermehrter politischer Glücks-Schmid, *etc.* pt. 3. 1697. 12°.   **1104. b. 55.**

—— The Copie of a Letter sent out of England to Don Bernardin Mendoza, Ambassadour in France for the King of Spaine, declaring the state of England . . . Found in the chamber of one Richard Leigh . . . [By W. Cecil, Baron Burghley.] Whereunto are adioyned certaine late Aduertisements, concerning the losses and distresses happened to the Spanish Nauie, *etc.* 2 pt. 𝕭.𝕷. 1588. 4°. *See* ENGLAND. *[Appendix.—History and Politics.—*II. 1588.]   **C.123.c.17.(2.)**

—— [Another copy.]   **440. i. 16.**

—— [Another copy.]   **292. e. 9. (3, 2.)**

—— [Another copy.]   **C. 33. b. 5.**

—— [Another copy.]   **G. 6148.**

—— [Another edition.] 1588. 4°. *See* ENGLAND. *[Appendix.—History and Politics.—*II. 1588.]   **9510. c. 4.**

—— [Another edition.] pp. 36. 1641. 8°. *See* ENGLAND. *[Appendix.—History and Politics.—*II. 1588.]   **9505. bb. 6.**

—— [Another copy.]   **E. 131. (27.)**

—— [Another copy.]   **G. 6068. (2.)**

—— [Another copy.]   **G. 6147.**

—— [Another edition.] 1744. 8°. *[Harleian Miscellany.* vol. 1.] *See* ENGLAND. *[Appendix.—History and Politics.—*II. 1588.]   **185. a. 5.**

—— [Another edition.] The State of England in 1588. In a letter from a priest at London to the Spanish Ambassador at Paris, *etc.* pp. viii. 56. 1746. 8°. *See* ENGLAND. *[Appendix.—History and Politics.—*II. 1588.]   **1445. f. 16.**

—— [Another edition.] The Copie of a Letter, *etc.* 1752. 4°. *[SOMERS (John) Baron Somers. A Fourth Collection of Scarce and Valuable Tracts, etc.* vol. 1.] *See* ENGLAND. *[Appendix.—History and Politics.—*II. 1588.]   **184. a. 13.**

—— [Another edition.] 1808. 4°. *[Harleian Miscellany.* vol. 1.] *See* ENGLAND. *[Appendix.—History and Politics.—*II. 1588.]   **2072.g.**

—— [Another edition.] 1809. 4°. *[SOMERS (John) Baron Somers. A Collection of Scarce and Valuable Tracts, etc.* vol. 1.] *See* ENGLAND. *[Appendix.—History and Politics.—*II. 1588.]   **750. g. 1.**

CECIL (WILLIAM) *Baron Burghley.*

—— Copije van eenen Brief wt Engelandt ghesonden aen Don Bernardin Mendosa . . . verclarende den staet van Enghelandt, *etc.* [1588.] 4°. *See* ENGLAND. *[Appendix.—History and Politics.—*II. 1588.]   **1197. d. 35. (2.)**

—— La Copie d'vne lettre enuoyée d'Angleterre à Dom Bernardin de Mendoze . . . [par] laquelle est déclaré [l'estat] du Roiaume d'Angleterre, *etc.* pp. 64. 1588. 8°. *See* ENGLAND. *[Appendix.—History and Politics.—*II. 1588.]   **C.123.c.17.(1.)**

—— [Another edition.] pp. 67. [1590?] 8°. *See* ENGLAND. *[Appendix.—History and Politics.—*II. 1588.]   **G. 6079.**

—— Essempio d'vna Lettera mandata d'Inghilterra a Don Bernardino di Mendozza . . . nella quale si dichiara, lo stato del reame d'Inghilterra, *etc.* pp. 104. 1588. 8°. *See* ENGLAND. *[Appendix.—History and Politics.—*II. 1588.]   **C. 55. b. 14.**

—— [Another copy.]   **G. 6078.**

—— A Copy of the Devise for the Alteratione of Religione, at the first year, of Q. Eliz. [By W. Cecil, Baron Burghley?] 1751. 4°. *[SOMERS (John) Baron Somers. A Fourth Collection of Scarce and Valuable Tracts.* vol 2.] *See* DEVISE.   **184. a. 13.**

—— A Copy of the Devise for the Alteratione of Religione, at the first year of Q. Eliz. [By W. Cecil, Baron Burghley?] 1809. 4°. *[SOMERS (John) Baron Somers. A Collection of Scarce and Valuable Tracts.* vol. 1.] *See* DEVICE.   **750. g. 1.**

—— A Declaration of the fauorable dealing of her Maiesties Commissioners appointed for the Examination of certaine Traitours, and of tortures vniustly reported to be done vpon them for matters of religion. [By W. Cecil, Baron Burghley.] 𝕭.𝕷. MS. NOTES. 1583. 4°. *See* ENGLAND. *Commissioners appointed for the Examination of certain Traitors.*   **C. 33. b. 6.**

—— [Another copy.]   **G. 6141.**

—— A Declaration of the Fauorable Dealing of Her Maiesties Commissioners, appointed for the Examination of certaine Traitours, *etc.* 1745. 4°. *[Harleian Miscellany.* vol. 3.] *See* ENGLAND.—*Commissioners appointed for the Examination of certain Traitors.*   **185. a. 7.**

—— A Declaration of the Favourable Dealing of Her Majestie's Commissioners, appointed for the Examination of certaine traitours, *etc.* 1809. 4°. *[Harleian Miscellany.* vol. 3.] *See* ENGLAND.—*Commissioners appointed for the Examination of certain Traitors.*   **2072.g.**

—— The Execution of Iustice in England for maintenaunce of publique and Christian peace, against certeine stirrers of sedition, *etc.* 1583. 4°. *See* ENGLAND. *[Appendix.—Law.]*   **C. 33. b. 35.**

—— [Another edition.] Execution of Justice in England, not for religion, but for treason. *See* COLLECTION. A Collection of Several Treatises concerning the . . . Penal Laws, *etc.* 1688. 4°.   **T. 2230. (34, 35.)**

—— [Another edition.] *See* JESUITS. *[Appendix.]* The Jesuits' Loyalty, *etc.* 1677, *etc.* 4°.   **860. k. 6.**

—— [Another edition.] *See* POPERY. A Preservative against Popery, *etc.* vol. 3. 1738. fol.   **478. f. 13.**

—— [Another edition.] 1745. *See* HARLEIAN MISCELLANY. The Harleian Miscellany, *etc.* vol. 2. 1744, *etc.* 4°.   **185. a. 6.**

—— [Another edition.] 1849. *See* GIBSON (Edmund) successively *Bishop of Lincoln* and *of London.* A Preservative against Popery, *etc.* vol. 17. 1848. 8°.   **3940. k. 6/17.**

CECIL (WILLIAM) *Baron Burghley.*

—— [Another edition.] 1809. *See* HARLEIAN MISCELLANY The Harleian Miscellany, *etc.* vol. 2. 1808, *etc.* 4°.
2072.g.

—— [Another edition.] [A facsimile of the edition of 1583.] *New York,* [1936.] 4°. [*Scholars' Facsimiles & Reprints.*]
W.P. 9530/3.

—— D'executie van Iustitie tot onderhoudinge vande publicke eñ christelicke vrede in Engelandt . . . Ouergheset vuyt het Enghelsche. 1584. 4°. *See* ENGLAND. [*Appendix.—Law.*]
C. 33. b. 24. (10.)

—— L'Execution de Justice faicte en Angleterre, pour maintenir la Paix publique et Chrestienne, *etc.* pp. 66. 1584. 8°. *See* ENGLAND. [*Appendix.—Law.*]
9510. aaa. 6.

—— Atto della Giustitia d'Inghilterra, esseguito, per la consueratione della commune & christiana pace . . . Traslatato d'Inglese in vulgare, *etc.* pp. 115. 1584. 8°. *See* ENGLAND. [*Appendix.—Law.*]
598. a. 31.

—— Iustitia Britannica : per quam liquet perspicue, aliquot in eo regno perditos ciues, seditionis et armorum ciuilium authores, regniq; hostium propugnatores acerrimos, vt communi Ecclesiæ Reiq; publicæ paci, cautius prospiceretur, morte mulctatos esse : propter religionem vero, aut cærimonias Romanas, neminem in capitis discrimen vocatum : licet ab aduersariis multo, & admodum malitiose publicetur. Prescriptum primum in nostrate lingua, deinde versum in Latinam. pp. 75. 1584. 8°. *See* BRITISH JUSTICE.
C.122.d.25.

—— [Another copy.]
808. c. 12.

—— [Another edition.] *See* BARLOW (Thomas) *Bishop of Lincoln.* Papismus regiæ potestatis eversor, *etc.* 1682. 8°.
1025. a. 28.

—— *See* ENGLAND. [*Appendix.—Law.*] Ad persecutores Anglos . . . contra falsum, seditiosum & contumeliosum libellum inscriptum : Justitia Britannica . . . responsio, *etc.* [1584 ?] 8°.
3932.dd.9.

—— *See* ENGLAND. [*Appendix.—Law.*] A true sincere and modest defence [by Cardinal William Allen] of English Catholiques that suffer for their faith . . . against a . . . libel intituled : " The Execution of justice in England." [1584.] 12°.
3938. aaa. 45.

—— A Memorial, presented to Queen Elizabeth . . . to prevent her Majesty's being engrossed by any particular favourite. *See* WOLSEY (Thomas) *Cardinal.* The Memoirs of that great favourite, Cardinal Woolsey, *etc.* 1706. 8°.
1124. d. 3.

—— [Another edition.] *See* JAMES I., *King of Great Britain and Ireland.* [*Extracts.*] The Prince's Cabala, *etc.* 1715. 12°.
522. a. 34.

—— [Another edition.] *See* ESSAYS. Occasional Essays on various subjects, *etc.* 1809. 8°.
521. h. 25.

—— Ordinances made by Sir W. Cecill . . . for the order and governement of xiij. poore men, whereof one to be the Warden of the Hospitall at Stanford Baron, *etc.* [1597.] *s. sh.* fol.
G. 6463. (349b.)

—— Bibliotheca Illustris : sive catalogus variorum librorum . . . bibliothecæ viri cujusdam prænobilis ac honoratissimi olim defuncti (William Cecil). pp. 94. *Willis : London,* [1687.] 4°.
821. i. 13. (2.)

—— [Another copy.] MS. NOTES OF PRICES. **821. i. 8. (1.)**

—— [Another copy.] MS. NOTES OF PRICES. **124. f. 17.**

CECIL (WILLIAM) *Baron Burghley.*

—— The Complete Statesman, exemplified in the life and actions of Sir W. Cecil. *See* PECK (Francis) *Antiquary.* Desiderata curiosa, *etc.* vol. 1. 1779. 4°. **2072.g.**

—— The Life of that Great Statesman William Cecil, Lord Burghley . . . Published from the original manuscript wrote soon after his Lordship's death . . . To which is added, his Character by the learned Camden, and an extract of his last will and testament. With memoirs of the family of Cecil, faithfully collected from records, manuscripts, and other authorities. By Arthur Collins. pp. xi. 118. *Robert Gosling ; Thomas Wotton : London,* 1732. 8°.
275. l. 3.

—— [Another copy.]
G. 14103.

—— Memoirs of the Life and Administration of William Cecil Baron Burleigh . . . Including a parallel between the state of government then and now. To which is prefixed a preface to the People of Britain. Together with an appendix of original papers. [Signed : R. C., i.e. Ralph Courteville.] 1738. 4°. *See* C., R.
G. 2149.

—— Reasons pro and con : being a Debate at the Council-Table between the Treasurer [Lord Burghley] and the General [the Earl of Essex] for making a Peace, or carrying on the war, in the reign of Queen Elizabeth ; wherein the force of the General's arguments prevailed against the sophistry of the Treasurer's. pp. 15. *S. Popping : London,* 1712. 8°.
8122. cc. 3.

—— William Cecil, Lord Burghley. (Part I. Historical Monograph. By the Rev. A. Jessopp . . . Part II. The Homes of the Cecils. By J. A. Gotch . . . Part III. The Portraits of the Cecils. By J. L. Caw . . . Part IV. The Genealogy and Arms of the Cecils. By A. C. Fox-Davies.) pp. xii. 142. *T. C. & E. C. Jack : London,* 1904. fol. [*Historical Monograph Series.*]
L.R. 31. b. 9.

—— William Cecil, Lord Burleigh. 1520–1598. *See* BRITISH STATESMEN. Lives of Eminent British Statesmen. vol. 1. 1831, *etc.* 8°.
12203. tt. 1/29.

CECIL (WILLIAM) *Baron Ros.* A Relation of the late Entertainement of . . . the Lord Roos his Majesties Embassador extraordinarie to the King of Spaine : his entrie into Madrid, *etc.* *E. Griffin, for N. Butter : London,* 1617. 4°.
1103. e. 30.

CECIL (WILLIAM) *Earl of Exeter.* Tempus putationis : or, the Ripe almond gathered. A sermon appointed to be preached at the funeral of . . . the Earl of Exeter in the Abby Church at Westminster. [*London,* 1665 ?] fol.
1418. k. 11.

A fragment, " Sermon XLII," *pp.* 485–492, *of an edition of " *Θρηνοικος*, The house of mourning."*

CECIL (WILLIAM) *M.A., Rector of Longstanton St. Michael, Cambridgeshire.* *See* CECIL (Richard) Elementary Religious Truths . . . compiled [by W. Cecil] from . . . sermon-notes of . . . R. Cecil, *etc.* 1881. 8°.
4465. k. 14.

—— The Church Choir Hymn Book for public or family worship : with appendix, containing miscellaneous moral pieces, *etc.* pp. xvi. 315. xxiv. *Seeley & Co. : London,* 1845. 24°.
3435. d. 38.

—— A Solemn Appeal to . . . the Bishop, and . . . the Clergy of the diocese of Ely on the disorder and profaneness, exhibited at the parish church of St. Michael's, Cambridge, on occasion of the Confirmation held there, June 20, 1833. pp. 85. *W. Metcalfe : Cambridge,* 1833. 8°.
4323. aaaa. 16.

CECIL (*Lady* WILLIAM) *See* CECIL (Mary R. M.) *Lady William Cecil.*

CECIL (*Lord* WILLIAM GASCOYNE) *See* CECIL (*Lord* Rupert W. E. G.)

CECIL (WILLIAM THOMAS BROWNLOW) 5*th Marquis of Exeter.*
—— *See* ENGLAND.—*Lords Lieutenants of Counties.* Guide to the Duties of Lieutenants of Counties in England, Scotland & Wales. [With a preface by the Marquis of Exeter.] [1948.] 8°.ᵇ **9930. cc. 29.**

—— *See* PETERBOROUGH, *Soke of.*—*County Council.* [A volume presented to W. T. B. Cecil, 5th Marquis of Exeter, in commemoration of his services as County Alderman and Chairman of the Soke of Peterborough County Council. With a portrait.] [1950.] 4°. **010368. t. 5.**

CÉCILE. [For Saints, Sovereigns and Princesses of Sovereign Houses of this name :] *See* CECILIA.

—— Cécile, drame en trois actes et en prose. [By — de Bruix. With an engraving.] pp. viii. 69. *Londres; Paris*, 1776. 8°. **11738. aa. 19. (5.)**

—— [Another copy.] **11738. aa. 12. (1.)**
Imperfect ; wanting the engraving.

—— Cécile, fille d'Achmet III Empereur des Turcs, née en 1710. [A romance. By J. La Vallée.] 2 tom. *Constantinople* [*Paris*], 1787. 12°. **1208. d. 25.**

—— Cécile, ou la Nouvelle Félicia. 2 tom. *Paris*, 1806. 8°. **1093. aa. 8.**

—— Mémoires de Cécile, écrits par elle-même, revûs par M. de la Place. [By Éléonore Guichard.] 4 tom. *Paris*, 1751. 12°. **012551. de. 60.**

—— [Another edition.] 4 tom. *Paris*, 1752. 12°. **12512. ccc. 14.**

—— The Bracelet: or, the Fortunate discovery. Being the history of Miss Polly * * * * *. Translated, with some alterations, from a French work, entituled, Mémoires de Cécile [by E. Guichard]. 2 vol. *F. Noble; J. Noble: London*, [1759.] 12°. **12611. b. 6.**

CECILE, *Herald to Alphonso V., King of Aragon. See* SICILE.

CECILE, *Mother, of the Community of the Resurrection of Our Lord, Grahamstown* [ANNIE CECILIA RAMSBOTTOM ISHERWOOD]. *See* KATE, *Sister.* Mother Cecile . . . With four illustrations [including a portrait]. 1922. 8°. **W.P. 6559/2.**

—— *See* ROBINS (Margaret W.) Mother Cecile of Grahamstown, South Africa, *etc.* 1911. 16°. **4902. a. 36/7.**

—— Mother Cecile in South Africa, 1883–1906, Foundress of the Community of the Resurrection of Our Lord. Compiled by a Sister of the Community. [With plates, including portraits.] pp. ix. 308. *S.P.C.K.: London*, 1930. 8°. **4908. i. 16.**

CÉCILE (JEAN BAPTISTE THOMAS MÉDÉE) *See* CÉCILLE.

CECILIA. Cecilia; or, Memoirs of an heiress. By the author of Evelina [i.e. Frances Burney, afterwards d'Arblay]. 5 vol. *T. Payne & Son; T. Cadell: London*, 1782. 12°. **94. a. 5–9.**

—— The fourth edition. 5 vol. *T. Payne & Son; T. Cadell: London*, 1784. 12°. **12611. e. 12.**

—— The fifth edition. 5 vol. *T. Payne & Son; T. Cadell: London*, 1786. 12°. **12614. aaa. 8.**

—— A new edition. 2 vol. *W. Emans: London*, 1820. 8°. **12614. i. 3.**
With an additional titlepage, engraved.

CECILIA.

—— Cecilia ; or, the Eastern lovers. A novel. Translated from the French. pp. 187. *Printed for the Author: London*, 1773. 12°. **1154. i. 12.**

—— Cecilia's Choice. (By the author of Rachel's Reward.) pp. 204. *William Stevens: London*, [1901.] 8°. [*Family Story-Teller.* no. 154.] **012600. ee. 154.**

CECILIA [SOBRINO], *del Nacimiento.*

—— *See* ALONSO-CORTÉS (B.) Dos Monjas Vallisoletanas Poetisas (las Madres María de San Alberto y Cecilia del Nacimiento), *etc.* 1944. 8°. **11866. c. 6.**

—— A la Madre Cecilia del Nacimiento, gloria del Carmelo y de España, en el III centenario de su muerte, 1646–1946. [The poems of Cecilia del Nacimiento, edited with an introduction by Emeterio de Jesús Maria.] *Burgos*, 1946. 8°. [*El Monte Carmelo.* Numero extraordinario. abril/sept. 1946.] **P.P. 210. lac.**

CECILIA, *Madame, Religious of St. Andrew's Convent, Streatham. See* BIBLE. [*Polyglott.*] Catholic Scripture Manuals . . . With introduction and annotations by Madame Cecilia. 1904, *etc.* 8°. **03051. k.**

—— *See* BOLO (H.) The Beatitudes . . . Translated by Madame Cecilia. 1906. 8°. **4378. ff. 12.**

—— *See* BOUFFIER (G.) The Annual Retreat . . . Translated . . . by Madame Cecilia. 1906. 8°. **3457. bbb. 88.**

—— *See* DAHLMANN (J.) Outline Conferences for Children of Mary . . . With a preface by Madame Cecilia. 1905. 8°. **3456. dd. 63.**

—— *See* LELONG (E. A.) *Bishop of Nevers.* [La Sainte religieuse.] The Nun . . . Translated . . . by Madame Cecilia, *etc.* 1914. 8°. **4061. ee. 19.**

—— *See* PLUS (R.) The Ideal of Reparation . . . Translated by Madame Cecilia. [1921.] 8°. **04403. f. 72.**

—— At the Feet of Jesus. pp. 279. *Burns & Oates: London*, 1900. 8°. **4227. df. 19.**

—— Second edition. pp. ii. 279. *Burns & Oates: London*, 1904. 8°. **4227. de. 19.**

—— From the Sepulchre to the Throne. pp. xv. 426. *Burns & Oates: London*, 1914. 8°. **4223. h. 33.**

—— Girls' Clubs & Mothers' Meetings. pp. ix. 163. *Burns & Oates: London*, 1911. 8°. **4193. ff. 32.**

—— Looking on Jesus, the Lamb of God. pp. xiii. 431. *R. & T. Washbourne: London*, 1912. 8°. **4223. h. 3.**

—— Mater Mea. Thoughts for Mary's Children. Written and compiled by Madame Cecilia. pp. vii. 133. *R. & T. Washbourne: London*, 1904. 16°. **3455. aaa. 54.**

—— More Home Truths for Mary's Children. pp. 268. *Burns & Oates: London*, 1902. 8°. **04403. ee. 5.**

—— Reference Catalogue of Selected Works of Wholesome Fiction. pp. 60. *Burns, Oates & Co.: London*, 1923. 8°. **011904. aaa. 46.**

—— The Retreat Manual. A handbook for the annual retreat and monthly recollection, *etc.* pp. 208. *Burns & Oates: London*, 1901. 8°. **3455. h. 19.**

—— Short Spiritual Readings for Mary's Children. [With a preface by Gilbert Higgins.] pp. xv. 238. *R. & T. Washbourne: London*, 1906. 8°. **04403. ee. 29.**

—— Spiritual Gleanings for Marian Sodalists, *etc.* pp. x. 216. *Longmans & Co.: London*, 1913. 8°. **04376. ee. 8.**

CECILIA, *Madame, Religious of St. Andrew's Convent, Streatham.*

—— The Training of Girls in their Teens. pp. viii. 61. *Burns & Oates: London*, 1911. 8°.   **08415. e. 9.**

CECILIA [VASA], *Margravine of Baden-Rodemachern. See* BELL (James) *Prebendary of Wells.* Queen Elizabeth and a Swedish Princess. Being an account of the visit of Princess Cecilia of Sweden to England, *etc.* 1926. 8°.   **C. 102. i. 1/8.**

—— *See* ÖDBERG (F.) Om prinsessan Cecilia Wasa, *etc.* 1896. 8°.   **10761. h. 22.**

CECILIA, *of the Dominican Convent of San Sisto in Rome* [— CESARINI ?].

—— Die "Miracula beati Dominici" der Schwester Cäcilia. Einleitung und Text. [Edited by Angelus M. Walz.] *Lat. In:* Miscellanea Pio Paschini. vol. 1. pp. 293–326. 1948. 8°.   **Ac.2002.u.**

—— Legend of S. Dominic. *In:* GIRARDUS, *de Fracheto.* Lives of the Brethren of the Order of Preachers, *etc.* pp. 273–295. 1896. 8°.   **4782. bb. 21.**

CECILIA, *Saint. See* A., L. Invocacion cuotidiana á la augusta vírgen y martyr Santa Cecilia. 1833. *s. sh.* 4°.   **9180. dd. 7. (10.)**

—— *See* BOSIO (Antonio) *Antiquarian.* La Chasteté victorieuse en l'admirable conuersion de S. Valerian espoux de saincte Cécile, *etc.* 1617. 8°.   **860. h. 8. (2.)**

—— *See* BOSIO (Antonio) *Antiquarian.* Histori vom Leyden der heiligen Jungfrawen vñ Martyrin Cæciliæ, *etc.* 1604. 4°.   **3906. cc. 22.**

—— *See* CLICHTOVEUS (J.) [In hoc opusculo agitur de laudibus Sancti Ludovici . . . de laudibus sacratissimae virginis et martyris Ceciliae.] 1516. 4°.   **9040. c. 1. (2.)**

—— *See* FISCHER (Johann W.) Geschichte und Beschreibung der grossen Orgel in der Haupt- und Pfarr-Kirche . . . in Breslau, nebst Denkwürdigkeiten aus dem Leben der heiligen Cäcilie, *etc.* 1821. 8°.   [MISSING.]

—— *See* GOERRES (G.) Das Leben der heiligen Cäcilia in drei Gesängen. [1843.] 16°.   **11526. a. 24.**

—— *See* GÓMEZ RODELES (C.) Vida de Santa Cecilia, *etc.* 1882. 8°.   **4829. a. 38.**

—— *See* GUÉRANGER (P. L. P.) Histoire de Sainte Cécile, *etc.* 1849. 8°.   **4825. c. 22.**

—— *See* GUÉRANGER (P. L. P.) Life of Saint Cecilia, *etc.* 1866. 8°.   **4826. aaa. 14.**

—— *See* GUÉRANGER (P. L. P.) Sainte Cécile et la société romaine aux deux premiers siècles, *etc.* 1874. 4°.   **4828. g. 11.**

—— —— 1878. 8°.   **4825. ee. 3.**

—— *See* KIRSCH (J. P.) Die heilige Cäcilia in der römischen Kirche des Altertums, *etc.* 1910. 8°. [*Studien zur Geschichte und Kultur des Altertums.* Bd. 4. Hft. 2.]   **Ac. 2026/9.**

—— *See* LADERCHI (G.) S. Cæciliæ, Virg. et Mart., acta et Transtyberina Basilica seculorum singulorum monumentis asserta, *etc.* 1722, *etc.* 4°.   **659. h. 18, 19.**

—— *See* POIRÉE (E.) Sainte Cécile . . . Quarante-deux illustrations. [1921.] 8°.   **W.P. 6017/7.**

—— *See* RIBADENEIRA (P. de) Buhé Santès Cécile, *etc.* [1867.] 12°.   **887. g. 22.**

CECILIA. *Saint.*

—— *See* RIGOLA (G. F. A.) La Consonanza delle virtù. Orazione sacra in lode di S. Cecilia, *etc.* [1700.] 4°.   [MISSING.]

—— *See* SHERIDAN (Thomas) *D.D.* A Letter to the Rev. Dr. T. Sheridan . . . To which is added the history of the life of St. Cæcilia. 1731. 8°.   **4165. b. 93.**

—— Cæcilia. A Roman drama, *etc.* [In verse.] pp. 81. *D. & J. Sadleir & Co.: New York*, 1865. 12°.   **11791. bb. 11.**

—— The Choice of St. Cecilia; a selection of fashionable songs. pp. 70. *Oliver & Boyd: Edinburgh*, [1830 ?] 24°.   **11622. a. 8. (7.)**

—— Guerzen é inour Santès Cécile. *Gùénèd*, [1870 ?] 16°.   **887. g. 20. (5.)**

—— The Legend of S. Cecilia. pp. 8. *Mowbray & Co.: Oxford*, [1896.] 16°.   **4823. a. 14. (3.)**

—— Life and Martyrdom of the Holy and Glorious Martyr . . . Cecilia, and those who were with her, SS. Valerian, Tiburtius and Maximus. Translated from the ancient Acts [by E. F. Bowden]. pp. 32. *John Hodges: London*, 1887. 8°.   **4829. a. 43.**

—— The Life of St. Cecilia, from MS. Ashmole 43 and MS. Cotton Tiberius E. VII. With introduction, variants, and glossary by Bertha Ellen Lovewell. pp. 139. *Boston*, 1898. 8°. [*Yale Studies in English.* no. 3.]   **Ac. 2692. ma/3.**

—— An Ode, perform'd on St. Cecilia's Day, 1717 . . . And a mad dialogue by Mr. Leveridge and Mrs. Thurmond, *etc.* pp. 11. *Jonas Browne: London*, 1718. 4°.   **11631. bb. 11.**

—— Principaux épisodes de la vie de Sainte Cécile. Scène lyrique sur paroles tirées de l'Office du Bréviaire romain et des actes du martyre de la Vierge romaine. Oratorio avec accompagnement de grand orchestre composé par P.-L. Torchet, *etc.* pp. 15. *Meaux*, [1855.] 8°.   **11739. d. 5.**

—— Puy de musique, érigé à Évreux, en l'honneur de madame sainte Cécile; publié d'après un manuscrit du XVIᵉ siècle par MM. Bonnin . . . et Chassant. pp. ii. 88. *Évreux*, 1837. 8°.   **7895.c.33.**

—— [Another copy.]   **785. g. 20.**

—— [Another copy.] L.P.   **1400. k. 38.**

—— La Rapresentatione di Santa Cecilia Vergine, & Martire. Nouamente ristampata. [In verse.] *Fiorenza*, [1580 ?] 8°.   **11426. cc. 25.**

—— [Another edition.] *Appresso G. Baleni: Firenze*, 1586. 8°.   **11426. dd. 88.**

—— [Another edition.] [*Florence*, 1590 ?] 4°.   **11426. dd. 87.**

—— [Another edition.] Di nuouo ricorretta. *Alla Loggia del Papa: Siena*, 1606. 8°.   **11426. dd. 89.**

—— [Another edition.] Di nuouo riuista da Francesco d'Anibale, da Ciuitella. *Alla Loggia del Papa: Siena*, 1620. 4°.   **11426. dd. 78.**

—— Saint Cecilia. [By Lady Amabel Kerr.] pp. 24. *Catholic Truth Society: London*, [1902.] 8°.   **3943. aa. 6. (2.)**

—— A Song for St. Cecilia's Day. [By John Dryden.] *See* ACIS. Acis and Galatea, *etc.* 1768. 4°.   **11630. d. 4. (16.)**

CECILIA. *Saint.*

—— St. Cecilia ; or, the British Songster. A new and select collection of the best Scots and English songs, *etc.* pp. 324. *P. Anderson: Edinburgh,* 1782. 12º. **11622. aaa. 13.**

CECILIA, *Sister.*

—— The Deliverance of Sister Cecilia. By Sister Cecilia, as told to William Brinkley. [An account of the author's experiences in Czechoslovakia and of her escape from the Communist police.] pp. viii. 344. *Longmans, Green & Co.: London,* 1955. 8º. **4869. e. 7.**

CECILIA AUGUSTA MARY, *Consort of Frederick William, Crown Prince of Germany.* See NEUMANN-STRELA (C.) Festschrift zur Hochzeit des Kronprinzen-Paares, *etc.* 1905. 8º. **010708. h. 56.**

—— See RADZIWILL (C.) *Princess,* afterwards KOLB, afterwards DANVIN (C.) The Disillusions of a Crown Princess, *etc.* [With portraits.] 1920. 8º. **010704. ff. 19.**

—— Erinnerungen. [With plates, including portraits, and a genealogical table.] pp. 236. *Leipzig,* [1930.] 8º. **010706. k. 43.**

—— The Memoirs of the Crown Princess Cecilie, *etc.* (Translated by Emile Burns.) [With plates, including portraits.] pp. 256. *Victor Gollancz: London,* 1931. 8º. **010705. k. 35.**

—— Erinnerungen an den deutschen Kronprinzen. [With plates, including portraits.] pp. 215. *Biberach an der Riss,* [1952.] 8º. **10711. a. 16.**

—— Sommer an der See. [With a portrait.] pp. 31. *Berlin,* 1923. 8º. **12359. a. 37** *No. 10 of fifty copies autographed by the author.*

—— Sommer an der See. [With a portrait.] pp. 31. *Berlin,* 1924. 8º. **012352. aa. 30.**

CECILIA RENATA, *Queen Consort of Vladislaus IV., King of Poland.* See OPITZ VON BOBERFELD (M.) Felicitati augustae honorique nuptiar. serenissimor. principum Vladislai IV. Pol. Suec.que Regis, et Caeciliae Renatae, Archiducis Austriae. 1637. 4º. **12301. dd. 5. (7.)**

—— See OSSĘDOWSKI (S.) Cythara Nouoduorsciana, in . . . aduentum Cracouiam . . . Vladislai IV., Regis Poloniæ . . . et . . . Cæciliæ Renatæ, Reginæ Poloniæ, *etc.* 1638. 8º. **11409. h. 11.**

CECILIA (GIOVANNI FRANCESCO) See VANNUTELLI (G.) Cronica della vita di G. F. Cecilia. 1841. 8º. **10630. d. 46. (2.)**

CECILIAN. Das Kirchenlied. Eine kleine Festgabe für Kirchenchöre . . . Von einem Cäcilianer. pp. 12. *Paderborn,* [1912.] 8º. [*Kleines Theater.* Hft. 439.] **11747. d. 38. (1.)**

CECILIAN SOCIETY. See SYDNEY.—*Australian Cecilian Society.*

CECILIANE. See SICILIANE.

CECILIE. En kort, men oprigtig Beretning om den saa kaldede smukke Cecilies hastige Fløttetid . . . Samt Nymphens meget rørende Svane-Sang og Afskeeds Aria, *etc.* [By Martin Brun.] pp. 16. *Kiøbenhavn,* 1772. 8º. **1881. b. 46. (8.)**

CECILIE, *pseud.* Nogle Blade, skrevne til Clara Raphael [i.e. Mathilde Lucie Fibiger, on her work entitled " Clara Raphael "] fra Cecilie. pp. 32. *Kjøbenhavn,* 1851. 8º. **8415. c. 55. (1.)**

CECILIO, *pseud.?* La Conciliazione. Osservazioni sui pensieri di un uomo politico [in a work entitled " Le Condizioni dello Stato e la pace religiosa in Italia "]. [By " Cecilio."] pp. 69. *Roma,* [1898.] 8º. **8033. c. 2.**

CECILIO (GAIO PLINIO) See PLINIUS CAECILIUS SECUNDUS (C.)

CECILIUS (GULIELMUS) *Baron Burghley.* See CECIL (William)

CECILL (JOHN) See CECIL.

CECILL (WILLIAM) *Baron Burghley.* See CECIL.

CECILLE, *Herald to Alphonso V., King of Aragon.* See SICILE.

CÉCILLE (JEAN BAPTISTE THOMAS MÉDÉE)

—— See DELAMARCHE (F. A.) and DUPRÉ (M. J.) Campagne dans les mers de l'Inde et de la Chine à bord de la frégate L'Érigone commandée en 1841, 1842 et 1843 par M. Cécile [*sic*], *etc.* 1847, *etc.* 8º. **10055. e. 19.**

CECILY. Cecily's Birds, by the author of " Our Valley " . . . Illustrated by F. Dadd. pp. 256. *S.P.C.K.: London,* [1887.] 8º. [MISSING.]

CECILY, *Duchess of York.* See PAGET (Thomas G. F.) The Rose of Raby . . . A life of Cecily Nevile, Duchess of York. 1937. 8º. **10884. cc. 20.**

CECINA (LORENZO AULO) Notizie istoriche della città di Volterra, alle quali si aggiunge la serie de' podestà, e capitani del popolo di essa. Opera . . . data in luce, illustrata con note, ed accresciute di altre notizie istoriche dal cavaliere Flaminio dal Borgo. pp. xxviii. 331. *Pisa,* 1758. 4º. **663. b. 32.**

—— [Another copy.] **178. i. 23.**

CECINA RICA Y FERGEL (PABLO) Medula eutropelica calculatoria, que enseña a jugar a las damas con espada y broquel, *etc.* pp. 223. *Sevilla,* [c. 1740.] 8º. **7913. de. 21.**

CECIONI (ADRIANO) Scritti e ricordi. Con lettere di G. Carducci, F. Martini, ecc., e con prefazione e note di G. Uzielli. pp. xv. 484. *Firenze,* 1905. 8º. **12227. e. 14.**

CECIRE (ANTONIO MARIA) La Dottrina della chiesa sulle indulgenze esposta e difesa . . . per dimostrare il valore delle indulgenze contenute nella Bolla-Crociata pe' Regni delle due Sicilie. pp. 360. *Napoli,* 1791. 8º. **1356. b. 14. (2.)**

CECKIUS (JOHANNES) See ZECCHIUS.

CECO, *d'Ascoli.* See STABILI (F. degli) called CECCO D'ASCOLI.

CECONI (ANGELO) Scritti in onore del prof. Angelo Ceconi in occasione del trentesimo anno di insegnamento, *etc.* pp. xii. 407. *Torino,* 1936. 4º. **7320. tt. 4.**

CECOSLOVACCHIA. See CZECHOSLOVAKIA.

CÉCYL (AYMÉ) *pseud.* [i.e. ADRIENNE DEPUICHAULT.] La Famille Hobby, histoire villageoise. pp. 108. *Tours,* 1870. 8º. **12809. aaa. 19.**

—— Histoire du royaume de Bois-Belle. pp. 307. *Paris; Bourges,* 1863. 12º. **12515. b. 3.**

—— Noble et martyr. [A tale.] pp. 72. *Lille, Paris,* [1871.] 12º. [MISSING.]

—— La Science des petits . . . Deuxième édition. pp. 141. *Bourges,* 1864. 12º. **8704. aaa. 10.**

CECYL (EDWARD) *Viscount Wimbledon.* See CECIL.

CECYLL (John)   *See* Cecil.

CEDAM.   *See* Casa Editrice Dott. Antonio Milani.

CEDAR, *County of, Iowa.* The History of Cedar County, Iowa . . . Illustrated. pp. 729.   *Western Historical Company: Chicago,* 1878.   8°.   **10409. k. 14.**

CEDAR CHEST. The Cedar Chest, and other poems. pp. 40.   *A. S. Nicol: Perth,* 1909.   8°.
11646. df. 28. (5.)

CEDAR CREEK. Cedar Creek; from the shanty to the settlement. A tale of Canadian life. [By Elizabeth H. Walshe.] pp. 296.   *R.T.S.: London,* [1863.] 16°.
[MISSING.]

—— [Another edition.] pp. 383. *R.T.S.: London,* [1888.] 8°.
[MISSING.]

—— [A reissue.]   *London,* [1902.] 8°.   **04429.h.8.**

CEDAR LIBRARY.
—— Cedar Library.   *Lutterworth Press: London,* 1952– . 8°.   **W.P. a. 337.**

CEDARS. "The Cedars": a poem. By W. H. [i.e. William Henderson.] [1872.] 12°. *See* H., W.
11649. df. 44. (12.)

—— Goodly Cedars: a child's Sunday book. pp. 142. *John Morgan: London,* [1862.] 16°.   **4409. bb. 11.**

CEDARS, *Upper Canada.* An Authentic Narrative of Facts relating to the exchange of prisoners taken at the Cedars . . . With remarks upon the report and resolves of the American Congress on that subject. pp. 50. *T. Cadell: London,* 1777. 8°.   **103. c. 27.**

—— Narration authentique de l'échange des prisonniers faits aux Cèdres pendant la guerre américaine de 1775. Traduit de l'anglais par Marcel Ethier. *See* Verreau (H.) Invasion du Canada, *etc.* 1873. 8°.   **9555. eee. 11.**

CEDED DISTRICTS COLLEGE.   *See* Anantapur.

CEDEL (Sigismundus) *Resp.* De juramento paupertatis. 1743. *See* Strykius (S.) Viri quondam illustris . . . S. Strykii . . . opera omnia, *etc.* vol. 4.   1743, *etc.* fol.
498. g. 6.

CEDEÑO (E. Arévalo) *See* Arévalo Cedeño.

CEDEÑO (Matías) Copia de Carta escrita de . . . Ceuta à . . . Sevilla, de 16. de Junio . . . de 1674. Donde dà quenta del feliz sucesso que el . . . Marques de Trucifal tuvo contra las Agarenas armas el dia doze de dicho mes, *etc. F. de Ochoa: Granada,* 1674. 4°.   **1323. g. 1. (9.)**

CEDERBERG (Arno Rafael)

—— *See* Finland. [*Miscellaneous Public Documents, etc.*] Suomen maaherrojen valtiopäiväkertomukset 1755-1756. Landshövdingarnas i Finland riksdagsberättelser 1755-1756. Toimittanut . . . A. R. Cederberg. 1950. 8°. [*Suomen historian lähteitä.* no. 7.]   Ac. **7814/7.**

—— *See* Finland.—*Läntinen Tutkijakunta.* Läntisen ja Itäisen tutkijakunnan asiakirjoja w. 1725-1727 . . . Toimittaneet A. R. Cederberg, K. O. Alho. 1939. 8°. [*Suomen historian lähteitä.* no. 3.]   Ac. **7814/7.**

—— Heinrich Fick. Ein Beitrag zur russischen Geschichte des XVIII. Jahrhunderts. pp. iv. 103. 160*. *Tartu-Dorpat,* 1930. 8°. [*Eesti Vabariigi Tartu Ülikooli toimetused.* B. 17.] Ac. **1091/4.**

CEDERBERG (Arno Rafael)

—— Jaakko Stenius vanhempi. Kappale 18:nnen vuosisadan suomalaista sivistyshistoriaa. pp. 285. *Helsingissä,* 1928. 8°. [*Suomen Kirkkohistoriallisen Seuran toimituksia.* no. 24.]   Ac. **2049.**

—— Maamme kirkonarkistot. Opas kirkonarkistojen käyttäjille . . . Toinen painos. pp. 92. *Helsinki,* 1936. 8°. [*Suomen Kirkkohistoriallisen Seuran toimituksia.* no. 14.]   Ac. **2049.**

—— Pehr Wargentin als Statistiker. Untersuchungen in der Geschichte der Bevölkerungsstatistik während der zweiten Hälfte des 18. Jahrhunderts. pp. v. 185. *Helsinki,* 1919. 8°. [*Suomalaisen Tiedeakatemian toimituksia.* sarja B. nid. 4. no. 4.]   Ac. **1094. c.**

—— Pohjois-Karjalan kauppaolot vuosina 1721-1775. Yliopistollinen väitöskirja. pp. vii. 213. *Helsinki,* 1911. 8°. [*Suomen Historiallinen Seura. Historiallinen arkisto.* pt. 23. 1. no. 2.]   Ac. **7814/3.**

—— Suomalaiset ja inkeriläiset yliopilaat Tarton ja Tarton-Pärnun yliopistossa v. 1632-1710. 1939. *See* Helsinki. —*Suomen Sukututkimusseura.* Suomen sukututkimusseuran vuosikirja, *etc.* no. 33. 1919, *etc.* 8°.
Ac. **5948.**

—— Suomen historia vapaudenajalla. [With plates.] 2 vol. *Porvoo, Helsinki,* 1942, 47. 8°.   **09456. i. 8.**

CEDERBERG (Björn) Bland vindskupor. En julhistoria. pp. 34. *Stockholm,* 1887. 16°.   [*Öreskrifter för folket.* no. 140.]   **12206. cc.**

CEDERBERG (Eino Edvard Augustinus)

—— *See* Finland.—*Suomen Kirjailijaliitto.* Suomen Runotar . . . Toimittanut Suomen Kirjailijaliiton asettama toimituskunta: J. V. Lehtonen, E. Cederberg, *etc.* 1931. 8°.   **011586. n. 22.**

CEDERBERG (Johan Antero) *See* Liturgies.—*Latin Rite.—Rituals.—*II. *Åbo.* "Manuale Aboense" . . . jonka vuonna 1522 painetun ensimmäisen painoksen mukaan uudestaan julkaisi J. A. Cederberg. 1894. 8°.
[MISSING.]

—— *See* Liturgies.—*Lutheran Churches.—Finland.* Jaakko Suomalaisen Wirsikirja . . . Kopion tehnyt J. A. Cederberg. 1893. 8°. [*Bidrag till kännedom af Finlands natur och folk.* hft. 52. no. 1.]   Ac. **1094/4.**

—— Lehtiä Turun tuomiokapitulin historiasta . . . Katoolinen aikakausi. pp. vii. 248. *Turku,* 1892. 8°. **4685. g. 32.**

CEDERBERG (Lauri Antero) Försäkringsgivarens regressrätt. 1923. *See* Helsinki.—*Juridiska Föreningen i Finland.* Tidskrift, *etc.* 1923. 1910, *etc.* 8°.
Ac. **2145.**

CEDERBERG (Solfrid)

—— Daniel Larsson och Brita Sigridsdotter samt deras efterkommande, *etc.* 1940. *See* Helsinki.—*Suomen Sukututkimusseura.* Suomen Sukututkimusseuran vuoskirja, *etc.* vol. 24. 1919, *etc.* 8°.   Ac. **5948.**

CEDERBLAD (Albert) Göteborg. Skisserade skildringar af Sveriges andra stad . . . Med en karta, *etc.* pp. 281. *Göteborg,* 1884. 8°.   **10280. ee. 18.**

CEDERBLAD (Carin)

—— *See* Cederblad (J. G.) Edvard Grieg. Från norskt manuskript av C. Cederblad. 1946. 8°.   **7900. c. 46.**

CEDERBLAD (CARL) *See* FOGELKLOU, afterwards FOGEL-KLOU-NORLIND (E. M.) Vad man tror och tänker inom svenska folkrörelser. Carl Cederblads enquêtematerial, 1930, *etc.* 1934. 8º.   **8081. e. 30.**

CEDERBLAD (HILDA FREDRICA) Svarta gestalten på Thorsborg. Bilder och minnen från första tredjedelen af vårt århundrade. [By H. F. Cederblad.] 2 dl. 1850. 8º. *See* THORSBORG.   **12580. bbb. 1.**

CEDERBLAD (JOHANNE GRIEG)

—— Edvard Grieg. Från norskt manuskript av Carin Cederblad. [With plates, including portraits.] pp. 159. *Stockholm,* 1946. 8º.   **7900. c. 46.**

—— Sangen om Norge. Edvard Grieg og hans samtid. [With portraits.] pp. 119. *Oslo,* 1948. 8º. **10761. l. 4.**

CEDERBLAD (SVEN)

—— Meridian Observations of Miscellaneous Stars, *etc.* pp. 34. *Stockholm,* 1954. 4º. [*Kungl. Svenska Vetenskapsakademiens handlingar.* ser. 4. bd. 5. no. 2.]   **Ac. 1070.**

CEDERBLAD (SVEN TRYGGVE)

——   Studier i Stagnelii romantik. Akademisk avhandling, *etc.* pp. ix. 327. *Uppsala & Stockholm,* 1923. 8º.   **011851. k. 32.**

CEDERBLOM (GERDA) *See* HILLESTRÖM (P.) Pehr Hilleström som kulturskildrare. Utgivare G. Cederblom. 1927. 4º.   **7862. v. 22.**

—— Nordiska Museet. Svenska allmogedräkter . . . Med illustrationer efter original av E. von Walterstorff. pp. 79. pl. XLVIII. 1921. 4º. *See* STOCKHOLM.—*Nordiska Museet.*   **7743. d. 37.**

—— Svenska folklivsbilder. Utgivna av G. Cederblom. pp. 40. pl. 100. 1923. 4º. *See* STOCKHOLM.—*Nordiska Museet.*   **7854. v. 18.**

CEDERBLOM (JOHAN ERIK) Skridskoåkning. pp. 42. *See* VINTERIDROTT. Vinteridrott, *etc.* 1889. 8º. [*Illustreradt bibliotek för idrott.* no. 9.]   [MISSING.]

CEDERBORG (CARL AUGUST) Boken och svärdet. Historisk roman från Sveriges medeltid. pp. 322. *Göteborg,* 1932. 8º.   **12584. p. 21.**

—— Kungens kurir. Blad ur Karl X. Gustavs hjältesaga. pp. 293. *Göteborg,* 1931. 8º.   **12583. v. 15.**

—— Lyckoringen. Historisk roman från Gustav III:s tid. pp. 312. *Göteborg,* 1933. 8º.   **12584. pp. 36.**

CEDERBORGH (FREDRIK) *See also* DOLK, *Friherre, pseud.* [i.e. F. Cederborgh.]

—— *See* BÖÖK (M. F. C.) Fredrik Cederborgh. Minnesteckning. 1925. 8º.   **010760. df. 4.**

—— *See* EHNMARK (E.) Studier i svensk realism. 1700-talstraditionen och Fredrik Cederborgh, *etc.* 1930. 8º.   **11854. w. 9.**

—— Ottar Trallings lefnads-målning. Ur enke-prostinnan Skarps gömmor benäget meddelad. Ny upplaga. pp. 139. *Stockholm,* 1864. 8º.   **12581. bbb. 40.**

—— Ungdoms tidsfördrif. 3 bd. *Stockholm,* 1834. 8º.   **1207. d. 15.**

—— [Selections.] 1908. *See* LEVERTIN (O. I.) Sveriges national-litteratur, 1500–1900. vol. 12. 1907, *etc.* 8º.   **011852. cc. 1/12.**

CEDERBORGH (FREDRIK REINHOLD) Om mjölk hushållning och smörberedning. pp. 45. *Stockholm,* 1868. 8º. [*Smärre samlade skrifter i landthushållningen.* no. 9.]   **7076. aa. 5.**

—— Den Tillförlitlige kogubben. Handbok i nötboskapsskötseln, eller alfabetiskt ordnadt sammandrag af läran om nötkreaturs uppfödande, utfodring, wård, *etc.* pp. iv. 186. *Örebro,* 1863. 8º.   **7079. a. 6.**

CEDERBOURG (ERIC) En Kort beskrifning öfwer den wid wästra hafwet belägna . . . siö-handel- och stapulstaden Götheborg, *etc.* pp. 231. *Götheborg,* 1739. 4º.   **8229. bbb. 69.**

CEDERCREUTZ (CARL)

—— *See* FREY (R. K. H.) Iter entomologicum et botanicum ad insulas Madeiram et Azores anno 1938 a Richard Frey, Ragnar Storå et Carl Cedercreutz factum. 1940, *etc.* 8º. [*Commentationes biologicae.* vol. 8.]   **Ac. 1094. (2.)**

—— Beitrag zur Kenntnis der Süsswasseralgen auf den Azoren. pp. 36. *Helsingfors ; Leipzig,* 1941. 8º. [*Commentationes biologicae.* vol. 8. no. 9.]   **Ac. 1094. (2.)**

—— Beitrag zur Kenntnis der Gefässpflanzen auf den Azoren. pp. 29. *Helsingfors ; Leipzig,* 1941. 8º. [*Commentationes biologicae.* vol. 8. no. 6.]   **Ac. 1094. (2.)**

CEDERCREUTZ (HERMAN) *Baron.* Sverige under Ulrica Eleonora och Fredric I, eller ifrån 1718 till 1751. Efter den, af framledne . . . friherre Cedercreutz, författade handskrift. Ett inledande bihang till skriften Tessin och tessiniana. pp. 278. *Stockholm,* 1821. 8º.   **1451. f. 5.**

CEDERCRONA (DANIEL GUSTAF) Sweriges rikes ridderskaps och adels wapen bok. *Stockholm,* 1746. fol.   **9917. k. 3.**

—— [Another copy.]   **135. e. 2.**

CEDERGREN (CARL AXEL HUGO)

—— *See* BENGTSON (B.) and CEDERGREN (C. A. H.) Prins Oscar Bernadotte . . . Under redaktion av B. Bengtson och H. Cedergren, *etc.* 1953. 8º.   **10764. b. 8.**

CEDERGREN (G. R.)

—— *See* STOCKHOLM.—*Svensk Botanisk Förening.* Svensk botanisk tidskrift, *etc.* (Generalregister. årg 1–20. Uprättat av T. Arwidsson och G. R. Cedergren.) 1907, *etc.* 8º.   **Ac 3280.**

CEDERGREN (HUGO) *See* CEDERGREN (C. A. H.)

CEDERGREN (KARL GUSTAF)

—— Svenska skråsigill. K. G. Cedergrens efterlämnade anteckningar, redigerade och kompletterade av Gösta von Schoultz. [With plates.] pp. 64. *Stockholm,* 1944. 8º. [*Nordiska Museets handlingar.* no. 20.]   **W.P. 5376/20.**

CEDERHAMN (PETRUS) Catalogus dissertationum, quæ ad illustrandas res svecicas faciunt, præsertim in argumentis historicis, ecclesiasticis, juridicis, *etc.* [By P. Cederhamn.] pp. 214. 1765. 4º. *See* CATALOGUES.   **271. f. 1.**

CEDERHIELM (CARL GUSTAF) [Poems.] *See* HANSELLI (P.) Samlade vitterhetsarbeten af svenska författare, *etc.* dl. 11. pt. 2. 1871. 8º.   **11557. g.**

CEDERHIELM (CARL WILHELM) *See* VOLTAIRE (F. M. A. de) [*Brutus.*] Brutus, sorge-spehl, *etc.* [Translated by C. W. Cederhielm.] 1871. 8º. [*Samlade vitterhetsarbeten af svenska författare.* dl. 11. pt. 2.]   **11557. g.**

CEDERHIELM (Carl Wilhelm)

—— Carl Wilhelm Cederhielms Tal, om wilda träns plantering, i Swerige; hållit för Wetenskaps Academien, *etc.*
Upsala, [1740.] 8°.   965. i. 16. (3.)

—— Rede von der Pflanzung der wilden Bäume in Schweden, *etc. See* Gruner (G. S.) Auserlesene Sammlung zum Vortheil der Staatswirthschaft, *etc.* Bd. 1.
1763. 8°.   966. h. 6.

CEDERHIELM (Germund) [Poems.] *See* Hanselli (P.) Samlade vitterhetsarbeten af svenska författare, *etc.* dl. 11. pt. 2. 1871. 8°.   11557. g.

CEDERHIELM (Joannes) Faunae ingricae prodromus, exhibens methodicam descriptionem insectorum, agri Petropolensis. Præmissa mammalium, avium, amphibiorum et piscium enumeratione, *etc.* pp. xviii. 348. pl. iii. *Lipsiae*, 1798. 8°.   956. c. 23.

—— [Another copy.]   1258. g. 11.

CEDERHIELM (Josias) *See* Hassinger (E.) Zwei Denkschriften Josias Cederhielms und die preussisch-russischen Beziehungen in den Jahren 1710/11. [With the text.] 1938. 8°. [*Karolinska Förbundets årsbok.* 1938.]
Ac. 1068. b.

—— Josias Cederhielms bref till sin broder Germund, 1707–1722 (Juni 1700–1701 samt 1706). [With a portrait.] 1912, 13. *See* Quennerstedt (A.) Karolinska krigares dagböcker. bd. 6, 8. 1901, *etc.* 8°.   9431. h. 14.

—— Josias Cederhielms dagboksanteckningar 1700–1706, 1709. Meddelade av F. Wernstedt. 1926. *See* Sweden. —*Karolinska Förbundet.* Karolinska Förbundets årsbok. 1927. 1911, *etc.* 8°.   Ac. 1068. b.

CEDERHJELM (Carl Gustaf) *See* Cederhielm.

CEDERHJELM (Carl Wilhelm) *See* Cederhielm.

CEDERHJELM (Germund) *See* Cederhielm.

CEDERHJELM (Hugo Montgomery) *See* Montgomery Cederhjelm.

CEDERHOLM (Boris) *See* Vrede (V. A.) Флагъ Адмирала. (Разсказы А. А. Гефтера . . . Б. Л. Седерголма, *etc.*) [Edited by V. A. Vrede.] [1930.] 8°.
012591. k. 57.

—— Въ разбойномъ станѣ. Три года въ странѣ концессій и "Чеки." 1923–1926. [With a portrait.] pp. 317. *Pu̇ea*, 1933. 8°.   010290. eee. 82.

—— In the Clutches of the Cheka. Translated . . . by F. H. Lyon. [With plates, including portraits.]   *G. Allen & Unwin: London*, 1929. 8°.   010291. ee. 26.

CEDERHOLM (Hanna) Vi människor. Episoder. pp. 129. *Helsingfors*, 1921. 8°.   012352. dd. 24.

CEDERKREUTZ (Emil)

—— Yksinäisyyttä ja ihmisvilinää. Muistelmia. [With portraits.] pp. 300. *Jyväskulä, Helsinki,* 1939. 8°.
W.P.3933/6.
[*Satakunnan Kirjallisen Kerhon julkaisuja.* no. 6.]

CEDERLÖF (Carl) *See* Thimm (C. A.) Swedish Self-Taught . . . Edited by W. F. Harvey . . . Second edition. Revised by C. Cederlöf. 1908. 8°.
012902. eee. 33/10.

—— —— 1918. 8°.   012902. eee. 33/75.

—— —— [1932.] 8°.   012902. eee. 33/112.

CEDERLÖF (Johannes)

—— *See* Takolander (A.) Ekenäs stads historia. (dl. 2. [By] J. Cederlöf.) 1930, *etc.* 8°.   W.P. 2329.

—— ——   Det Finländska prästerskapets ekonomiska ställning intill sjuttonde seklet. pp. xvi. 371. *Helsingfors*, 1934. 8°.   [*Skrifter utgivna av Svenska Litteratursällskapet i Finland.* vol. 239.]   Ac. 9082.

—— [Another copy.]   20043. b. 28.

CEDERLÖF (Olof) Oeconomiska anmärkningar vid skånska karp-dammar, *etc. Praes.* C. B. Trozelius. pp. 19. *Lund,* [1766.] 4°.   B. 403. (10.)

CEDERMARK (Johan Harald)

—— Über Verlauf, Symptomatologie und Prognose kraniozerebraler Verletzungen. Klinisch-statistische Analyse eines Materials von durch stumpfe Gewalt Verletzten. pp. 199. *Stockholm*, 1942. 8°. [*Acta chirurgica scandinavica.* vol. 86. suppl. 75.]   P.P. 3081. b. (1.)

CEDERQWIST (Aaron) Exercitium academicum de Helicone musarum, *etc. Praes.* O. Celsius. pp. 27. *Upsalis*, [1712.] 8°.   T. 1937. (2.)

CEDERSCHIÖLD (Fredrik Johan) Allmän inledning till apriorsk, eller rationel, pligt-lära. pp. xv. 191. *Lund,* 1821. 8°.   8405. bbb. 22.

CEDERSCHIÖLD (Gunnar) *See* Cederschiöld (Mattias G.)

CEDERSCHIÖLD (Gustaf Johan Christofer) *See* Bandamenn. Bandamanna saga . . . utgifven af G. Cederschiöld. [1873.] 4°. [*Acta Universitatis Lundensis.* tom. 10.]   Ac. 1067.

—— *See* Clarus. Clarus saga . . . Islandicè et latinè edidit G. Cederschiöld. 1879. 4°.   12431. v. 14.

—— *See* Clarus. Clári Saga. Herausgegeben von G. Cederschiöld. 1907. 8°. [*Altnordische Saga-Bibliothek.* no. 12.]   2346. g. 4.

—— ——   *See* Einarr Skulason. Geisli eða Óláfsdrápa ens helga, er Einarr orti Skúlason . . . utgifven af G. Cederschiöld. [1873.] 4°. [*Acta Universitatis Lundensis.* tom. 10.]   Ac. 1067.

—— *See* Erec, *Knight of the Round Table.* Erex saga. Efter handskrifterna utgifven af G. Cederschiöld. 1880. 8°. [*Samfund til Udgivelse af gammel nordisk Litteratur.* Publications. no. 3.]   Ac. 9057.

—— *See* Jomsvikings. Jómsvíkinga saga . . . utgifven af G. Cederschiöld. [1874.] 4°. [*Acta Universitatis Lundensis.* tom. 11.]   Ac. 1067.

—— Altnordische Saga-Bibliothek. Herausgegeben von G. Cederschiöld, Hugo Gering und Eugen Mogk (Finnur Jónsson, Emil Olson). 18 Hft. *Halle*, 1892–1929. 8°.
2346. g. 4.

—— Fornsögur Suðrlanda. Isländska bearbetningar af främmande romaner från medeltiden. Efter gamla handskrifter utgifna af G. Cederschiöld. (Magus saga jarls.— Konrads saga.—Bærings saga.—Flovents saga.—Bevers saga.) pp. 273. cclii. [*Lund,* 1877–83.] 4°. [*Acta Universitatis Lundensis.* tom. 13–15, 18, 19.]   Ac. 1067.

—— [Another issue.] pp. cclii. 273. *Lund,* 1884. 4°.
12403. b. 22.

—— Fresta duger, jämte andra uppsatser. pp. 257. *Stockholm*, 1914. 8°.   12972. m. 20.

CEDERSCHIÖLD (Gustaf Johan Christofer)

—— Kalfdråpet och vänpröfningen, ett bidrag till kritiken af de isländska sagornas trövärdighet. pp. 41. *Lund,* 1890. 8°. **011824. f. 67. (3.)**

—— Konung Sverre. pp. xi. 188. *Lund,* 1901. 8°. **10761. f. 35.**

—— Medeltidsberättelser. Sagor, legender ock anekdoter från fornisländskan. pp. 155. *Stockholm,* 1885, 91. 8°. [*Nyare bidrag till kännedom om de svenska landsmålen ock svenskt folklif.* bd. 5. no. 6.] **P.P.5044.g. (1.)**

—— Om Erikskrönikan, et historiskt epos från folkungatiden. pp. 265. *Göteborg,* 1899. 8°. [*Populärt vetenskapliga föreläsningar vid Göteborgs Högskola.* no. 11.] **Ac. 2651. d/2.**

—— Om grundtalens lexikaliska behandling. pp. 59. *Göteborg,* 1897. 8°. [*Göteborgs Högskolas årsskrift.* bd. 3. no. 12.] **Ac. 2651. d.**

—— Om svenskan som skriftspråk. pp. viii. 354. *Göteborg,* 1897. 8°. [*Populärt vetenskapliga föreläsningar vid Göteborgs Högskola.* no. 4.] **Ac. 2651. d/2.**

—— Andra upplagan. pp. viii. 326. *Lund,* 1902. 8°. **Ac. 2651. d/2.**

—— Rimlista till Eufemiavisorna och Erikskrönikan. pp. xiv. 275. *Göteborg,* 1903. 8°. [*Göteborgs Högskolas årsskrift.* bd. 8. no. 3.] **Ac.2651.d.**

—— Rytmens trollmakt. Några bidrag till människans historia. pp. 187. *Stockholm,* 1905. 8°. [*Populärt vetenskapliga föreläsningar vid Göteborgs Högskola. Ny följd.* no. 1.] **Ac. 2651. d/2.**

—— Språk i språket. 2 pt. *Stockholm,* 1909. 8°. [*Studentföreningen Verdandis småskrifter.* 163, 164.] **08282. c. 1/163, 164.**

—— Studier öfver isländska kyrkomåldagar från fristatstiden. 1887. *See* Copenhagen.—*Kongelige Nordiske Oldskrift-Selskab.* Annaler, *etc.* (Aarbøger, *etc.* række 2. bd. 2.) [1837, *etc.*] 8°. **Ac. 5538/4.**

—— Studier öfver verbalabstrakterna i nutida svenska. pp. 132. *Göteborg,* 1908. 8°. [*Göteborgs Högskolas årsskrift.* bd. 14. no. 3.] **Ac.2651.d.**

CEDERSCHIÖLD (Maria) En Banbryterska. Skildringar från Ellen Fries' studentår i Uppsala. Ur hennes bref och anteckningar samlade och utgifna af M. Cederschiöld. pp. 107. *Stockholm,* 1913. 8°. **10602. ppp. 3. (2.)**

—— Läsarne i Småland. Ett utkast efter naturen. [By M. Cederschiöld.] pp. 40. 1854. 8°. *See* Småland. **3925. bbb. 36. (3.)**

CEDERSCHIÖLD (Mattias Gunnar)

—— Elsass-Lothringen. Studier. [With illustrations.] pp. 84. *Lund,* 1918. 8°. **10196. g. 25.**

—— I skärselden och på andra ställen . . . Med teckningar av författaren. pp. 195. *Stockholm,* 1931. 8°. **12583. v. 9.**

—— Tretton år med Ivar Kreuger. [With plates, including portraits.] pp. 183. *Stockholm,* 1937. 8°. **10762. b. 11.**

CEDERSCHIÖLD (Staffan Fredrik Robert Pehr) *See* Hagen (A. L. van der) and Cederschiöld (S. F. R. P.) Svenska aktiebolag med begränsad ansvarighet, *etc.* 1875. 4°. **08228. g. 44.**

CEDERSCHJÖLD (Fredrik August) *See* Cederschjöld (P. G.) Några blad ur P. G. Cederschjölds efterlemnade anteckningar, utgifne af F. A. Cederschjöld. 1857. 12°. **7440. a. 6.**

—— Är svenska folket verkligen så fysiskt och moraliskt förderfvadt, som Herr Prof. M. Huss antyder uti sin afhandling: "Om Sveriges endemiska sjukdomar"? Recension. pp. 64. *Stockholm,* 1854. 8°. **10281. d. 21.**

—— Belysning af Hr. Professor G. Brantings "Upplysningar." pp. 35. *Stockholm,* 1864. 8°. **7441. aaa. 63. (4.)**

—— Om läkekonst och quacksalveri, föredrag hållet vid Svenska Läkare-Sällskapets högtidsdag den 6 oktober 1857. pp. 137. *Stockholm,* 1857. 8°. **7391. a. 10.**

CEDERSCHJÖLD (Pehr Gustaf) Handbok för riksdagsmän . . . Tredje, tillökta upplagan. pp. iv. 98. *Stockholm,* 1839. 12°. **1391. b. 43.**

—— Några blad ur P. G. Cederschjölds efterlemnade anteckningar, utgifne af F. A. Cederschjöld. pp. 151. *Stockholm,* 1857. 12°. **7440. a. 6.**

—— Svenska riksdagarne imellan åren 1719 och 1772. Första Riksdagen år 1719 med ett bihang. (Bihang till Riksdagen i Stockholm år 1719, innehållande protocoller och handlingar hörande till actionen emot baron v. Görtz.) 2 bd. 1825, 26. 8°. *See* Sweden.—*Riksdagen.* **1056. d. 21.**

CEDERSCHÖLD (J. A.) *Resp. See* Wieselgren (P.) De claustris Svio-Gothicis, *etc.* 1832. 4°. **4785. g. 13.**

CEDERSTOLPE (Th. von) Sagen von Luxemburg, poetisch bearbeitet . . . Zweite unveränderte Auflage. pp. x. 272. *Luxemburg,* 1852. 12°. **11527. de. 34.**

CEDERSTRÖM (Adelina Maria Clorinda) *Baroness. See* Patti (A. M. C.) afterwards Cederström (A. M. C.) *Baroness.*

CEDERSTRÖM (Bror) *Baron. See* Cederström (C. G. B.) *Baron.*

CEDERSTRÖM (Carl Gustaf) *Baron. See* Juel (C. A.) Om Dana-Arf. Academisk afhandling . . . framstället af C. A. Juel och C. G. Cederström, *etc.* [1851.] 8°. [missing.]

—— Om de i trakten af Carlstad förekommande fogelarter. Akademisk afhandling, *etc.* Praes. J. P. Areschoug. pp. 16. *Upsala,* [1851.] 8°. **1257. e. 14.**

—— Om hafsluft och hafsbad vid Sverges vestra kust i physiologiskt och therapeutiskt hänseende. pp. 37. *Stockholm,* 1860. 8°. **7689.aa.21.**

—— Om insjöfisket och insjöfiskaren. pp. 22. *Stockholm,* 1899. 8°. [*Studentföreningen Verdandis småskrifter.* no. 76.] **08282. c. 1/76.**

—— Råd och anvisningar till Sverges insjöfiskare. pp. 32. *Stockholm,* 1901. 8°. [*Studentföreningen Verdandis småskrifter.* no. 98.] **08282. c. 1/98.**

—— Wermlands läns fiskevatten. 3 dl. *Karlstad,* 1895, 96. 8°. **7290. aaa. 30.**

CEDERSTRÖM (Carl Gustaf Bror) *Baron.* Anteckningar ang. Kronprinsens Husarreg:te, 1813–1913. *See* Stille (A. G. H.) Striden vid Bornhöft i Holstein, *etc.* 1913. 4°. **9431. l. 3.**

CEDERSTRÖM (Carl Olof Rudolf) *Baron.* Livrustkammarens Lützenminnen. *See* Jacobson (C. G. E.) Minnesalbum över Gustaf II. Adolf, *etc.* 1932. fol. **1765. f. 19.**

CEDERSTRÖM (CARL OLOF RUDOLF) *Baron.*

—— De Svenska riksregalierna och kungliga värdighetstecknen, *etc.* (Redaktion: Karl Erik Steneberg.) [With illustrations including portraits.] pp. 351. 1942. 4°. *See* STOCKHOLM.—*Nordiska Museet.*—*Kungliga Livrustkammaren.* **C. 119. h. 8.**

CEDERSTRÖM (CARL OLOF RUDOLF) *Baron,* and **MALMBORG** (BROR OTTO GÖSTA)

—— Den äldre Livrustkammaren, 1654. Utgiven av R. Cederström och G. Malmborg. Åtföljd av en sammanfattande del på engelska språket [by G. A. Urquhart]. [With plates.] 2 pt. 1930. fol. *See* STOCKHOLM.—*Nordiska Museet.*— *Kungliga Livrustkammaren.* [MISSING.]

CEDERSTRÖM (CARL RUDOLF HENRIK) *Baron. See* EYVINDR, *Skaldaspillir.* Försök till tolkning och förklaring af Hákonar-mál. Akademisk afhandling af R. Cederström. 1860. 8°. **11565. cc. 40. (3.)**

CEDERSTROM (D. J.)

—— Geology and Ground-Water Resources of St. Croix, Virgin Islands. [With a map.] pp. vi. 117. pl. 6. *Washington,* 1950. 8°. [*U.S. Department of the Interior. Geological Survey Water-Supply Paper.* no. 1067.] **A.S. 212.**

CEDERSTRÖM (GUSTAF CARL ULRIK) *Baron. See also* AGRICOLA (Claudius) *pseud.* [i.e. Baron G. C. U. Cederström.]

—— Fiskodling och Sveriges fiskerier, *etc.* pp. 269. *Stockholm,* 1857. 8°. **8244. b. 54.**

—— Naturhistoriska betraktelser och iakttagelser innefattande hänvisningar till lämpliga sätt att forska för att kunna tillförlitligt utreda sillfiskarnes tillhåll och vandringar, sam en derpå grundad framställning om hvad som kan göras till silfiskeriernas förbättring. pp. 23. 46. *Stockholm,* 1871. 8°. **7204. aaa. 6. (7.)** *The date in the colophon is* 1872.

—— Små-plancher till ledning vid fisk-odling. Af C . . . . [i.e. G. C. U. Cederström]: m. fl. pp. 19. pl. XIV. 1859. 8°. *See* C . . . . **7290. a. 42.**

CEDERSTRÖM (GUSTAF OLOF) *Baron. See* QUENNERSTEDT (A.) Indelte soldaten . . . Med teckningar af G. Cederström. 1887. 4°. **8825. g. 16.**

—— *See* ROMDAHL (A. L.) Gustaf Cederström. [With plates.] 1935. 4°. **7863. s. 5.**

—— Minnen. [With illustrations.] pp. 316. *Stockholm,* 1913. 8°. **010761. k. 10**

CEDERSTRÖM (RUDOLF) *Baron, Intendent och Föreståndare för Livrustkammaren. See* CEDERSTRÖM (Carl O. R.)

CEDERSTRÖM (RUDOLF) *Baron, Kammarherre hov drottning Lovisa. See* CEDERSTRÖM (Carl R. H.) *Baron.*

CEDERSTRÖM (RUDOLPH) Minnes-sång öfver konung Carl XIV Johan. pp. 37. *Stockholm,* 1846. 8°. **11565. c. 50. (2.)**

CEDERVALLER (THILDA) *See* THILDA [Cedervaller].

CEDERWALL (KARIN)

—— *See* EKART (A.) Direct från Ryssland, *etc.* (Översättning av K. Cederwall.) 1948. 8°. **10293. bb. 8.**

CEDILLIUS (ALPHONSUS) *See* ORTIZIUS (B.) Summi Templi Toletani . . . descriptio. [With a preface by A. Cedillius.] 1549. 8°. **C. 63. e. 5.**

CEDILLO, LUIS LOPEZ DE AYALA ALVAREZ DE TOLEDO Y DUSMET, *Count de. See* LOPEZ DE AYALA ALVAREZ DE TOLEDO Y DUSMET.

CEDMON. *See* CÆDMON.

CEDO, *pseud.* [i.e. C. D'ORCHIMONT.] Betraktelser öfver Europas närvarande ställning i orientaliska frågan, af Cedo. pp. 57. *Stockholm,* 1855. 8°. **8028. a. 38. (2.)**

CEDOLIM (PIERRE) successively *Bishop of Nona* and *of Lesina. See* CEDOLINI (Pietro)

CEDOLINI (PIETRO) successively *Bishop of Nona* and *of Lesina.* Discorso . . . fatto alla Santità di nostro Sign. Clemente Ottavo, per la difesa contra il Turco l'anno 1594. *See* TESORO. La terza parte del Tesoro politico, *etc.* [1605.] 8°. **521. c. 22.**

—— [Another edition.] *See* TESORO. Del tesoro politico. pt. 3. 1612. 4°. **521. d. 16.**

—— Discours . . . faict à la Saincteté du Pape Clement VIII pour la deffence contre le Turc, l'an 1594. *See* TESORO. Trésor politique, *etc.* livre 3. 1611. 4°. **C. 80. a. 6.**

CÉDONT (JULES) Remarques sur la fièvre jaune, *etc.* pp. 58. *Paris,* 1863. 4°. [*Collection des thèses soutenues à la Faculté de Médecine de Paris.* An 1863. tom. 2.] **7373. e. 5.**

CEDORS (DE) *See* TASSONI (A.) *Count.* Le Seau enlevé, *etc.* [The translator's dedication signed: D. C., i.e. — de Cedors.] 1759, *etc.* 12°. **1063. b. 30.**

CÉDOZ (F. M. TH.) Un Couvent de religieuses anglaises à Paris de 1634 à 1884, *etc.* pp. xx. 479. *Paris; Burns & Oates: Londres,* 1891. 8°. **4629. aaa. 25.**

CEDRENUS (GEORGIUS) *See* DELISLE (L. V.) Feuillets d'un manuscrit de Cedrenus, *etc.* 1881. 8°. **820. f. 43. (8.)**

—— *See* ZONARAS (J.) Ioannis Zonaræ Annales, aucti additionibus G. Cedreni. 1567. fol. [*AYMINIUS (J.) Corpus vniuersæ historiæ.*] **C. 74. e. 8.**

—— Georgii Cedreni Annales, siue Historiæ ab exordio mundi ad Isacium Comnenum usque compendium: nunc primùm . . . Græcè & Latinè editi: Guilielmo Xylandro Augustano interprete, qui annotationes etiam addidit, & tabellas chronologicas, *etc. Gr. & Lat.* pp. 662. coll. 663–714. *Per I. Oporinum et Episcopios Fratres: Basileæ,* [1566.] fol. **589. l. 1.**

—— [Another copy.] **C. 47. l. 5.**

—— Γεωργιου του Κεδρηνου Συνοψις ιστοριων. Georgii Cedreni Compendium historiarum. Ex versione Guillelmi Xylandri, cum eiusdem annotationibus. Accedunt . . . præter lacunas . . . expletas, notæ in Cedrenum P. Iacobi Goar . . . & Caroli Annibalis Fabroti . . . glossarium ad eundem Cedrenum. Item, Ioannes Scylitzes . . . excipiens ubi Cedrenus desinit, nunc primùm Græcè editus, *etc. Gr. & Lat.* 2 tom. *E Typographia regia: Parisiis,* 1647. fol. [*Corpus byzantinæ historiæ.*] **196. h. 5, 6.**

—— [Another edition.] 2 tom. pp. 679. 56. *Venetiis,* 1729. fol. [*Corpus byzantinæ historiæ.*] **804. i. 2/4.**

—— [Another edition.] Georgius Cedrenus Ioannis Scylitzæ ope ab Immanuele Bekkero suppletus et emendatus. 2 tom. *Bonnae,* 1838. 8°. [*Corpus scriptorum historiae byzantinae.*] **2071. h. 24.**

CEDRENUS (GEORGIUS)

—— [Another edition.] (Accedunt Michaelis Pselli opera quæ reperiri potuerunt omnia.) *Gr. & Lat.* 2 tom. *Paris*, 1864. 4°. [*Patrologiæ cursus completus.* Series græca. tom. 121, 122.] **2002. a.**

CÈDRES, *Les. See* CEDARS.

CEDRI (SETTIMIO) *See* FRANCUCCI (C. M.) All'illustrissimi . . . Monsignori Canale . . . Sceriman . . . Romana reparationis riparum Tyberis. Tra l'illm̄i signori possessori delli beni adjacenti alle ripe del fiume Tevere, e la Rev. Camera Apostolica, Ristretto di fatto, *etc.* [By C. M. Francucci, S. Cedri and A. Clari.] 1761. fol.
T. 86*. (15.)

—— Septimii Cedri . . . Responsum juris pro veritate in causa Leodiensis electionis. *See* CLEMENT WENCESLAUS, *Elector and Archbishop of Treves.* Sacra congregatione consistoriali . . . Leodien. electionis. Pro regio serenissimo principe Clemente è Saxonia, *etc.* 1764. 4°. **1230. e. 25.**

CEDRIC. Cedric's Diaries and Letters from America. [The preface signed: C. C. B., i.e. Cedric Clifton Brown. With illustrations, including portraits.] 1928. 8°. *See* B., C. C. **010410. g. 44.**

—— Cedric's [i.e. Cedric Clifton Brown's] Letters during the Great War, 1914–1919. [With a portrait.] pp. ix. 162. *Printed for private circulation: London & Beccles,* 1926. 8°.
010902. f. 41.

CEDRIC, *pseud.* The Distribution of the National Wealth, considered in its bearings upon the several questions now before the public, more especially those of the Corn Laws, and restriction in general. By Cedric. pp. 104. *Robert Jennings: London,* 1827. 8°. **T. 1175. (8.)**

CEDRIC II., *pseud.* [i.e. HERBERT HULME.] The Poet Gray and Knutsford. An unpublished pedigree [of the family of Antrobus, Gray's maternal ancestors]. Containing also " Elegy written in a Country Churchyard." By Cedric II. Nine illustrations. (Reprinted from the " Knutsford Division Guardian.") pp. 12. [*Knutsford,* 1911.] 8°. **9903. aaa. 30.**

CEDRIŅŠ (VILIS)

—— *See* ULMĀNIS (K. A.) *President of Latvia.* Kārla Ulmaņa 60 gadi. 1877 . . . 1937. Svētku raksti. (Grāmatu sakārtojis V. Cedriņš.) [1937.] 8°. **12357. m. 36.**

CEDRINUS, *pseud.* [i.e. J. FRIEDRICH RADIKE.] *See* ALBRECHT (H. C.) Geheime Geschichte eines Rosenkreuzers [i.e. Cedrinus], *etc.* 1792. 8°. **4783. bb. 5.**

CEDRON (J. DE) Carlistes et libéraux. pp. 27. *Paris,* 1875. 8°. **8042. e. 43. (2.)**

CEDROWSKI (JAN)

—— Dwa pamiętniki z XVII wieku, Jana Cedrowskiego i Jana Floriana Drobysza Tuszyńskiego. Wydał i wstępem poprzedził Adam Przyboś. pp. xxxviii. 122. *Wrocław, Kraków,* 1954. 8°. **10796. cc. 39.**

—— Pamiętnik J. Cedrowskiego własną jego ręka spisany w XVII wieku. *See* BALIŃSKI (M.) Pamiętniki historyczne, *etc.* 1859. 8°. **9475. bbb. 13.**

CEDRÚN DE LA PEDRAJA (GONZALO) La Niñez de Menéndez y Pelayo . . . Discurso, *etc.* pp. 26. *Madrid,* 1912. 8°. **10600. bb. 24. (4.)**

CEDRUS DEODARA, *pseud.* Twenty-four Excursions and Routes in the Himalaya Mountains . . . With an appendix containing a brief guide to some other sanitaria in India. By Cedrus Deodara. pp. 179. XII. *Wyman & Co.: Calcutta,* 1877. 8°. **10055. df. 7.**

CEDRY. *See* PERIODICAL PUBLICATIONS.—*Beyrout.*

CEDULIUS (COELIUS) *See* SEDULIUS.

CÉE (JEAN PAUL) Avant-projet d'un code des lois morales fondé sur les principes démocratiques et socialistes, *etc.* pp. viii. 185. *Paris,* 1890. 8°. **8285. cc. 41.**

CEE (KAY) *pseud.* Is Israel a Nation in the World To-day ? pp. 29. *Covenant Publishing Co.: London,* 1934. 8°.
04033. de. 90.

CEELY (CHRISTOPHER) [For editions of " Sir Francis Drake revived ", partly based on the reports of C. Ceely, Ellis Hixom and others :] *See* NICHOLS (Philip) *Preacher.*

CEELY (ROBERT) Further Observations on the Variolæ Vaccinæ . . . Reprinted from the " Transactions of the Provincial Medical and Surgical Association," *etc. See* CROOKSHANK (Edgar M.) History and Pathology of Vaccination, *etc.* vol. 2. 1889. 8°. **2255. g. 2.**

—— Health Officers, their appointment, duties, and qualifications . . . With prefatory remarks by R. Ceely. pp. 30. *T. Richards: London,* 1873. 8°. **C.T. 331. (5.)**

—— Observations on the Variolæ Vaccinæ . . . Reprinted from the " Transactions of the Provincial Medical and Surgical Association," *etc. See* CROOKSHANK (Edgar M.) History and Pathology of Vaccination, *etc.* vol. 2. 1889. 8°. **2255. g. 2.**

CÉFALE. *See* CEPHALUS.

CEFALI (SEBASTIANO) Relacya o stanie politycznym i wojskowym Polski . . . z roku 1665, z notami dodanemi przez hr. Krzystofa Masini, *etc. See* RYKACZEWSKI (E.) Relacye nuncyuszów apostolskich, *etc.* tom 2. 1864. 8°.
4695. ee. 28.

CEFALONIA. *See* CEPHALONIA.

CEFALÙ, FRANCESCO, *Bishop of.* [1587–1593.] *See* GONZAGA.

——, OCTAVIUS, *Bishop of.* [1633–1638.] *See* BRANCIFORTIUS.

CEFFALONIE (MARIN CARBURI DE) *Count. See* CARBURI (Marin) *Count,* calling himself *Chevalier de Lascary.*

CEFFI (FILIPPO) *See* COLONNE (G. delle) *Begin.* [fol. 2 recto :] Incomincia il prologo sopra la historia di troia, *etc.* [Translated by F. Ceffi.] 1481. fol. **IB. 21297.**

—— *See* COLONNE (G. delle) La Storia della guerra di Troia tradotta in lingua volgare da M. G. delle Colonne [or rather by F. Ceffi], *etc.* 1665. 4°. **1074. c. 23.**

—— —— 1868. 8°. **12403. ff. 19.**

—— Le Dicerie (da imparare a dire a uomini giovani e rozzi) di Ser Filippo Ceffi . . . pubblicate da Luigi Biondi. pp. cii. 87. *Torino,* 1825. 8°. **8405. g. 3.**

—— [Another copy.] L.P. **1387. i. 10.**

CEFFINO (ZANOBIO) La triomphante entrata di Carlo .v. Imperadore Augusto: in Lalma Citta di Roma: con il significato delli Archi Triomphali: ꝛ delle Figure Antiche in prosa ꝛ versi Latini. [1536.] 4°. **C. 33. h. 7.**

—— [Another edition.] [1536.] 4°. **9930. f. 71. (2.)**

—— La Triumphante entree de l'empereur . . . Charles le cincqiesme . . . faicte en la . . . cite de Rome, auecq les significations des Epitaphes triumphantz ꝛ figures auctenticques, *etc.* G.L. *Imprimebat I. Steelsius: Antuerpiæ,* 1536. 4°. **C. 33. e. 23.**

—— Ein Sendtbrieff, so der Edel Herr Zanobio Ceffino dem . . . Hertzogen zu Florentz, [von] dem Triumphlichenn einzug dess . . . Römischen Kaisers Caroli des Fünfftē . . . in die Hochlobliche Stat Rom . . . zierlich vnd ordenlich zugeschriben. Mit allem fleiss auss Wellsch jnns Teutsch gepracht. [1536.] 4°. **9930. bbb. 33.**

CEFFINO (ZANOBIO)

—— Un Poemetto inedito del secolo XVI in onore di San Tommaso Moro. (Stäze di Zanobio Ceffino, cittadino fiorentino, sopra l'eresia del re d'Inghilterra e sopra la morte di Tommaso Moro, Gran Cancellero.) [Edited by A. Castelli. Reprinted from " Aevum."] *Milano,* [1938.] 8⁰. **11859. i. 13.**

CEFISIO (FILODEMO) *pseud.* [i.e. GIUSEPPE MANCINI.] *See also* MANCINI (G.) *Archbishop of Siena.*

—— *See* PETRARCA (F.) [*Two or more Works.—Latin and Italian.*] F. Petrarchae Poëmata minora, *etc.* (Sette epistole a soggetti diversi ed elogio in morte della madre volgarizzati da F. Cefisio.) vol. 3. 1829, *etc.* 8⁰. **11421. dd. 20.**

CEFN CHRONICLE YEAR BOOK AND ALMA-NACK. *See* PERIODICAL PUBLICATIONS.—Cefn.—*Cefn Chronicle.*

CEFN COCH MSS. The Cefn Coch MSS.: two MSS. of Welsh poetry written principally during the XVIIth century. Edited by the Rev. J. Fisher. [With facsimiles.] pp. xxviii. 460. *I. Foulkes : Liverpool,* 1899. 8⁰. **11595. f. 34.**

CEGA (ANTONIO CELIO) *See* CELIO CEGA.

CEGANI (GAETANO) Il Canale di Suez, lezione tenuta nell'Istituto Industriale di Venezia. pp. 45. *Milano,* 1869. 16⁰. **8235. aa. 38.**

—— Canali e ferrovie d'America. Pensieri. pp. 32. *Venezia,* 1870. 8⁰. **8235. cc. 44. (6.)**

CEGDESSA (MARTIUS À CASA) *Marsiliensis, pseud. See* CASA CEGDESSA.

CEGIELSKI (GASPAR JÓZEF HIPOLIT)

—— *See* GROT (Z.) Hipolit Cegielski. [With portraits.] 1947. 8⁰. **10797. g. 25.**

—— *See* KUEHNER (R.) Grammatyka języka greckiego. Podług Kuehnera wyłożona przez H. Cegielski. 1843. 8⁰. **12923. bb. 2.**

—— Nauka poezyi, zawierająca teoryą poezyi i jéj redzajów, oraz znaczny zbiór najcelniejszych wzorów poezyi polskiéj do Teoryi zastósowany [*sic*] . . . Wydanie drugie. pp. viii. 647. *Poznań,* 1851. 8⁰. **11826. f. 1.**

—— O Pisowni Pana L. Rzepeckiego i towarzyszów. pp. 49. *Poznań,* 1868. 8⁰. **12976. c. 32. (9.)**

—— *See* SZCZĘSNY, *pseud.* W sprawie pisowni odpowiedź Panu H. Cegielskiemu . . . na jego broszurę pod tytułem : "O pisowni Pana L. Rzepeckiego i to-warzyszów" napisał Szczęsny. 1868. 8⁰. **12976. i. 19. (7.)**

—— O słowie Polskiem i konjugacyach jego, wraz z wstępem-krytycznym. pp. 91. *Poznań,* 1852. 8⁰. **12976. i. 20. (2.)**

—— Die zweckmässigsten Ackergeräthe und landwirthschaft-lichen Maschinen ihrer Construction und Gebrauchsweise nach beschrieben und in 156 Abbildungen dargestellt von Dr. H. Cegielski. pp. 82. *Posen,* 1858. 4⁰. **7077. i. 19.**

—— Życie i zasługi Doktora K. Marcinkowskiego. Rzecz, *etc.* pp. 43. *Poznań,* 1866. 8⁰. **10601. d. 8. (2.)**

CEGIELSKI (HIPOLIT) *See* CEGIELSKI (Gaspar Józef Hipolit)

CEGLIŃSKI (JULIAN) *See* WARSAW. Album des vues de Varsovie et de ses environs, dessinées . . . et lith. par J. Cegliński, *etc.* [1861 ?] *obl.* 4⁰. **Maps 28. a. 46.**

CEGNAR (FRANCE) *See* NĚMCOVÁ (B.) Babica . . . Po-slovenil F. Cegnar. 1862. 16⁰. **12591. a. 10.**

—— *See* SCHILLER (J. C. F. von) [*Maria Stuart.—Slove-nian.*] Marija Stuart . . . Poslovenil F. Cegnar. 1861. 16⁰. **11748. aa. 55.**

—— *See* SCHILLER (J. C. F. von) [*Wilhelm Tell.—Slovenian.*] Viljem Tell . . . Poslovenil F. Cegnar. 1862. 16⁰. **11748. aa. 57.**

—— Pesmi. pp. 164. *v Celovcu,* 1860. 16⁰. **11585. aaa. 10.**

CÉGRÉTIN (PAUL) Étude sur Claude Tillier, *etc.* pp. 51. *Clamecy,* 1880. 8⁰. **10604. e. 14. (1.)** *Imperfect ; wanting the " portrait-frontispice."*

ČEH ( ) [For the Bohemian surname of this form :] *See* ČECH.

CEHEL. *See* CETHEL.

CÉHEL (PÉGÉ DE) *pseud.* [i.e. PROSPER GAUTHIER DE CLAGNY.] *See* PÉGÉ DE CÉHEL.

CEHELSKYJ (LONGIN) *See* TSEHEL'SKY (L'.)

ČEHOV ( )

—— [For the Russian surname of this form :] *See* CHEKHOV.

ČEHOVA (MIRA)

—— *See* SOBOLEV (L. S.) Морска душа. (Превела М. Чехова. 1947. 8⁰. **12594. aaa. 24.**

CEI (FRANCESCO) Sonecti, capituli, canzone, sextine, stanze et strambocti . . . in laude di Clitia. ff. 58. *Impresso per P. di Giunta : Firenze,* 1514. 8⁰. **239. b. 8.**

—— [Another edition.] Opera noua composta per . . . F. Cei . . . in laude de Clitia. Opera . . . nouamente stäpata. [In verse.] *Impresso per G. di Rusconi : Venetia,* 1518. 8⁰. **11427. df. 2.**

CEI (LEONIERO) Locomobili e trebbiatrici. Note per gli ispettori e istruzioni ai conduttori . . . Quarta edizione riveduta ed ampliata, *etc.* pp. xix. 458. *Milano,* 1919. 16⁰. **12199. i. 18.** *One of the " Manuali Hoepli."*

—— Il Motorista d'aviazione. Descrizione, governo e manu-tenzione dei motori per l'aviazione, *etc.* pp. xvi. 535. *Milano,* 1920. 16⁰. **12199. i. 26.** *One of the " Manuali Hoepli."*

CEILIOCHUIR (MUIRERTACH) *See* KELIHER (Murtogh).

CEILLIER (EUGÈNE) Les Bouquets. Comédie en un acte. 1880. *See* THÉÂTRE. Théâtre de campagne, *etc.* sér. 6. 1876, *etc.* 12⁰. **2296. a. 7.**

CEILLIER (LAURENT) Roger-Ducasse. Le musicien—l'œuvre. [With portraits.] pp. 87. *Paris,* [1920.] 8⁰. **7894. aaa. 35.**

CEILLIER (REMI) *Benedictine. See* BARBEYRAC (J.) Traité de la morale des Pères de l'Église ; où en défendant un article de la préface sur Puffendorf contre l'Apologie de la morale des Pères du P. Ceillier . . . on fait diverses réflexions sur plusieurs matières importantes. 1728. 4⁰. **6. d. 11.**

—— *See* BEUGNET (A.) Étude biographique et critique sur Dom Remi Ceillier. 1891. 8⁰. [*Mémoires de la Société des Lettres, Sciences et Arts de Bar-le-Duc.* sér. 2. tom. 10.] **Ac. 271.**

CEILLIER (Remi) *Benedictine.*

—— Histoire générale des auteurs sacrés et ecclésiastiques, *etc.* tom. 1–22. *Paris*, 1729–58. 4º.
130. c. 2–16. & 131. c. 1–7.
Imperfect; wanting tom. 23 and the Index.

—— Nouvelle édition . . . revue, corrigée, complétée et terminée . . . par un directeur de grand séminaire [i.e. L. M. F. Bauzon]. 16 tom. *Paris*, 1858–69. 8º.

—— Table générale des matières . . . Rédigée par Laur.-Ét. Rondet . . . revue, corrigée et augmentée par M. l'abbé Bauzon. 2 tom. *Paris*, 1868, 69. 8º.
4999. f.

CEILLIER (Rémi) *Prestidigitateur.* Manuel pratique d'illusionnisme et de prestidigitation, *etc.* 2 tom. *Paris*, 1935, 36. 8º. [MISSING.]

CEINIOGWERTH. Y Geiniogwerth. *See* Periodical Publications.—*Denbigh.*

CEINTURE. Ceinture du monde. *See* Vaudoyer (J. L.)

CEIONIUS COMMODUS, afterwards **LUCIUS AELIUS CAESAR,** *Adopted Son of the Emperor Hadrian. See* Lucius Aelius Caesar.

CEIRIOG, *Rural District of.*

—— Official Guide to the Rural District of Ceiriog, Denbighs. Second [*etc.*] edition. [By L. Elgar Pike.] [1951– .] 8º. *See* Pike (Leslie E.) 010370. a. 43.

CEIRIOG, *Bardic name of John Hughes. See* Hughes (John Ceiriog)

CEIRIOG MEMORIAL INSTITUTE. *See* Glyn-ceiriog.

CEIRIOG (Gwilym) *Bardic name of William Roberts. See* Roberts (William) called *Gwilym Ceiriog.*

CÉIS CORAINN. *See* Keshcorran.

CEIST. The Important Question answered . . . A'Cheist chudthromach air a freagairt. [1860?] 12º. *See* Question. [MISSING.]

CEIT, *Mhòr.*

—— Ceit Mhòr agus Maighstir Lachun Minister Lochacaroin. [By Thomas M. Fraser. A religious tale.] pp. 16. *Duncan Macvean: Glasgow,* 1848. 16º. 4411. aa. 48. (4.)

CEITA (João de) Quadragena segunda em que se contem os dous sanctos tempos do anno: conuem a saber, Aduento, & Quaresma; com seus introitos, *etc.* pp. 546. *L. Craesbeeck: Euora,* 1625. fol. [MISSING.]

CÉITINN (Seathrún) *See* Keating (Geoffrey) *D.D.*

CEJADOR Y FRAUCA (Julio) *See* Alemán (M.) Primera (segunda) parte de Guzman de Alfarache . . . Edición transcrita y revisada por J. Cejador. 1913, *etc.* 8º. 12489. p. 22.

—— *See* Calisto. [*Spanish.*] Fernando de Rojas. La Celestina . . . Edición y notas de J. Cejador y Frauca. 1913, *etc.* 8º. 11728. bb. 16.

—— *See* Gomez de Quevedo Villegas (F.) [*Works.*] Quevedo. (II. Los Sueños. Edición y notas de J. Cejador y Frauca.) 1911, *etc.* 8º. W.P. 750.

—— *See* Gracián (Lorenzo) *pseud.* El Criticón . . . Edición transcrita y revisada por J. Cejador. 1913. 8º. 12489. p. 21.

CEJADOR Y FRAUCA (Julio)

—— *See* Horatius Flaccus (Q.) [*Works.—Spanish.*] Horacio . . . vuelto en lengua castellana por D. J. Cejador y Frauca. 1928. 8º. 11355. d. 30.

—— *See* Lazarillo, *de Tormes.* [*Spanish.*] La Vida de Lazarillo de Tormes . . . Edición y notas de J. Cejador y Frauca. 1914. 8º. 12490. pp. 10.

—— *See* Menéndez y Pelayo (M.) Mamarrachos Académicos . . . Prólogo de D. J. Cejador. [1924.] 8º. 012942. bb. 11.

—— *See* Ruiz (Juan) *Archpriest of Hita.* Libro de Buen Amor. Edición y notas de J. Cejador y Frauca. 1913, *etc.* 8º. 011451. eee. 61.

—— El Cantar de Mio Cid y la epopeya castellana. 1920. *See* Periodical Publications.—*Paris.* Revue hispanique, *etc.* tom. 49. 1894, *etc.* 8º. P.P. 4331. aea.

—— Cintarazos. Artículos inéditos, *etc.* 3 tom. *Madrid,* 1927. 8º. 012352. bbb. 7.

—— ¡ De la Tierra—! Colección de artículos. pp. ii. 336. *Madrid,* 1914. 8º. 12354. pp. 4.

—— Diccionario Etimológico-Analítico Latino-Castellano. pp. 541. *Madrid,* 1926. 8º. 012941. cc. 4.

—— Epítome de Literatura Latina. pp. 66. *Madrid,* 1914. 8º. 11313. f. 5.

—— [Another edition.] pp. 63. *Madrid,* 1923. 8º. 11313. aa. 14.

—— Fraseología o Estilística Castellana. 4 pt. pp. 748. 697. *Madrid,* 1921–25. 8º. 012941. dd. 10.

—— Historia de la Lengua y Literatura Castellana. 14 tom. *Madrid,* 1915–22. 8º. 12942. v. 2.

—— Ibérica. 2 vol. *Barcelona, Madrid,* 1926, 28. 8º. 07708. k. 55.

—— La Lengua de Cervantes. Gramática y diccionario de la lengua castellana en el ingenioso hidalgo Don Quijote de la Mancha. [With a preface by Rufino J. Cuervo.] 2 tom. *Madrid,* 1905, 06. 8º. 12941. l. 9.

—— *See* Revilla (M. G. A.) El Lenguaje Popular y el Erudito. Replica a Don Julio Cejador y Frauca, autor de la "Gramática de la Lengua de Cervantes." 1921. 8º. 12941. c. 31.

—— El Lenguaje. Sus trasformaciones, su estructura, su unidad, su orígen, su razon de ser, *etc.* 12 tom. *Salamanca,* 1901–14. 8º. 012901. i. 41.

—— Miguel de Cervantes Saavedra. Biografía, bibliografía, crítica. pp. 77. *Madrid,* 1916. 8º. 10632. t. 26.

—— Origen del Lenguaje y Etimología Castellana, *etc.* pp. xi. 349. *Madrid,* 1927. 8º. 012941. cc. 7.

—— El Quijote y la Lengua Castellana . . . Conferencia, *etc.* pp. 24. *Madrid,* 1905. 8º. 011853. i. 53. (8.)

—— Recuerdos de mi Vida. Obra póstuma. Prólogo de Ramón Pérez de Ayala. [With a portrait.] pp. xvii. 85. *Madrid,* 1927. 8º. 10634. dd. 24.

—— Refranero Castellano. 3 vol. *Madrid,* 1928, 29. 8º. 012941. dd. 18.

—— Tierra y Alma Española. [With illustrations.] pp. 404. *Madrid,* [1924.] 8º. 10161. dd. 23.

CEJADOR Y FRAUCA (JULIO)

—— Toponimia Hispánica hasta los Romunos inclusive, para cotejarla con la Bascongada y completar la obra de Humboldt (Prüfung der Untersuchungen über die Urbewohner Spaniens, vermittelst der baskischen Sprache), *etc.* [With a preface by Julio Broutá.] pp. xv. 142. *Madrid*, 1928. 8°.   010160. de. 31.

—— Trazas del Amor. Novela psicológica. pp. 284. *Madrid*, 1914. 8°.   12490. pp. 9.

—— La Verdadera Poesía Castellana. Floresta de la antigua lírica popular, recogida y estudiada por D. J. Cejador y Frauca. 5 tom. *Madrid*, 1921–24. 8°.   11453. aa. 11.

—— Vocabulario Medieval Castellano. pĻ 414. *Madrid*, 1929. 8°.   012941. dd. 19.

ČEJCHAN (VÁCLAV)

—— Bakunin v Čechách. Příspěvek k revolučnímu hnutí českému v letech 1848–1849. S dvěma přilohami [i.e. Meine Vertheidigung an Herrn Advokat Franz Otto, and Druhé provolání k slovanům, by M. A. Bakunin. With a portrait and a summary in French], *etc.* pp. xiv. 200. 1928. 8°.   [*Spisy Vojenského archivu RČS.* řada 2. čís. 1.]   09315. i. 28/2. (1.)

—— 1000 let. Kronika československo-ruských styků slovem i obrazem. (Sestavili V. Čejchan, M. Rampasová a V. Vymětal.) [With plates.] pp. 107. 1947. 8°.   *See* CZECHOSLOVAKIA.—*Ministerstvo Informací.* S. R. 58/28.

ČEJCHAN (VÁCLAV) and MÁGR (ANTONIN STANISLAV)

—— Прага-Москва—Москва-Прага. Тысячелетний календарь культурной связи. (Составили В. Чейхан и А. Ст. Марр.) [With illustrations.] pp. 102. *Прага*, 1946. 8°.   8289. b. 51.

ČEJKA (JOSEF) Dr. *See* SHAKESPEARE (W.) [*Works.— Bohemian.*] Dramatická Díla Williama Shakespeara. [Translated in verse by J. Čejka, F. L. Čelakovský and others.] 1856, *etc.* 8°.   11762. bbb. 25.

—— *See* SHAKESPEARE (W.) [*Romeo and Juliet.—Bohemian.*] W. Shakespeare'a Romeo a Julie. Přeložil Dr. J. Čejka. 1861. 8°.   11765. aa. 42. (4.)

—— Kytice ze španělských romancí. Přeložili J. Čejka a V. Nebeský. [Collected by J. Čejka and V. Nebeský, and edited by the latter.] pp. xii. 186. *v Praze*, 1864. 8°.   11452. b. 9.

ČEJKA (JOSEF) Miller, of Humenec. *See* ADÁMEK (K. V.) Josef Čejka, Český emigrant a Uherský emissař evangelický, *etc.* 1910. 8°.   4805. gg. 19. (2.)

ČEJKA (THEODOR) Slovníčky esperantsko-český a českoesperantský. pp. 149. [1908.] 8°. *See* VYMAZAL (F.) Mezinárodní řeč Esperanto, *etc.* pt. 2. [1908.] 8°.   12901. aaa. 34.

CEJNEK (JOSEF) Österreichische Münzprägungen von 1705 bis 1935. pp. 93. *Wien*, 1935. 8°.   Dept. of Coins & Medals.

—— Österreichische, ungarische, böhmische und schlesische Münzprägungen v. 1519–1705. pp. xv. 144. *Wien*, [1936.] 8°.   Dept. of Coins & Medals.

CEJNEK (RAJMUND) Z dějin moravského studentstva v Praze . . . Otisk z "Moravské Orlice." pp. 97. *v Brně*, 1905. 8°.   8357. bb. 47.

CEJNOWA (STANISŁAW FLORJAN) *See* CENÔVA.

CEJP (KAREL)

—— *See* KAVINA (K.) and PILÁT (A.) Atlas hub evropských, *etc.* (sv. 4. Omphalia (Fr.) Quél. Kalichovka. Napsal K. Cejp.) 1935, *etc.* 8°.   **7084.c.1.**

—— Monografie hydnaceí Republiky Československé, *etc.* pp. 107. pl. II. *v Praze*, 1928. 8°.   [*Fauna et flora čechoslovenica.* sv. 2.]   Ac. 799/45.

CEJUDO (ANGEL CARRERA) *See* CARRERA CEJUDO.

CEJUDO (FRANCISCO) *See* INCHAURRANDIETA (R.) Sifones del Canal de Isabel II. Memoria escrita por R. Inchaurrandieta, J. Sanz . . . y F. Cejudo. 1858. 8°.   8776. d. 25. (2.)

CEJUDO (GERONIMO MARTIN CARO Y) *See* CARO Y CEJUDO.

CEJUDO (JOSÉ) En la Inauguracion del Conservatorio Nacional de Declamacion de México, el director general D. J. Cejudo, á los alumnos de ambos secsos matriculados en la primera época. pp. 8. *México*, 1853. 12°.   12301. a. 4.

CEKA (EMU) *pseud.* [i.e. F. MUCK.] *See* EMU CEKA, *pseud.*

ČEKIĆ (MILUTIN) Jugoslawien am Scheidewege. Das serbo-kroatische Problem und Jugoslawiens Aussenpolitik. (Übertragen von Josef Bobek.) pp. vii. 138. *Leipzig*, [1939.] 8°.   8028. dd. 38.

—— Jugoslawien am Scheidewege. Das serbo-kroatische Problem und Jugoslawiens Aussenpolitik. (Übertragen von Josef Bobek.) pp. vii. 138. *Leipzig*, [1939.] 8°.   08028. i. 121.

CEKOTA (A.) The Technique of Inventive Work. pp. 32. *Efficiency Magazine: London*, [1939.] 8°. [*Up-to-Date Bulletins for Business Men.* no. 92.]   W.P. 78/92.

CEKOTA (ANTHONY) *See* CEKOTA (Antonín)

CEKOTA (ANTONÍN)

—— *See* MASEFIELD (John E.) Volání moře. (Přeložil A. Cekota.) 1938. 8°.   C. 106. e. 1.

—— The Battle of Home. Some problems of industrial community . . . Illustrated by Joseph Lenhard. [An account of the establishment by Czech immigrants of the Canadian village of Batawa.] pp. xiv. 373. *Macmillan Co. of Canada: Toronto*, 1944. 8°.   8289. cc. 33.

CEKUK (COHÉ) Effendi, *pseud.* [i.e. PAUL PANCKOUCKE.] *See* COHÉ-CEKUK, *Effendi, pseud.*

CELA.

—— Cela est fort aisé à dire. pp. 7. [1791.] 8°.   R. 207. (11.)

CELA (AMARO FERNÁNDEZ PARDO DE) *See* FERNÁNDEZ PARDO DE CELA.

CELA (CAMILO JOSÉ) *See* CELA Y TRULOCK (C. J.)

CELA (MANUEL RODRÍGUEZ DE) *See* RODRÍGUEZ DE CELA.

CELADA (ANTONIO CAPO) *See* CAPO-CELADA.

CELADA (BENITO)

—— Números sagrados derivados del siete. Contribución a la historia del siete, la semana y el sábado. *In:* Sefarad. año 8. fasc. 1, 2. 1948. 8°.   Ac. 132. f/4.

CELADA (DIEGO DE) De benedictionibus Patriarcharum electa sacra: commentario litterali, et morali illustrata, *etc.* [With the text of Genesis i, ix, xii. 1–9, xxvi. 1–5, xxvii, xlviii, xlix.] pp. 404. *Apud P. Balleonum: Venetiis*, 1642. fol.   1215. l. 7.

CELADA (DIEGO DE)

—— Editio altera, ab eodem auctore, & correctior, & auctior, etc. pp. xli. 472. *P. Borde, L. Arnaud & C. Rigaud: Lugduni*, 1657. fol. **L.16.c.6.**
The titlepage is engraved.

—— R.P. Didaci de Celada . . . in Estherem commentarij litterales & morales, cum duplici tractatu appendice, altero de Assueri conuiuio mystico, id est, eucharistico: altero de Esthere figuratâ . . . Editio vltima à mendis expurgata. [With the text.] pp. 790. *P. Borde, L. Arnaud & C. Rigaud: Lugduni*, 1658. fol.
3166. h. 6.

—— R.P. Didaci de Celada . . . in Rutham commentarij litterales et morales. Cum duplici tractatu appendice, altero de Boozi conuiuio mystico . . . altero de Ruth figuratâ, *etc.* [With the text.] pp. 604. *Apud H. Verdussium & H. Aertssens: Antuerpiæ*, 1652. fol.
L.17.e.8.(1.)

—— Judith illustris perpetuo commentario literali & morali . . . Auctore R.P. D. de Celada . . . Editio tertia ab eodem auctore & accuratè correctior, & copiosè auctior. pp. 710. 1648. fol. *See* BIBLE.—*Apocrypha.—Judith.* [*Latin.*] **L.17.e.8.(2.)**

CELADENUS (ALEXIUS) *Bishop of Gallipoli. See* CELADONI.

CELADON. Celadon; or, the Bright example; a pastoral on the death of His Royal Highness the P. of Denmark. pp. 13. *Printed for the Author: London*, 1708. 8º.
11602. i. 26. (1.)

—— Celladon's Garland; containing three new songs, *etc.* pp. 8. *B. Deacon: London*, [1750?] 12º.
1076. l. 25. (30.)

—— [Another edition.] pp. 8. [*Newcastle-upon-Tyne?* 1750?] 12º. **11621. b. 60. (6.)**

CELADON, *Pegnesischer Blum-Genosse, pseud.* [i.e. CHRISTOPH ADAM NEGELEIN.] *See* BIBLE.—*Psalms.* [*German.—Metrical Versions.*] Die alte Zions-Harpfe . . . verneuet angestimmet, von dem Pegnesischen Blum-Genossen Celadon. 1693. 12º.
3090. i. 26.

—— Abraham, der Gross-Glaubige; und Isaac der Wunder-Gehorsame. In einem Sing-Spiel vorgestellet von dem Pegnesischen Blum-Genossen Celadon. pp. 53. *J. J. Felsecker: Nürnberg*, 1682. 12º. **11746. de. 13.**

—— [Another copy.] **11746. ee. 2.**

CELADON, *von der Donau, pseud.* [i.e. JUSTUS SUSART.] Der Deutschen dreyssig-jähriger Krieg, poetisch erzählet durch Celadon von der Donau. [*Vienna?*] 1657. 8º.
11515. a. 8. (1.)

CELADONI (ALEXIS) *Bishop of Gallipoli.* Alexij Celadeni . . . Oratio ad sacrum Cardinalium senatum ingressurum ad nouum Pont. eligendum. [*J. Besicken: Rome*, 1503.] 4º. **12301. e. 50.**

CELADORES. Castiguense á los Zeladores que roban á los pobres vendedores, ó sea diálogo entre varios zeladores y muchos de la Plaza. pp. 4. *México*, 1833. 4º.
9770. bb. 22. (6.)

CELAGE. *See* PERIODICAL PUBLICATIONS.—*Mexico.*

ČELAKOVSKÝ (FRANTIŠEK LADISLAV) *See* BAČKOVSKÝ (F.) Několik rozprav o F. L. Čelakovském . . . S podobiznou. 1887. 8º. [*Bibliotéka paedagogická.* sv. 120.]
12216. l.

—— *See* GOETHE (J. W. von) [*Geschwister.—Bohemian.*] Marinka. Hra . . . přeložená od F. L. Čelakowského. 1827. 16º. **11746. b. 21.**

ČELAKOVSKÝ (FRANTIŠEK LADISLAV)

—— *See* HANUŠ (I. J.) Literatura příslovnictví slovanského a německého, či předchůdcové F. L. Čelakovského v " Mudrosloví národu slovanského v příslovích," *etc.* 1853. 8º. [*Bibliotheka slovanského příslovnictví.* sv. 1.]
12305. d. 34.

—— *See* MIKHAILO IVANOVICH, *Potok.* Potok Michajlo Iwanowić. Powěst staroruská. [Translated into Bohemian by Č., i.e. F. L. Čelakovský.] 1827. 12º. [*RHESA (L. F.) Litewské národnj pjsně.*]
11585. a. 54. (2.)

—— *See* NOWAKOWSKI (J. F.) Czelakowski Franciszek Ładysław. 1862. 8º. **10601. g. 2. (1.)**

—— *See* PERIODICAL PUBLICATIONS.—*Königgratz.* Dennice . . . Sebránjm J. Chmely . . . a F. L. Čelakowského. [1824.] 16º. **P.P. 4835. r.**

—— *See* RHESA (L. F.) Litewske národnj pjsně . . . přeložené a wydané od F. L. Čelakowského. 1827. 12º.
11585. a. 54. (1.)

—— *See* SCOTT (*Sir* W.) *Bart.* [*The Lady of the Lake.*] Panna Gezernj . . . přeložil F. L. Čelakowský. 1828. 12º. **11641. b. 42.**

—— *See* SHAKESPEARE (W.) [*Works.—Bohemian.*] Dramatická Díla Williama Shakespeara. [Translated into verse by J. Čejka, F. L. Čelakovský and others.] 1856, *etc.* 8º.
11762. bbb. 25.

—— *See* VLADYKA (J.) F. L. Čelakovský, *etc.* 1949. 8º. **10790. de. 18.**

—— *See* VRANSKA (Ts.) Фр. Л. Челаковски и славянското народно творчество, с особен оглед към българските народни песни и пословици, *etc.* pp. 93. 1945. 8º. [*Годишник на Софийския Университет. Историко-филологически Факултет.* том. 41.] **Ac. 1137. (1.)**

—— F. L. Čelakovského sebrané listy. 9 seš. pp. 539. v Praze, 1865 [1863–65]. 8º. **10921. c. 18.**

—— Z let probuzení . . . Listy F. L. Čelakovského a Bohuslavy Rajské 1844–1845. pp. 147. 1872. *See* RAJSKÁ, afterwards ČELAKOVSKÁ (A. B.) Z let probuzení, *etc.* kn. 2. 1872, *etc.* 8º. [*Ženská bibliotéka.* část 2.] **8416. i. 11.**

—— Korrespondence a zápisky . . . Vydal František Bílý. (sv. 4. část. 1. K tisku připravil a poznamkami opatřil Václav Černý.) sv. 1– sv. 4 část. 1. *V Praze*, 1907–33. 8º. [*Sbírka pramenův k poznání literarního života československého. Skup. 2. čís. 10, 14, 17, 21, 27.*] **Ac. 799/5.**

—— Rejstřík. Sestavil Jaroslav Šťastný. pp. 219. v Praze, 1939. 8º. [*Sbírka pramenů, etc.* skup. 2. čís. 28.] **Ac. 799/5.**

—— Aus Franz Ladislaw Čelakowsky's Dichtungen. *See* WENZIG (J.) Kränze aus dem böhmischen Dichtergarten. [1856.] 16º. **11585. a. 48.**

—— Česká čítací kniha pro druhou třídu nižšího gymnasia. Sestavil Dr F. L. Čelakovský. Vydání šesté. pp. 289. v Praze, 1875. 8º. **12202. f. 16.**

—— Čtení o počátcích dějin vzdělanosti a literatury národův slovanských, jež na Vysokých školách Pražských měl F. L. Čelakovský. pp. 230. v Praze, 1877. 8º. [*Nowočeská bibliotéka.* čís. 21.] **Ac. 800/10.**

—— Františka Ladislava Čelakovského Čtení o srovnavací mluvnici slovanské na Universitě Pražské, *etc.* [Edited by P. J. Šafařík.] pp. vii. 357. v Praze, 1853. 8º. [*Nowočeská bibliotéka.* čís. 17.] **Ac. 800/10.**

ČELAKOVSKÝ (František Ladislav)

—— Dodavky ke Slovniku Josefa Jungmanna. Sebral a vydal
Dr. F. J. Čelakovský. pp. 66. *v Praze*, 1851. 4°.
827. eee. 6.

—— Malý výbor z veškeré literatury české . . . Druhé
rozmnožené vydání. pp. 642. *v Praze,* 1872 . 8°.
12265. g. 2.

—— Mudrosloví národu slovanského ve příslovích. Připojena
jest sbírka prostonárodních českých pořekadel. Uspořádal a vydal F. L. Čelakovský. pp. 644. *v Praze*,
1852. 8°. [*Nowočeska biblioteka.* čís. 14.]
Ac. 800/10.

—— Fr. Lad. Čelakovského Mudrosloví národu slovanského
v příslovích. Vydání druhé, jež uspořádal Dr J. V. Novák.
25 seš. pp. xv. 783. *v Praze*, 1891–93. 8°. **8467. i. 3.**

—— Ohlas pjsnj ruských. pp. 95. *w Praze*, 1829. 12°.
11585. c. 12.

—— Ohlasy. Ohlas písní ruských. Ohlas písní českých, *etc.*
pp. 159. *v Praze*, [1945 ?] 8°. **11588. a. 87.**
Světová knihovna. no. 67–68.

—— Nachhall Russischer Lieder von Fr. Lad. Čelakowský.
Ger. See Wenzig (J.) Blüthen neuböhmischer Poësie,
etc. 1833. 8°. **11747. de. 17. (3.)**

—— Fr. Lad. Čelakowskjeho Wothlós pěsni ruskich. Do
Łužisko-Serbskjeje rečje přełožištaj J. E. Smoleŕ a J. A.
Warko. pp. 70. *Prazy*, 1846. 8°. **11585. c. 53. (4.)**

—— Остатки Языка Славянъ Полабскихъ, собранные и
объясненные Ф. Л. Челаковскимъ. Издалъ В. А.
Францевъ. pp. 21. *Санктпетербургъ*, 1901. 8°.
[*Сборникъ Отдѣленія Русскаго Языка и Словесности
Императорской Академіи Наукъ.* том. 7. прил. no. 3.]
Ac. 1125/39.

—— Františka Ladislava Čelakovského Růže Stolistá.
Báseň a pravda. Výkladem a rozborem opatřil F.
Bílý. S podobiznou. Druhe, rozhojněné vydání. pp. 112.
v Praze, 1894. 8°. **011586. h. 17.**

—— Slowanské národnj pjsně sebrané Frant. Lad. Čela-
kowským. [With musical notes.] 3 djl. *w Praze*,
1822–27. 8°. **11585. c. 11.**
The collective titlepage is engraved.

—— Smjšene Básně Frant. Ladisl. Čelakowskýho. pp. 104.
w Praze, 1822. 12°. **11585. a. 13.**
*With an autograph note of presentation to Sir John
Bowring.*

—— Druhé rozmnožené vydání. pp. 163. *w Praze*,
1830. 8°. **11585. c. 13.**

—— F. L. Čelakovského Spisů básnických knihy šestery.
pp. 404. *w Praze*, 1847. 8°. [*Nowočeská biblioteka.*
čís. 9.] **Ac. 800/10.**

ČELAKOVSKÝ (Jaromír) *See* Bohemia. [*Collections of
Laws, etc.—*I.] Codex juris municipalis . . . Vydává
. . . J. Čelakovský. 1886, *etc.* 8°. **05549. k. 18.**

—— Sborník příspěvků k dějinám král. hlav. města Prahy
. . . za redakce prof. dr. Jaromíra Čelakovského. (díl 2, 3.
Za redakce Josefa Teige.—díl 4, 6. Za redakce Václava
Vojtíška.) díl 1–4, 6. 1907–30. 8°. *See* Prague.—
Obec. **9315. f. 20.**

—— De vernaculis et extraneis registris, praecipue de his,
quae ad Bohemicam et alias Austriacas Aulicas Cancel-
larias pertinent. O domácich a cizích registrech, *etc.*
Boh. pp. 142. *v Praze*, 1890. 4°. [*Königlich-Böhmische
Gesellschaft der Wissenschaften. Rozpravy Král. České
Společnosti Nauk.* Třída filosoficko-historicko-filologická.
řada 7. sv. 3. čís. 6.] **Ac. 801.**

ČELAKOVSKÝ (Jaromír)

—— Klášter Sedlecký, jeho statky a práva v době před
válkami Husitskými . . . K vydání připravil Václav
Vojtíšek. pp. iv. 142. *v Praze*, 1916. 8°. [*Rozpravy
České Akademie Císaře Františka Josefa, etc.* Třída 1.
čís. 58.] **Ac. 799/2.**

—— O účasti právníkův a stavů ze zemí českých na kodifikaci
občanského práva Rakouského. [1753–1811.] pp. 60.
v Praze, 1911. 8°. [*Rozpravy České Akademie Císaře
Františka Josefa, etc.* Třída 1. čís. 45.] **Ac. 799/2.**

—— Das Heimfallsrecht auf das freivererbliche Vermögen
in Böhmen. Ein Beitrag zur böhmischen Rechtsgeschichte. (Übersetzung und zum Teile Umarbeitung
einer . . . Monografie [*sic*] " Právo odůmrtné k statkům
zpupným v Čechách." pp. 85. *Prag*, 1882. 8°.
5551. cc. 3.

ČELAKOVSKÝ (Ladislav František) Die Myxomyceten
Böhmens, *etc.* pp. 80. pl. 5. *Prag*, 1893. 8°. [*Archiv
der naturwissenschaftlichen Landesdurchforschung von
Böhmen.* Bd. 7. no. 5.] **Ac. 2915.**

—— Ueber die Aufnahme lebender und todter verdaulicher
Körper in die Plasmodien der Myxomyceten. 1892. *See*
Ratisbon.—*Regensburgische Botanische Gesellschaft.* Flora,
etc. Bd. 76. 1818, *etc.* 8°. **Ac. 3258/3.**

ČELAKOVSKÝ (Ladislav Jozef) Rozpravy o Darwinowě
theorii a o vývojí rostlinstva. [A reprint of " Úvahy
přírodovědecké o Darwinově theorii " and of " Vyvinování
se rostlinstva s ohledem na Darwinovu theorii," with
corrections, and of an abstract of " O zákonech fyloge-
netického vývoje rostlinstva."] pp. 243. *v Praze*,
1894. 8°. **7006. g. 6.**

—— Analytická květena česká. Na základě " Prodromu
květeny české." pp. xxx. 412. *v Praze*, 1879. 8°.
7033. bb. 9.

—— Analytická květena Čech, Moravy a Rak. Slézska
. . . Druhé rozmnožené vydání Analytické květeny
české. pp. xxxiv. 430. *v Praze*, 1887. 8°. **7029. bb. 16.**

—— Třetí rozmnožené vydání, *etc.* pp. xlviii. 456.
v Praze a ve Vídni, 1897. 8°. **07028. k. 37.**

—— Arbeiten der botanischen Section in den Jahren 1864–
1868. *Prag*, 1869. 8°. [*Archiv der naturwissenschaftlichen
Landesdurchforschung von Böhmen.* Bd. 1. Sect. 3.]
Ac. 2915.

—— Die Gymnospermen. Eine morphologisch-phylogene-
tische Studie, *etc.* pp. 148. *Prag*, 1890. 4°. [*Abhandlungen der Königlich-Böhmischen Gesellschaft der Wissenschaften.* Siebente Folge. Bd. 4. B. no. 1.] **Ac. 801.**

—— Květena okolí Pražského. Seznam všech okolo Prahy
samorostlých a vůbec pěstovaných druhů a plemen rostlin
cévnatých a jejich stanovisk, *etc.* pp. 164. *v Praze*,
1870. 8°. [*Společnost Wlastenského Museum w Čechach.*
Živa. pt. 4.] **Ac. 800/6.**

—— Nauka o květenstvích na základě deduktivním, srovná-
vacím a fylogenetickém, *etc.* [With a résumé in German.]
pp. 88. pl. iv. *v Praze*, 1892. 8°. [*Rozpravy České
Akademie Císaře Františka Josefa, etc.* třída 2. roč. 1.
čís. 20.] **Ac. 799/2.**

—— Neue Beiträge zur Foliolartheorie des Ovulums, *etc.*
pp. 42. pl. ii. *Prag*, 1884. 4°. [*Abhandlungen der
Königlich-Böhmischen Gesellschaft der Wissenschaften.*
Sechste Folge. Bd. 12. B. no. 8.] **Ac. 801.**

ČELAKOVSKÝ (LADISLAV JOZEF)

—— O abnormálních metamorfosách květů tulipánových. Příspěvek k morfologii srovnávací, *etc.* [With a resumé in German.] pp. 32. pl. II. *v Praze*, 1892. 8°. [*Rozpravy České Akademie Císaře Františka Josefa, etc.* třída 2. roč. 1. čís. 44.] Ac. **799**/2.

—— O chlorofyllu. Úryvek z fysiologie rostlin. pp. 63. *v Praze*, 1881. 8°. [*Sbírka přednášek a rozprav.* ser. 2. čís. 3.] **12209.** w. **1/13.**

—— O kladodiích Asparageí—rodů Danaë, Semele, Ruscus a Asparagus. Srovnávací morfologická studie, *etc.* [With a resumé in German.] pp. 66. pl. IV. *v Praze*, 1893. 8°. [*Česká Akademie Císaře Františka Josefa. Rozpravy.* třída 2. roč. 2. čís. 27.] Ac. **799**/2.

—— O listech šitých a exkrescenčních. Teratologické příspěvky k morfologii listů, *etc.* [With a resumé in German.] pp. 28. pl. II. *v Praze*, 1892. 8°. [*Česká Akademie Císaře Františka Josefa. Rozpravy.* třída 2. roč. 1. čís. 41.] Ac. **799**/2.

—— O některých zrůdnostech na habru a smrku se objevujících, *etc.* [With a resumé in German.] pp. 50. pl. II. *v Praze*, 1893. 8°. [*Česká Akademie Císaře Františka Josefa. Rozpravy.* třída 2. roč. 2. čís. 37.] Ac. **799**/2.

—— O působení nedostatku kyslíka na pohyby některých organismů aërobních, *etc.* pp. 31. *v Praze*, 1899. 8°. [*Česká Akademie Císaře Františka Josefa. Rozpravy.* třída 2. roč. 8. čís. 1.] Ac. **799**/2. *Imperfect; wanting the titlepage.*

—— O významu a původu věnce, paracorolla, Narcisovitých, *etc.* pp. 29. pl. IV. *v Praze*, 1898. 8°. [*Česká Akademie Císaře Františka Josefa. Rozpravy.* třída 2. roč. 7. čís. 13.] Ac. **799**/2.

—— Příspěvky k fyllotaxii květů, *etc.* pp. 30. pl. II. *v Praze*, 1898. 8°. [*Česká Akademie Císaře Františka Josefa. Rozpravy.* třída 2. roč. 7. čís. 22.] Ac. **799**/2.

—— Prodromus der Flora von Böhmen, enthaltend die wildwachsenden und allgemein kultivirten Gefässpflanzen des Königreiches. (Vierter Theil, enthaltend die Nachträge bis 1880 nebst Schlusswort, Verzeichnissen und Register.) 4 Tl. pp. viii. 955. *Prag*, 1867–81. 8°. [*Archiv der naturwissenschaftlichen Landesdurchforschung von Böhmen.* Bd. 1–4.] Ac. **2915.**

—— Úvahy přírodovědecké o Darwinově theorii . . . Zvláštní otisk z časopisu " Osvěta " 1877. pp. 60. *v Praze*, 1877. 8°. **7006.** f. **8.** (1.)

—— Vyvinování se rostlinstva s ohledem na Darwinovu theorii. pp. 48. *v Praze*, 1869. 8°. [*Společnost Wlastenského Museum w Čechach. Živa.* pt. 1.] Ac. **800**/6.

—— Zur Kritik der Ansichten von der Fruchtschuppe der Abietineen. Nebst einem morphologischen Excurse über die weiblichen Blüthen der Coniferen . . . Mit einer Tafel, *etc.* pp. 62. *Prag*, 1882. 4°. [*Abhandlungen der Königlich-Böhmischen Gesellschaft der Wissenschaften.* Sechste Folge. Bd. 11. B. no. 6.] Ac. **801.**

ČELAKOWSKÁ (ANTONINA) *See* RAJSKÁ, afterwards ČELAKOVSKÁ (A. B.)

ČELAKOWSKÁ (BOHUSLAVA) *See* RAJSKÁ, afterwards ČELAKOVSKÁ (Antonina B.)

ČELAKOWSKÝ (FRANTIŠEK LADISLAV) *See* ČELAKOVSKÝ.

CELAN (PAUL)

—— Mohn und Gedächtnis. [Poems.] pp. 75. *Stuttgart*, [1952.] 8°. **Cup.500.a.13.**

CELANDER, *pseud.* [i.e. JOHANN GEORG GRESSEL.] Celanders verliebte-galante, sinn-vermischte und Grab-Gedichte. pp. 472. *Hamburg & Leipzig*, 1716. 8°. **11525.** df. **22.**

CELANDER (HILDING) *See* CELANDER (K. H.)

CELANDER (KARL HILDING)

—— *See* HOLTSMARK (A. E.) Ordforrådet i de eldste norske håndskrifter . . . På grunnlag av materiale samlet av H. Celander, *etc.* 1955. 8°. **12974.** i. **25.**

—— Förkristen jul enligt norröna källor. Mit einer deutschen Zusammenfassung. pp. 91. *Stockholm*, 1955. 8°. [*Göteborgs universitetets årsskrift.* vol. 61. no. 3.] Ac. **2651.** d.

—— Lokes mytiska ursprung. 1911. *See* UPSALA.—*Regia Academia Upsaliensis.* Upsala Universitets årsskrift. 1910. 1861, *etc.* 8°. Ac. **1075**/6.

—— Några danska och svenska julvisor, *etc.* pp. 111. *Göteborg*, 1946. 8°. [*Göteborgs kungl. Vetenskaps- och Vitterhets-Samhälles handlingar.* följd. 6. ser. A. bd. 3. no. 2.] Ac. **1063.**

—— Närkiska folkminnen från Lillkyrka ock Vinön, *etc.* pp. 91. *Stockholm*, 1922. 8°. [*Bidrag till kännedom om de svenska landsmålen ock svenskt folkliv.* bd. 16. no. 3.] P.P. **5044.** g. (1.)

—— Om övergången av ð>d i fornisländskan och fornnorskan. Akademisk avhandling, *etc.* pp. 93. *Lund*, 1906. 8°. **12972.** n. **19.**

—— Stjärngossarna, deras visor och julspel . . . With an English summary. pp. 500. *Stockholm*, 1950. 8°. [*Nordiska Museets handlingar.* no. 38.] W.P. **5376/38.**

CELANDER (TH.) and PALM (B.) *Lexicographer.*

—— Liliput Dictionary : English-Swedish. pp. 730. [*Schmidt & Gunther: Frankfurt-on-Main*, 1955.] 64°. Cup. **550.** a. **16.** *Liliput Dictionary.* no. 81.

—— Liliput-ordbok : svensk-engelsk. pp. 633. *Schmidt & Gunther: Frankfurt/Main*, [1955.] 64°. Cup. **550.** a. **15.** *Liliput ordbok.* no. 80.

CELANI (ENRICO) *See* ARAGONA (T. d') Le Rime di Tullia d'Aragona . . . Edite a cura e studio di E. Celani. 1891. 8°. **12226.** de. **15.** (3.)

—— *See* BELLATRECCIA (B.) Manifestazioni spiritiste intorno al cattolicismo di Dante nelle sue relazioni con Dio e con la civile società. Per cura e con prefazione di E. Celani. 1912. 8°. **011420.** a. **1/56.**

—— *See* BURCHARDUS (J.) *Bishop of Città Castellana and Orte.* Johannis Burckardi liber notarum . . . A cura di E. Celani. 1906, *etc.* 8°. [*MURATORI (L. A.) Rerum italicarum scriptores, etc.* tom. 32. pt. 1.] **9168.** l.

—— *See* CERROTI (F.) Bibliografia di Roma medievale e moderna . . . accresciuta a cura di E. Celani. 1893, *etc.* 4°. **2330.** f. **19.**

—— *See* LUBIN (A.) Abbatiarum Italiae brevis notitia . . . Additiones . . . nunc primum editae curante Henrico Celani. 1895. 8°. **4571.** g. **2.**

—— *See* MICHELI (B.) Sonetti romaneschi . . . Editi a cura di E. Celani. 1889. 8°. **11429.** g. **10.**

—— *See* MURATORI (L. A.) Lettere inedite . . . al P. G. Bianchini, per E. Celani. 1890. 8°. [*Atti e memorie delle Reali Deputazioni di Storia Patria per le Provincie Modenesi.* ser. 3. vol. 5.] Ac. **6520.**

CELANI (ENRICO)

—— See PANVINIO (O.) "De gente Sabella", manoscritto inedito. [Edited by E. Celani.] 1891, etc. 4º. [Studi dell'Accademia di Conferenze Storico-Giuridiche. anno 12, 13.] Ac. **6541.**

—— See PERIODICAL PUBLICATIONS.—Spalato. Bullettino di archeologia e storia dalmata, etc. (Indice generale compilato da E. Celani.) 1878, etc. 8º. P.P. **1897. h.**

—— See ROME.—The City.—Accademia di Conferenze Storico-Giuridiche. Studi e documenti, etc. (Indice generale compilato da E. Celani. Volume I–XXI—anno 1880–1900.) 1880, etc. 4º. Ac. **6541.**

—— See TASSO (Torquato) [Postille alla Divina Commedia.] Postille alla Divina Commedia edite . . . da E. Celani, etc. 1895. 8º. **011420. a. 1/16.**

—— Una Pagina di feudalismo. La signoria dei Peretti-Savelli-Sforza-Cesarini sulla contea di Celano e baronia di Pescina, 1591–1806. pp. vi. 199. Città di Castello, 1893. 8º. **10132. g. 21.**

—— R. Biblioteca Angelica. [By E. Celani, continued by S. Vitale.] 1915, 34. 8º. [Inventari dei manoscritti delle biblioteche d'Italia. vol. 22, 56.] See ROME.—The City.—Bibliotheca Angelica. **011900. dd. 20.**

CELANI (PIETRO) Saggio di fisico-matematica, etc. pp. 16. Roma, [1845?] 8º. **898. d. 5. (17.)**

CELANO (CARLO) See NAVARRA (T.) Un Oscuro imitatore di Lope de Vega: Carlo Celano, etc. 1919. 8º. **011851. cc. 21.**

—— Degli avanzi delle poste. pp. 335. G. Zini: Venetia' 1677. 12º. **721. b. 33**

—— Notitie del bello, dell'antico e del curioso della città di Napoli . . . divise in diece giornate, etc. [With a prefatory epistle by F. A. Sabbatini d'Anfora.] 10 pt. G. Raillard: Napoli, 1692. 12º. **574. a. 12–17.**

—— [Another copy.] C. **47. b. 2.** With the arms of Pope Innocent XII. stamped on the binding. In this copy the "Giornata decima" differs from the preceding in the titlepage and list of "Errori."

—— Delle notizie del bello dell'antico e del curioso della citta di Napoli . . . In questa terza edizione corrette, ed accresciute. Giornata quinta (–decima). 6 pt. Napoli, 1759. 12º. **010136. aa. 26.**

—— Quarta edizione, in cui si è aggiunto tutto ciò, che si è di nuovo fatto in Napoli . . . con un ristretto della vita dell'autore. [With a portrait.] 5 vol. Napoli, 1792. 8º. **10131. bbb. 40.**

CELANO (TOMMASO DA) See THOMAS, de Celano.

CÉLAPHON, Frère, pseud. See B****, J.B., Mr., D.M. La Maçonnerie mesmérienne, ou les leçons prononcées par Fr. Mocet . . . Célaphon, etc. 1784. 8º. **4783. c. 2.**

CELARAIN (JUAN PABLO) Itinerarios y leguarios que proceden de Mérida, capital del Estado de Yucatan á las vigias de su parte litoral, etc. [By J. P. Celarain and others.] pp. 32. Merida, 1851. 12º. **10480. aa. 15.**

CELARIÉ (HENRIETTE)

—— Alice Ozy, dame de beauté, dame galante. In: Les Œuvres libres. Nouvelle série. no. 85. pp. 175–210. 1953. 8º. **12208. ee. 310.**

CELARIÉ (HENRIETTE)

—— Celle qui fut presque impératrice. Marguerite Bellanger. In: Les Œuvres libres. Nouvelle série. no. 108. mai 1955. pp. 234–258. 1955. 8º. **12208. ee. 333.**

—— En esclavage. Journal de deux déportées. Publié par Henriette Celarié. pp. 342. Paris, Barcelone, [1918.] 8º. **09082. d. 24.**

—— Slaves of the Huns. The experiences of two girls of Lille . . . Translated from the French by Maude M. C. Ffoulkes. pp. vi. 243. Cassell & Co.: London, [1918.] 8º. **9083. aa. 42.**

—— Éthiopie, xxᵉ siècle. pp. 252. [Paris,] 1934. 8º. **10094. a. 33.**

—— Une Lionne: Cora Pearl, etc. 1947. See PERIODICAL PUBLICATIONS.—Paris. Les Œuvres libres, etc. Nouvelle série. no. 19. 1921, etc. 8º. **12208. ee. 245.**

—— Le Martyre de Lille. pp. 257. Paris, Barcelone, 1919. 8º. **09083. a. 92.**

The date on the wrapper is 1920.

—— Un Mois au Maroc. Ouvrage illustré de quarante-huit gravures et de quatre cartes. pp. 254. Paris, [1923.] 8º. **010097. de. 51.**

—— Un Mois en Algérie et en Tunisie. Ouvrage illustré de quarante et une gravures et de seize cartes. pp. 247. Paris, [1924.] 8º. **010097. de. 50.**

—— Un Mois en Corse. Ouvrage illustré, etc. pp. 231. Paris, [1920.] 8º. **010171. e. 45.**

—— Monique la romanesque. pp. 262. Paris, 1921. 8º. **012547. b. 33.**

—— La Prise d'Alger. pp. 127. [Paris, 1929.] 8º. [Récits d'autrefois.] **012202.c.2/12.**

—— Promenades en Indochine. pp. 282. Paris, [1937.] 8º. **010056. a. 57.**

—— Sous les obus. Souvenirs d'une jeune lorraine, 1914–1915. Illustrations de L. Comte. pp. 236. Paris, [1916.] 8º. **9082. h. 19.**

—— La Vie vagabonde et tumultueuse de Lola Montès. In: Les Œuvres libres. Nouvelle série. no. 51. pp. 177–208. 1950. 8º. **12208. ee. 276.**

CELATA, pseud. [i.e. MARY ANN OWEN.] The Early Blossom; or the Young inquirer . . . By Celata. [In verse.] pp. xv. 199. Houlston & Stoneman: London, 1854. 12º. **11649. c. 28.**

CELATUS, pseud [i.e. OWEN OWEN.] The Modern Theme of Education, the People's Right and a Nation's Glory: being the substance of a lecture on the British system. By Celatus. pp. xvi. 176. John Johnstone: London, 1847. 16º. **8305. a. 8.**

—— [A reissue.] Houlston & Stoneman: London, 1854. 8º. **8307. f. 82.**

—— The Public Pearl; or, Education the people's right and the nation's glory . . . By Celatus, etc. pp. 326. Houlston & Stoneman: London, 1854. 12º. **8307. f. 81.**

CELAURO (PIETRO) William Wordsworth. (Poeta e filosofo della letteratura inglese, 1770–1850.) [With plates, including a portrait.] pp. 189. Palermo, 1935. 8º. **11857. c. 51.**

ÇELAYA (Andrés)

—— *See* DAROCA. Historia dc la ciudad de Daroca. Dictada por un eclesiástico, en el año 1629, a ruego de A. Çelaya, para la librería manuscrita del conde de Guimerá. 1878. 8°. **10161. aa. 15.**

CELAYA (Gabriel)

—— Las Cartas boca arriba. [Poems.] pp. 86. *Madrid*, 1951. 8°. **11453. e. 30.**
Adonais. vol. 74.

CELAYA (Joannes de) Dialectice ĩtroductiones magistri Ioannis de celaya . . . cū nonnulis Magistri Ioannis ribeyro . . . additionibus recenter impresse : et per eundem sue integritati restitute. **G.L.** *Edibus L. Fardelet: Aureliacii*, [1516?] 4°. **1134. g. 36. (1.)**

—— Expositio magistri ioannis de Celaya . . . in libros Aristotelis : de generatione et corruptione : cum questionibus eiusdem. [With the text.] ff. xxxix. 1518. fol. *See* ARISTOTLE. [*De Generatione et Corruptione.—Latin.*] **8705. g. 1. (3.)**

—— Expositio magistri ioannis de Celaya . . . in octo libros phisicorum Aristotelis : cum questionibus eiusdem, scďm triplicem viam beati Thome realium et nominalium. [With the Latin version of J. Arguropoulos.] ff. cci. 1517. fol. *See* ARISTOTLE. [*Physica.—Latin.*] **8705. g. 1. (1.)**

—— Expositio magistri ioannis de Celaya . . . in quattuor libros de celo ⁊ mundo Aristotelis : cum questionibus eiusdem. [With the Latin version of J. Arguropoulos.] ff. lx. 1518. fol. *See* ARISTOTLE. [*De Coelo.—Latin.*] **8705. g. 1. (2.)**

—— Clarissimi . . . Doctoris . . . Ioannis a Celaia . . . scripta . . . in quartū volumē sentētiaⱬ [of Petrus Lombardus] . . . Textus etiam eiusdem quarti voluminis Magistri sententiarum suis locis insertus, *etc.* **G.L.** ff. cccxviii. MS. NOTES. *I. Ioffre*: [*Valencia*,] 1528. 4°. **3837. bb. 55.**

—— Clarissimi . . . Doctoris . . . Ioannis a Celaya . . . scripta . . . ſm triplicē viã diui Thome Realiū & Nominaliū in primū (scďȝ) lĩbrū Snīarū [of Petrus Lombardus]. [With the text.] **G.L.** 2 tom. *Cura G. Costilla:* [*Valencia*,] 1531. 4°. **C. 63. c. 31.**

—— Clarissimi . . . doctoris Parisiēsis magistri Ioannis a Celaia Valentini scripta . . . intertium volumē sententiarū [of Peter Lombard]. Quę in Valentino gymnasio die veneris decimo Kalēdas Nouembris . . . Inchoata sunt. Anno a Christo nato 1526, *etc.* **G.L.** ff. cclxiiii. *Cura Ioannis Ioffredi:* [*Valencia*,] 1530. 4°. **1477. bb. 42.**

CELAYA (José María de) Breve reseña histórica del Convento-colegio de Santo Domingo de Ocaña y de los hijos ilustres del mismo. [With plates.] pp. 105. *Madrid*, [1926.] 8°. **04782. eee. 17.**

CELA Y TRULOCK (Camilo José)

—— Ávila. [With plates.] pp. 24. *Barcelona*, [1952.] 8°. **10163. e. 5.**

—— Baraja de invenciones. pp. 256. *Valencia*, 1953. 8°. **12362. b. 2.**
Part of the series " Prosistas contemporáneos."

—— Café de artistas. pp. 64. [*Madrid*, 1953.] 8°. [*La Novela del sábado.* año 1. no. 6.] **P.P. 4074. dcd.**

—— Caminos inciertos.
1. La Colmena. pp. 252. 1951. **W.P. B. 271/1.**

Buenos Aires, 1951– . 8°. **W.P. B. 271.**
Part of a series called " Grandes novelistas."

CELA Y TRULOCK (Camilo José)

—— [La Colmena.] The Hive . . . With an introduction by Arturo Barea. (Translated by J. M. Cohen in consultation with A. Barea.) pp. 255. *Victor Gollancz: London*, 1953. 8°. **12492. dd. 16.**

—— Del Miño al Bidasoa. Notas de un vagabundaje. pp. 275. *Barcelona*, 1952. 8°. **010160. k. 19.**

—— Esas nubes que pasan... Segunda edición. pp. 180. *Madrid*, 1953. 8°. **12493. a. 22.**

—— La Familia de Pascual Duarte. [A novel.] (Quinta edición.) pp. 226. *Barcelona*, 1951. 8°. **12492. e. 29.**
Colección Áncora y delfín. vol. 63.

—— [La Familia de Pascual Duarte.] Pascual Duarte's Family . . . Translated . . . by John Marks. pp. vi. 128. *Eyre & Spottiswoode: London*, 1946. 8°. **12491. d. 42.**

—— El Gallego y su cuadrilla, y otros apuntes carpetovetónicos. pp. 242. *Madrid*, 1949. 8°. **10163. de. 4.**

—— Mrs. Caldwell habla con su hijo. pp. 231. *Barcelona*, 1953. 8°. **12492. de. 11.**
Colección " Áncora y delfín." vol. 83.

—— Nuevas andanzas y desventuras de Lazarillo de Tormes y Siete puntos carpetovetónicos. [With a portrait.] pp. 292. [*Madrid?* 1953.] 8°. **12492. e. 18.**
Selecciones Airon. no. 10.

—— Pabellón de Reposo. Novela. Ilustraciones de Suárez del Árbol. pp. 240. *Madrid*, 1944. 8°. **12491. aa. 24.**

—— Pisando la dudosa luz del día, *etc.* (Poemas de una adolescencia cruel.) *Barcelona*, 1945. 8°. **11452. i. 40.**

—— Siete puntos carpetovetónicos. *See supra*: Nuevas andanzas y desventuras de Lazarillo de Tormes, *etc.*

—— Timoteo, el incomprendido, *etc.* pp. 78. *Madrid*, [1952.] 8°. **12487. p. 37.**
Novelistas de hoy. vol. 6.

CELBA (Ant.) Jiráskovo padolí, Hronov, a jeho okolí. (II. změněné vydání.) pp. 39. *v Hronově*, 1924. 8°. **10201. c. 20.**

CELDONI. [For Saints of this name :] *See* CELEDONIUS.

CELE TREI CRIȘURI. *See* PERIODICAL PUBLICATIONS. —*Oradea.*

ČELE (Madikane) Songs and Tales of the Zulu Tribe . . . Recorded from the singing and the sayings of Madikane Čele. *See* SIMANGO (C. K.) Songs and Tales from the Dark Continent, *etc.* [1920.] 8°. **12431. v. 9.**

CELEBES. Het Muntwezen op Celebes . . . Overgedrukt uit het Makassaarsch Handels- en Advertentie-Blad, *etc. Makassar*, [1864.] 8°. **8246. bb. 9.**

ČELEBIJA (Čatib) *See* MUŠTAFĀ IBN 'ABD ALLĀH, called KATIB CHELEBĪ, *etc.*

CELEBRATED CRIME SERIES. Celebrated Crime Series. (Mellifont Celebrated Crime Series.) 28 . Vol. *Mellifont Press: London*, [1936–38.] 8°. **6059. aaa. 9.**

CELEBRATION BULLETIN. *See* PERIODICAL PUBLICATIONS.—*London.*

CELEBRINO (EUSTACHIO) *See* TAGLIENTE (G. A.) Lo presento libro insegna la vera arte . . . delo excellēte scriuere, *etc.* (Intagliato per E. Cellebrino.) 1525. 4°.
[MISSING.]

—— Il Modo di imparare di scrivere lettera Merchantescha, *etc.* [A facsimile.] *See* MORISON (Stanley) Eustachio Celebrino da Udene, *etc.* 1929. 8°. **Cup.510.ee.12.**

—— Nouella de vno Prete, *etc.* [In verse.]
Stampata per F. Bindoni & M. Pasini : Venetia, 1535. 8°.
G. **10651.**

—— Opera noua che insegna apparechiar vna mensa a vno cōuito : ꝛ etiã a tagliar in tauola de ogni sorte carne ꝛ dar li cibi secondo lordine che vsa no gli scalchi p far honore a forestieri. Intitulata Refetorio, *etc.* *Cesena,* [1530 ?] 8°. [MISSING.]

—— Opera noua piaceuole laquale insegna di far varie cōpositione odorifere per adornar ciascuna donna intitulata Venusta. ff. 14. [*Venice ?*] 1525. 8°.
[MISSING.]

—— [Another edition.] ff. 15. *F. Bindoni & M. Pasini : Vinegia,* 1550. 8°. **1168.** e. 8. (1.)

—— Regimeno mirabile : ꝛ verissimo a conseruar la sanita in tempo di peste con li remedij necessarij : Da piu valenti medici experimentati : ꝛ per Eustachio celebrino da Udene insieme racolti in vn volume intitulato. Optimo remedio de sanita. *Ad instantia de H. Soncino : Cẹsena,* 1527. 8°. **7561.** a. **32.**

—— Il Successo de tutti li fatti che fece il Duca di Borbon con la presa di Roma. [By E. Celebrino.] [1528 ?] 8°. *See* CHARLES, *Duke o Bourbon, Constable of France.*
239. b. **11.**

—— [Another edition.] 1535. 8°. **1071.** g. **22.** (8.)

—— [Another edition.] *Stampata per G. A. Vauassore & Florio fratello : Vinegia,* 1542. 8°. G. **10653.**

—— [Another edition.] La Presa di Roma. *See* CAMOLLIA. La Guerra di Camollia, *etc.* 1886. 8°. **12226.** de. **6.** (1.)

CÉLÉBRITÉS. Célébrités catholiques. *See* CATHOLIC CELEBRITIES.

—— Célébrités contemporaines. 42 pt. *Paris,* 1882–88. 8°.
10658. c. **20-23.**

—— Célébrités lyonnaises. *See* LYONESE CELEBRITIES.

—— Célébrités révolutionnaires. Les régicides. Par Ch. de B * * *. 1865. 8°. *See* B * * * (Ch. de)
10661. bbb. **34.**

CELEBRITIES. Celebrities of the Day. *See* PERIODICAL PUBLICATIONS.—*London.*

—— Celebrities of the Stage. [Portraits with accompanying text.] no. 1. pp. 62. *Louis & Bernard : Manchester,* [1925.] 8°. **11796.** bb. **34.**
No more published.

—— Historical Celebrities. Oliver Cromwell, George Washington, the Emperor Napoleon, Duke of Wellington. [Reprinted from " Chambers's Papers for the People."] pp. 288. *W. & R. Chambers : London & Edinburgh,* 1887. 8°. **10601.** bbb. **9.**

—— Literary Celebrities. Biographies of Wordsworth— Campbell—Moore—Jeffrey. [Reprinted from " Chambers's Papers for the People."] pp. 288.
W. & R. Chambers : London & Edinburgh, 1887. 8°.
10803. bb. **7.**

ČELEDA (JAROSLAV)

—— *See* GABRIEL (J.) František Benda . . . Z obsáhlé monografie Fr. Bendy od J. Čeledy vyňal a upravil J. Gabriel. [1926.] 8°. **10796.** a. **27.**

—— Josef Mysliveček. Tvůrce pražského nářečí hudebního rokoka tereziánského. [With illustrations, including portraits.] pp. 285. *v Praze,* 1946. 8ᶜ **7900.** c. **32.**

—— Smetanův druh sděluje. Život a dílo Josefa Srba-Debrnova, *etc.* [With an edition of J. Srb's " Paměti," and portraits.] pp. 230. *Praha,* 1945. 8°.
10795. pp. **35.**

CELEDON (RAFAEL) Gramática, catecismo i vocabulario de la lengua Goajira, *etc.* pp. 52. iv. 179. *Paris,* 1878. 8°. [*Coleccion linguística americana.* tom. 5.]
12907. dd. **17.**

—— Gramática de la lengua Kŏggaba, con vocabularios y catecismos. pp. xxxiv. 129. *Paris,* 1886. 8°. [*Coleccion linguística americana.* tom. 10.] **12907.** dd. **17.**

CELEDONIUS, *Saint. See* ABAD (J. I.) Historia dels sants martyrs Hermenter y Celdoni, *etc.* [1800 ?] 8°.
4827. a. **7.**

CELEJOWICZ (MATHIAS PAULUS) Fastigium tiarati honoris excelsum . . . in magno meritorum herede principe . . . Georgio Albrachto Comite à Denhoff . . . Episcopo Cracoviensi . . . assurgens ; dum auspicato ingressu, Cracoviam Sarmatiæ & Episcopatûs Cracoviensis primariam sedem . . . antistes ingrederetur, *etc.* *Cracoviæ,* [1701.] fol. **12301.** m. **9.**

CELEN (VITAL)

—— *See* SWAEN (M. de) Werken . . . Uitgegeven door Dr. V. Celen, *etc.* 1928, *etc.* 8°. **20001.** b. **38.**

—— *See* WALSCHAP (A.) Het Letterkundig werk van Alfons Walschap . . . Ingeleid en uitgegeven door V. Celen, *etc.* 1952. 8°. **10099.g.7/7.**

CELENIO (INARCO) *pseud.* [i.e. LEANDRO FERNÁNDEZ DE MORATIN.] *See also* FERNÁNDEZ DE MORATIN (L.)

—— *See* B., D. C. C. T. D. D. U. D. F. D. Exámen de la tragedia intitulada Hamlet . . . traducida al castellano por I. Celenio, *etc.* 1800. 8°. **11765.** b. **31.**

—— *See* MOLIÈRE (J.B.P.*de*) [*Le Médecin malg.. lui.—Spanish.*] El Medico á Palos, comedia . . . imitada por I. C. [i.e. I. Celenio], *etc.* 1815. 4°.
T. **1736.** (23.)

—— —— 1817. 4°. **1342.** e. **12.** (1.)

—— —— 1820. 8°. **243.** l. **4.**

—— —— 1863. 4°. **2298.** i. **2.**

—— *See* SHAKESPEARE (W.) [*Hamlet.—Spanish.*] Hamlet. Tragedia . . . traducida . . . por I. Celenio, *etc.* 1798. 4°. **840.** f. **10.**

—— El Baron. Comedia en dos actos, en verso. pp. 134. *Madrid,* 1803. 8°. **11728.** de. **17.**

—— El Baron. Comedia en dos actos, en verso. pp. 34. *Madrid,* 1817. 4°. **1342.** e. **6.** (53.)

—— The Baron : a comedy in two acts, translated . . . by Fanny Holcroft. 1805. *See* PERIODICAL PUBLICATIONS. —*London.* The Theatrical Recorder, *etc.* vol. 2. 1805, *etc.* 8°. [MISSING.]

CELENIO (INARCO) *pseud.* [i.e. LEANDRO FERNÁNDEZ DE MORATIN.]

—— La Comedia nueva. Comedia en dos actos, en prosa. pp. 128. **L.P.** *Parma*, 1796. 8⁰.   **11726.** i. **7.**

—— La Mogigata. Comedia en tres actos, en verso. pp. 40. *Madrid*, 1817. 4⁰.   **1342.** e. **6.** (52.)

—— El Si de las Niñas. Comedia en tres actos, *etc.* pp. 36. *Madrid*, 1817. 4⁰.   **1342.** e. **6.** (51.)

—— La Sombra de Nelson. [A poem.] pp. 8.   *Madrid*, 1805. 8⁰.   **11450.** bbb. **32.**

—— El Viejo y la Niña. Comedia en tres actos, en verso. pp. 36. [*Madrid*, 1817.] 4⁰.   **1342.** e. **6.** (50.)

CELENTANO (BERNARDO) *See* SETTEMBRINI (L.) Il Tasso dipinto da B. Celentano. 1864. 8⁰.   [MISSING.]

CELENTANO (LUIGI) Intorno all'arte del cantare in Italia nel secolo decimonono. pp. 47. *Napoli*, 1867. 8⁰.   [MISSING.]

CELENTANO (VINCENZO) Per la reale amministrazione di beneficenza di Capitanata contro lo appaltatore e garanti della edificazione dell'Orfanotrofio Maria Cristina in Foggia e gl'ingegneri direttori dell'opera. Consiglio d'intendenza. pp. 67. *Foggia*, 1857. 4⁰. **8276.** i. **6.** (3.)

CELENZA (GIULIA) *See* SHAKESPEARE (William) [*A Midsummer Night's Dream.—English and Italian.*] Sogno d'una notte d'estate. Versione . . . di G. Celenza . . . Un profilo di G. Celenza di Mario Praz. 1934. 8⁰.   **11767.** a. **28.**

CELER (LYSIPONIUS) *pseud.* [i.e. JOANNES GROENEVELT.] The Late Censors deservedly Censured; and their spurious litter of libels against Dr. Greenfield [i.e. Groenevelt] and others, justly expos'd to contempt: by the following answer to all, but especially the last, intituled, A Reply to the Reasons against the Censors of the College of Physicians &c. . . . By Lysiponius Celer. pp. 28. *Printed for the Author; London*, 1698. 4⁰.   **550.** b. **5.**

CÉLÉRIER (JEAN)

—— Maroc . . . Deuxième édition, revue et augmentée. [With maps and plates.] pp. 196. *Paris*, 1954. 8⁰.   **010093.** de. **85.**

    Part of the series " L'Union franç⸗se."

CÉLÉRIER (LÉON M.) Rapport sur les boissons fermentées, par MM. Célérier et Grosfils. pp. 100. *Paris*, 1881. 8⁰. [*Exposition Universelle de 1878. Rapports du Jury International.* Groupe 7. Classe 75.]   [MISSING.]

CÉLÉRIER (LODOÏS) Essai sur la chlorose. Thèse, *etc.* pp. 45. *Montpellier*, 1845. 4⁰.   **1182.** d. **11.** (12.)

CELERINO (M.)

—— *See* SHAW (George B.) [*Single Plays.*] [Too True to be Good.] Troppo vera per esser buona . . . Unica traduzione autorizzata di C. Castelli e M. Celerino. 1933. 8⁰.   **11783.** df. **24.**

CELESIA (   ) *Minister of the Republic of Genoa. See* F. DE LA C., *Madame de.* Mémoire de Madame de F. de la C. [i.e. Mme Falques de la Cépèdes] contre Mr. C. M. de la R. de G. [i.e. Mr. Celesia, Ministre de la République de Gènes.] 1758. 8⁰.   **1080.** k. **17.**

CELESIA (DOROTHEA) *See* VOLTAIRE (F. M. A. de) [*Tancrède.*] Almida, a tragedy. [Founded on Voltaire's " Tancrède."] By a Lady [i.e. D. Celesia], *etc.* 1771. 8⁰.   **11777.** f. **8.**

CELESIA (DOROTHEA)

—— Indolence; a poem. By the author of Almida [i.e. D. Celesia]. pp. 23. 1772. 4⁰. *See* INDOLENCE.   **840.** l. **11.** (2.)

CELESIA (EMANUELE) *See* ISNARDI (L.) Storia della Università di Genova . . . fino al 1773. (Continuata fino a' dì nostri per E. Celesia.) 1861, *etc.* 8⁰.   **8355.** dd. **37.**

—— Valdimagra.—Le sei giornate di Genova. 1849. *See* BROFFERIO (A.) Tradizioni italiane, *etc.* vol. 3. 1847, *etc.* 8⁰.   **12470.** g. **38.**

—— Alla generosa guardia nazionale di Genova; inno di guerra. [*Genoa*, 1848.] *s. sh.* fol.   **804.** k. **13.** (283.)

—— L'Altare e la patria. Inni. pp. 37. *Torino*, 1848. 8⁰.   **11436.** c. **50.** (5.)

—— Il Canzoniere di Emanuele Celesia. pp. 380. *Genova*, 1879. 8⁰.   **11436.** f. **5.**

—— La Congiura del conte Gianluigi Fieschi. Memorie storiche del secolo XVI, cavate da documenti originali ed inediti. pp. 328. *Genova*, 1864. 8⁰.   **9150.** d. **8.**

—— The Conspiracy of Gianluigi Fieschi, or, Genoa in the sixteenth century. Translated . . . by David H. Wheeler. [With a portrait.] pp. xxxii. 343. *Sampson Low & Co.: London*, 1866. 8⁰.   **9150.** d. **23.**

—— Dante in Liguria. pp. 74. *Genova*, 1865. 4⁰.   **11422.** g. **21.** (1.)

—— Dell'antichissimo idioma de' Liguri. pp. 107. *Genova*, 1863. 8⁰.   **12902.** ee. **7.**

—— Della rivoluzione di Genova nell'aprile del 1849 esposta nelle sue vere sorgenti. Memorie e documenti di un testimonio oculare [i.e. E. Celesia]. pp. 154. 1850. 16⁰. *See* GENOA.   **1316.** d. **1.**

—— Intelletto e amore. Racconto. pp. 178.   *Firenze*, 1846. 12⁰.   **12470.** e. **14.**

—— Linguaggio e proverbi marinareschi. pp. 173. *Genova*, 1884. 8⁰.   **12304.c.43.**

—— Nuove liriche. pp. 165. *Genova*, 1846. 8⁰.   **11436.** c. **11.**

—— Petrarca in Liguria. pp. 73. *Genova*, 1874. 8⁰.   **10631.** g. **2.**

—— Savignone e Val di Scrivia. Passeggiate apennine. pp. 138. *Genova*, 1874. 8⁰.   **10132.** b. **8.**

—— Storie genovesi del secolo XVIII. pp. xi. 256. *Genova*, 1855. 8⁰.   **1318.** g. **7.**

CELESIA (ERNESTO H.) Federalismo Argentino. Apuntes históricos, 1815–1821. Córdoba. 3 vol. *Buenos Aires*, 1932. 8⁰.   **9774.** dd. **6.**

CELESIA (G. B.) Pel dì del fausto imeneo tra la signora Angela Celesia ed il signor Rafaello Samengo. [In verse.] pp. 7. *Genova*, 1835. 8⁰.   **T. 2490.** (7.)

CELESIA (PAOLO) Della " Suberites domuncula " e della sua simbiosi coi Paguri. 1893. *See* GENOA.—*Società Ligustica di Scienze Naturali, etc.* Atti. vol. 4. 1890, *etc.* 8⁰.   **Ac. 2809.** b.

—— Sul differenziamento delle proprietà inibitorie e delle funzioni coordinatrici nella catena gangliare dei crostacei decapodi. 1897. *See* GENOA.—*Società Ligustica di Scienze Naturali, etc.* Atti. vol. 8. no. 1. 1890, *etc.* 8⁰.   **Ac. 2809.** b.

CELESIA (Pietro Geremia Michelangelo) *Cardinal.*
See Olive, *Saint.* Acta sanctæ Olivæ . . . submissa ab
. . . P. J. M. A. Cardinali Celesia. 1885. 8º.
4824. de. 19. (17.)

—— Elogio del Santo Padre Pio Nono, *etc.* pp. 35.
Palermo, 1878. 8º. **4856. h. 2.**

—— Lo Spirito del cattolicismo. Considerazioni. pp. 502.
Palermo, 1875. 8º. **4061. bbb. 9.**

CELESIA (Pietro Paolo) *See* Bianchi (Agostino) Éloge
historique de Pierre Paul Celesia, *etc.* 1809. 8º.
B. 702. (10.)

CELESTA. Celesta. Romantische Tragödie . . . von E.
v. W. 1847. 8º. *See* W., E. v. **11746. e. 49.**

CELESTE. The Manœuvres of Celeste. By M. E. G.
1912. 8º. *See* G., M. E. **012623. a. 54.**

CÉLESTE (Raymond) Louis Machon . . . Nouvelles recherches sur sa vie et ses œuvres. 1600–1672. pp. 68.
Bordeaux, 1883. 8º. **11840. k. 40. (2.)**

CELESTIAL ALMANACK. *See* Ephemerides.

CELESTIAL JOURNAL. *See* Ephemerides.

CELESTIAL OBSERVATIONS. *See* Ephemerides.

CELESTIAL TELEGRAPH. *See* Ephemerides.

CELESTIALS.

—— The Celestials. *See* Glasgow.—*Trinity College.*

CELESTIN. History of Celestin with the Ass's Head.
Histoire de Célestin la tête d'âne. *Eng. & Fr.* ff. 16.
Darton & Hodge: London; Paris [printed], [1863.] 8º.
12806. f. 6.

CÉLESTIN (Claude) *See* Caelestinus (Claudius)

CELESTIN (Franjo Jurjevič) Russland seit Aufhebung
der Leibeigenschaft. pp. 388. *Laibach,* 1875. 8º.
8094. b. 2.

CELESTIN (Jack) *See* De Leon (J.) and Celestin
(J.) Line Engaged, *etc.* [1936.] 8º
11784.f.1/37.

—— *See* De Leon (J.) and Celestin (J.) The Silent Witness,
etc. [1936.] 8º. **11784.f.1/32.**

CELESTIN (Jack) and **DE LEON** (Jack)

—— The Man at Six. A detective
play in three acts. pp. 74. *New York, London,*
[1929.] 8º. [*French's Acting Edition.*] **11791. tt. 1/113.**

—— *See* De Leon (J.) The Man at Six. A story . . .
from the . . . play by J. Celestin and J. de Leon.
[1930.] 8º. **012600. h. 7.**

CÉLESTIN (L.) Méthode anglaise. Keepsake didactique,
dédié à la jeunesse, ouvrage divisé en 8 séries et 125
tableaux. Renfermant des notions curieuses et instruc-
tives sur toutes les branches des connaissances humaines.
pp. 155. *Paris,* [1858.] 12º. **12202. c. 10.**

CELESTINA. [For editions and translations of " Celestina:
tragicomedia de Calisto y Melibea ":] *See* Calisto.

—— Célestina, ou la Philosophe des Alpes. Histoire récente
. . . publiée par Mr. D. . . . . . 1789. 12º. *See* D. . . . .,
Mr. **12511. d. 12.**

—— The Delightful History of Celestina the Faire: Daughter
to the King of Thessalie . . . Done out of French into
English. pp. [244.] *A.I. for William Barley: London,*
1596. 4º. **C. 122. bb. 21.**
The last leaf is mutilated.

CELESTINE. [For editions of the play of Calisto and
Melibea bearing the title " Celestine ":] *See* Calisto.

—— Célestine, ou l'Aveugle de Pâturages (Célestine Darscott),
etc. 1838. 24º. *See* Darscott (C.) **4888. a. 19. (6.)**

—— Célestine, suivie de Jésus à Rome et de la Procession
expiatoire au Capitole. Traduit de l'allemand. Cinquième édition. Mis en vers par Leibsteinn—Suisse.
Poème héroïque en trois chants, composé par l'avocat de
Jésus de l'Académie helvétique. (Imitation du Tartuffe
de Molière.) pp. 30. *Genève,* 1866. 8º.
011483. bbb..11. (1.)

CELESTINE I., *Pope, Saint.* S. Cœlestini 1. Papæ
Epistolæ et decreta, *etc.* 1773. *See* Gallandius (A.)
Bibliotheca veterum patrum, *etc.* tom. 9. 1765, *etc.* fol.
469. h. 9.

—— Epistola . . . ad Cyrillum.—Epistola . . . ad Nestorium.
—Epistola . . . ad Theodosium.—Epistola . . . ad Cyrillum.
—Commonitorium . . . episcopis et presbyteris euntibus
ad Orientem.—Epistola ad Ephesinam Synodum.—
Epistola . . . post damnationem Nestorii ad sanctam
Synodum Ephesinam scripta.—Epistola . . . ad Theo-
dosium . . . post Synodum.—Epistola ad clerum et
plebem Constantinopoli constitutam post Synodum. *See*
Cigheri (A. M.) Sanctae matris nostrae Catholicae
Ecclesiae dogmatum et morum ex selectis veterum patrum
operibus veritas demonstrata, *etc.* tom. 4. 1791. 4º.
699. i. 2.

—— S. Cœlestini 1 Papæ Epistolæ et decreta. 1846. *See*
Migne (J. P.) Patrologiæ cursus completus, *etc.* tom. 50.
1844, *etc.* 4º. **2000. b.**

—— Coelestini Epistolae selectae. 1872. *See* Hurter (H.
von) Sanctorum patrum opuscula selecta, *etc.* vol. 18.
1874, *etc.* 16º. **3622. a. 1/18.**

—— Commonitorium episcopis et presbyteris euntibus ad
Orientem. *See* Lupus (C.) Ad Ephesinum Concilium
variorum patrum epistolæ, *etc.* 1682. 4º. **1124. g. 24.**

—— Caelestini . . . De gratia Dei, epistola ad Galliarum
episcopos. *See* Cigheri (A. M.) Sanctae matris nostrae
Catholicae Ecclesiae dogmatum et morum ex selectis
veterum patrum operibus veritas demonstrata, *etc.* tom. 8.
1791. 4º. **699. i. 4.**

—— A Discourse on the Archangel Gabriel. *Coptic & Eng.*
See Budge (*Sir* Ernest A. T. W.) *Keeper of Egyptian and
Assyrian Antiquities, British Museum.* Miscellaneous
Coptic Texts in the Dialect of Upper Egypt, *etc.* 1915. 8º.
07705.aa.25.

CELESTINE II., *Pope* [Guido di Castello]. *See* Certini
(A.) Vita di Papa Celestino Secondo, *etc.* 1716. 8º.
658. a. 27.

—— *See* Foglietti (R.) Per le origini di Macerata. Un
Papa maceratese [Celestine II.]. 1905. 8º.
10151. dd. 16.

—— Epistolæ Cœlestini II. Papæ. 1808. *See* Bouquet (M.)
Recueil des historiens des Gaules, *etc.* tom. 15.
1738, *etc.* fol. **Circ.8–9.b. .**

CELESTINE III., *Pope* [Giacinto Bobo]. Epistolæ
Cœlestini III. Papæ. 1833. *See* Bouquet (M.) Recueil
des historiens des Gaules, *etc.* tom. 19. 1738, *etc.* fol.
Circ.8–9.b.

—— Coelestini III. Pontificis Romani Epistolæ et privi-
legia, *etc.* 1855. *See* Migne (J. P.) Patrologiæ cursus
completus, *etc.* tom. 206. 1844, *etc.* 4º. **2001. a.**

CELESTINE IV., *Pope* [GOFFREDO CASTIGLIONE]. *See*
KOEHLER (Carl) *Dr. phil.* Das Verhältnis Kaiser
Friedrichs II. zu den Päpsten seiner Zeit [Innocent III.,
Celestine IV.], *etc.* 1888. 8º. [*Untersuchungen zur deut-
schen Staats- und Rechtsgeschichte.* no. 24.] [MISSING.]

CELESTINE V., *Pope, Saint* [PIETRO DI MORRONE]. *See*
PETER CELESTINE.

CÉLESTINE, *pseud.* [i.e. CATHERINA FELICIA VAN REES.]
Open brief aan hare vrouwelijke landgenooten, van
Celestine. [Advocating the emancipation of women.]
pp. 16. *Arnhem*, 1870. 8º.   **8415. df. 20. (2.)**

CELESTINE-EDWARDS (S. J.) *See* EDWARDS.

CELESTINI (C.) *See* SODINI (A.) L'Anima umbra . . .
Con tredici vedute . . . riprodotte da acqueforti di C.
Celestini. [1923.] 4º.   **L.R. 28. b. 18.**

CELESTINO. [For Saints and Popes of this name :] *See*
CELESTINE.

CELESTINO, *an Augustinian. See* AGUDO (G.) and
CELESTINO, *an Augustinian.* Complemento de los documentos del folleto de 14 de noviembre de . . . 1863,
sobre cuestiones de curatos. 1863. 8º.   **4183. h. 6. (2.)**

—— *See* AGUDO (G.) and CELESTINO, *an Augustinian.* Im-
portantisima cuestion que puede afectar gravemente á la
existencia de las Islas Filipinas. 1863. fol.
                               4183. h. 6. (1.)

CELESTINO [COLLEONI], *F. Sacerdote Capuccino.* Historia
quadripartita di Bergomo et suo territorio . . . da diuersi
auttori stampati, e manuscritti, raccolta per F. Celestino.
2 pt. *V. Ventura: Bergomo, Brescia*, 1617, 18. 4º.
                               176. d. 8–10.

—— [Another copy of p. 1.]   **795. f. 1.**

CELESTINO (ANTONIO BERBEGAL Y) *See* BERBEGAL Y
CELESTINO.

CELESTINO (BARTOLOMMEO) Bartholomæi Cælestini
Elogium Gregorii Tifernatis. 1764. *See* CALOGIERÀ (A.)
Nuova raccolta d'opuscoli scientifici, *etc.* tom. 11.
1755, *etc.* 12º.   **247. a. 11.**

CELESTINO SOARES (JOSÉ AUGUSTO) *See* BRAZ DE
OLIVEIRA (J.) Modelos de Navios existentes na Escola
Naval . . . Apontamentos para um catalogo . . . Tra-
ducção franceza de J. A. Celestino Soares. 1896. fol.
                               8808. h. 29.

CELESTINUS. [For Saints and Popes of this name :]
See CELESTINE.

CELESTINUS, *Monasterii Verulamiensis Monachus. See*
PRIAPIC POEM. Auctoris ignoti carmen priapeium, a
Celestino quodam, Monasterii Verulamiensis monacho,
notis opisthographis antiquitus explanatum . . . in lucem
edidit A.B.C. [The text of an unpublished ballad attributed to W. M. Thackeray, with a Latin translation by
W. C. A. Ker.] 1896. 8º.   **C. 57. e. 67.**

CELEUSMA. Celeusma, seu Clamor, ad theologos Hier-
archiæ Anglicanæ . . . Per quem justâ & sanctâ indigna-
tione permoventur, excitanturꝗ ad sociandas vires &
jungendas dextras, cum patribus abeuntibus ab eis in
disciplina, *etc.* [By William Jenkyn.] pp. 111.
Londini, 1679. 4º.   **T. 714. (1.)**

—— *See* GROVE (Robert) *Bishop of Chichester.* Roberti
Grovii . . . Responsio ad nuperum libellum qui
inscribitur Celeusma, *etc.* 1680. 4º.   **T. 714. (2.)**

CELEUSMA.

—— *See* GROVE (Robert) *Bishop of Chichester.* Re-
futatio cujusdam scripti hoc insigniti lemmate, Roberti
Grovii Responsio ad . . . libellum qui inscribitur,
Celeusma . . . Per authorem Celeusmatis edita.
1681. 4º.   **T. 714. (3.)**

—— *See* GROVE (Robert) *Bishop of Chichester.* Roberti
Grovii . . . Defensio suæ responsionis ad . . .
libellum, qui inscribitur Celeusma, *etc.* 1682. 4º.
                               T. 714. (4.)

CELEYRON (HENRY) Faculté de Droit de Paris. Thèse
pour la licence. (Jus romanum. De exercitoria actione,
etc.—Droit français . . . Du louage, *etc.*) pp. 67. *Paris*,
1858. 8º.   **5406. aaa. 5. (11.)**

CELHABE (B.) Cantua [beginning : Entꝗunic espantutan
Indien berria]. *Basque, dialect of Labourd. See* URRUGNE.
Urruñaco phestetan lehen precioa eraman duen cantua,
etc. [1855 ?] 4º.   **885. l. 2.**

CELI (ALFONSO) Monografia storica su Camico in Agrigento.
pp. viii. 28. *Girgenti*, 1900. 8º.   **9006. e. 23. (3.)**

—— Sulla probabile ubicazione della piscina degli antichi
Agrigentini. Osservazioni alle note del dottor Giulio
Schubring [in his "Historische Topographie von
Akragas"]. pp. 18. *Girgenti*, 1889. 8º.   [MISSING.]

CELI (ETTORE) L'Abbicì dell'agricoltore. Principii dell'
arte agraria . . . Seconda edizione . . . accresciuta, *etc.*
pp. viii. 484. *Modena*, 1865. 8º.   **7077. bbb. 12.**

CELI (ETTORE) and **ZANELLI** (ANTONIO)

——   Regno d'Italia. Le lane
italiane alla Esposizione di Parigi nel 1878. pp. 43.
Roma, 1878. 8º.   [MISSING.]

CELI (GIUSEPPE) Ricerche sulla biologia e filogenesi del
fico ed inquadramento delle relative razze italiane meri-
dionali—Ficus carica L. Memoria. 1908. *See* NAPLES.
—*Reale Istituto d'Incoraggiamento di Napoli.* Atti, *etc.*
ser. 6. vol. 59. 1888, *etc.* 8º.   **Ac. 2815.**

CELIA. Celia in Search of a Husband. By a modern
antique [i.e. Miss Byron ?]. 2 vol. *A. K. Newman & Co.:
London*, 1809. 8º.   **1152. f. 8.**

—— Second edition. 2 vol.   *A. K. Newman & Co.:
London*, 1809. 8º.   **12612. ff. 7.**

—— Celia ; or, the Force of example. pp. 100. *American
Sunday School Union: Philadelphia*, [1886.] 12º.
                               12808. eee. 6.

—— Celia Suited, or the Rival heiresses ; comprising new
sketches of modern female habits and manners, religion
and morals. ⫝ 2 vol. *H. Colburn: London*, 1810. 8º.
       [By Jane Best.]   **12612. ff. 6.**

—— Celia's Answer to the Lover's Complaint. [A ballad.]
For Charles Barnet: [*London*, 1700 ?] *s. sh.* fol.
                               C. 39. k. 6. (32.)

—— Celia's Complaint for the Loss of her Virginity. [A
song.] ℬ.ℒ.   *For Charles Passenger: London*,
[1695 ?] *s. sh. obl.* fol.   **Rox. II. 50.**

—— Celia's New Garland : compos'd of eight new songs, *etc.*
pp. 19. *Edw. Midwinter: London*, [1728 ?] 12º.
                               11621. b. 4. (1.)

—— Celia's Triumph, or, Venus dethron'd, *etc.* [A ballad.]
ℬ.ℒ. *For P. Brooksby:* [*London*, 1678 ?] *s. sh. obl.* fol.
                               C. 22. f. 6. (35.)

CELIA.

—— The Enchanted Lover; or, Celia triumphant . . . Conquered by Love enchanted Strephon sings, *etc.* [1675?] fol. *See* STREPHON. Rox. II. **139**.

—— The Happy Lover; or, Celia won by Aminta's loyalty: a new song in great request at court. [By Thomas Durfey. With the music.] *For J. Blare: London*, [1685?] *s. sh.* fol. C. **40. m. 9. (96.)**

—— Loves Triumph over Bashfulness: or, the Pleas of honour and chastity over-ruled. Being a pleasant new play-song, by way of dialogue between Celia and Strephon. 𝔅.𝔏. [*London*, 1680?] *s. sh.* fol. Rox. II. **312**.

—— Repentance too late: being fair Celia's complaint for the loss of her virginity . . . Being a pleasant new play-song. 𝔅.𝔏. *For F. Coles, etc.: London*, [1680?] *s. sh. obl.* fol. Rox. IV. **28**.

—— Romance de la Bella Celia, que adora, y su respuesta. *See* ALARCOS, *Count*. Relacion del Conde Alarcos. 1764. 4°. T. **1953. (1.)**

CELIA, *Hertogin*. Hertoginne Celia en Grave Prospero. Bly-eynde-spel. [In verse. By Theodoor Rodenburgh.] *J. Pietersz.: Amsterdam*, 1617. 4°. **11755. bb. 81. (1.)**

CELIA, *Madonna*. Lettere amorose di Madonna Celia gentildonna Romana. Scritte al suo amante. ff. 76. *Appresso A. degli Antonii: Venetia*, 1562. 8°. G. **10101**.

—— Nuouamente . . . ristampate, rauuedute & ricorrette. ff. 76. *Appresso A. Reuenoldo & B. Rubino: Vinegia*, 1565. 12°. **1084. d. 16. (2.)**

—— [Another edition.] ff. 70. *Appresso I. Simbeni: Venetia*, 1572. 8°. **246. d. 43. (1.)**

CELIA, *pseud. See* GRÉVILLE (Henry) *pseud*. Dosia . . . Translated . . . by Celia. [1881.] 8°. **12518. l. 6.**

CELIA, *pseud.* [i.e. CECYLJA MIKLASZEWSKA.] Antek. Opowiadanie przez Celią. pp. 74. *Warszawa*, 1891. 8°. **012589. i. 7. (3.)**

CÉLIANNE. Célianne, ou les Amans séduits par leurs vertus. [By F. A. Benoit.] pp. 8. 126. *Paris*, 1768. 8°. **012551. df. 8.**

CELIANO (LIVIO) Rime. *See* LICINO (G. B.) Rime di diuersi celebri poeti dell'età nostra, *etc.* 1587. 8°. **84. b. 4.**

CELIBACY. Celibacy of Priests, Monks, and Nuns. pp. 4. *R.T.S.: London*, [1865.] 12°. **4406. g. 2. (115.)**

—— Clerical Celibacy. A plea for the wider recognition of the vocation. By a Missionary Priest of the Anglican Church. pp. 46. *Mowbray & Co.: Oxford, London*, [1891.] 8°. **4108. de. 32. (9.)**

CÉLIBAT.

—— Du célibat religieux. Rapport et discussion sur un ouvrage intitulé Nature et virginité; considérations physiologiques sur le célibat religieux, par Jean-Ennemond Dufieux. Par M. Th. Perrin, rapporteur, et MM. Diday, Brachet, Devay, Gromier et Bonnet. [c. 1855.] 8°. **7640. e. 29. (3.)**

CÉLIBATAIRE. Le Célibataire, comédie en cinq actes et en vers, *etc.* [By C. J. Dorat.] pp. 90. *Paris*, 1776. 8°. **11738. d. 35. (1.)**

—— [Another edition.] pp. 95. *Paris*, 1776. 8°. [*Recueil général des opéra bouffons.* tom. 10.] **11735. b. 2.**

CÉLIBATAIRE.

—— Réflexions philosophiques sur le plaisir; par un Célibataire [i.e. A. B. L. Grimod de Lareynière]. pp. 80. *Neufchâtel*, 1783. 8°. T. **2389. (2.)**

—— Seconde édition. pp. 80. *Neufchâtel, Paris*, 1783. 8°. **1102. e. 1.**

CELIBATE. The Sentimental Celibate. By the Husband of one Wife. pp. 89. *Faith Press: London*, 1922. 8°. **12628. ccc. 10.**

CELIBILICRIBRIFACIUS, *pseud.* Jungfer Robinsone, oder die verschmitzte Junge-Magd, worinne deroselben . . . Lebens-Wandel . . . erzehlet . . . werden . . . Vorgestellet von Celibilicribrifacio. pp. 136. *Hall in Schwaben*, [1724?] 8°. **012554. f. 28. (2.)** *Pp. 5–14 are mutilated.*

CÉLICE (LÉON) Dissertation sur les urines dans l'état pathologique. pp. 56. *Paris*, 1874. 4°. [*Collection des thèses soutenues à la Faculté de Médecine de Paris.* An 1874. tom. 4.] **7374. a. 9.**

CELICHIUS (ANDREAS) Brotmangel, oder, woher es sich verursache, das allerley Thewrung vnd Hungersnoth so gewaltiglich einreisset, *etc.* [A sermon.] *Bey J. Francken: Magdeburg*, 1581. 8°. [MISSING.]

—— Kurtze, deutliche vnd richtige Fragestücke, von der Himmelfart . . . Jesu Christi. *W. Kirchner: Magdeburg*, 1580. 4°. [MISSING.]

—— XIX Predigten von der Historia des Leidens vnd sterbens Jesu Christi. ff. 190. *H. Kraffts Erben: Wittemberg*, 1586. 4°. [MISSING.]

—— Predigt am Sonntag Esto mihi. [1866.] *See* KOCH (E. E.) Evangelische Hauskanzel, *etc.* 1866, *etc.* 8°. [MISSING.]

CELICHOWSKI (ZYGMUNT) *See* COLOMBO (C.) List K. Kolumba o odkryciu Ameryki. W polskim przekładzie ogłosił Dr. Z. Celichowski, *etc.* 1892. 8°. **9004. gg. 30. (5.)**

—— *See* KWIATKOWSKI (M.) M. Kwiatkowskiego Książeczki rozkoszne o poczciwem wychowaniu dziatek 1564 . . . Wydał Dr. Z. Celichowski. 1889. 8°. [*Bibljoteka pisarzów polskich.* no. 3.] Ac. **750/45.**

—— *See* LATIN-POLISH DICTIONARY. Słowniczek łacińsko-polski wyrazów prawa magdeburskiego z wieku XV. Przedruk . . . objaśnił Dr. Z. Celichowski. 1875. 4°. **12976. i. 27.**

—— *See* LELEWEL (J.) Korespondencya J. Lelewela z Tytusem Hr. Działyńskim. Wydał Dr. Z. Celichowski. 1884. 8°. **010910. d. 1. (1.)**

—— *See* LONDON. — IV. [*Appendix. — Miscellaneous.*] Historya prawdziwa która się stała w Landzie [i.e. London] mieście niemieckiem. 1588. Wydał Dr. Z. Celichowski. 1891. 8°. [*Bibljoteka pisarzów polskich.* no. 13.] Ac. **750/45.**

—— *See* MROWIŃSKI PŁOCZYWŁOS (J.) J. Mrowińskiego Płoczywłosa Stadło małżeńskie. 1561. Wydał Dr. Z. Celichowski. 1890. 8°. [*Bibljoteka pisarzów polskich.* no. 12.] Ac. **750/45.**

—— *See* PUSSMAN (K.) Krzysztofa Pussmana Historya barzo cudna o stworzeniu nieba i ziemi. 1551. Wydał Dr. Z. Celichowski. 1890. 8°. [*Bibljoteka pisarzów polskich.* no. 10.] Ac. **750/45.**

CELICHOWSKI (ZYGMUNT)

—— *See* SEKLUCYAN (J.) J. Seklucyana Oeconomia albo gospodarstwo. 1546. Wydał Dr. Z. Celichowski. 1890. 8°. [*Biblijoteka pisarzów polskich.* no. 9.] Ac. **750**/45.

—— *See* STANISŁAW, *of Szczodrkowice.* Stanisława ze Szczodrkowic Rozmowa pielgrzyma z gospodarzem o niektórych ceremoniach kóscielnych. 1549. Wydał Dr. Z. Celichowski. 1900. 8°. [*Biblioteka pizarzów polskich.* no. 37.] Ac. **750**/45.

—— *See* VLADISLAUS II., Jagellon, *King of Poland.* Cronica conflictus Wladislai regis Poloniae cum Cruciferis anno Christi 1410. Z rękopisu . . . wydał Dr. Z. Celichowski. 1911. 8°. **09004**. aa. **15**. (2.)

—— *See* ZAMOYSKI (W.) *Count.* Jenerał Zamoyski, 1803–1868. [His reminiscences with a connecting narrative by Z. Celichowski.] tom 1. 1803–1830. 1910. 8°. **10790**. h. **37**.

—— Przyczynki do dziejów panowania Zygmunta Starego. [Historical documents, edited by Z. Celichowski.] zesz. 1, 2. *Poznań,* 1900, 02. 8°. **9476**. i. **29**.

—— Ars Moriendi. Rozprawa bibliograficzna. [With the Latin text of the edition of 1450 and the variants from the copy in the library at Kórnik.] (Osobne odbicie z tomu XVII Rozpraw Wydziału Filologicznego Akademii Umiejętności w Krakowie.) *w Krakowie,* 1892. 8°. **011907**. i. **15**. (1.)

—— De fontibus qui ad abdicationem Joannis Casimiri et electionem Michaëlis Wisniowiecii pertinent, 1668–1669. [By Z. Celichowski.] pp. 94. 1871. 8°. *See* JOHN CASIMIR, *King of Poland.* **9476**. f. **15**.

CELIDONIO ERRANTE, *pseud. See* ERRANTE.

CELIDONIO (CARLO) Relazione della venuta e dimora in Milano . . . della Serenissima Maria Teresa Arciduchessa d'Austria . . . e del serenissimo Francesco III . . . Granduca di Toscana col serenissimo suo fratello Principe Carlo di Lorena nel mese di maggio . . . 1739, *etc.* pp. 72. *Milano,* 1739. 4°. **9930**. f. **41**.

CELIDONIO (GIUSEPPE) La Diocesi di Valva e Sulmona. 4 vol. *Casalbordino, Sulmona,* 1909–12. 8°. **4606**. f. **5**.

CÉLIE. Amour de Célie avec la [*sic*] comte Bonarelli. Nouvelle galante. pp. 238. *Cologne,* 1721. 12°. **012551**. de. **48**.

The running title reads: "Dissertation sur le double amour de Célie."

—— Celie. Nouuelle. [The privilege made out to Jean Bridou.] 1663. 8°. *See* BRIDOU (J.) **12512**. ccc. **25**.

—— Les Soirées de Célie, ou Recueil de chansons en vaudevilles et arriettes, *etc. See* EPHEMERIDES.

CELIER (ALEX.) Le Révérend père Dom Paul Piolin. [With a portrait.] pp. 192. *Laval, Paris,* [1896.] 18°. **4864**. b. **12**.

CELIER (ELIZABETH) *See* CELLIER.

CELIER (LÉONCE) *See* FRANCE.—*Chancellerie.* Recueil des documents concernant le Poitou contenus dans les registres de la Chancellerie de France. Publiés par P. Guérin (L. Celier). 1881, *etc.* 8°. [*Archives historiques du Poitou.* tom. 11, 13, 17, 19, 21, 24, 26, 29, 32, 35, 38, 41, 50, 56, e tc.] Ac. **6887**

—— *See* MANS, *Diocese of.* Catalogue des actes des évêques du Mans jusqu'à la fin du XIIIe siècle. Avec une introduction par L. Celier. 1910. 4°. **4999**. e. **41**.

CELIER (LÉONCE)

—— Les Dataires du XVe siècle et les origines de la Daterie Apostolique. [With an appendix of documents.] pp. 173. *Paris,* 1910. 8°. [*Bibliothèque des Écoles Françaises d'Athènes et de Rome.* fasc. 103.] Ac. **5206**/2.

—— Les Filles de la Charité. pp. 271. [*Paris,*] 1929. 8°. [*Les Grands Ordres Monastiques.* no. 8.] W.P. **9331**/8.

—— St. Charles Borromée, 1530–1584 . . . Deuxième édition. pp. xii. 205. *Paris,* 1912. 8°. **4826**. ee. **41**.

CÉLIÈRE (PAUL) *See* CÉLIÈRES.

CÉLIÈRES (ANDRÉ) *See* MÉRAS (E. A.) and CÉLIÈRES (A.) Contes populaires, *etc.* [1938.] 8°. W.P. **11961**/2.

—— Victor Cherbuliez. Romancier, publiciste, philosophe. [With a bibliography.] pp. 578. *Paris,* 1936. 8°. **10655**. i. **40**.

CÉLIÈRES (ÉDOUARD) Thèse pour le doctorat en médécine, *etc.* (Questions sur diverses branches des sciences médicales.) pp. 41. *Paris,* 1841. 4°. [*Collection des thèses soutenues à la Faculté de Médecine de Paris.* An 1841. tom. 3.] **7371**. c. **3**.

CÉLIÈRES (J. L.) Considérations sur le tétanos en général, et particulièrement sur le tétanos traumatique, *etc.* pp. 42. *Paris,* 1810. 4°. **1182**. h. **7**. (1.)

CÉLIÈRES (P. JOSEPH) Des tumeurs érectiles et de leur traitement. Thèse, *etc.* pp. 77. *Montpellier,* 1852. 4°. **7379**. b. **8**. (23.)

CÉLIÈRES (PAUL) Les Bêtes noires du capitaine. Comédie en quatre actes, en prose. pp. 103. *Paris,* 1874. 12°. **11739**. aaa. **6**.

—— Le Chef-d'œuvre de Papa Schmeltz. pp. 366. *Paris,* 1881. 12°. **12518**. k. **11**.

—— Contez-nous cela ! [Tales.] pp. 375. *Paris,* 1876. 12°. **12512**. cc. **9**.

—— Un Dîner de huit couverts ; charade en trois parties. pp. 22. *Paris,* 1882. 18°. **11740**. e. **15**. (3.)

—— Domino ! Comédie en un acte, en vers. pp. 60. *Paris,* 1872. 12°. **11740**. b. **5**. (3.)

—— Une Exilée. pp. 332. *Paris,* 1887 [1886]. 12°. **12491**. o. **8**.

—— Les Héroïnes du devoir, *etc.* pp. 210. *Paris,* 1886. 8°. **12491**. o. **22**.

—— Une Heure à lire. [Tales.] pp. 342. *Paris,* 1878. 12°. **12517**. f. **27**.

—— Les Mémorables aventures du docteur J. B. Quiès. Illustré de 125 dessins par F. Lix. pp. 284. *Paris,* 1886. 4°. **12513**. m. **26**.

—— The Startling Exploits of Dr. J. B. Quiès, from the French . . . By Mrs. Cashel Hoey and Mr. J. Lillie, *etc.* pp. xi. 328. *Sampson Low & Co.: London,* 1886. 8°. **12491**. p. **1**.

—— Quand il pleut . . . Vignettes, *etc.* pp. 368. *Paris,* 1883. 18°. **12518**. l. **13**.

—— Le Roman d'une mère . . . Deuxième édition. pp. 372. *Paris,* 1883. 18°. **12510**. k. **9**.

—— Le Théâtre chez soi. Le Gibier de Son Altesse : charade en trois parties. pp. 29. *Paris,* [1885.] 12°. **11740**. bb. **40**. (2.)

—— Trente-cinq ans de bail, comédie en un acte, *etc.* pp. 20. *Paris,* [1874.] 8°. **11739**. dd. **2**.

CELINDA. Celinda's Last Gasp; or, Her farewel to false Coridon. [A ballad.] 𝔅.𝔏. *For J. Deacon: London,* [1690?] *s. sh.* fol. Rox. II. 45.

CÉLINE (LOUIS FERDINAND) *pseud.* [i.e. LOUIS F DESTOUCHES.]

—— *See* HINDUS (Milton) [Crippled Giant.] L. F. Céline tel que je l'ai vu, *etc.* 1951. 8º. 10666. b. 8.

—— Bagatelles pour un massacre. [Chiefly attacking the Jews.] pp. 379. *Paris,* [1937.] 8º. 04034. k. 53.

—— Casse pipe. pp. 150. *Paris,* 1949. 8º. 12519. e. 5.

—— Entretiens avec le professeur Y. pp. 153. [*Paris,*] 1955. 8º. 12520. c. 11.

—— Féerie pour une autre fois. 2 pt.
1. Féerie pour une autre fois. pp. 327. 1952.
2. Normance. pp. 375. 1954.
[*Paris,*] 1952, 54. 8º. X. 908/826.

—— Guignol's band. Roman. pp. 314. [*Paris,*] 1952. 8º. 012551. pp. 11.

—— [Guignol's Band.] Guignol's Band . . . Translated . . . by Bernard Frechtman and Jack T. Nile. pp. 256. *Vision: London,* 1954. 8º. 12519. g. 9.

—— Mea culpa, suivi de la vie et l'œuvre de Semmelweis. pp. 124. *Paris,* [1936.] 8º. 010709. de. 42.

—— Mea Culpa and The Life and Work of Semmelweis . . . Translated by Robert Allerton Parker. pp. 175. *G. Allen & Unwin: London,* 1937. 8º. 010709. k. 3.

—— Mort à crédit. Roman. pp. 697. *Paris,* 1936. 8º. 12514. s. 25.

—— Death on the Instalment Plan. (Translated by John Marks.) pp. 587. *Chatto & Windus: London,* 1938. 8º. 012548. k. 2.

—— Voyage au bout de la nuit. Roman. pp. 623. *Paris,* 1933. 8º. 012547. ccc. 52.

—— Journey to the End of the Night. (Translated by John Marks.) pp. 543. *Chatto & Windus: London,* 1934. 8º. 12514. s. 6.

—— [Another edition.] pp. 509. *Little, Brown & Co.: Boston,* 1934. 8º. 12514. s. 5.

—— Journey to the End of the Night . . . Translated . . . by John H. P. Marks. pp. 509. *Vision: London,* 1950. 8º. 012550. m. 21.

—— Normance. *See supra*: Féerie pour une autre fois.

CELIO (ATTILIO)

—— Zur Pathologie der chronischen, stenosierenden Diverticulitis coli sog. Diverticulitistumor. Inaugural-Dissertation, *etc.* (Erschienen in " Helvetica Chirurgica Acta.") pp. 27. *Basel,* 1951. 8º. 7643. f. 12.

CELIO (GASPARE) Memoria fatta dal signor Gaspare Celio dell'habito di Christo. Delli nomi dell'artefici delle pitture, che sono in alcune chiese, facciate, e palazzi di Roma. [A photographic facsimile of the edition published by S. Bonino at Naples in 1638.] pp. 152. [1939.] 12º. L.R. 263. aa. 21.

CELIO (LODOVICO) *Rodigino. See* RICHERIUS (Ludovicus C.)

CELIO (SEBASTIAN B. DE MIER Y) *See* MIER Y CELIO.

CELIO CEGA (ANTONIO) Vittorio Alfieri. Saggio letterario, *etc. See* GORIZIA.—*Kaiserlich-Königliches Ober-Gymnasium.* Siebzehnter Jahresbericht, *etc.* [1867.] 8º. 10630. bb. 39. (10.)

CELIR (C.) Thirty Years After. pp. 96. *Hornsey Journal Printing Works: London,* 1937. 8º. [*F.P. Racing Novels.* no. 232.] 012614. aaa. 1/232.

CELIS (CAMILO DE) Escala por donde fue elevado al trono . . . Agustin Primero. pp. 4. *Puebla,* 1822. fol. 9770. k. 6. (92.)

Cropped.

CELIS (GAB.) Volkskundige kalender voor het Vlaamsche land. pp. 336. *Gent,* 1923. 8º. 12450. pp. 11.

CELIS (ISIDORO MARÍA HILARIO HOYOS Y DE LA TORRE RUBIN DE) *Marquis. See* HOYOS Y DE LA TORRE RUBIN DE CELIS.

CELIS (ISIDORO PEREZ DE) *See* PEREZ DE CELIS.

CELIS (MICHEL RUBIN DE) *See* RUBIN DE CELIS.

CELIS (PEDRO) *See* ARGUINDEGUI (J. M.) Los Militares de la provincia de Carabobo. [A reply to remarks contained in a pamphlet by General Bermudez upon the revolutionary movement in Venezuela. Signed by J. M. Arguindegui, P. Celis, and others.] pp. 12. 1826. 8º. 8180. e. 5. (3.)

CELIS (PEDRO COSSIO Y) *See* COSSIO Y CELIS.

CELIS BRICEÑO (PABLO) Elementos de Derecho Constitucional de la República. pp. 268. *Caracas,* 1939. 8º. [MISSING.]

CELISIA (DOROTHEA) *See* CELESIA.

CELISTO TEGEATICO, *pseud.* [i.e. GALEAZZO FONTANA.] *See* TEGEATICO (C.)

CELIUS (GEORGIUS HENRICUS) Cataclysmus Thuringiacus, vulgo die Thüringische Sündfluth, *etc.* Praes. G. H. Goetze. pp. 38. *Typis J. Gollneri: Jenæ,* 1677. 4º. 1054. h. 18. (14.)

—— [Another edition.] pp. 40. *Typis J. Gollneri: Jenæ,* 1690. 4º. 897. d. 6. (4.)

—— Extract aus der . . . disputatione academica de cataclysmo Thuringiaco. *See* LAGE (G. W. von der) Die vollständigen Acta der Thüringischen Sünd-Fluth des Jahres 1613. 1720. 4º. 8755. bbb. 21.

CELIUS (LUDOVICUS) *Rhodiginus. See* RICHERIUS (L. C.)

CELIUS (MICHAEL) *See* CAELIUS.

CÉLIZ (FRANCISCO) Diary of the Alarcón Expedition into Texas, 1718–1719 . . . Translated by Fritz Leo Hoffman. pp. 124. pl. x. 1935. 8º. *See* UNITED STATES OF AMERICA.—*Quivira Society.* Ac. 8534/2.

CELJE.

Druga Gimnazija v Celju.

—— Letno poročilo II. Gimnazije v Celju za šolsko leto 1951/52. Izšlo ob 500-letnici mesta Celja. pp. 48. [*Celje,*] 1952. 8º. 8356. p. 32.

—— *Družba Sv. Mohorja v Celju.* Grundriss der Volksglaubens und Volksbrauchs der Serbokroaten. Von Dr. Edmund Schneweis . . . Mit 45 Abbildungen. pp. 267. *Celje,* 1935. 8º. 20010. g. 10.

CELJE.

—— *Evangelische Andreaskirche. See* ANDREW, *Saint and Apostle.*—[*Churches and Institutions.*]—*Cilli.*—*Evangelische Andreaskirche.*

Mestni Ljudski Odbor Celje.

—— Predlog družbenega plana za leto 1953 [*etc.*] z dokumentacijo. *Celje*, 1953– . 4°.　　　P.P. **1423**. pwb.

Okrajni Ljudski Odbor Celje-Okolica.

—— Predlog družbenega plana Okrajnega ljudskega odbora Celje-okolica za leto 1953 [*etc.*] za diskusijo.　[*Celje*, 1953– .] 8°.　　　　　P.P. **1423**. pw.

Prva Gimnazija v Celju.

—— Poročilo (Letno poročilo) za šolsko leto 1951/52 [*etc.*]. *Celje*, 1952– . 8°.　　　　　P.P. **1213**. cla.

Ribarska Zadruga v Celju.

—— Pravilnik o izvrševanju ribolova Ribarska zadruge z o. j. v Celju. pp. 16. *v Celju*, [1951.] 16°.　　5759. de. **16**.

Šola za Trgovske Učence v Celju.

—— Letopis Šole za Trgovske Učence v Celju. 1951/52, *etc. Celje*, 1952– . 8°.　　　　　P.P. **2459**. xgh.

CELJE, *Counts of.*

—— 　　　　　Chronica der edlen Grafen von Cilli, *etc.* 1726. *See* HAHN (S. F.) D. Simonis Friderici Hahnii ... Collectio monumentorum, *etc.* tom. 2. 1724, *etc.* 8°.　　　　　　　　　　　123. k. **18**.

—— [Another edition.] Chronicon triplex Celejanum, seu Chronica der gefürsteten Graven von Cilly, *etc.* 1777. *See* CAESAR (A. J.) Annales ducatus Styriæ, *etc.* tom. 3. 1768, *etc.* fol.　　　　　170. i. **12**.

—— *See* KRONES VON MARCHLAND (F. X.) Die Cillier Chronik. Kritische Untersuchungen ihres Textes und Gehaltes. 1873. 8°.　[*Archiv für österreichische Geschichte*. Bd. 50.]　　　　Ac. **810**/8.

CELL.

—— The Cell. *See* CAMBRIDGE.—*University of Cambridge.*— *Colleges.*—*Selwyn College.* The Sell.

CELL (ERHARD) *See* CELLIUS (Erhardus)

CELL (GEORGE CROFT) *See* BIBLE.—*New Testament.* [*English.*] John Wesley's New Testament. Compared with the Authorized Version. With an introduction by G. C. Cell. [1938.] 8°.　　　　3048. e. **7**.

—— The Rediscovery of John Wesley. [With a portrait.] pp. xviii. 420. *H. Holt & Co.: New York*, [1935.] 8°.　　　　　　　　　　　20029. eee. **23**.

CELL (JOHANN ERHARD) *Resp. See* SCHICKARD (W.) *the Elder.* Bechinath Happeruschim, hoc est; Examinis commentationum Rabbinicarum in Mosen Prodromus, *etc.* 1624. 4°.　　　　　4033. aa. **34**.

CELL (JOHN WESLEY)

—— Analytic Geometry ... Second edition. pp. xii. 326. *John Wiley & Sons: New York; Chapman & Hall: London*, 1951. 8°.　　　　　08535. eee. **24**.

—— Engineering Problems illustrating Mathematics. A project of the Mathematics Division of the Society for the Promotion of Engineering Education. J. W. Cell, Chairman of Committee. pp. xi. 172. 1943. 8°. *See* UNITED STATES OF AMERICA.—*Society for the Promotion of Engineering Education.*—*Mathematics Division.* 　　　　　　　　　　　08535. b. **61**.

CELLA, *pseud.* [i.e. JACOBA C. A. DE VOS.] Langs verschillende paden. Een verhaal door Cella. Met een woord vooraf van F. Haverschmidt. Tweede druk.　　pp. 351. *Tiel*, [1889.] 8°.　　　　　012581. e. **4**.

CELLA MARIANA. *See* MARIAZELL.

CELLA (ALBERTO DELLA) *See* ITALY. [*Collections of Laws, etc.*] Raccolta di leggi e disposizioni relative all'esercito ed agli impiegati civili ... Compilata per cura di V. Bodrero e A. della Cella. 1867. 8°.　　5326. a. **7**.

—— Cortona antica. Notizie archeologiche, storiche ed artistiche, raccolte e pubblicate da A. della Cella. pp. 315. *Cortona*, 1900. 8°.　　　　　10131. dd. **12**.

CELLA (ANGELO DELLA) Cenno storico diretto al sig. dottore Bancalari. [On certain surgical operations.] pp. 23. *Genova*, 1839. 8°.　　　　T. **2490**. (11.)

CELLA (ANSELMUS) and CELLA (CHRISTOPHORUS) Europæ descriptio ... per A. atꝗ C. Cellæ.　Prognosticon Antonii Torquati ... ab anno MCCCCLXXX vsꝗ ad annum MDXXXVIII ... De fide et moribus Æthiopum (per Franciscum Titelmannum), *etc.　In ædibus I. Steelsij, typis I. Graphæi: Antuerpiæ*, 1535. 8°.　G. **7072**. (2.)

—— [Another edition.] *In ædibus I. Steelsii; typis I. Graphei: Antuerpiæ*, 1536. 8°.　　　　10026. a. **14**.

CELLA (ANTONIO) Tropotipo, cio è à dire Norma de costumi.　Dialogo ... fatto in versi [by A. Cella] ... e dato in luce ad instanza del signor Calimerio Cigola. pp. 78. [1591.] 8°. *See* TROPOTIPO.　11429. aa. **15**.

CELLA (CHRISTOPHORUS) *See* CELLA (A.) and CELLA (C.) Europæ descriptio, *etc.* 1535. 8°.　G. **7072**. (2.)

—— —— 1536. 8°.　　　　　10026. a. **14**.

CELLA (JACOPO DELLA) Al preclarissimo amico Giampaolo Maggi. [A eulogy of *Cristoforo Poggiali.*] pp. 15. [*Parma?* 1803.] 4°.　　　　　L.R. **233**. b. **39**.

—— Della famiglia Anguissola elogio storico. pp. 47. *Piacenza*, 1779. 8°.　　　　　9917. d. **5**.

CELLA (PAOLO DELLA) Viaggio da Tripoli di Barberia alle frontiere occidentali dell'Egitto fatto nel 1817. [With a map.] pp. 222. *Genova*, 1819. 8°.　　B. **507**. (5.)

—— Narrative of an Expedition from Tripoli in Barbary, to the Western Frontier of Egypt, in 1817, by the Bey of Tripoli ... With an appendix, containing instructions for navigating the great Syrtis. Translated ... by Anthony Aufrere. [With a map.] pp. xv. 238. *J. & A. Arch: London*, 1822. 8°.　　1047. h. **4**.

—— [Another copy.]　　　　　G. **15741**.

—— Voyage en Afrique, au royaume de Barcah et dans la Cyrénaïque ... Traduit [from P. della Cella's " Viaggio da Tripoli, *etc.*"] et augmenté ... par Adolphe Pezant. [With plates and a map.] pp. xvi. 432. 1840. 8°. *See* AFRICA.　　　　　789. b. **10**.

CELLA (SCIPIONE DELLA) Rime dell'eccellente dottore Scipione de' Signori della Cella. Raccolte doppo sua morte [by G. B. Sessa], *etc.* pp. 203. *M. T. Malatesta: Milano*, 1609. 8°.　　　　　11427. df. **12**.

—— [Another edition.] [Edited by Petronio Ruinetti.] pp. 200. *G. Recaldini: Bologna*, 1674. 12°.　　　　　　　　　　　11427. de. **39**.

CELLACH, *Saint.* Caithréim Cellaig. Edited by Kathleen Mulchrone. pp. xix. 55.　*Stationery Office: Dublin*, 1933. 8°. [*Mediaeval and Modern Irish Series*. vol. 4.]　　　　　　　　　　　Ac. **9955**. b.

CELLACHAN, *of Cashel.* Caithreim Cellachain Caisil. The victorious career of Cellachan of Cashel, or the wars between the Irishmen and the Norsemen in the middle of the 10th century. The original Irish text, edited, with translation and notes, by Alexander Bugge. pp. xix. 171. 1905. 8°. *See* OSLO.—*Norsk Historisk Kjeldeskrift—institutt.* Ac. **5561**/16.

CELLACTITE AND BRITISH ÚRALITE, LTD.
—— The Corrugated Chronicle, etc. no. 1–4. July, Aug., Oct., Dec. 1944. vol. 2. no. 1, *etc.* Nov. 1947, *etc.* *London*, 1944– . fol. & 4°. P.P. **5793.** nod.
No. 1–4 reproduced from typewriting. Not published between Dec. 1944 and Nov. 1947.

CELLADON. *See* CELADON.

CELLAI (GAETANO) *See* LEGENDRE (Adrien M.) Elementi di geometria . . . con note . . . tradotte in italiano da G. Cellai, *etc.* 1862. 8°. **08533.** df. **25.**

CELLAMARE, ANTONIO GIUDICE, *Prince of.* *See* GIUDICE.

CELLAR WORK. Cellar Work at a glance. Instructions to licensed victuallers, barmen, etc., by a Retired Licensed Victualler. pp. 24. *The Author: London*, 1896. 12°.
[MISSING.]

CELLARD (ANTONIN) De l'asphyxie laryngée dans la variole. pp. 79. *Paris*, 1874. 4°. [*Collection des thèses sontenues à la Faculté de Médecine de Paris.* An 1874. tom. 4.] **7374.** a. **9.**

CELLARD (FÉLIX) Des indications que présentent les différentes espèces de difformités du bassin dans l'accouchement, *etc.* pp. 41. *Paris,* 1843. 4°. [*Collection des thèses soutenues à la Faculté de Médecine de Paris.* An 1843. tom. 3.] **7371.** d. **13.**

CELLARIER (FÉLIX) Études sur la raison. pp. 279. *Paris*, 1889 [1888]. 8°. **8470.** bbb. **49.**

—— Rapports du relatif et de l'absolu. pp. vi. 419. *Paris*, 1890. 8°. **4375.** cc. **6.**

CELLARIER (P. M. E.) Introduction à l'étude de Guy de Chauliac. Thèse, *etc.* pp. 278. *Montpellier*, 1856. 4°. **7379.** d. **1.** (7.)

—— [Another copy, with a different titlepage.] *Montpellier*, 1856. 8°. **7321.** f. **9.**

CELLARIO (CRISTOFANO) *See* CELLARIUS (Christophorus) *the Elder.*

CELLARIO (JACOBUS) Specimen analyticum circa inflammationis elementa, dissertatio inauguralis, *etc.* pp. 28. *Ticini Regii,* [1829.] 8°. **7383*.** b. **1.** (3.)

CELLARIO (LEOPOLDO) Le Truppe alpine e la difesa delle Alpi. Idee, *etc.* pp. 36. *Torino*, 1881. 8°. **10108.** aa. **38.** (5.)

CELLARIUS, *pseud.* [i.e. SAMUEL BUTLER.] Darwin among the Machines, *etc.* [Signed: Cellarius. A cutting from "The Press" of Christchurch, N.Z.] [*Christchurch, N.Z.,* 1863.] *s. sh.* fol. **1856.** g. **14.** (36.)

CELLARIUS, *pseud.* [i.e. THOMAS WELBANK FOWLE.] A New Analogy between Revealed Religion and the Course and Constitution of Nature. By Cellarius. pp. viii. 295. *Macmillan & Co.: London*, 1881. 8°. **4018.** g. **7.**

CELLARIUS (ANDREAS) Harmonia Macrocosmica, seu Atlas universalis et novus totius universi creati cosmographiam generalem et novam exhibens, *etc.* 2 pt. *Apud J. Janssonium: Amstelodami*, 1660. fol.
Maps C. **6.** c. **2.**
With an additional titlepage, engraved.

CELLARIUS (ANDREAS)

—— [Another issue.] *Apud J. Janssonium: Amstelodami,* 1661. fol. **49.** i. **10.**

—— [Another edition of the plates.] *Amstelodami,* 1708. fol. Maps **18.** e. **5.**

—— Regni Poloniæ, Magnique Ducatus Lituaniæ, omniumque regionum juri Polonico subjectorum, novissima descriptio, *etc.* pp. 605. *Apud A. Janssonium: Amstelodami,* 1659. 12°. **572.** a. **13.**

CELLARIUS (BALTHASAR) *Praes.* *See* BORN (S. F.) Disputatio theologica de ecclesia, *etc.* 1650. 4°. **1363.** b. **6.** (6.)

—— *Praes.* *See* ENCKHUSEN (J.) Disputatio secunda de divina rerum scientia, *etc.* 1659. 4°. **700.** h. **17.** (13.)

—— *Praes.* *See* ROSA (B.) Positiones theologicæ de præcipuis fidei orthodoxæ controversiis, *etc.* 1657. 4°. **585.** c. **30.** (6.)

—— D. Balthasaris Cellarii Tabellæ physicæ . . . in usum studiosæ juventutis typis excusæ. *Impensis J. Bielkii; excudebat J. J. Bauhoferus: Jenæ,* 1670. fol. **536.** l. **3.**

CELLARIUS (CASPAR) Disputatio inauguralis de negligentia, *etc.* pp. 48. *J. H. Schönnerstædt: Altdorphj,* [1672.] 4°. **897.** d. **4.** (57.)

CELLARIUS (CHRISTIANUS) De incendio excitato in ciuitate Delpht . . . carmen. [With other poems.] *G. Spyridipœus: Antuerpiæ,* 1536. 8°. **11409.** e. **14.**

—— Oratio pro pauperibus, vt eis liceat mendicare. *Per Henricum Petri Middelburgensem: Antuerpiæ,* 1530. 8°. **113.** a. **52.**

CELLARIUS (CHRISTOPHORUS) *the Elder.* [For dissertations at which C. Cellarius acted as Praeses :]
See ANTONIUS (A.)   BOEDENBURG (C. F.)
    BAIER (Johann W.) *the*   BREITHAUPT (A. C.)
     Younger.   CELLARIUS (S.)
    BARTH (Christophorus G.)   DORNMEIER (A. J.)
    BEICHE (G.)   HOLLENHAGEN (J. F.)
    BERENS (B.)   PETERSEN (Fridericus A.)
    BLUMENROEDER (D.)   RAHT (J. C.)

—— *See* BIBLE.—*Old Testament.*—*Selections.* [*Polyglot.*] Excerpta Veteris Testamenti syriaci, cum latina interpretatione noua & annotationibus C. Cellarii. 1682. 4°. **219.** f. **8.** (7.)

—— *See* BIBLE. — *Pentateuch.* — *Selections.* [*Polyglot.*] Christophori Cellarii . . . Horæ samaritanæ, hoc est, excerpta Pentateuchi samaritanæ versionis, cum latina interpretatione noua & annotationibus perpetuis: etiam grammatica samaritana . . . et glossarium, *etc.* 1682. 4°. **1014.** c. **21.**

—— *See* BIBLE.—*New Testament.*—*Selections.* [*Polyglot.*] Excerpta Noui Testamenti syriaci, cum latina interpretatione . . . Auctore C. Cellario. 1682. 4°. **219.** f. **8.** (8.)

—— *See* BURCKHARD (J.) De . . . Christophori Cellarii obitu epistola, *etc.* [1707.] 4°. **819.** f. **26.** (5.)

—— *See* BURCKHARD (J.) Viri celeberrimi Christophori Cellarii lucubrationum, ab a. CIƆIƆCLXXII ad a. CIƆIƆCCVII editarum, catalogus. [1707.] 4°. **819.** f. **26.** (6.)

—— *See* CAESAR (C. J.) [*Works.*—*Latin.*] C. Julii Cæsaris commentarii . . . E recensione C. Cellarii, cumque selectis ejusdem notis, *etc.* 1797. 8°. **1307.** b. **9.**

CELLARIUS (Christophorus) *the Elder.*

—— *See* Caesar (C. J.) [*Works.—Latin.*] C. Iulii Caesaris commentarii . . . Post Cellarium et Morum denuo curavit I. I. Oberlinus. 1805. 8°.　　　**587. d. 6.**

—— *See* Caesar (C. J.) [*Works.—Latin and Italian.*] I Comentarj di C. Giulio Cesare . . . Con le note di C. Cellario. 1782. 8°.　　　**196. a. 5–7.**

—— *See* Cellarius (S.) Salomonis Cellarii . . . Origines et antiquitates medicæ . . . emendatiores auctioresque editæ a C. Cellario. 1701. 8°.　　　**550. a. 4.**

—— *See* Cicero (M. T.) [*Letters.—Ad Familiares.—Latin.*] M. Tullii Ciceronis epistolarum ad diversos . . . libri xvi. C. Cellarius recensuit et annotationibus illustravit, *etc.* 1722. 8°.　　　**1082. e. 7.**

—— —— 1771. 8°.　　　**160. k. 23.**

—— *See* Cunaeus (P.) Petri Cunæi IC. Orationes argumenti varii, ejusdemque alia latina opuscula . . . C. Cellarius notas et obseruationes adiecit, *etc.* 1693. 8°.　　　**1090. e. 3. (1.)**

—— —— 1735. 8°.　　　**1091. b. 1.**

—— *See* Curtius Rufus (Q.) Q. Curtii Rufi De rebus Alexandri Magni historia superstes. C. Cellarius recensuit, *etc.* 1696. 12°.　　　**585. a. 31.**

—— *See* Curtius Rufus (Q.) Q. Curtii Rufi De rebus gestis Alexandri Magni . . . libri superstites. Cum omnibus supplementis . . . F. Modii . . . C. Cellarii, *etc.* 1724. 4°.　　　**1322.1.30.**

—— *See* Eutropius (F.) Eutropii Breviarium Romanæ historiæ . . . Cum metaphrasi græca Pæanii. C. Cellarius . . . recensuit, *etc.* 1678. 8°.　　　**9039. aaa. 35.**

—— —— 1698. 8°.　　　**9040. a. 41. (1.)**

—— —— 1726. 8°.　　　**9040. b. 15.**

—— *See* Eutropius (F.) Eutropii Breviarium historiæ Romanæ, cum metaphrasi græcâ Pæanii, et notis integris E. Vineti . . . item selectis C. Cellarii. Accedunt Sexti Rufi Breviarium cum notis integris C. Cellarii, *etc.* 1729. 8°.　　　**197. a. 8.**

—— *See* Eutropius (F.) Eutropii Breviarium Romanæ historiæ . . . C. Cellarius recensuit, *etc.* 1741. 8°.　　　**588. c. 23.**

—— *See* Eutropius (F.) Eutropii Breviarium historiæ Romanæ cum . . . notis integris . . . C. Cellarii, *etc.* 1762. 8°.　　　**197. a. 5.**

—— *See* Eutropius (F.) Eutropii Breviarium historiæ Romanæ cum metaphrasi græca Pæanii, et notis integris E. Vineti . . . C. Cellarii . . . Accedit Rufus Festus, cum notis integris F. Sylburgii, C. Cellarii, *etc.* (Libellus provinciarum Romanarum in lucem olim productus a cl. v. A. Schonhovio, emendatior editus & notis illustratus a C. Cellario.) 1793. 8°.　　　**802. k. 32.**

—— *See* Faber (B.) Basilii Fabri . . . Thesaurus eruditionis scholasticae . . . Novam hanc editionem . . . C. Cellarius . . . correxit, et . . . locupletavit. 1696. fol.　　　**12932. ff. 10.**

—— —— 1726. fol.　　　**70. g. 3.**

—— —— 1710. fol.　　　**631. m. 3.**

—— —— 1735. fol.　　　**12932. h. 2.**

—— —— 1749. fol.　　　**1890. d. 21.**

CELLARIUS (Christophorus) *the Elder.*

—— *See* Lactantius (L. C. F.) [*Works.*] Lucii Coelii siue Cæcilii Lactantii Firmiani opera omnia, quæ exstant. C. Cellarius recensuit et adnotationibus illustrauit. 1698. 8°.　　　**1017. c. 24.**

—— —— 1736. 8°.　　　**3670. df. 11.**

—— —— 1739. 8°.　　　**3627. aaa. 27.**

—— *See* Lactantius (L. C. F.) [*Phoenix.*] Firmiani Lactantii Carmen de phœnice. Subjiciuntur notæ criticæ C. Cellarii, *etc.* 1824. 8°. [*Lemaire* (N. E.) *Bibliotheca classica latina, etc.* vol. 135.]　　　**11305. m. 5.**

—— *See* Minucius Felix (M.) M. Minucii Felicis Octauius: et C. Cypriani De vanitate idolorum liber: vterque recensitus et illustratus a C. Cellario. 1699. 8°.　　　**846. e. 19.**

—— *See* Nepos (C.) Cornelius Nepos . . . De vita excellentium imperatorum novis commentariis . . . et tabulis geographicis illustratus ab C. Cellario, *etc.* 1750. 12°.　　　**609. c. 4.**

—— *See* Panegyrici. Duodecim Panegyrici veteres . . . recensiti et adnotationibus illustrati a C. Cellario, qui et indices copiosiores rerum et verborum adiecit. 1703. 8°.　　　**835. d. 26.**

—— *See* Pico della Mirandola (G.) *Count della Concordia, the Elder.* Ioannis Pici Mirandulæ . . . Epistolarum liber recensitus & illustratus a C. Cellario. 1682. 8°.　　　**1083. i. 5.**

—— *See* Plinius Caecilius Secundus (C.) [*Works.—Latin.*] C. Plinii Cæcilii Secundi Epistolæ et Panegyricus. Recensuit ac nouis commentariis illustrauit, etiam . . . tabulis geographicis auxit C. Cellarius, *etc.* 1711. 12°.　　　**1067. e. 26.**

—— —— 1737. 12°.　　　**1477. d. 2.**

—— *See* Plinius Caecilius Secundus (C.) [*Epistolae.— Latin.*] Caii Plinii Cæcilii Secundi Epistolarum libros decem cum notis selectis I. M. Catanæi . . . C. Cellarii aliorumque . . . recensuerunt . . . C. Cortius et P. D. Longolius, *etc.* 1734. 4°.　　　**636. k. 2.**

—— *See* Prudentius Clemens (A.) [*Works.*] Aurelii Prudentii Clementis quae exstant. Recensuit et adnotationibus illustrauit C. Cellarius, *etc.* 1703. 8°.　　　**166. c. 12.**

—— *See* Rufus (S.) Breviarium . . . de victoriis ac provinciis populi Romani . . . cum annotationibus C. Cellarii. 1679. 8°.　　　**C. 45. c. 3.**

—— *See* Rufus (S.) Breviarium . . . de victoriis et provinciis populi Romani . . . Accedit Libellus provinciarum Romanarum ex sæculo . . . Theodosiano. C. Cellarius utrumque recensuit et adnotationibus illustravit. 1698. 8°.　　　**9040. a. 41. (2.)**

—— —— 1698. 8°.　　　**589. b. 18.**

—— *See* Schoensleder (W.) Apparatus eloquentiæ . . . cum præfatione C. Cellarii, *etc.* 1710. 8°.　　　**827. b. 5.**

—— *See* Sedulius (C.) Cælii Sedulii . . . Mirabilium diuinorum libri, Paschale carmen dicti, et hymni duo. C. Cellarius . . . recensuit et adnotationibus illustrauit. 1704. 8°.　　　**1001. b. 17.**

—— *See* Sedulius (C.) C. Sedulii Carminis paschalis libri v. et hymni duo. Cum notis C. Barthii, C. Cellarii . . . aliorumque, *etc.* 1761. 8°.　　　**1002. i. 18.**

CELLARIUS (CHRISTOPHORUS) *the Elder.*

—— *See* SICHEMITES. Epistolæ samaritanæ Sichemitarum ad Jobum Ludolfum, *etc.* [Edited by C. Cellarius.] 1688. 4°. **219. f. 8. (13.)**

—— *See* SIGONIO (C.) Caroli Sigonii opera omnia, *etc.* (tom. 4. Palestinæ parallelismus alphabeticus ex N. Sansonii, atque H. Relandi, tum abecedariis, tum tabulis; ex Christophori verò Cellarii, A. Calmeti . . . tabulis tantum excerptus.) 1732, *etc.* fol. **657. h. 4.**

—— *See* SILIUS ITALICUS (C.) C. Silii Italici . . . De bello punico secundo libri XVII. C. Cellarius recensuit et notis et tabulis geographicis . . . illustravit. 1695. 8°. **1001. b. 30.**

—— *See* STRABO. Στραβωνος Γεωγραφικων βιβλοι ιζ'. . . . Accedunt . . . notæ . . . selectæ . . . ex scriptis P. Merulæ . . . C. Cellarii, *etc.* 1707. fol. **10001. h. 3.**

—— *See* STRABO. Strabonis rerum geographicarum libri XVII. (Cum notis selectis C. Cellarii.) 1796, *etc.* 8°. **10005. cc. 16.**

—— *See* ZOSIMUS, *the Historian.* Ζωσιμου . . . Ἱστορια νεα. Zosimi . . . Historia nova . . . Accurante C. Cellario. 1679. 8°. **294. e. 10.**

—— Christophori Cellarii Programmata varii argumenti oratoriis exercitiis in Citicensi Lyceo præmissa. Eiusdemque orationes ibidem in illustriore consessu recitatæ, *etc.* pp. 616. *Sumtu I. F. Gleditschii: Lipsiæ,* 1689. 8°. **1090. h. 9.**

—— Christophori Cellarii . . . Geographia antiqua, iuxta & noua, recognita . . . et plurimis locis aucta ac immutata. 2 pt. *Sumtu I. Bielckii: Ienæ,* 1692, 86. 12°. **568. b. 19.** *With an additional titlepage, engraved. The titlepage of pt. 2 reads: "Christophori Cellarii . . . Geographia antiqua . . . Cizæ, sumptu I. Bielkii . . . typis F. Hetstedii. 1686."*

—— [Another edition.] 2 pt. *Sumtu I. Bielckii: Ienæ,* 1698, 97. 12°. **571. a. 24.** *With an additional titlepage, engraved.*

—— Christophori Cellarii Dissertationes academicæ, varii argumenti in summam redactæ cura et studio Io. Georgii Walchii, qui et dissertationem de auctoris vita et scriptis . . . adiecit. [With a portrait.] 2 vol. *Lipsiæ,* 1712. 8°. **246. i. 33, 34.**

—— Christophori Cellarii Orationes academicæ, collectæ opera Ioannis Georgii Walchii qui et præfatione de fatis oratoriæ inter Græcos, Romanos, et Germanos, copiose edisseruit. pp. 317. *Lipsiæ,* 1714. 8°. **236. a. 19.**

—— Suada Cellariana, id est Orationes selectae Hallenses, quas de argumentis singularibus et illustrissimis, ductu Cellarii . . . in Academia Hallensi recitarunt iuvenes . . . Præfationem adiecit Nicol. Hieron. Gundlingius, *etc.* [With a portrait.] pp. 603. *Halæ Magdeburgicæ,* 1716. 8°. **1090. h. 10.**

—— Christophori Cellarii Epistolæ selectiores et præfationes. Conlegit Io. Georgius Walchius, qui et copiosiorem diatriben de dedicationibus librorum veterum latinorum præmisit. [With a portrait.] pp. 290. *Lipsiæ,* 1715. 8°. **246. i. 12.**

—— Breviarium antiquitatum Romanarum Cellario-Freyerianum suppletum & recognitum. [Edited by J. P. Anchersen.] pp. 188. *Havniæ,* 1743. 8°. **1103. b. 28. (4.)**

—— [Another edition.] Accurante Hieronymo Freyero. pp. 147. *Groningæ,* 1751. 8°. [MISSING.]

CELLARIUS (CHRISTOPHORUS) *the Elder.*

—— Editio decima. pp. 144. *Halæ Magdeburgicæ,* 1778. 8°. [MISSING.]

—— *See* VASLET (L.) Introduction à la connoissance des antiquitez romaines, traduite en partie d'un . . . ouvrage latin de Cellarius [i.e. "Breviarium antiquitatum Romanarum"], *etc.* 1723. 8°. **575. c. 29.**

—— Christophori Cellarii Canones de linguæ sanctæ proprietatibus . . . Nunc denuo reuisi, aucti, atque emendati tertiùm eduntur, *etc.* pp. 40. *Prostant in Bibliopolio Bielckiano: Ienæ,* 1679. 4°. **219. f. 8. (3.)**

—— מרינתא רבבל siue Chaldæa in tres prouincias, I. Grammaticam chaldaicam, II. Vsum chaldaismi triplicem, III. Messiologiam targumicam, diuisa. pp. 90. *Sumtu I. Bielkii: Cizæ,* 1678. 4°. **219. f. 8. (5.)**

—— Christophori Cellarii Chaldaismus, siue Grammatica noua linguæ chaldaicæ, *etc.* pp. 32. *Sumtu Bielckiano: Cizæ,* 1685. 4°. **219. f. 8. (4.)**

—— Christophori Cellarii Collectanea historiæ Samaritanæ, quibus præter res geographicas, tam politia huius gentis, quam religio et res literaria explicantur. pp. 48. *Sumtu I. Bielkii: Cizæ,* 1688. 4°. **219. f. 8. (12.)**

—— [Another edition.] 1759. *See* UGOLINUS (B.) Thesaurus antiquitatum sacrarum, *etc.* vol. 22. 1744, *etc.* fol. **686. l. 2.**

—— Christophori Cellarii Compendium antiquitatum Romanarum. Nunc ex manuscripto libro integrum editum et adnotationibus illustratum a M. Io. Ern. Imman. W[alc]hio. pp. 648. *Halæ Magdeburgicæ,* 1748. 8°. [MISSING.] *The titlepage is slightly mutilated.*

—— חכמת בני קדם sive Compendium philologiæ sacræ . . . auctore & præside M. C. Cellario, *etc.* (Respondendo defendere susceperunt Godofredus Wog, Godofredus Lübichen.) pp. 52. *Literis Hildebrandianis: Leucopetrae,* 1671. 4°. **1363. b. 6. (2.)**

—— Christophori Cellarii . . . Curæ posteriores de barbarismis et idiotismis sermonis latini. Recognitæ et plurimis locis auctæ. pp. 432. *Sumtu I. Bielckii: Ienæ,* 1687. 12°. **12935. aaaa. 10. (2.)** *With an additional titlepage, engraved.*

—— [Another edition.] Tertium recognitæ et plurimis locis auctæ. pp. 432. *Ienæ,* 1700. 12°. **623. a. 22. (1.)** *With an additional titlepage, engraved. Cropped.*

—— [Another edition.] pp. 528. *Panormi,* 1707. 16°. **827. a. 4.**

—— [Another edition.] Quintum recognitæ et plurimis locis auctæ. pp. 432. *Ienæ,* 1718. 12°. **623. a. 23. (1.)** *With an additional titlepage, engraved.*

—— *See* BORRICHIUS (A.) Appendix ad Curas posteriores . . . Christophori Cellarii . . . Post nouo titulo insignita A. B. Obseruationes singulares circa latinam linguam . . . Accedit Christophori Cellarii Discussio et examen huius Appendicis et Obseruationum. 1718. 12°. **623. a. 23. (2.)**

—— *See* BORRICHIUS (Olaus) *Højesteretsassessor.* Dissertatio philologica, de Curis posterioribus . . . C. Cellarii, *etc.* [1682.] 4°. **625. c. 25. (6.)**

—— De latinitate mediæ et infimæ ætatis liber, siue Antibarbarus, recognitus denuo & innumeris locis auctus. pp. 280. *Sumtu Bielckiano: Ienæ,* 1682. 12°. **12935. aaaa. 10. (1.)**

CELLARIUS (Christophorus) *the Elder.*

—— [Another edition.] Recognitus tertium et innumeris locis auctus. pp. 268. *Sumtu Bielkiano: Ienæ*, 1695. 12°. **623. a. 21. (1.)**

—— [Another edition.] Recognitus quartum & pluribus locis auctus . . . Editio v. pp. 268. *Sumtu I. F. Bielckii: Ienæ*, 1723. 12°. **623. a. 23. (3.)**

—— [Another edition.] pp. 160. *See* POPMA (A.) Ausonii Popmæ . . . De differentiis verborum, *etc.* 1779. 8°. **625. f. 22.**

—— De processu juris Romani antiquo. *See* infra: Dissertatio inauguralis sistens processum iuris Romani antiquum, *etc.*

—— Christophori Cellarii De studiis Romanorum litterariis in urbe et provinciis dissertatio. 1719. *See* SALLENGRE (A. H. de) Novus thesaurus antiquitatum Romanarum, *etc.* tom. 3. 1716, *etc.* fol. **588. l. 16.**

—— [Another edition.] 1735. *See* SALLENGRE (A. H. de) Novus thesaurus antiquitatum Romanarum, *etc.* tom. 3. 1737. fol. **145. i. 4.**

—— Christophori Cellarii Discussio Appendicis danicæ ad Curas suas posteriores, nuper nouo titulo Obseruationum singularium circa latinam linguam prænotatæ [by A. Borrichius]. pp. 98. *Sumtu Bielckiano: Jenæ*, 1695. 12°. **623. a. 21. (2.)**

—— [Another edition.] Iterum auctior edita. pp. 102. *Jenæ*, 1700. 12°. **623. a. 22. (2.)**

—— Christophori Cellarii Dissertatio de amœnitatibus historicis et geographicis ex itineribus S. Pauli Apostoli collectis. 1747. *See* UGOLINUS (B.) Thesaurus antiquitatum sacrarum, *etc.* vol. 7. 1744, *etc.* fol. **686. k. 7.**

—— Christoph. Cellarii Dissertatio de Cn. Pompeii M. expeditione judaica, *etc.* 1763. *See* UGOLINUS (B.) Thesaurus antiquitatum sacrarum, *etc.* vol. 26. 1744, *etc.* fol. **686. l. 6.**

—— Christophori Cellarii Dissertatio de excidio Sodomæ. 1747. *See* UGOLINUS (B.) Thesaurus antiquitatum sacrarum, *etc.* vol. 7. 1744, *etc.* fol. **686. k. 7.**

—— Dissertatio inauguralis sistens processum iuris Romani antiquum, *etc.* Praes. J. S. Strykius. pp. 65. *Literis C. Henckelii: Halæ Magdeb.*, [1698.] 4°. **501. e. 9. (11.)**

—— [Another edition.] De processu juris Romani antiquo. 1750. *See* STRYKIUS (S.) Viri quondam illustris . . . S. Strykii . . . necnon . . . J. S. Strykii opera omnia, *etc.* vol. 12. 1743, *etc.* fol. **498. g. 14.**

—— Christoph. Cellarii Dissertatio, qua Flavii Josephi de Herodibus historia a νοθείας suspicione contra v. cl. Johannem Harduinum justis vindiciis adseritur et nummis antiquis conciliatur. 1763. *See* UGOLINUS (B.) Thesaurus antiquitatum sacrarum, *etc.* vol. 26. 1744, *etc.* fol. **686. l. 6.**

—— A Dissertation . . against Hardouin, wherein Josephus's history of the Herods is defended by unexceptionable arguments, and from ancient coins. *See* JOSEPHUS (F.) [*Works.—English.*] The Works of Flavius Josephus, *etc.* 1733. fol. **4515. g. 10.**

—— Christophori Cellarii Elementa astronomiæ, ad interpretandos poetas aliosque veteres scriptores accommodata; cum . . . Guilielmi Schickardi Astroscopio, hoc est Schemate cœlum concauum repræsentante, *etc.* pp. 60. *Lipsiæ*, 1705. 8°. **531. e. 4. (7.)**

CELLARIUS (Christophorus) *the Elder.*

—— [Another edition.] *See* MANILIUS (M.) Marci Manilii Astronomicon, *etc.* 1743. 8°. **165. n. 8.**

—— [Erleichterte lateinische grammatica.] Краткая латинская грамматика . . . исправленная и умноженная Господиномъ Геснеромъ; съ нѣмецкаго на россійской языкъ переведена . . . Антономъ Барсовымъ. pp. 220. [*Moscow*,] 1762. 8°. **12933. bbb. 29.**

—— Christophori Cellarii . . . Geographia antiqua, *etc.* pp. 264. *Sumtu I. Bielkii: Cizæ*, 1686. 12°. **795. a. 50. (2.)**

—— [Another edition.] Recognita denuo . . . & quinta editione plurimis locis aucta & immutata. Huic demum sextæ editioni tot chartas ex majori auctoris Geographia antiqua quot ad minorem hanc illustrandam requirebantur, duplicemque indicem . . . addidit, totam recensuit, & scholarum usui accommodavit Samuel Patrick. pp. vii. 180. *S. Ballard, etc.: Londini*, 1731. 8°. **10005. c. 24.**

—— Editio altera & castigatior. pp. 180. *S. Ballard, etc.: Londini*, 1745. 8°. **304. h. 21.**

—— [Another edition.] pp. 180. *J. & T. Pote, etc.: Londini*, 1764. 8°. **10005. bbb. 9.**

—— [Another edition.] pp. 180. *J. & T. Pote, etc.: Londini*, 1782. 8°. **568. e. 43.**

—— [Another edition.] pp. 180. *J. & T. Pote, etc.: Londini*, 1786. 8°. **10005. cc. 15.**

—— [Another edition.] pp. 180. *E. Ballard, etc.: Londini*, 1790. 8°. **10003. cc. 24.**

—— [Another edition.] pp. 180. *W. & W. Ginger, etc.: Londini*, 1802. 8°. **10004. d. 3.**

—— Editio nova et castigatior. pp. 180. *F. C. & J. Rivington, etc.: Londini*, 1812. 8°. **10004. d. 4.**

—— General View of Geography, Ancient and Modern: or, an Attempt to impress on the mind of a school-boy a general idea of Cellarius's Ancient and Guthrie's Modern Maps . . . For the use of Rugby School. 2 pt. *N. Rollason: Coventry*, 1789. 8°. **12201. b. 1. (5.)** *Imperfect; wanting all after the second leaf of pt. 2. Cropped.*

—— Christophori Cellarii Geographia antiqua in compendium redacta novis praefationibus nunc exornata. A Francisco Tirolio et Joanne Baptista Ghisio . . . amplioribus tabulis aucta et accuratioribus catalogis locupletata. pp. 40. *Romae*, 1774. fol. **Maps 37. e. 2.** *The titlepage is engraved.*

—— Christophori Cellarii Glossarium Syro-Latinum, nuper vulgatis vtriusque Testamenti excerptis accommodatum. pp. 48. *Sumtu I. Bielckii: Cizæ*, 1683. 4°. **219. f. 8. (9.)**

—— Christofori Cellarii Grammatica ebraea in tabulis synopticis . . . Editio secunda, cui . . . accessit noua et perspicua institutio rabbinismi. 2 pt. *Sumtu I. Bielckii: Cizae*, 1684. 4°. **12903. c. 21.**

—— Tertia editione auctiori accedit separatim noua et perspicua institutio rabbinismi. pp. 45 [54]. *Sumtu I. Bielckii: Jenæ*, 1699. 4°. **219. f. 8. (2.)** *Imperfect; wanting the "Institutio rabbinismi."*

—— Christophori Cellarii . . . Historia antiqua multis accessionibus aucta et emendata, cum notis perpetuis et tabulis synopticis. Editio sexta, *etc.* pp. 242. *Ienæ*, 1719. 12°. **9006. aa. 6.** *Interleaved.*

CELLARIUS (Christophorus) *the Elder.*

—— Christophori Cellarii Historia explicandis epistolis Ciceronis accommodata, post auctoris mortem edita a Io. Michæle Heusingero. *See* FABRICIUS (Franciscus) *Marcoduranus.* Francisci Frabricii . . . Historia M. Tullii Ciceronis, *etc.* 1727. 8⁰.   **610. b. 7.**

—— Christophori Cellarii . . . Historia medii æui a temporibus Constantini Magni ad Constantinopolim a Turcis captam deducta, et cum notis perpetuis ac tabulis synopticis iterum edita. pp. 287.   *Sumptu I. Bielkii: Ienæ,* 1698. 12⁰.   **582. a. 13.**

—— [Another edition.] Sextum auctior et emendatior edita. pp. 275. COPIOUS MS. NOTES. *Ienæ,* 1718. 12⁰.
          580. a. 19.
Interleaved.

—— Christophori Cellarii Historia noua, hoc est XVI et XVII sæculorum, cum initio seculi XVIII, ad hæc tempora vsque qua eiusdem auctoris Historiæ, antiqua et medii æui, ad nostra tempora continenti ordine proferuntur, cum notis perpetuis, tabulis synopticis et indice rerum. Editio sexta producta cura Burcardi Gotthelfii Struuii. pp. 569. MS. NOTES. *Ienæ,* 1720. 12⁰.   **580. a. 20.**

—— [Another edition.] Christophori Cellarii Historia vniuersalis breuiter ac perspicue exposita, in antiquam, et medii æui ac nouam diuisa . . . Editio VII. Prioribus multo emendatior et summariis aucta, *etc.* pp. 552. *Ienae,* 1727. 12⁰.   **9004. aaa. 11.**
With a "Prœmium generale" followed by a second titlepage, reading "Christophori Cellarii Historia noua, etc."

—— [Another edition.] Christophori Cellarii Historia vniuersalis . . . Editio IX., *etc.* pp. 575. *Ienæ,* 1735. 12⁰.
          580. a. 21.
With the "Prœmium generale" and the second titlepage, as in the preceding.

—— Isagoge in linguam arabicam, ad ductum præstantissimorum grammaticorum recognita et aucta. pp. 70. *Sumtibus I. Bielkii: Cizæ,* 1686. 4⁰.   **219. f. 8. (11.)**

—— Chr. Cellarii Iudicium de Vindiciis latinæ linguæ Borrichianis nuperrime Hafniæ Danorum in lucem editis. [A reply to A. Borrichius' criticisms of Cellarius' "Discussio Appendicis danicæ ad Curas posteriores."] pp. 84. *Ienæ,* 1704. 12⁰.   **624. a. 35. (3.)**

—— Christophori Cellarii kurtze historische Nachricht von dem Stapel-Recht der alten Stadt Magdeburg, worinnen zugleich von denen ehmaligen Burggrafen, und deren . . . Befugnüssen und Gerechtigkeiten gehandelt, und die in D. Benjamin Leubers' Magdeburgischen Stapel-Unfug enthaltene Fehler und Irrthümer entdecket . . . werden, *etc.* pp. 132. *Magdeburg,* 1741. 4⁰.
          5510. c. 8.

—— I. C. Cellarii Latinitatis liber memorialis, in usum scholarum belgicarum conversus. [Edited by J. F. Reitz, assisted by J. H. Reitz.] Editio sexta. *Lat. & Dutch.* pp. 296. *Lugduni Batavorum,* 1794. 8⁰.
          625. a. 35.

—— [Latinitatis liber memorialis.] Христофора Целларія краткой латинской лексиконъ съ россійскимъ и нѣмецкимъ переводомъ. 2 pt.   *въ Санктпетербургѣ,* 1746. 8⁰.   **12935. df. 4.**

—— Целларіевъ латинскій лексиконъ. Primitiva latina. *See* RHENIUS (J.) Первые начатки латинскаго языка, *etc.* 1767. 8⁰.   **624. a. 3.**

—— Notitia orbis antiqui, siue Geographia plenior, ab ortu rerumpublicarum ad Constantinorum tempora orbis terrarum faciem declarans. C. Cellarius ex vetustis . . . monimentis collegit, & nouis tabulis geographicis . . . illustrauit, *etc.* [With a portrait.] 2 tom. *Lipsiæ,* 1701, 06. 4⁰.   **569. f. 24.**

CELLARIUS (Christophorus) *the Elder.*

—— [Another edition.] [With a portrait.] 2 tom. *Impensis Joannis Oweni: Cantabrigiæ,* 1703, 06. 4⁰.
          214. a. 14, 15.
The imprint in tom. 2 is "Casparus Fritsch: Amstelædami."

—— [Another copy.]   **677. e. 13, 14.**

—— [Another edition.] Alteram hanc editionem annotationibus . . . illustrauit & auxit L. Io. Conradus Schwartz, *etc.* [With a portrait.] 2 tom. *Lipsiæ,* 1731, 32. 4⁰.
          570. f. 4, 5.

—— [Another edition.] [With a portrait.] 2 tom. *Lipsiæ,* 1773. 4⁰.   **214. a. 12, 13.**

—— Christophori Cellari[j] . . . Nucleus historiæ inter antiquam & novam mediæ, hoc est, ab Augusto Cæsare a[d] Carolum M. in occidente: & ad captam a Turcis Constantinopolim in oriente productæ, cum notis & tabulis synopticis. pp. 89.   *Impensis J. Bielckii: Ienæ,* 1676. 12⁰.   **800. a. 15.**
The titlepage is slightly mutilated.

—— Oratio qua supremo suo curatori . . . Paulo a Fuchs . . . mortalitate intercepto Fridericiana Academia officium supremum . . . persoluit, verba faciente C. Cellario, *etc. Berolini,* [1704.] fol.   **10706. m. 16. (5.)**

—— Christophori Cellarii Orthographia latina ex vetustis monumentis excerpta . . . Editio secunda auctior. pp. 156. *Halæ Magdeburgicæ,* 1704. 8⁰.   **827. d. 13.**

—— Editio tertia auctior. pp. 98 [132]. *Ienæ,* 1710. 8⁰.
          12932. b. 24.

—— Editio prima Patauina, vltimis Ienensibus emendatior. pp. 117. *Patauii,* 1724. 8⁰.   **236. c. 19.**

—— Editio quinta. pp. 132. FEW MS. NOTES. *Ienæ,* 1729. 8⁰.   **827. d. 14.**

—— Editio II Patauina. pp. 117. *Patauii,* 1739. 8⁰.
          625. b. 19.

—— Christoph. Cellarii Orthographia latina . . . quam denuo recensuit, emendauit, obseruationibus Longolii . . . Heumanni . . . Heusingeri, Schurzfleischii suisque auxit; et Cortii disputationes de vsu orthographiæ cum orthographia Norisiana typis repetendas curauit Theoph. Christophorus Harles. Cum præfatione Christiani Adolphi Klotzii. 2 tom. *Altenburgi,* 1768. 8⁰.   **12933. c. 14.**

—— [Another copy.]   **72. b. 3.**

—— Christophori Cellarii Porta Syriæ patentior, siue Grammaticæ nouæ . . . editio secunda, *etc.* pp. 95. *Sumtu I. Bielckii: Cizæ,* 1682. 4⁰.   **219. f. 8. (6.)**

—— Programma exercitii oratorii de humana Christi natura contra hæreticos quosvis defendenda. *See* GLASS (S.) Salomonis Glassii . . . opuscula. Christologia Mosaica . . . et Christologia Davidica, *etc.* 1700. 4⁰.   **3109. c. 12.**

—— Clarissimi viri Christophori Cellarii Rabbinismus, sive Institutio grammatica, rabbinorum scriptis legendis & intelligendis accommodata. pp. 96. *See* RELAND (A.) Adriani Relandi Analecta rabbinica, *etc.* 1702. 8⁰.
          621. c. 11.

—— [Another edition.] pp. 96. *See* RELAND (A.) Hadriani Relandi Analecta rabbinica, *etc.* 1723. 8⁰.   **621. c. 12.**

—— Christophori Cellarii Sciagraphia philologiæ sacræ . . . Editio secunda, emendata, & vsu arabismi etymologico aucta. pp. 72.   *Prostat in bibliopolio Bielkiano: Ienæ,* 1678. 4⁰.   **219. f. 8. (1.)**

CELLARIUS (CHRISTOPHORUS) *the Younger.* Origines et successiones Comitum Wettinensium, *etc.* pp. 52.
I. F. Gleditsch: Halæ Magdeburgicæ, 1697. 4°.
1054. h. 20. (10.)

CELLARIUS (CHRISTOPHORUS JULIUS) Christoph. Julii Cellarii, JC. De principum domaniis liber. [1701.] *See* FRISE (C.) Jus domaniale, *etc.* pt. 2. 1701, *etc.* fol.
503. i. 2.

CELLARIUS (CUNRADUS) *Praes. See* BARDILI (C.) Fatum mathematicum, *etc.* 1621. 12°. **8562. a. 29.**

—— Partitiones meteorologicæ, *etc.* pp. 595. *Typis Werlinianis: Tubingæ,* 1627. 8°. **538. a. 9.**

CELLARIUS (EDUARD) Zur Reformfrage des deutschen Schwurgerichts, nebst einem Entwurf, das Verfahren bei dem Schwurgericht und dem Einzelrichter betreffend. pp. 44. *Alsfeld,* [1871.] 8°. **5656.e.6.**

CELLARIUS (FRIDERICUS) Disputatio medica de hernia, *etc. Praes.* H. Meibomius. *Apud H. Hessium: Helmstadii,* [1686.] 4°. **1179. b. 11. (14.)**

CELLARIUS (GEORGIUS FRIDERICUS) Respirationis læsiones hypochondriaco-scorbuticas . . . publicæ censuræ exponit G. F. Cellarius, *etc. Typis J. Nisii: Jenæ,* [1677.] 4°. **1185. d. 9. (21.)**

CELLARIUS (HELMUT) Die Reichsstadt Frankfurt und die Gravamina der deutschen Nation. pp. xii. 102. *Leipzig,* 1938. 8°. [*Schriften des Vereins für Reformationsgeschichte.* Jahrg. 55. Hft. 1.] **Ac. 2027.**

CELLARIUS (HENRI) La Danse des salons . . . Dessins de Gavarni, *etc.* pp. 174. *Paris,* 1847. 8°.
7915.ee.16.

—— La Danse des salons . . . Deuxième édition. [With plates.] pp. 174. *Paris,* 1849. 8°. Hirsch **1739.**

—— The Drawing Room Dances. pp. xi. 140. pl. VII. *E. Churton: London,* 1847. 8° **1042. e. 48.**

—— Fashionable Dancing . . . With twelve illustrations by Gavarni. pp. 144. *David Bogue: London,* [1847.] 4°. **7913. f. 9.**
A different translation from the preceding.

CELLARIUS (HENRICUS) Dissertationem hanc inauguralem de affectu hypochondriaco . . . publico philiatrorum examini submittit H. Cellarius, *etc. Praes.* G. Rolfinck. pp. 28. *Typis J. J. Bauhoferi: Jenæ,* 1671. 4°. **1185. f. 20. (13.)**

—— [Another copy.] **7306. i. 14. (3.)**

CELLARIUS (J.) *Dramatist.* Die Isispriester in den letzten Tagen von Pompeji. Drama in fünf Aufzügen. [In verse.] pp. 69. *Leipzig,* [1883.] 8°. **11748. bb. 3. (1.)**

CELLARIUS (JACOBUS) *Jesuit. See* KELLER (Jacob)

CELLARIUS (JACOBUS) *Professor of Moral Philosophy at Lauingen.*
—— *See* GREEK-LATIN LEXICON. Λεξικον ἑλληνορωμαϊκον: hoc est, Dictionarium graeco-latinum . . . a I. Cellario & N. Hönigero . . . emendatum, *etc.* [1584.] 8°. **12924. i. 7.**

CELLARIUS (JEAN DAVID) Dissertation sur la pneumonie ataxique, *etc.* pp. 23. *Strasbourg,* 1802. 4°. [*Collection générale des dissertations de l'École Spéciale de Médecine de Strasbourg.* tom. 3.] **7381.*b.**

CELLARIUS (JEREMIAS CUNRADUS) De anevrysmate, disputatio, *etc. Praes.* G. B. Metzger. pp. 20. *Typis J. Heinii: Tubingæ,* 1679. 4°. **1179. d. 14. (6.)**

—— Dissertatio medica de acidularum usu externo, *etc. Praes.* E. R. Camerarius. pp. 37. *Literis Heinianis: Tubingæ,* 1677. 4°. **1179. d. 4. (14.)**

CELLARIUS (JOANNES) *Gnostopolitanus.* Ad Volphangum Fabritiū Capitonem . . . De vera et constanti serie theologice disputationis Lipsiace epistola. G.L.
[*M. Landsberg: Leipsic,* 1519.] 4°. T. **2213. (6.)**

—— Elogium famossissimi viri Neminis Montani, Terre filii, Noctis et Cocyti fratris, publici Vittenberge iuuenū eruscatoris, ac vtriusꝗ lingue inscientissimi, a Joanne Cellario Gnostopolitano concinnatum, qui interim Nullū agit. G.L. *Ex ædibus Vuolffgangi Monacensis: Lipsiæ,* 1519. 4°. **3905. c. 143. (1.)**

—— Iudicium Ioannis Cellarij de Martino Luthero. [*M. Lotter: Leipsic,* 1520.] 4°. **698. e. 40.**

CELLARIUS (JOHANNES) *Budissinus.* In Christianissimi Galliarum Regis Caroli IX. imaginem. [Elegiac verses. With a portrait.] *Apud G. Brunonem: Witebergæ,* 1571. fol. **1879.cc.15.(110.)**

CELLARIUS (JOHANNES GEORGIUS) Dissertatio inauguralis medica de transpiratione insensibili et sudore, *etc. Praes.* J. A. Wedelius. pp. 27. *Ienæ,* 1728. 4°. **1185. e. 10. (35.)**

—— Epistola gratulatoria, qua caussam efficientem secretionis, et excretionis periphericæ . . . Johanni Georgio Cellario summos facultatis medicæ honores in Academia Jenensi . . . capessenti sistit amicus quidam integer. *Vinariæ,* [1728.] 4°. T. **525. (32.)**

CELLARIUS (JOHANNES JACOBUS) *See* MAAGIUS (J. H.) and CELLARIUS (J. J.) Physicæ sacræ specimen de locustis, *etc.* 1724. 4°. **446. b. 16. (6.)**

CELLARIUS (JOHANNES JUSTUS) *See* MEINHART (G. F.) Disputationem metaphysicam de potentia naturali et libera . . . submittunt præses M. J. J. Cellarius . . . & respondens G. F. Meinhart, *etc.* [1675.] 4°.
525. d. 10. (34.)

CELLARIUS (JUSTUS) *Praes. See* BEHRENS (C. B.) Disputatio physica de penetrabili efficacia effluviorum, *etc.* 1681. 4°. **1179. b. 10. (16.)**

—— *Praes. See* FISCHBECK (A. W.) Dissertatio academica de viventibus sponte nascentibus, *etc.* [1679.] 4°.
B. **429. (8.)**

—— *Praes. See* SCHRADER (Fridericus) *Professor of Medicine at Helmstadt.* Exercitatio . . . de natura panis, *etc.* [1676.] 4°. **1179. b. 10. (5.)**

—— *Praes. See* SELLEN (C. H.) Exercitatio academica de antiquo funerum ritu, *etc.* [1682.] 4°. **585. c. 30. (5.)**

—— Abdanckungs-Rede. *See* FROELINGIUS (A.) Spiegel der Eitelkeit in irdischen Dingen, *etc.* [1681.] 4°.
853. g. 2. (4.)

—— Iusti Cellarii De ratione liberè philosophandi in pervestigandis cum primis rebus naturalibus oratio. *Typis H. D. Mulleri: Helmæstadii,* 1674. 4°. **536. e. 8. (16.)**

—— Justi Cellarii . . . Programma quo liberalis doctrinæ in Academia Julia studiosi ad publicas prælectiones invitantur. *Typis H. D. Mulleri: Helmæstadii,* 1674. 4°.
619. e. 2. (8.)

CELLARIUS (JUSTUS)

—— Panegyricus serenissimis ac potentissimis principibus . . . Dn. Georgio Wilhelmo, Dn. Rudolpho Augusto ducibus Brunsvicensium ac Luneburgensium regentibus post felicem expugnationem Stadensis civitatis triumphatoribus, *etc. Typis H. D. Mulleri: Helmestadii,* 1676. fol.
731. l. 7. (7.)

CELLARIUS (MARTINUS) *See* BORRHAUS (Martin)

CELLARIUS (MAXIMILIAN JOSEPH) Ueber die Noth der kleinern Gewerbe und die Mittel zu gründlicher Abhülfe, *etc.* pp. 44. *Ulm,* 1845. 8°. **8275. d. 7. (3.)**

CELLARIUS (SALOMO) Dissertatio inauguralis medica de ictero, *etc.* Praes. J. H. Schulze. pp. 28. *Halæ Magdeburgicæ,* [1732.] 4°. **7306. e. 19. (15.)**
The titlepage is cropped.

—— Origines et antiquitates medicas ad disputandum proponit . . . S. Cellarius. *Praes.* C. Cellarius. *Literis C. Henckelii: Halæ Magdeburgicæ,* [1696.] 4°.
T. 506. (2.)

—— [Another edition.] Salomonis Cellarii . . . Origines et antiquitates medicæ . . . emendatiores auctioresque editæ a Christophoro Cellario. [With a portrait.] pp. 62. *Ienæ,* 1701. 8°. **550. a. 4.**

—— [Another copy.] **T. 412. (1.)**

CELLARIUS (VALENTINUS) *Resp.* Manuductionis aphoristicæ ad discursum artium et disciplinarum methodicum sectio sexta in qua continetur historica, *etc. See* EBERTUS (T.) M. Theodori Eberti . . . Manuductionis aphoristicæ . . . sectiones sedecim, *etc.* [1620.] 4°. **819. f. 6.**

CELLE. Zellisches Stadt-Recht, aufs neue übersehen, und mit . . . Anmerkungen erläutert . . . Mit einer . . . Abhandlung vom Schosse, und einer Nachricht von der Stadt Zelle ersteren Ursprung und einigen deren Fatis . . . Zweyte verbesserte Auflage. [Compiled by C. L. Bilderbeck.] 3 pt. *Zelle,* 1739. 4°. **711. e. 29. (1.)**

—— Das Zellesche Stadtrecht. Von neuem herausgegeben und durchgehends mit erläuternden practischen Anmerkungen begleitet vom Ober-Appellationsrath T. Hagemann. pp. viii. 286. *Hannover,* 1800. 8°.
[MISSING.]

—— Adresse der Bürger und Einwohner der Stadt Celle an Sr. [*sic*] Majestät den König von Hannover. [A petition for constitutional reform.] *Celle,* 1848. 4°.
8072. f. 96. (1.)

Lithographed.

—— Gedenkfeier des 18. Octobers. Sämmtliche Festreden [by Adelbert Herrmann and others], welche bei der öffentlichen Erinnerungsfeier zu Celle am 18. October 1863 gehalten worden. (Mit . . . im Festzuge gedrucktem Gedichte.) pp. 16. [*Celle,* 1863.] 8°. **9386. aaa. 7.**

—— Gedenkfeier des 18. Octobers. Vollständiges Programm der Feier in Celle 1863, *etc.* pp. 20. [*Celle,* 1863.] 8°.
9386. b. 29.

—— Historisch-topographisch-statistische Beschreibung der Stadt Celle im Königreiche Hannover, *etc.* [The preface signed: E. S., i.e. E. P. J. Spangenberg.] 1826. 8°. *See* S., E. **10230. cc. 17.**

—— Die Schreckenstage des Aufruhrs zu Celle am 18. und 19. Juli 1866. pp. 14. *Celle,* [1866.] 8°. **9335. a. 15.**

Amt für Bodenforschung Hannover.

—— Erdöl und Tektonik in Nordwestdeutschland. Sammelband enthaltend die Vorträge der Erdöltagung in Hannover vom 9. bis 11. September, 1947 . . . Herausgegeben von A. Bentz, *etc.* [With a map.] pp. 387. pl. XIV. *Celle,* 1949. 8°. **07107. p. 21.**

CELLE.

—— *Anwaltskammer.* Gutachten über den Entwurf erster Lesung einer allgemeinen deutschen Civilprocessordnung, mit besonderer Berücksichtigung der Hannoverschen Bürgerlichen Processordnung . . . Dem Königl. Justizministerio in Hannover von dem Ausschusse der Anwaltskammer in Celle erstattet. Mit einer Inhaltsübersicht herausgegeben von F. Meyersburg. pp. viii. 80. *Celle,* 1866. 8°. [MISSING.]

—— *Bibliothek des Königlich-Hannoverschen Ober-Appellations-Gerichts. See* HANOVER.—*Ober-Appellations-Gericht.* —*Bibliothek.*

—— *Celler Conferenzen. See infra: Celler Versammlung von Geistlichen und Vertrauensmännern.*

—— *Celler Kirchliche Versammlung. See infra: Celler Versammlung von Geistlichen und Vertrauensmännern.*

—— *Celler Versammlung von Geistlichen und Vertrauensmännern.* Verhandlungen der Celler Versammlung von Geistlichen und Vertrauensmännern am 22. April 1863. Nach stenographischen Aufzeichnungen . . . Dritte Auflage. pp. 68. *Celle,* 1863. 8°. **8073. ee. 83.**

—— *See* CHUEDEN (F. W.) Die Petition der Celler kirchlichen Versammlung vom 22. April 1863 . . . nach ihrer Quelle beleuchtet, *etc.* 1863. 8°.
3913. bbb. 45.

—— Was ist's mit den Celler Conferenzen? Wachtruf an Hannoverland. Fünfte Auflage. pp. 16. *Leipzig & Dresden,* 1862. 8°. **3913. aaa. 55.**

Deutsches Heinrich Schütz-Fest.

—— Zweites deutsches Heinrich Schütz-Fest . . . 1929 in Celle. Gestaltet von der Musikgemeinde . . . Celle. In Verbindung mit der Heinrich Schütz-Gesellschaft . . . Dresden. [A programme, with the text of the songs and with the music of the choruses.] pp. 16. [1929.] 8°. *See infra: Musikgemeinde.* Hirsch **4571.**

—— *Gymnasium.* Sechster Jahresbericht über das Gymnasium der Stadt Celle das Jahr 1836 umfassend, womit zu der öffentlichen Prüfung sämmtlicher Klassen der Anstalt . . . die Beschützer und Freunde des hiesigen Schulwesens pflichtmässig einladet . . . Dr. Ernst Kästner. Voran geht eine Abhandlung des Collaborators Dr. Berger: De usu modorum temporumque apud Homerum in comparationibus. pp. 31. *Celle,* 1837. 4°.
8355. d. 18.

—— *Hof-Apotheke.* Consignatio, et taxa omnium medicamentorum . . . quæ in officina pharmaceutica Cellensi prostant. Verzeichniss und Tax, aller Arzeneyen . . . welche in der Zellischen Hoff-Apotheke zu finden. *Lat. & Ger.* pp. 147. *Andreas Holwein: Zelle,* 1682. 4°. **777. c. 20. (2.)**

—— *Lyceum.* Zweiter Jahres-Bericht über das Lyceum der Stadt Celle. Womit zu der Prüfung . . . einladet Dr. L. Ph. Hüpeden, Director. Praemittitur: De usu atque natura infinitivi historici apud Latinos commentatio grammatica. Scripsit H. L. O. Mueller. pp. 33. *Celle,* 1833. 4°. **T. 6*. (11.)**

Musikgemeinde.

—— Zweites deutsches Heinrich Schütz-Fest . . . 1929 in Celle. Gestaltet von der Musikgemeinde . . . Celle. In Verbindung mit der Heinrich Schütz-Gesellschaft . . . Dresden. [A programme, with the text of the songs and with the music of the choruses.] pp. 16. *Kassel,* [1929.] 8°. Hirsch **4571.**

Schloss Celle.

—— Kostbarkeiten alter Kunst, *etc.* (Ausstellung. Katalog.) [With plates.] *Celle,* [1954.] 8°. **7960. h. 43.**

CELLE, *Dukes of.* [For official acts and documents issued by Dukes of the Celle branch of the House of Brunswick:] *See* BRUNSWICK-CELLE.

CELLE (DE) *Baron.* Vers adressés à Mr. le Baron de Celle, d'Hove, &c. le 21 septembre 1787. [1787.] *s. sh.* 12°. **8079. c. 8. (8.)**

CELLE (EUGÈNE**)** Thèse pour le doctorat en médecine, *etc.* (Questions sur diverses branches des sciences médicales.) pp. 21. *Paris*, 1840. 4°. [*Collection des thèses soutenues à la Faculté de Médecine de Paris.* An 1840. tom. 3.] **7371. b. 4.**

—— Hygiène pratique des pays chauds, ou Recherches sur les causes et le traitement des maladies de ces contrées. pp. 384. *Paris*, 1848. 8°. **7410. c. 15.**

CELLE (G. F. S. DI REVILIASCO E**)** *Count. See* REVILIASCO E CELLE.

CELLE (GIOVANNI DALLE**)** *See* BARTOLOMMEO [Granchi], *da San Concordio, Pisano.* Principio del Maestruzzo [i.e. of the "Summa magistrutia"], *etc.* [Translated by G. dalle Celle.] 1868. 8°. **3833. b. 25.**

—— *See* CICERO (M. T.) [*Two or more Works.—Italian.*] Volgarizzamento inedito di alcuni scritti di Cicerone (Sogno di Scipione—Paradossi) e di Seneca (Trattato delle quattro virtù morali—De' costumi) fatto per G. dalle Celle, ed alcune lettere dello stesso, *etc.* 1825. 8°. **T. 2493. (4.)**

—— *See* CICERO (M. T.) [*Two or more Works.—Italian.*] Opuscoli di Cicerone volgarizzati, *etc.* [The "Somnium Scipionis" and "Paradoxa" translated by G. dalle Celle.] 1850. 8°. **11396. h. 6.**

—— Lettere del Beato Don G. dalle Celle . . . e d'altri . . . recate a miglior lezione dal P. Bartolommeo Sorio. pp. 83. 1845. *See* GIGLI (O.) Biblioteca classica sacra, *etc.* secolo 14. tom 3. 1844, *etc.* 4°. **3622. d. 1.**

CELLE (J. A. D. D.**)** Extract from the Hanover Magazine, No. 4, January 12, 1765. Answer to a question . . . concerning the spawning of fish. *See* JACOBS (S. L.) Translation of a Letter from the Hanover Magazine, *etc.* 1778. 8°. **B. 581. (7.)**

CELLE (NICCOLÒ**)** Nuovi elementi fisio-patologici di medicina eclettica. 3 pt. *Pisa*, 1841. 8°. **1405. h. 8.**

CELLE (PIERRE DE**) *Bishop of Chartres. See* PETRUS I., *Bishop of Chartres.*

CELLEBRINO (EUSTACHIO**)** *See* CELEBRINO.

CELLENIO (ROSMIRO**)** *P.A., pseud.* [i.e. CLAUDIO TEDESCHI.] All'eminentissimo . . . Cardinale Gian Maria Riminaldi nella solenne assunzione alla sacra porpora. Sonetto. [Signed: Rosmiro Cellenio, P. A.] *Roma*, 1785. *s. sh.* fol. **1897. c. 2. (3.)**

CELLEONIBUS (THOMAS EX CAPITANEIS DE**)** *See* CAPITANEIS DE CELLEONIBUS.

CELLEOR (ELIZABETH**)** *See* CELLIER.

CELLEPA ( ) Encore les Jacobins! Peuple, qu'en veux-tu faire? L'origine du nom des Jacobins, et tous les crimes qu'ils ont commis depuis le 9 thermidor, *etc.* pp. 8. [*Paris*, 1794?] 8°. **935. b. 12. (23.)**

—— [Another copy.] **F. 352. (3.)**

CELLER CONFERENZEN. *See* CELLE.—*Celler Versammlung von Geistlichen und Vertrauensmännern.*

CELLER (LUDOVIC**) *pseud.* [i.e. LUDOVIC LECLERC.] *See* MOLIÈRE (J. B.) [*Le Mariage Forcé.—French.*] Le Mariage forcé. Comédie-ballet en 3 actes . . . Nouvelle édition publiée . . . par L. Celler, *etc.* 1867. 8°. **11736. c. 45.**

—— Contes. La visite du docteur Méplat. Une vengeance photographique. L'homme de bronze. pp. 189. *Paris*, 1875. 12°. **12517. ff. 2.**

—— Les Décors, les costumes, et la mise en scène au XVIIe siècle—1615–1680. pp. 162. *Paris*, 1869. 12°. **11795. ccc. 8.**

—— Études dramatiques. 3 pt. *Paris*, 1870–75. 12°. **11795. de. 27.**

—— Les Origines de l'opéra et le Ballet de la Reine, 1581 [of B. da Belgiojoso]. Étude sur les danses, la musique, les orchestres et la mise en scène au XVIe siècle, *etc.* pp. vii. 364. *Paris*, 1868. 12°. 18°. **11795. ccc. 29.**

—— [Another copy.] Les Origines de l'opéra et le Ballet de la Reine, *etc. Paris*, 1868. 18°. **Hirsch 1830.**

—— La Semaine sainte au Vatican. Étude musicale et pittoresque. Texte et musique. 2 pt. *Paris*, 1867. 12°. **3477. bb. 8.**

CELLÉRIER (CHARLES**)** Démonstration d'un théorème fondamental relatif aux facteurs primitifs des nombres premiers. Applications au théorème de Fermat et à la recherche des facteurs primitifs. pp. 61. *Genève*, 1896. 4°. [*Mémoires de la Société de Physique et d'Histoire Naturelle de Genève.* tom. 32. no. 7.] **Ac. 2870.**

—— Mémoire sur les variations des excentricités et des inclinaisons. pp. 208. 1894. *See* PARIS.—*Académie des Sciences.* Mémoires présentés par divers savans, *etc.* tom. 31. 1833, *etc.* 4°. **Ac. 425.**

—— Note sur l'impossibilité de faire passer de la chaleur d'un corps plus froid dans un corps plus chaud sous forme rayonnante. pp. 15. *Genève*, 1891. 4°. [*Mémoires de la Société de Physique et d'Histoire Naturelle de Genève.* vol. supplémentaire. no. 5.] **Ac. 2870.**

—— Note sur la théorie des halos. pp. 73. *Genève*, 1887. 4°. [*Mémoires de la Société de Physique et d'Histoire Naturelle de Genève.* tom. 29. no. 9.] **Ac. 2870.**

—— Note sur les mouvements des corps électrisés. pp. 71. *Genève*, 1888. 4°. [*Mémoires de la Société de Physique et d'Histoire Naturelle de Genève.* tom. 30. no. 5.] **Ac. 2870.**

CELLÉRIER (GUSTAVE**)** Étude numérique des concours de compensation de chronomètres faits à l'Observatoire de Genève en 1884 et 1886. pp. 45. *Genève*, 1887. 4°. [*Mémoires de la Société de Physique et d'Histoire Naturelle de Genève.* tom. 29. no. 6.] **Ac. 2870.**

—— Réfraction cométaire. pp. 20. *Genève*, 1883. 4°. [*Mémoires de la Société de Physique et d'Histoire Naturelle de Genève.* tom. 28. no. 5.] **Ac. 2870.**

—— Théorèmes généraux de thermodynamique et leur application aux corps élastiques. pp. 59. *Genève*, 1894. 4°. [*Mémoires de la Société de Physique et d'Histoire Naturelle de Genève.* tom. 32. no. 5.] **Ac. 2870.**

CELLÉRIER (HENRY**)** La Politique fédéraliste, *etc.* pp. xviii. 268. *Paris*, 1916. 8°. **08052. a. 31.**

CELLÉRIER (JACOB ÉLISÉE**)** *See* CELLÉRIER (J. I. S.) Recueil de prières chrétiennes . . . complété et publié par J. E. Cellérier fils. 1845. 8°. **1220. k. 27.**

CELLÉRIER (Jacob Élisée)

—— De l'origine authentique et divine de l'Ancien Testament. Discours, *etc.* pp. iii. v. 282. *Genève; Paris*, 1826. 12º. **1107**. b. **1**.

—— [Another copy.] **3127**. bb. **12**. (**1**.)

—— A Discourse on the Authenticity and Divine Origin of the Old Testament . . . Translated . . . by the Rev. John Reynell Wreford. pp. xvi. 286. *Simpkin & Marshall, etc.: London*, 1830. 8º. **690**. b. **25**.

—— De l'origine authentique et divine du Nouveau Testament. Discours, *etc.* pp. vi. 415. *Genève; Paris*, 1829. 12º. **3127**. bb. **12**. (**2**.)

—— The Authenticity of the New Testament. Translated . . . by a Sunday School Teacher. pp. xiv. 254. *Weeks, Jordan & Co.: Boston*, 1838. 8º. **4017**. e. **30**.

—— L'Église de Satigny, ou Discours prononcés le 6 août 1848 a la visite consistoriale de cette paroisse. [By J. E. Cellérier and —— Collodon.] pp. 31. *Genève*, 1848. 8º. **4481**. b. **39**. (**5**.)

—— Élémens de la grammaire hébraïque . . . Suivie des Principes de la syntaxe hébraïque, traduits librement de l'allemand de Wilhelm Gesenius. Seconde édition augmentée et considérablement modifiée. pp. viii. 296. *Genève*, 1824. 8º. **12903**. cc. **19**.

—— Esprit de la législation mosaïque. 2 tom. *Genève; Paris*, 1837. 8º. **863**. m. **26**.

—— Essai d'une introduction critique au Nouveau Testament, ou Analyse raisonnée de l'ouvrage intitulé: Einleitung in die Schriften des N.T. . . . par J. L. Hug, *etc.* pp. xiv. 524. *Genève*, 1823. 8º. **1107**. d. **16**.

—— Introduction à la lecture des livres saints, à l'usage des hommes religieux et éclairés . . . Ancien Testament. pp. 547. *Genève; Paris*, 1832. 8º. **1107**. d. **17**.

—— Manuel d'herméneutique biblique. pp. xviii. 381. *Genève; Paris; [Stuttgart* printed,] 1852. 8º. **3127**. e. **37**.

—— Qu'est-ce qu'un serviteur de Jésus-Christ? Trois discours, *etc.* pp. 128. *Genève; Paris*, 1832. 8º. **4426**. cc. **4**. (**1**.)

—— Christ washing His Disciples' Feet, *etc.* [A sermon.] *See* Pons (J. S.) The Doctrine of the Church of Geneva illustrated, *etc.* ser. 1. 1825, *etc.* 8º. **1005**. dd. **6**.

—— On the Method to be pursued in the Study of the Holy Scriptures. [A sermon.] 1832. *See* Pons (J. S.) The Doctrine of the Church of Geneva illustrated, *etc.* ser. 2. 1825, *etc.* 8º. **1005**. dd. **6**.

—— On the Study of the Holy Scriptures. [A sermon.] 1832. *See* Pons (J. S.) The Doctrine of the Church of Geneva illustrated, *etc.* ser. 2. 1825, *etc.* 8º. **1005**. dd. **6**.

CELLÉRIER (Jean Isaac Samuel) *See* Bruniquel (E.) Étude sur la prédication de J. I. S. Cellérier, *etc.* 1864. 8º. **3678**. bb. **14**. (**7**.)

—— *See* France.—*Reformed Churches.* La Confession de Foi faite . . . par les Églises Réformées . . . précédée de Réflexions générales sur la nature, le légitime usage, et la nécessité des Confessions de Foi par MM. Cellérier, père, et Gaussen, *etc.* 1859. 12º. **3506**. b. **46**.

—— *See* Heraesiae Mastix, *pseud.* The Reviewer reviewed; or Remarks occasioned by a review of M. Cellérier's Sermons in the "Christian Observer." 1821. 8º. **4105**. bb. **24**.

CELLÉRIER (Jean Isaac Samuel)

—— Discours familiers d'un pasteur de campagne. pp. 494. *Genève; Paris*, 1818. 8º. **4426**. bb. **10**.

—— Seconde édition. Corrigée et augmentée. pp. 529. *Genève*, 1820. 8º. **1360**. k. **6**.

—— Quatrième édition corrigée d'après les notes laissées par l'auteur et augmentée d'un sermon inédit. pp. vi. 326. *Paris*, 1845. 8º. **4425**. e. **20**.

—— Homélies sur divers textes, *etc.* 2 tom. *Genève; Paris*, 1825. 8º. **4426**. dd. **9**.

—— [Another edition.] Nouveaux sermons, ou Homélies sur divers textes, *etc.* 2 tom. *Paris*, 1831. 8º. **1360**. k. **12**.

—— Nouveaux discours familiers d'un pasteur de campagne. 2 tom. *Genève*, 1827. 8º. **1360**. k. **3**.

—— Recueil de prières chrétiennes pour le culte domestique par J. I. S. Cellérier . . . mis en ordre, complété et publié par J. E. Cellérier fils. pp. iv. 252. *Paris*, 1845. 8º. **1220**. k. **27**.

—— Sermons et prières pour les solennités chrétiennes (Sermons et prières pour les dimanches ordinaires). Seconde édition, revue et augmentée. 3 tom. *Genève; Paris*, 1824. 8º. **1360**. k. **11**.

—— Sermons, homélies, discours familiers et prières . . . Nouveau recueil, avec une notice biographique par M. le professeur Diodati. pp. vi. cviii. 435. *Paris*, 1845. 8º. [MISSING.]

—— Trois sermons sur la lecture de l'Écriture sainte. pp. 134. *Genève*, 1819. 8º. [MISSING.]

—— Pensées pieuses sur divers sujets. [Selections from several works.] pp. 7. 280. *Paris*, 1830. 16º. **4403**. b. **55**.

—— [Another edition.] pp. vii. 306. *Paris*, 1844. 8º. **4410**. bb. **8**.

—— [Twelve sermons, abridged and translated into English.] *See* Luscombe (Matthew H. T.) *Bishop of the Scotch Episcopal Church.* Sermons from the French, *etc.* 1825. 8º. **1025**. k. **9**.

—— On the Christian Faith. [A sermon.] *See* Pons (J. S.) The Doctrine of the Church of Geneva illustrated, *etc.* vol. 1. 1825, *etc.* 8º. **1005**. dd. **6**.

CELLÉRIER (Lucien) Étude sur les sociétés anonymes en France et dans les pays voisins. pp. xvi. 564. *Paris*, 1905. 8º. **08226**. cc. **38**.

CELLERNO (Odoardo) Vita di San Luigi Bertrando . . . raccolta da processi fatti per la sua canonizatione, *etc.* pp. 316. *N. A. Tinassi: Roma*, 1671. 4º. **4828**. b. **14**.

CELLES (François Bédos de) *See* Bédos de Celles.

CELLES (J. René) *See* René-Celles.

CELLES (Jean de) Malherbe. Sa vie, son caractère, sa doctrine, *etc.* [With a portrait.] pp. 287. *Paris*, 1937. 8º. **010664**. ee. **48**.

CELLESI (Camillo) [For official documents issued by C. Cellesi as Presidente delle Strade:] *See* States of the Church.—*Tribunale delle Strade.*

—— Bando di subasta [of property belonging to C. Cellesi]. [Dated: 20 Nov. 1717.] *Roma*, 1717. *s. sh.* fol. **1896**. d. **18**. (**185**.)

CELLESI (CAMILLO)

—— Proroga di subasta [of property belonging to C. Cellesi]. [Dated: 5 March 1718.] *Roma,* 1718. *s. sh. obl.* 4°.
1896. d. 19. (37.)

CELLESI (DONATO) Sei fabbriche di Firenze disegnate e incise da D. Cellesi. pl. XXIV. *Firenze,* 1851. fol.
1261. d. 10.

Lithographed throughout.

CELLESI (JACOPO) *See* GALLUCCIUS (A.) Historia della guerra di Fiandra . . . volgarizzata da I. Cellesi, *etc.* 1673. 4°.
156. d. 4, 5.

CELLESI (MARIA ALMA AURORA) Applauso poetico per la sacra solenne velazione di D. M. A. A. Cellesi [and others] . . . religiose dell'ordine di S. Benedetto nel venerabil monastero di S. Pietro di Pistoja, quest' anno 1730. pp. 12. *Pistoja,* [1730.] 4°.
11431. c. 59. (13.)

CELLESIUS (JACOBUS) *See* CELLESI (Jacopo)

CELLI (A. C.) In Memoriam. H.R.H. Prince Leopold, *etc.* [A poem.] pp. 3. [*London,* 1884.] 8°.
11650. e. 18. (6.)

—— (2nd edition.) pp. 3. [*London,* 1884.] 8°.
11650. e. 18. (7.)

CELLI (ANGELO) *See* MARCHIAFAVA (E.) and CELLI (A.) On the Alterations in the Red Globules in Malaria Infection, and on the Origin of Melanæmia, *etc.* 1888. 8°. [KLEBS (E.) *and* TOMMASI-CRUDELI (C.) *On the Nature of Malaria.*]
Ac. 3838/50.

—— *See* ROME.—*The City.—Reale Università di Roma.—Istituto d'Igiene Sperimentale.* Annali . . . Pubblicati per cura del prof. A. Celli. 1891, *etc.* 8°.
Ac. 104. b.

—— La Malaria secondo le nuove ricerche. Con tavole e figure . . . 2ª edizione accresciuta, *etc.* [With a bibliography.] pp. xv. 224. *Roma,* [1900.] 8°.
7561. l. 15.

—— Quarta edizione intieramente rifatta. pp. xvi. 384. *Torino,* 1910. 8°.
7561. l. 16.

—— Malaria according to the New Researches . . . Translated from the second Italian edition by John Joseph Eyre . . . With an introduction by Dr. Patrick Manson . . . With maps and illustrations. pp. xxiv. 275. *Longmans & Co.: London,* 1900. 8°.
07687. h. 4.

—— New edition. pp. xxiv. 275. *Longmans & Co.: London,* 1901. 8°.
[MISSING.]

—— Malaria according to the New Researches . . . Translated from the second Italian edition by John Joseph Eyre . . . New edition, 1901. Reissue. pp. xiv. 275. *Longmans & Co.: London,* 1904. 8°.
7689. b. 33.

—— Storia della malaria nell'Agro romano. Opera postuma con . . . una carta topografica. [With plates.] *Città di Castello,* 1925. 4°. [*Memorie della R. Accademia Nazionale dei Lincei.* Classe di scienze fisiche, *etc.* ser. 6. vol. 1. fasc. 3.]
Ac. 102/11.

—— The History of Malaria in the Roman Campagna from ancient times . . . Edited and enlarged by Anna Celli-Fraentzel, *etc.* [With a bibliography.] pp. viii. 226. *J. Bale & Co.: London,* 1933. 8°.
07688. ee. 12.

—— In onore del Prof. Angelo Celli, nel 25° anno di insegnamento. [With illustrations.] pp. iv. 832. *Torino,* 1913. 8°.
07306. k. 13.

CELLI (ANGELO) and **SCALA** (ALBERTO)

—— Sull'acqua del Tevere. Studio dal punto di vista dell'igiene. 1891. *See* ROME. —*The City.—Accademia Medica, etc.* Atti, *etc.* ser. 2. vol. 5. 1876, *etc.* 8°.
Ac. 3707.

CELLI (DOMENICO) Poema piacevole in versi estemporanei . . . per l'esultanze popolari avvenute nei faustissimi giorni 17. 18. & 19. luglio in occasione del solenne perdono concesso dall'immortale pontefice Pio Nono . . . coll'aggiunta di un canto in terza rima per l'elevazione al sommo pontificato del medesimo. pp. 16. *Roma,* 1846. 8°.
899. c. 9. (5.)

CELLI (FAITH) *See* MURRAY (Faith) calling herself FAITH CELLI.

CELLI (GAETANO) Pel fausto ritorno in Roma di Nostro Signore Papa Pio VII. P.O.M. stanze, *etc.* *Roma,* 1814. 4°.
898. i. 5. (10.)

CELLI (LUIGI) Storia della sollevazione di Urbino contro il duca Guidobaldo II Feltrio della Rovere dal 1572 al 1574, *etc.* pp. viii. 304. *Torino, Roma,* 1892. 8°.
9166. ee. 12.

CELLI (PIETRO) Del principio di nazionalità nella moderna società europea. pp. 285. *Pavia,* 1867. 8°.
8007. ee. 12.

—— Del riordinamento della pubblica beneficenza. Studio. pp. 58. *Milano,* 1883. 8°.
8276. aaa. 50. (9.)

—— L'Estensione del suffragio politico e la rappresentanza parlamentare delle minoranze. Pensieri e proposte. pp. 38. *Milano,* 1878. 8°.
8032. b. 10. (8.)

—— Sistema di diritto internazionale moderno. pp. 226. *Firenze,* 1872. 8°.
6955.f.20.

CELLIER (A.) *of Saint-Quentin-sur-Coole.* Propositions de médecine et de chirurgie; thèse, *etc.* pp. 27. *Paris,* 1833. 4°.
1184. e. 11. (34.)

CELLIER (ALEXANDRE) L'Orgue moderne . . . Suivi d'un supplément sur l'orgue expressif ou harmonium . . . Préface de Louis Vierne. [With plates.] pp. 135. *Paris,* 1913. 8°.
7896. w. 8.

—— Les Passions et l'Oratorio de Noël de J. S. Bach. Précédé d'une notice biographique. [With plates, including a portrait.] pp. 212. *Paris, Bruges* [printed], 1929. 8°. [*Collection des grandes œuvres musicales.*]
W.P. 8853/5.

CELLIER (ALEXANDRE) and **BACHELIN** (HENRI)

—— L'Orgue. Ses éléments— son histoire—son esthétique, *etc.* [With illustrations.] pp. 254. *Paris,* 1933. 4°.
[MISSING.]

CELLIER (AMÉDÉE) Faculté de Droit de Paris. Thèse pour la licence, *etc.* (Jus romanum. Depositi vel contra. —Droit français. Du prêt.) pp. 70. *Paris,* 1859. 8°.
5406. b. 11. (9.)

CELLIER (ANDRÉ)

—— La Viticulture française et les projets d'Office national du vin. Thèse, *etc.* pp. 272. *Montpellier,* 1938. 8°.
8234. g. 68.

CELLIER (ANTOINE) Opuscula nova anatomica. Thomæ Petruccij, Casparis Bartholini, et Joannis Verle. [Edited by A. Cellier.] pp. 179. *A. Cellier: Lugduni,* 1680. 12°.
780. c. 3.

CELLIER (CHARLES ÉLIE) Réflexions sur la révolution genevoise et en particulier sur l'insurrection du 19 juillet 1794 et ses suites. pp. 16. [*Geneva*, 1794.] 8º.
8074. i. 13. (21.)

CELLIER (EDMOND) Histoire économique de la poterie de grès dans la Puisaye de 1700 à 1870. pp. 118. *Lille*, 1932. 8º.
8230. cc. 27.

CELLIER (ELIZABETH) *See* CRESSWELL ( ) *Madam.* A Letter from the Lady Creswell to Madam C. the Midwife (Madam Cellier), on the publishing her late Vindication, &c. Also A Whip for Impudence: or, a lashing repartee to the snarling midwifes Matchless Rogue, *etc.* [1680.] fol.
1881. c. 3. (28.)

—— *See* DANGERFIELD (T.) The Case of Tho. Dangerfield: with some remarkable passages that happened at the tryals of Elizabeth Cellier . . . and the Earl of Castlemain, *etc.* 1680. fol.
[MISSING.]

—— *See* DANGERFIELD (T.) Mr Tho. Dangerfeild's Second Narrative: wherein is contained a faithful charge against the Lady Powis, Mr. Stamford . . . and Mrs. Cellier, *etc.* 1680. fol.
T. 94*. (4.)

—— *See* OSBORNE (Thomas) 1st *Duke of Leeds.* The New Popish Sham-Plot discovered: or, the Cursed contrivance of the Earl of Danby, Mrs. Celier, with the Popish Lords, and Priests, in the Tower and Newgate, fully detected, *etc.* [1681?] *s. sh.* fol.
T. 3*. (49.)

—— *See* W., W., *Sir.* Newgate Salutation; or, a Dialogue between Sir W. W. [i.e. Sir William Waller] and Mrs. Cellier. [1680.] *s. sh.* fol.
1872. a. 1. (133.)

—— Malice Defeated: or a Brief relation of the accusation and deliverance of Elizabeth Cellier, wherein her proceedings . . . are particularly related, and the mystery of the meal-tub fully discovered. Together with an abstract of her arraignment and tryal, written by her self, *etc.* pp. 46. *For Elizabeth Cellier: London*, 1680. fol.
T. 2*. (27.)

—— [Another copy.]
T. 96*. (1.)

—— [Another copy.]
515. l. 1. (11.)

—— [Another edition.] pp. 48. *For Elizabeth Cellier: London*, 1680. fol.
515. l. 1. (10.)

—— [Another copy.]
102. i. 19.
Imperfect; wanting all after p. 44.

—— —— *See* DANGERFIELD (T.) Tho. Dangerfield's Answer to a certain . . . Pamphlet, entituled, Malice Defeated, *etc.* 1680. fol.
T. 1*. (74.)

—— —— *See* PRANCE (Miles) Mr. Prance's Answer to Mrs. Cellier's Libel [i.e. "Malice Defeated"], *etc.* 1680. fol.
T. 1*. (75.)

—— —— The Midwife Unmask'd; or, the Popish design of Mrs. Cellier's meal-tub plainly made known; being a second answer to her scandalous libel, *etc.* pp. 4. *For T. Davies: London*, 1680. fol.
T. 2*. (9.)

—— —— Modesty triumphing over Impudence. Or, Some notes upon a late romance published by E. Cellier [i.e. "Malice Defeated"] . . . Together with the depositions of Richard Adams . . . against her, before his Majesty, *etc.* pp. 19. *For Jonathan Wilkins: London*, 1680. fol.
[MISSING.]

CELLIER (ELIZABETH)

—— The Scarlet Beast Stripped Naked, being the mistery of the meal-tub the second time unravelled; or a brief answer to the Popish-midwives scandalous narrative, intituled Mallice Defeated, *etc.* pp. 4. 4. *Printed by D. Mallet:* [1680.] fol.
T. 1*. (105.)

—— [Another copy.]
515. l. 18. (18.)

—— To the Praise of Mrs. Cellier the Popish Midwife; on her incomparable book. [Verses.] *For Walter Davis: London*, 1680. *s. sh.* fol.
C. 20. f. 2. (133.)

—— [Another copy.]
Lutt. III. 130.

—— A Scheme for the Foundation of a Royal Hospital, and raising a revenue of five or six-thousand pounds a year, by, and for the maintenance of a corporation of skilful midwives, and such foundlings or exposed children, as shall be admitted therein, *etc.* 1745. *See* HARLEIAN MISCELLANY. The Harleian Miscellany, *etc.* vol. 4. 1744, *etc.* 4º.
185. a. 8.

—— [Another edition.] 1751. *See* SOMERS (John) *Baron Somers.* A Fourth Collection of Scarce and Valuable Tracts, *etc.* vol. 2. 1752, *etc.* 4º.
184. a. 14.

—— [Another edition.] 1809. *See* HARLEIAN MISCELLANY. The Harleian Miscellany, *etc.* vol. 4. 1808, *etc.* 4º.
2072. g.

—— [Another edition.] 1813. *See* SOMERS (John) *Baron Somers.* A Collection of Scarce and Valuable Tracts, *etc.* vol. 9. 1809, *etc.* 4º.
750. g. 9.

—— To Dr ----- an Answer to his Queries, concerning the Colledg of Midwives. pp. 8. [*London*, 1688.] 4º.
1178. h. 2. (2.)

—— The Complaint of Mrs Celiers, and the Jesuits in Newgate, to the E. of D. [i.e. the Earl of Danby] and the Lords in the Tower, concerning the discovery of their new sham-plot. *For T. Benskins: London*, [1680?] *s. sh.* fol.
1897. c. 20. (18**.)

—— The Devil pursued: or, the Right saddle laid upon the right mare; a satyr upon Madam Celliers standing in the pillory . . . By a Person of Quality. [In verse.] *For T. Davies: London*, 1680. *s. sh.* fol.
C. 20. f. 2. (134.)

—— [Another copy.]
Lutt. II. 58.

—— Maddam Celliers Lamentation standing on the Pillory. [In verse.] *See* INNOCENT XI., *Pope.* The Popes Letter, to Maddam Cellier in relation to her great sufferings for the Catholick Cause, *etc.* 1680. *s. sh.* fol.
1897. c. 19. (50.)

—— Mistriss Celier's Lamentation for the Loss of her Liberty. (Her Cordial. [In verse.]) *For S. J.: London*, 1681. *s. sh.* fol.
1881. c. 3. (37.)

—— The Tryal and Sentence of Elizabeth Cellier; for writing, printing, and publishing a scandalous libel, called Malice Defeated, *etc.* pp. 39. *For Thomas Collins: London*, 1680. fol.
T. 96*. (2.)

—— [Another copy.]
515. l. 1. (9.)

—— The Triall of Elizabeth Cellier . . . June the 11th. 1680. pp. 17. 1680. *See* CARE (Henry) The Trial of Henry Carr, *etc.* 1681, *etc.* fol.
[MISSING.]

CELLIER (ELIZABETH)

—— A True Copy of a Letter of Consolation sent to Nat. the Printer, near the Pope's keys in Fetter-Lane, from the Meal-Tub Midwife, in New-gate. *For W. Johnson: London,* 1681. *s. sh.* fol. **700. l. 24.**

CELLIER (EUGÈNE) De l'udosadénite—eczéma. pp. 39. *Paris,* 1833. 4°. [*Collection des thèses soutenues à la Faculté de Médecine de Paris.* An 1853. tom. 4.] **7372. f. 6.**

CELLIER (FRANÇOIS) De la division labiale de naissance, vulgairement nommé bec-de-lièvre, *etc.* [A thesis.] pp. 59. *Paris,* an XI [1803]. 8°. **1182. b. 19. (5.)**

CELLIER (FRANÇOIS ARSÈNE) and **BRIDGEMAN** (CUNNINGHAM) Gilbert, Sullivan, and D'Oyly Carte. Reminiscences of the Savoy and the Savoyards . . . With 63 portrait and other illustrations and 6 facsimile letters. pp. xxiii. 443. *Sir I. Pitman & Sons: London,* 1914. 8°. **011795. cc. 20.**

—— Second edition. pp. xxiii. 443. *Sir I. Pitman & Sons: London,* 1927. 8°. **010855. eee. 25.**

CELLIER (HENRI) *See* CHARTON (E. T.) Guide pour le choix d'un état . . . Rédigé par MM. Bourguignon . . . Cap . . . Cellier, *etc.* 1842. 8°. **789. bb. 28.**

CELLIER (HONORÉ) Leis Artistos, oou Dernier trin de San-Just. Scèno histouriquo et coumiquo. [In verse.] pp. 4. *Marseille,* [1858.] 8°. **11498. f. 59. (11.)**

CELLIER (JEAN) Das Verhältnis des Parlaments zum Volke, mit besonderer Berücksichtigung des schweizerischen Staatsrechtes. Dissertation, *etc.* pp. 124. *Zürich,* 1936. 8°. **08073. dd. 5.**

CELLIER (JULES) Le Bienheureux J.-B. de la Salle, *etc.* pp. x. 416. *Montreuil-sur-Mer,* 1896. 8°. **4865. dd. 23.**

—— Pour et contre les Juifs. pp. iii. 351. *Saint-Amand,* 1896. 8°. **4033. h. 44.**

CELLIER (L. M.) and **DESPREZ** (A. B.) Accord de la raison et de la tradition sur la légitimité des opérations de l'Assemblée nationale, concernant le clergé. 2 pt. pp. 288. *Chaalons,* 1792. 8°. **F.R. 158. (8.)**

CELLIER (LÉON)

—— L'Epopée romantique. pp. 276. *Paris,* 1954. 8°. **11872. b. 4.** *Université de Grenoble. Publications de la Faculté des Lettres.* no. 11.

CELLIER (LOUIS)

——   Antoine Watteau, son enfance, ses contemporains, *etc.* [With a portrait.] pp. 110. *Valenciennes,* 1867. 8°. **10660. dd. 24.**

—— Essai biographique. La famille de Pujol. (Extrait du Courrier du Nord.) pp. 151. *Valenciennes,* 1861. 8°. **9904. b. 11.**

—— Essai sur l'atelier monétaire de Valenciennes et sur le monogramme de la monnaie des comtes de Hainault. pp. 32. *Valenciennes,* 1869. 8°. **7756. de. 7. (4.)**

—— Glossaire topographique de l'arrondissement de Valenciennes. pp. 95. *Valenciennes,* 1859. 8°. **10173. bbb. 5.**

—— Notre-Dame de Saint-Cordon. Souvenir de l'an 1864. pp. 66. *Valenciennes,* 1864. 8°. **10171. g. 29.**

CELLIER (MAURICE MÖCKLI) *See* MOECKLI-CELLIER.

CELLIER (NOÉMI) Courte notice sur la vie et la mort de Mlle N. Cellier. pp. 64. *Montpellier,* 1865. 12°. **4863. bbb. 34. (2.)**

CELLIER (REGN. LAURENT) *See* OUDIN (F.) Ludovici Magni equus triumphalis, *etc.* (Le Statue équestre: traduction [by R. L. Cellier].) 1725. 4°. **T. 1776. (3.)**

CELLIER (VICTOR AMÉDÉE SÉCHERET) *See* SÉCHERET-CELLIER.

CELLIER-DUFAYEL (NARCISSE HONORÉ) Athénée national de Paris. Inauguration du nouveau local, place Vendôme, 12. Séance du 10 juin 1852. Discours d'ouverture, prononcé par . . . N.-H. Cellier Du Fayel. pp. 8. *Paris,* 1852. 8°. **8355. e. 13.**

—— Morale conjugale et style épistolaire des femmes; appréciation des lettres de Madame la duchesse de Praslin. pp. 103. *Paris,* 1850. 8°. **10910. g. 22.**

—— Noblesse et préjugés. pp. 308. *Paris,* 1852. 8°. **8008. e. 5.**

—— Origine commune de la littérature et de la législation chez tous les peuples démontrée par l'examen comparatif des monuments littéraires des Hébreux, des Hindous, des Chinois, des Mahométans, *etc.* pp. xii. 388. *Paris,* 1843. 8°. **817. c. 10.**

CELLIÈRE (LOUIS) Traité élémentaire de peinture en céramique . . . Quatrième édition, revue, *etc.* pp. 128. *Paris,* 1883. 12°. **7858. bb. 27.**

CELLIERS (JAN F. E.) *See* HALT (Marie R.) Mannie. Geoutoriseerde Afrikaanse vertaling van "Histoire d'un petit homme" . . . deur J. F. E. Celliers, *etc.* 1925. 8°. **012582. c. 60.**

—— *See* MÉRIMÉE (P.) Colomba . . . Vertaal . . . deur J. F. E. Celliers. 1920. 8°. **12516. pp. 9.**

—— Die Groot geheim. [A poem.] pp. 44. *Pretoria,* 1924. 8°. **011557. k. 80.**

—— Heldinne van die oorlog. Twede hersiene druk. Tooneelstuk in vier bedrywe, *etc.* pp. 40. *Pretoria,* 1924. 8°. **011755. g. 43.**

—— Jopie Fourie, en ander nuwe gedigte. pp. 106. *Kaapstad,* 1920. 8°. **011556. eee. 40.**

—— Kuns in lewe en kultur. 'n Eenvoudige bespreking van enige grondbegrippe. pp. 161. *Kaapstad & Bloemfontein,* 1933. 8°. **[MISSING.]**

—— Die Lewenstuin, en ander gedigte. pp. 116. *Pretoria,* 1923. 8°. **011557. l. 52.**

—— Liefde en plig . . . 'n Toneelspel in vier bedrywe, *etc.* pp. 64. *Kaapstad; Pretoria, Amsterdam,* 1920. 8°. [*Die Suidafrikaanse toneel.* no. 23.] **11756. aa. 30/23.**

—— Liefdelewe. [Verses.] pp. 90. *Pretoria,* 1924. 8°. **011557. i. 35.**

—— Martje . . . [A poem.] Met voorberig van Dr. Leo Fouché. pp. ix. 116. *Kampen,* [1912.] 8°. **011556. e. 41.**

—— Tweede hersiene druk. pp. 106. *Amsterdam; Kaapstad,* 1916. 8°. **11556. cc. 67.**

—— Ou Gawie, en ander verhale en sketse. pp. 171. *Pretoria,* 1924. 8°. **12582. pp. 8.**

—— Die Saaier, en ander nuwe gedigte. pp. 108. *Pretoria, Amsterdam; Kaapstad,* 1918. 8°. **011557. l. 54.**

CELLIERS (Jan F. E.)

—— De Vlakte en ander gedigte, insluitende " Die Rivier " en " Unie-Kantate " . . . Vyfde druk, *etc.* pp. 145. *Kaapstad*, 1920. 8°.　　　　　**011557. i. 40.**

—— Jan Celliers. [Extracts. With a portrait.] pp. 74. *Kaapstad*, [1925.] *obl.* 12°.　　　　　**011557. de. 9.**

CELLIEZ (Adelaïde) Les Impératrices. France, Russie, Autriche, Brésil . . . Ouvrage illustré de seize dessins à deux teintes par MM. Y. et H. Grenier. pp. vi. 616. *Paris*, [1860.] 8°.　　　　　**10604. f. 7.**

—— Les Reines d'Angleterre. [With plates.] pp. xiv. 617. *Paris*, 1852. 8°.　　　　　**10805. f. 10.**

—— Les Reines d'Espagne, suivies des reines de Portugal. [With plates.] pp. v. 361. *Paris*, [1856.] 8°.　　　　　**10632. f. 18.**

—— Les Reines de France . . . Nouvelle édition ornée de . . . portraits, *etc.* pp. 524. *Paris*, [1886.] 8°.　　　　　**10659. g. 3.**

—— Scènes de l'histoire contemporaine. Évènements, anecdotes, souvenirs, personnages depuis la Révolution jusqu'à nos jours . . . Ouvrage illustré de 16 dessins à deux teintes [by] MM. Y. et H. Grenier. pp. ii. 630. *Paris*, [1861.] 8°.　　　　　**09008. d. 3.**

CELLIEZ (Adelaïde Joséphine Charlotte) Historique de l'instruction du Chinois qui a été présenté au Roi, le 8 octobre 1821, par M. Philibert, capitaine de vaisseau, *etc.* pp. 20. *Blois*, 1822. 4°.　　　　　**821. ee. 29.**

CELLIEZ (Henry) *See* Le Senne (C.) Code du théâtre . . . Avant-propos par M. H. Celliez. 1878. 12°.　　　　　**5423. b. 7.**

—— Dictionnaire usuel de législation commerciale et industrielle, *etc.* pp. 700. *Paris*, 1836. 8°.　　**1374. f. 7.**

—— M. Libri n'est pas contumax. Consultation de Me H. Celliez . . . sur la pétition adressée au Sénat, suivie de l'adhésion de Me Édouard Laboulaye . . . et d'une adresse des députés au Parlement italien. pp. 14. *Paris*, 1861. 8°.　　　　　**10602. dd. 14. (1.)**

—— Mémoire sur les irrégularités de la procédure criminelle suivie contre M. Libri, et sur l'application de l'art. 441 du Code d'instruction criminelle pour la révision de cette procédure,*etc.* pp. iv. 92. *Paris*, 1861. 8°.　[MISSING.]

CELLIEZ (L. J. B.) Thèse pour le doctorat en médecine, *etc.* (Questions sur diverses branches des sciences médicales.) pp. 31. *Paris*, 1839. 4°. [*Collection des thèses soutenues à la Faculté de Médecine de Paris.* An 1839. tom. 4.]　　　　　**7371. a. 4.**

CELLIEZ (P. C.) Réflexions philosophiques sur la méthode à employer pour parvenir à la connoissance de la maladie. pp. 22. *Montpellier*, [1801.] 4°.　　**1180. d. 9. (21.)**

CELLI-FRAENTZEL (Anna) *See* Celli (A.) The History of Malaria in the Roman Campagna from ancient times . . . Edited and enlarged by A. Celli-Fraentzel, *etc.* 1933. 8°.　　　　　**07688. ee. 12.**

CELLINI (Adolfo) La Questione romana al tribunale di Dante Alighieri. Dal periodico senese " Religione e civiltà," *etc.* pp. xii. 61. *Siena*, 1914. 8°.　　　　　**11421. g. 42.**

CELLINI (Benvenuto) *the Artist.* Opere. 3 vol.
　　vol. 1, 2. Vita di Benvenuto Cellini . . . da lui medesimo scritta . . . Ora per la prima volta ridotta a buona lezione ed accompagnata con note da Gio. Palamede Carpani. 1806, 11.
　　vol. 3. Due trattati . . . uno dell'oreficeria, l'altro della scultura. Coll'aggiunta di altre operette (Lettere, discorsi e poesie), *etc.* pp. lx. 417. 1811.
Milano, 1806, 11. 8°. [*Collezione de' classici italiani.* vol. 142–144.]　　**12201.p.1/142–144.**
Imperfect; wanting pp. 353–368 of vol. 3, the place of which is taken by the corresponding pages of vol. 2.

—— [Another copy.]　　　　　**277. f. 6–8.**

—— [Another copy of vol. 1, 2.]　　**564. b. 20, 21.**

—— Vita di Benvenuto Cellini . . . scritta da lui medesimo, restituita alla lezione originale sul manoscritto Poirot ora Laurenziano ed arricchita d'illustrazioni e documenti inediti dal dottor Francesco Tassi. (vol. 3. Ricordi, prose e poesie di Benvenuto Cellini, con documenti la maggior parte inediti, *etc.*) 3 vol. *Firenze*, 1829. 8°.　　　　　**563. a. 22–24.**

—— Opere. (vol. 1, 2. Vita di Benvenuto Cellini . . . scritta da lui medesimo, giusta l'autografo pubblicato dal Tassi. Con cinque tavole in rame.—vol. 3. Trattati e discorsi . . . Con una tavola in rame.) 3 vol. *Lipsia*, 1833, 35. 12°.　　　　　**12226. b. 19.**
The collective title " Opere " appears only on the half-title of vol. 3.

—— Le Opere di Benvenuto Cellini, arricchite di note ed illustrazioni. pp. 600. *Firenze*, 1843. 4°.　　　　　**12226. g. 10.**
Part of the " Collezione generale dei classici italiani."

—— La Vita di Benvenuto Cellini, seguita dai trattati dell'oreficeria e della scultura e dagli scritti sull'arte. Con 196 illustrazioni. Prefazione e note di Arturo Jahn Rusconi e A. Valeri. pp. xviii. 857. *Roma*, 1901. 8°.　　　　　**10633. h. 9.**

—— Discorso . . . dell'architettura. *See* Nani (G.) I Codici manoscritti volgari della libreria Naniana, *etc.* 1776. 4°.　　　　　**620. i. 10. (2.)**

—— Due trattati, vno intorno alle otto principali arti dell' oreficeria. L'altro in materia dell'arte della scultura, *etc.* (Poesie toscane, et latine sopra il Perseo statua di bronzo, e il Crocifisso statua di marmo fatte da Messer Benuenuto Cellini.) ff. 47 [61]. *Per V. Panizzij & M. Peri: Fiorenza*, 1568. 4°.　　　　　**1044. d. 7.**

—— [Another copy.]　　　　　**57. c. 5.**

—— [Another copy.]　　　　　**G. 6201.**

—— Due trattati, *etc.* (Frammento di un discorso di Benvenuto Cellini sopra i principj e 'l modo d'imparare l'arte del disegno.) pp. xxvii. 156. *Firenze*, 1731. 4°.　　　　　**562*. c. 4. (1.)**

—— [Another edition.] pp. xxxii. 162. 13.　　*Firenze*, 1731. 4°.　　　　　**G. 16557.**

—— I Trattati dell'oreficeria e della scultura di Benvenuto Cellini, nuovamente messi alle stampe secondo la originale dettatura del codice Marciano per cura di Carlo Milanesi. Si aggiungono: i discorsi e i ricordi intorno all'arte. Le lettere e le suppliche. Le poesie. pp. lviii. 487. *Firenze*, 1857. 8°.　　　　　**12226. b. 9.**

—— The Treatises of Benvenuto Cellini on Goldsmithing and Sculpture. (Made into English from the Italian of the Marcian codex by C. R. Ashbee.) [With plates.] pp. xiv. 164. *Edward Arnold: London*, 1898. 4°.　　　　　**C. 99. k. 4.**

CELLINI (Benvenuto) *the Artist.*

—— Abhandlungen über die Goldschmiedekunst und die Sculptur . . . Übersetzt und verglichen mit den Parallelstellen aus Theophilus' Diversarum artium schedula von Justus Brinckmann. pp. vi. 193. *Leipzig*, 1867. 8º.
[MISSING.]

—— Racconti di Benvenuto Cellini, ora per la prima volta pubblicati. (Per occasione delle nobilissime nozze del conte Giovanni Cittadella con la contessa Laura Maldura.) [Edited by B. Gamba from a MS. in the Biblioteca di San Marco at Venice, with the full text of the introduction to Cellini's "Trattato dell'oreficeria" from the same MS. and an additional "racconto" reprinted from the preface to the 1731 edition of the "Due trattati." With a dedication by A. Dondiorologio Amai.] pp. 47. *Venezia*, 1828. 8º. **10630. dd. 8.**

—— Le Rime di Benvenuto Cellini. Pubblicate ed annotate per cura di Adolfo Mabellini. pp. 282. *Torino*, 1890. 8º. **11429. f. 19.**
No. 55 of an edition of 100 copies. The date in the colophon and on the wrapper is 1891.

—— Vita di Benvenuto Cellini . . . da lui medesimo scritta . . . tratta da un'ottimo manoscritto, *etc.* [The dedication by the editor, A. C. Cocchi, signed: Seb. Artopolita.] pp. 318. *Pietro Martello: Colonia* [*Naples*], [1728.] 4º. **134. a. 11**

—— [Another copy.] **673. h. 15.**

—— [Another copy.] **G. 1704.**

—— Vita di Benvenuto Cellini . . . da lui medesimo scritta. 2 vol. pp. x. 632. *Milano*, 1805. 4º. **1329. f. 14.**

—— Vita di Benvenuto Cellini . . . da lui medesimo scritta. Ridotta a buona lezione ed illustrata da Gio. Palamede Carpani. (Ricordi di Benvenuto Cellini.—Lettere, discorsi e poesie.) 3 vol. *Milano*, 1821. 8º. **611. g. 17–19.**
Vol. 1–3 of a series entitled " Vite di uomini illustri scritte da loro medesimi."

—— Vita di Benvenuto Cellini scritta da lui medesimo, tratta dall'autografo per cura di Giuseppe Molini. Con brevi annotazioni. pp. viii. 562. *Firenze*, 1830. 12º. **1043. a. 5.**
With an additional titlepage, engraved.

—— Edizione seconda, collazionata di nuovo coll'originale e ricorretta con brevi annotazioni e una scelta di documenti. 2 tom. pp. xii. 734. *Firenze*, 1832. 8º. **563. a. 25.**

—— Vita di Benvenuto Cellini . . . scritta per lui medesimo . . . Edizione eseguita su quella della Società Editrice Fiorentina, arricchita di moltissime note ed illustrazioni. 2 vol. *Torino*, 1852. 8º. **10630. a. 9.**
Part of the " Nuovo biblioteca popolare."

—— La Vita di Benvenuto Cellini, scritta da lui medesimo, ridotta alla lezione originale del codice Laurenziano, con note e documenti illustrativi e con un saggio delle sue rime. Aggiuntevi le notizie pubblicate dal marchese Giuseppe Campori intorno alle relazioni del Cellini col cardinale Ippolito d'Este, ed . . . a' suoi allievi Paolo Romano e Ascanio da Tagliacozzo, novamente accresciute e corrette. Seconda edizione. [Edited by E. Camerini.] pp. 414. *Milano*, 1874. 8º. **10631. bbb. 11.**
No. 5 of the " Biblioteca classica economica."

—— Vita di Benvenuto Cellini scritta da lui medesimo. [Edited by Guido Biagi.] pp. ix. 634. *Firenze*, 1883. 32º. **20003. aa. 71.**

CELLINI (Benvenuto) *the Artist.*

—— La Vita di Benvenuto Cellini scritta da lui medesimo, restituita esattamente alla lezione originale, con osservazioni filologiche e brevi note dichiarative ad uso dei non Toscani per cura di B. Bianchi . . . Nuova edizione. pp. viii. 626. *Firenze*, 1886. 8º. **10629. aaa. 47.**
Part of the " Biblioteca nazionale economica."

—— La Vita di Benvenuto Cellini scritta da lui medesimo. Nuovamente riscontrata sul codice Laurenziano, con note e illustrazioni di Gaetano Guasti. pp. xxvii. 672. *Firenze*, 1890. 8º. **10629. cc. 28.**

—— Vita di Benvenuto Cellini. Testo critico, con introduzione e note storiche per cura di Orazio Bacci. Col ritratto del Cellini e con altre illustrazioni. pp. xci. 451. *Firenze*, 1901. 8º. **10631. dd. 1.**

—— La Vita di Benvenuto Cellini. Illustrata da note di Attilio Butti. Adorna di 32 grandi incisioni e 35 riproduzioni fotografiche dei migliori lavori. pp. 645. *Milano*, 1910. 8º. **10632. p. 1.**

—— The Life of Benvenuto Cellini : a Florentine artist . . . Written by himself . . . and translated from the original by Thomas Nugent, *etc.* 2 vol. *T. Davies: London*, 1771. 8º. **786. g. 4, 5.**

—— [Another copy.] **277. g. 2, 3.**

—— [Another edition.] 2 vol. *R. & T. Desilver: Philadelphia*, 1812. 12º. **10631. b. 4.**

—— Memoirs of Benvenuto Cellini . . . written by himself . . . A new edition. Corrected and enlarged from the last Milan edition. With the notes and observations of G. P. Carpani, now first translated by Thomas Roscoe. 2 vol. *H. Colburn & Co.: London*, 1822. 8º. **563. a. 20, 21.**

—— The Life of Benvenuto Cellini . . . Written by himself. Translated by Thomas Nugent, *etc.* 2 vol. *Hunt & Clarke: London*, 1828. 12º. [*Autobiography.* vol. 16, 17.] **010602. a. 3/2.**

—— [Another copy.] **1154. a. 12.**

—— Memoirs of Benvenuto Cellini . . . written by himself . . . Now first collated with the new text of Giusippe [*sic*] Molini and corrected and enlarged from the last Milan edition, with notes and observations of G. P. Carpani. Translated by Thomas Roscoe. pp. viii. 504. *London*, 1847. 8º. [*Bohn's Standard Library.*] **2504. a. 14.**

—— [Another edition.] pp. viii. 504. *H. G. Bohn: London*, 1850. 8º. **20019. aa. 57.**

—— The Life of Benvenuto Cellini, newly translated into English by John Addington Symonds. With engraved portrait and eight etchings by F. Laguillermie, also eighteen reproductions of the works of the master. 2 vol. *J. C. Nimmo: London*, 1888 [1887]. 8º. **2262. c. 12.**

—— [Another copy.] **L.P.** **10629. g. 8.**
No. 99 of 100 copies printed on large paper, with etchings as India proofs.

—— Second edition. 2 vol. *J. C. Nimmo: London*, 1888. 8º. **10629. c. 7.**

—— Third edition. With a mezzotint portrait. pp. liv. 514. *J. C. Nimmo: London*, 1889. 8º. **10629. f. 40.**

—— Fourth edition, *etc.* pp. liv. 464. *J. C. Nimmo: London*, 1896. 8º. **10629. dd. 27.**

CELLINI (BENVENUTO) *the Artist.*

—— [Another edition.] (Seen through the press by C. J. Holmes and decorated by C. S. Ricketts.) 2 vol. *Printed at the Ballantyne Press: London; sold by Hacon & Ricketts: London; John Lane: New York,* 1900. fol.
C. **99**. k. **8**.

—— The Life of Benvenuto Cellini written by himself. Translated out of the Italian, with an introduction, by Anne Macdonell. 2 vol.   *J. M. Dent & Co.: London; E. P. Dutton & Co.: New York,* 1903. 8º. [*Temple Autobiographies.* vol. 1, 2.]   **10600**. e. **12/2**.

—— Benvenuto Cellini. Memoirs written by himself. Translated by Thomas Roscoe. [Revised by Luigi Ricci.] pp. 527.   *Unit Library: London & New York,* 1903. 8º. [*Unit Library.* no. 24.]   **012209**. ee. **3/20**.

—— [A reissue.] Memoirs of Benvenuto Cellini. Written by himself. The translation of Thomas Roscoe revised by Luigi Ricci. With illustrations in photogravure. **L.P.** *London,* 1904. 8º.   **10633**. ee. **1**.

—— Autobiography of Benvenuto Cellini. Translated by Thomas Roscoe. pp. viii. 571.   *George Newnes: London; C. Scribner's Sons: New York,* 1904. 8º. **10629**. aa. **68**.

—— The Life of Benvenuto Cellini . . . Translated . . . by John Addington Symonds. Fifth edition, *etc.* pp. liv. 464.   *Macmillan & Co.: London,* 1905. 8º.
010632. bb. **20**.
Previous edition 1896.

—— The Memoirs of Benvenuto Cellini written by himself. Translated by Thomas Roscoe, *etc.* pp. 527. *Hutchinson & Co.: London,* 1906. 8º.   [*Library of Standard Biographies.*]   **10602**. e. **25/3**.
A reissue of the " Unit Library " edition of 1904.

—— [Another issue.]   *J. M. Dent & Co.: London; E. P. Dutton & Co.: New York,* [1906.] 8º. [*Everyman's Library.*]   **12206.p.1/107.**

—— The Life of Benvenuto Cellini. A new version by Robert H. Hobart Cust. (Bibliography of Cellini literature contributed by Sydney J. A. Churchill . . . and list of Cellini's works.) [With plates.] 2 vol.   *G. Bell & Sons: London,* 1910. 8º.   **10633**. a. **3**.

—— The Life of Benvenuto Cellini . . . written by himself. Translated . . . by Anne Macdonell . . . Illustrated with . . . drawings . . . and . . . portraits. pp. xiv. 368. *J. M. Dent & Sons: London & Toronto,* 1926. 8º.
10634. df. **15**.

—— Benvenuto Cellini: Memoirs written by himself. Roscoe's translation revised throughout. pp. xviii. 535. *Oxford University Press: London,* 1927. 8º.   [*World's Classics.* no. 300.]   **012209**. df. **204**.

—— The Life of Benvenuto Cellini. A new version by Robert H. Hobart Cust. [With plates.] 2 vol. *Navarre Society: London,* 1927. 8º.   **10634**. bbb. **17**.
A reissue of the edition of 1910.

—— [A reissue, with the addition of a prefatory note.] *London,* 1935. 8º.   **20019**. c. **31**.

—— The Life of Benvenuto Cellini, written by himself. (Translated by John Addington Symonds. Introduced and illustrated by John Pope-Hennessy.) [With plates.] pp. xiv. 498. *Phaidon Press: London,* 1949. 8º.
10630. k. **23**.
Previous edition 1905.

CELLINI (BENVENUTO) *the Artist.*

—— The Autobiography of Benvenuto Cellini. Translated and with an introduction by George Bull. pp. 396. *Penguin Books: Harmondsworth,* 1956 [1955]. 8º. [*Penguin Classics.* no. L 49.]   W.P. **513/49**.

—— Mémoires de Benvenuto Cellini. Traduction de D. D. Farjasse. Nouvelle édition illustrée de 60 gravures. pp. 343. *Paris,* 1875. 4º.   **10629**. g. **7**.

—— Mémoires de Benvenuto Cellini . . . écrits par lui-même et traduits par Léopold Leclanché. pp. vii. 492. *Paris,* [1844.] 12º.   **1402**. b. **41**.

—— La Vie de Benvenuto Cellini, écrite par lui-même. Traduction Léopold Leclanché. Notes et index de M. Franco. Illustrée de neuf eaux-fortes par F. Laguillermie et de reproductions des œuvres du maître. pp. 624. *Paris,* 1881. 8º.   **10629**. f. **12**.

—— Benvenuto Cellini. Eine Geschichte des XVI. Jahrhunderts. (Nach dem Italien'schen. Von J. W. von Göthe.) 3 Tl. *Braunschweig,* 1798. 8º. **10631**. aaa. **19**.
The titlepage is engraved.

—— [Another edition.] Leben des Benvenuto Cellini . . . von ihm selbst geschrieben. Übersezt und mit einem Anhange herausgegeben von Goethe. 2 Tl.   *Tübingen,* 1803. 8º.   **10631**. bb. **45**.
The titlepage of Tl. 1 *is engraved.*

—— [Another edition.] Benvenuto Cellini von Goethe. Mit einer Einleitung von Ernst Hermann. pp. xxii. 376. *Berlin,* 1872. 8º.   **10631**. aaa. **27**.

—— [Another edition.] Benvenuto Cellini, deutsch von Goethe, mit Steinzeichnungen von Max Slevogt. pp. 423. *Berlin,* 1913. 4º.   Dept. of Prints & Drawings.

—— Benvenuto Cellini önéletírása olaszból fordította, bevezetéssel és jegyzetekkel ellátta Szana Tamás. Számos önálló . . . képpel. 2 köt.   *Budapest,* 1890, 91 [1889–91]. 8º.   **10629**. cc. **23**.
Published in parts.

—— Benvenuto Cellini à Paris sous François Iᵉʳ. [An extract from the " Vita " translated into French.] Notes de Ch. Gailly de Taurines, *etc.* pp. 182. pl. III.   *Paris,* 1908. 8º.   **10633**. g. **36**.

—— [Vita.] Mitt liv. På norsk ved Tryggve Norum. Med illustrasjoner og etterord av Per Palle Storm. pp. 487. *Oslo,* 1945. 4º.   **10635**. h. **1**.

—— *See* TULLIO (G.) Saggio critico sullo stile nella " Vita " di Benvenuto Cellini. 1906. 8º.
10633. i. **25**.

—— Le Più belle pagine di Benvenuto Cellini. Scelte da Adolfo Venturi. [With a portrait.] pp. ix. 316. *Milano,* 1929. 12º. [*Le più belle pagine degli scrittori italiani.* vol. 47.]   **012226**. a. **1/47**.

APPENDIX.

—— *See* ANTONIADE (C.) Trois figures de la Renaissance. Pierre Arétin, Guichardin, Benvenuto Cellini. [With a portrait.] [1937.] 8º.   **20013**. c. **22**.

—— *See* BOUCHARD (P. de) Benvenuto Cellini. (Conférence.) 1903. 8º.   **10632**. df. **29**.

—— *See* BOYER D'AGEN (A. J.) Raymond de Lodève et Benvenuto Cellini. Le miniaturiste et le relieur du " Livre d'heures " de Charles-Quint. 1923. 8º.
07805. dd. **3**.

—— *See* CHURCHILL (Sidney J. A.) Bibliografia Celliniana. 1907. 8º.   **011908**. k. **5**.

CELLINI (BENVENUTO) *the Artist.*

—— *See* CORTISSOZ (R.) Benvenuto Cellini, Artist and Writer. 1906. 8°.   **10601. t. 1. (9.)**

—— *See* COURBON (P.) Étude psychiatrique sur Benvenuto Cellini, 1500–1571. 1906. 8°.   **10633. i. 12.**

—— *See* CUST (Robert H. H.) Benvenuto Cellini, *etc.* 1912. 8°.   **07806. df. 6/32.**

—— *See* DIMIER (L.) Benvenuto Cellini à la cour de France. Recherches nouvelles. 1898. 8°.   **10632. g. 16. (7.)**

—— *See* EGGENSCHWYLER (R.) Saggio sullo stile di Benvenuto Cellini, *etc.* 1940. 8°.   **11867. c. 28.**

—— *See* FOCILLON (H.) Benvenuto Cellini . . . Biographie critique, illustrée de vingt-quatre planches, *etc.* [1911.] 8°.   **2266. bb. 58.**

—— *See* GIRAUD (Jean Baptiste) *Conservateur des Musées archéologiques de la ville de Lyon.* Le Sceau de Benvenuto Cellini pour le cardinal de Ferrare, *etc.* 1882. 8°.   **7709. bbb. 20. (4.)**

—— *See* GUASTI (G.) Del crocefisso d'argento attribuito a Benvenuto Cellini, *etc.* 1893. 8°.   **[MISSING.]**

—— *See* HUBBARD (Elbert) Little Journeys to the Homes of Eminent Artists : Cellini. [With a portrait.] 1902. 8°.   **Cup.510.pa.3.**

—— *See* KIRBY, *afterwards* GREGG (Mary) *and* KIRBY (E.) The Italian Goldsmith ; or, the Story of Cellini. 1861. 8°.   **10630. a. 17.**

—— —— [1877.] 16°.   **10602. aaaa. 14/7.**

—— *See* KLAPSIA (H.) Benvenuto Cellini. [With reproductions.] [1943.] 8°.   **7812. pp. 26.**

—— *See* LAMARTINE DE PRAT (M. L. A. de) Benvenuto Cellini. 1866. 12°.   **10630. aa. 4.**

—— *See* MABELLINI (A.) Delle rime di Benvenuto Cellini. 1885. 8°.   **11840. aaa. 35.**

—— *See* MOLINIER (E. C. L. M.) Benvenuto Cellini. [1894.] 8°.   **2264. d. 2.**

—— *See* PLON (E.) Benvenuto Cellini . . . Recherches sur sa vie, sur son œuvre et sur les pièces qui lui sont attribuées, *etc.* 1883, *etc.* 4°.   **1809. b. 1.**

—— *See* POTTER (Frederick S.) A Wonderful Goldsmith—Benvenuto Cellini. [1882.] 8°.   **[MISSING.]**

—— *See* POWER (*Sir* D'Arcy) *K.B.E.* The Medical Experiences of Benvenuto Cellini. [1898.] 8°.   **07305. e. 31. (12.)**

—— *See* REUMONT (A. von) Benvenuto Cellini's letzte Lebensjahre. 1847. 8°.   *[Historisches Taschenbuch.* Neue Folge. Jahrg. 8.]   **P.P. 3625.**

—— *See* SUPINO (I. B.) L'Arte di Benvenuto Cellini. Con nuovi documenti sull'oreficeria fiorentina del secolo XVI. 1901. 8°.   **[MISSING.]**

—— *See* THADDEUS (Victor) Benvenuto Cellini and his Florentine Dagger. [With portrait.] [1933.] 8°.   **20019. ff. 10.**

—— *See* VIENNA.—*Kaiserlich-Königliches Münz- und Antiken-Cabinet.* Die Cinque-Cento-Cameen und Arbeiten des Benvenuto Cellini und seiner Zeitgenossen im k.k. Münz- und Antiken-Cabinette zu Wien. 1858. fol.   **1756. c. 15.**

CELLINI (BENVENUTO) *the Artist.*

—— Chisel, Pen & Poignard ; or, Benvenuto Cellini, his times and his contemporaries. By the author of " The Life of Sir Kenelm Digby " [i.e. Thomas Longueville], *etc.* pp. x. 159. pl. XVIII.   *Longmans & Co. : London,* 1899. 8°.   **10630. bb. 51.**

—— Münzen und Medaillen des Benvenuto Cellini. [By Julius Friedländer.] pp. 8. *Berlin,* [1855.] 4°.   **7755. e. 3. (3.)**

CELLINI (BENVENUTO) *Literary Critic.*

—— *See* GREENE (Robert) *the Poet.* Friar Bacon and Friar Bungay. John of Bordeaux . . . Testo critico con introduzione e commento di B. Cellini. 1952. 8°.   **11770. g. 17.**

——   Marlowe. *Roma,* 1937– . 8°.   **W.P. 12613.**

—— Thomas Love Peacock. pp. 284. *Roma,* 1937. 8°.   **10825. eee. 37.**

CELLINI (FRANCESCO) Cenno sui pozzi modanesi detti artesiani. [With a plan.] pp. 15. *Roma,* 1841. 8°.   **8207. f. 26. (8.)**

CELLINI (GIUSEPPE) *See* ANNUNZIO (G. d') [*Single Works.*] Laudi del cielo, del mare, della terra e degli eroi. (Ioseph Cellini ornavit.) 1903, *etc.* 4°.   **2284. g. 7.**

CELLINI (I.) *See* RUSCELLI (G.) Indice degl'uomini illustri, *etc.* [Edited by I. Cellini.] 1572. 4°. **611. e. 2.**

CELLINI (JOSEPH) *See* CELLINI (Giuseppe)

CELLINI (MARIANO) Pel giorno XXIV giugno 1871 in Firenze. [A memoir of G. P. Vieusseux.] pp. 27. [*Florence ?* 1871 ?] 8°.   **10630. aaa. 35. (3.)**

—— Ricordi storici intorno Giampetro Vieusseux e il tempo nostro, riuniti in questa da altre edizioni e giornali [by M. Cellini]. pp. 248. *Firenze,* 1869. fol. *One of an edition of* 100 *copies.*   **Cup.1254.d.23.**

CELLINI (MARIANO) *and* GHIVIZZANI (GAETANO)

—— Dante e il suo secolo. XIV maggio MDCCCLXV. [Essays by various writers. Edited by M. Cellini and G. Ghivizzani.] 2 vol. pp. xvi. 956. *Firenze,* 1865. 4°.   **1871. d. 9.**

CELLIO (MARCO ANTONIO) Il Fosforo o' vero la pietra bolognese preparata per rilucere frà l'ombre. pp. 102. *Il Vannacci : Roma,* 1680. 12°.   **1036. a. 27.**

CELLIUS (ERHARDUS) Carmen seculare in laudem Dei, honorem illustrissimæ Domus Wirtembergicæ, & commendationem inclytæ Academiæ Tubingensis, ante annos centum . . . fundatæ, *etc.* pp. 71.   *Excudebat G. Gruppenbachius : Tubingæ,* 1578. 4°.   **C. 68. h. 8. (3.)**

—— Eques auratus Anglo-Wirtembergicus : id est ; Actus . . . quo . . . Iacobus . . . Rex Angliæ . . . Fridericum Ducem Wirtembergicum . . . in . . . Regij Ordinis Garterij societatem . . . singularibus quibusdam ceremonijs recepit . . . Descriptus libris VIII., *etc.* pp. 270. MS. NOTES [by Sir William Dethick].   *Typis auctoris : Tubingæ,* 1605. 4°.   **1054. d. 2. (1.)**

—— Imagines professorum Tubingensium . . . qui, hoc altero Academiæ Seculo, anno 1577. inchoato, in ea & hodie . . . viuunt . . . & intereà mortui sunt . . . elegiis ἰσαριθμοστοίχοις, singulorum vitam breuiter recensentibus, illustratæ, *etc.* (Elegia in aulam nouam Academiæ Tubingensis, coloribus illustratam, sub finem anni Domini, M.D.XCIII. continens omnes, hoc tempore, professores academicos : et singulorum professiones.) 2 pt.   *Typis auctoris : Tubingæ,* 1596. 4°.   **11408. bb. 51.**

CELLIUS (ERHARDUS)

—— Oratio de vita et morte . . . clarissimi viri . . . Dn. M. Samuelis Heilandi, *etc.* [With Greek and Latin verses by various authors, and a portrait.] pp. 51. *Apud G. Gruppenbachium: Tubingæ,* 1592. 4°. **1126. h. 29.**

—— Württembergisch New Jahr das ist, Vber die nachfolgende Bildtnuss . . . Herrn Friderichs Hertzogens zu Württemberg . . . Geschlechts, Lebens, Regierungs, vnd gantzen Landts Wurttembergs kurtzer Lob: Ehrn: vnnd Wunsch Spruch, *etc. See* RATHGEB (J.) Warhaffte Beschreibung zweyer Raisen, *etc.* 1603. 4°.
C. 32. b. 31.

—— [Another edition.] *See* RATHGEB (J.) Warhaffte Beschreibung zweyer Raisen, *etc.* 1604. 4°. **1045. g. 22.**

CELLIUS (GEORGIUS FRIDERICUS) Disputatio inauguralis medica de mictione pultacea. *Praes.* E. R. Camerarius. pp. 32. *Typis J.-H. Reisii: Tubingæ,* 1683. 4°.
T. 587. (7.)

—— [Another copy.] **1179. d. 14. (17.)**

—— Disquisitio medica, quale signum in morbis præbeat urina, *etc. Praes.* E. R. Camerarius. pp. 16. *Typis J.-H. Reisii: Tubingæ,* 1680. 4°. **1179. d. 14. (9.)**

CELLIUS (JOHANNES ERHARDUS) *See* CELL (Johann E.)

CELLIUS (JOHANNES FRIDERICUS) De terra magnete . . . disputabunt Georgius Christoph. Gebhardi . . . & J. F. Cellius, *etc.* *Literis D. B. Starckii: Gryphiswaldiæ,* 1692. 4°. **536. f. 10. (7.)**

CELLONESE (ANDREA) Specchio simbolico, ouero Delle armi gentilitie, *etc.* pp. x. 184. *G. F. Paci: Napoli,* 1667. 4°. **9904. cc. 7.**
With an additional titlepage, engraved.

CELLORRITI, *pseud.* [i.e. G. B. TORRICELLI.] *See* TORRICELLI (G. B.)

CELLOT (LOUIS) Ludouici Cellotii . . . opera poetica. pp. 644. *S. Cramoisy: Parisiis,* 1630. 8°.
11712. c. 65.

—— Mauritiados Andegauensis libri III. [In verse.] pp. 122. *G. Laboe & M. Guyot: Flexiæ,* 1628. 4°. **11409. g. 12.**
With an additional titlepage, engraved.

—— R.P. Ludovici Cellotii . . . Orationes panegyricæ, *etc.* (R.P. Nicolai Caussini . . . Angelus Pacis, *etc.*) 2 pt. *Apud J. W. Friessem: Coloniæ Agrippinæ,* 1674. 12°.
1090. d. 3.

CELLOTIUS (LUDOVICUS) *See* CELLOT (Louis)

CELLULE.

—— La Cellule. Recueil de cytologie et d'histologie générale, *etc. See* CARNOY (J. B.)

—— *Petit-Séminaire de Saint-Sauveur.* Souvenirs de Saint-Sauveur, ou Essais littéraires des élèves du Petit-Séminaire de Cellule. pp. xxxi. 144. *Paris,* [1872.] 12°. **12239. c. 3.**

CELLY (FURIO LOPEZ) *See* LOPEZ-CELLY.

CELLY (RAOUL) Répertoire des thèmes de Marcel Proust [in " A la recherche du temps perdu "], *etc.* [With an appendix referring to his other works.] pp. 382. *Paris,* 1935. 8°. [*Les Cahiers Marcel Proust.* no. 7.]
W.P. 2209/7.

CELMAN (MIGUEL JUAREZ) *President of the Argentine Republic. See* JUAREZ CELMAN.

CELMIRA. Tragedia. La Celmira. En cinco actos. Traducida del frances, al castellano [by P. A. J. de Olavide y Jáuregui]. [In verse.] pp. 32. *Barcelona,* [1790?] 4°. **1342. e. 1. (45.)**

CELMS (MĀRTIŅŠ)

—— Rīga: rokas grāmata ekskursantiem. [With illustrations and a map.] pp. 120. *Rīgā,* 1926. 8°.
010290. ff. 35.

CELNART (ÉLISABETH FÉLICIE) *See* BAILLY (A. D.) Choix d'anecdotes anciennes et modernes . . . Cinquième édition, considérablement augmentée, et mise en ordre par Mme Celnart. 1828. 18°. **12207. a. 1/4.**

—— *See* PARISET ( ) *Madame.* Nouveau manuel complet de la maîtresse de maison . . . suivi d'un appendice par Mesdames Gacon-Dufour, Celnart, *etc.* 1852. 18°.
12207. a. 1/277.

—— *See* PARISET ( ) *Madame,* and CELNART (E. F.) Nouveau manuel complet de la maîtresse de maison, *etc.* 1913. 18°. **12207. a. 1/575.**

—— Du progrès social et de la conviction religieuse, *etc.* pp. viii. 500. *Paris,* 1840. 8°. **1141. e. 10.**

—— Manuel complet des domestiques, ou l'Art de former de bons serviteurs; savoir: maîtres-d'hôtel, cuisiniers, cuisinières . . . etc.; contenant d'importants détails sur le service des malades, et beaucoup d'utiles recettes d'économie domestique. pp. viii. 224. *Paris,* 1836. 18°. [*Encyclopédie-Roret.*] **12207. a. 1/115.**

—— Manuel des dames, ou l'Art de l'élégance, sous le rapport de la toilette, des honneurs de la maison, des plaisirs, des occupations agréables . . . Seconde édition, revue, corrigée, augmentée et ornée de figures. pp. 272. *Paris,* 1833. 18°. [*Encyclopédic-Roret.*] **12207. a. 1/10.**

—— Manuel des demoiselles, ou Arts et métiers qui leur conviennent . . . Ouvrage orné de planches. Quatrième edition revue, corrigée et augmentée. pp. iv. 308. *Paris,* 1830. 12°. **1420. a. 6.**

—— Cinquième édition, revue, augmentée, *etc.* *Bruxelles,* 1830. 12°. [MISSING.]

—— Nouveau manuel complet des demoiselles, ou Arts et métiers qui leur conviennent, et dont elles peuvent s'occuper avec agrément . . . Nouvelle édition, entièrement renouvelée et augmentée, *etc.* pp. iii. 280. pl. IV. *Paris,* 1837. 18°. [*Encyclopédie-Roret.*]
12207. a. 1/132.

—— Manuel des habitans de la campagne et de la bonne fermière, ou Traité complet d'économie rurale et domestique . . . Seconde edition, entièrement refondue. pp. iii. 232. *Paris,* 1834. 18°. [*Encyclopédie-Roret.*]
12207. a. 1/69.

—— Nouveau manuel complet d'économie domestique, contenant toutes les recettes les plus simples et les plus efficaces sur l'économie rurale et domestique . . . Troisième édition, entièrement refondue et considérablement augmentée, *etc.* pp. 284. *Paris,* 1837. 18°. [*Encyclopédie-Roret.*] **12207. a. 1/116.**

—— Nouveau manuel complet de la bonne compagnie, ou Guide de la politesse et de la bienséance . . . Nouvelle édition, augmentée et entièrement refondue. pp. vi. 246. *Paris,* 1845. 18°. [*Encyclopédie-Roret.*] **12207. a. 1/38.**

—— [Another copy.] **12207. a. 1/273.**

—— Nouveau manuel complet de la broderie, *etc.* pp. 309. *Paris,* 1840. 18°. [*Encyclopédie-Roret.*]
12207. a. 1/52.

—— Atlas. *obl.* 8°. **12207. a. 2/3.**

CELNART (Élisabeth Félicie)

—— Nouveau manuel complet des jeux de société . . . avec des poésies fugitives . . . Nouvelle édition, revue, corrigée et augmentée, *etc.* pp. viii. 334. *Paris*, 1846. 18º. [*Encyclopédie-Roret.*] **12207. a. 1/188.**

—— Manual completo de juegos de sociedad o tertulia, y de prendas . . . 2ª edición: corregida y aumentada, *etc.* [Translated by Mariano de Rementería y Fica.] pp. 272. *Madrid*, 1839. 8º. **7918. a. 81.**

—— Nouveau manuel complet du parfumeur . . . Nouvelle édition, entièrement renouvellée et très-augmentée, *etc.* pp. viii. 297. *Paris*, 1845. 18º. [*Encyclopédie-Roret.*] **12207. a. 1/123.**

—— Nouvelle édition, *etc.* pp. viii. 307. *Paris*, 1854. 18º. [*Encyclopédie-Roret.*] **12207. a. 1/292.**

—— Perfumery: its manufacture and use. With instructions in every branch of the art, and recipes . . . From the French of Celnart and other late authorities. With additions and improvements, by Campbell Morfit. pp. 285. *Carey & Hart: Philadelphia*, 1847. 12º. **1400. c. 1.**

—— Nouveau manuel du fleuriste artificiel, ou l'Art d'imiter d'après nature toute espèce de fleurs . . . suivi de l'art du plumassier . . . Nouvelle édition augmentée. pp. 284. *Paris*, 1838. 18º. [*Encyclopédie-Roret.*] **12207. a. 1/133.**

—— Nouveau manuel complet du fleuriste artificiel . . . Nouvelle édition revue et augmentée, *etc.* pp. viii. 344. *Paris*, 1901. 18º. [*Encyclopédie-Roret.*] **12207. a. 1/506.**

—— Nouveau manuel de la ménagère parfaite et de la maîtresse de maison . . . Nouvelle édition . . . entièrement renouvelée et très-augmentée. pp. ii. 320. *Paris*, 1839. 18º. [*Encyclopédie-Roret.*] **12207. a. 1/70.**

CELNER (L.) Geschichte des Feldzugs in Russland im Jahre 1812. Nach grösseren Werken in Auszug bearbeitet, *etc. Reutlingen*, 1839. 12º. **9076. a. 14.**

CELONI (Tertulliano)

—— Compendio storico della musica antica e moderna estratto dai migliori autori e compilato da T. Celoni . . . Susseguito da un prontuario di armonia pratica e dimostrativa. pp. 54. *Firenze*, 1842. 8º. **7901. bb. (1.)**
Containing the first part only.

CELORIA (Giovanni) *See* Lockyer (*Sir* Joseph N.) K.C.B. Astronomia . . . Nuova versione . . . di G. Celoria, *etc.* 1895. 8º. **012200. i. 23.**

—— *See* Lorenzoni (G.) Operazioni eseguite nell'anno 1875 negli osservatorii astronomici di Milano, Napoli e Padova . . . per determinare le differenze di longitudine fra Genova, Milano, Napoli e Padova. Resoconto dei professori G. Lorenzoni, G. Celoria, *etc.* 1883. fol. [*Pubblicazioni del Reale Osservatorio di Brera.* no. 24.] **8752. h. 1.**

—— *See* Respighi (L.) and Celoria (G.) Operazioni eseguite nell'anno 1879 per determinare la differenza di longitudine fra gli Osservatori astronomici del Campidoglio in Roma e di Brera in Milano. Resoconto dei professori L. Respighi, G. Celoria. 1882. fol. [*Pubblicazioni del Reale Osservatorio di Brera.* no. 21.] **8752. h. 1.**

—— *See* Schiaparelli (G. V.) and Celoria (G.) Posizioni medie per 1870, 0 di 1119 stelle . . . determinate . . . negli anni 1860–1872. 1901. fol. [*Pubblicazioni del Reale Osservatorio di Brera.* no. 41.] **8752. h. 1.**

CELORIA (Giovanni)

—— *See* Schiaparelli (G. V.) and Celoria (G.) Resoconto dell'operazioni fatte a Milano . . . per determinare la differenza di longitudine dell'Osservatorio di Brera coll'Osservatorio di Neuchâtel, *etc.* 1875. fol. [*Pubblicazioni del Reale Osservatorio di Brera.* no. 8.] **8752. h. 1.**

—— *See* Uzielli (G.) La Vita e i tempi di Paolo dal Pozzo Toscanelli . . . con un capitolo . . . sui lavori astronomici del Toscanelli di G. Celoria. 1893. fol. **1764. e. 2.**

—— Operazioni eseguite nell'anno 1881 per determinare la differenza delle longitudini fra gli Osservatori del Dépôt général de la Guerre à Montsouris presso Parigi, del Mont Gros presso Nizza, di Brera in Milano . . . Resoconto delle operazioni fatte da G. Celoria. pp. 96. *Milano*, 1887. fol. [*Pubblicazioni del Reale Osservatorio di Brera.* no. 29.] **8752. h. 1.**

—— Sopra alcuni scandagli del cielo eseguiti all'Osservatorio reale di Milano, e sulla distribuzione generale delle stelle nello spazio. Annotazioni. pp. 48. *Milano*, 1878. fol. [*Pubblicazioni del Reale Osservatorio di Brera.* no. 13.] **8752. h. 1.**

—— Sugli eclissi solari totali del 3 giugno 1239 e del 6 ottobre 1241. Memoria. pp. 20. *Milano*, 1876. fol. [*Pubblicazioni del Reale Osservatorio di Brera.* no. 11.] **8752. h. 1.**

—— Sul grande commovimento atmosferico avvenuto il 1º di agosto 1872 nella Bassa Lombardia e nella Lomellina. Annotazioni. pp. 12. *Milano*, 1873. fol. [*Pubblicazioni del Reale Osservatorio di Brera.* no. 1.] **8752. h. 1.**

—— Sull'eclissi solare totale del 3 giugno 1239. Memoria. pp. 26. *Milano*, 1875. fol. [*Pubblicazioni del Reale Osservatorio di Brera.* no. 10.] **8752. h. 1.**

—— Sulle variazioni periodiche e non periodiche della temperatura nel clima di Milano. Memoria. pp. 86. *Milano*, 1874. fol. [*Pubblicazioni del Reale Osservatorio di Brera.* no. 4.] **8752. h. 1.**

—— La Terra astro dell'universo. Conferenza. pp. 31. *Milano*, 1888. 8º. **8562. ff. 30. (6.)**

CELORIA (Giovanni) and **LORENZONI** (Giuseppe)

—— Resoconto delle operazioni fatte a Milano ed a Padova, nel 1875 . . . per determinare le differenze di longitudine fra gli Osservatorj astronomici di Milano e di Padova, e quelli di Vienna e di Monaco. pp. 81. *Milano*, 1879. fol. [*Pubblicazioni del Reale Osservatorio di Brera.* no. 14.] **8752. h. 1.**

CELORIA (Giovanni) and **PERROTIN** (J.)

—— Détermination de la différence de longitude . . . entre Milan et Nice. 1887. *See* Nice. —*Observatoire de Nice.* Annales, *etc.* tom. 2. 1887, *etc.* 4º. **8567. i. 4.**

CELORIA (Giovanni) and **RAJNA** (Michele)

—— Differenza delle longitudini fra Milano, Osservatorio astronomico di Brera, e Crea, punto trigonometrico di 1º ordine della rete geodetica italiana. Osservazioni di G. Celoria e M. Rajna, calcoli di L. Gabba. pp. 60. *Milano*, 1909. fol. [*Pubblicazioni del Reale Osservatorio di Brera.* no. 45.] **8752. h. 1.**

CELORICO.—*Câmara da Vereação.* Acordão da Camara, ou Senado consulto da vereaçaõ de C. dos Bebados; o qual mandou ao conselho de Portugal em Madrid, sobre os negocios da guerra, e estado, anno de 1623. *Lisboa*, 1820. 8º. **8005. aa. 1. (5.)**

CÉLORON DE BLAINVILLE ( ) Question des Transatlantiques. M. de Kerhallet et le Port de la Pointe-à-Pitre. pp. 49. *Pointe-à-Pitre*, 1862. 8º.
8155. cc. 50. (1.)

CELOS (GEORGES) La Genèse des figures. Études de symbolique. L'anneau—l'épée dans la tétralogie de Richard Wagner. pp. 123. *Paris*, 1912. 8º.
7897. p. 4.

CELOSSE (JOHANNES) Disputatio medica inauguralis, de asthmate, *etc.* A. *Elzevier: Lugduni Batavorum*, 1689. 4º.
1185. g. 19. (7.)

CELOSTÁTNÍ KONFERENCE.
—— Celostátní Konference Dělnických Dopisovatelů. *See* PRAGUE.

CELOSTÁTNÍ PRACOVNÍ KONFERENCE.
—— Celostátní Pracovní Konference Analytických chemiků. *See* PRAGUE.

CELOSTÁTNÍ SJEZD.
—— Celostátní Sjezd Katolického Duchovenstva. *See* PRAGUE.

CELOTTI (JOHANNES BAPTISTA) De praecipuis fundamentis diagnoseos morborum columnae vertebralis dissertatio inauguralis, *etc.* pp. 16. *Patavii*, 1829. 8º.
7306. b. 6. (49.)

CELOTTI (LIBERALIS) De sudore morboso disceptatio academica, *etc.* pp. 20. *Patavii*, 1828. 8º.
7306. b. 5. (8.)

CELOTTI (LUIGI)
—— Notice d'une collection de tableaux. Dont la vente aura lieu le . . . 14 novembre [1814], *etc.* [The collection ascribed in a MS. note to — Celotti.] pp. 8. MS. PRICES. 1814. 8º. *See* CATALOGUES. **562. e. 31. (8.)**

—— Notice des curiosités, consistant en tableaux et miniatures . . . sculptures et bronzes . . . etc.; le tout recueilli par M. * * * [identified in a MS. note as — Celotti.] La vente de ces objets aura lieu les 30, 31 août et 1er. septembre 1819, *etc.* pp. 36. MS. NOTES AND PRICES. [1819.] 8º. *See* CATALOGUES. **562. e. 43. (7.)**

—— Per le nozze Concini-Malanotti. Anacreontica. *Treviso*, 1824. *s. sh.* fol.
1870. d. 1. (225*.)

CELOTTI (NICCOLA) Sacra novena in onore di S. Vincenzo Ferrerio, *etc.* pp. 134. *Venezia*, 1763. 8º.
4828. a. 13.

CELOTTI (PELLEGRINO NICCOLA) *See* MINGARELLI (F.) Ferdinandi Mingarellj . . . Epistola qua cl. Celotti emendatio ɴ. xvi. Matth. c. ɪ. rejicienda ostenditur. 1763. 12º. [*CALOGIERÀ* (*A.*) *Nuova raccolta d'opuscoli, etc.* tom. 10.] **247. a. 10.**

—— —— 1764. 4º. **3205. c. 6.**

—— Ragionamento sopra alcuni punti di varia erudizione antica, *etc.* 1764. *See* CALOGIERÀ (A.) Nuova raccolta d'opuscoli, *etc.* tom. 11. 1755, *etc.* 12º. **247. a. 11.**

CELOTTUS (NICOLAUS PEREGRINUS) *See* CELOTTI (Pellegrino N.)

CELS (ALPHONSE) Éléments d'anthropologie. Notion de l'homme comme organisme vivant et classification des sciences anthropologiques fondamentales. tom. 1. pp. viii. 202. *Bruxelles*, 1884. 8º. **7406. h. 18.** *No more published.*

—— Évolution géologique de la terre et ancienneté de l'homme. pp. 247. *Bruxelles*, 1909. 8º. **07109. g. 39.**

CELS (JACQUES MARTIN) *See* CUVIER (G. L. C. F. D. de) *Baron.* Recueil des éloges historiques, *etc.* tom. 1. (Jacques-Martin Cels.) 1819, *etc.* 8º. **611. f. 24.**

—— *See* SINCLAIR (*Right Hon. Sir* John) *Bart.* Projet d'un plan pour établir des fermes expérimentales, *etc.* (Rapport sur le projet précédent [by H. A. Tessier and J. M. Cels].) [1800.] 4º. **733. g. 11. (11.)**

—— *See* VENTENAT (E. P.) Description des plantes nouvelles et peu connues, cultivées dans le jardin de J. M. Cels, *etc.* (Note du citoyen Cels, sur ses cultures.) 1800. fol.
451. k. 14.

CELS (JACQUES MARTIN) and **LOTTIN** (AUGUSTIN MARTIN)
—— Coup-d'œil éclairé d'une bibliothèque, à l'usage de tout possesseur de livres. Par Mr * * * [i.e. J. M. Cels and A. M. Lottin]. pp. x. 415. 1773. 8º. *See* COUP. **272. i. 17.**

CELSANUS (BARNABAS) *See* CLAUDIANUS (C.) *Begin.* [fol. 2 *recto:*] Barnabas Celsanus Bartholomæo paiello Equiti Vicentino. S.P.D. [fol. 102 *verso:*] Finis operum Cl. Claudiani, *etc.* [Edited by B. Celsanus.] 1482. fol.
IB. 31862.

—— *See* OVIDIUS NASO (P.) [*Works.—Latin.*] *Begin.* [pt. 1. fol. 2 *recto:*] P. Oui. Nasonis . . . Heroidum alias Epistolarum: liber unicus incipit, *etc.* *End.* [pt. 2. fol. 167 *verso:*] Barnabas Celsanus Vicentinus Habes humanissime lector Opera P. Ouidii a nobis . . . emendata, *etc.* 1480. fol. **IB. 31816.**

—— —— 1484. fol. **IB. 21975.**

CELSE. *See* CELSUS.

CELSE (AURÈLE CORNÉLIUS) *See* CELSUS (Aulus C.)

CELSI (GIACOMO) Vna Lettera . . . al . . . Ambasiator Veneto presso la S. di N. S. Papa Pio Quinto, sopra la presa di Sopoto in Albàia, & altri logi de Turchi, *etc.* *Mātoua*, [1570.] 12º. **1313. a. 16. (4.)**

CELSI (MINO) *See* CELSUS (Minus)

CELSING (GUSTAF) Gustaf Celsings dagbok. Utgiven av Thede Palm. 1933. *See* SWEDEN.—*Karolinska Förbundet.* Karolinska Förbundets årsbok. 1932/33. 1911, *etc.* 8º.
Ac. 1068. b.

CELSIUS (ANDERS) [For dissertations at which A. Celsius acted as Praeses:]
See AMNELL (E. J.)   NORLIN (J. B.)
BERCH (Anders) *the Elder.*   SPARSCHUCH (J.)
COLLIANDER (E.)   TÖRNER (J. J.)
GIÖRANSSON (I. V.)   VALLERIUS (I.)
HELLANT (A.)

—— *See* HÖPKEN (A. J. von) *Count.* Åminnelse-tal öfver . . . herr Anders Celsius, *etc.* 1752. 8º. **965. i. 2. (3.)**

—— *See* MOREAU DE MAUPERTUIS (P. L.) La Figure de la terre, déterminée par les observations de Messieurs de Maupertuis, Clairaut . . . accompagnés de M. Celsius, *etc.* 1738. 8º. **716. d. 3.**

—— —— 1738. 12º. **972. d. 8.**

CELSIUS (ANDERS)

—— *See* NORDENMARK (N. V. E.) Anders Celsius, *etc.*
[With portraits.] 1936. 4°. [*Lychnos-bibliotek.* vol. 1.]
Ac. **1074/2.**

—— De observationibus pro figura telluris determinanda in
Gallia habitis, disquisitio. pp. 20. *Upsaliæ,* [1738.] 4°.
536. f. 4. (20.)

—— [Observationer om twänne beständiga grader på en
thermometer.] Beobachtungen von zween beständigen
Graden auf einem Thermometer. *See* OETTINGEN (A. J.
von) Abhandlungen über Thermometrie von Fahrenheit,
Réaumur, Celsius, *etc.* 1894. 8°. **8706. eee. 1/57.**

—— Andreae Celsii . . . Oratio de mutationibus generaliori-
bus quae in superficie corporum coelestium contingunt,
etc. See LINNAEUS (C.) Caroli Linnaei . . . Oratio de
telluris habitabilis incremento, *etc.* 1744. 8°.
953. e. 2.

—— A. Celsii Tanckar om cometernes igenkomst.
Stockholm, 1735. 4°. **8562. cc. 36. (8.)**

—— CCCXVI. observationes de lumine boreali, ab A. MDCCXVI.
ad A. MDCCXXXII. partim a se, partim ab aliis, in Svecia
habitas, collegit A. Celsius. pp. 48. *Norimbergæ,*
1733. 4°. **717. k. 14. (5.)**

CELSIUS (HUGO) *Dissutus Cavillonus. See* DISSUTUS
(Celsus H.) *Canon of Chalon-sur-Saône.*

CELSIUS (MAGNUS NICOLAI)

——
Praes. See
AURIVILLIUS (J.) Dissertatio philosophica de natura
piscium, *etc.* [1676.] 4°. B. **426. (13.)**

——
See KARLSTRÖM
(S.) De Thule veterum dissertatio, *etc.* [1673.] 8°.
151. a. 5.

—— Magni Celsii . . . Computus ecclesiasticus, *etc.* pp. 349.
Sumptu auctoris excudebat H. Curio: Upsaliæ, 1673. 8°.
8561. aaa. 28.

CELSIUS (MAGNUS OLAI) afterwards **CELSE** (MAGNUS
VON)

—— Apparatus ad historiam Sveo-Gothicam . . . Sectio prima,
bullarii Romano-Sveo-Gothici recensionem sistens.
pp. 222. *Holmiæ,* 1782. 4°. **590. h. 13.**

—— [Another copy.] **205. a. 2.**

—— *See* LINDHULT (H. G.) Ad bullarium Romano-
Sveogothicum a Magno von Celse . . . editum ac-
cessio nova, *etc.* 1854. 4°. **4532. g. 10. (3.)**

—— Bibliothecæ Regiæ Stockholmensis historia brevis et
succincta. pp. 210. *Holmiæ,* 1751. 8°. **271. a. 21.**

—— Monasterium Sko in Uplandia, dissertatione academica
breviter descriptum, *etc. Praes.* E. Alstrin. pp. 45.
Stockholmiæ, [1728.] 4°. **296. l. 17. (1.)**

CELSIUS (NICOLAUS) [For dissertations at which N. Celsius
acted as Praeses :]
See ACRELIUS (J. J.)   HOLENIUS (Z.)
    BÖÖK (L.)   RUDA (S.)
    FRISENDAHL (E.)   SEPELIUS (L.)
    GRANAGRIUS (I.)   WALLINUS (J.)
    HEIDMAN (J.)

CELSIUS (OLOF) *the Elder.* [For dissertations at which
O. Celsius acted as Praeses :]
See ÅKERMAN (J.)   HALLMAN (J. G.)
    ÄLFWIK (L.)   HEDLIND (P.)
    ALROT (E.)   KIÄLLMAN (E.)
    ARNELL (L.)   MAGELIUS (J.)
    BÆCKNER (A.)   NOHRBORG (O.)
    BÅNG (A.)   NOREEN (E.)
    BERGGREN (J.)   ODHELIUS (O.)
    BERGROT (O.)   ODHELIUS (T.)
    BREANDER (P.)   SCARIN (A.)
    CEDERQWIST (A.) SERENIUS (J.)
    EKEWALL (J.)   SETTHELIUS (H.)
    EKORN (J.)   TORGER (N.)
    FRONDEL (E.)   TOUSCHIER (J.)
    GESTRINIUS (S.) WAHLMAN (A.)
    GRANHOLM (J.) WETTERSTEN (P.)
    GRÖNDELL (P.)

—— *See* BÄCK (Abraham) Åminnelse-tal öfver . . . hr. doct.
Olof Celsius, *etc.* 1758. 8°. **965. i. 2. (17.)**

—— *See* UPSALA.—*Archbishops.* Incerti scriptoris Sveci
chronicon primorum in ecclesia Upsalensi Archiepisco-
porum, *etc.* [Edited by O. Celsius.] 1705. 12°.
296. g. 35.

—— אבטחים sive Melones Ægyptii, ab Israëlitis desiderati
. . . quinam & quales fuerint, *etc.* pp. 28.
Lugduni Batavorum, 1726. 8°. B. **422. (14.)**

—— Olavi Celsii De monumentis quibusdam runicis, epistola
ad amicum. pp. 16. *Upsaliæ,* 1727. 4°. T. **2212. (3.)**

—— Dissertatio philosophica de natura avium, *etc. Praes.*
J. Schwede. pp. 41. *H. Keyser: Upsalæ,* [1690.] 8°.
1090. d. 8. (11.)

—— [Another copy.] B. **656. (3.)**

—— Olavi Celsii Hierobotanicon, sive De plantis Sacræ
Scripturæ dissertationes breves, *etc.* 2 pt. *Upsaliæ,*
1745, 47. 8°. **3126. cc. 26.**

—— [Another copy, with a different titlepage.]
Amstelædami, 1748. 8°. **452. c. 12, 13.**

—— [Another copy.] **672. e. 23, 24.**

—— قصص على اللفه وعلم العرب sive Historia linguæ & eruditionis
Arabum, *etc. Praes.* G. P. Lilljenblad. pp. 199.
H. Keyser: Upsaliæ, [1694.] 8°. **11825. aa. 10.**

—— Runæ Medelpadicæ ab importuna crisi breviter vindi-
catæ, auctore O. C. [i.e. O. Celsius.] pp. 36. 1726. 4°.
See C., O. T. **2218. (8.)**

CELSIUS (OLOF) *the Younger, Bishop of Lund.* [For dissertations at which O. Celsius acted as Praeses :]
See ARENIUS (J. E.)   STENBECK (P.)
    BÅNGE (D.)   STRICKER (J. C.)
    BERG (O. E.)   TIDSTRÖM (A.)
    BRÖTTLING (E.) TILLMAN (J.)
    HEDENBERG (E.) WAHLSTEDT (J.)
    ISRAELSSON (J.) WALLMANN (J.)
    LUNDSTRÖM (E.) ZIERVOGEL (E.)
    ROSENSTIERNA (H.)

—— *See* ÖDMANN (Samuel) *the Elder.* Åminnelse-tal, öfver
. . . herr doctor Olof Celsius, *etc.* 1796. 8°.
965. i. 9. (7.)

—— Åminnelse-tal, öfver . . . herr baron Salomon von
Otter, *etc.* pp. 24. *Stockholm,* [1747.] 8°. **965. i. 1. (3.)**

—— Åminnelse-tal, öfver . . . herr Carl Reinhold Berch,
etc. pp. 38. *Stockholm,* 1781. 8°. **965. i. 7. (2.)**

CELSIUS (OLOF) *the Younger, Bishop of Lund.*

—— Åminnelse-tal öfver . . . herr gr. Fredrich Sparre, *etc.*
pp. 16. *Stockholm*, 1749. 8°.   965. i. 1. (7.)

—— Åminnelse-tal öfver . . . herr grefve Carl Gyllenborg,
etc. pp. 28. *Stockholm,* [1747.] 8°.   965. i. 1. (4.)

—— Åminnelse-tal öfver . . . herr Lars Benzelstierna, *etc.*
pp. 30. *Stockholm,* [1758.] 8°.   965. i. 2. (16.)

—— Åminnelse-tal öfver . . . herr Olof von Dalin, *etc.*
pp. 49. *Stockholm*, 1764. 8°.   965. i. 3. (10.)

—— Åminnelse-tal, öfver . . . herr Pehr Elvius, *etc.* pp. 36.
Stockholm, 1750. 8°.   965. i. 2. (4.)

—— Bibliothecae Upsaliensis Historia. pp. 153.
Upsaliæ, 1745. 8°.   273. d. 28. (2.)

—— —— Anonymi in Bibliothecae Upsaliensis historiam,
Regiae Academiae Upsal. impensis MDCCXLV. editam,
stricturae. [By A. Norrelius.] pp. 71. *Upsaliæ*,
1746. 8°.   273. d. 28. (1.)

—— *See* BREITHOLTZ (L. G.) Våra första fransk-klassiska
dramer. Celsius' Ingeborg och Dalins Brynilda.
1944. 8°.   11798. aa. 18.

—— Konung Erik den Fjortondes historia, sammanskrefwen
efter gamla handlingar . . . Andra, af forfattaren ökta
och förbättrade uplagan. pp. 343. *Lund*, 1795. 8°.
                                              1199. f. 23.

—— Histoire d'Eric xiv. Roi de Suède . . . Traduite . . .
par M. Genet le fils. (Continuation de l'Histoire des
révolutions de Suède, de M. l'abbé de Vertot.) 2 tom.
Paris, 1777. 12°.   154. a. 22.

—— [Another copy.]   C. 67. c. 6.
*With the arms of Charles Gravier, Count de Vergennes,
stamped on the binding.*

—— Geschichte König Erichs des Vierzehnten . . . Aus dem
Schwedischen. [Translated by Johann G. P. Moeller.]
pp. 381. *Flensburg & Leipzig*, 1777. 8°. 10761. bb. 42.

—— Konung Gustaf den Förstes historia, *etc.* 2 dl.
Stockholm, 1746, 53. 8°.   1448. b. 25.

—— Tredie uplagan. pp. 812. *Lund*, 1792. 8°.
                                              10759. c. 17.

—— Geschichte Königs Gustavi des Ersten . . . aus dem
Schwedischen übersetzt. Tl. 1. pp. 512. *Copenhagen
& Leipzig*, 1749. 8°.   154. c. 8.

—— Monumenta politico-ecclesiastica ex archivo Palm-
skiöldiano nunc primum in lucem edita quæ, præside
O. Celsio submittit C. Enstedt (J. Lindblad, A. Lithzenius
[and others]). pp. 262. *Upsaliæ*, [1750–53.] 4°.
                                              295. k. 7.

—— Observata quædam de dignitate ducali in Suecia, *etc.*
Praes. J. Ihre. pp. 48. *Upsaliæ*, [1740.] 4°.
                                              229. h. 16. (7.)

—— Svea Rikes kyrko-historia. dl. 1. pp. 176.
Stockholm, 1767. 4°.   206. a. 9.

—— Herr vice Bibliothecariens Olof Celsii tal, hollit vid dess
inträde i Kongl. Vetenskaps Academien, *etc. See*
BENZELIUS (H.) successively *Bishop of Lund* and *Arch-
bishop of Upsala.* Tal, holne uti Kongl. Vetenskaps
Academien, då . . . Henric Benzelius och . . . Olof
Celsius derstädes intogo sina säten, *etc.* 1746. 8°.
                                              965. i. 11. (4.)

—— Tal om smak uti den Svenska, så bundna, som obundna
vältaligheten: hållit i Kongl. Vetensk. Academien, *etc.*
pp. 64. *Stockholm*, 1768. 8°.   965. k. 4. (8.)

CELSIUS (OLOF) *the Younger, Bishop of Lund.*

—— Anmärkningar öfver . . . Olof Celsii tal, om smak
uti den svenska så bundna, som obundna vältaligheten.
[By C. Manderström.] pp. 16. *Stockholm*, 1768. 8°.
                                              965. k. 4. (9.)

CELSO. [For Saints of this name:] *See* CELSUS.

CELSO, *di Bologna. See* FALEONI (Celso)

CELSO MARIA, *da Verona. See* BONAVENTURA, *Saint,
Cardinal, etc.* [*Single Works.—De Sex Alis Seraphim.*]
Delle sei ale dei Serafini . . . Prima versione italiana
. . . di F. C. M. da V. [i.e. Fra Celso Maria da Verona],
etc. 1875. 16°.   3832. aaa. 4.

CELSO (AFFONSO) *Count. See* CELSO DE ASSIS FIGUEIREDO.

CELSO (HUGO DE) *See* DESCOUSU (Celse H.)

CELSO DE ASSIS FIGUEIREDO (AFFONSO) *Count.*
Camões. Edição commemorativa do terceiro centenario
da morte de Camões, *etc.* pp. 111. *S. Paulo*, 1880. 8°.
                                              10632. aa. 12.

—— Um Invejado. [A novel.] 2 vol. *Rio de Janeiro*,
1894, 95. 8°.   12489. c. 30.

—— José Vieira Couto de Magalhães. Subsidios para uma
biographia. *In:* RIO DE JANEIRO.—*Instituto Historico e
Geographico Brasileiro.* General Couto de Magalhães, *etc.*
pp. 13–36. 1938. 8°.   10888. e. 17.

—— Oito Annos de Parlamento. Reminiscencias e notas.
pp. 315. *Rio de Janeiro*, 1901. 8°.   9903. b. 23.

—— Porque me ufano do meu paiz. 2ª edição revista.
pp. 202. *Rio de Janeiro*, 1901. 8°.   8180. aa. 34.

—— Porque me ufano do meu paiz . . . 5ª edição revista.
pp. 203.   *Rio de Janeiro, Paris; Chartres* [printed],
[c. 1910.] 8°.   08042. e. 2.

—— Reforma Administrativa e Municipal. Parecer e pro-
jectos do Senador A. Celso. 1930. *See* RIO DE JANEIRO.
—*Instituto Historico e Geographico Brasileiro.* Revista,
etc. tom. 107. 1839, *etc.* 8°.   P.P. 3937.

—— Visconde de Ouro Preto. Excerptos biographicos-
[Containing a reprint of " O Assassinato do Coronel
Gentil de Castro," by Count A. Celso de Assis Figueiredo.
With selections from the works of the Viscount de Ouro
Preto, and a portrait.] pp. 579. *Rio de Janeiro*, 1929. 8°.
[*Revista do Instituto Historico e Geographico Brasileiro.*
tom. 103.]   P.P. 3937.

—— [Another edition.] Visconde de Ouro Preto . . . Com
acrescimos e annexos, entre os quaes o " Advento da
Dictadura Militar no Brasil " [by the Viscount de Ouro
Preto]. [With portraits.] pp. 438. *Pôrto Alegre*,
1935. 8°.   010886. g. 28.
*Without the selections from the works of the Viscount de
Ouro Preto contained in the first edition.*

CELSO DE ASSIS FIGUEIREDO (AFFONSO) *Viscount
de Ouro Preto. See* FLEIUSS (Max) Ouro-Preto. [With
portraits.] 1931. 8°.   P.P. 3937. a. (3.)

—— Advento da Dictadura Militar no Brazil. pp. 232.
Paris, 1891. 8°.   8180. e. 13.

—— [Another edition.] [With a biography by Count
Affonso Celso de Assis Figueiredo, and portraits.] *See*
CELSO DE ASSIS FIGUEIREDO (A.) *Count.* Visconde de
Ouro Preto, *etc.* 1935. 8°.   010886. g. 28.

—— A Marina d'Outr'ora. Subsidios para a historia.
pp. xi. 467. v. *Rio de Janeiro*, 1894. 8°.   8804. cc. 19.

CELSO DE ASSIS FIGUEIREDO (AFFONSO) *Viscount de Ouro Preto.*

—— Questions de l'esclavage au Brésil. Discours prononcé à la Chambre des Députés. pp. 16.   *Rio de Janeiro,* 1886. 8°.   **8156. df. 37.**

—— [Selections from the works of the Viscount de Ouro Preto. With a portrait.] *See* CELSO DE ASSIS FIGUEIREDO (A.) *Count.* Visconde de Ouro Preto, *etc.* 1929. 8°. [*Revista do Instituto Historico e Geographico Brasileiro.* tom. 103.]   **P.P. 3937.**

CELSPIRIUS (Z.) *pseud.* [i.e. CHRISTIAN SERPILIUS.] Z. Celspirii de anagrammatismo libri II, quorum prior theoriam, posterior anagrammatographos celebriores, cum appendice selectorum anagrammatum, exhibet. pp. 303. *Ratisponæ*, 1713. 8°.   **12305. bb. 28.**

CELSUS, *Christian Apologist.* Ad Vigilium Episcopum de Judaica incredulitate, Celsi cujusdam in altercationem Jasonis & Papisci, præfatio. *See* CYPRIAN, *Saint, Bishop of Carthage.* Sancti Caecilii Cypriani opera, *etc.* 1726. fol.   **11. f. 11.**

—— [Another edition.] *See* CYPRIAN, *Saint, Bishop of Carthage.* S. Cæcilii Cypriani . . . opera, *etc.* tom. 2. 1782. 8°.   **3670. aaa. 23.**

CELSUS, *the Philosopher. See* CUNNINGHAM (Francis) *Vicar of Lowestoft.* A Dissertation on the Books of Origen against Celsus, *etc.* 1812. 8°.   **3805. b. 15.**

—— *See* FENGER (Johan F.) *the Elder.* De Celso, Christianorum adversario, *etc.* 1828. 8°.   **4825. b. 10.**

—— *See* HARRIS (James Rendel) Celsus and Aristides, *etc.* 1921. 8°.   **3624. bb. 8.**

—— *See* HAUPT (W.) *Prediger.* Der Celsus des zweiten Jahrhunderts verglichen mit dem herrschenden Geiste des 19. Jahrhunderts. 1878. 16°.   **[MISSING.]**

—— *See* JUSTIN, *Martyr, Saint.* [*Appendix.*] Justinus, Celsus, Origenes . . . glæde sig over, at den Danske Geistlighed sagtnes, *etc.* 1785. 8°.   **830. b. 6. (21.)**

—— *See* JUSTIN, *Martyr, Saint.* [*Appendix.*] Aftvunget Svar paa tvende nye Spotte-Skrifter: det eene: Justinus, Celsus, *etc.* 1785. 8°.   **830. b. 6. (20.)**

—— *See* KIND (A.) Teleologie und Naturalismus in der altchristlichen Zeit. Der Kampf des Origenes gegen Celsus um die Stellung des Menschen in der Natur. 1875. 8°.   **8463. d. 2. (7.)**

—— *See* KOETSCHAU (P.) Die Textüberlieferung der Bücher des Origenes gegen Celsus in den Handschriften dieses Werkes und der Philokalia, *etc.* 1889. 8°. [*Texte und Untersuchungen zur Geschichte der altchristlichen Literatur.* Bd. 6. Hft. 1.]   **3628. d. 1/6.**

—— *See* LAGRANGE (F.) *Bishop of Chartres.* La Raison et la foi, ou Étude sur la controverse entre Celse et Origène au sujet du christianisme, *etc.* 1856. 8°.   **4015. d. 22.**

—— *See* MIURA-STANGE (A.) Celsus und Origenes. Das Gemeinsame ihrer Weltanschauung nach den acht Büchern des Origenes gegen Celsus, *etc.* 1926. 8°. [*Beihefte zur Zeitschrift für die neutestamentliche Wissenschaft.* no. 4.]   **P.P. 103. lf.**

—— *See* MOSHEIM (J. L. von) Dissertazione . . . sopra l'opera di Origene contro il filosofo platonico Celso, *etc.* 1786. 8°.   **528. l. 12.**

—— *See* MUTH (J. F. S.) Der Kampf des heidnischen Philosophen Celsus gegen das Christentum, *etc.* 1899. 8°.   **4015. f. 9.**

CELSUS, *the Philosopher.*

—— *See* ORIGEN. Origen : Contra Celsum, *etc.* 1953. 8°.   **3628. b. 8.**

—— *See* ORIGEN. Origenis contra Celsum liber I, *etc.* *Gr.* 1860. 8°.   **3627. d. 22.**

—— *See* ORIGEN. Origenis contra Celsum libri I–IV., *etc.* *Gr.* 1876. 8°.   **3805. b. 1.**

—— *See* ORIGEN. Origenis contra Celsum libri VIII., *etc.* *Gr. & Lat.* 1605. 4°.   **854. k. 1.**

—— *See* ORIGEN. Ὠριγενης κατα Κελσου . . . Origenis contra Celsum libri octo, *etc.* 1658. 4°.   **3805. b. 13.**

—— —— 1677, *etc.* 4°.   **1009. b. 11.**

—— *See* ORIGEN. *Begin.* [fol. 1 *verso :*] Theodorus Gazinus Constantinopolita. Xφoforo psona : S. P. D. [fol. 3 *recto :*] Origenis proaemium contra Celsum, *etc.* 1481. fol.   **IB. 19156.**

—— *See* ORIGEN. Origen against Celsus. [1660 ?] 8°.   **3627. b. 40.**

—— *See* ORIGEN. Traité d'Origène contre Celse, *etc.* 1700. 4°.   **691. f. 5.**

—— —— 1843. 8°. [GENOUD (A. E.) *Les Pères de l'Église,* *etc.* tom. 8.]   **1125. d. 18.**

—— —— 1843. 8°. [MIGNE (J. P.) *Démonstrations évangéliques.* tom. 1.]   **1350. i. 3.**

—— *See* ORIGEN. Origenis Adamantii Tractatus contra Celsum analysis. 1791. 4°. [CIGHERI (A. M.) *Sanctae Matris nostrae Catholicae Ecclesiae dogmatum et morum . . . veritas demonstrata, etc.* tom. 1. pt. 1.]   **699. i. 1.**

—— *See* PATRICK (John) *D.D., Professor of Biblical Criticism in the University of Edinburgh.* The Apology of Origen in reply to Celsus, *etc.* 1892. 8°.   **3805. bb. 18.**

—— *See* PÉLAGAUD (E.) Un Conservateur au second siècle. Étude sur Celse, *etc.* 1878. 8°.   **8462. cc. 4.**

—— *See* PHILIPPI (F. A.) De Celsi adversarii Christianorum philosophandi genere. 1836. 8°.   **T. 2069. (9.)**

—— *See* ROUGIER (Louis) *Professeur agrégé de philosophie.* Celse, ou le Conflit de la civilisation antique et du christianisme primitif. 1926. 8°.   **04530. e. 10.**

—— *See* WIFSTRAND (A.) Die wahre Lehre des Kelsos. 1942. 8°. [*Kungl. Humanistiska Vetenskapssamfundet i Lund. Årsberättelse.* 1941–1942.]   **Ac. 1068.**

—— Der Ἀληθης Λογος des Kelsos. Von Robert Bader. [With the text.] pp. xi. 216.   *Stuttgart-Berlin,* 1940. 8°.   **04018. i. 8.**

—— [Another copy.] Der Ἀληθης Λογος des Kelsos. *Stuttgart, Berlin,* 1940. 8°.   **04018. i. 11.**

—— Celsus' Wahres Wort. Ælteste Streitschrift antiker Weltanschauung gegen das Christenthum vom Jahr 178 n. Chr. Wiederhergestellt, aus dem Griechischen übersetzt, untersucht und erläutert, mit Lucian und Minucius Felix verglichen von Dr. Theodor Keim. pp. xv. 293. *Zürich,* 1873. 8°.   **4516. ee. 2.**

—— Arguments of Celsus, Porphyry, and the Emperor Julian against the Christians; also extracts from Diodorus Siculus, Josephus and Tacitus, relating to the Jews. Together with an appendix containing the oration of Libanius in defence of the temples of the heathens, translated by Dr. Lardner, *etc.* [By Thomas Taylor, the Platonist.] pp. xiv. 116.   *Thomas Rodd : London,* 1830. 12°.   **4015. a. 7.**

CELSUS, *pseud.* Medical and Surgical Directions for Cottagers, *etc.* [The preface signed : Celsus.] pp. 59. *W. Freeman ; Whiteley & Co.: London*, 1864. 16°.
7390. a. 65. (6.)

CELSUS, *Saint. See* DELUCCHI (P.) Della vita dei . . . martiri Nazario e Celso, *etc.* 1877. 8°. **4827. bbb. 20.**

—— *See* PURICELLI (G. P.) De SS. martyribus Nazario et Celso . . . dissertatio, *etc.* 1656. fol. **487. l. 9.**

—— *See* SAVIO (C. F.) La Leggenda dei santi Nazario e Celso. 1897. fol. [AMBROSE, *Saint, Bishop of Milan.—Appendix. Ambrosiana, etc.*] **4827. h. 4**

—— Celse Martyr, tragedie latine et Les Terreurs paniques comedie françoise, qui seront représentées . . . avril 1712, *etc.* [Programmes, with the text of the " Intermedes de musique."] pp. 12. *See* ROUEN.—*Société de Bibliophiles Normands.* Ancien théâtre scolaire, *etc.* fasc. 3. 1904. 4°. **Ac. 8938/57.**

—— SS. Celsus et Julianus martyres. Tragoedia. Acta . . . in Gymnasio Soc: Jesu Ratisbonæ . . . M.DC.XCI. Sigreicher Glauben- und Todts-Kampff, *etc.* [A summary.] *Lat. & Ger. Regenspurg*, [1691.] 4°. **840. e. 4. (27.)**

CELSUS, *Veronensis. See* MAFFEUS (C.)

CELSUS ( ) *Jurist. See* UBALDIS (B. de) [*In Justiniani Codicem.*] Baldi Perusini in primum(—undecimum) codicis prælectiones. Annotarunt Alexander Imol., Celsus, *etc.* 1561. fol. **C. 73. i. 4.**

CELSUS (ANGELUS) *Cardinal. See* ROME, *Church of.—Rota.* Decisiones Sacræ Rotæ Romanæ coram . . . A. Celso, *etc.* 1668. fol. **5327. g. 8.**

CELSUS (ARRUNTIUS) De proprietate et differentiis Latini sermonis. *See* ISIDORE, *Saint, Bishop of Seville.* [*Etymologiae.*] Isidori . . . originum libri viginti, *etc.* [1577.] fol. **456. d. 11.**

—— [Another edition.] *See* VULCANIUS (B.) Thesaurus utriusque linguæ, *etc.* 1600. fol. **623. l. 12.**

CELSUS (AULUS CORNELIUS)

WORKS.

Latin.

—— A. Cornelii Celsi quae supersunt. Recensuit Fridericus Marx. pp. cxiv. 484. *Lipsiae & Berolini*, 1915. 8°. [*Corpus medicorum latinorum.* vol. 1.] **2025.h.**

SINGLE WORKS.

DE ARTE DICENDI.

Latin.

—— Aurelii Cornelii Celsi . . . De arte dicendi libellus, primum in lucem editus, curante Sixto à Popma. 1722. *See* FABRICIUS (J. A.) Jo. Alberti Fabricii . . . Bibliotheca latina, *etc.* vol. 3. 1721, *etc.* 8°. **011902. e. 36.**

—— [Another edition.] *See* FABRICIUS (J. A.) Jo. Alberti Fabricii Bibliotheca latina, *etc.* tom. 2. 1728. 4°. **680. c. 18.**

DE MEDICINA.

Latin.

—— *Begin.* [fol. 1 *verso:*] Bartholomeus Fontius Saxetto suo. S. [fol. 2 *recto:*] Cornelii Celsi de medicina liber incipit. [fol. 188 *verso:*] Cornelii Celsi de medicina liber finit, *etc.* [fol. 189 *recto:*] Primo libro Cornelii Celsi. de medicina haec continentur. *End.* [fol. 195 *verso:*] Finit tabula. [Edited by Bartholomaeus Fontius.] *A Nicolao* [*Laurentii*] *impressus: Florentiae*, 1478. fol. & 4°. **IB. 27079.**
196 *leaves, the last blank. Sig.* [*⁶] a⁴ b–i⁶ l–z⁶ &⁶ aa–gg⁶ hh⁴ A⁸. *34 lines to a page.*

CELSUS (AULUS CORNELIUS) [SINGLE WORKS.—DE MEDICINA.—*Latin.*]

—— [Another copy.] **167. d. 1.**
Without the blank leaf.

—— [Another copy.] **G. 9003.**
Without the blank leaf.

—— *Begin.* [fol. 2 *recto:*] Aurelii Cornelii Celsi medicinae liber primus incipit. [fol. 144 *verso:*] Cornelii celsi de medicina Liber finit, *etc.* [fol. 145 *recto:*] Primo libro Cornelii Celsi de medicina haec continentur. *End.* [fol. 151 *verso:*] Finis tabulae. *Per Leonardum pachel & Vlderichum sinczenzeler: Mediolani*, 1481. 4°. **C. 14. b. 8.**
152 *leaves, the first and last blank. Sig.* a–i⁸ K⁸ l–s⁸ [*⁸]. 39 *lines to a page. Without the blank leaves. Fol.* 2 *is mutilated by the removal of a capital.*

—— *Begin.* [fol. 2 *recto:*] Aurelii Cornelii Celsi medicinae liber primus incipit. [fol. 59 *verso:*] Cornelii celsi de medicina Finis, *etc.* [fol. 60 *recto:*] In primo libro Cornelii Celsi de medicina haec continentur. *Ioannes rubeus Vercellensis: Venetiis, die* viii. *mensis Iulii*, 1493. fol. **IB. 23159.**
62 *leaves, the first blank,* 7–60 *so numbered. Sig.* a–i⁶ k⁴ l⁴. 61 *lines to a page. Without the blank leaf.*

—— [fol. 2 *recto:*] Aurelii Cornelii Celsi medicinae liber primus incipit. *End.* [fol. 91 *recto:*] facile noxæ postea pateat. In primo libro Cornelii Celsi de medicina hęc cõtinēt. *Per Philippum pinzi. Sumptibus Benedicti fontana: Venetiis, die* .vi. *Mai*, 1497. fol. **IB. 23676.**
94 *leaves,* 9–91 *so numbered. Sig.* A⁸ b–l⁸ m⁶. 46 *lines to a page.*

—— [Another copy.] **167. d. 2. (1.)**

—— [Another copy.] **G. 9026**
Bound in stamped brown morocco with gilt roundels and a coloured plaquette design in the centre of each cover. This copy belonged to J. Grolier, and has an inscription in the lower cover: " Est mei Io. grolier Lugd' & amicorum."

—— [Aurelij cornelij celsi medicine libri octo nouiter emēdati et inpressi, *etc.*] ᴮᴸ. ff. cvi. FEW MS. NOTES. *Impressor S. beuelaqua fuit: Lugduni*, 1516. 4°. **540. f. 1.**
Imperfect; wanting the titlepage and the last four leaves, forming part of the index.

—— Cornelius Celsus cum tabula. A. C. Celsi . . . Medicine libri octo . . . collatis q̃pluribus exemplaribus manuscriptis accurate recogniti, *etc.* ᴮᴸ. ff. 45. FEW MS. NOTES. *Impēsis L. A. Junta: Venetijs*, 1524. fol. **541. g. 21.**

—— [Another edition.] Accessit huic thesaurus ueriùs, quàm liber, Scribonij Largi, titulo Compositionū Medicamentorum: nunc primùm tineis, & blattis ereptus industria Ioannis Ruellij. 2 pt. MS. NOTES. *Apud C. Vuechel: excudebat S. Siluius; Parisijs*, 1529, 28. fol. **541. g. 10.**

—— In hoc uolumine hæc continentur. Aurelij Cornelij Celsi Medicinæ libri .VIII. . . . Quinti Sereni Liber de medicina . . . Accedit index in Celsum, et Serenum quam copiosus. [Edited by G. B. Cipelli under the pseudonym of J. B. Egnatius.] ff. 164. MS. NOTES. *In ædibus Aldi & A. Asulani: Venetijs*, 1528. 8°. **C. 19. c. 2.**

—— [Another copy.] **165. l. 24.**

—— Aurelii Cornelii Celsi, De Re Medica, libri octo eruditissimi. Q. Sereni Samonici præcepta medica, uersibus hexametris. Q. Rhemnij Fannij Palæmonis, de ponderibus & mensuris, liber . . . Hos libros D. Ioan. Cæsarius . . . castigavit, *etc.* 2 pt. *Per I. Secerium: Haganoæ*, 1528. 8°. **1477. a. 18.**

CELSUS (AULUS CORNELIUS) [SINGLE WORKS.—DE MEDICINA.—*Latin.*]

—— [Another edition.] 2 pt. MS. NOTES.
I. Soter excudebat: Salingiaci, 1538. 8º.   **774. b. 3.**

—— [Another edition.] Omnia ex diuersorum codicum . . .
collatione castigata. pp. 476. FEW MS. NOTES.
Apud S. Gryphium: Lugduni, 1542. 8º.   **541. a. 27.**

—— [Another edition.] pp. 581.   *Apud I. Tornæsium &*
G. Gazeium: Lugduni, 1549. 12º.   **1068. b. 26.**

—— Aurelij Cornelij Celsi, de arte Medica libri octo . . .
Gulielmi Pantini . . . in duos quidem priores libros
commentarij & in reliquos annotationes breuiores . . .
Accessit quoꝗ . . . locupletiss. index. pp. 564.
Per I. Oporinum: Basileæ, 1552. fol.   **C. 47. i. 21.**
The titlepage is mutilated.

—— Aurelij Cor. Celsi De re medica libri viii. Item Qu.
Sereni liber de medicina. Qu. Rhemnij Fannij
Palæmonis de pond. & mensuris liber, *etc.* pp. 581.
Apud I. Tornæsium & G. Gazeium: Lugduni, 1554. 12º.
549. a. 9.

—— [Another edition.] Cum adnotationibus & correctioni-
bus R. Constantini. pp. 499. FEW MS. NOTES. *Apud*
G. Rouillium: Lugduni, 1566. 8º.   **541. a. 10.**

—— Aurelii Cornelii Celsi De re medica libri octo, *etc. See*
ESTIENNE (H.) *le Grand.*   Medicæ artis principes,
post Hippocratem & Galenum, *etc.* tom. 2. 1567. fol.
39. f. 5.

—— Aurelij Cornelij Celsi De re medica libri octo. Accessere
in primum eiusdem Hieremiæ Thriueri Brachelij com-
mentarij doctissimi: in reliquos verò septem, Balduini
Ronssei . . . enarrationes. pp. 752. MS. NOTES.
Apud F. Raphelengium; ex officina Plantiniana:
Lugduni Batavorum, 1592. 4º.   **541. c. 6.**

—— A. Cornelii Celsi De re medica libri octo. Item Q. Sereni
liber de medicina. Q. Rhemmij [*sic*] Fannij Palæmonis de
ponderibus & mensuris liber. Vindiciani Carmen. Omnia
. . . castigata, additis ad marginem varijs lectionibus.
pp. 575. *Apud I. Tornæsium: [Lyons,]* 1608. 16º.
549. a. 10.

—— A. Cornelii Celsi De medicina lib. I(–VIII). *See* NARDI
(G.) Noctes geniales, *etc.* 1656. 4º.   **543. e. 5.**

—— A. Corn. Celsi De medicina libri octo, ex recognitione
Joh. Antonidæ vander Linden. pp. 558.   *Apud*
J. Elsevirium: Lugduni Batav., 1657. 12º.   **G. 17203.**
With an additional titlepage, engraved.

—— Aurel. Cornel. Celsi De medicina libri octo. Cum
præfatione Georg. Wolffg. Wedelii, et indice locupletissimo. (Aurelii Cornelii Celsi vita a Joanne Rhodio
conscripta.) pp. 590. *Jenæ*, 1713. 8º.   **774. b. 4.**

—— Aur. Cornelii Celsi De medicina libri octo breuioribus
Rob. Constantini, Is. Casauboni, aliorumque scholiis
ac locis parallelis illustrati. Cura & studio Th. J. ab
Almeloveen . . . Editio ultima, *etc.* (Jo. Baptistæ
Morgagni . . . in Aur. Corn. Celsum epistola, *etc.*—In
Celsum prolegomena. [By J. A. van der Linden.]—
Aurelii Cornelii Celsi vita a . . . Joanne Rhodio con-
scripta.—Q. Sereni Samonici de medicina præcepta
saluberrima, *etc.*—Jo. Baptistæ Morgagni . . . in Q.
Serenum Samonicum epistola, *etc.*—Q. Rhemnii Fannii
Palæmonis de ponderibus et mensuris liber.) [Edited by
J. B. Vulpius.] 2 pt. *Patavii*, 1722. 8º.   **46. m. 5.**

CELSUS (AULUS CORNELIUS) [SINGLE WORKS.—DE MEDICINA.—*Latin.*]

—— Aur. Corn. Celsi De medicina libri octo breuioribus
Rob. Constantini, Is. Casauboni, aliorumque scholiis . . .
illustrati. Cura & studio Th. J. ab Almeloveen . . .
Accedunt Joh. Rhodii vita C. Celsi, item contenta
capitum . . . Editio ultima prioribus multo auctior &
emendatior. 2 tom. *Lugduni Batavorum*, 1730. 12º.
1165. c. 20.

—— Aur. Corn. Celsi De medicina libri octo. Cum notis
integris Joannis Caesarii, Roberti Constantini, Josephi
Scaligeri, Isaaci Casauboni, Joannis Baptistae Morgagni.
Ac locis parallelis. Cura & studio Th. J. ab Almeloveen
. . . Accedunt J. Rhodii vita C. Celsi, variae lectiones
ex tribus antiquis editionibus, itemque loci aliquot
Hippocratis et Celsi ab Henrico Stephano παραλλήλως
concinnati. [Edited by J. B. Vulpius.] pp. 749.
Lugduni Batavorum, 1746. 8º.   **58. n. 3.**

—— Ex recensione Leonardi Targæ. (Epistolæ aliquot in
A. Cornelium Celsum.) pp. 586. *Patavii*, 1769. 4º.
41. h. 19.

—— Aur. Cornelii Celsi De medicina libri octo, ad editionem
Patavinam, quam anno DMCCL. [*sic*] Vulpius dedit et
nuperiorem Lipsiensem, nunc cura Alberti von Haller
denuo editi. Indicem auctiorem reddidit P. R. Vicat.
2 tom. *Lausannæ*, 1772. 8º.   **541. c. 7.**

—— A. Cornelii Celsi De re medica libri octo. Ex fide manuscriptorum codicum & vetustissimorum librorum . . .
recensuit J. Valart. pp. xx. 553. *Parisiis*, 1772. 12º.
678. a. 23.

—— A. Cornelii Celsi Medicinae libri octo. Ex recensione
Leonardi Targae. Accedunt notae variorum, item,
quae nunc primum prodeunt, J. L. Bianconii dissertatio
de Celsi aetate, et Georgii Matthiae lexicon Celsianum.
(Epistolae aliquot in A. Cornelium Celsum Jo. Baptistae
Morgagni.) 2 pt. *Lugduni Batavorum*, 1785. 4º.
541. f. 3.

—— [Another copy.]   **G. 9004.**

—— A. Corn. Celsi De medicina libri octo, ad optimas
editiones collati. Præmittitur notitia literaria, studiis
Societatis Bipontinæ. (A. Corn. Celsi vita a Joanne
Rhodio conscripta.) pp. xxiv. 553. *Biponti*, 1786. 8º.
159. g. 10.

—— A. Corn. Celsi De medicina libri octo. Ex recensione et
cum notis Leonardi Targae. Praemittitur Ioan. Lud.
Bianconii epistola de Celsi aetate. Accedunt indices.
2 vol. pp. lx. 506. *Argentorati*, 1806. 8º. **159. g. 11, 12.**

—— A. Cornelii Celsi De re medica libri octo. Editio nova,
à S. Pariset . . . emendata. 2 pt. *Parisiis*, 1808. 16º.
7321. a. 31.

—— A. C. Celsi De re medica libri octo. Editio nova,
curantibus P. Fouquier . . . et F. S. Ratier. pp. 431.
Parisiis; Lipsiæ, 1823. 12º.   **7321. aa. 1.**

—— A. Corn. Celsi Medicinae libri octo. Ex recensione
Leonardi Targae. Quibus accedunt tituli marginales
. . . annotationes criticae . . . tabulae characterum,
ponderum, mensurarum, aliae; indices materiae medicae
Celsianae . . . praefixa de Celsi vita dissertatione. Con-
cinnavit Eduardus Milligan. pp. lxviii. 639.   *Apud*
Maclachlan & Stewart: Edinburgi; apud Baldwin, Cradock
& Joy: Londini, 1826. 8º.   **541. c. 8.**

CELSUS (Aulus Cornelius) [Single Works.—De Medicina.—*Latin.*]

—— A. Corn. Celsi De medicina libri octo, quos potissimum ad Leon. Targae recensionem in scholarum usum accommodatos additis quibusdam indicibus edidit Ioan. Henr. Waldeck. pp. 289. *Monasterii Guestphalorum,* 1827. 12°.
1168. e. 22.

—— A. Corn. Celsi Medicinae libri octo. Ex recensione Leonardi Targæ, accurante Joan. Gul. Underwood. pp. 276. *Apud W. Joy: Londini,* 1830. 12°. **541. a. 15.**

—— Editio nova ex recensione Leo. Targæ, curante G. F. Collier . . . Accedit lexicon Celsianum breve. 4 vol. *S. Highley: Londini,* 1830. 12°. **549. a. 11, 12.**
The titlepages are engraved.

—— [Another edition.] Ex recensione Leon. Targæ. Accedunt J. Rhodii dissertatio de Celsi vita. Schillingii quæstio de Celsi ætate, L. Targæ præfatio et index libb. mss. editorumque, excerpta de balneis, de ponderibus et mensuris Romanis monitum breve, cum conspectu capitum. Præfixis characterum, balnearum, instrumentorumque tabulis. Editio secunda, accuratissime emendata. Opera et studio Georgii Frederici Collier. [With a plate.] pp. xl. 342. *Apud Simpkin & Marshall: Londini,* 1831. 12°. **541. a. 11.**

—— A. Cornelii Celsi Medicina. Ediderunt, brevi annotatione indicibusque . . . instruxerunt F. Ritter et H. Albers. pp. xxxvi. 401. *Coloniae ad Rhenum,* 1835. 12°.
1168. e. 27.

—— A. Corn. Celsi Medicinae libri octo . . . diligentissime emendati . . . cura et studio Georgii Futvoye. pp. xvi. 334. *J. T. Cox & E. Portwine: Londini,* 1837. 8°. **541. a. 18.**

—— A. C. Celsi De medicina opera, e recensione Leonardi Targæ. Edente et curante I. Steggall. pp. 349. *Apud J. Churchill: Londini,* 1837. 12°. **541. a. 12.**

—— A. Cornelii Celsi De medicina libri octo . . . Recensuit adnotatione critica indicibusque instruxit C. Daremberg. pp. xlviii. 405. *Lipsiae,* 1859. 8°. **2047. f. 7.**
Part of the "Bibliotheca scriptorum graecorum et romanorum Teubneriana."

Latin and English.

—— The Eight Books on Medicine of A. C. Celsus. With a literal and interlineal translation . . . by J. W. Underwood. 2 vol. pp. 538. *Printed for the Author: London,* 1830. 12°. **541. a. 16.**

—— Aur. Corn. Celsus on Medicine, in eight books, Latin and English. Translated from L. Targa's edition, the words of the text being arranged in the order of construction. To which are prefixed, a life of the author (by J. Rhodius), tables of weights and measures, with explanatory notes . . . By Alex. Lee. 2 vol. *E. Cox: London,* 1831, 36. 8°. **541. c. 9.**

—— De medicina. With an English translation by W. G. Spencer. 3 vol. *William Heinemann: London; Harvard University Press: Cambridge, Mass.,* 1935, 38. 8°. [*Loeb Classical Library.*] **2282. d. 138.**

Latin and French.

—— A. C. Celsi De medicina. Traité de la médecine. [The French translation by H. Ninnin.] 1837. *See* Bayle (A. L. J.) Encyclopédie des sciences médicales, *etc.* (Septième division.) 1834, *etc.* 8°. **07305. cc. 3/12.**

—— Traité de la médecine. [The French translation by A. Chaales des Étangs.] 1852. *See* Nisard (J. M. N. D.) Collection des auteurs latins, *etc.* 1850, *etc.* 8°.
11306. m. 19.

CELSUS (Aulus Cornelius) [Single Works.—De Medicina.]

Latin and Italian.

—— Auli Cornelii Celsi De medicina libri octo ex recensione Leonardi Targae; quibus accedunt versio italica; de Celsi vita et opere; pharmacopœa et armamentarium chirurgicum; bibliotheca Celsiana latina et italica; adnotationes . . . indices . . . et lexicon Celsianum. Curante Salvatore de Renzi. 2 tom. *Neapoli,* 1851, 52. 8°. **541. f. 15, 16.**

English.

—— A. Cornelius Celsus Of Medicine, in eight books; translated, with notes critical and explanatory, by James Greive, *etc.* pp. xxxii. 519. *D. Wilson & T. Durham: London,* 1756. 8°. **42. e. 10.**

—— A Translation of the Eight Books of Aulus Cornelius Celsus. From the text of Leo. Targa, with a brief explanatory lexicon, by G. F. Collier. 4 vol. *S. Highley: London,* 1830. 16°. **549. a. 13, 14.**
The titlepages are engraved.

—— A. Cornelius Celsus Of Medicine, in eight books. Translated, with notes critical and explanatory by James Greive . . . Revised, with additional notes, by George Futvoye. Third edition. pp. xxviii. 468. *T. Chidley: London,* 1837. 12°. **541. a. 19.**

German.

—— A. C. Celsus acht Bücher von der Arzneikunde. Aus dem Lateinischen in's Deutsche übertragen, mit Beigabe von Celsus Biographie und erläuternden Bemerkungen von Bernhard Ritter. pp. xxxii. 605. *Stuttgart,* 1840. 8°. **7306. aa. 7.**

—— Aulus Cornelius Celsus über die Arzneiwissenschaft, in acht Büchern, übersetzt und erklärt von Eduard Scheller . . . Nebst Bianconi's Briefe über Celsus. 2 Tl. *Braunschweig,* 1846. 8°. **541. e. 29.**

—— Zweite Auflage nach der Textausgabe von Daremberg neu durchgesehen von Walther Frieboes . . . Mit einem Vorworte von R. Kobert . . . Mit einem Bildnis . . . und 4 Tafeln. pp. xlii. 862. *Braunschweig,* 1906. 8°.
7679. g. 19.

Italian.

—— Della medicina di A. C. Celso libri otto. Portati nella lingua italiana, secondo l'esemplare latino dato al pubblico, da Teodoro Jansenio d'Almeloveen . . . Fatica dell'abate Chiari da Pisa, *etc.* (Breve notizia della vita dell'autore.) 2 tom. *Venezia,* 1747. 8°. **236. k. 41, 42.**

De Medicina.—Selections and Extracts.
Latin.

—— Flosculi in medicina ex C. Celso extracti. *See* Hunain ibn Ishāk, al-'Ibādī. Liber Hysagoge, *etc.* [1510?] 8°.
539. c. 34.

—— Flosculi medicinales ex C. Celso extracti. *See* Articella. Articella nuperrime impressa, *etc.* 1519. 8°.
544. b. 8.

—— [Another edition.] *See* Articella. Articella nuperrime impressa, *etc.* 1525. 8°. **544. b. 9.**

—— [Another edition.] *See* Articella. Articella nuperrime impressa, *etc.* 1534. 8°. **544. b. 10.**

—— Aurelij Cornelij Celsi De sanitate tuenda liber plurimis in locis antea nemini suspectis, castigatus & commentarijs illustratus per Hieremiam Thriuerum. *Apud M. Crommium: Antuerpiæ,* 1539. 8°. **774. b. 8. (1.)**

CELSUS (Aulus Cornelius) [Single Works.—De Medicina.—Selections and Extracts.]

—— [Another copy, with a different titlepage.]
C. 60. b. 3.
Without the date in the imprint.

—— Flosculi medicinales selecti ex libris A. Cornelij Celsi. *See* Ryff (W. H.) Medicinæ theoricæ et practicæ breue . . . enchiridion, *etc.* 1542. 12°.   544. a. 5.

—— Insigniores aliquot sententiæ selectæ ex libris A. C. Celsi. *See* Hippocrates. [*Two or more Works.—Latin.*] Hippocratis aphorismi, *etc.* 1555. 8°.   539. a. 4.

—— Commentarij de sanitate tuenda in primum librum de Re medica Aurel. Cornelij Celsi . . . Autore Iodoco Lommio. [With the text.] ff. 141.   *Apud A. M. Bergagne: Louanij,* 1558. 8°.   774. b. 8. (2.)

—— De febribus liber. *See* Febres. De febribus opus sane aureum, *etc.* 1576. fol.   777. i. 40.

—— Cornelii Celsi aliquot aphorismorum Hippocratis Latina conuersio.—Cornelii Celsi prognosticorum aliquot Hippocr. Latina conuersio. *See* Hippocrates. [*Two or more Works.—Latin.*] Diuini Hippocratis Aphorismorum . . . paraphrasis poëtica, *etc.* 1579. 8°.   539. d. 19. (1.)

—— Insigniores aliquot sententiæ selectæ ex libris A. C. Celsi. *See* Hippocrates. [*Aphorismi.—Greek and Latin.*] Hippocratis Aphorismi, *etc.* 1595. 8°.   539. a. 6.

—— A. Cornelij Celsi De re medica liber octavus. Ejus priora quatuor capita commentarijs illustrata à Petro Paaw. *See* Hippocrates. [*De Capitis Vulneribus.— Greek and Latin.*] Petri Paaw . . . succenturiatus anatomicus, *etc.* 1616. 4°.   541. a. 6.

—— Insigniores aliquot sententiæ selectæ ex libris Aurelij Cornelij Celsi. *See* Hippocrates. [*Two or more Works.— Greek and Latin.*] Hippocratis aphorismi et prognostica, Ioanne Butino interprete, *etc.* 1625. 8°.   539. a. 30.

—— [Another edition.] *See* Hippocrates. [*Two or more Works.—Greek and Latin.*] Hippocratis Aphorismi, *etc.* 1631. 12°.   539. a. 11.

—— De positu et figura ossium totius humani corporis. *See* Galenus (C.) [*De Ossibus, etc.—Greek and Latin.*] Galenus de ossibus, *etc.* 1665. 12°.   540. b. 11.

—— Ex libris de re medica Aurelii Cornelii Celsi quædam describuntur, unde colligi possit, in quo Latinus ille Hippocrates cum altero consentiat vel dissentiat, *etc. See* Hippocrates. [*Aphorismi.—Latin.*] Tripus medicinæ, oracula Hippocratica divulgans, *etc.* 1681. 12°.
540. a. 32.

—— Insigniores aliquot sententiæ, selectæ ex libris Aurelii Cornelii Celsi, *etc. See* Hippocrates. [*Aphorismi.— Greek and Latin.*] Ἱπποκρατους ἀφορισμοι, *etc.* 1685. 16°.   7320. aaaa. 5.

—— Jodoci Lommii . . . Commentarii de sanitate tuenda in primum librum de re medica A. C. Celsi, *etc.* [With the text.] pp. 326. *Lugduni Batavorum,* 1724. 8°.
540. b. 36.
Previous edition 1558.

—— Aurel. Cornelius Celsus. Lib. IV. cap. VI. *See* Triller (D. W.) Dan. Wilh. Trilleri . . . Succincta commentatio de pleuritide, *etc.* 1740. 8°.   T. 390. (1.)

—— [Insigniores sententiae.] *See* Hippocrates. [*Two or more Works.—Latin.*] Manuale medicorum, *etc.* 1739. 12°.   539. b. 31.

—— Iodoci Lommii . . . Commentarii de sanitate tuenda, in primum lib. de re medica Aurel. Cornelii Celsi . . . Editio nova, *etc.* [With the text.] pp. 325.
Amstelodami, 1745. 12°.   1169. d. 3. (3.)
Previous edition 1724.

—— [Another copy.]   **1039.g.21.**

CELSUS (Aulus Cornelius) [Single Works.—De Medicina.—Selections and Extracts.]

—— Celsi libri VIII varietates scripturae e codice Laurentiano. *See* Nicetas, *the Physician.* Graecorum chyrurgici libri, *etc.* 1754. fol.   **L.20.a.8.(1,2.)**

—— Jodoci Lommii Commentarii in Aurel. Cornel. Celsum. [With the text.] Novam editionem curavit, et praecipua Graecorum et Romanorum in diaeteticam merita recensuit Josephus Eyerel. pp. lx. 384. *Vindobonæ,* 1794. 8°.   1405. f. 25.
Previous edition 1745.

—— Lectiones Celsianæ et Gregorianæ; or, Lessons in Celsus and Gregory, consisting of passages from those authors syntactically arranged, with copious observations . . . and a lexicon of the words. To which is added a succinct and comprehensive grammar . . . By William Cross. pp. vii. 169. *J. Wilson: London,* 1831. 12°.   774. b. 7.

Latin and English.

—— A. C. Celsi De re medica: liber primus et tertius. Accedunt translatio et ordo verborum cura Ioannis Steggall. pp. 173. *Apud J. Churchill: Londini,* 1833. 12°.
541. a. 13.

—— A Literal Interlinear Translation of the First and Third Books of Celsus; with "ordo," and the text of Targa. By Charles Gerard. Revised and amended, with an introduction . . . by Robert Venables. pp. xii. 250. *J. T. Cox; Edward Portwine: London,* 1834. 8°.
C.T. 30.

—— The First Four Books of A. C. Celsus De re medica, with an ordo verborum and literal translation. By John Steggall. pp. 517.   *John Churchill: London,* 1837. 12°.
541. a. 14.

—— Second edition. pp. 377.   *John Churchill: London,* 1853. 12°.   541. a. 29

English.

—— The Flowers of Celsus containing many aphorismes, *etc. See* Valentinus (P. P.) *pseud.* Enchiridion medicum, *etc.* 1612. 4°.   774. d. 4.

—— Some Very Remarkable Sentences collected from the writings of . . . Aurelius Cornelius Celsus. *See* Hippocrates. [*Aphorismi.—English.*] The Aphorisms of Hippocrates, and the Sentences of Celsus, *etc.* 1708. 8°.
541. a. 2.

—— [Another edition.] *See* Hippocrates. [*Aphorismi.— English.*] The Aphorisms of Hippocrates, *etc.* 1735. 8°.
541. a. 3.

—— A. Cornelius Celsus on Medicine. *See* Gregory (James) *M.D.* A Literal Translation of those parts of Gregory's Conspectus Medicinae Theoreticae and Celsus De medicina which have been fixed upon by the Court of Apothecaries for the examination of candidates. 1831. 12°.
774. b. 6.

German.

—— Kritischer Versuch einer deutschen Uebersetzung der acht Bücher des Aurel. Cornel. Celsus von der Arzneykunst, von D. Johann Heinrich Lange. [Selected passages, with an introduction.] pp. 126.   *Lüneburg,* 1768. 8°.   541. c. 10.

—— Grundriss der Wund-Arzneykunst in den ältern Zeiten der Römer. Oder: A. Cornel. Celsus siebentes und achtes Buch von der Arzneykunst . . . ins Deutsche übersetzt, und mit Anmerkungen versehen von J. C. Jäger, *etc.* pp. 264. *Frankfurt,* 1789. 8°.   1168. e. 19.

CELSUS (Aulus Cornelius)

APPENDIX.

—— *See* Baier (J. J.) *Professor of Medicine at Altdorf.* I. I. Baieri Schediasma quo institutum suum de A. C. Celso . . . commendat. [1720.] 4º. **1179. k. 15. (8.)**

—— *See* Brolén (C. A.) De elocutione A. Cornelii Celsi. 1872. 8º. [*Upsala Universitets årsskrift.* 1872.] Ac. **1075/6.**

—— *See* Broca (P. P.) Conférences historiques de la Faculté de Médecine. Celse, *etc.* 1865. 8º. **10600. ff. 1. (2.ꞌ**

—— *See* Champier (S.) Symphonia Galeni ad Hippocratem, C. Celsi ad Avicennam, *etc.* [1528.] 8º. **774. b. 9. (2.)**

—— *See* Chifflet (J. J.) Acia C. Celsi propriæ significationi restituta, *etc.* 1633. 4º. **836. f. 20. (3.)**

—— —— 1688. 4º. [*Miscellanea Chifletiana.* vol. 1.] **604. e. 3.**

—— *See* Choulant (J. L.) Prodromus novæ editionis Auli Cornelii Celsi librorum octo de medicina . . . Inest apparatus critici Celsiani tentamen bibliographicum. 1824. 4º. **823. i. 7. (6.)**

—— *See* Dalechamps (J.) Chirurgie Françoise, *etc.* (Les passages d'Aëce Grec, C. Celsus . . . qui concernent la matiere traictée de Paul. [The passages of Celsus being marginal notes based on his " De medicina."]) 1570. 8º. **549. b. 16.**

—— —— 1610. 4º. **549. i. 3.**

—— *See* Hippocrates. [*Two or more Works.—Greek and Latin.*] Hippocratis . . . Jusiurandum. Aphorismorum sectiones VIII . . . C. Celsi versione calci subdita, *etc.* 1587. 8º. **539. a. 24. (1.)**

—— *See* Hippocrates. [*Aphorismi.—Greek and Latin.*] Hippocratis aphorismorum genuina lectio . . . His accesserunt adnotationes in C. Celsum . . . Per I. Morisotum. 1547. 8º. **539. c. 2. (1.)**

—— *See* Hippocrates. [*Aphorismi.—Greek and Latin.*] Ἱπποκρατους ἀφορισμοι . . . Accedunt . . . loca parallela ex ipso Hippocrate, ut et Celso, petita. [1675?] 12º. **539. c. 8.**

—— *See* Hippocrates. [*Aphorismi.—Greek and Latin.*] Ἱπποκρατους ἀφορισμοι . . . Variorum auctorum maxime Hippocratis & Celsi locis parallelis illustrati, *etc.* 1685. 16º. **7320. aaaa. 5.**

—— —— 1784. 12º. **57. k. 7.**

—— *See* Hippocrates. [*Aphorismi.—Latin.*] Hippocratis Aphorismi, cum locis parallelis Celsi, *etc.* 1807. 16º. **779. a. 6.**

—— *See* Introductio. Introductio in vitalem philosophiam. Cui cohaeret omnium morborum . . . additis Veterum placitis, Hippocratis, Galeni, Celsi . . . explicatio, *etc.* 1623. 4º. **718. e. 37.**

—— *See* Kissel (C.) A. Cornelius Celsus. Eine historische Monographie, *etc.* 1844. 8º. **551. c. 41.**

—— *See* Krause (C. C.) A. C. Celsi De re medica libros quatuor posteriores emendat . . . C. C. Krause, *etc.* [1762.] 4º. **T. 507. (20.)**

—— *See* Loescher (C. I.) Dissertatio . . . de morbo coeliaco singulari a C. Celso descripto, *etc.* [1765.] 4º. **7306. h. 11. (15.)**

—— *See* Lutheritz (C. F.) Hippokrates . . . und Celsus Systeme der Medizin, *etc.* 1810. 8º. **773. g. 27.**

CELSUS (Aulus Cornelius) [Appendix.]

—— *See* Morgagni (G. B.) Jo. Baptistæ Morgagni . . . in Aur. Corn. Celsum et Q. Ser. Samonicum . . . epistola, *etc.* 1724. 4º. **541. c. 12.**

—— —— 1735. 4º. **41. g. 15. (1.)**

—— *See* Reiche (P.) Der Umfang der intern-medizinischen Kenntnisse des Celsus, *etc.* 1934. 8º. [missing.]

—— *See* Rhodius (J.) J. Rhodii De acia dissertatio ad C. Celsi mentem. 1639. 4º. **7482. bbb. 20.**

—— —— 1672. 4º. **603. c. 27.**

—— *See* Rorarius (N.) Contradictiones . . . in libros . . . Celsi, *etc.* 1572. 12º. **774. b. 21.**

—— *See* Rubeus (H.) Annotationes in libros octo Cornelij Celsi de re medica, *etc.* 1616. 4º. **541. c. 11.**

—— *See* Sabbadini (R.) Guarino Veronese e gli archetipi di Celso e Plauto, *etc.* 1886. 8º. **11312. bbb. 27.**

—— *See* Sabbadini (R.) Storia e critica di testi latini. Cicerone . . . Celso, *etc.* 1914. 8ᶜ. **011313.de.1/10.**

—— *See* Scalinci (N.) La Oftalmiatria di Aulo Cornelio Celso, *etc.* 1940. 8º. **7612. d. 15.**

—— *See* Schoeman (I. F. X.) Commentatio de lithotomia celsiana critico-chirurgica, *etc.* 1841. 4º. **7421. g. 38.**

—— *See* Sepp (S.) Pyrrhonëische Studien . . . Die philosophische Richtung des Cornelius Celsus, *etc.* 1893. 8º. **8460. e. 29.**

—— *See* Wellmann (M.) A. Cornelius Celsus. Eine Quellenuntersuchung. 1913. 8º. **012901. dd. 1/23.**

CELSUS (Aurelius Cornelius) *See* Celsus (Aulus C.)

CELSUS (Cornelius) *See* Celsus (Aulus C.)

CELSUS (Joannes) Princeps ex C. Tacito. 1670. *See* Melles (S. de) Steph. de Melles . . . novum totius philosophiæ syntagma, *etc.* vol. 5. 1669, *etc.* 12º. **526. b. 14.**

CELSUS (Julius) *See* Caesar (C. J.) [*De Bello Gallico.—Latin.*] *Begin.* [fol. 1 *recto:*] [G]ay Iuly cesaris dictatoris exordia. Vt pleracꝫ mortaliũ fragilia, *etc.* [The life of Caesar sometimes attributed to J. Celsus, but in fact written by Francesco Petrarca. Followed by Caesar's De bello gallico, of which bk. 8 is here attributed to J. Celsus.] 1473. fol. **C. 2. c. 8.**

—— *See* Dodwell (Henry) *the Elder.* Annales Velleiani, *etc.* (Appendix dissertationum duarum . . . quarum I. agitur Julii Cæsaris vitâ per J. Celsum [or rather, by F. Petrarca] nuper editâ à A. Grævio.) 1698. 8º. **609. f. 4.**

—— *See* Rossetti (D. de) Petrarca, Giul. Celso, e Boccaccio ; illustrazione bibliologica delle vite degli uomini illustri del primo, di C. Giulio Cesare attribuita al secondo, *etc.* 1828. 8º. **11421. f. 28.**

—— [For editions of " Commentarii de vita Caesaris," otherwise " Historia Julii Caesaris," sometimes attributed to J. Celsus, but in fact written by F. Petrarca :] *See* Petrarca (F.) [*De Viris Illustribus.*]

CELSUS (Juventius) *See* Stella Maranca (F.) Intorno ai frammenti di Celso. 1915. 8º. **5206. g. 9.**

CELSUS (Minus)

—— *See* Schellhorn (J. G.) Dissertatio epistolaris de M. Celso Senensi rarissimæ disquisitionis, in hæreticis coercendis quatenus progredi liceat, auctore, *etc.* 1748. 4º. **1371. g. 20.**

CELSUS (Minus)

—— In hæreticis coercendis, quatenus progredi liceat . . . Disputatio. [The preface of the editor, J. Fischart, headed: S. I. F. D. M. D.] ff. 229. *Christlingæ* [*P. Perna: Basle*], 1577. 8°. **857. f. 3.**

—— [Another edition.] Mini Celsi . . . De hæreticis capitali supplicio non afficiendis. Adjunctæ sunt eiusdem argumenti Theodori Bezæ & Andreæ Duditii epistolæ duæ contrariæ. Cum indice satis copioso & accurato. ff. 260. 1584. 8°. **857. f. 5.**

—— [Another edition.] Henoticum Christianorum, seu Disputationis M. Celsi . . . quatenus in hæreticis coërcendis progredi liceat? lemmata potissima . . . Recensita à D. Z. [i.e. Daniel Zwicker], *etc.* pp. 48. *Amsterodami*, 1662. 8°. **3906. b. 4. (1.)**

—— [Another copy.] **3925. aaa. 10. (2.)**

—— Nozze Franco–Cave-Bondi. XXVI giugno MCMIV. Una lettera inedita di Mino Celsi senese al vescovo Claudio Tolomei. [Edited by Gustavo Boralevi.] pp. 22. *Livorno*, 1904. 8°. **10910. cc. 40.**

CELT. *See* Periodical Publications.—*London.* The Imperial & Colonial Magazine . . . Edited by " Celt " and E. F. Benson. [1900, *etc.*] 4°. **P.P. 3773. ga.**

—— The Celt. A magazine devoted to Irish interests. *See* Periodical Publications.—*Dublin.*

—— The Celt. A weekly periodical of Irish national literature. *See* Periodical Publications.—*Dublin.*

—— Y Celt. The magazine of the Porth Higher Grade School. *See* Porth.—*Porth Higher Grade School.*

—— Cymru Fydd Gymru Rydd, or the National Movement in Wales. By a Celt. pp. 85. *Welsh National Press Co.: Carnarvon*, 1895. 8°. **8139. de. 6.**

—— The Cynic's Autograph Book. Compiled by " Celt ". [The preface signed: J. F.] 2 pt. 1910, 13. 8°. *See* F., J. **12352. p. 37.**

—— The Cynic's Cyclopædia. By Celt. pp. 167. *Hutchinson & Co.: London*, [1922.] 8°. **012305. i. 34.**

—— Woman. The good and the bad in her. The dicta of famous people of all times; collected, with additions, by " Celt." pp. 119. *Gay & Hancock: London*, 1912. 8°. **08415. e. 11.**

—— Woman, Wedlock, and the World. A confession book of borrowings from various classics, with some modern instances by " Celt." Second edition. pp. 111. *Gay & Hancock: London*, 1911. 8°. **08415. e. 7.**

CELT (Marek) *pseud.* [i.e. Tadeusz Chciuk.]

—— By Parachute to Warsaw. pp. 88. *D. Crisp & Co.: London*, 1945. 8°. **9101. ee. 56.**

CELTA (Sincerus) Zwey neue Jesuitische Meister-Stücke [i.e. " Funffzehen Motiva, welche alle guthertzige Lutheraner, bey gegenwärtiger Gefahr, viel lieber sich mit der Römisch-Catholischen Kirche zu vereinigen, als die in 15. projectirten Puncten bestehende Religions-Allianz mit den Calvinern einzugehen wohl bewegen könten, per quendam Theologum Polonum " and " Leicht und kräfftiges Mittel die unruhigen Gemüther zu stillen, das ist den neulich entstandenen Federstreit zwischen den Herrn D. Valent. Ernestus Löscher und seine Wiedersacher glücklich aufzuheben, per quendam Theologum Polonum," both by Gottfried Hannenberg] . . . beleuchtet und nach Verdienst abgefertigt von S. Celta. pp. 167. 1724. 8°. **4092. bbb. 4.**

CELTES (Conradus) *See* Apuleius (L.) *Madaurensis.* [*De Mundo.*—*Latin.*] Lucij Apulei . . . Epitoma diuinū de mundo Seu Cosmographia ductu Conradi Celtis' impressū Vienne, *etc.* [1497?] fol. **IB. 51521.**

—— *See* Aschbach (J. von) Die früheren Wanderjahre des Conrad Celtes und die Anfänge der von ihm errichteten gelehrten Sodalitäten. 1869. 8°. **10601. ff. 10. (2.)**

—— *See* Aschbach (J. von) Roswitha und Conrad Celtes, *etc.* 1868. 8°. **11824. h. 29. (5.)**

—— *See* Bradish (J. A. von) Der ' Erzhumanist ' Celtes und das Wiener ' Dichter-Kollegium,' *etc.* [1936.] 8°. **11871. g. 4.**

—— *See* Guntherus, *Cisterciencis.* Ligurini de gfstis [*sic*] Imp. Cæsaris Friderici primi Augusti libri decē . . . nnper [*sic*] . . . a C. Celte reperti postliminio restituti, *etc.* 1507. fol. **C. 47. i. 15.**

—— *See* Hartmann (B.) Konrad Celtis in Nürnberg. Ein Beitrag zur Geschichte des Humanismus in Nürnberg. 1889. 8°. **10602. dd. 14. (9.)**

—— *See* Kluepfelius (E.) De vita et scriptis C. Celtis Protucii, *etc.* 1827. 4°. **816. l. 6.**

—— *See* Moth (C. F.) Conradus Celtis Protucius, *etc.* 1898. 8°. **010708. e. 17.**

—— *See* Roswitha. Opera Hrosvite . . . nuper · a Conrado Celte inuenta. 1501. fol. **77. h. 4. (1.)**

—— *See* Tritonius (P.) Melopoiæ, siue Harmoniæ tetratenticæ super xxii genera carminum heroicorū elegiacorū lyricorum & ecclesiasticorū hymnorū . . . ductu C. Celtis impresse, *etc.* 1507. fol. **M.K. 1. i. 17.**

—— Conradi celtis Panegyris ad duces batuarie. [In verse.] [fol. 4 *recto*:] Ejusdē oratio in gymnasio in jngelstadio publice recitata. G.L. [*Erhard Ratdolt: Augsburg*, 1492?] 4°. **IA. 6733.** 12 *leaves, the last blank. Without signatures.* 38–40 *lines to a page.*

—— [Another copy.] **IA. 6733a.**

—— Conradis Celtis Protucij . . . quatuor libri amorum secundum quatuor latera Germaniæ feliciter incipiunt. (Conradi Celtis de origine situ moribus et institutis Norimbergae libellus incipit.) *Norībergæ*, 1502. fol. **C. 57. g. 11.**

—— Fünf Bücher Epigramme . . . Herausgegeben von Dr. Karl Hartfelder. pp. xviii. 125. *Berlin*, 1881. 8°. **11409. gg. 8.**

—— Der Briefwechsel des Konrad Celtis. Gesammelt, herausgegeben und erläutert von Hans Rupprich. pp. xxii. 678. *München*, 1934. 8°. [*Veröffentlichungen der Kommission zur Erforschung der Geschichte der Reformation und Gegenreformation. Humanistenbriefe.* Bd. 3.] Ac. **714/13. (1.)**

—— Ars versificandi et carminum conradi celtis protucii poete laureati. G.L. [*Martin Landsberg: Leipsic*, 1495?] 4°. **IA. 8067.** 20 *leaves. Sig.* A⁶ B⁶ C⁸. 43 *lines to a page.*

—— Conradi Celtis . . . de origine, situ, moribus, & institutis Norinbergæ libellus incipit fœliciter. *See* Irenicus (F.) Germaniæ exegeseos volumina duodecim, *etc.* 1518. fol. **C. 78. d. 3. (1.)**

—— [Another edition.] Conradi Celtis Protucij . . . De origine, situ, moribus et institutis Norimbergæ libellus. *See* Pirckheimer (B.) V. illustris Bilibaldi Pirckheimeri . . . opera, *etc.* 1610. fol. **631. l. 10.**

CELTES (Conradus)

—— [Another edition.] *See* Irenicus (F.) Francisci Irenici . . . Exegesis historiæ Germaniæ, *etc.* 1728. fol.
156. h. 2.

—— [Another edition.] Conrad Celtis und sein Buch über Nürnberg. [Edited, with introduction and notes, by Albert Werminghoff.] pp. vi. 245. *Freiburg i. B.*, 1921. 8°. **10256. dd. 19.**

—— Conradi Celtis Protucij De situ ꝛ moribus Germanie fragmenta. [In verse.] *See* Tacitus (P. C.) [*Germania. —Latin.*] Cornelij Taciti . . . de situ Germanie ꝛ incolarū, *etc.* [15]15. 4°. **1314. e. 6.**

—— [Another edition.] *See* Schardius (S.) Historicum opus, *etc.* tom. 1. [1574.] fol. **9366. i. 11.**

—— [Another edition.] *See* Bildius (B.) *Rhenanus.* Beati Rhenani . . . Rerum Germanicarum libri tres, *etc.* 1610. 8°. **1054. b. 13.**

—— [Another edition.] *See* Schardius (S.) Schardius redivivus, *etc.* tom. 1. 1673. fol. **9366. l. 6.**

—— *Begin.* Aeternitati imperii: et felicitati inclytę domus austrię dedicatum. (In hoc libello continentur. Diuo Maximiliano Augusto Chunradi Celtis ῥαψωδια laudes et victoria de Boemannis per septem Electores et Regem. Phoebum. Mercurium et Bachum et nouem Musas personatas publico spectaculo Vienne acta. Anno M.D.IIII.) [With woodcuts.] *ꝑ Mgr̄m Ioann: Otmar: Auguste: Vinde:, 1505.* 4°. **C. 57. i. 1.**

—— Cōradi Celtis Economia. [In verse.] 𝔊.𝔏. [*Johann Winterburg: Vienna, 1500?*] 4°. IA. **51573.** *4 leaves, without signatures. 37–39 lines to a page.*

—— Epitoma in vtrāꝗ Ciceronis rhetoricā cū arte memoratiua noua ꝛ modo epistolandi vtilissimo. 𝔊.𝔏. [*Ingolstadt, 1492?*] 4°. IB. **13523.** *23 leaves. Sig. a⁹ b⁸ c⁶. 40–42 lines to a page.*

—— Ludus Diane in modum Comedie coram Maximiliano Rhomanorum Rege . . . actus. [By C. Celtes] 1501. 4°. *See* Diana, *the Goddess.* **C. 57. c. 3.**

—— [Another copy.] **C. 57. c. 50.**

—— [Another copy.] Ludus Diane, *etc.* [By C. Celtes.] 1501. 4°. *See* Diana, *the Goddess.* Hirsch III. **684.**

—— Methodus conficiendarum epistolarum. *See* Vives (J. L.) De conscribendis epistolis libellus, *etc.* 1537. 8°. **1084. g. 2.**

—— [Another edition.] De conscribendis epistolis. *See* Vives (J. L.) Linguae Latinae exercitatio, *etc.* 1541. 8°. **C. 47. b. 17. (2.)**

—— [Another edition.] Methodus conficiendarum epistolarum. *See* Vives (J. L.) Ioan. Ludouici Viuis . . . De conscribendis epistolis, *etc.* 1547. 8°. **1480. a. 11.**

—— [Another edition.] *See* Brandolinus (A.) called *Lippus.* Lippi Brandolini De ratione scribendi libri tres, *etc.* 1549. 8°. **10905. aaa. 12.**

—— Conradi Celtis Protucij, primi in Germania poetę coronati, libri Odaꝵ quatuor, cum Epodo, & sæculari carmine, diligēter & accurate impræssi, & hoc primū typo in studiosoꝵ emolumentū editi. [Edited by J. Vadianus.] *Ex officina Schüreriana, ductu Leonhardi & Lucę Alantsee fratrum: Argentorati, 1513.* 4°. **11408. c. 71.**

CELTES (Conradus)

—— [Another edition.] Libri odarum quattuor. Liber epodon. Carmen saeculare. Edidit Felicitas Pindter. pp. vi. 137. *Lipsiae; Szeged* [printed], 1937. 8°. [*Bibliotheca scriptorum medii recentisque aevorum.*]
012208.1.2/15.

—— Oratio in gymnasio in Ingelstadio publice recitata cum carminibus ad orationem pertinentibus. Edidit Iohannes Rupprich. pp. vi. 20. *Lipsiae; Szeged* [printed], 1932. 8°. [*Bibliotheca scriptorum medii recentisque aevorum.*]
012208.1.2/22.

—— Conradi Celtis proseuticum ad diuū. Fridericum terciū pro laurea Appollinari. [In verse.] 𝔊.𝔏. *per F. kreusner: nurmberg,* [1487?] 4°. IA. **7673.** *Six leaves, without signatures. 32, 33 lines to a page.*

—— Quattuor libri amorum secundum quattuor latera Germaniae. Germania generalis. Accedunt carmina aliorum ad libros amorum pertinentia. Edidit Felicitas Pindter. pp. vi. 127. *Lipsiae; Karcag* [printed], 1934. 8°. [*Bibliotheca scriptorum medii recentisque aevorum.*]
012208.1.2/5.

—— In hoc libello Continentur Septenaria sodalitas litteraria Germanie. [By C. Celtes.] Ausonij Sententie septem Sapientum septenis versibus explicate. Eiusdem Ausonij ad drepanum de ludo septem sapientum. Epistola sancti Hieronymi ad magnū Oratorem vrbis de legendis ꝛ audiēdis poetis. 𝔊.𝔏. 1500. 4°. *See* Germany. [*Appendix.—Miscellaneous.*] IA. **51525.**

—— [Poems.] *See* G., A. F. G. Delitiæ poetarum germanorum, *etc.* pt. 2. 1612. 12°. **238. i. 15.**

—— Selections from Conrad Celtis, 1459–1508. Edited with translation and commentary by Leonard Forster. pp. xii. 122. pl. III. *Cambridge University Press: Cambridge,* 1948. 8°. **11410. b. 66.**

CELTIA. *See* Dublin.—*Celtic Association.*

CELTIBÈRE, *pseud. See* Leconte (E.) *Publisher.* Notre Dame de Paris, recueil contenant 80 planches . . . et une notice archéologique où l'on a recherché la nature, l'origine, & la raison d'être de toutes les parties du monument par Celtibère. [1841.] fol. **1265. i. 15.**

CELTIBERIA.

—— Celtiberia. Revista. *See* Soria, *Town of.—Centro de Estudios Sorianos.*

CELTIBERIAN RANGES. Zur Tektonik der Keltiberischen Ketten . . . Von C. Hahne, G. Richter und E. Schröder. pp. 180. pl. 8. *Berlin,* 1930. 8°. [*Abhandlungen der Gesellschaft der Wissenschaften zu Göttingen. Math.-phys. Klasse. Neue Folge. Bd. 16. no. 3.*]
Ac. **670. (2.)**

CELTIC. *See* Celtic Language.

CELTIC ANNUAL. *See* Dundee.—*Dundee Highland Society.* Year Book.

CELTIC ANTIQUITIES. Celtische Alterthümer zu Erläuterung der ältesten Geschichten und Verfassung Helvetiens. [By G. Walther.] pp. xxvi. lxiv. 192. 23. *Bern,* 1783. 8°. **1054. c. 1.**

CELTIC ASSOCIATION. *See* Dublin.

CELTIC CONFERENCE. *See* Celtic Congress.

CELTIC CONGRESS.

—— [Birkenhead, 1917.] The Celtic Conference, 1917. Report of the meetings held at Birkenhead . . . together with the papers by Mr. T. Gwynn Jones . . . Dr. S. P. MacEnri [and others] . . . Compiled by D. Rhys Phillips, etc. pp. 137. *Milne, Tannahill & Methven: Perth,* 1918. 8°. Ac. **9948.**

—— [Neath, 1918.] Transactions of the Celtic Congress, 1918. Report of the meetings held at Neath . . . Compiled by D. Rhys Phillips. [With plates.] pp. 116. *Swansea,* 1918. 8°. Ac. **9948/2.**

—— [Edinburgh, 1920.] Transactions of the Celtic Congress, 1920. Report of the meetings held at Edinburgh . . . Compiled by D. Rhys Phillips. pp. 186. *Milne, Tannahill & Methven: Perth,* 1921. 8°. Ac. **9948/3.**

—— [Douglas, 1921.] Transactions of the Celtic Congress, 1921. Containing the papers read at the Douglas Congress, with a report of the meetings. Compiled by D. Rhys Phillips. [With plates.] pp. 216. *Swansea,* 1923. 8°. Ac. **9948/4.**

—— [Quimper, 1924.] Congrès panceltique de Quimper . . . 1924. [Report of proceedings. With plates.] pp. 381. *Redon,* [1925.] 8°. Ac. **9948/5.**
The title on the wrapper reads " Les Celtes à Quimper . . . 1924."

CELTIC DIGEST. *See* NEW YORK.—*Columbia University.—Celtic Society.*

CELTIC FOLK TALES. Celtic Folk Tales. Child lore. Folk tales and rhymes. Gaelic, Irish, Welsh, Norse, German, etc. (Re-issued.) pp. 128. *A. Maclaren & Sons: Glasgow,* 1938. 32°. **944.** c. **35.**

CELTIC LANGUAGE. Specimen of an Etimological Vocabulary; or, Essay, by means of the analitic method, to retrieve the antient Celtic. By the author of a pamphlet entitled The Way to Things by Words, and to Words by Things [i.e. John Cleland]. pp. xvi. 231. *L. Davis & C. Reymers: London,* 1768. 8°. **439.** g. **25.**

—— [Another copy.] **69.** b. **21.** (1.)

—— [Another copy.] MS. NOTES. G. **17838.** (2.)

—— Additional Articles to the Specimen of an Etimological Vocabulary; or, Essay by means of the analytic method to retrieve the ancient Celtic. By the author of a pamphlet entitled The Way to Things by Words [i.e. John Cleland]. pp. xvii. 46. *Lockyer Davis: London,* 1769. 8°. **69.** b. **21.** (2.)

—— [Another copy.] MS. NOTES. G. **17838.** (3.)

—— The Way to Things by Words, and to Words by Things; being a sketch of an attempt at the retrieval of the antient Celtic, to which is added, a succinct account of the Sanscort, or learned language of the Bramins; also two essays, on the origin of the musical waits at Christmas; and on the real secret of Free Masons. [By John Cleland.] pp. vii. 123. *L. Davis & C. Reymers: London,* 1766. 8°. B. **693.** (2.)

—— [Another copy.] **69.** b. **19.**

—— [Another copy.] MS. NOTES. G. **17838.** (1.)

—— [Another copy.] G. **17839.**

CELTIC LIBRARY. The Celtic Library. 4 vol. *P. Geddes & Colleagues: Edinburgh,* 1896. 8°. **012202.** eee. **2**

CELTIC MAGAZINE. *See* PERIODICAL PUBLICATIONS. —*Inverness.*

CELTIC MONTHLY. *See* PERIODICAL PUBLICATIONS.— *Glasgow.*

CELTIC ORNAMENT. Examples of Celtic Ornament —reduced—from the Books of Kells and Durrow. 1892. 4°. *See* BIBLE.—*Appendix.—Gospels.* [*Pictorial Illustrations.*] **7709.**c.**10.**

CELTIC ORNAMENTS. Celtic Ornaments from the Book of Kells. 1895 [1892–95]. 4°. *See* BIBLE.—*Appendix.—Gospels.* [*Pictorial Illustrations.*] K.T.C. **6.** b. **11.**

CELTIC PHILOLOGY.

—— Progrès des études classiques et du moyen âge, philologie celtique, numismatique, etc. pp. viii. 154. *Paris,* 1868. 8°. [*Recueil de rapports sur l'état des lettres et les progrès des sciences en France.*] S. **267.** (10.)

CELTIC REVIEW. *See* PERIODICAL PUBLICATIONS.— *Edinburgh.*

CELTIC SOCIETY.

—— *See also* NEW YORK.—*Columbia College, afterwards Columbia University.*

—— Celtic Society. [Dublin.] *See* DUBLIN.

—— Celtic Society. [Edinburgh.] *See* EDINBURGH.

—— Celtic Society of Montreal. *See* MONTREAL.

CELTIC TINKER. The Celtic Tinker, and other poems. By " D." 1918. 8°. *See* D. **011648.** eee. **81.**

CELTIC VERSE.

—— A Second Little Garland of Celtic Verse. *Thomas B. Mosher: Portland, Maine,* 1903. 16°. [*The Bibelot.* vol. 9. no. 5.] P.P.**8001.**ea.**(34.)**

CELTIC WHO'S WHO. The Celtic Who's Who. Names and addresses of workers who contribute to Celtic literature, music or other cultural activities, etc. [Edited by Lachlan Macbean.] pp. iii. 12–170. *Fifeshire Advertiser: Kirkcaldy,* 1921. 8°. **010603.** de. **7.**

CELTIC YEAR. *See* PERIODICAL PUBLICATIONS.— *London.*

CELTICA.

—— *See also* DUBLIN.—*Dublin Institute for Advanced Studies.*

—— *See also* PERIODICAL PUBLICATIONS.—*Paris.*

CELTICUS, *pseud. See* VALLANCEY (Charles) An Essay on the Antiquity of the Irish Language . . . And, Remarks on the Essay . . . addressed to the printer of the London Chronicle, in the year 1772 [signed: Celticus]. 1818. 8°. G. **16669.**

—— Gallicae res! Skizzen über Frankreichs Wehrkraft von Celticus. pp. iv. 107. *Leipzig,* 1888. 8°. **8823.** i. **34.**

—— *See* GALLUS, *pseud.* Choses d'Allemagne. Coup d'œil sur les forces militaires de l'Allemagne. Réponse à Gallicæ res, etc. 1888. 8°. **8074.** ee. **33.**

—— Jenseits der Vogesen. Neue Bilder aus dem französischen Soldatenleben vom Verfasser der Gallicae res. [The preface signed: Celticus.] pp. vi. 104. *Leipzig,* 1888. 8°. **8823.** m. **52.**

CELTIS (CONRADUS) *See* CELTES.

CELTIS (EMOLIBIE DE) *pseud.* [i.e. M. L. O'Byrne.] *See* EMOLIBIE DE CELTIS.

CELTIS (KONRAD) *See* CELTES (Conradus)

CELTISCHE ALTERTHUEMER. *See* CELTIC ANTIQUITIES.

CELTOPHILE. Ereuna; or, an Investigation of the etymons of words and names, classical and scriptural, through the medium of Celtic: together with some remarks on Hebræo-Celtic affinities. By a Celtophile [i.e. Francis Crawford]. pp. viii. 176. *Williams & Norgate: London, Edinburgh*, 1875. 8°. **12902. b. 1.**

CELTS. The Celts. A prize poem, recited in Rugby School, June 29, MDCCCXLVIII. [By George Joachim Goschen.] pp. 10. *Crossley & Billington: Rugby*, 1848. 8°. **C. 57. d. 10. (14.)**

—— "De Geestelijke cultuur van Kelten en Germanen."— Superieur of inférieur? [The preface signed: E. W. G.] [1931.] 8°. *See* G., E. W. **010006. i. 38.**

—— Wild Scenes amongst the Celts. The penitent and the fugitive. pp. vi. 114. *J. Henry & J. Parker: London*, [1859.] 8°. **4414. dd. 32.**

CELURCA.

—— Celurca. The Arraignment of Venus. [By] T. L. P. [i.e. Thomas L. Paton.] [Poems.] [1926.] 8°. *See* P., T. L. **011644. e. 67.**

CELY, *Family of.* The Cely Papers. Selections from the correspondence and memoranda of the Cely Family, Merchants of the Staple, A.D. 1475–1488. Edited . . . by Henry Elliot Malden. [With a facsimile.] pp. liii. 214. 1900. 4°. *See* LONDON.—III. *Historical Society of Great Britain.* [*Camden Third Series. vol. 1.*] Ac. **8118/7.**

CELY (ANTONIO MEDINA) *See* MEDINA CELY.

CELY (MICHAEL) Black Wings. A story of adventure in the air. With four illustrations . . . by A. Mason Trotter. pp. 255. *Cassell & Co.: London*, 1933. 8°. **20053. aa. 26.**

—— Canada Calling! A story of adventure in the air . . . Illustrated by L. F. Lupton. pp. 240. *F. Warne & Co.: London & New York*, [1943.] 8°. **12827. eee. 47.**

—— The Flight of the Scarlet Eagle. pp. 256. *F. Warne & Co.: London & New York*, [1937.] 8°. **20059. g. 21.**

—— Plane no. 21. pp. 254. *F. Warne & Co.: London & New York*, [1938.] 8°. **12820. f. 9.**

—— Round the World in Eighty Hours. pp. 288. *F. Warne & Co.: London & New York*, [1936.] 8°. **20055. h. 19.**

CELY COLAJANNI (G.) Emo. Melodramma tragico in quattro atti. Da rappresentarsi nel Real Teatro S. Carlo. pp. 31. *Napoli*, 1846. 8°. **905. d. 5. (4.)** *Imperfect; wanting pp.* 19–30.

CEM BIBLIÓFILOS.

—— Cem Bibliófilos do Brasil. *See* RIO DE JANEIRO.— *Sociedade dos Cem Bibliófilos do Brasil.*

CEMA (M. B.) *pseud.* The Barrier, and other stories. pp. 32. *A. H. Stockwell: London*, 1936. 8°. **04412. de. 98.**

CEMACH (ALEXANDER ISAAK) [Chirurgische Diagnostik in Tabellenform.] Surgical Diagnosis in Tabular Outline . . . Authorized translation, with additions and notes, by Edward L. Bortz, *etc.* pp. x. pl. 112. *F. A. Davis Co.: Philadelphia*, 1928. 4°. **07481. i. 25.**

CEMACH (HARRY PAUL)

—— The Elements of Punched Card Accounting. pp. x. 137. *Sir Isaac Pitman & Sons: London*, 1951. 8°. **8219. de. 17.**

CEMAES, *Rural District of.*

—— Official Guide to Cemaes Rural District, North Pembrokeshire, *etc.* [By Dillwyn Miles. Various editions.] [1951– .] 8°. *See* MILES (Dillwyn) **010370. i. 43.**

CEMALEDDINUS. *See* 'UMAR IBN AḤMAD, called IBN al-'ADĪM.

CEMELE. *See* CIMIEZ.

CEMENT. Cement and Cement Manufacture. *See* PERIODICAL PUBLICATIONS.—*London.* Concrete and Constructional Engineering.

CEMENT AND CONCRETE ASSOCIATION. *See* ENGLAND.

CEMENTATION COMPANY.

—— Cementation News. no. 1–7. 4 Oct.—15 Nov. 1954. *London*, 1954. 4°. **P.P. 5793. eab.** *Reproduced from typewriting.*

CEMENTATION NEWS.

—— Cementation News. *See* CEMENTATION COMPANY.

CEMENTED-CARBIDE TOOLS.

—— Cemented-Carbide Tools, *etc.* [By Donald H. Shute.] pp. 62. *Machinery Publishing Co.: London*, [1935.] 8°. [*Machinery's Yellow Back Series.* no. 6.] **W.P. 567/6.**

CEMENTES (JÁNOS) *See* HERZFELDER (A. D.) A Kolozsvári codex [by J. Cementes]. Egy XVI-ik századbeli chemiai kézirat ismertetése, *etc.* 1897. 8°. **8906. cc. 29.**

ĆEMERLIĆ (HAMDIJA) Les Systèmes électoraux en Yougoslavie. pp. 175. *Paris*, 1937. 8°. **08073. bb. 62.**

CEMETERY. The Cemetery. A brief appeal to the feelings of society in behalf of extra-mural burial. [A poem.] pp. vii. 33. *William Pickering: London*, 1848. 8°. **11645. a. 70.**

—— The Cemetery; or, "Consecrated or unconsecrated?" pp. 12. *S.P.C.K.: London*, [1871.] 8°. **4420. i. 1. (28.)**

—— Shall our Cemetery be Consecrated? pp. 4. [1897.] 8°. **4109. b. 25. (2.)**

CEMLYN-JONES (ELIAS WYNNE) *See* JONES.

CEMOVIĆ (MARKO P.) Современныя славянскія проблемы *etc.* pp. 115. *Петроградъ*, 1915. 8°. **8095. f. 7.**

CEMPINI (LEOPOLDO) *See* RIDOLFI (C.) *Marquis.* Toscana ed Austria. Scritto dei signori marchese C. Ridolfi . . . L. Cempini, *etc.* 1859. 8°. **8032. d. 71. (7.)**

CEMPIS, *Tomais à.* *See* HAEMMERLEIN (T.) *à Kempis.*

CEMPLA (JÓZEF)

—— Wawel. Komnaty królewskie. 16 plansz. Rysował J. Cempla. Wstępem opatrzył dr Adam Mściwujewski. pp. 6. pl. 16. *Kraków*, 1954. fol. **7870. l. 10.**

CEMPOALLAN. *See* ZEMPOALA.

CEMPUIS.—*Orphélinat Prévost.* Bulletin. sér. 1. no. 1—sér. 3. no. 6. nov. 1882—nov.-déc. 1890. *Cempuis,* 1882–90. 8°.
[Continued as :]
L'Éducation intégrale. Bulletin de l'Orphélinat Prévost, *etc.* sér. 4. no. 1—sér. 5. no. 6. jan.-févr. 1891—nov.-déc. 1894. *Cempuis,* 1891-94. 8°. **08355. g. 3.**
"L'Éducation intégrale" was published from 1895 onwards by the "Association Internationale de l'Éducation Intégrale."

—— Fêtes pédagogiques à l'orphélinat Prévost. Sessions normales de pédagogie pratique. 1890-1891-1892 (1893). 2 vol. *Cempuis,* 1893. 8°. **08355. g. 2.**

CENA. La Cena. Diario de la Habana. *See* PERIODICAL PUBLICATIONS.—*Havanna, Cuba.*

—— La Cena de le ceneri. Descritta in cinque dialogi, *etc.* [By G. Bruno.] pp. 128. [*John Charlewood: London,*] 1584. 8°. **C. 37. c. 14. (2.)**

—— La Cena magica. Farsa giocosa . . . da rappresentarsi nel Teatro Gallo a S. Benedetto la stazione autunnale 1855. pp. 19. *Venezia,* [1855.] 8°. **905. c. 1. (13.)**

—— Saynete nuevo, intitulado : La Cena de Carnaval, *etc.* [In verse.] pp. 7. *Valencia,* 1816. 4°. **11728. b. 100.**

CENA (CARLO) La Nostra alleanza colla Germania. La pace mediante retrocessione dell'Alsazia e della Lorena, *etc.* pp. 13. *Roma,* 1893. 8°. **8027. bbb. 32. (2.)**

CENA (GIOVANNI) Opere complete. (Edizione definitiva con notizia.) [Edited by Leonardo Bistolfi, Annibale Pastore and Eugenia Balegno.] 5 vol. *Torino,* 1928, 29. 8°. **11436. d. 59.**

—— Poesie . . . Edizione completa, con ritratto e notizia. pp. xi. 343. *Firenze,* 1922. 8°. **11427. i. 1.**

—— Gli Ammonitori. Romanzo. pp. 215. *Roma,* 1904. 8°. **12471. t. 23.**

—— The Forewarners . . . Translated . . . by Olivia Agresti Rossetti. With a preface by Mrs. Humphry Ward. pp. xii. 291. *Smith, Elder & Co.: London,* 1908. 8°. **12471. p. 31.**

—— In umbra. Versi. pp. 159. *Torino,* 1899. 8°. **11429. e. 45.**

—— Leonardo Bistolfi. Dalla Nuova antologia, *etc.* [With a portrait and reproductions.] pp. 24. *Roma,* 1905. 8°. **7877. b. 41.**

—— Madre. [A poem.] pp. 76. *Torino,* 1897. 8°. **11429. cc. 22.**

CENA (MIECZYSŁAW)

—— Badania porównawcze czynników fizycznych klimatu pomieszczeń zwierzęcich. pp. 60. *Wrocław,* 1952. 8°. [*Prace Wrocławskiego Towarzystwa Naukowego.* ser. B. no. 53.] **Ac. 868. b/2.**

CENAC (J. T. HENRI)

—— Résumé clinique d'un service de fiévreux à l'hôpital militaire de Strasbourg pendant l'année 1861, *etc.* pp. 27. *Strasbourg,* 1861. 4°. [*Collection générale des dissertations de la Faculté de Médecine de Strasbourg.* sér. 2. tom. 27.] **7381. e.**

CENAC (JEAN PIERRE BLAIZE) Considérations sur le goître endémique, *etc.* pp. 29. *Montpellier,* 1821. 4°. **1180. i. 16. (11.)**

CENAC (MATHIEU RAYMOND JEAN FRANÇOIS) Considérations sur la dysenterie, *etc.* pp. 11. *Montpellier,* 1822. 4°. **1181. c. 4. (21.)**

CENAC (MICHEL) Quelques considérations pratiques sur les tumeurs blanches. Thèse, *etc.* pp. 93. *Montpellier,* 1861. 4°. **7379. e. 8. (7.)**

CENACCHI (MARIO)

—— Biblioteca Gozzadini. 2 vol. 1937. 8°. [*Inventari dei manoscritti delle biblioteche d'Italia.* vol. 65, 66.] *See* BOLOGNA.—*Biblioteca Comunale dell'Archiginnasio.—Biblioteca Gozzadini.* **011900. dd. 20.**

CENACCHI (ORESTE) Vecchia Bologna. Echi e memorie, *etc.* pp. xiv. 206. *Bologna,* 1926. 8°. **010151. eee. 37.**

—— Vecchi motivi di critica. Note e ricerche, *etc.* pp. viii. 280. *Bologna,* 1905. 8°. **11825. bb. 32.**

CÉNAC-MONCAUT (JUSTIN ÉDOUARD MATHIEU) Les Chrétiens ; ou, la Chute de Rome. Poëme en douze chants. pp. 187. *Paris,* 1865. 18°. **11482. bb. 11.**

—— Le Colporteur des Pyrénées, ou les Aventures de Pierre Ardisan, *etc.* pp. 278. *Paris,* 1866. 8°. **12515. ee. 11.**

—— Le Congrès des brochures, ou le Droit ancien et le droit nouveau. pp. 16. *Paris,* 1860. 8°. [MISSING.]

—— Contes populaires de la Gascogne. pp. xviii. 222. *Paris,* 1861. 12°. **12513. aa. 6.**

—— Dictionnaire gascon-français, dialecte du département du Gers, suivi d'un abrégé de grammaire gasconne. pp. vii. 143. *Paris,* 1863. 8°. **12953. bbb. 15.**

—— L'Église romaine et la liberté ; ou, Introduction historique à l'avénement de Pie IX. pp. xii. 299. *Paris, Lyon,* 1848. 8°. **4570. d. 6.**

—— Éléments d'économie sociale . . . avec un appendice sur la question des subsistances. pp. 82. *Paris,* 1847. 8°. **8205. ccc. 56. (4.)**

—— Seconde édition. pp. 185. *Paris, Auch,* 1848. 12°. **8275. b. 12**

—— L'Espagne inconnue. Voyage dans les Pyrénées de Barcelone à Tolosa. Avec une carte routière. pp. iv. 374. *Paris,* 1861. 12°. **10161. b. 31.**

—— L'Europe et l'Orient ; poème en six chants. pp. 116. *Paris,* 1857. 8°. **11481. f. 9.**

—— La France et l'Europe latine. Le Pape et l'Italie. Questions de droit supérieur. pp. 32. *Paris,* 1860. 8°. **8032. g. 39. (4.)**

—— Histoire de l'amour dans l'antiquité chez les Hébreux, les Orientaux, les Grecs et les Romains. pp. 392. *Paris,* 1862. 12°. **8415. bb. 34.**

—— Histoire de l'amour dans les temps modernes, chez les Gaulois, les chrétiens, les barbares, et du moyen âge au dix-huitième siècle. pp. 418. *Paris,* 1863. 8°. **08415. de. 65.**

—— Histoire des Pyrenées et des rapports internationaux de la France avec l'Espagne . . . Annales de la Catalogne, de l'Aragon, de la Navarre, *etc.* 5 tom. *Paris,* 1853–55. 8°. **1322. e. 6–10.**

—— Histoire du charactère et de l'esprit français depuis les temps les plus reculés jusqu'à la renaissance. 2 vol. *Paris,* 1867. 8°. **12352. bbb. 40.**

—— Introduction à la politique rationnelle, ou Théorie du gouvernement représentatif . . . avec un appendice sur les devoirs de l'homme. pp. 53. *Paris,* 1847. 8°. **8052. g. 16.**

CÉNAC-MONCAUT (Justin Édouard Mathieu)

—— Jérôme Lafriche, ou le Paysan gentilhomme. [A novel.] pp. 257. *Paris*, 1859. 8º.   **12513. bb. 38.**

—— Lettre à M. Paul Meyer . . . sur l'auteur de la chanson de la croisade albigeoise (Guilhem de Tudela) en particulier et sur certains procédés de critique en général. pp. 40. *Paris*, 1869. 8º.   **11482. k. 21. (10.)**

—— Lettres à MM. Gaston Paris et Barry sur les Celtes et les Germains, les chants historiques basques et les inscriptions vasconnes des Convenae, à propos de l'histoire du caractère et de l'esprit français, *etc.* pp. 56. *Paris*, 1869. 8º.   **11852. i. 18. (4.)**

—— Littérature populaire de la Gascogne. Contes, mystères, chansons historiques . . . recueillis dans l'Astarac, le Pardiac, le Béarn et le Bigorre. Texte patois, avec la traduction en regard, et la musique des principaux chants. pp. xviii. 513. *Paris*, 1868. 12º.   **12236. b. 9.**

—— Percement des Pyrénées. Chemins de fer et routes internationales en cours d'exécution, richesses naturelles . . . Avec une carte géographique. pp. 31. *Paris*, 1861. 8º.   **8235. h. 15.**

—— Les Révolutions imminentes et l'attitude de la France à leur égard. pp. 32. *Paris*, 1861. 8º.   **8010. e. 29. (6.)**

—— Les Richesses des Pyrénées françaises et espagnoles, *etc.* pp. viii. 256. *Paris*, 1864. 8º.   **10172. ee. 21.**

—— L'Ultrascientifisme, ou l'Église romaine et la société moderne, considérées d'un point de vue autre que celui de M. Quinet. pp. 175. *Toulouse*, 1845. 8º.   **4051. e. 9.**

—— Voyage archéologique et historique dans l'ancien comté de Bigorre. pp. 104. *Tarbes ; Paris*, 1856. 8º.   **10172. c. 6.**

—— Voyage archéologique et historique dans l'ancien comté de Comminges et dans celui des Quatre-Vallées. pp. 170. *Tarbes ; Paris*, 1856. 8º.   **10173. c. 18.**

—— Voyage archéologique et historique dans l'ancien royaume de Navarre. pp. 147. *Tarbes ; Paris*, 1857. 8º.   **10173. c. 16.**

—— Voyage archéologique et historique dans l'ancienne vicomté de Béarn. pp. 118. *Tarbes ; Paris*, 1856. 8º.   **10172. c. 5.**

—— Voyage archéologique et historique dans le Pays Basque, le Labour, et le Guypuscoa. pp. 116. *Tarbes ; Paris*, 1857. 8º.   **10173. c. 5.**

—— Voyage archéologique et historique dans les anciens comtés d'Astarac et de Pardiac. Suivi d'un essai sur la langue et la littérature gasconne. pp. 250. *Paris ; Mirande*, 1856. 8º.   **10172. c. 4.**
  The date on the wrapper is 1857.

CENACULO. O Cenaculo. *See* Periodical Publications.—*Lisbon.*

CENÁCULO VILAS-BOAS (Manuel do) *See* Villas Boas (M. do Cenáculo) successively *Bishop of Beja and Archbishop of Évora.*

CENAD. *See* Cennad.

CENADWR. *See* Cenhadwr.

CENADWRI. Nefol Gennadwri ; neu copi o lythyr, yr hwn a gafwyd dan garreg, yn mha un y mae amryw gynghorion da a buddiol ; eithr yn fwyaf enwedigol yn

CENADWRI.

nghylch cadw y Sabbath. At yr hyn y 'chwanegwyd ymddiddanion a fu rhwng Adrian, Ymmerawdr Rhufain, ac Epig ddoeth ; sef y ddau ŵr callaf yn y byd, *etc.* pp. 16. *T. Williams : Dolgelleu*, [1800 ?] 12º.   **875. c. 32.**

CEÑAL (Enrique G.) *See* Cáceres y Prat (A.) El Vierzo, *etc.* [With a preface by E. G. Ceñal.] 1883. 8º.   **10161. bb. 14.**

CENALIS (Robertus) successively *Bishop of Vence, of Riez and of Avranches.* *See* Alliaco (P. de) *Cardinal.* [*Posteriora.*] Posteriora . . . cuʒ additiōibus magistri roberti cenalis. 1518. fol.   **C. 62. ee. 15.**

—— *See* Bridges (John) *Bishop of Oxford.* A Defence of the Gouernment established in the Church of Englande . . . Aunswering to the argumentes of . . . Cænalis, *etc.* 1587. 4º.   **1353. f. 1.**

—— *See* Bucer (M.) [*Single Works.*] Defensio aduersus axioma catholicum, id est, criminationem R.P. Roberti Episcopi Abrincēsis, *etc.* 1534. 12º.   **3908. aa. 81.**

—— Ad sacramentiorum huius seculi hæreticorum . . . petulantiam euertendam præsentissima antidotus. Huic accedit in excæcatos Caluinicæ familiæ tenebriones Apologia. 2 pt. *Apud G. Iulianum : Parisiis*, 1558. 8º.   **3906. a. 52.**

—— De liquidorum leguminumque mensuris, ex variis sacræ Scripturæ et authorū veterum, ac recentiorum locis congestæ observatiunculæ, *etc.* pp. 35. *Ex officina R. Stephani : Parisiis*, 1532. 4º.   **1015. b. 5.**

—— De vera mensurarum ponderumque ratione, opus de integro instauratū a . . . Roberto Senali, *etc.* pp. 119. *Apud I. Roigny : Parisiis*, 1535. 8º.   **602. a. 38.**

—— [Another copy.] few ms. notes.   **1401. b. 3. (2.)**

—— [Another edition.] Liber iā tertiò auctus & recognitus ab authore. Accedunt & paralipomena quædā. pp. 16. ff. 173. *Apud I. Roigny : Parisiis*, 1547. 8º.   **8503. aaa. 23.**

—— [Another edition.] 1699. *See* Graevius (J. G.) Thesaurus antiquitatum Romanorum, *etc.* tom. 11. 1694, *etc.* fol.   **L.R.302.a.1/11.**

—— Bayeux et ses environs . . . traduit du latin et annoté par F. de Barghon Fort-Rion. [An extract from "Historia Gallica."] pp. 31. *Caen ; Paris*, 1860. 8º.   **10170. cc. 21.**

—— Opus quadripartitum super compescenda hereticorum petulantia. ff. 239. *Apud I. Keruer : Parisiis*, 1557. 8º.   **699. c. 1. (1.)**

—— Pro tuendo sacro coelibatu axioma catholicum, *etc.* pp. 219. *Apud I. Roigny : Parisiis*, 1545. 8º.   **1020. d. 5. (1.)**

CENAMI (Fabrizio) Orazione politica morale detta nella sala del Senato della . . . Repubblica di Lucca, *etc.* *Lucca*, 1742. 4º.   [missing.]

CENAMI (Valeria) La Divina Commedia nelle traduzioni di H. W. Longfellow e di H. F. Cary. pp. 60. *Lucca*, 1933. 8º.   **011420. aa. 27.**

CENAMI ARNOLFINI (Lavinia Felice) *See* Bambacari (C. N.) Descrizione delle azioni e virtù dell'illustrissima Signora L. F. Cenami Arnolfini, *etc.* [With a portrait.] 1715. 4º.   **1224. i. 14.**

CENAMOR VAL (Hermógenes) Los Españoles y la Guerra. Neutralidad ó intervención? pp. 230. *Madrid*, 1916. 8º.   **08027. df. 17.**
The date on the wrapper is 1917.

CENAR (Edmund) Gry piłką z rycinami. pp. 27. *Lwów*, 1896. 8º.   [Missing.]

CÉNAR (Jules de) *pseud.* [i.e. Jules de Carné.] *See also* Carné (J. de)

—— Pécheurs et pécheresses. [Tales.] pp. 305. *Paris*, 1862. 12º.   **12512. bbb. 38.**

CÉNAS (F. G.) Le Topinambour offert comme moyen d'améliorer les plus mauvais terrains . . . 3me édition . . . augmentée. pp. 31. *Grenoble*, 1863. 8º.   **7075. dd. 17.**

CENAT DE L'HERM (Théodore) *See* Peter [Garavito], *of Alcantara, Saint.* Traité de l'oraison et de la méditation . . . Traduit de l'espagnol par l'abbé Cenat de l'Herm. 1845. 4º. [*Theresa* [*de Cepeda*], *de Jesus, Saint. Œuvres très complètes, etc.* tom. 3.]   **481. f. 17.**

CENATI (Bernardino) La Silvia errante. Arcicomedia capriciosa morale, con li intermedi in versi. pp. 156. *S. Combi: Venetia*, 1605. 12º.   **638. b. 5. (1.)**

CENCELLI (Agostino) Compendio storico della vita e miracoli del Beato Francesco Caracciolo, fondatore de' Cherici Regolari Minori. pp. xvi. 254. *Roma*, 1769. 4º.   **709. c. 21.**

—— [Another edition.] pp. ix–xvi. 254. *Roma*, 1805. 4º.   **1231. d. 13.**

CENCELLI (Valentino Orsolini) *See* Orsolini-Cencelli.

CENCELLI-PERTI (Alberto) Macchine agricole, *etc.* pp. viii. 215. *Milano*, 1889. 8º.   **012200. h. 40.**
One of the " Manuali Hoepli."

CENCETTI (Giorgio)

—— Gli Archivi dello Studio bolognese a cura del . . . dott. G. Cencetti. pp. 134. 1938. 8º. *See* Bologna.—*Università di Bologna.*   **Ac. 6496. d.**

—— Note paleografiche sulla scrittura dei papiri latini dal i al iii secolo d.C. *In:* Accademia delle Scienze dell'Istituto di Bologna. Classe di scienze morali. Memoire. ser. 5. vol. 1. pp. 1–54. 1951. 8º.   **Ac. 2802/4.**

CENCI, *Family of. See* Bertolotti (A.) Francesco Cenci e la sua famiglia, *etc.* 1879. 8º.   **10631. de. 15.**

—— *See* Brigante Colonna (G.) and Chiorando (E.) Il Processo dei Cènci, 1599. [With portraits.] 1934. 8º.   **9917. cc. 43.**

—— *See* Fraschetti (C.) I Cenci. Storia e documenti dalle origini al secolo xviii. 1935. 8º.   **9907. p. 15.**

—— Contemporaneous Narrative of the Trial and Execution of the Cenci. [With a preface by Sir John Simeon.] [1858.] *See* London.—iii. *Philobiblon Society.* Bibliographical & Historical Miscellanies. vol. 4. 1854, *etc.* 8º.   **Ac. 9120.**

CENCI (Antonius) De remediorum administratione, dissertatio medica inauguralis, *etc.* pp. 30. *Ticini Regii*, [1823.] 8º.   **7383*. c. 2. (15.)**

CENCI (Beatrice) *See* Angelis (N. de) Beatrice Cenci, o il Parricidio, *etc.* 1885. 8º.   **10601. a. 9. (4.)**

CENCI (Beatrice)

—— *See* Barbiellini Amidei (A.) Beatrice Cenci. Historical recollections of her life and family. 1905. 8º.   **10630. a. 53.**

—— —— 1909. 8º.   **10629. de. 9.**

—— *See* Bardi (U.) *pseud.* Beatrice Cenci, dramma storico, *etc.* (Notizie storiche sopra Beatrice Cenci e il secolo decimosesto.) 1879. 8º.   **11714. b. 11. (4.)**

—— *See* Cenci (Giacomo) *Brother of Beatrice Cenci.* Narrazione della morte di Giacomo e Beatrice Cenci, *etc.* 1821. 8º.   **11779. e. 48. (2.)**

—— *See* Cenci (Giacomo) *Brother of Beatrice Cenci.* Relation de la mort de Giacomo et de Béatrix Cenci, *etc.* *Fr. & Ital.* 1822. 8º. [*Mélanges publiés par la Société des Bibliophiles Français.* tom. 2.]   **Ac. 8933/5. (2.)**

—— *See* Diguet (C.) Beatrice Cenci, *etc.* [1884.] 12º.   **10633. b. 6.**

—— *See* Farinaccius (P.) Translation of the Pleading of Prospero Farinacio in defence of Beatrice Cenci and her relatives. 1838. 8º. [*Bowyer* (*Sir George*) *A Dissertation on the Statutes of the Cities of Italy, etc.*]   **5325. bbb. 11.**

—— *See* Guardione (F.) Difendendo Beatrice Cenci. [1924.] 8º.   **10633. d. 34.**

—— *See* Montenovesi (O.) Beatrice Cenci davanti alla giustizia dei suoi tempi e della storia, *etc.* 1928. 8º.   **10634. cc. 27.**

—— *See* Ricci (C.) Beatrice Cenci. 1923. 8º.   **10633. d. 33.**

—— *See* Ricci (C.) Beatrice Cenci . . . Translated, *etc.* 1926. 8º.   **10634. bb. 20.**

—— *See* Ricci (C.) The Cenci. A study in murder. [An abridged translation of C. Ricci's " Beatrice Cenci."] By Sir L. Cust. 1929. 16º.   **10633. b. 42.**

—— *See* Rinieri (I.) Beatrice Cenci secondo i costituti del suo processo. Storia di una leggenda. 1909. 8º.   **10633. bb. 9.**

—— *See* Scolari (Filippo) *Dottore in Legge.* Beatrice Cenci, causa celebre criminale del secolo xvi, *etc.* 1855. 8º.   **5373. ee. 3.**

—— *See* Torrigiani (A.) Clemente viii e il processo criminale della Beatrice Cenci, *etc.* 1872. 8º.   **4855. cc. 17.**

—— Letter of Beatrice Cenci [dated 22 Aug. 1599], with remarks on her portrait by Guido. Communicated by Mr. Edward Cheney. pp. 8. [1861.] *See* London.—iii. *Philobiblon Society.* Bibliographical and Historical Miscellanies. vol. 6. 1854, *etc.* 8º.   **Ac. 9120.**

—— Beatrice Cenci romana. Storia del secolo xvi. pp. 245. *Livorno*, 1863. 16º.   **12470. aaa. 7.**

—— Beatrice Cenci romana. Storia del secolo xvi. raccontata dal D. A. A. Seconda edizione. [With a frontispiece.] pp. 192. 1869. 12º. *See* A., A.   **10629. de. 8.**

—— La Bella Beatrice Cenci. Racconto storico di F. B., *etc.* 1874. 16º. *See* B., F.   **12471. aaa. 20.**

CENCI (Carlos B.) [A report upon the condition and prospects of the English immigrants at the Government Colony of Cananéa, Brazil.] pp. 23. [1874.] 8º.   **8156. bb. 5.**

CENCI (Donato Antonio) *See* Anacleto, *da Sandonato, Minore Riformato* [D. A. Cenci].

CENCI (FRANCESCO) *See* BERTOLOTTI (A.) Francesco Cenci e la sua famiglia, *etc.* 1879. 8°. **10631. de. 15.**

—— *See* DUBRETON, afterwards LUCAS-DUBRETON (J.) L'Assassinat de Francesco Cenci. 1950. 8°. [*Les Œuvres libres. Nouvelle série.* no. 47.] **12208. ee. 272.**

CENCI (GIACOMO) *Brother of Beatrice Cenci.* Narrazione della morte di Giacomo e Beatrice Cenci, e di Lucrezia Petronia Cenci, loro matregna, patricidi in Roma, nel pontificato di Clemente P.P. VIII. . . . 11 settembre, 1599. pp. 24. *J. Moyes: Londra*, 1821. 8°. **11779. e. 48. (2.)**

—— Relation de la mort de Giacomo et de Béatrix Cenci, et de Lucrèce Petroni, leur belle-mère; arrivée à Rome, sous le pontificat de Clément VIII, le 11 septembre, 1599. (La Funesta morte di Giacomo et Beatrice Cenci, *etc.*) [Edited by Alphonse de Malartic.] *Fr. & Ital.* pp. 62. 1822. *See* PARIS.—*Société des Bibliophiles Français.* Mélanges, *etc.* tom. 2. 1820, *etc.* 8°. Ac. 8933/5. (2.)

CENCI (GIACOMO) *Gentiluomo Romano.* Gli Errori. Comedia, *etc.* [Edited by G. da la Gatta.] *C. de Nicolini: Vinegia*, [1535?] 8°. **C. 62. a. 10.**

CENCI (LUCREZIA) *See* CENCI (Giacomo) *Brother of Beatrice Cenci.* Narrazione della morte di Giacomo e Beatrice Cenci, e di L. Petronia Cenci, *etc.* 1821. 8°. **11779. e. 48. (2.)**

—— *See* CENCI (Giacomo) *Brother of Beatrice Cenci.* Relation de la mort de Giacomo et de Béatrix Cenci, et de Lucrèce Petroni, *etc.* *Fr. & Ital.* 1822. 8°. [*Mélanges publiés par la Société des Bibliophiles Français.* tom. 2.] **Ac. 8933/5. (2.)**

CENCI (PIO)
—— [Il Cardinale Raffaele Merry del Val.] Cardinal Merry del Val. By Monsignor Vigilio Dalpiaz. Translated by a Benedictine of Stanbrook Abbey. [Adapted and translated from "Attraverso una porpora", an abridged version by V. Dalpiaz of P. Cenci's "Il Cardinale Raffaele Merry del Val." With a portrait.] pp. vii. 272. *Burns, Oates & Co.: London*, 1937. 8°. **4856.k.4.**

CENCI GOGA, *Family of.* *See* CENCI GOGA (B.) Memorie storiche e genealogiche della famiglia dei Cenci Goga, *etc.* 1934. 8°. **09915. l. 29.**

CENCI GOGA (BENIAMINO) Memorie storiche e genealogiche della famiglia dei Cenci Goga di Perugia dal secolo XII al XX. Con notizie su di alcune famiglie perugine ed altre imparentate con i Cenci. pp. 236. *Perugia*, 1934. 8°. **09915. l. 29.**

CENCINIUS (FRANCISCUS) *See* OLEA (A. de) Additiones aureae D. Alphonsi de Olea . . . ad eius tractatum de cessione iurium et actionum, cum decisionibus Sacræ Rotæ Romanæ excerptæ à corpore operis Lugduni in 5. editione nuper impressi . . . a D. F. Cencinio. 1675. fol. **5323. ee. 12.**

CENCIO, *del Prefetto Stefano.* *See* CENCIUS, *de Praefecto.*

CENCIUS, *de Praefecto.*

—— *See* BORINO (G. B.) Cencio del prefetto Stefano l'attentatore di Gregorio VII. 1952. 8°. [*Studi gregoriani.* vol. 4.] **W.P. 2735.**

CENCIUS, *de Sabellis, Cardinal.* *See* HONORIUS III., *Pope* [Cencio Savelli].

CENCUREERING. *See* CENSUREERING.

CENDAÑA (SILVERIO M.) Studies in the Biology of Coccophagus, Hymenoptera, a genus parasitic on Nondiaspidine Coccidae. *Berkeley*, 1937. 8°. [*University of California Publications in Entomology.* vol. 6. no. 14.] **Ac. 2689. g/31.**

CENDRARS (BLAISE) *pseud.* [i.e. FRÉDÉRIC SAUSER.]

—— *See* BRINGOLF (H.) [Der Lebensroman des Leutnant Bringolf.] ¶ Have no Regrets . . . Edited by B. Cendrars, *etc.* 1931. 8°. **10655. c. 29.**

—— *See* JENNINGS (Alphonso J.) [Through the Shadows with O. Henry.] Hors la loi ! . . . Traduction et adaptation . . . par B. Cendrars. 1936. 8°. **010885. ff. 24.**

—— *See* LEPAGE (A.) Blaise Cendrars, *etc.* 1926. 8°. **11825. b. 42.**

—— *See* LÉVESQUE (J. H.) Blaise Cendrars. Avec une anthologie des plus belles pages de l'œuvre de B. Cendrars, une bibliographie complète, *etc.* [With portraits.] 1947. 8°. **12240. a. 23.**

—— Anthologie nègre. [With a bibliography.] pp. 320. *Paris*, 1921. 8°. **12431. tt. 16.**

—— The African Saga. Translated from L'Anthologie nègre by Margery Bianco, *etc.* pp. 378. *Payson & Clarke: New York*, 1927. 8°. **12450. r. 5.**

—— Aujourd'hui. pp. 246. *Paris*, 1931. 8°. **12349. p. 21.**

—— La Banlieue de Paris. Texte de Blaise Cendrars sur 130 photos de Robert Doisneau. pp. 54. pl. 135. *Paris; Lausanne* printed, 1949. 8°. **10175. d. 13.**

—— Bourlinguer. [Reminiscences.] pp. 400. *Paris*, 1948. 8°. **10655. l. 36.**

—— D'Oultremer à Indigo. pp. 269. *Paris*, 1940. 8°. **12549. g. 33.**

—— Dans le silence de la nuit, *etc.* 1945. *See* PERIODICAL PUBLICATIONS.—*Paris.* Les Œuvres libres, *etc.* Nouvelle série. no. 4. 1921, *etc.* 8°. **12208. ee. 230.**

—— Dan-Yack. Le plan de l'aiguille. Les confessions de Dan-Yack. Roman. Nouvelle édition. pp. 326. *Paris*, 1946. 8°. **012550. p. 9.**

—— Dix-neuf poèmes élastiques, *etc.* *Paris*, 1919. 8°. **011483. c. 64.**

—— Feuilles de route. 1. La Formose. Dessins de Tarsila. pp. 75. *Paris*, 1924. 16°. **010026. e. 21.** *No more published.*

—— Histoires vraies. pp. 273. *Paris*, [1938.] 8°. **12358. b. 27.**

—— Le Lotissement du Ciel. pp. 344. *Paris*, 1949. 8°. **010665. n. 33.**

—— La Main coupé. [With a portrait.] pp. 325. *Paris*, 1946. 8°. **9102. a. 26.**

—— Moravagine. Roman. pp. 362. *Paris*, 1926. 8°. **12516. pp. 23.**

—— L'Or. La merveilleuse histoire du général Johann August Suter. pp. 277. *Paris*, 1925. 8°. **012547. dd. 62.**

—— Sutter's Gold . . . Translated . . . by Henry Longan Stuart. [With plates.] pp. 179. *Harper & Bros.: New York & London*, 1926. 8°. **12547. h. 14.**

—— [Another copy, with a different titlepage.] *William Heinemann: London; printed in U.S.A.*, [1927.] 8°. **012547. d. 30.**

CENDRARS (BLAISE) *pseud.* [i.e. FRÉDÉRIC SAUSER.]

—— Petits contes negres pour les enfants des blancs. pp. 109. *Paris*, 1928. 8º. [*Le Coffret de l'âge heureux.*]
12549. k. 3/2.

—— Little Black Stories for Little White Children. Translated . . . by Margery Bianco. [With woodcuts by Pierre Pinsard.] pp. 138. *Payson & Clarke: New York,* 1929. 4º. 12801. gg. 41.

—— [Le Plan de l'aiguille.] Antarctic Fugue, *etc.* pp. 171. *Pushkin Press: London,* 1948. 8º. 012550. a. 93.

—— Profond aujourd'hui . . . Dessins de Monsieur A. Zarraga. *Paris*, [1918.] 8º. 12330. s. 30.

—— Rhum. L'aventure de Jean Galmot. pp. 246. *Paris,* 1930. 8º. 10655. aaa. 17.

—— Vin de Samos. [1948.] *See* PERIODICAL PUBLICATIONS. —*Paris.* Les Œuvres libres, *etc.* no. 251. 1921, *etc.* 8º. 12208. ee. 251.

—— Blaise Cendrars. Une étude par Louis Parrot, un choix de poèmes et de textes, une bibliographie établie par J.-H. Levesque, des inédits, des manuscrits, des dessins, des portraits. pp. 258. [*Paris,*] 1948. 16º. [*Poètes d'aujourd'hui.* no. 11.] W.P. 1567/11.

CENDRATA (LUDOVICUS) *See* JOSEPHUS (F.) [*Two or more Works.—Latin.*] *Begin.* [fol. 1 *recto:*] Ludouicus Cendrata . . . Antonio donato . . . salutem. [fol. 4 *recto:*] Iosephi . . . de Bello Iudaico, *etc.* [Edited by L. Cendrata.] 1480. fol. IB. 30733.

CENDRÉ (Loïs)
—— Les Flammes et les voiles. Prose. pp. 001 [100]. *Lausanne,* 1915. 8º. 12360. cc. 46.

CENDRECOURT (MARIE CAROLINE ROSALIE RICHARD DE) *Dame de Saint-Surin.* *See* RICHARD DE CENDRECOURT.

CENDRES. Cendres végétatives. [A prospectus.] [*Caen ?* 1810 ?] *s. sh.* fol. B. 273. (29.)

CENDREY (CAMILLE DE) *See* COLLINS (William W.) [Readings and Writings in America. The Frozen Deep, *etc.*] La Mer glaciale. Roman traduit . . . par C. de Cendrey. 1877. 8º. 12604. df. 3.

—— *See* COLLINS (William W.) [Hide and Seek.] Cache-cache . . . Roman traduit . . . par C. de Cendrey. 1877. 8º. 12604. df. 4.

—— *See* COLLINS (William W.) [The Law and the Lady.] La Piste du crime. Traduit . . . par C. de Cendrey. 1875. 12º. 12603. c. 16.

CENDRILLON. *See* CINDERELLA.

CENDRIN. Les Regrets de Cendrin [on the state of France]. pp. 16. [*Paris ?*] 1615. 8º. 8050. bbb. 20. (15.)

CENE, *de la Chitarra, d'Arezzo.* *See* BENCIVENE, *dalla Chitarra, d'Arezzo.*

CENEAU (ROBERT) *successively Bishop of Vence, of Riez and of Avranches.* *See* CENALIS (Robertus)

CENECH, *pseud.* [i.e. THOMAS CENECH DAVIES.] Cerddi'r Encil. [With plates, including a portrait.] pp. 112. *Gwasg Gymraeg Foyle: Llundain,* 1931. 8º. 11595. dd. 20.

CENEDA. Statuta civitatis Cenetæ, recentioribus sanctionibus adiectis. pp. 84. [*Venice,*] 1772. 4º. 5357. f. 4.

CENEDA, ALBERTINO, *Bishop of.* [1653–1667.] *See* BARISONI.

——, FRANCESCO, *Bishop of.* [1710–1725.] *See* TREVISANI.

——, FRANCISCUS, *Bishop of.* [1498–1508.] *See* BREVIUS.

——, GIOVANNI AGOSTINO, *Bishop of.* [1768–1774.] *See* GRADENIGO.

——, JACOPO, *Bishop of.* [1822–1827.] *See* MONICO.

——, MICHAEL, *Bishop of.* [1547–1586.] *See* TURRIANUS.

——, PIETRO ANTONIO, *Bishop of.* [1786–1792.] *See* ZORZI.

CENEDELLA (GIACOMO ATTILIO) *See* UBERTI (G.) Guida nell'uso pratico delle acque minerali di Pejo . . . Con nuove analisi del dottor A. Cenedella. [1847.] 8º. 7462. ee. 2. (5.)

—— Analisi chimica dell'acqua termale di Monfalcone. [With a chart.] pp. 65. L.P. *Udine,* 1862. 4º. 7470. i. 11.

—— Analisi chimica della nuova acqua minerale . . . de Torrebelvicino, *etc.* pp. 57. *Lonigo,* 1851. 8º. 7462. e. 9. (6.)

CENEK (EDVARD)

—— Bohuslav Ečer: Jak jsem je stíhal. Reportážní pásmo E. Cenka. [With plates, including portraits.] pp. 258. *Praha,* 1946. 8º. 6058. pp. 37.

ČENĚK (JAN) *See* PRAGUE.—*Československý Pedagogický Ústav J. A. Komenského.* Z našeho pokusného školství . . . Sestavil prof. J. Čeněk. Essais d'innovation dans l'enseignement tchécoslovaque . . . Rédigé par J. Čeněk. 1924. 8º. Ac. 2619. (1.)

CENERELLI (G.) Lettere inedite alla celebre Laura Bassi, scritte da illustri Italiani e stranieri, con biografia. [The biography by A. Garelli. Edited by G. Cenerelli.] pp. 232. *Bologna,* 1885. 8º. 10909. i. 20.

CENERI (ANGELO MARIA) L'Uso dello strumento geometrico detto là tavoletta pretoriana . . . Opera postuma . . . Aggiuntavi la pratica del paralellogrammo trigonometrico, *etc.* pp. 72. pl. 11. *Bologna,* 1728. 4º. 60. e. 15.

CENERI (GIUSEPPE) *See* AGLEBERT (A.) Del collegio di Spagna, e dei diritti della città di Bologna. Relazione di A. Aglebert e voto legale degli Ill^mi Sigg Prof. O. Regnoli e G. Ceneri. 1881. 8º. 8033. g. 19. (4.)

—— Opere. vol. 1–4. *Bologna,* 1891–1900. 8º. 12226. g. 18.
Imperfect; wanting vol. 5–7.

—— Gl'Internazionalisti e l'articolo 426 del Codice penale. Difesa . . . al tribunale di Forlì. Udienza 6. Ottobre, 1879. pp. 29. *Bologna,* 1879. 8º. 5359. b. 11. (1.)

—— Nuovi ricordi di foro; con appendice. pp. 442. *Bologna,* 1887. 8º. 5359. ee. 8.

—— Varia di G. Ceneri. pp. 166. *Bologna,* 1884. 8º. 8032. bb. 24.

CENETA. *See* CENEDA.

CENETE, *Marquisate del.*

—— Documentos Árabes del Cenete. [Documents issued under the authority of the Cadi of Guadix, relating to districts afterwards forming part of the Marquisate del Cenete. Edited by C. A. González Palencia.] 1940. [*Al-Andalus.* vol. 5. fasc. 2.] *See* GUADIX. Ac. 147.

CENETE, Rodrigo Mendoza, *Marquis del.* *See* Mendoza.

CENHADWR. Y Cenhadwr. Cylchgrawn, etc. *See* Periodical Publications.—*Carnarvon.*

—— Ceńadwr Eglwysig. *See* Periodical Publications.— *London.*

CENHINEN.

—— [For the Welsh word sometimes spelt thus:] *See* Ceninen.

CENI (Antonio) Annuario della pubblica istruzione della Provincia di Parma. [With tables.] pp. 255. *Parma*, 1867. 8º. **8309. ee. 3.**

CENIA, Pedro Cotoner y Verí Allende-Salazar y Fortuny, *Marquis de la. See* Cotoner y Verí Allende-Salazar y Fortuny.

CENICEROS (José Ángel) Address by José Ángel Ceniceros . . . Mexico City, July 23, 1935. *See* Portes Gil (E.) *President of the Republic of Mexico.* Addresses by E. Portes Gil . . . and J. A. Ceniceros. 1935. 8º. **12301. p. 46.**

CENICEROS Y VILLARREAL (Rafael) Obras. [With a portrait.] 2 tom. *México*, 1908, 09. 8º. **12231. de. 3.** *Part of the "Biblioteca de Autores Mexicanos."*

CENINEN. Y Geninen. *See* Periodical Publications.— *Carnarvon.*

CENISE (Rochat) *See* Rochat-Cenise.

CENITAGOYA (Vicente de)

—— Los Machiguengas. (Contribución para el estudio de la etnografía de las razas amazónicas.) [With illustrations and a map.] pp. 211. *Lima*, [1943.] 8º. **010007. e. 72.**

CENIVAL (Pierre de)

—— *See* Castries (H. de) *Count.* Les Sources inédites de l'histoire du Maroc de 1530 à 1845. (Publiées par P. de Cenival; P. de Cossé Brissac.) 1905, *etc.* 8º. **9062. dd. 1.**

—— *See* Fernandes (Valentim) Description de la côte d'Afrique, *etc.* [Translated and edited by P. de Cenival and T. Monod.] 1938. 8º. **Ac.6917/2.(a6.)**

—— *See* Lopes (D.) Mélanges d'études luso-marocaines dédiés à la mémoire de David Lopes et Pierre de Cenival. [With portraits.] 1945. 8º. **12357. tt. 22.**

—— *See* Rome, *Church of.* [*Popes.*]—Alexander iv. Les Registres d'Alexandre iv. Recueil des bulles . . . publiées ou analysées . . . par MM. Bourel de la Roncière (P. de Cenival), *etc.* 1902, *etc.* 4º. [*Bibliothèque des Écoles Françaises d'Athènes et de Rome.* sér. 2. no. 15.] **Ac. 5206/2.**

—— *See* Santa Cruz do Cabo de Gué. Chroniqüe de Santa-Cruz du Cap de Gué, Agadir. Texte portugais . . . traduit et annoté par P. de Cenival. 1934. 8º. **010093. i. 11.**

—— Bibliographie marocaine, 1923–1933. [Compiled by P. de Cenival, Christian Funck-Brentano and Marcel Bousser.] pp. 606. [1937.] 8º. *See* Rabat.—*École Supérieure de Langue Arabe et de Dialectes Berbères, etc.* **Ac. 17/2.**

CENKALSKA (Krystyna)

—— *See* Żywulska (K.) [Przeżyłam Oświęcim.] I came back. [Translated by K. Cenkalska.] [1951.] 8º. **10796. dd. 19.**

ČENKOV (Emmanuel) *pseud. See* Čenkova (E. z)

ČENKOV (Emmanuel de) *pseud. See* Čenkova (E. z)

ČENKOVA (Emmanuel z) *pseud.* [i.e. Emanuel Stehlík.] *See* Régamey (J.) and Régamey (F.) Nos frères de Bohème, *etc.* [With a prefatory letter by E. z Čenkova.] [1908.] 8º. **10210. bb. 51.**

—— Domovem i cizinou. Z rozptýlených listů. 1900–1910. Básně. pp. 99. iii. *Praha*, 1910. 8º. **011586. ff. 66. (2.)**

—— Oslava Victora Huga v Paříži roku 1902. Paměti poselstva Král. Hlavního-města Prahy. Sestavil E. ryt. z Čenkova. pp. 115. 1902. 4º. *See* Prague.—*Rada.* **10659. h. 28.**

CENLOOT (Creslah) *pseud.* [i.e. Charles Colton?] Panthea. A poetical tragedy. By Creslah Cenloot. pp. 36. *Wyman & Sons: London*, 1888. 8º. **11781. g. 35.**

CENNAD. Cennad Catholig Cymru. *See* Periodical Publications.—*Llanrwst.*

—— Cennad Hedd. *See* Periodical Publications.— *Merthyr Tydfil.*

CENNADWRI. *See* Cenadwri.

CENNER (Lajos) and SCHMIEDT (Ferencz) A mi könyvünk. Irták és kiadják Cenner L. és Schmiedt F. (Vannak benne komoly vallásos elbeszélések, társadalmi rajzok, humoros történetek, *etc.*—A komoly elbeszéléseknek Schmiedt F., a humoros résznek Cenner L. a szerzőjük.) pp. viii. 296. *Budapest*, 1897. 8º. **012591. k. 11.**

CENNI. Cenni intorno all'origine della scrittura alfabetica. [By O. Barbieri.] pp. 64. *Bologna*, 1884. 8º. **12902. ccc. 7. (5.)**

—— Cenni sopra lo Statuto fondamentale del 4. marzo, 1848 . . . di F. G. [1848.] 8º. *See* G., F. **8032. g. 44. (1.)**

—— Cenni storici e teoretici sulle comete e particolarmente su quelle dell'anno 1832, *etc.* pp. vii. 127. pl. ii. *Milano*, 1832. 8º. **717. f. 34.**

—— Cenni sulla Santissima Sindone, sulle principali sue pubbliche ostensioni, e su quella che ha luogo addì 4 maggio di quest' anno 1842. [With illustrations.] pp. 34. *Torino*, [1843.] 8º. **7703. e. 12. (7.)**

—— Vari cenni statistici. [*Lucca?* 1840?] 16º. **10136. de. 2. (16.)** *Forming part of a larger work.*

CENNI (Angiolo) *See also* Risoluto, *pseud.* [i.e. A. Cenni.]

—— Il Ciarlone, cioe uno che canta in bancho, & conta come ha medicine, & rimedi a molte infirmita, & come caua un dente a un villano . . . Composto per il Resoluto Sanese della congrega de Rozi [i.e. A. Cenni]. [In verse.] [1550?] 8º. *See* Ciarlone. **11427. b. 27.**

—— Il Romito Negromante, comedia pastorale. [By A. Cenni.] [1547.] 8º. *See* Romito. **162. e. 48.**

CENNI (Enrico) Della libertà considerata in sè stessa, in relazione al diritto, alla storia . . . e al progresso dell' umanità. pp. 589. *Napoli*, 1891. 8º. **8009. i. 31.**

—— Della mente e dell'animo di Roberto Savarese. Studio. *See* Savarese (R.) Scritti forensi, *etc.* 1876. 8º. **5373. h. 14.**

—— Delle presenti condizioni d'Italia, e del suo riordinamento civile. pp. 276. *Napoli*, 1862. 8º. **8032. h. 10.**

CENNI (ENRICO)

—— Il Divorzio considerato come contro natura ed anti-giuridico. pp. xii. 115. *Firenze*, 1881. 8º.
5176. cc. 11.

—— Napoli e l'Italia. Considerazioni, *etc.* pp. 112. *Napoli*, 1861. 8º. **8033. bb. 37. (3.)**

—— S. Benedetto e la civiltà; discorso, *etc.* pp. 86. *Napoli*, 1879. 8º. **4828. df. 18.**

—— Scritti varii di filosofia politica. pp. 453. *Siena*, 1879. 8º. **8010. de. 7.**

—— Uno Sguardo sul medio evo. pp. 101. *Napoli*, 1878. 8º. **9073. df. 10.**

CENNI (GAETANO) *See* LATERAN COUNCILS. [769.] Concilium Lateranense Stephani III. A. 769 nunc primum in lucem editum . . . studio C. Cennii. 1735. 8º.
5015. ee. 18.

—— *See* MURATORI (L. A.) Dissertazioni sopra le antichità italiane . . . Nuova edizione accresciuta di prefazioni e note dall' abate G. Cenni. 1765, *etc.* 4º.
1317. h. 13–15.

—— *See* ORSI (G. A.) *Cardinal.* Della origine del dominio e della sovranità de' Romani Pontefici . . . Seconda edizione accresciuta d'alcune note e dell'esame del diploma di Lodovico Pio dall'abate G. Cenni. 1754. 8º.
1123. g. 14.

—— —— 1789. 8º. **4051. e. 32.**

—— *See* SEVILLANO (N.) Primatus Hispaniarum vindicatus, sive Defensio Primatus Ecclesiæ Toletanæ . . . Latine reddita a C. Cenni. 1729. fol. **476. i. 12.**

—— De antiquitate Ecclesiæ Hispanæ dissertationes, in duos tomos distributæ. Iis præmittitur Codex veterum canonum Ecclesiæ Hispanæ ex genuina . . . collectione S. Isidori Hispalensis, quo illustratur antiquitas Ecclesiæ, præsertim Occidentalis. [With a portrait of Cardinal A. G. M. de Rohán.] 2 tom. *Romæ*, 1741. 4º.
205. a. 7.

—— *See* SCARMALLIUS (G. M.) Vindiciae antiquitatum monasticarum Hispaniae adversus C. Cennium. 1753. 4º. **1367. k. 4.**

—— Dissertazioni sopra varj punti interessanti d'istoria ecclesiastica, pontificia, e canonica . . . Raccolte, e pubblicate . . . da Gio. Bartolomeo Colti. (Dissertazioni sopra varj punti interessanti d'istoria romana, *etc.*) 2 tom. *Pistoja*, 1778, 79. 4º. **5107. c. 8.**

—— Monumenta dominationis pontificiæ, sive Codex Carolinus juxta autographum Vindobonense, epistolæ Leonis III. Carolo Augusto, diplomata Ludovici, Ottonis et Henrici, chartula comitissæ Mathildæ et Codex Rudolphinus ineditus, chronologia, dissertationibus et notis illustrata, opera et studio C. Cennii. 2 tom. *Romæ*, 1760, 61. 4º. **1230. f. 2, 3.**

CENNI (GIACOMO MARIA) Della vita di Gaio Cilnio Mecenate . . . libri due. pp. 239. *F. de Lazari: Roma*, 1684. 12º. **610. a. 12.**

—— Per la conquista di Buda fatta dall'armi Cesaree sotto la condotta del Sereniss. Sig. Duca de Lorena, l'anno M.DC.LXXXVI. Oda, *etc.* pp. 10. *I. Paci: Lucca*, 1686. 4º. **838. m. 22. (116.)**

CENNI (GIOVANNI) *Cavalier.* Dilucidazioni relative alla condotta serbata dal già Intendente di Catanzaro Cavalier D. G. Cenni in ordine agli ultimi politici avvenimenti. pp. 15. [*Naples*, 1848.] 8º. **8033. b. 10.**

CENNI (GIOVANNI) *of Ravenna.* Il Dramma di Alfredo Oriani, *etc.* (Vita di un precursore.) [With a portrait.] pp. vii. 311. *Ravenna*, 1935. 8º. **20003. c. 15.**

CENNI (ITALO) *See* SCHIAPARELLI (C.) La Battaglia del Piave . . . Con illustrazioni originali . . . di I. Cenni, *etc.* 1922. 8º. **9084. cc. 24.**

—— L'Esercito italiano. 16 tavole a colori, 150 uniformi. I. Cenni dispose e disegnò. *Milano*, 1914. *obl.* fol.
14001. d. 16.

CENNI (QUINTO) *See* ARCHINTI (L.) Custoza 1848–66. Album storico artistico militare composto ed eseguito da Q. Cenni, *etc.* [1878, *etc.*] *obl.* fol. **1763. b. 8.**

—— *See* MODERNI (P.) L'Assedio di Roma nella guerra del 190... Con illustrazioni di Q. Cenni, *etc.* [1900.] 8º.
12470. ff. 25.

—— *See* TAPPARELLI D'AZEGLIO (M.) *Marquis.* Niccolò de' Lapi . . . Con illustrazioni di Q. Cenni. 1883. 4º.
12470. k. 16.

—— Album della guerra italo-turca e della conquista della Libia, 1911–12. Quinto Cenni, pittore. dispensa 3, 4. *Milano*, [1913.] *obl.* fol. **1862. a. 7.**

—— Atlante militare. Organizzazione, uniforme e distintivi degli eserciti e delle armate d'Europa . . . Illustrazioni, *etc.* pp. 67. *Milano*, [1890.] 8º. **8829. k. 30.**

—— I Bersaglieri. Numero unico illustrato per cura di Q. Cenni. (In occasione del primo cinquantenario dei Bersaglieri.) pp. 28. *Milano*, 1886. fol. **1850. b. 20.**

CENNICK (JOHN)

—— *See* HUTTON (Joseph E.) John Cennick. A sketch. [With a portrait.] [1906.] 8º. **4902. de. 17.**

—— *See* ROCHE (John) *of Dublin.* Moravian Heresy. Wherein the principal errors of that doctrine, as taught . . . by . . . Mr Cennick . . . are . . . refuted, *etc.* 1751. 12º. **4139. b. 81.**

—— Twenty Discourses on . . . Important Subjects, *etc.* 2 vol. *M. Lewis: London*, 1762 [1765?]. 8º.
4455. a. 9. (2.)
A reissue with general titlepages and prefaces, of discourses published separately between 1753 and 1765.

—— [Another edition.] 2 vol. *M. Lewis: London*, 1770 [1773?]. 8º. **4453. b. 7.**
A collective reissue similar to the preceding, but the separate discourses are of different editions.

—— [Another edition.] 2 vol. *H. Trapp: London*, 1777. 12º. **4454. bbb. 16.**
A collective reissue similar to the preceding. Sermons 15 and 16 of vol. 2 are mutilated.

—— [Another edition.] (The Life of Mr. J. Cennick . . . Written by himself . . . The fourth edition.) vol. 1. *H. Trapp: London*, 1790 [1793?]. 12º. **4454. bbb. 17.**
A collective reissue similar to the preceding. Imperfect; wanting vol. 2.

—— Sermons, selected from the Works of . . . J. Cennick. To which are added two . . . sermons by . . . Jonathan Edwards . . . At the end . . . are annexed some letters, by . . . Mrs A — s [Margaret Magdalen Althans], *etc.* pp. 308. *C. Adams: Bath*, 1796. 12º. **4454. b. 5.**

—— Discourses on Important Subjects . . . A new edition [of " Twenty Discourses "] . . . To which is prefixed, the Life of the author revised and enlarged by Matthew Wilks. [With a portrait.] 2 vol. *H. D. Symonds; T. Williams: London*, 1803. 12º. **1113. b. 14, 15.**

CENNICK (**John**)

—— [Another edition.] Village Discourses on Important Subjects; particularly adapted to domestic worship . . . To which are prefixed, the Life of the author, revised and enlarged, and a recommendatory preface by Matthew Wilks. [With a portrait.] 2 vol. *Sherwood, Neely & Jones: London,* 1819. 12°.　　　**4461. c. 8.**

—— A new edition. [With a portrait.] pp. iv. 420. *Thomas Johnson: Liverpool,* 1840. 12°.　　**4461. bb. 8.**

—— An Account of a Late Riot at Exeter. pp. 30. *J. Lewis: London,* 1745. 8°.　　　　**4139. b. 24.**

—— An Account of the Conversion of Edward Lee, a malefactor who was executed at Haverford-West . . . for a robbery. In a letter from Mr. Cennick, *etc.* (The Confession of Edward Lee, *etc.*) pp. 22.　*M. Lewis: London,* 1756. 12°.　　　　　　**4474. aaa. 15.**

—— [Another edition.] pp. 22.　　*H. Trapp: London,* 1789. 8°.　　　　　　**4455. a. 8. (21.)**

—— [Another copy.]　　　　　　**1417. c. 6.**

—— The Assurance of Faith; or, the Experience of a true Christian. Being the substance of a discourse delivered at Glenevy . . . in the year 1754. pp. 24.　*M. Lewis: London,* 1756. 12°.　　　　**4474. aaa. 16.**

—— The third edition. pp. 24.　　*H. Trapp: London,* 1786. 8°.　　　　　　**4455. a. 8. (16.)**

—— The Beatific Vision; or, Beholding Jesus crucified; being the substance of a discourse preached in Ballymenagh . . . in the year 1755. pp. 19.　*M. Lewis: London,* 1756. 12°.　　　**4474. aaa. 17.**

—— The third edition. pp. 19.　　*H. Trapp: London,* 1786. 8°.　　　　　　**4455. a. 8. (20.)**

—— The Beatitudes; being the substance of a discourse delivered in Dublin, December the 21st, 1753 . . . The second edition. pp. 24.　*M. Lewis: London,* 1756. 12°.　　　　　　**4474. aaa. 18.**

—— The fifth edition. pp. 24.　*M. Trapp: London,* 1791. 8°.　　　　　　**4455. a. 8. (4.)**

—— The Benefits of the New-Testament. Being the substance of a discourse delivered in London in the year 1745 . . . The second edition. pp. 16.　*M. Lewis: London,* 1756. 8°.　　　　**4475. aa. 25.**

—— The Benefits of the New-Testament . . . The second edition. pp. 16.　*M. Lewis: London,* 1771. 8°.　　　　　　**03440. h. 36. (13.)**

A different edition from that of 1756.

—— The third edition. pp. 16.　　*H. Trapp: London,* 1784. 8°.　　　　　　**4474. aaa. 36.**

—— The Best Foundation. Being the substance of a discourse delivered in Biddiford . . . the year 1744 . . . The second edition. pp. 20.　*M. Lewis: London,* 1756. 8°.　　　　　　**4475. aa. 23.**

—— The Best Foundation . . . The third edition. pp. 20. *M. Lewis: London,* 1775. 8°.　**03440. h. 36. (8.)**

—— The Bloody Issue healed: being the substance of a sermon preached at the Tabernacle, London, on . . . October 10, 1743 . . . The second edition. pp. 16.　*M. Lewis: London,* 1772. 8°.　　**03440. h. 36. (5.)**

—— The Dæmoniac. Being the substance of a discourse delivered in Haverford-West, in May, 1753 . . . The second edition. pp. 19.　*M. Lewis: London,* 1756. 12°.　　　　　　**4474. aaa. 19.**

CENNICK (**John**)

—— The fifth edition. pp. 19.　*H. Trapp: London,* 1790. 8°.　　　　　　**4455. a. 8. (5.)**

—— The Danger of Infidelity; or, the Necessity of a living faith in Christ. The substance of a discourse deliver'd in Bristol, in the year 1742. pp. 20.　　*John Hart: London,* 1753. 8°.　　　　**4476. aa. 109. (5.)**

—— The second edition. pp. 20.　*M. Lewis: London,* 1758. 8°.　　　　　　**4016. b. 15.**

—— The Danger of Infidelity . . . The fourth edition. pp. 20. *M. Lewis: London,* 1772. 8°.　**03440. h. 36. (3.)**

—— Deliverance from Death. Being the substance of a discourse preached at Kingswood . . . March 25, 1753. pp. 16.　*M. Lewis: London,* 1756. 12°.　**4474. aaa. 20.**

—— The third edition. pp. 16.　　*H. Trapp: London,* 1787. 8°.　　　　　**4455. a. 8. (11.,**

—— Dives and Lazarus. Being the substance of a discourse delivered in Dublin, in the year 1753 . . . The second edition. pp. 16.　*M. Lewis: London,* 1756. 12°.　　　　　　**4474. aaa. 21.**

—— The fifth edition. pp. 16.　　*H. Trapp: London,* 1790. 8°.　　　　　　**4455. a. 8. (6.)**

—— The Divinity of Christ. Being the substance of a discourse deliver'd in Dublin, in the year 1746. pp. 20. *John Hart: London,* 1753. 12°.　　**4474. aaa. 12.**

—— The second edition. pp. 20.　*M. Lewis: London,* 1759. 8°.　　　　　　**4224. b. 33.**

—— The Divinity of Christ . . . The fourth edition. pp. 20. *M. Lewis: London,* 1773. 8°.　**03440. h. 36. (14.)**

—— The Fall and Redemption. Being the substance of a sermon preached at Ballynahone . . . in the year 1752 . . . The second edition. pp. 24.　*M. Lewis: London,* 1756. 12°.　　　　　**4474. aaa. 22.**

—— The Fall and Redemption . . . The third edition. pp. 24. *M. Lewis: London,* 1775. 8°.　**03440. h. 36. (19.)**

—— The First Principles of Christianity. Being the substance of a discourse delivered in the North of Ireland in the year 1752 . . . The second edition. pp. 36.　*M. Lewis: London,* 1756. 12°.　　　　**4474. aaa. 23.**

—— The fifth edition. pp. 36.　*M. Trapp: London,* 1791. 8°.　　　　　**4455. a. 8. (2.)**

—— The Gift and Office of the Holy Ghost. Being the substance of a discourse delivered . . . in Little Somerford . . . in the year 1740 . . . The second edition. pp. 20.　*M. Lewis: London,* 1756. 12°.　**4474. b. 18.**

—— The Gift and Office of the Holy Ghost . . . The third edition. pp. 20.　*M. Lewis: London,* 1771. 8°.　　　　　　**03440. h. 36. (1.)**

—— The fourth edition. pp. 20.　　*H. Trapp: London,* 1783. 12°.　　　　　**4474. aaa. 35.**

—— The Good Samaritan: being the substance of a sermon preach'd at the Tabernacle in London, in the year 1744. pp. 16.　*Printed for the Author, and sold by John Lewis: London,* 1744. 8°.　　**03440. h. 36. (9.)**

—— The Good Shepherd. Being the substance of a discourse delivered at St. Ginnis in Cornwall in the year 1744. The second edition. pp. 16.　*M. Lewis: London,* 1756. 8°.　　　　　　**4474. b. 19.**

CENNICK (JOHN)

—— The Good Shepherd . . . The third edition. pp. 16. *M. Lewis: London*, 1775. 8°.   03440. h. **36**. (**7**.)

—— The Great Sacrifice. Being the substance of a discourse delivered in Bath, in the year 1753 . . . The second edition. pp. 18. *M. Lewis: London*, 1756. 12°.
4474. aaa. **24**.

—— The third edition. pp. 20. *H. Trapp: London*, 1787. 8°.
4455. a. **8**. (**9**.)

—— The Hidden Treasure. Being the substance of a discourse delivered at Philbatch . . . in South Wales in the year 1753 . . . The second edition. pp. 16. *M. Lewis: London*, 1756. 12°.   **4474**. aaa. **25**.

—— The fifth edition. pp. 16. *H. Trapp: London*, 1791. 8°.
4455. a. **8**. (**7**.)

—— A Letter to the Little Children: especially to those who want to know how to go to heaven . . . The fifth edition. pp. 8. *H. Trapp: London*, [1783?] 12°.
4403. cc. **11**.

—— [Another edition.] pp. 16. *R.T.S.: London*, [1830?] 16°.
864. a. **4**. (**2**.)

—— A new edition, corrected. pp. 12.   *G. Norman: London*, 1838. 12°.   T. **2295**. (**4**.)

—— The Life of Mr. J. Cennick . . . Written by himself . . . The second edition. pp. vi. 42.   *Printed for the Author: Bristol*, 1745. 12°.   **4455**. a. **9**. (**1**.)

—— [Another copy.]   1416. a. **34**. (**1**.)

—— [Another copy.]   G. **14668**. (**1**.)

—— The Linsey-Woolsey Garment. Being the substance of a discourse delivered at Drumargen . . . in the year 1754. pp. 21. *M. Lewis: London*, 1756. 12°.
4474. aaa. **26**.

—— The third edition. pp. 21. *H. Trapp: London*, 1786. 8°.
4455. a. **8**. (**17**.)

—— The Lost Sheep, Piece of Silver, and Prodigal Son. Being the substance of a discourse delivered in the county of Antrim . . . in the year 1750 . . . The second edition. pp. 24. *M. Lewis: London*, 1756. 8°.
4475. aa. **26**.

—— The Lost Sheep, Piece of Silver, and Prodigal Son . . . The second edition. pp. 24.   *M. Lewis: London*, 1770. 8°.   03440. h. **36**. (**16**.)
A different edition from the preceding.

—— Lot's Flight. Being the substance of a discourse deliver'd in Pembroke, on . . . October 14, 1753. pp. 20 *John Hart: London*, 1754. 12°.   **4474**. aaa. **14**.

—— The third edition. pp. 20.   *M. Lewis & Son: London*, 1767. 12°.   **4475**. a. **38**.

—— The fifth edition. pp. 20.   *H. Trapp: London*, 1788. 8°.   **4455**. a. **8**. (**10**.)

—— The Marriage of Isaac. A discourse delivered at Exeter, in the year 1744 . . . The second edition. pp. 24. *M. Lewis: London*, 1772. 8°.   03440. h. **36**. (**11**.)

—— Naaman Cleansed. Being the substance of a sermon preached at Smiths-Hall, Bristol . . . The fourth edition. [With an address to the reader, signed: G. Whitefield.] pp. 16. *M. Lewis: London*, 1760. 8°.   **4475**. aa. **31**.

—— Naaman cleansed . . . The fifth edition. pp. 16. *M. Lewis: London*, 1774. 8°.   03440. h. **36**. (**4**.)

CENNICK (JOHN)

—— **The seventh edition. pp. 18.**   *M. Trapp: London*, 1793. 8°.   **4476**. aa. **14**.

—— The New Birth. Being the substance of a discourse delivered at Malmsbury . . . in the year 1741. pp. 15. *M. Lewis: London*, 1775. 8°.   03440. h. **36**. (**2**.)

—— The New Birth. Being the substance of a discourse delivered at Malmsbury . . . in the year 1741 . . . The fifth edition. pp. 15. *H. Trapp: London*, 1788. 12°.
4474. aaa. **37**.

—— Nunc Dimittis. Some lines of the Reverend Mr. Cennick's . . . which he wrote some time ago, and carried with him in his pocket-book, where they were found after his decease. pp. 7. *M. Lewis: London*, 1756. 12°.
11631. aa. **6**.

—— [Another edition.] pp. 6.   *M. Lewis: [London,]* 1757. 12°.   **11631**. aa. **7**.

—— [Another edition.] pp. 8.   *H. Trapp: London*, 1783. 12°.   **11632**. aa. **13**.

—— [Another edition.] pp. 8.   *H. Trapp: London*, 1787. 12°.   **1416**. a. **34**. (**2**.)

—— [Another edition.] pp. 8.   *H. Trapp: London*, 1791. 8°.   **4455**. a. **8**. (**22**.)

—— [Another edition.] *See* HOGG (Reynold) Scriptural Supports, *etc.* 1823. 8°.   **4408**. h. **19**

—— The Offices of the Messiah. Being the substance of a discourse delivered in Haverford-West . . . in the year 1753. pp. 20. *M. Lewis: London*, 1756. 12°.
4474. aaa. **27**.

—— The fifth edition. pp. 20. *H. Trapp: London*, 1789. 8°.
4455. a. **8**. (**8**.)

—— The Patterns of Mercy. Being the substance of a discourse delivered at Ballinderry . . . in the year 1754 . . . The second edition. pp. 24.   *M. Lewis: London*, 1756. 12°.   **4474**. aaa. **28**.

—— The fifth edition. pp. 24. *M. Trapp: London*, 1791. 8°.
4455. a. **8**. (**13**.)

—— The Privilege of Believers. Being the substance of a discourse delivered at Grogun . . . in the year 1754 . . . The second edition. pp. 16.   *M. Lewis: London*, 1756. 12°.   **4474**. aaa. **29**.

—— The fifth edition. pp. 16. *M. Trapp: London*, 1791. 8°.
4455. a. **8**. (**12**.)

—— The Reproach of the Cross. A discourse delivered at Gloonen . . . in the year 1754. pp. 18.   *M. Lewis: London*, 1756. 12°.   **4474**. aaa. **30**.

—— The third edition. pp. 18. *H. Trapp: London*, 1786. 8°.
4455. a. **8**. (**18**.)

—— Sacred Hymns for the Children of God, in the Days of their Pilgrimage. By J. C. [i.e. J. Cennick.] pp. xxxii. 220. 1741. 12°. *See* C., J.   **3436**. e. **24**.

—— The second edition. pp. xxxii. 343. 1741. 12°.   *See* C., J.   **3436**. e. **1**. (**1**.)

—— Sacred Hymns for the Children of God, in the Days of their Pilgrimage. By J. C. [i.e. John Cennick.] [A different collection from the preceding.] 2 pt. 1742. 12°. *See* C., J.   **3436**. e. **1**. (**2**.)

—— Sacred Hymns, for the Use of Religious Societies, *etc.* [With six hymns by Joseph Humphreys.] 3 pt. *Felix Farley: Bristol; M. Lewis: London*, 1743-64. 12°.
3435. c. **44**.
Imperfect; wanting pp. 33–40 of pt. 2. *Pt.* 3 *was printed in London.*

CENNICK (JOHN)

—— [Another copy of pt. 1 and 2.] **3434. b. 46.**

—— The Safety of a True Christian. Being the substance of a discourse delivered in London, in the year 1744. pp. 18. *M. Lewis: London,* 1756. 12⁰. **4474. aaa. 31.**

—— The third edition. pp. 18. *H. Trapp: London,* 1786. 8⁰. **4455. a. 8. (15.)**

—— St. Paul's Conversion. Being the substance of a sermon preached at Plymouth . . . in the year 1744 . . . The third edition. pp. 16. *M. Lewis: London,* 1760. 8⁰. **4475. aa. 32.**

—— St. Paul's Conversion . . . The third edition. pp. 16. *M. Lewis: London,* 1775. 8⁰. **03440. h. 36. (6.)**

—— The Shadows of Christ. Being the substance of a discourse delivered in the North of Ireland in the year 1751 . . . The second edition. pp. 28. *M. Lewis: London,* 1756. 8⁰. **4475. aa. 27.**

—— The Shadows of Christ . . . The second edition. pp. 28. *M. Lewis: London,* 1771. 8⁰. **03440. h. 36. (18.)**
A different edition from the preceding.

—— A Short Catechism, chiefly design'd for the instructing of little children in the doctrines of Jesus Christ. pp. 51. *Printed for the Author: London,* 1744. 12⁰. **4136. c. 7. (30.)**

—— Simon and Mary. Being the substance of a sermon preach'd in Exeter, in the year 1744 . . . The second edition. pp. 23. *M. Lewis: London,* 1759. 8⁰. **4475. aa. 29.**

—— Simon and Mary . . . The third edition. pp. 23. *M. Lewis: London,* 1772. 8⁰. **03440. h. 36. (10.)**

—— The Sower. Being the substance of a discourse delivered in the County of Antrim . . . in the year 1748. pp. 23. *S. Powell: Dublin,* 1754. 8⁰. **03440. h. 36. (15.)**

—— The Sower. Being the substance of a discourse delivered in the County of Antrim in the year 1748 . . . The second edition. pp. 23. *M. Lewis: London,* 1756. 8⁰. **4475. aa. 28.**

—— The Sufferings and Satisfaction of Christ. Being the substance of a discourse deliver'd in the North of Ireland in the year 1752. pp. 28. *John Hart: London,* 1753. 12⁰. **4474. aaa. 13.**

—— [Another edition.] pp. 28. *M. Lewis: London,* 1758. 8⁰. **4225. b. 16.**

—— The third edition. pp. 28. *H. Trapp: London,* 1791. 8⁰. **4455. a. 8. (3.)**

—— The Syrophenician: or, a Pattern of invincible faith. Delivered in a discourse at London in the year 1750 . . . The second edition. pp. 19. *M. Lewis: London,* 1759. 8⁰. **4475. aa. 30.**

—— The Syrophenician . . . The third edition. pp. 19. *M. Lewis: London,* 1773. 8⁰. **03440. h. 36. (17.)**

—— A Treatise of the Holy Ghost: wherein is proved, that the Spirit of God was in the Prophets and Apostles, and is in every true believer, to the end of the world. pp. 84. *J. Lewis: London,* 1742. 12⁰. **4256. aaa. 8.**

—— The Two Covenants. Being the substance of a discourse delivered in London, in the year 1745 . . . The second edition. pp. 24. *M. Lewis: London,* 1756. 8⁰. **4475. aa. 24.**

CENNICK (JOHN)

—— The Two Covenants . . . The third edition. pp. 24. *M. Lewis: London,* 1771. 8⁰. **03440. h. 36. (12.)**

—— The Vision of Dry Bones. Being the substance of a discourse delivered in Dublin, in the year 1754. pp. 18. [*Dublin ?* 1754 ?] 12⁰. **4474. aa. 10.**

—— The second edition. pp. 20. *M. Lewis: London,* 1756. 12⁰. **4474. aaa. 32.**

—— The fifth edition. pp. 20. *H. Trapp: London,* 1789. 8⁰. **4455. a. 8. (14.)**

—— The Widow of Nain. Being the substance of a discourse delivered in * * *, in the year 1755. pp. 18. *M. Lewis: London,* 1756. 12⁰. **4474. aaa. 33.**

—— The third edition. pp. 18. *H. Trapp: London,* 1786. 8⁰. **4455. a. 8. (19.)**

—— The Woman of Samaria. Being the substance of a discourse delivered at Scoles . . . in the year 1752 . . . The second edition. pp. 20. *M. Lewis: London,* 1756. 12⁰. **4474. aaa. 34.**

—— The fourth edition. pp. 19. *H. Trapp: London,* 1789. 8⁰. **4455. a. 8. (1.)**

CENNINI (BERNARDO) *See* COEN (G.) L'Arte tipografica in Italia nell' ultimo decennio. Parole lette il 24. giugno 1871 nella festa letteraria in onore di B. Cennini. 1871. 12⁰. **11899. b. 40. (5.)**

—— *See* FANTOZZI (F.) Notizie biografiche originali di B. Cennini, *etc.* 1839. 8⁰. **819. i. 32.**

—— *See* OTTINO (G.) Di Bernardo Cennini e dell'arte della stampa in Firenze . . . Sommario storico, *etc.* 1871. 8⁰. **11899. ff. 34. (3.)**

—— *See* OTTINO (G.) Il IV centenario di Bernardo Cennini, *etc.* 1871. 8⁰. **10631. e. 42. (14.)**

—— Le Feste del IV Centenario Cenniniano. Relazione di Piero Barbèra. Bernardo Cennini e il suo tempo. Discorso di Andrea Bertolotto. Un Pensiero alla stampa. Discorso del professor Carlo Fontanelli. pp. 31. *Firenze,* 1871. 8⁰. **10631. e. 42. (12.)**

CENNINI (CENNINO) Di Cennino Cennini. Trattato della pittura. Messo in luce la prima volta con annotazioni dal cavaliere Giuseppe Tambroni. pp. lii. 171. *Roma,* 1821. 8⁰. **1402. e. 16.**

—— Il Libro dell'arte, o Trattato della pittura . . . Di nuovo pubblicato, con molte correzioni e coll'aggiunta di più capitoli tratti dai codici fiorentini, per cura di Gaetano e Carlo Milanesi. pp. xxix. 207. *Firenze,* 1859. 8⁰. **7855. b. 26.**

—— Il Libro dell'Arte. Text edited by Daniel V. Thompson, Jr. (The Craftsman's Handbook. Translated . . . by D. V. Thompson, Jr.) [With facsimiles.] *Ital. & Eng.* 2 vol. *Yale University Press: New Haven; Oxford University Press: London,* 1932, 33. 8⁰. [*Louis Stern Memorial Fund. Publications.*] **Ac. 2692. mhc. (8.)**

—— A Treatise on Painting . . . Translated by Mrs Merrifield. With an introductory preface . . . notes and illustrations, *etc.* pp. lxx. 177. pl. 9. *Edward Lumley: London,* 1844. 8⁰. **1402. k. 7.**

—— The Book of the Art of Cennino Cennini. A contemporary practical treatise on quattrocento painting. Translated . . . with notes on mediæval art methods by Christiana J. Herringham. pp. xxxviii. 288. *George Allen: London,* 1899. 8⁰. **7858. e. 28.**

CENNINI (CENNINO)

—— Traité de la peinture . . . Mis en lumière pour la première fois avec des notes par le chevalier G. Tambroni. Traduit par Victor Mottez. pp. xxviii. 160.   *Paris, Lille*, 1858. 8°.   [MISSING.]

—— Le Livre de l'art; ou, Traité de la peinture . . . Traduit par Victor Mottez. Nouvelle édition [by Henry Mottez] augmentée de dix-sept chapitres nouvellement traduits, précédée d'une lettre d'Auguste Renoir, et d'une préface inédite du traducteur, suivie de notes et d'éclaircissements sur la fresque par Victor Mottez. pp. xxxvi. 151. *Paris*, 1911. 8°.   **7875. s. 24.**

—— Das Buch von der Kunst, oder Tractat der Malerei . . . Übersetzt, mit Einleitung, Noten und Register versehen von Albert Ilg. pp. xxiii. 188.   *Wien*, 1871. 8°. [*Quellenschriften für Kunstgeschichte . . . des Mittelalters und der Renaissance.* Bd. 1.]   **2262. b.**

—— *See* BORRADAILE (Viola) and (R.) The Student's Cennini. A handbook for tempera painters (presenting, in concise form, the information concerning egg tempera contained in Cennini's ' Libro dell'Arte '). 1942. 8°.
                                          7867. a. 32.

CENNINUS (PETRUS) *See* SERVIUS MAURUS HONORATUS. *Begin.* [fol. 1 *recto*:] [B]Vcolica ut ferunt dicta sunt a custodia boum, *etc.* [The commentary of Servius upon the works of Virgil, edited by P. Cenninus.] 1471, *etc.* fol.
                                          IC. **27010.**

CENNIUS (CAJETANUS) *See* CENNI (Gaetano)

CENNO. Cenno sulle cause ed effetti dell'attual condizione delle nostre principali derrate. Di C. D. V. 1830. 8°. *See* V., C. D.   **8207. e. 2. (12.)**

CENNUS (CAJETANUS) *See* CENNI (Gaetano)

CENO (ASCANIO MORI DA) *See* MORI (A. de')

CENOBIO.

—— Cenobio. Rivista mensile di cultura. *See* PERIODICAL PUBLICATIONS.—*Lugano.*

CENOMANENSIS (HILDEBERTUS) *See* HILDEBERTUS successively *Bishop of Le Mans* and *Archbishop of Tours.*

CENOMANNIS. *See* MANS.

CENOMANNUM. *See* MANS.

CENOMANNUS (GULIELMUS PLANTIUS) *See* PLANTIUS.

CENOMANUS (GUIDO JUVENALIS) *See* JOUENNEAUX (Gui)

CENOMANUS (MARINUS LIBERGIUS) *See* LIBERGE (Marin)

CENÔVA (FLORJAN) *See* CENÔVA (Stanisław F.)

CENÔVA (STANISŁAW FLORJAN) *See also* KASZUBA, *gburczan, pseud.* [i.e. S. F. Cenôva.]

—— *See also* WOJKASEN, *pseud.* [i.e. S. F. Cenôva.]

—— *See also* WÓJKASIN, ze Sławósena, *pseud.* [i.e. S. F. Cenôva.]

—— *See* BUKOWSKI (A.) Florian Cenowa, twórca regionalizmu kaszubskiego, *etc.* 1947. 8°.   **10797. c. 31.**

—— Skôrb Kaszébskosłovjnskjè mòvé . . . Védêł Dr. F. Cenôva. [With two supplements in Polish.] no. 1–13. pp. 198. 16. 16. 15. *Svjecè*, 1866–68. 8°. **12304. g. 32.**

—— [Another copy of no. 1–3.]   **12976. c. 31. (7.)** *Imperfect; wanting the titlepage.*

CENÔVA (STANISŁAW FLORJAN)

—— Zarés do Grammatikj Kaśébsko-Słovjnskjè Mòvé napjesêł é védêł Dr. F. Cenôva wòjkasin ze Sławòséna. (Entwurf zur Grammatik der kassubisch-slovinischen Sprache . . . Wörterbuch der kassubisch-slovinischen und deutschen Sprache.) pp. 96. *w Poznaniu*, 1879. 8°.
                                    12902. b. 52. (2.)

—— [Another copy.]   **12903. c. 51. (5.)**

CENOWA (FLORIAN) *See* CENÔVA (S. F.)

CENSALE (GIROLAMO) Il Forzato. [A poem.] ff. 97. *Nella Stampa del Cacchio; per Marino d'Alessandro: Napoli*, 1577. 12°.   **11426. a. 27.**

CENSER. A Golden Censer. [An exposition of the Book of Revelation.] pt. 1, 3. *J. H. Batty: London*, [1870.] 8°.
                                    764. m. 5. (8.)
Pt. 2 was never published. The imprint of pt. 1, apparently reading " — Jackson: London," has been cut away.

—— [Another copy of pt. 3.]   **3185. de. 27.**

CENSEUR. Le Censeur, ou Examen des actes . . . qui tendent à détruire ou à consolider la constitution de l'État, *etc. See* PERIODICAL PUBLICATIONS.—*Paris.*

—— Le Censeur des censeurs. *See* PERIODICAL PUBLICATIONS.—*Paris.*

—— Le Censeur des journaux. *See* PERIODICAL PUBLICATIONS.—*Paris.*

—— Le Censeur européen. *See* PERIODICAL PUBLICATIONS.—*Paris.* Le Censeur, *etc.*

ČENSKÝ (FERDINAND) Kurzgefasste praktische Grammatik der böhmischen Sprache für Deutsche. Mit besonderer Berücksichtigung der Militär-Terminologie, *etc.* pp. 182. *Prag*, 1871. 8°.   **12976. cc. 27. (7.)**

—— Zweite vermehrte und verbesserte Auflage. pp. 302. *Prag*, 1878. 8°.   **12976. cc. 31.**

—— Vojenská čítanka . . . Militärisches Lesebuch . . . Praktischer Anhang zu der . . . Kurzgefassten Grammatik der böhmischen Sprache, *etc.* pp. 154. *v Praze*, 1871. 8°.
                                    8829. bbb. 29.

CENSOR. The Censor. *See* PERIODICAL PUBLICATIONS.—*London.*

—— The Censor. [1771, 72.] *See* PERIODICAL PUBLICATIONS. —*Boston, Massachusetts.*   **Mic. A. 137. (3.)**

—— The Censor: a weekly review of satire, politics, *etc. See* PERIODICAL PUBLICATIONS.—*London.*

—— El Censor. Obra periódica. *See* PERIODICAL PUBLICATIONS.—*Madrid.*

—— Der Censor, oder: Beweis, dass die Büchercensur und alle Einschränkungen des Büchergewerbes . . . höchst nachtheilige Veranstaltungen sind . . . Ein kleiner Beytrag zum gerechtfertigten Nachdrucker. pp. 80.   *Frankfurt & Leipzig*, 1775. 8°.   **818. c. 20. (1.)**

—— The Censor, or Citizen's journal. *See* PERIODICAL PUBLICATIONS.—*Dublin.*

—— The Censor, or Covent-Garden journal. *See* PERIODICAL PUBLICATIONS.—*Dublin.* The Covent-Garden Journal.

—— El Censor, periódico político y literario. *See* PERIODICAL PUBLICATIONS.—*Madrid.*

CENSOR.

—— A Short Account of divers Falsehoods contained in a pamphlet lately publish'd, entituled, The Censor censur'd, &c. *See* ROSE (William) *Apothecary.* Observations upon the Case of William Rose, *etc.* 1704. 4°.
1418. c. 47.

—— Waarom de censor de mails opent. pp. 12.
G. B. Dibblee: London, 1917. 8°. **09084. c. 4.**

CENSOR, *Dramaticus, pseud.* A Complete History of the Drama, from the earliest periods to the present time. By Censor Dramaticus. pp. [1]–140. *T. Wilkins: London*, 1793. 8°. **11857. b. 76.**
No more published.

—— [Another copy.] **840. g. 24.**

CENSOR, *pseud.* [i.e. OLIVER BELL BUNCE.] *See also* BUNCE (Oliver B.)

—— Don't: a manual of mistakes & improprieties more or less prevalent in conduct & speech. By Censor. Unmutilated and authorised edition. pp. 96. *Field & Tuer: London*, [1883.] 16°. [*Vellum-Parchment Shilling Series of Miscellaneous Literature.* no. 9.] **12206. cc. 40.**

—— (Second edition.) pp. 96. *Field & Tuer: London*, [1883.] 16°. [*Vellum-Parchment Shilling Series of Miscellaneous Literature.* no. 9.] **12206. cc. 41.**

—— (Third edition.) pp. 96. *Field & Tuer: London*, [1883.] 16°. [*Vellum-Parchment Shilling Series of Miscellaneous Literature.* no. 9.] **12206. cc. 42.**

—— [Another edition.] pp. 77. *Griffith & Farran: London*, 1884 [1883]. 16°. **8411. aaa. 27.**

—— (Fourth edition.) pp. 96. *Field & Tuer: London*, [1884.] 16°. **8410. aa. 29.**

—— [Another edition.] pp. 94. *D. Appleton & Co.: New York*, 1884. 16°. **8411. aaa. 33.**

—— [Another edition.] pp. 64. *Ward, Lock & Co.: London*, [1884.] 8°. **8411. aaa. 31.**

—— [A reissue.] Don't: a Manual of Mistakes, *etc. New York*, 1886. 16°. **8409. a. 47.**

—— (New & enlarged edition.) pp. 72. *Ward, Lock & Co.: London, New York*, [1888.] 8°. **8411. aa. 36.**

—— [Another edition.] pp. 68. *Ward, Lock & Co.: London*, 1912. 8°. **8410. k. 23.**

—— Revised and enlarged edition. pp. 96. *Ward, Lock & Co.: London & Melbourne*, [1938.] 8°. **8408. k. 44.**

—— Don't . . . Revised and enlarged edition. pp. 64. *Ward, Lock & Co.: London & Melbourne*, [1953.] 8°. **8412. df. 28.**

CENSOR (C.) *pseud.* The Thespian Mirror, or Poetical strictures; on the professional characters of Mr. Cooke [and other actors] . . . of the Theatres Royal, Manchester, Liverpool, and Chester. By C. Censor. pp. 40. *Printed for the Author: [Manchester,]* 1793. 8°.
12354. h. 22. (1.)
Imperfect; wanting pp. 9–32.

CENSORI (VINCENZO) Dei criteri educativi di Gian Giacomo Rousseau in relazione con i progressi della scienza . . . 2ª edizione con aggiunte. pp. 156. *Tivoli*, 1895. 8°. **8311. b. 37.**
The place of publication given on the wrapper is Palermo.

CENSORINI, *Signor, pseud.* Riflessioni sul Discorso istorico-politico dell'origine, del progresso, e della decadenza del potere de' chierici su le signorie temporali [by G. Capecelatro, Archbishop of Taranto] . . . Dialogo del signor Censorini italiano, col signor Ramour francese. pp. 94. *Filadelfia [Naples ? 1788 ?]* 8°.
1356. b. 16. (2.)

—— [Another edition.] *See* DISCORSO. Discorso istorico-politico dell'origine, del progresso, e della decadenza del potere de' chierici, *etc.* 1820. 8°. **1364. k. 3.**

CENSORINUS. *See* MODIUS (F.) Franc. Modij . . . Nouantiquae lectiones . . . in quibus . . . Silius, Censorinus . . . Statius, alij supplentur, emendantur, *etc.* 1584. 8°. **1089. h. 5.**

—— Index librorum: qui in hoc uolumine continentur. Censorinus de die natali. Tabula Cebetis. Dialogus Luciani. Enchiridion Epicteti. Basilius. Plutarchus de Inuidia & Odio. [fol. 1 *verso:*] Ad nobilem Bartholomeum blanchinum Philippi Beroaldi Boñ. epistola. [fol. 2 *recto:*] Censorini opusculum: de die natali, *etc.* [fol. 16 *recto:*] Cebetis Thebani tabula: e Graeco in Latinum conuersa per Ludouicum Odaxium Patauinum. [fol. 20 *recto:*] Luciani philosophi Graeci dialogus de virtute conquerēte cum Mercurio. a Carolo aretino græco in latinū traductus. [Attributed also to Leone Battista Alberti.] [fol. 21 *recto:*] Angeli Politiani in Epicteti Stoici Enchiridion e graeco a se interpretatum ad Laurentium Medicem epistola. [fol. 21 *verso:*] Epicteti Stoici Enchiridion. [fol. 29 *recto:*] Sancti Basilii de liberalibus studiis et ingenuis moribus liber per Leon. Ar. [i.e. L. Bruni] ex Gre. in Latinum conuersus. [fol. 34 *recto:*] Basilii Oratio de inuidia e Graeco in Latinum conuersa per Nicolaum Perotum incipit. [fol. 37 *recto:*] Plutarchi libellus de differentia inter odium et inuidiam incipit foeliciter. [Edited by P. Beroaldus.] *per Benedictum hectoris: Bononiæ*, quarto idus Maii [12 May], 1497. fol.
Maps **C. 7. b. 12. (4–9.)**
38 leaves. Sig. a⁶ b⁶ c–f⁴ g⁸ h². *40 lines to a page.*

—— [Another copy.] **G. 8297.**

—— [Another copy.] Index librorum: qui in hoc uolumine continentur. Censorinus de die natali, *etc. Bononiæ*, 1497. fol. **Hirsch 1. 112.**

—— Index librorum: qui in hoc uolumine continentur. Censorinus de die natali. Ad Q. Cerellium. Tabula Cebetis per Lodouicū Odaxiū e græco cōuersa. Plutarchus de Inuidia & Odio. Basilii Oratio de Inuidia per Nicolaū Perottū traducta. Basilii Epistola de Vita solitaria ad Gregorium Nazanzenum per Franciscum Filelphum e græco traducta. [With a prefatory letter by P. Beroaldus.] *[Bernardinus Venetus, de Vitalibus: Venice,* 1500 ?] 4°. **IA. 24363.**
42 leaves. Sig. a–i⁴ k⁶. *30 lines to a page.*

—— Index operum quæ in hoc uolumine continentur. Censorini de die natali liber aure⁹ . . . antiquæ lectioni restitutus. Neruæ Traianicȝ & Adriani Cæsaris uitæ ex Dione in latinum uersæ: a G. Merula. Item Vesæui montis conflagratio ex eodem Merula interprete. Cebetis Thebani tabula (in Latinum conuersa per Lodouicum Odaxium). Plutarchi libellus de differentia inter odium & inuidiam. Basilii oratio de inuidia (in Latinum conuersa per N. Perotum). Basilii epistola de uita solitaria (per Franciscum Filephum . . . traducta). [With a prefatory epistle by Tristanus Calchus.] *Jo. Jacomo e Frat. de Legnano: [Milan,* 1503 ?] 4°. **IA. 24356. (1.)**
The printers' names are given in a woodcut on the titlepage.

—— Censorini opusculum, De die natali, ad Q. Cerellium. *See* MACROBIUS (A. T.) Macrobius Aurelius integer, *etc.* 1519. fol. **11350. g. 2.**

—— [Another edition.] *See* CONSENTIUS (P.) Disciplinarum liberalium orbis, *etc.* 1528. 4°. **12933. b. 20.**

CENSORINUS.

—— Censorini opusculum De die natali, *etc.* (Additis ex uetusto exemplari nonnullis, quæ desiderabantur.) *See* MACROBIUS (A. T.) Macrobij in Somnium Ciceronis . . . explanatio, *etc.* 1528. 8°.　　　　**682. a. 17.**

—— Censorini De die natali liber . . . ab Aldo Mannuccio emendatus, & notis illustratus. pp. 84.　*Apud Aldum: Venetiis*, 1581. 8°.　　　　**8610. a. 25.**

—— [Another copy.] Censorini de die natali liber, *etc. Venetiis*, 1581. 8°.　　　　Hirsch 1. **113.**

—— Noua editio, Lud. Carrione recensente augente, & pristino ordini suo restituente. Ejusdem argumenti fragmētum incerti scriptoris antea cum eodem Censorini . . . libro continenter impressum, nunc vero ab eodem Lud. Carrione separatum, correctiusque, & . . . auctius editum. pp. 55. 27.　　*Apud Æ. Beysium: Lutetiæ*, 1583. 8°.　　　　**721. d. 4.**

—— [Another copy.]　　　　**8610. aaa. 16. (2.)**

—— [Another edition.] pp. 44. 19.　MS. NOTES [by I. Casaubon]. *Apud F. Le Preux: Lugduni*, 1593. 8°.
　　　　589. a. 15. (2.)

—— —— Censorini liber de die natali. Henricus Lindenbrogius recensuit, & notis illustravit. (Fragmentum incerti scriptoris antea Censorino tributum . . . editum a Lud. Carrione.) pp. 174 [176].　*In Bibliopolio Heringiano: Hamburgi*, 1614. 4°.　　　　**C. 69. aa. 16.**

—— Censorini De die natali liber . . . Ab E. Puteano Bamelrodio publice Lovanii explicandus. pp. 87. *Typis P. Dormalii: Lovanii*, 1628. 4°.　　**721. f. 20.**

—— Censorinus De die natali. Henric. Lindenbrogius recensuit; et notis, iterata hac editione passim adauctis, illustravit. (Fragmentum incerti scriptoris, antea Censorino tributum . . . editum a Lud. Carrione.) pp. 250. *I. Maire: Lugduni Batavorum*, 1642. 8°.　　**720. b. 29.**

—— [Another copy.]　　　　**721. b. 27.**

—— Censorinus De die natali. Henricus Lindenbrogius recensuit, et notis illustravit. (Fragmentum incerti scriptoris, antea Censorino tributum . . . editum a Lud. Carrione.) Quibus . . . accedunt Nunnesii in Fragmentum notæ, cum spicilegio annotationum . . . Salmasii, Scaligeri, &c. Opus . . . denuo recognitum atque auctum. pp. 212. *Ex officina Joh. Hayes; impensis Tho. Dawson jun.: Cantabrigiæ*, 1695. 8°.　　　**977. a. 40.**

—— Censorini liber de die natali cum perpetuo commentario Henrici Lindenbrogii, nec non notarum spicilegio collecto ex Scaligeri . . . aliorumque scriptis, ut et C. Lucilii, Satyrarum quae supersunt reliquiae cum notis & animadversionibus Franc. Jan. F. Douzae, ex recensione Sigeberti Havercampi, *etc.* (Fragmentum incerti scriptoris, antea Censorino tributum . . . editum a Lud. Carrione.) [Edited by E. and A. Havercamp. With plates.] pp. 448. *Lugduni Batavorum*, 1743. 8°.　　**674. b. 13.**

—— Censorinus De die natali. Ex recensione Andreae Goetzii. Editio altera. pp. x. 66.　*Altorphii*, 1744. 8°.
　　　　787. a. 69.

—— Censorini liber de die natali, cum perpetuo commentario Henrici Lindenbrogii, *etc. Lugduni Batavorum*, 1767. 8°.
　　　　721. f. 21.
　　A reissue of the Leyden edition of 1743.

—— [Another copy.]　　　　**51. l. 12.**

CENSORINUS.

—— Censorini De die natali liber. Recensuit et emendavit Otto Jahn. (Fragmentum Censorino adscriptum.) pp. xxiv. 109.　*Berolini*, 1845. 8°.　　**8610. d. 17.**

—— Censorini De die natali liber. Recensuit Fridericus Hultsch. pp. xiii. 98.　*Lipsiae*, 1867. 8°.　　**2048. a. 9.** *Part of the " Bibliotheca scriptorum graecorum et romanorum Teubneriana."*

—— Censorini De die natali liber. Ad codicum denuo collatorum fidem recensuit Johannes Cholodniak. pp. 79. *Petropoli*, 1889. 8°.　　　　**8562. dd. 23.**

—— Livre . . . sur le jour natal, traduit . . . en français par M. J. Mangeart. *Lat. & Fr.* pp. 133.　　*Paris*, 1843. 8°. [*Bibliothèque latine-française.* sér. 2.]
　　　　11306. k. 12.

—— Censorin. [The " Liber de die natali " with a French translation by T. C. E. Baudement.] 1852. *See* NISARD (J. M. N. D.) Collection des auteurs latins, *etc.* 1850, *etc.* 8°.　　　　**11306. m. 19.**

—— De die natale. " The Natal Day." By Censorinus . . . Life of the Emperor Hadrian by Ælianus Spartianus . . . Translated . . . by William Maude. 2 pt.　*Cambridge Encyclopedia Co.: New York*, 1900. 8°.　　**8563. cc. 8.**

—— Aureum aliud ex Censorino de Musica caput. [An extract from " De die natali liber."] *See* TERENTIANUS, *Maurus.* Terentiani Mauri venustissimus de literis syllabis et metris Horati liber. 1510. 8°.　　**625. c. 5.**

—— Aureum Ex Censorini De Musica Collectaneum. [Extracts from the fragment by an unknown writer published as part of the " De die natali liber " in early editions of this work.] *See* TERENTIANUS, *Maurus.* Terentiani Mauri venustissimus de literis syllabis et metris Horati liber. 1510. 8°.　　　　**625. c. 5.**

—— Fragmentum scriptoris incerti, antea Censorino tributum, & cum eius De die natali libro . . . impressum, nunc correctius, & . . . auctius editum, a Lud. Carrione. *See* PROCLUS, *Diadochus.* [*Chrestomathia Grammatica.*] Procli Chrestomathia poetica, *etc.* 1615. 4°.　　**77. f. 11.**

—— Censorino adscriptum fragmentum de metris.　*See* PUTSCHIUS (H.) Grammaticæ Latinæ auctores antiqui, *etc.* 1605. 4°.　　　　**67. c. 15.**

CENSORINUS, *Novatus. See* NOVATUS (C.)

CENSORINUS PHILALETHES, *pseud. See* PHILALETHES (Censorinus) *pseud.*

CENSORINUS (Q. MODERATUS) Q. Moderati Censorini De vita, et morte latinae linguae paradoxa philologica criticis nonnullis dissertationibus exposita, asserta, et probata. Praemittuntur . . . colloquia inter eruditum civem Ferrariensem & Hispanos aliquot . . . Omnia dialogi fide ab uno Hispanorum narrata. [Purporting to be edited by M. Aimerich, but in fact written by him.] pp. 232. *Ferrariae*, 1780. 8°.　　**12932. bbb. 17.**

CENSORSHIP. Censorship and Trade. pp. 24.　*Eyre & Spottiswoode: London*, 1916. 8°.　　**08028. h. 35.**

CENSUR. Die Censur des Landwirths durch das richtige Soll und Haben der doppelten Buchhaltung nebst Betriebsrechnung einer Herrschaft von 2200 Morgen für den Zeitraum vom 1. Juli 1859 bis 1. Juli 1860. Bearbeitet von einem schlesischen Rittergutsbesitzer. pp. 156. *Breslau*, 1861. 8°.　　　　**8505. cc. 5.**

—— Ueber die Censur. [By G. W. C. Lochner.] pp. 39. *München*, 1843. 8°.　　　　**818. h. 3. (5.)**

CENSUR-FLUECHTLINGE. Censur-Flüchtlinge. Zwölf Freiheitslieder. [By R. von Gottschall.] pp. 50. *Zürich & Winterthur*, 1843. 8°. **11525. f. 46. (2.)**

CENSUR-KALENDER. Censur-kalender. Samling af skeppsbrutet gods, tillhörigt den finska pressen, jemte skizzer från de finska censurförhållendenas område. [Edited by E. von Quanten.] Hälfte 1. pp. 160. *Stockholm*, 1861. 8°. **11851. bb. 12.** *No more published.*

CENSURA. Censura cleri; or a Plea against scandalous ministers. 1660. 4°. *See* ENGLAND.—*Church of England.* —*Clergy.* [*Appendix.*] **111. b. 13.**

—— Censura Literaria. Containing titles, abstracts, and opinions of old English books, *etc.* 1805, *etc.* 8°. *See* BRYDGES (*Sir* Samuel E.) *Bart.* [*Works.*] **1091. h. 15.**

—— Censura temporum. *See* PERIODICAL PUBLICATIONS.— *London.*

CENSURE. *See* C., F. E. A. Response d'vn ecclésiastique à vn de ses amis . . . Sur vne Censure publiée . . . contre la probabilité des opinions dans la morale, *etc.* [On the "Censure d'un livre anonyme, intitulé Apologie pour les Casuistes . . . Faite par Messeigneurs les Evesques d'Alet, Pamiés, *etc.*"] [1658.] 4°. **860. l. 18. (11.)**

—— A Brotherly and Friendly Censure of the errour of a dear friend . . . in an answer to his four Questions [concerning Excommunication and Suspension from the Sacrament], *etc.* 1645. 4°. *See* QUESTIONS. **E. 265. (4.)**

—— The Censure of a loyall Subject: vpon certaine noted Speach and behauiours, of those fourteene . . . Traitors [i.e. John Ballard, Anthony Babington and others], *etc.* [The dedication signed: G. W., i.e. George Whetstone.] [1587.] 4°. *See* W., G. **600. c. 23.**

—— A Censure of Three Scandalous Pamphlets. 1. A Defence of Dr. Crisp, against the Charge of Mr. Edwards of Cambridg, by Esquire Edwards in Wales [i.e. "A Short Review of some Reflections . . . upon Dr. Crisp's sermons . . . By Thomas Edwards"], *etc.* 1699. 8°. *See* EDWARDS (Thomas) *Esq.* **4152. aa. 56. (10.)**

—— La Censure, petit conte, extrait d'une grande épître. [By — Desarps. In verse.] pp. 8. *Paris*, 1814. 8°. **8052. k. 10. (26.)**

CENSUREERING. De Verzonnene cencureering, en gevolgen der onafgevergde logen, omtrent het danssen eener menuet. [A comedy in verse, by Elizabeth Bekker, afterwards Wolff.] pp. 32. [1780?] 8°. **011556. g. 30. (13.)**

CENSUS. The Census. [A religious tract. Signed: F. B., i.e. Francis Bourdillon.] [1861.] 8°. *See* B., F. **4406. g. 1. (115.)**

—— The Census. *S.P.C.K.: London*, [1871.] 8°. **4420. i. 1. (15.)** *A different work from the preceding.*

—— Census Catholicus: or, a Project of a tax . . . as large and extensive as a general excise . . . With some brief remarks on a book, entitled, An Essay for a General Tax . . . written by . . . Monsieur Vauban. Humbly submitted to the consideration of this present Parliament. *Printed for the Author: London*, 1711. fol. **816. m. 6. (94.)** *Imperfect; wanting all after p. 12.*

—— Census of Partial Employment, Unemployment, and Occupations. *See* UNITED STATES OF AMERICA.

—— Census of Production Committee. *See* ENGLAND.— *Board of Trade.*

CENSUS AND STATISTICS MONTHLY. *See* CANADA.—*Dominion Bureau of Statistics.*

CENSUS BULLETIN. *See* UNITED STATES OF AMERICA. —*Census Office.*

CENSUS COMMITTEE. *See* BERMUDA.

CENSUS DIRECTORY. *See* DIRECTORIES.—*Philadelphia.*

CENSUS LIBRARY PROJECT. *See* UNITED STATES OF AMERICA.

CENSUS MONOGRAPH SERIES.

—— *See* UNITED STATES OF AMERICA.—*Social Science Research Council.*—*Committee on Census Monographs.*

CENSUS OF DISTRIBUTION COMMITTEE. *See* ENGLAND.—*Board of Trade.*

CENT BIBLIOPHILES. *See* PARIS.

CENT-VINGT COURT. Le 120 "Court." Revue d'un jeune bataillon de Chasseurs. *See* FRANCE.—*Army.*— *Chasseurs à Pied.*—*120ᵉ Bataillon.*

CENT (NEHEMIA) *pseud.* A Word to London's Provinciall Assembly. Or, a View of some passages in the Ministers late Vindication of their Government. To which is added a vindication of the Covenant against all intruders and opposers. By Nehemia Cent. pp. 40 [48]. *Printed for the Author: London*, 1650 [1649]. 4°. **E. 586. (1.)**

CENT (PIERRE) En Afrique française. Blancs & noirs. Bourreaux & victimes. [With special reference to the Savorgnan de Brazza mission of enquiry into the administration of the Congo under Gentil.] pp. 52. *Paris*, 1905. 8°. **010095. f. 25.**

CENT (SION) *See* KENT (John) *Welsh Poet.*

CENTANI (GIACOMO) *See* CERTANI (G.)

CENTANNI (EUGENIO) *See* TIZZONI (G.) and CENTANNI (E.) Modo di preparare siero antirabbico ad alto potere curativo, *etc.* 1895. 4°. [*Memorie della R. Accademia delle Scienze dell'Istituto di Bologna.* ser. 5. tom. 5.] **Ac. 2802.**

CENTANNI (LUIGI)

—— Le Spogliazioni di opere d'arte fatte alle Marche sotto il primo Regno italico. *In:* Deputazione di Storia Patria per le Marche. Atti e memorie. ser. 7. vol. 5. pp. 73–124. 1950. 8°. **Ac. 6508/3.**

CENTANNIUS (VALENCIUS) *See* GALEN. [*Works.*— *Latin.*] Cl. Galeni . . . omnia . . . opera; in Latinam linguam conuersa, *etc.* (Cl. Galeni de paruæ pilæ exercitio V. Centannio interprete.) 1550. fol. **L.20.a.1.**

—— —— 1562, *etc.* fol. **L.20.a.2.**

—— —— 1609. fol. **L.20.b.1.**

CENTAR.

—— Centar za Tehničku i Naučnu Dokumentaciju. *See* JUGOSLAVIA.—*Jugoslovenski Centar za Tehničku i Naučnu Dokumentaciju.*

CENTAUR.

—— Centaur. [Selections from famous authors.] *Centaur: London*, 1946– . 8°. **W.P. 1662.**

CENTAUR.

—— The Centaur not Fabulous. In five letters to a friend on the life in vogue. [By Edward Young.] pp. xvi. 378. *A. Millar; R. & J. Dodsley: London,* 1755. 8°. **525. i. 3.**

—— The third edition, corrected. pp. xii. 281. *A. Millar; R. & J. Dodsley: London,* 1755. 12°. **8407. bbb. 16**

—— The fourth edition, corrected. pp. xii. 281. *A. Millar; J. Dodsley: London,* 1765. 12°. **8410. bbb. 44.**

—— Three Letters concerning Systematic Taste, exemplified in The Centaur not Fabulous [by Edward Young]: Laicus's Letter of June 7th, 1755 London Evening-Post, and the Bishop of London's [Thomas Sherlock's] second volume of Discourses. [By Caleb Fleming.] pp. 58. *C. Henderson: London,* 1755. 8°. **699. h. 12. (5.)**

CENTAUR, H.M.S.
Loss of His Majesty's Ship Centaur . . . the 23d of September, 1782; and miraculous preservation of the pinnace, with the Captain, Master, and ten of the crew. [By John Nicholson Inglefield.] Also, the Explosion of the French East-India Company's vessel the Prince . . . July, 1752, *etc.* pp. 28. *Thomas Tegg: London,* [1818.] 8°. **10026. b. 1. (9.)**

—— Wonderful Escape from Shipwreck. An account of the loss of His Majesty's Ship Centaur. [An abridgment of the narrative of John Nicholson Inglefield.] pp. 12. *S. Hazard: Bath,* [1795.] 12°. **4422. dd. 1. (7.)**

CENTAUR BIBLIOGRAPHIES.
The Centaur Bibliographies of Modern American Authors. *See* AMERICAN AUTHORS.

CENTAUR BOOKLET.
Centaur Booklet Number One (—Four, Six). 5 no. *Centaur Press: London,* 1934. 8°. **Cup. 510. c. 1.**
" Silver Wedding " by Lady O'Conor, probably intended to be Centaur Booklet Number Five, was published separately.

CENTAURE.
Le Centaure. Recueil trimestriel de littérature et d'art. *See* PERIODICAL PUBLICATIONS.—*Paris.*

—— Le Centaure. Revue illustré du sport. *See* PERIODICAL PUBLICATIONS.—*Paris.*

CENTAURUS.

—— Centaurus. International magazine of the history of science and medicine. *See* PERIODICAL PUBLICATIONS.—*Copenhagen.*

CENTAZZI (GUILHERME)
A Alma do Justo. Romance original portuguez precedido de duas palavras sobre a vida do author. 2 tom. *Lisboa,* 1861. 16°. **12491. aa. 5.**

—— Beatriz e o Aventureiro. 2 tom. *Lisboa,* 1848. 16°. **12491. aa. 17.**

—— Considérations générales sur l'action des exercices gymnastiques sur l'économie animale . . . Thèse, *etc.* pp. 18. *Paris,* 1834. 4°. **1184. f. 12. (24.)**

—— O Estudante de Coimbra, ou Relampago da historia portugueza, desde 1826 ate 1838. [With a portrait.] 3 tom. *Lisboa,* 1840, 41. 12°. **10632. a. 3.**

—— As Sete Pennadas. [In verse.] pp. 160. *Lisboa,* 1852. 16°. **11452. aaa. 23.**

CENTELLAS ( ) Captain.
Las Dictaduras y el Señor Cambó. pp. 184. *Madrid,* 1929. 8°. **08042. a. 24.**

CENTELLAS (JOACHIN DE)
Les Voyages et conquestes des Roys de Portugal es Indes d'Orient, Ethiopie, Mauritanie d'Afrique & Europe: auec l'origine, succession & descente de leurs maisons, iusques au Sereniss. Sebastian, nagueres atterré en la bataille qui il eust contre le Roy de Fez . . . Le tout recueilly de fideles tesmoings . . . du Sieur I. de Centellas. [With a map.] ff. 60. *Par I. d'Ongoys: Paris,* 1578. 8°. **1195. a. 41.**
The running title reads " Dernier voyage en Afrique."

—— [Another copy.] **G. 7067.**

CENTELLI (ATTILIO)
See TIEPOLO (G. B.) Gli Affreschi di G. B. Tiepolo . . . Con uno studio di A. Centelli. [1895.] fol. **Dept. of Prints & Drawings.**

—— L'Oriente d'oggi, da Brindisi a Beikòs. pp. viii. 278. *Milano,* 1892. 8°. **10125. aaa. 20.**

—— Caterina Cornaro e il suo regno. Con tre ritratti, *etc* pp. 173. *Venezia,* 1892. 8°. **10632. df. 21.**

CENTELLI (GIOVANNI BATTISTA)
Alla Sagra Congregazione dell'Acque . . . Per l'Illmo . . . Signor Prencipe D. Luigi Pio di Savoia, contro l'Illmi Signori interessati Bolognesi nella ripresa del fiume Idice. Memoriale di fatto col sommario. [*Rome,*] 1739. fol. **658. k. 16. (14.)**

—— Alla Sagra Congregazione dell'Acque . . . per l'Illmo . . . Signor Prencipe D. Luigi Pio di Savoia. Contro l'Illmi Signori interessati Bolognesi nella ripresa del fiume Idice. Risposta con sommario. [*Rome,*] 1739. fol. **658. k. 16. (13.)**

CENTEN (SEBASTIAAN)
See BRANDT (G.) *the Elder.* Historie der vermaerde zee- en koop-stadt Enkhuisen . . . Den tweede druk met een vervolg vermeerdert door S. Centen. 1747. 4°. **10271. c. 15.**

—— *See* VELIUS (T.) Chronyk van Hoorn . . . met aantekeningen vermeerdert door S. Centen. 1740. 4°. **1300. e. 15.**

CENTENAIRE.
Les Derniers soupirs d'un centenaire, sur les malheurs de sa patrie. pp. 16. [1789?] 8°. **F. 418. (3.)**

—— Nouveaux mélanges de littérature, d'histoire et de philosophie d'un centenaire, *etc.* pp. vi. 253. 1769. 8°. **12356. i. 11.**

CENTENAIRES ALGÉRIENS.
See ALGERIAN CENTENARIES.

CENTENARI (NARDO NALDONI)
See NALDONI-CENTENARI.

CENTENARY.
The First Centenary of a Series of Concise and Useful Tables of all the Complete Decimal Quotients, which can arise from dividing an unit, or any whole number less than each divisor, by all integers from 1 to 1024. pp. xiv. 18. [1825?] 4°. **530. k. 32.**

CENTENARY BOOKLETS.
Centenary Booklets. *Drummond Book Depot: Stirling,* [1938- .] 16°. **W.P. 13373.**

CENTENARY CELEBRATIONS JOINT RETAILERS' SUB-COMMITTEE.
See OLDHAM.

CENTENARY CONFERENCE.
Centenary Conference on the Protestant Missions of the World. *See* LONDON.—III.

CENTENARY SERIES.

—— Centenary Series. [Temperance tracts.] *Hope Press: Westminster,* [1955- .] 16°. **W.P. D. 310.**

CENTENARY SUNDAY-SCHOOL SOUVENIR.
Centenary Sunday-School Souvenir. [Twelve illustrations, with a short account of the Sunday-School movement by Homer Herbert.]   *Sunday School Union:*
London, 1880. *obl.* 16°.   **4223. a. 3.**

CENTENERA, CARLOS DE IBARRA, *Viscount de. See*
IBARRA.

CENTENERA (MARTIN DEL BARCO) *See* BARCO CEN-
TENERA.

CENTENNIAL MEMORIAL TEMPLE. *See* NEW
YORK.

CENTENNIUS (RALPH) *pseud.* The Dominion [of
Canada] in 1983. pp. 30. *Toker & Co.: Peterborough, Ont.,*
1883. 8°.   **8154. b. 12. (2.)**

CENTENO.—*Eastern Caribbean Farm Institute.*

—— First [*etc.*] Report of the Governing Body, Provisional,
covering the years 1952 and 1953 [*etc.*].   [*Bridgetown,*]
1955– . fol.   **C.S. F. 54/28.**

CENTENO (ADÁN HERMOSO) *See* HERMOSO CENTENO.

CENTENO (ALONSO DE ESPINOSA) *See* ESPINOSA CENTENO.

CENTENO (AMARO) Historia de Cosas del Oriente . . .
Traduzido y recopilado de diuersos y graues historiadores, *etc.* ff. 138.   *Impresso en casa de D. Galuan, a*
costa de M. Rodriguez: Cordoua, 1595. 4°.   **279. c. 25.**

—— [Another copy.]   **G. 6949.**

CENTENO (ANSELMO) Manifestacion de los servicios,
mérito y patriotismo del Ilmo. Sr Dr D. Mariano Chacon
y Becerra, *etc.* [Edited by A. Centeno.] pp. 39.
Lima, 1864. 4°.   **4866. aaa. 42. (3.)**

CENTENO (AUGUSTO)

—— The Intent of the Artist. By Sherwood Anderson,
Thornton Wildes, Roger Sessions, William Lescaze.
Edited, with an introduction, by A. Centeno.
pp. 162. pl. 8.   *Princeton University Press: Princeton,*
1941. 8°.   **11863. cc. 30.**

CENTENO (FERNANDO)

—— Signo y mensaje. Poema. (Ilustraciones de F
Amighetti.) pp. 31. *San José, Costa Rica,* 1959. 4°.
                                   11454. f. 5.

CENTENO (FRANCISCO) *See* ARGENTINE REPUBLIC. [*Collections of Laws, etc.*] República Argentina. Tratados,
convenciones, protocolos, actos y acuerdos internacionales.
Publicación oficial. [Edited by F. Centeno.] 1911, *etc.* 8°.
                                   [MISSING.]

—— *See* BORRERO (F.) Descripcion de las Provincias del
Rio de la Plata, *etc.* [Edited by F. Centeno.] 1911. 8°.
                                   010480. h. 14.

—— *See* FERRÉ (P.) Epistolario de los Generales Ferré y
Paz, *etc.* [Edited by F. Centeno.] 1923. 8°.
                                   10906. c. 11

—— Catálogo de documentos del Archivo de Indias en Sevilla
referentes á la historia de la República Argentina 1778–
1820. [Edited by F. Centeno.] tom. 3. 1910. 8°. *See*
ARGENTINE REPUBLIC.—*Ministerio de Relaciones*
Exteriores.   **11908. h. 22.**

—— Catálogo de la Biblioteca, Mapoteca y Archivo.
Apéndice. Servicios prestados en la carrera diplomática
y administrativa, 1810–1910. [By F. Centeno, assisted
by J. B. Dizak. Third edition.] pp. xvii. 1053.
1910. 8°. *See* ARGENTINE REPUBLIC.—*Ministerio de*
Relaciones Exteriores.   **11906. k. 5.**

CENTENO (FRANCISCO)

—— Digesto de relaciones exteriores, 1810–1913. [With
plates.] pp. 385. 1913. 8°. *See* ARGENTINE REPUBLIC.
—*Ministerio de Relaciones Exteriores.*   **8179. f. 41.**

—— Precursores de la Diplomacia Argentina. Diputaciones
a Chile de Alvarez Jonte, Vera y Pintado y Paso, 1810–
1814. De la Revista de derecho, historia y letras, *etc.*
pp. vi. 4–253. *Buenos Aires,* 1920. 8°.   **9773. dd. 7.**

—— Virutas Históricas, 1810–1928. [A collection of documents from the archives of the Argentine Department of
Foreign Affairs. Edited by F. Centeno. With a portrait.]
3 vol. *Buenos Aires,* 1929, 35. 8°.   **9773. v. 1.**

CENTENO (GASPAR DE VILLALPANDO) *See* VILLALPANDO
CENTENO.

CENTENO (JOACHIN DE VILLALPANDO) *See* VILLALPANDO
CENTENO.

CENTENO (LÚCAS) *See* SALGUERO (P.) Vida del venerable padre . . . Fr. Diego Basalenque . . . Nuevamente
impressa con los autos de su translacion al Convento de
Santa María de Gracia de . . . Valladolid en la Nueva
España, por . . . L. Centeno, *etc.* 1761. 4°.
                                   4985. de. 18.

CENTENO (PEDRO) *See* CROISET (J.) Año Cristiano . . .
Adicionado con las vidas de los santos . . . que çelebra
la Iglesia de España, y que escribieron los PP. Fr. P.
Centeno y Fr. J. de Rojas, *etc.* 1853, *etc.* 8°.
                                   3456. ff. 1.

—— Oracion que en la solemne accion de gracias que tributa-
ron á Dios en la iglesia de San Felipe el Real de esta corte,
las pobres Niñas del Barrio de la Comadre asistentes á su
escuela gratuita, por haberlas vestido y dotado S. M. con
motivo de su exâltacion al trono . . . dixo . . . Fr. P.
Centeno . . . el dia 20 de setiembre de 1789. pp. 28.
Madrid, [1789.] 4°.   **12301. e. 3. (14.)**

CENTENO GRAÜ (M.) *See* VENEZUELA.—*Ministerio de*
Hacienda. Bosquejo Histórico de la Vida Fiscal de
Venezuela, *etc.* [With a preface by M. Centeno Graü.]
1924. 8°.   **8244. dd. 35.**

—— *See* VENEZUELA.—*Ministerio de Hacienda.* Historical
Sketch of the Fiscal Life of Venezuela, *etc.* [With a
preface by M. Centeno Graü.] 1925. 8°.   **8224. g. 26.**

—— Acueductos de Caracas. [With illustrations and diagrams.] pp. 38. *Caracas,* [1918.] fol.   **1763. a. 20.**

CENTENO Y GARCÍA (JOSÉ) Memoria geológico-
minera de las Islas Filipinas. [With a map.] pp. viii. 61.
1876. 8°. *See* SPAIN.—*Ministerio de Ultramar.*
                                   07109. m. 2. (8.)

CENTEOLA. Centeola, and other tales, by the author of
" Green Mountain Boys " [i.e. Daniel Pierce Thompson],
etc. pp. 312. *Carleton: New York,* 1864. 12°.
                                   12707. ccc. 21.

CENTER. *See* CENTRE.

CENTER (ALLEN HARRY)

—— *See* CUTLIP (Scott M.) and CENTER (A. H.) Effective
Public Relations, *etc.* 1953. 8°.   **8290. k. 9.**

CENTER (JOHN GILBERT BEEBE) *See* GARDINER (Harry N.)
Feeling and Emotion . . . By H. M. Gardiner . . .
J. G. Beebe-Center. [1937.] 8°.   **W.P. 11124/4.**

—— The Psychology of Pleasantness and Unpleasantness.
pp. viii. 427. *D. Van Nostrand Co.: New York,* 1932. 8°.
                                   08466. ff. 25.

CENTER (STELLA STEWART) The Worker and his Work. Readings in present-day literature . . . Compiled by Stella S. Center . . . Illustrated. pp. 350. *Philadelphia & London*, [1920.] 8º. [*Lippincott's School Text Series.*] **20019. c. 32/1.**

CENTER (STELLA STEWART) and PERSONS (GLADYS L.)

—— Teaching High-School Students to Read. A study of retardation in reading. [With plates.] pp. xviii. 167. *D. Appleton-Century Co.: New York, London,* [1937.] 8º. [*National Council of Teachers of English. English Monograph.* no. 6.] **W.P. 9202/6.**

CENTERS (RICHARD)

—— The Psychology of Social Classes. A study of class consciousness. pp. xii. 244. *Princeton University Press: Princeton, N.J.,* 1949. 8º. [*Studies in Public Opinion.* no. 1.] **W.P. 3560/1.**

CENTERWALL (BROR AUGUST) Konsten att resa. Teckningar av Gösta Chatham. pp. 195. *Stockholm,* 1932. 8º. **10026. cc. 32.**

—— Thespiskärran. Skildringar från landsortsteatern. pp. 98. *Malmö,* 1914. 8º. **12581. b. 47.**

CENTERWALL (JULIUS EBBE) *See* CICERO (M. T.) [*Orations.—Two or more Orations.—Swedish.*] Valda tal af Marcus Tullius Cicero. I svensk öfversättning J. Centerwall. 1871, *etc.* 8º. **11304. c. 8.**

—— *See* SPARTIANUS (A.) Spartiani Vita Hadriani commentario illustrata. Disputatio prior. Scripsit J. Centerwall. [With the text.] 1870. 8º. [*Upsala Universitets årsskrift.* 1870.] **Ac. 1075/6.**

—— Från Hellas och Levanten. Ströftåg till lands och vatten . . . Med 63 illustrationer . . . samt 8 kartor. pp. 421. *Stockholm,* 1888. 8º. **10125. de. 17.**

—— Romas kristna katakomber. pp. 130. *Stockholm,* 1881. 8º. [*Ur vår tids forskning.* no. 27.] **08709. d. 10. (27.)**

—— Romas ruiner. Vandringar inom den eviga stadens murar . . . Med . . . tonplanscher, *etc.* pp. 252. *Stockholm,* 1889. 8º. **7706. c. 43.**

—— En Slump. Komedi i tre akter, på vers. pp. 68. *Upsala,* 1867. 8º. **11754. bbb. 82. (3.)**

CENTGRAF (ALEXANDER)

—— Martin Luther als Publizist. Geist und Form seiner Volksführung. [With facsimiles.] pp. 94. viii. 1940. 8º. *See* BERLIN. — *Friedrich-Wilhelms-Universität.* — *Institut für Zeitungswissenschaft.* **3910. f. 46.**

CENTI (ANGELO) Cenni storici di Vezzano Ligure. (Statuti municipali di Vezzano Ligure, tradotti dall'originale latino-curialesco dal P. A. Centi.) pp. 304. *Genova,* 1898. 8º. **10132. e. 23.**

CENTI (ANTONIO CAVANILLES Y) *See* CAVANILLES Y CENTI.

CENTIFOLIEN. Centifolien. 100 auserlesene Vorträge . . . Gesammelt und herausgegeben von W. J. [1870.] 8º. *See* J., W. **11528. b. 50.**

CENTIFOLIUM. Centi-Folium Stultorum in Quarto. Oder Hundert ausbündige Narren, in Folio. Neu aufgewärmet, und . . . mit hundert schönen Kupfer-Stichen . . . aufgesetzt, *etc.* pp. 404. *J. C. Megerle: Wienn,* [1709.] 4º. **1456. f. 12.**

CENTINELA. El Centinela. *See* PERIODICAL PUBLICATIONS.—*Mexico.*

—— Centinela Alerta, o Argos americano en favor de su patrio suelo. [Signed: C. A. G.] 1821. 4º. *See* G., C. A. **9770. bb. 6. (31.)**

—— Centinela contra serviles. [Signed: F. M., i.e. F. Merino.] 1820. 4º. *See* M., F. **9770. bb. 27. (12.)**

—— Noticia estraordinaria del reconocimiento de la independencia de México por España. [Signed: El Centinela.] *México,* 1833. *s. sh.* fol. **9770. k. 11. (174.)**

CENTINUS (MARCELLUS) Marcelli Centini Ode in D. Petrum Riccium. *See* RICCIUS (P.) *Archipresbyter S. Hieronymi Illyricorum.* Oratorij ac poetici plausus, *etc.* 1615. 4º. **10630. e. 13. (7.)**

CENTIO (ALESSANDRO) L'Amico infedele. Comedia. pp. 156. *P. Saluioni: Macerata,* 1617. 12º. **638. a. 22. (2.)**

—— Il Padre afflitto, commedia, *etc.* ff. 87. *Appresso S. Martellini: Macerata,* 1578. 8º. **162. f. 23.**

—— [Another edition.] ff. 84. *A. dei Vecchi: Venetia,* 1606. 12º. **638. a. 22. (1.)**

—— [Another copy.] **162. a. 41.**

CENTKIEWICZ (CZESŁAW JACEK)

—— *See* CENTKIEWICZÓWNA (A.) and CENTKIEWICZ (C. J.) W lodach Eisfiordu. 1953. 8º. **010460. pp. 20.**

—— Wyspa mgieł i wichrów. Pierwsza polska ekspedycja narodowa roku polarnego 1932/33. pp. 313. *Warszawa,* 1934. 8º. **010460. f. 31.**

CENTKIEWICZÓWNA (ALINA) and CENTKIEWICZ (CZESŁAW JACEK)

—— W lodach Eisfiordu. pp. 300. *Warszawa,* 1953. 8º. **010460. pp. 20.**

CENTLIVER (SUSANNA) *See* CARROLL, afterwards CENTLIVRE.

CENTLIVRE (SUSANNA) *See* CARROLL, afterwards CENTLIVRE.

CENTLIVRES (ROBERT)

—— Nicolas de Flue. L'histoire et la légende. [With illustrations.] pp. 143. *Genève,* 1947. 8º. **4830. h. 67.**

CENTNER (ÉDOUARD) Faculté de Droit de Paris. Droit romain. Du legs de la dot, et en général de la chose due. Droit français. Le divorce et la séparation de corps en droit international privé . . . Thèse pour le doctorat, *etc.* pp. 241. *Paris,* 1893. 8º. **5406. e. 6.**

CENTNERSZWEROWA (R.)

—— *See* GALSWORTHY (John) Saga rodu Forsytów. (Tłumaczyła R. Centnerszwerowa.) 1948, *etc.* 8º. **W.P. 3641.**

CENTNERUS (GODOFREDUS) Q. Septimii Florentis Tertulliani quæ supersunt omnia in Montanismo scripta videri . . . edisseruit G. Centerus. 1853. *See* TERTULLIANUS (Q. S. F.) [*Works.—Latin.*] Quinti Septimii Florentis Tertulliani quæ supersunt omnia, *etc.* tom. 3. 1853, *etc.* 8º. **3627. e. 12.**

CENTO. The Cento: a selection of approved pieces, from living authors. pp. ix. 312. *John Richardson: London,* 1822. 8º. **12350. f. 12.**

CENTO.

—— The Cento: being a collection of choice extracts, from the most approved authors, *etc.* pp. 161.   *J. Fox: Pontefract*, 1798. 8°.   **8408. b. 25.**

—— Centonis κακορραφια. [By S. Curtaudus? In reply to the " Navicula solis " of J. Bérault.] pp. 4. [1645 ?] 4°.   **551. b. 8. (3.)**

—— Centonis κακορραφιας diffibulatio, in qua pleraque diplomata Pontificia & Regia Academiæ Monspeliensis falsi conuincuntur. [By René Moreau. In reply to " Centonis κακορραφια," sometimes attributed to S. Curtaudus.] pp. 31.   *Parisiis*, 1646. 4°.   **551. b. 8. (4.)**

—— Appendix ad Centonis κακορραφιας diffibulationem. [By René Moreau.] pp. 11. 1646. 4°.   **551. b. 8. (4*.)**

CENTO. Le Pitture di Cento, con alcuni ritratti e costumi de' celebri pittori centesi. *Bologna*, 1792. 12°.   [MISSING.]

—— *Biblioteca Comunale.* Cenni storici sulla Biblioteca comunale di Cento. Bibliografia delle opere rare, *etc.* [By A. Pellegrini.] pp. 61.   *Lucca*, 1901. 8°.   **011907. i. 7.**

—— Gli Incunabuli della Biblioteca comunale di Cento, con l'aggiunta di alcuni codici ed incunabuli posseduti dal comm. Antonio Maiocchi. [By L. Sighinolfi.] pp. viii. 58.   *Bologna*, 1906. 8°.   **11909. r. 8. (6.)**

CENTO (FERNANDO) La Pedagogia nel pensiero di Dante Alighieri, *etc.* pp. xx. 84.   *Macerata*, [1921.] 8°.   **011420. c. 23. (7.)**

—— [Another edition.] Il Pensiero educativo di Dante. 2ª edizione riveduta, *etc.* pp. xix. 88.   *Milano*, 1925. 8°.   **011420. dd. 26.**

CENTO (VINCENZO) Religione e morale nel pensiero di Giovanni Gentile. [With a portrait.] pp. 92.   *Roma*, 1923. 8°. [*Quaderni di " Bilychnis."* no. 15.]   **P.P. 23. ebc. (2.)**

CENTOCULI (ARGUS) *pseud.* Old England; or, the Broadbottom Journal. By Argus Centoculi. no. 179–193, 140–366. 4 Oct. 1746—30 March 1751. 1746–51 *See* PERIODICAL PUBLICATIONS.—*London.* Old England or, the Constitutional Journal, *etc.* 1743, *etc.* fol.   Burney.

CENTOFANTI (LEOPOLDI TANFANI) *See* TANFANI CENTO-FANTI.

CENTOFANTI (SILVESTRO) *See* BIONDI (D.) Un Dimenticato. Silvestro Centofanti nella vita e nell'opera letteraria. 1921. 8°.   **011850. aa. 23.**

—— *See* GALLI (A.) Ricordi di illustri Italiani . . . Silvestro Centofanti, A. Vannucci, *etc.* 1886. 8°.   **10629. a. 25.**

—— La Letteratura greca, dalle sue origini fino alla caduta di Constantinopoli, e Studio sopra Pitagora. pp. 425. *Firenze*, 1870. 12°.   **11852. bbb. 17.**

—— Al Commento di Francesco da Buti sopra la Divina Commedia introduzione. pp. 20.   *Pisa*, 1858. 4°.   **11420. g. 19. (1.)**

—— Alla santità di Pio IX, pontefice massimo, e al popolo romano dopo la congiura felicemente scoperta e vinta Silvestro Centofanti con animo italiano ed in versi inspirati dalle cose congratulando applaudiva. pp. 13. *Pisa*, 1847. 8°.   **11436. c. 48. (5.)**

CENTOFANTI (SILVESTRO)

—— La Civiltà e la poesia nella Divina Commedia. Discorso. *See* DANTE ALIGHIERI. [*General Appendix.—Biography and Criticism.*] Dante e il suo secolo. vol. 1. 1865, *etc.* 4°.   **1871. d. 9. (10.)**

—— Dante autore e maestro alla Italia della sua nazionale letteratura. Discorso, *etc.* 1866. *See* DANTE ALIGHIERI. [*General.—Biography and Criticism.*] Dante e il suo secolo. vol. 2. 1865, *etc.* 4°.   **1871. d. 9. (44.)**

—— Un Preludio al corso di lezioni su Dante Alighieri. [An essay " Pei giovani poeti italiani " followed by " Stanze su Dante Alighieri già scritte in occasione del monumento inalzato in S. Croce " and " A Vittore Hugo. Ode."] pp. lxx. 50.   *Firenze*, 1838. 8°.   **11422. ff. 29. (1.)**

—— [Another copy.]   **1062. g. 23.**

—— [Another copy.]   **011420. d. 34.**

—— Saggio sulla vita e sulle opere di Plutarco. pp. cxc. *See* PLUTARCH. [*Vitae Parallelae.—Italian.*] Le Vite parallele di Plutarco, *etc.* vol. 1. 1845, *etc.* 12°.   **10605. c. 1.**

—— Sopra Frate Ilario. Lettera . . . ad Alessandro Torri. *See* DANTE ALIGHIERI. [*General Appendix.—Biography and Criticism.*] Studi inediti su Dante Alighieri, *etc.* 1846. 8°.   **1463. g. 9.**

—— Sopra un luogo (Inferno, canto 1, versi 8 e 9) diversamente letto nella Divina Commedia. Lettera, *etc.* (Estratto dai N. 20, 21, 22 e 23 dello Spettatore.) pp. 82. *Firenze*, 1856. 16°.   **11420. aa. 4. (1.)**

—— Sull'indole e le vicende della letteratura greca. Discorso. *See* GREEK POETS. I Poeti greci, *etc.* 1841. 4°.   **1338, n. 1.**

—— Sulla Vita nuova di Dante. Lezione ultima. (Dall'Euganeo.) pp. 20.   *Padova*, 1845. 8°.   **011421. bbb. 19.**

CENTOFLORENIUS (LUDOVICUS) *See* LAURO (G.) Ciuitatis Nouæ in Piceno delineatio . . . vna cum disputatione D. Abbatis Ludouici Centoflorenij super dubio an idem locus sit vere ciuitas, quamuis sede episcopali careat. 1630. 4°.   **659. c. 12. (7.)**

—— Clypeus Lauretanus aduersus hæreticorum sagittas. pp. 204.   *Typis F. Caballi: Romæ*, 1643. 4°.   **1230. c. 38.**

The titlepage is engraved.

CENTOLA (LUIGI) La Pena del duella estesa ai militari e la riforma del tribunale militare in tribunale misto, *etc.* pp. xviii. 80.   *Roma*, 1875. 8°.   **08425. e. 6.**

CENTOLINUS (FAMIANUS) *See* ROME, Church of.—*Rota.* Decisiones Rotæ CXL . . . Quibus etiam accesserunt additiones . . . F. Centolini, *etc.* 1606. fol.   **495. k. 5. (2.)**

—— —— 1682. fol.   [*Dn. Prosperi Farinacii . . . opera omnia, etc.* vol. 4.]   **711. g. 8.**

CENTOMO (LUIGI) Cenni sulla difteria curata coi solfiti. Memoria, *etc.* pp. 105.   *Vicenza*, 1869. 8°.   **7561. h. 39.**

CENTON (FRANCESCO) Oratione. *See* MICHELE (A.) Le Glorie immortali del Serᵐᵒ Prencipe di Vinegia Mariano Grimani descritte in dodici . . . orationi, *etc.* 1596. 4°.   **T. 2279. (1.)**

CENTONA (PROBA) *See* FALCONIA PROBA (V.)

CENTONE (HIERONYMO) *See* PETRARCA (F.) [*Canzoniere.—Italian.*] *Begin.* [pt. 1. fol. 2 *recto*:] Tabula. Per informatione & dechiaratione di questa tabula, *etc. End.* [pt. 2. fol. 101 *verso*:] Finisse gli sonetti di Misser Franceschо Petrarcha coreti & castigati per me Hieronymo Centone, *etc.* 1490. fol.   **C. 4. i. 5.**

CENTONE (HIERONYMO)

—— —— 1492. fol.   IB. 20866.

—— —— 1492, etc. fol.   86. k. 17.

—— —— 1494. fol.   IB. 24159.

—— —— 1497. fol.   IB. 23725.

CENTONZA (RAFFAELE) I Più comuni vocaboli e modi errati della lingua italiana raccolti . . . sulle opere di Rodinò, Ugolini . . . ed altri filologi. pp. 72. *Napoli,* 1879. 16°.   **12941. a. 47.**

CENTORE-BINEAU (D.) Saint-Just, 1767-1794 . . . Avec un fac-similé et douze gravures [including portraits], *etc.* pp. 292. *Paris,* 1936. 8°.   **010665. h. 17.**

CENTORIE (ASCAIGNE) *See* CENTORIO DEGLI HORTENSII (Ascanio)

CENTORIO-D'AVOGADRE (LOUIS) *Count. See* LE TOUZÉ DE LONGUEMAR (A.) Coup d'œil sur une correspondance inédite . . . contenant les lettres du comte Louis Centorio d'Avogadre, *etc.* 1860. 8°. **8828. i. 23.**

CENTORIO DEGLI HORTENSII (ASCANIO) *See* BANDELLO (M.) *Bishop of Agen.* [*Novelle.—Collections.*] Il Primo(—terzo) volume delle nouelle del Bandello . . . Con vna aggiunta d'alcuni sensi morali dal S. A. Centorio de gli Hortensii, *etc.* 1560. 8°.   **1074. f. 18-20.**

—— —— 1566. 4°.   **1074. g. 17.**

—— Le Amorose Rime di M. Ascanio Centorio. ff. 47. *Per M. Pagan: Venetia,* 1553. 8°.   **239. c. 30.**

—— I Cinque Libri degl'Auuertimenti, Ordini, Gride, et Editti: fatti, et osseruati in Milano, ne' tempi sospettosi della peste; ne gli anni MDLXXVI. et LXXVII. . . . Raccolte dal cavagliero A. Centorio de' Hortensii, *etc.* pp. 454. *Appresso G. & G. P. Giolito de' Ferrari: Vinegia,* 1579. 4°.   **26. h. 6.**

—— [Another edition. With a dedication by G. B. Bidelli.] pp. 380. *G. B. Bidelli: Milano,* 1631. 4°.   **1167. k. 34.**

—— Commentarii della guerra di Transilvania . . . ne quali si contengono tutte le cose, che successero nell'Vngheria dalla rotta del re Lodouico XII. sino all'anno MDLIII, *etc.* (La seconda parte de' Commentarii delle guerre, & de' successi più notabili, auuenuti così in Europa come in tutte le parti del mondo dall'anno MDLIII fino à tutto il MDLX, *etc.*) 2 pt. MS. NOTES. *Appresso G. Giolito de' Ferrari: Vinegia,* 1566, 69. 4°.   **281. i. 15.**

—— [Another copy of pt. 1.] FEW MS. NOTES. **1056. l. 4.**

—— Commentarii della guerra di Transilvania. Riproduzione fotografica con un saggio introduttivo di Ladislao Gáldi. [A facsimile of the edition of 1566.] pp. xi. 266. *Budapest,* 1940. 8°.   **09315. l. 15.**

—— Memoires de la guerre de Transilvanie & de Hongrie entre l'Empereur Leopold I & le Grand Seigneur Mehemet IV, Georges Ragotski & les autres successeurs Princes de Transilvanie. [By A. Centorio degli Hortensii.] 2 tom. 1680. 12°. *See* TRANSYLVANIA. [*Appendix.— Historical.*]   **9314. a. 2.**

—— Harangues militaires . . . recueillies des quatre liures de la guerre de Transsyluanie. *See* BELLEFOREST (F. de) Harangues militaires, *etc.* 1572. fol. **M.L.tt.4.**

—— Il Primo(—quinto) Discorso di Messer Ascanio Centorio sopra l'ufficio d'un capitano generale di essercito. 5 pt. *Appresso G. Giolito de Ferrari: Vinegia,* 1558-62. 4°.   **58. e. 8.**

—— Discorsi di guerra . . . diuisi in cinque libri, *etc.* 5 pt. *Gabriel Giolito de' Ferrari: Vinegia,* 1568, 59, 62. 4°.   **1476. aaa. 42.**
Pt. 1–3 are reissues of the edition published in 1566. Pt. 4, 5, which were not printed again after 1559 and 1562 respectively, are taken from the editions of those years.

CENTORIO DEGLI HORTENSII (ASCANIO)

—— [Another copy.] Discorsi di guerra . . . divisi in cinque libri, *etc. Vinegia,* 1568. 4°.   **1481. c. 38.** *Imperfect; containing Discorso 1–3 only.*

—— I Grandi apparati e feste fatte in Melano dalli Illust. & Eccell. S. il S. Duca di Sessa . . . & S. Marchese di Pescara . . . in casa dell'Illustr. S. Gio. Battista Castaldo, Marchese di Cassano. ff. 32. *Appresso di G. Antonio di gli Antonij: Melano,* 1559. 8°.   **9930. a. 18.** [*sic.*]

—— L'Aura soaue di M. Ascanio Centorio. pp. 226. *Appresso G. Giolito de' Ferrari & Fratelli: Vinegia,* 1556. 8°.   **241. d. 10.**

CENTRAAL-AMERIKA. *See* AMERICA, *Central.*

CENTRAAL BUREAU. Centraal Bureau voor de Kennis van de Provincie Groningen en Omgelegen Streken. *See* GRONINGEN.—*Natuurkundig Genootschap te Groningen.*

—— Centraal Bureau voor de Statistiek. *See* NETHERLANDS. —*Kingdom of the Netherlands.*

—— Centraal Bureau voor Maatschappelijk Hulpbetoon. *See* AMSTERDAM.

—— Centraal Bureau voor Nederlandse en Friese Dialecten. *See* AMSTERDAM.—*Koninklijke Akademie van Wetenschappen,* afterwards *Koninklijke Nederlandse Akademie van Wetenschappen.*

—— Centraal Bureau voor Schimmelcultures. *See* BAARN.

—— Centraal bureau voor Sociale Adviezen. *See* NETHERLANDS.—*Kingdom of the Netherlands.*

CENTRAAL INSTITUUT.

—— Centraal Instituut voor Industrieontwikkeling. *See* NETHERLANDS.—*Kingdom of the Netherlands.*

—— Centraal Instituut voor Landbouwkundig Onderzoek. *See* WAGENINGEN.

—— Centraal Instituut voor Materiaalonderzoek. *See* NETHERLANDS. [Kingdom of the Netherlands.]—*Nederlandse Centrale Organisatie voor Toegepast-Natuurwetenschappelijk Onderzoek.*

CENTRAAL MUSEUM. Centraal Museum te Utrecht. *See* UTRECHT.

CENTRAAL PLANBUREAU.   *See* NETHERLANDS. [*Kingdom of the Netherlands.*]

CENTRAAL TECHNISCH INSTITUUT.

—— Centraal Technisch Instituut T.N.D. *See* NETHERLANDS. [Kingdom of the Netherlands.]—*Nederlandse Centrale Organisatie voor Toegepast-Natuurwetenschappelijk Onderzoek.*

CENTRAAL VEE-ARTSENIJKUNDIG GENOOTSCHAP. *See* NETHERLANDS.—*Nederlands Veeartsenijkundig Genootschap.*

CENTRAL. The Central. *See* LONDON.—III. *City and Guilds of London Institute for the Advancement of Technical Education.—City and Guilds (Engineering) College.—Old Students' Association.*

CENTRAL-. *See also* ZENTRAL-.

CENTRAL ADVISORY COUNCIL.

—— Central Advisory Council for Education (England). *See* ENGLAND.—*Board of Education,* afterwards *Ministry of Education.*

CENTRAL ADVISORY COUNCIL.

—— Central Advisory Council for the Spiritual Care of the Deaf and Dumb. *See* ENGLAND.—*Church of England.—National Assembly.*

—— Central Advisory Council of Training for the Ministry. *See* ENGLAND.—*Church of England.—National Assembly.*

CENTRAL ADVISORY WATER COMMITTEE. *See* ENGLAND.—*Board of Agriculture and Fisheries.*

CENTRAL AEROHYDRODYNAMICAL INSTITUTE.

—— Central Aerohydrodynamical Institute in the Name of prof. Joukovsky. *See* MOSCOW.—*Центральный Аэрогидродинамическій Институтъ имени Н. Е. Жуковскаго.*

CENTRAL AFRICA. *See also* AFRICA, *Central.*

—— Central Africa; a monthly record of the work of the Universities' Mission. *See* AFRICA, *Central.—Universities' Mission to Central Africa.*

CENTRAL AFRICAN AND EAST AFRICAN WHO'S WHO.

—— The Central African, and East African, Who's Who. *See* PERIODICAL PUBLICATIONS.—*Salisbury, Southern Rhodesia.*

CENTRAL AFRICAN ARCHIVES.

Government Archives of Southern Rhodesia, 1935–1946.
Central African Archives, 1946– .

—— Central African Archives in Retrospect and Prospect. (Archives in a New Era.) A report by the Chief Archivist (V. W. Hiller) for the years ending 31 August 1947. (30 June 1954.) [With plates.] *Salisbury,* 1947–55. 8°.
C.S. c. **610.**

—— Oppenheimer Series. *London,* 1945– . 8°.
W.P. **8538.**

—— The Story of Nyasaland. Told in a series of historical pictures to commemorate the diamond jubilee of Nyasaland, 1891–1951. Descriptive souvenir and catalogue. (Produced by V. W. Hiller.) [With plates.] pp. 95. [*Salisbury, Rhodesia;*] *Glasgow* printed, 1951. 8°.
09062. cc. **26.**

CENTRAL AFRICAN CLASSIFIED DIRECTORY. *See* DIRECTORIES.—*Africa, Central.*

CENTRAL AFRICAN COUNCIL.

—— Fauna of British East and Central Africa. Proceedings of a Conference held at the Victoria Falls on 18th and 19th September, 1950. pp. 52. *Lusaka,* 1950. 8°.
C.S.D.634.

—— Report of the Central African Council. Presented to the Legislative Assembly [of Southern Rhodesia], 1947 pp. 32. 1947. fol. *See* RHODESIA, *Southern.* [*Miscellaneous Official Publications.*] C.S. D. **331/13.**

—— Regional Organisation of Research in the Rhodesias and Nyasaland. A report to the Central African Council by Dr. J. E. Keyston. pp. 91. *Salisbury,* 1948. fol.
C.S.D.634/2.

Standing Committee on African Housing.
—— Report on African Housing. [With plans.] pp. 20. [*Salisbury,*] 1949. fol. **C.S.D.640.**

CENTRAL AFRICAN JUBILEE. A Central African Jubilee, *etc.* [An account of the F. S. Arnot Jubilee Conference at Muchacha.] [1932.] 8°. *See* MUCHACHA. —*F. S. Arnot Jubilee Conference.* **4764.** bb. **28.**

CENTRAL AFRICAN MISSION. *See* AFRICA, *Central.—Universities' Mission to Central Africa.*

CENTRAL AFRICAN STATISTICAL OFFICE. *See* RHODESIA, *Southern.*

CENTRAL AGRICULTURAL BOARD.

—— Central Agricultural Board of Trinidad. *See* TRINIDAD AND TOBAGO, *Colony of.*

CENTRAL ALLIANCE. Central Alliance of Transylvanian Saxons of the United States. *See* UNITED STATES OF AMERICA.

CENTRAL AMERICA. *See* AMERICA, *Central.*

CENTRAL AMERICAN. Reflexiones sobre la Necesidad de una Reforma política en Centro-América. Escritas por un Centro-Americano [i.e. Marquis J. J. de Aycinena]. pp. 16. *New-Amsterdam,* 1832. 8°. **8180.** cc. **2.** (3.)

—— Otras Reflexiones sobre Reforma política en Centro-América. [Signed: Un Centro-Americano, i.e. Marquis J. J. de Aycinena.] pp. 21. [*Philadelphia,* 1833.] 8°.
8180. cc. **2.** (4.)

—— Otras Reflexiones sobre Reforma política en Centro-América. [Signed: Un Centro-Americano, i.e. Marquis J. J. de Aycinena.] pp. 45. [1834.] 8°. *See* AYCINENA (J. J. de) *Marquis.* **8180.** cc. **2.** (5.)

CENTRAL AMERICAN PEACE CONFERENCE. *See* WASHINGTON, *D.C.*

CENTRAL AND ASSOCIATED CHAMBERS OF AGRICULTURE. *See* LONDON.—III. *Central Chamber of Agriculture.*

CENTRAL AND EASTERN EUROPEAN CONFERENCE.

—— Human Freedom is being crushed. The story of deportations behind the Iron Curtain. pp. 80. *Washington,* 1951. 8°. **8029.** g. **16.**

CENTRAL AND SOUTH AMERICAN COMMISSION. *See* UNITED STATES OF AMERICA.

CENTRAL AND SOUTH-EAST SCOTLAND REGIONAL PLANNING ADVISORY COMMITTEE. *See* SCOTLAND.

CENTRAL ANTI-MAYNOOTH COMMITTEE. *See* LONDON.—III.

CENTRAL-ARCHIV. *See* CENTRALARCHIV.

CENTRAL ASIA.

—— Архитектура республик Средней Азии, *etc.* 1951. 8°. *See* VEIMARN (B. V.) Ac. **1106.** k/7. (1.)

CENTRAL ASIAN MISSION. *See* LONDON.—III.

CENTRAL ASIAN PIONEER MISSION.
See LONDON.—III. *Central Asian Mission.*

CENTRAL ASIAN PRAYER FELLOWSHIP. *See* LONDON.—III.

CENTRAL ASIAN QUESTION. The Central Asian Question, from an Eastern stand-point. pp. 85. *Williams & Norgate: London,* 1868. 8°. **8028.** bb. **25.** *Printed for private circulation.*

CENTRAL ASIAN QUESTION.

—— [Another edition.] pp. 112.   *Williams & Norgate :* London, 1869. 8°.   **8022. bbb. 29.**

CENTRAL ASIAN RESEARCH CENTRE.   *See* LONDON.—III.

CENTRAL ASIAN REVIEW. *See* LONDON.—III. *Central Asian Research Centre.*

CENTRAL ASIAN SOCIETY. *See* LONDON.—III.

CENTRAL ASIATIC JOURNAL. *See* PERIODICAL PUBLICATIONS.—*The Hague.*

CENTRAL ASSOCIATION. Central Association, Cape Colony. *See* CAPE OF GOOD HOPE.—*Central Farmers Association.*

—— Central Association for Mental Welfare. *See* ENGLAND. —*Central Association for the Care of the Mentally Defective, etc.*

—— Central Association for Stopping the Sale of Intoxicating Liquors on Sunday. *See* ENGLAND.

—— Central Association for the Care of the Mentally Defective. *See* ENGLAND.

—— Central Association in Aid of Soldiers' Wives and Families. *See* LONDON.—III.

—— Central Association of Accountants. *See* LONDON.—III.

—— Central Association of Agricultural and Tenant-Right Valuers. *See* ENGLAND.

—— Central Association of Agricultural Valuers. *See* ENGLAND.—*Central Association of Agricultural and Tenant-Right Valuers,* afterwards *Central Association of Agricultural Valuers.*

—— Central Association of Miners' Permanent Relief Societies. *See* ENGLAND.

—— Central Association of Photographic Societies affiliated with the Royal Photographic Society of Great Britain. *See* ENGLAND.

—— Central Association of University Extension Students. *See* LONDON.—III. *University Extension Guild.*

—— Central Association Volunteer Regiments. *See* LONDON. —III. *Central Association Volunteer Training Corps.*

—— Central Association Volunteer Training Corps. *See* LONDON.—III.

CENTRAL-AUSSCHUSS. *See* CENTRALAUSSCHUSS.

CENTRAL AUSTRALIA. *See* AUSTRALIA, *Central.*

CENTRAL AUSTRALIAN MUSEUM.

—— Central Australian Museum (Scientific). *See* ALICE SPRINGS.

CENTRAL BANK.

—— Central Bank of Ceylon. *See* CEYLON.

—— Central Bank of Ireland. *See* IRELAND.—*Irish Free State.*

CENTRAL BANK OF CEYLON BULLETIN. *See* CEYLON.—*Central Bank of Ceylon.*

CENTRAL BIBLE TRUTH DEPOT. *See* LONDON. —III.

CENTRAL-BIBLIOTHEK. *See* CENTRALBIBLIOTHEK.

CENTRAL-BLATT. *See* CENTRALBLATT.

CENTRAL BOARD. Central Board for Conscientious Objectors. *See* LONDON.—III.

—— Central Board for the Relief of Destitution in the Highlands and Islands of Scotland. *See* SCOTLAND.

—— Central Board of Health. *See* ENGLAND.

—— Central Board of Health of Jamaica. *See* JAMAICA.

—— Central Board of Missions. *See* ENGLAND.—*Church of England.*

—— Central Board of the Trade Protection Societies. *See* LONDON.—III.

CENTRAL BRITISH FUND.

—— Central British Fund for Jewish Relief and Rehabilitation. *See* ENGLAND.

CENTRAL BRITISH RED CROSS COMMITTEE. *See* LONDON.—III.

CENTRAL BUREAU. Central Bureau for Animal Husbandry and Dairying. *See* INDIA.—*Department of Agriculture.*

—— Central Bureau for Church Crusades. *See* ENGLAND.— *Industrial Christian Fellowship.—Church Crusades Committee.*

—— Central Bureau for the Employment of Women. *See* LONDON.—III.

—— Central Bureau of Hospital Information. *See* LONDON. —III.

—— Central Bureau of Minorities. *See* GENEVA.—*Bureau Central des Minorités.*

—— Central Bureau of Political Information. *See* LONDON. —III.

CENTRAL BUSINESS COLLEGE. *See* TORONTO.

CENTRAL BUSINESS DISTRICT COUNCIL. *See* WASHINGTON, *D.C.—Urban Land Institute.*

CENTRAL CAMPAIGN COMMITTEE. Central Campaign Committee for the Disestablishment of the Church of England in Wales. *See* LONDON.—III.

CENTRAL CATHOLIC LIBRARY ASSOCIATION. *See* DUBLIN.

CENTRAL CHAMBER. Central Chamber of Agriculture. *See* LONDON.—III.

CENTRAL CHINA WESLEYAN METHODIST LAY MISSION. *See* CHINA.

CENTRAL CHINA WESLEYAN MISSION PRAYER UNION. *See* CHINA.

CENTRAL CHURCH COMMITTEE. Central Church Committee for Defence and Instruction. *See* ENGLAND.— *Church of England.—Church Committee for Church Defence and Church Instruction, etc.*

CENTRAL CHURCH FUND. *See* ENGLAND.—*Church of England.*

CENTRAL CHURCHES GROUP. *See* ENGLAND.

CENTRAL-COMITÉ. *See* CENTRALCOMITÉ.

CENTRAL COMMISSION.

—— Central Commission for Investigation of German Crimes in Poland. *See* POLAND.—*Główna Komisja Badania Zbrodni Niemieckich.*

CENTRAL COMMITTEE. Central Committee for Church Crusades. *See* ENGLAND.—*Industrial Christian Fellowship.—Church Crusades Committee.*

—— Central Committee for Jewish Education. *See* LONDON.—III. *Jewish War Memorial.*

—— Central Committee for National Patriotic Organizations *See* LONDON.—III.

—— Central Committee for the Care of Cripples. *See* LONDON.—III.

—— Central Committee for the Holy Year, 1950. *See* VATICAN.—*Comitato Centrale per l' Anno Santo, 1950.*

—— Central Committee for the Protection of Churches. *See* ENGLAND.—*Church of England.—Central Council for the Care of Churches.*

—— Central Committee for the Survey and Study of British Vegetation. *See* ENGLAND.

—— Central Committee, Lower Provinces, for the Collection of Works of Industry and Art for the Paris Universal Exhibition of 1867. *See* BENGAL.

—— Central Committee of Mining Researches. *See* RUSSIA.—*Центральный Комитетъ Промышленныхъ Развѣдокъ.*

—— Central Committee of Poor Law Conferences. *See* ENGLAND.

—— Central Committee of Schoolmasters. *See* LONDON.—III.

—— Central Committee of Scottish Business Clubs. *See* EDINBURGH.

—— Central Committee of the Citizens' Advice Bureaux. *See* ENGLAND.

—— Central Committee of Women's Church Work. *See* ENGLAND.—*Church of England.*

—— Central Committee on Camping Legislation. *See* LONDON.—III.

—— Central Committee on Policy and Political Education. *See* ENGLAND.—*National Union of Conservative and Constitutional Associations.*

CENTRAL CONCESSIONS COMMITTEE. Central Concessions Committee of the U.S.S.R. *See* RUSSIA.—*Совѣтъ Труда и Обороны.—Главный Концессіонный Комитетъ.*

CENTRAL CONFERENCE. Central Conference of American Rabbis. *See* UNITED STATES OF AMERICA.

—— Central Conference of Women Workers. *See* ENGLAND.—*National Council of Women of Great Britain.*

CENTRAL CONFERENCE COUNCIL.

—— Central Conference Council of the National Union of Women Workers. *See* ENGLAND.—*National Council of Women of Great Britain.*

CENTRAL CONTROL BOARD (LIQUOR TRAFFIC). *See* ENGLAND.

CENTRAL CO-OPERATIVE AGENCY. *See* LONDON.—III.

CENTRAL CO-OPERATIVE BOARD. *See* MANCHESTER.

CENTRAL CO-ORDINATING COMMITTEE.

—— Central Co-ordinating Committee of Refugee Welfare Organisations in Great Britain. *See* ENGLAND.

CENTRAL CO-ORDINATING COMMITTEE.

—— Central Co-ordinating Committee of Societies within the Church of England. *See* ENGLAND.—*Church of England*

CENTRAL COUNCIL. Central Council for District Nursing in London. *See* LONDON.—III.

—— Central Council for Health Education. *See* LONDON.—III.

—— Central Council for Jewish Education in the United Kingdom and Eire. *See* ENGLAND.

—— Central Council for Jewish Refugees. *See* CENTRAL COUNCIL FOR JEWISH REFUGEES.

—— Central Council for Rivers Protection. *See* ENGLAND.

—— Central Council for School Broadcasting. *See* ENGLAND.

—— Central Council for the Care of Churches. *See* ENGLAND.—*Church of England.*

—— Central Council for the Care of Cripples. *See* LONDON.—III.

—— Central Council for Women's Church Work. *See* ENGLAND.—*Church of England.*

—— Central Council for Works and Buildings. *See* ENGLAND.—*Ministry of Works.*

—— Central Council of Anglo-Polish Societies. *See* LONDON.—III.

—— Central Council of Church Bell Ringers. *See* LONDON.—III.

—— Central Council of Economic Leagues. *See* LONDON.—III.

—— Central Council of English, Scottish and Irish Railway Stockholders' Protection Associations. *See* LONDON.—III.

—— Central Council of Jewish Religious Education in the United Kingdom and Eire. *See* ENGLAND.—*Central Council for Jewish Religious Education, etc.*

—— Central Council of National Dog Week. *See* LONDON.—III. *National Dog Week Council.*

—— Central Council of Physical Recreation. *See* LONDON.—III.

—— Central Council of Recreative Physical Training. *See* LONDON.—III.

—— Central Council of the Church for Religious Education. *See* ENGLAND.—*Church of England.—National Society for Promoting the Education of the Poor in the Principles of the Established Church, etc.*

—— Central Council of Trade Unions of the U.S.S.R. *See* RUSSIA.—*Всероссійскій Центральный Совѣтъ Профессіональныхъ Союзовъ.*

—— Central Council of Voluntary Social Services. *See* KINGSTON, *Jamaica.*

CENTRAL COUNCIL FOR JEWISH REFUGEES.

Council for German Jewry, 1936–39.
Central Council for Jewish Refugees, 1939–44.
Incorporated in the Central British Fund for Jewish Relief and Rehabilitation, 1944.

CENTRAL COUNCIL FOR JEWISH REFUGEES.

—— Council for German Jewry. Report for 1936(–1938).
3 pt. [*London*, 1937–39.] 4º.
[Continued as :]
Central Council for Jewish Refugees. Report for 1939
(1940). 2 pt. *London*, [1940, 41.] 4º. P.P. **954.** caf.

CENTRAL CRIMINAL COURT. *See* LONDON.—
II. *Sessions.*

CENTRAL DORSETSHIRE COMMITTEE. *See*
DORSET.

CENTRAL ELECTRICITY AUTHORITY. *See*
ENGLAND.

CENTRAL ELECTRICITY BOARD. *See* ENGLAND.

CENTRAL EMPLOYMENT BUREAU. Central Employment Bureau for Women. *See* LONDON.—III. *Central
Bureau for the Employment of Women, etc.*

CENTRAL EUROPE. *See* EUROPE, *Central.*

CENTRAL EUROPEAN FEDERALIST.

—— The Central European Federalist. *See* NEW YORK.
Czechoslovak-Polish Research Committee.

CENTRAL EUROPEAN TRADE REVIEW.

—— *See* LONDON.—III. *British-Central European Chamber of
Commerce.* Bulletin.

CENTRAL EXPERIMENTAL FARM, *Ottawa.* *See*
OTTAWA.

CENTRAL FARMERS ASSOCIATION, *Cape Colony.*
See CAPE OF GOOD HOPE.

CENTRAL FEDERATION. Central Federation of
Nippon Culture. *See* JAPAN.—*Nippon Cultural Federation.*

CENTRAL FILM LIBRARY. *See* ENGLAND.—*Central
Office of Information.*

CENTRAL FIRE BRIGADES ADVISORY COUNCIL. *See* ENGLAND.—*Home Office.*

CENTRAL FOUNDATION GIRLS' SCHOOL. *See*
LONDON.—III.

CENTRAL GAELIC COMMITTEE. *See* EDINBURGH.
—*Educational Institute of Scotland.*

**CENTRAL GEOLOGICAL AND PROSPECTING
INSTITUTE.** *See* RUSSIA.—*Центральный Научно
Исследовательский Геолого-Разведочный Институт.*

CENTRAL GRAIN COMPANY. Private Grain Code.
pp. 32. *Central Grain Co.: Winnipeg*, [1915.] 8º.
8757. aaa. 62

CENTRAL HALL. Central Hall of Arts and Sciences.
See LONDON.—III.

CENTRAL HEALTH SERVICES COUNCIL. *See*
ENGLAND.—*Ministry of Health.*

CENTRAL HILL CHAPEL, *Upper Norwood.* *See*
LONDON.—III.

CENTRAL HOUSING ADVISORY COMMITTEE.
See ENGLAND.

CENTRAL IGBO PRIMER.

—— Central Igbo Primer I [*etc.*]. *Macmillan & Co.: London ;
Dublin* printed, [1952– .] 8º. W.P. A. **130.**

CENTRAL INDIAN ASSOCIATION. Central Indian
Association of Malaya. *See* KUALA LUMPUR.

CENTRAL INFORMATION BUREAU. Central Information Bureau for Educational Films. *See* LONDON.
—III.

CENTRAL INSTITUTE.

—— Central Institute of Art and Design. *See* ENGLAND.

—— Central Institute of Statistics. *See* ITALY.—*Istituto
Centrale di Statistica.*

CENTRAL INSTITUTION. *See* LONDON.—III. *City
and Guilds of London Institute for the Advancement of
Technical Education.—Central Technical College, etc.*

CENTRAL-INTELLIGENZBLATT. Central-Intelligenzblatt für Land-, Forstwirthschaft und verwandte
Zweige. *See* PERIODICAL PUBLICATIONS.—*Prague.* Jechl's
land- und volkswirthschaftliches Wochenblatt, etc.

CENTRAL ISLAMIC SOCIETY. *See* LONDON.—III.

CENTRAL JAPAN PIONEER. *See* LONDON.—III.
Central Japan Pioneer Mission.

CENTRAL JAPAN PIONEER MISSION. *See*
LONDON.—III.

CENTRAL JOINT ADVISORY COMMITTEE.
—— Central Joint Advisory Committee on Tutorial Classes.
See LONDON.—III.

CENTRAL-KOMMISSION. *See* CENTRALKOMMISSION.

CENTRAL LAND ASSOCIATION.

—— *See* LONDON.—III. *Country Landowners' Association.*

CENTRAL LAND BOARD. *See* ENGLAND.

CENTRAL LANDOWNERS' ASSOCIATION.

—— *See* LONDON.—III. *Country Landowners' Association.*

CENTRAL-LANDWIRTHSCHAFTS-SCHULE. *See*
WEIHENSTEPHAN.

CENTRAL LAW JOURNAL. *See* PERIODICAL PUBLICATIONS.—*Saint Louis, Mo.*

CENTRAL LIBRARY.

—— Central Library for Animal Diseases. *See* LONDON.—III.
Royal College of Veterinary Surgeons.—Memorial Library.

—— Central Library for Students. *See* LONDON.—III.
National Central Library.

—— Central Library of Baroda. *See* BARODA.

CENTRAL LITERARY ASSOCIATION. *See* BIRMINGHAM.—*Birmingham Central Literary Association.*

CENTRAL LITERARY MAGAZINE. *See* BIRMINGHAM.—*Birmingham Central Literary Association.*

CENTRAL LONDON ELECTRICITY, LTD.
London Associated Electricity Undertakings, 1935–
1938.
Central London Electricity Ltd., 1938–1948.
Subsequently incorporated in the London Electricity
Board.

—— L.A.E.U. Staff Journal. vol. 1. no. 1–7. June—Dec.
1936. [*London*,] 1936. 8º.
[Continued as :]
Contact. vol. 1. no. 8—vol. 13. no. 4. Jan. 1937—
April 1948. *London*, 1937–48. 8º. P.P. **5793.** nla.

CENTRAL LONDON GROUP. Central London Group of the Kodak Fellowship. *See* KODAK FELLOWSHIP. – *Central London Group.*

CENTRAL LONDON OPHTHALMIC HOSPITAL. *See* LONDON.—III.

CENTRAL LONDON THROAT, NOSE AND EAR HOSPITAL. *See* LONDON.—III.

CENTRAL LUNATIC ASYLUM, *Virginia. See* VIRGINIA, *State of.*

CENTRAL MEDICAL SCHOOL. *See* SUVA.

CENTRAL MEDITERRANEAN FORCE. *See* ENGLAND.

CENTRAL METEOROLOGICAL OBSERVATORY. *See* TOKYO.

CENTRAL MIDWIVES BOARD. Central Midwives Board. *See* ENGLAND.

—— Central Midwives Board for Scotland. *See* SCOTLAND.

CENTRAL MINE RESCUE COMMITTEE. *See* ENGLAND.—*National Coal Board.*—*East Midlands Division.*

CENTRAL MINING-RAND MINES GROUP.
Health Department.

—— Report for the year 1936, together with a review of the work of the Department since 1914. (Report for the year 1937 [etc.].) [*Johannesburg,* 1937– .] 4°. A.R. 612.

CENTRAL MORTGAGE AND HOUSING CORPORATION. *See* CANADA.

CENTRAL MUSIC LIBRARY. *See* LONDON.—III.

CENTRAL NATIONAL COUNCIL.

—— Central National Council for Applied Scientific Research in the Netherlands. *See* NETHERLANDS. [Kingdom of the Netherlands.]—*Nederlandse Centrale Organisatie voor Toegepast-natuurwetenschappelijk Onderzoek.*

—— Central National Council of the Dobrudja. *See* DOBRUJA.

CENTRAL NEW YORK BUSINESS DIRECTORY. *See* DIRECTORIES.—*New York, State of.*

CENTRAL NEWS. *See* PERIODICAL PUBLICATIONS.—*Johannesburg.*

CENTRAL NONCONFORMIST COMMITTEE. *See* BIRMINGHAM.

CENTRAL NOTTINGHAM CONSERVATIVE ASSOCIATION. *See* NOTTINGHAM.

CENTRAL NOTTINGHAM NEWS.

—— Central Nottingham News. *See* NOTTINGHAM.—*Central Nottingham Conservative Association.*

CENTRAL NOTTINGHAM YOUNG CONSERVATIVE ORGANISATION. *See* ENGLAND.—*National Union of Conservative and Constitutional Associations.*—*Young Conservatives.*

CENTRAL OFFICE.

—— Central Office of Information. *See* ENGLAND.

CENTRAL OFFICE OF INFORMATION REFERENCE PAMPHLET. *See* ENGLAND.—*Central Office of Information.*

CENTRAL-ORGAN. *See* CENTRALORGAN.

CENTRAL ORGANISATION. Central Organisation for a Durable Peace. *See* HAGUE.—*Organisation Centrale pour une Paix Durable.*

CENTRAL ORTHOGRAPHY COMMITTEE. *See* AFRICA, South.—*Union of South Africa.*

CENTRAL PACIFIC RAILROAD COMPANY. The American Overland Route. The Union and Central Pacific Railways across the American Continent, *etc.* 1876. 8°. *See* UNION PACIFIC RAILROAD COMPANY.
P.P. 3904. k.

—— The Lands of the Central Pacific Railroad Co. of California with general information on the resources of the country through which the railroad takes its way. June 1, 1880. pp. 68. *H. S. Crocker & Co.: San Francisco,* 1880. 8°. 10409. c. 1. (3.)

—— Union & Central Pacific R.R. Line, *etc.* [An illustrated map and time-table of the Union Pacific and Central Pacific Railroads between Omaha and San Francisco.] [1871.] 8°. *See* UNION PACIFIC RAILROAD COMPANY. 8235. aaa. 42.

CENTRAL PATHOLOGICAL LABORATORY.

—— Central Pathological Laboratory of the London County Mental Hospitals, Maudsley Hospital, Denmark Hill. *See* LONDON, *County of.*—*County Council.*

CENTRAL PENINSULAR RAILWAY COMPANY OF PORTUGAL. A Refutation of the Report of the Contractors of the Railway from Lisbon to Santarem, founded upon the analysis of the facts that preceded the suspensions of the works by said contractors. pp. 24. *Lisbon; London* [printed], 1855. 8°. 08235. dd. 8. (1.)

CENTRAL PLANNING BUREAU.

—— Central Planning Bureau of the Netherlands. *See* NETHERLANDS. [*Kingdom of the Netherlands.*]—*Centraal Planbureau.*

CENTRAL POOR LAW CONFERENCE. *See* LONDON.—III.

CENTRAL PRESS ASSOCIATION. *See* BUNDORAN.

CENTRAL PRISONERS OF WAR COMMITTEE.

—— Central Prisoners of War Committee of the British Red Cross and the Order of St. John. *See* ENGLAND.—*British Red Cross Society.*

CENTRAL PROTESTANT DEFENCE ASSOCIATION. *See* DUBLIN.

CENTRAL PROVINCES.

This heading includes the official publications of the Central Provinces, 1862–1903, and those of the Central Provinces and Berar, 1903 onwards. Official publications of Berar issued before 1st October 1903 are entered under BERAR. *Publications issued after 1948 are entered under* MADHYA PRADESH.

LAWS.—I. GENERAL COLLECTIONS.

—— The Central Provinces Code: consisting of the Bengal Regulations and Local Acts of the Governor General in Council in force in the Central Provinces. pp. vi. 253. 1881. 8°. *See* INDIA.—*Legislative Department.*
I.S. 364/10.

—— [Another edition.] With appendices comprising . . . a list of the acts which have been applied to the scheduled districts of the Central Provinces by notification under the Scheduled Districts Act, 1874. Second edition. pp. xi. 393. 1891. 8°. *See* INDIA.—*Legislative Department.*
I.S. 364/18.

—— Third edition. pp. iii. 454. 1905. 8°. *See* INDIA.—*Legislative Department.*
I.S. 364/28.

CENTRAL PROVINCES.

—— Central Provinces Act No. 1 of 1914 (—no. IX of 1940). [With indexes.] [*Nagpur*, 1914–40.] 8°. I.S. C.P. **115/4.** *Imperfect; wanting No. 1 of 1922, No. V of 1923, the whole of 1924–1940 except No. 1 of 1925, no. 17 of 1936, and no. 79 of 1940, and the Indexes for 1924–1926, 1935, 1936, 1940.*

—— The Central Provinces Code . . . Fourth edition. pp. iv. 496. 1918. 8°. *See* INDIA.—*Legislative Department.* I.S. **364/40.**

—— Fifth edition. pp. vi. 600. 1924. 8°. *See* infra: LEGISLATIVE DEPARTMENT. I.S. C.P. **115/9. (1.)**

—— Sixth edition. 2 vol. 1934, 35. 8°. *See* infra: LEGISLATIVE DEPARTMENT. I.S. C.P. **115/9. (2.)**

LAWS.—II. COLLECTIONS OF LAWS ON SPECIAL SUBJECTS.

—— [*Berar.*] British Enactments in force in Berar . . . Compiled by C. S. Findlay. pp. 197. *Nagpur*, 1916. 8°. I.S. C.P. **123/4. (1.)** *The half-title reads: " The Berar Code."*

—— [Another edition.] The Berar Code. Provisional edition. pp. 123. *Nagpur*, 1927. 8°. I.S. C.P. **123/4. (2.)**

—— Second edition. pp. 183. *Nagpur*, 1931. 8°. I.S. C.P. **123/4. (3.)**

—— [*Local Rules and Orders.*] Compilation—Revised—of Local Rules and Orders made under Enactments applying to the Central Provinces . . . Corrected up to the 31st December 1903. 2 pt. *Nagpur*, 1904. 8°.

—— Amendment to the preface to the Compilation of Local Rules and Orders. *Nagpur*, [1906.] *s. sh.* 8°.

—— Addenda and Corrigenda, *etc.* no. 1–31. [*Nagpur*, 1906–08.] 8°. I.S. C.P. **115.**

LAWS.—IV. SEPARATE LAWS.

—— Notification . . . No. 387. [Central Provinces Motor-Vehicles Rules made by the Chief Commissioner under the Indian Motor-Vehicles Act, VIII of 1914. Dated: 1 April 1915.] pp. 7. *Nagpur*, [1915.] fol. I.S. C.P. **55.**

—— Notification . . . No. 504. [Central Provinces Motor-Vehicles Rules made by the Chief Commissioner under the Indian Motor-Vehicles Act, VIII of 1914. Dated: 8 May 1915. Cancelling the Rules of 1 Apr. 1915.] pp. 7. *Nagpur*, [1915.] fol. I.S. C.P. **55/2.**

—— The Central Provinces Tenancy Act. Being the Act 1 of 1920 . . . with comments, explanatory notes, notifications, rules, charts of inheritance and up-to-date rulings of High Courts. By D. V. Gokhale . . . Second edition. pp. 27. 10. 419. 171. 31. *D. V. Gokhale: Khandwa*, [1931.] 8°. **5310. bb. 29.**

—— Central Provinces Act No. 1 of 1920. The Central Provinces Tenancy Act, 1920. [The text of the Act, together with an extract from the Central Provinces Tenancy-Amendment-Act of 1939.] pp. 54. [*Nagpur*, 1940.] 8°. I.S. C.P. **115/11.**

—— The Central Provinces and Berar Tenancy Act. [The text of the Central Provinces Tenancy Act, 1920, together with an extract from the Central Provinces Tenancy-Amendment-Act of 1939, and an introductory essay.] pp. 94. [*Nagpur*, 1941.] 8°. I.S. C.P. **115/10.**

MISCELLANEOUS OFFICIAL PUBLICATIONS.

—— Annual Public Health Report, *etc. See* infra: Annual Sanitary Report, *etc.*

CENTRAL PROVINCES. [MISCELLANEOUS OFFICIAL PUBLICATIONS.]

—— Annual Report of the Income-Tax Department, *etc. See* infra: Report on the Administration of the Income-Tax Act, *etc.*

—— Annual Report of the Sanitary Commissioners, *etc. See* infra: Annual Report on Vital Statistics, *etc.*

—— Annual Report on Hospitals and Dispensaries, *etc. See* infra: Notes on the Annual Statements of the Hospitals and Dispensaries, *etc.*

—— [Annual Report on Inland Emigration in the Central Provinces for the year ending 30th June 1904.] pp. 6. *Nagpur*, 1904. fol. I.S. C.P. **54.**

—— Annual Report on the Administration of the Central Provinces (Report on the Administration of the Central Provinces). For the year 1861-62(–1902-03). 43 pt. [*Calcutta ;*] *Nagpur*, [1862]–1903. 4°, 8°. & fol. I.S. C.P. **1 & 116.** *This set includes both 4° and 8° editions of the report for 1862-63.*

—— Report on the Administration of the Central Provinces & Berar for the year 1903-04(–1920-21). 18 pt. *Nagpur*, 1904–22. fol. & 8°. [Continued as :] Central Provinces and Berar. A review of the administration of the province. 1921-22(–1936-37). (Triennium Report of the General Administration of the province for the years 1937–1940.) 18 pt. *Nagpur*, 1923–41. 8°. I.S. C.P. **1/3 & 116/3.** *Wanting the " Review " for 1933–34.*

—— Annual Report on the Administration of the Indian Companies Act, *etc. See* infra: Report on the Working of the Indian Companies Act, *etc.*

—— Annual Report on the Lunatic Asylums (on the Mental Hospital), *etc. See* infra: Report on the Lunatic Asylums, *etc.*

—— Annual Report on the Rail-borne Traffic, *etc. See* infra: Report on the Rail-borne Traffic, *etc.*

—— [Annual Report on the Working of the Assam Labour and Emigration Act in the Central Provinces for the years ending the 30th June 1920, 1922, 1924, 1925.] 4 pt. *Nagpur*, [1920–25.] fol. I.S. C.P. **54/2.**

—— Annual Report on Vital Statistics and Sanitary Condition of the Central Provinces for the year 1868. (Second Annual Report of the Sanitary Commissioner for the Central Provinces, 1869.—Annual Report of the Sanitary Commissioner . . . 1870[–1890].—Report of the Sanitary Commissioner . . . for the year 1891[–1895].—Annual Sanitary Report of the Central Provinces, for the year 1896[–1902].) 35 pt. [*Nagpur ;*] *Allahabad*, [1869]–1903. fol. I.S. C.P. **35.**

—— Annual Sanitary Report (Annual Public Health Report) of the Central Provinces and Berar for the year 1903 (–1934). 32 pt. *Nagpur*, 1904–36. fol. & 8°. I.S. C.P. **35/3 & 128/2.**

—— [Annual Reports on Municipal Operations—Reports on the Working of the Municipal Committees—in the Central Provinces.] 1874-75–1878-79, 1891-92–1902-03. 16 pt. [*Nagpur ;*] *Allahabad*, [1877]–1903. fol. I.S. C.P. **25.**

—— [Annual Reports of the Municipal Committees of the Central Provinces and Berar for the year 1903-04– 1909-10.] (Resolution reviewing the Reports on the Working of Municipal Committees . . . during the year 1910-1911[–1918-19; 1921-22–1926-27; during the year ending 31st March 1928—year ending 31st March 1935].) 30 pt. *Nagpur*, [1904]–37. fol. & 8°. I.S. C.P. **25/3 & 121/3.** *Imperfect; wanting the reports for 1919-20, 1920-21.*

CENTRAL PROVINCES. [MISCELLANEOUS OFFICIAL PUBLICATIONS.]

—— Annual Sanitary Report, *etc. See* supra: Annual Report on Vital Statistics, *etc.*

—— Annual Statement of the Income Tax Act, *etc. See* infra: Report on the Administration of the Income Tax Act, *etc.*

—— Annual Statements of the Income Tax Act, *etc. See* infra: Report on the Administration of the Income Tax Act, *etc.*

—— Arboricultural Returns, *etc. See* infra: Review by the Chief Commissioner on Arboricultural Operations, *etc.*

—— Assessment Groups and Group Rate Report of the First Revision Settlement of 103 Izara Villages in the Wun Taluq of the Yeotmal District. 1928. [By G. B. Despāṇḍe. With maps.] pp. 2. 39. *Nagpur,* [1928.] fol. I.S. C.P. **19/44. (4.)**

—— Assessment Groups and Group Rates Report of the Akola Taluq in the Akola District. [By D. R. Dongre. With a map.] pp. 2. 2. 35. *Nagpur,* [1927.] fol. I.S. C.P. **19/45. (1.)**

—— Assessment Groups and Group Rates Report of the First Revision Settlement of 19 Izara Villages in the Mangrul Taluq of the Akola District for the year 1926. [By G. B. Despāṇḍe. With a map.] pp. 2. 36. *Nagpur,* [1927.] fol. I.S. C.P. **19/45. (3.)**

—— Assessment Groups and Group Rates Report of the First Revision Settlement of 71 Izara Villages in the Yeotmal Taluq of the Yeotmal District in the year 1928. [By G. B. Despāṇḍe. With maps.] pp. 2. 40. *Nagpur,* [1928.] fol. I.S. C.P. **19/44. (5.)**

—— Assessment Groups and Group Rates Report of the First Revision Settlement of 64 Izara Villages in the Darwha Taluq of the Yeotmal District for the year 1927. [By G. B. Despāṇḍe. With maps.] pp. 2. 30. *Nagpur,* [1927.] fol. I.S. C.P. **19/44. (1.)**

—— Assessment Groups and Group Rates Report of the First Revision Settlement of 28 Izara Villages in the Pusad Taluq of the Yeotmal District for the year 1926. [By G. B. Despāṇḍe. With maps.] pp. 2. 25. *Nagpur,* [1927.] fol. I.S. C.P. **19/44. (3.)**

—— Assessment Groups and Group Rates Report of the Second Revision Settlement in the Akot Taluq of the Akola District. [By D. R. Dongre. With a map.] pp. 3. 46. *Nagpur,* [1928.] fol. I.S. C.P. **19/45. (2.)**

—— Assessment Groups and Group Rates Report of the Second Revision Settlement of the Chikhli Taluq in the Buldana District for the year 1926-27. [By D. R. Dongre. With a map.] pp. 2. 41. *Nagpur,* [1927.] fol. I.S. C.P. **19/46.**

—— The Berar Explosives, Petroleum and Motor Vehicles Manual, containing the Indian Explosives Act, 1884, the Indian Petroleum Act, 1899, the Indian Motor Vehicles Act, 1914, as applied to Berar, and Rules and Orders issued thereunder. Corrected up to 31st March 1918. pp. 227. *Nagpur,* 1918. 8°. I.S. C.P. **115/6.**

—— The Berar Explosives Rules, *etc. See* infra: [Rules under the Indian Explosives Act, *etc.*]

—— The Berar Revenue Manual, volume II. As corrected up to the 1st August, 1920, *etc.* [A collection of " revenue book circulars."] pp. iv. 456. viii. *Nagpur,* 1921. 8°. I.S. C.P. **110/4. (1.)**

—— [Another edition.] Corrected up to the 1st May 1931, *etc.* pp. 327. *Nagpur,* 1931. 8°. I.S. C.P. **110/4. (2.)**

CENTRAL PROVINCES. [MISCELLANEOUS OFFICIAL PUBLICATIONS.]

—— Book Circular No. XLVI. [Report by the Sanitary Commissioner on Vital Statistics in the Central Provinces. Dated: 27 July 1868.] pp. 23. [*Nagpur,* 1868.] fol. I.S. C.P. **38.**

—— Book of Municipal Forms, *etc. See* infra: Municipal Manual, *etc.*

—— Catalogue of Books &c. issued . . . in the Central Provinces and registered . . . during the quarter ending 30th September 1875 (during the quarter ending 30th June 1878; during the quarter ending 31st March 1882; during the quarter ending 30th June 1882; during the quarter ending 31st December 1883; during the quarter ending 31st March 1884; during the quarter ending 30th June 1892—the quarter ending 31st March 1904). 54 pt. [*Nagpur,* 1875]–1904. fol. I.S. C.P. **45.**

—— Catalogue of Books (of Books and Pamphlets) registered in the Central Provinces (and Berar) during the quarter ending the 30th June 1904(—the quarter ending 31st March 1907; during the quarter ending 30th September 1907—the quarter ending the 31st December 1932; during the quarter ending the 30th June 1933 [*etc.*]). *Nagpur,* 1904– . fol. & 8°. I.S. C.P. **45/3 & 131.**

—— Catalogue of Sanskrit & Prakrit Manuscripts in the Central Provinces and Berar. By Rai Bahadur Hiralal. pp. 2. 5. lv. 808. 8. *Nagpur,* 1926. 8°. **14096.** ddd. 4.

—— Census of the Central Provinces, 1881. 2 vol. *Bombay,* 1882, 83. fol. I.S. C.P. **5.**

—— Central Provinces and Berar. A review of the administration of the province. *See* supra: Report on the Administration of the Central Provinces & Berar, *etc.*

—— Central Provinces' Census 1872. 2 pt. [*Nagpur,* 1873.] fol. I.S. C.P. **4.**

—— The Central Provinces Court of Wards Manual, containing the Act and Rules thereunder having the force of law, and section v of the Revenue Manual. pp. 20. 106. *Nagpur,* 1902 [1903]. 8°. I.S. C.P. **118.**

—— Second edition. pp. 139. *Nagpur,* 1914. 8°. I.S. C.P. **118/2.**

—— Central Provinces (and Berar) District Gazetteers . . . Edited by R. V. Russell (A. E. Nelson). 65 vol.

(1) Akola District.
A volume. Descriptive. By C. Brown. General editor . . . A. E. Nelson. [With plates and a map.] pp. xxi. 398. 1910.
B volume. Statistical Tables. 1891–1907. Edited by A. E. Nelson. pp. 139. 1909.
B volume. Statistical Tables. 1891–1911. pp. 146. 1912.
—— Addenda and Corrigenda to the B volume Tables . . . for the year 1913-14(–1922-23, 1924-25). no. 1–12, 14. [1915–26.]

(2) Amraoti District.
A volume. Descriptive. Edited by S. V. Fitzgerald . . . and A. E. Nelson. [With plates and maps.] pp. xx. 437. 1911.
B volume. Statistical Tables. 1891–1907. Edited by A. E. Nelson. pp. 139. 1910.
B volume. Statistical Tables. 1891–1911. pp. 139. 1913.
—— Addenda and Corrigenda to the B volume Tables . . . for 1913-14 and 1914-15(–1924-25). no. 2–11. [1917–26.]

(3) Balaghat District.
A volume. Descriptive. By C. E. Low. [With plates and a map.] pp. xviii. 334. 1907.
B volume. Statistical Tables. 1891–1901. Edited by R. V. Russell. pp. 93. 1905.
—— Addenda (Corrigenda) to the B volume Statistical Tables, *etc.* 5 pt. [1908–10.]
B volume. Statistical Tables. 1891–1914. pp. 98. 1916.
—— Addenda and Corrigenda to the Tables of the B volume . . . for the years 1914-15 and 1915-16 (–1924-25). no. 1–11, 13. [1917–26.]

(4) Betual District.
A volume. Descriptive. Edited by R. V. Russell. [With plates and maps, and an erratum leaf.] pp. xiv. 265. 1907, [o8.]
B volume. Statistical Tables. 1891-1907. Edited by R. V. Russell. pp. 99. 1904.
—— Addendum (Addenda and Corrigenda) to the B volume Statistical Tables, etc. 4 pt. [1909?-11.]
B volume. Statistical Tables. 1891-1914. pp. 102. 1916.
—— Addenda and Corrigenda to the B volume Gazetteer, etc. 1914-15-1923-24. no. 1-10. [1917-25.]

(5) Bhandara District.
A volume. Descriptive. Edited by R. V. Russell. [With plates and maps.] pp. xvi. 243. 1908.
B volume. Statistical Tables. 1891-1901. Edited by R. V. Russell. pp. 112. 1905.
—— Amendments (Addenda) to the B volume Statistical Tables, etc. 3 pt. [1909-11.]
B volume. Statistical Tables. 1891-1915. pp. 120. 1917.
—— Correction List (Addenda and Corrigenda) to B volume Gazetteer . . . for 1915-16(-1925). no. 1-11. [1918-26.]

(6) Bilaspur District.
A volume. Descriptive. Edited by A. E. Nelson. [With plates, including maps.] pp. xvii. 341. 1910.
B volume. Statistical Tables. 1891-1901. Edited by R. V. Russell. pp. 98. 1905.
—— Addenda (Corrigenda) to the B volume Tables, etc. 5 pt. [1908-11.]
B volume. Statistical Tables. 1891-1911. pp. 104. 1913.
—— Addenda and Corrigenda to the B volume Tables . . . for 1912-13 (1915-1924-25). no. 1, 3-11. [1914-26.]

(7) Buldana District.
A volume. Descriptive. Edited by A. E. Nelson. [With plates and maps.] pp. xxv. 470. 1910.
B volume. Statistical Tables. 1891-1907. Edited by A. E. Nelson. pp. 145. 1909.
B volume. Statistical Tables. 1891-1911. pp. 136. 1914.
—— Addenda and Corrigenda to the B volume Tables . . . for the year 1913-14(-1924-25). no. 2-10, 13. [1915-26.]

(8) Chanda District.
A volume. Descriptive. By L. F. Begbie . . . Edited by A. E. Nelson. [With plates and maps.] pp. xxi. 477. 1909.
B volume. Statistical Tables. 1891-1901. Edited by R. V. Russell. pp. 115. 1905.
—— Addenda (and Corrigenda) to the B volume Tables, etc. 5 pt. [1908-11.]
B volume. Statistical Tables. 1891-1915. pp. 149. 1916.
—— Addenda and Corrigenda to the Tables of the B volume . . . for 1915-16(-1917-18, 1919-20-1922-23, 1924-25). no. 1-4, 6-9, 11. [1917-26.]

(9) Chattisgarh Feudatory States. Written by E. A. DeBrett. [With plates.] pp. xxvi. 354. 1909.

(10) Chhindwara District.
A volume. Descriptive. Edited by R. V. Russell. [With plates and a map.] pp. xiii. 342. 1907.
B volume. Statistical Tables. 1891-1901. Edited by R. V. Russell. pp. 105. 1904.
—— Addendum (Corrigendum) to the B volume . . . up to 1905-06(-1909-10). 5 pt. [1908-11.]
B volume. Statistical Tables. 1891-1914. pp. 109. 1917.
—— Correction Lists (Addenda and Corrigenda) to the Tables of the B volume . . . for 1914-15 and 1915-16 (-1919-20, 1921-22-1923-24). no. 1-9. [1918-25.]

(11) Damoh District.
A Volume. Descriptive. Edited by R. V. Russell. [With a map.] pp. xiv. 216. 1906.
B volume. Statistical Tables. 1891-1901. Edited by R. V. Russell. pp. 75. 1904.
—— Addenda and Corrigenda to the B volume Tables, etc. 6 pt. [1909-11.]
B volume. Statistical Tables. 1891-1911. pp. 87. 1914.
—— Addenda and Corrigenda to the B volume Tables . . . for 1913-14(-1924-25). no. 1-13. [1916-26.]

(12) Drug District.
A volume. Descriptive. Edited by A. E. Nelson. [With plates and maps.] pp. xv. 210. 1910.
B volume. Statistical Tables. 1906-1912. pp. 71. 1913.
—— Addenda and Corrigenda to the B volume Tables . . . for the year 1912-13(-1924-25). no. 1-12, 14. [1915-26.]

(13) Hoshangabad District.
A volume. Descriptive. By G. L. Corbett . . . and R. V. Russell. [With plates and maps.] pp. xvi. 364. 1908.
B volume. Statistical Tables. 1891-1901. Edited by R. V. Russell. pp. 118. 1904.
—— The Amendments (Addenda) to the B volume Tables, etc. 5 pt. [1908-11.]
B volume. Statistical Tables. 1891-1911. pp. 122. 1914.
—— Addenda and Corrigenda to the B volume tables . . . for the year 1913-14(-1924-25). no. 1-12. [1915-26.]

(14) Jubbulpore District.
A volume. Descriptive. Edited by A. E. Nelson. [With plates and maps.] pp. xix. 393. 1909.
B volume. Statistical Tables. 1891-1901. Edited by R. V. Russell. pp. 90. 1904.
—— Corrigendum (Addenda and Corrigenda) to the B volume Tables, etc. 8 pt. [1908-11.]
B volume. Statistical Tastes. 1891-1911. pp. 112. 1914.
—— Addenda and Corrigenda to the B volume Tables . . . for 1913-14(-1918-19, 1920-21-1921-22, 1923-24, 1925-26). no. 1-7, 9-12. [1916-27.]

(15) Mandla District.
A volume. Descriptive. By F. R. R. Rudman. [With plates and maps.] pp. xvi. 260. 1912.
B volume. Statistical Tables. 1891-1901. Edited by R. V. Russell. pp. 80. 1904.
—— Addenda (Corrigenda) to the B volume Tables, etc. 4 pt. [1908-11.]
B volume. Statistical Tables. 1891-1911. pp. 86. 1913.
—— Addenda and Corrigenda to the B volume Tables . . . for the year 1913-14(-1922-23, 1924-25). no. 2-12, 14. [1915-26.]

(16) Nagpur District.
A volume. Descriptive. Edited by R. V. Russell. [With plates and maps.] pp. xiv. 345. 1908.
B volume. Statistical Tables. 1891-1901. Edited by R. V. Russell. pp. 127. 1905.
—— Corrigendum (Addenda and Corrigenda) to the B volume Tables, etc. 7 pt. [1908-10.]
B volume. Statistical Tables. 1891-1915. pp. 171. 1916.
—— Addenda and Corrigenda to the Tables of the B volume . . . for the year 1915-16(-1922-23, 1924-25). no. 1, 3-10, 12. [1917-26.]

(17) Narsinghpur District.
A volume. Descriptive. Edited by R. V. Russell. [With a map.] pp. xiv. 241. 1906.
B volume. Statistical Tables. Edited by R. V. Russell. pp. 90.
—— Addenda (and Corrigenda) to B volume Tables, etc. 5 pt. [1907 ?-11.]
B volume. Statistical Tables. 1891-1911. pp. 88. 1912.
—— Addenda and Corrigenda to the B volume Tables . . . for the year 1914-15(-1922-23, 1924-25). no. 3-11, 13. [1916-26.]

(18) Nimar District.
A volume. Descriptive. Edited by R. V. Russell. [With plates, including a map. pp. xvi. 261. 1908.
—— Amendment, etc. [1922.]
B volume. Statistical Tables. 1891-1901. Edited by R. V. Russell. pp. 96. 1904.
—— Corrigendum (Addenda) to the B volume Statistical Tables, etc. 6 pt. [1908-10.]
B volume. Statistical Tables. 1891-1913. pp. 96. 1915.
—— Addenda and Corrigenda to B volume . . . for 1913-14 and 1914-15(-1924-25). no. 1-12. [1917-26.]

(19) Raipur District.
A volume. Descriptive. Edited by A. E. Nelson [With plates and maps.] pp. xxi. 351. 1909.
B volume. Statistical Tables. 1891-1901. Edited by R. V. Russell. pp. 113. 1905.
—— [Addenda and corrigenda.] 5 pt. [1908-11.]
B volume. Statistical Tables. 1891-1911. pp. 103. 1913.

CENTRAL PROVINCES. [MISCELLANEOUS OFFICIAL PUBLICATIONS.]

—— Addenda and Corrigenda to the B volume Tables . . . for the year 1914-15(–1923-24, 1925-26). no. 1, 4–13. [1916–26.]

(20) Saugor District.
A volume. Descriptive. Edited by R. V. Russell. [With a map.] pp. xvi. 267. 1906.
B volume. Statistical Tables. 1891–1901. Edited by R. V. Russell. pp. 106. 1905.
—— Addenda (and Corrigenda) to the B volume Tables, *etc.* 7 pt. [1908–11.]
B volume. Statistical Tables. 1891–1911. [With a map.] pp. 110. 1913.
—— Addenda and Corrigenda to the B volume Tables . . . for 1912-13(–1924-25). no. 1–13. [1915–26.]

(21) Seoni District.
A volume. Descriptive. Edited by R. V. Russell. [With plates and a map.] pp. xii. 197. 1907.
B volume. Statistical Tables. 1891–1901. Edited by R. V. Russell. pp. 84. 1904.
—— List of Addenda (Corrigenda) to the B volume Tables, *etc.* 5 pt. [1908–11.]
B volume. Statistical Tables. 1891–1911. pp. 85. 1913.
—— Addenda and Corrigenda to the B volume Tables . . . for 1912-13(–1924-25). no. 1–13. [1914–26.]

(22) Wardha District.
A volume. Descriptive. Edited by R. V. Russell. [With a map.] pp. xiii. 271. 1906.
B volume. Statistical Tables. 1891–1901. Edited by R. V. Russell. pp. 117. 1905.
—— Addenda to the B volume Tables, *etc.* 3 pt. [1908 ?–10.]
B volume. Statistical Tables. 1891–1914. pp. 144. 1916.
—— Addenda and Corrigenda to the Tables of the B volume . . . for the years 1914-15 and 1915-16 (–1922-23, 1924-25). no. 1–6, 7, 10. [1917–26.]

(23) Yeotmal District.
A volume. Descriptive. By C. Brown . . . and R. V. Russell. [With plates and maps.] pp. xvii. 242. 1908.
B volume. Statistical Tables. 1891–1911. pp. 105. 1914.
—— Addenda and Corrigenda to the B volume Tables . . . for 1913-14(–1915-16, 1917-18, 1920-21–1923-24, 1925-26). no. 1–10. [1916–26.]

Allahabad, etc., 1904–27. 8°.   I.S. C.P. **114. (1–23.)**
The Sambalpur District B volume which was published in this series is placed with the Bengal District Gazetteers.

—— The Central Provinces Forest Manual . . . Second edition. pp. iv. 228. *Nagpur,* 1907. 8°.
I.S. C.P. **120. (1.)**

—— Third edition. pp. xiii. 331. *Nagpur,* 1915. 8°.
I.S. C.P. **120. (2.)**

—— Fourth edition. pp. ix. 315. *Nagpur,* 1921. 8°.
I.S. C.P. **120. (3.)**

—— The Central Provinces & Berar Forest Manual. Fifth edition. 2 vol. *Nagpur,* 1932. 8°.   I.S. C.P. **120. (4.)**

—— The Central Provinces Inland Emigration Manual, 1904. [Containing the Assam Labour and Emigration Act, VI of 1901, with Rules, Forms and Schedules issued thereunder.] pp. xviii. 152. *Allahabad,* 1904. 8°.
I.S. C.P. **125. (1.)**

—— [Another edition.] Containing the Assam Labour and Emigration Act, VI of 1901, as amended by the Assam Labour and Emigration Acts, XI of 1908 and VIII of 1915, and Rules and Orders issued thereunder. Corrected up to 1st November 1917. pp. 140. *Nagpur,* 1917. 8°.
I.S. C.P. **125. (2.)**

—— The Central Provinces Revenue Manual . . . Containing the Revenue Acts and Rules thereunder. Sixth edition. 4 vol. *Nagpur,* 1921. 8°. I.S. C.P. **110/3. (1.)**

—— Seventh edition, *etc.* 4 vol. *Nagpur,* 1933, 32, 35. 8°.
I.S. C.P. **110/3. (2.)**

CENTRAL PROVINCES. [MISCELLANEOUS OFFICIAL PUBLICATIONS.]

—— District Council Manual for the Central Provinces . . . 1910. Second edition. pp. 2. iv. 110.   *Nagpur,* [1911.] 8°.   I.S. C.P. **121.**

—— The Explosives, Petroleum and Motor Vehicles Manual. Containing the Indian Explosives Act, 1884 ; the Indian Petroleum Act, 1899 ; the Indian Motor Vehicles Act, 1914 ; and rules and orders issued thereunder. Corrected up to 1st March 1916. pp. ii. 241. *Nagpur,* 1916. 8°.   I.S. C.P. **115/7.**

—— The Factories Manual of the Central Provinces and Berar, containing the Indian Factories Act, XII of 1911, together with notifications, rules and circulars thereunder. pp. ii. 65. *Nagpur,* 1914. 8°.   I.S. C.P. **115/8.**

—— Final Report of the Land Revenue Settlement of the Bhandora District in the Central Provinces effected during the years 1916–1921. [By Eyre Gordon. With a map.] pp. 5. 4. 60. 74. *Nagpur,* 1922 [1923]. fol. I.S. C.P. **19/38.**

—— Final Report of the Land Revenue Settlement of the Mandla District, 1904–1910. [By H. F. E. Bell. With a map.] pp. 6. 2. 2. 156. 3. *Nagpur,* 1911 [1913]. fol.
I.S. C.P. **19/21.**

—— Final Report on the Land Revenue Settlement of the Bilaspur—Khalsa—District of the Central Provinces. [By J. E. Hance. With a map and charts.] pp. 2. 5. v. 115. 65. *Nagpur,* 1914. fol.   I.S. C.P. **19/31.**

—— Final Report on the Land Revenue Settlement of the Chandarpur, Padampur and Malkharoda, &c., Portion of Sambalpur District left in the Central Provinces. [By Francis Dewar. With a map.] pp. 2. 14. 5. *Nagpur,* 1912 [1913]. fol.   I.S. C.P. **19/23.**

—— Final Report on the Land Revenue Settlement of the Drug District in the Central Provinces. [By H. E. Hemingway. With a map.] pp. 4. 3. 2. 20. 66. 4. *Nagpur,* 1912 [1913]. fol.   I.S. C.P. **19/26.**

—— Final Report on the Land Revenue Settlement of the Hoshangabad District in the Central Provinces effected during the years 1913 to 1918. [By H. C. Gowan. With a map.] pp. 3. 2. iii. 53. 79. *Nagpur,* 1919 [1920]. fol.
I.S. C.P. **19/36.**

—— Final Report on the Land Revenue Settlement of the Melghat Taluq in the Amraoti District effected during the years 1925–1927. [By R. M. Crofton. With a map.] pp. 3. 33. *Nagpur,* [1928.] fol.   I.S. C.P. **19/47.**

—— Final Report on the Land Revenue Settlement of the Narsinghpur District in the Central Provinces effected during the years 1923–1926. (By J. G. Bourne.) [With maps.] pp. 3. viii. 95. 39. *Nagpur,* [1927.] fol.
I.S. C.P. **19/43.**

—— Final Report on the Land Revenue Settlement of the Nimar District in the Central Provinces effected during the years 1911 to 1914. [By A. E. Nelson. With a map.] pt. 3. 9. 3. 7–58. 35. *Nagpur,* 1915 [1916]. fol.
I.S. C.P. **19/32.**

—— Final Report on the Land Revenue Settlement of the Phuljhar Zamindari of the Raipur District in the Central Provinces. [By Francis Dewar. With a map.] pp. 2. 16. 16. *Nagpur,* 1912 [1913]. fol. I.S. C.P. **19/24.**

—— Final Report on the Land Revenue Settlement of the Raipur District in the Central Provinces. [By H. E. Hemingway. With a map.] pp. 4. 3. 2. 2. 47. 42. *Nagpur,* 1912. fol.   I.S. C.P. **19/22.**

CENTRAL PROVINCES. [MISCELLANEOUS OFFICIAL PUBLICATIONS.]

—— Final Report on the Land Revenue Settlement of the Wardha District in the Central Provinces effected during the years 1908 to 1912. [By Alan Kenyon Smith. With a map.] pp. 3. 6. 3. 65. 40. *Nagpur*, 1913 [1914]. fol.
I.S. C.P. **19/29**.

—— Final Report on the Land Revenue Settlement of the Zamindari Estates of the Bilaspur District in the Central Provinces. [By C. U. Wills. With maps.] pp. 3. 3. 115. ix. *Nagpur*, 1912 [1913]. fol.
I.S. C.P. **19/25**.

—— Final Report on the Land Revenue Settlements of the Chanda District in the Central Provinces effected during the years 1897–06. [By Percy Hemingway. With maps.] pp. 2. 6. 8. 3. ii. 83. 235. *Nagpur*, 1910 [1912]. fol.
I.S. C.P. **19/20**.

—— Final Report on the Resettlement of Drug District. By Mr. P. S. Rau. [With a map and a diagram.] pp. 2. iii. 102. [*Nagpur*, 1933.] fol.
I.S. C.P. **19/53**.

—— Final Report on the Re-settlement of the Betul District in the Central Provinces effected during the years 1916–1921. [By C. G. C. Trench. With a map.] pp. 3. 2. 66. *Nagpur*, 1923. fol.
I.S. C.P. **19/39**.

—— Final Report on the Resettlement of the Chhindwara District in the Central Provinces during the years 1913–17. [By C. J. Irwin. With a map.] pp. 3. 4. 109. *Nagpur*, 1918 [1919]. fol.
I S. C.P. **19/35**.

—— Final Report on the Resettlement of the Khalsa of the Bilaspur District, 1927–1932. By Rai Bahadur Chhotelal Verma. [With maps.] pp. 2. iii. 37. 48. *Nagpur*, 1932. fol.
I.S. C.P. **19/52**.

—— Final Report on the Re-settlement of the Raipur & Drug Zamindaris in the Central Provinces during the years 1921–24. [By C. F. Waterfall. With a map.] pp. 3. 85. *Nagpur*, 1926. fol.
I.S. C.P. **19/41**.

—— Final Report on the Re-settlement of the Sironcha and Garchiroli Tahsils of the Chanda District in the Central Provinces during the years 1922–24. [By D. Lakshamaṇa Svāmī.] pp. 6. 31. 49. *Nagpur*, 1926. fol.
I.S. C.P. **19/42**.

—— Final Report on the Re-settlement of the three cis-Wainganga Tahsils of the Chanda District in the Central Provinces. [By Raghu-nātha Sadā-ṣiva Ṭhākura. With a map.] pp. ii. 3. 106. *Nagpur*, 1924. fol.
I.S. C.P. **19/40**.

—— Final Report on the Revised Settlement of the Seoni District in the Central Provinces effected during the years 1916–1920. [By K. L. B. Hamilton. With a map.] pp. 3. 4. ii. 98. *Nagpur*, 1921 [1922]. fol.
I.S. C.P. **19/37**.

—— Final Report on the Revision of the Land Revenue Settlement of the Phuljhar, Bilaigarh-Katgi and Bhatgaon Zamindaris of the Raipur District in the Central Provinces effected during the years 1930–31. [By Chintāmaṇ Dvārakānātha Deṣa-mukha. With a map.] pp. 2. ii. 23. 30. *Nagpur*, 1931. fol.   I.S. C.P. **19/48**.

—— Final Report on the Revision of the Land Revenue Settlement of the Raipur District—khalsa—in the Central Provinces effected during the years 1926–1931. [By Chintāmaṇ Dvārakānātha Deṣa-mukha. With a map and a chart.] pp. iii. 129. *Nagpur*, 1932. fol.
I.S. C.P. **19/51**.

CENTRAL PROVINCES. [MISCELLANEOUS OFFICIAL PUBLICATIONS.]

—— Final Settlement and Assessment Report on the Baihar Ryotwari Tract of the Balaghat District. [By Francis Dewar. With a map.] pp. 2. 2. 53. *Nagpur*, [1913.] fol.
I.S. C.P. **19/28**.

—— Forest Account Rules for the Central Provinces, *etc.* pp. iv. 89. *Nagpur*, 1916. 8°.   I.S. C.P. **120/3**.

—— Gazetteer of the Central Provinces. [Compiled by A. C. Lyall, P. Dods and C. A. R. Browning.] pp. iii. 192. *Nagpore*, 1867. 8°.   I.S. C.P. **114/2**.

—— A Grammar of the Chhattisgarhi Dialect of Eastern Hindi . . . By Hira Lal Kavyopadhyaya . . . Translated by Sir George A. Grierson . . . Revised and enlarged by Pandit Lochan Prasad Kavya-vinod, *etc.* pp. ix. 225. *Calcutta*, 1921. 8°.   **12906**. h. **41**.

—— History of Services of Gazetted (and other) Officers in the Civil Department in the Central Provinces. Corrected up to 1st July, 1892(–1908). 16 pt. *Nagpur*, 1892–1908. 8°.   I.S. C.P. **122/5**.
Imperfect; wanting the issue for July 1903.

—— Income-Tax Report and Returns. *See infra*: Report on the Administration of the Income-Tax Act, *etc.*

—— Memorandum on the Precautions to be taken against Cholera. [Dated: 9 March 1869.] pp. 3. [*Nagpur*, 1869.] fol.   I.S. C.P. **35/6**.

—— Mining Manual of the Central Provinces and Berar. (Compiled by C. E. Low.) pp. 4. 116. *Nagpur*, [1908.] 8°.   I.S. C.P. **109/3**. (**1.**)

—— Revised edition. pp. vii. 160. *Nagpur*, 1915. 8°.
I.S. C.P. **109/3**. (**2.**)

—— Third edition. [With a map.] pp. vii. 268. *Nagpur*, 1921. 8°.   I.S. C.P. **109/3**. (**3.**)

—— Fourth edition. [With a map.] pp. 13. xxxi. 266. *Nagpur*, 1928. 8°.   I.S. C.P. **109/3**. (**4.**)

—— Minute, by R. Temple, Esq. . . . on a Project for the Formation of a Reservoir on the River Pench. pp. 10. *Nagpore*, 1864. 8°.   I.S. C.P. **133/4**.

—— Minute on the Projected Extension of the Great Indian Peninsular Railway, from its present terminus at Nagpore, on to Kamptee, in the Central Provinces. By R. Temple. pp. 9. ix. *Nagpore*, 1863. 8°.   I.S. C.P. **140**.

—— A Monograph on the Iron and Steel Industry in the Central Provinces. By L. F. Begbie. [With plates.] pp. iv. 61. *Nagpur*, 1908. 4°.   I.S. C.P. **16/2**.

—— A Monograph on the Wire and Tinsel Industry in the Central Provinces. By B. N. De. [With plates.] pp. 29. *Nagpur*, 1910. 4°.   I.S. C.P. **16/3**.

—— Municipal Manual for the Central Provinces . . . 1910. Second edition. 9 pt. *Nagpur*, [1911.] 8°.

—— Book of Municipal Forms issued as a supplement to the Municipal Manual, *etc.* pp. 96.
MS. CORRECTIONS. *Nagpur*, [1913.] fol.
I.S. C.P. **121/2**.

—— Note on Fruit Culture in the Central Provinces. pp. 4. *Nagpur*, [1913.] fol.   I.S. C.P. **28/4**.

—— Note on the Annual Statements of the Stamp Revenue, *etc. See infra*: Report, with the Chief Commissioner's Remarks, on the Stamp Revenue, *etc.*

CENTRAL PROVINCES. [Miscellaneous Official Publications.]

—— Note on the Stamp Revenue, *etc.* *See* infra: Report, with the Chief Commissioner's Remarks, on the Stamp Revenue, *etc.*

—— Note on the Working of the Stamp Department. *See* infra: Report, with the Chief Commissioner's Remarks, on the Stamp Revenue, *etc.*

—— Note on Vaccination, *etc.* *See* infra: Report on the Vaccine Operations conducted by the special Vaccination Department, *etc.*

—— Notes on the Annual Statements of the Government Charitable Dispensaries, *etc.* *See* infra: Report on the Working of Government Charitable Dispensaries, *etc.*

—— Notes on the Annual Statements of the Hospitals and Dispensaries (Triennial Report on the Government Charitable Dispensaries—on Hospitals and Dispensaries) in the Central Provinces and Berar for the year 1903(–1928). (Annual Report—Triennial Report—on Hospitals & Dispensaries in the Central Provinces and Berar for . . . 1929[–1936].) 32 pt. *Nagpur,* 1904–37. fol. & 8°. I.S. c.p. **21/3** & **128/5.**
The reports issued every third year from 1904 onwards take the place of the annual statements for the years in which they are issued. Imperfect; wanting the reports for 1920 and 1933.

—— Notes on the Annual Statements on the Lunatic Asylums (of the Mental Hospital), *etc.* *See* infra: Report on the Lunatic Asylum, *etc.*

—— Notes on the Annual Statements on Vaccine Operations, *etc.* *See* infra: Report on the Vaccine Operations, *etc.*

—— Notes on Vaccination, *etc.* *See* infra: Report on the Vaccine Operations conducted by the special Vaccination Department, *etc.*

—— A Primer of Co-operative Credit. By H. R. Crosthwaite. pp. iv. 140. *Nagpur,* 1910. 8°. I.S. c.p. **117.**

—— Progress Report of the Forest Administration, *etc.* *See* infra: Report with the Chief Commissioner's Review on the Forest Administration, *etc.*

—— Report by the Sanitary Commissioner, *etc.* *See* supra: Book Circular No. XLVI.

—— Report of the Sanitary Commissioner, *etc.* *See* supra: Annual Report on Vital Statistics, *etc.*

—— Report on Coins dealt with under the Treasure Trove Act during the year 1907-08(–1930-31). (Triennial Report . . . for the years 1931-32, 1932-33 and 1933-34; for the years 1934-35, 1935-36 and 1936-37.) 26 pt. *Nagpur,* 1908–37. fol. & 8°. I.S. c.p. **13** & **135.**

—— Report on Education, *etc.* *See* infra: Review on Education, *etc.*

—— Report on Roadside Arboriculture, *etc.* *See* infra: Review by the Chief Commissioner on Arboricultural Operations, *etc.*

—— Report on Scarcity in the Jubbulpore Division of the Central Provinces during the year 1913-14, and on the operations undertaken for the relief of distress. pp. 26. *Nagpur,* [1915.] fol. I.S. c.p. **44/4.**

—— [Report on Sugar Production in the Central Provinces. 22 Aug. 1883.] pp. 13. [*Nagpur,* 1883.] fol. I.S. c.p. **28.**

—— Report on the Administration of the Central Provinces, *etc.* *See* supra: Annual Report on the Administration of the Central Provinces, *etc.*

CENTRAL PROVINCES. [Miscellaneous Official Publications.]

—— Report on the Administration of the Feudatory States of the Central Provinces for the year 1894 (1912–1929). 19 pt. *Nagpur,* 1895–1930. fol. & 8°.
Imperfect; wanting the reports for 1895–1911.
[Continued as:]
Report on the Administration of the Central Provinces States for . . . 1930 (1931). 2 pt. *Nagpur,* 1931, 32. 8°. I.S. c.p. **1/8** & **116/4.**

—— Report on the Administration of the Income Tax Act for the year 1891-92(–1899-1900). ([Annual Statements of the Income Tax Act for the year 1900-01.]—Report on the Administration of the Income Tax Act for the triennium ending 31st March 1902.—Annual Statements . . . for the year 1902-03, 1903-04.) 13 pt. *Nagpur,* 1892–1904. fol. I.S. c.p. **15.**

—— Report on the Administration of the Income-Tax Act [in the Central Provinces and Berar] for the triennium ending 31st March 1905. (Annual Statements of the Income Tax Act—of the Income-Tax and the Super-Tax Acts—Income-Tax Report and Returns—Annual Report of the Income-Tax Dept.—for the year 1905-06 [–1923–24].) 17 pt. *Nagpur; Calcutta,* 1905–24. fol. & 8°. I.S. c.p. **15/2.**
The reports issued every third year from 1905 onwards take the place of the annual statements for the years in which they are issued. Imperfect; wanting the statements for 1906-07, 1908-09 and 1920-21.

—— Report on the Administration of the Land Revenue Department of the Central Provinces for the year 1874-75 (1878-79, 1880-81, 1881-82). 8 pt. *Nagpur,* 1875–83. 8° & fol.
Imperfect; wanting the report for 1879-80. Previous reports form part of the " Review by the Chief Commissioner of the Revenue Administration."
[Continued as:]
Review of the Administration of the Land Revenue Department . . . for the revenue year ending 30th September 1883 (1884). (Review of the Agricultural and Revenue Reports for the year 1884-85. By the Chief Commissioner.) 3 pt. [*Nagpur,* 1884]–86. fol.
[Continued as:]
Resolution (Report) on the Revenue Administration of the Central Provinces for the year 1885-86(–1913-14). 29 pt. *Nagpur,* 1887–1915. fol.
[Continued as:]
Reports (Resolution) on the Revenue Administration (on the Land Revenue Administration) and on the Operations of the Land Records and Settlement Departments in the Central Provinces during the year 1914-15 (–1926-27; for the year ending the 30th September 1928—year ending the 30th September 1935). 21 pt. *Nagpur,* 1916–36. fol. & 8°. I.S. c.p. **110** & **20.**
Previous reports on the operations of the Land Records and Settlement Departments were issued separately and are entered under DEPARTMENT OF LAND RECORDS.

—— Report on the Agra and Bombay Road. By Lieut.-Col. H. Goodwyn. pp. 32. *Agra,* 1851. 8°. I.S. c.p. **133/6.**

—— Report on the Assessment Groups and Group Rates of the First Revision Settlement of 93 Izara Villages in the Kelapur Taluq of the Yeotmal District for the year 1927. [By G. B. Despande. With maps.] pp. 2. 35. *Nagpur,* [1927.] fol. I.S. c.p. **19/44.** (2.)

—— Report on the Census of the Central Provinces effected on the 5th November 1866. [With tables.] pp. 19. *Nagpore,* [1867.] 8°. I.S. c.p. **105.**

CENTRAL PROVINCES. [MISCELLANEOUS OFFICIAL PUBLICATIONS.]

—— Report on the Cholera Epidemic of 1868. By Dr. S. C. Townsend. [With maps and tables.] pp. 3. v. 85. [*Nagpur*,] 1869. fol.   I.S. C.P. **35/4**.

—— [Report on the Cultivation of and Trade in Cotton in the Central Provinces for the year 1880-81.] pp. 2. [*Nagpur*, 1882.] fol.   I.S. C.P. **28/2**.

—— Report on the District of Nimar, by R. Temple. pp. iii. 29. *Nagpore*, 1864. 8°.   I.S. C.P. **112**.

—— Report on the Excise Revenue in the Central Provinces (of the Central Provinces), for the year 1871-72(–1873-74, 1875-76–1879-80, 1881-82–1902-03). 30 pt. *Nagpur; Allahabad*, 1872–1903. fol.   I.S. C.P. **9**. *Imperfect; wanting the reports for 1874-75 and 1880-81.*

—— Report on the Excise Revenue (on the Excise Administration) of the Central Provinces (and Berar) for the year 1903-04(–1921-22; for the year 1922–1935). 33 pt. *Nagpur*, 1904–36. fol. & 8°. I.S. C.P. **9/3** & **137**.

—— Report on the Famine in the Central Provinces in 1896 and 1897. By R. H. Craddock, *etc.* (vol. 3. Appendices v & vi—P.W.D. Section—by E. E. Oliver.) [With maps.] 3 vol. *Nagpur*, 1898. fol.   I.S. C.P. **44**.

—— Report on the Famine in the Central Provinces in 1899-1900. [Compiled by A. H. L. Fraser.] (vol. 3. Appendix IV—P.W.D. Section—by the Hon'ble L. M. St. Clair.) [With maps.] 3 vol. *Nagpur*, 1901. fol.   I.S. C.P. **44/2**.

—— Report on the Forest Administration, *etc. See* infra: Report with the Chief Commissioner's Review on the Forest Administration, *etc.*

—— Report on the Industrial Survey of the Central Provinces and Berar, 1908-09. [By C. E. Low.] pp. 94. *London*, 1910. 8°.   I.S. C.P. **109/2**.

—— Report on the Jails in the Central Provinces for the year 1869(–1902). 34 pt. *Nagpore; Allahabad*, 1870–1903. fol.   I.S. C.P. **22**.

—— Report on the Jails of the Central Provinces (and Berar) for the year 1903(–1935). 33 pt.   *Nagpur*, 1904–36. fol. & 8°.   I.S. C.P. **22/3** & **123/10**.

—— Report on the Judicial Administration—Civil—of the Central Provinces for the year 1869(–1902). 34 pt. *Nagpore; Allahabad*, 1870–1903. fol.   I.S. C.P. **6**.

—— Report on the Judicial Administration—Civil—of the Central Provinces (and Berar) for the year 1903(–1935). 33 pt. *Nagpur*, 1904–36. fol. & 8°.   I.S. C.P. **6/3** & **123/8**.

—— Report on the Judicial Administration—Criminal—of the Central Provinces for the year 1869(–1903). 34 pt. *Nagpore; Allahabad*, 1870–1903. fol.   I.S. C.P. **7**.

—— Report on the Judicial Administration—Criminal—of the Central Provinces (and Berar) for the year 1903(–1935). 33 pt. *Nagpur*, 1904–36. fol. & 8°. I.S. C.P. **7/4** & **123/9**.

—— Report on the Land Revenue Settlement of British Nimar; a district of the Central Provinces. Effected by Captain J. Forsyth . . . 1868-69. [With a map.] pp. 13. xiv. 356. *Nagpore*, 1870. 8°.   I.S. C.P. **108/11**.

—— Report on the Land Revenue Settlement of the Baitool District, Nerbudda Division, Central Provinces. Effected by W. Ramsay . . . 1866. [With a map.] pp. 158. *Bombay*, 1867. 8°.   I.S. C.P. **108/2**.

CENTRAL PROVINCES. [MISCELLANEOUS OFFICIAL PUBLICATIONS.]

—— Report on the Land Revenue Settlement of the Balaghat District in the Central Provinces effected during the years 1895–1898. [By James R. Scott. With a map.] pp. 2. 2. 4. iii. 56. 59. *Nagpur*, 1901 [1902]. fol.   I.S. C.P. **19/12**.

—— Report on the Land Revenue Settlement of the Betul District in the Central Provinces effected during the years 1894 to 1899. [By B. P. Standen. With a map.] pp. 2. 3. 4. viii. 140. 59. *Nagpur*, 1901 [1903]. fol.   I.S. C.P. **19/13**.

—— Report on the Land Revenue Settlement of the Bhandara District in the Central Provinces effected during the years 1894 to 1899. [By A. B. Napier. With a map.] pp. 5. 6. 2. 45. 79. *Nagpur*, 1902 [1904]. fol.   I.S. C.P. **19/14**.

—— Report on the Land Revenue Settlement of the Bilaspur District of the Central Provinces, effected during the years 1886 to 1890. [By Parshotam Dās. With a map and a sheet of corrigenda.] pp. 8. 5. iii. 162.   *Nagpur*, 1892 [1895], [1901 ?] fol.   I.S. C.P. **19/3**.

—— Report on the Land Revenue Settlement of the Chindwara District, Nerbudda Division, Central Provinces, effected by W. Ramsay. [With a map.] pp. 8. xvii. 164. *Nagpore*, 1869. 8°.   I.S. C.P. **108/7**.

—— Report on the Land Revenue Settlement of the Damoh District in the Central Provinces effected during the years 1908 to 1913. [By C. G. C. Trench. With a map.] pp. 3. 4. 62. 4. *Nagpur*, 1914 [1915]. fol.   I.S. C.P. **19/30**.

—— Report on the Land Revenue Settlement of the Damoh District of the Central Provinces, effected during the years 1889 to 1891. [By J. B. Fuller. With a map.] pp. 2. 7. 2. 78. *Nagpur*, 1893 [1901]. fol. I.S. C.P. **19/4**.

—— Report on the Land Revenue Settlement of the Drug Tahsil in the Raipur District of the Central Provinces effected during the years 1896 to 1902. [By E. R. K. Blenkinsop. With a map.] pp. ii. 3. 5. 72. 42. *Nagpur*, 1903 [1907]. fol.   I.S. C.P. **19/17**.

—— Report on the Land Revenue Settlement of the Dumoh District, Jubbulpoor Division, Central Provinces, effected by A. M. Russell . . . 1866. [With a map.] pp. 127. *Bombay*, 1867. 8°.   I.S. C.P. **108/3**.

—— Report on the Land Revenue Settlement of the Hoshangabad District in the Central Provinces effected during the years 1891–1898 [*sic*, for 1896]. [By F. G. Sly. With a map.] pp. 5. 8. iii. 66. lvii. *Nagpur*, 1905. fol.   I.S. C.P. **19/19**.

—— Report on the Land Revenue Settlement of the Jubbulpore District in the Central Provinces effected during the years 1886 to 1894. [By Aulād Ḥusain. With a map.] pp. 3. 18. 2. 50. 73. *Nagpur*, 1896 [1901]. fol.   I.S. C.P. **19/6**.

—— Report on the Land Revenue Settlement of the Jubbulpore District, in the Jubbulpore Division, Central Provinces, effected by Major W. Nembhard . . . and A. M. Russell. [The report compiled by A. M. Russell. With tables.] pp. 14. iv. 90. *Nagpore*, 1869. 8°.   I.S. C.P. **108/8**.

—— Report on the Land Revenue Settlement of the Jubbulpore District in the Central Provinces effected during the years 1907 to 1912. [By H. R. Crosthwaite. With a map.] pp. 3. 6. 117. *Nagpur*, 1912 [1913]. fol.   I.S. C.P. **19/27**.

CENTRAL PROVINCES. [MISCELLANEOUS OFFICIAL PUBLICATIONS.]

—— Report on the Land Revenue Settlement of the Mundlah District of the Central Provinces, effected by Captain H. C. E. Ward, 1868–69. pp. 5. ix. 162. *Bombay*, 1870. 8°. I.S. C.P. **108/10.**

—— Report on the Land Revenue Settlement of the Nagpore District, in the Nagpore Division, Central Provinces, effected by A. B. Ross. [With "Supplement to the Settlement Report of the Nagpore District, being copy of an article on that district written for the Central Provinces' Gazetteer, by M. Low," and with tables.] 2 pt. *Nagpore*, 1869. 8°. I.S. C.P. **108/9.**

—— Report on the Land Revenue Settlement of the Nagpur District in the Central Provinces effected during the years 1890 to 1895. [By R. H. Craddock. With a map.] pp. 5. 2. 7. xvii. 229. 68. *Nagpur*, 1899 [1900]. fol. I.S. C.P. **19/9.**

—— Report on the Land Revenue Settlement of the Nagpur District in the Central Provinces effected during the years 1912 to 1917. [By J. F. Dyer. With a map, and an erratum slip.] pp. 3. 4. 4. 73. 66. *Nagpur*, 1917 [1919], [1930.] fol. I.S. C.P. **19/33.**

—— Report on the Land Revenue Settlement of the Narsingh-pur District ni [*sic*] the Central Provinces effected during the years 1885 to 1894. [By E. A. De Brett. With a map.] pp. 2. 6. 2. 53. 29. *Nagpur*, 1896 [1902]. fol. I.S. C.P. **19/7.**

—— Report on the Land Revenue Settlement of the Nimar District in the Central Provinces effected during the years 1895 to 1899. [By C. W. E. Montgomerie. With a map.] pp. 3. 4. 4. iv. 37. 45. *Nagpur*, 1903 [1905]. fol. I.S. C.P. **19/16.**

—— Report on the Land Revenue Settlement of the Nursing-pore District, Nurbudda Division, Central Provinces, effected by C. Grant . . . 1866. [With tables.] pp. viii. 103. *Nagpore*, [1867.] 8°. I.S. C.P. **108.**

—— Report on the Land Revenue Settlement of the Raipur District of the Central Provinces, effected during the years 1885 to 1889. [By L. S. Carey. With a map and an amendment.] pp. 7. 5. iv. 185. *Nagpur*, 1891 [1895], [1901 ?] fol. I.S. C.P. **19.**

—— Report on the Land Revenue Settlement of the Sambal-pur District of the Central Provinces, effected during the years 1885 to 1889. [By J. B. Fuller. With a map, and a sheet of corrigenda.] pp. 7. iii. 91. *Bombay*, 1891 [1893], [1901 ?] fol. I.S. C.P. **19/2.**

—— Report on the Land Revenue Settlement of the Saugor District in the Central Provinces effected during the years 1887–1897. [By E. A. DeBrett. With a map.] pp. 3. 4. 71. 52. *Nagpur*, 1902 [1904]. fol. I.S. C.P. **19/15.**

—— Report on the Land Revenue Settlement of the Saugor District, Jubbulpore Division, Central Provinces, 1867, effected by Lt. Coll. J. N. H. Maclean. [With tables.] pp. 13. viii. 105. xii. *Nagpore*, 1867. 8°. I.S. C.P. **108/4.**

—— Report on the Land Revenue Settlement of the Seonee District, on [*sic*] the Central Provinces. Effected by W. B. Thomson . . . 1867. [With maps.] pp. 14. xv. 112. *Bombay*, 1867. 8°. I.S. C.P. **108/5.**

—— Report on the Land Revenue Settlement of the Seoni District in the Central Provinces effected during the years 1894 to 1898. [By Aulād Ḥusain. With a map.] pp. 5. 2. 71. 95. *Nagpur*, 1900 [1902]. fol. I.S. C.P. **19/11.**

CENTRAL PROVINCES. [MISCELLANEOUS OFFICIAL PUBLICATIONS.]

—— Report on the Land Revenue Settlement of the Wardha District in the Central Provinces effected during the years 1891 to 1894. [By Parshotam Dās. With a map.] pp. 2. 4. 2. 79. 46. *Nagpur*, 1896 [1904]. fol. I.S. C.P. **19/8.**

—— Report on the Land Revenue Settlement of the Wurdah District of the Central Provinces, 1867, effected by H. Rivett-Carnac. [With tables.] pp. 16. xi. 122. *Nagpore*, 1867. 8°. I.S. C.P. **108/6.**

—— Report on the Land Revenue Settlement of the Zamindari Estates in the Raipur District of the Central Provinces. Effected during the years 1899–1902. [By James R. Scott. With a map.] pp. 4. 9. 27. 32. *Nagpur*, 1904 [1906]. fol. I.S. C.P. **19/18.**

—— Report on the Lunatic Asylums in the Central Provinces, for the year 1874(–1895). (Annual Report—Triennial Reports—Notes on the Annual Statements—on the Lunatic Asylums—on the Lunatic Asylum—in the Central Provinces for the year 1896–1922.—Triennial Report on the Working of the Mental Hospital in the Central Provinces and Berar . . . for the years 1921, 1922, 1923. —Notes on the Annual Statements of the Mental Hospitals —Annual Report on the Mental Hospital—in the Central Provinces and Berar . . . for the year 1924–1935.) 58 pt. *Nagpur; Allahabad*, 1875–1936. fol. & 8°. I.S. C.P. **24 & 128/4.**

The reports issued every third year from 1902–1923 take the place of the annual statements for the year in which they are issued. No annual report was issued in 1900 or 1901. Imperfect; wanting the triennial report for 1920 and the annual statement for 1921.

—— Report on the Management by Government of Private Estates, etc. *See infra*: Review of the Reports on Estates under Government Management, etc.

—— **Report on the Police Administration of the Central Provinces for the year 1869(–1896, 1898–1902). 33 pt.** *Nagpore; Allahabad*, 1870–1903. fol. I.S. C.P. **26.** *Imperfect; wanting the report for 1897.*

—— Report on the Police Administration of the Central Provinces (and Berar) for the year 1903(–1936). 34 pt. *Nagpur*, 1904–37. fol. & 8°. I.S. C.P. **26/3 & 127/4.**

—— Report on the Progress of Education, etc. *See infra*: Review on Education, etc.

—— Report on the Projected Tramway between Nagpore and the Eastern Districts of the Central Provinces. By R. Temple. pp. vii. 36. iv. *Nagpore*, 1863. 8°. I.S. C.P. **140/2.**

—— [Report on the Railway-borne Traffic (Annual Report on the Rail-borne Traffic) of the Central Provinces for the year 1883-84(–1902-03).] 20 pt. *Nagpur*, 1903. fol. I.S. C.P. **42.**

The title on the wrapper of the report for 1883-84 reads "Report on the Trade and Resources of the Central Provinces."

—— Annual Report on the Rail-borne Traffic of the Central Provinces and Berar for the official year 1903-04, ending the 31st March 1904(—the year ending the 31st March 1922; the year ending the 31st March 1924—the year ending the 31st March 1933). 29 pt. *Nagpur*, 1904–34. fol. I.S. C.P. **42/3.**

Imperfect; wanting the report for the year ending the 31st March 1923.

—— Report on the Reformatory School, Jubbulpore . . . for the year 1898(–1909). *Allahabad; Nagpur*, 1899–1910. fol. I.S. C.P. **17.**

CENTRAL PROVINCES. [MISCELLANEOUS OFFICIAL PUBLICATIONS.]

—— Report on the Revision of the Land Revenue Settlement of the Bilaspur Zamindaris in the Bilaspur District of the Central Provinces effected during the years 1928–1930. [By T. C. S. Jayaratnam. With plates and maps.] pp. 3. ii. 103. *Nagpur*, 1931. fol. I.S. C.P. **19/50.**

—— Report on the Revision of the Land Revenue Settle ment of the Chhindwara District in the Central Provinces effected during the years 1891 to 1895. [By C. W. E. Montgomerie. With a map.] pp. 3. 5. vii. 103. 151. *Nagpur*, 1900 [1902]. fol. I.S. C.P. **19/10.**

—— Report on the Revision of the Land Revenue Settlement of the Saugor District in the Central Provinces effected during the years 1911 to 1916. [By G. L. Corbett. With a map.] pp. 3. 4. v. 204. *Nagpur*, 1918 [1919]. fol. I.S. C.P. **19/34.**

—— Report on the Revision on the Land Revenue Settlement of the Mandla District in the Central Provinces effected during the years 1927–1930. [By C. J. W. Lillie. With maps.] pp. 3. ii. 24. 56. *Nagpur*, 1931. fol. I.S. C.P. **19/49.**

—— Report on the River Godavery and its Feeders: their navigable capabilities; the resources and trade of the adjacent countries; and the projected navigation works. By R. Temple. pp. iv. 87. *Nagpore*, 1863. 8°. I.S. C.P. **133/3.**

—— Report on the River Mahanuddy and its Tributaries: the resources and trade of the adjacent countries; and the proposed works for the improvement of navigation and irrigation. By R. Temple. pp. viii. 66. vii. *Nagpore*, 1863. 8°. I.S. C.P. **133/2.**

—— Report on the Stamp Revenue, *etc*. *See* infra: Report, with the Chief Commissioner's Remarks, on the Stamp Revenue, *etc*.

—— Report on the State and Progress of Education, *etc*. *See* infra: Review on Education, *etc*.

—— Report on the Summary Land Revenue Settlement of the Mandla District of the Central Provinces, effected during the years 1888–90. [By J. B. Fuller.] pp. 3. 26. *Nagpur*, 1894 [1895]. fol. I.S. C.P. **19/5.**

—— Report on the Trade and Resources of the Central Provinces, for the year 1863-4(–1866-67, 1868-69; for the years 1869-70, 1870-71 and 1871-72; for the year 1872-73–1878-79, 1880-81–1882-83). 16 pt. *Nagpore*, 1864–83. fol. & 8°. I.S. C.P. **111 & 41.**
Imperfect; wanting the reports for 1867–68 and 1879–80.

—— Report on the Vaccine Operations conducted by the special Vaccination Department, Central Provinces, for the year 1868 (1869). (Report on the Vaccine Operations in the Central Provinces for the year 1870 [1871, 1872-73, 1873-74, 1878-79–1886-87].—Notes on the Annual Statements—Report—on Vaccine Operations . . . for the year 1887-88[–1895-96].—Note (Notes)—Triennial Report —on Vaccination . . . for the year 1896-97[–1902-03].) 31 pt. *Nagpore; Allahabad*, 1870–1903. fol I.S. C.P. **40.**
The reports issued every third year from 1890 onwards cover the preceding triennium and take the place of the notes for the years in which they are issued.

—— Notes (Triennial Report) on Vaccination in the Central Provinces (and Berar) for the season 1903-1904(–1919-20, 1921-22–1928-29). 25 pt. *Nagpur*, 1904–29. fol. & 8°. I.S. C.P. **40/3 & 128/3.**
The triennial reports issued for 1902–05 onwards take the place of the notes for the years in which they are issued. Imperfect; wanting the notes for 1920-21.

CENTRAL PROVINCES. [MISCELLANEOUS OFFICIAL PUBLICATIONS.]

—— Report on the Working of Government Charitable Dispensaries in the Central Provinces for the year 1869(–1886). 18 pt. *Nagpore*, 1870–87. fol. [Continued as:] Notes on the Annual Statements (Triennial Report on the Working) of the Government Charitable Dispensaries in the Central Provinces for the year 1887(–1902). 16 pt. *Nagpur; Allahabad*, 1888–1903. fol. I.S. C.P. **21.**
The reports issued every third year from 1889 onwards take the place of the annual statements for the years in which they are issued.

—— Report on the Working of the Cotton Duties Acts, XVII of 1894 and II of 1896, in the Central Provinces, for the financial year 1895–96. (Report on the Working of the Cotton Duties Act, II of 1896 . . . for the financial year 1896-97[–1898-99].) 4 pt. *Nagpur; Allahabad*, 1897–99. fol. I.S. C.P. **16.**

—— Report on the Working of the District Post Office for the year 1870-71. pp. 2. 2. *Nagpur*, 1872. fol. I.S. C.P. **27.**

—— Report on the Working of the Indian Companies Act, VI of 1882 in the Central Provinces and Berar during the year 1911-12(–1913-14). (Report on the Working of the Indian Companies Act, VII of 1913 . . . during the year 1914-15[–1926-27].—Report—Annual Report—on the Administration of the Indian Companies Act . . . during the year 1927-28[—the year ending 31st March 1934].) 23 pt. *Nagpur*, 1912–34. fol. & 8°. I.S. C.P. **15/3 & 117/2.**

—— Report upon Malaria in the Central Provinces. By Major W. H. Kenrick. [With maps.] pp. 191. *Nagpur*, 1914. fol. I.S. C.P. **37.**

—— Report, with the Chief Commissioner's Remarks (Review), on the Stamp Revenue of the Central Provinces for the year 1869-70(–1876-77, 1879-80–1882-83, 1883, 1884, 1885-86). (Report on the Stamp Revenue . . . for the year 1886-87–1899-1900.—Note on the Annual Statements of the Stamp Revenue . . . for the year 1900-1901.—Report on the Stamp Revenue . . . for the triennium ending 31st March 1902.—Note on the Stamp Revenue . . . for the year 1902-1903). 32 pt. *Nagpore; Allahabad*, 1870–1903. fol. I.S. C.P. **39.**
Imperfect; wanting the Reports for 1877–78 and 1878–79.

—— Report (Note) on the Stamp Revenue (Note on the Working of the Stamp Department) of the Central Provinces (and Berar) for the year 1903-1904(–1927-28; for the triennium ending 31st March 1929; for the year ending the 31st March 1930—the year ending the 31st March 1936). 33 pt. *Nagpur*, 1904–36. fol. & 8°. I.S. C.P. **39/3 & 138.**
The reports issued every third year from 1905 onwards cover the preceding triennium and take the place of the annual notes for the years in which they are issued.

—— Report with the Chief Commissioner's Review on Education, *etc*. *See* infra: Review on Education, *etc*.

—— Report with the Chief Commissioner's Review on the Forest Administration of the Central Provinces, for the year 1869-70. (Progress Report of the Forest Administration . . . for 1876-77, *etc*.—Report on the Forest Administration . . . for the year 1890-91[–1901-02].) 14 pt. *Nagpore; Allahabad*, 1870–1902. fol. & 8°. I.S. C.P. **11.**
The reports for 1870-71–1876-77 were issued in the Forest Administration Reports of India.

—— Report on the Forest Administration of the Central Provinces (and Berar) for the year 1902-03(–1927-28; for the year ending 31st March 1929—the year ending 31st March 1938). 54 pt. *Nagpur*, 1903–39. fol. & 8°. I.S. C.P. **11/3 & 120/4.**
The reports for 1919-20 onwards were issued in two parts, the "Report on the Administration" or "Administration Report" and the "Statistical Statements."

CENTRAL PROVINCES. [MISCELLANEOUS OFFICIAL PUBLICATIONS.]

—— Report on the Working (on the Administration) of the Workmen's Compensation Act, VIII of 1923, in the Central Provinces and Berar during the year 1926 [etc.].
Nagpur, [1927– .] 8°.   I.S. C.P. **129/2**.
From 1953 onward published by the Government of Madhya Pradesh. Wanting the issues between 1936 and 1951.

—— Reports on the Revenue Administration, etc. *See* supra : Report on the Administration of the Land Revenue Department, etc.

—— [Reports on the Working of District Councils and Local Boards in the Central Provinces for 1891-92–1902-03.] 12 pt. *Nagpur; Allahabad,* [1892]–1903. fol.
            I.S. C.P. **18**.

—— [Reports on the Working of District Councils and Local Boards in the Central Provinces and Berar for 1903-04–1926-27 ; for the year ending 31st March 1928—the year ending 31st March 1935.] 32 pt. *Nagpur,* 1904-37. fol. & 8°. I.S. C.P. **18/3 & 121/4**.

—— [Reports on the Working of the Factories Act during the year ending the 31st December 1898; during the year ending the 31st December 1900.] 2 pt. *Nagpur,* [1899,] 1901. fol.   I.S. C.P. **12**.

—— [Reports on the Working of the Indian Factories Act in the Central Provinces and Berar for the year 1910–1935.] 26 pt. *Nagpur,* [1911]–36. fol. & 8°.
         I.S. C.P. **12/3 & 104**.

—— [Reports on the Working of the Lock Hospitals for 1876–1889.] 14 pt. [*Nagpur,* 1877–90.] fol.
            I.S. C.P. **23**.

—— Reports on the Working of the Municipal Committees, etc. *See* supra : Annual Reports on Municipal Operations, etc.

—— Resolution on the Management by Government of Private Estates, etc. *See* infra : Review of the Reports on Estates under Government Management, etc.

—— Resolution on the Revenue (on the Land Revenue) Administration, etc. *See* supra : Report on the Administration of the Land Revenue Department, etc.

—— Resolution reviewing the Reports on the Working of Municipal Committees, etc. *See* supra : Annual Reports on Municipal Operations, etc.

—— Returns of Railway Borne Traffic (of the Rail-borne Traffic) during the quarter ending 30th September 1885 [or rather, 31st December 1884] (during the quarter ending 30th June 1890; during the quarter ending 31st December 1891—the quarter ending 31st December 1895 ; during the quarter ending 30th June 1896—the quarter ending 30th June 1900). 28 pt. [*Nagpur,* 1885]–1900. fol.   I.S. C.P. **43**.

—— Review by the Chief Commissioner on Arboricultural Operations in the Central Provinces, for the years 1871-72 and 1872-73. (Arboricultural Returns 1882-83.—Report on Roadside Arboriculture . . . for the year ending 31st March 1884.) 3 pt. *Nagpur,* 1874–84. fol.
          I.S. C.P. **2**.
The report for 1883–84 was issued by the Department of Agriculture.

—— Review of the Administration of the Land Revenue Department, etc. *See* supra . Report on the Administration of the Land Revenue Department, etc.

—— Review of the Agricultural and Revenue Reports, etc. *See* supra : Report on the Administration of the Land Revenue Department, etc.

CENTRAL PROVINCES. [MISCELLANEOUS OFFICIAL PUBLICATIONS.]

—— Review of the Reports on Estates under Government Management in the Central Provinces, during the year ending September 30th, 1885. (Resolution on the Management by Government of Private Estates . . . during the year ending September 30th, 1886[—the year ending 30th September 1894 ; the year ending 30th September 1896—the year ending 30th September 1899]. —Report on the Management by Government of Private Estates . . . for the revenue year ending 30th September 1900[—the year ending 30th September 1934].) 49 pt. *Nagpur,* 1886–1935. fol. & 8°. I.S. C.P. **8 & 118/3**.
Imperfect ; wanting the report for 1894-95.

—— Review on Education (Report with the Chief Commissioner's Review on Education—Report on Education—Report on the Progress of Education—Report on the State and Progress of Education) in the Central Provinces during the year 1865-66 (1869-70–1902-03). 35 pt. *Nagpore; Allahabad,* 1866–1903. fol. I.S. C.P. **29**.
In 1897 and 1902 reports for the preceding quinquennium take the place of the annual reports.

—— Report on the State and Progress of Education in the Central Provinces (and Berar) for the year 1903-04(–1920-21, 1924-25, 1925-26; for the quinquennium ending 31st March 1927 ; for the year ending 31st March 1928—the year ending 31st March 1935). 29 pt. *Nagpur,* 1904–36. fol. & 8°. I.S. C.P. **29/3 & 136**.
From 1907 onwards every fifth report deals with the preceding quinquennium and takes the place of the annual report for the year in which it is issued. Imperfect ; wanting the report for the quinquennium ending 31st March 1922 and the annual reports for 1922-23 and 1923-24.

—— Review, with the Chief Commissioner's Remarks, on the Stamp Revenue, etc. *See* supra : Report, etc.

—— [Rules to regulate the Transport of Explosives in Berar. With Amendments.] pp. 11. *Nagpur,* [1909.] fol.
          I.S. C.P. **50/2**.

—— [Rules under the Indian Explosives Act, 1884, as applied to Berar, for the manufacture, possession and sale of explosives.] pp. 29. *Nagpur,* [1908.] fol. I.S. C.P. **50**.

—— [The Berar Explosives Rules, 1914. Made by the Chief Commissioner, Central Provinces.] pp. 57. *Nagpur,* 1914. fol.   I.S. C.P. **50/4**.

—— Selection of Letters written in the first quarter of the year 1865, by order of the Chief Commissioner, Central Provinces, to the address of the Commissioner, Nagpore Division, regarding local improvements in the districts of that Division. pp. 39. [*Nagpur ? 1865 ?*]
          I.S. C.P. **133/5**.

—— Statement of Rural and Urban Wages prevailing in the Central Provinces and Berar for the year ending the 30th June 1910(—the year ending the 30th June 1924). 15 pt. *Nagpur,* [1911–24.] fol. I.S. C.P. **47**.

—— Treasury Manual for the Central Provinces. Fifth edition. Corrected up to 31st December 1906. (Reprinted.) pp. 442. *Nagpur,* 1912. 8°. I.S. C.P. **119**.

—— Triennial Report on Coins dealt with under the Treasure Trove Act, etc. *See* supra: Report, etc.

—— Triennial Report on the Government Charitable Dispensaries (on Hospitals and Dispensaries), etc. *See* supra: Notes on the Annual Statements of the Hospitals and Dispensaries, etc.

—— Triennial Report on the Working of the Government Charitable Dispensaries, etc. *See* supra : Report on the Working of the Government Charitable Dispensaries, etc.

CENTRAL PROVINCES. [Miscellaneous Official Publications.]

—— Triennial Report on the Working of the Mental Hospital, *etc.* *See* supra: Report on the Lunatic Asylums, *etc.*

—— Triennial Report on Vaccination, *etc. See* supra: Report on the Vaccine Operations of the special Vaccination Department, *etc.*

—— Triennial Reports on the Lunatic Asylums, *etc. See* supra: Report on the Lunatic Asylums, *etc.*

LEGISLATIVE COUNCIL.

—— **Effect of Legislation by the Chief Commissioner of the Central Provinces in Council** (by the Legislative Council of the Governor—by the Local Legislature—by the Legislative Council for the year 1915 (1917, 1918, 1920–23, 1927–35, for the years 1936 and January to March 1937). 17 pt. *Nagpur*, 1917–38. 8°.   I.S. C.P. **115/5.**

—— Proceedings of the Legislative Council of the Chief Commissioner of the Central Provinces, 1914[–1920], *etc.* 7 vol. *Nagpur*, 1915–[20]. fol.
[Continued as:]
Proceedings of the Legislative Council of the Governor of the Central Provinces, *etc.* 1921. vol. 1—1930. vol. 1. *Nagpur*, [1921]–30. fol. & 8°.
[Continued as:]
Legislative Council Proceedings . . . First(—thirteenth) Session of the Fourth Legislative Council. Official Report. 13 vol. *Nagpur*, 1930–36. 8°.
        I.S.C.P.36.& 115/3.

DEPARTMENTS OF STATE AND PUBLIC INSTITUTIONS.

CENTRAL PROVINCES AND BERAR UNIVERSITY COMMITTEE.

—— Report, *etc.* pp. xxii. 108. *Nagpur*, 1915. fol.
        I.S. C.P. **53.**

CIVIL MEDICAL DEPARTMENT.

—— Annual Report of the Chemical Examiner and Bacteriologist to the Governments of the North-Western Provinces and Oudh (of the United Provinces of Agra and Oudh) and of the Central Provinces. For the year 1894(–1935). 1895–1936. fol. *See* AGRA AND OUDH, *United Provinces of.—Office of the Chemical Examiners to Government.*
        I.S. UP. **6 & 167.**

—— The Central Provinces Medical Manual, *etc.* pp. 119. 46. xii. *Nagpur*, 1912. 8°.   I.S. C.P. **128.**

CIVIL VETERINARY DEPARTMENT.

—— Manual of the Civil Veterinary Department, Central Provinces & Berar. pp. 94. *Nagpur*, 1916. 8°.
        I.S. C.P. **130/3.**

—— Report (Annual Report) on the Working of the Civil Veterinary Department of the Central Provinces and Berar during the year 1925-26(—the year ending the 31st March 1941). *Nagpur*, 1926–41. 8°. I.S. C.P. **130/2.**
Imperfect; wanting the report for 1927-28.

COTTON DEPARTMENT.

—— Report on the Cotton Department [of the Central Provinces and Berar] for the year 1867-68 (1868-69). By Harry Rivett-Carnac. 2 pt. *Bombay*, 1869. 8°.
        I.S. C.P. **109.**

COURT OF THE JUDICIAL COMMISSIONER.

—— *See* infra: COURTS OF JUSTICE.

COURTS OF JUSTICE.

Court of the Judicial Commissioner.

—— Civil Circulars of the Judicial Commissioner, Central Provinces. Revised edition. 1912. 5 pt. *Nagpur*, 1912. 8°.   I.S. C.P. **123/2. (1.)**

CENTRAL PROVINCES. [Departments of State and Public Institutions.]

—— Revised edition. 1920. 5 pt. *Nagpur*, 1920. 8°.
        I.S. C.P. **123/2. (2.)**

—— Reprint. 1929. 5 pt. *Nagpur*, 1929. 8°.
        I.S. C.P. **123/2. (3.)**

—— Criminal Circulars of the Judicial Commissioner, Central Provinces. Revised edition. 1915. 4 pt. *Nagpur*, 1915. 8°.   I.S. C.P. **123/3. (1.)**

—— Revised edition. 1929. 4 pt. *Nagpur*, 1929. 8°.
        I.S. C.P. **123/3. (2.)**

—— The Nagpur Law Reports: containing cases determined by the Court of the Judicial Commissioner at Nagpur and by the Judicial Committee of the Privy Council on appeal from that Court. vol. 24—vol. 31. suppl. 5. Jan. 1928—May 1936. *Nagpur*, 1928–36. 8°.
        P.P. **1351. ahf.**

No more published.

—— Rules made by the Court of the Judicial Commissioner, Central Provinces, with the previous approval of the Local Government under section 125 of the Code of Civil Procedure, 1908, as amended. (Supplement, *etc.*) 2 pt. [*Nagpur*, 1930, 31.] 8°.   I.S. C.P. **123/5. (1.)**

—— Rules made by the Court of the Judicial Commissioner, Central Provinces . . . Corrected up to the 1st October 1933. pp. 13. [*Nagpur*, 1933.] 8°. I.S. C.P. **123/5. (2.)**

High Court.

—— The Indian Law Reports . . . Nagpur series: containing cases determined by the High Court at Nagpur and by the Judicial Committee of the Privy Council on appeal from that Court, *etc.* Sept. 1936—Feb. 1937. 6 pt. *Nagpur*, 1936, 37. 8°.   P.P. **1351. aho.**

DEPARTMENT OF AGRICULTURE.

—— Agricultural Ledger Series, Central Provinces. No. 1. (Bulletin no. 2–9.) *Nagpur*, 1895–1902. 8°. I.S. C.P. **124.**

—— [Bulletin.] no. 1–5. [*Nagpur*,] 1908–16. 8°.
        I.S. C.P. **124/2.**

—— Annual Reports of Experimental Farms, Akola and the Experimental Farm attached to the Agricultural College, Nagpur, for the year 1925-1926 (1926-1927; for the year ending 31st March 1928—the year ending 31st March 1931). 6 pt. *Nagpur*, 1927–32. 8°.   I.S. C.P. **113/8.**

—— Annual Reports of Experimental Farms of the Southern and Eastern Circles, Tharsa and Raipur, for the year 1925-1926 (for the year ending 31st March 1927—the year ending 31st March 1931). 6 pt.   *Nagpur*, 1927–32. 8°.   I.S. C.P. **113/5.**

—— Annual Reports on Experimental Farms, Nagpur, Akola, Powarkhera, Adhartal, Chhindwara, Tharsa, and Raipur, for the year ending 31st March 1932. (Annual Reports on Experimental Farms, Nagpur, Akola, Adhartal, Chhindwara, Powarkhera and Raipur, for the year ending 31st March 1933—the year ending the 31st March 1935.) 4 pt. *Nagpur*, 1934, 35. 8°.   I.S. C.P. **113/9.**

—— Annual Reports on Experimental Farms of the Northern and Plateau Circles, Powarkhera, Adhartal, Chhindwara, with that of cattle-breeding stations attached thereto, for the year 1925-1926 (for the year ending 31st March 1927—the year ending 31st March 1931). 6 pt. *Nagpur*, 1927–32. 8°.   I.S. C.P. **113/7.**

—— Comments by the Director of Agriculture on the Return of Expenditure of the Provincial and District Gardens in the Central Provinces and Berar for the year ending 30th June 1917. pp. 6. *Nagpur*, [1917.] fol.
        I.S. C.P. **3/10.**

—— Report of the Department of Land Records and Agriculture, Central Provinces. For the year 1892-93(—the
year ending the 30th September 1901). 9 pt. *Nagpur,*
1894-1902. fol. I.S. C.P. **3.**
*Later reports were issued separately by the Department of
Land Records and the Department of Agriculture.*

—— Report on the Department of Agriculture (Report on
the working of the Department of Agriculture) for the
year 1901-02(—the year ending the 31st March 1936).
34 pt. *Nagpur,* 1903-37. fol. & 8°. I.S. C.P. **3/11 & 124/4.**

—— Report on Demonstration Work carried out in the
Eastern Circle during the year ending 30th June 1922
(1923; during the year 1923-24, 1924-25). (Report on
Demonstration Work carried out in the Eastern Circle,
together with reports on the seed and demonstration
farms . . . with that of the cattle breeding stations
attached thereto, for the year 1925-26 [1926-27; for the
year ending 31st March 1928—the year ending the
31st March 1935].) 14 pt. *Nagpur,* 1923-35. 8°.
I.S. C.P. **113.**

—— Report on Demonstration Work carried out in the
Plateau Sub-circle, together with reports on seed and
demonstration farms . . . for the year 1925-26 (1926-27;
for the year ending 31st March 1928—the year ending
31st March 1930). 5 pt. *Nagpur,* 1927-31. 8°.
I.S. C.P. **113/6.**

—— Report on Roadside Arboriculture . . . for the year
ending 31st March 1884. 1884. *See* supra: MISCEL-
LANEOUS OFFICIAL PUBLICATIONS. Review by the Chief
Commissioner on Arboricultural Operations, *etc.*
1874, *etc.* fol. I.S. C.P. **2.**

—— Report on the 1. Agricultural Collége at Nagpur,
2. Botanical and Chemical Research, 3. Central Museum,
Nagpur, 4. Maharajbagh Menagerie, Nagpur for the year
1914-15, *etc.* (Report on the 1. Agricultural College,
Nagpur, 2. Botanical and Chemical Research, 3. Entomo-
logical Work, 4. Central Museum, Nagpur, 5. Maharaj
Bagh Menagerie, for the year ending the 30th June 1916.—
Report on the 1. Agricultural College, Nagpur, 2. Botanical and Chemical Research, 3. Maharaj Bagh Menagerie,
for the year ending the 30th June 1916 [or rather, 1917]
(–1920).—Report on the 1. Agricultural College, Nagpur,
2. Botanical, Chemical and Mycological (and Entomo-
logical) Research, 3. Maharaj Bagh Menagerie, 4. Agricultural Engineer's Section, for the year ending the
30th June 1921(–1923; for the year 1923-24–1926-27;
for the year ending 31st March 1928–1936). 22 pt.
Nagpur, 1915-36. fol. & 8°. I.S. C.P. **3/9 & 124/6.**

—— Report on the Agricultural Stations in the Central
Provinces (and Berar) for the year 1905-1906(–1913-14),
etc. 9 pt. [*Nagpur,*] 1906-15. 4° & fol. I.S. C.P. **10/3.**

—— Report on the Agricultural Stations in the Eastern
Circle for the year ending the 30th June 1922 (1923; for
the year 1923-24, 1924-25). 4 pt. *Nagpur,* 1923-26. fol.
I.S. C.P. **10/6.**

—— Report on the Agricultural Stations in the Northern
Circle for the year ending the 30th June 1915(–1923; for
the year 1923-24, 1924-25). 11 pt. *Nagpur,* 1915-26. fol.
I.S. C.P. **10/4.**

—— Report on the Agricultural Stations in the Southern
Circle for the year ending the 30th June 1915(–1922; for
the year ending the 31st March 1923; for the year 1923-24,
1924-25). 11 pt. *Nagpur,* 1915-26. fol. I.S. C.P. **10/5.**

—— Report on the Agricultural Stations in the Western
Circle for the year 1914-15(—the year ending the 30th
June 1918; for the year ending the 30th June 1920—the
year ending the 30th June 1924; for the year 1924-25).
10 pt. *Nagpur,* 1915-26. fol. I.S. C.P. **10/7.**
Imperfect; wanting the report for 1918-19.

—— Report on the Cattle-Breeding Operations in the Central
Provinces and Berar for the year ending the 30th June
1923 (for the year 1923-24[–1929-30]). 8 pt. *Nagpur,*
1924-31. 8°. I.S. C.P. **130.**

—— Report on the Demonstration Work carried out in the
Northern Circle for the year 1914-15(–1924-25). (Report
on Demonstration Work carried out in the Northern
Circle, together with reports on seed farms and demonstration farms, for the year 1925-26 [1926-27; for the year
ending 31st March 1928—the year ending the 31st March
1935].) 21 pt. *Nagpur,* 1915-35. fol. & 8°.
I.S. C.P. **3/6 & 113/2.**

—— Report on the Demonstration Work carried out in the
Southern Circle for the year 1914-15(–1924-25). (Report
on Demonstration Work carried out in the Southern
Circle, together with reports on the seed and demonstration farms . . . and the cattle-breeding farm . . . for
the year 1925-26 [for the year ending 31st March 1927—
the year ending the 31st March 1935].) 21 pt. *Nagpur,*
1915-35. fol. & 8°. I.S. C.P. **3/7 & 113/3.**

—— Report on the Demonstration Work carried out in the
Western Circle for the year 1914-15(—the year ending the
30th June 1918; during the year ending 30th June 1920
—the year ending 30th June 1923; during the year
1923-24, 1924-25). (Report on Demonstration Work
carried out in the Western Circle, together with reports on
the seed, demonstration and cattle-breeding farms . . .
for the year 1925-26 [1926-27; for the year ending
31st March 1928—the year ending the 31st March 1935].)
22 pt. *Nagpur,* 1915-35. fol. & 8°.
I.S. C.P. **3/8 & 113/4.**
*Imperfect; wanting the report for the year ending the
30th June 1919. The reports for 1925-26–1930-31 were
issued in two parts each year.*

—— Report on the Experimental Farms in the Central
Provinces for the year 1903-04 (1904-05), *etc.* 2 pt.
Nagpur, 1904, 05. fol. I.S. C.P. **10/2.**

—— Report on the Nagpur Model Farm (the Nagpur Experimental Farm) for the year 1882-83(–1887-88, 1890-91–
1902-03). (Report on the Experimental Farm attached
to the Agricultural College, Nagpur, for the year ending
30th June 1915[–1923, for the year 1923-24–1924-25].)
Nagpur, 1883-1926. fol. I.S. C.P. **10.**
*Reports for 1903/04 and 1904/05 are included in the Re-
ports on the Experimental Farms. Continued by the Annual
Reports of Experimental Farms, which are entered above.*

—— Report on the Working of the Co-operative Credit
Societies (of the Co-operative Societies) in the Central
Provinces & Berar for the year 1907-08(–1926-27; for
the year ending 30th June 1928—the year ending 30th
June 1935). 28 pt. *Nagpur,* 1908-36. fol. & 8°.
I.S. C.P. **46 & 117/3.**

DEPARTMENT OF INDUSTRIES.

—— [For the Annual Reports on the Rail-borne Traffic of the
Central Provinces and Berar, of which those for 1919-20
were issued by the Department of Industries:] *See* supra:
MISCELLANEOUS OFFICIAL PUBLICATIONS.

CENTRAL PROVINCES. [DEPARTMENTS OF STATE
AND PUBLIC INSTITUTIONS.]

—— Report on the Working of the Department of Industries
. . . for the year ending 30th September 1919 (for the
year ending 31st December 1920—the year ending the
31st December 1933; for the period of 15 months ending
the 31st March 1935; for the year ending the 31st March
1936). 17 pt. *Nagpur*, 1919–36. fol. & 8º.
I.S. C.P. **52 & 129.**

—— Cost of Living Index Numbers for the Industrial Workers
at Nagpur and Jubbulpore (for the Industrial Workers at
Nagpur) for the month of July 1932 [*etc.*]. *Nagpur*,
1932– . *obl.* 8º. I.S. C.P. **134.**
*From 1950 onward issued by the Department of Industries,
Madhya Pradesh.*

DEPARTMENT OF LAND RECORDS.

—— Report on the Operations of the Land Records and
Settlement Departments in the Central Provinces during
the year 1902-03(–1915-16). 14 pt. *Nagpur*,
1903–16. fol. I.S. C.P. **20/3.**
Earlier reports are entered under DEPARTMENT OF AGRI-
CULTURE. *Later reports were issued with the reports on the
Land Revenue Administration and are entered under*
MISCELLANEOUS OFFICIAL PUBLICATIONS.

—— Season and Crop Report of the Central Provinces and
Berar for the year 1908-09(–1919-20; 1921-22—the year
ending the 31st May 1935). 26 pt. *Nagpur*,
1909–35. fol. & 8º. I.S. C.P. **3/4 & 124/5.**
Imperfect; wanting the report for 1920-21.

DEPARTMENT OF LAND RECORDS AND AGRICULTURE.

—— *See* supra: DEPARTMENT OF AGRICULTURE.

DEPARTMENT OF LAND RECORDS AND SETTLEMENT, BERAR.

—— Report on the Operations of the Land Records and
Settlement Departments in Berar during the year 1903-
1904(–1915-16). 13 pt. *Nagpur*, 1904–16. fol.
I.S. C.P. **20/5.**
*Later Reports form part of the " Reports on the Revenue
Administration of Berar," which are entered below under*
REVENUE DEPARTMENT.

ETHNOLOGICAL COMMITTEE.

—— Report of the Ethnological Committee on Papers laid
before them and upon examination of specimens of
aboriginal tribes brought to the Jubbulpore Exhibition
of 1866-67. [Compiled by A. C. Lyall.]
pp. 12. 10. 120. 22. 9. *Nagpore*, 1868. 8º. I.S. C.P. **106.**

FOREST DEPARTMENT.

—— [For the Reports on the Forest Administration of the
Central Provinces and Berar:] *See* supra: MISCEL-
LANEOUS OFFICIAL PUBLICATIONS.

HIGH COURT.

—— *See* supra: COURTS OF JUSTICE.

IRRIGATION DEPARTMENT.

—— *See* infra: PUBLIC WORKS DEPARTMENT.—*Irrigation
Branch.*

LEGISLATIVE DEPARTMENT.

—— The Central Provinces Code, consisting of the Bengal
Regulations, Local Acts of the Governor General in
Council, Acts of the Chief Commissioner of the Central
Provinces in Council and of the Legislative Council of
the Governor of the Central Provinces in force in the
Central Provinces . . . Fifth edition. pp. vi. 600.
Nagpur, 1924. 8º. I.S. C.P. **115/9. (1.)**

—— Sixth edition. 2 vol. *Nagpur*, 1934, 35. 8º.
I.S. C.P. **115/9. (2.)**

CENTRAL PROVINCES. [DEPARTMENTS OF STATE
AND PUBLIC INSTITUTIONS.]

OFFICE OF THE COMPTROLLER, afterwards OFFICE OF THE ACCOUNTANT-GENERAL.

—— Manual of Appointments & Allowances of Gazetted &
Departmentally Gazetted Officers in the Central Provinces
and Berar. Second edition. pp. 4. xv. 149. *Allahabad*,
1907. 8º. I.S. C.P. **122/6. (1.)**

—— Second edition (reprinted). pp. xv. 190. *Nagpur*,
1913. 8º. I.S. C.P. **122/6. (2.)**

—— Manual of Appointments and Allowances of Gazetted
Officers in the Central Provinces and Berar. Third
edition. pp. xi. 162. *Nagpur*, 1917. 8º.
I.S. C.P. **122/6. (3.)**

—— Fourth edition. pp. iv. 188. *Nagpur*, 1923. 8º.
I.S. C.P. **122/6. (4.)**

—— Fifth edition. pp. iii. 226. *Nagpur*, 1928. 8º.
I.S. C.P. **122/6. (5.)**

—— Manual of Appointments and Allowances of Non-
Gazetted Officers in the Central Provinces and Berar.
pp. iv. 49. *Nagpur*, 1916. 8º. I.S. C.P. **122/7. (1.)**

—— Second edition. pp. 40. *Nagpur*, 1925. 8º.
I.S. C.P. **122/7. (2.)**

—— The Quarterly Civil List for the Central Provinces . . .
Corrected up to 1st July 1893(—up to 1st October 1908),
etc. no. 83–144. *Nagpur*, 1893-1908. 8º. I.S. C.P. **122/4.**
*Imperfect; wanting no. 84, 85, 87–91, 95, 96, 103, 104,
107, 108, 119, 120, 124, 127, 135–137, 139 and 142.*

POLICE DEPARTMENT.

—— Lectures on some Criminal Tribes of India and Religious
Mendicants. Second edition. By G. W. Gayer.
pp. iii. 139. [*Nagpur*,] 1910. fol. I.S. C.P. **26/5.**

—— The Police Manual for the Central Provinces, *etc.*
pp. vii. 413. *Nagpur*, 1914. 8º. I.S. C.P. **127/2.**

PROVINCIAL BANKING ENQUIRY COMMITTEE.

—— Report of the Central Provinces Provincial Banking
Enquiry Committee, 1929–30. 4 vol. *Nagpur, Calcutta*,
1930. 8º. I.S. C.P. **119/6.**

PROVINCIAL CO-OPERATIVE CONFERENCE.

—— Proceedings of the First (Second) Provincial Co-operative
Conference, Central Provinces & Berar. Held . . .
14th December 1912 (15th & 16th September, 1913). 2 pt.
Jubbulpore, 1913. fol. I.S. C.P. **46/2.**

PUBLIC WORKS DEPARTMENT.

—— Annual Progress Report of the Public Works Department in the Central Provinces for the year 1871-72
(1873-74–1876-77), *etc.* 5 pt. *Nagpur*, 1872–77. fol.
I.S. C.P. **31.**
Imperfect; wanting the report for 1872-73.

—— The Central Provinces, Public Works Department,
Manual of Orders. 3 vol. [*Nagpur*, 1915.] 8º.
I.S. C.P. **133. (1.)**

—— [Another edition.] Corrected up to 1st August 1919.
3 vol. *Nagpur*, [1920.] 8º.

—— Appendix xxx . . . Volume III. List of Standard
Plans and Estimates in the Central Provinces and
Berar as corrected up to 31st December 1920. pp. 27.
Nagpur, [1921.] 8º. I.S. C.P. **133. (2.)**

—— State Railways. Chief Engineer's Annual Progress
Report for 1874-75. pp. 17. *Nagpur*, 1875. fol.
I.S. C.P. **32.**
*A separate issue of chap. 6 of the Annual Progress Report
of the Public Works Department.*

CENTRAL PROVINCES. [DEPARTMENTS OF STATE AND PUBLIC INSTITUTIONS.]

Irrigation Branch.

—— Administration Report of the Irrigation Branch of the Public Works Department in the Central Provinces (and Berar) for the year 1908-09(–1918-19). 11 pt. *Nagpur*, 1909–20. fol.   I.S. C.P. **31/3.**

—— Review of the Work of the Irrigation Department, Central Provinces, for the year 1918-19 (1919-20). 2 pt. *Nagpur*, 1919, 20. fol.   I.S. C.P. **31/4.**

PUBLICITY DEPARTMENT.

—— The Central Provinces & Berar Government at Work. From 15th March to 15th July 1938 (15th July to 15th October 1938; 15th October 1938 to 31st January 1939). vol. 1. no. 2, 3; vol. 2. no. 1.   *Nagpur*, 1938, 39. 8°.   I.S. C.P. **116/5.**

REGISTRATION DEPARTMENT.

—— Report on the Working of the Registration Act, xx. of 1866, in the Central Provinces . . . for the year 1869-70 (1870-71). (Report on the Working of the Registration Department in the Central Provinces, for the year 1871-72[–1878-79; 1879–1884; 1885-86, 1886-87].) 18 pt. *Nagpore*, 1870–87. fol.
[Continued as:]
Notes on the Annual Statements (Report on the Working) of the Registration Department for the year 1887-88 (–1896-97, 1898-99–1901-02; during the calendar year 1902). 15 pt. *Nagpur; Allahabad*, 1888–93. fol.   I.S. C.P. **33.**

The reports issued every third year from 1890 onwards take the place of the annual statements for the year in which they are issued. Imperfect; wanting the note on the annual statements for 1897-98.

—— Note on the Working (Report—Triennial—on the Working) of the Registration Department in the Central Provinces (and Berar) during the calendar year 1903(–1917-19; 1921–1924; 1926; 1926–28–1929–31; 1933–1935). 29 pt. *Nagpur*, 1904–36. fol. & 8°.   I.S. C.P. **33/3 & 139.**
The triennial reports issued for 1904–06 onwards take the place of the annual note for the last year which they cover. Imperfect; wanting the annual notes for 1920, 1927 and 1932 and the triennial report for 1923–25.

REVENUE DEPARTMENT.

—— Report on the Revenue Administration of Berar for the year 1904-05(–1913-14). 10 pt. *Nagpur*, 1906–15. fol.
[Continued as:]
Reports (Report) on the Revenue Administration and on the Operations of the Land Records and Settlement Departments in Berar (in the Berar Division) during the year 1914-15[–1934-35]. *Nagpur*, 1916–36. fol. & 8°.   I.S. C.P. **20/2 & 110/2.**
Previous reports are entered under BERAR.

STAMP DEPARTMENT.

—— Note on the Working of the Stamp Department in the Central Povinces and Berar, *etc. See supra*: MISCELLANEOUS OFFICIAL PUBLICATIONS. Report (Note) on the Stamp Revenue, *etc.*

APPENDIX.

—— States of the Central Provinces. List of Chiefs and Leading Families. pp. 18. 1926. 8°.   *See* INDIA. [*Miscellaneous Official Publications.*]   I.S. **351/13.**

CENTRAL PROVINCES AND BERAR UNIVERSITY COMMITTEE. *See* CENTRAL PROVINCES.

CENTRAL PROVINCES PIECES. C. P. Pieces [i.e. Central Provinces Pieces] and other verse by S. 1899. 8°. *See* S.   **011651. k. 51.**

CENTRAL PUBLIC HOUSE TRUST ASSOCIATION. *See* LONDON.—III.

CENTRAL RADIO WAVE OBSERVATORY. *See* JAPAN.—*Radio Regulatory Commission.*

CENTRAL RAILROAD OF NEW JERSEY. Guide-Book of the Central Railroad of New Jersey, and its connections through the coal-fields of Pennsylvania. pp. 120. *Harper & Bros.: New York*, 1864. 8°. **10412. bbb. 32.**

CENTRAL RELIEF COMMITTEE. Central Relief Committee of the Society of Friends. *See* DUBLIN.

CENTRAL SCHOOL.

—— Central School of Arts and Crafts. [Birmingham.] *See* BIRMINGHAM.—*College of Arts and Crafts.*

—— Central School of Arts and Crafts. [London.] *See* LONDON.—III.

—— Central School of Science and Technology, Stoke-on-Trent. *See* STOKE-ON-TRENT.

CENTRAL SCHOOL ASSOCIATION. *See* LONDON.—III.

CENTRAL SCHOOL TEACHER. The Central School Teacher. The magazine of the National Association of Teachers in Selective Central Schools. *See* ENGLAND.—*National Association of Teachers in Selective Central Schools.*

CENTRAL SCIENTIFIC INSTITUTE. Central Scientific Institute of Fisheries (of Fishery Industries). *See* RUSSIA.—*Народный Комиссаріатъ Снабженія.—Центральный Научный Институтъ Рыбнаго Хозяйства, etc.*

CENTRAL SCIENTIFIC LIBRARY. Central Scientific Library of Charkow. *See* KHARKOV.—*Императорскій Харьковскій Университетъ, etc.—Библіотека, afterwards Харківська Центральна Наукова Бібліотека.*

CENTRAL SOCIETY. Central Society for Higher Religious Education. *See* ENGLAND.

—— Central Society for Women's Suffrage. *See* LONDON.—III. *Fawcett Society.*

—— Central Society of Architecture of Belgium. *See* BRUSSELS.—*Société centrale d'Architecture de Belgique.*

—— Central Society of Education. *See* LONDON.—III.

—— Central Society of Sacred Study. *See* ENGLAND.—*Church of England.*

CENTRAL SOUDAN MISSION. *See* TRIPOLI.

CENTRAL SOUTH LONDON FREE CHURCH COUNCIL. *See* LONDON.—III.

CENTRAL STATISTICAL ADMINISTRATION.

—— Central Statistical Administration of the U.S.S.R. Council of Ministers. *See* RUSSIA.—*Центральное Статистическое Управление.*

CENTRAL STATISTICAL OFFICE. *See* ENGLAND.

CENTRAL SUNDAY CLOSING ASSOCIATION. *See* ENGLAND.—*Central Association for Stopping the Sale of Intoxicating Liquors on Sunday.*

CENTRAL SYNAGOGUE. *See* London.—III.

CENTRAL TECHNICAL COLLEGE. *See* London.—III. *City and Guilds of London Institute for the Advancement of Technical Education.*

CENTRAL TEMPERANCE LEGISLATION BOARD. *See* London.—III.

CENTRAL TENUVA. *See* Palestine.—*Federation of "Tenuva" Agricultural Cooperative Marketing Associations.*

CENTRAL - THIERARZNEISCHULE. Central-Thierarzneischule zu München. *See* Munich.—*Koeniglich-Bayerische Central-Thierarzneischule.*

CENTRAL TIME TABLE. The Central Time Table of Railway, Steamer and Coach Routes in Great Britain and Ireland. *See* Periodical Publications.—*Dublin.*

CENTRAL TRANSLATIONS INSTITUTE. *See* London.—III.

CENTRAL TRANSPORT CONSULTATIVE COMMITTEE. *See* England.

CENTRAL TRIBUNAL. Central Tribunal appointed under the Military Service Act, 1916. *See* England.

CENTRAL TURKEY COLLEGE. *See* Aintab.

CENTRAL (UNEMPLOYED) BODY FOR LONDON. *See* London.—II.

CENTRAL UNION. Central Union of Chinese Students. *See* England.

CENTRAL UNION GAZETTE. *See* England.—*Central Union of Chinese Students, etc.*

CENTRAL VALUATION COMMITTEE. *See* England.—*Ministry of Health.*

CENTRAL-VERBAND. *See* Centralverband.

CENTRAL-VEREIN. *See* Centralverein.

CENTRAL VIGILANCE COMMITTEE FOR THE REPRESSION OF IMMORALITY. *See* London.—III.

CENTRAL WARD GAZETTE. Central Ward Gazette. Official organ Central Ward Residents' Association. *See* Merton and Morden, —*Central Ward Residents' Association.*

CENTRAL WARD RESIDENTS.
—— Central Ward Residents' Association. *See* Merton and Morden.

—— Central Ward Residents' Club. *See* Morden.

CENTRAL WARD RESIDENTS' ASSOCIATION GAZETTE. *See* Merton and Morden.—*Central Ward Residents' Association.* Central Ward Gazette.

CENTRAL WELFARE COUNCIL.
—— Central Welfare Council of Malaya. *See* Malaya. [Malayan Union, 1946-48.]

CENTRAL WELSH BOARD. *See* Wales.

CENTRAL WOOL COMMITTEE. *See* Australia.

CENTRAL WORKERS' CONSUMERS' CO-OPERATIVE SOCIETY AT KHARKOV. *See* Kharkov —*Харківсьъкий Центральний Робітничий Кооператив.*

CENTRAL YOUTH COUNCIL. *See* England.—*Church of England.*

CENTRAL YOUTH COUNCIL REVIEW. *See* England.—*Church of England.—Central Youth Council.*

CENTRAL YOUTH EMPLOYMENT EXECUTIVE. *See* England.—*Ministry of Labour.*

CENTRAL-ZEITUNG. *See* Centralzeitung.

CENTRAL ZIONIST ARCHIVES. *See* Jerusalem.

CENTRALARCHIV. Central-Archiv der fortschreitenden landwirthschaftlichen Erfahrung. *See* Periodical Publications.—*Konigsberg.*

—— Centralarchiv des fürstlichen Hauses Thurn und Taxis. *See* Ratisbon.

—— Centralarchiv für Gesetzgebung, Verwaltung und Statistik. *See* Vienna.

CENTRALAUSSCHUSS. Centralausschuss der Demokraten Deutschlands. *See* Germany.

—— Centralausschuss für die innere Mission der deutschen evangelischen Kirche. *See* Germany.—*Evangelical Church.*

CENTRALBIBLIOTHEK. Central-Bibliothek der Literatur, Statistik und Geschichte der Pädagogik und des Schulunterrichts. *See* Periodical Publications.—*Halle.*

CENTRALBLATT. *See also* Zentralblatt.

—— Centralblatt. Ein Organ sämmtlicher deutscher Vereine für Volksbildung und ihre Freunde. *See* Periodical Publications.—*Leipzig.*

—— Central-Blatt der Abgaben-, Gewerbe- und Handels-Gesetzgebung und Verwaltung in den Königlich Preussischen Staaten. *See* Prussia.—*Finanzministerium.*

—— Centralblatt der Land- und Forstwirthschaft in Böhmen. *See* Prague.—*Císařsko-Královská Vlastenecko-Hospodářská Společnost.*

—— Centralblatt für allgemeine Pathologie u. pathologische Anatomie. *See* Periodical Publications.—*Jena.*

—— Centralblatt für Anthropologie, Ethnologie und Urgeschichte. *See* Periodical Publications.—*Breslau.*

—— Centralblatt für Bacteriologie und Parasitenkunde. *See* Periodical Publications.—*Jena.*

—— Centralblatt für Bibliothekswesen. *See* Periodical Publications.—*Leipzig.*

—— Centralblatt für Chirurgie. *See* Periodical Publications.—*Leipzig.* Centralblatt für die gesammte Medicin.

—— Centralblatt für das gewerbliche Unterrichtswesen in Österreich. *See* Periodical Publications.—*Vienna.*

—— Central-Blatt für das Deutsche Reich. *See* Germany.—*Reichskanzler-Amt.*

—— Centralblatt für die gesammte Landeskultur. *See* Prague. — *Císařsko-Královská Vlastenecko-Hospodářská Společnost.* Centralblatt der Land- und Forstwirthschaft in Böhmen.

—— Centralblatt für die gesammte Medicin. *See* Periodical Publications.—*Leipzig.*

—— Centralblatt für die mährischen Landwirte. *See* Brunn.—*Kaiserlich-Königliche Mährisch-Schlesische Gesellschaft zur Beförderung des Ackerbaues, der Natur- und Landeskunde.* Mittheilungen, etc.

CENTRALBLATT.

—— Centralblatt für die medicinischen Wissenschaften. *See* PERIODICAL PUBLICATIONS.—*Berlin.*

—— Centralblatt für Eisenbahnen und Dampfschiffahrt in Oesterreich. *See* PERIODICAL PUBLICATIONS.—*Vienna.*

—— Centralblatt für Gynäcologie. *See* PERIODICAL PUBLICATIONS.—*Leipʒig.* Centralblatt für die gesammte Medicin.

—— Centralblatt für innere Medicin. *See* PERIODICAL PUBLICATIONS.—*Leipʒig.* Centralblatt für die gesammte Medicin.

—— Centralblatt für klinische Medicin. *See* PERIODICAL PUBLICATIONS.—*Leipʒig.* Centralblatt für die gesammte Medicin.

—— Centralblatt für Mineralogie, Geologie und Palæontologie. *See* PERIODICAL PUBLICATIONS.—*Stuttgart.*

—— Centralblatt für Naturwissenschaften und Anthropologie. *See* PERIODICAL PUBLICATIONS.—*Leipʒig.*

—— Centralblatt für Physiologie. *See* PERIODICAL PUBLICATIONS.—*Vienna.*

—— Centralblatt für praktische Augenheilkunde. *See* PERIODICAL PUBLICATIONS.—*Leipʒig.*

—— Centralblatt für Rechtswissenschaft. *See* PERIODICAL PUBLICATIONS.—*Stuttgart.*

—— Centralblatt für slavische Literatur und Bibliographie. *See* PERIODICAL PUBLICATIONS.—*Bautzen.*

CENTRALBUREAU.

—— Centralbureau der internationalen Erdmessung. *See* EUROPAEISCHE GRADMESSUNG.

—— Centralbureau für Meteorologie und Hydrographie im Grossherzogthum Baden. *See* BADEN.

CENTRALCOMITÉ. Central-Comité der deutschen Vereine vom Rothen Kreuz. *See* GERMANY.

CENTRALCOMMISSION. *See* CENTRALKOMMISSION.

CENTRALE.

—— Centrale Belge de Documentation. *See* BRUSSELS.

—— Centrale des Coopératives de Production et de Consommation de Roumanie. *See* BUCHAREST.

—— Centrale Féderale de l'Économie de Guerre. *See* SWITZERLAND.

CENTRALE ADVIESCOMMISSIE.

—— Centrale Adviescommissie voor de Prijspolitiek. *See* NETHERLANDS. [Kingdom of the Netherlands.]—*Ministerie van Economische Zaken.*

CENTRALE BOEREN VEREENIGING, *Cape Colony.* *See* CAPE OF GOOD HOPE.—*Central Farmers Association.*

CENTRALE COMMISSIE.

—— Centrale Commissie voor de Filmkeuring. *See* NETHERLANDS.—*Kingdom of the Netherlands.—Centrale Commissie voor de Keuring van Films.*

—— Centrale Commissie voor de Keuring van Films. *See* NETHERLANDS.—*Kingdom of the Netherlands.*

—— Centrale Commissie voor de Statistiek. *See* NETHERLANDS.—*Kingdom of the Netherlands.*

CENTRALE COMMISSIE.

—— Centrale Commissie voor het Boekdrukkers- en Rasterdiepdrukbedrijf. *See* NETHERLANDS. [*Kingdom of the Netherlands.*]

—— Centrale Commissie .voor Onderzoek van het Nederlandse Volkseigen. *See* AMSTERDAM.—*Koninklijke Akademie van Wetenschappen,* afterwards *Koninklijke Nederlandse Akademie van Wetenschappen.*

CENTRALE CULTUURTECHNISCHE COMMISSIE. *See* NETHERLANDS. [Kingdom of the Netherlands.] —*Directie van den Landbouw.*

CENTRALE DIRECTIE.

—— Centrale Directie van de Wederopbouw en de Volkshuisvesting. *See* NETHERLANDS. [Kingdom of the Netherlands.]

CENTRALE GEZONDHEIDSRAAD. *See* NETHERLANDS.—*Kingdom of the Netherlands.*

CENTRALE ORGANISATIE.

—— Centrale Organisatie T. N. O. *See* NETHERLANDS. [Kingdom of the Netherlands.]—*Nederlandse Centrale Organisatie voor Toegepast-Natuurwetenschappelijk Onderzoek.*

CENTRALE VEREENIGING. Centrale Vereeniging, Cape Colony. *See* CAPE OF GOOD HOPE.—*Central Farmers Association.*

—— Centrale Vereeniging voor Openbare Leeszalen en Bibliotheken. *See* NETHERLANDS. [*Miscellaneous Institutions and Societies.*]

CENTRALHOCHSCHULE. Die Centralhochschule. Lustspiel in Versen in drei Aufzügen. [By J. A. Maehly.] pp. 80. *Basel*, 1854. 8º.
11745. c. 15.

CENTRALIAN.

—— The Centralian. Magazine of the Central School, Watford. *See also* WATFORD.—*Watford Central School. Watford Central School Magazine.*

—— The Centralian. Saint Elizabeth's Central School Magazine. *See* LIVERPOOL.—*Saint Elizabeth's Central School.*

CENTRALISMO. Centralismo y despotismo todo viene a ser lo mismo. *México*, 1835. *s. sh.* fol.
9770. k. 12. (123.)

—— Pocos quieren Centralismo y los mas Federalismo, ó sea Representacion que el pueblo de Guadalajara dirige al Escmo. sr. presidente de la república para que se restablezca el orden constitucional en el estado de Jalisco. pp. 4. *Guadalajara*, 1834. fol. 9770. k. 12. (74.)

—— O muertos o federados quieren ser los arrancados. O sea Impugnacion al folleto titulado: Pocos quieren centralismo y los mas federalismo. *Guadalajara*, 1834. fol. 9770. k. 12. (57.)

CENTRALIZACYA. Centralizacya Związku Zagranicznego Socyalistów Polskich. *See* LONDON.—III.

CENTRALIZING CHRISTIAN SCHOOL BOOK SOCIETY. *See* BENARES.

CENTRALIZZAZIONE. La Centralizzazione progressista ed il reggime municipale retrogrado. Cenni d'un amico dell'ordine scritti nel 1851. pp. xiii. 253. *Torino*, 1871. 8º.
8033. aaa. 14.

CENTRALKOMMISSION. *See* also ZENTRALKOMMIS-
SION.

—— Central Commission für die Rhein-Schiffahrt. *See* COM-
MISSION CENTRALE POUR LA NAVIGATION DU RHIN.

—— Centralkommission für schweizerische Landeskunde.
See BERNE.

—— Centralkommission für wissenschaftliche Landeskunde
von Deutschland. *See* STUTTGART

—— Central-Commission zur Erforschung und Erhaltung
der Baudenkmale. *See* AUSTRIA.—*Ministerium für Cultus
und Unterricht.*

CENTRALLEITUNG. Centralleitung des Wohlthätigkeitsvereins in Stuttgart (Württemberg). *See* STUTTGART.
—*Zentralleitung des Wohlthätigkeitsvereins, etc.*

CENTRALNA KOMISJA.
—— Centralna Komisja Regulaminowa. *See* POLAND.—
Ministerstwo Obrony Narodowej.

CENTRALNA RADA.
—— Centralna Rada Związków Zawodowych. *See* POLAND.

CENTRALNA ŻYDOWSKA KOMISJA.

—— Centralna Żydowska Komisja Historyczna. *See* POLAND.
—*Centralny Komitet Żydów Polskich.*

CENTRALNE BIURO.
—— Centralne Biuro Wystaw Artystcznych. *See* POLAND.

CENTRALNY KOMITET. Centralny Komitet Obrony
Narodowej w Ameryce. *See* CHICAGO.

—— Centralny Komitet Żydów Polskich. *See* POLAND.

CENTRALNY NARODOWY KOMITET. Centralny
Narodowy Komitet Polski. *See* WARSAW.

CENTRALNY URZĄD.
—— Centralny Urząd Szkolenia Zawodowego. *See* POLAND.

CENTRALNY ZARZĄD.
—— Centralny Zarząd Lasów Państwowych. *See* POLAND.

—— Centralny Zarząd Przemysłu Hutniczego. *See* POLAND.

—— Centralny Zarząd Przemysłu Sklarskiego. *See* POLAND.

CENTRALORGAN. Central-Organ für den deutschen
Handelsstand. *See* PERIODICAL PUBLICATIONS.—*Cologne.*

CENTRALSTELLE. *See* also ZENTRALSTELLE.

—— Centralstelle für Arbeiter-Wohlfahrtseinrichtungen. *See*
BERLIN.

—— Centralstelle für das internationale Hochschulwesen.
See MUNICH.

CENTRALVERBAND. *See* also ZENTRALVERBAND.

—— Centralverband deutscher Industrieller. *See* GERMANY.

—— Central-Verband deutscher Tonkünstler und Tonkünstler-
Vereine. *See* GERMANY.

CENTRALVEREIN. *See* also ZENTRALVEREIN.

—— Centralverein der Bergwerksbesitzer Österreichs. *See*
VIENNA.

—— Central-Verein der Stenographen des österreichischen
Kaiserstaates zu Wien. *See* VIENNA.

CENTRALVEREIN.

—— Centralverein deutscher Staatsbürger jüdischen
Glaubens. *See* GERMANY.

—— Central-Verein deutscher Zahnaerzte. *See* VIENNA.

—— Centralverein für das Wohl der arbeitenden Klassen.
See BERLIN.

—— Centralverein für Handelsgeographie und Förderung
deutscher Interessen im Auslande. *See* BERLIN.

—— Centralverein für Hebung der deutschen Fluss- und
Kanalschifffahrt. *See* BERLIN.

—— Centralverein homöopathischer Ärzte. *See* GERMANY.
—*Deutscher Zentralverein homöopathischer Ärzte.*

CENTRALZEITUNG. Central-Zeitung für Optik und
Mechanik, *etc. See* GERMANY.—*Deutscher Optiker-Ver-
band.*

CENTRE. The Centre. *See* PERIODICAL PUBLICATIONS.—
Edinburgh.

—— *See* also PERIODICAL PUBLICATIONS.—*Radlett.*

—— The Centre. (Official organ of the Slough Social Centre
Club.) *See* SLOUGH.—*Slough Social Centre Club.*

—— The Centre, Bedford. *See* BEDFORD.

—— The Centre. The social centre in relation to unemployment and national health. A study by five independent
observers. pp. vii. 29. *P. S. King & Son: London,*
1933. 8°. **8286. bb. 2.**

—— Centre Basque et Gascon d'Études Régionales. *See*
BAYONNE.

—— Centre Belge d'Études Économiques et Sociales. *See*
BRUSSELS.

—— Centre belge de recherches mathématiques. *See* BELGIUM.

—— Centre Bibliographique Canadien. *See* CANADA.—*Public
Archives.—Canadian Bibliographic Centre.*

—— Centre Catholique des Intellectuels Français. *See*
FRANCE.

—— Centre Catholique International de Documentation et
Statistiques. *See* PARIS.

—— Centre d'Enseignement Supérieur Aérien. *See* FRANCE.

—— Centre d'Étude des Problèmes Humains. *See* PARIS.

—— Centre d'Études Cathares. *See* TOULOUSE.—*Institut
d'Études Occitanes.*

—— Centre d'Études Culturelles, Économiques et Sociales.
See STRASBURG.

—— Centre d'Études de Chimie Métallurgique. *See* FRANCE.
Centre National de la Recherche Scientifique.

—— Centre d'Études de la Révolution. *See* PARIS.—*Université de Paris.—Faculté des Lettres.*

—— Centre d'Études de " Paix et Démocratie." *See* PARIS.

—— Centre d'Études de Politique Étrangère. *See* PARIS.

—— Centre d'Études et Recherches des Charbonnages de
France. *See* VERNEUIL.

—— Centre d'Études Européennes. *See* STRASBURG.—*Université de Strasbourg.*

CENTRE.

—— Centre d'Études Hongroises en France. *See* PARIS.

—— Centre d'études kurdes. *See* PARIS.

—— Centre d'Études Médiévales. *See* NAMUR.

——. Centre d'Études Politiques. *See* NEUCHÂTEL.

—— Centre d'études polonaises. *See* PARIS.—*Bibliothèque Polonaise de Paris.*

—— Centre d'Études pour la Réforme de l'État. *See* BRUSSELS.

—— Centre d'Études Russes Istina. *See* PARIS.

—— Centre d'Information de la Recherche d'Histoire de France. *See* FRANCE.—*Archives Nationales.*

—— **Centre d'Information et de Documentation.** *See* POLAND.—*Ministerstwo Informacyi i Dokumentacyi.*

—— Centre d'Information et de Documentation du Congo Belge et du Ruanda-Urundi. *See* BELGIUM.

—— Centre d'Information Interprofessionnel. *See* FRANCE.

—— Centre d'Information Législative Internationale. *See* GENEVA.—*International Legislative Information Centre.*

—— Centre de Coopération Scientifique de l'UNESCO pour le Moyen-Orient. *See* UNITED NATIONS EDUCATIONAL, SCIENTIFIC AND CULTURAL ORGANISATION.—*Science Co-operation Office for the Middle East.*

—— Centre de coopération scientifique du moyen orient. *See* UNITED NATIONS EDUCATIONAL, SCIENTIFIC AND CULTURAL ORGANIZATION.—*Middle East Science Cooperation Office.*

—— Centre de Cultura Valenciana. *See* VALENCIA.

—— Centre de Documentation. *See* YUGOSLAVIA.—*Jugoslovenski Centar za Tehničku i Naučnu Dokumentaciju.*

—— Centre de Documentation Cartographique et Géographique. *See* FRANCE.—*Centre National de la Recherche Scientifique.*

—— Centre de Documentation Chimique. *See* PARIS.

—— Centre de Documentation Juive Contemporaine. *See* PARIS.

—— Centre de Documentation Sociale. *See* PARIS.—*École Normale Supérieure.*

—— Centre de Documentation Technique et Économique sur les Plantes Médicinales Aromatiques et Similaires. *See* FRANCE.—*Office National des Matières Premières Végétales pour la Droguerie, la Pharmacie, la Distillerie et la Parfumerie.*

—— Centre de Hautes Études d'Administration Musulmane. *See* PARIS.

—— Centre de Hautes Études Internationales. *See* BUCHAREST.—*Institut Social Românesc.—Centru de Inalte Studii Internaţionale.*

—— Le Centre de l'amour, decouvert soubs divers emblesmes galans et facetieux. [Engravings reproduced from two works by P. Rollos, "Vita Corneliana," and "Euterpe soboles." With explanatory verses in French.] pp. 92. pl. 92. *Chez Cupidon: Paris,* [1650?] *obl.* 4°.
12305. aaa. 1.

CENTRE.

—— Centre de Recherches Archéologiques. *See* ANTWERP.—*Centrum voor Archeologische Vorschingen.*

—— Centre de Recherche Culturelle de la Route des Indes. *See* INSTITUT FRANÇAIS D'AFRIQUE NOIRE.—*Centre I.F.A.N. Djibouti.*

—— Centre de Recherches et de Déontologie Médicales. *See* MOUVEMENT INTERNATIONAL DES INTELLECTUELS CATHOLIQUES.

—— Centre Européen du Rœrich Museum. *See* NEW YORK.—*Roerich Museum.—Centre Européen.*

—— Centre Européen Universitaire. *See* NANCY.

—— Centre Excursionista de Catalunya. *See* BARCELONA.

—— Centre Fédératif du Crédit Populaire en France. *See* FRANCE.

—— Centre for Courses in International Affairs. *See* LONDON.—III. *University of London.*

—— **Centre for Information and Documentation.** *See* POLAND.—*Ministerstwo Informacyi i Dokumentacyi.*

—— Center for Research in Child Health and Development. *See* CAMBRIDGE, *Massachusetts.—Harvard University.—Harvard School of Public Health.*

—— Center for Research on World Political Institutions. *See* PRINCETON, *New Jersey.—Princeton University.*

—— Center for Safety Education. *See* NEW YORK.—*University of the City of New York.*

—— Centre Français d'Information sur l'Éducation de Base. *See* PARIS.

—— Centre Franco-Chinois d'Études Sinologiques. *See* PEKIN.

—— Centre Franco-Polonais de Recherches Historiques de Cracovie. *See* CRACOW.

—— Centre international d'études de la formation religieuse. *See* BRUSSELS.—*International Centre for Studies in Religious Education.*

—— Centre International d'Études sur l'Architecture et l'Urbanisme. *See* PARIS.—*International Studies Centre for Architecture and Town Planning.*

—— Centre International d'Études sur le Fascisme. *See* LAUSANNE.—*International Centre of Fascist Studies.*

—— Centre International de Dialectologie Générale. *See* LOUVAIN.

—— Centre International de Documentation Classique. *See* PARIS.

—— Centre International de l'Enfance. *See* INTERNATIONAL CHILDREN'S CENTRE.

—— Centre International de Sylviculture. *See* BERLIN.

—— Centre International de Synthèse. *See* PARIS.

—— Centre International des Syndicalistes Libres en Exil. *See* PARIS.

CENTRE.

—— Centre International du Tabac. *See* ROME.—*The City*.

—— Centre National d'Étude des Télécommunications. *See* FRANCE.—*Ministère des Postes, Télégraphes et Téléphones*.

—— Centre National d'Information Économique. *See* FRANCE.

—— Centre National de Documentation Pédagogique. *See* PARIS.

—— Centre National de la Cinématographie Française. *See* FRANCE.

—— Centre National de la Recherche Scientifique. *See* FRANCE.

—— Centre National de Recherches " Primitifs Flamands." *See* BELGIUM.

—— Centre National du Commerce Extérieur. *See* FRANCE.

—— Centre National Néerlandais de Documentation pour l'Histoire de l'Art et l'Iconographie. *See* HAGUE.— *Rijksbureau voor Kunsthistorische Documentatie*.

—— Center of International Studies. *See* PRINCETON, *New Jersey.—Princeton University*.

—— Centre Polonais de Recherches Scientifiques de Paris. *See* PARIS.

—— Centre Polytechnicien d'Études Économiques. *See* PARIS.

—— A Literary Centre of a Literary Capital [i.e. Edinburgh]. pp. 27. *Robert Grant & Son : Edinburgh*, 1946. 4°.
11857. d. 49.

CENTRE BROADSHEET. *See* PERIODICAL PUBLICATIONS.—Edinburgh.—*The Centre*.

CENTRE COURT, *pseud.* Badminton. By " Centre Court." pp. 64. *London & New York*, [1928.] 8°. [*Warne's " Recreation " Books*. no. 13.] W.P. **7651/13.**

CENTRE NEWS. *See* SLOUGH.—*Slough Social Centre Club*. The Centre.

CENTRE SAFEGUARDING. *See* PERIODICAL PUBLICATIONS.—*Edinburgh*.

CENTREBOARD, *pseud.* [i.e. C. A. GRANT.] How to Sail a Dinghy. What every boy and girl should know. pp. 30. *Printed for the Author : London*, [1930.] 8°.
08806. a. 45.

—— (Second edition, enlarged.) pp. 52. *C. A. Grant : London*, 1931. 8°. **8808. de. 11.**

—— (Third edition, revised and enlarged.) pp. 60. *G. Wilson & Co.: London*, 1934. 8°. **8808. e. 3.**

—— (Fourth edition.) pp. 70. *G. Wilson & Co.: London*, 1936. 8°. **8808. e. 44.**

CENTRO.

—— Centro Académico Democracia Cristã. *See* COIMBRA.— *Universidade de Coimbra*.

—— Centro Alpinistico Italiano. *See* TURIN.—*Club Alpino Italiano*.

—— Centro Bibliografico Medico. *See* ROME.—*The City*.

CENTRO. Centro Bibliographico. *See* RIO DE JANEIRO.

—— Centro da Lavoura e Commercio. *See* RIO DE JANEIRO.

—— Centro de Cooperación Científica de la Unesco para América Latina *See* UNITED NATIONS EDUCATIONAL SCIENTIFIC AND CULTURAL ORGANIZATION.—*Science Cooperation Office for Latin America*.

—— Centro de Cultura Paraguaya " General Bernardino Caballero." *See* ASUNCIÓN, *Paraguay*.

—— Centro de Cultura Valenciana. *See* VALENCIA.—*Centre de Cultura Valenciana*.

—— Centro de Defensa Social. *See* MADRID.

—— Centro de Documentação Científica. *See* LISBON.— *Instituto de Alta Cultura*.

—— Centro de Documentación Científica, Técnica y Económica. *See* MONTEVIDEO.

—— Centro de Estudios Asturianos. *See* OVIEDO.

—— Centro de Estudios Cooperativos de Venezuela. *See* CARACAS.

—— Centro de Estudios Extremeños. *See* BADAJOZ.

—— Centro de Estudios Filosoficos. *See* MEXICO, *City of.— Universidad Nacional Autónoma de México.—Facultad de Filosofía y Letras*.

—— Centro de Estudios Histórico-Militares del Perú. *See* LIMA.

—— Centro de Estudios Históricos. *See* MADRID.—*Junta para Ampliación de Estudios e Investigaciones Científicas*.

—— Centro de Estudios Históricos. *See also* MEXICO, *City of.* —*Colégio de México*.

—— Centro de Estudios Históricos de Granada y su Reino. *See* GRANADA.

—— Centro de Estudios Históricos Internacionales. *See* BARCELONA.—*Universidad de Barcelona*.

—— Centro de Estudios Históricos y Geográficos del Azuay. *See* CUENCA, *Ecuador*.

—— Centro de Estudios Literarios. *See* MEXICO, *City of.— Colegio de México*.

—— Centro de Estudios Psicalógicos de Montevideo. *See* MONTEVIDEO.

—— Centro de Estudios Sorianos. *See* SORIA, *Town of*.

—— Centro de Estudos Archeológicos. *See* RIO DE JANEIRO.

—— Centro de Estudos da Guiné Portuguesa. *See* BISSAU.

—— Centro de Estudos de Química e Física. *See* COIMBRA.— *Instituto para a Alta Cultura*.

—— Centro de Estudos Humanísticos. *See* OPORTO.—*Universidade do Pôrto*.

—— Centro de Historia de Santander. *See* BUCARAMANGA.

—— Centro de Historia del Norte de Santander. *See* SAN JOSÉ DE CÚCUTA.

—— Centro de Investigaciones Antropológicas de México. *See* MEXICO, *City of*.

CENTRO.

—— Centro de Investigaciones Científicas. *See* CARACAS.—*Fundación Biogen.*

—— **Centro de Investigaciones Especiales o Laboratorio de Estadística. *See* SPAIN.—*Instituto Nacional de Estadística.***

—— Centro de Investigaciones Históricas. *See* GUAYAQUIL.

—— Centro de la Union Ibero-Americana en Vizcaya. *See* BILBAO.

—— Centro de Pesquisas Folclóricas Mário de Andrade. *See* SÃO PAULO.—*Conservatório Dramático e Musical de São Paulo.*

—— Centro delle Arti " Quo Vadis." *See* ROME.—*The City.*

—— Centro di Cultura e Civiltà della Fondazione Giorgio Cini. *See* VENICE.—*Centro di Cultura e Civiltà.*

—— Centro di Demodossalogia. *See* ROME.—*The City.*

—— Centro di Ricerche Teatrali. *See* ITALY.

—— Centro di Studi Archeologici ed Artistici del Piemonte. *See* TURIN.—*Deputazione Subalpina di Storia Patria.*

—— Centro di studi coloniali. [Before 1940.] *See* FLORENCE.—*Reale Istituto di Scienze Sociali e Politiche " Cesare Alfieri," etc.*

—— [From 1940 onwards.] *See* FLORENCE.—*Università di Firenze.*

—— **Centro di Studi di Slavistica. *See* NAPLES.—*Università degli Studi.—Instituto Superiore Orientale.***

—— Centro di Studi Filologici e Linguistici Siciliani. *See* PALERMO.

—— Centro di Studi Filosofici Cristiani. *See* GALLARATE.

—— Centro di Studi per l'Albania. *See* ROME.—*The City.—Reale Accademia d'Italia.*

—— Centro di Studi per la Geografia Antropica. *See* ITALY.—*Consiglio Nazionale delle Ricerche.*

—— Centro di Studi per la Preparazione agli Affari. *See* MILAN.

—— Centro di Studi Preistorici e Archeologici. *See* VARESE.—*Civici Musei di Varese.*

—— Centro di Studi Sociali. *See* ROME.—*The City.*

—— Centro di Studi Tassiani. *See* BERGAMO.

—— Centro di Studio per la Svizzera Italiana. *See* ROME.—*The City.—Reale Accademia d'Italia.*

—— Centro Español de Londres. *See* LONDON.—III.

—— Centro Europeo di Scienze Storiche. *See* TRENT.

—— Centro Fililógico " Andrés Bello." *See* GUATEMALA, City of.

—— Centro " Gabriela Mistral." *See* SAN JOSE DE CÚCUTA.—*Colegio Cúcuta.*

—— Centro Histórico Larense. *See* BARQUISIMETO, *City of.*

CENTRO.

—— Centro Interamericano de Vivienda. *See* ORGANIZATION OF AMERICAN STATES.—*Inter-American Housing Centre.*

—— Centro Internazionale delle Arti e del Costume. *See* VENICE.

—— Centro Internazionale di Cultura e Civiltà della Fondazione Giorgio Cini. *See* VENICE.—*Centro di Cultura e Civiltà.*

—— Centro Internazionale di Studi Umanistici. *See* ROME.—*The City.*

—— Centro Israelita de Cuba. *See* CUBA.

—— Centro Italiano di Documentazione. *See* MILAN.

—— Centro Italiano di Studi e Pubblicazioni per la Riconciliazione Internazionale. *See* ROME.—*The City.*

—— Centro Italiano di Studi sull'Alto Medioevo. *See* SPOLETO.

—— Centro Mexicano de Escritores. *See* MEXICO, *City of.*

—— Centro Nacional de Investigaciones de Café. *See* CHINCHINÁ.

—— Centro Nazionale d'Informazioni Bibliografiche. *See* ROME.—*The City.—Biblioteca Nazionale Centrale Vittorio Emanuele.—Centro Nazionale per il Catalogo Unico delle Biblioteche Italiane e per le Informazioni Bibliografiche.*

—— Centro Nazionale di Documentazione Scientifico Tecnica. *See* ITALY.—*Consiglio Nazionale delle Ricerche.*

—— Centro Nazionale di Studi Alfieriani. *See* ASTI.

—— Centro Nazionale di Studi di Storia dell'Architettura. *See* ITALY.

—— Centro Nazionale di Studi Manzoniani. *See* MILAN.

—— **Centro Nazionale di Studi sul Rinascimento. *See* FLORENCE.—*Istituto Nazionale di Studi sul Rinascimento.***

—— Centro Oficial de Estudios Americanistas de Sevilla. *See* SEVILLE.

—— Centro per la Storia del Movimento Contadino. *See* MILAN.

—— Centro Protector de la Mujer. Proyecto por D. L. A. de la T. 1876. 8°. *See* T., D. L. A. de la, *Presbítero, Abogado del Ilustre Colegio de Madrid.* **8416. f. 16. (6.)**

—— Centro Rio-Grandense de Estudos Históricos. *See* RIO GRANDE DO SUL.

—— Centro Social Obrero. *See* SANTO DOMINGO.

—— Centro Studi e Indagini sull'Opinione Pubblica. *See* ROME.—*The City.—Centro di Demodossalogia.*

—— Centro Studi per l'Africa Orientale Italiana. *See* ROME.—*The City.—Reale Accademia d'Italia.*

—— Centro Studi per l'Albania. *See* ROME.—*The City.—Reale Accademia d'Italia.—Centro di Studi per l'Albania.*

—— Centro Studio Pittori nell'Arte del Vetro. *See* VENICE.

—— Centro Vallecaucano de Historia y Antigüedades. *See* CALI.

CENTRO-AMERICANO. *See also* CENTRAL-AMERICAN.

—— El Centro-Americano. *See* PERIODICAL PUBLICATIONS.
—*Guatemala.*

CENTROSOJUS, LTD. Кооперативный календарь,
etc. 1920. pp. 104. *Москва*, [1919.] 8°.
P.P. **2456.** id.

—— Общее дѣло (дело), *etc.* год. изд. 3. no. 10–15.
20 іюн.—31 авг. 1918. год. изд. 5. no. 1–6. март.—
авг. 1920. *Москва*, 1918, 20. 8°. P.P. **1423.** pho.

—— Объединеніе, *etc.* год. изд. 8. no. 10–16. *Москва*,
1918. 8°. P.P. **1423.** pho. (2.)

—— Творцы кооперации и их думы . . . С 51 портретами
работы . . . П. Я. Павлинова. pp. 280. *Москва*,
1919. 8°. **010790. e. 53.**

—— "Труды Центросоюза." Непериодические сборники.
год. изд. 2. вып. 4. окт. 1919. pp. 210. *Москва*,
1919. 8°. **08248. i. 63.**

*Всероссійское Собраніе Уполномоченныхъ
Центросоюза.*

—— Ко II Всероссійскому Собранію уполномоченных
Центросоюза. Резолюции I Всероссійского Собрания
Уполномоченных Центросоюза, 1, 2 и 3-й Сессии Совета
Центросоюза. pp. 32. *Москва*, 1921. 8°. **08282. k. 32.**

Закавказскіе Конторы.

—— Известия Центросоюза. Информационно-экономи-
ческий двухнедельник. 1920. no. 5, 6 ; 1921. no. 8–9.
Тифлис, 1920, 21. 8°. P.P. **1423.** php.

Инструкторскій Отдѣлъ.

—— Бюллетень . . . Непериодическое издание. no. 1, 2.
июль, авг. 1919. *Москва*, 1919. 8°. **8287. d. 7.**

Организаціонное Управленіе.

—— Кооперация о самой себе . . . Со вступительной
статьей Д. И. Илимского-Кутузова. pp. 136. *Москва*,
1921. 8°. **08276. cc. 47.**

Сельско-хозяйственный Отдел.

—— Краткий каталог сельско-хозяйственных машин и
орудий. pp. 7. *Москва*, 1922. 8°. **1865. c. 14. (33.)**

Совѣтъ.

—— IV-я сессия Совета Центросоюза. Стенографический
отчет 15-21 ноября 1921 г. pp. 214. *Москва*, 1921. 8°.
8282. g. 51.

English Branch.

—— Торговая библиотека Центросоюза. no. 1–7.
в Лондоне, 1923–25. 12°. **8233. a. 28**

CENTRU. Centru de Înalte Studii Internaţionale. *See*
BUCHAREST.—*Institut Social Românesc.*

CENTRUM.

—— Centrum Documentationis Medicae. *See* CZECHOSLO-
VAKIA.—*Zdravotnické Dokumentační Středisko.*

—— Centrum voor Archeologische Vorschingen. *See* ANT-
WERP.

—— Centrum voor de Geschiedenis van de Textiele Kunsten
en van de Tapijtkunst. *See* GHENT.

—— Centrum Zrzeszenia Przyjaciół Żołnierza Polskiego. *See*
DETROIT.—*Friends of Polish Soldiers Committee, Inc.*

CENTRUM.

—— Nationaal Centrum voor Navorsingen over de Vlaamse
Primitieven. *See* BELGIUM.—*Centre National de Recherches
" Primitifs Flamands."*

CENTRUMSFRACTION. Die Centrumsfraction und die
politischen Parteien. pp. 47. *Berlin*, 1882. 8°.
8074. e. 14. (3.)

CENTURIA.

—— Centuria. 1890. [Sonnets. By George John Romanes.]
pp. 108. *London*, [1890 ?] 8°. **11657. b. 84.**
Privately printed.

—— Centuria chymica, hoc est, Tractatus aureus
de lapide philosophorum carmine conscriptus ab authore
anonymo. pp. [32.] [*Leipsic ?*] 1652. 4°. **1034. k. 41.**
Several leaves are slightly mutilated.

—— Centuria Mirabilis : or, the Hundred heroes of the
British Plutarch, who have flourished since the Reformation, *etc.* [By Francis Wrangham.] pp. 8. *Privately
printed : Scarborough*, [1816 ?] 4°. **10604. h. 18. (1.)**
One of an edition of fifty copies.

—— Centuria rariorum problematum historico-medico-physi-
corum. pp. 136. [*Frankfort ? 1690 ?*] 4°.
1172. f. 6. (2.)

—— Centuria variarum quæstionum, oder Ein hundert
Fragen, von allerley Materien und Sachen. Samt un-
vorgreifflicher Antwort darauff, *etc.* [By Martin Zeiler.]
pp. 397. *G. Wildeisen : Ulm*, 1658. 8°. **12355. a. 32.**

—— Centuria III. variarum quæstionum, oder, das dritte
hundert Fragen, von allerley Materien vnd Sachen, samt
vnvorgreifflicher Antwort darauff, *etc.* [By Martin Zeiler.]
pp. 491. *G. Wildeysen : Ulm*, 1659. 8°. **721. c. 31.**

CENTURIA, BONIFACIO A., *Bishop of.* [1874–1896.] *See*
TOSCANO (B. A.) successively *Bishop of Pamplona,
Colombia and of Centuria.*

——, JOHN, *Bishop of.* [1790–1812.] *See* DOUGLASS.

——, VALENTIN FAUSTINO, *Bishop of.* [1857–1861.] *See*
BERRIO-OCHOA (V. F. de)

CENTURIER (ALBERT) *See* BERNARD (Tristan) and CEN-
TURIER (A.) L'École des charlatans, *etc.* 1930. fol. [*La
Petite Illustration.* Théâtre. no. 259.]
P.P. **4283. m. (2.)**

CENTURIES. Between the Centuries. [In verse. Signed :
J. E. S., i.e. Joseph Edwin Saunders.] [1901.] 8°. *See*
S., J. E. **011652. k. 112.**

—— The Centuries. A chronological synopsis of history on
the " space-for-time " method, *etc.* [The compiler's
preface signed : J. H., i.e. Jonathan Hutchinson.]
1897. 8°. *See* H., J. **9004. m. 14.**

—— "The First Six Centuries." Reprinted from The
Church Intelligencer. pp. 7. *Church Association :
London*, [1905.] 8°. **4109. i. 19. (3.)**

—— The Great Centuries of Painting. *See* SKIRA (A.)

CENTURINI (JOSEPH BERRA) *See* BERRA CENTURINI.

CENTURINI (LUIGI) Cogoleto non è la patria di Cristoforo Colombo . . . Lettera prima(—quinta) aperta al
Sig. Gio. Bartolomeo Fazio. [In answer to " Della patria
di Cristoforo Colombo," by G. B. Fazio.] 5 pt.
Genova, 1892. 8°. **10601. e. 21. (4.)**

—— Giuoco degli scacchi. Del finale di torre e cavallo contro
torre. Esempi diversi con note ed aggiunte. [The postscript signed : L. C., i.e. L. Centurini.] pp. 30. 1853. 8°.
See C., L. **7906. aaa. 19.**

CENTURIO (JOANNES BAPTISTA) *See* JOANNES MARIA, *à Sancto Josepho, Carmelita* [G. B. Centurione].

CENTURION. Ante-Room Ballads. By Centurion. pp. 88. *G. Routledge & Sons: London*, 1905. 8°.
011651. h. 45.

—— Army Administration. A business view. By Centurion. pp. 104. *A. Constable & Co.: Westminster*, 1900. 8°.
8832. aa. 36.

—— Centurion's Letter on the Present Government of India. pp. 46. *Thacker, Spink & Co.: Calcutta*, [1852.] 8°.
8022. d. 13.

—— Christian Dogma: being an enquiry into the cause of the increasing rejection of the testimony of Holy Scripture as the result of the higher criticism. By "Centurion." pp. 61. *A. H. Stockwell: London*, [1903.] 8°.
4380. e. 20.

—— An Essay on Practical Federation. By Centurion [i.e. Sir Graham John Bower]. pp. 37. *Hatchards: London*, 1887. 8°.
8155. df. 3. (8.)

—— A Few Words on the Military Organization of Great Britain. By Centurion. pp. 19. *James Ridgway: London*, 1860. 12°.
8828. bbb. 29. (7.)

—— Gentlemen at Arms. By "Centurion" [i.e. John Hartman Morgan.] pp. xii. 274. *William Heinemann: London*, 1918. 8°.
09082. d. 27.

—— Hints to Young Officers of the Volunteer Service. By Centurion. pp. 48. *W. J. Johnson: London*, 1883. 16°.
8831. a. 49.

—— John Neville: Soldier, Sportsman, and Gentleman. A novel. By a Centurion, *etc.* 2 vol. *Tinsley Bros.: London*, 1865. 8°.
12623. a. 3.

—— The Man who Didn't Win the War. An exposure of Lloyd Georgism. By Centurion. [Articles reprinted from the "National Review."] pp. 174. *"National Review": London*, 1923. 8°.
08139. a. 45.

—— Men whose Fathers were Men. A story of a hobby. By Centurion. pp. 99. *A. H. Baldwin & Sons: London*, 1925. 8°.
08821. d. 10.

—— Our Army as it should be. By Centurion. pp. 32. *T. Richards: [London,]* 1871. 8°.
8824. bb. 65. (7.)

—— "Short" and "Long" Service. A reply to Sir Garnet Wolseley. By Centurion. pp. 31. *W. H. Allen & Co.: London*, 1881. 8°.
8831. b. 15. (12.)

CENTURION, *Ship.* The Valiant and most laudable fight performed in the Straights, by the Centurion of London, against fiue Spanish gallies. Who is safely returned this present moneth of May. anno. D. 1591. (Present at this fight, Maister John Hawes Marchant, and sundry other of good account.) 𝔅.𝔏. pp. 6. [*London?* 1591?] 4°.
C. 32. d. 12.

CENTURION (ADAM) *Marquis de Estepa.* *See* CENTURION Y CÓRDOBA (Adan)

CENTURION (ANDRES SQUARZAFIGO Y) *See* SQUARZAFIGO Y CENTURION.

CENTURION (JORGE SQUARZAFIGO Y) *See* SQUARZAFIGO Y CENTURION.

CENTURION (JOSÉ AHUMADA Y) *See* AHUMADA Y CENTURION.

CENTURIÓN (JOSÉ GÓMEZ) *See* GÓMEZ CENTURIÓN.

CENTURION (LEOPOLDO AUGUSTO DE) El Conde de Montemolin. Historia de la vida pública y privada de D. Carlos Luis de Borbon y de Braganza, primogenito de D. Carlos Maria Isidro . . . Segunda edicion. Corregida y considerablemente aumentada. [With a portrait.] pp. 248. *Madrid*, 1848. 8°.
10632. a. 4.

CENTURION (LUIS) *See* POLO (P.) Por Pedro Polo tesorero de las alcabalas y rentas reales de la villa de Talauera. Con L. Centurion heredero de Bernabe Centurion, y con el señor Fiscal. [1650?] fol.
1322. l. 7. (23.)

CENTURION (OCTAVIO) *Marquis de Monesterio. Begin.* [fol. 2 *recto:*] y consultaron con su superior, *etc.* [A paper addressed by the Marquis de Monesterio to the Nuns of the Capuchin Convent at Madrid, 13 April 1641.] [*Madrid*, 1641.] fol.
1322. l. 9. (29.)
Imperfect; wanting fol. 1.

CENTURION (RAMON DE AHUMADA Y) *See* AHUMADA Y CENTURION.

CENTURIONE (AGOSTINO) Stanze. 1785. *See* RUBBI (A.) Parnaso italiano, *etc.* tom. 10. 1784, *etc.* 8°.
240. g. 10.

CENTURIONE (GIOVANNI AGOSTINO) *See* LABERIO (G. B.) Il Preteso possesso dell'Eccellentissimo Signor G. A. Centurione prouato ad euidenza non manutenibile, *etc.* 1713. fol.
501. g. 19. (30.)

CENTURIONE (GIOVANNI BATTISTA) *See* JOANNES MARIA, *à Sancto Josepho, Carmelita* [G. B. Centurione].

CENTURIONE (PAOLETTO) *See* PIERLING (P.) L'Italie et la Russie au XVI° siècle. Voyages de P. Centurione à Moscou, *etc.* 1892. 8°.
9078. bb. 28.

CENTURIONS. The Centurions; or Scripture portraits of Roman officers. pp. xvi. 250. *R. B. Seeley & W. Burnside: London*, 1841. 8°.
1218. a. 18.

CENTURION Y CÓRDOBA (ADAN) *Marquis de Estepa.* *See* ARIAS GUERRERO (R.) Relacion sumaria de la Iornada que el Marques de Estepa . . . hizo a la villa de Hardales, *etc.* [1647.] fol.
1322. l. 9. (27.)

—— Informacion para la Historia del Sacro Monte llamado de Valparaiso y antiguamente Illipulitano junto a Granada . . . Primera parte. ff. 156. *Bartolome de Lorençana: Granada*, 1632. 4°.
487. f. 19.

—— *Begin.* Señor. El Marques de Estepa, señor de la casa de Albornoz, dize, *etc.* [Petitioning the King of Spain to confer upon him the title of Duke.] pp. 12. [1650?] fol.
1322. l. 4. (39.)

—— [Another edition.] ff. 4. [1650?] fol.
1322. l. 9. (28.)

CENTURY. The Century. Illustrated monthly magazine. *See* PERIODICAL PUBLICATIONS.—*New York.* Scribner's Monthly, *etc.*

—— A Century of Creepy Stories. pp. 1178. *Hutchinson & Co.: London*, [1934.] 8°.
012604. d. 44.

—— A Century of Detective Stories. With an introduction by G. K. Chesterton. pp. 1019. *Hutchinson & Co.: London*, [1935.] 8°.
12626. r. 1.

—— A Century of Dishonor; a sketch of the United States government's dealings with some of the Indian tribes. By H. H. [i.e. Helen Hunt, afterwards Jackson], *etc.* 1881. 8°. *See* H., H.
8176. aaa. 28.

—— A Century of Entertainment. pp. 251. *Hutchinson & Co.: London*, [1938.] 8°.
012643. n. 83.

CENTURY.

—— A Century of Ghost Stories. pp. 1013.
Hutchinson & Co.: London, 1936. 8°.　　**12602. w. 4.**

—— A Century of Hymns for general use, *etc.* [The editor's preface signed: J. T.] 1861. 12°. *See* T., J.
　　3437. c. 40.

—— A Century of Law Reform. Twelve lectures on the changes in the law of England during the nineteenth century. Delivered at the request of the Council of Legal Education, *etc.* [By W. B. Odgers, Sir H. B. Poland, and others.] pp. ix. 431.　*Macmillan & Co.: London*, 1901. 8°.　　**06005.de.14.**

—— A Century of Nature Stories, *etc.* pp. 1024.
Hutchinson & Co.: London, [1937.] 8°.　　**7208. b. 18.**

—— A Century of Sayings to help our Doings. By a man in the crowd. *W. & F. G. Cash: London*, 1856. 18°.
　　8406. b. 31.

—— A Century of Suggestions addressed to the Sleepy. By one of themselves. pp. 51.　*Mountcastle's Library: London*, [1858.] 8°.　　**8138. c. 27.**

—— A Century of Surgeons on Gonorrhœa, and on Strictures of the Urethra. pp. viii. 184.　*G. B. Whittaker: London*, 1825. 12°.　　**1174. b. 34.**

—— A Century of Thrillers from Poe to Arlen, *etc.* [With illustrations.] pp. 1087.　*Daily Express Publications: London*, 1934. 8°.　　**12601. t. 43.**

—— A Century of Thrillers. Second series. pp. 896.　*Daily Express Publications: London*, 1935. 8°.　**12626. r. 13.**

—— [A reissue.] *London*, [1935.] 8°.　　**12625. ppp. 9.**

—— A Century of Wrong. Issued by F. W. Reitz . . . With preface by W. T. Stead. [A translation of "Een Eeuw van onrecht," by the Right Hon. J. C. Smuts.] pp. xxiii. 152. *"Review of Reviews": London*, [1900.] 8°.
　　8155. cc. 8.

—— The First Century and the Nineteenth. By the Wandering Jew. pp. 201. *Leadenhall Press: London*, [1893.] 8°.
　　4376. de. 10.

—— Our First Century. pp. 54.　*Thomas Scott: London*, [1873.] 8°.　　**4017. e. 2. (3.)**

—— The Second Century of Humour. With illustrations by Fougasse, *etc.* pp. 1019.　*Hutchinson & Co.: London*, 1936. 8°.　　**12315. ppp. 7.**
A similar collection entitled " A Century of Humour " is entered under WODEHOUSE (P. G.).

CENTURY ARITHMETICS. The Century Arithmetics. 16 pt. *Blackie & Son: [London*, 1889–95.] 8°.
　　8535. aa. 14.

CENTURY ASSOCIATION. *See* NEW YORK.

CENTURY BIOLOGICAL SERIES. *See* HEGNER (Robert W.)

CENTURY BOOKS. The Century Books of Useful Science. *See* BOND (Alexander R.)

CENTURY CALENDAR. The Circular Century Calendar. 1797 to 1903. *Waterlow & Sons: London*, [1877.] 4°.　　**1899.b.20.(152.)**
A card.

CENTURY CATHOLIC COLLEGE TEXTS. *See* LAPP (John A.)

CENTURY CHEMISTRY SERIES. *See* KENDALL (James) *Professor of Chemistry, Columbia University.*

CENTURY CHILDHOOD LIBRARY. *See* ANDERSON (John E.)

CENTURY CLASSICS. The Century Classics. 5 pt. *Century Co.: New York*, 1900. 8°.　　**012208. f. 33.**
Imperfect; containing only " The Essays of Francis Bacon," Bunyan's " Pilgrim's Progress," Defoe's " Journal of the Plague Year," Goldsmith's " Vicar of Wakefield " and " Poems of Robert Herrick."

CENTURY COOK BOOK. *See* RONALD (Mary) *pseud.*

CENTURY DATE CARD. Century Date Card. *J. F. Nock: St. Leonards*, 1901. 8°.　　**9504. aa. 10.**

CENTURY DEVOTIONAL LIBRARY. *See* SUTER (John W.) *the Younger.*

CENTURY DICTIONARY. The Century Dictionary. An encyclopedic lexicon of the English language. *See* WHITNEY (William D.)

—— The New Century Dictionary of the English Language. *See* EMERY (Hulbert G.) and BREWSTER (K. G.)

CENTURY EARTH SCIENCE SERIES. *See* MATHER (Kirtley F.)

CENTURY EDUCATION SERIES. The Century Education Series. 3 vol. *Century Co.: New York & London*, [1929–35.] 8°.　　**12213.f.6.**

CENTURY FOREIGN TRADE SERIES. The Century Foreign Trade Series. 2 vol. *Century Co.: New York*, 1920. 8°.　　**08235. aaa. 36.**

CENTURY GEOGRAPHICAL HANDBOOKS. The Century Geographical Hand Books. no. 3–7. *Blackie & Son: [London*, 1891.] 8°.　　**10003. aaa. 18.**
No. 1, 2 were not published.

CENTURY GEOGRAPHICAL READERS. The Century Geographical Readers. 12 pt. *Blackie & Son: London*, 1890–92. 8°.　　**10004. aa. 47.**
Imperfect; wanting Course " S," Standard 3.

CENTURY GUILD. *See* LONDON.—III.

CENTURY GUILD HOBBY HORSE. *See* LONDON. —III. *Century Guild.*

CENTURY HISTORICAL HANDBOOKS. Century Historical Handbooks. 5 pt. *Blackie & Son: London*, [1891.] 8°.　　**9503. bb. 38.**

CENTURY HISTORICAL READERS. The Century Historical Readers. 8 pt. *Blackie & Son: London*, 1891 [90, 91]. 8°.　　**9503. d. 29.**

CENTURY HISTORICAL SERIES. *See* BURR (George L.)

CENTURY (ILLUSTRATED) HOTEL GUIDE. The " Century "—Illustrated—Hotel Guide to the United Kingdom, *etc. See* DIRECTORIES.—*Hotels, Boarding Houses, etc.* [*Great Britain.*]

CENTURY INFANT READER. *See* CENTURY READERS.

CENTURY LIBRARY. The Century Library. [Novels.] 4 pt. *T. Fisher Unwin: London*, 1895, 96. 8°.
　　12602. c. 44.
Imperfect; wanting " The Donce Family " by Edith Johnstone and " An Altruist " by Ouida. Separate issues of these two books are entered under JOHNSTONE (E.) *and* OUIDA *respectively.*

—— The Century Library. *Eyre & Spottiswoode: London*, 1947– . 8°.　　**W.P. 10489.**

CENTURY LIBRARY.

—— Century Library of American Antiques. *See* BROWNE (Waldo R.)

CENTURY MAGAZINE. *See* PERIODICAL PUBLICATIONS.—*New York.* Scribner's Monthly, *etc.*

CENTURY MODERN LANGUAGE SERIES. *See* MACKENZIE (Kenneth) *Ph.D.*

CENTURY NEW WORLD SERIES. *See* WILLOUGHBY (William F.)

CENTURY PHILOSOPHY SERIES. *See* LAMPRECHT (Sterling P.)

CENTURY PRESS.

—— Century Press Books for Young Enthusiasts. *See* CORBLUTH (Arnold)

—— Century Press Health and Hygiene Books. *London, New York,* [1948– .] 8°. **W.P. 13188.**

—— Century Press Popular Series of Guide Books. *Century Press: London,* [1950– .] 8°. **W.P. 2818.**

CENTURY PRIMERS. *See* CENTURY READERS.

CENTURY PSYCHOLOGY SERIES. *See* ELLIOTT (Richard M.)

CENTURY READERS. The Century Readers. 15 pt.

> The Century Primers. no. 1, 2.
> The Century Infant Reader.
> The Century Readers. no. 1-6.
> The Century Readers. Home Lesson Book. no. 1-6.

Blackie & Son: London, 1888, 89. 8°. **12203. ee. 19.**

CENTURY READINGS. Century Readings in the English Essay. *See* WANN (Louis)

CENTURY RURAL LIFE BOOKS. *See* GALPIN (Charles J.)

CENTURY SCIENCE SERIES. *See* ROSCOE (*Right Hon. Sir* Henry E.)

CENTURY SOCIAL SCIENCE SERIES. The Century Social Science Series. *Century Co.: New York & London,* 1923– . 8°. **W.P. 7349.**

CENTURY STAMP AND COIN COMPANY.

—— Price List no. 2. pp. 16. *Century Stamp & Coin Co.: Minneapolis,* 1894. 8°. **Crawford 243. (8.)**

CENTURY STUDIES. The Century Studies in Economics. *See* KIEKHOFER (William H.)

—— Century Studies in Education. *See* UHL (Willis L.)

CENTURY TELEGRAPHIC CODE. The Century Telegraphic Code. (Dictionary Code. Appendix to the Century Telegraphic Code.) pp. viii. 56. *Telegraphic Code Co.; Spottiswoode & Co.: London; Longmans & Co.: New York,* [1906.] fol. **1805. b. 6.**

CENTURY VOCATIONAL SERIES. *See* PROSSER (Charles A.)

CENTVINC (JEAN) Sous les ruines de la Cour des Comptes. Illustrations de F. Bac. pp. 145. *Paris,* 1897. 8°. **012551. b. 4.**

CENTYMCA. *See* LONDON.—III. *Young Men's Christian Association.*

CENTYMCA BULLETIN. *See* LONDON.—III. *Young Men's Christian Association.*

CENTZ (P. C.) *pseud.* [i.e. BERNARD J. SAGE.] Davis and Lee: a vindication of the Southern States, citizens, and rights, by the Federal Constitution and its makers, *etc.* pp. 80. *Van Evrie, Horton & Co.: New York; London* printed, 1866. 8°. **8175. aaa. 75. (8.)**

—— The Republic of Republics; or, American federal liberty . . . Fourth edition. pp. xxvii. 606. *Little, Brown & Co.: Boston,* 1881. 8°. **8175. cc. 2.**

CENYPRES, LTD.

—— Cenypres Trade Index of the United Nations. *See* DIRECTORIES.—*Commerce.*

CENZATO (GIOVANNI)

—— *See* MASCAGNI (P.) Cinquantenario della " Cavalleria Rusticana " . . . Le lettere ai librettisti, *etc.* [Edited by G. Cenzato.] [1940.] 4°. **7891. dd. 6.**

—— La Casa di riposo per musicisti in Milano. (Nuova edizione.) [With illustrations.] pp. 67. 1951. fol. *See* MILAN.—*Casa di Riposo per Musicisti.* **Hirsch 1333.**

—— Itinerari provinciali, *etc.* pp. xv. 286. *Milano,* 1932. 8°. **010151. f. 26.**

CENZATTI (GEMMA) Alfonso de Lamartine e l'Italia. pp. 116. *Livorno,* 1903. 8°. **9165. ccc. 13.**

CEO (MARIA DO) *See* MARIA, *do Ceo.*

CEO (VIOLANTE DO) *See* VIOLANTE, *do Ceo.*

CEÓL-SÍDHE. Ceól-Síḋe . . . Irish Songs. pp. 96. *Irish Book Co.: Dublin,* 1902, 05. 8°. [Léiġeaⁿ Éiⱡeaⁿ Series. no. 4, 14.] **872. m. 24.**

CEOLA (MARIO) Guerra nostra, 1915–1918. Con particolare studio sui giudizi degli alleati e dei nemici al valore delle truppe italiane. Con 18 illustrazioni inedite e 4 cartine. pp. 325. *Milano,* 1933. 8°. **09081. aaa. 25.**

CEOLDO (PIETRO) Albero della famiglia Papafava nobile di Padova, compilato con le sue prove da P. Ceoldo. [With a folding plate.] pp. 4. xv. 179. *Venezia,* 1801. 4°. **1328. k. 10.**

—— Memorie della chiesa ed abbazia di S. Stefano di Carrara nella diocesi di Padova esposte da D. P. Ceoldo. [With a plan.] pp. iv. viii. 290. *Venezia,* 1802. 4°. **1487.k.18.**

CEOLFRIDUS, *Abbot of Wearmouth and Jarrow. See* BEDE, *the Venerable, Saint.* [*Smaller Collections of Works.*] Venerabilis Bedæ Epistolæ duæ, necnon Vitæ Abbatum Wiremuthensium & Girwiensium [i.e. of Ceolfridus and others], *etc.* 1664. 8°. **857. d. 9.**

—— Ceolfridi . . . Epistola ad Naitanum Regem Pictonum, pro catholico: Pascha et Romana tonsura. 1850. *See* MIGNE (J. P.) Patrologiæ cursus completus, *etc.* tom. 89. 1844, *etc.* 4°. **2000. d.**

—— The Life of Ceolfrid, Abbot of the Monastery at Wearmouth and Jarrow. By an unknown author of the eighth century. Translated from the original, and edited (with introductory essay and notes) by Douglas Samuel Boutflower . . . To which is added a reprint of an article on the Codex Amiatinus by the late Rev. J. L. Low, *etc.* pp. 120. *Hills & Co.: Sunderland; Simpkin, Marshall & Co.: London,* 1912. 8°. **4902. h. 21.**

ČEOVIĆ (IVO)

—— Lov u pitanjima i odgovorima. 2 izdanje. pp. 229. *Zagreb,* 1952. 8°. **7921. a. 86.** *Mala lovačka biblioteka.* sv. 19, 20.

CEP (SYLVAIN) Considérations sur l'hémorragie utérine tenant à l'insertion du placenta sur l'orifice de la matrice. Tribut académique, *etc.* pp. 19. *Montpellier,* 1834. 4°.
1181. g. 5. (15.)

CEPAGATI, FEDERICO VALIGNANI, *Marquis di.* *See* VALIGNANI.

CEPARI (VIRGILIO) Essercitio della presenza di Dio. pp. 500. *G. B. Bidelli: Milano,* 1621. 12°.
4400. l. 26.

—— Vita del beato Luigi Gonzaga della Compagnia di Giesu, *etc.* (Meditatione de gl'angeli santi . . . composta dal beato L. Gonzaga.) pp. 341. *L. Zannetti: Roma,* 1606. 4°. **485. a. 21. (3.)**

—— [Another edition.] pp. 447. *P. P. Tozzi: Vicenza,* 1615. 8°. **862. g. 8.**

—— [Another edition.] Vita di San Luigi Gonzaga della Compagnia di Gesu, scritta dal padre V. Cepari. Con la terza parte nuovamente composta da un altro religioso della medesima Compagnia. pp. 520. *Milano,* 1728. 8°. **1125. a. 24.**

—— [Another edition.] pp. 176. 144. *Venezia,* 1839. 8°. **4828. a. 14.**

—— The Life of B. Aloysius Gonzaga . . . translated into English by R. S. pp. 518. *Paris; [St. Omer* printed], 1627. 8°. **G. 1304.**
The titlepage is engraved.

—— Life of Saint Aloysius Gonzaga . . . New translation [of the German translation by Friedrich Schroeder] with notes from original sources, letters and documents. Edited by Father Francis Goldie. pp. xxvi. 432. *Benzinger & Co.: Einsiedeln,* 1891. 8°. **4829. df. 25.**

—— Life of St. Aloysius Gonzaga, S.J. Translated . . . by a Priest of the same Society. (Abridged.) pp. 105. *M. H. Gill & Son: Dublin,* 1891. 8°. **4823. aa. 4.**

—— Het Leven van den salighen Lodewyck Gonzaga . . . Verduytscht door P. Leonardus de Fraye. pp. 382. *G. van Wolsshaten & H. Aertssen: Antwerpen,* 1615. 8°. **4827. df. 5.**

—— [Another copy.] Het Leven vanden Salighen Lodewyck Gonzaga, *etc.* *Antwerpen,* 1615. 8°. **1481. de. 21.**

—— Vie de saint Louis de Gonzague . . . Traduite par M. Calpin . . . Nouvelle édition, corrigée par A. M. D. G * * * [i.e. J. N. Loriquet]. pp. viii. 340. *Avignon,* 1820. 12°. **4827. df. 11.**

—— Das Leben des hl. Aloysius Gonzaga . . . Ins Deutsche übersetzt und durch einen Nachtrag vervollständigt von Friedrich Schröder. [With a portrait.] pp. xxx. 468. *Einsiedeln,* 1891. 8°. **4829. df. 28.**

—— De vita beati Aloysii Gonzagæ . . . libri tres, *etc.* [Translated from the Italian.] pp. 518. *Sumptibus B. Gualtheri: Coloniæ Agrippinæ,* 1608. 8°.
4827. a. 14.

—— [Another copy, with a different titlepage, engraved, and with a portrait and three leaves containing the index and errata.] **862. g. 7.**

—— Vita B. Aloysii Gonzagæ . . . Hac secunda editione accuratius in capita et paragraphos distincta. [With a portrait.] pp. 452. *I. Veruliet: Valencenis,* 1609. 8°. **4825. a. 9.**

—— [Another copy, with a different titlepage.] *Apud I. Keerbergium: Antuerpiæ,* 1609. 8°. **862. g. 6. (1.)**
Imperfect; wanting the portrait.

CEPARI (VIRGILIO)

—— *See* LOUIS [Gonzaga], *Saint.* The Life of St. Aloysius Gonzaga, of the Society of Jesus. (Grounded upon Cepari's work.) [1885.] 8°. [*Library of Religious Biography.* vol. 1.] **4823. bbb. 15.**

—— Vita del venerabile servo di Dio Giovanni Berchmans, fiammingo, religioso della Compagnia di Gesù . . . Quinta edizione. [With a portrait.] pp. 193. *Roma,* 1751. 4°. **1124. i. 22.**

—— The Life of the Blessed Berchmans . . . Adapted from the Italian of Father Joseph Boero [or rather, from Boero's edition of the life by V. Cepari]. pp. vii. 99. 1868. 16°. *See* BOERO (G.) **4867. a. 11.**

—— Leben des gottseeligen Joannis Berchmanns der Gesellschaft Jesu, aus weitläuffiger Erzählung P. Virgilii Ceparii S.J. in einen kurtzen Begriff zusammen gezogen, und in das Teutsch übersetzt. Von einem Priester bemeldter Gesellschaft. [With a portrait.] pp. 204. *München,* 1707. 12°. **862. g. 28.**

—— Vita Ioannis Berchmanni flandro-belgæ religiosi Societatis Iesu . . . Latine reddita a P. Hermanno Hugone. [With a portrait.] pp. 285. *Ex officina Plantiniana B. Moreti: Antuerpiæ,* 1630. 8°. **862. e. 10.**

—— [Another copy.] **C. 67. e. 2.**
Imperfect; wanting the last leaf bearing the publisher's device.

—— *See* GOLDIE (Francis) The Life of the Blessed John Berchmans. [Founded on the life by V. Cepari.] 1873. 8°. **3605. dd. 7.**

—— Vita della serafica vergine S. Maria Maddalena de' Pazzi . . . Con aggiunta delle lettere inedite della santa, dettate in estasi. pp. 540. *Prato,* 1884. 8°. **4823. b. 6.**

—— The Life of St. Mary Magdalene of Pazzi, Carmelitess. (Translated from the Italian.) pp. xiv. 428. *T. Richardson & Son: London,* 1849. 8°. [*The Saints and Servants of God.*] **4826. bbb. 18.**

—— Vie de Ste Marie-Magdeleine de Pazzi . . . traduite par l'Abbé Prau. pp. 288. *Tournai,* 1856. 8°. **4831. a. 51.**

—— Vita di S. Francesco Borgia terzo Generale della Compagnia di Gesù. 2 vol. *Monza,* 1884. 16°.
4827. de. 32.

—— Res à B. Francisco Borgia, ex Duce Gandiæ, III. Societatis Iesu Generale gestæ, quas e V. Ceparii . . . compendio Italicè vulgato And. Schottus . . . Latinè conscripsit. [With a portrait.] pp. 306. *Sumptibus H. Mylii: Coloniæ,* 1626. 12°. **858. a. 18.**

CEPARO (VINCENTIUS) De urticaria dissertatio inauguralis, *etc.* pp. 8. *Patavii,* 1828. 8°. **7306. b. 5. (9.)**

CEPA Y ESTEVEZ (PEDRO) Discurso pronunciado en la Universidad Central por el licenciado en Medicina, *etc.* (Filosofia medica española durante el periodo arábigo.) pp. 16. *Madrid,* 1857. 8°. **8355. f. 32. (3.)**

CEPEDA (ALEJANDRO DE) Xacara nueva, de un xaque, que haze relacion a otro amigo suyo de lo que le sucedio una tarde passeandose por Madrid. *See* FERNANDEZ DE MATA (G.) Soledades de Aurelia, *etc.* 1737. 8°.
12490. aa. 2.

CEPEDA (ALFONSO SANCHEZ DE) *See* SANCHEZ DE CEPEDA.

CEPEDA (ANTONIO GUILLÉN RODRÍGUEZ DE) *See* GUILLÉN RODRÍGUEZ DE CEPEDA.

CEPEDA (BALTASAR DE) Relaciõ de algunas Processiones, y fiestas en Conuentos, y Parroquias, que á hecho la famosa ciudad de Seuilla, a la Inmaculada Concepciõ de Maria Virgen, Señora nuestra, etc. [In verse.]
A. Rodriguez: Seuilla, 1615. 4º. C. **63**. b. **27**. (8.)

—— Testimonio en relacion, que da el Tiempo del estado q̄ oy tiene el pleyto de la Inmaculada Cõcepciõ de la Virgē nuestra señora. [In verse.] *A. Gamarra: Seuilla,* [1617 ?] 4º. C. **63**. b. **27**. (20.)

CEPEDA (FERNANDO DE) *See* GOMEZ DE MORA (A.) El Doctor A. Gomez de Mora, Fiscal de su Magestad, contra Don F. de la Torre (Don F. de Cepeda . . . sobre auer induzido, pagado, y supuesto testigos ; intentando prouar graues delitos al dicho señor Fiscal), etc. [1641 ?] fol.
9771. h. **1**. (6.)

—— *Begin.* Señor, Con orden que he tenido del Marquès de Cadereyta, virrey desta Nueua España, etc. [A memorial to the King of Spain, relating to the naval affairs of the Spanish possessions in the Indies, etc.] *Madrid,* 1639. fol. **1324**. i. **5**. (11.)

—— *Begin.* Señor. Con orden, que he tenido del Marques de Cadereyta, Virrey desta Nueua España, etc. [A report of the safety of the Spanish galleons after an engagement with the Dutch fleet.] ff. 10. [*Mexico,* 1638.] fol.
9771. h. **2**. (10.)

—— [Another edition.] ff. 10. *F. Salbago: Mexico,* 1638. fol. **9770**. k. **1**. (1.)

CEPEDA (FERNANDO DE) and **CARRILLO ALTA-MIRANO** (FERNANDO ALFONSO)

—— Relacion vniversal legitima, y verdadera del sitīo en que esta fundada la . . . ciudad de Mexico . . . Dispuesta, y ordenada por . . . D. F. de Cepeda . . . y D. F. A. Carrillo. Corregida, ajustada, y concertada con el Licenciado Don Iuan de Albares Serrano. (Relacion . . . contra ella por parte de Don Antonio Vrrutia de Vergara, etc.) 2 pt. *F. Salbago: Mexico,* 1637. fol.
145. e. **15**.

CEPEDA (FRANCISCO) Conferencias de Abuli, celebradas con . . . R. M. de Labra sobre política antillana, etc. pp. xxxii. 304. *Ponce,* 1890. 8º. **8042**. aaa. **28**.

CEPEDA (FRANCISCO DE) Resumpta Historial de España desde el Diluuio hasta el Año de 1642, etc. ff. 160.
P. Taço: Madrid, 1643. 4º. **9180**. e. **17**.
The titlepage is engraved.

ÇEPEDA (FRANCISCO NUÑEZ DE) *See* NUÑEZ DE ÇEPEDA.

CEPEDA (GABRIEL DE) Historia de la Milagrosa, y Venerable Imagen de N. S. de Atocha, Patrona de Madrid, etc. pp. 475. *Imprenta Real: Madrid,* 1670. 4º.
487. g. **24**. (1.)

CEPEDA (HILARIO NÚÑEZ DE) *See* NÚÑEZ DE CEPEDA.

CEPEDA (JOAQUIN ROMERO DE) *See* ROMERO DE CEPEDA.

CEPEDA (RAFAEL RODRÍGUEZ DE) *See* RODRÍGUEZ DE CEPEDA.

CEPEDA (RAMON) Ensayos políticos. Contestacion á un libro [" Las Nacionalidades "] del Sʳ Pí y Margall. 1877. 8º. **8042**. b. **11**.

CEPEDA (TERESA SANCHEZ DE) *See* THERESA [de Cepeda], de Jesus, Saint.

CEPEDA DÁVILA Y AHUMADA (TERESA SANCHEZ DE) *See* THERESA [de Cepeda], de Jesus, Saint.

CEPEDA Y AHUMADA (TERESA SANCHEZ DE) *See* THERESA [de Cepeda], de Jesus, Saint.

CEPEDA Y GOROSTIZA (MARIA DEL ROSARIO) Elogio de la Reyna N.S. . . . leido . . . el Sabado 15 de Julio de 1797. pp. 16. *Madrid,* 1797. 4º. **12301**. e. **5**. (2.)

CÉPÈDE (CASIMIR)

—— La Circulation automobile à gazogène, la carbonisation des bois et l'avenir de la forêt française. 1942. *See* TOULOUSE.—*Académie des Sciences, Inscriptions et Belles-Lettres. Mémoires, etc.* sér. 13. tom. 4. 1901, etc. 8º.
Ac. **555**.

CEPEDES (GONZALO DE) *See* CESPEDES Y MENESES.

CEPERLLI (DE BARTO) *See* BARTO CEPERLLI.

CEPHA (MOSES BAR) *Bishop of Bēth-Rāmān, Bēth-Kiyōnāya and Mosul. See* MOSES BAR KĒPHĀ.

CÉPHALAS (CONSTANTINE) *See* KEPHALAS (Konstantinos)

CEPHALION. Cephalionis fragmenta. *Gr.* 1849. *See* MUELLER (*Karl*) *Historian,* and MUELLER (Theodor) Fragmenta historicorum græcorum, etc. vol. 3. 1841, etc. 8º. **011306.cc.5**.

—— Cephalionis historiographi græci : de regno Assyriorum. *Lat. & Ital.* 1824. *See* MARTINETTI (G. G.) Collezione classica, ossia Tesoro delle antichità giudaiche, etc. tom. 2. 1824, etc. 8º. **1305**. c. **6**.

CEPHALLIGNIUS (ANTONIUS) *See* WOODHEAD (Anthony)

CEPHALONIA. Καταθεσεις και διαδικασιαι επι των εν Κεφαλληνια κατα το ετος 1849 συμβαντων. Depositions and proceedings relative to the events which occurred in Cephalonia in the year 1849. Deposizioni e procedimenti, etc. *Mod. Gr., Eng., & Ital. Corfù,* [1849.] 8º.
8028. b. **18**.

—— *Begin.* Noi Proueditor di Ceffalonia, etc. [A bill of health for issue to ships leaving the port of Cephalonia, filled in for an English vessel.] [1709.] *s. sh. obl.* fol.
L.R.404.a.4.(14.)
Engraved.

CEPHALUS. Cephalus and Procris. A dramatic masque. With a pantomime interlude, call'd, Harlequin Grand Volgi, etc. pp. 20. *J. Watts: London,* 1733. 8º.
841. b. **58**.

—— Le Rauissement de Cefale. Representé à Florence aux nopces royales. [By G. Chiabrera.] Traduit de l'italien . . . Par N. Chrétien : . . Auec vn cantique presenté à Monseigneur le Dauphin, le iour de son baptesme. pp. 40. *T. Reinsart: Rouen,* 1608. 12º. [*Les Tragedies de N. Chretien, Sieur des Croix.*] **163**. b. **13**.

CEPHALUS (ARIOPONUS) *See* COPUS (Martinus)

CEPHALUS (SIGISMUNDUS) Warer Grundt vnnd beweisung, das die vnrecht handlen, die jren Predigern verbieten, das Antichristisch Bapstumb mit seinen grewеln zustraffen, etc. MS. NOTES. *Getruckt durch C. Rhödinger: Magdeburg,* 1551. 4º. **3905**. f. **29**.

CEPHAS. Cephas, the Young Sailor ; a warning to youth, and an incentive to the faith of pious but discouraged parents. By his father . . . Second edition. pp. 102. *T. Ward & Co.: London,* 1835. 12º. **694**. b. **41**.

CEPHAS, *pseud.* Christel, a Christmas poem ; and sonnets, by Cephas. pp. 26. *Slatter & Rose: Oxford ; G. Bell: London,* [1855.] 8º. **11648**. d. **38**.

CEPHAS, *pseud.*

—— A New Social Order. By Cephas. pp. 54 *Cornish Bros.: Birmingham,* 1942. 8º. **08286**. d. **109**

CEPHAS, *M.G.Y.M.S.*, *pseud.* Voluntary Verses; or Rhyme and reason regarding religious establishments. By Cephas, M.G.Y.M.S. pp. 12. *W. R. M'Phun: Glasgow*, 1835. 12°. **908. c. 5. (10.)**

CEPHISODORUS. [Fragments.] *Gr.* See KOCK (T.) Comicorum atticorum fragmenta, *etc.* vol. 1. 1880, *etc.* 8°. **2047.i.**

CEPHYRIUS (ERNESTUS) De fractione panis in sacrosancto Eucharistiæ sacramento. Disputatio theologica, *etc. Praes.* G. Mylius, *etc.* pp. 31. *Witebergae*, [1700?] 4°. **4326. aaa. 11.**

CEPIANUS (JOANNES) *See* MACER (J.) Ioannis Macri . . . de prosperis Gallorum successibus Libellus . . . Cum scholiis I. Blondi . . . & I. Cepiani. 1555. 8°. **1058. a. 3. (2.)**

ČEPIČKA (ALEXEJ)

—— *See* POMER. O nový pomer cirkvi k štátu. [Speeches by A. Čepička and others.] 1950. 8°. **3915. aaa. 2.**

ČEPINAC (NIKOLA) *See* RUSSELL (Bertrand A. W.) *Earl Russell.* О воспитању, нарочито у раном детињству. С енглеског превео Др. Н. Чепинац. 1931. 8°. **08308. cc. 21.**

ČEPINSKIS (VINCAS) Elektronine valentingumo teorija. pp. 88. *Kaunas*, 1928. 8°. [*Lietuvos Universiteto Matematikos-Gamtos Fakulteto leidinys.*] Ac. **1157. h. (4.)**

—— Fizinė chemija. II [*etc.*] dalis. *Klaipėdoje*, 1930– . 8°. [*Lietuvos Universiteto Matematikos-Gamtos Fakulteto leidinys.*] Ac. **1157. h. (7, 8, 12, *etc.*)**

CEPIO (CN. FANNIUS) *See* FANNIUS (C.)

CEPIO (CORIOLANUS) *See* CIPPICUS.

CEPNIK (HENRYK) *See* FREDRO (Aleksander) *Count.* Nieznana komedya A. Fredry " Intryga na prędce." Wydał . . . H. Cepnik. 1917. 8°. **11758. r. 13.**

—— Józef Piłsudski, twórca niepodległego Państwa Polskiego. Zarys życia i działalności, 5. XII. 1867–12. v. 1935. [With a portrait.] pp. 316. *Warszawa*, 1936. 8°. **10796. aa. 21.**

—— Teatr polski w Wiedniu. Rzecz o występach Dramatu lwowskiego na scenie " Bürgertheater " w Wiedniu w dniach od 1. do 8. maja 1910 roku . . . Z ilustracyami. pp. 87. *we Lwowie*, 1910. 8°. **11805. m. 15.**

CEPNIK (KAZIMIERZ) Edward Śmigły Rydz, generalny inspektor sił zbrojnych. Zarys życia i działalności. [With a portrait.] pp. 199. *Warszawa*, 1936. 8°. **20013. bb. 16.**

CEPOLLA (BARTHOLOMAEUS) *See* CAEPOLLA.

CEPORINUS (JACOBUS) *See* BIBLE.—*New Testament.* [*Greek.*] Της Καινης Διαθηκης Άπαντα. Noui Testamenti omnia. [Corrected by J. Ceporinus.] 1524. 8°. **218. d. 20.**

—— *See* DIONYSIUS, *Periegetes.* Διονυσιου Οἰκουμενης περιηγησις. Ἀρατου Φαινομενα. Προκλου Σφαιρα . . . Cum scholijs Ceporini. 1523. 8°. **1067. i. 10.**

—— *See* PINDAR. [*Greek.*] Πινδαρου Ὀλυμπια, Πυθια, Νεμεα, Ἰσθμια, *etc.* [Edited by J. Ceporinus.] 1526. 8°. **1067. k. 10.**

—— Compendium Grammaticæ Græcæ Iacobi Ceporini, iam tertium de integr[o] ab ipso authore & castigatum & locupletatum. Hesiodi Georgicon, ab eodem Ceporino breui Scholio adornatum . . . Epigrammata quædam . . . adiecta. pp. 198. *Apud C. Froschouer: Tiguri*, 1526. 8°. **12923. aa. 19.**

CEPORINUS (JACOBUS)

—— [Another edition.] Ex postrema authoris editione, nunc primum opera Ioannis Frisii Tigurini castigatum & auctum. pp. 227. *Excudebat Ioannes Windet: Londini*, 1585. 8°. **1211. a. 38.**

CEPORINUS (JOHANNES) *See* VENRAY (J. van)

CEPPARI (VIRGILIO) *See* CEPARI.

CEPPI (MARC) *See* AUCASSIN. [*Modern French.*] Aucassin et Nicolette . . . With questionnaire, exercises and vocabulary by M. Ceppi. 1926. 8°. **12951. e. 13.**

—— *See* BISSCHOP (E. de) [Kaimiloa.] The Voyage of the Kaimiloa . . . Translated by M. Ceppi. 1940. 8°. **010498. d. 11.**

—— *See* BRUEYS (D. A. de) and PALAPRAT (J.) *Sieur de Bigot.* L'Avocat Patelin . . . Abridged and edited . . . by M. Ceppi. 1909. 8°. **012238. aa. 1/13.**

—— *See* COPPÉE (F. E. J.) Récits en prose et en vers . . . Edited with marginal notes on reform lines, conversational questions, and materials for free composition by M. Ceppi. 1919. 8°. **12952. r. 37/7.**

—— *See* COUSTENOBLE (H.) and CEPPI (M.) A Pronunciation Dictionary of the French Language, *etc.* 1929. 8°. [*GASC* (*F. E. A.*) *Gasc's Concise Dictionary, etc.*] **12951. de. 8.**

—— —— [1933.] 8°. [*GASC* (*F. E. A.*) *Gasc's Concise Dictionary, etc.*] **12951. ee. 38.**

—— *See* DESHUMBERT (M.) and CEPPI (M.) Grammaire française moderne. 1914. 8°. **12953. p. 7.**

—— *See* DESSAGNES (P. A.) A Concise French Course. Adapted by M. Ceppi, *etc.* 1922. 8°. **12951. aaa. 47.**

—— *See* DUMAS (A.) *the Elder.* [*Le Comte de Monte-Cristo.*] Edmond Dantès. Founded on an episode from " Monte Cristo " . . . Adapted by M. Ceppi. 1909. 8°. **12239.de.7/13.**

—— *See* DUMAS (A.) *the Elder.* [*Mes Mémoires.*] La Pistole. Récit tiré des Mémoires d'Alexandre Dumas. Edited by M. Ceppi. 1910. 8°. **012202. ff. 4/7.**

—— *See* DUMAS (A.) *the Elder.* [*Selections, Extracts, etc.*] Récits de chasse . . . Edited with marginal notes on reform lines, conversational questions, and materials for free composition by M. Ceppi. 1910. 8°. **12952. r. 37/8.**

—— *See* DUMAS (A.) *the Elder.* [*Selections, Extracts, etc.*] Récits de théâtre . . . Edited with marginal notes on reform lines, conversational questions, and materials for free composition by M. Ceppi. 1923. 8°. **12952. r. 37/9.**

—— *See* DUMAS (A.) *the Elder.* [*Selections, Extracts, etc.*] Tales by Dumas . . . Edited by M. Ceppi, *etc.* 1930, *etc.* 8°. **12238. de.**

—— *See* GASC (F. E. A.) Gasc's Concise Dictionary of the French & English Languages, *etc.* [With a supplement of new words by M. Ceppi.] 1929. 8°. **12951. de. 8.**

—— —— 1933. 8°. **12951. ee. 38.**

—— *See* GASC (F. E. A.) A Dictionary of the French and English Languages . . . New edition, with revised and enlarged supplement of new words and meanings [by M. Ceppi]. 1931. 8°. **2278. f. 10.**

—— *See* GASC (F. E. A.) Gasc's Little Gem Dictionary of the French and English Languages. Edited by M. Ceppi. 1911. 16°. **12952. de. 51.**

CEPPI (Marc)

—— *See* Guyon (C.) Nouveaux récits héroïques . . . Edited by M. Ceppi. 1918. 8º.   **12951. aaa. 10.**

—— *See* Guyon (C.) Récits héroïques . . . Edited by M. Ceppi. 1916. 8º.   **12953. p. 13.**

—— *See* Hugo (V. M.) *Viscount*. [*Les Misérables.*] Gavroche. Épisode tiré de " Les Misérables " . . . Adapted and edited by M. Ceppi. 1911. 8º. **012955.a.1/6.**

—— *See* Hugo (V. M.) *Viscount*. [*Les Misérables.*] Cosette. Épisode tiré de " Les Misérables " . . . Adapted and edited by M. Ceppi. 1912. 8º.   **012955.a.1/5.**

—— *See* Maupassant (H. R. A. G. de) Trois contes . . . Edited with marginal notes on reform lines, conversational questions, and materials for free composition by M. Ceppi. 1913. 8º.   **12952. r. 37/6.**

—— *See* Molière (J. B. P. de)   [*Selections.— French.*] Tales from Molière. Arranged and edited by M. Ceppi. 1912. 8º.   **11736. bb. 37.**

—— *See* O'Connor (Daniel S.) [Peter Pan Picture Book.] L'Histoire de Peter Pan . . . Traduction de M. Ceppi. 1916. 8º.   **012807. dd. 23.**

—— *See* Reynard the Fox. [*French.*] Les Aventures de Maître Renard. [Selections.] Edited by M. Ceppi, *etc.* [1913.] 8º.   **12548. pp. 12.**

—— *See* Toepffer (R.) Le Lac de Gers. Edited, with introduction, French-English vocabulary . . . by M. Ceppi. 1913. 8º.   **12199. d. 1/15.**

—— L'Aventure de Ted Bopp. pp. 62. *London*, 1930. 8º. [*Bell's Junior French Series.*]   **12955. de. 35/3.**

—— Bell's Junior French Series. Edited by M. Ceppi. 8 vol. *G. Bell & Sons: London*, 1929-36. 8º.   **12955. de. 35.**

—— Bell's New French Picture Cards. Illustrations by H. M. Brock . . . Text by M. Ceppi. 2 sets. *G. Bell & Sons: London*, [1930.] 8º.   **12955. a. 30.**

—— Bell's Sixpenny French Texts. Edited by M. Ceppi. 6 vol. *G. Bell & Sons: Londres*, 1914. 8º.   **12950. de. 47.**

—— Bell's Standard French Plays. Edited by M. Ceppi. 6 vol. *G. Bell & Sons: London*, 1913. 8º.   **11740. l. 20.**

—— Bell's Standard French Texts. Edited by M. Ceppi. 8 vol. *G. Bell & Sons: London*, 1914, 15. 8º.   **12951. eee. 4.**

—— A Book of French Verse, chosen and arranged for school use. pp. viii. 124. *G. Bell & Sons: London*, 1923. 8º.   **011483. a. 38.**

—— Le Casque invisible. pp. 63. *London*, 1936. 8º. [*Bell's Junior French Series.*]   **12955. de. 35/8.**

—— C'est la guerre. Six nouvelles. pp. vi. 107. *G. Bell & Sons: Londres*, 1915. 8º.   **012551. a. 48.**

—— Contes brefs. pp. viii. 113.   *G. Bell & Sons: London*, 1939. 8º.   **12955. de. 1.**

—— Contes faciles. Popular tales and legends re-written in easy French for elementary classes. Compiled and edited . . . by M. Ceppi. pp. vi. 98.   *London*, 1913. 8º. [*Hachette's New Series of French Readers on the Direct Method.*]   **12952. r. 37/3.**

—— Contes français, anciens et modernes. Edited by M. Ceppi. (Questionnaires and Exercises.) 2 pt. *G. Bell & Sons: London*, 1911. 8º.   **012548. a. 25.**

CEPPI (Marc)

—— Contes imaginaires. pp. 96.   *G. Bell & Sons: London*, 1950. 8º.   **012955. a. 30.**

—— Contes mythologiques. pp. vii. 136.   *G. Bell & Sons: London*, 1928. 8º.   **12951. eee. 28.**

—— Easiest French Reader. pp. vii. 103.   *G. Bell & Sons: London*, 1918. 8º.   **12950. bbb. 36.**

—— [Another edition.] Transcribed into phonetic script. pp. 92. *G. Bell & Sons: London*, 1924. 8º.   **12951. bbb. 3.**

—— Easy Exercises in French Prose. pp. viii. 124. *G. Bell & Sons: London*, 1925. 8º.   **12951. aa. 63.**

—— Les Emplois de Pierre Quiroule. [With exercises and vocabulary.] pp. vii. 86.   *G. Bell & Sons: London*, 1938. 8º.   **12951. c. 38.**

—— Encore des petits contes. pp. viii. 114. *G. Bell & Sons: London*, 1929. 8º.   **12951. e. 39.**

—— Ernest, Ernestine et Cie . . . Reprinted from " L'Echo de France." pp. viii. 140.   *G. Bell & Sons: London*, 1924. 8º.   **12951. bbb. 4.**

—— First Year French Reader. pp. 63.   *London*, 1932. 8º. [*Bell's Junior French Series.*]   **12955. de. 35/7.**

—— Flips et Compagnie. [Tales.] pp. vii. 123. *G. Bell & Sons: London*, 1917. 8º.   **12547. p. 22.**

—— French by yourself. A quick course in reading for adult beginners and others. pp. 271.   *G. Bell & Sons: London*, 1949. 8º. [' *By Yourself' Language Series.*]   **012902.r.15/4.**

—— A French Dramatic Reader. Compiled by M. Ceppi. pp. 204. *G. Bell & Sons: London*, 1913. 8º.   **11735. bbb. 27.**

—— French Lessons on the Direct Method. 4 vol. *Hachette & Co.: London, Paris*, 1907-14.   **12950. pp. 41.**

—— French for Young Beginners, *etc.* pp. 152. *G. Bell & Sons: London*, 1928. 8º.   **12951. eee. 23.**

—— French Passages for Translation or Dictation. pp. 48. *G. Bell & Sons: London*, 1937. 8º.   **12953. pp. 24.**

—— Hachette's New Phonetic French Reader. Short graduated extracts in prose and verse . . . printed in the phonetic symbols of the Association Phonetic Internationale, with the corresponding ordinary script on opposite pages. Compiled and edited for the use of elementary and intermediate classes by M. Ceppi. pp. 64.   *Hachette & Co.: London, Paris*, 1913 [1912]. 8º.   **12952. s. 30.**

—— Hachette's New Series of French Readers on the Direct Method . . . General editor: M. Ceppi. 9 vol. *Hachette & Co.: London, Paris*, 1910-23. 8º.   **12952. r. 37.**

—— L'Image expliquée. pp. 64. *London*, 1929. 8º. [*Bell's Junior French Series.*]   **12955. de. 35/1.**

—— Lectures françaises. Choisies et adaptées par M. Ceppi. pp. viii. 208. *G. Bell & Sons: London*, 1933. 8º.   **12951. g. 8.**

—— Modern French Course, *etc.* 4 vol.   *G. Bell & Sons: London*, 1931, 32. 8º.   **12951. ff. 19.**

—— Additional Exercises for Modern French Course. pp. 72. *G. Bell & Sons: London*, 1935. 8º.   **12951. cc. 28.**

—— Additional Exercises for Modern French Course, second year. pp. 15. *G. Bell & Sons: London*, [1935.] 8º.   **12951. cc. 27.**

CEPPI (MARC)

—— Morceaux choisis des auteurs contemporains, prose et vers. Graduated and self-contained extracts from French writers of the nineteenth and twentieth centuries. Edited . . . by M. Ceppi. pp. iv. 152. *Hachette & Co.: London, Paris,* 1912 [1911]. 8°. **12236.** bb. **33.**

—— Nos lycéens. pp. 59. *London,* 1931. 8°. [*Bell's Junior French Series.*] **12955. de. 35/5.**

—— Notes on the Teaching of French, and passages for dictation. pp. vii. 119. *G. Bell & Sons: London,* 1935. 8°. **12951. cc. 34.**

—— Nouveaux contes faciles. Popular tales and legends re-written in easy French for elementary classes. Compiled and edited . . . by M. Ceppi. pp. vii. 81. *London,* 1915. 8°. [*Hachette's New Series of French Readers on the Direct Method.*] **12952. r. 37/4.**

—— Nouveaux contes français. pp. 175. *G. Bell & Sons: London,* 1922. 8°. **012547. a. 19.**

—— Petits contes pour les petits. A very simple reader. pp. 79. *G. Bell & Sons: London,* 1937. 8°. **12952. pp. 41.**

—— Un Peu de français. Earliest lessons & practice in phonetics, *etc.* pp. vi. 119. *G. Bell & Sons: London,* 1924. 8°. **12951. b. 48.**

—— Renard le fripon . . . Illustrated. pp. 88. *Edwin Arnold: London,* [1914.] 8°. **012548. a. 32.**

—— Simple French Stories. Compiled by M. Ceppi. pp. 111 *G. Bell & Sons: London,* 1913. 8°. **012551. a. 24.**

—— Toujours des petits contes. pp. viii. 119. *G. Bell & Sons: London,* 1934. 8°. **12951. g. 39.**

—— Trente petits dialogues. pp. viii. 135. *G. Bell & Sons: London,* 1931. 8°. **12951. f. 38.**

—— Trente-deux petits contes. pp. iv. 124. *G. Bell & Sons: London,* 1927. 8°. **12951. eee. 14.**

—— Twelve French Plays for Schools. A conversational reader. pp. 128. *G. Bell & Sons: London,* 1936. 8°. **12953. pp. 20.**

CEPPI (MARC) and **CARRÉ** (ALBERT LUCIEN)

—— Nouveau cours de français . . . Première (—quatrième) année. 4 pt. *G. Bell & Sons: London,* 1950, 52. 8°. **12957. a. 9.**

CEPPI (MARC) and **JONES** (LLEWELYN JOHN)

—— Le Français. A practical French course. 2 pt. *G. Bell & Sons: London,* 1920, 21. 8°. **12951. b. 16.**

—— Le Français. Cours pratique. 1ère partie. pp. xii. 218. *G. Bell & Sons: London,* 1921. 8°. **12955. aa. 46.** *No more published.*

CEPPITELLI (GIUSEPPE) Gli Applausi di Roma verso l'augusta persona di sua A. R. l'Arciduca Massimiliano d'Austria . . . Terzine. [With " Sonetto del Signor Dottor Martelli."] pp. iv. [*Rome,* 1775 ?] 4°. **T. 44*. (21.)**

—— Celebrandosi la solenne festività del glorioso martire S. Lorenzo nel suo Oratorio dalla venerabile Archiconfraternità del Santissimo Sagramento in S. Lorenzo in Lucina . . . Sonnetto. *Roma,* 1778. *s. sh.* fol. **T. 101*. (15.)**

—— Per il fausto possesso che prende nella basilica di San Giovanni in Laterano la Santità di Nostro Signore Papa Pio VI . . . Sonetto. *Roma,* 1775. *s. sh.* fol. **T. 101*. (11.)**

CERA (VINCENZO LEONARDO) Progetto di un ospedale clinico per le malattie della mente . . . Memoria accompagnata da progetto architettonico di Francesco Paolo Capaldo. pp. 40. *Napoli,* 1868. fol. **1831. a. 10.**

—— Sulla alimentazione forzata dei folli sitofobi. pp. 135. *Napoli,* 1888. 8°. [MISSING.]

CERACCHI (ERCOLE) Relazione agl'onorevoli Deputati al Parlamento italiano, *etc.* pp. 22. *Rieti,* 1865. 8°. **8033. e. 18. (6.)**

CERACCHI (GIUSEPPE) *See* FERNAND-HUE (G.) Un Complot de police sous le Consulat. La conspiration de Ceracchi et Aréna, *etc.* 1909. 8°. **09225. f. 30.**

—— *See* MERVILLE (D. de) Procès instruit . . . contre Demerville, Céracchi . . . et autres, prévenus de conspiration contre la personne du premier Consul, *etc.* [1801.] 8°. **878. i. 5.**

CERADINI (ADRIANO) *See* CERADINI (G.) Opere. [Edited by A. Ceradini.] 1906. 4°. **12226. i. 14.**

CERADINI (CARLOTTA) *See* CERADINI (G.) A proposito dei due globi mercatoriani, *etc.* [With a preface by C. Ceradini.] 1894. 4°. **10001. e. 8.**

CERADINI (GIULIO) *See* LORIA (L.) Block-sistema automatico del prof. G. Ceradini in esperimento presso l'amministrazione delle strade ferrate dell'Alta Italia, *etc.* 1882. fol. **8767. m. 22.**

—— *See* LUCIANI (L.) Giulio Ceradini, *etc.* [A biographical sketch.] 1894. 8°. **10603. d. 15. (5.)**

—— *See* SCARTAZZI (A.) Block-sistem automatico con nuovi apparecchi a corrente periodica del dott. G. Ceradini, *etc.* 1899. fol. **8767. m. 21.**

—— Opere. [Edited by Adriano Ceradini. With a portrait.] 2 vol. *Milano,* 1906. 4°. **12226. i. 14.**

—— A proposito dei due globi mercatoriani, 1541–1551. Appunti critici sulla storia della geografia nei secoli XV e XVI, *etc.* [With a preface by Carlotta Ceradini.] pp. xxii. 301. MS. NOTES. *Milano,* 1894. 4°. **10001. e. 8.**

—— Difesa della mia memoria intorno alla scoperta della circolazione del sangue, contro l'assalto dei signori H. Tollin . . . e W. Preyer . . . e qualche nuovo appunto circa la storia della scoperta medesima. pp. 168. *Genova,* 1876. 8°. [MISSING.]

—— Il Meccanismo delle valvole semilunari del cuore . . . Con una tavola, *etc.* pp. 62. *Firenze,* 1873. 8°. **7419. bb. 6.**

—— La Scoperta della circolazione del sangue. Appunti storico-critici . . . Nuova edizione . . . aumentata. pp. 335. *Milano,* 1876. 8°. [MISSING.]

CERALDI (CINTIO)

—— Apollo in Apolline. Cena del Sig. Co. Astorre Orsi. All'eminentiss. sig. card. Sacchetti. [A description of the theatrical entertainments offered at this dinner, with the text of the songs.] pp. 52. *Per Nicolò Tebaldini: Bologna,* 1639. 4°. **Hirsch IV. 1325.**

CÉRALE (ÉDOUARD)

—— Essai sur la mélanose vraie. Thèse, *etc.* pp. 56. *Montpellier,* 1880. 4°. **7379. m. 3. (3.)**

CERALE (LEOPOLDO ACHILLE) Définir la contagion, établir les différences qui peuvent exister entre la contagion et l'infection : doit-on admettre des maladies contagieuses ? . . . Thèse, *etc.* pp. 31. *Montpellier,* 1841. 4°. **1182. c. 5. (11.)**

CERAM (C. W.) *pseud.* [i.e. KURT W. MAREK.]

—— Enge Schlucht und schwarzer Berg. Entdeckung des Hethiter-Reiches. pp. 248. pl. XLVIII. *Hamburg,* 1955. 8°. **07705. p. 23.**

—— [Götter, Gräber und Gelehrte.] Gods, Graves, and Scholars. The story of archæology . . . Translated . . . by E. B. Garside. pp. xii. 433. pl. XXXII. *Victor Gollancz ; Sidgwick & Jackson : London,* 1952. 8°. **07704. aaa. 17.**

CÉRAMANO (CHARLES FERDINAND)

—— *See* BOCQ (E.) Céramano, peintre naturiste. [With reproductions and a portrait.] 1908. 4°. **7867. aa. 38.**

CERAME (F. RUSSO DE) *See* RUSSO DE CERAME.

CERAMEUS (CASPAR) *See* VELTKIRCH (J.) Epitomae physicae libri quatuor, *etc.* [Edited by C. Cerameus.] 1538. 8°. **536. a. 1.**

CERAMEUS (THEOPHANES) *Archbishop of Taormina. See* THEOPHANES, *Cerameus, etc.*

CERAMI (CHARLES AUGUST)

—— Successful Leadership in Business. pp. xiv. 224. *Prentice-Hall : New York,* 1955. 8°. **8231. h. 103.**

CERAMIC DIGEST. *See* PERIODICAL PUBLICATIONS.— *Saint Albans.*

CERAMIC GAZETTE. *See* PERIODICAL PUBLICATIONS. —*Teddington.*

CERAMIC SOCIETY. *See* STOKE-ON-TRENT.—*British Ceramic Society.*

CERÁMICA.

—— C.E.R.A.M.I.C.A. [A series.] *See* C.E.R.A.M.I.C.A.

CERAMICS. *See* PERIODICAL PUBLICATIONS.—*Leighton Buzzard.*

—— Ceramics in Art and Industry. *See* DOULTON AND CO.

CÉRAMIQUE.

—— Céramique . . . Études céramologiques. *See* GENEVA.— *Académie Internationale de la Céramique.*

CERAMIUS (MICHAEL) *Resp.* Propositiones de dono miraculorum : contra Mirabiliarios Papistas, *etc. Praes.* J. Pappus. *Typis N. Vyrioti :* [*Strasburg,*] 1574. 4°. **700. h. 16. (1.)**

CÉRAN (LÉON DE) *pseud.* [i.e. JÉRÔME LÉON VIDAL.] *See* BARTHÉLEMY, *pseud.* L'Épée, le bâton et le chausson, vaudeville . . . Par MM. Barthélemy, Lhérie et L. de Céran, *etc.* 1830. 8°. **11738. h. 31. (3.)**

—— *See* BARTHÉLEMY, *pseud.* Le Mort sous le scellé, folie . . . Par MM. Barthélemy, Lhérie et Céran, *etc.* 1832. 8°. **11738. h. 31. (7.)**

—— *See* BRUNSWICK ( ) *pseud.* Les Croix et le charivari, à-propos . . . Par MM. Brunswick, Lhérie et de Céran, *etc.* 1831. 8°. **11738. h. 31. (8.)**

—— *See* MARION DUMERSAN (T.) Gothon du passage Delorme, imitation . . . de Marion Delorme, burlesque . . . par MM. Dumersan, Brunswick et Céran, *etc.* 1831. 8°. **11738. dd. 31. (11.)**

CÉRAN-LEMONNIER (LOUIS) *See* ROUSSEAU (Louis) *Zoologist,* and CÉRAN-LEMONNIER (L.) Promenades au Jardin des Plantes, *etc.* 1837. 8°. **970. a. 33.**

CÉRAN-LEMONNIER (LOUIS)

—— Atlas de la géographie des trois règnes de la nature. Distribution des animaux, des végétaux, des minéraux, à la surface du globe. [Three maps, with letterpress.] *Paris,* 1837. fol. **Maps 49. e. 7.**

—— Programme de l'enseignement de l'histoire naturelle dans les collèges, adopté par le Conseil royal de l'Instruction publique, disposé en tableaux méthodiques . . . Deuxième édition. [Forty-nine plates.] *Paris,* 1837. fol. **443. i. 12.** *Engraved throughout.*

—— Thèse pour le doctorat en médecine, *etc.* (Questions sur diverses branches des sciences médicales.) pp. 34. *Paris,* 1838. 4°. **1184. i. 6. (10.)**

CERASI (FILIPPO) Raccolta di memorie mediche, edite ed inedite. vol. 1. (Del parassitismo nella pertosse epidemica di Roma nel 1867, *etc.*) pp. 52. *Roma,* 1874. 8°. **7320. dd. 10.**

No more published.

CERASIANUS (JOANNES) Repetitio famosissimi c. Sentētiaȝ sanguinis bona ⁊ vtilis sub ti. Ne. cle. vel mo. in qua plenissime ⁊ plucide tractatur omnis materia irregularitatis Clericis permaxime necessaria. [fol. 56 *recto:*] Repetitū ⁊ resumptū est hoc. c. Sententiā sanguinis in alma vniuersitate Liptzensi Ex cōmissione et mādato . . . Iohānis de Breytenbach . . . Per . . . Iohannē Cerasiauu [*sic*], *etc.* G.ᴸ. ⁊ Melchiorem Lotter : [*Leipsic,*] 1499. 4°. **IA. 12119.**

56 leaves. Sig. A–H⁶ I⁸. 42 lines to a page.

CERASINUS (JOANNES KIRSTEYN) *See* CERAZYN (Jan)

CERASIO (GIOVANNI PIETRO) Methodo dello spetiale . . . Nel quale . . . si tratta del vero modo di perfettamente formare qual si voglia composto medicinale. pp. 132. *I. de gli Antonij : Milano,* 1611. 8°. **1038. d. 35. (6.)**

CERASIUS (JOANNES ANDREAS) Io. Andreae Cerasii Trebiatis de agro Reuerendi D. Alexandri Valentis Prothonotarij Apostolici et Comitis Palatini ad viatorem carmen. *Apud P. Petrutium : Perusiæ,* 1579. 4°. **11405. d. 14.**

ČERAŠKA (L.)

—— Provizorinis Lietuvos hydracariną sąrašas. Die provisorische Liste der Hydracarinen Litauens. 1932. *See* KAUNAS.—*Lietuvos Universitetas, etc.* Lietuvos Universiteto Matematikos Gamtos fakulteto darbai. t. 6. sąs. 3. 1923, *etc.* 8°. **Ac. 1157/2.**

CERASOLI (FRANCESCO) *See* ROME, *Church of.*—[*Popes.*] —Clement VI. [1342–1352.] Clemente VI e Giovanna I di Napoli. Documenti inediti, *etc.* [Edited by F. Cerasoli.] 1896, *etc.* 8°. [*Archivio storico per le province napoletane.* anno 21, 22.] **Ac. 6534.**

—— *See* ROME, *Church of.*—[*Popes.*]—Clement VI. [1352–1362.] Clemente VI e Casa Savoia. Documenti vaticani trascritti da F. Cerasoli, *etc.* 1900. 8°. [*Miscellanea di storia patria.* tom. 36.] **Ac. 6550.**

—— *See* ROME, *Church of.*—[*Popes.*]—Innocent VI. [1352–1362.] Innocenzo VI e Giovanna I regina di Napoli. Documenti inediti, *etc.* [Edited by F. Cerasoli.] 1897, *etc.* 8°. [*Archivio storico per le province napoletane.* anno 22, 23.] **Ac. 6534.**

—— *See* ROME, *Church of.*—[*Popes.*]—Gregory XI [1370–1378.] Gregorio XI e Giovanna I regina di Napoli. Documenti inediti, *etc.* [Edited by F. Cerasoli.] 1898, *etc.* 8°. [*Archivio storico per le province napoletane.* anno 23–25.] **Ac. 6534.**

CERASOLI (Leone Mattei) *See* Mattei-Cerasoli.

CERASTUS CORNANUS (Cornelius) *pseud. Praes. See* Crufenas (C. T.) *pseud.* Themata medica de Beanorum, Archibeanorum, Beanulorum & Cornutorum . . . affectibus, *etc.* [1626?] 4°.   **1179. d. 9. (17.)**

—— —— 1642. 12°. [*Nugae venales, etc.*] **12330.aa.2.**

—— —— [1650?] 4°.   **1179. d. 9. (18.)**

—— —— [1650?] 4°.   **12330. ccc. 39. (3.)**

—— —— 1662. 12°. [*Nugae venales, etc.*]   **12314. e. 6.**

—— —— 1689. 12°. [*Nugae venales, etc.*]   **245. b. 18.**

—— —— 1720. 12°. [*Nugae venales, etc.*]   **12315. a. 18.**

CERATI (A.) *Abbé. See* Barberi (G. P.) Grand dictionnaire français-italien et italien-français . . . Continué et terminé par MM. Barti et Cerati. 1838, *etc.* 4°.   **828. h. 7.**

—— Des usurpations sacerdotales, ou Du clergé en opposition avec les principes actuels de la société et du besoin de ramener le culte catholique à la religion primitive ; précédé du récit de la mission du P. Farina à Ajaccio. Publié par Saint-Edme. pp. xxxv. 184. *Paris*, 1828. 8°.   **1119. f. 15.**

CERATI (Antonio) *Count. See also* Filandro, *Cretense, pseud.* [i.e. *Count* A. Cerati.]

—— *See* Bible.—*Genesis.* [*Italian.*] La Genesi. Versione di monsignor D. G. Cerati. [With a life of the translator by Count A. Cerati.] 1807. 8°.   **1063. e. 8.**

—— *See* Tonani (R.) Ellogium Comitis . . . Antonii Cerati, *etc.* 1816. 4°.   **L.R. 233. b. 30.**

—— Alla Santità di Pio VII. nel suo passagio per Parma dopo l'incoronazione da lui fatta in Parigi di Napoleone Buonaparte Imperadore de' Francesi e Re d'Italia umilia Antonio Cerati i seguenti sonetti. *Co' Tipi Bodoniani : Parma*, 1805. 4°.   **L.R. 233. b. 10. (3.)**

—— [Another copy.]   **L.R. 233. b. 26.**

—— Elogio del cardinale Sforza Pallavicino, *etc. See* Rubbi (A.) Elogj italiani. tom. 11. [1782.] 8°.   **276. g. 25.**

—— Elogio del signor marchese Prospero Manara. pp. 100. [*Parma*,] 1801. 8°.   **1161. d. 5.**

—— Elogio dell'abate Carlo Innocenzo Frugoni. *See* Frugoni (C. I.) Poesie, *etc.* tom. 1. 1779, *etc.* 8°.   **12227. bbb. 1.**

—— [Another edition.] *See* Rubbi (A.) Elogj italiani. tom. 3. [1782.] 8°.   **276. g. 21.**

—— Elogio di monsignor Gasparo Cerati, patrizio parmigiano, *etc.* pp. xxxii. 122. *Parma*, 1778. 8°.   **277. f. 5.**

—— [Another edition.] pp. 122. *See* Rubbi (A.) Elogj italiani. tom. 5. [1782.] 8°.   **276. g. 22.**

—— Elogio funebre recitato . . . nelle solenni esequie di S.E. il signor conte Aurelio Bernieri Terrarossa . . . celebrate nella cattedrale di Parma il giorno IV. d'agosto MDCCXCV. Aggiuntevi alcune poesie melanconiche dell'autore. pp. 80. *Parma*, 1797. 8°.   **10602. h. 13. (1.)**

—— La Magreide, ghiribizzo poetico, e l'Ipocondria, scherzo misto di versi, e di prosa, di Filandro Cretense (Conte A. Cerati). pp. 77. *Parma*, 1781. 8°.   **T. 2276. (3.)**

—— [Another copy.]   **1463. i. 28. (2.)**

CERATI (Antonio) *Count.*

—— Per la beatificazione del venerabile Lorenzo da Brindisi, Gener. dell'Ord. de' Cappuccini, festeggiata . . . nella chiesa de' Padri Cappuccini del convento di Parma. Panegirico in versi sciolti di Filandro Cretense (A. Cerati). pp. 23. *Parma*, 1784. 8°.   **1463. i. 28. (5.)**

—— I Sanvitali. Prosa e versi di Filandro Cretense (A. Cerati). pp. 128. *Parma*, 1787. 8°.   **1463. i. 28. (1.)**

—— La Villa di Forci. Poemetto. *See* Italian Poems. Poemetti italiani. vol. 12. 1797. 12°.   **1062. f. 12.**

—— Le Ville Lucchesi, con altri opuscoli, in versi ed in prosa di Filandro Cretense, Pastor Arcade (A. Cerati). pp. viii. 194. **L.P.** *Parma*, 1783. 8°.   **83. d. 1.**

CERATI (Francesco) Tragedie. pp. 268. *G. P. Pinelli : Venetia*, 1638. 12°.   **641. b. 19.**

CERATI (Gasparo Gaetano Francesco) *See* Cerati (A.) *Count.* Elogio di monsignor Gasparo Cerati, *etc.* 1778. 8°.   **277. f. 5.**

—— —— [1782.] 8°. [*Rubbi (A.) Elogj italiani.* tom. 5.]   **276. g. 22.**

CERATI (Gregorio) *Bishop of Piacenza. See* Bianchi (Giovanni) *of Piacenza.* La Vita e i tempi di monsignor Gregorio Cerati, *etc.* 1893. 8°.   **4866. de. 14.**

—— *See* Bible.—*Genesis.* [*Italian.*] La Genesi. Versione di monsignor D. G. Cerati, *etc.* 1807. 8°.   **1063. e. 8.**

CERATINUS (Jacobus) Iacobi Ceratini de sono literarum, præsertim Græcarum, libellus. *See* Greek Language. De vera pronuntiatione Gr. et Latinæ linguæ, commentarii, *etc.* 1587. 8°.   **236. g. 33.**

—— [Another edition.] *See* Haverkamp (S.) Sylloge scriptorum, qui de linguæ Græcæ . . . pronuntiatione commentarios reliquerunt, *etc.* 1736. 8°.   **623. e. 8.**

CERATO (Margherita) Caterina Sforza. Conferenza tenuta all'Accademia dell'Arcadia, il 4 maggio 1903. pp. 33. *Roma*, 1903. 8°.   **10629. g. 22.**

CERAULO (Giovanni Battista) Passato ed avvenire religioso in relazione alla politica. Studi storici. vol. 1. pt. 1. pp. clxl. 411. *Palermo*, 1868. 8°.   **4017. df. 15.** *No more published.*

—— Il Passato e lo avvenire religioso in relazione alla politica. Studi storici. pt. 1. disp. 1. pp. 1–24. *Palermo*, 1866. 8°.   **3902. dd. 10.** *Imperfect ; wanting all after p. 24. A different work from the preceding.*

—— La Vita politica di Vittorio Emanuele II a traverso la unificazione degli stati italiani. vol. 1, 2 ; vol. 3. pp. 1–120. *Palermo*, 1879–82. 4°.   **8032. m. 11.**

CERAUNIO (Araste) *pseud.* [i.e. Filippo Marcheselli.] —— Rime. 1717. *See* Rome.—*The City.—Arcadia.* Rime degli Arcadi, *etc.* tom. 6. 1716, *etc.* 12°.   **240. k. 9.**

CERAUSIO (Egone) *pseud.* [i.e. Pietro Giubelei.] Rime. 1717. *See* Rome.—*The City.—Arcadia.* Rime degli Arcadi, *etc.* tom. 6. 1716, *etc.* 12°.   **240. k. 9.**

ČERAZ (Minas)

—— Armenia . . . Reprinted from the "Journal of the Manchester Geographical Society." [With a map.] pp. 3. [1891.] 8°.   **10077. i. 21. (6.)**

—— Homère et les Arméniens. (Extrait des Mélanges Charles de Harlez.) *Leide*, [1895.] 4°.   **11335. k. 7. (4.)**

Č'ERAZ (MINAS)

—— L'Orient inédit. Légendes et traditions arméniennes, grecques et turques, recueillies et traduites. pp. 328. *Paris*, 1912. 8°. [*Collection de chansons et de contes populaires.* tom. 39.] **2348. aaa. 39.**

—— Saïat Nova, sa vie et ses chansons . . . From the " Journal of the Royal Asiatic Society." [1893.] 8°. **10601. d. 32. (14.)**

—— Poètes arméniens, *etc.* [Selections from the works of various authors.] pp. xi. 155. *Paris*, 1913. 8°. **17046. a. 1.**

CERAZYN (JAN) Enchiridion aliquot locorum communium Iuris Maidenburgeñ. per J. K. Cerasinum . . . obiter explicatorum. *See* MAGDEBURG. Porządek Sądów y Spraw Mieyskich Práwá Máydeburskiego, *etc.* 1619. 4°. **716. c. 36.**

—— [Another edition.] *See* MAGDEBURG. Porządek sądow y spraw mieyskich prawa Maydeburskiego, *etc.* 1760. 4°. [MISSING.]

CERBANTES (   )

—— [For the Spanish surname of this form :] *See* CERVANTES.

CERBANUS.

—— *See* JOHN, *of Damascus, Saint.* Translatio latina Ioannis Damasceni—De orthodoxa fide l. III. c. 1–8—saeculo XII in Hungaria confecta [by Cerbanus], *etc.* 1940. 8°. [*Magyar-görög tanulmányok.* no. 13.] **Ac. 821. f/2.**

—— *See* MAXIMUS, *Saint, Abbot and Confessor.* Translatio latina Sancti Maximi Confessoris—De Caritate ad Elpidium l. I–IV.—saeculo XII. in Hungaria confecta [by Cerbanus], *etc.* 1944. 8°. [*Magyar-görög tanulmányok.* no. 25.] **Ac. 821. f/2.**

CERBARO. *See* CERBERUS.

CERBELAUD (GEORGES) and **DUMONT** (GEORGES) Le Génie civil et les travaux publics à l'Exposition universelle de 1878 . . . sous la direction de M. E. Cahen. pp. xvi. 581. *Paris*, 1879. 8°. [MISSING.]

CERBELLON (GASPAR MERCADER Y DE) *Count. See* MERCADER Y DE CERBELLON.

CERBELLÓN DE LA VERA (EUSTAQUIO)

—— Dialogo harmonico, sobre el Theatro critico universal [of B. G. Feyjóo y Montenegro]: en defensa de la musica de los templos, *etc.* pp. 64. *Madrid*, 1726. 4°. **7889. b. 65.**

CERBELLON DE SANTACRUZ (RODRIGO) *Begin.* El Doctor D. R. Cerbellon de Santacruz, Presbytero, *etc.* [A memorial of his services and of those of his ancestors, *etc.*] MS. ADDITION. [*Madrid ?* 1630 ?] fol. **1324. i. 2. (121.)**

—— [Another copy.] MS. ADDITION. **1324. i. 2. (122.)**

CERBELLONO (FABRIZIO) *See* SERBELLONI (F.) *Governor of Avignon.*

CERBERUS. Cerbaro inuoco [by Simone Sardini]. et contra Cerbaro. Con la disperata de M. Antonio Tibaldeo. [Three poems. With a woodcut.] [*Florence ?* 1520 ?] 4°. **11422. d. 31.**

CERBERUS, *pseud. See* PERIODICAL PUBLICATIONS.— *London.* The Theatrical Inquisitor . . . By Cerberus. 1812, *etc.* 8°. [MISSING.]

CERBERUS DIABOLUS, *pseud.* *See* DIABOLUS (C.) *pseud.*

CERBERUS (ANGELUS) *pseud.* Die ästhetische Prügeley oder der Freymüthige im Faustkampf mit den Eleganten. Zweyaktige Posse in gewogenen Versen, von Angelus Cerberus, *etc.* (Eine gegen Goethe gerichtete satirische Schrift.) *See* GEIGER (L.) Firlifimini, *etc.* 1885. 8°. **12249. ee. 2.**

CERBIDIO, *Afrodisiense, pseud.* [i.e. — CIPRIANI.] Notizie del governo della Sabina, *etc.* pp. xxxi. *Roma*, 1768. 4°. **658. i. 22. (3.)**

CERBINO. La nouella di Cerbino. [In verse. With a woodcut.] [*Lorenzo Morgiani: Florence*, 1495 ?] 4°. **IA. 27908.**

6 leaves, without signatures. Double columns, four and a half eight-line stanzas to the column.

—— [Another edition.] [Edited by Teodorico Landoni.] pp. 38. *Bologna*, 1862. 8°. **12226. bbb. 3. (9.)**

CERBONEY DUBARRY (JOSEPH MARIE CÉLESTIN) Sur le choléra ; thèse, *etc.* pp. 26. *Paris*, 1832. 4°. **1184. e. 8. (32.)**

CERBONI (CARLO) Cenni storici sulla Repubblica Argentina, 1515–1860. [With a preface by A. Colocci.] pp. xii. 247. *Buenos Aires*, 1891. 8°. **9781. e. 11.**

—— Leggenda elbana. pp. 43. *Roma*, 1882. 8°. **12471. ccc. 17.**

CERBONI (DOMINICUS DE) successively *Patriarch of Grado* and *of Venice.* Epistola Dominici Patriarchæ Venetiarum, ad Petrum Antiochiæ Patriarcham. (Γραμμα Δομινικου, *etc.*) Gr. & Lat. 1681. *See* COTELERIUS (J. B.) Ecclesiæ Græcæ monumenta. tom. 2. 1677, *etc.* fol. **491. g. 2.**

—— [Another edition.] *See* WILL (C. J. C.) Acta et scripta quae de controversiis ecclesiae Graecae et Latinae . . . extant, *etc.* 1861. 4°. **4520. e. 8.**

CERBONI (FABIO) Il Cimitero di San Miniato al Monte illustrato. [With epitaphs and tables.] pp. 110. *Firenze*, 1865. 8°. **10630. bb. 16.**

CERBONI (GIUSEPPE) *See* CUCCOLI (G.) Sulla logismografia. Nuovo sistema di contabilità del comm. G. Cerboni. Tre letture, *etc.* 1877. 8°. **8507. b. 5.**

—— *See* VIGLEZZI (V.) La Logismografia. Progetto di scrittura a partita doppia del comm. G. Cerboni . . . Esposizione teorico-pratica, *etc.* 1877. 4°. **8505. h. 3.**

—— Cagioni che impedirono ed impediscono lo assetto della contabilità delle imposte dirette. [With tables.] pp. 166. *Firenze*, 1869. 8°. **8228. e. 37.**

—— Sull'ordinamento della contabilità dello Stato. [With a table.] pp. 59. *Firenze*, 1866. 8°. **8226. ff. 30. (4.)**

—— Conferenze intorno alla vita e alle opere di Giuseppe Cerboni. Edite per cura del comitato esecutivo per le onoranze cerboniane, *etc.* pp. vii. 253. *Roma*, 1914. 8°. **10632. p. 19.**

CERBONI (IPPOLITO) Discorso accademico contro la poesia de' vani poeti . . . fatto . . . per ischerzo ne l'Academia de gli Affidati di Pauia, *etc.* pp. 16. *C. Ventura: Bergamo*, 1613. 4°. **1074. g. 20. (5.)**

—— L'Urania. Anagogici misteri sopra il nome santiss. Maria. Con due madrigali sopra ciascheduno mistero. I primi di diuersi nobili ingegni, e' secondi dell'autore. pp. 112. MS. NOTES. *C. Ventura: Bergamo*, 1609. **11427. e. 10.**

CERBONIUS (HIERONYMUS)

—— *See* URSUS (Robertus) De obsidione Tifernatum. [Edited by H. Cerbonius.] 1538. 4°. **C. 107. bb. 13.**

CERBU (Eman.)

—— *See* Rosetti (R. D.) Cartea dragostei, *etc.* [Compiled by R. D. Rosetti, in collaboration with E. Cerbu.] [1923.] 8º.   **11587. b. 1.**

CERC. Cerc de Studii Social-Creştine " Solidaritatea." *See* Bucharest.

—— Cercu de Studii Social-Economice al Basarabiei. *See* Kishinev.

CERCA CENTRAL OFFICE. *See* Commonwealth Air Transport Council.

CERCAMON. Les Poésies de Cercamon. Editées par Alfred Jeanroy. pp. ix. 36. *Paris*, 1922. 8º.   [*Les Classiques français du moyen âge.*]   **012207. cc. 1/27.**

CERCEAU (   ) *Curé et Maire de Congis.* La Constitution vengée des inculpations des ennemis de la Révolution. Discours, *etc.* pp. 16. [*Paris*, 1790.] 8º.
F. 798. (5.)

—— [Another copy.]   **F. 160. (13.)**
Imperfect; wanting pp. 7–10.

CERCEAU (G.) L'Âme d'un grand catholique. Esprit de foi de Louis Veuillot . . . d'après sa correspondance. L'homme public. 2 tom. *Paris*, [1910.] 8º.
4864. b. 17.

—— L'Âme d'un grand chrétien. Esprit de foi de Louis Veuillot d'après sa correspondance. L'homme intime. pp. xv. 344. *Paris*, [1908.] 8º.   **4863. cc. 34.**

CERCEL (Petru) *See* Esarcu (C.) Petru Cercel. Documente descoperite in arhivele Venetiei. 1874. 8º.
10795. d. 39.

—— *See* Tocilescu (G. G.) Petru Cercellu, *etc.* 1874. 16º.
9136. bb. 8. (2.)

CERCELLŬ (Petru) *See* Cercel.

CERCETĂRI.

—— Cercetări filozofice. *See* Bucharest.—*Academia Republicii Populare Romîne.—Institut de Filosofie.*

—— Cercetări privind istoria veche a RPR. *See* Bucharest. —*Academia Republicii Populare Romîne.*

CERCHA (Maksymilian) *See* Kopera (F.) Pomniki Krakowa M. i S. Cerchów, *etc.* [1900, *etc.*] fol.
1704. a. 19.

CERCHA (Stanisław) *See* Kopera (F.) Pomniki Krakowa M. i S. Cerchów, *etc.* [1900, *etc.*] fol.
1704. a. 19.

—— Baśni ludowe, zebrane we wsi Przebieczanach, w powiecie wielickim. 1896. *See* Cracow.—*Akademya Umiejętności.* Zbiór wiadomości do antropologii krajowej, *etc.* (Materyały antropologiczno-archeologiczne, *etc.* tom 1.) 1877, *etc.* 8º.   **Ac. 750/155.**

—— Poszukiwania archeologiczne w guberni mohilewskiej, w powiatach rohaczewskim, bychowskim i mohilewskim . . . dokonane w latach 1892–4. 1896. *See* Cracow.— *Akademya Umiejętności.* Zbiór wiadomości do antropologii krajowej, *etc.* (Materyały antropologiczno-archeologiczne, *etc.* tom 1.) 1877, *etc.* 8º.   **Ac. 750/155.**

—— Przebieczany, wieś w powiecie wielickim. Opisał pod względem etnograficznym S. Cercha. 1900. *See* Cracow. —*Akademya Umiejętności.* Zbiór wiadomości do antropologii krajowej, *etc.* (Materyały antropologiczno-archeologiczne, *etc.* tom 4.) 1877, *etc.* 8º.   **Ac. 750/155.**

CERCHA (Stanisław) and KOPERA (Feliks)

—— Nadworny rzeźbiarz Króla Zygmunta Starego Giovanni Cini z Sieny i jego dzieła w Polsce. Z 112 ilustracyami w tekscie. pp. 120. *Kraków*, [1916.] 8º.   **7877. de. 6.**

CERCHI (Bindaccio de') La Battaglia di Monte Aperti. *See* Henricus, *Septimellensis.* Trattato contro all'avversità della fortuna, *etc.* 1829. 12º.   **8404. aa. 33.**

CERCHI (Giovanni Maria) *See* Cecchi.

CERCHI (Vieri) Delle lodi del Gran Duca di Toscana Cosimo secondo. Orazione . . . Recitata pubblicamente . . . nella Accademia degli Alterati. Il dì xiij. di febbraio 1621. [With portraits of Cosmo II. and Ferdinand I. de' Medici.] pp. 47. *I Giunti: Firenze,* [1621.] 4º.
113. e. 16.

—— [Another edition.] 1731. *See* Dati (C. R.) Prose fiorentine, *etc.* pt. 1. vol. 6. 1716, *etc.* 8º.
659. b. 20.

—— [Another edition.] *See* Dati (C. R.) Prose fiorentine, *etc.* tom. 4. pt. 2. 1735. 4º.   **629. i. 17.**

—— Orazione . . . Delle lodi di Don Francesco Medici de' Principi di Toscana. 1731. *See* Dati (C. R.) Prose fiorentine, *etc.* pt. 1. vol. 6. 1716, *etc.* 8º.
659. b. 20.

—— [Another edition.] *See* Dati (C. R.) Prose fiorentine, *etc.* tom. 4. pt. 2. 1735. 4º.   **629. i. 17.**

CERCHIARI (G. Luigi) Fisionomia e mimica. Note curiose. Ricerche storiche e scientifiche, *etc.* pp. xii. 336. pl. xxxiii. *Milano*, 1905. 16º.
012200. i. 116.
One of the " Manuali Hoepli."

—— Motoaratura e motocoltura. Con un questionario sull'importanza e sull'avvenire della motoaratura, *etc.* pp. xv. 370. *Milano*, 1920. 16º.   **12199. i. 25.**
One of the " Manuali Hoepli."

CERCHIARI (Gioachino) Sulle acque minerali imolesi dette del Monte Castellaccio . . . Seconda edizione, *etc.* pp. 90. *Imola*, 1839. 8º.   **7462. e. 7. (4.)**

CERCHIARI (Giulio Cesare) Ristretto storico della città d'Imola, *etc.* pp. 230. *Bologna*, 1847. 8º.
10130. bb. 32.

CERCHIARI (Paris) *See* Saavedra Fajardo (D. de) L'Idea del principe politico christiano . . . trasportata dalla lingua spagnuola dal sig. dottor P. Cerchiari. 1684. 12º.   **637. b. 18.**

CERCHIARI (Tomasino de') *See* Grion (G.) Tomasino de' Cerchiari, poeta cividalese del duecento. Cenno. [1892 ?] 8º.   **10631. df. 51.**

CERCHIARIUS (Joannes Aloysius) Orationes. *Mediolani*, 1659. 24º.   **4425. a. 29. (1.)**

—— Poesis. *Mediolani*, 1659. 24º.   **4425. a. 29. (2.)**

CERCHIIS (Raphael de) *Begin.* [fol. 1 *recto:*] Libellus qui uulgari sermone nuncupat el Birraccino: compositus p Raphaelem Petri de Cerchiis notarium peritissimum Florentinum. *Impressum per Laurētium de Morgianis impensa Petri de Pacinis: Florentiæ,* xii. Kal. Maias [20 April], 1497. 4º.   **IA. 27840.**
42 leaves. Sig. a–d⁸ e¹⁰. *37–39 lines to a page.*

—— [Another edition.] Libellus q vulgari sermone nuncupatur el Birracino. *Ad instātiā Io. Alexādri: Senis,* 1530. 8º.   **5359. a. 12.**

CERCHIIS (Raphael de)

—— [Another edition.] Il Birraccino. Libellus nuncupatus, il Birraccino. In quo continētur oēs ordines, & Actus: quos iudices, & eorum notarii, oēsᖅ alii officiales ī officio cōstituti obseruare, & facere debeant. Nouiter cum summa diligentia impressus. ff. 71.　　*per N. de Aristotelibus dictum Zoppinum: Venetiis,* 1533. 8º.
　　　　　　　　　　　　　　　　　　　　　　　Voyn. 17.

CERCIÀ (Raffaele) C'è l'inferno? Discussione fra l'abate Don Pompilio e la signora Almerinda Contessa di Valleoscura. pp. iv. 111. *Napoli,* 1882. 8º.
　　　　　　　　　　　　　　　　　　　　　　4257. g. 13.

—— De sanctissimae Trinitatis mysterio tractatus dogmatico-scholasticus. pp. iv. 274. *Neapoli,* 1880. 8º.
　　　　　　　　　　　　　　　　　　　　　　4225. f. 3.

CERCIDAS. Meliambs, Fragments, and Cercidea. *Gr. & Eng. See* Herodas. Herodes, Cercidas and the Greek Choliambic Poets, *etc.* 1929. 8º. [*Loeb Classical Library.*]　　　　　**2282. d. 109.**

—— [Cercidea. The text, with a translation.] *See* Knox (Alfred D.) The First Greek Anthologist, *etc.* 1923. 8º.
　　　　　　　　　　　　　　　　　　　　　11313. aa. 13.

CERCIELLO (Giuseppe) Uno Sguardo al Montenegro. Cenno storico. pp. 36. *Napoli,* 1896. 8º.
　　　　　　　　　　　　　　　　　　　　09004. cc. 2. (6.)

CERCLE. Le Cercle. (Le Second Cercle.—Le Troisième Cercle.) [Dialogues on the political state of the Netherlands.] 3 pt. [*Brussels,* 1789?] 8º.　　**106. b. 29.**

—— Cercle Archéologique de Mons. *See* Mons.

—— Cercle Archéologique de Termonde. *See* Dendermonde.

—— Cercle Archéologique du Pays de Waes. *See* Saint-Nicolas.—*Oudheidskundige Kring van het Land van Waes.*

—— Cercle Archéologique, Littéraire et Artistique de Malines. *See* Mechlin.—*Cercle Royal Archéologique, Littéraire et Artistique de Malines.*

—— Cercle Belge de la Librairie, de l'Imprimerie, et des Professions qui s'y rattachent. *See* Brussels.

—— Cercle d'Études Commerciales de Limoges. *See* Limoges.

—— Cercle de la Jeunesse. *See* Port Louis.

—— Cercle de la Librairie, de l'Imprimerie, de la Papeterie, *etc. See* Paris.

—— Cercle de la Russie Neuve. *See* Paris.

—— Cercle de Rose Hill. *See* Rose Hill, *Mauritius.*

—— Cercle des Amitiés Latines. *See* Paris.

—— Cercle des Beaux-Arts. *See* Paris.

—— Cercle des Étudiants des Facultés Catholiques de Lille. *See* Lille.

—— Le Cercle des femmes. Comédie. [The dedication signed: C., i.e. Samuel Chappuzeau.] [1662?] 12º. *See* C.　　　　　　　　　　**11736. aa. 20.**

—— Cercle des Relations Intellectuelles. *See* Lyons.

—— Cercle Descartes. *See* Paris.

—— Cercle Floral d'Anvers. *See* Antwerp.

—— Cercle Franco-Américain. *See* Paris.

CERCLE.

—— Cercle Historique et Archéologique de Gand. *See* Ghent.—*Geschied- en Oudheidkundige Kring.*

—— Cercle historique et archéologique de Gand. *See* Ghent. —*Maatschappij voor Geschiedenis en Oudheidkunde.*

—— Cercle Joseph de Maistre. *See* Paris.

—— Cercle La Tour du Pin. *See* Paris.

—— Cercle Linguistique de Copenhague. *See* Copenhagen. *Lingvistkredsen.*

—— Cercle Linguistique de Prague. *See* Prague.—*Pražský Linguistický Kroužek.*

—— Cercle Littéraire. *See* Brussels.

—— Cercle Littéraire de Port-Louis. *See* Port Louis.

—— Cercle Littéraire " Hebraeo." *See* Paris.

—— Cercle Médical Liégeois. *See* Liége.

—— The Circle; or, Conversations on love & gallantry; originally in French. Now Englished [and slightly abridged, from " Le Cercle, ou les Conversations galantes " by François Salvat, Sieur de Montfort]. And since augmented with several new songs, illustrated with musical notes, both treble & bass. By Nath. Noel. pp. 254. 1676. 8º. *See* Circle.　　**12330. b. 40.**

—— Cercle Pratique d'Horticulture et de Botanique de l'Arrondissement du Havre. *See* Havre-de-Grâce.

—— Cercle Royal Archéologique, Littéraire et Artistique de Malines. *See* Mechlin.

—— Le Cercle sacré et Le Tambour du chef. [A translation of " The Forbidden Circle and Drummer and the Chief," by Esma Rideout Booth.] pp. 16.　*Sheldon Press: London,* [1946.] 8º. [*Bibliothèque de la famille africaine.* no. 13.]　　　　　　**W.P. 561/13.**

—— Cercle Savoisien de la Ligue de l'Enseignement. *See* Chambéry.

—— Cercle Social pour la Confédération Universelle des Amis de la Vérité. *See* Paris.

CERCLER (René)
—— Mathieu de Dombasle, 1777–1843. Avec un portrait hors texte. pp. xii. 194. *Paris,* 1946. 8º.
　　　　　　　　　　　　　　　　　　　　10656. k. 55.

CERCLET (A.) *See* France. [*Laws, etc.*—II.] Code des chemins de fer, ou Recueil complet des lois ... concernant l'établissement, l'administration, la police et l'exploitation des chemins de fer. Par A. Cerclet. 1845. 8º.
　　　　　　　　　　　　　　　　　　　　5425. e. 5.

CERCOETIUS (Antonius) *Amoricus, pseud. See* Kerkoetius.

CERDA (　Mexia de la) *See* Mexia de la Cerda.

CERDA (Agustin Antonio Roca y) *See* Roca y Cerda.

CERDA (Ana de Gomez de Silva Mendoza y la) *Princess de Éboli* and *Duchess de Pastrana. See* Gomez de Silva Mendoza y la Cerda.

CERDA (Bernarda Ferreira de la) *See* Ferreira de la Cerda.

CERDA (Bernardus) *See* Schneegans (E.) *of Strasburg.* Die Quellen des sogenannten Pseudo-Philomena und des Officiums von Gerona zu Ehren Karls des Grossen, *etc.* [With the text of the latter as transcribed by Bernardus Cerda.] 1891. 8º.　　　　　**011840. l. 53.**

CERDA (C. Granzow de la) *See* Granzow de la Cerda.

CERDA (Cayetano de la) El Coronel C. de la Cerda comandante jeneral interino del Estado, al público. [A reply to a pamphlet published by M. Diez de la Bonilla entitled: "Contestaciones entre el Gobierno Nacional de Centro-América y el Ministro Plenipotenciario de los E. U. Mexicanos sobre los insultos hechos á este."] [*Guatemala*, 1832.] fol. **9770. k. 10. (112.)**

—— *See* S. (Francisco de P. G. de) Vindicacion á favor de la persona del Escmo. Señor D. M. Diez de la Bonilla, *etc.* [A reply to two pamphlets, the one by F. Mejia, the other by C. de la Cerda and entitled: "El Coronel C. de la Cerda . . . al público."] 1832. 4º. **9770. bb. 21. (54.)**

CERDA (Cristobal Colon de la) Tratado de Particion de la Corona de España celebrado entre la Francia y el Austria en vida de Carlos II. Discurso. *Madrid*, 1860. 8º. [MISSING.]

CERDA (Domingo Hidalgo de Torres y la) *See* Hidalgo de Torres y la Cerda.

CERDÁ (Elías) Don Quijote en la Guerra. Fantasía que pudo ser historia. pp. 194. *Madrid*, [1915.] 8º. **12490. pp. 20.**

CERDA (Emilio de la) Ensayos Poeticos. [Edited by Antonio Luis Carrion.] pp. xiv. 141. *Malaga*, 1868. 8º. **11450. ccc. 30.**

CERDA (Fernando Correa de la) *Bishop of Oporto. See* Correa de la Cerda.

CERDA (Gerardo Mullé de la) *See* Mullé de la Cerda.

CERDA (Gilberto)

—— Vocabulario español de Texas. Por G. Cerda, B. Cabaza y J. Farias. pp. vii. 347. *University of Texas Press: Austin*, 1953. 8º. **12944. h. 21.** *University of Texas Hispanic Studies.* vol. 5.

CERDA (Gundisalvus de la) F. Gundisalui de la Cerda . . . Commentaria in Epistolam D. Pauli Apostoli, ad Romanos. [With the text.] pp. 347. 1583. fol. *See* Bible.—*Romans.* [*Latin.*] [MISSING.]

CERDA (Joannes Ludovicus de la) *See* Calepinus (A.) Ambrosii Calepini Dictionarium . . . adornatum a R.P. I. L. de la Cerda, *etc.* 1647. fol. **12903. k. 5.**

—— —— 1663. fol. **629.n.14.**

—— *See* Solomon, *King of Israel.* Ψαλτηριον Σολομωντος. Psalterium Salomonis. J. L. de la Cerda interprete. (J. L. de la Cerda Scholia in Psalterium Salomonis.) *Gr. & Lat.* 1713. 8º. [*Fabricius* (J. A.) *Codex pseudepigraphus Veteris Testamenti, etc.* vol. 1.] **691. a. 15.**

—— *See* Virgilius Maro (P.) [*Works.*] P. Virgilii Maronis priores sex (posteriores sex) libri Aeneidos (Bucolica et Georgica) argumentis, explicationibus, notis illustrati, auctore J. L. de la Cerda, *etc.* 1612, *etc.* fol. **11352. i. 2.**

—— —— 1628. fol. **74. h. 9–11.**

—— —— 1647, *etc.* fol. **11352. h. 14.**

—— —— 1680. 8º. **159. d. 5.**

—— *See* Virgilius Maro (P.) [*Works.*] P. Virgilius Maro qualem omni parte illustratum publicavit C. G. Heyne; cui Servium . . . (pariter et Cerdam) et variorum notas cum suis subjunxit N. E. Lemaire. 1819, *etc.* 8º. **11305. m. 4.**

CERDA (Joannes Ludovicus de la)

—— Io. Ludouici de la Cerda . . . Aduersaria sacra . . . Accessit, eodem autore, Psalterij Salomonis ex Græco MS. codice peruetusto Latina versio, & ad Tertulliani librum de Pallio commentarius auctior [with the text]. Prodeunt . . . nunc primum. 3 pt. *Sumpt. Ludovici Prost Hæredis Rouille: Lugduni*, 1626. fol. **6. g. 6.** *The titlepage is engraved.*

—— *See* Salas (P. de) Compendium latino-hispanum . . . Accedunt verba sacra, ex Adversariis Joannis L. de la Cerda diligenter excerpta, *etc.* 1779. 4º. **1478. b. 5.**

—— Aelii Antonii Nebrissensis de institutione grammaticæ libri quinque . . . denuo recogniti. [Or rather, a compilation by J. L. de la Cerda, based on the "Grammatica latina" of Antonio de Lebrixa and the "Minerva" of F. Sanchez.] pp. 279. 1652. 8º. *See* Antonio, *de Lebrixa, the Elder.* [*Grammatica Latina.*] **12935. b. 30.**

—— [Another edition.] Novissime . . . mendis . . . expurgati, pristinamque ferme ad puritatem restituti a D. Petro del Campo et Lago, *etc.* pp. 320. 1804. 8º. *See* Antonio, *de Lebrixa, the Elder.* [*Grammatica Latina.*] **12935. de. 18.**

—— Nova editio. pp. 229. 1855. 12º. *See* Antonio, *de Lebrixa, the Elder.* [*Grammatica Latina.*] **12934. b. 29.**

—— Nova editio. pp. 239. 1857. 12º. *See* Antonio, *de Lebrixa, the Elder.* [*Grammatica Latina.*] **12932. b. 48.**

—— Nova editio. pp. 323. 1859. 8º. *See* Antonio, *de Lebrixa, the Elder.* [*Grammatica Latina.*] **12932. aaa. 39.**

—— *See* Zamora (S. de) Prosodia . . . Segun el libro quinto del arte del P. J. L. de la Cerda [i.e. of his "De institutione grammaticae"], *etc.* 1785. 12º. **12932. a. 60.**

—— De excellentia coelestium spirituum; imprimis de angeli custodis ministerio liber. pp. 557. *S. Cramoisy: Parisiis*, 1631. 8º. **847. k. 22.**

CERDÁ (Joaquín)

—— *See* Martínez de Zamora (F.) La "Margarita de los pleitos," de Fernando Martínez de Zamora. [Edited, with an introduction, by J. Cerdá.] 1950. 8º. [*Anuario de historia del derecho español.* tom. 20.] **Ac. 145. c/15.**

CERDA (José María de la Cueva y la) *Duke de Alburquerque. See* Cueva y la Cerda.

CERDA (Joseph de la) *successively Bishop of Almeria and of Badajoz. See* Bible.—*Judith.* [*Latin.*] Reverend. et illustr. M.D.D. Ioseph de La Zerda . . . in sacram Iudith historiam commentarius, *etc.* 1653. fol. **3165. h. 8.**

CERDA (Juan de la) *4th Duke de Medinaceli, Viceroy of Sicily.* Advertencias que el duque de Medinaceli dejó á D. García de Toledo sobre el gobierno del reino de Secilia . . . 1565. 1856. *See* Fernandez de Navarrete (M.) Colección de documentos, *etc.* tom. 28. 1842, *etc.* 8º. **9195. ccc.**

—— Documentos relativos al nombramiento de gobernador y capitan general de los Paises-Bajos de D. Juan de la Cerda, duque de Medinaceli, desde 1571 á 1573. 2 pt. 1859, 60. *See* Fernandez de Navarrete (M.) Colección de documentos, *etc.* tom. 35, 36. 1842, *etc.* 8º. **9195. d.**

—— La Relazione del vicerè Juan de la Cerda Duca di Medinaceli a Garcia de Toledo, 1565. [Edited by Rosa Guccione Scaglione.] *Span. In:* Archivio storico siciliano. ser. 3. vol. 5. fasc. 1. pp. 35–108. 1953. 8º. **P.P. 3556. u.**

CERDA (JUAN DE LA) 5th *Duke de Medinaceli*. Los Conceios y Vezinos de los lugares del Ducado de Medina Celi. Con Don Iuan de la Cerda, Duque del dicho Ducado. ff. 34. 1605. fol. **1322. l. 4. (1.)**

CERDA (JUAN DE LEYBA Y DE LA) *Marquis de Leyba and de Ladrada, Viceroy of Mexico*. See LEYBA Y DE LA CERDA.

CERDA (LUIS DE BAÑUELOS Y DE LA) *See* BAÑUELOS Y DE LA CERDA.

CERDÁ (MANUAL) *See* CERDÁ DE VILLARESTÁN.

CERDA (MARIA DE LA) *See* MARIA [Fernandez Coronel], *de Jesus, de Agreda*.

CERDA (MARIA ISIDRA QUINTINA GUZMAN Y LA) *See* GUZMAN Y LA CERDA.

CERDA (MARTIN DE LA) *See* SPAIN.—*Consejo de Guerra*. Sentencia que dieron los Señores del Consejo Supremo de Guerra al Alcayde del Peñon [M. de la Cerda]. 1617. fol. **1322. l. 9. (23.)**

CERDA (MELCHIOR DE LA)

—— Apparatus latini sermonis per Topographiam, Chronographiam, & Prosopographiam, perque locos communes, ad Ciceronis normam exactus, *etc.* 2 pt. *Excudebat Rodericus Cabrera: Hispali,* 1598. 4°. **C. 125. b. 10.**

—— Camporum eloquentiæ, in causis, enumeratione partium, genere, coniugatis, adiunctis, longe lateque patentium, volumen primum . . . Editio tertia, nunc correctius edita, *etc.* pp. 531. *Apud I. Kinchium: Coloniæ Agrippinensium,* 1637. 8°. **C. 67. c. 24.**

—— Consolatio ad Hispanos propter classem in Angliam profectam subita tempestate submersam . . . anno M.D.LXXXVIII. pp. 24. [*Ingolstadt?*] 1621. 4°. **8042. b. 33.**

—— [Another copy.] **G. 6077.**

CERDA (MIGUEL DE LA) *See* PHILIP III., *King of Spain*. Lo que se asienta y concierta entre su Magestad y el Doctor B. Vellerino de Villalobos cerca de la labor de la moneda, con los ingenios que inventaron M. de la Cerda difunto, y el dicho Doctor Vellerino. [1599.] fol. **1323. k. 17. (1.)**

CERDA (PEDRO MESSÍA DE LA) *See* MESSÍA DE LA ZERDA.

CERDA (PEDRO VALLE DE LA) *See* VALLE DE LA CERDA.

CERDA (RODRIGO SARMIENTO DE SILVA VILLANDRANDO Y LA) *Duke de Hijar*. *See* SARMIENTO DE SILVA VILLANDRANDO Y LA CERDA.

CERDA (RUI GOMEZ DE SILVA MENDOZA Y LA) *Duke de Pastrana*. *See* GOMEZ DE SILVA MENDOZA Y LA CERDA.

CERDÁ DE VILLARESTÁN (MANUEL) Catalogo de las Monedas arábigo-españolas pertenecientes à la coleccion numismática de M. Cerdá de Villarestán. *pp. 15.* *Madrid,* 1853. 8°. D. **7758.b.28.**

—— Catálogo general de las antiguas monedas autónomas de España, con noticia de sus leyendas, tipos, simbolos y pueblos a que corresponden. 6 pt. *Madrid,* 1858. 8°. **7758.c.17.**

—— Repertorio histórico para uso de los institutos y colegios del Reino. pp. 128. *Madrid,* 1855. 16°. **9006. b. 6.**

CERDA ENRIQUEZ DE RIBERA (JUAN FRANCISCO TOMÁS LORENZO DE LA) *Duke de Medinaceli*. Atributos de el Sol parangonados . . . con los desvelos del . . . Duque de Medina-Zeli . . . Soneto. [By Fermin de Sarasa y Arce?] [*Madrid?* 1680?] *s. sh.* fol. **T. 22*. (41.)**

CERDAN (JEAN PAUL DE) *Count*. *See* N., N. Politisches Bedencken [by N. N.] über das Schreiben des also genanten Grafen von Sardan . . . [J. P. de Cerdan] dessen Titul ist, Von wem und durch wen der Keyser und das Reich verrathen. 1681. 4°. **8073. b. 82.**

—— L'Europe esclave, si l'Angleterre ne rompt ses fers. [By Count J. P. de Cerdan.] pp. 106. 1677. 12°. *See* EUROPE. **G. 16109. (2.)**

—— [Another edition.] Augmenté, *etc.* 2 pt. 1678. 12°. *See* EUROPE. **8027. a. 1.**

—— Nouvelle édition. pp. 72. 1689. 12°. *See* EUROPE. **8122. a. 56. (7.)**

—— [Another edition.] pp. 90. 1702. 12°. *See* EUROPE. **8010. a. 12. (2.)**

—— L'Europe esclave, si l'Angleterre ne rompt ses fers. Das zur Dienstbarkeit gebrachte Europa, *etc.* *Fr. & Ger.* [1678.] 4°. [*Philemeri Irenici Elisii Diarium Europæum.* Tl. 36. vol. 2.] *See* EUROPE. **301. g. 9.**

—— Europe a Slave, unless England break her chains: discovering the grand designs of the French-Popish party in England for several years past. pp. 94. 1681. 12°. *See* EUROPE. **8122. a. 36.**

—— The second edition. pp. 94. 1683. 16°. *See* EUROPE. **8122. a. 37.**

—— Europa tot slavin gemaecht, soo Engelandt niet haer boeyen breeckt. Uyt het Frans vertaelt. pp. 28. 1677. 4°. *See* EUROPE. **8122. ee. 9. (8.)**

—— [Another edition.] pp. 28. 1678. 4°. *See* EUROPE. **8122. aaa. 20. (9.)**

—— The Kingdom of Sweden restored to its true Interest. A political discourse. [By Count J. P. de Cerdan.] pp. 32. 1682. 4°. *See* SWEDEN. [*Appendix.—History and Politics.—*II.] **4106. cc. 10. (3.)**

—— [Another copy.] The Kingdom of Sweden restored, *etc.* [By Count J. P. de Cerdan.] 1682. 4°. *See* SWEDEN. [*Appendix.—History and Politics.—*II.] **114. i. 2.**

—— La Suède redressée dans son veritable interest. [By Count J. P. de Cerdan.] Traduit de l'alleman, *etc.* pp. 68. 1682. 12°. *See* SWEDEN. [*Appendix.—History and Politics.—*II.] **1193. b. 5.**

CERDÁN DE LANDA SIMON PONTERO (AMBROSIO) Disertacion preliminar a los apuntamientos históricos de los mas principales hechos y acaecimientos de cada uno de los señores Gobernadores, Presidentes y Vireyes del Perú, *etc.* *See* PERU.—*Acts of Viceroys*. Memorias de los Vireyes, *etc.* tom. 1. 1859. fol. **9771. g. 9.**

—— Tratado jeneral sobre las aguas que fertilizan los valles de Lima. pp. 127. *Lima,* 1828. 4°. **1304. e. 1.**

CERDAN DE TALLADA (TOMAS) Verdadero gouierno desta Monarchia, tomado por su proprio subjecto la conseruacion de la paz, *etc.* ff. 181. *Vendense en casa de M. Borras; impresso en casa de la viuda de P. de Huete: Valencia,* 1581. 8°. **8008. a. 9.**

—— Veriloquium en Reglas de Estado, segun derecho diuino, natural, canonico, y ciuil, y leyes de Castilla . . . Iuntamente con segunda impression de la Visita de Carcel, *etc.* pp. 515. *I. C. Garriz: Valencia,* 1604. 4°. **878. i. 20.**

CERDANUS ET RICUS (FRANCISCUS) *See* CERDÁ Y RICO (Francisco)

CERDAN Y ANTILLON (BALTASAR LOPEZ DE GURREA XIMENEZ) *Count del Villar*. *See* LOPEZ DE GURREA XIMENEZ CERDAN Y ANTILLON.

CERDÁN Y PONTÉRO (AMBROSIO) *See* CERDÁN DE LANDA SIMON PONTERO.

CERDÁ RUIZ-FUNES (JOAQUÍN)

—— *See* ARIAS DE BALBOA (V.) *Bishop of Plasencia.* Las Glosas de Arias de Balboa al Fuero Real de Castilla. [Edited by J. Cerdá Ruiz-Funes.] 1951, 52. 8°. [*Anuario de historia del derecho español.* tom. 21/22.]
Ac. **145**. c/**15**.

CERDA SILVA Y MENDOZA (GASPAR DE SANDOVAL) *Count de Galve. See* SANDOVAL CERDA SILVA Y MENDOZA.

CERDA Y BAYONA (JOAQUÍN ARGAMASILLA DE LA) *See* ARGAMASILLA DE LA CERDA Y BAYONA.

CERDA Y CAETANO (FERNANDO DE MONCADA ARAGON LA) *Duke de San Juan. See* MONCADA ARAGON LA CERDA Y CAETANO.

CERDA Y DE ARAGÓN (LUIS FRANCISCO DE LA) *Duke de Medinaceli. See* RAMÍREZ DE VILLA-URRUTIA (W.) *Marquis de Villa-Urrutia.* La Embajada del Marqués de Cogulludo a Roma en 1687. 1920. 8°.
9181. cc. **33**.

—— —— 1927. 8°.
9181. ff. **9**.

—— *See* ROUQUILLO BRICEÑO (P.) Correspondencia entre dos embajadores, Don Pedro Rouquillo y el Marqués de Cogolludo, 1689–1691, *etc.* 1951, *etc.* 8°. Ac. **6630/39**.

CERDA Y DE LAS BÁRCENAS (TOMÁS DE LA) La Negación de España. Esbozo de la crísis de nuestra nacionalidad. pp 127. *Madrid*, 1934. 8°.
08042. b. **50**.

CERDÁ Y RICO (FRANCISCO) *See* ALPHONSO XI., *King of Castile and Leon.* Cronica de D. Alfonso el Onceno . . . Segunda edicion . . . ilustrada con apendices y varios documentos por Don F. Cerdá y Rico. 1787. 4°. [*Coleccion de las cronicas . . . de los Reyes de Castilla.* tom. 7.]
179. d. **11***.

—— *See* CERVANTES DE SALAZAR (F.) Obras que F. Cervantes de Salazar ha hecho glossado i traducido, *etc.* [Edited by F. Cerdá y Rico.] 1772. 4°.
98. l. **1**.

—— *See* GENESIUS DE SEPULVEDA (J.) Joannis Genesii Sepulvedae . . . opera, cum edita, tum inedita, accurante Regia Historiae Academia. [Edited with a biographical introduction by F. Cerdá y Rico and others.] 1780. .4°.
88. f. **6–9**.

—— *See* GIL POLO (G.) La Diana Enamorada, *etc.* [Edited by F. Cerdá y Rico.] 1778. 8°.
12491. e. **16**.

—— —— 1802. 8°.
1208. d. **24**.

—— *See* GONZÁLEZ PALENCIA (C. A.) Don Francisco Cerdá y Rico, *etc.* 1928. 8°.
10634. dd. **36**.

—— *See* LOUBAT DE BOHAN (F. P.) *Baron.* [Principes pour monter et dresser les chevaux de guerre.] Principios para montar é instruir los caballos de guerra . . . Traducidos . . . por Don F. Cerda y Rico, *etc.* 1827. 8°.
07288.aa.52.

—— *See* MENDOZA IBAÑEZ DE SEGOVIA Y PERALTA (G. de) *Marquis de Mondexar.* Memorias historicas de la vida y acciones del Rey D. Alonso el Noble . . . ilustradas con notas y apendices por F. Cerdá y Rico. 1783. 4°. [*Coleccion de las cronicas . . . de los Reyes de Castilla.* tom. 4.]
179. d. **9**.

—— *See* MENDOZA IBAÑEZ DE SEGOVIA Y PERALTA (G. de) *Marquis de Mondexar.* Memorias historicas del Rei D. Alonso el Sabio, *etc.* [Edited by F. Cerdá y Rico.] 1777. fol.
181. f. **3**.

CERDÁ Y RICO (FRANCISCO)

—— *See* UREÑA Y SMENJAUD (Rafael de) Las Ediciones del Fuero de Cuenca. [With special reference to the edition of F. Cerdá y Rico.] 1917. 8°.
011904. i. **7**.

—— Correspondencia entre Cerdá y Rico y Don Fernando José de Velasco. [Edited, with an introduction, by A. González Palencia.] *In:* Boletín de la Real Academia de la Historia. tom. 124, cuaderno 1, 2. 1949. 8°.
Ac. **6630/7**.

—— Clarorum Hispanorum opuscula selecta et rariora, tum Latina, tum Hispana, magna ex parte nunc primum in lucem edita a F. Cerdano et Rico. vol. 1. pp. liv. 630. 94. *Matriti*, 1781. 4°.
830. g. **1**.
No more published.

—— [Another copy.]
90. h. **21**.

—— Francisci Cerdani Commentarius de praecipuis rhetoribus Hispanis.—Appendix triplex: I. De rhetoribus antiquis cum Graecis, tum Latinis. II. De Hispanis purioris Latinitatis cultoribus. III. De iis, qui Hispane tersius et elegantius sunt loquuti. *See* VOSSIUS (G.) *Canon of Canterbury.* G. J. Vossii Rhetorices contractae . . . libri quinque, *etc.* 1781. 8°.
237. h. **29**.

CERDA Y SALABERT (LUÍS JESÚS MARIA FERNÁNDEZ DE CÓRDOVA-FIGUEROA DE LA) *Duke de Medinaceli. See* FERNÁNDEZ DE CÓRDOVA-FIGUEROA DE LA CERDA Y SALABERT.

CERDD. Cerdd ddigrif, am deulu a gollodd rifedi yr wythnos. *See* GWYDR. Y Gwydr Glas. [1840?] 8°.
C.**116**.b.**25**.(**80**.)

—— Cerdd o hanes am ddau Bladurwyr, wrth ladd Haidd a ffrwyth yr Heidden a'u tafloedd hwythau i lawr. [With: "Can. Hen Wlad fy Nhadau." By E. James.] pp. 3. [1860?] 8°.
C.**116**.b.**25**.(**37**.)

—— Cerdd y Tea. [By Dyn Gwirion.] pp. 2. [1790?] 8°.
C.**117**.bb.**16**.(**59**.)

—— Cerdd ynghylch y Rhyfel, *etc. See* JONES (William) *Writer of Ballads.* Dwy Gerdd, *etc.* [1805?] 8°.
C.**117**.bb.**16**.(**61**.)

—— Cerdd yr Hen Amser Gynt. Ar y dôn Albanaidd "Auld Lang Syne." [By John Blackwell.] *See* ELEN. Cerdd Elen y Glyn, *etc.* [1850?] *s. sh.* 8°.
C.**116**.b.**25**.(**57**,)

—— [Another edition.] *See* ELEN. Cerdd Elen y Glyn. [1850?] *s. sh.* 8°.
C.**116**.b.**25**.(**79**.)

—— Dwy gerdd ddiddan. Y gyntaf, Cerdd am Balas a losgodd yn Sir Amwythig. Yr ail, Ymddiddan rhwng Gŵr Ifangc a'i Gariad. III. Penill i annerch ar Swit Richard. [Signed: M. Roberts.] pp. 8. *Argraphwyd tros Mary Fychan:* [*Trefriw?* 1790?] 8°.
C.**117**.bb.**16**.(**51**.)

—— Dwy gerdd newydd, y gyntaf, Cerdd o fawl i Filitia swydd Aberteifi, ynghyd a'r Officers, gan roddi iddynt glod fel y maent yn ei haeddu. [By Richard Roberts.] Yr ail, Cerdd a anfonodd Ellis Rober[ts] at Thomas Edwards, ar D[dull] ymofyn pa achos fod cymmaint Llygredd a Dallineb yn Eglwys Loegr, &c. pp. 8. *W. Edwards: Croesoswallt*, 1794. 8°.
C.**117**.bb.**16**.(**15**.)
Imperfect; wanting pp. 3–6. The titlepage is mutilated.

—— Dwy cerdd newydd. Y gyntaf, yn rhoi hanes rhyfeddol am Frenhin yn Scotland a ymwnaeth hyd eithaf ei allu, i sefyll yn erbyn ei Dynged sef priodi yr hon oedd yn digwydd iddo, drwy geisio ei bywyd mewn amryw ffyrdd. Yn ail, Hanes dwy eneth a foddodd yn Afon Ogwen [signed: Abraham Williams]. pp. 8. *M. & Ellin Dafis:* [*Trefriw?* 1789?] 8°.
C.**117**.bb.**16**.(**41**.)

CERDDI. Dwy o gerddi newyddion. I. O drymder galarus am Royal George yr hon a suddodd yn ei harbwr gyda mil o bobl oedd arni, lle yr aeth tri chant o ferched i'r gwaelod a phlant gyda nhw. [Signed: E. Roberts.] II. O fawl i Ferch. [Signed: Robert Gruffudd.] (Tri Englyn ir Cynhauaf gwlyb. [Signed: Ellis Roberts.] —"Llawenydd beunydd di baid," etc. [An "englyn," signed: D. F.]) pp. 8. *Dafydd Jones: Trefriw*, 1782. 8°.
C.117.bb.16.(5.)

—— Dwy o gerddi newyddion. Yn gyntaf. Cerdd newydd ar Gwel yr Adeilad. Yr ail. Cerdd newydd ar Crimson Velvet. pp. 8. [*Stafford Prys: Shrewsbury*, 1780?] 8°.
C.117.a.47.(1.)

—— [Dwy] o gerddi newyddion. I. Yn rhoi byrr hanes Dynes a wnaeth weithred ofnadwy ymhlwy Llansantffraid glyn Conwy, sef diheunyddio ffrwyth ei bry ai ado fe rhwng bwystfilod y ddaear. [Signed: Ellis Roberts.] II. Cerdd ar ddioddefaint Crist, wedi ei throi or Groeg ir Gymraeg. [Signed: Sion ap Howell.] (Hymn. [Signed: Dewi Fardd.]) pp. 8. *Dafydd Jones, tros Harri Owen: Trefriw*, 1784. 8°.
Cropped. **C.117.bb.16.(9.)**

—— Hen gerddi gwleidyddol: 1588–1660 . . . a argreffir yn awr am y waith gyntaf. pp. 45. *Caerdydd*, 1901. 4°. [*Cymdeithas Llen Cymru. Publications.* ser. 1. no. 2.]
Ac. 8220.

—— Tair o gerddi newyddion. I. Yn gosod yn fyrr Ryfeddod Angylion, happusrwydd Dynion, a blinder Cythreiliaid, sef Iechydwriaeth trwy Grist, ar esgeulusdra o weddio am ran ym Mhren y Bywyd. [Signed: John Roberts.] II. Yn mynegi fel y digwyddodd i Wr ifangc feichiogi merch, ac yn gweddio am edifeirwych am ei bechod. III. Fel y bu i wr ifangc garu merch, ac fo faeliodd ei chael yn briod: ar yr achos hwnnw fe a ganodd fel y mae 'n canlyn. [Signed: John Williams.] pp. 8. *Dafydd Jones: Trefriw*, 1783. 8° **C.117.bb.16.(7.)**

—— Tair o gerddi newyddion. Yn gyntaf, Cerdd er dwyn ar gôf i ddynion ddyll y poennau y mae 'r enaid colledig yn i ddiodde yn Uffern gida Dysyñiad ar ddynion aniwiol ddychwelyd att Dduw. Iw chanu ar Grimson Velfett. [Signed: Hugh Roberts.] Yn ail, Dechre Cerdd ar Loath y Part y fordd hwyaf o ymddiddan rhwng dynn ai gydwybod. Bob yn ail pennill. [Signed: Ellis Roberts.] Yn drydydd, Cerd [about Tea] iw channu ar Susan Lygad-ddy, etc. [Signed: Dyn Gwirion.] pp. 8. *Ynghaerlleon gan Elizabeth Adams, tros Petter Maurrice: Bala*, [1755?] 8°. **C.117.bb.16.(63.)**

CERDDOR. Y Cerddor. Cylchgrawn misol. *See* PERIODICAL PUBLICATIONS.—*Wrexham.*

—— Cerddor Cymreig. *See* PERIODICAL PUBLICATIONS.—*Wrexham.*

—— Cerddor y Cymry. *See* PERIODICAL PUBLICATIONS.—*Llanelly.*

CERDEIRA (ELEUTÉRIO) *See* PERES (D.) História de Portugal . . . Direcção artística de E. Cerdeira. [1928, etc.] fol. **9088.n.5.**

CERDEÑA. *See* SARDINIA.

CERDEÑO Y MONÇON (LUIS DE) *See* MOLINA (M. de) and CERDEÑA Y MONÇON (L. de) Por Don J. A. Fernandez de Cordova y Sosa . . . Con Doña F. Fernandez de Cordova, Condesa de Casapalma . . . Sobre el estado de Guadalcázar. [1672?] fol. **1322. l. 8. (3.)**

—— Por Don Diego de Hiprando Gilimon de la Mota . . . con Don Juan de Solorzano, y Don Luis de Peralta y Velasco . . . Sobre la tenuta de los Mayorazgos que fundaron los Señores Don Baltasar Gilimon de la Mota . . . y Doña Gregoria de la Vega su muger, en los años de mil y quinientos, y noventa y nueve, mil y seiscientos y veinte, y mil y seiscientos y veinte y nueve. ff. 11. [1680?] fol. **1322. l. 8. (12.)**

CERDEÑO Y MONÇON (LUIS DE)

—— Por Don Nicolas Romero de Mella, Contador de tributos, y azogues de la Nueua España. En el pleyto que trata con el señor Fiscal. Sobre la restitucion del dicho oficio; y en satisfacion de los cargos que le hizo . . . Don Pedro de Galuez . . . el año de 53. en la visita de los Ministros y oficiales Reales del Reyno de Mexico. [*Mexico?* 1653?] fol. [MISSING.]

CERDIC, *King of the West-Saxons. See* HILL (Geoffry) Cerdic's Landing Place. [1911.] 8°. **09008. c. 5. (8.)**

CERDÓ (FRANCISCO) El Castillo de Caldora. Drama tragico en tres jornadas. pp. 69. *Palma*, 1842. 8°. **1342. c. 8.**

—— Juan Angelats, drama histórico, original, en tres actos. pp. 52. *Palma*, 1862. 8°. **11726. aa. 33. (7.)**

CERDO (JOANNES)

—— Oratio hec est funebris. In laudem Joannis Cerdonis. Quam nominauimus Vademecum Quia cum emeris tunc portas tecum Cum duabus epistolis clarorū virorum Quas nequaꝗ dices imperitorum. **G.L.** [1518?] 4°.
12315. b. 33.

CERDÓ (MIGUEL OLIVÉR Y) *See* OLIVÉR Y CERDÓ.

CERDÓ (RAPHAEL) Essai sur les embarras des premières voies considérés comme irritations gastriques. Dissertation, etc. pp. 21. *Montpellier*, 1824. 4°.
1181. c. 17. (18.)

—— Essai sur les fractures de l'humerus. Tribut académique, etc. pp. 19. *Montpellier*, 1824. 4°. **1181. c. 18. (3.)**

CERDONI (GIOVANNI) *See* NONNANUCI (Egidio) *pseud.* [i.e. G. Cerdoni.]

CERDONIO (DESIDERIO) El Ropavejero Literario, en las ferias de Madrid, etc. pp. 149. *Madrid*, 1796. 4°.
1480. a. 25.

CÈRE (ÉMILE) *See* DUCOR (H.) Aventures d'un marin de la Garde Impériale . . . Préface de E. Cère. [1895.] 8°.
10105. aa. 4.

—— *See* FIGUEUR, afterwards SUTTER (T.) La Vraie Madame Sans-Gêne . . . Préface de M. E. Cère, etc. 1895. 12°.
010663. f. 43.

—— Madame Sans-Gêne (Thérèse Figueur) et les femmes soldats. 1792–1815. pp. 320. *Paris*, [1894.] 12°.
010663. f. 16.

CÉRÉ (JEAN LUCIEN) Dissertation sur le choléra-morbus asiatique; thèse, etc. pp. 27. *Paris*, 1833. 4°.
1184. e. 11. (4.)

CÈRE (PAUL J.) De l'enseignement primaire. Les Frères de la doctrine chrétienne et les instituteurs laïques. pp. iv. 130. *Paris*, 1847. 8°. **8307. e. 17.**

—— La Décentralisation administrative. pp. 158. *Paris*, 1865. 8°. **8052. dd. 11.**

—— Manuel du fonctionnaire chargé de la police judiciaire, administrative et municipale, etc. pp. iv. 448. *Paris*, 1854. 12°. **5425. aa. 8.**

—— Manuel du juge de paix et du justiciable de la justice de paix. pp. 452. *Paris*, 1854. 12°. **5405. a. 15.**

—— Les Populations dangereuses et les misères sociales. pp. 378. *Paris*, 1872. 8°. **8276. bb. 33.**

CEREAL SYNONYM COMMITTEE. *See* ENGLAND.

CEREALI (Francesco) Ritratto del sacerdote Christiano . . . nel quale si discrivono gli officij . . . dell'istesso sacerdote, *etc.* pp. 360. *Appresso B. di Zanni : Cremona,* 1599. 12º. **4499. a. 8.**

CEREALIS, *Bishop of Castellum Ripense.* Cerealis Episcopi contra Maximinum Arianum. *See* Sichardus (J.) Antidotum contra diuersas omnium fere seculorum hæreses. 1528. fol. **474. d. 12.**

—— [Another edition.] *See* Heroldt (J.) *Basilius.* Hæreseologia, *etc.* 1556. fol. **472. e. 1.**

—— [Another edition.] 1610. *See* La Bigne (M. de) Bibliothecæ veterum patrum . . . tomi octo, *etc.* tom. 4. 1609, *etc.* fol. **C. 79. i. 2.**

—— [Another edition.] 1618. *See* La Bigne (M. de) Magna bibliotheca veterum patrum, *etc.* tom. 5. pt. 3. 1618, *etc.* fol. **469. e. 5.**

—— [Another edition.] *See* La Bigne (M. de) Magna bibliotheca veterum patrum, *etc.* tom. 4. pt. 1. 1654. fol. **3624. e.**

—— [Another edition.] 1847. *See* Migne (J. P.) Patrologiæ cursus completus, *etc.* tom. 58. 1844, *etc.* 4º. **2000. b.**